Moonis Ali   Richard Dapoigny (Eds.)

Advances in Applied Artificial Intelligence

19th International Conference on
Industrial, Engineering and Other Applications of
Applied Intelligent Systems, IEA/AIE 2006
Annecy, France, June 27-30, 2006
Proceedings

 Springer

Series Editors

Jaime G. Carbonell, Carnegie Mellon University, Pittsburgh, PA, USA
Jörg Siekmann, University of Saarland, Saarbrücken, Germany

Volume Editors

Moonis Ali
Texas State University-San Marcos
Department of Computer Science
601 University Drive, San Marcos, TX 78666-4616, USA
E-mail: ma04@txstate.edu

Richard Dapoigny
Université de Savoie
LISTIC/ESIA
Domaine Universitaire, BP 806, 74016 Annecy Cedex, France
E-mail: richard.dapoigny@univ-savoie.fr

Library of Congress Control Number: 2006927485

CR Subject Classification (1998): I.2, F.1, F.2, I.5, F.4.1, D.2, H.4, H.2.8, H.5.2

LNCS Sublibrary: SL 7 – Artificial Intelligence

ISSN   0302-9743
ISBN-10   3-540-35453-0 Springer Berlin Heidelberg New York
ISBN-13   978-3-540-35453-6 Springer Berlin Heidelberg New York

Springer is a part of Springer Science+Business Media

springer.com

© Springer-Verlag Berlin Heidelberg 2006
Printed in Germany

Typesetting: Camera-ready by author, data conversion by Scientific Publishing Services, Chennai, India
Printed on acid-free paper   SPIN: 11779568   06/3142   5 4 3 2 1 0

Lecture Notes in Artificial Intelligence   4031

Edited by J. G. Carbonell and J. Siekmann

Subseries of Lecture Notes in Computer Science

Preface

> "Intelligent Design and complex problem solving
> are twined like wife and husband."

In the current competitive global industrial environment there are many problems which need intelligent systems technology for optimal solutions. The central theme of the 19th International Conference on Industrial, Engineering & Other Applications of Applied Intelligent Systems (IEA/AIE 2006) is to focus on the research methodologies and practical implementations of these methodologies for intelligent solutions of problems in real-world applications.

We are pleased to present the papers in these proceedings which cover various aspects of applications of applied intelligent systems. We received more than 330 papers from many countries and each paper was reviewed by at least two reviewers. Only 134 papers were selected for presentation in the normal and special sessions. The normal sessions cover the following topics: planning and scheduling, multi-agent systems, fuzzy logic, data mining and knowledge discovery, genetic algorithms, decision support, expert systems, neural networks, computer vision, speech recognition, systems for real-life applications, machine learning, model-based reasoning, heuristic search, and knowledge engineering.

We also organized several special sessions in the areas of bioinformatics, ontology, knowledge discovery, intelligent control systems, intelligent industrial systems, and applications of data mining. The conference program also included four invited lecturers given by Fausto Giunchiglia, Erik Sandewall, Sylviane Gentil and Trevor Martin.

Many people have contributed in various ways to the successful organization of this conference. We would like to express our sincere thanks to the authors, Program Committee members and chairs, special session chairs, reviewers and organizers for their hard work. We would also like to thank Ms. Valerie Braesch and Ms. Joelle Pellet for their efficiency in dealing with several issues related to conference organization and management. There are many other participants whose role was of crucial importance in the organization of the conference. The present conference would not have been possible without their valuable support.

Annecy, June 2006

Moonis Ali
Richard Dapoigny

Organization

IEA/AIE 2006 was organized by the department of Computer Science, University of Savoie and ISAI (International Society of Applied Intelligence) in cooperation with LISTIC/ESIA, AAAI, ACM/SIGART, AFIA, CSCSI/SCEIO, ECCAI, ENNS, INNS, JSAI, TAAI and Texas State University - San Marcos.

Conference Organization

General Chair	Moonis Ali
	(Texas State University - San Marcos, USA)
Program Chair	Richard Dapoigny
	(University of Savoie, France)
Program Co-chairs	Patrick Brézillon
	(Paris VI University, France)
	Laurent Foulloy
	(University of Savoie, France)
Organizing Committee	Patrick Barlatier
	(University of Savoie, France)
	Sylvie Galichet
	(University of Savoie, France)
	Gilles Mauris
	(University of Savoie, France)
	Eric Benoit
	(University of Savoie, France)
Conference Secretariat	Valérie Braesch
	(University of Savoie, France)
	Joelle Pellet
	(University of Savoie, France)

Program Committee

F. Alexandre	E.K. Burke	G. Dreyfus
V. Aubergé	B. Chaib-draa	F. Esposito
P. Barlatier	C.W. Chan	L. Foulloy
F. Belli	J. Chen	C. Freksa
E. Benoit	S.M. Chen	S. Galichet
L. Berrah	P. Chung	H.W. Guesgen
L. Borzemski	F.S. Correa da Silva	M.T. Harandi
P. Brézillon	R. Desimone	H. Hattori

T. Hendtlass	J. Mira	C. Roche
G. Horvath	L. Monostori	L. Saitta
M.P. Huget	K. Morik	M. Sánchez-Marré
T. Ito	H. Munoz-Avila	K. Suzuki
S. Iwata	Y.L. Murphey	T. Tanaka
F. Jacquenet	B. Neumann	J. Treur
L. Jain	N.T. Nguyen	S. Vadera
C. Jonker	T. Nishida	P. Valckenaers
K. Kaikhah	H.G. Okuno	M. Valtorta
F. Kabanza	B. Orchard	J. Vancza
Y.L. Karnavas	C. Pellegrini	X.Z. Wang
L. Kerschberg	S. Pesty	S. Watanabe
T. Kinosihta	F.G. Pin	G. Williams
A. Kumar	W. Don Potter	T. Wittig
R.L. Loganantharaj	S. Ramaswamy	C. Yang
K. Madani	M.C. Randall	Y. Yang
M.M. Matthews	R. Ranon	
G. Mauris	V.J. Rayward-Smith	

Additional Reviewers

S. Sakurai	A. Garrido	J.L. Lin
D. Jiang	B.C. Csaji	J. Liu
C.S. Lee	B. Sekeroglu	J. Sun
F. Honghai	B. Kadar	K.W. Chau
E. Gutieriez	C. Araz	K. Zhang
L. Wang	C.C. Wang	K. Dimililer
C.S. Ho	C.H. Chang	K.H. Kim
B.C. Chien	C.Y. Chang	K. Rim
T.P. Hong	C. Nguyen	K.R. Ryu
A. Khashman	D. Krol	L. Tarassenko
A. Pfeiffer	D.A. Clifton	M.G. Garcia-Hernandez
L.H. Wang	E. Onaindia	M. Galetakis
H.M. Lee	G.S. Kukla	M. Shan
C.H. Cheng	H. Selim	M.S. Oh
M. Nakamura	H. Rau	P.R. Bannister
D.L. Yang	H. Hesuan	P.J. Chen
M. Mejia-Lavalle	H.M. Chiang	R. Garcia-Martinez
N.C. Wei	I. Ozkarahan	S. Lee
F. Liu	J. Kang	T. Arredondo
S. Li	J. Rezaei	T.Y. Lee
J.S. Aguilar-Ruiz	M. Jerzy	W. Weidong
A. Lim	J. Jianyuan	W.A. Tan

Table of Contents

Invited Contributions

Multi-agent Systems

Decision-Support

Genetic Algorithms

Heuristic Search

Data-Mining and Knowledge Discovery

Planning and Scheduling

Fuzzy Logic

Computer Vision

Case-Based Reasoning

Knowledge Engineering

Machine Learning

Model-Based Reasoning

Speech Recognition

Special Session on Bioinformatics

Special Session on Ontology and Text

Special Session on Data for Discovery in Engineering

Special Session on Intelligent Control Systems

Special Session on Intelligent Systems for Industry

Special Session on Applications of Data Mining

Managing Diversity in Knowledge

Fausto Giunchiglia

Department of Information and Communication Technology University of Trento,
38050 Povo di Trento, Italy

We are facing an unforeseen growth of the complexity of data, content and knowledge. Here we talk of complexity meaning the size, the sheer numbers, the spatial and temporal pervasiveness of knowledge, and the unpredictable dynamics of knowledge change, unknown at design time but also at run time.

In knowledge engineering and management the "usual" approach is to take into account, at design time, all the possible future dynamics. The key idea is to design a "general enough" reference representation model, expressive enough to incorporate all the possible future variations of knowledge.

The approach proposed here is somewhat opposite. Instead of taking a top-down approach, where the whole knowledge is designed integrated, with a pure a-priori effort, we propose a bottom-up approach where the different knowledge parts are kept distinct and designed independently.

The key idea is to consider diversity as a feature which must be maintained and exploited and not as a defect that must be cancelled or absorbed in some general "universal-looking" schema. People, organizations, communities, populations, cultures build diverse representations of the world for a reason, and this reason lies in the local context. What context exactly, is hard to say. However it can be safely stated that context has many dimensions: time, space, contingent goals, short term or long term goals, personal or community bias, environmental conditions, ., and so on.

We will present and discuss the ideas above comparing, as an example, how the notions of context and of ontology have been applied in the formalization of knowledge (for instance in the Semantic Web). We will then argue that a context-based approach to managing diversity in knowledge must be studied at three different levels:

1. Representation level, dealing with all the issues related to how local and global knowledge are represented, to their semantics, and to the definition of the operations which allow to manipulate them.
2. Organization level, dealing with the organization and interaction of inter-connected knowledge parts and systems manipulating them.
3. Social level, dealing with the problem of how systems (incrementally) reach agreement, thus creating (sub)communities of shared or common knowledge.

M. Ali and R. Dapoigny (Eds.): IEA/AIE 2006, LNAI 4031, p. 1, 2006.
© Springer-Verlag Berlin Heidelberg 2006

Artificial Intelligence for Industrial Process Supervision

S. Gentil

Laboratoire d'Automatique de Grenoble
UMR 5528 CNRS-INPG-UJF
BP 46, F-38402 Saint Martin d'Hères Cedex
sylviane.gentil@inpg.fr

Abstract. This paper presents some difficulties of complex industrial process supervision and explains why artificial intelligence may help to solve some problems. Qualitative or semi-qualitative trend extraction is mentioned first. Then fault detection and fault supervision are evoked. The necessity for intelligent interfaces is explained next and distributed supervision is finally mentioned.

Keywords: Supervision, Model-based Diagnosis, Prognosis, Trend extraction, Causal Reasoning, Multi-agents systems, Decision Support, Fuzzy Logic.

1 Introduction

Nowadays, automation is the most important factor for complex industrial plant development. A complex process (transportation system, plane, thermal or nuclear power plant, electrical network, water treatment plant …) is a process in an open environment, where uncertainty and dynamical phenomena play an important role and decision making is difficult. These processes involve many measured variables. Their automation needs managing an important amount of heterogeneous information, distributed among interconnected sub-systems.

Controlling such plants is done with a SCADA (Supervisory Control and Data Acquisition system). It is a reactive system connected on line to the process with real time constraints. It may have various objectives. A first set of objectives concerns the production performances: product quality, deadlines and manufacturing costs. A second set of objectives concerns safety. Industrial accidents resulting in human victims or environmental damages are no more accepted. Moreover, cost reduction requires a permanent availability of the production tool. Guarantying plant safety has been relying for a long time only on hardware redundancy. Some functionality is now replaced by analytical redundancy.

Automation concerns a plant with various functioning modes: normal operating mode, start up and shut down modes and failure modes, corresponding to the different system states when the plant suffers a failure or a malfunction. These modes are quite difficult to predict. They may need either to stop the process immediately or to change the control laws (changing control loops set point or even the control architecture).

Supervision objective is to manage the control effect on the process. This means verifying that the process is in its normal mode. If it is not the case, a reaction has to be found at least to avoid damages and to limit shuts downs, and if possible to

M. Ali and R. Dapoigny (Eds.): IEA/AIE 2006, LNAI 4031, pp. 2–11, 2006.
© Springer-Verlag Berlin Heidelberg 2006

guaranty production continuity. Depending on circumstances, multiple tasks may be envisaged [1]. Supervision vocabulary related to failure modes is now clarified.

A **failure** is a permanent interruption of the system or of a component function while a **malfunction** is an intermittent one. A **fault** is a deviation of at least one characteristic feature of the system behaviour from the normal condition. A fault can be observed thanks to a **fault indicator**, computed with measured variables. **Monitoring** refers to the possibility to recognize a fault mode. In its basic version, it consists in checking variables with regard to thresholds, generally empirically set by process engineers, and in generating alarms if necessary. In case of danger, the supervisor triggers an appropriate counteraction automatically. In more advanced versions of monitoring, a mathematical model can be used to generate fault indicators or rough measurements can be processed to obtain features relevant for classification. In the classical diagnostic procedure, two steps are recognized. **Detection** consists in using a set of fault indicators to generate qualitative symptoms (Boolean or fuzzy values). **Isolation** or **classification** consists in deducing from a set of symptoms a minimal set of physical components whose malfunction or failure is sufficient in order to explain the symptoms. Isolation is difficult because secondary faults may be observed that are only consequences of primary faults related to a component failure. The abnormal component set must be precise (i.e. contain the right abnormal components) and as small as possible (i.e. not contain many normal components). When the faulty components are isolated, the plant has to be stopped if safety is at stake or a redundant component can be started, or a different control strategy has to be used (fault tolerant control).

Nevertheless, it is impossible to anticipate every situation in a complex system and to plan the corresponding counteraction. One has to bring into play many varied procedures that are not linked in a deterministic manner but in function of the context. This explains why **human operators** are still in charge of large industrial installations. A human' important quality is to know how to manage unforeseen uncertain situations and to design relevant strategies when dysfunction occurs. Excluding human operators from control rooms is not planned, even for highly automated processes. Thus supervision must be designed with a man/machine cooperation point of view. Human operator is always the ultimate link in the decisional chain. The supervisory system must justify its choices, explain them to the human operator and support human reasoning in the final decision-making. This is when artificial intelligence may play an important role. Considering the present supervision tools it is to be noted that operators are provided with quantities of data, but no analysis about these data and their relations. In a cascading faulty situation the adequacy between the alarms flow and the time required by the operator to analyze it on-line is not respected any more. Supervision support functionalities are mainly concerned in a man-machine interface ergonomics, which is obviously a major step but not sufficient. It is necessary to conceive on-line systems able to manage the information combinatory, to link and to structure data—to sum up, to achieve all the tasks for which human reasoning is rapidly limited [2]. Monitoring, alarm filtering, fault detection and isolation, diagnosis and action advice are features to be provided to operators.

In the following sections, solutions to some of the above mentioned problems will be presented, inspired by AI techniques. The present paper does not pretend to be a survey of AI for supervision [3], but rather presents some realizations with an AI user point of view. Fuzzy clustering or expert systems for diagnosis will not be described. We have rather chosen to describe applications where control theory and artificial intelligence are intimately mixed.

2 Semi-qualitative Trend Extraction for Monitoring or Prognosis

Trend analysis is a useful approach to extract information from numerical data and represent it symbolically, in a qualitative or semi-qualitative way. A qualitative trend is a description of the evolution of the qualitative state of a variable, in a time interval, using a set of symbols called primitives. Generally, a small set of primitives is used to create episodes: an episode is an interval of uniform behaviour. A qualitative trend is consequently a qualitative history that is represented by a sequence of consecutive (contiguous and non-overlapping) episodes. The trend can be further interpreted by the operator in function of the specific system under study, thanks to his/her expert knowledge. Process trends have particularly been considered in the chemical process industry [4] and in medical applications. Often, the use of a semi-qualitative trend is preferred to a purely qualitative one, to allow representing quite precisely numerical data.

2.1 Semi-qualitative Trend Extraction

This paragraph presents a methodology for semi-qualitative trend extraction as an example [5]. Data acquired on line on the process are first described by successive linear segments. The segmentation algorithm determines on line the moment when the current linear approximation is no longer acceptable and when a new segment should be computed. Two consecutive segments may be discontinuous. The segment i ends at time $t_e(i)$, one sampling time before the next one starts $t_0(i+1)$. Corresponding data amplitude is denoted by y.

The new segment is used with the preceding one to form a shape. Seven temporal primitives are used for this classification: *Increasing, Decreasing, Steady, Positive Step, Negative Step, Increasing/Decreasing Transient, Decreasing/Increasing Transient*. The shape associated with the segment i starts at time $t_b(i)=t_0(i)-1$. The classification of the segment into a temporal shape provides symbolic information meaningful to the operator.

A semi-quantitative episode is described by [*Primitive*, $t_b(i)$, $y_b(i)$, $t_e(i)$,$y_e(i)$]. To obtain an easily understandable trend, only three basic primitives are used for the episodes: {*Steady, Increasing, Decreasing*}. If a shape is in {*Steady, Increasing, Decreasing*}, the symbolic information is obviously converted into one of the symbolic primitives. If the shape is *Step* or *Transient*, it is split into two parts. A Positive Step for instance becomes [*Increasing*, $t_e(i-1)$, $y_e(i-1)$,$t_0(i)$, $y_0(i)$] , [*Steady*, $t_0(i)$, $y_0(i)$, $t_e(i)$, $y_e(i)$].

The aggregation of episodes consists in associating the most recent episode with the former ones to form the longest possible episode. In the case of two *Steady* episodes, the result can be *Steady, Increasing* or *Decreasing* following the increase of the global sequence.

On line, the four steps are achieved using the current segment (i) to extract a temporary trend. Later, when a new linear approximation will have been calculated, the current segment will become the previous segment and will now be completely defined. It will be aggregated with the definitive trend and a temporary trend will be calculated using the new current segment.

2.2 Trend Analysis for Prognosis

Trend analysis can be used in different ways to inform the operator about the future behaviour of a given signal. The qualitative information such as variable is *Steady* or *Increasing* is by itself a useful tool. Moreover, the semi-quantitative episodes can be used to predict the value of the monitored variables in a time window. The segmentation algorithm provides the linear model that better describes the present behaviour of the signal. If an alarm threshold is known, then the model can be used to solve the problem: how much time is needed for the signal to arrive at this threshold?

A two-tank system is used to illustrate the method (Fig. 1). The system has been modelled using physical relations implemented with Simulink. The simulator allows

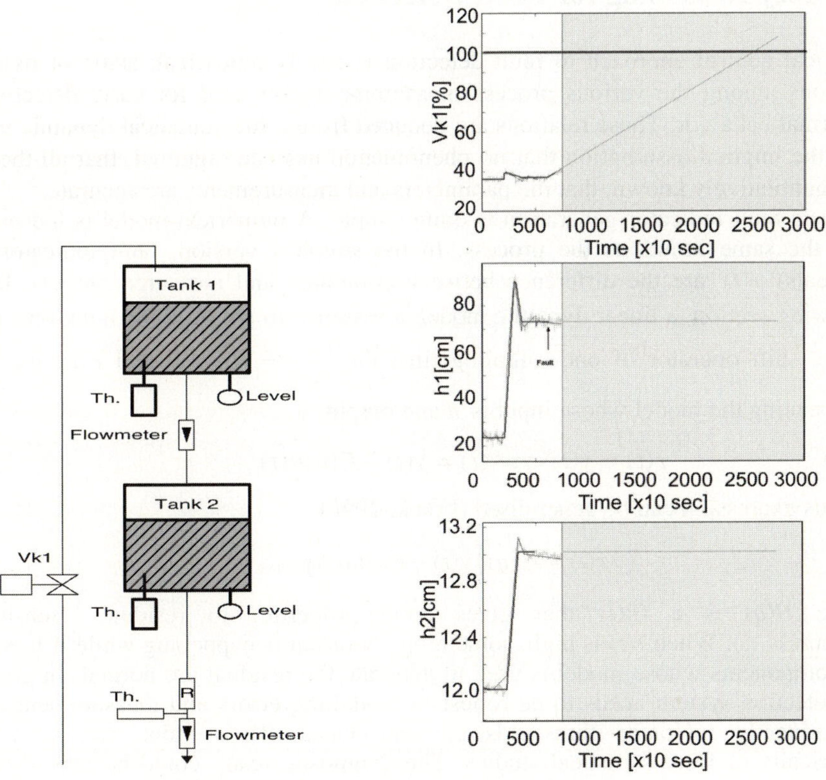

Fig. 1. The two-tank system example

the simulation in normal as well as in faulty conditions. Noise is added to simulated variables. The lower tank level is controlled by the servo-valve *Vk1*. Measurements available to the control and supervision systems are the water levels *h1*, *h2* and output flow *q1*, *q2* of each tank.

The fault scenario described in Fig. 1 starts with an *h2* level set-point change at time 0, followed by a failure at time 6000 sec. A ramp leakage is introduced in tank 1, simulating a progressive failure. The control system compensates the leakage, maintaining the tank levels equal to their reference values by increasing the valve opening. The operator can see on the interface the variable trends and their prediction (grey background). This prediction is based on the last episode, which is extrapolated on a long time horizon. The prediction allows seeing level *h1* remaining constant for a long time thanks to the regulation loop; but this will no longer be the case when the valve reaches its saturation level (100%). The operator has an idea about the time left before this saturation and can thus perform a counteraction (a reduction of the set point value for level *h2*, or a programmed shutdown, or a call to the maintenance service).

3 Fuzzy Reasoning for Fault Detection

Classical control approach to fault detection is purely numerical: static or dynamic relations among the various process measurements are used for early detection of abnormal behavior. These relations are deduced from a mathematical dynamic model with the implicit assumption that no phenomenon has been ignored, that all the data are quantitatively known, that the parameters and measurements are accurate.

Basic fault indicator generation is quite simple. A numerical model is fed on line with the same inputs as the process. In the simplest version, fault indicators (or residuals) $r(t)$ are the difference between computed and measured outputs. In the following section, a linear dynamic model is assumed to simplify the notations. Let q be the shift operator of one sampling time ($q^{-1}y(t) = y(t-1)$) and $F(q)$ the filter representing the model whose input is $\breve{u}$ and output y^*

$$r(t) = \breve{y}(t) - y^*(t) = \breve{y}(t) - F(q)\breve{u}(t) \tag{1}$$

This expression can be generalised (Frank, 1996)

$$r(t) = H(q)\left[\breve{y}(t) - F(q)\breve{u}(t)\right] \tag{2}$$

where $H(q)$ is a filter that gives good properties to residuals (sensitivity, robustness…). When *r(t)* is high, something abnormal is happening while if it is zero, the components whose model is used to generate the residual are normal. In practice, the detection system needs to be robust to modelling errors and measurement noise. Consequently tolerance thresholds are introduced. Their value can be chosen empirically or from statistical studies. The diagnostic result could be very different depending on whether the fault indicator is equal to a specified threshold plus or minus epsilon, regardless of the amplitude of epsilon, which can lead to unstable detection. This is why many people chose to adopt a fuzzy reasoning for detection.

This allows a gradual decision. Moreover, fuzzy reasoning allows taking into account more information than a simple numerical value, for instance the residual variation. Fuzzification with symmetric trapezoidal membership functions and using traditional notations lead to fuzzy descriptions for the residual and its variation that are used in the following inference rule

$$\text{if } r_i(k) \text{ is } A \text{ and } \Delta r_i(k) \text{ is } B \text{ then variable state is } S \tag{3}$$

The conclusion $S \in \{OK, AL\}$; OK means that the variable behaviour is normal while AL means that an alarm must be triggered. The symbolic rule base is presented in Table 1. Choosing product and sum as fuzzy operators expressing this rule base, a simple matrix product can express the inference, which results in short real time processing [6].

Table 1. Fuzzy inference for detection

		$\Delta r_i(k) = r_i(k) - r_i(k-1)$		
		N	Z	P
	NN	0/OK+1/AL	0/OK+1/AL	0.2/OK+0.8/AL
	N	0/OK+1/AL	0.4/OK+0.6/AL	0.6/OK+0.4/AL
$r_i(k)$	Z	0.8/OK+0.2/AL	1/OK+0/AL	0.8/OK+0.2/AL
	P	0.6/OK+0.4/AL	0.4/OK+0.6/AL	0/OK+1/AL
	PP	0.2/OK+0.8/AL	0/OK+1/AL	0/OK+1/AL

Two kinds of decisions have been proposed to aggregate partial conclusions over a time window of M sampling periods: a robust decision D^- and a sensitive decision D^+

$$D^-(AL) = H^-\left(S_1(AL)...S_M(AL)\right) \tag{4}$$

$$D^-(OK) = H^+\left(S_1(OK)...S_M(OK)\right) \tag{5}$$

$$D^+(AL) = H^+\left(S_1(AL)...S_M(AL)\right) \tag{6}$$

$$D^+(OK) = H^-\left(S_1(OK)...S_M(OK)\right) \tag{7}$$

H^+ is a disjunction (max for instance) and H^- is a conjunction (min for instance). $D^-(OK)$ (respectively $D^+(OK)$) represents the maximal (minimal) bound for the state normal and $D^+(AL)$ (respectively $D^-(AL)$) represents the maximal (minimal) bound for the alarm state.

4 Causal Reasoning for Fault Isolation

After fault detection, potential causes have to be isolated. Causality occupies a central position in human cognition. Informal descriptions of real world in the form A causes B, are exceedingly common. AI community has been working for a long time on representations of causality. Causal descriptions are the source of various reasoning modes. B can be predicted or explained using A. A could be deduced from B. Causality plays an essential role in human decision-making [7]. Diagnosis is also a causal process, because it consists in designating the faulty components that have caused, and can explain, the observed malfunctions. A causal structure is a qualitative description of the effect or influence that system entities (variables, faults, etc.) have on other entities. It may be represented by a directed graph (digraph). A causal graph represents a process at a high level of abstraction. In the logical theory of abductive diagnosis, diagnosis is formalized as reasoning from effects to causes. Causal knowledge is represented as logical implications of the form causes • effects where causes are usually abnormalities or faults. The pieces of causal knowledge can be organized in a directed graph. This abductive type of reasoning contrasts with deductive reasoning from causes to effects.

Causality, assimilated to calculability, has also been used to represent the physical behaviour of a system. Influence graphs are another type of causal approach to diagnosis. The graph nodes represent the system variables; the directed arcs symbolize the normal relations among them (see Fig. 2 for an example). Influence graphs avoid fault modelling, which could be unfeasible in the case of a complex system. They provide a tool for reasoning about the way in which normal or abnormal changes propagate and are suitable for physical explanations of the dynamical evolution of variables, whether normal or abnormal. No a priori assumption is made about the type of relations labelling each arc. They could be qualitative or quantitative. The simplest influence graph structure is the signed digraph (SDG). The branches are labelled by signs: "+" (or "-") when the variables at each end of the arc have the same (or opposite) trends.

All influence-graph-based diagnostic methods implement the same basic principle. The objective is to account for deviations detected in the evolution of the variables with respect to the normal behaviour, using a minimum of malfunctions at the source. Malfunctions can be related to physical components, so as to obtain a minimal diagnosis. If significant deviations are detected, primary faults, directly attributable to a failure or an unmeasured disturbance, are hypothesized. The propagation paths in the directed graph are analyzed to determine whether this fault hypothesis is sufficient to account for secondary faults, resulting from its propagation in the process over time. The algorithm is a backward/forward procedure starting from an inconsistent variable. The backward search bounds the fault space by eliminating the normal measurements causally upstream. Then each possible primary deviation generates a hypothesis, which is forward tested using the states of the variables and the functions of the arcs.

Arcs can be labelled with dynamic quantitative relations, which is justified from the diagnostic needs of industrial plants [8]. This leads to a combined method for diagnosis that takes advantage of the precision of FDI fault indicators because it uses a quantitative model. Simultaneously, it benefits from the logical soundness of AI approaches through the use of a causal structure that supports the diagnostic reasoning [9,10]. This method has been applied successfully to an industrial process during the European project CHEM [11].

5 Interface

Skilled operators generally take the proper decision when the failure is clearly identified. With the current control systems, the execution of actions is not problematic. Their main problem comes from the difficulty in linking the behaviour of correlated variables (e.g. in control loops or when the temporal delays between the deviations in both behaviours are significant). In addition when a failure mode does not correspond to an abrupt change but rather to a slow drift, they can hardly detect the fault. The several kinds of reasoning that have been presented in the previous sections are very well adapted to a cooperative interface allowing quick understanding of the process state.

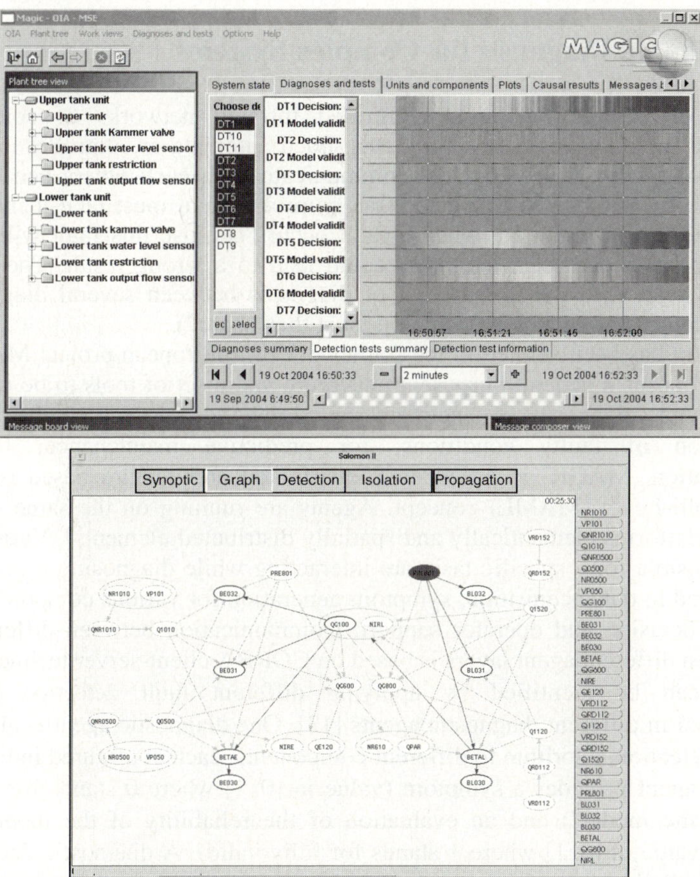

Fig. 2. Interface: detection (upper part); causal graph for isolation (lower part)

In the interface screen presented in Fig. 2, each line is associated with a variable, and each column is associated with a sampling time. Columns close to the left side represent earlier time samples. The information display is inspired by the concept of mass data display. Each decision (detection, isolation) is associated with a colour. The results of fuzzy detection and isolation reasoning are defuzzified into an index associated with a colour shade. In the detection view, the detection decisions are defuzzified into an index of a colour map from green (normal state) to red (faulty state). In the isolation view, the decisions are defuzzified into an index of a colour map from blue (upstream fault) to red (local fault).

The causal graph representation is also well adapted to an interface explaining the source of the observed faults (Fig. 2). The output of the isolation reasoning is displayed in the graph in the following way. If the node is not red, the variable is in a normal state. If the contour of the node is red, the alarm corresponds to a secondary fault. If the interior of the node is red then the variable is isolated as a primary fault. The fault path is also shown in red. The fault path in the causal graph can be seen as a justification module that explains the alarm chain to the operators.

6 Distributed Diagnosis for Complex Systems

Diagnosis of complex systems, controlled through networks of controllers or automata, plants interesting new problems. Each automata or controller is connected to a particular subsystem and must communicate with each others because, as the components are physically connected, the control system must take it into account. This is specifically important when a fault occurs because this fault will propagate along the process and local diagnosis could lead to a wrong result. The theoretical problem is related to the distribution of diagnosis between several diagnosers and their communication (which information must they share?).

A solution has been studied in the framework of a European project MAGIC [12]. MAGIC proposes a general purpose architecture and a set of tools to be used for the detection and diagnosis of incipient or slowly developing faults; for early identification of faulty conditions; for predictive maintenance; for system reconfiguration. MAGIC is based on a distributed architecture based on a Multi-Agents-Multi-Level (MAML) concept. Agents are running on the same or separate computer platforms (semantically and spatially distributed elements). Various agents, each responsible for a specific task, are interacting while diagnosing a plant. Agents are dedicated to data acquisition, symptom generation for various components, global diagnostic decision and operator support. Communication between different agents and between different agent layers is based on CORBA client-server technology.

Faults can be identified by applying different fault detection algorithms, implemented in different diagnostic agents [13]. One diagnostic agent is able to apply the same detection algorithm to different components, each configured individually. A diagnostic agent provides a symptom (value in [0..1] where 0 stands for "behaviour similar to the model") and an evaluation of the reliability of the model used for detection (value in [0..1] where 1 stands for fully valid). A diagnostic decision agent centralizes all the symptoms. Its objective is to provide a final decision about the components' state, integrating symptoms covering different overlapping subsystems or merging different symptoms about the same sub-system, using a signature table or fuzzy logic. This project is just a first step towards a generic distributed diagnostic solution. Industrial solutions should adopt normalized agents systems.

References

1. Iserman R., Fault Diagnosis Systems, Springer Berlin Heidelberg, 2006.
2. Gentil S., Montmain J., Hierarchical representation of complex systems for supporting human decision making, Advanced Engineering Informatics, 18/3 (2004) 143-159.
3. de Kleer J., Kurien J., Fundamentals of Model-based Diagnosis, IFAC Symposium Safeprocess 2003 Washington (USA).
4. Venkatasubramanian, V,. Process Fault Detection and Diagnosis: Past, Present and Future. 4th Workshop On-Line Fault Detection and Supervision in the Chemical Process Industries 2001, Seoul (Korea).
5. Charbonnier S., Garcia-Beltran C., Cadet C., Gentil S., Trends extraction and analysis for complex system monitoring and decision support, Engineering Applications of Artificial Intelligence, 18/1 (2004) 21-36.
6. Evsukoff A., Gentil S., Montmain J., Fuzzy Reasoning in Co-operative Supervision Systems, Control Engineering Practice 8 (2000) 389-407.
7. Montmain J., Gentil S., Causal modelling for supervision, 14th IEEE International Symposium On Intelligent Control/Intelligent Systems and Semiotics, ISIC 1999 Cambridge (USA).
8. Montmain J., Gentil S., Dynamic causal model diagnostic reasoning for on-line technical process supervision, Automatica 36 (2000), 1137-1152.
9. Gentil S., Montmain J., Combastel C., Combining FDI and AI Approaches within Causal-Model-based Diagnosis, IEEE Transactions SMC-Part B, 34 (5) (2004) 2207-2221.
10. M.-O. Cordier, Dague P., Lévy F., Montmain J., Staroswiecki M., Travé-Massuyès L., Conflicts versus Analytical Redundancy Relations : A comparative analysis of the model-based diagnostic approach from the artificial intelligence and automatic control perspectives, IEEE Transactions on Systems, Man and Cybernetics - Part B., 34 (5) (2004) 1992-2206.
11. Heim, S. Gentil, S. Cauvin, L. Trave-Massuyes, B. Braunschweig, Fault diagnosis of a chemical process using causal uncertain model, Workshop PAIS Prestigious Applications of Intelligent Systems, 15th European Conference on Artificial Intelligence ECAI 2002, Lyon (FR).
12. B. Köppen-Seliger, T. Marcu, M. Capobianco, S. Gentil, M. Albert, S. Latzel, 2003, Magic: an integrated approach for diagnostic data management and operator support, IFAC Symposium Safeprocess 2003 Washington (USA).
13. S. Lesecq, S. Gentil, M. Exel, C. Garcia-Beltran, 2003, Diagnostic Tools for a Multi-agent Monitoring System IMACS IEEE Multi-Conference CESA 2003, Lille (Fr.).

Fuzzy Ambient Intelligence in Home Telecare

Trevor Martin

Department of Engineering Mathematics, University of Bristol, Bristol BS8 1TR UK

Telecare is the use of communication and/or sensor technologies to detect remotely the requirements of people in need of medical care or other assistance. Typically, but not exclusively, the users of telecare systems are elderly people who would otherwise need residential or nursing support. There is growing interest in the use of telecare, particularly in countries where facing growth in the proportion of elderly people in the population (with consequent increases in care requirements). Both socially and financially, it is generally preferable for the elderly to remain in their own homes for as long as possible. A number of research projects have looked into home-based telecare and telemedicine systems as a way of increasing quality of life for the elderly as well as reducing the cost of care. We can distinguish telemedicine as a subfield of telecare, where the specific aim is to remotely monitor physiological parameters of a person (such as blood sugar levels, blood pressure, etc) whereas telecare is a less specific form of monitoring looking to generate alerts in emergency situations.

Telecare is not a new idea - simple alarms operated by pull-cords or pendants have been available for 30 or more years. We refer to these as first generation systems, typically used as panic-alarms to summon help in the case of a fall or other emergency. Whilst such systems have obvious benefits, they become useless when the user is unable to raise the alarm (e.g. because of unconsciousness) or does not recognise the need to signal an alarm. Second generation telecare systems make use of sensors to detect emergency situations. These sensors can be worn on the body, measuring factors such as respiration, pulse, etc, or can be sited around the home, detecting movement, possible falls, etc.

Second generation systems are obviously far more sophisticated than the first generation and may require substantial computation and a degree of ambient intelligence to establish when an emergency situation arises. As with the first generation, an alarm can be triggered to summon help.

In both first and second generation systems, the aim is to detect an emergency and react to it as quickly as possible. Third generation telecare systems adopt a more pro-active approach, giving early warning of possible emergency situations. In order to do this, it is necessary to monitor the well-being of a person - defined in terms of their physical, mental, social and environmental status. By detecting changes in the daily activities of the person, it is possible to detect changes in their well-being which may not be immediately observable, but can be detected over a longer period of time. Advances in sensor design and the continuing increase in processing power make it possible to implement such an ambient intelligence system, and we will describe the implementation of a third generation telecare system which has been tested in homes of elderly clients over a long term (6 to 18 months).

M. Ali and R. Dapoigny (Eds.): IEA/AIE 2006, LNAI 4031, pp. 12–13, 2006.
© Springer-Verlag Berlin Heidelberg 2006

The system is installed within a home as a customised sensor network, able to detect a persons movements and their use of furniture and household items. The sensors are designed to operate discreetly, such that the occupant need not interact directly with any component. We will focus particularly on the intelligent processing which enables the system to take low level data (e.g. kitchen sensor activated; cold water run for 20 seconds; kettle switched on for 60 seconds; fridge door opened) and answer questions such as is the occupant eating regularly, is the occupants social interaction increasing or decreasing, has the occupants sleep pattern changed significantly in the past few months etc. This is a very substantial inference and learning task and the nature of the data and queries make a soft computing approach a natural choice. Initial trials of the system indicate that intelligent data analysis and reasoning enables us to make plausible inferences of this type with a high degree of accuracy.

Modeling and Multi-agent Specification of IF-Based Distributed Goal Ontologies

Nacima Mellal, Richard Dapoigny, Patrick Barlatier, and Laurent Foulloy

LISTIC-ESIA, BP 806
University of Savoie
74016 Annecy, France
{nacima.mellal, richard.dapoigny, patrick.barlatier,
Laurent.foulloy}@univ-savoie.fr

Abstract. The concept of service is central in the design of distributed systems. In this approach for example, the web is developing web services and grid services. Nowadays, it is essential to take into account the crucial aspects of the dynamic services, that is to say their ability to adapt and to be composed in order to complete their task. To this end, the first part of the present paper aims to describe the implementation of a methodology which deals the automatic composition of services in distributed systems. Each service is related to a goal and is represented by a functional model called an Ontology. The model relies on a core reasoning process between interacting functional components of the complex system following the Information Flow (IF) approach. Afterwards, in the second part, we propose an algorithm describing the mechanism of the dynamic composition, basing on the first part and using Multi Agent System (MAS), where the agents support the functional components of the complex systems.

1 Introduction

Embedded computing systems must offer autonomous capabilities in the often hostile environment in which they operate. Moreover, these systems are becoming more and more complex such as distributed intelligent components which are able to communicate and to reason about actions. Such systems include command and control systems, industrial process-control plants, automotive systems, data-acquisition and measurement systems, just to name a few. Although these systems are dedicated to design-defined tasks, they must offer some level of intelligence to cope with the dynamic and unpredictable environment with which they interact. A computational model powerful enough to capture the intensional knowledge within distributed systems and expressive enough to serve as a basis for reasoning and planning is required. Upon the teleological assumption a formal model based on goal structures has been proposed [4]. These structures are elaborated with the mechanisms of Formal Concept Analysis (FCA) during the design phase and results in domain ontologies able to be coordinated at run-time within an Information Flow (IF)-based framework. Web Services foster an environment where complex services that are composed of a number of tasks can be provided. With its modularity and its ability to

M. Ali and R. Dapoigny (Eds.): IEA/AIE 2006, LNAI 4031, pp. 14–23, 2006.

support communication standards, the concept of service seems appropriate for the present model, each service being related to a high-level goal. The inter-dependencies between goal ontologies related to each service are deduced from an IF-based process implemented in a group of autonomous agent programs. These agents communicate asynchronously over a network to compose the desired high level goal.

In the second section, the semantics for goal fusion is presented through the goal ontology and the process of fusion. The third section describes the major features of the MAS implementation. The fourth section is dedicated to future works and conclusion.

2   The Semantics for Goal Fusion

2.1   The Goal Ontology

In the design of distributed intelligent system, as well as in the run-time process, the service-based model plays a central role. The proposed approach relates each service with a top-level goal. This approach allows dividing complex systems functionality into elementary functional components (externally a service is seen as a group of sub-services). The design process involves the composition of sub-services, the fusion of services and to check if the composition and/or fusion fulfill the requirements. Architectures using services are widely applied in the domain of web services or telecommunications and more recently, in the engineering domain (e.g., automotive applications) [13]. For many engineering applications, the results must be abstracted in terms of the functions (teleological approach). The functional knowledge is an expression of the teleological knowledge on which the system can reason. Any functional concept is described by a goal definition which is related to the intentional aspect of function [11] and some possible actions (at least one) in order to fulfill the intended goal [8] [10].

Inside a given service, the causal decomposition of a high-level goal is exclusively an AND decomposition. It relies on dependencies in the *lambda-calculus* style. However, the OR decomposition can be expressed at several abstraction levels. The alternative dependencies of a given goal (OR-type goal) are either expressed at the highest level (i.e., the service level, since a single goal is active at a given time inside a given process) or at a finest one by splitting the goal into several actions guarded by pre-conditions (way of achievement).

The teleological basis introduced in [3] relates the structure and behavior of the designed system to its goals. The goal modeling requires to describe a goal representation (i.e., a conceptual structure), and to define how these concepts are related. For our purpose, a classification of goals is built on the basis of two sorts, i) the goal type which requires an action verb, a physical role with a set of location types and ii) a physical context including the physical role with the location where the role has to be considered.

Definition 1. Given R, a finite set of physical roles and Ψ, the finite set of physical entity types, a physical context type is a tuple: $\xi_i = (r, \mu(r), \psi_1, \psi_2, ... \psi_{\mu(r)})$, where $r \in R$, denotes its physical role (e.g., a physical quantity), $\mu: R \rightarrow Nat$, a function assigning to each role its arity (i.e., the number of physical entity types related to a *given role) and $\{\psi_1, \psi_2, ... \psi_{\mu(r)}\} \subseteq \Psi$, a set of entity types describing the spatial location types where the role has to be taken.*

A similar definition holds for physical contexts tokens c_i by replacing physical entity types with physical entity tokens.

Definition 2. *A goal type is a pair(A, Ξ), where A is an action symbol and Ξ is a non-empty set of physical context types.*

In [5], since the goal types appear to be components of a hierarchical structure, it is worth describing them by means of a subsumption hierarchy (i.e., a concept lattice). A formal context is built, from which a concept lattice is extracted using the Formal Concept Analysis tool (FCA). Pruning techniques based both on standard FCA-based techniques [7] and applicative works [3], extract the goal hierarchy in which each node is a concept labeled with the appropriate goal. Using the results of FCA about hierarchies of conceptual scales together with a definition of ontology, we produce a domain ontology of goal types. This ontology reflects the intentional knowledge concerning the interaction of a given service with the physical system. Unlike hierarchies, ontologies have a richer conceptual structure and can be accessed through well-defined standard languages such as OWL-S. The nature of a primitive goal relationship is inferrable from the physical or control equations where variables v_i are inter-connected through their physical contexts ξ_i .

Definition 3. *A goal γ_i influences functionally γ_j iff the only way to achieve γ_j is to*

have already achieved γ_i , with the notation:

$$\gamma_i < \gamma_j \tag{1}$$

An important consequence is that the different levels of abstraction are able to cope with the complexity of the system.

Let us develop an example extracted from [5] which represents the concept lattice of a system controlling the velocity and the level of a water channel and having two input sensors for pressure measurement and an actuator able to regulate the water level. In addition the system is able to communicate through a network with other similar systems. The atomic goal types for this system are:

```
γ₁ =({to acquire},{(pressure, 1, liquid volume)})
γ₂ =({to compute},{(velocity, 1, channel part)})
γ₃ =({to compute},{(level, 1, channel part)})
γ₄ =({to send},{(velocity, 1, channel part), (level, 1, channel part)})
γ₅ =({to receive},{(velocity,1, channel_part), (level,1, channel_part)})
γ₆ =({to compute},{(level, 2, {channel part, channel part})})
γ₇ =({to compute},{(offset, 1, actuator)})
γ₈ =({to receive},{(offset, 1, actuator)})
γ₉ =({to act upon},{(position, 1, actuator)})
```

The three goal types (static services) related to the services (i.e., the hierarchies), namely $\Gamma 1$, $\Gamma 2$ and $\Gamma 3$ respectively describe a measurement, a manual and a control services. For each goal, the user must specify in a design step the appropriate service including local influences (see *Figure.1*).

```
Γ₁ =({to measure},{(velocity,1,channel_part),(level,1,channel_part)})
Γ₂ =({to control},{(level, 1, channel part)})
Γ₃ =({to manually-Move},{(position, 1, actuator)})
```

Ontological definition includes concepts (goal types) together with basic ontological axioms. Goal types are the basic concepts and their relations are defined through three core notions: the functional part-of ordering relation, the overlap between goals, and the sum (fusion) of goal types. The first relation concerns the partial order notion. In the spirit of the typed λ-calculus we will consider only the *undirect* functional part-of for which transitivity holds. Therefore, the functional part-of relation on concepts, denoted as $\subseteq_\Gamma$, is reflexive, anti-symmetric and transitive. The overlap is referred by the binary relation O between goal types and specified with the following ontological axiom:

$$\gamma_i O \gamma_j \equiv \exists \gamma_k (\gamma_k \subseteq \gamma_j \wedge \gamma_k \subseteq \gamma_j) \qquad (2)$$

Definition 4. *A functional part-of hierarchy F is described by the following tuple:*
$F = (\Gamma, \subseteq_\Gamma, O, +)$, where Γ is a finite set of goal types, $\subseteq_\Gamma$ is a partial order on Γ, O is the overlap relation, and +, the fusion relation on Γ.

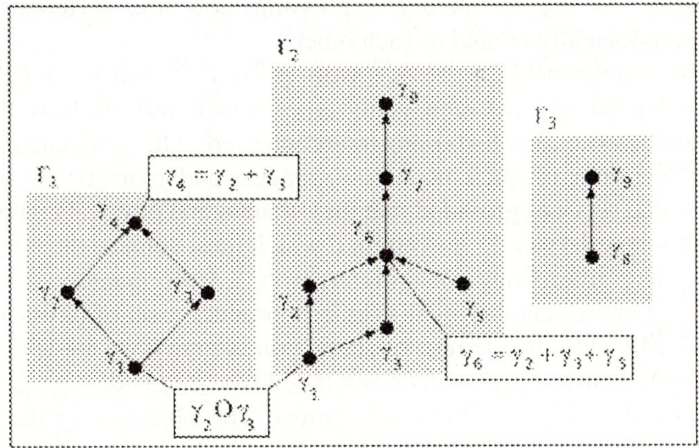

Fig. 1. The Goal Ontologies

2.2   The Fusion Process of Goal Ontologies

As a crucial topic, information exchange between functional hierarchies must occur in a semantically sound manner. Major works stem from the idea that a classification of information (types versus tokens) must exist in each of the components of a distributed system [1], [9]. Of particular relevance for us is the work in Information Flow (IF) and its application to context-dependent reasoning. Therefore, we follow the IF mathematical model which describes the information flow in a distributed system. It is based on the understanding that the information flow results from spacio-temporal connections of event tokens in the system. Classifications are connected via infomorphisms. The basic construct of channel theory is that of an *IF channel* between two IF classifications which models the information flow between components. Local logics express physical constraints through Gentzen sequents. Therefore there is a need to consider distributed IF logics of IF channels. Recent IF-based works such as [14] which tackle the ontology coordination problem have demonstrated that IF channels can accommodate with ontological descriptions. IF theory describes how information can flow through channels to convey new information under first order logic. Reasoning about goals is based on their extensional properties, i.e., on their physical context tokens, namely c_i. The semantic integration of goal types from separate systems is achieved through a process including several steps. This process described in [8], uses IF classifications where the classification relation is in fact a subsumption relation. We have extent this work to goal hierarchies where the classification relation expresses the functional dependency. The reader is supposed to be familiar with the IF formalism and notations (for a deeper understanding of channel theory, see [1]).

Given multiple functional hierarchies $F_i^{(0)}$ ... $F_j^{(k)}$ in a distributed application, where 0 stands for the requesting computing system, k for the remote one, and i, j, for the respective services S_i, S_j on these systems, an IF theory can be computed on the core resulting from the disjoint union of hierarchies. The semantic interoperability of hierarchies relies on the IF theory expressing how the different types from classifications are logically related to each other.

For example, a sequent like $\gamma_q^{(k)} \vdash \gamma_p^{(0)}$ with $\gamma_p^{(0)} \in F_i^{(0)}$ and $\gamma_q^{(k)} \in F_j^{(k)}$ represents the functional dependency between goals types which reflects how the tokens of different hierarchies (i.e., contexts) are interconnected. The associated core logic is distributed on the sum of each node (co-product) and extracts all goal sequents between distributed services provided that they share some physical context(s) [6].

Let us begin with a service S_i, on system 0 which must achieve the purpose referred by its related goal γ_i and its functional hierarchy $F_i^{(0)}$. Unfortunately, to complete this goal, the service requires another goal(s) able to produce a set of physical contexts c_i, .with $1 \leq i \leq n$. In addition, the remote service on system k we are looking for, must include goal type(s) such as $\gamma_q^{(k)} = (\{to\_send\}, \xi_i)$ where c_i is of type ξ_i, and $\gamma_r^{(k)} \vdash \ldots$ since it must satisfy additional local constraints. The objective of the composition process is to demonstrate that the requesting system (i.e., $F_i^{(0)}$), is able to automatically select the appropriate goal from the remote system (i.e., $F_j^{(k)}$), to complete its task (in the case of different ontologies, it requires first an ontology alignment).

From the goal hierarchies, we can derive the IF theories for each potential service. The theory for each service is divided in two parts, a set Σ_h covering syntactical constraints with respect to the ontological relations (see def. 4) and a set Σ_s describing semantic constraints within a given application. The goal types are classified on the basis of their physical context (extensional). In order to construct the IF channel, we must first extract from each potential hierarchy the physical context that matches the required pattern. This equivalence can be formalized with a classification M such as $|typ(M)| = n$. The types $\{ \alpha, \beta, \ldots \}$ of classification M represents the common domain of physical contexts (i.e., the partial alignment) and all their possible tokens. To relate the physical context classification with the goal classification it is useful to introduce the flip of goal classifications where flipping amounts to interchanging rows and columns. In order to satisfy the context correspondences, the flips of classifications $F_i^{(0)\perp}$ ..., $F_j^{(k)\perp}$ are introduced, which give rise to the respective couples of infomorphisms $\zeta_i^{(0)}$, ... $\zeta_{sj}^{(k)}$.

Each pair of channels $F_i^{(0)\perp}$ -M- $F_j^{(k)\perp}$ capture the information flow of the context alignment. The partial alignment of physical contexts is performed through the classification M where relations such as $\zeta_i^{(0)\wedge}(\alpha) = c_p^{(0)}$ and $\zeta_j^{(k)\wedge}(\alpha) = c_q^{(k)}$ mean that $c_p^{(0)}$ and $c_q^{(k)}$ represent identical types in the respective classifications $F_i^{(0)\perp}$ and $F_j^{(k)\perp}$. Given the flips of classifications and the type functions $\zeta_i^{(0)\wedge}$ and $\zeta_j^{(k)\wedge}$, we are able to express the token functions $\zeta_i^{(0)\vee}$, $\zeta_j^{(k)\vee}$ since they must verify the fundamental property of infomorphisms (see [1]). To express how the high level goal type from the classification $F_i^{(0)}$ can be related to a classification $F_j^{(k)}$, we introduce the conjunctive power for the flips $F_i^{(0)\perp}$ and $F_j^{(k)\perp}$, namely $\wedge F_i^{(0)\perp}$ and $\wedge F_j^{(k)\perp}$. The conjunctive power classifies goal types to sets of physical contexts whenever their entire context is in the set. This gives rise to conjunction infomorphisms:

$$\kappa_i^{(0)}: F_i^{(0)\perp} \to \wedge F_i^{(0)\perp} \text{ and } \kappa_j^{(k)}: F_j^{(k)\perp} \to \wedge F_j^{(k)\perp}$$

Finally, the information flow between the requesting classification (i.e., $F_i^{(0)}$) and potential candidate classifications (i.e., $F_j^{(k)}$), is captured by the colimit of the distributed system, that is the resulting classification C with the pair of infomorphisms:

$$g_i^{(0)}: \wedge F_i^{(0)\perp} \to C \text{ and } g_j^{(k)}: \wedge F_j^{(k)\perp} \to C$$

The types of the classification in C are elements of the disjoint union of types from $\wedge F_i^{(0)\perp}$ and $\wedge F_j^{(k)\perp}$ and the tokens are pairs of goal types $(\gamma_p^{(0)}, \gamma_q^{(k)})$. A token of $\wedge F_i^{(0)\perp}$ is connected to a token of $\wedge F_j^{(k)\perp}$ to form the pair $(\gamma_p^{(0)}, \gamma_q^{(k)})$ iff $\zeta_i^{(0)\vee}(\gamma_p^{(0)})$ and $\zeta_j^{(k)\vee}(\gamma_q^{(k)})$ are of the same type in M.

The IF classification on the core results from the distributed classifications. It captures both goal capabilities and the identification of some physical contexts. The sequents of the IF theory on the core are restricted to those sequents which respect

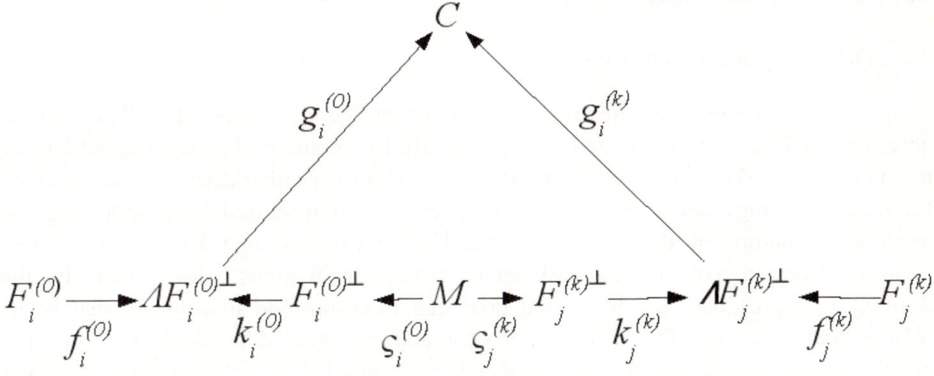

Fig. 2. Construction of the core channel from classifications

goal capabilities and physical contexts identifications. Given the logic $Log(C)=$ L on the core C, the distributed logic $DLog_c$ (L) on the sum of goal hierarchies $F_i^{(0)} + F_j^{(k)}$ is the inverse image of $Log(C)$ on this sum. The logic is guaranteed to be sound on those tokens of the sum that are sequences of projections of a normal token of the logic in C. In other words, the inverse image of IF logic in C is the result of the co-product of $F_i^{(0)}$ and $F_j^{(k)}$ with the morphism $[f_i^{(0)} \circ g_i^{(0)}, f_j^{(k)} \circ g_j^{(k)}]^{-1}$. We obtain sequents like $\gamma_p^{(0)}$, $\gamma_q^{(k)}$ relating goal(s) on remote systems to the local goal(s). From here it is straightforward to extend goal dependencies to dependencies between higher-level goal, and finally between distributed services. A scenario-based example with a full description of this process is available in [5].

3   The Goal Fusion with MAS

3.3   The MAS Features

Agent-based systems are of increasing importance. They are regarded as a new paradigm enabling an important step forward in empirical sciences, technology and theory. Cooperative agents can be equipped with different properties which do not all appear to be necessary or useful in every application, such as Autonomous Behavior, Cooperative ability, Intelligent or Emergent Behavior. Multi-Agents Systems (MAS) models are considered as programming paradigms as well as implementation models for complex information processing systems. More precisely, in distributed systems, the MAS paradigm is often useful, since each agent is able to locally process data and exchange only high-level information with other parts. Savings in bandwidth and transmission times are important features of such an architecture.

In this paper, we will exploit the high-level and dynamic nature of multi-agent interactions which is appropriate to open systems where the constituent components and their interaction patterns are continuously changing. The IF-based mechanism of searching for goal dependencies is typically that of distributed problem solving systems, where the component agents are explicitly designed to cooperatively achieve a given goal. Modularity is achieved by delegating control to autonomous components which can better handle the dynamics of the complex environment and can reduce their interdependencies.

3.2   The MAS Implementation

A variety of architectures are available for multi-agent systems [16]. The method described in §2.2 is implemented through the BDI formalism [12], each agent having its own knowledge base. This architecture exhibits deliberative reasoning (feed forward, planning) while its version includes here a modified loop reflecting the teleological nature of the formal model. Unlike the classical BDI model where goalsare deduced from beliefs, we derive beliefs from goals. More precisely, the desires are represented by the global goal that is committed to achieve, that is, its related goal ontology. The IF-based process acquires goal dependencies from other agents. As a consequence, the belief set is represented by the set of influencing goals since its is an expression of the teleological knowledge. The ongoing work turns out to map goals onto computational resources and we must consider the temporal constraints which is not the case in major of planning's models and the problem become more complex. This knowledge reflects the intentions, that is the intended sequences of actions in order to achieve the above sequence of goals. The agent implementation of the dependency search is detailed below in the algorithm and summarized in fig 3.

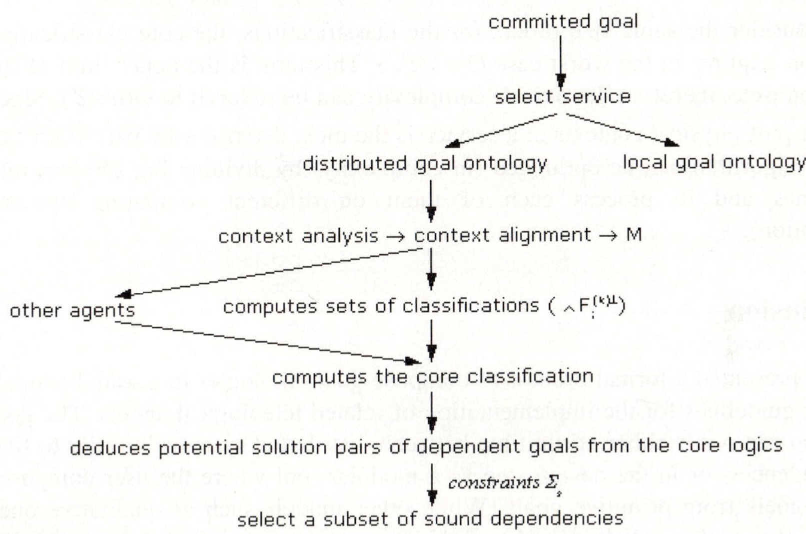


```
Begin : ' to achieve service Γᵢ ' in System (0),
   If (Γᵢ is not achievable locally), Then,
       Agent0 (A₀) gets the ontology (Fᵢ⁽⁰⁾ ) of Γi.
       A₀ derives the IF theory of Γi.
       A₀ forms the IF classification of Γi
       A₀ extracts the physical context cᵢ and generates M
       A₀ broadcasts a request to all agents working with typ(cᵢ ).
   If (no agent answers) Then service aborted
   Else,
       A₀ identifies the candidate agents Aₖ .
       A₀ builds a classification .
       A₀ computes the flip of Fᵢ⁽⁰⁾: Fᵢ⁽⁰⁾⊥, and ∧Fᵢ⁽⁰⁾⊥ .
       Aₖ computes the flip of Fⱼ⁽ᵏ⁾: Fⱼ⁽ᵏ⁾⊥ and ∧Fⱼ⁽ᵏ⁾⊥ .
       A₀ merges the results of Aₖ,, builds the classification C .
       //Tokens of C are pairs of goal types (γₚ⁽⁰⁾ , γ_q⁽ᵏ⁾) and types
are elements of the disjoint union of types from ∧Fᵢ⁽⁰⁾⊥ and ∧Fⱼ⁽ᵏ⁾⊥
       If γₚ⁽⁰⁾ , γ_q⁽ᵏ⁾ are of the same type in M,
       Then, A₀ computes Log(C), connects (γₚ⁽⁰⁾ , γ_q⁽ᵏ⁾), and
deduces the distributed logic.
       A₀ applies the constraints Σₛ for goal selection.
End: Fusion of the ontologies of the local goal with the remote one.
```

Fig. 3. The Fusion Algorithm

The algorithm complexity depends on the significant phases. The context analysis and alignment is not significant. The computation of classifications is O(nK(p)) with n, the number of goal types and p, the number of physical contexts in a service. The value of K(p) results from the conjunctive power of classifications and we have obviously

$$K(p) = \sum_{p'=1}^{p} \binom{p}{p'}. \text{ It is also trivial to see that : } K(p) = \sum_{p'=1}^{p} \binom{p}{p'} < \sum_{p'=0}^{p} \binom{p}{p'} = 2^p .$$

If we consider the same size orders for the classifications, the core classification computation requires in the worst case $O(n^2 \times 2^{p+1})$. This term is the upper limit of the computation time, therefore the overall complexity can be reduced to $O(n^2 \times 2^p)$. Since the number p of physical contexts in a service is the most deterministic part $(O(n^2) \subset O(2^n))$, the algorithm can be optimized (in complexity) by dividing big services into smaller ones and to process each of them on different computing systems (parallelization).

4 Conclusion

This paper presented a formal process to compose goal ontologies in a sound manner with major guidelines for the implementation of related teleological agents. The goal composition can occur either at run-time between distributed systems in order to find goal dependencies or in the design step as a modular tool where the user composes high-level goals from primitive goals. While other models such as qualitative ones (either causal models or abstraction hierarchies) generates spurious solutions, the IF-based approach avoids this problem through the use of sound distributed logics. Such a process must not be considered as a simple pattern matching process, since the resulting goal dependencies must respect the sum of the local logics both on the syntactic and the semantic level.

The agent specification meant to be simple enough to be used in the development of reusable and maintainable agent architectures for agent-oriented systems in engineering environments. The notion of dependence between agents is a challenging problem [2]. Some authors have proposed a graph structure to formalize the relationships between agents [15]. In this work, the IF-based approach tackles the problem of building these dependencies from distributed logics. The dependences are dynamic and their types of are AND-based. Concerning the ongoing work, the behavioral model based on the Event Calculus maps each goal to possible actions guarded with pre-conditions (we clearly separate goals from their way of achievement). The more adapted architecture for this step is the hybrid architecture combining deliberative and reactive reasoning. The reactive part is necessary since it allows re-planning in case of failure during the execution phase. We plan the MAS implementation with the Cognitive Agent Architecture (Cougaar) with the mechanisms for building distributed agent systems, it provides a rich variety of common services to simplify agent development and deployment. Cougaar seems a good compromise.

References

1. Barwise J., Seligman J.: Information Flow. Cambridge tracts in Theoretical Computer Science, 44, (1997) Cambridge University Press.
2. Castefranchi C., Cesta A., Miceli M.: Dependence Realtions in Multi-agent systems. In Y. Demazeau and E. Werner eds., Decentralized AI, Elsevier (1992)
3. Dapoigny R., Benoit E., Foulloy L.: Functional Ontology for Intelligent Instruments.Foundations of Intelligent Systems. LNAI 2871 (Springer) (2003) pp 88–92
4. Dapoigny R., Barlatier P., Benoit E., Foulloy L.: Formal Goal generation for Intel-ligent Control systems. 18th International Conference on Industrial & Engineering Applications of Artificial Intelligence & Expert Systems LNAI 3533 Springer (2005) pp. 712-721
5. Dapoigny R., Barlatier P., Mellal N., Benoit E., Foulloy L.: Inferential Knowledge Sharing with Goal Hierarchies in Distributed Engineering Systems. Procs. of IIAI'05, Pune (India) (2005)
6. Dapoigny R., Barlatier P., Benoit E., Foulloy L.: Formal Goal generation for Intelligient Control systems. 18th International Conference on Industrial & Engineering Applications of Artificial Intelligence & Expert Systems. LNAI 3533 Springer (2005) pp 712-721.
7. Dapoigny R., Barlatier P., Mellal N., Benoit E., Foulloy L., Goal integration for service inter-operability of engineering systems, Int. Conf. on Conceptual Structures (ICCS 2005), Kassel, de, July 2005, pp. 201-202
8. Ganter B., Wille R.: Formal concept analysis - mathematical foundations. (1999) Springer
9. Hertzberg J., Thiebaux S.: Turning an Action Formalism into a Planner:a case Study. Journal of Logic and Computation, 4, (1994) pp 617-654
10. Kent R.E.: Distributed Conceptual Structures. The relational methods in Computer Science, LNCS 2561, pp 104-123, (2002)
11. Lifschitz V.: A Theory of Actions. Procs. of the tenth International Joint Conference on Artificial Intelligence, Morgan Kaufmann eds., (1993) pp 432-437
12. Lind M.: Modeling Goals and Functions of Complex Industrial Plant.Journal of Applied Artificial Intelligence 8 (1994) pp 259–283
13. Rao A.S., and Georgeff M.P. : BDI Agents: from Theory to Practice. In Procs. of the 1rst Int. Conf. on Multi-agent Systems (ICMAS'95) pp 312--319 (1995)
14. Schätz B.: Towards Service-based Systems Engineering: Formalizing and checking service specifications, Tech. Report TUMI-0602 München (2002)
15. Schorlemmer M., Kalfoglou Y.: Using information-flow theory to enable semantic interoperability. In 6e Congres Catala en Intelligencia Artificial, Palma de Mallorca, Spain, (2003)
16. Sichman J.S., Conte R. : Multi-Agent Dependence by Dependence Graphs. Procs. of AAMAS'02 pp 483--490 (2002)
17. Zambonelli F. Jennings N.R., Wooldridge M. : Developing MultiAgent Systems: The Gaia Methodology. ACM Transactions on Software Engineering and Methodology, 12(3), (2003), pp 317–370.

Agent-Based Approach to Solving Difficult Scheduling Problems

Joanna Jędrzejowicz[1] and Piotr Jędrzejowicz[2]

[1] Institute of Mathematics, Gdańsk University,
Wita Stwosza 57, 80-952 Gdańsk, Poland
`jj@math.univ.gda.pl`
[2] Department of Information Systems, Gdynia Maritime University,
Morska 83, 81-225 Gdynia, Poland
`pj@am.gdynia.pl`

Abstract. The paper proposes a variant of the A-Team architecture called PLA-Team. An A-Team is a problem solving architecture in which the agents are autonomous and co-operate by modifying one another's trial solutions. A PLA-Team differs from other A-Teams with respect to strategy of generating and destroying solutions kept in the common memory. The proposed PLA-Team performance is evaluated basing on computational experiments involving benchmark instances of two well known combinatorial optimization problems - flow shop and job-shop scheduling. Solutions generated by the PLA-Team are compared with those produced by state-of-the-arts algorithms.

1 Introduction

Recently, a number of agent-based approaches have been proposed to solve different types of optimization problems [8]. One of the successful approaches to agent-based optimization is the concept of A-Teams. An A-Team is composed of simple agents that demonstrate complex collective behavior.

The A-Team architecture was originally developed by Talukdar [13]. A-Teams have proven to be successful in addressing hard optimization problems where no dominant algorithm exists. Within the A-Team multiple agents achieve an implicit cooperation by sharing a population of solutions. The design of the A-Team architecture was motivated by other architectures used for optimization including blackboard systems and genetic algorithms. In fact, the A-Team infrastructure could be used to implement most aspects of these other architectures. The advantage of the A-Team architecture is that it combines a population of solutions with domain specific algorithms and limited agent interaction. In addition, rich solution evaluation metrics tend to result in a more diverse set of solutions [9].

According to [13] an A-Team is a problem solving architecture in which the agents are autonomous and co-operate by modifying one another's trial solutions. These solutions circulate continually. An A-Team can be also defined as a set of

M. Ali and R. Dapoigny (Eds.): IEA/AIE 2006, LNAI 4031, pp. 24–33, 2006.

agents and a set of memories, forming a network in which every agent is in a closed loop.

An asynchronous team (A-Team) is a strongly cyclic computational network. Results are circulated through this network by software agents. The number of agents can be arbitrarily large and the agents may be distributed over an arbitrarily wide area. Agents cooperate by working on one another's results. Each agent is completely autonomous (it decides which results it is going to work on and when). Results that are not being worked on accumulate in common memories to form populations. Randomization (the effects of chance) and destruction (the elimination of weak results) play key roles in determining what happens to the populations.

A-Team architecture allows a lot of freedom with respect to designing procedures for communication between agents and shared memories as well as creation and removal of individuals (solution) from common memories. In this paper an approach to construct a team of agents, further on referred to as a PLA-Team, is proposed and validated. The approach makes use of the idea which has been conceived for the population learning algorithm. An effective search for a solution of computationally hard problems requires a cocktail of methods applied to a population of solutions, with more advanced procedures being applied only to more promising population members. Designing and implementing a PLA-Team is seen as an extension of the range of available agent-based optimization tools.

In Section 2 of the paper, a PLA-Team architecture is described and some details of the proposed approach are given. In Sections 3 and 4 experiment results are reported. The approach has been used to solve benchmark instances of the two well known and difficult combinatorial problems: the flow shop and job-shop scheduling. The solutions obtained by the proposed PLA-Team are compared with the performance of state-of-the-art algorithms including parallel ones. The conclusions contain an evaluation of the proposed approach and some suggestions for future research.

2   The Proposed Agent-Based Approach

The proposed agent-based approach is a variant of the A-Team architecture. Its origin can be traced to the idea of the population learning algorithm (PLA) and hence it is further on called the PLA-Team. Population learning algorithm was proposed in [4] as yet another population-based method, which can be applied to support solving difficult decision-making and optimization problems. Thus far PLA has been effectively applied to solving a variety of difficult scheduling problems. The algorithm has proven successful in finding better lower bounds than previously known for numerous instances of benchmark problems maintained in the OR-LIBRARY (`http://people.brunel.ac.uk/~mastjjb/jeb/info.html`) including, for example permutation flowshop scheduling, due-date scheduling or task scheduling on a single machine with total weighted tardiness as a criterion [5], [6]. The algorithm proved also successful in the domain of ANN training [3], producing high quality neural networks in a competitive time. The computational intelligence embedded within a population learning algorithm scheme is based on the following heuristic rules:

- To solve difficult computational problems use agents applying a cocktail of methods and techniques including random and local search techniques, greedy and construction algorithms, etc., building upon their strengths and masking weaknesses.
- To escape getting trapped in a local optimum generate or construct an initial population of solutions called individuals, which in the following stages will be improved, thus increasing chances for reaching a global optimum. Another mean of avoiding getting trapped in local optima is to apply, at various stages of search for a global optimum, some random diversification algorithms.
- To increase effectiveness of searching for a global optimum divide the process into stages retaining after each stage only a part of the population consisting of "better" or "more promising" individuals. Another mean for increasing effectiveness is to use at early stages of search improvement algorithms with lower computational complexity as compared to those used at final stages.

Although PLA has been producing high quality solutions its main disadvantage is, in most cases, an extensive demand for the computational power resulting in long computation times. To increase efficiency of the approach a parallel version of the PLA was proposed [3]. The parallel PLA is based on the co-operation between the master agent (server) whose task is to manage computations and a number of agents - autonomous PLA processes, who act in parallel. A set of the following rules governs the PLA:

- Master agent defines the number of working agents and the size of the initial population for each of them.
- Each working agent uses the same, described earlier, learning and improvement procedures.
- Master agent activates a parallel processing.
- After completing each stage agents inform master agent about the best solution found so far.
- Master agent compares the received values and sends out the best solution to all agents replacing their current worst solution.
- Master agent can stop computations if the desired quality level of the objective function has been achieved. Alternatively, computations are stopped after the predefined number of iterations at each PLA stage, has been executed.
- Each working agent can also stop computations if the above condition has been met.

The approach suggested in this paper uses a similar parallel architecture with different rules for communication between a variety of learning and improvement procedures employed to find a solution. The idea is to use identical procedures as in case of "classic" PLA with different agent roles and functionalities. This time an agent is not necessarily a complete PLA implementation but rather a simple local search procedure, a metaheuristic, or even a set of agents, aiming to find a solution to a problem at hand and representing one of the original PLA procedures.

The proposed team of agents consists of a number of autonomous and asynchronous agents of n kinds, where n is a number of learning and improvement procedures employed. The number of agents of each kind is not limited and depends on the availability of computational resources. There is, however an identical number of agents of each kind within a population of agents. An additional element of the proposed system is a common memory which contains a number of individuals representing feasible solutions to the problem at hand. Each agent acts independently executing a sequence of computation steps. A single computation step for an agent includes the following:

- Copying a number of individuals from the common memory, which is represented as a list of randomly generated individuals (feasible solutions). Individuals in the discussed examples are either permutations of jobs or permutations of tasks.
- Executing learning and improvement procedure upon thus drawn individuals.
- Returning the improved individuals to the common memory through discarding worst individuals in the common memory and replacing them with the improved ones.

There is no master agent nor any centralized control. Stopping condition for a group of agents working as a PLA-Team is set beforehand by the user. It could be either an amount of time the agents are allowed to work or a number of common memory calls performed by a selected agent.

It should be noted that within the proposed approach, the main idea of PLA, which is using more computationally complex learning/improvement procedures as a number of individuals within the population of solutions decreases is, indirectly, preserved. This is achieved through setting agent properties during its fine-tuning. Each agent, notwithstanding which local search procedure or metaheuristic it uses, is set to execute a similar number of evaluations of the goal function and hence, performing a single computation step in a comparable time. The number of evaluations of the goal function is controlled by allocating to an agent a number of individuals (solutions), which are drawn from the common memory and which an agent tries to improve at a given computation step. Consequently agents executing more computationally complex learning and improvement procedures would be drawing, at a single step, less individuals than agents executing less complex procedures. General scheme of the PLA-Team is shown in the following pseudo-code:

```
PLA-Team
begin
Initialize the common memory by using a random mechanism to produce
P individuals (here feasible solutions of the problem at hand);
Set within a parallel and distributed environment n×m agents, where
n is a number of improvement procedures employed and m is a number
of agents of each kind;
For each agent kind set a number of individuals that an agent can draw
in a single step from the common memory to assure a comparable number
of the goal function evaluations in a single computation step;
repeat for each agent
Draw randomly the allowed number of individuals from P and copy them
into working memory;
Improve individuals in the working memory by executing learning and
improvement procedures;
Replace worse individuals in P by comparing pair-wise best-one currently
produced with the currently worst-one in P, second best-one produced
with the currently second worst-one in P, etc.
After each comparison an individual from P is replaced by the improved
one if the latter is better;
until stopping criterion is met
Select best individual from P as a solution
end
```

3   Flowshop Scheduling Using a PLA-Team Architecture

In the permutation flowshop scheduling problem (PFSP) there is a set of n jobs. Each of n jobs has to be processed on m machines in the order $1 \ldots m$. The processing time of job i on machine j is p_{ij} where p_{ij} are fixed and nonnegative. At any time, each job can be processed on at most one machine, and each machine can process at most one job. The jobs are available at time 0 and the processing of a job may not be interrupted. In the PFSP the job order is the same on every machine. The objective is to find a job sequence minimizing schedule makespan (i.e., completion time of the last job).

The PLA-Team applied to solving the PFSP instances makes use of the standard evolutionary algorithm with a cross-over and mutation, tabu search and simulated annealing. The above learning and improvement procedures have been previously used by the authors within the PLA implementation. A detailed description of these procedures can be found in [6]. Problem instances are represented as text files in exactly the same format as they appear in the OR-LIBRARY.

The computational experiment was designed to compare the performance of the PLA-Team with other state-of-the art techniques. It has been decided to follow the experiment plan of [11] to assure comparability. The experiment involving PLA has been carried on a PC computer with the 2.4 GHz Pentium 4 processor and 512 MB RAM. The PLA-Team consisted of 3 agents working in a parallel environment on a cluster of 3 PC computers with P4 1.9 GHz processors

Table 1. The average deviation from the currently known upper bound (%)

instance	NEHT	GA	HGA	SAOP	SPIRIT	GAR	GAMIT	PLA	PLA-Team
20 × 5	3.35	0.29	0.20	1.47	5.22	0.71	3.28	0.03	**0.00**
20 × 10	5.02	0.95	0.55	2.57	5.86	1.97	5.53	0.58	**0.32**
20 × 20	3.73	0.56	0.39	2.22	4.58	1.48	4.33	0.42	**0.26**
50 × 5	0.84	0.07	0.06	0.52	2.03	0.23	1.96	0.07	**0.03**
50 × 10	5.12	1.91	1.72	3.65	5.88	2.47	6.25	0.77	**0.71**
50 × 20	6.20	3.05	2.64	4.97	7.21	3.89	7.53	1.67	**1.62**
100 × 5	0.46	0.10	0.08	0.42	1.06	0.18	1.33	0.03	**0.01**
100 × 10	2.13	0.84	0.70	1.73	5.07	1.06	3.66	0.72	**0.52**
100 × 20	5.11	3.12	2.75	4.90	10.15	3.84	9.70	1.09	**1.35**
200 × 10	1.43	0.54	0.50	1.33	9.03	0.85	6.47	0.56	**0.41**
200 × 20	4.37	2.88	2.59	4.40	16.17	3.47	14.56	1.05	**1.04**
500 × 20	2.24	1.65	1.56	3.48	13.57	1.98	12.47	1.13	**1.09**
Average	3.33	1.33	1.15	2.64	7.15	1.84	6.42	0.68	**0.61**

with 512 MB RAM. The results obtained by applying the PLA and the PLA-Team are compared with the following results reported in [11]: NEHT - the NEH heuristic with the enhancements, GA - the genetic algorithm, HGA - the hybrid genetic algorithm, SAOP - the simulated annealing algorithm, SPIRIT - the tabu search, GAR - another genetic algorithm and GAMIT - the hybrid genetic algorithm.

For evaluating the different algorithms the average deviation from the currently known upper bound is used. Every algorithm has been run to solve all 120 benchmark instances from the OR-LIBRARY and the data from a total of 10 independent runs have been finally averaged. As a stopping criteria all algorithms have been allocated 30 seconds for instances with 500 jobs, 12 seconds for instances with 200 jobs, 6 seconds for instances with 100 jobs, 3 seconds for instances with 50 jobs and 1.2 seconds for instances with 20 jobs. In case of the PLA-Team common memory included 100 individuals, the evolutionary algorithm was allowed to draw 50 instances in each computation step, the tabu search algorithm - 20 instances and the simulated annealing - 10 instances. PLA-Team was iterating until the allowed time has elapsed. The results obtained for all 120 instances from the OR-LIBRARY benchmark sets averaged over 10 runs are shown in Table 1.

PLA-Team does also outperform the state of the art ant-colony algorithms reported in [10]. These authors propose two ant colony algorithms M-MMAS and PACO. Both are generating 40 ant-sequences and use some local search algorithms to improve solutions. M-MMAS reportedly required less than one hour of computational time on a Pentium 3 computer with 800 MHz for solving all 20, 50 and 100 job instances from the OR-Library. It is worth noting that the PLA-Team required 306 seconds for the same task, albeit using the above described cluster of 3 Pentium 4 computers. Comparison of the ant-colony algorithms and the PLA-Team are shown in Table 2. PLA-Team worked using the same settings as previously reported. Data for M-MMAS and PACO are taken from [10].

Table 2. The average deviation from the currently known upper bound (%)

instance	M-MMAS	PACO	PLA-Team
20 × 5	3.35	0.29	**0.00**
20 × 10	5.02	0.95	**0.32**
20 × 20	3.73	0.56	**0.26**
50 × 5	0.84	0.07	**0.03**
50 × 10	5.12	1.91	**0.71**
50 × 20	6.20	3.05	**1.62**
100 × 5	0.46	0.10	**0.01**
100 × 10	2.13	0.84	**0.52**
100 × 20	5.11	3.12	**1.35**

From the experiment results it can be easily observed that PLA-Team can be considered as a useful state-of-the-art tool for the permutation flowshop scheduling.

4   Job-Shop Scheduling Using a PLA-Team Architecture

An instance of the job-shop scheduling problem consists of a set of n jobs and m machines. Each job consists of a sequence of n activities so there are $n \times m$ activities in total. Each activity has a duration and requires a single machine for its entire duration. The activities within a single job all require a different machine. An activity must be scheduled before every activity following it in its job. Two activities cannot be scheduled at the same time if they both require the same machine. The objective is to find a schedule that minimizes the overall completion time of all the activities.

In this paper a permutation version of the job-shop scheduling problem is used. That is, given an instance of the job-shop scheduling problem, a solution is a permutation of jobs for each machine defining in a unique manner a sequence of activities to be processed on this machine. For a problem consisting of a set of n jobs and m machines a solution is a set of m permutations of n elements each. A feasible solution obeys all the problem constraints including precedence constraints.

The PLA-Team applied to solving the job-shop scheduling problem instances makes use of the standard evolutionary algorithm with a cross-over and mutation, the tabu search and the simulated annealing. The above learning and improvement procedures are exactly the same as in case of the permutation flow shop described in previous section.

The computational experiment carried out was designed to compare the performance of the PLA-Team with other approaches including agent-based or distributed algorithms. The PLA-Team again consisted of 3 agents, one for each of the learning and improvement procedures used, working in a parallel environment on a cluster of 3 PC computers with P4 1.9 GHz processors with 512 MB RAM. In Table 3 the results obtained by PLA-Team are compared with the

Table 3. PLA-team versus A-team

	A-Team			PLA-Team		
	Av.result	St. dev.	Av. deviat.	Av.result	St. dev.	Av. deviat.
FT10	958.40	12.35	3.05%	952.00	0.00	**2.37 %**
ABZ5	1238.00	0.00	0.00%	1221.00	0.00	**-1.05%**
ABZ6	948.00	0.00	0.53%	943.00	0.00	**0.00%**
LA16	949.75	6.50	0.50%	964.20	4.66	**2.03%**
LA17	787.00	0.00	0.38%	792.00	0.00	**1.02%**
LA18	856.67	6.13	1.02%	854.75	2.25	**0.79%**
LA19	852.00	9.09	1.19%	850.50	1.50	**1.01%**
LA20	906.67	3.68	0.52%	907.00	0.00	**0.55%**
ORB1	1108.00	11.43	4.63%	1080.00	0.00	**1.98%**
Average	-	5.46	1.31%	-	0.93	**0.96%**

A-Team results of [1] on a set of 10×10 instances from the OR-LIBRARY. These results have been generated by a team consisting of agents using two variants of the simulated annealing, three variants of the tabu search, two variants of the hill climbing algorithm and a genetic algorithm plus a destroying server. A-team was allowed to work until 10,000,000 evaluations with a population size of 500. In case of the PLA-Team common memory included 100 individuals, the evolutionary algorithm was allowed to draw 30 instances in each computation step, the tabu search algorithm 10 instances and the simulated annealing 5 instances. PLA-Team was allowed to iterate for 30 computation steps of the simulated annealing agent. All results are averaged over 5 independent runs.

A further experiment aimed at comparing the PLA-Team performance with the state of the art algorithms. In this experiment common memory included 50 individuals, the evolutionary algorithm was allowed to draw 15 instances in each computation step, the tabu search algorithm 10 instances and the simulated annealing 5 instances. PLA-Team was allowed to iterate for 10 computation steps of the simulated annealing agent. All results were averaged over 10 independent

Table 4. Average deviation from the optimum (%) and average computation time (s)

	SAT		KTM		KOL		MSA		PLA-Team	
Instan.	Av.dv	Av.t	Av.dv	Av.t	Av.dv	Av.t	Av.dv	Av.t	Av.dv	Av.t
ABZ7	4.55	5991	x	x	x	x	3.08	1445	3.34	521
ABZ8	9.40	5905	x	x	x	x	7.71	1902	10.97	732
ABZ9	7.71	5328	x	x	x	x	7.16	1578	7.68	555
LA21	1.53	1516	0.38	1720	0.48	594	0.23	838	0.57	213
LA24	1.50	1422	0.75	1170	0.58	509	0.49	570	1.08	196
LA25	1.29	1605	0.36	1182	0.20	644	0.08	1035	0.46	387
LA27	2.28	3761	1.00	919	0.76	3650	0.84	982	1.34	396
LA29	5.88	4028	3.83	3042	3.47	4496	4.65	1147	3.98	487
LA38	1.87	3004	1.21	3044	0.54	5049	1.56	1143	1.28	465
LA40	1.72	2812	0.96	6692	0.59	4544	0.59	1894	1.34	630

runs. The PLA-Team performance was compared with a rescheduling based simulated annealing and a tabu search based approach denoted, respectively as SAT and KTM and reported in [12], the hybrid genetic algorithm simulated annealing of [7] denoted KOL, and a parallel modular simulated annealing [1]. Comparison results are shown in Table 4.

It can be observed that the PLA-Team, while not being the best performer among the compared approaches, achieves reasonably good or even good solutions in a competitive time. On the 10×10 set of benchmark instances the PLA-Team has produced consistently very good results.

5   Conclusions

PLA-Team architecture seems to be a useful approach which can produce effective solutions to many computationally hard combinatorial optimization problems. Extensive experiments that have been carried show that:

- A team of agents sharing common memory and solving problem instances using different learning and improvement strategies achieves a synergic effect producing better results than each of the individual procedures could obtain in a comparable time.
- PLA-Team can be considered as a competitive approach as compared with many alternative algorithms.
- Agents co-operating within a PLA-Team demonstrate a complex collective behavior.
- Effectiveness of the proposed approach can be attributed to diversity of learning and improvement procedures, diversification introduced by the population-based approach, parallel computations and a unique strategy of controlling computation cycle time through differentiation of a number of individuals each kind of agents is working with.

The approach needs further investigation. An open question is how will a PLA-Team perform with the increased number of replicated agents and how such systems should be designed. It would be also interesting to introduce some advanced mechanisms allowing a team of agents to escape from local optima. At present the fine-tuning phase of the PLA-Team elements is rather intuitive and should be, in future, based on scientifically established rules.

References

1. Aydin, M.E., Fogarty, T.C.: Teams of autonomous agents for job-shop scheduling problems: An Experimental Study, Journal of Intelligent Manufacturing, 15(4), (2004), 455–462
2. Aydin, M.E., Fogarty, T.C.: A simulated annealing algorithm for multi-agent systems: a job-shop scheduling application, Journal of Intelligent Manufacturing, 15(6), (2004), 805–814

3. Czarnowski, I., Jędrzejowicz, P.: Application of the Parallel Population Learning Algorithm to Training Feed-forward ANN. In: P.Sincak (ed.) Intelligent Technologies - Theory and Applications, IOS Press, Amsterdam, (2002)10–16
4. Jędrzejowicz P.: Social Learning Algorithm as a Tool for Solving Some Difficult Scheduling Problems, Foundation of Computing and Decision Sciences, 24 (1999) 51–66
5. Jędrzejowicz, J., Jędrzejowicz, P.: PLA-Based Permutation Scheduling, Foundations of Computing and Decision Sciences 28(3) (2003) 159–177
6. Jędrzejowicz, J., Jędrzejowicz, P.: New Upper Bounds for the Flowshop Scheduling Problem, In:M. Ali, F. Esposito (ed.)Innovations and Applied Artificial Intelligence, LNAI 3533 (2005),232–235
7. Kolonko, M.: Some new results on simulated annealing applied to job shop scheduling problem, European Journal of Operational Research, 113, (1999), 123–136.
8. Parunak, H. V. D.: Agents in Overalls: Experiences and Issues in the Development and Deployment of Industrial Agent-Based Systems, Intern. J. of Cooperative Information Systems, 9(3) (2000), 209–228
9. Rachlin, J., Goodwin, R., Murthy, S., Akkiraju, R., Wu, F., Kumaran, S., Das, R. : A-Teams: An Agent Architecture for Optimization and Decision-Support J.P. Muller et al. (Eds.): ATAL'98, LNAI 1555 (1999), pp. 261–276
10. Rajendran, Ch., Ziegler, H. : Ant-colony algorithms for permutation flowshop scheduling to minimize makespan/total flowtime of jobs, European Journal of Operational Research 1555(2004) 426–438.
11. Ruiz, R., Maroto, C., Alcaraz, J.: New Genetic Algorithms for the Permutation Flowshop Scheduling Problems, Proc. The Fifth Metaheuristic International Conference, Kyoto, (2003) 63-1–63-8
12. Satake, T., Morikawa, K., Takahashi, K., Nakamura, N. : Simulated annealing approach for minimizing the makespan of the general job-shop, International Journal of Production Economics, 60-61, (1999) 515–522.
13. Talukdar, S., Baerentzen, L., Gove, A., de Souza, P. : Asynchronous Teams: Cooperation Schemes for Autonomous, Computer-Based Agents, Technical Report EDRC 18-59-96, Carnegie Mellon University, Pittsburgh, (1996)

Development of the Multiple Robot Fish Cooperation System

Jinyan Shao, Long Wang, and Junzhi Yu

Center for Systems and Control, Department of Mechanics and Engineering Science
Peking University, Beijing 100871, P.R. China
jyshao@mech.pku.edu.cn

Abstract. In this paper, we present the development of the Multiple Robotic Fish cooperation System (MRFS), which is built on the basis of a series of radio-controlled, multi-link biomimetic fish-like robots designed in our lab. The motivation of this work is that the capability of one single fish robot is often limited while there are many complex missions which should be accomplished by effective cooperation of multiple fish robots. MRFS, as a novel test bed for multiple robotic fish cooperation, can be applied to different types of complex tasks. More importantly, MRFS provides a platform to test and verify the algorithms and strategies for cooperation of multiple underwater mobile robots. We use a disk-pushing task as an example to demonstrate the performance of MRFS.

1   Introduction

In recent years, biomimetic robotics has emerged as a challenging new research topic, which combines bioscience and engineering technology, aiming at developing new classes of robots which will be substantially more compliant and stable than current robots. Taking advantage of new developments in materials, fabrication technologies, sensors and actuators, more and more biologically inspired robots have been developed. As one of the hot topics, robotic fish has received considerable attention during the last decade [1]-[7]. Fish, after a long history's natural selection, have evolved to become the best swimmers in nature. They can achieve tremendous propulsive efficiency and excellent maneuverability with little loss of stability by coordinating their bodies, fins and tails properly. Researchers believe that these remarkable abilities of fish can inspire innovative designs to improve the performance, especially maneuverability and stabilization of underwater robots.

By now, the research on robotic fish mainly focus on design and analysis on individual robot fish prototype, while seldom is concerned with the cooperation behaviors of the fish. As we know, fish in nature often swim in schools to strive against the atrocious circumstances in the sea. Similarly, in practice, the capability of a single robot fish is limited and it will be incompetent for achieving complex missions in dynamic environments. Thus, for real-world (ocean based) applications, a cooperative multiple robot fish system is required, which is the motivation of this work.

In this paper, we provide the development of the Multiple Robot Fish cooperation System (MRFS), which is built on the basis of a series of radio-controlled, multi-link biomimetic robot fish. There are two features in MRFS: first, this cooperative platform

M. Ali and R. Dapoigny (Eds.): IEA/AIE 2006, LNAI 4031, pp. 34–43, 2006.

is general and can be applied to different types of cooperative tasks; second, high-level tasks are eventually decomposed into two reactive motion controllers, which are designed under full consideration on the inertia of fish and the hydrodynamic forces of surrounding water.

The remaining of the paper is organized as follows. In Section 2 we present the establishment of the platform for MRFS. Based on the hardware and software platform, a four-level hierarchical control architecture is provided in Section 3. In Section 4, a cooperative dish-pushing task is used as an example to demonstrate the performance of MRFS and corresponding experimental results are shown. Finally, we conclude the paper and outline some future work in Section 5.

2 Design and Implementation of MRFS Platform

Before introducing MRFS, we first present the robotic fish prototypes developed in our laboratory. Figure 1 shows some of them. For technical details on design and implementation of the robotic fish, the readers are referred to [1] [2]. We can't elaborate on them here due to space limitation.

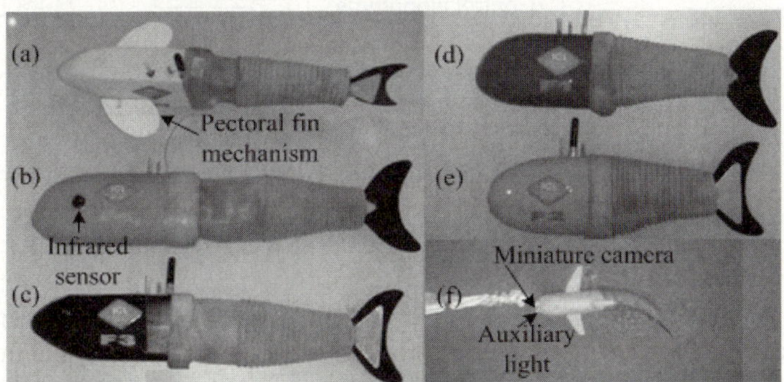

Fig. 1. Prototypes of different robot fishes. (a) Up-down motioned, 3-link robot fish, 380 mm in length. (b) 4-link robot fish with infrared sensors, 450 mm in length. (c) 4-link, 2-D motioned robot fish, 400 mm in length. (d) 3-link, 2-D motioned robot fish, 380 mm in length. (e) 2-link robot fish with infrared sensors, 280 mm in length. (f) 3-link robot fish with miniature wireless camera, 400 mm in length.

As mentioned above, a single fish is often limited both in capabilities and movement range. It will be incompetent for many complex tasks in dynamic environments. In this case, a multi-robot fish cooperative system becomes a desired solution. Inspired by the technology of multi-agent system and the approaches developed for cooperation of ground mobile robots, we establish the hardware platform of MRFS as depicted in Figure 2. The whole system can be decomposed into four subsystems: robot fish subsystem, image capturing subsystem, decision making and control subsystem and wireless communication subsystem.

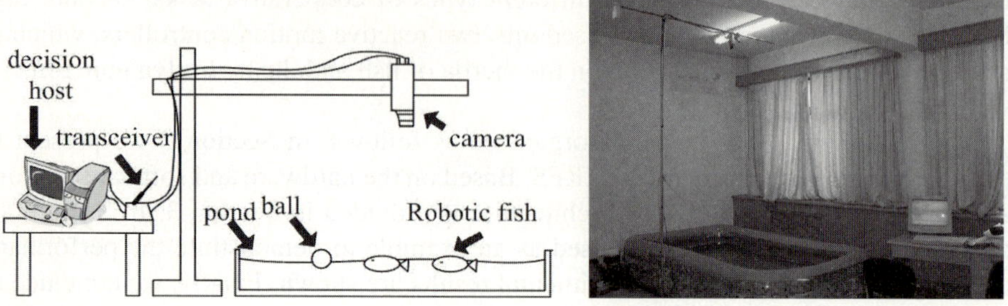

Fig. 2. Hardware platform for MRFS

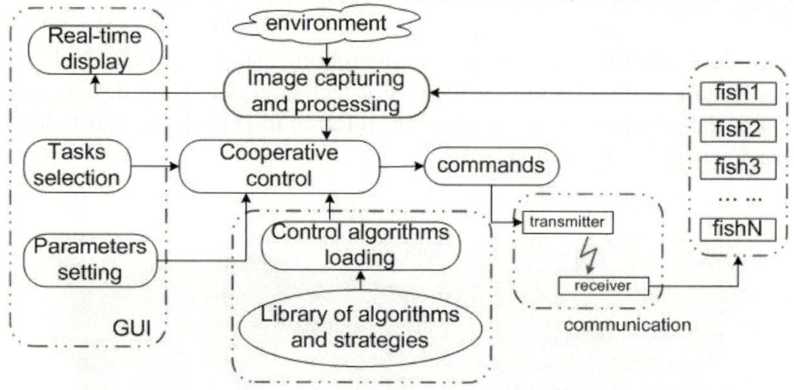

Fig. 3. Architecture of software platform

The information about fish and their surroundings are captured by an overhead camera and after being effectively processed, they are sent to the decision making and control subsystem as inputs. Then, based on input signals and specific control strategies for different tasks, the decision making subsystem produces corresponding control commands and transmits them to every robotic fish through the wireless communication subsystem. Since a global vision is adopted, MRFS should be basically categorized into centralized control system and so global planning and optimization can be obtained as a result.

Based on the hardware architecture, we also develop a task- oriented software platform, on which we can implement various functions associated with cooperative task, such as task selection, environmental parameters setting, real-time display, image processing, control algorithm loading and commands executing.

Figure 3 shows the schematic diagram of the software system architecture. It consists of GUI (Graphics User Interface), image processing module, algorithm module, communication module and fish module. Through GUI, users can choose different tasks, set parameters of environment (goals, obstacles, etc.). In image processing module, a global image information is captured and processed. After that, useful information is abstracted and used for making decision. Algorithm module contains the algorithms and strategies, determining how the fished cooperate with each other. Communication module transmits every control command to the fish module which are the actuators of MRFS.

3 Hierarchical Control Algorithm for Cooperative Applications

In this section, we propose a hierarchical control algorithm for cooperative application on MRFS. A four-level hierarchical architecture is developed: The first level is task planner level. In this level, the required task is decomposed into different roles. During the decomposition, it should be guaranteed that these roles are necessary and sufficient for achieving the task. After producing different roles we should select the most qualified candidate of robotic fish for each role according to some proper rules. Aiming at requirements of different tasks, we introduce both static and dynamic role assignments mechanism. In static assignments, once roles are determined at the beginning of the task, they will not change during the task; while in the dynamic mechanism, the fish may exchange their roles according to the progress of the task. The third level is the action level. In this level, a sequence of actions are designed for each role. By action, we mean an intended movement of fish, such as turning, advancing, and so on. The fourth level, which is called the controller level, is the lowest one. In this controller level, we give a sufficient consideration to some unfavorable factors when control due to the speciality of fish.

- When the fish swims, the interaction between it and its surrounding water will result in resonance at certain frequency. Moreover, the fish can't stop immediately even if the oscillating frequency is set to zero. Hydrodynamic forces and the fish's inertia will make it drift a short distance along its advancing direction.
- In our design, the fish's orientation is controlled by modulating the first two joints' deflection (ϕ_1, ϕ_2). However, it is quite difficult to adjust the deflection accurately, because the drag force produced by surrounding water is an unstructured disturbance and we can't get its precise model.

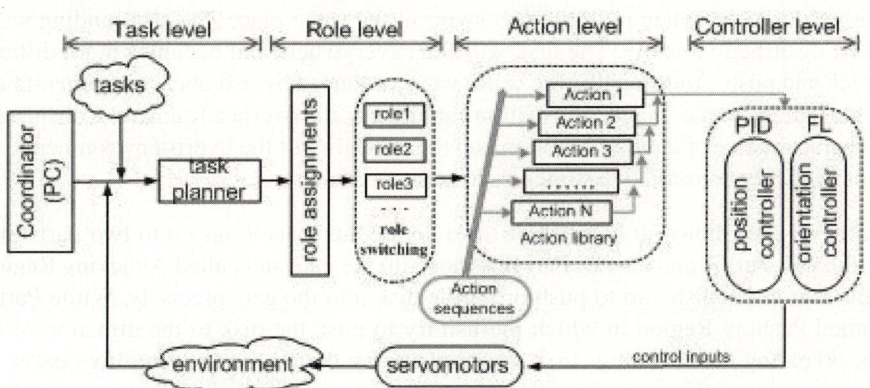

Fig. 4. The block diagram of the hierarchical architecture

Based on the above conditions, we adopt a PID controller for piecewise speed control and a fuzzy logic controller for orientation control, which are presented particularly in our previous work [3].

Figure 4 illustrates the block diagram of cooperative control architecture consisting of four levels.

4   Application: Three-Fish Cooperative Disk-Pushing

In this section, we will utilize a cooperative disk-pushing task to demonstrate the performance of MRFS and the hierarchial control architecture. We conduct the experiments in a swimming tank with three biomimetic robotic fish as shown in Figure 5 (a). There is a 25cm diametical disk floating on the water and a 30cm wide gate in the right side of the tank. The objective for the three fish is to push the disk into the gate.

It seems that this task is quite simple, one fish may be enough to achieve it. In fact, the fish's head is only 40mm wide and the disk drifts with the fluctuant water, it is difficult for a fish to touch and push the disk exactly in the expected point. Moreover, as we mentioned in Section 2, because of its inertia and hydrodynamic forces, the fish can't stop immediately even if the oscillating frequency is set to zero. It will drift along its current direction and thus, overshot occurs. When this happens, the fish must turn back and re-adjust its relative position to the disk, which will take a long time. Additionally, while the fish swims back and adjusts its attitudes, it will inevitably disturb the surrounding water. As a result, the disk may float away before the fish approaches it, which will increase difficulty to the task.

4.1   Cooperative Strategies

In order to push the disk more stably and precisely, the fish are expected to help each other and work cooperatively. However, as the number of the fish increases, more problems may occur. First, because of space limitation, the fish may collide with each other. In order to deal with such circumstance, the fish must adopt some collision avoiding strategies at the same time push the disk, which will debase the performance of cooperation. Moreover, when multiple fish swim in the same place, the surrounding water will be disturbed violently. The disk will float everywhere and becomes more difficult to track and push. Additionally, the water wave produced by fish may cause uncertainty and inaccuracy to the image information captured by the overhead camera. Considering the characteristics of the fish's motion and the speciality of the hydro-environments, we adopt relatively conservative strategies to achieve this task.

Strategy I: As shown in Figure 5 (b), we divide the space (tank) into two parts in X coordinates: Part A and Part B. Part B is closer to the gate and called Attacking Region. in this region, the fish aim to push or hit the disk into the gate precisely. While Part A is called Pushing Region in which the fish try to push the disk to the direction of the gate, preparing for attacking. In Y coordinates, we divide the tank into five parts: I - V, representing different regions that the three fish take charge of. We use such kind of region-responsibility strategy with main intent to avoid collisions between the fish.

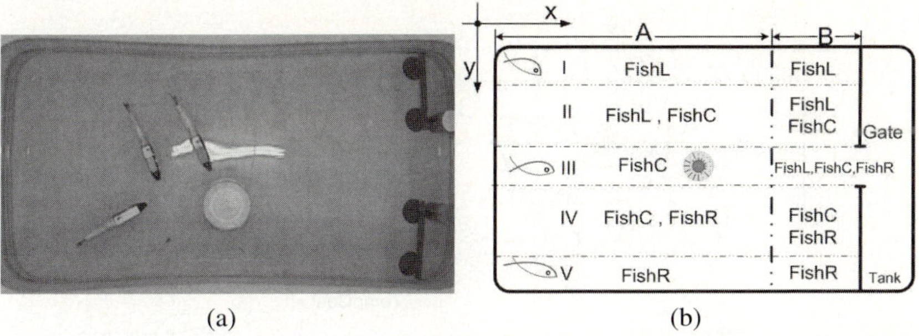

Fig. 5. The experiment setting and region division

For each fish, if the disk is not in the region that it is responsible for. It will still swim restrictively within its region and cannot invade other regions to disturb other fish.

Strategy II: We prefer slowing down than overshooting. When controlling the fish, we intent to slow down the fish to some extent, especially when it approaches the disk.

Strategy III: As we mentioned, the fish can't stop immediately even you send stop command. It will drift a short distance out of control. So, in practice, even when the fish is idle, we will let the fish wander or move very slowly instead of using stop command to halt it.

4.2   Task Decomposition and Responsibility Assignments

Based on the region division shown in Figure 5 (b), we define three roles: one is main attacker(FishC), the other two are (left and right) assistant attackers(FishL and FishR). The role assignments are static, and they will not change during the task. When the disk is not in the region that one fish takes charge of, it will swim restrictively in its region and can not invade to other regions to disturb other fish. Figure 5 (b) indicates region division and allocation of responsibility for three roles.

4.3   Actions Design

When a fish pushes the disk, it may use either its head, middle-body or even its tail. Also it can disturb the surrounding water in a proper way and let the disk drift closer to the gate. Hence, we designed the following primitive actions for fish individuals:

Action 1: As depicted in Figure 6, the first action for the fish is to swim approaching the disk and hit the disk exactly along the direction from the disk to the gate. where (x_F, y_F, α) denotes the pose of the fish, (x_D, y_D) and (x_C, y_C) stand for the center of the disk and the position of the gate, β is the expected direction from the disk to the gate, l_1 indicates the expected moving direction of the disk. Considering the fish's bodylength and its inertia, we choose a point G (x_G, y_G) which locates at the extended line of l_1 as the pushing-point. l_2 is the section connecting the fish to G, and l_3 represents the perpendicular of l_1 which pass through point G.

   As illustrated in Figure 6 (a), if the pushing-point G locates between the fish and the disk, i.e. $(x_D - x_F) \times (x_C - x_D) > 0$, we define the perpendicular bisector l_4 for section

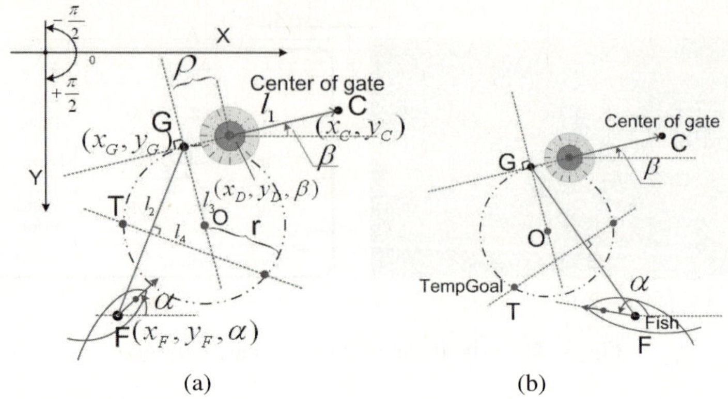

(a)   (b)

Fig. 6. The action of pushing disk along the exact direction to the gate

l_2. Then using r as radius, we make a circle C which is tangental to l_1 at point G. If the circle intersects l_4 at one point, we chose this point as a temporary goal for the fish, or if they are two intersections, we chose the point with small x-coordinates, namely T, as the temporary goal. While, if the fish is far away from the disk and there is no intersection between C and l_1, G will be the temporary goal point for the fish. As the fish moves, a series of temporary goals will be obtained, which will lead the fish swim gradually to the pushing-point.

After some geometrical analysis, The positions of intersection points can be calculated by the following equation:

$$(x - x_D - \rho\cos\beta - r\sin\alpha)^2 + (y - y_D - \rho\sin\beta + r\cos\alpha)^2 = r^2$$
$$y - \frac{1}{2}(y_G + y^F) = \frac{x_F - x_G}{y_G - y_F}(x - \frac{1}{2}(x_G + x_F)) \tag{1}$$

Figure 6 (b) depicts the case when the fish is between the disk and the goal, i.e. $(x_D - x_F) \times (x_C - x_D) < 0$.

Action 2: Although when determining the pushing-point, we give sufficient consideration for the dynamics of the fish and the difficulty when controlling it, we still can't guarantee the fish reach its destination in the expected attitudes, especially its orientation. Once it gets to the pushing-point with large orientation error, it may miss the disk. In this case, we design the following action which allows the fish to push the disk by throwing head.

As shown in Figure 7 (a), if the fish approaches the pushing-point (in a small neighbor region) and its orientation satisfies the following condition, it will take a sharp turn to the direction of the disk.

$$\begin{cases} (x_F, y_F) \in \{\|(x_G, y_G) - (x_F, y_F)\| \leq \delta\} \\ \alpha \in \{|\alpha - \beta| \geq \zeta\} \end{cases} \tag{2}$$

where δ and ζ are the bounds for position error and orientation error, which are determined empirically experiments. In our experiment, we choose $\delta = 5cm$ and $\zeta = \frac{\pi}{15}$.

Action 3: In particular, this action takes full advantage of the agility of fish's tail. Figure 7 (b) indicates the fish pats the disk by its tail.

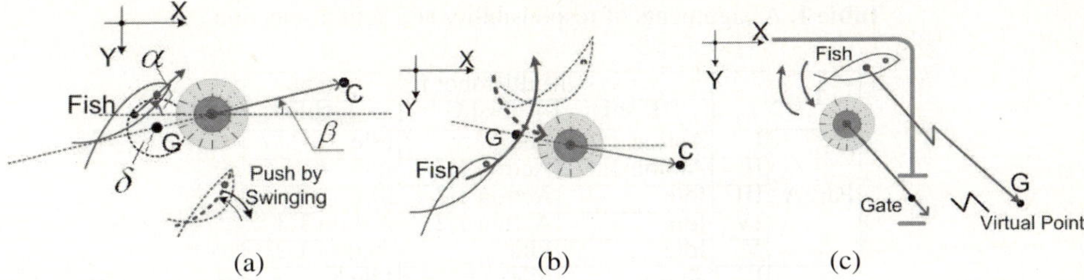

Fig. 7. Three actions: a)pushing disk by shaking(throwing) head, b) pushing the disk by tail and c) swimming towards a virtual pushing-point

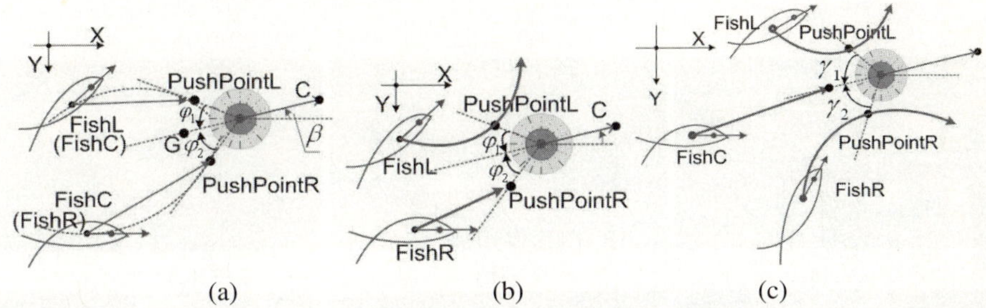

Fig. 8. Cooperative actions: a) two fish both use *Action 1*, (b) one takes *Action 1* and the other use *Action 3* and c)one use *Action 1* and the other two use *Action 4*

Action 4: Action 4 will be implemented when the disk floats very close to the gate and in the corner of the tank. This action allows the fish to move the disk slowly towards the goal by oscillating. As shown in Figure 7 (c), in this action, we design a point outside the tank as a virtual pushing-point. Thus the fish will always try to swim to that virtual destination, although it can never reach it. During moving (or struggling), its body, especially posterior body, oscillates continually, which disturbs the water and makes the disk float towards the gate.

In addition, based on the above four basic actions, some cooperative action can be obtained naturally. Figure 8 presents three of them.

According to the above assignments for responsibility and cooperative actions designed, we sum up the corresponding strategies for each fish individual when the disk is in different situations:

Figure 9 describes the scenario of one experiment. We conduct extensive experiments for this task on MRFS. The results are not very perfect but successful and promising. For more pictures and videos of MRFS and the experimental results, please visit http :// www.mech.pku.edu.cn/robot/MRFS.html.

Now, we are carrying out more experiments and searching better methods to reduce the impact of fish's inertia and the disturbance from surrounding water more effectively. Also, our ongoing work includes adopting other strategies and comparing them using some criteria and finally choosing the most efficient one.

Although the above cooperative task may be quite simple, it is very heuristic for further research on more complex cooperation of multiple fish. In fact, this study involves

Table 1. Assignments of responsibility and action selection

Disk		Multi-robot fish		
		FishL	FishC	FishR
Part A	I	Action 1,2	Idle	Idle
	II	Action 1,3	Action 1,2	Idle
	III	Idle	Action 1,2	Idle
	IV	Idle	Action 1,2	Action 1,3
	V	Idle	Idle	Action 1,2
Part B	I	Action 4	Idle	Idle
	II	Action 1,3	Action 1,2	Idle
	III	Action 4	Action 1,2	Action 4
	IV	Idle	Action 1,2	Action 1,3
	V	Idle	Idle	Action 4

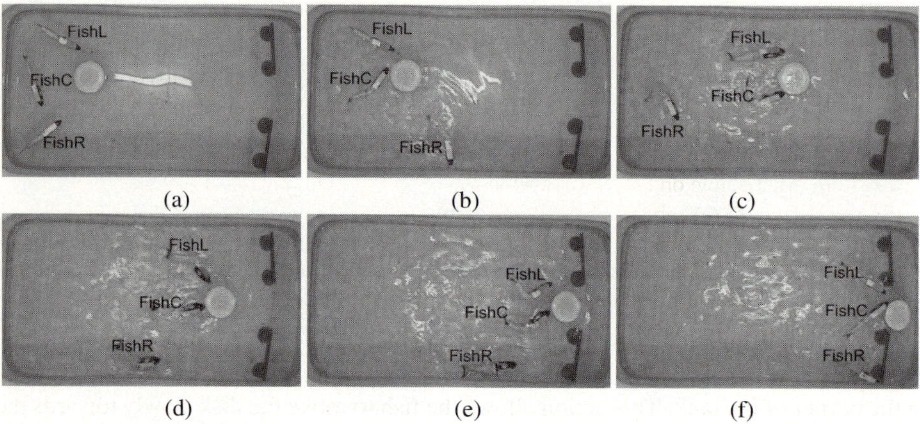

Fig. 9. Sequences of overhead images, order is left to right and top to down

a spectrum of problems, ranging from cooperative strategies, self-organizing mechanism, task allocation, collective swarming behavior, control laws, and so on. In our experiments, only three fish are used, which is because the tank is not large enough to accommodate more. When a larger space is available, more fish will swim freely in the tank, and other complicated tasks such as self-organized schooling and cooperative formation can be designed and tested.

5   Conclusions and Future Work

This paper concentrates on the multi-robot fish cooperation problem. It describes the design and implementation of MRFS and evaluates its performance using a cooperative disk-pushing task. Corresponding experimental results show that higher efficiency and much greater capabilities can be obtained when the fish cooperate with each other properly. It is observed that MRFS provides a useful and effective platform to design and achieve cooperative tasks for multiple robot fish.

Of course, there is still a long time before employing the fish to implement some practical tasks in the sea. Future work will focus on the following two aspects. On the one hand, we plan to add some sensors like ultrasonic and infrared detectors to the fish body to improve its autonomy and efficiency. On the other hand, more complex tasks will be designed and tested on MRFS. Next, we will attempt to organize competitive games. Similar to Robocup, we can expect water polo matches between seven autonomous robotic fish and seven manually controlled fish to imitate the real polo game by following the same rules. The results of such kind of attempts will be presented soon.

References

1. Yu, J., Wang, L., Tan, M.:A framework for biomimetic robot fish's design and its realization, in Proc. American Control Conf. Portland, USA. (2005)1593-1598
2. Yu, J., Wang, L.:Parameter optimization of simplified propulsive model for biomimetic robot fish, in Proc. IEEE Int. Conf. Robotics and Automation. Barcelona, Spain,(2005)3317-3322
3. Yu, J., Wang, S., Tan, M.:Basic motion control of a free-swimming biomimetic robot fish, in Proc. IEEE Conf. Decision and Control, Maui, Hawaii USA, (2003)1268-1273
4. Triantafyllou, M. S., Triantafyllou,G. S.: An efficient swimming machine. Sci. Amer. **272** (1995)64-70
5. Lighthill, M. J.: Note on the swimming of slender fish. J. Fluid Mech. **9** (1960)305–317
6. Barrett, D., Grosenbaugh, M., Triantafyllou, M.: The optimal control of a flexible hull robotic undersea vehicle propelled by an oscillating foil, in Proc. IEEE AUV Symp. **24** (1999)1-9
7. Terada, Y.: A trial for animatronic system including aquatic robots, J. Robot. Soc. Jpn. **18**(2000)195-197
8. Domenici, P., Blake, R. W.: The kinematics and performance of fish fast-start swimming, J. Exper. Biol., **200** (1997)1165-1178

Introducing Social Investors into Multi-Agent Models of Financial Markets

Stephen Chen[1], Brenda Spotton Visano[2], and Ying Kong[2]

[1] Information Technology Program, Atkinson Faculty, York University
4700 Keele Street, Toronto, Ontario M3J 1P3
sychen@yorku.ca
[2] Economics Program, Atkinson Faculty, York University
4700 Keele Street, Toronto, Ontario M3J 1P3
spotton@yorku.ca, ykong@yorku.ca

Abstract. Existing models of financial market prices typically assume that investors are informed with economic data and that wealth maximization motivates them. This paper considers the social dimensions of investing and the effect that this additional motivation has on the evolution of prices in a multi-agent model of an equity market. Agents in this model represent both economically informed investors and socially motivated investors who base their decision to invest solely on the popularity of the investment activity itself. The new model captures in a primitive but important way the notion of frenzy associated with speculative manias and panics, and it offers further insight into such anomalies as market bubbles and crashes.

Keywords: Multi-Agent Model, Financial Market Modelling, Social Investors, Herding, Signalling Games.

1 Introduction

Recent attempts to model complex financial market dynamics through simulation by multi-agent models have focused primarily on investors who base their decisions to trade on economic information alone [2][4][18]. While we are also interested in the effects of differing but interdependent agent motivations on the time path of market prices, we will also consider the social motivations of investors. The actions of social investors can add a unique and highly destabilizing influence to the dynamics of a financial market. One of the goals of this study is to examine how the corridor of stability between efficient markets and markets that lead to bubbles/crashes is affected by the introduction of social investors.

A multi-agent model (MAM) of a financial market with two classes of agents which include economically informed (traditional) investors and socially motivated investors has been developed. Economic data informing the traditional investors include the current market price of the stock, the expected future value of the stock, and the recent rate of change in the observed market price. Therefore, the agents which represent the traditional investors in our MAM will capture the behavioural effects of both the fundamentals traders (who trade on fundamental value only) and the noise traders (who trade on price trends). A socially motivated investor will base his or her

M. Ali and R. Dapoigny (Eds.): IEA/AIE 2006, LNAI 4031, pp. 44–53, 2006.

trading decisions on the popularity of the investment activity alone. If a social investor sees a large number of other investors buying, then a social investor will buy as well. Conversely and symmetrically, a social investor seeing a large number of sellers will sell.

It is useful to highlight the differences between noise traders and social investors. Noise traders are usually very sophisticated investors who may use charts and technical analysis to exploit (short-term) price trends. In exploiting (i.e. following) price trends, the actions of noise traders tend to exaggerate price fluctuations in a financial market [2][4][18]. Social investors are typically poorly informed investors – their investment decisions are not based on any financial information at all. The effects of social investors on a financial market are less predictable, and these effects will be studied in our paper.

Compared to existing financial market MAMs that are designed to reproduce aggregate market data [2][4][18], the purpose of the new MAM is to reproduce singularities in market dynamics. Existing models of event singularities are static and thus can neither expose conditions that may aid prediction of a market bubble nor inform any intervention strategies designed to mitigate its effects. The newly developed multi-agent model is a first attempt to address these shortcomings – it promises a tool that will enable our observation of the market dynamics that characterize periods of instability.

Although primitive in its characterization of equity markets, we have been able to replicate the basic results of the extant models, and thus provide a basis for comparison of price dynamics with and without the social investor. We explore the sensitivity of the price dynamics to agent behaviours by altering the number of social investors and tracking the time path of prices under different assumptions about the behaviour of the economically informed investors. For example, the developed MAMs are able to meaningfully model the situation where the fundamental value of the underlying asset is known with certainty by the economically informed investor. In this situation, the system remains stable with even a relatively large number of social investors. When the fundamental value is not known with certainty and economically informed investors adjust their estimate of the true market price by including recent price movements (in a manner that reflects noise trading behaviour), the threshold level of social investors required to drive the system unstable declines.

With only a small number of social investors, the stable dimensions of the first two models reproduce the efficient market hypothesis and mean reversion dynamics of extant models respectively. The introduction of "noise" trading in the second model causes temporary overshooting, but trading guided by estimates of fundamentals operates to dampen the deviations over time such that the price again converges on the fundamental value. Trading by a dominance of fundamentals-informed speculators thus ensures that speculation will stabilize markets in the way analysed by Friedman [9].

In the presence of social investing behaviour, the stability of the MAM is conditional on the number of social investors, and the stability threshold is sensitive to both the trading behaviour of the economically informed investor and the size of any shock to fundamental values. With a "small" number of social investors (where "small" varies depending on the behaviour of the economically informed investor), the system is stable. As the number of social investors increases, the system hits a threshold beyond which the system is unstable in the sense that deviations from the fundamental increase, rather than decrease, over time. As such, the model captures the notion of a corridor of stability outside of which the model becomes dynamically unstable [3][15]. We are also able to demonstrate the manner in which the threshold level of stability determined by the degree of social investing is also sensitive to the size of any shock to fundamental values through the new MAMs.

One of the economic and financial questions that the developed MAM allows us to address is the determination of the threshold size of social investing relative to the innovation (shock to the fundamental value) that pushes the model outside of its corridor of stability. The MAM also supports the analysis of how sensitive this threshold is to the type of economically informed trading behaviours, and to the size of a shock to the underlying fundamental value of the asset. The economic background for these explorations is developed in the following section before the basic multi-agent model is developed in section 3. Sections 4 through 6 examine the model parameters corresponding to efficient markets, noise trading, and price shocks. Section 7 discusses the results and directions for future research, and section 8 summarizes.

2 Background

In conventional models of prices in competitive financial markets, the price of equities reflects fully and accurately the existing information on the income earning potential of an asset. This "efficient market" outcome as explored by Fama [5][6][7][8] suggests that the present discounted value of the expected future income over the life of the asset—its "fundamental value"—will ultimately govern the asset's market price. Deviations from this so-called "fundamental value" will only be temporary – speculators capable of estimating the true fundamental value will quickly arbitrage away any implicit capital gains. Deviations may appear as the result of new information about future profitability and, as such, represent the disequilibrium adjustment to a new equilibrium with prices again equal to the now altered fundamental value.

Although intuitively appealing and consistent with a long-standing tradition in finance that acknowledges the importance of "value investing" [26], actual price movements and the resulting distribution of returns do not appear to adhere to the strict predictions of the efficient markets hypothesis. Explanations for persistent deviations from estimated fundamental values include various explanations for a "bubble" in stock prices. A "bubble" occurs when competitive bidding, motivated by repetitive and self-fulfilling expectations of capital gains, drives up a given asset's price in excess of what would otherwise be warranted by a fundamental value. The bubble may be driven by the presence of "noise" traders. Noise traders attempt to exploit short-term momentum in the movement of stock prices, and their actions (e.g. buying when prices are rising and selling when prices are falling) can exaggerate any movement in prices.

The presence of noise traders alters, however, neither the ultimate equilibrium market price for stocks nor the fact that the market will eventually reach it. In the extant literature, the formal introduction of "noise" traders creates a mean-reverting market dynamic to explain temporary deviations from fundamentals [16][17]. The presence of noise traders can confound market dynamics to such an extent that under some conditions or for some time, it is profitable for the more sophisticated traders to disregard the intrinsic value of the asset, follow the herd, and thus contribute to the asset bubble that results [10]. It has also been suggested that herding may explain the excess kurtosis observable in high-frequency market data [2].

Both the "fundamentals" trader and the "noise" trader base their decision to trade on economic information alone. The fundamentals trader estimates expected future profitability of the underlying firm and extracts capital gains by trading when current market prices deviate from the estimate. The noise trader will "chart" the past history of prices to predict future movements (assuming repetitive time trends). These charts allow noise traders to indirectly capture a "herding" market psychology that may move markets independently, if temporarily, away from fundamental values.

Since these traders base their decisions solely on objective market information, the more traditional financial models exclude by assumption the possibility that the investment activity may also be a social activity. In situations where individuals are motivated to belong to a group, the possibility of fads, fashions, and other forms of collective behaviour can exist. Visano [25] suggests that investing in equity markets is not immune from social influences, especially when investors face true uncertainty. Consistent with the early views of financial markets as "voting machines" when the future is uncertain [13][25], Visano's result explains the fad and contagion dimensions of investing which relate to Lynch's [19] explanations of the recent internet "bubble".

When objective information is incomplete and individuals base investment decisions on social rather than economic information, outcomes become contingent on the collective assessment of the objective situation, and these outcomes are no longer uniquely identifiable independent of this collective opinion. Attempts to model this heterogeneity of investment behaviour and multiplicity of interdependent outcomes render the mathematics so complex as to threaten the tractability of the typical highly aggregated dynamic model. By presenting an opportunity to analyze the effects of different agent behaviours, there are significant potential benefits in using a multi-agent model to simulate the actions of a financial market.

3   Model Assumptions

All of the following multi-agent models have the same basic parameters. Ten thousand agents each have the opportunity to choose to own or not own a stock. A decision to change from owning to not owning will cause the agent to sell, and a decision to change from not owning to owning will cause the agent to buy. During each time period of the simulation, each agent will be activated in a different random order. When activated, an agent will observe the current conditions and determine if it should own or not own the stock.

Informed investors will base their decisions on the price of the stock and a calculated value of the stock. Depending on the model, this calculation may include the fundamental value of the stock, the current price of the stock, price trends, and derivatives of price trends. (See Appendix A for calculation details.) Social investors will base their decisions on the actions of other investors. Examining a random sample of

100 other investors, seeing a large number invested will lead to a decision to own, seeing a small number invested will lead to a decision to not own, and seeing a number in between will lead to no change in their previous decision.

A decision by an agent to buy or sell will affect the market price of the stock. In the following multi-agent models, the market price is determined by assuming a primitive linear supply and demand function. (Each unit of demand causes the price to increase by one unit such that the price is equal to the number of agents who own the stock.) At the beginning of the model, 50% of each class of investor own the stock and the remaining agents do not own the stock. The initial market price is thus 5000, and the fundamental price of the stock is set at 5100.

4   Model 1 – Efficient Markets

The efficient market hypothesis (which assumes there are only economically informed investors with perfect information) predicts a market price equal to the fundamental value of the stock. Further, the introduction social investors should have no effect since any deviation between the market price and the fundamental value will cause the informed investors to engage offsetting trades until the market price again matches the fundamental value. We reproduce these results in our base-line system below in Figure 1.

Fig. 1. A market with investors who have perfect information is inherently stable. This stability is not affected by the introduction of social investors.

5   Model 2 – Noise Trading

The assumptions underlying the base-line model are stringent – estimates of underlying fundamental asset values are rarely identifiable as uniquely and unambiguously as the efficient market hypothesis assumes. When the possibility is introduced that an investor knows her or his information is less than perfect and that others may possess better information, an incentive is created for the investor to follow the herd. Following the herd can help investors achieve capital gains when other investors are also accumulating capital gains (i.e. not selling). However, herding can also drive prices away from the true underlying fundamental value, so the risk of capital loss becomes possible. To capture some of these strategic investment considerations, we adapt the base-line model by adding the first and second price derivative to the investment decisions of the economically informed traders.

The second multi-agent model is again stable if it has only informed investors who base their future price expectations on both the first and second derivative of a stock's price (see Figure 2). This MAM is also stable if a small number of social investors is added to the system. Although there is greater price volatility due to the price momentum created by the noise trading behaviour, this price momentum does not cause instability for a relatively small number of social investors (see Figure 2). However, this price momentum does lead to market instability if the market influence of social investors is large enough.

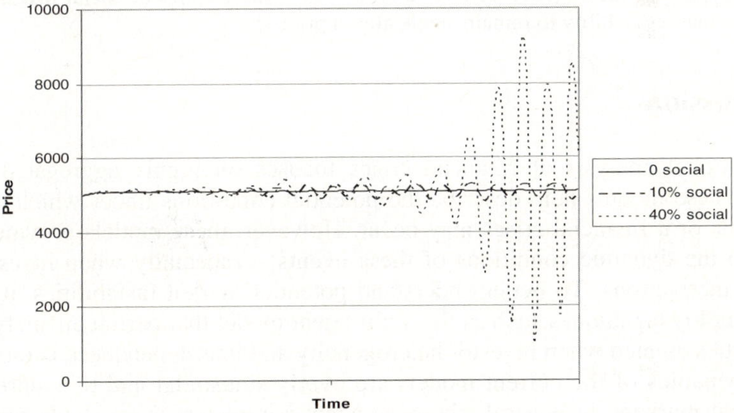

Fig. 2. A market with informed investors who balance the rewards of short-term capital gains with the risks of returning to the fundamental value should be stable. However, this balance can be easily affected by the addition of social investors.

6   Model 3 – Price Shocks

Historically, the onset of a market bubble is stimulated by a shock to the asset's underlying fundamental value. For example, a new technology like the internet increases the future profitability of a stock by an unknown amount. In this situation, informed investors become more reliant on market signals to determine the future fundamental value. With only informed investors participating in the market, this determination can eventually be made (see Figure 3). However, the addition of even a small number of social investors can distort the price signals enough to cause instability.

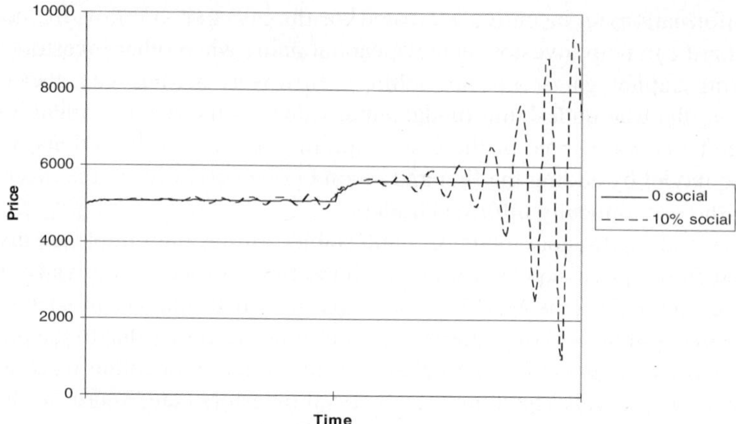

Fig. 3. A price shock occurs at the tick mark on the Time axis. Before this time, the fundamental price is 5100, and it is 5600 after. A market with only informed investors can handle this price shock, but the introduction of even a relatively small number of social investors greatly reduces the market's ability to remain stable after a price shock.

7 Discussion

The traditional analysis of financial crises focuses on highly aggregated dynamic models. These models help describe the potential conditions under which a speculative bubble or a financial crises may occur. However, these models provide little insight into the dynamic conditions of these events – especially when investors have different motivations. To better understand potential market instabilities, it is necessary to employ techniques such as the multi-agent model that permit an analysis of the complexities created when investor heterogeneity and interdependence is introduced.

The dynamics of the current models are overly sinusoidal and thus unrepresentative of real markets. In general, choosing agent parameters for a stable market (e.g. Model 1) is easy and straightforward. However, finding a set of agent parameters that are on the boundary of stability (e.g. Models 2 and 3) has been more difficult. Traditional economic models provide little insight into the specification of these parameters, so the current multi-agent models represent a foundation for the coordinated exploration and development of computational and economic models.

In particular, the developed multi-agent model suggests a signalling game. In a game theory model, players make their decisions based on payoffs that depend on the actions of the other players. The likely behaviour of the players in a game can be determined by identifying a Nash equilibrium. In a Nash equilibrium, a decision by one player will make a specific decision the most beneficial to the other player, and this decision by the other player will make the original decision the most beneficial to the first player. Since this set of decisions is stable, the game model is in equilibrium.

The previous MAMs of financial markets [2][4][18] could not be easily analyzed with game theory. In these models, noise investors (players) who observe a stock price that is rising on fundamentals will decide to buy the stock because of its upward price trajectory, and this decision may subsequently cause the stock to rise above its fundamental price. When the stock price is above its fundamental value, fundamentalist investors (players) will decide to sell. Since a decision by fundamentalists to buy can lead to a decision by noise investors to also buy which can then lead to a decision by fundamentalist investors to sell, these models do not have a Nash equilibrium.

The new multi-agent model which introduces social investors has two Nash equilibria. The first equilibrium involves the buying decisions of informed investors being seen by the social investors which leads them to buy, and this decision will drive up the price expectations of the informed investors which maintains their decision to buy. A Nash equilibrium where all of the players are buying represents the actions of market participants during a speculative frenzy. The second Nash equilibrium involves the converse situation where a decision to sell by informed investors leads the social investors to sell which confirms the decision of informed investors to sell.

Between these two Nash equilibria which represent market bubbles and crashes, the actions of the informed and social investors can create the dynamics of an efficient market. In a signalling game, a signal (like the price shock in our MAM) can change the equilibrium outcome of a game model. Signaling models have been widely used in economics [24] to explain phenomena such as uninformative advertising [21][23], limit pricing [20], dividends [1][12] and warranties [11][22]. In these games, a player with private information (the informed player) sends a signal of his private type to the uninformed player before the uninformed player makes a choice. In our MAMs, the informed player can be viewed as the economically informed (traditional) investors while the uninformed player can be viewed as the socially motivated investors.

The informed investors will make a decision and pass a signal to the socially motivated investors. The socially motivated investors will make a decision based on this signal. This game can have different equilibriums which depend on the nature of the informed investors. If the informed investors act as one person and all make the same decision, a pooling equilibrium is reached. Conversely, a separating equilibrium will be generated if the informed investors make different investment decisions. To create the possibility that the signaling game can represent an efficient market, it is necessary that some signals will lead to a separating equilibrium where some investors buy and some investors sell. The insight gained from choosing agent parameters that lead to marginally stable MAMs will be of great value in designing new signaling game models.

8 Summary

A series of multi-agent models for financial markets has been developed. These computational models provide a valuable tool for the evaluation and development of economic models that represent the conditions and events of financial crises. A key focus of the models in development is the role of social investors – an investor class that cannot be meaningfully handled by the assumptions of traditional economic models.

References

1. Battacharya, S.: Imperfect information, dividend policy and the 'bird in the hand' fallacy. Bell Journal of Economics 9(1):259-70. (1979)
2. Cont, R., Bouchard, J.-P.: Herd Behavior and Aggregate Fluctuations in Financial Markets. Macroeconomic Dynamics 4:170-196. (2000)
3. Dimand, R.W.: Fisher, Keynes, and the Corridor of Stability. American Journal of Economics and Sociology 64(1):185-199. (2005)
4. Eguiluz, V.M., Zimmermann, M.G.: Transmission of Information and Herd Behavior: An Application to Financial Markets. Physical Review Letters 85:5659-5662. (2000)
5. Fama, E.F.: The Behavior of Stock Market Prices. Journal of Business 38:34-105. (1965)
6. Fama, E.F.: Efficient Capital Markets: A Review of Theory and Empirical Work. Journal of Finance, 25:383-416. (1970)
7. Fama, E.F.: Foundations of Finance. Basic Books, New York. (1976)
8. Fama, E.F.: Efficient Markets: II. Journal of Finance 46(5):1575-1617. (1991)
9. Friedman, M.: The Case for Flexible Exchange Rates. In Friedman, M. (ed), Essays in Positive Economics, University of Chicago Press, pgs 157-203. (1953)
10. Froot, K.A., Scharfstein, D.S., Stein, J.C.: Herd on the Street: Informational Inefficiencies in a Market with Short-Term Speculation. Journal of Finance 47:1461-1484. (1992)
11. Gal-Or, E.: Warranties as a signal of quality. Canadian Journal of Economics 22(1):50-61. (1989)
12. John, K., Williams, J.: Dividends, dilution and taxes: A signalling equilibrium. Journal of Finance 40(4):1053-1069. (1985)
13. Keynes, J.M.: The General Theory of Employment, Interest and Money. Reprinted Prometheus Books. (1936, 1997)
14. Kindleberger, C.P.: Manias, Panics, and Crashes. Basic Books, New York. Revised edition issued in 1989. (1978)
15. Leijonhufvud, A.: Effective Demand Failures. Swedish Journal of Economics 75: 27-48. (1973) Reprinted in Leijonhufvud, A., Information and Coordination: Essays in Macroeconomic Theory, Oxford University Press. (1981)
16. De Long, J.B., Schleifer, A., Summers L.H., Waldman, R.J.: Noise Trader Risk in Financial Markets. Journal of Political Economy 98:703-738. (1990)
17. De Long, J.B., Schleifer, A., Summers L.H., Waldman, R.J.: Positive Feedback Investment Strategies and Destabilizing Rational Speculation. Journal of Finance 45(2):379-395. (1990)
18. Lux, T., Marchesi, M.: Scaling and criticality in a stochastic multi-agent model of a financial market. Nature 397:498-500. (1999)
19. Lynch, A.: Thought Contagions in the Stock Market. Journal of Psychology and Financial Markets 1:10-23. (2000)
20. Milgrom, P., Roberts., J.: Limit pricing and entry under incomplete information: An equilibrium analysis. Econometrica 50:443. (1982)
21. Milgrom, P., Roberts., J.: Price and advertising signals of product quality. Journal of Political Economy 94(4):796-821. (1986)
22. Miller, M.H., Rock, K.: Dividend policy under asymmetric information. Journal of Finance 40:1031. (1985)
23. Nelson, P.: Advertising as information. Journal of Political Economy, 82(4):729-54. (1974)
24. Riley, J.G.: Silver signals: Twenty- years of screening and signalling. Journal of Economic Literature 39:432-478. (2001)

25. Visano, B.S.: Financial Crises: Socio-economic causes and institutional context. Routledge, London. (forthcoming)
26. Williams, J.B.: The Theory of Investment Value. Reprinted Augustus M. Kelley, New York. (1938, 1965)

Appendix A – Investor Models

For a series of artificial market prices, the future market price calculated by the informed investors is shown in Table 1. In model 1, the calculated price is always equal to the fundamental value (e.g. 51). In models 2 and 3, the price calculation includes a time-based multiplier and a second derivative of the current trend. If the difference in the past trends have the same sign as the current trend, then it is also multiplied by 0.8. Therefore, the price calculated at time 2 is 42.5% of 51 plus 57.5% of (47 + (-2)/0.8 + (-1)/1.6 + [(-2)-(-1)]*0.8) and it is 42.5% of 51 plus 57.5% of (47 + (-2)/1.6 + (-1)/2.4 + [0-(-2)]) at time 3. For the social investors, the examined sample size is 100 investors, and the large number that causes buying is 60 and the small number that causes selling is 42.

Table 1. Future price expectations calculated by the informed investors in each model for a series of artificial market prices

Time	Market Price	Model 1	Models 2 and 3
0	50	51	51
1	49	51	48.4
2	47	51	46.4
3	47	51	48.9
4	48	51	50.0
5	50	51	52.7
6	51	51	52.1
7	51	51	51.4
8	54	51	57.0
9	53	51	51.4

Cross-Organisational Workflow Enactment Via Progressive Linking by Run-Time Agents

Xi Chen and Paul Chung

Computer Science Department, Loughborough University
Loughborough, Leicestershire, United Kingdom LE11 3TU
{X.Chen, P.W.H.Chung}@lboro.ac.uk

Abstract. Driven by popular adoptions of workflow and requirements from the practice of virtual enterprise (VE), research in workflow interoperability is currently on the increase. Nonetheless, it is still in its early stage compared with the maturity of individual workflow technology. Some attempts have been tried, however results are not satisfactory especially in a VE context, where many of the partnerships are dynamic and temporary. Reasons include the rigidity and high initial coordination cost inherently associated with top-down modelling and enactment approaches. Therefore, this paper proposes a bottom-up and WfMS [1] -independent approach towards cross-organisational workflow enactment, which is via progressive linking enabled by run-time agents. This is expected to pave the way for further cross-organisational workflow needs.

Keywords: Multi-Agent Systems, Workflow Interoperability, Virtual Enterprise.

1 Introduction

Business processes are at the core of productivity for an organisation. They control and describe how business is conducted in terms of "a set of one or more linked procedures or activities which collectively realise a business objective or policy goal, normally within the context of an organisational structure defining functional roles and relationships" [1]. To support mobility and dynamism, individual business processes are vital for a company to react faster and be more flexible in running its daily business in a constantly changing environment [2]. However, the idea of virtual enterprises (VE) blurs the boundaries between organisations and requires cross-organisational interactions, which brings in many challenges.

Workflow was born to tackle the issue of business process automation and is proven, to date, as a mature technology. It is carried out with the support of workflow management system (WfMS) that provides complete design, execution and management services to workflow. The essential strategy of workflow is the separation of business logic from software applications. Although being separated, they are still linked in the form of 'activities' that represent logical steps within a process [1]. Centred around a set of activities, an activity-based workflow is constructed in contrast to an

---

[1] WfMS is the acronym for workflow management system [1].

M. Ali and R. Dapoigny (Eds.): IEA/AIE 2006, LNAI 4031, pp. 54–59, 2006.

entity-based workflow [3]. Each activity can be either manual or automatic depending on the task to be carried out, where the automatic ones are, mostly, implemented as applications.

The problem of workflow interoperability has been identified due to adoptions of diverse WfMS products between organisations and the inevitability of interconnections for the purpose of cooperation across organisational boundaries. Three basic interoperation patterns, namely, chained process, nested synchronous sub-process, and event synchronised process [4] should be tackled, among which more concerns are put on the first two [5]. Due to inherent complexity, event synchronisation, although encountered very often in real business, has not received much attention by WfMC itself [6]. A number of research projects have been carried out in the area of workflow interoperability, nevertheless results are not satisfactory when applied in a VE context because of their rigidity and the high initial coordination cost imposed by top-down approaches. This project proposes a more effective approach, which addresses enactment of cross-organisational workflow from a bottom-up view and in the form of a progressive linking mechanism supported by run-time agents. It is expected the success of such an approach will shed light on and facilitate the formalisation and execution of cross-organisational workflow. This paper identifies challenges of workflow enactment in the context of VE, describes the approach, presents a possible way of implementation, discusses its effectiveness and highlights the future work.

2   Challenges

Workflow interoperability is commonly examined from a top-down view [7,8,9], which intends to start from the concept of traditional workflow and extend it beyond organisational boundaries in order to keep the control flow manageable. However, as a technology-driven approach, it brings in much initial cost in terms of a detailed and rigid pre-definition that does not reflect the run-time nature of agile interactions within VEs where many of the partnerships are dynamic and temporary. However, if centralised control is removed due to the choice of a bottom-up modelling approach, there seems to be no way of propagating control flow from one workflow to another at run time.

Real-life interoperation always poses a tightly-interwoven control flow structure. Also, many existing business processes are mobile and ever-changing because of their dynamic nature. The dynamism should be dealt with effectively by the cross-organisational workflow to minimise disturbance to cooperation, which implies a loosely-coupled interaction mechanism. Therefore, the realisation of tightly-interwoven processes by means of a loosely-coupled mechanism is identified as a challenge.

According to the Workflow Reference Model [6] initiated by WfMC, Interface 4 is the standard interface dedicated for the purpose of interoperability and has attracted much attention. Although standardisation provides a solution with regard to interoperability, the practical value is discounted in the face of the diversity of standards [10] and the reality towards their acceptance. Therefore, standardisation cannot be fully relied on.

Moreover, approaches that require substantial effort, e.g., dialogue definition [5], workflow view [7,11], Interworkflow [9], agent-based workflow [12], and standardisation [13,14], are unlikely to be adopted widely in the near future.

3 Progressive Linking Approach

For the purpose of simplicity, interoperation discussed in this section is confined to participation between two organizations but not any particular two. It is assumed that when a workflow is invoked it will always instantiate a new process instance.

3.1 Interoperation Modelling

At least, three aspects, namely, control flow, data flow and communication, should be addressed in order for two workflows to interoperate with each other. For control flow, other measures must be taken to route control due to the lack of a centralised architecture. To facilitate the discussion, the concept of interaction point is introduced here. An interaction point can be defined as from (or to) which, a request (or response) is emitted (or targeted). Since workflow engines are state machines, an appropriate sequence of interaction can be ensured at run time [7] as long as interaction points are correctly specified in both participating processes. Synchronisation is achieved by a process sending request and waiting for a response from the other process[5]. Activity-level modelling for interaction point is chosen in order to make the approach adaptive to all interoperability patterns. An interaction point is therefore modelled as an interface activity, which is further implemented in the form of a generic workflow activity. This activity is configured to synchronously (letting the process wait while the application is executing) invoke software agent as an external run-time application, which makes it an agent-enhanced approach [15]. Control token [16] is passed back and forth among WfMSs and agents.

Data flow is managed by the semantics of 'sending' and 'waiting', which are implicitly indicated by the type (incoming or outgoing) of data being exchanged by the two workflow engines through this interface activity. Basic interoperability patterns are all modelled at the activity level by employing the concepts of interface activity, incoming and outgoing data, which is illustrated in Fig. 1.

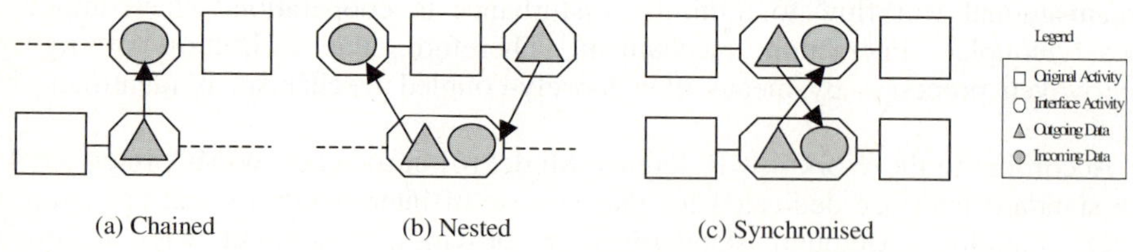

Fig. 1. Interoperation patterns modelling using interface activities

Mediated communication [7] is used due to the loosely-coupled approach is adopted. Semantic service descriptions extracted from individual processes are used for message routing. Thus, agents on the one side pass outgoing data from the interface activity to the mediator, whilst agents on the other side check whether desired incoming data arrives and deliver it to the corresponding interface activity accordingly.

3.2 Compatible Workflow

At build time, based on a common agreement, the workflows involved should be modelled and tuned into compatible ones and interface activities are inserted into the processes at desired positions to make both processes ready to go. Semantic service descriptions (in the form of interaction identifiers) are also attached to each pair of outgoing and incoming data belonging to the interface activities on both sides.

3.3 Form Filling

At run time, an empty form is created and two compatible workflows begin their interoperation by filling the form jointly in sequence. Using Fig. 1 (a) as an example, when the first interface activity (only containing outgoing data) from Organisation A is executed, Agent A is invoked and puts the source activity ID (A2), interaction identifier (PurchaseOrder), data (PO200511) and attached document (if any) associated with this activity as well as the identifier of the partner process (Process B) into the form. The occurrence of information in the form triggers Agent B who arranges the instantiation of a new process on the side of Organisation B. After being instantiated, Process B reaches its first interface activity (only containing incoming data) who calls Agent B to register its interaction identifier as a mark of interest. Agent B looks at the form and checks whether there is such an identifier in an unfinished entry. If yes, it writes the activity ID (B1) into the entry and transfers the data and the document (if any) to Process B for consumption. Table 1 gives the headings of the form and an example entry.

Table 1. Heading of communication form and an example entry

Seq.	Source	Target	Interaction ID	Message	Doc	Iteration
1	A2	B1	PurchaseOrder	PO200511	attached	NIL
...						

By doing so, the form shows the current progress of the interoperation. Apart from making a loosely-coupled structure possible, in case of exception, it can be used to trace and locate the trouble spot. When all interactions finish, the completed form can be saved as a historical record.

The progressively filled form is also able to handle event synchronisation and iterative cases effectively through reasoning based on recorded data and progressive status of the form filling. For example, the appearance of two successive uncompleted entries with a blank Source and Target field in each means a rendezvous point is reached; a completed entry with the Source and Interaction ID fields exactly the same as the ones in a previous entry implies an occurrence of iteration, in which case, the entry needs to be marked in the field of Iteration to draw the attention to the recipient.

4 Implementation

Implementation of the approach is underway. A client/server system archetecture is chosen. General characteristics of WfMS are fully exploited in order to achieve a WfMS-independent solution and avoid undue complexity. Both interoperation triggering and acceptance will utilise the workflow application invocation mechanism. To support the mediated communication among software agents, a blackboard system [17] will be adopted. This is due to the structure and functionalities provided by the blackboard system architecture match the proposed approach very well. Knowledge sources (KSs) can be implemented as agents on the client side whilst the blackboard (BB) can be used to hold the form on the server. KS-trigger mechanism can be used as well to bring attention to agents on both sides when something happens to the form.

5 Discussion and Future Work

The approach of progressive linking is developed by using artificial intelligence technology based on a comprehensive investigation of workflow model in terms of control flow, data flow, activity model and application invocation mechanism. It addresses the challenges identified in Section 2. Firstly, this approach reflects realistic cooperation between processes. The complexity of cross-organisational control flow is wrapped in the procedure of invoking mediated software agents, which enable interoperation without a centralised control mechanism. Secondly, loosely-coupled interaction mechanism is provided by the run-time progressive interaction. The tightly-interwound process is dealt with by activity-level interaction modelling that provides a general method for all interoperability patterns. Thirdly, interoperability standards are avoided as much as possible in terms of the agent invocation through application invocation interface rather than workflow interoperability interface. Finally, since the substantial work is implemented in the form of external software agents, there is no structural change imposed on involving WfMSs, which brings in a WfMS-independent solution.

However, since this approach relies on compatible workflows, the issue of compatibility has yet to be addressed. Obviously, cross-organisational workflow compatibility cannot be solved by means of cross-organisational workflow enactment alone but the idea of progressive linking paves the way for a possible direction for achieving it by letting the intelligent agents progressively negotiate the flow of interoperation from scratch within an intelligent framework for cross-organisational cooperation. Internal processes are exposed as services, which allows software agents to negotiate and pick up the desired ones on the fly to dynamically construct cross-organisational workflow. These will be addressed in the future work. It is expected that the progressive linking approach enabled by run-time agents will facilitate intelligent interoperation that will benefit B2B e-business among VEs.

References

1. Workflow Management Coalition: Terminology & Glossary, Technical Report WFMC-TC-1011. Workflow Management Coalition (1999)
2. International Business Machines Corporation: IBM WebSphere MQ Workflow Version 3.6 – Concepts and Architecture. 8th edn. IBM Corp. (2005)
3. Guillaume, F.: Trying to Unify Entity-based and Activity-based Workflows. < http://www.zope.org/Wikis/DevSite/Projects/ComponentArchitecture/TryingToUnifiyWorkflowConcepts>. (accessed 3.7.2005)
4. Workflow Management Coalition: Workflow Standard – Interoperability Abstract Specification, Technical Report WFMC-TC-1012. Workflow Management Coalition (1999)
5. Biegus, L., Branki, C.: InDiA: a Framework for Workflow Interoperability Support by Means of Multi-Agent Systems. Engineering Applications of Artificial Intelligence 17 (7) (2004) 825-839
6. Workflow Management Coalition: The Workflow Reference Model, Technical Report WFMC-TC-1003. Workflow Management Coalition (1995)
7. Schulz, K.A., Orlowska, M.E.: Facilitating Cross-Organisational Workflows with a Workflow View Approach. Data & Knowledge Engineering 51 (1) (2004) 109-147
8. Leymann, F., Roller, D.: Production Worklow – Concepts and Techniques. Prentice Hall, New Jersey (2000)
9. Workflow Management Coalition: Interworkflow Application Model: The Design of Cross-Organizational Workflow Processes and Distributed Operations Management, Technical Report WFMC-TC-2102. Workflow Management Coalition (1997)
10. Bernauer, M., Kappel, G., Kramler, G., Retschitzegger, W.: Specification of Interorganizational Workflows – A Comparison of Approaches. Vienna University of Technology White Paper. Vienna (2002) < http://www.big.tuwien.ac.at/ research/ publications/2003/0603.pdf>. (accessed 1.11.2005)
11. Chiu, D.K.W., Cheung, S.C., Karlapalem, K., Li, Q., Till, S.: Workflow View Driven Cross-Organizational Interoperability in a Web-service Environment. Information Technology and Management 5 (2004) 221-250
12. Jennings, N., Norman, T., Faratin, P., O'Brien, P., Odgers, B.: Autonomous Agents for Business Process Management. International Journal of Applied Artificial Intelligence 14(2) (2000) 145-189
13. Workflow Management Coalition: Workflow Standard – Interoperability Wf-XML Binding, Technical Report WFMC-TC-1023. Workflow Management Coalition (2001)
14. O'Riordan, D.: Business Process Standards For Web Services. < http://www.webservicesarchitect.com/content/articles/BPSFWSBDO.pdf>. (accessed 6.7.2005)
15. Shepherdson, J., Thompson, S., Odgers, B.: Cross Organisational Workflow Coordinated by Software Agents. Proceedings of WACC Workshop on Cross-Organisational Workflow Management and Co-ordination, San Francisco. (1999)
16. Aalst, W.v.d. and Hee, K.v.: Workflow Management: Models, Methods, and Systems. MIT Press, Cambridge (2002)
17. Corkill, D.: Blackboard Systems. AI Expert 6(9) (1991) 40-47

Comparison and Analysis of Expertness Measure in Knowledge Sharing Among Robots

Panrasee Ritthipravat[1], Thavida Maneewarn[1],
Jeremy Wyatt[2], and Djitt Laowattana[1]

[1] FIBO, King Mongkut's University of Technology Thonburi, Thailand
`{pan, praew, djitt}@fibo.kmutt.ac.th`
[2] School of Computer Science, University of Birmingham, United Kingdom
`jlw@cs.bham.ac.uk`

Abstract. Robot expertness measures are used to improve learning performance of knowledge sharing techniques. In this paper, several fuzzy Q-learning methods for knowledge sharing i.e. Shared Memory, Weighted Strategy Sharing (WSS) and Adaptive Weighted Strategy Sharing (AdpWSS) are studied. A new measure of expertise based on regret evaluation is proposed. Regret measure takes uncertainty bounds of two best actions, i.e. the greedy action and the second best action into account. Knowledge sharing simulations and experiments on real robots were performed to compare the effectiveness of the three expertness measures i.e. Gradient (G), Average Move (AM) and our proposed measure. The proposed measure exhibited the best performance among the three measures. Moreover, our measure that is applied to the AdpWSS does not require the predefined setting of cooperative time, thus it is more practical to be implemented in real-world problems.

1   Introduction

Reinforcement learning notoriously requires a long learning period, particularly when applied with a complicated task. Additionally, it is difficult for a robot to explore huge state and action spaces in a short time. To alleviate these problems, multiple mobile robots have been served to learn a task by exploring different part of state and action spaces simultaneously. During a learning period, they may share the knowledge they have learnt. Unfortunately, most reinforcement learning techniques require auxiliary methods to integrate external knowledge sources into the robot's knowledge. In general, knowledge gained from one robot is possibly different from that of the others, even if the robots have the same mechanism and learn the same task. This happens because the robots have different experiences and properties. Therefore, knowledge sharing among robots is one of the most challenging topics in robotic research.

Knowledge sharing among reinforcement learning robots has been extensively studied in order to utilize and gain benefit from multiple knowledge sources, which can be obtained from other robots or even human being. However, the robot would gain more benefit when the knowledge is shared from the more competent sources than the less competent one. We believe that knowledge sharing

M. Ali and R. Dapoigny (Eds.): IEA/AIE 2006, LNAI 4031, pp. 60–69, 2006.
© Springer-Verlag Berlin Heidelberg 2006

techniques should achieve better performances if robots can identify the expertness of the knowledge source. Hence the robots can effectively determine the appropriate amount of the acquired knowledge from the source. Previous research shows that knowledge sharing can be carried out in several ways. They can be classified as direct and indirect methods.

The direct method focuses on direct integration all available sources of shared knowledge into robot's knowledge. Various techniques were studied. For example, the 'Policy Averaging' [1] is the method which averaged all policies into the new knowledge. The 'Weighted Strategy Sharing: WSS' [2] is the method in which weights were assigned to all knowledge sources according to the robot expertise or compatibility of agent state spaces [3] and then summed into the new knowledge. The 'Same-policy' [1] is the method in which all agents used and updated the same policy.

In the indirect method, external knowledge sources will be used to guide the robot's decision making, but they will not be integrated into robot's learning directly. Most works used shared knowledge to bias action selection. The robot selects an action according to the resulting probabilities. Techniques were 'Skill Advice Guided Exploration (SAGE)' [4], 'Supervised Reinforcement Learning (SRL)' [5] etc.

2   Knowledge Sharing Techniques

Knowledge sharing techniques investigated in this paper are summarized as follows.

2.1   Shared Memory: SM

This technique is inspired from the 'Same-policy' [1]. After interaction with an environment, the robots use and update the same set of state-action values. Since all robots have the same brain, each individual robot's experiences directly affects the overall robots' decision making. For learning a task with n robots, action values will be updated n times in each iteration. Learning should be faster than individual learning since n robots explore various states simultaneously.

2.2   Weighted Strategy Sharing: WSS

The WSS method [2] is composed of two phases: individual learning and cooperative learning phases. Initial all robots are in the individual learning phase. They learn a task separately. At a predefined end of learning trials, all robots switch to the cooperative learning phase which allows the robots to share the learned state-action values. In this phase, the action values of all robots will be weighted and summed as the new knowledge for every robot as shown in Eq. 1

$$Q^{new}(s, a) = \sum_{m=1}^{n} W_m Q^m(s, a), \tag{1}$$

where $Q^{new}(s, a)$ is a new set of state-action values initialized for all n sharing robots. Superscript m indicates the mth robot's. W_m is weight calculated from robots' expertise as presented in Eq. 2

$$W_m = \frac{expertness_m}{\sum\limits_{p=1}^{n} expertness_p}, \qquad (m = 1, \ldots, n), \qquad (2)$$

where $expertness_m$ is the mth robot expertness value. Therefore, at the end of cooperative learning phase, all robots have homogeneous set of state-action values. The individual learning phase will then be continued thereafter. These phases will switch back and forth at every cooperative time. The cooperative time is set at every predefined end of learning trials. It will determine how often sharing knowledge is carried out. Frequent sharing means the robots have less time for being in the individual learning phase. This results in low diversity of robots' knowledge. On the contrary, infrequent sharing means that high diversity of the robots' knowledge can be achieved. However, the robot rarely takes benefit from them. Setting the suitable cooperative time is quite difficult. Additionally, all robots have to finish their individual learning phase before the cooperative learning phase can start. If a robot finishes its individual learning phase before the other robots, it has to wait for other robots to finish their individual learning phase. Then they can share their knowledge. Therefore, the WSS does not support asynchronous knowledge sharing in multiple robots. Problems of setting the suitable cooperative time and waiting for the other robots have made the WSS impractical for real-world implementation. The idea of adaptively selecting the suitable cooperative time is inspired from [6]. We will introduce the new method named Adaptive Weighted Strategy Sharing in the next subsection.

2.3 Adaptive Weighted Strategy Sharing: Adaptive WSS

This strategy allows each robot to make a decision whether to share knowledge with the other $n - 1$ robots by itself. The robot is presumed to perceive all the other robots' knowledge and their expertness values at any time t. At the end of robot learning trial, the robot will assign weights to all sources of shared knowledge as computed from Eq. 2. Difference between the robot's weight, W_i, and that of the other robots, W_j where $j \underset{j \neq i}{\in} n - 1$ will be employed to determine probability of sharing, $Prob_{sharing}$, as shown in Eq. 3.

$$Prob_{sharing} = \begin{cases} 0 & \text{if } |W_i - W_j| \leq Th_1, \\ 1 & \text{if } |W_i - W_j| \geq Th_2, \quad and \\ \frac{|W_i - W_j| - Th_1}{Th_2 - Th_1} & \text{otherwise.} \end{cases} \qquad (3)$$

In Eq. 3, two thresholds Th_1 and Th_2 will be set. In this paper, they are 0.1 and 0.5 respectively. If the difference is less than Th_1, sharing will not be occurred. In the contrary manner, if the difference is higher than the Th_2, the sharing probability will be 1. In this manner, each robot is able to determine which sharing robots are. Once sharing robots have been determined, a new knowledge can be obtained from Eq. 1. After the sharing, all sharing robots will have the same level of expertise. Therefore new expertness value for all sharing robots can be computed from an average of the sharing robot expertness values. Unlike the WSS method, the robot will update its knowledge and the expertness value immediately while the other sharing robots are learning a task. The new knowledge and the expertness value will be kept in robots' memories. Once robot's learning trial is finished, they will be employed for the next learning trial.

From the techniques presented above, weights play an important role in knowledge sharing among robots. Weight will be used not only to determine whether the knowledge from the sources should be used but also how much the knowledge from the source should be contributed to the new knowledge. In this paper, weight which is determined from the robot expertness will be studied. A new robot expertness measure based on regret evaluation is proposed.

3   Measure of Expertness

The robot expertness indicates how well its current policy is. Two expertness measures previously proposed by Ahmadabadi's team were Gradient (G) and Average Move (AM) measures. The expertness value evaluated by the G measure takes accumulated rewards since each individual learning phase has begun in order to be less biased from long history of experiences. However, the G measure suffers when it has negative value. The higher negative value of G could have two possible meanings, either it has sufficiently learned to indicate which actions should not be executed or it is exploring improper actions. In the second case, the use of this measure can degrade the robot learning performance. Another measure is the Average Move (AM). The AM takes an average number of moves that the robot executed before achieving the goal into consideration. The lower number of moves that the robot has done, the higher expertness value is. However, when the robot randomly explores an environment, the AM cannot be used to represent the robot expertise.

As described above, previous measures are inefficient to represent the robot expertness measure. In this paper, we proposed a new measure of expertise based on regret evaluation. The regret measure is formed from the uncertainty bounds of the two best actions, i.e. the greedy action and the second best action. Bounds of both actions will be compared. If the lower limit of the bound of the greedy action is higher than the upper limit of the bound of the second best action, it is more likely that the greedy action is the best action. The regret measure given state s at time $t + 1$ is calculated from:

$$regret(s_{t+1}) = -(lb(Q(s_{t+1}, a_1)) - ub(Q(s_{t+1}, a_2))), \tag{4}$$

where $lb(Q(s_{t+1}, a_1))$ is the lower limit of estimated state-action value given state s at time $t + 1$ of the greedy action. $ub(Q(s_{t+1}, a_2))$ is the upper limit of approximated state-action value given state s at time $t + 1$ of the second best action. They are approximated from past state-action values sampled from time

$t-k+1$ to t as: $\{Q_T(s_T,a)\}_{T=t-k+1}^{t} = \{Q_{t-k+1}(s_{t-k+1},a),\ldots,Q_t(s_t,a)\}$ where k is a number of samples. Due to the fact that normal distribution in each state-action value is assumed, the uncertainty bounds of the sampled state-action values, $Bound(Q_t(s_t,a))$, can be estimated from:

$$Bound(Q_t(s_t,a)) = \overline{Q}_T(s_T,a) \pm t_{\frac{\alpha}{2},k-1}\frac{\hat{s}}{\sqrt{k}}, \qquad (5)$$

where $\overline{Q}_T(s_T,a)$ is the mean of the k samples of the estimated state-action values. $\hat{s}$ is sample standard deviation. $(1-\alpha)$ is the confidence coefficient and $t_{\frac{\alpha}{2},k-1}$ is student's t-distribution providing an area of $\frac{\alpha}{2}$ in the upper tail of a t distribution with $k-1$ degrees of freedom. Mapping the regret measure into the expertise value given state s at time t can be defined as follows:

$$expertness_m(s_t) = 1 - \frac{1}{1+exp(-b*regret(s_t))}. \qquad (6)$$

From Eq. 6, the regret value is mapped into a flipped sigmoid function ranges between [0 1]. b is slope of the mapped function. The large negative regret measure causes the expertness value to approach one. Illustrative examples of positive and negative regret measure are shown in Figs. 1(a) and 1(b).

In Figs. 1(a) and 1(b), a state composed of 5 possible actions is taken into consideration. Each action has its corresponding uncertainty bound as presented by three horizontal lines. The upper and lower lines are the upper and lower limits of the bound. The lines labeled with the numbers indicate limits considered. The middle line represents average of estimated state-action values. Small circles represent possible greedy actions. As seen in Fig. 1(a), there exist two possible greedy actions, i.e. actions a_3 and a_4. If the greedy action is a_4, the robot may decide that the action a_4 is the best action. However, action a_3 has a higher average of estimated state-action values. It is more likely to be the best action. Therefore, when uncertainty bounds of two best actions are overlapped, the best action cannot be explicitly determined. In this case, whatever the greedy action is, the regret measure will have a positive value. It represents that the robot

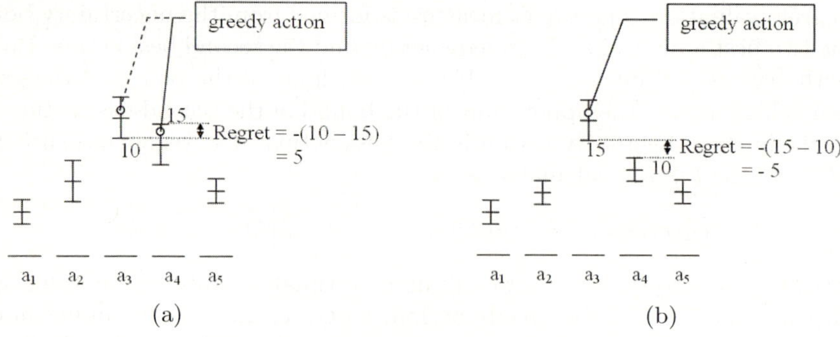

Fig. 1. Examples of regret measure (a) positive regret (b) negative regret

lacks the confidence whether the greedy action is the best action. In Fig. 1(b), the greedy action is definitely the action a_3 and it has a high chance of being the best action. The regret measure will have a negative value. Thus, the measured regret can represent how confidence the robot has in taking the greedy action.

4   Simulation

Eight techniques were used to test effectiveness of our proposed expertness measure within the scope of two problems: knowledge sharing among robots that learn a task from scratch and among robots that relearn the transferred knowledge. Fuzzy Q-learning technique used in this paper follows unmodified version presented in [7]. These techniques are 1.)'SP'; Separate learning or learning without sharing knowledge. 2.) 'SM': Shared Memory. 3.)'WSS': Weighted Strategy Sharing with G expertness measure 4.) 'WSSAM': WSS with AM measure 5.) 'WSSR': WSS with regret measure. 6.) 'AdpWSS': Adaptive WSS + G. 7.) 'AdpWSSAM': Adaptive WSS + AM 8.) 'AdpWSSR': Adaptive WSS + regret. For the WSS based algorithms, 5 cooperative times are studied. They are at every 20, 40, 60, 80, and 100 learning trials. The best results will be selected and compared with the other algorithms.

For the first problem, intelligent goal capturing behaviour is simulated. The goal will avoid being captured once it realizes that the distance between the goal and the robot is lower 30 cm. and the orientation of the goal w.r.t the robot is in between -45° and 45°. It will run in a perpendicular direction to the robot's heading direction. 1000 trials are tested for a single run. For the second problem, two robots relearn knowledge gained from a static obstacle avoidance to form the dynamic obstacle avoidance behaviour. Two robots learn to approach a goal which has two opponents moving in opposite direction. Learning parameters for all problems are summarized in table 2. The discount factor and learning rate are 0.9 and 0.1 for all problems respectively. Parameters were tuned for each algorithm by hand. The accumulated reward, averaged over trial in each run,

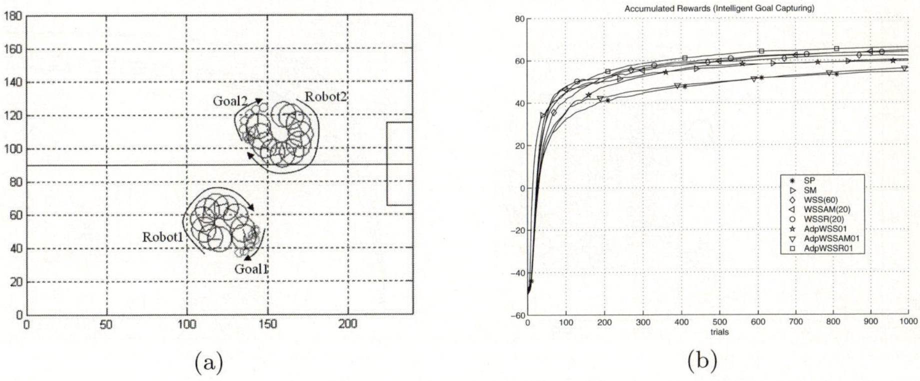

(a)   (b)

Fig. 2. Intelligent goal capturing (a) robots' path (b) accumulated rewards

is recorded. Their averages over 50 runs are used to compare the learning performance of these algorithms. From the simulation results, accumulated rewards and collision rates of these behaviours are summarized in table 1. For the WSS based algorithm, the best results are selected to compare with the other algorithms. The best cooperative time will be presented in the parenthesis. As an example, the WSS (20) is the WSS algorithm with the cooperative time is set at every 20 learning trials. Robot's path and accumulated rewards averaged over trial of the first and the second problems are shown in Figs. 2 and 3 respectively.

In Fig. 2(a), two robots learn to capture their goals in separated environment. The robots are presented by the bigger circles with lines indicated their heading direction. In Fig. 3(a), two robots learn to move to the goal while avoiding collision with dynamic obstacles in the same environment. Two opponents move in opposite direction presented by arrow lines as to obscure the robots. The robots have to avoid both opponent robots and their teammate. The simulation results showed that, the WSSR gave the best performances. The second best algorithm is the WSSAM. However, the AM measure is not suitable when applying to the Adaptive WSS. As seen in Figs. 2(b) and 3(b), the AdpWSSAM was only slightly better than the separate learning method. The SM was better than the AdpWSS and the AdpWSSAM. However it converged to suboptimal accumulated rewards in both problems. The AdpWSSR gave the superior performances for the first problem. However, it has slightly inferior performances compared to the WSS based algorithms in the second problem. As seen from the simulation results, our proposed expertness measure based on regret evaluation resulted in better performance than other expertness measures. For the WSS based algorithm, the best cooperative time depended on task and algorithms. Setting the suitable time for real-world implementation makes the algorithms are impractical. Additionally, it is not support asynchronous learning in multiple robots since the robot has to wait for all other robots to finish their individual learning phase. Therefore, only the AdpWSSR, SM and SP methods are suitable to be implemented into real-world robot learning problem. The results from the real-world knowledge sharing experiment are shown in the next section.

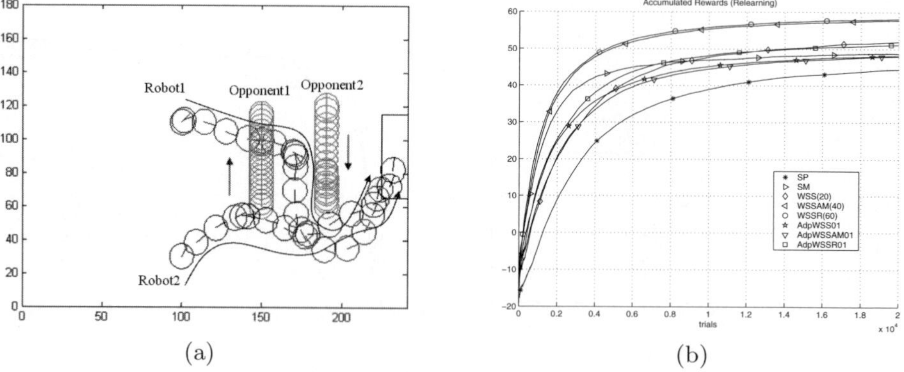

Fig. 3. Dynamic obstacle avoidance (a) robots' path (b) accumulated rewards

Table 1. Simulation results (average over two behaviours)

(a) General method			(b) WSS based method			(c) AdpWSS based method		
Methods	Accum. Rewards	Collision rate	Methods	Accum. Rewards	Collision rate	Methods	Accum. Rewards	Collision rate
SP	49.4209	**0.1274**	WSS	58.3409	0.1122	AdpWSS	53.8814	0.1215
SM	**54.5071**	0.1287	WSSAM	61.1725	0.0970	AdpWSSAM	51.9866	0.1229
—	—	—	WSSR	**61.2822**	**0.0846**	AdpWSSR	**58.6398**	**0.1035**

Table 2. Parameter setting

Parameters	Problem 1	Problem 2
Inputs of the FIS	'd_g' , 'o_g'	'd_g', 'o_g', 'd_{ob}', 'o_{ob}'
Outputs of the FIS	Gains of linear and angular velocities with candidate actions are [0, 0.25, 0.5] and [-1, 0, 1] respectively	
Centre positions of Membership functions	'd_g': {0, 15, 40} cm. 'o_g': {-0.4, 0, 0.4} rad.	'd_g': {20, 60, 140} cm. 'o_g': {-0.4, 0, 0.4} rad 'd_{ob}': {15, 30, 10}cm. 'o_{ob}': $\{-\frac{\pi}{2}, -\frac{\pi}{4}, 0, \frac{\pi}{4}, \frac{\pi}{2}\}$ rad.
Spans of Membership functions	'd_g': {5, 5, 15} cm. 'o_g': {0.15, 0.2, 0.15} rad.	'd_g': {15, 15, 30} cm. 'o_g': {0.15, 0.2, 0.15} rad. 'd_{ob}': {5, 5, 5} cm. 'o_{ob}': {0.25, 0.25, 0.25, 0.25, 0.25}rad.
$\varepsilon - probability$	$\varepsilon = 0.1$	$\varepsilon = \begin{cases} \frac{1}{(success)+1} & \text{if } \varepsilon > 0.1 \\ 0.1 & \text{otherwise} \end{cases}$
Reward function	$r_1(t) = \begin{cases} 100 & \text{success} \\ -0.1 & \text{otherwise} \end{cases}$	$r_2(t) = \begin{cases} 100 & \text{success} \\ -100 & \text{collide} \\ 0 & \text{otherwise} \end{cases}$

where 'd_g' is distance from a goal to a robot
 'o_g' is orientation of the goal with respect to the robot reference frame
 'd_{ob}' is distance from the closest obstacle to the robot
 'o_{ob}' is orientation of the closest obstacle with respect to the robot reference frame

5 Experiments

In this section, knowledge gained from robotic simulators is transferred to real robots. The robots learn a dynamic obstacle avoidance behaviour in the same environment within 1300 learning trials. Experiments were performed on the robotic soccer platform. However, to avoid frequent collision among robots, the problem is simplified. The opponent will stop moving if there is an obstacle within 5 cm. Three algorithms are implemented into real robots. They are 'SP', 'SM' and 'AdpWSSR'. Experimental results are shown in Figs. 4(a) and 4(b).

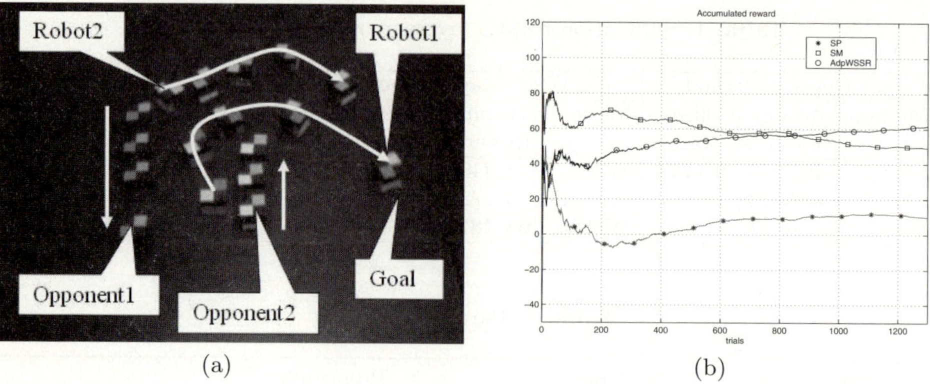

Fig. 4. Experimental results (a) robots' path (b) accumulated rewards

In Fig. 4(a), robots' path was shown. Two opponents moved in the opposite direction as presented by arrows. The robot1 moved to the goal successfully while avoiding collision with the robot2 and the opponent2. The robot2 was moving to the goal. As seen in Fig. 4(b), the AdpWSSR gave higher accumulated rewards averaged over trial in a long run. In the beginning of relearning period, the SM gave the best results. This was corresponding to the simulation results showed in Fig. 3(b). However learning performance of the SM was decreased when learning period was extended. Both knowledge sharing techniques gave better performances than learning without sharing knowledge.

6   Discussion

From the simulation results, the WSSR gave the best performances averaged over two behaviours. However, it is impractical for implementation in the real robot since it requires predefined setting of cooperative time. Additionally, it does not support asynchronous knowledge sharing among robots because the robot has to wait for all other robots to finish their individual learning phase before the cooperative learning phase can begin. Though using AM measure with the WSS based algorithm seems to work properly, it is not suitable when it is applied to the Adaptive WSS algorithm. Additionally, the AM measure cannot be used effectively when the robot randomly explores the states. SM gave the lowest performances compared to the other knowledge sharing algorithms. Its problem arises when a local minimum is encountered. It is difficult for the robots to get out from such situation. This happened because the robots use common decision making policy. It is difficult to achieve different solutions from the group's judgment. Therefore, the proposed measure of expertise gave the best results among all measures since it truly represents the robot expertness. Moreover, the robot expertness value measured by our method is varied over state space according to robot's experiences. This is different from weights assigned by previous measures in which the robot's expertise is treated to be equal in each state. Treating in this manner results in low diversity of the robots' learning after knowledge sharing is arisen. The experimental results showed that the knowledge gained from robotic simulators can be seamlessly transferred to the real robots. The Adaptive WSS with regret measure is practical for real-world implementation since it does not require the predefined setting of cooperative time and it also supports asynchronous learning in multiple robots.

7 Conclusion

In this paper, various knowledge sharing algorithms are studied. A new expertness measure based on regret evaluation is proposed. Simulation results showed that our proposed measure when applied to various investigated algorithms gave the best performances compared to the other previously proposed measures. Additionally, the Adaptive WSS with our proposed regret measure is practical for real-world implementation since the setting of suitable cooperative time is not required and it also supports asynchronous knowledge sharing among robots. Experimental results showed that knowledge gained from robotic simulators can be seamlessly transferred to real robots. However, learning time still needs to be improved. Extension to other knowledge sharing methods should be explored in the future works.

Acknowledgement

This work was supported by the Thailand Research Fund through the Royal Golden Jubilee Ph.D Program (Grant No. PHD/1.M.KT.43/C.2). Matlab software was supported by TechSource System (Thailand).

References

1. Tan, M.: Multi-agent reinforcement learning: Independent vs cooperative agents. In: Proc. 10th Int. Conf. Machine Learning (1993)
2. Ahmadabadi, M.N., Asadpour, M.: Expertness Based Cooperative Q-Learning. IEEE Trans. SMC.–Part B. **32**(1) (2002) 66–76
3. Bitaghsir, A.A., Moghimi, A., Lesani, M., Keramati, M.M., Ahmadabadi, M.N., Arabi, B.N.: Successful Cooperation between Heterogeneous Fuzzy Q-learning Agents. IEEE Int. Conf. SMC. (2004)
4. Dixon, K.R., Malak, R.J., Khosla, P.K.: Incorporating Prior Knowledge and Previously Learned Information into Reinforcement Learning Agents. Tech. report. Institute for Complex Engineered Systems, Carnegie Mellon University (2000)
5. Moreno, D.L., Regueiro, C.B., Iglesias, R., Barro, S.: Using Prior Knowledge to Improve Reinforcement Learning in Mobile Robotics. Proc. Towards Autonomous Robotics Systems. Univ. of Essex, UK (2004)
6. Yamaguchi, T., Tanaka, Y., Yachida, M.: Speed up Reinforcement Learning between Two Agents with Adaptive Mimetism. IEEE Int. Conf. IROS. (1997) 594–600
7. Ritthipravat, P., Maneewarn, T., Laowattana, D., Wyatt, J.: A Modified Approach to Fuzzy Q-Learning for Mobile Robots. In: Proc. IEEE Int. Conf. SMC. (2004)

Multiagent Realization of Prediction-Based Diagnosis and Loss Prevention

Rozália Lakner[1], Erzsébet Németh[1,2],
Katalin M. Hangos[2], and Ian T. Cameron[3]

[1] Department of Computer Science, University of Veszprém, Veszprém,
Hungary
[2] Systems and Control Laboratory, Computer and Automation Research Institute,
Budapest, Hungary
[3] School of Engineering, The University of Queensland,
Brisbane, Australia 4072

Abstract. A multiagent diagnostic system implemented in a Protégé-JADE-JESS environment interfaced with a dynamic simulator and database services is described in this paper. The proposed system architecture enables the use of a combination of diagnostic methods from heterogeneous knowledge sources. The process ontology and the process agents are designed based on the structure of the process system, while the diagnostic agents implement the applied diagnostic methods. A specific completeness coordinator agent is implemented to coordinate the diagnostic agents based on different methods. The system is demonstrated on a case study for diagnosis of faults in a granulation process based on HAZOP and FMEA analysis.

1 Introduction

For complex multiscale process systems that are difficult to model, a combination of model-based analytical and heuristic techniques is usually needed to develop a diagnostic system [1]. The approach of multiagent systems (MAS) [2] which emerged in AI represents a promising solution for such a diagnosis task, being based on information from heterogeneous knowledge sources [3]. A multiagent system can then be used for describing the system model, the observations, the diagnosis and loss prevention methods with each element being established through formal descriptions. This work investigates the use of the architecture and algorithms of multiagent systems for diagnosing faults in process plants when both dynamic models and heuristic operational knowledge of the plant are available. In particular, we consider a granulation process and the advice to operators in order to reduce potential losses. The significance of this work lies in a coherent fault detection and loss prevention framework based on a well-defined formalization of complex processes and the diagnostic procedures.

M. Ali and R. Dapoigny (Eds.): IEA/AIE 2006, LNAI 4031, pp. 70–80, 2006.
© Springer-Verlag Berlin Heidelberg 2006

2   Main Processes and Techniques in Fault Detection and Diagnosis

2.1   Fault Detection, Diagnosis and Loss Prevention

Early detection and diagnosis of process faults while the plant is still operating in a controllable region can help avoid abnormal events and reduce productivity loss. Therefore diagnosis methods and diagnostic systems have practical significance and strong traditions in the engineering literature.

The diagnosis of process systems is usually based on symptoms. *Symptoms* are deviations from a well-defined "normal behaviour", such as $T_{low} = (T < T_{min})$ which is defined by using a measurable temperature variable T. In the case of a dynamic system the measurable quantities are time-varied, so the symptoms related to these variables will also change with time.

In model-based fault detection and diagnosis one usually assigns a so-called *root cause* to every faulty mode of the system, the variation of which acts as a cause of the fault.

In the case of a fault it is usually possible to take actions in the initial phase of the transient to avoid serious consequences or to try to drive the system back to its original "normal" state. Dedicated *input signal(s)* serve this purpose for each separate fault (identified by its root cause) where the preventive action is a prescribed scenario for the manipulated input signal.

2.2   HAZOP and FMEA Analysis

The information available for the fault detection and diagnosis task is typically derived from a variety of sources which have varying characteristics. These sources include conceptual design studies and risk analyses as well as detailed dynamic models for parts of the system or for specific operating modes [4]. Heuristic operational experience is often elicited from operators and other plant personnel. The heuristic information can be collected with systematic identification and the analysis of process hazards, as well as the assessment and mitigation of potential damages using so-called Process Hazard Analysis (PHA). There are several methods used in PHA studies such as Failure Modes and Effects Analysis (FMEA), Hazard and Operability Analysis (HAZOP), Fault Tree Analysis (FTA) and Event Tree Analysis (ETA).

The Hazard and Operability study is the most widely used methodology for hazard identification. HAZOP [5] is a systematic procedure for determining the causes of process deviations from normal behaviour and the consequences of those deviations. This works on the fundamental principle that hazards and operational problems can arise due to deviations from normal behaviour. It addresses both the process equipment, operating procedures and control systems (in this case, known as CHAZOP).

Failure mode and effect analysis (FMEA) [6] is a qualitative analysis method for hazard identification, universally applicable in a wide variety of industries. FMEA is a tabulation of each system component, noting the various modes by which the equipment can fail, and the corresponding consequences (effects) of the failures. FMEA focuses on individual components and their failure modes. HAZOP and FMEA provide a comprehensive analysis of the key elements that help constitute an effective diagnostic system. The incorporation of failure modes can greatly enhance the tool's capabilities.

2.3   Prediction-Based Diagnosis

Prediction of a system's behaviour is used for deriving the consequences of a state of the system in time that is usually performed in process engineering by dynamic simulation. With the help of prediction, however, the faulty mode of the system can also be detected based on the comparison between the real plant data and the predicted values generated by a suitable dynamic model. This type of fault detection and diagnosis is called prediction-based diagnosis [7]. Because process systems are highly nonlinear and their models can be drastically altered depending on the actual fault mode, simple reduced models are needed for prediction-based diagnosis.

3   Knowledge Representation of the Diagnostic System

The proposed framework for a multiagent diagnostic system consists of an ontology design tool and a multiagent software system. The domain specific knowledge is represented as modular ontologies using the ontology design tool Protégé [8]. This knowledge is integrated into a multiagent software system where different types of agents cooperate with each other in order to diagnose a fault.

3.1   Process-Specific Ontology

The process-specific ontology describes the concepts, their semantical relationships and constraints related to the processes in question, similar to the general ontology for process systems given by OntoCAPE [9]. The process-specific ontology has two different parts, namely the common knowledge of the general behaviour of the process systems and the application-specific knowledge. This description defines the structure of a general process model for the process in question and enables the construction of a concrete process model realization which can be used as a dynamic simulation both in real-time simulation and in prediction-based diagnosis.

3.2   Diagnostic Ontology

The knowledge from human expertise and operation about the behaviour of the system in the case of malfunction, together with the reasons, consequences and possible corrections is described here. The diagnostic ontology contains the semantic knowledge on diagnostic notions (e.g. symptoms, root causes), different kind of tools such as FMEA and HAZOP tables and procedures such as reasoning based on FMEA or HAZOP knowledge.

3.3   Real-Time Database

Both the process-specific ontology and the diagnostic ontology contain time-varying elements such as process variables, actuator variables and their related variables. The values of these variables can be supplied by either a real process or a simulator and can be stored in the real-time database.

4   The Multiagent Diagnostic System

4.1   The Main Elements of the Multiagent Diagnostic System

Similar to the ontology classification described above, the agents of the diagnostic system belong to three main categories such as process-related, diagnostic-related and real-time service related agents.

The process agents. Process agents assist the user and the other agents in modelling and simulation of the process in question. This can be performed under different, faulty and non-faulty circumstances. Some types of process agents and their main tasks are as follows:

- *Process output predictors (PPs)* provide prediction by using dynamic simulation with or without preventive action(s).
- The *prediction accuracy coordinator (PAC)* checks the accuracy of the prediction result and calls additional agents to refine the result if necessary.
- *Model parameter estimators* can be associated with each of the PPs. The PAC may call this agent by requesting a refinement of the model parameters when the accuracy of the agent is unsatisfactory.

The diagnostic agents. Diagnostic agents perform measurements, symptom detection, fault detection [7], fault isolation and advice generation for avoiding unwanted consequences. These agents may perform logical reasoning and/or numerical computations. Some types of diagnostic agents and their main tasks are as follows:

- The *symptom generator and status evaluator* is based on non-permissible deviations that checks whether a symptom is present or not.
- The *state and diagnostic parameter estimators (SPEs)* are advanced symptom generators that use several related signals and a dynamic state space model of a part of the process system to generate a symptom.
- *Fault detectors (FDs)* use the services provided by SPEs or PPs to detect the fault(s) by using advanced signal processing methods.
- *Fault isolators (FIs)* work in the case of the occurrence of a symptom to isolate the fault based on different techniques (fault-tree, HAZOP, FMEA, fault-sensitive observers etc.).
- *Loss preventors (LPs)* suggest preventive action(s) based on different techniques that have been used for the HAZID and remedial actions (HAZOP, prediction, etc.).

- The *completeness coordinator* checks completeness of the result (detection, isolation or loss prevention) and calls additional agents if necessary.
- The *contradiction or conflict resolver (CRES)* calls additional agents in case of contradiction to resolve it.

The real-time agents. Beside the two main categories, the diagnostic system contains the following real-time agents for controlling and monitoring the process environment:

- *Monitoring agents* access and/or provide data from real world or from simulation.
- *Pre-processor agents* detect the non-permissible deviations which can be the possible symptoms.
- *Control agents* control the process in case of preventive actions.
- *Corroborating agents* act on requests from diagnostic agents and provide additional measured values or information.

4.2   The Structure of the Multiagent Diagnostic System

Several agent construction and simulation tools have been proposed in the literature by a number of researchers and commercial organizations. A non-exhaustive list includes: ABLE [10], AgentBuilder [11], FIPA-OS [12], JADE [13] and ZEUS [14]. The JADE (Java Agent DEvelopment Framework) has been chosen as the

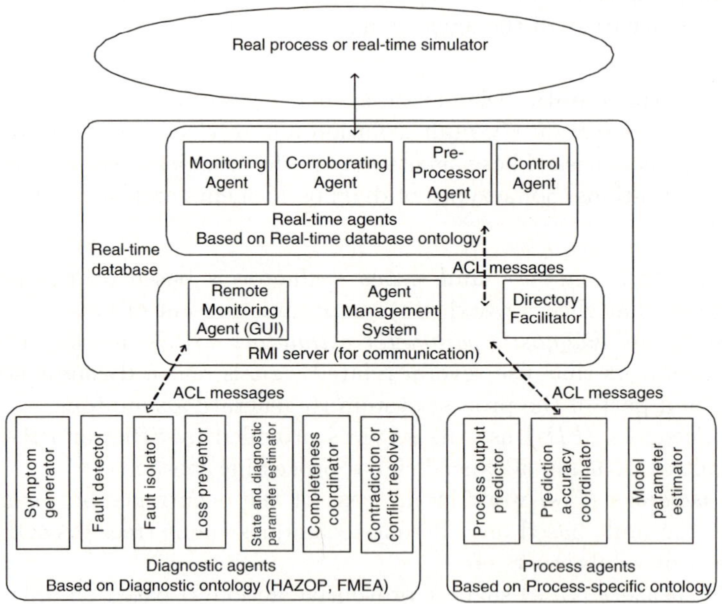

Fig. 1. The structure of the multiagent diagnostic system

multiagent implementation tool, that has integration facilities with the Protégé ontology editor and the Java Expert System Shell (JESS) [15]. The JADE agent platform can be split into several containers which are separate JAVA virtual machines and contain agents implemented as JAVA threads. The communication among the agents is performed through message passing represented in FIPA Agent Communication Language (FIPA ACL).

JADE does not support inferencing techniques but it can be integrated with some reasoning systems, such JESS and Prolog. JESS is a rule engine and scripting environment written in the JAVA language. It possesses both a very efficient forward chaining mechanism using the Rete algorithm as well as a backward chaining mechanism.

The dynamic models for the simulations are implemented in MATLAB. MATLAB serves to generate real-time data of the simulated process system and it contains the simplified models for prediction. The communication between MATLAB and JADE is solved by the TCP/IP protocol. For storing the huge amount of archive data a MySQL database is used. The connection between JADE and MySQL databases is realized by MySQL Connector/J.

The main elements and the software structure of the proposed multiagent diagnostic system implemented in JADE can be seen in Figure 1.

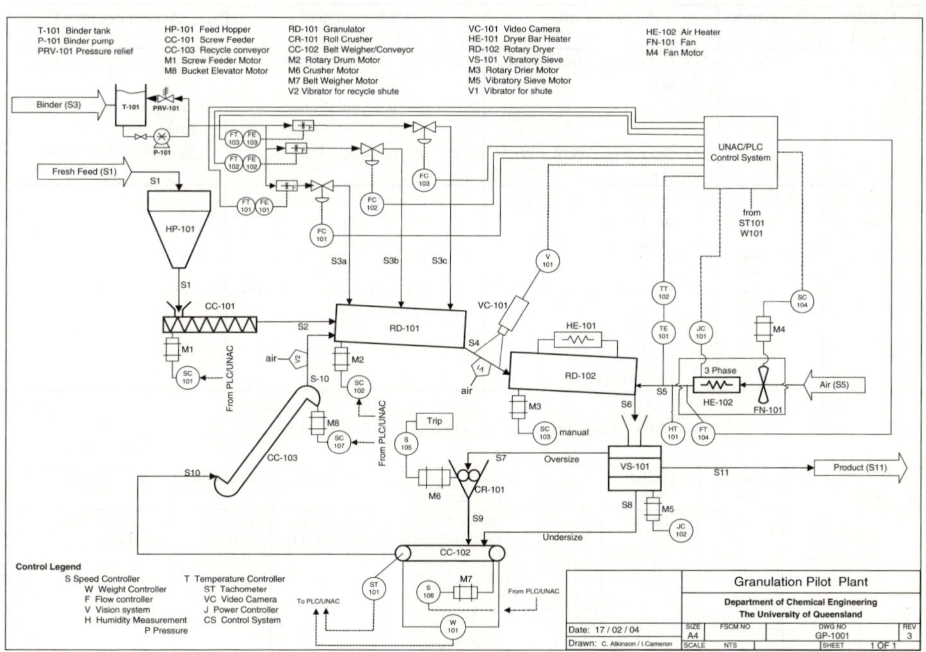

Fig. 2. Granulation pilot plant schematic

5   Case Study

The proposed methods and the prototype diagnostic system are demonstrated on a commercial fertilizer granulation system [16]. The simplified flowsheet of the plant with the variables used by the diagnostic system is shown in Fig. 2. The aim of the case study was to investigate the cooperation of the diagnostic agents, therefore we have selected a case when the diagnostic result can only be obtained by a combination of different fault detection and isolation methods.

5.1   Knowledge Elements of the Granulation Diagnostic System

There are two different types of knowledge elements in the granulator diagnostic system. The dynamic process models that contain traditional engineering knowledge of a process plant in the form of a set of differential-algebraic equations and the systematically collected heuristic knowledge that originates from a HAZOP or FMEA analysis.

The results of the HAZOP analysis are collected in a HAZOP result table, the structure of which is shown in Fig. 3. It defines logical (static) cause-consequence relationships between symptoms and potential causes that can be traced to root

Guide-word	Deviation	Possible causes	Consequences	Action required
Mean Particle Diameter (D50)	LESS	(1) Decrease in fresh feed size (2) Decrease/loss of slurry flow	* decrease in system holdup * change in granulation condition * change in recycle PSD	a) increase fresh feed size b) change to original feed type c) increase slurry flow
Slurry feed flow	LESS	(1) operator error in setting the flowrate (2) failure in valve actuator (3) failure in valve causing closure (4) reduced slurry production in preneutralizer	* reduced liquid phase in granulator * lack of granulation * lower product size range flow from granulator	

The structure of a HAZOP result table

Com-ponent	Descrip-tion	Failure mode	Possible causes	Effects		Detection	Criticality	Action
				Local	System			
FCV	Slurry flow control valve	Stuck Closed Open	maintance failure corrosion	loss of flow control lower or no flow	potential product quality impacts no growth D50 reduces in product	indirectly via product quality	MEDIUM quality reduction in product	- review maintenance procedures

The relevant part of the FMEA table

Fig. 3. HAZOP and FMEA result tables

causes of the deviation. The table in Fig. 3 illustrates two related symptoms with at least two different causes each.

A possible cause is regarded as a *root cause* if it refers to a failure mode of a physical component in the system, for example cause (2) in the second row of the HAZOP table. When such a root case is found we can complement or refine the diagnosis result by using the corresponding item from the FMEA table also shown in Fig. 3.

5.2   Simulation Results

In order to illustrate the operation of the proposed agent-based diagnostic system, only a part of the system, namely the diagnostic agent-set, based on logical reasoning is demonstrated. The structure of the agent-system can be seen in the left-hand side of Figure 4. Apart from the built-in main-container's agents, the agent platform contains three containers: the first for the real-time agents (MonitoringAgent and PreProcessorAgent), the second for the diagnostic agents (SymptomGeneratorAgent, FaultIsolatorAgents - based on both HAZOP and FMEA analysis, CompletenessCoordinatorAgent and LossPreventorAgent) and the third for a process agent (ProcessOutputPredictor). The main behaviour of the diagnostic agents is the logical reasoning based on heuristic knowledge (HAZOP, FMEA) with the help of the JESS rule engine. The communication and the operation of the diagnostic agent sub-system can be seen in the right-hand side of Figure 4. Based on the variable-values supplied by the MonitoringAgent the PreProcessorAgent determines the deviances in the system. In the case of deviance the SymptomGeneratorAgent checks the presence of symptoms and informs the CompletenessCoordinatorAgent. It calls the FaultIsolator- and LossPreventorAgent to determine the possible faults and suggest preventive actions. In case

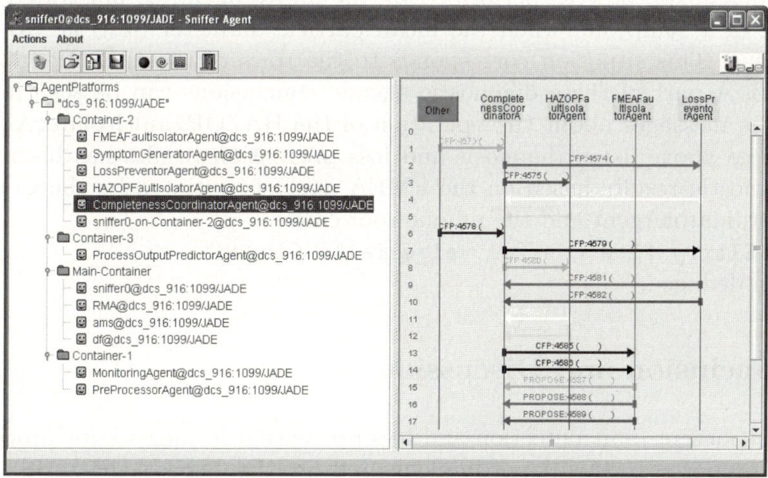

Fig. 4. The structure and the communication of the agent system

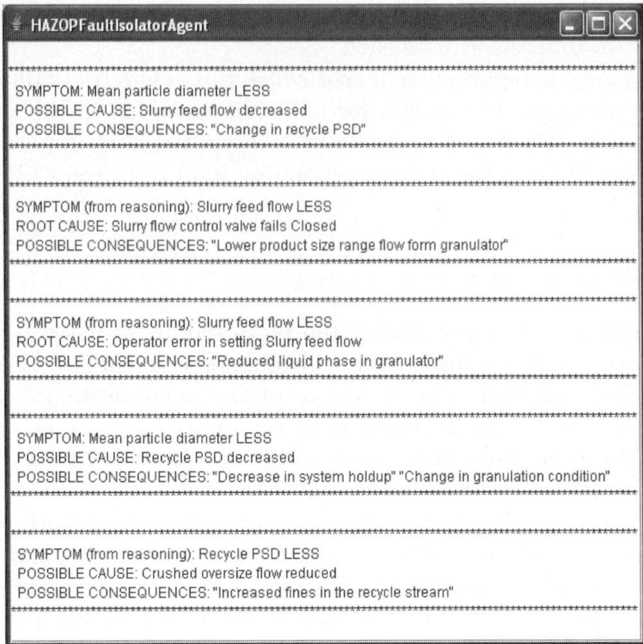

Fig. 5. The HAZOPFaultIsolatorAgent's conclusion

of multiple faults the FMEAFaultIsolatorAgent refines the result. Based on the suggestions of these agents the CompletenessCoordinatorAgent orders the operation of the ProcessOutputPredictor for predicting the behaviour of the system with the preventive action.

The diagnostic process performed by the above agents is illustrated on the example of a symptom, when the mean particle diameter (d_{50}) is less than a limit value. This situation corresponds to the rows of the HAZOP table seen in Fig. 3. A part of these diagnostic agents' conclusions can be seen in Fig. 5 where the messages about the operation of the HAZOPFaultIsolatorAgent are listed. The above listed diagnosis and loss prevention results has been refined the diagnostic results based on the FMEA analysis initiated by the CompletenessCoordinatorAgent and the unique root cause

```
"Slurry flow control valve fails Closed"
```
has been deduced.

6   Conclusion and Discussion

A novel coherent fault detection and loss prevention framework for process systems is proposed in this paper implemented in a Protégé-JADE-JESS environment that has clearly shown the advantages of such a technology in building complex diagnostic systems based on heterogeneous knowledge sources. The process ontology and the process agents based thereon have been designed following the structure of process systems that is first explored in [17] where a Coloured Petri Net-based diagnosis system is described. The diagnostic procedures based on model-based reasoning have been developed for a G2-based intelligent diagnostic system in [18] where the need for combining the different fault isolation methods to refine the diagnosis has arisen.

Acknowledgements

This research has been supported by the Hungarian Research Fund through grants T042710 and T047198, which is gratefully acknowledged, as well as the Australian Research Council International Linkage Award LX0348222.

References

1. Blanke, M., Kinnaert, M., Junze, J., Staroswiecki, M., Schroder, J., Lunze, J., Eds, Diagnosis and Fault-Tolerant Control. Springer-Verlag. (2003)
2. Jennings, N., R.,Wooldridge, M., J.: Agent Technology, Springer-Verlag, Berlin. (1998)
3. Wörn, H., et al.: DIAMOND: Distributed Multi-agent Architecture for Monitoring and Diagnosis, Production Planning and Control. **15** (2004) 189–200
4. Cameron, I.T., Raman, R.: Process Systems Risk Management. Elsevier, (2005)
5. Knowlton, R., E.: Hazard and operability studies : the guide word approach, Vancouver: Chematics International Company (1989)
6. Jordan, W.: Failure modes, effects and criticality analyses. In: Proceedings of the Annual Reliability and Maintainability Symposium, IEEE Press (1972) 30–37
7. Venkatasubramanian, V., Rengaswamy, R., Kavuri, S., N.: A review of process fault detection and diagnosis Part II: Qualitative models and search strategies. Computers and Chemical Engineering **27** (2003) 313–326
8. The Protégé Ontology Editor and Knowledge Acquisition System, (2004) http://protege.stanford.edu
9. Yang, A., Marquardt, W., Stalker, I., Fraga, E., Serra, M., Pinol, D.: Principles and informal specification of OntoCAPE, Technical report, COGents project, WP2. (2003)
10. Agent Building and Learning Environment (ABLE). http://www.research.ibm.com/able
11. Reticular Systems. AgentBuilder - An integrated Toolkit for Constructing Intelligence Software Agents. (1999) http://www.agentbuilder.com.
12. FIPA-OS. http://www.nortelnetworks.com/products/announcements/fipa/index.html.
13. JADE - Java Agent DEvelopment Framework. http://jade.tilab.com.
14. Nwana, H., S., Ndumu D., T., Lee L., C.: ZEUS: An advanced Tool-Kit for Engineering Distributed Multi-Agent Systems. In: Proc of PAAM98, (1998) 377–391
15. JESS, the Rule Engine for the Java platform. http://herzberg.ca.sandia.gov/jess/
16. Balliu, N.: An object-oriented approach to the modelling and dynamics of granulation circuits, PhD Thesis, School of Engineering, The University of Queensland, Australia 4072. (2004)

17. Németh, E., Cameron, I. T., Hangos, K. M.: Diagnostic goal driven modelling and simulation of multiscale process systems. Computers and Chemical Engineering **29** (2005) 783-796.
18. Németh, E., Lakner R., Hangos K. M., Cameron I. T.: Prediction-based diagnosis and loss prevention using model-based reasoning. In: Lecture Notes in Artificial Intelligence, Vol. **3533**, Springer-Verlag, (2005) 367-369.

Emergence of Cooperation Through Mutual Preference Revision

Pedro Santana[1] and Luís Moniz Pereira[2]

[1] IntRoSys S.A.
[2] Universidade Nova de Lisboa,
Quinta da Torre, Campus FCT-UNL
2829-516 - Portugal

Abstract. This paper proposes a method allowing an agent to perform in a socially fair way by considering other agents' preferences. Such a balanced action selection process is based on declarative diagnosis, which enables the removal of contradictions arising as all agents' preferences are confronted within the deciding agent. Agents can be negatively affected when some of their preferences are not respected for the sake of a global compromise. The set of preferences to be yielded by agents in order to remove all contradictions in a balanced way (i.e. the diagnosis that better manages how each agent is to be affected) is determined by minimising a cost function computed over application independent features. By respecting the resulting non-contradictory preferences set, the deciding agent acts cooperatively.

Keywords: Preference revision, multi-agent systems, cooperative behaviour.

1 Introduction

Preference criteria are subject to be modified when new information is brought to the knowledge of the individual, or aggregated when we need to represent and reason about the simultaneous preferences of several individuals. As a motivating example, suppose you invite three friends Karin, Leif and Osvald to go and see a movie. Karin prefers thrillers to action movies. Leif, on the other hand, prefers action movies to thrillers. Finally, Osvald is like Leif and prefers action movies to thrillers. Suppose you need to buy the tickets. Which movie do you choose?

One way to consider preferences in Multi-Agent scenarios, is to devise a strategy for removal of contradictions, which may arise when the preferences of all agents are put together. For instance, if *agent A prefers a to b* and agent B the other way around, then we have a contradiction (a synonym of conflict in this context). Removing the referred contradiction is another way of saying that at least one of the agents will have to *relax* its own preferences so a trade-off is achieved.

This paper proposes a methodology along this line of reasoning, that can be used as an agent mental process to allow the agent to perform in a fair manner. For instance, an agent engaged in a task that requires to make some choices, like selecting a TV programme, may choose to act fairly by considering others' preferences as well. Another possible application for the method set forth herein is to help a *broker* (i.e. an agent

M. Ali and R. Dapoigny (Eds.): IEA/AIE 2006, LNAI 4031, pp. 81–90, 2006.

responsible for distributing work) to allocate agents to those tasks that better suit them; in this case preferences can involve skills as well.

Other work on preferences revision can be found in [1,2], where the authors study the preservation of properties by different composition operators of preference relations definable by first-order formulas. In terms of preferences aggregation [3] handles different types of relationships that take into account the relative importance of the interacting agents, whereas [4] extended CP nets to handle preferences of several agents based on the notion of voting. In [5], a stimulating survey of opportunities and problems in the use of preferences, reliant on AI techniques, is presented.

2   Approach Overview

This paper presents some of the concepts presented in [6], which proposes an adapted version of the contradiction removal method defined for the class of normal logic programs plus integrity constraints, as proposed in [7], which transforms a given program into its revisable form. Then, it follows that each of the stable models of the revisable program specifies which preferences minimally need to be yielded or added for that program model to be consistent. Finally, from all preference revision minimal stable models, the one that is *fairest* (i.e. seeking highest cooperation while minimising losses) is selected and proffered to the end-user.

The proposed method involves the following steps: (1) set the preferences for each agent; (2) integrate all agents' preferences into a single *merged program*; (3) extend the *merged program* into a *revisable program* form; (4) determine the minimal stable models of the *revisable program* so as to generate all possible revision hypotheses; (5) from the set of minimal stable models select the most *fair* one, taking into account present and past iterations; and (6) repeat the whole process as desired.

3   Background Concepts

3.1   Stable Models

Let $\mathcal{L}$ be a first order language. A literal in $\mathcal{L}$ is an atom A in $\mathcal{L}$ or its default negation *not A*. A Normal Logic Program (NLP) P over $\mathcal{L}$ (sometimes simply called program) is a finite set of rules of the form $H \leftarrow B_1, B_2, \cdots, B_n, not\ C_1, not\ C_2, \cdots, not\ C_m$, with $(n \geq 0, m \geq 0)$ comprising positive literals H, and B_i, and default literals not C_j. $\mathcal{L}_P$ denotes the language of P.

Models are 2-valued and represented as sets of those positive literals which hold in the model. The set inclusion and set difference are with respect to these positive literals. Minimality and maximality too refer to this set inclusion.

Definition 1. *[8] Let P be a NLP and I a 2-valued interpretation. The* GL-transformation *of P modulo I is the program* $\frac{P}{I}$, *obtained from P by (1) removing from P all rules which contain a default literal not A such that $A \in I$ and (2) removing from the remaining rules all default literals. Since* $\frac{P}{I}$ *is a definite program, it has a unique least model J. Define* $\Gamma_P(I) = J$. *Stable models are the fixpoints of* Γ_P, *and they do not always exist (namely when a finite program contains loops over an odd number default negations).*

3.2 Preference Relation

Given a set N, a preference relation $\succ$ is any binary relation on N. Given two elements a and b in N, $a \succ b$ means that a is preferred to b. We assume that N contains at least two elements. We restrict $\succ$ to satisfy the properties of a strict partial order, which involves:

$$Irreflexivity : \forall x, x \nsucc x$$
$$Asymmetry : \forall x \forall y, x \succ y \Rightarrow y \nsucc x$$
$$Transitivity : \forall x \forall y \forall z, (x \succ y \wedge y \succ z) \Rightarrow x \succ z$$

Let us call the above properties integrity constraints, which are employed to detect preference contradictions (others could be added); they can be described in logic programming as follows:

$$\bot \leftarrow p(x, x). \qquad \bot \leftarrow p(x, y), p(y, x). \qquad \bot \leftarrow p(x, y), p(y, z), not\, p(x, z).$$

where x, y, and z are variables, $\bot$ represents a contradiction, when present in a model of a program, and $p(a, b)$ represents a preference of type $a \succ b$. An agent i can define its preferences by adding facts of type $p_i(x, y)$. As previously stated, the preferences of all agents have to be merged into a *merged program*. As a consequence, we have to add the following clause to the integrity constraints set: $p(x, y) \leftarrow p_i(x, y)$. Thus, there will exist a p predicate rule for each corresponding p_i predicate. If one of the integrity constraints rules succeeds, then there is a contradiction in the *merged program*.

3.3 Declarative Diagnosis

In this section we adopt the definitions set forth in [6]. Given a contradictory program P, i.e. with a contradictory stable model, to revise (i.e. eliminate) the contradiction symbol ($\bot$) from its models we need to modify P by adding and removing rules. In this framework, the diagnostic process reduces then to finding such combinations of rules. To specify which rules in P may be added or removed, we assume given a set C of predicate symbols in $\mathcal{L_P}$. C induces a partition of P into two disjoint parts: a changeable one P_c and stable one P_s. P_c contains the rules in P defining predicate symbols in C, while P_s contains the rules in P defining predicate symbols not belonging to C. P_c is the part subject to the diagnosis process.

Definition 2. *Let P be a program and C a set of predicate symbols in $\mathcal{L_P}$. Let D be a pair $\langle U, I \rangle$ where U is a set of atoms, whose predicate symbols are in C and $I \subseteq P_c$. Then, D is a diagnosis for P iff $(P - I) \bigcup U \nvDash \bot$. The pair $\langle \{\}, \{\} \rangle$ is called empty diagnosis.*

Intuitively, a diagnosis specifies the rules to be added and removed from the changeable part of P to revise its contradiction $\bot$. In order to minimise the number of changes, one should consider minimal diagnosis.

Definition 3. *Let P be a program and $D = \langle U, I \rangle$ a diagnosis for P. Then, D is a minimal diagnosis for P iff there exists no diagnosis $D_2 = \langle U_2, I_2 \rangle$ for P such that $(U_2 \bigcup I_2) \subseteq (U \bigcup I)$.*

Let us now clarify what P_c and P_s are. P_s (the stable partition of program P) refers to the integrity constraints and preferences that agents consider as non-negotiable (i.e. those preferences agents do no accept to discard at the cost of rejecting further cooperation). In this work we only considered negotiable preferences. On the other hand, P_c refers to the agents' preferences that will be subject to revision (i.e. that can be yielded). As an example, let us assume that there are two agents, one with a single preference and another one with two preferences; these define P_c:

$$P_c = \begin{pmatrix} p_1(a,b) \\ p_2(b,a) \\ p_2(c,b) \end{pmatrix} \quad P_s = \begin{pmatrix} \bot \leftarrow p(x,x) \\ \bot \leftarrow p(x,y), p(y,x) \\ \bot \leftarrow p(x,y), p(y,z), not\, p(x,z) \\ p(x,y) \leftarrow p_1(x,y) \\ p(x,y) \leftarrow p_2(x,y) \end{pmatrix}$$

which contains those rules (i.e. preferences) that can be removed as well as those rules that have been added so as to guarantee consistency. In this case, one possibility would be to remove $p_1(a,b)$ because it contradicts $p_2(b,a)$ (non-reflexivity) whereas a rule $p(c,a)$ would be added to ensure transitivity. Another possibility, which is simpler and so preferable, would be to remove $p_2(b,a)$ and no further change would be required.

Now it is necessary to extend P so it has a suitable form for contradiction removal. To do that, we have to consider the *revisable set*, which includes default atoms, *not A*, whose CWA (Closed World Assumption) makes them initially true, can be revised by adding A to P. By so doing, one can disable rules having such defaults in their body, and, as a consequence, remove some contradictions. Also, the positive atom A, being initially false, can be made true by adding it as a fact. This will enable rules with A introduced in their body.

Definition 4. *The revisables of a program P is a subset of the set of atoms A (with $A \neq \bot$) for which there are no rules defining A in P.*

Definition 5. *Let P be a program and V a set of revisables of P. A set $Z \subseteq V$ is a revision of P with respect to V iff $P \bigcup Z \nvDash \bot$.*

Definition 6. *Let P be a program and C a set of predicate symbols in $\mathcal{L}_P$. The transformation Γ that maps P into a program P' is obtained by applying to P the following two operations: (1) add $not\, incorrect(A \leftarrow Body)$ to the body of each rule $A \leftarrow Body$ in P_c and (2) add, for each predicate p with arity n in C, the rule $p(x_1, \cdots, x_n) \leftarrow uncovered(p(x_1, \cdots, x_n))$.*

In our example, the *revisable program* would be:

$$\Gamma(P) = \begin{pmatrix} \bot \leftarrow p(x,x) & p_1(a,b) \leftarrow not\, incorrect(p_1(a,b)) \\ \bot \leftarrow p(x,y), p(y,x) & p_2(b,a) \leftarrow not\, incorrect(p_2(b,a)) \\ \bot \leftarrow p(x,y), p(y,z), & p_2(c,b) \leftarrow not\, incorrect(p_2(c,b)) \\ \quad not\, p(x,z) & \\ p(x,y) \leftarrow p_1(x,y) & p_1(x,y) \leftarrow uncovered(p_1(x,y)) \\ p(x,y) \leftarrow p_2(x,y) & p_2(x,y) \leftarrow uncovered(p_2(x,y)) \end{pmatrix}$$

The transformation Γ preserves the truths of program P. Then, by adding instances of *incorrect*/1, one can eliminate unsound answers of predicate rules and, by adding instances of *uncovered*/1, one can complete predicates with missing answers.

4   Proposed Approach

The proposed approach considers that, in opposition to definition 6, the *uncovered* literal is applied to $p_i/2$ instead of $p/2$. That is to say, that those added preferences relate to the group (i.e. $p/2$) and not to an agent i in particular. With this alteration, the number of even loops is reduced, and as a consequence complexity as well. In addition, the preference to be added is usually related to the group and not to an agent in particular. Let us imagine a scenario where one agent prefers a to b whereas another prefers b to c. So that *transitivity* holds in that scenario, it is necessary to state that a is preferred to c. However, this information does not refer to any agent in particular - it belongs to the group as a whole. If considered otherwise, the addition of a preference could not be exploited as a metric of *unhappiness*; how could one assume that an agent has been disadvantaged with the addition of a preference that might be true (i.e. the referred agent may in fact prefer a to c)?

The stable models of $\Gamma(P)$, minimal with respect to the revisables, that do not lead to a contradiction are potential candidates for the *best diagnosis*. Let us focus on how cooperation among agents is polarised by choosing which preferences have to be *minimally* yielded by each agent, *in a fair way*. From the set of such minimal stable models (i.e. in the set of possible minimal diagnoses), we have to select the *best diagnosis*.

Since the entire process describes a mental process to be reiterated each time a task and/or the environment require, we need to take into account all previous losses an agent had in prior iterations (i.e. by recording every time some agent had to *yield* a preference). Therefore, the *best diagnosis* will be one determined by following a criterion of *fairness*. This is achieved by a cost function that weighs a given diagnosis in a *fair* way, i.e. by taking into account previous decisions, is minimised over the whole set of available diagnoses.

4.1   *Yielding* a Preference

Let us analyse what *yielding a preference* formally means.

Definition 7. *Let P be a program containing all preferences of all agents involved in a given iteration, $D = \langle U, I \rangle$ a diagnosis for P, $P_A \subseteq P$ a program with all preferences for agent A and $p(x,y)$ a preference of x over y. For each $incorrect(p(x,y)) \in I$, an agent A has 'yielded' a preference if $p_A(x,y) \in P_A$. For each $uncovered(p(x,y)) \in U$, an agent A has 'yielded to add' a preference.*

Computing the number of times an agent has to *yield* or *yield to add* a preference in a given diagnosis gives us an idea of how much displeased that agent will be with the solution trade-off. The presence of *yielding to add* preferences in a given solution may result in erroneous assumptions about others' preferences; as such, solutions including such assumptions are to be penalised. Still, *yielding* a preference and *yielding to add* a preference have not the same weight in the unhappiness of the agent. Therefore, we consider different weights for each type, w_y and w_{ya} respectively. In the experimental part of this paper $w_y = 2$ and $w_{ya} = 1$ are considered; that is to say that, *yielding* a preference is twice worse than *yielding to add* a preference, which intuitively makes sense. The exact proportion should be subject to further analysis, but out of the scope of this paper.

Notice the cost of *yielding* a preference only affects the agent in question, whereas the cost of *yielding to add* a preference affects all agents in the same amount. This means that *yielding* a preference increases the *dispersion* of *unhappiness* among agents, whereas *yielding to add* preferences increases the average number of *unhappiness*.

4.2   Diagnosis Assessment

The goal is to determine which diagnosis (i.e. which minimal stable model) is less *expensive* in terms of the "yieldings" agents have to endorse. In order to do so, the cost of a diagnostic D is assessed via a cost function. Two main components are considered, namely: the *average of yieldings*, $a(D)$, and the *dispersion of yieldings*, $d(D)$. The *average of yieldings* is defined by $a(D) = \frac{1}{n} \cdot \sum_{a \in A} w_{yield}(a, D)$, where D is the diagnostic in question, A is the set of agents involved in the process, n is the number of agents in A, and $w_{yield}(a, D)$ returns the total cost of agent a in diagnosis D.

The total cost of an agent a in a diagnosis D is $w_{yield}(a, D) = w_y \cdot n_y(a, D) + w_{ya} \cdot n_{ya}(a, D)$, where w_y and w_{ya} are the weights of *yielding* and *yielding to add* a preference, respectively, $n_y(a, D)$ and $n_{ya}(a, D)$ are the number of *yield* and *yield to add* preferences respectively in diagnosis D (see definitions 7).

The *dispersion* of a diagnosis D, $d(D) = \sqrt{\frac{1}{n} \cdot \sum_{a \in A} (w_{yield}(a, D) - a(D))^2}$, refers to the concept of standard deviation from statistics. It is worth emphasising the quadratic term in the standard deviation definition, which increases the cost of a diagnosis quadratically, in relation to its displacement from the average. Accordingly, as the *unfairness* of solutions increases, their related cost increases at a faster pace.

The standard deviation concept is used to measure how much *unfair* a diagnosis is for a given agent; in other words, the more disparate is the sacrifice of a given agent when compared to the average sacrifice, the more unfair the diagnosis is. The purpose of the cost function is to reduce the sacrifice of all agents as well as to avoid that some agents be much more sacrificed than the average. The next formula describes the minimising of the cost function in order to obtain the *best diagnosis* of the current iteration, $b_d[n]$:

$$b_d[n] = \min_D \left(\frac{w_{win}}{w_{all}} (\beta_d \cdot d(D) + \beta_a \cdot a(D)) \right) \tag{1}$$

where w_{win} is the quantity of accumulated victories of the agent less sacrificed (i.e. with smaller w_{yield}) in D, w_{all} is the quantity of accumulated victories the agent with greater amount of accumulated victories has, and β_a and β_d are weights. An agent accumulates a victory each time it is the one with smaller w_{yield} in the *best diagnosis* of a given iteration. It is assumed that the preferences of agents may change between iterations.

The $\frac{w_{win}}{w_{all}}$ component endows the system with memory, which allows to take into account previous iterations. This way, the selection of the *best diagnosis* takes into consideration that some agents may have been more sacrificed in the past than others. Intuitively, the possibilities of accepting the diagnosis in question as the *best diagnosis*, increase if the winning agent has less victories than the one with more victories, proportionally. As a result, all agents gradually converge into an homogeneous number of victories.

5   Experimental Results

The proposed method has been implemented in the XSB-Prolog[1] using the XSB-XASP Package[2], which implements the Answer Set semantics (cf. [9] for other application examples) and allows computing the stable models of a given program.

In this section we will briefly go over some implementation details. To do so, some (simplified for presentation purposes) XSB-PROLOG code will be exhibited. With the purpose of creating several scenarios that can be covered by different stable models, it is necessary to create even loops over default negation (where *tnot* is XSB-Prolog's tabled *not*), such as:

```
covered(X):-tnot(uncovered(X)).    incorrect(X):-tnot(correct(X)).
uncovered(X):-tnot(covered(X)).    correct(X):-tnot(incorrect(X)).
```

where each loop allows for its two opposite stable models solutions. The integrity constraints have been defined as follows (a two agent scenario has been considered):

```
false(X,_,_)  :- p(X,X).           false(X,Y,_)  :- p(X,Y), p(Y,X).
false(X,Y,Z)  :- p(X,Y), p(Y,Z), X \= Z, tnot( p(X,Z) ).
```

Agents' preferences can be defined in this manner (note that *incorrect*/1 literals have already been added):

```
p(son,X,soaps)  :- tnot( incorrect(p(son,X,soaps)) ).
p(son,cinema,X)  :- tnot( incorrect(p(son,cinema,X)) ).
```

which states that the son prefers to see anything in the TV to soaps, and prefers cinema to anything else. This code allows creating scenarios where new preferences are added (i.e. where *uncovered*/1 literals are inserted):

```
p(X,Y):-p(agent_1,X,Y).                     p(X,Y)  :- p(agent_2,X,Y).
p(X,Y):-not p(agent_1,X,Y),not p(agent_2,X,Y),uncovered(p(X,Y)).
```

The following code generates several hypotheses (i.e. stable models), which are then considered for the selection of the *best diagnosis*), by performing a call to the XSB-XASP package so it computes in *Res* the stable models with *ok* as the top goal; *ok* succeeds only if a given scenario does not fail to cope with each integrity constraint:

---

¹ http://xsb.sourceforge.net
² http://xsb.sourceforge.net/packages/xasp.pdf

```
ok :- tnot( notok ).
notok :- option(X), option(Y),option(Z), notok(X,Y,Z).
notok(X,Y,Z) :- false(X,Y,Z).
pstable_model(ok,Res,1) % Top goal call
```

An everyday multi-agent conflict resolution scenario is the one we can find in our houses when all family members have to cooperate (at least it is so expected) to decide on which TV programme they will watch. A simple version of such a scenario has been implemented with these characteristics:

Involved Agents: Father, mother, and son;
Available TV Programmes: Soaps, news, cinema, and documentaries;
Weights: $\beta_1 = 1$ and $\beta_2 = 3$. β_2 should be greater than β_1 in order to guarantee that the solutions converge to a small amount of yielded preferences. As long as this proportion between the two parameters is kept, the final results are not very sensitive to parameter variation.
Son's preferences: $cinema \succ x$; $documentaries \succ news$
Mother's preferences: $soaps \succ x$; $cinema \succ news$; $documentaries \succ news$
Father's preferences: $x \succ soaps$; $news \succ x$; $documentaries \succ news$

Starting with the accumulated victories as $(mother, father, son) = (1, 1, 1)$, the selected TV program (such that no other is preferred to in the *best diagnosis*) is cinema, the accumulated victories change to $(mother, father, son) = (1, 1, 2)$, and the explanation is ("inc" represents "incorrect"):

```
[inc(p(son,cinema,cinema)),inc(p(father,news,cinema)),
 inc(p(father,news,news)),inc(p(mother,soaps,cinema)),
 inc(p(mother,soaps,news)),inc(p(father,soaps,soaps)),
 inc(p(mother,soaps,soaps))]
```

The son is the one yielding less preferences and as a result he wins. Cinema is the only TV programme such that no other is preferred to in the *best diagnosis* and so it is selected. All preferences leading to contradiction are said to be incorrect. For instance, the son prefers cinema to anything, but he may not prefer cinema to cinema itself (irreflexivity). The father prefers news to anything else, but since the son prefers cinema to anything else (including news), the father has to yield the preference of news over cinema in particular (asymmetry). Other solutions exist, such as adjusting son's preferences so the father could see what he most prefers. However, those solutions are not so balanced (i.e. *fair*) than the selected one, in the current context.

In a subsequent iteration the selected TV programme is soaps, the accumulated victories become $(mother, father, son) = (2, 1, 2)$, and the explanation is:

```
[inc(p(son,cinema,cinema)),inc(p(father,cinema,soaps)),
 inc(p(son,cinema,soaps)),inc(p(father,news,cinema)),
 inc(p(father,news,news)),inc(p(father,news,soaps)),
 inc(p(father,soaps,soaps)),inc(p(mother,soaps,soaps))]
```

Although seeing soaps increases the total number of preferences to be yielded (i.e. now the son has to yield two preferences), soaps is preferred because the mother was in disadvantage in terms of victories. If the past had not been considered, at this iteration the result would be the same as in the previous iteration. In a third iteration, the selected TV programme is soaps, the accumulated victories become $(mother, father, son) = (2, 2, 2)$ and the explanation is:

```
[inc(p(son,cinema,cinema)),inc(p(son,cinema,news)),
 inc(p(mother,cinema,news)),inc(p(son,cinema,soaps)),
 inc(p(father,news,news)),inc(p(mother,soaps,cinema)),
 inc(p(mother,soaps,news)),inc(p(father,soaps,soaps)),
 inc(p(mother,soaps,soaps))]
```

A new *best diagnosis* is produced, which is caused by the disadvantage of the father. From this sequence of three examples, one can observe the evolution of the solution so as to maintain everybody happy.

In a second experiment a new son's preference, $x \succ soaps$, which is going to augment the displeasure in watching soaps (the father also prefers anything to soaps), has been added. Resetting the accumulated victories to $(mother, father, son) = (1, 1, 1)$ we obtain cinema as the selected TV programme, $(mother, father, son) = (1, 1, 2)$ as the new accumulated victories, and the following explanation:

```
[inc(p(son,cinema,cinema)),inc(p(father,news,cinema)),
 inc(p(father,news,news)),inc(p(mother,soaps,cinema)),
 inc(p(mother,soaps,soaps)),inc(p(father,soaps,soaps)),
 inc(p(son,soaps,soaps)),inc(p(mother,soaps,soaps))]
```

In line with the victory of the son, cinema is selected. Running a new the selected TV program is cinema, $(mother, father, son) = (2, 1, 2)$ is the new set of accumulated victories, and the explanation is as follows:

```
[inc(p(son,cinema,cinema)),inc(p(father,news,cinema)),
 inc(p(father,news,news)),inc(p(father,news,soaps)),
 inc(p(son,news,soaps)),inc(p(mother,soaps,cinema)),
 inc(p(father,soaps,soaps)),inc(p(son,soaps,soaps)),
 inc(p(mother,soaps,soaps))]
```

This time the mother wins since she was at a disadvantage in terms of victories; nevertheless, cinema is seen rather than soaps. In a last iteration we get news as the selected programme, $(mother, father, son) = (2, 2, 2)$ as the new accumulated victories, and the following explanation:

```
[inc(p(son,cinema,cinema)),inc(p(son,cinema,news)),
 inc(p(mother,cinema,news)),inc(p(father,news,news)),
 inc(p(mother,soaps,cinema)),inc(p(mother,soaps,news)),
 inc(p(father,soaps,soaps)),inc(p(son,soaps,soaps)),
 inc(p(mother,soaps,soaps))]
```

The father wins because he was at a disadvantage in terms of victories and, as a consequence, news is the selected programme. This experience demonstrates that it is not enough to be disadvantaged in terms of victories to obtain what one desires. More concretely, the mother was at a disadvantage and, as a result, she won the second iteration; still, soaps was not the chosen programme category. This occurred because the son also made clear that he would prefer to see anything but soaps.

6   Concluding Remarks

A method for preference revision in a multi-agent scenario has been presented. Instead of considering explicit priorities among agents and/or preferences, the method proposes a dynamic approach. A cost function that considers generic features of the solution (e.g. the quantity of preferences yielded by agents) has been employed to obtain a general approach, avoiding parameters too application dependent. Introducing memory in the revision process enables the emergence of cooperation as iterations unfold. Cooperation shows up in the form of an homogeneous amount of victories amongst all agents.

Assessing which preferences one should add or remove in the way prescribed in this paper, allows us to enact a flexible method for preference revision. If instead priorities among preferences are to be considered as the sole method for preference revision, intensive and tedious parameter tuning is going to be required so as to guarantee that preferences are conveniently revised. In such a memory-less solution, the system is not able to evolve towards cooperation as iterations unfold, resulting in fully deterministic and static solutions. On the contrary, we consider our approach of special interest for dynamic environments.

We have employed the two-valued Stable Models semantics to provide meaning to our logic programs, but we could just as well have employed the three-valued Well-Founded Semantics [10] for a more skeptical preferential reasoning. Also, we need not necessarily insist on a strict partial order for preferences, but have indicated that different constraints may be provided.

References

1. Chomicki, J.: Preference formulas in relational queries. ACM Transactions on Database Systems **28** (2003) 427–466
2. Andreka, H., Ryan, M., Schobbens, P.Y.: Operators and laws for combining preference relations. Journal of Logic and Computation **12** (2002) 13–53
3. Yager, R.R.: Fusion of multi-agent preference ordering. Fuzzy Sets and Systems **117** (2001) 1–12
4. Rossi, F., Venable, K.B., Walsh, T.: mCP nets: representing and reasoning with preferences on multiple agents. In: Procs. of the 19th Conf. on Artificial Intelligence, LNCS 749, AAAI Press (2004) 729–734
5. Doyle, J.: Prospects for preferences. Computational Intelligence **20** (2004) 111–136
6. Dell'Acqua, P., Pereira, L.M.: Preference revision via declarative debugging. In: Progress in Artificial Intelligence, Procs. 12th Portuguese Int. Conf. on Artificial Intelligence (EPIA'05), Covilhã, Portugal, Springer, LNAI 3808 (2005)
7. Pereira, L.M., Damásio, C., Alferes, J.J.: Debugging by diagnosing assumptions. In Fritzson, P., ed.: Procs. of the 1st Int. Workshop on Automatic Algorithmic Debugging (AADEBUG'93), Springer–Verlag, LNCS 749 (1993) 58–74
8. Gelfond, M., Lifschitz., V.: The stable model semantics for logic programming. In: Procs. of the 5th Int. Logic Programming Conf., MIT Press (1998)
9. Baral, C.: Knowledge Representation, Reasoning and Declarative Problem Solving. Cambridge U.P. (2003)
10. Gelder, A.V., Ross, K.A., Schlipf, J.S.: The well-founded semantics for general logic programs. J. ACM **38** (1991) 620–650

Running Contracts with Defeasible Commitment

Ioan Alfred Letia and Adrian Groza

Technical University of Cluj-Napoca
Department of Computer Science
Baritiu 28, RO-400391 Cluj-Napoca, Romania
`{letia, adrian}@cs-gw.utcluj.ro`

Abstract. Real life contracts imply commitments which are active during their running window, with effects on both normal runs as well as in the case of exceptions. We have defined defeasible commitment machines (DCMs) to provide more flexibility. As an extension to the task dependency model for the supply chain we propose the commitment dependency network (CDN) to monitor contracts between members of the supply chain. The workings of the DCMs in the CDN is shown by a simple scenario with supplier, producer, and consumer.

Keywords: Multi-agent systems, Autonomous agents, Internet applications.

1   Introduction

Although contracts are a central mechanism for defining interactions between organizations, there is currently inadequate business support for using the information provided by these contracts. The current requirements of the supply chains [1] demand a more outward view on contract management for each entity within the chain. The emerging services science deals with such issues: 1) services contract specifications, cases, and models; 2) service level agreements; 3) automatic and semi-automatic services contract generation and management; 4) legal issues in services contract and operations; 5) decision support systems for contracts operations. Our work [2] belongs to the above trend, based on the temporalised normative positions in defeasible logic [3] using a special case of the nonmonotonic commitment machines [4].

In the supply chain context a contract breach can be propagated over the entire chain, with rules imposed by law that help agents to manage perturbations in the supply chain. Each agent has more than one way to respond to a perturbation, following remedies that are adequate for an efficient functionality of the supply chain: expectation damages, opportunity cost, reliance damages, and party designed damages [5].

The main contribution of this paper consists in showing how the defeasible commitment machines (DCMs) can be used within a commitment dependency network (CDN). In the next section we describe the temporalised normative positions that we use in section 3 to define DCMs and contracts. In the section 4

M. Ali and R. Dapoigny (Eds.): IEA/AIE 2006, LNAI 4031, pp. 91–100, 2006.

we show for a simple scenario how contracts are executed and the section 5 discusses how exceptions can be captured in our framework.

2   Temporalised Normative Positions

We are using the temporalised normative positions [3]: A *normative defeasible theory* (NDL) is a structure $(F, R_K, R_I, R_Z, R_O, \succ)$ where F is a finite set of facts, R_K R_I R_Z R_O are respectively a finite set of persistent or transient rules (strict, defeasible, and defeaters) for knowledge, intentions, actions, and obligations, and $\succ$ representing the superiority relation over the set of rules.

A rule in NDL is characterized by three orthogonal attributes: strength, persistence, modality. R_K represents the agent's theory of the world, R_Z encodes its actions, R_O the normative system (obligations), while R_I and the superiority relation capture the agent's strategy or his policy. The conclusion of a *persistent rule* holds at all instants of time after the conclusion has been derived, unless a superior rule has derived the opposite conclusion, while a *transient rule* establishes the conclusion only for a specific instance of time [3].

Whenever the premises of *strict rules* are indisputable then so is the conclusion, while *defeasible rules* are rules that can be defeated by contrary evidence. *Defeaters* are rules that cannot be used to draw any conclusions, their only use is to prevent some conclusions, as in "if the customer is a regular one and has a short delay for paying, we might not ask for penalties". This rule cannot be used to support a "not penalty" conclusion, but it can prevent the derivation of the penalty conclusion.

$\rightarrow_X^t$, $\Rightarrow_X^t$ and $\rightsquigarrow_X^t$ are used for transient rules (strict, defeasible respectively defeaters), $\rightarrow_X^p$, $\Rightarrow_X^p$ and $\rightsquigarrow_X^p$ for persistent rules (strict, defeasible respectively defeaters), where $X \in \{K, I, Z, O\}$ represents the modality. A conclusion in NDL is a tagged literal where $+\Delta_X^\tau q : t$ means that q is definitely provable of modality X, at time t in NDL (fig. 1) and $+\partial_X^\tau q : t$ means q is defeasibly provable of modality X, at time t in NDL (fig. 2, 3). Similarly, $-\Delta_X^\tau q : t$ means that q is not definitely provable of modality X and $-\partial_X^\tau q : t$ says that q is not defeasibly provable of modality X. Here $\tau \in \{t, p\}$, t stands for transient, while p for a persistent derivation.

A strict rule $r \in R_s$ is $\Delta_X - applicable$ if $r \in R_{s,X} \forall a : t_k \in A(r) : a_k : t_k$ is $\Delta_X - provable$, and is $\Delta_X - discarded$ if $r \in R_{s,X} \exists a_k : t_k \in A(r) : a_k : t_k$ is $\Delta_X - rejected$. Conditions for $\partial_X - applicable$ and $\partial_X - discarded$ are similar, with Δ replaced by ∂.

The conditions for concluding whether a query is transient or persistent, definitely provable is shown in the figure 1. For the transient case, at step $i + 1$ one can assert that q is definitely transient provable if there is a strict transient rule $r \in R_s^t$ with the consequent q and all the antecedents of r have been asserted to be definitely (transient or persistent) provable, in previous steps. For the persistent case, the persistence condition (3) allows us to reiterate literals definitely proved at previous times. For showing that q is not persistent definitely provable, in addition to the condition we have for the transient case, we

$+\Delta_X^t$: If $P(i+1) = +\Delta_X^t q : t$ then
   $q : t \in F$, or
   $\exists r \in R_{s,X}^t [q : t]$ r is $\Delta_X - applicable$

$+\Delta_X^p$: If $P(i+1) = +\Delta_X^p q : t$ then
   $q : t \in F$, or
   $\exists r \in R_{s,X}^p [q : t]$ r is $\Delta_X - applicable$ or
   $\exists t' \in \Gamma : t' < t$ and $+\Delta_X^p q : t' \in P(1..i)$.

Fig. 1. Transient and persistent definitely proof for modality X

$+\partial_X^t$: If $P(i+1) = +\partial_X^t q : t$ then
   (1) $+\Delta_X q : t \in P(1..i)$ or
   (2) $-\Delta_X \sim q : t \in P(1..i)$ and
      (2.1) $\exists r \in R_{sd,X}[q : t]$: r is ∂_X-applicable and
      (2.2) $\forall s \in R[\sim q : t]$: s is ∂_X-discarded or
           $\exists w \in R(q : t)$: w is ∂_X-applicable or $w \succ s$

Fig. 2. Transient defeasible proof for modality X

$+\partial_X^p$: If $P(i+1) = +\partial_X^t q : t$ then
   (1) $+\Delta_X^p q : t \in P(1..i)$ or
   (2) $-\Delta_X \sim q : t \in P(1..i)$, and
      (2.1) $\exists r \in R_{sd,X}^p [q : t]$: r is ∂_X-applicable, and
      (2.2) $\forall s \in R[\sim q : t]$: either s is ∂_X-discarded or
           $\exists w \in R(q : t)$: w is ∂_X-applicable or $w \succ s$; or
   (3) $\exists t' \in \Gamma : t' < t$ and $+\partial_X^p q : t' \in P(1..i)$ and
      (3.1) $\forall s \in R[\sim q : t"], t' < t" \leq t$, s is ∂_X-discarded, or
           $\exists w \in R(q : t")$: w is ∂_X-applicable and $w \succ s$.

Fig. 3. Persistent defeasible proof for modality X

have to assure that, for all instances of time before now the persistent property has not been proved. According to the above conditions, in order to prove that q is definitely provable at time t we have to show that q is either transient, or persistent definitely provable [3].

Defeasible derivations have an argumentation like structure [3]: first we choose a supported rule having the conclusions q we want to prove, second we consider all the possible counterarguments against q, and finally we rebut all the above counterarguments showing that, either some of their premises do not hold, or the rule used for its derivation is weaker than the rule supporting the initial conclusion q. $\sim q$ denotes the complementary of literal q (if q is the positive p then $\sim q$ is $\neg p$; if q is $\neg p$ then $\sim q$ is p). A goal q which is not definitely provable is defeasibly transient provable if we can find a strict or defeasible transient rule for which all its antecedents are defeasibly provable, $\sim q$ is not definitely provable and for each rule having $\sim q$ as a consequent we can find an antecedent which does not satisfy the defeasible provable condition (fig. 2).

For the persistence case, the aditional clause (3) (fig. 3) verifies if the literal $q : t$ has been persistent defeasibly proved before, and this conclusion remained valid all this time since there has been no time t'' when the contrary $\sim q$ was proved by the rule s, or that rule was not stronger than the one sustaining q.

3   Defeasible Commitment Machines

Commitment machines were proposed as a formalism for declarative specification of protocols. We view a contract as a protocol binding different parties to their commitments by specifying the type of services agreed upon, the obligations, and the remedies in case of breach. Contracts are represented by defeasible commitment machines (DCM), that is a theory in the normative defeasible logic (NDL) consisting of two parts. The first part captures the representation of commitments and the operations on them in NDL (section 3.2) as a contract independent theory, while the second is contract dependent and includes rules describing specific contractual clauses (section 3.3).

3.1   Standard Commitments

We use the notion of commitment for the clauses of the contract, translated into facts, definitions, or normative rules. The commitments capture the obligations of one party towards the nother. Realistic approaches attach deadlines to commitments in order to detect their breach or satisfaction.

A *base-level commitment* $C(x, y, p : t_{maturity}) : t_{issue}$ binds a debtor x to a creditor y for fulfilling the proposition p until the deadline $t_{maturity}$. A *conditional commitment* $CC(x, y, q : t'_{maturity}, p : t_{maturity}) : t_{issue}$ denotes that if a condition q is brought about at $t'_{maturity}$, then the commitment $C(x, y, p : t_{maturity}) : t_{issue}$ will hold. In the conditional commitment $CC(s, b, pay(P_c) : t_{maturity}, deliver(g_i) : t_{maturity} + 3) : t_{issue}$ the agent s (representing the seller agent or the debtor) assumes the obligation to agent b (representing the buyer or the creditor) to deliver the item g_i in three days after the buyer has paid the price P_c. A commitment may be in one of the following states: active (between t_{issue} and $t_{maturity}$ and $\neg breach$), violated ($t_{maturity} \leq t_{current}$ and the commitment was not discharged or released) or performed (if the debtor executes it until $t_{maturity}$).

The operations for the manipulations of commitments [6] are:

- $Create(x, C) : t_{issue}$ - the debtor x signs the commitment C at time t_{issue} (can only be performed by the C's debtor x);
- $Cancel(x, C) : t_{breach}$ - the debtor x will no longer satisfy its obligation (this can usually[1], be performed only by C's debtor x);

---

[1] The current practice in law decommits an agent from its obligations in some special situations (i.e. the creditor has lost his rights). Hence, the normative agent that monitors the market can also cancel some commitments.

- $Release(y, C) : t_x$ - releases C's debtor x from commitment C (performed by the creditor y);
- $Assign(y, z, C) : t_x$ - replaces arbitrarily y with z as C's creditor (performed by the creditor y);
- $Delegate(x, z, C) : t_x$ - replaces x with z as C's debtor (performed by the debtor x);
- $Discharge(x, C) : t_x$ - C's debtor x fulfills the commitment.

These operations cannot be carried out arbitrarily. They are subject to rules that govern the electronic market and which set the power of agents within that market [4]. An agent has power when one of its actions determines a normative effect. For instance, the agents must have the power to delegate or assign a commitment, otherwise their operations have no normative consequence.

3.2   Commitments in Temporalised Normative Positions

We enhanced the task dependency network model [1, 5] used to model the supply chain. A commitment dependency network (CDN) is a graph (V,E) with vertices $V = G \cup A$, where: $G =$ the set of commitments, $A = S \cup P \cup C$ the set of agents, $S =$ the set of suppliers, $P =$ the set of producers, $C =$ the set of consumers, and a set of edges E connecting agents with their input and output commitments. An output commitment for agent a is a commitment in which a is the debtor, while an input commitment for agent a is a commitment in which a is the creditor. With each agent a we associate an input set $I_a = \{c \in C | \langle c, a \rangle \in E\}$ containing all the commitments where a is creditor and an output set $O_a = \{c \in C | \langle a, c \rangle \in E\}$ containing all the commitments where a is debtor. Agent a is a supplier if $I_a = 0$, a consumer if $O_a = 0$, and a producer otherwise. Such a multi-party commitment network is satisfiable if all the commitments may be discharged [7].

Following the steps in [4], we have defined [2] the defeasible commitment machine (DCM) using the normative defeasible logic instead of the causal logic with the goal to increase the flexibility of the commitments. Commitments in NDL are declared persistent knowledge $\rightarrow_K^p C(x, y, p) : t_i, \rightarrow_K^p CC(x, y, q, p) : t_i$. The rules of a DCM (fig. 4) capture the meaning of the operations, where t_m stands for $t_{maturity}$, representing the deadline attached to the commitment. Persistent conclusions remain valid until a more powerful derivation retracts them (for instance $r_2 \succ r_1$).

For the life cycle of a commitment, cancellation means an exception which appears in contract execution (rules r_3 and r_4). Usually, cancellation is compensated by activating another commitment or a contrary-to-duty obligation. The debtor may propose another commitment which is more profitable for both partners in the light of some arising opportunities on the market or just recognizes its incapacity to accomplish the task. The sooner the notification, the lower the damages. In some situations, a commitment may be active even after it is breached [6], expressed here by the defeasible rule r_3. Therefore, a normative agent can block the derivation of that conclusion in order to force the execution of a specific commitment. The same reason is valid for the rules r_{13} and r_{14} when the debtor does not execute its commitment until the deadline t_m. However, a

$$r_1 : Create(x, y, p : t_m) : t_{issue} \rightarrow_K^p C(x, y, p : t_m) : t_{issue}$$
$$r_2 : Discharge(x, y, p : t_m) : t_{perf} \rightarrow_K^p \neg C(x, y, p : t_m) : t_{perf}$$
$$r_3 : Cancel(x, y, p : t_m) : t_{breach} \Rightarrow_K^p \neg C(x, y, p : t_m) : t_{breach}$$
$$r_4 : Cancel(x, y, p : t_m) : t_{breach} \Rightarrow_K^p C(x, y, contrary\_to\_duty : t'_m) : t_{breach}$$
$$r_5 : Release(x, y, p : t_m) : t_{release} \rightarrow_K^p \neg C(x, y, p : t_m) : t_{release}$$
$$r_6 : Delegate(x, y, p : t_m, z) : t_{delegate} \Rightarrow_K^p \neg C(x, y, p : t_m) : t_{delegate}$$
$$r_7 : Delegate(x, y, p : t_m, z) : t_{delegate} \Rightarrow_K^p C(z, y, p : t_m) : t_{delegate}$$
$$r_8 : Assign(x, y, p : t_m, z) : t_{assign} \Rightarrow_K^p \neg C(x, y, p : t_m) : t_{assign}$$
$$r_9 : Assign(x, y, p : t_m, z) : t_{assign} \Rightarrow_K^p C(x, z, p : t_m) : t_{assign}$$
$$r_{10} : CCreate(x, y, q : t_m, p : t_m + \tau) : t_{issue} \rightarrow_K^p CC(x, y, q : t_m, p : t_m + \tau) : t_{issue}$$
$$r_{11} : CDischarge(x, y, q : t_m, p : t_m + \tau) : t_{perf} \rightarrow_K^p \neg CC(x, y, q : t_m, p : t_m + \tau) : t_{perf}$$
$$r_{12} : CDischarge(x, y, q : t_m, p : t_m + \tau) : t_{perf} \rightarrow_K^p C(x, y, p : t_m + \tau) : t_{perf}$$
$$r_{13} : t_{current} > t_m \wedge C(x, y, p : t_m) : t_m \Rightarrow_K^p \neg C(x, y, p : t_m) : t_m$$
$$r_{14} : t_{current} > t_m \wedge C(x, y, p : t_m) : t_m \Rightarrow_K^p C(x, y, contrary\_to\_duty : t'_m) : t_m$$
$$r_2 \succ r_1, \; r_3 \succ r_1, \; r_5 \succ r_1, \; r_6 \succ r_1, \; r_8 \succ r_1, \; r_{11} > r_{10}$$

Fig. 4. Defeasible commitment machine

$$r_{18} : SendRequest : t_x \rightarrow_K^p request : t_x$$
$$r_{19} : SendOffer : t_x \rightarrow_K^p offer : t_x$$
$$r_{20} : SendOffer : t_x \rightarrow_Z^t CCreate(M, C, acceptC : t_m, goods : t_m + 2) : t_x$$
$$r_{21} : SendAccept : t_x \rightarrow_K^p accept : t_x$$
$$r_{22} : accept : t_x \wedge CC(M, C, acceptC : t_m, goods : t_m + 3) : t_x$$
$$\rightarrow_Z^t CDischarge(M, C, acceptC : t_m, goods : t_m + 3) : t_x$$
$$r_{23} : SendAccept : t_x \rightarrow_Z^t CCreate(C, M, goods : t_m, pay : t_m + 2) : t_x$$
$$r_{24} : SendGoods : t_x \Rightarrow_K^p goods : t_x + 2$$
$$r_{25} : SendGoods : t_x \rightarrow_Z^t CCreate(M, C, pay : t_m, receipt : t_m + 1) : t_x$$
$$r_{26} : goods : t_x \wedge CC(C, M, goods : t_m, pay : t_m + 2) : t_x$$
$$\rightarrow_Z^t CDischarge(C, M, goods : t_m, pay : t_m + 2) : t_x$$
$$r_{27} : goods : t_x \wedge C(M, C, goods : t_m) \rightarrow_Z^t Discharge(M, C, goods : t_m) : t_x$$
$$r_{28} : SendPayment : t_x \rightarrow_K^p pay : t_x + 1$$
$$r_{29} : pay : t_x \wedge CC(M, C, pay : t_m, receipt : t_m + 1) : t_x$$
$$\rightarrow_Z^t CDischarge(M, C, goods : t_m, pay : t_m + 2) : t_x$$
$$r_{30} : pay : t_x \wedge C(C, M, payC : t_m) : t_x \rightarrow_Z^t Discharge(C, M, payC : t_m) : t_x$$
$$r_{31} : SendReceipt : t_x \Rightarrow_K^p receipt : t_x + 1$$
$$r_{32} : receipt : t_x \wedge C(M, C, receipt : t_m) : t_x \rightarrow_Z^t Discharge(M, C, receipt : t_m) : t_x$$

Fig. 5. Contracts in Temporalised Normative Positions

commitment cannot be active after it is satisfied (rule r_2). Note that *assign* and *delegate* are defeasible, because agents need special power to execute them.

3.3   Contract Specification in DCM

The rules in the figure 5 use the DCM for representing a specific contract between two agents, expressing actions that spread over more instances of time (i.e rules r_{24}, r_{28}, r_{31}). For instance, the rule r_{24} says that the seller agent starts the action *SendGoods* at time t_x, but the items reach the destination only after two days, when the fluent *goods* becomes true. The same rules are also defeasible, meaning that if an unpredictable event appears (i.e. an accident), their consequent fluents may be retracted. The execution of the contract may start from any state, because there is no specific order of actions. This can be useful for the supply chain, where long time business relationships suppose that the first steps in contract negotiation are no longer needed.

4   Running the Contracts

In the simple scenario of figure 6 the supplier A commits to deliver the item g_1 no later than the deadline t_m. The producer B commits to pay the item in maximum 3 days after receiving it, and also commits to deliver g_2 until t'_m. The consumer C commits to pay no later than 2 days after obtaining the product. The commitment dependency network specifies which commitments are in force at a particular instance of time. The picture illustrates the instance t_1 of time from the figure 7, which traces an execution in this scenario.

At time t_0 the consumer C notifies agent B that it intends to buy the item g_2 paying the price P'_c in 2 days after the shipment was made. Consequently, producer B asks the supplier A for delivering the item g_1 at the price P_c. At time t_1 agent A commits to deliver its output item, and at time t_2 it executes the action $SendGoods(g_1)$. Since it is a transient derivation, the agent will send it just once. According to rule r_{25}, the consequence of the operation is the commitment $\rightarrow^p_K CC(A, B, P_c : t_m, receipt : t_m+1) : t_2$. At time t_4, according to rule r_{24}, the items arrive ($\Rightarrow^p_K g_1 : t_4$) and agent B pays the price P_c for them. This defeasible derivation can be defeated by an unpredictable event. The fluent $g_1 : t_4$ fires the rule r_{26}, the conditional commitment is discharged and applying rule r_{12} a base-level commitment is created ($\rightarrow^p_K C(B, A, P_c : t_7) : t_4$). At time t_{10} all fluents are true showing that the goods g_1 and g_2 were delivered, the amounts P_c and P'_c were paid and both receipts were sent, meaning that the system has reached a *desirable state* [8].

The goal of executing a contract does not consist in just performing certain sequences of actions, but to reach a desirable state. Observe that not all the possible commitments specifying the contract had been activated. Such situations often arise when the agents are running a long time business relationships and they do no initiate their interactions from a start state. This is an argument for

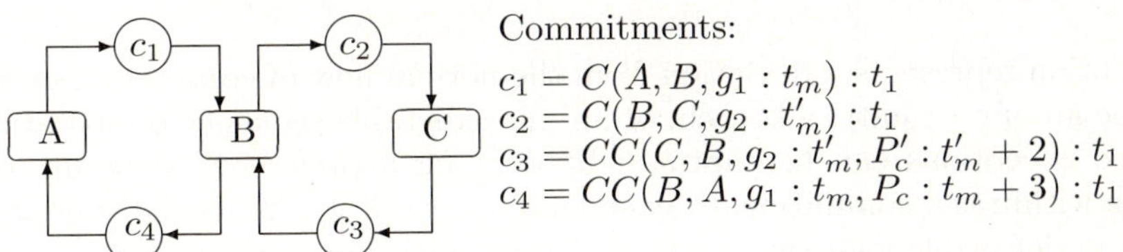

Fig. 6. Commitment dependency network: supplier A, producer B, consumer C

t_0	$B:$	$\rightarrow^t_Z Create(B, A, g_1 : t_n, P_c : t_n + 3) : t_0$	
	$C:$	$\rightarrow^t_Z Create(C, B, g_2 : t'_n, P'_c : t'_n + 2) : t_0$	
	$DCM:$	$\Rightarrow^p_K CC(B, A, g_1 : t_n, P_c : t_n + 3) : t_0$	$\Rightarrow^p_K CC(C, B, g_2 : t'_n, P'_c : t_n + 2) : t_0$
t_1	$A:$	$\rightarrow^t_Z Create(A, B, g_1 : t_m) : t_1$	
	$B:$	$\rightarrow^t_Z Create(B, C, g_2 : t'_m) : t_1$	
	DCM	$\Rightarrow^p_K C(A, B, g_1 : t_m) : t_1$	$\Rightarrow^p_K C(B, C, g_2 : t'_m,) : t_1$
		$CC(B, A, g_1 : t_n, P_c : t_n + 3) : t_1$	$CC(C, B, g_2 : t'_n, P'_c : t_n + 2) : t_1$
t_2	$A:$	$\rightarrow^t_Z SendGoods(g_1) : t_2$	
	$DCM:$	$\rightarrow^p_K CC(A, B, P_c : t_m, receipt : t_m + 1) : t_2$	
		$CC(B, A, g_1 : t_n, P_c : t_n + 3) : t_2$	$CC(C, B, g_2 : t'_n, P'_c : t_n + 2) : t_2$
		$C(A, B, g_1 : t_m) : t_2$	$C(B, C, g_2 : t'_m,) : t_2$
t_3	$DCM:$	$CC(A, B, P_c : t_m, receipt : t_m + 1) : t_3$	$CC(B, A, g_1 : t_n, P_c : t_n + 3) : t_3$
		$CC(C, B, g_2 : t'_n, P'_c : t_n + 2) : t_3$	$C(A, B, g_1 : t_m) : t_3$
		$C(B, C, g_2 : t'_m,) : t_3$	
t_4	$B:$	$\rightarrow^t_Z SendPay(P_c) : t_4$	
	$DCM:$	$\Rightarrow^p_K g_1 : t_4$	$\rightarrow^p_K C(B, A, P_c : t_7) : t_4$
		$CC(A, B, P_c : t_m, receipt : t_m + 1) : t_4$	$CC(C, B, g_2 : t'_n, P'_c : t_n + 2) : t_4$
		$C(B, C, g_2 : t'_m,) : t_4$	
$\vdots$			
t_9	$B:$	$\rightarrow^t_Z SendReceipt(receipt') : t_9$	
	$DCM:$	$\Rightarrow^p_K P'_c : t_9$	$\rightarrow C(B, C, receipt' : t'_{10}) : t_9$
		$g_2 : t_9$	$receipt : t_9$
		$P_c : t_9$	$g_1 : t_9$
t_{10}	$DCM:$	$\Rightarrow^p_K receipt' : t_{10}$	$P'_c : t_{10}$
		$g_2 : t_{10}$	$receipt : t_{10}$
		$P_c : t_{10}$	$g_1 : t_{10}$

Fig. 7. Trace of running the contracts in DCM

using our framework for the supply chain context. Note also that there are no base-level commitments, so the system is in a *final state*, where the interactions may end. But the interaction can continue from such a state by activating any of the commitments of the contract. A well-formed contract is one in which both final and undesirable states[2] do not occur at the same time.

In the supply chain the majority of actions are repetitive, a requirement easily captured by our approach. The agents have only to derive persistently and defeasibly their actions (i.e. $\Rightarrow^p_Z SendGoods : t_x$). In the case of perturbations in the supply chain, agents can rebut the above rule by activating a stronger one which specifies more or less items to be delivered (changing the superiority relation over the set of rules).

5   Exceptions

An exception represents a deviation from the normal flow of contract execution. It can be an opportunity, a breach, or an unpredictable sequence of operations. Expected exceptions can be captured by defining a preference structure over the runs within the commitment dependency network [9]. With the superiority relation in defeasible logic, we can easily define such a structure.

---

[2] States in which at least one fluent is not true.

In our view, unexpected exceptions can be managed in two ways: by introducing exception patterns or, when there is no domain dependent information, by applying principles of contract law. Contracts can be more or less elaborate, with several levels. Using well-defined exception patterns, one can generate more robust contracts. Moreover, it is considered that 80% of actual judicial cases follow the same classes of exception patterns [10]. We can provide a taxonomy of template contracts and a taxonomy of exceptions. When there are no explicit contrary-to-duty rules and no dependent domain information, the solution is to apply principles of contract law in order to compute the remedy, such as expectation damages, reliance damages, and opportunity costs. The amount of expectation damages must place the victim in the same position as if the actual contract had been performed. The amount of reliance damages must place the victim in the same position as if no contract had been signed. The amount of opportunity-cost damages must place the victim in the same position as if the best alternative contract had been performed [11, 5].

By tracking the life cycle of the commitments within a CDN one can detect and anticipate exceptions in contract execution, and therefore design proactive agents for such a market. An active base-level commitment represents a hard constraint for the debtor agent, while proposing a conditional commitment denotes a more risk-averse attitude. Moreover, inner commitments are permitted in a defeasible commitment machine. This opens the possibility of designing agents with different levels of risk attitude [2].

6   Related Work and Conclusions

Nonmonotonic commitment machines have been defined [4] using causal logic, while in DCMs deadlines have been attached to commitments, which represents a more realistic approach. Moreover, defeasible logic is more suitable than causal logic for capturing exceptions. Contracts have been already represented with defeasible logic and RuleML [12], but, by introducing DCMs between members of the supply chain, we offer a more flexible solution for contract monitoring. Capturing exceptions in the commitment machines of [9] is not performed with deadlines, needed for detecting the breach of a contractual clause. Exceptions in a semantic perspective [13] have used courteous logic which is a subset of defeasible logic. Commitments between a network of agents have also been analyzed [7], but without time constraints.

The main contribution of this paper consists in introducing DCMs in the execution of contracts, to obtain two main advantages. On the one hand, agents can reason with incomplete information. Therefore, contracts represented as DCMs are more elaboration tolerant [4]. Also, this property of nonmonotonic logics allows us to model confidential contractual clauses. On the other hand, our long term research goal is to manage exceptions in contract execution. We argue that using DCMs and the expressiveness of defeasible logic it is easier to catch both expected and unexpected exceptions. The novelty regarding commitments

consists in attaching deadlines to each commitment by using the temporalised
normative defeasible logic [3].

Acknowledgments

We are grateful to the anonymous referees for useful comments. Part of this work
was supported by the grant 27702-990 from the National Research Council of
the Romanian Ministry for Education and Research.

References

1. Walsh, W., Wellman, E.: Decentralized supply chain formation: A market protocol
   and competitive equilibrium analysis. Journal of Artificial Intelligence Research
   19 (2003) 513–567
2. Letia, I.A., Groza, A.: Agreeing on defeasible commitments. In: Declarative Agent
   Languages and Technologies, Hakodate, Japan (2006)
3. Governatori, G., Rotolo, A., Sartor, G.: Temporalised normative positions in defeasible logic. In: 10th International Conference on Artificial Inteligence and Law,
   Bologna, Italy (2005)
4. Chopra, A.K., Singh, M.P.: Nonmonotonic commitment machines. In: International Workshop on Agent Communication Languages and Conversation Policies,
   Melbourne, Australia (2003)
5. Letia, I.A., Groza, A.: Automating the dispute resolution in a task dependency
   network. In Skowron, A., ed.: Intelligent Agent Technology, Compiegne, France
   (2005) 365–371
6. Mallya, A.U., Yolum, P., Singh, M.P.: Resolving commitments among autonomous
   agents. In: International Workshop on Agent Communication Languages and Conversation Policies, Melbourne, Australia (2003)
7. Wan, F., Singh, M.: Formalizing and achieving multiparty agreements via commitments. In: 4th International Joint Conference on Autonomous Agents and
   Multiagent Systems, Utrecht, The Netherlands, ACM Press (2005) 770–777
8. Winikoff, M., Liu, W., Harland, J.: Enhancing commitment machines. In: Declarative Agent Languages and Technologies. LNCS 3476, Springer-Verlag (2005) 198–
   220
9. Mallya, A.U., Singh, M.P.: Modeling exceptions via commitment protocols. In: 4th
   International Joint Conference on Autonomous Agents and Multiagent Systems,
   Utrecht, The Netherlands, ACM Press (2005) 122–129
10. Bibel, L.W.: AI and the conquest of complexity in law. Artificial Intelligence and
    Law **12** (2004) 159–180
11. Craswell, R.: Contract law: General theories. In Bouckaert, B., Geest, G.D., eds.:
    Encyclopedia of Law and Economics, Volume III. The Regulation of Contracts.
    Cheltenham (2000) 1–24
12. Governatori, G.: Representing business contracts in RuleML. Journal of Cooper-
    ative Information Systems **14** (2005)
13. Grosof, B.: Representing E-Commerce rules via situated courteous logic programs
    in RuleML. Electronic Commerce Research and Applications **3** (2004) 2–20

A Self-organized Energetic Constraints Based Approach for Modelling Communication in Wireless Systems

Jean-Paul Jamont[1] and Michel Occello[2]

[1] Institut National Polytechnique de Grenoble, LCIS, 26000 Valence, France
[2] Université Pierre Mendès, LCIS/INPG, 26000 Valence, France
{jean-paul.jamont, michel.occello}@esisar.inpg.fr

Abstract. Open physical artificial systems often involve wireless autonomous entities under high constrainted energetic policies. Their features naturally lead to apply multiagent techniques to ensure both the autonomy of entities and the best whole system organization. We propose a multiagent approach for wireless communication robust management for such physical systems using self-organization mechanisms.

1 Introduction

A physical complex system can be defined as composed of many software/hardware elements which interact each other and with their environment These interactions are often non-linear and generally contain feedback loops. These systems are characterized by the emergence at a global level of new properties and of a new dynamic which is not easily predictible from the observation and the analysis of the elementary interactions.

Working with these systems like in collective robotics or massive instrumentation imposes the use of wireless technology. The features of such complex cognitive physical system leads to naturally apply multiagent techniques to ensure both the autonomy of entities and the best organization of the whole system [4].

This paper presents the different steps of the design of an energy efficient middleware based on the MWAC model (Multi-Wireless-Agent Communication). In a the first section is discussed the necessity to adopt a message oriented middleware (MOM) for our applications. We then propose our multiagent approach based on self-organization to manage the communication of these decentralized embedded nodes networks. We give finally an insight to some quantitative results showing the benefit of a multiagent approach compared to traditional protocols in a real world application of intrumentation of an underground instrumentation.

2 A Multiagent Approach to Design an Energy Efficient Message Oriented Middleware

Our research works deal with embedded multiagent systems like collective robotics or physical instrumentation. Considering complex embedded control

M. Ali and R. Dapoigny (Eds.): IEA/AIE 2006, LNAI 4031, pp. 101–110, 2006.

systems as networks of decentralized cooperative nodes is an attractive way to design physical intelligent applications [10, 4].

Multihop communication. In wireless networked systems, communication between two hosts is generally not direct. To communicate, entities require help from other hosts (multihop communication). Such a requirement creates an important routing problem because updating the location of neighbors is difficult. All adapted wireless routing protocols use flooding techniques. In a flooding technique, a host gives the message to all its neighbors which do the same.

Limited power ressources. Hosts have limited power ressources. One of the whole system aims is so to reduce as much as possible the energy expense. When they have nothing to do generally for sparing energy they enter in a sleep mode. When they communicate they must use good routing protocols and optimal ways (generally the criteria are the number of hops). But they must decrease as much as possible the flooding scheme because the associated power cost is very high. An agressive environment like an underground river system (as for one of our applications) can cause some internal faults for agent. The communication infrastructure must be very adaptive, fault tolerant and self-stabilized: an agent failure must not have an important impact on the system. This system must provide reliable communications and must adapt to "real-time" constraints. Furthermore, in the case of mobile devices the infrastructure of systems are not persistent.

Message oriented middleware. We need to design a mobile communication management layer to manage the wireless communications between the different agents of the system. This layer must increase interoperability, portability and flexibility of an application by allowing the application to be distributed over heterogenous multiple agents. It must reduce the complexity of development of the agents. This layer will be a Message Oriented Middleware (MOM) (fig. 1).

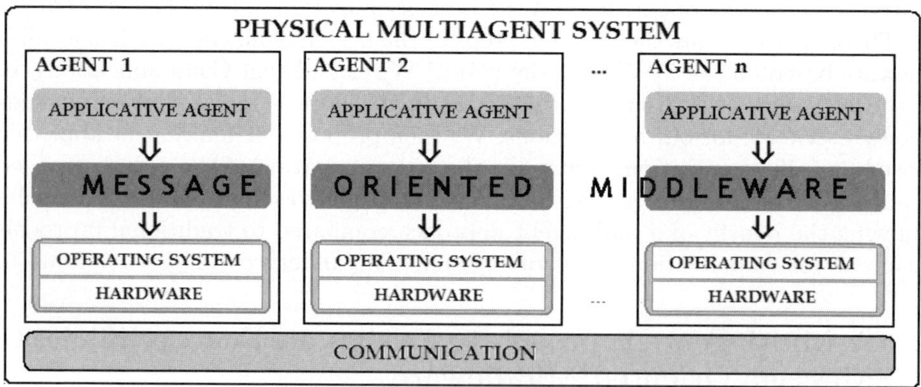

Fig. 1. Our embedded multiagent system architecture

Multiagent approach The distributed and open nature of wireless networks means that the multiagent approach is an adapted answer. Another advantage of this approach is the external representation of the interactions and of the organization. External representations offer multiple possibilities such as the monitoring by an external observer. A few works reaching the same objectives show that the approach is interesting : they are described in [5]. Our MOM must be economic in an energy point of view : this constitutes one of the main differences with the other works on multiagent based middleware [1, 9].

We are thereafter going to be interested in the AEIO decomposition [2]. We will follow the method of multiagent design discussed in [11], associated to this multiagent decomposition. It proposes a decomposition according to four aspects collectively accepted today. The *agent aspect* (A) gathers all elements together for defining and constructing these entities. Our agents have hybrid architectures, i.e. a composition of some pure types of architectures. Indeed, the agents will be of a cognitive type in case of a configuration alteration, it will be necessary for them to communicate and to manipulate their knowledge in order to have an efficient collaboration. On the other hand, in a normal use case it will be necessary for them to be reactive (stimuli/response paradigm) to be most efficient. All the agents have the same communication capabilities but the communicated data depend of their roles. The *environment aspect* (E) for dealing with the analysis of environment elements and with capability such as the perception of this environment and the actions one can do on it. The environment will be made of measurable information. It is deterministic, non episodic, dynamic and continuous. Agents can move in this physical environment but don't know their position. The *interaction aspect* (I) includes all elements which are in use for structuring the external interactions among the agents (agent communication language, interaction protocols). The *organization aspect* (O) allows to order agent groups in organization determined according to their roles. The MWAC model focus on the two last aspects.

3   The MWAC Model

Organization and interaction aspect. In this type of application no one can control the organization a priori. Relations between agents are going to emerge from the evolution of the agents'states and from their interactions.

Our organizational basic structures are constituted by (see fig 2) : one and only one *group representative agent* (r) managing the communication in its group, some *connection agents* (c) which know the different representative agents and can belong to several groups, some *simple members* (s) which are active in the communication process only for their own tasks (They don't ensure information relay). With this type of organizational structure, the message path between the source (a) and the receiver (b) is generally $((a, r),^* [(r, c), (c, r)], (r, b))$.

Because a representative agent is the most sollicited agent in a group, the best one is the one having the most important level of energy and the most important number of neighbors. We use a role allocation based self-organization

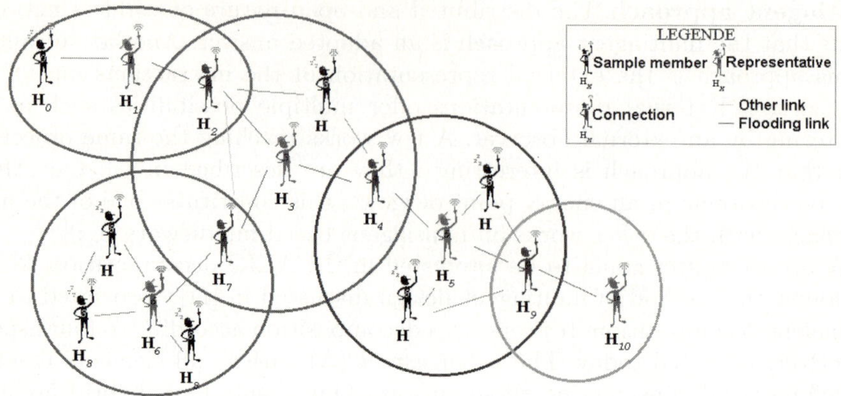

Fig. 2. Group organization

mechanism involving the election of a representative agent based on a function which estimates the adequation between its desire to be the manager and its capacity to be.

The energy saving is obtained owing to the fact that the flooding is only directed to the representative agents of the groups and to some connection agents. However, networks with an organizational structure must pay attention to the maintenance of their routing table. Generally, the adaptive features of these tables come from periodical exchanges between the different nodes. In our approach we do not wish to use this technique to ensure the maintenance of coherence. Indeed, our principle will be "if we do not need to communicate, it is useless to spend energy to ensure the coherence maintenance". However, we will thus use eavesdropping of surrounding agent communications. We extract knowledge from these messages exchanges to update our beliefs about our neighbors. Moreover, our self-organization mechanism will integrate an energy management policy.

The MWAC formal description. We propose here a formal description of our model. The notation find their sources in the work described in [8].

Identifier. Hosts of the network are modeled by agent. Each agent have an identificator i. We note A_i the agent identified by i.

The multiagent system. The multiagent system Γ is the set of agents $\Gamma = \{A_1, A_2, ..., A_i, ..., A_n\}$ with $card(\Gamma) = n$. Our multiagent system is open : hosts can enter or leave the system.

Time. We note $\mathbb{T}$ the ordered set with the operator $<$ and an element $-\infty$ with $\forall t \in \mathbb{T}, t < -\infty$. So $\mathbb{T} = \mathbb{N} \cup \{-\infty\}$.

Groups. 1) An agent group is noted $\mathcal{G}$. In our organization, a group is identified by its representant Identifier. The group where the representant is A_R is noted $\mathcal{G}_R$. All groups are part of the system : $\mathcal{G}_R \in \mathcal{P}(\Gamma)$.
(2: intention) A group has a finite time to live (with a lower and a higher limit).

The lower limit is the most interesting (the group birth) : we note $[A_R, t_0]$ the group created by A_R at t_0 with $(A_R, t_0) \in \Gamma \times \mathbb{T}$.

(3: belief in extension) We note $[A_R, t_0]^{A_j, t_1}$ the set of agents that A_j think members of the group $[A_R, t_0]$ at t_1.

(4: extension) We note $[A_R, t_0]^t$ the set of agents really in $[A_R, t_0]$ at t. We note $[A_R, t_0]^t$ the group composition $\mathcal{G}_R$ created at t_0 at the given date t. This knowledge can be defined from the belief of the agents:

$$[A_R, t_0]^t \ = \ \{A_j \in \Gamma \ | \ A_j \in [A_R, t_0]^{A_j, t} \ \wedge \ A_j \in [A_R, t_0]^{A_R, t}\} \tag{1}$$

Belief. $\mathcal{B}_{A_i} \ \varphi$ minds that the agent A_i thinks φ, in other words it thinks that φ is true. To highlight the recursive feature of the group definition given in 1, we can note that $(A_j \in [A_R, t_0]^{A_i, t}) \ \equiv \ (\mathcal{B}_{A_i} \ (A_j \in [A_R, t_0]^t))$.

Desir. $\mathcal{D}_{A_i} \ \varphi$ minds that the agent A_i desires φ, in other words it wants to verify φ.

Knowledge. $\mathcal{K}_{A_i} \ \varphi$ minds that the agent A_i knows φ.

Roles. *(1)* We note $role(A_i, t)$ the function that returns the role of the agent A_i at the date t with $(A_i, t) \in \Gamma \times \mathbb{T}$. A role can be R_R for a representant, R_C for a connection agent and R_S for a simple member. When an agent is initialized, he has no role. The function $role$ can then return $\emptyset$ to signify that the agent has no role.

(2: simplification of writing) We note $role_t(A_i)$ the last role taken by A_i.

(3: choice of a role) Each agent chooses a role depending on its neighborhood. So, choosing a role leads to notify the new role to neighbors and modify its knowledge about its own role. So $\mathcal{K}_{A_i}(role(A_i, t_v) \ = \ R_R)$ can be understood following different way. Firstly, we learn simply that the agent A_i is representant, but if $\mathcal{K}_{A_i}(role(A_i, t_{v-1}) \neq role(A_i, t_v))$ then the agent A_i has modified his role to be representant.

Power supply. *(1)* We note $power(A_i, t)$ the function which returns the energy level (a percentage) of the agent A_i at the date t with $(A_i, t) \in \Gamma \times \mathbb{T}$.

(2: simplification of writing) We note $power(A_i)$ the current energy level of the agent A_i.

Neighborhood. We note N_{A_i} the neighborhood that A_i knows. It is a set of agents in the emission range of the agent A_i not including itself. So, $N_{A_i} \in \mathcal{P}(\Gamma)$. An agent knows a neighbor by its unique identifier but can access to its role and its group ($\forall A_j \in N_{A_i}, \ \mathcal{K}_{A_i} \ role(A_j) \wedge \mathcal{K}_{A_i} \ group(A_j)$) with $group$ the function defined similar to $role$ but $group(A_j)$ returns the group identifier of the agent A_j. We can notice that if $\mathcal{K}_{A_i} \ [A_R, t_0]^{A_j, t_1}$ then $\mathcal{K}_{A_i} \ group(A_j) = R$. The reciprocal is not true because there is an uncertainty about the time.

Formalized description of the role attribution. Choosing a role depends firstly on its neighborbood (*basic algorithm*). However, because our power level is low, an agent can not desire to be representant (*energetic constraint*). The decision processes of agents are not synchronized. Two neighbors can take the same decision at the same time. It is possible that two close agents choose a representative role: there is a *representant conflict* which must be detected and corrected. It is possible to have two closer groups which don't include a connection agent between them: there is an *inconsistency* which must be detected and corrected.

We begin by focusing on our algorithm which allows to the agent A_i to choose a role in function of its neighborhood N_{A_i}.

Basic algorithm. 1) There is no neighbor : the concept of role doesn't make sense. $(N_{A_i} = \emptyset) \Rightarrow (\mathcal{K}_{A_i}(role(A_i) = \emptyset))$

2) Neighbors exist $(N_{A_i} \neq \emptyset)$.
$(\mathcal{K}_{A_i}(card(\ \{A_j \epsilon N_{A_i}\ |\ role(A_j) = R_R\}\ ) = 0)\ \Rightarrow (\mathcal{K}_{A_i}(role(A_i) = R_R))$

$\mathcal{K}_{A_i}((card(\ \{A_j \epsilon N_{A_i}\ |\ role(A_j) = R_R\}\ ) = 1)\ \Rightarrow (\mathcal{K}_{A_i}(role(A_i) = R_S))$

$\mathcal{K}_{A_i}((card(\ \{A_j \epsilon N_{A_i}\ |\ role(A_j) = R_R\}\ ) > 1)\ \Rightarrow (\mathcal{K}_{A_i}(role(A_i) = R_C))$

Energetic constraint. Generally, the role of representative or connection make that the agents take an active part in the management of communications. From this fact, consumption of energy is higher. So, $(power(A_i) < trigValue) \Rightarrow (\mathcal{K}_{A_i}(role(A_i) = R_S))$.

Detecting and correcting a representant conflict. *(1: Conflict detection)* An agent A_i detects a conflict with other agents if $\mathcal{K}_{A_i}(N_{A_i} \neq \emptyset) \wedge \mathcal{K}_{A_i}(role(A_i) = R_R) \wedge \mathcal{K}_{A_i}((card(\ \{A_j \epsilon N_{A_i}\ |\ role(A_j) = R_R\}\ ) >= 1)$.
(2: Conflict correction) A_i has detected a conflict with other agents. he sends a *ConflictRepresentativeResolution* message (see the interaction aspect) to its representative neighbors. This message contains the score of the agent A_i. The agents, which receive this message, calculate their own score. Agents with an inferior score leave their role and choose another. An agent with a better score sends its score to its neighbors.

An exemple of *score* function can be simply expressed. The following function supports an agent with a high energy level and a significant neighbor (the interest is to have dense groups in order to limit the flooding volume). $score(A_i) = power(A_i).card(N_{A_i})$

Detecting and correcting an inconsistency. *(1: Inconsistency detection)* An inconsistency can be detected only by one representative starting from beliefs of one of its members. This detection needs an interaction between an agent A_i and its representative A_R (message *VerifyNeighborGroupConsistency*).

The agent A_i will send the list of the groups of its neigborhood of which it does not know if its representative knows the proximity.

We define $N_{A_i,L} = \{A_k \epsilon N_{A_i}\ |\ role(A_k) = R_C\}$.

A connection agent is member of many groups, so, if $A_L \epsilon N_{A_i} \wedge role(A_L) = R_C \wedge [A_\alpha, t_\alpha]^{A_L,t_a} \wedge [A_\beta, t_\beta]^{A_L,t_b}$. then $\mathcal{K}_{A_i}(group(A_L) = \alpha)$ et $\mathcal{K}_{A_i}(group(A_L) = \beta)$. We define $\zeta_{A_i} = \{A_j \epsilon N_{A_i}\ |\ group(A_j) \neq group(A_i) \wedge (\ \nexists A_k \epsilon N_{A_i,L}\ / (group(A_k) = group(A_j) \wedge group(A_k) = group(A_i))\ )\}$.

The inconsistency is found by A_i if $card(\zeta_{A_i}) = 0$. The representative agent A_R of A_i receives a message with ζ_{A_i}. For $\forall A_n \epsilon \zeta_{A_i}$, if $card(\{A_y \epsilon N_{A_R,L}\ |\ group(A_y) = n\}) = 0$ then there is a real inconsistency.

(2: Inconsistency correction) In this case several strategies can be used. We judge that if a path with a low energy cost is available, one will support a stability of the organization to a reorganization. A search for path towards one of the groups soft will thus be sent with a TTL (Time to Live) relatively low.

If a path exists, the organization does not change. If not, the representative proposes to A_i, if $role(A_i) = R_C$, to be a representant (*ISuggestYouToBeRepresentative*). The agent A_i can refuse to become representative (if its energy level is too low) but in all the case, the representant A_R leaves its role.

About belief and knowledge of its neighborhood. We have seen that the reasoning is based on the belief/knowledge on the neighbors. In our system a belief is a recent knowledge (on which no reasoning has been yet applied). If an agent receives an information σ, it is a belief. If it does not find a contradiction with this knowledge then σ becomes a knowledge. If not, a message *WhoAreMyNeighbors* can be sent to verify some knowledge.

An agent A_i which receives the information σ, can be the receiver or can just be a relay of a communication which takes place in our range of communication. In this last case, we talk about eavesdropping. Eavesdropping allows to an agent to verify some information about a neighbor (identifier) without using a specific message... without extra energy expense.

The agents will interact only with the agents in acquaintance. Agents interact by asynchronous exchange of messages (without rendez vous). Among the different protocols that we use, the choice of an introduction protocol is essential. Indeed, this protocol allows to the agents to be known, i.e. to bring their knowledge and their know-how to the agents' society. An other important protocol is the *best representant election* protocol seen previously. These protocols are an arrangement of some of the different types of small messages defined in [5].

4 Implementation and Evaluation in the Case of an Underground River System Instrumentation

Implementation. Therefore, we will demonstrate the feasibility of our approach in the case of the instrumentation of an underground hydrographic system (the EnvSys project [6]). In a subterranean river system, the interesting parameters to measure are numerous: temperature of the air and the water, air pressure and if possible water pressure for the flooded galleries, pollution rate by classical pollutants, water flow, draft speed, etc. All these information will be collected at the immediate hydrographic network exit by a works station like a PC. These data will be processed to activate alarms, to study the progress of a certain pollution according to miscellaneous measuring parameters, to determine a predictive model of the whole network by relating the subterranean parameters measures of our system with the overground parameter measures more classically on the catchment basin.

We have chosen for sensors a classical three-layers embedded architecture (physical layer/link layer/applicative layer).

We use the physical layer which is employed by NICOLA system, a voice transmission system used by the French speleological rescue teams [3]. This layer is implemented in a digital signal processor rather than a full analogic system. Thereby we can keep a good flexibility and further we will be able to apply a signal processing algorithm to improve the data transmission. The link layer used is a CAN (Controller Area Network) protocol stemming from the motorcar industry and chosen for its good reliability. The applicative layer is constituted by the agents' system. A hybrid architecture enables to combine the strong features of each of reactive (to the message) and cognitive capabilities (to detect inconsistency and re-organisation). The ASTRO hybrid architecture [10] is especially adapted to a real time context. The integration of deliberative and reactive capabilities is possible through the use of parallelism in the structure of the agent. Separating Reasoning/Adaptation and Perception/Communication tasks allows a continuous supervision of the evolution of the environment. The reasoning model of this agent is based on the Perception/Decision/Reasoning/Action paradigm. The cognitive reasoning is thus preserved, and predicted events contribute to the normal progress of the reasoning process.

In this application, the agent must transmit periodically measures to the workstation. The *communication module* calls the MAS middleware services supplied through a component. The agent must use a `WCommunication` package, written in Java langage and translated into C++ langage because a lot of physical plateforms use this langage. This package contents two abstracts classes (`Identifier` and `Message`) and two main classes called `Communication` and `BitField`. In the `Message` abstract class the designer must implement the primitives to convert the message in a bit field (`BitField MessageToBitField(Message m)` and the recipocal primitive `Message BitFieldToMessage(BitField b)`). In the Identifier abstract class the designer must implement the type of identifier and two primitives `BitField IdentifierToBitField()` and `Message BitFieldToMessage(BitField b)`. The primitive to convert the identifier in a bit field must be implemented by the designer. The Communication class contains a list of couples (`Identifier,Message`) for the emission and the reception. This list is private and must be accessed via `Bool SendMessage(identifier, Message)` and `CoupleIdentifierMessage ReceiveMessage()`.
The package must be connected to the operating system. The operating system must give the battery energy level (primitive `SetBatteryLevel(Float l)` to the `Communication` class and must give the bit field which arrives. In an other hand, the middleware gives to the operating system the bit field to send by calling `BitField GetBitFieldToSend()`.

These agents are embedded on autonomous processor cards. These cards are equipped with communication modules and with measuring modules to carry out agent tasks relative to the instrumentation. These cards supply a real time kernel. The KR-51(the kernel's name) allows multi-task software engineering for C515C microcontroller. We can produce one task for one capability. We can then quite easily implement the parallelism inherent to agents and satisfy the real-time constraints.

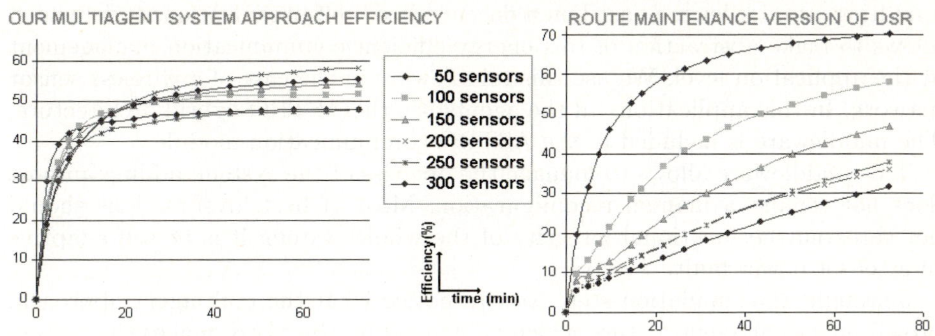

Fig. 3. Approach comparison for the uni directionnal use case

Evaluation. In order to evaluate and improve such agents' software architectures and the cooperation techniques that they involve, we introduce a simulation stage in our development process. The simulation first allowed us to experiment our approach and the software solutions that we provide for the various problems. We have compared our MAS to three traditionnal solution based on ad-hoc protocols. The DSDV protocol (Destination-Sequenced Distance-Vector protocol [12]) and the natural DSR protocol (Dynamic Source Routing protocol [7]) do not appear in this comparison because its efficiency were lower than the ehanced version of DSR which uses a route maintenance (memorization of the main route). We thereafter call efficiency the ratio between the theoretical useful volume of the optimal way divided by the volume of each transmitted communication.

In the EnvSys project, all agents communicate only with the workstation situated at the end of the undergound river system : it is a unidirectionnal protocol. In this case, messages are small. For this example, three messages are sent by five seconds. The same scenario is applied for the different protocols.

We can see that the benefit (fig 3) of our approach is important in the EN-VSYS case. Our routing method can deliver quickly all messages with a good efficiency. Higher is the number of sensors better is the reactivity of our approach. We must note that if the system knows no pertubation or mobility variation of DSR will be better from an efficiency point of view is normal because in this case DSR learns all the routes (succession of sensors) allowing to communicate with the workstation. It is not really the case of our approach which reasons about the group and not from the sensors. One consequence is that the routes used by the messages with our approach are not optimal. We can see that our approach support the addition of a lot of sensors. The number of groups don't explose with the number of sensors but their density increases.

5   Conclusion

We have presented in this paper a multiagent system to manage wireless communication between agents in respect to energy constraints. We have proposed a multiagent middleware based on a decentralized self-organization model which allows to make abstraction of this energy efficient communication management at the application level. We use this middleware in the case of a wireless sensor network. In this application, all the agents use the ASTRO hybrid architecture. The middleware is included in the ASTRO communication module.

This middleware allows to manage the openess of the system: adding an host does not require a manual reconfiguration. Most of hosts'dysfunctions should not threaten the functional integrity of the whole system: it is be self-adaptive to a sensor power fault.

Throught the simulation step, we can notice what the multiagent approach, providing an emergent feature which is inferred by the MAS, makes the system fault tolerant to changes of the environment in which it evolves. Generic aspects of agents allow us to envisage differents applications for this middleware such as diagnosis, risk management, data fusion...

References

1. Calisti, M. et al. An agent-based middleware for adaptative roaming in wireless networks. In *Workshop on Agents for Ubiquitous Computing*, 2004.
2. Y. Demazeau. From interactions to collective behavior in agent-based systems. In *European Conference on Cognitive Science*, 1995.
3. N. Graham. The Nicola Mark II a New Rescue Radio for France. In *The CREG Journal*, volume 38, pages 3–6, December 1999.
4. J.-P. Jamont and M. Occello. Using self-organization for functionnal integrity maintenance of wireless sensor networks. In *Proceedings of IEEE International Conference on Intelligent Agent Technology*. IEEE Computer Society, 2003.
5. J.-P. Jamont and M. Occello. An adaptive multiagent infrastructure for self-organized physical embodied systems. In *IEEE International Symposium on Advanced Distributed Systems*, volume LNCS 3061. Springer Verlag, January 2004.
6. J.-P. Jamont, M. Occello, and A. Lagreze. A multiagent system for the instrumentation of an underground hydrographic system. In *Proceedings of IEEE International Symposium on Virtual and Intelligent Measurement Systems*, 2002.
7. D.-B. Johnson and D.-A. Maltz. Dynamic source routing in ad hoc wireless networks. In *Mobile Computing*, pages 153–181. Kluwer Academic Publishers, 1996.
8. F. Legras and C. Tessier. Lotto: group formation by overhearing in large teams. In *Proceedings of the Second International Joint Conference on Autonomous Agents and Multiagent Systems, AAMAS 2003*, pages 425–432, Australia, July 2003. ACM.
9. M. Mamei and F. Zambonelli. Self-organization in multi-agent systems : a middleware approach. In *AAMAS 2003 Workshop on Engineering Self-Organising Systems*, pages 233–248, 2003.
10. M. Occello, Y. Demazeau, and C. Baeijs. Designing organized agents for cooperation in a real time context. In *Collective Robotics*, volume LNCS/LNAI 1456, pages 25–73. Springer-Verlag, March 1998.
11. M. Occello and J.L. Koning. Multi-agent based software engineering: an approach based on model and software reuse. In *From Agent Theory to Agent Implementation II - EMCSR 2000 Symposium*, pages 645–657, Vienna, April 2000.
12. C.E. Perkins, E.M. Royer, and S. Das. Highly dynamic destination-sequenced distance-vector (dsdv) routing for mobile computers. In *ACM SIGCOMM'94*, 1994.

Evaluation of Several Algorithms in Forecasting Flood

C.L. Wu and K.W. Chau

Department of Civil and Structural Engineering, Hong Kong Polytechnic University,
Hunghom, Kowloon, Hong Kong, People's Republic of China
cekwchau@polyu.edu.hk

Abstract. Precise flood forecasting is desirable so as to have more lead time for taking appropriate prevention measures as well as evacuation actions. Although conceptual prediction models have apparent advantages in assisting physical understandings of the hydrological process, the spatial and temporal variability of characteristics of watershed and the number of variables involved in the modeling of the physical processes render them difficult to be manipulated other than by specialists. In this study, two hybrid models, namely, based on genetic algorithm-based artificial neural network and adaptive-network-based fuzzy inference system algorithms, are employed for flood forecasting in a channel reach of the Yangtze River. The new contributions made by this paper are the application of these two algorithms on flood forecasting problems in real prototype cases and the comparison of their performances with a benchmarking linear regression model in this field. It is found that these hybrid algorithms with a "black-box" approach are worthy tools since they not only explore a new solution approach but also demonstrate good accuracy performance.

1 Introduction

Numerical models for flood propagation in a channel reach can broadly be classified into two main categories: conceptual models [1-5]; and, empirical models based on system analysis or "black-box" approach. Huge amount of data are usually required for calibration of these conceptual models. In many cases, a simple "black-box" model may be preferred in identifying a direct mapping between inputs and outputs. During the past decade, several nonlinear approaches, including artificial neural network (ANN), genetic algorithm (GA), and fuzzy logic, have been employed to solve flood forecasting problems. Smith and Eli [6] applied a back-propagation ANN model to predict discharge and time to peak over a hypothetical watershed. Tokar and Johnson [7] compared ANN models with regression and simple conceptual models. Liong *et al.* [8] employed an ANN approach for river stage forecasting in Bangladesh. Cheng and Chau [9] employed fuzzy iteration methodology for reservoir flood control operation. Chau and Cheng [10] performed a real-time prediction of water stage with ANN approach using an improved back propagation algorithm. Chau [11] calibrated flow and water quality modeling using GA. Cheng *et al.* [12] combined a fuzzy optimal model with a genetic algorithm to solve multiobjective rainfall-runoff model calibration. Chau [13-14] performed river stage forecasting and rainfall-runoff correlation with particle swarm optimization technique. Cheng *et al.* [15] carried out long-term prediction of discharges in Manwan Reservoir using ANN models.

M. Ali and R. Dapoigny (Eds.): IEA/AIE 2006, LNAI 4031, pp. 111 – 116, 2006.
© Springer-Verlag Berlin Heidelberg 2006

In this paper, two hybrid algorithms, namely, genetic algorithm-based artificial neural network (ANN-GA) and adaptive-network-based fuzzy inference system (ANFIS), are applied for flood forecasting in a channel reach of the Yangtze River. To the knowledge of the authors, these types of algorithms have never been applied to hydrological and water resources problems. The new contributions made by this paper are the application of these two algorithms on flood forecasting problems in real prototype cases and the comparison of their performances with a benchmarking linear regression (LR) model in this field.

2   Genetic Algorithm-Based Artificial Neural Network (ANN-GA)

A hybrid integration of ANN and GA, taking advantages of the characteristics of both schemes, may be able to increase solution stability and improve performance of an ANN model. A genetic algorithm-based artificial neural network (ANN-GA) model is developed here wherein a GA [16] is used to optimize initial parameters of ANN before trained by conventional ANN. In the GA sub-model, the objective function used for initializing weights and biases is represented as follows:

$$\min J(W,\theta) = \sum_{i=1}^{p} \left| Y_i - f(X_i, W, \theta) \right| \tag{1}$$

where W is the weight, θ is the bias or threshold value, i is the data sequence, p is the total number of training data pairs, X_i is the ith input data, Y_i is the ith measured data, and $f(X_i, W, \theta)$ represents simulated output. The main objective of the sub-model is to determine optimal parameters with minimal accumulative errors between the measured data and simulated data.

3   Adaptive-Network-Based Fuzzy Inference System (ANFIS)

In this study, the output of each rule is taken as a linear combination of input variable together with a constant term. The final output is the weighted averaged of each rule's output. The fuzzy rule base comprises the combinations of all categories of variables. As an illustration, the following shows a case with three input variables and a single output variable. Each input variable (x, y, and z) is divided into three categories. Equally spaced triangular membership functions are assigned. The categories are assigned: "low," "medium," and "high." The number of rules in a fuzzy rule base is c^n, where c is the number of categories per variable and n the number of variables. The optimal number of categories is obtained through trials and performance comparison. The format of the rule set contains an output $o_{i,j,k}$ for a combination of category i of input variable x, category j of input y, and category k of input variable z, respectively.

If a rule is triggered, the corresponding memberships of x, y, and z will be computed. The weight $w_{i,j,k}$ to be assigned to the corresponding output $o_{i,j,k}$ will be furnished by the result of a specific T-norm operation. Multiplication operation is adopted here. A single weighted average output will then be acquired by combining the outputs from all triggered rules as follows:

$$o = \frac{\sum w_{i,j,k} \cdot o_{i,j,k}}{\sum w_{i,j,k}} \qquad (2)$$

For this flood forecasting model, some parameters, including each triangular membership function and the consequence part of each rule, have to be obtained through learning by ANN. The algorithm is able to enhance the intelligence when working in uncertain, imprecise, and noisy environments and to accomplish faster convergence. It possesses the characteristics of both the neural networks, including learning abilities, optimization abilities, and connectionist structures, and the fuzzy control systems, including human like "if-then" rule thinking and ease of incorporating expert knowledge, etc. In this system, the parameters defining the shape of the membership functions and the consequent parameters for each rule are determined by the back-propagation learning algorithm and the least-squares method, respectively.

4 Application Case

The studied channel reach from Luo-Shan to Han-Kou is located at the middle of the Yangtze River. The water elevation at Luo-Shan station ranges from 17.3m during the non-flooding period to 31.0m during the flooding period whilst the mean levels are 20.8m and 27.1m during the non-flooding and flooding periods, respectively. The key objective of this study is to forecast water stages of the downstream station, Han-Kou, on the basis of its counterparts at the upstream station, Luo-Shan.

For the ANN-GA model, a three-layer network is adopted with three input nodes and one output node. As an initial data preprocessing, the input and output data are normalized to be ranging between 0 and 1, corresponding to the minimum and the maximum water stages, respectively. ANN-GA models are trained with different number of nodes in the hidden layer so as to determine the optimal network geometry for these data sets. A testing set is incorporated so as to avoid the overfitting problem. Training is stopped when the error learning curve of the testing set starts to increase whilst that of the training set is still decreasing. It is found that, amongst them, the architecture with 3 nodes in the hidden layer is the optimal.

For an ANFIS model, more number of categories will furnish higher accuracy, but at the same time will have the disadvantages of larger rule bases and higher computation cost. Trial and error procedure is performed with a view to selecting the appropriate number of variable categories. Careful treatment is also made to avoid overfitting, though it is anticipated that more subspaces for the ANFIS model might result in better performance. An optimal number of categories of 3 is adopted, after having taken into consideration of the computational time, root mean square error in training (RMSE_tra), and root mean square error in validation (RMSE_vali).

5   Results and Analysis

The performance comparison of the LR, ANN-GA, and ANFIS models in forecasting 1-day lead time water levels at Han-Kou on the basis of the upstream water levels at Luo-Shan station during the past three days is shown in Figure 1. The fluctuation of absolute error is the largest for the LR model and is smallest for the ANFIS model. Table 1 shows the performance comparison using RMSE_tra, RMSE_vali, training time, and number of parameters. The ANFIS model is able to attain the highest accuracy, yet requires less training time than ANN-GA model. However, it should be noted that the ANFIS model involves more number of parameters than the other two models.

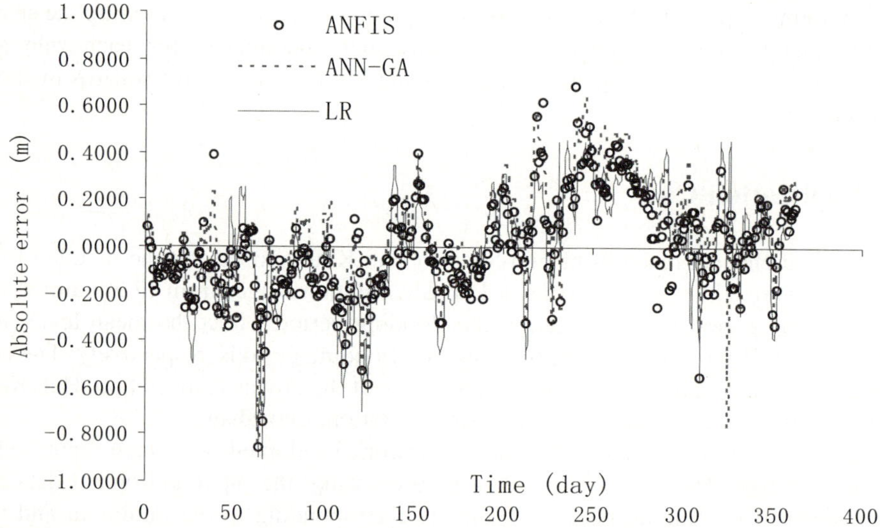

Fig. 1. Performance comparison in terms of absolute errors for different algorithms

Table 1. Performance comparison for different models in flood prediction

Models	RMSE_tra (m)	RMSE_vali (m)	Training time (s)	Number of parameter
LR	0.238	0.237	Nil	4
ANN-GA	0.213	0.226	135	16
ANFIS	0.204	0.214	49	135

Their differences in performance can be explained somewhat by the fact that the LR model can only fit a linear function to input-output data pairs whilst both the ANN-GA and ANFIS models can contort themselves into complex forms in order to handle non-linear problems. It is justifiable that an ANN-GA model with 16 parameters is more flexible than LR model with 4 parameters since the coupling of ANN and GA can take advantage of the local optimization of ANN and the global optimization of GA. The results indicate that the local approximation approach of the ANFIS model has better performance in mapping the connectivity of input-output data pairs than the global approximation approach of the ANN-GA model. More importantly, the ANN-GA model entails more training time than the ANFIS model due to the time consuming searching nature of GA. Nevertheless, with the recent rate of development of computer technology, it will not be a major constraint. As such, it is trusted that hybrid algorithms, including ANN-GA and ANFIS, will have significant potentials as alternatives to conventional models in solving hydrological problems.

6   Conclusions

In this paper, two hybrid "black-box" models are applied for real flood forecasting. Both ANN-GA and ANFIS models are able to produce accurate flood predictions of the channel reach between Luo-Shan and Han-Kou stations in the Yangtze River. Amongst them, the ANFIS model, having the characteristics of both ANN and FIS, is the optimal in terms of the simulation performance, yet requires a larger amount of parameters in comparison with the benchmarking LR model. The ANN-GA model adequately combines the advantage of ANN with the advantage of GA, yet consumes most computation cost. Both ANN-GA and ANFIS models could be considered as feasible alternatives to conventional models. The new contributions made by this paper are the application of these two algorithms on flood forecasting problems in real prototype cases and the comparison of their performances with a benchmarking model in this field.

Acknowledgement

This research was supported by the Internal Competitive Research Grant of Hong Kong Polytechnic University (A-PE26).

References

1. Chau, K.W., Jiang, Y.W.: 3D Numerical Model for Pearl River Estuary. Journal of Hydraulic Engineering ASCE **127(1)** (2001) 72-82
2. Chau, K.W., Jin, H.S.: Numerical Solution of Two-Layer, Two-Dimensional Tidal Flow in a Boundary Fitted Orthogonal Curvilinear Coordinate System. International Journal for Numerical Methods in Fluids **21(11)** (1995) 1087-1107
3. Chau, K.W., Jin, H.S., Sin, Y.S.: A Finite Difference Model of Two-Dimensional Tidal Flow in Tolo Harbor, Hong Kong. Applied Mathematical Modelling **20(4)** (1996) 321-328

4. Chau, K.W., Lee, J.H.W.: Mathematical Modelling of Shing Mun River Network. Advances in Water Resources **14(3)** (1991) 101-124
5. Chau, K.W., Lee, J.H.W.: A Microcomputer Model for Flood Prediction with Application. Microcomputers in Civil Engineering **6(2)** (1991) 109-121
6. Smith, J., Eli, R.N.: Neural-Network Models of Rainfall-Runoff Process. Journal of Water Resources Planning and Management, ASCE **121(6)** (1995) 499-508
7. Tokar, A.S., Johnson, P.A.: Rainfall-Runoff Modeling using Artificial Neural Networks. Journal of Hydrologic Engineering, ASCE **4(3)** (1999) 232-239
8. Liong, S.Y., Lim, W.H., Paudyal, G.N.: River Stage Forecasting in Bangladesh: Neural Network Approach. Journal of Computing in Civil Engineering, ASCE **14(1)** (2000) 1-8
9. Cheng, C.T., Chau, K.W.: Fuzzy Iteration Methodology for Reservoir Flood Control Operation. Journal of the American Water Resources Association **37(5)** (2001) 1381-1388
10. Chau, K.W., Cheng, C.T.: Real-time Prediction of Water Stage with Artificial Neural Network Approach. Lecture Notes in Artificial Intelligence **2557** (2002) 715-715
11. Chau, K.W.: Calibration of Flow and Water Quality Modeling using Genetic Algorithm. Lecture Notes in Artificial Intelligence **2557** (2002) 720-720
12. Cheng, C.T., Ou, C.P., Chau, K.W.: Combining a Fuzzy Optimal Model with a Genetic Algorithm to solve Multiobjective Rainfall-Runoff Model Calibration. Journal of Hydrology **268(1-4)** (2002) 72-86
13. Chau, K.W.: River Stage Forecasting with Particle Swarm Optimization. Lecture Notes in Computer Science **3029** (2004) 1166-1173
14. Chau, K.W.: Rainfall-Runoff Correlation with Particle Swarm Optimization Algorithm. Lecture Notes in Computer Science **3174** (2004) 970-975
15. Cheng, C.T., Chau, K.W., Sun, Y.G., Lin, J.Y.: Long-Term Prediction of Discharges in Manwan Reservoir using Artificial Neural Network Models. Lecture Notes in Computer Science **3498** (2005) 1040-1045
16. Goldberg, D.E., Kuo, C.H.: Genetic Algorithms in Pipeline Optimization. Journal of Computing in Civil Engineering ASCE **1(2)** (1987) 128-141

Simulation Analysis for On-Demand Transport Vehicles Based on Game Theory

Naoto Mukai[1], Jun Feng[2], and Toyohide Watanabe[1]

[1] Department of Systems and Social Informatics,
Graduate School of Information Science, Nagoya University
Furo-cho, Chikusa-ku, Nagoya, 464-8603, Japan
`naoto@watanabe.ss.is.nagoya-u.ac.jp`,
`watanabe@is.nagoya-u.ac.jp`
[2] Hohai University, Nanjing, Jiangsu 210098, China
`fengjun-cn@vip.sina.com`

Abstract. In these years, on-demand transportations (such as demand-bus) are focused as new transport systems. Vehicles in the on-demand transport systems must take reasonable actions in various situations to increase their profits. However, it is difficult to find convincing solutions in such situations because there are uncertainties about customers and other transport vehicles. Therefore, in this paper, we focus on two issues: "how to control risk?" and "how to compete (or cooperate) with another transport vehicle?". Moreover, we show the decision-making processes for the transport vehicles on the basis of game theory. The profits for transport vehicles are classified into assured and expected rewards. The former represents scheduled customers in advance. The latter represents undetermined customers. Transport vehicles set their routes in consideration of the balancing between the rewards (i.e., risk). The transport vehicles are classified into several types based on risk policies and transport strategies. Finally, we report results of simulation experiments.

1 Introduction

A transport system is one of the main functions in a city life. Thus, numerous effort to improve the system has been continuously. Technological advances in recent years are ready to change the scene surrounding the transport systems. In other words, many people own mobile devices instrumented GPS functions and can inform their positions to transport companies (or vehicles). Hence, strategies for transport vehicles will change to more dynamic plans. In fact, it appears that most of traditional strategies is static: e.g., bus systems incorporate fixed bus routes (fixed bus stops). In recent years, new strategies called on-demand transportations [1, 2, 3] are introduced into some local towns. On-demand transportation system requires no specific routes because transport vehicles of the system visit positions of customers according to occasion demands. However, there are some problems in the on-demand transportations. Especially, the route decision problem of the on-demand transportation is more difficult than traditional static transportation systems [4, 5] due to conflicts with other transport systems and uncertainties about

M. Ali and R. Dapoigny (Eds.): IEA/AIE 2006, LNAI 4031, pp. 117–126, 2006.

other vehicles (which include trains) and customers. For the reason, current managements of the system are limited to local areas and small customers.

Our purpose is to establish more effective framework of on-demand transportation systems for companies and customers. Therefore, in this paper we focused on two issues: "how to control risk?" and "how to compete (or cooperate) with another transport vehicle?". It is obvious that the risk for transport vehicles (companies) concerns to their profits. The profits can be classified into assured and expected rewards. The former represents scheduled customers in advance. The latter represents undetermined customers. It seems that the setting for travel routes in consideration of the expected reward in addition to the assured reward is useful for transport vehicles although they involve risks in varying degrees. Hence, we introduce policies against the risk which control the balancing between two rewards. Moreover, it appears that each transport vehicle has a different transport strategy (i.e., answers for "which route should be selected?") which affects their profits. It is not always possible to plan better transport strategies than other vehicles because one strategy influences results of other strategies. Hence, we clarify the decision-making processes in environments where different strategies compete with each other on the basis of game theory. In the results, we classify the transport vehicles into three risk policies (neutral, risk-avoiding, and risk-taking) and three transport strategies (mixed, competitive, and Nash). We also performed simulation experiments and show the characteristics of the transport vehicles.

The remainder of this paper is as follows: Section 2 formalizes transport areas and vehicles for simulation experiments. Section 3 describes the risk policies which control the balancing between assured and expected rewards. Section 4 describes the transport strategies based on the game theory [6]. Section 5 reports results of the simulation experiments. Finally, Section 7 concludes and offers our future works.

2   Environment

In this section, we formalize an environment surrounding transport systems for simulation experiments.

2.1   Transport Area

A transport area A for transport systems is represented by a graph structure which includes nodes N and edges E as Equation (1). A node n represents a picking place (like a bus stop) and the number of waiting customers at n at time t is given by $|c(n,t)|$. An edge e represents a route with length $|e|$ between the picking places. The nodes include one or more depots D for transport vehicles. Basically, vehicles set their transport routes according to occasion demands in advance their departures. After the setting, the transport vehicles depart from their depots. Finally, the transport vehicles return their depots through their traveling routes. In this simulation experiment, we deal with pick-up transportation problems and the transport area is a two-way circular graph.

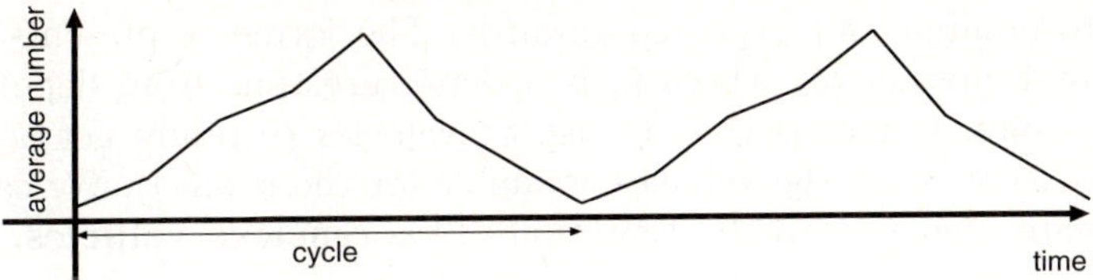

Fig. 1. Example of trend function

$$
\begin{cases}
R = (N, E) \\
N = \{n_1, n_2, \cdots\} \\
E = \{e(n, n')|n, n' \in N\} \\
D = \{d_1, d_2, \cdots\} \in N
\end{cases}
\tag{1}
$$

Generally, occasion patterns of transport demands are not always the same due to uncertainties of customers. However, it appears that there is a trend depending on locations or time of day. For example, at the start of office hours, people move from housing area to business area. Hence, we formalize such occasion trends as a distribution function $d(n, t)$ in Figure 1. The function represents an average number of occurrence demands on node n at time t. The function also has a *cycle* like time of day. Moreover, the uncertainty of the trend is given by a normal probability distribution with average $d(n, t)$ and variance σ^2. In other words, if the variance σ^2 is small, the number of occurrence demands is almost the same with the average number $d(n, t)$. If not so, the number of occurrence demands varies widely.

2.2   Transport Vehicle

A transport vehicle v is given by five parameters as Equation (2). The *depot* is a depot of the vehicle. The *speed* is a traveling speed of the vehicle so that the traveling time between n and n' is represented by $|e(n, n')|/speed$. The *capacity* is a maximum riding number of customers at the same time. If the number of customers $|c(n, t)|$ is more than the maximum number, the overlimit customers $(|c(n, t)| - capacity)$ must wait for arrival of the next vehicle. Moreover, if two vehicles visit the same node at the same time, the half number of customers $|c(n, t)|/2$ is assigned to each vehicle. The *policy* and *strategy* are a risk policy and a transport strategy of the vehicle. These two parameters are discussed in the following sections.

$$
v = (depot, speed, capacity, policy, strategy)
\tag{2}
$$

3   Risk Policy

It appears that the risk for transport vehicles concerns to their rewards. In this simulation, the rewards for transport vehicles are regarded as the number of riding customers in one traveling (i.e., from start to return). We can classify the rewards into assured and expected rewards. The former represents scheduled customers as Equation (3) where t_d is a departure time from depot and R is a traveling route. It means that transport vehicles certainly get a reward r_a at node n (except when the vehicles scramble for the reward). We call vehicles which estimate their rewards by Equation (3) as **reactive vehicles**.

$$r_a = \sum_{n \in R} |c(n, t_d)| \tag{3}$$

The latter represents undetermined customers as Equation (4) where t_r is a return time to the depot. As described above, the function $d(n, t)$ includes uncertainty represented by a normal probability distribution with variance σ^2. Thus, it means that transport vehicles maybe get a reward r_e at the node n in addition to the reward r_a (except when the vehicles scramble for the reward).

$$r_e = \sum_{n \in R} \int_{t_d}^{t_r} |d(n, t)| dt \tag{4}$$

It seems that the setting for travel routes in consideration of the expected reward in addition to the assured reward maybe increase the profit of vehicles although they involve risks in varying degrees. Hence, we introduce a weight function $w(\sigma^2)$ $(0 \leq w(\sigma^2) \leq 1)$ of the expected reward as a policy against risks so that the total of reward can be estimated as Equation (5). We call vehicles which estimate their rewards by Equation (5) as **proactive vehicles** [7, 8].

$$r = r_a + w(\sigma^2) \cdot r_e \tag{5}$$

In this paper, we adopt Equation (6) as the weight function. The parameter α $(\alpha \geq 0)$ dictates attitudes of vehicles against the risks. Figure 2 shows three types of the weight function. If α is 1, the attitudes of vehicles are **neutral**. The degree of variance σ^2 is inversely proportional to the weight of the expected reward. If α is more than 1, the attitudes of vehicle are **risk-taking**. The curve of the risk-taking is distorted on the upper side. Hence, risk-taking vehicles prefer gambles even though the uncertainty (i.e., variance σ^2) is high. If α is less than 1, the attitudes of vehicles are **risk-avoiding**. The curve of the risk-avoiding is distorted on the lower side. Hence, risk-avoiding vehicles prefer assuredness even though the uncertainty (i.e., variance σ^2) is low.

$$w(\sigma^2) = -\sigma^{2\alpha} + 1 \tag{6}$$

4   Transport Strategy

In this section, we consider a competitive game, which is called synchro game in the field of the game theory, between two transport vehicles. Transport strategy is classified into three types: **mixed**, **competitive**, and **Nash**. We show decision-making processes between two vehicles with specific strategies by using simple

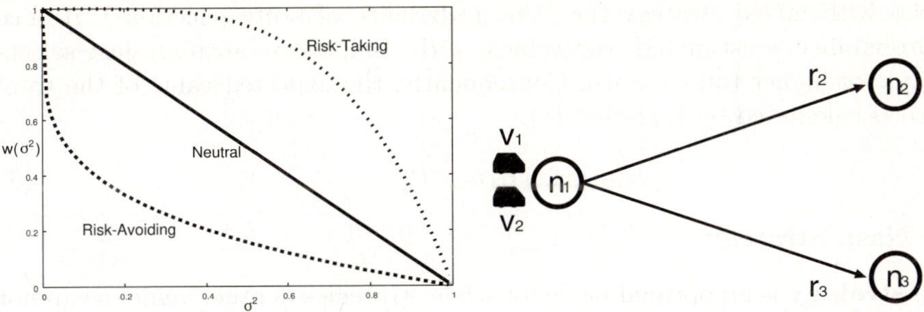

Fig. 2. Three types of weight function   **Fig. 3.** Situation of route selection

Table 1. Profit matrix for v_1 and v_2

		v_2	
		n_2	n_3
v_1	n_2	$(r_2/2 : r_2/2)$	$(r_2 : r_3)$
	n_3	$(r_3 : r_2)$	$(r_3/2 : r_3/2)$

situation shown in Figure 3. In the situation, there are two vehicles (v_1 and v_2) at n_1. They must select from n_2 and n_3 as the next node. For simplicity, we assume that both vehicles adopt the same risk policy: i.e., their estimation rewards are the same value. Hence, estimate rewards of n_2 and n_3 are given by r_2 and r_3, respectively. A profit matrix for v_1 and v_2 is shown in Table 1. The profit matrix represents the rewards between the two vehicles in all possible combinations of their choices. For example, if v_1 selects n_2 and v_2 also selects n_2, the rewards of v_1 and v_2 are $r_2/2$ (half of r_2).

4.1   Mixed Strategy

Mixed strategy is a simple probabilistic behavior for transport vehicles. In the situation, v_1 selects n_2 at the probability p and n_3 at the probability $(1 - p)$. In the same way, v_2 selects n_2 at the probability q and n_3 at the probability $(1 - q)$. The probability can be determined in advance because the probabilities are independent of strategies of other vehicles. For example, if p is 0.5, v_1 visits n_2 and n_3 evenly. If p is 1, v_1 always visits n_2 only. The expected value of the total reward is calculated by Equation (7) where $R(n_2)$ and $R(n_3)$ are expected values when v_1 selects n_2 and n_3, respectively.

$$\begin{cases} R & = p \cdot R(n_2) + (1 - p) \cdot R(n_3) \\ R(n_2) = q \cdot \frac{r_2}{2} + (1 - q) \cdot r_2 \\ R(n_3) = q \cdot r_3 + (1 - q) \cdot \frac{r_3}{2} \end{cases} \tag{7}$$

4.2   Competitive Strategy

Competitive strategy is an optimal behavior against the mixed strategy. Hence, a vehicle with competitive strategy needs to estimate behaviors of rival vehicles with mixed strategy (i.e., the probability of route selections). If once the probability is estimated, the vehicle with competitive strategy just selects the node of higher total reward. Consequently, the expected value of the total reward is calculated by Equation (8).

$$R = \max\left(R(n_2), R(n_3)\right) \tag{8}$$

4.3   Nash Strategy

Nash strategy is an optimal behavior when strategies of other vehicles can not be estimated. Thus, this strategy is also independent of strategies of other vehicles as well as the mixed strategy. The probability is based on Nash Equilibrium in the field of game theory. It means that the expected value of total reward for v_2 cannot over than v_1 even if v_2 selects n_2 or n_3. Hence, the probability is calculated by equality $R(n_2) = R(n_3)$, and its calculation result is shown in Equations (9) and (10). Consequently, the expected value of the total reward is calculated by Equation (11). Nash strategy also can be regarded as **Cooperative strategy** because the expected values of both vehicles are the same.

$$p = \frac{2r_2 - r_3}{r_2 + r_3} \tag{9}$$

$$(1 - p) = \frac{-r_2 + 2r_3}{r_2 + r_3} \tag{10}$$

$$R = \frac{3}{2} \cdot \frac{r_2 \cdot r_3}{r_2 + r_3} \tag{11}$$

4.4   Example

Consider the next specific situation. Let r_2 be 3, and r_3 be 2. Vehicle v_1 adopts mixed strategy with $p = 0.5$: i.e., v_1 selects n_2 and n_3 evenly. What strategy should the vehicle v_2 adopt? Figure 4 shows the expected value of total reward for v_2 when

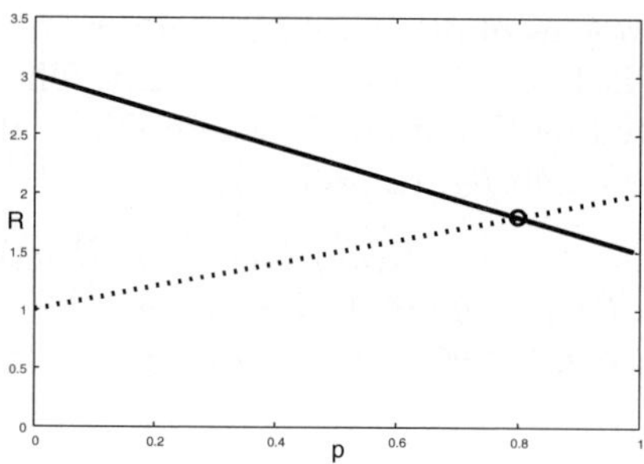

Fig. 4. Expected value of total reward

p is from 0 to 1. The $R(n_2)$ is the straight line, and $R(n_3)$ is the broken line. If v_2 can estimate that the probability p is 0.5, v_2 should select n_2 as the next node. This is because $R(n_2)$ is more than $R(n_3)$. If v_2 can not estimate the probability p, v_2 should select the probability 0.8 that line $R(n_2)$ intersects line $R(n_3)$. This is because the value of v_1 can not over than v_2 even if v_1 selects n_2 or n_3.

5   Simulation Experiments

In this section, we report two results of simulation experiments. The first simulation experiment compares three risk policies: neutral, risk-avoiding, and risk-taking. The second simulation experiment compares three transport strategies: mixed, competitive, and Nash.

5.1   Simulation Environment

The environment in this simulation experiment is as follows. The transport area is a two-way circulate graph which includes 1 depot, 10 nodes, and 5 two-way branches. The lengths of all edges are set to the same value with the speeds of vehicles (i.e., all vehicles move from a current node to all link-nodes in a unit time). The values of distribution function of the area are set from 1 to 5 randomly, and the cycle of the distribution function is set to 10. The cycle is repeated 1000 times. As described above, we deal with synchro games between two vehicles. Thus, in this simulation experiments, two vehicles departure from the same depot at the same time and return to the same depot at the same time. The graphs of the simulation results show the average profit (the number of riding customers) for each vehicle when the capacity of vehicles is set from 10 to 19.

5.2   Risk Policy

We investigate effects of attitudes of vehicles against risks on their profits. The variance σ^2 of occasion patterns is set to 0.1 and 0.5. Figure 5 shows the results of reactive and proactive vehicles. These results indicate that the proactivity of vehicles improves their profits, and enough capacity of vehicles maximizes its performance. However, the uncertainty of the occasion patterns makes the performance less effective. Figure 6 shows the results of three risk policies: neutral($\alpha = 1$), risk-avoiding($\alpha = 1/3$), and risk-taking ($\alpha = 3$). In the result(a), there is no difference among the three risk policies because the risk is very low. In the result(b), the risk-taking vehicle shows a good result. This reason is that the average of the distribution function is set to small value so that the number of waiting customers (who cannot ride the previous vehicle) is also small. Hence, the expected reward becomes more important factor for their profits.

5.3   Transport Strategy

We investigate effects of transport strategies on their profits. The variance σ^2 of occasion patterns is set to 0.1. Figure 7 shows the results of the three transport

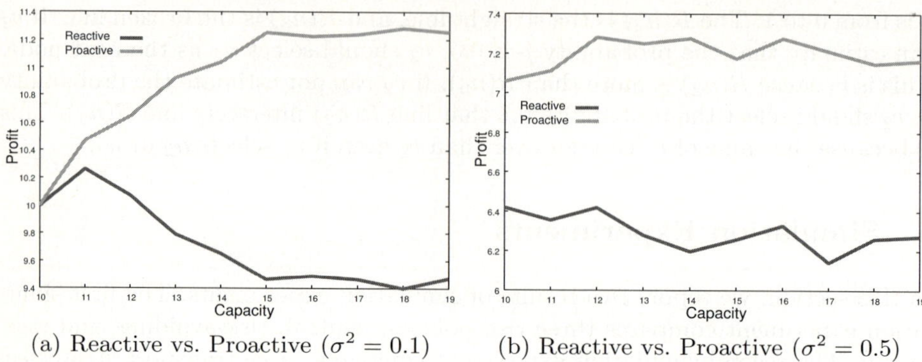

(a) Reactive vs. Proactive ($\sigma^2 = 0.1$)   (b) Reactive vs. Proactive ($\sigma^2 = 0.5$)

Fig. 5. Comparing between reactive and proactive vehicles

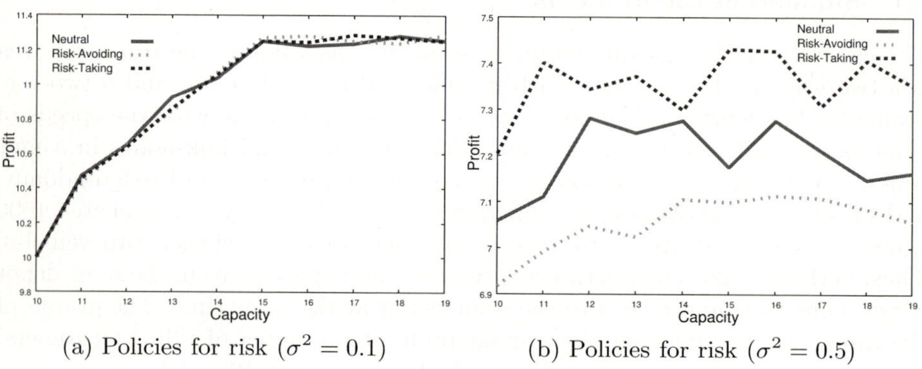

(a) Policies for risk ($\sigma^2 = 0.1$)   (b) Policies for risk ($\sigma^2 = 0.5$)

Fig. 6. Comparing among three risk policies

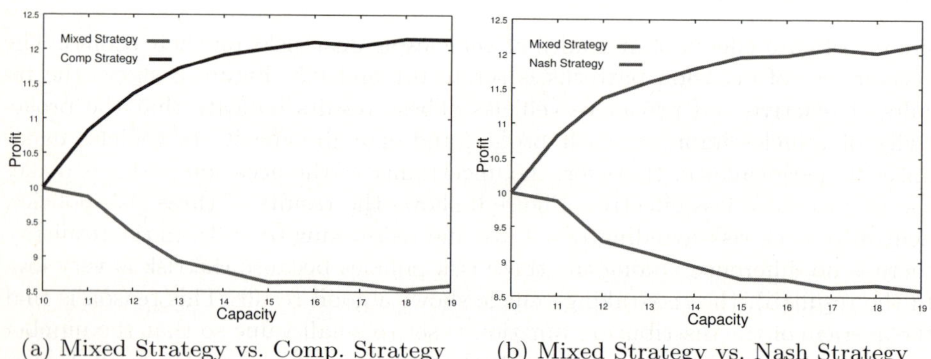

(a) Mixed Strategy vs. Comp. Strategy   (b) Mixed Strategy vs. Nash Strategy

Fig. 7. Simulation results for transport strategy

strategies: mixed, competitive, and Nash. These results indicate that competitive and Nash strategies naturally show good results, and enough capacity of vehicles maximizes its performance. At the first view, two curves of competitive and Nash strategies are almost the same. However, we can see that the curve of competitive strategy slightly increases earlier than the curve of Nash one. This fact suggests that vehicles should adopt Nash strategy while learning actions of rival vehicles to estimate their strategies if the capacity is not so enough. Additionally, after the learning actions of rival vehicles, the vehicles should adopt competitive strategy.

6 Conclusion

In this paper, we focused on on-demand transportation systems. The service of traditional systems is limited due to conflicts with other transport systems and uncertainties about other transport vehicles. Therefore, we formalized the risk for transport vehicles and classified the policy against the risk into three types: neutral, risk-avoiding, and risk-taking. Furthermore, we showed decision-making processes based on the game theory and classified strategy for transport vehicles into three types: mixed, competitively, and Nash. Finally, we reported the results of simulation experiments. The results indicate that the appropriate risk policy and transport strategy for the environment can improve the profits of transport systems even though there are conflicts and uncertainties.

In the future work, we must consider alternate games among transport vehicles (i.e., differential arrival time). Moreover, we would like to extend our theory to actual environments.

Acknowledgment

We would like to thank Japan Society for the Promotion of Science (JSPS). And, we acknowledge to Prof. Naohiro Ishii of Aichi Institute of Technology.

References

1. Ohta, M., Shinoda, K., Noda, I., Kurumatani, K., Nakashima, H.: Usability of demand-bus in town area. Technical Report 2002-ITS-11-33, Technical Report of IPSJ (2002) in Japanese.
2. Noda, I., Ohta, M., Shinoda, K., Kumada, Y., Nakashima, H.: Is demand bus reasonable in large scale towns? Technical Report 2003-ICS-131, Technical Report of IPSJ (2003) in Japanese.
3. Harano, T., Ishikawa, T.: On the vakidity of cooperated demand bus. Technical Report 2004-ITS-19-18, Technical Report of IPSJ (2004) in Japanese.
4. Desrochers, M., Lenstra, J., Savelsbergh, M., F.Soumis: Vehicle routing with time windows: Optimizatin and approximation. Vehicle Routing: Methods and Studies (1988) 65–84
5. Solomon, M., Desrosiers, J.: Time window constrained routing and scheduling problems. Transportations Science **22** (1988) 1–13
6. Gibbons, R.: Game Theory for Applied Economics. Princeton Univ Pr (1992)

7. Mukai, N., Feng, J., Watanabe, T.: Dynamic construction of routine patterns for transport vehicles based on ant colony system. IPSJ Journal **46** (2005) to be appeared in this November.
8. Mukai, N., Feng, J., Watanabe, T.: Proactive route planning based on expected rewards for transport systems. In: Proceedings of IEEE International Conference on Tools with Artificial Intelligence. (2005) to be appeared in this November.

A Set Theoretic View of the ISA Hierarchy

Yee Chung Cheung, Paul Wai Hing Chung, and Ana Sălăgean

Department of Computer Science
Loughborough University
Loughborough, UK
P.W.H.Chung@lboro.ac.uk, A.M.Salagean@lboro.ac.uk

Abstract. The ISA (is-a) hierarchies are widely used in the classification and the representation of related objects. In terms of assessing similarity between two nodes, current distance approaches suffer from its nature that only parent-child relationships among nodes are captured in the hierarchy. This paper presents an idea of treating a hierarchy as a set rather than as a tree in the traditional view. The established set theory is applied to provide the foundation where the relations between nodes can be mathematically specified and results in a more powerful and logical assessment of similarity between nodes.

Keywords: fuzzy matching, information retrieval, knowledge representation.

1 Introduction

The ISA hierarchies are widely used to classify and represent domain concepts. In its tree structure, the root represents the most general concept and its child nodes represent more specific concepts. Each node can be further decomposed as necessary. In a hierarchy the parent-child relation is the only one that is explicitly represented between nodes. The mainstream approaches to assess the similarity between nodes in a hierarchy are developed based on the idea of conceptual distance. The conceptual distance between two nodes is defined in terms of the length of the shortest path that connects the nodes in a hierarchy (Rada, [5]). However, similarity assessment based on conceptual distance does not always provide satisfactory results. This paper describes an alternative approach that views a hierarchy as a set which enables richer information to be specified. In this view the established set theory can be applied to both hierarchy specification and similarity assessment. The next section gives a brief description of similarity assessment based on conceptual distance. The third section presents the set theoretic approach. The application of the set theoretic view to similarity assessment is demonstrated in section four. A number of examples of capability matching are used throughout the paper. The paper ends with a discussion and conclusion section.

M. Ali and R. Dapoigny (Eds.): IEA/AIE 2006, LNAI 4031, pp. 127–136, 2006.

2   Conceptual Distance Approaches

Figure 1 is a simple capability ontology of programming skills represented as a hierarchy. For example, the term Object-Oriented represents the general concept of object-oriented programming skills; the term VB means Visual Basic programming skills. The parent-child relation between Object-Oriented and VB can be interpreted as VB programming skill is a kind of Object-Oriented programming skill. This capability ontology can be used to describe the skills of agents and the required capability to perform specific tasks.

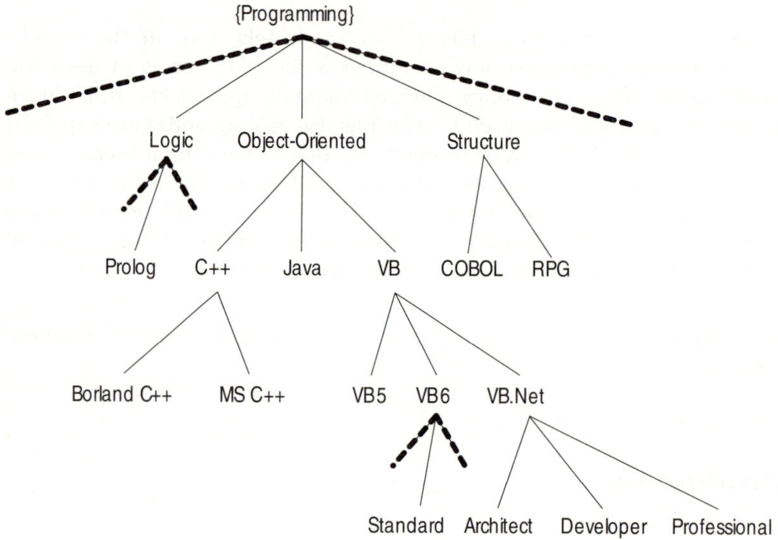

Fig. 1. A simple ISA hierarchy of programming skills

To identify the most appropriate agent for a given task, it is required to assess the goodness of fit (GOF) of an agent's skills against the required capability. The GOF is represented as a number in the interval $[0, 100]$ where the upper limit 100 implies a perfect match. In the following examples, o_a refers to the capability of an available agent and o_r refers to the required capability for performing a task. The following equation, taken from [4], defines GOF based on the distance approach:

$$\text{GOF} = \left(1 - \frac{IP + EP}{IR + ER}\right) \times 100$$

where IP is the number of edges on the path between o_r and the common ancestor of o_r and o_a; EP is the number of edges of the path between o_a and the common ancestor of o_r and o_a; IR is the number of edges on the path between o_r and the root of the hierarchy; ER is the number of edges on the path between o_a and the root of the hierarchy.

Table 1 shows the results of applying this equation to a few examples based on Figure 1. From these examples, it can be seen that this approach does not always produce appropriate GOF values. Consider examples 2 and 3: if the required capability is Java, both available capabilities VB and C++ have the same GOF with value 50. However, an agent who knows C++ may require less effort to learn Java than another agent who knows VB. Another problem can be found in examples 4 and 5. In example 5, the required capability is C++ and the availability is general capability in Object-Oriented. However, it has the same GOF as example 4 where the required capability is any Object-Oriented skills and the available capability is C++. Finally, examples 6 and 7 show a serious problem: when either o_a or o_r is the root, the GOF value is always 0.

Table 1. Examples GOF using traditional distance approach

Example	o_a	o_r	$\text{GOF}(o_a, o_r)$
1	Java	Java	100
2	VB	Java	50
3	C++	Java	50
4	C++	Object-Oriented	66
5	Object-Oriented	C++	66
6	MS C++	Programming	0
7	Programming	MS C++	0

Chung and Jefferson suggested in [3] that different types of relationship between two nodes in a hierarchy have to be dealt with appropriately. They identified four different categories in matching domain concepts in a hierarchy, which are:

1. o_a is the same as o_r;
2. o_a is a descendant of o_r in the hierarchy;
3. o_a is an ancestor of o_r in the hierarchy;
4. o_a and o_r are on different branches in the hierarchy.

In category 1, as o_a is the same as o_r, i.e. $o_a = o_r$, it is obvious that $\text{GOF}(o_a, o_r) = 1$. In category 2, o_a is a concept of o_r. Therefore, if a task requires o_r then someone who knows o_a is suitable, and thus $\text{GOF}(o_a, o_r) = 1$. In category 3, o_a is more general than o_r. It means that o_a may or may not be what the user is required. A general rule for the domain is required. In category 4, o_a and o_r are on different branches in the hierarchy. Their investigation concludes that it is inappropriate to apply a general rule to determine the GOF value in this category. Nodes on different branches in a hierarchy may or may not be related. It is up to the domain experts to determine how closely two nodes are related or not related at all.

On the other hand, in [6] Sussna identified that besides the length of the path, the specificity of two nodes in the path (measured by the depth in the hierarchy) is an important parameter that affects the distance measure. In his work, a weight is assigned to each edge in the hierarchy and the total weight of the path between two nodes is calculated. The weights try to capture the fact that for the same path length, nodes lower in the hierarchy seem to be conceptually closer. In another similar work, [2], Agirre and Rigau took the density of concepts in the hierarchy into consideration: concepts in a deeper part of the hierarchy should be ranked closer, and the Conceptual Density [1] formula is used to provide more accurate results. Although the above works improve the assessment of similarity, they still suffer from the nature of the ISA hierarchy where only the parent-child relation is captured.

3   Set Theoretic Approach

We propose to view a hierarchy as a collection of sets and their inclusion relationships. Namely to each node in the tree we associate a set and each edge from a parent S to a child A represents the fact that the set A is included in the set S, i.e. $A \subseteq S$. This corresponds to the intuition that the notion A is conceptually included in the more general notion S. Different children of the same parent may or may not overlap. This also corresponds intuitively to the fact that the concepts may or may not have some degree of similarity.

We also quantify the "size" of the sets by defining a measure function on the set of all subsets of the root set. For each such set A its measure is a real number $\mu(A)$ with $\mu(A) \geq 0$. As usual the measure function will have the properties:

1. $\mu(\emptyset) = 0$ (The empty set has size 0)
2. If $A \subseteq B$ then $\mu(A) \leq \mu(B)$
3. If A and B are disjoint then $\mu(A \cup B) = \mu(A) + \mu(B)$.

We are interested not so much in the sizes of the sets but rather in their relative sizes. For each set A except the root we define the quantity $P(A)$ representing the relative size of A against the size of its parent set S, i.e. $P(A) = \mu(A)/\mu(S)$. Intuitively this quantifies what proportion of the general concept S is covered by the concept A. Obviously, since $A \subseteq S$, we have $0 \leq P(A) \leq 1$. For each parent S having children $A_1, A_2, \ldots, A_k$ we assume we are given $P(A_1), P(A_2), \ldots, P(A_k)$ and $P(A_{i_1} \cap A_{i_2} \cap \ldots \cap A_{i_t})$ for all $2 \leq t \leq k$ and $1 \leq i_1 < i_2 < \ldots < i_t \leq k$.

We make an important simplifying assumption, namely that each child is, in a sense "uniformly distributed" throughout its parent set. More precisely, if a node S has children A_1 and A_2 which are not disjoint (i.e. $A_1 \cap A_2 \neq \emptyset$) and furthermore A_1 has children B_1 and B_2, then say B_1 appears in the same proportion in $A_1 \cap A_2$ as in A_1, that is $\mu(B_1 \cap A_1 \cap A_2)/\mu(A_1 \cap A_2) = P(B_1)$. In the sequel we will call this assumption "the uniformity property".

We are now ready to define $\mathrm{GOF}(o_a, o_r)$ for our model. Intuitively, we want to measure what proportion of the required notion o_r is covered by the available notion o_a. Therefore, we define

$$\mathrm{GOF}(o_a, o_r) = 100 \frac{\mu(o_a \cap o_r)}{\mu(o_r)}. \tag{1}$$

We will look in more detail at how can this be computed according to the positions of o_a and o_r in the hierarchy. A summary will be given in Table 2.

If $o_r = o_a$ or $o_r \subset o_a$ then $o_a \cap o_r = o_r$ so (1) becomes $\text{GOF}(o_a, o_r) = 100$. This fits well with the intuition that we have a perfect match in this case.

If $o_a \subset o_r$ then $o_a \cap o_r = o_a$ so (1) becomes $\text{GOF}(o_a, o_r) = 100\mu(o_a)/\mu(o_r)$. This can be computed as follows: assume the path in the tree from o_a to its ancestor o_r consists of the sets $o_a \subseteq B_1 \subseteq B_2 \subseteq \ldots \subseteq B_u \subseteq o_r$. Then

$$\text{GOF}(o_a, o_r) = 100\frac{\mu(o_a)}{\mu(o_r)} = \frac{\mu(o_a)}{\mu(B_1)} \cdot \frac{\mu(B_1)}{\mu(B_2)} \cdots \frac{\mu(B_u)}{\mu(o_r)}$$

hence

$$\text{GOF}(o_a, o_r) = 100P(o_a)P(B_1)\cdots P(B_u)$$

Finally we have the case when none of o_a and o_r are included in the other. We look first at the situation where o_a and o_r are siblings, i.e. both are children of the same parent S. We have:

$$\text{GOF}(o_a, o_r) = 100\frac{\mu(o_a \cap o_r)}{\mu(o_r)} = 100\frac{\frac{\mu(o_a \cap o_r)}{\mu(S)}}{\frac{\mu(o_r)}{\mu(S)}} = 100\frac{P(o_a \cap o_r)}{P(o_r)}$$

For the more general case when none of o_a and o_r are included in the other and they are not siblings, $\text{GOF}(o_a, o_r)$ can be computed as follows: let S be the common ancestor of o_a and o_r and let the path from o_a to S consist of the sets $o_a \subseteq B_1 \subseteq B_2 \subseteq \ldots \subseteq B_u \subseteq S$ and the path from o_r to S consist of the sets $o_r \subseteq C_1 \subseteq C_2 \subseteq \ldots \subseteq C_v \subseteq S$. Then, as before, we have $\frac{\mu(o_a)}{\mu(B_u)} = P(o_a)P(B_1)\cdots P(B_{u-1})$. Due to the uniformity property, o_a occupies uniformly a proportion $\mu(o_a)/\mu(B_u)$ of any subset of B_u, in particular of $B_u \cap o_r$. This means

$$\frac{\mu(o_a \cap o_r)}{\mu(B_u \cap o_r)} = \frac{\mu(o_a \cap B_u \cap o_r)}{\mu(B_u \cap o_r)} = \frac{\mu(o_a)}{\mu(B_u)}$$

so $\mu(o_a \cap o_r) = \mu(B_u \cap o_r)\mu(o_a)/\mu(B_u)$. We still have to compute $\mu(B_u \cap o_r)$. Since $o_r \subseteq C_v$ we have $\mu(B_u \cap o_r) = \mu(B_u \cap C_v \cap o_r)$. Again by the uniformity property, $B_u \cap C_v$ occupies uniformly a proportion $\mu(B_u \cap C_v)/\mu(C_v)$ of any subset of C_v, in particular of o_r. Hence

$$\frac{\mu(B_u \cap o_r)}{\mu(o_r)} = \frac{\mu(B_u \cap C_v \cap o_r)}{\mu(o_r)} = \frac{\mu(B_u \cap C_v)}{\mu(C_v)}$$

so $\mu(B_u \cap o_r) = \mu(o_r)\mu(B_u \cap C_v)/\mu(C_v)$. So we can compute

$$\text{GOF}(o_a, o_r) = 100\frac{\mu(o_a \cap o_r)}{\mu(o_r)} = 100\frac{\mu(B_u \cap o_r)\mu(o_a)}{\mu(B_u)\mu(o_r)} = 100\frac{\mu(B_u \cap C_v)\mu(o_a)}{\mu(C_v)\mu(B_u)}$$

and finally

$$\text{GOF}(o_a, o_r) = 100\frac{P(B_u \cap C_v)}{P(C_v)}P(o_a)P(B_1)\cdots P(B_{u-1}).$$

Table 2. Formulae for GOF in the set approach

	$\mathrm{GOF}(o_a, o_r)$	Explanations
General formula	$100\dfrac{\mu(o_a \cap o_r)}{\mu(o_r)}$	
$o_a = o_r$	100	
$o_a \supset o_r$	100	
$o_a \subset o_r$	$100P(o_a)P(B_1)\cdots P(B_u)$	$o_a \subseteq B_1 \subseteq \ldots \subseteq B_u \subseteq o_r$
o_a and o_r siblings	$100\dfrac{P(o_a \cap o_r)}{P(o_r)}$	
o_a and o_r arbitrary	$100\dfrac{P(B_u \cap C_v)}{P(C_v)}P(o_a)P(B_1)\cdots P(B_{u-1})$	$o_a \subseteq B_1 \subseteq \ldots \subseteq B_u \subseteq S$ $o_r \subseteq C_1 \subseteq \ldots \subseteq C_v \subseteq S$

Table 2 summarises the formulae for computing GOF using the set approach. Examples of computations of GOF using this definition will be given in the next section.

We note that storing at each node all the quantities $P(A_{i_1} \cap A_{i_2} \cap \ldots \cap A_{i_t})$ for all $1 \le t \le k$ and $1 \le i_1 < i_2 < \ldots < i_t \le k$ can lead to excessive memory usage. It also provides a level of detailed information that often will be neither available nor needed. We can simplify the representation as follows. For each parent S having children $A_1, A_2, \ldots, A_k$ we assume we are given $P(A_1 \cap A_2 \cap \ldots \cap A_k)$ and, optionally $P(A_1), P(A_2), \ldots, P(A_k)$ and $P(A_{i_1} \cap A_{i_2} \cap \ldots \cap A_{i_t})$ for all $2 \le t < k$ and $1 \le i_1 < i_2 < \ldots < i_t \le k$. If we are not given $P(A_{i_1} \cap A_{i_2} \cap \ldots \cap A_{i_t})$ for some t and some $1 \le i_1 < i_2 < \ldots < i_t \le k$, we assume by default that $A_{i_1} \cap A_{i_2} \cap \ldots \cap A_{i_t} = A_1 \cap A_2 \cap \ldots \cap A_k$, and therefore $P(A_{i_1} \cap A_{i_2} \cap \ldots \cap A_{i_t}) = P(A_1 \cap A_2 \cap \ldots \cap A_k)$. If $P(A_1), P(A_2), \ldots, P(A_k)$ are not given then we assume by default that $P(A_1) = P(A_2) = \ldots = P(A_k)$ and $S = A_1 \cup A_2 \cup \ldots A_k$. We can then deduce the values $P(A_i)$ using the inclusion-exclusion formula:

$$\mu(A_1 \cup A_2 \cup \ldots A_k) = \sum_{i=1}^{k} \mu(A_i) - \sum_{1 \le i_1 < i_2 \le k} \mu(A_{i_1} \cap A_{i_2}) + \ldots +$$

$$+(-1)^{t+1} \sum_{1 \le i_1 < i_2 < \ldots < i_t \le k} \mu(A_{i_1} \cap \ldots \cap A_{i_t}) + \ldots +$$

$$+(-1)^{k+1}\mu(A_1 \cap A_2 \cap \ldots \cap A_k)$$

Dividing by $\mu(S)$ we obtain

$$1 = \sum_{i=1}^{k} P(A_i) - \sum_{1 \le i_1 < i_2 \le k} P(A_{i_1} \cap A_{i_2}) + \ldots +$$

$$+(-1)^{t+1} \sum_{1 \le i_1 < i_2 < \ldots < i_t \le k} P(A_{i_1} \cap \ldots \cap A_{i_t}) + \ldots +$$

$$+(-1)^{k+1}P(A_1 \cap A_2 \cap \ldots \cap A_k) \tag{2}$$

When only $P(A_1 \cap A_2 \cap \ldots \cap A_k)$ is given we have therefore $1 = kP(A_1) - (k - 1)P(A_1 \cap A_2 \cap \ldots \cap A_k)$, hence for all i we have

$$P(A_i) = \frac{1 + (k - 1)P(A_1 \cap A_2 \cap \ldots \cap A_k)}{k}. \tag{3}$$

4   Example

The hierarchy given in Figure 1 can be enriched using some sample similarity figures, obtaining the hierarchy given in Figure 2.

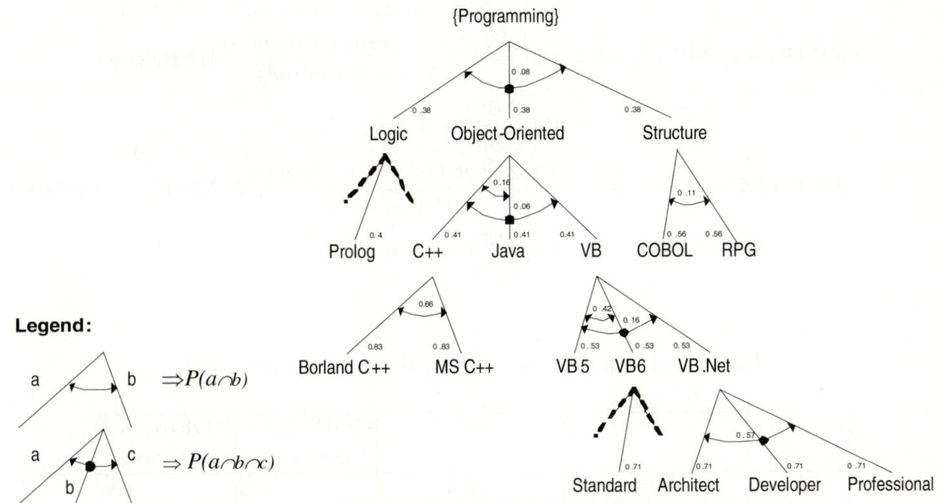

Fig. 2. Enriched hierarchy

The numerical values given in Figure 2 are obtained as follows. Take for example the concept Object-Oriented and its three children, the concepts C++, Java and VB. We assume that the three children have the same size i.e. $P(\text{C++}) = P(\text{Java}) = P(\text{VB}) = x$. The amount of overlap of the concepts has to be obtained from domain experts. Assume the experts indicate that C++ and Java are 40% similar, i.e. $P(\text{C++} \cap \text{Java}) = 0.4P(\text{Java}) = 0.4x$ and that the similarity of all the three notions is 15%, i.e. $P(\text{C++} \cap \text{Java} \cap \text{VB}) = 0.15P(\text{Java}) = 0.15x$. The similarity of VB with C++ and of VB with Java are not given so it is assumed that they equal the similarity of all the three concepts, i.e. $P(\text{C++} \cap \text{VB}) = P(\text{Java} \cap \text{VB}) = P(\text{C++} \cap \text{Java} \cap \text{VB}) = 0.15x$. Using formula (2) we can then compute

$$1 = P(\text{C++}) + P(\text{Java}) + P(\text{VB}) - P(\text{C++} \cap \text{Java}) - P(\text{Java} \cap \text{VB}) -$$
$$-P(\text{C++} \cap \text{VB}) + P(\text{C++} \cap \text{Java} \cap \text{VB})$$
$$= 3x - 0.4x - 0.15x - 0.15x + 0.15x = 2.45x$$

Hence $x = 1/2.45 = 0.41$, $P(\text{C++} \cap \text{Java}) = 0.4x = 0.16$ and $P(\text{C++} \cap \text{Java} \cap \text{VB}) = 0.15x = 0.06$.

We compute GOF for several combinations of o_a and o_r using the formulae introduced in the previous section.

$$\text{GOF}(\text{Java}, \text{Java}) = 100$$

$$\text{GOF}(\text{VB}, \text{Java}) = 100\frac{P(\text{VB} \cap \text{Java})}{P(\text{Java})} = 100\frac{0.06}{0.41} = 15$$

$$\text{GOF}(\text{C++}, \text{Java}) = 100\frac{P(\text{C++} \cap \text{Java})}{P(\text{Java})} = 100\frac{0.16}{0.41} = 39$$

$$\text{GOF}(\text{MS C++}, \text{Programming}) = 100P(\text{MS C++})P(\text{C++})P(\text{Object-oriented})$$

$$= 100 \times 0.83 \times 0.41 \times 0.38 = 13$$

$$\text{GOF}(\text{Prolog}, \text{MS C++}) = 100\frac{P(\text{Logic} \cap \text{Object-Oriented})}{P(\text{Object-Oriented})}P(\text{Prolog})$$

$$= 100\frac{0.08}{0.39}0.4 = 8$$

$$\text{GOF}(\text{MS C++}, \text{Prolog}) = \frac{P(\text{Object-Oriented} \cap \text{Logic})}{P(\text{Logic})}P(\text{MS C++})P(\text{C++})$$

$$= 100\frac{0.08}{0.39}0.83 \times 0.41 = 7.$$

Table 3. Examples GOF using the set view approach

Example	o_a	o_r	GOF(o_a, o_r) Distance	GOF(o_a, o_r) Set view
1	Java	Java	100	100
2	VB	Java	50	15
3	C++	Java	50	39
4	C++	Object-Oriented	66	41
5	Object-Oriented	C++	66	100
6	MS C++	Programming	0	13
7	Programming	MS C++	0	100
8	Prolog	MS C++	0	8
9	MS C++	Prolog	0	7

These results and a few more are summarised in Table 3. We note that the results obtained using the set approach are more reasonable than the ones using distance. Examples 2 and 3 show that in the set theoretic approach we can model the fact that C++ is more similar to Java than VB is to Java. In examples 4 through to 7, one of the concepts is a descendant of the other. While the distance approach was unable to differentiate between the situation when the required concept is a descendant of the available one or the other way around, the set approach does, yielding a GOF of 100 in the first case and an intermediate GOF in the converse situation. Also, in the latter situation, the set approach GOF will be progressively lower as the available concept is further down the tree from the required concept (compare examples 4 and 6). When one of the concepts is the root of the tree, the distance approach yields a GOF of 0, which is certainly not the expected behaviour, while the set theoretic view gives again a GOF of 100 in the case when the required concept is a descendant of the available one, and an intermediate GOF in the converse situation. Finally, in examples 8 and 9 the common ancestor of the two concepts is the root. The distance approach produces a GOF of 0 in all such situations, while the set approach produces some small GOF as intuitively expected, as the two concepts, although distantly related, do still have some small degree of similarity.

5   Group Matching

Supporting group matching that assesses the GOF of a group of objects against another group is an additional advantage of the set theoretic view. Agent selection for tasks is an example of such matching. To perform a task an agent may require multiple capabilities which form a capability set. Similarly, each agent may possess a set of capabilities. To find out who is the most appropriate agent for a given task, the capability sets possessed by the agents have to be matched against the required capability set.

If an agent has capabilities $A_1, \ldots, A_k$ and the required capabilities are $R_1, \ldots, R_t$ then GOF will be defined as the proportion of the union of required capabilities which is covered by the union of the available capabilities, i.e.

$$\mathrm{GOF}(\cup_{i=1}^{k} A_i, \cup_{j=1}^{t} R_j) = 100 \frac{\mu((\cup_{i=1}^{k} A_i) \cap (\cup_{j=1}^{t} R_j))}{\mu(\cup_{j=1}^{t} R_j)}$$

The computation is in this case more complex and will be the subject of further work.

6   Discussion and Conclusion

The is-a hierarchy is a useful representation that is widely used. However, in terms of assessing the similarity between nodes, it is limited by its nature that the parent-child relation is the only one that is explicitly represented. The set theoretic view is therefore proposed as a solution to this problem.

The basic idea is viewing a hierarchy as a universal set and the child nodes are subsets of this universal set. The similarity is represented by the overlapping between sets. This approach offers a number of advantages over the traditional hierarchy.

First, well-established set theory can be applied to describe hierarchies and the relation between nodes. It allows the similarity between the nodes to be precisely specified while traditional hierarchy only has parent-child connections.

Secondly, the set theory can be used to assess the similarity between any two nodes for which the similarity is not given directly. The outcomes are more reasonable as a result of the enrich relation provided in a set-based description.

Thirdly, the set theoretic approach supports group matching. Current distance based approaches support only one to one matching and lack a theory to support combining the individual results.

Fourthly, the hierarchy description and set description can both be used in the same application. The tree view in hierarchy provides a simple visual explanation to the user and the set description enables a precise assessment at the back end.

The above sections demonstrate how a set theoretic view can improve the traditional hierarchy. Providing appropriate similarity figures is critical to generating a precise set-based description for a hierarchy. Experience shows that reasonable similarity values between different nodes can be obtained from domain experts. Although the given figures vary slightly between experts, the trends are similar. For example, there is general agreement that the similarity between C++ and Java is higher than between C++ and VB.

In conclusion, the set theoretic approach enables more precise description and accurate assessment over the traditional distance-based approaches. As the hierarchical and set theoretic views can both be used in the same application, the simplicity of hierarchies will not be impaired while the set theoretic view provides additional support.

References

1. E. Agirre and G. Rigau. A proposal for word sense disambiguation using conceptual distance. In *International Conference on Recent Advances in Natural Language Processing, Tzigov Chark, Bulgaria*, September 1995.
2. E. Agirre and G. Rigau. Word sense disambiguation using conceptual density. In *Proceedings of COLING-96*, 1996.
3. P.W.H. Chung and M. Jefferson. A fuzzy approach to accessing accident databases. *Applied Intelligence*, 9:129–137, 1998.
4. Cognitive Systems Inc., Boston. *ReMind Reference Manual*, 1992.
5. R. Rada, H. Mili, E. Bicknell, and M. Blettner. Development an application of a metric on semantic nets. *IEEE Transactions on Systems, Man and Cybernetics*, 19(1):17–30, 1989.
6. M. Sussna. Word sense disambiguation for free-text indexing using a massive semantic network. In *Proceedings of the Second International Conference on Information and knowledge Management*, Arlington, Virginia USA, 1993.

Tale of Two Context-Based Formalisms for Representing Human Knowledge

Patrick Brézillon[1] and Avelino J. Gonzalez[2]

[1] LIP6, Box 169, University Paris 6, 8 rue du Capitaine Scott, 75015 Paris, France
`Patrick.Brezillon@lip6.fr`
`http://www-poleia.lip6.fr/~brezil/`
[2] ECE Department, University of Central Florida, Orlando, FL 32816, USA
`Gonzalez@pagasus.cc.ucf.edu`

Abstract. This paper describes an investigation that compared and contrasted Context-based Reasoning (CxBR) and Contextual Graphs (CxG), two paradigms used to represent human intelligence. The specific objectives were to increase understanding of both paradigms, identifying which, if either, excels at a particular function, and to look for potential synergism amongst them. We study these paradigms through ten different aspects, with some indication of which one excels at this particular facet of performance. We point out how they are complementary and finishes with a recommendation for a new synergistic approach, followed by an example of an application of the new approach to tactical

1 Introduction

Context has always played an important, if little understood, role in human intelligence. This is especially true in human communications and decision making. One's awareness of his/her context as well as that of others with whom she/he interacts, permits many assumptions to be made about the environment and/or problem at hand. Otherwise, all assumptions would have to be explicitly spelled out. Thus, a context can be said to bring with it much knowledge about the situation in which the problem is to be solved and/or the environment in which it must be solved. Context, therefore, allows many important aspects of human interaction to remain implicit when the communicants are in a common, or in a shared and commonly understood context.

There is not yet a commonly accepted definition of context [4]. Nevertheless, a consensus begins to appear around "Context is what constrains a problem solving without intervening in it explicitly" [8]. This definition suggests that the context is always let implicit and tacit, and is rarely mentioned explicitly.

Context models provide knowledge managers with a very valuable tool. The recognition of its context can give a problem-solving agent a means to prune the search for solutions, or influence the solution selected or decision made. *Context-based Reasoning* (CxBR) and *Contextual Graphs* (CxG) are two popular emerging context-driven paradigms for representing human intelligence. They have been amply and thoroughly described in the literature. In the interest of space, we omit a description and refer the readers to [12], [5] for detailed descriptions of CxBR and CxG respectively.

M. Ali and R. Dapoigny (Eds.): IEA/AIE 2006, LNAI 4031, pp. 137 – 145, 2006.

2 Presentation of the Context-Based Formalisms of Representation

2.1 Context-Based Reasoning (CxBR)

CxBR was specifically designed to model human behaviour in *tactical missions*. Gonzalez [11] defines *tactical behaviour* as "the continuous and dynamic process of decision making by a performing agent (human or otherwise) who interacts with its environment while attempting to carry out a mission in the environment." Decisions are made at several levels during the execution of the mission.

2.2 Contextual Graphs (CxGs)

Contextual graphs are oriented without circuits, with exactly one input and one output, and a general structure of spindle. A path (from the input to the output of the graph) represents a practice (or a procedure), a type of execution of the task with the application of selected methods. There are as many paths as practices. Figure 1 presents an example drawn from [7].

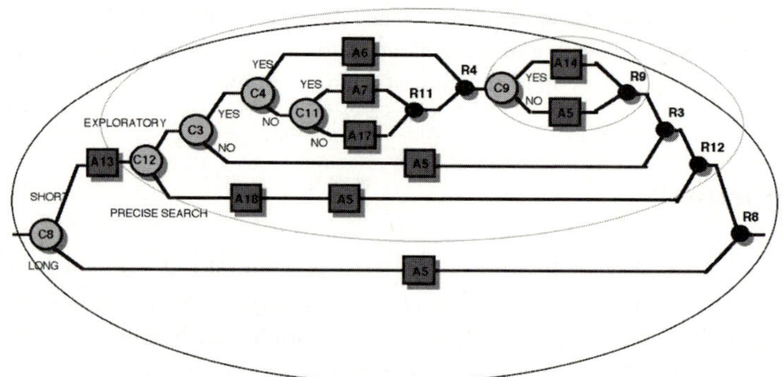

Fig. 1. Contextual Graph Organization (from [7])

2.3 Commonalities Among CxBR and CxG

The first and most obvious similarity is that CxBR and CxGs both generally attempt to provide emulate human-like intelligence by using context as the basic modelling element. Secondly and less obviously, both are activity-based paradigms. This is in sharp contrast to several popular cognitive architectures such as SOAR [17], ACT-R [2] and others that are goal-based. These rely on the agent setting a goal for the system to find a production or some other knowledge piece that allows the agent to achieve that goal or sub-goal. In CxG, the goals are implicit in the context being experienced because one tries to model the user's behaviour and infers their goals. Moreover, the global goal is the problem solving represented in a contextual graph is known ("Find the solution of problem X"). CxBR introduces its mission goals in the non-control *mission context*, of which there is only one. The intermediate goals of the agent in the mission are defined by a plan consisting of a sequence of major-contexts with the transition criteria defined.

3   Comparative Analysis with Ten Metrics

3.1   Class of Application Domains

CxBR is designed to interface tightly with the environment in which the agents will be operating. The problem solving is developed in real time in a continuously changing environment. Problem solving and environment interact and may modify the other. CxBR can be conceivably applied to higher level tasks such as strategic or policy level tasks. However, this has not been verified via example. Past successful application areas of CxBR include automobile driving [16], [9], [10], [13], [18], armor warfare [3], submarine warfare [12], Maritime navigation [15], and anti-submarine warfare [19].

Contextual graphs give a representation of problems already solved by humans. Thus, environmental changes are known in advanced and correspond to different instantiations of contextual elements. Generally, enterprises develop procedures to cover class of problems, when actors of the enterprise develop practices, which are contextualization of the procedures. CxGs allow to deal with practices (and procedures) and have been successfully applied to provide decision support for incident management in the Paris metro system [6], in other domains [7] and to provide program management assistance at the US National Science Foundation [20].

3.2   Context Organization and Granularity

CxBR organizes the knowledge relevant to a particular situation as a hierarchy of contexts (see Figure 2). At the highest level is the *mission context* that defines the mission to be undertaken. Major contexts represent the gross contextual situations and are the main means of agent control. Context is refined though the definition of minor

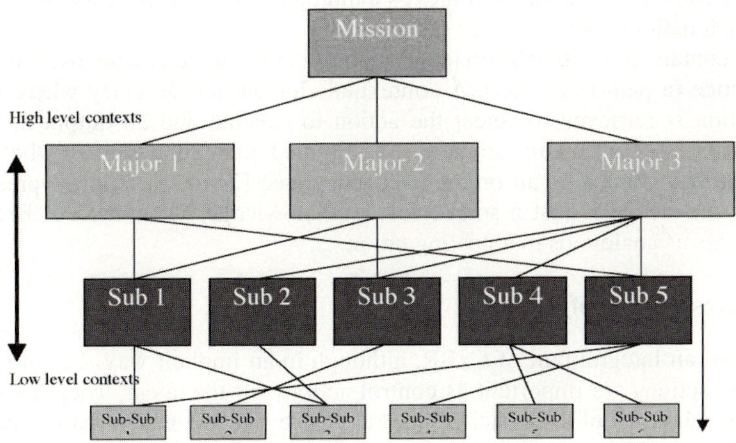

Fig. 2. CxBR Hierarchical Context Organization

contexts. Minor contexts can occupy several levels in the hierarchy (e.g., sub-context, sub-sub-context etc.). A context contains all the knowledge that defines it.

CxGs also organize the knowledge, but not in a hierarchy. First, they propose a uniform representation of elements of reasoning and of contexts at the granularity at which is considered the problem solving (although the use of subgraphs like activities introduce a notion of granularity). Second, contextual elements constitute a heterogeneous population because they do not necessarily correspond to the domain. Three, the accumulation of practices (methods for the problem solving) leads to a kind of refinement of the context by specialization. Figure 3 depicts an abstracted view of how the granularity of a context and organization of contextual elements is represented in the graph of Figure 1.

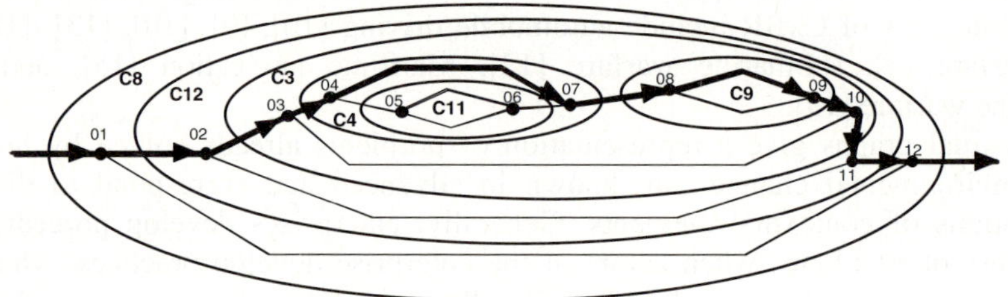

Fig. 3. Context organization in CxGs

3.3 Representation of Contextual Knowledge

In CxBR, contexts are "self-contained control modules" containing knowledge that allows the agent to manage the current situation it is facing. This knowledge is composed of two general types of knowledge, and this is applicable to both, high-level and low-level contexts: (a) The action knowledge to manage the current situation successfully; and (b) The "situationally awareness" to know when they are irrelevant. The second refers to context movement. The knowledge found at the different levels is: (a) High-level: which major context should be active; and (b)Low-level: what to do within each major context

CxGs contain contextual knowledge such as contextual elements used at least once in a practice (a path in a CxG). A contextual element has an entry where its current instantiation is retrieved to select the action to execute and an output at which the instantiation does not matter anymore. Instantiated contextual elements belong to the proceduralized context as an ordered sequence (see [7] for a complete presentation). External knowledge is just a source for new knowledge when needed. Brezillon [5] presents this as analogous to a peeling onion.

3.4 Representation of Actions

Actions are an integral part of CxBR, although in an implicit way. Given its application class, actions are important as control actions for the agent. They are embedded in control functions of a physical/temporal nature that are inside major contexts and minor contexts. There is no distinction between parallel, sequential and iterative activities – all are relegated to *action functions* and handled equally well. Implicit representation of actions introduces flexibility in how action functions are implemented, as no specific way to represent activities is specified.

Actions and activities are also an integral part of CxGs in an explicit representation. This allows to contrast the choice of a method (a sequence of actions) on another with respect to the contextual elements used. CxGs easily represent sequential activities and also parallel activities with *parallel action groupings* (introduced like a kind of a complex structure of context, may be at a different level of representation). However, CxGs do not represent iterative (looping) activities. CxG's explicit representation of actions in the architecture is an advantage.

3.5 Context Dynamics

In CxBR, context is dynamic because it changes as the situation changes. Contextual movement occurs through transition knowledge, most often implemented as *Sentinel Rules*, that monitors the environment for situational criteria that signal a change in situation warranting a change in context. Environmental criteria typically determine which context is active in CxBR. An analogy is made to a polar bear jumping between ice floes seeking its prey. It hopes onto the ice floe that best fits the situation in relation to its objective. Context shifts occur discretely and definitively and the movement is *horizontal* (e.g. from one major context to another one). *Vertical* shifts – the further specification of the context – are done through the context hierarchy. Knowledge within the major contexts determines when the minor contexts should be activated and de-activated.

In CxGs, the main form of dynamics comes from the instantiation of contextual elements on a path (the practice development). According to the instantiation of the contextual element, a path is chosen and an action is preferred on another one. The instantiated contextual element moves from the contextual knowledge to the proceduralized context., and from the proceduralized context to the contextual knowledge when the corresponding action or activity is realized. This corresponds to a *vertical* motion. The dynamics is related to the change of status of one contextual element at a time. Thus the movement is more continuous than discrete. No horizontal movement (i.e. from one path or practice to another path or another practice) is possible. The unique possibility would be a shift toward another contextual graph (another solving of the problem). This does not exist now in CxGs, except towards an activity that is itself a CxG.

3.6 Interaction with the Environment

Interaction with environment is a critical aspect of tactical missions. Therefore, CxBR agents are highly interactive with the real or simulated environment in which they are situated. Their environment generally is unpredictable, and complete information from the environment is generally not available. Furthermore, decisions change the environment. The environment, to a large degree dictates the active major context. The interface with the environment is done through two fact bases that reflects the world as seen by the agent: (a) a local one that reflects only those things about the environment perceivable by the individual agent, and (b) a global fact base that reflects things about the environment that are known by all agents (weather, the score, etc.).

CxGs do not address a real time environment directly because they bring only a knowledge base structured by users' experience for an intelligent assistant. The environment representation concerns what users can perceive and interpret and translate in practices through contextual elements, availability of tools at the given moment, etc.

3.7 Representation of Time

In CxBR, time is inherently represented implicitly, and can be also represented explicitly if desired by the modeller. A tactical mission develops over time, so time is inherent. Furthermore, major contexts are active for a time period, and then become inactive. Lastly, the environment, whether simulated or real, by necessity, incorporates the concept of time – real time. Time can also be explicitly represented in CxBR if the modeller desires. Functions can be written to make use of time as variable. Since the environment with which it interacts is in real time, it facilitates defining real time functions when they are necessary. While CxBR is best at handling time on a real, continuous basis, it can also be handled, at least conceptually, on a discrete event basis.

In CxGs, time is implicitly represented by the ordering of actions and activities in a practice. The user/agent comes in and out of contexts over time, but this is not necessarily real time. Furthermore, all time must be occupied by some activity – a delay is considered like a waiting activity (Action "Wait 30 seconds"). CxG handles time equally well on a continual or discrete basis. Time being an event of the environment, an intelligent assistant would need an external means for handling time, like a simulator.

3.8 Incremental Knowledge Acquisition and Practice Learning

Learning is a very important aspect of human behaviour and context facilitate learning. If the context in which something is to be learned can be identified, the learning process can be made effective as well as efficient. The more specific the context, the more knowledge is already implicit. CxBR has no natural means to acquire knowledge or learn, only indirect ones with CITKA [14], GenCL [10], and Reinforcement CxBR [1].

CxGs are enriched by users, when the system using them fails to solve the problem. Then, the system acquires incrementally new knowledge and its context of validity (from the external knowledge) and learns accordingly a new practice. This is a kind of explanation from the user to the machine. Both tasks, incremental acquisition and learning, are intertwined with the task at hand (the problem solving).

3.9 Uncertainty and Unpredictability

CxBR is used in applications that often contain uncertainty as well as unpredictability. Uncertainty can come from the environment (events) as well as from the knowledge itself. Lastly, all information may not be available at the time the decision is to be made. Conceptually, CxBR is naturally adaptable for handling uncertainty and unpredictability within its action functions and within its Sentinel Rules. However, current implementations of CxBR have not incorporated uncertainty or impreciseness, so this has not been validated at this time.

CxGs do not naturally handle uncertainty and unpredictability because practices are already developed by users and introduced in the system. The closest situation would be when the system does not have the relevant elements of reasoning and of contexts. However, then incremental acquisition of knowledge and learning of the new practice fix the problem. Handling uncertainty and unpredictability, however, is not one of CxGs strengths at the moment.

3.10 Providing Explanations

Explanations in CxBR have not been explored because explanations are not considered critical in tactical mission domain, other than possibly for after-action review of trainee performance. Explanations could be conceivably generated quickly and easily by displaying the major and minor contexts active at any one time – currently, or in a chronological record of the past. This explanation could include the sentinel rule that fired to activate the currently active context or any context that had previously been active.

CxGs use contextual information to generate explanations. An explanation is a presentation of the context in which an action was realized, alternatives abandoned and the reasons of this, who introduced the practice, etc. Introducing explanatory elements does not represent a burdensome overhead to the developer in terms of extra definitions because explanatory elements are introduced in a contextual graph at the time of the incremental knowledge acquisition. The initial explanation from the user to the system, is reproduced later from the system to other users when needed and with additional information automatically collected by the system (creator, date of creation, etc.).

3.11 Summary

Clearly, both CxBR and CxG succeed to emulate human-like intelligence by using context as the basic modelling element. However, they do not seem good in the same dimensions. First, this comes from the fact that CxBR and CxG work on different types of application, real time for cxBR and not for CxG, environment impact the current reasoning (CxBR) or not (CxG). Second , models have different nature, discrete for CxBR (with polar bear metaphor) or continuous for CxG (with the pelling onion metaphor). Third, the introduction of context in reasoning modelling allow to handle with the task at hand other intertwined tasks like incremental acquisition of knowledge, practice learning and explanation generation in CxG and not in CxBR.

However, the most interesting finding is that both appear complementary, CxBR at a global level (mission) when CxG is efficient at the operational level.

It is also important to note that both techniques employ "context movement" to reflect changes in the situation or in the amount of knowledge available about a problem. This is recognition of the fact that contexts always change, and one important criterion for the success of an agent is to be able to recognize the changes in context.

4   Conclusions

This investigation has carefully analyzed the Contextual Graph and Context-based Reasoning, paradigms to better understand them and draw some parallels as well as distinctions. It compared how each treats aspects of human intelligence and behavior. The investigation provided several deep insights into contextual reasoning in general.

It is clear from the research that, in spite of some key but general commonalities, these two paradigms are quite different in how they approach problems as well as the kinds of problems they address. The main difference concerns the approach of the reasoning: In CxBR, the task is considered at a high level (Go and observe the enemy) and details are not considered, while CxGs focus more on details (if there is a hill, first go behind, etc.). In that sense, both approaches are complementary. Their treatment of contexts, however, is somewhat similar, and most importantly, synergistic. Therefore, the results have led to the proposal of a new architecture, the result of the best features of both being integrated into one called the context-driven modeling architecture for human intelligence. This is the type of application commonly associated with CxBR. This is also close from the approach of intelligent assistant systems. Future research includes the implementation of this architecture into a prototype system, and evaluate the improvement in performance of the resulting system with one implemented solely in each of the two paradigms.

References

Aihe, D. and Gonzalez, A. J., "Context-driven Reinforcement Learning", Proceedings of the Second Swedish-American Workshop on Modeling and Simulation, Cocoa Beach, FL, February2-3, 2004.

Anderson, J. R., Matessa, M., & Lebiere, C. (1997). "ACT-R: A theory of higher level cognition and its relation to visual attention", Human Computer Interaction, 12(4), pp. 439-462.

Barrett, G. C. and Gonzalez, A. J., "Expanding Knowledge Representation within Context Based Reasoning to Facilitate Modeling Collaborative Behaviors", Proceedings of the European Simulation Interoperability Workshop, Euro-SIW, June 2004, Edinburgh, Scotland.

Bazire, M. and Brézillon, P. (2005) Understanding context before to use it. Modeling and Using Context (CONTEXT-05), A. Dey, B.Kokinov, D.Leake, R.Turner (Eds.), Springer Verlag, LNCS 3554, pp. 29-40.

Brezillon, P., "Modeling and Using Contexts: Past, Present and Future," Research Report, Laboratoire d'Informatique de Paris 6, Pierre and Marie Curie University, Paris, France, 2002

Brezillon, P., "Representation of Procedures and Practices in Contextual Graphs", The Knowledge Engineering Review, 2004.

Brezillon, P. "Task-realization models in Contextual Graphs." In: Modeling and Using Context (CONTEXT-05), A. Dey, B.Kokinov, D.Leake, R.Turner (Eds.), Springer Verlag, LNCS 3554, pp. 55-68, 2005.

Brézillon P and Pomerol J-Ch "Contextual knowledge sharing and cooperation in intelligent assistant systems." *Le Travail Humain*, 1999, 62, 3, 223-246.

Brown, J., ""Application and Evaluation of the Context-based Reasoning Paradigm", Master's Thesis, Department of Electrical and Computer Engineering, University of Central Florida, July 1994.

Fernlund, H. (2004), "Evolving Models from Observed Human Performance" Doctoral dissertation, Department of Electrical and Computer Engineering, University of Central Florida, Spring, 2004.

Gonzalez, A. J. and Ahlers, R., "Context-based Representation of Intelligent Behavior in Training Simulations", Transactions of the Society of Computer Simulation, Vol. 15, No. 4, 1998, pp. 153-166.

Gonzalez, F. G., Grejs, P. and Gonzalez, A. J., "Autonomous Automobile Behavior through Context-based Reasoning, Proceedings of the International FLAIRS Conference, Orlando, FL, May 2000

Gonzalez, A. J., Gerber, W. J. and Castro, J., "Automated Acquisition of Tactical Knowledge through Contextualization", Proceedings of the 2002 Conference on Computer Generated Forces and Behavior Representation", Orlando, FL, May 2002.

Gonzalez, A. J., Presentation to faculty at Air Force Institute of Technology, December, 2004, Wright-Patterson Air Force Base

Gumus, I., "A Threat Prioritization Algorithm for Multiple Intelligent Entities in a Simulated Environment", Master's Thesis, Department of Electrical and Computer Engineering, University of Central Florida, Summer 1999

Henninger, A, E. and Gonzalez, A, J., "Automated Acquisition Tool for Tactical Knowledge", Proceedings of the 10th Annual Florida Artificial Intelligence Research Symposium, May 1997, pp. 307-311.

Laird, J. E., Newell, A. and Rosenbloom, P. S., "Soar: An Architecture for General Intelligence", Artificial Intelligence, 33(1), 1987, pp. 1-64.

Norlander, L., "A Framework for efficient Implementation of Context-Based Reasoning in Intelligent Simulations", Master's Thesis, Department of Electrical and Computer Engineering, University of Central Florida, 1998.

Proenza, R., "A Framework for Multiple Agents and Memory Recall within the Context-based Reasoning Paradigm", Master's Thesis, Department of Electrical and Computer Engineering, University of Central Florida, Spring 1997.

Sherwell, B. W., Gonzalez, A. J. and Nguyen, J., "Contextual Implementation of Human Problem-solving Knowledge in a Real-World Decision Support System", Proceedings of the Conference on Behavior Representation in Modeling and Simulation, Los Angeles, CA, May 2005.

Some Characteristics of Context

Patrick Brézillon

LIP6, case 169, 8 rue du Capitaine Scott, 75015 Paris, France
Patrick.Brezillon@lip6.fr
http://www-poleia.lip6.fr/~brezil/

Abstract. Drawn from the lessons learned in an application for the subway company in Paris, we pointed out that operators used practices instead of the procedures developed by the company, practices appearing like contextualization of the procedures taking into account specificity of the task at hand and the current situation. This leads us to propose, first, a working definition of context at a theoretical level, and, second, its implementation in a software called Contextual Graphs. In this paper, we present the results of the complete loop, showing how the theoretical view is intertwined with the implemented one. Several results of the literature are discussed too. Beyond this internal coherence of our view on context, we consider knowledge acquisition, learning and explanation generation in our framework. Indeed, these tasks must be considered as integrated naturally with the task at hand of the user.

1 Introduction

Contextual graphs are used in several domains such as medicine, ergonomics, psychology, army, information retrieval, computer security, road safety, etc. [1]. The common factor in all these domains is that the reasoning is described by procedures established by the enterprise. These procedures are tailored by actors that take into account the context in which they have to deal with the focus. Thus actors create practices as contextualizations of procedures. A practical reasoning is not a logical and theoretical reasoning for which the action leads to a conclusion. In a practical reasoning, the conclusion cannot be detached from the premises, i.e. take a meaning out of these premises.

Thus, each actor develops his own practice to address a focus in a given context, and one observes almost as many practices as actors for a given procedure because each actor tailors the procedure in order to take into account the current context, which is particular and specific.

If it is relatively easy to model procedures, the modeling of practices is not an easy task because they are as many practices as contexts of occurrence of a given focus. Moreover, procedures cannot catch the high interaction between the task at hand and the related tasks that are generated by the task itself.

Hereafter, the paper is organized in the following way. Section 2 presents the lessons learned on context up to now, from our working definition to an example of the contextual graphs we have implemented. Section 3 discusses how context appears in a

M. Ali and R. Dapoigny (Eds.): IEA/AIE 2006, LNAI 4031, pp. 146–154, 2006.
© Springer-Verlag Berlin Heidelberg 2006

contextual-graph representation through some elements such as its related focus, the representation as contextual elements, the enrichment of a contextual graph, and the building of the proceduralized context in contextual graphs. Section 4 concludes by giving a global coherent picture of context and points out, as a new axe of research how an item of contextual graphs could be the result of a mixing of levels of representation.

2   Lessons Learned on Context

2.1   Our Working Definition

For a given focus of an actor, Brézillon and Pomerol [2] consider context as the sum of three types of knowledge. First, there is the part of the context that is relevant at this step of the decision making, and the part that is not relevant. The latter part is called **external knowledge**. External knowledge appears in different sources, such as the knowledge known by the actor but let implicit with respect to the current focus, the knowledge unknown to the actor (out of his competence), contextual knowledge of other actors in a team, etc.

The former part is called **contextual knowledge**, and obviously depends on the actor and on the focus at hand. However, the frontier between external and contextual knowledge is porous and evolves with the progress of the focus.

For addressing the current focus, the actor selects a sub-set of the contextual knowledge, assembles, organizes and structures it for addressing the current focus. We call the result the **proceduralized context**. When an element of the contextual knowledge moves in the proceduralized context, this means that we consider explicitly its current instantiation and its particular position with respect to other contextual elements already in the proceduralized context.

Sometimes, the building of a proceduralized context fails to account for the current focus of the actor. Then, the actor must provide new (external) knowledge to allow the system to learn a new practice. There are simultaneously an incremental acquisition of new contextual elements and the learning of a new practice. With this joint acquisition and learning tasks, the system is fed with the specific context of occurrence.

This triple aspect—context growth by integration of external knowledge in the PC building, by integration of a new "chunk of knowledge" in the contextual knowledge, and context change by the movement between the body of contextual knowledge and proceduralized contexts—illustrates the dynamic dimension of context [1]. Without an explicit representation of this dynamic dimension, it is not possible to catch entirely context in an application.

Once the current focus is satisfied, the proceduralized context becomes a piece of contextual knowledge. This "chunk of knowledge" [7] will exist with its building blocks (the contextual-knowledge items retained initially and the way in which they have been assembled).

2.2 Contextual-Graph Representation

A contextual graph is a context-based representation of all the practices that have been used in a problem solving. Contextual graphs are oriented, acyclic, with exactly one input and one output, and a general structure of spindle. A path (from the input to the output of the graph) represents a practice (or a procedure), a type of execution of the task with the application of selected methods. A contextual graph is an acyclic graph because user's tasks are generally in ordered sequences. For example, the activity "Make the train empty of travelers" is always considered at the beginning of an incident solving on a subway line, never at the end of the incident solving.

Elements of a contextual graph are: actions, contextual elements, sub-graphs, activities and parallel action groupings.

- An **action** is the building block of contextual graphs. It must be understood in the spirit of task.
- A **contextual element** is a couple of nodes, a contextual node has one input and N outputs (branches) corresponding to N known instantiations of the contextual element, and a recombination node [N, 1] from which the instantiation does not matter anymore. The contextual element is instantiated only between the contextual node and the recombination node.
- A **sub-graph** is itself a contextual graph. It is mainly used for obtaining different displays of the contextual graph on the graphical interface by some mechanisms of aggregation and expansion like in Sowa's conceptual graphs [9].
- An **activity** is a particular sub-graph (and thus also a contextual graph by itself) that is identified by actors because appearing in several contextual graphs. This recurring sub-structure is generally considered as a complex action.
- A **parallel action grouping** expresses the fact (and reduce the complexity of the representation) that several groups of actions must be accomplished in parallel or in any order before to continue the practice application. The parallel action grouping is a kind of complex representation of contexts. This item expresses a problem of representation of items at a too low level of granularity.

Indeed, we distinguish between these elements, and their instances in contextual graphs. For example, the action A5 in Figure 1 appears several times on different branches (and thus different contexts).

Right now, there is a software for visualizing contextual graphs and incrementally acquiring new practices. There are already a number of functions (zoom, handling of parts of a graph, change of language, etc.) for handling contextual graphs and the current development concerns the introduction of explanations. The use of this software in a number of applications shows that if the software itself cannot be separated from its interface (because of the incremental acquisition capability), the software is really independent of the applications already developed.

2.3 An Example

Figure 1 presents an Activity in the contextual graph given in [2]. This contextual graph represents the different practices that can be used during the information exploitation on a link target during a Web search. Square boxes represent actions,

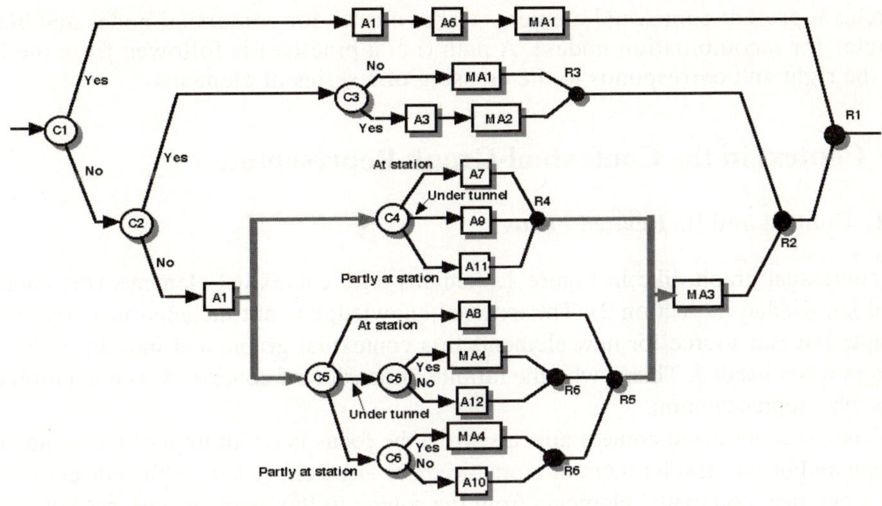

Fig. 1. Evacuation of a damaged train

Table 1. Evacuation of a damaged train [2]: Meaning of the items appearing in Figure 1 with C for contextual elements and A for actions

	Actions
1	Residual traffic regulation
2	Damaged train continues with travelers
3	Damaged train continues with travelers until a steep incline
4	Damaged train restarts without travelers
5	Stable damaged train at end station
6	Repair damage
7	Exit of travelers out of the damaged train
8	Exit of travelers out of next train
9	Exit of travelers out of damaged train via available cars
10	Exit of travelers out of next train via available cars
11	Exit of the travelers out of damaged train via track
12	Exit of travelers out of next train via track
13	Next train joins damaged train
14	Link both trains
15	Convoy return to end station
16	Disassemble convoy
17	Next train goes to next station

	Contextual elements
C1	Immediate repair possible?
C2	Enough motor coaches available?
C3	Is there a steep incline between the damaged train and end station
C4	Position of the damaged train?
C5	Position of the following train?
C6	Presence of a station between the two trains?

	Macro-actions
MA1	Damaged train continues service (Actions A2 – A5)
MA2	Damaged train stops service (Actions A7 – A4 – A5)
MA3	Make a convoy with damaged train and next train (Actions 13, 14, 15, 5 and 16)
MA4	Empty next train at a station (Action A17 – A8)

circles represent contextual elements (large circles for contextual nodes and black circles for recombination nodes). A path (i.e. a practice) is followed from the left to the right and corresponds to the crossing of a series of elements.

3 Context in the Contextual-Graph Representation

3.1 Context and Its Related Focus

A contextual graph, like in Figure 1, contains only contextual elements (the contextual knowledge in Section 2). The external knowledge is not included in a contextual graph, but is a source for new elements in a contextual graph, and introduced by the actors when needed. This is why the infinite dimension of context [5] is not a problem in such a representation.

The proceduralized context appears when the focus is on an item of the contextual graph and/or the development of a practice. For any item (where is the current focus) on a practice, contextual elements from the source to this item are instantiated, if the recombination node has not been crossed equally. The proceduralized context corresponds to an ordered sequence of instantiated contextual elements.

If the focus concerns a given item of the practice, say action A6 in Figure 1, then one has a static context with two pieces of contextual knowledge (C9 and C11), and an ordered sequence of instantiated contextual elements corresponding to the proceduralized context (C8 with the value "Short", C12 with the value "Exploratory", C3 with the value "Yes", and C4 with the value "Yes").

If the focus concerns the practice itself, then by the play of the contextual elements entering the proceduralized context, say at C4 in Figure 1, or leaving it such as at R4, the context of the practice presents a dynamic. We will see in the following that there is another type of dynamics coming from the incremental acquisition of knowledge.

3.2 Representation of Context Like Contextual Elements

Contextual knowledge is represented by contextual elements. As shown in Table 1, contextual elements constitute a heterogeneous population of elements (coming from different domains), and there is no real hierarchy, at least in the semantic sense. The organization of the contextual elements is more oriented by the problem solving itself.

The branches between a contextual node and a recombination node are exclusive, each corresponding to a given instance of the contextual element. However, if a contextual element appears on a branch on another contextual element (say C4-R4 on the branch "Yes" of the contextual element 3), the contextual element must exist only on the branch of the other contextual element. Thus a contextual element is always defined (embedded) with respect to another contextual element, as already said by McCarthy [5]. We have been a step further with the onion metaphor [4, 6] by showing that contextual elements are organized by layers around actions.

By their position, contextual elements are more related to the relationships between the elements of reasoning (the actions) that on the elements themselves.

3.3   Enrichment of a Contextual Graph

When the system fails to represent the practice used by an actor (given as a sequence of actions such as A13-A6-A14 for the upper path), the system presents the actor the practice the nearest of the actor's practice, exhibits the differing part between the practices, and ask for an explanation. For example, in Figure 2, there was A13 followed, say, by action A7 according to the contextual element C3 (implicitly the type of search was supposed to be exploratory).

However, an actor may decide to look for the phone number of a colleague on the Web and gives very precise keywords and has his answer in the first link provided by the search engine. The actor then explains the system that the contextual element C12 "types of search?" must be introduced because the treatment is different from the previous one, i.e. an exploratory search. A new practice is generally introduce in a contextual graph as a variant of an existing practice differing from the previous one by few element (generally a contextual element and an action or an activity). Thus, a system using a contextual-graph presentation incrementally acquires new knowledge and, simultaneously, learns a new practice when it fails to account for user's practice.

By accumulation of all the practices used for a problem solving, a contextual graph could be assimilated to a kind of "micro-corporate memory" for the problem solving represented by this contextual graph. A contextual graph is living, it can be used for monitoring, diagnosis, simulation, explanation, etc. Although, we have not work in this direction, a base of contextual graphs can cover all a domain and thus bring a solution to knowledge management.

3.4   Context Structures

If we represent contextual elements of Figure 1 by ovals alone, without the actions and paths, we obtain Figure 2. There are some observations to make.

First, a contextual element is always embedded in another contextual element (or several ones). Contextual elements never intersect. Thus, a contextual element, as a focus, is itself in a context. In a contextual graph, the dimension of context is finite, limited by the number of practices learnt by the system.

About the infinite dimension of context pointed out by McCarthy [5], we observe that the dimension of context is infinite in two senses: any contextual element may contain another contextual element (e.g. C4 contains C11) and is contained in another contextual element (e.g. C4 is contained in C3). This is recursive and only limited by the record of experience. A contextual graph representing a unique problem solving, the number of methods that can be used for problem solving is limited. However, we have not yet explored the possibility of the solving of highly complex problems.

Second, the development of a practice is a series of input/output of contextual elements according to the law "last in, first out." There is some similarity with the work of Giunchiglia's team (e.g. see [8]). For example, in C3 we go first in C4 and them in C9 (without excluding the possibility to avoir C4 or C9). In contextual graph, on the one hand, contextual elements are embedded, but discrete as in Giunchiglia's work.

On the other hand, the "bridging rules" in the Italian work correspond to instantiation of the context at the upper level (e.g., the instantiation of C3). This is a new path to explore to developing contextual graphs as a formalism of representation of the knowledge and the reasoning.

Third, contextual elements are knowledge pieces in various domains and just assembled by an individual (e.g. see definitions of C3, C4, C9 in Table 1). Thus, there is a refinement of practices by taking increasingly into account contextual elements. The organization of contextual elements in a contextual graph is more related to the growth of the contextual graph from the initial procedure than to an intrinsic property (like an ontology on contextual elements). This is very similar of our experimental finding five years ago in the application for the subway company in Paris [4] such as represented in Figure 3.

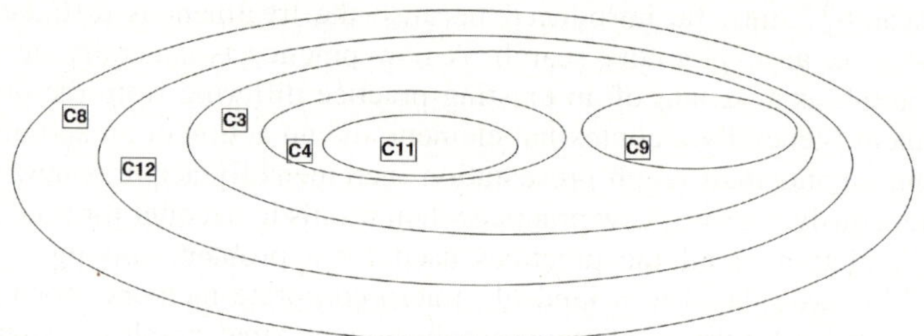

Fig. 2. Organization of the contextual elements in Figure 1

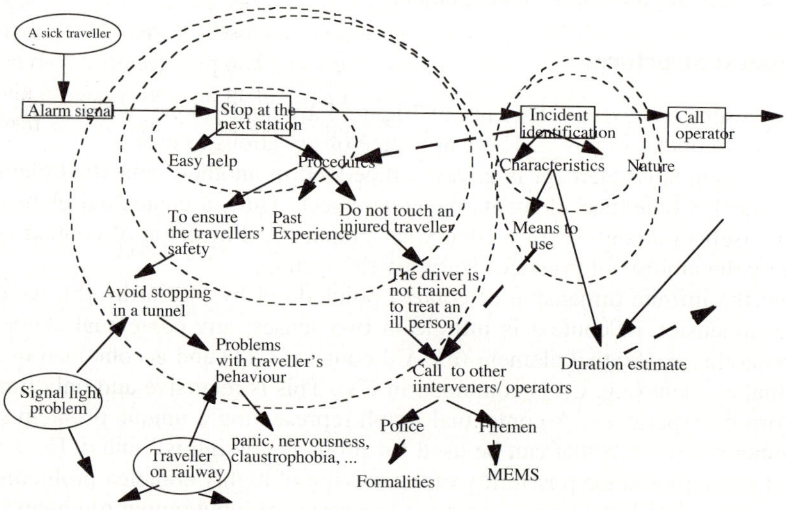

Fig. 3. Context organization in the SART application (Brézillon et al., 2000)

4 Conclusion

Contextual graphs offer a uniform representation of elements of reasoning and contextual elements at the same level. Context in our formalism intervenes more at the levels of the links between actions than actions themselves. Contextual elements being organized in contextual graphs in the spirit of "nest of dolls", we have not a hierarchy of context because a given contextual element is itself contextualized and can appear encompassed in different other contextual elements. Rather, a contextual element is a factor of knowledge activation.

We show that contextual issues cannot be addressed in a static framework only and that eliciting and sharing contextual knowledge in a dynamic way is a key process in addressing and understanding context problems.

The introduction of the item "Parallel Action Grouping" (PAG) simplifies the representation of contextual graphs. However, if an activity is assimilated to a complex action, a PAG is more than a complex contextual element. An activity sums up a complexity at the same level of representation. A parallel action grouping generally represents (as a simplification) a complex entanglement of contextual elements corresponding to a low level of description of the problem solving modeled in the contextual graph. In the popular example of the coffee preparation given in UML manuals, it is said that we must take the coffee and the filter in one order or the other (or in parallel). However, according to the type of coffee machine (e.g. we must put it apart to fill the reservoir with water), the piece of the coffee machine where must be put the filter can be independent of the coffee machine, mobile on the coffee machine or fixed into the coffee machine. Each situation would be considered independently, but all situations will conclude on a unique action: "Put the coffee in the filter." Thus, instead of making complicated a contextual graph for representing its (natural) complexity, which is at a lower level of detail, we use parallel action groupings.

Information can be drawn from a contextual graph, such as the way in which it has been developed, which actors has developed a given part of the contextual graph. It is possible to have an evaluation of the distance between two practices (i.e. two paths in the contextual graphs). Contextual graphs are a formalism of representation allowing the description of decision making in which context influences the line of reasoning (e.g. choice of a method for accomplishing a task). This formalism has been already used in different domains such as medicine, incident management on a subway line, road sign interpretation by a driver, computer security, psychology, cognitive ergonomics, usual actions in a house (preparing hard-boiled eggs, change of an electric bulb, etc.). The extensions that will be given to this work concerns: (1) its introduction in an intelligent assistant system for providing suggestions to the actor, (2) the management of the database (operations on the items, regrouping contextual elements, etc.) in order to produce robust procedures; statistics on the development, use of a given path; and (3) the introduction of a module of explanation generation of different types and at different levels of details.

References

1. Brézillon, P.: Representation of procedures and practices in contextual graphs. The Knowledge Engineering Review, 18(2) (2003) 147-174.
2. Brezillon, P. "Task-realization models in Contextual Graphs." In: Modeling and Using Context (CONTEXT-05), A. Dey, B.Kokinov, D.Leake, R.Turner (Eds.), Springer Verlag, LNCS 3554, pp. 55-68, 2005.
3. Brézillon, P. and Pomerol, J.-Ch.: Contextual knowledge sharing and cooperation in intelligent assistant systems. *Le Travail Humain*, **62**(3), Paris: PUF, (1999) pp 223-246.

4. Brézillon, P., Cavalcanti, M., Naveiro, R. and Pomerol, J-Ch.: SART: An intelligent assistant for subway control. Pesquisa Operacional, Brazilian Operations Research Society, 20(2) (2000) 247-268.
5. McCarthy, J.: "Notes on formalizing context", Proceedings of the 13th IJCAI (1993) Vol. 1, 555-560.
6. Pasquier, L., Brézillon, P. and Pomerol, J.-Ch.: Chapter 6: Learning and explanation in a context-based representation: Application to incident solving on subway lines. In: R. Jain, A. Abraham, C. Faucher and J. van der Zwaag (Eds.) Innovations in Knowledge Engineering. International Series on Advanced Intelligence, 2003, pp. 129-149.
7. Schank, R.C.: *Dynamic memory, a theory of learning in computers and people* Cambridge University Press (1982).
8. Serafini, L., Giunchiglia, F., Mylopoulos, J. and Bernstein, P.: Local relational model: A logical formalization of database coordination. In: P. Blackburn, C. Ghidini, R. Turner, F. Giunchiglia (Eds.), Modeling and Using Context, Springer Verlag, LNAI 2680, pp. 286-299 (2003)
9. Sowa, J.F.: Knowledge Representation: Logical, Philosophical, and Computational Foundations. Brooks Cole Publishing Co., Pacific Grove, CA (2000).

Signal and Image Representations Based Hybrid Intelligent Diagnosis Approach for a Biomedicine Application

Amine Chohra, Nadia Kanaoui, Véronique Amarger, and Kurosh Madani

Images, Signals, and Intelligent Systems Laboratory (LISSI / EA 3956), Paris-XII University, Senart Institute of Technology, Avenue Pierre Point, 77 127 Lieusaint, France
{chohra, amarger, madani}@univ-paris12.fr

Abstract. Fault diagnosis is a complex and fuzzy cognitive process, and soft computing methods as neural networks and fuzzy logic, have shown great potential in the development of decision support systems. Dealing with expert (human) knowledge consideration, Computer Aided Diagnosis (CAD) dilemma is one of the most interesting, but also one of the most difficult problems. Among difficulties contributing to challenging nature of this problem, one can mention the need of fine classification and decision-making. In this paper, a brief survey on fault diagnosis systems is given. From the classification and decision-making problem analysis, a hybrid intelligent diagnosis approach is suggested from signal and image representations. Then, the suggested approach is developed in biomedicine for a CAD, from Auditory Brainstem Response (ABR) test, and the prototype design and experimental results are presented. Finally, a discussion is given with regard to the reliability and large application field of the suggested approach.

1   Introduction

A *diagnosis system* is basically one which is capable of identifying the nature of a problem by examining the observed symptoms. The output of such a system is a diagnosis (and possibly an explanation or justification) [1]. In many applications of interest, it is desirable for the system to not only identify the possible causes of the problem, but also to suggest suitable remedies (systems capable of advising) or to give a reliability rate of the identification of possible causes. Recently, several decision support systems and intelligent systems have been developed [2], [3] and the diagnosis approaches based on such intelligent systems have been developed for industrial applications [1], [4], [5], and biomedicine applications [6], [7], [8], [9], [10]. Currently, one of the most used approaches to feature identification, classification, and decision-making problems inherent to fault detection and diagnosis, is soft computing implying mainly neural networks and fuzzy logic [1], [3], [4], [5], [6], [9], [10].

Over the past decades, new approaches based on artificial neural networks have been developed aiming to solve real life problems related to optimization, modeling, decision-making, classification, data mining, and nonlinear functions (behavior) approximation. Inspired from biological nervous systems and brain structure, artificial

M. Ali and R. Dapoigny (Eds.): IEA/AIE 2006, LNAI 4031, pp. 155 – 165, 2006.

neural networks could be seen as information processing systems, which allow elaboration of many original techniques covering a large application field based on their appealing properties such as learning and generalization capabilities [11], [12], [13].

Another aspect of increasing importance, and strongly linked to data processing and the amount of data available concerning processes or devices (due to the high level of sensors and monitoring), is the extraction of knowledge from data to discover the information structure hidden in it. Several approaches have been developed to analyze and classify biomedicine signals: electroencephalography signals [7], electrocardiogram signals [8], and particularly signals based on Auditory Brainstem Response (ABR) test, which is a test for hearing and brain (neurological) functioning, [6], [14], [15], [16]. Traditionally, biomedicine signals are processed using signal processing approaches, mainly based on peak and wave identification from pattern recognition approaches, such as in [6], [7], [8], [14], [15], [16]. The main problem is then to identify pertinent parameters. This task is not trivial, because the time (or frequency) is not always the variable that points up the studied phenomena's features leading then to a necessity of multiple knowledge representations (signal, image, ...).

This paper deals with pattern recognition (classification) and decision-making based on Artificial Intelligence using soft computing implying neural networks and fuzzy logic applied to a biomedicine problem. The aim of this paper is absolutely not to replace specialized human but to suggest a decision support tool with a satisfactory reliability degree for Computer Aided Diagnosis (CAD) systems. Thus, a brief survey on fault diagnosis systems is given in Sect. 2. Afterwards, the decision-making problem from the results of two neural classifications is stated and a hybrid intelligent diagnosis approach is suggested in Sect. 3. In Sect. 4 and Sect. 5, the suggested approach is developed for a computer aided auditory diagnosis, from signal and image representations, in order to achieve a diagnosis tool able to assert auditory pathologies based on ABR test which provides an effective measure of the integrity of the auditory pathway. Then, the prototype design and experimental results are presented, and a discussion is given with regard to the reliability and large application field.

2   Fault Diagnosis Systems

Globally, the main goals of fault diagnosis systems for Computer Aided Diagnosis (CAD) [5], [10] are: to detect if a fault is in progress as soon as possible, to classify the fault in progress, to be able to suggest suitable remedies (systems able of advising) or to give a reliability rate of the identified fault through a Confidence Index (CI).

CAD is an attractive area leading to future promising fault diagnosis applications. However, dealing with expert (human) knowledge consideration, the computer aided diagnosis dilemma is one of most interesting, but also one of the most difficult problems. The fault diagnosis help is often related to the classification of several information sources implying different representations. Fault diagnosis can be obtained from the classification of only one kind of information (knowledge) representation. However, experts use several information to emit their diagnosis. Then, an interesting way to built efficient fault diagnosis system can be deduced from this concept in order to take advantage from several information. More, experts can use several information sources, in various forms; qualitative or quantitative data, signals, images, to emit their diagnosis. Thus, these information could be issued from different information sources and/or from different representations of a same test. For instance, in case of diagnosis of the same fault classes set, one can consider that these information are independently, in parallel, classified and after the decision-making of their results gives then final results as shown in Fig. 1. Final results gives the fault classes set and suitable remedies or a reliability rate of the possible identified fault class.

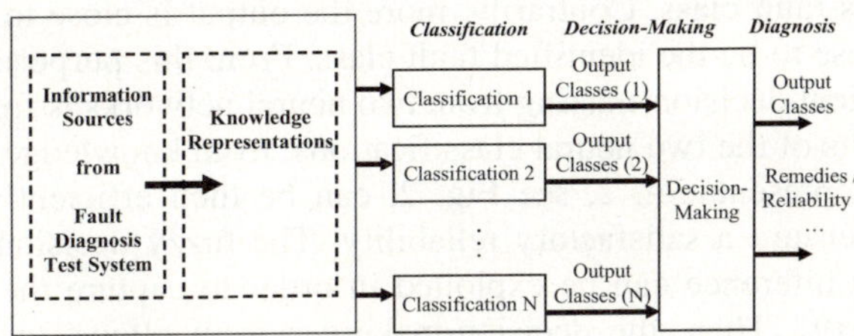

Fig. 1. Global diagnosis synopsis of the same fault classes set

3   Hybrid Intelligent Diagnosis Approach

In order to study the decision-making phase of the approach suggested in Fig. 1, two different knowledge representations have been considered from only one information source, as shown in Fig. 2. This configuration in the case of diagnosis of the same fault classes set leads to two different classifications. More, if such classifications are handled by neural networks, which are known to be appropriate for classification [11], [12], [13], [17] the decision-making appears to be difficult particularly in CAD. In such cases, CAD can be useful and efficient only if the results are given with a reliability parameter (e.g., a CI on each fault classes set result).

The nature of neural classification results (neural outputs) of the neural architectures used for classification are, in general, not binary values. In fact, for instance, the typical MultiLayer feedforward Perceptron networks (MLP) used for classification with sigmoïdal outputs give output class values between [0, 1]. This makes difficult the problem of the decision-making from two neural networks. Another neural architecture is based on Radial Basis Function networks (RBF).

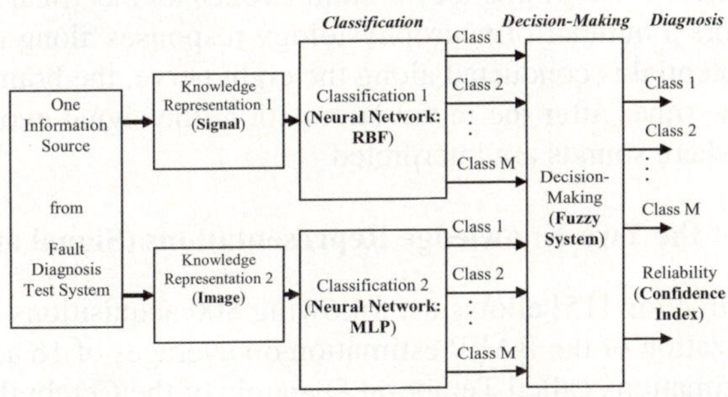

Fig. 2. Decision-making from two neural classifications (diagnosis of the same fault classes set)

The analysis of neural classifier outputs shows that, in case of MLP, more the output is close to 1 and more this output will be close to be the identified fault class. Contrarily, more the output is close to 0 and more this output will be far to be the identified fault class. In case of RBF, the outputs are distances from RBF centers. In this case with a new scale of outputs it is easily to make output class values varying between [0, c], where c is a constant to be determined (e.g., see Sect. 5.1, Fig. 7). Then, more the output which is a distance is close to c and more this output will be far to be identified as fault class. Contrarily, more the output is close to 0 and more this output will be close to be the identified fault class. From this purpose, one interesting way to built efficient decision-making from two neural networks is fuzzy logic [18].

Thus, the results of the two neural classifications, from knowledge representation 1 and knowledge representation 2, see Fig. 2, can be then efficiently exploited in a fuzzy system to ensure a satisfactory reliability. The fuzzy decision-making system based on a fuzzy inference can be exploited in order to capture the expert (human) knowledge [2], [19]. Then, the decision-making system allows to decide the fault classes diagnosis among: Class 1, Class 2, ..., and Class M, and its usefulness and efficiency are better traduced with the associated CI on its decision. Contrary to a time or frequency (signal) based representation, the image based one, taking benefit from it's 2-D nature, offers advantage a richer representation alowing to take into account more complex features (shapes, particular information, ...).

4   Biomedicine Application: Computer Aided Auditory Diagnosis

The ABR test involves attaching electrodes to the head to record electrical activity from the auditory nerve (the hearing nerve) and other parts of the brain. This recorded electrical activity is known as brainstem auditory evoked potentials (BAEP).

4.1   Brainstem Auditory Evoked Potentials (BAEP) Clinical Test

When a sense organ is stimulated, it generates a string of complex neurophysiology processes. BAEP are electrical response caused by the brief stimulation of a sense system. The stimulus gives rise to the start of a string of action's potentials that can be recorded on the nerve's course, or from a distance of the activated structures. BAEP are generated as follows (see Fig. 3 (a)): the patient hears clicking noise or tone bursts through earphones. The use of auditory stimuli evokes an electrical response. In fact, the stimulus triggers a number of neurophysiology responses along the auditory pathway. An action potential is conducted along the eight nerve, the brainstem, and finally to the brain. A few times after the initial stimulation, the signal evokes a response in the area of brain where sounds are interpreted.

4.2   Extraction of the Two Knowledge Representations (Signal and Image)

A technique of extraction [15] allows us, following 800 acquisitions such as described before, the visualization of the BAEP estimation on averages of 16 acquisitions. Thus, a surface of 50 estimations called Temporal Dynamic of the Cerebral trunk (TDC) can be visualized. The average signal, which corresponds to the average of the 800 acquisitions, and the TDC surface could then be obtained. Those are then processed into a signal representation as shown in Fig. 3 (b). In this figure, an example of TDC surface for a patient is shown. The average signal (named signal representation) is presented in front of TDC surface which is better shown in Fig. 3 (c). The signal to image conversion (named image representation), shown in Fig. 5, is obtained after a processing of TDC surface signal and image processing [9], [20].

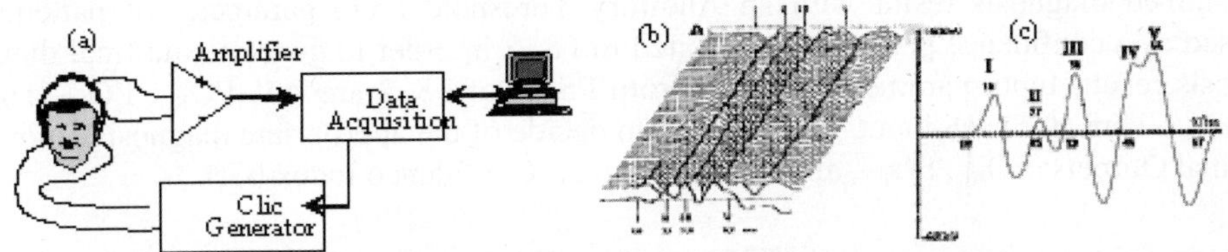

Fig. 3. (a) BAEP clinical test. (b) TDC surface. (c) Average signal processing.

Three patient classes are studied: Retro-cochlear auditory disorder's patients (Retro-cochlear Class: RC), Endo-cochlear auditory disorder's patients (Endo-cochlear Class: EC), healthy patients (Normal Class: NC). Fig. 4 (a), Fig. 4 (b) and Fig. 4 (c) show examples of signal representations for two patients: RC, EC, and NC.

Fig. 5 presents image representations for the same six patients. These figures (Fig. 4 and Fig. 5) illustrate the fact that, signal or image representations could be very similar for patients belonging to different classes, and they could be very different for patients belonging to a same class, demonstrating the difficulty of their classification.

4.3 Suggested Hybrid Intelligent Diagnosis System

The hybrid intelligent diagnosis system suggested in Fig. 6 is built of data processing stage, classification stage, primary fuzzy decision-making stage leading to a primary diagnosis, and final fuzzy decision-making stage leading to the final diagnosis. Note that this suggested diagnosis system is deduced from the synopsis of classification and decision-making presented in Fig. 2.

The data processing stage consists of extracting signal and image representations from data source (signals: TDC surface) and deducing the signal data and image data.

The classification stage consists of the signal classification which is based on RBF networks while the image classification is based on MLP networks. In fact, MLP are *neural global* approximators, whereas RBF are *neural local* approximators [11].

The primary and final fuzzy decision-making stages consists of the Fuzzy System 1 (FS_1) and Fuzzy System 2 (FS_2), respectively. These fuzzy decision-making systems are used to capture the decision-making behavior of a human expert while giving the appropriate diagnosis [2], [17], i.e., it must mimic the input/output mapping of this human expert. Note that the two fuzzy inferences of FS_1 and FS_2, based on Mamdani's fuzzy inference, are developed as detailed in the diagnosis approach using only image representation described in [9] with the simplification detailed in [21]. From this simplification, the fuzzy rule base of FS_1 which is built of $3^6 = 729$ rules will make in use only $2^6 = 64$ rules in each inference, while the fuzzy rule base of FS_2 which is built of $3^4 = 81$ rules will make in use only $2^4 = 16$ rules in each inference.

160   A. Chohra et al.

Thus, the double classification, from signal representation and image representation, is exploited in FS_1 to ensure a satisfactory reliability for a computer aided auditory. Input parameters, obtained from the two neural networks, of FS_1 are RC_S, EC_S, NC_S, RC_I, EC_I, and NC_I. Thus, for each input, FS_1 is able to decide of appropriate diagnosis among Primary Outputs PO_{RC}, PO_{EC}, and PO_{NC}.

The diagnosis reliability obtained from the FS_1 is reinforced (enhanced) using the obtained diagnosis result with an Auditory Threshold (AT) parameter of patients, used as a confidence parameter, exploited in FS_2 in order to generate the final diagnosis result. Input parameters, issued from FS_1, of FS_2 are AT, PO_{RC}, PO_{EC}, and PO_{NC}. Thus, for each input, FS_2 is able to decide of the appropriate diagnosis among Final Outputs: FO_{RC}, FO_{EC}, and FO_{NC} with their Confidence Index (CI).

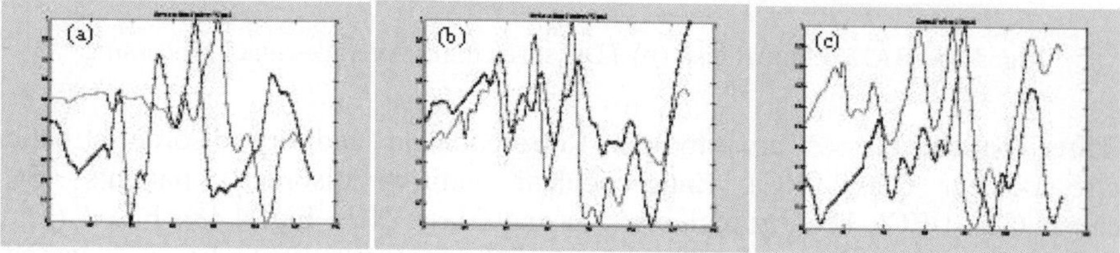

Fig. 4. Two examples of signal representations for patients: (a) RC. (b) EC. (c) NC.

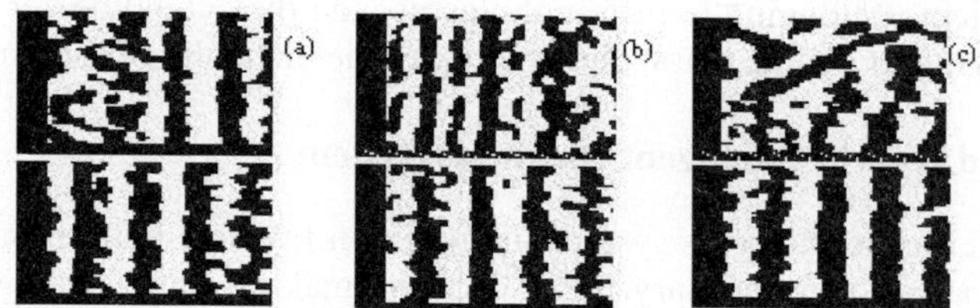

Fig. 5. Two examples of image representations for patients: (a) RC. (b) EC. (c) NC.

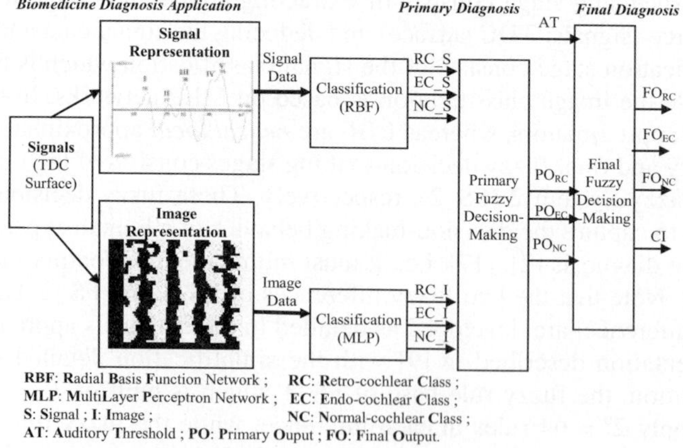

Fig. 6. Hybrid intelligent diagnosis system synopsis for auditory diagnosis help

Table 1. Signal neural classification results (RBF)

Signal Results (RBF)	Learning Rate	Generalization Rate
Retro-cochlear	100 %	44.44 %
Endo-cochlear	100 %	52.11 %
Normal	100 %	58.33 %

Table 2. Image neural classification results (MLP)

Image Results (MLP)	Learning Rate	Generalization Rate
Retro-cochlear	100 %	29.62 %
Endo-cochlear	100 %	35.21 %
Normal	100 %	70.23 %

5 Prototype Design and Experimental Results

For the validation of the suggested intelligent system, in the case of auditory diagnosis help, the used data base is issued from a specialized center in functional explorations in oto-neurology CEFON[1] [15]. It is built of 11 Retro- cochlear patients, 6 Endo-cochlear patients, and 7 Normal patients for learning base, while 27 Retro-cochlear patients, 71 Endo-cochlear patients, and 84 Normal patients for generalization base.

5.1 Prototype Design

The neural classification results are presented in Table 1 for signal classification and in Table 2 for image classification. Learning database has successfully been learnt by the two classifications. Global correct classification rate is quite similar for the two classifications, 51.62 % for signal one and 45.02 % for image one. However, correct classification rate is more homogeneous in case of signal classification. Image classification allows to obtain as far as 70.23 % of correct classification for NC. Obtained rates for RC and EC are then low and quite similar. With the two classifications, if EC are incorrectly classified by neural classifications, the obtained class is NC (in majority). And, if NC are incorrectly classified by neural classifications, obtained class is EC (in majority). For FS_1 and FS_2, membership functions of RC_S, EC_S, NC_S, RC_I, EC_I, NC_I, have been defined in Fig. 7 (a), (b), (c), (d), (e), and (f), and those of AT, PO_{RC}, PO_{EC}, and PO_{NC} in Fig. 8 (a), (b), (c), and (d), respectively.

5.2 Auditory Diagnosis Results

Table 3 and Table 4 present the results obtained by fuzzy decision-making systems FS_1 and FS_2, respectively. Rates written between brackets (x %) represent the generalization rates calculated taking into account patients classified simultaneously in

---

[1] Centre d'Explorations Fonctionnelles Oto-Neurologiques (CEFON), Paris, France.

two classes. In majority of cases, these simultaneous classifications are obtained for EC and NC. For all classes, the generalization rate of FS_2 is higher than this of FS_1, showing the pertinent rule of the auditory threshold. Generalization rate of normal class is clearly higher for fuzzy decision-making system FS_2 than for the two classifications, achieving a value of 84.52 % (89.28 %). Obtained rates for RC and EC are higher than these obtained by image classification but quite similar than those obtained by signal classification.

An important contribution of the FS_2 is that it gives each fault diagnosis associated with a CI. This is illustrated through the following result example with a high CI: the fuzzy output = { μ_{FORC}, μ_{FOEC}, μ_{FONC}, μ_{CI} } = {0.05, 0.94, 0.05, 0.96}. Then, defuzzified output = Max{ μ_{FORC}, μ_{FOEC}, μ_{FONC} },

$$= Max\{ 0.05, 0.94, 0.05 \} = \mu_{OEC} = 0.94.$$

And final result is then, in this example, μ_{OEC} and μ_{CI} equal to 0.94 and 0.96, respectively. This result means that the identified fault (pathology) diagnosis (0.94) is EC with a high CI (0.96).

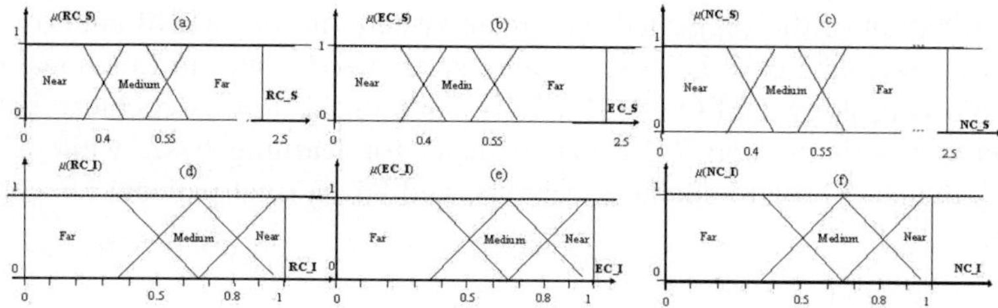

Fig. 7. Membership functions of: (a) RC_S. (b) EC_S. (c) NC_S. (d) RC_I. (e) EC_I. (f) NC_I.

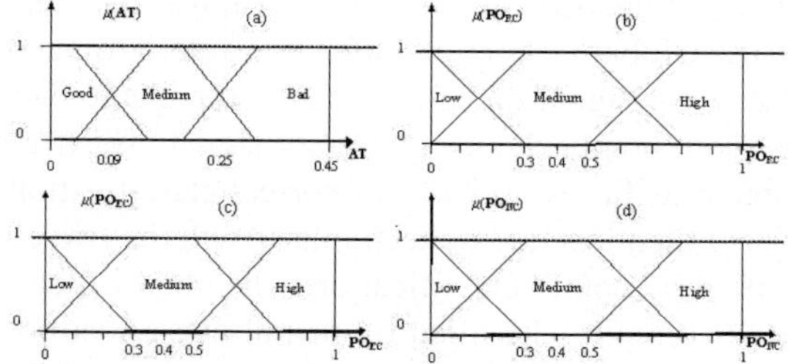

Fig. 8. Membership functions of: (a) Auditory Threshold (AT). (b) PO_{RC}. (c) PO_{EC}. (d) PO_{NC}.

Table 3. Fuzzy decision-making system FS_1 results

Fuzzy System (FS_1) Results	Learning Rate	Generalization Rate
Retro-cochlear	100 %	33.33 % (37.03 %)
Endo-cochlear	100 %	29.57 % (42.25 %)
Normal	100 %	63.09 % (77.38 %)

Table 4. Fuzzy decision-making system FS_2 results

Fuzzy System (FS_2) Results	Learning Rate	Generalization Rate
Retro-cochlear	100 %	40.74 % (51.85 %)
Endo-cochlear	100 %	49.29 % (59.15 %)
Normal	100 %	84.52 % (89.28 %)

6 Discussion and Conclusion

In this paper, a hybrid intelligent diagnosis approach for computer aided auditory diagnosis, based on neural classifications and fuzzy decision-making systems has been suggested. In fact, the double classification is exploited in FS_1, for a primary diagnosis, to ensure a satisfactory reliability. Second, this reliability is reinforced using a confidence parameter AT with the primary diagnosis result, exploited in FS_2, in order to generate the final diagnosis giving the appropriate diagnosis with a CI. In fact, the aim is then to achieve an efficient and reliable CAD system for three classes: two auditory pathologies RC and EC and normal auditory NC. A signal and an image, issued from ABR test, are used as the two initial data representations. Implementation and experimental results were presented and discussed. The generalization rate of NC is clearly higher for FS_1 and FS_2 than for the two classifications. The obtained rates for RC and EC are higher than obtained by image classification but quite similar than those obtained by signal classification. An important contribution of the final fuzzy system FS_2 is that it gives each fault diagnosis associated with a CI.

It is pertinent to notice that a large number of signal issued representations could be converted in image representations. More, the image representation offers benefit of a richer information representation than the signal one. In fact, such approach take advantage from features which are unreachable from unidimensional signal.

This approach could be applied to other diagnosis problem in biomedicine, where signal and image representation could be extracted from clinical tests. Elsewhere, it could be used for industrial domain, e.g., mechatronic system as illustrated in Fig. 9, where a revolving machine is presented and two information (knowledge) representations are shown: a signal representation and an image representation. For industrial diagnosis problems, the suggested hybrid intelligent diagnosis approach can be used. In fact, the same classification and decision-making processing architecture of the approach can be used with corresponding specific pertinent parameters and mainly modifications will be in FS_1 and FS_2 rule bases from specific experimental data.

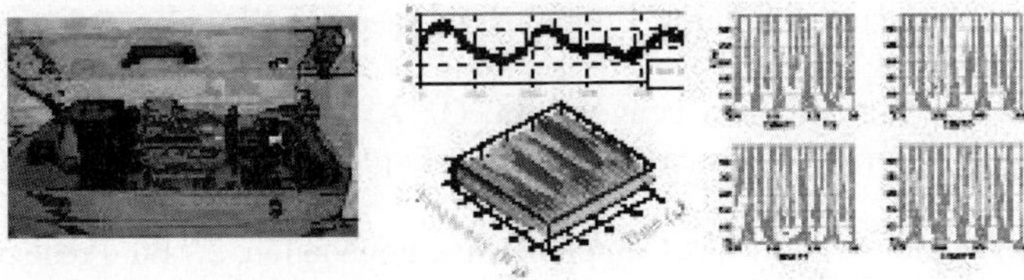

Fig. 9. Example of industrial diagnosis system and signal and image representations

However, before that, a number of current system's aspects could be investigated in order to enhance the final results. For this purpose, a fine tuning of fuzzy rules is necessary as well as a more detailed presentation of the results (the results presented are those only with a high CI).

Another important point concerns the number of classes in the suggested approach i.e, only three output classes (fault classes set). In fact, this approach could be generalized to many output classes exploiting the concept of modular neural networks [3]. Such concept allows to avoid to deal with a huge number of fuzzy rules in case of a great number of output classes.

References

1. Balakrishnan, K., Honavar, V.: Intelligent Diagnosis Systems. Technical Report, Iowa State University, Ames, Iowa 50011-1040, U.S.A (1997)
2. Turban, E., Aronson, J.E.: Decision Support Systems and Intelligent Systems. Int. Edition, Sixth Edition, Prentice-Hall (2001)
3. Karray, F. O., De Silva, C.: Soft Computing and Intelligent Systems Design, Theory, Tools and Applications. Addison Wesley, ISBN 0-321-11617-8, Pearson Ed. Limited (2004)
4. Meneganti, M., Saviello, F.S., Tagliaferri, R.: Fuzzy Neural Networks for Classification and Detection of Anomalies. IEEE Transactions on Neural Networks, 9, No. 5, (1998) 848-861
5. Palmero, G.I.S., Santamaria, J.J., de la Torre, E.J.M., Gonzalez, J.R.P.: Fault Detection and Fuzzy Rule Extraction in AC Motors by a Neuro-Fuzzy ART-Based System. Engineering Applications of Artificial Intelligence, 18, Elsevier, (2005) 867-874
6. Piater, J.H., Stuchlik, F., von Specht, H., Mühler, R.: Fuzzy Sets for Feature Identification in Biomedical Signals with Self-Assessment of Reliability: An Adaptable Algorithm Modeling Human Procedure in BAEP Analysis. Comput. and Biomedical Resear., 28, (1995) 335-353
7. Vuckovic, A., Radivojevic, V., Chen, A.C.N., Popovic, D.: Automatic Recognition of Alertness and Drowsiness from EEG by an Artificial Neural Network. Medical Engineering & Physics, 24 (5), (June 2002) 349-360
8. Wolf, A., Barbosa, C.H., Monteiro, E.C., Vellasco, M.: Multiple MLP Neural Networks Applied on the Determination of Segment Limits in ECG Signals. 7th International Work-Conf. on Artificial and Natural NN, Proc. Part II, Mao, Menorca, Spain, June 2003, LNCS 2687, Springer-Verlag Berlin Heidelberg, (2003) 607-614
9. Chohra, A., Kanaoui, N., Amarger, V.: A Soft Computing Based Approach Using Signal-To-Image Conversion for Computer Aided Medical Diagnosis (CAMD). Information Processing and Security Systems, Edited by K. Saeed and J. Pejas, Springer, (2005) 365-374
10. Yan, H., Jiang, Y., Zheng, J., Peng, C., Li, Q.: A Multilayer Perceptron-Based Medical Support System for Heart Disease Diagnosis. Exp. Syst. with App., Elsevier, (2005) in press
11. Haykin, S.: Neural Networks: A Comprehensive Foundation, 2nd Ed. Prentice-Hall (1999)
12. Zhang, G.P.: Neural Networks for Classification: A Survey. IEEE Trans. on Systems, Man, and Cybernetics – Part C: Applications and Reviews, vol. 30, no. 4, (2000) 451-462
13. Egmont-Petersen, M., De Ridder, D., Handels, H.: Image Processing with Neural Networks – A Review. Pattern Recognition, 35, (2002) 2279-2301

14. Don, M., Masuda, A., Nelson, R., Brackmann, D.: Successful Detection of Small Acoustic Tumors using the Stacked Derived-Band Auditory Brain Stem Response Amplitude. The American Journal of Otology 18, 5, (1997) 608-621
15. Vannier, E., Adam, O., Motsch, J.F.: Objective Detection of Brainstem Auditory Evoked Potentials with a Priori Information from Higher Presentation Levels. Artificial Intelligence in Medicine, 25, (2002) 283-301
16. Bradley, A.P., Wilson W.J.: On Wavelet Analysis of Auditory Evoked Potentials. Clinical Neurophysiology, 115, (2004) 1114-1128
17. Azouaoui, O., Chohra, A.: Soft Computing Based Pattern Classifiers for the Obstacle Avoidance Behavior of Intelligent Autonomous Vehicles (IAV). Int. J. of Applied Intelligence, Kluwer Academic Publishers, 16, no. 3, (2002) 249-271
18. Zadeh, L.A.: The Calculus of Fuzzy If / Then Rules. AI Expert, (1992) 23-27
19. Lee, C.C.: Fuzzy Logic in Control Systems: Fuzzy Logic Controller – Part I & Part II. IEEE Trans. On Systems, Man, and Cybernetics, 20, no. 2, (1990) 404-435
20. Gonzalez, R.C., Woods, R.E.: Digital Image Processing. 2nd Edition Prentice-Hall (2002)
21. Farreny, H., Prade, H.: Tackling Uncertainty and Imprecision in Robotics. 3rd Int. Symposium on Robotics Research, (1985) 85-91

Handling Airport Ground Processes Based on Resource-Constrained Project Scheduling

Jürgen Kuster and Dietmar Jannach

Department of Business Informatics and Application Systems,
University of Klagenfurt, Universitätsstraße 65-67, 9020 Klagenfurt, Austria
{jkuster, dietmar}@ifit.uni-klu.ac.at
http://ifit.uni-klu.ac.at

Abstract. This paper describes how the Resource-Constrained Project Scheduling Problem (RCPSP) can be used as a basis for real-time decision support in the disruption management of the aircraft turnaround, the most typical airport ground process. For this purpose, the RCPSP is extended by the possibility to describe alternative activities, which can be used to model potential process modifications. An evolutionary approach is presented for solving this generalized problem, considering both basic rescheduling possibilities as well as the option of exchanging activities. The work presented in this paper is based on the results of a study conducted in collaboration with Deutsche Lufthansa AG, concerned with the analysis of the elementary requirements of decision support systems for turnaround process management.

1   Introduction

Managing disruptions of airport ground processes is a complex task: This is mainly due to the particularly high level of time and resource dependencies (among processes), the huge amount of parallel and interrelated activities as well as the often incomplete, unstable and deficient information, which forms the basis for the selection of appropriate repair activities. Moreover, the decision on a process intervention typically has to be made within little time, since the airport represents a highly dynamic and volatile environment with continuously changing resource and time availabilities.

In the current situation, it is usually the human operators who are responsible for disruption management (DM, see [1] for example) in the turnaround process. They make their decisions based on the available information and their individual experience. The improvement of the former element is targeted by the concepts of Collaborative Decision Making (CDM, see [2, 3] for example), which focus on the augmentation of information awareness and information sharing. However, air traffic organizations are also particularly interested in the enhancement of the latter, the rather subjective foundation of respective decisions. We have therefore studied the elementary requirements of turnaround-related decision support systems (DSS) in collaboration with Deutsche Lufthansa AG. The work presented herein is based on the respective insights and findings.

M. Ali and R. Dapoigny (Eds.): IEA/AIE 2006, LNAI 4031, pp. 166–176, 2006.
© Springer-Verlag Berlin Heidelberg 2006

Basically, the problem of providing decision support in management of disruptions in time- and resource-bound processes (such as the turnaround process but also any other time-critical production process) comes down to the selection of appropriate options of *rescheduling* and *process modification*: The respective set of interventions is required to be actually applicable and is considered optimal if it minimizes the costs associated with both the previous and the pending disruptions. Its execution shall furthermore produce a schedule as similar as possible to the original plan. Whereas the aspect of rescheduling has been discussed extensively in the literature, little work has been done on the options of structural modifications in flexible processes. The principal challenge consists in modelling this flexibility and in considering it in an algorithm which is able to provide good solutions in real-time.

We claim that the conceptual framework of the Resource-Constrained Project Scheduling Problem (RCPSP, see [4] for example) is perfectly suited for the resolution of the part of the problem concerned with rescheduling. The associated model provides possibilities to describe time and resource dependencies on a relatively high level, which makes the RCPSP intuitive and easily describable. Based on the respective elements, schedules for the contained activities can be generated and optimized in an efficient manner: Especially the possibility to use various forms of metaheuristics (as opposed to the application of exact mathematical programming) makes it possible to solve even problems of realistic size in reasonable time.

However, the current versions of the RCPSP provide a relatively weak support for structural flexibility and almost no possibilities to evaluate process modifications or alternative process paths. Even though the Multi-Mode RCPSP (MRCPSP, see [5] for example) introduces elementary forms of flexibility by making it possible to vary resource requirements and duration values, we argue that this is not sufficient for the application of the RCPSP to DM in realistic problems. This is mainly due to the fact that the human operator typically requires (and actually has) more options than the mere temporal shift of starting times and the simple modification of activity execution modes. He might, in particular, want to change the order of activities, insert or remove supporting tasks, or even parallelize activities which have been planned for serial execution (or vice versa).

This paper therefore introduces the *x-RCPSP* (where *x* stands for *ex*tended) as a generalization of the classical RCPSP. It provides possibilities to define alternative activities, which can be used to describe potential process modifications within a comprehensive process model. The remainder of the paper is structured as follows: In Section 2, a simplified version of the turnaround process is introduced along with three exemplary forms of potential modifications. Section 3 describes the *x-RCPSP* approach by defining a formal model and by outlining its application to the problem of disruption management. Section 4 provides an overview on related approaches before, finally, Section 5 summarizes the contribution of this paper and gives an outlook on future work.

2   The Turnaround Process

In general, the turnaround process combines all activities carried out at an airport while the respective aircraft is on ground. The simplified version considered for exemplary purposes in this paper, is structured as follows: After the plane reaches its final position, first the passengers leave the aircraft before it is fuelled, cleaned and catered simultaneously. After the last of these activities has finished, the outgoing passengers enter the plane which then leaves its position, heading for the runway. Figure 1 illustrates an instance of this process, where a disruption has occurred during deboarding, leading to deviations of the predicted (white) from the planned (gray) process times and finally causing a delay.

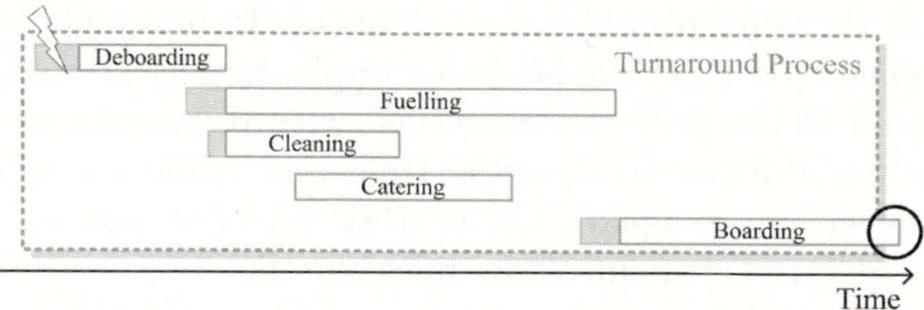

Fig. 1. Simplified Version of the Turnaround Process with Disruption

We assume that – apart from simply rescheduling (i.e. temporally shifting) the process – various forms of structural intervention are available to eliminate the pending delay. First, it is possible to accelerate deboarding by assigning additional buses. Second, it is possible to shorten cleaning, if in exchange the cabin is additionally inspected by the cabin crew prior to boarding. And finally, it is possible to parallelize fuelling and boarding if the fire brigade is available for supervision. Equipped with these options, the task of DM is the identification of a combination of rescheduling and process modification activities, which minimizes the departure delay and (in particular) the associated costs. Under the assumption that the original plan was optimal, the aim is to get back on track: The number of schedule modifications shall therefore also be minimized.

3   Using the RCPSP for Disruption Management

In this section, a generalization of the RCPSP is introduced, which can provide the basis for DSS in the area of process DM by supporting alternative activities and variable process execution paths. After the formal description of the model, an exemplary heuristic approach based on an evolutionary algorithm is sketched.

3.1   Extended Model

The extension proposed in this section is based on the idea of placing an abstract layer at the top of the elementary constructs of the classical RCPSP. Instead of having only one fixed set of activities, associated precedence constraints and resource requirements, we distinguish two different levels by introducing respective supersets for these fundamental elements. The supersets contain all elements which can but do not have to be considered in schedule generation, whereas the subjacent sets of *active* elements are actually and definitively considered: They form the basis for the final schedule.

Accordingly, the Extended Resource-Constrained Project Scheduling Problem *x-RCPSP* can be described as follows: Each project is defined by a set of potential activities $\mathcal{A}^+ = \{0, 1, ..., a, a+1\}$, where 0 and $a+1$ represent abstract start and end activities of the project, having a duration of 0 and no resource requirements associated. The currently *active* activities form a subset $\mathcal{A} \subseteq \mathcal{A}^+$. Correspondingly, $\mathcal{A}^+ \setminus \mathcal{A}$ represents the set of *inactive* activities, which shall not be contained in the final schedule. Let furthermore be $\mathcal{A}^0 \subseteq \mathcal{A}^+$ the set of those activities which jointly form the reference (i.e. standard) process and which shall be executed preferably. For the execution of the activities, a set of renewable resource types $\mathcal{R} = \{1, ..., r\}$ is available, with u_k units available for type k. For the definition of various forms of dependencies, the following constructs can be used to describe activity details:

- A duration d_i is associated with an activity i and describes how long its execution lasts. The respective value must not be negative: $d_i \geq 0 \quad \forall i \in \mathcal{A}^+$
- Precedence constraints can be used to order activities: A precedence constraint $p_{i,j}$ states that activity i has to be finished at or before the start of activity j. As regards the grouping of such constraints, a two-leveled approach is used, corresponding to the classification of activities: $\mathcal{P}^+$ contains all potential precedence constraints linking the elements of $\mathcal{A}^+$, whereas *active* precedence constraints form the subset $\mathcal{P} = \{p_{i,j} \in \mathcal{P}^+ \mid i, j \in \mathcal{A}\}$. If we introduce β_i as the starting time of activity i, the following statement has therefore to be true: $\beta_i + d_i \leq \beta_j \quad \forall p_{i,j} \in \mathcal{P}$
- Resource requirements describe the relationship between activities and resources: An activity i requires $q_{i,k}$ units of type k throughout its execution. Again, two sets can be distinguished: $\mathcal{Q}^+$ contains one requirement definition for any combination of an activity $i \in \mathcal{A}^+$ and a resource type $r \in \mathcal{R}$, whereas $\mathcal{Q} = \{q_{i,k} \in \mathcal{Q}^+ \mid i \in \mathcal{A}\}$ groups only the requirements describing *active* activities. Resources are constrained the way that the respective requirements must not exceed the availabilities at any time t. If we suppose $\mathcal{A}_t$ to be the set of activities carried out at t, the following statement has to be true for any t: $\sum_{i \in \mathcal{A}_t} q_{i,k} \leq u_k \quad \forall k \in \mathcal{R}$

Li et al. [6] used several indices to describe alternative *resources* in scheduling problems: Apart from the description of exchange possibilities, they also considered mutual dependencies in their model. We adapt this methodology for the description of alternative *activities* by introducing the following constructs:

- Alternative Activity Index $\mathcal{X}^+$. This index describes potential substitutes for an activity: $x_{i,j} \in \mathcal{X}^+$ states that activity i can be *deactivated* (i.e. removed from $\mathcal{A}$) if activity j is *activated* (i.e. added to $\mathcal{A}$). Note, that the matrix formed this way is not necessarily symmetric, since the possibility to replace activity i with activity j does not automatically imply the possibility to substitute j with i.

- Mutual Dependency Index $\mathcal{M}^+$. This index groups all definitions of activity interdependency. Basically, the following two types of binary and non-commutative relationship between elements of $\mathcal{A}^+$ can be distinguished:
  - Mutual Exclusion. $m_{i,j}^{\ominus} \in \mathcal{M}^+$ implies that activity j can and shall be removed from the schedule upon *activation* of activity i.
  - Mutual Inclusion. $m_{i,j}^{\oplus} \in \mathcal{M}^+$ states that i and j are linked and that activity j shall also be added to $\mathcal{A}$ if activity i is *activated.*

Equipped with these constructs, the *x-RCPSP* can be used to describe potential *structural modifications.* Basically, each possible form of respective intervention introduces a choice point into the process model, where it is possible to select either the activity of the reference process or a potential alternative. In this context, the switch from a previously chosen execution path to a valid alternative corresponds to a structural modification. For the simplified version of the turnaround process and the associated forms of intervention (see Sect. 2), the resulting model is illustrated in Figure 2: Solid lines visualize the structure of the reference process whereas dashed lines show alternative activities and respective precedence constraints. The encircled *or*-nodes symbolize choice points.

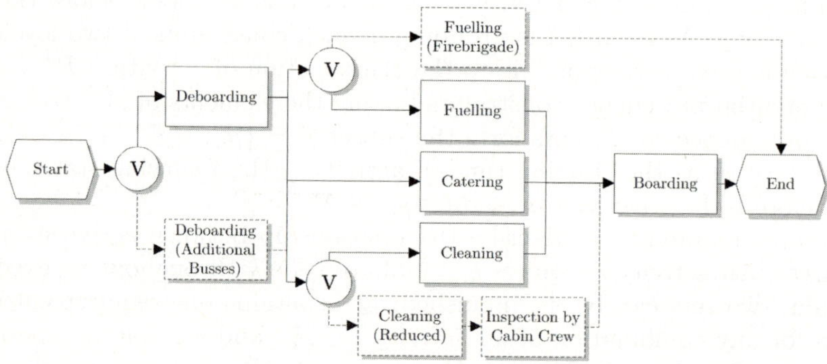

Fig. 2. Turnaround Process with Modification Possibilities

Correspondingly, we might define the elements of the *x-RCPSP* as given in Table 1. Note, that for improved readability a simplified form of notation is used in the following: $i \rightarrow j$ defines that $p_{i,j} \in \mathcal{P}^+$, $i \triangleright n \times k$ defines that $q_{i,k} = n \in \mathcal{Q}^+$, $i \Rightarrow j$ defines that $x_{i,j} \in \mathcal{X}^+$, $i \Leftrightarrow j$ defines that $x_{i,j}, x_{j,i} \in \mathcal{X}^+$, $i \oplus j$ defines that $m_{i,j}^{\oplus} \in \mathcal{M}^+$ and $i \ominus j$ defines that $m_{i,j}^{\ominus} \in \mathcal{M}^+$.

3.2   An Evolutionary Algorithm for Disruption Management

In the context of time- and resource-bound processes, disruption management is concerned with the continuous adaptation of a schedule (defining the starting times of future activities) to the dynamic and stochastic real-world environment.

Table 1. Formal Description of the Exemplary Turnaround Process

Set	Content
$\mathcal{R}$	Bus, Firebrigade
$\mathcal{A}^0$	Start, Deb, Fue, Cat, Cle, Boa, End
$\mathcal{A}^+$	Start, Deb, Deb^{Bus}, Fue, Fue^{Par}, Cat, Cle, Cle^{Red}, Ins, Boa, End
$\mathcal{P}^+$	Start $\to$ Deb, Start $\to$ Deb^{Bus}, Deb $\to$ Fue, Deb $\to$ Fue^{Par}, Deb $\to$ Cat, Deb $\to$ Cle, Deb $\to$ Cle^{Red}, Deb^{Bus} $\to$ Fue, Deb^{Bus} $\to$ Fue^{Par}, Deb^{Bus} $\to$ Cat, Deb^{Bus} $\to$ Cle, Deb^{Bus} $\to$ Cle^{Red}, Fue $\to$ Boa, Fue^{Par} $\to$ End, Cat $\to$ Boa, Cle $\to$ Boa, Cle^{Red} $\to$ Ins, Ins $\to$ Boa, Boa $\to$ End
$\mathcal{Q}^+$	Deb $\triangleright$ 1 $\times$ Bus, Deb^{Bus} $\triangleright$ 2 $\times$ Bus, Fue^{Par} $\triangleright$ 1 $\times$ Firebrigade
$\mathcal{X}^+$	Deb $\Leftrightarrow$ Deb^{Bus}, Fue $\Leftrightarrow$ Fue^{Par}, Cle $\Leftrightarrow$ Cle^{Red}
$\mathcal{M}^+$	Cle^{Red} $\oplus$ Ins, Cle $\ominus$ Ins

In a comprehensive view, not only rescheduling (i.e. the rearrangement of contained activities) but also potential structural interventions (i.e. the exchange of alternative activities) have to be considered. This section illustrates how the model described above can serve as the basis for respective DM.

For this purpose we apply an evolutionary algorithm, where optimization is accomplished in the continuous evolution of a population: The fittest individuals survive and their children are generated through recombination and mutation. As a metaheuristic approach, it provides good results in shorter time than exact optimization approaches of mathematical programming. In the following, an appropriate form of representation, an approach for the generation of an initial population, a potential fitness function and selection scheme and, particularly, specific crossover and mutation operators are described. As regards respective interrelations, a basic understanding of evolutionary algorithms is assumed.

Encoding. A schedule causing higher costs than originally intended represents the starting point for the evolutionary algorithm. As opposed to direct representation, where a solution itself represents an individual, we use the indirect form of activity list representation: The reason for this is the difficulty of directly representing and modifying the schedule's time values [7]. An activity list λ corresponds to a correctly (with respect to precedence constraints) sorted vector of all elements in $\mathcal{A}$. It defines the order in which activities shall be added to the schedule and can therefore be converted into a final set of starting times unambiguously. Respective Schedule Generation Schemes (SGS) have been described by Kolisch et al. [8] and Hindi et al. [7], for example. Note, that the scheduling process is thus split into two steps: λ respects all precedence relations, whereas only the finally derived schedule takes resource constraints into consideration.

Initial Population. The original schedule shall represent the progenitor of all members of the initial population. Since it is assumed to respect any precedence constraint, the respective timetable can be converted into an activity list λ by simply sorting all elements $i \in \mathcal{A}^+$ which have been considered in the schedule according to their starting times. All other members of the initial population are deduced from this original solution (which corresponds to the option of *not* intervening at all) through the application of the mutation operator (as discussed below). For the considered example, $\langle$Deb, Fue, Cle, Cat, Boa$\rangle$ represents a potential first member, from which other activity sequences such as $\langle$Deb, Cle, Fue, Cat, Boa$\rangle$ or $\langle$Deb, Fue, Cle^{Red}, Ins, Cat, Boa$\rangle$ can be generated.

Fitness and Selection. The fitness function evaluates the quality of an activity list through the assessment of the associated interventions and the analysis of the implied schedule. In the reduction of a potential solution to a simple numeric quality value, the function has to consider all objectives for schedule optimization: Whereas most scheduling approaches for the classical RCPSP focus on the makespan property, disruption management is rather concerned with the implications of earliness and tardiness, costs for interventions as well as the dissimilarity to the original plan. Accordingly, a turnaround-related fitness function typically combines the costs associated with predicted departure delays and the costs of intervening, considering the fact that higher costs imply lower quality.

If the members of an existing population do not fulfill specific optimization criteria, the best solutions form the next generation along with the offspring created through recombination and mutation (as discussed below): Respective parents are selected with a probability proportional to their (relative) fitness.

Crossover Operator. A method for the combination of two parent solutions is summarized in Alg. 1. Whereas the case of both elements being based on the same set of activities can be handled by the operators which have been defined for the classical RCPSP [7], we particularly focus on the description of how crossover can look like if the activity sets are distinct. The basic idea for our approach is that one parent λ_a prescribes which activities shall be contained in the child and the other one, λ_b, defines their order. To cope with different elements, we use a transition set $\mathcal{T} \subseteq \mathcal{X}^+$ which describes the conversion from activity list λ_b to λ_a. If $\mathcal{X}_a$ is assumed to be the set of modifications which led from the original sequence to a solution a, $\mathcal{T}$ is intended to define one transition for every element which exists only in either $\mathcal{X}_a$ or $\mathcal{X}_b$. Note, that respective elements of $\mathcal{X}_a$ can be applied directly, whereas the direction of the transition has to be inverted for elements of $\mathcal{X}_b$: Unless all elements can be converted this way, the parent solutions are considered incompatible and the algorithm returns without a result (line 5). Otherwise, each activity $i \in \lambda_b$ is appended to the child sequence λ if it is also contained in λ_a: Precedence constraints are considered in the way that all successors of i (as well as their successors) are shifted to the end of the vector. If $i \notin \lambda_a$ and a valid transition is defined in $\mathcal{T}$, the respective exchange operation is executed, taking into account all mutual dependencies: Afterwards the loop is resumed considering j in the next iteration. If i neither is contained in λ_a nor can be converted (consider activities which will be removed later on due to an exclusive dependency), the method proceeds.

As regards the turnaround process, consider two parent nodes $\lambda_1 = \langle$Deb^{Bus}, Fue, Cle, Cat, Boa$\rangle$ and $\lambda_2 = \langle$Deb^{Bus}, Cat, Cle^{Red}, Ins, Boa, Fue$^{Par}\rangle$. If $\lambda_a \leftarrow$

Algorithm 1. Crossover (λ_a, λ_b)

1: **if** $\mathcal{A}_a = \mathcal{A}_b$ **then**
2:     generate λ through the application of an RCPSP-related crossover operator
3: **else**
4:     $\mathcal{T} \leftarrow (\mathcal{X}_a \setminus \mathcal{X}_b) \cup \{x_{i,j} \in \mathcal{X}^+ | x_{j,i} \in (\mathcal{X}_b \setminus \mathcal{X}_a)\}$
5:     **if** $|\mathcal{T}| < |\mathcal{X}_a \bigtriangleup \mathcal{X}_b|$ **then** return *false*
6:     **for all** i in λ_b **do**
7:         **if** $i \in \lambda_a$ **then** append(λ, i)
8:         **elseif** $\exists\, x_{i,j} \in \mathcal{T}$ **then** replace i with j in λ_b and **proceed** with j
9:         **else proceed**
10:     **end for**
11: **end if**
12: return λ

λ_1 and $\lambda_b \leftarrow \lambda_2$, the transition set $\mathcal{T} = \{\text{Cle}^{Red} \Rightarrow \text{Cle}, \text{Fue}^{Par} \Rightarrow \text{Fue}\}$ groups the inversions of the elements exclusively contained in $\mathcal{X}_b$. According to the order prescribed by λ_b, activity list $\lambda = \langle \text{Deb}^{Bus}, \text{Cat}, \text{Cle}, \text{Fue}, \text{Boa}\rangle$ is created as a child. If alternatively $\lambda_a \leftarrow \lambda_2$ and $\lambda_b \leftarrow \lambda_1$, the sequence $\lambda = \langle \text{Deb}^{Bus}, \text{Fue}^{Par}, \text{Cle}^{Red}, \text{Ins}, \text{Cat}, \text{Boa}\rangle$ can be generated (under the assumption that mutually inclusive activities are placed at their earliest possible positions).

Mutation Operator. In order to avoid early convergence to local minima, a mutation operator is used (with a certain probability) to slightly modify a generated child and to extend the space of considered options thereby. A potential realization is summarized in Alg. 2: Given an activity list λ, mutation means that activities are either shifted (i.e. rescheduled) or exchanged: θ corresponds to the probability of applying the former, $1 - \theta$ to the probability of applying the latter form of modification. Methods for mutating an activity list by shifting the contained elements have been described in the context of the RCPSP (see [7], for example). We therefore focus on the exchange option herein: For the respective modification, first an arbitrary $x_{i,j} \in \mathcal{X}^+$ is selected for any $i \in \lambda$. Then, i and all elements excluded by j are removed from the activity list, before finally j and all linked activities are added at the former position of i or after their last predecessor: All associated successors (with subsequent successors) have to be shifted to the right-hand side of the inserted element.

Algorithm 2. Mutate (λ)

1: **if** a randomly generated value $\leq \theta$ **then**
2:     rearrange λ through the application of an RCPSP-related mutation operator
3: **else**
4:     select an arbitrary $x_{i,j} \in \mathcal{X}^+ | i \in \lambda$
5:     remove i and $\{k | m_{j,k}^{\ominus} \in \mathcal{M}^+\}$ from λ
6:     insert j and $\{k | m_{j,k}^{\oplus} \in \mathcal{M}^+\}$ at the former position of i or after the last predecessor, and shift all successors to the right-hand side
7: **end if**
8: return λ

As far as the example of the turnaround process is concerned, consider the activity list $\lambda = \langle \mathrm{Deb}^{Bus}, \mathrm{Cat}, \mathrm{Cle}, \mathrm{Fue}, \mathrm{Boa} \rangle$: A simple rescheduling operation can transform this sequence into $\langle \mathrm{Deb}^{Bus}, \mathrm{Cle}, \mathrm{Cat}, \mathrm{Fue}, \mathrm{Boa} \rangle$ or $\langle \mathrm{Deb}^{Bus}, \mathrm{Fue}, \mathrm{Cle}, \mathrm{Cat}, \mathrm{Boa} \rangle$, for example. The exchange operator defined before, might mutate λ into $\langle \mathrm{Deb}^{Bus}, \mathrm{Cat}, \mathrm{Cle}, \mathrm{Fue}^{Par}, \mathrm{Boa} \rangle$ if $\mathrm{Fue} \Rightarrow \mathrm{Fue}^{Par}$ is chosen from $\mathcal{X}^+$, or into $\langle \mathrm{Deb}^{Bus}, \mathrm{Cat}, \mathrm{Cle}^{Red}, \mathrm{Ins}, \mathrm{Fue}, \mathrm{Boa} \rangle$ upon the selection of $\mathrm{Cle} \Rightarrow \mathrm{Cle}^{Red}$.

4 Related Work

As an individual research area, disruption management originally and traditionally focused on aircraft and crew scheduling (see [1, 9] for example): The Descartes project, which is concerned with the efficient rescheduling of respective entities in case of disruptions, represents the main contribution to the development and application of respective concepts [10, 11]. Currently, DM is also being adapted for various other areas: Production planning [12, 13] as well as supply chain management [14] represent examples of respective domains of application.

Disruption management for the RCPSP has been described by Zhu et al. [15]: They confine the possibilities of interventions to the classical options such as rescheduling as well as a modification of durations and resource assignments. For the resolution of the mathematically formulated problem a hybrid mixed-integer programming/constraint programming procedure is applied. Thus, Zhu et al. focus on the identification of an optimal solution for classical forms of modification, whereas the approach described herein is intended to identify (only) good solutions in a wider space of options and within a shorter time horizon.

As regards the idea of providing the RCPSP with additional flexibility, little research has been done so far. To the best of our knowledge, only Artigues et al. [16] and Elkhyari et al. [17] have made respective proposals. The former is concerned with the dynamic insertion of activities, where each occurrence of an unexpected activity corresponds to a disruption. The latter provides possibilities to handle over-constrained networks based on the excessive use of so-called explanations. And also the concept of alternative activities has received only little attention in the scheduling domain: Only Beck et al. [18] proposed an approach, in which a Probability of Existence (PEX) can be defined for any activity.

5 Conclusions and Future Work

This paper illustrated how the concept of the RCPSP can be used as a basis for turnaround process disruption management. For this purpose, a generalization has been introduced, which is able to cope with alternative activities and potential forms of process modifications. The x-$RCPSP$ provides several advantages: First, it supports comprehensive flexibility in complex process structures. Second, the underlying concept is intuitive, which makes it easy to define and maintain respective models. And finally, the possibility to apply metaheuristic search methods makes it possible to use it for real-time decision support in realistic DM:

Although the time required for the identification of the optimal solution might be high, good results can be obtained even if optimization is cut off.

An unoptimized version of the presented algorithms has been implemented in a Java-based prototype: It illustrates the effectiveness of the proposed methods and their practical applicability to DSS in turnaround process DM. As regards performance results, comparative evaluation is difficult since there are no respective publications considering similar problem classes. Nonetheless, future tasks include the further optimization of the respective procedures, research on potential reductions of the search space (following Bean et al. [19], for example) and the generation of benchmarkable results for realistic problem sizes.

Acknowledgement. This work has been carried out in the context of the *cdm@airports* project, which is partly funded by FFF, Austria.

References

1. Clausen, J., Hansen, J., Larsen, J., Larsen, A.: Disruption Management. ORMS Today **28** (2001) 40–43
2. Wambsganss, M.: Collaborative Decision Making through Dynamic Information Transfer. Air Traffic Control Quarterly **4** (1997) 107–123
3. Hoffman, R., Ball, M., Odoni A., Hall W., Wambsganss M.: Collaborative Decision Making in Air Traffic Flow Management. Technical Report, UC Berkeley (1999)
4. Brucker, P., Drexl, A., Mohring, R., Neumann, K., Pesch, E.: Resource-constrained project scheduling: Notation, classification, models, and methods. European Journal of Operational Research **112** (1999) 3–41
5. Hartmann, S.: Project Scheduling with Multiple Modes: A Genetic Algorithm. Annals of Operations Research **102** (2001) 111–135
6. Li, R.K-Y., Willis, R.J.: Alternative resources in project scheduling. Computers and Operations Research **18** (1991) 663–669
7. Hindi, K.S., Yang, H., Fleszar, K.: An Evolutionary Algorithm for Resource-Constrained Project Scheduling. IEEE Evolutionary Computation **6** (2002) 512–518
8. Kolisch, R., Hartmann, S.: Heuristic Algorithms for solving the Resource-Constrained Project Scheduling Problem: Classification and Computational Analysis. In: Project scheduling: Recent models, algorithms and applications (1999) 147–178
9. Thengvall, B., Bard, J.F., Yu, G.: Balancing user preferences for aircraft schedule recovery during irregular operations. IIE Operations Engineering **32** (2000) 181–193
10. Kohl, N., Larsen, A., Larsen, J., Ross, A., Tiourine, S.: Airline Disruption Management - Perspectives, Experiences and Outlook. Technical Report 2004-16, IMM, Technical University of Denmark (2004)
11. Clausen, J., Larsen, A., Larsen, J.: Disruption Management in the Airline Industry - Concepts, Models and Methods. Technical Report 2005-01, IMM, Technical University of Denmark (2005)
12. Yang, J., Qi, X., Yu, G.: Disruption management in production planning. Naval Research Logistics **52** (2005) 420–442
13. Xia, Y., Yang, M.H., Golany, B., Gilbert, S., Yu, G.: Real-time disruption management in a two-stage production and inventory system. IIE Transactions **36** (2004)

14. Xu, M., Qi, X., Yu, G., Zhang, H., Gao, C.: The demand disruption management problem for a supply chain system with nonlinear demand functions. Journal of Systems Science and Systems Engineering **12** (2003) 82–97
15. Zhu, G., Bard, J.F., Yu, G.: Disruption management for resource-constrained project scheduling. Journal of the Operational Research Society **56** (2005) 365–381
16. Artigues, C., Michelon, P., Reusser, S.: Insertion techniques for static and dynamic resource constrained project scheduling. European Journal of OR **149** (2003)
17. Elkhyari, A., Guéret, C., Jussien, N.: Constraint Programming for Dynamic Scheduling Problems. In: ISS'04 Int. Scheduling Symposium (2004) 84–89
18. Beck, J.C., Fox, M.S.: Constraint Directed Techniques for Scheduling with Alternative Activities. Artificial Intelligence **121** (2000) 211–250
19. Bean, J.C., Birge, J.R., Mittenthal, J., Noon, C.E.: Matchup Scheduling with Multiple Resources, Release Dates and Disruptions. OR **39** (1991) 470–483

Distribution System Evaluation Algorithm Using Analytic Hierarchy Process

Buhm Lee[1], Chang-Ho Choi[2],*, Nam-Sup Choi[1], Kyoung Min Kim[1], Yong-Ha Kim[3], Sang-Kyu Choi[4], and Sakis A. Meliopoulos[5]

[1] Dept. of Electrical and Semiconductor Engineering, Chonnam National University,
San 96-1, Dundeok-Dong, Yeosu City, Jeollanam-do, Korea 550-749
{buhmlee, nschoi, kkm}@yosu.ac.kr
[2] Dept. of Transportation, Chonnam National University,
San 96-1, Dundeok-Dong, Yeosu City, Jeollanam-do, Korea 550-749
jc1214@yosu.ac.kr
[3] Dept. of Electrical Engineering, University of Incheon,
177 Dohwa-Dong, Incheon City, Korea 402-749
yhkim@incheon.ac.kr
[4] School of Electronic, Communication, and Information, Anyang Technical College,
San 39-1, Anyang 3-Dong, Anyang City, Gyeongki-do, Korea 430-749
cskm@aytc.anyang-c.ac.kr
[5] School of Electrical and Computer Enginering, Georgia Institute of Technology,
Atlanta, GA 30332-0250, USA
sakis.meliopoulos@ee.gatech.edu

Abstract. This paper presents a methodology based on the Analytic Hierarchy Process to calculate unified power quality index which provide an overall assessment of the distribution system performance. To obtain the unified power quality index, we propose the use of the AHP model which has three states: [Best] - [Real] - [Worst]. The proposed method is especially useful and effective for planning. We have applied the proposed method to an actual relatively large system. The method identified the pareto-optimal expansion plan.

1 Introduction

Consumers of power systems require a reliable and high quality power supply. The practice today is to address the two issues, reliability and power quality, separately. Distribution system planners or operators assess the reliability of load points by means of reliability indices and evaluate the power quality in terms of voltage sags, voltage drops, harmonics, etc..

The reliability of a distribution system is quantified with a set of reliability indices. These indices are the well known SAIFI, SAIDI, ASIFI, ASIDI, MAIFI, etc. which are addressed in the IEEE Std 1366[1], including computational processes for these indices. The distribution reliability indices evaluate the reliability of the distribution system at a specified point. Similarly but independently, the IEEE Std P1564[2,3]

---

* Corresponding author.

M. Ali and R. Dapoigny (Eds.): IEA/AIE 2006, LNAI 4031, pp. 177–186, 2006.

addresses power quality indices and their computation, such as SARFI. The power quality indices quantify the effects of voltage sags, etc. at a specific point of the distribution system. The voltage sags are typically computed by loadflow techniques that are used as the main computational tool for voltage sags indices. Finally, the IEEE Std 519[4] addresses the impact of harmonics in power quality. It defines indices such as THD, TIF, etc. The harmonic based power quality indices are typically computed by harmonics loadflow tools. These indices also computed for a specific point of the distribution system. The calculated power quality indices, characterize the power quality at a specified point of the system, and can be repeated for any bus of the system. Evaluation of the overall power quality of the system is not provided.

This paper presents a new methodology to obtain unified power quality index which can assess the performance of the distribution system. Among power quality indices, reliability and voltage sag indices are based on distribution system. That means we can get indices directly by using IEEE Std 1366 and IEEE Std P1564 for distribution system. On the contrary, there are no indices related to voltage drops. And, there are harmonic indices, such as THD, by using IEEE Std 519 are based on each bus, not system. So, we developed a model based on Analytic Hierarchy Process (AHP)[5,6] to obtain system indices from voltage drops and harmonic indices on each bus. We propose the use of three states, such as [Best] - [Real] - [Worst]. By using eigenvalue analysis, we can compare the attributes of the various alternatives and compute the unified index value of a system.

To Whom It May Concern: obtain the unified item index, such as unified reliability index, unified voltage sag index, unified voltage deviation index, and unified harmonics index, for the system, we present an AHP model to get unified item index from various indices. Finally, to get unified power quality index, we present an AHP model. By using presented these methodology, we can get unified power quality index which can show the power quality of the distribution system. Especially, this method is effective on planning. For example, decision-maker can build alternatives of expansion plan, and can choose a best one among power quality alternatives.

We applied the proposed method to the real system planning, and we show it can provide a unified power quality index.

2 Evaluation Methodology

2.1 Evaluation of Power Quality at Load Point

The power quality of a system is quantified by the following attributes: reliability (interruptions), voltage sag, voltage drops, and harmonics. A discussion of each individual attribute is provided following by the proposal of a unified index.

(1) Reliability

Reliability is quantified by the number of interruptions N_i and their durations r_i at each load point i, and we need to measure it at each load point[1]. It is practically impossible to measure reliability. We relay on probability models[7], to predict reliability. Specifically, consider eq.(1) which relates N_i to λ_i.

$$N_i = \lambda_i N_{T\,i} \tag{1}$$

Where,

λ_i : Failure rate at load point i [fr/yr]

$N_{T\,i}$: Number of loads at load point i [ea]

By using eq.(1), we can calculate λ_i and r_i at every load point using the failure and duration of equipment of the system(assuming that the component probability model in known). After calculation of λ_i and r_i, we convert it to N_i and r_i of each load point.

(2) Voltage Sag

The voltage sag $N_{x\,i}$ is defined as the percentage x [%] of undervoltage at each load point i [3]. We employ a probabilistic model to predict voltage sags. Specifically, consider eq.(2) which relates $N_{x\,i}$ to $\lambda_{x\,i}$.

$$N_{x\,i} = \lambda_{x\,i} N_{T\,i} \tag{2}$$

Where,

$\lambda_{x\,i}$: x [%] sag rate at load point i [fr/yr] (x =50, 70, 90).

To the transition rates $\lambda_{x\,i}$ at any load point can be computed with Monte carlo simulations assuming specific probabilities of events that cause voltage sags.

(3) Voltage drops

Voltages of load point can be calculated by loadflow. From voltages of load point, we calculate voltage deviation V_i^{err} as eq.(3).

$$V_i^{err} = |V_i - 1| \tag{3}$$

Where,

V_i : Actual voltage at load point i [PU]

(4) Harmonics

Harmonic spectrum and indices can be calculated by harmonic loadflow and IEEE Std 519[4]. We calculate THD_i^V , TIF_i for indices of harmonics as eq.(4).

$$THD_i^V = \frac{\sqrt{\sum_{h=2}^{50} V_h^2}}{V_1} \qquad TIF_i = \frac{\sqrt{\sum_{h=2}^{50} (T_h Z_h I_h)^2}}{V_1} \tag{4}$$

Where,

V_i : h^{th} harmonic line-to-neutral voltage (1th : fundamental)

T_h : Telephone interference factor

Z_h : Power system impedance at harmonic order h

I_h : Harmonic current into power system.

2.2 System Wide Indices

We propose the use of system wide indices to characterize the overall power quality of the entire system. We calculate reliability and voltage sags indices using IEEE Std 1366 and IEEE Std P1564, and voltage drops and harmonics indices using newly developed AHP model. This model provides a framework for quantifying the overall performance of the system.

2.2.1 Proposed AHP Model
(1) Proposed states of AHP model
Although the AHP model allows for creating any number of states, we propose the use of three states, defined as [Best], [Real], and [Worst] in this AHP model. [Best] means the best states, [Real] means calculated states, and [Worst] means the worst states for the user. By using these three states, we create an AHP model which inherently quantifies the system performance indices in a unified manner. An example structure of the AHP model for THD is shown at Fig. 1.(a).

[Example of these states]
Guess, the voltage of a load point is 0- ∞ [Volt]. Even though, voltage of load point can vary 0- ∞ [Volt], it is meaningless. You can only load at this load point under -20 - 20[%] of voltage deviation, because your equipment cannot run over $\pm$ 20[%] voltage deviation. So, 20[%] of voltage deviation is [Worst]. And, [Best] is 0[%] which has no voltage deviation. Of course, [Best] should not be zero, but should be the usual variations, for example [-0.05 to 0.05] etc. Here, if voltage deviation of current state is 3[%], [Real] is 3[%].

(2) Assessment of alternatives using eigenvalues
We proposed a comparative evaluation method of alternatives using eigenvalues. The object of AHP[5,6] is evaluation of alternatives by using competing attributes. The AHP procedure contain eigenvalues which are obtained at limiting procedure to compare competing attributes of alternatives. These eigenvalues can show the competing scale of alternatives. We employ the competing scale as index, and use their degrees of [Real] between [Best] - [Real] - [Worst] as [0] - [Index] - [1]. Here, index [0] means best state and [1] means worst state.

2.2.2 Calculation of Indices
(1) Reliability and voltage sags
Reliability indices calculations are based on the IEEE Std 1366[1], and voltage sag indices calculations are based on the IEEE Std P1564[3].

$$SAIFI = \frac{\sum N_i}{N_T} \qquad SAIDI = \frac{\sum r_i N_i}{N_T} \qquad ASIFI = \frac{\sum L_i}{L_T} \qquad (5)$$

$$ASIDI = \frac{\sum r_i L_i}{L_T} \qquad MAIFI = \frac{\sum ID_i N_i}{N_T} \qquad SARFI_x = \frac{\sum N_{xi}}{N_T}$$

Where,

$$N_T = \sum N_i, \quad L_T = \sum L_i$$

SAIFI : System Average Interruption Frequency Index
SAIDI : System Average Interruption Duration Index
ASIFI : Average System Interruption Frequency Index
ASIDI : Average System Interruption Duration Index
MAIFI : Momentary Average Interruption Frequency Index
SARFI : System Average RMS variation Frequency Index
L_i : Load at load point i [kW]

ID_i : Average monetary interruptions per sustained interruption at load point i

(2) Voltage drop and harmonics

To get V_{sys}^{err}, THD_{sys}^{V}, and TIF_{sys} directly is not possible. So, we use a proposed AHP at 2.2.1 to calculate these indices at system level. Structure of THD AHP model is shown at Fig. 1.(a).

2.3 Item Wide Indices

From calculated indices at 2.2, such as reliability indices, voltage sag indices, voltage deviation index, harmonic indices, we calculate unified reliability index, voltage sag

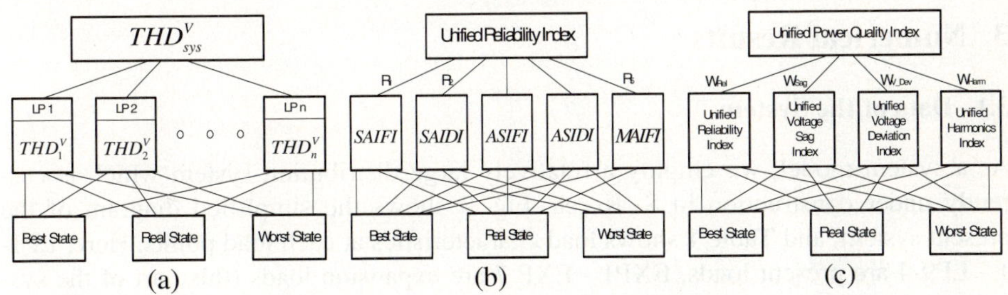

Fig. 1. Structure of AHP models to unify indices

index, voltage deviation index, and harmonics index by using proposed AHP at 2.2.1. Because voltage deviation index is only one, we use V_{sys}^{err} directly as a voltage deviation index. Structure of Reliability AHP model is shown at Fig. 1.(b).

2.4 Unified index of Power Quality for the Distribution System

From unified reliability index, voltage sag index, voltage deviation index, and harmonics index at 2.3, we calculate unified power quality index by using proposed AHP at 2.2.1. This value shows the power quality for the system. Structure of AHP model is shown at Fig. 1.(c).

Fig. 2 illustrates the overall procedure of the proposed method.

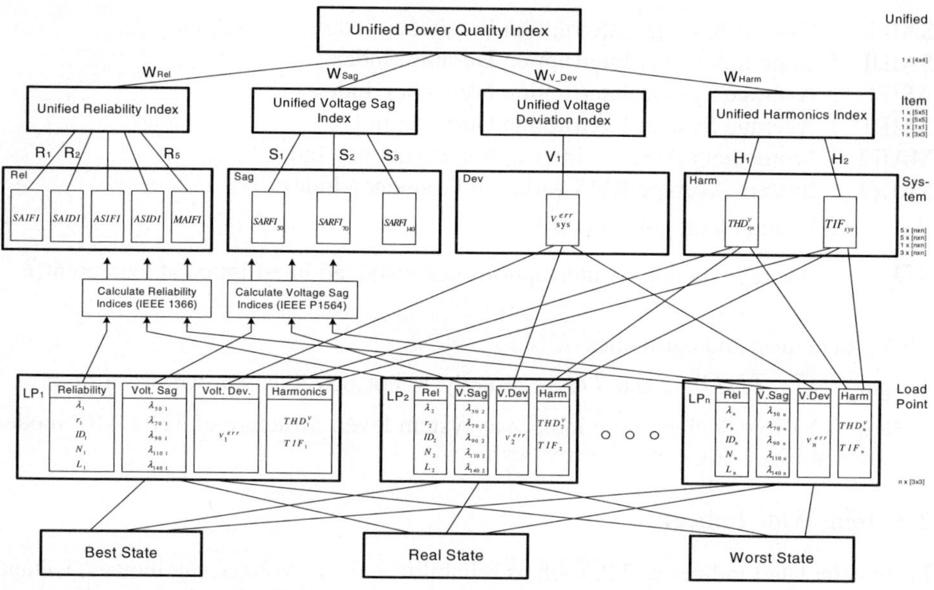

Fig. 2. Structure of unified index by using AHP

3 Numerical Results

3.1 Data of the System

As a system model, we employ a relatively large distribution system which is currently under construction in S. Korea. Fig. 3 shows the simplified diagram of the present system, and Table 1 shows load characteristics at each load points. Here, LP1-1 - LP9-4 are present loads, EXP1 - EXP 7 are expansion loads (this part of the system is under construction). We seek to determine the best system (from the power quality point of view) for serving these new loads.

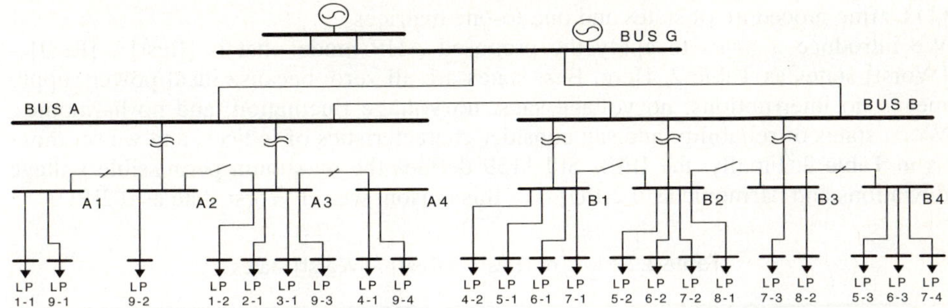

Fig. 3. Simplified diagram of present system

Table 1. Load characteristics at each load points

Load Point	Load [kVA]	[ea]	Load Point	Load [kVA]	[ea]	Load Point	Load [kVA]	[ea]
LP1-1	10000	13	LP6-3	1274	100	EXP1	29000	25
LP1-2	6000	8	LP7-1	10168	900	EXP2	10000	80
LP2-1	5000	5	LP7-2	5084	450	EXP3	29000	30
LP3-1	10000	77	LP7-3	5084	450	EXP4	24000	50
LP4-1	12000	100	LP7-4	5084	450	EXP5	19000	100
LP4-2	12000	100	LP8-1	6130	78	EXP6	33000	25
LP5-1	12000	60	LP8-2	6130	78	EXP7	12000	180
LP5-2	9000	45	LP9-1	5346	68			
LP5-3	14500	73	LP9-2	5042	111			
LP6-1	11080	100	LP9-3	7032	148			
LP6-2	5610	100	LP9-4	8578	22			

3.2 Procedure and Results

We consider three alternative expansion plans for serving the loads EXP1 - EXP7. The plans are illustrated in Fig. 4. Alternative 1 uses the existing substations A and B which are expanded with additional transformers to feed the new loads. Alternative 2 and 3 are based on constructing a new substation C which is fed by a single circuit (Alternative 2) or with two circuits (Alternative 3).

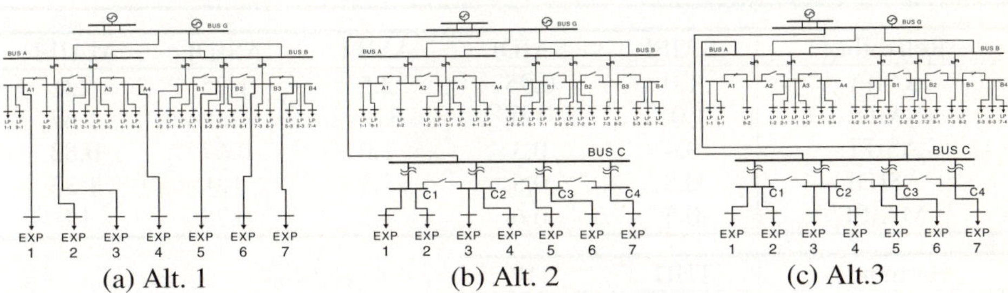

Fig. 4. Alternatives for expansion plans

(1) Define procedure of states and one-to-one matrices

We introduce 3-states to apply the proposed AHP model that is [Best] - [Real] - [Worst] states as Table 2. Here, Best states are all zero, because ideal power supply means no interruptions, no voltage sags, no voltage fluctuation, and no harmonics. Worst states of reliability and sag consider characteristics of indices, and we set those as in Table 2. Finally, the IEEE Std 1159 defines the maximum permissible voltage deviations and harmonic as 0.2[PU]. For this reason, we set Worst state as 0.2[PU].

Table 2. Setting of [Best] - [Real] - [Worst] states

Indices			[Best]	[Real]	[Worst]
System Level indices	Reliability	SAIFI	0.	Calculated	1.
		SAIDI	0.	Calculated	200.
		ASIFI	0.	Calculated	1.
		ASIDI	0.	Calculated	200.
		MAIFI	0.	Calculated	2.
	Volt. Sag	$SARFI_{50}$	0.	Calculated	3.
Load Point Level indices	Volt. Dev.	V_i	0.[PU]	Actual	0.2[PU]
	Harmonics	THD_i	0.[PU]	Actual	0.2[PU]
		TIF_i	0.[PU]	Actual	0.2[PU]

To build AHP model, we built one-to-one matrix, and show it in Table 3. The one-to-one matrix is computed with the following attributes: system level reliability, voltage sags, voltage deviation and harmonics to consider kWh of loads. One-to-one matrix of item level, reliability and harmonics are made to consider usage of indices at field. Finally, one-to-one matrix of unified power quality level is made to consider importance of power quality at field. Here, all one-to-one matrices are arbitrary. Different system designers may use different one-to-one matrices.

Table 3. One-to-One matrix for each level

Unified Index	Reliability	Volt. Sag	Volt. Dev.	Harmonics
Reliability	1.0	5.0	0.2	1.33
Volt. Sag	0.2	1.0	0.05	0.2
Volt. Dev.	5.0	20.0	1.0	4.0
Harmonics	0.75	5.0	0.25	1.0

Reliability	SAIFI	SAIDI	ASIFI	ASIDI	MAIFI
SAIFI	1.0	0.95	2.5	1.25	2.0
SAIDI	1.05	1.0	3.33	2.0	1.67
ASIFI	0.4	0.3	1.0	0.67	0.83
ASIDI	0.8	0.5	1.5	1.0	1.33
MAIFI	0.5	0.6	1.2	0.75	1.0

Harmonics	THD	TIF
THD	1.0	5.0
TIF	0.2	1.0

(2) Results of unified power quality index
Fig. 4 and Tables 2,3 suggest that it is possible to calculate each eigenvalue as indices, such as unified power quality index, item indices, and system indices. The results by using AHP procedure are shown in Table 4.

Table 4. Calculated indices

	Indices		Alt. 1	Alt. 2	Alt. 3
	Unified Power Quality Index		0.19786	0.10386	0.09434
Item Level Unified Indices		Reliability	0.13073	0.12416	0.10810
		Volt. Sag	0.17245	0.16223	0.13990
		Vot. Dev.	0.21506	0.07366	0.06770
		Harmonics	0.19853	0.20643	0.19059
System Level Indices	Reliability	SAIFI	0.12934	0.12167	0.10492
		SAIDI	0.10762	0.10718	0.10563
		ASIFI	0.18836	0.16289	0.09747
		ASIDI	0.11256	0.11099	0.10496
		MAIFI	0.16167	0.15209	0.13115
	Volt. Sag	$SARFI_{50}$	0.17245	0.16223	0.13990
	Volt. Dev.	V_{sys}	0.21506	0.07366	0.06770
	Harmonics	THD_{sys}	0.21388	0.22623	0.20741
		TIF_{sys}	0.12179	0.10741	0.10649

The results of Table 4 show that the best solution is Alt. 3. It means that additional construction of high voltage substation is useful to increase power quality. In system level, reliability and voltage sag are slightly better at Alt. 3.(Alt.1<Alt.2<Alt.3), and harmonics is nearly same. , But voltage deviation is absolutely better at Alt. 2 and Alt. 3. In item level, except harmonics all is better at Alt. 3. Finally, unified power quality index shows Alt.1 < Alt. 2 < Alt. 3.

(3) Tradeoffs between power quality and cost
In an actual operation of the distribution system, operating cost is as important attribute as power quality. For this reason, we compare power quality .vs. operating cost. The results are shown in Table 5. The operating costs are the investment cost/lifetime of each power circuit.

Table 5. Power quality indices and operating cost

	Unified Power Quality Index	Operating cost [$/yr]
Alt. 1	0.19786	6,280,000
Alt. 2	0.10386	6,795,000
Alt. 3	0.09434	6,875,000

From Table 5, Alt. 1 shows worst power quality but lease expensive operating cost. On the contrary, Alt. 3 shows best power quality with most expensive operating cost. Here, Table 5 shows these alternatives are in pareto-optimal, and choose the best alternative is responsible for decision-maker. The presented data are useful for decision makers as it reveals the tradeoffs.

4 Conclusion

This paper presents a power quality evaluation methodology by means of unified index. The contributions of the paper are:

(1) A new AHP model is proposed with the classification of [Best], [Real], and [Worst] states. The proposal can unify system reliability indices and power quality indices. In the course of AHP procedure, we extract eigenvalues which can shows competition, and evaluate power quality at each level. Finally, we can obtain unified index of power quality.

(2) The proposed methodology has been applied to a relatively large distribution system which is under expansion. The study case shows the process for selecting the best system in terms of improving power quality. The methodology is useful for planning of distribution system.

(3) The study case shows the tradeoffs between operating cost and power quality. The methodology identifies the pareto-optimal solution. This information is very useful to decision-makers.

We plan to continue improvements of the methodology addressing the issue of realistically quantifying the cost of power quality.

Acknowledgement

This work was financially supported by Chonnam National University.

References

1. IEEE: IEEE Guide for Electric Power Distribution Reliability Indices, IEEE Std 1366 (2001)
2. IEEE: IEEE Recommended Practice for Monitoring Electric Power Quality, IEEE Std 1159 (1995)
3. Math H. J. Bollen, D. Daniel Sabin, Rao S. Thallam: Voltage-Sag Indices – Recent Developments in IEEE P1564 Task Force. (2003) 34-41
4. IEEE: IEEE Recommended Practices and Requirements for Harmonic Control in Electrical Power Systems, IEEE Std 519 (1992)
5. Thomas L. Satty: The Analytic Network Process. RWS Publications (1996)
6. Marija D. Ilic, Shell Liu: Hierarchical Power Systems Control – Its Value in a Changing Industry. Springer (1996)
7. Roy Billinton, Ronald N. Allen: Reliability Evaluation of Power Systems. Plenum Press (1984)

A Hybrid Robot Control System Based on Soft Computing Techniques

Alfons Schuster

School of Computing and Mathematics, Faculty of Informatics, University of Ulster
Shore Road, Newtownabbey, Co. Antrim BT37 0QB, Northern Ireland
`a.schuster@ulster.ac.uk`

Abstract. This paper describes the so-called *RobSim* robot control system software. *RobSim* is a hybrid system based on soft computing techniques and includes a genetic algorithm component, a fuzzy logic component, and a component utilizing features derived from chaos theory. The presented system is an extension of our previous work. A new component of the system exploits the principle of self-similarity found in chaos theory via so-called adaptive fuzzy sets for problem solving. Compared to earlier versions the current system provides increased functionality, adaptability, and flexibility, extending the problem solving potential of the system to a wider range of applications.

Keywords: genetic algorithms, fuzzy logic.

1   Introduction

This paper continuous our earlier work on the *RobSim* robot control system software [1], [2]. The high-level view of the system given in Figure 1 illustrates how the current system potentially could be employed in the future.

Sensors allow the system to interface with an environment. In an ideal scenario *RobSim* reacts to incoming signals in a meaningful way, providing positive feedback to the environment. In order to achieve this task *RobSim* employs a problem solving strategy. Figure 1 indicates that this strategy involves a fuzzy logic controller and a component using measures from chaos theory, both embedded within a genetic algorithm (GA). The principles of a GA are well known, and in *RobSim* there are no significant deviations from standard procedures. The GA in Figure 1 generates a start population with a predefined number of fuzzy control systems (FCSs). *RobSim* uses measures from chaos theory to establish the problem solving potential (i.e., the fitness) of each FCS in a population. The usefulness of these measures is documented in more detail in our previous work [1], [2]. The GA iterates through a loop with predefined exit conditions. In each loop the quality of every FCS is determined. *RobSim* uses well-known GA procedures to select and modify solutions that indicate as being better than other solutions in order to achieve further improvement. The GA stops when the exit conditions are met. In the current setup a system developer would evaluate the

M. Ali and R. Dapoigny (Eds.): IEA/AIE 2006, LNAI 4031, pp. 187–196, 2006.

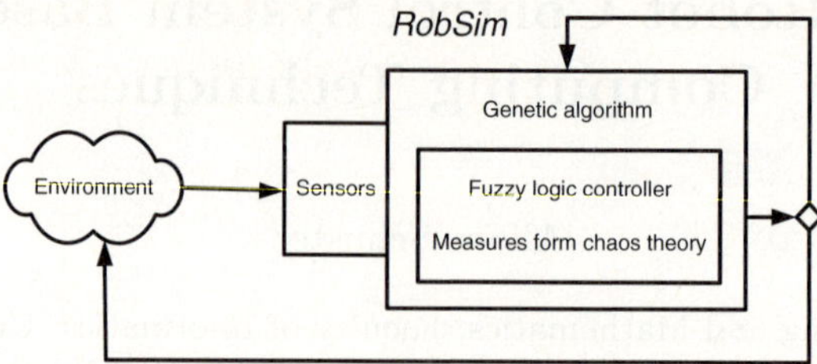

Fig. 1. High-level view of the *RobSim* robot control system software

final proposal of the system. The process illustrated in Figure 1 can be implemented at different levels of complexity. For example for rule base generation, rule weight assignment, or the shaping of fuzzy sets. The general strategy is to continuously increase the level of quality and complexity and to learn from the problems emerging at different levels.

The problem on which *RobSim* is put to the test involves a tracking task. In this task two objects A and B are positioned in a conventional x, y coordinate system. The task for object B is to track and finally catch object A. This is illustrated in Figure 2. Note that this illustration actually is taken from an example application provided with the commercial fuzzy logic tool CubiCalc 2.0 that was used in this study.

Object A moves on a specifiable trajectory, and the trajectory for object B is produced by the control software. Figure 2 illustrates two scenarios. Object A moves on a straight line in both scenarios. For object B there are two trajectories, one relatively smooth, and the other more ragged or jagged. Figure 2 indicates that following either trajectory object B finally approaches object A, and so both trajectories provide a solution to the given task. The solution finally selected however could be the FCS that produces the trajectory that is less jagged, because for many problems FCS designers prefer a system that converges towards a solution with some smoothness [3]. Our previous work dealt with this problem in some way. This earlier work had some limitations however. We mentioned earlier that the process in Figure 1 can be implemented at different levels of complexity. Previously we concentrated on the shaping of fuzzy sets for the fuzzy controller, for example. It turned out that the way in which this process

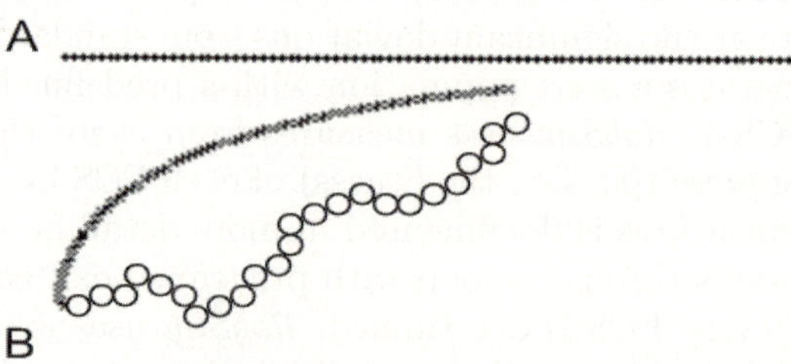

Fig. 2. A tracking problem where an object B has to approach and finally catch object A. Two trajectories are shown for object B.

was implemented was not ideal. This paper describes the improvements we made to the system in order to overcome this problem. The solution to the problem is based on so-called adaptive fuzzy sets. The paper describes how this solution is derived from the concept of self-similarity used in chaos theory.

The remaining sections of this document are organized as follows. Section 2 describes the shortcomings of the previous system and also proposes a solution to these shortcomings. This solution exploits the feature of self-similarity found in chaos theory via so-called adaptive fuzzy sets. Section 3 provides results from experimental applications of our approach. Section 4 includes a discussion. This discussion also reports on the findings of a preliminary study where we investigated the usefulness of the Lego MindStorms Robot kit as a potential implementation platform for our system. Section 5 ends the paper with a summary.

2   Shortcomings of Previous Systems

A description of the proposed solution requires a bit more detail about our previous work. The tracking problem illustrated in Figure 2 is a task where an object B chases an object A by adjusting its azimuth in accordance with the relative direction of object A. The rational of the system is simple: correct object B's azimuth in direct proportion to a tracking error. Overall the control system for this task is not too complex. It contains one input variable called *TrackingError*, and one output variable called *AzimuthAdjust*. The rule base of the system contains five rules of the form: "If *TrackingError* is *LargePositive* then make *AzimuthAdjust LargePositive*", for example. The input and the output variable are represented by fuzzy sets. The task for *RobSim* is to automatically generate a FCS solution suitable for this task. We mentioned before that this task may involve different levels of complexity. Obviously, the generation of a FCS from the ground up involving the production of all fuzzy sets, the rule base, relationships between input and output variables, as well as the selection of fuzzification and defuzzification techniques, for example, is the most complex level. Our earlier work didn't go that far. *RobSim* was applied to the sub-task of shaping the fuzzy sets for input and output variables. This shaping process involves a random element and starts with the (random) generation of fuzzy sets for the input and output variables. Figure 3-(a) illustrates a set of randomly generated fuzzy sets for the variable *TrackinError* mentioned earlier.

RobSim then alters the shape of these fuzzy sets in order to arrive at an improved solution to the problem via the process illustrated earlier in Figure 1. Figure 3-(b) illustrates a typical outcome of this shaping process. Figure 3-(c) illustrates how this outcome compares with an "ideal" solution. Note that this ideal solution is taken from an example application provided with the CubiCalc 2.0 tool mentioned earlier. Figure 3 is quite instructive. For example, Figure 3-(c) illustrates that, from left to right, the "correct" order of the fuzzy sets is *LargeNegative, SmallNergative, AlmostZero, SmallPositive,* and *LargePositive*. Note that this sequence is determined by the location of the middle points of the fuzzy sets. Figure 3-(a) indicates that in the initial, randomly generated

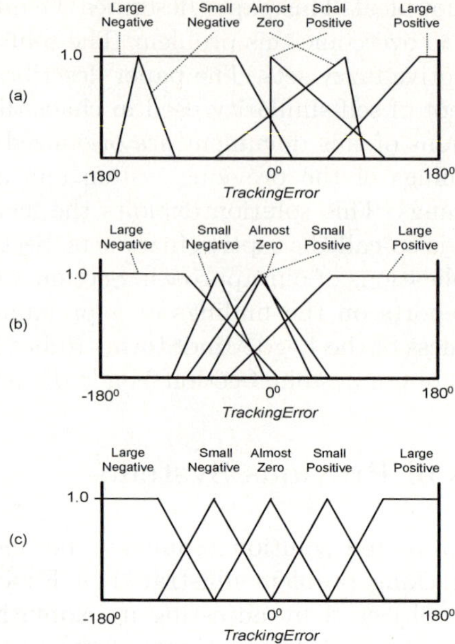

Fig. 3. Process of shaping of fuzzy sets, (a) random generation of fuzzy sets for the variable *TrackinError*, (b) a typical outcome of the shaping process, (c) solution provided by commercial CubiCalc 2.0 tool

arrangement the two fuzzy sets *AlmostZero* and *SmallPositive* are not in the correct order. The shapes of the fuzzy sets in Figure 3-(a) are also quite different from the configurations of their ideal counterparts. Figure 3-(b) indicates that the system eventually comes up with an improved configuration. One conclusion of our earlier studies was that the system over time indeed generated increasingly better solutions [2]. Although this was encouraging in our view, under closer inspection it turned out that the process of shaping fuzzy sets in this form was an over-complication. The remainder of this section identifies this over-complication and also describes an approach to simplify the process.

Figure 3-(a) indicates that the sequence of fuzzy sets from left to right is *SmallNegative*, *LargeNegative*, *SmallPositive*, *AlmostZero* and, *LargePositive*. This sequence does not make too much sense. Chen and Hwang, for example, mention that there almost always is a logical order for linguistic variables [4]. For instance, in a particular temperature context a logical order could be: *very cold, cold, warm, very warm*, and not: *cold, very warm, very cold, warm*. Similarly, the logical order for the linguistic terms for variable *TrackingError* is: *LargeNegative, SmallNegative, AlmostZero, SmallPositive*, and *LargePositive*. Another observation indicates that in many FCS applications the shape of the fuzzy sets is either symmetrical or has the form of a trapezoid. For example, the boundary sets *LargeNegative* and *LargePositive* in Figure 3-(c) are trapezoidal, and the in-between sets *SmallNegative*, *AlmostZero*, and *SmallPositive* in the same figure are symmetrical. Fuzzy sets are also usually arranged evenly over the domain of a variable. An arrangement as in Figure 3-(c) is typical, for example. Another finding considers the labelling of fuzzy sets. For the variable *TrackingError* in Figure 3 these labels are *LargeNegative*, *SmallNegative*, *AlmostZero*, *SmallPositive*, and *LargePositive*. These labels make the system more understandable, but in the end, a label is only a label, it does not really determine the functioning of the system. For example, it is possible to replace these labels by the labels A, B, C, D, and E. If all labels are replaced consistently then the behavior of the system wouldn't change a bit. These observations combined lead us towards adaptive fuzzy sets and self-similarity.

2.1 Adaptive Fuzzy Sets and Self-similarity

This section uses Figure 4 below to introduce the concepts of adaptive fuzzy sets and self-similarity. Later in this section we describe how *RobSim* aims to exploit these concepts in future realizations.

Figure 4 illustrates various scenarios where linguistic variables are modelled via a collection of fuzzy sets. For example, Figure 4-(a) illustrates that the same set of labels and the same set of fuzzy sets (in terms of shape and arrangement) can be used for the description of two entirely different concepts, namely the variable *TrackingError*, but also a scenario involving an *AccountBalance* variable. Figure 4-(b) illustrates a case where the shape and arrangement of fuzzy sets remains static, but the domain of a variable undergoes change. In both cases the variable is called *Speed*, but in case one the variable domain is

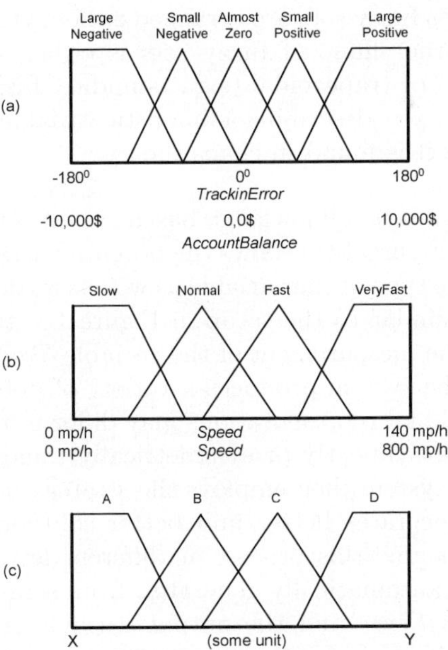

Fig. 4. Various linguistic variables and arrangements of fuzzy sets demonstrating the concepts of adaptive fuzzy sets and self-similarity

[0, .., 140] mp/h, whereas in case two it is [0, .., 800] mp/h. The first domain might be useful for indicating the speeds of vehicles on a highway, whereas the second domain might be useful for indicating the speeds of faster vehicles, an aeroplane, for example. It is possible to say then that the set of fuzzy sets for this variable is similar under different scales of magnification, where magnification relates to different domains. In chaos theory this feature is interpreted as self-similarity. The concept of self-similarity achieved recognition when it emerged in the analysis of the question: "How long is the coast line of England?" Since then it was studied in many contexts including Cantor sets, the famous Koch snowflake, neural networks, fractals, and fuzzy logic, for example [5], [6], [7]. Figure 4-(a) and Figure 4-(b) also illustrate the main characteristics and the main working of adaptive fuzzy sets. In general we can say that adaptive fuzzy sets are a collection of fuzzy sets that adjust to particular changes in an adaptive, dynamic way, for example, by changing the domain of a variable, the type of a variable, or both. Figure 4 reveals even more. From experience we know that in many FCS applications the arrangement of fuzzy sets representing a variable is either symmetric or linear. For example, in Figure 4-(a) the fuzzy sets are arranged symmetrically around the value zero, whereas in Figure 4-(b) the arrangement is linear (from 0 to 140 mp/h, or from 0 to 800 mp/h). These findings can be summarized as follows:

- There is almost always a logical order for linguistic variables.
- Good labelling is a good practice in many applications. But, for correct functioning labelling is not essential.
- In most applications fuzzy sets are arranged either symmetrically or linearly.
- In many systems the shape of fuzzy sets is either symmetrical (e.g., in-between fuzzy sets) or trapezoidal (e.g., boundary fuzzy sets).
- A collection of fuzzy sets describing a linguistic variable may show the feature of self-similarity as it is found in chaos theory.

Figure 4-(c) indicates how a knowledge-based system such as *RobSim* can exploit this information. Figure 4-(c) shows the potential arrangement of fuzzy sets for a variable. So far the type of the variable as well as its domain are not defined. Imagine now a setup similar to the setup in Figure 1 with a system having an integrated sensor for the measurement of the variable *TrackingError* introduced earlier. In this setup the system produces a variety of potential representations for this variable. Individual representations may differ in their variable domain, the domain arrangement (linearly or symmetrically), and the number of fuzzy sets, for example. The system then employs the strategy described earlier where a GA incrementally generates better and better solutions to the problem. It is possible again to imagine this process at different levels of complexity. The system presented here automatically generates, from scratch, fuzzy sets for the input variable *TrackingError* and the output variable *AzimuthAdjust* for the tracking scenario mentioned in Section 1.

3   Application Development and Results

The current system is implemented using the Delphi programming language.
The system was tested in several experimental investigations. In these tests the
main GA parameters were set to: number of iterations = 35, number of FCSs in
a population = 30, crossover rate = 20, mutation rate = 5, time series produced
by FCS = 100 data points. Table 1 below provides a snapshot illustrating some
of the data produced in these investigations.

Table 1. Some of the data generated in the *RobSim* study. Please note that the values
in this table stand representatively for our study.

Variable	Start population (random settings)	Final population (GA driven)
Arrangement input	linear	symmetric
Arrangement output	symmetric	symmetric
Number of fuzzy sets input	4	4
Number of fuzzy sets output	4	4
Left border input	-32^0	-112.4
Right border input	158.6^0	112.4
Left border output	-24^0	-94.1
Right border output	24^0	94.1
...	...	...

Table 1 contains three columns. Column one identifies some of the FCS variables involved in the modelling task. Column two and column three hold particular values for these variables. The difference between the two columns is that
the values in column two are taken from a FCS produced in the start population
(i.e., they are generated by a process involving a random element). On the other
hand, the values in column three are taken from the final population, and so
should be driven to higher quality by the GA. Essentially, the FCSs produced in
the final population are the solutions proposed by *RobSim*. For example, Table 1
illustrates that in one of the FCSs generated in the start population the arrangement of the fuzzy sets for variable *TrackingError* is "linear", and "symmetric"
for variable *AzimuthAdjust*. According to column two both variables are modelled by four fuzzy sets. Column two also indicates domain $[-32^0, .., 158.6^0]$ for
variable *TrackingError*, and domain $[-24^0, .., 24^0]$ for variable *AzimuthAdjust*.
Table 1 illustrates different values for the FCS produced in the final population.
Compared with the values for the start population these values represent an improvement. For example, the study behind Table 1 started with a *TrackingError*
of -60^0. This value is not covered by the domain $[-32^0, .., 158.6^0]$ given for the
FCS from the start population. One feature of *RobSim* is to consider cases like
this. In the current situation *RobSim* adjusts the domain for this particular FCS
"on the fly" in a predefined way. The GA ensures that FCSs indicating as being
better than other FCSs are propagated with a higher probability to forthcoming

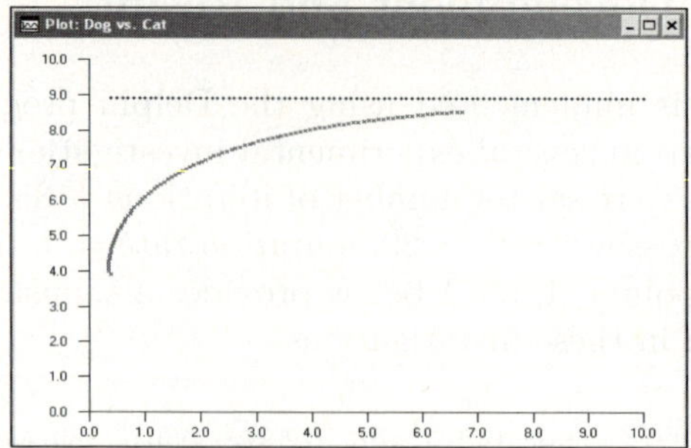

Fig. 5. Dynamic behavior of a solution generated by *RobSim* in the final population

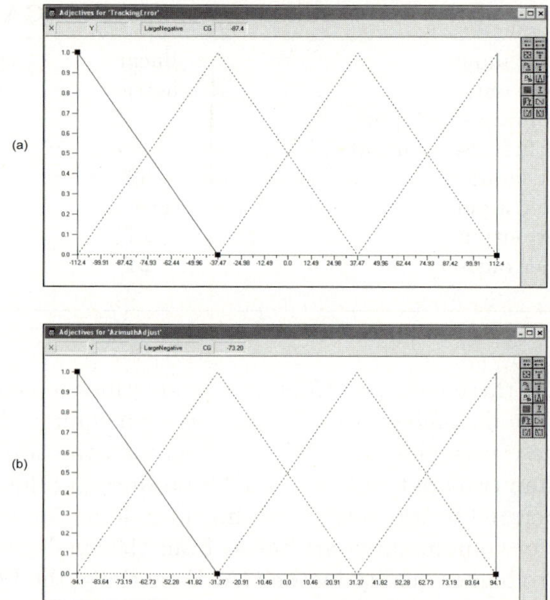

Fig. 6. Fuzzy sets for (a) input variable *TrackingError*, and (b) output variable *AzimuthAdjust*. The fuzzy sets are generated by *RobSim* in the final population.

populations. Our previous work described in detail the measures (measure of convergence, fractal dimension measures) *RobSim* employs for this task. A discussion of them therefore is omitted here. Anyway, in Table 1 we can see that the domain $[-112.4^0, .., 112.4^0]$ given for the FCS from the final population covers the value -60^0.

Earlier we mentioned that a final assessment of the quality of proposed solutions generated by *RobSim* is undertaken by the system developers. This assessment includes analysis of various data items produced by *RobSim*. For example, *RobSim* records relevant data for all FCSs (start population, intermediate populations, and final population). This data was compared against data that was available through the commercial CubiCalc software tool. Our analysis indicated in all instances that, on average, the FCSs in the final population were superior to the FCSs in the start population. Usually, several of the FCSs in the final population compared quite favorably in terms of their dynamic behavior to the solution provided by the commercial CubiCalc tool. For example, Figure 5 illustrates the dynamic behavior for the FCS from the final population in Table 1. Note that in order to generate this view the recorded data was imported into the commercial CubiCalc tool.

Further, Figure 6-(a) and Figure 6-(b) illustrate the variables *TrackingError* and *AzimuthAdjust* generated from data recorded for the FCS from the final population (Table 1). We want to emphasize again that the solutions illustrated in Figure 5, Figure 6-(a), and Figure 6-(b) stand representatively for the FCSs produced in the final population.

4 Discussion

One aspect that comes to mind is the fact that the current system exists as a software simulation where the environment and its problems are hard-coded in the simulation. The system therefore exhibits the problems typically associated with so-called micro-worlds [8]. To some extent we envisage our current efforts as a learning exercise. Our overall strategy is to learn and move from simple examples towards more complex and challenging applications. Ultimately we envisage the *RobSim* approach running on a real robot. We have undertaken preliminary steps into this direction already by investigating the potential of the commercial Lego MindStorms Robot kit as a potential platform for our system [9], [10]. These investigation revealed several limitations. The lack of sufficient memory in particular made the Lego kit unsuitable for our work. The Palm Pilot Robotic Kit developed by Carnegie Mellon robotics research groups appeares to be a more appropriate environment [11]. In this discussion we also want to acknowledge the huge amount of work, current and past, in the fields of robotics and soft computing. We feel that the *RobSim* approach presented here is a useful contribution to the field due to its unique character and value. *RobSim* is unique in its selection and combination of techniques, such as using fractal dimension measures and a measure of convergence, both derived from chaos theory, for the generation of a GA fitness value, for example. The relationship between adaptive fuzzy sets and self-similarity also represents an interesting feature of the system. Finally, it is not only the combination of these techniques that make *RobSim* and interesting R&D project, it is also the positive and encouraging results we have generated in our study that motivate us to further develop the system.

5 Summary

This paper presented the so-called *RobSim* system. *RobSim* is a hybrid robot control system, and is based on soft computing techniques. The system presented in the paper is an extension of previous work. The paper concentrated on a particular aspect of the system, the dynamic construction of various parts of a FCS. We presented results from various experimental investigations on the bases of a working *RobSim* implementation. These results are encouraging in our view. Compared to earlier versions the current system demonstrates increased functionality, increased adaptability, and greater flexibility, extending the problem solving potential of the system to a wider range of applications. The paper also reported briefly on how the current *RobSim* simulation may be moved into a more realistic environment in the form of commercial robot kits available today.

References

1. Schuster, A., Blackburn, W.T., Segu Prieto, M.: A study on fractal dimensions and convergence in fuzzy control systems. Journal of Telecommunication and Information Technology, **3** (2002) 30–36
2. Schuster, A.: "Using chaos theory for the genetic learning of fuzzy controllers". Proceedings of 17th International Conference on Industrial and Engineering Applications of Artificial Intelligence and Expert Systems IEA/AIE'04, Ottawa, Canada. Eds: Orchard B., Yang C., and Moonis A. Lecture Notes in Artificial Intelligence LNAI. **3029** (2004) 382–391
3. Ross, T.J.: Fuzzy logic with engineering applications. McGraw-Hill, New York, London, (1995)
4. Chen, S.J., Hwang, C.L.: Fuzzy multiple attribute decision making, methods and applications. Springer Verlag, Berlin, Heidelberg, (1992)
5. Mandelbrot, B.B.: The fractal geometry of nature. Freeman W.H. and Company, New York, (1977)
6. Kaye, B.H.: A random walk through fractal dimensions. Ed. Weinheim, Cambridge, New York, NY, VCH, (1989)
7. Grim, P.: Self-reference and chaos in fuzzy logic. IEEE Transactions on Fuzzy Systems, **1:4** (1993) 237–253
8. Brighton, H., Selina, H., Appignanesi, R.: Introducing artificial intelligence. Totem Books, (2004)
9. Kelly, S., Schuster, A.: Application of a fuzzy controller on a Lego MindStorms robot. 1st International Conference on Automation, Control and Instrumentation IADAT-aci2005, Bilbao, Spain, 2-4 February (2005) 200–203
10. Lego MindStorms, `http://mindstorms.lego.com` (Accessed 10 Nov 2005)
11. Palm Pilot Robotic Kit, `http://www.cs.cmu.edu/~reshko/PILOT/` (Accessed 10 Nov 2005)

A Combination Genetic Algorithm with Applications on Portfolio Optimization

Jiah-Shing Chen and Jia-Leh Hou

National Central University, Jungli, Taiwan 320
{jschen, alexhou}@mgt.ncu.edu.tw

Abstract. This paper proposes a combination genetic algorithm (GA) for solving the combination optimization problems which can not be naturally solved by standard GAs. A combination encoding scheme and genetic operators are designed for solving combination optimization problems. We apply this combination GA to the portfolio optimization problem which can be reformulated approximately as a combination optimization problem. Experimental results show that the proposed combination GA is effective in solving the portfolio optimization problem.

1 Introduction

There are four common types of combinatorial problems: arrangement, permutation, combination, and combination with repetition. The sizes of their solution spaces are listed below.

Arrangement: There are n^r ways of ordering r of n distinct objects with repetitions.

Permutation: There are $P(n, r) = n!/(n - r)!$ ways of ordering r of n distinct objects without repetitions.

Combination: There are $C(n, r) = n!/r!(n-r)!$ ways of selecting r of n distinct objects without repetitions.

Combination with repetitions: There are $C(n + r - 1, r)$ ways of selecting r of n distinct objects with repetitions.

Arrangement problems can be solved naturally by standard genetic algorithms. Permutation genetic algorithms have been developed to solve permutation optimization problems. However, few studies have been done on using genetic algorithms for combination optimization problems.

This paper proposes a combination genetic algorithm for solving combination optimization problems. In particular, the combination genetic algorithm is applied to the portfolio optimization problem which can be reformulated approximately as a combination optimization problem.

Our experimental results show that the performances of our combination GA are better than those of uniform allocation on return and downside risk.

The rest of this paper is organized as follows. Section 2 summarizes various genetic algorithms. Section 3 reviews the research on the portfolio optimization problem. Section 4 describes our combination genetic algorithm. Section 5

M. Ali and R. Dapoigny (Eds.): IEA/AIE 2006, LNAI 4031, pp. 197–206, 2006.

presents the experimental design and results of our combination GA on the portfolio optimization problem. Section 6 gives our concluding remarks.

2 Overview of Genetic Algorithms

Genetic algorithms (GA) were proposed by Holland in 1975 from Darwin's theory of evolution: survival of the fittest [1]. Genetic algorithms uses an evolutionary process resulting in a fittest solution to solve a problem. The evolutionary process consists of several genetic operators: selection, crossover and mutation [2, 3, 4, 5, 6].

Genetic algorithms are computationally simple and powerful. Genetic algorithms are very good tool for optimization problems since they make no restrictive assumptions about the solution space.

The advantage of GAs is in their parallelism. GA searches a solution space using a population of individuals so that they are less likely to get stuck in local optimums. This is achieved with a cost, i.e., the computational time. GAs can be slower than other methods. However, the longer run time of GAs can be shortened by terminating the evolution earlier to get a satisfactory solution.

2.1 The Basic Genetic Algorithm

To solve a problem with genetic algorithms, an encoding mechanism must first be designed to represent each solution as a chromosome, e.g., a binary string. A fitness function is also required to measure the goodness of a chromosome. Genetic algorithms search the solution space using a population which is simply a set of chromosomes. During each generation, the three genetic operators: selection, crossover and mutation, are applied to the population several times to form a new population. Selection picks 2 chromosomes according to their fitness: a fitter chromosome has a higher probability of being selected. Crossover recombine the 2 selected chromosomes to form new offsprings with a crossover rate. Mutation randomly alters each position in each offspring with a small mutation rate. New population is then generated by replacing some chromosomes with new offsprings. This process is repeated until some termination condition, e.g., the number of generations, is reached. Figure 1 shows the pseudo code of the basic genetic algorithm. When the number of genetic applications (k) is half the population size $(n/2)$, the GA is called generational GA; when $k < n/2$, it is called steady-state GA.

There are many parameters and settings that can be implemented differently in genetic algorithms. The first question to ask is how to encode a solution as a chromosome. Selection, crossover, and mutation can also be done in several ways.

2.2 Encoding

Encoding of chromosomes is the first question to ask when starting to solve a problem with GA. Encoding depends on the problem heavily. The most common encoding in GA is binary encoding. Value encoding, permutation encoding and tree encoding have also been used.

```
procedure BasicGA
   Initialization: Generate a random population of n chromosomes
   while (termination condition is not satisfied)
      Evaluation: Evaluate the fitness of each chromosome in the population
      loop (do genetic applications k times for each generation)
         Selection: Select 2 chromosomes according to their fitness
         Crossover: Cross over selected chromosomes to form new offsprings with a crossover rate
         Mutation: Mutate each position in each new offspring with a mutation rate
      endloop
      Replacement: Replace chromosomes in parent population with new offsprings
   endwhile
   Report the best solution (chromosome) found
endprocedure
```

Fig. 1. The basic genetic algorithm

Binary encoding: Every chromosome is a string of bits, 0 or 1. Binary encoding is the most common one, mainly because the first research of GA used this type of encoding and because of its relative simplicity.

Value encoding: Every chromosome is a sequence of some values. Values can be anything connected to the problem, such as (real) numbers, chars or objects. Direct value encoding can be used in problems where some more complicated values such as real numbers are used. Use of binary encoding for this type of problems would be difficult.

Permutation encoding: Every chromosome is a permutation of numbers in which each number appears exactly once. Permutation encoding is useful for ordering problems, such as traveling salesman problem or task ordering problem.

2.3   Selection

The selection method determines how chromosomes are selected from the population to be parents for crossover. Better parents are usually selected with the hope that they have a better chance of producing better offsprings. There are many methods in selecting parent chromosomes. Examples are roulette wheel selection, rank selection, integral roulette wheel selection, and tournament selection.

2.4   Crossover

Crossover operates on selected genes from parent chromosomes to create new offsprings. Crossover methods depend on the underlying encoding of chromosomes.

Binary Encoding: Common crossover methods for binary encoding include one-point crossover, two-point crossover, n-point crossover, uniform crossover, and arithmetic crossover [4].

Value Encoding: All crossover methods for binary encoding can be used for value encoding.

Permutation Encoding: Special crossover operators are needed to ensure that the resulting offsprings are still valid permutations. Crossover operators for permutation encoding include order crossover (OX) [7], partially mapped crossover (PMX) [8], cycle crossover (CX) [9], and position based crossover (POS) [10].

2.5   Mutation

Mutation is intended to prevent all solutions in the population falling into a local optimum of the solution space. A mutation operator randomly changes the offspring resulted from crossover. The technique of mutation also depends on the encoding of chromosomes.

Binary Encoding: Mutation methods for binary encoding include bit inversion and re-initialization.
Value Encoding: For a real-valued gene, a random number from a suitable distribution is added.
Permutation Encoding: Mutation methods for permutation encoding include exchange mutation, insertion mutation, displacement mutation, simple inversion mutation, inversion mutation, and scramble mutation.

3   Background

3.1   Portfolio Optimization Problem

The portfolio optimization problem can be formulated as follows:

$$
\begin{aligned}
\max\ & \alpha \sum_i x_i r_i - (1 - \alpha) \sum_{ij} x_i x_j \sigma_{ij} \\
\text{subject to}\ & \sum_{i=0}^{n} x_i = 1,\ 0 \le x_i \le 1,\ x_i \in R,
\end{aligned}
\tag{1}
$$

where α is a real constant between 0 & 1, x_i is the proportion (between 0 & 1) of capital invested in instrument i, r_i is the expected return rate of instrument i and σ_{ij} is the risk (standard deviation) of instrument i. The objective is to find the optimal portfolio with maximum return and/or minimum risk).

Traditional approach to this portfolio problem is Markowitz's mean-variance analysis [11] which uses the Lagrange multiplier method to find the optimal static portfolio.

3.2   Genetic Algorithms on Portfolio Optimization Problem

The easiest way to use GAs on the portfolio problem is to encode each weight x_i as a nonnegative integer or floating number. Standard genetic operators can then be applied as usual. To enforce the $\sum_{i=0}^{n} x_i = 1$ constraint, normalization of each x_i by dividing their sum $\sum_{i=0}^{n} x_i$ is usually required [12].

One problem with this encoding method is that many chromosomes decode into the same portfolio. This multiplies the GA's search space and makes GA less efficient in finding the optimal portfolio. Another problem with normalization is that similar chromosomes may decode into very different portfolios which makes it more difficult for GA to produce better chromosomes from good chromosomes.

4   Combination Genetic Algorithms

The real number model of portfolio problem in (1) can be approximated by the following integer model with large m to achieve the desired precision.

$$\max \; \alpha \sum_i \frac{w_i}{m} \cdot r_i - (1 - \alpha) \sum_{ij} \frac{w_i}{m} \cdot \frac{w_j}{m} \cdot \sigma_{ij}$$

$$\text{subject to} \; \sum_{i=0}^{n} w_i = m, \; 0 \leq w_i \leq m, \; w_i \in Z, \tag{2}$$

where m is a large positive integer, w_i/m approximates the x_i in (1) and the constraints become $\sum_{i=0}^{n} w_i = m$, $0 \leq w_i \leq m$, & $w_i \in Z$. This turns the portfolio optimization problem into the combination optimization problem and reduces the search space to nonnegative integers such that $\sum_{i=0}^{n} w_i = m$, whose size is C_m^{n+m}.

Standard GAs are not suitable to solve the combination optimization problem. We therefore propose a combination GA to solve the combination optimization problem. Its encoding and genetic operators are developed accordingly.

4.1   Combination Encoding

The integer solutions for the constraint $\sum_{i=0}^{n} w_i = m$ have one-to-one correspondence with the $n + m$-bit strings containing exactly m 1's. We therefore use binary strings (of length $n + m$) with a fixed number (m) of 1's as encoding. For example, the chromosome 1110110 represents that $w_0 = 3$, $w_1 = 2$ and $w_2 = 0$.

The implication of this combination encoding scheme is that each chromosome must have a certain number (m) of 1's initially, after crossover, and after mutation. Initial chromosome can be easily generated by randomly m of $n + m$ bits to 1's. The exchange mutation, which exchanges two randomly selected genes, for permutation encoding can also be used for combination encoding. The crossover operator for combination encoding requires special attention to conform to the m 1's constraint.

4.2   Combination Crossover

Standard crossover operators for binary encoding have a high probability of violating the m 1's constraint. There are several ways to conform to the m 1's constraint. One way is to restrict the crossover points so that the crossovered sections have the same number of 1's. When the selected crossover points do not satisfy this condition, the crossover points are reselected until they do. This may require a large number of reselecting crossover points.

Another way to conform to the m 1's constraint is to repair the violating chromosomes after crossover. Assume that the violating chromosome has k 1's. If there are fewer than m 1's (i.e., $k < m$), then $m-k$ 0's are randomly selected to be changed to 1's. One the other hand, if there are more than m 1's (i.e., $k > m$), then $k - m$ 1's are randomly selected to be changed to 0's. Although the repair makes a chromosome feasible, it also makes the chromosome less similar to its parents.

Instead of the above two methods, we propose a shrinking crossover (SX). SX revises the two-point crossover to exchange the same number of 1's by moving the second crossover point leftward until there are equal number of 1's between the two crossover points as shown in Figure 2.

```
procedure SX(C1, C2, s, t)
    until (C1 and C2 have the same number of 1's between s & t)
        t = t-1
    enduntil
    for (i = s to t)
        Temp = C1 [i]
        C1 [i] = C2 [i]
        C2 [i] = Temp
    endfor
endprocedure
```

Fig. 2. Algorithm of the shrinking crossover (SX)

5   Experiments

The integer portfolio optimization as in (2) is basically a single period model as is the real number version in (1). To make the resulting portfolio changing with time, instead of designating each i to a fixed security, the designation is changed every period similar to the ordering technique in [12] which requires $r_i \geq r_{i+1}$.

To test our combination GA in solving the dynamic integer portfolio optimization problem, stock listed and traded in the Taiwan Stock Exchange are used as our targets. Two stock selection/ordering criteria are used: top price and top monthly price gain percentage. Portfolios are generated and evaluated by the sliding time window method [13] as shown in Figure 3. Portfolios are generated using ℓ months' historical data ($ell = 3 - 6$) and are tested for 1 month before new stocks are selected and new portfolios are generated again. This process is repeated to move with time every month for the whole $k = 36$ months of testing period. The returns are calculated after all transaction costs and taxes were deducted. In our simulations, the number n of selected stocks is 20 with each $i = 1 - 20$ designating the i-th selected stock and $i = 0$ designating the cash. The total capital is divided into $m = 50$ equal portions.

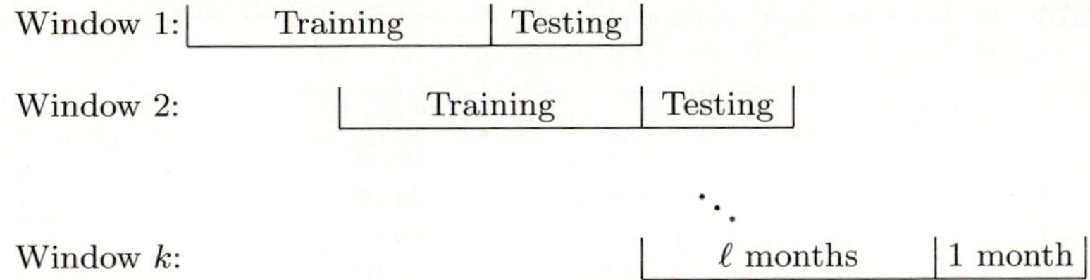

Fig. 3. Sliding time window simulation

5.1 Fitness Function

The fitness of a chromosome is evaluated by its performance in the training period. We use the final wealth as the fitness function of our combination GA, which is defined as

$$f(w_0, w_1, \ldots, w_n) = \prod_{t=1}^{\ell}(1 + r_p(t)),$$

where $r_p(t) = \sum_{i=0}^{n} w_i r_i(t)$ is the return of the portfolio during month t in the training period.

5.2 The GA Parameters

The settings used in our combination GA runs are described as follow.

The weights of a portfolio are represented in a chromosome as a 70-bit binary string with 50 1's. As a result, The GA search space becomes

$$C_{50}^{70} = \frac{70!}{50!20!} \approx 1.6 \times 10^{17}.$$

The population size is 200. The selection method is roulette wheel. The crossover method is our SX crossover with a crossover rate of 100%. The mutation method is exchange mutation with a mutation rate of 0.5% per bit. Termination condition is simply fixed generations and the number of generations is set to 500.

5.3 Experimental Results

We use two stock selection/ordering criteria: top price and top monthly price gain percentage. Each selection criterium is trained for 4 different training lengths, $\ell = 3 - 6$.

Table 1 shows the accumulated test period returns of the top $n = 20$ priced stocks selected every month for the 4 training periods. The returns range from 18% to 30% with an average of 22.85%, each of which is better than the uniform allocation's -35.97% return.

The testing period equity curves of the top $n = 20$ priced stocks selected every month for the 4 training periods is shown in Figure 4. The equity curves

Table 1. Accumulated testing period returns of top $n = 20$ priced stocks

Training length	Return (%)
$\ell = 3$	18.37
$\ell = 4$	24.98
$\ell = 5$	30.02
$\ell = 6$	18.03
Average	22.85
Uniform	-35.97

Table 2. Accumulated testing period returns of top $n = 20$ stocks of price gain percentage

Training length	Return (%)
$\ell = 3$	72.76
$\ell = 4$	100.09
$\ell = 5$	-17.33
$\ell = 6$	39.49
Average	48.75
Uniform	-46.42

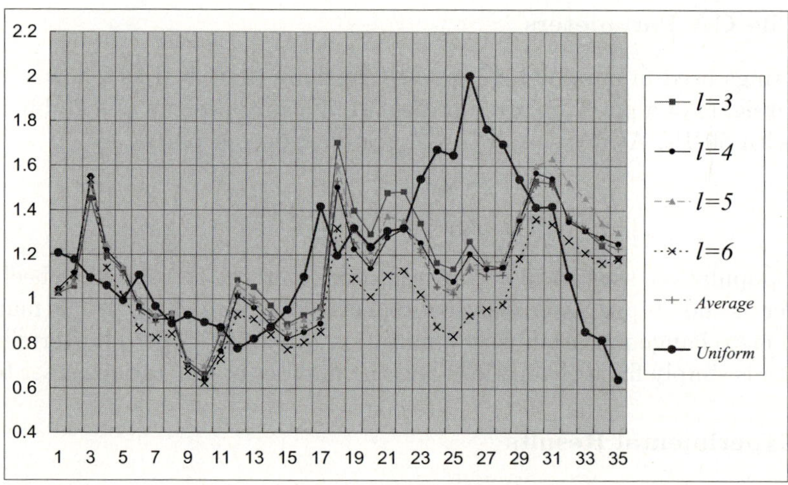

Fig. 4. Equity curves of top 20 priced stocks

of combination GA runs have a smaller fluctuation than that of the uniform allocation.

Table 2 shows the accumulated test period returns of the top $n = 20$ stocks of price gain percentage selected every month for the 4 training periods. The returns range from -17% to 100% with an average of 48.75%, each of which is better than the uniform allocation's -46.42% return.

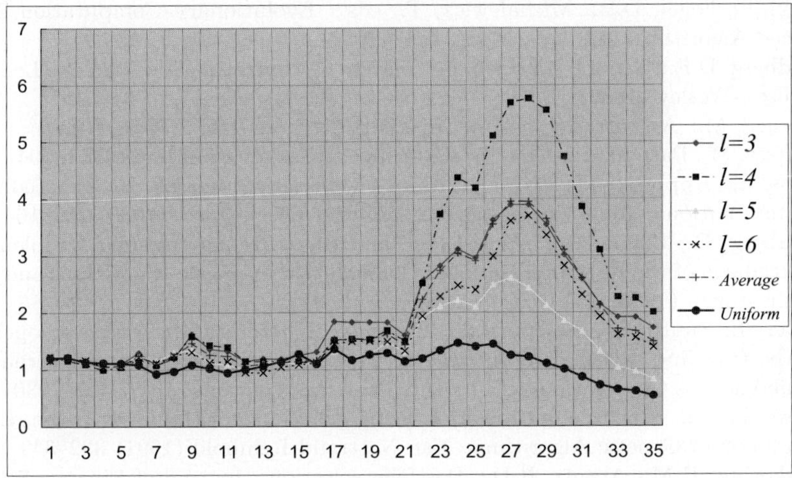

Fig. 5. Equity curves of top $n = 20$ stocks of price gain percentage

The testing period equity curves of the top $n = 20$ stocks of price gain percentage selected every month for the 4 training periods is shown in Figure 5. The equity curves of combination GA runs are mostly above the uniform allocation's during the whole testing period.

From the results of these two sets of experiments, there are evidences to indicate that the combination GA can produce higher returns and/or lower risks.

6 Conclusion

This study develops a combination genetic algorithm for combination optimization problems. The combination GA is applied to the integer portfolio optimization problem. The experimental results demonstrate the feasibility and effectiveness of the combination GA for the integer portfolio optimization problem. The success of combination GA on the integer portfolio optimization suggests it be applied to other combination optimization problems in general.

Future directions of this research include the development of other combination crossover and mutation operators. Designing more sophisticated selection and trading strategies for combination genetic algorithms on the portfolio optimization problem is another interesting direction.

References

1. Holland, J.H.: Adaptation in Natural and Artificial Systems: An Introductory Analysis with Applications to Biology, Control, and Artificial Intelligence. University of Michigan Press (1975)
2. Bäck, T., Fogel, D.B., Michalewicz, T., eds.: Evolutionary Computation 1: Basic Algorithms and Operators. IOP (2000)

3. Bäck, T., Fogel, D.B., Michalewicz, T., eds.: Evolutionary Computation 2: Advanced Algorithms and Operators. IOP (2000)
4. Goldberg, D.E.: Genetic Algorithm in Search, Optimization and Machine Learning. Addison-Wesley (1989)
5. Mitchell, M.: An Introduction to Genetic Algorithms. MIT Press (1996)
6. Srinivas, M., Patnaik, L.: Genetic algorithms: A survey. Computer **27** (1994) 17–26
7. Davis, L.: Applying adaptive algorithms to epistatic domains. In: Proceedings of the International Joint Conference on Artificial Intelligence. (1985) 162–164
8. Goldberg, D., Lingle, R.: Alleles, loci, and the traveling salesman problem. In: Proceedings of the First International Conference on Genetic Algorithms and Their Applications. (1985) 154–159
9. Oliver, I., Smith, D., Holland., J.: A study of permutation crossover operators on the traveling salesman problem. In: Proceedings of the Second International Conference on Genetic Algorithms and Their Applications. (1987) 224–230
10. Syswerda, G.: Schedule optimization using genetic algorithms. In Davis, L., ed.: Handbook of Genetic Algorithms. Van Nostrand Reinhold (1991) 332–349
11. Markowitz, H.M., Arnott, R.D.: Portfolio selection. Journal of Finance **7** (1952) 77–91
12. Xia., Y., Liu, B., Wang, S., Lai, K.K.: A model for portfolio selection with order of expected returns. Computers and Operations Research (2000) 409–422
13. Kimoto, T., Asakawa, K., Yoda, M., Takeoka, M.: Stock market prediction system with modular neural networks. In: Proceedings of the 1990 International Joint Conference on Neural Networks. (1990) 1–6

Genetic Algorithm-Based Improvement of Robot Hearing Capabilities in Separating and Recognizing Simultaneous Speech Signals[*]

Shun'ichi Yamamoto[1], Kazuhiro Nakadai[2], Mikio Nakano[2], Hiroshi Tsujino[2],
Jean-Marc Valin[3], Ryu Takeda[1], Kazunori Komatani[1],
Tetsuya Ogata[1], and Hiroshi G. Okuno[1]

[1] Graduate School of Informatics, Kyoto University, Japan
{shunichi, rtakeda, komatani, ogata, okuno}@kuis.kyoto-u.ac.jp
[2] Honda Research Institute Japan Co., Ltd., Japan
{nakadai, nakano, tsujino}@jp.honda-ri.com
[3] CSIRO ICT Centre, Ausralia
Jean-Marc.Valin@sciro.edu

Abstract. Since a robot usually hears a mixture of sounds, in particular, simultaneous speech signals, it should be able to *localize*, *separate*, and *recognize* each speech signal. Since separated speech signals suffer from spectral distortion, normal automatic speech recognition (ASR) may fail in recognizing such distorted speech signals. Yamamoto *et al.* proposed using the Missing Feature Theory to mask corrupt features in ASR, and developed the automatic missing-feature-mask generation (AMG) system by using information obtained by sound source separation (SSS). Our evaluations of recognition performance of the system indicate possibilities for improving it by optimizing many of its parameters. We used genetic algorithms to optimize these parameters. Each chromosome consists of a set of parameters for SSS and AMG, and each chromosome is evaluated by recognition rate of separated sounds. We obtained an optimized sets of parameters for each distance (from 50 cm to 250 cm by 50 cm) and direction (30, 60, and 90 degree intervals) for two simultaneous speech signals. The average isolated word recognition rates ranged from 84.9% to 94.7%.

Keywords: Robot-human interaction, Speech recognition, Sound source separation, Simultaneous Speakers, Microphone array, Robot audition.

1 Introduction

Since speech communications are essential in human-human interactions, robot-human interaction should also be based primarily on speech communications. Voiced speech signals in daily communications are usually superimposed with additional sounds including environmental noises. As people with normal hearing capabilities can hear

[*] This research was partially supported by the Ministry of Education, Culture, Sports, Science and Technology, Grant-in-Aid for Scientific Research and COE Program of Informatics Research Center for Development of Knowledge Society Infrastructure, and TAF and SCAT Grants.

M. Ali and R. Dapoigny (Eds.): IEA/AIE 2006, LNAI 4031, pp. 207–217, 2006.

many of these under various conditions, robots need to have similar capabilities for symbiosis to occur between robots and people in the real-world. In other words, *robot audition*, i.e., where a robot hears sounds with its own ears installed within its body [7], should be able to cope with simultaneous speech signals originating from various directions and distances. Tasaki *et al.* expanded the concept of *Proxemics*, which classifies the interaction distance into private, personal, social and public, to develop the *location-based interaction scheme* [9, 10]. Their scheme requires recognizing a mixture of speech signals originating from various locations in different directions and at different distances.

Robot audition requires sound source localization and separation, and the recognition of separated sounds. Although the number of research on robot audition has increased in recent years, most efforts have focused on sound source localization and separation. Only a few researchers have focused on simultaneous speech signals, sound source separation (SSS), and the recognition of separated sounds. The humanoid, *HRP-2*, uses a microphone array to localize and separate a mixture of sounds, and can recognize speech commands for a robot in noisy environments [4]. *HRP-2*, however, only focused on a single speech signal. The humanoid robot *SIG* uses a pair of microphones to separate multiple speech signals with the *Adaptive Direction-Pass Filter* and recognizes each separated speech signal by automatic speech recognition (ASR) [5]. When three speakers uttered words, *SIG* recognized what each speaker had said. Yamamoto *et al.* recently developed a new interfacing scheme between SSS and ASR based on the Missing Feature Theory (MFT), which uses missing-feature masks to avoid corrupt features, used in ASR's decoding process to improve recognition [12]. They demonstrated that their interfacing scheme worked well for different types of humanoids, i.e., *SIG-2*, *Replie*, and *ASIMO* with manually created missing-feature masks.

Yamamoto, and Valin *et al.* further developed *Automatic-missing-feature Mask Generation (AMG)* by using a microphone array system consisting of eight microphones to separate sound sources. Their SSS consisted of two components [11]:*Geometric Source Separation (GSS)* [8] and the *Multi-Channel Post-Filter (MCPF)* [11, 1]; the former separated each sound source by using an adaptive beamformer with the geometric constraints of microphones, while the latter refined each separated sound by taking channel-leak and background noises into account. They developed AMG by using information obtained with MCPF to generate missing-feature masks for all separated sounds.

In applying an MFT-based interface to a location-based interaction scheme, we found that ASR depended significantly on location, i.e., direction and distance. Recognition for speakers at around 200 cm from the center direction was the best, while that for speakers at peripherals or close locations was lowest. A preliminary experiment on changing one of the most important parameters revealed that recognition was improved by 10% from the default setting used by Yamamoto, *et al.* [13].

The purpose of this study was to optimize the parameters for separating sound sources and generating automatic missing feature masks to improve the recognition of simultaneous speech signals. Since interfering sounds such as speech signals dynamically change and common noise suppression techniques cannot thus be applied, we adopted the *Genetic Algorithm (GA)* [3] to optimize these parameters. The rest of the paper is organized as follows: Section 2 explains SSS and ASR, focusing on important parameters. Section 3 describes the GA to obtain a set of optimized parameters. Section 4 describes the experiments we did for evaluation, and Section 5 discusses the results and observations. Section 6 concludes the paper.

2 Recognition System of Simultaneous Speech Signals

The system recognizing system for simultaneous speech signals is described in this section in terms of parameters that should be optimized. The system [13] consists of two subsystems, *Microphone Array Source Separation (MASS)* and ASR. Both of them are integrated by MFT. There is an overview of the system in Fig. 1.

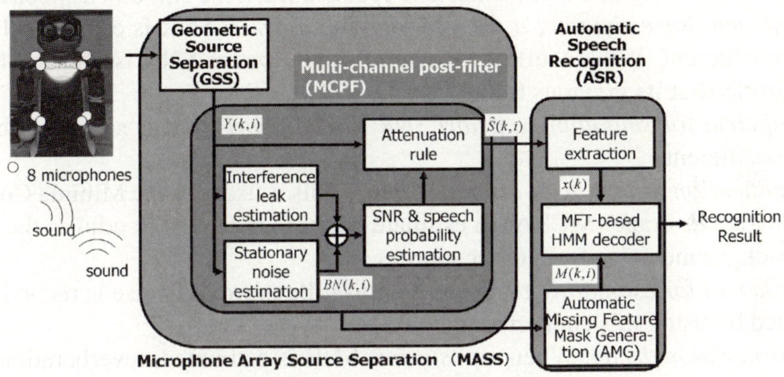

Fig. 1. System consists of sound source separation and automatic speech recognition

2.1 MASS (Microphone Array Source Separation)

MASS consists of GSS and MCPF. GSS was a linear separation system originally proposed by Parra *et al.* [8], and Valin *et al.* modified it to provide faster adaptation using a stochastic gradient and shorter time-frame estimates [11]. The initial separation by GSS was refined by MCPF, i.e., a generalization of beamformer post-filtering for multiple sources [1, 11]. This post-filter used adaptive spectral estimates of background noises and interfering sources to enhance the signal that was produced during the initial separation. The main idea is that, for each source of interest, the noise estimate is decomposed into stationary and transient components assumed to be due to leakage between the output channels at the initial separation stage. How stationary noise and nterference leaks are estimated is shown in Fig. 1.

We selected thirteen parameters for MASS; one for GSS, eleven for MCPF, and one for AMG (described later), as described below:

(1) *GSS adaptation rate*: This specifies how the separation matrix in GSS is updated. The larger it is, the faster the separation matrix meets specified constraints. However, if the adaptation rate is too large, the separation matrix cannot converge.

(2) *Leak-estimate factor*: This specifies how the interference from other sources is reduced in estimating leaks. It is likely to depend on the distances between sources and between the robot and the source.

(3) *Canceling rate of leak-estimate factor*: This adjusts the factor for estimating leaks in estimating leak noise.

(4) *Compensation for background noise*: This compensates for the estimated background noise in each frame. If it is large, the background noise is regarded as large.

(5) *Coefficient for smoothed spectrum*: The spectrum is recursively averaged in each time frame, and the leak is estimated from the spectrum. In smoothing, the smoothed spectrum is calculated from the output of GSS in the current frame and the smoothed spectrum in the previous frame. If the coefficient is large, the previous smoothed spectrum affects greatly the current smoothed spectrum.

(6) *Weight for reducing background noise*: The estimated background noise is multiplied by the weight, when the noise is reduced from the smoothed spectrum.

(7) *Coefficient for estimating a priori SNR*: The *a priori* SNR is estimated by using the coefficient. If the coefficient is small, the *a priori* SNR is affected by the *a priori* SNR at its previous frame.

(8) *Coefficient for smoothing a priori SNR* The *a priori* SNR is smoothed by using the coefficient.

(9) *Amplification rate for leak-estimate factor*: This is used for the Minima Controlled Recursive Average (MCRA) to estimate background noise. It adjusts the leakage of background noise from other sources.

(10) *Coefficient for estimating background noise*: Background noise is recursively averaged by using this coefficient.

(11) *Reverberation decay*: When *a posteriori* SNR is estimated, reverberation is used as a clue. This is calculated from the echo in the previous frame and the estimated source by GSS in the current frame. If reverberation time is long, reverberation decay should be small.

(12) *Instantaneous reverberation attenuation level*: This affects estimates of reverberation. If it is small, reverberation is regarded as small.

(13) *Threshold for AMG*: This is the most important factor, which will be explained in the next subsection.

2.2   MFT-Based ASR

AMG needs information about which spectral parts of a separated sound are distorted. This kind of information may be obtained by through MASS. We used post-filter gains as reference data to generate a missing-feature mask automatically. Since we used a feature vector with 48 spectral-related features, the missing-feature mask was a vector of 48 corresponding features. Each element of a vector represented the reliability of each feature [13]. We used a binary (1: reliable, or 0: unreliable) missing-feature mask.

Since MCPF is used to reduce the amount of interference in separated sounds, it also provides useful information about the amount of noise. We computed a missing-feature mask by comparing the input and output of MCPF. The feature is considered reliable for each mel-frequency band, if the ratio of output energy to input energy is greater than threshold T_{MFM}. The reason for this is that we assumed that the more noise present in a certain frequency band, the lower the post-filter gain would be for that band. A continuous missing- feature mask $m(k,i)$ is thus computed as:

$m(k,i) = \frac{S(k,i)+BN(k,i)}{Y(k,i)}$, where $Y(k,i)$ is the post-filter input and and $S(k,i)$ is the output energy both for frame k at mel-frequency band $i = 1, \cdots, \frac{N}{2}$, and $BN(k,i)$ is the background noise estimated for that band. The main reason for including noise estimate $BN(k,i)$ in the numerator of the equation is that it ensures that the missing-feature mask will be reliable (1) when no speech source is present. From continuous mask $m(k,i)$, we derive binary mask $M(k,i)$ as: $M(k,i) = 1$, if $m(k,i) > T_{MFM}$ and 0, otherwise. Here, T_{MFM} is the threshold for AMG. T_{MFM} mainly depends on interference leaks from other sources. For example, if the power level of a sound source is small, $m(k,i)$ may generally be small. Therefore T_{MFM} should be set to a large value.

2.3 ASR Based on MFT

MFT-based ASR is a variation of Hidden Markov Model (HMM) recognizers, which are commonly used by most ASRs [2]. The difference is only in the decoding process. In conventional ASR systems, estimating a path with maximum likelihood is based on state transition probabilities and the output probability in HMM. In the case of MFT-based recognition, estimating the output probability is different from conventional ASR systems. Let $M(i)$ be the MFM vector, which represents the reliability of acoustic features. Output probability $b_j(x)$ is given by

$$b_j(x) = \sum_{l=1}^{L} P(l|S_j) \exp \left\{ \sum_{i=1}^{N} M(i) \log f(x(i)|l, S_j) \right\}, \tag{1}$$

where $P(\cdot)$ is a probability operator, $x(i)$ is a feature vector, N is the size of the feature vector, and S_j is a jth state.

The Mel-Frequency Cepstrum Coefficient (MFCC) is commonly used in conventional ASR systems. However, we use Mel-Scale Log Spectral (MSLS) features, because AMG exploits estimates of corrupt spectral features.

3 Optimization of Parameters with GA

The optimization of parameters with GA [3] is discussed in this section. The parameters are detailed in Section 2. Alleles are generally fixed n the GA. However it was difficult to fix alleles in our case, because the ranges of the parameters were not sufficiently well known. To solve this, we adopted a method using an intentional bias.

3.1 Genotype: Representation of Each Individual

The representation of each individual, that is, a *genotype*, is defined by the lengths of the gene and alleles. In this paper, the length of the gene is fixed, and each allele is defined as a finite set. Since the goal was to search for parameters for our recognition system whose word correct rate (WCR) for ASR would be the highest in all cases, each locus was defined as each parameter as discussed in Section 2.1. Alleles were defined as all possible values of the parameter.

3.2   Genetic Algorithm: Cycle of Search for Optimization

The process to optimize the parameters with GA is as follows:

(1) *Initialization*: Let N be the size of the population. For an initial population, N individuals are generated, and all genes for each individual are decided at random.
(2) *Crossover*: M pairs of individuals are selected at random to produce $2M$ children, where M is the number of crossovers. Children are generated by uniform crossover. In crossing over, a bit sequence with the same length as a chromosome is generated at random. This bit sequence, called the mask pattern, is used to specify which parent's genes are passed on which child. Since generated children are added to the population, its size becomes $N + 2M$.
(3) *Mutation*: Each individual in the population mutates with mutation probability p_m. Each gene in our GA is replaced by an allele that is selected at random.
(4) *Calculation of fitness*: Fitness is defined as the WCR for ASR, which has parameters given by an individual, since our goal was to optimize parameters to obtain the best recognition for WCR.
(5) *Selection*: Since crossover increased the population to $N + 2M$, individuals are selected to decrease its size to N. Our method uses a combination of elite and roulette selection.
    (a) *Elite selection*: L Individuals with the highest fitness in the population ($N+2M$ individuals) are selected.
    (b) *Roulette selection*: $N - L$ individuals are selected from the remaining population. Individuals of higher fitness are selected with higher probability.
(6) *Evaluation of population*: If the mean fitness of all individuals in the current generation is close to that in the previous, i.e., the difference is less than T_{GA}, the population is considered to have converged and GA is terminated.

4   Experiments on Optimazing and Evaluating Parameters

The parameters in the experiments for the recognition system were optimized for WCR with GA. The benchmarks consisted of two and three simultaneous speech signals originating from various positions for different directions and at different distances.

4.1   Recording Conditions for Two and Three Simultaneous Speech Signals

We used Robovie-R2, which had eight microphones attached to its body (Fig. 1). Simultaneous speech signals were recorded in a room whose reverberation time was about 0.2 seconds (RT20) (see Fig. 3). All sounds were played through loudspeakers (Genelec 1029A), which were located at five different distances and in three different directions. The loudspeakers were located 50, 100, 150, 200, and 250 cm from the robot, and located every 30, 60, and 90 degrees. A set of loudspeakers was located at the same distance from the robot (see Fig. 2). Two simultaneous speech signals and three simultaneous speech signals were recorded under these conditions. In recording two simultaneous signals for one speaker and one piece of music, loudspeakers

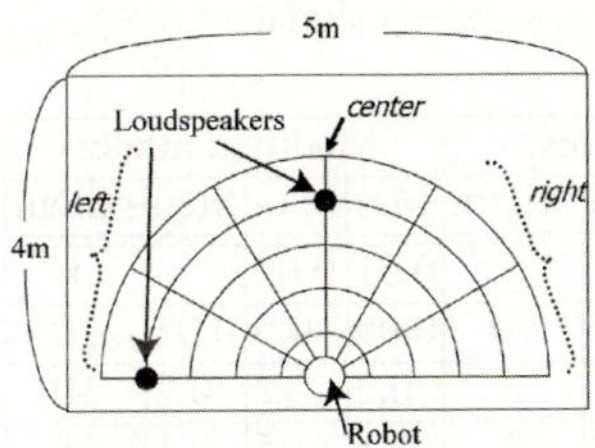

Fig. 2. Locations of Robovie-R2 and loudspeakers

Fig. 3. Three loudspeakers speaking to Robovie

Fig. 4. Three human speakers speaking to Robovie

were located 200 cm from the robot and located at 30, 60, and 90 degree intervals. There were 216 phonemically-balanced words playing from each loudspeaker.

Since one application of our system is the location-based interaction scheme proposed by Tasaki *et al.*, which chooses an appropriate person as an interaction partner and then faces her or him, we focused on recognition of the center speaker. Several scenarios for benchmarks were set up for this purpose. The recording data set were as follows:

[a] Two simultaneous speeches by speaker A at the left and speaker B in the center,
[b] Two simultaneous speeches by speaker C at the left and speaker A in the center,
[c] Three simultaneous speeches by speaker A at the left, speaker B in the center, and speaker D at the right,
[d] simultaneous speech by speaker A in the center and music A at the right,
[e] simultaneous speech by speaker A in the center and music B an the right,

where speakers A, B, and D were male, C was female, music A was Japanese pop music, music B was classical music. Only data set [a] was used to optimize parameters.

4.2 Speech Recognition by MFT-Based ASR

Multiband Julius was used for the MFT-based ASR [6]. Julius is a Japanese continuous speech recognizer with either stochastic language models or grammar-based language models. Multiband Julius is an extended Julius to recognize speech using MFT. We used a triphone in the experiments for the acoustic model with a grammar-based language model to recognize isolated words. The triphone is a HMM with three states and four mixtures in each state, and was trained on 216 phonemically balanced words developed by ATR. Vocabulary consisted of 200 words.

4.3 Parameters to Be Optimized Using GA

The genes for GA corresponded to the parameters of the recognition system and the alleles corresponding to the sets of possible values for it. They are listed in Table 1, where we can see the initial set of alleles and a modified set. The size of the population in the experiments, N, was 100, the number of crossovers, M, was 40, the number of elite selections, L, was 10, and the probability of mutation, p_m was 0.01.

Table 1. Parameters for system to recognize simultaneous speech signals

Genes (Parameters in recognition system)	Base-line	Initial alleles				Modified alleles			
		Min	Max	Step	#Elem	Min	Max	Step	#Elem
(1) *GSS adaptation rate*	0.01	0.01	0.05	0.01	5	0.01	0.01	–	1
(2) *Leak-estimate factor*	0.25	0.05	0.5	0.05	10	0.05	0.5	0.05	10
(3) *Canceling rate for leak-estimate factor*	1	0.6	2	0.2	8	0.2	2	0.2	10
(4) *Compensation for background noise*	1.2	0.6	8	0.2	2	0.1	1.5	0.1	15
(5) *Coefficient for smoothed spectrum*	0.5	0.5	1	0.1	6	0.1	0.8	0.1	8
(6) *Weight for reducing background noise*	0	0	1	0.1	11	0	1	0.1	11
(7) *Coefficient for estimating a priori SNR*	0.8	0.5	1	0.1	6	0.1	1	0.1	10
(8) *Coefficient for smoothed a priori SNR*	0.7	0.5	1	0.1	6	0.9	0.9	–	1
(9) *Amplification rate for leak-estimate-fact*	1.5	1	2	0.1	11	1	2	0.1	11
(10) *Coefficient for estimating BG-noise*	0.98	0.8	1	0.02	11	0.8	1	0.02	11
(11) *Reverberation decay*	0.5	0	0.9	0.1	10	0	0.5	0.05	11
(12) *Instantaneous reverb. attenuation level*	0.2	0	1	0.1	11	0	0.5	0.05	11
(13) *AMG threshold*	0.25	0	1	0.1	11	0	0.65	0.05	13

4.4 Results of Optimizing Parameters

The parameters for each location were only optimized for data set [a]. The progress of optimization in terms of fitness (WCR) are plotted in Fig. 5. The x-axis indicates generations, while the y-axis indicates the maximum fitness in the population. Sets of alleles are modified according to the results of the nineth generation in the tenth generation.

The results reveal that fitness was greatly improved even in the second generation in all cases except at 50 cm at 30 degree intervals. In addition, fitness increased and saturated after the tenth generation, because alleles were modified after taking the parameters in the ninth generation into consideration.

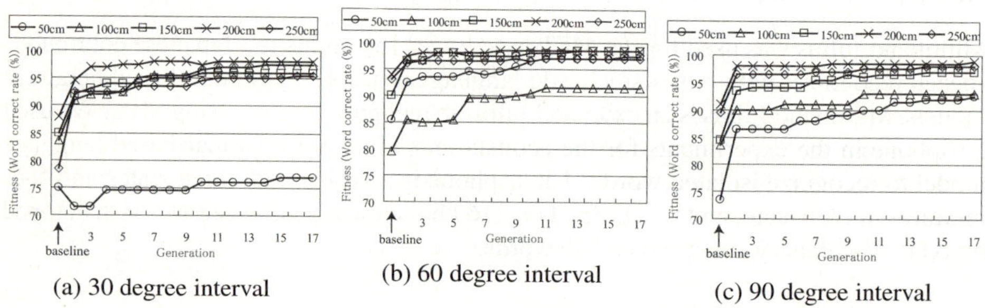

(a) 30 degree interval   (b) 60 degree interval   (c) 90 degree interval

Fig. 5. Progress in optimization in terms of fitness by applying GA on data set [a]

4.5 Evaluation of Optimized Parameters

All the data sets were recognized by using the optimized parameters obtained with GA on data set [a] as was mentioned in Sec. 4.4. Therefore, the benchmark for [a] is

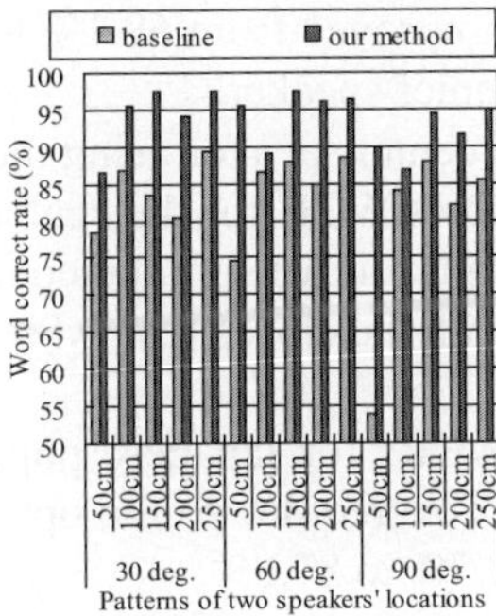

Fig. 6. *Closed*: Left speaker A with B

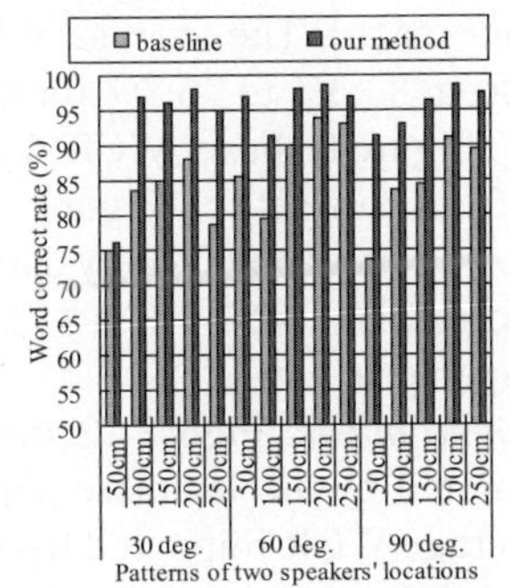

Fig. 7. *Closed*: Center speaker B with A

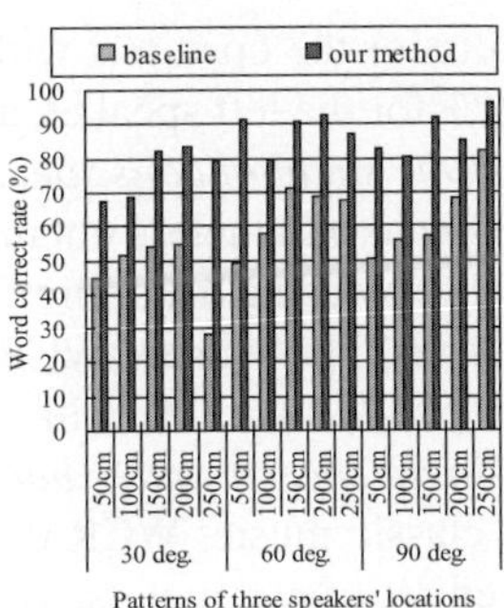

Fig. 8. *Closed*: Center speaker A with B and C

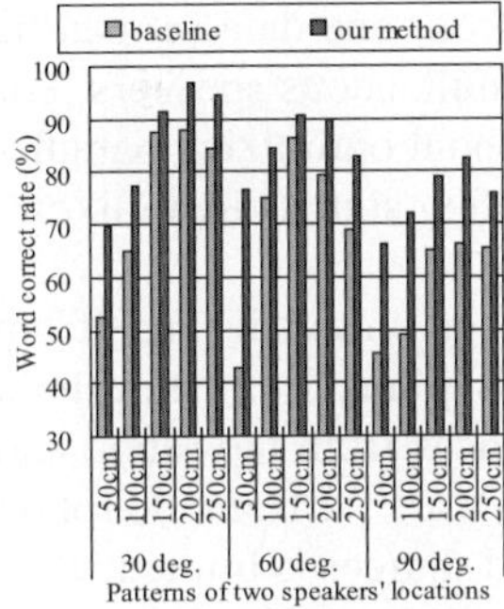

Fig. 9. *Open*: Left speaker C with A under *Fig.6–7*

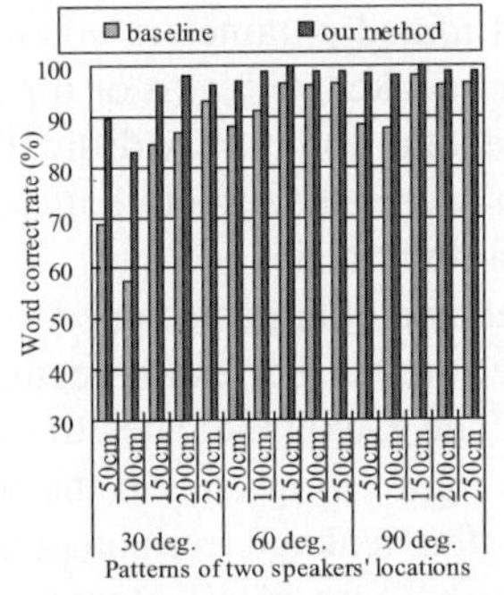

Fig. 10. *Open*: Center speaker A with C *under Fig.6–7*

Fig. 11. *Open*: Center speaker A with B and C under *Fig.6–7*

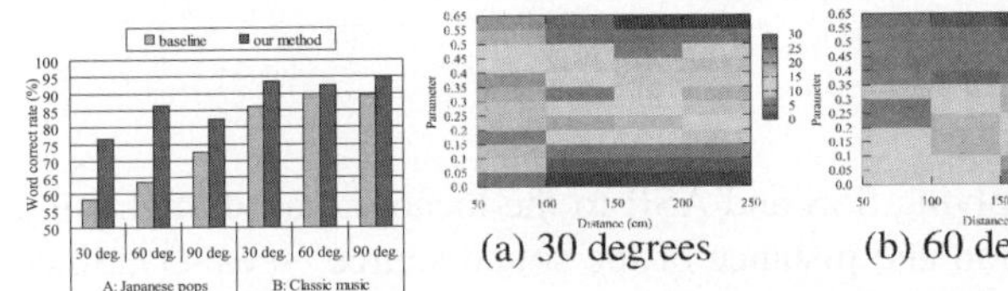

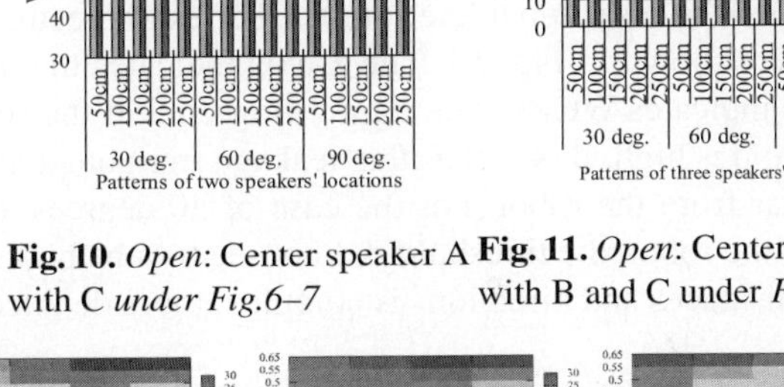

Fig. 12. Speech with background music

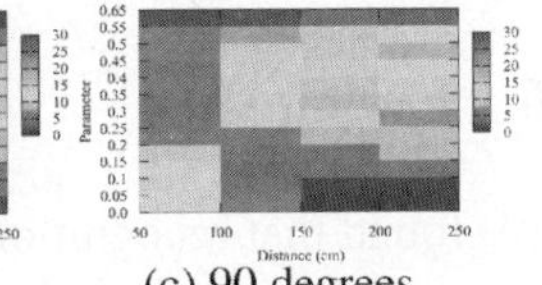

Fig. 13. Histogram of threshold for AMG

considered a *closed test*, while those on [b–e] are *open tests*. Another closed test was done on data set [c], i.e., three simultaneous speakers. The results for recognizing data sets [a] to [e] are shown in Figures 6–12. For comparison, baseline WCRs were obtained with the default values for all parameters listed in Table 1.

Two simultaneous speeches: Figures 6 and 7 show WCRs for left and center speakers for the closed test. The average WCR improved from 82.3% to 93.6% for the left speaker, and from 84.9% to 94.7% for the center speaker. Figures 9 and 7 show the results for the open test with data set [b]. The average WCR improved from 68.1% to 82.0% for the left speaker, and from 83.3% to 96.7% for the center speaker.

Three simultaneous speeches: Figure 8 shows WCR for the center speaker using the optimized parameters obtained from data set [c]. Figure 11 shows WCR for the center speaker by using the optimized parameters obtained by data set [a] for two simultaneous speeches. The average WCR improved from 57.4% to 83.9% with the closed test, while from 57.4% to 72.1% with the open test.

Single speech under background music: Figure 12 show WCRs for Japanese pops and classic music. WCR deteriorated by the Japanese pops recovered due to the optimized set of parameters. The average WCR improved from 76.7% to 87.8%.

5   Discussion

These results prove that the optimized parameters obtained from one data set can be transferred to at least the center speaker with two or three simultaneous speakers. For closer intervals and distances, recognition is very difficult without optimizing parameters. Such optimized parameters were also effective in separating signals in a mixture of one speech signal and one playing music.

The various sets of parameters we obtained seemed to depend on the distance from the robot and the direction to the sources. For example, the histograms for the threshold of AMG are shown in Fig. 13. The x-axis indicates the distances from the robot, and the y-axis indicates WCRs. The figure shows that if the sources are far from the robot, the threshold is high. Ihis means that leakage from other sound sources is limited when they are far from the robot. For the case of 30 degrees, however, even if the sources were near the robot, the threshold did not seem to be high. Thus, since the dependence between distances and directions is complex, more detailed analysis is necessary.

6   Conclusion

We found that recognition in applying SSS and ASR to the location-based interaction scheme, depended on the direction and distance of the sound source (speaker). Since numerous parameters for SSS and AMG are involved in improving these, we used genetic algorithms to optimize the parameters. Optimized parameters obtained for one data set could be transferred to other configurations of speakers at a location. Our system particularly recognizes the utterances of the center speaker without depending on the direction or the distance by selecting the appropriate set of parameters. To illustrate one potential application, we demonstrated that when *three real people* spoke to the robot to place a meal order at the same time (Fig. 4), it separated and recognized what all three had ordered and responded with total prices and individual orders.

Acknowledgements. We thank to Profs Jean Rouat and François Michaud of Université de Sherbrooke, Canada for permission to use their implementation of GSS and MCPF.

References

1. I. Cohen and B. Berdugo: Microphone Array Post-Filtering for Non-Stationary Noise Suppression, *Proc. of ICASSP-2002*, 901–904, IEEE, 2002.
2. M. Cooke, P. Green, L. Josifovski, and A. Vizinho: Robust Automatic Speech Recognition with Missing and Unreliable Acoustic Data, *Speech Communication*, Vol.34, 267–285 (2001).
3. D. Goldberg: *Genetic Algorithms in Search, Optimization and Machine Learning*, Addison-Wesley Pub. 1989.
4. I. Hara, F. Asano, H. Asoh, *et al.*: Robust Speech Interface based on Audio and Video Information Fusion for Humanoid HRP-2, *Proc. of IROS-2004*, 2404–2410, IEEE & RSJ, 2004.
5. K. Nakadai, H. G. Okuno, and H. Kitano: Robot Recognizes Three Simultaneous Speech by Active Audition, *Proc. of ICRA-2003*, 398–403, IEEE, 2003.
6. Y. Nishimura: Multiband julius. http://www.furui.cs.titech.ac.jp/mband_julius/.
7. H.G. Okuno, K. Nakadai, T. Lourens, H. Kitano: Sound and Visual Tracking for Humanoid Robot, *Proc. of IEA/AIE-2001*,LNAI 2070, 640-650, 2001.
8. L. C. Parra and C. V. Alvino: Geometric Source Separation: Mergin Convolutive Source Separation with Geometric Beamforming, *IEEE Trans. on SAP*, vol.10, no.6, 352–362, 2002.
9. T. Tasaki, S. Matsumoto, *et al.*: Distance Based Dynamic Interaction of Humanoid Robot with Multiple People, *Proc. of IEA/AIE-2005*, LNAI 3533, 111–120, 2005.
10. T. Tasaki, K. Komatani, T. Ogata, and H.G. Okuno: Spatially Mapping of Friendliness for Human-Robot Interaction, *Proc. of IROS-2005*, 521–526, IEEE, 2005.
11. J.-M. Valin, J. Rouat, and F. Michaud: Enhanced Robot Audition based on Microphone Array Source Separation with Post-Filter, *Proc. of IROS-2004*, IEEE & RSJ, 2004.
12. S. Yamamoto, *et al.*: Assessment of General Applicability of Robot Audition System by Recognizing three Simultaneous Speeches, *Proc. of IROS-2004*, 2111–2116, IEEE & RSJ.
13. S. Yamamoto, J.-M. Valin, *et al.*: Enhanced Robot Speech Recognition based on Microphone Array Source Separation and Missing Feature Theory, *Proc. of ICRA-2005*, 1489–1494, IEEE,

A Hybrid Genetic Algorithm
for the Flow-Shop Scheduling Problem

Lin-Yu Tseng and Ya-Tai Lin

Department of Computer Science, National Chung Hsing University,
250 Kuo Kuang Road, Taichung, Taiwan
lytseng@cs.nchu.edu.tw
http://oblab.cs.nchu.edu.tw

Abstract. The flow-shop scheduling problem with the makespan criterion is an important production scheduling problem. Although this problem has a simple formulation, it is NP-hard. Therefore many heuristic and metaheuristic methods had been proposed to solve this problem. In this paper, a hybrid genetic algorithm is presented for the flow-shop scheduling problem. In our method, a modified version of NEH with random re-start is used to generate the initial population. Also, a new orthogonal array crossover is devised as the crossover operator of the genetic algorithm. The tabu search is hybridized with the genetic algorithm and acts as the local search method. The proposed algorithm had been tested on two benchmarks. The results are compared with those of other methods that had also been tested on these benchmarks. The comparison shows that our method outperforms other methods on these benchmarks.

Keywords: Genetic Algorithms, Planning and Scheduling.

1 Introduction

The flow-shop scheduling problem is one of the best known production scheduling problem. There are several optimization criteria for this problem. The most common used criterion is to minimize the maximum completion time, i.e. the makespan. The flow-shop scheduling problem with the makespan criterion is defined as follows:

Suppose that there are n jobs and m machines. Each of n jobs is to be sequentially processed on machines $1, 2... m$. The processing time of job i on machine j is given as T_{ij}. At any time, each job can be processed on at most one machine and each machine can process at most one job. Also, once a job is processed on a machine; it cannot be terminated before completion. The sequence in which the jobs are to be processed is the same for each machine. And the objective is to find a permutation for jobs such that makespan is minimized.

The formulation of the problem is simple, yet the problem is NP-hand [4]. Since this problem is an important problem both in theory and in practice. Many methods had been proposed and they can be classified as in one of the following three classes.

(1) The exact methods [1]: Most of these methods use the branch-and-bound strategy. Although some easy instances having 200 jobs can be solved by these methods in reasonable time, the branch-and-bound scheme fails in finding the optimal

M. Ali and R. Dapoigny (Eds.): IEA/AIE 2006, LNAI 4031, pp. 218–227, 2006.
© Springer-Verlag Berlin Heidelberg 2006

solution of many hard instances with only 50 jobs and 20 machines[14]. The exact methods had reach their limit. The computation time for large instances and hard instances is not affordable.

(2) The heuristic methods[3][9]: These methods are constructive heuristic method. They in general are vary fast but suffer from poor solution quality. The best method among these methods is NEH [9]. But the mean relative error of the makespan provided by NEH to the lower bound of the optimal makespan is still above 5%.

(3) The metaheuristic methods: In recent years various metaheuristic methods had been applied to solve the flow-shop scheduling problem. These include simulated annealing [7][11], tabu search [6][10][15], genetic algorithm [12] and hybrid metaheuristic [13][16][17]. Metaheuristic methods in general obtain much better solution quality than heuristic methods do. And the computation time is much less than that of the exact methods.

Begin form Taillard [15], tabu search [5] had been applied to the flow-shop scheduling problem rather successfully. Following this line, Nowicki and Smutnicki [10] proposed the tabu search algorithm with back jump tracking (TSAB) based on a neighborhood structure defined by the blocks on the critical path. Grabowski and Wodecki [6] also used tabu search but they devised a method to estimate the lower bound of a local search operation in order that the time needed for local search can be reduced. Reeves and Yamada [13] hybridized the genetic algorithm and the path re-linking in solving this problem. Wang and Zheng [16] used genetic algorithm but they partitioned the population into subsets and applied different crossover operators to different subsets in order to sustain the diversity of the population. They also hybridized the simulated annealing with the genetic algorithm as a local search method. Another hybrid algorithm of the genetic algorithm and the ordinal optimization was proposed by Wang et al. [17].

In this paper, we proposed a hybrid algorithm for the flow-shop scheduling problem. This algorithm hybridizes the genetic algorithm, which acts as the global search method and the tabu search, which acts as the local search method. The proposed algorithm had been tested on the benchmark instances [2] and [12]. And the results are better than those reported by Wang and Zheng [16] and Wang et al. [17].

The remaining parts of the paper are organized as follows. In section 2, the orthogonal array crossover is described. In section 3, our hybrid algorithm is presented. Section 4 states the experimental results. Section 5 concludes this study and lists the future research works.

2   The Orthogonal Array Crossover

In this section, we briefly introduce the concept of orthogonal arrays which are used in experimental design methods. For more details, the reader may refer to [8]. After introducing the orthogonal array, we describe the orthogonal array crossover operator used in our genetic algorithm.

2.1 The Orthogonal Arrays

Suppose in an experiment, there are k factors and each factor has q levels. In order to find the best setting of each factor's level, q^k experiments must be done. Very often, it is not possible or cost effective to test all q^k combinations. It is desirable to sample a small but representative sample of combinations for testing. The orthogonal arrays were developed for this purpose. In an experiment that has k factors and each factor has q levels, an orthogonal array $OA(n,k,q,t)$ is an array with n rows and k columns which is a representative sample of n testing experiments that satisfies the following three conditions. (1) For the factor in any column, every level occurs the same number of times. (2) For the t factors in any t columns, every combination of q levels occurs the same number of times. (3) The selected combinations are uniformly distributed over the whole space of all the possible combinations. In the notation $OA(n,k,q,t)$, n is number of experiments, k is the number of factors, q is the number of levels of each factor and t is called the strength. Another often used notation for the orthogonal array is $L_n(q^k)$. In this notation t is omitted and is always set to 2. A $L_8(2^7)$ orthogonal array is shown in Table 1 as an illustrating example.

For an experiment, there are various orthogonal arrays available. After an orthogonal array is chosen, one may apply the following criterion to determine the best combinations of each factor's level in this experiment. Let E_i be the evaluation value of the ith experiment in the array. The main effect of factor j with level k, F_{jk} is defined

as $F_{jk} = \sum_{i=1}^{n} E_i A_{ijk}$, where A_{ijk} is 1 if factor j's level is k in the ith experiment and

A_{ijk} is 0 otherwise. After all F_{jk} had been computed, the level of factor j is chosen to be k if $F_{jk} = \max_{1 \le l \le q} F_{jl}$.

Table 1. $L_8(2^7)$ orthogonal array

Test No.	Factors							Evaluation Value (E_i)
	1	2	3	4	5	6	7	
1	0	0	0	0	0	0	0	E_1
2	0	0	0	1	1	1	1	E_2
3	0	1	1	0	0	1	1	E_3
4	0	1	1	1	1	0	0	E_4
5	1	0	1	0	1	0	1	E_5
6	1	0	1	1	0	1	0	E_6
7	1	1	0	0	1	1	0	E_7
8	1	1	0	1	0	0	1	E_8

2.2 The Orthogonal Array Crossover

In a flow-shop scheduling problem that has n jobs and m machines, the chromosome in our genetic algorithm is coded as a permutation of $1, 2,..., n$. The crossover operator applied for such chromosomes usually uses one or two cut point. But in this study, we use six cut points in the crossover operator by utilizing an orthogonal array $L_8(2^7)$ as shown in Table 1. The orthogonal array crossover operator is described in the following.

Step1. Given two parent chromosomes. Randomly choose six cut points for parents. So there are seven subsequences of each parent chromosome.

Step2. Consulting the ith row of the orthogonal array $L_8(2^7)$ to produce child i, C_i for $i=1, 2, \ldots, 8$. The jth subsequence of C_i comes from the jth subsequence of parent 1 if the jth factor has level 0 in the ith row. Otherwise, the jth subsequence of C_i comes from the jth subsequence of parent 2. When inheriting the jth subsequence from a parent, if a job in this subsequence has already been inherited by C_i, then this job will not be inherited and a space will occupy this position of C_i. After all subsequences were inherited, all space in C_i are filled by jobs not shown in C_i with the order that they appear in parent 1.

Step3. Compute the makespan for each child C_i. Take this value as the evaluation value E_i.

Step4. Compute the main effect of factor j with level k, F_{jk}, for j=1, 2, \ldots, 7 and k=0, 1.

Step5. Find the best combination of each factor's level. Use the best combination to produce child C_9. Evaluate the makespan of C_9.

Step6. Choose from C_1, C_2, \ldots, C_9 the one that has the best makespan as the child C of the crossover of parent 1 and parent 2.

3   The Hybrid Genetic Algorithm

In this section, we describe the proposed hybrid genetic algorithm for the flow-shop scheduling problem. The genetic algorithm acts as a global search method in this algorithm. Especially the orthogonal array crossover is used as the crossover operator in order to increase the strength of intensification. The tabu search is hybridized with the genetic algorithm in order to improve the local search ability. The proposed algorithm is described in the following.

Step1. Set population size P_s, mutation rate P_m , the number of Max_Stuck and set $S_l=0$.

Step2. Use NEH-RS-M to generate the initial population. (NEH-RS-M will be described in section 3.1).

Step3. Compute the makespan of each chromosome in the population. Let the best chromosome be π^* and its makespan be C^*.

Step4. For each chromosome P_1 in the population, randomly choose another chromosome P_2 (different from P_1). Apply orthogonal array crossover operator to P_1 and P_2 and obtain child C. If the makespan of C is better than that of P_1 or P_2, apply the local search to C and replace the worse one of P_1 and P_2 by C. (The local search is a tabu search and will be described in section 3.2).

Step5. Randomly choose P_s*P_m chromosomes. Apply mutation operator to each chosen chromosome. (The mutation operator will be described in subsection 3.3).

Step6. Compute the makespan of each chromosome in the population. Let the chromosome with the best makespan be π_1 and its makespan be C_1. If $C_1<C^*$ then $C^*\leftarrow C_1$ and $\pi^*\leftarrow\pi_1$. Otherwise, $S_l\leftarrow S_l+1$.

Step7. If $S_l > Max\_Stuck$ then stop else go to Step4.

3.1 NEH-RS-M

Selecting a good set of chromosomes as the initial population usually improves the performance of a genetic algorithm. In order to generate a good initial population for the genetic algorithm, a modified version NEH-RS-M of NEH-RS (NEH with random re-start) [18] is applied. This algorithm is stated as follows.

Step1. Compute the total processing time $T_i = \sum_{j=1}^{m} T_{ij}$ for each job i.

Step2. Sort T_i in nonascending order. Let L be the sorted list of jobs according to this ordering.

Step3. Randomly choose two jobs from the first half of L. Move these two jobs to $L[1]$ and $L[2]$. Find the best scheduling of $L[1]$ and $L[2]$, that is, a scheduling of these two jobs that has the best makespan. Denote this scheduling by S2.

Step4. For $i=3$ to n

choose job $L[i]$ and insert $L[i]$ into i possible positions in scheduling S_{i-1}. Among these i possible schedulings, find the one that has the least makespan.

Denote this best scheduling by S_i.

Step4. Return S_n.

The initial population is generated by iteratively appling NEH-RS-M to produce the chromosome.

3.2 The Local Search

The purpose of the local search is trying to find a better solution in a neighborhood of a solution. In this study, tabu search is used as the local search method. Tabu search was proposed by Glover in 1977 [5]. It uses tabu-list to avoid repetitive search of the same area and to escape from the local optima.

Neighborhood structures are used in the tabu search. A neighborhood $N(x)$ of solution x in the solution space is defined as the set of all solutions that are reachable by applying a move to the solution x. In the flow-shop scheduling problem, the usually used moves are the insertion operator and the exchange operator. It is pointed out by [15] that the insertion operator outperforms the exchange operator in the tabu search for the flow-shop scheduling problem. Nowicki and Smutnicki [10] observed that picking out a job in a critical block and inserting it in different position of the same block will not improve the makespan. They narrowed down the neighborhood by only allowing a job to be inserted in the previous critical block or the successive critical block. Grabowski and Wodecki [6] further narrowed down the neighborhood by restricting the insertion only in the last position of the previous critical block or the first position of the successive critical block. They also proposed a method to estimate the lower bound of the insertion in order to apply only those insertions that are likely to make profit. In this study we combine these two methods in our Find_Best_Move procedure.

The tabu search is described in the following and after that, the procedure Find_Best_Move is described.

```
program Tabu Search (π, C)
  var
    C*            : Integer;
    generation : Integer;
    stuck         : Integer;
  begin
    C* := C;
    generation := 0;
    stuck := 0;
    while generaion < max_generation do
    begin
      BestMove := Find_Best_Move(π, C);
      addToTabuList(BestMove);
      π := generateNewSchedule(BestMove);
      C := evaluation(π);
      if C < C* then
      begin
        π* := π;
        C* := C;
        Stuck := 0;
      end else begin
        Stuck := Stuck+1;
        if stuck >= max_Stuck then
        begin;
          perturbation();
          Stuck := 0;
        end;
      end;
    generation := generation+1;
    end;
  end.
```

Some notations are helpful in describing the procedure Find_Best_Move. They are given bellow.

1. π represents a solution. $\pi(i)$ denotes the job in the ith position.
2. S_j^a denotes the critical block immediately before the critical block in which job j resides. P_a represents the last position of S_j^a. $|S_j^a|$ is the size of S_j^a.
3. S_j^b denotes the critical block immediately after the critical block in which job j resides. P_b represents the first position of S_j^b. $|S_j^b|$ is the size of S_j^b.
4. *Ins(x, y)* represents the insertion operator by which the job in position x is inserted in position y.
5. *Exch(x, y)* represents the exchange operator by which the jobs in position x and position y are interchanged.

224   L.-Y. Tseng and Y.-T. Lin

Procedure Find_Best_Move (π, C)

Step1. Set $i=1$, $C_{best}=C$ and *BestMove=Ins(1,1)*.
Step2. Find a critical path of π and find the critical blocks.
Step3. If $i \leq n$ (n is the number of jobs) then go to Step4 else return *BestMove*.
Step4. Evaluate the lower bound of *Ins($\pi(i),\pi(P_a)$)*. If this lower bound ≤ 0 then go to
        Step5 else go to Step6.
Step5. Evaluate the makespan of π after applying *Ins($\pi(i),\pi(k)$)*, where k= P_a, P_a -1,...,
        P_a-min(α, $|S_j^a|$-1). If the best one among these schedulings has a makespan
        better than C_{best}, then update C_{best} and store that insertion operator in *BestMove*.
Step6. Evaluate the lower bound of *Ins($\pi(i),\pi(P_b)$)*. If this lower bound ≤ 0 then go to
        Step7 else go to Step8.
Step7. Evaluate the makespan of π after applying *Ins($\pi(i),\pi(k)$)*, where k= P_b, P_b
        +1,..., P_b+min(α, $|S_j^b|$-1). If the best one among these schedulings has a
        makespan better than C_{best}, then update C_{best} and store that insertion operator in
        BestMove.
Step8. i←i+1, go to step3.

The procedure perturbation( ) used in the tabu search is just the same as that in
Grabowski and Wodecki [6].

3.3 Mutation

The mutation operator is used to diversify the population in the genetic algorithm.
Suitable application of the proper mutation operator can prevent the premature convergence of the genetic algorithm. Since the insertion operator has been used in the
local search, we use the exchange operator as the mutation operator. Randomly
choose P_s*P_m chromosomes from the population, where P_s is the population size and
P_m is the mutation rate. For each chosen chromosome, apply *Exch(x, y)* t times, where
x, y are randomly chosen positions and $1 \leq t \leq T$ with T being a predefined number.

4 Experimental Results

The proposed hybrid algorithm had been implemented with C++ language on a personal computer whose CUP is AMD 1.83GHz and memory size is 512MB and the
operating system is Windows XP. The algorithm had been tested on two benchmarks
developed by Carlien [2] (Car1 to Car8) and by Reeves [12] (rec0, rec3,... rec41).
These two benchmarks include twenty-nine instances in total.

In this experiment, the parameters in our algorithm are set as follows: population
size P_s is 50; Mutation rate P_m is 0.1; the *max_generation* in the tabu search is 50; the
max_stuck in the tabu search is 3; α is set to 3 and the length of tabu list is 6.

The algorithm was tested on each instance twenty times. The results are summarized in Table 2. In Table 2, n is the number of jobs; m is the number of machines;

C_{opt} gives the makespan of the optimal solution; *maxStuck* is the number of maximum stuck allowed in the main program; T is the maximum number of the exchange operation; *min*, *max* and *avg* list the maximum, the minimum and the average makespans found in the twenty runs; *Avg Time* gives the average CPU time and *Opt.* gives number of the optimum findings within twenty runs.

In Table2, the entries for *maxStuck* and T are blank for Car1 to Car8 because the optimal solutions were found in the initial population. Wang et al.[16][17] had also tested their algorithms on these two benchmarks. So we compared our results with results of the better one (the order-based genetic algorithm, OGA [17]) of the two algorithms proposed by Wang et al. This comparison is stated in Table 3. In Table 3, WRE is the worst relative error (i.e. C_{worst}-C_{opt}/C_{opt} * 100%); BRE is the best relative error (i.e. C_{best}-C_{opt}/C_{opt}*100%) and ARE is the average relative error (i.e. $C_{average}$-C_{opt}/C_{opt} * 100%).

Table 2. The expeimental results of the proposed hybrid algorithm

Instance	n, m	C_{opt}	maxStuck	T	max	min	avg	Avg Time	Opt.
car1	11,5	7038			7038	7038	7038	0.00	20/20
car2	13,4	7166			7166	7166	7166	0.00	20/20
car3	12,5	7312			7312	7312	7312	0.00	20/20
car4	14,4	8003			8003	8003	8003	0.00	20/20
car5	10,6	7720			7720	7720	7720	0.00	20/20
car6	8,9	8505			8505	8505	8505	0.00	20/20
car7	7,7	6590			6590	6590	6590	0.00	20/20
car8	8,8	8366			8366	8366	8366	0.00	20/20
rec01	20,5	1247	3	3	1249	1247	1247	0.36	17/20
rec03	20,5	1109	3	3	1109	1109	1109	0.27	17/20
rec05	20,5	1242	3	3	1245	1242	1243	0.27	12/20
rec07	20,10	1566	3	3	1572	1566	1566	0.78	18/20
rec09	20,10	1537	3	3	1537	1537	1537	0.60	20/20
rec11	20,10	1431	3	3	1431	1431	1431	0.68	20/20
rec13	20,15	1930	3	3	1952	1932	1940	1.45	0/20
rec15	20,15	1950	3	3	1976	1951	1968	1.26	0/20
rec17	20,15	1902	3	3	1944	1902	1926	1.54	2/20
rec19	30,10	2093	6	3	2111	2099	2101	1.82	0/20
rec21	30,10	2017	6	3	2046	2026	2035	1.09	0/20
rec23	30,10	2011	6	3	2021	2014	2020	1.69	0/20
rec25	30,15	2513	6	3	2556	2523	2539	3.90	0/20
rec27	30,15	2373	6	3	2411	2392	2401	3.93	0/20
rec29	30,15	2287	6	3	2327	2302	2311	4.09	0/20
rec31	50,10	3045	6	5	3101	3053	3062	4.28	0/20
rec33	50,10	3114	6	5	3121	3114	3114	3.42	18/20
rec35	50,10	3277	6	5	3277	3277	3277	2.93	20/20
rec37	75,20	4951	6	5	5112	5050	5077	17.78	0/20
rec39	75,20	5087	6	5	5212	5131	5178	17.38	0/20
rec41	75,20	4960	6	5	5139	5046	5100	18.37	0/20

Table 3. Comparisons of the Hybrid GA and OGA

Instance	Hybrid GA			OGA		
	WRE	BRE	ARE	WRE	BRE	ARE
car1	0.00	0.00	0.00	0.00	0.00	0.00
car2	0.00	0.00	0.00	0.00	0.00	0.00
car3	0.00	0.00	0.00	0.00	0.00	0.00
car4	0.00	0.00	0.00	0.00	0.00	0.00
car5	0.00	0.00	0.00	0.00	0.00	0.00
car6	0.00	0.00	0.00	0.00	0.00	0.00
car7	0.00	0.00	0.00	0.00	0.00	0.00
car8	0.00	0.00	0.00	0.00	0.00	0.00
rec01	0.16	0.00	**0.00**	0.16	0.00	0.04
rec03	0.00	0.00	0.00	0.00	0.00	0.00
rec05	**0.24**	0.00	**0.08**	0.32	0.00	0.21
rec07	**0.38**	0.00	**0.00**	1.15	0.00	0.79
rec09	**0.00**	0.00	**0.00**	1.17	0.00	0.35
rec11	**0.00**	0.00	**0.00**	3.07	0.00	0.91
rec13	**1.14**	**0.10**	**0.52**	1.66	0.26	1.08
rec15	**1.33**	**0.05**	**0.92**	2.21	0.10	1.23
rec17	**2.21**	0.00	**1.26**	3.21	0.00	2.08
rec19	0.86	0.29	**0.38**	3.01	**0.14**	1.76
rec21	**1.44**	**0.45**	**0.89**	3.12	1.44	1.64
rec23	**0.50**	**0.15**	**0.45**	3.08	0.85	1.90
rec25	**1.71**	**0.40**	**1.03**	3.74	1.31	2.67
rec27	**1.60**	**0.80**	**1.18**	3.58	0.97	2.09
rec29	**1.75**	**0.66**	**1.05**	5.95	1.88	3.28
rec31	**1.84**	**0.26**	**0.56**	2.59	0.43	1.49
rec33	**0.22**	**0.00**	**0.00**	4.05	0.61	1.87
rec35	**0.00**	0.00	**0.00**	0.33	0.00	0.00
rec37	**3.25**	**2.00**	**2.54**	4.30	2.46	3.41
rec39	**2.46**	**0.86**	**1.79**	3.24	1.63	2.28
rec41	**3.61**	**1.73**	**2.82**	4.69	2.30	3.43

Table 3 reveals that our hybrid algorithm outperforms the order-based genetic algorithm.

5   Conclusions and Future Works

A hybrid genetic algorithm is presented to solve the flow-shop scheduling problem. In this algorithm, the genetic algorithm acts as the global search method. The performance of the genetic algorithm is enhanced by applying a modified version of NEH-RS to generate the initial population. The strength of intensification increases by utilizing the orthogonal array crossover operator. Tabu search is hybridized to act as the local search method. The experimental results show that the proposed algorithm is competitive.

Proper hybridization of global search methods and local search methods may be a good way of designing effective and efficient algorithms for optimization problems. But from problem to problem or even from instance to instance, there seems to reveal a fact that some problems (or instances) may need more global search than local search and on the contrary, other problems (or instances) may need more local search than global search. Our future research works include finding good hybridization of global search methods and local search methods and also designing an automatic adaptation scheme to better adjust the load of the two kinds of methods according to the problem (or instance) at hand.

References

1. Carlier, J., Rebai, Ï.: Two branch and bound algorithms for the permutation flow shop problem. Eur. J. Oper. Res. 90 (1996) 238-251.
2. Carlier, J.: Ordonnancements a contraintes disjunctives. RAIRO Recherche operationell/Oerations Research. 12 (1978) 333-351.
3. Dannenbring, D.: An evaluation of flow shop sequencing heuristics. Manag. Sci. 23 (1977) 1174-1182.
4. Garey, M. R., Johnson, D. S., Sethi, R.: The complexity of flowshop and jobshop scheduling. Math. Oper. Res. 1 (1976) 117-129.
5. Glover, F., Laguna, M.: Tabu Search. Kluwer Academic Publishers, Boston, MA. (1997).
6. Grabowski, J., Wodecki, M.: A very fast tabu search algorithm for the permutation flow shop problem with makespan criterion. Comput. Oper. Res. 31 (2004) 1891-1909.
7. Ishubuchi, M., Masaki, S., Tanaka, H.: Modified simulated annealing for the flow shop sequencing problems. Eur. J. Oper. Res. 81 (1995) 388-398.
8. Montgomery, D. C.: Design and Analysis of Experiments, 3rd ed. New York: Wiley. (1991).
9. Nawaz, M., Enscore, Jr. E., Ham, I.: A heuristic algorithm for the m-Machine, n-Job flow-Shop Sequencing Problem. Omega. 11 (1983) 91-95.
10. Nowicki, E., Smutnicki, C.: A fast tabu search algorithm for the permutation flow-shop problem. Eur. J. Oper. Res. 91 (1996) 160–175.
11. Ogub, F. A., Simith, D. K.: Simulated annealing for the permutation flowshop problem. Omega. 19 (1990) 64-67.
12. Reeves, C. R.: A genetic algorithm for flowshop sequencing", Comput. Oper. Res. 22 (1995) 5-13.
13. Reeves, C. R., Yamada, T.: Genetic algorithm, path relinking and the flowshop sequencing problem. Evol. Compu. 6 (1998) 45-60.
14. Taillard, E.: Benchmarks for basic scheduling problems. Eur. J. Oper. Res. 64 (1993) 278-285.
15. Taillard, E.: Some efficient heuristic methods for the flow shop sequencing problem. Eur. J. Oper. Res. 47 (1990) 65-74.
16. Wang, L., Zheng D. –Z.: A effective hybrid heuristic for flow shop scheduling. Int. J. Adv. Manuf. Technol. 21 (2003) 38-44.
17. Wang, L., Zheng, L., Zheng D. –Z.: A class of order-based genetic algorithm for flow shop scheduling. Int. J. Adv. Manuf. Technol. 22 (2003) 828-835.
18. Watson, J. P., Barbulescu, L., Whitley, L. D., Howe, A. E.: Contrasting structured and random permutation flow-shop scheduling problem: search-space topology and algorithm performance. Jour. Comput. 14 (2002) 98-123.

Solving a Large-Scaled Crew Pairing Problem by Using a Genetic Algorithm

Taejin Park and Kwang Ryel Ryu

Department of Computer Engineering, Pusan National University
Jangjeon-Dong San 30, Kumjeong-Ku, Busan 609-735, Korea
{parktj, krryu}@pusan.ac.kr

Abstract. This paper presents an algorithm for a crew pairing optimization, which is an essential part of crew scheduling. The algorithm first generates many pairings and then finds their best subset by a genetic algorithm which incorporates unexpressed genes. The genetic algorithm used employs greedy crossover and mutation operators specially designed to work with chromosomes of set-oriented representation. As a means of overcoming the premature convergence problem caused by greedy genetic operators, the chromosome is made up of an expressed part and an unexpressed part. The presented method was tested on real crew scheduling data.

1 Introduction

Given a timetable containing all the legs to be serviced for a day by a fleet of vehicles, the crew scheduling problem is the process of assigning individual crew members to legs with minimum cost. A pairing is a combination of legs that can be assigned to a crew as a daily duty. The crew scheduling problem is separated into two independent sub-problems [1]. The *pairing generation* problem is the process of generating many feasible pairings. The *pairing optimization* problem is the process of finding the best subset of all the generated pairings in such a way that all the legs are covered by the selected pairings at minimum cost. Pairing generation is relatively easily solved by an enumerative method. The number of pairings generated in a real problem, however, is huge, and thus the complexity of pairing optimization is very high.

Previous works on pairing optimization employed solution techniques such as Lagrangian relaxation [2], genetic algorithm [3] and column generation [4]. The first two methods are inefficient and thus are applicable only when there is a small number of feasible pairings. The column generation method is applicable to somewhat larger-scaled problems because it generates pairings dynamically as needed while finding the solution to pairing optimization. Because the column generation method is based on integer programming, however, the computation may take a prohibitively long time, and its applicability is limited to problems whose objective function and constraints are represented in linear forms. In our previous work [5] we developed a hybrid of tabu search and integer programming. The hybrid algorithm combines the advantages of both methods and thus can solve large-scaled crew pairing optimization problems more efficiently than either method alone can, and is free from linearity

M. Ali and R. Dapoigny (Eds.): IEA/AIE 2006, LNAI 4031, pp. 228 – 237, 2006.

constraints. In this paper, we solve pairing optimization by applying a genetic algorithm which incorporates unexpressed genes [6]. This algorithm employs greedy heuristics in crossover and mutation operators to improve the search's efficiency, and introduces a new chromosomal structure incorporating *unexpressed genes* as a means of maintaining the population's diversity.

Section 2 describes an example of the crew scheduling problem used in our empirical study. Section 3 explains the chromosomal structure and the greedy genetic operators, and Section 4 introduces unexpressed genes. Section 5 reports experimental results comparing the genetic algorithm's performance to that of other search methods. Finally, Section 6 gives some conclusions.

2 Example Crew Scheduling and Maximal Covering Problem

The problem we have experimented with in this research is the crew-scheduling problem of a subway line in real operation. As shown in the timetable of train trips of Figure 1 (a), the trains move back and forth between the two stations A and B where the two crew bases are located. Although there are many stations between A and B in the original timetable, only C is shown in the figure because it is the only station (except A and B) where crews can take a break and switch to a different train. There are four types of legs in this problem, i.e., $A \rightarrow C$, $C \rightarrow B$, $B \rightarrow C$, and $C \rightarrow A$, and the total number of legs is 634.

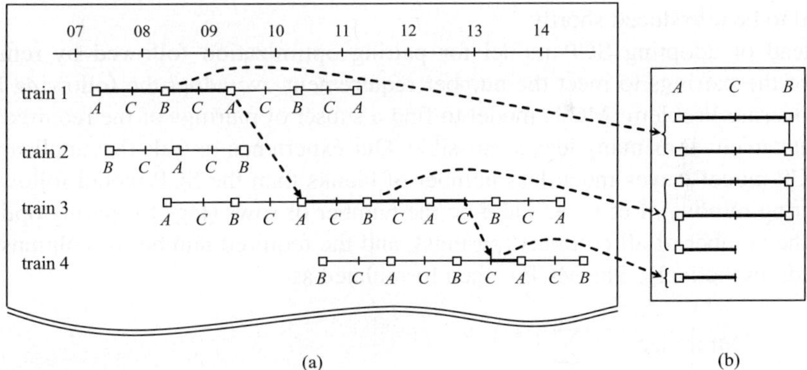

Fig. 1. A fragment of timetable showing daily train trips (a), and an example pairing (b)

Figure 1 (b) shows an example pairing which consists of a sequence of legs taken from the timetable of train trips. There are many rules that should be followed by each pairing as a daily duty. A pairing must start and finish at the same crew base (A or B) and should cover ten legs, which makes the train switch at station C inevitable. A crew cannot operate the vehicle continuously without break for longer than three hours for a safety reason, but the number of breaks (rest periods) allowed for a pairing is bounded by four because the crews prefer not to make too many train switches. We must find a set of pairings each of which satisfies these and many other constraints not mentioned here, so that all the legs in the timetable are covered.

There are also constraints and objectives that must be followed by the pairings collectively. The number of pairings is fixed to 65 of which 38 belong to crew base A and the rest to crew base B. Since there are 634 legs and each pairing covers 10 legs, we allow some of the legs to be covered by more than one pairing. When multiple pairings cover the same leg, those pairings except a designated one are said to contain a *deadhead* or deadhead leg, for which the crew does not work but is just transported as a passenger. One of the important objectives of this pairing optimization problem is to minimize the average work hour that is defined as the time interval from the start of the first leg (start time) to the finish of the last leg (finish time) of a pairing. Another objective is to minimize the number of pairings having four breaks.

In the pairing generation step, the pairings satisfying all the constraints can be generated relatively easily by an enumerative method. The problem is that there are simply too many feasible 10-leg pairings, which can be extracted from the 634-leg timetable. So, we provide with a pool of selected pairings whose size is not too big to be used for solving the pairing optimization problem within an acceptable time. An inevitable consequence of using a limited pool of pairings is a sacrifice of the solution quality; the result of pairing optimization based on SCP model is quite likely to contain more number of pairings than allowed. Therefore, some of the pairings should be removed from the resultant solution to meet the requirement on the number of pairings, which makes some of the legs left uncovered by any pairing. In our algorithm the uncovered legs, or what we call the *blanks*, are taken care of by a heuristic repair method to be introduced shortly.

Instead of adopting SCP model for pairing optimization followed by removing some of the pairings to meet the number requirement, we adopt the following Maximal Covering Problem (MCP) model to find a subset of pairings of the required number that can cover as many legs as possible. Our experience reveals that application of the MCP model leaves much less number of blanks than the SCP model followed by the pairing removal. Let m, n, and d be the number of rows (legs for paring optimization), the number of all columns (parings), and the required number of columns to be selected, respectively. The MCP is then formulated as

$$\text{Minimize} \quad \sum_{i=1}^{m} y_i \tag{1}$$

$$\text{subjected to} \quad \sum_{j=1}^{n} x_j = d \tag{2}$$

$$\sum_{j=1}^{n} a_{ij} x_j + y_i \geq 1, \quad i = 1, \ldots, m \tag{3}$$

$$x_j \in \{0,1\}, \quad j = 1, \ldots, n \tag{4}$$

$$y_i \in \{0,1\}, \quad i = 1, \ldots, m \tag{5}$$

where $x_j = 1$ if pairing j is selected, and 0 otherwise. $a_{ij} = 1$ if pairing j covers the ith leg (i.e. the ith leg is contained in pairing j), and 0 otherwise. The first constraint imposes the required number d of pairings to be selected. The second constraint forces the variable y_i to take the value 1 when the ith leg is a blank. When the ith leg is not a blank, y_i will take the value 0 so that the given summation is minimized.

After a subset of pairings of given number has been chosen by applying the above MCP model, the blanks that remain must be taken care of. The blanks are removed by applying a heuristic repair algorithm, which modifies or replaces some of the pairings in the chosen subset. Figure 2 illustrates the basic idea of a repair operation by modification. In the figure, a blank leg L_2 is repaired by having pairing P give up the leg L_1 and cover L_2 instead to become pairing P'. Note that in pairing P' the new leg L_2 does not interfere with any of the preceding or succeeding legs. If L_1 happens to be a deadhead leg, repair of L_2 is complete. Otherwise, the same process continues by modifying a series of pairings until a deadhead leg is encountered. Given a blank leg such as L_2, there can be more than one pairing that can be modified for blank repair. A breadth-first search or an iterative deepening search can be used to find a shortest path from the blank to a deadhead. A few variations of this operation and other heuristics including pairing replacement are used in the heuristic repair algorithm.

As there are more rows left uncovered in the given maximal covering solution, we observe a significant (more than linear) increase in time needed for the repair. Therefore, the pairing subset before heuristic repair should have as few blanks as possible. In the following sections, we describe how we apply a genetic algorithm for solving the maximal covering problem to minimize such blanks.

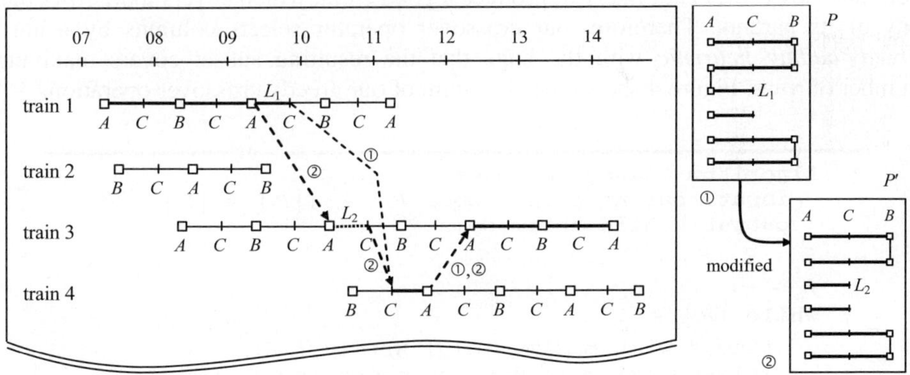

Fig. 2. Repair of a blank leg by modification of a pairing

3   Chromosome Representation and Greedy Genetic Operators

The solution to the MCP is the subset of d columns (i.e., pairings) selected from the n columns of a given matrix. The solution is evaluated by an objective function, which basically counts the number of rows covered by the selected d columns, and sometimes also considers the quality of the columns constituting the solution and other problem-specific constraints. Figure 3 shows the chromosome representation adopted for solving an MCP. It is just a string or set of indices of d selected columns where the order of the columns is meaningless.

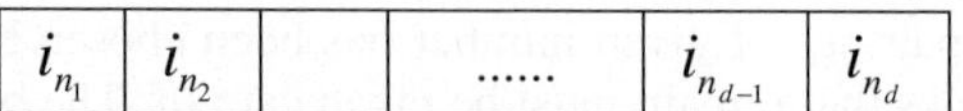

Fig. 3. Subset-oriented chromosome representation for MCP

Under this representation, n-point or uniform crossover produces illegal offsprings having repeated alleles. One may use penalty functions or apply post-crossover fix-ups to cope with these problems. For example, uniform crossover with fix-up (UXF) can be used for subset encoding [7]. However, UXF is a *locus-based* crossover operator although locus is meaningless when subset encoding is used. What we need is an operator, which chooses a subset of the columns from the selected parents. Radcliffe proposed improved crossover operators, RAR_w, for fixed-length subset problems, which are very useful for many applications [8]. However, it is not suitable for the problem where the size of the subset to be selected is much smaller than the size of the element pool from which to select. In our problem, there are 180,000 elements while the subset size is just 65.

The crossover operator that we use greedily selects a subset of columns from the selected parents. Given two parent chromosomes P_1 and P_2, our crossover operator produces a single child P_c by selecting d columns from $P_1 \cup P_2$. A random selection of columns, however, is not likely to produce a good child, which covers more rows than any of its parents. Therefore, our crossover operator selects columns by using a *greedy-adding heuristic* with the hope that the resulting subset covers maximum number of rows. Figure 4 shows the algorithm of our greedy crossover operation.

```
Algorithm GreedyCrossover
   input: parent chromosomes P₁, P₂ (|P₁| = |P₂| = d)
   output: child chromosome Pc
P = P₁ ∪ P₂;
Pc = ∅;
while |Pc| ≠ d
    find j with maximum δ(j) where j∈P;
    (tie-breaking is done by comparing Sp(j))
    Pc := Pc ∪ {j};
    P := P − {j};
return Pc;
```

Fig. 4. Algorithm of greedy crossover

$\delta(j)$ in the above algorithm heuristically measures the goodness of a column j in the following way:

$$\delta(j) = Eval(P_c \cup \{j\}) - Eval(P_c) \tag{6}$$

where $Eval(P)$ is the number of rows covered by the set of columns in P. The best column according to this heuristic is the one that, when added to the current subset, contributes the most to the increase in the number of rows covered. Although not shown formally in the above algorithm, there is an important tie-breaking strategy which plays a significant role in enhancing the performance of our genetic algorithm: When there are more than one columns with maximum $\delta(j)$, we select the column whose similarity to all the columns in P $(= P_1 \cup P_2)$ is the lowest. The similarity $S_P(j)$ of column j to all the columns in P (including j itself) is measured by calculating the inner product of the column vectors as follows:

$$S_P(j) = \sum_{v \in P} j \cdot v = j \cdot \sum_{v \in P} v \tag{7}$$

Note that the columns of any MCP are binary vectors. If the columns have almost the same number of 1s (which is often the case and also so in the MCPs of pairing optimization used in our experiments), then the value of the inner product of two such binary vectors j and v becomes bigger as the Hamming distance of the two gets smaller. $S_P(j)$ is calculated ahead of time for each of the columns before entering the **while** loop of the algorithm of Figure 4.

Given a set of columns P, a column with low $S_P(j)$ is the one that covers many rows which are different from those covered by the other columns in P. The reason for preferring the column with the lowest $S_P(j)$ for tie-breaking is that by selecting such a column it is expected that the columns to be selected in succession in the next iteration will be likely to cover more rows which are not covered by the columns selected so far. Suppose on the contrary that we select the column with the highest $S_P(j)$ among the columns with the same maximum $\delta(j)$. Then the column to be added in the next iteration would be so similar to the one just selected that it is not likely to cover more new rows.

For the mutation, a k-exchange method is used. This mutation first performs a mutation test by applying a predetermined mutation probability not at the level of individual genes (columns) but at the level of chromosome. Once the chromosome is determined to be mutated, k columns are removed randomly and then k new columns are inserted by the greedy-adding heuristic.

4 Adopting Unexpressed Genes for Diversification

While the greedy crossover described in the previous section is very good at producing individuals having good column combination of high coverage, the population as a whole rapidly loses over the generations those columns, which are not selected by the crossover. This loss of diversity leads to premature convergence. To overcome this premature convergence problem, we have tried to adopt popular niching methods, i.e., crowding operator [9] and fitness sharing [10]. Although these diversification schemes brought some improvement, the search performances were still much worse than the neighborhood search algorithms. It has been shown that incorporation of unexpressed genes is an effective means to diversify population and thus prevent premature convergence. Unexpressed genes preserve some columns, which are not selected by the crossover but suspected to be potentially useful in later generations.

Figure 5 shows the chromosome structure having unexpressed genes, where the chromosome C consists of the expressed part $E(C)$ with d columns and the unexpressed part $U(C)$ with r columns. Although only $E(C)$ is used when C is evaluated, both parts are involved when crossover is applied. Given the parents P_1 and P_2, the expressed part $E(P_c)$ of the child P_c is produced by the same greedy crossover operator described in Figure 4 except that this time d columns are selected from the pool of almost $2(d+r)$ different columns[1] of both the expressed and unexpressed parts of the two parents.

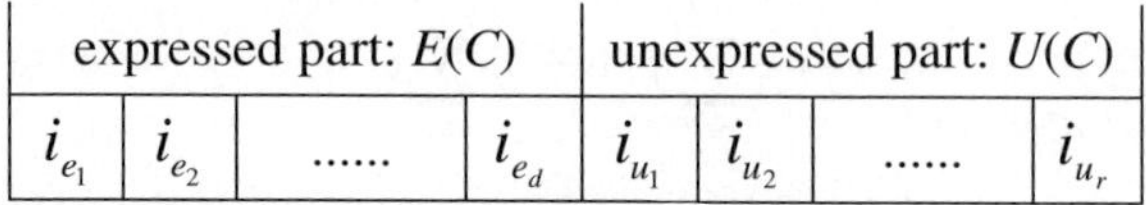

Fig. 5. Chromosome with unexpressed genes

After the columns for $E(P_c)$ is selected, the unexpressed part $U(P_c)$ is produced again from both the expressed and unexpressed parts of P_1 and P_2 by selecting the columns which are the most dissimilar to those already selected for $E(P_c)$. The similarity $S_{E(Pc)}(j)$ of column j to the columns in $E(P_c)$ is calculated similarly as in equation (7). By forcing the unexpressed part to become as different from the expressed part as possible, the resultant chromosome, when it becomes a parent, is expected to serve as a pool of more diverse columns from which better new children may be produced for the next generation. The unexpressed genes formed this way contribute a lot to prevention of premature convergence by maintaining the diversity of the population.

After the crossover, each part of the chromosome is mutated separately. The expressed part is mutated again by the k-exchange mutation, but the unexpressed part is mutated randomly by simply replacing each column by a randomly selected one.

5   Experimental Results and Discussions

We used a real subway crew scheduling data for the experiments, where $m = 634$, $n = 179,514$, $d = 65$, and each column covers exactly 10 rows.[2] All the experiments were done on a Pentium IV 2G Hz server with 1G RAM.

We implemented two versions of genetic algorithm: GA with unexpressed genes (GAUG) and GA without unexpressed genes (GA). For GAUG, the population size was set to 1,500 and 3-exchange mutation with the mutation rate of 0.01 was used. The mutation rate for the unexpressed part was 0.1 and the length of the unexpressed part was set to 80. For GA, the only difference was its population size of 3,346 considering the fact that the length of an individual chromosome is only 65 compared to 145 of GAUG ($3,346 \approx 1,500 \times 145/65$). The evaluation of each individual is made by counting the number of rows covered by the columns of only the expressed part, and

---

[1] The number of different columns can be smaller than $2(d+r)$ if the same column appears in both parents.

[2] We generated 179,514 columns by using an enumerative method. The number happens to be so after many experiments.

fitness scaling was not used. The initial population was generated not randomly but by using the greedy-adding heuristic. However, the columns for the unexpressed part were still selected randomly. For the selection, stochastic universal sampling method was used.

We also implemented two popular neighborhood search algorithms, i.e., tabu search (TS) and simulated annealing (SA), for performance comparison. To be fair, the initial solution for both algorithms was generated by using the greedy-adding heuristic, and neighborhood solutions were generated by using the k-exchange method, which is similar to the k-exchange mutation. However, it turned out to be better for the neighborhood search algorithms to have the value of k range from 1 to 5 instead of the fixed value of 3.

Each of the above algorithms was run for 10 times given 60 minutes of CPU time and the number of rows still left uncovered was counted. Table 1 shows the best, the worst, and the average results of these experiments. We can see that GAUG is a clear winner. This result is also better than that of the hybrid method [5] that left 10 rows uncovered in the best case.

Table 1. Experimental results with the subway crew scheduling MCP data

Algorithm	Best	Average	Worst
GAUG	**5**	**6.5**	**8**
GA	15	15.9	17
SA	7	8.0	10
TS	9	10.0	12

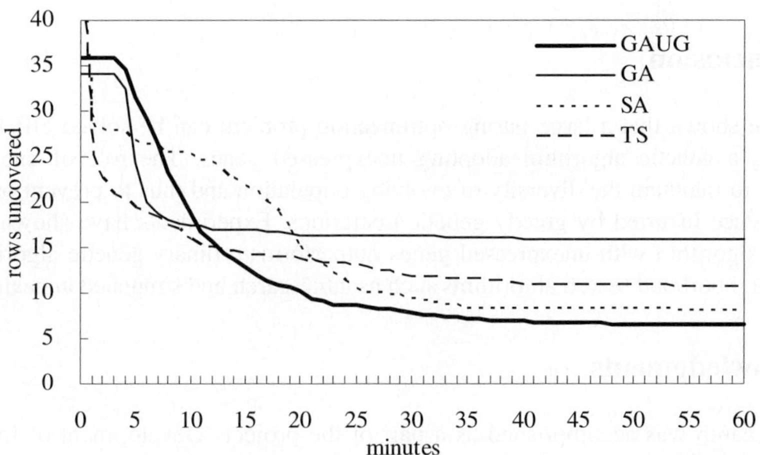

Fig. 6. Average search behaviors for the crew scheduling MCP data

Figure 6 compares the curves obtained by averaging at every minute the ten runs of the four algorithms for the given 60 minutes of CPU time. Although the quality of solution improves rather slowly during early iterations, GAUG eventually outperforms all the other methods. As can be seen by the curve of GA, however, genetic algorithm without the unexpressed genes performs the worst due to severely premature convergence. The reason for little improvement by both genetic algorithms at the beginning is that they were given relatively good initial populations by using the greedy-adding heuristic.

Table 2 compares the results of applying heuristic repair to the maximal covering solutions obtained by GAUG, GA, and SA. As seen from the bottom row of the table, it took only 18 minutes to repair 5 blanks, while it took 1 hour and 23 minutes and 3 hours to repair 7 and 15 blanks, respectively. We can see how important it is to remove as many blanks as possible in the maximal covering phase. The quality of the final solution produced by GAUG is also better than that by GA and SA. The solution is considered better when it has less number of breaks and has shorter average work hour.

Table 2. Results of heuristic repair after the maximal covering phase

	GAUG	GA	SA
Initial blanks	5	15	7
Final blanks	0	1	0
Avg. work hour	10h 39m	10h 43m	10h 49m
Number of pairing with 2, 3, and 4 breaks	52:11:2	23:34:8	32:26:7
CPU time	18m	3h	1h 23m

6 Conclusion

We have shown that a large paring optimization problem can be solved efficiently by applying a genetic algorithm adopting unexpressed genes. The role of unexpressed genes is to maintain the diversity of evolving population and thus to prevent premature convergence incurred by greedy genetic operations. Experiments have shown that the genetic algorithm with unexpressed genes outperforms ordinary genetic algorithm and other neighborhood search algorithms such as tabu search and simulated annealing.

Acknowledgments

This research was accomplished as a part of the project "Development of Intelligent Port and Logistics System for Super-Large Container Ships", which was sponsored by Ministry of Maritime and Fishery in Korea. The authors express their appreciation for the financial support.

References

1. Bodin, L., Golden, B., Assad, A., Ball, M.: Routing and scheduling of vehicles and crews: the state of the art. Computers and Operations Research, 10 (1983) 63-211.
2. Caparara, A., Fischetti, M., Guida, P.L., Toth, P., Vigo, D.: Solution of large-scale railway crew planning problems: The Italian experience. Technical Report OR-97-9, DEIS University of Bologna (1997).
3. Beasly, J.E., Chu, P.C.: A genetic algorithm for the set covering problem. European Journal of Operational Research, 94, (1996) 392-404.
4. Barnhart, C., Johnson, E.L., Nemhauser, G.L., Savelsbergh, M.W.P., Vance, P.H.: Branch and price: Column generation for huge integer programs. Operations Research, 46 (1998) 316-329.
5. Hwang, J., Kang, C. S., Ryu, K. R., Han, Y., Choi, H. R.: A Hybrid of Tabu Search and Integer Programming for Subway Crew Scheduling Optimization. *IASTED-ASC*, (2002) 72-7.
6. Park, T., Ryu, K. R.: Exploiting Unexpressed Genes for Solving Large-Scaled Maximal Covering Problems. 8th Pacific Rim International Conference on Artificial Intelligence. (2004) 342-351.
7. Crawford, K. D., Hoelting, C. J., Wainwright, R. L., Schoenefeld, D. A.: A study of fixed-length subset recombination. Foundsations of Genetic Algorithm 4 (1996).
8. Radcliffe, N. J.: Genetic set recombination. Foundations of Genetic Algorithms 2, Morgan Kaufmann (1993).
9. Mahfoud, S.W.: Crowding and preselection revisited. Proceedings Second Conference Parallel Problem Solving from Nature (1992).
10. Goldberg, D. E., Richardson, J.: Genetic algorithm with sharing for multimodal function optimization. Proceedings of the Second International conference on Genetic Algorithm (1987) 41-49.

Population Structure of Heuristic Search Algorithm Based on Adaptive Partitioning

Chang-Wook Han and Jung-Il Park

School of Electrical Engineering and Computer Science, Yeungnam University,
214-1 Dae-dong, Gyongsan, Gyongbuk, 712-749 South Korea
{cwhan, jipark}@yumail.ac.kr

Abstract. A random signal-based learning merged with simulated annealing (SARSL), which is serial algorithm, has been considered by the authors. But the serial nature of SARSL degrades its performance as the complexity of the search space is increasing. To solve this problem, this paper proposes a population structure of SARSL (PSARSL) which enables multi-point search. Moreover, adaptive partitioning method (APM) is used to reduce the optimization time. The validity of the proposed algorithm is conformed by applying it to a complex test function example and a general version of fuzzy controller design.

1 Introduction

To search an optimum of a function with continuous variables is difficult if there are many peaks and valleys. In these cases, traditional optimization methods are not competent. They will either be trapped to local optima or need much more search time. In recent years, many researchers have been trying to find new ways to solve these difficult problems, and stochastic approaches have attracted much attention [1-3].

Random signal-based learning merged with simulated annealing (SARSL) is a powerful optimization algorithm as proved in [3]. But it can not find the global optimum of complex problem very well because of its serial nature. In this paper, a population structure of SARSL (PSARSL) is proposed. PSARSL is an extended version of SARSL as a population structure. PSARSL enables the SARSL to explore the search space with various random initial states, and then each SARSL in the population exploits the search space with the help of SA. Besides, this paper considers an adaptive partitioning method (APM) to reduce the optimization time and enhance the accuracy. The performance of the proposed method is compared with other algorithms with respect to computational effort and accuracy. For this comparison, the test functions optimization and a fuzzy controller design for an inverted pendulum are considered.

2 Description of the Proposed Algorithm

Though, SARSL is a good optimization algorithm for a simple optimization problem, it may not be a good algorithm for a complex one because of its serial nature. To overcome this shortcoming, a population structure of SARSL (PSARSL), that is an extension of SARSL as a population structure, is proposed as described in Fig. 1. The

M. Ali and R. Dapoigny (Eds.): IEA/AIE 2006, LNAI 4031, pp. 238 – 243, 2006.

PSARSL can get the diversity of solution set by starting with different initial states, and then performs local search for each local area. Therefore, PSARSL can find more accurate solution than SARSL with lower computational effort, because PSARSL searches different local areas with corresponding initial states and SARSL (serial algorithm) is a good local search algorithm as proved in [3]. As shown in Fig. 1, each serial algorithm of PSARSL starts from corresponding initial states generated at random. These m serial algorithms search each local area and finally converge on the near global optima.

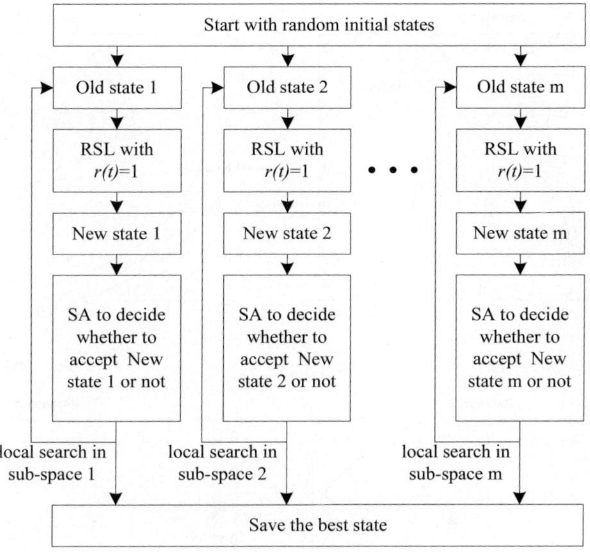

Fig. 1. The flowchart of PSARSL

In case of complex optimization problems, adaptive partitioning method (APM) is very helpful in the reduction of computational effort and enhancement of accuracy [4]. In this paper, the following APM is used to enhance the performance of PSARSL:

Step 1. The original search region is equally partitioned into K rectangles (subregions).
Step 2. Generate R uniformly distributed random states for each subregion, and then evaluate the performance index for all random states.
Step 3. The subregion that contains the best performed state is further equally partitioned into K subregions, and the best performed state is updated.
Step 4. If the partitioning has not been performed in the surrounding subregions (the subregions except the currently partitioning subregion) for S steps, go to next step, else go to Step 2.
Step 5. Use PSARSL in the most promising subregion that has taken from APM to find the global optimum, and additionally, apply simple genetic algorithm (SGA) with small population to the surrounding subregions (consider these subregions as one) because there is a little possibility to exist the global optimum.

Example 1. In this example, the following two-dimensional test function [1] is considered to clarify the APM described above:

$$F(x,y) = 0.5 - (\sin\sqrt{x^2 + y^2} - 0.5)^2 / (1 + 0.001(x^2 + y^2))^2 \qquad -1 \le x, y \le -4 . \tag{1}$$

This function has a global maximum in $(x, y)=(0, 0)$ as 1, and many local maxima, whose values are 0.990283, are around the global maximum. Fig. 2 describes the contours of the most promising subregions for each APM iterations, where $K=4$, $R=20$, and $S=4$.

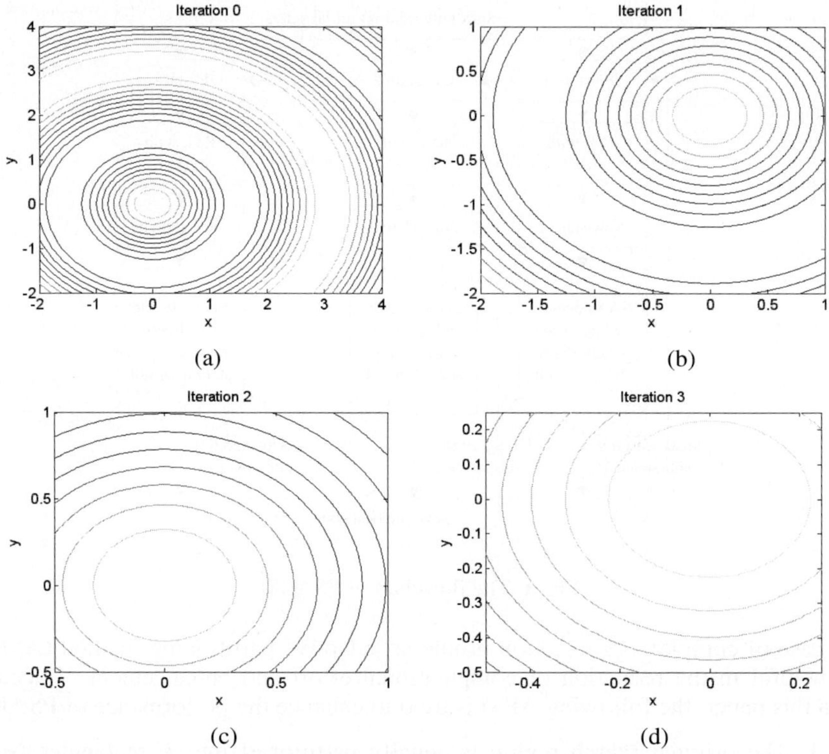

Fig. 2. Contours of the most promising subregions for each APM iterations: (a) Iteration 0=[-2, 4]x[-2, 4] (original region), (b) Iteration 1=[-2, 1]x[-2, 1] (subregion taken from the 1st iteration), (c) Iteration 2=[-0.5, 1]x[-0.5, 1] (subregion taken from the 2nd iteration), (d) Iteration 3=[-0.5, 0.25]x[-0.5, 0.25] (subregion taken from the 3rd iteration)

This APM has been performed 30 independent times, and finally, the subregion including global optimum is always survived in the last iteration step of APM as the most promising subregion. Once the most promising subregion has been taken from APM, the PSARSL can find the global optimum in the subregion, as shown in Fig. 2(d), more easily.

From this example we can expect that the complexity of the search space for the most promising subregion obtained by APM is much reduced than that of the original one, and the probability of containing the global optimum inside the obtained subregion is very high. This makes PSARSL to find the optimal state more effectively. Additionally, a SGA is used to explore the surrounding subregions with small population because there is a small possibility that the global optimum can be found in the surrounding subregions.

3 Experimental Results

To verify the effectiveness of the proposed method, we consider several benchmark test functions and a fuzzy controller design example. The parameters used in the experiment are set by trial and error, and are defined as follows: learning rate=0.01, cooling rate=0.98, initial temperature=0.1, population size of PSARSL and SGA=20, maximum number of parallel epoch for PSARSL and SGA=200, crossover rate=0.8, mutation rate=0.1, K=4, R=20, and S=4. The proposed method will be compared with PSARSL without APM. Moreover, in this simulation, standard version of genetic algorithm (GA), which is well-known population structure optimization algorithm, is considered as well. For the reasonable comparison the maximum number of parallel epoch for PSARSL and GA without APM=1000, and initial temperature for PSARSL without APM=1.0 (others are the same as above), and each algorithm is run 30 times independently.

3.1 Optimization of the Test Functions

We employ four real-valued benchmark test functions [1], given in Table 1, to demonstrate the mechanics of the proposed method. This table shows high dimensional problem (f1, f4) and low dimensional problem (f5, f6) together.

Table 1. Test functions and their specifications

Name	Function	Global optimum
f1	$f_1(\mathbf{x}) = \sum_{i=1}^{n} x_i^2$ where n=10, -4.12 < x_i < 5.12	0
f4	$f_4(\mathbf{x}) = \sum_{i=1}^{n} i \cdot x_i^4$ where n=10, -1.0 < x_i < 1.28	0
f5	$f_5(\mathbf{x}) = 1/(0.002 + \sum_{j=1}^{25} \dfrac{1}{j + \sum_{i=1}^{2}(x_i - a_{ij})^6})$ where -64.0 < x_1, x_2 < 65.356	0.998004
f6	$f_6(\mathbf{x}) = 0.5 - \dfrac{\mathrm{Sin}^2(\sqrt{x_1^2 + x_2^2}) - 0.5}{(1 + 0.001(x_1^2 + x_2^2))^2}$ where -1.0 < x_1, x_2 < -4.0	1

The results of optimization are summarized in Table 2. This table shows the percentage of global optimum (optimization accuracy) and the average number of function evaluation (optimization speed) to reach 10^{-5} error, respectively. The optimization accuracy of the proposed method and GA is very similar, while the optimization speed is very different, i.e. the proposed method is much faster optimization algorithm than GA in these four test functions because of using APM. In the proposed method, the most promising subregion obtained by APM contains a global optimum as 97.5% for all test function optimizations. The performance of PSARSL (without APM) is inferior to that of others as we expected above.

Table 2. Optimization results of the test functions

Name	Algorithms	% of global optimum	Average number of function evaluation to reach global optimum
f1	Proposed method	96.7	5317.5
f1	PSARSL without APM	76.7	12836.1
f1	GA	93.3	7162.6
f4	Proposed method	93.3	6024.7
f4	PSARSL without APM	73.3	15520.3
f4	GA	90	8317.9
f5	Proposed method	100	3492.3
f5	PSARSL without APM	80	10893.6
f5	GA	100	5351.1
f6	Proposed method	100	3016.8
f6	PSARSL without APM	86.7	7921.3
f6	GA	100	5719.6

3.2 Applications to Fuzzy Controller Design

To show the effectiveness of the proposed method, optimization of the fuzzy controller for balancing an inverted pendulum system [3] is considered. To simplify the problem, only the control of the pole is considered for the inverted pendulum system, that is, the considered states are angle, θ, and angular velocity, $\dot{\theta}$, of the pole with respect to the vertical axis. The fuzzy controller for this system consists of 25 possible rules that have antecedent parts with 5 fixed triangular membership functions (fuzzy sets) for each input variable, and 25 consequent part membership functions. The 25 centers and 25 widths of consequent part are considered to be optimized [3]. The same inverted pendulum parameters and performance index of [3] are used.

Table 3 describes the average simulation results (average over 30 independent simulations) for each algorithm. The maximum number of function (performance index) evaluation for each algorithm is 20000. This means that each algorithm has been performed with the same computational effort. In this table, the average best Q (performance index) and the average number of function evaluation to reach 1% of the best Q show the accuracy and speed, respectively. As can be seen, the proposed method is superior to other algorithms with respect to optimization accuracy and speed, but the more precise experiments are needed to compare in the future.

Table 3. Average simulation results

Algorithm	The avg. best Q	The avg. number of function evaluation to reach 1% of the best Q
Proposed method	12.01	10346.2
PSARSL without APM	15.12	15274.7
GA	12.27	12154.9

Fig. 3 shows the average control result of the inverted pendulum obtained by the 30 optimized fuzzy controllers for each algorithm. From this figure, we can see that the fuzzy controllers optimized by the proposed method control the inverted pendulum much better than other algorithms.

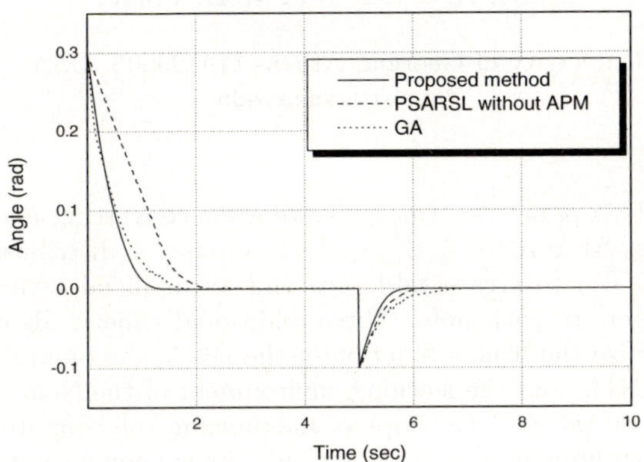

Fig. 3. Average control result of each algorithm

4   Conclusions

This paper proposed the APM based heuristic search algorithm to reduce the optimization time and enhance the accuracy. The APM finds the most promising subregion containing the global or near global optima to decrease the complexity of the search space. The PSARSL was applied to this subregion to find the optimum state, while a simple genetic algorithm was used to search the surrounding subregions to find the missing optimum state which may occur very rarely. The validity was confirmed by the optimization of the benchmark test functions and the fuzzy controller for the inverted pendulum. As is shown, the proposed method is superior to PSARSL and GA (without APM) with respect to optimization speed and accuracy. This means that APM is very effective to enhance the performance of PSARSL. For the further research, the more complex general problems should be considered, and the more deep theoretical analysis rather than heuristic approach is needed.

References

1. De Jong, K.: An Analysis of the Behavior of a Class of Genetic Adaptive Systems. Ph.D. dissertation, Dept. Computer Sci., Univ. Michigan, Ann Arbor, MI (1975)
2. Goldberg, D.E.: Genetic Algorithms in Search, Optimization and Machine Learning. Addison-Wesley, Reading, MA (1989)
3. Han, C.W., Park, J.I.: Design of a Fuzzy Controller using Random Signal-based Learning Employing Simulated Annealing. Proc. of the IEEE Conference on Decision and Control, Sydney, Australia (2000) 396-397
4. Tang, Z.B.: Partitioned Random Search to Optimization. Proc. of the American Control Conference, San Francisco (1993)

Generating Guitar Tablature with LHF Notation Via DGA and ANN

Daniel R. Tuohy and W.D. Potter

University of Georgia, Athens GA 30605, USA
daniel2e@uga.edu

Abstract. This paper describes a system for converting music to guitar tablature. At run time, the system employs a distributed genetic algorithm (DGA) to create tablature and an artificial neural network to assign fingers to each note. Three additional genetic algorithms are used to optimize the fitness function of the DGA, the operating parameters of the DGA, and the learning environment of the Neural Network. These steps are taken in the hope of maximizing the consistency of our algorithm with human experts. The results have been encouraging.

1   Introduction: The Guitar Fingering Problem

Stringed instruments suffer from a one-to-many relationship between notes and the positions from which they can be played. Figure 1 shows four different positions from which the same "E" can be produced. These are called fretboard positions and are described by two variables, a string and a fret. It is the burden of the performer to choose a fretboard position for every note in a piece of music. Tablature is a musical notation system that represents music as fretboard positions rather than as notes, freeing the performer from tedious decision making. Tablature is ordinarily created by humans. There have been commercial attempts to generate tablature automatically, but these are notorious for creating unnecessarily difficult or unplayable tablature [3] [11].

It is the goal of our system to be able to consistently generate tablature competitive with that created by humans. This problem has been given considerable attention in the last few years. Examples of three recent academic attempts to achieve a similar goal were conducted at the Universities of Doshisha, Victoria, and Torino, each with apparent weaknesses. The model from the University of Doshisha has been designed only for use on monophonic melodies, and cannot create tablature for pieces including chords [3]. The model from the University of Victoria is a learning algorithm that consults published tablature to learn different musical styles, and an assessment of performance on an independent test set is not provided [6]. We will only compare our results to those from the University of Torino, as this approach has the same aspirations as our own [5][4].

In this paper we will describe four genetic algorithms and one neural network. In section two we will describe TabGA, the distributed genetic algorithm

M. Ali and R. Dapoigny (Eds.): IEA/AIE 2006, LNAI 4031, pp. 244–253, 2006.

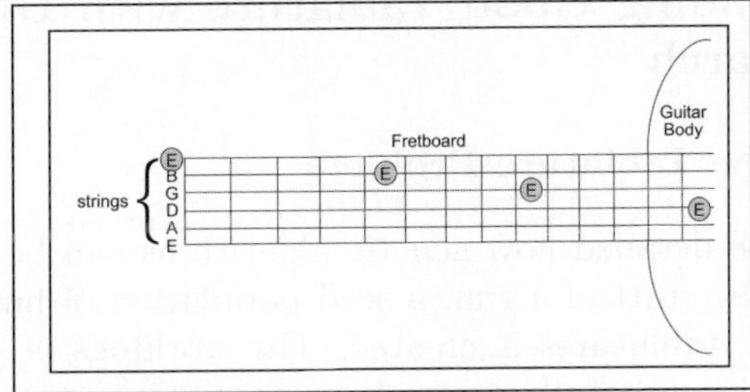

Fig. 1. Four different fretboard positions for a 330 hz "E"

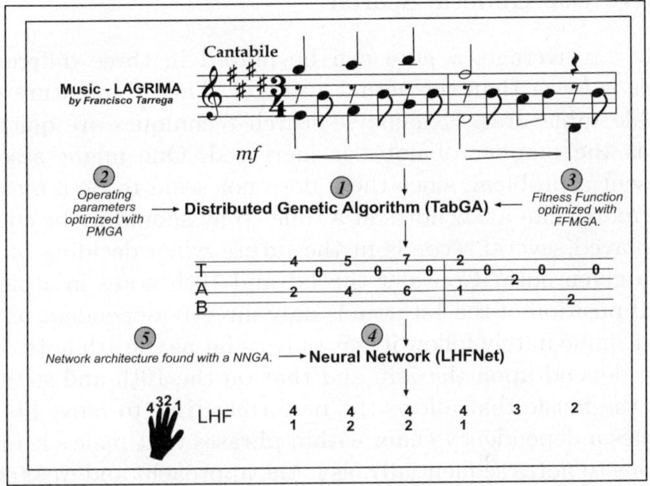

Fig. 2. An overview of our system and it's five components. (1) TabGA takes as input music and creates tablature. TabGA's operating parameters were set using (2) PMGA and the fitness function was optimized with (3) FFMGA. The resulting tablature is then used by (4) LHFNet to create left handed fingering notation. The architecture of LHFNet was discovered with (5) NNGA.

designed to create tablature from guitar music. Section 2 also provides an analysis of PMGA, a Meta GA for optimizing the operating parameters of TabGA. A Meta GA, as used in this paper, is defined as a GA that executes another GA in its fitness evaluations. Section three is an analysis of the fitness function of TabGA, upon which the ability to create tablature competitive with human experts is entirely dependent. In section four we describe FFMGA, a Meta GA used to tune the fitness function of TabGA. In section five we discuss LHFNet, the neural network we have implemented to determine appropriate left handed fingering for guitar tablature. Section 5 also will address NNGA, a GA used to determine the architecture for LHFNet. An overview of the entire system is illustrated in Figure 2.

2   TabGA: Finding Good Tablature with Distributed Genetic Search

2.1   A GA for the Tablature Problem

In previous work we detailed how genetic algorithms can be used to find good tablature [10]. At the start of a run, a seed population of hundreds of random, but musically valid, tablatures is created. The workings of genetic algorithms are well-known, and figure 3 illustrates how crossover and mutation function in this domain.

2.2   Why We Use Genetic Search

Suppose that, on average, a note can be played in three different fretboard positions (this is lower than the actual average). Then a tablature with n notes has 3^n possible tablatures. Exhaustive search techniques are quickly rendered impractical as the number of notes is increased. One might assert that this does not present a problem, since there does not seem to be a reason to create tablature for more than a few notes at a time. Why should we be concerned with notes to be played several seconds in the future when deciding on a fretboard position for a given note? Consider the 1st and 10th notes in a piece of music. The fretboard position of the 1st note is only directly dependent on those of the few notes that immediately follow it, say only as far as the 4th note. However, the 4th note may depend upon the 7th, and that on the 10th and so on until there is a break in the music that allows the performer time to move his hand freely. This establishes a dependency chain within phrases that makes it inadvisable to assign positions to notes sequentially, as is the approach (and weakness) of many commercial tablature generators. For this reason, we choose to break music into logical phrases manually, then process each phrase with the GA.

2.3   Genitor II Background

The DGA that we have implemented in TabGA is based on the Genitor II system devised by Whitley and Starkweather [14]. Genitor II is an implementation of a DGA, also called Island GAs. It was chosen because of its reliability for converging quickly on very good solutions over a wide variety of NP-hard problems [1]. Adherence to the steady-state and island paradigms is characteristic of Genitor II. A Steady State GA is one in which individuals are introduced into the population individually, rather than as a whole new generation. An Island GA is one in which the population is divided into separate sub-populations, each of which conducts genetic search independently. It is this aspect which provides the distributed nature of the DGA. Each island consists of a small population of individuals and uses a Steady State GA to evolve that population. Because of sampling bias inherent in the initial population of each island, the islands will naturally focus on different parts of the search space. The islands periodically swap their best individuals between one other, which encourages the sharing

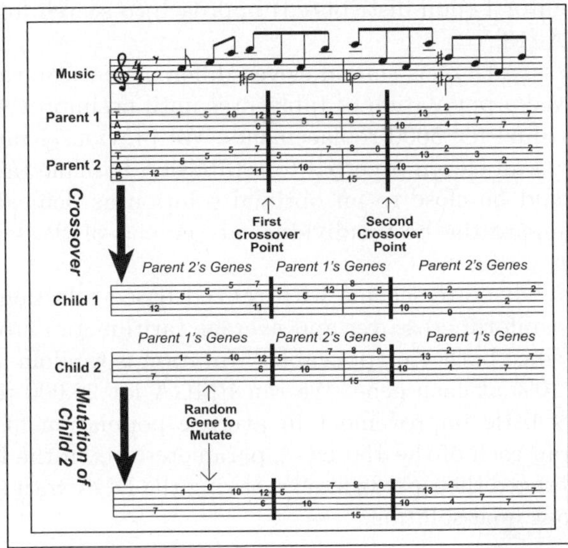

Fig. 3. Obtaining a child from two parents in a simple GA

of beneficial characteristics that might proliferate in distant parts of the search space.

Whitley specifically mentioned that problems with "multiple structurally incompatible solutions" are well-suited for exploitation by the Genitor II scheme. The application he has in mind is the optimization of weights in a neural network. Such problems may have many globally competitive solutions that, when recombined with each other, yield very poor results. This is exactly the problem that we face with tablature generation. Consider a piece of music that is optimally played low on the fretboard, but could be as easily played higher on the fretboard. Attempting to recombine a tablature of each type would result in an unplayable tablature. The results presented by Whitley and Starkweather on neural network optimization indicate that Genitor II is better suited to such problems than other genetic search techniques. The Genitor II scheme presents us with more operating parameters than would a simpler evolutionary search technique, so we again turn to genetic search to find good values for these parameters.

2.4   Optimization with the Parameter Meta GA (PMGA)

A set of DGA operating parameters can be represented as a chromosome composed of eight variables. These are the population size, the number of islands, the interval at which islands swap individuals, the number of individuals that are swapped, the linear bias of the ranked-based selection, two variables governing adaptive mutation, and a binary variable indicating whether to use one or two point crossover. In PMGA we have chosen to use a meta GA based loosely on Whitley's Genitor I (non-distributed) approach to search for the best set of values for TabGA [13].

To assess fitness, a DGA is run on eleven different musical excerpts. For each excerpt, we evolved a population of tablatures until no improvement was found in the best individual for 5000 replacements. We previously ran a hand tuned DGA 100 times on all eleven excerpts to establish a baseline tablature for each excerpt that should be close to an optimal solution as defined by our fitness function. We compare the best individual at the end of the evolution process with the baseline.

PMGA is a steady-state scheme with ranked based selection and a population size of 150. Uniform crossover and average (arithmetic) crossover are used interchangeably since both are applicable. Mutation is random and occurs with a probability of 10% at each gene. We ran PMGA for 20,000 replacements, at which point very little improvement in average population fitness was being made. We then ran each of the 150 DGA parameter sets in the final population ten times and averaged their performance, taking the DGA with the best average performance as our final solution.

3   An Overview of the TabGA Fitness Function for Evaluating Tablature Difficulty

The fitness function for our GA is required to assess the difficulty, or "playability", of tablature. We have elected not to use a system based on minimizing the distance traveled for each finger. This method was first detailed by Sayegh and has been expounded upon in other research [7] [6] [5]. Systems that adopt this paradigm analyze of the movement of each finger, and then use a cost function that penalizes each finger's movement. However, net finger movement alone does not constitute difficulty. Many other factors, some very difficult to articulate, are also important. We have implemented a fitness function based on the author's musical expertise. We have endeavoured to include in our fitness function as many relevant difficulty factors as possible, though none are dependent upon accurately accounting for each finger.

We will now provide an overview of our fitness function, which is quite lengthy. We will provide as much information as possible, but will summarize specific details for the sake of brevity. We have included as many metrics of difficulty as possible, and will allow a Meta GA (FFMGA) to decide the importance that each metric should be given.

3.1   Biomechanical Factors

There are twelve factors considered to be biomechanical in nature because they assess the physical difficulty of hand movement.

How the Hand Moves. The first eight biomechanical factors are concerned with the total amount of movement the hand must undertake. These are the number of times frets must be depressed, a reward for the number of times open strings are played, the total fretwise distance between sequential chords, a penalty for larger fretwise distances, total fretwise distance between each chord and the average of the six surrounding notes, a penalty if this distance is particularly large, total maximum fretwise distance within chords, and total largest fretwise distance between any two notes of sequential chords.

How the Hand is Held. The remaining four factors reward tablatures that allow the hand to remain in the same position as often as possible, allowing each finger to be lifted or pressed exactly once. We look for hand positions that cover the tablature to the maximum extent. For each position, there is a variable that holds the number of notes for which that position can be held and a variable that carries a penalty associated with the difficulty with holding the position.

3.2   Cognitive Factors

There are two other factors that are cognitive in nature, and assess the difficulty that may arise from the violation of certain accepted conventions of guitar performance unrelated to physical difficulty. Guitar players will be startled by tablatures which, even if physically less difficult, are not intuitive. The first of these conventions is that higher notes should be played on higher strings. In line with this convention, a tablature incurs a penalty if a note that is higher than the preceding note is played on a lower string, or a lower note on a higher string. A second convention gives a slight penalty to notes placed higher on the fretboard. This establishes a preference for positions lower on the fretboard in cases where two candidate fretboard positions are of similar difficulty.

4   Improving Fitness Assessments with the Fitness Function Meta GA (FFMGA)

We have a total of fourteen difficulty factors, and each has an associated weight that determines its contribution to tablature fitness. In previous work we tuned these weights manually, hoping to find a set of weights that would best capture the actual difficulty of tablature. We seek to improve upon our efforts with a Meta GA. The chromosome for a DGA in FFMGA is fourteen continuous valued variables corresponding to the weights of the difficulty factors. Each variable is given a range of possible values that we consider to be reasonable, either 0-30 or 0-3 depending on which order of magnitude we deem most appropriate for that variable. For assessing fitness we have taken from published tablature books and the web a selection of excerpts from 30 different pieces of music comprising a total of 751 notes and their corresponding fretboard positions. We selected the excerpts in a random fashion, though preference was given to excerpts that moved around the fretboard, thereby requiring a more intelligent approach to tablature creation. The fitness of a fitness function chromosome is the percentage of generated fretboard positions consistent with those assigned by human experts. The implementation of FFMGA is nearly identical to that of the PMGA, and was run for 20000 replacements.

5 LHFNet: A Neural Network for Left Handed Fingering Notation

Tablature sometimes includes information on which specific fingers to use at each fretboard position. This is known as Left Handed Fingering (LHF) notation, and further relieves the performer from having to decide on appropriate performance technique. We have employed a Neural Network to handle this task. We chose to use a Neural Network because of the vast number of inputs that are potentially viable. There is, for each learning pattern, a set of 59 variables that we consider and there is no obvious method for determining which are relevant and how they should be weighted. By using these variables as inputs to a neural network we free ourselves from having to make such determinations. The model we have adopted consults a neural network at every fretboard position in a tablature to determine the appropriate finger to be used. The outputs are values between .1 and .9 for each of the four fingers. We then assign whichever finger has the highest value as the finger for that fretboard position.

5.1 Training Data Acquisition

We trained the network with tablature from the web. Tablature was taken from the popular classical guitar tablature repository at www.classtab.org [16]. We chose thirty pieces of music that included LHF notation. The pieces are all classical, including works from Bach, Villa-Lobos, Tarrega, Sor, and others. In total we generated 6800 training patterns, one for each note, from the data.

5.2 Network Architecure and Inputs

For exploratory purposes, we used the neural network package NeuroShell to get an idea of what network architecture was most suitable for this problem [15]. We tested multilayer, Ward, and simple back-propagation architectures with several combinations of activation functions and layer sizes. The standard three-layer back-propagation architecture with sigmoid activation functions was found to fit the data the best. We will focus our search on networks of this type and use genetic search to determine hidden layer size, learning rate, momentum, and inputs. The neural networks are built with source code from the GAIL package developed by Brian A. Smith [8].

5.3 Optimizing LHFNet with the Neural Network GA (NNGA)

Network Inputs. For each note we have extracted a set of 59 possible network inputs. The first two are the fret and the string of the current note. The next twenty are comprised of attributes of the most recent note on which each finger was used. These are the fret, string, notes since, chords since, and a binary variable indicating if the note is in the same chord as the current note. There are then four binary variables indicating whether or not each finger is "free", which is dependent on how many notes have elapsed since the finger was last used, and if the string on which the finger was last used has been depressed by a different finger in the intervening time. The next 15 variables are the fret, string and finger of the previous five notes. The next 10 are the fret and string of the next five notes. The remaining eight variables detail the chord that the current note occupies. These are number of notes, number of notes on open strings, the highest string that is open, the number of notes higher than the lowest fret in the chord, the highest played string, the lowest played string, the highest played fret and the lowest played fret.

We extracted all of these features from the data because all are potentially valuable, but we do not know a priori which ones are important. We use NNGA to pare down the inputs for us.

Chromosome and Fitness. The chromosome for one of our networks is a bit string of length 59, two continuous valued variables for learning rate and momentum, and an integer for the number of hidden nodes. Each bit in the bit string determines whether or not an input is included. We set the range for learning rate at .05-.25, momentum at 0-.2 and hidden layer size at 8-17. These ranges were chosen based on what we have observed in exploratory testing with NeuroShell.

Network fitness is determined by accuracy on a production set, which comprises a randomly selected 15% of the 6800 patterns. This is also the size of the test set, and the remaining 70% are used for training. Training has concluded when no improvement in mean squared error has been found in 250000 events.

The GA. NNGA is similar to the Genitor I style used in PMGA and FFMGA. We set population size at 100, mutation rate at 7%, and use rank-based selection with uniform crossover. The GA was run for 30000 replacements.

6   Results

6.1   Optimized DGA vs. DGA vs. Simple GA

We are interested in comparing the effectiveness of the simple GA, the hand-tuned DGA, and the DGA found with PMGA. We ran the three GAs on each piece of music ten times for 20,000 replacements, which is sufficient time for convergence, and recorded how many times each algorithm found the baseline solution. Each GA was run with the parameter settings found to work best for that GA, either empirically or through testing, and all had the same population size.

The DGA parameter set found by PMGA seems to afford us only a marginal benefit, if any. The optimized DGA found the baseline solution in 74.7% of its runs, compared to 70% for the hand tuned DGA. However, there is a noticeable benefit to the DGA over the simple GA, which found the baseline solution only

40% of the time. When we consider only the "difficult" pieces, namely excerpts 5-11, the difference is even more remarkable. On these excerpts the optimized and hand tuned DGAs found the baseline solution in 60% and 56% of cases respectively, while the Simple GA found the solution in only 14.3% of the cases. As may have been expectd, no improvement upon the baseline solutions was made.

Table 1. Performance of 3 GAs on 11 musical excerpts. Number of times in 10 runs the baseline solution was found.

	1	2	3	4	5	6	7	8	9	10	11	*Total*
Optimized DGA (TabGA)	10	10	10	10	10	10	7	6	1	0	8	82
Hand Tuned DGA	10	9	10	10	10	10	7	2	1	1	7	77
Simple GA	10	7	7	10	4	3	2	0	0	0	1	44

6.2   Consistency of TabGA and LHFNet with Human Experts

The accuracy achieved by TabGA on our test set is 91.1%. That is, 91.1% of the fretboard positions in the generated tablature were consistent with the human-created tablature. This is a marked improvement over the DGA using our previous fitness function, which has an accuracy of 73% on the same set of data. In addition, deviations from published tablature did not result in significantly more difficult tablature. For LHF notation, the accuracy achieved by LHFNet on the independent test set was 80.6%.

The University of Torino reports accuracies of 98% and 90% respectively, but these numbers were achieved on a very different set of data. The best tablatures that we were able to find on the web for the same pieces of music on which their system was judged had the characteristic that nearly every note was placed at the lowest possible position. Tablatures of this nature are not particularly difficult to create, and our system achieved an accuracy of 98.9% on data from the same pieces of music. We could not test our neural network on this data, however, since left handed fingering notation for these pieces was not available to us. For most of the thirty excerpts on which our algorithm was run, tablature creation is much more difficult. For this reason, we contend that the versatility and validity of our approach can be justly asserted.

7   Further Directions

This system has been used in the development of a framework for creating arrangements of pieces of music never before written for guitar, with compelling results. It acts as part of an evaluation function for a guided heuristic search that distinguishes arrangements on the basis of both playability, as defined by TabGA, and musical merit[10].

References

1. Gordon, V.S., Whitley, D.: Serial and Parallel Genetic Algorithms as Function Optimizers. 5th International Conference on Genetic Algorithms (1993) 177–183
2. Heijink, H., Meulenbroek, R.G.J.: On the complexity of classical guitar playing: functional adaptations to task constraints. Journal of Motor Behaviour **34(4)** (2002) 339–351
3. Miura, M., Hirota, I., Hama, N., Yanigida, M.: Constructing a System for Finger-Position Determination and Tablature Generation for Playing Melodies on Guitars. Systems and Computers in Japan **35(6)** (2004) 755–763
4. Radicioni, D., Lombardo, V.: Guitar Fingering for Music Performance. Proceedings of the Internation Computer Music Conference. Barcelona, Spain. (2005)
5. Radicioni, D., Anselma, L., Lombardo, V.: A segmentation-based prototype to compute string instruments fingering. Proceedings of the Conference on Interdisciplinary Musicology. Graz, Austria. (2004)
6. Radisavljevic, A., Driessen, P.: Path Difference Learning for Guitar Fingering Problem. Proceedings of the International Computer Music Conference. Miami, USA. (2004)
7. Sayegh, S.: Fingering for String Instruments with the Optimum Path Paradigm. Computer Music Journal **13(6)** (1989) 76–84
8. Smith, B.: GAIL: Georgia Artificial Intelligence Library Neural Network Package. University of Georgia. (2004)
9. Tuohy, D., Potter, W.D.: A Genetic Algorithm for the Automatic Generation of Playable Guitar Tablature. Proceedings of the International Computer Music Conference. Barcelona, Spain. (2005)
10. Tuohy, D., Potter, W.D.: GA-based Music Arranging for Guitar. Submitted to IEEE Congress on Evolutionary Computation (2006).
11. Wang, J., Tsai-Yen, L.: Generating Guitar Scores from a MIDI Source. International Symposium on Multimedia Information Processing. Taipei, Taiwan. (1997)
12. Whitley, D.: Genetic Algorithms and Neural Networks. Genetic Algorithms in Engineering and Computer Science (1995) 1–15
13. Whitley, D., Kauth, J.: GENITOR: A Different Genetic Algorithm. Proceedings of the Rocky Mountain Conference on Artificial Intelligence.
14. Whitley, D., Starkweather, T.: GENITOR II: a distributed genetic algorithm. J. Expt. Theor. Artif. Intel. **2** (1990) 189–213
15. NeuroShell 2 Neural Network Kit by Ward Systems Group. http://www.wardsystems.com.
16. Classical Guitar Tablature. http://www.classtab.org
17. A-Z Guitar Tabs. http://www.guitaretab.com

Search Space Reduction as a Tool for Achieving Intensification and Diversification in Ant Colony Optimisation

Marcus Randall

School of Information Technology
Bond University, QLD 4229, Australia
Ph.: +61 7 55953361
mrandall@bond.edu.au

Abstract. The aim of adding explicit intensification/diversification measures to ant colony optimisation is so that it better samples the search space. A new and novel method of achieving this is based on the idea of search space reduction in which solution components are fixed during an intensification stage and certain values for some components are excluded during diversification. These phases are triggered as required throughout the search process. In comparison to an existing intensification/diversification scheme and a control ant colony solver, the results using the travelling salesman problem reveal that the new scheme offers a substantial improvement. It often achieves optimal results for benchmark problem instances. Additionally, this scheme requires few extra computational resources and is applicable to a range of combinatorial problems.

Keywords: heuristic search, ant colony optimisation.

1   Introduction

Search through combinatorial landscapes requires the ability, at different stages, to explore subsections of space more thoroughly as well as to discover promising new territories. These are referred to as *intensification* and *diversification* respectively and is an essential part of successful search strategies [7]. A relatively new combinatorial optimisation meta-heuristic strategy, known as ant colony optimisation (ACO) [3], has been applied to a wide range of problems. While it has some intensification/diversification features built into the underlying solution construction mechanism (see Randall [9] for a description of these), relatively little work has been carried out in developing and testing explicit intensification/diversification schemes. Representative work in this area is described below.

Gambardella, Taillard and Dorigo [6] propose a hybrid ant system for the quadratic assignment problem (QAP) that is known as HAS-QAP. It

M. Ali and R. Dapoigny (Eds.): IEA/AIE 2006, LNAI 4031, pp. 254–261, 2006.

incorporates simple intensification and diversification processes into the algorithm. HAS-QAP begins each iteration with a complete solution (rather than constructing it) and uses an ant system controlled local search. In an intensification phase, the initial solution it uses is the best solution found to date. When diversification is activated, both the pheromone matrix and the initial solution are reinitialised. In the case of the latter, the solution is a random solution (i.e., a random permutation for the QAP). Blum [1] follows similar ideas to the above by allowing the search to intensify around a set of elite solutions (intensification phase) and diversifying by having a number of restart phases and resetting the pheromone values to random levels.

Randall and Tonkes [11] outline a scheme based on ant colony system (ACS) in which the characteristic component[1] selection equations (see Equations 1 and 2 in the next section) are modified so that the level of pheromone, in relation to the heuristic information, is varied. The premise is that components having higher pheromone levels have shown in the past to be attractive and vice-versa. During an intensification phase, pheromone levels have a higher influence, while during diversification, components with large amounts of pheromone are actively discouraged. Meyer [8] extended this idea by introducing the concept of "α-annealing" based on simulated annealing. Like simulated annealing, diversity is highly encouraged at the beginning of the search process by controlling the relative weighting of the pheromone information. The paper reports encouraging initial results for small benchmark travelling salesman problems (TSPs).

More systematic approaches to intensification/diversification were given in Randall [9] and Randall [10]. The first analysed the frequency of incorporating components into the solution. In an intensification phase, frequently incorporated components were highly weighted while in a diversification phase their use was discouraged. These phases were triggered on the basis of the progress of the search. That is diversification was started if the search had not recently received improved costs while intensification was performed if the search was frequently receiving good solutions. Overall, improved solution costs were obtained for larger TSPs over a control ACS strategy. In the second work, ants within a particular colony (iteration) were explicitly forced to use different solution components at certain steps within an iteration. This allowed the ants to spread out in search space and not follow one another, thus implementing a diversification only strategy. Significantly improved solutions were produced (over a control strategy) for a variety of TSP and QAP instances.

The strategy outlined herein develops the notion of explicit intensification and diversification and integrates this within a search space reduction technique. The remainder of this paper is organised as follows. Section 2 outlines the standard mechanics of the ACS search paradigm in regards to the TSP while Section 3 outlines how the new intensification/diversification strategy can be used within ACS. Section 4 gives the computational results and Section 5 has the conclusions of this work.

---

[1] A component is the building block of a problem.

2 Ant Colony System for the Travelling Salesman Problem

ACO is modelled on the foraging behaviour of *Argentine* ants. The seminal work by Dorigo [2] showed that this behaviour could be used to solve discrete optimisation problems. ACO is in fact a collection of meta-heuristic techniques. This section gives a brief overview of one of these, ant colony system [4].

ACS can best be described with the TSP metaphor as it is a well understood optimisation problem. In addition, it will be used to test the new intensification/diversification strategy outlined in this paper. Consider a set of cities, with known distances between each pair of cities. The aim of the TSP is to find the shortest path to traverse all cities exactly once and return to the starting city. The ACS paradigm is applied to this problem in the following way. Consider a TSP with N cities. Cities i and j are separated by distance $d(i,j)$. Place m ants randomly on these cities $(m \ll N)$. In discrete time steps, all ants select their next city then simultaneously move to their next city. Ants deposit a substance known as *pheromone* to communicate with the colony about the utility (goodness) of the edges. Denote the accumulated strength of pheromone on edge (i,j) by $\tau(i,j)$.

At the commencement of each time step, Equations 1 and 2 are used to select the next city s for ant k currently at city r. Equation 1 is a greedy selection technique that will choose the city that has the best combination of short distance and large pheromone levels. Using the first branch of Equation 1 exclusively will lead to sub-optimal solutions due to its greediness. Therefore, there is a probability that Equation 2 will be used to select the next city instead. This equation generates a probability and then roulette wheel selection is used to generate s.

$$s = \begin{cases} \arg\max_{u \in J_k(r)} \left\{ \tau(r,u)[d(r,u)]^\beta \right\} & \text{if } q \leq q_0 \\ \text{Equation 2} & \text{otherwise} \end{cases} \tag{1}$$

$$s = R\left(\begin{cases} \dfrac{\tau(r,s)[d(r,s)]^\beta}{\sum_{u \in J_k(r)} \tau(r,u)[d(r,u)]^\beta} & \text{if } s \in J_k(r) \\ 0 & \text{otherwise} \end{cases} \right) \tag{2}$$

where R is the roulette wheel selection function, $q \in [0,1]$ is a uniform random number and q_0 is a parameter. To maintain the restriction of unique visitation, ant k is prohibited from selecting a city which it has already visited. The cities which have not yet been visited by ant k are indexed by $J_k(r)$. It is typical that the parameter β is negative so that shorter edges are favoured. The use of $\tau(r,s)$ ensures preference is given to edges that are well traversed (i.e., have a high pheromone level). The pheromone level on the selected edge is updated according to the local updating rule in Equation 3.

$$\tau(r,s) \leftarrow (1 - \rho) \cdot \tau(r,s) + \rho \cdot \tau_0 \tag{3}$$

Where:

ρ is the local pheromone decay parameter, $0 < \rho < 1$.
τ_0 is the initial amount of pheromone deposited on each of the edges.

Global updating of the pheromone takes place once all ants have constructed a solution. Edges that compose the best solution (so far) are rewarded with an increase in their pheromone level while the pheromone on the other edges is evaporated (decreased). This is expressed in Equation 4.

$$\tau(r, s) \leftarrow (1 - \gamma) \cdot \tau(r, s) + \gamma \cdot \Delta\tau(r, s) \tag{4}$$

$$\Delta\tau(r, s) = \begin{cases} \frac{Q}{L} & \text{if } (r, s) \text{ is an edge within the best solution} \\ 0 & \text{otherwise.} \end{cases} \tag{5}$$

Where:

$\Delta\tau(r, s)$ is used to reinforce the pheromone on the edges of the best solution (see Equation 5).
L is the length of the best (shortest) tour to date while Q is a constant.
γ is the global pheromone decay parameter, $0 < \gamma < 1$.

An in-depth pseudocode description of the ACS algorithm can be found in Dorigo and Gambardella [5].

3   Fixing and Restricting Solution Components During Intensification/Diversification Phases

The following description of the new intensification/diversification scheme is applied to the TSP. However, the principles are applicable to other combinatorial problems.

A matrix r is used to store the frequency and quality of solutions in which the available components appear. Specifically, for each component[2] of an ant's solution, r_{ij} (where i is the city and j is the position in the solution vector) is increased by an amount proportional to the quality of the solution. This is calculated by Equation 6 and applied after the ants have constructed their solutions within an iteration.

$$r_{ij} = r_{ij} + c\left(1 - \frac{cost_k}{U}\right) \qquad 1 \leq k \leq m \tag{6}$$

Where:

c is a scaling constant,
$cost_k$ is the cost of the solution constructed by ant k and
U is an upper bound on cost such as that constructed by the nearest neighbour heuristic.

It is necessary for both intensification and diversification to determine those components with the greatest r values for each position within the solution/tour. In intensification, these components can be fixed so that ants need only produce

---

[2] A component for a TSP is defined as a city at a position.

a partial solution for each of the phase's iterations. For diversification however, the values of the components are made tabu, forcing the ants to search elsewhere. The question of how these components are selected at certain times within the search process is an important one. While many methods to achieve this exist, the following approach is adopted as it does not require additional parameters. In essence, the cluster of the best performing components is sought. The largest gap between succeedingly ordered values of r is used to form the cluster. Algorithm 1 outlines the mechanics of this.

Algorithm 1. The algorithm to choose the intensification/diversification group of components. Note that vector f contains the set of final components.

1: Find the best city (in terms of r) for each position and assign these values to vector y
2: Remove duplicate city components from y (retaining the best city for each position)
3: Order y in descending order
4: $z =$ The index of the largest difference between each successive pair of items in y
5: Assign the components $y(1 \ldots z)$ to vector f
6: **return** z
7: **end**

Statement 2 of the algorithm is a necessary one for problems that require each solution component to have a unique value (e.g., permutation problems). For other problems, such as the generalised assignment problem (in which an agent may perform many jobs), it is unnecessary and can be removed.

In intensification, the components produced from Algorithm 1 are fixed and ants use the normal component selection rules to construct the rest of the (partial) solution. In diversification, the values of the components effectively receive a 0 probability of being selected. At the beginning of each phase r is set to all 0 entries.

The three phases of the search, namely, *normal, intensification* and *diversification* are triggered according to the rules established by Randall [9]. In summary, these are:

> *intensification* - If improved solutions are received at a frequency greater than *intens* iterations, this phase is initiated.
>
> *diversification* - If improved solutions cannot be found within *divers* iterations, this phase is initiated.

Note that each phase lasts for a fixed number of iterations (referred to as the *phase_length*) and that *intens* and *divers* are parameters of the process. The search reverts to the standard ACO algorithm (*normal*) after these phases have been completed.

4   Computational Experience

Twenty TSP problem instances are used to test the new intensification/diversification technique. As the problem instances and the way the search phases are triggered are the same as Randall [9], the results may be directly compared. The solvers used in the previous study are an ACS control strategy (i.e., one without the explicit intensification and diversification mechanisms) and a scheme implementing intensification/diversification based on frequency analysis (previously described). The test problems are from TSPLIB [12] and are given in Table 1. The computing platform used to perform the experiments is a 2.6 GHz Pentium 4. Each problem instance is run across ten random seeds.

The ACS parameter settings are $\{\beta = -2, \gamma = 0.1, \rho = 0.1, m = 10, q_0 = 0.9, intens = 20, divers = 200, phase\_length = 200, c = 0.0001\}$. The standard ACS values have been found to be robust by Dorigo and Gambardella [5] and the intensification/diversification settings have been used in Randall [9]. Three thousand iterations per run are used as this can be carried out in a reasonable amount of computational time and allow sufficient use of the intensification and diversification mechanisms.

The results of the three strategies are shown in Table 2. Results are shown in terms of relative percentage deviation (RPD) from the best known cost. This is calculated as $\frac{E-F}{F} \times 100$ where E is the result cost and F is the best known cost. In order to describe the range of costs gained by these experiments, the minimum (denoted "Min"), median (denoted "Med") and maximum (denoted "Max") are given. Non-parametric descriptive statistics are used as the data are highly non-normally distributed. For each of these measures, a bold entry indicates (for that solver) that it is the best of all the solvers.

Table 1. Problem instances used in this study

Name	Size (cities)	Best-Known Cost
gr24	24	1272
fri26	26	937
swiss42	42	1273
hk48	48	11461
eil51	51	426
berlin52	52	7542
st70	70	675
eil76	76	538
kroA100	100	21282
bier127	127	118282
si175	175	21407
d198	198	15780
ts225	225	126643
gil262	262	2378
pr299	299	48191
lin318	318	42029
pcb442	442	50778
si535	535	48450
u574	574	36905
rat575	575	6773

Table 2. The results for the three strategies. Note that "Indiv 1" refers to intensification/diversification strategy of Randall [9] and "Indiv 2" is the new scheme.

Problem	Control			Indiv 1			Indiv 2		
	Min	Med	Max	Min	Med	Max	Min	Med	Max
gr24	0	0.47	5.03	0	0.47	5.03	0	0	0
fri26	0	1.92	2.56	0	1.92	2.56	0	0	0
swiss42	0	2.71	7.54	0	3.18	7.54	0	0	0
hk48	0	0.42	2.71	0	1.61	3.62	0	0	0.11
eil51	0.23	2	5.87	0.23	2.11	6.81	0	0.23	0.23
berlin52	0	3.02	5.56	0	3.43	6.96	0	0	0
st70	0.89	2.59	6.81	1.04	3.41	6.81	0	0	0.89
eil76	2.23	3.72	5.58	2.42	3.72	5.95	0	0	1.12
kroA100	0.05	0.73	6.47	0.8	3.88	9.14	0	0	0.45
bier127	1.99	4.13	4.87	1.22	2.51	7.69	0	0.23	0.38
si175	8.1	8.95	9.28	1.63	8.57	9.28	0	0.02	0.05
d198	1.22	2.13	3.37	2.95	3.93	6.08	0	0.28	0.52
ts225	5.06	5.93	7.01	2.36	3.28	9.69	0	0	0
gil262	2.19	4.44	6.48	7.82	10.45	14.17	0.08	0.61	1.64
pr299	11.29	13.2	15.15	5.79	9.12	17.12	0.33	0.93	2.17
lin318	14.62	15.9	17.5	7.1	19.59	21.75	0	0.53	1.27
pcb442	20.47	21.43	23.27	5.91	22.7	25.91	0.33	0.93	2.17
si535	11.6	14.29	15.95	11.6	14.29	15.95	0.02	0.05	0.13
u574	24.11	26.44	28.59	7.4	12.6	29.44	13.88	14.49	15.33
rat575	17.6	20.02	21.69	10.87	14.87	22.87	1.23	1.27	1.92

It is evident that on the majority of occasions, the new intensification/diversification scheme outperforms the control and original intensification/diversification technique. It frequently finds the optimal solution, even for the largest size problems (up to lin318). The only problem on which its performance is marginally behind is u574, although its worst case behaviour is better than its counterparts.

In terms of the computational requirements, the new scheme adds relatively little to that of the overall algorithm. Its largest part is that of calculating the components that form the intensification/diversification group. However, the calculations need only be performed infrequently in a run. Additionally, in both intensification and diversification, the size of the explorable search space is reduced (especially for intensification).

5   Conclusions

In order to find and explore promising regions of the state space, it is often necessary to use intensification and diversification strategies. The one outlined in this paper identifies, at various stages within a run, groups of components that have been found to be good in the construction of solutions. In an intensification phase, these components are fixed while for diversification, the values of the components within the a group are excluded. The results show that this technique outperforms a previous strategy on a range of TSP instances.

Two issues that require further attention are a) the way in which the group of fixed components is selected and b) the method of triggering intensification, diversification and normal phases within the run. The former is particularly crucial so that the most promising sub-regions of space may be identified. The new technique will also need to be empirically tested across a range of problems.

References

1. C. Blum. ACO applied to group shop scheduling: A case study on intensification and diversification. In M. Dorigo, G. Di Caro, and M. Sampels, editors, *Third International Workshop on Ant Algorithms, ANTS 2002*, volume 2463 of *Lecture Notes in Computer Science*, pages 14–27, Brussels, Belgium, 2002. Springer-Verlag.
2. M. Dorigo. *Optimization, Learning and Natural Algorithms*. PhD. thesis, Politecnico di Milano, 1992.
3. M. Dorigo and G. Di Caro. The ant colony optimization meta-heuristic. In D. Corne, M. Dorigo, and F. Glover, editors, *New Ideas in Optimization*, pages 11–32. McGraw-Hill, London, 1999.
4. M. Dorigo and L. Gambardella. Ant colonies for the traveling salesman problem. *BioSystems*, 43:73–81, 1997.
5. M. Dorigo and L. Gambardella. Ant Colony System: A cooperative learning approach to the traveling salesman problem. *IEEE Transactions on Evolutionary Computation*, 1(1):53–66, 1997.
6. L. Gambardella, E. Taillard, and M. Dorigo. Ant colonies for the quadratic assignment problem. *Journal of the Operational Research Society*, 50:167–176, 1999.
7. F. Glover and M. Laguna. *Tabu Search*. Kluwer Academic Publishers, Boston, MA, 1997.
8. B. Meyer. On the convergence behaviour of ant colony search. In *Proceedings of the 7th Asia-Pacific Conference on Complex Systems*, pages 153–167, 2004.
9. M. Randall. A systematic strategy to incorporate intensification and diversification into ant colony optimisation. In H. Abbass and J. Wiles, editors, *Proceedings of the Australian Conference on Artificial Life*, pages 199–208, Canberra, Australia, 2003.
10. M. Randall. Maintaining diversity within individual ant colonies. In H. Abbass, T Bossamaier, and J. Wiles, editors, *Recent Advances in Artificial Life*, volume 3 of *Advances in Natural Computation*, pages 227–238. World Scientific, New Jersey, 2005.
11. M. Randall and E. Tonkes. Intensification and diversification strategies in ant colony optimisation. *Complexity International*, 9, 2002.
12. G. Reinelt. TSPLIB - A traveling salesman problem library. *ORSA Journal on Computing*, 3:376–384, 1991.

Truck Dock Assignment Problem with Operational Time Constraint Within Crossdocks

Andrew Lim[1,2], Hong Ma[1], and Zhaowei Miao[1,2]

[1] Dept of Industrial Engineering and Logistics Management
Hong Kong Univ of Science and Technology, Clear Water Bay, Kowloon, Hong Kong
[2] School of Computer Science & Engineering
South China University of Technology, Guang Dong, PR China

Abstract. In this paper, we consider a truck dock assignment problem with operational time constraint in crossdocks where the number of trucks exceeds the number of docks available. The objective is to find an optimal assignment of trucks that minimizes the operational cost of the cargo shipments and the total number of unfulfilled shipments. We combine the above two objectives into one term: the total cost, a sum of the total dock operational cost and the penalty cost for all the unfulfilled shipments. The problem is then formulated as an Integer Programming (IP) model. A genetic algorithm (GA), in which the operators relate to the IP model constraints, is then proposed. Computational experiments are conducted, showing that the proposed GA dominates the CPLEX Solver in nearly all test cases adapted from industrial applications.

1 Introduction and Problem Description

A crossdock can be thought of as a high-speed warehouse with several purposes. Most importantly it is a consolidation point that helps to reduce transportation costs. One of the key activities at crossdocks is the dock assignment for trucks. Trucks are assigned to docks for the duration of a time period during which the cargo and trucks are processed. Dock availability and times of arrivals/departures for each truck can change during the course of the planning horizon due to operational contingencies. Such changes in turn have impact on dock availability, since docks may become unavailable when required. Nowadays, a familiar scene at crossdocks is that arriving trucks are waiting to be processed, sometimes for a long time, before finally proceeding to their docks, because the docks are occupied by another truck. Therefore, it is necessary to schedule those docks well in order to increase the utilization and achieve better performance of the transshipment network. The large number of freight and the dynamic nature of the problem has also made it important for crossdock operators to use docks in the best possible way.

In classical models, transshipment is studied in the context of network flow [1, 6]. One such model where transshipment becomes an important factor is in crossdocking which has become synonymous with rapid consolidation and

M. Ali and R. Dapoigny (Eds.): IEA/AIE 2006, LNAI 4031, pp. 262–271, 2006.

processing. Napolitano has described various crossdocking operations which include manufacturing, transportation, distributor, transportation, retail and opportunistic crossdocking, all of which have the common feature of consolidation and short cycle times made possible by known pickup and delivery times [8]. Tsui and Chang used a bilinear program of assigning trailers to doors, where the objective was to minimize weighted distances between incoming and outgoing trailers [10]. Recently, a study by Bartholdi and Gue examined minimizing labor costs in freight terminals by properly assigning incoming and outgoing trailers to doors [2]. Although this cross-docking study has considered intra-terminal factors such as types of congestion that impact costs, they do not address actual dock assignments to arriving vehicles when considering the time window of trucks and capacity of crossdocks. Moreover, our problem is similar in some ways to the problem of gate assignments in airports, for which some analytical work exists. For instance, the basic gate assignment problem is a quadratic assignment problem and shown to be **NP**-hard [9]. Due to the **NP**-hardness, various heuristic approaches have been used by researchers. Recently, work has focused on the over-constrained airport gate assignment [3, 4, 7], where there is an excess of flights over gates. The objective was to minimize the number of flights without any gate assigned (i.e. those left on the ramp) and the total walking distance.

In this paper, we consider the over-constrained truck dock assignment problem with time window, operational time, and capacity constraint in a transshipment network through crossdocks where the number of trucks exceeds the number of docks available, and where the objective is to minimize the operational cost of the cargo shipment and the number of unfulfilled shipments. The two objectives are combined into one term: the total cost, a sum of the total dock operational cost and the total penalty cost for the unfulfilled shipments. The problem is then formulated as an Integer Programming (IP) model. Since the air gate assignment problem is **NP**-hard, our problem is also **NP**-hard, because the air gate assignment problem is a special case of our problem.

This work is organized as follows: in the next section, an IP model of the problem is developed. In Section 3, we propose a genetic algorithm and provide the computational results. We summarize our findings and suggest future work in Section 4.

2   IP Formulation

In this section, we provide an IP model for the problem. We have the capacity constraint, which means that the number of cargos inside the crossdock is limited by the total capacity. The other important constraint is the time window constraint. For example, if truck A at dock a is to receive cargos from truck B at dock b, truck A has to wait at dock a until the pallet with cargos arrives, i.e. truck B needs to send the cargos well in advance, taking the operational time for cargo shipment from dock a to dock b into consideration. Usually in the crossdock, the operational time is decided by the physical distance between the two docks. If it is found that some trucks cannot be assigned due to the limited number of docks, those trucks need to be rescheduled. The trucks can be postponed for one more day, or they can be rescheduled to other crossdocks where a vacancy is available. In such situations, a penalty cost is incurred for all the unfulfilled cargo shipments by these trucks. Figure 1 illustrates an outline of the crossdock and major elements of our problem.

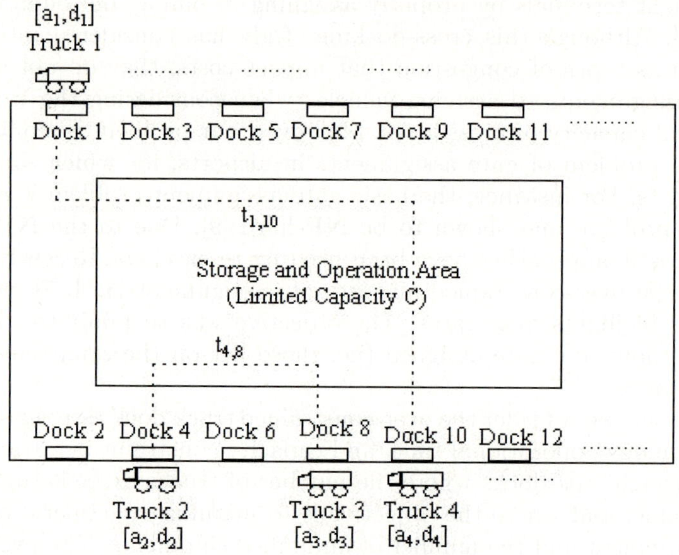

Fig. 1. Truck Dock Assignment Problem with Operation Time Constraint

In the IP model, the following notations are used:

N: set of trucks arriving at and/or departing from the crossdock;
M: set of docks available in the crossdock;
n: total number of trucks, that is $|N|$, where $|N|$ denotes the cardinality of N;
m: total number of docks, that is $|M|$;
a_i: arrival time of truck i ($1 \leq i \leq n$);
d_i: departure time of truck i ($1 \leq i \leq n$);
$t_{k,l}$: operational time for pallets from dock k to dock l ($1 \leq k, l \leq m$);
$f_{i,j}$: number of pallets transferring from truck i to truck j ($1 \leq i, j \leq n$;)
$c_{k,l}$: operational cost per unit time from dock k to dock l ($1 \leq k, l \leq m$);
$p_{i,j}$: penalty cost per unit cargo from truck i to truck j ($1 \leq i, j \leq n$;)
C: capacity of crossdock, i.e. the maximum number of cargos the crossdock can hold at a time.

We also define $x_{i,j} \in \{0, 1\}$: 1 iff truck i departs no later than truck j arrives; 0 otherwise. Then we set $x_{i,j}$ from the truck time window data (a_i, d_i) ($1 \leq i \leq n$). The decision variables are as follows:

$$y_{i,k} = \begin{cases} 1, & \text{if truck } i \text{ is assigned to dock } k \\ 0, & \text{otherwise.} \end{cases}$$

$$z_{ijkl} = \begin{cases} 1, & \text{if truck } i \text{ assigned to dock } k \text{ and truck } j \text{ assigned to dock } l \\ 0, & \text{otherwise.} \end{cases}$$

Note that $y_{i,k} = y_{j,k} = 1$ implies that $a_i > d_j$ or $a_j > d_i$ $(1 \leq i, j \leq n)$. Moreover, in order to make all data reasonable, some remarks of the parameters and setting are given as follows:

(1) $f_{i,j} \geq 0$, iff $d_j \geq a_i$ $(1 \leq i, j \leq n)$, otherwise $f_{i,j} = 0$ which means truck i transfers cargos to truck j iff truck j departs no earlier than truck i arrives ;
(2) $a_i < d_i$ $(1 \leq i \leq n)$ which means for each truck, the arrival time should be strictly smaller than departure time;
(3) $n > m$ which satisfies the over-constrained condition;
(4) capacity C is defined as follows: when truck i comes, then it will consume $\sum_{k=1}^{m} \sum_{l=1}^{m} \sum_{j=1}^{n} f_{i,j} z_{ijkl}$ units of capacity. On the other hand, only if when truck j leaves, then $\sum_{k=1}^{m} \sum_{l=1}^{m} \sum_{i=1}^{n} f_{i,j} z_{ijkl}$ units of capacity release;
(5) sort all the a_i's and b_i's in an increasing order, and let t_r $(r = 1, 2..., 2n)$ correspond to these $2n$ numbers such that $t_1 \leq t_2 \leq ... \leq t_{2n}$. Use this notation, we can easily formulate the set of capacity constraints later.

Our objective is to minimize the total cost: the sum of the operational cost and the penalty cost. The IP model is as follows:

$$\min\left(\sum_{k=1}^{m} \sum_{l=1}^{m} \sum_{i=1}^{n} \sum_{j=1}^{n} c_{k,l} t_{k,l} z_{ijkl} + \sum_{i=1}^{n} \left(\sum_{j=1}^{n} p_{i,j} f_{i,j} \left(1 - \sum_{k=1}^{m} \sum_{l=1}^{m} z_{ijkl}\right)\right)\right)$$

s.t.

$$\sum_{k=1}^{m} y_{i,k} \leq 1 (1 \leq i \leq n) \tag{1}$$

$$z_{ijkl} \leq y_{i,k} (1 \leq i, j \leq n, 1 \leq k, l \leq m) \tag{2}$$

$$z_{ijkl} \leq y_{j,l} (1 \leq i, j \leq n, 1 \leq k, l \leq m) \tag{3}$$

$$y_{i,k} + y_{j,l} - 1 \leq z_{ijkl} (1 \leq i, j \leq n, 1 \leq k, l \leq m) \tag{4}$$

$$x_{i,j} + x_{j,i} \geq z_{ijkk} (1 \leq i, j \leq n, i \neq j, 1 \leq k \leq m) \tag{5}$$

$$\sum_{k=1}^{m} \sum_{l=1}^{m} \sum_{i \in \{i:\ a_i \leq t_r\}} \sum_{j=1}^{n} f_{i,j} z_{ijkl} - \sum_{k=1}^{m} \sum_{l=1}^{m} \sum_{i=1}^{n} \sum_{j \in \{j:\ d_j \leq t_r\}} f_{i,j} z_{ijkl} \leq C (1 \leq r \leq 2n) \tag{6}$$

$$f_{ij}z_{ijkl}(d_j - a_i - t_{k,l}) \geq 0(1 \leq i, j \leq n, 1 \leq k, l \leq m) \tag{7}$$

$$y_{i,k} \in \{0,1\}, y_{j,l} \in \{0,1\}, z_{ijkl} \in \{0,1\}(1 \leq i, j \leq n, 1 \leq k, l \leq m) \tag{8}$$

The first term in the objective function is operational cost and the second term is the penalty cost. Constraints (1) ensures that each truck cannot be assigned to more than one dock. Constraints (2)-(4) jointly define the variable z which represent the logic relationship among $y_{i,k}$, $y_{j,l}$ and z_{ijkl}. Constraint (5) specifies that one dock cannot be occupied by two different trucks simultaneously. Constraint (6) is capacity constraint which means that for each time point t_r, the total number of pallets inside the crossdock cannot exceed the capacity C. Finally, constraint (7) says that the transfer process of cargoes from truck i at dock k to truck j at dock l takes place within the time windows, i.e. from the arrival time of truck i to the departure time of truck j.

3   Meta-heuristics: Genetic Algorithm

It is possible to solve the IP model developed in section 2 by the ILOG CPLEX Solver, but we find that as the problem size grows, the number of decision variables and constraints in the IP model multiplies astronomically. For a moderate problem size in our consulting work for the industry of 40 trucks and 8 docks, the number of decision variable $z_{i,j,k,l}$ reaches $102,400$, and the number of active constraints turns out to exceed $270,000$. Therefore, It is necessary to develop some meta-heuristic approaches to handle large real world cases efficiently.

Genetic algorithms (GA) have become a well-known and powerful meta-heuristic approach for hard combinatorial optimization problems [5]. Genetic algorithms are based on the ideas of natural selection, and have been applied to numerous combinatorial optimization problems successfully. In this section, we first describe the essential components of our proposed GA for the dock assignment problem, eg. solution representation, the crossover operator, etc. Then we outline the framework of the GA. Finally, we give the details of the experiments conducted and analysis of the results.

3.1   GA Components

Solution Representation. The chromosome is an important component in GA and has great influence on the algorithm output. We here represent the dock assignment solution by a chromosome sequence A of length n that defines an assignment of n trucks to the docks. The value of each gene is the dock gate number. The representation is depicted in Fig. 2. If the truck is not assigned to any of the docks when all the docks are occupied, the corresponding gene is set to 0. In case when a generated chromosome sequence from the initial population is infeasible due to constraint (5) and (7), or the capacity constraint (6) in the IP model, we simply drop it and generate a new one.

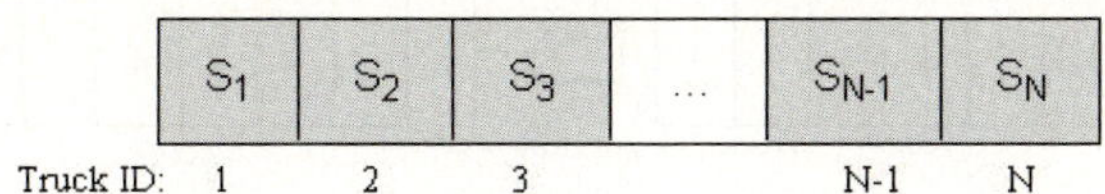

Fig. 2. The Solution Representation

Crossover. We implement two crossover operators: One-Point Crossover and Two-Point Crossover. In the One-Point Crossover, one random crossing site is selected. The first offspring is built from attaching the first part of the first parent to the second part of the second parent. Similarly, the second offspring is built from the first part of the second parent and the second part of the first parent. In the Two-Point Crossover, two random crossing sites are selected. The sequences between two crossing sites are swapped to produce offsprings. This is illustrated in the following example. The operators are illustrated in Fig. 3 and Fig. 4.

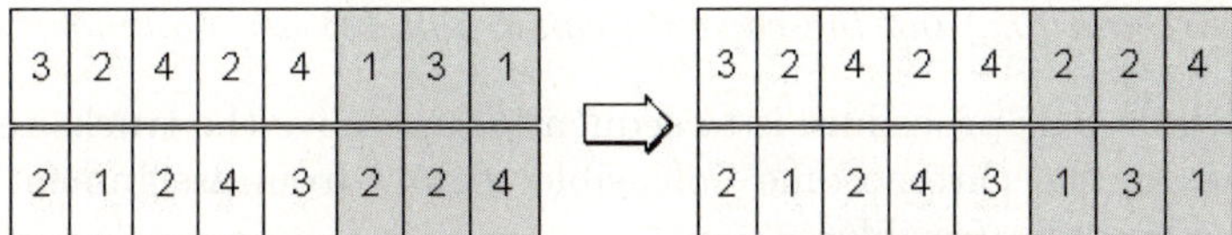

Fig. 3. The One-Point Crossover Operator

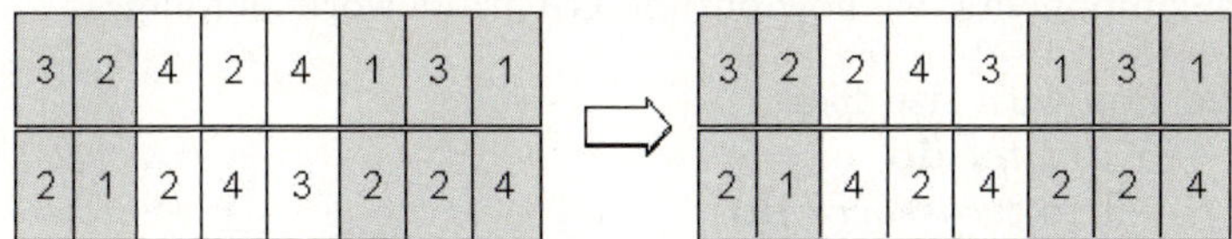

Fig. 4. The Two-Point Crossover Operator

In our proposed GA, we use both of the above-mentioned operators. During the crossing-over procedure, half of the new population is generated by the One-Point Crossover, and the other half is generated by the Two-Point Crossover.

Mutation. We chose the 'Swap Mutation' as our mutation operator, which selects two mutation sites at random and swaps the values at these two sites. An example is in Fig. 5.

Repair. It is obvious that the above crossover and mutation operator will generate infeasible chromosomes that violate some of the constraints in the model (see constraints (5), (6) and (7)). We next first define the 'infeasible region' of the infeasible chromosome, and then describe the repair operator based on Lemma 1.

Fig. 5. The Mutation Operator

Definition 1. *The 'infeasible region' of offsprings generated by the One-Point Crossover is defined as the shorter part separated by crossing site.*

Definition 2. *The 'infeasible region' of offsprings generated by the Two-Point Crossover is defined as the shorter part of the swapped part and the unswapped part separated by the two crossing sites.*

Definition 3. *The 'infeasible region' of offsprings generated by the 'Swap Mutation' consists only of two mutation sites.*

Lemma 1. *Removing the trucks from the assignment in the 'infeasible region' of the chromosome strictly reduces the chance of infeasibility. This is because once the truck is removed from the assignment, the truck related time window constraint (5) and (7), and the capacity constraint (6) are no longer active.*

Therefore, the repair procedure is to sequentially remove the trucks represented by the genes of the chromosome 'infeasible region' from assignment until the chromosome becomes feasible.

3.2 GA Framework and Parameter Settings

With these components, we now outline GA framework as follows.

> **Initialize** Pop with size $\sharp pop$
> **for** $iter \leftarrow 1$ to $\sharp iter$ **do**
>   **for** $off \leftarrow 1$ to $\sharp crossover$ **do**
>   Randomly select ParentA and ParentB
>   Crossover ParentA and ParentB to produce OffspringA and OffspringB
>   **end for**
>   **for** each newly-produced individual indv **do**
>   mutate indv with probability p_1
>   **end for**
>   repair the infeasible newly-produced individuals
>   evaluate each individual
>   select the best $\sharp pop$ individuals from all the individuals
>   update current best solution
> **end for**

In the algorithm, #pop, #crossover, #iter and p_1 are parameters. The following values are used in the experiments: $\sharp iter = 10^4$, $\sharp pop = 300$, $\sharp crossover = 500$. The mutation probability p_1 is taken to be 0.2. The maximum iteration is 10^5 and the termination condition was when the best solution did not improve within 500 iterations.

3.3   Experimental Results and Analysis

The algorithm is coded in Java and run on Intel P4 2.4GHz PC with 512M memory. As comparison, we use ILOG CPLEX 8.0 to solve the IP formulation presented in Section 2.

Test Data Generation. We chose a representative layout of a crossdock to have two parallel sets of terminals, where docks are symmetrically located in the two terminals shown in Fig. 6. Such a scheme is very common in crossdocks today. We set the distance between two adjacent docks within one terminal (e.g., dock 1 and dock 3) to be 1 unit and the distance between two parallel docks in different terminals (e.g., dock 1 and dock 2) to be 3 units. To simplify the problem, we assumed that forklift can only walk 'horizontally' or 'vertically', i.e., if one forklift wants to transfer one pallet from dock 3 to dock 2, the walking distance is 1+3=4 units. This is somewhat similar to the so-called Manhattan metric.

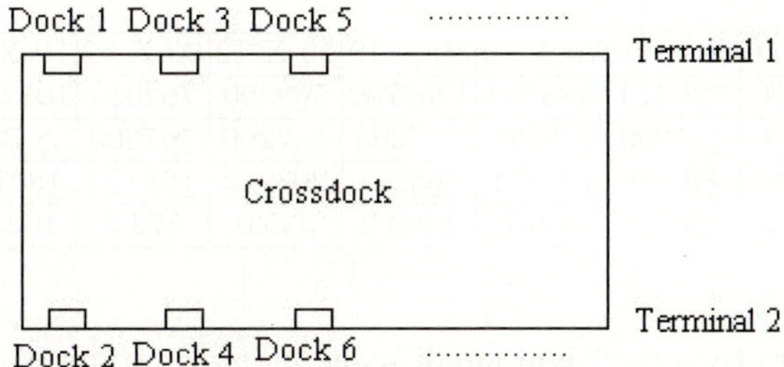

Fig. 6. Crossdock topology

The test data generation requires two parameters: the number of trucks n and the number of docks m. The n start points of truck time window $a_i(1 \leq i \leq n)$ were uniformly generated in the interval $[1, \frac{n*70}{m}]$. The end points of truck i time window d_i were generated as $d_i = a_i + [45, 74]$. The rectilinear walking distances between dock gates k and l is calculated and then proportionally converted to the corresponding operational time $t_{k,l}$. The number of shipping pallets $f_{i,j}$ is randomly generated in the interval $[6, 60]$ if $d_j \geq a_i$ (0 otherwise). The operational cost per unit time from dock k to dock l ($c_{k,l}$) are uniformly generated in the interval $[1, 4]$, while penalty cost per unit cargo from truck i to truck j ($p_{i,j}$) are generated in the interval $[8, 12]$. The total capacity of the crossdock is set to $C = \beta \sum_{1 \leq i,j \leq n} f_{i,j}$, where β is generated in the interval $[0.6, 0.9]$.

Results and Analysis. We designed three categories of instances to test the algorithm. The detailed results are presented in Table 1–3. Each category has 40 test cases, sorted into 8 groups where each group has 5 cases. The first row of the each table specifies the instance size. $n \times m$ denotes that there are n trucks and m docks for this instance group.

Table 1. Results of CPLEX and heuristics on random instances with small sizes

Size	12 X 4	14 X 4	16 X 4	18 X 4	12 X 6	14 X 6	16 X 6	18 X 6
CPlex	11622	6065	13024	36417	10154	6657	14607	23541
Time (s)	527	1712	6403	$\geq$ 7200	$\geq$ 7200	$\geq$ 7200	$\geq$ 7200	$\geq$ 7200
GA	11622	6065	13024	36359	10152	6655	13941	16675
Time (s)	46.8	104.1	36.1	61.2	33.1	81.0	116.2	148.2

Table 2. Results of CPLEX and heuristics on random instances with medium sizes

Size	20 X 6	25 X 6	30 X 6	20 X 8	25 X 8	30 X 8	35 X 8	40 X 8
CPlex	18369	64469	68001	40573	41075	200012	251004	349390
Time	$\geq$ 7200	$\geq$ 7200	$\geq$ 7200	$\geq$ 7200	$\geq$ 7200	$\geq$ 7200	$\geq$ 7200	$\geq$ 7200
GA	18538	64428	35121	38239	32977	39809	18306	102920
Time	50.2	67.1	279.6	76.6	119.4	218.7	182.8	323.8

Table 3. Results of CPLEX and heuristics on random instances with large sizes

Size	50 X 10	60 X 10	70 X 10	80 X 10	50 X 12	60 X 12	70 X 12	80 X 12
CPlex	535690	720610	973230	1257730	569390	762910	1012130	1294070
Time	$\geq$ 7200	$\geq$ 7200	$\geq$ 7200	$\geq$ 7200	$\geq$ 7200	$\geq$ 7200	$\geq$ 7200	$\geq$ 7200
GA	91844	83109	174671	365271	203929	164876	183716	204793
Time	1186.2	918.4	760.7	1493.2	335.0	572.3	1023.8	1265.1

1. Small Size Instances: Eight small scale instance groups are generated with the sizes ranging from 12×4 to 18×6. The results are shown in Table 1. The CPLEX solver gets optimal solutions for the three smallest groups within the time limit of 7200 seconds. For these three instance groups, GA obtains the optimal solutions within a much shorter runtime as well. For the rest groups, CPLEX solver fails to get optimum within the time limit, while GA obtains good solutions quickly.

2. Medium Size Instances: Eight groups which range from 20×6 to 40×8 are used here. CPLEX fails to get optimual solutions within the time limit for all the instance groups in Table 2. CPLEX beats GA only in the smallest instance group(20×6), while GA outperforms CPLEX in all other groups.

3. Large Size Instances: Eight large scale instance groups ranging from 50×10 to 80×12 are generated. The results are shown in Table 3. The CPLEX solver is merely able to obtain feasible dock-assignments within the time limit. GA continues to dominate in solution quality and runtime, solving all the large size test cases within an average of 6 minutes. Therefore, we find the the superiority of the proposed GA is more apparent in medium and large test instances. From the experiment observations, we believe that the proposed GA is an effective approach to tackle the truck dock assignment problem.

4   Conclusions and Future Work

In this paper, we consider the over-constrained truck dock assignment problem with operational time constraint in a transshipment network through crossdocks. The problem is adapted from our consulting work for an industrial application, where the objective is to minimize the number of unfulfilled shipments and the total shipment costs. Our main contribution is that we formulate it as an IP model to minimize the total weighted cost for the first time in literature, taking the operational time of each pallet into consideration and relating it to the respective truck serving time window. We also propose a genetic algorithm in which the operators relate to the IP model, because the astronomical problem size forbids the CPLEX Solver to handle the IP formulation well in many real-world test cases. Experiments are conducted by using a range of test data sets that reflect realistic scenarios. For some small-size instances, the IP model can be solved to optimality by the ILOG CPLEX Solver within a reasonable time. For medium-size and large-size instances, the GA is preferred in order to get quick and good solutions.

With the current problem, the service time windows of trucks are hard time windows, i.e. predetermined and fixed, so there are groups of trucks that are mutually exclusive for assignment, which inevitably causes lost shipments at last. One future study is to work on the soft time window scenario, i.e. the time windows that can be violated at a cost. In this scenario, we are able to slightly adjust the time windows to avoid lost shipments in case that conflicts exist.

References

[1] J.E. Aronson. A survey on dynamic network flows. *Annals of Operations Research*, 20:1–66, 1989.

[2] J. Bartholdi and K. Gue. Reducing labor costs in an ltl cross-docking terminal. *Operations Research*, 48:823–832, 2000.

[3] H. Ding, Andrew Lim, B. Rodrigues, and Yi Zhu. New heuristics for the over-constrained flight to gate assignments. *Journal of the Operational Research Society*, 55:760–768, 2004.

[4] H. Ding, Andrew Lim, B. Rodrigues, and Yi Zhu. The over-constrained airport gate assignment problem. *Computers and Operational Research*, 32:1867–1880, 2005.

[5] John H. Holland. *Adaptation in Natural and Artifical Systems*. University of Michigan Press, Ann Arbor, MI, 1975.

[6] B. Hoppe and E. Tardos. The quickest transshipment problem. *Mathematics of Operations Research*, 25(1):36–62, 2000.

[7] Andrew Lim, B. Rodrigues, and Yi Zhu. Airport gate scheduling with time windows. *Artificial Intelligence Review*, 24:5–31, 2005.

[8] M. Napolitano. Making the move to cross docking. Warehousing Education and Research Council, 2000.

[9] T. Obata. The quadratic assignment problem: Evaluation of exact and heuristic algorithms. Technical report, 2000.

[10] L. Tsui and C. Chang. Optimal solution to dock door assignment problem. *Computers and Indutrial Engineering*, 23:283–286, 1992.

A Hybrid Genetic Algorithm for Solving the Length-Balanced Two Arc-Disjoint Shortest Paths Problem

Yanzhi Li[1], Andrew Lim[1,2], and Hong Ma[1]

[1] Dept of Industrial Engineering and Logistics Management
Hong Kong Univ of Science and Technology, Clear Water Bay, Kowloon, Hong Kong
[2] School of Computer Science & Engineering
South China University of Technology, Guang Dong, P.R. China

Abstract. We consider a HAZMAT transportation problem, which is modeled as the length-balanced two arc-disjoint shortest paths problem (LB2SP). In LB2SP, we try to find two arc-disjoint paths on a given network. We hope to reach two objectives: a minimized sum of the path lengths, and a minimized length difference between the paths. These two objectives are independent and even conflicting. Therefore, the objective function of LB2SP is expressed as a weighted sum of two terms: sum of the path lengths and the length difference between the paths. LB2SP is known to be NP-Hard, and can be formulated as an Integer Programming (IP) model. We propose a genetic algorithm (GA) and hybridize a quick Lagrangian relaxation-based heuristic (LRBH) as a module with the proposed GA. Computational experiments are conducted to compare the performance of the hybrid GA with the CPLEX solver, showing that the GA with hybridization of LRBH is efficient for LB2SP.

Keywords: shortest path, length-balanced, Lagrangian relaxation.
Areas: heuristic search, industrial application of AI, genetic algorithms.

1 Problem Introduction

There has been great concern over hazardous materials (HAZMAT) transportation in the United States since September 11, 2001. Besides the worry about potential terrorist activity, transportation security must also address everyday incidents and risks such as natural disasters and roadway incidents. In fact, the most common emergencies that the U.S. Department of Transportation responds to are flooding, tornados, snow and ice emergencies, and culvert failures [7]. Therefore, a realistic transportation security strategy must be multi-layered and go beyond "guards and gates":

Assume the following situation. There is a road network, composed of intersections and roads connecting the intersections. A truck carrying HAZMATs is to travel from an origin to a destination. Assuming the risk en route is proportional to the tour length, a shortest path from the origin to the destination is

M. Ali and R. Dapoigny (Eds.): IEA/AIE 2006, LNAI 4031, pp. 272–281, 2006.

prepared for the truck driver in order to minimize the risk. A second alternative path is also required as a backup detour. When parts the of first path are reported not travelable due to natural disasters or traffic incidents, the driver should switch to the backup path. In addition to viewing our second path as a simple detour due to natural conditions, considerations of potential terrorist activity are a must. If the tour plan is leaked to terrorist groups, the transportation of HAZMAT is exposed to attacks. Thus we introduce randomness in choosing the tours, i.e. leave this decision to the truck driver just-in-time. The two paths under consideration possess the following two characteristics: 1. The lengths of the two paths need to be as short as possible in order to reduce risks en route. 2. The lengths of the two paths need to be well balanced, i.e. the difference in length of the two paths needs to be as small as possible.

1.1 Problem Definition and the Integer Programming Formulation

The problem was visited previously and shown to be NP-Hard [4]. We restate the definition of LB2SP and its Integer Programming (IP) model as follows.

Problem 1 (Length-Balanced Two Arc-disjoint Shortest Paths Problem). In a directed network $G = (V, A)$ with c_{ij} associated with each arc $(i, j) \in A$. The network has a distinct source node $V = 0$ and a distinct sink node $V = N$. We need to determine two arc-disjoint paths from the source node to the sink node. Two terms are related to the two paths. One is the sum of the two path lengths. The other is the difference of the two path lengths. The objective is to minimize the weighted sum of the two terms.

The IP Formulation

$$z = \min \alpha \left(\sum_{(i,j)\in A} c_{ij}x_{ij} + \sum_{(i,j)\in A} c_{ij}y_{ij} \right) + \beta \left(\sum_{(i,j)\in A} c_{ij}y_{ij} - \sum_{(i,j)\in A} c_{ij}x_{ij} \right)$$

s.t.:

$$\sum_{(i,j)\in A} c_{ij}x_{ij} \leq \sum_{(i,j)\in A} c_{ij}y_{ij} \qquad \text{for all } (i,j) \in A \qquad (1)$$

$$\sum_{j:(i,j)\in A} x_{ij} - \sum_{j:(i,j)\in A} x_{ji} = \begin{cases} 1 & \text{for } i = 1 \\ 0 & \text{for } i \in N - \{1, n\} \\ -1 & \text{for } i = n \end{cases} \qquad (2)$$

$$\sum_{j:(i,j)\in A} y_{ij} - \sum_{j:(i,j)\in A} y_{ji} = \begin{cases} 1 & \text{for } i = 1 \\ 0 & \text{for } i \in N - \{1, n\} \\ -1 & \text{for } i = n \end{cases} \qquad (3)$$

$$x_{ij} + y_{ij} \leq 1 \qquad \text{for all } (i,j) \in A \qquad (4)$$

$$x_{ij} = 0 \text{ or } 1 \qquad \text{for all } (i,j) \in A \qquad (5)$$

$$y_{ij} = 0 \text{ or } 1 \qquad \text{for all } (i,j) \in A \qquad (6)$$

$$u_i - u_j + nx_{ij} \leq n - 1 \qquad (7)$$

$$w_i - w_j + ny_{ij} \leq n - 1 \tag{8}$$

$$\alpha > 0 \text{ and } \beta > 0 \tag{9}$$

Decision variable x_{ij} and y_{ij} define two s-t paths. The objective function consists of two terms: the sum of the path lengths and length difference of the two paths. Parameter α and β measure the weight of the two terms. Constraints (2) and (3) are the network mass balance constraints corresponding to the shortest path (SP) problem. Constraint (4) states that there is no common arc in the two paths. In a way similar to the IP formulation of TSP [5], constraints (7) and (8) eliminate cycles in the two paths as well as possible subtours.

2   A Genetic Algorithm Approach

Genetic algorithms (GA) have become a well-known and powerful meta-heuristic approach for hard combinatorial optimization problems [2]. Genetic algorithms are based on the ideas of natural selection, and have been applied to numerous combinatorial optimization problems successfully. One possible approach to solving the stated IP model of LB2SP is to apply the branch and bound method at an expensive computational cost (e.g., by using the ILOG CPLEX Solver). Since many investigators have applied GAs to the SP routing problem successfully (see [6], [3]), in this section, we develop a genetic algorithm approach to the LB2SP. In the next section, a quick heuristic based on Lagrangian relaxation (LRBH) is combined with the proposed GA to considerably enhance the overall performance.

2.1   Genetic Representation

Since our solution consists of a pair of arc-disjoint paths, the chromosome is composed of two sequences of positive integer numbers. Each of them represents one path. An example of a chromosome is shown in Fig. 1. The gene of the first locus of each sequence is reserved for the source node, while the gene of the last is reserved for the destination node. The length of the chromosome is limited to $2N$, as the length of each path is not greater than N, where N is the total number of nodes of the network.

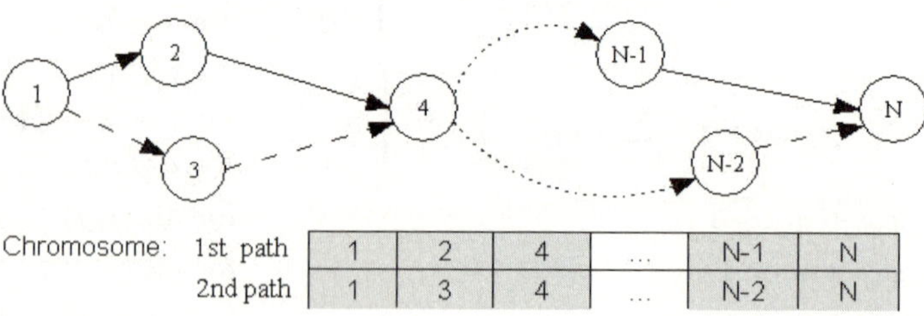

1st path	1	2	4	...	N-1	N
2nd path	1	3	4	...	N-2	N

Fig. 1. Example of a pair of paths and the encoding scheme

2.2 Evaluation Function

The evaluation function is the sole means of judging the quality of the evolved chromosomes. In the LB2SP, the fitness function f_i of chromosome i can be naturally defined as follows:

$$f_i = \frac{1}{z} = \frac{1}{\alpha f_1 + \beta f_2} \tag{10}$$

where z is the objective value in the IP model, f_1 is the length sum, and f_2 is the length difference. The goal is to minimize the objective function z, so the higher the value of the evaluation function, the better the fitness of the chromosome.

2.3 Crossover

Crossover, as a two-parent operator, combines two solutions from the current population to form hopefully a better solution. In the proposed GA for LB2SP, our crossover operator is specially designed, which consists of two steps: 1. Exchange one path of the two candidate solutions to generate two new offsprings; 2. In each offspring, cut and exchange the partial route at the "crossing sites" [1].

As shown in Fig. 2. A pair of solutions are randomly selected from the current population, and we are about to exchange one path between the two candidate solutions. There are two different possible schemes to make the exchange: the 1st path of the 1st chromosome is exchanged with the 1st path of the 2nd chromosome, or the 1st path of the chromosome is exchanged with the 2nd path of the 2nd chromosome. The two schemes lead to two different pairs of newly generated solutions respectively. Keeping in mind that one of our objectives is to minimize the path length difference, the scheme that may lead to a pair of paths with a smaller length difference is more likely to be selected according to

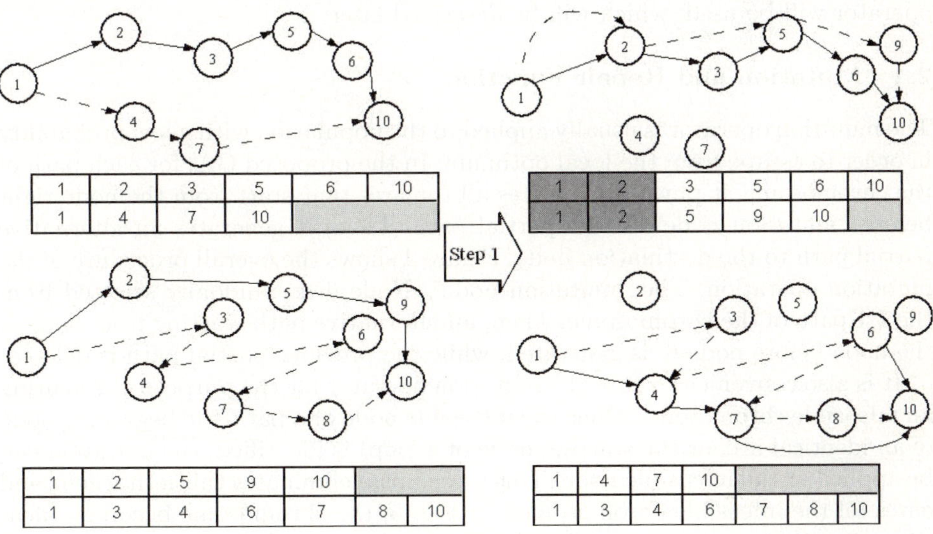

Fig. 2. Example of the crossover procedure: Step 1

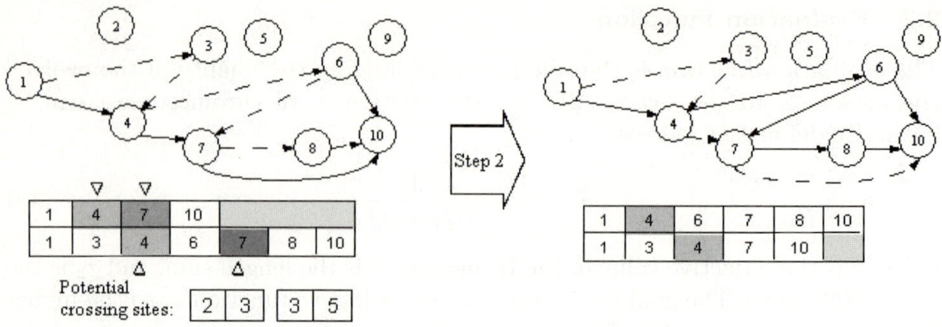

Fig. 3. Example of the crossover procedure: Step 2

a probability designated as p_e. In Fig. 2, by exchanging the 2nd path of the 1st chromosome with the 1st path of the 2nd chromosome, two new chromosomes are generated.

In the second step, we check for each offspring whether there is at least one common node in the two paths except for the source and destination nodes. It is not required that the common node be at the same position of the routing paths. As shown in Fig. 3, a set of pairs of positions that are commonly included in the two paths are identified: (2,3) for node 4 and (3,5) for node 7. Such pairs of positions are referred as the "potentially crossing sites". One crossing site is randomly selected and each partial route after the crossing site is cut and assembled. Thus, two new paths are produced.

It is possible that the two paths in a newly generated chromosome no longer satisfies the arc-disjoint property, as shown in Fig. 2, where the two paths of 1st new solution both consist of the arc (1,2). It is also possible loops are formed during the second step of the crossover operation. In both situations, a repair operator will be used, which will be described later.

2.4   Mutation and Repair Function

The mutation operator is usually applied to the population with a low probability in order to escape from the local optimum. In the proposed GA, for each path of the chromosome, it physically deletes all the arcs that start from the node right before "mutation node" in the partial path. Then, it generates an alternative partial path to the destination node. Figure 4 shows the overall procedure of the mutation operation. The "mutation node", Node 6, is randomly selected from the 1st path of the chromosome. Then, an alternative path starting from node 5, the node before node 6, is generated, while the previous partial path is deleted.

It is also convenient to use the mutation operator for the purpose of repairing an infeasible chromosome. Once the infeasible node of a path(the beginning node of an identical arc, or the starting node of a loop) is identified, the mutation can be applied at the infeasible node. This mechanism eliminates this lethal gene and cures all the infeasible chromosomes. In Fig. 5, the chromosome becomes infeasible after the crossover operation, because both of the paths have the identical

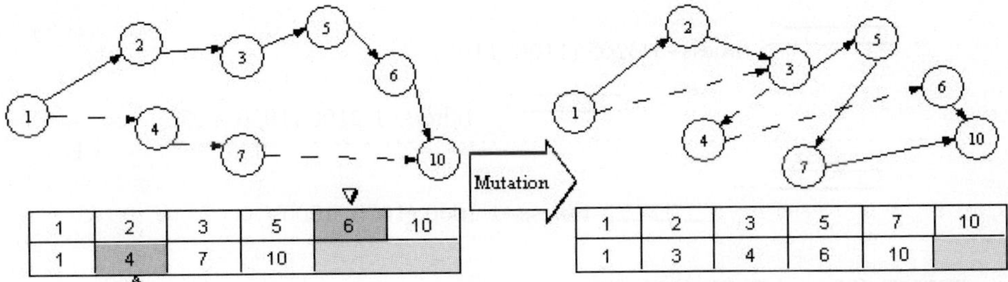

Fig. 4. Example of the mutation procedure

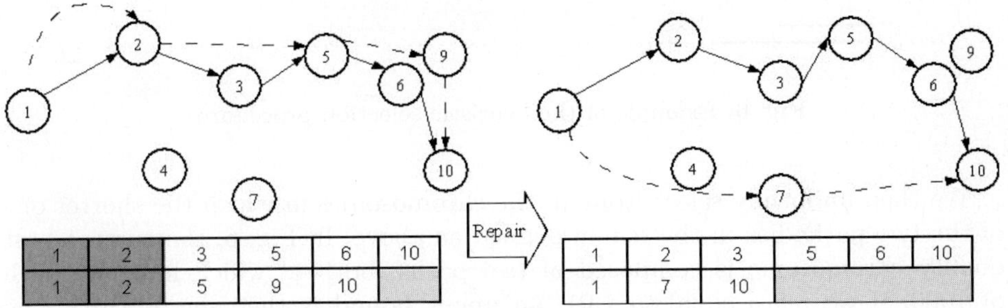

Fig. 5. Example of the repair procedure

arc (1,2). Thus, we set the mutation node at node 2 and apply the mutation operator. Node 2 and the related partial are deleted, and a new partial path which satisfies the arc-disjoint property is produced.

2.5   Selection

The common notion in GA uses μ to denote the number of parents and λ to denote the number of offspring. In the proposed GA, the first half size of the next population, $\mu/2$, is selected based on their evaluation function value in a deterministic manner. The second half size of the next generation is stochastically selected in a limited region of the whole current population $\mu + \lambda$. We observe in LB2SP that the evaluation function alone does not accurately reflect the rank of the quality of the chromosomes that are to be generated in the next population. Since each chromosome consists of two paths, the smaller the length difference between either pair of paths of the two chromosomes, the more likely the newly generated chromosome will have a high quality. Here we define two boundaries of the target region of the selection as follows:

Lower Bound[LB]: The length of the SP from the source node to the destination node of the network.

Upper Bound[UB]: The length of the longer path of the current best solution multiplied by a factor ρ.

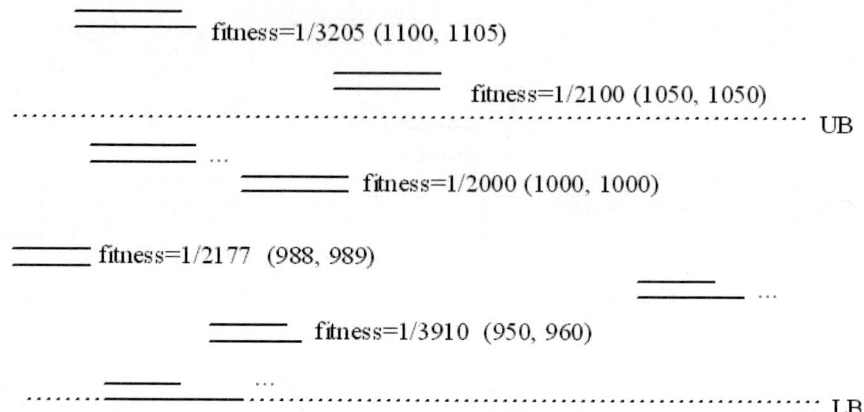

Fig. 6. Example of the heuristic selection procedure

We then uniformly select from all the chromosomes in which the shorter one of the two paths lies in the region defined as above. In Fig. 6, the current best quality chromosome is composed of two paths, both of which have a length of 1000. If we set ρ equal to 1.01, an upper bound is then set to 1010. The lower bound is always set to the shortest distance from the source node to the destination node. Between the two bounds, a population region is formed, which includes some chromosomes with very low fitness values and one desired short path at the same time. Those chromosomes above the upper boundary are excluded, as it is not likely they will improve the population quality if selected, although some of them have a relative high evaluation function value.

3   The LRBH and Hybridization with GA

In the current setting of LB2SP, as stated before, the solutions need to be provided on the fly, usually in seconds, not in minutes or hours. The quick convergence of GA is of paramount importance. Therefore, it is of our interest to elevate the performance of GA. The Lagrangian relaxation-based heuristic (LRBH) is an iterative method that generates LB2SP solutions quickly. In general, it turns LB2SP into two parametric SP problems, which essentially says we solve the SP problem in a new network where the arc costs have been adjusted by the Lagrangian multiplier μ_{ij}^1 and μ_{ij}^2. (Please refer to [4] for detail of the algorithm.) Since GA is also an iterative algorithm that simulates the natural evolution process, we are then able to execute them in parallel, introducing the quick solutions from the LRBH to the GA population base, with an emphasis on the balance of path length. Figure 7 illustrates the structure of the proposed GA with LRBH hybridization.

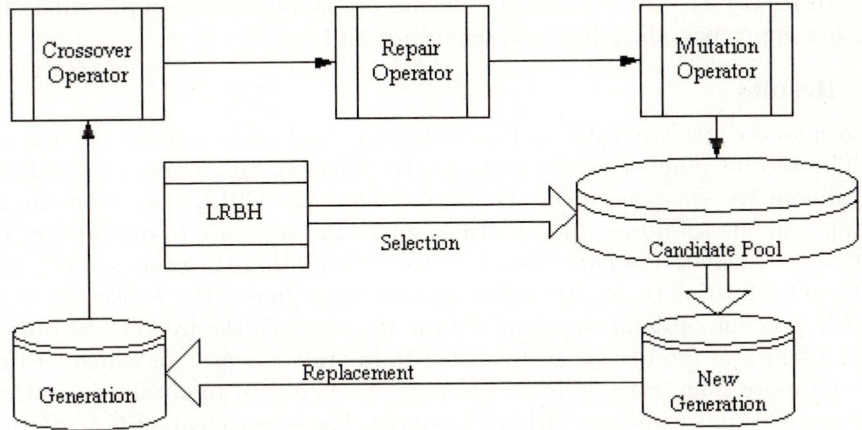

Fig. 7. Structure of the proposed GA with LRBH hybridization

4 Computational Experiments

Experiments are carried out on a Pentium IV 2.4Ghz machine with 512MB memory. The proposed GA and LRBH are coded in Java. ILOG CPLEX 8.0 is used to solved the IP formulation presented in section 2.

4.1 Test Data Generation and Parameter Setting

Because benchmark for this new problem is not available, test cases of geometric graphs with 50, 100, and 150 nodes are generated by the following procedure: At first, n random points are chosen in a 1000*1000 square. $n = 50$, 100, or 150. The value of a parameter γ, which measures the density of the graph, is randomly chosen between 0.3 and 0.6, where

$$\gamma = \frac{\text{the number of edges of the test graph}}{\text{the number of edges of a complete graph with } n \text{ nodes}} \tag{11}$$

If the graph is not connected, the necessary number of edges are added to make it connected. Then we use a simple greedy algorithm to do a preliminary test. The algorithm computes a first shortest path, removes its arcs from the network, and computes a second shortest path. If the length of the two shortest paths is found to be equal, the solution must be optimal for LB2SP. These trivial test cases are excluded in the experiment, because they can not be used to measure the true performance of the heuristics.

In the objective function, parameter β is specified at a value significantly large than parameter α. Here we set $\alpha = 1$ and $\beta = 200$, which means every unit difference between the two paths incurs a value of 200 units penalty from the total path length. The following values are used in the proposed GA: $\#iteration = 10^4$, $\#population = 300$ $\#crossover = 500$. The mutation probability is set to

$p_m = 0.05$. The crossover exchange scheme probability is set to $p_e = 0.8$. The selection upper boundary factor is set to $\rho = 1.01$.

4.2   Results

The results are given in Table 1. The first row of each table denotes the instance ID. The second number of the instance ID refers to the number of nodes in the random test case networks. We record both the CPLEX solutions in 180 seconds and the solutions when CPLEX solves the test case to optimality. The solution time is noted in parentheses. Table 1 shows that the proposed GA with LRBH hybridization performs well for all test cases. In 8 of the 9 cases for which CPLEX gets the optimal solutions within 180 seconds, the hybrid GA obtains optimal solutions too (except instance 9-10). In other 11 cases for which CPLEX takes far more time (ranging from 4 minutes to 33 hours) to obtain the optimal solutions, GA gets solutions within 2 minutes. The average gap of GA solutions to optimality for these 11 cases is within 2.7%. The table also shows these 11 GA solutions are unparalleled in quality by the CPLEX solutions when a time limit is imposed. We observe while the runtime of CPLEX tends to vary greatly for different cases, the proposed GA solves the problem within the time proportional to the case size in terms of the number of nodes of the network. Therefore, we believe that the hybrid GA is an effective approach to tackle LB2SP.

Table 1. Comparison between the CPLEX Solver and GA w/LRBH hybridization

test case	CPLEX					GA w/LRBH hybridization				
	path1	path2	obj	time(s)	opt(time)	path1	path2	obj	time(s)	% of opt
1-50	1163	1165	2728	180	2220(291s)	1110	1110	2220	33.7	100%
2-50	1081	1081	2162	62.2		1081	1081	2162	34.8	100%
3-50	1110	1111	2421	12.95		1110	1111	2421	15.7	100%
4-50	1198	1198	2396	14.05		1198	1198	2396	12.38	100%
5-50	1250	1250	2500	36.10		1250	1250	2500	29.49	100%
6-50	1116	1119	2835	180	2374(498s)	1112	1113	2425	38.7	97.85%
7-100	1022	1027	3049	180	2148(6216s)	1190	1190	2380	47.2	89.20%
8-100	1263	1273	4536	180	2372(19435s)	1207	1207	2414	39.93	98.13%
9-100	1101	1101	2202	61.75		1140	1140	2280	55.90	96.46%
10-100	1167	1170	2937	180	2352(445s)	1198	1198	2396	80.14	98.13%
11-100	1157	1159	2716	180	2348(399s)	1174	1174	2348	41.86	100%
12-100	1173	1174	2547	180	2124(1301s)	1178	1178	2156	28.67	98.49%
13-150	1027	1029	2456	180	2072(915s)	1031	1032	2263	60.17	90.78%
14-150	1019	1020	2239	180	2038(4440s)	1036	1036	2072	68.7	98.33%
15-150	983	984	2167	180	1976(875s)	988	988	1976	62.19	100%
16-150	1131	1132	2463	180	2290(1015s)	1154	1154	2308	118.53	99.21%
17-150	987	990	2577	180	1994(915s)	998	998	1996	48.48	99.90%
18-150	1009	1009	2018	11.61		1009	1009	2018	66.73	100%
19-150	1000	1000	2000	113.5		1000	1000	2000	64.48	100%
20-150	986	986	1972	116.1		986	986	1972	97.75	100%

5 Conclusion

We have studied the length-balanced two arc-disjoint shortest path problem (LB2SP), which offers the solution to a particular HAZMAT transportation problem. The objective of the study has double-edged effect at one time: (1) Provide two short paths for decision making. (2) Maintain a small length difference of the two paths. We propose a genetic algorithm and hybridize a Lagrangian relaxation based heuristic (LRBH) as a module with the genetic algorithm. Experiments indicate that the hybridization is successful. Computational results also show that the proposed GA with LRBH hybridization outperforms ILOG CPLEX, and is efficient for LB2SP.

References

[1] Chang Wook Ahn and R. S. Ramakrishna. A genetic algorithm for shortest path routing problem and the sizing of populations. *IEEE Trans. Evolutionary Computation*, 6(6):566–579, 2002.

[2] John H. Holland. *Adaptation in Natural and Artifical Systems*. University of Michigan Press, Ann Arbor, MI, 1975.

[3] Y. Leung, G. Li, and Z.B. Xu. A genetic algorithm for the multiple destination routing problems. *IEEE Trans. Evolutionary Computation*, 2(4):150–161, 1998.

[4] Y. Li, A. Lim, and H. Ma. A Lagrangian relaxation based heuristic for solving the length-balanced two arc-disjoint shortest paths problem. In *Proc. AI2005, LNAI 3809*, pages 1323–1326, 2005.

[5] C. E. Miller, A. W. Tucker, and R. A. Zemlin. Integer programming formulation of traveling salesman problems. *J. ACM*, 7(4):326–329, 1960.

[6] M. Munemoto, Y. Takai, and Y. Sato. A migration scheme for the genetic adaptive routing algorithm. In *Proc. IEEE Int. Conf. Systems, Man, and Cybernetics*, pages 2774–2779, 1998.

[7] U.S. Department of Transportation. Hazardous materials information system database. Office of Hazardous Materials Safety, U.S. Department of Transportation, Washington DC, Oct. 1999.

A Fast and Effective Insertion Algorithm for Multi-depot Vehicle Routing Problem with Fixed Distribution of Vehicles and a New Simulated Annealing Approach

Andrew Lim[1,2] and Wenbin Zhu[1]

[1] Dept of Industrial Engineering and Logistics Management
Hong Kong Univ of Science and Technology, Clear Water Bay, Kowloon, Hong Kong
[2] School of Computer Science & Engineering
South China University of Technology, Guang Dong, PR China

Abstract. Multi-depot Vehicle Routing Problem has great practical value to the logistics and supply chain management. The fixed distribution of vehicles variant (MDVRPFD) brings it one step closer to the practical use. Based on the simple fact that all sub-routes of an optimal route must be optimal, a new randomized best insertion (RBI) algorithm is proposed. The proposed insertion algorithm is highly effective in minimizing number of vehicles and fast. Compared to the best known result published for MDVRPFD variant, the solutions generated by this new insertion algorihtm require 20% fewer vehicles. Adopting a generalized n-op neighborhood operator, a Simulated Annealing approach yields a reduction of 12% in total distance compared to best known results of MDVRPFD.

Keywords: MDVRP, MDVRPFD, meta-heuristic, insertion algorithm, sub-route optimization.
Areas: meta-heuristic, vehicle routing, industrial applications of AI.

1 Introduction and Problem Description

Multi-depot vehicle routing problem (MDVRP) has great practical value. There has been a great deal of literature on MDVRP [4], [5], [6] etc. Little attention has been attracted to the more practical variant, MDVRPFD, proposed by [2] that limits the number of vehicle available at each depot. A good solver of MDVRPFD problem can immediately find applications in the logistics industry.

MDVRPFD proposed by [2] can be summarized as follows:

- There are M depots, each depot has limited number of vehicles.
- Each vehicle starts from its corresponding depot, serves a set of customers and returns to the same depot. The total demand of customers served by the vehicle must not exceed the capacity of the vehicle.
- All N customers are served, each customer is served by exactly one vehicle.
- the objective is to minimize the total distance travelled by the fleet.

M. Ali and R. Dapoigny (Eds.): IEA/AIE 2006, LNAI 4031, pp. 282–291, 2006.

Though [2] ignored the number of vehicles in its objective function, in practice, being able to minimize the number of vehicles reduces operational costs and/or brings more business oportunities (serving more customers with the existing fleet, for example). As such in this paper, we will consider minimizing number of vehicles as another objective and include it in the comparision.

This paper presents a new randomized best insertion (RBI) algorithm that is fast and generates high quality initial solutions which can then be fed to meta-heuristics to produce very good solutions to MDVRPFD problem. In this paper, the standard simulated annealing (SA) meta-heuristic is chosen. When applied to the initial solutions generated by RBI, it outperforms all algorithms implemented in [2] in 21 out of 22 instances by a large margin. Our solver solves all 22 instances in about 20 to 30 minutes.

We generated a set of large instances which is closer to the practical size and provided the computational results for further reference.

This paper starts by giving a detailed description of RBI in Section 2. Following that, the structure of SA is described in Section 3. We then highlight some of the implementation considerations, discuss how to choose effective parameters, and compare our results against the best published results in Section 4. The next section provides more information on how to generate large instances and lists our results. Section 6 concludes this paper.

2   The Randomized Best Insertion Algorithm

Our insertion algorithm tries to construct routes one by one and insert customers to routes until there is no customer left. It starts by randomly choosing a customer c as seed. Then finds the nearest depot d to the customer c that has available vehicle(s). Construct a route r with three nodes d, c, d (line 1.3 to 1.6, Algorithm 1). Then the algorithm tries to insert as many customers as possible to r (see the Repeat Until loop in Algorithm 1). Finally the route r is added to the solution. A new seed customer is randomly chosen to construct a new route. The process continues until all customers are inserted.

The question is in what order we shall insert customers? Consider a customer c, there are two alternatives: 1. insert c into the best position on current route r; 2. create a new route to serve the customer. Clearly, we favor the option that incurs less cost. However, we can not compare the two costs directly, as the structure of solution resulting from these two options is very different. Let us assume we can somehow convert the two costs, let λ be the convertion rate between the cost of option 2 and option 1. We can define a single combined metric $\lambda \cdot c2 - c1$ (similar idea has been proposed by [8] for VRPTW). The higher the value implies a higher cost for option 2, in other words, it favors option 1. We sort all customers using this metric and insert customers in the descending order.

It is easy to find the cost for option 2. It is, however, very expensive to calculate the exact cost of option 1, which is equivalent to optimally solving a TSP problem. To speed up the algorithm, we will use an estimation to approximate

Data: C is the list of customers to be inserted
Data: D is the list of depots
Data: g is the graph and $g(u, v)$ is the distance from customer u to v
Result: Solution S

1.1 Create an empty solution S;
1.2 **while** C *is not empty* **do**
1.3   Randomly choose a customer c, and delete it from C;
1.4   Find nearest depot d from D for c that has available vehicle(s);
1.5   Construct a route r consisting of three nodes $[d, c, d]$;
1.6   Decrease number of vehicle available at depot d by one;
1.7   **repeat**
1.8   // insert customers in descending order of $\lambda \cdot c2 - c1$;
1.9 $c2Max \leftarrow -\infty$, $bestC \leftarrow null$, $bestR \leftarrow null$;
1.10   **foreach** *customer c from C* **do**
1.11   **if** *adding c to r does not violate capacity constraint* **then**
1.12 $c1Min \leftarrow \infty$, $c1v \leftarrow null$;
1.13   **foreach** *consecutive pair of nodes (u, v) on route r* **do**
1.14 $c1 \leftarrow g(u, c) + g(c, v) - g(u, v)$;
1.15   **if** $c1 < c1Min$ **then** $c1Min \leftarrow c1$, $c1v \leftarrow v$;
1.16   **end**
1.17 $r_1 \leftarrow$ insert c into route r before $c1v$;
1.18 $r_2 \leftarrow$ `OptimizeRoute`$(r_1,$ *index of $c1v$*$)$;
1.19 $\delta \leftarrow$ the difference between total distance of r_2 and r;
1.20 $d \leftarrow$ nearest depot to customer c;
1.21 $c2 \leftarrow \lambda \cdot (g(d, c) + g(c, d)) - \delta$;
1.22   **if** $c2 > c2Max$ **then** $c2Max \leftarrow c2$, $bestC \leftarrow c$, $bestR \leftarrow r_2$;
1.23   **end**
1.24   **end**
1.25   **if** $bestC \neq null$ **then** $r \leftarrow bestR$, delete $bestC$ from C ;
1.26   **until** $bestC$ *is null* ;
1.27   add r to Solution S;
1.28 **end**

Algorithm 1. Randomized Best Insertion Algorithm

the cost. Line 1.12 to 1.16 in Algorithm 1 estimate the best location for insertion. Line 1.17 to 1.19 tries to insert the customer c into the estimated best location, invokes OptimizeRoute procedure (we will describe it shortly) to find an approximate solution to the TSP problem, then takes the difference between the distance of approximate TSP solution and the route before insertion as the cost for option 1.

Now the only unsolved puzzle is how to quickly generated a high quality approximate route. It is obvious that all sub-routes of an optimal route are optimal. In other words, if we are able to identify a sub-route $[u, ..., v]$ that is not optimal, then replace the sub-route by the corresponding optimal sub-route $[u, ..., v]$ (the start and end node are fixed, the intermidate nodes are rearranged) will reduce the total distance of the route (this idea is inspired by the E-op proposed by [1]). We can use the dynamic programming algorithm proposed by [7] to find the optimal solution of a sub-route. Imagine, there is a window of fixed size w that selects a sub-route for optimization. The window is inititally centered at the location where customer c is inserted. After the first rearrangement, if the nodes in the left half of the window are changed, we can slide the window to the left by $w/2$. The window will now include another $w/2$ nodes from route r. Reapply the TSP optimizer may further reduce the total distance of r. This process can continue until there is no more change or the left end of r is reached. Similarly, we can slide the window to the right and perform the optimization for the right part of r. (see Algorithm 2).

Data: r the route to be optimized
Data: i the location where a new customer is just inserted
Data: w number of nodes to be optimized at once
Result: r optimized route
2.1 $s \leftarrow \max(i - w/2, 0)$;
2.2 **while** $s \geq 0$ **do**
2.3   call dynamic TSP algorithm for sub-route $r[s, s + w)$;
2.4   **if** $r[s, s + w/2)$ *is changed* **then**
2.5 $s \leftarrow \max(s - w/2, 0)$;
2.6   **else**
2.7 $s \leftarrow -1$;
2.8   **end**
2.9 **end**
2.10 $rLen \leftarrow$ the number of nodes in r;
2.11 **if** $r[i, i + w/2)$ *is changed* **then**
2.12 $s \leftarrow i$;
2.13   **while** $s < rLen$ **do**
2.14   call TSP DP solver for sub-route $r[s, s + w)$;
2.15   **if** $r[s, s + w/2)$ *is changed* **then**
2.16 $s \leftarrow \min(s + w/2, rLen - w)$;
2.17   **else**
2.18 $s \leftarrow rLen$;
2.19   **end**
2.20   **end**
2.21 **end**

Algorithm 2. Optimize Route

3   The Simulated Annealing Algorithm

The overall solver for MDVRPFD problem is listed in Alogirhtm 3. First we use RBI to generate an initial solution S_0 (line 3.1). Then we apply the SA to find an improved solution S (line 3.2). At last, we optimize every route in S(line 3.3). For each route we use dynamic programming algorithm for TSP to optimize its sub-routes using a loop.

Input   : C the list of customers to be served
Input   : D the list of depots
Input   : g the distance metrics between
Output: S the solution to MDVRPFD problem

3.1 $S_0 \leftarrow$ `RandomizedBestInsertion`(C,D,g);
3.2 $S \leftarrow$ `SimulatedAnnealing`(S_0);
3.3 **foreach** *route r in S* **do**
3.4 $\quad n \leftarrow$ length of r;
3.5 $\quad$ **for** $s = 0$ **to** $n - w$ **do**
3.6 $\quad\quad e \leftarrow \min s + w, n$;
3.7 $\quad\quad$ call TSP DP solver to optimize sub-route $r[s, e]$;
3.8 $\quad\quad s \leftarrow s + w/2$;
3.9 $\quad$ **end**
3.10 **end**

Algorithm 3. Overall Solver

Our SA uses a simple cooling scheme. The outer loop (line 4.3 in Algorithm 4) controls the cooling process. In each iteration, the temperature is multiplied by cooling ratio c, a number very close to but smaller than one. The inner loop (line 4.5 in Algorithm 4) tries to find the equilibrium. Here, we simply consider K (a design parameter) successful applications of neighborhood operators or N (a design parameter) consecutive unsuccessful attempts as reaching the equilibrium.

The neighborhood operators we adopted are the generalized n-op operators proposed by [3] for VRPTW. There are four operators: 1. move a n-node sub-route from one route to a different random location on the same route (line 4.13); 2. move a n-node sub-route from one route to a random location on another route (line 4.22); 3. swap a m-node sub-route from one route to a different random location on the same route (line 4.15); 4. swap a m-node sub-route from one route with a n-node sub-route from another route (line 4.24). Both the location and the length of the sub-routes are randomly generated.

Our simulated annealing algorithm will accept moves/swaps that reduce the total distance. For moves/swaps that increase the total distance, we will accept it with a probability given by the formula $e^{-d/t}$, where e is the natural constant, d is the change of total distance, and t is the current temperature.

4   The Computational Experiments

4.1   Implementation Notes and Testing Environments

We implemented the algorithms presented in this paper in the Java^{TM} programming language using single thread.

We devoted a great deal of effort to code the dynamic programming algorithm for TSP very efficiently. Our implementation uses $14*(n-2)*2^{n-2}+16*(n-2)^2$

Data: S the initial solution
Data: T_0, T_e the initial and termination temperature
Data: c the cooling ratio $0 < c < 1$
Data: K the number of iterations at given temperature
Data: N the maximum unsuccessful consecutive attempts at given temperature
Result: *best* the best solution found.

```
4.1   t ← T_0;
4.2   best ← S;
4.3   while t > T_e and cpu time < preset limit do
4.4       i ← 0, n ← 0;
4.5       while i < K and n < N do
4.6           r_1 ← randomly choose a route from S;
4.7           r_2 ← randomly choose a route from S;
4.8           randomly select a sub-route sr_1 from r_1;
4.9           if r_1 = r_2 then
4.10              generate a random real number p ∈ [0, 1];
4.11              len ← number of nodes on r_1;
4.12              if p < 1/len then
4.13                  move sub-route sr_1 to a different random location on r_1;
4.14              else
4.15                  randomly select a different non-overlapping sub-route sr_2;
4.16                  swap sr_1 with sr_2;
4.17              end
4.18          else
4.19              generate a random real number p ∈ [0, 1];
4.20              len ← number of routes in S;
4.21              if p < 1/len then
4.22                  move sub-route sr_1 to a random location on r_2, if the
                      capacity constraint is not violated.;
4.23              else
4.24                  randomly select s sub-route sr_2 from r_2;
4.25                  swap sr_1 with sr_2, if the capacity constraints are not
                      violated.;
4.26              end
4.27          end
4.28          if S is changed then
4.29              d ← the change of total distance of S;
4.30              if d < 0 then
4.31                  accept the changes to S;
4.32                  try to update best, if S is better;
4.33              else
4.34                  accept the changes with a probability e^{-d/t}, otherwise
                      undo the changes;
4.35              end
4.36          end
4.37          if S is changed then  i ← i + 1, n ← 0 ;
4.38          else  n ← n + 1 ;
4.39      end
4.40      t ← t · c;
4.41  end
```

Algorithm 4. Simulated Annealing

bytes of memory and uses $3 * (n-2)^2 * 2^{n-2}$ double pricision (64-bit real number providied by Java) operations (including comparison, assignment and addition), where n is the number of nodes of a sub-route.

We used double precision throughout our implementation to track the cost of solutions. We took special care to avoid cummulative errors result from long sequence of double precision operations when calculating the cost of a route and/or solutions. There are at most $n + m$ cummulated double precision errors for the cost of a solution, where n is the number of customers and m is the number of routes in the solution.

All our experiments are conducted on a HP Proliant DL360 server with dual Xeon CPU at clock rate 3.0GHz, 2GB memory, running Debian Sarge linux operating system. The JDK installed is version 5.0 update 05 downloaded from Sun java official website.

4.2   Parameter Hunting

To determine the best random seed and λ for the RBI. We first fixed the λ to 0.48 (suggested by [8] for his insertion algorithm, whose cost metric is quite similar to ours) and varies random seed. For each random seed, we applied RBI to all 22 instances mentioned by [2] (which is a subset of instances posted on [9]). Table 1 shows the total distance, total number of vehicles and total CPU time in percentage using seed 3 as base. The result shows that the proposed insertion algorithm is relatively stable with respect to random seed. The total distance only varies by no more than 7% and total number of vehicles varies by only 0.3%. We chose 3 as seed for further experiments.

Then we verified the choice of λ by fixing random seed to 3 and varied λ. Again for each choice of λ we applied the solver to all 22 instances and summed up the results. Table 2 uses $\lambda = 0.1$ as base and compares the relative performance. It shows 0.4 to 0.6 is a promising region. We performed a more intensive search in that region and the result is shown in Table 3. It seems the best region will be $[0.48, 0.52]$. We finally chose 0.48, as this is proven to be effective ([1],[8]).

As the simulated annealing algorithm adopted in this paper is standard, and it is well known that the most important parameters are the initial temperature T_0, the cooling ratio c, and the equilibrium condition K. According to our experience, those parameters shall take size of input instances into account, otherwise the tuned solver will very likely perform badly when applied to new instances with different input size.

The T_0 determine the tolerance of worse moves in the initial phase. We set it to the average distance of routes in the initial solution produced by RBI. We varied K (in terms of multiples of number of customers) and c and applied the solver to all 22 instances. The result in Table 4 shows the relative performance (first row is the base). It shows increasing K and c will reduce the cost but decrease speed significantly, which accords with the general understanding to SA. K and c is diminished, yet it dramatically slow down the algorithm. We feel setting K to 3 times the number of input customers and c to 0.995 is a good compromise between performance and speed. The parameter N, the maximum

Table 1. Effect of Random Seed to RBI

seed	distance	vehicle No.	CPU time
3	100.00%	100.00%	100.00%
5	105.62%	100.30%	107.00%
7	104.47%	100.00%	94.00%
11	102.12%	100.00%	84.00%
13	106.28%	100.30%	92.00%
17	105.87%	99.70%	91.00%
19	104.58%	100.00%	93.00%

Table 2. Effect of λ to RBI Algorithm 1

λ	distance	vehicle No.	CPU time
0.1	100.00%	100.00%	100.00%
0.3	98.27%	100.30%	134.00%
0.4	98.08%	100.30%	172.00%
0.5	96.99%	100.00%	163.00%
0.6	99.42%	100.00%	173.00%
5	131.87%	100.00%	947.00%
10	149.50%	99.70%	942.00%

Table 3. Effect of λ to RBI Algorithm 2

λ	distance	vehicle No.	CPU time
0.4	100.00%	100.00%	100.00%
0.42	97.87%	100.00%	103.00%
0.44	96.72%	100.00%	97.00%
0.46	97.73%	100.00%	98.00%
0.48	95.87%	99.71%	95.00%
0.5	98.89%	99.71%	94.00%
0.52	98.64%	99.71%	95.00%
0.54	97.70%	99.71%	96.00%
0.56	98.55%	100.00%	97.00%
0.58	101.02%	100.00%	103.00%
0.6	101.37%	99.71%	100.00%

Table 4. Effect of K and c to SA algorithm

K	c	distance	vehicle No.	CPU time
2	0.99	100.00%	100.00%	100.00%
2	0.995	98.21%	100.00%	121.00%
3	0.99	99.39%	100.00%	108.00%
3	0.995	98.03%	100.00%	138.00%

unsuccessful consecutive attempts at given temperature, is set to 10 times the number of customers.

4.3   Results

Table 5 summarizes our computational results. The column *file* lists the input file names, the column *instance* lists the name of the instances, the *best* columns list best results from previous literature for MDVRPFD, the *RBI* columns list the results of our proposed RBI algorithm, the *SA* columns list results of our SA algorithm. The column *CPU* lists the CPU times in milliseconds. The second last row sums up the corresponding columns to give an overall comparision. The the last row compares our overall results against the best known results. From the table we can see, except instance SMALL-1, for all other 21 instances our proposed insertion algorithm requires fewer or equal number of vehicles to serve all customers. We can also see that, except instance SMALL-4, for all other 21 instances our proposed Simulated Annealing algorithm generates solutions with smaller distances. In total our proposed new insertion algorithm reduces number of vehicles required by about 20% and the proposed simulated annealing algorithm further reduces the distance and yields a total reduction of 12%. The total CPU time required to find the solutions for all 22 instances is less than 1728 seconds (or 29 minutes).

Table 5. Computational Results

file	instance	best distance	vehicle	RBI distance	vehicle	CPU	SA distance	vehicle	CPU
pr01	SMALL-1	891.54	4	1085.05	4	3169	889.70	4	6010
p02	SMALL-2	522.65	8	566.24	5	377	510.53	5	3059
p01	SMALL-3	690.27	16	746.91	10	109	586.78	10	3724
pr07	SMALL-4	1042.32	6	1441.26	5	8653	1124.71	5	15921
p03	SMALL-5	746.27	15	974.67	10	186	681.15	10	5675
p12	SMALL-6	1574.26	10	1758.15	8	4680	1327.82	8	10104
pr02	SMALL-7	1486.94	8	1696.33	7	11191	1331.96	7	22742
p05	MEDIUM-1	923.34	10	996.65	8	6818	792.36	8	16913
p04	MEDIUM-2	1289.22	16	1361.92	15	119	1042.69	15	11057
p06	MEDIUM-3	987.09	18	1444.00	15	106	941.91	15	10753
pr03	MEDIUM-4	1987.93	12	2717.04	10	39446	1919.72	10	61000
p15	MEDIUM-5	2975.8	20	3996.94	15	42336	2704.21	15	68599
pr04	MEDIUM-6	2722.12	16	3567.18	14	60420	2283.33	14	97798
pr09	LARGE-1	2719.84	18	3293.20	16	68085	2335.40	16	116716
pr05	LARGE-2	3036.06	20	3196.75	19	43675	2518.26	19	104404
p18	LARGE-3	4447.05	30	5541.18	22	115768	4190.58	22	172029
p08	LARGE-4	5460.78	28	5826.79	25	10578	4689.73	25	73657
p11	LARGE-5	4524.7	30	6189.98	25	11759	3821.18	25	80232
p10	LARGE-6	4677.37	32	5093.41	25	14740	3844.34	25	83105
p09	LARGE-7	5069.92	36	5880.91	25	18733	4141.50	25	86332
pr06	LARGE-8	3376.79	24	4121.58	22	113307	2832.50	22	198395
p21	LARGE-9	6553.46	45	8342.90	33	352003	6112.98	33	479344
	total	57705.72	422	69839.04	338	926258	50623.34	338	1727569
	compare to best			121.03%	80.09%		87.73%	80.09%	

5   New Problem Instances

We generated 27 new instances with 1000 customers, various depots (1,4,9,16,25) and various vehicle capacity (300,600,900). These 27 instances are divided into two categories. The first category has 15 instances with customers uniformly distributed, and the second category has 12 instances with customers clustered around depots.

The demand of customers is randomly generated in the range $[1, 60]$ with uniform distribution. The number of vehicles per depot is set to $\lceil 2 * N * d/n \rceil$, where N is number of customers, d is expected demand per customer, n is number of depots. For instance with n by n depots, all depots are arranged in an n by n grid. There are n by n squares of the same size centered at the depots. The size of the square is determined such that the gap between two adjacent squares is 20% of the size of the square. The lower, left corner of the lower left square is at coordinate (0,0) and the upper right corner of the upper right square is at coordinate (65535,65535). For the first category, all customers are uniformly distributed in the square (0,0) (65535,65535). For the second category, customers are distributed in the small squares associated with the depots. Each small square contains same number of customers (when the total number of customers is not dividable by n^2, the remaining customers are put in the lower left cluster) uniformly distributed within the square.

The data format is the same as MDVRP described by [9] with m in the first line indicates the number of available vehicles for each depot. Both input data and solutions can be downloaded from http://iwen.net/vrp/mdvrpfd/. We also make a binary version of our solver available on the same website.

6   Conclusion

This paper proposed to consider the number of vehicles as an objective, which brought the MDVRPFD one step closer to the practice. The computational results have shown the randomized best insertion method proposed in this paper is highly effective in producing high quality initial solutions. When combined with a standard simulated annealing meta-heuristics, it greatly improved both the total distance and number of vehicles required over previously reported best results. The core idea behind the proposed insertion algorithm is that all sub-routes of an optimal route must be optimal. The same idea may be applicable to other combinatorial optimization problems such as VRPTW. We also proposed a large set of instances and presented the computational results for future reference.

References

[1] A. Lim, and X. Zhang, *A Two-stage Heuristic with Ejection Pools and Generalized Ejection Chains for the Vehicle Routing Problem with Time Windows*. Informs Journal on Computing, accepted on 2005.

[2] A. Lim, and F. Wang. *Multi-Depot Vehicle Routing Problem: A One-Stage Approach*. IEEE Transactions on Automation Science and Engineering, Vol.2, No.4, October 2005.

[3] H. Li and A. Lim. *Local Search with Annealing-like Restarts to Solve the VRPTW*. EJOR, Vol 150, pp. 115-127, 2003.

[4] I. Giosa, I. Tansini, and I. Viera, *New assignment algorithms for the multi-depot vehicle routing problem*. Journal of Operational Research Society, Vol. 53, pp. 997-984, 2002.

[5] S. Salhi, and M. Sari, *A multi-level composite heuristic for the multi-depot vehicle fleet mix problem*. EJOR, vol 103, pp. 95-112, 1997.

[6] I-M. Chao, B. Golden, and E. Wasil. *A new heuristic for the multi-depot vehicle roting problem that improves upon best-known solutions*. American Journal of Mathematics and Magement Science, Vol 13, no. 3, pp. 371-406, 1993.

[7] Sniedovich M. - *A dynamic programming algorithm for the travelling salesman problem* APL Quote Quad, 23(4), 1-2, 1993.

[8] M. M. Solomon. *Algorithms for the Vehicle Routing and Scheduling Problems with Time Window Constraints*. OR, 35:254-265, 1987.

[9] MDVRP instances posted on vrpweb. *http://neo.lcc.uma.es/radiaeb/WebVRP/index.html?/Problem_Instances/MDVRPInstances.html*

On the Behaviour of Extremal Optimisation When Solving Problems with Hidden Dynamics

Irene Moser and Tim Hendtlass

Centre for Intelligent Systems and Complex Processes
Swinburne University of Technology, VIC 3122, Australia
{imoser, thendtlass}@ict.swin.edu.au

Abstract. Solving dynamic combinatorial problems poses a particular challenge to optimisation algorithms. Optimising a problem that does not notify the solver when a change has been made is very difficult for most well-known algorithms. Extremal Optimisation is a recent addition to the group of biologically inspired optimisation algorithms. Due to its extremely simple functionality, it is likely that the algorithm can be applied successfully in such a dynamic environment. This document examines the capabilities of Extremal Optimisation to solve a dynamic problem with a large variety of different changes that are not explicitly announced to the solver.

1 Introduction

Extremal Optimisation (EO) is based on the Bak-Sneppen model [1] conceived to explain natural phenomena through self-organising criticality. The authors argued that any system whose "worst" component is replaced by a random substitute – with the substitution having an influence on the quality of the component's neighbours – will experience long periods of stability punctuated with critical states in which the overall quality suddenly deteriorates before being gradually improved to a high level again.

The model has since been transformed into an algorithm that simply replaces one component of poor quality at a time. It has been used for solving engineering optimisation problems such as heat pipe design [8] and physics problems such as spin glasses, e.g. in [3]. The same authors have also used EO for solving the graph partitioning and travelling salesperson problems [4].

Although most endeavours in combinatorial optimisation concentrate on solving static problems, various authors have reported successful attempts at solving dynamic problems, using solvers such as Evolutionary Algorithms [6] or Ant Colony Optimisation [7]. Their work is mainly concerned with the question how the algorithm should be adapted to dynamic problems so that it reacts appropriately when a change becomes known. In this work, we examine the algorithm's behaviour in an dynamic environment where the solver is not explicitly advised when a change has been made.

M. Ali and R. Dapoigny (Eds.): IEA/AIE 2006, LNAI 4031, pp. 292 – 301, 2006.

2 Extremal Optimisation

Unlike Genetic Algorithms, which work on a population of solutions, EO improves a single solution using mutation. The solution is made of multiple components which are assigned individual fitness values. The initial implementation proposed in [5] only accepted the component with the worst fitness to be mutated and replaced by a random component. This method proved inefficient in that it produced suboptimal solutions that would not improve further.

Boettcher and Percus [4] introduce a probabilistic choice of component for mutation. The solution components are ranked according to their fitness values, using a rank of 1 for the worst-quality component and n for the best. A candidate component is chosen for mutation and confirmed with a probability of $r^{-\tau}$, where r is the fitness rank and τ is a small value between 1 and 10. The behaviour of the algorithm depends entirely on the choice of the τ value, which has been discussed in [2] and other works of the authors. For the current problems, preliminary experiments have yielded an ideal value of ~ 3.

3 Experiments

As Branke [6] points out, the implementation of a benchmark for a dynamic solver requires a problem which facilitates the variation of as many environmental variables as possible. Often, the designer is faced with a tradeoff between a natural unpredictability of variations and their measurability. In our experiments, we oscillate between two configurations; a base problem to measure the performance, and a variation which is solved during "disruptive" phases. Whether the solver, which keeps no explicit history, "remembers" earlier configurations is one of the features explored.

3.1 Problem

The choice of problem was inspired by the desire to design illustrative experiments with a broad variety of dynamics. Based on the standard knapsack problem, the composition problem used has components with a type attribute in addition to a cost and value. The number of components in the solution is restricted by a cost limit (the equivalent of the capacity of a knapsack). Introducing typed components provides the possibility of implementing type constraints such as proportions or mutual exclusion.

Consider a problem with a set C of $\{c_1(t_1)...c_x(t_k)\}$ typed components. The objective is to build a Solution S of $\{c_1...c_n\}$ components, maximising either of the alternative objective functions (equation 1 or 2).

$$\text{maximise} \sum_{i=1}^{n} v(c_i) \; / \tag{1}$$

$$\text{maximise n,} \tag{2}$$

$$\text{s.t.} \sum_{i=1}^{n} w(c_i) \leq l \,, \tag{3}$$

where

> v = value
> $w(c_i)$ = cost of component c_i

Equation 3 is the cost limit constraint all problems have in common. The type-related constraints of Equation 4 and 5 are alternatives and describe the rules for adding types of components proportionally (equation 4) or under the constraint of mutually exclusive types (Equation 5) where only one of the types may be present for the solution to be valid.

$$\forall c_i(t_j) \in S, \frac{p_i}{\sum_{i=1}^{k} p_i} \approx \frac{|c(t_i)|}{n} \, {}^1 \tag{4}$$

$$\left(|c(t_a)| = 0 \vee |c(t_b)| = 0 \right), \tag{5}$$

where

> x = complexity (number of items in problem)
> n = number of items in solution
> l = limit
> $S = \{c_1...c_n\}$ = solution
> $T = \{t_1...t_k\}$ = types
> $C = \{c_1(t_1)...c_x(t_k)\}$ = typed components
> k = number of types
> $P = \{p_1...p_k\}$ = proportions
> $e = \{t_a, t_b\}$ = mutually exclusive types

In our experiments, we chose two base problems which have the following values in common: $x = 500$, $l = 3000$ and $k = 5$. This allows for approximately 30 to 100 components to be part of a solution, as each component has a cost and a value which are set to random values between 1 and 400. Each of the component types is equally represented in the x components. One of the problems imposes constraints on the relative proportions of each type of (10:20:30:10:30 components) the other a pair $e=\{t_a, t_b\}$ of mutually exclusive types.

3.2 Problem Dynamics

As has been observed by Randall in [7], the possible types of changes an optimisation problem can undergo on a general level are variations of constraints and components

---

[1] The proportional constraint is an approximation as the smallest possible addition is unity.

as well as changes of the objective function. In our problems, these categories are represented by the implementations mentioned in Table 1.

Table 1. Implementations of change categories in the experiments on the composition problem

Category	Implementation
Change of constraints	Variation of cost limit
	Variation of type proportions
	Variation of mutually exclusive components
Change of components	Add/remove components
	Change component attributes
Change of objective function	Maximise value / maximise item count

Based on these aspects of change, 10 experiments were run between the base problems described in 3.1 (the problem imposing a constraint of mutual exclusion is only used in experiment 1) and the following variations:

Table 2. Variations of the problem used in the experiments with EO

Experiment	Problem Variation
1	Different pair of types $e \neq e'$ for mutual exclusion
2	Different objective function (equation 2)
3	Reduced cost limit to $l = 2500$
4	Reduced cost limit to $l = 1000$
5	Changed type proportions to $P = \{10:30:20:10:30\}$
6	Changed type proportions to $P = \{20:10:10:40:20\}$
7	Changed attributes (cost, gain) in 10% of the components
8	Changed attributes (cost, gain) in 80% of the components
9	Added an additional 10% to the base problem's components ($x = 550$)
10	Added an additional 80% to the base problem's components ($x = 900$)

The experiments have been designed to juxtapose the behaviour of the algorithm, when faced with major change, with its performance in a situation where minor variations can be expected to leave a previously found solution in the vicinity of a new optimum.

3.3 Algorithm

The core EO algorithm has been adapted to a composition problem and applied to the dynamic environment without changes. Some implementations (as in [4]) have reduced the algorithm complexity by rebuilding only the affected parts of the fitness table. When solving dynamic problems, this entails the risk of invalid fitness tables. In the current implementation, the complete fitness table is recalculated after each mutation. The algorithm steps for the composition problem are:

> 1. create an initial random solution
> 2. build a fitness table
> 3. choose a random component
> 4. confirm a component to mutate according to $r^{-\tau}$
> 5. remove the component
> 6. add components until cost limit is reached
> 7. repeat 2 – 6 for a given number of cycles

The representation of the problem components and their fitnesses in the solution are crucial to the quality of the outcome. In the model of the component problem used for our experiments, the presence of a component in the solution is a Boolean value and the fitness of a component is a solution-independent static value, obtained in two different ways according to the two objective functions:

– optimise value: fitness = component value/component cost
– optimise item count: fitness = (component cost)$^{-1}$

The algorithm obtains the correct fitness value for each component from the problem that is being solved. To account for possible changes between mutations, the fitnesses of the components in the solution are calculated after each mutation. This guarantees that the fitness table is correct in the current environment.

In all experiments, the problem under scrutiny (which is the variation described in Table 2, save for Experiment 2 where the original "base problem" of 0 is recorded) is run for 10000 cycles (mutations), while the alternate problem is run for 100 or 2000 cycles respectively. 2000 cycles should allow the algorithm to adapt the solution completely to the new environment, whereas 100 mutations are unlikely to eradicate all the traits useful for solving the observed problem to a good quality.

Most of the changes in Table 2 lead to a situation where the solution is invalid after the swap. The algorithm cannot know the solution is invalid, as the change of environment is hidden from the solver. When components are chosen randomly for mutation, invalid components are identified through a check with the problem and mutated with a probability of 1. In the case of very different problems, 100 cycles are conceivably not enough to produce a valid solution for the current problem instance.

4   Results

The comparison between the outcomes of different phases of the run aims at shedding light on the robustness of the algorithm when faced with severe changes that have to be assimilated over time. As there are no known best solutions to the problems, the benchmark results were obtained by an adaptation of Ant Colony System (ACS) working on one problem continuously for 10000 cycles for 1000 trials. In a static environment, ACS found better results for this type of problem than EO.

4.1   Random Initial Solution vs. Initial Solution Modelled on Alternate Solution

Here we compare running the algorithm from a random initial solution, as in the case of a static problem, with a start from a solution that was produced during 2000 cycles of solving the alternate problem.

In 7 experiments, the initial phase (phase 1) starting from a random solution achieves an average of over 98% of the best-known outcome. The worst result for this phase is obtained from Experiment 1, whose average over 1000 runs reaches only 93.3% of the best-known outcome. As the problem used is an instance of mutual exclusion, only the inclusion of the mutually exclusive type with the highest value can lead to the best-known solution. Whenever the conflicting type is included, no optimal result can be expected.

When this problem is solved in phase 2, i.e. after the alternate problem, 723 of 1000 results surpass the solutions achieved in phase 1. All experiments behave similarly in this respect: More than half – approximately 600 out of 1000 – of the results of phase 2 surpass their counterparts from phase 1.

Another interesting aspect is how many mutations are required for the algorithm to reach its best results in phase 1 compared to phase 2 (i.e. the "phase-best"). When there is little or no correlation between the problems, there will presumably be little difference between the curves, as the solution given to phase 2 as a start is as unrelated to the current problem as a random initial solution. As shown in Fig. 1, the best outcomes are found roughly at the same stages.

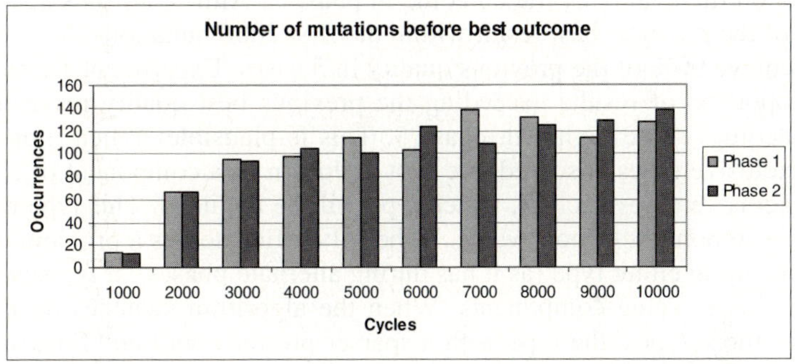

Fig. 1. Experiment 8 – histogram of how soon the 1000 instances find the phase-best outcome. Phase 1 is run from a random initial solution, phase 2 after 2000 cycles on the alternate problem.

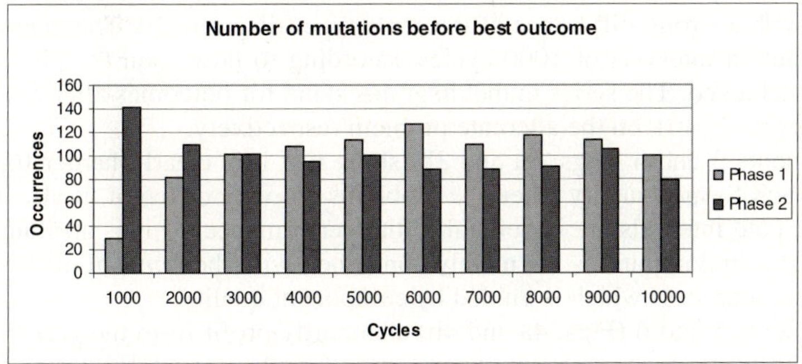

Fig. 2. Experiment 4 – mutations before best outcome (of phase) is reached. Problems are similar and phase 2 is given a good initial solution by a phase 1 run on the alternate problem.

All experiments on pairs of problems with similarities require fewer mutations in the second phase before finding the best result. The histogram in Fig. 2 is a typical example, although in this case the phenomenon may have a different explanation. The two problems used in experiment 4 – cost limit of 3000/1000 – may arguably be rather different, but the initial mutations of phase 2 are concerned with removing the redundant components that could be fitted in for the alternate problem. As removed components are chosen according to (lack of) fitness and additions are made at random, the algorithm here can be seen as "profiting from" a removal phase.

4.2 Reaching Previously Achieved Quality After Alternate Phase

To test the robustness of the algorithm, it is interesting to see how quickly it readjusts to a changed environment and achieves previous solution quality after a "disruptive" phase of work on the alternate problem. The experiments measure *if* and *after how many cycles* 90%, 95%, 99% and 100% previous (phase 1) best result has been reached again in phase 3 after a disruptive phase 2. The disruptive phase is run for 100 and 2000 mutations respectively.

For the vast majority of the experiments, the number of mutations in phase 2 has little impact on the quality of the outcome in phase 3. Almost all runs achieve results within 5% of the previous best result within the first 2000 mutations. Only experiment 1 fails to achieve 90% of the previous quality in 5 cases. Experiment 1 also shows the greatest proportion of results exceeding the previous best quality result in phase 3, half the outcomes score higher in phase 3. This is plausible: When a problem with mutually exclusive types is solved, the first inclusion of a component of either of the mutually exclusive types decides, which type will be included. This type may be represented by components of poor value. If the solver first solves a problem that has the option of including either type (as it has during alternate phases), it is likely to include more of the better-value components. When the algorithm switches back to mutual exclusion of these types, the type with a sparser presence will be "flushed" from the solution sooner and the more "valuable" type will remain.

The distance between the two problems solved has a greater impact on the readjustment of the solution to the current environment than the number of cycles the algorithm is given to run on the "disruptive" phase. The following histograms (Figs. 3-6) compare experiments on pairs of problems with a slight difference (diagrams a) and pairs with a strong difference of the same type (diagrams b). The diagrams group the outcomes in intervals of 1000 cycles according to how soon the phase-best outcome was achieved. The series in the diagrams stand for outcomes after runs with 100 and 2000 cycles' work on the alternate problem respectively.

Experiments 3 and 4 (Figs. 3a and 3b) show that it is clearly harder for the algorithm to reach former quality when the problems are very different. It also shows that longer alternate intervals are beneficial to the performance. This is attributable to the fact that the initial mutations are mainly concerned with the removal of the redundant components, a process which is guided by component quality.

Experiments 5 and 6 (Figs. 4a and 4b) also partly profit from the greediness of removal. Even in the case of severe change, only less than 50 of 1000 runs fail to produce 99% of the previous best outcome a second time in less than 10000 mutations.

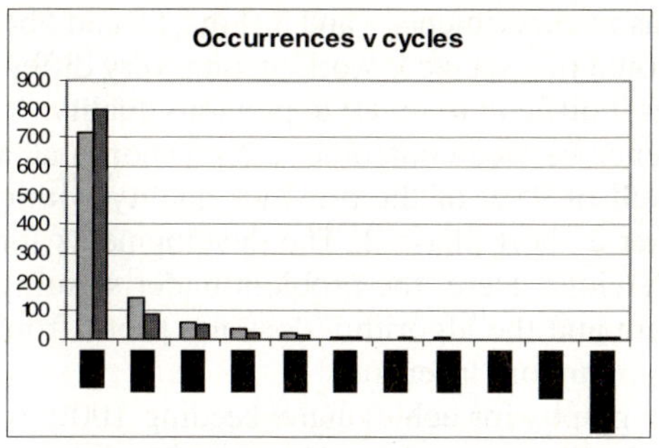

Fig. 3. (a) Experiment 3 (see Table 2)

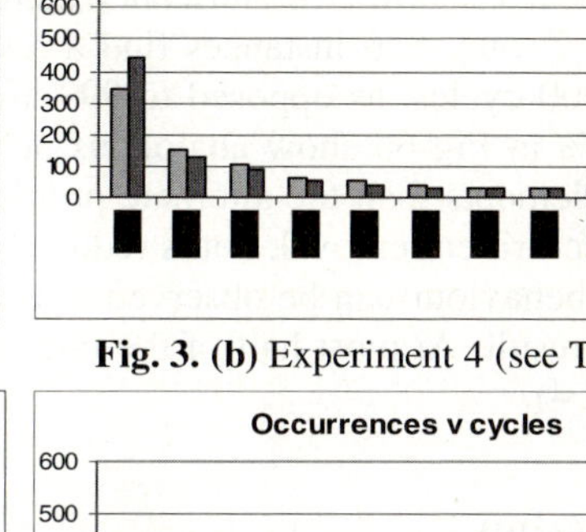

Fig. 3. (b) Experiment 4 (see Table 2)

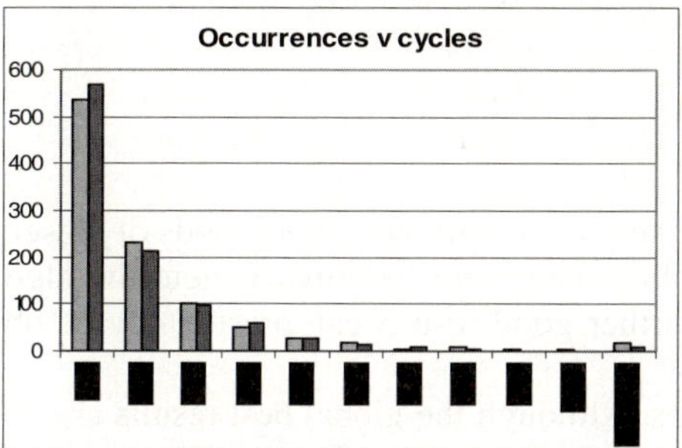

Fig. 4. (a) Experiment 5 (see Table 2)

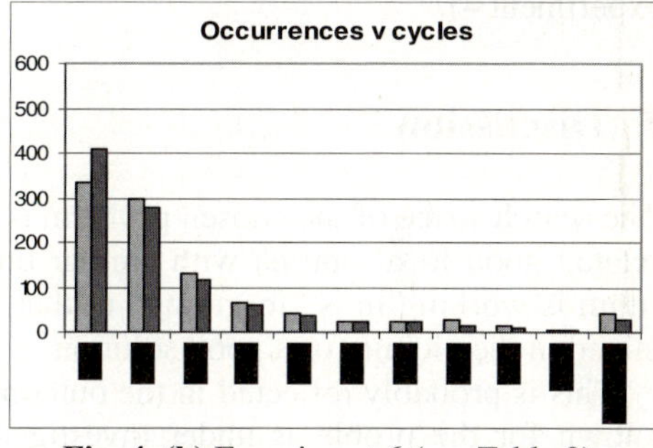

Fig. 4. (b) Experiment 6 (see Table 2)

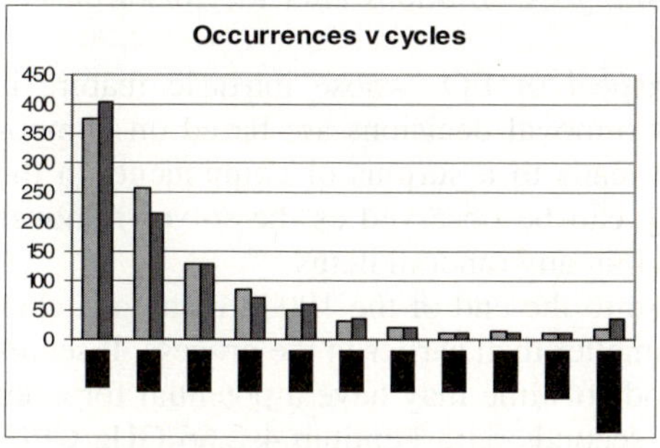

Fig. 5. (a) Experiment 7 (see Table 2)

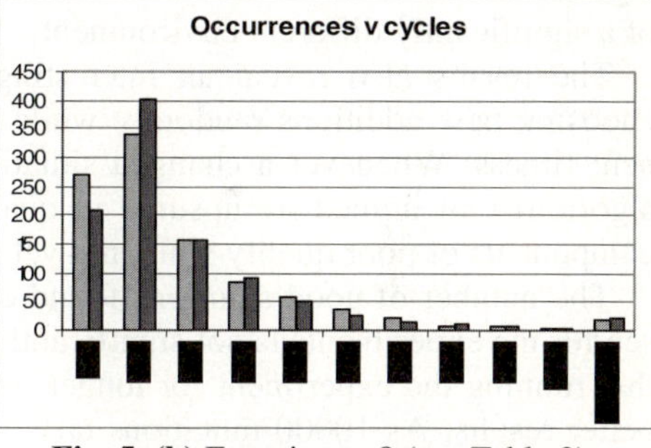

Fig. 5. (b) Experiment 8 (see Table 2)

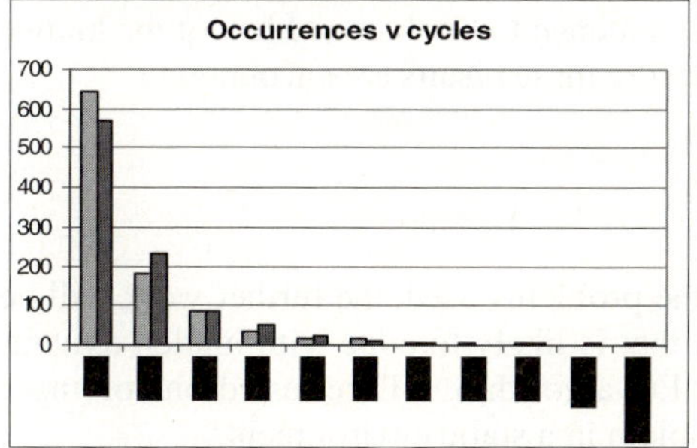

Fig. 6. (a) Experiment 9 (see Table 2)

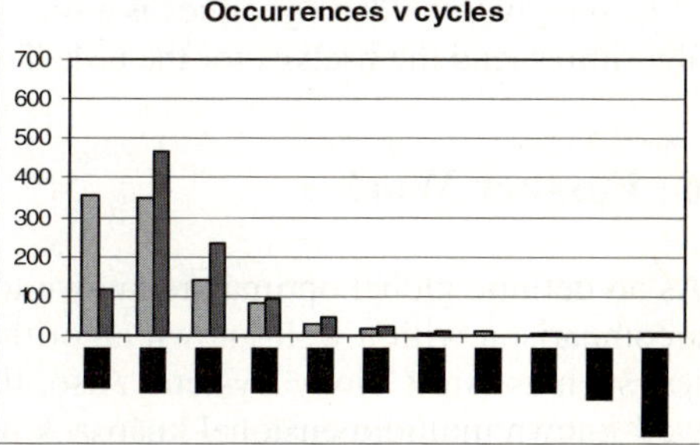

Fig. 6. (b) Experiment 10 (see Table 2)

Cycles needed to reach 99% of the previous best outcome after 100 (left bars) and 2000 (right bars) alternate runs

When component attributes are changed, as in experiments 7 and 8 (Figs. 5a and 5b), the development of the solution behaves as could be expected: working on a very different problem for a longer period of time makes it difficult to revert to previous quality.

Experiment 10 shows a significant difference between outcomes after a short and a long phase 2: only 836 instances find a result of 95% of the previous quality within the first 1000 cycles, as opposed to 999 after a short phase 2. The developments for finding 99% in Fig 6b show analogous behaviour. Here, the problem under scrutiny has more elements than the alternate problem and the algorithm does not profit from the heuristic-driven removal, but is reduced to random insertion.

Similar behaviour can be observed in the graphs for achieving/exceeding 100% of a previous result. At most half of the instances do not reach previous quality (case of experiment 4).

5 Discussion

The search space of the chosen problem is likely to contain neighbourhoods of closely related good local optima with similar quality. Therefore the environment the algorithm is working in is "forgiving" in that further good results can presumably be obtained in the vicinity of a good solution.

This is probably reflected in the outcomes. Although the global best results are not known for the problems under investigation, many good results are found and the algorithm shows a solid robustness in reaching good solutions after the "disturbance" of a significantly different environment.

The results also reveal an interesting aspect of EO, whose intrinsic feature is choosing new additions randomly while its removal decisions are based on component fitness. Whenever a changed situation leads to a surplus of components in the algorithms an immediate upsurge in quality can be observed as the solver removes components of poor quality while not yet adding any random items.

The number of good solutions found close to the end of the 10000 mutations chosen for the experiments is not significantly smaller than earlier in the process. It seems that running the experiment for longer periods of time may have a potential for even better results. As 10000 mutations take 1.5 seconds on a Pentium 4 2.66 GHz CPU, longer runs are not a serious performance problem.

Coping with hidden dynamics is a special challenge to a solver and few of the known algorithms lend themselves for the task. Therefore these results are encouraging.

6 Further Work

As no definite global optima are known to the problems used, the further work will be a comparison with a well-known algorithm that is likely to cope with hidden dynamics, such as Ant Colony System. Also, the EO algorithm will be tested on solving a well-known multidimensional knapsack problem in a static environment.

Our current experiments have not been useful in answering the question whether the problem dynamics are beneficial in helping the algorithm overcome local optima. Boettcher and Percus [301] suspect that the components of a solution may interlock even though a sufficiently small τ has been chosen. This seems unlikely, because the fitness values are static and the additions are made randomly. Nonetheless, the current results have revealed a number of best-known optima that could not be achieved during static runs. This may be an indication that forced variations of the environment may be beneficial for the solution quality.

References

1. Bak, P., Sneppen, K.: Punctuated equilibrium and criticality in a simple model of evolution, Phys. Rev. Let. 74, 4083-4086, (1993)
2. Boettcher, S., Percus, A.G.: Extremal optimization: an evolutionary local-search algorithm. In: Proceedings of the 8th INFORMS Computing Society Conference (2003)
3. Boettcher, S.: Extremal Optimization for Sherrington-Kirkpatrick Spin Glasses. European Physics Journal B 46 (2005) 501-505
4. Boettcher, S., Percus, A.: Nature's Way of Optimizing. Artificial Intelligence, Vol. 119, Number 1 (2000) 275-286
5. Boettcher, S., Percus, A.: Optimization with Extremal Dynamics. Physical Review Letters, Vol. 86 (2001) 5211-5214
6. Branke, J.: Evolutionary Optimization in Dynamic Environments. Kluwer Academic Publishers, Dordrecht, (2001)
7. Randall, M.: A Dynamic Optimisation Approach for Ant Colony Optimisation Using the Multiple Knapsack Problem. The Second Australian Conference on Artificial Life, Sydney (2005)
8. Sousa, F.L., Vlassov, V.V., Ramos, F.M.: Heat Pipe Design Through Generalized Extremal Optimization. Heat Transfer Engineering. ISSN 0145-7632, Volume 25, Number 7 (2004) 34-45

Local Search Algorithm for Unicost Set Covering Problem

Nysret Musliu

Vienna University of Technology, Karlsplatz 13, 1040 Vienna, Austria

Abstract. The unicost set covering problem is a NP-hard and it has many applications. In this paper we propose a new algorithm based on local search for solving the unicost set covering problem. A fitness function is proposed for this problem and different neighborhood relations are considered for the exploration of the neighborhood of the current solution. A new approach is introduced for effective exploration of the neighborhood during the improvement phase. This approach is based on the upper bound of the best cover, which is found during the search, and using only determined moves. Additionally, in order to avoid cycles during the search, a search history is used. The proposed algorithm is experimentally evaluated for 85 well-known random and combinatorial problems in the literature, and it gives very satisfactory results in a reasonable amount of time. The proposed algorithm improves the best existing solutions for 8 problems in the literature. For a class of combinatorial problems, the best existing results are improved significantly.

1 Introduction

For the set covering problem ([7]) we have given the finite set X and the family F of subsets of X. Each element of X belongs to at least one subset of F. The problem is to find the minimum size subset $C \subseteq F$ whose members cover all elements of X. The variant of the set covering problem in which all sets in F have the weight 1 is called the unicost set covering problem.

Many problems can be formulated as a set covering problem. Applications of a set covering problem include scheduling, testing, construction of optimal logical circuits, inspection of computer viruses, etc. The unicost set covering problem considered in this paper appeared in the problem of generation of generalized hypertree decompositions from tree decompositions. The importance of tree decompositions and hypertree decompositions lies in the fact that many constraint satisfaction and other NP-complete problems can be polynomially solved if their associated hypergraph has a low width for the chosen decomposition. Tree and hypertree decompositions are out of the main focus of this paper, and therefore the reader is refereed to [5] and [10] for definitions and further details on the importance of these concepts for solving constraint satisfaction problems.

Different methods have been proposed in the literature for the set covering problem. Examples of using exact methods are [1] and [2]. For solving larger instances of this problem, approximation algorithms and heuristic algorithms have been proposed. One of the best approximation algorithms is the greedy

M. Ali and R. Dapoigny (Eds.): IEA/AIE 2006, LNAI 4031, pp. 302–311, 2006.

algorithm [6]. The greedy algorithm finds a solution for the set covering problem by iteratively picking a set that covers as many remaining uncovered variables as possible. Grossman and Wohl [11] compared nine different algorithms for the set covering problem including different variants of the greedy algorithm, randomized algorithms, and neural networks. They reported that the best results were obtained by using the randomized greedy algorithm. This algorithm is identical to the greedy algorithm, except that in the phase of selection ties are broken randomly for sets which contain the same number of uncovered variables. The results obtained by the randomized greedy algorithm were obtained by iterating this algorithm 100 times.

Marchiori and Steenbeek [13] enhanced the greedy algorithm by introducing a new rule for breaking ties in the steps of adding and removing sets. Further, the simple optimization step was applied in the constructed solution by the enhanced greedy algorithm. An iterated algorithm is proposed that starts each run with partial cover obtained from the solution constructed by the enhanced greedy algorithm in the previous iteration. The authors reported very good results with this method and they improved the best results for many problems in the literature. Nonobe and Ibaraki [14] have proposed a tabu search algorithm for constraint satisfaction problems. This general tabu search problem solver has been applied for the set covering problem and the algorithm has been evaluated for the class of problems defined from Steiner triple systems. The tabu search approach has also been used in [12], here the authors compared their results for 70 problems to CPLEX, and report better results than those reported in [11]. However, the quality of results reported in [12] are worse than the results reported in [13]. Other metaheuristic approaches, such as genetic algorithms ([4]) have been proposed for solving this problem.

In this paper we propose a new method based on local search for solving the unicost set covering problem. We investigate the use of different neighborhood relations and propose a simple fitness function for this problem. The proposed algorithm includes a new method for the generation of the neighborhood during each iteration based on the knowledge of the number of sets of the current best known solution. Additionally, the algorithm uses a search history and a basic tabu search mechanism to avoid cycles during the search.

This paper is organized as follows: in the next section the local search algorithm for solving the unicost set covering problem is described. In section 2, its computational results on 85 problems are presented, before the final section which contains our conclusions and remarks.

2   Local Search Algorithm

In this section a local search based algorithm for unicost set covering problem is described. The algorithm is based on an iterative local improvement of the initial solution. In each iteration the neighborhood of the current solution is generated, and one solution from this neighborhood is selected for the next iteration. A basic variant of a local search is used for the selection criteria, in which the best solution of the neighborhood is selected for the next iteration. However, also the so called tabu mechanism to avoid the cycles during the search is introduced. If the solutions are obtained by moves, which are performed in a determined number of previous iterations, then they are considered as tabu solutions and will be accepted only if they fulfill particular criteria. For the generation and restriction of the neighborhood of the current solution, a unique method is applied. This method is based on the upper bound for the number of sets of the best solution found during the search. The basic elements of this local search procedure are described below in detail.

2.1 Neighborhood Structure

As described in Section 1 the solution for the set covering problem is a subset $C \subseteq F$ whose members cover all elements of X. Note that the solution, which in this case is the subset C, can be illegal in the beginning and also in the improvement phase, i.e. a solution which does not cover all elements of X. To generate the neighborhood of subset C two basic moves are applied:

$ADD\_SET(S)$ - a set S (which is not in C) from the family of sets F is added in C: $C \leftarrow C \cup S$

$REMOVE\_SET(S)$ - a set S is removed from C: $C \leftarrow C - S$

Another move, which has been used in the literature, swaps one set $S1$ in C with another set $S2$ not in C: $SWAP\_SETS(S1, S2)$

The whole neighborhood that is generated by only applying ADD_SET and $REMOVE\_SET$ moves contains $|F|$ solutions. If the $SWAP\_SETS$ move is applied the generated neighborhood is much larger. In this case the whole neighborhood contains $|C| * (|F| - |C|)$ solutions.

The $SWAP\_SETS$ move can be performed by the sequence of ADD_SET and $REMOVE\_SET$ moves:

$$SWAP\_SETS(S1, S2) = REMOVE\_SET(S1) + ADD\_SET(S2)$$

To avoid a very large number of solutions in the neighborhood we implemented a method which only applies ADD_SET and $REMOVE\_SET$ moves. We also experimented with all three moves mentioned above. The experiments showed that the moves ADD_SET and $REMOVE\_SET$ are sufficient to obtain very satisfactory solutions in a reasonable amount of time.

2.2 Restricting Neighborhood by Introducing an Upper Bound Parameter

We define the upper bound parameter as the number of sets of actual best legal solution. If only the ADD_SET and $REMOVE\_SET$ moves are applied, this upper bound can be used to restrict the neighborhood during the search. With this restriction the move ADD_SET can be applied in the current solution only if the number of sets in the current solution is less than $upperbound - 1$. The upper bound is calculated from the first legal solution, which covers all elements of X. If the legal solution is improved during the search, the upper bound parameter is updated automatically. The motivation for restricting the neighborhood during the search is given below. By using this restriction the search is intensified in the neighborhood (considering number of sets) of the current best solution by not allowing the exploration of the solutions which have more sets than the current best legal solution. However, this method does not restrict the exploration of solutions with worse fitness. Moreover, by using fitness function defined in section 2.3, with this restriction is enforced almost all the times during the improvement phase (the phase in which one cover is already known) that in one iteration the $REMOVE\_SET$ is performed, whereas in the next iteration ADD_SET move is performed. The move $REMOVE\_SET$ can be applied during each iteration, if the variables can be covered with less sets. Through alternate applying of ADD_SET and $REMOVE\_SET$ we mimic the $SWAP\_SETS$ move with much smaller neighborhood during each iteration.

Additionally, to make the search more effective, during the neighborhood exploration the following rule is applied: if the set is removed from C, in the next iteration for adding in C are considered only the sets which share elements with the set removed in the previous iteration. This requires storing of additional information for the problem, but makes the search more effective.

2.3 Fitness Function

A simple fitness function is used to calculate the quality of solution during the search. A penalty of value 1 for each uncovered element of set X and each set in C is given. The fitness of solution is equal with the sum of uncovered variables and the number of sets in C:

$$Fitness = NrOfUncoveredElements + |C|$$

The aim is to minimize this fitness function during the search, such that all elements of set X are covered.

To calculate the fitness efficiently, the fitness of neighborhood solutions is calculated only from the fitness of the previous solution and the change caused from the applied move.

2.4 Initial Solution

We experimented with the empty initial solution and the initial solution which is generated with the greedy algorithm [6]. The greedy algorithm finds a solution for the set covering problem by iteratively picking a set that covers as many remaining uncovered variables as possible. The results presented in this paper are obtained with the initial solution which is obtained by the greedy algorithm.

2.5 Using of the Search History

In order to avoid the cycles during the search, the search history is used. The information for the search are stored in a short term memory (tabu list). In this memory are stored the information for the sets which are removed or added in the past number of iterations *nIter*. For example, if the solution accepted for the next iteration is obtained by adding the set $S1$ in C, in the tabu list will be added the set $S1$. The moves $ADD\_SET(S1)$ and $REMOVE\_SET(S1)$ are made tabu (can not be applied) for several iterations depending on the length of the tabu list. We experimented with the different lengths for the tabu list. In the first variant the length of the tabu list is same for all examples independently from the size of the problem. In the second variant we experimented with the tabu length which depends from the number of sets in the solution generated by the greedy algorithm. Experimental results showed that the second variant gives better results for the problems we consider in this paper. The information for the length of the tabu list used in experiments are given in Section 3.

2.6   Selection Criteria

The solution is accepted for the next iteration based on the following criteria: the best solution (ties are broken randomly) from the neighborhood becomes the current solution in the next iteration, if it is not tabu solution. The solution is considered tabu, if it is obtained by applying of one of moves on the set which is in the tabu list. If the best solution from neighborhood is tabu, the aspiration criterion is applied. For the aspiration criteria, we use a standard version [9] according to which the tabu status of a move is ignored if the move has a fitness better than the current best solution.

2.7   The Algorithm

The pseudo code of the overall local search algorithm which was shown the best in the experimental evaluation is given below. This algorithm exploits the simple fitness function defined in the section 2.3, applies only ADD_SET and $REMOVE\_SET$ moves, and makes use of the short term memory. Additionally, the upper bound parameter is used to reduce the neighborhood.

Local Search Algorithm

1. Generate the initial solution
2. Initialize the tabu list and the UPPERBOUND parameter
3. Generate the neighborhood of the current solution as described in section 2.2 (apply only ADD_SET and $REMOVE\_SET$ moves)
4. Evaluate the neighborhood solutions
5. Select the solution for the next iteration (see section 2.6)
5. Update the tabu list and UPPERBOUND parameter
7. Go to step 3 if the stopping criteria is not fulfilled, otherwise go in step 8
8. Return the best legal solution.

3   Computational Results

The algorithms proposed in this paper are evaluated experimentally for 85 problems from the literature. These problems include random problems and the set covering problems which appeared in different combinatorial problems. Characteristics of these instances are presented in [13]. Instances 4-6, A-E and NRE-NRH are random generated instances. Instances 4-6 are from [1], A - E from [2], and NRE - NRH from [3]. All these instances are available from the OR-library (http://mscmga.ms.ic.ac.uk/jeb/orlib/scpinfo.html). These instances represent a weighted set covering problem, in which columns can have different costs. As in [11], [13], [12] the costs of columns are discarded when applying the algorithm to the unicost set covering problem. The results obtained in this paper are compared with the results from [11], [13], [12] and are not comparable with (except for instances $E.1 - E.5$) the results obtained by [1], [2], and [3] because they considered a weighted set covering problem.

The CYC and CLR instances are from [11] and arise from combinatorial problems. These instances are derived from two questions of Erdós and are described in detail in [11]. The STS instances are derived from Steiner triple systems ([8]), and they are known to be difficult set covering instances.

Our algorithms are implemented in C++ and the experiments are performed in a computer Pentum 4, 2,4GHZ, 512 MB RAM. For each problem 10 independent runs are executed.

The algorithm presented in Section 2.7, which has been shown to be very powerful for unicost set covering problem exploits the tabu list. The parameter for the length of the tabu list is found experimentally for each class of instances mentioned before. The tabu length depends from the number of sets in the solution that is obtained by the greedy algorithm (we denote this parameter as NrOfGreedySets). For each class of problems the length of the tabu list is obtained as follows: $TabuLength = TSFactor * NrOfGreedySets + 1$. The experiments with the following tabu length factor ($TSFactor$) were performed: 0, 0.05, 0.1, 0.15 and 0.2. The best tabu length for each class of problems was chosen based on the sum of the average number of sets in 10 runs (for all solutions of that particular class), and based on the average time for which the solutions are found.

In Tables 1, 2, and 3 are presented the results of the algorithm proposed in this paper for 85 problems from the literature. The results obtained with the previous approaches proposed in the literature are also presented in these tables. The ITEG algorithm [13] was tested on a multi-user Silicon Graphics IRIX Release 6.2 IP25, 194 MHZ MIPS R10000 processor, 512 MB RAM. The algorithms from [12] were tested on Dell Precision 530 Workstations with two 1.8 GHz Pentium Xeon processors and 1GB of RAM. First column of each table represents the problems for which the results are given. In the second column for each problem is presented the best solution obtained by the algorithms proposed in [11] (the number represents number of sets the solution contains). In the third and the fourth column are presented results from [12]. The best solution is presented in the third column, whereas the time for which the solution is found is presented in the fourth column (T). Next three columns represent results from [13] (best solution, averages number of sets for 10 runs, and average time used for each problem). The last three columns give the results obtained by the algorithm

Table 1. Comparison of the results for the class of problems 4,5,6,A,B,C,D,E

Example	[11] Best	[12] Best	[12] T	ITEG ([13]) Best	ITEG ([13]) Avg	ITEG ([13]) T(Avg)	Our algorithm Best	Our algorithm Avg(Stdev)	Our algorithm T(Avg/Stdev)
scp41.txt	41	38	938	38	38	10	38	38,1 (0,3)	0,5 (0,7)
scp42.txt	38	37	5	37	37	10	37	37 (0,0)	0 (0,0)
scp43.txt	40	38	1	38	38	10	38	38 (0,0)	0 (0,0)
scp44.txt	41	38	272	39	39,1	10	38	38,6 (0,5)	0,7 (1,1)
scp45.txt	40	38	23	38	38	10	38	38 (0,0)	0,4 (1,0)
scp46.txt	40	37	3	37	37,8	10	37	37,2 (0,4)	0,8 (0,9)
scp47.txt	41	38	413	38	38,4	10	38	38,4 (0,5)	1,1 (0,7)
scp48.txt	40	38	6	37	37,7	10	37	37,6 (0,5)	1 (1,3)
scp49.txt	40	38	35	38	38,1	10	38	38 (0,0)	1 (1,2)
scp410.txt	41	38	161	38	38,6	10	38	38,3 (0,5)	1,2 (1,4)
scp51.txt	35	35	5	34	34,9	10	34	34,7 (0,5)	1 (2,2)
scp52.txt	35	35	6	34	34,7	10	34	34,2 (0,4)	3,2 (2,6)
scp53.txt	36	34	39	34	34	10	34	34 (0,0)	0,8 (1,4)
scp54.txt	36	34	1182	34	34	10	34	34 (0,0)	1,6 (2,0)
scp55.txt	36	34	12	34	34,1	10	34	34,1 (0,3)	2,2 (3,0)
scp56.txt	36	34	989	34	34,5	10	34	34,1 (0,3)	3,1 (3,0)
scp57.txt	35	34	75	34	34	10	34	34 (0,0)	0,6 (1,1)
scp58.txt	37	34	74	34	34,9	10	34	34,4 (0,5)	2,2 (3,6)
scp59.txt	36	35	6	35	35	10	35	35,6 (1,0)	0,6 (1,0)
scp510.txt	36	34	1873	34	34,6	10	34	34,5 (0,5)	3,4 (3,6)
scp61.txt	21	21	5	21	21	60	21	21 (0,0)	0 (0,0)
scp62.txt	21	21	6	20	20,3	60	20	20 (0,0)	0,7 (0,8)
scp63.txt	21	21	10	21	21	60	21	21 (0,0)	0 (0,0)
scp64.txt	22	21	4	21	21	60	20	20,9 (0,3)	0,6 (1,9)
scp65.txt	22	21	25	21	21	60	21	21 (0,0)	0 (0,0)
scpa1.txt	40	39	337	39	39,1	30	39	39 (0,0)	3,2 (2,9)
scpa2.txt	41	39	79	39	39,1	30	39	39 (0,0)	4,7 (3,1)
scpa3.txt	40	39	179	39	39	30	39	39,1 (0,3)	1,8 (1,8)
scpa4.txt	40	38	1715	38	38	30	37	37,8 (0,4)	5,7 (6,6)
scpa5.txt	40	38	771	38	38,7	30	38	38,4 (0,5)	6,1 (4,5)
scpb1.txt	23	22	719	22	22	60	22	22 (0,0)	8,3 (8,8)
scpb2.txt	22	22	17	22	22	60	22	22 (0,0)	2 (4,2)
scpb3.txt	22	22	698	22	22	60	22	22 (0,0)	1,1 (3,5)
scpb4.txt	23	22	1910	22	22	60	22	22,1 (0,3)	11,6 (9,5)
scpb5.txt	23	22	46	22	22,2	60	22	22 (0,0)	12,1 (8,9)
scpc1.txt	45	43	1524	43	43,5	40	43	43,5 (0,5)	5,9 (5,7)
scpc2.txt	45	44	197	43	43,5	40	43	43,4 (0,5)	9,5 (8,5)
scpc3.txt	45	43	1029	43	43,6	40	43	43,4 (0,5)	10,2 (10,4)
scpc4.txt	46	43	1325	43	43,1	40	43	43,3 (0,5)	11,6 (9,2)
scpc5.txt	45	44	149	43	43,5	40	43	43,9 (0,3)	2,1 (2,0)
scpd1.txt	26	25	395	25	25	110	25	25,1 (0,3)	6,4 (10,7)
scpd2.txt	25	25	1890	25	25	110	25	25 (0,0)	2,2 (1,4)
scpd3.txt	25	25	91	25	25	110	24	24,9 (0,3)	21,6 (27,0)
scpd4.txt	26	25	226	25	25	110	25	25 (0,0)	17,7 (16,4)
scpd5.txt	26	25	200	25	25	110	25	25 (0,0)	24,1 (16,4)
scpe1.txt	5	5	-	5	5	10	5	5 (0,0)	0 (0,0)
scpe2.txt	5	5	-	5	5	10	5	5 (0,0)	0 (0,0)
scpe3.txt	5	5	-	5	5	10	5	5 (0,0)	0 (0,0)
scpe4.txt	5	5	-	5	5	10	5	5 (0,0)	0 (0,0)
scpe5.txt	5	5	-	5	5	10	5	5 (0,0)	0 (0,0)

Table 2. Comparison of the results for the class of problems NRE, NRF, NRG, NRH

	[11]	[12]		ITEG ([13])			Our algorithm		
Example	Best	Best	T	Best	Avg	T(Avg)	Best	Avg(Stdev)	T(Avg/Stdev)
scpnre1.txt	17	18	38	17	17	34	17	17,3 (0,5)	2,2 (3,0)
scpnre2.txt	17	18	27	17	17	34	17	17,1 (0,3)	1,5 (2,3)
scpnre3.txt	17	18	32	17	17	34	17	17,1 (0,3)	16,5 (38,8)
scpnre4.txt	17	17	54	17	17	34	17	17,2 (0,4)	5 (7,8)
scpnre5.txt	17	17	586	17	17,2	34	17	17 (0,0)	4,5 (4,6)
scpnrf1.txt	10	11	29	10	10,3	66	10	10,7 (0,5)	17,3 (28,9)
scpnrf2.txt	11	11	39	10	10,4	66	10	10,5 (0,5)	43,9 (63,3)
scpnrf3.txt	11	11	30	10	10,6	66	10	10,6 (0,5)	48,7 (112,6)
scpnrf4.txt	11	11	22	10	10,5	66	10	10,7 (0,5)	17,9 (31,5)
scpnrf5.txt	11	10	482	10	10,7	66	10	10,6 (0,5)	29,4 (73,5)
scpnrg1.txt	-	63	1089	62	62,4	26	61	62,4 (0,8)	27,3 (24,1)
scpnrg2.txt	-	61	3401	62	62,5	26	62	62,3 (0,5)	29,8 (34,4)
scpnrg3.txt	-	62	901	62	62,8	26	62	62,9 (0,6)	20,8 (24,5)
scpnrg4.txt	-	63	1045	62	63,7	26	62	63,1 (0,7)	41,8 (42,7)
scpnrg5.txt	-	63	406	62	62,7	26	62	62,8 (0,4)	40,2 (35,7)
scpnrh1.txt	-	35	2008	34	34,8	61	34	34,9 (0,6)	8,7 (16,3)
scpnrh2.txt	-	36	297	34	34,7	61	34	34,9 (0,3)	7,8 (21,2)
scpnrh3.txt	-	36	968	34	34,8	61	34	34,9 (0,3)	19,1 (32,2)
scpnrh4.txt	-	35	940	34	35	61	34	34,9 (0,6)	26,1 (67,7)
scpnrh5.txt	-	36	454	34	34,6	61	34	34,8 (0,4)	50,3 (150,0)

Table 3. Comparison of the results for the problems CYC, CLR and STS

	[11]	[12]		ITEG ([13])			Our algorithm		
Example	Best	Best	T	Best	Avg	T(Avg)	Best	Avg(Stdev)	T(Avg/Stdev)
scpcyc06.txt	60	-	-	60	61,4	0	60	60 (0,0)	0 (0,0)
scpcyc07.txt	144	-	-	144	148	1	144	144 (0,0)	0 (0,0)
scpcyc08.txt	352	-	-	348	351,8	5	342	343,8 (0,6)	11,1 (10,4)
scpcyc09.txt	816	-	-	825	827,6	19	774	791,9 (6,4)	110,4 (122,6)
scpcyc10.txt	1916	-	-	1858	1860,7	110	1820	1823,9 (2,9)	488,9 (189,7)
scpcyc11.txt	4268	-	-	4202	4218,3	500	4088	4144,9 (24,5)	1497,8 (67,2)
scpclr10.txt	28	-	-	25	25	10	25	25 (0,0)	0 (0,0)
scpclr11.txt	27	-	-	23	23	20	23	23 (0,0)	0 (0,0)
scpclr12.txt	27	-	-	23	23	50	23	23 (0,0)	3,7 (3,8)
scpclr13.txt	29	-	-	23	25,3	110	23	23,4 (0,5)	79 (64,9)
STS27.txt	-	-	-	18	18	1	18	18 (0,0)	0 (0,0)
STS45.txt	-	-	-	30	30,7	2	30	30 (0,0)	0,1 (0,3)
STS81.txt	-	-	-	61	61	11	61	62,4 (1,0)	0 (0,0)
STS135.txt	-	-	-	104	104	15	104	105,7 (1,2)	1,1 (3,5)
STS243.txt	-	-	-	198	202,2	100	198	199 (2,1)	29,6 (31,1)

proposed in this paper (see section 2.7). From these three columns the first column represents for each problem the best solution obtained in 10 runs. The second column gives the average and standard deviation of number of sets in 10 runs. Last column gives information for the average (and standard deviation) time for which the best solution is found. The time for all algorithms is given in seconds.

In [14] and [15] are given results only for STS class of problems. These results are not included here. To our best knowledge the tables given in this paper represent the best known results for the unicost set covering problems found in the literature. The only exception is the problem STS.135 for which a better solution (with value 103) is reported in [15].

Based on these tables we can conclude that the approach proposed in this paper gives better results compared to [11] for 52 problems. The methods proposed in [11] do not outperform our algorithm for any of problems. Compared to the methods proposed in [12] our approach gives better results for 24 problems. The only problem for which the approach proposed in [12] is better (for 1 set) is the problem $scpnrg2$. In [12] are not given results for CYC, CLR and STS problems. The ITEG algorithm proposed in [13] outperforms slightly our approach (considering average in 10 runs) in 22 examples, whereas our approach outperforms ITEG in 34 problems. Considering the best solution in 10 runs our approach gives better results for 9 problems compared to ITEG, and ITEG does not give better results than our approach for any of problems. The algorithm proposed in this paper improves the best known results in the literature for 8 problems (6.4, A.4, D.3. NRG1, CYC08 - CYC11) and can find the best known results for all problems, except for the problems NRG2 (62 instead of 61 obtained in [12]) and STS.135 (104 instead 103 obtained in [15]). The results for problems $CYC.08 - CYC.11$ are improved significantly by our algorithm. Note that with the individual tabu length for each problem (not the tabu length for the class of problems) our algorithm could also find better solution for the following problems: $NRE4(16)$, $A.2(38)$, and $D.1(24)$.

4   Conclusion

In this paper we presented a local search algorithm for solving the unicost set covering problem. We have used simple neighborhood relations and have introduced a unique approach for neighborhood exploration during the search. The neighborhood exploration is based on the upper bound of the number of sets in the best solution and restriction of particular add moves. This restriction is based on information about the removed set in the previous iteration. Additionally, we have used a search history to avoid possible cycles during the search. The proposed algorithm has been evaluated experimentally in 85 problems which appeared previously in the literature. Experimental results show that our local search algorithm gives very satisfactory results for problems appearing in the literature. In particular, our algorithm performs as well as the best results cited in the literature, except for two problems. The solutions generated by our algorithm for these two problems are only worse with respect to 1 set. For 8 problems from the literature our algorithm discovers better solutions. In the future work we are planning to analyze the use of the frequency based memory and to apply the adaptive tabu list for the unicost set covering problem.

Acknowledgments. This paper was supported by the Austrian Science Fund (FWF) project: *Nr. P17222-N04, Complementary Approaches to Constraint Satisfaction.*

References

1. E. Balas and A. Ho. Set covering algorithms using cutting planes, heuristics, and subgradient optimization: a computational study. *Mathematical Programming*, 12:37–60, 1980.
2. J. E. Beasley. An algorithm for set covering problems. *European Journal of Operational Research*, 31:85–93, 1987.
3. J. E. Beasley. A lagrangian heuristic for set covering problems. *Naval Research Logistics*, 37:151–164, 1990.
4. J. E. Beasley and P. C. Chu. A genetic algorithm for set covering problem. *European Journal of Operational Research*, 94:392–404, 1996.
5. H. L. Bodlaender. Discovering treewidth. In *In P. Vojtás, M. Bieliková, B. Charron-Bost, and O. Sýkora, editors, SOFSEM 2005: Theory and Practice of Computer Science, pages 116. Springer, Lecture Notes in Computer Science, vol. 3381, 2005.*
6. V. Chvátal. A greedy heuristic for the set-covering problem. *Math. of Oper. Res.*, 4/3:233–235, 1979.
7. T. H. Cormen, C. E. Leiserson, R. L. Rivest, and C. Stein, editors. *Introduction to Algorithms, 2nd ed.* The MIT Press, Massachusetts, 2001.
8. D.R. Fulkerson, G.L. Nemhauser, and L.E. Trotter. Two computationally difficult set covering problems that arise in computing the 1-width of incidence matrices of steiner triple systems. *Mathematical Programming Study*, 2:72–81, 1974.
9. Fred Glover and Manuel Laguna. *Tabu search*. Kluwer Academic Publishers, 1997.
10. G. Gottlob, N. Leone, and F. Scarcello. A comparison of structural csp decomposition methods. *Artificial Intelligence*, 124(2):243–282, 2000.
11. T. Grossman and A. Wool. Computational experience with approximation algorithms for the set covering problem. *European Journal of Operational Research*, 101:81–92, 1997.
12. G. Kinney, J.W. Barnes, and B. Colleti. A group theoretic tabu search algorithm for set covering problems. *Working paper, available from http://www.me.utexas.edu/ barnes/research/*, 2004.
13. Elena Marchiori and Adri Steenbeek. An iterated heuristic algorithm for the set covering problem. *Proceedings of WEA'98, Germany*, 1998.
14. K. Nonobe and T. Ibaraki. A tabu search approach to the constraint satisfaction problem as a general problem solver. *European Journal of Operational Research*, 106:599–623, 1998.
15. M.A. Odijk and H. van Maaren. Imporved solutions for the steiner triple covering problems. *Technical Report, TU Delft University, 11, 1996*, 1996.

Evaluating Interestingness Measures with Linear Correlation Graph

Xuan-Hiep Huynh, Fabrice Guillet, and Henri Briand

LINA CNRS 2729 - Polytechnic School of Nantes University
La Chantrerie BP 50609 44306 Nantes cedex 3, France
{xuan-hiep.huynh, fabrice.guillet, henri.briand}@univ-nantes.fr

Abstract. Making comparisons from the post-processing of association rules have become a research challenge in data mining. By evaluating interestingness value calculated from interestingness measures on association rules, a new approach based on the Pearson's correlation coefficient is proposed to answer the question: How we can capture the stable behaviors of interestingness measures on different datasets?. In this paper, a correlation graph is used to evaluate the behavior of 36 interestingness measures on two datasets.

1   Introduction

In the framework of data mining [5], association rules [1] are a key tool aiming at discovering interesting implicative patterns in data.

In this paper, we present a new approach and a dedicated tool ARQAT [9] (Association Rule Quality Analysis Tool) to study the specific behavior of a set of interestingness measures (IMs) in the context of a specific dataset and in an exploratory analysis perspective, reflecting the post-processing of association rules. More precisely, ARQAT is a toolbox designed to help a data-analyst to capture the best IMs and as a final purpose, the best rules within a specific ruleset. In addition, we focus our study on 36 objective IMs studied in the literature. We present a new approach based on the analysis of a correlation graph to clustering objective IMs. We apply this approach to compare and discuss the behavior of IMs on two prototypical datasets: a strongly correlated one (mushroom dataset [13]) and a lowly correlated one (synthetic dataset). Our objective is to find the stabilities and the differences between IMs.

The paper is structured as follows. In Section 2, we present related works on objective IMs for association rules. In Section 3, we propose the correlation graph clustering approach. Section 4 is dedicated to a specific study on two datasets in order to extract the stable correlations.

2   Related Works on Objective IMs

Many interesting surveys on objective IMs can be found in the literature. They mainly address two related research issues, the definition of the set of principles

M. Ali and R. Dapoigny (Eds.): IEA/AIE 2006, LNAI 4031, pp. 312–321, 2006.
© Springer-Verlag Berlin Heidelberg 2006

or properties that lead to the design of a good IM, and their comparison from a data-analysis point of view to study IM behavior in order to help the user to select the best ones.

Considering the principles of a good IM issue, Piatetsky-Shapiro [15] introduces a new IM, called Rule-Interest, and proposes three underlying principles for a good IM on a rule $a \rightarrow b$: (P1) 0 value when a and b are independent, (P2) monotonically increasing with $a \cap b$, (P3) monotonically decreasing with a or b. Hilderman and Hamilton [8] have proposed five principles: minimum value, maximum value, skewness, permutation invariance, transfer. Tan et al. [17] have defined five interestingness principles: symmetry under variable permutation, row/column scaling invariance, anti-symmetry under row/column permutation, inversion invariance, null invariance. Freitas [6] proposes an "attribute surprisingness" principle. Bayardo and Agrawal [3] concluded that the best rules according to any IMs must reside along a support/confidence border. The work allows for improved insight into the data and supports more user-interaction in the optimized rule-mining process. Kononenko [11] analyzes the biases of eleven IMs for estimating the quality of multi-valued attributes. The values of information gain, j-measure, gini-index, and relevance tend to linearly increase with the number of values of an attribute. Gavrilov et al. [7] studied the similarity IMs for clustering of similar stocks.

Some of these surveys also address the related issue of the IM comparison by adopting a data-analysis point of view. Hilderman and Hamilton [8] use the five proposed principles to rank summaries generated from databases and use sixteen diversity IMs and show that: (1) six IMs matched five proposed principles, (2) nine remaining IMs matched at least one proposed principle. By studying twenty-one IMs, Tan et al. [17] show that an IM cannot be adapted in all cases and use both a support-based pruning and standardization methods to select the best IMs and they found that, in some cases many IMs are highly correlated with each other. Eventually, the decision-maker will select the best IM by matching the five proposed properties. Vaillant et al. [18] evaluate twenty IMs to choose a user-adapted IM with 8 properties: (g_1) asymetric processing of A and B, (g_2) decrease with n_b, (g_3) independence, (g_4) logical rule, (g_5) linearity with $n_{a\bar{b}}$ around 0^+, (g_6) sensitivity to n, (g_7) easiness to fix a threshold, (g_8) intelligibility. Blanchard et al. [4] classify the eighteen objective IMs into four groups according to the evaluation of independence, balance, issued from descriptive or statistical type. Finally, Huynh et al. [10] introduce the first result of a new clustering approach for classifying thirty-four IMs with positive correlation.

3   Correlation Graph Approach

3.1   Principles

Let an association rule $a \rightarrow b$ where a and b are two disjoint sets of items (called itemset). Itemset a (resp. b) is associated with a subset of transactions $A = T(a)$ (resp. $B = T(b)$) with $T(a) = \{t \in T, a \subseteq t\}$, and T is the set of all transactions. The rule can be described by four cardinalities $(n, n_a, n_b, n_{a\bar{b}})$ where $n = |T|$,

$n_a = |A|$, $n_b = |B|$, $n_{ab} = |A \cap \overline{B}|$. The cardinal $n_{a\overline{b}}$ corresponds to the effective number of negative examples of the rule.

Let $R(D) = \{r_1, r_2, ..., r_p\}$ denote input data as a set of p association rules derived from a dataset D. Each rule $a \to b$ is described by its itemsets (a, b) and its cardinalities $(n, n_a, n_b, n_{a\overline{b}})$. Let M be the set of q available IMs for our analysis $M = \{m_1, m_2, ..., m_q\}$. Each IM is a numerical function on rule cardinalities: $m(a \to b) = f(n, n_a, n_b, n_{a\overline{b}})$.

For each IM $m_i \in M$, we can construct a vector $m_i(R) = \{m_{i1}, m_{i2}, ..., m_{ip}\}$, $i = 1..q$, where m_{ij} corresponds to the calculated value of the IM m_i for a given rule r_j.

The correlation value between any two IMs $m_i, m_j \{i, j = 1..q\}$ on the set of rules R will be calculated by using a Pearson's correlation coefficient CC [16], where $\overline{m_i}, \overline{m_j}$ are the average calculated values of vector $m_i(R)$ and $m_j(R)$ respectively.

$$CC(m_i, m_j) = \frac{\sum_{k=1}^{p} [(m_{ik} - \overline{m_i})(m_{jk} - \overline{m_j})]}{\sqrt{[\sum_{k=1}^{p} (m_{ik} - \overline{m_i})^2][\sum_{k=1}^{p} (m_{jk} - \overline{m_j})^2]}}$$

In order to interpret the correlation value, we introduce the two following definitions:

Definition 2. τ-*correlated.* Two IMs m_i and m_j are correlated with respect to the dataset D if their absolute correlation value is greater than or equal to a threshold τ: $|CC(m_i, m_j)| \geq \tau$.

Definition 3. θ-*uncorrelated.* Two IMs m_i and m_j are uncorrelated with respect to the dataset D if the absolute value of their correlation value is lower than or equal to a threshold value θ: $|CC(m_i, m_j)| \leq \theta$.

For θ-uncorrelated, we use a statistical test of significance by choosing a level of significance of the test $\alpha = 0.05$ for hypothesis testing, θ is then calculated by the following formula: $\theta = 1.960/\sqrt{p}$ in a population of size p [16]. Common values for α are: $\alpha = 0.1, 0.05, 0.005$, so we choose $\alpha = 0.05$. The assignment $\tau = 0.85$ of τ-correlated is used because this value is widely acceptable in the literature.

As correlation is symmetrical, the $q(q-1)/2$ correlation values can be stored in one half of the table $q \times q$. This table can also be viewed as the relation of an undirected and valued graph called correlation graph, in which a vertex value is an IM and an edge value is the correlation value between 2 vertices/IMs.

3.2   Example

For instance, Fig. 1 can be the correlation graph obtained on five association rules $R(D) = \{r_1, r_2, r_3, r_4, r_5\}$ extracted from a dataset D and three IMs $M = \{m_1, m_2, m_3\}$ which values and correlations are given in Tab. 1.

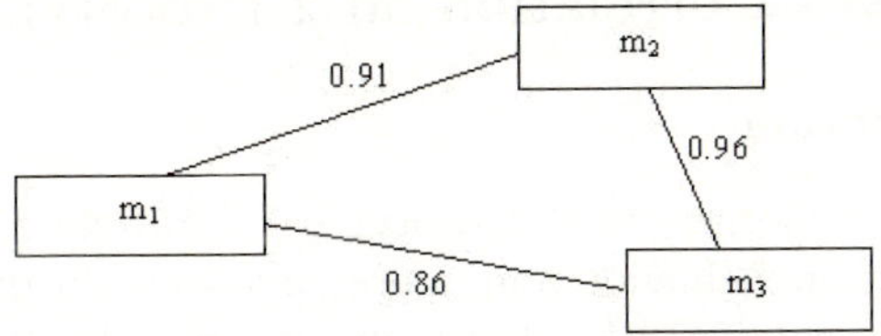

Fig. 1. An illustration of correlation graph

Table 1. Correlation values for three IMs and five association rules

$R(D)$	m_1	m_2	m_3
r_1	0.84	0.89	0.91
r_2	0.86	0.90	0.93
r_3	0.88	0.94	0.97
r_4	0.94	0.95	0.99
r_5	0.83	0.87	0.84

CC	m_1	m_2	m_3
m_1		0.91	0.86
m_2			0.96
m_3			

3.3   Correlated Versus Uncorrelated Graphs

Unfortunately, as the correlation graph is complete, it is not directly human-readable. We need to define two transformations in order to extract more limited and readable subgraphs. First, by using definition 2, we can extract the *correlated partial subgraph (CG+)*: the part of the graph where we only retain edges associated with a τ-correlated. Second, upon definition 3, we also introduce the *uncorrelated partial subgraph (CG0)* where we only retain edges associated with correlation values close to 0 (θ-uncorrelated).

These 2 partial subgraphs can be then processed in order to extract clusters of IMs. Each cluster is defined as a connected subgraph. In CG+, each cluster will gather correlated or anti-correlated IMs that may be interpreted similarly: they deliver a close point of view on data (see Fig. 2). Moreover, in CG0 each cluster will contain uncorrelated IMs: IMs that deliver a different point of view (see Fig. 3).

3.4   Extension to Graph of Stability

We introduce some extensions to define the stabilities between IMs.

Definition 4. τ-stable/θ-stable cluster. τ-stable/θ-stable cluster is a cluster in which each edge must have the τ-correlated/θ-uncorrelated over all the CG+/ CG0 graphs studied. The correlation value for each edge in a τ-stable/θ-stable cluster is the average value of all the τ-correlated/θ-uncorrelated obtained in the corresponding CG+/CG0 graph.

Definition 5. $\overline{CG+}/\overline{CG0}$ graph: is a graph contains only the τ-stable/θ-stable clusters.

4   Study of IM's Correlation on 2 Prototypical Datasets

4.1   Data Description

We have applied our method to 2 prototypical datasets: D_1 and D_2, in order to compare correlation behavior and more precisely, to discover some stable clusters. We use the categorical dataset mushroom (D_1) from Irvine machine-learning database repository and one synthetic dataset (D_2), the latter is obtained by stimulating the transactions of customers in retail businesses. We also generate the set of association rules (ruleset) R_1 (resp. R_2) from the dataset D_1 (resp. D_2) using the the algorithm Apriori [2]. R_2 has the typical characteristic of the Agrawal dataset T5.I2.D10k (T5: average size of the transactions is 5, I2: average size of the maximal potentially large itemsets is 2, D10k: number of items is 100). For an evaluation of the IM behavior of the "best rules" from these two rulesets, we have extracted R_1' (resp. R_2') from R_1 (resp. R_2) as the union of the first 1000 best rules ($\approx 1\%$, descending with interestingness values) issued from each IM (see Tab. 2).

Table 2. Description of the datasets

Dataset	Items (Avg. length)	Transactions	Number of rules (support thres.)	$R(D)$	θ	τ	$R(D)$
D_1	118 (22)	8416	123228	R_1	0.005	0.85	R_1
			10431	R_1'	0.020	0.85	R_1'
D_2	81 (5)	9650	102808	R_2	0.003	0.85	R_2
			7452	R_2'	0.023	0.85	R_2'

4.2   Used IMs

In our experiment we compared and analyzed 36 IMs studied in surveys [3] [8] [17], added with four complementary IMs: Implication Intensity (II), Entropic Implication Intensity (EII), TIC (informational ratio modulated by the contra-positive), and IPEE (probabilistic index of deviation from equilibrium). The formulas of 34 IMs are defined in [10] completed with two following IM formulas:

$$II = 1 - \sum_{k=max(0,n_a-n_b)}^{n_{a\bar{b}}} \frac{C_{n_b}^{n_a-k} C_{n_{\bar{b}}}^{k}}{C_n^{n_a}} \text{ and } IPEE = 1 - \frac{1}{2^{n_a}} \sum_{k=0}^{n_{a\bar{b}}} C_{n_a}^{k}.$$

We must notice that EII($\alpha = 1$) and EII($\alpha = 2$) are two entropic versions of the II measure .

4.3   Discussion

Our discussion aims at finding stable relations between the IMs studied over the four rulesets. We investigate in: (1) the $\overline{CG0}$ graphs in order to identify the IMs that do not agree for ranking the rules, (2) the $\overline{CG+}$ graph in order to find the IMs that do agree for ranking the rules.

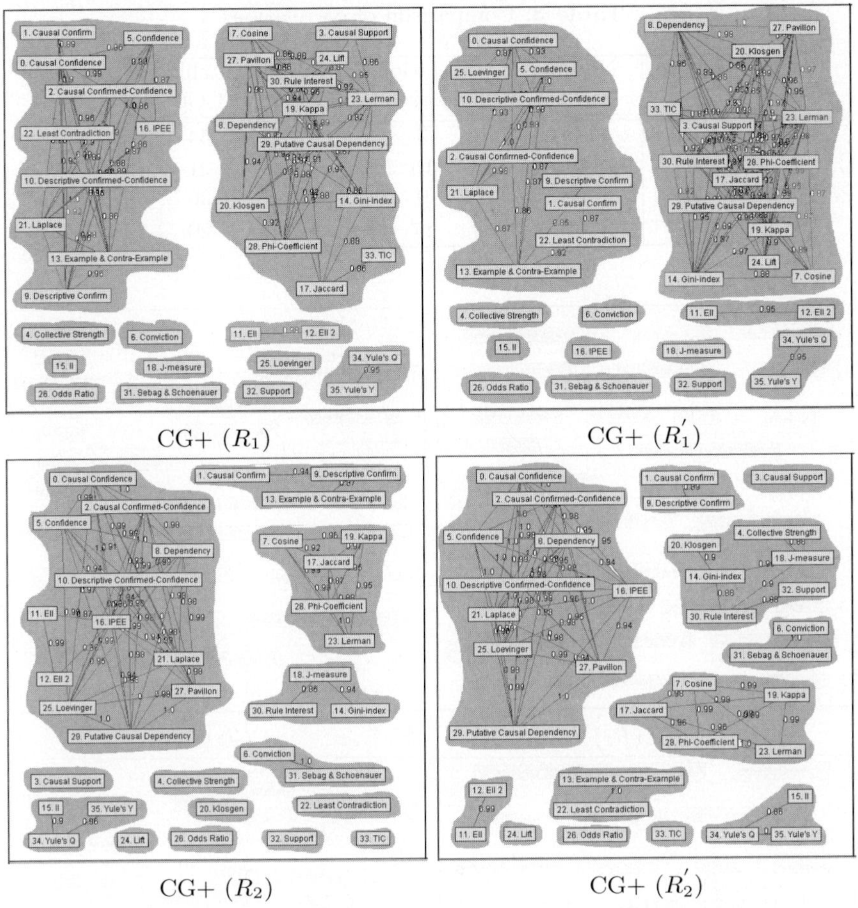

CG+ (R_1)   CG+ (R_1')

CG+ (R_2)   CG+ (R_2')

Fig. 2. CG+ graphs (clusters are highlighted in grey)

***CG+* and *CG*0.** Fig. 2 shows four $CG+$ graphs obtained from the four rulesets. As we saw, the sample rulesets and the original rulesets have close results so we can use the sample rulesets for representing the original rulesets. This observation is useful when we evaluate the CG+ graphs but not for CG0 graphs. For example, with the CG+ graph of R_1 (Fig. 2), the user can choose the largest cluster containing the 14 IMs (Causal Support, Pavillon, Lift, Lerman, Putative Causal Dependency, Rule Interest, Phi-Coefficient, Klosgen, Dependency, Kappa, Gini-index, Cosine, Jaccard, TIC) for his/her first choice. In this cluster we can also see the weak relation between TIC and the other IMs of the cluster. Tab. 3 also shows the two opposite tendencies obtained from the number of τ-correlated computed: $79(R_1) \rightarrow 91(R_1'), 65(R_2) \rightarrow 67(R_2')$.

With the four CG0 graphs (Fig. 3), we can easily see that the number of θ-uncorrelated increases when the best rules are selected: $2(R_1) \rightarrow 15(R_1'), 0(R_2) \rightarrow 17(R_2')$ (Fig. 3, Tab. 3).

Table 3. Comparison of correlation

Ruleset	Number of correlations		Number of clusters	
	τ-correlated	θ-uncorrelated	CG+	CG0
R_1	79	2	12	34
R_1'	91	15	12	21
R_2	65	0	14	36
R_2'	67	17	12	20

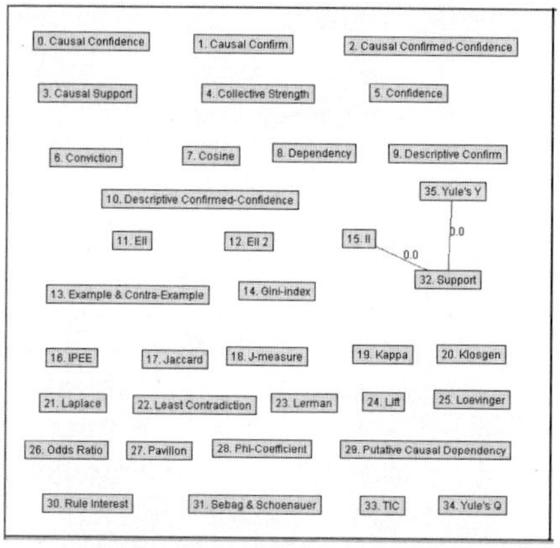

CG0 (R_1)

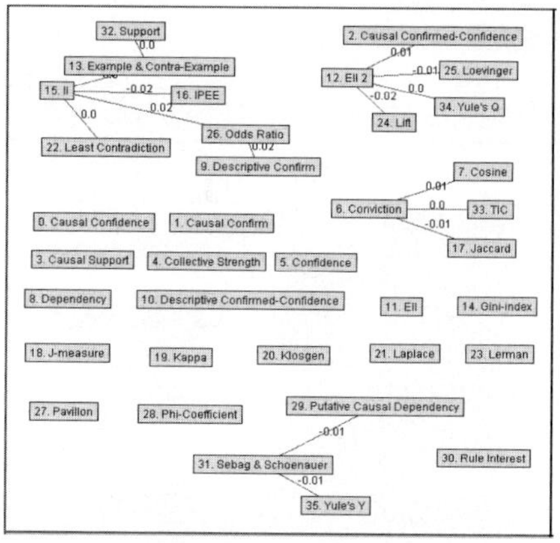

CG0 (R_1')

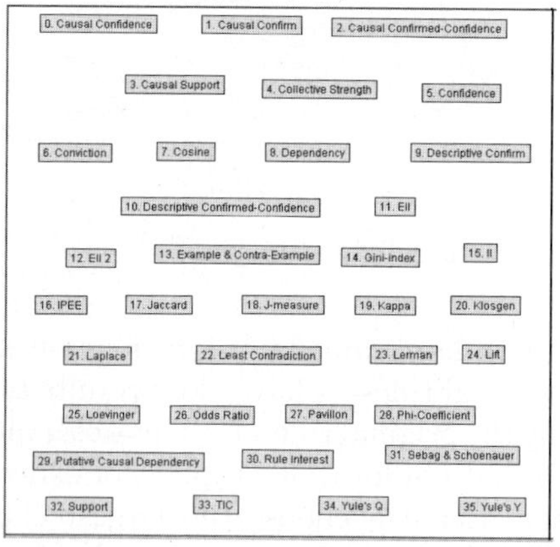

CG0 (R_2)

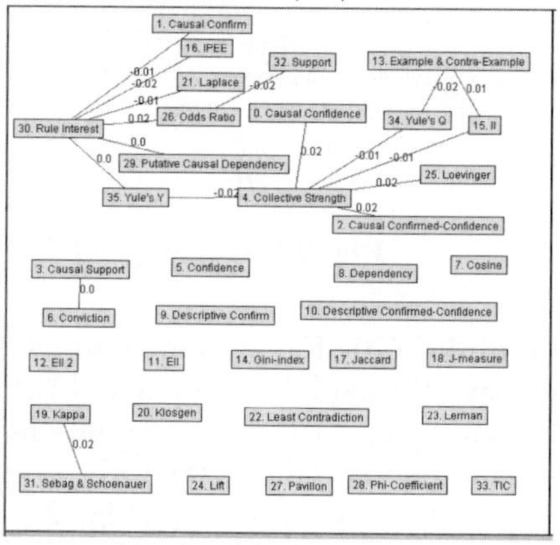

CG0 (R_2')

Fig. 3. CG0 graphs

$\overline{CG0}$ graphs: uncorrelated stability. Uncorrelated graphs first show that there are not θ-stable clusters that appear on the 4 rulesets studied in Fig. 3. Secondly, there is no $\overline{CG0}$ graph from these datasets. A close observation of four CG0 graphs shows that at least one IM in each cluster will later be clustered around in a τ-stable cluster of $\overline{CG+}$ graph (Fig. 3, Fig. 4) like Yule's Y, Putative

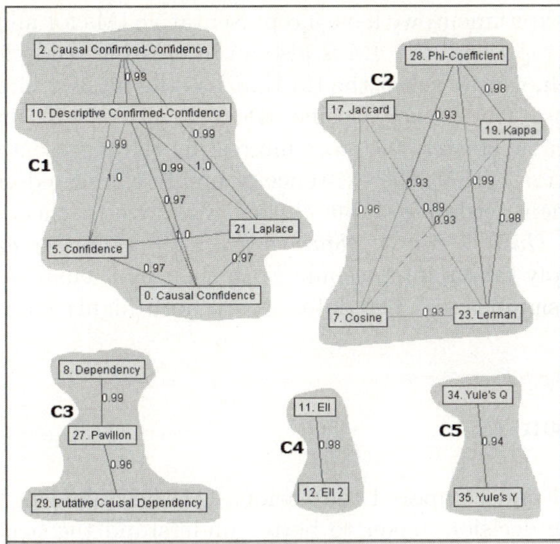

Fig. 4. $\overline{CG+}$ graph

Causal Dependency, EII($\alpha = 2$), Cosine, Laplace so that the stronger the θ-uncorrelated, the more interesting the IM participated in the θ-uncorrelated.

$\overline{CG+}$ **graph: correlated stability.** From Tab. 3, we can see that, R_1' approximately is twice as much correlated as R_2'. As seen in Fig. 4, five τ-stable clusters found come from the datasets studied.

By briefly analyzing these τ-stable clusters, we draw some interesting results.

(C1), the largest cluster, (Confidence, Causal Confidence, Causal Confirmed-Confidence, Descriptive Confirmed-Confidence, Laplace) has most of its IMs extended from Confidence measure. From this cluster, we can see a highly connected component - each vertex must have an edge with the other vertices - indicating the strong agreement of the five IMs.

(C2), another cluster, has two highly connected components which are formed by Phi-Coefficient, Lerman, Kappa, Cosine and Jaccard. The clusters gathers from similarity measures.

(C3), has three IMs (Dependency, Pavillon, Putative Causal Dependency) that are reasonably well correlated.

(C4), is a cluster formed by EII and EII 2, which are two IMs obtained with different parameters of the same original formula.

(C5), Yule's Q and Yule's Y, brings out a trivial observation because these IMs derived from Odds Ratio measure.

In looking for τ-stable clusters, we have found the τ-correlated that existing between various IMs and we have identified five τ-stable clusters. Each τ-stable cluster forms a subgraph in a $\overline{CG+}$ graph, also containing a highly connected component. Therefore, we can choose a representative IM for each cluster. For example, in our experiment, we have 5 representative IMs for all the 36 IMs. How we can choose a representative IM is also an interesting study for the future. In the first approach, we can select the IM that has the highest number of relations with others: Causal Confidence, Cosine, Klosgen, EII($\alpha = 2$), and Yule's Y. The stronger the τ-stable cluster, the more interesting the representative IM. An important observation is that, the existence of highly connected graphs represents a perfect agreement with a τ-stable cluster. We have reached significant information: *τ-stable clusters can be obtained from different IMs and rulesets.* The different IMs imply taking into account both their mathematical definitions and their respective significance. The datasets are both highly correlated and lowly correlated.

5 Conclusion

We have studied and compared the various IMs described in the literature in order to help the decision-maker to better understand the behavior of the IM. A new approach called correlation graph with two types: CG+ and CG0 is proposed to evaluate the association rule quality by using graphs as a graphical insight on the data. With this approach, the decision-maker receives a very small number of the IMs to decide and easily select the best rules to be examined. Our approach is strongly related to the dataset and the number of proposed IMs. This approach will be helpful in the domain of knowledge quality research.

Our future research will investigate the two following directions. First, we will improve the correlation analysis by introducing a better measure than Pearson coefficient whose limits are stressed in the literature. Second, we will also improve the IM clustering analysis with IM aggregation techniques to facilitate the user's decision making from the best IMs.

References

1. Agrawal, R., Imielinski, T., Swami, A.: Mining association rules between sets of items in large databases. Proceedings of 1993 ACM-SIGMOD International Conference on Management of Data. ACM Press, Washington DC, USA (1993) 207–216
2. Agrawal, R., Srikant, R.: Fast algorithms for mining association rules. VLDB'94, Proceedings of 20th International Conference on Very Large Data Bases. Morgan Kaufmann Publishers Inc., Santiago, Chile (1994) 487–499
3. Bayardo, Jr.R.J., Agrawal, R.: Mining the most interestingness rules. KDD'99, Proceedings of the 5th ACM SIGKDD International Confeerence On Knowledge Discovery and Data Mining. ACM Press, San Diego, CA, USA (1999) 145–154
4. Blanchard, J., Guillet, F., Gras, R., Briand, H.: Assessing rule interestingness with a probabilistic measure of deviation from equilibrium. ASMDA'05, Proceedings of the 11th International Symposium on Applied Stochastic Models and Data Analysis. Brest, France (2005) 191–200
5. Fayyad, U.M., Piatetsky-Shapiro, G., Smyth, P., Uthurusamy, R.: Advances in Knowledge Discovery and Data Mining, AAAI/MIT Press, 1996.

6. Freitas, A.A.: On rule interestingness measures. Knowledge-Based Systems, 12(5-6). Elsevier, (1999) 309–315

7. Gavrilov, M., Anguelov, D., Indyk, P., Motwani, R.: Mining the stock market: which measure is best?. KDD'00, Proceedings of the 6th International Conference on Knowledge Discovery and Data Mining. Boston, MA, USA (2000) 487-496.

8. Hilderman, R.J., Hamilton, H.J.: Knowledge Discovery and Measures of Interestingness. Kluwer Academic Publishers (2001)

9. Huynh, X.H., Guillet, F., Briand, H.: ARQAT: an exploratory analysis tool for interestingness measures. ASMDA'05, Proceedings of the 11th International Symposium on Applied Stochastic Models and Data Analysis. Brest, France (2005) 334–344

10. Huynh, X.H., Guillet, F., Briand, H.: Clustering interestingness measures with positive correlation. ICEIS'05, Proceedings of the 7th International Conference on Enterprise Information Systems. Miami, USA (2005) 248–253

11. Kononenco, I.: On biases in estimating multi-valued attributes. IJCAI'95, Proceedings of the Fourteenth International Joint Conference on Artificial Intelligence. Montreal, Canada, (1995) 1034–1040

12. Liu, B., Hsu, W., Mun, L., Lee, H.: Finding interesting patterns using user expectations. IEEE Transactions on Knowledge and Data Mining 11(6). IEEE Educational Activities Department, (1999) 817–832

13. Newman, D.J., Hettich,S., Blake, C.L., Merz, C.J.: [UCI] Repository of machine learning databases, http://www.ics.uci.edu/~mlearn/MLRepository.html. University of California, Irvine, Department of Information and Computer Sciences, (1998).

14. Padmanabhan, B., Tuzhilin, A. : A belief-driven method for discovering unexpected patterns. KDD'98, Proceedings of the 4th International Conference on Knowledge Discovery and Data Mining. ACM Press, New York, USA (1998) 94–100

15. Piatetsky-Shapiro, G.: Discovery, analysis and presentation of strong rules. Knowledge Discovery in Databases, G. Piatetsky-Shapiro and W. Frawley editors. MIT Press, Cambridge, MA (1991) 229–248

16. Ross, S.M.: Introduction to probability and statistics for engineers and scientists. Wiley, (1987)

17. Tan, P.N., Kumar, V., Srivastava, J.: Selecting the right objective measure for association analysis. Information Systems 29(4). Elsevier, (2004) 293–313

18. Vaillant, B., Lenca, P., Lallich, S.: A clustering of interestingness measures. DS'04, the 7th International Conference on Discovery Science, LNAI 3245. Springer-Verlag, Padova, Italy (2004) 290-297

Extended Another Memory: Understanding Everyday Lives in Ubiquitous Sensor Environments

Masakatsu Ohta, Sun Yong Kim, and Miyuki Imada

NTT Network Innovation Laboratories, NTT Corporation
3-9-11 Midori-cho, Musashino-shi, Tokyo 180-8585, Japan
{ohta.masakatsu, kim.sunyong, imada.miyuki}@lab.ntt.co.jp

Abstract. A lifetime recording agent that suggests unusual events to a user is proposed. The goal is to create a memory device that supports human memory by filtering, categorizing, and remembering everyday events. In ubiquitous sensor environments, the agent classifies users' experiences represented by surrounding objects and predicts typical events that a user will experience next. Unusual events are detected by the awareness of different characteristics as the human brain does. If the prediction is incorrect, the actual event is considered to be unusual. A recurrent neural network that autonomously alters its architecture is introduced to perform event prediction. Experiments confirm: (1) a suitable hierarchical level of event categories for a current situation can be obtained by estimating the event prediction performance, that is, the recall rate and (2) rehearsal sequences dynamically generated by the network can substitute for a sequence of actual events. Thus, the agent easily responds to new environments without forgetting previous memories.

1   Introduction

Recording an entire lifetime has been studied extensively in recent years. MyLifeBits [1] is the fulfillment of Vannevar Bush's Memex vision [2] and is intended to record a person's whole life by using photographs, movies, web pages browsed, e-mail, and phone calls and suggests useful records for supporting a user to solve some problems. Aizawa [3] has proposed a life log system that captures a user's experiences from a wearable camera and context information from wearable sensors such as a GPS receiver, acceleration sensor, gyro sensor and brainwave analyzer. The system uses sensor data as a key for video retrieval. Kern [4] has proposed a system that annotates a user's activities in meetings. It records actions such as walking, standing, sitting, and speaker changes from various sensor data. The annotation is implemented by a hidden Markov model trained with data labeled in advance with important activities. The UK Computing Research Committee [5] has discussed the Memories for Life project as a part of the Grand Challenge for Computing Science.

People are likely to present nearly the same behavior when they find themselves in the same or a similar situation; therefore, most records that are automatically captured are redundant. The question here is one of defining what

M. Ali and R. Dapoigny (Eds.): IEA/AIE 2006, LNAI 4031, pp. 322–331, 2006.

events need to be detected. Most studies, however, cannot assess which events catch a user's attention. Aizawa uses brain waves to evaluate whether a user is paying attention to the present event [3]. However, physiological reactions such as brain waves and heart rate are easily affected by a user's health and environment, which restrict the usage of these reactions. In Kern's supervised learning, activities that the system detects need to be defined and training data labeled with these activities need to be prepared in each environment, which is time consuming and unsuitable for lifetime recordings in various environments. The second question to be considered is how to specify a proper hierarchical level at which events are classified. When a system retrieves past events, which a user experienced nearby, the system has to specify the nearby area on a certain scale and retrieve the events classified into the category related to this area. The hierarchical level of categories changes according to situations, such as a user walking, jogging, or driving a car. However, the previous studies are assigned a fixed hierarchical level of categories and cannot flexibly adapt the hierarchical level to various situations. Thus, a user cannot retrieve from memory suitable events for the present situation.

In this paper, we propose a lifetime recording agent, ExAM (Extended Another Memory), that suggests unusual experiences to a user in various situations. In a ubiquitous sensor environment, ExAM classifies events that a user experiences and learns typical sequences of the events from only sensor data. Then it predicts successive events that the user will experience next. If a predicted event is incorrect, the actual event that the user experiences is assumed to be unusual. On the other hand, if the prediction is correct, the actual event is ignored. The hierarchical level of classifying events can be controlled to decrease prediction errors. Moreover, for new events, which a user has not experienced before, ExAM classifies events one-by-one and learns new sequences that they can follow without forgetting memories already learned from the previous sequences.

This paper is organized as follows. Section 2 describes prediction-based awareness of unusual events, which is inspired by a human memory system. Section 3 presents the implementation of ExAM. Section 4 introduces some experiments in the actual world: the classifying events, the sequence learning, and the performance of incremental learning. Finally, concluding remarks are given in Section 5.

2 Prediction-Based Awareness

A person tends to follow an invariant pattern of behavior in a similar situation. Thus, something that happens in an unexpected order can be an unusual event for him. For example, while walking to work, a person would be easily aware of a new shop, whether it is familiar or strange to him. On the other hand, most scenes hardly impress on his memory. Hawkins [6] has proposed a memory-prediction framework of the brain. Across all senses, the brain continuously makes predictions about what we will experience. This prediction is done unconsciously. Thus, if a prediction is correct, the predicted event will be outside awareness. If a prediction is incorrect, however, a person readily notes that something he sees and hears is odd. Learning typical sequences of events in the actual world, the brain gradually comes to form predictions about events in various environments. Therefore, an agent that reproduces autonomous learning and predictions using sensor data would specify unusual events in various environments.

3   ExAM

3.1   Event Explained with Objects

ExAM records an event on a photograph or a movie, and correlates the event to surrounding objects that are present when a user experiences the event. Some studies report that an object is suitable for explaining an event. Bartlett [7] pointed out that, in human memory, a person understands an event based on a schema. Brewer [8] demonstrated that a schema about a *room* is characterized by objects and affects remembering processes. Computational models also suggested that a schema represented by objects is suitable for understanding situations [9] and sharing experiences [10].

In a ubiquitous sensor environment, ExAM records surrounding objects by using its sensor and uses the objects to specify a user's experiences. For example, when a user has a meeting in a room, ExAM records the meeting scene, recognizes the objects in the meeting room, such as the white board, the table, and the projector, and distinguishes this meeting from other events.

3.2   Classifying Event

If examined in detail, all events are different from each other. Thus, an event is always new and unusual whenever a user experiences it. Moreover, sensor data has noise caused by external factors. This implies that a slight difference between events should be ignored and similar events should be classified into the same category. In a lifetime recording, it is impossible to define adequate categories in advance because many kinds of events will happen in various environments. For this reason, ExAM uses the Adaptive Resonance Theory [11] algorithm, which is an incremental clustering method, to classify events.

Consider classifying event k. Event k is expressed as $\boldsymbol{X}^k = (x_1^k, \cdots, x_q^k, \cdots)$, where $x_q^k = 1$ if object q is related to event k, otherwise $x_q^k = 0$. Category j is expressed by the prototype vector $\boldsymbol{W}^j = (w_1^j, \cdots, w_q^j, \cdots)$, where w_q^j denotes the weight of object q in category j and an object that has large w_q^j is a typical object in category j. The choice function,

$$J = arg \ \max_{j}(T^j = \mathcal{N}(\boldsymbol{X}^k)\boldsymbol{W}^j), \tag{1}$$

picks category J. Function $\mathcal{N}(\boldsymbol{X})$ normalizes vector $\boldsymbol{X}$ to unit length. If $T^J < \rho$, event k is classified into a new category and its prototype vector is initialized as follows:

$$\boldsymbol{W}^{new} = \mathcal{N}(\boldsymbol{X}^k). \tag{2}$$

Otherwise, event k is classified into category J and $\boldsymbol{W}^J$ is updated as follows:

$$\boldsymbol{W}^J = \mathcal{N}\left(\eta\mathcal{N}(\boldsymbol{X}^k) + (1-\eta)\boldsymbol{W}^J\right), \tag{3}$$

where parameter $\eta(0 < \eta \leq 1)$ is the learning rate. Typical event K in category j is also obtained as follows:

$$K = arg \ \max_{k}(T^k = \mathcal{N}(\boldsymbol{X}^k)\boldsymbol{W}^j). \tag{4}$$

$\rho(0 < \rho < 1)$ is called vigilance parameter and is concerned with the hierarchical level of categories. As ρ becomes larger, categories increases and events are classified in detail. ExAM obtains a proper ρ in each environment by estimating event prediction performance.

3.3   Sequence Learning

After classifying events, sequences of events are translated into those of typical events. ExAM predicts typical events following the current event. Before prediction, ExAM has to learn the regularity of the sequences. Recurrent neural networks, which retain previous outputs as a context, have been widely used for forecasting time series [12, 13, 14, 15]. ExAM uses the constructive backpropagation (CBP) algorithm [15], which can efficiently decide desirable network architecture, because the network should adapt its architecture to various environments that are not known in advance.

The i-th input unit and the i-th output unit denote category i. Thus, the numbers of input and output units equal the number of categories. A fragment of the sequence of typical events is expressed as a pattern of categories. Consider category sequence "12345" a fragment of which denotes the category related to its typical event. The patterns corresponding to the fragments are

$$10000 \ \ 01000 \ \ 00100 \ \ 00010 \ \ 00001.$$

The patterns are entered into the network according to sequences of typical events. The task for the network is to predict the next input pattern. The network is trained to map a pattern to the next pattern.

CBP adds new hidden units until a network yields an acceptable solution. When a new hidden unit is added, feedforward and recurrent connections from the previous hidden units are connected to the new hidden unit. In addition, recurrent connections from the new hidden unit are connected to both the previous hidden units and itself (Figure 1). CBP updates the weights of the connections with the h-th hidden unit to minimize the following error function,

$$E_p^h = \sum_{k} \left(T_{kp} - V_{kp}^h\right)^2. \tag{5}$$

T_{kp} is the desired value of the k-th output unit for the p-th training pattern. V_{kp}^h is the value of the k-th output unit for the p-th training pattern, supposing that there are h hidden units. Note that the h-th hidden unit does not see the effect

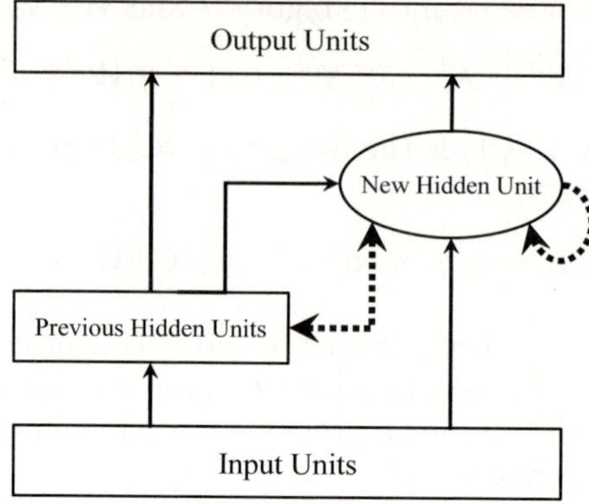

Fig. 1. Network Architecture in CBP Learning. Solid and Dashed lines denote feed-forward and recurrent connections, respectively.

of the following hidden units in the output error because the training is done in a hierarchical manner.

Turning now to obtaining a proper hierarchical level of categories, a ρ that is too large increases the number of possible categories of typical events following the current event and increases the variation of the sequences that need to be learned. This implies that the prediction error increases if an insufficient number of training patterns are prepared. Therefore, ExAM obtains the proper ρ, which is the largest in which prediction performance is above a threshold.

3.4 Incremental Learning

When new categories are created and environments change, the network has to learn new sequences again. After training with only the training patterns created from new sequences, it is generally observed that a neural network forgets its previous memories and failed to predict previous sequences. Using both new and all of the previous training patterns is the simplest approach to solve this problem. As the number of training patterns increases, however, the time required for training increases. Tani [16] has proposed consolidation learning that uses the training pattern dynamically generated by a recurrent neural network as a substitute for the previous actual training pattern. ExAM similarly uses consolidation learning. In addition, if new categories are created, ExAM adds input and output units corresponding to the new categories and connects these units to existing hidden units. Though the number of input and output units increases, ExAM attempts to adapt its architecture to new situations by adding hidden units.

4 Experiment

As an example of a lifetime recording, we considered that a user visits predefined locations in an office. We regarded this visit as an event that the user experiences.

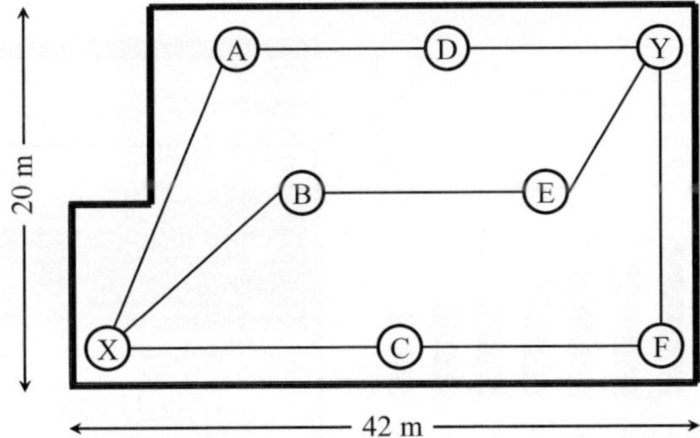

Fig. 2. Predefined Locations and Routes in the Office

Eight predefined locations in the office the size of which is 20 x 42 m (Figure 2) and four routes through the predefined locations are set as follows:

$$Route1 : X\ A\ D\ Y\ D\ A\ X$$
$$Route2 : X\ B\ E\ Y\ D\ A\ X$$
$$Route3 : X\ B\ E\ Y\ F\ C\ X$$
$$Route4 : X\ C\ F\ Y\ F\ C\ X.$$

In this experiment, we focused on the prediction performance of the recurrent neural network of ExAM.

Events were collected in the following way. At each predefined location we took a picture, which was used only for confirmations, and recorded the surrounding objects. For recording objects, we used the active RFID (Radio Frequency IDentification) tags attached to the company's property [17]. The tag ID sends out a signal every seven seconds but that is often not received because of external factors. Thus, we recorded the tag IDs for thirty seconds every event. Ten events were recorded at each predefined location. We created route sequences selected at random and obtained the sequence of the predefined locations from those routes. Next, we obtained event sequences randomly selected from the events recorded at the predefined location in the order corresponding to the sequences of predefined locations.

4.1 Event Prediction

We prepared a training sequence including 181 events obtained from a sequence of 30 routes and a test sequence including 121 events obtained from a sequence of 20 routes. On average, 60 objects were recorded per event. Next, we created a training sequence of typical events, classifying the events in the order corresponding to the training sequence. The test sequence of typical events was also created in the same manner. To investigate the effect of the hierarchical level of categories on prediction performance, ρ were set to 0.65, 0.70, 0.75, 0.80, and 0.85. As a result, the numbers of categories were 6, 7, 8, 12, and 33, respectively. At $\rho = 0.75$, the number of categories agreed with the number of predefined locations.

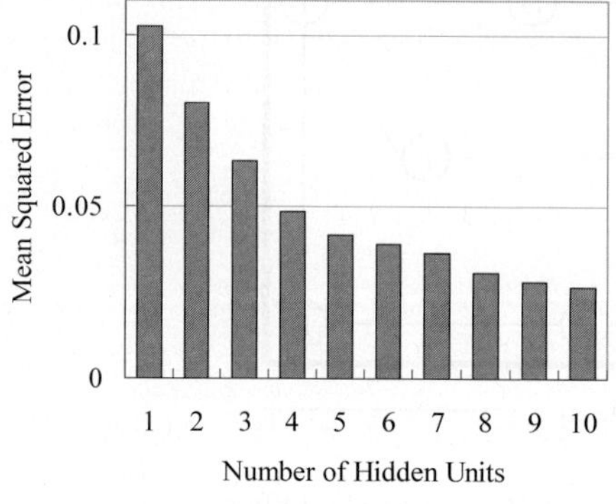

Fig. 3. Mean Squared Error vs. Number of Hidden Units. Vigilance value is 0.75.

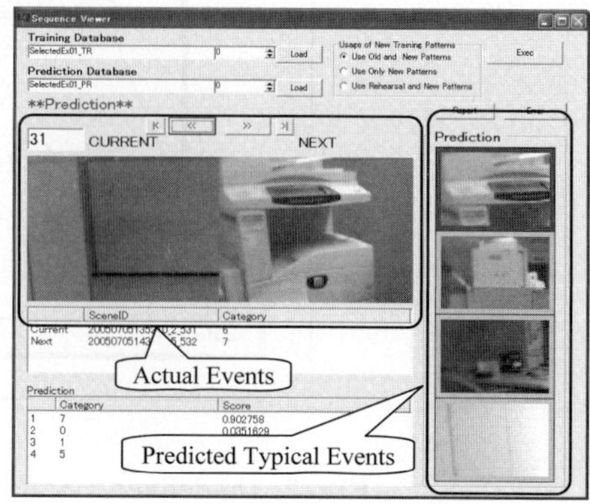

Fig. 4. Prediction of Typical Events

Next, the network attempted to learn the sequences of typical events created at the above ρs. The learning rate and the momentum term were set to 0.01 and 0.9, respectively. At each ρ, there was only one hidden unit at the beginning of training. The network was trained on 700 passes through the training sequence. If the last added hidden unit decreases the mean squared error(MSE) during the training sequence 5% more than the previous MSE, the network adds a new hidden unit and is trained again. On the other hand, if the decrease is negligible, the training is terminated. The dependency of MSE on the number of hidden units is shown in Figure 3. As the number of hidden units increases, the error decreases and the network architecture becomes more suitable for the given task. After training, the network predicted the next typical events for the test sequence. The predicted events that have output units, which generate large values, are shown in Figure 4.

Note that the prediction task is nondeterministic. The events next to predefined location X depend on the frequency of occurrence of each route. Similarly, in routes 2 and 3, the successors to predefined location Y depend on which route is selected at X. However, once the network knows the actual successors to X and Y, the network can make correct predictions afterward. This implies that we cannot use the value generated by output units to determine successors in a straightforward manner. For this reason, at each prediction step, a typical event was selected with a probability proportional to the values generated by output units. We repeated this sampling ten times and investigated whether the actual next event is included in the sampled events. If the actual next event is sampled, we supposed that the network could recall the correct event, and defined the recall rate as follows:

$$Recall\ Rate = \frac{the\ number\ of\ correct\ recalls}{sequence\ length}.$$

The recall rate plotted vs. vigilance value is shown in Figure 5. At each ρ, the network was trained ten times and these results were averaged. The four routes are cyclic; thus, the successor event depends on the present and former events. However, at small ρ, the network exhibited good performance because the recurrent neural network succeeded in retaining the patterns of the former events. As ρ increases, the number of categories increase and the variation pattern of sequences to be learned increases. Thus, the task becomes more complex. At $\rho = 0.85$, the prepared training sequence was not sufficient to reflect a typical sequence. Thus, the recall rate decreased significantly.

4.2   Incremental Learning

We examined a retraining of the network already trained under the condition of $\rho = 0.75$. Two new cyclic routes in another room were prepared. Three predefined locations exist in each route. A new training sequence of 135 events was created from new routes as mentioned above. Moreover, a test sequence of 226 events was created from the new and the previous four routes. The network needs to predict events not only in new routes but also in the previous four routes. The number of categories increased by five when classifying these new events at $\rho = 0.75$. The following trainings were studied.

Case 1. A new network was trained with the sequence of 316 events created by connecting the new training sequence to the previous sequence of 181 events used in the above subsection.

Case 2. The network was retrained with only the new training sequence.

Case 3. The created rehearsal sequence with the same length as the new training sequence was generated by the already trained network. After the input and hidden units were initialized at random, the network calculated the output values and returned them to the input units repetitively. The network was retrained with the sequence created by connecting the new training sequence to the created rehearsal sequence.

The weights of the connections between hidden and new inputs, and the connections between hidden and new output units were initialized at random. While retraining, the values of the new units in the rehearsal sequence were filled with 0. The network was retrained ten times and these results were averaged.

There were 10 hidden units in the already trained network. After the training, on average, there were 10, 13, and 14 hidden units in Case 1, Case 2, and Case 3, respectively. The suitability of the rehearsal sequence is shown in Figure 6. In Case 2, the new training sequence forced the network to forget the previous memories and decreased the recall rate. However, the performance of Case 3 was comparable to that of Case 1. This implies that the rehearsal sequence represented the actual previous training sequence and retained the previous memories. Five units were added in the input and output layers, and a significant alteration was imposed on the network. In Case 3, however, the network adapted itself to the new situation by adding these new hidden units.

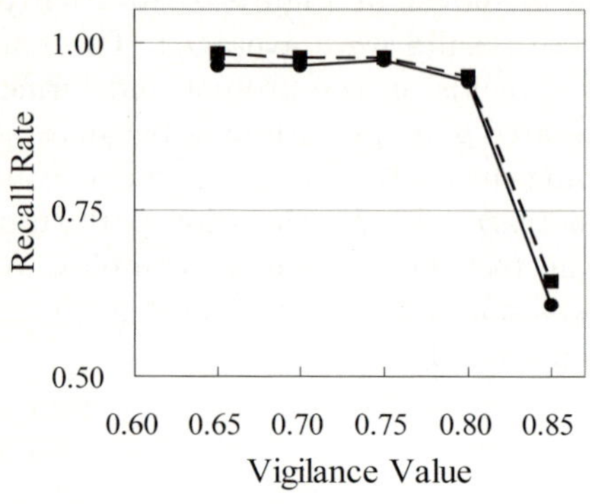

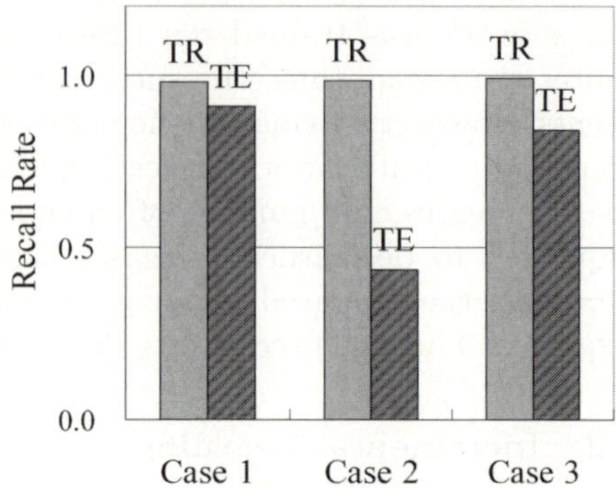

Fig. 5. Prediction Performance vs. Hierarchical Level of Categories. Dashed and Solid lines denote training and test, respectively.

Fig. 6. Performance of Created Rehearsal Sequence. TR and TE denote training and test, respectively. Vigilance value is 0.75.

5   Conclusion

We proposed a lifetime recording agent, ExAM, that suggests unusual events to a user. The detection of unusual events is based on the awareness of variations of human behavior and unusual events do not need to be defined in advance. An experiment using active RFID tags attached to objects indicated that the hierarchical level of event categories is controlled by the event prediction performance. Moreover, rehearsal sequences dynamically generated by the recurrent neural network are available for retaining previous memories. Thus, a user does not need to retain all past events for training a network and only needs to store unusual events. As a result, ExAM effectively learns and predicts new sequences in a new environment without forgetting previous memories.

In a lifetime recording, it is difficult to choose the hierarchical level of categories in advance. One approach to selecting the proper hierarchical level is to classify events with vigilance values at the same time and choose a suitable value for each situation estimating the performance of predictions. In addition, an event similar to an old event is often not classified into the category the old one was assigned to. This alternation depends on the sequences and frequency of events. A similar phenomenon is also observed in human memory [7, 18]. We think this modification is essential to develop a human-like memory system. However, most previous work on lifetime recordings has not been concerned with this phenomenon.

One interesting idea is to learn and predict typical events for collaboration between colleagues. In this case, many training sequences can easily be collected. At present, we focused on events represented by surrounding objects. Further studies to comprehend events that are more complex using other sensors and to evaluate the performance of ExAM in various situations are required.

References

1. Gemmell, J., Bell, G., Lueder, R., Drucker, S., Wong, C.: Mylifebits: Fulfilling the memex vision. In: ACM Multimedia'02. (2002) 235–238
2. Bush, V.: As we may think. The Atlantic Monthly **176** (1945) 101–108
3. Aizawa, K., Hori, T., Kawasaki, S., Ishikawa, T.: Capture and efficient retrieval of life log. In: Pervasive 2004 Workshop on Memory and Sharing Experiences. (2004) 15–20
4. Kern, N., Schiele, B., Junker, H., Lukowicz, P., Tröster, G.: Wearable sensing to annotate meetings recordings. In: ISWC. (2002) 186–193
5. UKCRC: Memories for life. (http://www.ukcrc.org.uk/grand_challenges/index.cfm)
6. Hawkins, J., Blakeslee, S.: On Intelligence. Times Books (2004)
7. Bartlett, F.C.: Remembering: A Study in Experimental and Social Psychology. Cambridge University Press (1932)
8. Brewer, W.F., Treyens, J.C.: Role of schemata in memory for places. Cognitive Psychology **13** (1981) 207–230
9. Rumelhart, D.E., Smolensky, P., McClelland, J.L., Hinton, G.E.: Schemata and sequential thought processing in pdp models. In McClelland, J.L., Rumelhart, D.E., Group, T.P.R., eds.: Parallel Distributed Processing. Volume 2. Cambridge, MA: MIT Press. (1986)
10. Lin, N., Mase, K., Sumi, Y.: An object-centric storytelling framework using ubiquitous sensor technology. In: Pervasive 2004 Workshop on Memory and Sharing of Experiences. (2004)
11. Carpenter, G.A., Grossberg, S., Rosen, D.B.: ART 2-A: An adaptive resonance algorithm for rapid category learning and recognition. Neural Networks **4** (1991) 493–504
12. Jordan, M.I.: Attractor dynamics and parallelism in a connectionist sequential machine. In: the Eighth Annual Meeting of the Cognitive Science Society. (1986) 531–546
13. Elman, J.L.: Finding structure in time. Cognitive Science **14** (1990) 179–211
14. Tani, J.: Model-based learning for mobile robot navigation from the dynamical systems perspective. IEEE Trans. on System, Man and Cybernetics Part B(Special Issue on Robot Learning) **26** (1996) 421–436
15. Lehtokangas, M.: Constructive backpropagation for recurrent networks. Neural Processing Letters **9** (1999) 271–278
16. Tani, J.: An interpretation of the "self" from the dynamical systems perspective: A constructivist approach. Journal of Consciousness Studies **5** (1998) 516–542
17. Tsubaki, T., Hayashi, H., Shimizu, M.: Asset tracking system using rfid tags. In: WPMC2003. Volume 3. (2003) 492–495
18. Linton, M.: Transformations of memory in everyday life. In Neisser, U., ed.: Memory observed: Remembering in natural contexts. San Francisco: W H Freeman (1982)

Incremental Clustering of Newsgroup Articles

Sascha Hennig and Michael Wurst

University of Dortmund, Department of Computer Science
Baroperstr. 301, 44221 Dortmund, Germany
`wurst@ls8.cs.uni-dortmund`

Abstract. Clustering text documents is a basic enabling technique in a wide variety of Information and Knowledge Management applications. This paper presents an incremental clustering system to organize and manage Newsgroup articles. It serves administrators and readers of a Newsgroup to archive important postings and to get a structured overview on current developments and topics. To be practically applicable, such a system must fulfill two conditions. First, it must be able to process rapidly changing text streams, modifying the cluster structure dynamically by adding, deleting and restructuring clusters. Second, it must consider the user in the incremental process. Severe changes in the organization structure are unacceptable for most users, even if they are optimal from the point of view of an abstract clustering criterion. We propose an approach to model the cost to accommodate to changes in the cluster structure explicitly. Users then may constraint, which changes are acceptable to them.

Keywords: data mining, internet applications, knowledge management.

1   Introduction

Newsgroups are one of the most important data and information sources on the Internet. The Usenet alone produces about 2 Terabyte of articles each day. To preserve this information and to make it accessible is a very challenging task. On the one hand, readers and administrators of newsgroups need a convenient structure to browse old, archived articles. On the other hand they need a structured view on current developments in the Newsgroup, such as new important topics and how they relate to each other. Both problems can be approached with text clustering methods. The aim of text clustering is to structure documents into (hierarchical) groups of similar documents. Text clustering is used in many Information and Knowledge Management applications to allow users to explore large text collections efficiently. However, there is an important obstacle to apply such algorithms to Newsgroups or similar data sources. Most clustering algorithms focus on rather slow growing *text collections*. To apply clustering to Newsgroups this paradigm has to be extended to cover *text streams*. Text streams differ from text collections in several points. First, new documents are added at a very high pace. Second, topics change constantly and new topics are introduced on a daily basis. Third, old documents often become obsolete after

M. Ali and R. Dapoigny (Eds.): IEA/AIE 2006, LNAI 4031, pp. 332–341, 2006.

a short period of time and should not influence the cluster structure any more. The same holds for more recent applications, as Blogs or RSS feeds.

Incremental clustering algorithms handle text streams in a natural way. Such algorithms are able to incorporate new documents as they arrive and modify the cluster structure correspondingly. There has been some research of how to extend clustering algorithms to be incremental [1], as well theoretical error bounds on incremental clustering [2]. Scientific work is mostly focused on the question, to which extent incremental algorithms can produce the same cluster quality as their non-incremental counterparts more efficiently. This is however only one aspect of the problem.

The other aspect is understanding the role of the user in the incremental clustering process. In Information and Knowledge Management applications, text clustering is applied to provide users with a convenient access structure to a document pool. This access structure must on the one hand represent the underlying data. On the other hand, it must reflect the preferences and habits of the user. This observation has a consequence on the application of incremental clustering. If the system constantly changes the access structure the user is familiar with, then the system will be of limited use, as the costs for the user to accommodate to a constantly changing structure are very high. Incremental clustering systems must take this cost into account explicitly. They must accommodate to new text documents adequately, while changing the underlying cluster structure only to a level accepted by the user.

In this work, we propose an incremental clustering system for newsgroups that takes the user directly into account. Users may specify to which degree modifications are acceptable to them. The system then modifies the cluster structure, given these constraints.

In section 2, we present the overall structure of our application. Section 3 introduces a variant of frequent term set clustering that is the point of departure for our method. Section 4 then describes the incremental extension of this algorithm. In section 5 we present an empirical evaluation of our approach.

2   Incremental Newsgroup Clustering

Our news organizer system should serve administrators and readers of a Newsgroup to archive important postings and to get a structured overview on current developments and topics. Preserving news articles is an important challenge, as news articles often contain highly valuable information in a very unstructured way. Imposing a hierarchical structure on these articles is an important step to uncover and activate this information. Typical use scenarios are administrators of (technical) Newsgroups writing FAQs, journalists looking for an overview on current discussions on a topic for an article or just casual readers of the group searching for specific information.

In our news organizer system, documents are structured in a cluster hierarchy as depicted in Fig. 2. Each document contains a thread, thus a discussion structure on an initial posting. As new articles and threads arrive, they are inserted

Table 1. Example for term occurrences in documents

xml	d1,d2,--,d4,d5,d6,--,d8,d9,d10
java	d1,d2,--,--,d5,d6,--,--,d9,--
linux	--,--,d3,d4,--,d6,d7,--,--,d10
db2	d1,--,--,--,--,d6,--,d8,d9,--

automatically to the appropriate position in the hierarchy. The user can edit threads and mark them as 'archive'. These documents are kept, while other threads are deleted after a predefined period of time. The cluster structure is adjusted using the algorithm described below as to reflect all current documents, as well as all archived documents. The idea is to cover current topics *and* topics that reflect a long term information need of the user.

The user can constraint structural changes by providing a level of maximal structural change. They may also select, whether the changes are performed automatically or whether the system only proposes changes. In the latter case, the user can accept these changes on an individual basis and select clusters that should be preserved in any case.

Sophisticated linguistic processing is not part of the system. However we use some preprocessing on the incoming news articles. Firstly, we delete standard signatures at the end of news articles. Secondly, quotes are deleted, as articles are aggregated to threads. Finally, stop words are removed.

3   Frequent Term Set Clustering

Clustering text data is very challenging. First, texts are usually represented in a very high dimensional space. Second, text data sets are often very large. Finally, text clustering demands for overlapping clusters, as documents can be assigned to more than one cluster or topic. Frequent Term Set (FTS) clustering is a state of the art approach to text clustering that can deal with these problems [3,4]. The general idea of FTS clustering is based on mining frequent items sets [5]. Each document is modeled as a set of terms. FTS are subsets of terms that co-occur in many documents. Formally, this can be written as follows. Let $D = \{D_1, \ldots, D_n\}$ be the set of all documents and $T = \{t_1, \ldots, t_k\}$ the set of all terms. Each document is represented by the terms it contains $D_j \subseteq T$. The set of all documents covered by a term set is defined as $cov(T') = \{D_i \in D | T' \subseteq D_i\}$, thus the set of documents that contains all terms in T'. The set of frequent term sets is then defined as $F = \{F_j \subseteq T | |cov(F_j)| \geq \alpha |D|\}$, where α defines a minimal support, thus a minimal fraction of documents in which a term set must occur to be frequent. In the example depicted in table 3, {xml}, {java}, {linux} and {xml,java} are frequent, while e.g. {db2} or {linux,java} are not, based on a minimal support of 50%.

FTS can be arranged by the subset relation: if T' is an FTS, then all $T'' \subset T'$ are FTS as well. Figure 1 shows an example. In FTS clustering, clusters are always frequent term sets. The key problem is how to chose the subset of FTS

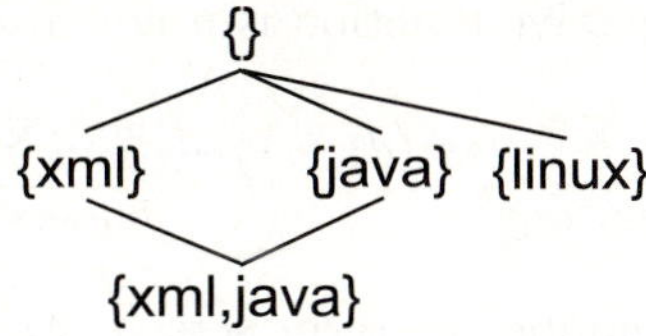

Fig. 1. An example fts hierarchy derived from table 3

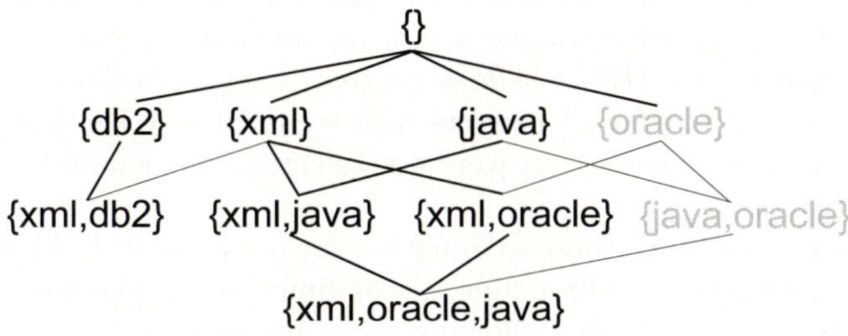

Fig. 2. An example for a cluster hierarchy derived from an FTS hierarchy. The black FTS and bold lines form the cluster hierarchy presented to the user. The thin lines and gray FTS are not selected and are hidden from the user.

that form the cluster hierarchy. In Fig. 2 the black terms sets are selected as clusters, the gray term sets are not. A document is assigned to each FTS it covers and that is part of the cluster hierarchy.

The selection of clusters from the FTS hierarchy is based on an objective function. Such a function assigns a performance measure to each possible subset $F' \subseteq F$. The optimal set is then selected by an optimization procedure.

This optimization can be performed level wise. For each FTS F_i, $N(F_i)$ denotes the set of direct successors of F_i in the FTS hierarchy. The task is then to chose for each F_i a set $M(F_i) \subseteq N(F_i)$ that is optimal concerning the objective function. In the above example {xml,oracle} and {xml,java} are chosen as successors for {xml}, while {xml,db2} is not used.

[3] and [6] propose objective functions that chose $M(F_i) \subseteq N(F_i)$ to minimize the document overlap between the clusters in $M(F_i)$. The idea is that two clusters with the same parent should have only minimal overlap. Also all documents should be covered by at least one FTS in $M(F_i)$.

In our practical experiments we found that overlap is not sufficient as objective function. The problem is, that on the one hand many documents are covered by only one FTS and on the other hand, many FTS cover only few documents. Thus many subclusters are introduced, as to cover all documents, leading to a very complex and incomprehensible cluster structure.

While this may be acceptable from a point of view of the data, it is clearly not acceptable for the user. We therefore introduce a misc cluster at each node. It contains all documents that were not covered by any of the selected subclusters.

The following extended objective function is used to select $M(F_i)$:

$$LCost(F_i) = \sum_{d \in C(d_i)} (m_i(d) - 1) + \sum_{d \in cov(F_i) \setminus C(d_i)} n_i(d) \tag{1}$$

where $m_i(d)$ denotes the number of term sets in $M(F_i)$ that contain d, thus the number of term sets covering d that are part of the cluster hierarchy. $n_i(d)$ denotes the number of term sets in $N(F_i)$ that cover d and are not element of $M(F_i)$. These are the term sets that could cover d but were not chosen for the cluster hierarchy. $C(d_i)$ denotes the set of all documents that are covered by at least one term set in $M(F_i)$. The objective function is thus constituted of two parts. First, the overlap of clusters and second the FTS that could cover documents in the misc cluster, but were not selected. We denote this latter ones as unused possibilities.

While $LCost(F_i)$ defines the cost function for one cluster F_i by chosing subclusters $M(F_i)$, we additionally define a cost function for the whole cluster hierarchy. This is achieved by the following recursive function:

$$GCost(F_i) = \frac{LCost(F_i)|cov(F_i)| + \sum_{F_j \in M(F_i)} GCost(F_j)|cov(F_j)|}{|cov(F_i)| + \sum_{F_j \in M(F_i) \wedge M(F_j) \neq \emptyset} |cov(F_j)|} \tag{2}$$

For leaf nodes the global cost is zero as there are no overlaps and no unused possibilities. For inner nodes the cost is a weighted average over the local costs and the costs of all subclusters. As weighting function, the number of documents is used. Note, that this formula does not normalize with respect to leaf nodes. Doing so would always lead to leaf nodes having optimal cost and thus to a flat cluster hierarchy.

Based on this objective function, we use a bottom-up procedure to find an optimal selection of FTS for the cluster hierarchy. The algorithm is based on a branch and bound procedure on each level that prunes the search to avoid unnecessary calculations.

Together with adequate preprocessing, this approach produces a user friendly cluster structure from an initial set of documents. The question is, how this structure can be updated as documents are added or deleted. To avoid unnecessary computations, the FTS hierarchy and all local and global costs are stored.

4   Incremental Frequent Term Set Clustering

The underlying document set can change as new documents arrive and old ones are deleted. Documents can easily be inserted into the existing cluster hierarchy, as they are described by the terms they contain. However, adding documents can render an existing cluster hierarchy invalid or suboptimal. A cluster becomes invalid, if the corresponding FTS does not have the minimal support any more. It

Table 2. Structural changes

SCP Allowed Modifications
0 Insertion of new documents
1 Reclustering of misc clusters and addition of new fts
2 Deletion of invalid clusters
3 Deletion of valid cluster leafs
> 3 Deletion of valid inner clusters

becomes suboptimal, if another choice of FTS would reduce the global cost. In both cases the cluster should be deleted from the cluster hierarchy. Also, FTS that reduce the overall cost should be added to the cluster hierarchy. For this purpose, the level-wise procedure as described above can be used. As the FTS structure is stored along with the current cluster hierarchy, this process only updates the parts of the hierarchy that are affected by changes. Changes to the cluster structure are performed in batches, thus the system only inserts documents until a certain amount of new documents in reached. Then restructuring is invoked.

Deleting and adding clusters is perfectly acceptable to keep the cluster hierarchy optimal. From the point of view of the user, such modifications are always connected with the cost to accommodate to the new structure. We therefore introduce the concept of structural change points (SCP). Each modification to the cluster structure is connected with a cost factor, capturing the cost for the user to accommodate to the modified structure. The user may then state which kinds of modifications are acceptable to her. We chose the following cost functions. Adding a new cluster has a cost of 1 SCP. Deleting an invalid cluster (a cluster with less than the minimal support) has a cost of 2 SCP. Deleting a valid leaf node has a cost of 3 SCP. Deleting an inner node has a cost that is defined recursively by the following formula:

$$scp_{del}(F_i) = max\{scp(F_j)|F_j \in M(F_i)\} + \begin{cases} 1, \; for \; |M(F_i)| = 1 \\ 2, \quad\quad else \end{cases} \quad (3)$$

The cost for deleting an inner node increases depending on the subtree. Nodes that have more than one successor produce higher costs than nodes with only one successor. If the users allows modifications of a maximum degree of 1 SCP, clusters can be added and leaf nodes can be deleted, however inner nodes cannot be deleted. Table 4 summarizes the possible changes.

The individual cost factors could be chosen in another way, however we found that the cost matrix presented above worked very well in our practical experiments.

The update procedure above is modified to be constrained by a maximum level of SCP. In the optimization, only such modifications are considered, that would not exceed this level. On the one hand, this assures, that only modifications are performed that are accepted by the user. On the other hand, the whole process of updating the cluster structure is much more efficient, as parts of the cluster

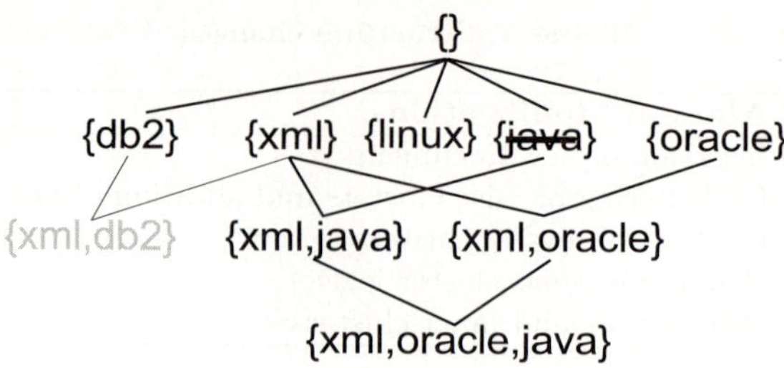

Fig. 3. An example for a cluster hierarchy after modifications to the structure. The black concept and bold lines form the new cluster hierarchy. The FTS {java} should be deselected, however the SCP level is not sufficient for this operation.

hierarchy that do not qualify for certain modifications can be directly omitted in the optimization process.

One current limitation of the system is, that while clustering is performed incrementally, FTS are generated non-incrementally using the Apriori algorithm. However, as this process only takes a few minutes even for large newsgroups it does not influence the performance of the system much.

Figure 3 shows an example of a modified cluster hierarchy. The FTS {linux} is added, as it is frequent now and {java, oracle} is removed, as it is not frequent any more. Also, {oracle} is selected for the FTS hierarchy. The FTS {db2,xml} becomes suboptimal and can be deleted based on a SCP level of 3. The FTS {java} becomes suboptimal and should be deselected, however this operation cannot be performed automatically, as 3 SCP are not sufficient to delete an inner cluster.

5   Evaluation

We evaluated our algorithm on four Newsgroups with different characteristics, as depicted in Table 3. The focus of the evaluation was on the following three questions: 1. How does the quality of incremental clustering differ from clustering the whole set of documents at once? 2. How does this quality depend on the user restrictions? 3. What is the influence of the batch size in this process?

Table 3. The Newsgroups used for the evaluation with number of documents (threads), number of documents for the initial clustering and the batch size for incremental clustering

Newsgroup	documents	initial	batch
microsoft.public.access	10556	6554	250
alt.politics	8676	5474	250
alt.philosophy	2506	1786	100
alt.comp.hardware	1411	935	50

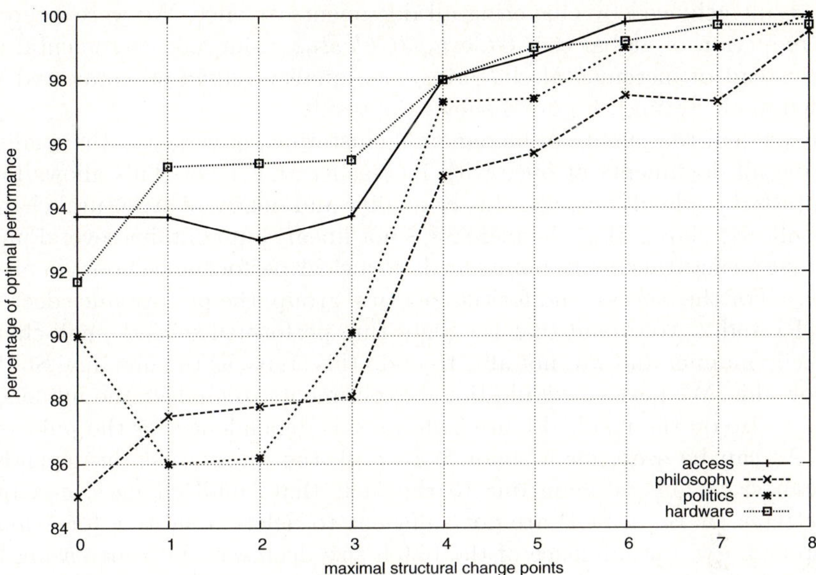

Fig. 4. Performance of incremental clustering compared to non-incremental clustering

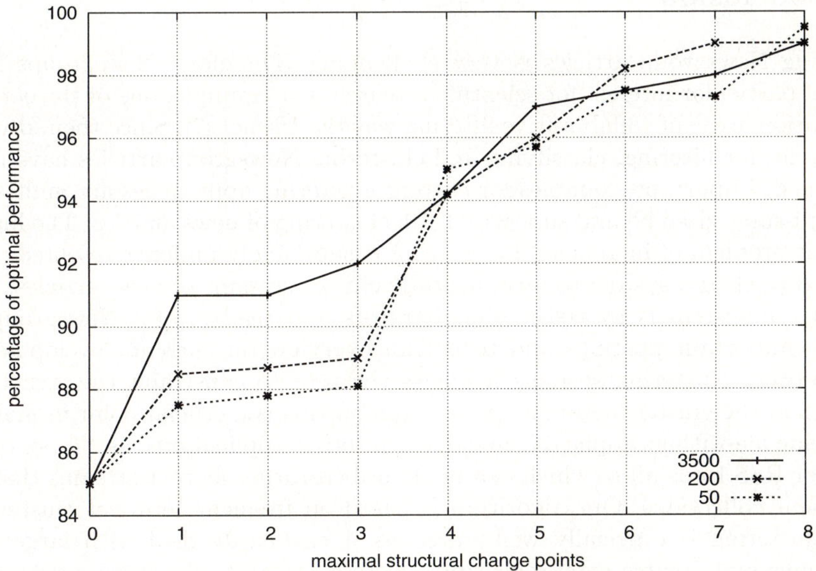

Fig. 5. The influence of the batch size on the result

The overall evaluation procedure was the following. For each Newsgroup, an initial clustering was generated using only a fraction of the documents. The remainder of the documents was added in batches. The batch size for each Newsgroup is depicted in table 3. The result of incremental clustering is compared to the result achieved by clustering all documents at once. We were interested in the reduction of global cost $GCost_{all}/GCost_{inc}$ using non-incremental clustering instead of incremental clustering (the quality reduction connected with incremental clustering). Figure 4 shows the result.

As expected, the quality of incremental clustering converges to the quality of clustering all documents at once with increasing SCP level. This allows for an user adjusted trade-off between cluster quality and degree of structural changes. The result also shows, that the increase is not linear, but contains several jumps. Using four structural change points leads to a clear performance boost in all four examples. For the 'access' and for the 'politics' group, the performance decreases for level 1 and 2. We found that the algorithm performed several small changes in a greedy manner and was not able to undo this steps, as the maximal SCP did not allow this. We performed additional experiments to analyze the influence of the batch size on the result. Figure 5 shows this dependency for the philosophy group. As can be seen, for a small SCP level, the quality clearly depends on the batch size. This is again due to the fact, that small changes, cannot be undone later, as the 2 SCP are not sufficient to delete a subtree for example. Correspondingly, the influence of the batch size decreases with increasing SCP level, as greedy changes can be corrected at a later step without problems.

6   Conclusion

Handling Newsgroup articles is very challenging. Therefore, Newsgroups have been of particular interest for scientific research. For example, one of the earliest application areas of collaborative filtering was the Usenet [7]. Since then, diverse techniques for filtering, classifying and clustering Newsgroup articles have been developed. Important examples for current clustering approaches are multi-way [8], semi-supervised [9] and supervised [10] clustering of news articles. The highly relevant problem of incremental clustering is suprisingly underrepresented.

We described a system to incrementally cluster streams of news articles. The aim of the system is to assist administrators and readers of a Newsgroup to archive important postings and to get an overview on current developments. Unlike other clustering systems it allows the user to constraint the structural changes in the cluster hierarchy. In our opinion this is a crucial point in making clustering algorithms applicable in current Internet applications, as Newsgroups, Blogs or RSS feeds all of which can be described rather as text streams than as document collections. Our algorithm is based on frequent term set clustering. FTS clustering is especially well suited as it can easily deal with large text collections and creates comprehensible clusters. Also, it allows for overlapping clusters, which is important as news articles can often be to several topics.

We analyzed the properties of the algorithm in an empirical evaluation. As expected, there is a trade off between cluster quality, batch size and the degree of allowed structural change. However, even with quite strict constraints, a high quality could be achieved compared with the non-incremental variant of the algorithm.

In our future work we intend to provide the user with the opportunity to influence the cluster structure even further by using algorithms for supervised and semi-supervised clustering [9], [10]. Such an extension allows the user to select, which clusters are most important for the access structure interactively. Also we plan to incorporate background knowledge in the clustering process [11], which could help to deal with very short articles, containing only very few terms.

References

1. Jain, A.K., Murty, M.N., Flynn, P.J.: Data clustering - a review. ACM Computing Surveys **31** (1999)
2. Charikar, M., Chekuri, C., Feder, T., Motwani, R.: Incremental clustering and dynamic information retrieval. SIAM Journal on Computing **33** (2004)
3. Beil, F., Ester, M., Xu, X.: Frequent term-based text clustering. In: Proceedings of the International Conference on Knowledge Discovery and Data Mining. (2002)
4. Fung, B.C.M., Wang, K., Ester, M.: Hierarchical document clustering using frequent items. In: Proceedings of the SIAM International Conference on Data Mining. (2003)
5. Agrawal, R., Imielinski, T., Swami, A.: Mining association rules between sets of items in large databases. In: Proceedings of the ACM SIGMOD International Conference on Management of Data. (1993)
6. Wang, K., Xu, C., Liu, B.: Clustering transactions using large items. In: Proceedings of the International Conceference on Information and Knowledge Management. (1999)
7. Konstan, J.A., Miller, B.N., Maltz, D., Herlocker, J.L., Gordon, L.R., Riedl, J.: GroupLens: Applying collaborative filtering to Usenet news. Communications of the ACM **40** (1997)
8. Bekkerman, R., El-Yaniv, R., McCallum, A.: Multi-way distributional clustering via pairwise interactions. In: Proceedings of the International Conference on Machine Learning. (2005)
9. Cohn, D., Caruana, R., McCallum, A.: Semi-supervised clustering with user feedback. Technical Report TR2003-1892, Cornell University (2000)
10. Finley, T., Joachims, T.: Supervised clustering with support vector machines. In: Proceedings of the International Conference on Machine Learning. (2005)
11. Hotho, A., Staab, S., Stumme, G.: Ontologies improve text document clustering. In: Proceedings of the International Conference on Data Mining. (2003)

Topic Detection Using MFSs

Ivan Yap[1], Han Tong Loh[1], Lixiang Shen[2], and Ying Liu[3]

[1] Department of Mechanical Engineering, Blk EA 07-08
National University of Singapore, 10 Kent Ridge Crescent, Singapore
`{g0202430, mpelht}@nus.edu.sg`
[2] Design Technology Institute Ltd, Faculty of Engineering, Blk E4 01-07,
National University of Singapore, 10 Kent Ridge Crescent, Singapore 119260
[3] Singapore MIT Alliance, E4-04-10, National University of Singapore, Singapore 119260
`mpeliuy@nus.edu.sg`

Abstract. When analyzing a document collection, a key piece of information is the number of distinct topics it contains. Document clustering has been used as a tool to facilitate the extraction of such information. However, existing clustering methods do not take into account the sequences of the words in the documents, and usually do not have the means to describe the contents within each topic cluster. In this paper, we record our investigation and results using Maximal Frequent word Sequences (MFSs) as building blocks in identifying distinct topics. The supporting documents of MFSs are grouped into an equivalence class and then linked to a topic cluster, and the MFSs serve as the document cluster identifier. We describe the original method in extracting the set of MFSs, and how it can be adapted to identify topics in a textual dataset. We also demonstrate how the MFSs themselves can act as topic descriptors for the clusters. Finally, the benchmarking study with other existing clustering methods, i.e. k-Means and EM algorithm, shows the effectiveness of our approach for topic detection.

1 Introduction

In different fields of work, there is a need to gather information from large collections of textual work, for example a database of engineering research paper abstracts, or a collection of newly submitted patent abstracts. Useful information includes, but is not restricted to, how many distinct topics are contained within the collection, the content of each of these clusters, and examples of documents that make up a cluster. Automated means of detection are necessary when faced with data collections even in the order of hundreds, as they are more consistent and efficient when compared to the human sieving of data.

Document clustering has been employed in previous work in the literature, as an initial step in determining the distinct topics from a document collection [4]. However, most of the clustering algorithms approach the problem from a feature-based perspective, i.e. using single words as features [11]. While phrases have long been used to supplement word-based indexing in IR system [8], they have not been widely applied to document clustering [6, 12]. Our approach in this paper is to cluster documents based on similar frequent word sequences, occurring across the dataset. In

M. Ali and R. Dapoigny (Eds.): IEA/AIE 2006, LNAI 4031, pp. 342–352, 2006.
© Springer-Verlag Berlin Heidelberg 2006

particular, we use the Maximal Frequent word Sequences (MFSs) of the dataset to group documents together. The MFS algorithm is explained in detail in Section 2. How the topics are detected and how the documents are clustered is described in Section 3. Results of our experiments are reported in Section 4. Section 5 concludes.

2   The MFS Algorithm and Equivalence Classes

The idea and method of discovering the set of MFSs out of a textual dataset was first proposed by Ahonen [2]. A MFS is a sequence of words that is "frequent in the document collection and, moreover, that is not contained in any other longer frequent sequence" [2]. A word sequence is frequent if it appears in at least σ documents, where σ is a pre-specified support threshold. The goal of the MFS algorithm is to find all maximal frequent phrases in the textual dataset.

The strength of the method is that it employs a versatile technique for finding sequential text phrases from full text, allowing, if desired, gaps between the words in a phrase [3]. For example, the word sequence *"product knowledge databases"* can be extracted as a frequent phrase even if its occurrence is in the form of:

- *"...product* management using *knowledge databases..."*
- *"...product* data in *knowledge databases..."*
- *"...product* specifications, *knowledge databases..."*

in the supporting documents. The maximum gap allowed between words of a sequence is determined by the maximal word gap parameter. Algorithm 1 explains the basic logic of MFS.

Algorithm 1: Discovery of all maximal frequent sequences in the documents

```
    Input:      S: a set of pre-processed documents,
                σ: a support threshold,
                g: maximal word gap
    Output:   Max: a set of maximal frequent sequences

            // Initial phase: collect all frequent pairs
    1.  For all the documents d ∈ S
    2.  Collect all the ordered pairs and occurrence information
        within d
    3.  Grams₂ = all ordered pairs that are frequent in S
            // Discovery phase: build longer word sequences by ex-
            panding and joining and store MFSs and occurrence infor-
            mation into Max
    4.  k := 2;
    5.  Max := ∅;
    6.  While Gramsₖ is not empty
    7.      For all grams g ∈ Gramsₖ
    8.          If g is not a subsequence of some m ∈ Max
    9.          If g is frequent
    10.             max := Expand(g);
    11.             Max := Max ∪ max;
    12.             If max = g
    13.                 Remove g from Gramsₖ;
```

```
14.          Else
15.                 Remove g from Grams_k;
16.      Prune(Grams_k);
17.      Grams_{k+1} := Join(Grams_k);
18.      k := k + 1;
19. Return Max
```

The algorithm starts with a set of ordered frequent word pairs, such as *ab* and *bc*. Then it searches for the MFSs in a bottom-up and greedy manner. It adds an item into a pair in a greedy manner by trying all possible choice, until the longer sequence is no longer frequent. As this process repeats, it only expands the sequences that are not contained in any of the existing maximal sequences. If some cannot be expanded, they are themselves maximal sequences. It stops until there are no grams left for expansion.

After the MFSs have been found, they will be grouped into equivalence classes. We explain how this can be done. Let A and B be two MFSs amongst a set of MFSs. The equivalence class of A, Eq_A, contains the set of MFSs that co-occur with A in almost the same documents, as given by a confidence parameter. Det_A is the set of MFSs that are determined by A, and is required in deciding which MFSs belong in Eq_A. For A and B, if:

$$\frac{Frequency(A, B\ co-occur)}{Frequency(A)} \geq Confidence \tag{1}$$

then we add B to the set Det_A; A itself is also included in Det_A. The other MFSs are tested in the same manner, and will be added to Det_A if they satisfy the above criterion. Eq_A is thus made up of all MFS X such that $Det_X = Det_A$.

In previous work on association rule mining [1, 7], the confidence parameter is a measure of the strength of the rule. The use of confidence here is similar; for each MFS, we find other MFSs that are associated to it (with a strength as determined by the confidence), and include them in its *Det* set. When we next group MFSs that have matching *Det* sets together, we are consolidating MFSs that are associated to the same set of MFSs, and this consolidated group of MFSs we term an equivalence class. Finally, an equivalence class is considered to be the representative of a topic, if the precision of the class is higher than a predefined threshold, say 0.7, i.e. at least 0.7 of the supporting documents of that class are from that same topic.

3 Using MFSs to Detect Topics and Cluster Documents

In Ahonen's work [2, 3], the method of discovering MFSs in a textual dataset, and using equivalence classes to reduce the number of MFSs, is introduced. We build upon the existing work, by using MFSs that have already been grouped into equivalence classes, and link them to the distinct topics in a textual dataset.

Given a textual dataset, the following step-by-step procedure is taken for topic detection. The procedure is illustrated in Figure 1:

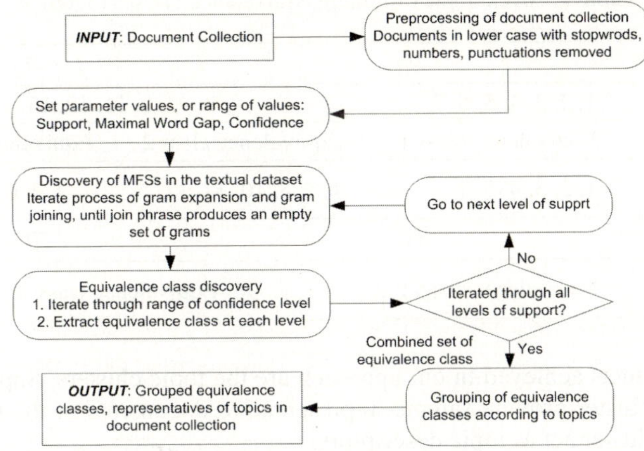

Fig. 1. The general flowchart of topic discovery in a document collection

In parameter settings, we depart from the literature [2, 3] in our use of support and confidence parameters; instead of using a single value for each, we choose a range of values. Thus, each level of support would yield its own set of MFSs. Likewise, each value of confidence would yield its own set of equivalence classes. The use of a range of values, instead of single values, is done to maximize the coverage of distinct topics amongst the output equivalence classes.

After the MFSs have been found, we group them into equivalence classes. In our implementation, the use of equivalence classes is slightly different from [3] as defined in Section 2; we no longer require that MFSs in an equivalence class be descriptive of "almost all the same documents", and we use a range of confidence values instead of a single value. Thus, in this step, we are using the same set of MFSs discovered as input, and iterating over a range of confidence values, with each confidence value yielding its own set of equivalence classes, which are not necessarily unique. Based on the returned results, we have equivalence classes across the range of topics that occur in the textual dataset. We then link an equivalence class to a topic based on how well the class matches the topic. The degree of match between a topic label and a class is defined as the number of instances that belong to both the topic label and the class [4]. Eventually, clusters of equivalence classes have become the representatives of topics in the dataset. Table 1 contains an example of linking equivalence classes to topics and how classes can be grouped together.

Looking at Table 1, we see that the dataset has two different topics, i.e. T_1 and T_2. Each topic has seven supporting documents. After processing, our method has found three equivalence classes and each class contains six supporting documents. For equivalence class 1, five of six documents belong to T_1. Therefore, class 1 will be interpreted as associated with topic T_1. As such, class 2 will be considered as associated with T_2, and class 3 is with T_1. Then we unite the classes which share the same topic labels, i.e. class 1 and 3. Finally, equivalence class 1 and 3 are formed as a single topic cluster to represent topic T_1, and equivalence class 2 is formed to represent topic T_2. Based on this approach, we are able to detect the distinct topics in the dataset.

Table 1. An example of linking equivalence classes to topics

Topics	T_1		T_2	
Document IDs	1, 2, 3, 4, 5, 6, 7		8, 9, 10, 11, 12, 13, 14	
Classes	Equivalence class 1	Equivalence class 2		Equivalence class 3
Supporting Document IDs	1, 2, 3, 4, 5, 7	1, 2, 8, 10, 11, 12		1, 2, 4, 6, 7, 12
Topic Clusters	TC_1		TC_2	
Supporting Classes	Equivalence class 1, 3		Equivalence class 2	

The end products achieved in our approach are the topic clusters. Supporting documents in each cluster provide sample, representative documents of the topic, and the MFSs in each cluster act as topic descriptors.

4 Experiments and Results

In this section, three experiments are conducted to show our method is able to perform as described. Our approach has been tested over two subsets of the Reuters-21578[1]. The first one, Reuters_261, is a single topic document collection consisted of 261 documents across a range of six topics[2]. The number of documents in each topic is between 41 and 46. The second one, Reuters_299_mixed, is a multi-topic document collection consisted of 299 documents from five topics[3]. The number of documents that had single topics is 224, and the number of documents tagged with two topics is 75. The goal of the first experiment is to choose a suitable range of parameters, which would yield a concise set of MFSs that would still cover all distinct topics in the dataset. The second experiment is a benchmarking study with two existing clustering methods, k-Means and Expectation Maximization (EM) algorithm, to test the effectiveness of our method. The last experiment is served to see whether our method works for multi-topic documents. The maximal word gap g is two in all three experiments.

The performance of either our approach or k-Means and EM algorithms are evaluated in terms of how well the documents belonging to each of the topic clusters match the documents belonging to the corresponding topics. After linking the equivalence classes to the topics and uniting the classes to form topic clusters, a contingency table for a topic cluster, as shown in Table 2, is then used to measure the results by means of the following five standard metrics [5, 9, 10]. In order to evaluate the global performance of the algorithm, we adopted the macro-averaged approach, which is to first compute the five metrics for each topic cluster and then average them.

Recall: $r = a/(a+c)$; Precision: $p = a/(a+b)$; F_1: $F_1 = 2pr/(p+r)$;

Miss: $m = c/(a+c)$; False Alarm: $f = b/(b+d)$

---

[1] http://www.daviddlewis.com/resources/testcollections/reuters21578/reuters21578.tar.gz
[2] Alum, grain, ipi, iron-steel, nat-gas, reserves.
[3] Alum, crude, grain, nat-gas, ship.

Table 2. A contingency table for evaluation in a binary setting, where 'a' is the number of items that match a method's outputs and target values, i.e. the number of outputs correctly clustered, 'b' and 'c' are the number of items that mismatch a method's outputs and target values respectively

	Expert Yes	Expert No
Output Yes	a	b
Output No	c	d

4.1 Topic Detection with Single-Topic Documents

Our criterion for appropriate values of support and confidence is as follows: among the equivalence classes generated from the target range of parameter values, all six topics of the dataset have to be represented.

To determine the appropriate levels of support to be used, we ran the MFS algorithm on the Reuters_261 dataset across high to low support levels. We started with a support of 25, which only produced MFSs that were two words long. From this starting value, we lowered support in steps of one, to a support level of five, the lower limit for how frequent a phrase had to be. For each level of support, we varied the level of confidence from 0.9 to 0.1, in steps of 0.1, and we examined the equivalence classes found. We looked at the equivalence classes for various levels of confidence, and chose combinations of support and confidence that had a wide spread of topics represented in the equivalence classes.

Table 3. Topic spread of equivalence classes, support nine to five and confidence 0.9 to 0.1

	Number of topics present				
Confidence	**support 9**	**support 8**	**support 7**	**support 6**	**support 5**
0.9	0	1	0	0	2
0.8	4	2	4	3	5
0.7	4	4	3	3	6
0.6	4	2	5	4	4
0.5	5	3	4	4	4
0.4	3	3	3	3	2
0.3	1	3	2	2	2
0.2	1	3	2	2	2
0.1	0	2	1	1	3
Topics found in confidence 0.8 to 0.5	1,3,4,5,6	2,3,4,5,6	2,3,4,5,6	2,3,4,5,6	1,2,3,4,5,6

The results from the Reuters_261 dataset are summarized in Table 3. Only the results for support nine to five are shown, where all six topics are represented. The results for the other levels of support are not shown because they do not have comprehensive topic representation. These combined results take into account the different confidence levels at each level of support. Looking at Table 3, for support levels between nine and five, the range of confidence values from 0.8 to 0.5 gives a complete spread of all topics in the dataset. This range is chosen because topic coverage has been maximized amongst the equivalence classes.

We noted that some equivalence classes were replicated across confidences and supports, so we took the union of the equivalence classes found from support nine to five, confidence 0.8 to 0.5, to form a combined set of distinct equivalence classes. Equivalence classes are useful to us only if they are representative of a topic. For some combinations of support and confidence, there are instances where bad equivalence classes are generated, i.e. the supporting documents are not distinctly from any one topic, and as such, are not representative of any topic. However, the error rate is low across most combinations, and so, the grouping of the good classes into clusters is relatively unhindered by the presence of the bad classes.

4.2 Comparison with k-Means and EM

In this section, we evaluate the performance of our proposed method against two existing clustering algorithms that have been previously used in topic detection, i.e. k-Means and EM algorithm [10].

For k-Means and EM algorithm, we need to specify the number of clusters, i.e. the parameter k. Since the dataset originally has only six topics, the ideal situation is that all documents can be partitioned into six clusters. Hence, we set k starting from six. For our proposed method using MFSs, when we vary the support and the confidence levels, our method identified an upper bound of 28 equivalence classes. If we assume that each equivalence class stands for one unique topic, then there would not be more than 28 clusters. Hence, in the k-Means and EM algorithms, we set k ending at 28.

To perform a fair comparison, we compared the performance of each method based on a single optimized set of parameters. In previous work [10], the optimal k is directly set as the number of topics in the original dataset. However, we do not assume that is the optimal parameter setting; instead we search for the optimal parameter(s). We search for k for k-Means and EM algorithm, and support and confidence for our method, by monitoring whether the setting can lead the algorithm to identify the most topics. The goal is that each topic has to be linked to at least one cluster from among the output clusters. For our proposed method, each topic has to be linked to at least one equivalence class from among the output classes. The evaluation measures miss, false alarm, precision and recall are macro-averaged for each method after ten runs of each different parameter setting. The statistic F_1 is then computed.

Table 4 shows the details of the benchmarking experiments among k-Means, EM and our method. The results for k-Means are not listed in Table 4, because even upon using different values of k and running from ten different initialization conditions, the six topics are still not fully represented in the output clusters of k-Means. This leads k-Means to dramatically underperform compared to others, and hence it is not reported here. Looking at the false alarm and precision measures in Table 4, we see that the MFS method outperforms EM significantly, suggesting that the equivalence classes returned by our proposed method contain accurate and concise collections of documents belonging to the various topics. However, looking at the miss and recall values, we see that the MFS method performs slightly poorer than EM. This is because the

MFS method recalls documents based on maximally frequent phrases. Not all documents of a topic may contain the maximally frequent phrases, and as such, not all documents are recalled.

Table 4. Macro-averaged evaluation measures for EM and MFS, k = number of clusters

Method	Settings	m	f	r	p	F_1
EM	$k=24$	0.517	0.096	0.483	0.663	0.540
	$k=25$	0.500	0.090	0.500	0.672	0.559
	$k=26$	0.564	0.103	0.436	0.641	0.573
	$k=27$	0.509	0.092	0.491	0.631	0.552
MFS	support=5 confidence=0.7	0.604	0.010	0.396	0.887	0.548

Other than the better quality of the equivalence classes, our method is also able to provide human readable phrases which act as topic descriptors, a feature that k-Means and EM do not offer, e.g. 'natural gas reserve' and 'cubic feet gas day' for topic 'nat-gas', and 'grain elevator' and 'grain ships loading waiting load' for topic 'grain'. These descriptors, i.e. the MFSs found, are taken directly from the text, and are highly representative of the document contents.

4.3 Topic Detection with Multi-topic Documents

It is seen that our method is effective in distinguishing single-topic documents, and is able to outperform traditional clustering methods in topic detection. In this section, we apply it to multi-topic documents, since real world document collections usually contain documents that span across a few topics.

We tested the suitability of the parameter values by repeating the experiments on the second dataset, Reuters_299_mixed, using the parameter values found previously. We examine the results returned by our method, and evaluate whether it is suitable for datasets that contain documents that overlap across topics.

As the dataset contained documents tagged with more than one topic, certain adaptations were made in evaluating the quality of an equivalence class. For supporting documents that are tagged with two topics, we treat them as supporting both topics. For example, in the equivalence class containing the MFSs "gas reserves" and "oil reserves", 15 of the 21 supporting documents have two topic tags attached to them. These documents are considered as supporting both topics. In evaluating the quality of this equivalence class, we adopted the criterion as specified in Section 2, i.e. at least 0.7 of the documents had to be from the same topic, for the class to be representative of that topic.

For Reuters_299_mixed, we followed the same procedure as illustrated in Figure 1, and re-used these parameter values/ranges: a maximal word gap of two, support from nine to five, and confidence from 0.8 to 0.5. Table 5 shows the number of topics represented for each combination of support and confidence that we used, as well as the breakdown of topics that are found at each level of support. Our method is able to detect all five distinct topics in the dataset.

Table 5. Topic spread of equivalence classes, support nine to five and confidence 0.8 to 0.5

	Number of topics present				
Confidence	**support 9**	**support 8**	**support 7**	**support 6**	**support 5**
0.8	2	0	2	2	3
0.7	3	2	3	3	3
0.6	3	1	5	3	3
0.5	2	2	5	3	4
Topics found in confidence 0.8 to 0.5	1,2,4	2,4	1,2,3,4,5	2,4,5	1,2,3,4,5

We then group MFSs into equivalence classes and link the classes to topics.

Table 6. Percentage of good equivalence classes, from support nine to five, confidence 0.8 to 0.5, for Reuters_299_mixed

Support 9

Condf.	N.o.G.	N.o.B.	T.o.C.	% GD
0.8	2	0	2	100
0.7	3	0	3	100
0.6	2	0	2	100
0.5	2	0	2	100

Support 8

Condf.	N.o.G.	N.o.B.	T.o.C.	% GD
0.8	0	0	0	n.a.
0.7	1	0	1	100
0.6	1	0	1	100
0.5	3	0	3	100

Support 7

Condf.	N.o.G.	N.o.B.	T.o.C.	% GD
0.8	3	0	3	100
0.7	6	0	6	100
0.6	7	0	7	100
0.5	8	0	8	100

Support 6

Condf.	N.o.G.	N.o.B.	T.o.C.	% GD
0.8	4	0	4	100
0.7	8	0	8	100
0.6	6	0	6	100
0.5	8	0	8	100

Support 5

Condf.	N.o.G.	N.o.B.	T.o.C.	% GD
0.8	6	2	8	75.0
0.7	8	2	10	80.0
0.6	8	2	10	80.0
0.5	12	1	13	92.3

Notes:
Condf.: Confidence;
N.o.G.: No. of good classes;
N.o.B.: No. of bad classes;
T.o.C.: Total No. of classes;
% GD: percentage of good classes

Table 6 shows the number of good and bad equivalence classes generated at each combination of support and confidence. The number of bad equivalence classes is once again a small percentage of the good equivalence classes, and so, the presence of the bad classes is not a major issue; the grouping of the good classes into topic clusters is still relatively unhindered.

In this multi-topic dataset, we have encountered the situation where one equivalence class can belong to two topics. For example, half of the supporting documents are associated with topic T_1, and another half documents are associated with topic T_2. In this case, we consider this equivalence class to be linked to both topics. A closer examination shows that such equivalence classes are indeed representative of both topics. They display the overlapping concepts, and are supported by the very documents that are associated with this overlap. This is useful if we want to detect which topics overlap, and if we want to find a representative set of documents that exhibit this topic-overlapping characteristic.

5 Conclusion

When using existing clustering methods to cluster documents of similar topics and further detect the distinct topics they contain, documents are usually represented by a term-by-document matrix without considering the order in which the words appear. Moreover, after the clustering, there are also no human-readable content descriptors to describe each cluster. In this paper, we have demonstrated how the MFS discovery algorithm can be adapted to discover distinct topics in documents. By varying the support and confidence parameters, we are able to discover MFSs and further group them into equivalence classes. By linking the equivalence classes with the topics based on the match rate and further grouping them into topic clusters, we are able to determine the number of topics in a collection. The benchmarking study with k-Means and EM algorithms shows the effectiveness of our approach.

References

1. Agrawal, R., Imieliński, T. & Swami, A.: Mining association rules between sets of items in large databases. Proceedings of the 1993 ACM SIGMOD international conference on Management of data, (1993)
2. Ahonen-Myka, H.: Finding All Frequent Maximal Sequences in Text. Proceedings of the 16th International Conference on Machine Learning ICML-99 Workshop on Machine Learning in Text Data Analysis, (1999)
3. Ahonen-Myka, H., Heinonen, O., Klemettinen, M. & Verkamo, A. I.: Finding Co-occurring Text Phrases by Combining Sequence and Frequent Set Discovery. Proceedings of 16th International Joint Conference on Artificial Intelligence IJCAI-99 Workshop on Text Mining: Foundations, Techniques and Applications, (1999)
4. Allan, J., Carbonell, J., Doddington, G., Yamron, J. & Yang, Y.: Topic Detection and Tracking Pilot Study Final Report. Proceedings of the DARPA Broadcast News Transcription and Understanding Workshop, (1998)
5. Baeza-Yates, R. & Ribeiro-Neto, B.: Modern information retrieval. Addison-Wesley Longman Publishing Co., Inc., Boston, MA, USA (1999)
6. Maarek, Y. S. & Wecker, A. J.: The Librarian's Assistant: automatically organizing on-line books into dynamic bookshelves. Proceedings of RIAO'94, Intelligent Multimedia, Information Retrieval Systems and Management, (1994)
7. Mannila, H., Toivonen, H. & Verkamo, I.: Efficient algorithms for discovering association rules. AAAI Workshop on Knowledge Discovery in Databases (KDD-94), (1994)
8. Salton, G. & Buckley, C.: Term Weighting Approaches in Automatic Text Retrieval. Information Processing and Management, Vol. 24, (1988) 513-523
9. Salton, G. & McGill, M. J.: Introduction to Modern Information Retrieval. McGraw-Hill, New York, USA (1983)

10. Seo, Y.-W. & Sycara, K.: Text Clustering for Topic Detection. CMU-RI-TR-04-03, Robotics Institute, Carnegie Mellon University (2004)
11. Willett, P.: Recent trends in hierarchic document clustering: a critical review. Information Processing and Management, Vol. 24, (1988) 577-597
12. Zamir, O. & Etzioni, O.: Web document clustering: a feasibility demonstration. Proceedings of the 21st annual international ACM SIGIR conference on Research and development in information retrieval, (1998)

A Rule Sets Ensemble for Predicting MHC II-Binding Peptides

Zeng An[1], Pan Dan[2], He Jian-bin[3], Zheng Qi-lun[3], and Yu Yong-quan[1]

[1] Faculty of Computer, Guangdong University of Technology, University Town,
Panyu District, Guangzhou, 510006 Guangdong, P.R. China
zengan@tom.com
[2] Guangdong Mobile Communication Co. Ltd., Guangzhou,
510100 Guangdong, P.R. China
pandan@gd.chinamobile.com
[3] South China University of Technology, Guangzhou, 510640 Guangdong, P.R. China

Abstract. Computational modeling of predicting which peptides can bind to a specific MHC molecule is necessary for minimizing the number of peptides required to synthesize and advancing the understanding for the immune response. Most prediction methods hardly acquire understandable knowledge and there is still some space for the improvements of prediction accuracy. Thereupon, Rule Sets Ensemble (RSEN) algorithm based on rough set theory, which utilizes expert knowledge of bindingïmotifs and diverse attribute reduction algorithms, is proposed to acquire understandable rules along with the improvements of prediction accuracy. Finally, the RSEN algorithm is applied to predict the peptides that bind to *HLA-DR4(B1*0401)*. Experimentation results show: 1) compared with the individual rule sets, the rule sets ensembles have significant reduction in prediction error rate; 2) in prediction accuracy and understandability, rule sets ensembles are better than the Back-Propagation Neural Networks (BPNN).

1 Introduction

Major histocompatibility complex (MHC) molecules are highly polymorphic cell surface molecules that present peptidic ligands to cells of the T cell compartment of the immune system [1]. Binding to MHC molecules is decisive in activating the immune system, and only a certain peptides can bind to specify MHC molecules. Therefore, predicting which peptides can bind to a specific MHC molecule could have great value for minimizing the number of peptides required to be synthesized and assayed and developing pharmaceuticals.

So far, the methods for predicting MHC binding peptides have been classified as 4 classes. 1) Motif-based prediction method. 2) Matrix-based prediction method [2]-[3]. The method assumes that each residue contributes independently of other residues to binding, while the recent findings reported both independent and inter-dependent binding of each amino acid within the peptide influences binding of peptides to MHC II molecules [4]. 3) Artificial Neural Networks (ANNs) -based prediction method [5]-[6]. The method utilizes the non-linearity processing capability of ANNs to deal with

M. Ali and R. Dapoigny (Eds.): IEA/AIE 2006, LNAI 4031, pp. 353–362, 2006.

the interactive effect among amino acids in all positions of the peptide. 4) Structure-based prediction method by X-ray crystallographic [7].

By comparison, ANNs-based prediction method has the highest prediction accuracy without the requirements of more conformational information of the peptides. But ANNs couldn't provide an explanation for the underlying reasoning mechanisms since "knowledge" embedded in the networks is cryptically coded as a large number of weights. In order to gain a better understanding of how ANNs solve the problems, most existing research works have focused on extracting symbolic rules from the trained ANNs [8]. But the works cannot completely solve the inherent "black-box" problem of ANNs yet.

The rough set theory (RS), which was advocated by Pawlak Z. [9] in 1982, gives an approach to automatic rule induction. The basic idea of RS used for rule induction is to derive the corresponding decision or classification rules through data reduction (attribute reduction and attribution value reduction) in a decision table under the condition of keeping the discernibility unchanged. The quality of the attribute reducts has a strong impact on the generalization capability of the rules based on these attributes reducts. The number of attributes in attribute reducts directly influences the complexity and the performance of the decision rules. Thereupon, a series of different attribute reduction algorithms, such as roughness, information entropy [10], and frequency function [11], have been designed.

In fact, the choices of attribute reduction algorithm strongly reply on the concrete datasets. The different attribute reduction algorithms have their own advantages respectively. Thus, a natural question is how to integrate the advantages of different attribute reducts acquired with different attribute reduction algorithms to improve the rules' generalization capability for solving classification problems.

It has been demonstrated in many applications that classification performance can be improved by combining multiple classifiers [12]. Through using an ensemble classifier, it is possible to reduce the mean error rate over that of the individual classifiers. Usually, the ensemble outperforms even the strongest individual member of the ensemble.

In this paper, we design the Rule Sets ENsemble (RSEN) algorithm, which combines the advantages of different attribute reduction algorithms and expert knowledge of binding motifs, to predict MHC class II-binding peptides.

2 Methodology

Before constructing the computational model that is used to predict MHC class II-binding peptides, we first convert an immunological question into a computational problem. The conversion scheme is called here for peptide pre-processing. Then we propose RSEN algorithm based on RS to acquire rules from the pre-processed peptides.

2.1 Peptide Pre-processing

The peptide-binding groove of class II molecules is open at both ends, allowing class II bound peptides to extend out of the cleft. As a result, peptides eluted from class II molecules may vary from 8 to 23 residues [13]. Analyses of binding motifs suggest only a core of nine amino acids within a peptide is essential for peptide/MHC binding [3].

The purpose of peptide pre-processing is to transform the peptides with different lengths into those with equal lengths, i.e., to obtain core sequences of nine amino acids (nonamer for short). It was found that certain peptide residues in anchor positions were highly conserved, and contributed significantly to the binding by their optimal fit to residues in the MHC binding groove [14]. Thereupon, one position corresponding to primary anchor is fixed in each nonamer and the alignment matrix is utilized to score each nonamer subsequence within the peptide. The highest scoring nonamer sequence is regarded as pre-processed result of the corresponding peptide. Meanwhile, every nonamer corresponds to its category of binding affinity (non-binder, low-, moderate-, and high-affinity binders). In this way, the problem of predicting MHC class II-binding peptides is converted into the classification problem.

2.2 Rule Sets ENsemble (RSEN) Algorithm

A decision table is composed of two parts: condition attributes and decision attribute. Here, we can form a decision table where every object represents a nonamer and the number of condition attributes and decision attribute is 180 (nine positions by 20 possible amino acids at each position) and one respectively. The values of condition attributes are composed of zeros and one, and the values of decision attribute correspond to peptide classes (0: no binding; 1: low affinity; 2: moderate affinity; 3: high affinity).

The RSEN algorithm is adopted to acquire the combination of multiple classifiers, which consists of three sub-algorithms.

1) Sub-algorithm1- producing candidates of base rule sets. It calls various attribute reduction algorithms to acquire different attribute reducts, and adopts the attribute value reduction algorithms to obtain the different rule sets based on these reducts.

2) Sub-algorithm2 - selecting base rule sets among candidates. It is used to choose the base rule sets through deleting those candidates with poor prediction performance.

3) Sub-algorithm3 - fusing decisions from base rule sets. It is mainly based on the majority voting.

2.2.1 Sub-algorithm1 - Producing Candidates of Base Rule Sets

The detailed steps of sub-algorithm1 are as follows:

1) Utilizing a variety of attribute reduction algorithms, such as AR-IERDCT (the attribute reduction algorithm based on information entropy [10] and Relative Difference Comparison Table [15]), attribute reduction algorithm based on contribution index [16], the improved algorithm for attribute reduct (AR1) and the enhanced algorithm for attribute reducts (AR2) [15], to acquire m different attribute reducts.

2) For each of m different attribute reducts, OAVRA® (renovated version for orderly attribute value reduced algorithm [15]) is called to obtained n

different rule sets with n different input sequences of training sample. Thus, $m \times n$ different rule sets can be acquired in all.

Owing to the limited pages, the detailed steps of AR-IERDCT and OAVRA® are omitted.

The rules in the candidates can be interpreted as follows: if specific amino acids appear at the specific positions and/or some never appear at the specific positions in a nonamer, we can deduce which class (non-binders, low-, moderate-, and high-affinity binders) the nonamer will belong to. Obviously, the rules will be meaningful to help experts advance the understanding of the immune response and reduce effectively the number of peptides required to be synthesized and assayed.

2.2.2 Sub-algorithm2 - Selecting Base Rule Sets Among Candidates

As usual, there could be some rule sets with poor performance in the obtained $m \times n$ candidates of base rule sets. The introduction of these candidates can disturb the prediction performance of rule sets ensemble. Hence, it is essential to select a part of candidates with good performance as the base rule set of a rule sets ensemble. Here, we rank each candidate rule set according to its ancillary estimator (the performance manifested on the evaluation set). The detailed description is as follows:

Assuming that there are k evaluation samples in the evaluation set.

1) Input k objects into the $m \times n$ different rule sets acquired with sub-algorithm1. Thus, the classification decision matrix comprising $m \times n$ columns and k rows is output. Here, each column is respectively corresponding to the classification outputs of a candidate rule set.

2) Compare every column in the classification decision matrix with the decision attribute column of the evaluation set to compute the estimated accuracy of every rule set on the evaluation set (ancillary estimator for short).

3) Select the h rule sets corresponding to the biggest ancillary estimators among $m \times n$ candidate rule sets as base rule sets to form a rule sets ensemble. Here, h $(1 \leq h \leq m \times n)$ is a preset integer.

2.2.3 Sub-algorithm3 - Fusing Decisions from Base Rule Sets

For a rule sets ensemble, the chances for reaching a full agreement are usually rather low. Therefore, it is necessary to develop a solution of fusing decisions from base rule sets. Here, Sub-algorithm3 is mainly based on majority voting and take some special measures to cope with the special cases such as a tie mixed with "unknown" decision. Owing to the limited pages, the detailed steps of Sub-algorithm3 are omitted.

3 Experiment Results and Discussions

The experimental data set is composed of 650 peptides to bind or not bind to *HLA-DR4 (B1*0401)*, which is provided by Dr. Vladimir Brusic. With the help of SYFPEITHI software [4], and the alignment matrix [5], each nonamer within the initial peptide after fixing the first position corresponding to the primary anchors can be scored. The pre-processed peptides are composed of the highest scoring nonamer sequence. Here, 915 pre-processed nonamers are obtained. There are some nonamers with unknown affinity and some uncertain nonamers (i.e., the same nonamers have different binding affinity) among the 915 nonamers.

After removing the uncertain or unknown nonamers from 915 pre-processed peptides, we have 764 nonamers remained (553 non-binders, 49 low-, 46 moderate- and 116 high-affinity binders). Here, all 764 nonamers are divided into three parts: the training part, the evaluation part and the test part, corresponding to P1, P2 and P3 in Table 1 respectively. The detailed distribution of the nonamers is shown in Table 1. And a 4-fold stratified cross-validation sample method is adopted.

Table 1. Detailed distribution of the 4-fold stratified cross-validation peptide sets

The i-th Fold	Number of peptides grouped by binding affinity											
	None (553)			Low (49)			Moderate (46)			High (116)		
	P 1	P 2	P 3	P 1	P 2	P 3	P 1	P 2	P 3	P 1	P 2	P 3
Fold 1	367	48	138	33	4	12	31	4	11	77	10	29
Fold 2	367	48	138	33	4	12	31	4	11	77	10	29
Fold 3	367	48	138	33	4	12	31	4	11	77	10	29
Fold 4	366	48	139	32	4	13	30	3	13	77	10	29

First, utilize the training samples to produce the candidates of base rule sets with sub-algorithm1. Here, ten different attribute reducts are acquired. The first attribute reduct is derived from the AR-IERDCT, the second is from the AR1 [15], the third is from the algorithm based on contribution-index [16], and the rest of attribute reducts come from the AR2 [15] where the initial attribute subsets are randomly set. For each of 10 different attribute reducts, OAVRA$^®$ is called to obtain two different rule sets with two different input sequences of training samples. Thus, 20 different candidates of base rule sets can be acquired in all.

Then, the base rule sets consisting of rule sets ensembles are obtained with sub-algorithm2. We use the evaluation part to obtain the ancillary estimators of 20 candidates respectively, and choose h (h = 4, 6, 8, 10, 12, 14, 16, 18 and 20) rule sets with the biggest ancillary estimators among 20 candidates as base rule sets to construct 9 rule sets ensembles respectively (see experiment number 1~9 in Table 2).

Finally, we make use of test part to examine the above-mentioned 9 rule sets ensembles. The test results are shown in Table 3 (see experiment number 1~9).

In addition, we utilized some RS-based and ANNs-based prediction methods to deal with the same 764 nonamers. For the sake of fair comparisons between the RSEN and those RS-based and ANNs-based methods, we merged the evaluation part P2 and the training part P1 in Table 1 to construct the *new* training part, i.e., all 764 nonamers are divided into two parts: the *new* training part and the test part. Similarly, a 4-fold stratified cross-validation sample method is adopted. The detailed descriptions of all of experiments and test results are respectively shown in Table 2 (experiment number 10~30) and Table 3 (experiment number 10~30). Table 4 shows a part of rules corresponding to experiment number 10.

Table 2. Descriptions of all of experiments

Experiment number	Descriptions
1~9	The rule sets ensembles in experiment 1~9 are correspondingly comprising 4, 6, 8, 10, 12, 14, 16, 18 and 20 rule sets with the biggest ancillary estimators among 20 rule sets with the help of sub-algorithm2. The distribution of data set is shown in Table 1.
10~11	In experiment 10~11, first, an attribute reduct of the *new* training part is obtain with the AR-IERDCT, then according to the resulting attribute reduct, two different rule sets are formed with two different input sequences of training samples in OAVRA®;
12~13	In experiment 12~13, the two individual rule sets for the *new* training part are obtained on the basis of the same attribute reduct acquired with AR1 and two different input sequences of training samples in OAVRA®;
14~15	In experiment 14~15, the two individual rule sets for the *new* training part are obtained on the basis of the same attribute reduct acquired with attribute reduction algorithm based on contribute index [16] and two different input sequences of training samples in OAVRA®;
16~29	In experiment 16~17, the two individual rule sets for the *new* training part are obtained on the basis of the same attribute reduct acquired with AR2 randomly and two different input sequences of training samples in OAVRA®; In experiment 18~29, the process of acquiring rule sets is the same as experiment 16~17; and so on.
30	In experiment 30, BPNN is used to obtain the classifier to predict the MHC II-binding peptides in the *new* training part. The structure of BPNN is 180-4-1 styles. The learning algorithm is error back-propagation, with a sigmoid activation function. Values for learning rate and momentum are 0.2 and 0.9 respectively.

Table 3. Test results with experiment number 1~30 in error rate (The numbers following '$\pm$' are the standard deviations)

Experiment number	None	Low	Moderate	High	Average
1	.069$\pm$.012	.794$\pm$.035	.770$\pm$.053	.467$\pm$.038	.218$\pm$.013
2	.052$\pm$.007	.800$\pm$.029	.778$\pm$.056	.466$\pm$.050	.207$\pm$.010
3	.044$\pm$.010	.798$\pm$.031	.780$\pm$.054	.452$\pm$.042	.199$\pm$.011
4	.041$\pm$.010	.808$\pm$.038	.780$\pm$.044	.440$\pm$.041	.196$\pm$.010
5	.041$\pm$.010	.808$\pm$.037	.772$\pm$.053	.441$\pm$.041	.195$\pm$.010
6	.037$\pm$.008	.812$\pm$.029	.785$\pm$.048	.439$\pm$.035	.193$\pm$.007
7	.036$\pm$.007	.812$\pm$.034	.785$\pm$.045	.434$\pm$.032	.191$\pm$.006
8	.036$\pm$.007	.806$\pm$.036	.787$\pm$.045	.440$\pm$.033	.192$\pm$.006
9	.035$\pm$.007	.812$\pm$.035	.783$\pm$.052	.440$\pm$.034	.191$\pm$.006
10	.122$\pm$.016	.714$\pm$.062	.680$\pm$.052	.427$\pm$.060	.251$\pm$.015

Table 3. (*continued*)

11	$.127 \pm .018$	$.737 \pm .049$	$.723 \pm .046$	$.452 \pm .055$	$.255 \pm .010$
12	$.159 \pm .014$	$.759 \pm .056$	$.741 \pm .034$	$.489 \pm .048$	$.282 \pm .011$
13	$.149 \pm .013$	$.757 \pm .045$	$.737 \pm .049$	$.492 \pm .045$	$.276 \pm .013$
14	$.162 \pm .026$	$.784 \pm .041$	$.724 \pm .036$	$.460 \pm .036$	$.281 \pm .017$
15	$.157 \pm .018$	$.806 \pm .036$	$.720 \pm .066$	$.445 \pm .048$	$.276 \pm .013$
16	$.166 \pm .014$	$.757 \pm .049$	$.748 \pm .038$	$.492 \pm .062$	$.289 \pm .012$
17	$.175 \pm .018$	$.749 \pm .044$	$.770 \pm .037$	$.522 \pm .051$	$.300 \pm .016$
18	$.184 \pm .017$	$.731 \pm .058$	$.774 \pm .046$	$.529 \pm .041$	$.307 \pm .015$
19	$.158 \pm .020$	$.747 \pm .071$	$.761 \pm .048$	$.525 \pm .054$	$.288 \pm .012$
20	$.171 \pm .027$	$.794 \pm .039$	$.763 \pm .046$	$.517 \pm .026$	$.299 \pm .019$
21	$.158 \pm .033$	$.788 \pm .041$	$.739 \pm .058$	$.510 \pm .025$	$.287 \pm .022$
22	$.168 \pm .018$	$.778 \pm .034$	$.778 \pm .047$	$.513 \pm .074$	$.296 \pm .016$
23	$.177 \pm .020$	$.782 \pm .041$	$.750 \pm .047$	$.523 \pm .049$	$.303 \pm .020$
24	$.171 \pm .013$	$.761 \pm .033$	$.746 \pm .034$	$.522 \pm .025$	$.297 \pm .010$
25	$.171 \pm .021$	$.782 \pm .048$	$.750 \pm .038$	$.516 \pm .046$	$.297 \pm .019$
26	$.173 \pm .026$	$.769 \pm .040$	$.770 \pm .060$	$.511 \pm .061$	$.299 \pm .022$
27	$.171 \pm .018$	$.776 \pm .030$	$.759 \pm .050$	$.511 \pm .042$	$.297 \pm .010$
28	$.154 \pm .021$	$.771 \pm .042$	$.750 \pm .067$	$.529 \pm .046$	$.286 \pm .020$
29	$.164 \pm .024$	$.780 \pm .036$	$.752 \pm .053$	$.524 \pm .055$	$.294 \pm .017$
30	$.100 \pm .016$	$.761 \pm .059$	$.757 \pm .051$	$.399 \pm .032$	$.228 \pm .014$

Table 3 shows the error rates for low-, moderate- and high-affinity binders are much higher than those for non-binder for all experiments, which results from two reasons: 1) there are too few nonamers for the three kinds of binders; 2) the borderlines among the low-, moderate- and high-affinity binders are slightly obscure.

From comparisons of the test results in error rates listed in Table 3, we can see as follows.

1) The rule sets ensembles corresponding to experiment 1~9 are obviously better than any individual rule sets in the prediction performance. In detail, the rule sets ensembles acquired with RSEN algorithm show significant reduction in the average error rate (approximately 13% -38%).

2) In all 30 experiments, the rule sets ensemble obtained in experiment 9, (i.e., the one comprising the all of 20 candidate rule sets) has the lowest average error rate (19.1%).

3) Compared with average error rate of BPNN, the average error rates of rule sets ensembles decreased by about 4%~16%. Much more importantly, the knowledge in rule sets ensembles is expressed in understandable rules and the decision-making process can be explained with logic reasoning in rule sets ensembles, while the weights in BPNN are hardly comprehended by human experts. What's more, the comprehensibility plays an important role in the prediction of MHC II-binders peptides. Thus, the rule sets ensembles are much better to predict MHC II-binders peptides than ANNs.

4)   From the comparisons of prediction error rates of 20 candidates, we can see the generalization capabilities of the rule sets based on different attribute reducts are obviously different. The input sequence of training samples has less influence on the generalization capability of the rule sets than attribute reducts have.

Table 4. A part of rules obtained with the AR-IERDCT and the OAVRA® corresponding to experiment number 10

Rule No.	Antecedents	Consequent
1	Y1(1)&L2(1)&A3(0)&E3(0)&K4(0)&M4(0)&Q4(0)&T4(0)&V4(0)&A5(0)&K5(0)&A6(1)&A7(0)&D7(0)&K7(0)&L7(0)&S7(0)&T7(0)&R8(1)&A9(0)&D9(0)&G9(0)&I9(0)&R9(0)&S9(0)&V9(0)	3
2	W1(0)&Y1(0)&R2(0)&A3(0)&T6(1)&R8(1)&S9(1)	0
3	Y1(0)&R2(0)&A3(1)&A6(1)&R8(0)&A9(0)&G9(0)&V9(0)	0
4	F1(0)&I1(0)&W1(0)&Y1(0)&A2(0)&L2(0)&R2(0)&S2(0)&A3(0)&E3(0)&M4(0)&Q4(0)&V4(0)&A5(0)&K5(0)&A6(0)&S6(0)&T6(0)&A7(0)&L7(0)&G8(1)&A9(0)&D9(0)&G9(0)&R9(0)&S9(0)&V9(0)	0
5	F1(0)&W1(0)&Y1(0)&A2(1)&A3(0)&M4(0)&A6(0)&T6(0)&R8(0)&A9(0)&G9(0)&S9(0)&V9(0)	0
6	F1(1)&N2(1)&A3(0)&E3(0)&K4(0)&M4(0)&Q4(0)&T4(0)&V4(0)&K5(1)&A6(0)&S6(0)&T6(0)&A7(0)&D7(0)&K7(0)&L7(0)&S7(0)&T7(0)&A8(0)&E8(0)&G8(0)&K8(0)&R8(0)&S8(0)&A9(1)	3
7	Y1(1)&A2(1)&A3(1)&M4(0)&V4(0)&A5(0)&A6(1)&L7(0)&K8(1)&A9(1)	3
8	F1(0)&W1(0)&Y1(0)&A2(0)&R2(0)&S2(0)&E3(1)&M4(0)&V4(0)&A5(0)&T6(1)&G8(0)&R8(0)&A9(0)&G9(0)&S9(0)&V9(0)	0
9	F1(0)&W1(0)&Y1(0)&A2(0)&R2(0)&A3(0)&M4(0)&A6(0)&T6(0)&L7(1)&G8(1)&A9(0)&G9(0)&S9(0)&V9(0)	0
10	I1(1)&A2(0)&L2(0)&R2(0)&S2(0)&A3(0)&E3(0)&M4(0)&Q4(0)&V4(0)&A5(0)&A6(0)&S6(0)&T6(0)&L7(0)&G8(0)&K8(0)&R8(0)&A9(0)&G9(0)&R9(0)&S9(0)&V9(0)	0
...	...	...

4 Conclusions

In order to minimize the number of peptides required to be synthesized and assayed and to advance the understanding for the immune response, people have presented many computational models mainly based on ANNs to predict which peptides can bind to a specific MHC molecule. Although the models work well in prediction performance, they cannot provide an explanation for the underlying reasoning mechanisms since "knowledge" embedded in the networks is cryptically coded as a large number of weights, while the comprehensibility is one of the very important requirements of reliable prediction systems of MHC binding peptides.

Thereupon, the RSEN algorithm based on RS theory is proposed to acquire the plain and understandable rules along with the improvements of prediction accuracy in this paper. The RSEN algorithm, which makes full use of the advantages of different attribute reducts, consists of three sub-algorithms. The sub-algorithm1 is used to produce candidates of base rule sets. Selecting base rule sets among candidates is the function of the sub-algorithm2. The sub-algorithm3 is for the decision fusion of base rule sets.

The experimental data set is composed of 650 peptides to bind or not bind to *HLA-DR4 (B1*0401)*, which is provided by Dr. Vladimir Brusic. For those pre-processed nonamers that bind or not bind to *HLA-DR4 (B1*0401)*, the conclusion as follows can be drawn through the analyses of the experimentation results: 1) the rule sets ensembles are much better than any individual rule set in the prediction accuracy. 2) Compared with the conventional BPNN, the rule sets ensembles not only show higher prediction accuracy, but also the knowledge embedded in the ensembles can be interpreted by human experts.

Acknowledgements

The authors gratefully acknowledge Dr. Vladimir Brusic for providing the data set used in this paper and Prof. Dr. Hans-Georg Rammensee for providing his paper. This work is supported in part by the Doctor Foundation of GDUT under Grant 063001 and the NSF of China under Grant 30230350.

References

1. Markus, S., Toni, W., Stefan, S.: Combining Computer Algorithms with Experimental Approaches Permits The Rapid and Accurate Identification of T Cell Epitopes from Defined Antigens. Journal of Immunological Methods. 257 (2001) 1–16
2. Hammer, J.: New Methods to Predict MHC-binding Sequences within Protein Antigens. Current Opinion Immunology. 7(1995) 263 –269
3. Rammensee, H., Bachmann, J., Emmerich, N.P., Bachor, O.A., Stevanovic, S.: SYFPEITHI: Database for MHC Ligands and Peptide Motifs. Immunogenetics. 50 (1999) 213–219
4. Raddrizzani, L., Sturniolo, T., Guenot, J., Bono, E., Galazzi, F., Nagy, Z.A., Sinigaglia, F., Hammer, J.: Different modes of peptide interaction enable HLA-DQ and HLA-DR molecules to bind diverse peptide repertoires. J. Immunol. 159 (1997) 703–711
5. Brusic, V., George, R., Margo, H., Jürgen, H., Leonard, H.: Prediction of MHC Class II-binding Peptides Using An Evolutionary Algorithm and Artificial Neural Network. Bioinformatics. 14 (1998) 121–130
6. Yu, K., Petrovsky, N., Schonbach, C., Koh, J.Y., Brusic, V.: Methods for Prediction of Peptide Binding to MHC Molecules: a Comparative Study. Mol. Med. 8 (2002) 137–48
7. Jun, Z., Herbert, R.T., George, B.R.: Prediction Sequences and Structures of MHC-binding Peptides: A Computational Combinatorial Approach. Journal of Compute-Aided Molecular Design. 15 (2001) 573–586

8. Andrews, R., Diederich, J., and Tickle, A.: Survey and Critique of Techniques for Extracting Rules from Trained Artificial Neural Networks". Knowledge Based System. 8 (1998) 373–389

9. Pawlak, Z.: Rough Sets. International Journal of Information and Computer Sciences. 11 (1982) 341–356

10. Wang, G.Y., Yu, H., and Yang, D.C.: Decision Table Reduction Based on Information Entorpy (in Chinese). Chinese Journal of Computers, 25 (2002) 759–766

11. Wang, J., Wang, J.: Reduction Algorithms Based on Discernibility Matrix: the Ordered Attributes Method. Journal of Computer Science and Technology, 16 (2001) 489–504

12. David, J.M., Lian, Y.: Critic-Driven Ensemble Classification. IEEE Transactions on Signal Processing. 47(1999) 2833–2844

13. Chicz, R.M., Urban, R.G., Lane, W.S., Gorga, J.C., Stern, L.J., Vignali, D.A., Strominger, J. L.: Predominant Naturally Processed Peptides Bound To HLA-DR1 Are Derived From MHC-related Molecules and Are Heterogeneous in Size. Nature. 358 (1992) 764

14. Madden, D.R.: The Three-dimensional Structure of Peptide-MHC Complexes. Annu Rev Immunol. 13 (1995) 587–622

15. Dan, P., Qi-Lun, Z., An. Z, Jing-Song, H.: A Novel Self-optimizing Approach for Knowledge Acquisition. IEEE Transactions on Systems, Man, And Cybernetics- Part A: Systems And Humans. 32 (2002) 505–514

16. Mak, B., Munakata, T.: Rule Extraction from Expert Heuristics: A Comparative Study of Rough Sets with Neural Networks and ID3. European Journal of Operational Research. 136 (2002) 212-229

Constructing Complete FP-Tree for Incremental Mining of Frequent Patterns in Dynamic Databases

Muhaimenul Adnan[1], Reda Alhajj[1,2], and Ken Barker[1]

[1] Department of Computer Science, University of Calgary, Calgary, AB, Canada
{adnanm, alhajj, barker}@cpsc.ucalgary.ca
[2] Department of Computer Science, Global University, Beirut Lebanon

Abstract. This paper proposes a novel approach that extends the FP-tree in two ways. First, the tree is maintained to include every attribute that occurs at least once in the database. This facilitates mining with different support values without constructing several FP-trees to satisfy the purpose. Second, the tree is manipulated in a unique way that reflects updates to the corresponding database by scanning only the updated portion, thereby reducing execution time in general. Test results on two datasets demonstrate the applicability, efficiency and effectiveness of the proposed approach.

1 Introduction

In general, most association rule mining models assume static input data and follow a fixed set of rules. They do not consider what the mining model should do when the database is updated. Database updates can however invalidate existing rules and might introduce new ones. Therefore, it is necessary for a mining model to consider the updated data. Most of the mining algorithms resolve this issue by rebuilding the whole mining model by scanning the entire old and new dataset. But this method is not feasible for applications where the database updates occur frequently or if the database evolves. It would have been very nice had there been a way to update the mining model to accommodate the new data without rebuilding the mining model from scratch. This is where the incremental mining algorithms play an important role. The target of these algorithms is to update the underlying mining model without scanning, or with minimal scanning of, the old data.

A formal definition of the association rule mining problem as given in [3, 14] can be stated as: Let $I = \{i_1, i_2, \ldots, i_m\}$ be a set of literals, called items. Let D be a set of transactions, where each transaction T is a set of items, such that $T \subseteq I$. Each transaction in D is given a unique identifier, denoted TID. A transaction T is said to contain itemset X if $X \subseteq T$. The support of an itemset X in D, denoted $\sigma_D(X)$, is the fraction of the total number of transactions in D that contain X. Let $\sigma (0 < \sigma < 1)$ be a constant called minimum support, mostly user-specified. An itemset X is said to be frequent on D if $\sigma_D(X) \geq \sigma$. The set of all frequent itemsets $L(D, \sigma)$ is defined formally as, $L(D, \sigma) = \{X : X \subset I, \sigma_D(X) \geq \sigma\}$. An Association rule is a correlation of the form "$X \Rightarrow Y$", where $X \subseteq I$, $Y \subseteq I$ and $X \cup Y = \phi$. The rule $X \Rightarrow Y$ has a support σ

M. Ali and R. Dapoigny (Eds.): IEA/AIE 2006, LNAI 4031, pp. 363–372, 2006.

in the transactional database D if $\sigma\%$ of the transaction in D contain $X \cup Y$. The rule $X \Rightarrow Y$ holds in the transactional dataset D with confidence c if $c\%$ of the transaction in D that contain X also contain Y. Given a set of transactions D, the problem of mining association rules is to generate all association rules that have support and confidence greater than the prespecified minimum support (σ) and minimum confidence (c), respectively. The association rule mining task can be broken into two steps: 1) identify all frequent k-itemsets from the database, where k is the cardinality of the itemset; and 2) generate rules from these large itemsets in a relatively straight forward manner.

For the problem of association rule mining, several incremental algorithms have been proposed, e.g., [6, 7, 8, 12, 16]. They can maintain mining models and can update the association rules if the database is updated without rebuilding the mining model for the whole updated database. But most of these incremental algorithms are level-wise in nature and depend on candidate generation and testing; hence require multiple database scans. On the other hand, *FP-growth* proposed by Han *et al* [15], is a novel approach that mines frequent patterns without explicitly re-generating the candidate itemsets. This approach uses a data structure called *FP-tree*, which is a compact representation of the original database. But, the problem with the FP-tree approach is that it is not incremental in nature.

In this paper, we present an incremental algorithm, which can update the FP-tree once the incremental database arrives without scanning the old transactional database. It actually uses a modified version of the FP-tree that keeps the information necessary and sufficient to minimize the number of database scans and to facilitate for mining with different threshold values without rebuilding the tree or keeping multiple FP-trees. Also, the proposed approach equally handles the addition of new transactions and the deletion of existing transactions without any need to rescan the old database.

The rest of the paper is organized as follows. Section 2 overviews the related work. Section 3 describes the handled problem. Section 4 presents the proposed algorithm. Section 5 reports test results. Section 6 is summary and conclusions.

2   Related Work

There are several incremental algorithms that update the association rules, and are basically *Apriori*-like (iterative) in nature. The FUP algorithm [6] is proposed for the maintenance of discovered association rules in large databases. The approaches described in [6, 7, 8] all belong to the same class of candidate generation and testing; they all require k scans to discover large itemsets with k as the length of the maximal large itemset. On the other hand, the work described in [16] proposes an incremental algorithm which requires at most one scan of the whole database to find the set of frequent patterns for the updated database. However, it was shown in the work described in [1] that the main bottleneck of the work described in [16] is that it has to generate negative border closure and the time required for that outweighs the time saving achieved by evading repeated database scans.

Most of the association rule mining processes differ in how the transaction subsets are projected. While *Apriori*-like algorithms do not materialize the projected transactions, other research efforts like Amir *et al* [2], Cheung *et al* [8] and Han *et al*

[15] rely on projecting the transactions or transactions subsets in one way or another. RARM [10] adopts a hybrid approach that combines the trie structure with the Apriori approach to generate the frequent patterns.

AFPIM [9] find new frequent itemsets with minimum recomputation when transactions are added to, deleted from, or modified in the transaction database. In AFPIM, the FP-tree structure of the original database is maintained in addition to the frequent itemsets. The authors claim that in most cases, without needing to re-scan the whole database, the FP-tree structure of the updated database is obtained by adjusting the preserved FP-tree according to the inserted and deleted transactions. The frequent itemsets of the updated database are mined from the new FP-tree structure. However, this claim is not supported by the approach as described in the paper. Actually, AFPIM is not a true incremental approach because it does not keep all the complete FP-tree, rather it is based on two values of support for constructing the FP-tree. It keeps in the tree only items with support larger than the minimum of the two kept support values, i.e., candidates to become frequent in the near future, this is not realistic and mostly requires full scan of the whole database almost every time it is updated.

3   Problem Statement

Assume at time t we have the transactional dataset D_t. Here, D_t is a set of transactions; each transaction is identified by a transaction identifier, denoted TID. Then, assume that at time $t+1$ the database is updated such that a set of transactions d_{t+1} is added to the database. So the resulting modified database *is*: $D_{t+1} = D_t \cup d_{t+1}$.

The incremental FP-tree construction algorithm can be defined as to find the FP-tree corresponding to the updated database D_{t+1} from the FP-tree which is valid for D_t by scanning only transactions in d_{t+1}.

Assume the FP-tree corresponding to the database D_t at time step t is represented as T_{D_t}. Our target is to construct the new FP-tree $T_{D_{t+1}}$ that corresponds to the updated database D_{t+1} at time step $t+1$. Moreover, we want to construct this updated FP-tree $T_{D_{t+1}}$ from the FP-tree T_{D_t} of the previous time step without scanning the old transactions of D_t and by scanning only transactions of d_{t+1}. Our proposal that makes this update possible is described next in Section 4.

We propose an algorithm for constructing the FP-tree incrementally. This algorithm updates the FP-tree for a certain time stamp t, by considering only the transactions of the next time stamp $t+1$, without scanning the old transactional database. Thereby, the proposed approach saves substantial amount of processor time.

When we add new transactions to the initial transaction set, some items that were previously infrequent may become frequent in the updated transaction set, and some items that were previously frequent may become infrequent in the updated transaction set. As we do not know which items are going to be frequent and which items are going to be infrequent, to be able to construct the FP-tree incrementally, we have to start with a complete FP-tree having absolute support threshold of 1, i.e., we have to preserve the complete history of the data in the FP-tree. So, for our algorithm to work, we always keep a complete FP-tree corresponding to the transactions that are valid at the current time. With this approach, we have the additional advantage that we do not need to build new FP-trees once we decide to mine frequent patterns for different support thresholds.

4 Incremental Construction of the FP-Tree

The proposed approach starts working from the initial FP-tree constructed at time t. When a new set of transactions d_{t+1} arrive at time $t+1$, the proposed algorithm first scans the incremental database d_{t+1} to collect the frequency of items in the incremental database d_{t+1}. Then, we combine the frequency of items both in the initial database D_t and the incremental database d_{t+1} to get the cumulative frequency list of the updated database D_{t+1}. After that we sort the items according to their cumulative frequency in descending ordering to get what we call the frequency list, denoted F_{t+1}-List. We then compare the old F_t-List and the new F_{t+1}-List, to find out which of the items changed their relative order in the sorted frequency ordering. We store these items in a separate list, called the S-List (shuffle list). So in essence, the S-List contains the set of items for which we need to change the order of the nodes in the FP-tree; because in the FP-tree the ordering of this set of items must be changed to reflect the addition of new transactions.

Before describing the proposed approach, we present a set of formal definitions of the basic terminology required for understanding the algorithm.

$Freq_t(a_{t,i})$: is defined as the fraction of transactions of the database state D_t at time t in which $a_{t,i}$ appears as an item.

F_t-List: represents the frequency list at time t; it contains the list of items sorted according to the frequency in descending ordering of items that appear in the transactions at time t. It is defined as the list $[a_{t,1}, a_{t,2}, ..., a_{t,n}]$, where n is the number of items in the database D_t, $a_{t,i}$ corresponds to an item in the database and $Freq_t(a_{t,i}) \geq Freq_t(a_{t,j})$ for $1 \leq i < j \leq n$.

$Pos_t(a_{t,i})$: is defined as the ordinal position of item $a_{t,i}$ in the frequency list F_t-List at time t.

S-List: The S-List is constructed from the F_{t+1}-List as follows:

1.   Take the first item, $a_{t+1,1}$ from the F_{t+1}-List.
2.   Insert item, $a_{t+1,1}$ into the S-List if $Pos_{t+1}(a_{t+1,1}) < Pos_t(a_{t,i})$, where there is an item $a_{t,i}$ in the F_t-List and $a_{t+1,1} = a_{t,i}$ for $1 \leq i \leq n$.
3.   Remove items $a_{t+1,1}$ and $a_{t,i}$ from the F_{t+1}-List, while maintaining the ordering of items.
4.   If there are more items in the F_{t+1}-List, go back to step 1.

Algorithm: *Incremental Update*

Input: FP-tree T_{D_t} at time t, and incremental transactions d_{t+1}.

Output: FP-tree $T_{D_{t+1}}$ at time $t+1$ for the updated database D_{t+1}.

Method: The FP-tree is updated by applying the following steps:

1.   Scan the incremental database d_{t+1} once to collect the frequencies of items.
2.   Combine the frequencies of the items in d_{t+1} and in D_t to get the cumulative frequency of the items in the updated database D_{t+1}.

3. Sort the items according to the cumulative frequency in descending ordering to get the F_{t+1}-List.
4. Compare the two lists: F_t-List and F_{t+1}-List. Identify items that have changed their order. These items constitute the S-List.
5. $T_{D_{t+1}} = shuffleTree(T_{D_t}, S\text{-List});$
6. $T_{D_{t+1}} = insertTree(T_{D_{t+1}}, d_{t+1});$
7. **Return** $T_{D_{t+1}}$

The Incremental Update algorithm has two important components – *shuffleTree* and *insertTree*. The former shuffles/rearranges the nodes of the initial FP-tree T_{D_t} to get a new FP-tree $T_{D_{t+1}}$, with the alteration of the ordering of nodes in the tree paths. Hence, the ordering of the items in the transactions now corresponds to the ordering of the cumulative frequency of items. Once we change the ordering of the nodes to get the modified FP-tree $T_{D_{t+1}}$, we can safely add the incremental transactions to this tree to get the desired FP-tree $T_{D_{t+1}}$.

Function: *ShuffleTree*

Input: FP-tree T_{D_t} at time t and ordered S-List.

Output: FP-tree $T_{D_{t+1}}$ in which nodes are ordered according to the cumulative frequencies of items

Method:

For each item in the S-List starting from the highest frequent item **do**

    Pull the node corresponding to the item to its *maximum attainable frequency peak* in the FP-tree T_{D_t} ;

    If two children of the same node correspond to a single item

  Then Recursively *Merge* the nodes that correspond to the same item and have the same parent.

  End If

End For

Function: *InsertTree*

Input: FP-tree $T_{D_{t+1}}$ and the incremental database d_{t+1}.

Output: Modified FP-tree $T_{D_{t+1}}$

Method:

For each transaction *Tran* in the database d_{t+1} **do**

    Sort the items in *Tran* according to the cumulative frequency in descending order.

    Add *Tran* to the tree $T_{D_{t+1}}$ while maintaining the prefix path property.

End For

The proposed incremental update algorithm calls two functions, namely *shuffleTree* and *insertTree*. The function *shuffleTree* rearranges nodes of the FP-tree T_{D_t} to get a new FP-tree $T_{D_{t+1}}$ in which the ordering of the nodes in the projected transactions represents the cumulative frequency in descending order of items.

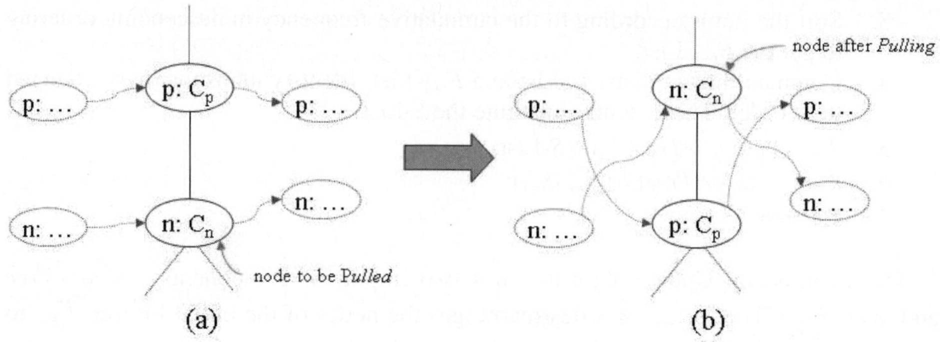

Fig. 1. Case-I ($C_n = C_p$)

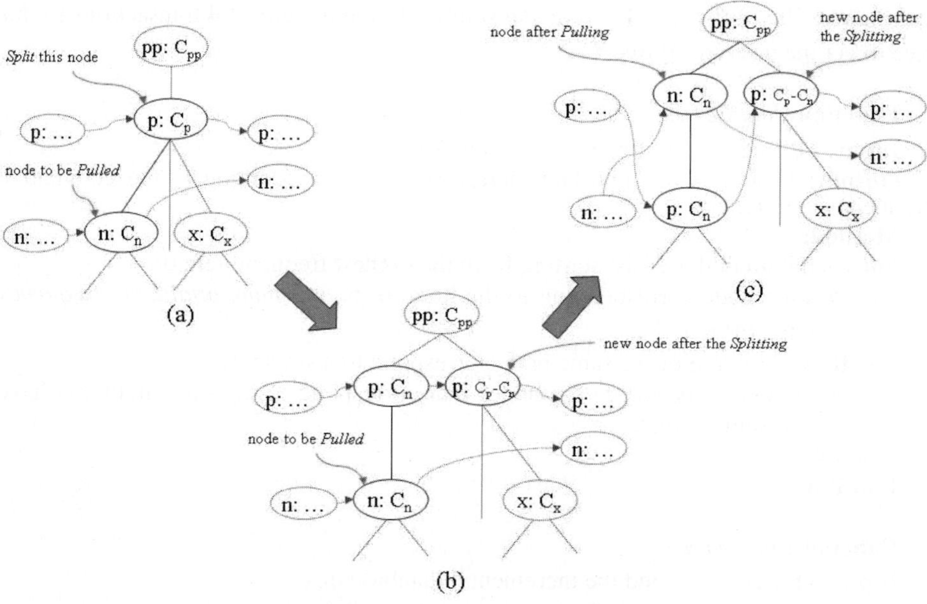

Fig. 2. Case-II ($C_n < C_p$)

We need to *pull* each node in the *S*-List to its *maximum attainable frequency peak* in the FP-tree. By *maximum attainable frequency peak* we mean the position in the FP-tree for which node frequency is higher than any node of the sub-trees below the peak. We start from the maximum frequent node in the *S*-List and pull subsequent frequent nodes in the *S*-List one by one. Depending on *item-count* C_n of the node to be *Pulled* and *item-count* C_p of its parent, there can be two situations to consider.

Case-I: $C_n = C_p$: In this case, the *item-count* of the node to be *pulled* is the same as the *item-count* of its parent. So we can safely assume that the parent has no other children other than the node to be *pulled*. Figure 1 shows an example of this case, and how the node is *pulled* in such situation. In this case, we can just swap the two nodes in question by swapping their *item-name*, *item-count* and *node-link* pointers.

Case-II: $C_n < C_p$**:** In this case, the *item-count* of the parent node is greater than the *item-count* of the node to be pulled. So, there is a strong possibility that either the node to be *pulled* has more that one sibling or the parent node was the last item for some transaction. In both cases, the *pulling* process starts by first *splitting* the parent node into two nodes. After the *split*, case-II reduces to case-I and the two nodes can be easily swapped to *pull* the desired node upwards.

The *Split* Operation: *Splitting* is done by creating one new node which corresponds to the same item as the parent node. We make this node as a sibling of the parent. We then adjust the *item-count* for the parent as C_n (the same count as for the node to be *pulled*) and make the *item-count* for the new node as C_p-C_n. Now we have to adjust the children of the parent node and the new node in question. This can be done by making all the siblings of the node to be *pulled* as children of the new node. This way, the parent node will contain only one child which is the node to be *pulled*. This successfully reduces case-II to a situation similar to case-I. Figure 2 shows one example of case-II and steps of the *pulling* operation.

We continue *pulling* recursively as long as the item frequency of the node to be pulled is greater than the item frequency of its parent. This condition is broken when we reach the *maximum attainable frequency peak corresponding* to the node and the node does not need to be pulled any farther; this is in fact the stopping criterion of the *pulling* operation.

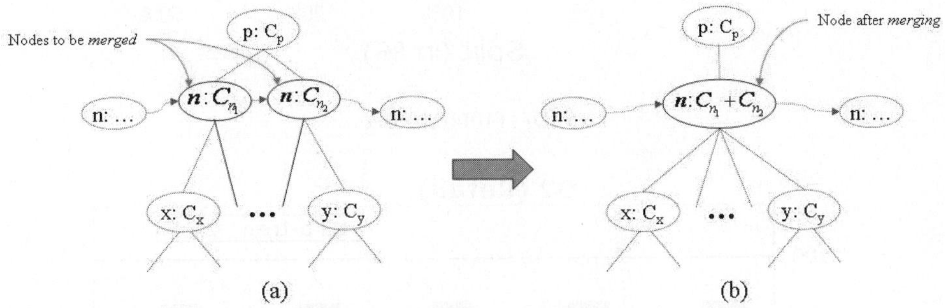

Fig. 3. *Merge* Operation

Once we have *pulled* the node to its *maximum attainable frequency peak* and because of the shuffling of nodes, there can be situations where the parent of the *pulled* node has two child nodes that correspond to the same item. In this case, we have to *merge* the two nodes to remain consistent with the definition of the FP-tree. We have to carry out this *merging* operation recursively, as there can be situations where two children of the *merged* node correspond to the same item. After the final *Merging* operation, we get a tree where the ordering of nodes corresponds to the cumulative frequency of items in descending order. The merge operation is demonstrated in Figure 3.

5 Experimental Results

In this section, we describe the performance of the proposed incremental update approach on real and synthetic datasets. The algorithm has been implemented in java

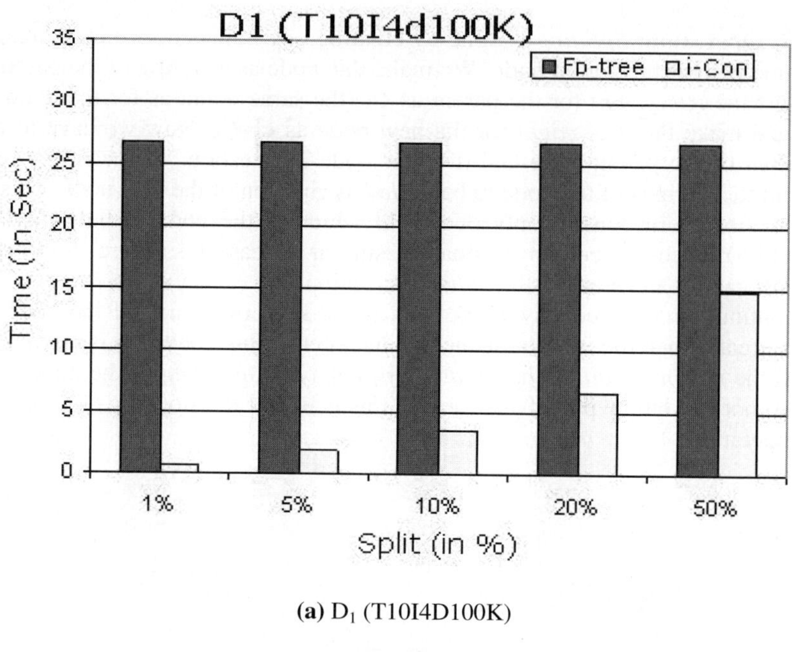

(a) D_1 (T10I4D100K)

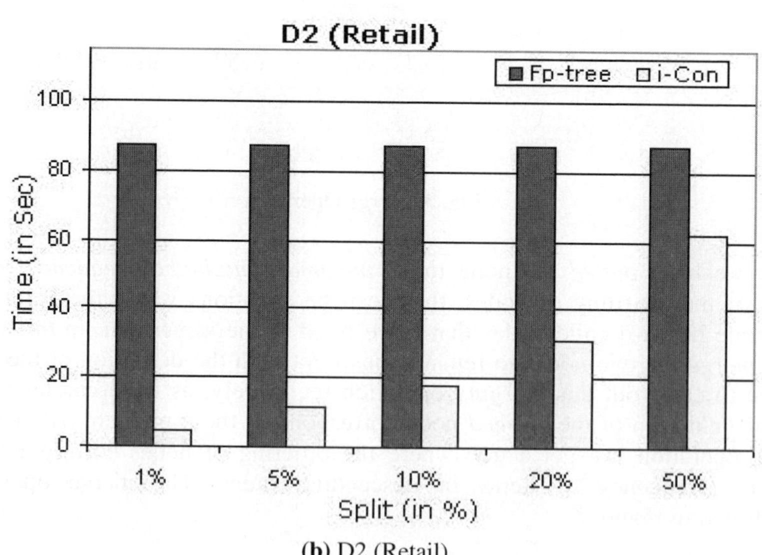

(b) D2 (Retail)

Fig. 4. Scalability with various sizes of incremental databases

and all the experiments have been conducted on an IBM Pentium IV machine with 2.0GHz CPU and 512MB main memory; running Windows-XP. The two datasets used in the experiments are: D_1 (T10I4D100K), which is synthetic with 1000 items and 100K transactions; and D_2 (Retail), which is real with 16,469 items and 88,162 transactions. The dataset D_1 (T10I4D100K) has been taken from the FIM dataset repository [13]. Dataset D_2 contains real data from some anonymous retail store and was donated by Tom Brijs [5]. It has been found that the proposed algorithm performs very well for each of these datasets.

We have tested the performance of the proposed approach against constructing the FP-tree from scratch for each of the two datasets, while varying the size of the incremental dataset. To construct the incremental dataset we have randomly chosen $x\%$ of the dataset to split the dataset into two parts. The part with $x\%$ of the transactions forms the incremental dataset, and the remaining part with $(100\text{-}x)\%$ of the transactions form the initial dataset for which the initial FP-tree is built. This initial FP-tree and the incremental dataset form the input to the proposed approach. In essence, we are measuring the time required to add $x\%$ of the transactions to the FP-tree representing $(100\text{-}x)\%$ of the transactions. In Figure 4, we present the time comparison of *the proposed approach* against constructing the FP-tree from scratch for the three datasets and for five different splits namely 1%, 5%, 10%, 20% and 50%. For each of these datasets, we have found that by adopting the incremental approach, we can save a substantial amount of time by not constructing the FP-tree from scratch whenever a database update occurs. Even when the split size is 50% of the original database, adopting incremental approach is considerably better that constructing the FP-tree from scratch.

6 Summary and Conclusions

In this paper, we described an incremental algorithm that can update the FP-tree incrementally without scanning the old dataset and with a minimal scanning (two scans) of the incremental database. Experimental results show that our approach performs considerably better compared to building the tree from scratch, and thereby achieves a huge amount of time saving. Following our approach, we can also mine for frequent patterns for any support threshold. For that we do not need to build FP-trees with different support thresholds. Our approach works for both addition and deletion of transactions. Currently, we are investigating whether it might be possible to keep part of the FP-tree disk resident and thereby minimize primary memory requirements and hence to be able to develop scalable approach.

References

1. M. Adnan and R. Alhajj and K. Barker, "Performance Analysis of Incremental Update of Association Rules Mining Approaches" *Proceedings IEEE INES*, Greece, Sep. 2005.
2. Amir, R. Feldman, and R. Kashi, "A New and Versatile Method for Association Generation," *Information Systems*, vol. 22, no. 6, pp.333-347, 1999.

3. R. Agrawal, T. Imielinski, and A. Swami, "Mining Association Rules between Sets of Items in Large Databases," *Proceedings of ACM-SIGMOD*, Washington D.C., pp.207-216, May 1993.

4. R. Agrawal and R. Srikant, "Fast Algorithms for Mining Association Rules," *Proceedings of VLDB*, pp.487-499, Sept. 1994.

5. T. Brijs, G. Swinnen , K. Vanhoof , and G. Wets, "The Use of Association Rules for Product Assortment Decisions: A Case Study," *Proceedings of ACM-KDD*, San Diego, pp.254-260, 1999.

6. D.W. Cheung, J. Han, V.T. Ng, C.Y. Wong, "Maintenance of Discovered Association Rules in Large Databases: An Incremental Updating Technique," *Proceedings of IEEE-ICDE*, pp.106-114, 1996.

7. D.W. Cheung, V.T. Ng, B.W. Tam, "Maintenance of Discovered Knowledge: A case in Multi-level Association Rules," *Proceedings of ACM-KDD*, pp.307-310, 1996.

8. D.W. Cheung, S.D. Lee, B. Kao, "A general Incremental Technique for Mining Discovered Association Rules," *Proceedings of DASFAA*, pp.185-194, 1997.

9. J.-L. Koh and S.-F. Shieh, An Efficient Approach for Maintaining Association Rules Based on Adjusting FP-Tree Structures, *Proceedings of DASFAA*, Korea, March 2004.

10. Das, W.K. Ng, and Y.K. Woon, "Rapid Association Rule Mining," *Proceedings of ACM-CIKM*, pp.474-481, 2001.

11. N.F. Ayan, A.U. Tansel, and E. Arkun, "An Efficient Algorithm to Update Large Itemsets with Early Pruning," *Proceedings of ACM SIGKDD*, 1999..

12. R. Feldman, Y. Aumann, A. Amir, and H. Mannila, "Efficient Algorithms for Discovering Frequent Sets in Incremental Databases," *Proceedings of the International Workshop Research Issues on Data Mining and Knowledge Discovery*, 1997.

13. http://fimi.cs.helsinki.fi/data/

14. V. Ganti, J. E. Gehrke, and R. Ramakrishnan, "DEMON: Mining and Monitoring Evolving Data," *IEEE TKDE*, Vol. 13, No.1, pp.50-63, 2001.

15. J. Han, J. Pei, and Y. Yin, "Mining Frequent Patterns without Candidate Generation," *Proc. of ACM-SIGMOD*, pp.1-12, Dallas, TX, May 2000.

16. S. Thomas, S. Bodagala, K. Alsabti, and S. Ranka, "An Efficient Algorithm for the Incremental Updation of Association Rules in Large Databases," *Proceedings of ACM-SIGKDD*, pp.263-266, 1997.

An Optimal Method for Multiple Observers Sitting on Terrain Based on Improved Simulated Annealing Techniques

Pin Lv, Jin-fang Zhang, and Min Lu

National Key Laboratory of Integrated Information System Technology,
Institute of Software, Chinese Academy of Sciences,
Beijing, 10080, China
{lvpin04, jinfang, lumin03}@ios.cn

Abstract. The problem of multiple observers sitting on terrain (MOST) is an important part in visibility-based terrain reasoning (VBTR), but it is difficult because of the unacceptable computing time. Recent developments in this field focus on involving spatial optimization techniques, such as a heuristic algorithm. In this paper, a new method is developed based on the Improved Simulated Annealing (ISA) algorithm through the analysis of different terrain characters. A new annealing function and a new state function are designed to make the improved algorithm fit the problem better. Experiment results show that without loss of precision, use of the ISA algorithm reduces time cost 50%~70% when compared with the traditional SA.

1 Introduction

Consider a given terrain, with an observer O at a certain height H. Define the viewshed as the specific terrain visible from O that lies within O's Region Of Interest (ROI), of radius R. The Multiple Observers Sitting on Terrain (MOST) problem consists of finding the fewest possible observers to make the united-viewshed of those observers cover a certain ratio area, given the kind of the observer (person, radar, etc.) and the characteristic of the observer (height, the radius of viewshed, etc.). The MOST problem has many applications, such as locating a telecommunication base station [2, 4, 8], protecting endangered species [3, 6], and locating wind turbines [15].

The current solving method for the MOST problem is to use a greedy algorithm, which compares all possible observer sets, in order to find the best one. The biggest disadvantage of this method is the fact that the computing cost rises exponentially with the increasing complexity of the problem, overrunning the computing capability of the existing computer. In order to solve this problem, W. Franklin et al. provided a toolkit which is based on the visibility-indexes of small cells and the swap algorithm [10, 11]; Rana [19] developed a method which only considers significant features of the terrain such as peaks or ridges; and Y.H. Kim [13] also provided a method based on the terrain features and heuristic algorithms such as a simulated annealing algorithm, a genetic algorithm and a swap algorithm. Y.H. Kim has also claimed that the traditional SA algorithm is the best one among all tested algorithms when considering the balance between time cost and accuracy [14].

M. Ali and R. Dapoigny (Eds.): IEA/AIE 2006, LNAI 4031, pp. 373–382, 2006.

In this paper, an optimal method that is based on an Improved Simulated Annealing (ISA) algorithm is developed. Experiment results show that without loss of precision, use of the ISA algorithm reduces time cost 50%~70% when compared with the traditional SA.

2 Modeling and Time Complexity Analysis

Suppose that the real terrain T is in an XYZ coordinate space. DEM is defined by a set of points $p \equiv (x_p, y_p, z_p)$ where (x_p, y_p) is the coordinate of one point in the X-Y plane, and z_p is the corresponding elevation of (x_p, y_p). Two points p_1 and p_2 are mutually visible (inter-visible) if every point $q \equiv (x, y, z) = p_1 + t(p_2 - p_1)$, $0 < t < 1$, lies above the corresponding point p_q of the terrain, i.e. $z > z_q$ [7, 9].

Suppose on the terrain which has n points, the number of the observers in an observer set be s. Then define the arbitrary observer set O_k which satisfies the condition above as:

$$O_k = \{o_{k,i} \mid o_{k,i} \in T, i = 1, 2, \cdots, s\} \tag{1}$$

Define the observer set's united viewshed as:

$$V(O_k) = \bigcup_{i=1}^{s} v(o_{k,i}) \tag{2}$$

where the $v(o_{k,i})$ is the view-shed of the observer o_i in the observer set O_k. The definition of MOST problems is

$$O_{opt} = \{O_k \mid MAX(V(O_k)), k = 1, 2, \cdots, C_n^s\} \tag{3}$$

where $MAX(V(O_k))$ is to get the maximum value of the united-viewshed of O_k.

To analyze the time complexity of MOST problems, suppose each observer's radius of viewshed R be n points and use a greedy algorithm. There are two main steps:

A : Compute the viewshed of each point on the terrain using the method described above. The time complexity is $O(n^2)$, according to [5].

B : Select all possible combinations of s observers from the n points, and for each combination, calculate the united-viewshed. The number of selections is

$$C_n^s = \frac{n!}{s!(n-s)!}$$

When n is very large and $n >> s$, this approximates to n^s. Caculating the united-viewshed is $O(n)$ for one combination. So the total time complexity is $n^s * O(n)$, which approximates to $O(n^{s+1})$. Because usually the $s >= 2$ commonly, $O(n^{s+1})$ is by far the larger of the two terms, the overall time complexity is $O(n^{s+1})$.

From analyses above, we can find that the time complexity of MOST problems is rising exponentially with the increase of the terrain area and the number of observers. With a problem of even moderate size, this suggests that the method based on a greedy algorithm will never be computationally tractable. Therefore, a new optimal method must be developed to find a solution of MOST which is both accurate and computationally feasible.

3 An Optimal Method for MOST

From the discussions above, it is clear to see that the key point of the solution for MOST is efficient comparison and selection of the multiple observers set.

Unfortunately, the selection of the best observer set from all possible ones is unfeasible. However, the MOST problem also can be treated as an optimal problem under some certain boundary conditions. Analogues to the solution of other optimal problems, using heuristic algorithms can make the solution feasible and get a nearly best observer set. Two typical heuristic algorithms, Simulated Annealing algorithm (SA) and Genetic Algorithm (GA), have been applied and the former one has been proven to be more suitable for MOST problems [14].

3.1 Principles of Simulated Annealing

Kirkpatrick et al. [16] introduced the conception of annealing in combinatorial optimization. This conception is based on a strong analogy between combinatorial optimization and the physical process of crystallization. This process has inspired Metropolis et al. [18] to propose a numerical optimization procedure known as Metropolis algorithm, which works as follows.

Starting from an initial situation whose 'energy level' is $f(0)$, a small perturbation of the state is made in the system. This brings the system into a new state with energy level $f(1)$. If $f(1)$ is smaller than $f(0)$, then the state change is accepted. Otherwise, if $f(1)$ is greater than $f(0)$, then the change is accepted with a certain probability. The probability of acceptance is given by the Metropolis criterion [1]:

$$P(accept\quad change) = \exp(\frac{f(0) - f(1)}{t_k})$$
(4)

where t_k is a control or freezing parameter. The Simulated Annealing process is ended when the temperature has become a small value [12].

A crucial element of the procedure is the gradual decrease of the freezing parameter t_k. Usually, this is done using a constant multiplication factor:

$$t_k = t_0 \bullet \lambda^k$$
(5)

where $0 < \lambda < 1$, k are the annealing iteration times in temperature stage decreasing, and t_0 is the initial temperature stage of the system. This effectively means that jumping to higher energy becomes less and less likely towards the end of the iteration procedure [18].

In the application of MOST, the energy level $f(\cdot)$ is a cost function which correlates with a state at a certain temperature stage. The initial temperature stage t_0, is obtained from the equation

$$t_0 = -|\Delta_{max}| / \ln p_r \tag{6}$$

where $|\Delta max|$ is the maximum difference of cost corresponding with a group of randomly selected states, and p_r is the initial accept probability, which is usually 0.5. The total number of iterations L per temperature stage is chosen by keeping the temperature stage constant until the cost function has reached a constant value or until it is oscillating around this constant value [20]. The annealing iteration times k are chosen by setting the final temperature stage to a minimal constant value.

3.2 Optimal Method Based on Improved SA

In this study, we developed an optimal method based on Improved Simulated Annealing (ISA) algorithm which consists of three steps as follows.

Step 1: According to the desired number of the observers s, partition the terrain into k average-sized smaller blocks and make each block contain s/k observers. The distribution of observers should be fairly uniform across the terrain.

Step 2: Pick s/k observers randomly and independently in each block. Compute each observer's viewshed and the united-viewshed coverage ratio of the observer set after the individual viewsheds have been combined.

Step 3: Let the result of Step 2 be the initial state, and apply the ISA to get the approximately best observer set. In our optimal method, we select 50 observer sets randomly, and get the original temperature stage of SA algorithm described in 3.1.

Table 1. The statistical information of six samples

	Min	Max	Diff	Mean	SD
Sample 1	693. 1	754. 2	61.1	712. 2	84. 28
Sample 2	939. 3	2531. 5	1592.2	1731. 2	250. 34
Sample 3	1197. 6	2452. 1	1254.5	1636. 8	470. 6
Sample 4	250. 0	461. 3	211.3	364. 4	1272. 6
Sample 5	2153. 5	2570. 1	416.6	2372. 7	2030. 2
Sample 6	930. 4	2481. 7	1551.3	2023. 6	3677. 1

3.3 The Improved Simulated Annealing Algorithm for MOST

For the MOST problem, we have done two analyses: The first analysis is the relationship between the distance separating two observers and the average increase of united-viewshed for these two observers compared to one observer. The second analysis is the relationship between the distance separating two observers and the ratio of the increased view-shed coverage for two observers, compared to one observer. In our analysis and in the following experiments, we assume that the observer height is H=1.6m, which is equal to the height of people's eyes.

3.3.1 The Improved New State Function

In order to get the relationships between the distance separating two observers and the average united-viewshed increase compared to one observer, three steps are included.

1. Select the first observer on the terrain randomly, and compute its viewshed.
2. Select the second observer randomly and let the new observer lie within the first one's neighbor domain whose radius is R. In our analysis, the R is average to 250 sample points (500 m). Compute the united-viewshed of the two observers, and then calculate the difference between the united viewshed and the viewshed of the single observer, as found in step 1. We refer to this resulting term as the "united-viewshed increase".
3. Repeat steps 1 and 2 50,000 times. Finally, get the relationships between the distances separating the two observers and their average united-viewshed increase compared to one observer's viewshed.

Repeat steps1 through 3 for six terrain samples, and get the result (See in Figure 1). The value given to the united-viewshed is the ratio between the number of the visible points in the united-viewshed and the total number of the points on the terrain.

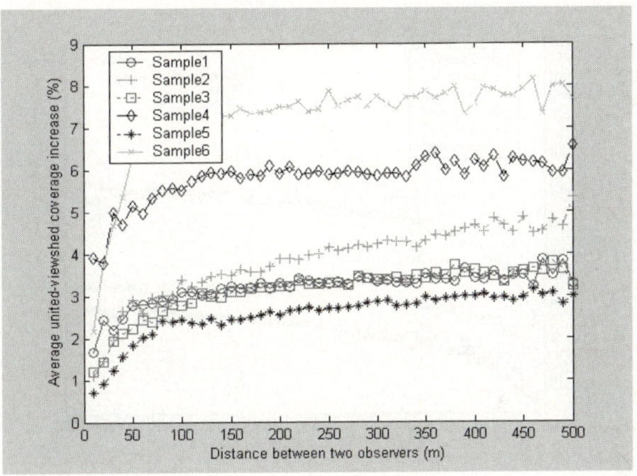

Fig. 1. The relationships between the distance separating two observers and their average united-viewshed increase compared to one observer's viewshed

The Figure 1 shows that the relationship curve between the distance separating two observers and their average united-viewshed increase compared to one observer's viewshed on different terrains is similar. That is, the united-viewshed increases with the distance between two observers. The rate of increase becomes slower and slower.

From the analysis above, we can see that if the observers are near, the average united-viewshed coverage of observer set decreases substantially. Therefore, the re-design of a new state function of SA algorithm should not only consider the average united-viewshed coverage ratio of new observer set but also consider the distance between observers. Accordingly, the new state function of new observer set O_k in an improved SA algorithm $\varphi(o_k)$ contains two parts:

$$\varphi(o_k) = f(o_k) + g(o_k), k = 1,2 \cdots n \tag{7}$$

where $f(o_k) = \dfrac{1}{\bigcup\limits_{k=1,2,\cdots n} v(o_k)}$, and $v(o_k)$ is the viewshed of observer k. $g(o_k)$ is a punish function. The degrees of punish increase as the average distance between observers decreases. Therefore, if the average distance is small, the new observer set solution cannot be accepted, and it prevents the occurrence of 'the assembling of the observers'.

3.3.2 The Improved Annealing Function

In order to show the relationship between the distance separating two observers and the variance ratio about the viewshed coverage of two observers compared to one, we compute the increase ratio at a certain distance based on the result in 3.3.1. The result is seen in Figure 2. The variance ratio is valued as the standard deviation (SD) of the united-viewshed increase.

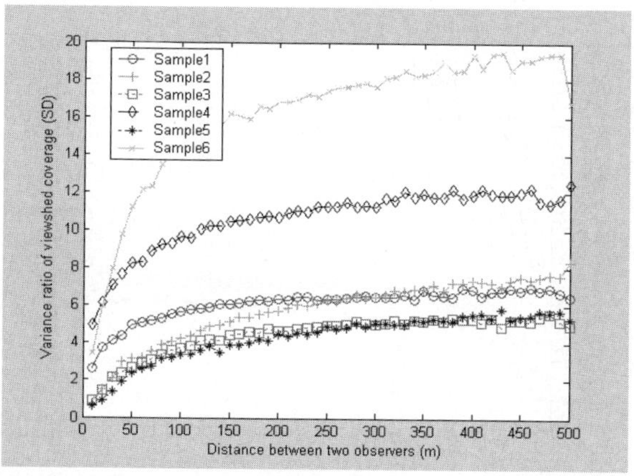

Fig. 2. The relationships between the distance separating two observers and the variance ratio about the viewshed coverage of two observers compared to one

Figure 2 shows that the variance of the united-viewshed mentioned in 3.3.1 increases with the distance between two observers, but the rate of increase slows. It is desirable to increase the annealing iteration times at a high temperature stage in order to help find the global optimal observer set, and to decrease the annealing iteration times at a low temperature stage for time cost savings. Therefore, it is necessary to redesign the annealing function to make it fit the MOST problem better.

Consider the annealing function of the traditional SA algorithm t_k [17], where t_0 is the original temperature stage, λ is the annealing factor, and k is the annealing iteration times. In order to increase the annealing iteration times at a high temperature and decrease the annealing iteration times at a low temperature, we introduce a temperature control function which can accommodate the origin annealing function in the traditional SA algorithm, and get the new annealing function t'_k , that is:

$$t'_k = \begin{cases} c \cdot (t_k^{\alpha})^{1/\gamma} & t_k <= 0.5 \\ \left[1 - c \cdot (1-t_k)^{\alpha}\right]^{1/\gamma} & t_k > 0.5 \end{cases} \tag{8}$$

where $c = \dfrac{1}{2} \cdot (0.5)^{\alpha}$.

Suppose that $\alpha/\gamma = \beta$, it can be proved that

$$\lim_{\gamma \to \infty} \{k_{max} \mid t_{k_{max}} = t_0\} = \log \frac{1/2^{\beta}}{\lambda^{\beta}} \tag{9}$$

where K_{max} is the maximum step that the annealing temperature stage can keep the same as the initial temperature stage t_0.

In order to control the annealing process, we introduce three boundary conditions:

1. Suppose in the traditional SA algorithm, when annealing temperature stage decreases to 70% of the original temperature stage, the annealing iteration times are k_1. Then in the improved SA, the annealing iteration times of achieving the same instance are $2 \cdot k_1$.
2. Suppose in the traditional SA algorithm, when annealing temperature stage decreases to 10% of the original temperature stage, the annealing iteration times are k_2. Then in the improved SA, the annealing iteration times of achieving the same instance are $k_2/2$.

According to the two conditions above, we can get $\alpha/\gamma \approx 3.98$ and k_{max} under different λ (see Table 2).

Table 2. The Max Annealing iteration times k_{max} Under Different λ

λ	0.5	0.6	0.7	0.8	0.9
k_{max}	1	1.35	1.9	3.1	6.6

3. Suppose in the improved SA algorithm, when annealing temperature stage decreases to 80% of the original temperature stage, the annealing iteration times is k_{max}.

According to the three conditions above, we can get the α and γ under different λ (see Table 3).

Table 3. Parameter α and γ Under Different λ

λ	0.5	0.6	0.7	0.8	0.9
α	11.43	10.81	9.09	11.43	12.06
γ	2.86	2.70	2.27	2.86	3.03

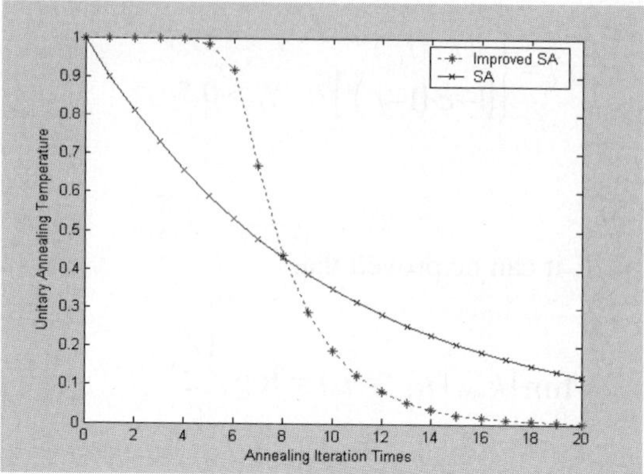

Fig. 3. The annealing function comparing traditional SA and improved SA of $\lambda = 0.9$

In Figure 3, it is clear to see that the annealing iteration times of improved SA is much longer than the traditional SA in high temperature stages: 6 times, compared to 1 time when the temperature decreases to 90% of the original temperature stage. In contrast, the instance in low temperature stage is opposite: 11 times, compared to 21 times when the temperature decreases to 10% of the initial temperature stage.

3.4 Experiment Result

We use our optimal method to solve the MOST problem for six representative terrains (described in 3.2) in two experiments. Each experiment is repeated 10 times for each terrain. The traditional SA algorithm is used in Step 3 of the optimal method in the first experiment; the Improved SA (ISA) algorithm is used in the second experiment. The two algorithms stop when the temperature decreases to 10% of the original temperature stage. All the experiments are done by using a 2.4 GHz Pentium PC and 1 Gbytes RAM to get the comparison of united-viewshed coverage and time cost between using SA and ISA. The experiment results are presented below:

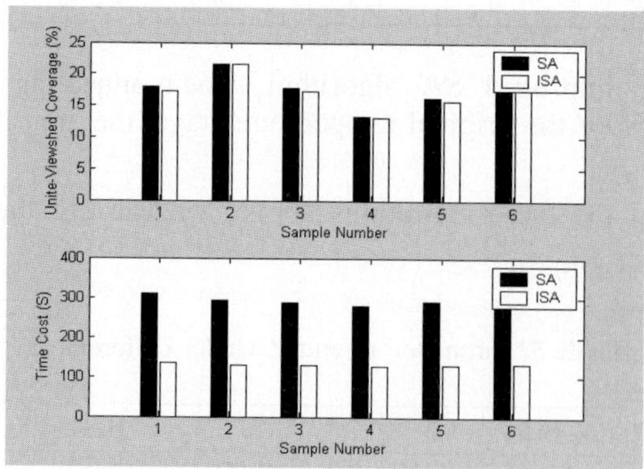

Fig. 4. 4 blocks ,1 observer per block, R=256 sample points, $\lambda = 0.9$, H=1.6m

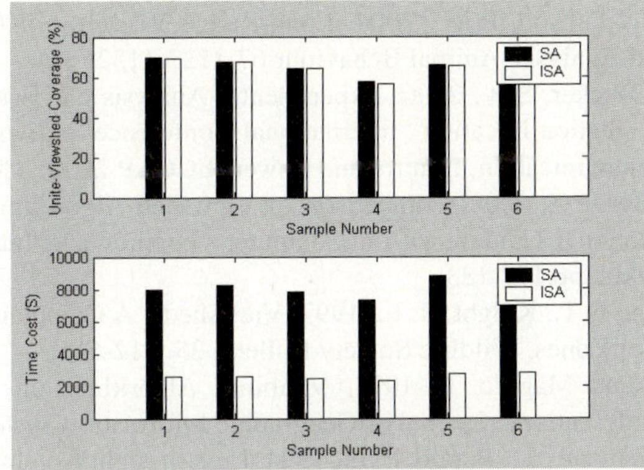

Fig. 5. 16 blocks , 8 observers per block, R=128 sample points, λ =0.9, H=1.6m

The ISA provides great time cost savings compared to the SA because when the annealing temperature decreases to 10% of the original temperature stage, the ISA uses only 11 iterations, while the SA uses 21. While the time cost savings of the ISA is great, the loss of accuracy is prevented by the greater number of annealing iterations at a high temperature (6, compared to 1), and the new state function. Figure 4 and figure 5 clearly show that without loss of precision, use of the ISA algorithm reduces time cost 50%~70% when compared with the traditional SA. The time cost savings become great as the number of observers increases.

4   Conclusions and Future

In visibility-based terrain reasoning, using a heuristic algorithm is an efficient method to solve the multiple observers sitting on terrain problem. However, if we use a general heuristic algorithm without any modification, it usually cannot get the best effect of the balance between precision and efficiency. Therefore, in this paper, an optimal method based on an Improved Simulated Annealing algorithm is developed after a problem-related analysis of six representative terrain samples. This improved algorithm reduces the time redundancy of the traditional SA algorithm.

Using the improved SA algorithm, it is hard to solve the MOST problem in a large terrain area with more observers and high precision in real time. More study is needed on the application of a multi-scale SA algorithm in multi-precision terrain data to solve MOST problems on large terrain. This method has great potential for the solution of MOST in real time.

References

1. Aarts, E.H.L. and Korst, J.H.M., 1989. Simulated annealing and Boltzmann machines, John Wiley and Sons,284 pp.
2. Anderson, H.R. and McGeehan, J.P., 1994. "Optimizing Microcell Base Station. Locations Using Simulated Annearing Techniques," in Proc. IEEE VTC. vol. 2. pp.858–862.

3. Aspbury, A.S. and Gibson, R.M., 2004. Long-Range Visibility of Greater Sage Grouse Leks: a GIS-based Analysis. Animal Behaviour 67:1127-1132.

4. Bhaskar, K. and Wicker, S.B., 2000. Experimental Analysis of Local Search Algorithms for Optimal Base Station Location. International Conference on Evolutionary Computing for Computer, Communication, Control and Power (ECCAP 2000), Chennai, India.

5. Branko, K. and Borut, Z. 2002. Comparison of Viewshed Algorithms on Regular Spaced Points. In: International Conference on Computer Graphics and Interactive Techniques, Budmerice, Slovakia. pp.177-183.

6. Camp, R.J., Sinton, D.T., Knight, R. L., 1997, Viewsheds: A Complementary Management Approach to Buffer Zones. Wildlife Society Bulletin 25: 612-615.

7. De Floriani, L., and Magillo, P. 1994. Visibility Algorithms on Triangulated Digital Terrain Models, International Journal of Geographic Information Systems 8(1),13-41.

8. De Floriani, L., Marzano, L., Puppo, P. E., 1994. Line-of-sight Communication on Terrain Models. International Journal of Geographical Information Systems 8 (4), 329-342.

9. De Floriani, L., Marzano, L., Puppo, P. E., 1999. Intervisibility on Terrains, Geographic Information System :Principles, Techniques, Management and Applications. John Wiley & Sons, pp.543-556.

10. Franklin, W.R and Vogt, C., 2004. Multiple ObserverSiting on Terrain with Intervisibility or Lo-Res Data. XXth Congress, International Society for Photogrammetry and Remote Sensing, Istanbul, Turkey, pp.12-23.

11. Franklin, W.R. and Vogt, C., 2004. Efficient Multiple Observer Siting on Large Terrain Cells, GIScience 2004 Third International Conference on Geographic Information Science. University of Maryland Conference Center, USA.

12. Jeroen, C.J. and Gerard, B.M.,2002. Using simulated annealing for resource allocation. Int.J.Geographical Information Science 16(6), 571-587.

13. Kim, Y.H. and Clarke, G., 2001. Exploring Optimal Visibility Site Selection Using Spatial Optimisation Tec-hniques. GIS Research UK, University of Glamorgan and University of Cardiff, Glamorgan, Wales, UK.

14. Kim, Y.H., Rana,, S., Wise, S., 2004. Exploring multiple viewshed analysis using terrain features and optimisation techniques. Computers and Geosciences,30 (9-10), pp. 1019-1032.

15. Kidner, D., Sparkes, A., Dorey, M., 1999. GIS and Wind Farm Planning. In Stillwell, J., Geertman,S.,and Openshaw, S. (Eds.), Geographical Information and Planning, Springer, London, pp. 203-223.

16. Kirkpatrick, C., Gelatt, D., Vecchi, M.P., 1983. Optimization by simulated annealing.Science,220(4598), 671-680.

17. Laarhoven, V., Aarts, E., 1987. Simulated Annealing: Theory and applications. Kluwer Academic, Norwell, 186 pp.

18. Metropolis, N., Rosenbluth, A., Rosenbluth, R., Teller, A., Teller, E., 1953. Equation of state calculations by fast computing machines. J.Chem.Phys 21, 1087-1092.

19. Rana, S., 2003. Fast approximation of visibility dominance using topographic features as targets and the associated uncertainty, Photogrammetric Engineering andRemote Sensing, 69 (8), 881-888.

20. Sundermann, E., 1995, PET image reconstruction using simulated annealing. In proceedings of the SPIE Medical Imaging Conference, Image Processing. San Diego, pp.378-386.

An On-Line Approach for Planning in Time-Limited Situations

Oscar Sapena and Eva Onaindía

Departamento de Sistemas Informáticos y Computación,
Universidad Politécnica de Valencia, Spain
{osapena, onaindia}@dsic.upv.es

Abstract. In this paper we present a novel planning approach, based on well-known techniques such as goal decomposition and heuristic planning, aimed at working in highly dynamic environments with time constraints. Our contribution is a domain-independent planner to incrementally generate plans under a deliberative framework for reactive domains. The planner follows the anytime principles, i.e a first solution plan can be quickly computed and the quality of the solution is improved as time is available. Moreover, the fast computation of the sequential actions allows the plan to start its execution before it is totally generated, thus giving rise to a highly reactive planning system.

1   Introduction

A planner aimed to generate behavior for an agent in complex dynamic and unpredictable environments, such as computer games or autonomous robots problems, often has to react within a limited period of time. In these type of applications, the goal is not to produce optimal plans, but to obtain a response that complies with the environment demands.

There are several planning approaches to deal with dynamic domains. Contingent planning [13], for example, generate plans where some branches are conditionally executed depending on the information obtained during the execution. Another approach is conformant planning [4], which allows to deal with uncertainty on the initial conditions and the action effects without monitoring the plan execution. However, these approaches cannot take into account all possible contingencies and the computation time is often prohibitive. In order to avoid the computational effort of considering all possible unexpected situations during planning time, the on-line planning approaches tackle these situations only when they appear. However, when precomputed behaviors are not available the planner has to react quickly to unexpected events. One of the common techniques to overcome this problem is to follow the anytime paradigm. Anytime algorithms give intelligent systems the capability to trade deliberation time for quality of results [16].

There are two main issues anytime algorithms deal with: interruptibility and quality. Interruptibility implies that the algorithm must be able to be interrupted at any time and provide some answer. The issue of quality implies that the solution is monotonically improved with respect to time. The *CASPER* planner [10], for example, starts with an

M. Ali and R. Dapoigny (Eds.): IEA/AIE 2006, LNAI 4031, pp. 383–392, 2006.
© Springer-Verlag Berlin Heidelberg 2006

empty plan and, at each iteration, tries to solve conflicts and to achieve new goals. The work discussed in [6] addresses the issue of integrating information about uncertainty into the planning process and also deals with time constraints. Unfortunately, these systems lack the ability to provide a first valid solution within an amount of time. The same problem occurs in the *PbR* algorithm [1], which assumes there is a polynomial algorithm to compute a valid initial plan for a particular problem. Other approaches, like the hierarchical planner proposed in [3], allows to limit the time for a first solution by means of a domain-dependent rule-based system. *A-UCMP* [8] is another hierarchical anytime planner that requires a library of reactive actions to execute plans containing abstract actions. To sum up, in general either real-time planners use domain-dependent information to have precompiled plans for quick reactions or they cannot provide an initial solution within a time interval.

2   Objectives

The goal of this paper is to present a domain-independent planner able to provide valid actions to an execution agent in environments with time constraints. Our proposal is a deliberative approach, unlike most of the current reactive planners that require a pre-computed behavior, usually implemented as a set of rules, to select an action according to the current world state [14]. This domain-dependent behavior is very costly to be computed or it is manually introduced into the planner.

Our approach is a novel combination of classical planning techniques such as goal decomposition and heuristic planning. This approach shows to be highly competitive when compared to other state-of-the-art planners, in terms of solution quality and time computation. Moreover, our approach follows the principles of the anytime algorithms:

- Interruptibility: time given to infer a single action is limited. Actually, the planner can compute a valid action (according to its current beliefs) in a few milliseconds. Consequently, if necessary, the plan execution can start almost immediately after the planning process has started. This way, we can get rapid reactions when an unexpected event occurs.
- Following the anytime computation, our planner attempts to find a better solution while time is available. This is currently done by artificially increasing the amount of time used to find a solution: the limit is initially set to a few milliseconds and it is successively increased to allow better solutions.

The contribution of this paper is to present and evaluate a novel fast deliberative planner, competitive with other well-known classical planners, and adaptable to reactive and dynamic domains: there is no need of pre-compiled plans, a first solution plan can be quickly computed and the solution is incrementally improved according to available time.

3   The Planning System

Our planning system is designed to react rapidly to unexpected events. The speed up of this process is achieved by focusing on the most immediate actions to execute rather than searching for a complete plan. An additional reason for this behavior is that plans often become invalid due to frequent changes in the dynamic environments.

The working scheme of the planner is quite simple. Given a state and a deadline, the planner searches for an action, executable in that state, which can successfully lead to a goal state. This process is repeated, starting from the resulting state after executing the last computed action, until a goal state is reached. This scheme is very flexible and it can be used in many different ways. The planning process, for example, can be carried out concurrently (or in an interleaved way) with the execution. This scheme offers many advantages like, for example, that the planner can take into account information which is only available during execution. However, working concurrently with the execution, implies the planner must make assumptions about the outcomes of action executions. Following the *assumption-based planning* approach [12], we have considered all actions as deterministic, replanning when an executed action has an unexpected outcome.

Our planner can also be used as an anytime planner, progressively improving a first initial solution while time is available. To obtain this behavior we gradually increase the maximum available time to compute the actions. Since there is no a systematic search process to explore all possible alternatives, there is a limit in the quality of the plans we can obtain. It would be feasible to incorporate this search process into the planner, but this improvement will be addressed in future works. Both utilization schemes, the on-line and the anytime, will be discussed in section 5.

4   The Planning Algorithm

The planning algorithm is based on a greedy action selection technique: the algorithm computes an individual plan for each top-level goal separately, and these plans are then ordered through a conflict-checking process in order to select the next action to execute. A planning problem $P = (O, I, G)$ is a triple where O is the set of operators, I the initial state and G the top-level goals. The algorithm starts from the current state S_0, which initially corresponds to I, and works in four stages:

The relaxed planning graph (*RPG*). The *RPG* is a graph based on a *GraphPlan*-like expansion [2] where delete effects are ignored. These type of graphs are commonly used in heuristic planners, like *FF* [9] or *LPG* [7], since they allow to compute accurate relaxed plans very fast. Our *RPG* includes some additional features such as metric optimization and support for sensing actions [15].

Calculation of the initial plans. In this stage, an incomplete plan is regressively computed for each non-achieved goal $g_i/g_i \in G \wedge g_i \notin S_0$. Therefore, P is decomposed in n planning subproblems $P_1 = (O, S_0, g_1)$, $P_2 = (O, S_0, g_2)$, ..., $P_n = (O, S_0, g_n)$, where n is the number of non-achieved goals.

The process for building an initial plan P_i starts from an empty plan and the set of subgoals SG which initially only contains the top-level goal g_i. In each iteration, the most costly (according to the *RPG*) literal, l, is selected from SG, as expanding firstly the most costly literals usually generates more informed plans. Then, the best-evaluated action, a, which produces l is added to the beginning of P_i. Actions are evaluated according to their cost and the number of conflicts that they cause (literals deleted by the

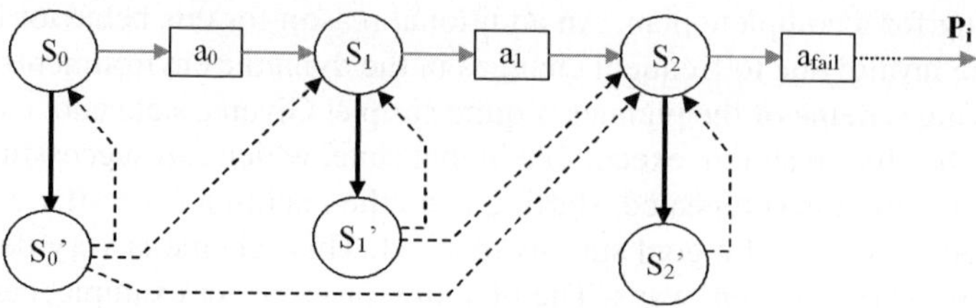

Fig. 1. Different alternatives to repair a precondition of a_{fail}

action and required for the next actions in the plan). Finally, the new set of subgoals SG will be formed with the preconditions of a that do not hold in S_0. This process continues until SG becomes empty.

An initial plan for a top-level goal is not necessarily executable since some of the actions in the sequence might not be applicable in their corresponding state. This is because the algorithm only takes into account one subgoal in each iteration. However, the objective of initial plans is accomplished: an incomplete plan is rapidly computed, the first action is directly executable, and it can be used as a good starting point for further refinements.

The refinement stage. Once P_i for each top-level goal g_i is computed, the refinement stage begins. Plans are improved while there is available time. If a plan P_i is not valid, then there is (at least) one action - which we call a_{fail} - in P_i with unsupported preconditions. In each iteration, an unsupported precondition, p, of a_{fail} is selected and repaired in order to achieve a more complete plan.

In order to repair precondition p of a_{fail}, a number of (incomplete) plans to achieve p are computed, in the same way that the initial plans. These new plans start from the states in P_i - which we call S_j - previous to action a_{fail} and lead to states S'_j in which p is true. These plans can be observed as bold arrows in Figure 1. In order to reuse the final part of plan P_i, from each state S'_j we compute new (incomplete) plans to reach an existing state in P_i, taking care not to delete literal p. The new plans (see dashed arrows in Figure 1) are also computed as initial plans.

The plans computed in this refinement stage provide different alternatives to repair precondition p. These alternatives can be observed in Figure 1 by following the arrows (plans) between the states. From all possible alternatives, the one that produces fewer conflicts (unsupported preconditions) is selected. When two alternatives produce the same number of conflicts, the one with the lowest cost (with regard to the problem metric) is selected.

Selection of the action to be executed. At this point, we have a plan P_i, which might not be totally executable, for each top-level goal g_i. When the executor requests the planner one action, the refinement stage is halted. The planner will return a_{next}, the first action of one or more plans (in case several plans share the same first action). In order to find out which plan must be executed in first place, we apply some criteria to rule out plans. These criteria are classified into:

– **Context criteria:** These criteria study the last executed actions in order to rule out those plans that do not make progress toward the goals, that is, plans that undo a previously achieved subgoal (inverse actions) or plans that cause an execution loop.
– *Mutex* **criteria:** These criteria study the *mutex* relations [2] between actions of different plans P_i. These relations are used to establish an order among plans in such a way that those plans that do not result ordered in first place are ruled out.
– **Least commitment criteria:** If a plan P_i can start its execution without affecting the later execution of other plan P_j, then P_j is ruled out. This way, we postpone the decision to later stages.

If the result of this filtering process is still a set of plans with different initial actions, then some additional criteria are applied. The first action a_{next} of the selected plan is sent to the executor, and the planner updates its environment model with the expected effects of a_{next}.

5   Results

First, we will show the obtained results from the perspective of the anytime behavior of our planner. We have chosen *LPG v1.2* [7] to test and compare our results because *LPG* is able to provide an initial solution very rapidly and then improve such a solution progressively. Tables 1, 2 and 3 show the successive solutions that our planner and *LPG* have generated for the *Blocksworld*, *Satellite* and *Numeric Depots* respectively (these results have been obtained using a 2 *Ghz. Pentium IV* computer with 512 *Mb.* of memory). *Numeric Depots* is the numeric version of the *Depots* domain, where some objects must be transported with trucks and arranged in stacks. In this domain, plan quality is not measured in number of actions but in units of consumed fuel. These problems can be found in the *IPC-3* (Third International Planning Competition, *http://planning.cis.strath.ac.uk/competition/*).

Results show that our planner is able to compute a first plan more rapidly than *LPG*. We must also take into account that, in our case, it is not necessary to wait for the

Table 1. Solutions found in 20 seconds per plan for several problems in the *Blocksworld* domain

Problem	Our solutions (plan length/time sec.)	LPG solutions (plan length/time sec.)
10	64/0.03, 34/0.06	100/0.28, 36/0.5, 34/2.28
11	128/0.05, 32/0.12	200/0.7, 40/1.15, 38/1,9, 36/4,1, 34/5.4, 32/6,52
12	56/0.03, 42/0.12, 38/0.21	154/0.59, 48/1.03, 44/1.21, 42/2.92, 40/3.98
13	72/0.04, 48/0.12, 42/0.19	174/3.06, 52/3.44, 44/4.67, 42/10.44
14	86/0.06, 44/0.18	130/0.77, 64/2.4, 48/2.6, 46/3.4, 44/3.55, 42/5.4
15	100/0.08, 52/0.18, 48/0.31	172/6.23, 50/13.41, 46/13.57
16	188/0.2, 80/0.53, 58/0.72, 54/1.3	192/14.16, 112/16.14, 60/17.27, 58/17.83
17	236/0.25, 68/0.47, 54/0.66	352/15.63, 62/19.9
18	310/0.35, 70/0.6, 62/1.7	-
19	128/0.18, 94/0.6, 86/1.3, 68/2.6, 64/4.4	-
20	106/0.16, 78/0.5, 66/2.7	-

Table 2. Solutions found in 20 seconds per plan for several problems in the *Satellite* domain

Problem	Our solutions (plan length/time)	*LPG* solutions (plan length/time sec.)
10	32/0.07, 31/0.47	32/0.09, 31/0.23, 29/4.48
11	35/0.09, 34/0.34	35/0.1, 34/0.16, 33/1.07, 31/1.7
12	43/0.15	51/0.21, 45/0.33, 43/0.5
13	58/0.29	67/0.36, 65/0.96, 59/2.11, 58/2.28, 57/2.46
14	45/0.17, 44/0.78	45/0.23, 43/0.62, 42/0.76, 41/7.23, 40/12.55
15	51/0.27, 50/1.22	74/0.34, 71/0.52, 64/0.62, 57/1.09, 51/1.31, 50/13.97
16	52/0.34, 49/1.2	54/0.33, 53/0.57, 51/1.31, 50/6.42
17	47/0.34, 46/1	55/0.43, 54/0.54, 53/0.86, 49/1.43, 47/5.32, 46/5.94
18	36/0.12	43/0.2, 41/0.32, 35/0.4, 33/9.88, 32/10.51
19	71/0.34, 65/1.3, 63/2.3	76/0.32, 73/0.54, 72/1.1, 69/1.45, 68/1.6, 64/8.6
20	89/0.5	108/0.4, 105/0.7, 102/1, 101/2, 99/3.4, 94/4, 88/16

Table 3. Solutions found in 30 seconds per plan for several problems in the *Numeric Depots* domain

Problem	Our solutions (fuel-cost/time sec.)	*LPG* solutions (fuel-cost/time sec.)
10	66/0.1	48/0.12, 47/0.18
11	160/0.68, 140/4.4, 120/7.9	159/4, 154/7, 134/9, 133/11, 123/21, 103/28
12	227/2.68, 125/5.28	288/9.1
13	56/0.08	107/0.16, 77/0.21, 68/0.33, 57/0.87
14	89/0.33, 78/1.51	99/1.92, 80/2.19, 78/2.96, 68/3.63
15	256/2.92, 134/13.16	204/28.59
16	57/0.23	79/0.33, 78/0.66, 68/0.8, 59/0.96, 58/1.1, 57/6.4
17	46/0.3	49/0.53, 48/1.44, 38/1.6
18	409/3.1, 113/7.9, 99/12.6, 86/29.4	167/5.17, 137/8.75
19	98/0.5	218/0.9, 201/1.4, 181/1.7, 180/2, 150/2.4, 100/5.6
20	226/6.24, 213/28.99	245/26.65

complete plan to be computed to start its execution. Moreover, our planner scales better than *LPG* in the presented domains. This can be also seen in Figure 2, where we show a comparison between the time needed by our planner and *LPG* to compute a first solution in the *ZenoTravel* domain. This domain, presented in the *IPC-3*, is a transportation domain, where objects are transported via aeroplanes. As for the plan quality, the first solutions of our planner are usually better than the ones of *LPG* and, in general, our planner finds equal or better quality solutions in less time than *LPG*.

Now, we will show the on-line behavior of our planner through the simulation of unexpected events and changes in the goals during the plan execution. For this purpose, we have defined a new robot manipulation domain in which a robot arm is used to pick up objects from some tables and to arrange them in a two-dimensional space around a central piece. The first proposed problem (see Figure 3) consists of ten objects (p1, ..., p10) stacked on five tables (table1, ..., table5) which must be arranged around a fixed central object C placed in a separated platform. An object can be assembled

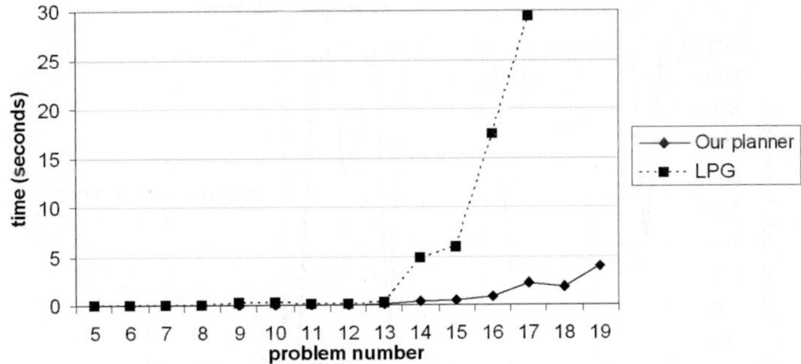

Fig. 2. Time to compute a first solution for our planner and *LPG* in the *ZenoTravel* domain

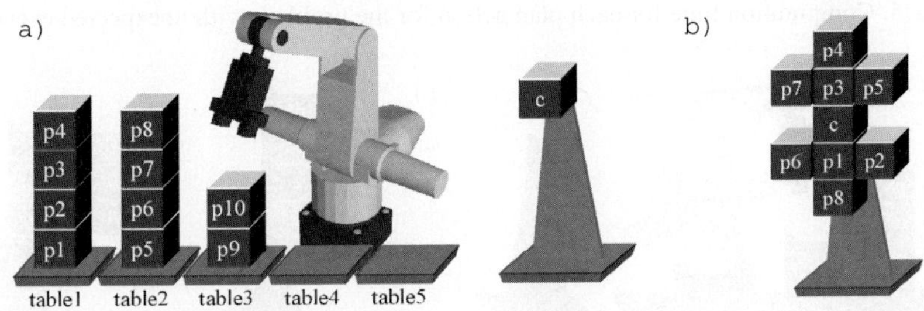

Fig. 3. a) Initial state and b) goal state for the first proposed problem

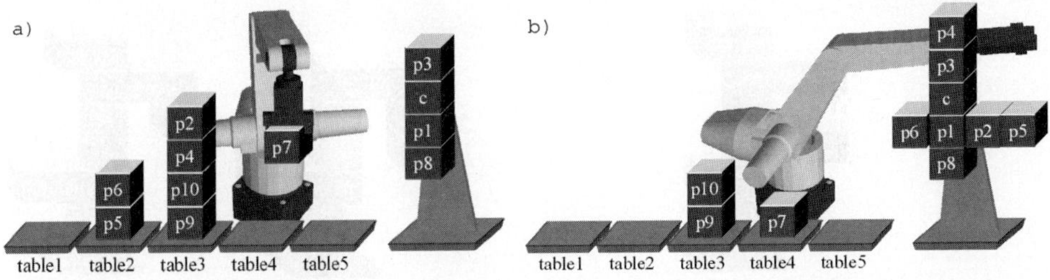

Fig. 4. a) First unexpected event: object *p7* falls on *table*4. b) Second unexpected event: *p5* is assembled to the right of *p2* instead of to the right of *p3*.

to the left, right, top or bottom of another object which has been already assembled. This problem is currently a challenge for many domain-independent planners: *LPG v1.2*, *SGPlan* [5] and *Metric FF* [9] take 2 minutes, 5 minutes and more than an hour respectively to find a solution (without considering unexpected events or goal changes because of their off-line nature).

For this problem, we have simulated two unexpected events during the execution (see Figure 4). The first unexpected event occurs when the robot has assembled p1, p3 and p8, and it is holding p7 (Figure 4a). At that moment, the robot detects that p7 has fallen onto table table4. The second unexpected event occurs when the robot tries to

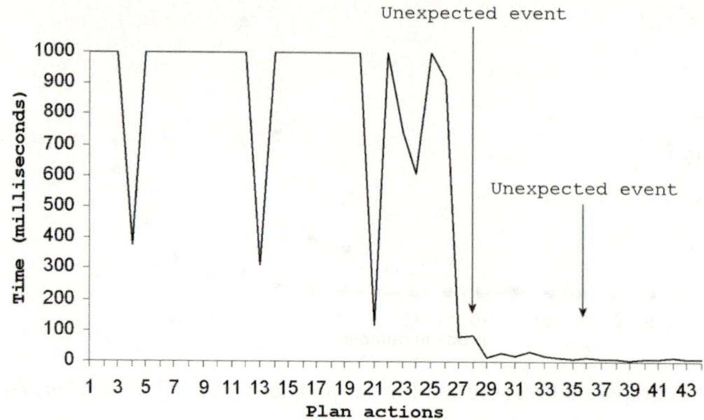

Fig. 5. Computation time for each plan action for the problem with unexpected events

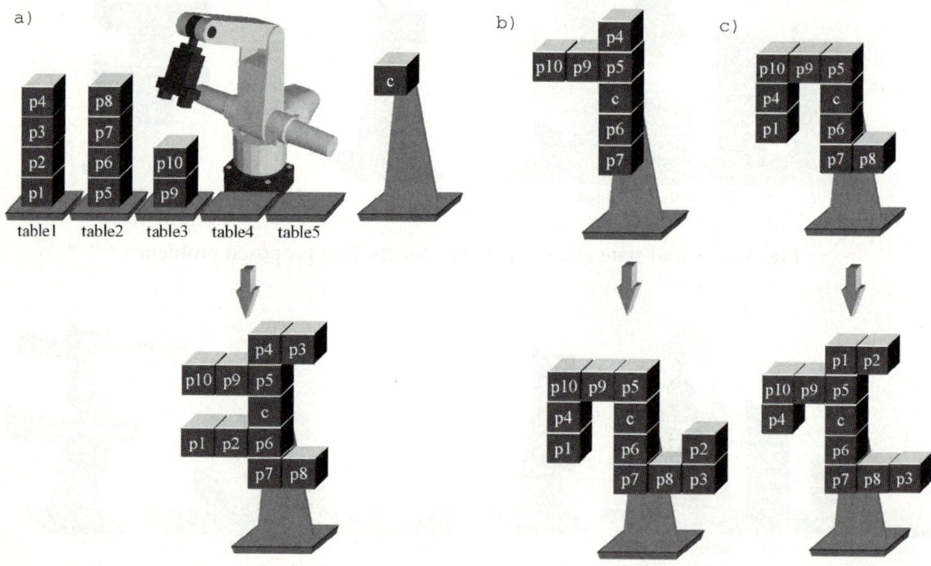

Fig. 6. a) Initial state (top) and goal state (bottom) for the second proposed problem. b) Current state (top) when the first change in the goals (bottom) occurs. c) Second change in the goals.

assemble p5 to the right of p3. An error causes that p5 is assembled to the right of p2. The robot arm can disassemble objects, so it must repair this error.

Figure 5 shows the computation time for each action in the plan. We have limited the available time to one second per action in order to obtain a smooth execution. This limitation together with the problem complexity causes the execution of some unnecessary actions. Firstly, it can be observed that the first actions in the plan are, in general, harder to compute since the distance to the goals is greater. On the contrary, when computing the last actions, the number of non-achieved goals may be very small since most of them

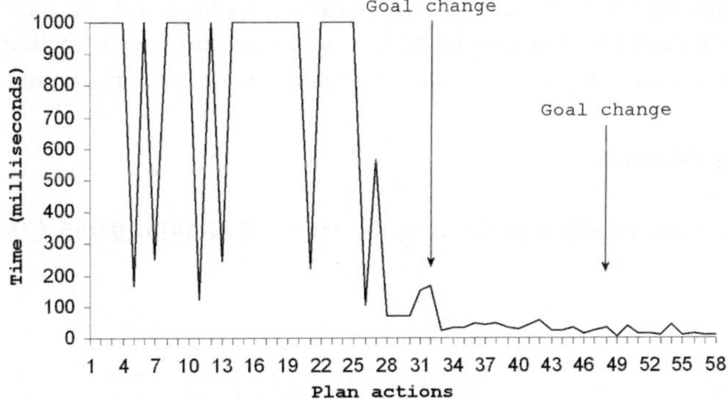

Fig. 7. Computation time for each plan action for the problem with goal changes

have already been accomplished. Consequently, the plans for each goal are shorter and need fewer refinement steps to be repaired.

It can also be observed that an unexpected event does not cause an appreciable increase in the computation time. This is due to the fact that the planner does not reuse previous calculations in order to compute an action. This way, the cost of computing the next action when everything goes as expected is very similar to the cost of computing a first action for a new situation.

In Figure 6 we show a second problem in order to illustrate the planner behavior when faced with changes in the goals. The top of this figure shows the current state of the assembly platform when the change in the goals occurs, whereas the bottom shows the new goal state to be achieved. Figure 7 shows the computation time to calculate each plan action and the instants at which a goal change occurs. It can be observed that a goal change has a similar effect to an unexpected event, that is, a negligible increase in the computation time. Unlike other replanning tools, the behavior of our system does not depend on how drastic the change is, but on the distance from the current state to the goals (actually, many replanners rely on the idea that the actual situation is only slightly different from the original one [11]).

6   Conclusions and Future Work

In this paper we have presented an anytime deliberative planner, designed to work in highly dynamic environments with time constraints. This planner is based on well-known techniques, such as goal decomposition and heuristic planning, but combined in a novel approach. Used as an on-line planner, our approach presents important advantages: our planner can obtain a first solution plan very rapidly and scales up very well in many domains. Also, plan execution can start after the first action has been computed, which can be done in a few milliseconds. This feature allows our planner fast reactions when unexpected events occur.

Our planner can also be used as an anytime planner by artificially increasing the available time to compute each action. Results show that plans obtained are quickly computed and have good quality. However, our planner is not complete, and there is a limit in the quality of the plans it can generate. Currently, we are interested in overcoming this limitation by including an additional search process when there is available time. This way, we can obtain a complete planner, able to produce better-quality plans.

Acknowledgements

This work has been partially supported by the *MCyT* TIN2005-08945-C06-06 (*FEDER*) project.

References

1. J.L. Ambite and C.A. Knoblock, 'Planning by rewriting', *JAIR*, **15**, 207–261, (2001).
2. A. Blum and M. Furst, 'Fast planning through planning graph analysis', *Artificial Intelligence*, **90**, 281–300, (1997).
3. W. Briggs and D.J. Cook, 'Anytime planning for optimal tradeoff between deliberative and reactive planning', *FLAIRS Conference*, 367–370, (1999).
4. D. Bryce and S. Kambhampati, 'Heuristic guidance measures for conformant planning', *Proceedings of ICAPS*, 365–375, (2004).
5. Y. Chen, C.W. Hsu, and B.W. Wah, 'SGPlan: Subgoal partitioning and resolution in planning', *IPC-4 Booklet (ICAPS)*, (2004).
6. T. Dean, L.P. Kaelbling, J. Kirman, and A. Nicholson, 'Planning under time constraints in stochastic domains', *Artificial Intelligence*, **76**(1-2), 35–74, (1995).
7. A. Gerevini, A. Saetti, and I. Serina, 'Planning through stochastic local search and temporal action graphs in LPG', *JAIR*, **20**, 239–290, (2003).
8. N. Hawes, 'Anytime planning for agent behaviour', *PLANSIG*, 157–166, (2001).
9. J. Hoffman and B. Nebel, 'The FF planning system: Fast planning generation through heuristic search', *Journal of Artificial Intelligence Research*, **14**, 253–302, (2001).
10. R. Knight, G. Rabideau, S.A. Chien, B. Engelhardt, and R. Sherwood, 'Casper: Space exploration through continuous planning', *IEEE Intelligent Systems*, **16**(5), 70–75, (2001).
11. S. Koenig, D. Furcy, and C. Bauer, 'Heuristic search-based replanning', *International Conference on Artificial Intelligence Planning and Scheduling (AIPS)*, 310–317, (2002).
12. S. Koenig, C.A. Tovey, and Y.V. Smirnov, 'Performance bounds for planning in unknown terrain', *Artificial Intelligence*, **147**(1-2), 253–279, (2003).
13. S.M. Majercik and M.L. Littman, 'Contingent planning under uncertainty via stochastic satisfiability', *Artificial Intelligence*, **147**(1-2), 119–162, (2003).
14. L. Pryor and G. Collins, 'Planning for contingencies: A decision-based approach', *Journal of Artificial Intelligence Research*, **4**, 287–339, (1996).
15. O. Sapena and E. Onaindía, 'Handling numeric criteria in relaxed planning graphs', *Proceedings of Iberamia (LNCS)*, **3315**, 114–123, (2004).
16. S. Zilberstein, 'Using anytime algorithms in intelligent systems', *AI Magazine*, **17**(3), 73–83, (1996).

Priority-Constrained Task Sequencing for Heterogeneous Mobile Robots

Metin Ozkan[1], Inci Saricicek[2], Osman Parlaktuna[1], and Servet Hasgul[2]

[1] Eskisehir Osmangazi University, Electrical and Electronics Engineering,
26480 Eskisehir, Turkey
{meozkan, oparlak}@ogu.edu.tr
[2] Eskisehir Osmangazi University, Industrial Engineering,
26480 Eskisehir, Turkey
{incid, shasgul}@ogu.edu.tr

Abstract. This paper presents an application of a technique for sequencing priority-constrained tasks which will be performed autonomously by a couple of heterogeneous mobile robots. Here the sequencing problem of sequentially-performed and separate tasks for multiple robots is considered. Two types of tasks are chosen. One type of tasks can be performed by only one robot. The second type of task requires completion of a part of the task by one robot and the rest of the task is completed by another robot due to nature of the tasks and abilities of the robots. It is assumed that tasks have been assigned to the robots, completion times and priorities of the tasks for each robot has been determined beforehand. In this paper, a technique is used for sequencing the tasks to produce a schedule with a minimum makespan. Real world experiments are presented to show the convenience of the proposed approach.

1 Introduction

In the recent years, many studies are focused on multiple mobile robot systems, with a variety of topics [1]. Many advantages of using multiple mobile robot systems have appeared for some tasks. It is possible to benefit from the advantages by improving methods to solve the problems which arise from using multiple robots. Groups of mobile robots are required to cooperate intelligently for successful task execution. The first step should be a feasible allocation of tasks to robots in the team. In the literature, many researches on multi-robot task allocation are addressed. The task allocation problem can be framed in the more general scheduling framework [2]. Scheduling has been well studied and the complexity of many scheduling problems has previously been established, and some algorithms have been developed [3, 4]. These scheduling algorithms suggested for different scheduling problems may be applicable for the multi-robot task allocation problem.

In this study, a technique for sequencing priority-constrained tasks for two-robot flow shop problem is proposed. In robotics, a flow shop has mobile robots in an environment, and all tasks are performed by these robots in the given sequence. However, the processing time for each task by each robot may vary. All tasks are assumed to be available at the beginning. Each robot performs its own subtask without concerning

M. Ali and R. Dapoigny (Eds.): IEA/AIE 2006, LNAI 4031, pp. 393 – 399, 2006.

about when the others will perform their own subtasks in a given task, and it continues performing the subsequent tasks or subtasks. The objective of this study is to develop a schedule that minimizes the makespan. For two-robot flow shop problem, a well-known scheduling algorithm, namely Johnson's rule, is used. A real world application by using well-equipped mobile robots is presented to show feasibility of the proposed approach.

The paper is organized as follows. Scheduling is explained in terms of robotics perspective in Section 2. The proposed task sequencing method is described in Section 3. The implementation of an application and results are given in Section 4. Finally, conclusion and further works are given in Section 5.

2   Scheduling – Robotics Perspective

Scheduling is a decision-making process that deals with the allocation of resources to tasks over time. It consists of planning and prioritizing activities that need to be performed in an orderly sequence of operations. The objective of scheduling for given tasks and resources may change according to requirements. It may be minimization of the completion time of the last task, minimization of the idle time of robots, balancing the loads of robots, task completion by using minimum resources, etc.

In classical scheduling problems, resources are generally machines in a production environment. Machines have a particular capacity and ability like robots; however, they can not move, perceive their environment, or react. The term *machine* and *job* called in the production planning terminology may be used like *robot* and *task* in the robotic terminology, respectively. The following explanations related to scheduling problem will use the terms *robot* and *task*.

In the production planning terminology, scheduling problems are classified extensively: single machine, flow shop, parallel machines, job shop, open shop, etc. Many algorithms are addressed as a solution to these problems in the literature. The same problems may be seen in groups of cooperative mobile robots. In the future, multiple mobile robots may be required to perform many tasks autonomously by satisfying the given objectives. For this, they need to schedule their activities according to required objectives. The scheduling algorithms may be used in the same way, modified to suit the requirements of robotics, or extended to include new features.

2.1   Framework and Notation

In all the scheduling problems considered, the number of tasks and robots are assumed to be finite. The number of tasks is denoted by n and the number of robots by m. Usually, the subscript j refers to a task (T_j, $j=1,...,n$), whereas the subscript i refer to a robot (R_i, $i=1,...,m$).

Processing time (p_{ij}) represents the processing time of task j by robot i. *Release date* (r_j) of task j may be referred to as the ready date which is the time the task arrives at the system. *Due date* (d_j) of task j represents the completion date. *Weight* (w_j) of task j is basically a priority factor, denoting the importance of task j relative to other tasks. The objective to be minimized is always a function of the completion times of the tasks depend on the schedule. The completion time of the operation of task j by robot i is denoted by C_{ij}. The time task j is completed is denoted by C_j. *Makespan* (C_{max}) is equivalent to the completion time of the last task to leave the system. It is denoted as $max(C_1, \ldots , C_n)$. A minimum makespan usually implies a high utilization of the robots.

3 Task Sequencing for Two Robots

Sequencing priority-constrained tasks performed by a couple of heterogeneous mobile robots is carried out by using a modified form of *Johnson's rule*. Johnson's rule is well-known in the scheduling literature, and it has been developed by Johnson [6]. In robotics, this rule may be applied to the simplest form of a flow shop arrangement which consists of only two robots, and each task is processed successively by these two robots: the first operation is performed by the first robot and the second one is performed by the second robot as seen in Fig. 1.

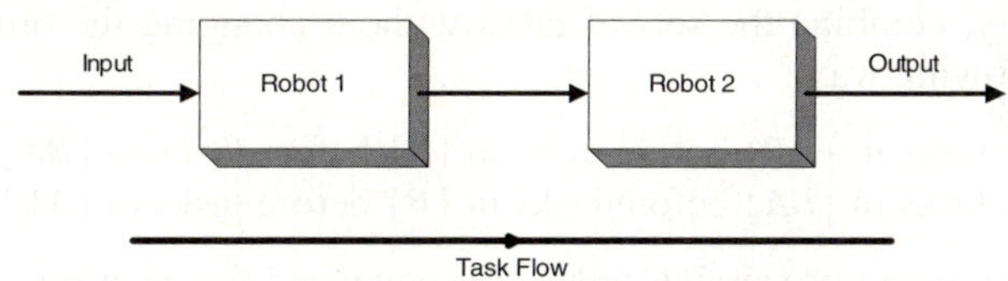

Fig. 1. The two-robot flow shop model

Let us define $A_j=p_{1j}$ and $B_j=p_{2j}$. The steps for Johnson's algorithm are as follows [5]:

Step1. Determine the minimum processing times of all A_j and B_j for the tasks to be sequenced.

Step2. If the minimum is associated with A_j, place the corresponding job in the earliest possible position in the sequence. If the minimum is associated with B_j, place the corresponding job in the latest possible position in the sequence.

Step3. Mark the task as being sequenced and scratch the associated A_j and B_j values.

Step4. If all tasks are placed in the sequence, go to *step 5*; otherwise go to *step 1*.

Step5. The optimum sequence has been obtained.

This algorithm is suitable for the two-robot flow shop scheduling problem. However, tasks may have different technological orderings. In this situation, the modified form of Johnson' rule may be appropriate. Jackson has shown that Johnson's algorithm may be modified to produce a minimum makespan sequence of n tasks with different orderings in a two-robot job shop [7]. The n tasks may be classified into four sets defined as follows and given in Fig.2:

{A}   : the set of tasks that are processed only by robot 1
{B}   : the set of tasks that are processed only by robot 2
{AB} : the set of tasks to be processed by robot 1 followed by robot 2
{BA} : the set of tasks to be processed by robot 2 followed by robot 1

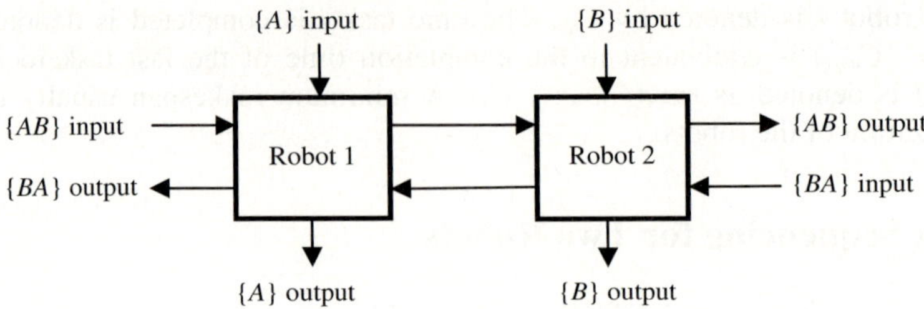

Fig. 2. Task flow diagram

Thus, the steps are

Step 1. Sequence the tasks in {*AB*} by Johnson's algorithm
Step 2. Sequence the tasks in {*BA*} by Johnson's algorithm
Step 3. Select any arbitrary sequence for the tasks in {*A*} and {*B*}
Step 4. Finally, combine the sets of tasks without changing the order within each set in the following way:

Robot 1 : tasks in {*AB*} before tasks in {*A*} before tasks in {*BA*}
Robot 2 : tasks in {*BA*} before tasks in {*B*} before tasks in {*AB*}

The tasks with given processing order are sequenced for each robot automatically by using the algorithm. Then, each robot performs their tasks according to the ordered sequence. The algorithm guarantees the completion of the tasks in required sequence without any conflict, and a minimum makespan will be produced. However, traveling times of the robots to the task locations are not considered. Traveling times are assumed to be negligible compared to processing times of the tasks.

4 Application

An application has been performed to show the effectiveness of the proposed approach. In this application, three mobile robots are used. Two of them perform the given tasks according to the scheduled sequence. They service a set of goal points with certain demands.

The third robot is used to determine the locations of service robots while they perform the tasks. For this purpose, colored cylindrical objects are placed at the top of service robots. Positions of the service robots are determined by using a PTZ camera and a laser range finder concurrently. The camera of the robot is used to recognize the service robots and determining their approximate direction. Then, the laser range finder is used to find the absolute location from the approximate direction. Finally, it sends the locations of the service robots to them by using previously developed communication scheme. The other duty of this robot is to distribute the sequenced tasks to the service robots.

4.1 Robot System

The application is implemented on two Pioneer 3-DX and one Pioneer 3-AT robots. Each one is equipped with a ring of 16 ultrasonic sensors, high precision encoders for dead-reckoning, electronic compass, onboard PC with wireless Ethernet, and Canon VCC4 camera with pan-tilt-zoom (PTZ). However, the robots have some different hardware. Pioneer 3-DX robots have a gripper to grasp and carry objects. Pioneer 3-AT is equipped with a SICK LMS200 laser range finder. The range finder scans a range of 180° of the environment with a resolution 1°.

4.2 Experiment

An application is carried out by the heterogeneous robot system. Two Pioneer 3-DX robots service a set of goal points with certain demands. Pioneer 3-AT robot determines the positions of the service robots. In addition, it calculates the task sequence of the robots. It conveys the position information and the sequenced tasks to the service robots by using a communication scheme.

Pink and green cylindrical objects are placed on the Pioneer 3-DX robots to identify them. In this manner, Pioneer 3-AT is able to recognize them, and determine their positions. All of the robots and task locations are given in Fig. 3. Robots use the proposed approach to implement the given tasks.

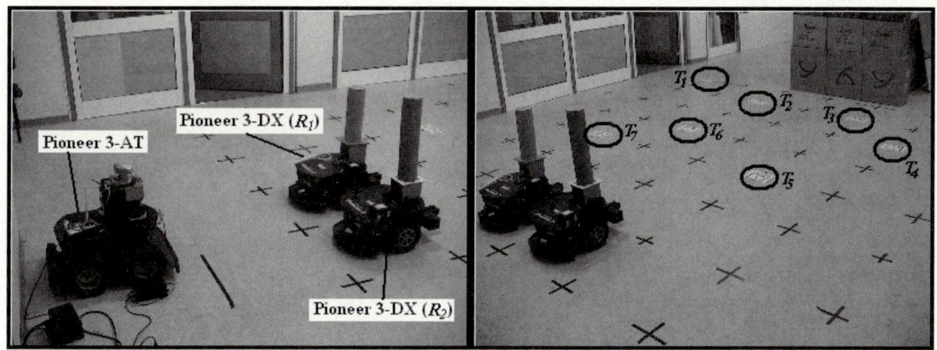

Fig. 3. The environment for the experiment

Tasks are sequenced by the Pioneer 3-AT by using modified Johnson's rule and distributed to the service robots. A set of sample tasks are presented in Table 1.

Table 1. The tasks to be performed by Pioneer 3-DX robots

Task no	First Operation		Second Operation		Task location	
	R_i	$p_{ij}(unit)$	R_i	$p_{ij}(unit)$	X(mm)	Y(mm)
1	R_1	8	R_2	2	5100	1800
2	R_1	7	R_2	5	4500	600
3	R_2	6	R_1	4	4500	-600
4	R_2	5	R_1	3	3900	-1200
5	R_1	7	-	-	2700	-600
6	R_2	1	-	-	3300	600
7	R_2	5	-	-	2700	1200

After the scenario is started, Pioneer 3-AT robot calculates the minimum makespan sequence for each service robot as follows:

$$R_1 \Rightarrow (\ T_2,\ T_1,\ T_5\ ,T_3\ ,T_4)$$
$$R_2 \Rightarrow (\ T_3,\ T_4,\ T_6\ ,T_7\ ,T_2,T_1)$$

The service robots visit the task locations in the given order, and wait at the task location during the processing times. The locations of the robots during their journey are plotted in Fig.4. As seen in the figure, the robots are just passing through their own task locations and no conflict arises at any task location.

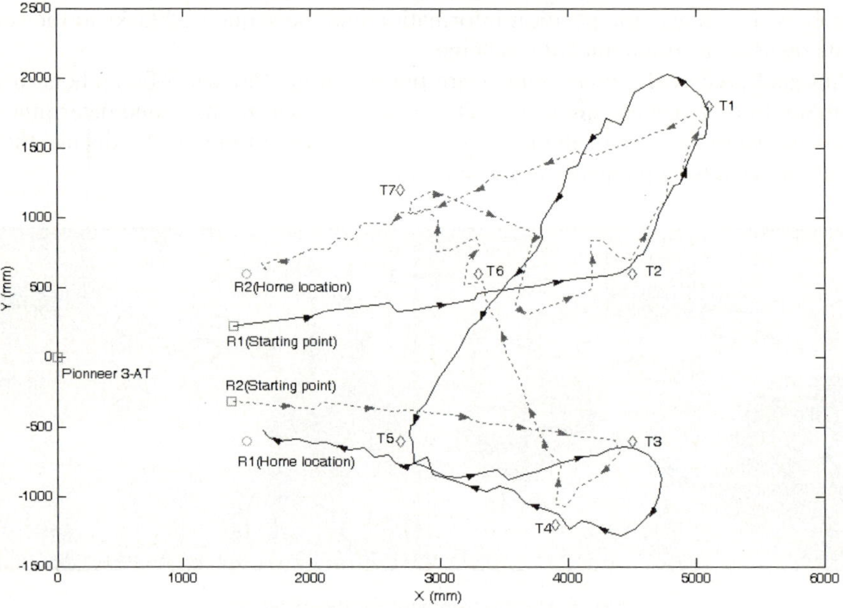

Fig. 4. The locations of robots while the tasks are performed

The experiment is recorded while the tasks are performed. Interested readers may watch the video which are served on the link "http://www.ai-robotlab.ogu.edu.tr".

5   Conclusion

In this study, priority-constrained tasks are scheduled using modified Johnson's rule. Proposed method is successfully applied to a two-robot flow shop problem. Since the algorithm guarantees the minimum makespan, the utilization of the robots is increased.

In this study cooperative works by mobile robots are not considered. In order to work cooperatively, robots should be at the same location at the same time. If a robot arrives to the job location earlier than the other it should wait. In this situation, it will be important that scheduling should minimize the waiting times of the robots to meet with the other robots for cooperation at the task location. In the future, we plan to study on this scenario. Additionally, we plan to include the traveling times of the robots to the task locations into the algorithm.

In the future, we intend to develop techniques for dynamic scheduling problems. Some tasks will be available at the beginning. Robots will schedule the existing tasks, and start to perform the tasks according to the schedule. However, if new tasks arrive, robots should reschedule the remaining tasks and newly added tasks. Additionally, we plan to increase the number of service robots.

Acknowledgements

This work is supported by the State Planning Organization of T.R. Prime Ministry (SPO) under the project "Accomplishing a given task by a homogeneous mobile robot group using dynamic role assignment".

References

1. Arai, T., E. Pagello, and L.E. Parker: Guest Editorial Advances in Multirobot Systems. IEEE Trans. on Robotics and Automation, 18(5), (2002) 655-661.
2. Torbjorn S. Dahl, Maja J. Mataric, and Gaurav S. Sukhatme: Scheduling with Group Dynamics: A Multi-Robot Task Allocation Algorithm Based on Vacancy Chains. Technical Report CRES-002-07, Center for Robotics and Embedded Systems, University of Southern California, (2002).
3. Peter Brucker: Scheduling Algorithms (Fourth Edition). Springer, (2004).
4. Michael Pinedo: Scheduling Theory, Algorithms, and Systems (Second Edition), Prentice Hall, (2002).
5. Dileep R. Sule: Industrial Scheduling. PWS Publishing, 1997.
6. S.M. Johnson: Optimal Two-and Three-Stages Production Schedules with Setup Times Included. Naval Research Logistics Quarterly, 1(1), (1954) 61-68.
7. L.A. Johnson and D.C. Montgomery: Operations Research in Production Planning, Scheduling and Inventory Control. John Wiley & Sons Inc., USA, (1974).

New Heuristics to Solve the "CSOP" Railway Timetabling Problem

L. Ingolotti[1], A. Lova[2], F. Barber[1], P. Tormos[2], M.A. Salido[1], and M. Abril[1]

[1] DSIC, Polytechnic University of Valencia, Spain
{lingolotti, fbarber, msalido, mabril}@dsic.upv.es
[2] DEIOAC, Polytechnic University of Valencia, Spain
{allova, ptormos}@eio.upv.es

Abstract. The efficient use of infrastructures is a hard requirement for railway companies. Thus, the scheduling of trains should aim toward optimality, which is an NP-hard problem. The paper presents a friendly and flexible computer-based decision support system for railway timetabling. It implements an efficient method, based on meta-heuristic techniques, which provides railway timetables that satisfy a realistic set of constraints and, that optimize a multi-criteria objective function.

Keywords: Constraint Satisfaction, Decision Support, Planning and Scheduling.

1 Introduction

The main motivations for this work are the need of obtaining an automatic timetabling process for railway companies, the hard requirement of using efficiently railway infrastructures and the challenge that this process implies for the application and research of techniques in the Artificial Intelligence field. The literature of the 1960s, 1970s, and 1980s relating to rail optimization was relatively limited. Compared to the airline and bus industries, optimization was generally overlooked in favor of simulation or heuristic-based methods. However, Cordeau et al. [1] point out greater competition, privatization, deregulation, and increasing computer speed as reasons for the more prevalent use of optimization techniques in the railway industry. Our review of the methods and models that have been published indicates that the majority of authors use models that are based on the Periodic Event Scheduling Problem (PESP) introduced by Serafini and Ukovich [7]. The PESP considers the problem of scheduling as a set of periodically recurring events under periodic time-window constraints. The model generates disjunctive constraints that may cause the exponential growth of the computational complexity of the problem depending on its size.

Schrijver and Steenbeek [5] have developed CADANS, a constraint programming-based algorithm to find a feasible timetable for a set of PESP constraints. The scenario considered by this tool is different from the scenario that we used; therefore, the results are not easily comparable. Nachtigall and Voget [4] also use PESP constraints to model the cyclic behavior of timetables and to consider

M. Ali and R. Dapoigny (Eds.): IEA/AIE 2006, LNAI 4031, pp. 400–409, 2006.

the minimization of passenger waiting times as the objective function. Their solving procedure starts with a solution that is obtained in a way similar to the one that timetable designers in railway companies use. This initial timetable is then improved by using a genetic algorithm. In our problem, the waiting time for connections is not taken into account because we only consider the timetabling optimization for a single railway line.

The train scheduling problem can also be modeled as a special case of the job-shop scheduling problem (Silva de Oliveira [8], Walker et al. [11]), where train trips are considered *jobs* that are scheduled on tracks that are regarded as *resources*. The majority of these works consider the scheduling of new trains on an empty network. However, infrastructure management railway companies usually also require the optimization of new trains on a line where many trains are already in circulation (that is, trains that have a fixed timetable). With this main objective, Lova et al. [2] propose a scheduling method based on *reference stations* where the priority of trains, in the case of conflict, changes from one iteration to another during the solving process.

2   Problem Specification

A railway line is composed by an ordered sequence of locations $\{l_0, l_1, ..., l_n\}$ which are linked by single or double track. The problem consists in scheduling a set of new trains (T_{new}), taking into account that the railway line may be occupied by other trains in circulation (T_C) whose timetables cannot be modified. The trains may belong to different operator types and their respective journeys may also be different from each other.

The timetable assigned to each new train must be feasible, i.e. it must fulfill the set of constraints defined in Section 2.1. Besides feasibility, two additional goals are pursued in this work: computational efficiency and optimality, which is measured according to the objective function defined in Section 2.2.

2.1   Feasibility of a Solution - Set of Constraints: CONS

The problem of obtaining a feasible and optimal railway timetabling can be defined as a Constraint Satisfaction and Optimization Problem (CSOP). Considering $T = T_{new} \cup T_C$, variables arr_i^t and dep_i^t represent the arrival/departure times of each train $t \in T$ from/to each station l_i of its journey. For each train $t \in T_C$, these variables are already instantiated, so that it is not necessary consider any constraint among them. A feasible railway timetable must satisfy a set of constraints CONS, which are defined by the Spanish Manager of Railway Infrastructure (ADIF).

Set of Constraints[1]

 - *Interval for the Initial Departure/Arrival Time* : given the intervals $[I_L^t, I_U^t]$ and $[F_L^t, F_U^t]$, each train $t \in T_{new}$ should leave/arrive its initial/final station $l_0^t / l_{n_t}^t$ at a time $dep_0^t / arr_{n_t}^t$ such that,

---

[1] In this work are described the main problem constraints, the rest of constraints that have been considered are detailed in [10].

$$I_L^t \leq dep_0^t \leq I_U^t \ . \tag{1}$$

$$F_L^t \leq arr_{n_t}^t \leq F_U^t \ . \tag{2}$$

- *Running Time*: for each track section $l_i^t \to l_{i+1}^t$, and for each train $t \in T_{new}$ is given a running time $\Delta_{i \to (i+1)}^t$ such that

$$arr_{i+1}^t = dep_i^t + \Delta_{i \to (i+1)}^t \ . \tag{3}$$

- *Commercial Stop*: each train $t \in T_{new}$ is required to remain in a station l_i^t of its journey at least C_i^t time units

$$dep_i^t \geq arr_i^t + C_i^t \ . \tag{4}$$

- *Headway Time*: if two trains, $\{t_i, t_j\} \subseteq T$, traveling in the same direction leave the same location l_k^t towards the location l_{k+1}^t, they are required to have a difference in their departure times of at least φ_k^d and a difference in their arrival times of at least φ_k^a. Particularly, when the blocking type in the track section is *Automatic* then $\varphi_k^d = \varphi_k^a$ and their values are determined by the user. When the blocking type of the track section is *Manual*, the second train must wait in the station until the first train arrives to the next open station.

$$|dep_k^{t_i} - dep_k^{t_j}| \geq \varphi_k^d \ . \tag{5}$$

$$|arr_{k+1}^{t_i} - arr_{k+1}^{t_j}| \geq \varphi_k^a \ . \tag{6}$$

- *Crossing*: A single-track section cannot be occupied at the same time by two trains going in the opposite directions. Considering that: T_D and T_U are the set of trains that travel in *down* and *up* direction respectively, $t \in T_D$, $t' \in T_U$ and $i \to j$ is a track section (down direction), this constraint is modeled by the following expression.

$$dep_j^{t'} > arr_j^t \vee dep_i^t > arr_i^t \ . \tag{7}$$

- *Reception/Expedition Time*: Crossing operations are performed in stations and they require to keep temporal safety margins (Reception and Expedition Time) between the involved trains. The difference between the arrival times/departure and arrival times of any two trains, $\{t', t\} \subseteq T \wedge \{t', t\} \nsubseteq T_D \wedge \{t', t\} \nsubseteq T_U$, in a same station l is defined by the expressions below, where R_t is the reception time specified for the train that arrives to l first and E_t is the expedition time specified for t.

$$arr_l^{t'} \geq arr_l^t \to arr_l^{t'} - arr_l^t \geq R_t \ . \tag{8}$$

$$|dep_l^{t'} - arr_l^t| \geq E_t \ . \tag{9}$$

- *Overtaking on the track section*: overtaking must be avoided between any two trains, $\{i, j\} \nsubseteq T_C \wedge (\{i, j\} \subseteq T_D \vee \{i, j\} \subseteq T_U)$, on any common track sections, $k \to (k+1)$, of their journeys:

$$(arr_{k+1}^i \geq arr_{k+1}^j) \leftrightarrow (dep_k^i \geq dep_k^j) \ . \tag{10}$$

– *Frequency*: The user can specify a given frequency among a subset of trains of T_{new}. Each subset of trains G must be composed by trains that have a same journey and that travel in a same direction. For each group, a different frequency may be specified, which must belong to an interval $[F_L^G, F_U^G]$, where the lower and upper bound may be the same. In this case a fixed frequency is specified for the group. For each station where a given frequency must be considered, the following expression must be satisfied

$$\{t', t\} \subset G \wedge dep_i^{t'} > dep_i^t \wedge (\nexists t'')_G (dep_i^t < dep_i^{t''} < dep_i^{t'})$$

$$\rightarrow F_L^G \leq dep_i^{t'} - dep_i^t \leq F_U^G \ . \tag{11}$$

2.2   Optimality of a Solution - Objective Function

We have defined the *Minimum Total Running Time* (Γ_{opt}^t) of each train $t \in T_{new}$, as the minimum time required by t to complete its journey, satisfying all the problem constraints in CONS but only taking into account the set of trains in circulation T_C; the trains $T_{new} \setminus t$ are ignored. We have two criteria to measure the quality of each solution: (i) the average delay (δ) of the new trains with respect the *Minimum Total Running Time*, and (ii) the deviation (σ) between the average delay of trains going in up direction (δ_U), and the average delay of trains going in down direction (δ_D). These values are computed according the following expressions:

$$\delta_t = \frac{arr_{n_t}^t - dep_0^t - \Gamma_{opt}^t}{\Gamma_{opt}^t}; \ \delta_U = \frac{\sum_{t \in T_U \cap T_{new}} \delta_t}{|T_U \cap T_{new}|}; \ \delta_D = \frac{\sum_{t \in T_D \cap T_{new}} \delta_t}{|T_D \cap T_{new}|}; \ \delta = \frac{\delta_U + \delta_D}{|T_{new}|}$$

The average delay deviation of each set of trains, up and down direction, with respect to the average delay of all new trains, is:

$$\sigma = \sqrt{\frac{(\delta_U - \delta)^2 + (\delta_D - \delta)^2}{2}}$$

A given weight, ω_{delay} and ω_{eq}, is assigned to each criterion respectively. The weight assigned to each one is determined by the railway planner. Finally, considering that *TTABLE* is one problem solution and therefore is the set of timetables for each new train, the objective function of this problem is formulated as:

$$f(TTABLE) = \text{MIN}(\omega_{delay} \times \delta + \omega_{eq} \times \sigma). \tag{12}$$

3   A Scheduling Order-Based Method (SOBM)

In order to obtain an optimal solution (timetables) in our CSOP, the process obtains successively different solutions, keeping the best one obtained each time. The search process of each solution is heuristically guided (Section 3.1), and a pruning process is applied to reduce the search time (Section 3.3). The process obtains new solutions iteratively until a given end condition is fulfilled (number of iterations, a given time interval, a minimum cost for the objective function, etc.). Each solution is obtained by repeating the following sequence of steps: select a train, assign a timetable to the selected train in a given track section of its journey and evaluate the partial solution to decide wether to continue or to prune, until a valid timetable had been assigned to every train in T_{new}; or until the current partial solution is discarded by the pruning process.

3.1   Heuristic Decision for the Priority Assignment

The disjunctive constraints are the main cause of the complexity of this problem. These constraints are due to the competition of two trains for the same resource, i.e. track section or track in a given station. When there is a conflict between two trains for the same resource, and one of them is a train in circulation, the train in circulation will always have higher priority, and the new train will always be delayed. However when the conflict occurs between two new trains, we use a heuristic based on the selection order of the trains to determine which of the two new trains will have higher priority on this resource. Each solution will be determined by this priorities assignment.

We consider the problem as a search tree whose root node (*initial node*) represents the empty timetabling. For each node where no successor is possible, there is an artificial terminal node (*final node*). Let T_{open} be the set of new trains whose timetables have not yet been completed ($T_{open} \subseteq T_{new}$). Each intermediate node is composed of a pair (t_i, s_j), which indicates that a feasible timetable must be found for the train $t_i \in T_{open}$ in its track section s_j. When the timetable of a train t_i is completed, this train is eliminated from the set T_{open}. Each level of the search tree indicates which part of the timetable of each train can be generated. The method must determine in each level, which of the nodes will be chosen. The problem consists of finding a path in the search tree, (from the *initial* node to the *final* node), so that the order of priorities established by this path produces the minimum cost according to the objective function.

In this point we describe how is selected each node that will compose the path of one solution. For each node (t_i, s_j) in a given level of the tree, consider that a feasible timetable was assigned to t_i from its initial station l_0^t until the station $l_{j_t}^t$. For each level, we measure the partial delay of each train $t \in T_{open}$ according to the following expression:

$$\delta_{partial}^t = \frac{arr_{j_t}^t - dep_0^t - \Gamma_{opt}^t}{\Gamma_{opt}^t} \tag{13}$$

Given that the minimum partial delay is $\delta_{min} = \min_{t \in T_{open}}(\delta_{partial}^t)$, the probability ρ_t, of train t being selected is computed according to the following expression:

$$\rho_t = \frac{(\delta_{partial}^t - \delta_{min} + \varepsilon)^\alpha}{\sum_{t \in T_{open}}(\delta_{partial}^t - \delta_{min} + \varepsilon)^\alpha} \tag{14}$$

A node is chosen according to the parameterized Regret-Based Biased Random Sampling (RBRS) [6] and [9], so that the train with higher priority is not necessarily the train chosen, due to the random component of the RBRS method.

If the node (t_i, s_j) is selected, then the next step will consist in setting the timetable for the train t_i in its track section s_j which is described in the next subsection.

3.2   Timetable Generation and Constraint Verification

Once a given node (t_i, s_j) has been selected, its computed a departure time for the train t_i from the location l_j^t $(s_j = l_j^t \rightarrow l_{j+1}^t)$ and an initial timetable is assigned in the track section s_j according to the constraints 3 and 4. From this initial timetable, the process proceeds to verify the rest of constraints in CONS in the track section s_j.

The constraints are verified taking into account the trains whose journeys include the track section under consideration. The new trains whose journeys include this track section but that have not yet been selected in s_j are not taken into account. Therefore, when the process indicates that train t_i has a conflict with another new train t' (violating constraints such as 7, 10, ... etc), it means that (t', s_j) has been selected before than (t_i, s_j). Thus, if the process detects a conflict between the train t_i and another train, it will delay to t_i, since the other train has been selected previously and therefore it has higher priority than t_i.

It important to remark that the order in which the new trains are selected influences the global scheduling. The order of selection determines the priority among the trains and the way that each conflict between two new trains (crossing, overtaking, capacity in stations, headway time,..., etc) will be solved.

3.3   Heuristic Decision for the Prune Process

Each time the process finishes building the timetable for a train t_i in a track section s_j, it estimates the objective function value corresponding to the current partial scheduling in the best of the cases (δ_{est}). In other words, when a train has not yet assigned a timetable from a given track section of its journey, the process estimates that this train will employ the minimum time possible, sum of running time plus commercial stop ($M_{i_t \rightarrow n_t}^t$), to go from this track section until its destination. The following expression shows how is computed δ_{est}.

$$\delta_{\text{est}} = \frac{\sum_{t \in \mathrm{T}_{\text{new}}} \delta_{\text{est}}^t}{|\mathrm{T}_{\text{new}}|} \tag{15}$$

$$\delta_{\text{est}}^t = \frac{arr_{i_t}^t - dep_0^t + M_{i_t \rightarrow n_t}^t - \Gamma_{\text{opt}}^t}{\Gamma_{\text{opt}}^t} \tag{16}$$

If the estimated cost for the current partial scheduling is greater than the best solution cost (obtained up to point), then the current iteration is aborted and the partial scheduling is discarded. The partial solution is not saved because a problem for a real environment would imply a very high spatial cost.

The method incorporates knowledge about the objective function of the problem in order to estimate when a solution might not be better than a previous one. It is a conservative technique because it does not risk a solution until it is sure that the solution will not be better than the best one obtained up to this point. We increase the method efficiency with this pruning process.

4   Results

The Spanish Manager of Railway Infrastructure (ADIF) provides us with real instances to obtain a realistic evaluation of the proposed heuristic. We describe ten problem instances in Figure 1.a (columns 2 to 9) by means of: the length of the railway line, number of single/double track sections, number of stations,number of trains and track sections (TS) corresponding to all these trains, for trains already in circulation and for new trains, respectively. The results are shown in Figure 1.b. This Table presents the best value of the objective function and the number of feasible solutions that were obtained for each problem (columns 2 and 3 for the RANDOM approach; columns 4 and 5 for the SOBM approach). The algorithm is implemented using C++ running on a Pentium IV 3,6 Ghz. The running time was of 300" for all the problems, and the parameters of the RBRS set to $\alpha=1$ and $\varepsilon=0,05$. The difference between the RANDOM approach and the SOBM approach is the way that the trains are chosen at each level of the search tree. In the first approach the trains are chosen randomly, in the second approach, the trains are chosen according to the method explained in Section 3. The results show that a guided heuristic such as SOBM explores regions in a more promising way in less time than the RANDOM approach does and this leads to better solutions.

MOM: A Decision Support System

We have developed a tool, MOM (*Modulo Optimizador de Mallas*), that provides solutions for the timetabling problem whose requirements have been given in

(a)

Problems	Infrastructure Despcription				In Circulation		New Trains	
	Km	1-Way	2-Way	Stat	Trains	TS	Trains	TS
1	209,1	25	11	22	40	472	53	543
2	129,4	21	0	15	27	302	30	296
3	177,8	37	4	25	11	103	11	146
4	225,8	33	0	23	113	1083	11	152
5	256,1	38	0	28	80	1049	15	235
6	256,1	38	0	28	81	1169	16	159
7	96,7	16	0	13	47	1397	16	180
8	96,7	16	0	13	22	661	40	462
9	298,2	46	0	24	26	330	11	173
10	401,4	37	1	24	0	0	35	499

(b)

Problems	RANDOM		SOBM	
	#of Solutions	Obj%	#of Solutions	Obj%
1	169	8,6	168	5,9
2	611	10,1	608	10
3	2185	21,1	3101	16
4	311	13,2	445	5,5
5	396	19,3	452	17,5
6	424	14,7	521	14,1
7	267	18	263	15,4
8	67	50,9	85	45,5
9	1112	11,5	1129	8,7
10	405	19,2	397	17,9

Fig. 1. Results obtained with the SOBM method

Section 2. MOM solves the problem using the SOBM method (Section 3). It is a tool that makes easier to railway planner the task of obtaining feasible and high quality timetables for the trains that must be added to a given railway line.

MOM allows the user to configure each problem instance as far as infrastructure, user requirements, solving process and quality of solutions is concerned.

- MOM interacts with the ADIF Database to obtain data related to the railway infrastructure (tracks in stations and sections, maintenance intervals, closing time, blocking type, etc.) and trains (journeys, commercial stops, etc. However, MOM allows the user modify the obtained data in order to provide the nearest scenario to every particular environment or user requirements, such that the given solutions are useful and significant. Moreover, MOM also allows to parameterize each train: intervals for departure and arrival times, running times in sections, frequency of departures, circulation days, specific safety margins (reception, expedition and headway time)in specific sections, etc.

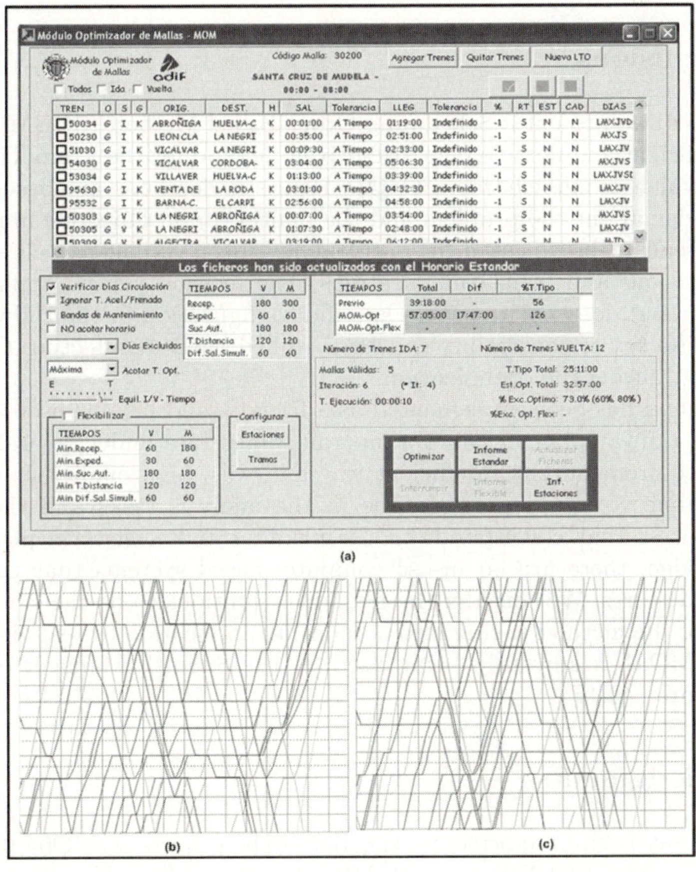

Fig. 2. A graphical example of solutions given by MOM

- MOM deals with hard and soft (i.e. *flexible*) constraints. That is, some given constraints (reception time, expedition time, etc.) can be relaxed within given bounds in order to obtain a better global scheduling (improvement in the objective function value). Any case, every relaxation should be finally validated by the user.
- In order to compute the quality of each solution, the objective function given in Section 2.2 takes into account: (i) the average delay of the trains with respect to the minimum running time, and (ii) the balance between the average delay of trains going in up and down direction respectively. The user specifies to MOM the weight that must be assigned to each criterion in the objective function.

In Figure 2.a is shown the MOM interface. The Figures 2.b and 2.c show two solutions. In the first one, the solving process has satisfied all the constraints without relax the variables domain. In the second solution, the problem was solved using the flexible mode. Certain constraints were relaxed and the average delay was 20% less than the average delay obtained in the first solution.

5   Conclusions

In this paper, we present a Scheduling Order-Based Method (SOBM) that proposes an efficient and flexible heuristic-driven method for the Train Timetabling Problem, which is modeled as a CSOP. Heuristic-decisions are based on both the knowledge about the problem and the multi criteria objective function.

Several realistic instances of the problem have been verified as well as different traffic conditions and train configurations. The method can be applied to any railway line and does not require a specific configuration in the railway infrastructure. The set of constraints can be modified without affecting the solving process used during the optimization.

The method has been implemented as a friendly and flexible user-aid system so that the railway planner can obtain train timetables under several scenarios and user requirements, in an efficient way and with high quality. It allows the railway planner to employ more time in the analysis tasks and the decision making process that corresponds to the medium and long term planning. To our knowledge, there are no in-use computer-based systems that consider all the shown features. We consider the main contributions to be the efficiency and flexibility of the method taking into account its application to real and complex scenarios. *MOM* is currently being used by the Spanish Manager of Railway Infrastructure (ADIF).

Acknowledgments

This work has been supported by the Research projects TIN2004-06354-C02-01 (MEC, Spain - FEDER) and GV04B/516 (Generalitat Valenciana, Spain). We are grateful to the Spanish Manager of Railway Infrastructure (ADIF) and to Jose Estrada Guijarro for give us the opportunity to interact with a real environment, for provide us with the instances presented in this paper, and for his effort and time to define the problem and evaluate the resulting schedules.

References

1. Cordeau, J., Toth, P. and Vigo, D. A survey of optimization models for train routing and scheduling. Transportation Science 32, 380-446 (1998)
2. Lova, A., Tormos, P., Barber, F., Ingolotti, L., Salido, M.A. and Abril, M. Intelligent Train Scheduling on a High-Loaded Railway Network. ATMOS 2004: Algorithmic Methods and Models for Optimization of Railways. Lecture Notes in Computer Science, LNCS (Springer Verlag). To appear. 2005
3. *MOM: Mdulo Optimizador de Mallas:*
   http://www.dsic.upv.es/users/ia/gps/MOM/
4. Nachtigall, K. and Voget, S. Minimizing waiting times in integrated fixed interval timetables by upgrading railway tracks 103, 610–627, (1997)
5. Schrijver, A., and Steenbeek, A. Timetable construction for railned. Technical Report, CWI, Amsterdam, The Netherlands (in Dutch), (1994)
6. Schirmer, A. and Riesenberg, S. Parameterized heuristics for project scheduling-Biased random sampling methods. Technical Report 456. Institute fr Betriebswirtschaftslehre der UNIVERSITT KIEL (1997)
7. Serafini, P. Ukovich, W. A mathematical model for periodic scheduling problems. SIAM Journal on Discrete Mathematics 2(4), 550–581, (1989)
8. Silva de Oliveira, E. Solving Single-Track Railway Scheduling Problem Using Constraint Programming. Phd Thesis. Univ. of Leeds, School of Computing (2001)
9. Tormos, P. and Lova, A. A Competitive Heuristic Solution Technique For Resource-Constrained Project Scheduling. Annals Of Operations Research 102, 65–81, (2001)
10. Tormos, P. et al. A Genetic Approach to Train Scheduling on a High-Traffic Railway Line. Algorithmic meThods and Models for Optimization of railwayS ATMOS 2005. Electronic Notes in Theoretical Computer Science. To be appear.
11. Walker, C., Snowdon, J. and Ryan, D. Simultaneous disruption recovery of a train timetable and crew roster in real time. Comput. Oper. Res. 32 (8), 2077–2094, (2005)

SEaM: Analyzing Schedule Executability Through Simulation

Riccardo Rasconi*, Nicola Policella, and Amedeo Cesta

ISTC-cnr
Institute for Cognitive Science and Technology
National Research Council of Italy
`name.surname@istc.cnr.it`

Abstract. Increasing attention is being dedicated to the problem of schedule execution management. This has encouraged research focused on the analysis of strategies for the execution of plans in real working environments. To this aim, much work has been recently done to devise scheduling procedures which increase the level of robustness of the produced solutions. Yet, these results represent only the first step in this direction: in order to improve confidence in the theoretical results, it is also necessary to conceive experimental frameworks where the devised measures may find confirmation through empirical testing. This approach also has the advantage of unveiling possible counter-intuitive insights of the proposed scheduling strategies, which otherwise might remain concealed. This paper presents: (a) an experimental platform designed to tackle the problem of schedule execution with uncertainty; (b) an analysis of a variety of schedule execution tests performed under variable environmental conditions.

1   Introduction

One of the most relevant issues in Scheduling regards schedule support at execution time; the dynamism and unpredictability which inherently permeate real-world application domains, make the ability to cope with unexpected events during the schedule execution phase an absolutely primary concern. The growing attention dedicated to this specific issue in research areas such as OR and AI is proved by the increasing number of single results and surveys [1, 2, 3, 4]. Notwithstanding the relatively recent developments, the whole topic still offers much room for investigation.

The aim of our work is to compare different approaches to schedule execution under uncertainty in a fair and controlled way, specifically focusing on Project Scheduling Problems [5]. These problems are characterized by a rich internal structure. They are based on a network of activities, among which it is possible to identify complex temporal relations that can be used to model a number of variably rigid causal links which normally constrain the tasks in a project. As a further source of complexity, several heterogeneous resources with different capacities serve the activities according to complex modalities.

This paper presents an experimental framework which allows us to carry out a series of reproducible experiments which aim at examining the behavior of schedules under

---

* PhD Student at DIST - University of Genova.

M. Ali and R. Dapoigny (Eds.): IEA/AIE 2006, LNAI 4031, pp. 410–420, 2006.
© Springer-Verlag Berlin Heidelberg 2006

execution, upon the occurrence of different kinds of unexpected disturbances. To show the possibilities opened by the framework we present a set of comparison on different state-of-the-art constraint based techniques. The experiments we present yield different results depending on a number of crucial factors, which range from the particular technique used to synthesize the initial solution (baseline schedule), to the type of rescheduling methodology employed for solution revision.

The paper is organized as follows: Section 2 briefly introduces the schedule execution problem we tackle, as well as the reference scheduling problem the whole framework is based upon; Section 3 describes the whole experimental infrastructure, giving special attention to the types of flexible solutions we use as baseline schedules and to the execution algorithm used to simulate their execution; Section 4 briefly introduces how uncertainty is modeled in the framework, while Section 5 describes the experiments and the obtained results. Section 6 concludes the paper.

2   The Scheduling Problem Under Uncertainty

In general terms, solving a scheduling problem for a given set of activities (or tasks) that have to be executed, basically means to find a suitable temporal allocation for each activity, so as to guarantee "good" performance relative to the optimization of an objective function, usually the project total completion time (*makespan*).

What follows is a brief description of the particular problem that we will refer to throughout all the paper, known as *Resource-Constrained Project Scheduling Problem with minimum and maximum time lags* (RCPSP/max) [6], which is basically composed of the following elements:

- **Activities.** $A = \{a_1, \ldots, a_n\}$ represents the set of activities or tasks. Every activity a_i is characterized by a processing time p_i;
- **Resources.** $R = \{r_1, \ldots, r_m\}$ represents the set of the resources necessary for the execution of the activities. Execution of each activity a_i can require an amount req_{ik} of one or more resources r_k for the whole processing time p_i;
- **Constraints.** The constraints are rules that limit the possible allocations of the activities. They can be divided into two types: (1) the *temporal constraints* impose limitations on the times the activities can be scheduled at; (2) the *resource constraints* limit the maximum capacity of each resource; at no time, the total demand level of any resource being assigned to one or more activities can exceed its maximum capacity.

This class of problems is interesting because it allows to model a broad range of real domains, that is, domains in which complex causal relations between activities and coordination between multiple steps must be enforced. These problems are characterized by a rich variety of time and resource constraints. The price for such expressiveness is that RCPSP/max is a complex problem; in fact, both optimization and feasibility are NP-hard[1].

---

[1] The reason for the NP-hardness lies in the presence of maximum time-lags, which inevitably imply the satisfaction of deadline constraints, thus transforming feasibility problems for precedence-constrained scheduling into scheduling problems with time windows.

Clearly, our goal is not limited to solving the RCPSP/max: in fact, regardless of the complexity related to finding a solution of a scheduling problem, other kinds of difficulties arise when we try to execute it in real working environments. The unpredictability which affects real world domains inherently entails a high level of uncertainty on the execution conditions. Therefore, unless some intelligent actions are taken during either the initial solving process and/or the execution phase, the solution is bound to lose its consistency, and therefore its usefulness.

Execution uncertainty in scheduling can be dealt with either *proactively* or *reactively*. The key point in the proactive approach is to synthesize solutions that are able to absorb the effects of unexpected events, thus minimizing the need to reschedule, while the reactive approach requires to exploit local or global online adjustments to the schedule, in order to re-gain consistency. As we will see, the difference between these two strategies is often very subtle; the objective of this paper is to investigate the possibilities offered by trading-off among simple adjustments, fixes to the baseline schedule, and new calls to problem solvers. To this aim, we have built an experimental environment targeted at studying how increasingly robust baselines can influence the reactive phase. Clearly, acting proactively requires a greater effort during the initial solving process in order to grant robustness to the solution, while acting reactively generally makes the execution phase more demanding, because of the higher number of necessary re-schedulings. In order to make the reactive approach computationally lighter, it is possible to bind the scope of the reaction within an arbitrarily wide neighborhood of the schedule conflicting area (local reaction). The global approach in general guarantees to find a higher quality solution with respect to a local method, though it exhibits a lack in reactivity, requiring more time for system reconfiguration. This paper addresses the issue of local vs. global re-scheduling within a particular set of constraint-based algorithms which are global in nature, but are forced to act locally by over-constraining the updated problem that the scheduler is called to reason upon.

It is worth noting that the problem of execution has been addressed in AI planning by several works [7, 8, 9], nevertheless those solutions are not directly applicable to project scheduling and differs from those described in this paper.

3   *SEaM:* The Scheduling Execution and Monitoring Framework

Fig. 1(a) shows the complete platform that we have set up in order to produce the experiments. It is composed of three blocks: the *solver* and the *generator* work off-line and have the job of, respectively, computing the initial solution (the baseline schedule), and generating the exogenous events, intended to disturb the schedule during its execution; the third block, called *SEaM* (for *Schedule Execution and Monitoring*), works on-line, and is responsible for performing a complete simulation of the execution of the initial solution. The disturbing events synthesized by the *generator* are injected during the simulated execution at specified times, and their effects are counteracted by the *SEaM* module, which is in charge of maintaining schedule consistency by exploiting a number of different *re-scheduling* policies.

The core of our work is represented by *SEaM* which is depicted in more detail in Fig. 1(b). This component accepts in input: (1) the initial solution (i.e. the schedule that

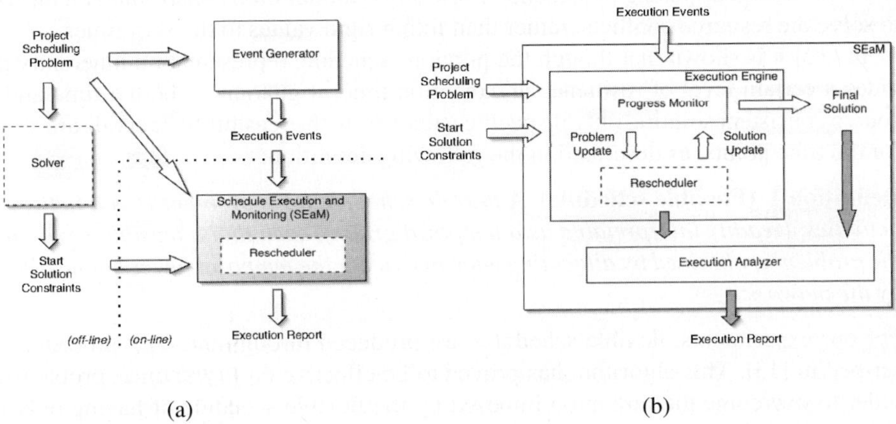

Fig. 1. The platform for comparing execution strategies (a), and detail of the *SEaM* module (b)

will be executed), in terms of the initial scheduling problem plus the constraints produced in the solving process, and (2) the exogenous events which have been produced by the event generator. Subsequently, the *Progress Monitor* module manages the schedule execution by simulating the advancement of time and dispatching the activities at their earliest possible start time, so as to minimize the global makespan. When an unexpected temporal event is acknowledged, the current problem is updated and passed to the *Rescheduler* which is in charge of producing the new solution that will act as the next baseline to continue execution. The cycle proceeds until either the execution is succesfully completed or a failure in delivering a new solution in encountered: in the latter case, the simulation is aborted. The figure shows also an additional module, the "Execution Analyzer", that is responsible for monitoring the whole execution process and finally generates the reports that describe the outcome of the experiments.

3.1 Solution Representation: Flexible Schedules vs. $\mathcal{POS}$s

Going back to Fig. 1(a), we can observe that the module in charge of enacting the strategy in order to deal with uncertainty is the off-line solver, which produces the baseline schedule. In contrast to most off-line schedulers, which deliver fixed-time solutions where the decision variables are represented by the start times of each activity, our approach is based on the general concept of "temporal flexibility" [10]. A temporally flexible solution can be described as a network of activities whose start times (and end times) are associated with a set of feasible values (feasibility intervals). Underlying the activity network there exists a second network (Temporal Constraint Network – TCN [11]), composed of all the start and end points of each activity (time points), bound to one another through specific values which limit their mutual distances. The search schema used in our approach focuses on decision variables which represent conflicts in the use of the available resources; the solving process proceeds by ordering pairs of activities until all conflicts in the current problem representation are removed. This approach is usually referred to as the Precedence Constraint Posting (PCP) [10], because it revolves around imposing precedence constraints (the *solution constraints*) on the TCN to solve the resource conflicts, rather than fixing rigid values to the start times.

In [12] it is shown that though the previous schedule representation inherently provides a certain level of resilience at execution time, it guarantees both a time and resource consistent solution only if specific values from the feasibility intervals are chosen for the time points, as described in the following definition:

Definition 1 (Flexible schedule). *A flexible schedule for a problem $\mathcal{P}$ is a network of activities, (readily interpretable as a temporal graph), such that a feasible solution for the problem is obtained by allocating each activity at the temporal lower bound allowed by the network.*

For our experiments, flexible schedules are produced through the ISES procedure described in [13]. This algorithm has proved to be effective on RCPSP/max problems. In order to overcome the limitation imposed by the flexible schedule of having only one consistent solution, a generalization of the TCN produced by a PCP phase is proposed in works such as [12, 14], in which methods for defining a set of both time and resource feasible solutions are presented. This new representation is called *Partial Order Schedule* [14]:

Definition 2 (Partial Order Schedule). *A Partial Order Schedule ($\mathcal{POS}$) for a problem $\mathcal{P}$ is an activity network, such that any possible temporal solution is also a resource-consistent assignment.*

A $\mathcal{POS}$ is a special case of a flexible solution and it can be obtained by replacing the solution constraints with a new set of constraints that impose a stronger condition on the TCN (*chaining constraints*). Fig. 2 shows an example of different types of scheduling solutions: the problem (a) is composed of four activities a, b, c, and d, all using the same resource, (maximum capacity = 2). Solution (b) represents a flexible schedule where the resource conflict has been solved by adding the solution constraint $d \prec c$; solution (c) represents a $\mathcal{POS}$ where two chaining constraints have been added: $b \prec c$ and $d \prec c$. It should be noted that the importance of choosing the RCPSP/max stems from the need to perform a fair comparison between flexible schedules and partial order schedules. In fact, in the absence of maximum time lags, a $\mathcal{POS}$ always represents an infinite and "complete" set of solutions, as it always allows to avoid a re-scheduling phase (propagating the changes that have occurred is sufficient). In the case of flexible schedules instead, propagation alone is not generally sufficient, as any unexpected change might introduce resource conflicts.

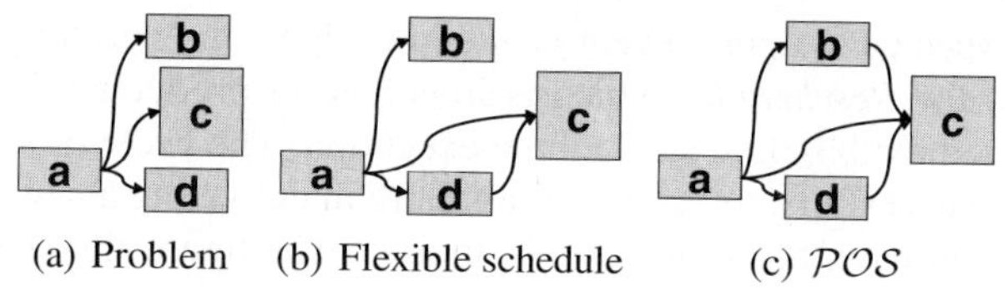

(a) Problem   (b) Flexible schedule   (c) $\mathcal{POS}$

Fig. 2. A problem and different solution representations

3.2 The Execution Algorithm

The details of the execution algorithm are illustrated in Algorithm 1. The algorithm is divided in an off-line and an on-line section; in the former, the initial solution can be

---

Algorithm 1. Solve a scheduling problem P and Execute one of its solution S

Input: problem P, policies parameter retract and pos
Output: Execution report

```
// off-line phase
S ← offlineScheduler(P)
```
if S *does not exist* **then**
   ⌊ STOP (SOLVER FAILURE)

if pos **then**
   ⌊ S ← createPOS(S)

```
// on-line phase
```
while *a disturb* E *exists* **do**
   if retract **then**
      if propagation(E, S) *fails* $\vee$ S *is not resource consistent* **then**
         S ← removeChoice(S)
         S ← onlineScheduler(S)
         if S *does not exist* **then**
            ⌊ STOP (EXECUTION FAILURE)
         if pos **then**
            ⌊ S ← createPOS(S)
   else
      if propagation(E,S) *fails* **then**
         ⌊ STOP (EXECUTION FAILURE)
      if S *is not resource consistent* **then**
         S ← onlineScheduler(S)
         if S *does not exist* **then**
            ⌊ STOP (EXECUTION FAILURE)

---

computed by the `offlineScheduler()` either as a flexible schedule (case FS) or as a $\mathcal{POS}$ (case POS) through the `createPOS()` procedure, depending on the value of the flag `pos`. In the latter, and regardless how the initial solution is produced, it is put into execution according to different modalities, depending on the value of the flag `retract`. At each step of the execution cycle, the environment is sensed for possible disturbs. Afterwards, if `retract` $= true$, the execution algorithm firstly removes all the constraints imposed in the previous solving process (`removeChoice()`), and secondly looks for a new solution (`onlineScheduler()`), possibly creating a new $\mathcal{POS}$. Note that the `onlineScheduler()` procedure implements the *Rescheduler* dotted box in Figs. 1(a) and 1(b). If `retract` $= false$, a new solution is searched leaving the previously imposed solution constraints untouched. In both cases, the algorithm initially checks for temporal consistency after each disturb is acknowledged through the `propagation()` procedure. Temporal consistency is in fact a condition that must be satisfied at all times, in order to continue schedule execution. The simulation is carried on until all the activities of the schedule are successfully executed, a temporal inconsistency is detected or the rescheduler fails to find an alternative solution.

4 Modeling the Uncertainty

The elements of uncertainty which usually impair the consistency of a schedule, may belong to one of the following types: (1) temporal changes, which exclusively pertain the temporal aspects of the problem; (2) resource variations, which modify the resource availability during the execution of a schedule; (3) causal changes, which involve the introduction of new constraints among the activities; (4) variations in the number of activities that have to be executed. In the present study, we focus our attention on the temporal aspects connected to the unpredictability of real environments: in particular, we will limit ourselves to the generation of temporal events, such as sudden delays of the activity start times and/or unexpected lengthening of the activity processing times, as depicted in Fig. 3:

delay of the activity start time: $e_{delay} = \langle a_i, \Delta_{st}, t_{aware} \rangle$
activity a_i undergoes a delay of Δ_{st} time units, at $t = t_{aware}$;

change of activity processing time: $e_p = \langle a_i, \Delta_p, t_{aware} \rangle$
activity a_i's processing time p_i is extended by Δ_p time units, at $t = t_{aware}$.

It is outside the scope of this paper to give a complete account on the event genera-tion: the interested reader should refer to [15] for further details. Yet, the aspect worth highlighting here is the rationale we have pursued in studying the generation of unex-pected events. In fact, though in the present work we produce the disturbances on top of the scheduling benchmark set described in [16], it should be remarked that the event-generating procedure we have devised is quite general, and can be used on a variety of different reference problems.

In the production of a benchmark set, we identified a number of fundamental fea-tures which characterize each unexpected event, such as the event type, the event qual-ity (or magnitude), as well as the its temporal distance from the previous event. The spacing of different exogenous events in each instance has been realized by adding the parameter t_{aware} in the definition of each event. This element specifies the "absolute" instant where the specific event is supposed to occur. By using the t_{aware} parameter it is possible to temporally sort all the generated events and to "fire" them in order of occurrence.

Fig. 3. Temporal changes: activities can last more than expected or they can undergo delays

5   Experimental Results

The comparison presented in this section is based on the analysis of known standard scheduling benchmarks in RCPSP/max combining each of them with four reactive scheduling benchmarks (world simulations). In this paper we present the results ob-tained from the $j30$ set [16]. This particular problem benchmark consists of one set of 270 scheduling problem instances of size 30×5 (number of activities $\times$ number of resources). Each instance of the reactive scheduling benchmark is composed of a set of unexpected events: each problem in the scheduling benchmark is associated with four instances of world simulations of different size (1, 2, 3, and 5 events each)[2]. In other

---

[2] All events represent either a delay on the start time, or a delay on the end time of the activities, and they are produced with the same probability throughout all the world simulations.

words, every scheduling problem will be put into four simulated executions, where each execution will be disturbed by, respectively, 1, 2, 3 and 5 exogenous events.

Table 1 shows the results of the executions on the j30 scheduling benchmark. We evaluate the different combinations of off-line/on-line policies — FS-NR (Flexible Schedule with No-Retraction), FS-R (Flexible Schedule with Retraction), POS-NR (POS with No-Retraction) and POS-R (POS with Retraction). In order to make the comparison more complete, we add a further execution mode based on the use of fixed time solutions where each activity is assigned a single start time instead of a set of alternatives. For each column in the table, we take into account the following aspects: the number of disturbances injected during each single execution (*number of disturbs*), the percentage (with respect to the number of initially solved problems) of the schedules which successfully completed the execution (*% executed*), the average makespan of the successfully executed schedules (*mk*), the average makespan deviation of the schedules before and after the execution (Δ *mk*), the percentage of the performed re-scheduling actions with respect to the number of the injected disturbances (*% resched.*), the average CPU time, in msecs, to compute the initial solution (*CPU Off-line*), the average CPU time spent to perform all re-schedulings during the execution (*CPU On-line*), the sensitivity of activity start time w.r.t. the execution process (ψ): this measure gives an assessment of how much the initial solution has been affected by the occurrence of the exogenous events during the execution[3].

With the exception of the *% executed* column, all data in the table are computed on the intersection set of all the succesfully executed problems.

5.1   Result Analysis

One of the most striking results that we observe regards the different abilities in preserving the executability of a solution. The outcome shows that the use of partial order schedules tends to lower the success rate in terms of completed executions (*% executed* column), mainly due to the dramatic increase in the number of rejected disturbs during the execution. This apparent anomaly can be explained as follows: the creation of a $\mathcal{POS}$ inherently involves a higher level of "constrainedness" in the TCN, in order to guarantee a resource conflict-free solution. This circumstance inevitably makes the TCN more reluctant in accepting new contraints, in the specific case, the constraints which model the exogenous events. Also, note how this effect gets worse as the number of the exogenous events increases (88,04% in the POS-NR case with 1 event, against 58,15% with 5 events).

Another important characteristic to be observed is the extremely low rate of necessary reschedulings exhibited by the POS-R/POS-NR policies (*% resched.* column): this result is all but surprising and confirms the theoretical expectations which motivated the study on the $\mathcal{POS}$. As shown, the need for schedule revision in case of $\mathcal{POS}$ utilization sensibly decreases by more than 75% in case of 5 disturbs. Note also the 100%

---

[3] This parameter is currently computed as follows $\psi = \sum_{i=1}^{N} \frac{|st_f(a_i) - st_0(a_i)|}{N}$. This measure gives an assessment of how much the initial solution has been affected by the occurrence of the exogenous events during the execution. The lower the value, the more the solution proved to be stable.

reschedulings figure relative to the case of *fixed time* schedules: in this case, a schedule revision is always needed: this is also confirmed by the extremely high *CPU on-line* values.

A very interesting aspect can be observed by comparing the *CPU on-line* values between the *Retraction* and *No Retraction* strategies. In general, the Retraction methods require a higher CPU on-line load because the removal of the solution constraints inevitably re-introduces some resource conflicts that must be solved by rescheduling. But the intriguing result lies in the fact that this difference in the CPU on-line rates stands *despite the comparable amount of performed reschedulings*. Let us look at the difference between the FS-R

Table 1. j30 Execution Results

method	number of disturbs	% executed	mk	Δmk	% resched.	CPU off-line	CPU on-line	ψ
FS-R		91.85%	103.43	4.29	27.27%	4478	77	2.55
POS-R		89.13%	102.63	3.60	5.19%	4613	15	1.84
FS-NR	1	91.85%	102.56	3.43	27.27%	4481	15	1.68
POS-NR		88.04%	102.14	3.10	5.19%	4612	2	1.55
fixed time		90.76%	106.29	7.16	100.00%	4480	300	5.04
FS-R		87.50%	106.99	8.02	34.21%	4106	150	4.32
POS-R		80.43%	104.91	6.03	4.51%	4242	20	2.92
FS-NR	2	88.59%	104.90	5.93	34.21%	4105	34	2.87
POS-NR		80.98%	104.83	5.95	4.51%	4239	4	2.83
fixed time		82.61%	107.35	8.38	100.00%	4109	501	5.57
FS-R		85.33%	109.55	9.73	26.90%	4506	190	5.40
POS-R		76.63%	108.11	8.36	5.85%	4647	37	4.30
FS-NR	3	83.15%	108.00	8.18	26.61%	4515	40	3.98
POS-NR		75.00%	107.83	8.09	5.85%	4646	8	4.02
fixed time		78.26%	109.95	10.12	100.00%	4512	848	6.45
FS-R		75.00%	119.30	16.19	26.43%	4282	267	8.48
POS-R		57.61%	116.44	13.37	5.24%	4414	73	6.48
FS-NR	5	74.46%	117.12	14.01	22.86%	4277	59	6.91
POS-NR		58.15%	115.86	12.79	5.00%	4410	12	6.15
fixed time		76.63%	118.33	15.23	100.00%	4286	1161	8.68

and FS-NR rates: it can be seen that, in the 5 events case, we have 267 ms. (FS-R) against 59 ms. (FS-NR), although the number of performed reschedulings is very close ($\approx 23\% \div 26\%$)! The same effect can be observed between the POS-R and POS-NR cases: 73 ms. against 12 ms., notwithstanding the same ($\approx 5\%$) number of reschedulings. This circumstance can be explained as follows: NR execution modes retain all the temporal constraints of the previous solution: hence, the rescheduler is bound to work on a smaller search space, finding the next solution almost immediately. The table also shows how inefficient the executions of fixed time solutions are (see the CPU on-line values).

One last word on schedule stability: the Δmk and ψ columns give a measure of the ability of a solution to remain stable during the execution. The former column takes into account solution continuity in terms of makespan preservation, while the latter accounts for stability in terms of maintainace of the activities' start times. As it can be seen, the highest stability during execution is obtained with the NR as opposed to R methodologies, because they maintain the structure of the initial solution for the whole execution. The most unstable solutions are produced in the fixed time case, as a direct consequence of the complete lack of temporal flexibility. In the cases where it is essential to maintain a high level of solution continuity, the No-Retraction methods are therefore to be preferred.

6   Conclusions

It is straightforward to assume that in order to face project scheduling problems, it is necessary to consider both the off-line solving phase, as well as a dynamical management, where the behaviour of the produced schedule is followed and analyzed throughout its whole lifespan. This paper discusses alternative approaches to the production, execution, monitoring and repairing of pre-defined schedules enforced in a constraint-based framework. We presented a platform, named *SEaM*, that simulates the execution of a baseline schedule, by maintaining an internal representation of the solution and updating this representation in order to (a) take into account the occurrence of exogenous events and (b) counteracting the effects of such events through proper rescheduling.

The *SEaM* allows us to obtain different insights on the combination of two aspects: (a) the use of different off-line scheduling techniques to increase proactive robustness and (b) the use of complementary re-scheduling policies to react to unexpected events. In particular we analyze two alternatives to the classical fixed time schedule – flexible schedules, containing a single point solution, and partial order schedules or $\mathcal{POS}$s. Moreover, we distinguish between the incremental modification of the initial schedule vs. the retraction of previously made decisions followed by a new resolution.

On the basis of well known project scheduling problem benchmarks, a set of exogenous events are produced *ad hoc* for each problem instance in order to maximize the possibility of dynamical event-acceptance. It is also worth remarking that the produced events are independent from the particular off-line scheduler used to provide the initial solution, as well as from the type of initial solution itself. The previous characteristics make it possible to use the *SEaM* framework to perform reproducible experiments.

A set of results support the usefulness of this analysis. Part of the outcome represents a direct confirmation of theoretical expectations from previous analysis; yet, the presence of counterintuitive insights in the results opens the way for further investigation and new perspectives.

Acknowledgments. The authors' work is partially supported by MIUR (Italian Ministry for Education, University and Research) under projects RoboCare (L. 449/97) and "Vincoli e Preferenze" (PRIN).

References

1. Davenport, A.J., Beck, J.C.: A Survey of Techniques for Scheduling with Uncertainty. accessible on-line at http://tidel.mie.utoronto.ca/publications.php on Feb, 2006. (2000)
2. Aytug, H., Lawley, M.A., McKay, K.N., Mohan, S., Uzsoy, R.M.: Executing production schedules in the face of uncertainties: A review and some future directions. European Journal of Operational Research **165** (2005) 86–110
3. Herroelen, W., Leus, R.: Robust and reactive project scheduling: a review and classification of procedures. International Journal of Production Research **42** (2004) 1599–1620
4. Verfaillie, G., Jussien, N.: Constraint solving in uncertain and dynamic environments – a survey. Constraints **10** (2005) 253–281
5. Brucker, P., Drexl, A., Mohring, R., Neumann, K., Pesch, E.: Resource-Constrained Project Scheduling: Notation, Classification, Models, and Methods. European Journal of Operational Research **112** (1999) 3–41

6. Bartusch, M., Mohring, R.H., Radermacher, F.J.: Scheduling project networks with resource constraints and time windows. Annals of Operations Research **16** (1988) 201–240
7. Schoppers, M.: Universal Plans for Reactive Robots in Unpredictable Environments. In: Proceedings of the Tenth International Joint Conference on Artificial Intelligence, IJCAI-87. (2005)
8. Ambros-Ingerson, J., Steel, S.: Integrating Planning, Execution and Monitoring. In: Proceedings of the Seventh National Conference on Artificial Intelligence, AAAI-88. (1988)
9. Beetz, M., McDermott, D.: Improving Robot Plans During Their Execution. In: Proceedings of the Second International Conference on AI Planning Systems, AIPS-94. (1994)
10. Cheng, C., Smith, S.F.: Generating Feasible Schedules under Complex Metric Constraints. In: Proceedings of the 12th National Conference on Artificial Intelligence, AAAI-94, AAAI Press (1994) 1086–1091
11. Dechter, R., Meiri, I., Pearl, J.: Temporal constraint networks. Artificial Intelligence **49** (1991) 61–95
12. Cesta, A., Oddi, A., Smith, S.F.: Profile Based Algorithms to Solve Multiple Capacitated Metric Scheduling Problems. In: Proceedings of the 4th International Conference on Artificial Intelligence Planning Systems, AIPS-98, AAAI Press (1998) 214–223
13. Cesta, A., Oddi, A., Smith, S.F.: An Iterative Sampling Procedure for Resource Constrained Project Scheduling with Time Windows. In: Proceedings of the 16th International Joint Conference on Artificial Intelligence, Morgan Kaufmann (1999) 1022–1029
14. Policella, N., Oddi, A., Smith, S.F., Cesta, A.: Generating Robust Partial Order Schedules. In: Principles and Practice of Constraint Programming, 10th International Conference, CP 2004. Volume 3258 of Lecture Notes in Computer Science., Springer (2004) 496–511
15. Policella, N., Rasconi, R.: Designing a Testset Generator for Reactive Scheduling. Intelligenza Artificiale (Italian Journal of Artificial Intelligence) **II** (2005) 29–36
16. Kolisch, R., Schwindt, C., Sprecher, A.: Benchmark Instances for Project Scheduling Problems. In Weglarz, J., ed.: Project Scheduling - Recent Models, Algorithms and Applications. Kluwer Academic Publishers, Boston (1998) 197–212

From Demo to Practice
the MEXAR Path to Space Operations

A. Cesta, G. Cortellessa, S. Fratini, A. Oddi, and N. Policella[*]

ISTC-CNR, Rome, Italy
Italian National Research Council
Institute for Cognitive Science and Technology

Abstract. This paper describes a software tool that synthesizes commands for data downlink from the on-board memory of the MARS EXPRESS spacecraft to the ground station. Some features of the tool are depicted, showing how AI techniques for planning, scheduling, domain modeling and intelligent interaction have been put into context in a challenging application environment. The system is the result of a two steps effort: a first study which produced a demonstration prototype able to capture the main aspects of the problem, and a second effort that has developed a fielded application completely integrated in operations environment. The tool is in daily use by the mission planning team of MARS EXPRESS at the European Space Agency since February 2005.

1   The Story: In Search of Real Data

In the period November 2000 - July 2002, authors research group has worked at the European Space Agency (ESA) study "Efficient Planning Algorithms for an Interplanetary Mission". This study was aimed at demonstrating Artificial Intelligence techniques for Planning and Scheduling applied to a mission planning problem within the MARS EXPRESS space program. An open problem, jointly identified by the research group and the MARS EXPRESS Mission Planning experts, has been studied and formalized as the Mars Express Memory Dump Problem (MEX-MDP). In May 2002, the group delivered to the ESA-ESOC center an advanced prototype called MEXAR, able to automate the generation of spacecraft operations for efficient on-board mass memory dumping. The software was composed of two main parts: (a) a Problem Solver able to address the MEX-MDP with different algorithms, and (b) and Interaction Module devoted to both facilitate user access to the solver, and provide a set of inspection functionalities over the solution. The various results have been presented in a series of official publications (see for example [1, 2, 3, 4]).

While developing MEXAR the group has acquired a substantial amount of background information on mission planning, difficult to obtain unless tightly cooperating with an operational space environment. On the other hand, MEXAR has provided the mission planning team a unique example of intelligent software technologies integration to address a problem in their daily activities. Nonetheless, a very important limitation plagued the first project: the unavailability of real data from the spacecraft or even from

---

* Contact: `amedeo.cesta@istc.cnr.it`. Authors are listed in alphabetical order.

M. Ali and R. Dapoigny (Eds.): IEA/AIE 2006, LNAI 4031, pp. 421–431, 2006.

a realistic simulation of the spacecraft's nominal work. As a consequence, although the study had a very positive outcome, it remained at the level of "nice demo". Its results remained unused at mission time because the tool was never validated against real mission data. In June 2004, contacts with the Mission Planning Team of MARS EXPRESS started again. It clearly emerged that during the first six months of spacecraft activities around Mars, the mission planners had faced serious manpower overload in addressing the Spacecraft Memory Dumping Problem. The downlink activities were synthesized mostly manually by a team of people continuously dedicated to this task. Authors proposed to start a specific study aimed at understanding the problem on the basis of real data analysis. Regular contacts with senior members of the ESOC Mission Planning Team allowed us to get acquainted with both those data and an amount of specific constraints that were introduced to cope with operational problems.

After three months, authors have been able to deliver to ESA an increasingly accurate operational version of a software able to cope with real problem instances, and real data files. During a subsequent period of three months the tool has been tested back to back against the previous semi-manual procedure developed within the team. Since February 2005 the new operational system called MEXAR2 is in continuous use at ESA-ESOC as the main tool to solve MEX-MDP instances. It directly synthesizes commands that implement the data downlink policy from on board memory to Earth.

In a more recent project titled "MEXAR2: A Software Tool for Continuous Support to Data Dumping Activities for MARS EXPRESS" authors have robustified the tool with additional functionalities and a user interface that facilitates its management. This paper is a short report on the "problem life cycle" MEXAR2 is inserted in, the features of the current tool, and an evaluation of its behavior.

2 Modeling the Problem and Automating Its Solution

In a deep-space mission like MARS EXPRESS data transmission to Earth represents a fundamental aspect. In this domain, a space-probe continuously produces a large amount of data resulting from the activities of its payloads and from on-board device monitoring and verification tasks (the so-called *housekeeping* data). All these data

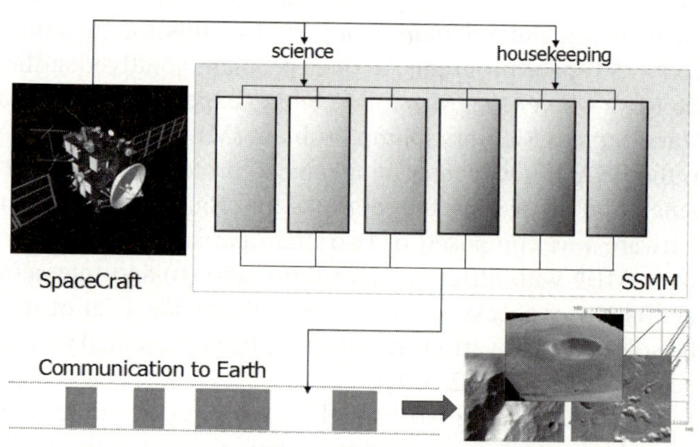

Fig. 1. The on-board vs. ground segment data flow

should be transferred to Earth during a number of downlink sessions. Moreover, in the case of MARS EXPRESS a single pointing system is present. This implies that, during regular operations, the space-probe either points to Mars, to performs payload operations, or points to Earth, to download the produced data. As a consequence, on-board data generally require to be first stored in a Solid State Mass Memory (SSMM) and then transferred to Earth. Therefore, the main problem to be solved consists in synthesizing sequences of spacecraft operations (*dump plans*) necessary to deliver the content of the on-board memory during the available downlink windows. This allows to save upcoming pieces of information without losing previously stored data and to optimize given objective functions.

In Fig. 1 the main data flow addressed in our work is shown: the spacecraft instruments produce data stored in the on-board memory subdivided into slots called *packet stores*. The problem goal is to create commands for downlinking such data to Earth during the interval in which the communication channel with the ground station is active. In general, synthesizing the plan involves managing the constraints due to the bounded on-board memory and the limited communication windows of different data transmission rates. The planned activities of the satellite are incrementally refined as soon as a specific operational period approaches. Same activities are not predicted in advance and a *short-term plan* is generated each one or two days. This two days plan is part of the set of commands uplinked to the satellite. Additionally due to differences in compression algorithms the amount of data produced by some of the activities cannot be exactly predicted in advance creating once in a while the need to recompute the short term plan very quickly before the commands uplink.

Domain entities. To model the problem we have subdivided the basic entities that are relevant to the MEX-MDP domain into *resources* and *activities*: resources represent domain subsystems able to give services, whereas activities model tasks to be executed using resources over time. We model two different types of resources: (a) the SSMM that is used to store both science and housekeeping data. The SSMM is subdivided into *packet stores*, $\{pk_1, pk_2, \ldots, pk_{np}\}$, each one with a fixed capacity, c_i, and priority, pr_i. Each packet store can be seen as a file of given maximum size that is managed cyclically, that is, previous pieces of information will be overwritten, and then lost, if the amount of stored data overflows the packet store capacity; (b) the *Communication Channel* that represents the downlink connections to Earth for transmitting data. This resource is characterized by a set of separated communication windows $CW = \{cw_1, cw_2, \ldots, cw_{nw}\}$ that identify intervals of time in which downlink connections can be established. Each element cw_j is a 3-tuple $\langle r_j, s_j, e_j \rangle$, where r_j is the available data rate during the time window cw_j and s_j and e_j are respectively the start and the end-time of this window.

Activities describe *how* resources can be used. Each activity a_i is characterized by a fixed duration, d_i, and two variables, s_i and e_i, which respectively represent its start-time and end-time. Two basic types of activity are relevant to MEX-MDP, store operations st_i and memory dumps md_i. Each store operation, st_i, "instantaneously" stores, at its end-time e_i, an amount of data q_i in a defined packet store, pk_i. Through a memory dump, $md_i = \langle pk_i, s_i, e_i, q_i \rangle$, an amount q_i of stored data is transmitted from the packet store pk_i to the ground station, during the interval $[s_i, e_i)$.

Two different data types are modeled using store operations: the *Payload Operation Request* (POR) and the housekeeping activities. *PORs* are scientific observations which generate a set of data distributed over the available packet stores. Housekeeping activities generate a flow of data with constant rate which has to be stored in the dedicated slots of the SSMM.

Algorithm 1. Generate down-link commands

Input: problem P, policies parameter robust and priority
Output: Down-link commands Cmd

```
// Data Dump Level
// Produce a data allocation over the communication channel
```
while S *incomplete* **do**
    S ← HousekeepingAllocation(P, priority)
    S ← MaxFlowAllocation(P, S, robust, priority)
    if *No more HK allocation* **then**
      └ break

```
// Packet Level
// Generate data commands
```
Cmd ← GenerateDownLink(S, priority)

return Cmd

Problem definition. A single MEX-MDP instance is composed of a set of scientific observations, a set of housekeeping productions, and a time horizon $\mathcal{H} = [0, H]$. The *solution* to a MEX-MDP is a set of dump commands $S = \{md_1, md_2, \ldots, md_{nd}\}$ *such that*:

- At each instant of $t \in \mathcal{H}$, the amount of data stored in each packet store pk_i does not exceed the packet store capacity c_i, i.e., overwriting is not allowed;
- The whole set of data is "available" on ground within the considered temporal horizon $\mathcal{H} = [0, H]$, except an amount of residual data for each packet store pk_i lower or equal to the capacity c_i;
- Each dump activity, md_i, is executed within an assigned time window cw_j which has a constant data rate r_j. Moreover, dump commands cannot mutually overlap.

Several additional constraints are considered by the solver. One of these constraints concerns the mentioned distinction between *housekeeping* and *science data* that have different relevance for mission planners and, for this reason, are stored in separate packet stores. The science devices allow to maintain on-board residual data, while housekeeping data have to be emptied by the end of each mission day because the status of the spacecraft should be checked continuously. A further constraint for the housekeeping packet stores requires to download them in a single dump, without preemption.

In general a solution should satisfy all the imposed constraints. A further goal is to find *high quality* solutions with respect to some specified metrics like *robustness, plan size*, etc. Informally, *a high quality plan delivers all the stored data and is able to "absorb" external modifications that might arise in a dynamic execution environment; contains the smallest number of dump activities and satisfies the priorities preferences imposed on the set of packet stores.*

The automated solver. To solve MEX-MDPs, a two levels abstraction has been introduced within the decision cycle: (a) a first level, *Data Dump level*, assesses the amount of data to dump from each packet store during each time window. (a) a second level, *Packet level*, generates the final dump commands from the result of the previous level.

The abstraction allows us to focus on the *dominant* aspects of the problem, i.e. data quantities, packets store capacities, and dump capability over the communication windows, without considering the problem of generating dump commands. It is worth remarking that the packet level step can be automatically accomplished once a solution for the Data Dump level is computed (no fail is possible) so we mainly have focused the attention on producing solutions for the Data Dump level.

A high level description of the solving process is shown in Algorithm 1. Following the abstraction into levels, it is subdivided in two steps. Goal of the first is to produce a data allocation over the communication channel: we select for each packet store and for each time window, the amount of data to download. The second step, generates the down-link commands starting from the allocation produced in the first step. The key aspect is the generation of the data dumps. This step is represented in Algorithm 1 by the *while* loop – which is entered with an empty initial solution S. Each iteration of the loop involves the two procedures:

- `HousekeepingAllocation` that aims at finding a consistent solution of the sub-set of the housekeeping packet stores. In fact these packet stores contain more important data for the probe safety, and as said before, neither residual data nor preemption are allowed.
- `MaxFlowAllocation` that, given a partial solution produced by the previous step, generates the data dumps from the remaining (scientific) packet stores. This procedure is based on a reduction of the problem P (included the solution of the previous step, S) to a Max-Flow problem: the former problem has a solution when the maximum flow of the latter equates the total amount of data to dump. For further details please see [5].

The max-flow approach involves the possibility of preemption, for this reason is not applied to the housekeeping packet stores. The `HousekeepingAllocation` is a backtracking search that generates at each step a possible dump plan for the housekeeping packets store. These two steps will be iterated until a complete solution is found or no alternative is possible (we thus check if there is any allocation available). The real problem required us to always generate a solution even if it implies data loss. Then, at the end of the while loop we will have a solution S that is used to generated the final list of dump commands.

It is worth observing that the whole procedure can use different parameters. The allocation in `HousekeepingAllocation` can be done considering the priority values of the housekeeping packets store (parameter **priority**). Additionally the procedure `GenerateDownLink` can consider the packets store priority values.

The procedure `MaxFlowAllocation` accepts a parameter **robust**. In this case we have an iterative max-flow based search that tries to flat possible peaks in the usage of the storage devices [5]. Broadly speaking robustness copes with the uncertainty on the exact amount of produced data. Sources of uncertainty stem mainly from the unpredictability of the scientific observations' outcome. For instance, the data volume produced by the High Resolution Stereo Camera (HRSC) – one of the most memory consuming payload – depends on the target and on the context. Thus the impossibility to have an exact estimation of the memory usage of each payload request leads to producing *brittle* solutions. Our aim has been to control the level of memory use in order to avoid possible loss of data due to overwriting. One possibility for overwriting can occur when a greater than expected volume of data has to be stored and there is not enough space in the packet store. For this reason we define as robust a solution in which a specified amount of space of each packet store is preserved in order to safeguard against overwriting. In other words, solutions robustness is related to the concept of distance to the overwriting state.

3   Exploiting Human Capabilities in the Solving Process

The more recent developments in MEXAR2 involved the design of an Interaction Module to facilitate users access to the system. In designing the interaction style of MEXAR2 we have pursued two objectives: (a) reproduce the usual problem solving cycle of real users, collecting in a unique tool all features and functionalities to guarantee their traditional problem solving style; (b) allow to exploit the domain expert abilities and foster her involvement and contribution to the problem solving. Indeed, the basic life cycle during the resolution of a MEX-MDP instance follows a continuous cycle among three phases: (a) *Problem Definition and Input Specification*; (b) *Automated Solution*; (c) *Inspection of Results*. When cycling to point (a) the user may tune a set of parameters that bias the problem solver behavior. In this way, for a given time interval, the user performs a *What-if Analysis* obtaining different solutions and, in the end, compares them according to different metrics choosing the best candidate for execution.

The general idea pursued with the system is to endow the user with an integrated tool able to relieve her from tedious and repetitive tasks preserving her traditional way of working, while providing an advanced environment which allows her to concentrate on strategic decisions preserving her control on the problem solving. The main layout of the MEXAR2

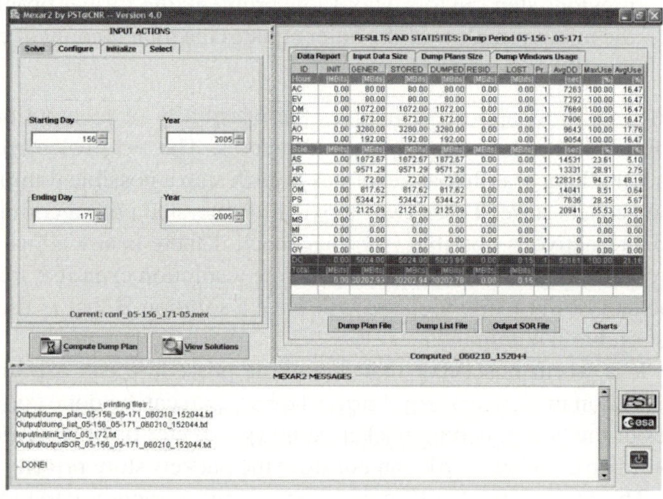

Fig. 2. MEXAR2 Interaction Module

interaction module is shown in Figure 2. It is subdivided into three main areas: the left part called "Input Actions" allows a user to activate the basic actions to access the MEXAR2 functionalities; the second pane, called "Results and Statistics", contains the results of a problem solving phase and a set of statistical information summarizing the current problem and its solution after the solving process. In the bottom of the interface a window called "MEXAR2 Messages" provides explanation messages and feedback from the current computation.

The basic actions to define a MEX-MDP problem consists of specifying the dump interval and checking the value corresponding to residual data in the packet stores. The first action entails to simply fill in the fields related to the starting and ending mission days (e.g, Starting Day: 156, 2005; Ending Day: 171, 2005). The second information is related to the amount of residual data which is still on each packet store from the previous dump period – the actual values of this data, are specified through the "Initialize" sub-pane. Then possible parameters for the solver are specified ("Select"). For example, the priority is activated or not, or the robustification algorithm is called into play after generating and initial solution. Through the "Configure" sub-pane the user can modify, at a detailed level, the operations to be served, and the domain representation of the spacecraft manipulated by the solver. This functionality gives access to the AI symbolic representation allowing expert users a good level of intervention in the solving process.

After specifying the needed context and the required parameters, the user may ask the solver to compute a dump plan for the specified period. The user has perception of the solver activity from the messages appearing in the MEXAR2 Messages pane.

Once the solver has generated a solution, the Interaction Module shows results as in Fig. 2. A set of statistics that gives aggregate information on the current solution are shown in the "Results and Statistics" pane. In particular a panel named "Data Report" is shown with entries subdivided into packet stores. This report gives the user an immediate view of the input/output data balance. For each packet store the data balance produced by the solution is shown through the columns: GENERATED, the total amount of data generated by the current set of requests; STORED, the amount of data actually stored; DUMPED, the amount of dumped data in the produced solution; RESIDUAL, the amount of data which remains in the packet store at the end of the last mission day; LOST, the amount of data lost in the corresponding packet store due to overwriting. Additionally, information is added that is useful for the solver functionalities, related to the current priority given to the packet store, the average turnover time for generated data on a specific dump plan; the maximum occupation peak on the packet store during the current plan and the average occupation of the packet store during the current dump plan. These last two data give the user feedback on the effectiveness of the robustification algorithm.

Apart the Data Report table the basic pane allows access to the three main files that are produced by the solver through three buttons ("Dump Plan", "Dump List", "Output SOR"). In this way we enable the basic problem life cycle of the users. Indeed these three files are the output needed to directly synthesizing the dump commands for the spacecraft.

It is worth commenting on the different role played by the Interaction Module in the two steps of our work. The MEXAR prototype from the first study [4] made a larger use of graphical interaction to show the internal structure of the symbolic model the solver was working on. The current MEXAR2 version is rather oriented toward serving the different features of the problem solver. During the first study the role of the interaction has been to convince users to trust not only the solver but the AI approach as a whole.

In the current operational tool, the interaction pursues a more "conventional" role of access facilitator.

4   Main Operative Results

The MEXAR2 tool helps the mission planners to solve MEX-MDP by reconciling several requirements as the large set of ground station allocation constraints, the limited communication bandwidth, the large amount of collected science data and the limited capacity of the on-board memory. The regular use of the tool has produced several and valuable results. First of all, it has improved the quality of the produced dump plans, as well as it has significantly reduced the time needed to create a dump plan, with a consequent reduction of manpower effort. A second and important result is the change of the *tasks* executed by the mission planners. In fact, with respect to the previous work practice, now the solving focus is shifted from level where many complex and repetitive tasks were the main issues, to an higher strategic level, where the main goal is to improve the quality of the produced solutions. In fact, as described in the previous sections, with the current version of the tool, it is possible to compute in few minutes several solutions, with different quality measures, by a simple setting of a number of control parameters. A full description of the MEXAR2 performance will go beyond the scope of this short paper, however we present here a synthetic analysis about the quality of the generated dump plans.

Test Data and Settings. We report the system performance on four sets of data, respectively labeled B1, B2, B3 and B4, which refer to different interval of real mission days within the first six months of 2005. Each period is represented by the format *[start-day year, end-day year]*. We have: B1: [014 05, 045 05], B2: [101 05, 120 05], B3: [142 05, 156 05], B4: [156 05, 171 05]. The four proposed benchmarks involve quite different values for the volumes of generated data in comparison with the overall communication channel dump capacity. Table 1 shows the duration of each input benchmark as number of mission days (*N.Days*) and compares the total volume of data generated (*VG*), in the interval of mission days with the maximal dump capacity of the communication channel (*DC*) in the same period (ratio *VG/DC*). Notice that the benchmark *B1* is the most critical and is the most probable candidate to lose data during the execution of the related dump plans.

Quantitative Performance. We report here a set of quantitative evaluations for MEXAR2 by using two different input parameters settings on the test data of Table 1. The two

Table 1. Volume of data generated [Mbits] vs. overall channel dump capacity [Mbits]

Benchmark	N.Days	Volume Generated (VG)	Dump Capacity (DC)	VG/DC
B1	31	78323.4	98268.1	0.80
B2	19	71938.6	114566.1	0.63
B3	14	22763.0	125516.2	0.18
B4	15	30747.2	155412.7	0.20

Table 2. Performances on S1 and S2 data. S2 differs for additional threshold settings.

	Benchmark	Stored	Dumped	Residual	Lost	Nstores	AvgPlanSize	MaxSize	Time
S1	B1	78323	78323	0	0	1534	17.8	57	209
	B2	71938	71938	0	0	1314	22.9	32	323
	B3	22763	22763	0	0	605	16.7	33	7
	B4	30747	30747	0	0	850	23.7	32	22
S2	B1	78323	78323	0	0	838	17.3	34	22
	B2	71938	71938	0	0	688	22.5	33	12
	B3	22763	22763	0	0	334	16.2	29	4
	B4	30747	30747	0	0	399	20.1	27	8

settings are labelled *S1* and *S2*. All the tests were executed with a Java2 Runtime Environment, Standard Edition (build 1.4.2_07-b05), on a SUN Ultra 10 with an Ultra Sparc IIi 440 Mhz processor and 256 MByte RAM, under Solaris 7. The following data are reported in tabular format for the evaluation: (a) Volumes of data stored (*Stored*), dumped (*Dumped*), residual in the packet store at the end of the dump period (*Residual*) and lost (*Lost*) (in [Mbits]); (b) Number of stores (*NStores*). It represents the total number of memory stores considered by the system as input data and it represents the size of the input data which can be directly related to the complexity of the solving algorithm, that is, its computational time and memory requirement. (c) The average plan size (*AvgPlanSize*) and the maximal size of a daily dump plan (*MaxSize*). We define the size of a daily dump plan, as the number of dump commands contained in a plan (included the commands for the housekeeping packet stores). (d) The total computation time (*Time* in seconds) to find a solution given an input benchmark set.

Table 2 compares the performance of MEXAR2 with respect to S1 and S2. The main difference between setting S1 and S2 are the so-called *threshold* values imposed on the reading of the input data records from the scientific instruments. In few words, each scientific observation, the POR, produces a sequence of data records (called ZD records) which represent the input stores for the solving algorithms described in the previous sections. A threshold value can be set for each packet store and represents a given percentage of its overall capacity. By setting a threshold to a value T, a sequence of many small data records targeted on the same packet store are grouped into a single cumulative record of size T and stored at the and of the grouped sequence. This fact has two advantages: (a) many small data records are grouped into a single one and dumped by a single command. In fact, if we observe S2, within the most critical input benchmark, B1, the longest plan is reduced from 57 to 34; (b) the number of input stores is also rather reduced (from 1534 to 838), as a consequence, the computation time is also reduced. As an example, for B1 the computational time is reduced from 209 seconds to 22 seconds. The use of thresholds in the packet stores is an example of the practical mechanisms that MEXAR2 has provided to the mission planners for tuning the input data and changing the behavior of the solving algorithm. This is a key aspect for allowing the users with the ability of exploring the solution space inserting hints from their experience in choosing the set of solving parameters.

5   Conclusions

This paper has described the main outcome of the MEXAR project that started from a research study for a specific open problem, in a space mission, usually solved with a lot of daily human effort, ended up producing an complete tool, MEXAR2, that endows the user with the ability to solve the problem easily and concentrate on high level decision making tasks.

The results of this work represents one of the few examples of problem solving tools based on AI planning and scheduling technology that is successfully being used in the operational phase of a space program. Most of previous examples are from the US space missions leaded by NASA and JPL [6, 7, 8, 9]. MEXAR2 is one of the few cases of operational use of such technology within an ESA program.

The authors experience started from the demonstration prototype that captured the problem features but was not tested on real data due to their unavailability. This preliminary experience has enabled an impressive speed up in the development of the actual operational prototype that is currently in use. It is worth saying that, even though a significant amount of work has been needed to interface the active part of the tool with the real data flow in the ESA mission control center, the path from theory to practice has been pursued completely. In addition, we have been able to transform the initial skepticism of ESA personnel with respect to new technology in huge satisfaction for the real enhancement of the quality of work that MEXAR2 guarantees.

Acknowledgements. This work has been sponsored by the the European Space Agency (ESA-ESOC) under contract No.18893/05/D/HK(SC). The authors would like to thank the MARS EXPRESS mission control team at ESA-ESOC for the valuable feedback on their work and in particular Erhard Rabenau and Alessandro Donati for their continuous assistance.

References

1. Oddi, A., Policella, N., Cesta, A., Cortellessa, G.: Generating High Quality Schedules for a Spacecraft Memory Downlink Problem. Lecture Notes in Computer Science **LNCS 2833** (2003)
2. Cesta, A., Cortellessa, G., Oddi, A., Policella, N.: A CSP-Based Interactive Decision Aid for Space Mission Planning. Lecture Notes in Artificial Intelligence **LNAI 2829** (2003)
3. Oddi, A., Policella, N.: A Max-Flow Approach for Improving Robustness in a Spacecraft Downlink Schedule. In: Proceedings of the 4th International Workshop on Planning and Scheduling for Space, IWPSS'04, ESA-ESOC, Darmstadt, Germany (2004)
4. Cortellessa, G., Cesta, A., Oddi, A., Policella, N.: User Interaction with an Automated Solver. The Case of a Mission Planner. PsychNology Journal **2** (2004) 140–162
5. Oddi, A., Policella, N.: Improving Robustness of Spacecraft Downlink Schedules. IEEE Transactions on Systems, Man, and Cybernetics–Part C: Applications and Reviews (2006) To appear.
6. Jonsson, A., Morris, P., Muscettola, N., Rajan, K., Smith, B.: Planning in Interplanetary Space: Theory and Practice. In: Proceedings of the Fifth Int. Conf. on Artificial Intelligence Planning and Scheduling, AIPS-00. (2000)

7. Smith, B.D., Engelhardt, B.E., Mutz, D.H.: The RADARSAT-MAMM Automated Mission Planner. AI Magazine **23** (2002) 25–36
8. Ai-Chang, M., Bresina, J., Charest, L., Chase, A., Hsu, J., Jonsson, A., Kanefsky, B., Morris, P., Rajan, K., Yglesias, J., Chafin, B., Dias, W., Maldague, P.: MAPGEN: Mixed-Initiative Planning and Scheduling for the Mars Exploration Rover Mission. IEEE Intelligent Systems **19** (2004) 8–12
9. S. Chien, S., Cichy, B., Davies, A., Tran, D., Rabideau, G., Castano, R., Sherwood, R., Mandl, D., Frye, S., Shulman, S., Jones, J., Grosvenor, S.: An Autonomous Earth-Observing Sensorweb. IEEE Intelligent Systems **20** (2005) 16–24

A New Method for Appraising the Performance of High School Teachers Based on Fuzzy Number Arithmetic Operations

Chih-Huang Wang and Shyi-Ming Chen

Department of Computer Science and Information Engineering
National Taiwan University of Science and Technology
Taipei, Taiwan, R.O.C.
smchen@et.ntust.edu.tw

Abstract. In recent years, some methods have been presented for appraising the performance of high school teachers. In this paper, we present a new method for appraising the performance of high school teachers based on simplified fuzzy number arithmetic operations. The proposed method uses fuzzy numbers to represent fuzzy grades, where the fuzzy weights of criteria are automatically generated from the opinions of evaluators. The proposed method can appraise the performance of high school teachers in a more flexible and more intelligent manner.

1   Introduction

In 1965, Zadeh proposed the theory of fuzzy sets [17]. In recent years, the application of the fuzzy set theory in education has begun [1], [2], [7], [8], [9], [10], [12], [14], [15], [16]. In [1], Biswas presented a fuzzy evaluation method (fem) and a generalized fuzzy evaluation method for students' answerscripts evaluation. In [2], Chang et al. presented a method for fuzzy assessment of junior high school students. In [7], Chen et al. presented new methods for students' evaluation using fuzzy sets. In [8], Cheng and Yang presented a method for the application of the fuzzy set theory in educational grading systems. In [9], Cheng et al. established the criteria for high school teachers appraisal. They used fuzzy linguistic questionnaires to appraise the performance of high school teachers and used fuzzy linguistic integrating operations to calculate teachers' fuzzy grades, and then used Lee-and-Li's method [13] and Chen-and-Cheng's method [3] to rank teachers' fuzzy grades.

In this paper, we present a new method to appraise the performance of high school teachers based on fuzzy number arithmetic operation. The proposed method appraises the performance of high school teachers based on simplified fuzzy number arithmetic. It can appraise high school teachers in a more flexible and more intelligent manner than the method presented in [9].

2   Simplified Fuzzy Arithmetic Operations Between Fuzzy Numbers

In 1965, Zadeh presented the theory of fuzzy sets [17]. A fuzzy number [11], [18] is a fuzzy set in the universe of discourse X that is both convex and normal. A trapezoidal

M. Ali and R. Dapoigny (Eds.): IEA/AIE 2006, LNAI 4031, pp. 432–441, 2006.

fuzzy number $\tilde{A}$ of the universe of discourse X can be characterized by a trapezoidal membership function parameterized by a quadruple (a, b, c, d) as shown in Fig. 1, where a, b, c and d are real values.

In Fig. 1, if b = c, then $\tilde{A}$ becomes a triangular fuzzy number, and it can be parameterized by a triplet (a, b, d). Let $\tilde{A}_1$ and $\tilde{A}_2$ be two triangular fuzzy numbers parameterized by the triplets (a_1, b_1, c_1) and (a_2, b_2, c_2), respectively. The simplified fuzzy number arithmetic operations between the triangular fuzzy numbers $\tilde{A}_1$ and $\tilde{A}_2$ are as follows [11]:

Fuzzy Number Addition $\oplus$:

$$(a_1, b_1, c_1) \oplus (a_2, b_2, c_2) = (a_1 + a_2, b_1 + b_2, c_1 + c_2). \tag{1}$$

Fuzzy Number Multiplication $\otimes$:

$$(a_1, b_1, c_1) \otimes (a_2, b_2, c_2) = (a_1 \times a_2, b_1 \times b_2, c_1 \times c_2). \tag{2}$$

Fuzzy Number Division $\oslash$:

$$(a_1, b_1, c_1) \oslash (a_2, b_2, c_2) = (a_1/c_2, b_1/b_2, c_1/a_2). \tag{3}$$

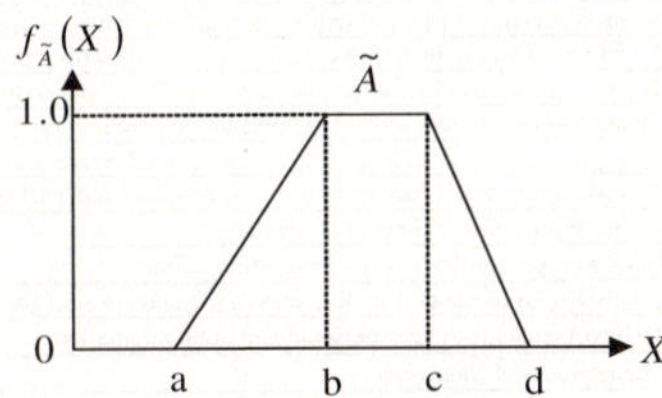

Fig. 1. A trapezoidal fuzzy number

3   A Review of Chen-and-Chen's Method for Ranking Fuzzy Numbers

In [6], Chen and Chen presented a method for ranking fuzzy numbers. The ranking value Rank($\tilde{A}$) of a generalized trapezoidal fuzzy number $\tilde{A}$, $\tilde{A}$ = (a_1, a_2, a_3, a_4), can be calculated as follows:

$$Rank(\tilde{A}) = x^*_{\tilde{A}} + (1 - y^*_{\tilde{A}})^{\hat{S}_{\tilde{A}}}, \tag{4}$$

where

$$x^*_{\tilde{A}} = \frac{y^*_{\tilde{A}}(a_3 + a_2) + (a_4 + a_1)(1 - y^*_{\tilde{A}})}{2}, \tag{5}$$

$$\hat{S}_{\tilde{A}} = \sqrt{\frac{\sum_{i=1}^{4}(a_i - \overline{a})}{3}}, \tag{6}$$

$$y_{\tilde{A}}^* = \begin{cases} \dfrac{1 \times \left(\dfrac{a_3 - a_2}{a_4 - a_1} + 2 \right)}{6}, & if\ a_1 \neq a_4 \\[4mm] \dfrac{1}{2}, & if\ a_1 = a_4 \end{cases} \qquad (7)$$

where $\bar{a} = \dfrac{a_1 + a_2 + a_3 + a_4}{4}$. The larger the value of Rank($\tilde{A}$), the better the ranking of $\tilde{A}$.

4 A New Method for High School Teachers' Appraisal

In this section, we present a new method for high school teachers' appraisal, where the criteria and the fuzzy linguistic questionnaires used for teacher appraisal used in [9] are adopted as shown in Table 1 and Table 2, respectively.

Table 1. The Criteria for Appraising the Performance of High School Teachers [9]

Criteria	Sub-criteria	Contents
X_1 (Teaching)	X_{11}	According to the standard of the course and the needs of the students to achieve the teaching goals
	X_{12}	To make teaching plans and to prepare teaching materials and tools properly
	X_{13}	To present teaching materials clearly and correctly with proper methods
	X_{14}	To bring the motivation of learning and testing and to increase students attention on lessons
	X_{15}	To express clearly in speaking (helpful for comprehension and learning.)
	X_{16}	To express clearly in writing (helpful for comprehension and learning.)
	X_{17}	To make good use of various of teaching methods and teaching media
	X_{18}	To make good use of time while teaching
	X_{19}	Giving proper feedback to students while teaching
X_2 (Class Managing)	X_{21}	Counseling students to obey the rules of life and develop good habits
	X_{22}	To direct students to keep personal and public sanitation
	X_{23}	Management of classroom
	X_{24}	Establishing an appropriate rule of class
	X_{25}	To praise and punish students properly
X_3 (Professional Attitude and Specialty)	X_{31}	To take care of students actively
	X_{32}	Working hard
	X_{33}	Researching and pursuing further education
	X_{34}	Being enthusiastic with working
X_4 (Cooperation in Administration and Relationship with People)	X_{41}	To build various kinds of students' files
	X_{42}	To join activities of school actively.
	X_{43}	To keep good relationship with co-workers in school
	X_{44}	To keep good relationship and interactions with students' parents
	X_{45}	Treating students fairly
	X_{46}	To keep good relationship with students
X_5 (Ability to Use Computers)	X_{51}	To be able to send and receive email
	X_{52}	To be able to design a web page interacting with students
	X_{53}	To be able to use word edit software to edit handouts and test papers
	X_{54}	To be able to search data on the web to be used in teaching

Table 2. A Fuzzy Linguistic Questionnaire for Appraising the Performance of A Teacher [9]

Fuzzy Linguistic Questionnaire				
Satisfaction Levels of the Criterion X_{ij}				
Low ←				→ High
VL	L	M	H	VH

In Table 2, five linguistic levels are used to evaluate teachers performance regarding the sub-criterion X_{ij}, i.e., very low (VL), low (L), middle (M), high (H) and very high (VH), where the triangular fuzzy numbers $\tilde{1}$, $\tilde{2}$, $\tilde{3}$, $\tilde{4}$ and $\tilde{5}$ corresponding to the linguistic satisfaction levels VL, L, M, H and VH are $\tilde{1} = (0, 1, 2)$, $\tilde{2} = (1, 2, 3)$, $\tilde{3} = (2, 3, 4)$, $\tilde{4} = (3, 4, 5)$ and $\tilde{5} = (4, 5, 6)$, respectively. The fuzzy grade $G(\tilde{x}_{ij})$ of the sub-criterion X_{ij} is calculated as follows:

$$G(\tilde{x}_{ij}) = \frac{\sum_{k=1}^{5} \tilde{x}_{ijk} f(\tilde{x}_{ijk})}{\sum_{k=1}^{5} f(\tilde{x}_{ijk})}, \tag{8}$$

where i denotes the index of the criterion, j denotes the index of the sub-criterion, k denotes the index of linguistic levels, $\tilde{x}_{ijk}$ denotes the kth linguistic satisfaction level of the criterion X_{ij}, $1 \le k \le 5$, $\tilde{x}_{ijk} \in \{\tilde{1}, \tilde{2}, \tilde{3}, \tilde{4}, \tilde{5}\}$, $f(\tilde{x}_{ijk})$ denotes the degree of percentage that the teacher satisfies the kth satisfaction level of the criterion X_{ij}, and $\sum_{k=1}^{5} f(\tilde{x}_{ijk}) = 1$. A fuzzy linguistic questionnaire for determining the weights of a criterion is shown in Table 3 [9]. The fuzzy weight $W(\tilde{x}_i)$ of the criterion X_i is calculated as follows:

$$W(\tilde{x}_i) = \frac{\sum_{k=1}^{5} \tilde{x}_{ik} f(\tilde{x}_{ik})}{\sum_{k=1}^{5} f(\tilde{x}_{ik})}, \tag{9}$$

where i denotes the index of the criterion, k denotes the index of linguistic levels, $\tilde{x}_{ik}$ denotes the kth linguistic satisfaction level of the criterion X_i, $1 \le k \le 5$, $\tilde{x}_{ik} \in \{\tilde{1}, \tilde{2}, \tilde{3}, \tilde{4}, \tilde{5}\}$, $f(\tilde{x}_{ik})$ denotes the degree of percentage that the criterion X_i satisfies the kth important level, and $\sum_{k=1}^{5} f(\tilde{x}_{ik}) = 1$.

Table 3. A Fuzzy Linguistic Questionnaire for Determining the Weight of the Criterion X_i [9]

Fuzzy Linguistic Questionnaire				
Importance Levels of the Criterion X_i				
Low				High
VL	L	M	H	VH

The proposed new method for high school teachers appraisal is now presented as follows:

Step 1: Determine the fuzzy weight of each criterion. Let each evaluator use the fuzzy linguistic questionnaire shown in Table 3 to evaluate the importance of each criterion. Then, use Eq. (9) to calculate the fuzzy weight of each criterion evaluated by each evaluator, where a fuzzy weight represented by a triangular fuzzy number (k, m, n) should satisfy the rules: "if k < 1, then let k = 1; if n > 5, then let n = 5". For example, assume that there are five evaluators E_1, E_2, E_3, E_4, E_5 and nine teachers A_1, A_2, A_3, A_4, A_5, A_6, A_7, A_8, A_9 being evaluated. After five evaluators fill out the fuzzy linguistic questionnaires, we get the result shown in Table 4. After applying Eq. (9) to calculate the fuzzy weight of each criterion evaluated by each evaluator, we get the calculation results as shown in Table 5.

Table 4. The Result after Five Evaluators Fill Out the Fuzzy Linguistic Questionnaires

Criteria	Evaluator E_1					Evaluator E_2					Evaluator E_3					Evaluator E_4					Evaluator E_5				
	VL	L	M	H	VH	VL	L	M	H	VH	VL	L	M	H	VH	VL	L	M	H	VH	VL	L	M	H	VH
X_1				80	20		10	80	10			20	60	20					70	30			80	10	10
X_2		10	70	20				40	60			30	60	10			20	70	10				5	15	80
X_3	20	80					20	70	10				70	30			20	70	10			20	80		
X_4		20	60	20			5	85	10			20	70	10			10	75	15			45	55		
X_5		30	50	20			40	40	20			20	70	10			20	30	50			20	70	10	

Table 5. The Fuzzy Weight of Each Criterion Evaluated by Each Evaluator

Fuzzy Weights / Criteria	E_1	E_2	E_3	E_4	E_5
X_1	(3.2, 4.2, 5)	(3, 4, 5)	(3, 4, 5)	(3.3, 4.3, 5)	(2.3, 3.3, 4.3)
X_2	(3.1, 4.1, 5)	(3.6, 4.6, 5)	(2.8, 3.8, 4.8)	(2.9, 3.9, 4.9)	(3.75, 4.75, 5)
X_3	(1.8, 2.8, 3.8)	(2.9, 3.9, 4.9)	(3.3, 4.3, 5)	(2.9, 3.9, 4.9)	(2.8, 3.8, 4.8)
X_4	(3, 4, 5)	(3.05, 4.05, 5)	(2.9, 3.9, 4.9)	(3.05, 4.05, 5)	(2.55, 3.55, 4.55)
X_5	(2.9, 3.9, 4.9)	(2.8, 3.8, 4.8)	(2.9, 3.9, 4.9)	(3.3, 4.3, 5)	(2.9, 3.9, 4.9)

Based on Eqs. (4)-(7), we rank the fuzzy weights with respect to each criterion X_i evaluated by the evaluators, where $1 \leq i \leq 5$, we drop the fuzzy weights with the smallest ranking value and the largest ranking value. Then, we calculate the average of the remaining fuzzy weights using the addition operations and the division operations of fuzzy numbers. Finally, we can get the fuzzy weighted vector $\tilde{W}$, where

$$\tilde{W} = \begin{bmatrix} \tilde{w}_1 \\ \tilde{w}_2 \\ \tilde{w}_3 \\ \tilde{w}_4 \\ \tilde{w}_5 \end{bmatrix},$$

$\tilde{w}_i$ denotes the average of the remaining fuzzy weights with respect to the ith criterion, and $1 \leq i \leq 5$. Therefore, the fuzzy weighted vector $\tilde{W}$ is as follows:

$$\tilde{W} = \begin{bmatrix} \tilde{w}_1 \\ \tilde{w}_2 \\ \tilde{w}_3 \\ \tilde{w}_4 \\ \tilde{w}_5 \end{bmatrix} = \begin{bmatrix} (3.07, 4.07, 5) \\ (3.2, 4.2, 4.97) \\ (2.87, 3.87, 4.87) \\ (2.98, 3.98, 4.97) \\ (2.9, 3.9, 4.9) \end{bmatrix} \cdot$$

Step 2: Establish the fuzzy grade matrix. Each evaluator uses the fuzzy linguistic questionnaire shown in Table 2 to evaluate the performance of high school teachers.

Then, use Eq. (8) to calculate the fuzzy grade of each sub-criterion of each teacher evaluated by each evaluator, where the fuzzy grade represented by the fuzzy number (k, m, n) should satisfy the rules: "if k < 1, then let k = 1; if n > 5, then let n = 5". For example, assume that the fuzzy grades evaluated by the five evaluators are as shown in Table 6, Table 7, Table 8, Table 9 and Table 10, respectively. Based on Eqs. (4)-(7), we rank the fuzzy grades of a teacher with respect to a sub-criterion evaluated by the evaluators, then drop the fuzzy grades with the smallest ranking value and the largest ranking value, and then calculate the average of the remaining fuzzy grades by using the addition operations and the division operations of fuzzy numbers to get the averaged fuzzy grade of the sub-cirterion. In the same way, we can get the averaged fuzzy grade of each sub-criterion of each teacher. Therefore, we can get the fuzzy grade of each teacher with respect to each sub-criterion to derive the averaged fuzzy grade table shown in Table 11.

Table 6. Fuzzy Grades Evaluated by the Evaluator E_1

Criteria	Sub-Criteria	Teacher A_1	Teacher A_2	Teacher A_3	Teacher A_4	Teacher A_5	Teacher A_6	Teacher A_7	Teacher A_8	Teacher A_9
X_1	X_{11}	(2.5,3.5,4.5)	(2,3,4)	(1.65,2.65,3.65)	(1.5,2.5,3.5)	(2.85,3.85,4.85)	(1.65,2.65,3.65)	(2.9,3.9,4.9)	(2.5,3.5,4.5)	(2.35,3.35,4.35)
	X_{12}	(3.2,4.2,5)	(1.45,2.45,3.45)	(2.9,3.9,4.9)	(2.8,3.8,4.8)	(1.5,2.5,3.5)	(4,5,5)	(1.8,2.8,3.8)	(1.5,2.5,3.5)	(1.8,2.8,3.8)
	X_{13}	(3.75,4.75,5)	(2.9,3.9,4.9)	(3.7,4.7,5)	(3.55,4.55,5)	(1,1.2,2.2)	(3.65,4.65,5)	(3.65,4.65,5)	(2.3,3.3,4.3)	(1.5,2.5,3.5)
	X_{14}	(1.8,2.8,3.8)	(1.25,2.25,3.25)	(2.9,3.9,4.9)	(3.35,4.35,5)	(1.5,2.5,3.5)	(1.65,2.65,3.65)	(3.35,4.35,5)	(1.7,2.7,3.7)	(2.35,3.35,4.35)
	X_{15}	(1,1.6,2.6)	(3.35,4.35,5)	(1,1.2,2.2)	(2.3,3.3,4.3)	(2.5,3.5,4.5)	(1,1.2,2.2)	(1.8,2.8,3.8)	(3.35,4.35,5)	(2.9,3.9,4.9)
	X_{16}	(1.5,2.5,3.5)	(3.7,4.7,5)	(2.45,3.45,4.45)	(1.7,2.7,3.7)	(1.45,2.45,3.45)	(2,3,4)	(3.55,4.55,5)	(1.65,2.65,3.65)	(3.35,4.35,5)
	X_{17}	(1.45,2.45,3.45)	(2.7,3.7,4.7)	(2.85,3.85,4.85)	(1,1.2,2.2)	(3.7,4.7,5)	(1.7,2.7,3.7)	(2.1,3.1,4.1)	(1,1.2,2.2)	(2.1,3.1,4.1)
	X_{18}	(1,1.1,2.1)	(1.6,2.6,3.6)	(2.9,3.9,4.9)	(4,5,5)	(1.25,2.25,3.25)	(1.7,2.7,3.7)	(1.95,2.95,3.95)	(2,3,4)	(1,1.2,2.2)
	X_{19}	(2.5,3.5,4.5)	(3.2,4.2,5)	(2.7,3.7,4.7)	(2.9,3.9,4.9)	(1.45,2.45,3.45)	(1.25,2.25,3.25)	(3.7,4.7,5)	(1.25,2.25,3.25)	(1.7,2.7,3.7)
X_2	X_{21}	(2.15,3.15,4.15)	(2.15,3.15,4.15)	(2.3,3.3,4.3)	(2.6,3.6,4.6)	(2.9,3.9,4.9)	(2.7,3.7,4.7)	(2.6,3.6,4.6)	(1.5,2.5,3.5)	(2.5,3.5,4.5)
	X_{22}	(2.7,3.7,4.7)	(3.2,4.2,5)	(2.6,3.6,4.6)	(1.8,2.8,3.8)	(2.15,3.15,4.15)	(2.15,3.15,4.15)	(1.45,2.45,3.45)	(2.35,3.35,4.35)	(2.9,3.9,4.9)
	X_{23}	(2.6,3.6,4.6)	(1.5,2.5,3.5)	(3.75,4.75,5)	(1.95,2.95,3.95)	(1.6,2.6,3.6)	(3.2,4.2,5)	(1.6,2.6,3.6)	(1.45,2.45,3.45)	(3.35,4.35,5)
	X_{24}	(2.55,3.55,4.55)	(2.6,3.6,4.6)	(2.55,3.55,4.55)	(2.6,3.6,4.6)	(1,1.2,2.2)	(2.6,3.6,4.6)	(1.5,2.5,3.5)	(1.25,2.25,3.25)	(2.9,3.9,4.9)
	X_{25}	(3.2,4.2,5)	(2.5,3.5,4.5)	(1.5,2.5,3.5)	(2.5,3.5,4.5)	(2.9,3.9,4.9)	(2,3,4)	(1.8,2.8,3.8)	(2.7,3.7,4.7)	(2.1,3.1,4.1)
X_3	X_{31}	(2.25,3.25,4.25)	(2.6,3.6,4.6)	(2.15,3.15,4.15)	(2.15,3.15,4.15)	(2.6,3.6,4.6)	(1.65,2.65,3.65)	(1.8,2.8,3.8)	(2.9,3.9,4.9)	(1.7,2.7,3.7)
	X_{32}	(1.7,2.7,3.7)	(1.8,2.8,3.8)	(2.6,3.6,4.6)	(3.75,4.75,5)	(3.75,4.75,5)	(1,1.1,2.1)	(2.5,3.5,4.5)	(2,3,4)	(1.45,2.45,3.45)
	X_{33}	(2.7,3.7,4.7)	(1.25,2.25,3.25)	(2.7,3.7,4.7)	(2.3,3.3,4.3)	(1,1.2,2.2)	(2.5,3.5,4.5)	(3.7,4.7,5)	(1.7,2.7,3.7)	(2.5,3.5,4.5)
	X_{34}	(2.6,3.6,4.6)	(2.15,3.15,4.15)	(1.7,2.7,3.7)	(2.85,3.85,4.85)	(1.45,2.45,3.45)	(3.75,4.75,5)	(3.55,4.55,5)	(1.6,2.6,3.6)	(1.5,2.5,3.5)
X_4	X_{41}	(2.6,3.6,4.6)	(2.75,3.75,4.75)	(2.25,3.25,4.25)	(2.7,3.7,4.7)	(2.35,3.35,4.35)	(3.65,4.65,5)	(2.15,3.15,4.15)	(3.7,4.7,5)	(1.7,2.7,3.7)
	X_{42}	(3.85,4.85,5)	(2.35,3.35,4.35)	(2.25,3.25,4.25)	(1.7,2.7,3.7)	(2.5,3.5,4.5)	(2.6,3.6,4.6)	(1.95,2.95,3.95)	(1.8,2.8,3.8)	(3.7,4.7,5)
	X_{43}	(2.6,3.6,4.6)	(2.55,3.55,4.55)	(1.45,2.45,3.45)	(1.45,2.45,3.45)	(1.8,2.8,3.8)	(1.25,2.25,3.25)	(1,1.2,2.2)	(2.9,3.9,4.9)	(1.6,2.6,3.6)
	X_{44}	(1.7,2.7,3.7)	(2.5,3.5,4.5)	(1.25,2.25,3.25)	(2.7,3.7,4.7)	(1.45,2.45,3.45)	(1.45,2.45,3.45)	(2.6,3.6,4.6)	(1,1.2,2.2)	(3.35,4.35,5)
	X_{45}	(2.6,3.6,4.6)	(2.15,3.15,4.15)	(2.6,3.6,4.6)	(2.35,3.35,4.35)	(2.6,3.6,4.6)	(2.6,3.6,4.6)	(2.9,3.9,4.9)	(2.35,3.35,4.35)	(1,1.2,2.2)
	X_{46}	(1.8,2.8,3.8)	(2.35,3.35,4.35)	(2.85,3.85,4.85)	(2.15,3.15,4.15)	(1.7,2.7,3.7)	(1.7,2.7,3.7)	(1.7,2.7,3.7)	(2.5,3.5,4.5)	(2.9,3.9,4.9)
X_5	X_{51}	(2.25,3.25,4.25)	(2.55,3.55,4.55)	(2.6,3.6,4.6)	(2.9,3.9,4.9)	(2.85,3.85,4.85)	(2.85,3.85,4.85)	(1.6,2.6,3.6)	(3.55,4.55,5)	(3.35,4.35,5)
	X_{52}	(1.45,2.45,3.45)	(2.7,3.7,4.7)	(2.15,3.15,4.15)	(2.35,3.35,4.35)	(2.9,3.9,4.9)	(2.9,3.9,4.9)	(1,1.2,2.2)	(1.5,2.5,3.5)	(1.45,2.45,3.45)
	X_{53}	(2.15,3.15,4.15)	(2.6,3.6,4.6)	(1.5,2.5,3.5)	(1.25,2.25,3.25)	(1.25,2.25,3.25)	(1.25,2.25,3.25)	(1.8,2.8,3.8)	(3.75,4.75,5)	(1,1.2,2.2)
	X_{54}	(2.35,3.35,4.35)	(1.6,2.6,3.6)	(2.85,3.85,4.85)	(1.8,2.8,3.8)	(2.9,3.9,4.9)	(2.9,3.9,4.9)	(1,1.2,2.2)	(2,3,4)	(1.25,2.25,3.25)

Table 7. Fuzzy Grades Evaluated by the Evaluator E_2

Criteria	Sub-criteria	Teacher A_1	Teacher A_2	Teacher A_3	Teacher A_4	Teacher A_5	Teacher A_6	Teacher A_7	Teacher A_8	Teacher A_9
X_1	X_{11}	(2.8,3.8,4.8)	(3.15,4.15,5)	(2.6,3.6,4.6)	(2.85,3.85,4.85)	(1.45,2.45,3.45)	(1.65,2.65,3.65)	(2.75,3.75,4.75)	(2.9,3.9,4.9)	(2.8,3.8,4.8)
	X_{12}	(2.6,3.6,4.6)	(1.8,2.8,3.8)	(3.7,4.7,5)	(2.85,3.85,4.85)	(2.35,3.35,4.35)	(2.6,3.6,4.6)	(2.7,3.7,4.7)	(1.8,2.8,3.8)	(2.35,3.35,4.35)
	X_{13}	(3.15,4.15,5)	(2.9,3.9,4.9)	(1.6,2.6,3.6)	(1.7,2.7,3.7)	(2.6,3.6,4.6)	(1,2,3)	(3.35,4.35,5)	(2.35,3.35,4.35)	(1,2,3)
	X_{14}	(2.5,3.5,4.5)	(2.7,3.7,4.7)	(1.8,2.8,3.8)	(3.65,4.65,5)	(3.75,4.75,5)	(1.8,2.8,3.8)	(2.75,3.75,4.75)	(3.15,4.15,5)	(2.75,3.75,4.75)
	X_{15}	(3.7,4.7,5)	(2.5,3.5,4.5)	(2.75,3.75,4.75)	(1.25,2.25,3.25)	(1.7,2.7,3.7)	(2.3,3.3,4.3)	(1.25,2.25,3.25)	(2.7,3.7,4.7)	(2.1,3.1,4.1)
	X_{16}	(2.6,3.6,4.6)	(2.85,3.85,4.85)	(2.5,3.5,4.5)	(2.6,3.6,4.6)	(1,1.2,2.2)	(3.15,4.15,5)	(2.1,3.1,4.1)	(1.95,2.95,3.95)	(2.9,3.9,4.9)
	X_{17}	(3.15,4.15,5)	(1.25,2.25,3.25)	(1.8,2.8,3.8)	(2,3,4)	(1.25,2.25,3.25)	(1.45,2.45,3.45)	(2.3,3.3,4.3)	(1.25,2.25,3.25)	(2.35,3.35,4.35)
	X_{18}	(1.25,2.25,3.25)	(3.15,4.15,5)	(1.5,2.5,3.5)	(2.7,3.7,4.7)	(3.7,4.7,5)	(2.6,3.6,4.6)	(1,1.1,2.1)	(2.1,3.1,4.1)	(1.45,2.45,3.45)
	X_{19}	(1.25,2.25,3.25)	(2.15,3.15,4.15)	(2.6,3.6,4.6)	(2.9,3.9,4.9)	(3.2,4.2,5)	(3.7,4.7,5)	(1.45,2.45,3.45)	(2.35,3.35,4.35)	(3.7,4.7,5)
X_2	X_{21}	(2.6,3.6,4.6)	(2.7,3.7,4.7)	(3.15,4.15,5)	(2.6,3.6,4.6)	(2.35,3.35,4.35)	(2.6,3.6,4.6)	(2.1,3.1,4.1)	(2.6,3.6,4.6)	(1.5,2.5,3.5)
	X_{22}	(2.7,3.7,4.7)	(2.6,3.6,4.6)	(1.5,2.5,3.5)	(1.25,2.25,3.25)	(3.7,4.7,5)	(2,3,4)	(3.7,4.7,5)	(3.35,4.35,5)	(2.75,3.75,4.75)
	X_{23}	(3.7,4.7,5)	(2.3,3.3,4.3)	(2.6,3.6,4.6)	(2.75,3.75,4.75)	(2.85,3.85,4.85)	(1,1.2,2.2)	(1.7,2.7,3.7)	(4,5,5)	(3.35,4.35,5)
	X_{24}	(1.25,2.25,3.25)	(3.15,4.15,5)	(1.8,2.8,3.8)	(2.1,3.1,4.1)	(1.5,2.5,3.5)	(3.55,4.55,5)	(1,1.2,2.2)	(2.35,3.35,4.35)	(2.9,3.9,4.9)
	X_{25}	(3.15,4.15,5)	(2.75,3.75,4.75)	(3.7,4.7,5)	(3.7,4.7,5)	(2.35,3.35,4.35)	(3.25,4.25,5)	(2.3,3.3,4.3)	(2.75,3.75,4.75)	(1.7,2.7,3.7)
X_3	X_{31}	(3.7,4.7,5)	(2.6,3.6,4.6)	(3.7,4.7,5)	(2.85,3.85,4.85)	(2.6,3.6,4.6)	(2.35,3.35,4.35)	(2.8,3.8,4.8)	(2.7,3.7,4.7)	(2.5,3.5,4.5)
	X_{32}	(2.1,3.1,4.1)	(2.8,3.8,4.8)	(3.15,4.15,5)	(2.35,3.35,4.35)	(2.3,3.3,4.3)	(2.3,3.3,4.3)	(2.7,3.7,4.7)	(2.9,3.9,4.9)	(3.35,4.35,5)
	X_{33}	(3.7,4.7,5)	(3.7,4.7,5)	(2.5,3.5,4.5)	(2.6,3.6,4.6)	(2.1,3.1,4.1)	(2.35,3.35,4.35)	(2.5,3.5,4.5)	(2.35,3.35,4.35)	(1.65,2.65,3.65)
	X_{34}	(2.3,3.3,4.3)	(2.5,3.5,4.5)	(2.85,3.85,4.85)	(1.8,2.8,3.8)	(3.15,4.15,5)	(3.65,4.65,5)	(3.15,4.15,5)	(1.5,2.5,3.5)	(2.5,3.5,4.5)
X_4	X_{41}	(2.5,3.5,4.5)	(1.5,2.5,3.5)	(2.6,3.6,4.6)	(2.7,3.7,4.7)	(1.8,2.8,3.8)	(2.9,3.9,4.9)	(1.8,2.8,3.8)	(2.9,3.9,4.9)	(1.45,2.45,3.45)
	X_{42}	(2.6,3.6,4.6)	(2.7,3.7,4.7)	(1.8,2.8,3.8)	(2.75,3.75,4.75)	(1.5,2.5,3.5)	(2.35,3.35,4.35)	(1.7,2.7,3.7)	(1,1.2,2.2)	(2.9,3.9,4.9)
	X_{43}	(3.7,4.7,5)	(1.25,2.25,3.25)	(2.75,3.75,4.75)	(2.5,3.5,4.5)	(3.75,4.75,5)	(1,1.2,2.2)	(2.5,3.5,4.5)	(2.5,3.5,4.5)	(3.35,4.35,5)
	X_{44}	(1.5,2.5,3.5)	(2.3,3.3,4.3)	(3.7,4.7,5)	(1.8,2.8,3.8)	(3.2,4.2,5)	(1.7,2.7,3.7)	(2.1,3.1,4.1)	(1.65,2.65,3.65)	(3.2,4.2,5)
	X_{45}	(2.7,3.7,4.7)	(1.5,2.5,3.5)	(3.2,4.2,5)	(2.35,3.35,4.35)	(2.9,3.9,4.9)	(1.25,2.25,3.25)	(1.45,2.45,3.45)	(3.7,4.7,5)	(1,1.1,2.1)
	X_{46}	(2.35,3.35,4.35)	(2.7,3.7,4.7)	(2.9,3.9,4.9)	(1.8,2.8,3.8)	(2.5,3.5,4.5)	(1.45,2.45,3.45)	(2.5,3.5,4.5)	(2.1,3.1,4.1)	(1.7,2.7,3.7)
X_5	X_{51}	(2.85,3.85,4.85)	(2.1,3.1,4.1)	(2.75,3.75,4.75)	(2.5,3.5,4.5)	(2.85,3.85,4.85)	(2,3,4)	(1,1.2,2.2)	(1.95,2.95,3.95)	(1.7,2.7,3.7)
	X_{52}	(1.8,2.8,3.8)	(1.25,2.25,3.25)	(2.9,3.9,4.9)	(1.45,2.45,3.45)	(2,3,4)	(1,1.2,2.2)	(1.8,2.8,3.8)	(2,3,4)	(3.35,4.35,5)
	X_{53}	(2.1,3.1,4.1)	(3.15,4.15,5)	(1.25,2.25,3.25)	(1.8,2.8,3.8)	(2.9,3.9,4.9)	(2.1,3.1,4.1)	(1.25,2.25,3.25)	(3.2,4.2,5)	(2,3,4)
	X_{54}	(2.8,3.8,4.8)	(2.5,3.5,4.5)	(2.15,3.15,4.15)	(2.85,3.85,4.85)	(2.5,3.5,4.5)	(1.7,2.7,3.7)	(1.5,2.5,3.5)	(1.45,2.45,3.45)	(1.25,2.25,3.25)

Table 8. Fuzzy Grades Evaluated by the Evaluator E_3

Criteria	Sub-criteria	Teacher A_1	Teacher A_2	Teacher A_3	Teacher A_4	Teacher A_5	Teacher A_6	Teacher A_7	Teacher A_8	Teacher A_9
X_1	X_{11}	(3.7,4.7,5)	(3.1,4.1,5)	(2.25,3.25,4.25)	(3.1,4.1,5)	(3.1,4.1,5)	(2.7,3.7,4.7)	(2.8,3.8,4.8)	(2.75,3.75,4.75)	(2.9,3.9,4.9)
	X_{12}	(2.6,3.6,4.6)	(2.15,3.15,4.15)	(3.15,4.15,5)	(3,55,4.55,5)	(2.35,3.35,4.35)	(2.95,3.95,4.95)	(2.1,3.1,4.1)	(3,35,4,35,5)	(3.65,4.65,5)
	X_{13}	(2.9,3.9,4.9)	(2.5,3.5,4.5)	(2.75,3.75,4.75)	(2.5,3.5,4.5)	(2.75,3.75,4.75)	(1.45,2.45,3.45)	(2.6,3.6,4.6)	(1.5,2.5,3.5)	(2.75,3.75,4.75)
	X_{14}	(1.45,2.45,3.45)	(1.8,2.8,3.8)	(2.8,3.8,4.8)	(1,2,3)	(3.7,4.7,5)	(1.25,2.25,3.25)	(0.2,1.2,2.2)	(2.3,3.3,4.3)	(2.1,3.1,4.1)
	X_{15}	(2.15,3.15,4.15)	(2.6,3.6,4.6)	(2.95,3.95,4.95)	(2.9,3.9,4.9)	(2.25,3.25,4.25)	(2.6,3.6,4.6)	(2.75,3.75,4.75)	(2.35,3.35,4.35)	(1.7,2.7,3.7)
	X_{16}	(2.3,3.3,4.3)	(3.65,4.65,5)	(3.65,4.65,5)	(3.1,4.1,5)	(2.6,3.6,4.6)	(3.7,4.7,5)	(2.7,3.7,4.7)	(2.95,3.95,4.95)	(1.95,2.95,3.95)
	X_{17}	(3.1,4.1,5)	(2.9,3.9,4.9)	(1.45,2.45,3.45)	(3.15,4.15,5)	(2.5,3.5,4.5)	(2.7,3.7,4.7)	(1.25,2.25,3.25)	(1.5,2.5,3.5)	(1,45,2.45,3.45)
	X_{18}	(2.85,3.85,4.85)	(1.8,2.8,3.8)	(3.7,4.7,5)	(2.95,3.95,4.95)	(3.1,4.1,5)	(1.7,2.7,3.7)	(2.35,3.35,4.35)	(0.2,1.2,2.2)	(2.9,3.9,4.9)
	X_{19}	(3.15,4.15,5)	(3.15,4.15,5)	(2.85,3.85,4.85)	(3.15,4.15,5)	(1,45,2.45,3.45)	(2,3,4)	(2.75,3.75,4.75)	(1,45,2.45,3.45)	(1.5,2.5,3.5)
X_2	X_{21}	(3.1,4.1,5)	(2.95,3.95,4.95)	(2.6,3.6,4.6)	(3.7,4.7,5)	(2.9,3.9,4.9)	(1.65,2.65,3.65)	(2.3,3.3,4.3)	(3.65,4.65,5)	(1.45,2.45,3.45)
	X_{22}	(1,2,3)	(2.75,3.75,4.75)	(2.5,3.5,4.5)	(1.8,2.8,3.8)	(2.6,3.6,4.6)	(2.7,3.7,4.7)	(1.8,2.8,3.8)	(1.25,2.25,3.25)	(2.1,3.1,4.1)
	X_{23}	(2.6,3.6,4.6)	(2.15,3.15,4.15)	(3.1,4.1,5)	(2.8,3.8,4.8)	(2,3,4)	(1.45,2.45,3.45)	(2.9,3.9,4.9)	(3.65,4.65,5)	(2.8,3.8,4.8)
	X_{24}	(2.25,3.25,4.25)	(3.15,4.15,5)	(2.85,3.85,4.85)	(2.6,3.6,4.6)	(3.2,4.2,5)	(2,3,4)	(3.75,4.75,5)	(1.45,2.45,3.45)	(3.65,4.65,5)
	X_{25}	(2.9,3.9,4.9)	(2.8,3.8,4.8)	(3.1,4.1,5)	(3.1,4.1,5)	(2.75,3.75,4.75)	(3.7,4.7,5)	(2.7,3.7,4.7)	(2.95,3.95,4.95)	(1.45,2.45,3.45)
X_3	X_{31}	(3.65,4.65,5)	(2.15,3.15,4.15)	(1.8,2.8,3.8)	(3.15,4.15,5)	(2.6,3.6,4.6)	(2.1,3.1,4.1)	(1,45,2.45,3.45)	(1.8,2.8,3.8)	(2.25,3.25,4.25)
	X_{32}	(1.25,2.25,3.25)	(3.65,4.65,5)	(2.95,3.95,4.95)	(1,2,3)	(0.1,1.1,2.1)	(2.5,3.5,4.5)	(2.8,3.8,4.8)	(1,2,3)	(1.7,2.7,3.7)
	X_{33}	(2.75,3.75,4.75)	(3.2,4.2,5)	(2.7,3.7,4.7)	(2.5,3.5,4.5)	(2.3,3.3,4.3)	(2.75,3.75,4.75)	(1.25,2.25,3.25)	(1.5,2.5,3.5)	(2.9,3.9,4.9)
	X_{34}	(2.95,3.95,4.95)	(2.6,3.6,4.6)	(2.1,3.1,4.1)	(3.1,4.1,5)	(2.35,3.35,4.35)	(1.45,2.45,3.45)	(1.8,2.8,3.8)	(2.75,3.75,4.75)	(1.25,2.25,3.25)
X_4	X_{41}	(2.85,3.85,4.85)	(2.95,3.95,4.95)	(2.7,3.7,4.7)	(1.8,2.8,3.8)	(3.1,4.1,5)	(2.9,3.9,4.9)	(0.2,1.2,2.2)	(2.95,3.95,4.95)	(2.85,3.85,4.85)
	X_{42}	(2.75,3.75,4.75)	(2.75,3.75,4.75)	(1.8,2.8,3.8)	(3.15,4.15,5)	(1.8,2.8,3.8)	(2.95,3.95,4.95)	(1,45,2.45,3.45)	(1.7,2.7,3.7)	(2.25,3.25,4.25)
	X_{43}	(3.65,4.65,5)	(1.7,2.7,3.7)	(2.75,3.75,4.75)	(3,55,4.55,5)	(3.2,4.2,5)	(3.7,4.7,5)	(2.85,3.85,4.85)	(1.7,2.7,3.7)	(0.1,1.1,2.1)
	X_{44}	(2.75,3.75,4.75)	(1,2,3)	(1.5,2.5,3.5)	(2.3,3.3,4.3)	(1.65,2.65,3.65)	(2.75,3.75,4.75)	(2.5,3.5,4.5)	(1.45,2.45,3.45)	(3.35,4.35,5)
	X_{45}	(3.65,4.65,5)	(1.8,2.8,3.8)	(1.5,2.5,3.5)	(3.2,4.2,5)	(2.25,3.25,4.25)	(2.8,3.8,4.8)	(2.5,3.5,4.5)	(3.75,4.75,5)	(1.7,2.7,3.7)
	X_{46}	(2.95,3.95,4.95)	(1.7,2.7,3.7)	(2.8,3.8,4.8)	(1.8,2.8,3.8)	(2.7,3.7,4.7)	(1.45,2.45,3.45)	(1.7,2.7,3.7)	(3.15,4.15,5)	(2.9,3.9,4.9)
X_5	X_{51}	(2.25,3.25,4.25)	(2.3,3.3,4.3)	(2.85,3.85,4.85)	(2.3,3.3,4.3)	(3.65,4.65,5)	(2.85,3.85,4.85)	(2.9,3.9,4.9)	(1,45,2.45,3.45)	(1.5,2.5,3.5)
	X_{52}	(1.8,2.8,3.8)	(2.25,3.25,4.25)	(1,1,2,2)	(3.1,4.1,5)	(1.8,2.8,3.8)	(1.7,2.7,3.7)	(1.5,2.5,3.5)	(1.5,2.5,3.5)	(0.2,1.2,2.2)
	X_{53}	(3.15,4.15,5)	(3.7,4.7,5)	(2,3,4)	(1,45,2.45,3.45)	(2.1,3.1,4.1)	(3.7,4.7,5)	(2,3,4)	(1.5,2.5,3.5)	(1.5,2.5,3.5)
	X_{54}	(2.9,3.9,4.9)	(1,45,2.45,3.45)	(2,3,4)	(1.7,2.7,3.7)	(3.15,4.15,5)	(1.5,2.5,3.5)	(2.1,3.1,4.1)	(0.2,1.2,2.2)	(3.75,4.75,5)

Table 9. Fuzzy Grades Evaluated by the Evaluator E_4

Criteria	Sub-criteria	Teacher A_1	Teacher A_2	Teacher A_3	Teacher A_4	Teacher A_5	Teacher A_6	Teacher A_7	Teacher A_8	Teacher A_9
X_1	X_{11}	(2.7,3.7,4.7)	(2.95,3.95,4.95)	(2.3,3.3,4.3)	(3.1,4.1,5)	(3.1,4.1,5)	(1,45,2.45,3.45)	(2.1,3.1,4.1)	(1.45,2.45,3.45)	(1.8,2.8,3.8)
	X_{12}	(2.3,3.3,4.3)	(2.7,3.7,4.7)	(2.35,3.35,4.35)	(2.85,3.85,4.85)	(1.45,2.45,3.45)	(2.75,3.75,4.75)	(2.3,3.3,4.3)	(1.95,2.95,3.95)	(2.8,3.8,4.8)
	X_{13}	(2.8,3.8,4.8)	(2.75,3.75,4.75)	(2.6,3.6,4.6)	(2.25,3.25,4.25)	(3.15,4.15,5)	(2.25,3.25,4.25)	(1,1,2,2)	(1.8,2.8,3.8)	(1.7,2.7,3.7)
	X_{14}	(2.7,3.7,4.7)	(2.3,3.3,4.3)	(2.1,3.1,4.1)	(2.7,3.7,4.7)	(2.75,3.75,4.75)	(1.8,2.8,3.8)	(2.25,3.25,4.25)	(2.75,3.75,4.75)	(1.7,2.7,3.7)
	X_{15}	(2.35,3.35,4.35)	(2.25,3.25,4.25)	(1,1,2,2)	(3.65,4.65,5)	(1.5,2.5,3.5)	(2.3,3.3,4.3)	(2.75,3.75,4.75)	(1.45,2.45,3.45)	(1.25,2.25,3.25)
	X_{16}	(3.65,4.65,5)	(3.2,4.2,5)	(2.75,3.75,4.75)	(1,1,2,2)	(2.5,3.5,4.5)	(1,45,2.45,3.45)	(3.15,4.15,5)	(1.8,2.8,3.8)	(2.85,3.85,4.85)
	X_{17}	(3.15,4.15,5)	(3.7,4.7,5)	(2.6,3.6,4.6)	(4,5,6)	(1,45,2.45,3.45)	(2.3,3.3,4.3)	(2.5,3.5,4.5)	(3.35,4.35,5)	(2.25,3.25,4.25)
	X_{18}	(3.7,4.7,5)	(2.75,3.75,4.75)	(3.1,4.1,5)	(2.25,3.25,4.25)	(1.8,2.8,3.8)	(1.65,2.65,3.65)	(2.35,3.35,4.35)	(1.45,2.45,3.45)	(3.35,4.35,5)
	X_{19}	(3.2,4.2,5)	(2.8,3.8,4.8)	(2.6,3.6,4.6)	(2.95,3.95,4.95)	(2.75,3.75,4.75)	(1.8,2.8,3.8)	(2.75,3.75,4.75)	(2.35,3.35,4.35)	(2.95,3.95,4.95)
X_2	X_{21}	(3.65,4.65,5)	(3.15,4.15,5.15)	(2.25,3.25,4.25)	(2.75,3.75,4.75)	(2,3,4)	(1,45,2.45,3.45)	(1.8,2.8,3.8)	(1,2,3)	(1.8,2.8,3.8)
	X_{22}	(2.6,3.6,4.6)	(2.6,3.6,4.6)	(2.3,3.3,4.3)	(1,2,3)	(1.8,2.8,3.8)	(2.25,3.25,4.25)	(2.3,3.3,4.3)	(1.8,2.8,3.8)	(2.25,3.25,4.25)
	X_{23}	(1,45,2.45,3.45)	(1,45,2.45,3.45)	(2.7,3.7,4.7)	(3.1,4.1,5)	(3.75,4.75,5)	(2.35,3.35,4.35)	(2.3,3.3,4.3)	(1.25,2.25,3.25)	(2.75,3.75,4.75)
	X_{24}	(2.75,3.75,4.75)	(1.8,2.8,3.8)	(3.2,4.2,5)	(3,55,4.55,5)	(1.8,2.8,3.8)	(2.25,3.25,4.25)	(2.25,3.25,4.25)	(2.35,3.35,4.35)	(1,45,2.45,3.45)
	X_{25}	(2.3,3.3,4.3)	(2.75,3.75,4.75)	(2.1,3.1,4.1)	(2.8,3.8,4.8)	(2.6,3.6,4.6)	(2.7,3.7,4.7)	(1.45,2.45,3.45)	(2.95,3.95,4.95)	(2.3,3.3,4.3)
X_3	X_{31}	(2.7,3.7,4.7)	(2.85,3.85,4.85)	(2.85,3.85,4.85)	(2.7,3.7,4.7)	(2.3,3.3,4.3)	(2.75,3.75,4.75)	(1.8,2.8,3.8)	(2.75,3.75,4.75)	(2.35,3.35,4.35)
	X_{32}	(3.7,4.7,5)	(2.25,3.25,4.25)	(2.75,3.75,4.75)	(1,1,2,2)	(2.75,3.75,4.75)	(1.7,2.7,3.7)	(2.25,3.25,4.25)	(1.8,2.8,3.8)	(1.65,2.65,3.65)
	X_{33}	(2.6,3.6,4.6)	(2.35,3.35,4.35)	(2.25,3.25,4.25)	(2.75,3.75,4.75)	(2.8,3.8,4.8)	(1.5,2.5,3.5)	(2.75,3.75,4.75)	(1.45,2.45,3.45)	(2.8,3.8,4.8)
	X_{34}	(1,45,2.45,3.45)	(1.8,2.8,3.8)	(2.6,3.6,4.6)	(2.7,3.7,4.7)	(1.25,2.25,3.25)	(1.25,2.25,3.25)	(1.5,2.5,3.5)	(2,3,4)	(2.85,3.85,4.85)
X_4	X_{41}	(2.25,3.25,4.25)	(3.15,4.15,5)	(2.25,3.25,4.25)	(2.7,3.7,4.7)	(1.8,2.8,3.8)	(3.1,4.1,5)	(2.9,3.9,4.9)	(2.85,3.85,4.85)	(1,45,2.45,3.45)
	X_{42}	(2.3,3.3,4.3)	(2.7,3.7,4.7)	(1.8,2.8,3.8)	(2.75,3.75,4.75)	(3.15,4.15,5)	(2.75,3.75,4.75)	(3.15,4.15,5)	(2.25,3.25,4.25)	(1,45,2.45,3.45)
	X_{43}	(2.25,3.25,4.25)	(2.75,3.75,4.75)	(3.15,4.15,5)	(3.1,4.1,5)	(1.7,2.7,3.7)	(1,1,2,1)	(2.5,3.5,4.5)	(1.65,2.65,3.65)	(3.35,4.35,5)
	X_{44}	(2.75,3.75,4.75)	(2.5,3.5,4.5)	(2.75,3.75,4.75)	(2.25,3.25,4.25)	(2.25,3.25,4.25)	(3.65,4.65,5)	(3.15,4.15,5)	(1,45,2.45,3.45)	(1.8,2.8,3.8)
	X_{45}	(2.5,3.5,4.5)	(2.1,3.1,4.1)	(1,45,2.45,3.45)	(3.1,4.1,5)	(3.7,4.7,5)	(3.15,4.15,5)	(1.7,2.7,3.7)	(2,3,4)	(2.1,3.1,4.1)
	X_{46}	(2.3,3.3,4.3)	(2.75,3.75,4.75)	(2.3,3.3,4.3)	(2.25,3.25,4.25)	(2.75,3.75,4.75)	(1.8,2.8,3.8)	(1,45,2.45,3.45)	(2.25,3.25,4.25)	(1,45,2.45,3.45)
X_5	X_{51}	(1.8,2.8,3.8)	(2.3,3.3,4.3)	(1,1,2,2)	(1.8,2.8,3.8)	(3.15,4.15,5)	(1,2,3)	(1,1,2,2)	(1.8,2.8,3.8)	(1.7,2.7,3.7)
	X_{52}	(2.85,3.85,4.85)	(2.75,3.75,4.75)	(1.5,2.5,3.5)	(2.75,3.75,4.75)	(2.75,3.75,4.75)	(1.8,2.8,3.8)	(1,45,2.45,3.45)	(2.9,3.9,4.9)	(1.5,2.5,3.5)
	X_{53}	(2.35,3.35,4.35)	(2.8,3.8,4.8)	(2.85,3.85,4.85)	(3.2,4.2,5)	(1.5,2.5,3.5)	(1,45,2.45,3.45)	(1,45,2.45,3.45)	(1,45,2.45,3.45)	(2,3,4)
	X_{54}	(3.65,4.65,5)	(2.25,3.25,4.25)	(2.75,3.75,4.75)	(2.25,3.25,4.25)	(2.1,3.1,4.1)	(1,1,2,2)	(3.15,4.15,5.15)	(2,3,4)	(3.35,4.35,5)

Table 10. Fuzzy Grades Evaluated by the Evaluator E_5

Criteria	Sub-criteria	Teacher A_1	Teacher A_2	Teacher A_3	Teacher A_4	Teacher A_5	Teacher A_6	Teacher A_7	Teacher A_8	Teacher A_9
X_1	X_{11}	(2.5,3.5,4.5)	(2.25,3.25,4.25)	(1.65,2.65,3.65)	(3.2,4.2,5)	(2.95,3.95,4.95)	(3.2,4.2,5)	(2.75,3.75,4.75)	(1.65,2.65,3.65)	(2.95,3.95,4.95)
	X_{12}	(3.7,4.7,5)	(1,45,2.45,3.45)	(3.15,4.15,5)	(3.65,4.65,5)	(2.75,3.75,4.75)	(1,45,2.45,3.45)	(1.65,2.65,3.65)	(3.9,4.9,9,5)	(2.25,3.25,4.25)
	X_{13}	(2.85,3.85,4.85)	(2.75,3.75,4.75)	(2.75,3.75,4.75)	(2.75,3.75,4.75)	(3.1,4.1,5)	(2.75,3.75,4.75)	(1,45,2.45,3.45)	(3.15,4.15,5)	(2.95,3.95,4.95)
	X_{14}	(3.7,4.7,5)	(2.25,3.25,4.25)	(1,45,2.45,3.45)	(2.25,3.25,4.25)	(2,3,4)	(1.5,2.5,3.5)	(2.5,3.5,4.5)	(1,45,2.45,3.45)	(1.65,2.65,3.65)
	X_{15}	(3.65,4.65,5)	(2.75,3.75,4.75)	(2.9,3.9,4.9)	(1.8,2.8,3.8)	(1,45,2.45,3.45)	(1.95,2.95,3.95)	(2.95,3.95,4.95)	(1.5,2.5,3.5)	(2.8,3.8,4.8)
	X_{16}	(2.25,3.25,4.25)	(2.95,3.95,4.95)	(2.75,3.75,4.75)	(3.2,4.2,5)	(2,3,4)	(3.3,4.3,5)	(2.85,3.85,4.85)	(1.95,2.95,3.95)	(2.95,3.95,4.95)
	X_{17}	(2.25,3.25,4.25)	(2.9,3.9,4.9)	(2.5,3.5,4.5)	(2.75,3.75,4.75)	(1.65,2.65,3.65)	(2.95,3.95,4.95)	(1,1.2,2.2)	(1,1.2,2.2)	(1,1.2,2.2)
	X_{18}	(1,45,2.45,3.45)	(1.7,2.7,3.7)	(3.1,4.1,5)	(1.95,2.95,3.95)	(2.75,3.75,4.75)	(3.2,4.2,5)	(1.8,2.8,3.8)	(1,45,2.45,3.45)	(3.35,4.35,5)
	X_{19}	(3.15,4.15,5)	(2.85,3.85,4.85)	(3,4,4,5)	(1.8,2.8,3.8)	(2.85,3.85,4.85)	(2.75,3.75,4.75)	(2.1,3.1,4.1)	(2.95,3.95,4.95)	(2.85,3.85,4.85)
X_2	X_{21}	(1.8,2.8,3.8)	(2.75,3.75,4.75)	(3.7,4.7,5)	(2.75,3.75,4.75)	(2.25,3.25,4.25)	(0.2,1.2,2.2)	(2.75,3.75,4.75)	(1.65,2.65,3.65)	(1,45,2.45,3.45)
	X_{22}	(1.5,2.5,3.5)	(1.65,2.65,3.65)	(3.15,4.15,5)	(3.6,4.6,5)	(2.5,3.5,4.5)	(1,45,2.45,3.45)	(1.8,2.8,3.8)	(2.8,3.8,4.8)	(1,45,2.45,3.45)
	X_{23}	(1,45,2.45,3.45)	(2.8,3.8,4.8)	(3.65,4.65,5)	(3,35,4,35,5)	(2.75,3.75,4.75)	(2.25,3.25,4.25)	(1.5,2.5,3.5)	(2.1,3.1,4.1)	(1,1.2,2.2)
	X_{24}	(1.8,2.8,3.8)	(1,45,2.45,3.45)	(3.2,4.2,5)	(2.8,3.8,4.8)	(2.75,3.75,4.75)	(2.8,3.8,4.8)	(1.25,2.25,3.25)	(1.5,2.5,3.5)	(1.7,2.7,3.7)
	X_{25}	(1,45,2.45,3.45)	(2.75,3.75,4.75)	(2.35,3.35,4.35)	(2.85,3.85,4.85)	(3.7,4.7,5)	(1.25,2.25,3.25)	(1.8,2.8,3.8)	(2.75,3.75,4.75)	(2.1,3.1,4.1)
X_3	X_{31}	(2.75,3.75,4.75)	(2.25,3.25,4.25)	(2.75,3.75,4.75)	(2.95,3.95,4.95)	(1,45,2.45,3.45)	(3.1,4.1,5)	(1.8,2.8,3.8)	(2.25,3.25,4.25)	(1.65,2.65,3.65)
	X_{32}	(1,45,2.45,3.45)	(1,45,2.45,3.45)	(1,45,2.45,3.45)	(2,3,4)	(4,5,5)	(3.15,4.15,5)	(2.8,3.8,4.8)	(1.7,2.7,3.7)	(2.25,3.25,4.25)
	X_{33}	(2.75,3.75,4.75)	(2.8,3.8,4.8)	(1.8,2.8,3.8)	(1.65,2.65,3.65)	(3.7,4.7,5)	(1.95,2.95,3.95)	(3.8,4.8,5)	(2.5,3.5,4.5)	(1.25,2.25,3.25)
	X_{34}	(1.8,2.8,3.8)	(2.75,3.75,4.75)	(3.7,4.7,5)	(2.75,3.75,4.75)	(3.35,4.35,5)	(1.8,2.8,3.8)	(3.7,4.7,5)	(2.85,3.85,4.85)	(2.1,3.1,4.1)
X_4	X_{41}	(2.75,3.75,4.75)	(3.15,4.15,5)	(1,45,2.45,3.45)	(3.15,4.15,5)	(1.5,2.5,3.5)	(1,45,2.45,3.45)	(1,45,2.45,3.45)	(1,45,2.45,3.45)	(2.8,3.8,4.8)
	X_{42}	(3.75,4.75,5)	(1,45,2.45,3.45)	(2.9,3.9,4.9)	(1,45,2.45,3.45)	(2.25,3.25,4.25)	(3.35,4,35,5)	(2.25,3.25,4.25)	(2.25,3.25,4.25)	(1.7,2.7,3.7)
	X_{43}	(3.65,4.65,5)	(3,4,5)	(2.75,3.75,4.75)	(2.75,3.75,4.75)	(3.2,4.2,5)	(1.65,2.65,3.65)	(3.35,4.35,5)	(1,45,2.45,3.45)	(2.8,3.8,4.8)
	X_{44}	(1,45,2.45,3.45)	(3.1,4.1,5)	(2.5,3.5,4.5)	(2.95,3.95,4.95)	(1.8,2.8,3.8)	(2.85,3.85,4.85)	(2.7,3.7,4.7)	(3.2,4.2,5)	(1.65,2.65,3.65)
	X_{45}	(1,45,2.45,3.45)	(2.75,3.75,4.75)	(1.65,2.65,3.65)	(1.95,2.95,3.95)	(3.7,4.7,5)	(1,45,2.45,3.45)	(3.6,4.6,5)	(2.8,3.8,4.8)	(2.1,3.1,4.1)
	X_{46}	(2.1,3.1,4.1)	(1.8,2.8,3.8)	(2.75,3.75,4.75)	(2.1,3.1,4.1)	(2.8,3.8,4.8)	(3.1,4.1,5)	(3.55,4.55,5)	(3.7,4.7,5)	(3.25,4.25,5)
X_5	X_{51}	(1.5,2.5,3.5)	(2.75,3.75,4.75)	(3.7,4.7,5)	(3.7,4.7,5)	(3.35,4.35,5)	(3.1,4.1,5)	(1.1,1,2.1)	(1.8,2.8,3.8)	(2.9,3.9,4.9)
	X_{52}	(2.8,3.8,4.8)	(3.15,4.15,5)	(1,45,2.45,3.45)	(2.5,3.5,4.5)	(3.95,4.95,5)	(1.65,2.65,3.65)	(2,3,4)	(1.95,2.95,3.95)	(1,1.2,2.2)
	X_{53}	(1.95,2.95,3.95)	(3.7,4.7,5)	(1,45,2.45,3.45)	(2.8,3.8,4.8)	(3.7,4.7,5)	(1,1.2,2.2)	(1,1.2,2.2)	(3.35,4.35,5)	(1.7,2.7,3.7)
	X_{54}	(1,45,2.45,3.45)	(1.65,2.65,3.65)	(2.1,3.1,4.1)	(1,1,1.2.1)	(3.35,4.35,5)	(2.7,3.7,4.7)	(2,3,4)	(1.5,2.5,3.5)	(1,1.2,2.2)

Table 11. The Averaged Fuzzy Grade Table

Criteria	Sub-criteria	Teacher A_1	Teacher A_2	Teacher A_3	Teacher A_4	Teacher A_5	Teacher A_6	Teacher A_7	Teacher A_8	Teacher A_9
X_1	X_{11}	(2.67,3.67,4.67)	(2.76,3.76,4.73)	(2.07,3.07,4.07)	(3.02,4.02,4.95)	(2.97,3.97,4.93)	(2,3,4)	(2.77,3.77,4.77)	(2.3,3.3,4.3)	(2.68,3.68,4.68)
	X_{12}	(2.8,3.8,4.73)	(1.8,2.8,3.8)	(3.07,4.07,4.97)	(3.07,4.07,4.9)	(2.07,3.07,4.07)	(2.77,3.77,4.77)	(2.07,3.07,4.07)	(2.37,3.37,4.25)	(2.47,3.47,4.47)
	X_{13}	(2.97,3.97,4.92)	(2.8,3.8,4.8)	(2.7,3.7,4.7)	(2.5,3.5,4.5)	(2.82,3.82,4.78)	(2.15,3.15,4.15)	(2.47,3.47,4.35)	(2.15,3.15,4.15)	(1.98,2.98,3.98)
	X_{14}	(2.33,3.33,4.33)	(2.11,3.11,4.11)	(2.23,3.23,4.23)	(2.77,3.77,4.65)	(2.82,3.82,4.67)	(1.65,2.65,3.65)	(2.5,3.5,4.5)	(2.25,3.25,4.25)	(2.05,3.05,4.05)
	X_{15}	(2.72,3.72,4.5)	(2.61,3.61,4.61)	(2.22,2.95,3.95)	(2.33,3.33,4.33)	(1.82,2.82,3.82)	(2.18,3.18,4.18)	(2.43,3.43,4.43)	(2.18,3.18,4.18)	(2.2,3.2,4.2)
	X_{16}	(2.38,3.38,4.38)	(3.26,4.26,4.98)	(2.78,3.78,4.78)	(2.47,3.47,4.43)	(1.98,2.98,3.98)	(2.82,3.82,4.67)	(2.9,3.9,4.85)	(1.9,2.9,3.9)	(2.9,3.9,4.9)
	X_{17}	(2.83,3.83,4.75)	(2.83,3.83,4.83)	(2.3,3.3,4.3)	(2.63,3.63,4.5)	(1.87,2.87,3.87)	(2.23,3.23,4.23)	(1.88,2.88,3.88)	(1.25,1.98,2.98)	(1.94,2.94,3.94)
	X_{18}	(1.85,2.85,3.85)	(2.08,3.08,4.08)	(3.03,4.03,4.97)	(2.63,3.63,4.63)	(2.55,3.55,4.52)	(2,3,4)	(2.03,3.03,4.03)	(1.63,2.63,3.63)	(2.57,3.57,4.45)
	X_{19}	(2.93,3.93,4.83)	(2.93,3.93,4.93)	(2.71,3.71,4.71)	(2.92,3.92,4.92)	(2.35,3.35,4.35)	(2.18,3.18,4.18)	(2.53,3.53,4.53)	(2.05,3.05,4.05)	(2.5,3.5,4.5)
X_2	X_{21}	(2.61,3.61,4.58)	(2.8,3.8,4.8)	(2.68,3.68,4.63)	(2.7,3.7,4.7)	(2.5,3.5,4.5)	(1.9,2.9,3.9)	(2.33,3.33,4.33)	(1.92,2.92,3.92)	(1.58,2.58,3.58)
	X_{22}	(2.26,3.26,4.26)	(2.65,3.65,4.65)	(2.46,3.46,4.46)	(1.62,2.62,3.62)	(2.42,3.42,4.33)	(2.13,3.13,4.13)	(1.97,2.97,3.97)	(2.32,3.32,4.32)	(2.37,3.37,4.37)
	X_{23}	(2.21,3.21,4.21)	(1.98,2.98,3.98)	(3.15,4.15,4.9)	(2.88,3.88,4.85)	(2.53,3.53,4.53)	(2.02,3.02,4.02)	(1.87,2.87,3.87)	(2.38,3.38,4.18)	(2.97,3.97,4.85)
	X_{24}	(2.2,3.2,4.2)	(2.51,3.51,4.46)	(3.06,4.06,4.8)	(2.67,3.67,4.67)	(2.02,3.02,4.02)	(2.55,3.55,4.55)	(1.67,2.67,3.67)	(1.77,2.77,3.77)	(2.5,3.5,4.5)
	X_{25}	(2.78,3.78,4.73)	(2.75,3.75,4.75)	(2.51,3.51,4.48)	(2.92,3.92,4.88)	(2.75,3.75,4.75)	(2.65,3.65,4.57)	(1.97,2.97,3.97)	(2.82,3.82,4.82)	(1.97,2.97,3.97)
X_3	X_{31}	(3.03,4.03,4.82)	(2.48,3.48,4.48)	(2.58,3.58,4.58)	(2.83,3.83,4.83)	(2.5,3.5,4.5)	(2.4,3.4,4.4)	(1.8,2.8,3.8)	(2.57,3.57,4.57)	(2.1,3.1,4.1)
	X_{32}	(1.75,2.75,3.75)	(2.28,3.28,4.28)	(2.76,3.76,4.76)	(1.78,2.78,3.78)	(3.75,4.75,5.75)	(2.17,3.17,4.17)	(2.67,3.67,4.67)	(1.83,2.83,3.83)	(1.87,2.87,3.87)
	X_{33}	(2.73,3.73,4.73)	(2.78,3.78,4.72)	(2.48,3.48,4.48)	(2.47,3.47,4.47)	(2.58,3.58,4.58)	(2.27,3.27,4.27)	(2.98,3.98,4.75)	(1.85,2.85,3.85)	(2.32,3.32,4.32)
	X_{34}	(2.23,3.23,4.23)	(2.41,3.41,4.41)	(2.51,3.51,4.51)	(2.77,3.77,4.77)	(2.32,3.32,4.27)	(2.3,3.3,4.08)	(2.83,3.83,4.6)	(2.12,3.12,4.12)	(2.03,3.03,4.03)
X_4	X_{41}	(2.61,3.61,4.61)	(2.95,3.95,4.9)	(2.36,3.36,4.36)	(2.7,3.7,4.7)	(1.98,2.98,3.98)	(2.97,3.97,4.93)	(1.8,2.8,3.8)	(2.9,3.9,4.9)	(1.98,2.98,3.98)
	X_{42}	(3.03,4.03,4.78)	(2.58,3.58,4.58)	(1.95,2.95,3.95)	(2.4,3.4,4.4)	(2.18,3.18,4.18)	(2.77,3.77,4.77)	(1.97,2.97,3.97)	(1.92,2.92,3.92)	(2.28,3.28,4.28)
	X_{43}	(3.3,4.3,4.87)	(2.33,3.33,4.33)	(2.75,3.75,4.75)	(2.78,3.78,4.75)	(2.73,3.73,4.6)	(1.3,2.03,3.03)	(2.62,3.62,4.62)	(1.95,2.95,3.95)	(2.58,3.58,4.47)
	X_{44}	(1,98,2.98,3.98)	(2.43,3.43,4.42)	(2.8,3.8,4.8)	(2.42,3.42,4.42)	(1.9,2.9,3.9)	(2.43,3.43,4.43)	(2.6,3.6,4.6)	(1.52,2.52,3.52)	(2.78,3.78,4.6)
	X_{45}	(2.6,3.6,4.6)	(2.01,3.01,4.01)	(1.95,2.95,3.95)	(2.6,3.6,4.57)	(3.07,4.07,4.83)	(2.18,3.18,4.18)	(2.37,3.37,4.37)	(2.95,3.95,4.72)	(1.6,2.33,3.33)
	X_{46}	(2.25,3.25,4.25)	(2.38,3.38,4.38)	(2.1,3.1,4.1)	(2.02,3.02,4.02)	(2.65,3.65,4.65)	(1.57,2.57,3.57)	(1.97,2.97,3.97)	(2.63,3.63,4.58)	(2.5,3.5,4.5)
X_5	X_{51}	(2.1,3.1,4.1)	(2.36,3.36,4.36)	(2.73,3.73,4.73)	(2.57,3.57,4.57)	(3.12,4.12,4.95)	(2.45,3.45,4.45)	(1.23,1.67,2.67)	(1.85,2.85,3.85)	(2.1,3.1,4.1)
	X_{52}	(2.13,3.13,4.13)	(2.56,3.56,4.56)	(1,7,2.7,3.7)	(2.47,3.47,4.47)	(2.55,3.55,4.55)	(1.72,2.72,3.72)	(1.58,2.58,3.58)	(1.82,2.82,3.82)	(1.32,2,3)
	X_{53}	(2.2,3.2,4.2)	(3.21,4.21,4.93)	(1.65,2.65,3.65)	(2.02,3.02,4.02)	(2.17,3.17,4.17)	(1.72,2.72,3.72)	(1.5,2.5,3.5)	(2.68,3.68,4.5)	(1.73,2.73,3.73)
	X_{54}	(2.68,3.68,4.68)	(1.81,2.81,3.81)	(2.33,3.33,4.33)	(1.92,2.92,3.92)	(2.85,3.85,4.88)	(1.73,2.73,3.73)	(1.87,2.87,3.87)	(1.65,2.65,3.65)	(1.95,2.95,3.83)

Then, we apply the simplified fuzzy numbers addition operations and division operations to the averaged fuzzy grade table shown in Table 11 to get the fuzzy grade of each criterion of each teacher with respect to each criterion. Finally, we can get the fuzzy grade matrix $\tilde{G}$ defined as follows:

$$\tilde{G} = \begin{matrix} & \mathbf{X}_1 & \mathbf{X}_2 & \cdots & \mathbf{X}_k \\ \mathbf{A}_1 \\ \mathbf{A}_2 \\ \vdots \\ \mathbf{A}_n \end{matrix} \begin{bmatrix} \tilde{g}_{11} & \tilde{g}_{12} & \cdots & \tilde{g}_{1k} \\ \tilde{g}_{21} & \tilde{g}_{22} & \cdots & \tilde{g}_{2k} \\ \vdots & \vdots & \ddots & \vdots \\ \tilde{g}_{n1} & \tilde{g}_{n2} & \cdots & \tilde{g}_{nk} \end{bmatrix},$$

where $\tilde{g}_{ij}$ denotes the fuzzy grade of the ith teacher A_i with respect to the jth criterion X_j, $1 \le i \le n$, $1 \le j \le k$, n denotes the number of teachers, and k denotes the number of criteria. Therefore, we can get the fuzzy grade matrix $\tilde{G}$, shown as follows:

$$\tilde{G} = \begin{matrix} & X_1 & X_2 & X_3 & X_4 & X_5 \\ A_1 \\ A_2 \\ A_3 \\ A_4 \\ A_5 \\ A_6 \\ A_7 \\ A_8 \\ A_9 \end{matrix} \begin{bmatrix} (2.61,3.61,4.55) & (2.41,3.41,4.40) & (2.44,3.44,4.38) & (2.63,3.63,4.52) & (2.28,3.28,4.28) \\ (2.58,3.58,4.54) & (2.54,3.54,4.53) & (2.49,3.49,4.47) & (2.45,3.45,4.45) & (2.49,3.49,4.42) \\ (2.57,3.54,4.52) & (2.77,3.77,4.65) & (2.58,3.58,4.58) & (2.32,3.32,4.32) & (2.10,3.10,4.10) \\ (2.70,3.70,4.65) & (2.56,3.56,4.54) & (2.46,3.46,4.46) & (2.49,3.49,4.48) & (2.25,3.25,4.25) \\ (2.36,3.36,4.33) & (2.44,3.44,4.43) & (2.79,3.79,4.78) & (2.42,3.42,4.36) & (2.67,3.67,4.64) \\ (2.33,3.33,4.20) & (2.25,3.25,4.23) & (2.29,3.29,4.23) & (2.20,3.20,4.15) & (1.91,2.91,3.91) \\ (2.40,3.40,4.38) & (1.96,2.96,3.96) & (2.57,3.57,4.46) & (2.22,3.22,4.22) & (1.55,2.41,3.41) \\ (2.01,2.98,3.97) & (2.24,3.24,4.24) & (2.09,3.09,4.09) & (2.31,3.31,4.27) & (2,3,3.96) \\ (2.37,3.37,4.35) & (2.28,3.28,4.25) & (2.08,3.08,4.08) & (2.29,3.24,4.19) & (1.78,2.70,3.67) \end{bmatrix}.$$

Step 3: Calculate the total fuzzy grade vector $\tilde{R}$, where

$$\tilde{R} = \tilde{G} \otimes \tilde{W} = \begin{bmatrix} \tilde{g}_{11} & \tilde{g}_{12} & \cdots & \tilde{g}_{1k} \\ \tilde{g}_{21} & \tilde{g}_{22} & \cdots & \tilde{g}_{2k} \\ \vdots & \vdots & \ddots & \vdots \\ \tilde{g}_{n1} & \tilde{g}_{n2} & \cdots & \tilde{g}_{nk} \end{bmatrix} \otimes \begin{bmatrix} \tilde{w}_1 \\ \tilde{w}_2 \\ \vdots \\ \tilde{w}_k \end{bmatrix} = \begin{bmatrix} \tilde{g}_{11} \otimes \tilde{w}_1 \oplus \tilde{g}_{12} \otimes \tilde{w}_2 \oplus \cdots \oplus \tilde{g}_{1k} \otimes \tilde{w}_k \\ \tilde{g}_{21} \otimes \tilde{w}_1 \oplus \tilde{g}_{22} \otimes \tilde{w}_2 \oplus \cdots \oplus \tilde{g}_{2k} \otimes \tilde{w}_k \\ \vdots \\ \tilde{g}_{n1} \otimes \tilde{w}_1 \oplus \tilde{g}_{n2} \otimes \tilde{w}_2 \oplus \cdots \oplus \tilde{g}_{nk} \otimes \tilde{w}_k \end{bmatrix} = \begin{bmatrix} \tilde{R}_1 \\ \tilde{R}_2 \\ \vdots \\ \tilde{R}_k \end{bmatrix}, \tag{10}$$

where $\tilde{R}_i$ denotes the total fuzzy grade of the ith teacher A_i and $1 \le i \le n$. Therefore, we can get the total fuzzy grade vector $\tilde{R}$, shown as follows:

$$\tilde{R} = \begin{bmatrix} \tilde{R}_1 \\ \tilde{R}_2 \\ \tilde{R}_3 \\ \tilde{R}_4 \\ \tilde{R}_5 \\ \tilde{R}_6 \\ \tilde{R}_7 \\ \tilde{R}_8 \\ \tilde{R}_9 \end{bmatrix} = \begin{bmatrix} (37.18, 69.57, 109.39) \\ (37.72, 70.29, 110.76) \\ (37.16, 69.4, 109.58) \\ (37.49, 69.57, 110.62) \\ (38.02, 70.72, 111.35) \\ (33.02, 64.02, 102.41) \\ (32.13, 62.30, 100.98) \\ (32.02, 62.57, 101.47) \\ (32.58, 62.84, 101.55) \end{bmatrix}.$$

Step 4: Use Eqs. (4)-(7) to rank the total fuzzy grades of the teachers. The larger the value of Rank($\tilde{R}_i$), the better the ranking of $\tilde{R}_i$ and the better the choice of teacher A_i, where $1 \le i \le n$ and n denotes the number of teachers. For example, after applying Eqs. (4)–(7) to rank the total fuzzy grades $\tilde{R}_1$, $\tilde{R}_2$, $\tilde{R}_3$, $\tilde{R}_4$, $\tilde{R}_5$, $\tilde{R}_6$, $\tilde{R}_7$, $\tilde{R}_8$ and $\tilde{R}_9$ obtained in Step 3, we can get the ranking results as shown in Table 12. From Table 12, we can see that Rank($\tilde{R}_5$) > Rank($\tilde{R}_2$) > Rank($\tilde{R}_4$) > Rank($\tilde{R}_1$) > Rank($\tilde{R}_3$) > Rank ($\tilde{R}_6$) > Rank($\tilde{R}_9$) > Rank($\tilde{R}_8$) > Rank($\tilde{R}_7$). Because $\tilde{R}_5$ has the largest ranking value, teacher A_5 is the best choice.

Table 12. Ranking Values of the Total Fuzzy Grades

Total Fuzzy Grades $\tilde{R}_i$	X*	Y*	$\hat{S}$	Rank($\tilde{R}_i$)
$\tilde{R}_1$	72.0467	0.3333	29.5575	72.04670624
$\tilde{R}_2$	72.9233	0.3333	29.9055	72.9233
$\tilde{R}_3$	72.0467	0.3333	29.6541	72.046706
$\tilde{R}_4$	72.6933	0.3333	29.9482	72.6933
$\tilde{R}_5$	73.3633	0.3333	30.0242	73.3633
$\tilde{R}_6$	66.4833	0.3333	28.4086	66.4833
$\tilde{R}_7$	65.1367	0.3333	28.2150	65.1367
$\tilde{R}_8$	65.3533	0.3333	28.4551	65.3533
$\tilde{R}_9$	65.6567	0.3333	28.2623	65.6567

5 Conclusions

In this paper, we have presented a new method for appraising the performance of high school teachers based on simplified fuzzy number arithmetic operations. The proposed method uses fuzzy numbers to represent fuzzy grades, where fuzzy weights of criteria are automatically generated from the opinions of evaluators. The proposed method can appraise the performance of high school teachers in a more flexible and more intelligent manner.

Acknowledgements

This work was supported in part by the National Science council, Republic of China, under Grant NSC-94-2213-E-011-003.

References

1. Biswas, R.: An application of fuzzy sets in students' evaluation. Fuzzy Sets and Systems 74 (1995) 187–194
2. Chang, D.F., Sun, C.M.: Fuzzy assessment of learning performance of junior high school students. Proceedings of the 1993 First National Symposium on Fuzzy Theory and Applications, Hsinchu, Taiwan, Republic of China (1993) 10–15
3. Chen, L.S., Cheng, C.H.: Selecting IS personnel using ranking fuzzy number by metric distance method. European Journal Operational Research 160 (2005) 803□820
4. Chen, S.M.: A weighted fuzzy reasoning algorithm for medical diagnosis. Decision Support Systems 11 (1994) 37–43
5. Chen, S.M.: A new approach to handling fuzzy decision making problems. IEEE Transactions on Systems, Man, and Cybernetics 18 (1988) 1012–1016
6. Chen, S.J., Chen, S.M.: A new method for handling multicriteria fuzzy decision-making problems using FN-IOWA operators. Cybernetics and Systems: An International Journal 34 (2003) 109–197
7. Chen, S.M., Lee, C.H.: New methods for students' evaluation using fuzzy sets. Fuzzy Sets and Systems 104 (1999) 209–218
8. Cheng, C.H., Yang, K.L.: Using fuzzy sets in education grading system. Journal of Chinese Fuzzy Systems Association 4 (1998) 81–89
9. Cheng, C.H., Wang, J.W., Tsai, M.F., Huang, K.C.: Appraisal support system for high school teachers based on fuzzy linguistic integrating operation. Journal of Human Resource Management 4 (2004) 73–89
10. Chiang, T.T., Lin, C.M.: Application of fuzzy theory to teaching assessment. Proceedings of the 1994 Second National Conference on Fuzzy Theory and Applications, Taipei, Taiwan, Republic of China (1994) 74–92
11. Kaufmann, A., Gupta, M.M.: Fuzzy Mathematical Models in Engineering and Management Science. North-Holland Amsterdam The Netherlands (1988)
12. Law, C.K.: Using fuzzy numbers in education grading system. Fuzzy Sets and Systems 83 (1996) 311–323
13. Lee, E.S., Li, R.L.: Comparison of fuzzy numbers based on the probability measure of fuzzy events. Computer and Mathematics with Applications 15 (1988) 887–896
14. Ma, J., Zhou, D.: Fuzzy set approach to the assessment of student-centered learning. IEEE Transactions on Education 43 (2000) 237–241
15. Nolan, J.R.: An expert fuzzy classification system for supporting the grading of student writing samples. Expert Systems with Applications 15 (1998) 59–68
16. Wu, M.H.: A research on applying fuzzy set theory and item response theory to evaluate learning performance. Master Thesis, Department of Information Management, Chaoyang University of Technology, Wufeng, Taichung Country, Republic of China (2003)
17. Zadeh, L.A.: Fuzzy sets. Information and Control 8 (1965) 338–353
18. Zimmermann, H.J.: Fuzzy Set Theory and It's Applications. Kluwer-Nijhoff, Dordrecht The Netherlands (1991)

New Methods for Evaluating the Answerscripts of Students Using Fuzzy Sets

Hui-Yu Wang[1] and Shyi-Ming Chen[2]

[1] Department of Education, National Chengchi University, Taipei, Taiwan, R.O.C.
`94152514@nccu.edu.tw`
[2] Department of Computer Science and Information Engineering, National Taiwan University of Science and Technology, Taipei, Taiwan, R.O.C.
`smchen@et.ntust.edu.tw`

Abstract. In this paper, we present new methods for evaluating the answerscripts of students, where the evaluating values are represented by fuzzy numbers, and an optimism index λ determined by the evaluator is used to indicate the degree of optimism of the evaluator for evaluating the answerscripts of students, where the value of λ is between zero and one. The universe of discourse is formed by a set of satisfaction levels. The fuzzy mark awarded to the answer of each question of the answerscript of a student is represented by a type-2 fuzzy set. The proposed methods can overcome the drawbacks of the existing methods. It can evaluate the answerscripts of students in a more flexible and more intelligent manner.

1 Introduction

In recent years, some methods have been presented for students' evaluation [1], [2], [5], [7]-[10], [13]-[17]. In [5], Chen and Lee have pointed out that the methods presented in [1] have the following drawbacks: (1) Because they used a matching function to measure the degrees of similarity between the standard fuzzy sets and the fuzzy marks of the questions, it will take a large amount of time to perform the matching operations. (2) Two different fuzzy marks may be translated into the same awarded grade and it is unfair for students' evaluation. Therefore, they presented two new methods for applying fuzzy sets in students' answerscripts evaluation to overcome the drawbacks of the ones presented in [1]. However, the drawbacks of the methods presented in [5] are that they can not deal with the situation that the evaluating values are represented by fuzzy numbers and they don't consider the degree of optimism of the evaluator in evaluating students' answerscripts. If we can allow the evaluating values to be represented by fuzzy numbers and can consider the degree of optimism of the evaluator in evaluating the students' answerscripts, then there is room for more flexibility.

In this paper, we present new methods for evaluating students' answerscripts, where the evaluating values are represented by fuzzy numbers and an optimism index λ[7] determined by the evaluator is used to indicate the degree of optimism of the evaluator for evaluating students' answerscripts, where $0 \leq \lambda \leq 1$. The fuzzy mark awarded to the answer of each question of a student's answerscript is represented by a

M. Ali and R. Dapoigny (Eds.): IEA/AIE 2006, LNAI 4031, pp. 442–451, 2006.

type-2 fuzzy set. The proposed methods can overcome the drawbacks of the methods presented in [1] and [5]. It can evaluate students' answerscripts in a more flexible and more intelligent manner.

2 Basic Concepts of Fuzzy Sets and Fuzzy Numbers

In the following, we briefly review basic concepts of fuzzy sets and fuzzy numbers from [4], [12], [19] and [20]. Let X be the universe of discourse, $X = \{x_1, x_2, \cdots, x_n\}$. A fuzzy set A of the universe of discourse X can be represented as follows:

$$A = \{(x_1, \mu_A(x_1)), (x_2, \mu_A(x_2)), \cdots, (x_n, \mu_A(x_n))\}, \tag{1}$$

where μ_A is the membership function of the fuzzy set A, $\mu_A(x_i)$ denotes the grade of membership of x_i belonging to the fuzzy set A, and $\mu_A(x_i) \in [0, 1]$. A fuzzy set A of the universe of discourse U is convex if and only if for all u_1, u_2 in X,

$$\mu_A(\lambda x_1 + (1 - \lambda)x_2) \geq Min(\mu_A(x_1), (\mu_A(x_2)), \tag{2}$$

where $0 \leq \lambda \leq 1$. If $\exists\ x_i \in X$, such that $\mu_A(x_i) = 1$, then the fuzzy set A is called a normal fuzzy set. A fuzzy number is a fuzzy set in the universe of discourse X that is both convex and normal. A triangular fuzzy number A of the universe of discourse X can be characterized by a triangular membership function parameterized by a triplet (a, b, c) as shown in Fig. 1. According to [4] and [12], the defuzzified value $DEF(A)$ of the trapezoidal fuzzy number A shown in Fig. 1 is as follows:

$$DEF(A) = \frac{a+b+b+c}{4}. \tag{3}$$

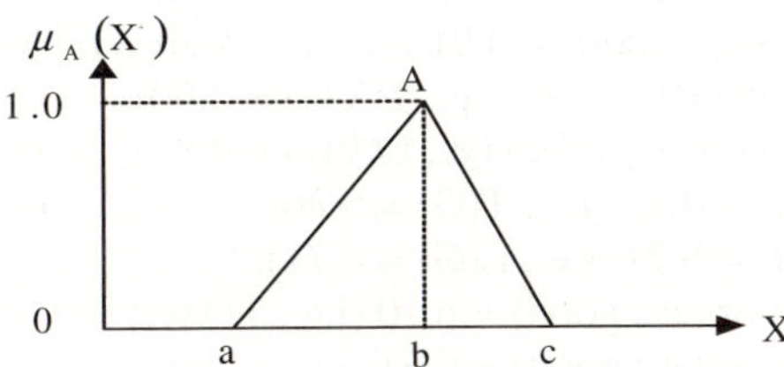

Fig. 1. A triangular fuzzy number A

3 A New Method for Student's Evaluation Using Fuzzy Numbers

In this section, we present a new method for students' answerscripts evaluation, where the evaluating values are represented by fuzzy numbers and an optimism index λ [7] determined by the evaluator is used to indicate the degree of optimism of the evaluator for evaluating students' answerscripts, where $\lambda \in [0, 1]$. If $0 \leq \lambda < 0.5$, then the evaluator is a pessimistic evaluator. If $\lambda = 0.5$, then the evaluator is a normal evaluator. If $0.5 < \lambda \leq 1.0$, then the evaluator is an optimistic evaluator. Eleven satisfaction levels shown in Table 1 [5] are used to evaluate the students' answerscripts regarding a question of a test/examination, where the corresponding degrees of satisfaction of the eleven satisfaction levels are shown in Table 1.

Table 1. Satisfaction Levels and Their Corresponding Degrees of Satisfaction [5]

Satisfaction Levels	Degrees of Satisfaction
extremely good (EG)	100% (i.e., 1.00)
very very good (VVG)	91%-99% (i.e., 0.91-0.99)
very good (VG)	81%-90% (i.e., 0.81-0.90)
good (G)	71%-80% (i.e., 0.71-0.80)
more or less good (MG)	61%-70% (i.e., 0.61-0.70)
fair (F)	51%-60% (i.e., 0.51-0.60)
more or less bad (MB)	41%-50% (i.e., 0.41-0.50)
bad (B)	25%-40% (i.e., 0.25-0.40)
very bad (VB)	10%-24% (i.e., 0.10-0.24)
very very bad (VVB)	1%-9% (i.e., 0.01-0.09)
extremely bad (EB)	0% (i.e., 0)

Let T and L be two mapping functions to map a satisfaction level to its maximum degree of satisfaction and its minimum degree of satisfaction shown in Table 1, respectively. Therefore, from Table 1, we can see that

$$
\begin{aligned}
&T(\text{extremely good}) = 1.00 \ (\text{i.e., } T(EG) = 1.00), \\
&L(\text{extremely good}) = 1.00 \ (\text{i.e., } L(EG) = 1.00), \\
&T(\text{very very good}) = 0.99 \ (\text{i.e., } T(VVG) = 0.99), \\
&L(\text{very very good}) = 0.91 \ (\text{i.e., } L(VVG) = 0.91), \\
&T(\text{very good}) = 0.90 \ (\text{i.e., } T(VG) = 0.90), \\
&L(\text{very good}) = 0.81 \ (\text{i.e., } L(VG) = 0.81), \\
&T(\text{good}) = 0.80 \ (\text{i.e., } T(G) = 0.80), \\
&L(\text{good}) = 0.71 \ (\text{i.e., } L(G) = 0.71), \\
&T(\text{more or less good}) = 0.70 \ (\text{i.e., } T(MG) = 0.70), \\
&L(\text{more or less good}) = 0.61 \ (\text{i.e., } L(MG) = 0.61), \\
&T(\text{fair}) = 0.60 \ (\text{i.e., } T(F) = 0.60), \\
&L(\text{fair}) = 0.51 \ (\text{i.e., } L(F) = 0.51), \\
&T(\text{more or less bad}) = 0.50 \ (\text{i.e., } T(MB) = 0.50), \\
&L(\text{more or less bad}) = 0.41 \ (\text{i.e., } L(MB) = 0.41), \\
&T(\text{bad}) = 0.40 \ (\text{i.e., } T(B) = 0.40), \\
&L(\text{bad}) = 0.25 \ (\text{i.e., } L(B) = 0.25), \\
&T(\text{very bad}) = 0.24 \ (\text{i.e., } T(VB) = 0.24), \\
&L(\text{very bad}) = 0.10 \ (\text{i.e., } L(VB) = 0.10), \\
&T(\text{very very bad}) = 0.09 \ (\text{i.e., } T(VVB) = 0.09), \\
&L(\text{very very bad}) = 0.01 \ (\text{i.e., } L(VVB) = 0.01), \\
&T(\text{extremely bad}) = 0 \ (\text{i.e., } T(EB) = 0).
\end{aligned}
\tag{4}
$$

Assume that an evaluator evaluates the students' answerscripts by using an extended fuzzy grade sheet as shown in Table 2, where $\tilde{y}_i$ denotes a fuzzy number defined in [0, 1] and $1 \leq i \leq 11$. In any row of Table 4, the columns from the second to the twelfth indicate the fuzzy mark awarded to the answer to the corresponding question in the first column, where the fuzzy mark is represented as a type-2 fuzzy set. The last (i.e., the thirteenth) column of the extended fuzzy grade sheet shown in Table 2 indicates the degree of satisfaction evaluated by the proposed method awarded to each question. The box at the bottom of the extended fuzzy grade sheet shown in Table 2 indicates the total mark awarded to the student. Let $\tilde{0}$, $\tilde{0}$, $0.\tilde{1}$, $0.\tilde{2}$, $0.\tilde{3}$, $0.\tilde{4}$, $0.\tilde{5}$, $0.\tilde{6}$, $0.\tilde{7}$, $0.\tilde{8}$, $0.\tilde{9}$ and $1.\tilde{0}$ be triangular fuzzy numbers, where

$$\tilde{0} = (0, 0, 0), \qquad 0.\tilde{1} = (0, 0.1, 0.2), \qquad 0.\tilde{2} = (0.1, 0.2, 0.3),$$
$$0.\tilde{3} = (0.2, 0.3, 0.4), \qquad 0.\tilde{4} = (0.3, 0.4, 0.5), \qquad 0.\tilde{5} = (0.4, 0.5, 0.6),$$
$$0.\tilde{6} = (0.5, 0.6, 0.7), \qquad 0.\tilde{7} = (0.6, 0.7, 0.8), \qquad 0.\tilde{8} = (0.7, 0.8, 0.9), \qquad (5)$$
$$0.\tilde{9} = (0.8, 0.9, 1.0), \qquad 1.\tilde{0} = (1.0, 1.0, 1.0).$$

Table 2. Fuzzy Mark Represented by Fuzzy Numbers of Question Q.i in An Extended Fuzzy Grade Sheet

Question No.	Satisfaction Levels											Degree of Satisfaction
	EG	VVG	VG	G	MG	F	MB	B	VB	VVB	EB	
⋮	⋮	⋮	⋮	⋮	⋮	⋮	⋮	⋮	⋮	⋮	⋮	⋮
Q.i	$\tilde{y}_1$	$\tilde{y}_2$	$\tilde{y}_3$	$\tilde{y}_4$	$\tilde{y}_5$	$\tilde{y}_6$	$\tilde{y}_7$	$\tilde{y}_8$	$\tilde{y}_9$	$\tilde{y}_{10}$	$\tilde{y}_{11}$	
⋮	⋮	⋮	⋮	⋮	⋮	⋮	⋮	⋮	⋮	⋮	⋮	⋮
												Total Mark =

For example, assume that an evaluator uses an extended fuzzy grade sheet to evaluate the fuzzy mark of the first question (i.e., Q.1) of a test/examination of a student, shown as follows:

$$FN_{Q.1} = \{(EG, \tilde{0}), (VVG, 0.\tilde{9}), (VG, 0.\tilde{8}), (G, 0.\tilde{5}), (MG, \tilde{0}),$$
$$(V, \tilde{0}), (MB, \tilde{0}), (B, \tilde{0}), (VB, \tilde{0}), (VVB, \tilde{0}), (EB, \tilde{0})\}.$$

For convenience, the fuzzy set $FN_{Q.1}$ can also be abbreviated into

$$FN_{Q.1} = \{(VVG, 0.\tilde{9}), (VG, 0.\tilde{8}), (G, 0.\tilde{5})\}.$$

It indicates that the satisfaction level of the student's answerscript with respect to the first question is: about 90% very very good, about 80% very good and about 50% good.

Assume that the fuzzy mark of the question Q.i of a student's answerscript evaluated by an evaluator is as shown in Table 2, where $\tilde{y}_i$ is a fuzzy number in the universe of discourse [0, 1] and $1 \leq i \leq 11$. Assume that the degree of optimism of the evaluator determined by the evaluator for evaluating students' answerscript is λ, where $\lambda \in [0, 1]$. If $0 \leq \lambda < 0.5$, then the evaluator is a pessimistic evaluator. If $\lambda = 0.5$, then the evaluator is a normal evaluator. If $0.5 < \lambda \leq 1.0$, then the evaluator is an optimistic evaluator. The proposed method for students' answerscripts evaluation based on fuzzy numbers is now presented as follows:

Step 1: Based on formula (3), defuzzify each fuzzy number $\tilde{y}_i$ in the extended fuzzy grade sheet shown in Table 2 into a crisp value DEF($\tilde{y}_i$), where DEF($\tilde{y}_i$)$\in [0, 1]$ and $1 \leq i \leq 11$, as shown in Table 3.

Table 3. Defuzzified Values of Fuzzy Marks of Question Q.i of Table 2

Question No.	Satisfaction Levels											Degree of Satisfaction
	EG	VVG	VG	G	MG	F	MB	B	VB	VVB	EB	
⋮	⋮	⋮	⋮	⋮	⋮	⋮	⋮	⋮	⋮	⋮	⋮	⋮
Q.i	DEF($\tilde{y}_1$)	DEF($\tilde{y}_1$)	DEF($\tilde{y}_1$)	DEF($\tilde{y}_1$)	DEF($\tilde{y}_1$)	DEF($\tilde{y}_1$)	DEF($\tilde{y}_1$)	DEF($\tilde{y}_1$)	DEF($\tilde{y}_1$)	DEF($\tilde{y}_1$)	DEF($\tilde{y}_1$)	
⋮	⋮	⋮	⋮	⋮	⋮	⋮	⋮	⋮	⋮	⋮	⋮	⋮
												Total Mark =

Step 2: From formula (4), we can see that T(EG) = 1, L(EG) = 1, T(VVG) = 0.99, L(VVG) = 0.91, T(VG) = 0.90, L(VG) = 0.81, T(G) = 0.80, L(G) = 0.71, T(MG) = 0.70, L(MG) = 0.61, T(F) = 0.60, L(F) = 0.51, T(MB) = 0.50, L(MB) = 0.41, T(B) = 0.40, L(B) = 0.25, T(VB) = 0.24, L(VB) = 0.10, T(VVB) = 0.09, L(VVB) = 0.01, T(EB) = 0 and L(EB) = 0. In this case, the degree of satisfaction D(Q.i) of the question Q.i of the student's answerscript can be evaluated by the function D,

$$D(Q.i) = \frac{DEF(\tilde{y}_1) \times [(1-\lambda)L(EG) + \lambda T(EG)] + DEF(\tilde{y}_2) \times [(1-\lambda)L(VVG) + \lambda T(VVG)] + ... + DEF(\tilde{y}_{11}) \times [(1-\lambda)L(EB) + \lambda T(EB)]}{DEF(\tilde{y}_1) + DEF(\tilde{y}_2) + ... + DEF(\tilde{y}_{11})}, \quad (6)$$

where DEF($\tilde{y}_j$) denotes the defuzzified value of the fuzzy number $\tilde{y}_j$, $1 \leq j \leq 11$, and $0 \leq D(Q.i) \leq 1$. The larger the value of D(Q.i), the higher the degree of satisfaction that the question Q.i of the student's answerscript satisfies the evaluator's opinion.

Step 3: Consider the situation that the total mark of a candidate's answerscript to a paper is 100 marks. Assume that there are n questions to be answered, i.e.,

TOTAL MARKS = 100,
Q.1 carries s₁ marks,
Q.2 carries s₂ marks,
⋮
Q.n carries s_n marks,

where $\sum_{i=1}^{n} s_i = 100$, $0 \leq s_i \leq 100$, and $1 \leq i \leq n$. Assume that the evaluated degree of satisfaction of the question Q.1, Q.2, $\cdots$, and Q.n are D(Q.1), D(Q. 2), $\cdots$, and D(Q.n), respectively, then the total mark of the student is evaluated as follows:

$$s_1 \times D(Q.1) + s_2 \times D(Q.2) + \cdots + s_n \times D(Q.n). \tag{7}$$

Put this total mark in the appropriate box at the bottom of the extended fuzzy grade sheet.

Example 3.1: Consider a candidate's answerscript to an examination of 100 marks. Assume that in total there are four questions to be answered:

TOTAL MARKS = 100,
Q.1 carries 20 marks,
Q.2 carries 30 marks,
Q.3 carries 25 marks,
Q.4 carries 25 marks.

Assume that an evaluator awards the students' answerscript by an extended fuzzy grade sheet as shown in Table 4 and assume that the optimism index λ of the evaluator is 0.6 (i.e., $\lambda = 0.6$).

Table 4. Extended Fuzzy Grade Sheet of Example 3.1

Question No.	Satisfaction Levels											Degree of Satisfaction
	EG	VVG	VG	G	MG	F	MB	B	VB	VVB	EB	
Q.1	$0.\tilde{8}$	$0.\tilde{9}$	$\tilde{0}$	$\tilde{0}$	$\tilde{0}$	$\tilde{0}$	$\tilde{0}$	$\tilde{0}$	$\tilde{0}$	$\tilde{0}$	$\tilde{0}$	
Q.2	$\tilde{0}$	$\tilde{0}$	$\tilde{0}$	$0.\tilde{6}$	$0.\tilde{9}$	$0.\tilde{5}$	$\tilde{0}$	$\tilde{0}$	$\tilde{0}$	$\tilde{0}$	$\tilde{0}$	
Q.3	$\tilde{0}$	$\tilde{0}$	$0.\tilde{8}$	$0.\tilde{7}$	$0.\tilde{5}$	$\tilde{0}$	$\tilde{0}$	$\tilde{0}$	$\tilde{0}$	$\tilde{0}$	$\tilde{0}$	
Q.4	$\tilde{0}$	$\tilde{0}$	$\tilde{0}$	$\tilde{0}$	$\tilde{0}$	$\tilde{0}$	$\tilde{0}$	$0.\tilde{5}$	$0.\tilde{9}$	$0.\tilde{2}$	$\tilde{0}$	
												Total Mark =

Step 1: From formula (5), we can see that $\tilde{0} = (0, 0, 0)$, $0.\tilde{2} = (0.1, 0.2, 0.3)$, $0.\tilde{5} = (0.4, 0.5, 0.6)$, $0.\tilde{6} = (0.5, 0.6, 0.7)$, $0.\tilde{7} = (0.6, 0.7, 0.8)$, $0.\tilde{8} = (0.7, 0.8, 0.9)$ and $0.\tilde{9} = (0.8, 0.9, 1.0)$. Based on formula (3), we can get DEF($\tilde{0}$) = 0, DEF($0.\tilde{2}$) = 0.2, DEF($0.\tilde{5}$) = 0.5, DEF($0.\tilde{6}$) = 0.6, DEF($0.\tilde{8}$) = 0.8, and DEF($0.\tilde{9}$) = 0.9. Therefore, the triangular fuzzy numbers shown in Table 4 can be defuzzified into crisp values as shown in Table 5.

Step 2: Because the optimism index λ of the evaluator is 0.6 (i.e., $\lambda = 0.6$), according to formula (4) and by applying formula (6), we can see that

$$D(Q.1) = \frac{DEF(0.\tilde{8}) \times [(1 - 0.6) \times L(EG) + 0.6 \times T(EG)] + DEF(0.\tilde{9}) \times [(1 - 0.6) \times L(VVG) + 0.6 \times T(VVG)]}{DEF(0.\tilde{8}) + DEF(0.\tilde{9})},$$

$$= \frac{0.8 \times [(1 - 0.6) \times L(EG) + 0.6 \times T(EG)] + 0.9 \times [(1 - 0.6) \times L(VVG) + 0.6 \times T(VVG)]}{0.8 + 0.9},$$

$$= \frac{0.8 \times (0.4 \times 1.0 + 0.6 \times 1.0) + 0.9 \times (0.4 \times 0.91 + 0.6 \times 0.99)}{0.8 + 0.9},$$

$$= 0.9778,$$

$$D(Q.2) = \frac{DEF(0.\tilde{6}) \times [(1-0.6) \times L(G) + 0.6 \times T(G)] + DEF(0.\tilde{9}) \times [(1-0.6) \times L(MG) + 0.6 \times T(MG)] + DEF(0.\tilde{5}) \times [(1-0.6) \times L(F) + 0.6 \times T(F)]}{DEF(0.\tilde{6}) + DEF(0.\tilde{9}) + DEF(0.\tilde{5})},$$

$$= \frac{0.6 \times [(1-0.6) \times L(G) + 0.6 \times T(G)] + 0.9 \times [(1-0.6) \times L(MG) + 0.6 \times T(MG)] + 0.5 \times [(1-0.6) \times L(F) + 0.6 \times T(F)]}{0.6 + 0.9 + 0.5},$$

$$= \frac{0.6 \times (0.4 \times 0.71 + 0.6 \times 0.80) + 0.9 \times (0.4 \times 0.61 + 0.6 \times 0.70) + 0.5 \times (0.4 \times 0.51 + 0.6 \times 0.60)}{0.6 + 0.9 + 0.5},$$

$$= 0.6690,$$

$$D(Q.3) = \frac{DEF(0.\tilde{8}) \times [(1-0.6) \times L(VG) + 0.6 \times T(VG)] + DEF(0.\tilde{7}) \times [(1-0.6) \times L(G) + 0.6 \times T(G)] + DEF(0.\tilde{5}) \times [(1-0.6) \times L(MG) + 0.6 \times T(MG)]}{DEF(0.\tilde{8}) + DEF(0.\tilde{7}) + DEF(0.\tilde{5})},$$

$$= \frac{0.8 \times [(1-0.6) \times L(VG) + 0.6 \times T(VG)] + 0.7 \times [(1-0.6) \times L(G) + 0.6 \times T(G)] + 0.5 \times [(1-0.6) \times L(MG) + 0.6 \times T(MG)]}{0.8 + 0.7 + 0.5},$$

$$= \frac{0.8 \times (0.4 \times 0.81 + 0.6 \times 0.90) + 0.7 \times (0.4 \times 0.71 + 0.6 \times 0.80) + 0.5 \times (0.4 \times 0.61 + 0.6 \times 0.70)}{0.8 + 0.7 + 0.5},$$

$$= 0.7790,$$

$$D(Q.4) = \frac{DEF(0.\tilde{5}) \times [(1-0.6) \times L(B) + 0.6 \times T(B)] + DEF(0.\tilde{9}) \times [(1-0.6) \times L(VB) + 0.6 \times T(VB)] + DEF(0.\tilde{2}) \times [(1-0.6) \times L(VVB) + 0.6 \times T(VVB)]}{DEF(0.\tilde{5}) + DEF(0.\tilde{9}) + DEF(0.\tilde{2})},$$

$$= \frac{0.5 \times [(1-0.6) \times L(B) + 0.6 \times T(B)] + 0.9 \times [(1-0.6) \times L(VB) + 0.6 \times T(VB)] + 0.2 \times [(1-0.6) \times L(VVB) + 0.6 \times T(VVB)]}{0.5 + 0.9 + 0.2},$$

$$= \frac{0.5 \times (0.4 \times 0.25 + 0.6 \times 0.40) + 0.9 \times (0.4 \times 0.10 + 0.6 \times 0.24) + 0.2 \times (0.4 \times 0.01 + 0.6 \times 0.09)}{0.5 + 0.9 + 0.2},$$

$$= 0.2170.$$

Table 5. Defuzzified Values of Fuzzy Numbers of the Extended Fuzzy Grade Sheet Shown in Table 4

Question No.	Satisfaction Levels											Degree of Satisfaction
	EG	VVG	VG	G	MG	F	MB	B	VB	VVB	EB	
Q.1	0.8	0.9	0	0	0	0	0	0	0	0	0	
Q.2	0	0	0	0.6	0.9	0.5	0	0	0	0	0	
Q.3	0	0	0.8	0.7	0.5	0	0	0	0	0	0	
Q.4	0	0	0	0	0	0	0	0.5	0.9	0.2	0	
												Total Mark =

Step 3: By applying formula (7), the total mark of the student can be evaluated as follows:

$$20 \times D(Q.1) + 30 \times D(Q.2) + 25 \times D(Q.3) + 25 \times D(Q.4)$$
$$= 20 \times 0.9778 + 30 \times 0.6690 + 25 \times 0.7790 + 25 \times 0.2170$$
$$= 19.556 + 20.07 + 19.475 + 5.425$$
$$= 64.526$$
$$\cong 65 \text{ (assuming that no half mark is given in the total mark).}$$

4   A Generalized Fuzzy Evaluation Method Using Fuzzy Numbers

In this section, we present a generalized fuzzy evaluation method for students' answerscripts evaluation using fuzzy numbers. Consider a candidate's answerscript to a paper of 100 marks. Assume that there are n questions to be answered:

$$\text{TOTAL MARKS} = 100,$$
$$\text{Q.1 carries } s_1 \text{ marks,}$$
$$\text{Q.2 carries } s_2 \text{ marks,}$$
$$\vdots$$
$$\text{Q.}n \text{ carries } s_n \text{ marks,}$$

where $\sum_{i=1}^{n} s_i = 100$, $0 \leq s_i \leq 100$, and $1 \leq i \leq n$. Assume that the degree of optimism of the evaluator is λ, where $\lambda \in [0, 1]$. If $0 \leq \lambda < 0.5$, then the evaluator is a pessimistic evaluator. If $\lambda = 0.5$, then the evaluator is a normal evaluator. If $0.5 < \lambda \leq 1.0$, then the evaluator is an optimistic evaluator. Assume that an evaluator evaluates the questions of students' answerscripts using the following four criteria [1]:

$$C_1: \text{Accuracy of information,}$$
$$C_2: \text{Adequate coverage,}$$
$$C_3: \text{Conciseness,}$$
$$C_4: \text{Clear expression,}$$

and assume that the weights of the criteria C_1, C_2, C_3 and C_4 are w_1, w_2, w_3 and w_4, respectively, where $0 \leq w_i \leq 1$ and $1 \leq i \leq 4$. Furthermore, assume that the evaluator can evaluate each question of students' answerscripts using the above four criteria based on the method described in Section 3. In this case, an evaluator can evaluate students' answerscripts using a generalized extended fuzzy grade sheet as shown in Table 6, where the evaluating values in Table 6 are represented by fuzzy numbers and the degrees of satisfaction of the question Q.i of a student's answerscript regarding to the criteria C_1, C_2, C_3 and C_4 evaluated by the proposed method presented in Section 3 are $D(C_{i1})$, $D(C_{i2})$, $D(C_{i3})$, and $D(C_{i4})$, respectively, where $0 \leq D(C_{i1}) \leq 1$, $0 \leq D(C_{i2}) \leq 1$, $0 \leq D(C_{i3}) \leq 1$, $0 \leq D(C_{i4}) \leq 1$, and $1 \leq i \leq n$.

The degree of satisfaction $P(Q.i)$ of the question Q.i of the student's answerscript can be evaluated as follows:

$$P(Q.i) = \frac{w_1 \times D(C_{i1}) + w_2 \times D(C_{i2}) + w_3 \times D(C_{i3}) + w_4 \times D(C_{i4})}{w_1 + w_2 + w_3 + w_4}, \tag{8}$$

where $0 \leq P(Q.i) \leq 1$ and $1 \leq i \leq n$. The total mark of the student can be evaluated and is equal to

$$s_1 \times P(Q.1) + s_2 \times P(Q.2) + \cdots + s_n \times P(Q.n). \tag{9}$$

Put this total score in the appropriate box at the bottom of the extended fuzzy grade sheet.

Table 6. A Generalized Extended Fuzzy Grade Sheet [5]

Question No.	Criteria	Satisfaction Levels											Degree of Satisfaction for Criteria	Degree of Satisfaction for Questions
		EG	VVG	VG	G	MG	F	MB	B	VB	VVB	EB		
Q.1	C_1												$D(C_{11})$	P(Q.1)
	C_2												$D(C_{12})$	
	C_3												$D(C_{13})$	
	C_4												$D(C_{14})$	
Q.2	C_1												$D(C_{21})$	P(Q.2)
	C_2												$D(C_{22})$	
	C_3												$D(C_{23})$	
	C_4												$D(C_{24})$	
$\vdots$	$\vdots$	$\vdots$	$\vdots$	$\vdots$	$\vdots$	$\vdots$	$\vdots$	$\vdots$	$\vdots$	$\vdots$	$\vdots$	$\vdots$	$\vdots$	$\vdots$
Q.n	C_1												$D(C_{n1})$	P(Q.n)
	C_2												$D(C_{n2})$	
	C_3												$D(C_{n3})$	
	C_4												$D(C_{n4})$	

$$\text{Total Mark} = s_1 \times P(Q.1) + s_2 \times P(Q.2) + \cdots + s_n \times P(Q.n)$$

5 Conclusions

In this paper, we have presented new methods for evaluating students' answerscripts, where the evaluating values are represented by fuzzy numbers, and an optimism index λ determined by the evaluator is used to indicate the degree of optimism of the evaluator for evaluating students' answerscripts, where $\lambda \in [0, 1]$. The universe of discourse is formed by a set of satisfaction levels. The fuzzy mark awarded to the answer of each question of a student's answerscript is represented by a type-2 fuzzy set. The proposed methods can overcome the drawbacks of the methods presented in [1] and [5]. It can evaluate students' answerscripts in a more flexible and more intelligent manner.

Acknowledgements

The authors would like to thank Professor Jason Chihyu Chan, Department of Education, National Chengchi University, Taiwan, Republic of China, for providing very helpful comments and suggestions.

References

1. Biswas, R.: An Application of Fuzzy Sets in Students' Evaluation. Fuzzy Sets and Systems 74 (1995) 187–194
2. Chang, D.F., Sun, C.M.: Fuzzy Assessment of Learning Performance of Junior High School Students. Proceedings of the 1993 First National Symposium on Fuzzy Theory and Applications, Hsinchu, Taiwan, Republic of China (1993) 10–15

3. Chen, S.M.: A New Approach to Handling Fuzzy Decisionmaking Problems. IEEE Transactions on Systems, Man, and Cybernetics 18 (1988) 1012–1016

4. Chen, S.M.: Evaluating the Rate of Aggregative Risk in Software Development Using Fuzzy Set Theory. Cybernetics and Systems: An International Journal 30 (1999) 57–75

5. Chen, S.M., Lee, C.H.: New Methods for Students' Evaluating Using Fuzzy Sets. Fuzzy Sets and Systems 104 (1999) 209–218

6. Chen, S.M., Wang, J.Y.: Document Retrieval Using Knowledge-Based Fuzzy Information Retrieval Techniques. IEEE Transactions on Systems, Man, and Cybernetics 25 (1995) 793–803

7. Cheng, C.H., Yang, K.L.: Using Fuzzy Sets in Education Grading System. Journal of Chinese Fuzzy Systems Association 4 (1998) 81–89

8. Chiang, T.T., Lin, C.M.: Application of Fuzzy Theory to Teaching Assessment. Proceedings of the 1994 Second National Conference on Fuzzy Theory and Applications, Taipei, Taiwan, Republic of China (1994) 92–97

9. Frair, L.: Student Peer Evaluations Using the Analytic Hierarchy Process Method. Proceedings of 1995 Frontiers in Education Conference 2 (1995) 4c3.1–4c3.5

10. Echauz, J.R.: Vachtsevanos, G.J.: Fuzzy Grading System. IEEE Transactions on Education 38 (1995) 158–165

11. Kaburlasos, V.G., Marinagi, C.C., Tsoukalas, V.T.: PARES: A Software Tool for Computer-Based Testing and Evaluation Used in the Greek Higher Education System. Proceedings of the 2004 IEEE International Conference on Advanced Learning Technologies (2004) 771–773

12. Kaufmann, A., Gupta, M.M.: Fuzzy Mathematical Models in Engineering and Management Science. North-Holland Amsterdam The Netherlands (1988)

13. Law, C.K.: Using Fuzzy Numbers in Education Grading System. Fuzzy Sets and Systems 83 (1996) 311–323

14. Ma, J., Zhou, D.: Fuzzy Set Approach to the Assessment of Student-Centered Learning. IEEE Transactions on Education 43 (2000) 237–241

15. McMartin, F., Mckenna, A., Youssefi, K.: Scenario Assignments as Assessment Tools for Undergraduate Engineering Education. IEEE Transactions on Education 43 (2000) 111-119

16. Pears, A., Daniels, M., Berglund, A., Erickson, C.: Student Evaluation in An International Collaborative Project Course. Proceedings of the 2001 Symposium on Applications and the Internet Workshops (2001) 74–79

17. Wu, M.H.: A Research on Applying Fuzzy Set Theory and Item Response Theory to Evaluate Learning Performance, Master Thesis, Department of Information Management, Chaoyang University of Technology, Wufeng, Taichung County, Republic of China (2003)

18. Xingui, H.: Weighted Fuzzy Logic and Its Applications. Proceedings of the 12th Annual International Computer Software and Applications Conference, Chicago, Illinois (1988) 485–489

19. Zadeh, L.A.: Fuzzy Sets. Information and Control 8 (1965) 338–353

20. Zimmermann, H.-J.: Fuzzy Set Theory and Its Applications. Kluwer-Nijhoff Dordrecht (1991)

Genetic Lateral and Amplitude Tuning with Rule Selection for Fuzzy Control of Heating, Ventilating and Air Conditioning Systems[*]

R. Alcalá[1], J. Alcalá-Fdez[1], F.J. Berlanga[2], M.J. Gacto[1], and F. Herrera[1]

[1] University of Granada, Dept. Computer Science and A.I., E-18071 Granada, Spain
{alcala, jalcala, herrera}@decsai.ugr.es, mjgacto@ugr.es
[2] University of Jaén, Dept. Computer Science, E-23071 Jaén, Spain
berlanga@ujaen.es

Abstract. In this work, we propose the use of a new post-processing method for the lateral and amplitude tuning of membership functions combined with a rule selection to develop accurate fuzzy logic controllers dedicated to the control of heating, ventilating and air conditioning systems concerning energy performance and indoor comfort requirements.

1   Introduction

Heating, Ventilating and Air Conditioning (HVAC) systems are equipments usually implemented to maintain satisfactory comfort conditions in buildings. The energy consumption as well as indoor comfort aspects of buildings are highly dependent on the design, performance and control of their HVAC systems. Therefore, the use of automatic control strategies, as Fuzzy Logic Controllers (FLCs), could result in important energy savings compared to manual control [1, 10].

FLCs in buildings are often designed using rules of thumb not always compatible with the controlled equipment requirements, energy performance and users expectations and demand. However, different criteria should be optimized for a good performance of the HVAC system and, due to the nature of the problem, a rational operation and improved performance of FLCs is required [10]. A way to improve the FLC performance is the tuning of Membership Functions (MFs).

Recently, a new linguistic rule representation was presented to perform a fine genetic Lateral and Amplitude tuning (LA-tuning) of MFs [3]. It is based on a new symbolic representation with three values (s, α, β), respectively representing a label, the lateral displacement and the amplitude variation of the support of this label. The tuning of both parameters involves a reduction of the search space that eases the derivation of optimal models respect to classical tuning. This work proposes to apply and to combine the LA-tuning with a rule selection [11, 12] to develop accurate FLCs dedicated to the control of HVAC systems.

This paper is arranged as follows. The next section presents the basics of the HVAC system control problem. Section 3 introduces the genetic LA-tuning and

[*] Supported by the Spanish Ministry of Science and Technology under Projects TIC-2002-04036-C05-01 and 04, and TIN-2005-08386-C05-01 and 03.

M. Ali and R. Dapoigny (Eds.): IEA/AIE 2006, LNAI 4031, pp. 452–461, 2006.

rule selection. Section 4 proposes the evolutionary algorithm for the LA-tuning with rule selection. Section 5 applies the proposed method to the HVAC control problem. And finally, Section 6 points out some concluding remarks.

2   The HVAC System Control Problem

An HVAC system is comprised by all the components of the appliance used to condition the interior air of a building. The HVAC system is needed to provide the occupants with a comfortable and productive working environment which satisfies their physiological needs. In Figure 1, a typical office building HVAC system is presented. This system consists of a set of components to be able to raise and lower the temperature and relative humidity of the supply air.

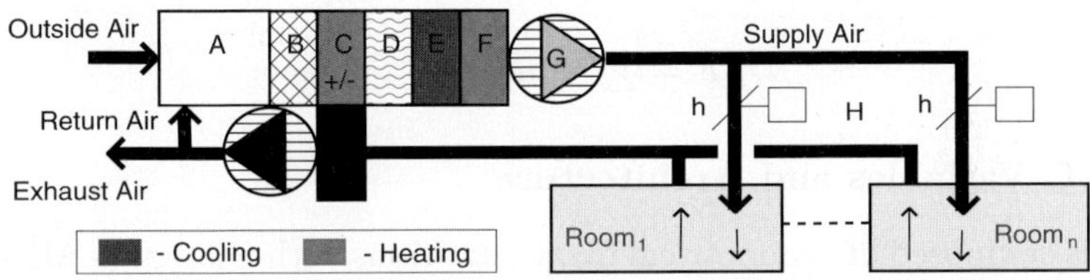

Fig. 1. Generic structure of an office building HVAC system

Some artificial intelligence techniques could be successfully applied to enhance the HVAC system capabilities [5, 10]. However, most works apply FLCs to individually solve simple problems such as thermal regulation (maintaining a temperature setpoint), energy savings or comfort improvements. On the other hand, the initial rule set is usually constructed based on the operator's control experience using rules of thumb, which sometimes fail to obtain satisfactory results [10]. Therefore, the different involved criteria should be optimized for a good performance of the HVAC System. Usually, *the main objective is to reduce the energy consumption while maintaining a desired comfort level.*

In our case, five criteria should be optimized improving an initial FLC obtained from human experience (involving 17 variables) by using the LA-tuning and rule selection. To do so, we consider the calibrated and validated models of a real test building. Both, the initial FLC and the simulation model were developed within the framework of the JOULE-THERMIE programme under the GENESYS [1] project (see [1, 4] for more information on this problem).

2.1   Objectives and Fitness Function

Our main optimization objective is the energy performance but maintaining the required indoor comfort levels, specifically to *minimize* the following five criteria:

---

[1] GENESYS Project: Fuzzy controllers and smart tuning techniques for energy efficiency and overall performance of HVAC systems in buildings, European Commission, Directorate-General XII for Energy (contract JOE-CT98-0090).

O$_1$ Upper thermal comfort limit[2]: *if $PMV > 0.5$, $O_1 = O_1 + (PMV - 0.5)$.*
O$_2$ Lower thermal comfort limit: *if $PMV < -0.5$, $O_2 = O_2 + (-PMV - 0.5)$.*
O$_3$ Indoor air quality: *if CO_2 conc. $> 800ppm$, $O_3 = O_3 + (CO_2 - 800)$.*
O$_4$ Energy consumption: $O_4 = O_4+$ Power at time t.
O$_5$ System stability: $O_5 = O_5+$ System change from time t to $(t - 1)$, where
system changes states for a change in the system operation.

These criteria are combined into one overall objective function by means of a vector of weights. When trustworthy weights are available, this approach reduces the size of the search space providing the adequate direction into the solution space and its use is highly recommended. In our case, trusted weights were obtained by the experts for the objective weighting fitness function: $w_1^O = 0.0083022$, $w_2^O = 0.0083022$, $w_3^O = 0.00000456662$, $w_4^O = 0.0000017832$ and $w_5^O = 0.000761667$. Finally, the fitness function to be minimized was computed as:

$$F = \sum_{i=1}^{5} w_i^O \cdot O_i \ .$$

2.2   FLC Variables and Architecture

The DB is composed of symmetrical fuzzy partitions with triangular MFs labeled from $L1$ to Ll_i (with l_i being the number of labels of the i-th variable). Figure 3 depicts the initial DB together with the tuned DB to optimize the paper size.

A hierarchical FLC architecture considering the PMV, CO_2 concentration, previous HVAC system status and outdoor temperature was proposed for the GENESYS site. The architecture, variables and initial Rule Base (RB) can be seen in Figure 4 together with the final selected rules again for the paper size. Figure 4 represents the decision tables of each module of the hierarchical FLC in terms of these labels. Each cell of the table represents a fuzzy subspace and contains its associated output consequent(s), i.e., the corresponding label(s). The output variables are denoted in the top left square for each module. Both, the initial RB and DB, were provided by experts.

3   LA-Tuning and Rule Selection

This section presents the two techniques that are combined to improve the FLC behavior in the HVAC control problem, the LA-tuning and the rule selection.

3.1   The LA-Tuning of Membership Functions

In [2], a new model of tuning of MFs was proposed considering the linguistic 2-tuples representation scheme introduced in [9], that allows the symbolic translation of a label by considering an only parameter per label. The LA-tuning [3]

---

[2] PMV is the more global Predicted Mean Vote thermal comfort index 7730 selected by the international standard organization ISO, incorporating relative humidity and mean radiant temperature (http://www.iso.org/iso/en/ISOOnline.frontpage).

is an extension of the lateral tuning to also perform a tuning of the support amplitude of the MFs. To adjust the displacements and amplitudes of the MF supports we propose a new rule representation considering two parameters, α and β, relatively representing the lateral displacement and the amplitude variation of a label. In this way, each label can be represented by a 3-tuple (s, α, β), where α is a number within the interval [-0.5, 0.5) that expresses the domain of a MF when it is moving between its two lateral MFs (as in the 2-tuples representation), and β is also a number within the interval [-0.5, 0.5) that allows an increase or decrease in the support amplitude of a MF by 50% of its original size. Let us consider a set of labels S representing a fuzzy partition. Formally, we have the triplet,

$$(s_i, \alpha_i, \beta_i), \quad s_i \in S, \ \{\alpha_i, \beta_i\} \in [-0.5, 0.5)$$

As an example, Figure 2 shows the 3-tuple represented label $(s_2, -0.3, -0.25)$ together with the lateral displacement and amplitude variation of the corresponding MF. Let c_{s_2} and a_{s_2} be the right and the left extreme of the s_i support, and Sup_{s_2} be its size. The support of the new label $s'_2 = (s_2, -0.3, -0.25)$, can be computed in the following way:

$$Sup_{s'_2} = Sup_{s_2} + \beta * Sup_{s_2} \quad , \text{with } Sup_{s_2} = c_{s_2} - a_{s_2}$$

In our case, the learning is applied to the level of linguistic partitions. In this way, the pair $(X_j$, label) takes the same tuning values in all the rules where it is considered. For example, X_j is (High, 0.3, 0.1) will present the same values for those rules in which the pair "X_j is High" was initially considered. Notice that, since symmetrical triangular MFs and a FITA (*First Infer, Then Aggregate*) fuzzy inference will be considered, a tuning of the amplitude of the consequents has no sense, by which the β parameter will be only applied on the antecedents.

In the context of the FLCs, we are going to see its use in the linguistic rule representation. Let us consider a control problem with two input variables, one

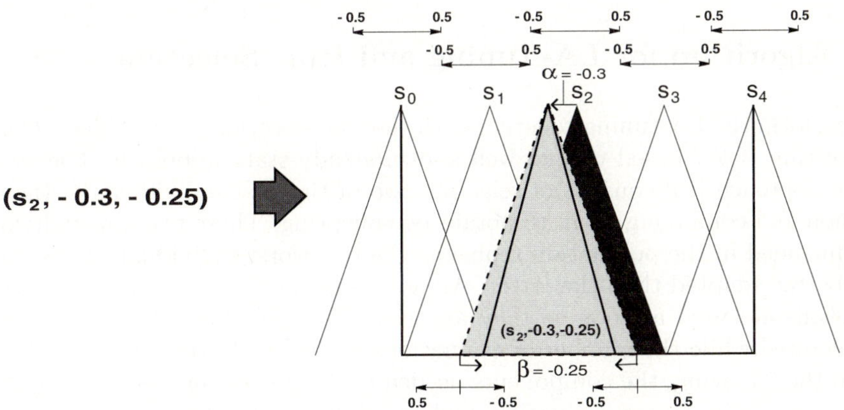

Fig. 2. LA-Variation of the MF Associated to s_2

output variable and a DB defined from experts determining the MFs for the following labels: *Error* and $\triangledown Error \rightarrow \{N, Z, P\}$, and *Power* $\rightarrow \{L, M, H\}$. Based on this DB definition, an example of a 3-tuples represented rule is:

If *Error* is (Zero,-0.3,0.1) and $\triangledown Error$ is (Positive,0.2,-0.4) then *Power* is (High,-0.1).

3.2   Rule Selection

Rule set reduction techniques try to minimize the number of rules of a given fuzzy rule-based system while maintain (or even improve) the system performance. To do that, erroneous and conflicting rules that degrade the performance are eliminated, obtaining a more cooperative fuzzy rule set and therefore involving a potential improvement of the system accuracy. Furthermore, in many cases the accuracy is not the only requirement of the model but also the interpretability becomes an important aspect. Reducing the model complexity is a way to improve the system readability, i.e., a compact system with few rules requires a minor effort to be interpreted.

Fuzzy rule set reduction is generally applied as a post-processing stage, once an initial fuzzy rule set has been derived. One of the most known fuzzy rule set reduction techniques is the rule selection. This approach involves obtaining an optimal subset of fuzzy rules from a previous fuzzy rule set by selecting some of them. We may find several methods for rule selection, with different search algorithms that look for the most successful combination of fuzzy rules [11, 12]. In [13], an interesting heuristic rule selection procedure is proposed where, by means of statistical measures, a relevance factor is computed for each fuzzy rule composing the fuzzy system to subsequently select the most relevant ones.

These kinds of techniques could be easily combined with other post-processing techniques to obtain more compact and accurate fuzzy models. In this way, some works have considered the rule selection together with the tuning of MFs by coding all of them (rules and parameters) in the same chromosome [7]. In this work, we combine the rule selection with the LA-tuning of MFs.

4   Algorithm for LA-Tuning and Rule Selection

To perform the LA-tuning together with the rule selection we consider a Genetic Algorithm (GA) based on the well-known steady-state approach. The steady-state approach [14] consists of selecting two of the best individuals in the population and combining them to obtain two offspring. These two new individuals are included in the population replacing the two worst individuals if the former are better adapted than the latter. An advantage of this technique is that good solutions are used as soon as they are available. Therefore, the convergence is accelerated while the number of evaluations needed is decreased.

In the following, the components needed to design this process are explained. They are: chromosome evaluation, coding scheme and initial gene pool, the genetic operators and a restarting approach to avoid premature convergence.

4.1 Evaluating the Chromosome

The fitness function (see Section 2.1) has been modified in order to consider the use of fuzzy goals that decrement the importance of each individual fitness value whenever it comes to its respective goal or that penalize each objective whenever its value is worse with respect to the initial solution. To do so, a function modifier parameter is considered, $\delta_i(x)$. A penalization rate, p_i, has been included in $\delta_i(x)$, allowing the user to set up priorities in the objectives (0 less priority and 1 more priority). With g_i being the goal value, i_i being the initial solution value and $q_i = max(g_i, i_i)$, the global fitness is evaluated as:

$$F' = \sum_{i=1}^{5} w_i^O \cdot \delta_i(O_i) \cdot O_i \ , \quad with \quad \delta_i(x) = \begin{cases} 0, & if\ x \le g_i \\[2mm] \dfrac{x - g_i}{i_i - g_i}, & if\ g_i < x < i_i \\[3mm] \dfrac{x - q_i}{x - x \cdot p_i} + 1, & if\ x \ge q_i \end{cases} \ .$$

4.2 Coding Scheme and Initial Gene Pool

To combine the rule selection with the LA-tuning, a double coding scheme for both *rule selection* (C_S) and *LA-tuning* (C_T) is used:

- For the C_S part, the coding scheme generates binary-coded strings of length m (with m being the number of fuzzy rules in the existing FLC). Thus, the corresponding part C_S^p for the p-th chromosome will be a binary vector that determines when a rule is selected or not (values '1' and '0' respectively),

$$C_S^p = (c_{S1}^p, \ldots, c_{Sm}^p) \mid c_{Si}^p \in \{0, 1\} \ .$$

- For the C_T part, a real coding is considered, i.e., the real parameters are the GA representation units (genes). This part is the joint of the parameters of the fuzzy partitions, lateral (C^L) and amplitude (C^A) tuning. Let us consider the following number of labels per variable: $(m^1, \ldots, m^n)$, with n being the number of system variables ($n - 1$ input variables and 1 output variable). Then, a chromosome has the following form,

$$C_T = (C^L + C^A) = (c_{11}^L, \ldots, c_{1m^1}^L, \ldots, c_{n1}^L, \ldots, c_{nm^n}^L) \ + $$
$$(c_{11}^A, \ldots, c_{1m^1}^A, \ldots, c_{(n-1)1}^A, \ldots, c_{(n-1)m^n}^A).$$

Finally, a chromosome C^p is coded in the following way: $C^p = C_S^p C_T^p$.

To make use of the available information, the initial FLC obtained from expert knowledge is included in the population as an initial solution. To do so, the initial pool is obtained with first individual having all genes with value '1' in the C_S part and having all genes with value '0.0' (no displacement or amplitude variation) in the C_T part. The remaining individuals are generated at random.

4.3   Genetic Operators

The crossover operator will depend on the chromosome part where it is applied:

- For the C_T part, the BLX-α crossover [6] and a hybrid between a BLX-α and an arithmetical crossover [8] are considered. In this way, if two parents, $C_T^v = (c_{T1}^v, \ldots, c_{Tk}^v, \ldots, c_{Tg}^v)$ and $C_T^w = (c_{T1}^w, \ldots, c_{Tk}^w, \ldots, c_{Tg}^w)$, are going to be crossed, two different crossovers are considered,
    1. Using the BLX-α crossover [6] (with $\alpha = 0.3$), one descendent $C_T^h = (c_{T1}^h, \ldots, c_{Tk}^h, \ldots, c_{Tg}^h)$ is obtained, with c_{Tk}^h being randomly generated within the interval $[I_{L_k}, I_{R_k}] = [c_{min} - I \cdot \alpha, c_{max} + I \cdot \alpha]$, $c_{min} = min(c_{Tk}^v, c_{Tk}^w)$, $c_{max} = max(c_{Tk}^v, c_{Tk}^w)$ and $I = c_{max} - c_{min}$.
    2. The application of the arithmetical crossover [8] in the wider interval considered by the BLX-α, $[I_{L_k}, I_{R_k}]$, results in the next descendent:
    $$C_T^h \text{ with } c_{Tk}^h = aI_{L_k} + (1 - a)I_{R_k},$$
    and with $a \in [0, 1]$ randomly generated each time this operator is applied.
- In the C_S part, the standard two-point crossover is used.

Finally, four offspring are generated by combining the two ones from the C_S part with the two ones from the C_T part. The mutation operator flips the gene value in the C_S part but, to improve the convergence no mutation is considered in the C_T part. Once the mutation is applied on the four generated offspring, the resulting descendents are the two best of these four individuals.

4.4   Restart Approach

Finally, to get away from local optima, this algorithm uses a restart approach. Whenever the population converges to similar results (practically the same fitness value), the entire population but the best individual is randomly generated within the corresponding variation intervals. It allows the algorithm to perform a better exploration of the search space and to avoid getting stuck at local optima.

5   Experiments

To evaluate the goodness of the approach proposed (LA-tuning with rule selection), the HVAC problem is considered to be solved. The FLCs obtained from the proposed approach will be compared to the performance of a classic On-Off controller and to the performance of the initial FLC (provided by experts). *The goals and improvements will be computed with respect to this classical controller as done in the GENESYS [3] project.* The intention from experts was to try to have 10% energy saving (O_4) together with a global improvement of the system behavior compared to On-Off control. Comfort parameters could be slightly increased if necessary (no more than 1.0 for criteria O_1 and O_2). The methods considered in this study are shown in Table 1.

The values of the parameters used are: 31 individuals, 0.2 as mutation probability per chromosome (except for GL and GLA without mutation) and 0.35

Table 1. Methods Considered for Comparison

Method, Ref.	Year	Description
S, [4]	2005	Rule Selection (C_S part of GLA-S)
CL, [1]	2003	Classical Tuning
GL, [2]*	2004	Global Lateral-tuning (C^L part of GLA-S)
CL-S, –	–	Classical Tuning (CL) + Rule Selection (S)
GL-S, –	–	Global Lateral-tuning (GL) + Rule Selection(S)
GLA, –	–	Global LA-tuning (C_T part of GLA-S)
GLA-S, –	–	Global LA-Tuning + Rule Selection

* The global lateral tuning proposed in [2] adapted to this problem.

Table 2. Comparison among the different methods

MODEL	#R	PMV O_1	O_2	CO$_2$ O_3	Energy O_4	%	Stability O_5	%
ON-OFF	–	0.0	0	0	3206400	–	1136	–
Initial FLC	172	0.0	0	0	2901686	9.50	1505	-32.48
$\overline{S}$	160	0.1	0	0	2886422	9.98	1312	-15.52
$\overline{C}$	172	0.0	0	0	2586717	19.33	1081	4.84
$\overline{C-S}$	109	0.1	0	0	2536849	20.88	1057	6.98
$\overline{GL}$	172	0.9	0	0	2325093	27.49	1072	5.66
$\overline{GL-S}$	113	0.7	0	0	2287993	28.64	800	29.58
$\overline{GLA}$	172	0.9	0	0	2245812	**29.96**	797	29.84
$\overline{GLA-S}$	**104**	0.8	0	0	2253996	29.70	634	**44.19**

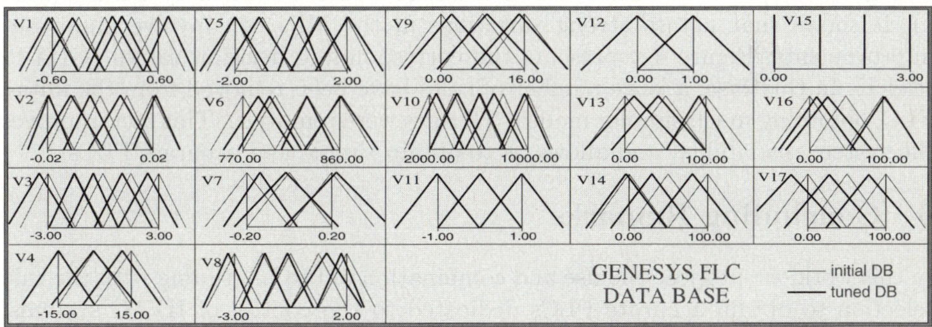

Fig. 3. Initial and Tuned DB of a Model Obtained with GLA-S (seed 1)

as factor a in the max-min-arithmetical crossover in the case of CL. The termination condition is to reach 2000 evaluations. To see the GA convergence, three runs have been performed with different seeds for the random number generator.

The results presented in Table 2 correspond to averaged results obtained from the three different runs, where % stands for the improvement rate with respect to the On-Off controller and #R for the number of rules. No improvement

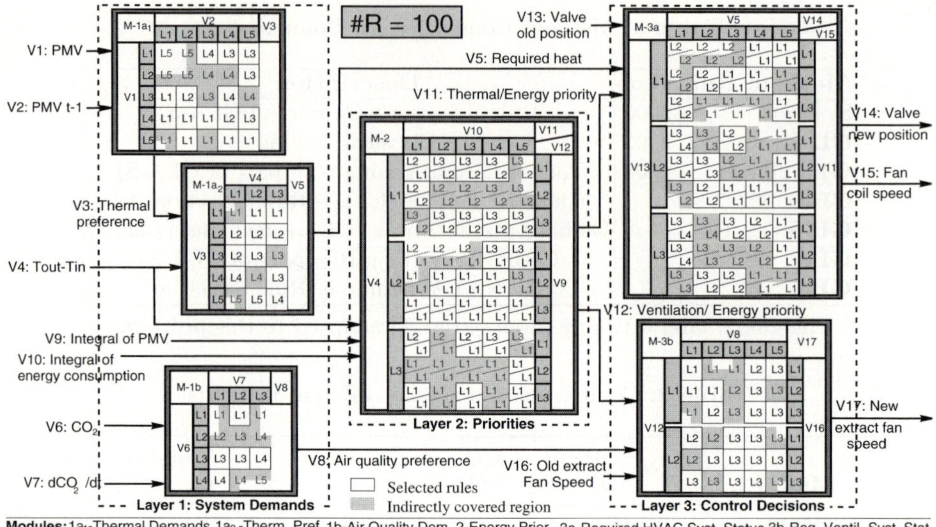

Modules: 1a₁-Thermal Demands, 1a₂-Therm. Pref., 1b-Air Quality Dem., 2-Energy Prior., 3a-Required HVAC Syst. Status, 3b-Req. Ventil. Syst. Stat.

Fig. 4. RB and final structure of a Model Obtained with GLA-S (seed 1)

percentages have been considered in the table for $O_1 \ldots O_3$, since these objectives always met the experts requirements (goals). A good trade-off between energy and stability was achieved by GLA-S. GLA-S presents improvement rates of about a 29.7% in energy and about a 44.2% in stability, with the remaining criteria for comfort and air quality within the requested levels. Moreover, the proposed algorithm presented a good convergence and seems to be robust.

Figure 3 depicts the initial and final DB of a FLC obtained by GLA-S (seed 1). It shows that not so strong variations in the MFs can involve important improvements. Figure 4 represents the corresponding decision tables (GLA-S, seed 1). In this case, a large number of rules have been removed from the initial FLC, obtaining much simpler models (72 rules were removed). This fact improves the system readability, and allows us to obtain simple and accurate FLCs.

6   Concluding Remarks

In this work, we propose the use and combination of the LA-tuning with the rule selection to obtain accurate FLCs dedicated to the control of HVAC systems. Techniques based on the LA-tuning, specially that including rule selection, have yielded much better results than the remaining approaches, showing their good behavior on these kinds of complex problems. It is due to the following reasons:

- The search space reduction that the LA-tuning involves in complex problems. It allows to these techniques to obtain more optimal FLCs.
- The complementary characteristics that the tuning approaches and the rule selection present. The ability of the rule selection to reduce the number of rules by only selecting those presenting a good cooperation is combined with the tuning accuracy improvement, obtaining accurate and compact FLCs.

As further work, we propose the use of multiobjective GAs in order to obtain even simpler FLCs maintaining a similar accuracy.

References

1. Alcalá R., Benítez J.M., Casillas J., Cordón O., Pérez R.: Fuzzy control of HVAC systems optimized by genetic algorithms. Applied Intelligence **18** (2003) 155–177
2. Alcalá R., Herrera F.: Genetic tuning on fuzzy systems based on the linguistic 2-tuples representation. Proc. of the IEEE Int. Conf. on Fuzzy Syst. **1** (2004) 233–238
3. Alcalá R., Alcalá-Fdez J., Gacto M.J., Herrera F.: Genetic lateral and amplitude tuning of membership functions for fuzzy systems. Proc. of the 2nd Int. Conf. on Machine Intelligence (ACIDCA-ICMI'2005) 589–595
4. Alcalá R., Casillas J., Cordón O., González A., Herrera F.: A genetic rule weighting and selection process for fuzzy control of HVAC systems. Engineering Applications of Artificial Intelligence **18:3** (2005) 279–296
5. Calvino F., Gennusa M.L., Rizzo G., Scaccianoce G.: The control of indoor thermal comfort conditions: introducing a fuzzy adaptive controller. Energy and Buildings **36** (2004) 97–102
6. Eshelman L.J., Schaffer J.D.: Real-coded genetic algorithms and interval-schemata. Foundations of Genetic Algorithms **2** (1993) 187–202.
7. Gómez-Skarmeta A.F., Jiménez F.: Fuzzy modeling with hybrid systems. Fuzzy Sets Syst. **104** (1999) 199–208
8. Herrera F., Lozano M., Verdegay J.L.: Fuzzy connectives based crossover operators to model genetic algorithms population diversity. Fuzzy Sets Syst. **92:1** (1997) 21–30
9. Herrera F., Martńez L.: A 2-tuple fuzzy linguistic representation model for computing with words. IEEE T. Fuzzy Syst. **8:6** (2000) 746–752
10. Huang S., Nelson R.M.: Rule development and adjustment strategies of a fuzzy logic controller for an HVAC system - Parts I and II (analysis and experiment). ASHRAE Trans. **100:1** (1994) 841–850, 851–856.
11. Ishibuchi H., Murata T., Türksen I.B.: Single-objective and two objective genetic algorithms for selecting linguistic rules for pattern classification problems. Fuzzy Sets Syst. **89:2** (1997) 135–150
12. Krone A., Krause H., Slawinski T.: A new rule reduction method for finding interpretable and small rule bases in high dimensional search spaces. Proc. of the IEEE Int. Conf. on Fuzzy Syst. **2** (2000) 693–699
13. Krone A., Taeger H.: Data-based fuzzy rule test for fuzzy modelling. Fuzzy Sets Syst. **123:3** (2001) 343–358
14. Whitley D., Kauth J.: GENITOR: A different genetic algorithm. Proc. of the Rocky Mountain Conf. on Artificial Intelligence (1988) 118–130

Fuzzy Motivations for Evolutionary Behavior Learning by a Mobile Robot

Tomás Arredondo V., Wolfgang Freund, Cesar Muñoz,
Nicolas Navarro, and Fernando Quirós

Universidad Técnica Federico Santa María, Valparaíso, Chile,
Departamento de Electrónica,
Casilla 110 V, Valparaíso, Chile
tarredondo@elo.utfsm.cl

Abstract. In this paper we describe a fuzzy logic based approach for providing biologically based motivations to be used in evolutionary mobile robot learning. Takagi-Sugeno-Kang (TSK) fuzzy logic is used to motivate a small mobile robot to acquire complex behaviors and to perform environment recognition. This method is implemented and tested in behavior based navigation and action sequence based environment recognition tasks in a Khepera mobile robot simulator. Our fuzzy logic based motivation technique is shown as a simple and powerful method for a robot to acquire a diverse set of fit behaviors as well as providing an intuitive user interface framework.

Keywords: Fuzzy logic, evolutionary, mobile robot, environment recognition, AEM.

1 Introduction

Providing more natural and intuitive interfaces between robots and people is clearly seen as desirable and beneficial. Much recent research has focused on providing more intuitive and natural interfaces for robotic control [1, 2].

Towards this goal we have developed a fuzzy logic based method that provides a natural interface in order to give a variety of motivations used in robotic learning. To test the validity of the proposed method we tested the fuzzy logic based method on behavior based navigation and environment recognition tasks within a Khepera robot simulator. The results show that the method has potential for improving human understanding of robotic behavior learning as well as provides a method for generating greater diversity of robotic behaviors. To the best of our knowledge fuzzy logic has not been used before in this manner in a robotics application.

In our experiments we studied two different tasks for testing with fuzzy based motivations in the Khepera robot simulator: basic behavior based navigation and action based environmental modeling (AEM).

Behavior based architectures (e.g. subsumption) in general do not use world models, representative or symbolic knowledge and there is a tight coupling between sensing and action (moving). This design philosophy promotes the idea

M. Ali and R. Dapoigny (Eds.): IEA/AIE 2006, LNAI 4031, pp. 462–471, 2006.

that robots should be inexpensive, robust to sensor and other noise, incremental, uncalibrated and without complex computers and communication systems. Planning actions based on internal world representations in not seen as something beneficial because of its inherent error and associated costs. Behavior based learning systems typically used include reinforcement learning, neural networks, genetic algorithms, fuzzy systems, case and memory based learning [3, 4]. Behavior based navigation as implemented in the Khepera simulator YAKS [5] inputs sensor values directly into a neural network that drives left and right motors for navigation in different rooms.

Action-based environmental modeling (AEM) also follows this less is more philosophy by using a simple mobile robot with local sensors in order to navigate and perform environment recognition in various scenarios (rooms). AEM uses a small action set (e.g. go straight, turn left, turn right, turn around) in order to perform a sequence of actions based on sensed states in a specific environment. The search space of suitable behaviors is huge and designing suitable behaviors by hand is very difficult therefore Yamada [6] has used a genetic algorithm within a Khepera simulator to find suitable behaviors for AEM.

In the training phase of the AEM procedure and for each room of the set of rooms being recognized the robot executes an action sequence which is converted into an environment vector. These vectors are repeatedly fed into a SOM [18] network in order for the neural network to learn without supervision which is the output node (r-node) that corresponds to each room. The environment vector used for each room and the winning output node is also stored as a room instance. The next step is a test phase in which the robot executes an action sequence in one of the rooms previously used and the r-node for the test room is determined using the previously trained SOM network. The robot then determines which room used during training has the minimum distance to the current test room by using 1-Nearest Neighbor with Euclidean distance. Fitness considerations include returning to his original starting neighborhood (homing), ability to identify the room it is in (accuracy), and using the shortest possible sequence (efficiency). Collision avoidance is implicit in the efficiency measure; the final fitness is the sum of all three [6].

In Section 2, we describe fuzzy logic in robotic control. Our method and how it was implemented is described in Section 3. In Section 4 and 5 we describe and summarize our test results. Finally, in Section 6 some conclusions are drawn.

2   Fuzzy Logic in Robotic Behavioral Control

Fuzzy logic systems produce actions using a set of fuzzy rules and variables. These variables are referred to as linguistic variables and indicate a degree of membership of the variable to a particular fuzzy set. The degree of membership (between 0 and 1) is defined by a membership function which maps a crisp input to a fuzzy output (fuzzifier). Fuzzy logic control systems consist of: fuzzifier, fuzzy rule base, fuzzy inference engine, and a defuzzifier. In many applications fuzzy logic provides a more natural interface that gives greater flexibility than traditional logic [7].

Fuzzy logic has been used widely in various robotic applications such as robotics behavioral fusion. Flakey and Marge are two robots that used fuzzy based implementations to blend different possible behaviors for things such as collision avoidance, goal seeking, docking, and wall following [8, 9]. These robots had issues with scalability and exponential growth in the rule base which they attempted to manage by: reduction of input spaces and using contexts with a limited world model [8], or by using independent distributed fuzzy agents and weighted vector summation via fuzzy multiplexers for producing the final command signals for its drive and steer mechanism [9]. More recently other fuzzy logic strategies have been used in mobile robotics including: neuro-fuzzy controllers for behavior design (based on direction, distance and steering) [10], fuzzy based modular motion planning [11], fuzzy integration of groups of behaviors [12], multiple fuzzy agents used in behavior fusion [13], GA based neuro fuzzy reinforcement learning agents used in training a walking robot [14], and behavior based fuzzy logic integration for robotic navigation in challenging terrain [15]. As far as our research shows fuzzy logic has not been previously used in robotics in terms of motivating actions and behaviors. We have implemented such motivations as fuzzy fitness functions for robotic behaviors.

3   Fuzzy Motivations for Robotic Learning

Motivation as currently viewed by psychologists as an internal state or condition (e.g. a need, desire or want) that serves to influence the intensity and direction of behavior. Motivation is generally accepted as involved in the performance of learned behaviors. That is a learned behavior may not occur unless it's driven by a motivation. There are many sources for motivations including: behavioral, social, biological, cognitive, affective, and spiritual [16]. Differences in motivations are key drivers in helping to produce a variety of behaviors which have a high degree of benefit (or fitness) for the organism.

In our experiments, we use motivation settings in order to determine the fuzzy fitness of a robot in various environments. In terms of robotic learning the motivations that we consider include: curiosity (C), homing (H), orientation (O), and energy (E, the opposite of laziness). The membership functions used for each of the four motivations in our experiment is shown in Fig. 1.

The Takagi-Sugeno-Kang (TSK) fuzzy logic model is used, TSK fuzzy logic does not require deffuzification as each rule has a crisp output that is aggregated as a weighted average [17]. As shown in Fig. 2, the fuzzy motivations considered include the parameters of C, H, O and E, which are used as input settings (between 0 and 1) prior to running each experiment, with the sum kept at one. A run environment (room) is selected and the GA initial robot population is randomly initialized. After this, each robot in the population performs its task (navigation and optionally environment recognition) and a set of fitness values (a, g, l, b) corresponding to the performed task are obtained.

The fitness criteria and the variables that correspond to them are: amount of area explored (a), proper action termination and escape from original

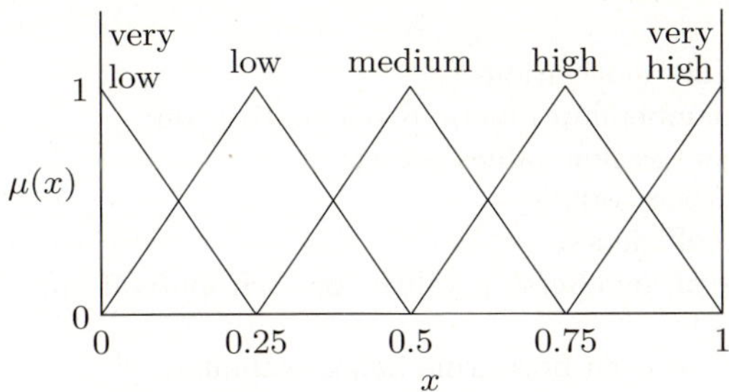

Fig. 1. Fuzzy membership functions

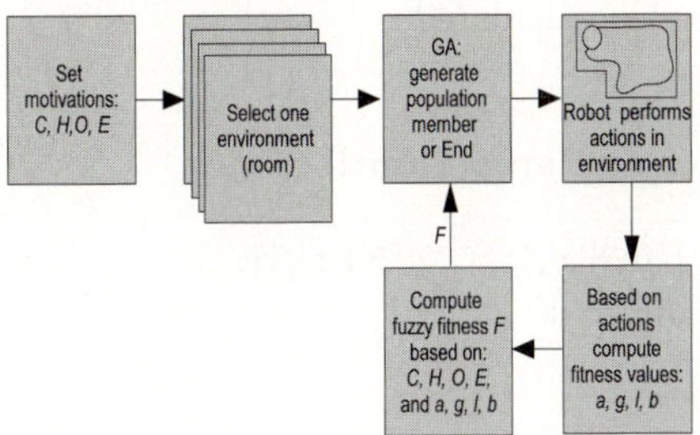

Fig. 2. System Overview

neighborhood area (g), environment recognition (l) and percent of battery usage (b). These fitness values are calculated after the robot completes each run. The a value is determined by considering the percentage area explored relative to the optimum, g is determined by

$$g = 1 - \frac{\text{final distance to the robot home}}{\text{maximum possible distance}},$$

l is currently not used and determined only off-line, finally b is the estimated total energy consumption of the robot considering each step.

The final fuzzy motivation fitness value (F) is calculated using TSK based fuzzy logic (four fuzzy variables with five membership functions each: $4^5 = 1024$ different fuzzy rules) as shown in Fig. 3 and using the membership functions from Fig. 1 to compute μ values. For the coefficient array C we used a linear function. A sample fuzzy rule (number 10) is given as follows:

if (Y[1] == V.H.) and (Y[2] == L) and (Y[3] == V.L.) and (Y[4] == V.L.) then
f[10] = X[1]Y[1]C[4]+X[2]Y[2]C[2]+X[3]Y[3]C[1]+X[4]Y[4]C[1].

3.1   Implementation Environment

We used the simulator YAKS (Yet Another Khepera Simulator) for our implementation. YAKS is a simple open source behavior based simulator [5] that uses neural networks and genetic algorithms in order to provide a navigation environment for a Khepera robot. Sensor inputs are directly provided into a multilayer

Algorithm FuzzyFitness
Input:
  N : number of fuzzy motivations;
  M : number of membership functions per motivation;
  $X[N]$: array of motivation values preset;
  $Y[N]$: array of fitness values;
  $C[N]$: array of coefficients;
  $\mu[N][M]$: matrix of membership values for each motivation;
Variables:
  $w[n]$: the weight for each fuzzy rule being evaluated;
  $f[n]$: the estimated fitness;
  $n, x_0, x_1, \ldots, x_N$: integers;
Output:
  F : the fuzzy fitness value calculated;
begin
  $n := 1$;
  for each $x_1, x_2, \ldots, x_N := 1$ **step** 1 **until** M **do**
  begin
    $w[n] := \min\{\mu[1][x_1], \mu[2][x_2], \ldots, \mu[N][x_N]\}$;
    $f[n] := \sum_{i=1}^{N} X[i]Y[i]C[x_i]$;
    $n := n + 1$;
  end;
  $F := (\sum_{i=1}^{N^M} w[i]f[i])/(\sum_{i=1}^{N^M} w[i])$;
end;

Fig. 3. Fuzzy Fitness Algorithm

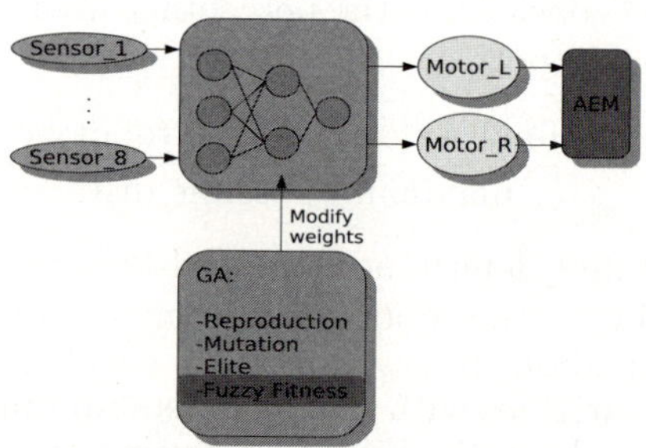

Fig. 4. Fuzzy fitness and AEM implementation

neural network in order to drive left and right wheel motors. A simple genetic algorithm is used with 200 members, 200 generations, mutation of 1%, and elite reproduction. Random noise (6%) is injected into motor actions and sensors to improve realism. The GA provides with a mechanism for updating neural network weights used by each robot in the population that is being optimized. Figure 4 shows where the fuzzy fitness algorithm and AEM are incorporated into the simulator.

As seen in Fig. 5, to implement AEM, we select a highly fit robot (corresponding to the neural network in Fig. 4) and make him navigate in all environments

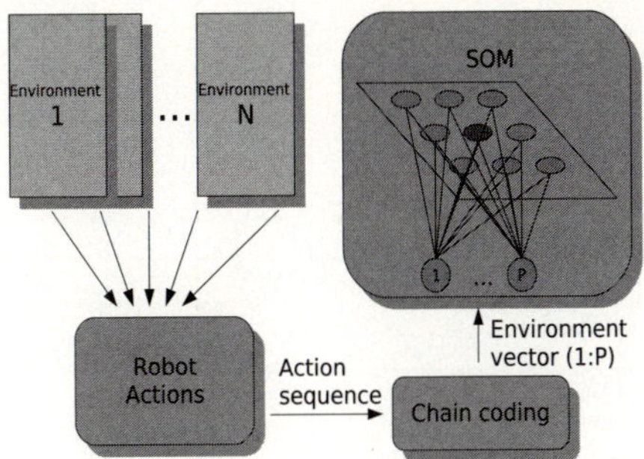

Fig. 5. AEM Overview

(rooms). This navigation produces actions which are saved as action sequences. These action sequences are converted using chain coding into an environment vector [6]. These vectors are fed into the SOM network for unsupervised learning. After learning the SOM network associates a vector with one of its output nodes (r-nodes).

For our implementation of SOM we select an input of 400 actions (steps) and a linear output layer of 128 nodes. The actions are obtained by converting each motor command (Motor_L and Motor_R) which is a real value between 0 and 1 into an action (left 30°, right 30°, turn 180°, go straight).

After training SOM we evaluate it by using the same robot and at random select a room for him to navigate in. The SOM network is evaluated by the ability of the robot to recognize which room (r-node) it navigates in. This ability could be fed as the orientation value in the fuzzy fitness calculation.

4 Navigation and Environment Recognition Experimental Results

4.1 Scenario 1: Navigation

We tested behavior based navigation in five different rooms. For comparison and as an example, we selected two sets of fuzzy motivation criteria. This scenario did not include environment recognition (AEM). In order to contrast the effect of curiosity, the first criterion (C, H, O, E) used was (.8, .1, 0, .1) and the second was (.5, .3, 0, .2). We stopped each experiment after 400 steps. As seen in the examples of Fig. 6, during the simulations performed average fuzzy fitness in the first generation was 0.1 and gradually increased. Figures 7 and 8 show some representative results of navigation by various robots after fuzzy fitness optimization.

4.2 Scenario 2: Environment Recognition

We tested behavior based environment recognition using five different rooms. For comparison we selected two sets of fuzzy motivation criteria (C, H, O, E),

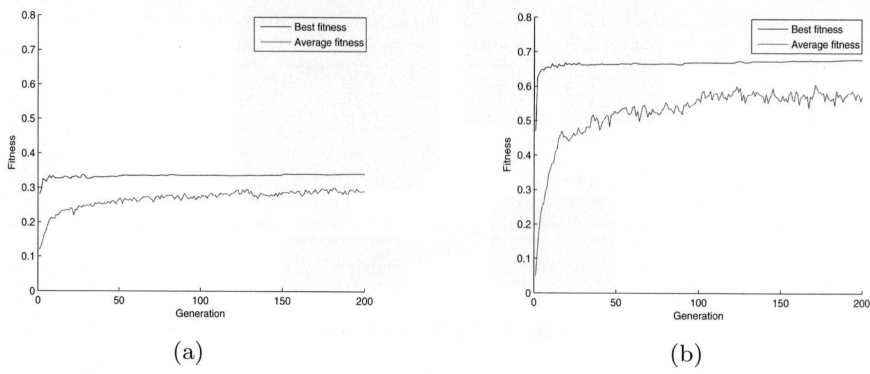

Fig. 6. Fitness Evolution Examples: (a) low curiosity (b) high curiosity

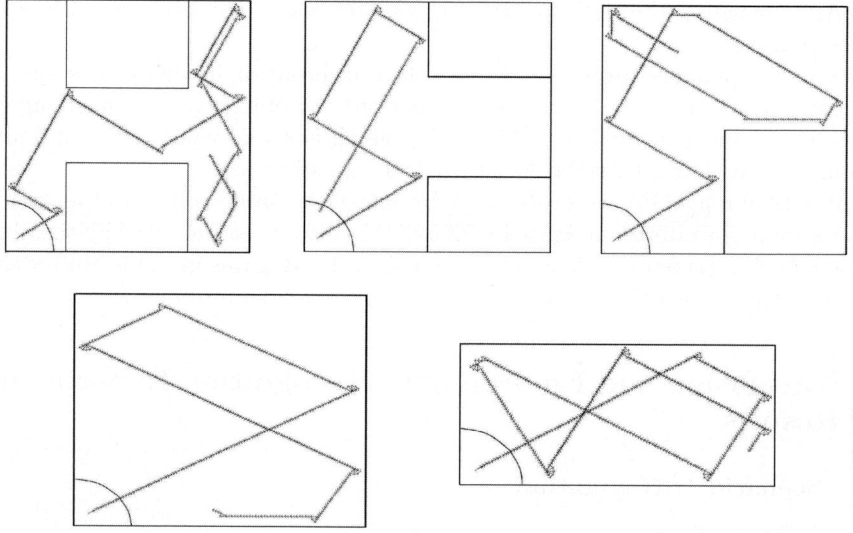

Fig. 7. Navigation with (C, H, O, E) as $(.8, .1, 0, .1)$

the first criterion used was $(.8, .1, 0, .1)$ and the second was $(.5, .3, 0, .2)$. We stopped each experiment after 400 steps.

During testing, the same robot (neural net) was made to navigate and recognize five rooms with the following shapes: H, T, L, Square and Rectangle. The procedure was repeated 10 times for each room. The threshold for r-node recognition was set at 10 nearest neighbor nodes in the SOM output layer. Environment recognition is the % recognition of which room the robot actually visited. Tables 1 and 2 show our results.

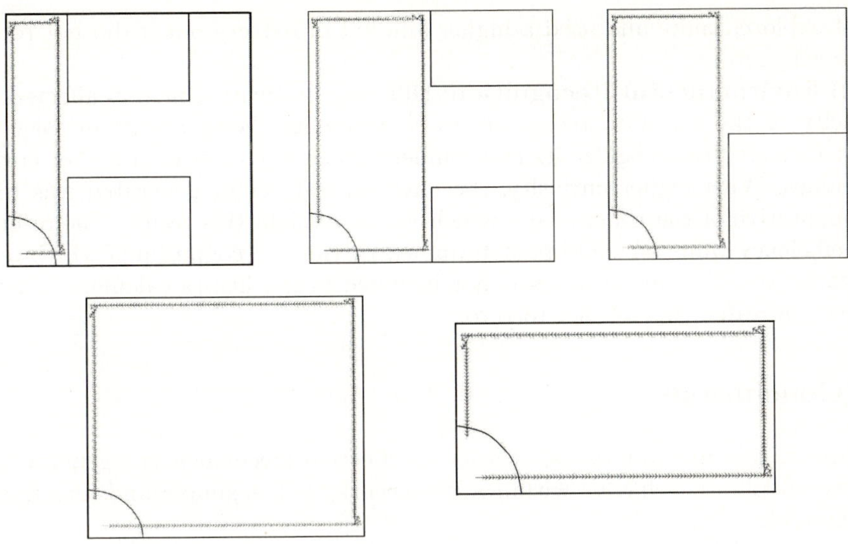

Fig. 8. Navigation with (C, H, O, E) as $(.5, .3, 0, .2)$

Table 1. Navigation and Environment Recognition with (C, H, O, E) as $(.8, .1, 0, .1)$

Room shape	Average Fitness	% of Optimal Exploration	% Recognition	% Battery usage
H	0.6421	93.84	80.00	79.19
T	0.6686	91.77	100.00	78.45
L	0.6507	97.04	100.00	79.58
Square	0.6699	99.88	100.00	79.56
Rectangle	0.6377	95.29	100.00	79.88

Table 2. Navigation and Environment Recognition with (C, H, O, E) as $(.5, .3, 0, .2)$

Room shape	Average fitness	% of Optimal Exploration	% Recognition	% Battery usage
H	0.2465	54.66	20.00	57.90
T	0.2694	57.84	0.00	59.66
L	0.2707	57.93	0.00	59.67
Square	0.3274	80.63	100.00	74.64
Rectangle	0.267	57.70	0.00	59.60

5   Discussion

The results of our experiments are summarized below:

(1) **Navigation:** By changing the different motivation factors the character-istics of robot navigation were changed. With lower curiosity and higher homing the robot conserved its battery (battery usage was around 50%) and the robot managed to explore only around 50% of the region. With higher curiosity the

robot explored more and used a higher amount of battery but it did not return home very often.

(2) **Environmental Recognition:** Different motivation factors affected the capacity of the robot to recognize its environment. With lower curiosity the robot managed to recognize its environment much less than with higher curiosity values. With higher curiosity, the environment vector generated was more representative of the room shape which would explain this result. The orientation efficiency value (l) could be determined by the % recognition of which room the robot actually ran in but was not included in the fitness calculation as the orientation value (O) was set to zero.

6 Conclusions

In general this method was shown as an effective mechanism for generating a variety of robotic behavior within a framework that is simple and intuitive to understand.

Future work includes: the integration of other motivations such as urgency for completing specific missions, integration of % recognition into the fuzzy fitness calculation, the construction of a low cost robot specifically designed to test this method, and the possible real-time extensions to this method.

Acknowledgements

This research was partially funded by Fundación Andes and by the research center (DGIP) of UTFSM. We would also like to thank Dr. Seiji Yamada for providing information about AEM.

References

1. Park, H., Kim, E., Kim, H.: Robot Competition Using Gesture Based Interface. In: Moonis, A. Esposito, F. (eds): Innovations in Applied Artificial Intelligence. Lecture Notes in Artificial Intelligence, Vol. 3353. Springer-Verlag, Berlin (2005) 131-133.
2. Tasaki, T., Matsumoto, S., Ohba, H., Toda, M., Komatani, K., Ogata, T., Okuno, H.: Distance-Based Dynamic Interaction of Humanoid Robot with Multiple People. In: Moonis, A. Esposito, F. (eds): Innovations in Applied Artificial Intelligence. Lecture Notes in Artificial Intelligence, Vol. 3353. Springer-Verlag, Berlin (2005) 111-120.
3. Brooks, R.: A Robust Layered Control System for a Mobile Robot. IEEE Journal of Robotics and Automation, Vol. RA-2, No. 1 (1986) 14-23.
4. Arkin, R.: Behavior-Based Robotics, MIT Press, Cambridge, (1998).
5. YAKS simulator website: http://r2d2.ida.his.se/
6. Yamada, S.: Evolutionary behavior learning for action-based environment modeling by a mobile robot. Applied Soft Computing, 5 (2005) 245-257
7. Jang, J., Chuen-Tsai, S., Mitzutani, E.: Neuro-Fuzzy and Soft Computing, Prentice Hall, NJ, (1997).

8. Konolige, K., Meyers, K., Saffiotti, A.: FLAKEY, an Autonomous Mobile Robot. SRI technical document, July 20 (1992)
9. Goodrige, S., Kay, M., Luo, R.: Multi-Layered Fuzzy Behavior Fusion for Reactive Control of an Autonomous Mobile Robot. Proceedings of the Sixth IEEE International Conference on Fuzzy Systems (July 1997) 573-578
10. Hoffman, F.: Soft computing techniques for the design of mobile robot behaviors. Information Sciences, 122 (2000) 241-258
11. Al-Khatib, M., Saade, J.: An efficient data-driven fuzzy approach to the motion planning problem of a mobile robot. Fuzzy Sets and Systems, 134 (2003) 65-82
12. Izumi, K., Watanabe, K.: Fuzzy behavior-based control trained by module learning to acquire the adaptive behaviors of mobile robots. Mathematics and Computers in Simulation, 51 (2000) 233-243
13. Martnez Barber, H., Gmez Skarmeta, A.: A Framework for Defining and Learning Fuzzy Behaviours for Autonomous Mobile Robots, International Journal of Intelligent Systems, 17(1) , (2002) 1-20
14. Zhou, C. : Robot learning with GA-based fuzzy reinforcement learning agents, Information Sciences, 145 (2002) 45-68
15. Seraji, H., Howard, A.: Behavior-Based Robot Navigation on Challenging Terrain: A Fuzzy Logic Approach, IEEE Trans on Robotics and Automation, V.18, No.3 (June 2002) 308-321
16. Huitt, W.: Motivation to learn: An overview. Educational Psychology Interactive. Valdosta State University.: http://chiron.valdosta.edu/whuitt/col/motivation/motivate.html, (2001).
17. Jang, J.-S, Sun, C.-T., Sun, Mizutani, E.: Neuro-Fuzzy and Soft Computing: a computational approach to learning and machine intelligence, Prentice Hall, NJ, (1997).
18. Kohonen Teuvo: The self-organizing map. Proceedings of the IEEE, 79(9): 1464-1480, (1990)

Optimization of Self-organizing Fuzzy Polynomial Neural Networks with the Aid of Granular Computing and Evolutionary Algorithm

Ho-Sung Park[1], Sung-Kwun Oh[2], and Tae-Chon Ahn[1]

[1] School of Electrical Electronic and Information Engineering, Wonkwang University,
344-2, Shinyong-Dong, Iksan, Chon-Buk, 570-749, South Korea
`{neuron, tcahn}@wonkwang.ac.kr`
[2] Department of Electrical Engineering, The University of Suwon, San 2-2 Wau-ri,
Bongdam-eup, Hwaseong-si, Gyeonggi-do, 445-743, South Korea
`ohsk@suwon.ac.kr`

Abstract. In this study, we introduce and investigate a class of intelligence architectures of Self-Organizing Fuzzy Polynomial Neural Networks (SOFPNN) that is based on a genetically optimized Fuzzy Polynomial Neurons(FPNs), develop a comprehensive design methodology involving mechanisms of genetic algorithms and information granulation. With the aid of the information granulation, we determine the initial location (apexes) of membership functions and initial values of polynomial function being used in the premised and consequence part of the fuzzy rules respectively. The GA-based design procedure being applied at each layer of SOFPNN leads to the selection of preferred nodes with specific local characteristics (such as the number of input variables, the order of the polynomial, a collection of the specific subset of input variables, and the number of membership function) available within the network.

1 Introduction

The challenging quest of how to construct models that come with significant approximation and generalization abilities as well as are easy to comprehend has been within the community for decades [1]. GMDH-type algorithms have been extensively used since the mid-1970's for prediction and modeling complex nonlinear processes [2]. While providing with a systematic design procedure, GMDH comes with some drawbacks. To alleviate the problems associated with the GMDH, Self-Organizing Neural Networks (SONN, called "SOFPNN") were introduced by Oh and Pedrycz [3], [4], [5] as a new category of neural networks or neuro-fuzzy networks.

In this study, in considering the above problems coming with the conventional SOFPNN, we introduce a new structure and organization of fuzzy rules as well as a new genetic design approach. The new meaning of fuzzy rules, information granules melt into the fuzzy rules. That is, we determine the initial location (apexes) of membership functions in the premise part and the initial values of polynomial function of consequence part of the fuzzy rules by information granulation. In a nutshell, each fuzzy rule describes the related information granule. The determination of the optimal

M. Ali and R. Dapoigny (Eds.): IEA/AIE 2006, LNAI 4031, pp. 472–477, 2006.

values of the parameters available within an individual FPN (viz. the number of input variables, the order of the polynomial, a collection of preferred nodes, and the number of MF) leads to a structurally and parametrically optimized network through the genetic approach.

2   The Conventional SOFPNN with Fuzzy Polynomial Neuron (FPN) and Its Topology

The FPN consists of two basic functional modules. The first one, labeled by **F**, is a collection of fuzzy sets that form an interface between the input numeric variables and the processing part realized by the neuron. The second module (denoted here by **P**) is about the function – based nonlinear (polynomial) processing. The detailed FPN involving a certain regression polynomial is shown in Table 1.

Table 1. Different forms of regression polynomial building a FPN

| | No. of inputs | 1 | 2 | 3 |
| Order of the polynomial | | | | |
Order	Type			
0	Type 1	Constant	Constant	Constant
1	Type 2	Linear	Bilinear	Trilinear
2	Type 3	Quadratic	Biquadratic-1	Triquadratic-1
	Type 4		Biquadratic-2	Triquadratic-2

1: Basic type, 2: Modified type

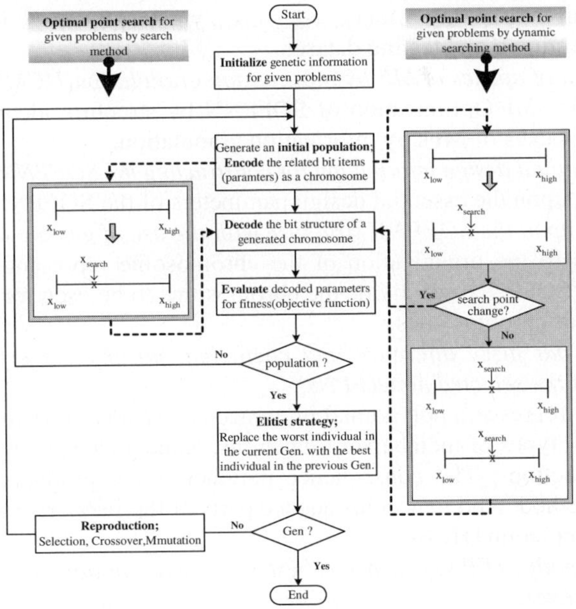

Fig. 1. Optimization of SOFPNN parameter by GA with dynamic searching range

3   The Optimization of SOFPNN

3.1   Optimization of SOFPNN by Structure Identification

With aid of GAs [6], optimal structure design available within FPN (viz. the number of input variables, the order of the polynomial, a collection of the specific subset of input variables, and the number of MFs) lead to a structurally optimized network. Furthermore, we determine the initial location (apexes) of membership functions in the premise part and the initial values of polynomial function of consequence part of the fuzzy rules by IG [7] (using HCM [8]).

3.2   Optimization of SOFPNN by Parameter Identification

For the parametric identification, we obtained the effective model that the axes of MFs are identified by GA to reflect characteristic of given data. Especially, the genetically dynamic search method is introduced in the identification of parameter as shown in Fig. 1. It helps lead to rapidly optimal convergence over a limited region or a boundary condition.

4   The Algorithm and Design Procedure of SOFPNN

Step 1. *Determine system's input variables.*
Define system's input variables $x_i(i=1, 2, \ldots, n)$ related to the output variable y.
Step 2. *Form training and testing data.*
The input-output data set $(x_i, y_i)=(x_{1i}, x_{2i}, \ldots, x_{ni}, y_i)$, $i=1, 2, \ldots, N$ is divided into two parts, that is, a training and testing dataset.
Step 3. *Decision of apexes of MF by Information granulation(HCM).*
As mentioned in '3.1 Optimization of SOFPNN by structure identification', we obtained the new apexes of MFs by information granulation.
Step 4. *Decide initial design information for constructing the SOFPNN structure.*
Here we decide upon the essential design parameters of the SOFPNN structure.
Step 5. *Decide upon the SOFPNN structure with the use of genetic design.*
When it comes to the organization of the chromosome representing (mapping) the structure of the SOFPNN, we divide the chromosome to be used for genetic optimization into four sub-chromosomes.
Step 6. *Carry out fuzzy inference and coefficient parameters estimation for fuzzy identification in the selected node(FPNs).*
At this step, the regression polynomial inference is considered. In the fuzzy inference, we consider two types of membership functions, namely triangular and Gaussian-like membership functions. The consequence parameters are produced by the standard least squares method. And new consequence parts of the fuzzy rule are constructed by information granulation (HCM).
Step 7. *Select nodes (FPNs) with the best predictive capability and construct their corresponding layer.*

The nodes (FPNs) are generated through the genetic design. In GAs, we calculate the fitness function as following Eq. (1).

$$F(\text{fitness function}) = 1/(1+EPI) \tag{1}$$

Where, EPI denotes the performance index for the testing data (or validation data).

Step 8. *Check the termination criterion.*

As far as the performance index is concerned (that reflects a numeric accuracy of the layers), a termination is straightforward and comes in the form,

$$F_1 \leq F_* \tag{2}$$

Where, F_1 denotes a maximal fitness value occurring at the current layer whereas F_* stands for a maximal fitness value that occurred at the previous layer. In this study, we use one measure that is the Mean Squared Error (MSE).

Step 9. *Determine new input variables for the next layer.*

If (2) has not been met, the model is expanded. The outputs of the preserved nodes $(z_{1i}, z_{2i}, \ldots, z_{Wi})$ serves as new inputs to the next layer $(x_{1j}, x_{2j}, \ldots, x_{Wj})(j=i+1)$.

The SOFPNN algorithm is carried out by repeating steps 4-9.

5   Experimental Studies

We illustrate the performance of the network and elaborate on its development by experimenting with data coming from the gas furnace process [9]. The delayed terms of methane gas flow rate, $u(t)$ and carbon dioxide density, $y(t)$ are used as system input variables such as $u(t\text{-}3)$, $u(t\text{-}2)$, $u(t\text{-}1)$, $y(t\text{-}3)$, $y(t\text{-}2)$, and $y(t\text{-}1)$. The output variable is $y(t)$. We consider the MSE given by (3) to be a pertinent performance index. Table 2 summarizes the list of parameters used in the genetic optimization of the networks.

Table 2. Computational overhead and a list of parameters of the GAs and the SOFPNN

	Parameters		1st layer	2nd layer	3rd layer
GAs	Maximum generation	S.O	150	150	150
		P.O		100	
	Total population size	S.O	100	100	100
		P.O	300*No. of Node in 1st layer		
	Selected population size (S.O)		30	30	30
	Crossover rate		0.65	0.65	0.65
	Mutation rate		0.1	0.1	0.1
SOFP NN	String length		3+3+30+5 +90	3+3+30+5	3+3+30+5
	Maximal no. of inputs to be selected(Max)		$1 \leq l \leq \text{Max}(2\text{~}3)$	$1 \leq l \leq \text{Max}(2\text{~}3)$	$1 \leq l \leq \text{Max}(2\text{~}3)$
	Polynomial type (Type T) of the consequent part of fuzzy rules		$1 \leq T^* \leq 4$	$1 \leq T \leq 4$	$1 \leq T \leq 4$
	Membership Function (MF) type		Triangular Gaussian	Triangular Gaussian	Triangular Gaussian
	No. of MFs per each input(M)		2 or 3	2 or 3	2 or 3

l, T, Max: integers, S.O : Structure Optimization, P.O : Parameter Optimization.

Table 3 summarizes the results: According to the information of Table 2, the selected input variables (Node), the selected polynomial type (T), the selected no. of MFs (M), and its corresponding performance index (PI and EPI) were shown when the genetic optimization for each layer was carried out.

Table 3. Performance index of SOFPNN for gas furnace process(S.O : Structure Optimization, P.O : Parameter Optimization)

| | | In case of selected input | | | | | | In case of entire system input | | | | | | |
| | | | S.O | | P.O | | | | S.O | | P.O | | |
MF	Max	Node(M)	T	PI	EPI	PI	EPI	Node(M)	T	PI	EPI	PI	EPI
Tri	2	8(2) 29(3)	3	0.010	0.115	0.011	0.111	5(2) 6(3)	2	0.006	0.116	0.007	0.108
	3	15(2) 25(3) 0	4	0.013	0.120	0.013	0.105	20(2) 28(3) 0	2	0.006	0.118	0.007	0.117
Gau	2	9(2) 10(2)	3	0.010	0.122	0.011	0.120	11(2) 12(3)	2	0.006	0.121	0.006	0.124
	3	4(2) 20(3) 0	4	0.012	0.113	0.013	0.103	7(2) 15(3) 0	2	0.005	0.122	0.005	0.114

Fig. 2 illustrates the optimization process by visualizing the values of the performance index obtained in successive generation of GAs (the Max of inputs to be selected is set to 2 with the structure composed of 3 layers, PI=0.007 and EPI=0.108).

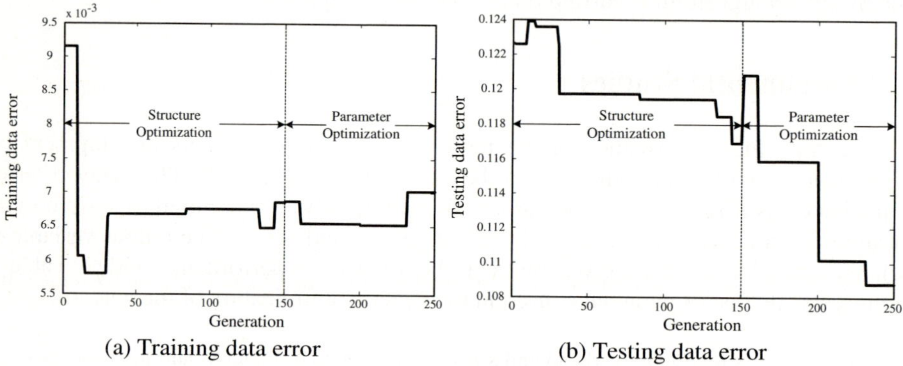

(a) Training data error   (b) Testing data error

Fig. 2. The optimization process quantified by the values of the performance index

Table 4 includes a comparative analysis of the performance of the proposed network with other models.

Table 4. Comparative analysis of the performance of the network; considered are models reported in the literature

Model			PI	PI_s	EPI_s
Box and Jenkin's model [9]			0.710		
Sugeno and Yasukawa's model [10]			0.190		
Oh and Pedrycz's model [11]			0.123	0.020	0.271
Kim, et al.'s model [12]				0.034	0.244
Lin and Cunningham's model [13]				0.071	0.261
SONN [5]	Gaussian-like	CASE I (5th layer)		0.016	0.133
		CASE II (5th layer)		0.018	0.131
Our model	Triangular	3rd layer (Max=2)		0.007	0.108
		3rd layer (Max=3)		0.013	0.105
	Gaussian-like	3rd layer (Max=2)		0.006	0.124
		3rd layer (Max=3)		0.013	0.103

6 Concluding Remarks

In this study, we introduced and investigated a new architecture and comprehensive design methodology of Self-Organizing Fuzzy Polynomial Neural Networks (SOFPNN), and discussed their topologies. With the aid of the information granulation, we determine the initial location (apexes) of membership functions and initial values of polynomial function being used in the premised and consequence part of the fuzzy rules respectively. And GA-based design procedure applied at each stage (layer) of the SOFPNN leads to the selection of these optimal nodes with local characteristics (such as the number of input variables, the order of the consequent polynomial of fuzzy rules, input variables, and number of membership function) available within SOFPNN. Most importantly, through the proposed framework of genetic optimization we can efficiently search for the optimal network architecture (structurally and parametrically optimized network) and this becomes crucial in improving the performance of the resulting model.

Acknowledgement. This paper was supported by Wonkwang University in 2005.

References

1. Cherkassky, V., Gehring., Mulier, F..: Comparison of adaptive methods for function estimation from samples. IEEE Trans. Neural Networks. **7** (1996) 969-984
2. Ivakhnenko, A.G..: Polynomial theory of complex systems. IEEE Trans. on Systems, Man and Cybernetics. SMC-**1** (1971) 364-378
3. Oh, S.K., Pedrycz, W..: The design of self-organizing Polynomial Neural Networks. Information Science. **141** (2002) 237-258
4. Oh, S.K., Pedrycz, W., Park, B.J.: Polynomial Neural Networks Architecture: Analysis and Design. Computers and Electrical Engineering. **29** (2003) 703-725
5. Oh, S.K., Pedrycz, W.: Fuzzy Polynomial Neuron-Based Self-Organizing Neural Networks. Int. J. of General Systems. **32** (2003) 237-250
6. Jong, D.K.A.: Are Genetic Algorithms Function Optimizers?. Parallel Problem Solving from Nature 2, Manner, R. and Manderick, B. eds., North-Holland, Amsterdam (1992)
7. Zadeh, L.A.: Toward a theory of fuzzy information granulation and its centrality in human reasoning and fuzzy logic. Fuzzy sets and Systems. **90** (1997) 111-117
8. Bezdek, J.C.: Pattern Recognition with Fuzzy Objective Function Algorithms. New York. Plenum (1981)
9. Box, D. E., Jenkins., G. M.: Time Series Analysis, Forecasting and Control, California. Holden Day. (1976)
10. Sugeno. M., Yasukawa., T.: A Fuzzy-Logic-Based Approach to Qualitative Modeling. IEEE Trans. Fuzzy Systems. **1** (1993) 7-31
11. Oh, S.K., Pedrycz, W.: Identification of Fuzzy Systems by means of an Auto-Tuning Algorithm and Its Application to Nonlinear Systems. Fuzzy sets and Systems. **115** (2000) 205-230
12. Kim, E. T., et al.: A simple identified Sugeno-type fuzzy model via double clustering. Information Science. **110** (1998) 25-39
13. Lin, Y., Cunningham III, G. A.: A new approach to fuzzy-neural modeling. IEEE Trans. Fuzzy Systems. **3** (1995) 190-197

Fuzzy Clustering-Based on Aggregate Attribute Method

Jia-Wen Wang and Ching-Hsue Cheng

Department of Information Management,
National Yunlin University of Science and Technology,
123, section 3, University Road, Touliu, Yunlin 640, Taiwan, R.O.C.
{g9220803, chcheng}@yuntech.edu.tw

Abstract. This paper, we propose a fuzzy clustering-based on aggregate attribute method for classification tasks, which comprises three phases: (1) Calculate the aggregate attribute values. (2) Apply fuzzy clustering to cluster the aggregate values. (3) Predict the testing data's class. For verifying proposed method, we use two datasets to illustrate our performance, the datasets are: (1) Iris; (2) Wisconsin-breast-cancer dataset. Finally, we compare with other methods; it is shown that our proposed method is better than other methods.

1   Introduction

To assign new instances from a domain to one class of mutually exclusive classes based on the observed attributes of the instance is a common problem that occurs in the sciences, social sciences and business. The increasing complexity and dimensionality of classification problems, it is necessary to deal with structural issues of the identification of classifier systems. Selecting the important attributes and determining effective initial discretization of the input domain are important tasks [2, 7]. But the problems are difficulty and complexity problem in the real world.

In this paper, we propose a fuzzy clustering-based on aggregate attribute method for classification tasks. An aggregate attribute value is composed of a set of attributes [15]. We obtain aggregate value by beta coefficient, and use fuzzy c-means to build clusters by aggregate values. In order to verify our method, we use two databases: (1) Iris dataset; (2) Wisconsin-breast-cancer dataset. Moreover, estimating accuracy is important that it allows one to evaluate how accurately a given classifier will label future data, that is, data on which the classifier has not been trained [7]. Therefore, we partition the dataset as training/testing data for estimating accuracy. Finally, the result presented the accuracy of the proposed method is better than the existing methods.

The rest of this paper is organized as follows. In Section 2, we briefly review literature. In section 3, we describe the proposed method in detail. In section 4, we present some actual example to verify our method and compare with other methods. Finally, section 5 is conclusion.

2   Preliminary

In this section, we describe about the fuzzy clustering method and regression, and beta coefficient.

M. Ali and R. Dapoigny (Eds.): IEA/AIE 2006, LNAI 4031, pp. 478–487, 2006.
© Springer-Verlag Berlin Heidelberg 2006

2.1 Fuzzy Cluster Method

Clustering has been obtaining popularity as an efficient tool of data analysis to under-stand and visualize data structures. The different types of clustering algorithms can be classified into hierarchical, partitional, categorical and large DB. In partitional cluster-ing algorithms, there are many clustering algorithm such as Squared error clustering algorithm, K-means clustering, PAM (partitioning around medoides) algorithm, Bond energy algorithm (BEA), clustering with genetic algorithms, clustering with neural networks etc [7].

The prevalent formulation of this task is to use C feature vectors $v_j (j = 1, 2, ..., C) \in R^C$ to represent the C clusters such that a sample x_k is classified into the jth cluster according to some measure of similarity and its corresponding objective function. Two types of clustering techniques are usually of consideration, namely, hard (or crisp) clustering and fuzzy (or soft) clustering. Formally, hard clus-tering divides U into subsets $A_1, A_2, ..., A_C$, such that $A_1 \cup A_2 \cup ... \cup A_C = U$ and $A_i \cap A_j = \varnothing, \forall i \neq j, i, j = 1, 2, ..., C$. On the contrary, fuzzy clustering derives a number of subsets $A_1, A_2, ..., A_C$ of U such that $A_1 \cup A_2 \cup ... \cup A_C = U$ and $A_i \not\subset A_j, \forall i \neq j, i, j = 1, 2, ..., C$.

Fuzzy C Mean (FCM), is the most famous and basic fuzzy clustering algorithm. FCM attempts to find a fuzzy partition of the data set by minimizing the following within group least-squares error objective function with respect to fuzzy memberships u_{ik} and center v_i:

$$J_m(X, U, V) = \sum_{i=1}^{c} \sum_{k=1}^{n} u_{ik}^m d^2(x_k; v_i) \tag{1}$$

where $m > 1$ is the fuzziness index used to tune out the noise in the data, n is the number of feature vectors x_k, $c > 2$ is the number of clusters in the set and $d(x_k; v_i)$ is the similarity measure between a datum and a center. Minimizing J_m under the following constraints:

$$(1) 0 \leq u_{ik} \leq 1, \forall i, k,$$

$$(2) 0 < \sum_{k=1}^{n} u_{ik} \leq n, \forall i, \tag{2}$$

$$(3) \sum_{i=1}^{c} u_{ik} = 1, \forall k,$$

yields an iterative minimization pseudo-algorithm well known as the FCM algorithm. The components v_{il} of each center v_i and the membership degrees u_{ik} are updated according to the expressions

$$v_{il} = \frac{\sum_{k=1}^{n} u_{ik}^{m} x_{kl}}{\sum_{i=1}^{n} u_{ik}^{m}} \tag{3}$$

and

$$u_{ik} = \frac{1}{\sum_{j=1}^{c} (\frac{d(x_k; v_i)}{d(x_k; v_j)})^{2/m-1}} \tag{4}$$

The membership matrix $U(c,n)$ is initialized randomly or by defining $U^{(0)}(c,n)$ as follows:

$$U^{(0)} = (1 - \frac{\sqrt{2}}{2})U_u + \frac{\sqrt{2}}{2}U_r \tag{5}$$

where $U_u = [1/c]$ and U_r is a random hard partition of data.

2.2 Regression

In multiple regression analysis, we study the relationships among three or more variables. We write the multiple regression model as follows [6]:

$$y_i = \beta_0 + \beta_1 x_{1j} + \beta_2 x_{2j} + \cdots + \beta_k x_{kj} + e_j \tag{6}$$

where y_i is a typical value of Y, the dependent variable, from the population of interest; $\beta_0, \beta_1, ..., \beta_k$ are the population partial regression coefficients; and $x_{1j}, x_{2j}, ..., x_{kj}$ are observed values of the independent variables $X_1, X_2, ..., X_k$, respectively. e_j are assumed to be random and normal distribution $N(0, \sigma^2)$, $j = 1, 2, \cdots, n$.

2.2.1 Beta Coefficient

The standardized the coefficients are called beta coefficients. The steps of the beta coefficients are [6]:

(1) Standardized all of your variables $y_1 = (y - \bar{y})/S_y$, denote y_1 is the standardized of the y, $\bar{y}$ is the mean of the y. and S_y is the standard deviation of y.

(2) Assume z_1 is standardized of the X_1, z_2 is standardized of the X_2.

(3) Then, we can obtain the regression model. $y_1 = \beta_1 \times z_1 + \beta_2 \times z_2$.

The advantage of Beta coefficients (as compared to regression coefficients which are not standardized) is that the magnitude of these Beta coefficients allows you to compare the relative contribution of each independent variable in the prediction of the dependent variable.

3   Fuzzy Clustering-Based on Aggregate Attribute Method

In this section, we proposed a method based on fuzzy clustering technique and the aggregate attribute. Assume there are n attributes var_1, var_2, ..., var_n. We use the beta coefficient to calculate the aggregate values, and then we use the fuzzy clustering method to cluster the value. The concept is shown in figure 1.The advantage of Beta coefficients is: (1) eliminates the problem of dealing with different units of measurement (2) allows you to compare the relative contribution of each independent variable in the prediction of the dependent variable. The section 3.1 is the steps of this process, and the section 3.2 is the algorithm for the proposed method.

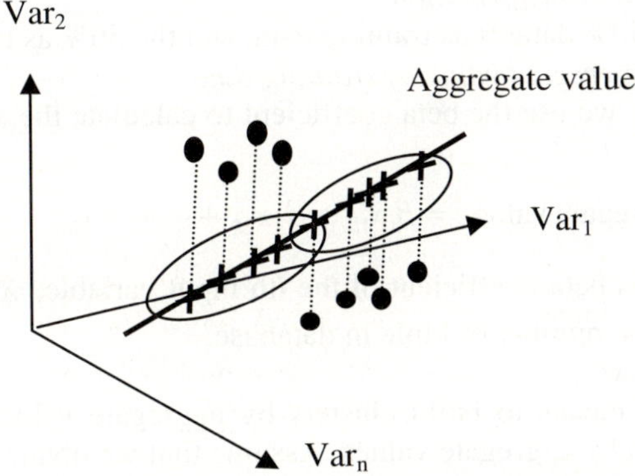

Fig. 1. The concept of the proposed method

The steps of this process are described below:

A. ***Data selection & transformation:*** Extract features (Selection input variable and class variable), transform or consolidate into appropriate forms. The fundamental task of variable selection must be performed by the analyst. Moreover, the selection of a dependent variable is many times dictated by the research problem and the research target.

B. ***Calculate the aggregate value:*** Different input variables have different influence on the class variable. We calculate the aggregate value between the attributes by Beta coefficient.

C. ***Cluster the aggregate value:*** Use the fuzzy cluster method to cluster the aggregate value.

D. ***Evaluation:*** Compare accuracy with the past research.

3.1 The Algorithm for Proposed Method

In this section, we present the algorithm for proposed method. Assume an n tuples relation database including 6 attributes is shown as Table 1. The attributes "X_1", "X_2", "X_3" and "X_4" are called input variables and the attribute "Class" is called a class variable. And the NO is the tuple's number.

Table 1. A relation database

NO	X_1	X_2	X_3	X_4	Class
O_1	X_{11}	X_{21}	X_{31}	X_{41}	C_1
O_2	X_{12}	X_{22}	X_{32}	X_{42}	C_2
$\vdots$	$\vdots$	$\vdots$	$\vdots$	$\vdots$	$\vdots$
O_n	X_{1n}	X_{2n}	X_{3n}	X_{4n}	C_n

Step 1: *Data selection & transformation:*
   We use the 50% dataset as training data, and the 50% as testing data.
Step 2: *Calculate the aggregate value by training data:*
   In this paper, we use the beta coefficient to calculate the aggregate attribute value.

$$\text{The aggregate value}_n = \beta_1 x_{1k} + \beta_2 x_{2k} + \cdots + \beta_i x_{in} \tag{7}$$

Where the β_i is beta coefficient of the ith input variable, X_{in} is the ith input variable. n is the number of tuple in database.
Step 3: *Building clusters:*
   Use fuzzy c-means to build clusters by aggregate values. This step is to build clusters by aggregate values. Assume that we obtain k clusters (i.e., $C_1, C_2, \ldots, C_k$) shown as below:

$$C_1 = \{a_{1,1}, a_{1,2}, \ldots, a_{1,P_1}\} \cdots C_i = \{a_{i,1}, a_{i,2}, \ldots, a_{i,j}\} \cdots C_k = \{a_{k,1}, a_{k,2}, \ldots, a_{k,j}\} \tag{8}$$

where a_{ij} denotes the jth aggregate value of C_i.
Step 4: *Predict the testing data's class:*
   Calculate the Euclidean distance $Dist_i$ between the tuple of testing data and C_i.

$$Dist_i = \sqrt{\left(C_{i\_center} - a_{ij}\right)^2} \tag{9}$$

where C_{i_center} is the ith cluster center, and the minimal $Dist_i$ denotes "The tuple belongs to C_i."
Step 5: *Evaluation:* Compare accuracy with the past research.
   For verifying proposed method, we use two public datasets to illustrate our performance, the datasets are: (1) Iris dataset; (2) Wisconsin-breast-cancer dataset.

4   Numerical Simulations and Results

For verification and comparison, we use two datasets: (1) Iris dataset; (2) Wisconsin-breast-cancer dataset. The two examples are the well-known classification problem, and the data is freely available in the internet [4, 10, 11].

4.1   Iris Dataset

There are three species (or class labels) in the class variable: setosa, versicolor, and virginica. From each species there are 50 observations for sepal length (SL), sepal width (SW), petal length (PL), and petal width (PW) in cm. The dataset is shown in Table 2. (1)From step 1 we partition the dataset, the 50% dataset as training data and others as testing data. (2) Secondly, we obtain aggregate value (see Table 4) from the proposed method. The beta coefficient (see Table 3) is shown in table. (3) Thirdly, use fuzzy c-means to build clusters by aggregate values. We can obtain the cluster center. It is shown in Table 5. (4) Finally, we can use the training's cluster to predict the testing data's class by equation (9).

The experimental result is shown in Table 6. The proposed model is compared with Chen and Yu's algorithm [5], Wu and Chen's algorithm [16], and Hong and Lee's algorithm [8]. From Table 6, the results indicate the proposed algorithm is the best performance in testing data, and the accuracy rate is 97.3333%.

Table 2. Iris dataset

Data no	Sepal length	Sepal width	Petal length	Petal width	Class
1	5.1	3.5	1.4	0.2	1
2	4.9	3	1.4	0.2	1
⋮					
149	6.2	3.4	5.4	2.3	3
150	5.9	3	5.1	1.8	3

Note. The class values: 1 is setosa; 2 is versicolor; 3 is virginica.

Table 3. Beta coefficient

Variables	Beta coefficients
Sepal_length	-0.11092
Sepal_width	-0.02342
Petal_length	0.488904
Petal_width	0.568151

Note. [a] Dependent Variable: Class.

Table 4. Aggregate attribute

Data no	sepal length	sepal width	petal length	petal Width	Aggregate value
1	5.1	3.5	1.4	0.2	-0.11121
2	4.9	3	1.4	0.2	-0.06234
...	...	...	...	...	...
74	6.3	2.7	4.9	1.8	2.332041
75	6.7	3.3	5.7	2.1	2.800344

Table 5. Cluster center

Fuzzy c-means cluster center
-0.03307
1.773493
2.661606

Table 6. Comparison results with other methods for iris dataset

Algorithms	Classification accuracy rate
The proposed algorithm (75 training instances and 75 testing instances)	**97.3333%**
Chen and Yu's algorithm (75 training instances and 75 testing instances)	96.3427%
Wu and Chen's algorithm (75 training instances and 75 testing instances)	96.2100%
Hong and Lee's algorithm (75 training instances and 75 testing instances)	95.5700%

4.2 Wisconsin-Breast-Cancer Dataset

The second numerical example concerns the determination of the breast cancer in humans from Wisconsin University hospital in Madison, USA. This is also freely available in the Internet via anonymous ftp from ics.uci.edu in directory/ pub/ machine-learning-databased/ Wisconsin-breast-cancer. This problem has 9 features/input attributes which determine whether a patient is benign or malign. The 9 features are: (a) Clump Thickness (b) Uniformity of Cell Size (c) Uniformity of Cell Shape (d) Marginal Adhesion (e) Single Epithelial Cell Size (f) Bare Nuclei (g) Bland Chromatin

(h) Normal Nucleoli (i) Mitoses. There are 683 samples/patterns. This data has been used in the past by Mangasarian et al. [10, 11] and Bennet et al. [4]. The dataset is shown in Table 7. The beta coefficient is shown in Table 8.

We use the 50% dataset as training data, and the 50% as testing data. The result of the breast cancer classification problem is shown in Table 9. As the error estimates are either obtained from 10-fold cross validation or from testing the solution once by using the 50% of the data as training set. The related methods [1, 12, 13, 14] are compared with the proposed model. From Table 9, the proposed model is the best performance and the accuracy rate is 98.2%.

Table 7. The Wisconsin-breast-cancer dataset

ID	Clump Thickness	Uniformity of Cell Size	Uniformity of Cell Shape	Marginal Adhesion	Single Epithelial Cell Size	Bare Nuclei	Bland Chromatin	Normal Nucleoli	Mitoses	Class
63375	9	1	2	6	4	10	7	7	2	2
128059	1	1	1	1	2	5	5	1	1	1
⋮										
160296	5	8	8	10	5	10	8	10	3	2

Note. The class values: 1 is benign, 2 is malign.

Table 8. The beta coefficient

Variables	Beta Coefficients
Clump Thickness	0.26101
Uniformity of Cell Size	0.032392
Uniformity of Cell Shape	0.143727
Marginal Adhesion	0.094532
Single Epithelial Cell Size	0.074322
Bare Nuclei	0.345085
Bland Chromatin	0.03087
Normal Nucleoli	0.09801
Mitoses	0.013683

Note. [a] Dependent Variable: Class.

Table 9. Comparison results with other methods for wisconsin-breast-cancer dataset

Algorithms	Classification accuracy rate
The proposed model (342 testing instances)	**98.2%**
Konstam's algorithm (342 testing instances)	97.5%
Setiono's algorithm (2000)	97.36
Setiono's algorithm (2000)	98.1
Pena-Reyes and Sipper(2000)	97.36
Pena-Reyes and Sipper(2000)	97.07
Nauck and Kruse(1999)	95.06

5 Conclusions

For solving classification problems, we have proposed a fuzzy clustering-based on aggregate attribute method. From two datasets' experiment results; we can see that the accuracy of the proposed method is better than the existing methods. That is, the proposed method can get better estimated accuracy than the existing methods. In the future, we could consider other aggregate attribute methods to improve the performance.

Acknowledgements

The authors would like to thank: (1) the University of Wisconsin Hospitals, Dr. William H. Wolberg, provided the dataset. (2) the anonymous referees whose comments have improved the presentation of the paper.

References

1. Konstam, A., Group classification using a mix of genetic programming and genetic algorithms, ACM Press, (1998)
2. Abonyi, J., Roubos, J.A., Szeifert, F. Data-driven generation of compact, accurate, and linguistically sound fuzzy classifiers based on a decision-tree initialization, International Journal of Approximate Reasoning 32, (2003) 1-21
3. Arnold, S.F.: Mathematical Statistics, Prentice-Hall, Englewood Cliffs NJ (1990)
4. Bennett, K.P. & Mangasarian, O.L., Robust linear programming discrimination of two linearly inseparable sets, Optimization Methods and Software 1 (1992) 23±34.
5. Chen, S.M., & Yu, C.A., new method to generate fuzzy rules from training instances for handling classification problems. Cybernetics and Systems: An International Journal, 34(3), (2003) 217-232.

6. Draper, N.R., Smith, H.: Applied Regression Analysis, John Wiley and Sons, New York (1998).

7. Han, J. & Kamber, M.: Data Mining: Concepts and Techniques, Morgan Kaufmann (2001)

8. Hong, T. P., & Lee, C. Y. Induction of fuzzy rules and membership functions from training examples. Fuzzy Sets and Systems, 84(1), (1996) 33-47.

9. MacQueen, JB.: Some methods for classification and analysis of multivariate observations, Proceedings of the Fifth Berkeley Symposium on Mathematical Statistics and Probability, (1967) 281-297.

10. Mangasarian, O.L. & Wolberg, W.H., Cancer diagnosis via linear programming, SIAM News 23 (1990) 1-18.

11. Mangasarian, O.L., Setiono, R. and Wolberg, W.H. Pattern recognition via linear programming: Theory and application to medical diagnosis, in: T.F. Coleman, Y. Li (Eds.), Large-scale numerical optimization, SIAM Publications, Philadelphia, 1990, pp. 22±30.

12. Nauck, D., Kruse, R. Obtaining interpretable fuzzy classification rules from medical data, Artif. Intell. Med. 16, (1999) 149-169.

13. Peña-Reyes, C.A., Sipper, M. A fuzzy genetic approach to breast cancer diagnosis, Artif. Intell. Med. 17, (2000) 131-155.

14. Setiono, R., Generating concise and accurate classification rules for breast cancer diagnosis, Artif. Intell. Med. 18, (2000) 205-219.

15. Subtil, P., Mouaddib, N. and Foucaut O. A fuzzy information retrieval and management system and its applications, Proceedings of the 1996 ACM symposium on Applied Computing, (1906) 537-541.

16. Wu, T. P., & Chen, S.M., A new method for constructing membership functions and fuzzy rules from training examples. IEEE Transactions on Systems, Man and Cybernetics-Part B, 29(1), (1999) 25-40.

Recurrent Neural Network Verifier for Face Detection and Tracking

Sung H. Yoon[1], Gi T. Hur[2], and Jung H. Kim[3]

[1] Computer Science Dept., North Carolina A&T State University, NC 27411, USA
[2] Multimedia Contents Dept., DongShin University, South Korea
[3] Electrical Engineering Dept., North Carolina A&T State University, NC 27411, USA

Abstract. This paper presents a new method for face verification for vision applications. There are many approaches to detect and track a face in a sequence of images; however, the high computations of image algorithms, as well as, face detection and head tracking failures under unrestricted environments remain to be a difficult problem. We present a robust algorithm that improves face detection and tracking in video sequences by using geometrical facial information and a recurrent neural network verifier. Two types of neural networks are proposed for face detection verification. A new method, a three-face reference model (TFRM), and its advantages, such as, allowing for a better match for face verification, will be discussed in this paper.

Keywords: face tracking; face verification; Hopfield neural networks; annealing; geometrical feature, video sequence.

1 Introduction

Pattern recognition and computer vision theory have been considerably improved during the last decade, such that, the appearance of an automated vision system seems very close to our future. However, because of the higher computational burden of understanding image algorithms, applications of face recognition to multi-context images are still limited to the restricted environment. Face detection and recognition have been an important issue in video sequence applications because different facial views and varied illumination cause problems when detecting and recognizing a human face. There are many approaches to detect and verify a human face in video sequences [1]-[8]. Some methods are based on feature invariants, which are used to find out structural features. Some are based on template matching, which uses a stored pattern to track head positions. Others include an appearance-based method that utilizes a trained model from a set of images to capture the representative variability of a facial appearance. The face detection and tracking approach developed in this study is based on using feature invariants: color, gradient and geometrical facial features[9].

We use geometric feature points for face verification based on neural networks. The feature points are usually detected in a curvature function space by capturing all the local extrema whose curvature values are above a certain threshold value. Geometric feature points can generate useful local features such as angles between neighboring corners and distances between every pair of corners. In addition, the geometric feature

M. Ali and R. Dapoigny (Eds.): IEA/AIE 2006, LNAI 4031, pp. 488–499, 2006.

points are appropriate for constructing neural networks. To extract reliable features, it is very important to detect consistent feature points invariant under translation, rotation, and scale. Our procedure for face detection finds candidates for face regions using color and gradient, and then extracts geometric features inside the face region. We model the face (mouth, nose, eyes) and use geometrical facial information for face verification. Geometrical facial feature properties change depending on image quality and size of a face.

The inherent parallelism of neural networks allows rapid pursuit of many hypotheses in parallel with high computation rate [10][11]. Moreover, it provides a great degree of robustness or fault tolerance compared to conventional computers because of many processing nodes, each of which is responsible for a small portion of the task. Damages to a few nodes or links thus do not impair overall performance significantly. For this reason, a Hopfield style neural network has been proposed to solve matching problems for face detection and recognition. It is one of the popular neural computations used in real world applications. Its popularity is due to its simple architecture and well-defined time-domain behavior. The Hopfield neural network (HNN) is composed of single-layer neurons with fully connected feedback connections. The neurons have the sigmoid gain characteristic, while the connectivity matrix corresponding to the connection is symmetric and the diagonal terms of the matrix are zero. Such networks always move in the direction of decreasing the energy of the networks and get stable states at the local minimum of energy.

In a complex background, there are many clutters. We use an innovative neural network based verifier for face detection. This technique can be further used for face recognition when it is required. In this paper, we propose a component-based approach to face detection and recognition in video sequences using a neural network verifier. Identifying a face with large tolerance proves the robustness of the algorithm. In Section 2, we describe the overall system description and the hybrid color scheme. In Section 3, we review the HNN, feature extraction and graph formation. In Section 4, we present our simulation results and the results are obtained. In Section 5, we state our conclusions.

2   Approach

2.1   Overall System Description

Under very restricted conditions, it is possible to track the human face with each modality alone. However, single modality results in substantial tracking failures in unconstrained environments. We have created a head tracking system that achieves robust performance via the integration of multiple visual features. By combining these modules in simple ways, we can build a system that attains overall robust performance [8]. We describe our system using three visual modalities: intensity gradient, skin color model, and geometrical face information.

In our experiment, tracking with color and gradient gives good results in restricted conditions [9]. However, it sometimes fails in unrestricted and complex environments. If we make use of a geometrical feature in addition to color and gradient, it can provide more robust head tracking results. Potential face regions detected from color and gradient are then verified by a geometrical feature. The geometrical feature of a face will enhance the detection rate of a face when it is used with color and gradient. It is sometimes difficult to accurately extract geometrical features from a face. We use a recurrent neural network for robust verification. Neural network based verification performs very well, even when some feature points are missing or off true positions. The following shows the overall description of the system. Figure 1 describes our algorithm to overcome the problem of frequent inaccurate predictions of a fast moving face's next position. The first step is to extract potential face regions using skin color and gradient. The next step is to extract facial features from the potential face regions. The final step is to verify if it is a true face region using the proposed neural network. A detailed description of each module is as follows:

We use the notation M for the current head's state and location. The following equation explains how to find the best head state and location within a search window.

$$M^* = \arg\max_{M_i}(\alpha(M_i) + \beta(M_i)) \tag{1}$$

where $\alpha(M_i)$, $\beta(M_i)$ are the matching scores based on intensity gradients and color histograms, respectively. The search space M is the set of all states within some range of the predicted location with simple linear prediction.

The candidates that have high matching scores are then verified by a neural network. This verification method is one of the major contributions of this research. This verification method is so robust that it could verify a face and non-face without accurate geometrical features. This verification technique can be further used for face recognition if the quality of an image is good enough to extract accurate feature points.

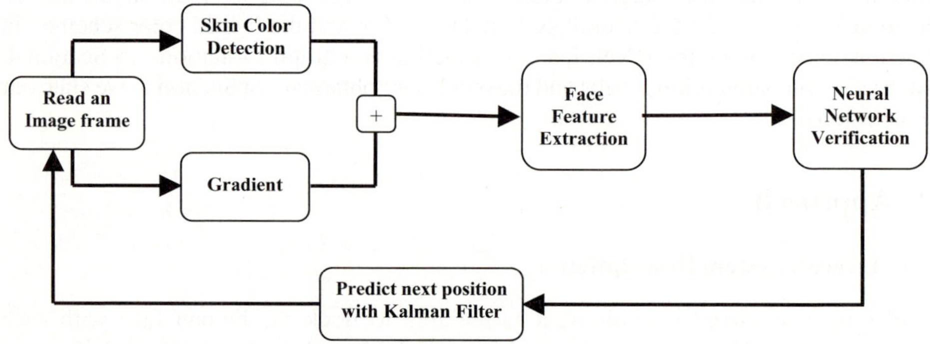

Fig. 1. Head tracking algorithm using image segmentation and Kalman Estimation

2.2 Neural Network Based Verification

The appearance of an automated vision system seems very close to our future because pattern recognition and computer vision theory has been considerably improved during the last decade. However, because of the higher computational burden of understanding image algorithms, applications of face recognition to multi-context images are still limited to the restricted environment. The Hopfield neural network is one of the popular neural computations used in real world applications. Its popularity is due to its simple architecture and well-defined time-domain behavior. The Hopfield neural network is composed of single-layer neurons with fully connected feedback connections. The neurons have the sigmoid gain characteristic, while the connectivity matrix corresponding to the connection is symmetric and the diagonal terms of the matrix are zero. Such networks always move in the direction of decreasing the energy of the networks and get stable states at the local minimum of the energy. The face verification problem is constructed as an optimization problem, which can be solved by neural networks. In the following subsections, we will present Hopfield neural network based verification methods.

2.2.1 Geometrical Feature Extraction and Graph Formation

To obtain the required facial features, a binary image is obtained by using a proper threshold value. It is essential to find the proper threshold value to distinguish the eyes, nose and mouth from the other face regions. There are many available methods to calculate the optimal threshold value [15] [16]. The methods showed a good result detecting facial components such as eyes, noses, and mouth. In our early study [17], we developed an algorithm that detects corner points of the facial components. We use the corner points of each facial component for extracting facial features. Corner points are important since the information of the shape is concentrated at the points having high curvatures. From the corner points, we can extract useful features. They are a local feature (an angle between neighboring corners) and relational features (distances between the corners). These two features, which are invariant under transnational and rotational changes, are used for the robust description of shape of facial components. A graph can be constructed for an object model using corner points as nodes of the graph. Each node has a local feature as well as relational features with other nodes. For the matching process, a similar graph is constructed for the input image which may consist of one or several overlapped objects. Each model graph is then matched against the input image graph to find the best matching subgraph.

2.2.2 Hopfield Neural Networks for Face Verification

The Hopfield neural network is constructed by connecting a large number of simple processing elements (neurons) to each other. A two dimensional array is constructed to apply a face matching problem into a neural network as shown in Figure 2. The columns of the array label the nodes of a face model, and the rows indicate the nodes of an input face. Therefore, the state of each neuron represents the measure of match between two nodes from each graph. For example, a white neuron in Figure 2 represents a successful match between corresponding feature points between the model and input. A shaded neuron represents a mismatch between corresponding feature points between the model and input. In general, for the ith node in the input image and the kth node in the object model, the ik^{th} processing neuron located in the ith row and ki^{th} column.

The output of the ik^{th} neuron is fed to the input of the jl^{th} neuron by connection of strength C_{ijkl}. In addition, each neuron has external inputs (an offset bias) of I_{ik} to its input. The states of the neurons can be expressed by U_{ik}, the outputs by V_{ik}, the

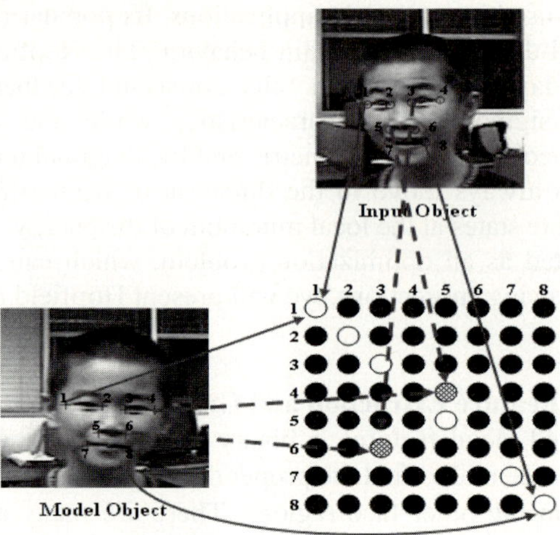

Fig. 2. 2-D array for Hopfield neural networks

connection strengths by C_{ikjl}, and the external inputs by I_{ik}. The matching process can be characterized as minimizing the following energy function:

$$E = -\frac{A}{2}\sum_{i}\sum_{j}\sum_{k}\sum_{l}C_{ijkl}V_{ik}V_{jl}$$

$$+\frac{B_1}{2}\sum_{i}\sum_{k}\sum_{l\neq k}V_{ik}V_{il} + \frac{B_2}{2}\sum_{k}\sum_{i}\sum_{j\neq i}V_{ik}V_{jl}$$

$$(2)$$

where V_{ik} is a binary variable which converges to "1" if the ith node in the input image matches the kth node in the object model; otherwise, it converges to "0". The first term in equation (2) is a compatibility constraint. Local and relational features which have different measures are normalized to give tolerance for ambiguity of the features. The last two terms are included to enforce the uniqueness constraint so that each node in the object model eventually matches only one node in the input image and the summation of the outputs of the neurons in each row or column is no more than 1. C_{ikjl} is normalized by a fuzzy function so that it helps us obtain good solutions. Therefore the coefficient A is supposed to be more emphasized in the matching problem. The comparability measure C_{ikjl} is expressed as follows:

$$C_{ikjl} = W_1 \times F(f_i, f_k) + W_2 \times F(f_j, f_l)$$

$$+ W_3 \times F(r_{ij}, r_{kl})$$

$$(3)$$

The fuzzy function $F(x, y)$ has a value 1 for a positive support and -1 for a negative support. The value of $F(x, y)$ is defined such that if the absolute value of the difference between x and y is less than a threshold, then $F(x, y)$ is set to 1, otherwise $F(x, y)$ is set to -1. The first term is related to the local feature of (i, k)th neuron. If the ith node of a model and the kth node of an input have similarity in their local features, then the value of the fuzzy function $F(f_i, f_k)$ is set to 1, otherwise set to 0. The second term is related to the local feature of (j, l)th neuron. $F(f_j, f_l)$ is set to 0 or 1 by the procedure as explained above. The third term is related to the relational feature between two neurons. If the relational feature between ith and jth node in a model is similar to the relational feature between kth and lth node, then $F(r_{ij}, r_{kl})$ is set to 1, otherwise set to 0.

The coefficient W_i would add to 1. Therefore the value of C_{ikjl} is normalized from - 1 to 1. The performance of the algorithm is significantly influenced by the weight and the tolerance of the fuzzy function. As the tolerance 0 in the fuzzy function is larger, robustness of the algorithm is increased but mismatching may occur. On the other hand, as the tolerance θ is smaller, the algorithm becomes very sensitive to the noise level of an input so that a matchable node may not be detected. However, the mismatching rate will be decreased. For example, when the current comer detection algorithm is applied to a noisy image or a blurred image, comer points can be displaced by the smoothing effect. In this case, the tolerance should be increased even though it causes mismatching. The weight W_i is decided by the significance of the features. In this graph matching, local features do not contribute to interactions between neurons but relational features do. Therefore, relational features are more emphasized than local features in the neural network application, i.e. the weight of the relational feature W_3 has a larger value than other weights. The second term of the energy function of the matching problem is represented by a quadratic function so that it can be cast into the Hopfield energy function. The third term also has the same formation as the second term of the energy function. Therefore, equation (2) can be cast into a Hopfield style energy function as follows:

$$E = -\frac{1}{2}\sum_i \sum_j \sum_k \sum_l C_{ikjl} V_{ik} V_{jl} - \sum_i \sum_j I_{ik} V_{ik}$$

(4)

$$C_{ikjl} = AC_{ikjl} - B_1 \delta_{ij} - B_2 \delta_{kl} + (B_1 + B_2)\delta_{ij}\delta_{kl}$$

where $\delta_{ij} = 1$ when $i = j$, otherwise $\delta_{ij} = 0$. Hopfield proved that the energy function is a Liapunov function. Thus the energy function converges to a local minimum when the states of neurons converge to stable states. The matching process is based on global information of the image which provides excitatory or inhibitory supports for matching local features. The simulation is a random process which will arrive at a stable state when the energy function of equation (14) is at its minimum.

2.2.3 Three Face Reference Model

One of the challenging problems is recognizing a face with different poses. We use three face reference model (TFRM) that covers the frontal view, left view, and right view of a face. There are many advantages to using a TFRM for face verification. The TFRM covers all pose changes allowing for a better match for face verification. Different images from the database can be selected to represent the TFRM, allowing more comparisons, providing a more comprehensive matching process for face verification. The TFRM is robust; mismatching 2 out of 3 models do not affect overall performance. Face verification can still be obtained even if 2 of the 3 models do not match. If at least one reference model match, face verification is a success. The TFRM has a higher success rate than a reference model based on a single view because the image can be compared against three images with different angles of view instead of one single image. In our experiment, TFRM will be compared to SFRM.

3 Simulation Results

Our face verification method has been evaluated using a face image database containing 400 sequences of images. Each image contains the same face with variations in position, scale, and facial expression. Our algorithm verifies a face within an image by comparing it to a reference model. For face verification, images in the database will be used as input images and as reference models.

We use two methods to select images for face verification; face verification by comparing randomly selected images or face verification by selecting two neighboring images. For random comparison of images, we use the three face reference model (TFRM). It consists of three images of three different facial poses selected from our image database; frontal view, right view, and left view. If the input image matches at least one of these three images, verification is a success.

The following is a successful face verification example using a three face reference model (TFRM). In Figure 3, the facial image is compared to the frontal, right and left face views using the Hopfield neural network. Table 1 shows the matching results of the images. When the tolerance is set to 5, face verification fails when the 15th image in the database is compared to the frontal and right view of the TFRM; however, face verification is successful when compared to the left view. Face verification for this image is a success because it matches one of the TFRM.

(a)   (b)

Fig. 3. (a) Input image (b) Three face reference model (TFRM): frontal view, right view, left view

Neural networks provide good matching results between a model and input image. Its algorithm is applied for matching feature points of the face using a 2-dimensional array (rows represent the model image, columns represent input image). Two points are used to detect each facial component; eyes, nose, and mouth, therefore, 8 feature points are used to recognize a face. Feature points 1 and 2 represent the corner points on each side of the left eye. Feature points 3 and 4 represent the corner points on each side of the right eye. Feature points 5 and 6 represent the corner points on each side of the nose.

Feature points 7 and 8 represent the corner points on each side of the mouth. Each feature point in the model is compared to all feature points of the input image.

Figure 4 is an example of a successful and unsuccessful single model case for face verification. The following is a success case using a single model. Straight lines indicate the matching of feature points of similar facial components and dotted lines indicate the matching of feature points of dissimilar facial components. The eyes, nose, and mouth of a model image are compared to an input image by matching their feature points. All feature points match between the model and input image. Eight diagonal 1's are located in the (1,1), (2,2), (3,3), (4,4), (5,5), (6,6), (7,7), and (8,8) position of the array indicating the matching of feature points between similar facial components. 0's in the array indicate other feature points in the image do not match. Face verification is a success because at least 5 feature points must match between corresponding components and this image has 8 matching feature points. The graphical image of the 2-dimensional array shows 8 diagonal white squares representing matched feature points and black squares representing unmatched feature points.

The following is an example of a single model case failure. The eyes, nose, and mouth of a single model image and an input image are compared by matching their feature points. Three pairs of feature points, 2 (right corner point of eye), 6 (right corner point of nose), and 8 (right corner point of mouth), match between the model and input image. A 2-dimensional array is used to represent matching of feature points. Three diagonal 1's are located in the (2,2), (6,6) and (8,8) position of the array indicating the matching of feature points between similar facial components. 1's located outside the diagonal, located in positions (3,5) and(7,4) indicates a matching of feature points of dissimilar facial components (i.e. (3,5) indicates matching of left corner point of eye and left corner point of nose). 0's indicate feature points in the image do not match. Face verification fails for this input image because at least 5 feature points must match

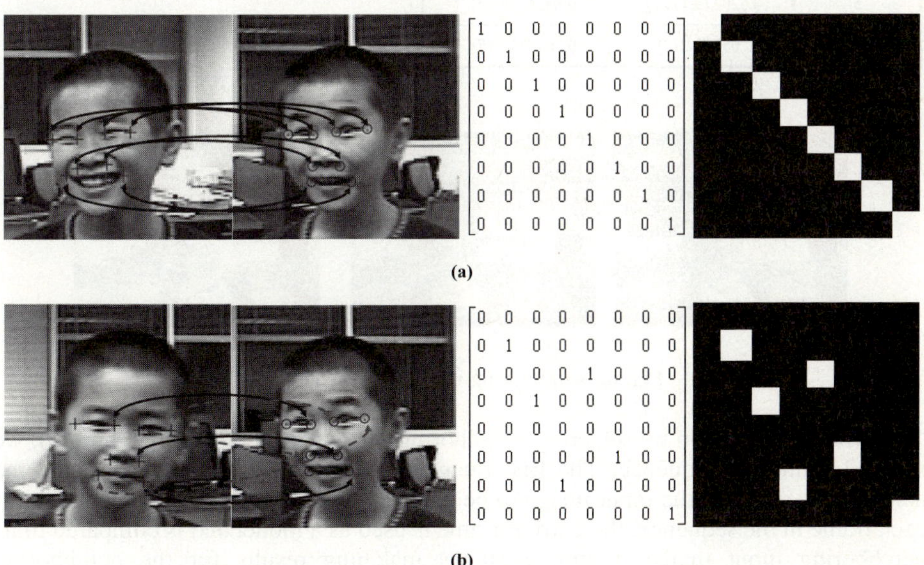

(a)

(b)

Fig. 4. (a) Success case (b) Failure case

between similar components, however, this image has only 3 matching corresponding feature points indicated by 3 diagonal 1's in the array. The graphical image of the 2-dimensional array shows 3 diagonal white squares indicating failure. Also, 2 white squares are located outside the diagonal indicating a matching of feature points of dissimilar facial components.

In Table 1, we present matching ratio results of the face verification method applied to the face image database using HNN. Matching ratio is defined as the ratio of the number of images that match a reference model to the total number of images input. Table 1 is used to measure the performance of two types of reference models using random images. A matching ratio is simulated on 17 images. With an optimum tolerance of 4, 16 out of 17 images match the single face reference model (SFRM) resulting in a matching ratio of 94.12%. However, 17 out of 17 images match the TFRM which has a greater matching rate of 100%. In Figure 5, the results show that the TFRM has a higher matching rate for face verification than SFRM.

Table 1. Matching Ratio using HNN (SFRM vs TFRM)

Tolerance	Matching Ratio	
	SFRM	TFRM
1	0.5294 (9/17)	0.5294 (9/17)
2	0.8824 (15/17)	0.9412 (16/17)
3	0.9412 (16/17)	0.9412 (16/17)
4	0.9412 (16/17)	1.0000 (17/17)
5	0.5294 (9/17)	0.8824 (15/17)
6	0.7059 (12/17)	0.7647 (13/17)

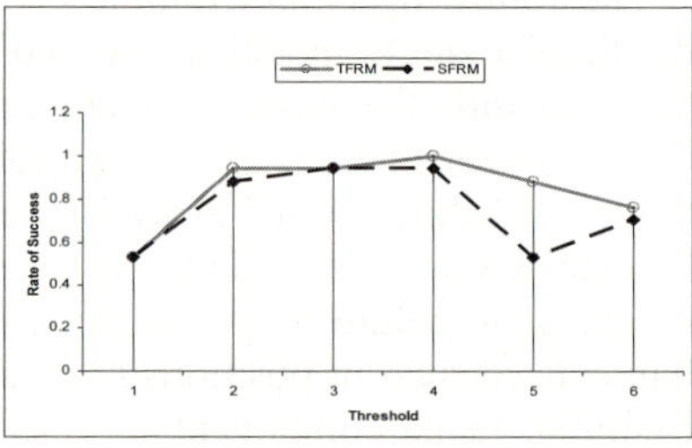

Fig. 5. Three face reference model (TFRM) using HNN

Fig. 6. Neighboring images in a sequence

For face verification by selecting neighboring images in a sequence (Figure 6), we select 2 frames in sequence. The first image is the reference model image and the neighboring image is the input image to be compared against the reference model. For each frame in the sequence, the current frame is used as a model and is compared to its neighboring input image. Figure 7 shows matching results for the neighboring sequence. The results show that with tolerances 3 and 4, a matching result was 100%. Using neighboring frame as a reference model yielded better results than using a fixed single face reference model. The advantage of face verification using neighboring images is that we can have a better success rate than a fixed reference model. However, it has a problem with a drift. Tracking will fail if a severe drift occurs due to the result of poor segmentation.

Extracting feature points is not reliable under unrestricted and poor lighting conditions. Some points may not be detected or may be off from true position. We created situations where a few feature points were missing or off from true position to test our neural network based verifiers. The first simulation uses an image missing two feature points from the same facial component, (i.e. a feature point missing on each side of the right eye, therefore, right eye not detected in the image). The second simulation uses an image missing two feature points, one from a different facial component, (i.e. one feature point missing from the right side of the left eye, one feature point missing from the left side of the nose). If four or more feature points of the image match the reference model, a successful match is obtained. The matching ratio results are based on 170 experiments.

After calculating the matching ratios for images missing combinations of feature points and images missing two feature points from the same facial component, the average matching ratio results were calculated. Table 2 presents the HNN matching

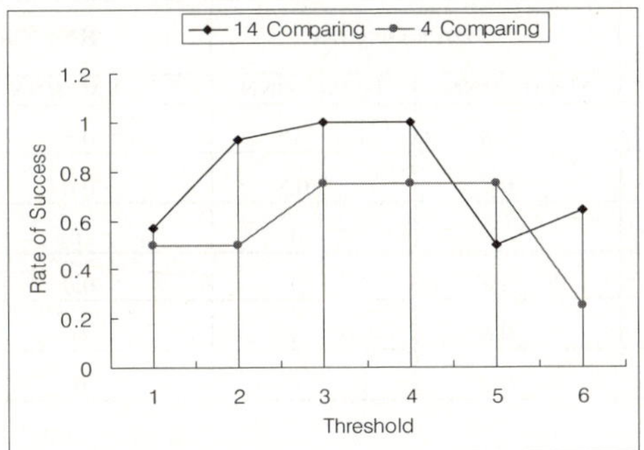

Fig. 7. Neighboring sequence

Table 2. Measures HNN average performance

Tolerance	Matching Ratio	
	SFRM - HNN	TFRM - HNN
1	0.3628	0.3799
2	0.6155	0.6544
3	0.6253	0.7059
4	0.6863	0.7451
5	0.5907	0.7427
6	0.5651	0.5651

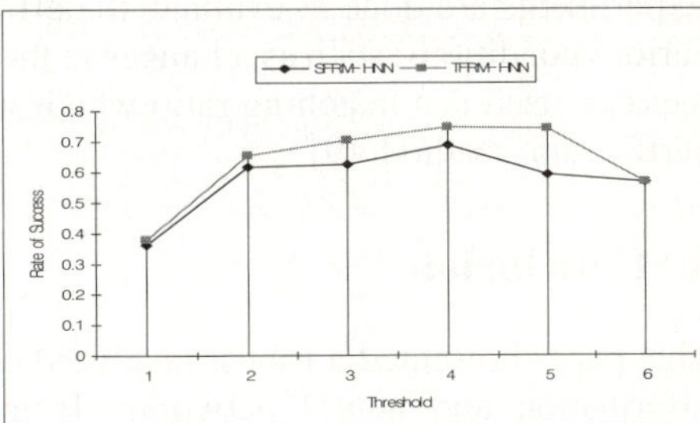

Fig. 8. Compares HNN average performance of SFRM and TFRM

ratio averages for the SFRM and the TFRM. With an optimum tolerance set at 4, the SFRM results in an average matching ratio of 68.63%, and the TFRM results in a higher average matching ratio of 74.51%. Comparing the SFRM to the TFRM and applying the HNN, the TFRM averages are constantly higher (Figure 8).

In the third simulation, two feature points are forced to locate off the true positions. This image is referred to as a poorly segmented image. For face verification and recognition, a comparison is made between each of the 8 feature points in the reference model and the 8 feature points in the poorly segmented image. The results of the simulation show images with changed features points have a lower matching ratio than original images; images with feature points located at original positions.

Tables 3 measures the HNN matching ratios for original images and poorly segmented images, respectively. When using a TFRM, both images have a 100% matching ratio when the tolerance is set at 3 and 4. In general, higher matching ratios result when both types of images are compared to the TFRM. Both images are compared to the SFRM in Figure 1 and the TFRM in Figure 2. The graphs indicate matching original images to a TFRM results in higher matching ratios.

Table 3. Measures HNN performance using points off from true positions

Tolerance	HNN-Original		HNN-Changed Points	
	SFRM - HNN	TFRM - HNN	SFRM -HNN	TFRM - HNN
1	0.8	0.8	0.6	0.8
2	0.8	0.8	0.6	0.6
3	1	1	1	1
4	0.6	1	0.6	1
5	0.6	1	0	0.4
6	0.2	0.4	0	0.2

Yet again, comparing original images to TFRM achieve the best results. Overall, HNN show good performance under poor pre-processing conditions such as mission points or false detection of points. Algorithms have been implemented in Matlab. Experiments are done to evaluate the efficiency of our face verification method under various conditions, such as, changes in the types of reference models. The performance measure used is a matching ratio which verifies the excellent performance of our face verification method. [9]

4   Conclusion

This paper presented a robust face verification method that utilized geometrical facial information and neural networks. If multiple visual modalities such as gradient intensity, color, and geometrical features, are combined well, we could expect more robust results. A HNN based verifier has been presented. It shows good performance in terms of matching ratios. Our simulation results show that our face detection approach performed well using a three face reference model. Our technique can be extended to face recognition without modification of neural network based verification.

References

[1] Ming-Hsuan Yang, David J. Kriegman, Narendra Ahuja, "Detecting Faces in Images: A Survey", *IEEE Transactions on Pattern Analysis and Machine Intelligence*, Vol. 24, No. 1, January 2002

[2] J. Yang, A. Waibel, A real-time face tracker, In Proc. of WACV'96, (1996) 142-147.

[3] S. Birchfield, Elliptical Head Tracking Using Intensity Gradients and Color Histograms, *Proc. of the IEEE Conference on Computer Vision and Pattern Recognition*, Santa Barbara, CA pp 232-237, June 1998.

[4] Szu-Hao Huang, and Shang-Hong Lai, "Detecting Faces from Color Video by Using Paired Wavelet Features", *Computer Vision and Pattern Recognition Workshop*, 27-02, pp. 64-64, Jun. 2004

[5] Y.Rodriguez, F.Cardinaux, S.Bengio, and J. Mariethoz, "Estimating the quality of face localization for face verification", *Proceedings of International Conference on Image Processing (ICIP '04)*, vol.1, no.22-27, pp. 581-584, Oct. 2004

[6] Ming-Jung Seow, D.Valaparla, and V.K. Asari, "Neural network based skin color model for face detection", *Applied Imagery Pattern Recognition Workshop, 2003. Proceedings. 32nd*, pp.141-145, Oct. 2003

[7] Q.Yang, X.Ding, and Z.Chen, "Discriminant local feature analysis of facial images", *Proceedings of International Conference on Image Processing (ICIP '03)*, vol 2, pp. II - 863-6 vol.3, Sept. 2003

[8] T. Darrell, et. al., "Integrated person tracking using stereo, color, and pattern detection," *Conference on Computer Vision and Pattern Recognition, Santa Barbara*, CA, 601—608, June 1998.

[9] Gwang M. Kim, DongCheng Lin, Jung H. Kim, and Sung H. Yoon, "Robust Head Tracking Based on Hybrid Color Histogram and Random Walk Kalman Filter," *In The Multi-modal Speech Recognition Workshop*, Greensboro, NC, June 2002.

[10] R.P. Lippman, "An introduction to computing with neural networks," *IEEE ASSP*, pp4-22, 1987.

[11] M. Takeda and J. W. Goodman, "Neural networks for computation: Number representations and programming complexity," *Applied Optics,* (25) 18, Sept. 15, 1986.

[12] S. German, D. German, "Stochastic relaxation, Gibbs distributions, and the Bayesian restoration of images," *IEEE Trans. Pattern Anal. Mach. Intell. PAMI-6,* 721-741, 1984.

[13] G. Bilbro, W. Snyder, "Applying mean field annealing to image noise removal," *Journal of Neural Network Computation.* pp5-17, 1990.

[14] E. Van Den Bout, T. K. Miller III, "Graph partitioning using annealed neural networks, " *IEEE Trans. Neural Networks* 1 (2192-203, 1990.

[15] Li Zhuang, Guang-you Xu, Haizhou Ai, and Gang Song, " Detection and tracking of facial features under a complex background" *Human Vision and Electronic Imaging* VII, June 2002, pp. 448-454.

[16] T.C. Chang, T.S. Huang, and C. Novak, "Facial feature extraction from color images", *Proc. the 12th IAPR International Conference on Pattern Recognition*, Vol. 2, pages 39-43, 1994

[17] Gwang Kim, Jung H. Kim, Sung Ho Yoon and Gi Taek Hur, "Lip Boundary Detection Techniques Using Color and Depth Information", Proceedings of SPIE 2002 International Symposium on Electronic Imaging, San Hose, CA, USA.

[18] Chow, T.Y. and Lam, K.M., "Mean-shift based mixture model for face detection in color image" *Proceedings of International Conference on Image Processing (ICIP '04)*, pp601-604, 2004

[19] V.V. Starovoitov1, D.I Samal1, D.V. Briliuk1, Three Approaches for Face Recognition", *The 6-th International Conference on Pattern Recognition and Image Analysis*, Russia, pp. 707-711 October, 2002

Automatic Gait Recognition by Multi-projection Analysis

Murat Ekinci

Computer Vision Lab.
Dept. of Computer Engineering,
Karadeniz Technical University, Trabzon, Turkey
ekinci@ktu.edu.tr

Abstract. Human identification at a distance by analysis of gait patterns extracted from video has recently become very popular research in biometrics. This paper presents multi-projections based approach to extract gait patterns for human recognition. Binarized silhouette of a motion object is represented by 1-D signals which are the basic image features called the distance vectors. The distance vectors are differences between the bounding box and silhouette, and extracted using four projections to silhouette. Based on normalized correlation on the distance vectors, gait cycle estimation is first performed to extract the gait cycle. Second, eigenspace transformation is applied to time-varying distance vectors and the statistical distance based supervised pattern classification is then performed in the lower-dimensional eigenspace for human identification. A fusion strategy developed is finally executed to produce final decision. Experimental results on four databases demonstrate that the right person in top two matches 100% of the times for the cases where training and testing sets corresponds to the same walking styles, and in top three-four matches 100% of the times for training and testing sets corresponds to the different walking styles.

1   Introduction

Gait recognition is the term typically used in the computer community to refer to the automatic extraction of visual cues that characterize the motion of a walking person in video and is used for identification purpose in surveillance [2][3][1][6]. Often in surveillance applications, it is difficult to get face information at the resolution required for recognition. As for gait is one of the few biometrics and a behavioral biometric source that can be measured at a distance.

Gait recognition methods can be broadly divided into two groups, model based and silhouette based approaches. Model based approaches [3][14] recover explicit features describing gait dynamics, such as stride dimensions and the kinematics of joint angles. The silhouette approach [6][7][8][2], characterizes body movement by the statistics of the patterns produced by walking. These patterns capture both the static and dynamic properties of body shape.

In this paper, it is attempted to develop a simple but effective representation of silhouette for gait-based human identification using silhouette analysis. Similar

M. Ali and R. Dapoigny (Eds.): IEA/AIE 2006, LNAI 4031, pp. 500–509, 2006.

observations have been made in [7][8][2], but the idea presented here implicitly captures both structural (appearances) and transitional (dynamics) characteristics of gait. A more robust approach for gait cycle estimation which is very important step in gait recognition is also presented. Instead of width/length time signal of bounding box of moving silhouette usually used in existing gait period analysis [3][9][10][2], here we analyze four projections extracted directly from differences between silhouette and the bounding box, and further convert them into associated four 1D signals. The novel approach presented is basically to produce the distance vectors, which are four 1-D signals are extracted for each projections, they are top-, bottom-, left-, and right-projections. Then normalized correlation-based a similarity function is executed to estimate gait cycle of moving silhouette. As following main purpose, depending on four distance vectors, PCA based gait recognition algorithm is first performed. A statistical distance based similarity is then achieved to obtain similarity measures on training and testing data. Next, fusion strategies on that similarities are calculated to produce final decision. Robust results for human identification have been obtained at the experiments on four different databases.

2   Gait Feature Extraction and Classification

Given a sequence of images obtained from a static camera, the moving person is first detected and tracked to compute the corresponding sequence of motion regions in each frame. Motion segmentation is achieved via background modeling/subtraction using a dynamic background frame estimated and updated in time, more details are given in [5]. Then a morphological filter operator is applied to the resulting images to suppress spurious pixel values. Once a silhouette generated, a bounding box is placed around silhouette. Silhouettes across a motion sequence are automatically aligned by scaling and cropping based on the bounding box.

2.1   Gait Signature Extraction

Silhouette representation is based on the projections to silhouette which is generated from a sequence of binary silhouette images $bs(t)= bs(x,y,t)$, indexed spatially by pixel location (x,y) and temporally by time t. There are four different image features called the distance vectors. They are top-, bottom-, left- and right-distance vectors. The distance vectors are the differences between the bounding box and the outer contour of silhouette. An example silhouette and the distance vectors corresponding to four projections are shown in the middle of figure 1. The distance vectors are separately represented by four 1D signals. The size of 1D signals is equal to the height or to the width of the bounding box for left- and right-distance vectors or for top- and bottom-distance vectors, respectively. The values in the signals for both left- and right-projections are computed as the difference in the locations of the bounding box and left-most and right-most boundary pixels, respectively, in a given row. The other projections along a given column are also computed as the differences from the top of

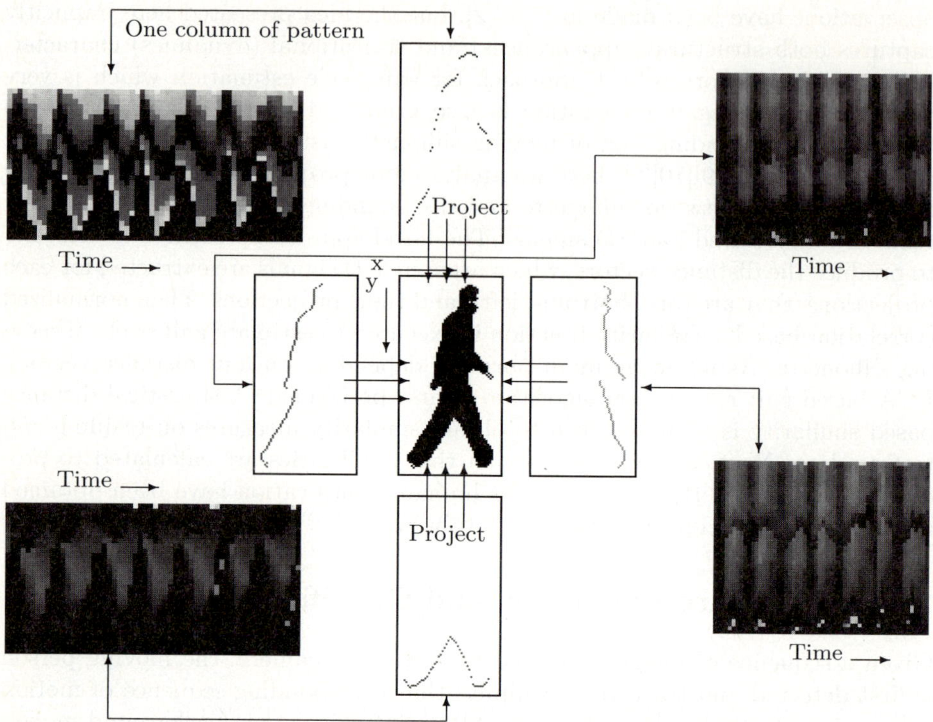

Fig. 1. Silhouette representation. **(Middle)** Silhouette and four projections, **(Left)** temporal plot of the distance vectors for top and bottom projections, **(Right)** temporal plot of the distance vectors for left and right projections.

the bounding box to the top-most of silhouette for top-projection, from the bottom of the box to the bottom-most of silhouette pixels for bottom-projections, respectively.

From a new 2D image $F_T(x,t) = \sum_y bs(x,y,t)$, where each column (indexed by time t) is the top-projections (row sum) of silhouette image $bs(t)$, as shown in figure 1 top-left. Each value $F_T(x,t)$ is then a count of the number of the row pixels between the top side of the bounding box and the outer contours in that columns x of silhouette image $bs(t)$. The result is a 2D pattern, formed by stacking top projections together to form a spatio-temporal pattern. A second pattern $F_B(x,t) = \sum_{-y} bs(x,y,t)$ can be constructed by stacking bottom projections, as shown in figure 1 bottom-left. The third pattern $F_L(y,t) = \sum_x bs(x,y,t)$ is also constructed by stacking with using the differences produced from the left projections and the last pattern $F_R(y,t) = \sum_{-x} bs(x,y,t)$ is finally constructed by stacking the right projections, as shown in figure 1 top-right and bottom-right 2D patterns, respectively. The variation of each component of the distance vectors can be regarded as gait signature of that object. From the temporal distance vector plots, it is clear that the distance vector is roughly periodic and gives the extent of movement of different part of the subject. The brighter a pixel in 2D patterns in figure 1, the larger value is the value of the distance vector in that position.

2.2   Training

The representation of 2D silhouette shape by four 1D signals, called distance vectors, significantly reduces the subsequent computational cost. To eliminate the influence of spatial scale and signal length of the distance vectors, the algorithm scales these distance vector signals with respect to magnitude and size through the sizes of the bounding boxes. Next, eigenspace transformation based on Principal Component Analysis (PCA) is applied to time varying distance vectors derived from a sequence of silhouette images to reduce the dimensionality of the input feature space. The training process similar to [2][4] is illustrated as follows:

Given k class for training, and each class represents a sequence of the distance vector signals of a person in one gait cycle. Multiple sequences of each person can be separately added for training. Let $V_{i,j}^w$ be the jth distance vector signal in the ith class for w projection to silhouette and N_i the number of such distance vector signals in the ith class. The total number of training samples is $N_t^w = N_1^w + N_2^w + ... + N_k^w$, as the whole training set can be represented by $[V_{1,1}^w, V_{1,2}^w, .., V_{1,N_1}^w, V_{2,1}^w, ..., V_{k,N_k}^w]$. The mean m_v^w and the global covariance matrix $\sum^w$ of w projection training set can easily be obtained by

$$m_v^w = \frac{1}{N_t^w} \sum_{i=1}^{k} \sum_{j=1}^{N_i^w} V_{i,j}^w \tag{1}$$

$$\sum{}^w = \frac{1}{N_t^w} \sum_{i=1}^{k} \sum_{j=1}^{N_i^w} (V_{i,j}^w - m_v^w)(V_{i,j}^w - m_v^w)^T \tag{2}$$

Here each V^w represents the distance vectors, F_w, for w projection (Top-Bottom-Left-Right) as explained in section 2.1. If the rank of matrix $\sum$ is N, then the N nonzero eigenvalues of $\sum$, $\lambda_1, \lambda_2, .., \lambda_N$, and associated eigenvectors $e_1, e_2, .., e_N$ can be computed based on theory of *singular value decomposition* [4]. The first few eigenvectors correspond to large changes in training patterns, and higher-order eigenvectors represent smaller changes [2]. As a result, for computing efficiency in practical applications, those small eigenvalues and their corresponding eigenvectors are ignored. Then a transform matrix $T^w = [e_1^w, e_2^w, .., e_s^w]$ to project an original distance vector signal $V_{i,j}^w$ into a point $P_{i,j}^w$ in the eigenspace is constructed by taking only $s < N$ largest eigenvalues and their associated eigenvectors for each projections to silhouette. Therefore, s values are usually much smaller than the original data dimension N. Then the projection average $A_i{}^w$ of each training sequence in the eigenspace is calculated by averaging of $P_{i,j}^w$.

2.3   Pattern Classification

Statistical distance. measuring has initially been selected for classification. The accumulated distance between the associated centroids A^w (obtained in the process of training) and B^w (obtained in the process of testing) can be easily computed by

$$d_S(A, B) = \sqrt{(\frac{A_1 - B_1}{s_1})^2 + ... + (\frac{A_p - B_p}{s_p})^2} = \sqrt{(A - B)^t S^{-1}(A - B)} \quad (3)$$

Where $S = diag(s_1^2, ..., s_p^2)$. In the distance measure, the classification result for each projection is then accomplished by choosing the minimum of d. The classification process is carried out via the nearest neighbor classifier. The classification is performed by classifying the test sequence into class c that can minimize the similarity distance between the test sequence and all training sequences by

$$c = arg_i \ min \ d_i(T, R_i) \quad (4)$$

where T represents a test sequence, R_i represents the ith training sequence, d is the similarity measures described in above.

A fusion task includes two different strategies is finally developed. In **the strategy 1**, each projection is separately treated. Then the strategy 1 is combining the distances of each projections at the end by assigning equal weight. The final similarity using strategy 1 is calculated as follows:

$$D_i = \sum_{j=1}^{4} \alpha_j * d_{ji} \quad (5)$$

where D_i is the fused distance similarity value, j is the algorithm's index for projection, α its normalized weight, d_i its single projection distance similarity value and 4 is the number of projections (left, right, top, bottom). As conclusion, if any two distance similarity vectors in four projections give maximum similarities for same person, then the identification is determined as positive. This fusion strategy has rapidly increased the recognition performance in the experiments.

At the experiments, it has been seen that some projection has given more robust results than others. For example, while human moves in lateral view with respect to image plane, the back side of human can give more individual characteristics in gait. So, the projection corresponding to that side can give more reliable results. We called dominant feature to this case. As a result, **the strategy 2** has also been developed to further increase the recognition performance. In the strategy 2, if the projection selected as dominant feature gives positive or at least two projections of others give positive for an individual, then identification by fusion process is to be positive. The dominant feature in this work is automatically assigned by estimating the direction of motion objects under tracking. At the next section, the dominant features determined by experimentally for different view points with respect to image plane are also given.

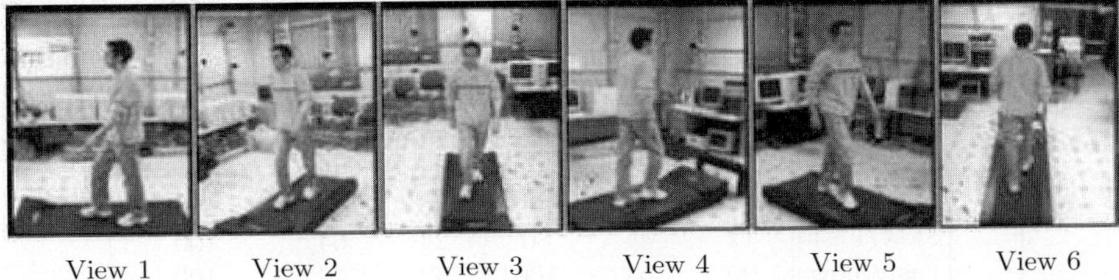

View 1   View 2   View 3   View 4   View 5   View 6

Fig. 2. The six CMU database viewpoints

3 Experiments and Results

We evaluate the performance of the method on CMU's MoBo database[12], NLPR gait database [2], our database, and USF database [6]. The Viterbi algorithm was used to identify the test sequence, since it is efficient and can operate in the logarithmic domain using only additions [11]. The performance of the algorithm presented is evaluated on four different databases of varying of difficulty. The gait cycle is automatically estimated by using the algorithm presented in the previous work in [13].

CMU Database. This database has 25 subjects (23 males, 2 females) walking on a treadmill. Each subject is recorded performing four different types of walking: slow walk, fast walk, inclined walk, and slow walk holding ball. There are about 8 cycles in each sequence, and each sequences is recorded at 30 frames per second. It also contains six simultaneous motion sequences of 25 subjects, as shown in figure 2.

One of the cycle in each sequence was used for testing, others for training. First, we did the following experiments on this database: **1)** train on slow walk and test on slow walk, **2)** train on fast walk and test on fast walk, **3)** train on walk carrying a ball and test on walk carrying a ball, **4)** train on slow walk and test on fast walk, **5)** train on slow walk and test on walk carrying a ball, **6)**

Table 1. Classification performance on the CMU data set for viewpoint 1

Test/Train	All projections: equal				Dominant: Right projection		
	Rank 1	Rank 2	Rank 3	Rank 4	Rank 1	Rank 2	Rank 3
Slow/Slow	72	100	100	100	84	100	100
Fast/Fast	76	100	100	100	92	100	100
Ball/Ball	84	100	100	100	84	100	100
Slow/Fast	36	92	100	100	52	100	100
Fast/Slow	20	60	100	100	32	88	100
Slow/Ball	8	17	33	58	42	96	100
Fast/Ball	4	13	33	67	17	50	88
Ball/Slow	8	17	38	67	33	88	100
Ball/Fast	13	29	58	92	29	63	100

Table 2. Classification performance on the CMU data set for all views. Eight gait cycles were used, seven cycles for training, one cycle for testing.

View	Test/Train	All projections equal			Dominant: Right projection		
		Rank 1	Rank 2	Rank 3	Rank 1	Rank 2	Rank 3
4	Slow/Slow	76	100	100	84	100	100
	Fast/Fast	84	100	100	96	100	100
	Slow/Fast	12	44	80	24	64	100
	Fast/Slow	20	64	100	32	76	100
					Dominant: Left projection		
5	Slow/Slow	80	100	100	80	100	100
	Fast/Fast	88	100	100	88	100	100
	Slow/Fast	16	44	80	24	64	100
	Fast/Slow	24	56	96	32	68	100
					Dominant: Right projection		
3	Slow/Slow	80	100	100	88	100	100
	Fast/Fast	72	100	100	76	100	100
	Slow/Fast	20	64	100	28	76	100
	Fast/Slow	24	56	92	28	68	100
					Dominant: Right projection		
6	Slow/Slow	72	100	100	84	100	100
	Fast/Fast	76	100	100	80	100	100
	Slow/Fast	16	44	88	36	76	100
	Fast/Slow	16	40	72	24	56	100

train on fast walk and test on slow walk, **7)** train on fast walk and test on walk carrying a ball, **8)** train on walk carrying a ball and test on slow walk, **9)** train on walk carrying a ball and test on fast walk.

The results obtained using the proposed method are summarized on the all cases **1)-9)** in Table 1. It can be seen that the right person in the top two matches 100% of times for the cases where testing and training sets correspond to the same walk styles. When the strategy developed in the fusion as dominant feature (projections) is used, the recognition performance is increased, as seen in Table 1. For the case of training with fast walk and testing on slow walk, and vice versa, the dip in performance is caused due to the fact that for some individual as biometrics suggests, there is a considerable change in body dynamics and stride length as a person changes his speed. Nevertheless, the right person in the top three matches 100% of the times for that cases, and dominant projection strategy has also increased the recognition performance for Ranks 1 and 2. For the case of training with walk carrying ball and testing on slow and fast walks, and vice versa, encouraging results have also been produced by using the proposed method, and the dominant feature property has still increased the recognition performance, as given in Table 1.

For the other view points, the experimental results are also summarized on the cases **1)-4)** in Table 2. When the all experimental results for the different view points are considered, it can be seen that, the right person in the top two matches 100% and in the top four matches 100% of the times for the cases **1)-2)**

| Lateral view | Oblique view | Frontal view |

Fig. 3. Some images in the NLPR database

and for the cases **3)-4)**, respectively. It is also seen that, when the dominant feature is used, gait recognition performance is also increased. Consequently, the proposed method for gait recognition can easily be seen that, it is view-invariant.

NLPR Database. The *NLPR* database [2] includes 20 subjects and four sequences for each viewing angle per subject, two sequences for one direction of walking, the other two sequences for reverse direction of walking. For instance, when the subject is walking laterally to the camera, the direction of walking is from right to left for two of four sequences, and from right to left for the remaining. Those all gait sequences were captured as twice (we called two experiments) on two different days in an outdoor environment. All subjects walk along a straight-line path at free cadences in three different views with respect to the image plane, as shown in figure 3, where the white line with arrow represents one direction path, the other walking path is reverse direction.

We did the following experiments on this database: **1)** train on one image sequence and test on the remainder, all sequences were produced from first experiment, **2)** train on two sequences obtained from first experiment and test on two sequences obtained from second experiment. This is repeated for each viewing angle, and for each direction of walking. The results for the experiments along with cumulative match scores in three viewing angle are summarized in Table 3. When the experimental results are considered, the right person in the

Table 3. Performance on the NLPR data set for three views

Walking Direction	View	Training	Test	Rank1	Rank2	Rank3
One Way Walking	Lateral	Exp. 1	Exp. 1	65	100	100
		Exp. 1	Exp. 2	55	100	100
	Frontal	Exp. 1	Exp. 1	60	100	100
		Exp. 1	Exp. 2	35	100	100
	Oblique	Exp. 1	Exp. 1	40	90	100
		Exp. 1	Exp. 2	30	60	100
Reverse Way Walking	Lateral	Exp. 1	Exp. 1	60	100	100
		Exp. 1	Exp. 2	50	100	100
	Frontal	Exp. 1	Exp. 1	60	100	100
		Exp. 1	Exp. 2	40	100	100
	Oblique	Exp. 1	Exp. 1	45	100	100
		Exp. 1	Exp. 2	35	75	100

Table 4. Performance on our data set: (The abbreviation: L⇒ R : From Left to Right)

Direction	Outdoor(15 person)		Indoor(7 person)		All(22 person)		
	Rank 1	Rank 2	Rank 1	Rank 2	Rank 1	Rank 2	Rank 3
L⇒ R	67	100	86	100	68	95	100
R⇒ L	67	100	71	100	68	100	100

top two matches 100% of times for lateral and frontal viewing angles, and in the top three matches 100% of times for oblique view.

Our Database. The database established for gait recognition has 22 people (2 females, 20 males), and subjects are walking laterally to the camera, the directions of walking is from left to right, and from right to left. The database includes two sequences for each subject. One sequence includes 3 gait cycle for each direction, and the length of each gait cycle varies with the pace of the walker, but the average is about 26 frames. The subjects walk along a straight-line path at free cadences, and 15 subjects were walking outside, seven subjects were walking inside. The results for the experiments along with cumulative match scores in lateral view are also summarized in Table 4. Three gait cycles were used, two cycles for training, one cycle for testing. Walking from left to right and the other direction are separately tested to achieve initial experimental results. When the results of each projection based distance vectors are re-implemented by using dominant feature strategy as explained in section 2.3, significantly improvements on the gait recognition has also been achieved. This is the robust implementation and is one of the novelty presented by this paper.

USF Database. Finally, the USF database [6] is considered. The database has variations as regards viewing direction, shoe type, and surface type. At the experiments, one of the cycle in each sequence was used for testing, others (3-4 cycles) for training. Different probe sequences for the experiments along with the cumulative match scores are given in Table 5 for the algorithm presented in this paper and three different algorithms [15][2][7]. The same silhouette data from USF were directly used. These data are noisy, e.g., missing of body parts, small holes inside the objects, severe shadow around feet, and missing and adding

Table 5. Performance on the USF database for four algorithm.

Exp.	The method			Baseline[15]		NLPR[2]		UMD[7]	
	Rnk 1	Rnk 2	Rnk 3	Rnk 1	Rnk 5	Rnk 1	Rnk 5	Rnk 1	Rnk 5
GAL[68]	35	80	100	79	96	70	92	91	100
GBR[44]	34	82	100	66	81	58	82	76	81
GBL[44]	25	55	91	56	76	51	70	65	76
CAL[68]	39	90	100	30	46	27	38	24	46
CAR[68]	30	66	100	29	61	34	64	25	61
CBL[41]	30	78	100	10	33	14	26	15	33
CBR[41]	29	66	100	24	55	21	45	29	39
GAR[68]	34	60	90	–	-	-	-	-	-

some parts around the border of silhouettes due to background characteristics. In Table 5, G and C indicate grass and concrete surfaces, A and B indicate shoe types, and L and R indicate left and right cameras, respectively. The number of subjects in each subset is also given in square bracket. It is observed that, the proposed method has given the right person in top three matches 100% of the times for training and testing sets corresponding to the same camera.

4   Conclusion

This paper has described a novel gait recognition approach that uses multi projections of silhouettes as the basic feature for classification. The approach on gait cycle estimation and on gait recognition is view-invariant and is fully automatic for real time applications. The performance of the gait recognition method proposed was also illustrated using different gait databases.

References

1. G. V. Veres,*et.al*, What image information is important in silhouette-based gait recognition? Proc. IEEE Conf. on Computer Vision and Pattern Recognition, 2004.
2. L. Wang, T. Tan, H. Ning, W. Hu, Silhouette Analysis-Based Gait Recognition for Human Identification. IEEE Trans. on PAMI Vol.25, No. 12, Dec.,2003.
3. C. BenAbdelkader, R. G. Cutler, L. S. Davis, Gait Recognition Using Image Self-Similarity. EURASIP Journal of Applied Signal Processing, April, 2004.
4. P. Huang, C. Harris, M. Nixon, Human Gait Recognition in Canonical Space Using Temporal Templates. IEE Proc. Vision Image and Signal Proc. Conf., 1999.
5. M. Ekinci, E. Gedikli, Background Estimation Based People Detection and Tracking for Video Surveillance. Springer LNCS Vol. 2869, pp:421-429, November, 2003.
6. S. Sarkar, *et al* The HumanID Gait Challenge Problem: Data Sets, Performance, and Analysis. IEEE Trans. on Pat. Anal. and Mach. Intell., Vol.27, No. 2, 2005.
7. A. Kale, *et. al.*, Identification of Humans Using Gait. IEEE Trans. on Image Processing, Vol.13, No.9, September 2004.
8. Yanxi Liu, R. T. Collins, T. Tsin, Gait Sequence Analysis using Frieze Patterns. Proc. of European Conf. on Computer Vision, 2002.
9. C. BenAbdelkader, *et.al*, Stride and Cadence as a Biometric in Automatic Person Identification and Verification. Proc. Int. Conf. Aut. Face and Gesture Recog.,2002.
10. R. Collins, R. Gross, and J. Shi, Silhouette-Based Human Identification from Body Shape and Gait. Proc. Int. Conf. Automatic Face and Gesture Recognition, 2002.
11. J. Phillips *et.al*, The FERET Evaluation Methodology for Face recognition Algorithm. IEEE Trans. Pattern Analysis and Machine Intell. Vol.22, no.10, Oct.2000.
12. R. Gross, J. Shi, The CMU motion of body (MOBO) database. Tech. Rep. CMU-RI-TR-01-18, Robotics Institute, Carnegie Mellon University, June 2001.
13. M. Ekinci, E. Gedikli A Novel Approach on Silhouette Based Human Motion Analysis for Gait Recognition. Springer Verlag LNCS Vol.3804, pp.219-226, Dec.2005.
14. A. I. Bazin, M. S. Nixon, Gait Verification Using Probabilistic Methods. IEEE Workshop on Applications of Computer Vision, 2005.
15. P. Phillips, et.al., Baseline Results for Challenge Problem of Human ID using Gait Analysis. Pro. Int. Conf. Automatic Face and Gesture Recognition, 2002.

A Novel Image Retrieval Approach Combining Multiple Features of Color-Connected Regions[*]

Yubin Yang[1], Shifu Chen[1], and Yao Zhang[2]

[1] State Key Laboratory for Novel Software Technology, Nanjing University,
Nanjing 210093, P.R. China
[2] Department of Information Management, Nanjing University,
Nanjing 210093, P.R. China

Abstract. This paper proposes a novel image retrieval method MCM (Multi-component Co-occurrence Matrices), which combines the color-connected regions in an image with their corresponding visual features in a region-growing like manner. Experimental results have shown that the MCM method has good retrieval performance and efficiency, due to the capability of integrating color composition, color spatial layout and texture characteristics into its coarse-granule region representation.

1 Introduction

Image feature extraction techniques in CBIR (Content-based Image Retrieval) studies generally fall into two categories: global feature extraction and region-based (local) feature extraction. Global features are fast and easy to compute, however, their practicability are limited because the user's goal is, in many cases, to retrieve similar regions, rather than similar images as the whole. At the same time, the approaches based on regional features can localize regions and then use the region information to retrieve the images containing similar regions, which are more intuitive, accurate and consistent with human's visual perception. Consequently, region-based image retrieval has now been playing more dominant roles in CBIR studies. However, semantically accurate image segmentation is still an open problem in computer vision. And in some cases, where a fine-granule matching is not feasible, such as fast searching and filtering in an image database, it is not effective to retrieve images based on their delicate segmentation results. To address the above issues, some researchers have proposed CBIR methods that only use "Coarse Region" information, aiming to guarantee the retrieval performance by utilizing rough region information, and lower the costs by avoiding the intractable image segmentation problem as well [1, 2].

In this paper, a novel image retrieval method MCM is proposed. The MCM can retrieve images by combining the coarse-granule color-connected regions in an image with their corresponding visual features in a region-growing like manner. The rest of this paper is organized as follows. Related work is briefly reviewed in Section 2. In Section 3, the basic definitions about color-connectivity

---

[*] This work was supported by the National Natural Science Foundation of P.R. China under Grant No. 60505008.

M. Ali and R. Dapoigny (Eds.): IEA/AIE 2006, LNAI 4031, pp. 510–519, 2006.
© Springer-Verlag Berlin Heidelberg 2006

texture are introduced, and the feature extraction algorithm is then presented. The similarity measure process is proposed in Section 4. Experimental results and comparisons are then presented in Section 5. Finally, concluding remarks and future work are given in Section 6.

2   Related Work

The co-occurrence matrix is generally used as an underlying structure for storing the textural content of images [3]. It is the most noticeable characteristic that it works well for stochastic textures and small window sizes [4]. However, gray level co-occurrence matrix cannot sufficiently handle color composition and color spatial layout information in images. Moreover, due to its dependency on the gray level numbers, the efficiency reduces significantly when the examined images contain a large number of gray levels, which is usually the case for color images.

In order to use co-occurrence matrix to retrieve color images more accurately and efficiently, many extensions of gray level co-occurrence matrix have been proposed. For example, Vassili et al. [5] firstly quantized the color values of each RGB color image, and then computed a color co-occurrence matrix in the same way as gray level co-occurrence matrix computation. Takahashi et al. [6] subdivided an image into several sub-blocks and extracted the gray level co-occurrence matrices of each sub-block, to compute seven statistical values as image feature vector.

3   Color-Connectivity Texture

A new image feature descriptor, color-connectivity texture, is proposed in this paper, which is represented as a set of color co-occurrence matrices of color-connected regions. Due to the limitation of the current image segmentation techniques in generality, efficiency and reliability, an image is firstly partitioned into several sub-blocks in pre-defined size, as a simple substitution to delicate image segmentation process. After that, the dominant color feature of each sub-block is extracted.

3.1   Dominant Color Extraction

For each image sub-block, the dominant color is computed in order to search color-connected regions. To provide multi-resolution retrieval capabilities, the number of sub-blocks can be specified by users at a range of N^2 (N=2,3,4,8). In our experiments, the default value of N is 4 (16 sub-blocks).

Suppose that the dimension of a color image T=$f(x, y)$ is $X \times Y$, and image T is subdivided into N^2 (N=2,3,4,8) sub-blocks with same size, then the following definitions are given:

Definition 1 (mosaic block T_{ij})

$$T_{ij} = \{f(x,y) | i \cdot \tfrac{X}{N} \leq x < (i+1) \cdot \tfrac{X}{N}, j \cdot \tfrac{Y}{N} \leq y < (j+1) \cdot \tfrac{Y}{N}\} \qquad (1)$$

where $0 \leq i \leq N-1, 0 \leq j \leq N-1$.

Definition 2 (mosaic dominant color). *For each mosaic block $T_{ij}(0 \leq i \leq N-1, 0 \leq j \leq N-1)$, a quantized color bin in HSV color space is defined as the mosaic dominant color of T_{ij}, extracted using the following algorithm:*

Algorithm 1. *mosaic dominant color extraction*

Step 1. Quantize the HSV color values of each mosaic block T_{ij} using $8 \times 3 \times 3$ quantization algorithm in [7], then compute the HSV color histogram $H_{ij} = [h_1, h_2, \cdots, h_{72}]$;

Step 2. For each mosaic block T_{ij}, compute a dominant color range (range width=3) as follows:

```
Max ←0;
Index ← 0;   //Index: the index of dominant color range
for n = 1 to 69
begin   //compute the dominant color range
      count ← 0;
      for m = n to n+2   //range width is 3
      begin
            count ← count+h_m;
            //h_m is the number of pixels with the m-th color
      end
      if (count > Max) then
      begin
            Max ← count;
            Index ← n;
      end
end
```

Step 3. Find out the HSV color value with the maximum pixel frequency in range [Index, Index+2] as the dominant color of mosaic block T_{ij};

Step 4. End of algorithm.

Fig. 1 shows the mosaic dominant colors of the same image with different mosaic blocks. As can be seen from Fig. 1, the more mosaic blocks, the more accurate and detailed color composition and color spatial layout can be represented. In that way, the mosaic dominant color is able to satisfy both "coarse-granule" and "fine-granule" image retrieval tasks.

Fig. 1. Dominant colors in different partitions (Left: original image, Middle: 4×4 dominant colors, Right: 8×8 dominant colors)

3.2   Color-Connected Region

In order to accurately localize color-connected regions, a new definition of dominant color similarities, which reflects human's visual perception, is proposed as follows.

Definition 3 (correlated color). *For a pair of colors (C_i, C_j) in quantized HSV color space Q, where C_i is represented as (h_i, s_i, v_i) and C_j is represented as (h_j, s_j, v_j), we define $C_i(or, C_j)$ as a correlated color of $C_j(or, C_i)$, if any of the following conditions is satisfied:*

(I) C_i and C_j belong to the same color bin in quantized HSV color space, i.e. $h_i = h_j$, $s_i = s_j$, and $v_i = v_j$;
(II) C_i and C_j belong to different color bins but satisfied any of the following conditions:
  (a) $s_i * 3 + v_i = s_j * 3 + v_j$, and $|h_i - h_j| = 1$;
  (b) $h_i = h_j, s_i = s_j$, and $v_i, v_j \in \{0, 1\}$.

On the basis of Def. 3, the following definitions related to the "color connectivity" are then derived:

Definition 4 (color connectivity). *Suppose that a color image T is subdivided into N^2 mosaic blocks, then for each mosaic block $T_{ij}(0 \le i \le N - 1, 0 \le j \le N - 1)$, compute its mosaic dominant color C_{ij} using Algorithm 1 discussed in Section 3.1. For each pair of 4-connected mosaic block T_{ij} and T_{kl} $(|i - k| = 1$ and $j = l$; or $|j - l| = 1$ and $i = k)$, if their mosaic dominant colors are correlated colors satisfying Def. 3, then T_{ij} and T_{kl} are defined as a mosaic block pair with color connectivity.*

Definition 5 (color-connected region). *The new region, which is composed of all the mosaic blocks with the same color connectivity in terms of 4-connectivity principle, is defined as a color-connected region.*

Definition 6 (color-connected region set). *All the color-connected regions in an image T compose an exclusive color-connected region set $S = \{R_i\}(1 \le i \le M$, where M is the number of color-connected regions in image T), which satisfies the following constraints:*

1. $\bigcup_{i=1}^{M} R_i = T$;
2. $R_i \cap R_j = \phi(i \ne j, 1 \le i, j \le M)$;
3. $R_i(1 \le i \le M)$ is a color-connected region;
4. R_i and $R_j(i \le j, 1 \le i, j \le M)$ is not with the same color-connectivity.

Fig. 2 illustrates an instance of color-connected region set.

3.3   Texture Feature Computation

As an image is represented as a color-connected region set, the discriminative visual features of the entire image are then extracted, to combine the texture

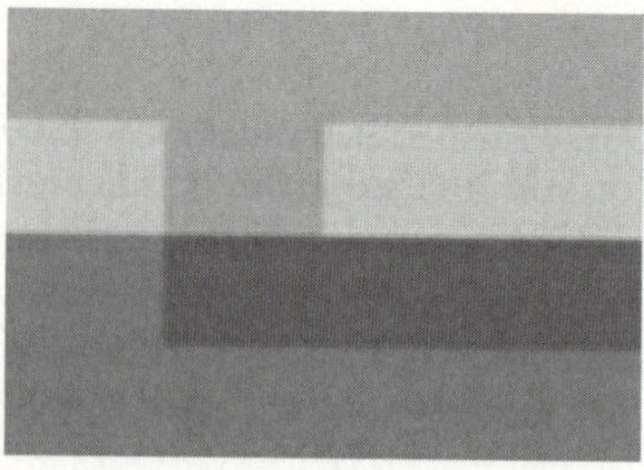

Fig. 2. Instance of color-connected region set. The right image shows the five color-connected region set corresponding to the left original image.

characteristics in different color channels. They are represented as a set of color co-occurrence matrices. Each color co-occurrence matrix depicts the color spatial interdependence and distribution of the pixels in a local color-connected region.

The co-occurrence matrices of each color-connected region are then computed for the following four color components: (1) R (Red), G (Green) components of RGB color space, a basic color representation mechanism. B (Blue) component is not included since the RGB color space is linear correlated. (2) H (Hue) component of HSV color space, a color representation mechanism mostly consistent with human's visual perception for colors. H is used to describe different colors. (3) Intensity component I, which describes the brightness and is given with an experiential equation [8]:

$$I = 0.21I + 0.72G + 0.07B \tag{2}$$

All the four color co-occurrence matrices are computed for each color-connected region, where distance between the pixels in each pair, i.e. displacement, is 1 and the directions are $0^0, 45^0, 90^0$ and 135^0 respectively. The algorithm is described as follows:

Algorithm 2. *color co-occurrence matrices computation*
Step 1. Determine the color-connected region set $S = \{R_i\}(1 \leq i \leq M)$ of image T;
Step 2. Extract color component matrices of R, G, H and I from the pixel array of image T, with a quantization level of D=8;
Step 3. For each color-connected region, compute the normalized co-occurrence matrices of R, G, H and I components to extract the following statistical values, which are common descriptors reflecting texture characteristics very well [9]:

$$\text{(a) } Energy : E = \sum_{i=1}^{D} \sum_{j=1}^{D} m(i,j)^2 \tag{3}$$

where 'Energy' is a measure of texture homogeneity and $m(i,j)(1 \leq i,j \leq n)$ are the elements of each co-occurrence matrix.

$$\text{(b) } Inertia : I = \sum_{i=1}^{D} \sum_{j=1}^{D} (i-j)^2 \cdot m(i,j) \tag{4}$$

where 'Inertia' is a measure of the moment of inertia about its main diagonal in each co-occurrence matrix, representing the contrast of an image.

$$(c)\ Entropy: S = -\sum_{i=1}^{D}\sum_{j=1}^{D}(m(i,j)\cdot logm(i,j)) \tag{5}$$

where 'Entropy' is a measure of texture complexity. A high entropy value implies a high degree of image complexity.

$$(d)\ Homogeneity: H = \sum_{i=1}^{D}\sum_{j=1}^{D}\frac{m(i,j)}{1+(i-j)^2} \tag{6}$$

where 'Homogeneity' indicates the degree to which similar gray levels tend to be neighbors.

Thus, we can compose a 16-dimension feature vector $F_i = [F_{Ri}, F_{Gi}, F_{Hi}, F_{Ii}] = \{f_{i1}, \cdots, f_{i16}\}$ for each region R_i;

Step 4. Suppose that the number of mosaic blocks contained in each color-connected region R_i is B_i, to keep the rotation invariance of the feature descriptors, we design the feature vector of the entire image T as $F = [F_R, F_G, F_H, F_I] = \{f_1, ..., f_{16}\}$, where each normalized vector element f_k $(1 \le k \le 16)$ can be computed as follows:

$$f_k = \frac{\sum_{i=1}^{M} f(i_k)\cdot \frac{B_i}{N^2}}{\max_{1\le i\le M}(f_{i_k})} \tag{7}$$

Step 5. End of algorithm.

4   Similarity Measurement

Assume that the feature vectors of two images A and B, are represented as $F_A = [F_{RA}, F_{GA}, F_{HA}, F_{IA}] = \{f_{A1}, \cdots, f_{A16}\}$ and $F_B = [F_{RB}, F_{GB}, F_{HB}, F_{IB}] = \{f_{B1}, \cdots, f_{B16}\}$. Since different parts describe different aspects of the image, they have different contributions to the image similarity, which should be integrated using appropriate weight combination. Consequently, the distance (dissimilarity) between two images A and B can be defined as:

$$D(A, B) = w_1 \cdot D_E(F_{RA}, F_{RB}) + w_2 \cdot D_E(F_{GA}, F_{GB})$$
$$+ w_3 \cdot D_E(F_{HA}, F_{HB}) + w_4 \cdot |F_{IA}, F_{IB}| \tag{8}$$

where D_E denotes the Euclidean distance in vector space, used for R, G and H color components in three-dimension RGB and HSV color space, while $|\cdot|$ denotes the Manhattan distance in vector space, dealing with one dimensional gray level component. The parameter w_i is a weight factor, which is set to indicate the significance of each similarity measure in the combined measure, satisfying $0 \le w_i \le 1, \sum_{i=1}^{4} w_i = 1$.

There are many ways of choosing weights w_i $(i=1,2,3,4)$. For example, in a uniform weighting scheme, we assume each similarity measure is equally important and effective. Another choice is to assign the weights according to the relative importance of each component. In the *MCM* method, we assign different weight values to different color components, in order to take into account their diverse contributions to the image retrieval task. However, finding the appropriate combination is not a trivial task. In our experiments, these values are set empirically. By default, the weight combination is: $w_1 = 0.3, w_2 = 0.3, w_3 = 0.3,$ and $w_4 = 0.1$, aiming to attach more importance to color information.

We have also noticed that, although the Euclidean distance and the Manhattan distance both measure differences between image feature vectors, they have different value coverage. Specifically, for our normalized texture features based on color co-occurrence matrices, the value range of the Manhattan distance is [0,2], while the value range of the Euclidean distance is $[0,\sqrt{2}]$. To measure the image similarity more accurately, we normalize the distance function in Eq. (8) and give the following similarity measure:

$$S(A, B) = w_1 \cdot \frac{\sqrt{2} - D_E(F_{RA}, F_{RB})}{\sqrt{2}} + w_2 \cdot \frac{\sqrt{2} - D_E(F_{GA}, F_{GB})}{\sqrt{2}}$$
$$+ w_3 \cdot \frac{\sqrt{2} - D_E(F_{HA}, F_{HB})}{\sqrt{2}} + w_4 \cdot \frac{2 - |F_{IA}, F_{IB}|}{2} \tag{9}$$

Thus, utilizing the overall image-to-image similarity measurement function S(A, B), the images can be retrieved according to their contents, represented as coarse region information and low-level features.

5   Experimental Results

5.1   Experiment Setup

The performance of a CBIR system is typically measured using "Recall" and "Precision". These measures are usually represented in the form of "Precision-Recall" (P-R) curve [7]. "Recall" defines the percentage of true similarity matches with respect to the overall similar images that actually exist in the image database, while "Precision" is the percentage of similarity matches with respect to all of the matches given by the CBIR system. Assume that N_c is the number of correct matches, N_m is the number of missed matches, N_f is the number of false matches, then we have:

$$Recall = N_c/(N_c + N_m) \tag{10}$$

$$Precision = N_c/(N_c + N_f) \tag{11}$$

In order to evaluate the retrieval performance of the *MCM* method, we implemented it in our experimental image retrieval system @IMAGE [7]. Different retrieval experiments were carried out using the QBE (Query-By-Example) querying interface provided in @IMAGE system. The test image databases cover different types of images, which contain almost 5,000 general-purpose images including mountains, seas, buildings, trademarks, texture patterns, forests, vegetation, human beings, airplanes, automobiles, animals and flowers etc. Each image is 24-bit RGB color image accessed in .JPG file format, with different image sizes. we also compare our retrieval approach with other two approaches presented in [5] and [6], which are both based on co-occurrence matrix feature representation and reported better retrieval performance than the global co-occurrence matrix feature.

5.2   Comparisons of Retrieval Precisions

Firstly, to observe how well the *MCM* method represents the coarse-granule shape, color composition, and color spatial layout characteristics, the retrieval precisions for the following five image categories: "Mountains", "Flowers", "Automobiles", "Textures" and "Buildings" are tested. In this kind of experiments, we randomly picked 5 query images from each different category. For each query example, a retrieved image is considered a correct match if and only if it is in the same category as the query. Only the top 10 matches to each query are included in the calculation, and the average precision of all the five query images are listed and compared in Table 1.

Table 1. Comparisons of image retrieval precisions

Image categories	*Takahashi* approach	*Vassili* approach	*MCM* approach
Mountains	80.6%	83.2%	94.3%
Flowers	69.6%	76.2%	88.3%
Automobiles	81.2%	82.0%	85.1%
Textures	74.3%	82.8%	93.3%
Buildings	65.9%	72.1%	84.3%

As we can see from Table 1, *MCM* has the best retrieval precisions for all the image categories. In particular, the retrieval precisions of *MCM* for "Textures" and "Mountain" images, where texture characteristics play dominating role in describing image content, are both higher than those of other image categories, which shows its effectiveness on texture representation. On the other hand, although the color-connectivity texture feature is able to integrate color spatial layout information, it is still in a "coarse-granule" resolution and cannot achieve very satisfactory retrieval precisions on "Building" and "Automobile" images. However, the performance of *MCM* is still much higher than those in [5] and in [6]. As for the "Flower" images, where both color and texture should be considered, *MCM* and *Vassili* approaches both utilize color information in their feature descriptors. The *MCM* approach has relatively better performance, because it includes both color composition and color spatial layout information. This also proves the feasibility and effectiveness of the color-connectivity texture features.

Moreover, in all experimental results shown in Table 1, the retrieval precisions of *MCM* are all higher than *Takahashi* approach, which used gray level co-occurrence matrices. This reveals that integration of multiple low-level features in Content-based Image Retrieval can achieve better performance than individual low-level feature.

5.3   Comparison of P-R Curves

The comparison of the P-R performance curves of all the three approaches is provided in this section. The query image is randomly selected from the image database without any pre-defined category, and the query results are observed according to the relevance of the image semantics, not just the rough category. Since the relevance of image semantics differs from different users, we select five different users, each to make retrieval experiments for 50 randomly selected query images, and the average precision and recall are calculated to make a comparison. Fig. 3 gives P-R curves of all the three image retrieval approaches on the whole test image databases.

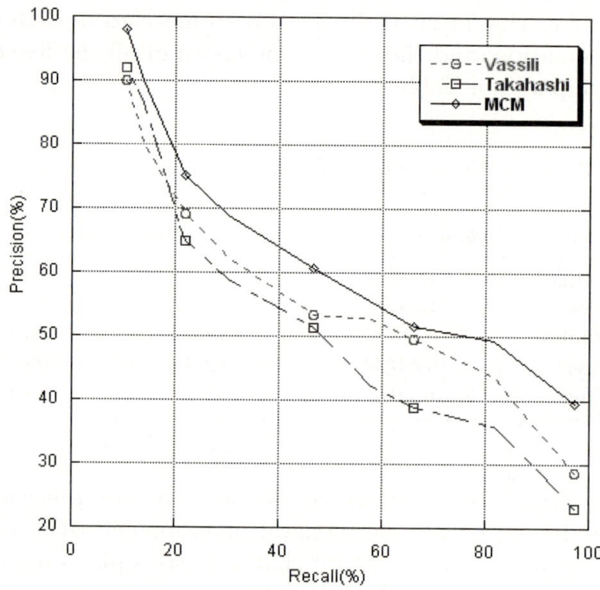

Fig. 3. P-R curves of three image retrieval approaches

We learn from Fig. 3 that the overall performance of *MCM* is more accurate and robust than *Takahashi* approach and *Vassili* approach. The color-connectivity texture feature is effective in representing image texture distribution. It also generalizes better than other two approaches because of the integration of color composition and color layout information.

6   Conclusions

This paper proposes a novel image retrieval method *MCM* (Multi-component Co-occurrence Matrices). *MCM* is able to combine image region information with the corresponding visual features, by performing a coarse but fast localization of color-connected regions in a region-growing like manner. Experimental results have shown that the *MCM* method has satisfactory retrieval performance without increasing of computational cost.

In our future research, a more refined quantization level of image colors will be explored, aiming to increase the resolution of color-connected regions and enhance its discriminative power. Designing robust region-based similarity measurement, to obtain better retrieval performance and alleviate the impact from segmentation-related uncertainties, is also another important issues. Furthermore, establishing a good automatic weight-choosing scheme to combine different similarity metrics, is also important for more accurate similarity measure.

References

1. Malki J, Boujemaa N, Nastar C, and Winter A (1999) Region queries without segmentation for image retrieval by content. In: Proceedings of Visual Information and Information Systems, Amsterdam, The Netherlands, June 2-4, 1999, pp 115-122
2. Fauqueur J, Boujemaa N. Image retrieval by regions: coarse segmentation and fine color description(2002) In: Proceedings of International Conference on Visual Information System (VISUAL'2002), Hsin-Chu, Taiwan, March 2002, pp 24-35
3. Haralick RM (1979) Statistical and structural approaches to texture. In: Proceedings of the IEEE, Vol. 67, May 1979, pp 786-804
4. Whelan PF, Molloy D (2001) Machine vision algorithms in Java: techniques and implementation. Springer-Verlag
5. Vassili K, Stephan V (1998) Color co-occurrence descriptors for querying-by-example. In: Proceedings of International Conference on Multimedia Modeling, Lausanne, Switzerland, October 12-15, pp 32-37
6. Takahashi N, Iwasaki M, Kunieda T, et al (2000) Image retrieval using spatial intensity features. Signal Processing: Image Communication, Vol. 16, pp 45-57
7. Yang YB (2003) Research and applications on the key techniques of content-based image retrieval. Ph.D. Thesis, Nanjing University, Nanjing, P. R. China (in Chinese)
8. Gaurav S. (1997) Digital color Imaging. IEEE Transactions On Image Processing, Vol. 6-7, pp 901-932
9. Conners RW, Harlow CA (1980) A theoretical comparison of texture algorithms. IEEE Transactions on Pattern Analysis and Machine Intelligence, Vol. 2, pp 204-222

An Application of Random and Hammersley Sampling Methods to Iris Recognition

Luis E. Garza Castañón[1], Saúl Montes de Oca[2],
and Rubén Morales-Menéndez[1]

[1] Department of Mechatronics and Automation, ITESM Monterrey Campus
`{legarza, rmm}@itesm.mx`
[2] Automation Graduate Program Student, ITESM Monterrey Campus
`saul_montesdeoca@yahoo.com.mx`
Av. Eugenio Garza Sada Sur No. 2501
Monterrey, N.L. 64849 México

Abstract. We present a new approach for iris recognition based on a sampling scheme. Iris recognition is a method to identify persons, based on the analysis of the eye iris. A typical iris recognition system is composed of four phases: image acquisition and preprocessing, iris localization and extraction, iris features characterization, and comparison and matching. The main contribution in this work is in the step of characterization of iris features by using sampling methods and accumulated histograms. These histograms are built from data coming from sampled subimages of iris. In the comparison and matching step, a comparison is made between accumulated histograms of couples of iris samples, and a decision of accept/reject is taken based on samples differences and on a threshold calculated experimentally. We tested two sampling methods: random and Hammersley, and conduct experiments with UBIRIS database. Under certain conditions we found a rate of successful identifications in the order of 100 %.

1   Introduction

Iris recognition is related to the area of biometrics. The main intention of biometrics is to provide reliable automatic recognition of individuals based on the measuring of a physical characteristic or personal trait. Biometrics can be used for access control to restricted areas, such as airports or military installations, access to personal equipments such as laptops and cellular phones, and public applications, such as banking operations [11]. A wide variety of biometrics systems have been deployed and resulting systems include different human features such as: face, fingerprint, hand shape, palmprint, signature, voice and iris [7]. The last one may provide the best solution by offering a much more discriminating power than the others biometrics. Specific characteristics of iris such as a data-rich structure, genetic independence, stability over time and physical protection, makes the use of iris as biometric well recognized.

M. Ali and R. Dapoigny (Eds.): IEA/AIE 2006, LNAI 4031, pp. 520–529, 2006.

In last years, there have been different implementations of iris recognition systems. Daugman's system [2] used multiscale quadrature wavelets (Gabor filters) to extract texture phase structure information of the iris to generate a 2,048-bit iris code and compared the difference between a pair of iris representations by their Hamming distance. In [10] iris features are extracted by applying a dyadic wavelet transform with null intersections. To characterize the texture of the iris, Boles and Boashash [1] calculated a one dimension wavelet transform at various resolution levels of a concentric circle on an iris image. In this case the iris matching step was based on two dissimilarity functions. Wildes [13] represented the iris texture with a Laplacian pyramid constructed with four different resolution levels and used the normalized correlation to determine whether the input image and the model image are from the same class. A Similar method to Daugman's is reported in [9], but using edge detection approach to localize the iris, and techniques to deal with illumination variations, such as histogram equalization and feature characterization by average absolute deviation. In [6] a new method is presented to remove noise in iris images, such as eyelashes, pupil, eyelids and reflections. The approach is based on the fusion of edge and region information. In [3] an iris recognition approach based on mutual information is developed. In that work, couples of iris samples are geometrically aligned by maximizing their mutual information and subsequently recognized.

Most of the previous work rely on some sort of filtering or transformation of iris data, and this step can be time consuming. We present an approach where direct information from selected areas of iris is used to build a set of features. In our work we apply standard techniques as integro-differential operators to locate the iris, and histogram equalization over extracted iris area to compensate for illumination variations. The main contribution of our work is in the feature extraction step, where we sample square subimages of iris, and build an acummulated histogram for each subimage. Every iris is represented by a set of features, and each feature is an accumulated histogram. The number and the size of square subimages were calculated experimentally. The comparison between iris sample and irises in database is done by computing the Euclidean distance between histograms, and a decision to accept or reject iris sample is taken based on a threshold calculated also experimentally.

We ran experiments with UBIRIS database [12] and tested two different sampling schemes: random and Hammersley. We have found under certain conditions a rate of succesful matching in the order of 100 %.

2   The Proposed Approach

The implementation of our approach relies on the use of colored eyes images from UBIRIS database. Eyes images include samples where iris is free from any occlusion, and others with moderate obstruction from eyelids and eyelashes (Fig. 1). We transform the images color representation to just grey level pixels, because this process is sufficient to reveal the relevant features of iris.

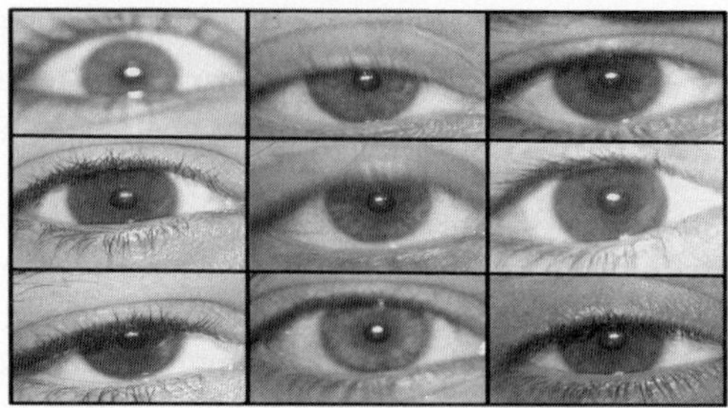

Fig. 1. Eyes samples with noise (moderate obstruction)

2.1   Iris Localization

The search of limbic and pupilar limits is achieved with the use of the integro-differential operator shown in eqn 1.

$$\overset{max}{(r, x_0, y_0)} = \left| \frac{\partial}{\partial r} G(r) * \oint_{r, x_c, y_c} \frac{I(x, y)}{2\pi r} ds \right| \tag{1}$$

where $I(x, y)$ is an image containing an eye.

The operator behaves as an iterative circular edge detector, and searches over the image domain (x, y) for the maximum in the partial derivative with respect to an increasing radius r, of the normalized contour integral of $I(x, y)$ along a circular arc ds of radius r and center coordinates (x_0, y_0). The symbol $*$ denotes convolution and $G_\sigma(r)$ is a smoothimg function, tipically a Gaussian of scale σ.

This operator behaves well in most cases with moderate noise conditions, but requires some fine tuning of parameters, in order to deal with pupil reflections, obscure eyes and excess of illumination. Heavy occlusion of iris by eyelashes or eyelids needs to be handled by other methods. In our work, eye images with heavy occlusion were discarded.

The extracted iris image has to be normalized to compensate for pupil dilation and contraction under illumination variations. This process is achieved by a transformation from cartesian to polar coordinates, using equations 2 and 3.

$$x(r, \theta) = (1 - r)x_p(\theta) + rx_s(\theta) \tag{2}$$

$$y(r, \theta) = (1 - r)y_p(\theta) + ry_s(\theta) \tag{3}$$

where $x(r, \theta)$ and $y(r, \theta)$ are defined as a linear combination of pupil limits $(x_p(\theta), y_p(\theta))$ and limbic limits $(x_s(\theta), y_s(\theta))$. r is defined in the interval $[0, 1]$, and θ in the interval $[0, 2\pi]$.

2.2   Strip Processing

The iris image strip obtained in previous step, is processed by using an histogram equalization method, to compensate for differences in illumination conditions.

The main objective in this method is that all grey levels (ranging from 0 to 255) have the same number of pixels. Histogram equalization is obtained by working with the accumulated histogram, shown in eqn 4.

$$H(i) = \sum_{k=0}^{i} h(k) \qquad (4)$$

where $h(k)$ is the histogram of the kth grey level.

A flat histogram, where every grey level has the same number of pixels, can be obtained by eqn 5.

$$G(i') = (i' + 1)\frac{N_r * M_c}{256} \qquad (5)$$

Where N_r and M_c are the image dimensions and 256 is the number of grey levels.

2.3   Iris Sampling

Sampling strategies have been applied recently with certain degree of success in texture synthesis [4, 8]. The main idea in our work is to extract relevant features of iris, by sampling a set of subimages from the whole image. In our case we tested two sampling strategies: random and Hammersley. In the first strategy we randomly generate a set of coordinates (x, y) where the subimage is centered. In the second strategy we generate a more uniform sampling of coordinates by using Hammersley sequence sampling.

Hammersley sampling [5] is part of to the *quasi*-Monte Carlo methods, or low-discrepancy sampling family. The *quasi*-prefix refers to a sampling approach that employs a deterministic algorithm to generate samples in an n-dimensional space. These points are as close as possible to a uniform sampling. Discrepancy refers to a quantitative measure of how much the distribution of samples deviates from an ideal uniform distribution (i.e. low-discrepancy is a desired feature).

Quasi-Monte Carlo methods as Hammersley sequences show lower error bound in multidimensional problems such as integration. Error bounds for pseudo-Monte Carlo Methods are $\mathcal{O}(N^{-1/2})$, and for classical integration is $\mathcal{O}(N^{-2/n})$. However, Hammersley sequences has lower error bound with $\mathcal{O}(N^{-1}(log_{10}N)^{n-1})$ where N is the number of samples and n is the dimension of the design space. Usually, as n grows up Hammersley shows better results, note that pseudo-Monte Carlo error bound is a probabilistic bound.

Hammersley Algorithm. This algorithm generates N points using the radix-R notation of an integer. A specific integer, q, in radix-R notation can be represented as in eqn 6.

$$q = q_m q_{m-1}...q_2 q_1 q_0$$
$$q = q_0 + q_1 R + q_2 R^2 + \cdots + q_m R^m \qquad (6)$$

where $m = [log_R(q)] = [ln(q)/ln(R)]$, and the square brackets, [ ], denote the integer portion of the number inside the brackets. The inverse radix number function constructs a unique number on the interval $[0, 1]$ by reversing the order of the digits of q around the decimal point. The inverse radix number function is:

$$\phi_R(q) = q_0 q_1 q_2 ... q_m$$
$$\phi_R(q) = q_0 R^{-1} + q_1 R^{-2} + \cdots + q_m R^{-m-1} \tag{7}$$

The Hammersley sequence of $n-$dimensional points is generated as

$$x_n(q) = \left(\frac{q}{N}, \phi_{R_1}(q), \phi_{R_2}(q), \ldots, \phi_{R_{n-1}}(q) \right) \tag{8}$$

where $q = 0, 1, 2, \ldots, N - 1$ and the values for $R_1, R_2, \ldots, R_{n-1}$ are the first $n - 1$ prime numbers $(2, 3, 5, 7, 11, 13, 17, \ldots)$. This algorithm generates a set of N points in the $n-$dimensional design space $[0, 1]^N$.

Fig. 2 shows the samples generated by a random and Hammersley algorithms over iris strip. Uniformity properties can be appreciated in a qualitative fashion. Hammersley points have better uniformity properties because the algorithm exhibits an optimal design for placing n points on a k-dimensional hypercube.

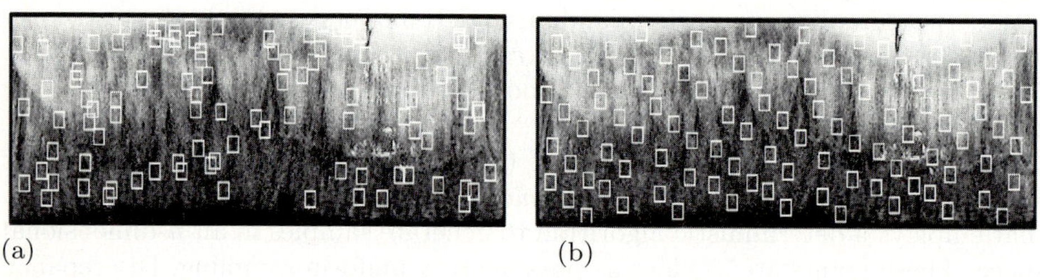

(a)   (b)

Fig. 2. Qualitative comparison of random (a) and Hammersley samplings (b), over an iris strip

2.4   Comparison and Matching

In our method, the iris features are represented by a set of accumulated histograms computed from sampled selected square subimages of iris strip. An accumulated histogram represents a feature and is built by using equation 4. The complete iris is represented by a set of accumulated histograms, one of them for every subimage. The optimal size of the number of features and subimage size, were determined empirically by experiments. A decision to accept or reject the iris sample is done according to the minimum Euclidean distance calculated from the comparison of iris sample and irises database, and also according to a threshold. Figure 3 shows the structure of this phase.

We can formalize the method as follows: Let I be an image, representing an iris strip, and $p \in I$ be a pixel and $\omega(p) \subset I$ be an square image patch of width S_f centered at p. We built iris features by forming a set of accumulated histograms with k bins, $P_m(i)$ $i = 1 \cdots k$, $m = 1 \cdots N_f$, from a set of N_f sampled patches

$$\{\Omega = \omega(p_1), \cdots, \omega(p_{Nf})\}.$$

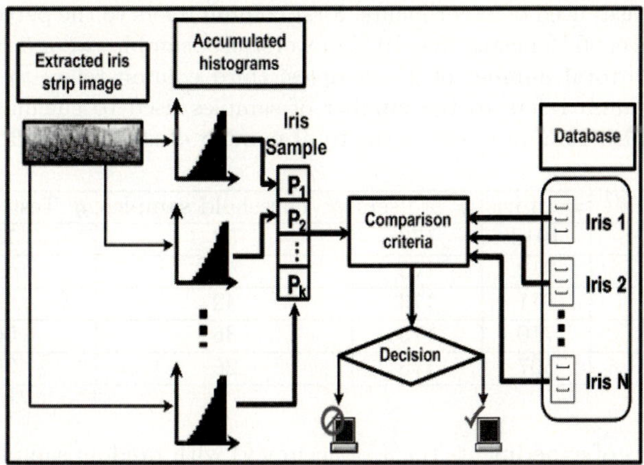

Fig. 3. The process of comparison and matching

The features of every iris in database are represented by a set of accumulated histograms $\{P_{DB_1}(i), P_{DB_2}(i), \cdots, P_{DB_{Nf}}(i)\}$.

An iris sample features set $\{P_{SMP_1}(i), P_{SMP_2}(i), \cdots, P_{SMP_{Nf}}(i)\}$ is compared against every iris features set in a database of size ℓ, according to the norm:

$$L = \min_n \sqrt{\sum_j \sum_i (P_{DB_j}(i) - P_{SMP_j}(i))^2} \tag{9}$$

with $n = 1 \cdots \ell$, $i = 1 \cdots k$, $j = 1 \cdots N_f$.

A decision to accept o reject the sample is taken based on the rule $L < \delta$, with δ being a threshold computed experimentally.

3 Experiments

Experiments were ran for UBIRIS database. Images with too much occlusion and noise were discarded, because the difficulty to locate the iris region with integro-differential operators. Then, our experimental database was built with 1013 samples coming from 173 users. With this database, we perform some experiments with 100 % of samples and others experiments where worst user samples were discarded. Table 1 shows the different databases used.

In table 2 the results of experiments from random sampling are shown. Every result is the average of 10 experiments performed. We can see that best results were obtained for cleaner databases. In table 3 the results of experiments from Hammersley sampling are shown. We can see that better results were obtained by using Hammersley sampling than for random sampling.

In Fig. 4 we can see the ROC curves for the different databases used in experiments with Hammersley sampling. databases with cleaner iris samples

Table 1. Databases used of experiments. First column refers to the percent of database used. For instance, 90 % means that 10 % of worst user samples were discarded. Second column refers to total number of iris samples, third column refers to the number of users, fourth column refers to the number of samples used to calculate the decision threshold, and fifth column refers to the total number of samples used for testing.

DB Size (%)	# of iris	# of users	# Threshold samples	# Test samples
100	1013	173	52	788
90	912	173	46	693
80	811	173	42	596
70	710	173	36	501
50	507	173	26	308

Table 2. Results of experiments (in % of accuracy) with random sampling, and different size (S_f) and number (N_f) of subimages

DB Size(%)	$N_f = 100$ $S_f = 5$	$N_f = 100$ $S_f = 15$	$N_f = 100$ $S_f = 25$	$N_f = 150$ $S_f = 5$	$N_f = 150$ $S_f = 15$	$N_f = 150$ $S_f = 25$	$N_f = 200$ $S_f = 5$	$N_f = 200$ $S_f = 15$	$N_f = 200$ $S_f = 25$
100	90.8	91.14	92.72	90.81	92.79	92.38	91.83	92.07	92.98
90	92.48	93.96	93.78	93.32	94.23	94.05	94.34	95.29	93.99
80	96.58	97.40	96.83	98.59	98.59	97.59	98.18	98.4	98.4
70	98.25	99.48	99.44	99.63	99.59	99.52	99.89	99.7	99.85
50	99.94	100.0	100.0	100.0	100.0	100.0	100.0	100.0	100.0

Table 3. Results of experiments (in % of accuracy) with Hammersley sampling, and different size (S_f) and number (N_f) of subimages. Highlighted results show the improvement over random sampling strategy.

DB Size(%)	$N_f = 100$ $S_f = 5$	$N_f = 100$ $S_f = 15$	$N_f = 100$ $S_f = 25$	$N_f = 150$ $S_f = 5$	$N_f = 150$ $S_f = 15$	$N_f = 150$ $S_f = 25$	$N_f = 200$ $S_f = 5$	$N_f = 200$ $S_f = 15$	$N_f = 200$ $S_f = 25$
100	90.47	92.12	93.14	90.48	93.0	93.64	92.12	92.76	93.64
90	92.56	93.85	94.42	94.29	94.64	94.42	94.21	95.07	94.37
80	97.87	98.72	98.34	98.84	99.0	98.5	99.09	99.13	98.31
70	99.48	99.85	99.52	99.85	99.74	99.59	99.96	100.0	99.85
50	100.0	100.0	100.0	100.0	100.0	100.0	100.0	100.0	100.0

reflects better results. In Fig. 5 we can see the distribution curves of accumulated histograms distance for two databases used in experiments with Hammersley sampling. The Overlapping between distribution curves ing Fig. 5 (b) leads to worst results.

4   Comparison to Previous Work

Daugman's system [2] has been tested thoroughly with databases containing thousands of samples, and reports of 100 % of accuracy have been given. In [10],

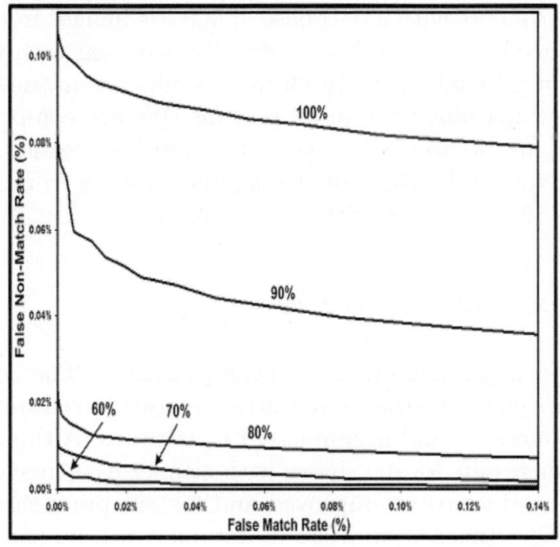

Fig. 4. Hammersley sampling ROC curve for different database sizes

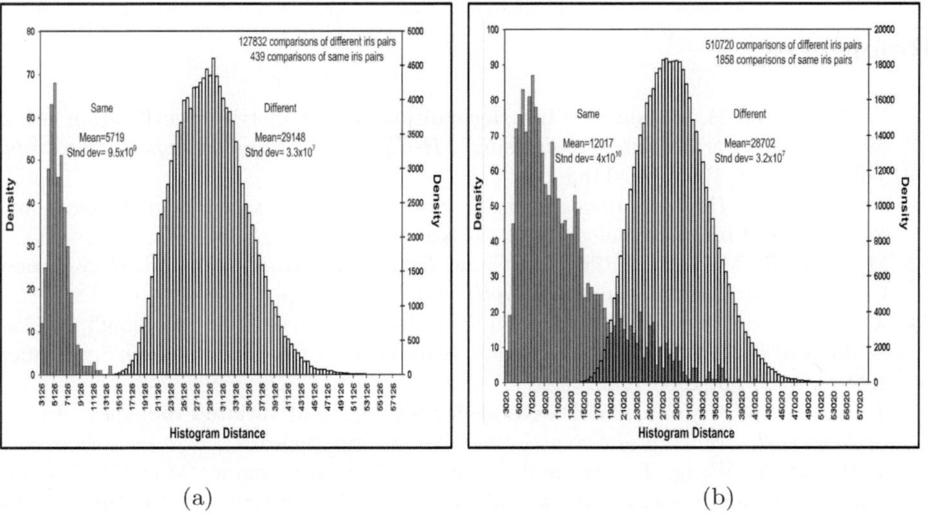

(a)   (b)

Fig. 5. Distribution of accumulated histograms distance (L), in Hammersley sampling, for 50 % database (a), and 100 % database (b)

the experimental results given are in the order of 97.9 %, by working with a database of 100 samples from 10 persons. Boles and Boashash [1] report best results in the order of 100 % but working with very small sets of images. Wildes [13] report results in the order of 100 % by working with a database of 600 samples coming from 40 individuals. In [9], a report is given about a performance of 99.09 % in experiments with a database of 500 iris images from 25 individuals. In [6] the results are between 98 % and 99 % by working with CASIA database (2255 samples from 213 subjects). In [3] best results are in the order of 99.05 % with a database of 384 images from 64 persons. We are competitive with most of the methods mentiond above. In comparison our best results, are in the order of 100 % working with a database of 308 samples coming from 173 persons, and in the order of 99 % and higher with 501 samples.

5   Conclusions and Future Works

A new approach for iris recognition has been presented. The novel contribution relies on the feature characterization of iris by the use of two sampling techniques, random and Hammersley, and accumulated histograms. Although experimental results show better results for databases with cleaner eyes images, we claim that our method will conduct to an improved and faster approach where just a few samples of subimages taken from irises in database will be necessary to discard most of them in a first step, and then concentrate the effort of comparison and matching in a very reduced set of iris samples. This potential approach will lead us to test bigger databases.

References

1. W. Boles and B. Boashash, "Iris Recognition for Biometric Identification using dyadic wavelet transform zero-crossing", *IEEE Transactions on Signal Processing*, Vol. 46, No. 4, 1998, pp. 1185-1188.
2. J. Daugman, "How Iris Recognition Works", *IEEE Transactions on Circuits and Systems for Video Technology*, Vol. 14, No. 1, 2004, pp. 21-30.
3. M. Dobes, L. Machala, P. Tichasvky, and J. Pospisil, "Human Eye Iris Recognition Using The Mutual Information", *Optik*, No. 9, 2004, pp. 399-404.
4. A. Efros, and T. Leung, "Texture Synthesis by Non-Parametric Sampling", in *Proceedings of the 7th IEEE International Conference on Computer Vision*, September 1999, Vol. 2, pp. 1033-1038.
5. J. Hammersley, "Monte Carlo Methods for Solving Multivariate Problems", *Annals of New York Academy of Science*, 1960, No. 86, pp. 844-874.
6. J. Huang, Y. Wang, T. Tan, and J. Cui, "A New Iris Segmentation Method for Iris Recognition System", In *Proceedings of the 17th International Conference on Pattern Recognition*, 2004, pp. 554-557.
7. A. Jain, A. Ross, A. Prabhakar, "An Introduction to Biometric Recognition", *IEEE Transactions on Circuits and Systems for Video Technology*, Vol. 14, No. 1, 2004, pp. 4-20.
8. L. Liang, C. Liu, Y. Xu, B. Guo, and H. Shum, "Real-time Texture Synthesis by Patch-based Sampling", *ACM Transactions on Graphics*, Vol. 20, No. 3, July 2001, pp. 127-150.
9. L. Ma, Y. Wang, T. Tan, and D. Zhang, "Personal Identification Based on Iris Texture Analysis", *IEEE Transactions on Pattern Analysis and Machine Intelligence*, Vol. 25, No. 12, 2003, pp. 1519 - 1533.

10. D. de Martin-Roche, C. Sanchez-Avila, and R. Sanchez-Reillo, "Iris Recognition for Biometric Identification using dyadic wavelet transform zero-crossing", In *Proceedings of the IEEE 35th International Conference on Security Technology*, 2001, pp. 272-277.
11. M. Negin, Chmielewski T., Salganicoff M., Camus T., Cahn U., Venetianer P., and Zhang G. "An Iris Biometric System for Public and Personal Use ", *Computer*, Vol. 33, No. 2, 2000, pp. 70-75.
12. H. Proenca, and L. Alexandre,"UBIRIS: A Noisy Iris Image Database", in *Proceedings of the International Conference on Image Analysis and Processing 2005*, Vol. 1, pp. 970-977.
13. R. Wildes, "Iris Recognition: An Emerging Biometric Technology", *Proceedings of the IEEE*, Vol. 85, No. 9, 1997, pp. 1348-1363.

Biometric-Iris Random Key Generator Using Generalized Regression Neural Networks

Luis E. Garza Castañón[1], MariCarmen Pérez Reigosa[1],
and Juan A. Nolazco-Flores[2]

[1] Department of Mechatronics and Automation, ITESM Monterrey Campus
`legarza@itesm.mx`
[2] Computer Science Department, ITESM Monterrey Campus
`jnolazco@itesm.mx`
Av. Eugenio Garza Sada Sur No. 2501
Monterrey, N.L. 64849 México

Abstract. In this work, we present a new approach to generate cryptographic keys from iris biometric. The main challenge of the general research is to find a suitable method to generate a cryptographic-iris-key every time the same iris information is analyzed, and this key should be different to the key generated for other users. Some problems to reach this goal are the imperfections that occurs in the biometric acquisition process, the features extraction selection and the matching algorithms. In our work, the key is calculated in four steps. First, the iris is located by use of the integrodifferential operators. Second, a set of features are computed by the use of Gabor filtering. Third, these features are divided in groups, depending on number of bits to be generated. In the final step, we generate a bit for each group of features by using a set of generalized regression neural net classifiers. We develop our experiments using a set of noisy images from the UBIRIS database, and the experimental results are very promising.

1   Introduction

The field of biometrics has received a lot of attention lately. Biometrics use physiological or behavioral characteristics unique to every individual. Examples of biometris includes: gait, DNA, ear, face, facial thermogram, hand thermogram, hand vein, fingerprint, hand shape, palmprint, signature, voice and iris [4]. From all biometrics mentioned before, iris has been proved to be reliable mainly due to specific characteristics such as a data-rich structure, genetic independence, stability over time and physical protection [3].

Biometrics can be used for person verification, person identification and for enabling cryptographic systems. When used for person verification, the persons biometric is known and the system requires the person to introduce his information to compare with the persons model. Person verification can be used for access control to restricted areas, such as airports or military installations, and public applications, such as banking operations [6]. When used for person identification, the person does not claim to be a person, but the system tries to

M. Ali and R. Dapoigny (Eds.): IEA/AIE 2006, LNAI 4031, pp. 530–539, 2006.
© Springer-Verlag Berlin Heidelberg 2006

identify who the person is. Person identification can be used in forensics. When used to enable cryptosytems, the biometric is used to generate random numbers needed to enable cryptographic systems, such as secure telephone calls, file storage, voice e-mail retrieval, digital signature, digital right management, etc. In this work we concentrate on the use of iris to generate these random numbers. The necessity of having a key which can not be forgotten, and that can be kept secure is one of the main goals of today key generation systems.

Although the incorporation of biometrics seems a natural step to improve security in user authentication systems, there are several challenges involved in combining biometrics and cryptographic systems. The reasons are the variations in the representations of a biometric identifier and the imperfect process of biometric feature extraction and matching algorithms [10]. These issues are translated to the generation of the correct and unique key for every user.

Related work to ours is given in [2], where a general framework for iris based user authentication is presented, although no experimental data are provided, which allow practical issues to be analyzed. In [5] an invariant key generation method based on a reference pattern and filters is proposed. To obtain invariance to the variant biometric data acquisition condition, Hamming distance data is converted to a regular form which is defined by a reference pattern. The reference pattern is designed as a lattice structured bit pattern. This work report results using False Reject Ratio in the order of 1 %, with a database of 50 users and 10 iris images per user.

In our work, the key are calculated in four steps. First, the iris is located by use of the integrodifferential operators. Second, a set of features are calculated by the use of Gabor filtering. Third, these features are divided in groups, depending on number of bits generated. In the final step, we generate a bit for each group of features by using the Generalized Regression Neural Net (GRNN) classifiers. Integrodifferential operators and Gabor filters are standard techniques used in automated iris recognition systems. Finally, the generation of the cryptographic keys is made by the use of a set of generalized regression neural net classifiers. The advantages of using GRNN classifiers is the short time to learn the model parameters and that they require just one tuning parameter. This work is organized as follows. In section 2, the architecture approach is described. In section 3, the experiments and results are described. In section 4 some comments and conclusions are given.

2   Architecture Approach

The architecture of our approach is shown in Fig. 1. The user eye image is preprocessed by histogram equalization, to compensate for illuminations variations. Next, we use integrodifferential operators to locate the iris region. The output of this step is a rectangular strip containing only the iris area. After this, we apply a bank of Gabor filters to extract relevant characteristics of iris. In this step, a set of Gabor coefficients are generated and translated to a matrix of features. This matrix is split in a set of vectors, which in turn are going to be used to train and test a set of neural network classifiers. Each classifier consists of a general regression neural network adapted for classification purposes. Every classifier will produce a binary key, and the complete cryptographic key will be formed by appending the keys generated by all the classifiers. The next sections will explain in more detail every step.

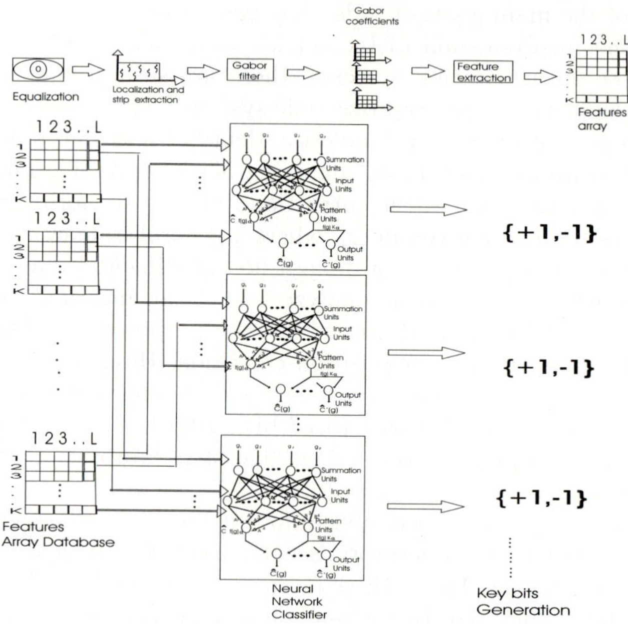

Fig. 1. Architecture of the iris based cryptographic system

2.1   Iris Localization

The finding of limbic and pupilar limits on the user eye image is achieved with the use of the integrodifferential operator shown in eqn 1.

$$\max_{(r, x_0, y_0)} = \left| \frac{\partial}{\partial r} H_\gamma(r) * \oint_{r, x_c, y_c} \frac{I(x, y)}{2\pi r} ds \right| \tag{1}$$

where $I(x, y)$ is an image containing the user eye.

The operator behaves as an iterative circular edge detector, and searches over the image domain (x, y) for the maximum in the partial derivative with respect to an increasing radius r, of the normalized contour integral of $I(x, y)$ along a circular arc ds of radius r and center coordinates (x_0, y_0). The symbol $*$ denotes convolution and $H_\gamma(r)$ is a smoothing function, typically a Gaussian of scale γ.

This operator behaves well in most cases with moderate noise conditions, but requires some fine tuning of parameters, in order to deal with pupil reflections, obscure eyes and excess of illumination. Heavy occlusion of iris by eyelashes or eyelids needs to be handled by other methods.

The extracted iris image has to be normalized to compensate for pupil dilation and contraction under illumination variations. This process is achieved by a transformation from cartesian to polar coordinates, using eqns 2 and 3. Where $x(r, \theta)$ and $y(r, \theta)$ are defined as a linear combination of pupil limits $(x_p(\theta),\ y_p(\theta))$ and limbic limits $(x_s(\theta),\ y_s(\theta))$. r is defined in the interval $[0, 1]$, and θ in the interval $[0, 2\pi]$.

$$x(r, \theta) = (1 - r)x_p(\theta) + rx_s(\theta) \tag{2}$$

$$y(r, \theta) = (1 - r)y_p(\theta) + ry_s(\theta) \tag{3}$$

The output of this transformation is a rectangular image strip. This strip is later enhanced by the application of an histogram equalization method.

2.2 Features Extraction

The user iris image is processed by a set of 2D Gabor filters, in order to generate a set of features. Gabor elementary functions are Gaussians modulated by sinusoidal functions. An important property of the family of the 2D Gabor filters family is their achievement of the theoretical lower bound of joint uncertainty in the domains of visual space and spatial frequency. This means that Gabor filters achieve the maximal possible joint resolution in the conjoint 2D visual space and 2D Fourier domains [1]. A 2D even Gabor filter can be represented by the following equation in the spatial domain:

$$G(x, y; \theta, \omega) = exp\left(-\frac{1}{2}\left[\frac{x'^2}{\delta_{x'}^2} + \frac{y'^2}{\delta_{y'}^2}\right]\right) cos(2\pi\,\omega\,x) \tag{4}$$

where
$$x' = x\,cos\theta + y\,sin\theta \tag{5}$$

$$y' = y\,cos\theta - x\,sin\theta \tag{6}$$

ω is the frequency of the sinusoidal plane wave along the direction θ from the x-axis, $\delta_{x'}$, and $\delta_{y'}$ are the space constants of the Gaussian envelope along x' and y' axes respectively.

The frequency parameter ω is often chosen to be a power of 2. In our experiments, the frequencies used are 2, 4, 8, 16, 32, and 64 cycles/degree. For each frequency ω, filtering is performed at $\theta = 0°$, $45°$, $90°$ and $135°$. So there are a total of 24 Gabor filters with different frequencies and directions. The output of this phase, for an image I of $N \times M$ pixels, is a set of 24 arrays, of complex coefficients $\{g_1, g_2, ..., g_{N \times M}\}$. We reduce the amount of data by dividing every array in square windows of size w and taking the average $\hat{g}$ of every window. For instance for iris images of size 720×200, a set of 3,456,000 Gabor coefficients are produced. With a window size of $w = 5$, the set of features is reduced to 138,240.

The set of features is split in feature vectors $\mathbf{F} = \{f_1, f_2, ..., f_K\}$, each of size L. From an image I of size $N \times M$, the number of feature vectors K is given by:

$$K = \frac{N \times M \times 24}{w^2 \times L} \tag{7}$$

This K features vectors of size L are used to train and test the GRNN classifiers. For every feature vector in the set $\mathbf{F} = \{f_1, f_2, ..., f_K\}$ with $f = \{\bar{g}_1, \bar{g}_2, ..., \bar{g}_L\}$, a GRNN classifier is trained to produce one unique binary key $C = +1$ or $C = -1$ for every user. That is, the ith GRNN classifier is trained and tested with the set of vectors composed by the ith feature vector of each user $\mathbf{\Phi}_i = \{f_i^1, f_i^2, ..., f_i^U\}$, where U is the number of users, $i = 1, 2, ..., K$, and K is the number of feature vectors. Then, the cryptographic key generated for the jth user is $\mathbf{C}^j = \{C_1^j, C_2^j, ..., C_K^j\}$, where $j = 1, 2, ..., U$.

2.3 General Regression Neural Network Classifier

We adapt a general regression neural network for classification purposes. An advantage of GRNNs is the fast learning time and that they require just one tuning parameter. The GRNN provides estimates of continuous variables and converges to the underlying (linear or nonlinear) regression surface [9].

Assume that $f(\mathbf{g}, c)$ represents the known joint continuous probability density function of a vector random variable $\mathbf{g}$, and a scalar random variable c. Let $\mathbf{G}$ be a measured value of random variable $\mathbf{g}$. The conditional mean of c given $\mathbf{G}$ is given by:

$$E[c|\mathbf{G}] = \frac{\int_{-\infty}^{\infty} c\, f(\mathbf{G}, c)\, dc}{\int_{-\infty}^{\infty} f(\mathbf{G}, c)\, dc} \tag{8}$$

when the density $f(\mathbf{g}, c)$ is not known, it must usually be estimated from a sample of observations of $\mathbf{g}$ and c. For a nonparametric estimate of $f(\mathbf{g}, c)$, a good choice is the class of consistent estimators proposed by Parzen. The probability estimator $\hat{f}(\mathbf{G}, C)$ is based upon sample values $\mathbf{G}^i$ and C^i of the random variables $\mathbf{g}$ and c, where n is the number of sample observations and p is the dimension of the vector variable $\mathbf{g}$:

$$\hat{f}(\mathbf{G}, C) = \frac{1}{(2\,\pi)^{(p+1)/2}\,\sigma^{(p+1)}} \cdot \frac{1}{n} \sum_{i=1}^{n} exp\left[-\frac{(\mathbf{G} - \mathbf{G}^i)^T (\mathbf{G} - \mathbf{G}^i)}{2\sigma^2}\right]$$

$$\cdot exp\left[-\frac{(C - C^i)^2}{2\sigma^2}\right] \tag{9}$$

The interpretation of the probability estimate $\hat{f}(\mathbf{G}, C)$ is that assigns sample probability of width σ for each sample $\mathbf{G}^i$ and C^i, and the probability estimate is the sum of those sample probabilities. The variable σ is a smoothing parameter that can be made large enough to smooth out noisy data, or small to allow estimated regression surface to be as nonlinear as is required to fit the observed values of C^i.

Combining the above two equations and performing the indicated integrations yields the following:

$$\hat{C}(\mathbf{G}) = \frac{\sum_{i=1}^{n} C^i \, exp\left(-\frac{D_i^2}{2\sigma^2}\right)}{\sum_{i=1}^{n} exp\left(-\frac{D_i^2}{2\sigma^2}\right)} \tag{10}$$

with the scalar function D_i^2

$$D_i^2 = (\mathbf{G} - \mathbf{G}^i)^T (\mathbf{G} - \mathbf{G}^i) \tag{11}$$

For some problems, the number of observations $(\mathbf{G}, C)$ may be small enough that is desired to use all the data obtainable directly in the above estimator. In other problems, the number of observations obtained can become sufficiently large that is no longer practical to assign a separate node to each sample. In this case various clustering techniques can be used to group samples so that the group can be represented by only one node that measures distance of inputs vectors from the cluster center. The above equation can be rewritten as:

$$\hat{C}(\mathbf{G}) = \frac{\sum_{i=1}^{m} A^i \, exp\left(-\frac{D_i^2}{2\sigma^2}\right)}{\sum_{i=1}^{m} B^i \, exp\left(-\frac{D_i^2}{2\sigma^2}\right)} \tag{12}$$

with

$$A^i(t) = A^i(t-1) + C^j \tag{13}$$

$$B^i(t) = A^i(t-1) + 1 \tag{14}$$

where $m < n$ is the number of clusters, and $A^i(t)$ and $B^i(t)$ are the values of the coefficients for cluster i after t observations. Fig. 2 shows the block diagram of a GRNN implementing eqn 12. The input units provide all of the input variables to the neurons on the second layer, the pattern units. The pattern unit is dedicated to one cluster center. When a new input vector is entered into network, it is subtracted from the stored vector representing each cluster center. The values of differences are summed and fed into a nonlinear activation function. The activation function normally used is the exponential. The pattern unit outputs are passed on to the summation units. The summation units perform a dot product between a weight vector and a vector composed of the signals from the pattern units, that is $f(\mathbf{G})\alpha$. α is a constant determined by the Parzen window used, but is not data dependent and does not need to be computed. The output unit merely divides $\hat{C}f(\mathbf{G})\alpha$ by $f(\mathbf{G})\alpha$ to yield the desired estimate of C.

We adapt the GRNN estimator for classification purposes in a simple manner. Before training, a random binary key is produced for every feature vector of every user. After this, Every GRNN estimator is trained to learn the correct key for every user. During testing, the estimation $\hat{C}$ given by each GRNN is converted to the closest binary class $C = \{+1, -1\}$.

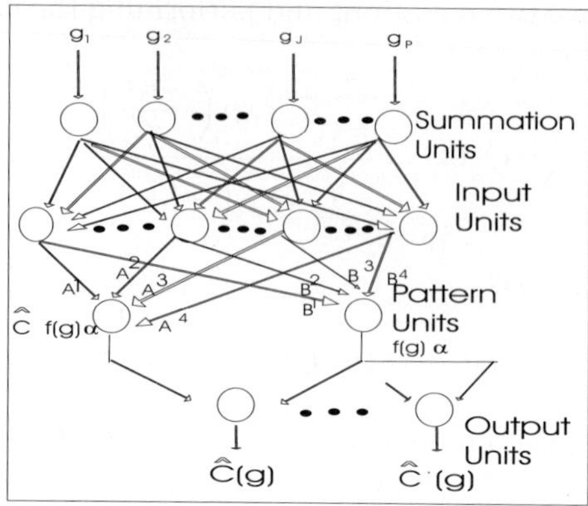

Fig. 2. A generalized regression neural network structure

3   Experiments and Results

In order to test our approach samples from UBIRIS database [8] were used. Our database contains three images from 100 different persons. Eyes images include 33 % of samples where iris is free from any occlusion, and 67 % of samples where iris shows moderate obstruction from eyelids and eyelashes and also noisy images with reflections and bad focusing, as is shown in Fig. 3.

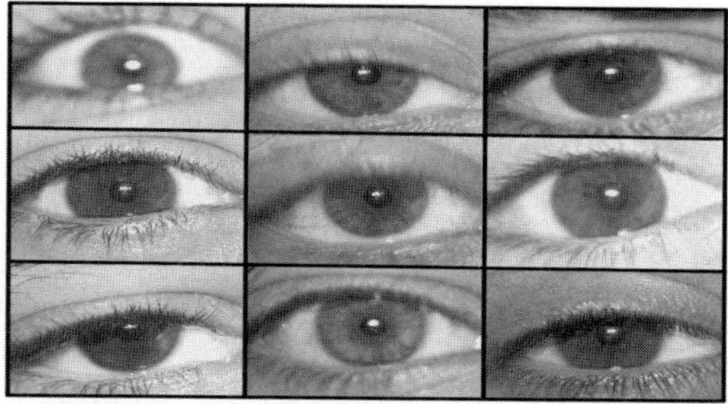

Fig. 3. Eyes samples with noise (moderate obstruction)

In this work two sets of Experiments were designed. In the first set of experiments one sample for each user was used to train the GRNN classifiers, and another sample to test the system. In a second set of experiments two samples for each user were used for training and another sample to test the system.

To measure the efficiency, we use the indexes η_1 and η_2. η_1 measures the percent of correct keys generated for all users. η_2 measures the percent of users to whom a complete correct key (of length=K) was generated. Tables 1 and 2 we show the best results obtained for these experiments From these experiments, we can conclude that η_1 is not highly affected by the number of users. On the other hand, we can also observe that η_2 is moderated affected by the number of users.

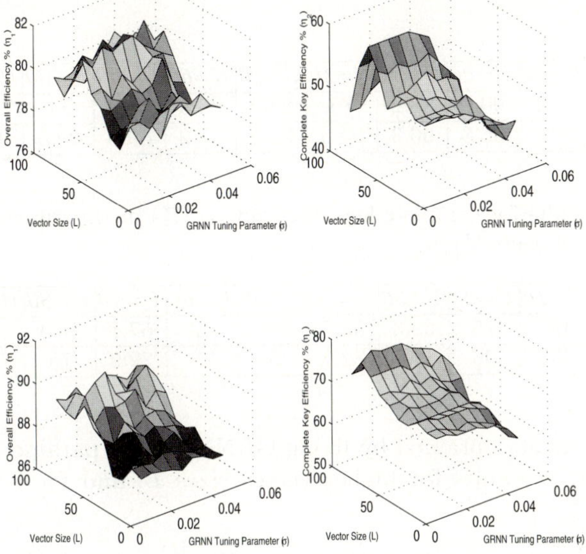

Fig. 4. Efficiency for $U = 100$ users with different features vector size L and grnn tuning parameter σ

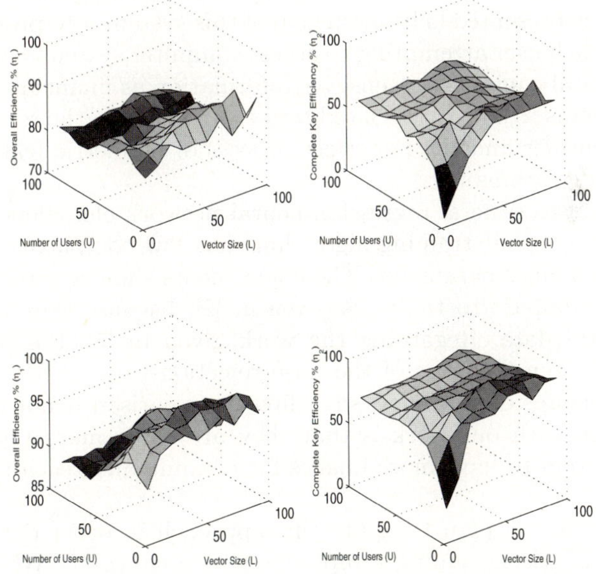

Fig. 5. Efficiency for $\sigma = 0.02$ with different number of users U and features vector size L

Fig. 4 shows the performance of our system for the whole set of users. Best results were obtained by using higher vector sizes (L), and seems to be not very sensitive to changes in the GRNN tuning parameter σ. In Fig. 5 we show the

Table 1. Best results for overall efficiency η_1 (%) in experiments 1 and 2, with different number of users U

Experiment	U=10	U=20	U=30	U=40	U=50	U=60	U=70	U=80	U=90	U=100
1	89.1	90.6	88.2	86	84.2	83.6	79.9	81	82.7	81.2
2	94.6	96.8	96.3	94.5	91.4	91.2	89.9	90.5	90.2	89.8

Table 2. Best results for complete key efficiency η_2 (%) in experiments 1 and 2, with different number of users U

Experiment	U=10	U=20	U=30	U=40	U=50	U=60	U=70	U=80	U=90	U=100
1	60	75	63.3	52.5	58	60	57.1	56.3	57.8	57
2	90	90	90	82.5	78	75	72.9	70	75.6	72

results of experiments obtained by fixing GRNN tuning parameter σ. Again we can observe better results for higher vectos sizes L, and for lower number of users U.

4   Conclusions and Future Works

In this work a Biometric-iris random key generator using generalized regression neural network is presented. The main goal of this system is to produce a random key unique for each user attempting to access computer system resources, such as copyrighted digital contents, or sensitive information as financial or health data. The main problems to solve are related to the variations in the representations of a biometric identifier and the imperfect process of biometric feature extraction and matching algorithms.

Our method uses general regression neural network classifiers, because they have the advantage that training algorithms has low complexity and also they just handle one tuning parameter. The experiments show acceptable results.

We can not compare to the work given in [2], because they do not provide any experimental data. Regarding the work given in [5], the performance of their system is given in terms of the false rejection ratio (FRR), while we are using other measures of efficiency, so a direct comparison is not possible. However a difference with our work is that they are using more images per user, allowing the system to have more images for training and reach higher levels of accuracy.

In future works, we plan to apply this approach in other databases with a higher number of users training samples as it is done in [5]. We are also planning to apply principal component analysis (PCA) or Independent Component Analysis (ICA) to our set of features. We want also to compare these results with other classification techniques such as back propagation Neural Networks, Support Vector Machines, and Bayesian networks.

References

1. D. Clausi and M. Jernigan, "Designing Gabor Filters for Optimal Texture Separability", *Pattern Recognition*, Vol. 33, 2000, pp. 1835-1849.
2. G. Davida, Y. Frankel, and B. Matt "On Enabling Secure Applications through Off-line Biometric Identification", *IEEE Symposium on Security and Privacy*, 1998, pp. 148-157.
3. J. Daugman, "How Iris Recognition Works", *IEEE Transactions on Circuits and Systems for Video Technology*, Vol. 14, No. 1, 2004, pp. 21-30.
4. A. Jain, A. Ross, A. Prabhakar, "An Introduction to Biometric Recognition", *IEEE Transactions on Circuits and Systems for Video Technology*, Vol. 14, No. 1, 2004, pp. 4-20.
5. H. Lee, S. Noh, K. Bae, K. park, and J. Kim "Invariant Biometric Code Extraction", in *Proceedings of the International Symposium on Intelligent Signal Processing and Communication Systems ISPACS 2004*, pp. 181-184
6. M. Negin, Chmielewski T., Salganicoff M., Camus T., Cahn U., Venetianer P., and Zhang G. "An Iris Biometric System for Public and Personal Use ", *Computer*, Vol. 33, No. 2, 2000, pp. 70-75.
7. L. O'Gorman, "Comparing Passwords, Tokens, and Biometrics for User Authentication", *Proceedings of the IEEE*, Vol. 91, No. 12, 2003, pp. 2021-2040.
8. H. Proenca, and L. Alexandre,"UBIRIS: A Noisy Iris Image Database", in *Proceedings of the International Conference on Image Analysis and Processing 2005*, Vol. 1, pp. 970-977.
9. D. Specht, "A General Regression Neural Network", *IEEE Transactions on Neural Networks*, Vol. 2, No. 6, November 1991, pp. 568-576.
10. U. Uludag, S. Pankanti, S. Prabhakar, and A. Jain "Biometric Cryptosystems: Issues and Challenges", *Proceedings of the IEEE* , Vol. 92, No. 6, 2004, pp. 948-960.

Head Detection and Tracking for the Car Occupant's Pose Recognition

Jeong-Eom Lee[1], Yong-Guk Kim[3], Sang-Jun Kim[1,2], Min-Soo Jang[1],
Seok-Joo Lee[4], Min Chul Park[5], and Gwi-Tae Park[1,*]

[1] Dept. of Electrical Engineering,
[2] Interdisciplinary Programs of Mechatronics,
Korea University, Seoul, Korea
*gtpark@korea.ac.krT
[3] School of Computer Engineering, Sejong University, Seoul, Korea
ykim@sejong.ac.krT
[4] Hyundai Autonet Co. Ltd., Korea
[5] Systems Technology Division, KIST, Korea

Abstract. This paper describes a Vision-based Occupant Pose Recognition (VOPR) system, which can ensure a safe airbag deployment. Head detection and its tracking are necessary for occupant's pose recognition in the car, since the position of occupant's head provides valuable information, such as his pose, size, position, and so on. We use the stereo cameras to extract a disparity map. Against variable lighting conditions including the night drive, we adopt infrared illumination as well as normal one. Results suggest that VOPR system is reliable and performs reasonably well.

1 Introduction

Airbags have played an important role for automotive safety. Although airbags have saved many lives, wrong deployment of them can lead to a fatal injury. Recently, National Highway Traffic Safety Administration (NHTSA) has amended Federal Motor Vehicle Safety Standard (FMVSS) No. 208, asking to install some smart airbags in the cars. This law aims to improve protection of the occupants for different height and weight, regardless of whether they use their seat belts, while minimizing the risk to infants, children, and other occupants of deaths and injuries caused by airbags [1]. In fact, risk to out-of-position occupants has been reduced, since various occupant sensing technologies are adopted into vehicle occupant protection systems by major automakers and suppliers [10]. But to improve safety inside the car, it is necessary to develop more reliable methods. In this study, we present a vision-based technology that enables to capture diverse information about occupant such as class, pose, distance from occupant to the dash board.

Several researchers have studied vision-based technology and proposed algorithms that can classify the occupant and control intensity of airbag deployment according to class, posture of occupant [6, 7, 8, 9]. In this paper, we particularly focus on head

M. Ali and R. Dapoigny (Eds.): IEA/AIE 2006, LNAI 4031, pp. 540–547, 2006.

detection and tracking method for the occupant's pose recognition to ensure safe airbag deployments. Detecting the head is relatively easier than other human body and its position provides valuable information about the occupant, such as pose, size, position, and so on. So, measuring the accurate position of occupant's head is critical for the smart airbag system. Our system for pose recognition consists of three parts: head detection, head tracking and head localization. The head detection is based on motion information and uses contour models and support vector machines (SVM) classifier [2]. The head tracking is based on edge information and use template matching. As the position of the detected or tracked head provides only 2-D information, we use 3-D disparity information extracted from the stereo images for head localization.

Section 2 of this paper provides more details of head detection and tracking method. And section 2 also describes how the position of the head on the image coordinates (2-D coordinate) is transformed into a camera coordinate (3-D coordinate). Result of experiments is described in section 3. Finally, we summarize our results and discuss the performance of the whole system in section 4.

2 Vision-Based Occupant Pose Recognition (VOPR) System

Our VOPR system consists of three parts: head detection, tracking and localization part. For the head detection and tracking in a car environment, several methods based on motion and color information are proposed [6, 7, 8, 9]. Considering diverse illumination condition within the car, it is difficult to take advantage of the color information. Moreover, since the infrared illumination is utilized to capture the occupant in the night, our method is based upon using only the grey image.

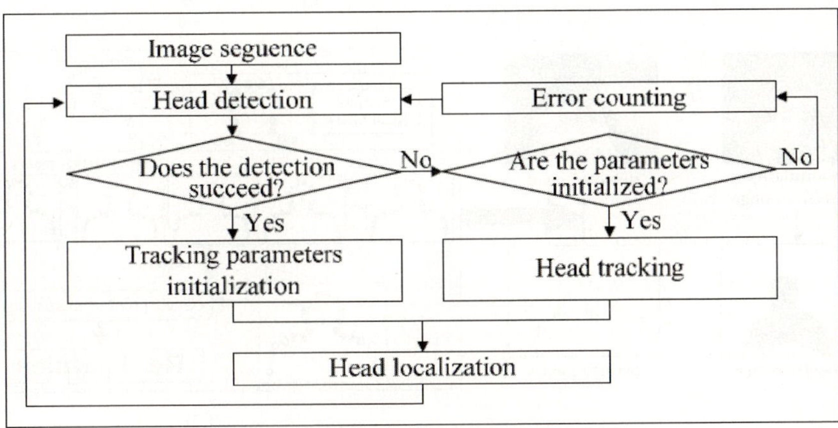

Fig. 1. A block diagram of the pose recognition system architecture

Difference images from the motion information are used for the head detection task and then, accurate head position is obtained by applying contour models and consequently an SVM classifier. However, when the occupant's motion is not significant, it is difficult to detect the head. On the other hand, head tracking works pretty well in such

case if parameters for head tracking have been initialized. Therefore, head detection and tracking should be used in complementary ways. **Fig. 1** shows a schematic diagram of our VOPR system architecture. In this figure, an error means that VOPR system is not initialized or it doesn't work. It is just prepared against the extremeness cases.

And the position of the detected or tracked head doesn't present a real position in the car since the detection and tracking are carried out only on 2-D image of a left charge coupled device (CCD) camera. By combining them with stereo information, we can obtain 3-D information of the occupant's head and then can control triggering and intensity of the air bag deployments.

The following sections describe the details of the head detection, head tracking and head localization.

2.1 Head Detection

This paper augments our previous work [15] which used head-shoulder contour model and support vector machines (SVM) classifier for head detection. In this previous paper, to get motion information, we first make an accumulative difference image of sequential images from the single camera. And a silhouette image is obtained after applying binary morphological operations. And then, feature points to consist of a contour are extracted from silhouette. These points are used as input for the SVM classifier. The public domain implementation of SVM, called LibSVM, was used for this study [3]. The head-shoulder contour model can be derived from the feature points and describe the shape of occupant's head, regardless of the orientation of the occupant's face. A procedure of head detection is depicted in **Fig. 2**.

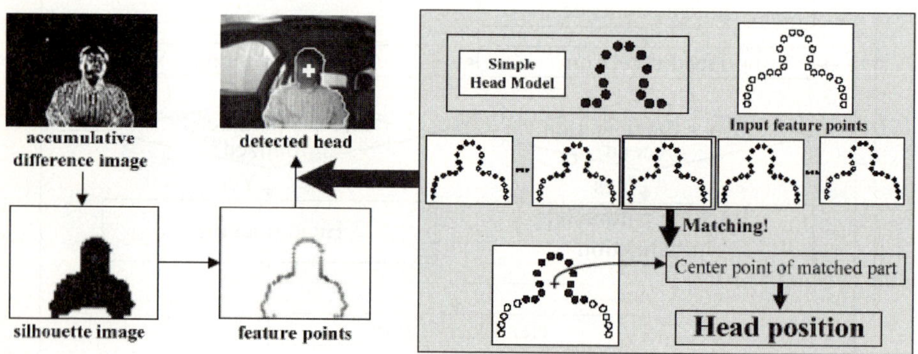

Fig. 2. A procedure of Head detection

2.2 Head Tracking

Our head tracking algorithm consists of two parts: initialization part and tracking part as shown in **Fig. 3**. In the first part, initial searching area for the template model is set up by using the position of the detected head. In the second part, a Ω shaped template is fitted to the head area and then updates the searching area.

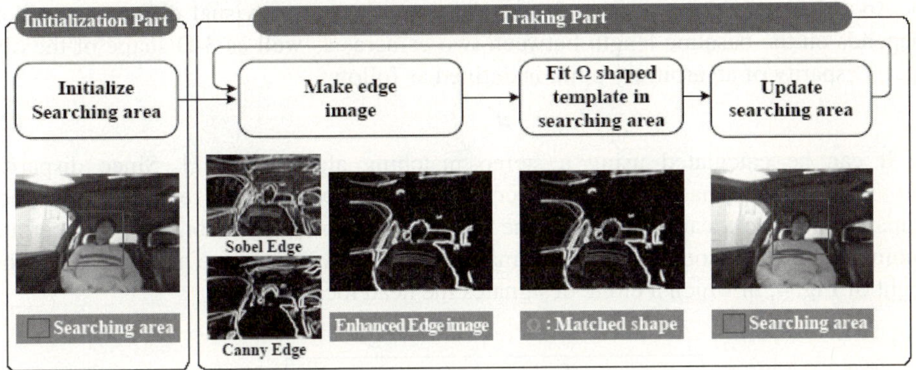

Fig. 3. A procedure of Head tracking

Here, the head tracking algorithm is based on edge method to improve computational efficiency. As shown **Fig. 3**, the edge detector is a combination of the *Sobel* [5] and the *Canny* operation [14]. In such way, we can obtain an edge image which contains the fine details around occupant's head and yet removes unwanted edge fragments. As a result, the enhanced edge image has only gray level which is similar to skin color.

The next step is to fit a model to the enhanced edge image. The model adopted here is a Ω-shaped model proposed in [12]. In fact, the Ω-shaped model is very similar to the head-shoulder contour model. The goal of such fitting is to find the most similar part by modifying scale and translation parameters. Namely, a matched template is adjusted to maximize a value between the Ω-shaped model and the edge image within the searching area. Such value can be calculated by using an equation:

$$f(I) = \sum_{x,y \in T_O} |I(x,y)| + \sum_{x,y \in T_I} |255 - I(x,y)|$$

(1)

$\mathbf{T}_O$: *a set of pixels on template,* $\mathbf{T}_I$: *a set of pixels on interior of template*

Here, $f(I)$ is increased when pixels on a boundary of template are close to white value and pixels within the template are close to black value. After the matched template is found, a center of the searching area is changed into a center of the matched template and its size is updated in proportion to the size of the matched template.

2.3 Head Localization

In this section, we describe how real position of the occupant's head can be obtained from the detected (or tracked) head. As stated in section 2.1 and 2.2, the position of the detected head is the central point of head-shoulder contour model or Ω-shaped model. Although the head detection and tracking method gives us useful information on the present position of the occupant's head, it doesn't provide 3-D pose information of the head, since the detection and tracking are carried out only on 2-D image. In the present study, we aim to combine the head detection with stereo information to acquire the pose information of the occupant within the car.

An object seen from a pair of stereo cameras leads to a visual difference, which depends on the baseline length between two cameras as well as 3-D shape of the object. Disparity of an arbitrary point is defined as follow:

$$d = u - u'$$
(2)

It can be calculated using a stereo matching algorithm [11]. Since disparity provides 3-D information of the object [6], we can recognize the real position of occupant's head in a car. To display the location that the head belongs to at a certain moment, a camera coordinate can be marked on a top-view picture as illustrate on the right of **Fig. 4**, in which a circle designates the head location.

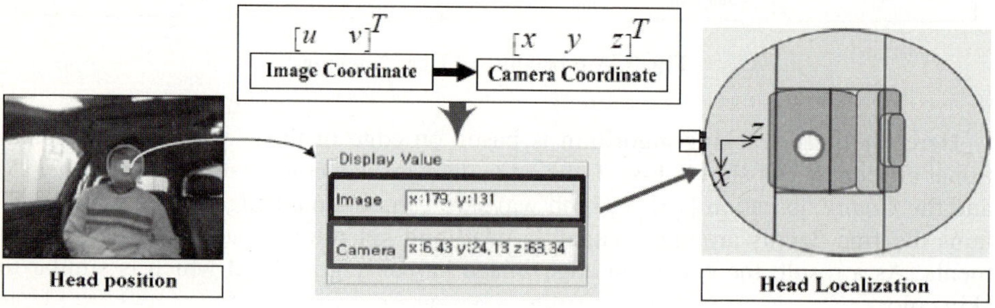

Fig. 4. Head localization

3   Results

3.1   Video Database for Test

The performance of the VOPR system is evaluated with our video database, which consists of sequential image sets captured within a car at 15fps (frame per second). **Table 1** shows the image database adopted in this study. In order to include the night drive case, we also took the infrared images for Image Sequence III and Image Sequence IV.

Table 1. The video database (unit:frame)

	Number of frame	Remark
Image Sequence I	235	•
Image Sequence II	212	•
Image Sequence III	122	Infrared
Image Sequence IV	196	Infrared
Total	765	

3.2 Performance of the Algorithm

In real-time demo, the head indicated as a circle drifts around different areas as the occupant move his head and body around the seat. However, the experiments were carried out with an off-line basis for four different video databases. We only counted it as a correct image frame when the system is able to assign the occupant's head position to the ground-truth among those 6 areas (see **Fig. 4**). Since the tolerance of the error was 7.5 cm that is radius of the typical human head, any image frames having an error larger than this tolerance are counted as the incorrect frames. **Table 2** summarizes the result of the analysis. **Fig. 5** shows graphs for the trial error, where the error is varied as the frame goes by time.

Table 2. Experimental Result (unit: frame)

	Video frames	Correct frames	Incorrect frames	Success rate
Image Sequence I	235	218	17	92.8%
Image Sequence II	212	180	32	84.9%
Image Sequence III	122	109	13	89.3%
Image Sequence IV	196	163	33	83.2%
Total	765	670	95	87.6%

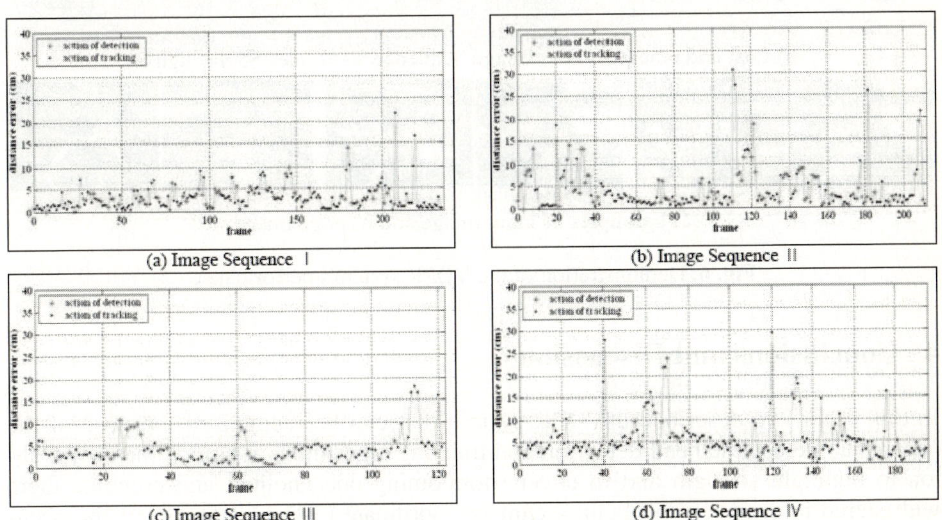

(a) Image Sequence I

(b) Image Sequence II

(c) Image Sequence III

(d) Image Sequence IV

Fig. 5. Graphs for the trial errors

As showed in **Table 2**, the total success rate of our system was 87.6%. Spikes in **Fig. 5** indicate false positives that are happened by wrong detection. However, you can observe that such spikes are corrected within a few frames. Besides, occlusion is the cause of errors. Although detection or tracking is accurate in 2-D images, occlusion caused errors when the image coordinates (2-D coordinate) is transformed into the camera coordinate (3-D coordinate). When the occupant's head is located closely to camera, a few pixel differences in 2-D images bring about wide differences in camera coordinate. This is the reason why errors occurred from 20th to 40th frames for Image Sequence Ⅱ. Demonstration of the VOPR system is shown in **Fig. 6**. **Fig. 6**(a) shows some errors caused by occlusion. **Fig. 6**(b) shows ability to re-acquire the subject by head detection when the occupant returned to the camera's field of view. **Fig. 6**(c) is some examples of edge images obtained from input images.

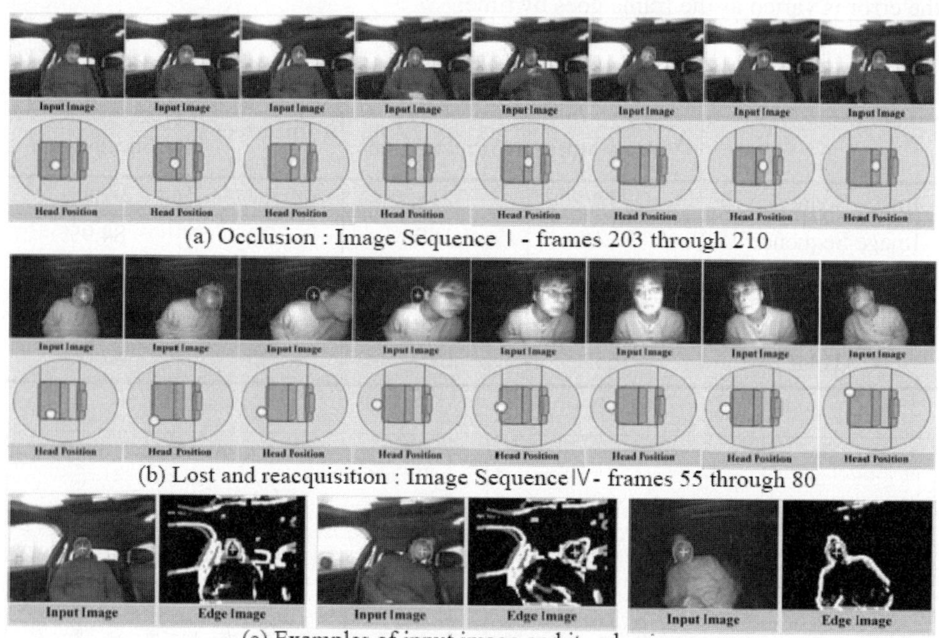

(a) Occlusion : Image Sequence Ⅰ - frames 203 through 210

(b) Lost and reacquisition : Image Sequence Ⅳ - frames 55 through 80

(c) Examples of input image and its edge image

Fig. 6. Demonstration of the VOPR system's performance

4 Conclusions and Discussion

In this paper, we described a VOPR system that can be recognized the pose of the occupant. We use the head detection and tracking algorithms in complementary fashion to highlight strength and to cover shortcoming one another, and combine them with stereo information to obtain a camera coordinate (3-D coordinate) of the occupant's head position. The disparity of the occupant's head position is calculated from the stereo image captured using a stereo camera. Because of computation time, the stereo matching algorithm is performed in the determined region. We plan to carry out such intensive computation using a specialized hardware such as FPGA. Our VOPR system just consists of two CCD cameras and infrared illumination. In video databases for test, the VOPR system successfully found the occupant's head and maintained appropriate performance. Experimental result confirms that our system is feasible and the performance is satisfactory. In the future, we will work on adding prediction scheme to solve problems caused by occlusion and false positives.

References

1. http://www.nhtsa.dot.gov
2. V. Vapnik, "The Nature of Statistical Learning Theory," Springer-Verlag, NY, USA, 1995
3. http://www.csie.ntu.edu.tw/~cjlin/libsvm/index.html
4. A. Blake and M. Isard, "Active Contours," Springer-Verlag, London, 1998
5. G. Baxes, "Digital Image Processing: principles and applications," John Wiley & Sons, New York, USA, 1994
6. Marcus Klomark, "Occupant Detection using computer vision," master's thesis, 2000
7. Y. Owechkp, N. Srinivasa, S. Medasani, and R. Boscolo, "Vision-Based Fusion System for Smart Airbag Applications," IEEE, Intelligent Vehicle Symposium, vol. 1, pp. 245-250, 2002
8. B. Alefs, M. Clabian, H. Bischof, W. Kropatsh, and F. Khairallah, "Robust Occupancy Detection from Stereo Images," IEEE Intelligent Transportation Systems Conference, 2004
9. M. M. Trivedi, S. Cheng, E. Childers, S. Krotosky, "Occupant Posture Analysis with Stereo and Thermal Infrared Video: Algorithms and Experimental Evaluation," IEEE Transactions on Vehicular Tech. Special Issue on In-Vehicle Vision Systems, Volume: 53, Issue: 6, 2004
10. L. Zhang, L. Chen, A. Vertiz, and R. Balci, "Survey of Front Passenger Posture Usage in Passenger Vehicles," 2004 SAE World Congress, 2004
11. C. Sun, "A Fast Stereo Matching Method," Digital Image Computing: Techniques and Applications, pp.95-100, 1997
12. R. Patil, P. E. Rybski, T. Kanade, and M. M. Veloso, "People Detection and Tracking in High Resolution Panoramic Video Mosaic," IEEE/RSJ International Conference on Intelligent Robots and Systems(IROS 2004), vol. 1, pp. 1323-1328, 2004
13. S. Birchfield, "Elliptical Head Tracking Using Intensity Gradients and Color Histograms," IEEE Conference on Computer Vision and Pattern Recognition, pp. 232-237, June 1998
14. J. Canny, "A Computational Approach to Edge Detection," IEEE Trans. On Pattern Analysis and Machine Intelligence, vol. 8, pp. 679-698, 1986
15. YG Kim, JE Lee, SJ Kim, SM Choi, and GT Park, "Head Detection of the Car Occupant based on Contour Models and Support Vector Machines," LNAI, Vol. 3533, pp. 59-61, 2005

Prediction of Construction Litigation Outcome
– A Case-Based Reasoning Approach

K.W. Chau

Department of Civil and Structural Engineering, Hong Kong Polytechnic University,
Hunghom, Kowloon, Hong Kong
cekwchau@polyu.edu.hk

Abstract. Since construction claims are normally affected by a large number of complex and interrelated factors, it will be advantageous to the parties to a dispute to know with some certainty how the case would be resolved if it were taken to court. The application of recent artificial intelligence technologies can be cost-effective in this problem domain. In this paper, a case-based reasoning (CBR) approach is adopted to predict the outcome of construction claims, on the basis of characteristics of cases and the corresponding past court decisions. The approach is demonstrated to be feasible and effective by predicting the outcome of construction claims in Hong Kong in the last 10 years. The results show that the CBR system is able to give a successful prediction rate higher than 80%. With this, the parties would be more prudent in pursuing litigation and hence the number of disputes could be reduced significantly.

1   Introduction

The construction industry is inherently prone to litigation since claims are normally affected by a large number of complex and interrelated factors. The disagreement between the involving parties can arise from interpretation of the contract, unforeseen site conditions, variation orders by the client, acceleration and suspension of works, and so on. The main forums for the resolution of construction disputes are mediation, arbitration, and the courts [1]. However, the consequence of any disagreements between the client and the contractor may be far reaching. It may lead to damage to the reputation of both sides, as well as inefficient use of resources and higher costs for both parties through settlement. The litigation process is usually very expensive since it involves specialized and complex issues. Thus, it is the interest of all the involving parties to minimize or even avoid the likelihood of litigation through conscientious management procedure and concerted effort.

It will be advantageous to the parties to a dispute to know with some certainty how the case would be resolved if it were taken to court. This would effectively help to significantly reduce the number of disputes that would need to be settled by the much more expensive litigation process. The use of artificial intelligence (AI) technologies can be cost-effective in the prediction of outcomes of construction claims, on the basis of characteristics of cases and the corresponding past court decisions. Some of these AI techniques have been used to identify the hidden relationships among various interrelated factors and to mimic decisions that were made by the court [2-3].

M. Ali and R. Dapoigny (Eds.): IEA/AIE 2006, LNAI 4031, pp. 548–553, 2006.

In this paper, a case-based reasoning (CBR) approach is employed for prediction of the outcome of construction litigation in Hong Kong, on the basis of characteristics of real cases and court decisions in the last 10 years. The focus of the present study is on the codification of simulation results and the assessment of the assumptions which have been used to evaluate the interaction of factors determining the litigation outcomes.

2 Nature of Construction Disputes

The nature of construction activities is varying and dynamic, which can be evidenced by the fact that no two sites are exactly the same. Thus the preparation of the construction contract can be recognized as the formulation of risk allocation amongst the involving parties: the client, the contractor, and the engineer. The risks involved include the time of completion, the final cost, the quality of the works, inflation, inclement weather, shortage of materials, shortage of plants, labor problems, unforeseen ground conditions, site instructions, variation orders, client-initiated changes, engineer-initiated changes, errors and omissions in drawings, mistakes in specifications, defects in works, accidents, supplier delivery failure, delay of schedule by subcontractor, poor workmanship, delayed payment, changes in regulations, third-party interference, professional negligence, and so on.

Prior to the actual construction process, the involving parties will attempt to sort out the conditions for claims and disputes through the contract documents. However, since a project usually involves thousands of separate pieces of work items to be integrated together to constitute a complete functioning structure, the potential for honest misunderstanding is extremely high. The legislation now in force requires that any disputes incurred have to be resolve successively by mediation, arbitration, and the courts.

3 Case-Based Reasoning (CBR)

CBR is the essence of human reasoning on the basis of experience, through the development of a case-memory representation of previously solved problems [4-8]. It utilizes the specific knowledge of previously experienced and concrete problem situations, which are termed cases. By searching for and reusing a similar past case, a new problem can be solved. Moreover, it represents an incremental and sustained learning since the retention of a new experience in the problem-solving process will enrich the case base for future usage. CBR has various advantages over alternative AI techniques, such as artificial neural network and knowledge-based system, for this particular domain problem in that similar reasoning process is exercised in practice. Whilst construction litigation is resolved principally by the interpretation of the law and the reference to legal precedents, CBR retrieves similar past cases for the solution of the new problems.

CBR comprises principally four steps: (1) retrieving past cases that resemble the existing problem; (2) adapting past solutions to the target situation; (3) applying these adapted solutions and evaluating the results; and (4) modifying and updating the case

Table 1. Definition of input features

Feature Name	List of alternatives				
Type of contract	Remeasure-ment	Lump sum	Design and build		
Contract value	Low	Medium	High		
Parties involved	Client	Contract-or	Sub-contractor	Engineer	Supplier
Plaintiff	Client	Contract-or	Sub-contractor	Engineer	Supplier
Defendant	Client	Contract-or	Sub-contractor	Engineer	Supplier
Resolution technique used	Yes	No			
Interpretation of documents	Yes	No			
Misrepresentat-ion of site	Yes	No			
Radical change in scope	Yes	No			
Directed changes	Yes	No			
Constructive changes	Yes	No			
Liquidated damages	Yes	No			
Late payment	Yes	No			

base. One of the key functions is the similarity measurement in the comparison between a pairs of features from the target case and the past cases.

3.1 Case Retrieval

The case base is first developed based on the past cases. Cases are then retrieved from the case base in similar future situations, together with the corresponding similarity score. For a CBR system, the speed and accuracy in retrieving pertinent cases are determined largely by case indexing, which is related to the appropriate type of feature matching as well as a suitable type of similarity assessment.

3.2 Feature Matching

Feature matching represents the requirement on the rigorousness of the match between the features of the target cases and their counterparts in the case base. Different matching alternatives should be used for different types of features. In this study, exact matching, which is appropriate for the "one of a list" or "yes or no" types, is used for all features.

3.3 Similarity Score Evaluation

Two methods are adopted in the similarity assessment of this study, namely, an inductive reasoning indexing method and a manual adaptation method.

By employing the inductive reasoning indexing method, a complex decision tree, which comprises tree branches representing all the feature alternatives, is built according to the input cases. The tree generated is then used to determine weights for the features. A similarity score is then assigned to all the cases that are retrieved from the case base. The score, representing the overall similarity measurement of all features, is used to rank these cases. The outcome of the retrieved highest-scoring case is selected to be the predictor. A key advantage of this method is its ability to analyze the cases automatically, objectively and speedily. The difficult task to determine the weights of various features does not need to be borne by the analysts. However, it requires a sufficient amount of cases in order to generate accurate results [9].

In the manual adaptation method, the weights of the features are specified by the experts after a comprehensive study and iterative trials with different priorities on these features. A similarity score is also determined, yet by manual method. The demanding nature of the task to make good and subjective decisions on the weightings is noted. In this method, the inductive reasoning indexing method is used as a preparation and guideline, rather than virtually from scratch.

3.4 Case Base Updating

The predicted case is then added to enrich the representation of the case base, which will be useful for further prediction. The constant update of the case base is essential for the real application of a system to retrieve a past case and adapt it to the needs of a new problem as time arises. This will facilitate the retrieval process which begins with the search engine selecting from the system's case base only those cases which have comparable similarity score for the target problem in hand.

4 The Study

The system is applied to study and predict the outcome of construction claims in Hong Kong. The data from 1991 to 2000 are organized case by case and the dispute characteristics and court decisions are correlated. Through a sensitivity analysis, 13 case elements that seem relevant in courts' decisions are identified. They are, namely, type of contract, contract value, parties involved, type of plaintiff, type of defendant, resolution technique involved, legal interpretation of contract documents, misrepresentation of site, radical changes in scope, directed changes, constructive changes, liquidated damages involved, and late payment.

All the 13 case elements can be expressed using "one of a list" or "yes or no" format. For example, 'type of contract' could be remeasurement contract, lump sum contract, or design and build contract. Table 1 shows the definition of input features in this case base. The outcome of court decisions is organized as an output feature from a list of 5 alternatives: client, contractor, engineer, sub-contractor, and supplier.

In total, 1105 sets of construction-related cases were available, of which 825 from years 1991 to 1997 were used for building the case base, and 280 from years 1998 to 2000 were used for testing.

Tests are performed to reduce the number of features used in the research. Two sets of input features are employed to experiment with various similarity assessment methods to test the rate of prediction of the system. Apart from the complete set of 13 input features, a restricted set of 10 input features is tried. Table 2 shows the comparison of prediction results by different methods.

Table 2. Comparison of prediction results with different methods

Method of similarity assessment	Complete set of features		Restricted set of features	
	Coefficient of correlation	Prediction rate	Coefficient of correlation	Prediction rate
Inductive reasoning indexing	0.969	0.77	0.964	0.72
Manual adaptation	0.987	0.84	0.979	0.81

5   Results and Discussions

Table 2 shows comparison of the prediction results with different methods of similarity assessments against complete or restricted set of features. The prediction rate of the inductive reasoning indexing method of similarity assessment for the complete set of features is 0.77 and the coefficient of correlation is 0.969 whilst, for the restricted set of features, the corresponding values are 0.72 and 0.964, respectively. When the manual adaptation of similarity assessment is used for the complete set of features, the prediction rate is 0.84 and the coefficient of correlation is 0.969. For the restricted set of features, the corresponding values are 0.81 and 0.979, respectively. The best prediction is obtained by using the manual adaptation of similarity assessment for the complete set of features. It can be seen that employing inductive reasoning indexing method as a preparation for manual adaptation is rather preferable. Moreover, better prediction results are in general attained with the complete set of features than those with the restricted set of features.

It is noted that the CBR is able to give a successful prediction rate of higher than 80%, which is much higher than by pure chance. It is believed that, if the involving parties to a construction dispute become aware with some certainty how the case would be resolved if it were taken to court, the number of disputes could be reduced significantly.

6   Conclusions

This paper presents a CBR approach for prediction of outcomes of construction litigation on the basis of the characteristics of the individual dispute and the corresponding past court decisions. Comparison is made of the prediction results with different methods of similarity assessments against complete or restricted set of features. Amongst various methods that are tried, the best prediction is obtained by using the manual adaptation of similarity assessment for the complete set of features. Moreover, better prediction results are in general attained with the complete set of features than those with the restricted set of features. It is demonstrated that the novel approach, which is able to provide model-free estimates in deducing the output from the input, is an appropriate prediction tool. The method presented in this study is recommended as an approximate prediction tool for the parties in dispute, since the rate of prediction is higher than 80%, which is much higher than chance. It is, of course, recognized that there are limitations in the assumptions used in this study. Other factors that may have certain bearing such as cultural, psychological, social, environmental, and political factors have not been considered here. Nevertheless, this initial study shows that it is worthwhile pursuing this method further for more detailed investigation on its effectiveness and capability.

References

1. Chau, K.W.: Resolving Construction Disputes by Mediation: Hong Kong Experience. Journal of Management in Engineering, ASCE **8(4)** (1992) 384-393
2. Arditi, D., Oksay, F.E., Tokdemir, O.B.: Predicting the Outcome of Construction Litigation Using Neural Networks. Computer-Aided Civil and Infrastructure Engineering **13(2)** (1998) 75-81
3. Chau, K.W.: Predicting Construction Litigation Outcome using Particle Swarm Optimization. Lecture Notes in Artificial Intelligence **3533** (2005) 571-578
4. Barletta, R.: An Introduction to Case-Based Reasoning. AI Expert **6(8)** (1991) 42-49
5. Kolodner, J.L.: An Introduction to Case-Based Reasoning. Artificial Intelligence Review **6(1)** (1992) 3-34
6. Aamodt, A., Plaza, E.: Case-Based Reasoning: Foundational Issues, Methodological Variations, and System Approaches. AICOM **7(1)** (1994) 39-59
7. Gupta, U.G.: How Case-Based Reasoning solves New Problems. Interfaces **24(6)** (1994) 110-119
8. Watson, I., Marir, F.: Case-Based Reasoning: A Review. The Knowledge Engineering Review **9(4)** (1994) 327-354
9. Quinlan, J.R.: Induction of Decision Trees. Machine Learning **1(1)** (1986) 81-106

Component Retrieval Using
Knowledge-Intensive Conversational CBR

Mingyang Gu and Ketil Bø

Department of Computer and Information Science, Norwegian University of Science
and Technology, Sem Saelands vei 7-9, N-7491, Trondheim, Norway
{mingyang, ketilb}@idi.ntnu.no

Abstract. One difficulty in software component retrieval comes from
users' incapability to well define their queries. In this paper, we propose
a conversational component retrieval model (CCRM) to alleviate this
difficulty. CCRM uses a knowledge-intensive conversational case-based
reasoning method to help users to construct their queries incrementally
through a mixed-initiative question-answering process. In this model,
general domain knowledge is captured and utilized in helping tackle the
following five tasks: feature inferencing, semantic similarity calculation,
integrated question ranking, consistent question clustering and coherent
question sequencing. This model is implemented, and evaluated in an
image processing component retrieval application. The evaluation result
gives us positive support.

1   Introduction

Component retrieval, how to locate and identify appropriate components for
current software development, is one of the major problems in component reuse
[1]. This problem becomes more critical with the emergence of several component architecture standards, such as, CORBA, COM, DCE, and EJB. These
standards make software components inter-operate more easily. Therefore component reuse surpasses the limitation of a single software company. Instead of
getting components from an in-house component library, users search for desired
components from component markets [2] (web-based software component collections provided by vendors or third parties), which separate component users and
component developers from each other. In addition, a large and rapidly increasing number of reusable components put more strict demands on the retrieval
efficiency [3].

Several methods have been put forward to address the component retrieval
problem [4], such as the free-text-based retrieval method, the pre-enumerated
vocabulary method, the signature matching method, the behavior-based retrieval
method, and the faceted selection method. Most of them assume that users
can define their component queries clearly and accurately, and get their desired
components based on such well defined queries. However, before users know the
components available for them to choose, they often lack clear ideas about what
they need, and usually can not define their queries accurately. In addition, the
huge number of available components prevents users from knowing all of them.

M. Ali and R. Dapoigny (Eds.): IEA/AIE 2006, LNAI 4031, pp. 554–563, 2006.

One promising solution to this problem can be that we invite an expert (or construct an intelligent system) who knows the characteristics of all the components. If one user needs a component, she can consult this expert. The expert extracts the requirement information from the user through conversation, and suggests appropriate components for her. Conversational case-based reasoning can be used to construct such an intelligent component retrieval system.

Case-Based Reasoning (CBR) is a problem solving method [5]. The main idea underlying CBR is that when facing a new problem, we search in our memory to find the most similar previous problem, and reuse the old solution to help solve the current problem. Conversational case-based reasoning (CCBR) [6] is an interactive form of CBR. It is proposed to deal with problems where users can not pose well defined queries (new cases) or where constructing well-defined new cases are expensive. CCBR uses a mixed-initiative dialog to guide users to facilitate the case retrieval process through a question-answering sequence. CCBR has been probed in several application domains, for instance, in the troubleshooting domain [7, 8], in the products and services selection [9, 10], and recently in workflow management [11].

In our research, we apply the CCBR method to software component retrieval, and propose a conversational component retrieval model (CCRM), where each component is described as a stored case, and a component query is formatted as a new case [4]. This CCRM model can help users construct their component queries incrementally through a dialog process, and find the appropriate components for them. In this paper, we identify six tasks in the component retrieval application, and extend the CCBR method to satisfy these identified tasks through incorporating general domain knowledge.

The rest of this paper is organized as follows. In Section 2, we present the framework of CCRM; in Section 3, comparing with the traditional CCBR process, a set of tasks are further identified in the software component retrieval application; in Section 4, we describe the design of CCRM focusing on how to solve the identified tasks; in Section 5, an implementation of CCRM is described and evaluated in an image processing software component retrieval application; at the end, related research is described and compared with our method in Section 6.

2   CCRM Overview

As illustrated in Fig. 1, the conversational component retrieval model (CCRM) includes six parts: a knowledge base, a query generating module, a similarity calculation module, a question generating and ranking module, a component displaying module, and a question displaying module.

The knowledge base stores both component-specific knowledge (cases) and general domain knowledge. After a user provides her initial requirement specification (arrow A), the query generating module uses it to construct a component query. Given a query, the similarity calculation module calculates the similarities between the query and each stored component, and returns a set of components whose similarities surpass a threshold (the threshold is pre-defined and can be

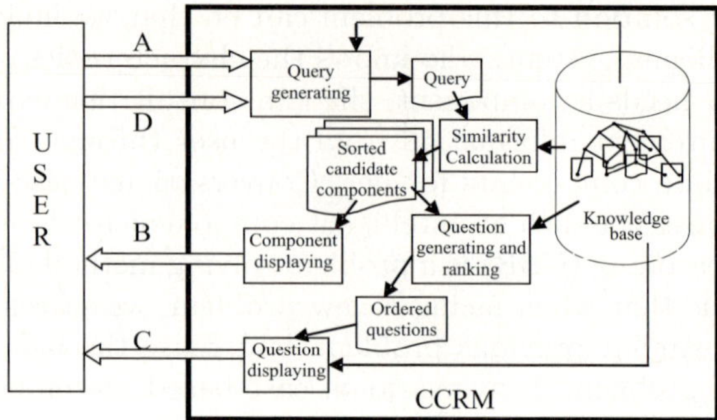

Fig. 1. The architecture of conversational component retrieval model (CCRM)

adjusted following the execution). In the question generating and ranking module, discriminative questions are identified from the returned components and ranked. The component displaying module displays the returned components, ordered by their similarities, to the user (arrow B). The question displaying module displays the ranked questions (arrow C). If the user finds her desired component in the displayed components, she can select it and terminate the retrieval process. Otherwise, she chooses a question, and provides the answer to the system (arrow D). Then the query generating module combines the previous query and the newly gained answer to construct a new query, and a new round of retrieving and question-answering is started until the user finds her desired component (success) or there are no questions left for her to choose (fail).

3   Requirements for Conversational CBR to Support Software Component Retrieval

3.1   Supporting Component Retrieval Using Generalized Cases

Most of the applications in CCBR assume that on each feature, there is either missing value or one discrete value (so called point cases, PC). However, for the cases used in CCRM (either a new case or a stored case), it is necessary to have multiple values on some features. The semantic for a stored case with multiple values for one feature is that the corresponding component has the capability to function in several situations, specified by multiple values for that feature. The multiple values on one feature in a new case means the user demands all the requirements specified by these values to be satisfied. The cases that can have multiple values on some features are named generalized cases (GC) [12]. In [13], we discussed how to support GCs in conversational CBR in a knowledge-poor context. In this paper, we will show how the GCs can be represented and utilized in a knowledge-intensive context.

To our knowledge, most of the applied CCBR methods are, to a large extent, knowledge-poor, that is, they only take the syntactical information or statistical metrics into account. The potential that general domain knowledge has for playing a positive role in the conversation process is little explored. In our research, we identify the following five tasks in CCRM, for which general domain knowledge is able to help controlling and improving the conversation process.

3.2   Feature Inferencing

In CCBR, the features that appear in the returned cases but not in the new case are selected and transformed into discriminative questions. However, if one feature can be inferred from the current features of a new case, this feature should be added to the new case automatically, instead of repeatedly inquiring it from the user. Users are likely not to trust a communicating partner who asks for information that is easy to infer, and the conversation efficiency will also be decreased by asking such "repeating" questions. Feature inferencing [14] is designed to extend a new case by adding the features that can be inferred by the current new case description.

3.3   Knowledge-Intensive Similarity Calculation

Selecting components based on their semantic similarities to user's query rather than syntactical similarities only is an active research topic [3, 15]. However, existing research concerned this topic mainly use domain knowledge to refine user's query before the searching process. In our research, besides the query refinement process (feature inferencing), we are using abductive inference [16] to exploit the general domain knowledge during the similarity calculation process. The similarity calculation process is divided into two steps: in the first step, similarities are calculated syntactically based on how high percentage of features specified in the query are matched by those in a component. In the second step, the abductive inference mechanism is adopted to exploit the general domain knowledge to construct the possible explanation paths trying to bridge the unmatched features [17].

3.4   Integrated Question Ranking

In CCBR, a main research topic is how to select the most discriminative questions and prompt them in a natural way to alleviate users' cognitive load. The feature inferencing process removes the questions that can be answered implicitly. Before the remaining questions are displayed to users, they need to be ranked intentionally. Currently, most of the question ranking metrics are knowledge-poor, for example, information metric, occurrence frequency metric, importance weight metric, and feature selection strategies [13]. The general domain knowledge, particularly the semantic relations between questions, can also be used to rank the discriminative questions. For example, if the answer to question B can be inferred from that of question A, or the answer to question A is easier or cheaper to obtain than that to question B, question A should be prompted to users before question B. In CCRM, an integrated question ranking method is designed, which uses not only the superficial statistical metrics of questions, but also the semantic relations among them.

Even though an integrated question ranking module outputs a set of sorted questions, their screen arrangement and questioning sequence should not be decided by such a sorted order alone. The main reason lies in that people always hope to inspect or answer questions in a natural way. They would prefer to see a set of questions, connected by some semantic relations, grouped together, and answered in an uninterrupted sequence. These requirements are captured by the following two tasks:

3.5   Consistent Question Clustering

The arrangement of questions on the screen should be consistent, that is, the questions with some semantic relations among them should be grouped and displayed together. For example, the questions having dependency relations among them should be grouped and displayed together. The order of the questions in each group should be decided intentionally.

3.6   Coherent Question Sequencing

The questions asked in the sequential question-answering cycles should be as related as possible, that is, the semantic contents of two sequential questions should avoid unnecessarily switching. For example, if in the previous question-answering cycle a more general question in an abstraction taxonomy is asked, the downward more specific question should be asked in the succeeding cycle rather than inserting other non-related questions between them.

4   CCRM Design

4.1   Knowledge Representation Model

In CCRM, knowledge is represented on two levels. The first is the object-level, in which both general domain knowledge and case-specific knowledge are represented within a single representation framework. The second is the meta-level, which is used to organize the semantic relations to complete the knowledge-intensive tasks identified above.

Object-Level Knowledge Model. A frame-based knowledge representation model, which is a part of the CREEK system [17], is adopted in CCRM. In this representation model, both case-specific knowledge and general domain knowledge are captured as a network of concepts and relations. Each concept and relation is represented as a frame in a frame-based representation language. A frame consists of a set of relationships, representing connections with other concepts or non-concept values, e.g. numbers. A relationship is described using an ordered triple $< C_f, T, C_v >$, in which C_f is the concept described by this relationship, C_v is another concept acting as the value of this relationship (value concept), and T designates the relation type. Viewed as a semantic network, a concept corresponds to a node and a relation corresponds to a link between two nodes.

Both a new case and stored cases are represented as concepts, and the features inside a case are represented as relationships starting from the concept representing this case. In CCRM, it is permitted for one case concept to have more than one of the same type of relationships in order to support generalized cases. The semantic relations among concepts are also represented using relationships, which can be used to support knowledge-intensive reasoning, for example, feature inferencing and semantic question ranking.

Meta-Level Knowledge Model. To organize general domain knowledge (semantic relations) to complete the knowledge-intensive tasks, we design a meta-level knowledge model. In this model, the semantic relations are defined as the subclasses of the meta-level relations, each of which corresponds to a knowledge-intensive task. So we only need to define the properties and operations once on a super-class meta-level relation, all its subclass semantic relations can inherit these properties and operations automatically. The separation of this meta-level representation model from the object-level model makes CCRM easy to be extended through introducing new semantic relations as the subclasses of some meta-level relations, and easy to be transplanted between different component retrieval application domains.

4.2   Explanation-Boosted Reasoning Process

An explanation-boosted reasoning process [14] is adopted in CCRM to complete the five knowledge-intensive tasks. This process can be divided into three steps: ACTIVATE, EXPLAIN and FOCUS. These three steps, which constitute a general process model, were initially described for knowledge-intensive CBR [17]. Here this model is instantiated for the identified five knowledge-intensive CCBR tasks. ACTIVATE determines what knowledge (including case-specific knowledge and general domain knowledge) is involved in one particular task, EXPLAIN builds up explanation paths to explore possible knowledge-intensive solutions for that task, and FOCUS evaluates the generated explanation paths and identify the best one/ones for that particular task.

5   Implementation and Evaluation

5.1   CCRM Implementation

We have implemented CCRM within the TrollCreek system [17]. TrollCreek is a knowledge-intensive case-based reasoner with a graphical knowledge model editor, where the knowledge-intensive similarity calculation has been realized. Our implementation adds the conversational process into the retrieval phase, and extends it to support generalized cases and complete the other four knowledge-intensive tasks.

In this implementation, a conversational retrieval process contains one or several conversation sessions. As illustrated in Fig. 2, in the computer interface there

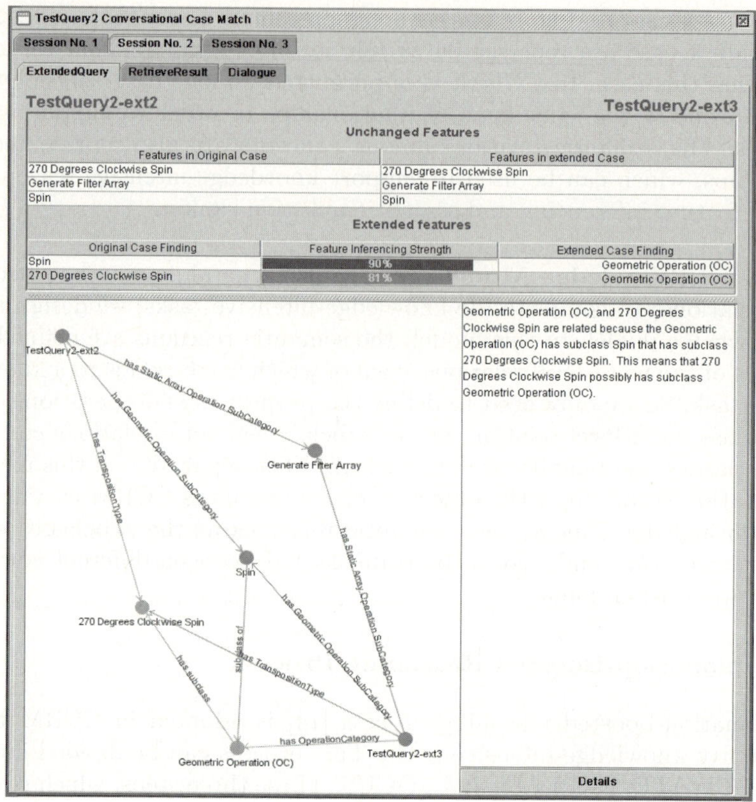

Fig. 2. The conversational retrieval process implemented in TrollCreek

are three window panes to move between within each session. The "Extended-Query" pane is used to display the original query and the extended query, and show the detailed explanation about how a feature is inferred from the original features. Based on the extended query, the similarity calculation module retrieves a set of components, and displays them in the "RetrieveResult" pane. In this pane a user can inspect the explanations about how the similarity is computed between each retrieved component and the extended query. If the user is not satisfied with the retrieved components, she can go to the "Dialogue" pane, where the discriminative questions are ranked using the integrated question ranking process, and adjusted by the consistent question clustering and the coherent question sequencing processes. After the user selects a discriminative question and submits the answer, a new conversation session is started based on a constructed new query through combining the provided answer with the previous query.

5.2   Evaluation

We choose image processing software component retrieval, particularly the components in the DynamicImager system [4], as the evaluation application.

DynamicImager is a visualization and image processing development environment, in which different image processing components can be combined in various ways. Currently, the components in the system are categorized according to their functions, and users select each component by exploring through the category structure manually.

A knowledge base is constructed by combining the image processing domain knowledge and 118 image processing components extracted from DynamicImager. In this knowledge base, there are 1170 concepts, 104 features and 913 semantic relationships.

For the evaluation of CCRM, we choose a relatively weak evaluation method, so called direct expert evaluation [18]. We invited two experts from the image processing domain and two experts from the software engineering domain to test our system. Given a set of image processing tasks, these domain experts were asked to retrieve image processing components using both a one-shot CBR-based retrieval method and the multiple shots knowledge-intensive CCBR based method (CCRM). After that, they were required to fill in a form to describe their subjective evaluation of the implemented system. The resulting analysis of the collected feedback forms shows us that:

- Based on the same initial new case, the CCRM method can achieve more useful results;
- The reasoning transparency provided by the explanation mechanisms in CCRM improves users' confidence in the retrieved results;
- The feature inferencing, consistent question clustering and coherent question sequencing mechanisms provide users' with a natural question-answering process, which helps to alleviate their cognitive loads in retrieving components interactively;
- The straight-forward question-answering query construction process is able to reduce users' cognitive load to guess the query, and help users with limited domain knowledge to retrieve the suitable components.

6   Related Research and Conclusion

Software is used to solve practical problems, and software components are existing solutions to previous problems, so component reuse can be described as "trying to use the solutions to previous similar problems to help solving the current problem". Therefore, it is very natural to use the CBR method to support component reuse. Various types of CBR methods have been explored and found useful for component reuse.

Object Reuse Assistant (ORA) [19] is a hybrid framework that uses CBR to locate appropriate components in an object-oriented software library (small-talk component library). In this framework, both small-talk classes and small-talk methods take the form of stored cases. The concepts in small-talk, for instance, c-class, c-method and c-data-spec, and their instantiated objects are connected together as a conceptual hierarchy. Though the conceptual hierarchy can be seen as a representation method combining case-specific knowledge and general knowledge, the retrieval process is knowledge-poor (a new case is compared with stored cases based on how many attributes two cases have in common).

IBROW [20] is an automated software configuration project. Users' tasks (queries) can be decomposed into sub-tasks by matched task decomposers, and sub-tasks can be decomposed further. Tasks or subtasks can finally be solved by matched software components. Both task decomposers and components are referred to as PSMs (problem solving methods). CBR is used at two levels in IBROW. The high level is called constructive adaptation. In this level, PSMs take the form of cases, which are represented using feature terms, and a knowledge-poor matching method (term subsumption) is adopted when searching the possibly applied PSMs. At the low level, CBR is used as a heuristic algorithm to realize the best-first searching strategy. Previously solved configurations are stored as cases, and represented as feature terms. In an intermediate stage of a configuration task, for each possible further configuration, C, the PSM, through applying which C is produced, is considered. The stored configurations in which the same PSM appears as a part are identified, and the similarities between each of these configurations and the semi-finished configuration C are calculated. The most similar configuration is selected, and its similarity value is taken as the heuristic value for this PSM to be applied. As the ORA system, IBROW uses a knowledge-poor retrieval process and only supports tentative and manual interactions between users and the system.

Comparing with these two CBR-based component retrieval systems, CCRM has two advantages: providing a conversational process helping users to construct their component queries incrementally and find out their desired component at the same time; providing integrated knowledge-intensive solutions to identified knowledge-intensive tasks: feature inferencing, knowledge-intensive similarity calculation, integrated question ranking, consistent question clustering and coherent question sequencing.

A limitation of our method is its dependence on knowledge engineering. The knowledge base combining both component specific knowledge and general domain knowledge is assumed to exist initially. The construction of this knowledge base puts a significant workload on the knowledge engineering process.

Our future work focuses on integrating this CCRM into the DynamicImager system to help users constructing their queries and finding out their desired components through a conversation process instead of manually searching through the categories.

References

1. Mili, A., Mili, R., Mittermeir, R.: A survey of software reuse libraries. Annals of Software Engineering **5** (1998) 349 – 414
2. Ravichandran, T., Rothenberger, M.A.: Software reuse strategies and component markets. Communications of the ACM **46** (2003) 109 – 114
3. Klein, M., Bernstein, A.: Searching for services on the semantic web using process ontologies. In: The First Semantic Web Working Symposium, Stanford, CA, (2001).

4. Gu, M., Aamodt, A., Tong, X.: Component retrieval using conversational case-based reasoning. In : Procedings of International Conference on Intelligent Information Processing, (2004).

5. Aamodt, A., Plaza, E.: Case-based reasoning: Foundational issue, methodological variations, and system approaches. AI Communications **7** (1994) 39–59

6. Aha, D.W., Breslow, L., Muñoz-Avila, H.: Conversational case-based reasoning. Applied Intelligence: The International Journal of Artificial Intelligence, Neural Networks, and Complex Problem-Solving Technologies **14** (2001) 9

7. Gupta, K.M.: Knowledge-based system for troubleshooting complex equipment. International Journal of Information and Computing Science **1** (1998) 29–41

8. Cunningham, P., Smyth, B.: A comparison of model-based and incremental case-based approaches to electronic fault diagnosis. In: Case-Based Reasoning Workshop, Seattle, USA (1994)

9. Cunningham, P., Bergmann, R., Schmitt, S., Traphoner, R., Breen, S., Smyth, B.: Websell: Intelligent sales assistants for the world wide web. KI - Kunstliche Intelligenz **1** (2001) 28–31

10. Shimazu, H.: Expertclerk: A conversational case-based reasoning tool for developing salesclerk agents in e-commerce webshops. Artificial Intelligence Review **18** (2002) 223 – 244

11. Weber, B., Rinderle, S., Wild, W., Reichert, M.: Ccbr-driven business process evolution. In: Case-Based Reasoning Research and Development, Proceedings of the 6th International Conference on Case-Based Reasoning, (2005).

12. Maximini, K., Maximini, R., Bergmann, R.: An investigation of generalized cases. In: 5th International Conference on Case-Based Reasoning, (2003), 261 – 275

13. Gu, M.: Supporting generalized cases in conversational cbr. In : Proceedings of the Fourth Mexican International Conference on Artificial Intelligence, (2005).

14. Gu, M., Aamodt, A.: A knowledge-intensive method for conversational cbr. In : Case-Based Reasoning Research and Development, Proceedings of the 6th International Conference on Case-Based Reasoning, (2005).

15. Sugumaran, V., Storey, V.C.: A semantic-based approach to component retrieval. The DATA BASE for Advances in Information Systems **34** (2003) 8–24

16. Öztürk, P.: Abductive inference - an evidential approach. In: A knowledge level model of context and context use in diagnositic domains - Doctoral Thesis. Norwegian University of Science and Technology (2000) 49 – 60

17. Aamodt, A.: Knowledge-intensive case-based reasoning in creek. In : Proceedings of the 7th European Conference on Case-Based Reasoning. Madrid, Spinger (2004)

18. Cohen, P.R., Howe, A.E.: How evaluation guides ai research. AI Mag. **9** (1988) 35–43

19. Fernández-Chamizo, C., González-Calero, P.A., Gámez-Albarrán, M., Hernández-Yáñez, L.: Supporting object reuse through case-based reasoning. In: EWCBR '96: Proceedings of the Third European Workshop on Advances in Case-Based Reasoning, London, UK, Springer-Verlag (1996) 135–149

20. IBROW-project: http://www.swi.psy.uva.nl/projects/ibrow/home.html (2005)

Identification of Characteristics After Soft Breakdown with GA-Based Neural Networks

Hsing-Wen Wang

National Changhua University of Education, College of Management,
Department of Business Administration, Changhua 500, Taiwan, R.O.C.
shinwen@cc.ncue.edu.tw

Abstract. In this research, we analyze the low-frequency noise power spectrum of drain current (S_{id}) in electrically stressed S_iO_2 film, and then propose the evolutionary neural networks-based model named ENN-SBD to identify the highly nonlinear degraded characteristics of low frequency noise around the soft breakdown (SBD). The S_{id} data follow the $1/f^\gamma$ relationship with different value of power exponent γ. The spatial oxide traps distribution is proposed to account for the different γ value. It is found that the S_{id} correlates closely with the gate fluctuations via the trapping and detrapping processes and hence it is feasible to build the model represents the behavior of soft breakdown. The results also indicate that ENN-SBD has more precisely identification capability than typical Lorentzian spectrum method. Besides, it is superior to the backpropagation neural networks-based model (BNN-SBD) while the system identification is proceeding. This paper is helpful for breakdown detection and saving the cost of testing from quality assurance in the process of advanced CMOS technology.

Keywords: Low-frequency noise, evolutionary neural networks, CMOS, soft breakdown, degraded characteristics.

1 Introduction

System modeling or system identification based on the conventional mathematical skills (e.g. differential equations) isn't suited for dealing with uncertain, non-structure or ill-define systems [1], [2]. The degraded characteristics of low frequency noise around the soft breakdown are typical problems known as the highly nonlinear and data-oriented while modeling its degradation characteristics. In fact, it costs much in the testing processes of quality assurance, especially for advanced CMOS technology. The reliability of thin S_iO_2 film used as gate dielectrics is one of the most concerned issues for advanced CMOS technology. When the gate oxide thickness is less than 5nm, there is new anomalous degradation and breakdown characteristics, called quasi-breakdown [3] or soft breakdown [4]. After the occurrence of SBD, the fluctuation phenomena are observed in the time evolution of the gate voltage or the gate current. It has been reported that the gate fluctuations are due to the trapping and detrapping of electrons in gate oxides [5]. Moreover, in thinner oxides the so-called carrier-number fluctuation model is that the trapping and detrapping processes within the gate oxide can modulate the underlying channel potential [6].

M. Ali and R. Dapoigny (Eds.): IEA/AIE 2006, LNAI 4031, pp. 564–572, 2006.

However, neither the experimental evidence in support of the carrier-number fluctuation model found yet nor the SBD model built. In this paper, during high-field stress we explore the noise power spectrum of drain current (S_{id}) characterization. In other words, the S_{id} data in fresh, stress-induced leakage current (SILC) and SBD mode are presented. We also discuss that for thinner gate oxide the S_{id} correlates with the gate current fluctuations and present the evolutionary neural networks-based SBD model.

Neural networks have been played an important role in attacking bottlenecks of advanced semiconductor technologies because of its distinguishing characteristic [7], [8], [9], [10], [11]. Ling et al (2003) demonstrates that the self-evolving neural networks contain the capability of fault tolerance to filter out the noise and provide high degree of accuracy of nonlinear function used to produce the model identification [12]. In view of this, this paper has adopted the ENN model to perform the non-parametric estimation with evolutionary process which systematical determines the optimal networks structure to obtain the global optimal solution instead of local optimal solution using traditional neural networks, and hence to obtain soft breakdown model with degraded characteristics of low frequency noise.

2 Evolutionary Neural Networks: Architectures and Algorithms

As to the type of ENN model adopted, it should be one where the users can easily define its exogenous variables or can add new elements to the ENN for system identification. In addition, the user should not have to worry about the problems of setting initial values to the weights of neurons, the number of neurons, the number of hidden layers and the neuron connections, etc., as attention can be devoted to optimizing the structure of networks on their own through genetic algorithms in the neural network learning process. Genetic algorithms are very effective at finding near global optimal solutions to a highly nonlinear function and a wide variety of problems [13], [14].

The ENN model used in this research is briefly described as follows. Chromosomes are used to express the neural network architecture and the parameters of the structure as presented in Fig. 1.

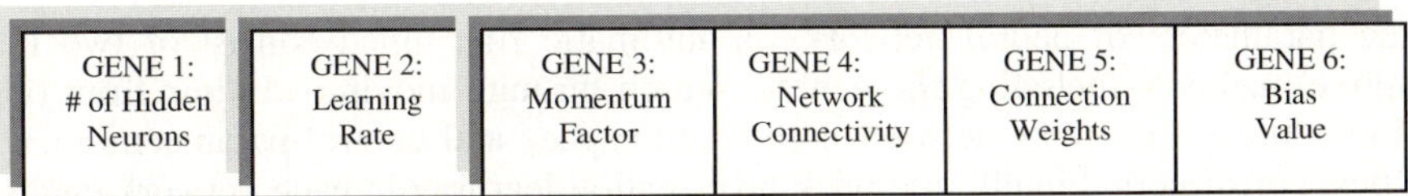

Fig. 1. Structure of chromosomes

The formation of each gene within a chromosome and the length of the chromosome can be determined depending on the cases. The network's evolutionary process is demonstrated in Fig. 2, and includes a training cycle and an evolutionary cycle. The steps for each stage are summarized below: (1) Initiate networks: randomly produce the initial networks' structure. (2) Training cycle: networks are built through genetic rules and a combination of weighted tuning. Training time is utilized in exchange for

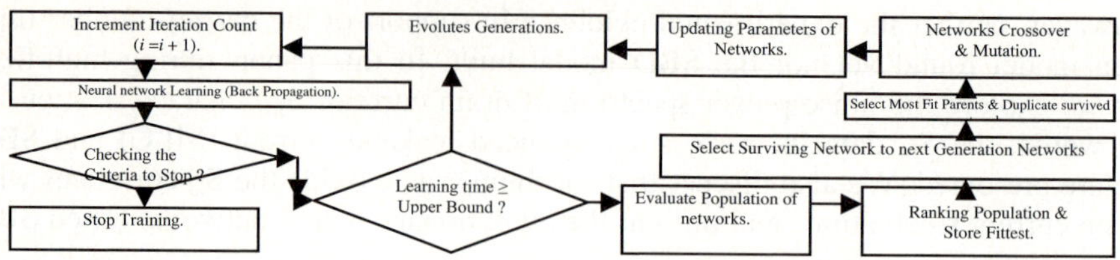

Fig. 2. The architecture of evolutionary cycle with nested training cycle for the ENN

the quality of an approximate optimal solution until the upper bound of the learning numbers can be reached. (3) Evolutionary cycle: the level of suitability of various networks for evaluating the fitness function is based on the mean square error, and the evolution of the networks then commences. In addition, based on the surviving networks which are decided by the suitability of the various networks, the reproduction, crossover and mutation of the surviving networks can be performed so as to generate a new generation of networks. (4) Return to Step (2) to conduct new generation network training until a satisfactory learning result or a pre-set termination condition is reached. We conclude the four stage operations of ENN as a pseudo code in Fig. 3:

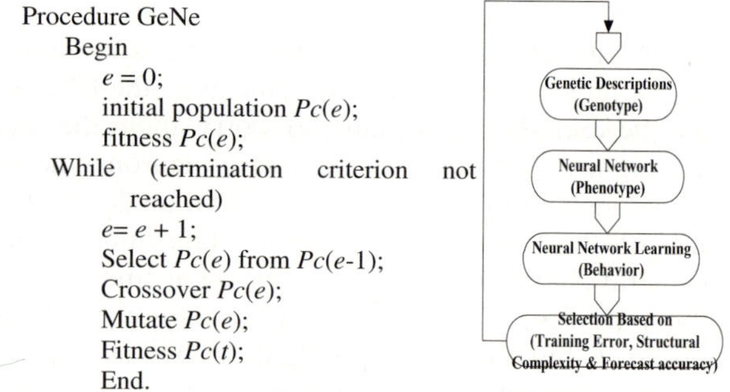

Fig. 3. The pseudo code of ENN

The parameters of neural networks is automatic fine tuned consist of two major adaptive methods, including the genetic search through moving window from observations, forecast horizon, network architecture space and control parameters to select the best performers. Finally, the back-propagation learning in each network evaluates the selected architectures to complete the evolution cycle.

We make good use of three criteria to measure the learning, testing and estimation accuracy in the ENN model so called performance indices, including R^2, *NRMSE* and *MAE*. The R^2 measures the interpretive capability of the SBD model to the real observations which is given as *Eq.* (1). It's more and more correlative to the real observations while R^2 is closer to 1. The NRMSE (Normalized Root Mean Square Errors) and MAE (Mean Absolute Errors) here is set to be the objective function for minimizing the tracking errors between the model outcomes and observations for SBD using ENN, which is given as *Eq.* (2) and *Eq.* (3).

$$R^2 = (n\sum_{i=1}^{n} x_i y_i - (\sum_{i=1}^{n} x_i)(\sum_{i=1}^{n} y_i))^2 \Big/ (n\sum_{i=1}^{n} x_i^2 - (\sum_{i=1}^{n} x_i)^2 (n\sum_{i=1}^{n} y_i^2 - (\sum_{i=1}^{n} y_i)^2) \tag{1}$$

$$RMSE = (\sum_{i=1}^{n} (y_i - x_i)^2 \Big/ \sum_{i=1}^{n} (y_i - (mean(y_i)))^{0.5} \tag{2}$$

$$MAE = \sum_{i=1}^{n} |y_i - x_i| \Big/ n \tag{3}$$

Where x_i: input variables; y_i: estimation results by ENN model (output variable); n: # of observations.

3   Experiments and System Identification

In the experiment part, the n-channel MOSFET used in the study was fabricated in a 0.18 um process. In this process, the physical gate oxide thickness was determined to be 3.3 nm by using a C-V method. A constant gate voltage of 5.5V was adopted to stress the gate oxide, with source, drain, and substrate tied to ground. The high-field stress was interrupted several times for characterization of S_{id}. The S_{id} measurement set-up comprised a HP 35665A dynamic signal analyzer, BTA 9603 FET noise analyzer and HP4156B semiconductor parameter analyzer, as illustrated in the Fig. 4. The transistor with gate oxide area of 10×10 um^2 was measured at the inversion condition (V_{DS}=0.1V and V_{GS}=1V). The frequency range of S_{id} was from 1 Hz to 1K Hz. Three noise filters were used to eliminate the residual noise in all bias sources.

In the modeling part, when considering the behavior of soft breakdown, the factors are induced into the ENN model. On account of the significant correlation on drain

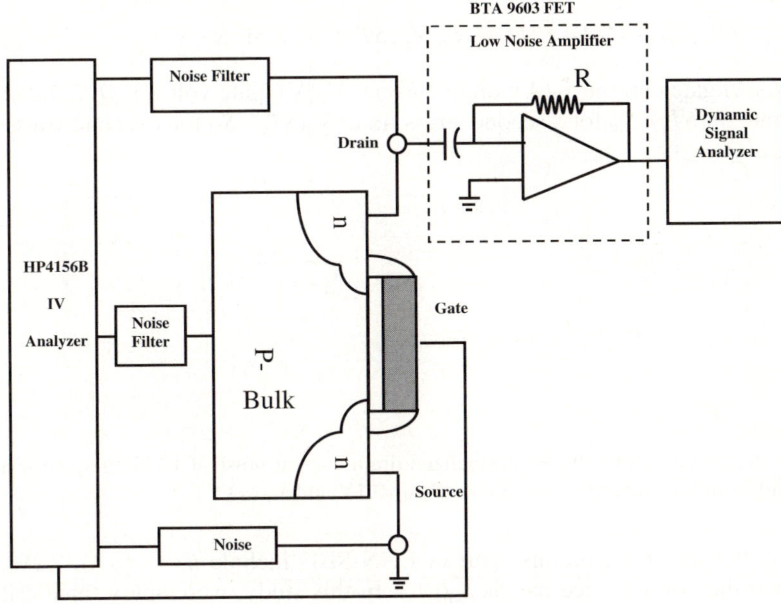

Fig. 4. Schematic diagram of the drain current noise measurement system

current in electrically stressed S_iO_2 film between various frequencies for several stress times before hard breakdown during from 1 Hz to 16.5 Hz (see Panel A, Table 1) which is also can be verified as exhibiting in Fig. 5. Fig. 5 shows that a significant correlation plot, that is, the normalization of noise power ($=S_{id}/I_D^2$) versus the gate current I_G, can serve as supporting evidence of the model since the S_{id} can be adequately traced to the gate current. A striking phenomenon of the gate current reduction in the SILC mode can be drawn herein. We can attribute it to the accumulation of the tunneling electrons trapped in the oxide.

Table 1. Correlation coefficient matrix for several stress times

Panel A. 1 Hz $\leq Q \leq$ 16.5 Hz, *Q*: frequency			
	Fresh	10 sec	30 sec
Fresh	1	0.5885*	0.7301*
10 sec	0.5885*	1	0.7934*
30 sec	0.7301*	0.7934*	1
Panel B. 17 Hz $\leq Q \leq$ 1K Hz, *Q*: frequency			
	Fresh	10 sec	30 sec
Fresh	1	0.3316	0.1428
10 sec	0.3316	1	0.3652
30 sec	0.1428	0.3652	1

On the contrary, they trap insignificant correlation while the frequency increases into 1K Hz (see Panel B, Table 1). The auxiliary variables, I_G(A), I_D(A) and V_G(V) is necessary to induced jointly in our model as *Eq.* (4)

$$S_{id}(ST_y) = F(Q, I_G, I_D, V_G, ST, S_{id}(ST_x)), x \neq y. \tag{4}$$

where, I_G(A):gate current; I_D(A): drain current; V_G(V): gate voltage; *Q*: frequency; *ST*: stress time; $S_{id}(ST_x)$: S_{id} for *x* second stress time; $S_{id}(ST_y)$: S_{id} for *y* second stress time.

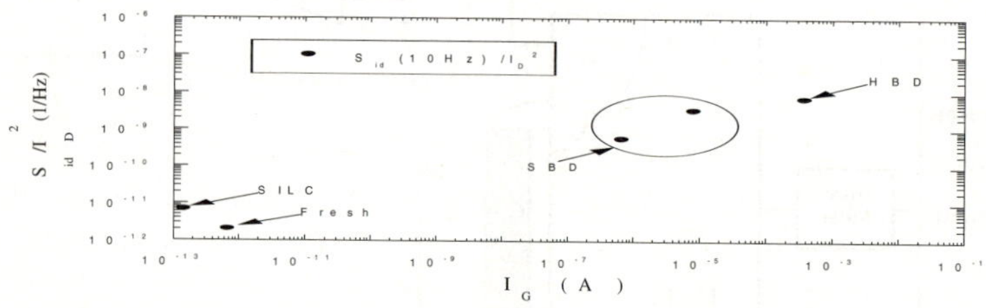

Fig. 5. A correlation plot between normalized drain current noise at 10 Hz frequency and gate current, all from the same bias condition of V_{DS}=0.1V and V_{GS}=1V

Hence, the factors of premise part of ENN-SBD include I_G(A), I_D(A), V_G(V), *Q*, *ST*, $S_{id}(ST_x)$ and the consequence part is $S_{id}(ST_y)$. In this study, we employ three criteria to stop training and testing. One is training epochs is equal to 50,000 times, the other is the training error doesn't change in late 1,000 times, error tolerance is less than 10^{-24}

or divergence happened. ENN would stop evolution and learning process automatically provided either of these criteria stands.

4 Experimental Results and Discussions

The time evolution of the gate current IG during constant voltage stress depicted in Fig. 6, showing two distinct events: SILC and SBD. After the occurrence of SBD, the gate current exhibits fluctuation phenomena as partially magnified in the insert of Fig. 6. The current fluctuations arise from the trapping and detrapping processes in and around SBD damaged region. Moreover, the high-field stress is interrupted several times to observe the characterization of S_{id}.

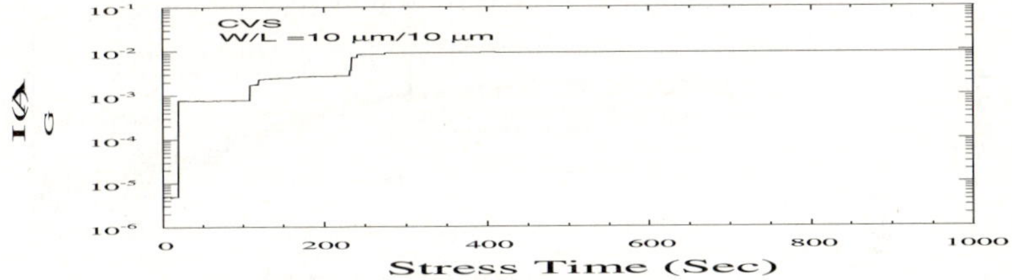

Fig. 6. Measured gate current versus stress time under a constant voltage stress

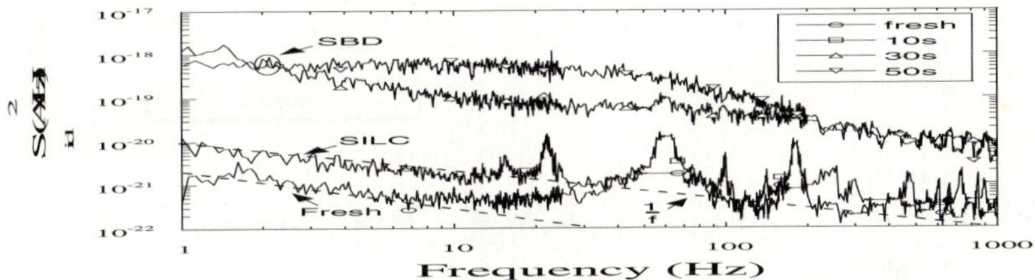

Fig. 7. Measured drain current noise power spectrum (S_{id}) for several stress times

Fig. 7 shows the measured S_{id} for different stress times. The S_{id} data follow the $1/f^{\gamma}$ relationship with different value of power exponent γ. The spatial traps distribution within the gate oxide can account for different γ value. The interpretation is similar to a literature model report [15]. Firstly, for S_{id} in the SILC mode the γ of 1 indicates that the traps are spatially uniform distribution within the gate oxide. Also, the oxide traps number increases with the time. The amount of oxide traps reflects the S_{id} magnitude increase. Subsequently, we observe a typical Lorentzian spectrum component after the occurrence of SBD. This component mainly arises from the trapping and detrapping processes in the localized oxide damage region, that is, a non-uniform oxide traps distribution. The inference is analogous to a Lorentzian spectrum observation on the small area device [16]. The area of the localized oxide damage region of around 0.3 nm^2 is proposed to account for this [17].

In addition, the time constant of the Lorentzian spectrum is estimated to be 3.5 *ms*, as shown in the Fig. 8. The time constant in S_{id} is associated with the net effect of the interaction between the oxide traps within the localized SBD damaged region and the underlying channel carrier, which is accounting for the carrier-number fluctuation model.

Fig. 8 shows ten fitting models for soft breakdown identification for 50 sec tress time, including linear, logarithmic, power, interpolate, polynomial, moving average, exponential, cubic-spline, $1/f^{\gamma}$ and ENN-SBD. This is consistent with the observation in Table 1. For most of the fitting models, they are all lose efficacy during the damage higher low-frequency region occurs area except the ENN. Besides, ENN has more precisely identification capability than typical Lorentzian spectrum method ($1/f^{\gamma}$).

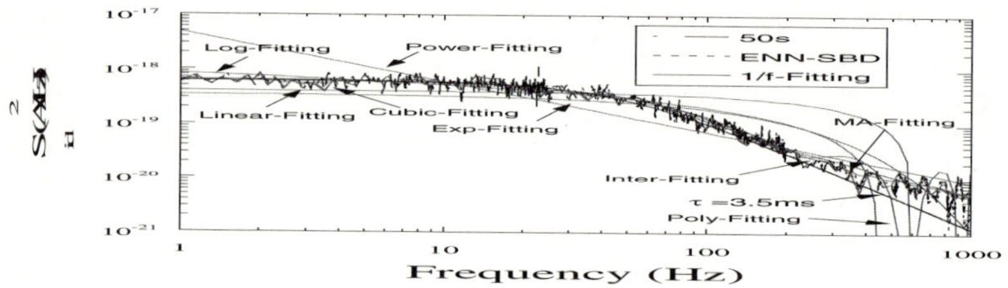

Fig. 8. Extracted the time constant of the Lorentzian spectrum from the data in Fig. 7

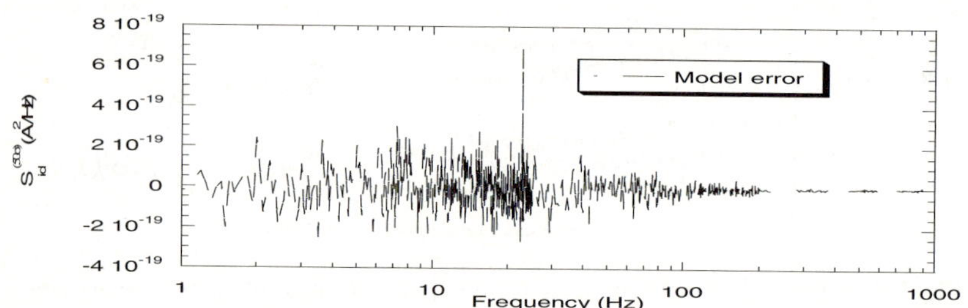

Fig. 9. ENN-SBD estimation error versus frequency

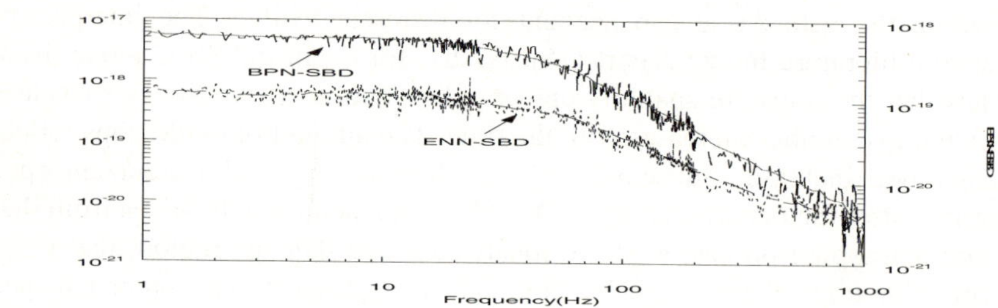

Fig. 10. Model comparisons between ENN-SBD and BPN-SBD for different frequency

In Fig. 9, there are 735 observations for each input/output variable. The moving window technique is employed to rolling the observations for batch learning in case of stress time is 50 sec. The first 485 pairs (training set) was used for training the ENN while the remaining 200 pairs for testing (used for validating the identified model), and 50 pairs for estimating. The resulting 111 neurons are generated after stop learning. It is quit unusual to observe the phenomenon that $RMSE_{train} \leq RMSE_{test}$ during the training process. Considering both the $RMSE$'s are very small, we conclude that: (1) the ENN has captured the essential components of the underlying dynamics; (2) the training data contains the effects of the initial conditions which might not be easy accounted for by the essential components identified by the ENN. As a comparison, we performed the same estimation by using the BPN with the same number of observations.

Fig. 10 shows the model comparisons between ENN-SBD and BPN-SBD with various frequencies. Obviously, ENN-SBD has a better performance than BPN-SBD in spite of committing to convergence at the end. It might indicate that the ENN can easily capture the spirit of "rule of thumb" used by humans, from another angle, it's more adaptive than BPN through genetic algorithms in the architecture.

5 Conclusions and Extensions of Current Work

First of all, during high-field stress, the origins of the S_{id} data in the SILC and SBD mode have been presented. The S_{id} data follow the $1/f'$ relationship with different value of power exponent γ. The spatial oxide traps distribution has been proposed to account for the different γ value. In addition, the Lorentzian spectrum is associated with the net effect of the interaction between the oxide traps within the localized SBD damaged region and the underlying channel carrier, that is, accounting for the carrier-number fluctuation model. It has pointed out that the S_{id} correlates closely with the gate fluctuations via the trapping and detrapping processes. Secondly, we have described the ENN-SBD mechanisms with case studies for the behavior inference of the degraded characteristics of low frequency noise after soft breakdown. By employing a hybrid learning procedure, the proposed model can refine the architecture to describe a complex CMOS system and has better performance than original Lorentzian spectrum method and BPN mechanism. Fabs build our model could thereby perform the simulation work instead of hardware operation and testing to reduce the reverent testing time and the costs.

Another important issue in the breakdown identification is how to modeling the hard breakdown which is even more difficult to estimate because it is tends to be an uncertainty problem. However, it would be more valuable to prevent the catastrophic hard breakdown occurs.

Acknowledgements

This paper was supported by the National Science Council under contract number NSC-94-2516-S-018-017. In addition, the author is very grateful to Dr. Kang for his valuable supports and the anonymous reviewers for their suggestions and comments.

References

1. Rietman, Edward A., Whitlock, Stephen A., Andrew Roy, Milton Beachy and Willingham, Timothy L. A System Model for Feedback Control and Analysis of Yield: A Multistep Process Model of Effective Gate Length, Poly Line Width, and IV Parameters. IEEE Transactions on Semiconductor Manufacturing. 14:1 (2001) 32-47.
2. Newnes, Linda B., Mileham, Tony R. and Doniavi, Ali. A Systems Approach to Semiconductor Optimization. IEEE Transactions on Electronics Packaging Manufacturing. 24:3 (2001) 171-177.
3. Lee, S. H., Cho, B. J., Kim, J. C., and Choi, S. H. Quasi-breakdown of ultrathin gate oxide under high field stress. IEDM Tech. Dig. (1994) 605-608.
4. Depas, M., Nigam, T., and Heyns, M. M. Soft breakdown of ultra-thin gate oxide layers. IEEE Trans. Electron Devices. 43 (1996) 1499-1504.
5. Houssa, M., Vandewalle, N., Nigam, T., Ausloos, M., Mertens, P. W., and Heyns, M. M. Analysis of the gate voltage fluctuations in ultra-thin gate oxides after soft breakdown. IEDM Tech. Dig. (1998) 909-912.
6. Weir, B. E., Silverman, P. J., Monroe, D., Krisch, K. S., Alam, M. A., Alers, G. B., Sorsch, T. W., Timp, G. L., Baumann, F., Liu, C. T., Ma, Y., and Hwang, D. Ultra-thin gate dielectrics : they break down, but do they fail? IEDM Tech. Dig. (1997) 73-76.
7. Braha, Dan and Shmilovici, Armin. Data Mining for Improving a Cleaning Process in the Semiconductor Industry. IEEE Transactions on Semiconductor Manufacturing, 15:1 (2002) 91-101.
8. Baker, M. D., Himmel, C. D. and May, G. S. Time series modeling of reactive ion etching using neural networks. IEEE Transactions on Semiconductor Manufacturing. 8:1 (1995) 62–71.
9. Rietman, E. A. and Lory, E. R. Use of neural networks in modeling semiconductormanufacturing processes: An example for plasma etch modeling. IEEE Transactions on Semiconductor Manufacturing. 6 (1993) 343–347.
10. Rietman, E. A. A neural network model of a contact plasma etch process for VLSI production. IEEE Transactions on Semiconductor Manufacturing. 9 (1996) 95–100.
11. Han, S. S. and May, G. Using neural networks process models to perform PECVD silicon dioxide recipe synthesis via genetic algorithms. IEEE Transactions on Semiconductor Manufacturing. 10 (1997) 279–287.
12. Ling, S.H., Leung, F.H.F., Lam, H.K., Yim-Shu Lee and Tam, P.K.S. A novel genetic-algorithm-based neural network for short-term load forecasting. Industrial Electronics, IEEE Transactions. 50: 4 (2003) 793 – 799.
13. Wong, F. and Lee, D. A Hybrid Neural Network for Selection. Proc. of the 2nd Annual Int. Conf. on Neural Networks (1993).
14. Wong, F., Tan, P. and Zhang, X. Neural Networks, Genetic Algorithms and Fuzzy Logic for Forecasting. Proceedings of the 3rd Int. Conf. on Advanced Applications and World-wide (1992).
15. Surya, C. and Hsiang, T. Y. Theory and experiment on the $1/f$ noise in p-channel metal-oxide-semiconductor field-effect transistors at low drain bias', Phys. Rev. B, 33 (1986), 4898-4905.
16. Uren, M. J., Day, D. J., and Kirton, M. J. $1/f$ and random telegraph noise in silicon metal-oxide-semiconductor field-effect transistors. Appl. Phys. Lett., 47 (1985) 1195-1197.
17. Chen, M. J., Kang, T. K., Liu, C. H., Chang, Y. J., and Fu, K. Y. Oxide thinning percolation statistical model for soft breakdown in ultrathin gate oxides. Appl. Phys. Lett. 77 (2000) 555-557.

Integrating Organizational Knowledge into Search Engine

Hiroshi Tsuji[1], Ryosuke Saga[1], and Jugo Noda[2]

[1] Graduate School of Engineering, Osaka Prefecture University
1-1 Gakuencho, Sakai, Osaka Japan 599-8531
`{tsuji@cs, saga@mis.cs}.osakafu-u.ac.jp`
[2] Software Division, Hitachi, Ltd.
`jugo.noda@hitachi.com`

Abstract. This paper presents a method for integrating organizational knowledge into general purpose search engine. The basic design concept is to provide front-end search agent, called SCIA/SF. SCIA/SF allows organizational people to externalize their findings from searches into pieces of relational-type knowledge, and to combine those pieces in a database. In addition, the organizational people have chance to internalize knowledge from SCIA/SF and collaborate with others by exchanging knowledge. SCIA/SF also receives feedback from people on the usefulness of relational-type knowledge in order to enforce its availability.

1 Introduction

Search is a typical application of computer. Specifically, web searching has been widely used after URL collection robots were invented [3]. By not using manual efforts, first stage search engines had provided powerful knowledge for Internet users. In fact, most people ask search engines when they have questions about anything.

To enhance search engines, much research has been done in such areas as natural language interface [16] and visualization technique [8]. This paper reviews three types of enhancement at first [15] [10] [14]. These enhancements concern supplementing search engines. Then we identifies that their efforts have not concerned on human-machine collaboration. For human-machine collaboration for search, we would like to follow SECI model proposed by [11]: socialization, externalization, combination and internalization.

To exclude failures made by search engine, we have tried to tame search engines as followings: when a person in an organization finds a solution from many search results, he let other persons of the same group release the effort to find the solution. We regard this activity as knowledge externalization. The more effort done by group members, the more knowledge is shared among them. This activity is regarded as knowledge combination.

However, externalized knowledge is not always available for others. Sometimes it fails to work well. The learning from successes and failures is an important task for us and depends on situations, status of work and BA. The activity of acquiring tacit

M. Ali and R. Dapoigny (Eds.): IEA/AIE 2006, LNAI 4031, pp. 573–582, 2006.

knowledge from combined knowledge is called internalization. Then the people who internalized the combined knowledge discuss when the knowledge works well. This action is referred to socialization. We would like to call such spiral activities "collaborative and intensive".

To integrate search engine power and human power, we present an agent system with knowledge called shortcut. The shortcut, which is maintained day by day, is a relationship between a specific term (sometimes a concept) and its unique pointers including URLs, rules and human professionals. Referring to the shortcut, the proposed agent works as a front end for the search engine. The paper also describes a prototype agent, called SCIA/SF (Shortcut Integrated Agent for Search Front), with its desirable attributes.

2 Reviews for Architecture of Traditional Search Engines

The basic architecture of traditional search engine is shown in Fig. 1. A search robot collects URLs and stores them in a database [3]. The engine finds related URLs and places them in order when a user specifies a search term. While the main concerns with search engines have involved increasing precision in the form of "search" and decreasing noise in the form of "rank", search engines are still limited in their abilities if human does not collaborate with the search engine.

For example, the search engine shows the same result for the same term. This means that search engines repeat the same failure even if users notify that some misses and/ or noises occurred in search results. However, it is true that misses and noise for a person are not always the same for others, even if the same search term is specified.

To customize a search, there is idea called re-search. The basic premise under the design of re-search is that useful URLs for a person in a group are also useful for others in the group [15]. So, referred URLs by group members are indexed in a local log database. Then the search engine allows finding out the most frequently accessed page or most recently accessed page. Further it allows the query like "Which pages did John and Mary access this week?" However, this architecture is not designed for explicit human assistance for the searches. (Note that the local database in [15] is stored in a proxy server for information sharing).

To define a solution for a search term beforehand, there is idea called sponsor-search. This idea is to prepare a special database for the sponsor and it is applied to advertisement. The basic assumption is that an authorized sponsor can maintain the special database. While it works well for advertisements, the solution is not robust. Even if a user dislikes solutions, he can not avoid nor modify them.

Another approach exists for supporting search users. A typical idea is to provide a thesaurus that defines term relationships including a hierarchy [10]. The basic idea is that broader terms will avoid missing solutions and narrower terms will help exclude noise. Using synonym works also for avoiding miss. Another idea is using co-occurrence terms [14] [9] and association rules for search terms [17]. However, there are no rooms for collaboration among users.

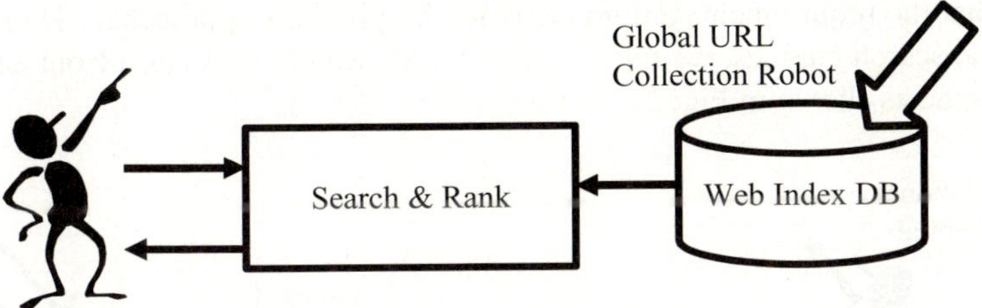

Fig. 1. Architectural Comparison on Supplementing Search Engine

3   Requirement Analyses for Taming Search Engine

Organizations increasingly create massive internal digital repositories of product development, department roles, varieties of rule and collaborative knowledge. Because open internet standards present unprecedented opportunities for implementing knowledge management solutions, most organizations have built web-centric system [12].

To find related documents from volumes of web pages, a search engine is used. Because the search engine collects web pages indices and maintains them automatically, it is powerful for sharing codified knowledge.

However, reviewing the approaches in the previous section, there have been requirements as follows: when a person in a group finds a solution from many search results, he should transfer his experience as knowledge to others in his group. Further, when we interviewed people in an organization, we found the interesting requirement as follows:

1. For proper noun such as the names of people or departments, users often request unique solutions for terms while search engines provide many pages.
2. For tacit knowledge (that is, knowledge that cannot be expressed in web pages), users request information about "who knows the matter" or "which rules specifies the matter. A related requirement is also discussed elsewhere [1]. This requirement implies the search interface for web and those for other applications should be integrated.
3. Because it is difficult to externalize the person's interest, their term-solution relationship (let us call it shortcut) can not always be defined beforehand. Rather such relationship should be accumulated and combined step by step.
4. Even if a shortcut is defined once, it may degrade over time. Further, its availability depends on the person's situation and status. So, the shortcut knowledge definition should be maintenance free. In other words, modifying knowledge when someone finds a wrong shortcut should not be time consuming task.
5. Even if shortcuts work well for a group, they sometimes do not work for others. Then, the granularity of the group becomes an issue. Then the level of personalization should be carefully designed [2].
6. Once shortcut knowledge does work well for an organization, it should be evaluated. If an incentive for knowledge provision exists, people will not hesitate to disclose their knowledge. The necessity of rewards for incentive is also discussed in [13].

Note that the requirements are not satisfied by previous approaches. Then, in order to tame the search engines, we introduce SCIA/SF which works as a front end for any search engine as shown in Fig. 2.

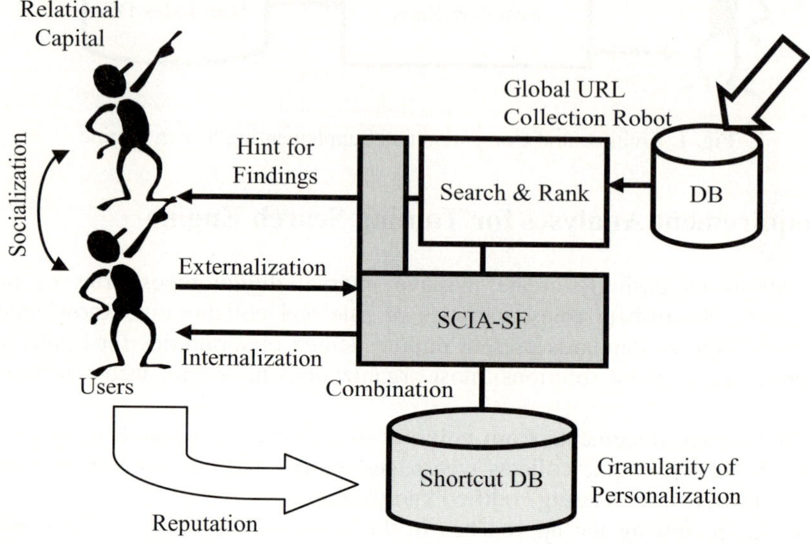

Fig. 2. Basic Idea on SCIA-SF

4   SCIA/SF: A Prototype System

To satisfy the requirements, a search engine should be tamed by persons. Further, functions should be provided for group collaboration. Once people in a group have a chance to collaborate on knowledge finding and externalization, the knowledge sharing can be intensive.

As shown in Fig. 3, SCIA/SF consists of four components and two databases. Let us introduce them in detail.

4.1   Components of SCIA/SF

There are four components in SCIA/SF: Front end term receiver, Bi-pass search, dynamic dictionary maintenance and static dictionary maintenance.

1. **Front end term receiver:** when it receives a search term from a user, it checks whether the term is defined as a shortcut. If it is, this component passes the shortcut to Bi-pass search component. Otherwise, it passes the search term to the general-purpose search engine. For our prototype, the search engine is Google but not limited to it. This stores the term log in a database.

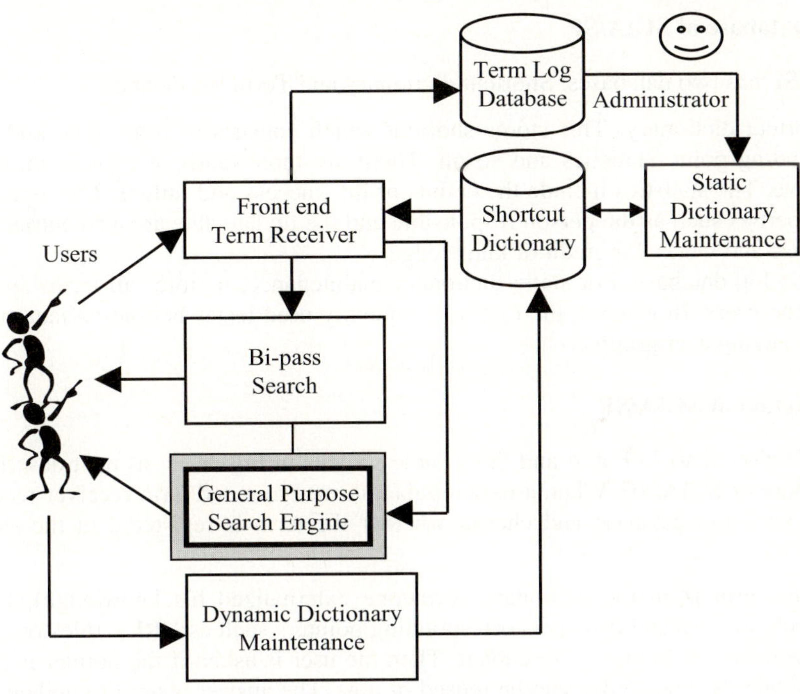

Fig. 3. Components of SCIA/SF

2. **Bi-pass search:** When it receives a shortcut from Front end term receiver, it shows the corresponding pointer to the user. There are three kinds of pointer in our proto-type: URLs, personal or department names with contact information, and organiza-tion rule. For URLs, it displays the corresponding page. This works for personal or department name. For the terms concerning procedures or applications, shortcuts to the contact information for people or departments who are responsible for the work is appreciated. If written rules for work exist, pointer to the rule book is useful for users. Our prototype system is restricted that one term cannot have more than one object.

3. **Dynamic dictionary maintenance:** It keeps the robustness of SCIA/SF by accept-ing the evaluation of users. If a shortcut for a term exists, users can not only ex-press whether it works or not but also modify it. Otherwise, users can create new shortcuts. Of course, users are not forced to do either of these. A detailed procedure for this is discussed later. This component also helps store statistics on successes and failures.

4. **Static dictionary maintenance:** This shows user statistics on search terms. Then users of SCIA/SF can find the knowledge sharing status. Users can add shortcuts for frequently used terms and also remove shortcuts if they do not work well (from user's feedback, it is verified whether the users do or do not appreciate the short-cut). A detailed flow is also shown later.

4.2 Database of SCIA/SF

SCIA/SF has two databases: Shortcut dictionary and Term log database.

1. Shortcut dictionary: This stores shortcut which consists of term, type and corresponding point, statistics and so on. There are three kinds of type as introduced above. The statistics include the counts of hit, success and failure. The registration properties such as the person responsible and the update date are also entries in database and works for credit of knowledge.
2. Term log database: For static dictionary maintenance, it stores all terms specified by the users. In general, the rank of frequently used terms is time-variant and differs among user groups.

4.3 Action of SCIA/SF

Using action chart in Fig. 4 and the sample screens in Fig. 5, let us next describe the procedure of SCIA/SF. When a user inputs a term, Front end term receiver records it in the term log database and checks whether the term is registered in the shortcut dictionary.

1. If the term is in the dictionary (someone externalized his knowledge), Bi-pass search initiates and displays corresponding pointers such as URLs, rules or contact information of human professional. Then the user is asked if the pointer is correct (whether the knowledge can be reused or not). The answer is used to update statistics in the shortcut dictionary by Dynamic dictionary maintenance. Such actions contributes to reputation of shortcut dictionary.

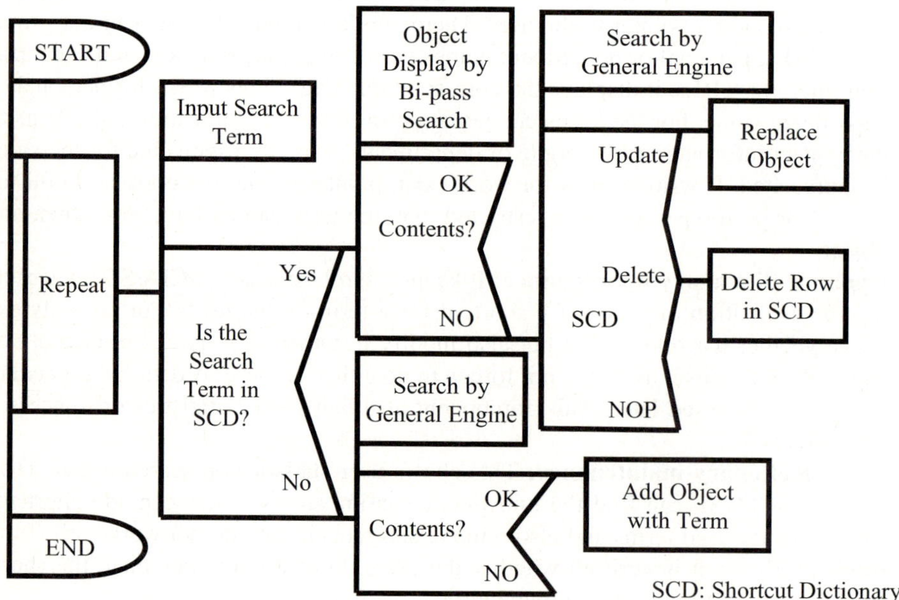

Fig. 4. General Flow of SCIA/SF

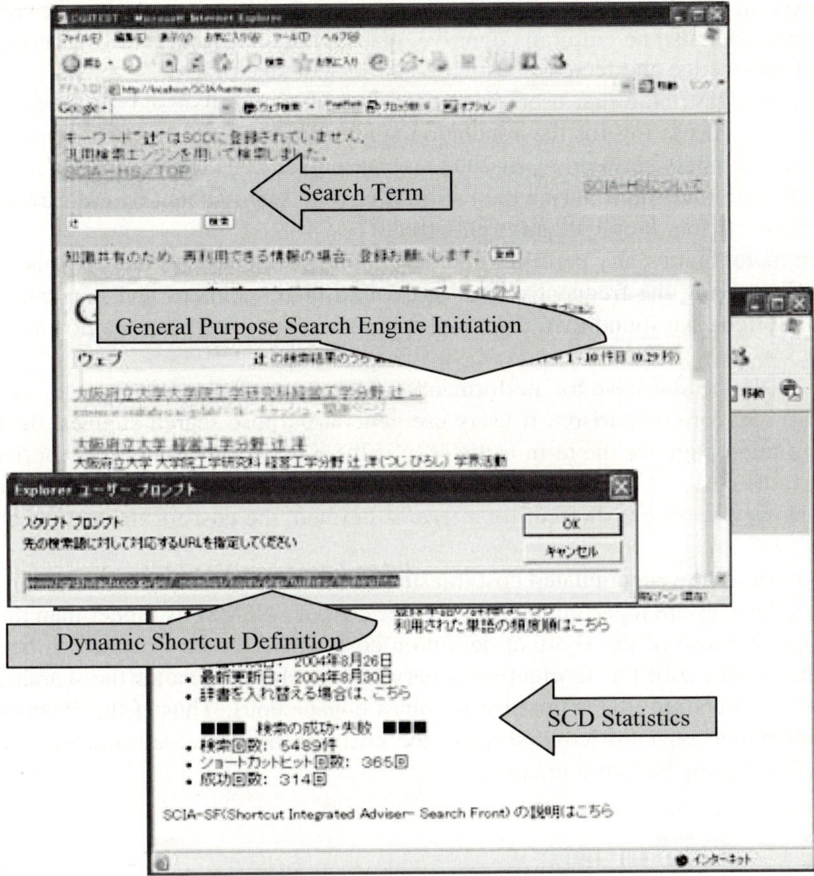

Fig. 5. Example Screens of SCIA/SF

2. If the pointer is not correct, the term will be passed to the general-purpose search engine. If the user finds a pointer to the term then, there is a chance to update Shortcut dictionary (he can capture new knowledge for others).
3. If the term is not there, the general-purpose search engine works as shown in Fig. 5. Similarly, if the user finds a pointer to the term after navigating the retrieved pages, the user is requested to add a shortcut into the dictionary as shown in Fig. 5 (c) (he is asked for knowledge externalization).

The term log database represents what the interesting matters are for the users (novel knowledge finding). The shortcut dictionary stores the statistics of precision on shortcuts (knowledge reputation). Viewing them, the authorized user maintains the dictionary statically (knowledge release).

5 Performance Assessment

To yield technical advances based on practical application, we are going to work on the laboratory level experimentation using Google as general-purpose search engine.

Such experimentation will be a good starting point for exploring the issues not only on technical but also on cultural, cognitive, managerial approach. However, collecting shortcut knowledge and feedback using SCIA/SF will take time.

Therefore, assuming that users have used SCIA/SF, we assessed the performance by analyzing access log for the simulation study. We had 1,975 search cases by our laboratory members between April 2004 and December 2004. Forty terms were specified more than four times during the period. The total search count by their frequently used terms was four hundred and twenty three.

Then more than twenty percent of the searching was done with the frequently used terms. Classifying the frequently used terms into the candidates and non-candidates for the shortcut, we found that about eighty five percent of terms were potential candidates.

Let us define the cost for performance assessment. There are Google cost and SCIA/SF cost for comparison. If users use general-purpose search engines, the order of the solution page for the term is the cost: if the n-th ranked page is appropriate for the term, the cost is n while the cost is forty if no appropriate pages exist for a search result. However, once a shortcut for a term is defined, the cost for the term is always one.

Fig. 6 shows the accumulated cost transition of Google and SCIA/SF. Note that the scales of the axes are logarithmic. Initially, the cost of SCIA/SF is higher than the cost of Google because of the shortcut definition cost. Then, the cost difference between them disappears until the shortcut dictionary grows. However, after the search count exceeds one hundred, the difference becomes conspicuous. Thus if the group members collaborate on knowledge sharing, the cost can be decreased and the level of knowledge sharing becomes intensive.

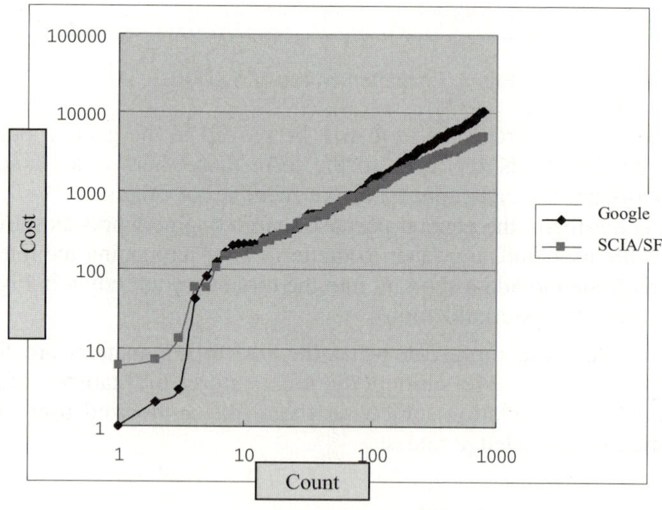

Fig. 6. Performance Assessment

6 Discussion and Concluding Remarks

While this paper has presented a new idea for integrating organizational knowledge into a general-purpose search engine, this paper has also shown how the general-purpose search engine provides a ubiquitous medium for seamlessly integrating human knowledge on internal organization. In our current prototype, the human contact information is only a written e-mail address and phone number. However, real-time remote consulting discussed in [7] [18] is another candidate for integrating knowledge into SCIA/SF.

The basic premise under this research is that search engine and people should collaborate for knowledge sharing and can do. Based on our framework, we have identified several desirable attributes of SCIA/SF:

    i. As a web-based system, SCIA/SF is platform free and has good portability.

    ii. As a front-end system, SCIA/SF is independent from search engines.

    iii. By enhancing bi-pass search component, SCIA/SF will integrate with legacy and existing systems.

    iv. Changing one shortcut dictionary for another, SCIA/SF supports heterogeneous group work.

    v. Collaborating with the general-purpose search engine, SCIA/SF is robust.

    vi. By viewing statistics, SCIA/SF allows evaluation of the level of knowledge sharing and provides the opportunities for incentives.

Thus, the presented framework induces knowledge sharing in an efficient and cost-effective way. In fact, implementing the prototype system took only a couple of months.

Much technical research has concentrated on knowledge management and information sharing. While the presented shortcut is a memory on success, failure database is also important as pointed out by [5]. Because the shortcuts are defined and accumulated by the group with the similar interests, they act as a kind of community computing [6]. From this aspect, there may be also future issues on knowledge management.

References

1. Ackerman, M. S., D. W. McDonald: Answer Garden 2- Merging Organizational Memory with Collaborative Help, Proc of ACM Computer-Supported Cooperative Work (1996)

2. Bush, A. A., A. Tiwana: Designing Sticky Knowledge Networks, Communication of the ACM, Vol. 48, No. 5, pp.67-71 (2005)

3. Chen, F.: Internet Agents, New Riders (1996)

4. Fruchter, R. and P. Demian: CoMem: Designing an Interaction Experience for Reuse of Rich Contextual Knowledge from Corporate Memory, AIEDAM, 16, pp.127-147 (2003)

5. Hatamura, Y., M. Nakao, and K. Iino: Prototyping a Failure Knowledge Database, Journal of IPSJ, 44, 7, PP733-739 (2003)

6. Ishida, T.: Towards Computation over Communities, in Community Computing and Support Systems, Springer (1998)

7. Koga, A., H. Mizuno, H. Tsuji: Intelligent Guidance Method for Remote Consultation Systems using History of User's Reference, IEEE/System Man and Cybernetics□Vol. IV, pp.117-122 (1999)

8. Mizuno, H., Y. Taniguchi, H. Tsuji, H. Yajima, and N. Komoda: A Method of Data Queries Based on Data Visualization Techniques, SIC Journal, Vol. 7, No.2 (1998)

9. Morimoto, H. Mase, C. Hirai, H. Tsuji, K. Kinugawa: Operator Navigation System for Help Desk, World Multiconference on Systemics, Cybernetics and Informatics, pp.173-178 (2000)

10. Nishikawa, N. H. Tsuji: Allowing Multiple Experts to Revise a Thesaurus Database, Proc. Human Computer Interaction '97, pp.371-374 (1997)

11. Nonaka, I. and H. Takeuchi: The Knowledge-Creating Company: How Japanese Companies Create the Dynamics of Innovation, Oxford University Press, Inc. (1995)

12. Tiwana, A.: Integrating Knowledge on the Web, IEEE Internet Computing, May, pp.32-39 (2001)

13. Tiwana, A.: Affinity to Infinity in Peer-to-Peer Knowledge Platforms, Communications of the ACM, 46, 5, pp.77-80 (2003)

14. Tokuda, T., H. Mase, H. Tsuji, Y. Niwa: Experimental Evaluation on Associative Keyword Reminder by Thesaurus, Proc. of 7th IFAC Symposium on Analysis, Design and Evaluation of Man-Machine Systems, pp.161-166 (1998)

15. Tsuji, H., H. Yajima: Man-Machine Cooperation in Information Retrieval, Filtering and Access, Proc. of 7th IFAC Symposium on Analysis, Design and Evaluation of Man-Machine Systems, pp.131-136 (1998)

16. Tsuji, H., Y. Morimoto, Y. Namba, H. Mase, H. Kinukawa, and H. Endoh: User Guidance Function in Natural Language Interface for Document Query and Handling, Proc. of Flexible Query-Answering System '96, pp.105-118 (1996)

17. Tsuji, H. and H. Hashimoto: Expert System for Transferring Programming Know-how from Skilled to Unskilled Programmers, Journal of Japanese Society for Artificial Intelligence, Vol.3, No.6, pp.755-764 (1988)

18. Yajima, H., T. Tanaka, H, Mizuno, and H. Tsuji: Interactive Consultation System with Asymmetrical Communications between Users and Expert Staff in an Electronic Community, In "Community Computing and Support Systems"(Toru Ishida, ED), p.268-281 (1998)

Ontology for Long-Term Knowledge

A. Dourgnon-Hanoune[1], P. Salaün[1], and Ch. Roche[2]

[1] EDF Research and Development, Performance Optimization of Industrial Process
Department, 6, Quai Watier – BP 49, 78401 Chatou Cedex - France
[2] Université de Savoie - Campus Scientifique, 73 376 Le Bourget du Lac cedex - France

Abstract. This article presents experience feedback regarding one of the
methods EDF uses for the reappropriation of ontological concepts in the field of
control and instrumentation. The final approach used here has enabled us to
check out these problems in a satisfactory manner. It has enabled us to obtain
consistent and consensual ontology capitalizing on the knowledge involving the
concepts impacting the field of production plant instrumentation and control.

Keywords: Instrumentation and Control (I&C); Industrial IT; Knowledge
Management; Competence Network; Collaborative Network; Ontology; CMS;
Portal.

The lengthening of the operating life of electricity generation power stations [3] is
leading to problems of maintaining the implemented knowledge and each transmission
to the upcoming generations in the long term. The problem is all the more difficult in
that this knowledge is not directly accessible in usable form but is spread out through
various bodies of knowledge, describing more their uses than their structures.

For several years now, we have been endeavoring to transmit knowledge about the
control and instrumentation of electricity generation power stations [4]. This article
presents experience feedback regarding one of the methods EDF uses for the
reappropriation of ontological concepts in the field of control and instrumentation.

1 Introduction

An approach to the management of knowledge presupposes from the outset an overall
approach defining all the external and internal parameters. We have opted for the
overall *entovation* methods supported by experts all over the world (www. entovation.
com) and which therefore benefits from considerable experience feedback. With
guidance from this approach, we have revealed that EDF control and instrumentation
experts communicate via concepts to be found in original design documents but
which, over the decades, have been disseminated to disappear almost entirely from
the current documents to the benefit of a "user" language.

Therefore, it was essential to locate this link which is missing from the current
documents and which underlies the expertise of the entire domain.

In the following examples, we will look at electromagnetic relays which are very
widely used in older control and instrumentation mechanisms.

M. Ali and R. Dapoigny (Eds.): IEA/AIE 2006, LNAI 4031, pp. 583 – 589, 2006.
© Springer-Verlag Berlin Heidelberg 2006

2   Finding the Concepts Again

2.1   When the Concepts Disappear to the Benefit of the Function

Some original concepts are to be found in the design and qualification documents resulting from engineering or R&D. On/Off relays are indicated as such. In later documents (essentially operating documents), the concept disappeared to the benefit of *logic control relays* where the logic control is the generic function that these relays handle.

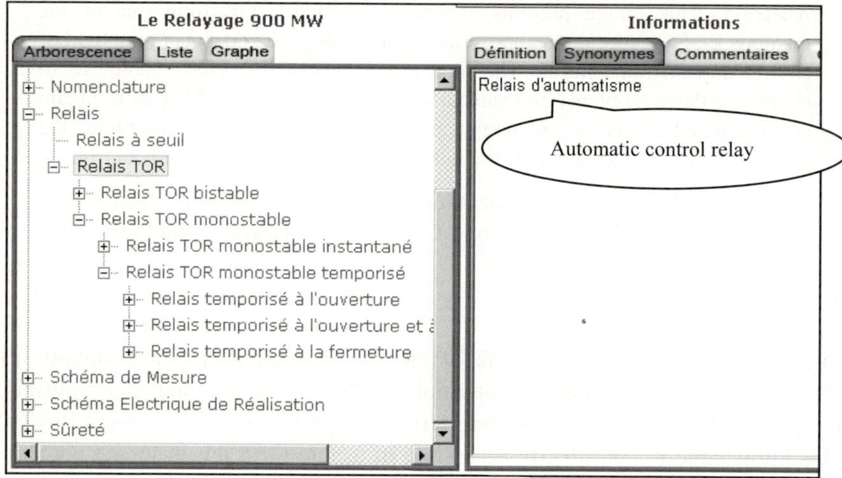

Fig. 1. Association of a synonym

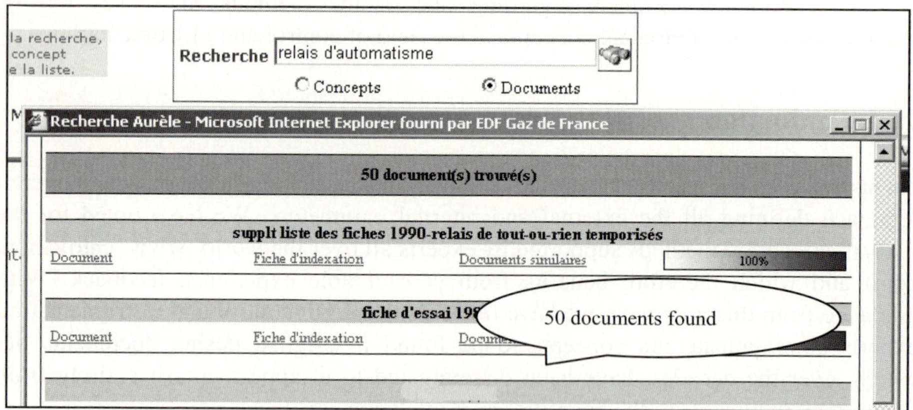

Fig. 2. Search for documents from a user word

Similarly, the *threshold relays* differ from *on/off relays* by their type of input, and are often referred to as *protection relays*; in reality, most of the time, they provide protection (of voltage sources, etc.).

The same object can therefore be designated in various manners depending on where the emphasis is placed: on the structural point of view or the functional one. The two points of view correspond to two different ontologies. Within the framework of our application field, the "structural" ontology has been retained because it is more independent of uses.

In this ontology, we have two types of relays: *On/Off relays* and *threshold relays,* and we associate the user words or synonyms with them (not to be understood in the linguistic meaning of the word but rather as "with reference to" or as "used for" in the thesaurus) corresponding to their function.

Experts then therefore interrogate the system in the user language and beginners recreate the knowledge that had become implicit.

2.2 When the Use Has Simplified the Language

The extraction of knowledge from a body of knowledge, that is to say from user words appearing in the text, poses a number of problems. Indeed, the structure of the vocabulary does not overlie the structure of the ontology concepts. Let us consider the example of *voltage* relays, which are mentioned in many operating documents. A first reflex could be to categorize them as a third sort of relay in the same way as the previous relays. But expertise informs us that *voltage relays* are *threshold relays* whose threshold value is a voltage. There are also *current relays, power relays* and so on which actually designate (user words) current threshold relays, power threshold relays, etc.

Accordingly, we have to understand the text and reconstruct the expertise to transmit it on the one hand and to allow relevant research on the other. In fact, research into *threshold relays* must be able to include research into *voltage relays (voltage threshold relays), power relays*, etc.

If we refer back to the ontological model described in [9], a concept "is defined by the essence of the object it subsumes". This gives us the following concepts: relays, on/off relays, threshold relays, voltage threshold relays, etc.

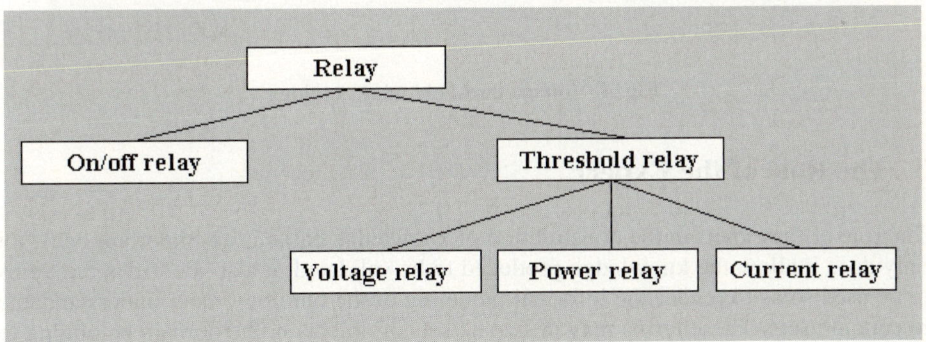

Fig. 3. Relay ontology

2.3   When the Language Is Ambiguous

Let us continue this example with voltage relays. Under *overvoltage relays* and *undervoltage relays*, we have what could be inferred as one being exclusive of the other: anything that is not *over* voltage is *under* voltage and vice versa. But things are not that simple. There are *undervoltage and overvoltage relays.*

The ontological model [9] defines differences as being "elementary units from which the meaning of terms is built. [...] Differences have some sense in the sense that they participate in the definition of conceptual terms". This gives us the following concepts: *overvoltage* and *undervoltage.*

"Differences are defined by [a] couple of opposite differences". In the example of Fig. 4, anonymous concepts C1 and C2 are defined from concept *voltage threshold relays* with the opposite difference to *undervoltage* and *not undervoltag'*.

This gives us the following tree in which all branches are exclusive of one another.

In this way, the search for documents referring to *undervoltage relays* will only refer to corresponding documents and not those referring to *undervoltage and overvoltage relays.*

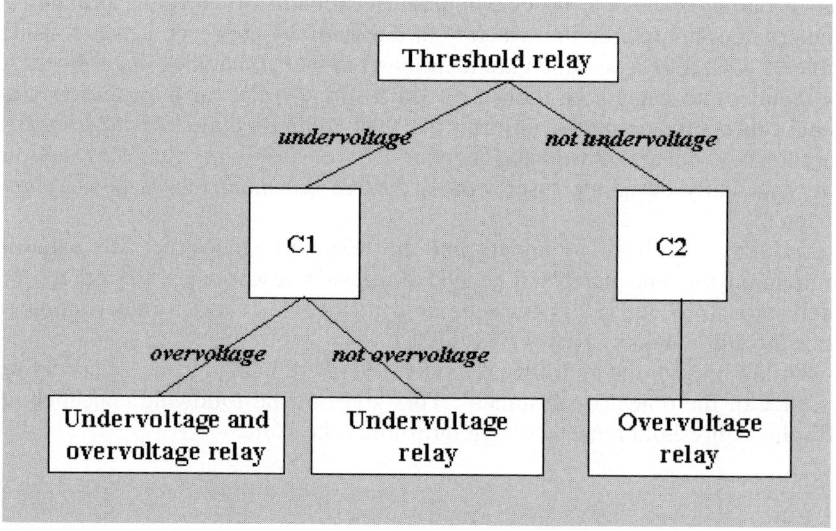

Fig. 4. Voltage threshold relay ontology

3   The Role of the Expert

The role of the expert in the construction of knowledge bases is an important one. Not only does it allow the knowledge produced to be validated, it also identifies the terms to be used so as to render the informal modeling of the ontology more understandable to certain users. These terms may designate sets of objects in the domain belonging to different concepts as opposed to a new concept in the domain to be added to the ontology.

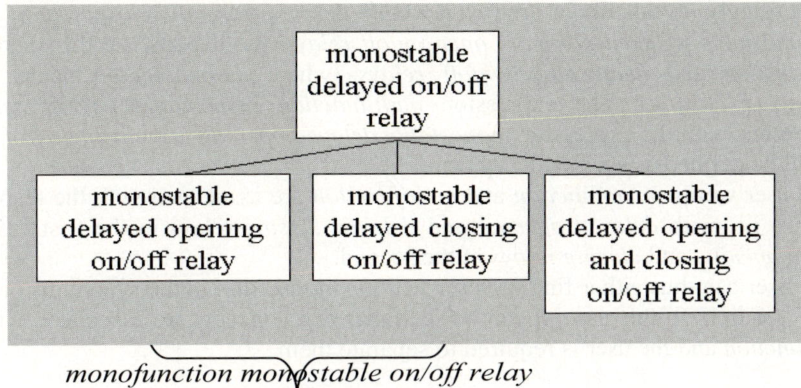

Fig. 5. Set of monofunction monostable on/off relays

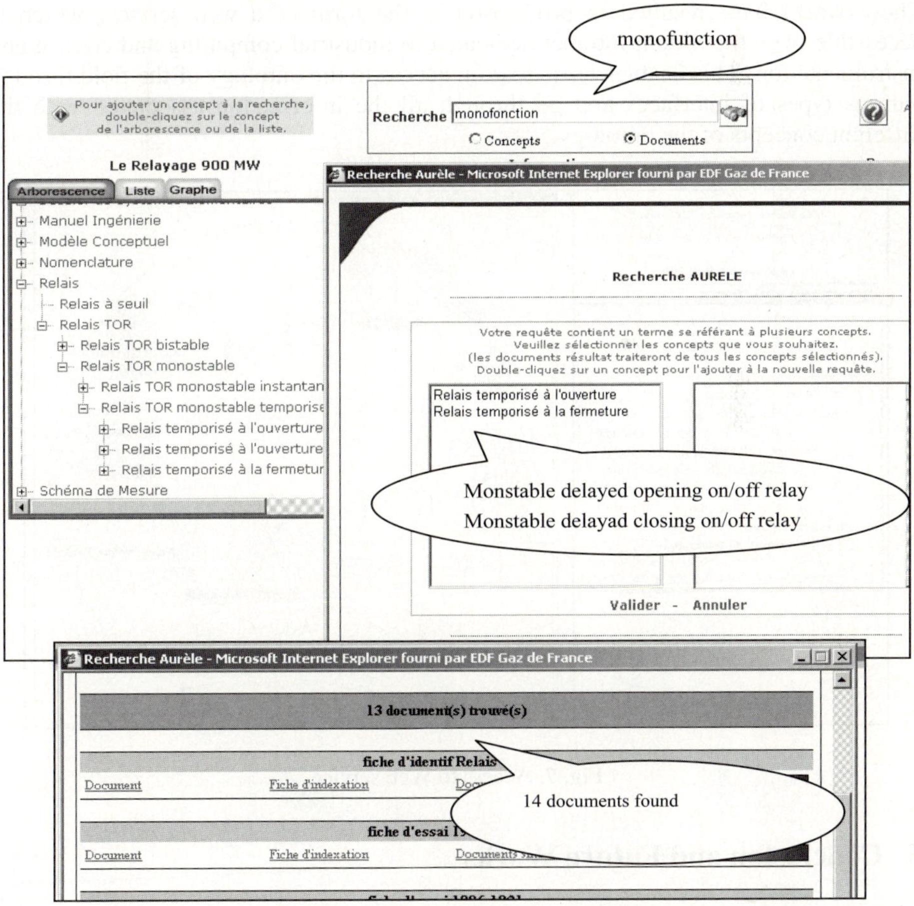

Fig. 6. Search for monofunction relays

Accordingly, to talk about <u>both</u> *monostable delayed normally closed on/off relays* and *monostable delayed normally open on/off relays,* the experts use the expression *monofunction* and *monostable on/off relays* (where *monofunction* means either *opening* or *closing*). The expression *multifunction monostable On/Off relay* is synonymous with the expression *monostable delayed opening* and *closing on/off relay* and will be defined as such in the system.

The user words *monofunction* and *multifunction* are associated with the respective concepts, i.e. with *delayed opening* and *delayed closing* relays in the first case and *delayed opening* and *closing relays* in the second.

The user can thus either find the user word *monofunction* in the synonyms or use it during a search. In this case, it can be seen that two concepts are associated with the *monofunction* and the user is required to separate them.

4   Implementation

These works have resulted in production in the form of a web service, which is accessible from the Sidoni intranet dedicated to industrial computing and control and instrumentation. This enables users to gain access to the ontology of the field through various types of interfaces and go through all the information associated with the different concepts of the ontology.

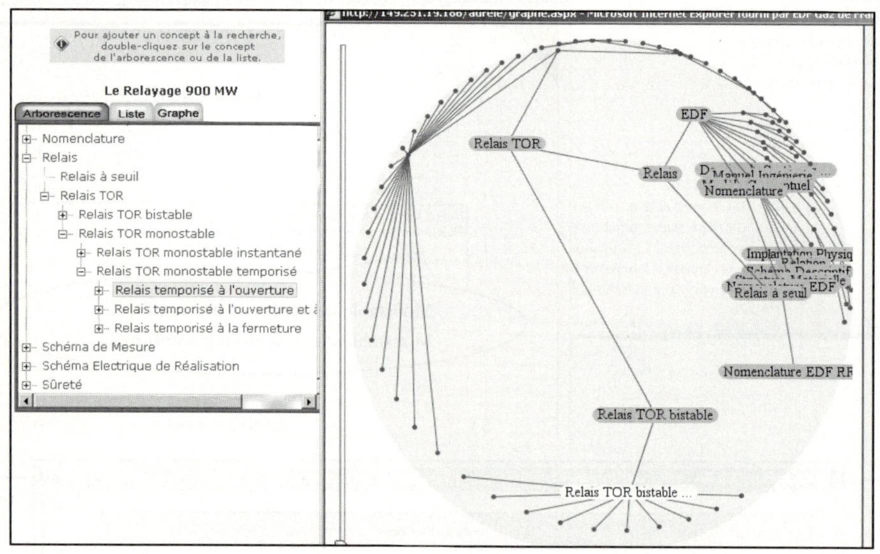

Fig. 7. Access to Web service

5   Conclusion and Future Works

The extension of the operating life of electricity generation power stations has raised the problem of reappropriating the implemented knowledge. The problem is all the more difficult in that most of the sources of information consist of bodies of knowledge whose main objective is not the description of the knowledge but the description of their uses. This means that we have to make a distinction between the structural and functional knowledge, two points of view which, although complementary, cannot be merged into one and the same ontology. We also need to clear up any ambiguities inherent in the "natural" language (even if constrained by our specialty area), if we want to get an ontology that can be used for managing our knowledge. The formal approach used here has enabled us to check out these problems in a satisfactory manner. It has enabled us to obtain a consistent and consensual ontology capitalizing on the knowledge involving concepts in the field of control and instrumentation of generation power stations while taking into consideration the user words appearing in the various documents.

References

[1] *Stephan E. Arnold,* Content Management: Role and Reality, http://www.arnoldit.com/articles/cmkoenigJuly2002.pdf

[2] *J-F. Ballay*, Firme et individu : qui apprend le plus ?, L'expansion Management Review, sept. 2004.

[3] *Ch. Bataille et Cl. Biraux,* Rapport sur la durée de vie des centrales nucléaires et les nouveaux types de réacteurs, Office parlementaire d'évaluation des choix scientifiques et technologiques, Mai 2003

[4] *A. Dourgnon-Hanoune, E. Mercier-Laurent, Ch. Roche*, How to value and transmit nuclear industry long-term Knowledge, ICEIS 2005.

[5] *Gomez et al.*, Ontological Engineering: with examples from the areas of Knowledge Management, e-Commerce and the Semantic Web, by Asuncion Gomez-Perez, Oscar Corcho, Mariano Fernandez-Lopez Springer, 2004

[6] *A. Réquilé-Romanczuk, A. Cechich, A. Dourgnon-Hanoune, J-C. Mielnik,* Towards a Knowledge-Based Framework for COTS Component Identification, *MPEC 2005.*

[7] *C. Roche*, Ontology: a Survey, 8th Symposium on Automated Systems Based on Human Skill and Knowledge, IFAC, September 22-24 2003, Göteborg, Sweden

[8] *C. Roche,* The 'Specific-Difference' Principle: a Methodology for Building Consensual and Coherent Ontologies, IC-AI'2001 2000, Las Vegas, USA, June 25-28 2001,

[9] *C. Roche,* Corporate ontologies and concurrent engineering, Journal of Materials Processing 107 (200) 187-193

[10] *Staab et al.*, Handbook on Ontologies by Steffen Staab (Editor), Rudi Studer (Editor), Springer, 2004

[11] *M. Uschold and R. Jasper*, A Framework for Understanding and Classifying Ontology Applications, IJCAI99 Workshop on Ontologies   and Problem-Solving Methods, Stockholm, Sweden, August 1999.

Introducing Graph-Based Reasoning into a Knowledge Management Tool: An Industrial Case Study

Olivier Carloni[1,2], Michel Leclère[1], and Marie-Laure Mugnier[1]

[1] LIRMM, CNRS - Université Montpellier 2
161 rue Ada, F-34392 Montpellier cedex 5 - France
{carloni, leclere, mugnier}@lirmm.fr
[2] Mondeca, 3 cité Nollez,
F-75018 Paris - France
http://www.mondeca.com

Abstract. This paper is devoted to an industrial case study focused on the issue of how to enhance ITM, a knowledge management tool, with reasoning capabilities, primarily by introducing a semantic query mechanism. ITM knowledge representation language is based on topic maps. We show that these topic maps (and especially those describing the domain ontology and the annotation base) can be naturally mapped to the SG family, a sublanguage of conceptual graphs. As this mapping is reversible, ITM can be equipped with a graph-based query language equivalent to conjunctive queries and it can be enriched with inference rules.

1   Introduction

In the last decade, there has been a massive flow of knowledge into organizations to meet with requirements of (1) capitalization of the knowledge and know-how of their members in order to build up a corporate memory (i.e. a disembodied representation of their expertise) and (2) implementation of their information systems at the "knowledge level", i.e. exploiting semantics of exchanged information. This evolution from information systems to knowledge systems has given rise to true knowledge engineering, which aims at eliciting knowledge (e.g. the semantics of exchanged information content). This elicitation is performed by way of a knowledge representation language and is controled by ontologies (domain ontologies for the conceptual vocabulary and representation ontologies for the language constructs) which are semantic referentials that delineate the meaning of symbols used by these languages. This issue arises again within the framework of the semantic web, which endeavors to describe the content of web resources in order to facilitate their access and use.

Mondeca is a software publisher that is developing ITM (Intelligent Topic Manager), a knowledge management tool based on these principles. The core of this software is a three-level knowledge base (cf. fig. 1):

M. Ali and R. Dapoigny (Eds.): IEA/AIE 2006, LNAI 4031, pp. 590–599, 2006.
© Springer-Verlag Berlin Heidelberg 2006

- the highest level is a meta-model of all ITM knowledge bases; it consists of a representation ontology reflexively specifying the semantics of all representations used by ITM;
- the intermediate level is composed of models that specify the vocabulary used to describe customer data managed by ITM; it generally comprises a domain ontology describing the conceptual vocabulary used to annotate the content of the customer's resources, some (representation) ontologies defining primitives related to specific data structures enabling ITM services (primitives for representing the thesaurus or the logical organization of documents);
- the lowest level contains the instances, which are clustered into workspaces (each workspace being "controlled" by an ontology of the intermediate level): annotations describing the content of information managed by ITM (data, documents), terminological resources (thesaurus) used to index this information, description of the logical organization of documents, etc.

ITM provides many services based on its knowledge base: indexing of documents from the thesaurus, creation of annotations controled by the domain ontology, semi-automatic building of document annotations, semantic navigation through the annotation base, searching the annotation base by a querying mechanism.

The representation language in ITM is based on the Topic Map (TM) paradigm in which knowledge is described by *topics*, representing entities of the modelized domain, and *associations* connecting topics and identifying the *role* played by each topic in the association [ISO00]. Topics can be identified by *names* and characterized by *occurrences* (kinds of attribute-value pairs). Two specific

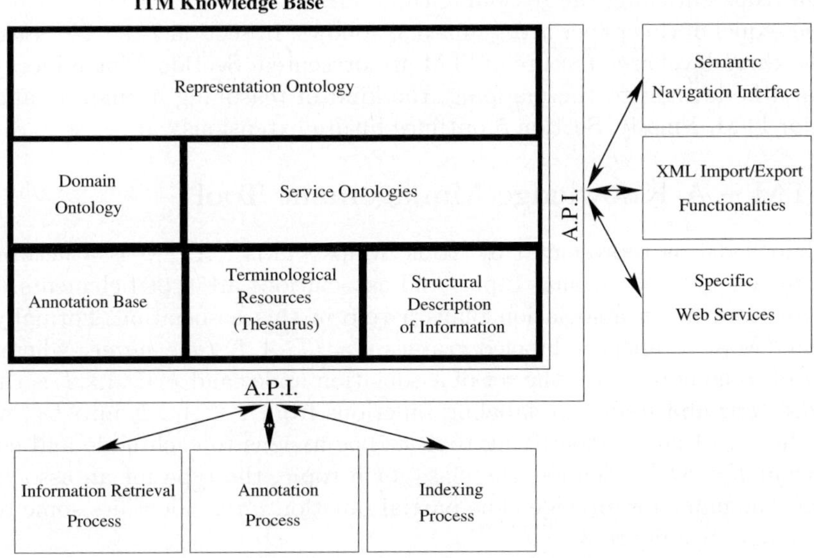

Fig. 1. Workspaces and modules in ITM

binary associations are standardized for any TM: *class-instance* association and *superclass-subclass* association [Top01]. TMs can be formalized as labeled graphs (or hypergraphs) [AdMRV02] where the vertices come from topics and associations and an edge between a topic and an association indicates the role played by the topic in this association (cf. section 2).

LIRMM and Mondeca are collaborating in a research project which aims at introducing reasoning on the knowledge represented in ITM knowledge bases. Formal semantics of representations used by ITM have thus to be defined in order to specify the desired reasonings. Despite the lack of formal semantics within the TM paradigm, its closeness to the conceptual graph model [Sow84] and especially to the $\mathcal{SG}$-family [BM02] – a TM is naturally transformed into a simple conceptual graph (SG) – has led us to map ITM representations into this family. By assimilating TMs to SGs it is possible: to provide ITM with formal semantics since the $\mathcal{SG}$ family is logically based; to incorporate inference rules in ITM bases since the $\mathcal{SG}$ family manages this kind of knowledge (as well as constraints, type definitions, etc); to use the reasoning schemes of the $\mathcal{SG}$ family, which are graph-based (thus operate directly on the knowledge defined by the user) while being sound and complete with respect to the predicate logic; to benefit from efficient algorithms developed for these graph operations and based on combinatorial techniques; and finally to tap the GPL library CoGITaNT, which is dedicated to developing applications based on conceptual graphs and implements the $\mathcal{SG}$ family [Gen97].

In this paper, we present mapping of ITM topic maps to SGs and the query language - as well as the answering mechanism - which is obtained via this mapping, thus equipping ITM with a formally based reasoning module. We then show that these initial results are easily extended to take inference rules into account, thus enriching the reasoning capabilities.

The sequel of this paper is organized as follows. In section 2 the TM language and the three-level architecture of ITM are presented. Section 3 introduces SGs. Section 4 is devoted to the mapping, the kind of reasoning it enables, and the gains for ITM. Finally, Section 5 outlines future extensions.

2   ITM – A Knowledge Management Tool

ITM knowledge is represented by Topic Maps (TMs). A TM is a network of topics linked by associations. Topics and associations are typed elements. Each topic involved in an association plays a role in this association. Formally, we define a TM as a bipartite labeled graph $tm = (T, A, E, type, name)$ where T is the set of topic nodes, A is the set of association nodes and $E \subseteq A \times T$ is the set of edges. *type* and *name* are labeling functions from $T \cup A \cup E$ into L_T, where L_T is the set of labels identifying topics. *type* assigns to each node and edge a label from L_T, which denotes the class for a topic, the type for an association and the role name for an edge. The partial function *name* identifies some topics with a name. See figure 2.

Each topic can be further described by a set of occurrences expressing relevant information about the topic. Each occurrence is composed of a value, a data type (called physical type in ITM) and a topic representing the type of the occurrence (called logical type in ITM). We denote by occ the mapping from T into $2^{V \times D \times L_T}$ which assigns to a topic its occurrence set, where D is the data type set and V is the set of values for types in D. Finally, we call ref the mapping which assigns to a TM the subset of L_T labels returned by the functions $type$ and occ. A TM tm is said to be self-content if each label l from $ref(tm)$ is assigned to a topic by the $name$ function. An ITM knowledge base is a self-content TM structured in three levels, namely the meta level TM, the model level TM and the instance level TM. These three levels fulfill the following constraints:

- the meta level TM is self-content;
- the set of labels obtained by ref to the model level TM (resp. instance level TM) is included in the set of labels assigned by $name$ on the meta level topics (resp. model level TM).
- all meta level topics and model level topics have a name.

The meta level TM defines modeling primitives. These primitives are interpreted by ITM and provide semantics of knowledge in all levels:

- an association of type `allowed association type` linking three topics t_c, t_a and t_r specifies that every topic of class t_c is allowed to play a role t_r in an association of type t_a. For example, the model level in Figure 2 authorizes a topic of class `Company` to play the role `Acquiring` in an association of type `Acquisition` at instance level;
- an association of type `allowed occurrence type` linking t_c and t_o specifies that a topic of class t_c may have an occurrence with logical type t_o;
- an association of type `has physical type` linking t_o and t_p specifies that all occurrences with logical type t_o have the physical type t_p. ITM uses the physical type to correctly interpret the value of the occurrence (as an integer, a date, a string or a pointer).
- the association of type `class-subclass` defines a partial order on topics; the `allowed association type` and `allowed occurrence type` associated with classes of topics are inherited according to this order.

3   Simple Conceptual Graphs

This section is devoted to an informal presentation of basic conceptual graphs. For further details the reader is referred to [CM92] or [BM02] (this latter paper studying the whole $\mathcal{SG}$ family).

A *simple conceptual graph (SG)* is a bipartite labeled graph: one class of nodes, called *concept* nodes, represents entities and the other, called *relations* nodes represents relationships between these entities or properties of them. E.g. the graph G_1 of Figure 3 can be seen as expressing the following knowledge: "A corporation specialized in food-processing acquires the company $S1$; $S1$ controls the company $S2$, which is specialized in food-processing as well". The node labels come from a vocabulary called a *support*, which can be more or less rich. The

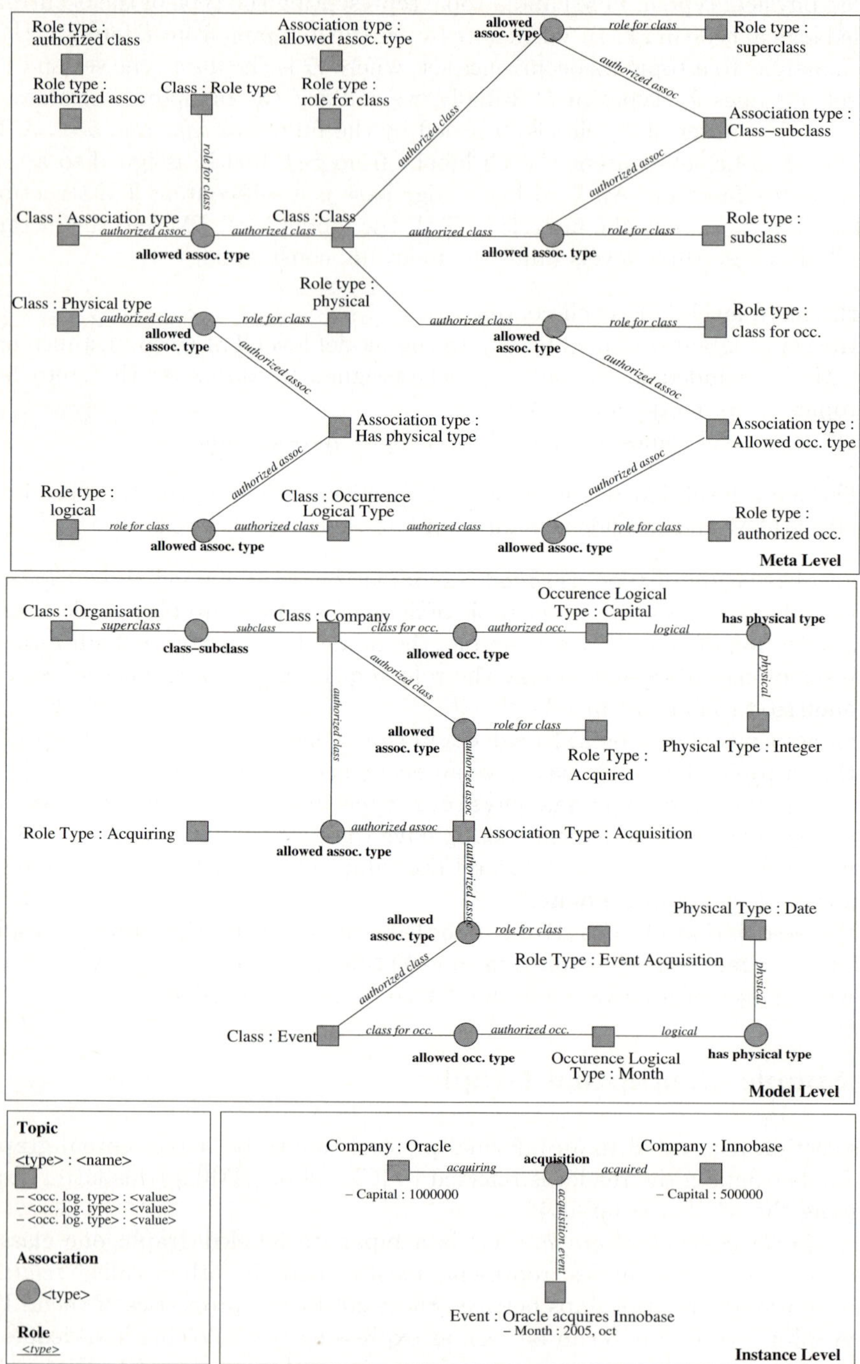

Fig. 2. A (partial) knowledge base with its meta, model and instance levels

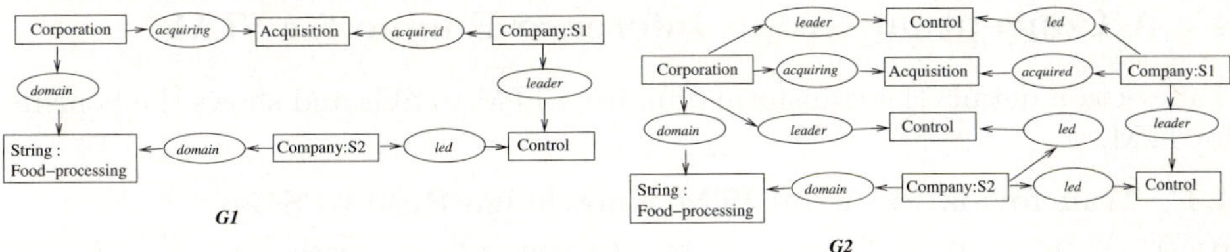

Fig. 3. Two SGs. As relations are all binary here the edge numbering is replaced by directed edges. The generic marker is not represented.

support considered here is a structure $S = (T_C,\ T_R,\ I,\ \sigma)$, where T_C is a set of concept types and T_R is a set of relations with any arity (the arity is the number of arguments of the relation). T_C and T_R are partially ordered. The partial order represents a specialization relation ($t' \leq t$ is read as "t' is a specialization of t"). I is a set of individual markers. σ is a mapping assigning to each relation a signature specifying its arity and the maximal type for each of its arguments. The support can be seen as a rudimentary ontology and SGs encode assertions called *facts*: they assert the existence of entities and relations among these entities.

In a SG a concept node is labeled by a couple $t : m$ where t is a concept type and m is a marker. If the node represents an unspecified entity its marker is the generic marker, denoted by $*$, and the node is called a *generic* node, otherwise its marker is an element of I, and the node is called an *individual* node. E.g. in the SG G_1 of Figure 3, the node [Company:S1] refers to "the" company $S1$, while the node [Corporation:*] refers to "a" corporation. A relation node is labeled by a relation r and, if n is the arity of r, it is incidental to n totally ordered edges. Classically, concept nodes are drawn as rectangles and relation nodes as ovals and the order on edges incidental to a *n-ary* relation node are numbered from 1 to n. A SG is denoted by $G = (C_G, R_G, E_G, l_G)$ where C_G and R_G are respectively the concept and relation node sets, E_G is the set of edges and l_G is the mapping labeling nodes and edges.

The fundamental notion for comparing SGs is a mapping from a SG to another called a *projection*. In graph terms it is a graph homomorphism. Intuitively a projection from G to H proves that the knowledge represented by G is included in (or implied by) the knowledge represented by H. More specifically, a projection π from G to H is a mapping from C_G to C_H and from R_G to R_H which preserves edges (if there is an edge numbered i between r and c in G then there is an edge numbered i between $\Pi(r)$ and $\Pi(c)$ in H) and may specialize labels. E.g. see Figure 3: there is a projection from G_1 to G_2 (which is particular since it is injective and does not change labels). See also the SG Q of Figure 5 (where '?' has to be replaced by $*$): there is a projection from Q to G_2 (knowing that Corporation < Company) but not from Q to G_1. Conceptual graphs are provided with a semantics in first order logic that we do not present here due to space limitations. The fundamental result of *projection soundness and completeness* shows the equivalence between projection checking and deduction checking on the formulas assigned to SGs ([Sow84] for the soundness and [CM92] for the completeness).

4   A Conceptual Graph Inference Engine for ITM

This section details the transformation from ITM to SGs and shows the benefits for ITM.

4.1   Transformation from ITM Knowledge Base to SGs

We denote by f the transformation from an ITM base to SGs. This transformation encodes the domain ontology into a support and the annotation base into a SG (or a set of SGs). It is illustrated by Figure 4.

Transformation of a domain ontology into a support.   Let us recall that the domain ontology is a TM of the model level.

1. Three concept types C (for topic classes), AT (association types) and OPT (occurrence physical types) are created as subtypes of a universal type $\top$. To each topic t with $type$ `class`, `association type` or `physical type`, f assigns a concept type with label $name(t)$ subtype of C, AT or OPT resp. The partial order on T_C is induced by the `class-subclass` association.
2. Two relations RT and OLT, with signature $\sigma(RT) = (C, AT)$ and $\sigma(OLT) = (C, OPT)$ resp., are created and represent in the support the supertypes of the role types and the occurrence logical types resp. Each topic t with type `role type` involved in a ternary association of type `allowed association type` connecting t to topics c and a becomes a relation with label $name(t)$, subrelation of RT; its signature is $\sigma(name(t)) = (f(c), f(a))$. Recall that each topic t with type `occurrence logical type` is linked by an association with type `has physical type` to a topic opt and by an association with type `allowed occurrence type` to a topic c; t becomes a relation, subrelation of OLT, with label $name(t)$ and signature $\sigma(name(t)) = (f(c), f(opt))$.

Transformation of an annotation base into a SG.   Let us recall that the annotation base is a TM of the instance level.

1. Each named topic t (i.e. $name(t)$ is defined) becomes an individual concept node labeled by $f(type(t)) : name(t)$; furthermore $name(t)$ is inserted as an individual marker into I.
2. Each unnamed topic t (resp. association a) becomes a generic concept node labeled by $f(type(t)) : *$ (resp. $f(type(a)) : *$).
3. Each edge e connecting an association a and a topic t becomes a relation node labeled by $f(type(e))$. Its two incident edges labeled 1 and 2 are resp. linked to $f(t)$ and $f(a)$;
4. Each occurrence $o = (v, opt, olt)$ in a topic t becomes a relation node labeled by $f(olt)$. Its two incident edges labeled 1 and 2 are resp. linked to a concept node $f(t)$ and to an individual concept node labeled $f(opt) : v$ (this individual node is created only if it does not exist yet).

f is a coding mapping, in the sense that it is *injective* on the set of annotations that can be defined relative to a domain ontology. This property makes it *reversible* and thus enables returning infered knowledge (e.g. an answer to a query) to ITM.

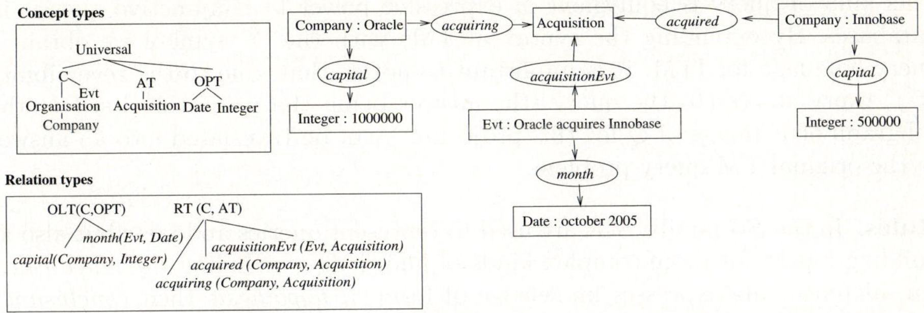

Fig. 4. The transformation f applied to the knowledge represented in Figure 2

4.2   Enhancing ITM Representation and Reasoning Capabilites

What are the gains for ITM? First, f indirectly provides formal semantics to ITM, which is that of conceptual graphs. Second, it enables enriching ITM by two features: a declarative query language, and inference rules integrated into the query answering mechanism. As f is reversible these enrichments are straightforward.

Query language. ITM search functions are able to search substructures of the network restricted to one topic or one association and its neighbors. On the other hand, SGs come with a search mechanism based on projection, which is able to find substructures of *any* shape. Let us consider a knowledge base K composed of a support and a fact base F. Given a query Q represented by a SG, K answers to Q if there is a projection from Q to F, i.e. Q can be deduced from K. Every projection from Q to F can be seen as an answer to Q. More generally, a query may include distinguished (generic concept) nodes. In this case the answer is restricted to these nodes. Classically, these nodes are marked by a '?' symbol (See Figure 5: Q asks for couples of compagnies satisfying certain conditions).

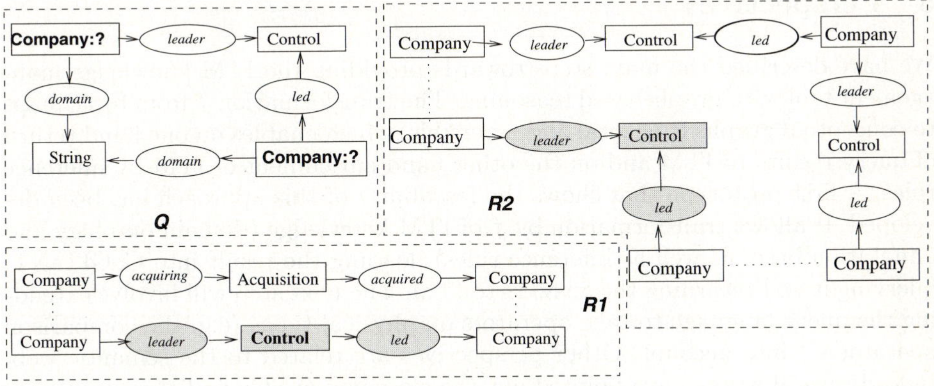

Fig. 5. A query and two rules

This kind of query is equivalent in expressive power to conjunctive queries in databases. By extending the syntax of TMs with the '?' symbol we obtain a query language for ITM. It is important to notice that, due to the reversibility of f, every answer to the query (the answer being the projection itself or the subgraph of F image of Q for this projection) can be translated into an answer to the original TM query problem.

Rules. In the $\mathcal{SG}$ family, SGs are used to represent queries and facts but also as building blocks for more complex kinds of knowledge, including *inference rules*. An inference rule expresses knowledge of form "if *hypothesis* then *conclusion*", where hypothesis and conclusion are both SGs. In Figure 5 two rules are represented. Each dotted line connects a node in the hypothesis and a node in the conclusion; these nodes are called *connection* nodes. The nodes of the conclusion which are not connection nodes are colored in gray. The rules express properties of the concept type "control": acquiring a company leads to control it ($R1$) and exercising control is transitive ($R2$).

A rule R can be applied to a SG F if there is a projection from its hypothesis to F. Applying R to F according to such a projection π consists in "attaching" to F the conclusion of R by merging each connection node of the conclusion with the image by π of the corresponding connection node in the hypothesis. See Figures 5 and 3: if $R1$ is applied to G_1 (using `Corporation` $<$ `Company`) and $R2$ to the resulting SG, one obtains G_2. Since a knowledge base is now composed of a support, facts (say F) and a set of rules (say $\mathcal{R}$), the query mechanism has to take implicit knowledge coded in rules into account. The knowledge base answers to a query Q if a SG F' can be derived from F using the rules of $\mathcal{R}$ such that Q can be projected to F'. Let us consider again Figures 3 and 5 : the base containing the fact G_1 and the rules $R1$ and $R2$ answers to Q; indeed Q can be projected to G_2, which is derived from G_1 by $R1$ and $R2$. Forward and backward chaining schemes have been defined, which are sound and complete with respect to logical deduction [SM96]. As previously, a simple extension of TM syntax and transformation f enables representation and processing of rules.

5   Perspectives

We have described the main steps towards providing the ITM knowledge management tool with graph-based reasoning. The transformation f from topic maps to conceptual graphs is natural and reversible, which enables on one hand return of query results to ITM and on the other hand enrichment of ITM by inference rules. A first prototype that shows the feasability of this approach has been developed. It allows transformation by f of ITM knowledge (domain ontology and annotation base, as well as inference rules), loading the result into CoGITaNT, querying it and returning the answers to ITM. The next step will involve extending the query language to take operators on physical types (e.g. the comparison operator $<$) into account. Other perspectives are related to the semantic web. Indeed several works have pointed out the closeness of SGs and the annotation language RDF/S proposed by the W3C [Hay04]. In particular it has been proved that SG projection is sound and complete with respect to deduction in RDF/S [Bag05]. f could thus be used as a base for defining an RDF/S exchange format for ITM knowledge that would be consistent with its SG semantics, and could be extended to inference rules.

References

[AdMRV02]   P. Auillans, P. Ossana de Mendez, P. Rosenstiehl, and B. Vatant. A formal model for topic maps. In *Proc. of ISWC'02*, volume 2342, pages 69–83, 2002.

[Bag05]   J.-F. Baget. Rdf entailment as a graph homomorphism. In *Proc. of ISWC'05*, 2005.

[BM02]   J.-F. Baget and M.-L. Mugnier. Extensions of Simple Conceptual Graphs: The Complexity of Rules and Constraints. *JAIR*, 16:425–465, 2002.

[CM92]   M. Chein and M.-L. Mugnier. Conceptual Graphs: Fundamental Notions. *Revue d'Intelligence Artificielle*, 6(4):365–406, 1992.

[Gen97]   D. Genest. Cogitant. http://cogitant.sourceforge.net, 1997.

[Hay04]   P. Hayes. Rdf semantics. Recommandation, W3C, 2004.

[ISO00]   ISO/IEC:13250. Topic maps: Information technology – document description and markup languages. `http://www.y12.doe.gov/sgml/sc34/` `http://www.y12.doe.gov/sgml/sc34/`

[SM96]   E. Salvat and M.-L. Mugnier. Sound and Complete Forward and Backward Chainings of Graph Rules. In *Proc. of ICCS'96*, volume 1115 of *LNAI*, pages 248–262. Springer, 1996.

[Sow84]   J. F. Sowa. *Conceptual Structures: Information Processing in Mind and Machine*. Addison-Wesley, 1984.

[Top01]   TopicMaps.Org. Xml topic maps (xtm) 1.0. `http://www.topicmaps.org/xtm/1.0/`, 2001.

Retaining Consistency in Temporal Knowledge Bases

Franz Wotawa and Bibiane Angerer[*]

Graz University of Technology, Institute for Software Technology,
8010 Graz, Inffeldgasse 16b/2, Austria
{wotawa, bangerer}@ist.tugraz.at
http://www.ist.tugraz.at/wotawa/

Abstract. Retaining consistency for large knowledge bases is a difficult task. This holds especially in the case where the knowledge base comprise temporal knowledge and where the knowledge comes from independent and unreliable sources. In this paper we propose the use of temporal logics, i.e., CTL, to describe the background theory and the corresponding Kripke Structure to store the temporal knowledge. Moreover, we introduce a declarative formalization of belief revision which is necessary to keep the knowledge base in a consistent state. Finally, we discuss how the structure of CTL formulas can be used to implement belief revision. The research described in the paper is motivated by a project that deals with automating the analysis of meetings, e.g., to provide meeting summaries, where cameras, microphones, and other sources of knowledge has to be integrated.

Keywords: Knowledge-processing, KBS methodology, temporal reasoning.

1 Introduction

The handling of information that comes from different independent sources is a difficult task. One reason for this observation is the fact that the given information is inconsistent because different sources deliver contradicting information. In computer science this problem becomes worst when considering the following situation. Given a set of sensors which are used for gaining information from a certain situation. Each of these sensors delivers a specific view on the situation. Because of reliability issues and different methodologies used the views are very likely to be inconsistent. Consider for example a meeting situation where several people are interacting (see Figure 1) together. During the meeting the participants present ideas, discuss them, and agree or disagree on results. Usually a meeting is more or less structured. Now assume that we want to have a system that allows for automatically analyzing a meeting with the purpose of providing a meeting summary or to allow for answering questions regarding the meeting

---

[*] Authors are listed in reverse alphabetical order.

M. Ali and R. Dapoigny (Eds.): IEA/AIE 2006, LNAI 4031, pp. 600–609, 2006.
© Springer-Verlag Berlin Heidelberg 2006

and its content. Figure 2 presents the structure of such a system. The meeting analysis system (MAS) has two different sensing devices and a number of other information sources like meeting invitations and schedules, or presentation materials to be used during the meeting. The sensing devices are an audio device which delivers the audio signals together with estimations of the position of the audio source and a video system which allows for recognizing meeting participants and their positions. Moreover, we assume the existence of a system that converts audio data into a textual representation.

In order to provide meeting summaries or to answer given questions the MAS has to store all information gained from the sensing devices, the modules attached to the system, and available background knowledge. Because of unreliable sensors and conversion routines like speech-to-text the observed information is very unlikely to be consistent with the background knowledge. Hence, providing a consistent world model which should be the final result of the information integration module is difficult. Beside consistency we face the problem that the observed information is not complete with respect to the available information a human can gain when listening to the audio and watching the available video information.

The objective of this paper is to provide a knowledge representation schema together with reasoning mechanisms that allow for:

1. checking and ensuring consistency, and
2. preserving as much information as possible and gaining new one.

Fig. 1. A classical meeting situation

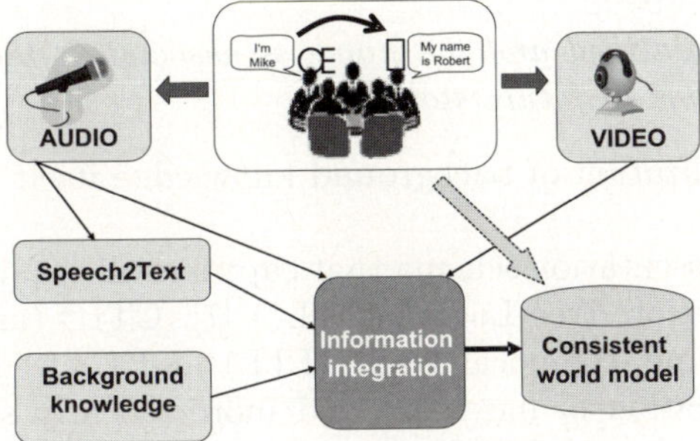

Fig. 2. Information sources

Based on this knowledge representation schema other applications like automated meeting analyzing tools are possible. Such applications require some sort of query language that enable the extraction of the needed information from the consistent knowledge base.

2   Representing the World

The information integration module (Fig. 2) obtains events and state information that represent the current state of a meeting from the attached sensors like audio or video. This information usually comprises a proposition like the number of participants which are detected by the video system together with some measure indicating the confidence about the proposition. Although the confidence can be high the proposition does not have to be true in the real world at the current point in time. Moreover, due to the fact that audio and video sensors exchange information directly they may deliver contradicting input to the information integration module. These contradictions which may not be detected at a certain state but later have to be identified and removed. The removal of contradictions can be done by removing propositions from world states such that the world state together with the underlying background theory are consistent again. Unfortunately, there can be several solutions for one problem and we have to deal with alternative world states in order to avoid loosing any information gathered by the sensors.

A knowledge representation schema that is capable to represent all information about an evolving situation like the mentioned meeting situation together with alternatives has to fulfill the following requirements:

1. Consider the storage of temporal knowledge.
2. Allow representation of background knowledge.
3. Handle alternative scenarios within the same schema.
4. Enable consistency checks.

Regarding background knowledge we want to specify sentences like the following.

"It cannot be the case that the number of participants changes over time when nobody is leaving the room."

"If a person is identified and the name is associated, then the name of the person does not change in future states."

Hence, the formalization of background knowledge itself requires to capture temporal aspects.

A knowledge representation schema that captures all requirements is the temporal logic Computation Tree Logic* (CTL*) [7]. CTL* (and in particular its fragments Linear Time Temporal Logic (LTL) and CTL) have been successfully used for verification of hardware and more recently software [4, 10]. For our purpose CTL can be used to formalize the background theory. The consistency check is done by checking the background theory against the current world model which is basically a state transition diagram. Each state comprises a set

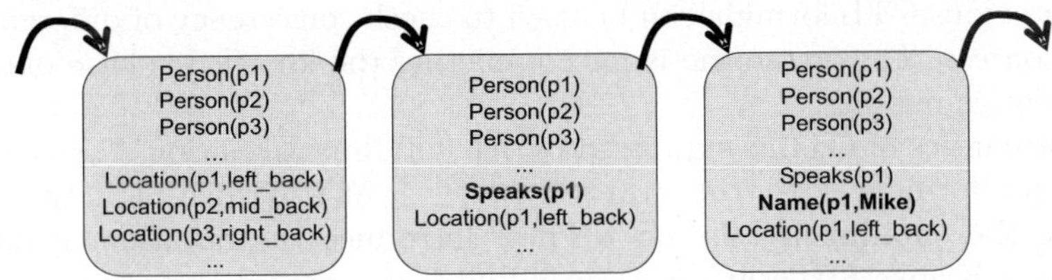

Fig. 3. Parts of a evolving world model

of proposition that are true. States are connected via directed edges. Going from one state to its successor state corresponds to advancing time. Each state corresponds to a time interval in the real world where the given set of propositions do not change. Figure 3 shows a part of a world model.

Formally, the world model is represented as a Kripke Structure $K = (A, S_0, S, R, L)$ where A is a finite set of atomic propositions, S is a finite set of states, $S_0 \subseteq S$ is a set of initial states, $R \subseteq S \times S$ is a relation which represents the edges between the states, and $L : S \mapsto 2^A$ is a mapping assigning each state of S a set of atomic propositions true in that state. L is called label function. For example, the label function L for the leftmost state in Fig. 3 comprises the propositions $Person(p1)$, $Location(p1, left_back)$ and others.

In order to be self contained we briefly introduce CTL and its semantics. In CTL we distinguish between state formulas and path formulas. Path formulas allow to speak about temporal issues whereas state formulas represent knowledge about one state. CTL formulas can use the branching time operators **A** and **E** which stand for every respectively some computational path and linear-time operators as well as operators from standard propositional logic. The linear time operators are **X** (next time), **U** (until), and **V** (unless). Formally, CTL formulas are state formulas which are inductively defined as follows:

1. Any atomic proposition $a \in A$ is a state formula.
2. If ϕ and ρ are state formulas, then $\neg\phi$, $\phi \wedge \rho$, and $\phi \vee \rho$ are state formulas.
3. If ϕ and ρ are state formulas, then $\mathbf{X}\phi$, $\phi\mathbf{U}\rho$, and $\phi\mathbf{V}\rho$ are path formulas.
4. If ϕ is a path formula, then $\mathbf{E}\phi$ and $\mathbf{A}\phi$ are state formulas.

Other operators like **F** (finally) and **G** (globally) can be expressed as $\mathbf{F}\phi \leftrightarrow$ **true U** ϕ and $\mathbf{G}\phi \leftrightarrow$ **false V** ϕ respectively.

For example, saying that a particular person cannot have different names during the meeting is represented by the following CTL formula:

$$AG\neg\,(Name(X,Y) \wedge Name(X,Z) \wedge Y \neq Z)$$

We also can express the fact that knowing a person's name in one state allows us to derive the person's name in the next state.

$$AG\,(Name(X,Y) \rightarrow X\,Name(X,Y))$$

The previous CTL formula can be used to check consistency of different information sources. The latter one is for completing the knowledge base once some information is missing.

The semantics of CTL is expressed by the entailment relation $K, s \models \phi$ which means that formula ϕ is true in a state $s \in S$ of a Kripke Structure K. To formalize the entailment relation we first introduce the notation of paths. A path π of a Kripke Structure K is an infinite sequence of states $\langle s_0, s_1, s_2, \ldots \rangle$ such that each successive pair of states (s_i, s_{i+1}) is an element of R, i.e., there exists an edge between s_i and s_{i+1} in the Kripke Structure. $\pi(i)$ denotes the i-th element of π ($i \geq 0$), and π^j denotes a suffix of π starting at element j, i.e., $\pi^j = \langle \pi(j), \pi(j+1), \ldots \rangle$.

1. $K, s \models a$ if $a \in L(s)$, for any atomic proposition $a \in A$.
2. $K, s \models \neg\phi$ if $K, s \not\models \phi$
3. $K, s \models \phi \wedge \rho$ if $K, s \models \phi$ and $K, s \models \rho$
4. $K, s \models \phi \vee \rho$ if $K, s \models \phi$ or $K, s \models \rho$
5. $K, s \models \mathbf{A} \ \phi$ if $K, \pi \models \phi$ for all paths π with $\pi(0) = s$.
6. $K, s \models \mathbf{E} \ \phi$ if there exists a path π with $\pi(0) = s$ such that $K, \pi \models \phi$.
7. $K, \pi \models \phi$ if $K, \pi(0) \models \phi$
8. $K, \pi \models \mathbf{X} \ \phi$ if $K, \pi^1 \models \phi$
9. $K, \pi \models \phi \ \mathbf{U} \ \rho$ if there exists an integer $k \geq 0$ such that $K, \pi^k \models \rho$ and $K, \pi^j \models \phi$ for all $0 \geq j < k$.
10. $K, \pi \models \phi \ \mathbf{V} \ \rho$ if for every integer $k \geq 0$, $K, \pi^j \not\models \phi$ for all $0 \geq j < k$ implies $K, \pi^k \models \rho$.

If $K, s_0 \models \phi$ for all initial states $s_0 \in S_0$, then we write $K \models \phi$. We say that ϕ is contradicting the Kripke Structure if $K \not\models \phi$.

3 Constructing the World Model

We consider an information integration module that is connected with sensors. The sensors send events at certain points in time. The first step that has to be provided by the information integration module is to store the received events as corresponding atomic propositions into a Kripke Structure. For this purpose we assume that the sensors send an event E, or $\neg E$ at time t_E whenever a specific feature is detected or vanishes respectively. Hence, if E is received by the information integration model a corresponding atomic proposition is added to the current state. If $\neg E$ is received the corresponding atomic proposition is removed from the current state. A new state is generated whenever time t from one of the sensors advances. In this case the current state becomes the old one. A new current state is generated. This state comprises all atomic formulas from the old state. A directed edge between the old and the current state is added to the Kripke Structure. Formally, the algorithm for constructing the initial world model looks like follows:

1. **Initialization**
   (a) Initialize the Kripke Structure $K = (A, S_0, S, R, L)$. A is set to all atomic propositions that are used in the given background theory, $S_0 := S := \{s_0\}$, $L(s_0) := \emptyset$, $R := \emptyset$.
   (b) Set the current state s to s_0 and the current time t to 0.
2. **Event handling:** If an event or its negation $\psi \in \{E, \neg E\}$ is received from one of the sensors, do the following:
   (a) if $t_E > t$ then let the old state be the current one, i.e., $o := s$, generate a new current state s, add (o, s) to R, set $t := t_E$, and let $L(s) := L(o)$. Otherwise, do nothing.
   (b) If ψ is of the form E, then add the corresponding atomic proposition a_E to $L(s)$.
   (c) If ψ is of the form $\neg E$, then remove the corresponding atomic proposition a_E from $L(s)$.

Step 2 of the algorithm is executed as long as events come from the sensors or whenever the algorithm is stopped by an external event, i.e., the user of the MAS stops analyzing the meeting. The result of the algorithm is a Kripke Structure, i.e., the initial world model, which captures all observations. Because of the algorithm the initial world model has the same structure like a linked list. No alternative paths are represented and neither consistency nor completeness (wrt. the background knowledge) can be guaranteed.

4   Revising the World Model

The most important objective of the information integration module is to provide a consistent and complete world model with respect to the given background knowledge. For this purpose the initial world model has to be checked. In case of detected inconsistencies we are interested in changing the Kripke structure (i.e., the initial world model) such that the contradiction cannot be derived anymore. Moreover, in the particular application context we have to find a Kripke Structure which represents the model of the real world, e.g., a meeting, that is not in contradiction with all given CTL formulas representing the background theory. This problem is well known in literature and referred as belief revision problem. Buccafurri and colleagues [3] presented a solution to the belief revision problem of Kripke Structures. Their approach deals with changing the connections between the states of the Kripke Structure, focusing mainly on the repair of concurrent programs, and is based on other program repair approaches like Console and colleague's work [6].

Although the basic idea behind belief revision can be adapted to solve the belief revision problem for temporal knowledge bases in our area, there is one important difference which have to be taken into account. Changing the connections between the states of the Kripke Structure is not enough. There is one important reason that supports this observations. First, when starting to build the knowledge base from observations the resulting Kripke Structure is hardly complete and consistent with respect to the given background knowledge. In order to ensure consistency, atomic propositions have to be removed from the states or new states representing alternative worlds and their corresponding connections have to be constructed. Moreover, for ensuring completeness new atomic propositions have to be added to the Kripke Structure. Hence, the label function of states, the set of states and their connectivity relation have to be updated.

In order to define formally the belief revision we first introduce the concept of update operators. An update operator either add an object to or remove an object from a part of the Kripke Structure. Depending on the part of the Kripke Structure, i.e., the states, the label function, or the state relation, we have different operators.

L-updates. The L-update operator $L^+(s, a)$ $(L^-(s, a))$ adds (removes) an atomic proposition a from the label function $L(s)$.

S-updates. The S-update operator $S^+(s)$ $(S^-(s))$ adds (removes) the state s from the set of states S of the Kripke Structure.

R-updates. The R-update operator $R^+(s, s')$ $(R^-(s, s'))$ adds (removes) the tuple (s, s') from the set R.

$K|u$ denotes the application of an update operator u to a Kripke Structure K. Note that the update operators cannot be applied in an arbitrary order. For example trying to apply the L-update operator to a non-existing state will not change the Kripke structure. Moreover, after introducing a state it has to be connected to another state.

We now define an update U to a Kripke Structure $K = (A, S_0, S, R, L)$ as a sequence $\langle u_1, \ldots, u_n \rangle$. The result of applying U to K is inductively defined by:

1. $K|\langle u_1 \rangle = K|u_1$
2. $K|\langle u_1, u_2, \ldots u_n \rangle = (K|\langle u_1 \rangle)|\langle u_2, \ldots, u_n \rangle$

We define an update U as sound and complete iff the following rules are fulfilled:

- No single update operator of U tries to update a nonexistent part of the Kripke Structure during its application.
- After applying the U the following property must hold for the resulting Kripke Structure K'. For all states s in K' there must be a path from the initial state to s.
- The Kripke Structure must be consistent with the background theory T which is a CTL formula, i.e., $K, s_0 \models T$.

Of course, when given an initial model and a background theory, we are only interested in finding sound and complete updates. Unfortunately, searching for such an update is intractable because all possible combinations have to be checked. In order to speed up computation we suggest the use of heuristics that take care of the structure of the CTL formulas used in the background theory.

For example, consider the previously introduced formulas

$$AG \neg \left(Name(X,Y) \wedge Name(X,Z) \wedge Y \neq Z\right) and$$
$$AG\left(Name(X,Y) \rightarrow X Name(X,Y)\right).$$

The first one is for checking consistency within a state whereas the latter is for ensuring completeness of atomic propositions along a path. In this case, the formular says that the name of the person remains the same in the next state. If we detect an inconsistency with respect to these formulas, we have to change the Kripke structure in order to distinguish two cases. Either the assigned name in the first occurrence is correct or the name in a later state is correct. A similar situation is depicted in Fig. 4(a). In this case the number of participants (*no_part*) is not allowed to change. A different correction is necessary for the situation in Fig. 4(b) where the consistency within one particular state is not ensured. In this example a detector delivers the observation that there is no noise (*no_noise*) but someone is speaking (*speaks*) which is obviously a case that cannot occur. The solution for this situation would be to introduce a new state to handle the inconsistency. Fig. 4(c) describes the situation where not all information is provided by the sensors. This information has to be restored by adding the necessary atomic propositions to the states. The computation of an update using the ideas described above would comprise the following steps. First, find out the reason for a detected inconsistency, e.g., a formula describing consistency requirements for a state is responsible for the inconsistency. Second, apply rules for adding new update operations. These rules have to correspond to the detected reason. For example, if a state inconsistency is detected, then it is necessary to introduce alternative states. These alternative states comprise

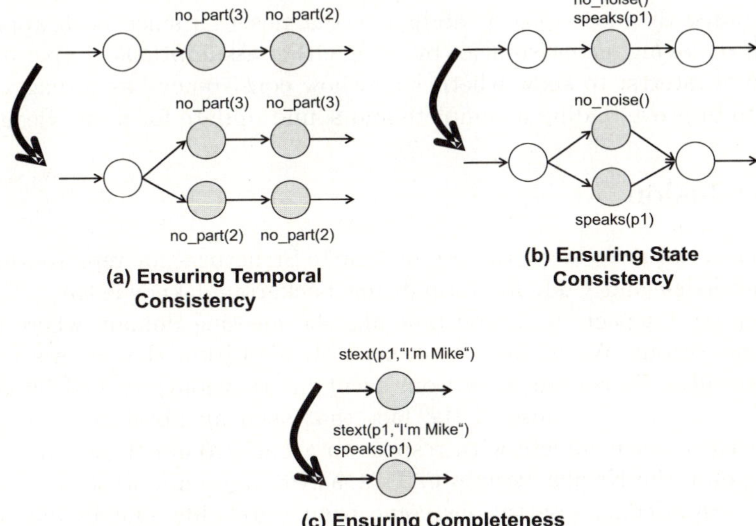

Fig. 4. Revising the knowledge base

all atomic propositions like the original state, except those propositions that are responsible for the conflict. For these propositions only one is allowed to occur in the original state and its alternative states. Third, use the modified Kripke Structure to check consistency again. If all consistencies are removed, the process stops and the update together with the finally created Kripke Structure is given back as result. Otherwise, a new reason has to be detected and so forth. Of course without further restrictions there is no guarantee that the proposed computation of the update halts. Future research has to deal with this issue.

5   Related Research

To our knowledge the use of Kripke Structures for representing world states together with CTL formulas for representing background knowledge is new. Previous research in this domain has mainly focused on using Kripke Structures and CTL for verification purposes, e.g., [4, 10]. The update or belief revision of Kripke Structures has been described before by Buccafurri et al. [3]. However, the authors introduce update only for the state relationship which seems to be enough for their purpose. Moreover, [3] is a very good source for reading about the relationship between the Kripke Structure revision and abductive reasoning for belief revision.

The work of Buccafurri et al. [3] makes use of the introduction of update operators like the work done by Console et al. [6]. In their paper and successor papers like [1, 2, 8] and most recently [9] the update operator is used in the context of debugging, namely fault detection, correction, repair. In their work there has been no necessity to handle temporal aspects which distinguishes their papers from ours.

There are of course also relationships to diagnosis approaches. Both to consistency-based diagnosis [11] or abductive diagnosis [5] since both approaches deal with removing inconsistencies by using either assumptions or operations. It would be of interest to show whether and how consistency-based diagnosis can be used to improve finding a complete and sound update for a knowledge base.

6   Conclusion

In this paper we introduced the use of Kripke Structures for representing temporal knowledge and CTL for formalizing background knowledge in domains where temporal aspects are important like the meeting domain where our examples come from. We further introduced an algorithm that allows for computing an initial knowledge base from event information provided by external sources like sensors. Because of the fact that such an obtained knowledge is neither correct nor complete with respect to a background theory, it is important to update the Kripke Structure. This is even more important in situations where the knowledge/observations come from unreliable sources like sensors. Therefore, we first introduced conceptually the concept of updating the initial knowledge which extends previous research. Second, we introduced heuristics for computing the update which is based on the structure of the formulas within the background knowledge. A pattern matching approach would give us back the required changes. There are open problems which have to be solved. It is unclear whether the heuristics can be adapted and used for all formulas that occur in practice. Furthermore, requirements that allow the use of the heuristics have to be obtained. Moreover, a proof of concept study has to be carried out.

Acknowledgement

The project results have been developed in the MISTRAL project (http://www.mistral-project.at). MISTRAL is financed by the Austrian Research Promotion Agency (http://www.ffg.at) within the strategic objective FIT-IT under the project contract number 809264/9338.

References

1. G. W. Bond and B. Pagurek. A Critical Analysis of "Model-Based Diagnosis Meets Error Diagnosis in Logic Programs". Technical Report SCE-94-15, Carleton University, Dept. of Systems and Computer Engineering, Ottawa, Canada, 1994.
2. Gregory W. Bond. *Logic Programs for Consistency-Based Diagnosis.* PhD thesis, Carleton University, Faculty of Engineering, Ottawa, Canada, 1994.
3. Francesco Buccafurri, Thomas Eiter, Georg Gottlob, and Nicola Leone. Enhancing model checking in verification by ai techniques. *Artificial Intelligence*, 1999.
4. E.M. Clarke, E.A. Emerson, and A.P. Sistla. Automatic Verification of Finite-State Concurrent Systems Using Temporal Logic Specifications. *ACM Transactions on Programming Languages and Systems*, 8(2):244–263, April 1986.
5. Luca Console, Daniele Theseider Dupré, and Pietro Torasso. On the relationship between abduction and deduction. *Journal of Logic and Computation*, 1(5):661–690, 1991.
6. Luca Console, Gerhard Friedrich, and Daniele Theseider Dupré. Model-based diagnosis meets error diagnosis in logic programs. In *Proceedings 13th International Joint Conf. on Artificial Intelligence*, pages 1494–1499, Chambery, August 1993.
7. E. Allen Emerson. Temporal and modal logic. In *Handbook of Theoretical Computer Science, Volume B: Formal Models and Sematics (B)*, pages 995–1072. J. van Leeuwen, North-Holland, 1990.
8. Alexander Felfernig, Gerhard Friedrich, Dietmar Jannach, and Markus Stumptner. Consistency based diagnosis of configuration knowledge bases. In *Proceedings of the European Conference on Artificial Intelligence (ECAI)*, Berlin, August 2000.
9. G. Friedrich and K. Shchekotykhin. Diagnosis of description logic knowledge bases. In *Working Notes of the IJCAI-05 Workshop on Model-Based Systems*, Edinburgh, Scotland, August 2005.
10. Kenneth L. McMillan. *Symbolic Model Checking.* Kluwer Academic Publishers, 1993. ISBN 0-7923-9380-5.
11. Raymond Reiter. A theory of diagnosis from first principles. *Artificial Intelligence*, 32(1):57–95, 1987.

Locality-Convolution Kernel and Its Application to Dependency Parse Ranking

Evgeni Tsivtsivadze, Tapio Pahikkala, Jorma Boberg, and Tapio Salakoski

Turku Centre for Computer Science (TUCS)
Department of Information Technology, University of Turku
Lemminkäisenkatu 14 A, FIN-20520 Turku, Finland
`firstname.lastname@it.utu.fi`

Abstract. We propose a Locality-Convolution (LC) kernel in application to dependency parse ranking. The LC kernel measures parse similarities locally, within a small window constructed around each matching feature. Inside the window it makes use of a position sensitive function to take into account the order of the feature appearance. The similarity between two windows is calculated by computing the product of their common attributes and the kernel value is the sum of the window similarities. We applied the introduced kernel together with Regularized Least-Squares (RLS) algorithm to a dataset containing dependency parses obtained from a manually annotated biomedical corpus of 1100 sentences. Our experiments show that RLS with LC kernel performs better than the baseline method. The results outline the importance of local correlations and the order of feature appearance within the parse. Final validation demonstrates statistically significant increase in parse ranking performance.

1 Introduction

With availability of structured data applicable for statistical and machine learning techniques, application of kernel methods (see e.g. [1, 2]) is shown to have an important role in Natural Language Processing (NLP). Recently, several papers have presented and applied new kernels to NLP problems with promising results. Collins and Duffy [3] described convolution kernels for various discrete structures, encountered in NLP tasks, which allow high dimensional representations of these structures in feature vectors. Suzuki et al. [4] introduced the Hierarchical Directed Acyclic Graph (HDAG) kernel for structured natural language data. It was shown that rich representation of the features through directed graphs in parse, improves performance in various NLP applications. A statistical feature selection approach for the above mentioned kernels was proposed in [5]. This work has been motivated not only by rapidly developing field of the kernel methods and their successful applications in NLP, but also by the importance of incorporating domain knowledge for improving the performance of the learning algorithms.

In this study, we address the problem of dependency parse ranking in the biomedical domain. The parses are generated by the Link Grammar (LG) parser

M. Ali and R. Dapoigny (Eds.): IEA/AIE 2006, LNAI 4031, pp. 610–618, 2006.
© Springer-Verlag Berlin Heidelberg 2006

[6] which was applied to the Biomedical Dependency Bank (BDB) corpus[1] containing 1100 annotated sentences. The LG parser is a full dependency parser based on a broad-coverage hand-written grammar. It generates all parses allowed by its grammar and applies the built-in heuristics to rank the parses. However, its ranking performance has been found to be poor when applied to biomedical text [7].

Recently, we proposed a method for dependency parse ranking [8] that uses Regularized Least-Squares (RLS) algorithm [9] and grammatically motivated features. The method, called RLS ranker, worked notably better giving 0.42 correlation compared to 0.16 of the LG heuristics. In this paper, we propose a Locality-Convolution (LC) kernel that provides a correlation of 0.46 when used in RLS algorithm. In all experiments, we applied the F-score based parse goodness function [8], and evaluated the ranking performance with Kendall's correlation coefficient τ_b described in [10].

The LC kernel addresses the problem of parse ranking through the following characteristics. Firstly, it possesses the convolution property described by Haussler [11], and operates over discrete structures. Secondly, it calculates similarity between windows spanning over the closely located features. Furthermore, it makes use of the position sensitive function, which takes into account the positions of the features within the windows. The LC kernel function can be considered as a specific instance of the convolution kernels and can be included in many methods, such as the RLS algorithm that we are using in this study.

The paper is organized as follows: in Section 2, we describe the RLS algorithm; in Section 3, we present grammatically motivated features for parse representation; in Section 4, we discuss convolution kernels, in Section 5, we define notions of locality windows, position sensitive feature matching, and finally introduce the LC kernel; in Section 6, we evaluate the applicability of the LC kernel to the task of dependency parse ranking and benchmark it with respect to previous baseline method; we conclude this paper in Section 7.

2   Regularized Least-Squares Algorithm

Let $\{(x_1, y_1), \ldots, (x_m, y_m)\}$, where $x_i \in P, y_i \in \mathbb{R}$, be the set of training examples. We consider the Regularized Least-Squares (RLS) algorithm as a special case of the following regularization problem known as Tikhonov regularization (for a more comprehensive description, see e.g. [9]):

$$\min_f \sum_{i=1}^{m} l(f(x_i), y_i) + \lambda \|f\|_K^2, \tag{1}$$

where l is the loss function used by the learning machine, $f : P \to \mathbb{R}$ is a function, $\lambda \in \mathbb{R}_+$ is a regularization parameter, and $\| \cdot \|_K$ is a norm in a Reproducing Kernel Hilbert Space defined by a positive definite kernel function K. Here P can be any set, but in our problem, P is a set of parses of the sentences of

---

[1] `http://www.it.utu.fi/~BDB`

the BDB corpus. The target output value y_i is calculated by a parse goodness function, that is, $y_i = f^*(x_i)$, and is predicted with the RLS algorithm. We used the F-score based function f^* as defined in [8]. The second term in (1) is called a regularizer. The loss function used with RLS for regression problems is called least squares loss and is defined as

$$l(f(x), y) = (y - f(x))^2.$$

By the Representer Theorem (see e.g. [12]), the minimizer of equation (1) has the following form:

$$f(x) = \sum_{i=1}^{m} a_i K(x, x_i),$$

where $a_i \in \mathbb{R}$ and K is the kernel function associated with the Reproducing Kernel Hilbert Space mentioned above.

Kernel functions are similarity measures of data points in the input space P, and they correspond to the inner product in a feature space H to which the input space data points are mapped. Formally, kernel functions are defined as

$$K(x, x') = \langle \Phi(x), \Phi(x') \rangle,$$

where $\Phi : P \to H$.

3　Features for Parse Representation

In the case of parse ranking problem, where parses are represented within dependency structure, particular attention to the extracted features is required due to the sparseness of the data. In [8] we proposed features that are grammatically relevant and applicable even when relatively few training examples are available. Grammatical features extracted from a dependency parse, contain information about the linkage consisting of pairwise dependencies between pairs of words (bigrams), the link types (the grammatical roles assigned to the links) and the part-of-speech (POS) tags of the words. An example of a fully parsed sentence is shown in Figure 1.

As in [8], we define seven feature types representing important aspects of the parse, consisting of the following grammatical structures:

Grammatical bigram feature is defined as a pair of words connected by a link. In the linkage example of Figure 1, the extracted grammatical bigrams are *absence—of, of—alpha-syntrophin*, etc.

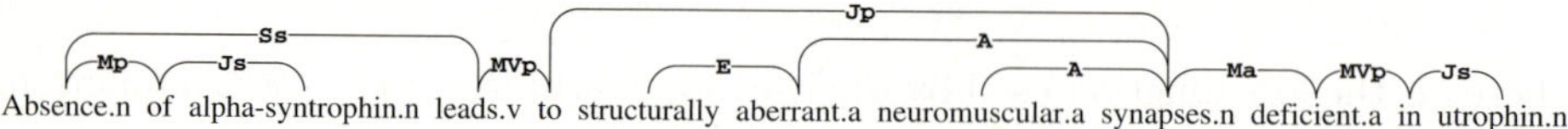

Fig. 1. Example of parsed sentence

Word & POS tag feature contains the word with the POS tag assigned to the word by the LG parser. In Figure 1, the extracted word & POS features are *absence.n, alpha-syntrophin.n* etc.

Link type feature represents the type of the link assigned by the LG parser. In the example, they are *Mp, Js*, etc.

Word & Link type feature combines each word in the sentence with the type of each link connected to the word, for example, *absence—Mp, absence—Ss*, etc.

Link length feature represents the number of words that a link in the sentence spans. In Figure 1, the extracted features of this type are *1, 1*, etc.

Link length & Link type feature combines the type of the link in the sentence with the number of words it spans. In Figure 1, the extracted features of this type are *1—Mp, 1—Js*, etc.

Link bigram feature extracted for each word of the sentence is a combination of two links connected to the word, ordered leftmost link first. In the example, the link bigrams are *Mp—Ss, Mp—Js*, etc.

As a natural continuation of [8], we propose projecting parses into feature sequences in order to take into account local correlations between parses. To avoid sparsity, for each parse, we make one sequence consisting of homogeneous features per each type instead of a single sequence containing the features of all types. We define these homogeneous feature sequences as follows. Let r be the number of types, and let $\{t_1, \ldots, t_r\}$ be the set of types. In our case, $r = 7$ and the corresponding feature types are described above. For example, t_1 is the grammatical bigram type consisting of all the grammatical bigram features of the particular parse. Let us consider a parse $p \in P$, and let $p_j, 1 \leq j \leq r$, be the sequence of the features of type t_j in the parse p in the order of their appearance. For example, in the case of Figure 1, $p_1 = $ *absence—of, absence—leads, of—alpha-syntrophin*, etc. The order of features is also preserved for all other types: $p_3 = $ *Mp, Ss* etc. or $p_4 = $ *absence—Mp, absence—Ss, of—Mp, of—Js* etc. For the basic types – POS tag, Word, Link type, and Link length features – as well as for the complex features representing conjunctions of the basic types, the order of appearance is determined by the indices of the words they are related to. For example, if there exist two grammatical bigrams having a common first word, the decision of the feature positions within the sequence is based on the index of the second word.

Now we can define a mapping Φ from the parse space P to the feature space H, $\Phi : P \rightarrow H$, representing parses through the sequences of the features as follows: $\Phi(p) = (p_1, \ldots, p_r)$. If we denote $p_j = (f_1^{t_j}, \ldots, f_{|p_j|}^{t_j})$, we get

$$\Phi(p) = ((\underbrace{f_1^{t_1}, \ldots, f_{|p_1|}^{t_1}}_{p_1}), \ldots, (\underbrace{f_1^{t_r}, \ldots, f_{|p_r|}^{t_r}}_{p_r})). \tag{2}$$

Here, the length of the sequences p_j, denoted as $|p_j|$, as well as the individual features $f_i^{t_j}$ depend on the parse p. We call the sequences p_j subparses of $p \in P$.

4   Convolution Kernels

The convolution kernels are usually built over discrete structures. They are defined between the input objects by applying convolution sub-kernels for the parts of the objects. Following [11], we briefly describe convolution kernel framework. Let us consider $x \in X$ as a composite structure such that $x_1, \ldots, x_N$ are its parts, where x_n belongs to the set X_n for each $1 \leq n \leq N$, and N is a positive integer. We consider $X_1, \ldots, X_n$ as countable sets, however, they can be more general separable metric spaces [11]. Let us denote shortly $\widehat{x} = x_1, \ldots, x_N$. Then the relation "$x_1, \ldots, x_N$ are parts of x" can be expressed as a relation R on the set $X_1 \times \ldots, X_N \times X$ such that $R(\widehat{x}, x)$ is true if $\widehat{x}$ are the parts of x. Then we can define $R^{-1}(x) = \{\widehat{x} : R(\widehat{x}, x)\}$. Now let us suppose that $x, y \in X$ and there exist decompositions such that $\widehat{x} = x_1, \ldots, x_N$ are the parts of x and $\widehat{y} = y_1, \ldots, y_N$ are the parts of y. If we have some kind of kernel functions

$$K_n(x_n, y_n) = \langle \Phi(x_n), \Phi(y_n) \rangle, 1 \leq n \leq N,$$

to measure similarity between elements of X_n, then the kernel $K(x, y)$ measuring the similarity between x and y is defined to be the following generalized convolution:

$$K(x, y) = \sum_{\widehat{x} \in R^{-1}(x)} \sum_{\widehat{y} \in R^{-1}(y)} \prod_{n=1}^{N} K_n(x_n, y_n). \tag{3}$$

There have been several different convolution kernels reported and applied in NLP, for example, string kernel [13], tree kernel [3], word-position kernel ([14], [15]) and HDAG kernel [5]. The LC kernel function proposed in this paper satisfies the properties of the above convolution approach and it is built over discrete and homogeneous sequences of the features described in the Section 3.

5   Locality-Convolution Kernel

The Locality-Convolution kernel has the following properties that we believe are of importance for the ranking task: i) the use of feature sequences extracted in the order of the appearance in the parse, ii) construction of locality window around matching features, and iii) position sensitive evaluation of the features within the window. Below we define these properties formally.

Let us consider parses $p, q \in P$ and let $p_j = (f_1^{t_j}, \ldots, f_{|p_j|}^{t_j})$ and $q_j = (g_1^{t_j}, \ldots, g_{|q_j|}^{t_j})$ be their subparses. They consist of the features of the same type t_j as described in Section 3. Next we consider how to define a similarity between the subparses p_j and q_j. For the sake of simplicity, we write in the feature sequences supersript j instead of t_j.

The similarity of the subparses p_j and q_j is obtained with the following kernel:

$$K(p_j, q_j) = \sum_{s \in S_j} \kappa(s) = \sum_{i=1}^{|p_j|} \sum_{k=1}^{|q_j|} \kappa(f_i^j, g_k^j) \delta(f_i^j, g_k^j), \tag{4}$$

where $S_j = \left\{ (f_i^j, g_k^j) | 1 \le i \le |p_j|, 1 \le k \le |q_j|, f_i^j = g_k^j \right\}$ is the set of all equal pairs of the features present in the subparses p_j and q_j, κ is a kernel, and

$$\delta(x, y) = \begin{cases} 0, & \text{if } x \neq y \\ 1, & \text{if } x = y. \end{cases}$$

If we set $\kappa \equiv 1$, then the equation (4) equals to $|S_j|$. To weight more those cases where there are exact matches near each other within a certain locality window, we define κ as follows. First, for each $s = (f_i^j, g_k^j) \in S_j$, we create a window around f_i^j and g_k^j of length w, and define

$$w_s = \left\{ (f_m^j, g_l^j) | \; s = (f_i^j, g_k^j) \in S_j, |m - i| \le \left\lfloor \frac{w}{2} \right\rfloor, |l - k| \le \left\lfloor \frac{w}{2} \right\rfloor, (f_m^j, g_l^j) \in S_j \right\}.$$

A simple realization of the weighting idea would be:

$$\kappa(s) = |w_s|, \tag{5}$$

where $|w_s|$ is the number of all identical feature pairs between two locality windows. As another alternative, we construct a function that requires the matching feature positions to be exactly the same:

$$\kappa(s) = \sum_{(f_m^j, g_l^j) \in w_s} \delta(m, l). \tag{6}$$

The kernel (4) with exact position matching κ described in (6) is related to the locality improved kernel proposed in [16]. However, if we would not require strict position matching, but rather penalize the features that match but have a different position within the windows, one can use the following position sensitive version of the kernel function:

$$\kappa(s) = \prod_{(f_m^j, g_l^j) \in w_s} \left(e^{-\left(\frac{(m-l)}{\theta} \right)^2} + 1 \right), \tag{7}$$

where $\theta \ge 0$ is a parameter. Note that (5), (6), and (7) become equal to 1, 1, and 2, respectively, when the length of the locality window is one. The choice of an appropriate κ might be a matter closely related to the domain of the study. In Section 6 we show that additional information captured with (7) is useful and improves the ranking performance. Drawing a parallel between the proposed kernel and the convolution approach, one can distinguish between "structures" and "different decompositions" constructed by our kernel. By substituting the position sensitive κ defined in (7) into (4), we obtain:

$$K_{LC}(p_j, q_j) = \sum_{s \in S_j} \prod_{(f_m^j, g_l^j) \in w_s} \left(e^{-\left(\frac{(m-l)}{\theta} \right)^2} + 1 \right), \tag{8}$$

which we call the Locality-Convolution kernel. Conceptually, the LC kernel enumerates all the substructures representing pairs of windows built around the matching features in the subparses and calculates their inner product. The LC kernel is able to treat not only exact matching of the features, but also matching within the locality windows, therefore making the similarity evaluation more precise.

To measure the similarity between whole parses, we measure the correspondence of their subparses within each type and then sum them up:

$$K(p,q) = \sum_{j=1}^{r} K_{LC}(p_j, q_j).$$ (9)

Finally, we wrap the kernel inside a Gaussian function $K^{\mathcal{G}}$ in the following way:

$$K^{\mathcal{G}}(p,q) = e^{\left(-\frac{K(p,p) - 2K(p,q) + K(q,q)}{\sigma^2}\right)},$$ (10)

where σ is a parameter controlling the width of Gaussian function. The wrapping has also a normalization effect, which is useful because the size of the parses, that is, the total number of features in the parse is not a constant. Expression (10) represents the kernel function used in the experiments of this study.

6   Experiments

The performance of the RLS ranker with the LC kernel proposed in this paper was compared to the baseline method, the RLS ranker described in [8]. Throughout our experiments we have been using BDB corpus which consists of 1100 annotated sentences. It was split into two datasets containing 500 and 600 sentences. The first dataset was used for the parameter estimation and the second one was reserved for the final validation. For each sentence, there is a certain amount of parses generated by the LG parser. Due to the computational complexity, we restricted the number of parses per sentence to 5 in training and to 20 in testing. When more parses were available for a sentence, we sampled randomly the necessary amount, when fewer were available, all parses were used.

We used the Kendall's correlation coefficient τ_b [10] as a performance measure in all experiments. The parse goodness function that determines the true ranks of the parses and the ranking procedure are described in [8].

The RLS algorithm has the regularization parameter λ that controls the trade-off between the minimization of the training error and the complexity of the regression function. In addition, the LC kernel uses θ parameter that determines the width of the position sensitive function and w, the size of the locality window, constructed around the matching features in both subparses. Finally, σ controls the width of the Gaussian function, into which the LC kernel is wrapped. The appropriate values of these parameters were determined by grid search with 10-fold cross-validation.

6.1   Evaluation of LC Kernel

The evaluation of the kernel function was conducted on the dataset consisting of 500 sentences. We observed a stable performance of the RLS ranker with the LC kernel providing a correlation of 0.45 against 0.42 of the RLS ranker reported in [8]. The values of the parameters found by grid search are: $\lambda = 2^{-10}$, $w = 3$, $\sigma = 155$, and $\theta = 0.5$. The small value of θ for the LC kernel in equation (8) indicates that the positional matching of the features inside the locality window is more important contributor than the position insensitive one. The optimal size of the window appeared to be small. To find out whether some of the feature types would prefer longer windows, we also tried different sizes for different features. There was, however, no notable improvement in performance.

6.2 Final Validation

In order to test the statistical significance of the ranking performance difference between the two methods, we conducted a two-tailed paired t-test. The rankers were trained on the parameter estimation data and the 600 sentences reserved for the final validation were considered as independent trials. The performance of the RLS ranker with the LC kernel on the validation data is 0.46 and the improvement is statistically significant ($p < 0.05$) when compared to 0.42 correlation obtained using the RLS ranker as reported in [8].

7 Conclusions

This paper introduces the Locality-Convolution (LC) kernel and its application to the dependency parse ranking with Regularized Least-Squares algorithm. The proposed LC kernel uses feature sequences extracted in the order of the appearance in the parse, constructs local windows around matching features in the sequences in order to capture local correlations between the parses, and performs position sensitive evaluation of the features within the window. The usage of the LC kernel is not restricted for the parse ranking tasks, but can be applied everywhere where dependency structures, position sensitive matching, or local correlations play an important role.

We compared the ranking performance with the proposed kernel function to the results reported in our previous work [8]. The results show statistically significant improvement from 0.42 to 0.46 in correlation. A straightforward way to obtain even higher correlations is to increase the number of training examples. In [8], we show that by increasing the number of parses per sentence it is possible to achieve a better performance, however, the improvement obtained by increasing the number of sentences is larger.

In the future, we plan to investigate the task of dependency parse ranking by learning the ranks directly instead of regressing the parse goodness function. We also aim to consider the convolution properties of the LC kernel on a more basic level of features by conducting different projections and to explore graph kernels that are able to evaluate locality relations within dependency parse structures.

Acknowledgments

We would like to thank CSC, the Finnish IT center for science, for providing us extensive computing resources. This work has been supported by Tekes, the Finnish National Technology Agency.

References

1. Shawe-Taylor, J., Cristianini, N.: Kernel Methods for Pattern Analysis. Cambridge University Press, New York, NY, USA (2004)
2. Scholkopf, B., Smola, A.J.: Learning with Kernels: Support Vector Machines, Regularization, Optimization, and Beyond. MIT Press, Cambridge, MA, USA (2001)
3. Collins, M., Duffy, N.: Convolution kernels for natural language. In Dietterich, T.G., Becker, S., Ghahramani, Z., eds.: NIPS, MIT Press (2001) 625–632
4. Suzuki, J., Hirao, T., Sasaki, Y., Maeda, E.: Hierarchical directed acyclic graph kernel: Methods for structured natural language data. In: ACL. (2003) 32–39
5. Suzuki, J., Isozaki, H., Maeda, E.: Convolution kernels with feature selection for natural language processing tasks. In: ACL. (2004) 119–126
6. Sleator, D.D., Temperley, D.: Parsing english with a link grammar. Technical Report CMU-CS-91-196, Department of Computer Science, Carnegie Mellon University, Pittsburgh, PA (1991)
7. Pyysalo, S., Ginter, F., Pahikkala, T., Boberg, J., Järvinen, J., Salakoski, T., Koivula, J.: Analysis of link grammar on biomedical dependency corpus targeted at protein-protein interactions. In Collier, N., Ruch, P., Nazarenko, A., eds.: Proceedings of the JNLPBA workshop at COLING'04, Geneva. (2004) 15–21
8. Tsivtsivadze, E., Pahikkala, T., Pyysalo, S., Boberg, J., Mylläri, A., Salakoski, T.: Regularized least-squares for parse ranking. In: Proceedings of the 6th International Symposium on Intelligent Data Analysis, Springer-Verlag (2005) 464–474 Copyright Springer-Verlag Berlin Heidelberg 2005.
9. Poggio, T., Smale, S.: The mathematics of learning: Dealing with data. Amer. Math. Soc. Notice **50** (2003) 537–544
10. Kendall, M.G.: Rank Correlation Methods. 4. edn. Griffin, London (1970)
11. Haussler, D.: Convolution kernels on discrete structures. Technical Report UCSC-CRL-99-10, UC Santa Cruz (1999)
12. Schölkopf, B., Herbrich, R., Smola, A.J.: A generalized representer theorem. In Helmbold, D., Williamson, R., eds.: Proceedings of the 14th Annual Conference on Computational Learning Theory and and 5th European Conference on Computational Learning Theory, Berlin, Germany, Springer-Verlag (2001) 416–426
13. Lodhi, H., Saunders, C., Shawe-Taylor, J., Cristianini, N., Watkins, C.J.C.H.: Text classification using string kernels. Journal of Machine Learning Research **2** (2002) 419–444
14. Pahikkala, T., Pyysalo, S., Ginter, F., Boberg, J., Järvinen, J., Salakoski, T.: Kernels incorporating word positional information in natural language disambiguation tasks. In Russell, I., Markov, Z., eds.: Proceedings of the Eighteenth International Florida Artificial Intelligence Research Society Conference, Menlo Park, Ca., AAAI Press (2005) 442–447 Copyright AAAI Press, http://www.aaai.org/.
15. Pahikkala, T., Pyysalo, S., Boberg, J., Mylläri, A., Salakoski, T.: Improving the performance of bayesian and support vector classifiers in word sense disambiguation using positional information. In Honkela, T., Könönen, V., Pöllä, M., Simula, O., eds.: Proceedings of the International and Interdisciplinary Conference on Adaptive Knowledge Representation and Reasoning, Espoo, Finland, Helsinki University of Technology (2005) 90–97
16. Zien, A., Ratsch, G., Mika, S., Scholkopf, B., Lengauer, T., Muller, K.R.: Engineering support vector machine kernels that recognize translation initiation sites. Bioinformatics **16** (2000) 799–807

Intrusion Detection Based on Behavior Mining and Machine Learning Techniques

Srinivas Mukkamala, Dennis Xu, and Andrew H. Sung

Department of Computer Science, New Mexico Tech, Socorro, NM 87801
Institute for Complex Additive Systems and Analysis, Socorro, NM 87801
`{srinivas, dennisxu, sung}@cs.nmt.edu`

Abstract. This paper describes results concerning the classification capability of unsupervised and supervised machine learning techniques in detecting intrusions using network audit trails. In this paper we investigate well known machine learning techniques: Frequent Pattern Tree mining (FP-tree), classification and regression tress (CART), multivariate regression splines (MARS) and TreeNet. The best model is chosen based on the classification accuracy (ROC curve analysis). The results show that high classification accuracies can be achieved in a fraction of the time required by well known support vector machines and artificial neural networks. TreeNet performs the best for normal, probe and denial of service attacks (DoS). CART performs the best for user to super user (U2su) and remote to local (R2L).

1 Introduction

Since the ability of an Intrusion Detection System (IDS) to identify a large variety of intrusions in real time with high accuracy is of primary concern, we will in this paper consider performance of unsupervised and supervised machine learning-based IDSs with respect to classification accuracy and false alarm rates.

AI techniques have been used to automate the intrusion detection process; they include neural networks, fuzzy inference systems, evolutionary computation, machine learning, support vector machines, etc [1-6]. Often model selection using SVMs, and other popular machine learning methods requires extensive resources and long execution times [7,8]. In this paper, we present a few machine learning methods (FP-Tree, MARS, CART, TreeNet) that can perform model selection with higher or comparable accuracies in a fraction of the time required by the SVMs.

Frequent-pattern tree is an extended prefix-tree structure for storing compressed, crucial information about frequent patterns, and develop an efficient FP-Tree based mining method, *FP-growth*, for mining *the complete set of frequent patterns* by pattern fragment growth [9]. MARS is a nonparametric regression procedure that is based on the "divide and conquer" strategy, which partitions the input space into regions, each with its own regression equation [10]. CART is a tree-building algorithm that determines a set of *if-then* logical (split) conditions that permit accurate prediction or classification of classes [11]. TreeNet a tree-building algorithm that uses stochastic gradient boosting to combine trees via a weighted voting scheme, to achieve accuracy without the drawback of a tendency to be misled by bad data

M. Ali and R. Dapoigny (Eds.): IEA/AIE 2006, LNAI 4031, pp. 619 – 628, 2006.

[12,13]. We performed experiments using Fp-Tree, MARS, CART, Treenet for classifying each of the five classes (normal, probe, denial of service, user to super-user, and remote to local) of network traffic patterns in the DARPA data.

The dataset used for analysis is described in seection 2. An introduction to frequent pattern tree based adaptive behaviour mining and results obtained on the DARPA dataset are given in section 3. A brief introduction MARS and model selection is given in section 4. CART and a tree generated for classifying normal vs. intrusions in DARPA data is explained in section 5. TreeNet is briefly described in section 6. In section 7, we analyze classification accuracies of MARS, CART, TreeNet using ROC curves. Conclusions of our work are given in section 8.

2 Data Used for Analysis

A subset of the DARPA intrusion detection data set is used for offline analysis. In the DARPA intrusion detection evaluation program, an environment was set up to acquire raw TCP/IP dump data for a network by simulating a typical U.S. Air Force LAN. The LAN was operated like a real environment, but being blasted with multiple attacks [14,15]. For each TCP/IP connection, 41 various quantitative and qualitative features were extracted [16] for intrusion analysis. Attacks are classified into the following types. The features extracted fall into three categorties, "intrinsic" features that describe about the individual TCP/IP connections; can be obtained from network audit trails, "content-based" features that describe about payload of the network packet; can be obtained from the data portion of the network packet, "traffic-based" features, that are computed using a specific window (connection time or no of connections). As DOS and Probe attacks involve several connections in a short time frame, whereas R2U and U2Su attacks are embedded in the data portions of the connection and often involve just a single connection; "traffic-based" features play an important role in deciding whether a particular network activity is engaged in probing or not.

In our experiments, we perform 5-class classification. The (training and testing) data set contains 11982 randomly generated points from the data set representing the five classes, with the number of data from each class proportional to its size, except that the smallest class is completely included. The set of 5092 training data and 6890 testing data are divided in to five classes: normal, probe, denial of service attacks, user to super user and remote to local attacks. Where the attack is a collection of 22 different types of instances that belong to the four classes (Probe, DoS, U2Su and R2L), and the other is the normal data. Note two randomly generated separate data sets of sizes 5092 and 6890 are used for training and testing FP-Tree, MARS, CART, and TreeNet respectively. Section 3 and section 7 summarizes the classifier accuracies.

3 Adaptive Behavior Mining by FP-Tree

Mining frequent patterns with a frequent pattern tree (FP-tree in short) avoids costly candidate generation and repeatedly occurrence frequency checking against the support threshold. Our method is largely based on mining frequent patterns without candidate generation [9]. The benefits of this method are highly condensed yet complete for frequent pattern mining, avoid costly database scanning. More important, it allows us to create an unsupervised rule generator. Most popular rule generators, are based on supervised learning, which are not capable for adaptive profiling.

To profile user behaviour, a frequent pattern tree (FP-tree) structure is used to store compressed, crucial information about frequent pattern, from which association rules are generated. We construct the FP-tree by accumulating the occurrences of the features in all transactions of normal activity in a time period. Transaction features are extracted from transaction database. By mining the FP-tree, we can find all the conditional rules that correlate the presence of one set of features with that of another set of features.

FP-tree structure is a combination of a general prefix tree and a linked list table. Figure 1 shows an example of creating a tiny FP-tree structure, which is constructed from a set of transaction data shown in table 1. It stores quantitative information about frequent patterns. The tree nodes are arranged in such a way that more frequently occurring nodes will have better chance of sharing nodes than less ones. From every tree node to the root node, the path is a frequent pattern. Table 1 shows five transactions for a typical online transaction system. Each transaction includes the class of purchased products, weekday, daypart, grouped IP address and grouped purchased amount. The abbrevations: ET-entertainment, BK-book, CL-clothes, ST-Saturday, SU-Sunday, MO-Monday, EV-evening, MR-morning, L#-less than # of dollars.

Table 1. Sample transaction data

TID	Transaction data	Frequent Items
1	ET, ST, EV, 129.138, L50	ST, 129.138, EV, ET
2	ET, ST, EV, 202.55, L10	ST, ET, L10
3	ET, SU, MR, 129.138, L50	129.138, ET
4	BK, ST, EV, 129.138, L10	ST, 129.138, EV, L10
5	CL, ST, EV, 129.138, L10	ST, 129.138, EV, L10

An FP-tree is then constructed as follows:

Create an empty root of the tree, figure 1.a. Scan database a second time. The items in each transaction are processed in L order, and a branch is created for each transaction. For example, the scan of the first transaction, T1 is "ET, ST, EV, 129.138, L50", which contains four items (ST, 129.138, EV, ET) in L order, shown in the first data row of table 1, leads to the construction of the first branch of the tree with four tree nodes: ({ST}:1,{129.138} :1, {EV}:1, {ET }:1), where {ST} is linked as a child of the root, {129.138} is linked to {ST}..., shown in figure 1.b. The second transaction, T2 is "ET, ST, EV, 202.55, L10", which contains {ST}, {ET} and {L10} in L order. These items would result in a branch where {ST} is linked to the root and {ET} is linked to {ST}, {L10} is linked to {ET}. However this branch would share a common prefix, {ST}, with the existing path for T1. Therefore we should increase the count of the {ST} node by 1, and create two new tree nodes, {ET}:1 and {L10}, which are linked as a child tree of {ST}:2, figure 1.c. In general, when considering the branch to be added for a transaction, the count of each node along a common prefix is increased by 1, and nodes for the items following the prefix are created and linked accordingly.

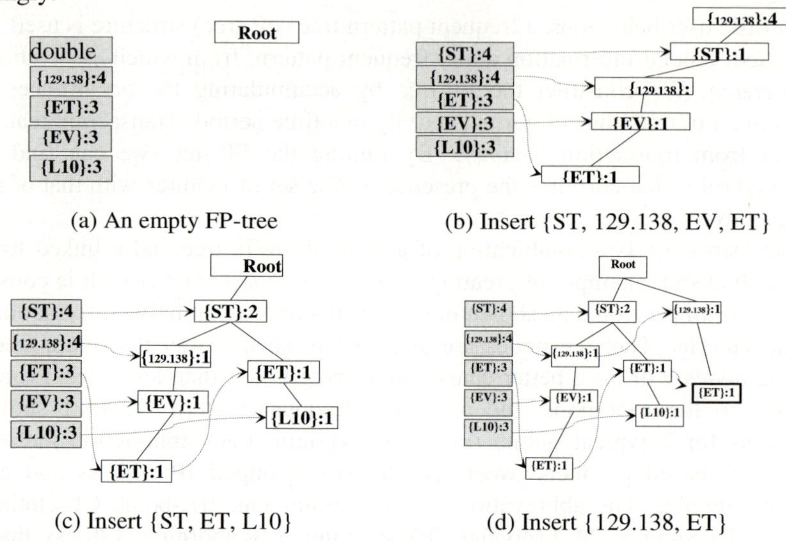

(a) An empty FP-tree   (b) Insert {ST, 129.138, EV, ET}

(c) Insert {ST, ET, L10}   (d) Insert {129.138, ET}

Fig. 1. An example of an FP-tree construction

To make tree traversal easy, an item header table is built so that each item pointer points to its occurrences in the tree via a chain of node links. The items in header table are absolutely same as the element in *L*. We can get all association rules under the condition of a particular frequency item by following its node link chain in header table. For example, we can get rules for {L10} by following node link chain of {L10}:3 in header table.

The results of FP-Tree based anomaly detection on DARPA dataset are given in Table 2 and ROC curves of this approach on different classes' of the dataset are given in Figure 2.

Table 2. Performance of FP-Tree

Class	Testing time (sec)	Accuracy
Normal	0.140	97.32%
Probe	0.266	99.01%
DOS	0.139	98.59%
U2R	0.019	98.36%
R2L	0.087	99.25%

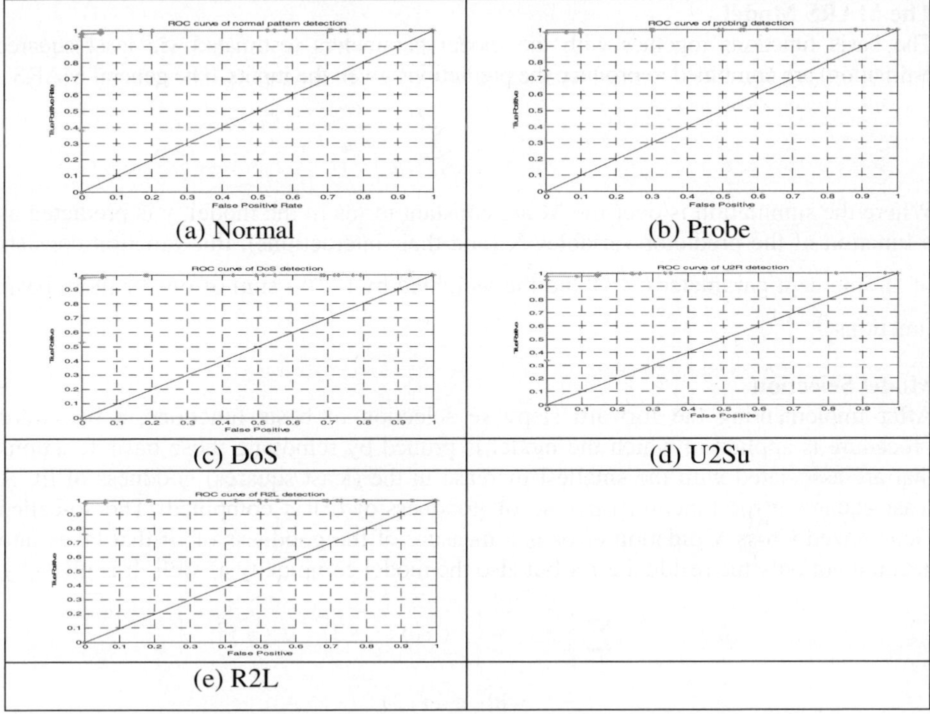

Fig. 2. ROC curves for DARPA dataset using (FP-Tree)

4 Multivariate Adaptive Regression Splines (MARS)

Multivariate Adaptive Regression Splines (MARS) is a nonparametric regression procedure that makes no assumption about the underlying functional relationship between the dependent and independent variables. Instead, MARS constructs this relation from a set of coefficients and basis functions that are entirely "driven" from the data. The method is based on the "divide and conquer" strategy, which partitions the input space into regions, each with its own regression equation. This makes MARS particularly suitable for problems with higher input dimensions, where the curse of dimensionality would likely create problems for other techniques.

Basis functions: MARS uses two-sided truncated functions of the form as basis functions for linear or nonlinear expansion, which approximates the relationships between the response and predictor variables. A simple example of two basis functions (t-x)+ and (x-t)+[10,12]. Parameter t is the knot of the basis functions (defining the "pieces" of the piecewise linear regression); these knots (parameters) are also determined from the data. The "+" signs next to the terms *(t-x)* and *(x-t)* simply denote that only positive results of the respective equations are considered; otherwise the respective functions evaluate to zero.

The MARS Model

The basis functions together with the model parameters (estimated via least squares estimation) are combined to produce the predictions given the inputs. The general MARS

$$y = f(x) = \beta_0 + \sum_{m-1}^{M} \beta_m h_m(X)$$

Where the summation is over the M nonconstant terms in the model, y is predicted as a function of the predictor variables X (and their interactions); this function consists of an intercept parameter (β_o) and the weighted by (β_m) sum of one or more basis functions $h_m(X)$.

Model Selection

After implementing the forward stepwise selection of basis functions, a backward procedure is applied in which the model is pruned by removing those basis functions that are associated with the smallest increase in the (least squares) goodness-of-fit. A least squares error function (inverse of goodness-of-fit) is computed. The so-called Generalized Cross Validation error is a measure of the goodness of fit that takes into account not only the residual error but also the model complexity as well. It is given by

$$GCV = \sum_{i=1}^{N} (y_i - f(x_i))^2 / (1 - c/n)^2$$

with $C = 1 + cd$

Where N is the number of cases in the data set, d is the effective degrees of freedom, which is equal to the number of independent basis functions. The quantity c is the penalty for adding a basis function. Experiments have shown that the best value for C can be found somewhere in the range 2 < d < 3 [10].

5 Classification and Regression Trees (CART)

CART builds classification and regression trees for predicting continuous dependent variables (regression) and categorical predictor variables (classification) [11,12].

The decision tree begins with a root node t derived from whichever variable in the feature space minimizes a measure of the impurity of the two sibling nodes. The measure of the impurity or entropy at node t, denoted by i(t), is as shown in the following equation:

$$i(t) = -\sum_{f=1}^{k} p(w_j / t) \log p(w_j / t)$$

Where p(wj | t) is the proportion of patterns xi allocated to class wj at node t. Each non-terminal node is then divided into two further nodes, tL and tR, such that pL , pR are the proportions of entities passed to the new nodes tL, tR respectively. The best division is that which maximizes the difference given in:

$$\Delta i(s,t) = i(t) - pi_L(t_L) - pi_R(t_R)$$

The decision tree grows by means of the successive sub-divisions until a stage is reached in which there is no significant decrease in the measure of impurity when a further additional division **s** is implemented. When this stage is reached, the node **t** is not sub-divided further, and automatically becomes a terminal node. The class wj associated with the terminal node t is that which maximizes the conditional probability p(wj | t). No of nodes generated and terminal node values for each class are for the dataset described in section V are presented in Table 3.

Table 3. Summary of tree splitters for all five classes

Class	No of Nodes	Terminal Node Value
Normal	23	0.016
Probe	22	0.019
DoS	16	0.004
U2Su	7	0.113
R2L	10	0.025

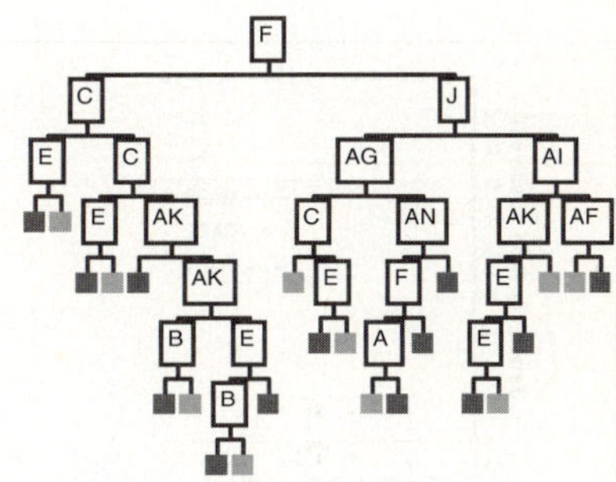

Fig. 3. Tree for classifying normal vs. intrusions

Figure 3 represents a classification tree generated for DARPA data described in section 2 for classifying normal activity vs. intrusive activity. Each of the terminal node describes a data value; each record is classifies into one of the terminal node through the decisions made at the non-terminal node that lead from the root to that leaf.

6 TreeNet

In a TreeNet model classification and regression models are built up gradually through a potentially large collection of small trees. Typically consist from a few dozen to several hundred trees, each normally no longer than two to eight terminal nodes. The model is similar to a long series expansion (such as Fourier or Taylor's series) - a sum of factors that becomes progressively more accurate as the expansion continues. The expansion can be written as [12,13]:

$$F(X) - F_0 + \beta_1 T_1(X) + \beta_2 T_2(X)... + \beta_M T_M(X)$$

Where T_i is a small tree.

Each tree improves on its predecessors through an error-correcting strategy. Individual trees may be as small as one split, but the final models can be accurate and are resistant to overfitting.

7 Roc Curves

Detection rates and false alarms are evaluated for the five-class pattern in the DARPA data set and the obtained results are used to form the ROC curves. The point (0,1) is the perfect classifier, since it classifies all positive cases and negative cases correctly. Thus an ideal system will initiate by identifying all the positive examples and so the curve will rise to (0,1) immediately, having a zero rate of false

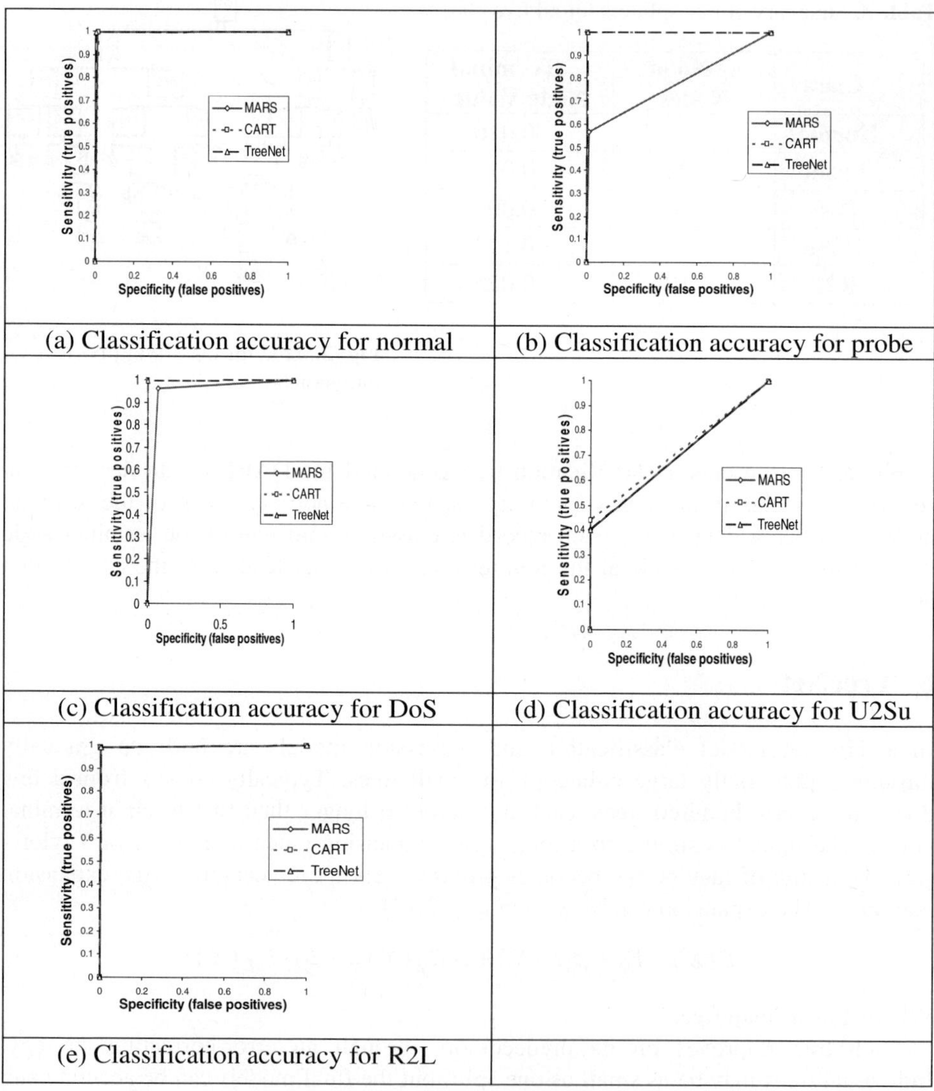

Fig. 4. ROC curves for DARPA dataset using (MARS, CART, TreeNet)

positives, and then continue along to (1,1). Figures 4 show the ROC curves of the detection models by attack categories as well as on all intrusions. In each of these ROC plots, the x-axis is the false positive rate, calculated as the percentage of normal connections considered as intrusions; the y-axis is the detection rate, calculated as the percentage of intrusions detected. A data point in the upper left corner corresponds to optimal high performance, i.e, high detection rate with low false alarm rate. Area of the ROC curves, no of false positives and false negatives are presented in Table 4.

Table 4. Performance (MARS, CART, and TreeNet) on DARPA Dataset

	MARS			CART			TreeNet		
Class	CA	FP	FN	CA	FP	FN	CA	FP	FN
Normal	0.993	56	4	0.991	75	5	0.997	18	0
Probe	0.777	64	305	0.998	24	0	0.999	14	0
DoS	0.945	185	169	0.998	1	16	0.998	3	9
U2Su	0.700	3	15	0.720	3	14	0.699	7	16
R2L	0.992	17	7	0.993	15	6	0.992	19	7

8   Conclusions

A number of observations and conclusions are drawn from the results reported in this paper:

- It is evident in this set of experiments that the training and testing times of FP-Tree based method outperform supervised machine learning techniques. However the accuracy of supervised machine learning techniqes (MARS, CART, TreeNet, SVMs) outperforms FP-Tree based mining.
- TreeNet easily achieves high detection accuracy (higher than 99%) for each of the 5 classes of DARPA data. Treenet performed the best for normal with 18 false positives (FP) and 0 false negatives (FP), probe with 14 FP and 0 FN, and denial of service attacks (DoS) with 3 FP and 9 FN.
- CART performed the best for user to super user (U2su) with 3 FP and 14 FN and remote to local (R2L) with 15 FP and 6 FN.

We demonstrate that using these fast execution machine learning methods we can achieve high classification accuracies in a fraction of the time required by the well know machine learning techniques.

References

1. S. Mukkamala, G. Janowski, A. H. Sung, Intrusion Detection Using Neural Networks and Support Vector Machines. Proceedings of IEEE International Joint Conference on Neural Networks 2002, IEEE press, pp. 1702-1707, 2002.
2. M. Fugate, J. R. Gattiker, Computer Intrusion Detection with Classification and Anomaly Detection, Using SVMs. International Journal of Pattern Recognition and Artificial Intelligence, Vol. 17(3), pp. 441-458, 2003.
3. W. Hu, Y. Liao, V. R. Vemuri, Robust Support Vector Machines for Anamoly Detection in Computer Security. International Conference on Machine Learning, pp. 168-174, 2003.
4. K. A. Heller, K. M. Svore, A. D. Keromytis, S. J. Stolfo, One Class Support Vector Machines for Detecting Anomalous Window Registry Accesses. Proceedings of IEEE Conference Data Mining Workshop on Data Mining for Computer Security, 2003.
5. A. Lazarevic, L. Ertoz, A. Ozgur, J. Srivastava, V. Kumar, A Comparative Study of Anomaly Detection Schemes in Network Intrusion Detection. Proceedings of Third SIAM Conference on Data Mining, 2003.
6. S. Mukkamala, A. H. Sung, Feature Selection for Intrusion Detection Using Neural Networks and Support Vector Machines. Journal of the Transportation Research Board of the National Academics, Transportation Research Record No 1822: 33-39, 2003.
7. S. J. Stolfo, F. Wei, W. Lee, A. Prodromidis, P. K. Chan, Cost-based Modeling and Evaluation for Data Mining with Application to Fraud and Intrusion Detection. Results from the JAM Project, 1999.
8. S. Mukkamala, B. Ribeiro, A. H. Sung, Model Selection for Kernel Based Intrusion Detection Systems. Proceedings of International Conference on Adaptive and Natural Computing Algorithms (ICANNGA), Springer-Verlag, pp. 458-461, 2005.
9. J. Han, J. Pei and Y. Yin. Mining Frequent Patterns Without Candidate Generation. Proceedings of ACM SIGMOD International Conference on Management of Data (SIGMOD'00), pp. 1-12, 2000.
10. T. Hastie, R. Tibshirani, J. H. Friedman, The elements of statistical learning: Data mining, inference, and prediction. Springer, 2001.
11. L. Breiman, J. H. Friedman, R. A. Olshen, C. J. Stone, Classification and regression trees. Wadsworth and Brooks/Cole Advanced Books and Software, 1986.
12. Salford Systems. TreeNet, CART, MARS Manual.
13. J. H. Friedman, Stochastic Gradient Boosting. Journal of Computational Statistics and Data Analysis, Elsevier Science, Vol. 38, PP. 367-378, 2002.
14. K. Kendall, A Database of Computer Attacks for the Evaluation of Intrusion Detection Systems. Master's Thesis, Massachusetts Institute of Technology (MIT), 1998.
15. S. E. Webster, The Development and Analysis of Intrusion Detection Algorithms. Master's Thesis, MIT, 1998.
16. W. Lee, S. J. Stolfo, A Framework for Constructing Features and Models for Intrusion Detection Systems. ACM Transactions on Information and System Security, Vol. 3, pp. 227-261, 2000.

Tractable Feature Generation Through Description Logics with Value and Number Restrictions

Nicola Fanizzi, Luigi Iannone, Nicola Di Mauro, and Floriana Esposito

Dipartimento di Informatica, Università degli Studi di Bari
Campus Universitario, Via Orabona 4, 70125 Bari, Italy
{fanizzi, iannone, ndm, esposito}@di.uniba.it

Abstract. In the line of a feature generation paradigm based on relational concept descriptions, we extend the applicability to other languages of the Description Logics family endowed with specific language constructors that do not have a counterpart in the standard relational representations, such as clausal logics. We show that the adoption of an enhanced language does not increase the complexity of feature generation, since the process is still tractable. Moreover this can be considered as a formalization for future employment of even more expressive languages from the Description Logics family.

1   Introduction

Many interesting tasks in AI such as natural language processing, computer vision, and planning require adequate relational representations. Examples include the problem of identifying relations of interest, identifying a speaker given the conference schedule, answering to free-form questions given relevant text, detecting people in an image or defining a policy for planning. Hence, multi-relational representations must be taken into account. The challenge is to provide the necessary expressivity, meeting the strong tractability constraints posed by such tasks.

The problem with learning unbiased relational representations is their intractability [1] which has led to the investigation of ways to impose some bias in order to make deductive and inductive reasoning more efficient. In order to overcome the inherent intractability, an increasing interest lately has been devoted to approaches based on *propositionalization* [2], whose final aim is to exploit the efficiency of propositional learning for inducing relational classifiers.

This work follows the approach to propositionalization that employs concept representations for abstracting relational structures by generating new relevant features through an efficient *generating function* (see [3]). Rather than during the learning process, features are intended to be generated before learning takes place.

Various relational representations which may serve as a starting point for feature construction, such as *concept graphs* and *frame systems*, have been unified in the framework of *Description Logics* (henceforth DLs) [4]. They are well suited for this purpose, indeed DLs descriptions are employed in KRR as a means for expressing concepts (as classes of individuals) and their properties. Besides, this family of languages is endowed with well-founded semantics and reasoning services (mostly for deductive inference) descending from a long research line.

M. Ali and R. Dapoigny (Eds.): IEA/AIE 2006, LNAI 4031, pp. 629–638, 2006.
© Springer-Verlag Berlin Heidelberg 2006

Differently from other techniques for propositionalization, in the proposed approach DLs representations constitute intermediate (rich) languages for transforming domain elements into new features expressed in a new lexicon based on DLs through *feature generating functions* [3]. The results of this transformation may then be piped as the input for general-purpose propositional learners especially those that can handle examples with a variable number of (relevant) features which is much less than the total number of (possibly infinite) features [5] for inducing structures that are described like functions mapping propositional variables to DLs descriptions.

In this paper we aim at generalizing this approach in terms of more expressive DLs. Differently from the mentioned work introducing DLs in the paradigm [3], where, for the sake of tractability, a very simple DL language, the *Feature Description Logic* (FDL) is employed. Actually FDL is a very simple language supporting only existential attributes and conjunction which are well suited for existential descriptions like in an ILP context. Yet, with the advent of the Semantic Web it is likely that many other KBs expressed in DLs will be made available for interoperation.

However existential representations are not always well suited. Indeed, consider features as a sort of types defined like in frame-based systems, E-R models and object-oriented models [6], they have to be regarded as constructed on different constructors, namely those based on universal restrictions. Therefore, we extend the original feature construction framework towards different DLs which are still endowed with efficient reasoning services requested by the paradigm. Particularly, we propose a method based upon the $\mathcal{ALN}$ logic [7, 8, 4] thus yielding more expressiveness for the relational descriptions that are abstracted by the elicited features. These features, in turn, can be acquired to enrich the starting knowledge base building up a new representation.

The original algorithm for feature extraction produces only active features acting as positive examples for the adopted propositional learners, thus making a sort of Closed World Assumption, which contrasts with the mainstream in DLs reasoning: an inactive feature should be explicitly inferred from the knowledge base. By allowing negation in the language, it becomes natural to represent also negative examples.

The paper is organized as follows. In Sect. 2 the representation language is presented. The learning framework is illustrated in Sect. 3 and it is discussed in Sect. 4. Possible developments of the method are examined in Sect. 5.

2 The $\mathcal{ALN}$ Description Logic

$\mathcal{ALN}$ is a DLs language which allows for the expression of universal features and numeric constraints [4]. It has been adopted because of the tractability of the related reasoning services [9]. In order to keep this paper self-contained, syntax and semantics for the reference representation is briefly recalled with the characterization of the descriptions in terms of concept graphs.

In DLs, primitive *concepts* $N_C = \{A, \ldots\}$ are interpreted as subsets of a certain domain of objects and primitive *roles* $N_R = \{R, S, \ldots\}$ are interpreted as binary relations on such a domain. In $\mathcal{ALN}$, more complex concept descriptions are built using atomic concepts and primitive roles by means of the constructors presented in Table 1. Their meaning is defined by an *interpretation* $I = (\Delta^I, \cdot^I)$, where Δ^I is the *domain* of the

Table 1. Constructors and related interpretations for $\mathcal{ALN}$.

NAME	INTENSION	EXTENSION
top concept	$\top$	Δ
bottom concept	$\bot$	$\emptyset$
primitive concept	A	$A^I \subseteq \Delta$
primitive negation	$\neg A$	$\Delta \setminus A^I$
concept conjunction	$C_1 \sqcap C_2$	$C_1^I \cap C_2^I$
value restriction	$\forall R.C$	$\{x \in \Delta \mid \forall y\ (x,y) \in R^I \to y \in C^I\}$
at-most restriction	$\leq n.R$	$\{x \in \Delta \mid \ |\{y \in \Delta \mid (x,y) \in R^I\}| \leq n\}$
at-least restriction	$\geq n.R$	$\{x \in \Delta \mid \ |\{y \in \Delta \mid (x,y) \in R^I\}| \geq n\}$

interpretation and the functor $\cdot^I$ stands for the *interpretation function* mapping the intension of concept and role descriptions to their extension.

A *knowledge base* $\mathcal{K} = \langle \mathcal{T}, \mathcal{A} \rangle$ contains two components: a T-box $\mathcal{T}$ and an A-box $\mathcal{A}$. $\mathcal{T}$ is a set of concept definitions $C \equiv D$, meaning $C^I = D^I$, where C is the concept name and D is a description given in terms of the language constructors. Differently from ILP, each (non primitive) concept has a single definition. Moreover, the DLs definitions are assumed not to be recursive, i.e. concepts cannot be defined in terms of themselves.

The A-box $\mathcal{A}$ contains extensional assertions on concepts and roles, e.g. $C(a)$ and $R(a,b)$, meaning, respectively, that $a^I \in C^I$ and $(a^I, b^I) \in R^I$. Note that, differently from the examples in the ILP setting, the concept description C can be more complex than LP facts. For instance they could assert a universal property of the an individual: $(\forall R.(A \sqcap \neg B))(a)$ that is, role R relates a exclusively to individuals[1] that are instances of the concept $A \sqcap \neg B$.

Example 2.1. Examples of $\mathcal{ALN}$ descriptions are [2]:
Polygamist $\equiv$ Person $\sqcap \forall$isMarriedTo.Person $\sqcap \geq 2$.isMarriedTo
Bigamist $\equiv$ Person $\sqcap \forall$isMarriedTo.Person $\sqcap = 2$.isMarriedTo
MalePolygamist $\equiv$ Male $\sqcap$ Person $\sqcap \forall$isMarriedTo.Person $\sqcap \geq 2$.isMarriedTo

The notion of *subsumption* between DLs concept descriptions can be given in terms of the interpretations defined above:

Definition 2.1 (subsumption). *Given two concept descriptions C and D, C subsumes D iff it holds that $C^I \supseteq D^I$ for every interpretation I. This is denoted denoted by $C \sqsupseteq D$. The induced equivalence relationship, denoted $C \equiv D$, amounts to $C \sqsupseteq D$ and $D \sqsupseteq C$.*

Note that this notion is merely semantic and independent of the particular DLs language adopted. It is easy to see that this definition also applies to the case of role descriptions.

The most important difference between DLs and clausal logics arises. Indeed, while in the context of DLs reasoning the *Open World Assumption* (OWA) is adopted, in ILP the *Closed World Assumption* (CWA) is generally required.

---

[1] It holds even in case no such $R-$filler is given.
[2] Here $(= n.R)$ is an abbreviation for $(\leq n.R \sqcap \geq n.R)$.

Example 2.2. Considering again the concepts described in Ex. 2.1, the assertions:

$$\mathcal{A} = \{ \, \text{Person(Bob)}, \text{Person(Meg)}, \text{Person(Pam)}, \text{Male(Bob)}, \neg\text{Male(Meg)},$$
$$\neg\text{Male(Pam)}, \text{isMarriedTo(Bob, Meg)}, \text{isMarriedTo(Bob, Pam)} \, \}$$

would entail that Bob is an instance of Polygamist if the CWA is adopted; otherwise also $\forall$isMarriedTo.Person(Bob) should be known for Polygamist(Bob) to hold.

Semantically equivalent (yet syntactically different) descriptions can be given for the same concept. However they can be reduced to a canonical form by means of equivalence-preserving rewriting rules, e.g. $\forall R.C_1 \sqcap \forall R.C_2 \equiv \forall R.(C_1 \sqcap C_2)$ (see [7, 4]). The normal form employs the notation needed to access the different parts (*sub-descriptions*) of a concept description C:

- $\text{prim}(C)$ denotes the set of all (negated) concept names occurring at the top level of the description C;
- $\text{val}_R(C)$ denotes conjunction of concepts $C_1 \sqcap \cdots \sqcap C_n$ in the value restriction of role R, if any (otherwise $\text{val}_R(C) = \top$);
- $\text{min}_R(C) = \max\{n \in \mathbb{N} \mid C \sqsubseteq (\geq n.R)\}$ (always a finite number);
- $\text{max}_R(C) = \min\{n \in \mathbb{N} \mid C \sqsubseteq (\leq n.R)\}$ (if unlimited then $\text{max}_R(C) = \infty$).

Definition 2.2 ($\mathcal{ALN}$ normal form). *A concept description C is in $\mathcal{ALN}$ normal form iff $C = \top$ or $C = \bot$ or*

$$C = \bigsqcap_{P \in \text{prim}(C)} P \sqcap \bigsqcap_{R \in N_R} (\forall R.C_R \sqcap \geq n.R \sqcap \leq m.R)$$

where $C_R = \text{val}_R(C)$, $n = \text{min}_R(C)$ and $m = \text{max}_R(C)$.

The complexity of normalization is polynomial [4]. Besides, subsumption can be checked in polynomial time too [9]. Note also that we are considering the case of subsumption with respect to empty terminologies that suffices for our purposes. Otherwise deciding this relationship may be computationally more expensive.

Although subsumption between concept descriptions is merely a semantic relationship, a more syntactic relationship can be found for a language of moderate complexity like $\mathcal{ALN}$ that allows for a structural characterization of subsumption [10].

Proposition 2.1 (subsumption in $\mathcal{ALN}$). *Given two $\mathcal{ALN}$ concept descriptions C and D in normal form, it holds that $C \sqsupseteq D$ iff all the following relations hold between the sub-descriptions:*

- $\text{prim}(C) \subseteq \text{prim}(D)$
- $\forall R \in N_R: \text{val}_R(C) \sqsupseteq \text{val}_R(D)$
- $\text{min}_R(C) \leq \text{min}_R(D) \wedge \text{max}_R(C) \geq \text{max}_R(D)$

Hence subsumption checking is accordingly polynomial like $O(n \log n)$, where n is the size of concept C. In the following we will refer to concepts descriptions in normal form unless a different case is explicitly stated.

The tree-structured representation of concept description are defined as follows [7]:

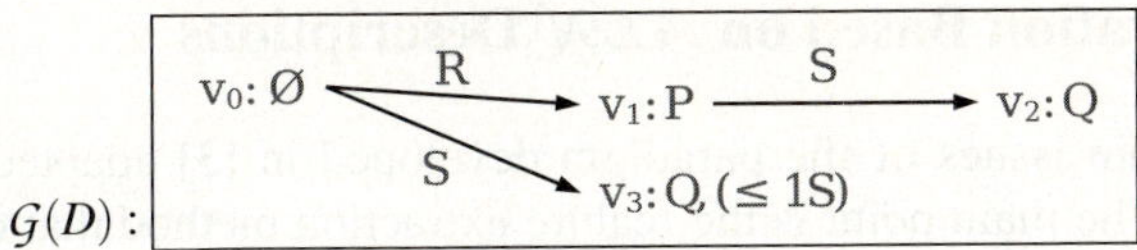

Fig. 1. The concept $D \equiv \forall R.(P \sqcap \forall S.Q) \sqcap \forall S.(Q \sqcap \leq 1S)$ as a description tree

Definition 2.3 (description tree). *A description tree for a concept C in $\mathcal{ALN}$ normal form is a tree $\mathcal{G}(C) = (V, E, v_0, l)$ with root v_0 where:*

- *each node $v \in V$ is labelled with a finite set $l(v) \subseteq N_C \cup \{\neg A \mid A \in N_C\} \cup \{\geq n.R \mid n \in \mathbb{IN}, R \in N_R\} \cup \{\leq n.R \mid n \in \mathbb{IN}, R \in N_R\}$*
- *each edge in E is labelled with $\forall R$, where $R \in N_R$.*

Proposition 2.2 (equivalence). *An $\mathcal{ALN}$ description C is semantically equivalent to an $\mathcal{ALN}$ description tree $\mathcal{G}(C)$ of size polynomial in the size of C, which can be constructed in polynomial time.*

Proof. Let C be a concept description C in $\mathcal{ALN}$ normal form. It corresponds to the tree $\mathcal{G}(C) = (V, E, v_0, l)$ defined recursively on the depth d of nested restrictions in C:

$(d = 0)$ $\mathcal{G}(C) = (\{v_0\}, \emptyset, v_0, l)$ with $l(v_0) = \text{prim}(C) \cup \bigcup_{R \in N_R}(\geq n.R \sqcap \leq m.R)$
$(d > 0)$ let $N_R(C)$ the names of roles at the top level of C. For any $R \in N_R(C)$, let
$\mathcal{G}(C_R) = (V_R, E_R, v_{0R}, l_R)$ be the description tree of $C_R = \text{val}_R(C)$, where w.l.o.g. the V_R's are pairwise disjoint and $v_0 \notin \bigcup_{R \in N_R} V_R$. Then:
- $V = \{v_0\} \cup \bigcup_{R \in N_R} V_R$
- $E = \{v_0 R v_{0R}\} \cup \bigcup_{R \in N_R} E_R$
- if $v = v_0$ then $l(v) = \text{prim}(C) \cup \bigcup_{R \in N_R}(\geq n.R \sqcap \leq m.R)$
  otherwise $l(v) = l_R(v)$ (being $v \in V_R$).

Example 2.3. The concept description $D \equiv \forall R.(P \sqcap \forall S.Q) \sqcap \forall S.(Q \sqcap \leq 1S)$ is equivalent to the tree depicted in Fig. 1.

Instance checking can be characterized in terms of homomorphisms between trees and graphs [7]:

Definition 2.4 (A-box description graph). *Let $\mathcal{A}$ be an $\mathcal{ALN}$ A-box, a be an individual occurring in $\mathcal{A}$ $(a \in \text{Ind}(\mathcal{A}))$ and $C_a = \bigsqcap_{C(a) \in \mathcal{A}} C$. Let $\mathcal{G}(C_a) = (V_a, E_a, a, l)$ denote the description tree of C_a. $\mathcal{G}(\mathcal{A}) = (V, E, l)$ is a A-box description graph with:*

- $V = \bigcup_{a \in \text{Ind}(\mathcal{A})} V_a$
- $E = \{aRb \mid R(a,b) \in \mathcal{A}\} \cup \bigcup_{a \in \text{Ind}(\mathcal{A})} E_a$
- $l(v) = l_a(v)$ *for all $v \in V_a$*

Subsumption and instance checking can be used to translate an individual of the domain (an instance of the target concept) into a set of features suitable for propositional algorithms. Thus DLs that allow for efficient subsumption procedures, such as $\mathcal{ALN}$, are to be preferred.

3 Feature Generation Based on $\mathcal{ALN}$ Descriptions

Now we recall the main issues of the paradigm developed in [3] adapted to a more generic DLs context. The main point is the feature extraction method that can be used to generate propositional formulae in terms of expressive features through subsumption queries from arbitrarily complex data represented by concept graphs.

Assertions in an A-box are described in terms of the relational language (primitive concept and role names). The aim is then producing a classifier that predicts new assertions to hold for selected elements. The adopted propositional learning algorithm requires examples to be generated on the basis of the available relational assertions in the A-box. These examples make up a set of *active* propositions (features) holding for the target concepts. The propositions can be thought of as ground assertions described in terms of the adopted DLs language.

Since the negation of primitive concepts is also allowed in this DLs language, it is possible to represent explicitly also negative information of instances of the target concept, something that was not possible in the original feature extraction paradigm [3]. This method actually works with the adoption of the CWA which is something unusual for dealing with DLs representations. The method can generate a large number of features belonging to a limited number of types represented by DLs descriptions. Thus the propositional learning algorithm to be employed has to be able to deal with this kind of situations.

Definition 3.1 (feature). *Given a concept description D, a feature F_D is a function $F_D : W \longmapsto \{0,1\}$ mapping interpretations to truth values. The feature F_D is said to be active in an interpretation $I \in W$ when it evaluates to* 1.

In the following, we will employ the canonic interpretation $I_{\mathcal{A}}$ of an A-Box $\mathcal{A}$, where the set of individuals stand for themselves.

Example 3.1. The description $D \equiv \forall \mathsf{isMarriedTo.Person}$ is active for the canonic interpretation $I_{\mathcal{A}}$ of the A-box presented in Ex. 2.1.

Active features may be employed as the input for efficient propositional learning systems, such as SNoW [11]. In a *learning from entailment* setting, the central point is the definition of efficient functions that are able to translate interpretations into sets of features [3], thus expressing relational qualities of the individuals that stand as instances of the target concepts.

Definition 3.2 (feature generating function). *Let I be a model for an A-box $\mathcal{A}$ and let $\mathcal{D}$ be a set of descriptions. A feature generating function (FGF), denoted with χ, determines sets of features as follows: $\chi(I, \mathcal{D}) = \{F_D \mid D \in \mathcal{D}, F_D(I) = 1\}$.*

Thus, the FGF χ performs a change of representation for I into the (subsumers of) description D. Now an interpretation can be regarded as a description graph in which each element involved is in the extension of some node. To restrict the range of possible interpretations, a particular one $I_{\mathcal{A}}$ can be regarded as the canonical model related to the A-box $\mathcal{A}$ [10] where each individual name stands for itself. This interpretation, in turn, can be represented as the very description graph $\mathcal{G}(\mathcal{A})$ (by Def. 2.4).

function $\chi_{\mathsf{msc}}(I, D)$: *Features*
input: I: interpretation,
                 D: $\mathcal{ALN}$ description
output: *Features*: feature set

begin
Features $\leftarrow$
for each $a \in \mathsf{Ind}(\mathcal{A})$ **do**
          begin
          $M_a \leftarrow msc^k_{\mathcal{A}}(a)$
          for each $D \in \mathcal{D}$ **do**
                  if $D \sqsupseteq M_a$ **then**
                              Features $\leftarrow$ *Features* $\wedge F_D$
          end
return *Features*
end

Fig. 2. A simple FGF algorithm for $\mathcal{ALN}$

A non-standard inference service for DLs computes the *most specific concept* of an individual a with respect to an A-box $\mathcal{A}$, denoted $msc_{\mathcal{A}}(a)$, which is the most specific concept description (with respect to subsumption) whose extension contains a with respect to all of the models for $\mathcal{A}$ [8]. The generation of the features based on the *msc* may be performed through the simple algorithm reported in Fig. 2. For each individual, the *msc* with respect to the A-box must be computed[3]. This is similar to the most specific subsumer (*mss*) employed in [3], where the language admitted ground (and partially ground) descriptions. We preferred the *msc* since it is well-known and investigated in the KRR community and can be performed through *instance checking* which is supported by existing reasoners.

Example 3.2. Let a generating description be:

$$D \equiv \mathsf{Male} \sqcap \, \leq 2.\mathsf{isMarriedTo} \sqcap \forall \mathsf{isMarriedTo}.\neg\mathsf{Male}.$$

In the canonical interpretation of the A-box in Ex 2.1, the feature F_D is active. This holds for all the assertions subsumed by D, such as $msc(\mathsf{Bob})$.

This inference is not possible in all the DLs. When the A-boxes are cyclic only approximations of the *msc* can be computed. The problem arises when the DLs language is endowed with existential restrictions (such as FDL) or number restrictions (like $\mathcal{ALN}$). For example consider a very simple $\mathcal{ALN}$ A-box $\mathcal{A} = \{R(a,a), (\leq 1.R)(a)\}$. The *msc* for a: $\forall R. \cdots \forall R.(\leq 1.R \sqcap \geq 1.R)$ makes an infinite descending chain of descriptions. Something similar can be obtained also with numeric restrictions.

A solution could be recurring to a different semantics allowing for recursive descriptions. However, it has been shown that such a solution may compromise the tractability of the overall method, since in that case computing the *msc*'s has an exponential cost. Another possible wayout is to allow for approximated *msc*'s [8], for example up to a certain depth related to the maximum cycle in the A-box [12].

---

[3] In case of cyclic A-boxes, the k-approximation of the *msc* is considered.

ABox $\mathcal{A}$ = { Person(Meg), ¬Male(Meg), (∀isMarriedTo.⊥)(Meg), Parent(Meg,Bob), Parent(Meg,Pat),
        Person(Bob), Male(Bob), Parent(Bob,Ann),
        Person(Pat), Male(Pat), (∀isMarriedTo.⊥)(Pat), Parent(Pat,Gwen),
        Person(Gwen), ¬Male(Gwen), (∀isMarriedTo.⊥)(Gwen),
        Person(Ann), ¬Male(Ann), Parent(Ann,Sue), isMarriedTo(Ann,Tom),
        Person(Sue), ¬Male(Sue),
        Person(Tom), Male(Tom) }

BK descriptions for feature generation $\mathcal{T}_{BK}$
        Single ≡ Person⊓ ≤ 0.isMarriedTo;
        Mother ≡ ¬Male ⊓ ∀Parent.Person⊓ ≥ 1.Parent;
GrandParent ≡ Person ⊓ ∀Parent.(Person ⊓ ∀Parent.Person ⊓ ≥ 1.Parent)⊓ ≥ 1.Parent

Positive (resp. negative) instances for the target concept: I^+ = {Meg, Gwen} (I^- = {Ann, Pat}).
Generated examples: $P = \{p_1, p_2\}$ and $N = \{n_1, n_2\}$ where

$$
\begin{aligned}
p_1 &= \text{Single} \wedge \text{Mother} \wedge \text{GrandParent} && \text{(for Meg)} \\
p_2 &= \text{Single} \wedge \text{Mother} && \text{(for Gwen)} \\
n_1 &= \neg\text{Single} \wedge \text{Mother} && \text{(for Ann)} \\
n_2 &= \text{Single} \wedge \neg\text{Mother} && \text{(for Pat)}
\end{aligned}
$$

whose easy generalization is: Single ∧ Mother.

Fig. 3. Toy example: a kinship learning problem

Example 3.3 (Kinship learning problem). Fig, 3 contains an ABox, $\mathcal{A}$, and a background TBox, $\mathcal{T}_{BK}$, with some descriptions employed for feature generation that are typical in a kinship learning problem. In particular, the description Single concerns an individual that is *non-married person*, Mother describes an individual that is *a non-male (female) parent of at least one person*, and GrandParent regards an individual that is *a person that is parent of at least a person that is parent of at least another person*.

Now, if Meg and Gwen are deemed as positive instances for the target concept, and Ann and Pat as negative instances, the corresponding examples for the propositional learning problem are to be generated; e.g., to generate features related to Gwen, one has to check whether $msc_{\mathcal{A}}(\text{Gwen}) = (Person \sqcap \neg\text{Male} \sqcap \forall\text{isMarriedTo}.\bot)$ is subsumed by some BK description, obtaining the example p_2 reported in Fig. 3. After the feature generation phase, it is easy to see how the two positive examples may be generalized in order to induce a consistent propositional description.

4 Applicability

We intend to discuss the efficiency of the feature generation method in this setting and its applicability. The overall algorithm including the FGF as a preprocessing phase would act as follows. Each interpretation is processed using a set of generating descriptions as a background knowledge of *types*. After the preliminary feature generation phase, a vector of active features is generated per interpretation which is then passed to the learning algorithm. As mentioned before, an algorithm that can work in variable-length vector of features is more suitable [5] (there could be an unlimited number).

Just like the original method, the adaptation to $\mathcal{ALN}$ presented here is tractable. Indeed, similarly to that paradigm, the following result holds:

Theorem 4.1 (FGF complexity). *Let I be an interpretation and let D be an $\mathcal{ALN}$ generating description. There is a FGF χ_{msc}, based on the msc operator, that is capable of generating all of the active features in polynomial time.*

Proof. Let I be an interpretation that is the canonical model of an A-box $\mathcal{A}$. The algorithm presented in Fig. 2 computes all the active features by finding the msc of each individual and performing a subsumption query. When the input description D subsumes such an msc the corresponding feature can be considered as being active.

Now, the description $M = msc_{\mathcal{A}}(a)$ can be recursively constructed as follows:

$$\mathsf{prim}(M) = \prod_{C(a)\in\mathcal{A}} C$$
$$\mathsf{val}(M) = \prod_{R\in N_R} \prod_{R(a,b)\in\mathcal{A}} \mathsf{msc}_{\mathcal{A}}(b)$$
$$\mathsf{max}(M) = \mathsf{min}(M) = |\{b \in \mathsf{Ind}(\mathcal{A}) \mid R(a,b) \in \mathcal{A}\}|$$

It is easy to see that computing the msc is linear in the depth of the A-box graph.

The algorithm is dominated by the construction of the msc and by the subsumption which are both polynomial in $\mathcal{ALN}$ (provided that no cycle occurs in the A-box).

In the original framework on using DLs for feature generation [3], the simple language FDL was adopted which is roughly equivalent with $\mathcal{EL}$ [10] with a *concrete domain* [4] for expressing attributes as datatype properties. This DL is basically endowed with two constructors: conjunction and qualified existential restriction ($\exists R.C$). As previously discussed, theoretically also this setting may suffer of the presence of cycles in the graph representing the interpretation.

As regards the problem of cyclic A-boxes, the characterization of concept descriptions is terms of regular languages should be exploited [8]. Besides, a change of semantics should be made in order to take into account cyclic definitions. However, the computation of *msc*'s would not be tractable unless recurring to approximations [12].

Learning directly $\mathcal{ALN}$ representations may compromise the effectiveness of the whole process. Indeed the standard generalizing operator for such description, the *least common subsumer (lcs)* applied to *msc*'s [13], is known to yield poorly predictive generalizations. In our case, the exploitation of a tractable feature generation method allows the application of efficient algorithms for propositional representations which can handle cases with very large number of features [5, 11].

5   Conclusions and Future Work

In the line of the paradigm for feature generation employing a DLs knowledge base as a collection of relational types, we have shown a method where a standard DLs language like $\mathcal{ALN}$ is adopted. This extends the applicability to different features with respect the original paradigm, namely universal and numeric restrictions, maintaining the tractability of feature generation process. Moreover this can also be considered a base for future extensions of the method toward even more expressive languages in the DLs family.

This work could be extended towards more expressive languages endowed with union and full negation in order to support completely the semantic concept models mentioned before [6]. This would allow for the exploitation of available pieces of knowledge encoded in DLs to be used as a sort of background knowledge in the manner indicated in the paper. Besides, the adoption of DLs languages with concrete domains [4] may help to constrain more the search space, thus augmenting the efficiency of the learning process. The next step will include investigation on the employment of feature construction techniques in order to automatize the setup of the generating features, e.g. concept learning algorithms applicable to DLs descriptions.

References

[1] Valiant, L.G.: Robust logics. In: Proceedings of the 31st Annual ACM Symposium on the Theory of Computing. (1999) 642–651

[2] Kramer, S., Lavrač, N., Džeroski, S.: Propositionalization approaches to relational data mining. In Džeroski, S., Lavrač, N., eds.: Relational Data Mining. Springer (2001)

[3] Cumby, C.M., Roth, D.: Learning with feature description logics. In Matwin, S., Sammut, C., eds.: Inductive Logic Programming, 12th International Conference, ILP2002. Volume 2583 of LNCS., Springer (2002) 32–47

[4] Baader, F., Calvanese, D., McGuinness, D., Nardi, D., Patel-Schneider, P., eds.: The Description Logic Handbook. Cambridge University Press (2003)

[5] Blum, A.: Learning boolean functions in an infinite attribute space. Machine Learning **9** (1992) 373–386

[6] Calvanese, D., Lenzerini, M., Nardi, D.: Unifying class-based representation formalisms. Journal of Artificial Intelligence Research **11** (1999) 199–240

[7] Molitor, R.: Structural subsumption for $\mathcal{ALN}$. Technical Report LTCS-98-03, LuFg Theoretical Computer Science, RWTH Aachen, Germany (1998)

[8] Baader, F., Küsters, R.: Computing the least common subsumer and the most specific concept in the presence of cyclic $\mathcal{ALN}$ concept descriptions. In Herzog, O., Güenter, A., eds.: Proceedings of the 22th Annual German Conference on Artificial Intelligence. Volume 1504 of LNAI., Springer (1998) 129–140

[9] Donini, F.M., Lenzerini, M., Nardi, D., Nutt, W.: The complexity of concept languages. Information and Computation **134** (1997) 1–58

[10] Küsters, R., Molitor, R.: Approximating most specific concepts in description logics with existential restrictions. In Baader, F., Brewka, G., Eiter, T., eds.: Proceedings of the Joint German/Austrian Conference on Artificial Intelligence, KI/ÖGAI01. Volume 2174 of LNCS., Springer (2001) 33–47

[11] Carleson, A., Cumby, C., Rosen, J., Roth, D.: The SNoW learning architecture. Technical Report UIUCDCS-R-99-2101, CS Dept., University of Illinois at Urbana-Champaign (1999)

[12] Mantay, T.: Commonality-based ABox retrieval. Technical Report FBI-HH-M-291/2000, Department of Computer Science, University of Hamburg, Germany (2000)

[13] Cohen, W.W., Borgida, A., Hirsh, H.: Computing least common subsumers in description logic. In: Proceedings of the 10th National Conference on Artificial Intelligence, AAAI92, MIT-Press (1992)

Diagnosing Program Errors with Light-Weighted Specifications

Rong Chen[1] and Franz Wotawa[2,*]

[1] College of Computer Science and Technology, Dalian Maritime University,
Linghai 1, 116026 Dalian, China
[2] Technische Universität Graz, Institut for Software Technology,
Inffeldgasse 16b/2, A-8010 Graz, Austria
{chen, wotawa}@ist.tugraz.at

Abstract. During the last decade many computer-aided debugging tools have been developed to assist users to detect program errors in a software system. A good example are model checking tools that provide counterexamples in case a given program violates the specified properties. However, even with a detailed erroneous run, it remains difficult for users to understand the error well and to isolate its root cause quickly and cheaply. This paper presents object store models for diagnosing program errors with light-weighted specifications. The models we use can keep track on object relations arising during program execution, detect counterexamples that violate user-provided properties, and highlight statements responsible for the violation. We have used the approach to help students to locate and correct the program errors in their course works.

1   Introduction

Building reliable software is often an onerous task in the real development process. Quite often, bugs in software systems can take days or weeks to debug. To reduce human debugging time, many computer-aided debugging systems [8, 2, 5, 1, 12, 3] have been developed to help users find program errors in various cases. In particular, program verification tools [1, 3] aid users to check whether a software system meets the properties. They detect program errors in various cases and reveal the violation of properties by providing the user with detailed counterexamples. However, manual inspection of program failures is time consuming, even with a detailed trace of a failure in hand.

A tool that helps programmers quickly diagnose program failures is desirable in terms of time to the market and costs for software development. We are interested in *Fault localization* that provides a way to aid users in moving from a trace of failure to an understanding of the error, and even perhaps to a correction of the error. A basic notion shared by researchers in the area of fault localization [4, 12, 1, 6, 9] is that to explain something is to identify its cause[6].

* The work presented in this paper was funded by the National Natural Science Foundation of China (NSFC) Project 60203015 and the Austrian Science Fund (FWF) P15265-N04.

M. Ali and R. Dapoigny (Eds.): IEA/AIE 2006, LNAI 4031, pp. 639–649, 2006.

Several approaches have been proposed to localize program errors automatically. Among them are counterexample explanation [1, 6], specification-assisted error localization [4], delta debugging [12], and model-based software debugging (MBSD) [9, 11]. Counterexample explanation identifies the root cause of a detected bug by examining the differences between an erroneous run and the correct run which is close to the erroneous one. In delta debugging [12] possible error locations are highlighted by conducting a modified binary search between a failing and a succeeding run of a program. The Archie system [4] localize the error of data structure inconsistency by minimizing the distance between the error and its manifestation as observably incorrect behavior.

We have developed a Model-Based Software Debugging (MBSD) which applies a model-based diagnosis technique [10] to fault localization. Given a program and a test case to witness the failure, the MBSD compiles the input program into component networks where each statement is mapped to a component whose behavior captures the statement's semantics. The logic behind the MBSD is that components are blamed since assuming the correctness of their statements leads to a failing run. In the MBSD framework, the functional dependency model (FDM) [11] and the value-based model (VBM) [9] handle the code very well and successfully localize the statements responsible for the incorrect program behavior, but they diagnose property violations poorly because they cannot handle the structural properties and their implications very well.

In this paper we propose a program model for diagnosing property violations with light-weighted specifications. This model handles run-time object relations and their compile-time abstractions. It provides users a means to specify structural properties and returns a quality diagnosis of property violations.

The rest of the paper is organized as follows. In Section 2 we introduce our approach by using a motivating example. Then we introduce the specification in Section 3 and the generation of the program model in Section 4. The experimental results given in Section 5 reveal that the program model provides a useful means for diagnosing common structural errors for some classes of programs. Finally, we summarize the paper.

2   A Motivating Example

We present in this section an example to show how a generated program model assist users in understanding the essence of a failing run that violates required properties.

To motivate and illustrate our technique, we use a Java program in Figure 1, which operates on a linked list. The list is implemented by the class *LinkedList* that provides methods to insert elements, remove elements, and reverse elements. This simple data structure comes with a structural constraint as follows:

Property 1. *List l is always acyclic.*

The code is truly simple. However we have already seeded a bug in the code. What can go wrong is that the *insert*(v) does not respect Property 1; it creates a cyclic list when it is ever called on a list with a single element.

```
class LinkedList {                          void insert(Object v) {
  LinkedList next;                            LinkedList c = this;
  Object value;                               LinkedList p = this;
  ...                                         while (!c.nextIsEmtpy()&&(v>c.value)){
  LinkedList(Object o){                         p = c;
    next = null;                                c = c.next;
    value = o;                                }
  }                                           if (p.nextIsEmpty()||(v!=p.value)){
  boolean nextIsEmpty(){                        p.next = new LinkedList();
    return (this.next == null)                  p = p.next;
  }                                             p.value = v;
  ...                                           p.next = c;
                                              }
                                            }
                                          }
```

Fig. 1. A Java example of *LinkedList*

Invoking the buggy *insert(v)* method on a list possibly corrupts the list. However, the corrupted list can grow further with new elements. So we have to wait even longer until the corrupted list manifests itself as observably incorrect behavior.

To see where it goes wrong, we write a *demo(b)* method in Figure 2(a), where the corrupted list l manifests itself as an infinite loop because the *size()* method is going through the entire list to calculate the length.

Our approach on fault localization is an application of the standard Model-Based Diagnosis [10]. Formally, a diagnosis system is a tuple $(SD, STMNTS, SPEC)$, where SD is a logical description of the program behavior, $STMNTS$ the set of statements, and $SPEC$ denotes the light-weighted specification of correctness. For instance, a test case specifies the input data and the expected output data. The program fault on the other hand is a set of system components, i.e., statements or expressions, which are responsible for the failure.

To illustrate the resulting description, Figure 2(b) displays the graphical representation of the system description of the statements $1 \sim 5$, where each statement

```
void demo(boolean b){
1. LinkedList l = new LinkedList(2);
2. if (b) {
     3. l.insert(20);
     4. l.insert(3);
     5. l.insert(5);
   }
/*@l.next.next.next.next!=l@*/
/*@¬ cyclic(l) @*/
6. l.size();
}
```

(a) The code

(b) The program model

Fig. 2. A Java example of *LinkedList*

is mapped to a component, and connection l_i holds the value of the list l after statement i. These components are connected because they manipulate the same list. In this way, the program model is defined by the structure of a component network and behaviors of all components. While the structural part corresponds to syntactic entities, the behavior part implements the language semantics.

The diagnosis process is a process of searching for possible bug locations by assuming how statements might behave. We represent the *correctness assumptions* about the behavior of statements in terms of predicates assigning appropriate modes to the statements. Formally, the diagnosis process is a searching process to find a set of assumptions that is consistent with the given specification:

Definition 1 (Mode Assignment)

A mode assignment for statements $\{S_1, ..., S_n\} \subseteq STMNTS$, each having an assigned set of modes ms and a default mode $default$ such that $default \in mc(S_i)$ for each $S_i \in STMNTS$, is a set of predicates $\{m_1(S_1), ..., m_n(S_n)\}$ where $m_i \in mc(S_i)$ and $m_i \neq default\ (S_i)$.

Consider the $demo(b)$ method, statements have the modes $\neg AB$ (not abnormal) and AB (abnormal), referring to the assumption of correct and incorrect behavior respectively. The goal of the diagnosing process is to find a set of assumptions that is consistent with the given specification.

Definition 2 (Diagnosis)

A set $\Delta \subseteq STMNTS$ is a diagnosis for a diagnosis problem $(SD, STMNTS, SPEC)$ iff $SD \cup SPEC \cup \{\neg AB(S) \mid S \in STMNTS \setminus \Delta\}$ is consistent.

Given the test case, input and output values are propagated forward and backward throughout the network. A contradiction is raised in the diagnosis system when (1) a variable gets two or more different values from different components, or (2) a certain property is violated at the output ports but not at the input ports. A conflict is defined by a set of components causing the contradictions.

Choosing $\neg AB$ mode as the default mode, we cannot assume statements 1 $\sim$ 5 in our example work correctly because the output list l_2 after statement 2 violates Property 1, i.e., $\neg cyclic(l)$ in Figure 2(b). To diagnosis this failing execution trace $[1, 2, 3, 4, 5]$, we start from the last statement 5, go back through all statements $[1, 2, 3, 4, 5]$, compute the witness $cyclic(l)$ at each statement, and thus to see where the data structure inconsistency actually originates. A contraction is thus raised at connection l_3, marked by X in Figure 2(b). This is because component $l.insert(20)$ receives an acyclic list but sends a cyclic list. So we cannot assume statements 1, 2 and 3 work correctly at the same time. Thus we have three single fault diagnoses $\{AB\ (1)\}$, $\{AB\ (2)\}$, and $\{AB\ (3)\}$. The diagnoses pinpoint the flaw in the $insert(v)$ method, i.e., the list become cyclic when it is used to insert the second element. This is informative for the user, giving a hint on how the flaw could be corrected.

In contrast, the VBM is less informative. An assertion $l.next.next.next.next\,! = l$ is used to specify the expected behavior of the $demo(b)$ method. Surely this assertion is violated. The VBM's diagnosis is that all statements 1, 2, 3, 4, 5 are possibly faulty because they influence the value of the assertion. Of course, the diagnosis is not false, but it obscures the original source of error.

3   Specification over Object Store

Structural properties are formulas defined over object relations. Since objects have types, object relations are thus typed.

Definition 3 (Object Relation)
An object relation R with type $(T_1 \to ... \to T_k)$, denoted by $R : T_1 \to ... \to T_k$, is a set of tuples $(o_1, ..., o_k)$ such that for $1 \le i \le k$, object o_i is of type T_i.

Let's call an object relation with k-tuples a *k-relation*. 1-relations and 2-relations are said to be *unary* and *binary*.

Example 1. *We think of a unary relation as a table with a single column, a binary relation as a table with two columns.*

1. *Let x be a program variable that references an object o of type T. Then $x : T$ is a unary relation of type T, which is a singleton set $\{(o)\}$.*
2. *Let A be a set of objects of type T. Then $A : T$ is a unary object relation of type T, which is a set $\{(o) \mid o \in A\}$.*
3. *The next field of a LinkedList makes a binary relation next : LinkedList $\to$ LinkedList.*

A data structure explicitly declares various binary relations. For any field f of an object x, f is a binary relation because $x.f$ can access at most one object. So we have:

Corollary 1. *Let $x.f$ be a field access that represents an object. f is a binary relation.*

Set operators and relational operators provide us a means to derive new relations. The relational operators in our concern are *concatenate* and *join*[1].

Definition 4 (Concatenate Operator)
Let $p : T_1 \to ... \to T_k$ and $q : T_1' \to ... \to T_m'$ be two relations. The concatenate $p \oplus q$ of relations, with type $(T_1 \to ... \to T_k \to T_2'... \to T_m')$, is a set $\{(p_1, ..., p_k, q_2, ..., q_m) \mid (p_1, ..., p_k) \in p$, there is a tuple $(q_1, ..., q_m) \in q$, such that $p_k = q_1$ and $T_k = T_1'\}$.

Definition 5 (Join Operator)
Let $p : T_1 \to ... \to T_k$ and $q : T_1' \to ... \to T_m'$ be two relations. The join $p \circ q$ of relations, with type $(T_1 \to ... \to T_{k-1}, \to T_2'... \to T_m')$, is a set $\{(p_1, ..., p_{k-1}, q_2, ..., q_m) \mid (p_1, ..., p_k) \in p$, there is a tuple $(q_1, ..., q_m) \in q$, such that $p_k = q_1$ and $T_k = T_1'\}$.

---

[1] Essentially they generalize the standard *product* and *join* operators.

If we apply the *concatenate* operator and *join* operator on the same input relations, the *join* contains less columns. For example, a *Tree* class declares two binary relations: *left* : *Tree* → *Tree* and *right* : *Tree* → *Tree*. Whereas *left* ⊕ *right* is a 3-relation that concatenates *left* and *right*, *left* ∘ *right* is a binary relation. Moreover, let A : *Tree* be a unary relation holding a set of objects of type *Tree*, the joint A ∘ *left* is a set of objects accessed by the objects in A through the field *left*.

By repeatedly applying the *join* operator, we can compute the **transitive closure** of a binary relation R, denoted by R^*. Given binary relations, we can create new k-relations by concatenating them and joining them. Therefore, we just keep track on binary relations when modeling the input program.

Putting them together, we write structural properties as formulas. For example, Property 1 is represented by:

$$\forall x \in l \circ next^* \Rightarrow x \notin x \circ next^* \tag{3.1}$$

which says that a list l is acyclic if there is no element in list l that can access itself.

Object relations have their origins and histories; they are like variables in that they have different values at different program points. So a relation is said to be a **parent relation** if it is the origin of other relations. An object relation is a **child** if it has a parent relation. Moreover, we introduce the term **relation variable**.

Definition 6 (Relation Variable)
A relation variable is a variable $T.f$, where f is a binary relation $f : T \rightarrow T'$. The value assigned to a relation variable is a set of pairs in the form (i_1, i_2) where i_1 and i_2 are of type T and T' respectively.

Since we implement a set of methods to perform a consistency checking on a relation variable, the violation of structural properties is detected if we know the variable value.

Definition 7 (Object Store)
An Object Store is a collection of relation variables and their values.

4   Model Building Process

In this section, we present the algorithm for generating object store models. Throughout this section, L is abbreviated for *LinkedList*.

To compile the program into models, we assume each syntactic entity has a function *buildOSM* which maps itself into a component, links its input ports, possibly propagate forwards static information, and returns its output connection. Statement by statement, we convert classes and methods successively and return a set of components defining the diagnosis system.

The static information in our model are location pairs, denoted by pairs of numbers that abstract the run-time objects and approximate the semantics of

ObjectCreation ::= $buildOSM(v = \textbf{new } C, env)$
    $v = \text{new } C$ $c = newComp(assignment, \textbf{new } C, env)$
             for all $v_p \in parent(env, v)$
                $c' = newRelation(c, pointstoRelation, v_p, env)$
                $propagate(c')$
             endfor

ObjectAssignment ::= $buildOSM(v = w, env)$
    $v = w$ $c = newComp(assignment, w, env)$
             for all $v_p \in parent(env, v)$
                $c' = newRelation(c, pointstoRelation, v_p, env)$
                $propagate(c')$
             endfor

FieldAccess ::= $buildOSM(v.f, env)$
    $v.f$ $c = \textbf{new } C_{fieldaccess}$
             $addComp(env, c)$
             $in(c) = conn(env, v)$
             $out(c) = conn(env, v.f)$
             for all $v_p \in parent(env, v)$
                $c' = newRelation(c, v_p, objectRelation, env)$
                $propagate(c')$
             endfor

FieldAssignment ::= $buildOSM(v.f = w, env)$
    $v.f = w$ $c = newComp(fieldassignment, w, env)$
             for all $v_p \in parent(env, v)$
                $c' = newRelation(c, objectRelation, v_p, env)$
                $propagate(c')$
             endfor

IfStatement ::= $buildOSM(\textbf{if } (Exp)\ S_1\ \textbf{else } S_2, env)$
    if Expr $c = \textbf{new } C_{if}$
       S_1 $addComp(env, c)$
    else $cond = buildOSM(Exp, env)$
       S_2 $oldpath = path(env)$
             $path(env) = path(env) + 1$
             Let env' be a copy of env
             $buildOSM(S_2, env')$
             $path(env) = path(env) + 1$
             Let env'' be a copy of env
             $buildOSM(S_1, env'')$
             create an input port of c and connect it to $cond$
             Let $A = modifiedConn(env') \cup modifiedConn(env'')$
             for all $x \in A$
                if $x \in modifiedConn(env')$
                    create an input port of c and connect it to x
                endif
                if $x \in modifiedConn(env'')$
                    create an input port of c and connect it to x
                endif
                create an output port of c and connect it to a new
                    connection x' named by x
                remove x from $modifiedConn(env)$
                add x' into $modifiedConn(env)$
             endfor
             $path(env) = oldpath$

Fig. 3. Algorithm for model building

four syntactic entities: class creation, object variable assignment, field access and field assignment. To describe the history of a relation, we introduce indexed relation variables as follows:

Definition 8 (Indexed Relation Variable)
An indexed relation variable is $NAME[PATH]_{IDX}$, where $NAME$ is a relation variable name, $PATH$ is a sequence of numbers denoting execution branches, and IDX is an index.

Similar to [9], the algorithm maps loops and method calls to hierarchic components with inner sub-models. The loop component contains two sub-models: M_C and M_B, where M_C denotes the sub-model of the loop condition, and M_B the sub-model of the loop body (represented as a nested if-statement[2].

We further assume that env represents the working environment of components, connections, and the indices assigned to variables. The algorithm is summarized in Figure 3, where c denotes a component and the following auxiliary functions are used:

- Function $addComp(env, c)$ adds a component c into the environment env.
- $in(c)$ denotes the input connections of c.
- $out(c)$ denotes the output connections of c.
- Function $propagate(c)$ receives the static information from the input ports of a component c, stores the input instance, unifies it with the value of the parent relation, and propagates them to the output port of c.
- Function $conn : (ENV, EXP \cup Var) \mapsto CONNS$ maps expressions or variables to connections by using an environment.
- Function $parent : (ENV, EXP) \mapsto CONNS$ looks up in the environment for a set of parent relations named by the input expression[3]. If none, a parent relation is created.
- Function $modifiedConn(env)$ returns a set of connections denoting variables with new values.
- $path(env)$ is a number denoting the current branch.
- $newComp(type, exp, env)$ is a function that returns a new component of $type$, which is initialized by the following steps:
  1: $c = \textbf{new} \ \ C_{type}$
  2: $addComp(env, c)$
  3: $out(c) = conn(env, exp)$
  4: $in(c) = buildOSM(exp, env)$
  5: $return \ c$
- $newRelation(c, v_p, type, env)$ is a function that returns a new relation component of $type$, which is initialized by the following steps:

---

[2] The nesting size is obtained by computing all pairs shortest path in a dependency graph (see [11]).

[3] For an object variable w, the name is $T.pt$, where T is w's class type. For a field access $v.f$, the name is in the form of $T.f$ where T is w's class type.

1: $c' = \textbf{new}\ \ C_{type}$
2: $addComp(env, c')$
3: $out(c') = conn(env, v_p)$
4: $in(c') = \{v_p\} \cup out(c) \cup in(c)$
5: $return\ c'$

5 Experimental Results

The experiments are performed on students' programs for the identical assignments in a programming course. Most of the assignments requires various data structures such as linked list, stack, tree, etc. All programs involve various control flows, virtual method invocation, and object-oriented language notations, such as multiple objects, class creations, instance method calls, class and instance variables, etc.

Given properties and test cases, fifty students are grouped into three groups: G1, G2 and G3, where G1 members are asked to locate and eliminate the errors in their programs using traditional debugging tools, while G2 and G3 are assisted with the debugging tool we developed, using the VBM and object store models respectively. Table 1 presents the average number of minutes used by each group to locate and correct the identical program errors.

We also compare the performance of the VBM and object store models running against the identical programs with seeded errors in Table 2, where we depict the elapse time for modeling (M-G column), the elapsed time for computing diagnoses (T-D column), and the number of diagnosis (N-D column). The right column lists the result obtained by diagnosing with a VBM. Compared with the VBM, it is shown that the number of diagnosis candidates is reduced and all diagnosis candidates are in the VBM's diagnosis. This accounts for why members in G3 use less time than those in G2 to locate and eliminate the identical program errors.

Table 1. Error corrections

Group	Error 1 in Shape	Error 2 in Stack	Error 3 in Expression Tree
G1	5	3	11
G2	3.5	1	8
G3	2.5	0.5	4

Table 2. Comparison of the program models

Program	M-G [sec.]	T-D [sec.]	N-D [#]	VBM N-D
LinkedList	0.6	0.3	3	10
Stack	0.6	0.4	1	4
	0.9	0.4	2	4
Shape	2.3	0.3	1	5
ExpressionTree	7.2	2.5	4	9

6 Related Work

During the last decade many computer-aided debugging tools have been developed to assist users to find program errors in a software system. The error detection techniques used by these tools are static and dynamic analysis, program slicing, symbolic execution and model checking.

In [8] Jackson introduces Aspect, an efficient specification-assisted approach for error detection. The Aspect specification is in the form of abstract dependencies, and its scheme is to check dependencies required by the specification against those implied by the source code. It is good at catching errors of missing variables.

The PREfix tool [2] detects anomalies by symbolic execution of code. It uses path-sensitive analysis to explore multiple execution paths in a function, with the goal of finding path conditions under which undesirable properties like null pointers hold. Carefully heuristics are needed to detect errors without generating too many spurious reports.

ESC [5] uses a powerful tailored theorem prover to check code against user-supplied annotations. It has been successfully applied to a particular class of program errors such as out-of-bounds array access, null pointer dereferencing and unsound use of locks.

Using program slicing and shape analysis, the Bandera project [3] is developing a toolkit that extracts finite state machines from code, which can thus be used by model checkers. The SLAM project combines symbolic execution and model checking to produce error traces in order to localize the fault in the source code [1]. Groce and Visser [7] attempt to extract information from a single counterexample produced by model checking in order to facilitate the understanding of malfunctioning systems.

The Archie system [4] successfully localize the error of data structure inconsistency. But there is no guarantee that the original source of all data structure corruption errors are captured in Archie because the consistency checker is invoked periodically.

7   Conclusion

In this paper, we present object store models to diagnose data structure inconsistencies. Our approach handles both the structural properties and their implications by reasoning about object relations arising from the program execution. We have used the approach to help students to locate and correct the program errors in their course works.

We will work on extending the model to handle programs with exceptions, threads and recursive method calls, and exploring how static analysis can assist us to rank user-provided properties.

References

1. T. Ball, M. Naik, and S.K. Rajamani. From symptom to cause: localizing errors in counterexample traces. In *Proc. of POPL*, pages 97–105. ACM Press, 2003.
2. William R. Bush, Jonathan D. Pincus, and David J. Sielaff. A static analyzer for finding dynamic programming errors. *Software Practice and Experience*, 30(7): 775–802, 2000.

3. James C. Corbett. Using shape analysis to reduce finite-state models of concurrent Java programs. *ACM Transactions on Software Engineering and Methodology*, 9(1):51–93, January 2000.
4. Brian Demsky and Martin Rinard. Automatic detection and repair of errors in data structures. *ACM SIGPLAN Notices*, 38(11):78–95, 2003.
5. David L. Detlefs, K. Rustan M. Leino, Greg Nelson, and James B. Saxe. Extended static checking. Technical Report SRC-RR-159, HP Laboratories, 1998.
6. A. Groce. Error explanation with distance metrics. In *TACAS*, volume 2988 of *Lecture Notes in Computer Science*. Springer, 2004.
7. A. Groce and W. Visser. What went wrong: Explaining counterexamples. In *10th International SPIN Workshop on Model Checking of Software*, 5 2003.
8. Daniel Jackson. Aspect: Detecting Bugs with Abstract Dependences. *ACM TOSEM*, 4(2):109–145, 1995.
9. W. Mayer, M. Stumptner, D. Wieland, and F. Wotawa. Can ai help to improve debugging substantially? debugging experiences with value-based models. In *Proc. ECAI*, pages 417–421. IOS Press, 2002.
10. Raymond Reiter. A theory of diagnosis from first principles. *Artificial Intelligence*, 32(1):57–95, 1987.
11. D. Wieland. *Model-Based Debugging of Java Programs Using Dependencies*. PhD thesis, Vienna University of Technology, Institute of Information Systems (184), Nov. 2001.
12. Andreas Zeller and Ralf Hildebrandt. Simplifying and isolating failure-inducing input. *IEEE Transactions on Software Engineering*, 28(2), 2002.

Diagnosis of Power System Protection

Rui D. Jorge[1] and Carlos V. Damásio[2]

[1] EFACEC Sistemas de Electrónica S.A., Carnaxide, Portugal
`rdjorge@se.efacec.pt`
[2] Centria, Universidade Nova de Lisboa, Portugal
`cd@di.fct.unl.pt`

Abstract. Power systems are naturally exposed to several fault conditions, namely short-circuits. Automatic protection and control systems are responsible for selective tripping of faulted devices and their subsequent reconnection.

An application to automatically diagnosing abnormal conditions in power distribution network substations is described in this work. It is based on a model of the power network and the associated protection and control system. Its main purpose is to assist in the analysis of protection device records, explain the observed operations and detect possible misbehavior. This application is specified and implemented using a combination of Logic Programming tools and techniques, in particular non-monotonic reasoning. The model is structured in several abstraction levels and a set of strategies and preferences is used to guide the diagnosis process.

The developed application was tested with several substation configurations, including sequences of events recorded at real installations.

1   Introduction

Power transmission networks are exposed to several types of fault conditions. Among these, the most common are short-circuits. In order to minimize the consequences of those disturbances, power networks are complemented with protection and control systems that are responsible for operating as soon as possible in emergency situations and for restoring normal operating conditions. These systems are normally installed at substations, where the switching devices that connect and disconnect power equipment are located (Fig. 1).

Every power system disturbance, namely those for which more equipment than the strictly necessary was disconnected, must be explained. This diagnosis procedure is executed, in the first place, at the Control Center (CC) responsible for the operation of the whole network, in order to restore as soon as possible the energy supply. At a second stage, the fault condition should be analyzed in detail at an Engineering Center (EC) to diagnose not only the fault location but also possible protection device failures or setup errors. The diagnosis task can be slow and difficult due to the amount of information produced. In the last years several automatic diagnosis applications have been proposed, most concerned real-time operation at CC, where temporal requirements are more

M. Ali and R. Dapoigny (Eds.): IEA/AIE 2006, LNAI 4031, pp. 650–659, 2006.
© Springer-Verlag Berlin Heidelberg 2006

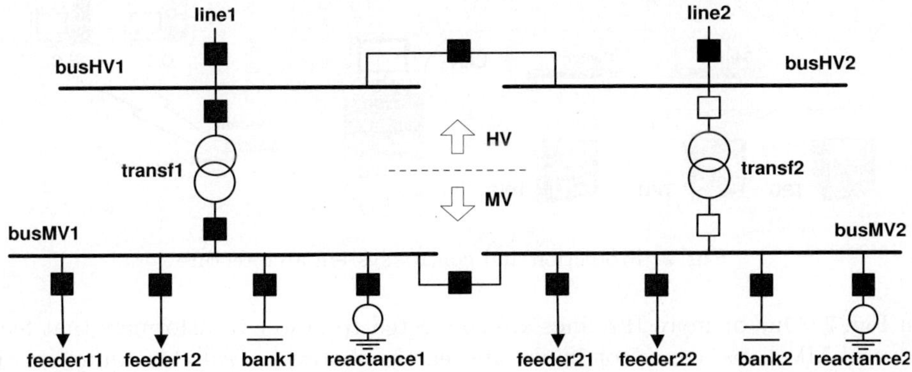

Fig. 1. Typical configuration of a distribution network substation

stringent ([11], [15]). Most of these applications use heuristic-based systems, but some incorporate also model-based techniques ([3], [9]).

This paper describes the implementation of a fault diagnosis application for power distribution substations, that provides detailed explanations of protection system operation and uses all the available information. Its main goal is to assist the *post-mortem* disturbance analysis at an EC.

The structure and behavior model of the target system being known, a model-based diagnosis approach was chosen. This choice assures a bigger adaptability and an easier way of handling complexity. In order to formally characterize the set of solutions of a diagnosis problem, both the model and the diagnosis process are specified and represented using Logic Programming. The notion of abduction as a technique to obtain explanations is exploited. The `Smodels` [12] and `XSB Prolog` [16] systems were used to develop the application.

In a first stage, the system was modeled through a set of rules, including the relevant portion of the power network and the protection devices. The diagnosis process was defined and implemented next, according to a set of strategies and preference criteria. Finally, integration issues were taken into account, namely data input and output. The developed application was tested with existing sub-station configurations and sequences of events related to real disturbances or obtained by simulation.

The rest of the paper is structured as follows. First, the system being modeled is presented and the basic concepts of model-based diagnosis theory are introduced. The model and the diagnosis process are briefly described in the next chapters. The analysis of the application architecture follows and some illustrative results are presented. Finally, conclusions and future work are discussed.

2   System Description

Distribution substations connect high voltage (HV) transport and medium voltage (MV) distribution networks. Their configuration is usually represented like

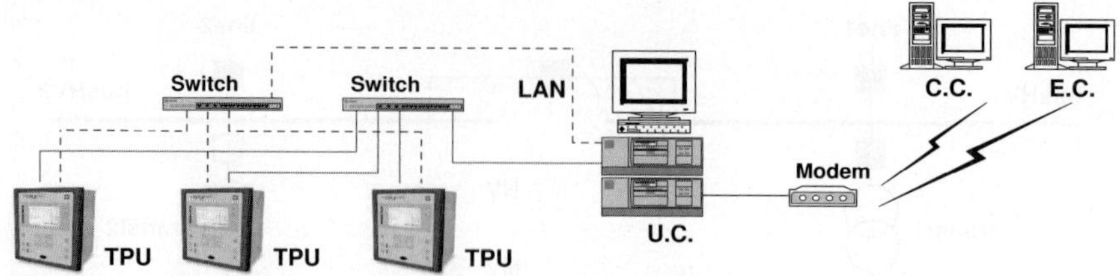

Fig. 2. Protection and control system architecture

in Fig. 1. One or more HV lines are connected to power transformers that feed several MV lines, capacitor banks and earth reactances. All this equipment is connected through buses.

Each of the previous components may be connected or disconnected by circuit breakers (in Fig. 1 black squares if closed, white squares if opened).

The protection and control system (Fig. 2) is mainly composed of several terminal protection units (TPU), connected among them and to a central unit (UC) through a local area network (LAN). Each protection device continuously monitors and protects a specific power device or network zone, in a relatively autonomous way. The UC interfaces the hierarchically superior network management centers. The LAN allows communication between units and the exchange of real-time information to the supervision and control system (SCADA).

3   Diagnosis and Logic Programming

3.1   Model-Based Diagnosis

Whenever a sufficiently detailed model of the correct system and of the faulty behavior are available, then a model-based diagnosis approach can be used. Its basic principle is the now classic scheme represented in Fig. 3: the behavior predicted by a system model is compared to actual observations of the same system; from the contradictions detected, possible diagnoses can be inferred.

In its basic version, a model-based diagnosis system only needs information about the correct behavior of the device [14]. Fault models can be added to limit the number of solutions generated, some of them physically impossible.

Two distinct characterizations result from the way the contradiction in observations is removed: in the consistent approach to diagnosis [2], values different from observed ones can't be derived after changing the logical value of a set of explanations in the base theory; in the abductive approach to diagnosis [10], the

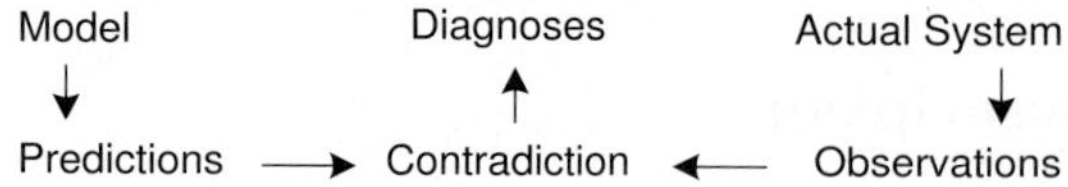

Fig. 3. Model-based diagnosis

observations should be derived from the same theory. In the work now described, a combination of both characterizations is used, since there is both a model of the system functioning correctly plus additional modeling of faulty behavior.

Struss [13] was the first to coin the idea of the diagnosis task as a dynamic process; in this approach, a set of working hypotheses is explicitly modeled and susceptible of being revised. Several strategies can be considered to control the diagnosis process by defining the active working hypotheses at each step. Additional criteria can be used to select preferential diagnoses. Some work tries to generalize these concepts: first, in a rather procedural way, Böttcher and Dressler [1]; then, in Damásio et al [4], a declarative representation of preferences and strategies using meta-programs is proposed.

3.2   Extended Logic Programming

The expressivity of declarative languages and, namely, of Logic Programming, can be used to represent and solve model-based diagnosis problems, as expressed in [8]. The approach is adopted in this work, as described next.

Extended logic programs are used to model the system, by making use of the two forms of negation available, which allow to express what is known to be false (explicit negation) and what is believed false (default negation). Given a first order language, an extended logic program is a set of rules and integrity constraints of the form:

$$H \leftarrow B_1, ..., B_n, not\, C_1, ..., not\, C_m (m \geq 0, n \geq 0) \ . \tag{1}$$

$H, B_1, ..., B_n, C_1, ..., C_m$ are objective literals. For integrity constraints, H corresponds to $\perp$ (contradiction). When $n = m = 0$, H is an alternative representation to the rule $H \leftarrow$ (fact). An objective literal is an atom A or its explicit negation $\neg A$, being $\neg\neg A = A$. $not\, L$ is a negative literal (default literal).

4   System Modeling

The substation model implemented uses Logic Programming to represent the structure of the system and the behavior of its components. System behavior depends on a set of hypotheses (abducibles) that correspond to open literals, whose logical value can be revised to assure the explanation of observations. The abducibles considered are: power network disturbances; circuit breaker open and close commands; protection device and circuit breaker behavior modes.

The model, described in [7], can be easily adapted to different system configurations. It is composed by the power network model, the protection device model and the circuit breaker model. It has 125 different rules, besides facts. For the example of Fig. 1, the number of instantiated rules is about 1600.

Because the system under analysis is dynamic, the sequences of observations for each diagnosis action are delimited by a time interval where the logical value of abducible hypotheses can be assumed constant. These sequences are triggered by the start signal of any protection device or a circuit breaker close command.

Temporal behavior is modeled in two different ways, according to the intended level of detail. The simplest time model considers only two instants: before and after protection operation. The detailed time representation employs a time resolution of 50 ms, which accommodates the inaccuracy inherent to protection operation time and the non-perfect clock synchronization among devices.

4.1   Network Model

The network model includes a description of the topology of the substation and of the associated faults. The relevant portion of the power system is described by a set of facts. These include: voltage levels (HV or MV), power devices (lines, transformers,...) and connections between them.

```
power_device(feeder11, feeder). connection(feeder11, busMV1, cb11, mt).
```

In order to express in the model the network propagation of fault effects, additional rules identify the equipments where each short-circuit (abducible `sc/3`) is observed for each time step (predicate `sc_visible/4`): locally at the faulted device if it is connected to some current source (`reaches_source/4`); and at any upstream power device connected between the faulted device and some source. This behavior is modeled by the two following rules, taken from the logic programming model of the system. Specific rules for `reaches_source/4` and `source_sc/5` are also included in the model.

```
sc_visible(Device, Net, FaultType, local, T) <-
   sc(Device, Net, FaultType ), reaches_source(Device, Net, FaultType, T).
sc_visible(DeviceUp, Net, FaultType, backup, T) <-
   source_sc(DeviceUp, DeviceDown, Net, FaultType, T),
   sc_visible(DeviceDown, Net, FaultType, _, T),
   not sc_visible(DeviceUp, Net, FaultType, local, T).
```

Other rules relate system disturbances and their effects, namely overcurrent, undervoltage and current and voltage asymmetry. For example, an overcurrent will be observed as a consequence of a short-circuit.

```
overcurrent(CB, phase_phase, Dist, T) <- sc_visible(CB, _, Dist, T).
```

4.2   Protection Model

Protection devices (TPU) are described by a set of facts, including its name and the associated circuit breaker. The list of internal functions for each device is also part of the model.

```
protection(prot_saida11). association(prot_saida11, disj_saida11).
```

Protection device behavior is modeled in three different ways, corresponding to three abstraction levels. Model activation is controlled by a set of working hypotheses (predicate `refined/1`). The rules associated with the protection model relate internal and external conditions to the predicted results of function operation (`obs/4`).

At the most abstract level, only the commands generated by the protection devices are modeled. The TPU is treated as a black box that opens and closes the associated circuit breakers by issuing manual or automatic commands. This abstraction level and the next one use the simplest time representation.

```
obs(Prot, func_cb, open_cmd, 1) <- open_command(Prot, manual).
obs(Prot, func_cb, open_cmd, 1) <- not refined(substation),
    open_command(Prot, automatic).
```

In the second level the predicted protection behavior for different network faults is modeled. There are rules to model the basic principles of protection: a protection must operate if a fault is observed in the respective protection zone, as long as the device is ok (mode ab_underoperation assumed false by default); it can also operate as backup of another faulty protection, as long as the disturbance is observed (fault mode ab_overoperation).

```
obs(Prot, func_cb, open_cmd, 1) <- refined(substation), not refined(Prot),
    time(T), association(Prot, CB), sc_visible(CB, _, local, T),
    not mode_func(Prot, ab_underoperation).
obs(Prot, func_cb, open_cmd, 1) <- refined(substation), not refined(Prot),
    time(T), association(Prot, CB), sc_visible(CB, _, backup, T),
    mode_func(Prot, ab_overoperation).
```

At the last level, the protection behavior is refined and each component function is described. This model uses the detailed time representation because protection operation is compared against its predefined settings.

4.3 Circuit Breaker Model

Switching devices associated with protection devices are modeled considering two possible failure modes (mode_func/2), one for open and one for close commands. Default negation is used to express that the circuit breaker is not abnormal by default. If the device is ok, the correct status should be attained after issuing the respective order (obs/4). This is only expected if the circuit breaker is previously in the opposite state (holds/4).

```
obs(Prot, func_cb, cb_closed, 1) <-
    association(Prot, CB), obs(Prot, func_cb, close_cmd, 1),
    not holds(Prot, func_cb, cb_closed, 0), not mode_func(CB, ab_close).
obs(Prot, func_cb, cb_closed, 0) <-
    association(Prot, CB), obs(Prot, func_cb, open_cmd, 1),
    holds(Prot, func_cb, cb_closed, ini), not mode_func(CB, ab_open).
```

To express negative observations (in case of failure) explicit negation is used:

```
-obs(Prot, func_cb, cb_closed, 1).
```

5 Diagnosis Process

The diagnosis problem presented in the last chapter exhibits a considerable dimension and complexity. For instance, the intermediate model for the substation in Fig. 1 has 138 abducibles, that generate a search space with 2^{138} states.

In order to reduce the time necessary to find the desired solutions a set of strategies and preferences guide the diagnosis process. A sequence of simpler steps is implemented, taking advantage of the several levels of abstraction of the model to reduce the overall complexity. At each step, some strategy - model refinement, addition of observations - is applied. Only the minimal solutions regarding set inclusion are given after each step. The process assures that no valid diagnoses are lost. At the end, the preference criteria are applied to present the final ordered solutions to the user. Figure 4 summarizes the implemented diagnosis process.

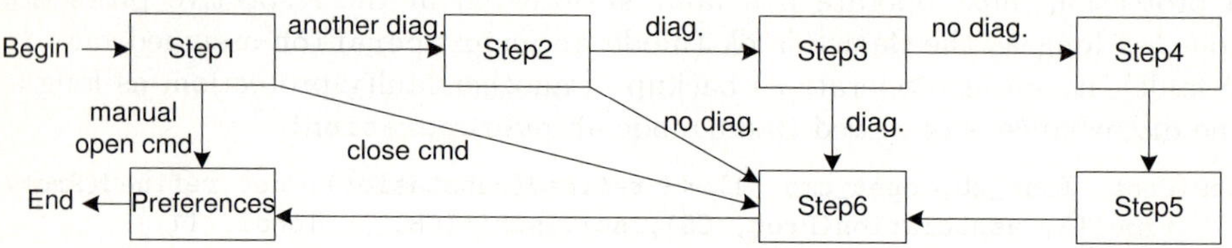

Fig. 4. Diagnosis process

5.1 Strategies

First, the least refined model is activated, which leads to one or more diagnoses. After this step, some simple hypotheses (manual open commands or close commands not followed by protection operation) are discriminated from other power system disturbances. In the first case the whole process may end immediately; in case a more complex network fault is diagnosed, the process proceeds to the next step, in which the intermediate model is activated. In this second step, these faults are detailed in a new set of diagnoses.

In the third step the strategy used is the addition of more observations in order to eliminate some invalid candidates. For each of the solutions from the previous step, all the abducibles associated with network faults are fixed. Because the diagnosis obtained from the previous step are restricted to minimal solutions, there is the possibility of ending the third step with no remaining valid candidates. In that case, the two previous steps are repeated, but without fixing network faults hypotheses (fourth and fifth steps).

Finally, in the sixth and last step, the most refined model is activated for the faulty components and the final solutions are presented with the greatest level of detail. If the two first steps don't produce any diagnoses this model is directly activated for every protection device.

5.2 Preferences

At the end, preference criteria are applied and final diagnoses are ordered according to them. These criteria could be very restrictive and eliminate some interesting solutions, namely simultaneous faults, if applied along the process.

The solutions are ordered according to the cardinality of faulty components, in the following way: first, the solutions with less power system faults (short-circuits, for instance) are considered; next, for the same number of faults, preference is given to diagnoses with less faulty protection devices. These criteria are based on the reduced probability of simultaneous faults in the network and the (expected) small rate of protection misbehavior.

To choose between diagnoses for which the previous criteria are not enough, a third preference criterium is considered based on the probability of different types of faults and fault locations.

6   Implementation and Results

6.1   Implementation

The described diagnosis process is specified and implemented in a declarative way using Logic Programming. The application has three distinct layers: the diagnosis layer, the strategies and preferences layer and the interface layer.

The inner layer solves, for a certain process step, a diagnosis problem, composed by the system model, a set of observations and a set of abducibles. This layer uses the `Smodels` system [12], to efficiently obtain the models of a normal logic program according to stable models semantics or, for extended logic programs, with explicit negation, the corresponding answer-sets [6]. A logic program, whose stable models correspond to the desired abductive solutions is obtained from the initial diagnosis problem through a program transformation [5].

In a second layer, the strategies and preferences are implemented. This layer is responsible for the sequence of partial diagnosis actions and the corresponding selection of working hypotheses, observations and abducibles. This process is executed till a satisfactory set of diagnoses is obtained. This layer is implemented using the `XSB Prolog` system, from which the inner layer can be automatically invoked to solve each of the partial diagnosis tasks.

The outer layer implements the application interface. It runs also under the `XSB Prolog` console, and is also responsible for the interaction with the database containing the system configuration and the set of observations.

6.2   Results

The developed application was tested with configurations of existing substations and sequences of events recorded during real power system disturbances. These examples have several configurations and dimensions. The number of power devices, protection and circuit breakers for each case are in Table 1. Other results were obtained by fault simulation, with the configuration presented in Fig. 1.

Test cases correspond to several types of faults, with distinct locations and sometimes with simultaneous occurrence of protection device or circuit breaker failures. Table 2 presents the time and the number of final diagnoses for each real disturbance. All tests were executed in a PC with 1.7 GHz clock frequency Intel Pentium IV processor, running the Windows operating system.

Table 1. Substation configuration

Substation	Pow/Prot/CB	Substation	Pow/Prot/CB
Aparecida (Brazil)	13 / 9 / 9	Turiz (Portugal)	8 / 7 / 7
Santa Elena (Chile)	11 / 9 / 9	Faro (Portugal)	16 / 15 / 15
Sr. Roubado (Portugal)	6 / 5 / 5	Central Tejo (Port.)	38 / 37 / 37

Table 2. Results

Test	N. of Diag.	Time[s]	Test	N. of Diag.	Time[s]
Aparecida (1st case)	1	5,8	Santa Elena	10	123,5
Aparecida (2nd case)	1	68,4	Faro (1st case)	2	813,7
Aparecida (3rd case)	1	71,2	Faro (2nd case)	14	892,7
Turiz (1st case)	1	41,3	Faro (3rd case)	2	145,4
Turiz (2nd case)	1	308,7	Sr. Roubado	1	21,4
Turiz (3rd case)	1	61,9	Central Tejo	1	593,3

Every test case was correctly diagnosed. The number of final solutions is usually small and often unique. A reasonable solution time is attained by employing the predefined set of strategies and preferences. Without the presented diagnosis process, the application showed to be infeasible.

Manual open and close commands (Aparecida, 1st case) are easily discriminated from other fault conditions. On the other hand, network disturbances demand more time to obtain sufficiently refined diagnoses. The two extra steps to search for non-minimal solutions are only needed in the case of simultaneous faults (Turiz, 2nd case); the option to use this strategy only if the previous ones fail is justified because this occurrence is relatively uncommon.

7   Conclusion

A first version of a distribution substation fault diagnosis application was developed. Non-monotonic reasoning techniques and tools are used and a model-based approach is followed. The main advantages are: a formal specification that can be validated and an easier way to handle system evolution and model refinement. Another strength of the proposed model is its applicability to several types of substations. However in some cases it is still necessary to add specific rules to the model. The nonexistence of an interface to the program that adds and validates rules provided by the user constitutes a present limitation.

The results obtained with real substation configurations confirm the feasibility of the proposed solution. The diagnosis tool is slightly slower than heuristic-based systems ([9], [11], [15]). However, this is not a critical issue because this application is intended to assist *post-mortem* record analysis, for which temporal requirements aren't so stringent. Besides that, heuristic-based systems are more difficult to maintain and upgrade.

Some future work will be: the development of a graphical user interface; the optimization of diagnostic process; the possibility of addition of user specific rules; the use of information from other substations to diagnose complex faults.

References

1. Böttcher, C., Dressler, O.: A framework for controlling model-based diagnosis systems with multiple actions. Ann. Math. A. I. (special issue on Model-based Diagnosis) **11** (1994)
2. de Kleer, J., Williams, B.: Diagnosing multiple faults. Artificial Intelligence **32**(1): 97–130, April 1987
3. Davidson, E., McArthur, S., McDonald, J.: A toolset for applying model-based reasoning techniques to diagnostics for power system protection. IEEE Trans. Power Systems **18**(2): 680–687, May 2003
4. Damásio, C., Nejdl, W., Pereira, L., Schroeder, M.: Model-based diagnosis preferences and strategies representation with meta-logic programming. In K. Apt and F. Turini, editors, Meta-logics and Logic Prog. **11**: 269–311, MIT Press, 1995
5. Eiter, T., Faber, W., Leone, N., Pfeifer, G.: The diagnosis frontend of the dlv system. Tech. Rep. DBAI-TR-98-20, Tech. Univ. Wien, Austria, November 1998
6. Gelfond, M., Lifschitz, V.: Logic programs with classical negation. Proc. 7th Int. Conf. on L.P., 579–597, MIT Press, 1990
7. Jorge, R.: Power network protection system diagnosis. Master Thesis (in portuguese), FCT, Univ. Nova. Lisboa, 2005
8. Pereira, L., Damásio, C., Alferes, J.: Diagnosis and debugging as contradiction removal. Proc. 2nd Int. Workshop on LP and Non-monotonic Reasoning, 334–348, Lisboa, Portugal, June 1993
9. Pfau-Wagenbauer, M., Nejdl, W.: Model/heuristic-based alarm processing for power systems. Journal on AI in Eng., Design and Manuf., **7**(1): 65–78, 1993
10. Poole, D.: Normality and faults in logic-based diagnosis. Proc. of 11th IJCAI, 1304–1310, Detroit, MI, August 1989
11. Sidhu, T., Cruder, O., Huff, G.: An abductive inference technique for fault diagnosis in electrical power transmission networks. IEEE Trans. Power Delivery **12**(1): 515–522, January 1997
12. Smodels system. version 2.27, http://www.tcs.hut.fi/softare/smodels/, 2003
13. Struss, P.: Diagnosis as a process. Work. Notes 1st Int. Workshop on Model-based diagnosis, Paris, 1989
14. Struss, P., Dressler, O.: Physical negation: integrating fault models into the general diagnostic engine. Proc. 11th IJCAI, 1318–1323, Detroit, MI, August 1989
15. Vale, Z., Moura, A.: An expert system with temporal reasoning for alarm processing in power system control centers. IEEE Trans. Power Systems **8**(3): 1307–1313, August 1993
16. XSB Logic Programming system. version 2.6, http://xsb.sourceforge.net/, 2003

Towards Lightweight Fault Localization
in Procedural Programs

Bernhard Peischl, Safeeullah Soomro, and Franz Wotawa

Technische Universität Graz
Intitute for Software Technology (IST)
Inffeldgasse 16b/2, A-8010 Graz, Austria
`{peischl, ssoomro, wotawa}@ist.tuGraz.at`

Abstract. In this paper we present a novel extension of a lightweight model for fault localization that allows for modeling procedural programs. The procedural programming paradigm is often used in (safety-critical) control software where a program's verification and subsequent fault localization is of utmost importance. In this article we present results from our recent case study relying on this kind of programs. Notably, our lightweight model is always able to localize the misbehavior's real cause.

Keywords: model-based software debugging, software debugging, control software, procedural abstraction.

1   Introduction

Detecting, localizing and correcting bugs is one of the most time consuming tasks in the software development. Verification technology has made considerable progress in the recent years. This has brought up tools like, for example, model checkers and nowadays we know successful applications of such tools in areas like hardware design or software development specifically in control engineering. However, today there is almost no tool support for localizing the misbehavior's real cause once it has been detected.

In this article we focus on fault localization in domains like control engineering where engineers often employ the procedural programming paradigm. Procedural programs are generally more computationally efficient than object-oriented programs, because there is less overhead to handle abstractions and the data structures more closely resemble the hardware that must manipulate them. Moreover, these programs are amendable to verification since they are inherently simpler due to avoidance of abstraction, dynamic dispatch and late binding of variables to values. Often control software is safety-critical and thus detection but also localization of bugs is of uttermost importance.

---

[1] Authors are listed in alphabetical order. The Austrian Science Fund (FWF) supports this work under project grant P17963-N04. The Higher Eductaion Comission (HEC), Pakistan, supports this work under its scholarship program.

M. Ali and R. Dapoigny (Eds.): IEA/AIE 2006, LNAI 4031, pp. 660–667, 2006.
© Springer-Verlag Berlin Heidelberg 2006

In [13, 14] we propose a model for fault localization that, in contrast to previous models, allows for taking advantage of arbitrary relationships between variables, and variables and constants. In software engineering invariants, or pre- and postconditions often capture such relationships. [10] points out that localization of structural faults requires such kind of design information. In this article we focus on a fault localization technique based on abstract dependences we proposed in [13, 14]. We (1) present first experimental results we obtained from this modeling approach and (2) extend our previous work by incorporating procedure calls. Thereby all advantages like the exploitation of specification artifacts and small model size remain.

2   Fault Localization with Abstract Dependences

Aspect [3] is a static analysis technique for detecting bugs in imperative programs. Aspect requires the user to specify the correct behavior in terms of abstract dependences between specific variables. Aspect's checker employs a dependence analysis to check code against the given specifications. In this way the Aspect system is able detect a program's erroneous behavior. Rather than for detecting a fault we employ abstract dependences to localize the real cause of misbehavior.

Abstract dependences are relations between variables of a program. We say that a variable x depends on a variable y iff a new value for y may causes a new value for x. For example, the assignment statement x = y + 1; implies such a dependence relation. Every time we change the value of y the value of x is changed after executing the statement. Another example which leads to the same dependence is the following program fragment:

```
if ( y < 10) then
       x = 1;
   else
       x = 0;
```

In this fragment not all changes applied to y cause a change on the value of x, although x definitely depends on y. The Aspect system now takes a program, computes the dependences and compares them with the specified dependences. If there is a mismatch the system detects a bug and notifies the user. However, the Aspect systems does not pinpoint the root-cause of the detected misbehavior to the user. In the following we explain the basic ideas using the following small program which implements the computation of the circumference and area of a circle. The program contains one fault in line 2 where a multiplication by Π is missing.

```
0. // pre true
1. d = r * 2;
2. a = d; // BUG! a = d * pi;
3. c = r * r * pi;
4. // post c = r² * pi,  a = 2 * r * pi
```

Informally, a program variable x depends on a variable y if a value for y potentially influences the value of x. In our small example program the variable d in the first line depends on the variable r. Hence, every statement of a program introduces new dependences. All defined variables of an assignment statement , i.e., variables occuring on the left side, depend on all variables of the right side of an assignment statement. Similar rules can be obtained for other statements as explained later on. These dependences solely are given by a statement whenever we assume that the statement is correct (wrt. the dependences). If a statement is assumed to be incorrect the dependences are not known. We express the latter fact by introducing a new type of variable, the so called model variables. Model variables are variables that work as placeholder for program variables. For example, if we assume statement 2 to be incorrect, we introduce a model that says that program variable a depends on model variable ξ_2 (where ξ_2 is unique).

The idea behind our approach is to find assumptions about the correctness and incorrectness of statements which do not contradict a given specification. What does this mean? In our running example, the specification is given as post-condition. From this post-condition we derive that a has to depend on r and pi. However, when assuming statement 1 and 2 to be correct, we derive that a depends on d and d in turn depends on r which leads to a depends on r but not on pi. Hence, the computed dependence contradicts the specified one. To get rid of this inconsistency, we might assume line 2 to be faulty. Hence, we can compute that a depends on model variable ξ_2. When now comparing the specification with the computed dependence we substitute ξ_2 by r and pi and we can no longer derive an inconsistency. Thus the statement in line 2 is a bug candidate since it explains the encountered misbehavior.

The interpretation of a dependence (x, y) of a relation $R \in \mathcal{D}$ is that x depends on y. The dependence relations for every line of our small program are:

$$
\begin{aligned}
&1.\ \texttt{d = r * 2;} \qquad && r_1 = \{(\texttt{d}, \texttt{r})\} \\
&2.\ \texttt{a = d;} \qquad && r_2 = \{(\texttt{a}, \texttt{d})\} \\
&3.\ \texttt{c = r * r * pi;} \quad && r_3 = \{(\texttt{c}, \texttt{r}), (\texttt{c}, \texttt{pi})\}
\end{aligned}
$$

Formally , we refer to the following definitions.

Definition 1 (Dependence Relation). *Given a program with variables V, and a set of model variables $M = \{\xi_1, \ldots\}$. A dependency relation is a subset of the set $\mathcal{D} = 2^{V \times (M \cup V)}$.*

For combining the dependences of two consecutive statments we define the following composition operator for dependence relations.

Definition 2 (Composition). *Given two dependence relations $R_1, R_2 \in \mathcal{D}$ on V and M. The composition of R_1 and R_2 is defined as follows:*

$$
R_1 \circ R_2 = \begin{aligned}
&\{(x, y) | (x, z) \in R_2 \wedge (z, y) \in R_1\} \cup \\
&\{(x, y) | (x, y) \in R_1 \wedge \nexists (x, z) \in R_2\} \cup \\
&\{(x, y) | (x, y) \in R_2 \wedge \nexists (y, z) \in R_1\}
\end{aligned}
$$

This definition ensures that no information is lost during computing the overall dependence relation for a procedure. Hence, the first line of the definition of composition handles the case where there is a transitive dependence. The second line states that all dependences that are not re-defined in R_2 are still valid. In the third line all dependences that are defined in R_2 are in the new dependence set provided that there is no transitivity relation.

Note that functional composition is not a commutative operation and that $\emptyset$ is the identity element of composition.

For example, the combined dependences of our running examples are: $r_1 \circ r_2 = \{(\mathtt{a}, \mathtt{r}), (\mathtt{d}, \mathtt{r})\} = r'$ and $r' \circ c_3 = \{(\mathtt{a}, \mathtt{r}), (\mathtt{d}, \mathtt{r}), (\mathtt{c}, \mathtt{r}), (\mathtt{c}, \mathtt{pi})\} = r''$.

In order to allow the direct comparison of specified dependences with the computed ones we introduce a projection operator which deletes all dependences for variables that are not of interest like the internal variable d.

Definition 3 (Projection). *Given a dependence relations $R \in \mathcal{D}$ and a set of variables $A \subseteq M \cup V$. The projection of R on A written as $\Pi_A(R)$ is defined as follows:*

$$\Pi_A(R) = \{(x, y) | (x, y) \in R \wedge x \in A \wedge y \in A\}$$

For example, $\Pi_{\{r,c,a,pi\}}(r'')$ is $\{(\mathtt{a}, \mathtt{r}), (\mathtt{c}, \mathtt{r}), (\mathtt{c}, \mathtt{pi})\}$ which is equivalent to the specification.

From here on we assume that the computed dependence relation is always projected onto the variables used within the specification before comparing it with the specification.

In [13, 14] we present a detailed formalization of this idea and show how to embed this idea into a model-based diagnosis framework [9, 1]. There we also present rules for the most important language artifacts like the assignment statement, the if-then-else statement, and while loop. Figure 1 and Figure 2 summarize these rules for correct ($\neg Ab$) and abnormal (Ab) behavior. In the

$$\neg Ab(x = e) \rightarrow D(x = e) = \{(\mathtt{x}, v) | v \in vars(e)\}$$

$$\neg Ab(\mathtt{if}\ e\ \mathtt{then}\ S_1\ \mathtt{else}\ S_2) \rightarrow$$
$$D(\mathtt{if}\ e\ \mathtt{then}\ S_1\ \mathtt{else}\ S_2) = D(S_1) \cup D(S_2) \cup ((M(S_1) \cup M(S_2)) \times vars(e))$$

$$\neg Ab(\mathtt{while}\ e\ \{\ S\ \}) \rightarrow$$
$$D(\mathtt{while}\ e\ \{\ S\ \}) = D(S)^* \cup (M(S) \times vars(e)) \circ D(S)^*$$

Fig. 1. The correct abstract behavior

$$Ab(x = e) \rightarrow D(x = e) = \{(x, \xi_\iota)\}$$

$$Ab(\mathtt{if}\ e\ \mathtt{then}\ S_1\ \mathtt{else}\ S_2) \rightarrow$$
$$D(\mathtt{if}\ e\ \mathtt{then}\ S_1\ \mathtt{else}\ S_2) = D(S_1) \cup D(S_2) \cup ((M(S_1) \cup M(S_2)) \times \{\xi_\iota\})$$

$$Ab(\mathtt{while}\ e\ \{\ S\ \}) \rightarrow$$
$$D(\mathtt{while}\ e\ \{\ S\ \}) = D(S)^* \cup (M(S) \times \{\xi_\iota\}) \circ D(S)^*$$

Fig. 2. The abstract behavior for buggy statement

next section we extend this work in showing how to deal with procedures and their corresponding parameters.

3   Abstract Dependences for Procedures

When dealing with programs relying on procedures we have to extend our model with rules for (1) mapping the formal to actual parameters, and (2) the treatment of return values. Note that we assume that parameters are passed on via call by value.

Definition 4 (Dependences for Procedure Body). *Let $proc(a_1, ..a_n)$ be a procedure with the actual parameters $a_1, ..., a_n$ and corresponding formal parameters $f_1, ..., f_n$. The dependence relation $D(proc(a_1, ..., a_n))$ is given by*

$$D(proc(a_1, ..., a_n)) = D(body(proc(f_1, .., f_n))) \circ \{(f_i, a_i) | i \in \{1..n\}\},$$

where $D(body(proc(f_1, .., f_n)))$ denotes the dependences of the procedure's body including the formal parameters $f_1, .., f_n$.

The program in Figure 3 invokes procedure *area* with the actual parameter $a1$ and assigns it to variable $ar1$.

```
0.  pi = 3.1415927
1.  ...
2.  // pre true
3.  procedure area (r)
4.  d = r * 2;
5.  ar = r*r*pi;
6.  return ar
7.  // post ar = r² · π
8.  ...
    ...
19. ...
20. ar1 = area(a1)
21. // post ar1 = a1² * pi
```

Fig. 3. Example program illustrating procedure invocation

For our small example, the dependences of the procedure are $D(body(area(r)))$ $= \{(d, r), (ar, r), (ar, pi)\}$. Thus the dependences after mapping actuals to formals yield to $D(area(a1)) = \{(d, a1), (ar, a1), (ar, pi)\}$. Note that pi is considered as a program variable herein.

Definition 5 (Invocation and Return Values of a Procedure). *Let $D(proc$ $(a_1, ..., a_n))$ the dependences obtained from a procedure invocation statement $t = proc(a_1, .., a_n)$ where t denotes a (optional) target variable, and let $return(proc)$ be a function returning all the variables appearing in the procedure's return statements. Let D^* be the transitive and reflexive closure of the dependence relation D. The rules for abnormal and correct behavior for invoking procedure proc are as follows:*

$$\neg Ab(t = proc(a_1, a_2, ..., a_n)) \rightarrow D(t = proc(a_1, a_2, ..., a_n)) =$$
$$\{t\} \times \{v | (x, v) \in D(proc(a_1, ..., a_n))^*, x \in return(proc)\}$$
$$Ab(t = proc(a_1, a_2, ..., a_n)) \rightarrow D(t = proc(a_1, a_2, ..., a_n)) = \{(t, \xi_\iota)\}$$

Revisiting our small example we obtain the following dependences $D(ar1 = proc(a1)) = \{ar1\} \times \{a1, pi\}$ which yields to $\{(ar1, a1), (ar1, pi)\}$. This treatment of return values reflects the fact that a developer would expect that variable $ar1$ depends on $a1$ after the procedure's invocation. Note that locals declared within a specific procedure do not appear in the specified dependences, thus we can remove all depenences involving these local variables.

4   Case Studies

The proposed model has been implemented in the Java programming language. For various example programs, we introduced a single fault, and afterwards computed all single-fault diagnoses. Table 1 present first empirical results. We solely considered small example programs ranging from 10 to 159 lines of code comprising several procedures. The second column in the table lists the total number of lines of code. The next column reports the number of reported diagnosis candidates, and the final column shows the amount of code that can be excluded by relying on our lightweight model.

Regarding the case studies summarized above, our model always appears to localize the real cause of misbehavior, that is – the diagnosis candidates contain the introduced erroneous statement. Notably, the running time required for computing all single-fault diagnoses is neglectable. The obtained results indicate that the lightweight approach herein is able to deal with procedural abstraction. However, depending on the structural properties of the program and the specific fault being introduced, in our examples, the amount of excludable code varies from 57 to 88 percent of the total number of statements. Note that in contrast to our previous value-level models [6, 8, 12], this model allows solely for localizing

Table 1. Results obtained from the case study

program name	tot. LOC	no. diagnosis cand.	excl. amount (perc.)
multiply	10	2	80.0
fibonacci	14	2	85.7
sum	16	7	56.3
ticket info	19	4	78.9
small example	15	3	80.0
extra example	22	5	77.3
arithmetics	28	7	75.0
tax comp.	34	12	64.7
calculator	38	16	57.9
converter	79	14	82.3
misc.	159	19	88.0

the misbehavior's cause at the granularity of statements rather than on the expression level.

5   Related Research

The author of [3] presents work which is closest to the work presented herein. This work employs abstract dependences for detecting rather than for localizing a fault. Furthermore in [5, 11] the authors employ the notion of dependences for fault localization. In contrast to the latter approach we do not employ detected differences in variable values at a certain line in code but make use of differences between specified and computed dependences and thus also incorporate the structural properties of program and specification.

In the recent past the authors of [12, 2, 4, 6] developed models for different languages at various abstraction levels in the model-based systems context. In general, abstract modeling approaches sacrifice detail in favor of computational complexity whereas more detailed value-level models [12, 7] provide accurate fault localization capabilities but on the other hand require considerable computational resources in terms of space and computing power.

The authors of [12, 2, 11, 8] solely make use of concrete values in incorporating design information (e.g. directly obtained from a test case revealing a certain malfunctioning). These models do not allow to take advantage of arbitrary relationships between several variables or variables and constants. Stumptner [10] shows that localizing structural faults requires exploiting such kind of design information like, for example, assertions, and pre- and post conditions.

6   Conclusion and Future Research

In this paper we extend a lightweight fault localization model towards the treatment of procedural abstractions and we present first case studies obtained from this model. Our experiments on small procedural programs indicate that this model is able to localize the misbehavior's real cause.

The model's extension to handle procedures and their corresponding parameters is important since, for example, control software often is developed using this paradigm. However, nowadays a vast amount of software is developed employing the object-oriented paradigm. Thus, to be generally applicable, the current model needs to be extended with abstract models for late binding, dynamic method dispatch, and abstraction.

References

1. Johan de Kleer and Brian C. Williams. Diagnosing multiple faults. *Artificial Intelligence*, 32(1):97–130, 1987.
2. Gerhard Friedrich, Markus Stumptner, and Franz Wotawa. Model-based diagnosis of hardware designs. *Artificial Intelligence*, 111(2):3–39, July 1999.

3. Daniel Jackson. Aspect: Detecting Bugs with Abstract Dependences. *ACM Transactions on Software Engineering and Methodology*, 4(2):109–145, April 1995.
4. Daniel Köb and Franz Wotawa. Introducing alias information into model-based debugging. In *16th European Conference on Artificial Intelligence (ECAI)*, pages 833–837, Valencia, Spain, August 2004. IOS Press.
5. Ron I. Kuper. Dependency-directed localization of software bugs. Technical Report AI-TR 1053, MIT AI Lab, May 1989.
6. Wolfgang Mayer and Markus Stumptner. Extending diagnosis to debug programs with exceptions. In *Proceedings 18th Int'l IEEE Conference on Automated Software Engineering*, pages 240–244, Montreal, Canada, October 2003.
7. Bernhard Peischl and Franz Wotawa. Model-based diagnosis or reasoning from first principles. *IEEE Intelligent Systems*, 18(3):32–37, May June 2003.
8. Bernhard Peischl and Franz Wotawa. Automated source-level error localization in hardware designs. In *IEEE Design & Test of Computers,* pages 8-19. IEEE Computer Society, January - February 2006.
9. Raymond Reiter. A theory of diagnosis from first principles, *Artificial Intelligence*, 32(1):57–95, 1987.
10. Markus Stumptner. Using design information to identify structural software faults. In *AI '01: Proceedings of the 14th Australian Joint Conference on Artificial Intelligence*, pages 473–486, London, UK, 2001. Springer-Verlag.
11. Dominik Wieland. *Model-Based Debugging of Java Programs Using Dependencies*. PhD thesis, Vienna University of Technology, Computer Science Department, Institute of Information Systems (184), Database and Artificial Intelligence Group (184/2), November 2001.
12. Franz Wotawa. Debugging hardware designs using a value-based Model. *Applied Intelligence*, 16(1):71–92, 2002.
13. Franz Wotawa and Safeeullah Soomro. Fault localization based on abstract dependencies. In *Proceedings of 18th International Conference on Industrial Engineering Applications of Artificial Intelligence Expert Systems*, Lecture Notes in Artificial Intelligence (LNAI), pages 357–359. Springer Verlag, 2005.
14. Franz Wotawa and Safeeullah Soomro. Using abstract dependencies in debugging. In *Proceedings of 19th International Workshop on Qualitative Reasoning QR-05*, pages 23–28, 2005.

On Adaptively Learning HMM-Based Classifiers Using Split-Merge Operations*

Sang-Woon Kim[1] and Soo-Hwan Oh[2]

[1] *Senior Member, IEEE.* Dept. of Computer Science and Engineering,
Myongji University, Yongin, 449-728 Korea
`kimsw@mju.ac.kr`
[2] Dept. of Computer Science and Engineering, Myongji University,
Yongin, 449-728 Korea
`ohsh@mju.ac.kr`

Abstract. In designing classifiers for automatic speech recognitions, one of the problems the user faces is to cope with an unwanted variability in the environment such as changes in the speaker or the acoustics. To overcome this problem, various adaptation schemes have been proposed in the literature. In this short paper, rather than selecting a single acoustic model as being representative of a category, we adaptively find the optimal or near-optimal number of hidden Markov models during the Baum-Welch (BW) learning process through *splitting* and *merging* operations. This scheme is based on incorporating the split-merge operations into the HMM parameter re-estimation process of the BW algorithm. In the *splitting* phase, an acoustic model is divided into *two* sub-models based on a suitable criterion. On the other hand, in the *merging* phase, *two* models are combined into a single one. The experimental results demonstrate that the proposed mechanism can efficiently resolve the problem by adjusting the number of acoustic models while increasing the classification accuracy. The results also demonstrate that the advantage gained in the case of multi-modally distributed data sets is significant.

Keywords: Automatic Speech Recognitions (ASR), Hidden Markov Models (HMM), Baum-Welch (BW) Algorithm, Splitting - Merging Techniques.

1 Introduction

Hidden Markov Models (HMMs) have been proven to be one of the most successful statistical modeling methods in the area of automatic speech recognition systems (ASR), especially of continuous speech recognition [7]. One of the problems in designing classifiers for ASR is that of coping with unwanted variability as is encountered when there are changes in the environment concerning the speaker or the acoustics. To overcome this problem, various adaptation schemes such as the deleted interpolation [2], the speaker adaptation [1], the corrective

* This work was generously supported by the Korea Research Foundation Grant funded by the Korea Government (MOEHRD-KRF-2005-042-D00265).

M. Ali and R. Dapoigny (Eds.): IEA/AIE 2006, LNAI 4031, pp. 668–673, 2006.

training [3], and the model clustering and splitting [6], have been proposed in the literature. Rather than selecting a single acoustic model (e.g., an HMM unit[1]) as representative of a particular category, the above schemes permit more than one acoustic model to be assigned to a category. However, typically the number of acoustic models is randomly determined in advance, and is decided by the number of pattern classes, or by resorting to a clustering of the training samples. The most popular training method for the parameter estimation of the acoustic module is the Baum-Welch (BW) algorithm based on the Maximum Likelihood (ML) criterion [7]. Other approaches are omitted here in the interest of brevity, but can be found in the literature including [4].

Motivated by the methods mentioned above, we investigate an adaptive learning method for HMM-based classifiers by using a splitting-merging technique. Our idea is to incorporate the split-merge operations into the BW learning process without resorting to any particular *transformation*. In the proposed method, the training data set is automatically clustered into multiple subsets through the split-merge operations of the BW learning process. With the *merging* operation, we combine similar data points which are close to their nearest neighbors, into a cluster. As opposed to this, in the *splitting* phase, we distribute two distant points into different clusters. As a criterion of merging or splitting, we utilize the differences in magnitude between the output probabilities of the models for the sample points and their representative values.

The main contribution of this paper is to demonstrate that the performance of HMM-based classifiers can be increased by employing an adaptive learning method - which is crucial in multi-modally distributed data sets. This has been done by incorporating a splitting-merging technique into the BW learning process and by demonstrating its power in classification accuracy. The reader should observe that this philosophy is *quite distinct* from those used in the recently-proposed SAT (Speaker Adaptive Training) [1] or the CAT (Cluster Adaptive Training) [5] strategies.

2   Adaptive Learning of HMM-Based Classifiers

We consider that the problem of attempting to recognize C different speech pattern classes. Then, an HMM-based classifier is designed with C HMMs to separate the C pattern classes. Each of the HMMs evaluate the output probability on the basis of the observed input vector strings. It then selects the largest output probability product and assigns the unknown input pattern to the corresponding class.

Consider a Markov chain with N states $\{q_1, \cdots, q_N\}$ and transition probabilities $P\{q_i \rightarrow q_j\} = a_{ij}$. Let $s(t)$ denote the state at time t. At each $t = 1, \cdots, T$, one of M output symbols or observations, $v_1, \cdots, v_M$, is generated with a probability $P\{v_k|s(t) = q_i\} = b_{ik}$. A hidden Markov model λ is specified by the $N \times N$ matrix $A = [a_{ij}]$, the $N \times M$ matrix $B = [b_{ik}]$, and the initial description

---

[1] In this paper, the "HMM unit" or "HMM module" represent a computational acoustic unit, which evaluates the output probability of an HMM-based classifier.

$\pi_i = P\{s(0) = q_i\}$. Given a model $\lambda = (A, B, \pi)$, the probability of a sequence of observations, $v_{y_1}, \cdots, v_{y_T}$ (each $y_t \in \{1, \cdots, M\}$), λ can be calculated by the *Forward-Backward* algorithm. In the case of the ML estimate criterion, the goal of the training is then to find the best set of parameters, λ^*, such that $\lambda^* = argmax_\lambda P_\lambda\{y_1^T\}$. The approach to iteratively maximize $P_\lambda\{y_1^T\}$ is referred to as Baum-Welch (BW) algorithm. Starting from initial guesses[2], the model parameters λ are iteratively updated according to the *Forward-Backward* algorithm so that $P_\lambda\{y_1^T\}$ is maximized at each iteration. Details of the algorithms are omitted here, but can be found in the well-known pieces of literature.

The problem we encounter in learning the HMM is to select the number of acoustic models required to optimize the HMM-based classifier for automatic speech recognition, as well as to estimate the parameter sets. We propose a systematic method for efficiently selecting the optimal or near-optimal *number* of HMM modules for each class. The selection is itself an iterative process and is achieved even as the HMM parameter set is estimated using the BW algorithm.

The procedure of the proposed algorithm can be formalized as follows:

1. *Initialization* : For every data sample, j, we initially train an HMM parameter set, λ_j, with the Baum-Welch algorithm. After this learning, the output probability, P_{λ_j}, (for each j), is used as the *representative* value, $P_{\lambda_{j0}}$, of the sample data point in the following steps;

2. *Splitting* : For every cluster, k, we train a model, λ_k, with the BW algorithm. In this learning[3], if the difference in magnitude between the output probability of a sample i, $P_{\lambda_k}(i)$, and its representative value, $P_{\lambda_{i0}}$, is greater than a threshold value ρ, namely, if $\|P_{\lambda_k}(i) - P_{\lambda_{i0}}\| > \rho$, then the data element i which has the greatest value in the cluster k is *split* as a new cluster, and the number of clusters is increased;

3. *Merging* : After clustering all of samples into clusters according to their output probabilities, we again train a HMM to get a parameter set for each cluster. In this learning, we consider all samples i and j of any two clusters, k and l, respectively. If the magnitudes of the different representative values, $P_{\lambda_{i0}}$ and $P_{\lambda_{j0}}$, and the output probabilities, $P_{\lambda_l}(i)$ and $P_{\lambda_k}(j)$, are smaller than the ρ, namely, if $\|P_{\lambda_l}(i) - P_{\lambda_{i0}}\| < \rho$ and $\|P_{\lambda_k}(j) - P_{\lambda_{j0}}\| < \rho$, then the two clusters, k and l, are *merged* into "a" cluster, and the number of clusters is decreased;

4. *Termination* : If *Splitting* or *Merging* step does not occur any more, then the process terminates. Otherwise, the above Steps 2 and 3 are repeated.

---

[2] In the *discrete* HMM, it is important to have a reasonable set of initial estimates. Empirical studies showed that we can use a uniform distribution to generate initial estimates.

[3] The learning has two versions: *Top-down* and *Bottom-up*. In the *Top-down* approach, we start the learning with 'a' cluster, in which all training samples are included. In the *Bottom-up* approach, on the other hand, initially the number of clusters is equivalent to the number of data samples. In this paper, we tested the experiments using the *Top-down* approach.

Table 1. The experimental learning steps for two speech data sets $C_1 = \{V_{1,i}\}_{i=0}^{9}$ and $C_2 = \{V_{2,i}\}_{i=0}^{9}$. In the notation of "$a : b$", the a's (which are integer values) are the serial numbers of the clusters, and the b's (real values) are the different magnitudes of the *representative* values and the output probabilities. The details of these terms can be found in the text.

# of epoch	data class	$V_{1,0}$ / $V_{2,0}$	$V_{1,1}$ / $V_{2,1}$	$V_{1,2}$ / $V_{2,2}$	$V_{1,3}$ / $V_{2,3}$	$V_{1,4}$ / $V_{2,4}$	$V_{1,5}$ / $V_{2,5}$	$V_{1,6}$ / $V_{2,6}$	$V_{1,7}$ / $V_{2,7}$	$V_{1,8}$ / $V_{2,8}$	$V_{1,9}$ / $V_{2,9}$
1	C_1	1: 93.8	1: 63.6	1: 73.1	1: 70.9	1: 38.1	1: 40.1	1: 47.8	1: 41.8	1: 57.9	1: 33.9
	C_2	1: 52.7	1: 44.8	1: 62.3	1: 51.5	1: 49.8	1: 26.6	1: 66.8	1: 56.9	1: 69.8	1: 39.7
2	C_1	2: 62.7	2: 38.4	2: 43.5	2: 44.7	2: 15.4	2: 28.2	1: 40.6	2: 20.1	2: 41.4	2: 21.6
	C_2	1: 51.1	1: 36.5	1: 65.8	1: 52.7	1: 39.8	1: 15.4	1: 48.0	1: 37.9	1: 47.1	1: 25.1
3	C_1	2: 62.7	2: 38.4	2: 43.5	2: 44.7	2: 15.4	2: 28.2	1: 35.8	2: 20.1	2: 41.4	2: 21.6
	C_2	1: 51.3	1: 35.7	3: 0.0	1: 52.4	1: 38.3	1: 13.4	1: 44.4	1: 33.7	1: 43.4	1: 22.9
4	C_1	4: 0.0	2: 37.6	2: 40.5	2: 44.6	2: 14.5	2: 27.3	1: 48.0	2: 21.4	2: 37.0	2: 21.9
	C_2	1: 51.3	1: 35.7	3: 0.0	1: 52.4	1: 38.3	1: 13.4	1: 44.4	1: 33.7	1: 43.4	1: 22.9

3   Experimental Results

The proposed algorithm has been tested and compared with conventional ones. This was first done by performing experiments on a naturally spoken data set, cited from the ETRI (Electronics and Telecommunications Research Institute, http://www.etri.re.kr/). The ETRI data set consists of a total of $1,150$ speech patterns, which correspond to the 115 kinds of bi-syllabic words spoken by ten speakers, five males and five females. The details of the pre-processing phases are omitted here, but can be found in the related manuals.

We report the run-time characteristics of the proposed algorithm for the speech data set. First of all, Table 1 shows an intermediate part of the learning steps (processes) for the two speech data sets $C_1 = \{V_{1,i}\}_{i=0}^{9}$ and $C_2 = \{V_{2,i}\}_{i=0}^{9}$. The speech data C_1 represents a Korean trisyllable phrase, "GaGeEa-", which means "at a store" in English, while the speech data C_2 is for a Korean quadri-syllabic phrase, "KwaGeoEaNun", which means "in the past" in English. We started the learning with a cluster each for both C_1 and C_2, i.e., by invoking *Top-down* learning. Here, the employed discrete HMM was the ergodic one, where the number of states and output symbols are 12 and 32, respectively. The threshold value was set as $\rho = 30$ [4].

From Table 1, we can see that optimal or near optimal number of HMM modules can be adaptively found in the learning process. We accomplished this by employing the *splitting-merging* strategy. First of all, consider the results for

---

[4] We selected this figure as the threshold value, ρ, after doing the experiment several times. It is doubtful whether the same threshold will work for various classes of speech recognition data. The choice of the threshold determines the number of clusters. A more valid choice would most probably be based on using a choice of threshold which would be some function of the data set to incorporate variability like noise conditions and male-female disparity. This choosing problem which will most probably arise in practical cases is currently being investigated.

Table 2. The experimental results for the speech data set. Here, Acc's are the classification accuracies (%), and t_1 and t_2 are the required processing CPU-times (in seconds) for the learning and the classification, respectively. The details of these terms can be found in the text.

Learning	# of States	# of Symbols	# of Clusters	Averaged # of Modules per a class	$t_1(sec)$	$Acc(\%)$	$t_2(sec)$
	8	32	115	1	901	86.51	40
CLM	8	64	115	1	1,526	92.64	70
	8	128	115	1	2,750	94.66	128
	8	32	313	3	1,322	86.16	110
PCM	8	64	357	3	2,158	90.28	216
	8	128	427	4	3,875	92.29	474
	8	32	788	7	2,150	96.15	277
ALM	8	64	955	8	4,279	98.42	578
	8	128	1,033	9	8,272	98.95	1,146

the first iteration (epoch), captioned '1'. All input patterns of C_1 and C_2 classes are regarded as those of the same cluster, namely, '1'. However, in the second iteration, the cluster of having the highest value (in the absolute sense), is *split* into a new cluster, and thus the $V_{1,0}$ of 93.8 is selected as a new cluster numbered as '2'. After this separation, the remaining words are classified into clusters '1' or '2' by invoking a clustering procedure. Identical comments can also be made about the other iteration steps. The reader should observe that the number of clusters, namely, *four*, can be automatically decided within *only* four iterations. As a consequence, we can design an HMM-based classifier that consists of four HMM modules even though the number of pattern classes is *two*.

Table 2 shows the experimental results of the proposed method for the ETRI speech data set. In *CLM* (the *Conventional Learning Method*), the classifiers that were designed processed just *one* HMM module per category as done for conventional classifiers. In *PCM* (the *Pre-Clustering Learning Method*), the number of HMM modules is determined by invoking a clustering algorithm before training the models. On the other hand, in the proposed *ALM* (*Adaptive Learning Method*), the number of modules is *adaptively* decided in the learning process [5].

From Table 2, we can see that an optimal or near optimal number of HMM modules for an HMM-based classifier can be selected adaptively. Consider the results of the *ALM* method. Here, three kinds of HMM-based classifiers were designed. The numbers of the states, namely, 8, are the same and the numbers of output symbols are 32, 64 and 128, respectively. The cluster numbers obtained from this learning are 788, 955, and 1,033, respectively. The reader should observe that these results are *automatically* determined (without a user-intervention) from the split-merge processes. Then, a comparison of the Acc's of *CLM*, *ALM*, and *PCM* shows that the HMM-based classifiers adaptively trained with *ALM* outperform the others. The comparison also shows that the results

---

[5] Evaluation is performed by using the *R*esubstitution (R) method, in which the same samples are used for both designing and testing the classifier.

obtained by PCM (worth than CLM) are not improved, and even worsened by the pre-clustering. Finally, it should be mentioned that the processing CPU-times of the proposed method is "marginally" higher. Approximately 5 to 10 fold increasing in processing time for *ALM* compared to *CLM* is based on the heavy iteration in the split-merge processes.

4   Conclusions

In designing classifiers for automatic speech recognitions, one of the difficult problems encountered is one of coping with an unwanted variability in the environment such as changes in the speaker or the acoustics. In this paper, we have proposed an adaptive learning mechanism to solve the problem using a *splitting-merging* technique. Rather than independently performing the clustering and the learning (estimation) processes, we have suggested a new scheme in which both processes are simultaneously incorporated. The experimental results demonstrate that the proposed scheme can efficiently resolve the problem of the unwanted variabilities by selecting an appropriate number of HMM acoustic models. Especially we emphasize that this adaptive learning method can be used advantageously for multi-modally distributed data sets. However the problems of reducing the processing CPU-time for the adaptive learning, and that of optimizing the experimental parameters of the method, are still open.

Acknowledgements. The authors would like to express their gratitude for the KRF Grant. They are also very grateful to Prof. B. J. Oommen who helped us in the preparation of this manuscript.

References

1. Anastasakos, T., McDonough, J., Schwartz, R., Kakhoul, J.: A compact model for speaker-adaptive training. *Proceedings of ICSLP*, 1137–1140, 1996
2. Bahl, L. R., Jelinek, F., Mercer, R. L.: A maximum likelihood approach to continues speech recognition. *IEEE Transactions on Pattern Analysis and Machine Intelligence*, **PAMI-5** 179–190, 1983.
3. Bahl, L. R., Brown, P. F., deSouzaBrown, P. V., Mercer, R. L.: A new algorithm for estimation of hidden Markov model parameters. *Proceedings of ICASSP'88*, New York, 493–496, April 1988.
4. Ben-Yishai, A., Burshtein, D.: A discriminative training algorithm for hidden Markov models. *IEEE Transactions on Speech and Audio Processing*, **12(3)** 204–217, May 2004.
5. Gales, M. J. F.: Cluster adaptive training for hidden Markov models. *IEEE Transactions on Speech and Audio Processing*, **8(4)** 417–428, July 2000.
6. Lee, K. F.: *Automatic Speech Recognition - The development of the SPHINX System.* Kluwer Academic Publishers, Boston, 1989.
7. Nakagawa, S.: A survey on automatic speech recognition. *IEICE Transactions on Information and Systems*, **E85-D(3)** 465–486, March 2002.

Comparative Study: HMM and SVM for Automatic Articulatory Feature Extraction

Supphanat Kanokphara, Jan Macek, and Julie Carson-Berndsen

UCD School of Computer Science and Informatics,
UCD Dublin, Belfield, Dublin, Ireland
{supphanat.kanokphara, jan.macek, julie.berndsen}@ucd.ie

Abstract. Generally speech recognition systems make use of acoustic features as a representation of speech for further processing. These acoustic features are usually based on human auditory perception or signal processing. More recently, Articulatory Feature (AF) based speech representations have been investigated by a number of speech technology researchers. Articulatory features are motivated by linguistic knowledge and hence may better represent speech characteristics. In this paper, we introduce two popular classification models, Hidden Markov Model (HMM) and Support Vector Machine (SVM), for automatic articulatory feature extraction. HMM-based systems are found to be best when there is good balance in the numbers of positive and negative examples in the data while SVM is better in the unbalanced data condition.

1 Introduction

HMMs are predominantly used as acoustic models in current speech recognition systems. The reason for this is that HMMs can normalize the time-variation of the speech signal and characterize the speech signal statistically and optimally. HMM-based speech recognition systems do not deal with the speech signal directly but rather deal with a specific kind of speech representation. Such speech representations have two roles in speech recognition systems. First, they reduce data for further speech recognition processing. Second, they ideally present only useful information from speech signal to the systems and ignore nonacoustic and/or nonlinguistic information such as speaking style, noise, emotion, etc.

For the reasons mentioned above, it is needless to say that the choice of speech representation can also greatly affect the accuracy of systems. Speech representations today are usually based on the acoustic information of the signal [1]. However, by relying only on this acoustic information, these speech representations seem to achieve only moderate success, especially, in adverse environments (noisy, out-of-task, out-of-vocabulary, etc). One of ways to solve this problem is to integrate linguistic knowledge as suggested in [2, 3].

Articulatory features (AF) have been shown to improve word recognition accuracy under variable conditions of speech signal production. For example, in a multilingual environment, feature recognizers trained on data from different languages were shown to have the capability of improving the overall performance

M. Ali and R. Dapoigny (Eds.): IEA/AIE 2006, LNAI 4031, pp. 674–681, 2006.

by ensemble recognizer or by crosslingual recognizer [4]. The AF representations have also proven to be good in noisy environment [5].

AF is thought to be a good compromise, offering better descriptions of the acoustic signal than phonemes yet still providing a linguistically interpretable symbolic annotation. Acoustic correlates of features have been described in the literature [6, 7]. The first detailed description of distinctive features [8] assumed that they had identifiable counterparts.

In this paper, two systems are introduced to extract articulatory features from the speech signal. The first system is based on an HMM. As mentioned previously, an HMM is designed to map a speech signal into a sequence of units. These units can be words, syllables, demisyllables, phones, etc. This approach is therefore suitable for articulatory feature extraction.

As a second approach to articulatory acoustic manner feature recognition we used Support Vector Machine (SVM) classifiers with a linear kernel in the SVM-Light implementation [9]. In contrast to the HMM approach, we run the SVMs in a static description setting, i.e. only parameters describing the recognized frame and four adjacent frames are used as a source of information for prediction. Although such a setting makes no use of contextual information we show that the achieved performance is better than HMMs in the highly skewed data condition.

Systematically, this paper is organized as follows. Section 2 explains the experimental details of the experimental paradigm used in this paper, i.e. the corpus, the evaluation method and the feature table. Section 3 describes the HMM-based AF extraction system while section 4 presents the SVM-based AF extraction system. Finally, discussion and conclusion work are presented in section 5.

2   Experimental Setup

2.1   The Corpus

The experiments use the standard TIMIT corpus [10] consisting of 6300 sentences, 10 sentences spoken by each of 630 speakers, of which 462 are in the training set and 168 are in the testing set. There is no overlap between the training and testing sentences, except 2 SA sentences that were read by all speakers. The training set contains 4620 utterances and the testing set contains 1680 utterances. The core test set, which is the abridged version of the complete test set, consists of 192 utterances, 8 from each of 24 speakers. In this paper, the full training set without SA sentences is used as the training set while only the core test set is used as the test set.

2.2   The Evaluation

The evaluation method used in this paper is a comparison of overall accuracy in terms of frame error rate (FER) together with recall and precision. FER is widely used for articulatory feature extraction evaluation [11]. This is because, in current speech technology, articulatory features are commonly used as an

Table 1. Assignment of articulatory manner feature classes to phonemes and their frequency in the TIMIT corpus

Manner feature	Frequency in corpus	Phone (TIMIT transcription used)
approximant	8.12%	axr, r, w, y
closure	9.68%	bcl, dcl, gcl, kcl, pcl, tcl
flap	0.78%	dx, nx
fricative	16.47%	ch, dh, f, hh, hv, jh, s, sh, th, v, z, zh
lateral approximant	3.37%	el, l
nasal	5.72%	em, en, eng, m, n, ng, nx
stop	16.22%	b, bcl, d, dcl, g, gcl, k, kcl, p, pcl, q, t, tcl
vocalic	37.99%	aa, ae, ah, ao, aw, ax, ax-h, ay, eh, er, ey, ih, ix, iy, ow, oy, uh, uw, ux

alternative or additional speech representation. The speech representation is a sequence of numeric vectors where each numeric vector represents speech in each time frame. Therefore, AF extraction systems are usually evaluated on the frame level. To understand the differences between achieved accuracies better under highly skewed data condition we present *precision* and *recall* rates in Tables 2 and 3. The precision is defined as the ratio

$$\frac{\text{\# of correctly classified instances of class } c}{\text{\# of instances classified as class } c}$$

and the recall is defined as the ratio

$$\frac{\text{\# of correctly classified instances of class } c}{\text{\# of instances of class } c}$$

Both measures analyse the correct classification for each feature class individually. It is important to mention the trade-off between precision and recall.

A true AF evaluation should compare between a reference (annotated at the feature level) and a hypothesized AF transcription. However, due to the cost and difficulty of corpus construction process, no feature annotated reference AF exists. In this paper, we directly convert reference phone transcriptions into AF transcriptions. These transcriptions lack the coarticulation properties which would be found in annotated. However, this is the only resource we have and it is widely accepted as the reference transcriptions for AF evaluation.

For our experiments we have been using the TIMIT corpus that is annotated at the phone level, thus for our task it was necessary to map from original phone annotations to articulatory acoustic features. The assignment of articulatory manner feature classes to phonemes is shown in Table 1.

3   The HMM-Based AF Extraction System

The HMM-based AF extraction system is actually a normal HMM-based phone recognizer. First the phone recognizer hypothesizes a phone sequence from the

Table 2. Frame Error Rates on TIMIT core test set for HMM for recognition of articulatory acoustic manner features

Manner Feature	Overall accuracy	Precision (for positive class)	Recall (for positive class)
Approximant	94.07%	66.00%	70.50%
Closure	95.27%	82.93%	84.01%
Flap	97.90%	36.22%	62.46%
Fricative	93.26%	85.75%	84.89%
Nasal	95.90%	77.31%	84.17%
Lateral Approximant	96.18%	49.69%	69.32%
Stop	92.10%	76.10%	87.54%
Vocalic	89.20%	90.36%	86.47%

input speech. The sequence is then mapped to AF sequences according to each individual tier from the feature table. The advantage of this system is that the information on different tiers can be used to help hypothesize the correct articulatory features which results in higher accuracy.

3.1   System Overview

The HMM-based articulatory feature extraction systems in this paper are constructed using HTK [12] which is now widely used for HMM based speech recognition experiments. The acoustic model training system starts by converting the speech signal into a sequence of vector parameters with a fixed 25 ms frame and a frame rate of 10 ms. Each parameter is then preemphasized with the filter $P(z) = 1 - 0.9z^{-1}$. The discontinuities at the frame edges are attenuated by using Hamming window. A fast Fourier transform is used to convert time domain frames into frequency domain spectra. These spectra are averaged into 24 triangular bins arranged at equal mel-frequency intervals (where $f_{mel} = 2595 \log_{10}(1 + f/700)$), where f denotes frequency in Hz. Then 12 dimensional mel-frequency cepstral coefficients (MFCCs) are obtained from cosine transformation and lifter. The normalized log energy is also added as the 13th frontend parameter. The actual acoustic energy in each frame is calculated and the maximum selected. All log energies are then normalized with respect to maximum and log energies below a silence floor (set to -50 dB) clamped to that floor.

These 13 frontend parameters are expanded to 39 frontend parameters by appending first and second order differences of the static coefficients. The chosen parameters have been used extensively and have proven to be a good choice for HMM-based speech recognition systems [13].

Each model contains 5 states with no skip state and the covariance matrices of all states are diagonal. After the context-independent HMMs have been trained, they are expanded to context-dependent HMMs using tree-based state tying technique [12] for crossphone network expansion. Maximum likelihood estimators are used to train HMM parameters. The number of training iterations after each change is determined automatically [14]. There is no mixture expansion. Only one mixture models are used in the experiment. For the recognition process, the Viterbi algorithm is used without any pruning factor and language model.

3.2 Experimental Result

According to the experimental results, HMM-based system works very well with AF extraction since all accuracies are averagely 94.24%. Considering precision and recall, HMM-based *flap* and *lateral approximant* extractors do not seem to work very well. The precision for *flap* is only 36.22% while it is only 49.69% for *lateral approximant*. The recall for *flap* is only 62.46% while it is only 69.32% for *lateral approximant*.

4 Articulatory Manner Features Recognition with SVMs

Support Vector Machines learn separating hyperplanes to classify instances in the feature space that is mapped from the input space of the classified data. The mapping from input space to feature space is performed with application of a kernel on the feature space. The dimension of the feature space is typically much higher than that of the original input space. The term 'feature' in this context is of course distinct from articulatory acoustic feature. The motivation for using SVMs comes from the pattern recognition community with mathematical properties of linear classifiers and from the statistical learning theory community with the structural risk minimization properties of SVMs [15, 16].

For a binary classification task with data points $\mathbf{x}_i$ ($i = 1, \ldots, n$) and labels y_i we have the decision function $f(\mathbf{x}) = \text{sign}(\mathbf{w} \cdot \mathbf{x} + b)$. If the dataset is separable we can find a w such that the decision function will assign value $f(\mathbf{x}_i) = y_i$ for every i. As the sign is invariant to positive scaling of the expression inside of the sign, we can define canonical hyperplanes such that $\mathbf{w} \cdot \mathbf{x} + b = 1$ for the closest points on one side and $\mathbf{w} \cdot \mathbf{x} + b = -1$ for the closest points on the other side. The separating hyperplane is then defined by $\mathbf{w} \cdot \mathbf{x} + b = 0$ and its normal is then $\mathbf{w}/|\mathbf{w}|_2$. The margin between the canonical hyperplanes can be found as a projection of distance between the two closest points on opposite sides ($\mathbf{x}_1$ and $\mathbf{x}_2$) on the normal of separating hyperplane. Since $\mathbf{w} \cdot \mathbf{x}_1 + b = 1$ and $\mathbf{w} \cdot \mathbf{x}_2 + b = -1$ the margin is $1/|\mathbf{w}|_2$.

The SVM approach to binary decision function learning is to maximize the margin $1/|\mathbf{w}|_2$ that is summarized in an optimization task formulation

$$\min \quad g(\mathbf{w}) = \frac{1}{2}|\mathbf{w}|_2^2 \quad subject\ to \quad y_i(\mathbf{w} \cdot \mathbf{x}_i + b) \geq 1 \text{ for all } i$$

and the learning task can be reduced to minimization of the primal lagrangian

$$L = \frac{1}{2}(\mathbf{w}^T \cdot \mathbf{w}) - \alpha_i(y_i(\mathbf{w} \cdot \mathbf{x}_i + b) - 1),$$

where α_i are Lagrangian multipliers.

Confidence measures for SVMs can be based on the value of $w \cdot x + b$. In our approach we used normalization of the SVM output into [0; 1] via normalization function $c(x) = 1 - \exp(-\sigma(\mathbf{w} \cdot \mathbf{x} + b)^2)$.

4.1   Experiments with SVMs for Articulatory Feature Recognition

We extracted 180 inputs for the SVM classifier. These were extracted for the current frame and two adjacent frames before and after the current frame, i.e. 5 frames in total. From each frame we extracted values of overall energy, overall entropy, 12 Mel-frequency Cepstral Coefficients with first and second order differences. The length of the frames was set to be 16 ms due to practical consideration of the speed of FFT on signals of length 2n. In our case we worked with 16 kHz data. The labels for each of the instances were converted from phoneme transcriptions of the speech signal. The distributions of classes vary significantly for different types of features. While the distribution of classes is almost equal (the case of AF vocalic) for half of the articulatory features, in the rest of the cases the positive classes are rare in the data. This has a strong influence on the recall of the positive classes although the overall accuracy remains high.

The SVMs were trained on all training data provided in TIMIT corpus and the evaluation of training was performed on the core test set of TIMIT corpus. Frame Error Rate (FER) was used to evaluate the performance and make it comparable with HMM approach mentioned above. Table 3 shows results for recognition of manner features based on FER on TIMIT core test set. The values of recall and precision are values for the positive class, i.e. for subset of instances with class of the respective manner feature. The N/A values in the Table 3 are caused by 0% recall of the positive class actually meaning that all instances were classified as negative class and leaving the precision value undefined.

In our experiments we tried to modify the training set to achieve better performance on the core test set to cope with significant differences in class distributions in data as is shown in Table 1. While only three of the manner feature classes occur in more than 15% of cases, five of the used feature classes imply highly unbalanced datasets. Although in the cases of *closure*, *fricative*, *stop* and *vocalic* the performance was influenced in a negative way, we did not obtain any change in the classifiers performance for the features *approximant*, *lateral approximant*, and *nasal*. The recall was positively influenced only in the case of the manner feature flap, but this change was an increased recall to the value of

Table 3. Frame Error Rates on TIMIT core test set for SVMs for recognition of articulatory acoustic manner features

Manner Feature	Overall accuracy	Precision (for positive class)	Recall (for positive class)
Approximant	91.88%	N/A	0%
Closure	94.20%	82.54%	56.36%
Flap	99.29%	N/A	0%
Fricative	88.51%	93.78%	36.10%
Nasal	96.26%	N/A	0%
Lateral Approximant	94.59%	N/A	0%
Stop	90.16%	81.41%	53.39%
Vocalic	82.23%	74.83%	80.17%

40.52% at precision rate of 7.75% and overall accuracy of 95.74%. These values were achieved for undersampling of the negative examples in the training set to 5% of the original count. Although approaches of over- and undersampling of under-/overrepresented classes in unbalanced data sets are standard and were reported to give good results [17, 18]. In our case we suspect that attributes used for description of the signal frames do not contain enough information to allow the SVM to separate them even after altering the original training dataset.

5   Conclusion

We presented two approaches to recognition of articulatory manner features that we use as a building block of a continuous speech recognizer. The comparison was made between the sequential method of Hidden Markov Models and the isolated frame recognition approach based on Support Vector Machines. Our results show high dependence of the performance on positive/negative class balance in the data whereby with increasing unbalance of the class distributions the performance of recognizers degrades.

According to the FER, the HMM outperformed SVMs in most of the cases except for the manner feature flap and nasal in terms of overall accuracy. This comparison is slightly unfair as the recall rates for both of these cases is 0%. Performance of the SVMs was highly dependent on the frequency of occurrence of positive classes in the data. It has not achieved good performance in terms of recall and accuracy in cases where the distribution of positive and negative classes was very unbalanced. Although we performed resampling of the original training data we did not observe useful positive change in the performance. We suspect this to be caused by poor discriminative power of the used parameters of the speech signal.

References

1. H. Hermansky: Mel Cepstrum, Deltas, Double-Deltas,-What Else is New? Proc. in Robust Methods for Speech Recognition in Adverse Conditions, Tampere, Finland (1999)
2. B. Launay, O. Siohan, A. C. Surendran, and C. H. Lee: Towards knowledge-Based Features for HMM Based Large Vocabulary Automatic Speech Recognition. In Proc. International Conference on Acoustics, Speech, and Signal Processing (ICASSP), Orlando (2002)
3. J. Carson-Berndsen: Time Map Phonology: Finite State Models and Event Logics in Speech Recognition. Dordrecht, Holland: Kluwer Academic Publishers (1998)
4. S. Stueker, T. Schulz, F. Metze, and A. Waibel: Multilingual Articulatory Features. In Proceedings of ICASSP, Vol. 1, (2003) 144-147
5. K. Kirchhoff: Robust Speech Recognition using Articulatory Information. Ph.D. thesis, University of Bielefeld (1999)
6. K. N. Stevens: Acoustic Correlates of some Phonetic Categories. Journal of the Acoustical Society of America (JASA), Vol. 68(3), (1980) 836-842
7. K. N. Stevens: Acoustic Phonetics. MIT Press: Cambridge (Ma), London (1998)

8. R. Jakobson, G. Fant, M. Halle. Preliminaries to Speech Analysis: The Distinctive Features and Their Correlates. MIT Press, 9th ed. 1969 (1952)

9. T. Joachims: Making large-Scale SVM Learning Practical. Advances in Kernel Methods - Support Vector Learning, B. Schlkopf, C. Burges, and A. Smola (ed.), MIT-Press, (1999)

10. J. S. Garofolo, L. F. Lamel, W. M. Fisher, J. G. Fiscus, D. S. Pallett, and N. L. Dahlgren: DARPA TIMIT Acoustic-Phonetic Continuous Speech Corpus CDROM, NIST (1993)

11. S. Chang, S. Greenberg, and M. Wester: An Elitist Approach to Articulatory-Acoustic Feature Classification. In Proc. 7th Eurospeech, Aalborg, Denmark (2001), 1725-1728

12. S. Young, G. Evermann, D. Kershaw, G. Moore, J. Odell, D. Ollason, D. Povey, V. Valtchev, and P. Woodland: The HTK Book, Microsoft Corporation and Cambridge Uni-versity Engineering Department (December 2002)

13. S. B. Davis and P. Mermelstein: Comparison of Parametric Representations for Monosyllabic Word Recognition in Continuously Spoken Sentences. IEEE Trans. Acoustic Speech and Signal Processing, Vol. 28(4), (1980), 357–366

14. P. Tarsaku and S. Kanokphara: A Study of HMM-Based Automatic Segmentations for Thai Continuous Speech Recognition System. In Proc. the Symposium on Natural Language Processing, (2002), 217–220

15. V. Vapnik: The Nature of Statistical Learning Theory, Springer. (1995)

16. C. J. C. Burges: A Tutorial on Support Vector Machines for Pattern Recognition, Data Mining and Knowledge Discovery, Vol. 2, Number 2, (1998), 121–167

17. M. A. Maloof: Learning when data sets are imbalanced and when costs are unequal and unknown. ICML-2003 Workshop on Learning from Imbalanced Data Sets II. (2003)

18. N. Lachiche and P. A. Flach: Improving accuracy and cost of two-class and multi-class probabilistic classifiers using ROC curves. In: Proc. 20th International Conference on Machine Learning (ICML'03), AAAI Press, (January 2003), 416–423

A Study on High-Order Hidden Markov Models and Applications to Speech Recognition*

Lee-Min Lee[1] and Jia-Chien Lee[2]

[1] Department of Electrical Engineering, Da Yeh University, Taiwan
`lmlee@mail.dyu.edu.tw`
[2] Department of Communication Engineering, Da Yeh University, Taiwan
`r9312023@mail.dyu.edu.tw`

Abstract. We propose high-order hidden Markov models (HO-HMM) to capture the duration and dynamics of speech signal. In the proposed model, both the state transition probability and the output observation probability depend not only on the current state but also on several previous states. An extended Viterbi algorithm was developed to train model and recognize speech. The performance of the HO-HMM was investigated by conducting experiments on speaker independent Mandarin digits recognition. From the experimental results, we find that as the order of HO-HMM increases, the number of error reduces. We also find that systems with both high-order state transition probability distribution and output observation probability distribution outperform systems with only high-order state transition probability distribution.

1 Introduction

The speech information is encoded as a phone sequence with each phone characterized by its spectral shape and duration. Hence, the speech signal presents approximately a short-time stationary property. The hidden Markov model (HMM) [1] with left to right state transition topology is fairly suited to model the characteristics mentioned above. The output of an HMM conditioned on a specific state sequence represent a piecewise stationary process and the state sequence itself represents an allocation of the phone durations. Speech recognition systems based on HMM are very popular not only because of its modeling power but also because there are powerful mathematical tools that can be used to efficiently estimate the model parameters, calculate the likelihood scores, and guide the design of systems.

However, the assumption that the state transition and output observation depend only on the current state does not exactly match the real speech process. The first order state transition dependency poorly models the state duration distribution [2][3], the piecewise stationary assumption does not go with the non-stationary nature of

* This research work was supported by National Science Council, Republic of China, under the Grant NSC93-2213-E-212-012. The Authors would like to thank National Center for High-performance Computing for providing computation power in this work. Thanks are also given to Chunghwa Telecom Laboratories, Chunghwa Telecom Co., Ltd., for providing the experimental database.

M. Ali and R. Dapoigny (Eds.): IEA/AIE 2006, LNAI 4031, pp. 682–690, 2006.

speech, and the independency of output observations violates the high correlations presented in successive speech frames. Arranging state numbers so that a state occupies only one or two frames can alleviate the deficiency of duration model. The constraint that the state sequence should match the initial and final state in isolated speech recognition further relieves this deficiency. The non-stationary problem can be also mitigated by short state duration model structure. Incorporating the dynamic feature [4] can mitigate the correlation problem. Channel adaptation methods such as cepstrum mean subtraction [5] remove the long-term correlation. Speaker adaptation such as maximum likelihood linear regression [6] and context dependent phone units [7] also implicitly deal with the short term correlation and make the observations more state-conditionally independent.

To overcome the shortages of the first order HMM, several refinements had been proposed. Mari *et al.* proposed a second order HMM for word recognition [8] and obtained a better model of state duration distribution. However, in their model, only the state transition depends on the instantaneous and previous states while an observation depends only on the instantaneous state. J. A. du Preez developed an algorithm to transform any high-order HMM to an equivalent first order HMM and proposed a fast incremental training algorithm to train the high-order HMM [9]. In that work, high-order dependency is considered only for state transition. Deng *et al.* used polynomial regression functions to model the trend of non-stationary states [10]. In their model, the output observation can be thought as depending on the state history, but the transition remained first order dependency.

In this paper, we propose the high-order hidden Markov model for speech recognition. In the proposed model, both the state transition probability and the output observation probability depend not only on the current state but also on several previous states. Viterbi style training and recognition algorithm were developed. The performance of the HO-HMM was investigated by conducting experiments on speaker independent Mandarin digits recognition. The rest of the paper is organized as follows. Section 2 presents the principles of HO-HMM and develops algorithms to train and recognize speech. In section 3, we conduct a series of experiments to investigate the performance gain of the HO-HMM. Conclusions and discussions are given in Section 4.

2   The High-Order Hidden Markov Model

The statistical speech recognition methods search for the most probable word or word sequence based on the observations. The diversity of spectrum and duration of the same phoneme makes speech recognition task difficult. Let $\mathbf{O}_1, \mathbf{O}_2, \cdots, \mathbf{O}_T$ be an observation sequence to be recognized, a statistical speech recognizer is to find a word or word sequence W such that

$$W = \arg\max_{w \in V^*} P\left(w \mid \mathbf{O}_1, \cdots, \mathbf{O}_T\right), \tag{1}$$

where V represent the vocabulary in the recognition task. Using Bayes' formula, (1) can be written as

$$W = \arg\max_{w \in V^*} P\left(\mathbf{O}_1, \cdots, \mathbf{O}_T \mid w\right) P(w), \tag{2}$$

where $P(\mathbf{O}_1,\cdots,\mathbf{O}_T \mid w)$ is the acoustic model probability and $P(w)$ is the prior word probability or the language model probability. For simplicity, we consider w as a word or a sub-word unit. Let the observation sequence $\mathbf{O}_1,\mathbf{O}_2,\cdots,\mathbf{O}_T$ produced by w be modeled by a stochastic sequence, where the sequence length T and observation vectors $\mathbf{O}_t$'s are all random. It is very complex and difficult to directly model the joint probability density function of the observation sequence. A reasonable approach is to group nearby observations of similar characteristics as being produced by the same state and then consider how do the states progress and how does a state sequence produce the observation sequence. Hence, the model is split into two parts, the first part considers the probability of a state sequence and the second part considers the observation sequence based on a state sequence. In HMM, the state transition is modeled as the first order Markov chain and the output observation at a particular time is modeled as a probabilistic function of the underlying state. This imprecise model works well if the prior topology constraint and sharing of parameters are carefully designed and tuned. However, it would be helpful if we model the acoustic model more precisely. By introducing state sequences, the acoustic model probability in (2) can be written as

$$P(\mathbf{O}_1,\cdots,\mathbf{O}_T \mid w) = \sum_{\substack{\text{all possiple}\\ q_1,\cdots,q_T}} P(\mathbf{O}_1,\cdots,\mathbf{O}_T,q_1,\cdots,q_T \mid w) \tag{3}$$

$$= \sum_{\substack{\text{all possiple}\\ q_1,\cdots,q_T}} \{ P(\mathbf{O}_1,\cdots,\mathbf{O}_T \mid q_1,\cdots,q_T,w) P(q_1,\cdots,q_T \mid w) \}$$

If we consider that state transition depends only on the previous d states and output depends only on the previous c states, then the model can be thought as an HO-HMM of order (d,c). The joint probability of state and observation sequences can be written as

$$P(\mathbf{O}_1,\cdots,\mathbf{O}_T,q_1,\cdots,q_T \mid w) \tag{4}$$
$$= P(q_1 \mid w)(\mathbf{O}_1 \mid q_1,w)P(q_2 \mid q_1,w)P(\mathbf{O}_2 \mid q_1,q_2,w)\cdots$$
$$\cdot P(q_t \mid q_{t-d},\cdots,q_{t-1},w)P(\mathbf{O}_t \mid q_{t-c+1},\cdots,q_t,w)\cdots$$
$$\cdot P(q_T \mid q_{T-d},\cdots,q_{T-1},w)P(\mathbf{O}_T \mid q_{T-c+1},\cdots,q_T,w)$$

From (4) we can see that there are an enormous number of parameters to be estimated (about N^d transition probabilities and N^c probability density functions for an N-state HO-HMM). Fortunately, the left to right structure used in speech recognition systems enable us to approximate the state history by the duration that the last state has stayed. Therefore, (4) can be further reduced to

$$P(\mathbf{O}_1,\cdots,\mathbf{O}_T,q_1,\cdots,q_T \mid w) \tag{5}$$
$$= P(q_1 \mid w)\cdot(\mathbf{O}_1 \mid q_1,d_1(q_1),w)\cdots P(q_t \mid q_{t-1},d_{t-1}(q_{t-1}),w)P(\mathbf{O}_t \mid q_t,d_t(q_t),w)\cdots$$
$$\cdot P(q_T \mid q_{T-1},d_{T-1}(q_{T-1}),w)P(\mathbf{O}_T \mid q_T,d_T(q_T),w)$$

where $d_t(q_t)$ represents the duration that state q_t has stayed up to time t, and when it exceeds the maximum dependency order D, it remains D. The model governed by (5) is the proposed duration HO-HMM in this research. Although it can be showed to be equivalent to a *DN*-state first order HMM, the proposed model is more structured so that acoustic knowledge can be more easily embedded into the parameter constraint and it allows the complex topology of equivalent first order HMM be automatically learned from the training data.

2.1   Extended Viterbi Algorithm

To train the model and recognize input utterance, we developed an extended Viterbi algorithm for HO-HMM. Let N denote the number of states in a model, D denote the order of dependency. The probability of transition from state i to itself after staying for d frames is denoted by $a(i,d)$. The observation probability density function for state i staying d frames is models as a Gaussian distribution function with mean vector and diagonal covariance matrix parameters $(\mu_{i,d}, \Sigma_{i,d})$. The log-likelihood score of an observation $\mathbf{O}$ under that condition is

$$L(\mathbf{O}; \mu_{i,d}, \Sigma_{i,d}) = -\tfrac{1}{2}\left\{ Dim \ln(2\pi) + \ln(|\Sigma_{i,d}|) + (\mathbf{O} - \mu_{i,d})^T \Sigma_{i,d}^{-1} (\mathbf{O} - \mu_{i,d}) \right\}, \tag{6}$$

where *Dim* is the dimension of the observation vector. We define the score of the candidate optimal partial path that, at time t, reaches and has stayed at state i for d frames as follows.

$$\delta(i,d,t) = \max_{q_1,\cdots,q_{t-d-1}} \ln\!\left(P\!\left(\mathbf{O}_1,\cdots,\mathbf{O}_t, q_1,\cdots q_{t-d-1}, q_{t-d} = i-1, q_{t-d+1} = \cdots = q_t = i \middle| w\right)\right), 0 < d < D \tag{7}$$

$$\delta(i,D,t) = \max_{q_1,\cdots,q_{t-D}} \ln\!\left(P\!\left(\mathbf{O}_1,\cdots,\mathbf{O}_t, q_1,\cdots, q_{t-D}, q_{t-D+1} = \cdots = q_t = i \middle| w\right)\right) \tag{8}$$

This score can be calculated recursively as described in the following algorithm. In that algorithm, the state at time t in the global optimal path is denoted by $s(t)$ and its staying time is denoted by $d_o(t)$. A non-emitting initial state (state 0) and final state (state $N+1$) are also included in the model.

2.2   HO-HMM Training

Initially, the training data are uniformly segmented according to the state number. The observation vectors belonging to the same state and staying time are grouped. The sample mean vector and covariance matrix are used as the maximum likelihood estimates for the observation probability density function. If mixture of Gaussian density functions is used to model the observation probability, then a clustering algorithm such as LBG algorithm [11] can be used to obtain the mixture weights, and the mean vector and covariance matrix for each mixture component. From the uniformly segmented state sequence, we can accumulate the state transition counts and then estimate state transition probabilities. Let $Count(i,d)$, $d \le D$, denote the times that state i has stayed d frames and let $Count(i,D+)$ denote the times that state i has stayed for more than D frames. Then, the state transition probabilities can be estimated by the following formulas.

Extended Viterbi Algoritm

step1 initialization:

for (t=1;t<=T;t++) for (d=1;d<=D;d++) $\delta(0,d,t)=-\infty$;

for (i=1;i<=N;i++) for (d=1;d<=D;d++) $\delta(i,d,1)=-\infty$;

$\delta(1,1,1)=L(\mathbf{O}_1;\boldsymbol{\mu}_{1,1},\boldsymbol{\Sigma}_{1,1})$;

step2 recursion:

for (*t*=2;*t*<=T;*t*++) for (i=1;i<=N;i++){

$$\delta(i,1,t)=\max_{1\le\tau\le D}\{\delta(i-1,\tau,t-1)+\ln(1-a(i-1,\tau))\}+L(\mathbf{O}_t;\boldsymbol{\mu}_{i,1},\boldsymbol{\Sigma}_{i,1})\ ;\ //d=1$$

for (d=2;d<D;d++) $\delta(i,d,t)=\delta(i,d-1,t-1)+\ln(a(i,d-1))+L(\mathbf{O}_t;\boldsymbol{\mu}_{i,d},\boldsymbol{\Sigma}_{i,d})$;

$$\delta(i,D,t)=\max_{D-1\le\tau\le D}\{\delta(i,\tau,t-1)+\ln(a(i,\tau))\}+L(\mathbf{O}_t;\boldsymbol{\mu}_{i,D},\boldsymbol{\Sigma}_{i,D})\ ;\ //d=D$$

}

step3 termination:

$$\delta_{opt}=\max_{1\le d\le D}\{\delta(N,d,T)+\ln(1-a(N,d))\}\ ;$$

$$d_o(T)=\arg\max_{1\le d\le D}\{\delta(N,d,T)+\ln(1-a(N,d))\}\ ;$$

step4 backtracking:

s(*T*)=N;

for (*t*=T-1;*T*>=1;*t*--) {

  if (1<d_o(*t*+1)<D) {

    s(*t*)= s(*t*+1);

    $d_o(t)=d_o(t+1)-1$;

  }

  if (d_o(*t*+1)==1) {

    s(*t*)= s(*t*+1)-1;

    $$d_o(t)=\arg\max_{1\le\tau\le D}\{\delta(s(t),\tau,t)+\ln(1-a(s(t),\tau))\}$$

  }

  if (d_o(*t*+1)==D) {

    s(*t*)= s(*t*+1);

    $$d_o(t)=\arg\max_{D-1\le\tau\le D}\{\delta(s(t),\tau,t)+\ln(a(s(t),\tau))\}$$

  }

}

$$a(i,d)=\frac{Count(i,d+1)}{Count(i,d)},1\le d<D \tag{9}$$

$$a(i,D)=\frac{Count(i,D+)}{Count(i,D)} \tag{10}$$

Once we have the initial model parameters, we can use the extended Viterbi algorithm to decode the training data and obtain the new optimal state sequences. Then, we can re-estimate the model parameters based on the new optimal state sequences. The decoding and re-estimation procedure is iterated until the likelihood score of the data converges or a prescribed number of iterations are reached.

3   Experiments on Mandarin Digits Recognition

A series of experiments on isolated Mandarin digits recognition was conducted to investigate the performance of proposed HO-HMM. The database includes sound from 100 speakers, 50 males and 50 females. There are five phases of recordings, and every speaker uttered the ten Mandarin digits in each phase. The database was divided into two parts; each part contains sounds from 25 male and 25 female speakers. One part was used for training and the other part for testing, and then the roles of these two parts were interchanged. The recognition error rate was then calculated based on all the 5000 utterances. The left to right topology is used for each word model. According to the estimated word duration, a word model contains 5 to 7 states and two boundary silence states that are shared for all word models. The feature vector consists of 12 mel-scale cepstral coefficients, one log energy, and the first and second order delta coefficients of the above features.

3.1   Experiments on Clean Speech Recognition

Two types of HO-HMM were used in clean speech recognition experiments. In the first type of HO-HMM, only the state transition depends on state staying time, while the output observation depends only on the current state regardless of the previous states. In the second type of HO-HMM, both the state transition and output observation depend on the state staying time. The output probability is represented by Gaussian or mixture of Gaussian probability density distributions. The performances of speech recognizers using HO-HMM of various order and mixture number were investigated. Fig. 1 shows the recognition error rates for HO-HMM with only high-order state dependency. From the experimental result, one can see that the increment of mixture number was the major contribution to performance gain. The error rate reduction was most prominent as the mixture number increased from 2 to 4, and the best was obtained at 8 mixture components. The performance drop at mixture 16 can be attributed to insufficiency of training data to reliably estimate the model parameters.

From fig. 1., one can see that high-order transition constraint only made slightly improvements in the case of single Gaussian component. This may due to that such constraint did not take account of the non-stationary trajectory of speech process. Increasing the number of mixture component could have the effect of allocating somecomponents to accommodate the trajectory at various staying time slots, and allocating some components to accommodate variations due to various speakers or environmental distortions. However, there are no explicit timing or environmental attribute associated with a particular mixture component. The timing constraint can be put at state level in HO-HMM with both high-order state transition and output

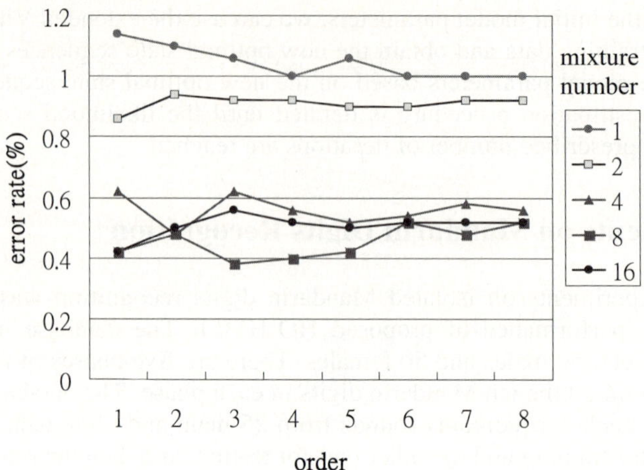

Fig. 1. Recognition error rates for HO-HMM with only high-order state dependency

dependencies. The experimental results for HO-HMM with both high-order depend-encies on state transition and output observation are shown in fig. 2. Comparing figs. 1 & 2, we can see that the error rate was further reduced for the further constrained system and the best performance was achieved when both mixture number and order of dependency were 4. Due to the growth of the parameter number and limited size of the training database, there was no sufficient number of speech frames to be used to estimate the density function of long staying state, the dependency order cannot be set too high. During the training procedure, speech frames allocated to some state may be reallocated to the neighboring states in the next iteration. This phenomenon may cause a state too short to accommodate high order dependency. In that case, non-uniform dependency order or parameter sharing technique may be employed.

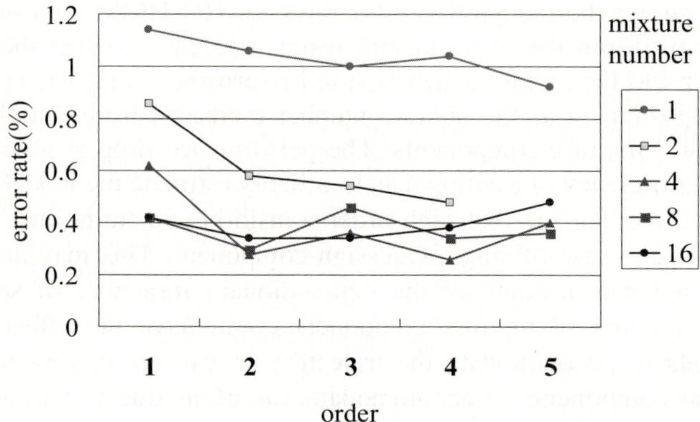

Fig. 2. Recognition error rates for HO-HMM with both high-order state transition and output observation dependencies

3.2   Experiments on Noisy Speech Recognition

To investigate the robustness of the propose HO-HMM we conducted experiments on noisy speech recognition. The models were trained from clean speech. White noise was added to testing speech with the SNR equaled to 20dB. The recognition results are shown in fig. 3 and 4. From the figures, we can find that HO-HMM with both high-order state transition and output observation dependencies are more robust than the traditional first order HMM and HO-HMM with only duration constraint.

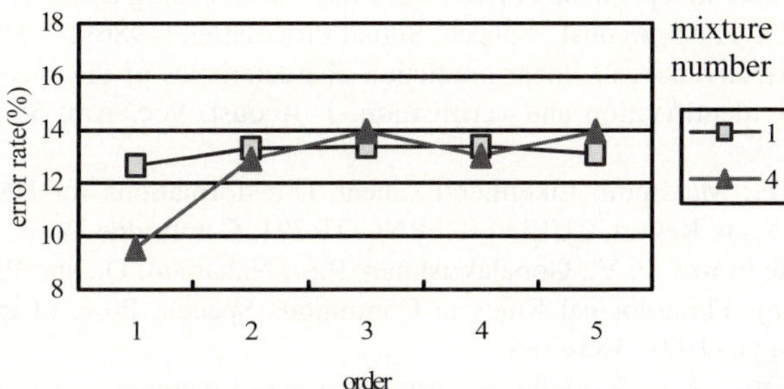

Fig. 3. Recognition error rates for HO-HMM with only high-order state transition dependency under noisy environment

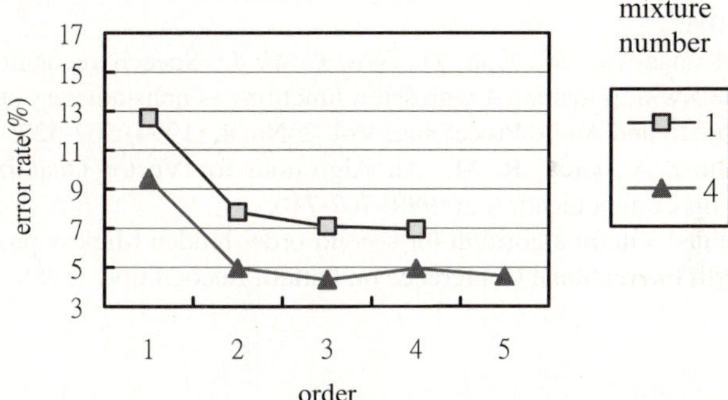

Fig. 4. Recognition error rates for HO-HMM with both high-order state transition and output observation dependencies under noisy environment

4   Conclusions

In this research, we propose HO-HMM for speech recognition. Both the state transition and output observation probabilities depend on a history of previous states so that the state duration and speech dynamic trajectory can be modeled more precisely. An extended Viterbi algorithm is proposed to score input speech against an HO-HMM and find out the best-matched state sequence that can be used to train the model. Experimental results on Mandarin digits recognition show that the proposed method can reduce the recognition error rate and is more robust against environmental noise.

References

1. Rabiner, L.: A tutorial on hidden Markov models and selected applications in speech recognition, Proc. IEEE, vol. 77, (1991) 257–285.
2. Levinson, S. E.: Continuously variable duration hidden Markov models for automatic speech recognition. Computer Speech and Language, vol. 1 no. 1, (1986) 29–45.
3. Russell, M. J., Cook, A.: Experimental evaluation of duration modeling techniques for automatic speech recognition, Proc. IEEE ICASSP (1987) 2376–2379.
4. Furui, S.: Speaker independent isolated word recognition using dynamic features of speech spectrum, IEEE Trans. Acoust., Speech, Signal Processing, (1986) 52–59.
5. Atal, B.S.: Effectiveness of linear prediction characteristics of the speech wave for automatic speaker identification and verification, J. Acoust. Soc. Am. 55 (6), (1974) 1304-1312.
6. Gales, M. J. F.: Maximum Likelihood Linear Transformations for HMM-based Speech Recognition, Tech. Report, CUED/FINFENG/TR291, Cambridge Univ., 1997.
7. Bahl, L. R., de Souza, P. V., Gopalakrishnan, P.S., Nahamoo, D., and Picheny, M.A.: Decision Trees for Phonological Rules in Continuous Speech, Proc. of the IEEE ICASSP, Toronto, Canada, (1991) 185--188.
8. Mari, J.-F., Haton, J.-P., Kriouile, A.: Automatic word recognition based on second-order hidden Markov models, IEEE Transactions on Speech and Audio Processing, vol. 5 no. 1, (1997) 22–25.
9. du Preez, J.A.: Algorithms for high order hidden Markov modeling, Proceedings of the IEEE South African Symposium on Communications and Signal Processing, 9-10 Sept., (1997) 101 -106.
10. Deng, L., Aksmanovic, M., Sun, D., Wu, C. F. J.: Speech recognition using hidden Markov models with polynomial regression functions as nonstationary states, IEEE Transactions on Speech and Audio Processing, Vol. 2, No. 4, (1994) 507-520.
11. Linde, Y., Buzo, A., Gray, R. M.: An Algorithm for Vector Quantizer Design, IEEE Transactions on Communications, (1980) 702-710.
12. He, Y.: Extended Viterbi algorithm for second-order hidden Markov process, Proceedings of the IEEE 9th International Conference on Pattern Recognition, (1988) 718–720.

Diagnostic Evaluation of Phonetic Feature Extraction Engines: A Case Study with the Time Map Model

Daniel Aioanei, Julie Carson-Berndsen, and Supphanat Kanokphara

School of Computer Science and Informatics,
University College Dublin, Belfield, Dublin 4, Ireland
{daniel.aioanei, julie.berndsen, supphanat.kanokphara}@ucd.ie
http://muster.ucd.ie

Abstract. This paper presents a framework for evaluating phonetic feature extraction engines in a phone identification task. The case study involves HMM-based feature extraction engines for fricative and vocalic which are evaluated both at the feature level and also on how they perform when coupled with a knowledge-based phone identification model. An exact comparison model is defined and performance of the feature extraction engines is measured with respect to the degradation in accuracy as each individual feature or combination of features are introduced incrementally into the input data. This type of diagnostic evaluation facilitates a more detailed investigation of how each feature impacts on the performance of the system as a whole and provides important insights for enhancing the performance of feature extraction engines in the context of automatic speech recognition.

Keywords: speech recognition, diagnostic evaluation, phonetic features.

1   Introduction

One of the key challenges faced by automatic speech recognition systems is the robust treatment of co-articulation phenomena (overlap of properties). One approach to tackling this problem is to use statistical context-dependent phone models, another approach is to use units smaller than the phone, namely phonetic features, and then apply rules to identify the phones, the syllables and ultimately the words defined by these features. One such model is the Time Map model [1] which uses an event logic and phonetic and phonological constraints to address the problem of co-articulation. In this case, statistical methods are used at a lower level to identify phonetic features rather than words, syllables or phones [2, 3, 4, 5]. Several implementations of the Time Map model have been proposed [6, 7], each of which uses a different technique to deal with underspecified and noisy input in order to identify the phones and syllables defined by the phonetic features. The common characteristic of these implementations is that they all accept as input parallel streams of phonetic features, known as a *multilinear representation* (see [7] for further details) which are detected from the speech signal by feature extraction engines.

M. Ali and R. Dapoigny (Eds.): IEA/AIE 2006, LNAI 4031, pp. 691–700, 2006.

This paper presents a framework that compliments the work referred to above by allowing the features which make up a multilinear representation to come from various sources using feature extraction engines of the type discussed in [8]. Given such an input, it is important that the higher-level phone and syllable identification components have some mechanism whereby they can evaluate the contribution of each of the features to the overall recognition process. For example, a system which takes information from feature extraction engines and produces figures on correctness and accuracy at the phone or syllable level does not allow for any evaluation of how each feature performs when integrated with the others.

In order to evaluate the contribution of features from various sources, it is first necessary to define a *comparison model*. In what follows, the *comparison model* is defined not in terms of a baseline but in terms of an exact model, i.e. a system which would achieve 100% accuracy if presented with *perfect data* (i.e 100% accuracy for each individual feature). The closest approximation to this is to use feature data which has been generated from the phoneme annotations using a phone-to-feature mapping and smoothing over adjacent occurrences of the same feature. Performance can then be measured with respect to the *comparison model* by incrementally replacing the perfect data for each feature with the feature extraction engine output. In other words, multilinear representations are compiled in a flexible step-by-step fashion using features from different sources (one source being the phoneme annotations and the other sources being the feature extraction engines). Unless a feature extraction engine is performing extremely well, a degradation in performance is expected with respect to the *comparison model* - each detected feature or combination of detected features is thus measurable and can provide detailed feedback to the designers of both the acoustic/articulatory feature extraction engines and the developers of the higher-level components.

In what follows, some experiments on the TIMIT corpus [9] are presented using HMM-based fricative and vocalic extraction engines together with the YASPER system [7], one specific implementation of the Time Map model. The architecture of the system used in these experiments is depicted in Figure 1. As can be seen from this figure the system consists of a *feature manager* set of feature extraction engines which provide input to an *interval manager*, the first component of YASPER. The extracted features are represented in terms of a multilinear representation of independent feature streams. YASPER also has a phonotactic manager and a lexicon manager which are not the focus of discussion in this paper. The interval manager deals with co-articulation and uses feature implication rules to deal with underspecified and noisy input. The multilinear representation of features is parsed to identify intervals of overlapping features. The intervals are then analysed and validated using feature implication rules. The feature implication rules are derived from a feature hierarchy, which captures the logical dependencies between the features in the phone-to-feature mapping used by the system [10]. Once the interval has been validated, the phone or the set of phones (in the case of underspecified input) defined by the features

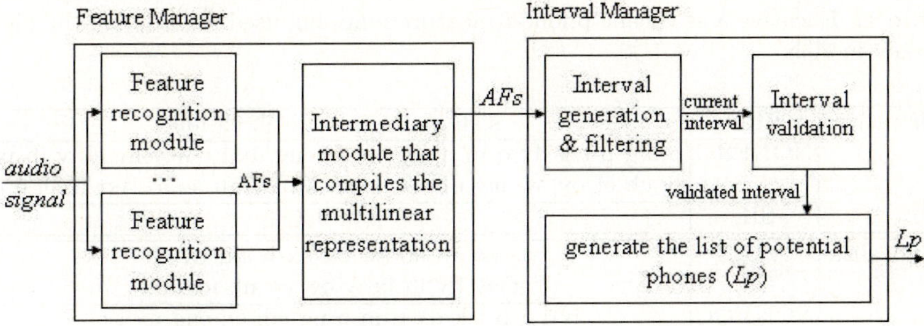

Fig. 1. Feature manager together with the interval manager of the YASPER system

in the current interval is identified. Subsequent phonotactic processing allows for syllable identification but the experiments described in later sections of this paper were designed to evaluate only the first stage of this process, namely the performance of the feature extraction engines in the phone identification task.

The next section presents two HMM-based feature extraction engines, one for fricative features and one for vocalic features. Section 3 presents an analysis of the extracted phonetic features and a heuristic which has been employed to improve on these results. Section 4 shows how the extracted features are used to compile a new *manner of articulation* tier by integrating the output of the fricative and vocalic feature extraction engines with the perfect data of the *comparison model*. The multilinear representation thus compiled is then given to YASPER which parses the multilinear representation and outputs the recognised phones. The training set of the TIMIT corpus has been used to train the HMM feature extraction engines, and the core test set to evaluate the feature recognition results. As YASPER is a knowledge-based system which does not need training, the core test set of the TIMIT corpus has been used to evaluate the phone recognition performance of YASPER as well. The core test set of TIMIT consists of the SX and SI sentences of 24 speakers, one female and two male for each of the 8 dialect areas of the corpus. The evaluation of the phone output is discussed in section 5 and some conclusions are drawn in section 6.

2   Feature Extraction Engines

Two phonetic feature extraction engines are used to illustrate the diagnostic evaluation framework in this paper. The phonetic extraction engines were built using HTK [11] and identify the presence of a feature, i.e. they look for FEA-TURE vs. NONFEATURE (everything else except silence) as defined in Table 1 for the features *fricative* and *vocalic*. The TIMIT training set was parametrised into 12 dimensional MFCCs, energy and their delta and acceleration (39 length front-end parameters). The feature models are trained from these parameters and the transcriptions converted from Table 1 accordingly. Each model contains 5 states and the covariance matrices of all states are diagonal.

Table 1. Fricative and vocalic phone-to-feature mapping used for training the hidden Markov models

fricatives	FRC	s sh z zh f th v dh jh ch hh
	NONFRC	b d g p t k dx q m n ng em en eng nx l r w y hv el iy ih ix ey eh er oy ow uw uh ux ae aa aw ay ah ao ax axr ax-h epi
	SIL	pau h#
vocalics	VOC	aa ae ah ao aw ax ax-h axr ay eh er ey hv ih ix iy ow oy uh uw ux
	NONVOC	b d g p t k dx q m n ng em en eng nx l r w y el s sh z zh f th v dh jh ch hh epi
	SIL	pau h#

Table 2. Fricative and vocalic feature extraction results

feature	% cor	% sub	% del	% ins	% acc
FRC	85.7	0.0	14.3	49.0	36.7
VOC	94.2	0.0	5.8	4.7	89.5

After the feature models have been trained, they are expanded to context-dependent models using a cross-word network. The back-off technique is used to determine the level of context dependency [12]. From the context-dependent HMMs, the number of model mixtures is incremented by 1 and the models are trained. This process continues until the number of mixtures is saturated. Eleven training processes are estimated using the maximum likelihood. The number of training iterations after each change is determined automatically in line with [13]. The language model is trained from the training set on each tier using back-off bigrams. For the recognition process, the Viterbi algorithm is used without any pruning factor. The grammar scale factor is 10.

Table 2 presents the fricative and vocalic feature extraction results based on the time-mediated alignment algorithm of NIST's sclite speech recognition scoring software [14].

3   Analysing the Feature Extraction Results

As can be seen from Table 2, the HMM-based feature extraction engine for the fricative feature performs fairly well in terms of correctness (85.7%) but very badly in terms of accuracy (36.7%), due to the fact that there are a large number of insertions. A closer look at the data revealed that one of the reasons why the insertion rate is so high is that in many cases the aspiration phases of stop bursts appeared to be recognized as fricatives. In order to verify this, the stop bursts in the evaluation reference files were replaced with fricatives and re-evaluated. The insertion rate went down from 49% to 5.9%. However, while manipulating the reference files obviously does not lead to any improvement

Table 3. TIMIT fricative and stop duration basic statistical measures

feature	Median	Mean	S.D.	Mean - S.D.
FRC	85.0 ms	88.6 ms	41.4 ms	47.3 ms
STP	44.1 ms	48.8 ms	27.8 ms	21.0 ms

Table 4. Fricative evaluation before and after smoothing

feature	% cor	% sub	% del	% ins	% acc
extracted FRC	85.7	0.0	14.3	49.0	36.7
smoothed FRC	84.5	0.0	15.5	39.5	45.0

in performance of the fricative extraction engine itself, it does highlight the necessity for a very good stop extraction engine, which can distinguish between closure phases and aspiration in stops, and an aspiration extraction engine which uses temporal information to distinguish fricative from aspiration phases. This insight facilitates fine tuning of the feature extraction engines.

Another avenue investigated to improve the results of the feature extraction engine is by means of a heuristic defined with respect to temporal data. Table 3 shows the arithmetic mean, median, and standard deviation values for the fricative and stop segment durations in the TIMIT corpus. More than half of the stops are outside the first standard deviation of the fricative durations ($Median_{STP} = 44.1ms < 47.3ms = Mean_{FRC} - S.D._{FRC}$). This provides a principled way of ignoring (or smoothing over) all fricative segments that have a duration shorter than the mean value minus the standard deviation. Combining this with the fricative extraction engine means that most short fricative segments that were recognised instead of aspirated stops, can be ignored without ignoring too many of the correctly recognised fricative segments. This insight facilitates the integration of temporal information into the feature extraction engines.

Table 4 shows the scoring results of the same extracted fricative features as in Table 2 but after smoothing over the short segments has been applied - the extracted FRC feature results are presented for comparison. The insertion rate has decreased significantly, while the deletion rate has increased only slightly. One reason for this could be that most short fricative segments are not detected by the fricative extraction engine in any case.

The next section demonstrates how smoothed fricative features and extracted vocalic features are integrated with the perfect data of the *comparison model* to compile a new *manner of articulation* tier which will allow the performance of the individual feature extraction engines to be evaluated in a phone identification task.

4   Compiling a New *Manner of Articulation* Tier

The outputs of the fricative and vocalic extraction engines are used to compile a new *manner of articulation* tier of the multilinear representation, which is combined with the perfect data of the comparison model; it is this representation which is passed to the interval manager component of YASPER for phone identification. On the comparison model data YASPER performs as expected with 100% accuracy and correctness. In compiling a multilinear representation which allows evaluation of the performance of individual feature extraction engines, *perfect* occurrences of a feature are replaced incrementally with the instances of that particular feature extracted from the speech signal. The impact of this feature on the overall performance of the system can then be measured in terms of a percentage degradation in overall performance (i.e. down from 100%). This is illustrated with the FRC and VOC feature extraction engines.

The first step in compiling a new multilinear representation is to delete all occurrences of the FRC feature in the perfect data and replace them with a special label called the *empty* feature, indicating the absence of any feature for those specific intervals. Then the FRC-free perfect manner tier and the FRC features extracted from the speech signal are merged. Here the best feature extraction engines is used for this merger, i.e. smoothed FRC. The insertion of the smoothed FRC feature always preserves its start and end time values which means that the start and/or end time values of the neighbouring features on the manner tier may have to be adjusted to those of the inserted FRC features. The *empty* features that are not overwritten by the smoothed FRC features remain on the manner tier as evidence of the imperfections of the fricative extraction engine, effectively modelling the deletions introduced.

Similarly, the *perfect* VOC features and indeed any other features can be replaced on the manner tier. When the extracted VOC features are inserted on the manner tier after the smoothed FRC features, manner tier compilation is performed giving the extracted VOC features a higher priority than the smoothed FRC features. The motivation for favouring the extracted VOC features over the FRC features is that the VOC features are extracted with higher accuracy. Figure 2 shows a small example of manner tier compilation that displays the *comparison model* manner tier at the top, followed by the smoothed FRC features, the extracted VOC features, and the resultant compiled manner tier at the bottom. Note that the extracted VOC features preserve their boundaries so that the smoothed FRC features and the STP feature remain in the portion not covered by extracted features.

The next section presents the YASPER phone output evaluation together with a new interval filtering methodology for improving performance of the phone identification task.

5   Phone Recognition Results

Table 5 shows the evaluation results of the phones output by YASPER in three cases:

- Case 1: YASPER phone output based on the *perfect* manner tier with only the smoothed FRC features inserted.

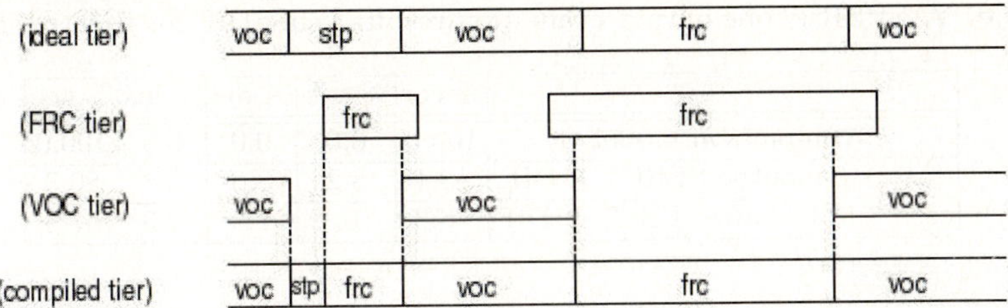

Fig. 2. Example *comparison model* manner tier (on top), plus the smoothed FRC and the extracted VOC features, which gives the compiled manner tier on the bottom

Table 5. YASPER phone output evaluation results

	% cor	% sub	% del	% ins	% acc
comparison model	100.0	0.0	0.0	0.0	100.0
case 1 (smoothed FRC)	84.5	13.1	2.4	15.1	69.4
case 2 (extracted VOC)	92.2	6.5	1.3	8.0	84.2
case 3 (VOC after FRC)	77.8	19.0	3.2	16.1	61.6

- Case 2: YASPER phone output based on the *perfect* manner tier with only the extracted VOC features inserted.
- Case 3: YASPER phone output based on the *perfect* manner tier with the extracted VOC features inserted after the smoothed FRC features.

Aioanei et al [7] discusses in more detail how YASPER parses the multilinear representation into intervals of overlapping features for the purposes of phone boundary identification. The segmentation procedure specifies that an interval can have one and only one feature on each of the tiers and the interval is chosen such that it spans the shortest feature on any tiers (i.e. the endpoint of each interval is defined by a change of feature on one of the tiers). As a result, intervals may be generated which are considerably shorter than a typical phone segment. YASPER addresses this through the use of an operation called Dynamic Interval Filtering (DIF), which uses knowledge about the temporal structure of features such as that mentioned in Table 3 above. For example, intervals that have the FRC feature on the manner tier cannot be shorter than $47.3ms = Mean_{FRC} - S.D._{FRC}$ (because short FRC segments have already been smoothed). Table 6 shows the evaluation results of the phone output of YASPER with Dynamic Interval Filtering for fricative features. Table 6 shows a clear improvement over the results in Table 5 (DIF for vowels did not lead to any improvements and thus is not discussed here).

Table 7 shows the confusion pairs for the phone output of YASPER when given only extracted FRC features (integrated with the perfect manner tier), compared to the case when given smoothed FRC features with DIF. The table shows the improvement brought by the smoothing algorithm and by the Dynamic

Table 6. YASPER phone output evaluation results using DIF for fricative features

	% cor	% sub	% del	% ins	% acc
comparison model	100.0	0.0	0.0	0.0	100.0
case 1 (smoothed FRC) + DIF	83.1	8.2	8.6	2.8	80.3
case 3 (VOC after FRC) + DIF	76.3	16.1	7.6	8.5	67.8

Table 7. Confusion pairs for fricatives

confusion pairs	extracted FRC without DIF	smoothed FRC with DIF
stops → fricatives	10.2%	6.6%
vowels → fricatives	1.8%	0.7%
nasals → fricatives	0.7%	0.2%
silence → fricatives	0.5%	0.1%
approximants → fricatives	0.3%	0.2%

Table 8. Confusion pairs for vocalic sounds

approximants → vowels	4.9%
stops → vowels	0.9%
nasals → vowels	0.5%
fricatives → vowels	0.2%

Table 9. Confusion pairs for FRC + VOC

confusion pairs	extracted FRC+ extracted VOC without DIF	smoothed FRC+ extracted VOC with DIF
stops → fricatives	9.6%	6.8%
stops → vowels	1.8%	1.8%
approximants → fricatives	0.6%	0.3%
approximants → vowels	5.1%	5.2%
nasals → fricatives	0.8%	0.2%
nasals → vowels	0.5%	0.7%
silence → fricatives	0.5%	0.8%

Interval Filtering component, and also confirms that the FRC feature extraction engine mostly confuses stops with fricatives, which is reflected in the phone output of the system.

Table 8 shows the confusion pairs for the phone output of YASPER given only the extracted VOC features (integrated with the perfect manner tier). The VOC feature extraction engine confuses mostly approximant segments with vocalic segments. This is not surprising since approximant sounds behave more like vowels than like consonants. Table 9 shows the confusion pairs for the phone output of YASPER when the *manner of articulation* tier is compiled by integrating the extracted VOC features after the extracted FRC features and then by integrating the extracted VOC features after the smoothed FRC features with DIF. This table confirms the improvements brought by the smoothing algorithm and by the DIF component. Tables 5 through 9 also show how the step-by-step procedure presented in this paper allows for detailed study of the merits of each component of the phone recogniser.

6 Conclusion

In this paper, a framework was presented for evaluating phonetic feature extraction engines in a phone identification task. The case study using two HMM-based phonetic feature extraction engines demonstrated how this approach facilitates a more detailed investigation of how each feature impacts on the performance of the system as a whole. An exact comparison model was defined and performance of the feature extraction engines was measured with respect to the degradation in accuracy as each individual feature or combination of features are introduced incrementally into the multilinear representation which serves as input to the knowledge-based recognition system. This type of diagnostic evaluation provides important insights for enhancing the performance of feature extraction engines in the context of automatic speech recognition. Future work is concerned with applying this evaluation technique to other feature extraction engines such as those defined in [8].

Acknowledgements

This material is based upon works supported by the Science Foundation Ireland under Grant No. 02/IN1/I100. The opinions, findings and conclusions or recommendations expressed in this material are those of the authors and do not necessarily reflect the views of Science Foundation Ireland.

References

1. Carson-Berndsen, J.: Time Map Phonology: Finite State Models and Event Logics in Speech Recognition. Kluwer Academic Publishers, Dordrecht, Holland (1998)
2. Juneja, A., Espy-Wilson, C.: An event-based acoustic-phonetic approach to speech segmentation and e-set recognition. In: Proceedings of the 15th International Congress of Phonetic Sciences, Barcelona (2003)
3. Ali, A., van der Spiegel, J.: Acoustic-phonetic features for the automatic classification of fricatives. Journal of the Acoustical Society of America **109** (2001) 2217–2235
4. Chang, S., Greenberg, S., Wester, M.: An elitist approach to articulatory-acoustic feature classification. In: Proceedings of Eurospeech. (2001) 1725–1728
5. Frankel, J., Wester, M., King, S.: Articulatory feature recognition using dynamic Bayesian networks. In: Proceedings of ICSLP. (2004)

6. Walsh, M.: Recasting the time map model as a multi-agent system. In: Proceedings of the 15th International Congress of Phonetic Sciences, Barcelona (2003)
7. Aioanei, D., Neugebauer, M., Carson-Berndsen, J.: Efficient phonetic interpretation of multilinear feature representations for speech recognition. In: Proceedings of the 2nd Language & Technology Conference, Adam Mickiewicz University, Poznan, Poland (2005)
8. Macek, J., Kanokphara, S., Geumann, A.: Articulatory-acoustic feature recognition: Comparison of machine learning and HMM methods. In: Proceedings of the 10th International Conference on Speech and Computer (SPECOM2005), Patras, Greece (2005) 99–102
9. Garofolo, J., Lamel, L., Fisher, W., Fiscus, J., Pallett, D., Dahlgren, N.: The DARPA TIMIT Acoustic-Phonetic Continuous Speech Corpus CDROM. NIST (1993)
10. Neugebauer, M.: Machine Learning and Phonological Classification. In: Proceedings of the TAAL Postgraduate Conference, University of Edinburgh (2003)
11. Young, S., Evermann, G., Hain, T., Kershaw, D., Moore, G., Odell, J., Ollason, D., Povey, D., Valtchev, V., Woodland, P.: The HTK Book (for HTK Version 3.2.1) (2002)
12. Kanokphara, S., Carson-Berndsen, J.: Better HMM-based articulatory feature extraction with context-dependent model. In: Proceedings of the 18th International Florida Artificial Intelligence Research. (2005)
13. Tarsaku, P., Kanokphara, S.: A study of HMM-based automatic segmentations for thai continuous speech recognition system. In: Proceedings of the Symposium on Natural Language Processing. (2002) 217–220
14. NIST: sctk-1.3 speech recognition scoring toolkit. In: www.nist.gov/speech/tools. (1996)

Soft Computing for Assessing the Quality of Colour Prints*

Antanas Verikas[1,2], Marija Bacauskiene[2], and Carl-Magnus Nilsson[1]

[1] Intelligent Systems Laboratory, Halmstad University,
Box 823, S-30118 Halmstad, Sweden
[2] Department of Applied Electronics, Kaunas University of Technology,
Studentu 50, LT-51368, Kaunas, Lithuania
`antanas.verikas@ide.hh.se/marija.bacauskiene@ktu.lt/cmn@ide.hh.se`

Abstract. We present a soft computing techniques based option for assessing the quality of colour prints. The values of several print distortion attributes are evaluated by employing data clustering, support vector regression, and image analysis procedures and then aggregated into an overall print quality measure using fuzzy integration. The experimental investigations performed have shown that the print quality evaluations provided by the measure correlate well with the print quality rankings obtained from the experts. The developed tools are successfully used in a printing shop for routine print quality control.

1   Introduction

Offset lithographic printing is the most widely used commercial printing technology. Multicolour pictures in offset lithographic printing are represented by cyan (C), magenta (M), yellow (Y), and black (K) dots of varying sizes on thin metal plates. The two left-most images in Fig. 1 provide an example of an image taken from an offset-printed picture and an enlarged view of a small area of the picture, respectively. The four-colour dots are clearly seen in this figure. An image comprised of such dots is usually called a halftone image. Since four colours are used in the printing process, four halftone images are created.

Fig. 2 illustrates the flowchart of the graphical process resulting into a newspaper page. A colour camera and a scanner are the main tools used to obtain colour images that are later used in offset colour printing. The images, called original in this paper, are usually recorded in the RGB colour space, see Fig. 2. Since C, M, Y, and K colours are used to print colour pictures, the so-called colour separation process, converting images from the RGB to the CMYK colour space, is applied. Next, by applying some half-toning procedure, each of the obtained C, M, Y, and K images is converted into the halftone counterpart. Printing plates are then easily obtained from the halftone images by applying the so-called computer-to-plate (CTP) technology. The colour observed in a small local area of such pictures depends on the actual proportions of the amount of the four

---

* We gratefully acknowledge the support we have received from the Foundation for Knowledge and Competence Development, Sweden.

M. Ali and R. Dapoigny (Eds.): IEA/AIE 2006, LNAI 4031, pp. 701–710, 2006.

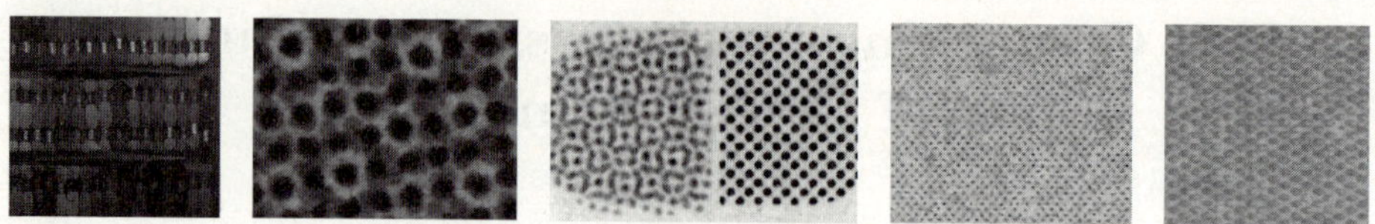

Fig. 1. A newspaper picture and an enlarged view of a small part of the picture (*left*). An example of the double grey-bar (*middle*). Two images exemplifying various quality aspects of printed dots (*right*).

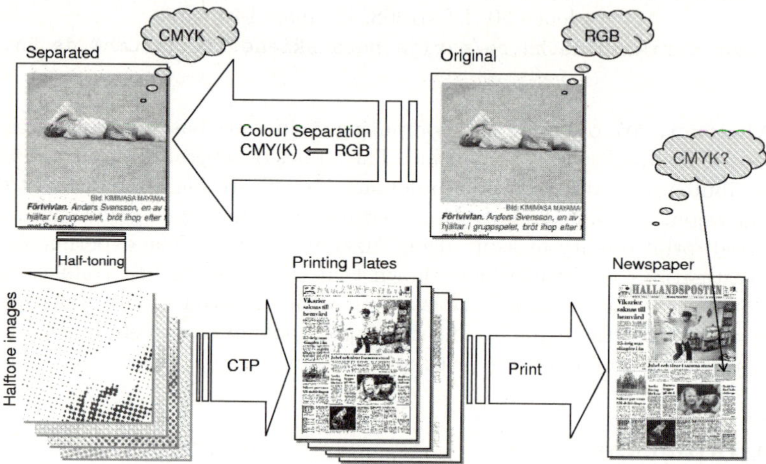

Fig. 2. The flowchart of the graphical process

inks deployed on that local area of paper—the CMYK values,—which have to be estimated by performing some measurements on the printed result (observe the question mark in Fig. 2). To obtain high quality prints, a relatively high precision of maintaining the beforehand determined ink proportions is required. The ability to print dots of the desired constant quality—size, shape, the degree of periodicity, ink density—is a key factor in obtaining the desired ink proportions in a small local area. The two rightmost images presented in Fig. 1 illustrate quality variations of printed dots. Thus, to assure high quality prints, a procedure for automatic print quality assessment is required. To enable the measurements required for assessing the print quality, a small test area is usually printed. Fig. 1 (*middle*) presents an example of such an area, the co-called double grey-bar.

Nonetheless of the current practice of using manual inspection of overall quality of complex colour prints in the printing industry, image analysis techniques are increasingly used for assessing various quality aspects of prints. Since manual procedures are tedious, time consuming, and the results are subjective as they depend on personal skills and mood, automated printing quality inspection systems are highly appreciated.

In general, various parameters are used to characterize print quality. The ones used most often are: ⋆ *dot deformation*—roundness, the degree of periodicity;

⋆ *dot gain*—the difference between the supposed average dot size and the actual measured average dot size; ⋆ *ink density deviation* from the required density level; ⋆ *edge sharpness*—the clarity of detail; ⋆ *the number of missing dots* (the parameter is only important in rotogravure printing).

A system attempting to simulate human print quality assessment for simple prints made by laser and ink jet printers is presented in [1]. Using simple print features characterizing noise level, edge sharpness, and tonal contrast the system is trained to categorize the prints into the *"bad quality"* and *"good quality"* classes. Another approach to the categorization of prints into the two classes was proposed in [2]. The categorization is based on moment invariants computed from a colour image histogram. A simple technique for measuring graininess when assessing print quality is presented in [3]. In [4], an approach to estimating the proportions of the four printing inks in a halftone image area was developed and used for printing quality monitoring in offset lithographic printing. Although there is a great interest in having a print quality measure integrating various quality aspects, the attempts to devise such a measure are very infrequent [5].

This paper is concerned with an attempt to develop such a measure for assessing the quality of offset lithographic prints. Several attributes characterizing distortion level of colour prints are estimated by employing data clustering, support vector regression, and image processing techniques and then aggregated into a print quality measure via Choquet fuzzy integral. To assess the offset printing quality we use the following print distortion attributes: the deviation of the *amount of C,M,Y,K inks* from the desired level, the *noise level*, the coefficient of variation of the *shape factor* of printed dots, the coefficient of variation of the *size* of the dots, and the coefficient of variation of *ink density*.

2 Estimating the Distortion Attributes

An image taken from a double grey-bar, as that shown in Fig. 1, is used as an information source to estimate the print distortion attributes. To evaluate the last three attributes, separate printed dots need to be detected and analyzed, while only a global analysis is required to estimate the first two. Next, we describe the main topics of the approach.

2.1 Estimating the Deviation of the Amount of Inks

The desired amount of the C, M, Y, and K inks in known in advance. Thus, estimation of the deviation amounts to estimation of the actual amounts of the inks. The average RGB values registered on the "black" part of the double grey-bar is the input information for estimating the amount of K. The amount of C, M, and Y is estimated from the average RGB values registered on the "coloured" part of the bar. Consequently, two mappings: $RGB \Rightarrow CMY$ and $RGB \Rightarrow K$ need to be determined. Since we use the approximately uniform $L^*a^*b^*$ colour space in the analysis, the mappings sought are $L^*a^*b^* \Rightarrow CMY$ and $L^*a^*b^* \Rightarrow K$. The $L^*a^*b^*$ values are easily obtained from RGB by applying the well known equations [6].

We use the support vector regression to discover the mappings sought. Let us assume that we have N colour patches spread over the whole colour gamut in question with known $L^*a^*b^*$—$\mathbf{x}$—and CMY—$\mathbf{y}$—values, the training set $S = \{(\mathbf{x}_1, \mathbf{y}_1), ..., (\mathbf{x}_N, \mathbf{y}_N)\}$. We collect the $\mathbf{x}$ vectors into the $N \times 3$ matrix $\mathbf{X}$ and the y vectors into the $N \times 3$ matrix $\mathbf{Y}$. Since we use the 1-norm ε-insensitive support vector regression, the optimization task is then to find $\boldsymbol{\alpha}^*$ by maximizing [7]

$$W(\boldsymbol{\alpha}) = \sum_{i=1}^{N} \alpha_i y_i - \varepsilon \sum_{i=1}^{N} |\alpha_i| - \frac{1}{2} \sum_{i,j=1}^{N} \alpha_i \alpha_j \kappa(\mathbf{x}_i, \mathbf{x}_j) \tag{1}$$

subject to

$$\sum_{i=1}^{N} \alpha_i = 0, \quad -C \le \alpha_i \le C, \quad i = 1, ..., N \tag{2}$$

with $\kappa(\mathbf{x}_i, \mathbf{x}_j)$ being a kernel, y_i is the target, and $C > 0$ is the regularization constant. Observe that a one-dimensional output is assumed in the above equations. The function f implementing the 1-norm ε-insensitive support vector regression is then given by

$$f(\mathbf{x}) = \sum_{j=1}^{N} \alpha_j^* \kappa(\mathbf{x}_j, \mathbf{x}) + b^* \tag{3}$$

where

$$b^* = -\varepsilon + y_i - \sum_{j=1}^{N} \alpha_j^* \kappa(\mathbf{x}_i, \mathbf{x}_j) \tag{4}$$

for i such that $0 < \alpha_i^* < C$.

In this study, we used polynomial $\kappa_p(\mathbf{x}_i, \mathbf{x}_j)$ and Gaussian $\kappa_g(\mathbf{x}_i, \mathbf{x}_j)$ kernels:

$$\kappa_p(\mathbf{x}_i, \mathbf{x}_j) = (1 + \mathbf{x}_i^T \mathbf{x}_j)^d \tag{5}$$

$$\kappa_g(\mathbf{x}_i, \mathbf{x}_j) = \exp\{-||\mathbf{x}_i - \mathbf{x}_j||^2/\sigma\} \tag{6}$$

with d and σ being parameters of the kernels. The mapping $L^*a^*b^* \Rightarrow K$ is found likewise, except that the output is one-dimensional.

The C, M, Y, and K values range between 0 and 100, where 0 means no ink and 100 stands for the area entirely covered by ink. Having the C, M, Y, and K values estimated, the distortion attribute Q_1 is then given by the average difference between the desired and the estimated actual values of the amount of inks.

2.2   Estimating the Noise Level

The "black" part of the bar is utilized to estimate the noise level. The estimation is based on the analysis of the Fourier power spectrum $P(u,v) = || F(u,v) ||^2 = R^2(u,v) + I^2(u,v)$ of a "dot image" $f(x,y)$, with $F(u,v)$ being the Fourier

transform of $f(x, y)$, and $R(u, v)$ and $I(u, v)$ are the real and imaginary components of $F(u, v)$, respectively. First, the central part of the power spectrum is
eliminated and three highest power peaks are then found in the upper part—the
first and the second quadrants—of the power plain.

Next, the power spectrum in the neighbourhood of each detected peak is
normalized to build a probability density function $p(\xi)$. Finally, the averaged
entropy, given by Eq.(7), is computed and used as a distortion attribute Q_2 to
quantify the noise level.

$$Q_2 = H = -\frac{1}{3 \log N_N} \sum_{j=1}^{3} \sum_{i=1}^{N_N} p_j(\xi_i) \log[p_j(\xi_i)] \tag{7}$$

where N_N is the size of the neighbourhood. Higher entropy H values are usually
computed for images of less regular dots.

2.3 Detecting the Printed Dots

We solve the task through unsupervised colour image segmentation. A relatively
simple fuzzy-clustering-based image segmentation technique can be used to segment an image taken from the "black" part of the bar [8]. However, a more
involved analysis is required to accurately segment the coloured part of the bar.
Eight combinations: *cyan, magenta, yellow, white, green (cy), blue (cm), red
(my)*, and *black (cmy)* are possible when printing C, M, and Y dots on each
other. Thus, the coloured part is segmented into these eight colour classes. Having the segmentation results, the C, M, and Y dots are easily recovered.

We segment an image by applying the mean shift procedure [9]. Pixels of a
colour image create a density distribution in the $L^*a^*b^*$ space. Pixels of similar
colours create modes of the distribution. If we can associate with each pixel of
the image the closest local mode of the distribution, we can use this information
to segment the image. The mean shift procedure provides this association.

Let us assume that $\{\mathbf{x}_i\}$, $i = 1, ..., N$ is a set of image pixels and $S_h(\mathbf{x})$ denotes
a hyper-sphere of radius h centered on $\mathbf{x}$ and containing $N_\mathbf{x}$ pixels. Then $M_h(\mathbf{x})$
given by

$$M_h(\mathbf{x}) = \frac{1}{N_\mathbf{x}} \sum_{\mathbf{x}_i \in S_h(\mathbf{x})} \mathbf{x}_i - \mathbf{x} \tag{8}$$

is called the *sample mean shift* [9]. The mean shift vector points towards the
maximum increase of the density. Thus, the mean shift procedure, obtained
by successive computation of $M_h(\mathbf{x})$ and translation of the window $S_h(\mathbf{x})$ by
$M_h(\mathbf{x})$ produces a path leading to a local density mode—convergence point.
Each pixel is associated with a convergence point representing a local density
mode in the 3-dimensional space. The convergence points of the procedure serve
as seed points for performing image segmentation. To obtain homogenous regions
in the segmented image, sufficiently close convergence points are merged. We do
the segmentation in the concatenated 5–dimensional *spatial-range* space. There
are two dimensions—x, y—in the spatial and three—$L^*a^*b^*$—in the range space.

Having the printed dots detected, the distortion attribute Q_3, related to dot size, is given by the coefficient of variation of the size

$$Q_3 = \sigma_S/m_S \tag{9}$$

with σ_S and m_S being the standard deviation and the mean value of the dot size S, respectively.

2.4 Estimating the Ink Density

We measure ink density with a colour camera via the local kernel ridge regression based reconstruction of a reflectance spectrum of a sample being measured [10]. Having the spectrum, the ink density D is evaluated as

$$D = -\lg \frac{\sum R(\lambda)S(\lambda)F(\lambda)}{\sum S(\lambda)F(\lambda)} \tag{10}$$

where λ stands for a wavelength, $R(\lambda)$ is the reflectance spectrum of a sample, $S(\lambda)$ is the relative power distribution of the light source, and $F(\lambda)$ is the spectral transmittance of the densitometer filter. The ink density is estimated for each printed dot and the distortion attribute Q_4, related to ink density, is then given by the coefficient of variation of the density $Q_4 = \sigma_D/m_D$.

2.5 Shape Factor

The dot shape factor ϑ we use is given by

$$\vartheta = S_d/P_d \tag{11}$$

where S_d and P_d are the dot area and perimeter, respectively. The distortion attribute Q_5, related to dot shape, is given by the coefficient of variation of the shape factor $Q_5 = \sigma_\vartheta/m_\vartheta$.

3 Fuzzy Integration of Distortion Attributes

In practice, distortion attributes are usually highly correlated. Therefore, when aggregating them into a quality measure it is desirable to assign weights not only to individual attributes, but also to groups of them. Aggregation based on fuzzy integrals—fuzzy integration—possesses this valuable property. In such schemes, different attributes are fused into a final quality measure by a fuzzy integral with respect to a fuzzy measure. A fuzzy measure represents weights on each attribute and also weights on each group of attributes.

3.1 Fuzzy Measure and Fuzzy Integral

Let Z be a non-empty finite set—a set of distortion attributes in our case—and 2^Z the power set of Z. A set function $g : 2^Z \rightarrow [0,1]$ is a *fuzzy measure* if $\bullet$ $g(\emptyset) = 0; g(Z) = 1$ and $\bullet$ if $A, B \subset 2^Z$ and $A \subset B$ then $g(A) \leq g(B)$.

The λ-fuzzy measure. Sugeno [11] introduced the so called λ-fuzzy measure, which satisfies the following additional property

$$g(A \cup B) = g(A) + g(B) + \lambda g(A)g(B) \tag{12}$$

for all $A, B \subset Z$ and $A \cap B = \emptyset$, and for some $\lambda > -1$. Let $Z = \{z_1, z_2, \ldots, z_L\}$ be a finite set, where L is the number of distortion attributes, and let $g^i = g(\{z_i\})$. When g is the λ-fuzzy measure, the values of $g(A_i)$ can be computed recursively:

$$g(A_1) = g(\{z_1\}) = g^1, \; g(A_i) = g^i + g(A_{i-1}) + \lambda g^i g(A_{i-1}), \text{ for } 1 < i \leq L.$$

We use the *discrete Choquet integral* to make the fuzzy integration. The discrete Choquet integral of a function h with respect to g is defined as

$$C_g(h(z_1), \ldots, h(z_L)) = \sum_{i=1}^{L} [h(z_i) - h(z_{i-1})]g(A_i) \tag{13}$$

where indices i have been permuted so that $0 \leq h(z_1)...h(z_L) \leq 1$, $A_i = \{z_i, ..., z_L\}$; $h(z_0) = 0$. In our case, the function $h(z)$ is a function of values of the distortion attributes. We adopted the following function $h(Q_i)$:

$$h(Q_i) = \exp\{-\theta_i Q_i\} \tag{14}$$

where θ_i is a parameter.

The g^i value reflects the importance of the ith distortion attribute. In this paper, the value was chosen to be proportional to the Spearman's correlation coefficient ρ between the quality rankings provided by the attribute and the expert. To evaluate the ranking obtained from the overall quality measure, we also used the Spearman's correlation coefficient:

$$\rho = \frac{\sum_{t=1}^{T} R[M(t)]R[E(t)] - T\left(\frac{T+1}{2}\right)^2}{\sqrt{\sum_{t=1}^{T} R^2[M(t)] - T\left(\frac{T+1}{2}\right)^2}\sqrt{\sum_{t=1}^{T} R^2[E(t)] - T\left(\frac{T+1}{2}\right)^2}} \tag{15}$$

where T is the number of images used, $R[E(t)]$ and $R[M(t)]$ are the quality rank given to the tth image by the expert and the measure, respectively.

4   Experimental Investigations

The experimental tests performed concern an offset newspaper printing process. An on-line printing process monitoring system has been used to capture the images of test areas used in the experiments. The system is equipped with a CCD colour camera of 1600×1200 pixels. The camera can be positioned with a high accuracy at any point across a newspaper page and is able to record high quality well-focused colour images from a web running at up to 15 m/s speed. An off-line version of the system is also available.

4.1   Choice of Parameters

The width of the kernel $\sigma = 0.2$ and the polynomial degree $d = 2$ turned to be a good choice for the kernel parameters. The value of the regression insensitivity parameter ε was chosen based on the process knowledge and was set to $\varepsilon = 0.015$. The regularization constant C was found by cross-validation and was equal to $C = 50$. Based on the values of the correlation coefficient ρ, the following importance weights g^i have been given to the the distortion attributes: $g^1 = 0.5$, $g^2 = 0.8$, $g^3 = 0.2$, $g^4 = 0.4$, and $g^5 = 0.2$. The values of $\theta_1 = 2$, $\theta_2 = 5$, $\theta_3 = 2$, $\theta_4 = 4$, and $\theta_5 = 2$ worked well in all the tests performed.

4.2   Estimating the Amount of Ink

To learn the mappings $L^*a^*b^* \Rightarrow CMY$ and $L^*a^*b^* \Rightarrow K$, a set of test colour patches were printed keeping the same ink density. For each cyan, magenta, and yellow inks, the average nominal ink coverage of a patch area—the dot size—was varied in 20% steps, namely, 0, 20, 40, 60, 80, and 100%. An example of 216 such pathes, with C, M, and Y varying from 0 to 100%, is shown in Fig. 3. The average ink coverage for the black ink was varied in 3% steps from 0 to 100%. In total, 216 test colour and 34 black patches were designed. Data from five of such prints were automatically recorded using the on-line system. One set of the data has been used to estimate the regression parameters, while the other four sets were allocated for testing.

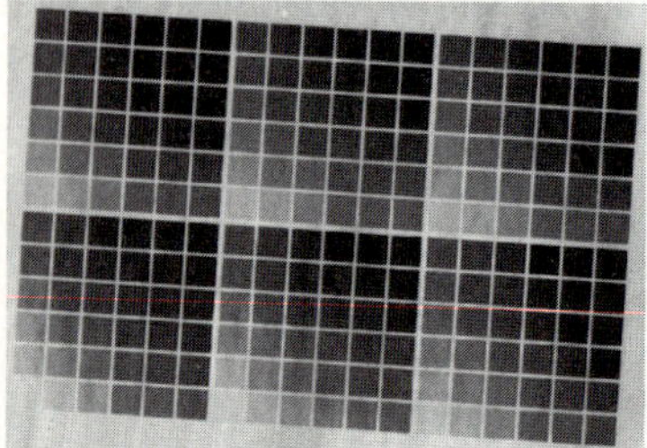

Colour	Gaussian	Polynom
C	1.12 (0.60)	1.17 (0.22)
M	1.09 (0.56)	1.18 (0.61)
Y	1.36 (0.77)	1.47 (0.59)
K	0.55 (0.37)	0.64 (0.39)

Fig. 3. An image taken from the 216 colour patches

Fig. 4. The average prediction error of the C, M, Y, and K values

To learn the mappings, the target values—the actual C, M, Y, and K values—are to be known. Though the nominal C, M, Y, and K values used to print the test patches are known, the actual values remain unknown, since halftone dots grow during the printing process. We estimated these values from the RGB values of the halftone series of the pure colours.

Fig. 4 presents the average absolute prediction error of the actual C, M, Y, and K values for the test data set using the Gaussian and polynomial kernels. In the parentheses, the standard deviation of the error is provided. Observe that C, M, Y, and K values range from 0 to 100. The prediction accuracy obtained is high enough for the approach to be used in practical applications. It is worth noting that evaluation of the prediction error is not an easy task, since the ground truth is not known. The actual C, M, Y, and K values used to estimate the regression parameters were evaluated using patches of single colours only (no overprints). Let us assume that the actual value of C=28 has been evaluated for the nominal C=20. It was then assumed that for all the overprints printed using the nominal value of C=20, the actual value of C was always 28, irrespective the proportions of the other two inks. It is clear that the assumption does not always holds in practice. Thus, we can expect that the estimation errors are even smaller, as the experience shows, than those observed in Fig. 4.

4.3   Assessing the Quality of Prints

The aim of the test was to compare the quality ranking given to different printed issues by human experts and by the integral quality measure. The quality of eight issues printed using different printing conditions and paper types has been ranked by 14 experts and the average ranking was obtained. Each issue contained test areas with the halftone bars. Images of the areas were recorded by the system and used to calculate the distortion attributes. The Spearman's correlation coefficient between the average ranking obtained from the expert and the rankings provided by the distortion attributes and the integral quality measure was then calculated.

Table 1 presents values of the correlation coefficient ρ computed for three distortion attributes yielding the highest values of the coefficient as well as the integral measure aggregating information available from all the attributes. The coefficient was evaluated separately for C, M, Y, and K inks. The Table also provides values of the probability p to obtain such correlation by chance.

Table 1. The Spearman's correlation coefficient ρ and the probability p.

Colour	Amount of Ink		Noise		Density		Integral	
	ρ	p	ρ	p	ρ	p	ρ	p
C	0.905	0.0020	0.976	0.0000	0.738	0.0366	0.976	0.0000
M	0.952	0.0003	0.976	0.0000	0.976	0.0000	0.952	0.0003
Y	0.929	0.0009	0.976	0.0000	0.738	0.0366	0.952	0.0003
K	0.905	0.0020	0.619	0.1017	0.905	0.0020	0.976	0.0000

The values of the Spearman's correlation coefficient computed for the rankings substantiate good correlation between the quality rankings obtained from the human experts and the overall quality measure. Lower values—not presented in Table 1—of the correlation coefficient were computed using rankings provided by the dot size and shape related attributes. A relatively low number of pixels, the printed dots consisted of, caused a rather high variance of the two aforementioned parameters. However, if the resolution is increased, the high variation of the dot size and shape seem to be good indicators of deficiencies in the printing process.

5   Conclusions

We presented a soft computing based option for assessing the quality of colour prints. Several attributes characterizing global as well as local distortion level of printed dots are estimated employing data clustering, support vector regression, and image processing techniques and then aggregated into an overall print quality measure via Choquet fuzzy integral.

The noise level, deviation of the actual amount of ink deposited on the paper from the desired level, and the variation coefficient of the average ink density level of different printed dots are the three most informative distortion attributes. Due to the relatively low resolution used to represent printed dots, the dot size and the shape related distortion attributes were less informative. However, if the resolution is increased, the high variation of the dot size and the shape become useful indicators of deficiencies in the printing process. The experimental investigations performed have shown that print quality evaluations provided by the proposed integral print quality measure correlate well with the print quality rankings obtained from the experts. The developed tools are successfully used in a printing shop for a routine print quality control.

References

1. Tchan, J., Thompson, R.C., Manning, A.: A computational model of print-quality perception. Expert Systems with Applications **17** (1999) 243–256
2. Luo, J., Zhang, Z.: Automatic colour printing inspection by image processing. Journal of Materials Processing Technology **139** (2003) 373–378
3. Trepanier, R.J., Jordan, B.D., Nguyen, N.G.: Specific perimeter: a statistic for assessing formation and print quality by image analysis. TAPPI Journal **81** (1998) 191–196
4. Verikas, A., Malmqvist, K., Bergman, L.: Neural networks based colour measuring for process monitoring and control in multicoloured newspaper printing. Neural Computing & Applications **9** (2000) 227–242
5. Verikas, A., Bacauskiene, M.: Image analysis and fuzzy integration applied to print quality assessment. Cybernetics and Systems **36** (2005) 549–564
6. Wyszecki, G., Stiles, W.S.: Color Science. Concepts and Methods, Quantitative Data and Formulae. 2nd edn. John Wiley & Sons, New York (1982)
7. Shawe-Taylor, J., Cristianini, N.: Kernel Methods for Pattern Analysis. Cambridge University Press, Cambridge, UK (2004)
8. Bergman, L., Verikas, A., Bacauskiene, M.: Unsupervised colour image segmentation applied to printing quality assessment. Image and Vision Computing **23** (2005) 417–425
9. Comaniciu, D., Meer, P.: Mean shift: A robust approach toward feature space analysis. IEEE Trans Pattern Analysis Machine Intelligence **24** (2002) 603–619
10. Verikas, A., Bacauskiene, M.: Estimating ink density from colour camera RGB values by the local kernel ridge regression. Engineering Applications of Artificial Intelligence **19** (2006)
11. Sugeno, M.: Fuzzy measures and fuzzy integrals: A survey. In Gupta, M.M., Saridis, G.N., Gaines, B.R., eds.: Fuzzy Automata and Decision Process. North-Holland Pub, Amsterdam (1977) 89–102

An Efficient Shortest Path Computation System for Real Road Networks

Zhenyu Wang[1], Oscar Che[2], Lijuan Chen[2], and Andrew Lim[1,2]

[1] School of Computer Science and Engineering, South China Univ of Technology,
Guangdong, China
[2] Dept of IELM, HKUST, Clear Water Bay, Kowloon, Hong Kong

Abstract. In this paper, we develop an efficient system to compute shortest paths in real road networks. An optimal shortest path algorithm is proposed based on a two-level hierarchical network structure. A pre-computation technique is used to improve the time efficiency. To further improve time efficiency and reduce memory requirement, we propose an algorithm to minimize the number of boundary nodes by relocating them between adjacent sub-networks. The performances of our approach with different network partition methods (with or without minimization of the number of boundary nodes) are compared in terms of both time efficiency and memory requirement. The experimental results on the real road network of Hong Kong demonstrated the efficiency of our method and the usefulness of minimizing of the number of boundary nodes.

Keywords: systems for real life applications, decision support, shortest path computation, hierarchical network structure.

1   Introduction

Efficient shortest path computations in real road networks are essential to *Intelligent Transportation System* (ITS) and other vehicle routing services. However, naive application of shortest path algorithms in real road networks always deteriorates because of the huge number of nodes. In the literature, various shortest path algorithms [13], [12] are available for route finding, of which the most popular one is Dijkstra's algorithm. Dijkstra's algorithm has a runtime complexity of $O(E + VlogV)$ for a network with E edges and V nodes. It performs well on a network with a small number of nodes. However, for a real road network with tens of thousands of nodes, the performance drops dramatically in term of time efficiency. Its application in the real road network thus requires some methods to reduce the number of nodes in consideration.

In the literature, a lot of work has been focused on the idea of hierarchical structures [4], [10], [3], [1]. The road network is organized into a hierarchical structure with the help of existing topographical knowledge, and heuristic methods are used to improve the time efficiency. Liu [10] partitioned the entire network into many small sub-networks by major roads. The shortest path algorithm was applied only to the sub-networks containing the origin or the destination and the

M. Ali and R. Dapoigny (Eds.): IEA/AIE 2006, LNAI 4031, pp. 711–720, 2006.

major road network. Jagadeesh *et al.* [3] proposed a heuristic improvement by using Euclidean distances, instead of real distances, in the origin and destination sub-network to improve the time efficiency. However, with these methods the results are not guaranteed to be optimal. Researchers have also developed optimal models for shortest path computation based on hierarchical network structures [4], [6]. Pre-computation was proposed as well to improve the time efficiency of shortest path queries. But pre-computation leads to another problem, i.e., the memory requirement is tremendous [11]. Ning *et al.* [4] stored all-pair shortest paths of each fragment graph rather than the shortest paths of the whole network. This approach balances time efficiency and memory requirement and is highly complimentary.

In a hierarchical approach, the partition method is of great importance because it directly influences the time efficiency. Habbal *et al.* [2] proved that the most favorable decomposition schemes are those in which the number of sub-networks is relatively small, the sub-networks are of equal size, the number of boundary nodes per sub-network is uniform and the total number of boundary nodes is as small as possible. Ning *et al.* [4], [5] developed a link-sorting partition algorithm which is efficient for large map fragmentation, and proposed the *Spatial Partition Clustering* (SPC) technique. Karypis and Kumar [8] presented a multilevel algorithm for multi-constraint graph partitioning such that the partitions satisfy a balancing constraint while aiming at minimizing the edge-cut.

In this paper, we present an efficient system for shortest path computation and queries in a real road network which guarantees the optimality. In our model, the hierarchical structure is adopted to reduce the number of nodes in consideration so as to improve the time efficiency. The pre-computation technique is applied to facilitate shortest path queries. The road network is partitioned into a number of sub-networks, and the trade-off between time efficiency and memory requirement is balanced by only storing all-pair shortest paths of each sub-network. To further improve time efficiency and reduce memory requirement, we propose an algorithm to minimize the number of boundary nodes by relocating them between adjacent sub-networks. To evaluate the performance of our approach, computational experiments were conducted on the Hong Kong road network with 13626 nodes and 28735 edges. The edge-node ratio is 2.11.

2 Methodology

2.1 Partitioning Tools

To partition the real road network appropriately, we studied the SPC method, the multilevel partitioning algorithm and a computer-aided partition method with topographical knowledge. SPC is a link-sorting based partitioning method, exploiting unique properties of transportation networks such as spatial coordinates and high locality. The algorithm is based on the *plane-sweep* technique commonly used in multi-dimensional spatial data operations. For the details of the algorithm, refer to [5]. In our implementation, the nodes, instead of the links, are partitioned into clusters, and the nodes of the same cluster are grouped together to form a sub-network. After all the nodes have been grouped into sub-networks, the entire network is successfully partitioned into a set of sub-networks and each node belongs to exactly a single sub-network. We also studied multi-level partitioning algorithms presented by Karypis and Kumar [8], [9], [7], and used the multilevel partitioning tool, METIS. METIS is a powerful software package for partitioning large graphs, partitioning large meshes, and computing fill-reducing orderings of sparse matrices.

The computer-aided partitioning method (CAP) is facilitated by human knowledge on the topographical respect of the real map. Through this approach, we divide the entire map into several sub-networks by manually selected boundary nodes. The selection of boundary nodes is subject to topographical knowledge of the map. When selecting the boundary nodes, we hope to isolate the regions with fewer roads connected with outside. For example, the Hong Kong Island is favorable to be isolated as a sub-map, which is connected with Kowloon through only 3 tunnels. So is the Lan Tau Island, which is linked with outside by the Tsing Ma Bridge. However, when it is difficult to further partition a dense sub-network, we have to select more boundary nodes. In such cases, it is necessary for us to study the specific region and then select as few boundary nodes as possible.

Moreover, a computer program was written to help us choosing the boundary nodes. The boundary nodes are selected one after another. After a boundary node is selected (or un-selected), the program displays the total number of sub-networks with current set of boundary nodes. For each sub-network, the program reports its size and the number of boundary nodes contained in it. This information is provided to help us deciding whether our previous choices of boundary nodes are good or not. With the help of the computer program and human knowledge, the Hong Kong road network was successfully partitioned into 74 components, each containing 52 to 309 nodes.

2.2   Optimal Shortest Path Computation Based on a Hierarchical Network Structure

We propose a shortest path algorithm based on a 2-level hierarchical network structure constructed by the SPC, METIS or computer-aided partitioning method. Our algorithm guarantees the optimality of the results. In order to explain the algorithm, we describe first the 2-level hierarchical network structure. After partitioning, the original network $G(V,E)$ is divided into sub-networks: SG_1, SG_2, ..., SG_n, called the *low-level* networks. In each sub-network, the nodes with an outgoing edge to or an incoming edge from other sub-networks is defined as *boundary nodes*. For example, consider Figure 1 where a digraph G and its sub-networks SG_1, SG_2 and SG_3 are shown. The boundary node set of SG_1, SG_2 and SG_3 is {E, F}, {G, H, J, L} and {M, N, O}, respectively.

We define the local shortest path between two boundary nodes computed within each sub-network as $SP_i(boundary_1, boundary_2, distance)$, where i corresponds to SG_i, the sub-network which the two boundary nodes belong to. Firstly, we apply Dijkstra's algorithm in each *low-level* network to compute all $SP_i(boundary_1, boundary_2, distance)$'s and store them. In Figure 1, for example,

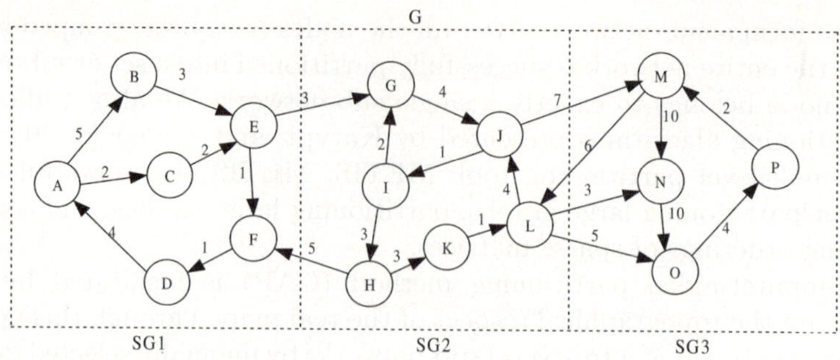

Fig. 1. A digraph G and its subgraph SG_1, SG_2 and SG_3

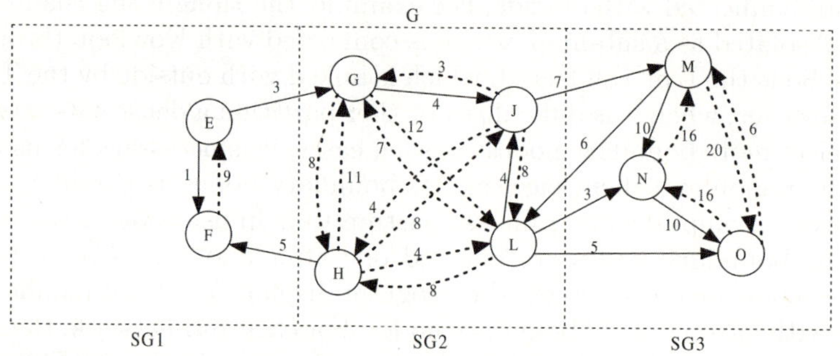

Fig. 2. The high-level network constructed from SG_1, SG_2 and SG_3

the local shortest path from boundary node E to F, computed within SG_1, is $SP_1(E, F, 1)$, the shortest path from G to H in SG_2 is $SP_2(G, H, 8)$, from M to N in SG_3 is $SP_3(M, N, 10)$, and so on.

We isolate all the boundary nodes, each two of which within the same sub-network are linked with two additional edges equivalent to the local shortest paths between them. Then add the outgoing or incoming edges to the corresponding boundary nodes. Thus we construct the *high-level* network, which is the connector of all the sub-networks. The high-level network together with the low-level sub-networks forms the 2-level network structure. The high-level network constructed from SG_1, SG_2 and SG_3 of Figure 1 is given in Figure 2, where the newly-added edges are represented by dashed arrows.

Apply the all-pair shortest path algorithm (that is, apply Dijkstra's algorithm repetitively) in the high-level network, and all-pair global shortest paths of the high-level network are determined, including the global shortest paths between each pair of boundary nodes that belong to the same sub-network. The shortest path between two boundary nodes computed in the high-level network is denoted as $SP_h(boundary_1, boundary_2, distance)$. The results are stored in memory. For example, the distance from M to N in the high-level network is $SP_h(M, N, 9)$, by going though L of SG_2.

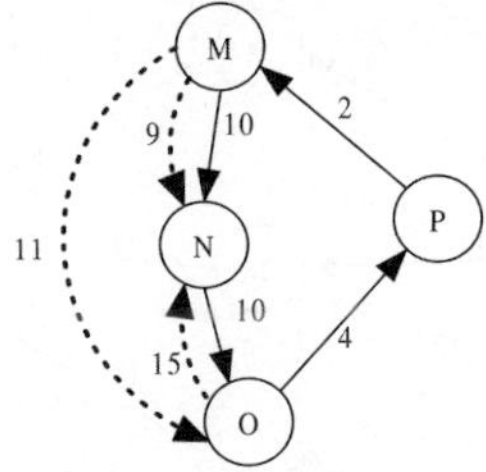

Fig. 3. The updated SG_3 with newly-added edges

Then we return to the low-level networks. Each pair of boundary nodes in the same sub-network SG_i are linked with an additional edge of weight $SP_h(boundary_1, boundary_2, distance)$, if $SP_h(boundary_1, boundary_2, distance)$ is less than $SP_i(boundary_1, boundary_2, distance)$. For example, the updated SG_3 is given in Figure 3, where the newly-added edges are represented by dashed arrows. After that we apply all-pair shortest path algorithm in each updated sub-network to compute global shortest paths between any two nodes of the sub-network. The results are then stored in memory. At the point, the global all-pair shortest paths for the high-level network and for each sub-network have been computed and stored. Thus, the all-pair shortest path initialization process is completed. Since there is a trade-off between time efficiency and memory requirement, we do not store all-pair shortest paths of the whole road network in our system. Instead, we only store all-pair shortest paths in each low-level network and the high-level network, which saves memory significantly without greatly compromising the time efficiency.

To retrieve the shortest path between two given nodes, s (the origin) and t (the destination), we should first check whether they are boundary nodes and where they are located. In the following, we denote the global shortest path from the origin to the destination as $SP(s, t, distance)$, and the set of boundary nodes of a sub-network SG_i as BN_i. There are 4 scenarios listed as follows.

Case 1: If the two nodes are both boundary nodes, $SP(s, t, distance) = SP_h(s, t, distance)$. For this case, retrieve the result from the high-level network.

Case 2: If the two nodes are located in the same low-level network, SG_i, $SP(s, t, distance)$ has already been computed and stored in SG_i. For this case, retrieve the result from SG_i.

Case 3: If s is inside a low-level network SG_i and t is a boundary node, we create a directed graph $G' = (V', E')$, where V' contains s, BN_i and t. For each boundary node, v, in BN_i, there is a directed edge in E' from s to v with weight $SP(s, v, distance)$, and another directed edge from v to t with weight $SP(v, t, distance)$. Then we apply Dijkstra's algorithm to obtain the shortest path from s to t in G'. Vise versa for the case that s is a boundary node but t is not. The auxiliary graph G' for computing $SP(P, L, distance)$ is given in Figure 4, from which we get $SP(P, L, 8)$.

Case 4: If s is inside a low-level network SG_i and t is inside a different low-level network SG_j , we create a directed graph $G' = (V', E')$, where V' contains

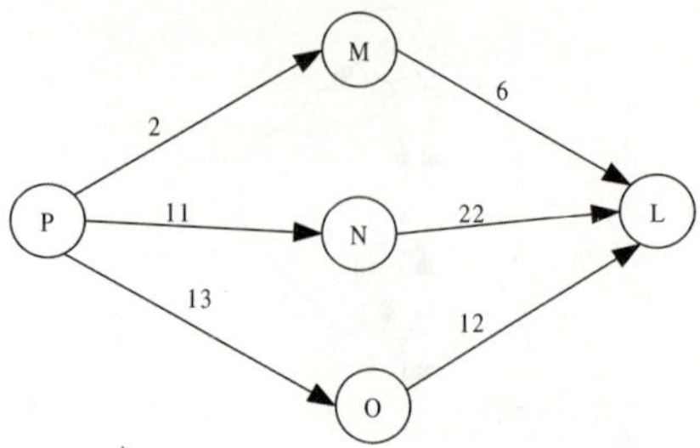

Fig. 4. The auxiliary graph G' for $SP(P, L, distance)$

s, BN_i, BN_j and t. For each boundary node, v, in BN_i, there is a directed edge in E' from s to v with weight $SP(s, v, distance)$. For each boundary node, v', in BN_j, there is a directed edge in E' from v' to t with weight $SP(v', t, distance)$. In addition, there is a directed edge from v to v' with weight $SP(v, v', distance)$. Then we apply Dijkstra's algorithm to obtain the shortest path from s to t in G'.

It is straight-forward to extend the above retrieval algorithm to retrieve the shortest paths from s to a set of destination nodes, $\{t_1, t_2, \ldots, t_n\}$. Thus, the description is omitted here.

2.3   Minimization of the Number of Boundary Nodes

From the algorithm described in the previous section, we realized that the number of boundary nodes affects both time efficiency and memory requirement. Since the boundary nodes are the entry/exit points of the low-level networks, the fewer they are, the fewer entry/exit points we need to consider in Case 3 and 4 of the retrieval algorithm. Moreover, in our implementation we pre-compute and store all-pair shortest paths of the high-level network, of which the nodes are exactly the boundary nodes. With fewer boundary nodes, less memory is required for the high-level network. Therefore, we took minimization of the number of boundary nodes into consideration and developed an algorithm for it. The algorithm improves the partitions generated by the methods as described in Section 2.1 by relocating the boundary nodes between different sub-networks.

Refer to Figure 1. The boundary node set of SG_1, SG_2 and SG_3 is {E, F}, {G, H, J, L} and {M, N, O}, respectively. If we move a boundary node from its native sub-network to another sub-network to which it is adjacent, we may reduce the number of boundary nodes. For example, if we move the boundary node L from SG_2 to SG_3, the resulting boundary node set for SG_2 and SG_3 is {G, H, J, K} and {L, M}, respectively. The number of boundary nodes is then reduced by 1.

To interpret the minimization algorithm formally, we define the *adjacent nodes* of a boundary node, v, as the nodes which are directly linked with v by an incoming or outgoing edge. An *adjacent sub-network* of v is a non-native sub-network which contains at least one of its adjacent nodes. In the native sub-network of v, there are two types of adjacent nodes: those adjacent nodes which are boundary nodes themselves (denoted as *native-boundary-nodes*) and those which are not (*native-regular-nodes*). In an adjacent sub-network of v, there are also two types of adjacent nodes: those linked with no other foreign boundary node except v (*single-linked-nodes*) and those linked with other foreign boundary nodes (*multi-linked-nodes*). If v is moved to an adjacent sub-network, the *native-boundary-nodes* will remain as boundary nodes, while the *native-regular-nodes* will become new boundary nodes. On the other hand, the *single-linked-nodes* in the target adjacent sub-network will become non-boundary nodes, while the *multi-linked-nodes* will remain as boundary nodes. v will become a non-boundary node only if it has only one adjacent sub-network and does not have any *native-boundary-node* or *native-regular-node*. Our minimization algorithm keeps on moving boundary nodes to their adjacent sub-networks as long as the total number of boundary nodes is reduced. It terminates at a local optimum where no further reduction is possible.

3   Computational Results

3.1   Comparison of Different Partitioning Methods

The partitioning methods (SPC, METIS and CAP) were tested on the Hong Kong road network. Figure 5 and 6 illustrate the all-pair shortest path computation time and memory usage of METIS, as the number of partitions, n_p, increases. The corresponding figures for SPC are omitted due to its poor performance. The best results for METIS, SPC and CAP are given in Table 1, where "+M" indicates that the partition method is enhanced by minimizing the number of boundary nodes.

The results indicate that the best value of n_p is about 90 for METIS and 50 for SPC. Table 1 clearly shows that METIS performed much better than SPC, while CAP is better than METIS. The memory requirement of CAP+M is about 4.82% less than METIS+M. More importantly, the all-pair shortest path computing time of CAP+M is over 1 second (28.62%) less than METIS+M, demonstrating the usefulness of topographic knowledge. Moreover, the results with minimization of the number of boundary nodes are always better than those without minimization, which demonstrates the strength of the minimization algorithm.

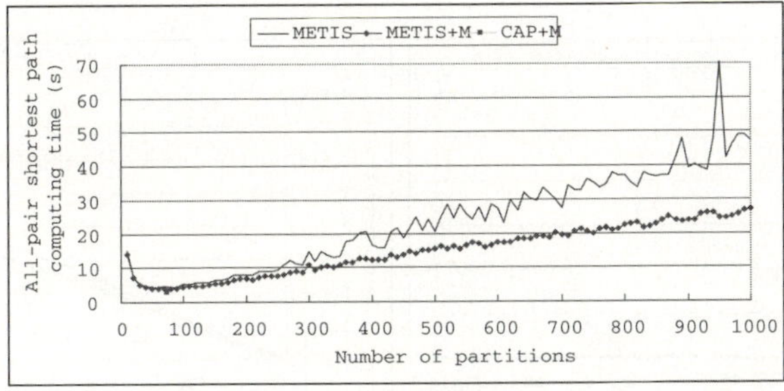

Fig. 5. All-pair shortest path computation time with METIS

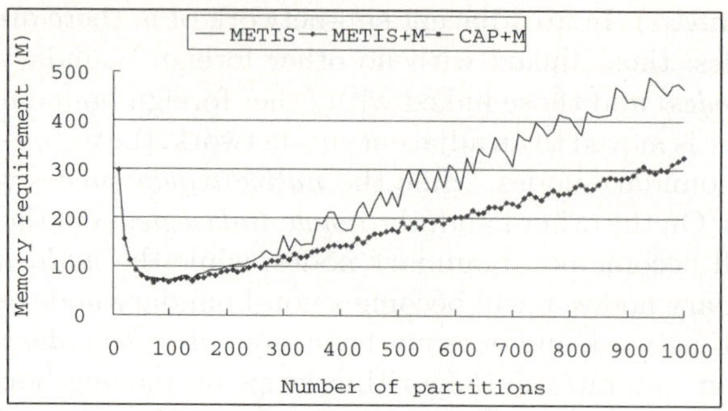

Fig. 6. Memory requirement with METIS

Table 1. The best results with METIS, SPC and CAP

Partition scheme	n_p	All-pair time(s)	n_p	Memory usage(M)
METIS	90	4.234	90	73.158
METIS+M	90	3.875	100	67.637
SPC	30	10.953	50	132.548
SPC+M	50	6.609	50	96.941
CAP	74	3.000	74	65.861
CAP+M	74	2.766	74	64.378

3.2 Time Comparison for One-One Shortest Path Computation

For one-one shortest path computation, our approach based on METIS+M
($n_p = 90$) and CAP+M was compared with direct application of Dijkstra's
algorithm. Figure 7 gives their average distance retrieval time, with the number
of queries ranging from 1 to 100. The computation time of our approach is at
the level of 10^{-3}s, much less than that of Dijkstra's algorithm, which indicates
the superiority of our approach. In addition, the distance time of CAP+M is less
than that of METIS+M, indicating the advantage of topographic knowledge in
partitions. Similarly, for the path retrieval time, Dijkstra's algorithm was much
worse than our approach, and CAP+M out-performed METIS+M again.

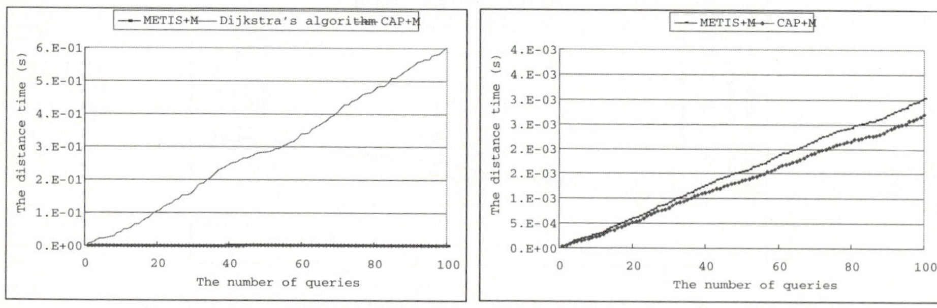

Fig. 7. Comparison of the path time

3.3   Time Comparison for Some-Some and All-All Shortest Path Computations

For some-some shortest path computation, we set the node pairs as 100-100, 200-200, 400-400, 600-600, 800-800, 1000-1000, 2000-2000, 4000-4000, 6000-6000, 8000-8000 and 10000-10000. The results of our approach with METIS+M and CAP+M are compared with those of the Dijkstra's algorithm in Table 2. The all-all results are given in Table 3. From Table 2 and 3, it is clear that the distance time of the Dijkstra's algorithm is more than that of our approach with METIS+M or CAP+M. Again, the distance time with CAP+M is less than METIS+M.

Further analysis of Table 2 and 3 reveals that, for n-n distance queries, the superiority of our approach decreases with the increasing of n. For example, the ratio of CAP+M time to the Dijkstra time increases from 3.76% to 65.90%. The underlining rationale is that each run of Dijkstra's algorithm always computes the shortest paths from a source node to all other nodes. Each 1-n query takes nearly the same time, regardless of the value of n. When n is small, most of the one-all shortest paths computed by the Dijkstra's algorithm are un-used and our approach with pre-computation is thus much more efficient. As n increases, the n-n Dijkstra time increases linearly with regard to n. For each 1-n query, our approach requires n 1-1 operations, if without optimization. By grouping queries with destination nodes in the same sub-network, we are able to improve our 1-n query processing. Even so, our retrieval time still increases much faster than the Dijkstra time. This explains why the time saving of pre-computation gradually decreases as n increases.

Table 2. Computation performance comparison for some-some shortest paths

Some-some	METIS+M(s)	CAP+M(s)	Dijkstra's algorithm(s)
100-100	0.093	0.047	1.250
200-200	0.235	0.187	2.500
400-400	0.734	0.500	4.969
600-600	1.281	0.922	7.453
800-800	1.891	1.406	10.000
1000-1000	2.578	1.969	12.406
2000-2000	6.969	5.453	24.781
4000-4000	19.969	15.797	49.031
6000-6000	38.328	30.453	73.532
8000-8000	62.375	49.828	98.094
10000-10000	92.078	72.843	122.485

Table 3. Computation performance comparison for all-all shortest paths

All-all	METIS+M(s)	CAP+M(s)	Dijkstra's algorithm(s)
13626-13626	137.14	110.813	168.141

4   Conclusion

In this paper, we developed an optimal shortest path algorithm, based on a two-level hierarchical network structure, to compute shortest paths in real road networks. Pre-computation was used to improve the time efficiency. We also proposed an algorithm to minimize the number of boundary nodes by relocating them between adjacent sub-networks. The experimental results on Hong Kong road network demonstrated the efficiency of our method and the usefulness of minimizing of the number of boundary nodes.

References

1. Ashok K. Goel, Todd J. Callantine, Murali Shankar, and B. Chandrasekaran. Representation, organization, and use of topographic models of physical spaces for route planning. In *Proc. the 7th IEEE Conference on Artificial Intelligence Applications*, pages 308–314. IEEE Computer Society Press, 1991. Miami Beach, Florida, February 1991.
2. Mayiz B. Habbal, Haris N. Koutsopoulos, and Steven R. Lerman. A decomposition algorithm for the all-pairs shortest path problem on massively parallel computer architectures. *Transportation Science*, 28(4):292–308, 1994.
3. G. R. Jagadeesh, T. Srikanthan, and K. H. Quek. Heuristic techniques for accelerating hierarchical routing on road networks. *IEEE Transactions on Intelligent Transportation Systems*, 3(4):301–309, 2002.
4. Ning Jing, Yun-Wu Huang, and Elke A. Rundensteiner. Hierarchical encoded path views for path query processing: An optimal model and its performance evaluation. *IEEE Transactions on Knowledge and Data Engineering*, 10(3):409–432, 1998.
5. Ning Jing, Yun-Wu Huang, and Elke A. Rundensteiner. Optimizing path query performance: Graph clustering strategies. *Transportation Research Part C*, 8(1-6):381–408, 2000.
6. Sungwon Jung and Sakti Pramanik. An efficient path computation model for hierarchically structured topographical road maps. *IEEE Transactions on Knowledge and Data Engineering*, 14(5):1029–1046, 2002.
7. George Karypis and Vipin Kumar. A fast and high quality multilevel scheme for partitioning irregular graphs. *University of Minnesota, Department of Computer Science/ Army HPC Research Center, Minneapolis, MN 55455 Technical Report No.95-035*, 1998.
8. George Karypis and Vipin Kumar. Multilevel algorithm for multi- constraint graph partitioning. *University of Minnesota, Department of Computer Science/ Army HPC Research Center, Minneapolis, MN 55455 Technical Report No.98-019*, 1998.
9. George Karypis and Vipin Kumar. Multilevel k-way partitioning scheme for irregular graphs. *University of Minnesota, Department of Computer Science/ Army HPC Research Center, Minneapolis, MN 55455 Technical Report No.95-064*, 1998.
10. Bing Liu. Route finding by using knowledge about the road network. *IEEE Transactions On Systems, Man, and Cybernetics-Part A: Systems and Humans*, 27(4):436–448, 1997.
11. Shashi Shekhar, Andrew Fetterer, and Brajesh Goyal. Materialization trade-offs in hierarchical shortest path algorithms. In *Proc. the 5th International Symposium on Advances in Spatial Databases*, pages 94–111, 1997.
12. F. Benjamin Zhan. Three fastest shortest path algorithms on real road networks: Data structures and procedures. *Journal of Geographic Information and Decision Analysis*, 1(1):69–82, 1997.
13. F. Benjamin Zhan and Charles E. Noon. Shortest path algorithms: An evaluation using real road networks. *Transportation Science*, 32(1):65–73, February 1998.

Automatic Topics Identification
for Reviewer Assignment

S. Ferilli, N. Di Mauro, T.M.A. Basile, F. Esposito, and M. Biba

Dipartimento di Informatica, University of Bari, Italy
{ferilli, ndm, basile, esposito, biba}@di.uniba.it

Abstract. Scientific conference management involves many complex and multi-faceted activities, which would make highly desirable for the organizing people to have a Web-based management system that makes some of them a little easier to carry out. One of such activities is the assignment of submitted papers to suitable reviewers, involving the authors, the reviewers and the conference chair. Authors that submit the papers usually must fill a form with paper title, abstract and a set of conference topics that fit their submission subject. Reviewers are required to register and declare their expertise on the conference topics (among other things). Finally, the conference chair has to carry out the review assignment taking into account the information provided by both the authors (about their paper) and the reviewers (about their competencies). Thus, all this subtasks needed for the assignment are currently carried out manually by the actors. While this can be just boring in the case of authors and reviewers, in case of conference chair the task is also very complex and time-consuming.

In this paper we propose the exploitation of intelligent techniques to automatically extract paper topics from their title and abstract, and the expertise of the reviewers from the titles of their publications available on the Internet. Successively, such a knowledge is exploited by an expert system able to automatically perform the assignments. The proposed methods were evaluated on a real conference dataset obtaining good results when compared to handmade ones, both in terms of quality and user-satisfaction of the assignments, and for reduction in execution time with respect to the case of humans performing the same process.

1   Introduction

Organizing scientific conferences is a complex and multi-faceted activity that often requires the use of a Web-based management system to make some tasks a little easier to carry out, such as the job of reviewing papers. Some of the features typically provided by these packages are: submission of abstracts and papers by Authors; submission of reviews by the Program Committee Members (PCMs); download of papers by the Program Committee (PC); handling of reviewers preferences and bidding; Web-based assignment of papers to PCMs for review; review progress tracking; Web-based PC meeting; notification of acceptance/rejection; sending e-mails for notifications. One of the hardest and most

M. Ali and R. Dapoigny (Eds.): IEA/AIE 2006, LNAI 4031, pp. 721–730, 2006.
© Springer-Verlag Berlin Heidelberg 2006

time-consuming tasks in Scientific Conferences organization is the process of assigning reviewers to submitted papers. Due to the many constraints to be fulfilled, carrying out manually such a task is very tedious and difficult, and does not guarantee to result in the best solution.

In the current practice, before the submission phase starts, the Chair usually sets up a list of research topics of interest for the conference, and all reviewers are asked to specify which of them correspond to their main areas of expertise. On the other hand, during the submission process, authors are asked to explicitly state which conference topics apply to their papers. Such an information provides a first guideline for associating reviewers to papers. One possible source of problems, in the above procedure, lies in the topics selected by the authors being sometimes misleading with respect to the real topic of the paper. For this reason, in order to make the assignment more objective, it would be desirable to automatically infer the paper topics rather than asking the authors to explicitly provide such an information.

While the topics selected by (or inferred for) a reviewer refer to his background competencies, in some cases the reviewers could have specific preferences about papers due to matter of taste or to other vague questions (e.g., the reviewer would like to review a paper just for curiosity; the abstract is imprecise or misleading, etc.). For this reason, the bidding preferences approach is sometimes preferred over the expertise one. We take into account both, but give priority to the one based on the reviewer expertise, assuming that if a paper bid by a reviewer does not match his topics of expertise, this should be considered as a warning. To this concerns, a small pattern language has been defined in the literature that captures successful practice in several conference review processes [8]. In this work two patterns are followed, indicating that papers should be matched, and assigned for evaluation, to reviewers who are competent in the specific paper topics (*ExpertsReviewPapers*), and to reviewers who declared to be willing to review those papers in the bidding phase (*ChampionsReviewPapers*).

This work aims at showing how this complex real-world domain can take advantage of intelligent techniques for indexing and retrieving documents and their associated topics. Specifically, it describes an intelligent component developed to be embedded in scientific Conference Management Systems that is able to automatically:

- identify paper topics, among those of interest for the conference, by exploiting the paper title and abstract;
- identify reviewers expertise, among the conference topics, by exploiting the title of the reviewers publications available in the Internet;
- assign reviewers to papers submitted to a conference.

The identification of paper topics and reviewers expertise is performed starting from the output of an automatic system for document analysis and then exploiting NLP methods for automatically extracting significant topics. Then, the assignment process is performed by an expert system that takes as input this information. Thus, the methods that we propose aim at exploiting intelligent techniques in the *ExpertsReviewPapers* pattern, that so far was applicable only if some steps were manually performed by the users.

2   Reviewers Assignment: The General Framework

In order to perform the assignment, the Chair needs to know both the conference topics selected for each submitted paper and the topics that better describe the reviewers expertise. In the following we show how it is possible to automatically acquire such a knowledge by means of the *Latent Semantic Indexing* (LSI) technique. As regards the papers, a system for the automatic processing of the submitted documents will be presented. It will be exploited in order to automatically extract the significant components, i.e. title and abstract, from the paper without the author do it manually. As concern the reviewers, the information needed from the application of the LSI was extracted from the online repository of their publications (at the moment this task is carried out manually). Successively, an expert system that automatically performs the assignments based on the extracted knowledge about the papers/reviwers topics will be presented.

2.1   Latent Semantic Indexing

A problem of most existing word-based retrieval systems consists of their ineffectiveness in finding interesting documents when the users do not use the same words by which the information they seek has been indexed. This is due to a number of tricky features that are typical of natural language. One of the most common concerns the fact that there are many ways (words) to express a given concept (*synonymy*), and hence the terms in a user's query might not match those of a document even if it could be very interesting for him. Another one is that many words have multiple meanings (*polysemy*), so that terms in a user's query will literally match terms in documents that are not semantically interesting to the user.

The LSI technique [3] tries to overcome the weaknesses of term-matching based retrieval by treating the unreliability of observed term-document association data as a statistical problem. Indeed, LSI assumes that there exists some underlying latent semantic structure in the data that is partially obscured by the randomness of word choice with respect to the retrieval phase and that can be estimated by means of statistical techniques. LSI relies on a mathematical technique called *Singular-Value Decomposition* (SVD). Starting from a (large and usually sparse) matrix of term-document association data, the SVD allows to build and arrange a semantic space, where terms and documents that are closely associated are placed near to each other, in such a way to reflect the major associative patterns in the data, and ignore the smaller, less important influences. As a result, terms that do not actually appear in a document may still end up close to it, if this is consistent with the major association patterns in the data. Position in the space thus serves as a new kind of semantic indexing, and retrieval proceeds by using the terms in a query to identify a point in the space, and returning to the user documents in its neighbourhood. It is possible to specify a reduction parameter that intuitively represents the number of different concepts to be taken into account, among which distributing the available terms and documents.

The large amount of items that a document management system has to deal with, and the continuous flow of new documents that could be added to the initial database, require an incremental methodology to update the initial LSI matrix. Indeed, applying from scratch at each update the LSI method, taking into account both the old (already analysed) and the new documents, would become computationally inefficient. Two techniques have been developed in the literature to update (i.e., add new terms and/or documents to) an existing LSI generated database: Folding-In [1] and SVD-Updating [9]. The former is a much simpler alternative that uses the existing SVD to represent new information but yields poor-quality updated matrices, since the information contained in the new documents/terms is not exploited by the updated semantic space. The latter represents a trade-off between the former and the recomputation from scratch.

2.2 The Document Management System

This section presents the current version of **DOMINUS** (DOcument Management INtelligent Universal System) [5], a system for automated electronic documents processing characterized by the intensive exploitation of intelligent techniques in each step of the document management process: acquisition, layout analysis, document image understanding, indexing, for categorization and information retrieval purposes. It can deal with documents in standard formats, such as PostScript (PS) or its evolution Portable Document Format (PDF).

The layout analysis process on documents in electronic format, sketched in Figure 1, is now reported along with the steps performed by the system going from the original PDF/PS document to the text extraction and indexing.

1. WINE: Rewrites basic PostScript operators to turn their drawing instructions into objects. It takes as input a PDF/PS document and produces (by an intermediate vector format) the initial document's XML basic representation, that describes it as a set of pages made up of basic blocks.
2. Rewriting rules: Identifies rewriting rules that could suggest how to set some parameters in order to group together rectangles (words) to obtain lines. Specifically, such a learning task was cast to a Multiple Instance Problem (MIP) and solved by exploiting the kernel-based method proposed in [4].
3. DOC: Collects semantically related basic blocks into groups by identifying frames that surround them based on whitespace and background structure analysis. This is a variant of Breuel's algorithm [2], that finds iteratively the maximal white rectangles in a page. The modification consisted in a bottom-up grouping of basic blocks into words and lines and in the empirical identification of a stop criterion to end the process before finding insignificant white spaces such as inter-word or inter-line ones.
4. Layout Correction: At the end of the previous step it could be possible that some blocks are not correctly recognized, i.e. background areas are considered

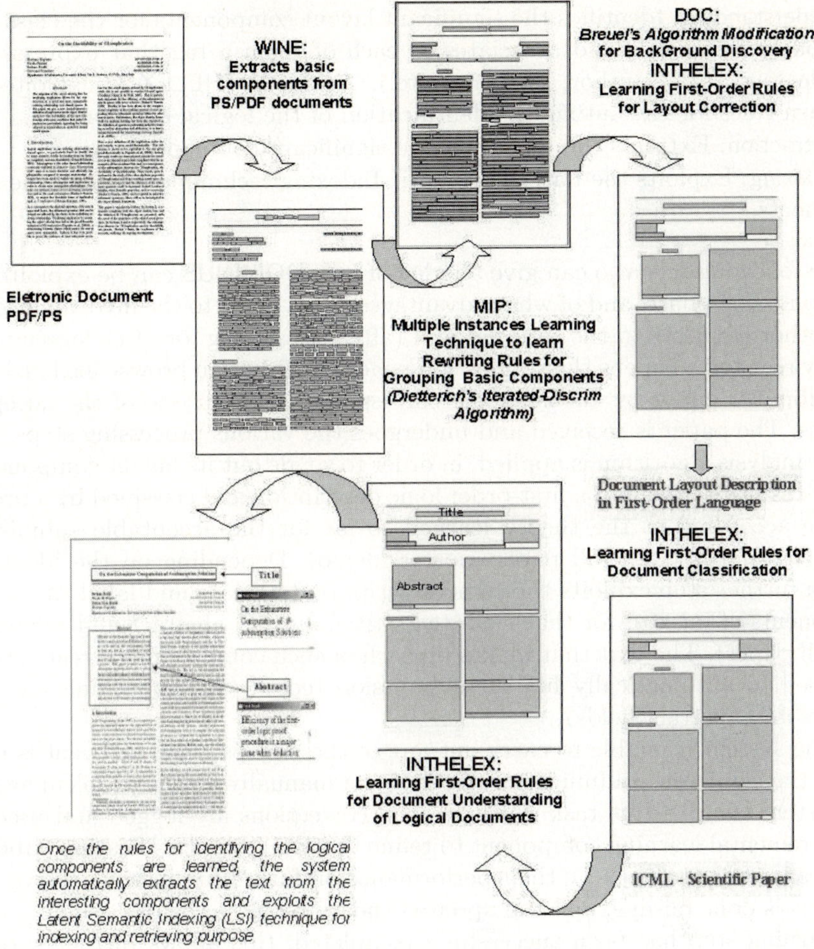

Fig. 1. Document Management System

content ones and vice versa. In such a case a phase of layout correction is needed, that is automatically performed in DOC by applying embedded rules automatically learned for this task. To this purpose, we firstly collect the manual corrections performed on some documents and describe them by means of a first-order language representing both the situations *before* and *after* the manual correction, then we exploit INTHELEX [6] (a first-order logic learner) on this training set in order to identify correction rules.

5. Classification: Associates the document to a class that expresses its type (e.g., scientific/newspaper article, etc.). Since the logical structure is obviously different according to the kind of document, classification of the document is a preliminary step before recognizing the relevant components for that document (e.g., a sender is significant for a mail but non for a newspaper article). INTHELEX is also exploited to learn rules for the automatic identification of the class.

6. **Understanding:** Identifies the significant layout components for the class previously recognized and associates to each of them a tag that expresses its role (e.g., title, author, abstract, etc.). Again, INTHELEX is exploited to learn rules for the automatic identification of the logical components.
7. **Extraction:** Extracts the text from the significant components.
8. **Indexing:** Exploits the Latent Semantic Indexing technique to index the documents.

The following scenario can give an idea of how DOMINUS can be exploited in the submission phase, and of what advantages it can bring to the involved people. An Author connects to the Internet and (after registering, or after logging in if already registered) opens the submission page, where he can browse his hard disk and submit a paper by choosing the corresponding file in one of the accepted formats. The paper is received and undergoes the various processing steps. The layout analysis algorithm is applied, in order to single out its layout components. Then, it is translated into a first-order logic description and classified by a proper module according to the theory learned so far for the acceptable submission layout standards (e.g., full paper, poster, demo). Depending on the identified class, a further step exploits the same description to locate and label the layout components of interest for that class (e.g., title, author, abstract and references in a full paper). The text that makes up each of such components is read, stored and used to automatically file the submission record (e.g., by filling its title, authors and abstract fields).

If the system is unable to carry out any of these steps, such an event is notified to the Conference administrators, that can manually fix the problem and let the system complete its task. Such manual corrections are logged and used by the incremental learning component to refine the available classification/labeling theories in order to improve their performance on future submissions. Nevertheless, this is done off-line, and the updated theory replaces the old one only after the learning step has been successfully completed: this allows further submissions to take place in the meantime, and makes the refinement step transparent to the Authors. Alternatively, the fixes can be logged and exploited all at once to refine the theory when its performance falls below a given threshold. Successively a categorization of the paper content according to the text read is performed, with the purpose of allowing to match the paper topics against the reviewers' expertise, in order to find the best associations for the final assignment. Specifically, the text contained in the title and abstract is exploited, since we assume they compactly summarize the subject and research field the paper is concerned with, respectively.

2.3   The Papers-Reviewers Assignment Phase

GRAPE (Global Review Assignment Processing Engine) [7], is an expert system, written in CLIPS, for solving the reviewers assignment problem, that takes advantage of both the papers content (topics) and the reviewers expertise and preferences (biddings). It could be used by exploiting, in addition to the papers topics, the reviewers expertise only, or both the reviewers expertise and biddings. In the following a brief description of the system is given.

Let $P = \{p_1, \ldots, p_n\}$ denote the set of n papers submitted to the conference C, regarding t topics (*conference topics*, TC), and $R = \{r_1, \ldots, r_m\}$ the set of m reviewers. The goal is to assign the papers to reviewers, such that the following basic constraints are fulfilled:

1. each paper is assigned to exactly k reviewers (usually, k is set to 3 or 4);
2. each reviewer should have roughly the same number of papers to review (the mean number of reviews per reviewer is equal to nk/m);
3. papers should be reviewed by domain experts;
4. reviewers should revise articles based on their expertise and preferences.

As regards constraint 2, **GRAPE** can take as input additional constraints indicating that some specific reviewer r must review at most h paper. These constraints override the general principle and must be taken into account for calculating the mean number of reviews for the other reviewers.

Two measures were defined to guide the system during the search of the best solutions: the *reviewer's gratification* and the *article's coverage*. The former represents the gratification degree of a reviewer, calculated on the basis of the papers assigned to him. It is based on the *confidence degree* between the reviewer and the assigned articles (the confidence degree between a paper p_i concerning topics Tp_i and the reviewer r_j expert in topics Tr_j is defined as the number of topics in common) and on the number of assigned papers that were actually bid by the reviewer. The article's coverage represents the coverage degree of an article after the assignments. It is based on the *confidence degree* between the article and the reviewers it was assigned to (the same as before), and the *expertise degree* of the assigned reviewers (represented by the number of topics in which they are expert, and computed for a reviewer r_j as Tr_j/TC). **GRAPE** tries to maximize both measures during the assignment process, in order to fulfil the basic constraints 3 and 4. To reach this goal a fundamental requirement is that each reviewer must provide at least one topic of preference, otherwise the article coverage degree would be always null.

The assignment process is carried out in two phases. In the former, the system progressively assigns reviewers to papers with the lowest number of candidate reviewers. At the same time, the system *prefers* assigning papers to reviewers with few assignments. In this way, it avoids to have reviewers with zero or few assigned papers. Hence, this phase can be viewed as a search for review assignments by keeping low the average number of reviews *per* reviewer and maximizing the coverage degree of the papers. In the latter phase, the remaining assignments are chosen by considering first the confidence levels and then the expertise level of the reviewers. In particular, given a paper p_i which has not been assigned k reviewers yet, the system tries to assign it to a reviewer r_j with a high confidence level between r_j and p_i. In case it is not possible, it assigns a reviewer with a high level of expertise.

The assignments resulting from the base process are presented to each reviewer, that receives the list A of the h assigned papers, followed by the list A' of the remaining ones, in order to actually issue his bidding. When all the reviewers have bid their papers, GRAPE searches for a new solution that takes into account these biddings as well, in addition to the information about expertise. In particular, it tries to change previous assignments in order to maximize both article's coverage and reviewer's gratification. By taking the article's coverage high, the system tries to assign the same number of papers bid with the same class to each reviewer. Then, the solution is presented to the reviewers as the final one.

The main advantage of GRAPE relies in the fact that it is a rule-based system. Hence, it is very easy to add new rules in order to change/improve its behavior, and it is possible to describe background knowledge, such as further constraints or conflicts, in a natural way. For example, one could insert a rule expressing the preference to assign a reviewer to the articles in which he is cited, assuming that he should be an expert in those fields.

3   Evaluation

The system was evaluated on a real-world dataset built by using data from the 18th Conference on Industrial & Engineering Applications of Artificial Intelligence & Expert Systems (IEA/AIE 2005), whose Call for Papers identified 34 topics of interest. The papers submitted were 264 and the reviewers 60. Since the objective was to assess the performance of the automatic topic recognition methodology, in this case only the reviewers' expertise, and not their bidding were exploited by the paper assignment system.

The following steps were carried out. Firstly, the layout of each paper was automatically analyzed in order to recognize the significant components. In particular, the abstract and title were considered the most representative of the document subject, and hence the corresponding text was read. The words contained therein were stemmed according to the technique proposed by Porter [10], resulting in a total of 2832 word stems, on which the LSI technique was applied in order to index the whole set of documents. Then, the same procedure was applied to index the reviewers, resulting in 2204 stems. In this case, the titles of their papers appearing in the DBLP Computer Science Bibliography repository (http://www.informatik.uni-trier.de/~ley/db/) were exploited. With respect to exploiting their homepages' information on research interests, this ensured a more uniform description. Compared to manually selecting the title of their publications, this ensured more completeness, even if at the cost of not having the abstracts available as well.

In both cases, the LSI parameters were set in such a way that all the conference topics were covered as different concepts. The experiment consisted in performing 34 queries, each corresponding to one conference topic, on both the papers and the reviewers in the database previously indexed, and then in associating to each paper/reviewer the topics for which it/he appears among the first l results. Specifically, the results on document topic recognition showed that 88 documents per query had to be considered, in order to include the whole set of documents. However, returning just 30 documents per query, 257 out of 264 documents (97.3%) were already assigned to at least one topic, which is an acceptable trade-off (the remaining 7 documents can be easily assigned by hand). Thus, 30 documents were considered a good parameter, and exploited to count the distribution of the topics between the documents. Interestingly, more than half of the documents (54.7%) concern between 2 and 4 topics, which could be expected both for the current interest of the researchers in mixing together different research areas and for the nature of the topics, that are not completely disjoint (some are specializations of others). Evaluated by the conference organizers, the result showed a 79% accuracy on average. As to the reviewers, even if taking $l = 6$ already ensured at least one topic for each of them, we adopted a more cautious approach and took $l = 10$, in order to balance the possible inaccuracy due to considering only the titles of their publications. The resulting accuracy was 65%.

Lastly, the topics automatically associated to papers and reviewers were fed to GRAPE in order to perform the associations, with the requirement to assign each paper to 2 reviewers. In order to have an insight on the quality of the results, in the following we present some interesting figures concerning GRAPE's outcome. In solving the problem, the system was able to complete its task in 120 seconds. GRAPE was always able to assign papers to reviewers by considering the topics only, except in two cases. In particular, except for those reviewers that explicitly asked to review less than 10 papers (*MaxReviewsPerReviewer* constraint), it assigned 10 papers to 40 reviewers, 9 to 2 reviewers, 8 to 3 reviewers, 7 and 6 to one reviewer. The experts considered the final associations made by GRAPE very helpful, since they would have changed just 7% of them.

4   Conclusions and Future Works

This paper proposed the application of intelligent techniques as a support to the various phases required for making automatic the task of paper-reviewer assignment in a scientific conference management. Experiments on a real domain prove the viability of the proposed approach.

Different future work directions are planned for the proposed system. First, the conference management system will be extended to cover other knowledge-intensive tasks currently in charge of the organizers, such as final presentations partition and scheduling according to the paper subject. Second, the automatic processing of the bibliographic references of the papers and of the publications of the reviewers will be faced. Furthermore, we plan to process the reviewers home page to discover all the information needed for their registrations in order to automatically fill in all the fields in the registration form (i.e., affiliation, research interests, etc.). Then, in a more general perspective, the proposed techniques will be applied to the problem of matching the documents in a digital library to the interests of the library users. The use of ontologies for improving matching effectiveness will be investigated as well.

References

1. Michael W. Berry, Susan T. Dumais, and Gavin W. O'Brien. Using linear algebra for intelligent information retrieval. *SIAM Rev.*, 37(4):573–595, 1995.
2. Thomas M. Breuel. Two geometric algorithms for layout analysis. In *Workshop on Document Analysis Systems*, 2002.
3. Scott C. Deerwester, Susan T. Dumais, Thomas K. Landauer, George W. Furnas, and Richard A. Harshman. Indexing by latent semantic analysis. *Journal of the American Society of Information Science*, 41(6):391–407, 1990.
4. Thomas G. Dietterich, Richard H. Lathrop, and Tomas Lozano-Perez. Solving the multiple instance problem with axis-parallel rectangles. *Artificial Intelligence*, 89(1-2):31–71, 1997.
5. Floriana Esposito, Stefano Ferilli, Teresa Maria Altomare Basile, and Nicola Di Mauro. Semantic-based access to digital document databases. In *Foundations of Intelligent Systems, 15th International Symposium (ISMIS 2005)*, volume 3488 of *Lecture Notes in Computer Science*, pages 373–381. Springer Verlag, 2005.
6. Floriana Esposito, Stefano Ferilli, Nicola Fanizzi, Teresa M.A. Basile, and Nicola Di Mauro. Incremental multistrategy learning for document processing. *Applied Artificial Intelligence: An Internationa Journal*, 17(8/9):859–883, September-October 2003.
7. Nicola Di Mauro, Teresa Maria Altomare Basile, and Stefano Ferilli. Grape: An expert review assignment component for scientific conference management systems. In *Innovations in Applied Artificial Intelligence: 18th International Conference on Industrial and Engineering Applications of Artificial Intelligence and Expert Systems (IEA/AIE 2005)*, volume 3533 of *Lecture Notes in Computer Science*, pages 789–798. Springer Verlag, 2005.
8. Oscar Nierstrasz. Identify the champion. In N. Harrison, B. Foote, and H. Rohnert, editors, *Pattern Languages of Program Design*, volume 4, pages 539–556. Addison Wesley, 2000.
9. Gavin W. O'Brien. Information management tools for updating an SVD-encoded indexing scheme. Technical Report UT-CS-94-258, University of Tennessee, 1994.
10. Martin F. Porter. An algorithm for suffix stripping. In J. S. Karen and P. Willet, editors, *Readings in information retrieval*, pages 313–316. Morgan Kaufmann Publishers Inc., San Francisco, CA, USA, 1997.

A Decentralized Calendar System Featuring Sharing, Trusting and Negotiating

Yves Demazeau, Dimitri Melaye, and Marie-Hélène Verrons

Équipe MAGMA, Laboratoire Leibniz-Imag – CNRS UMR 5522
INPG, 38031 GRENOBLE, France
{demazeau, melaye, verrons}@imag.fr

Abstract. This article presents a *decentralized* calendar system benefiting from the use of computational *trust*. In our system, each user is
represented by an agent in charge of the *scheduling* of events, either tasks
or meetings. Each event is characterized by two attributes: *importance*
and *urgency*. These notions are subjective: each agent has its own priorities and its own view of what is important and urgent. Timetables can
be *shared* with other agents according to the groups of the agents, thus
facilitating the scheduling of a meeting within a group. Nevertheless,
timetables do not have to be shared. So we introduce trust to support
this absence of information. These mechanisms use a generic trust model
permitting the calculation of trust from several sources. We stress on the
importance of the different sources for the emergence of *trust groups*.
When trust is not given between all participants in a meeting, *negotiation* is used to find a possible date.

1   Introduction

The expansion of distributed systems highlights new need: need to act in an
open dynamic unpredictable environment, need to guarantee security and need
to provide the best services for other services and users. In this paper, we are
interested in such a system: a decentralized calendar. Each user is represented
by an agent that is delegated to two tasks: the negotiation of meetings and the
sharing of the events of its calendar with the other agents of the system.

When calendars are shared between agents, finding a date for a meeting consists of solving a constraint satisfaction problem (CSP). But sharing its calendar
is not usually accepted. That's why we introduce the notion of trust to elicitate
the agents that will have access to one's calendar. If all participants of the meeting trust each other, the sharing of their calendars poses no problem and we go
back to a CSP. In the other case, we need a negotiation mechanism to find a
suitable date for each agent.

In a first section, we present our decentralized calendar. We are interested in
the addition of an event, especially an individual task, that takes into account
two notions: the importance and the urgency of the event. In a second section, we
discuss of the sharing of the calendars within groups that organize the agents of
the system. Then, we focalize on trust between agents in a third section. We show
how a trust model based on several trust sources can help the agent to manage

M. Ali and R. Dapoigny (Eds.): IEA/AIE 2006, LNAI 4031, pp. 731–740, 2006.

its calendar. The fourth section presents the negotiation model used to schedule meetings and the strategy used to negotiate them, and a discussion about the use of trust for negotiating meetings is made. The fifth section concludes the paper.

2   Decentralized Calendars

In this section we present the general architecture of the calendar system. We then concentrate on the addition of an event in the calendar according to its importance ans its urgency.

2.1   Architecture

The architecture of the calendar corresponds to a classic decentralised system. As Figure 1 illustrates it, each user is represented by an agent delegated to the management of calendar.

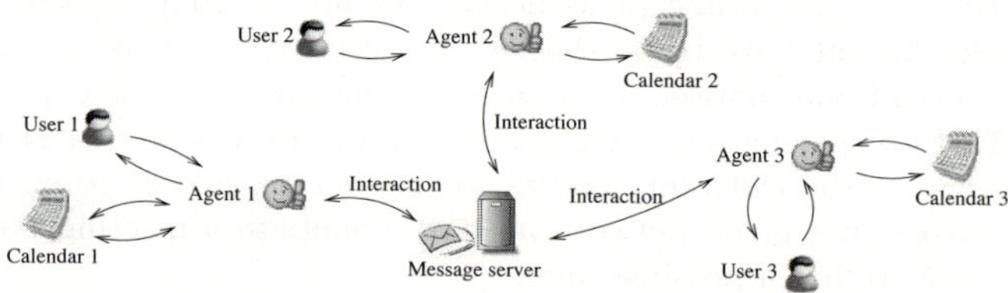

Fig. 1. Architecture of the decentralized calendar system

The calendar of an agent is stored locally in order to guarantee its privacy. The interactions are supported by a message server in charge of the transmission of the messages from an agent to one or several other agents. The server knows all agents by a directory. On the contrary, an agent does not know all agents necessarily. It can address the agents it knows directly, and it might interact with other through groups by broadcasting. In the subsection 3.1, we will precise this notion of group.

2.2   Addition of an Event

This section deals with the addition of an event in the calendar of an agent. An event is either a task or a meeting: a task is an individual event (that is to say an event involving no other participant), whereas a meeting is an event which requires the agreements of the participants. In both cases, the addition of the event is based on its importance and its urgency.

Importance and urgency. We ground our work on Covey's works [2] to organize the events of a calendar according to their priority. The idea is to consider the priority of an event according to two dimensions: its importance and its urgency. By default the importance is given greater place than urgency: Table 1

Table 1. Priorities by default according to the importance and the urgency

	High urgency	Low urgency
High importance	I	II
Low importance	III	IV

shows that an important and non-urgent event has priority over a non-important and urgent. However, the order of priority between importance and urgency is subjective. For example, an agent may prefer to schedule its urgent events before its important events. To simplify, in the remainder of this article, we assume that the priorities of the agents are the priorities by default (Table 1). Importance and urgency are two common scales used by all agents. Nevertheless, the vision of what is urgent and important is subjective and is not the same one for every agents. For instance, if an agent asks an urgent meeting, maybe it can appear not urgent for the others.

Formalization. We define an event as a product of six attributes: the agents participating to the event, the type of event, the importance of the event, the urgency of the event, the start date and the final date. These attributes correspond to the classic data of an event, except for the importance and the urgency which are specific to our system.

Let $\mathcal{A}$ be the set of the registered agents in the system. Let $\alpha \in \mathcal{A}$ be an agent. To simplify the notations, when it is not necessary, we do not specify in the remainder of this article that the objects are relating to a calendar of an agent α. Let the finite set $\mathcal{T}$ be the possible types of an event, and the infinite set $Date$ be the set of the possible dates. We do not define more precisely $Date$: for instance it could be the product of a year, a month, a day and an hour. Just we assume that the range of possible dates is infinite, countable (discretization of time by hour for example) and ordered by the relation $\leq_{time}$.

Let $\mathcal{E}$ be the set of the possible events. Let $\mathcal{E}^\alpha$ be the set of the events of α's calendar. Let $e_{A,t,i,u,d_1,d_2} \in \mathcal{E}^\alpha$ be an event of α's calendar where $A \in \mathcal{P}(\mathcal{A})$ is the set of the agents participating to the event, $t \in \mathcal{T}$ is the type of the event, $i \in \{0,1\}$ is the importance of the event (0 for low importance, 1 for high importance), $u \in \{0,1\}$ is the urgency of the event (0 for low urgency, 1 for high urgency), d_1 and $d_2 \in Date$ are the start date and the final date of the event. We equip $\mathcal{E}^\alpha$ with an order relation $\leq_e$ defined as $e_{A,t,i,u,d_1,d_2} \leq_e e'_{A',t,i',u',d'_1,d'_2}$ iff $d_1 \leq_{time} d'_1$.

Addition of a task. The organization of the events is based on their priority: a high priority event must be scheduled before a low priority event. The priority of an event is calculated according to its importance and its urgency. Indeed, it is easy to schedule the tasks systematically according to their priority, since it depends only on the importance and the urgency specified by the user. Formally, we define the following subset as the set of the tasks $\mathcal{T}^\alpha = \{e_{A,t,i,u,d_1,d_2} \in \mathcal{E}^\alpha \mid A = \emptyset\}$. Then, we define four sets corresponding to the four priorities described in Table 1: $T^\alpha_{0,0} = \{e_{A,t,i,u,d_1,d_2} \in \mathcal{T}^\alpha \mid i = 0, u = 0\}$,

$T_{0,1}^\alpha = \{e_{A,t,i,u,d_1,d_2} \in \mathcal{T}^\alpha \mid i = 0, u = 1\}$, $T_{1,0}^\alpha = \{e_{A,t,i,u,d_1,d_2} \in \mathcal{T}^\alpha \mid i = 1, u = 0\}$, and $T_{1,1}^\alpha = \{e_{A,t,i,u,d_1,d_2} \in \mathcal{T}^\alpha \mid i = 1, u = 1\}$. In the remainder of this article, we assume that the following constraint is supported: a more priority task cannot be scheduled after a less priority task. Formally, we have:

$$\forall i_1, j_1, i_2, j_2 \in \{0, 1\}, \text{ such that } i_1 + j_1 \leq i_2 + j_2 \text{ or } i_1 \leq i_2,$$
$$\forall e_1 \in T_{i_1,j_1}^\alpha, \forall e_2 \in T_{i_2,j_2}^\alpha, e_1 \leq_e e_2 \quad (1)$$

The user is responsible of the addition of a task by defining its attributes. The system checks that this task is scheduled after the tasks having a higher priority, that is to say that the constraint (1) is fulfilled. If it does not, the system can propose a solution (by changing the start date or by moving some event). We do not detail this mechanism that extends beyond the scope of this paper. When the task is added to the calendar, the sets $\mathcal{T}^\alpha, T_{0,0}^\alpha, T_{0,1}^\alpha, T_{1,0}^\alpha, T_{1,1}^\alpha$, are updated.

It is not so easy for the meetings, since their scheduling is a compromise solution depending on the other participants: a meeting may not correspond to the preferences of the user. In the next sections, we will show how the meetings can be scheduled according to sharing, trusting and negotiating.

3   Sharing Timetables

When timetables are shared, the meetings can be scheduled by well-known CSP. In this section we present the mechanism of knowledge sharing. This mechanism is based on the type of the event to share and on the groups of the agent.

3.1   Groups

In our system, the agents are organized according to groups. A group corresponds to a social structure, i.e. an arrangement of agents in defined relationships [10; 9]. Each agent belongs to at least one group. It is aware of it, and knows all other users in this group. When it knows another group, then it can interact with the agents of this group. Formally, let $\mathcal{A}$ be the set of the agents of the system, let $\mathcal{G}$ be the set of the groups registered in the system. We define $g \in \mathcal{G}$ as a set of agents registered in g.

We equip $\mathcal{G}$ with a non-total order relation leq_g. The order is pre-defined and is defined as a relation of subsumation between the social groups. In Figure 2, we instance an order with several different groups: on the one hand, one research institute is composed of its laboratories, the laboratories are composed of research teams; on the other hand, a family is composed of several family cells. Let us note that an agent can belong to several groups.

For the coherence of the system, if an agent belongs to a social group, then also it belongs to the including social group. For example, in Figure 2, if my agent belongs to the group "My team" and to the group "My family cell", it can interact with another member of "My family' or of "My research institute". Formally, we support the following constraint: $\forall a \in \mathcal{A}, (\exists h, g \in \mathcal{G} \text{ such that } h \leq_g g, a \in h) \Rightarrow a \in g$.

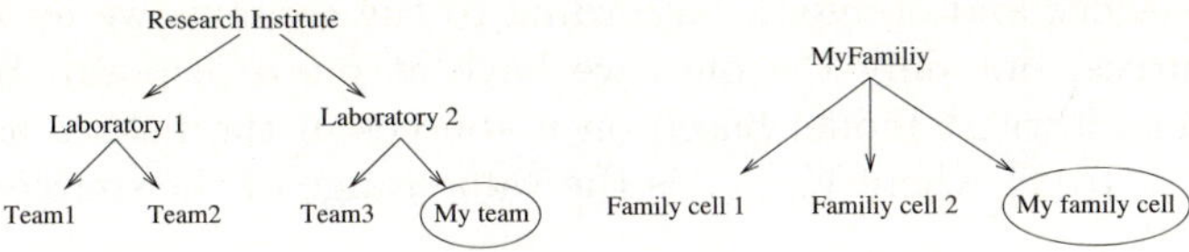

Fig. 2. Instance of a set of groups

3.2   Sharing and Groups

Knowledge can be shared with some agents. So an agent should be able to determine with which agents to share each event of its calendar. Formally, we define a function of sharing $shareAgent^\alpha : \mathcal{E}^\alpha \times \mathcal{A} \to \{0,1\}$. This function determines if an event is shared with a given agent. If $\forall a \in \mathcal{A}, shareAgent\alpha(e, a) = 0$, then the event e is private. If $\forall a \in \mathcal{A}, shareAgent\alpha(e, a) = 1$, then the event e is public. The interesting point is the case where the events can be shared with some agents, but not all. In accordance with this comment, in a first approach, knowledge can be shared according to groups. Formally, we define the function $shareGroup$ that associates a group and a type of event with a sharing binary value: $shareGroup : \mathcal{G} \times \mathcal{T} \to \{0,1\}$. The sharing value for an agent β can be calculated by combining the values of $shareGroup^\alpha$ for all groups of β (since an agent can belong to several groups). Inspired by [6], this combination can be optimistic or pessimistic, that is to say a (negative) positive sharing value is sufficient to have a (no) sharing of the event. Formally, we have: $shareAgent^\alpha(e_{A,t,i,u,d_1,d_2}, \beta) = Min_{g\in\mathcal{G} \; such \; that \; \beta\in g} shareGroup(g,t)$ or $shareAgent^\alpha(e_{A,t,i,u,d_1,d_2}, \beta) = Max_{g\in\mathcal{G} \; such \; that \; \beta\in g} shareGroup(g,t)$.

4   Trust in Agents

In this section, we show how trust can help an agent to go beyond a sharing based only on predefined groups. It can compensate the absence of information due to no sharing.

4.1   Trust Model

Trust is initially regarded as a central mechanism of coordination in situation of ignorance and a mechanism of social integration. We consider trust as a belief concerning an action to expect from another, in connection with something in a precise field or context. It is a hypothesis about a future behaviour and refers to a possibility of the realization of other's action. Our aim is to regard trust as a cognitive process and to take into account some of its dynamic aspects. A lot of trust models have been developed [11]. Their common point is that they can be viewed as a decision process. They are based on sources of trust and come to a binary trust act for a given field. At least four sources of trust can be distinguished: direct experience (personal experience of the trustier), categorization (properties of a more general category), reasoning and reputation (other's experience and opinion). According to the context, we have not to use all belief sources, but only the ones we have at one's disposal. Formally, we consider a generic trust model based on n sources in the field ω as a function $T_\omega : V_{Source}^n \rightarrow \{0, 1\}$ where V_{source} is the value range of the sources.

4.2 Sharing with Trust

In section 3.2, we have shown that an agent α determines the sharing of its calendar by calculating the function $shareAgent^\alpha : \mathcal{E}^\alpha \times \mathcal{A} \rightarrow \{0, 1\}$. We have proposed a way to calculate this function by associating the groups with a sharing value. However, it takes into account only general common sense rules about groups and is static. We propose to introduce trust to take into account user's preferences.

We instance a trust model in an agent based on two sources of trust: the individual interaction corresponding to an user's individual evaluation (the user gives a binary note to other users [3]) and the categorization source [1] corresponding to a general property of a group (for example, not sharing the private events with the research team's members). The trust model gives a trust function of an agent α in an agent about the sharing of α's event of a given type: $T_s^\alpha : \mathcal{T} \times \mathcal{A} \rightarrow \{0, 1\}$. We use this function to calculate α's sharing value of an event with an agent β: $shareAgent(e_{A,t,i,u,d_1,d_2}, \beta) = T_s^\alpha(t, \beta)$.

5 Negotiating Meetings

When the agents do not share their timetables (either they do not share according to the groups, or they do not trust each other), a negotiation system is necessary to take the meetings. In this section, we present the negotiation model and the strategy used to schedule meetings.

5.1 The Negotiation System

Organizing meetings is an activity where there are typically many negotiations. As a matter of fact, finding a date that fits everyone is difficult if calendars are kept private to their owners. For this application of calendar system, we need a negotiation framework that preserves users privacy by not sharing the calendars, allows negotiations between one and several agents, enables agents to retract themselves from a meeting previously taken and renegotiates automatically this meeting, and obviously lets us define our strategy to negotiate meetings. That's why we use *GeNCA* [7], a general negotiation API that has all the desired features. *GeNCA* has a three-level architecture that separates the communication level, the negotiation level and the strategic level of an application. This allows us to plug it in our application and define our negotiation strategies for meeting scheduling.

The negotiation level of *GeNCA* consists of a general negotiation protocol and a management of the agent's negotiations. The protocol allows an agent to propose contracts (here meetings) to other agents and to ask them counter offers in order to propose a new contract better fitting everyone. Several rounds of proposal and counter-proposals are possible and when a contract is confirmed, agents can retract themselves if the meeting is not possible any longer. In this case, the meeting is immediately negotiated again. The management system allows an agent to negotiate several meetings simultaneously and to negotiate sequencially meetings for the same date.

The strategic level is responsible for defining how meetings are to be negotiated. To help users define their strategies, *GeNCA* proposes to sort participants and resources (here time-slots) in order of preference (or importance) for each agent. So, when there is a conflict between two meetings, the agent can choose for example the one proposed by the most important person.

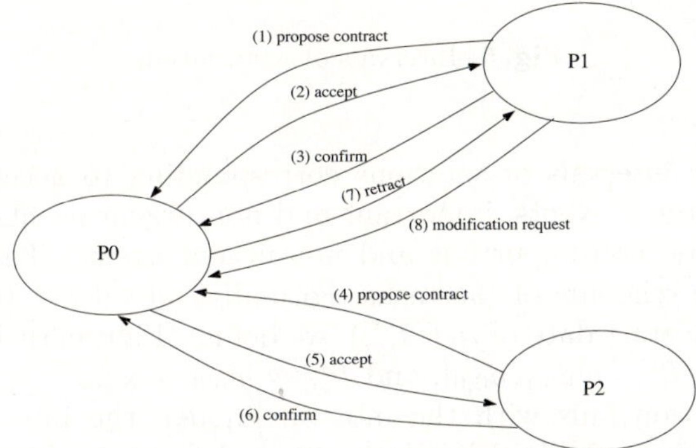

Fig. 3. A possible scenario of meeting negotiations

Figure 3 shows a possible scenario of negotiations of meetings between P_0, P_1 and P_2. In this example, P_0 thinks that P_2 is more important than P_1. First, P_1 proposes a meeting to P_0 who accepts. P_1 is the initiator and P_0 the participant. P_1 creates the contract (meeting) and sends P_0 the message *propose contract*. P_0 receives the contract, analyses it and sends an *accept* message to P_1 to tell him he agrees with the contract terms. Then P_2 proposes a meeting to P_0 at the same date. P_0, who considers P_2 more important than P_1, sends an *accept* message to P_2. P_2 confirms the contract (*confirm* message). Thus P_0 takes P_2's meeting and cancels P_1's (*retract* message). When P_1 receives this message, he decides to ask P_0 for a modification of the contract ie. another date for the meeting (*modification request* message).

5.2   Strategic Level for Adding a Meeting

In our system, each agent negotiates the date of the meeting inside an interval according to a strategy carried by the mechanism of negotiation. This interval is the acceptable range with it uses to offer and counteroffer during negotiation [4]. The negotiation can fail if the intervals of each agent are inconsistent. In that case, each agent recalculates its interval of possible solutions, and a new negotiation is carried out (Figure 4).

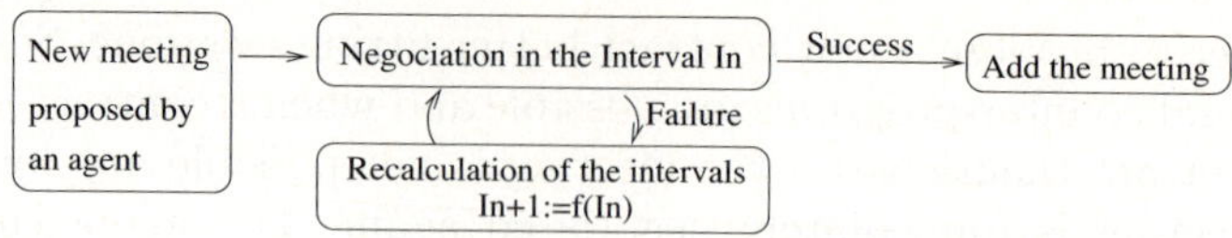

Fig. 4. Addition of a meeting

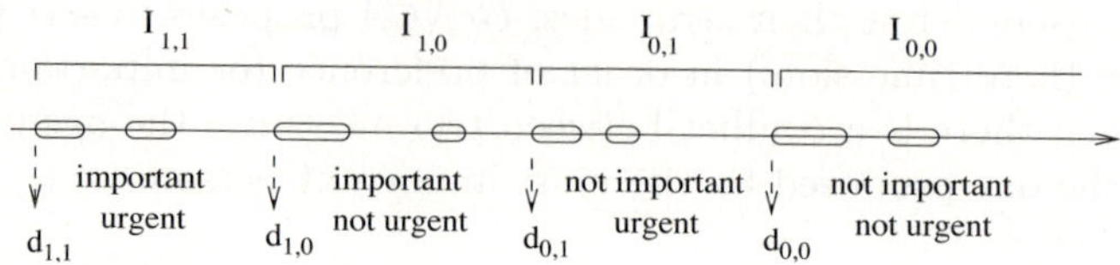

Fig. 5. Intervals of negotiation

We build four intervals of solutions corresponding to acceptable range for important and urgent events, important and non-urgent events, non-important and urgent events, non-important and non-urgent events. These intervals are derived from the schedule of the tasks. Formally, for all $i \in \{0, 1\}$, for all $j \in \{0, 1\}$, let $d_{i,j}$ the start date of $inf(T_{i,j}^{\alpha})$, we define (Figure 5): $I_{1,1}^{\alpha} = [d_{1,1}, d_{1,0}[$, $I_{1,0}^{\alpha} = [d_{1,0}, d_{0,1}[$, $I_{0,1}^{\alpha} = [d_{0,1}, d_{0,0}[$, and $I_{0,0}^{\alpha} = [d_{0,0}, +\infty[$.

If the negotiation fails with the interval $[d_1, d_2]$, the interval for the next negotiation becomes $f_{\tau}^{\alpha}([d_1, d_2])$ where f_{τ}^{α} is defined as $f_{\tau}^{\alpha}([d_1, d_2]) = [d_1 - \tau d_1, d_2 + \tau d_2]$. Formally, we define the function permitting an agent to determine the initial interval of solutions for a meeting proposed by an agent: $giveInterval^{\alpha} : \mathcal{E} \times \mathcal{A} \to \{I_{0,0}^{\alpha}, I_{0,1}^{\alpha}, I_{1,0}^{\alpha}, I_{1,1}^{\alpha}\}$.

5.3   Discussion

We discuss the introduction of trust for negotiating meetings. As we have explained in the previous subsection, the negotiation of meetings brings into play the importance and the urgency of the meeting to calculate some intervals of possible solutions. The importance, the urgency and the priorities are subjective: each agent has its own view of what it is important and urgent. Thus, when an agent proposes a meeting, trust in this agent can help to evaluate the effective importance and urgency of the meeting. In other words, the function $giveInterval^{\alpha}$ could be based on trust.

We consider two instances of trust model in an agent: an instance for the field "the agent has a good evaluation of the importance of the event" and an instance for the field "the agent has a good evaluation of the urgency of the event". Formally, we have two functions that return α's trust in an agent β: $T_i^{\alpha} : \mathcal{A} \to \{0, 1\}$ and $T_u^{\alpha} : \mathcal{A} \to \{0, 1\}$.

Like section 4.2, these both trust values are calculated from two sources. The first one is the individual interaction source. The second one is the categorization source and corresponds to some general properties of a group. For example, a student agent trusts in the professor agents, because these latter have more experience in the management of time. We assume we have a function that accounts for general trust in each group: $SourceGroup^\alpha_{negotiation} : \mathcal{G} \to V_{source}$. If an agent β proposes a meeting to the agent α and if α distrusts β in its evaluation of the importance or the urgency of the meeting, α tries to negotiate the meeting in an interval that does not correspond to β's evaluation of the importance and/or urgency of the meeting. Thus, the function $giveInterval$ is calculated as following:

$$giveInterval^\alpha(e_{A,t,i,u,d_1,d_2},\beta) = I^\alpha_{T^\alpha_i(\beta)+(1-T^\alpha_i(\beta))(1-i),T^\alpha_u(\beta)+(1-T^\alpha_u(\beta))(1-i)}$$

We would like to stress on the interest to use the individual interaction source. Firstly the individual interaction source supports the dynamic aspects of trust. It is submitted to some significant variations (for example the erosion of trust and the fragility of trust [5, 8]). If there would be only the categorization source, sharing would be similar to a static mechanism concerning general knowledge about groups Secondly, the individual interaction source permits the emergence of a complex trust network. Trust networks are groups based on trust relationship. These groups of trust are orthogonal with the social groups described in the previous section. If we want an agent to be able to handle such a network, each agent should have an internal representation of the trust relationship of all agents. Then the questions are: how to derive these relationships automatically? On whichinteractions are they are based in our calendar system? A partial solution is the capacity for an agent either to be able to observe the interactions between the other agents, or to have the opinions of the agents about other agents. But it asks two other questions: the privacy of the individual interactions and the social implication of the public or semi-public opinions.

6   Conclusion

We have presented a decentralized calendar benefiting from the use of computational trust. Each user is represented by an agent in charge of the scheduling of the events based on the importance and the urgency. Sharing, trusting and negotiating support this mechanism. This decentralized calendar has been implemented. Experiments and evaluation are in progress.

Our future works consists in the following three directions. Firstly, for the moment, the individual source of trust corresponds to the user's evaluation in the real life. A progress will be to build this source from the interactions between the agents in the framework of the calendar. But in the real life, the interactions can be private. So the question is which possible interactions are relevant to derive reliable evaluations. The second direction deals with the definition of the priorities in a more general framework: how to define the priorities if the importance and the urgency are not binary and if this multi-value scale is not shared by all agents. Thirdly, an agent should be able to build and exploit its own trust network. Such a building requires to derive the trust relationship existing between the other agents, and not only between it and the others. The addition of the reputation source could be the solution. However, it asks the question of the privacy and the social implication of an opinion. Such a trust network could be exploited during the negotiation of meetings: trust coalitions could be emerged to tip the scales in favour of a specific proposition.

Acknowledgements. We thank France Telecom R&D for supporting the research about trust as reported in this paper (CRE 46128855 France Telecom - CNRS).

References

1. C. Castelfranchi, R. Falcone, and G. Pezzulo. Trust in information sources as a source for trust: a fuzzy approach. In *Proceedings of AAMAS'02*, pages 89–96. ACM Press, 2003.
2. S. R. Covey. *The 7 Habits of Highly Effective People*. Simon & Schuster, 1989.
3. R. Guha. Open rating systems. Technical report, Stanford University, East Lansing, Michigan, 2003.
4. N. R. Jennings, P. Faratin, A. R. Lomuscio, S. Parsons, C. Sierra, and M. Wooldridge. Automated negotiation: prospects, methods and challenges. *International Journal of Group Decision and Negotiation*, 10(2):199–215, 2001.
5. C. M. Jonker and J. Treur. Formal analysis of models for the dynamics of trust based on experiences. In F. J. Garijo and M. Boman, editors, *Proceedings of MAA-MAW'99*, volume 1647, pages 221–231, Berlin, 1999. Springer-Verlag: Heidelberg.
6. S. Marsh. Optimism and pessimism in trust. In *Proceedings IB-ERAMIA94/CNAISE'94*. Ed. Ramirez, J. McGraw-Hill, 1994.
7. P. Mathieu and M.-H. Verrons. A General Negotiation Model using XML. *Artificial Intelligence and Simulation of Behaviour Journal (AISBJ)*, 1(6):523–542, 2005.
8. D. Melaye and Y. Demazeau. Bayesian dynamic trust model. In Springer, editor, *Proceedings of CEEMAS'05*, volume 3690 of *LNCS*, pages 480–489, 2005.
9. S. Ossowski. *Co-ordination in Artificial Agent Societies*. LNAI 1535, 1999.
10. A. Radcliffe-Brown. *Structure and function in primitive society*. Cohen & West, 1952.
11. S. D. Ramchurn, D. Huynh, and N. R. Jennings. Trust in multi-agent systems. *The Knowledge Engineering Review*, 19(1), 2004.

Unidirectional Loop Layout Problem with Balanced Flow

Feristah Ozcelik and A. Attila Islier

Eskişehir Osmangazi University, Department of Industrial Engineering
Bademlik, 26030, Eskisehir, Turkey
fdurmaz@ogu.edu.tr

Abstract. The unidirectional loop is an economical and flexible materials handling system transporting materials around a loop network in one direction only. There are n candidate locations around the loop to allocate n machines. This configuration is easily adaptable to changes in product mix and routing requirements. The challenge here is to find an assignment for machines to available sites to minimize the handling cost. If the material flow is conserved at each workstation, that is, if total inflow is equal to total outflow then such a loop is called as a balanced loop. This work addresses the unidirectional loop layout design problem with balanced flow. The problem is known to be NP-complete, and thus heuristic methods and artificial intelligence techniques are appropriate to solve such difficult problems in reasonable time. A hybrid Genetic Algorithm (GA) based on a move heuristic is developed to solve the problem. The performance of the GA is tested by using well known data sets from literature and considerable improvements are obtained.

1   Introduction

A loop network with machines arranged in a cycle and materials transported in only one direction around the cycle is one of the common layouts for flexible manufacturing systems (Fig. 1). These types of layouts are either served by loop conveyors, overhead monorail systems, or paths of unidirectional AGVs. A process plan is given for each part that specifies the sequence of machines the part must visit to complete its processing. When a part's operation is completed on a machine, it is moved to the routed machine on the unidirectional material-handling network. If the workstation is occupied, the part is stored in a local buffer, waiting for the workstation to become free. Alternatively discretely spaced carriers of the conveyor are used for temporary storage. Conveyor is used both for handling and storage purposes in this case. If any workstation is busy, part passes the workstation, makes complete tours until work station becomes available. The most commonly used operational strategy for such systems is that all parts enter and exit the system at a unique load/unload (L/U) station [1].

Unidirectional loop layouts are preferred to other configurations (single-row layout, double-row layout, cluster layout and circular layout) due to their relatively lower initial investment costs because they contain a minimal number of required material links to connect all workstations while providing a high degree of material handling flexibility [2]. Such configurations are able to satisfy all material handling requirements for the part types scheduled for manufacturing in the system as there is at least

M. Ali and R. Dapoigny (Eds.): IEA/AIE 2006, LNAI 4031, pp. 741–749, 2006.

one directed path connecting any pair of workstations. With these layouts, future introduction of new part types and process changes are easily accommodated.

The unidirectional loop layout problem is generally formulated as a Quadratic Assignment Problem (QAP) [3, 4, 5]. Given a flow matrix and a distance matrix, the problem is a special case of the QAP where the objective is to assign each workstation to one of the predetermined sites such that the total part transport distance per unit time is minimized.

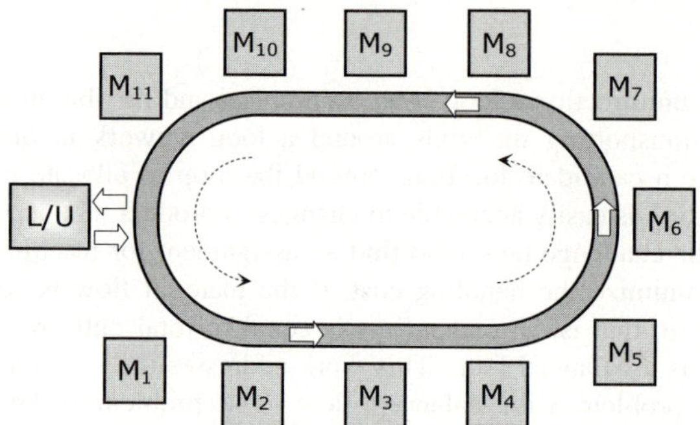

Fig. 1. Unidirectional loop layout with a single load/unload station

Two particular cases of unidirectional loop layout problem based on properties of the distance matrix (equidistant) and flow matrix (balanced) draw attention of researchers. In balanced case material flow is conserved at each workstation: total inflow is equal to total outflow [5]. If distances between candidate locations are all equal, the problem is named as equidistant unidirectional loop layout problem [3].

Afentakis was among the first to address the unidirectional loop layout problem [2]. Kouvelis and Kim have shown that this layout problem is NP-complete [1]. Both heuristics and exact methods are proposed to solve these difficult problems [4, 6, 7, 8, 9, 10].

The paper is structured as follows. Section 2 describes and models the balanced unidirectional loop layout problem. Section 3 introduces a hybrid Genetic Algorithm (GA) for the solution of unidirectional loop layout problem, while section 4 reports and discusses computational results of the experiments. Finally, section 5 summarizes the contribution of the paper.

2   Unidirectional Loop Layout Design Problem

Let n = {1, 2, ..., n} be the set of stations that will be located on a unicyclic material handling system. Let F_{nxn} be the part flow matrix where f_{ij} denotes the part flow from station i to station j. The matrix F can be calculated using part routings and production quantities.

Let $u_j = \sum_{i=1}^{n} f_{ji}$, the total flow from station j to other stations and $v_j = \sum_{i=1}^{n} f_{ji}$, the total flow from other stations to station j. In many cases, the number of parts coming into a station is equal to the number of parts leaving the station. This case will be called the *balanced case*, where $u_j = v_j, j = 1,2,...,n.$ The balanced case is particularly relevant in automated manufacturing, where no manual interruption is allowed to remove parts from the stations. When the flow matrix is balanced, distances between adjacent machines do not affect the problem solution [3, 5].

Kiran et.al. [5] developed an extended formulation for the balanced case. Because the actual distances between workstations is not important, the authors assumed the circuit length $\lambda=1$ and scaled the distances by dividing λ. Their binary integer linear programming formulation is as follows:

$$\min \sum_{\substack{i=1 \\ i \neq j}}^{n} \sum_{j=1}^{n} f_{ij} d_{ij} \qquad \text{s.t.} \tag{1}$$

$$\sum_{\substack{j=1 \\ j \neq i}}^{n} x_{ij} = 1 \qquad i = 1,....,n \tag{2}$$

$$\sum_{\substack{i=1 \\ i \neq j}}^{n} x_{ij} = 1 \qquad j = 1,....,n \tag{3}$$

$$d_{ij} + d_{ji} = 1 \qquad i, j = 1,...,n; i \neq j \tag{4}$$

$$d_{kj} \geq d_{ki} + d_{ij} + x_{ij} - 1 \qquad i, j, k = 1,...,n; i \neq j \neq k \tag{5}$$

$$x_{ij} = 0,1 \qquad i, j = 1,...,n; i \neq j \tag{6}$$

$$0 \leq d_{ij} \leq 1 \qquad i, j = 1,...,n; i \neq j \tag{7}$$

where d_{ij} denotes the transportation distance between location i and location j, and x_{ij} is a binary decision variable

$$x_{ij} = \begin{cases} 1 \text{ if workstation } j \text{ immediately follows workstation } i \text{ in an optimal layout} \\ 0 \text{ otherwise} \end{cases}$$

In this formulation, constraints (2) and (3) are exactly the assignment constraints and ensure that each workstation has exactly one predecessor and one successor. Constraints (4) and (5) define the properties of the distance matrix. Also (5) guarantees that $d_{ij} = d_{ik} + d_{kj}$ if workstation j immediately follows workstation k in the flow direction in an optimal layout. Kiran et al. [5] have shown that this is a valid BUCLP formulation. They also conjectured that it is in fact ideal and its linear programming relaxation gives always an integer optimal solution based on their test with 3600 random instances generated for n = 5–7 workstations. However, fractional solutions are possible for larger problems.

When the flow matrix is balanced, the sequence of stations completely determines the objective function value, regardless of the spacing between locations of machines. Consequently any formulation for the equal spaced unidirectional loop layout can be used in finding the sequence of the machines for balanced non-equal unidirectional loop layout problem.

Bozer and Rim proposed a linear programming relaxation for equidistant case and claimed that it solves the equidistant unidirectional loop layout problem optimally [3]. Altınel and Öncan simplified Bozer and Rim's relaxation by decreasing the number of constraints from $2n^3 + n^2 + 2n$ to $n^3 + n^2 + n$ [10]. Although their relaxation is equivalent to the Bozer and Rim's relaxation, it is faster than the former due to lower number of constraints.

$$\min \sum_{\substack{i=1}}^{n} \sum_{\substack{j=1 \\ i \neq j}}^{n} f_{ij} d_{ij} \qquad \text{s.t.} \tag{8}$$

$$d_{ij} + d_{ji} = n \qquad\qquad i, j = 1,...,n; \quad i \neq j \tag{9}$$

$$d_{ij} + d_{jk} \leq d_{ik} + n \qquad\qquad i, j, k = 1,...,n; \quad i \neq j \neq k \tag{10}$$

$$\sum_{\substack{j=1 \\ j \neq i}}^{n} d_{ij} = \sum_{\substack{j=1 \\ j \neq i}}^{n} d_{ji} \qquad\qquad i = 1,....,n \tag{11}$$

$$d_{ij} \geq 0 \qquad\qquad i, j = 1,...,n; \quad i \neq j \tag{12}$$

where d_{ij} denotes the transportation distance between location i and location j and f_{ij} denotes the average number of jobs to be moved from workstation i to workstation j over a given length of time.

Due to the combinatorial nature of the loop layout problem, an artificial intelligence technique seems to be appropriate to solve it in reasonable time. This paper introduces a hybrid GA to solve the balanced unidirectional loop layout problem.

3 Proposed Genetic Algorithm

Genetic algorithms are a particular class of evolutionary algorithms that use techniques inspired by evolutionary biology such as inheritance, mutation, natural selection, and recombination (or crossover). They are used to find approximate solutions to optimization problems.

Here a potential solution to a problem is inferred as an individual, which can be represented as a chromosome. Throughout the genetic evolution, due to selection, crossover and mutation mechanisms, high-quality offspring are produced from initial population of chromosomes. Generation by generation, the stronger individuals, as better solutions to the problem, are the survivors in a competitive environment. GAs have experienced increasing interest from the combinatorial optimization community and have shown great promise for performance in many industrial engineering areas [11].

Although GAs perform well in a global search, they take a relatively long time to converge to a local optimum [12]. Local improvement procedures, on the other hand, can find the local optimum in a small region of the search space but they are typically poor in a global search. Therefore, local search procedures can be incorporated into a

GA to improve its performance. This approach is named as *hybridization*. There are two possible ways to design hybrid genetic algorithms. One way is to interweave genetic algorithms with local search; another way is to invent new genetic operators inspired from local search techniques [13]. We adopt the second approach to design a move heuristic based mutation to find improved offspring.

3.1 Representation

Since the loop layout design problem attempts to find a permutation of machines by optimizing some measures, the solution itself can be used as a chromosome. For a 5-machine loop layout problem, the chromosome can be represented as **4 1 5 2 3**.

The loading/unloading station is not encoded in the chromosomes because it is assumed to be always prefixed to the list of machine permutation.

3.2 Crossover

Crossover is an operation to generate a new string (i.e., child) from two parent strings. In this study the maximal preservative crossover (MPX) operator which was introduced by [14] is used as a crossover operator.

Let two parent chromosomes be **1 2 3 4 5 6 7 8** and **2 4 6 8 7 5 3 1**. MPX first selects a random substring of the first parent, say **3 4 5**. Next, all the elements of the chosen substring are removed from the second parent. Second parent turns out to be **2 6 8 7 1**. Then, the substring chosen from parent 1 is copied into the first part of the offspring as **3 4 5**. Finally, the end of the offspring is filled up with genes in the same order as they appear in the second parent as **3 4 5 2 6 8 7 1**.

3.3 MOVE Mutation

Mutation changes the order of n machines in each string. This operation can be regarded as transition from a current solution to its neighborhood solution in local search algorithms. In this study, the idea of the MOVE heuristic suggested by Tansel and Bilen is used [7]. Thus a hybrid genetic algorithm that is capable to jump to a better solution (neighbor solution) is generated.

MOVE heuristic is based on comparing of the improvements obtained by exchanging of a certain workstation with all of the others one by one and adopting of the best move. Let the current assignment of n workstations to n available locations, describe a layout π. And let layout π_i is obtained by moving the i th element to the j the position, MOVE heuristic computes the change in the objective value by switching from π to π_i. This procedure is repeated for all i $\neq$ j and the improvements are recorded. Then the move resulting in the largest improvement is realized. The procedure is repeated until no improvement is possible. Moving workstation π_i from location i to location j causes a sequence of location changes. First workstation π_i is moved to location j. Then, if j<i workstations π_j , π_{j+1} , ..., π_{j-1} at locations j, j+1, ...,i-1, are shifted forward to locations j+1, j+2, ..., i. If i<j, backward shift occurs for workstations $\pi_{I+1,}$ $\pi_{I+2, ...,}\pi_j$, from locations i+1, i+2, ..., j to locations i, i+1, ... , j-1.

The proposed mutation operator works as follows. For all of the genes of the chromosome in the population, a random number is generated. If the random number is equal or less than mutation rate, this gene is moved to another position in the chromosome by MOVE approach. So for all of the positions that this gene can be moved the fitness value is calculated. And then the move with maximum fitness value is accepted. For example let the third gene of the chromosome (Fig. 2) is selected for mutation. Then by move mutation this gene is moved to the first, second, fourth, fifth, sixth, seventh and eighth positions of the chromosome. Then the neighbour solution that has the maximum fitness value is selected as child and that mutated chromosome replaces the unmodified solution in the population.

Parent and selected gene

2	4	6	8	7	5	3	1

Neighbourhood chromosomes

6	2	4	8	7	5	3	1
2	6	4	8	7	5	3	1
2	4	8	6	7	5	3	1
2	4	8	7	6	5	3	1
2	4	8	7	5	6	3	1
2	4	8	7	5	3	6	1
2	4	8	7	5	3	1	6

Fig. 2. Move mutation

3.4   The Implementation of the Hybrid Genetic Algorithm

The hybrid GA employed is simply as follows:

> *initialize;*
> *evaluate the individuals;*
> *repeat*
> > *select parents;*
> > *generate offspring;*
> > *mutate if enough solutions are generated;*
> > *copy the best fitted individuals into population as they were;*
> *until the population converges to a solution.*

Here, initialization is reading of the parameters such as population size, mutation rate and number of generations. Then the required feasible solutions are generated randomly. Evaluation is computing of the fitness power (total part transport distance per unit time here) of individuals. Parents to be crossed are selected taking into consideration of their performance and using the roulette wheel method. After selection of the fitted parents by this biased random process, they are matched to generate better offspring by a MPX process. The parent strings are changed with children to keep population size constant. Following a certain number of crossings, a randomly selected solution is mutated by changing the entry in a randomly selected position. At last, the best-fitted solutions are also added to the population to prevent the disappearance of good solutions (elitist strategy). If the best performing chromosomes remain unchanged within a certain number of generations (100 here) the population is considered to be converged. In fact, the chance for further improvement is very low, so the algorithm is stopped at this stage.

4 Computational Experience

To test the performance of the proposed algorithm, the data sets of [10] are used. The authors considered five different FMS environments with 10, 20, 30, 40 and 50 workstations interconnected by a unidirectional cyclic material handling system. They also fix the number of different part types to 50. In generating the random part flow matrices they imposed a constraint on the range of numbers in the matrix. They defined three ranges: 0-10, 0-50, 0-100 as low, medium and high variation part flows respectively and marked those instances with letters L, M and H to identify the type of variation they have. They generated 10 test problems per variation type. For example the package 20–M consists of ten test problems each with 20 workstations and medium variation in part flows. They generated balanced and unbalanced instanced that have these properties, which makes a test bed of 300 test instances. Because we consider balanced case we used the balanced test instances which make 150 instances.

Our computational results are summarized in tables 1 and 2. Table 1 includes averages of the relative percent deviations of the ten-problem test sets. The first columns of the table refer to the test sets. Each one of the remaining columns is associated with one of the heuristics explained by [10] and the proposed algorithm. Those authors compared their Exchange (EX), Relocation (RE), Sort and reverse (SR) and Move and reverse (MR) heuristics by KK3 [1], MOVE [7], pairwise interchange (SWAP), three-way interchange (3WI) and Lee–Huang–Chiang (LHC) heuristics. For more information on these heuristics refer to [10]. The column representing the new algorithm is emphasized as bold.

Table 1. Relative percent deviations from the lower bound

Instance	KK3	LHC	SWAP	SR	3WI	EX	MOVE	RE	MR	GA
10-L	3.08	1.75	1.27	1.46	0.36	1.20	0.30	0.30	0.03	**0.00**
10-M	1.69	1.53	1.12	0.47	0.37	1.12	0.09	0.13	0.00	**0.00**
10-H	2.72	1.94	1.44	1.76	0.92	1.42	0.22	0.36	0.14	**0.00**
20-L	5.66	4.84	3.89	3.00	2.57	2.42	0.90	0.90	0.79	**0.06**
20-M	5.44	4.31	4.12	2.25	2.39	2.28	0.99	0.99	0.48	**0.008**
20-H	5.63	4.21	4.15	2.81	2.74	2.51	1.62	1.44	0.81	**0.005**
30-L	7.18	6.26	5.12	4.87	4.31	3.59	2.13	1.95	1.93	**0.54**
30-M	8.07	6.16	5.70	4.45	4.24	3.45	2.38	2.01	1.76	**0.47**
30-H	8.31	6.38	6.35	4.97	4.37	3.85	2.52	2.19	1.60	**0.68**
40-L	10.20	7.97	7.62	5.80	5.98	5.15	4.39	4.38	3.58	**1.25**
40-M	10.49	7.75	7.80	6.31	5.94	5.90	3.65	3.46	2.99	**1.52**
40-H	10.23	7.61	7.46	6.36	5.81	5.11	3.39	3.36	3.35	**1.55**
50-L	11.89	9.66	9.34	8.18	7.60	7.14	5.64	5.60	4.81	**3.16**
50-M	12.70	9.52	9.48	8.02	7.55	7.29	5.78	5.57	5.27	**3.22**
50-H	12.65	9.55	10.24	8.26	7.64	7.36	5.66	5.56	5.29	**2.64**
Aver	7.73	5.96	5.67	4.60	4.19	3.99	2.64	2.55	2.19	**1.007**
MinAver	5.56	3.70	3.68	2.93	2.34	1.48	1.57	1.52	1.28	**0.58**
MaxAver	10.05	8.34	7.79	6.51	6.09	5.85	4.25	4.21	3.30	**1.47**

The last three rows of table 1 is respectively the column average (Aver), and the average of the smallest (MinAver) and largest (MaxAver) values. They are obtained with the ten instances of the test sets. The columns of table 1 are sorted in decreasing order of the column averages.

Table 2. Average number of generations

Instance	Generation	Instance	Generation	Instance	Generation
10-L	4,8	20-H	25,8	40-M	61,1
10-M	4,6	30-L	41,5	40-H	58,2
10-H	5,2	30-M	44	50-L	71,1
20-L	22,5	30-H	42,8	50-M	64
20-M	19,5	40-L	52,5	50-H	67,4

The relative differences are computed by using of the following formula

$$100 * \frac{(Upper\ bound - Lower\ bound)}{(Lower\ bound)} \tag{13}$$

where, Upper Bound is the total flow cost obtained by the corresponding heuristic, and Lower Bound is the optimal objective value of the Altınel and Öncan's relaxation. This model solved by CPLEX v. 8.0.

From Table 1, we see that GA provides higher quality solutions than the other heuristics from literature for all of the problems. Besides the average values, the max and the min percent deviations are better than the others.

All the test problems are solved on a Pentium IV PC with 256 MB Ram and 40 GB hard disk. Table 2 lists average number of generations. Since the CPU time is hardware and code depended, the average numbers of generations are preferred to compare the performances.

5   Conclusions

A common layout for flexible manufacturing systems is a loop network with machines arranged in a cycle and materials transported in only one direction around the cycle. We studied this layout problem with a single L/U station and balanced flow. We developed a hybrid GA based on a move heuristic. We tested the proposed algorithm by using 150 test problems from literature. Because the actual distances between machines are not important when part flow is balanced, a LP relaxation proposed for equidistant case is used to determine the lower bounds. The results showed that GA outperforms all of the compared heuristics. Because we compared the solutions with lower bounds instead of optimal solutions, the success of the algorithm is more than shown in the table. For problem sizes 10 and 20 we reached the LP solution (not LP relaxation).

Hybridization of GA with MOVE heuristic improved the local search capability so led to higher performance. The proposed heuristic seems to be capable to solve more complex versions (multi L/U stations, bidirectional systems, etc.) of the problem satisfactorily. The success of the algorithm encourages us to study on the other forms of the problem such as equidistant with balanced and unbalanced flow.

Acknowledgements

The authors thanks to Altınel and Öncan for their contribution by data set.

References

1. Kouvelis, P., Kim, M.W.: Unidirectional loop network layout problem in automated manufacturing systems, Operations Research, 40, 3 (1992) 533-550.
2. Afentakis, P.: A loop layout design problem for flexible manufacturing systems, International Journal of Flexible Manufacturing Systems, 1, 2 (1989) 175-196.
3. Bozer, Y. A., Rim, S.C.: Exact solution procedures for the circular layout problem, Technical Report 89-33, University of Michigan, USA (1989)
4. Kiran, A.S., Karabati, S.: Exact and approximate algorithms for the loop layout problem, Production Planning&Control, 4, 3 (1993) 253-259.
5. Kiran, A.S., Unal, A.T., Karabati, S.: A location problem on unicyclic networks: Balanced case, European Journal of Operational Research, 62 (1992) 194-202.
6. Kaku, B.K., Rachamadugu, R.: Layout design for flexible manufacturing systems, European Journal of Operational Research, 57 (1992) 224-230.
7. Tansel, B.C., Bilen, C.: Move based heuristics for the unidirectional loop network layout problem, European Journal of Operational Research, 108 (1998) 36-48.
8. Lee, S., Huang, K., Chiang, C.: Configuring layout in unidirectional loop manufacturing systems, International Journal of Production Research, 39, 6 (2001) 1183-1201.
9. Malakooti, B.: Unidirectional loop network layout by a LP heuristic and design of telecommunications networks, Journal of Intelligent Manufacturing, 15 (2004) 117-125.
10. Altınel, İ. K., Öncan, T.: Design of unidirectional cyclic layouts, International Journal of Production Research, 43, 19 (2005) 3983-4008.
11. Gen M, Cheng R.: Genetic algorithms and engineering design. New York: Wiley; (1997)
12. Wang H.F., Wu, K.Y.: Hybrid genetic algorithm for optimization problems with permutation property, Computers & Operations Research, 31 (2004) 2453-2471.
13. Cheng, R., Gen, M.: Loop layout design problem in flexible manufacturing systems using genetic algorithms, Computers and Industrial Engineering, 34, 1 (1998) 53-61.
14. Mühlenbein, H., GorgesSchleuter, M., Krämer, O.: Evolution algorithms in combinatorial optimization. Parallel Computing 7 (1988) 65–85.

A Heuristic Load Balancing Scheduling Method for Dedicated Machine Constraint

Arthur M.D. Shr[1], Alan Liu[1], and Peter P. Chen[2]

[1] Department of Electrical Engineering, National Chung Cheng University,
Chia-Yi 621, Taiwan, R.O.C.
arthurshr@gmail.com, aliu@ee.ccu.edu.tw
[2] Department of Computer Science, 298 Coates Hall, Louisiana State University,
Baton Rouge, LA 70803, U.S.A.
pchen@lsu.edu

Abstract. The dedicated machine constraint for the photolithography process in semiconductor manufacturing is one of the new challenges introduced in photolithography machinery due to natural bias. With this constraint, the wafers passing through each photolithography process have to be processed on the same machine. The purpose of the limitation is to prevent the impact of natural bias. However, many scheduling policies or modeling methods proposed by previous research for the semiconductor manufacturing system have not discussed the dedicated machine constraint. We propose the Load Balancing (LB) scheduling method based on a Resource Schedule and Execution Matrix (RSEM) to tackle this constraint. The LB method uses the RSEM as a tool to represent the temporal relationship between the wafer lots and machines. The LB method is to schedule each wafer lot at the first photolithography stage to a suitable machine according to the load balancing factors among photolithography machines. In the paper, we present an example to demonstrate the LB method and the result of the simulations to validate our method.

1 Introduction

Semiconductor manufacturing systems are different from the traditional manufacturing systems, such as a flow-shops manufacturing system in assembly lines or a job-shops manufacturing system. In a semiconductor factory, one wafer lot passes through hundreds of operations, and the processing procedure takes a few months to complete. Fig. 1 shows the concept of the process flow of a semiconductor manufacturing system.

One of the challenges in the semiconductor manufacturing systems is the dedicated photolithography machine constraint which is caused by the natural bias of the photolithography machine. Natural bias will impact the alignment of patterns between different layers. The smaller the dimension of the IC products, the more difficult they will be to align between different layers. This is the case especially when we move on to a smaller dimension IC for high technology products. The wafer lots passing through each photolithography stage have to be processed on the same machine. The purpose of the limitation is to prevent the impact of natural bias and to keep a good

M. Ali and R. Dapoigny (Eds.): IEA/AIE 2006, LNAI 4031, pp. 750–759, 2006.

yield of the IC product. A study discussing the performance improvements for photolithography process terms the dedicated constraint as machine dedication policies [1]. Fig. 2 describes the dedicated machine constraint.

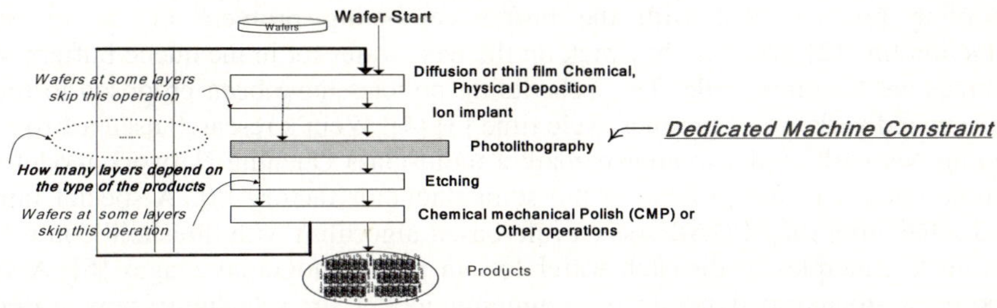

Fig. 1. The operations of semiconductor manufacturing incrementally develop an IC product layer by layer. The *dedicated machine constraint* is in the *photolithography* process area.

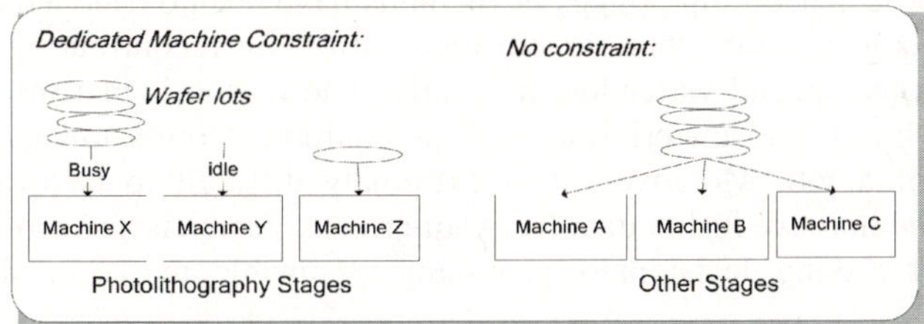

Fig. 2. When wafer lots enter each photolithography operation stage (layer), with this constraint, the wafer lots dedicated to machine *X*, they need to wait for machine *X*, even if there is no wafer lot waiting for machine *Y*, which is idle. On the other hand, when wafer lots enter into other operation stages, without any machine constraints, the wafer lots can be scheduled to any machine of *A*, *B* or *C* as long as it becomes idle.

The constraint is the most important challenge to improve productivity and fulfill the request for customers, as well as the main contributor to the complexity and uncertainty of semiconductor manufacturing. Moreover, the photolithography process is the most important process in semiconductor manufacturing. The yield of IC products is always dependent on a good photolithography process, while at the same time the process can also cause defects. Not surprisingly, the performance of the factory will rely on the photolithography machines. A factory's performance can be measured by the mean and variance of the manufacturing process time for products. The manufacturing lead-time, called the cycle time, is measured from the time when the wafer lot enters the production line until the time the wafer lot completes the process and exits the production system. When the production process starts, each wafer lot is assigned an estimated time of exiting the factory. Reducing the variance of cycle time can improve the ability to meet the delivery dates or due dates which have been committed to customers. A small variance of cycle time means the system can accurately predict the time a product will complete production. Some efficient scheduling policies have been proposed to reduce the mean and variance of product cycle time. A small variance of cycle time means the system can accurately predict the time a product will complete production.

Many Queuing Network scheduling polices or methods have been published to formulate the complexity of semiconductor manufacturing problems. These scheduling policies deal with the buffer competing problem in the re-entrant production line [2], wherein they pick up the next wafer lot in the queue buffers when machines are becoming idle. Two scheduling policies have been proposed to reduce the mean and variance of product cycle time [3] [4]. Wein's research used a Brownian Queuing Network model to approximate a multi-class Queuing Network model with dynamic control to the process in the semiconductor factory [5]. A special family-based scheduling rule, SDA-F uses a rule-based algorithm with threshold control and least slack principles to dispatch wafer lots in photolithography stages [6]. A study proposed a stochastic dynamic programming model for scheduling new wafer lot release and bottleneck processing by stage in the semiconductor factory [7]. One another research used the Petri Net approach to modeling, analysis, simulation, scheduling and the control of the semiconductor manufacturing system [8].

Although these scheduling polices or methods have been developed and applied in the semiconductor factories, there is still much effort for reconfiguring the system or rescheduling some special wafer lots manually. The reason is that the differences in operators, machines, and material, as well as equipment breakdown, will affect the effectiveness of a job. Moreover, it is extremely difficult to have algorithms for transforming the massive influx data from equipment, products and process status into information for making decisions or providing reasonable and acceptable scheduling strategies.

This load balancing issue is derived mainly from the dedicated photolithography machine constraint. This happens because once the wafer lots have been scheduled to one of the machines at the first photolithography stage, they must be assigned to the same machine in the subsequent photolithography stages until they have passed the last photolithography stage. Therefore, the short time of unexpected abnormal events or breakdown of one machine will cause a pile-up of many wafer lots waiting for the machine and make the machine critical to the factory. Some of the photolithography machines will become idle and remain so for a while, due to the fact that no wafer lots can be processed, and the other will always be busy while many wafer lots in the buffer limited to this machine are awaiting processing. As a result, some wafer lots will never be delivered to the customer on time, and the performance of the factory will have been decreased and impacted.

Recently, a study concerning the load balancing issue developed a load balance allocation function by applying a dynamic programming method to the tool constraint in the photolithography machines [9]. Two approaches were reported to use simulations to model the photolithography process, and one of them proposed a Neural Network approach to develop an intelligent scheduling method according to a qualifying matrix and the lot scheduling criteria to improve the performance of the photolithography machines [10]. The other one is to decide the wafer lots assignment of the photolithography machines at the time when the wafer lots were released to the manufacturing system to improve the load balancing problem [11]. However, their proposed scheduling methods did not concern the dedicated machine constraint, either.

In practical semiconductor manufacturing, the wafer lots of a load unbalancing factory usually need to be switched from the highly congested machines to the idle machines. This takes much time and relies on experienced engineers to manually handle alignment problems of the wafer lots with a different situation off-line. It is inefficient to determine, one lot at a time, which wafer lot and machine need to be switched. Moreover, this method cannot meet the fast-changing market of the semiconductor industry.

In this paper, motivated by the issues described above, we propose a heuristic Load Balancing (LB) scheduling method based on a Resource Schedule and Execution Matrix (RSEM) to tackle the dedicated machine constraint. By selecting a wafer lot which has the biggest waiting step for one machine, and by selecting a wafer lot which has the smallest load for one photolithography machine, we could schedule each wafer lot at first and unconstrained photolithography stage to a suitable photolithography machine.

The paper is organized as follows: Section 2 introduces the proposed RSEM and depicts its algorithm. An example of semiconductor factory applying the LB scheduling method is described in Section 3. Section 4 shows the simulation results that validated our approach. Section 5 discuses the conclusion and intended future work.

2 Resource Schedule and Execution Matrix (RSEM)

The RSEM consists of three modules including the *Task Generation, Resource Calculation*, and *Resource Allocation* modules. The first module is to model the tasks for the scheduling system. For example, in the semiconductor factory, the tasks are the procedures of processing wafer lots, starting from the raw material until the completion of the IC products. We generate a two-dimensional matrix for the tasks that are going be processed by machines. One dimension is reserved for the tasks, t_1, t_2, ..., t_n, the other is to represent the periodical time event (or step) s_1, s_2, ...,s_m. Each task has a sequential pattern to represent the resources it needs during the process sequence from the raw material to a product. We define each type resource as r_1, r_2, ..., r_o, where it means a particular task needs the resources in the sequence of r_1 first and r_2 following that until r_o is gained. Therefore, the matrix looks as follows:

$$
\begin{array}{c c c c c c c c c c c}
 & s_1 & s_2 & . & . & . & . & . & s_j & . & . & s_m \\
t_1 & r_1 & r_2 & r_3 & .. & .. & .. & r_{k.} & .. & .. & .. & .. \\
t_2 & & r_3 & r_4 & .. & .. & r_k & .. & .. & .. & .. & .. \\
. & & & & r_1 & r_3 & & & r_k & .. \\
t_i & & & & r_3 & r_4 & .. & .. & r_k & .. \\
. & & & & & & . & . \\
t_n & & & & .. & .. & r_k & .. & .. & ..
\end{array}
$$

The symbol r_k in the Matrix $[t_i, s_j]$ is to represent that the task t_i needs the resource (or machine) r_k at the time s_j. If t_i starts to be processed at s_j, and the total step number of t_i is p, we will fill its pattern into the matrix from $[t_i, s_j]$,..., to $[t_i, s_{j+p-1}]$. All the tasks, $t_1,...t_n$, follow the illustration above to form a task matrix in the *Task Generation* module. To represent the dedicated machine constraint in the matrix for this research, the symbol r_k^x, a replacement of r_k, is to represent that t_i has been dedicated to number x of k machine at s_j. The symbol w_k is to represent the wait situation when r_k cannot serve t_i at s_j. We will insert this symbol in the *Resource Allocation* module later.

The *Resource Calculation* module is to summarize the value of each dimension as the factors for the scheduling rule of the *Resource Allocation* module. For example, we can determine how many steps t_i needed to be processed by counting task pattern of t_i dimension in the matrix. We can also realize how many wait steps t_i has had by counting w_k from starting step to current step of t_i dimension in the matrix. Furthermore, if we count the r_k^x in s_j dimension, we can know how many tasks will need the machine m_x of resource r_k at s_j.

Before we can start the execution of the *Resource Allocation* module, we need to generate the task matrix, obtain all the factors for the scheduling rules, and build up the rules. The module is to schedule the tasks to the suitable resource according to the factors and predefined rules. To represent the situation of waiting for r_k; i.e., when t_i cannot take the resource of r_k at s_j, then we will not only insert w_k in the pattern of t_i, but will also need to shift the following pattern to the next step in the matrix. Therefore, we can obtain the updated factor for how many tasks wait for r_k at s_j only if we have counted w_k by the dimension s_j. We can also obtain the factor for how many wait steps that t_i has had only if we have counted w_k, $1 \leq k \leq o$ by t_i dimension in the matrix. To better understand our proposed scheduling process, the flowchart of RSEM is shown in Fig. 3.

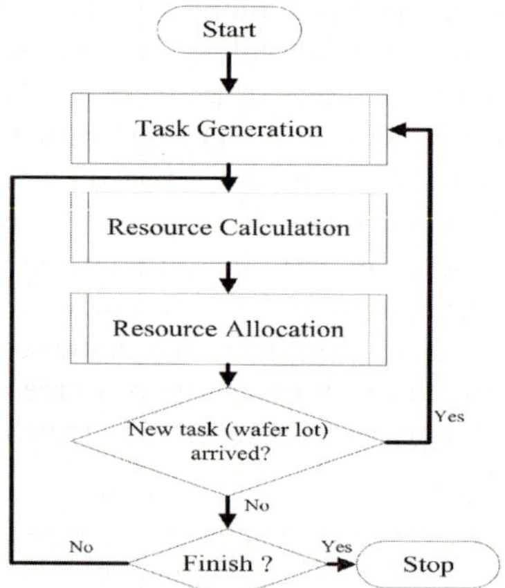

Fig. 3. The process of using the RSEM starts from the *Task Generation* module, and it will copy the predefined task patterns of tasks into the matrix. Entering the *Resource Calculation* module, the factors for the tasks and resources will be brought out at the current step. This module will update these factors again at each scheduling step. The execution of the scheduling process is in the *Resource Allocation* module. When we have done the schedule for all the tasks for the current step, we will return to check for new tasks and repeat the whole process again by following the flowchart. We will exit the scheduling process when we reach the final step of the last task if there is still no new task appended to the matrix. After that, the scheduling process will restart immediately when the new tasks arriving in the system.

3 Load Balancing Scheduling Method

In this section, we apply the Load Balancing (LB) scheduling method to the dedicated machine constraint of the photolithography machine in semiconductor manufacturing. The proposed LB method uses the RSEM as a tool to represent the temporal relationship between the wafer lots and machines during each scheduling step.

3.1 Task Generation

After obtaining the process flow for customer product from the database of semiconductor manufacturing, we can use a simple program to transform the process flow into our matrix representation. There exist thousands of wafer lots and hundreds of process steps in a typical factory. We start from transforming the process pattern of wafer lots into a task matrix. We let r_2 represent the photolithography machine and r represent non-photolithography machines. The symbol r_2^x in the Matrix$[i,j]$ is to represent the wafer lot t_i need of the photolithography machine m_x at the time s_j with dedicated machine constraint, while r_k^x $(k \neq 2)$ is to represent the wafer lot t_i need of the machine type k and the machine m_x at $s_{j'}$ $(j \neq j')$ without dedicated machine constraint. There is no assigned machine number for the photolithography machine before the wafer lot has passed first photolithography stage. Suppose that the required resource pattern of t_1 is as follows: $r_1r_3r_2r_4r_5r_6r_7r_2r_4r_5r_6r_7r_8r_9r_1r_3r_2r_4r_5r_6r_7r_3r_2r_8r_9$, and starts the process in the factory at s_1. We will fill its pattern into the matrix from Matrix$[t_1,s_1]$ to Matrix$[t_1,s_{25}]$, which indicates that the total number of the steps for t_1 is 25. The task t_2 in the matrix has the same required resource pattern as t_1 but starting at s_3; meanwhile, t_i in the matrix starts from s_8, and then it requires the same type resource, the photolithography machine, but does not the same machine as t_2 at s_{10}. This represents that t_2 needs the machine m_1, while t_i has not been dedicated to any machine yet. Moreover, two tasks, t_2 and t_i might compete with the same resource r_4 at s_{11} if r_4 is not enough for them at s_{11}. The following matrix depicts the patterns of these tasks.

	S_1	S_2	S_3	S_4	S_5	S_6	S_7	S_8	S_9	S_{10}	S_{11}	S_{12}	S_{13}	S_{14}	S_{15}	S_{16}	S_{17}	S_{18}	S_{19}	S_{20}	S_{21}	S_{22}	S_{23}	S_{24}	S_{25}	..	..	S_j	..	S_m
t_1	r_1	r_3	r_2	r_4	r_5	r_6	r_7	r_2	r_4	r_5	r_6	r_7	r_8	r_9	r_1	r_3	r_2	r_4	r_5	r_6	r_7	r_3	r_2	r_8	r_9			.		
t_2			r_1	r_3	r_2	r_4	r_5	r_6	r_7	r_2^{i}	r_4	r_5	r_6	r_7	r_8	r_9	r_1	r_3	r_2	r_4	r_5	r_6	r_7	r_3	r_2	r_8	r_9			
t_i								r_1	r_3	r_2	r_4	r_6	r_5	..	..	..	..	..	..	..	..	..	..	..	..	..	..	..	..	..
..													..	..																

3.2 Resource Calculation

The definitions and formulae of these factors for the LB scheduling method in the *Resource Calculation* module are as follows:

> *W: wafer lots in process,*
> *P: numbers of photolithography machines,*
> *K: types of machine (resource)*

- *How many wafer lots will need the k type machine (photolithography machine, k = 2) at s_j:*

$$RR(r_k^x, s_j) = \sum_{t_i \in W} Matrix[t_i, s_j] = r_k^x, 1 \le x \le P \tag{1}$$

- *How many wait steps t_i has had before s_j:*

$$WaitStep(t_i) = \sum_{j=start}^{current\ step} Matrix[t_i, s_j] = w_k, 1 \leq k \leq K \tag{2}$$

- *How many steps t_i has had before s_j:*

$$Steps(t_i) = \sum_{j=start}^{current\ step} Matrix[t_i, s_j] \neq "" \tag{3}$$

- *How many steps t_i will have.*

$$Steps(t_i) = \sum_{j=start}^{end\ step} Matrix[t_i, s_j] \neq "" \tag{4}$$

- *The load factor of machine m_x, wafer lots * remaining photolithography stages*

$$Load(m_x, s_j) = \sum_{t \in W} \{t_i * R(t_i) \mid pm(t_i) = m_x\} \tag{5}$$

- *How many remaining photolithography stages for t_i:*

$$R(t_i) = \sum_{j=start}^{end\ step} Matrix[t_i, s_j] = r_k^x, 1 \leq x \leq P, k = 2 \tag{6}$$

$pm(t_i)$: the number x of dedicated photolithography machine of t_i:

Load is defined as the wafer lots limited to machine m multiplied by their remaining layers of photolithography stage. *Load* is a relative parameter, representing the load of the machine and wafer lots limited to one machine compared to other machines. The larger load factor means that the more required service from wafer lots has been limited to this machine. The LB scheduling method uses these factors to schedule the wafer lot to a suitable machine at the first photolithography stage which is the only photolithography stage without the dedicated constraint.

3.3 Resource Allocation

The process flow of the Resource Allocation module for the example is described in this section. Suppose we are currently at s_j, and the LB scheduling method will start from photolithography machine. We check to determine if there is any wafer lot which is waiting for the photolithography machines at the first photolithography stage. The LB method will assign the m_x with smallest $Load(m_x, s_j)$ for them, one by one. After that, these wafer lots will be dedicated to a photolithography machine. For each m_x, the LB method will select one of the wafer lots dedicated to m_x which has the largest $WaitStep(t_i)$ for it. $Load(m_x, s_j)$ of m_x will be updated after these two processes. The other wafer lots dedicated to each m_x which cannot be allocated to the m_x at current step s_j will insert a w_2 for them in their pattern. For example, at s_{10}, t_i has been assigned to m_1, therefore, t_{i+1} will have a w_2 being inserted into at s_{10}, and then all the following required resources of t_{i+1} will shift one step. All the other types of machines will have the same process without need of being concerned with the dedicated machine constraint. Therefore, we assigned one of the wafer lots which has the largest $WaitStep(t_i)$, then the second largest one, and so on for each machine r_k. Similarly, the LB method will insert a w_k for the wafer lots which will not be assigned to machines r_k at this current step. Therefore, $WaitStep(t_i)$ is to represent the delay status of t_i.

		s_9	s_{10}	s_{11}	s_{12}	s_{13}	s_{14}	..	..	s_j	..	s_m
						..	..					
t_i	..		r_2^1	r_4	r_5	r_6	r_7	..	..			
$t_{i+1'}$	..		w_2	r_2	r_4	r_6	r_5	..	..	..	..	
..			↑	→	→	→	→					

3.4 Discussion

Realistically, it is not difficult to approach the real cases on a smaller scale time step. Another issue is that the machines in the factory have capacity limitation due to the capital invention, which is the resource constraint. How to make the most profit for the invention mostly depends on optimal resource allocation techniques. However, most scheduling polices or methods can provide neither the exact allocation in accepted time, nor a robust and systematic resource allocation strategy. We use the RSEM to represent complex tasks and allocate resources by the simple matrix calculation. This reduces much of the computation time for the complex problem.

Our LB scheduling system provides two kinds of functions. One is that, to define the resource allocation rules and factors according to expert knowledge, we can quickly obtain the resource allocation result at each step by the factors summarized from task matrix. The other is that we could predict the bottleneck or critical situation quickly by executing proper steps forward. This can also evaluate the predefined rules to obtain better scheduling rules for the system at the same time.

4 Simulation Result

We have done two types of simulations for a Least Slack (LS) time scheduling policy and our LB scheduling method. The LS time scheduling has been developed in the research, Fluctuation Smoothing Policy for Mean Cycle Time (FSMCT) [12] in which the FSMCT is for re-entrant production lines. The entire class of LS policies has been proven stable in a deterministic setting [3] [13]. The LS scheduling policy sets the highest priority to a wafer lot whose slack time is the smallest in the queue buffer of one machine. When the machine is going to idle, it will select the highest priority wafer lot in the queue buffer to service next. However, the simulation result shows that the proposed LB is better than the LS method. For simplifying the simulation to easily represent the scheduling methods, we have made the following assumptions:

1. *Each wafer lot has the same process steps and quantity.*
2. *All photolithography and other stages have the same process time.*
3. *There is no breakdown event in the simulations.*
4. *There is unlimited capacity for non-photolithography machines.*

We implemented a simulation program in Java and have run the simulations on the NetBeans IDE 4.1. Our simulation was set with 3 photolithography machines, 5 to 12 photolithography layers, and 500 wafer lots. In the task patterns, the symbol r represents the non-photolithography stage; and r_2 the photolithography stage. The basic task pattern for 5 layers is: "$rrr_2rrrrr_2rrrrrrrrr_2rrrrrr_2rrr_2rr$". Then the task pattern for each added layer after 5 layers is: "r_2rr". Therefore, the task pattern for 6 layers is: "$rrr_2rrrrr_2rrrrrrrrr_2rrrrrr_2rrr_2rrr_2rr$", the task pattern for 7 layers is: "$rrr_2rrrrr_2rrrrrrrrr_2rrrrrr_2rrr_2rrr_2rrr_2rr$",…, and the task pattern for 12 layers is: "$rrr_2rrrrr_2rrrrrrrrr_2rrrrrr_2rrr_2rrr_2rrr_2rrr_2rrr_2rrr_2rrr_2rr$". We simulate the wafer arrival rate between two wafer lots as a Poisson distribution. The simulation result is shown in Fig. 4 and the task matrix for 12 layers looks as follows:

Task Matrix (12 photolithography layers):

s_1...s_m

t_1:$rrr_2rrrrr_2rrrrrrrrr_2rrrrrr_2rrrr_2rrr_2rrr_2rrr_2rrr_2rrr_2rrr_2rr$

t_i: $rrr_2rrrrr_2rrrrrrrrr_2rrrrrr_2rrrr_2rrr_2rrr_2rrr_2rrr_2rrr_2rrr_2rr$

t_{500}:

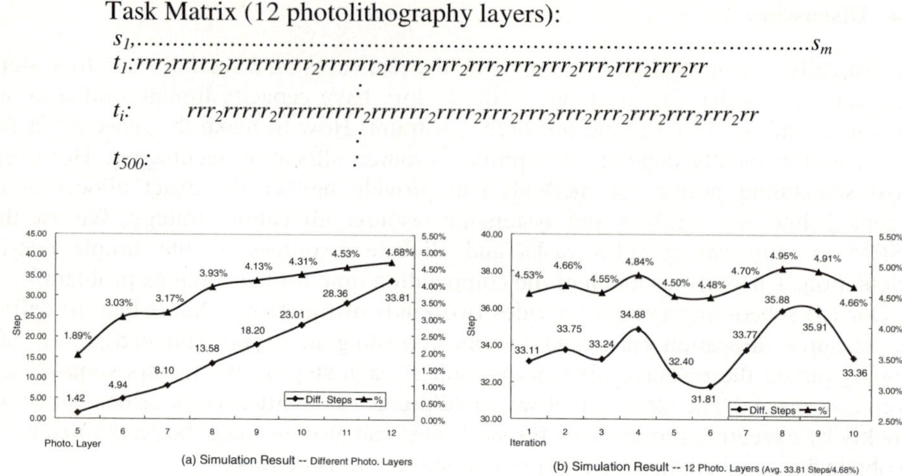

(a) Simulation Result -- Different Photo. Layers

(b) Simulation Result -- 12 Photo. Layers (Avg. 33.81 Steps/4.68%)

Fig. 4. By comparing the mean of cycle time of the case using different photolithography layers and ten iterations, the LS method has an average 33.81 steps more than the LB method. In other words, the LB method is better than the LS method 4.68% on average in the simulation. The simulations result of different photolithography layers indicates that the more the photolithography layers, the better the LB method performs than the LS method does.

We applied the LS and LB methods in the simulations. When the wafer lot needs to wait for its dedicated machine, we will insert a w in the process pattern of the wafer lot to represent the situation. After completing the simulations, we count the pattern of wafer lots to know how much time they have used. Although the simulations are simplified, they reflect the real situation we have met in the factory. It is not difficult to extend the simulation with more machines, wafer lots, and photolithography or non- photolithography stages. We can use different numbers of r_2 together, e.g., r_2, r_2r_2, or $r_2r_2r_2r_2$,..., for the task patterns to represent different process time of different photolithography stages. After applying the LS method to the above simulations and counting the required resource (formula (1), x = 1 and 2) for the photolithography machines at each step, we can realize that the load of two machines becomes unbalanced during the simulations, as well as the thrashing phenomenon that happens in the simulations.

5   Conclusion

To provide the solution to the issue of dedicated machine constraint, the proposed Load Balancing (LB) scheduling method has been presented. Along with providing the LB scheduling method to the dedicated machine constraint, we have also presented a novel model—the representation and manipulation method for the task patterns. In addition, the simulations have also shown that the proposed LB scheduling method was better than the LS method. The advantage of the LB method is that we could easily schedule the wafer lots by simple calculation on a two-dimensional matrix.

Acknowledgement

This research was supported in part by the Ministry of Education under grant EX-91-E-FA06-4-4 and the National Science Council under grant NSC-94-2213-E-194-010 and NSC-92-2917-I-194-005. This research was also partially supported by the U.S. National Science Foundation grant No. IIS-0326387. One of us, A. Shr, is grateful to Ms. Victoria Tangi for English proofreading.

References

1. Akcalt, E. Nemoto, K., and Uzsoy, R.: Cycle-time improvements for photolithography process in semiconductor manufacturing. IEEE Transactions on Semiconductor Manufacturing, Vol. 14, No. 1 (2001) 48-56.
2. Kumar, P. R.: Re-entrant Lines. In Queuing Systems: Theory and Applications, Special Issue on Queuing Networks, Vol. 13, Nos. 1-3 (1993) 87-110.
3. Kumar, P. R.: Scheduling Manufacturing Systems of Re-Entrant Lines. Stochastic Modeling and Analysis of Manufacturing Systems, David D. Yao (ed.), Springer-Verlag, New York (1994) 325-360.
4. Lu, S. C. H., Ramaswamy, D., Kumar, P. R.: Efficient Scheduling Policies to Reduce Mean and Variance of Cycle-time in Semiconductor Manufacturing Plants. IEEE Transactions on Semiconductor Manufacturing, Vol. 7, No. 3 (1994) 374-385.
5. Wein, L. M.: Scheduling Semiconductor Wafer Fabrication. IEEE Transactions on Semiconductor Manufacturing, Vol. 1, No. 3 (1988) 115-130.
6. Chern , C. and Liu, Y.: Family-Based Scheduling Rules of a Sequence-Dependent Wafer Fabrication System. IEEE Transactions on Semiconductor Manufacturing, Vol. 16, No. 1 (2003) 15-25.
7. Shen, Y. and Leachman, R. C.: Stochastic Wafer Fabrication Scheduling. IEEE Transactions on Semiconductor Manufacturing, Vol. 16, No. 1 (2003) 2-14.
8. Zhou, M. and Jeng, M. D.: Modeling, Analysis, Simulation, Scheduling, and Control of Semiconductor Manufacturing System: A Petri Net Approach. IEEE Transactions on Semiconductor Manufacturing, Vol. 11, No. 3 (1998) 333-357.
9. Miwa, T. Nishihara, N., and Yamamoto, K.: Automated Stepper Load Balance Allocation System. IEEE Transactions on Semiconductor Manufacturing, Vol. 18, No. 4 (2005) 510-516.
10. Arisha, A. and Young, P.: Intelligent Simulation-based Lot Scheduling of Photolithography Toolsets in a Wafer Fabrication Facility. Winter Simulation Conference (2004) 1935-1942.
11. Mönch, L., Prause, M., and Schmalfuss V.: Simulation-Based Solution of Load-Balancing Problems in the Photolithography Area of a Semiconductor Wafer Fabrication Facility. Winter Simulation Conference (2001) 1170-1177.
12. Kumar, S., Kumar, P. R.: Queuing Network Models in the Design and Analysis of Semiconductor Wafer Fabs. IEEE Transactions on Robotics and Automation, Vol. 17, No. 5 (2001) 548-561.
13. Lu, S. H., Kumar, P. R.: Distributed Scheduling Based on Due Dates and Buffer Priorities. IEEE Transactions on Automatic Control (1991) 1406-1416.

An Adaptive Control Using Multiple Neural Networks for the Variable Displacement Pump

Ming-Hui Chu[2], Yuan Kang[1], Yuan-Liang Liu[1],
Yi-Wei Chen[2], and Yeon-Pung Chang[1]

[1] Department of Mechanical Engineering, Chung Yuan Christian University
Chung Li, Taiwan 32023, R.O.C.
yk@cycu.edu.tw
[2] Department of Automation Engineering, Tung Nan Institute of Technology
Taipei 222, Taiwan, R.O.C.

Abstract. A model following adaptive controller made-up by neural networks is proposed to control the angular displacement of swashplate in a variable displacement axial piston pump (VDAPP), which consists of multiple neural networks including a direct neural controller, a neural emulator and a neural tuner. The controls of swashplate angle are investigated by simulation and experiment, serve its model-following characteristics can be evaluated and compared with other methods.

1 Introduction

The VDAPP is important for large efficiency since it can transmit specific powers with less bypass power lose. The flow and pressure of VDAPP are changing by control of the swashplate angle, which utilizes an electro-hydraulic proportional valve (EHPV). Absolutely, the VDAPP with an EHPV is used for saving energy.

The VDAPP is inherently nonlinear, time delay, and time variant as enduring varied pressure load. It is necessary that the adaptive control is used to enhance the adaptability and stability for the VDAPP control system. Several studies have been conducted in an attempt to improve the dynamics and controls of VDAPP. Akers and Lin [1] developed dynamic model of VDAPP and applied optimal control algorithms for motions of the swashplate angle. Their algorithms were simulated but difficult to implement. Recently, many learning architectures for neural control system have been presented. However, the direct control strategy with specialized learning architecture is easily implemented without off-line training, but the Jacobian of the plant need to be available prior. It is usually difficult to obtain the Jacobian of a nonlinear plant. Lin and Wai [2] proposed the δ adaptation law, they used a linear combination of the error and error's differential to approximate the back propagation error (BPE). Chu, etc. [3] established the dynamic model of VDAPP with an EHPV and presented a model-following direct neural controller to control the swashplate angle. In both studies, no specified method had been proposed to determine the parameters of linear combination. They used only tuning by try and error. However, it is necessary to develop algorithms for tuning the parameters of linear combination in direct neural controller.

M. Ali and R. Dapoigny (Eds.): IEA/AIE 2006, LNAI 4031, pp. 760–769, 2006.

Omatu and Yoshioka [4] proposed a PID controller whose parameters are tuned by neural network for the stable and fast response of an inverted pendulum. Omatu etc. [5] used the same method for the stable response of a single-input multi-output control system with double inverted pendulums. Moreover, it has been proven that the parameters of PID controller can be tuned by neural network for many other dynamical systems.

A novel model-following adaptive algorithm, using multiple neural networks, is proposed to control the swashplate angle to follow a reference model, which consists of a direct neural controller, a neural tuner and a neural emulator. The neural tuner is designed to adjust the parameters of the direct neural controller. The neural emulator is used to imitate the nonlinear model of the VDAPP to replace the Jacobian in control phase, which is also used for numerical simulation.

2 Adaptive Control Using Multiple Neural Networks

The illustration of VDAPP is shown in Fig. 1, two hydraulic actuators with different pistons area drive the swashplate, the bigger one is main actuator, which is controlled by an EHPV, and the other is bias actuator. A linear PD controller is used to control the spool displacement of EHPV with a PWM driver. A hall sensor measures the angular displacement of swashplate.

The swashplate dynamics can be expressed by a nonlinear third-order model and defined as

$$\alpha_P(n) = f\left(u_P(n-1),\ u_P(n-2), u_P(n-3),\ \alpha_P(n-1), \alpha_P(n-2), \alpha_P(n-3) \right) \qquad (1)$$

where $f(\cdot)$ is a nonlinear function, α_p is the angular displacement of VDAPP, u_p is the control input, and n represents the n-th sampling interval. The nonlinear model described by Eq.(1) can be emulated by a BPNN, which is called emulator and denoted by N_2.

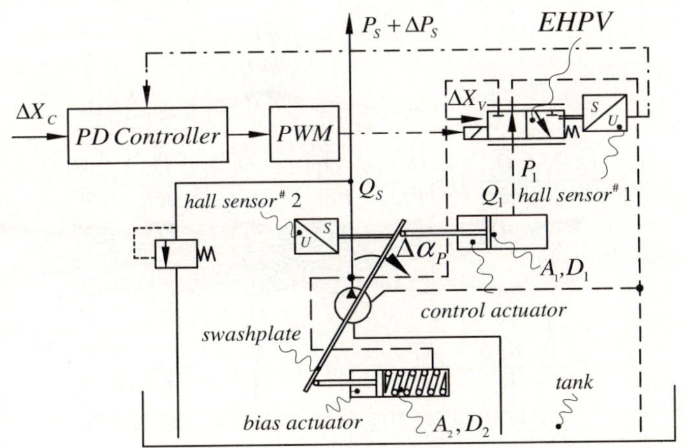

Fig. 1. Illustration of a VDAPP with three-way EHPV

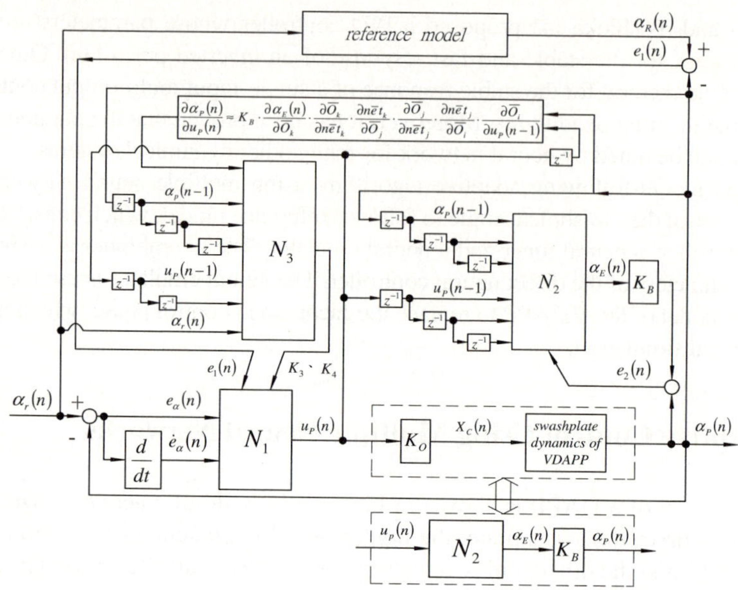

Fig. 2. The MNNACS for angle control of VDAPP swashplate (the original diagram is used for illustrating experiments or practices of a real VDAPP, when the diagram is used for design and simulation, the original block is replaced by N_2 block)

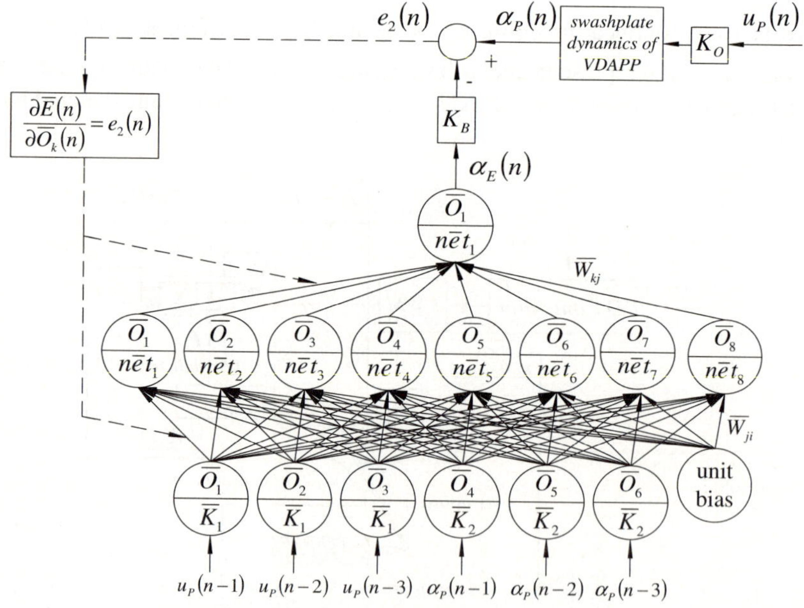

Fig. 3. The construction of neural emulator N_2

The proposed model-following adaptive control system using multiple neural networks (MNNACS) for the swashplate angular displacement of VDAPP is shown in Fig. 2, including a neural controller N_1, neural emulator N_2, and neural tuner N_3. The neural network N_2 is required to be trained priori, and used to emulate the nonlinear model of the VDAPP, which is applied to simulate the Jacobian in control phase. The detailed algorithms of N_2 have been presented by Narendra and Parthasarathy [6]. The construction of neural emulator N_2 is shown in Fig.3.

All networks N_1, N_2 and N_3 has three layers including input layer (subscripted by "i"), hidden layer (subscripted by "j") and output layer (subscripted by "k"). The hyperbolic tangent function is used for both N_1 and N_2 in the hidden and output layers, and the sigmoid function and unity are used for N_3 as the activation function for the nodes in the hidden layer and the output layer, respectively.

The network N_1 has two inputs, one output and five hidden nodes. Inputs are both errors e_α and $\dot{e}_\alpha$ between angle command α_r and actual angle α_p of swashplate. The input signals are normalized within ± 1 by using normalized factors K_1' and K_2'. The output u_p of neural controller is normalized by multiplying a scaling factor K_O, which is used as the displacement command of EHPV spool. The weights of N_1 are updated by BPE which is approximated by a linear combination of error e_1 and its differential $\dot{e}_1$ by multiplying the parameters K_3 and K_4, respectively [3]. The error e_1 is the difference between outputs of reference model α_R and actual swashplate angular displacement α_P (ie. $e_1 = \alpha_R - \alpha_P$). The appropriate parameters K_3 and K_4 are tuned by N_3. In this paper, a linear second order dynamic model whose parameters satisfying performance indexes, which depend on the industrial requirements, is designed to be the reference model.

The reference model is designed according to the characteristics of close-loop control system, which can perform the required dynamics and ideal outputs.

The neural network N_3 has 8 hidden nodes, 6 input nodes and 2 output nodes. The two outputs are denoted by K_3 and K_4 as the appropriate parameters. The six inputs are $\alpha_P(n-1)$, $\alpha_P(n-2)$, $\alpha_P(n-3)$, $u_P(n-1)$, $u_P(n-2)$, and $\alpha_r(n)$ with respect to plant output, input and the command signals, where n represents the n-th sampling interval, which are normalized by using $\hat{K}_1$, $\hat{K}_2$ and $\hat{K}_3$.

3   Weights Updating of BPNN for Neural Networks

Both algorithms of N_1 and N_2 are presented by Narendra and Parthasarathy [6]. While, the algorithm for the neural tuner is not same as the one for neural controller or emulator. The detailed descriptions of the algorithm for N_3 are presented in this study.

764 M.-H. Chu et al.

The variables and parameters of the three neural networks used in following analysis are denoted by superscript $'$ 、$-$ 、$\wedge$ respect to N_1 、 N_2 and N_3 . The weights-update quantities of the neural tuner are defined by:

$$\Delta\hat{W}_{kj}(n) = -\hat{\eta} \cdot \frac{\partial\hat{E}(n)}{\partial\hat{W}_{kj}(n)}, \quad k = 3, 4, \quad j = 1\sim8 \tag{2}$$

$$\Delta\hat{W}_{ji}(n) = -\hat{\eta} \cdot \frac{\partial\hat{E}(n)}{\partial\hat{W}_{ji}(n)}, \quad i = 1\sim6, \quad j = 1\sim8 \tag{3}$$

where the error energy function $\hat{E}(n)$ is defined by

$$\hat{E}(n) = \frac{1}{2}(\alpha_R(n) - \alpha_P(n))^2 = \frac{1}{2}e_1(n)^2 \tag{4}$$

The gradient of $\hat{E}(n)$ respects to the change of $\hat{W}_{kj}(n)$ can be determined by

$$\frac{\partial\hat{E}(n)}{\partial\hat{W}_{kj}(n)} = \frac{\partial\hat{E}(n)}{\partial\hat{net}_k(n)} \cdot \frac{\partial\hat{net}_k(n)}{\partial\hat{W}_{kj}(n)} = \hat{\delta}_k(n) \cdot \hat{O}_j(n) = \hat{\delta}_k(n) \cdot f(\hat{net}_j), \quad k = 3, 4 \tag{5}$$

where $f(\cdot)$ is the activation function, and $\hat{\delta}_k(n)$ can be determined by

$$\hat{\delta}_k(n) = \frac{\partial\hat{E}(n)}{\partial\hat{net}_k(n)} = \frac{\partial\hat{E}(n)}{\partial\alpha_P(n)} \cdot \frac{\partial\alpha_P(n)}{\partial u_P(n)} \cdot \frac{\partial u_P(n)}{\partial\hat{O}_k(n)} \cdot \frac{\partial\hat{O}_k(n)}{\partial\hat{net}_k(n)}$$

$$= -e_1(n) \cdot \frac{\partial\alpha_P(n)}{\partial u_P(n)} \cdot \frac{\partial u_P(n)}{\partial K_k} \cdot 1, \quad k = 3, 4 \tag{6}$$

where $\hat{O}_k(n) = \hat{net}_k(n)$ since unity is the activation function of output neurons, and the Jacobian of the swashplate dynamic is evaluated by

$$\frac{\partial\alpha_P(n)}{\partial u_P(n)} \approx K_B \cdot \sum_{j=1}^{8} \frac{\partial f(\overline{net}_k(n))}{\partial\overline{net}_k(n)} \cdot \overline{W}_{kj}(n) \cdot \frac{\partial f(\overline{net}_j(n))}{\partial\overline{net}_j(n)} \cdot \overline{W}_{ji}(n) \cdot \overline{K}_1(n) \tag{7}$$

where K_B is the gain for network N_2 , and $\overline{K}_1$ is the normalization factors for inputs of network N_2 .

The differential of E' with respect to the network output O'_k defined to be the BPE is approximated by a linear combination of the error and its differential. The $(n-1)$-th weight-update of the output layer for neural network N_1 is

$$\Delta W'_{kj}(n-1) = \eta' \cdot (K_3 \cdot e_1(n-1) + K_4 \cdot \dot{e}_1(n-1)) \cdot \frac{\partial f(net'_k(n-1))}{\partial net'_k(n-1)} \cdot O'_j(n-1) \tag{8}$$

where K_3 and K_4 are positive constants.

The differentials of the nth weight-update with respect to K_3 and K_4 are:

$$\frac{\partial W'_{kj}(n)}{\partial K_3} = \frac{\partial W'_{kj}(n-1)}{\partial K_3} - \eta' \cdot e_1(n-1) \cdot \frac{\partial f\left(net'_k(n-1)\right)}{\partial net'_k(n-1)} \cdot O'_j(n-1) \qquad (9)$$

$$\frac{\partial W'_{kj}(n)}{\partial K_4} = \frac{\partial W'_{kj}(n-1)}{\partial K_4} - \eta' \cdot \dot{e}_1(n-1) \cdot \frac{\partial f\left(net'_k(n-1)\right)}{\partial net'_k(n-1)} \cdot O'_j(n-1) \qquad (10)$$

respectively. And the differentials of plant input with respect to K_3 and K_4 is

$$\frac{\partial u_P(n)}{\partial K_k} = \frac{\partial u_P(n)}{\partial O'_k(n)} \cdot \frac{\partial O'_k(n)}{\partial net'_k(n)} \cdot \frac{\partial net'_k(n)}{\partial W'_{kj}(n)} \cdot \frac{\partial W'_{kj}(n)}{\partial K_k}$$

$$= \frac{\partial f\left(net'_k(n)\right)}{\partial net'_k(n)} \cdot O'_j(n) \cdot \frac{\partial W'_{kj}(n)}{\partial K_k}, \quad k = 3, \ 4 \qquad (11)$$

Substituting Eqs. (10) and (11) into Eq. (12) gives a result and substituting this result into Eq. (7) yields $\hat{\delta}_3$ and $\hat{\delta}_4$, which are then substituted into Eq. (6), the gradient of $\hat{E}$ with respect to the weights $\hat{W}_{ji}$ of N_3 can be obtained as

$$\frac{\partial \hat{E}(n)}{\partial \hat{W}_{ji}(n)} = \frac{\partial \hat{E}(n)}{\partial \hat{net}_j(n)} \cdot \frac{\partial \hat{net}_j(n)}{\partial \hat{W}_{ji}(n)} = \hat{\delta}_j(n) \cdot \hat{O}_i(n) \qquad (12)$$

where $\hat{\delta}_j(n)$ is defined by

$$\hat{\delta}_j(n) = \frac{\partial \hat{E}(n)}{\partial \hat{net}_j(n)} = \sum_{k=3}^{4} \frac{\partial \hat{E}(n)}{\partial \hat{net}_k(n)} \cdot \frac{\partial \hat{net}_k(n)}{\partial \hat{O}_j(n)} \cdot \frac{\partial \hat{O}_j(n)}{\partial \hat{net}_j(n)}$$

$$= \sum_{k=3}^{4} \hat{\delta}_k(n) \cdot \hat{W}_{kj}(n) \cdot \frac{\partial f\left(\hat{net}_j(n)\right)}{\partial \hat{net}_j(n)} \qquad (13)$$

Thus, the weights $\hat{W}_{kj}(n+1)$ and $\hat{W}_{ji}(n+1)$ can be determined from the time step from n to $n+1$ by using

$$\hat{W}_{kj}(n+1) = \hat{W}_{kj}(n) + \Delta \hat{W}_{kj}(n), \ k = 3, \ 4, \ j = 1 \sim 8 \qquad (14)$$

$$\hat{W}_{ji}(n+1) = \hat{W}_{ji}(n) + \Delta \hat{W}_{ji}(n), \ i = 1 \sim 6, \ j = 1 \sim 8. \qquad (15)$$

4 Numerical Simulation

The input signals $u_P(n)$ are randomly within an interval from 0 to 4 volts in constant duration 0.02 sec, which is used to excite the angular responses of swashplate. The corresponding angular responses $\alpha_P(n)$ are measured and together with inputs $u_P(n)$ served as training data pairs for priori training of N_2. The initial weights of N_2 are chosen between ± 0.5 randomly. The weights-update of N_2 is convergent after 3×10^6 iterations in training process till the MSE is smaller than 0.001 volts.

A linear second-order reference model with $\varsigma = 1$ and $\omega_n = 200$ Hz is shown as

$$\frac{\alpha_R(z)}{\alpha_r(z)} = \frac{0.0173z - 0.01459}{z^2 - 1.6375z + 0.67032} \tag{16}$$

The discharge volume of a VDAPP is fixed at 10.6 liters. The maximum angle of swashplate is 0.2618 rad meaning 100% of angular displacement. The swashplate actuators are supplied with internal supply. A pressure control valve is applied to control the pump outlet pressure. The pump outlet pressure is priori adjusted at 1 MPa respect to angular displacement = 0.00524 rad. The outlet pressure will increase to 1.5 MPa when the swashplate angle up to 0.10472 rad. In this simulation, the pump outlet pressure varies between 1 and 1.5 MPa.

The proposed MNNACS with 8 V step command are simulated. The time responses for swashplate angle with operation pressures of 2, 14 and 21MPa are shown in Fig. 4. It shows the time response for swashplate angle become faster as the outlet pressure increasing.

The DNCS using the appropriate parameters K_3 and K_4, which have been trained by MNNACS, is simulated. The parameters K_3 and K_4 are actually trained during control phase of MNNACS with the PRBS command. The simulation result is shown in Fig. 5. It is proven that the appropriate K_3 and K_4 can be obtained by the control phase of MNNACS. However the DNCS with simple structure can save much CPU time and easily be implemented, so that the DNCS using the well trained parameters K_3 and K_4 can be applied to control the swashplate angle. It enhances the adaptability and stability with favorable model following performance.

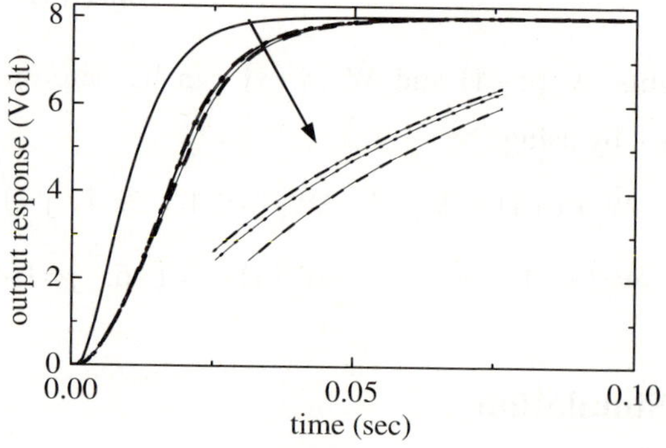

Fig. 4. Time responses for swashplate angle with MNNACS (reference model : —————— ; 2 MPa : — — — — — ; 14 MPa : •—•—•—•—• ; 21 MPa : —•—•—•—•)

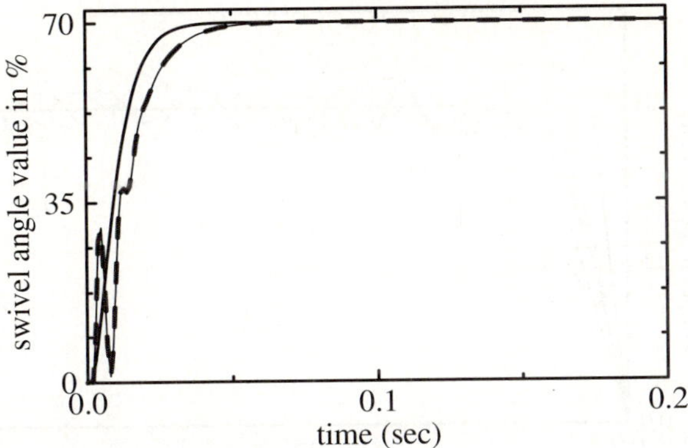

Fig. 5. Time responses for swashplate angle with DNCS using appropriate parameters K_3 and K_4 trained by MNNACS (reference model : ———— ; 2 MPa : ▬ ▬ ▬ ▬)

5 Experiments

The Rexroth A10VSO variable displacement axial piston pump is applied in the experiments. The output of neural controller is multiplied by $K_o = 3\,\mathrm{Volt}$, then converted to the analog voltsage between ± 3 V by a 12 bits bipolar D/A converter. The analog signal regards as the spool displacement command for EHPV system. Two Pentium PC with a 12 bits AD/DA interface and Labview AT-MIO16E-1 data acquisition interface are used to converter the output voltsage of hall sensor to numerical digitals with the sampling time of 0.01sec. The sampling time adopted in the experiments is 0.001sec, which is synchronized by a crystal oscillator.

A hydraulic cylinder having 10 liters used as discharge volume of pump, and a pressure control valve are mounted at the pump outlet. The actuators of swashplate utilize internal supply. The pump outlet pressure is controlled by a pressure control valve, the pump outlet pressure is priori adjusted to 0.1MPa, and the relief pressure is adjusted to 1MPa.

The proposed MNNACS, MNNACS without N_2, direct neural control system (DNCS) and indirect neural control system (INCS) are implemented to control the swashplate angle. The appropriate values of both parameters $K_3 = 2.91$, $K_4 = 0.003$ for DNCS are obtained by the control phase of MNNACS in simulation process. The maximum command input α_r is 10 volts, and the maximum output of the hall sensor is 10 volts. The step signals of amplitude 1 and 4 Volts are used as the command signals, and the experiment results are shown in Fig. 6(a) and (b). The phenomena of swashplate disturbed by pressure fluctuation can be observed. The control systems need more settling time for following the reference model, when the command increased. The experiment results show the DNCS with appropriate values of both parameters K_3 and K_4 has favorable model following characteristics. It is suggested that applied the DNCS to VDAPP with the appropriate parameters K_3 and K_4, which are trained by

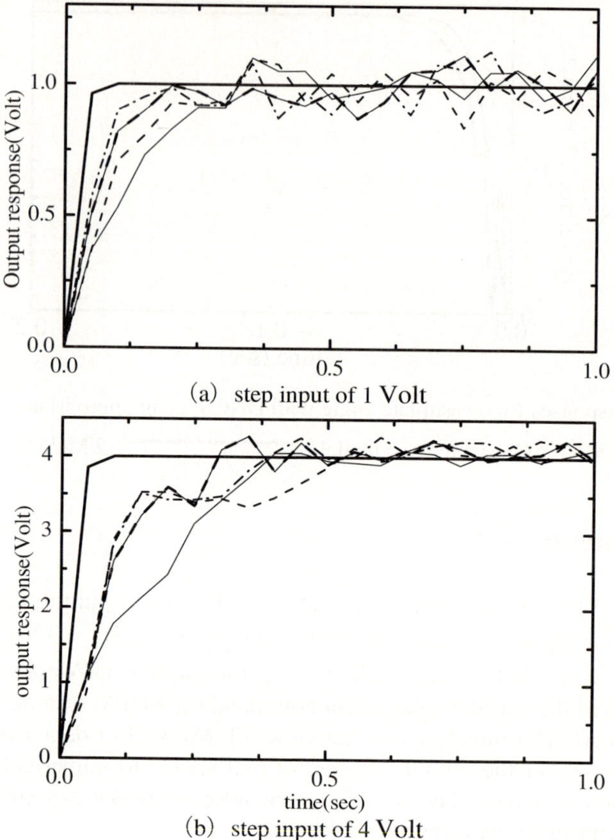

(a)   step input of 1 Volt

(b)   step input of 4 Volt

Fig. 6. Experiment results (reference model : ————— ; DNCS : — · — · — · — ; INCS : — — — — — ; MNNACS with N_2 : ▬ ▬ ▬ ▬ ; MNNACS without N_2 : —————)

control phase of MNNACS. By the method proposed by this study, the real time control system is easily implemented with favorable model- following performance.

6   Conclusion

In this paper, the DNCS, INCS and MNNACS applied to control the swashplate angle of the VDAPP are implemented. The simulation results of MNNACS show that the parameters determinations of control system will be convergent, and favorable model-following characteristics can be obtained. The swashplate angle control system applies the DNCS with the appropriate parameters K_3 and K_4, which are trained by MNNACS, still has favorable model-following performance. By the method proposed by this study, the real time control system for VDAPP is easily implemented.

References

1. Akers, A. and Lin, S. J., "Optimal Control Theory Applied to a Pump with Single-Stage Electrohydraulic Servovalve," Transaction of the ASME, Journal of Dynamical system, Measurement and Control, Vol. 110, No. 2, pp. 120-125, 1988.
2. Lin, F. J. and Wai, R. J., "Hybrid Controller using a Neural Network for a PM Synchronous Servo-Motor Drive," IEE, Proceedings of Electric Power Applications, Vol. 145, No. 3, pp. 223-230, 1998.
3. Chu, M. H., Kang, Y., Chang, Y. F., Liu, Y. L. and Chang, C. W., "Model-Following Controller Based on Neural Network for Variable Displacement Pump," JSME, International Journal (series C), Vol. 46, No. 1, pp. 176-186, 2003.
4. Omatu, S. and Yoshioka, M., "Self-Tuning Neuro-PID Control and Applications" IEEE, International Conference on Systems, Man, and Cybernetics, Computational Cybernetics and Simulation, Vol. 3, pp. 1985-1989, 1997.
5. Omatu, S., Fujinaka, T. and Yoshioka, M., "Neuro-PID Control for Inverted Single and Double Pendulums," IEEE, International Conference on Systems, Man, and Cybernetics, Vol. 4, pp. 2685-2690, 2000.
6. Narendra, K. S. and Parthasarathy, K., "Identification and control of dynamical systems using neural networks," IEEE, Neural Networks, Vol. 1, No. 1, pp. 4-27, 1990.

An Elaborated Goal Production Module for Implementing a Virtual Inhabitant

Se-Jin Ji, Jung-Woo Kwon, and Jong-Hee Park

E10-506, Electronics Dept., Kyungpook Nat'l University
1370 Sankyuk-Dong, Puk-gu, Daegu, Korea
{husty, zen98, jhpark}@eecs.knu.ac.kr
http://aimm.knu.ac.kr

Abstract. A Virtual Inhabitant is a kind of believable agent proposed to endow attractive features of human-controlled characters, especially the diverse behaviors, to the computer-controlled characters. To behave diversely, goal production module of a Virtual Inhabitant should be designed to produce wide variety of goals semi-automatically which are fit for general situations in contrast to the previous character's goal production models which are devised for handling very restricted situation based on fixed form goal description methods such as script, state-machine. In this paper, we elaborate the goal production module by categorizing diverse drive stimuli, devising extending and matching methods for those stimuli, and introducing additional methods for supporting the features stressed in psychological field and habitual/routine behavior of a Virtual Inhabitant. We expect that the proposed goal production module can be used for the characters in the open-ended games, on-line games, virtual communities, and so on.

1 Introduction

The current popularities of many on-line games and virtual communities[1-4] are largely based on the diverse actions of other user and social relationships among the users which computer controlled characters hardly provide. Computer-controlled characters which use finite state machines, rule bases, neural networks, and so on as their control mechanism show very restricted behaviours assigned at their creation time and these restricted behaviours of characters make the user's interest reduced seriously when he/she uses the application repeatedly. In contrast, human-controlled characters can behave differently under the exactly same situation according to the human user's operation and show more elaborated behaviours as the human user becomes more familiar to the applications. Because of these attractive features, the diverse and varied behaviours of human-controlled characters are very important source for inducing unceasing interest of the user despite of his/her repetitive use of the applications.

To overcome the restriction of computer-controlled characters and to utilize these attractive features of human-controlled characters, we proposed an agent architecture in [5] for implementing a computer controlled agent (characters) which is called Virtual Inhabitant[5] who behaves diversely as a human-controlled characters does and make social relationships with other characters. The Virtual Inhabitant is a kind of

M. Ali and R. Dapoigny (Eds.): IEA/AIE 2006, LNAI 4031, pp. 770–779, 2006.
© Springer-Verlag Berlin Heidelberg 2006

believable agent[5] who behaves diversely, lives long in the virtual environment, makes social relationships with others, keeps the relationships in his life time, and has continual self-updating abilities to behave in a diverse and adaptive manner.

To achieve these requirements, each module of Virtual Inhabitant should be designed to effectively diversify the behavior, and among those modules, the goal production module plays most important role for diversifying the Virtual Inhabitant's behavior by providing wide variety of goals. The computer-controlled characters in traditional on-line games[1, 2] have very restricted and fixed goal pools because they are designed to select their goals based on the hard-wired type goal description methods such as state-machine, rule, script. The characters based on these methods can not provide wide variety of behaviors, though they are very good for the restricted tasks such as guards for castle gate, merchant in the town. Characters in the SIMS[3], a kind of open-ended game, produce their goal according to their preference when there is no command from their user. This makes him/her somewhat realistic, but can not endow him/her with diverse behavior. Some previous academic agents such as [6-9] introduce some advanced mechanism such as the emotional drive, neural network, value ontology, directed improvisation for more elaborated goal production. However, these agent models can not achieve the requirements of Virtual Inhabitant because they just support one or two drive stimulus as the basis for their goal production and reflect little human features such as value, personality, social relation, emotion which are stressed in the psychological research field of motivation.

To overcome these drawbacks and fully utilize the good features of the goal production methods of the previous models, and fully support the stressed features in the psychological motivation research results[10-13] such as personality, sociality, emotion, value, cultural difference, we propose an elaborate goal production module. To appropriately design the proposed goal production module, we first categorize the diverse drive stimulus[10] and devise extending method for that stimulus. Next, we introduce the matching methods between the drive stimulus and the appropriate goal from the Virtual Inhabitant's action hierarchy. Lastly, we provide additional methods for supporting the features stressed in psychological field and habitual/routine behavior as a good source for the extra believability and diversity of Virtual Inhabitant's behavior.

The rest of this paper is organized as follows. In section 2, we briefly describe the overall architecture of Virtual Inhabitant. In section 3, the structure and operation of goal production module will be shown. In the last section, conclusion and future works will be presented.

2   Overall Architecture of Virtual Inhabitant

In this section, we briefly explain the overall architecture and behavioral module structure of Virtual Inhabitant. (For more detailed, see [5])

In the Fig.1 (a), the architecture of Virtual Inhabitant is roughly divided into four sub modules – behavioral module, memory structure, perceptions and actuation module, learning module. Each sub module consists of several more specific sub modules, for example, as shown in the Fig.1 (b), the behavioral module has goal production module, planning module, execution module, scheduler, and value system. (The arrows between two modules represent the flow of information).

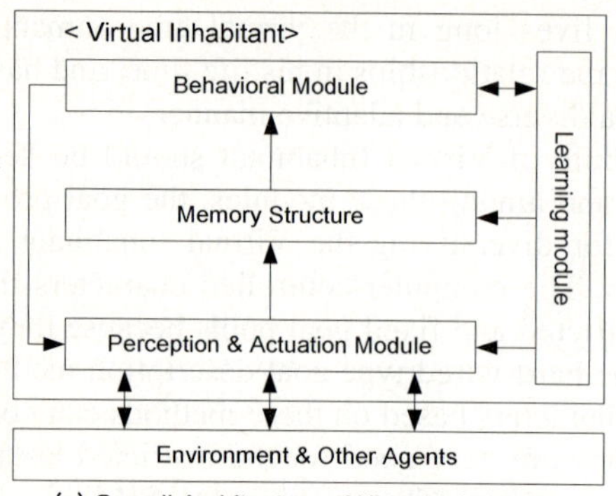

(a) Overall Architecture of Virtual Inhabitant

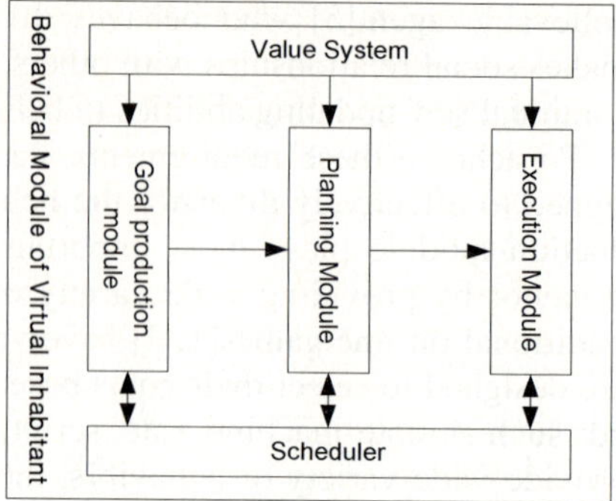

(b) Behavioral Module of Virtual Inhabitant

Fig. 1. Overall Architecture and Behavioral Module of Virtual Inhabitant

Perception and actuation module is a medium for a Virtual Inhabitant to interact with his/her environment. The facts perceived by perception module are delivered to the memory structure and become concepts (including entity, relationship, activity, and pure concept) through the recognition and inference process. The recognized concepts are quantified/qualified and stored in the appropriate place in the multi-layered memory structure. The memory structure is designed to efficiently support various aspect of knowledge such as social, historical, emotional and to be able to be used as a basis for diverse and believable manner of the Virtual Inhabitant's behavior. The behavioral module semi-automatically produces diverse goals based on the current state, expectation, association, evaluation, attribution for the stored concepts, decides which one will be executed among the produced goals, makes plan for the selected goal, and execute the constructed plan. Actuation module changes the virtual environment in which the Virtual Inhabitant dwells through the motion or speech. The learning module modifies each other module according to the executed result of behavior in order to make the Virtual Inhabitant more adaptive, believable, and diverse.

This paper mainly focuses on the goal production module in the behavioral module of a Virtual Inhabitant. Some other modules which should interact with the goal production module during the goal production process and their interaction process are briefly described at the level of detail required for the explanation of goal production module.

3   Goal Production Module – Structure and Operation

The goal production module is the most important module for diversifying a Virtual Inhabitant's behavior because the goal is the starting point of every behavior and the critical factor for determining the behavior trend of the Virtual Inhabitant. In this section, in order to design the goal production module which can produce diverse and believable goals, we analyze the cause of the drawbacks of previous models, present the improvement criteria, describe the overall function and structure of goal production module, and present the extending and matching methods between drive stimulus and goals.

3.1   Improvement Criteria

We analyzed that the restricted behavior of previous computer-controlled characters, academic agents for multimedia applications is originated from the over-simplified drive stimulus supported by their goal production process. The previous models[1-4, 6-9] use only one or two drive stimuli as their source for the goal production. With the simplified drive stimulus, a computer-controlled character is not able to behave in human-like and believable manner in the general situation to which the Virtual Inhabitant targets. Moreover the received drive stimulus is directly connected to the specific goal and never extended or converted to the form suitable for producing other available goals. Therefore the goal production process is simple one-to-one matching between simple drive stimulus and fixed goal. However, the real goal production process tends to be a form of m-to-n matching. For example, a goal, 'eat something', can be induced from various drive stimulus such as hunger(internal state), seeing of food(external factor), asking of eating by another person(external induction), and usual lunch time(habitual induction). In contrast, a drive stimulus, 'seeing a football', can induce several goals such as 'play football'(direct), 'play football video game'(by association), 'buy a football'(by evaluation). To appropriately support this m-to-n matching between drive stimulus and goal, we categorize the drive stimulus into five categories – internal/external factor, internal/external induction, habitual induction – according to the source and characteristics of the drive stimulus. The categorized drive stimulus is extended to another form in accordance with the method appointed for each category in order to diversify the goal and support the m-to-n matching process. Lastly we introduce some converting and filtering methods which exploit the support of other modules especially value system and social & emotional module for providing human-like features stressed in the psychological research of motivation such as personality, cultural motivation, learned motivation to the virtual inhabitant.

3.2   Overall Description of Goal Production Module

In this paper, we define a goal as 'an activity the Virtual Inhabitant wish(or need) to execute'. The phrase, 'the Virtual Inhabitant wish(or need) to execute', means 'stored in the scheduler and ready to be sent to the planning and execution module'. Goal production module produces a goal from the received drive stimulus. The goal production module is represented as a function like as follow.

Goal Production Function, GP
GP:Drive Stimulus→Goal
Domain of GP: cosmic element
Range of GP: capability of individual Virtual Inhabitant

The drive stimulus can be in the form of a cosmic element(including entity, relationship, activity)[15] existing in the virtual environment. The drive stimulus acquired by perception or communication is matched to the appropriate activity as a goal. The goal is selected from the elements in the set of the Virtual Inhabitant's capabilities. (The capability of individual Virtual Inhabitant is defined as an activity which have direct link to the self instance on instance layer of memory structure and quantified as 'capable'. See [5], [14], and [15].) The abstraction levels for each produced goal are varied according to the category of drive stimulus and GP function used in the production process. Some goals produced in the form of abstract action (higher position in the action hierarchy[14, 15]) with sparsely filled parameters while some other goals given in the form of concretized action(lower position in the action hierarchy) with almost fully filled parameters. For example, an abstract goal 'play' does not give any parameters and procedures for the action while a concrete goal 'play video games with Jack in the game center' provide some parameters for the action. The abstract goals will be concretized at the planning module later. The difference of the abstraction level gives another chance to be diversified once again during the planning process to the produced goals.

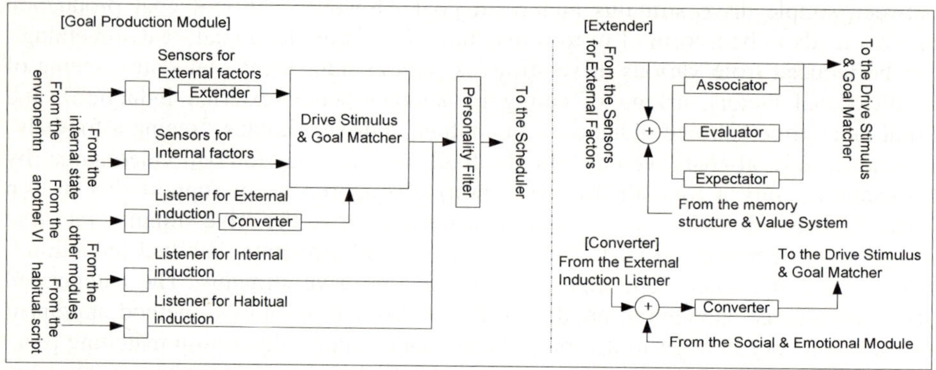

Fig. 2. Structure of Goal Production module

As shown in the Fig. 2, the goal production module consists of five sensor/listener for each drive stimulus category, drive-stimulus & goal matcher with extender and converter of the drive stimulus, and personality filters. Each information flow path in the goal production module produces goals based on its unique GP function. The received drive stimulus can be matched to more diverse goals by extending and converting process for the stimulus. The matching process of GP function and extending and converting process of each drive stimulus category will be described more detailed in the section 3.3.

3.3   Goal Production Process for Each Drive Stimulus Category

As mentioned in the section 3.1, the drive stimuli are organized into five categories. Each category has different goal matching process and extending/converting process for the received drive stimulus.

3.3.1   Goal Production Based on Internal Factors

The sensor for internal factors receives the change of the internal state of an individual Virtual Inhabitant. The operation process of GP function for this drive stimulus is as follows. If a certain internal state changes, the goal production module sends a request for evaluation of the changed state to the value system. The value system responds to the result by evaluating the state based on the value recorded in itself and stored in the value/preference layer[14, 15] of the Virtual Inhabitant's memory structure and the result is 'positive effect' or 'negative effect'. Then the goal production module choose one of the two goals, 'reinforce the state' and 'remedy the state' according to the evaluation result. if there is no action directly associated with the transition link between the original state and changed state on the Virtual Inhabitant's memory structure. If there is an action directly associated with the transition link quantified as 'causal' with direction from the changed state to the original state, the action is selected as a goal. The goal production based on internal factors seems to be very similar to the previous state-machine based goal production, however, they differ in that the former has potential to be diversified during the concretization process at the planning module and to be easily personalized due to the selection based on the personalized knowledge base and value system.

3.3.2 Goal Production Based on External Factors

The sensor for external factors receives the cosmic elements in the situation acquired by perception. The received cosmic elements are sent to the drive stimulus and goal matcher not only in the direct form but also in the form extended by association, expectation and evaluation. The extended factors can provide the matcher with the ability to match one drive stimulus to the various goals. For example, a drive stimulus 'seeing apple' can induce the various goal such as 'eat the apple', 'read the Snow White' by association, 'prevent the apple from the others' occupation' by expectation. The matching process between external factors and the goal is mainly based on the use of knowledge structure and value system of the Virtual Inhabitant. See [14, 15] for more detailed about the modules.

The GP function for the external factor in the direct form match those stimuli to the appropriate goals by finding the action directly linked to the factor and quantified as 'function'. If there is no action fulfilling the condition, the GP select the action linked to the received cosmic element with the highest weight for the link as the goal. Because quantification of the link and weight between two cosmic element are different for every individual Virtual Inhabitant according to the various reasons such as his/her parent(a Virtual Inhabitant for setting up initial state of him/her), experience in the virtual environment, the goal produced by this process can be different for each Virtual Inhabitant even though the received factor is the same one.

The extension of the received external factors with association is based on the mental connections between concepts in the Virtual Inhabitant knowledge structure. The association process occurs with respect to three disciplines – association through generalization hierarchy, association through similar attribute, association through connection link among concepts. The association through generalization hierarchy produces new goals by using the concepts of the received concept as a new drive stimulus. The association through similar attribute uses the concept which has similar properties with the received concept as the new drive stimulus. The association through connection link among concepts uses the concept directly connected to the received concept as new drive stimulus. In this case, due to the massiveness of the associated concepts, some selection policy is required. At this stage, we just use biased random selection based on the weight for the link between concepts. To prevent the divergence, only the direct form of goal is produced for the selected concept as new drive stimulus.

The extension by expectation is only applied to the activity and the state of cosmic element. For the activity, the extender sends a request to evaluate the activities described the effect slot in that activity to the value system and then produce extended goal 'Reinforce the activity' for the activities evaluated as positive effect and 'Prevent the activity' for the activities evaluated as negative effect. For the received state, the extender does similar process to the activities linked to the state with leaving link quantified as 'causal'[16]. For positive and negative evaluation, the extender produces new goals 'Reinforce the state' and 'Prevent the state'.

The extension by evaluation produces new goals 'Promote' and 'Prevent' according to the evaluation result from value system. The extender sends request to evaluate the concept whenever it receives new drive stimulus. Every concept in a Virtual Inhabitant's memory structure has quantified value for his/her preference for the concept determined through his/her experience in the virtual environment. The value system of a Virtual Inhabitant has a table which stores the weighting factor for each concept according to his/her cultural, familial, national value system. The value system evaluate the concept based on the composition of the preference value in the memory structure and weighting factor in it and return the evaluate value in the form of 'positive valence' and 'negative valence'. The extender assign new goals 'promote' and 'prevent' for the 'positive valence' and 'negative valence' respectively.

3.3.3 External Induction

External induction listener receives the question, order, encouragement from another character. The goal produced by GP function for this drive stimulus category is the same action received from another character or the action converted from the received one.

The order and encouragement from another character is sent to the scheduler directly when the Virtual Inhabitant decides to accept the request or in the converted form such as 'Reject the order', 'Resist the order' when the Virtual Inhabitant does not want to accept. Whether the Virtual Inhabitant accepts the request or not is determined based on the four factors – emotional attitude to the speaker, speaker's attitude of request, social relationship between two characters, and social position between two characters. In current stage, we simply give the same weight to the four factors and decide the result by comparing the normalized sum of those weight and normalized random number. If the normalized random number is greater than the weight sum, the Virtual Inhabitant accepts the request. In contrast, if the random number is less than the half of weight sum, the Virtual Inhabitant resist to the speaker. The question of another character is always converted to the goal 'Answer the question' or 'Ignore the question' and sent to the scheduler. The condition that 'Ignore' is selected is the same as the condition that 'Resist' for order is selected.

3.3.4 Internal Induction

The internal induction listener receives the drive stimulus originated from other modules of a Virtual Inhabitant. The drive stimulus received by internal induction listener and produced goal by that stimulus are differed according to from which module the induction is sent. Because the received drive stimulus already has the form of goal, the GP function for this stimulus category merely deliver the received goal to the scheduler. The representative internal inductions are 'attribution', 'analysis', 'exercise', 'cautious perception', 'improve/worsen social relationship', 'favor/harm other characters', and so on. Because the stimulus drives included in this category has no dependency to the goal production module, they can be freely extendable as the need of author of the Virtual Inhabitant.

'Attribution' from memory structure is the goal for inference for uncertain and unknown part of knowledge structure. This goal is induced by the existence of instance incompletely filled its concept templates on the instance layer. 'Analysis' is another goal requested from the memory structure. This goal is induced by the repetitive pattern which is abstracted and stored in the schema layer by this goal and by the uniqueness of instance in the instance layer. The 'attribution' and 'analysis' is very important goals simply by themselves, but they have more importance in that behavior for achieving them expands the knowledge in the memory structure so that the range of a Virtual Inhabitant's behavior become wider.

Social relationship described in the social module will induce the goal 'Favor/Harm other characters(Virtual Inhabitant and human-controlled character). The emotional result of interaction with other characters also can induce the same goal. If a Virtual Inhabitant has positive relationship or emotional attitude with a certain character, the Virtual Inhabitant produces the goal 'Favor the character'. If negative relationship and emotional attitude exist between the Virtual Inhabitant and the character, the produced goal will be 'Harm the character'. Emotional attitude can induce another type of goals 'Improve/Worsen Social Relationship'. The positive emotional attitude to a certain character will induce 'Improve Social Relationship with the character' while negative emotional attitude will produce 'Worsen Social Relationship with the character' These goals are concretized at the planning module necessarily and, as a result, instantiated as diverse behavior in the situation.

Cautious perception' is induced from the drive stimulus 'incomplete perception' of perception module. During the a Virtual Inhabitant perception process on his/her environment, there can be some incomplete result due to the interferences such as handicap of sensory organ, unsatisfied condition of sensing action, obstacles for perception. In this case a Virtual Inhabitant do more cautious perception in order to remove those interferences and get more precise and sufficient information.

'Exercise' is the goal induced from the drive stimulus 'failed action' by execution module. A Virtual Inhabitant can make a mistake in his execution of an action as a kind of discrepancy[14] which implies the difference between his/her conceptuality and reality. He/she will do exercise for the failed action in order to be more adaptive and competitive one in the virtual environment when his/her execution module is in idle state.

Planning module and execution module also induce many goals during the planning and execution phase. During the planning phase, many sub goals for achieving super goal are produced. Similarly, in the execution phase, several sub goals for removing interferences for execution and subtle adjustment for the original plan. However, because these goals are produced directly from the planning and execution module and managed as a child node in a plan tree of super goal, the goal production module does not care for them.

3.3.5 Habitual Induction

The habitual induction listener receives the drive stimulus from routine behavior, habit, hobby, tendency, etc. For example, a Virtual Inhabitant could have goals such as 'eat something' induced by his/her routine meal time, 'take a picture' induced by his/her hobby, 'smoke' induced by his/her addiction, 'clean some place' induced by his/her tendency. These goals make the Virtual Inhabitant more human-like, intimate, and believable because the behaviors based on them are everyday occurrence of human.

The input and output of the habitual induction sensor is the action described in the habitual script [5, 14] of the Virtual Inhabitant. Because the habitual script is personalized for each Virtual Inhabitant through the experience and learning in his/her life time[14], the goal based on it can make the Virtual Inhabitant's behavior reflect his/her personality and tendency stressed in the motivation research in psychology, though it is originally devised for reducing the planning cost of a Virtual Inhabitant.

The habitual induction has no additional matching process because the input is already in the form of action(i.e. goal). Instead of the matching process, the habitual induction has several triggering conditions – triggering routinely, randomly, and by tendency. The habitual induction can be triggered routinely according to the repetitive pattern described in the habitual script. For checking the triggering condition, the habitual induction listener periodically does polling the habitual script whether there are some behaviors on habitual script which are assigned for the current time. The randomly triggered habitual induction reflects the behaviors according to the hobby, addiction, habit such as 'smoking', 'scratching one's hair when speaking'. Checking for randomly triggered habitual induction occurs only when the execution module of a Virtual Inhabitant is in idle state. This make the Virtual Inhabitant more believable by showing personalized behavior pattern at the time there is no critical goals to execute. The habitual induction triggered by tendency of a Virtual Inhabitant such as 'love of cleanliness', 'love of order; 'love of collecting' reflect the behavior trend established strongly based on his/her personality and personal experience. This habitual induction can set a consistent basis of a Virtual Inhabitant and make him/her more individual one. The checking of this induction is triggered when the perceived state of situation fulfills the precondition of actions associated with the tendency or is the opposite state of the tendency.

4 Conclusion and Future Works

Previously we proposed an elaborated autonomous and believable agent which is called Virtual Inhabitant to endow a computer-controlled character with the attractive features of human-controlled character.[5] In this paper, we propose an improved goal production module in order to effectively support the diverse and human-like behavior which is the key requirements for the Virtual Inhabitant.

The proposed module can diversify the Virtual Inhabitants behavior because it can support various drive stimuli by categorizing the stimulus and m-to-n matching between those stimuli and goals based on the extension and conversion of the received stimulus. Moreover, the goal production module generates new goals semi-automatically because the goal executed as behavior can produce another goal through internal induction. The proposed module can be easily extendible because the large portion of goal production process is based on the other modules such as knowledge structure, value system which are independently modifiable to the goal production module. With these advantages, we expect that the proposed goal production can be used for implementing human-like computer-controlled character in many multimedia applications such as on-line games, open-ended games, virtual community, and intelligent tutoring system.

We are working on implementing the proposed module for verifying the model. Simultaneously with the implementation, we will reify and add additional dimensions for the GP function and design the effective personality filter. The scheduling process of the produced goal is also the topic of our further research.

References

1. Ultima Online, http://www.uo.com
2. Lineage Official Homepage, http://www.lineage.co.kr/
3. Home of the SIMS, http://thesims.ea.com/
4. Cyworld.Com, http://www.cyworld.com
5. Se-Jin Ji, Byung-Joo Kim, and Jong-Hee Park: An Agent-Architecture for Implementing a Virtual Inhabitant. In: MMM 04', Jan, Brisbane, Australia(2004), 316-322
6. Rousseau, D., and Hayes-Roth, B.: Improvisational Synthetic Actors with Flexible Personalities. Stanford Knowledge Systems Laboratory Report KSL-97-10, (1997).
7. Nick Hawes: Anytime Deliberation for Computer Game Agents, PhD thesis, School of Computer Science, The University of Birmingham, (2003)
8. Roxana Moreno, Rich Mayer, and James Lester: Life-Like Pedagogical Agents In: Constructivist Multimedia Environments: Cognitive Consequences of Their Interaction. Proceedings of the World Conference on ED-MEDIA, Montreal, (2000) , 741-746
9. Barry G. Silverman: More Realistic Human Behavior Models for Agents in Virtual Worlds: emotion, Stress, and Value Ontologies, *Technical Report*, ACASA/Systems Engineering Dept., University of Pennsylvania, Philadelphia, PA, (2001)
10. Hull, C.L.:A Behavior System. New Haven, Yale University (1952)
11. Doug-woong Hahn : Psychology of Human Motivation. Park-Young Sa, Seoul Korea (2004)
12. Weiner, B.: Human Motivation. Holt, Rinehart, and Winston, New York (1980)
13. Lewin, K.: Field Theory in Social Science. Harper, New York (1951)
14. Se-Jin Ji, Jeong-Woo Kwon, and Jong-Hee Park: An Elaborated Knowledge Structure for Implementing a Virtual Inhabitant. In:AIA 06'(Accepted)
15. Jong-Hee Park: Semantics of Concept. Technical Report, AIMM Lab, Kyungpook Nat'l University, Daegu, Korea(2004)
16. Se-Jin Ji: A Structure Causal Graph-based Model for Event Development. MS Thesis, Kyungpook Nat'l University(2001)

Agent-Based Prototyping of Web-Based Systems

Aneesh Krishna, Ying Guan, Chattrakul Sombattheera, and Aditya K. Ghose

Decision Systems Laboratory, School of IT and Computer Science
University of Wollongong, NSW 2522, Australia
{aneesh, yg32, cs50, aditya}@uow.edu.au

Abstract. Agent-oriented conceptual modelling in notations such as the $i*$ framework [13] have gained considerable currency in the recent past. Such notations model organizational context and offer high-level social/ anthropo-morphic abstractions (such as goals, tasks, softgoals and dependencies) as modelling constructs. It has been argued that such notations help answer questions such as what goals exist, how key actors depend on each other and what alternatives must be considered. Our contribution in this paper is to show an approach to executing high-level requirements models represented in the $i*$ agent-oriented conceptual modelling language. We achieve this by translating these models into sets of interacting agents implemented in the 3APL language. This approach enables us to analyze early phase system models by performing rule-/consistency-checking at higher-levels of abstraction. We show how this approach finds special application in the analysis of high-level models of a web-based system.

1 Introduction

Web-based systems are playing a more and more important role in the modern society nowadays. Based on the persistent nature and the colossal user population, a variety of existing software engineering approaches need to be adapted for web engineering. The design and development of a web-based system may include many business, technology and user challenges. Understanding and satisfying the critical requirements of these challenges will decide the success of a web-based systems commercial application. Web-based systems are more scalable and available to remote users, enabling utilities to better support decentralized operations during high-activity periods. A web-based system is a form of distributed systems architecture, essentially a collection of services. Web based system provides consistent interoperability and reuses existing services where possible. Implementing a web-based system can involve developing applications that use services and making applications available as services. Web services are self-describing software applications that can be advertised, located, and used across the Internet using a set of standards such as SOAP, WSDL [3] and UDDI [12]. Web services are built on the distributed environment of the Internet.

Agents are components that aim to communicate models motivated from real life [2]. The development of agent-based systems offers a new and existing paradigm for the creation of sophisticated programs in a dynamic and open environment, particularly in distributed domains such as a web-based systems and electronic commerce [10].

M. Ali and R. Dapoigny (Eds.): IEA/AIE 2006, LNAI 4031, pp. 780–789, 2006.

Current works on web services are closely entwined with work on agent-based systems. Agent-oriented techniques show a potential for web services, where agents are needed both to offer services and to make best use of the resources available [2]. Early-phase Requirement Engineering (RE) activities of web services are usually performed informally and without much tool support. The agent-oriented conceptual modelling notation as exemplified by the $i*$ framework [13] is a popular means of modelling proposed system requirements. Each component of a web service can be regarded as an agent and the whole web service can be viewed as composed of agent system. Hence, we feel that agent-oriented conceptual modelling technique $i*$ framework is suitable for modelling a web service. The $i*$ framework allows analysts to create agent-based prototypes of the proposed web services based on the preliminary requirements from the stakeholders. Such notations model organizational context and offer high level of social/anthropomorphic abstractions (such as goals, tasks, softgoals [4] and dependencies) as modelling constructs. It has been argued that such notations help to answer questions such as; what goals exist, how key actors depend on each other and what alternatives must be considered.

The objective of this paper is to show how agent-oriented conceptual modelling techniques (exemplified by the $i*$ framework) can be used to model web-based systems, and how these models can be executed by mapping $i*$ models into 3APL [9] agents. This approach makes use of the advantages of $i*$ for the early-phase of requirement engineering and validates the model by mapping it into an executable specification to see the design result in an emulation program.

The remainder of this paper is organized in the following manner. In Section 2, steps for modelling agent-based prototyping of web-based systems are given. We shall provide the executable specifications for the $i*$ framework in section 3. Section 3 also provides an example to illustrate the approach and section 4 presents some concluding remarks.

2   Modelling Web-Based Systems

Most of the available modelling techniques tend to address "late-phase" requirements while the vast majority of critical modelling decisions are arguably taken in early-phase requirements engineering [13]. Agent-oriented conceptual modelling offers an interesting approach in modelling the early-phase requirements. The $i*$ modelling framework is a semi-formal notation built on agent-oriented conceptual modelling. The central concept in $i*$ is the intentional actor agent. Intentional properties of an agent such as goals, beliefs, abilities and commitments are used in modelling requirements. The actor or agent construct is used to identify the intentional characteristics represented as dependencies involving goals to be achieved, tasks to be performed, resources to be furnished or softgoals (optimization objectives or preferences) to be satisfied. The $i*$ framework also supports the modelling of rationale by representing key internal intentional characteristics of actors/agents. The $i*$ framework consists of two modelling components: Strategic Dependency (SD) Models and Strategic Rationale (SR) Models. The SD model consists of a set of nodes and links. Each node represents an "actor", and each link between the two actors indicates that one actor depends on the other for something in order that the former may attain some goal. An SR model represents the internal intentional characteristics of each actor/agent via task decomposition links and means-end links. The task decomposition links provide details on the tasks and the (hierarchically decomposed) sub-tasks to be performed by each actor/agent while the means-end links relate goals to the resources or tasks required to achieve them. The SR model also provides constructs to model alternate ways to accomplish goals by asking why, how and how else questions. Readers are encouraged to read [13] for details on $i*$ framework.

Early Requirements Analysis: During the requirements elicitation phase, stakeholders and goals for individual service are first identified, then the functional and non-functional requirements of each of them are defined and finally the relationships between them are identified. In [6], the authors have proposed an approach based on the Tropos methodology [1], for designing web services. Our proposal is different from theirs in the sense that, we focus on to modeling web-based systems in the early requirement phase, and validate these models by executable specifications, while in [6], the authors have proposed the methodology for the whole requirement phase and they aim on implementing the web services.

We shall use the example of online shopping service throughout the rest of this paper to illustrate how to model a web service using $i*$ framework and consequently how these models can be executed. The online shopping service sells a range of products. Customers can buy goods through a website. After an order is placed, the retailer contacts the payment system to validate customer credits and also charge the customer from the customer's account. Once payment is processed, the retailer notifies the product management system to provide the necessary information. The product management system collects goods and ships them to the transport centre together with the delivery information. Eventually, the transport centre delivers the ordered products to the customer. Upon completion of the delivery, the retailer will get the confirmation of delivery. The modelling process includes following steps.

Step 1: Identify actors: Five actors are identified during this step. Customer/Web server, shops online through the website. Retail system, provides service for selling the products. Product management system offers goods and handles delivery. Transport system, delivers goods to the Customer. Payment system validates the Customer's credits and charges their account.

Step 2: Identify goals: After identifying the actors of a web service, their goals are defined simultaneously. In this case, the actor Customer/ Web server has the goal own product online and the actor Retailer system's goal is to sell product.

Step 3: Identify dependency relationships: The actor or agent construct is used to identify the intentional characteristics represented as dependencies involving goals to be achieved, tasks to be performed, resources to be furnished or softgoals (optimization objectives or preferences) to be satisfied [6]. Combining the results from steps 1 and 2, the output of this process is a Strategic Dependency (SD) model. Specifically, the customer has a goal to own products, shopping confirmation and softgoal to obtain products at the lowest price and assure the security of credit. He depends on the retail system to receive shopping confirmation. Conversely, the retail system depends on the web server to provide the order information for further transactions. The retail system also depends on the payment system and the product management system to fulfill charging customer Task dependency and the resource dependency providing products to customer respectively. Simultaneously, the payment system needs the customer credit information to charge customer. The product management system depends on the retail system to offer order information, which includes product information, and delivery information, and also depends on the Transport system to ship goods to customer on the condition that delivery information is provided together with goods (to be transported) to the transport system.

Step 4: Conduct means-end analysis and task-decomposition analysis: In the $i*$ framework, the Strategic Rationale (SR) model provides a more detailed level of modelling by looking "inside" actors to model internal intentional relationships. Intentional elements (goals, tasks, resources, and softgoals) appear in the SR model not only as external dependencies, but also as internal elements linked by task-decomposition and means-ends relationships (Figure 1). Task decomposition links provide details on the tasks and the (hierarchically decomposed) sub-tasks to be performed by each actor while the means-end links relate goals to the resources or tasks required to achieve them. The SR model also provides constructs to model alternate ways to accomplish goals by asking why, how and how else questions. During this step, goals are further decomposed. Tasks can also be decomposed into subtasks. The output of this step is a SR diagram for each actor. For example, the Customer/Web Server actor has an internal task to perform ShoppingOnline. This task can be performed by subtasks SelectProduct and PlaceOrder (these are related to the parent task via task decomposition links). The SelectProduct task is further decomposed into subtasks BrowseCatalog and SearchProduct.

Following the four steps that were mentioned, models of the proposed web service are generated. Our next step is to show how these agent-oriented models can be executed. In our proposal, we use 3APL as the programming language for generating executable specifications.

3 Mapping $i*$ Model to 3APL Agents

3APL (An Abstract Agent Programming Language) [9] [5] is a programming language for implementing cognitive agents. Agents written in 3APL language consist of goals, belief, practical reasoning rules and capabilities. A goal is a state of the system that the agent wants to achieve. A Belief is used to represent the current mental state of the agent. Practical reasoning rules are the means for the agent to manipulate the goals. Capabilities are the actions that can be performed by the agent. An action can only be performed if certain beliefs hold, this is called precondition of an action. In this paper, we adopt 3APL platform [5] to support our work. Our work is mainly based on 3APL definitions from [9] [5].

Definition 1 A 3APL agent is defined as a tuple n, B, G, P, A , where n is the name of the agent, B is a set of beliefs (Beliefbase), G is a set of goals (Goalbase), P is a set of practical reasoning rules (Rulebase) and A is a set of basic actions (Capabilities).

In [5], a set of programming constructs for goals are defined, namely BactionGoal, PreGoal, TestGoal, SkipGoal, SequenceGoal, IfGoal, WhileGoal and JavaGoal, which can be used in the body part of a practical reasoning rule and make 3APL more flexible.

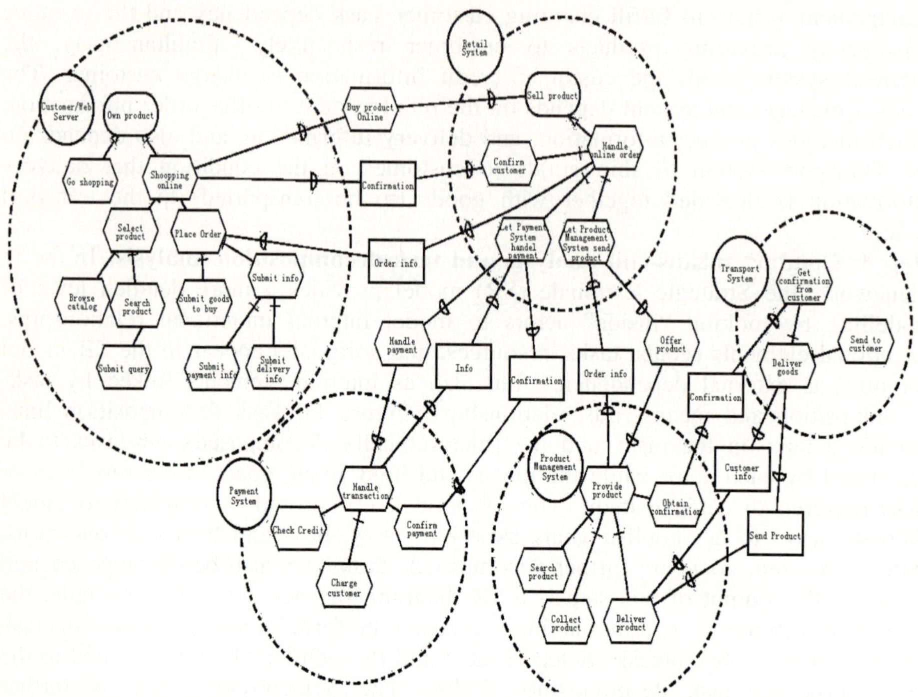

Fig. 1. Strategic Rationale Model of Online shopping service

In a 3APL agent, P is a set of rules in the form: $\pi_h <\text{-} \varphi \mid \pi_b$.

In this formula, π_h and π_b belong to a goal variable set, and φ is a belief. When the agent has goal π_h and believes φ then π_h is replaced by π_b.

For a 3APL agent, Beliefbase is dynamic. It is updated with executing basic actions from the set of capabilities. The structure of a basic action is shown below:

$$\{\varphi_1\}\ Action(X)\ \{\varphi_2\}$$

φ_1 is the pre-condition and φ_2 is the post-condition. Precondition and post-condition are belief formulas. It is possible to have an action that does not have any pre-condition or post condition. The execution of an action will result in the update of beliefbase through replacing preconditions by postconditions. The beliefbase can also be extended with a Prolog program (facts and rules) using the LOAD option [5]. In addition, beliefs can be generated from the communications between two agents (sent and received). 3APL has a mechanism to support the communications between agents. A message mechanism is defined in [5] to fulfill the communication between agents. The messages themselves have a specific structure, *Receiver/ Sender, Performative* are three compulsory elements in a message. Usually, there are three type of message: *send(Receiver, Performative, Content), sent(Receiver, Performative, Content), and received(Sender, Performative, Content).* This agent communication mechanism is described in details in [5]. In this paper we will not elaborate more on the syntax of 3APL, readers who may want more details are directed to [9] [5].

We view an i^* model as a pair $\langle SD, SR \rangle$ where SD is a graph denoted by $\langle Actors, Dependencies \rangle$ where *Actors* is a set of nodes (one for each actor) and *Dependencies* is a set of labeled edges. These edges can be of 4 kinds: *goal dependencies*(denoted by $D_G(SD)$), *task dependencies*(denoted by $D_T(SD)$), *resource dependencies*(denoted by $D_R(SD)$) and *softgoal dependencies*(denoted by $D_S(SD)$). Each edge is defined as a triple $\langle T_o, T_d, ID \rangle$, where T_o denotes the *depender*, T_d denotes the *dependum* and ID is the label on the edge that serves as a unique name and includes information to indicate which of the four kinds of dependencies that edge represents. SR is a set of graphs, each of which describes an actor. We adopt the concept of an environment simulator agent (*ESA*) defined in [11].

We define MAS is a pair $\langle Agents, ESA \rangle$ where $Agents = \{a_1, ..., a_n\}$, each a_i is a 3APL agent and *ESA* is a specially designated Environment Simulator Agent implemented in 3APL which holds the knowledge about the actions that might be performed by actors in SD model and the possible environment transformation after the executions of those actions. The environment agent can verify fulfillment properties (clearly defined in Formal Tropos [7]), which include conditions such as *creation conditions, invariant conditions, and fulfillment conditions* of those actions associated with each agent. Every action of each agent has those fulfillment properties. *ESA* is used to check whether those actions of all agents in this system satisfy corresponding conditions.

Each graph in an SR model is a triple $\langle SR\text{-}nodes, SR\text{-}edges, ActorID \rangle$. The *SR-nodes* consist of a set of goal nodes (denoted by N_G), a set of task nodes (denoted by N_T), a set of resource nodes (denoted by N_R) and a set of softgoal nodes (denoted by N_S). *SR-edges* can be of 3 kinds: means-ends links (denoted by the set *MELinks*), task-decomposition link (denoted by the set *TDLinks*) and softgoal contribution link (denoted by the set *SCLinks*). Each *MELink* and *TDLink* is represented as a pair, where the first element is the parent node and the second element is the child node. A *SCLink* is represented as a triple $\langle s, m, c \rangle$, where the first element is the parent node, the second element is the child node and the third element is the *softgoal contribution* which can be *positive* or *negative*.

Any MAS $\langle Agents, ESA \rangle$ obtained from an i^* model $m = \langle SD, SR \rangle$, where $SD = \langle Actors, Dependencies \rangle$ and *SR* is a set of triples of the form $\langle SR\text{-}nodes, SR\text{-}edges, ActorID \rangle$ (we assume that a such a triple exists for each actor in *Actors)* with $SR\text{-}nodes = N_G \cup N_T \cup N_R \cup N_s$ and $SR\text{-}edges = MELinks \cup TDLinks \cup SCLinks$ must satisfy the following conditions [8]:

1. For all a in *Actors*, there exists an agent in *Agents* with the same name. For example, in the Online Shopping System, *Retail system* is an actor in SR Model, therefore, there is an agent named "Retail System" in this 3APL agents system.
2. For every goal node or task node n in the SR diagram for that actor, the corresponding agent $\langle a, B, G, P, A \rangle$ in *Agents* must satisfy the property that $goal(n)$ or $task(n)$ in the G.
For example, goal *Sell product* and task *Handle Online Order* are in the boundary of actor *Retail System*, according to step 2, *SellProduct()* and *HandelOnlinOrder()* are in the goalbase of agent *RetailSystem*.

3. For all *a* in *Actors* and for each *p* in N_G (parent node) for which a link $\langle p, c \rangle$ in *MELink* exists in the SR model for that actor, with *c* in N_T (children node), the corresponding agent $\langle a, B, G, P, A \rangle$ in *Agents* must satisfy the property that *goal(p)<-φ | SeqComp(T)* is an element of *P*. Here $T=\{c_1,...,c_n\}$, given that $<p,c_1>,...,<p, c_n>$ are all the task decomposition links that share the same parent *p*. *SeqComp(T)* is an operation that generates the body of the procedural reasoning rule referred to above by sequentially composing the goal or task children identified in each of the means-ends links with the same parent *p*. The *i** model in itself does not provide any information on what this sequence should be. This needs to be provided by the analyst or, by default, obtained from a left-to-right reading of the means-ends-links for the same parent in an SR diagram.

For example, in the SR diagram of actor *Retail System* of figure 1, task *Handle Online Order* and goal *Sell Product* are connected by a means-end link, therefore, rule *SellProduct()<-φ | HandelOnlineOrder()* can be added into the Rulebase of agent *RetailSystem*. Belief formula *φ* and parameters of goal and task can be specified according to the real case.

4. For all *a* in *Actors* and for each *p* in N_T for which a link $\langle p, c \rangle$ in *TDLink* exists in the SR model for that actor (where *c* in $(N_T \cup N_G)$), the corresponding agent $\langle a, B, G, P, A \rangle$ in *Agents* must satisfy the property that *goal(p)<- φ| SeqComp(T)* is an element of *P*. Here $T=\{c_1,...,c_n\}$, given that $<p,c_1>,...,<p, c_n>$ are all the task decomposition links that share the same parent *p*. *SeqComp(T)* is as defined in rule 3.

Note that, in the rules defined above, the execution orders of sub-tasks within the *Task-decomposition links* are from left to right as default. Belief formulas of each practical reasoning rule cannot be generated completely automatically; instead, those beliefs are specified by designers.

Take task *Handel Online Order* as the parent task node for example, this task is decomposed into three sub-tasks: *Confirm Customer, Let Payment System Handle Payment* and *Let Product Management System Send Product*. Using the above rule, will lead to:

```
HandleOnlineOrder() <- φ|
 BEGIN
   letpaymentsystemhandelpayment();
   confirmcustomer();
   letproductmanagementsystemsendproduct()
 END.
```

Note that, in the rules defined above, the execution orders of sub-tasks within the *Task-decomposition links* are from left to right as default. Belief formulas of each practical reasoning rule cannot be generated completely automatically; instead, those beliefs are specified by designers.

5. For all *a* in *Actors* and for each triple $\langle s, m, c \rangle$ in *SCLinks* in the SR model for that actor, the corresponding agent $\langle a, B, G, P, A \rangle$ in *Agents* must satisfy the property that *belief(m, s, c)* is an element of *B*. We do not describe how beliefs about softgoal contributions are used in agent programs for brevity – we will flag however that they can plan a critical role in selecting amongst procedural reasoning rules.

For example, there are two ways to achieve goal *Own Product* for an actor, one is *Go Shopping*, the other is *Shopping Online*. On the assumption that task *GoShopping*

has positive contribution to softgoals low effort, convenient and *time saving* while task *ShoppingOnline has positive effects on those three softgoals.*
6. For all dependencies $\langle T_o, T_d, ID \rangle$ in SD, there exist agents $\langle T_o, B_o, G_o, P_o, A_o \rangle$, $\langle T_d, B_d, G_d, P_d, A_d \rangle$ in Agents, such that if $\langle T_o, T_d, ID \rangle$ is in $D_G(SD)$, then goal(ID) is an element of G_o,

Notice that these rules require that the creation conditions be communicated by the depender agent to the ESA agent. The ESA monitors all of the actions/tasks performed by each agent, all of the messages exchanged and all of the beliefs (usually creation conditions for dependencies) communicated by individual agents for consistency and for constraint violations (e.g. the FormalTROPOS-style conditions associated with dependencies). When any of these is detected, the ESA generates a user *alert.*

We shall select one task-dependency and one resource-dependency related to agent *Retail* System in order to illustrate rule 6. Actor *Customer* depends on actor *Retail System* to perform task *Buy Product Online* and to provide *Confirmation* of buying. According to rule 6, for agent *Customer, BuyProductOnline*() is in the Goalbase. Rules shown below are in its Rulebase:

Request(confirmation) <-
  product(P) AND needconfirmation(P) |
  BEGIN
    send(retailsystem, request, requestProvide(confirmation));
    send(ESA, inform ,believe(needconfirmation))
  END
Task(BuyProductOnline) <-
  needtobuyproductonline |
  BEGIN
    send(retailsystem, request, requestPerform(BuyProductOnline));
    send(ESA, inform ,believe(φ)) END are in Rulebase.

For agent *RetailSytem*, two rules are generated for these two dependencies relationships.
received(customer, request, requestProvide(confirmation)) |
  BEGIN
    send(customer, request, offer(confirmation));
    send(ESA, inform, believe(Offered(confirmation))
  END
received(customer, request, requestPerform (BuyProductOnline)) |
  BEGIN
    Perform(BuyProductOnline);
    send(ESA, inform, believe(Performed(BuyProductOnline))
  END

Notice that these rules require that the creation conditions be communicated by the depender agent to the ESA agent. The ESA monitors all of the actions/tasks performed by each agent, all of the messages exchanged and all of the beliefs (usually creation conditions for dependencies) communicated by individual agents for consistency and for constraint violations (e.g. the FormalTROPOS-style conditions associated with dependencies). When any of these is detected, the ESA generates a user *alert.*

We shall select one task-dependency and one resource-dependency related to agent *Retail* System in order to illustrate rule 6. Actor *Customer* depends on actor *Retail*

System to perform task *Buy Product Online* and to provide *Confirmation* of buying. According to rule 6, for agent *Customer*, *BuyProductOnline*() is in the Goalbase. Rules shown below are in its Rulebase:

Request(confirmation) <-
  product(P) AND needconfirmation(P) |
BEGIN
  send(retailsystem, request, requestProvide(confirmation));
  send(ESA, inform ,believe(needconfirmation))
END
Task(BuyProductOnline) <-
  needtobuyproductonline |
BEGIN
  send(retailsystem, request, requestPerform(BuyProductOnline));
  send(ESA, inform ,believe(φ)) END are in Rulebase.

   For agent *RetailSytem*, two rules are generated for these two dependencies relationships.

received(customer, request, requestProvide(confirmation)) |
 BEGIN
  send(customer, request, offer(confirmation));
  send(ESA, inform, believe(Offered(confirmation))
 END
received(customer, request, requestPerform (BuyProductOnline)) |
 BEGIN
  Perform(BuyProductOnline);
  send(ESA, inform, believe(Performed(BuyProductOnline))
 END

   Fig. 2 (provided below) is a snapshot for the Online Shopping 3APL agent System. It provides insight into the communication messages and flow of the desired system.

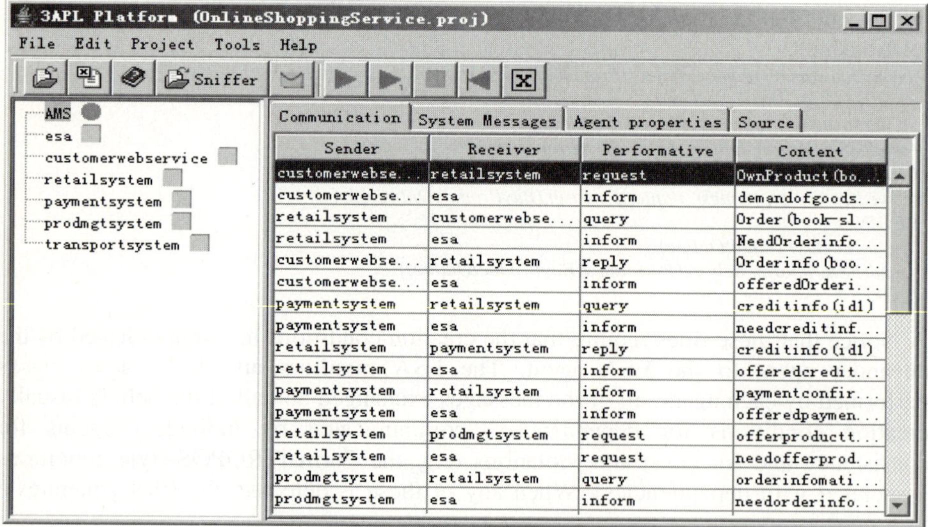

Sender	Receiver	Performative	Content
customerwebse...	retailsystem	request	OwnProduct (bo...
customerwebse...	esa	inform	demandofgoods...
retailsystem	customerwebse...	query	Order (book-sl...
retailsystem	esa	inform	NeedOrderinfo...
customerwebse...	retailsystem	reply	Orderinfo (boo...
customerwebse...	esa	inform	offeredOrderi...
paymentsystem	retailsystem	query	creditinfo (id1)
paymentsystem	esa	inform	needcreditinf...
retailsystem	paymentsystem	reply	creditinfo (id1)
retailsystem	esa	inform	offeredcredit...
paymentsystem	retailsystem	inform	paymentconfir...
paymentsystem	esa	inform	offeredpaymen...
retailsystem	prodmgtsystem	request	offerproductt...
retailsystem	esa	request	needofferprod...
prodmgtsystem	retailsystem	query	orderinfomati...
prodmgtsystem	esa	inform	needorderinfo...

Fig. 2. Communication messages

4   Conclusions

This paper has shown how agent-oriented conceptual modelling techniques such as *i** framework can be employed to model web-based systems. Along with this we have suggested an approach to executing *i** models by translating these into a set of interacting agents (services) implemented in the 3APL language. This approach makes use of the advantages of *i** for the early-phase of requirement engineering and validates the model by mapping it into an executable specification to see the design result in an emulation program. We are working towards automating the approach proposed in this paper. Furthermore, we also believe in the co-evolution approach in which models are composed of *i** model and 3APL agents. How to co-evolve *i** model and 3APL agents remains for future works.

References

1. Castro, J., Kolp, M., Mylopoulos, J., Towards requirements-driven information systems engineering: the Tropos project, *Information Systems Journal*, 2002, 27(6), pp. 365-389
2. Chen, F., Yang, H., Guo, H., Xu, B. Agentification for web services, *Proceedings of the 28th Annual International Computer Software and Applications Conference*, 2004, pp. 514 – 519
3. Chinnici, R. Web Service Description Language (WSDL) Version 1.2, World Wide Web Consortium, 2002, www.w3.org/TR/wsdl12/
4. Chung, L., Nixon, B., Yu, E., Mylopoulos, J. *Non-Functional Requirements in Software Engineering*, Kluwer Academic Publishing, 2000
5. Dastani, M. 3APL Platform User Guide November 16, *Utrecht University*, 2004
6. Diana, L., Mylopoulos, M. Designing Web Services with Tropos, *Proceedings of ICWS'04*, San Diego, USA, 2004. IEEE Computer Society Press
7. Fuxman, A., Liu, L., Pistore, M., Roveri, M., Mylopoulos, J. Specifying and Analyzing Early Requirements in Tropos, *Requirements Engineering Journal*, 2004, 9(2), pp. 132-150
8. Guan, Y., Ghose, A. K. Executable specifications for agent-oriented conceptual modeling. *Proceedings of the IEEE/WIC 2005 International Conference on Intelligent Agent Technology*, France, 2005
9. Hindriks, K. V., De Boer, F. S., Van der, H. W., Meyer, J. Agent programming in 3APL. *Autonomous Agents & Multi-Agent Systems*, 1999, 2(4), pp. 357- 401
10. Lohse, G., Spiller, P. (1998) "Electronic shopping", *Communications of the ACM*, July 1998, 41(7), pp. 81–87
11. Salim, F., Chang, C., Krishna, A., Ghose, A. K. Towards executable specifications: Combining *i** and AgentSpeak (L). *Proceedings of 17th International Conference on Software Engineering and Knowledge Engineering (SEKE-2005)*, Taipei, Taiwan, July, 2005
12. *Universal Description, Discovery and Integration*, Organization for Advancement of Structured Information System, (2002), www.uddi.org/specification.html
13. Yu, E. Modelling Strategic Relationships for Process Reengineering. *PhD Thesis, Graduate Department of Computer Science, University of Toronto, Toronto*, Canada, 1995, pp. 124

High-Dimensional Micro-array Data Classification Using Minimum Description Length and Domain Expert Knowledge

Andrea Bosin, Nicoletta Dessì, and Barbara Pes

Università degli Studi di Cagliari, Dipartimento di Matematica e Informatica,
Via Ospedale 72, 09124 Cagliari
andrea.bosin@dsf.unica.it,
{dessi, pes}@unica.it

Abstract. This paper reports on three machine learning methods, i.e. Naïve Bayes (NB), Adaptive Bayesian Network (ABN) and Support Vector Machines (SVM) for multi-target classification on micro-array datasets involving a large feature space and very few samples. By adopting the Minimum Description Length criterion for ranking and selecting relevant features, experiments are carried out to investigate the accuracy and effectiveness of the above methods in classifying many targets as well as to study the effects of feature selection on the sensitivity of each classifier. The paper also shows how the knowledge of a domain expert makes it possible to decompose the multi-target classification in a set of binary classifications, one for each target, with a substantial improvement in accuracy. The effectiveness of the MDL criterion to decide on particular feature subsets is asserted by empirical results showing that MDL is comparable with entropy based feature selection methodologies reported by earlier works.

Keywords: Data Mining & Knowledge Discovery, Machine Learning, Bioinformatics.

1 Introduction

DNA micro-arrays are novel biotechnologies that are being used increasingly in cancer research [1]. Micro-arrays measure the expression levels of a large number of genes in a biological sample. Since the samples come from patients whose pathological condition (e.g. cancer or non-cancer) has already been diagnosed by a doctor, the correlations between genes and pathologies can be studied. Hence, datasets derived from micro-arrays are very interesting to analyse, as they can be used to build diagnostic classifiers.

Because of the high cost of micro-array production, the number of samples is often limited while the large number of gene expressions requires a careful computational analysis. In this extreme of few observations on many features, the construction of a classifier generally proceeds by selecting a small informative set of genes that can distinguish among the various classes of pathology (feature selection), by choosing an appropriate mathematical model for the classifier, by estimating the parameters of the

M. Ali and R. Dapoigny (Eds.): IEA/AIE 2006, LNAI 4031, pp. 790–799, 2006.

model based on the "training set" of samples whose classification is known in advance. Finally, the accuracy and the sensitivity of the classifier is tested on an independent set of samples not used in training the classifier. In this paper, all these distinct steps are globally referred as *main classification task* (MCT).

Previous studies [2][3] have shown that the accuracy of the classifier can be greatly improved by reducing the number of features used as input to the classification model, since (1) many genes are not at all correlated with the pathology, and (2) the high level of correlation between the expression levels of many genes makes much of the information redundant. The relevance of good feature selection methods has been discussed, for example, by Guyon and colleagues [4].

As witnessed by recent literature [5][6][7], Bayesian networks and Support Vector Machines techniques may be useful to identify expression patterns in micro-array data, while the MDL criterion [8] is recognized as a new foundation both for feature selection and for classifier optimization. Specifically, we explore the role of MDL in building and evaluating the performance of three classifiers, i.e. Naïve Bayes (NB), Adaptive Bayesian Network (ABN) and Support Vector Machines (SVM).

The Acute Lymphoblastic Leukemia (ALL) dataset [9] provides an interesting testbed for the experiments presented here, whose goals are to:

a) evaluate the effectiveness of MDL principle as criterion for selecting features and comparing classifiers;
b) investigate the accuracy and effectiveness of the above classifiers (NB, ABN, SVM) in handling many ALL sub-types;
c) study the effects of feature selection on the accuracy and the sensitivity of classifiers;
d) investigate whether it is possible to increase the performance of classifiers, taking advantage from the diagnostic knowledge gleaned from a human expert.

In general, finding good classifiers is known to be a difficult task when gene expression profiles are used as complex biomarkers defining many different classes of cancer (multi-target classification). To maintain the feasibility of this study, we pursued a 2-stage design:

• *at stage I*, we attempted a multi-target classification involving all considered ALL sub-types;
• *at stage II*, we focused on decomposing the problem in a set of binary classification problems, one for each ALL sub-type.

Feature selection and classification methods, when applied to ALL gene expression data, assume as target classes the specific ALL sub-types, while features correspond to the expression levels measured for each gene.

The paper is organized as follows. Section 2 illustrates the feature selection heuristic, while Section 3 provides some insight on the classification algorithms. Section 4 presents the experimental study case and the related results. Results are further discussed in Section 5. Finally, Section 6 outlines conclusions.

2 Feature Selection Heuristic

Feature selection methods can be classified as *filters* and *wrappers* [10][11]. The essential difference between these approaches is that a wrapper method makes use of the algorithm that will be employed in building the final classifier, while a filter method does not. Filters only look at intrinsic characteristics of the data, by addressing the feature selection problem in isolation from the classifier design. Conversely, wrappers methods search through the space of all possible feature subsets and estimate the quality of a particular subset by measuring the predictive accuracy of a classifier built on this subset. Thus, wrappers rely on some classification algorithm while filters are independent of the classification method and may be used in conjunction with any classifier.

While more practical and easy to implement, filters don't explicitly select features, leaving the final choice to the user. Besides, they evaluate features independently on one another and hence result unable to handle correlation between them. Wrappers, on the other hand, may be too slow when applied to high-dimensional datasets.

We adopt a mixed strategy which consists in (i) ranking features according to the strength of their correlation with the target and (ii) applying a wrapper approach on a reduced search space, where only top-ranked features are included.

Specifically, the first step (i) is performed using a scoring metric derived from the MDL principle [8]. Basically, it states that the best theory to infer from training data is the one that minimizes the length (i.e. the complexity) of the theory itself and the length of the data encoded with respect to it. MDL provides a criterion to judge the quality of a classification model and, as a more particular case, it can be employed to address the problem of feature selection, by considering each feature as a simple predictive model of the target class.

So, as described in [12], we rank each feature according to its description length, that reflects the strength of its correlation with the target class. To this end, we use the MDL measure given by [13]:

$$\text{MDL} = \sum_j \log_2 \binom{N_j + C - 1}{C - 1} - \sum_j \sum_{i=1}^{N_j} \log_2(p_{ji}) \tag{1}$$

where N_j is the number of training instances with the j-th value of the given feature, C is the number of target class values, and p_{ji} is the probability of the value of the target class taken by the i-th training instance with the j-th value of the given feature (estimated from the distribution of target values in the training data). More details can be found in [5].

In the subsequent wrapper step (ii), we start with the set of the N top-ranked features (e.g. $N = 20$), build a classifier on this set of N features and test its accuracy. Then, we extend the set of features by adding the next k top-ranked features (e.g. $k = 10$), build a new classifier on the set of $N+k$ features, and again test its accuracy. This procedure is repeated until the accuracy of the classifier improves.

3   Classification Methods

Naïve Bayes is a very simple Bayesian network consisting of a special node, i.e. the target class, that is parent of all other nodes, i.e. the features, which are assumed conditionally independent given the value of the class. The NB network can be quantified against a training set of pre-classified samples, i.e. we can compute the probability associated to a specific value of each feature, given the value of the class. Then, any new sample can be easily classified by applying the Bayes rule.

Despite its strong independence assumption, that is clearly unrealistic in several application domains, NB has been shown to be competitive with more complex state-of-the-art classifiers [14][15][16]. In the last years, a lot of research has focused on improving NB classifiers by relaxing their full independence assumption. One of the most interesting approaches is based on the idea of adding correlation arcs between the features of a NB classifier. On these "augmenting arcs" are imposed specific structural constraints [14][15], in order to maintain computational simplicity on learning. The algorithm we evaluated, the Adaptive Bayesian Network [13], is a variant of the approach proposed in [15]. Specifically, ABN relaxes the NB full independence assumption according to a greedy approach based on MDL.

Support Vector Machines [17] have been successfully applied to a wide range of pattern recognition problems. A support vector machine finds an optimal separating hyperplane between members and non-members of a given class in an abstract space, that is represented by a kernel function. This technique avoids the computational burden of explicitly representing the feature vectors.

4   Experiments

The dataset used in this work is the Acute Lymphoblastic Leukemia dataset [9]. ALL is a heterogeneous disease consisting of various leukemia sub-types that remarkably differ in their response to chemotherapy [18]. The ALL dataset contains all known ALL sub-types (including T-ALL, E2A-PBX1, TEL-AML1, BCR-ABL, MLL, Hyperdip > 50) and consists of 327 samples, each one is described by the expression level of 12558 genes [9]. Specifically, the dataset includes 215 training samples and 112 testing samples.

The classifiers used in the experiments (namely NB, ABN, SVM) are trained and tested according to a *main classification task* (MCT), whose steps are defined as follows:

1.   Rank all features according to MDL feature selection.
2.   Select the set of the N top-ranked features (e.g. start with $N = 20$).
3.   Build a classifier from a training set D, filtered according to selected features.
4.   Test classifier accuracy on a test set T, filtered according to selected features.
5.   Extend the set from N to $N+k$ by adding the next k top-ranked features (e.g. $k = 10$)
6.   Repeat steps 2 to 5 until the accuracy of the classifier increases.

We denote as C(X, D, T) the MCT aiming to classify the sub-type X, on the training set D and on the test set T.

All the experiments have been carried out using standard data mining tools [21].

4.1 Stage I

At this stage, we perform a multi-target classification C(X,D,T) involving all considered ALL sub-types: the label X is the set of all six considered ALL sub-types, D includes the full 215 training samples and T includes the full 112 testing samples. Each sample is described by 12558 features.

The accuracy of NB, ABN and SVM classifiers is shown in Table 1 as the number N of top-ranked features increases. These results cannot unequivocally demonstrate which is the best classifier; however, they do give some evidence. The Bayesian classifiers outperform SVM when N < 200 while their accuracy is similar when N = 400. As can be seen, the number of features needed to achieve a stabilization in accuracy is very high (400), and the resulting classifiers have a high level of misclassifications (8-10%).

Table 1. Stage I: misclassifications of NB, ABN and SVM multi-target classifiers

C \ N	20	40	60	100	200	400
NB	29	21	18	18	12	11
ABN	27	22	15	12	9	9
SVM	39	45	58	38	23	9

4.2 Stage II

At this stage our methodology focuses on formalizing how the human expert approaches the ALL diagnosis and on integrating this approach in a machine learning process.

Essentially, the human experts, i.e. the physicians, use a divide-and-conquer approach based on clinical knowledge, experience and observation [18]. When analyzing a biological sample, they first look for evidence of the most common or unambiguous sub-type, T-ALL, against all the others (here referred as OTHERS1). If there is no T-ALL evidence, they look for the next most common or unambiguous sub-type, E2A-PBX1, against the remaining (here referred as OTHERS2). Then the process steps through TEL-AML1 vs. OTHERS3, BCR-ABL vs. OTHERS4, MLL vs. OTHERS5 and finally Hyperdip > 50 vs. OTHERS, that groups all samples not belonging to any of the previous sub-types.

As Figure 1 shows, this approach can be reproduced in a machine learning process that builds and evaluates six binary sub-models (one for each ALL sub-type) in turn. Being responsible for a single ALL sub-type, each binary model must be trained on a specific set that separates the samples belonging to its own target class from the samples belonging to other classes. At each level, the classification process C(X,D,T) is a binary classification whose label X is a single ALL sub-type.

Each C(X,D,T) gains information from the previous level because the ALL sub-types related to the latter are left out when the former is trained and tested. At each level of the decision tree, the classification process is carried out on different sub-types, starting from the original training and test sets that are progressively reduced from one level to the next, as shown in Table 2.

Table 3 shows the overall accuracy (i.e. the sum of misclassifications at each level) of the six binary NB, ABN and SVM classifiers as the number N of top-ranked features increases.

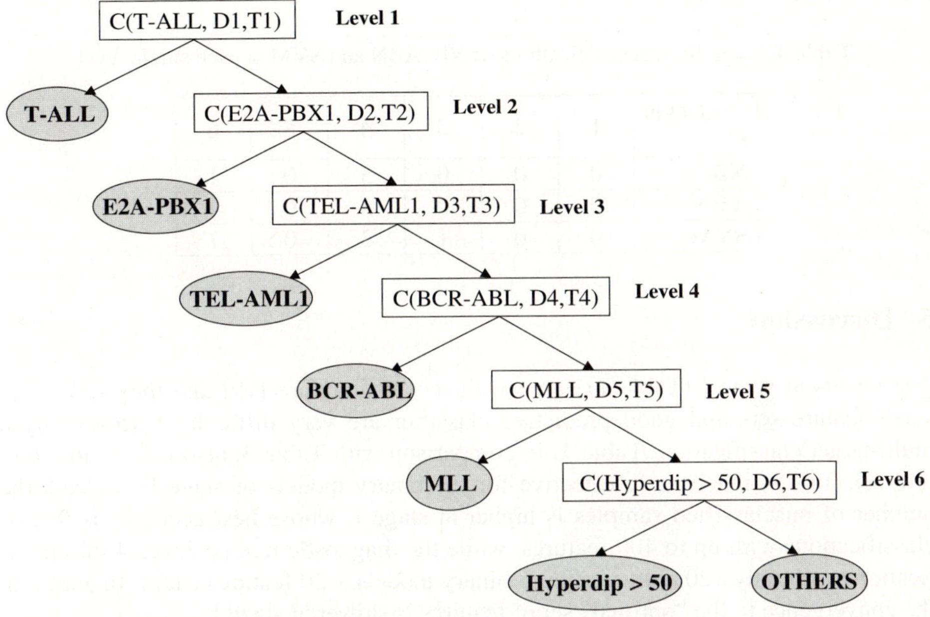

Fig. 1. Stage II: diagnostic decision tree

Table 2. Stage II: number of training (D) and test (T) samples at each level of the decision tree

Level	ALL subtype	D	T
1	T-ALL vs. OTHERS1	28 vs. 187	15 vs. 97
2	E2A-PBX1 vs. OTHERS2	18 vs. 169	9 vs. 88
3	TEL-AML1 vs. OTHERS3	52 vs. 117	27 vs. 61
4	BCR-ABL vs. OTHERS4	9 vs. 108	6 vs. 55
5	MLL vs. OTHERS5	14 vs. 94	6 vs. 49
6	Hyperdip > 50 vs. OTHERS	42 vs. 52	22 vs. 27

Table 3. Stage II: overall accuracy of NB, ABN and SVM

C \ N	10	20
NB	8	4
ABN	10	4
SVM	5	5

Table 4 summarizes the accuracy (i.e. the number of misclassifications) of NB, ABN and SVM classifiers at each level of the diagnostic decision tree. The results only refer to the classifiers built on the 20 top-ranked features, that turns out to be the "optimal" number of features since no improvement occurs when increasing the number of selected features.

Table 4. Stage II: misclassifications of NB, ABN and SVM at each single level

Level C	1	2	3	4	5	6
NB	0	0	0	3	0	1
ABN	0	0	0	3	0	1
SVM	0	0	1	3	0	1

5 Discussion

The results at stage I (Table 1) agree with recent literature [19] and they show that small feature sets and good predictive classifier are very difficult to achieve by a multi-target classification. Table 1, in comparison with Table 3, also reveals that feature selection is much more effective for the binary models of stage II. Indeed, the number of misclassified samples is higher at stage I, whose best accuracy is 9 misclassifications with up to 400 features, while the diagnostic tree achieves 4 misclassifications with only 120 features (i.e. 6 binary models x 20 features each). In addition, the convergence to the "optimal" set of features is slower at stage I.

At stage II, we have built NB, ABN, SVM binary classifiers at every single level L (L = 1, 2, 3, 4, 5, 6) and the best accuracy occurs with a set of 20 features at each single level. At stage I, we have built NB, ABN, SVM classifiers for an increasing number N of features (i.e. N = 20, 40, 60, 100, 200, 400) up to the "optimal" value of N = 400. In order to compare the effectiveness of both the proposed approaches, we look for the features common to both stages. Figure 2 shows, for each level (i.e. target) at stage II, the number of features in common with stage I.

As Figure 2 illustrates, there are many features in common for T-ALL, E2A-PBX1, TEL-AML1, but only a few in common for BCR-ABL, MLL, Hyperdip > 50. This seems to suggest that genes relevant to ALL sub-types T-ALL, E2A-PBX1, TEL-AML1 are promptly selected at both stages, but genes relevant to BCR-ABL, MLL, Hyperdip > 50 are hard to select at stage I.

A possible explanation is that the strength of the correlation of genes with a given ALL sub-type can be very different for different sub-types. Hence, if a single sub-type is assumed as target (stage II), the feature selection process top-ranks only those genes that are relevant for the target and discards all the others (even if they are strongly correlated with another sub-type). On the contrary, in the multi-target classification (stage I), all the genes most strongly correlated with any one of the sub-types are top-ranked, but the target they are mostly correlated to is not evident at all. Figure 2 shows that the "optimal" sets of features relevant to targets T-ALL, E2A-PBX1, TEL-AML1 at stage II are top-ranked at stage I, too, meaning that the correlation of each set with its target is similar in strength. This assertion is partially true for MLL and Hyperdip > 50, but definitely not true for BCR-ABL, meaning that the correlation is less strong.

Another interesting point emerging from the experiments at stage II, is that almost no overlap exists between the groups of 20 genes selected at each level. Specifically, only one overlapping gene has been found between levels 2-5, 3-4, 5-6, and this could suggest that very few genes (if any) are responsible for more than one sub-type of ALL.

The results presented in this paper can be compared with [20] where six different heuristics for feature selection, based on entropy theory, χ^2-statistics and t-statistics, are explored by learning NB and SVM classifiers on the ALL dataset [9]. In [20] the best feature selection heuristic ranks attributes according to their entropy and selects features "having an entropy value less than 0.1 if these exist, or the 20 features with the lowest entropy values otherwise", up to a maximum of 20 features. Table 5 shows a comparison between the two approaches.

The feature selection heuristic proposed in [20] allows for learning SVM and NB classifiers that respectively misclassify 5 and 7 samples. According to the heuristic proposed in this paper, which is based on MDL, the SVM classifiers (with 10 and 20 features) results in 5 misclassifications, while NB classifiers (with 20 and 10 features) results in 4 and 8 misclassifications.

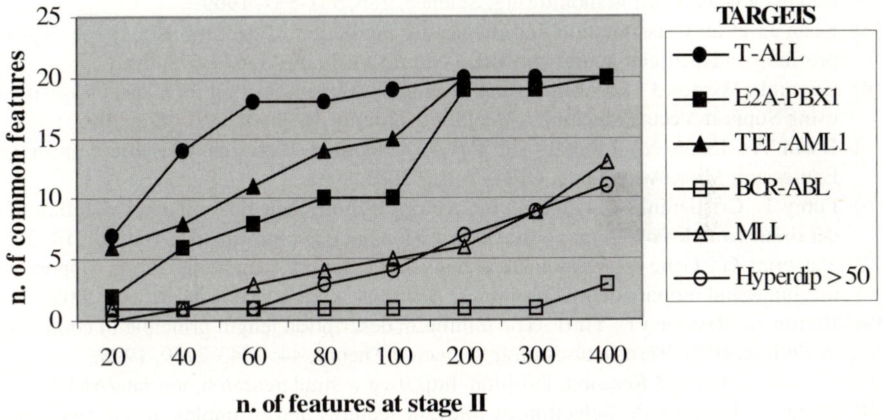

Fig. 2. Number of common features at stages I and II

Table 5. Comparison of different feature selection heuristics

	This work			Ref. [20]	
classifier	NB	ABN	SVM	NB	SVM
heuristic	MDL	MDL	MDL	entropy	entropy
errors	4	4	5	7	5

6 Conclusions

Our emphasis throughout this paper is on the practical application of MDL and hence we make extensive use of experiments on the considered data set [9]. As we see, MDL provides an objective framework under which rather disparate approaches to micro-array data classification can co-exist and be compared.

Specifically, we have shown that the effectiveness of MDL as a feature selection heuristic is comparable with the best heuristic (entropy) discussed in [20]. Our experiments also confirm that Bayesian networks can be used to build classifiers which result in a good accuracy, as proposed in [5]. In addition, both Bayesian networks and SVM classifiers greatly benefit from performing a feature selection based on MDL.

We have seen that the knowledge of a domain expert makes it possible to decompose a multi-target classification problem, and efficiently learn a set of binary classifiers, one for each target, with a substantial improvement in accuracy. This result highlights the relevance of the domain knowledge for decomposing multi-target classification problems in a structured set of binary classification problems.

References

[1] Hardimann G., Microarray methods and applications: Nuts & bolts. DNA Press, 2003.

[2] Golub T.R., et al.., Molecular classification of cancer: Class discovery and class prediction by gene expression monitoring. Science, 286, 531-537, 1999.

[3] Khan J., et al. Classification and diagnostic prediction of cancers using gene expression profiling and artificial neural networks. Nature Medicine, 7, 673-679, 2001.

[4] Guyon I., Weston J., Barnhill S., and Vapnik V., Gene Selection for Cancer Classification using Support Vector Machines. Machine Learning, 46 (1-3): 389 – 422, 2002.

[5] Bosin A., Dessì N., Liberati D., Pes B., Learning Bayesian Classifiers from Gene-Expression MicroArray Data, CIBB-WILF 2005.

[6] Furey T., Cristianini N. et al, Support vector machine classification and validation of cancer tissue samples using microarray expression data, Bioinformatics, 16:906-914, 2002.

[7] Valentini G., Gene expression data analysis of human lymphoma using support vector machines and output coding ensembles, Artificial Intelligence in Medicine, 2002.

[8] Barron A., Rissanen J., Yu B., The minimum description length principle in coding and modelling, IEEE Transactions on Information Theory, 44: 2743-2760, 1998.

[9] St. Jude Children's Research Hospital. http://www.stjuderesearch.org/data/ALL1/.

[10] Blum A., Langley P., Selection of relevant features and examples in machine learning, Artificial Intelligence, 97:245-271, 1997.

[11] Kohavi R., John G., Wrappers for feature subset selection. Artificial Intelligence, 97:273-324, 1997.

[12] Kononenko I., On biases in estimatine multi-valued attributes, IJCAI95, 1034-1040, 1995.

[13] Yarmus J.S., ABN: A Fast, Greedy Bayesian Network Classifier, 2003. http://otn.oracle.com/products/bi/pdf/adaptive_bayes_net.pdf.

[14] Friedman N., Geiger D., Goldszmidt M., Bayesian Network Classifiers, Machine Learning, 29: 131-161, 1997.

[15] Keogh E., Pazzani M.J., Learning the structure of augmented Bayesian classifiers, International Journal on Artificial Intelligence Tools, Vol. 11, No. 4, 587-601, 2002.

[16] Cheng G., Greiner R., Comparing Bayesian Network Classifiers, Proceedings of the Fifteenth Conference on Uncertainty in Artificial Intelligence, Morgan Kaufmann Publishers, Inc., San Francisco, 1999.

[17] Vapnik V., Statistical Learning Theory, Wiley-Interscience, New York, NY, USA, 1998.

[18] Yeoh E.J. et al., Classification, subtype discovery, and prediction of outcome in pediatric acute lymphoblastic leukemia by gene expression profiling, Cancer Cell, 1:133-143, 2002.

[19] Mukherjee S., Classifying Microarray Data Using Support Vector Machines, Understanding And Using Microarray Analysis Techniques: A Practical Guide. Kluwer Academic Publishers, Boston, MA, 2003.

[20] Liu H., Li J., Wong L., A Comparative Study on Feature Selection and Classification Methods Using Gene Expression Profiles and Proteomic Patterns, Genome informatics 13: 51-60, 2002.

[21] http://www.oracle.com

On Solving Edge Detection by Emergence

M. Batouche, S. Meshoul, and A. Abbassene

PRAI Group, LIRE Laboratory,
Mentouri University of Constantine
{batouche, meshoul, abbassene}@wissal.dz

Abstract. Emergence is the process of deriving some new and coherent structures, patterns and properties in a complex system. Emergent phenomena occur due to interactions (non-linear and distributed) between the elements of a system over time. An important aspect concerning the emergent phenomena is that they are observable on a macroscopic level, whereas they are produced by the interaction of the elements of the system on a microscopic level. In this paper, we attempt to grab some emergence and complexity principles in order to apply them for problem solving. As an application, we consider the edge detection problem a key task in image analysis. Problem solving by emergence consists in discovering the local interaction rules, which will be able to produce a global solution to the problem that the system faces. More clearly, it consists in finding the local rules which will have some awaited and adequate global behavior, to solve a given problem. This approach relies on evolving cellular automata using a genetic algorithm. The aim is to find automatically the rules that allow solving the edge detection problem by emergence. For the sake of simplicity and convenience, the proposed method was tested on a set of binary images,. Very promising results have been obtained.

1 Introduction

Many systems in nature produce complex patterns, which emerge from the local interactions of relatively simple individual components. Notably this type of emergent pattern formation often occurs without the existence of a central control [4]. Such systems consist of many components, with local interactions only and no central control. Examples of emergent pattern formation in such systems include the foraging and nest-building behavior of social insects, spiral waves in cultures of amoebae, synchronized oscillations in the brain, etc.

To simulate the behavior of complex systems, cellular automata (CA) have been used as a powerful mathematical [5]. CA have the advantage of being easy to understand and implement. To exploit all the power of CA (and consequently all the power of complex systems), one must take into account some paramount characteristics, especially the concept of emergence [4].

Emergence is the direct result of the complexity of interactions inside the system. The elements (components) of the system interact locally, the interactions between them are simple, but the significant number of elements and the feedback loop phenomenon (duplex interaction between the system and its environment) produces a complex and interesting behavior (see figure 1).

M. Ali and R. Dapoigny (Eds.): IEA/AIE 2006, LNAI 4031, pp. 800 – 808, 2006.

These local interactions occur on a micro level. But the observed phenomena occurring at the macro level (emergent) seem to not have any relationship with local interactions (surprising emergent phenomenon). Taking CA as modeling tools, we associate the system local interactions to the CA transition rules. These rules use local information to produce the future state of each cell [3]. CA can have very elaborate behaviors and even carry out calculations. It was proven than CA is a universal machine equivalent to a Turing machine [5].

If one wants to exploit all the power of this tool, he will have to understand the emergence phenomenon. The question is: What are the rules that provide the right global system behavior? This question is known as the "Inverse Problem" (see figure 2). A possible solution of the "Inverse Problem" is to use an optimization strategy, in order to find the appropriate CA that solves a given task. The search space would be the space of local interaction rules. Search is guided by a quality measure calculated at the global level, which would reflect the adequacy of the system to the problem [1]. A possible manner to deal with this problem is to use Genetic Algorithms (GAs) search scheme. The mixture of Cellular Automata and Genetic Algorithms known as Evolving Cellular Automata (EvCA) [6] provides a powerful and multi-purpose tool.

In this work, we try to solve the edge detection problem [9] in an emergent manner. We want to find a CA that will have a global behavior corresponding to edge detection task. Edge detection is a key problem in image analysis [9]. It is typically the primary task of any automatic image understanding process. The aim is to find border pixels between dissimilar regions using an Evolutionary Cellular Automaton. The local rule of this Cellular Automaton emerges (versus handmade) from the evolution of a population of candidate cellular automata by means of a Genetic Algorithm optimization strategy. A simple and efficient CA rule for border detection is revealed by the GA. This rule is run over a cellular automaton initialized by the pixel intensities of the image to be segmented. In this way, a simple, intrinsic parallel algorithm for border detection emerges.

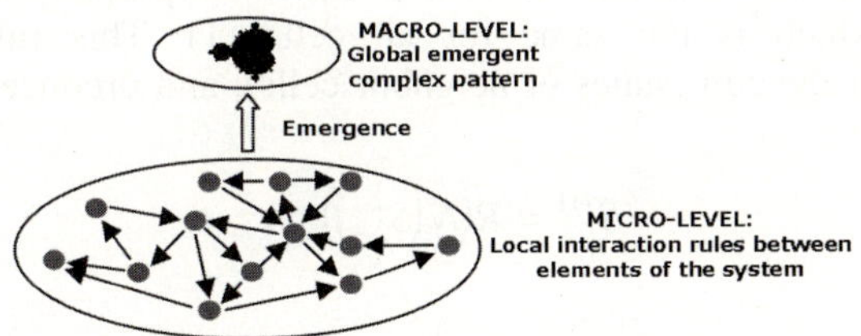

Fig. 1. Emergence of a global property from local interactions

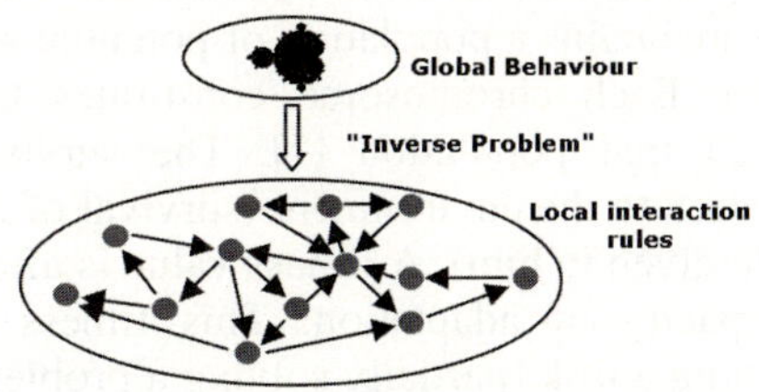

Fig. 2. The "Inverse Problem", Inversing the "Emergence Arrow"

2 Problem Formulation

A border is a frontier between two homogeneous areas of the image. A homogeneous zone is a part of the image containing pixels which exhibit similar characteristics (intensity, color, texture...). Inter-Zones contrast must be relatively strong. The border between two homogeneous areas constitutes what we call an "Edge" [2, 9]. In the "image processing" literature [9], we find many "edge detection" methods based on various algorithms. The mainstream of these methods are based on directional derivative calculations [9]. Other methods abolishing derivative calculations use preliminary knowledge concerning the nature and characteristics of the treated image, but these requirements limit the applicability of the method [2].

We propose here to construct an alternative method based on the evolution of CA population that uses simple local rules [5]. The aim is to obtain after an evolving process guided by a fitness function (edge detection quality value), a cellular automata able to segment an image and to detect significant edges by emergence.

3 Cellular Automata Principles

The Cellular Automata were invented by Stanislaw Ulam (1909-1984) and John von Neumann (1903-1957) at the end of the Forties in Los Alamos National Laboratory (United States) [5]. A CA is a D dimensional grid (lattice) composed of agents called cells. These cells interact and evolve in time, changing their states in a discontinuous way. The transition rules of each automaton (cell) are local and simple. They take into account only the state of the neighbor cells [3]. A Cellular Automaton is a discrete and dynamical system made up of a regular lattice of cells. Formally, it is a quintuplet $A = (L, D, S, NR, R)$. L is the D dimensional cellular lattice. At each discrete moment t, each cell can have only one state of the finite state set S. At each time step, all the cells update their states simultaneously. The transition process is driven by a local update rule R, which is the same for all cells (1). This rule takes the local neighborhood N of the cell (states of neighbor cells), and produce the future state of the cell [3].

$$S_{i,j}^{t+1} = R\big(N\big(S_{i,j}^{t}\big)\big). \tag{1}$$

4 Genetic Algorithms Principles

Genetic Algorithms GA [6] are stochastic search methods inspired by the "evolution species theory". The GA maintains a population of potential solutions, represented by chromosomes (genotype). Each chromosome constitutes the genetic code of an individual (phenotype) of that population [1]. The survival of an individual is conditioned by its adaptation to the environment (survival of the fittest – according to its adequacy with the role given to him). A fitness value is affected to each individual, which quantifies its capacity of adaptation. This fitness is proportional to the percentage of accomplishing a task (partially solving a problem). The fitness function

```
PO ← Initial Population;

Calculate_individual_fitness(PO);

WHILE not_end DO

P_tmp ← PO ∪ mutate(PO) ∪ crossover(PO);

Calculate_individual_fitness(P_tmp);

PO      ← select_best_fitness_from(P_tmp);

END
```

Fig. 3. Simplified Genetic Algorithm

is the individual selection criterion. The theory of the evolution suggests that some ratio of present generation (ancestor) can be selected to build the next generation (offspring). The new population is generated by the application of the genetic operators (crossover and mutation) [6]. An evolution process is applied trying to attain the optimal solution (or an approximate one). This solution will appear by combination and selection of individuals of the generations of candidate solutions. This process of optimization is frequently used to find approximate satisfactory solutions. Figure 3 shows the general scheme of a genetic algorithm.

5   Evolving Cellular Automata (EvCA)

The Evolving Cellular Automata (EvCA) is a methodology that takes advantage from the notion of evolutionary strategies. We apply this method as an optimization scheme, in the process of searching the best CA rule that is able to perform some computational task. An initial CA population, composed of chromosomes coding the local transition rule of each CA of the population, is randomly generated. After which, the GA evolve this initial population (Generation Zero), by applying the genetic operators: mutation and crossover. The selection of the individuals of the next generation is conditioned by the value of the fitness function [6]. This cyclic process makes the emergence of a set of interesting individuals. These individuals have a high fitness, and are thus most suited. They constitute the elite. One of them will be the chosen final solution [6]. It is important to choose well the chromosome's coding method, which corresponds to the local rule of the CA. Another serious point is the choice of the mutation and crossover operators. But the keystone remains the choice of the fitness function, which completely conditions the behaviour of the GA and the convergence of the evolution process towards an acceptable solution.

6   The Proposed Method

The proposed approach takes advantage of the capacity of Cellular Automata (CA) for generating and transforming a wide variety of patterns to implement the computational task of edge detection. Performing a computation with a CA means that the input to the computation (image to segment) is encoded as the initial configuration; the output (segmented image) is decoded from the configuration reached by the dynamics some later time step. The intermediate dynamical steps, that transform the input to the output, are taken as the steps in the computation. The computation emerges from the CA rule being obeyed locally by each cell [3]. Since it is very difficult to specify by hand a priori the particular dynamical rule suitable for a desired computation, an evolutionary process is applied in their search [4, 7, 8]. This calculation (edge detection task) must be an emerging phenomenon, produced by the execution of simple local rules by each cell of CA [3]. The proposed method can be summarized as follows. An Evolutionary Algorithm (Genetic Algorithm) is applied in the search for adequate CA dynamical rules that perform edge detection over a set of reference images and their segmented counterparts. The fitness function is a measure of quality of the edge detection process that results from the application of the CA on the set of reference images. The evolutionary process starts from a random initial population of CA rules. The result is a set of evolved local transition rules defining a CA edge detector.

6.1 The Rule Format

We represent the CA rule performing the edge detection task, as the concatenation of immediate neighborhood cells states of the cell to be updated (including this). And we add the next state of the central cell after update [7].

This rule can be run when its neighborhood part matches with a pixel patch (of the same size) in the image. Then we update the central pixel by the "next state" part of the rule. The matching between the neighborhood and the image patch is done modulo rotational operators (Rotate ($0°$, $90°$, $180°$ and $270°$); Flip-Flop (Horizontal, Vertical)). The rules are said to be rotational symmetric:

Simple rules cannot represent all possible pixel patch configurations in the image. Therefore, we assemble them into rules packets. In this manner, each individual in the GA population is represented by a chromosome. The chromosome is simply the rules packet.

We can introduce a weak matching criterion, by using a similarity threshold ε:

$$\textbf{difference(rule, pixel patch)} \leq \varepsilon \tag{2}$$

To make the CA determinist we introduce the following constraint: Each rule of the rules packet must be different from other rules, modulo the rotational operators and the similarity threshold.

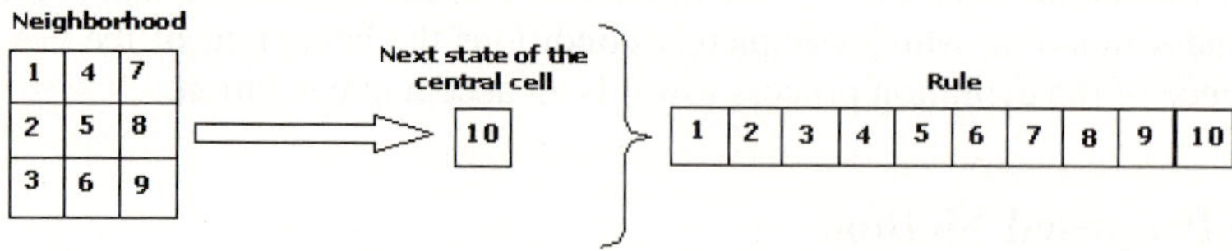

Fig. 4. CA rule formed by the neighborhood and the next state

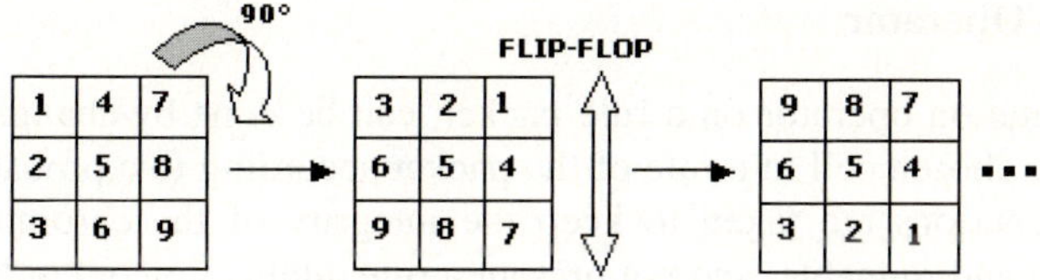

Fig. 5. Rotational equivalence

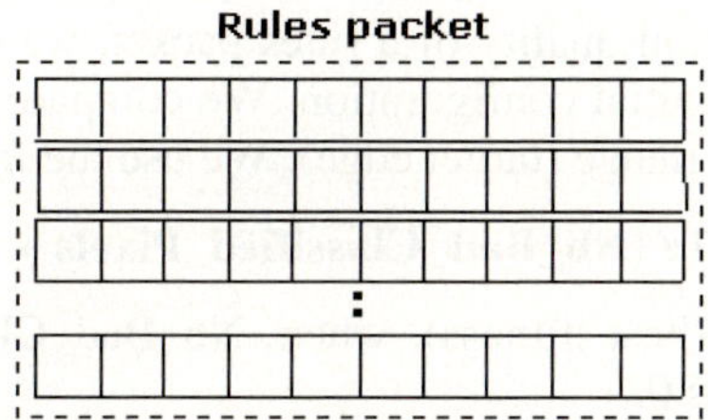

Fig. 6. Rules packet that forms an individual of the population

6.2 The Crossover Operator

Due to the chromosome (rules packet) form, we introduce two different crossover operators, a horizontal one and vertical one. They are applied in an equiprobable way.

6.2.1 Horizontal Crossover

This operator takes two parents rule packets and provides two children rule packets by interchanging some rules between them. This makes it possible to combine the best rules to obtain better individuals. This strategy keeps the cohesion and the stability of the crossover operator. The horizontal crossover operator adjusts and ameliorates the solutions obtained focussing on a local search area (exploitation).

6.2.2 Vertical Crossover

The vertical crossover operator exchanges rule parts between parent chromosomes. This allows obtaining children rules packets appreciably different from the parents. The vertical crossover operator explores a wider area of the search space. In this way, it has a comparable behaviour to a mutation operator, which diversifies the search process (exploration).

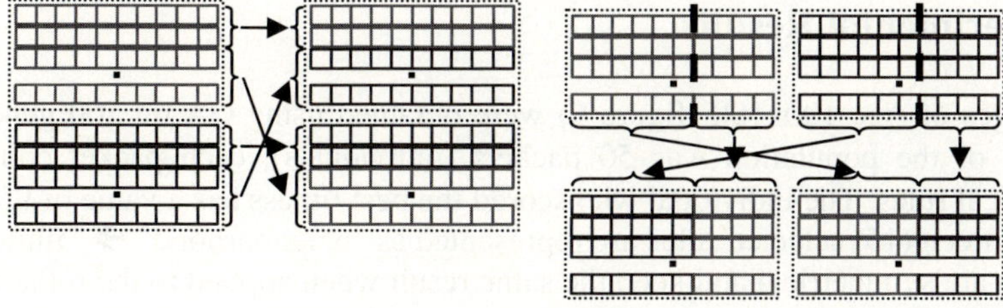

Fig. 7. Horizontal crossover operator   **Fig. 8.** Vertical crossover operator

6.3 Mutation Operator

Applying a mutation operator on a rule packet, can be done by changing the state of some randomly chosen cell in a rule of the packet according to a probability function. Of course precautions are taken to keep the integrity of the chromosome. It must always be valid and runnable, and not present a rule duplication or contradiction.

6.4 The Fitness Function and the Selection Operator

To evaluate the segmentation quality of a rules packet, we execute it on CA. Taking image pixel intensities as initial configuration. We compare the resulting pattern with the beforehand segmented image (target edge). We use the following fitness:

$$F = 1 / (Nb\_Bad\_Classified\_Pixels + 1) \tag{3}$$

This formula attains 1 (best fitness) when Nb_Bad_Classified_Pixels (wrongly classified edge) approaches 0.

The selection operator randomly chooses the most suited individuals from the current population (current generation). The probability of pulling some individual is proportional to the value of its fitness. Then, we apply the crossover and mutation operators on the selected individuals in order to build the new population (next generation).

Another fitness function could be used. It quantifies more accurately the quality of the segmentation. So, let us consider the following quantities [2]:

```
TP : True  Positive, correctly classified pixels;
FP : False Positive, incorrectly classified pixels;
FN : False Negative, unclassified pixels.
```

We calculate then the following values, **Building Detection Percentage (BDP)** (4), i.e. the percentage of correctly classified pixels in a particular class:

$$BDP = TP / (TP + FN) \tag{4}$$

We compute the **BDP** ratio for "edge" and for "non-edge" class pixels, respectively **BDP_Edge** and **BDP_background**. The selected fitness function would be calculated as the multiplication of these two values:

$$F = BDP\_Edge \times BDP\_background. \tag{5}$$

7 Experimental Results

The images of size 100x100 (figure 9) were obtained using GA on 500 generations. The size of the population was 50 packets (individuals); each packet contains 15 symmetrical rules. The individual who scored the best fitness has a value of 95,637%.

The fifteen (15) selected rules are represented as "neighborhood" ➜ "future state". The rules are symmetrical and keep the same result when applied to the rotated image.

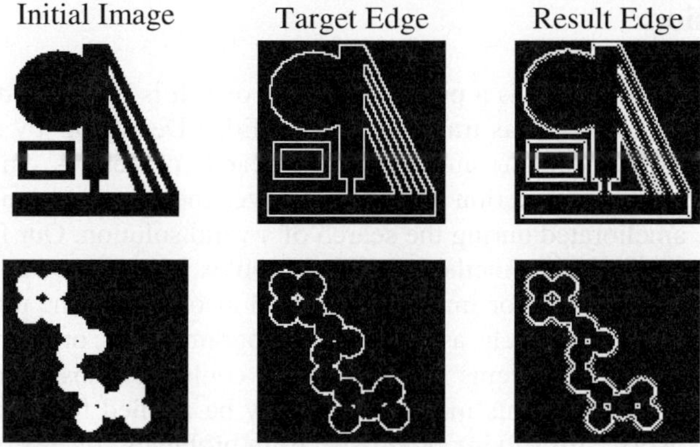

Fig. 9. Sample results from training set

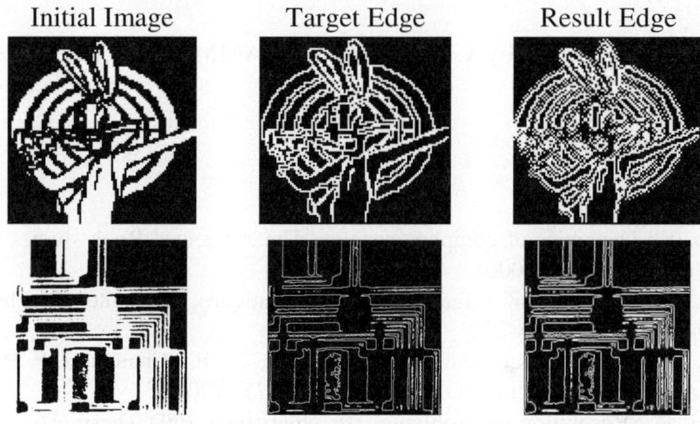

Fig. 10. Sample results from test

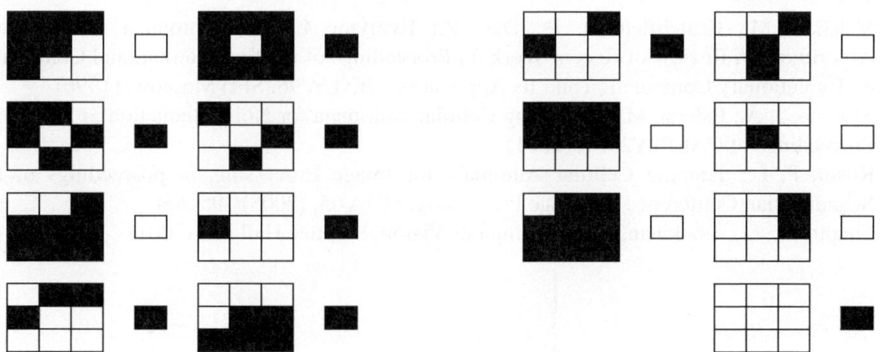

Fig. 11. GA final rules packet

8 Conclusion

The proposed methodology is a purely emergent one. It is based on the evolution and training principles. A CA was trained to solve "Edge Detection" by emergence. GAs were used to evolve cellular automata. The search process is enlightened by the optimization of a fitness function which symbolizes the segmentation quality. It is the criterion to be ameliorated during the search of a valid solution. Our future works will concern the extension of the method to more complex images such as 16 and 256 grey level images and also to color images. We could also explore the utilization of other evolutionary algorithms such as "Genetic Programming" or "Artificial Immune Systems". This approach seems promising and could be transposed to solve other general problems. Indeed, this methodology may be applied for building a powerful general "Framework", for solving broad-spectrum problems "by emergence".

Acknowledgments

This work was supported by CMEP – PROGRAMME TASSILI under Project 05 MDU 642.

References

1. Bar-Yam, Y.: Dynamics of complex systems, The Advanced Book studies in nonlinearity series, Westview Press, (2000)
2. Davis L. S.: A Survey of Edge Detection Techniques, Computer Graphics and Image Processing, 12 (1975) 248-270
3. Ganguly, N., Sikdar, B. K., Deutsch, A., Canright, G., P.P.Chaudhuri, P. P.: A Survey on Cellular Automata, Project BISON (IST-2001-38923), (2001)
4. Georgé, J. P. : Résolution de problèmes par émergence, PhD Thesis, Université Toulouse III, July 2004.
5. Langton, C. G.: Studying artificial life with cellular automata, Physica D., 22 (1986) 120-149
6. Mitchell, M., Crutchfield, J. P., Das, R.: Evolving Cellular Automata with Genetic Algorithms: A Review of Recent Work, in Proceedings of the first International Conference on Evolutionary Computation and Its Applications (EvCA'96, SFI) Moscow, (1996)
7. Moreno, J. A., Paletta, M. : Evolving Cellular Automata for Noise Reduction in Images, in Proceedings of CAEPIA'2001, (2001)
8. Rosin, P. L.: Training Cellular Automata for Image Processing, in proceedings of the Scandinavian Conference on Image Processing, SCIA'05, (2005) 195-204
9. Shapiro, L. G., Stockman, G. C.: Computer Vision, Prentice Hall inc. (2001)

Clustering Microarray Data Within Amorphous Computing Paradigm and Growing Neural Gas Algorithm

S. Chelloug, S. Meshoul, and M. Batouche

PRAI Group, LIRE Laboratory
Mentouri University of Constantine
{chelloug, meshoul, batouche}@wissal.dz

Abstract. The work described in this paper covers mainly the exploration of an important paradigm called amorphous computing. With the current smart systems composed of a great number of cognitive entities, amorphous computing offers useful tools and languages to emerge a coherent behavior relying on local communications and limited capabilities. In order to emphasize its capabilities, the problem of clustering microarray data has been solved within this new computing paradigm. Moreover, it is difficult and time consuming to deal with a large amount of noisy gene expression data. The core motivations of amorphous computing come from self-assembly property to emerge clusters of complex gene expressions. In particular, the process of clustering was applied with respect to the Growing Neural Gas algorithm (GNG), which is an incremental learning method and a visual technique. Although the GNG draws important features from the Self-Organizing map (SOM), it yields accurate results when no information about the initial distribution is available. This contribution considers a huge number of amorphous computing entities placed irregularly, each with a randomly selected reference vector. Using the GNG, the visualization of clusters of gene expressions is obtained by amorphous computing particles. The results obtained using the Netlogo platform are very encouraging and argue that self-organization by means of local interactions and irregularly placed particles will be qualified with performance in a real amorphous computing system.

1   Introduction

The current interest in parallel systems field appeared in the investigation of amorphous computing paradigm. Before its advent, parallel systems explored computational elements provided by some information: identities, coordinates and the configuration surrounding each element. To that effect, amorphous computing faces challenges from previous paradigms and considers a huge number of computational elements placed irregularly and communicating locally via broadcast. Also, these entities receive neither geometric information nor time synchronization. At the heart of success of amorphous computing, self-organization, self-healing and self-assembling properties are carried out with simple rules and mechanisms. In addition, one of the most studied technologies that raises considerable interest is called

M. Ali and R. Dapoigny (Eds.): IEA/AIE 2006, LNAI 4031, pp. 809–818, 2006.
© Springer-Verlag Berlin Heidelberg 2006

microarrays. From a material point of view, microarrays are microscopic slides that contain an ordered series of samples. They are used to determine the expression level of genes in a sample [1]. Hence, the most significant advantages of microarrays concern the extraction of new knowledge to help medical diagnosis. The amount of the data obtained is very large. A matrix represents it. Especially, each element of the matrix encodes the level of the gene under a specific condition. However, due the data size, errors and noise, the innovation of new techniques to analyse gene expressions is still under research. Since several clustering algorithms have been proposed, the choice of the appropriate technique is a problematic one. In this paper, the GNG algorithm is applied for clustering microarray data. It was advocated by Bernd Fritzke as an incremental learning technique that overcomes limitations of SOM. It creates successively more nodes based on simple concepts (reference vector, error, and neighborhood).

The contribution reported bellow suggests a new direction to cluster microarray data using amorphous computing and the GNG approach in quest of analyzing gene expressions by an in-deepth interpretation of the obtained results.

Thus, this paper includes six sections. In the first section, we present amorphous computing as a challenging paradigm. Next, we introduce microarrays. The GNG algorithm is explained in section 4. In addition, the proposed framework for clustering microarray data is described in section 5. Some experimental results are presented and discussed in section 6. Finally, conclusions and future work are driven.

2 Amorphous Computing

Actually, the state of artificial intelligence is very different to that of its earlier applications. While the first researchers designed theories and techniques to program the actions of a single cognitive entity, it was observed that new real problems involve distributed and open systems [2]. Hence, these systems are based on self-organization, self-healing and self-assembling properties that will enable the efficient development of complex applications. Using millions of tiny computing elements integrated with sensors and actuators and embed them into materials [3] is the principal characteristic behind this new vision. So far, the progress in robots has taken a radically different form that raises interest challenges. As explained in [4], the next robots will be built of a huge number of tiny programmable modules that could assemble themselves into different shapes and reconfiguring into a needed tool. In addition, the innovation of such systems is motivated by two factors: first biological systems exhibit remarkable robustness and self-healing properties relying on chemical substances and simple functions; second, nanotechnology has given support to such systems. In the context of sensor networks, which aim at providing a powerful solution to the monitoring and control of critical applications, paintable computing is described as computational elements that can be painted on an arbitrary surface and organize themselves to do an important task [5]. Namely, pushing computing is another progress, where the notion of self-assembly is a central one. It is defined as a set of pushing elements, which can sense and react to the physical world by means of installing, executing and passing a code [6]. In spite of the novelty of sensor networks and cellular engineering, important limitations are raised from the question of programming such systems. One way to overcome this problem is called amorphous computing. The attempt to introduce amorphous computing is to obtain a coherent behavior from the corporation of a mass of identical irregularly placed particles that may affect actions, might be mobile, have modest memory, are not synchronized and communicate with few neighbors. In addition, they are possibly faulty, sensitive to their environment, receive no time synchronization information and each particle's clock is initialized to a random time [7, 8]. So far, most approaches related to amorphous computing are described as languages. Furthermore, a global description is converted by an interpreter to low actions. The Origami Shape Language 'OSL' presented by Radhika Nagpal [9] encompasses the property of robustness by using average behavior rather than individual one. Also, the translation of a high description defined by means of six axioms to a low representation is done by gradients that produce good estimate of distance. Additionally, the Growing Point Language 'GPL' described by Daniel Coore [10] has used metaphors from Biology and makes it possible to define topological structures by the exploration of growing points that can split, die off and merge. Another lay of improvement in the field of amorphous computing is Resilient Serial Execution on Amorphous Computer 'RSEAM' based on a simple semantic of grouping nodes into cells [11]. Unlike the above languages, RSEAM draws heavily upon the problem of writing serial programs that are not aware of the underlying infrastructure and limitations of amorphous computing particles. The aim is to ensure that a program can be converted to a set of capsules interacting between them. Applied to the executing of a swarm of robots, the crucial issue for digital hormone model is to view robots as biological systems that can communicate and collaborate via hormones and receptors [12]. It inspired amorphous computing paradigm by relying on broadcast. Beside this approach, Stoy and Nagpal [13] have described a self-reconfigurable method used successively to move modules and arrive to a desired final configuration by a recruitment gradient generated to attract a wandering module. More specifically, the synthesis of 2D shapes using amorphous computing particles is possible by the compilation of a predetermined global shape into a program that instructs the agents to grow the shape. Kondacs [14] explained that replication and location based control mechanism are the two actions executed by amorphous computing entities to synthesis a 2D shape. Recently, Frost has taken ideas from biology and sensor networks and developed a decentralized approach for mapping unknown arbitrary 2D shapes. The developed method is very interesting. It is able to map shapes using simple actions [15].

3 Microarrays

Even though the idea of understanding cell's functions might be relatively old, only some important features of cells are successively explained. As noted in [16], the production of proteins stands out as a powerful mechanism that involves two steps: the transcription of the gene information into molecules of mRNA is the first phase. During the second one, mRNA molecules are translated into proteins within individual cells. Accordingly, biologist researches have defined the gene expression level as the measurement of the relative representation of a large number of mRNA species [17]. One of the differences that exist between actual and previous methods concerns the measurement of the expression level of thousand of genes simultaneously [18]. This is achieved by microarrays technology that forms a project, which is concerned with the investigation of electronic, mathematic, chemistry and computer science to study gene expressions. Already, [1] defines microarrays as a small surface, made in glass or nylon, and spotted in an organized order with a large number of probe DNA sequences. In such technology, the emphasis is characterized by four steps: the fabrication of microarrays, labeling of each mRNA, the transcription of the two mRNA samples into cDNA, which are both applied to the microarray and hybridize with arrayed probe DNA and then the extraction of the combined fluorescence from each mRNA with a scanner [16]. Obviously, there are good reasons for using microarrays: identify gene regulated in similar manner and characterize cellular differences between different cell types [1]. Beside these features, microarrays are widely used to deal with cancer research [19]. Once all steps are applied, microarrays provide a data matrix where the rows represent gene expressions, columns are experiment conditions and each element (i,j) is a real number indicating the value taken by the gene i in experiment j. As biologists are confronted with a large amount of complex gene expressions [18], generally including missing values and noise [20], the analysis of microarray data is an important issue.

4 Clustering

Clustering is the process of organizing a collection of K-dimensional vectors into groups whose members share similar features in some way [21]. In order to partition an initial input space, a wide range of clustering algorithms has been suggested in the literature. Each of them exhibits some advantages and problems. Clustering algorithms fall into two groups: supervised algorithms and unsupervised ones. Other authors distinguish hierarchical and non-hierarchical clustering techniques [22, 23]. Partitioning techniques choose the number of clusters before the actual process and frequently refer to the K-means algorithm. For a relatively more complex task, the SOM is a more suitable way that learns the topological mapping of n dimensional space. It is viewed as two layers of neurons. It is a more suitable way that learns the topological mapping of n dimensional space. Due to a competitive learning process that leads to a flexible net, SOM folds into a cloud formed by the input data [24]. For some cases, where neither the size of the map nor the organization of the map is available, the GNG seems a powerful solution. The GNG is among the recent clustering algorithms. It is motivated by a need to have a structure that is well suitable to represent the given input by modifying and extending the network architecture during learning. It appears quite different from SOM but it draws important features from it. Its principle is very simple: starting with two nodes, the algorithm constructs a graph that preserves the topology in a very general sense. During the process of clustering and for each input signal x an edge is inserted between the two closest nodes. Formally, each node k consists of a reference vector (w_k), a local accumulated error $(error_k)$ and a set of edges defining its topological neighbors. The basic algorithm can be found in [21], however, we describe here a few key aspects of the GNG. Once two randomly connected units are selected and connected by a zero age edge, the formation of clusters is obtained by an execution of a competitive Hebbian learning process. It proceeds in locating the closest nodes to each signal x and connecting them by an edge. Assume that s and t are the nodes of interest with $\|w_s-x\|^2$ as the smallest value and $\|w_t-x\|^2$ as the second smallest one, for all nodes k, the unit s will be translated to another position with a linear movement by updating its weight vector. The new error value is:

$$error_s \leftarrow error_s + \|w_s-x\|^2 \tag{1}$$

Jim Holmtrom explained that updating the error with squared distance is a way of detecting nodes that cover a large portion of the input distribution. So, the novel position of the winner and its topological neighbors is thus:

$$w_s \leftarrow w_s + e_w(x+w_s), \ e_w[0,1] \tag{2}$$

$$w_n \leftarrow w_n + e_n(x+w_n) \ \forall \, n \in neighbors(s) \ e_n \in [0,1] \tag{3}$$

The next step meant to maintain the Delaunay triangulation by incrementing the variable edge of s and all its topological neighbors. This process must be controlled during learning, so recent edges have their age reset to 0. More specifically, edges that should not be included in the Delaunay triangulation are moved. We identify them by looking to their age variable that becomes old. After a predefined number λ of iterations, a new node will be inserted between the node u with the largest error and its neighbor v with the second largest error. The insertion is done by respect to this equation:

$$w_r \leftarrow \frac{(w_u+w_v)}{2} \tag{4}$$

Due to node insertion, the errors of u and v will be invalid. To that effect, u, v and r must update their error's variable using the following formulas:

$$error_u \leftarrow \alpha \times error_u \tag{5}$$

$$error_v \leftarrow \alpha \ x \ error_v \tag{6}$$

$$error_r \leftarrow error_u \tag{7}$$

5   The Proposed Framework

Taking inspiration from the GNG, we propose a contribution that can be used to cluster microarrays data within the context of amorphous computing. The basic idea is that a massively distributed system of amorphous computing particles can dynamically change their links in a network. They communicate locally to accomplish the construction of a graph that represents well the input gene expressions. Using amorphous computing particles, one would have to investigate:

1. How can an amorphous computing particle consider itself as the winner that has the minimum distance to some stimulus or the maximum error?

2. How can amorphous computing particles create edges between them?
3. Assuming that the GNG algorithm is applied to mobile nodes, how can static amorphous computing entities affect the graph generated?

To answer these questions, we have conducted some adjustments to the GNG:

1. A related approach presented by Ellie D'Hondt [25] suggests the organization of a global task (in this case, the recognition of the winner) by the construction of an amorphous computing hierarchy. Theoretical and experimental results have shown that the amorphous computing hierarchy demonstrates general benefits. It minimizes cost, simplifies programming, facilities analysis, increases efficiency and termination is guaranteed [26]. So, amorphous computing particles organize themselves into clubs at different levels. At the first level of the hierarchy, the club algorithm proceeds by electing leaders. Each amorphous computing element chooses a random number and decrements it. If it reaches zero without being interrupted, it declares itself leader and diffuse a recruitment message to other particles. Thus, a particle that receives a message becomes member of the group and can eventually be recruited by further leaders. The higher level of the hierarchy is obtained by tree region algorithm. Its principle is similar to the above one but uses a parameter h to determine the bound of the region.

2. To apply the GNG, the second question can be solved by the attribution of relative coordinates to amorphous computing particles. In this context, Frost [17] has considers the problem of amorphous shape mapping and associates relative coordinates to the computational elements on the basis of the distance and orientation from a reference one.

3. Without moving, amorphous computing particles choose another one satisfying some conditions and pass it the past of the computation. We note that with irregularly placed particles, it is not always possible to find amorphous computing particles that satisfy equations (2, 3). We extend them as follow:

$$w_k = \left(w_s + e_w \left(x + w_s \right) \right) \pm \delta \tag{8}$$

$$w_n = \left(w_n + e_n \left(x + w_n \right) \right) \pm \delta \tag{9}$$

Interactions between a mass of amorphous computing particles are the principle key of this work. In particular, a mass of amorphous computing particles is placed randomly. Each of them is associated with a reference vector. In fact, the first step is a solution, which improves high performance to organize some tasks assigned to amorphous computing particles. If p is the highest leader of the hierarchy, it associates itself $(0,0)$ coordinates, alters its variable state to true and sends relative coordinates to others. On a more profound level, each amorphous computing particle is associated with a queue (msg-queue) to store received messages. In addition, an amorphous computing entity might be active or not depending on its active variable (active), which indicates if it is incorporated in the current graph. However, this pseudo-code proposed can be abstracted by the following actions: diffusion of a message by the root of the hierarchy, emission of the required information, modification of error's variable and then the selection of another particle to give it the past of the computation.

6 Experimental Results

An implementation of the proposed method has been made in order to conduct some experimental results. Netlogo 2.1 was the programming environment chosen. It is a programmable modeling environment for simulating natural phenomena. It can simulate a huge number of independent agents which act in parallel and execute their programs independently, if necessary interacting through local communication. It can take advantage of multiple processors by having multiple copies of Netlogo open, in separate virtual Java machines. However, it includes some built-in agents' variables that hold the initial values like the coordinates of the agents. In fact, it is necessary to hide some aspects of Netlogo and write our programs with respect to the constraints of amorphous computing paradigm. In order to cluster a relatively small number of gene expressions extracted freely from the PDR database available from: http://www.biologie.ens.fr/lgmgml/publication/pdr1gal/home.html.

3000 amorphous computing particles are randomly distributed; each runs asynchronously the amorphous GNG. Figure 1 illustrates the initial configuration of amorphous computing particles that are placed irregularly. As we can observe from table 1, λ is very small to increase the probability of finding a new particle satisfying equation (4).

In an attempt to test the technique and visualize the clusters obtained, we have referred to the U-Matrix (Unified matrix), usually constructed on the top of neurons. For the sake of terminology, if n is a neuron (amorphous computing particle), nn its set of immediate neighbors and w_n its reference vector [29]:

$$u-height(n)=\sum_{m \in NN(n)} d(w_n - w_m) \tag{10}$$

Fig. 1. Initial configuration of amorphous computing particles

Table 1. The considered parameters

e_w	e_n	α	β	age	λ	δ
0.25	0.23	0.75	0.6	20	2	0.8

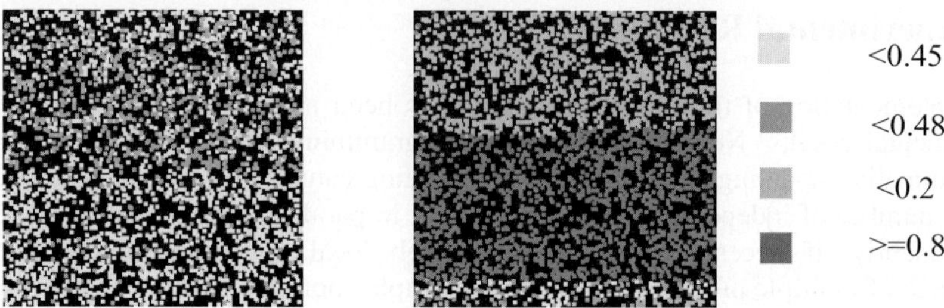

Fig. 2. Configuration after 1 iteration   **Fig. 3.** Visualization of clusters

Table 2. Clusters of gene expressions

Color of the cluster	Gene expressions	Number of entities	%
Cyan	YPR198W YAL010C YAL038W YAL004W YAL044C YAL043C YPR196W YPR193 YAL003W YAL002W YAL035W	1263	42.1
Magenta	YAL045C YAL039C YAL009W YAL047C YAL036C YAL011W YAL042W YAL048C YAL001C YPR194C YPR195C YPR199C YPR197C YAL049C YAL007C YAL037W YAL008W YAL043C-A YAL005C YAL040C YAL012W	1533	51.1
Yellow	YAL046C	114	4.73

The fundamental principal is to assign different colors to amorphous computing particle on the basis of the value obtained. The application of the U-Matrix after the first iteration does not show any cluster.

The pseudo-code executed leads to the modification of particles' reference vectors to visualize well the organization of the input gene expressions. In figure (3), amorphous computing articles have clearly cluster gene expressions and three clusters are illustrated. These results illustrated in table 2 show that a great number of genes have high level expression and are assigned to the second cluster. Only one gene has low level expressions and the others have important gene level expressions. Although the interpretation we have given is not sufficient, clustering gene expressions with amorphous computing provides a good scalability and time. Finally, the quality of the result is analyzed by the average quantization error (AQE):

$$\frac{1}{1+AQE} , AQE= \frac{1}{N}\sum \|x-w_c\| \tag{11}$$

x : An input vector, w_c : the reference vector of the winner.

After 1500 iterations, the quality of the map is 0,9722 that represents a very interesting value.

7   Conclusion

This work presents amorphous computing as a distributed control method that allows a coherent behavior to come from local interactions of irregularly placed particles. Combined with the GNG, it demonstrates that a mass of computational entities that receive neither geometric information nor time synchronization can self-organize to cluster gene expressions. Within the scope of this contribution, we show that a massive parallel system faced to limited information is a powerful tool in the first phase of knowledge extraction. If successful in a real amorphous computing system, this technique would also move complexity raised with microarray data. With regard to its limitations, this technique suffers from the problem related to the appropriate parameters, which is addressed by both clustering methods.

Acknowledgments

This work was supported by CMEP – PROGRAMME TASSILI under Project 05 MDU 642.

References

[1] T.Pasanen, J.Saarela, I.Saarikko, T.Toivanen, M.Tolvanen, M.Vihinen, G.Wong, 'DNA Microarray Data Analysis', Part 1, Editors Jarno Tuimala And M. Minna Laine CSC, ISBN 952-9821-89-1, 2003.

[2] K-P. Sycara, "Multiagent Systems", AI Magazine, Vol 19, No.2, 1998.

[3] R.Nagpal "Programmable Self-Assembly Using Biologically-Inspired Multiagent Control", AAMAS'02, Bologna (Italy), July 2002.

[4] R.Nagpal, M.Mamei, "Engineering Amorphous Computing Systems", Invited chapter in Methodologies and software engineering for agent systems, editors Bergenti, 2004.

[5] W. Buthera, "Programming a Paintable Computer", Phd thesis, Media Lab, MIT, Cambridge, 2002.

[6] J.Lifton, "Pushpin Computing: A Platform for Distributed Sensor Networks", Master's of Science in Media Arts and Sciences, MIT, September 2002.

[7] H. Abelson, D. Allen, D. Coore, C. Hanson, G. Homsy, T. Knight, Jr., R. Nagpal, E. Rauch, G.Sussman,R.Weiss,"AmorphousComputing", AI MEMO 1665, MIT, August 99.

[8] J.Beal, "A Robust Amorphous Hierarchy From Persistent Nodes", AI Memo 2003 - 012, MIT, May 2003.

[9] R.Nagpal, "Programming Self-Assembly: Constructing Global Shapes using Biologically-Inspired Local Interconnections and Orgami Mathematics", thesis, MIT, 2001.

[10] D.Coore, "Botanical Computing, a Development Approach to Generating Interconnect Topologies on an Amorphous Computer", thesis, MIT, February 1999.

[11] A. Sutherland, "Towards RSEAM: Resilient Serial Execution On Amorphous Machines", Master's thesis of engineering in electrical engineering and computer science, MIT, Cambridge, June 2003.

[12] W-M.Shen, P-Will, A.Galastyan, C-M.Chuong, "Hormone-Inspired Self-Organization and Distributed Control of Robotic Swarms", Autonomous Robots 17, 93-105, Netherlands, 2004

[13] K. Stoy, R. Nagpal, "Self-Repair trough Scale Independent Self-Reconfiguration", proceeding of 2004 IEEE/RSJ International Conference on Intelligent Robots and Systems, Sendai, 2004.

[14] A. Kondacs, "Biologically Inspired, Self-Assembly Of Two-Dimensional Shapes Using Global To Local Compilation", International Joint Conference On Artificial Intelligence (IJCAI), 2003.

[15] C.Frost, "Amorphous Mapping Objects", thesis in TCC, University of Virginia, May 2004.

[16] G.Grothaus,"Biologically Interpretable Disease Classification Based on Gene Expression Data", Master's thesis, Virginia Polytechnic Institute, May 2005.

[17] G.Unger, "Linear Separability and Classificability of Gene Expression Datasets", Master's thesis, Aviv University, February 2004.

[18] A.Mateos, J.Herrero, J.Tomames, J.Dopazo, "Supervised Neural Networks for Clustering Conditions in DNA array Data after Reducing Noise by Clustering Gene Expression Profiles", Center for Cancer Research (CNIO), Madrid, Spain, Microarray data analysis2, KluwerAcademic, Pp. 91-103.

[19] K.Aas, "Microarray Data Mining: Asurvey", SAMBA/02/01, January 2001.

[20] Cho, H.Won, "Machine Learning in DNA Microarray Analysis for Cancer Classification", Yonsei University, Korea, Asia-Pacific Bioinformatics Conference, Vol .19, Australia, 2003.

[21] J. Holmstrom, "Growing Neural Gas experiments with GNG, GNG with utility and supervised GNG", Uppsala Master's thesis in computer science, Uppsala University, Sweden, 2002.

[22] H.Jin, W-H.Shun, KS.Leung, M-L.Wong, "Expending Self-organizing map and Cluster Analysis", Chinese and Lingnan University, Elsevier 163(2004) 157-173, 2003.

[23] J. Neumann, "Holistic Processing of Hierarchical Structures in Connectionist Networks", Phd thesis, University of Edinburgh, 2001.

[24] T.Liao "Image Segmentation - Hybrid Method Combining Clustering and Region Merging", Thesis, Monash University, November, 2003.

[25] E.'Hondt, "Exploring the Amorphous Computing Paradigm", Master's thesis in computer science, Vrije University, Brussel, August 2000.

[26] D. Coore, R. Nagpal, R. Weiss, "Paradigms for structure in an amorphous computer", AI Memo No. 1614, October 97.

[27] A.Ultsech, "U*-Matrix: A tool to visualize clusters in high dimensional data", University of Marburg, Germany, December 2003.

Conflict-Directed Relaxation of Constraints in Content-Based Recommender Systems

Dietmar Jannach and Johannes Liegl

Institute for Business Informatics & Application Systems
University Klagenfurt, A-9020 Klagenfurt, Austria
dietmar.jannach@ifit.uni-klu.ac.at,
johannes.liegl@edu.uni-klu.ac.at

Abstract. Content-based recommenders are systems that exploit detailed knowledge about the items in the catalog for generating adequate product proposals. In that context, *query relaxation* is one of the basic approaches for dealing with situations, where none of the products in the catalogue *exactly* matches the customer requirements. The major challenges when applying query relaxation are that the relaxation should be minimal (or optimal for the customer), that there exists a potentially vast search space, and that we have to deal with hard time constraints in interactive recommender applications.

In this paper, we show how the task of finding adequate or customer optimal relaxations for a given recommendation problem can be efficiently achieved by applying techniques from the field of model-based diagnosis, i.e., with the help of extended algorithms for computing *conflicts* and *hitting sets*. In addition, we propose a best-effort search algorithm based on branch-and-bound for dealing with hard problems and also describe how an optimal relaxation can be immediately obtained when partial queries can be (pre-)evaluated.

Finally, we discuss the results of an evaluation of the described techniques, which we made by extending an existing knowledge-based recommender system and which we based on different real-world problem settings.

1 Introduction

Content-based recommender systems are a special class of recommendation systems that operate on the basis of explicit knowledge about customer requirements, product characteristics, and recommendation logic (typically some sort of "filter rules") that determines the set of products to be proposed, when given some specific customer requirements. One of the main problems of such content-based systems, however, is that situations can easily arise, where all of the existing products are filtered out and no adequate proposal can be made [1] as there exists no exact match. "*No products found*" is an undesirable system response in such situations, in which we would appreciate a more intelligent behaviour, i.e., an explanation of the situation or – even better – a list of products that fulfil as many as possible of the originally posted requirements. In that context, approaches based on Case-Based Reasoning (CBR) have the advantage that they are in principle capable of also retrieving products that

M. Ali and R. Dapoigny (Eds.): IEA/AIE 2006, LNAI 4031, pp. 819 – 829, 2006.

are *similar* to the user's query. Nonetheless, also these similarity-based approaches have their limitations, for example, that the most similar product might not be acceptable for the user, or that the means for explaining the proposal are limited [9].

Another approach of dealing with such situations is therefore to "relax" [10] the problem by giving up some of the requirements (i.e., remove parts of the query) and then test whether there exists a product that fulfils at least the remaining requirements. However, finding good relaxations is not a trivial problem, because typically many different alternative relaxations exist, the proposed relaxations should be minimal (or optimal for the user), and finally, the time-frame for finding such relaxations is strictly limited, because recommender systems are interactive applications. In this paper, we show how the task of finding adequate relaxations for a given recommendation problem can be efficiently achieved by applying techniques from the field of model-based diagnosis, i.e., with the help of extended algorithms for computing *conflicts* and *hitting sets*. After giving an introductory example, we develop a general and implementation-independent model of the recommendation problem and show how the relaxation problem can be mapped to a model-based diagnosis problem such that extended algorithms for conflict-identification and hitting set computation can be applied. In addition, we also propose a best-effort search algorithm based on branch-and-bound for dealing with hard problems and finally discuss experimental results which were achieved by extending an existing recommender system with these algorithms and by using different real-world test cases. The paper ends with a discussion of related and future work.

2 Example

In the following, we will give a simple example from the domain of digital cameras for illustrating the relaxation problem and the importance of conflict-directed search. Let us assume our product database (PDB) of digital cameras contains the following entries.

ID	USB	Firewire	Price	Resolution	Make
p1	true	false	400	5	Canon
p2	false	true	500	5	Canon
p3	true	false	200	4	Fuji
p4	false	true	400	5	HP

Our knowledge base of filter rules (FRS) comprises the following definitions.

f1: IF *the customer requires high-quality printouts of the pictures* THEN
    recommend cameras with a resolution of 5 mega-pixels.
f2: IF *the customer wants to have a cheap camera* THEN
    recommend cameras with a price smaller than 300.
f3: IF *customer needs a USB port* THEN
    recommend cameras with a USB port.
f4: IF *customer wants extended connectivity* THEN
    recommend cameras supporting Firewire.
f5: IN ANY CASE
    recommend cameras with a resolution higher than 3 mega-pixels.

Now, let us assume that a customer has the following requirements (REQ):

USB-support, extended-connectivity, only cheap cameras, high-quality printouts.

Given these requirements, the product database and the filter-rules, no single product will fulfil all the requirements. We can now try to relax (retract) some of the filter rules, in order to find products that fulfil as many of the customer's constraints as possible. A simple algorithm for finding an adequate relaxation is to compute all possible combinations of filters (the powerset of FRS) and check for each of these combinations whether products remain when these filter rules are retracted. Of course, such an algorithm will – in the worst case – require 2^n checks, which is inadequate for realistic settings, where response times below one second are required.

We therefore propose adopting a conflict-directed approach similar to Reiter's [13] Hitting-Set algorithm: If we look closer on the problem situation of our example, we see that there are two "minimal conflicts", $c_1 = \{f1, f2\}$ and $c_2 = \{f3, f4\}$, i.e., in any valid problem relaxation, at least one of the filters of c_1 and one of the filters of c_2 has to be removed. We also see that f5 is not involved in any conflict, which basically means that we do not have to take f5 into account when searching for relaxations. Furthermore, based on Reiter's general theory [13], we can conclude that computing the set of possible, minimal relaxations (i.e., *minimal diagnoses* in the sense of [13]) can be efficiently done by computing the *Hitting Set* of all minimal conflicts. In our example problem the set of minimal relaxations thus is the set:

$$\{\{f1, f3\}, \{f1, f4\}, \{f2, f3\}, \{f2, f4\}\}.$$

Given these conflicts, finding the *first* valid relaxation {f1,f3} thus involves only the examination of three paths ({f1},{f2},{f1,f3}), i.e., three queries to the database, when constructing the search tree in breadth-first manner (Fig. 1).

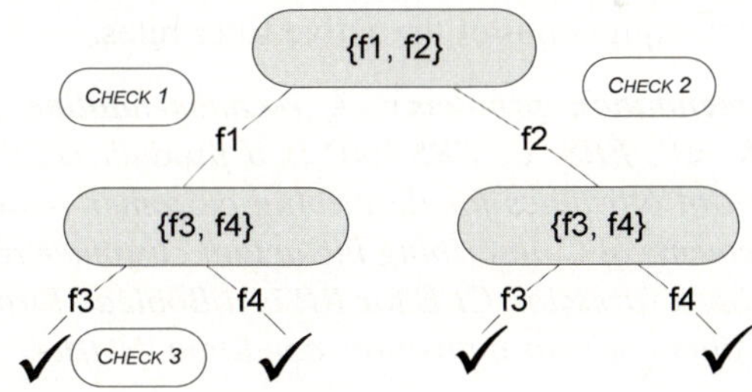

Fig. 1. Hitting set search tree for example problem

3   Conflict-Directed Filter Relaxation

In the following, we develop a basic formalization of content- or filter-based[1] recommender problems by mapping the problem of finding adequate products in a catalog to a selection-query for a relational database, which has the advantage that we

---

[1] We view "filter-based recommenders" [1] as a special class of content-based approaches.

can rely on an existing, well-established formalism. In addition, knowledge-based recommenders or simple product finders in fact work by dynamically constructing database queries for filtering the products. However, please note that the chosen formalisation does not necessarily imply that a database system has to be used; it is rather used here to clearly characterize the problem.

Content-based recommender systems rely on the existence of a product catalog that contains detailed descriptions of the items to be recommended. In general, such a product catalog can be described as a relational database table as follows.

Definition (Product catalog): *Items in a product catalog are described by a set of attributes A; each attribute $a_i \in A$ is assigned a domain d_i. A **product catalog** P is then a subset of the Cartesian product of the domains d_i, i.e. $P \subseteq d_1 \times ... \times d_n$.*

The set of suitable products for some given customer requirements is determined by a set of *filter rules*, which were informally sketched as "if-then" rules in the example section.

Definition (Filter rule): *Let C be the set of attributes for describing customer requirements. A filter rule f can be described by the two characteristics f.AC, and f.FE, where f.AC is a Boolean formula (activation constraint[2]) over customer requirements C which describes the condition, when the filter rule shall be applied. f.FE represents the actual filter expression on the elements of the catalog (subquery) and is a Boolean formula over constant values, attributes of the product catalog and attributes from C.*

Note that in our definition we allow the usage of variables (from C) in the filter expression, e.g. for modelling dynamic filter rules like "*In any case, propose only products whose price is equal or lower to the price the customer has specified.*"

The recommendation problem consists of finding a set of items from the catalog that fulfils all the filter expressions of the active filter rules.

Definition (Recommendation problem): *A recommendation problem RP can be described by a tuple <P, FRS, C, CRS>: P is a product catalog, FRS is the set of filter rules, C the set of attributes for describing customer requirements, and CRS a function over the elements of C describing the actual customer requirements.*

The compound filter expression CFE for RP is a Boolean formula defined to be the conjunction of the filters whose activation condition is true, given some customer requirements CRS, i.e,

$$CFE = \bigwedge\nolimits_{f \in FRS,\ f.AC\ =\ true} (f.FE).$$

*Finding a **solution** to **<P, FRS, C, CRS>** then corresponds to performing the database selection σ_{CFE} on the product catalog P.*

If none of the products in P satisfies all the compound expression CFE, we aim at finding a relaxation of the problem by retracting some of the filter rules, such that the selection results in a non-empty set of items from the catalog.

---

[2] The notion of "activation constraints" is inspired by the *Dynamic Constraint Satisfaction* approach, see e.g., [9]. We introduce that concept such that we can apply the approach also for "knowledge-based" recommenders, like, e.g., [7].

Definition (Valid relaxation): *Given a recommendation problem RP <P, FRS, C, CRS>, for which the size of the selection* $|\sigma_{CFE}(P)| = 0$, *a valid relaxation is a set RFRS $\subseteq$ FRS such that the solution for the modified recommendation problem RP' <P, FRS – RFRS, C, CRS> contains at least one element.*

Lemma: Given a recommendation problem *RP <P, FRS, C, CRS>* and $P \neq \varnothing$, a valid relaxation will always exist, because if we set *RFRS = FRS*, the selection query will be empty and all $p \in P$ are in the solution for *RP*.

In general, however, we are interested in finding optimal or minimal relaxations, e.g., we should try to find products that fulfil as many of the customer requirements as possible.

Definition (Minimal relaxation): *A relaxation RFRS for RP is said to be minimal if there exists no RFRS' $\subset$ RFRS such that RFRS' is a valid relaxation for RP.*

Computing minimal relaxations. One possible algorithm to compute possible relaxations is to compute the powerset of *FRS* and evaluate the value of the individual solutions. Because of the natural inefficiency of such an approach, we propose to apply a *conflict-directed* approach for finding relaxations: Given the definitions above, we can view the relaxation problem as a model-based diagnosis problem in the sense of [13] and correspondingly view the set of filter rules as the set of diagnosable and thus possibly faulty components of the system.

Definition (Conflict): *Given a recommendation problem RP<P, FRS, C, CRS>, a conflict CF is a subset of FRS such that there exists no solution for RP<P, CF, C, CRS>. A conflict CF is said to be minimal if there is no CF' $\subset$ CF which is also a conflict for RP<P, FRS, C, CRS>.*

Adapted Hitting-Set algorithm (sketch): Given a recommendation problem *RP<P, FRS, C, CRS>*, construct a HS-DAG[3] for the collection K of conflicts in breadth-first manner. Each node n of the HS-DAG is labelled with a conflict CS(n) $\in$ K. Edges leading away from n are labelled with a filter rule f $\in$ CS(n), the set of edge labels from the root to n is referred to as *H(n)*. Every call to the *Theorem Prover* TP [13] at a node n returns true when there exists a solution for the adapted recommendation problem RP <P, FRS – H(n), C, CRS> (meaning that n can be closed) or a conflict in the other case.

Computing minimal conflicts. If we are given a recommendation problem *RP<P, FRS, C, CRS>* whose result set is empty, the whole set of (active) filter rules of course represents a conflict. However, the size of the conflict sets directly influences the size of the resulting search tree, i.e., we are in general interested in finding small or minimal conflict sets. We therefore propose to use Junker's algorithm for efficiently computing such minimal conflicts [8]: QUICKXPLAIN is a recent, non-intrusive conflict detection algorithm that – based on a divide and conquer strategy – decomposes the overall problem based on the concept of "preferred constraints". The main advantage of the approach lies in its general applicability, i.e., it is not bound to

---

[3] Hitting Set Directed Acyclic Graph; according to [13], finding the set of minimal diagnoses corresponds to computing the *Hitting Set* of all minimal conflicts.

specific inference and dependency-tracking mechanisms in the underlying reasoning engine. In addition, QUICKXPLAIN also supports search for "preferred" conflicts for cases where not all elements of the conflict have the same priority. When applied to our problem, conflict detection means to identify minimal sets of active filter rules that have no products in common, i.e., which will lead to an empty result set.

Best-effort search for customer-optimal relaxations. When using Reiter's algorithm, we search for diagnoses in breadth-first manner, implicitly assuming that smaller diagnoses (relaxations) are preferable. In recommender applications, however, not all of the filter rules may have equal importance for the customer. On the one hand the domain engineer might annotate the rules in advance with some priority of application based on his/her expert knowledge; on the other hand we could allow the user to express his/her preferences on the importance of rules or derive it from other (external) data sources like from the behaviour of other users.

Definition (Optimal relaxation): Given a recommendation problem RP<P, FRS, C, CRS>, let RC be a function over the elements of FRS describing the costs of retracting a single filter f $\in$ FRS. Let COSTS be a function describing the costs of a relaxation as an integer number, which takes the set of retracted filters, the individual costs RC, and eventually also customer characteristics[4] into account. A relaxation RFRS for RP is said to be optimal if there exists no other set RFRS' $\subseteq$ FRS such that

$$COSTS(RFRS', CRS, RC) < COSTS(RFRS, CRS, RC).$$

For ensuring monotonicity of the COSTS function, COSTS(RFRS', CRS, RC) < COSTS(RFRS, CRS, RC), has to hold in cases where RFRS' $\subset$ RFRS

We introduce this general cost function, as minimal relaxations may not always be optimal, i.e., it might be better to relax two rules with lower importance than to relax one rule which is highly important for the customer. Applying breadth-first search is thus not reasonable in that context because a potentially many different conflicts have to be computed for finding the first solution; exhaustive search is only possible for very small problems. We therefore propose to explore the search space in depth-first manner, such that a first (non-optimal) relaxation can be found in very short time. After having found this initial solution, we proceed by applying a branch-and-bound search in which we prune those search paths that will definitely not lead to a better solution. We also propose to implement a time-constrained best-effort variant, where we define a maximum time (e.g., one second) for optimization. Of course, optimality of the result cannot be guaranteed then in general, but our experiments suggest that even rather complex problems can be solved in very short time or *good* relaxations can be found, e.g., when using a domain-independent, priority-based search heuristic.

Depth-first algorithm (sketch): Given a recommendation problem *RP<P, FRS, C, CRS>*, construct the HS-DAG for the collection K of *minimal*[5] conflicts in depth-first manner. Label edges and nodes similar to the algorithm described previously. As a general search heuristic, sort the elements of each conflict according to their weight in

---

[4] The cost function could, for instance, take personal preferences of the user into account.
[5] Note that we rely on *minimal* conflicts that are computed with QuickXPlain, which also means that tree pruning [13] is not required.

ascending order. Remember the value of the optimization function for the first valid relaxation as the currently best solution. When further exploring the search tree, always remember the value of the currently best solutions and prune those paths that will definitely result in solutions which are worse than the optimum found so far. In addition – since the relaxations that are found in the depth-first approach may be non-minimal – we need to minimize each relaxation that is found before proceeding with the search process. This minimization operation, however, requires at most n-1 additional consistency checks for a relaxation of size n, since we can check each of the elements of the actual relaxation individually.

4   Implementation and Discussion

In order to evaluate our approach, we have implemented the proposed algorithms in the knowledge-based Advisor Suite [7] system. Our particular aim was to demonstrate that the diagnosis approach is suitable given the hard real-time requirements of interactive recommender applications: in general, given a set of n diagnosable components, i.e., filter rules, the computational complexity of finding diagnoses of cardinality k is O(nk). From various real-world instantiations of the Advisor Suite system we know that a typical knowledge base contains about 40-70 filter rules; we also claim that the size of allowed relaxations should be limited to a maximum of five to seven filter rules for pragmatic reasons. From practical settings we know that users are not satisfied with proposals where for instance half of the rules (corresponding to the original wishes) could not be applied. The most costly and frequent operation during the construction of the HS-DAG and the computation of conflicts is to determine for a given set of filter rules whether these rules, if applied together, lead to an empty result set. For increased performance, we have chosen to perform a pre-processing step in which we evaluate the active filter rules individually, i.e., for each of the filter rules, we set up the list of products that fulfil the filter expression. For all of the filter rules that contain no variables in the filter expression, we can pre-compute the set of products that fulfil the expression. For all other rules, we have to set up the product list at run-time for each customer session. The results of these filters can be represented as bit-sets in compact way, i.e., for each product in the catalog we set a flag, if it is in the result or not (Fig. 2). The computation of the conjunction of the filter rules can then be efficiently done by applying a "bitwise and" on these bit-sets.

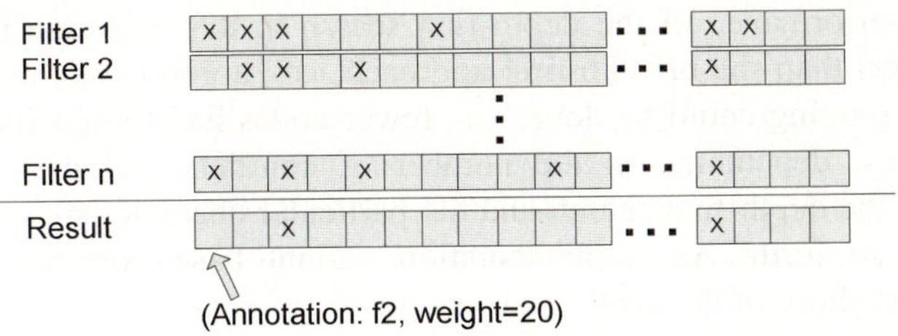

Fig. 2. Bit-set representation of filter rules

If the resulting bit-set contains no entries, we know that the result set is empty and we have to relax some of the filters. Note that this sort of representation is not mandatory for applying our approach but was actually implemented in the Java-based Advisor Suite system. Our measurements of the running times (see below) also include numbers for an implementation variant that does not rely on these pre-processing step but rather on individual database queries (HS/DBQ).

A particular side-effect when using the pre-processing technique is that we can directly determine the optimal or minimal relaxation without even constructing the HS-DAG: If we remember for each product the set of filter rules that had a "0" for the product and the sum of the weights of these rules (see Fig. 2) we only have to determine that product in the (empty) result set which minimizes the given optimization function. As such, the search for the best valid relaxation can be done by only evaluating each filter rule once, computing the conjunction of the bit-sets, and finding the minimum by scanning the result set (compare also the results of [6] for finding the first *maximal succeeding subquery*). We could therefore compute the optimal relaxation for all test cases in a few milliseconds (see column BSA in the table below). Still, this is only possible due to a very specific implementation in our system and is not as general as the described conflict-directed approach.

In the different test examples we varied the relaxation goal (cardinality only/optimization), the number of (active) filter rules, the number of products and conflicts, the average size of the conflicts, and the cardinality of the minimal diagnoses[6]. Our test databases contained up to 2.000 different products – the ramp up time for constructing the needed data structures is about 2 seconds on a Pentium IV desktop PC, which is not problematic since this has to be done only once during server start-up. The additional memory requirement for the data structures alone is *nbProducts * nbFilterRules* bits and thus strictly limited. The following tables show the average running times for a rather hard test case for one of our real-world knowledge bases that contains 70 filter rules. In the test cases, 25 of them were active for some given customer requirements. The number of and size of the conflicts was adequately increased with the size of the minimal relaxation that was to be found. The numbers in the table correspond to average running times in milliseconds for finding the first/best relaxation.

In that test case, all of the problems could be solved within the targeted time-frame of one second, even when using database queries instead of the bit-set representation. If no pre-computation of filter results was done, e.g., because all filter rules contain variables, the search process needed about 40 additional milliseconds in our test cases. The performance of the depth-first search in that test case is comparable (or slightly better) than the breadth-first approach, i.e., a good solution was found early and a lot of pruning could be done, i.e., fewer nodes had to be expanded. In general this will vary, depending on the number of conflicts and diagnoses, the search heuristic for the depth-first search and the particular characteristics of the importance factors and so forth. An implementation variant based on A* produced results comparable to those of the depth-first search.

---

[6] Note that a relaxation of size 10 is already rather unrealistic and of little help for the user.

Table 1. Breadth-first search for first diagnosis

Table 2. Depth-first / Branch & bound for optimal diagnosis

C	HS/BS	HS/DBQ	BSA	#N	#TP
1	12	177.1	10	1	15
3	14	345.6	10	4	22
5	14	416.6	10	23	75
7	18	472.9	10	95	99
10	67	861.2	10	1346	228

C	HS/BS	HS/DBQ	#N	#TP
1	12	164.5	1	15
3	15	338.5	6	22
5	16	414.6	19	75
7	16	465.8	62	99
10	35	697.1	471	187

C: Cardinality of smallest relaxation

HS/BS: HS-DAG construction, usage of bit-set representation

HS/DBQ: HS-DAG construction, usage of dynamically constructed queries

BSA: Analysis of bit-sets only (no HS-DAG)

#N: Number of search tree nodes

#TP: "Theorem prover" calls: DB-queries / Bit-set operations

5 Related Work and Conclusions

Related work. Query-relaxation for content-based recommenders was recently addressed in [9] and [10]. In this work, McSherry proposed an approach in which the user is incrementally presented individual explanations for the retrieval failure and the problem is iteratively solved. Such system behaviour can in principle also be implemented based on our approach if we compute a minimal conflict in each step and let the user decide how to proceed. Nonetheless, there might be many interactions required (e.g., if we need to relax many filters), the system will not be able to predict in general if the relaxation of the next sub-query will succeed, and no overall optimum can be guaranteed. In addition, the number of queries required for computing all conflicts before entering the recovery process may be too large for interactive applications in their approach. An comparable iterative repair approach is also implemented in our surrounding framework [7], where the user can interactively change the priorities of the rules according to his/her preferences.

The identification of the reasons for a failure of a query is also an issue in the area of Cooperative Query Answering. In [6], Godfrey shows complexity results for finding *Minimal Failing Sub-queries* MSF (correspond to *conflicts* in our approach) and *maximal succeeding queries* XSS (corresponding to our relaxed query) and proposes algorithms for finding one and enumerating all MSF/XSS. Our algorithms can be seen as alternatives to these basic mechanisms which are in addition capable of exploiting priorities for steering the (best-effort) search process and also incorporate recently developed algorithms for fast detection of minimal conflicts [8].

Incremental relaxation of overconstrained problems is also a well-known technique in the Constraint Satisfaction world, see e.g., [12] or [14], where *soft constraints* and *Partial Constraint Satisfaction* were introduced. These approaches, however, were designed to work in the context of some specific reasoning technique and cannot be easily applied to other problem solving or inference algorithms.

From the technological perspective, model-based diagnosis techniques for detecting problems in Software systems have been introduced e.g., in [2] or [4]. We see our approach in the general tradition of that work. Our future work includes the extension of the approach towards the computation of "repair alternatives": Instead of computing only possible relaxations, the goal will be to find a minimal set of changes in the user requirements such that a solution can be found. Finally, we also aim at evaluating approaches that exploit abstraction hierarchies within the knowledge base (see e.g., [3]), an approach that was also suggested as a tool for tackling the relaxation problem for recommenders in [11].

Conclusions. In this paper, we have shown how conflict-directed search can be used to significantly enhance the search for minimal relaxations of unsuccessful queries in filter-based recommender systems. The evaluation of the approach in a knowledge-based advisory framework has shown that even hard problem instances can be solved within the short time frames that are required in interactive recommender applications. Furthermore it was demonstrated how the usage of specialized data structures and pre-processing techniques can further reduce the number of required database queries and thus shorten response times. In our current work, we aim at generalizing this pre-processing approach and also extending it with a mechanism with which we can also compute relaxations (based on the bit-set matrix) that lead at least to n different products, which shall give the end user more choices when searching and comparing different items in a proposal.

References

[1] D. Bridge. Product recommendation systems: A new direction. In R. Weber and C. Wangenheim, eds., Proceedings of the Workshop Programme at the Fourth International Conference on Case-Based Reasoning, 2001, p. 79-86.

[2] L. Console, G. Friedrich, D. T. Dupré: Model-Based Diagnosis Meets Error Diagnosis in Logic Programs. IJCAI'1993, Chambéry, France, 1993, p. 1494-1501.

[3] A. Felfernig A., G. Friedrich, D. Jannach, M. Stumptner: Hierarchical Diagnosis of large configurator knowledge bases. In: S. McIlraith, D. T. Dupré (Eds.): 12th Intl. Workshop on Principles of Diagnosis, 2001, p. 55-62.

[4] A. Felfernig, G. Friedrich, D. Jannach, M. Stumptner. Consistency-based diagnosis of configuration knowledge bases, Artificial Intelligence, 152(2), 2004, p. 213-234.

[5] E. Freuder, R. J. Wallace: Partial Constraint Satisfaction, Artificial Intelligence (58), 1992.

[6] P. Godfrey. Minimization in Cooperative Response to Failing Database Queries, International Journal of Cooperative Information Systems Vol. 6(2), 1997, p. 95-149.

[7] D. Jannach. ADVISOR SUITE - A knowledge-based sales advisory system. In: Proceedings of ECAI/PAIS 2004, Valencia, Spain, IOS Press, 2004, pp. 720-724.

[8] U. Junker: QUICKXPLAIN: Preferred Explanations and Relaxations for Over-Constrained Problems. Proceedings AAAI'2004, San Jose, 2004, p. 167-172.

[9] D. McSherry, Explanation of Retrieval Mismatches in Recommender System Dialogues, ICCBR'03 Mixed-Initiative Case-Based Reasoning Workshop, Trondheim, Norway, 2003.

[10] D. McSherry, Incremental Relaxation of Unsuccessful Queries, Lecture Notes in Computer Science, Volume 3155, 2004, p. 331–345.

[11] N. Mirzadeh, F. Ricci and M. Bansal, Supporting User Query Relaxation in a Recommender System, Proceedings of 5th Intl. Conference on Electronic Commerce and Web Technologies, EC-Web '04, Zaragoza, Spain, 2004, p. 31-40.

[12] S. Mittal, B. Falkenhainer. Dynamic constraint satisfaction problems. In: Proceedings of the 8th National Conference on Artificial Intelligence, AAAI'89, 1989, p. 25-32.

[13] R. Reiter. A theory of diagnosis from first principles. Artificial Intelligence, 32(1), Elsevier, 1987, p. 57-95.

[14] T. Schiex, H. Fargier, and G. Verfaille. Valued constraint satisfaction problems: Hard and easy problems. In International Joint Conference on Artificial Intelligence IJCAI'95, Montreal, Canada, 1995, p. 631-639.

Modeling pH Neutralization Process Via Support Vector Machines

Dongwon Kim and Gwi-Tae Park[*]

Department of Electrical Engineering, Korea University, 1, 5-ka, Anam-dong, Seongbuk-ku,
Seoul 136-701, Korea
{upground, gtpark}@korea.ac.kr

Abstract. This paper discusses the use of support vector machines for modeling and identification of pH neutralization process. Support vector machines (SVM) and kernel method have become very popular as methods for learning from examples. We apply SVM to model pH process which has strong nonlinearities. The experimental results show that the SVM based on the kernel substitution including linear and radial basis function kernel provides a promising alternative to model strong nonlinearities of the pH neutralization but also to control the system. Comparisons with other modeling methods show that the SVM method offers encouraging advantages and has better performance.

1   Introduction

Process modeling is a very important step in the control, diagnosis and optimization of the process system. For most cases, the model is constructed from the data because first principle models are very difficult to be obtained. Neural networks, fuzzy systems, etc. can all be used to model chemical processes using historical data. Unfortunately, insufficient data hamper the accuracy of these models because they rely strongly on the data when inducing process behavior [1]. Many methods have been proposed to overcome this problem. As promising methods, there is support vector machine (SVM) which is introduced by Vapnik [2]. It is an elegant tool for solving pattern recognition and regression problems. Over the past few years, a lot of researchers from neural network and mathematical programming fields are attracted to devote themselves to the research on SVM. The basic theory is well understood and applications work successfully in practice. In many applications [3,4,5], SVM has been shown to provide higher performance than traditional learning machines [6] and has been introduced as powerful tools.

In this paper, SVM and kernel methods (KMs) are first applied to model and identify pH neutralization process. In the following, description of pH process and basic concepts of SVM will be described. In addition, we examine the feasibility of applying SVM in the strong nonlinearities of the pH neutralization process by comparing it with other techniques.

---

[*] Corresponding author.

M. Ali and R. Dapoigny (Eds.): IEA/AIE 2006, LNAI 4031, pp. 830–837, 2006.

2 pH Neutralization Process

To demonstrate the high modeling accuracy of the SVM, we apply it to a highly nonlinear process of pH neutralization of a weak acid and a strong base. This model can be found in a variety of practical areas including wastewater treatment, biotechnology processing, and chemical processing [7-9]. The pH is the measurement of the acidity or alkalinity of a solution containing a proportion of water. It is mathematically defined, for dilute solution, as the negative decimal logarithm of the hydrogen ion concentration [H+] in the solution, that is, pH=-log10[H+].

In the continuously stirred tank reactor (CSTR) [10] investigated, shown in Fig. 1, acetic acid (HAC) of concentration C_a flows into the tank at flow rate F_a , and is neutralized by sodium hydroxide(NaOH) of concentration C_b which flows into the tank at rate F_b . The equations of the CSTR can be described as follows.

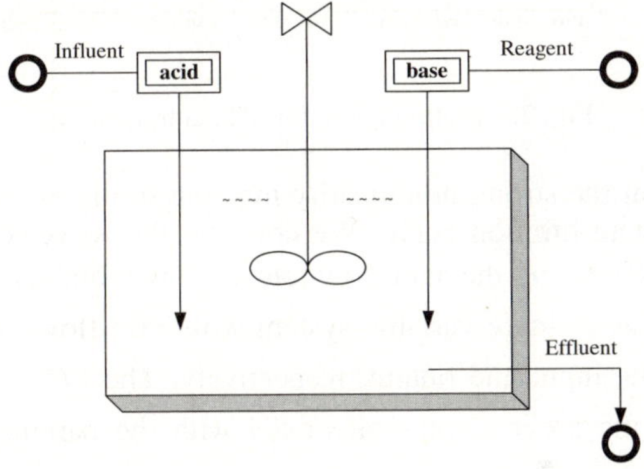

Fig. 1. Continuous tank reactor for pH neutralization

The process equations for the CSTR is given by

$$\frac{Vdw_a}{dt} = F_a C_a - (F_a + F_b)W_a$$

$$\frac{Vdw_b}{dt} = F_b C_b - (F_a + F_b)W_b \tag{1}$$

where the constant V is the volume of the content in the reactor, w_a and w_b are the concentrations of the acid and the base, respectively.

The above equation describes how the concentrations of w_a and w_b changes dynamically with time subject to the input streams F_a and F_b . To obtain the pH in the effluent, we need to find a relation between instantaneous concentrations w_a and w_b and pH values. This relationship can be described by a nonlinear algebra equation known as the titration or characteristic curve. Depending on the chemical species used, the titration curve varies. The static titration curve can be described as [9]

$$W_b + 10^{-pH} - 10^{pH-pK_w} - \frac{W_a}{1+10^{pK_a-pH}} = 0 \qquad (2)$$

where $pKa = -\log_{10} k_a$. The static relationship between base flow rate and pH in the reactor is plotted in Fig. 2.

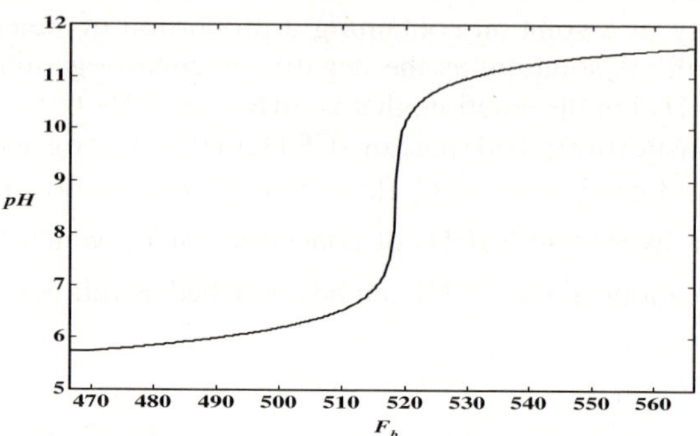

Fig. 2. Titration curve for pH neutralization

It can be seen that the strong nonlinearity inherent in the pH process is character-ized by its steady state titration curve. We consider the weak acid-strong base neu-tralization process. By fixing the acid flow-rate F_a (81cc/min) at a specific value, the process is regarded as a single variable system with base flow-rate F_b and the pH in the effluent being the input and output, respectively. The (F_b, y_{pH}) data pairs were produced by using the process physical model with the parameter values given in Table 1.

Table 1. Parameters and initial values for pH process

Variables	Meaning	Initial setting
V	Volume of tank	1000 cc
F_a	Flow rate of acid	81 cc/min
F_b	Flow rate of base	515 cc/min
C_a	Concentration of acid in Fa	0.32 mole/l
C_b	Concentration of base in Fb	0.05 mole/l
K_a	Acid equilibrium constant	$1.76*10^{-5}$
K_w	Water equilibrium constant	$1.0*10^{-14}$
$W_a(0)$	Concentration of acid	0.0435 mole/l
$W_b(0)$	Concentration of base	0.0432 mole/l

The base flow rate F_b was given by

$$F_b = 515 + 51.5\sin(2\pi t / 25) \quad for\ t \leq 150$$
$$F_b = 515 + 51.5\sin(2\pi t / 25) \quad for\ t \leq 150 \qquad (3)$$

For obtaining such a data pairs, we applied Newton-Raphson method that is given by Eqs. (4).

$$pH_{i+1} = pH_i - \frac{f(pH_i)}{f'(pH_i)}$$

(4)

The system inputs of the SVM structure consist of the delayed terms of $F_b(t)$ and $y_{pH}(t)$ which are input and output of the process, i.e.

$$\hat{y}_{pH}(t) = \varphi(F_b(t-3), F_b(t-2), F_b(t-1), y_{pH}(t-3), y_{pH}(t-2), y_{pH}(t-1))$$

(5)

where, $\hat{y}_{pH}$ and y_{pH} denote the SVM model output and the actual process output, respectively and 500 data pairs are generated. Further discussion on the process can be obtained in [9]

3 Support Vector Machine Modeling

The SVMs can be applied to regression problems by the introduction of an alternative loss function [2]. The basis idea in SVR is to map the input data x into a higher dimensional feature space via a nonlinear mapping Φ and then a linear regression problem is obtained and solved in this feature space. The following presents some basic concepts of SVR as described by prior research. A detailed explanation may be found in [3]. In SVM method, the regression function is approximated by the following function:

$$y = \sum_{i=1}^{l} w_i \Phi_i(x) + b$$

(6)

where $\{\Phi_i(x)\}_{i=1}^{l}$ are the feature of inputs, $\{w_i\}_{i=1}^{l}$ and b are coefficients. The coefficients are estimated by minimizing the regularized risk function.

$$R(C) = C\frac{1}{l}\sum_{i=1}^{l} L_\varepsilon(d_i, y_i) + \frac{1}{2}\|w\|^2$$

(7)

where

$$L_\varepsilon(d_i, y_i) = \begin{cases} 0 & \text{for} & |d-y| < \varepsilon, \\ |d-y| - \varepsilon & \text{otherwise} \end{cases}$$

(8)

and ε is a prescribed parameter.

In Eq. (7), $L_\varepsilon(d_i, y_i)$ is ε-insensitive loss function, which indicates that it does not penalize errors below ε. $\frac{1}{2}\|w\|^2$ is used as a flatness measurement of Eq. (6) and C is a regularized constant determining the tradeoff between the training error and the model flatness. Introduction of slack variables ζ, ζ^* leads Eq. (7) to the following constrained function

$$Minimize \quad R(w,\zeta^*) = \frac{1}{2}\|w\|^2 + C^*\sum_{i=1}^{l}(\zeta_i + \zeta_i^*) \tag{9}$$

$$s.t. \quad w\Phi(x_i) + b - d_i \leq \varepsilon + \zeta_i,$$
$$d_i - w\Phi(x_i) - b \leq \varepsilon + \zeta_i^*, \quad \zeta_i, \zeta_i^* \geq 0. \tag{10}$$

Thus, function (6) becomes the explicit form

$$f(x,\alpha_i,\alpha_i^*) = \sum_{i=1}^{l} w_i\Phi_i(x) + b = \sum_{i=1}^{l}(\alpha_i - \alpha_i^*)\Phi(x_i)^T\Phi(x) + b$$
$$= \sum_{i=1}^{l}(\alpha_i - \alpha_i^*)K(x_i,x) + b \tag{11}$$

In formula (11), Lagrange multipliers α_i and α_i^* satisfy the constraints $\alpha_i * \alpha_i^* = 0$, $\alpha_i \geq 0$, $\alpha_i^* \geq 0$ and they can be obtained by maximizing the dual form of function (9)

$$\Phi(\alpha_i,\alpha_i^*) = \sum_{i=1}^{l} d_i(\alpha_i - \alpha_i^*) - \varepsilon\sum_{i=1}^{l}(\alpha_i + \alpha_i^*)$$
$$- \frac{1}{2}\sum_{i=1}^{l}\sum_{j=1}^{l}(\alpha_i - \alpha_i^*)(\alpha_j - \alpha_j^*)K(\alpha_i,\alpha_j) \tag{12}$$

with constraints

$$\sum_{i=1}^{l}(\alpha_i - \alpha_i^*) = 0, \quad 0 \leq \alpha_i \leq C, \ 0 \leq \alpha_i^* \leq C \tag{13}$$

Based on the nature of quadratic programming, only a number of coefficients among α_i and α_i^* will be nonzero, and the data points associated with them refer to support vectors. The form $\Phi(x_i)^T\Phi(x)$ in Eq. (11) is replaced by kernel function with the form

$$K(x,y) = \Phi(x)^T\Phi(y) \tag{14}$$

There are some different kernels for generating the inner products to construct machines with different types of nonlinear decision surfaces in the input space. We employed three kind of kernel functions as follows

$$linear: \qquad K(x,y) = x^T y$$
$$RBF \qquad : \ K(x,y) = \exp(-\frac{1}{\sigma^2}\|x-y\|^2) \tag{15}$$

Using the two types of kernel functions such as linear, and radial basis function for SVR, approximated models are constructed and their results are compared. The accuracy was quantified in terms of mean squared error (MSE) values. With respect to the SVR modeling, we have considered two cases which inputs to the SVR consists of 4 inputs and 6 inputs, respectively. According to the kernel functions and number of inputs to the SVR, MSE values are summarized in Table 2. In addition, we can compare them at glance. As can be seen from the table, the RBF kernel provides the best results regardless of the number of inputs.

Table 2. Kernel functions and corresponding accuracy of pH process

kernel type	No. inputs	MSE
linear	4	0.925
	6	0.865
RBF	**4**	**0.0001**
	6	**0.0001**

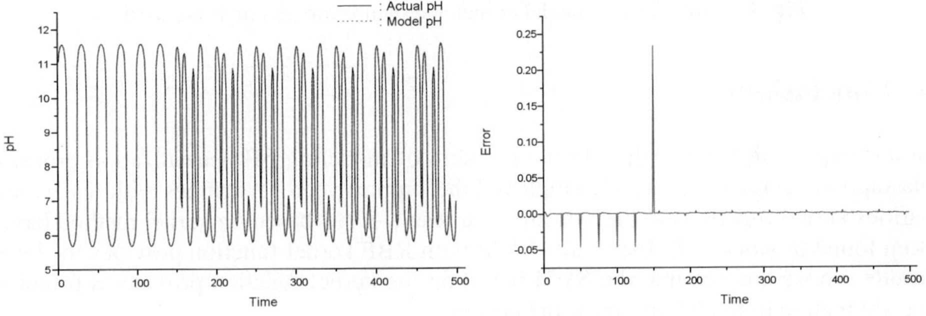

(a) Actual data and model data   (b) Errors between actual and model data

Fig. 3. Actual data vs. model output and their errors :4 inputs are used

Table 3. Performance comparison of various identification models

Model		MSE
		PI
[9]	USOCPN	0.230
	SSOCPN	0.012
SVR		0.0001

Figs. 3-4 show the results of the SVR with RBF kernel corresponding 4 and 6 inputs. When we employed 4 inputs for modeling of SVR, the actual data vs. model output and their corresponding errors are depicted in Fig. 3.

6 inputs are utilized for modeling; the results are shown in Fig. 4. In the figure, the actual pH data vs. model output and their corresponding errors can also be seen.

Table 3 provides a comparative analysis of other models. From the Table 3, it becomes obvious that the nonlinear pH process can be modeled reasonably well by the SVR and its accuracy outperforms other models.

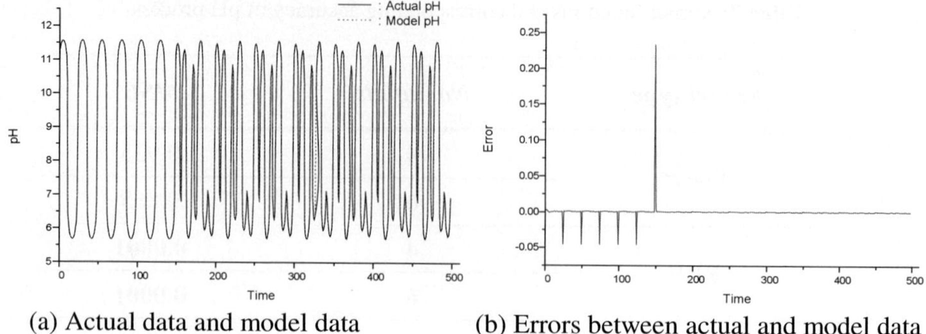

(a) Actual data and model data   (b) Errors between actual and model data

Fig. 4. Actual data vs. model output and their errors :6 inputs are used

4   Conclusions

In this paper, we have dealt with the problem of modeling pH neutralization process via support vector machine. We employed the support vector machines with respect to various kernel functions to the system. As a result, SVM based on kernel method have been found to work well. Especially SVM with RBF kernel function provides the best results. So we can see that the SVM based on the kernel function provides a promising alternative to model nonlinear pH process.

Acknowledgment

The authors would like to thank the financial support of the Korea Science & Engineering Foundation. This works was supported by grant No. R01-2005-000-11044-0 from the Basic Research Program of the Korea Science & Engineering Foundation.

References

1. Wang, Y., Rong, G., and Wang, S.: Hybrid fuzzy modeling of chemical processes. Fuzzy Sets and Systems. 130 (2002) 265-275.
2. Vapnik, V.: The Nature of Statistical Learning Theory. New York, John Wiley (1995).
3. Wang, W., Xu, Z.: A heuristic training for support vector regression. Neurocomputing. **61** (2004) 259-275.
4. Barzilay, O., Brailovsky, V.: On domain knowledge and feature selection using a support vector machine. Pattern Recognition Lett. **20** (1999) 475-484.
5. Drucker, H., Wu, D., Vapnik, V.: Support vector machines for span categorization. IEEE Trans. Neural Networ. **10** (1999) 1048-1054.
6. Burges, C.: A tutorial on support vector machines for pattern recognition. Data Min. Knowl. Discov. **2** (1998)
7. Shinskey, F.G.: pH and pION Control in Process and Waste Streams. New York, John Wiley (1973)

8. Hall, R.C., Seberg, D.E.: Modeling and Self-Tuning Control of a Multivariable pH Neutralization Process. Proc. ACC. (1989) 1822-1827.
9. Nie, J., Loh, A.P., Hang, C.C.: Modeling pH neutralization processes using fuzzy-neural approaches. Fuzzy Sets and Systems **78** (1996) 5-22.
10. McAvoy, T.J.: Time optimal and Ziegler-Nichols control. Ind. Engrg. Chem. Process Des. Develop **11** (1972) 71-78.

Generating Tutoring Feedback in an Intelligent Training System on a Robotic Simulator

Roger Nkambou[1], Khaled Belghith[2], and Froduald Kabanza[2]

[1] Université du Québec à Montréal
Montréal, Québec H3C 3P8, Canada
nkambou.roger@uqam.ca
[2] Université de Sherbrooke,
Sherbrooke, Québec J1K 2R1, Canada
khaled.belghith@usherbrooke.ca, kabanza@usherbrooke.ca

Abstract. Manipulating the Space Station Remote Manipulator (SSRMS), known as "Canadarm II", on the International Space Station (ISS) is a very challenging task. The astronaut does not have a direct view of the scene of operation and must rely on cameras mounted on the manipulator and at strategic places of the environment where it operates. In this paper, we present *Roman Tutor*, an intelligent robotic simulator we are developing to address this kind of problem. We also show how a new approach for robot path planning called FADPRM could be used to provide amazingly useful tutoring feedback for training on such a manipulator and under this big constraint of restricted sight.

1 Introduction

This paper presents *Roman Tutor*, an intelligent tutoring system to support astronauts in learning how to operate the Space Station Remote Manipulator (SSRMS), an articulated robot arm mounted on the international space station (ISS). Fig. 1-a illustrates a snapshot of the SSRMS on the ISS. Astronauts operate the SSRMS through a workstation located inside one of the ISS compartments. As illustrated on Fig. 1-b, the workstation has an interface with three monitors, each connected to a camera placed at a strategic location of the ISS. There are a total of 14 cameras on the ISS, but only three of them are seen at a time through the workstation. A good choice of the camera on each of the three monitors is essential for a correct and safe operation of the robot.

SSRMS can be involved in various tasks on the ISS, ranging from moving a load from one place of the station to another, to inspect the ISS structure (using a camera on the arm's end effector) and making repairs. These tasks must be carried out very carefully to avoid collision with the ISS structure and to maintain safety-operating constraints on SSRMS (such as avoiding collisions with itself and singularities). At different phases of a given manipulation such as moving a payload using the arm (Fig. 2), the astronaut must choose a setting of cameras that provides him with the best visibility while keeping a good appreciation of his evolution in the task. Thus, astronauts are trained not only to manipulate the arm per se, but also to recognize

M. Ali and R. Dapoigny (Eds.): IEA/AIE 2006, LNAI 4031, pp. 838–847, 2006.

visual cues on the station that are crucial in mentally reconstructing the actual working environment from just three monitors each giving a partial and restricted view, and to remember and be able to select cameras depending on the task and other parameters.

One challenge in developing a good training simulator is of course to build it so that one can reason on it. This is even more important when the simulator is built for training purpose [1]. Up until now, Simulation-Based Tutoring is possible only if there is an explicit problem space associated with tasks that are carried out during training to be able to track student actions and to generate relevant tutoring feedbacks [2,3]. Knowledge and model tracing are only possible in these conditions [4]. However, it is not always possible to explicitly develop a well-informed task structure in some complex domains, especially in domains where spatial knowledge is used, as there are too many possibilities to solve a given problem. This paper proposes a solution to this issue through a system called *RomanTutor* which uses a path planner to support spatial reasoning on a simulator and make it possible model tracing tutoring without an explicit task structure. We developed a simulator of the ISS and SSRMS with quite realistic rendering and kinematics constraints as with the real environment. The Simulator knowledge structure will be described later. Fig. 2 illustrates a snapshot of the simulator with SSRMS moving a payload from one place to another on the ISS. This simulates an operation that actually took place during the construction of the ISS.

As most complex tasks deal in one way or another with moving the SSRMS and for the simulator to be able to understand students' operations in order to provide feedback, it must itself be aware of the space constraints and be able to move the arm by itself. A path-planner that calculates arm's moves without collision and consistent with best available cameras views is the key training resource on which other resources and abstract tutoring processes hinge.

After a brief description of the path planner, we outline the different components of *Roman Tutor* and show how the FADPRM path planner is used to provide amazingly relevant tutoring feedback to the learner.

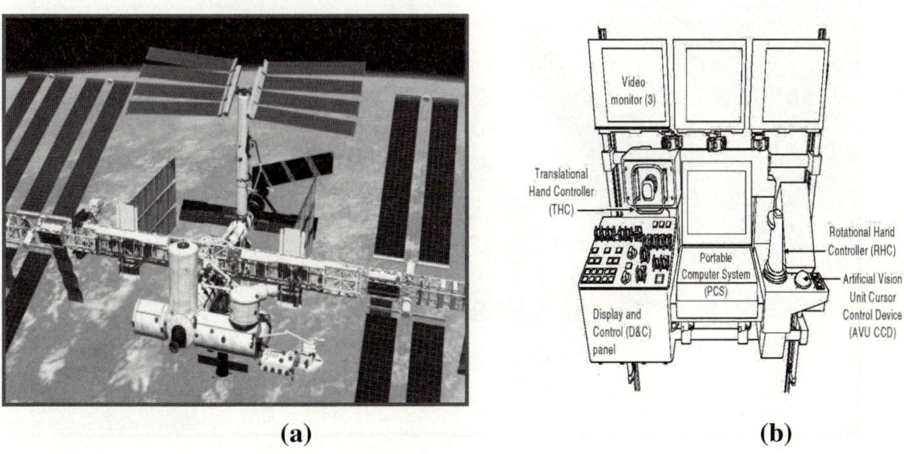

(a)   (b)

Fig. 1. ISS with SSRMS (a) and the workstation (b)

2   The FADPRM Path-Planner

In the literature, several approaches dealing with the path-planning problem for robots in constrained environments were found [5-7]. Several implementations were carried out on the basis of these various approaches and much of them are relatively effective and precise. The fact is that none of these techniques deals with the problem of restricted sight we are faced with in our case [8].

That's why we designed and implemented FADPRM [9] a new flexible and efficient approach for robot path planning in constrained environments. In more of the obstacles the robot must avoid, our approach holds account of desired and non-desired (or dangerous) zones. This will make it possible to take into account the disposition of the cameras on the station. Thus, our planner will try to bring the robot in zones offering the best possible visibility of the progression while trying to avoid zones with reduced visibility (Fig. 2).

FADPRM [9] allows us to put in the environment different zones with arbitrary geometrical forms. A degree of desirability dd, a real in [0 1] is assigned to each zone. The dd of a desired zone is then near 1, and the more it approaches 1, the more the zone is desired; the same for a non-desired zone where the dd is in [0 0.5]. On the international Space Station, the number, the form and the placement of zones reflect the disposition of cameras on the station. A zone covering the field of vision of a camera will be assigned a high dd (near 1) and will take a shape which resembles that of a cone (Fig. 2); whereas a zone that is not visible by any camera from those present on the station will be considered as an non-desired zone with a dd near to 0 and will take an arbitrary polygonal shape (a cube in Fig.2).

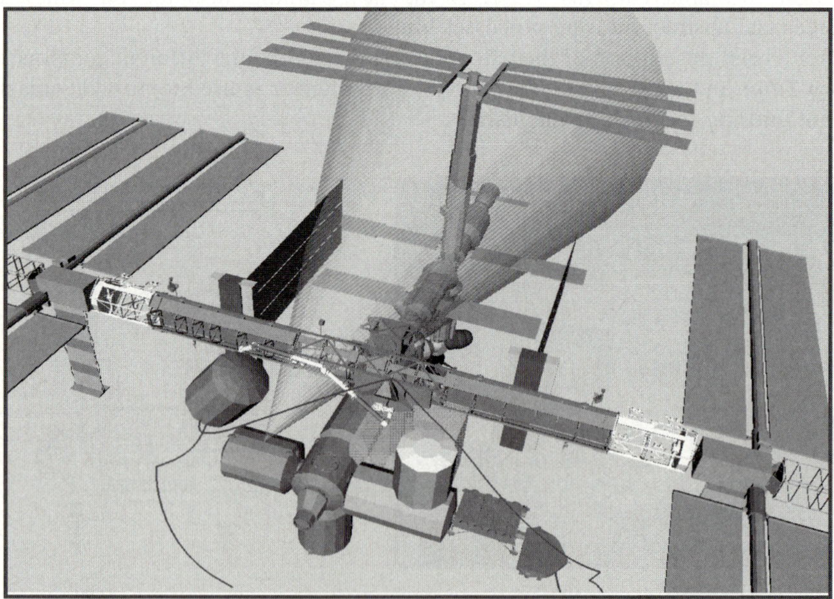

Fig. 2. SSRMS avoiding a non-desired zone (cube) and going through a desired zone (cone)

The robot workspace (the ISS environment here) is then preprocessed into a roadmap of collision-free robot motions in regions with highest desirability degree. More precisely, the roadmap is a graph such every node n is labeled with its corresponding robot configuration $n.q$ and its degree of desirability $n.dd$, which is the average of dds of zones overlapping with $n.q$. An edge (n,n') connecting two nodes is also assigned a dd equal to the average of dd of configurations in the path-segment $(n.q,n'.q)$. The dd of a path (i.e., a sequence of nodes) is an average of dd of its edges.

Following probabilistic roadmap methods (PRM) [10], we build the roadmap by picking robot configurations probabilistically, with a probability that is biased by the density of obstacles. A path is then a sequence of collision free edges in the roadmap, connecting the initial and goal configurations.

Following the Anytime Dynamic A* (AD*) approach [11], to get new paths when the conditions defining safe zones have dynamically changed, we can quickly re-plan by exploiting the previous roadmap. On the other hand, paths are computed through incremental improvements so the planner can be stopped at anytime to provide a collision-free path and the more time it is given, the better the path optimizes moves through desirable zones. Therefore, our planner is a combination of the traditional PRM approach [10] and AD* [11] and it is flexible in that it takes into account zones with degrees of desirability. This explains why we called it Flexible Anytime Dynamic PRM (FADPRM).

More precisely, FADPRM works as follows: The input is an initial configuration, a goal configuration, a 3D model of obstacles in the workspace, a 3D specification of zones with corresponding dd, and a 3D model of the robot. Given this input:

- To find a path connecting the input and goal configurations, we search backward from the goal towards the initial (current) robot configuration. Backward instead of forward search is done because the robot is moving, hence its current configuration, is not necessarily the initial configuration; we want to re-compute a path to the same goal when the environment changes before the goal is reached.
- A probabilistic queue *OPEN* contains nodes on the current roadmap's frontier (i.e., nodes are expanded because they are new or because they have previously been expanded but are no longer up to date w.r.t. to the desired path) and a list *CLOSED* contains non frontier nodes (i.e., nodes already expanded).
- Search consists of repeatedly picking a node from *OPEN*, generating its predecessors and putting the new ones or out of date ones in *OPEN*.
- The density of a node is the number of nodes in the roadmap with configurations that are a short distance away (proximity being an empirically set parameter, taking into account the obstacles in an application domain). The distance estimate to the goal takes into account the node's dd and the Euclidean distance to the goal.
- A node n in *OPEN* is selected for expansion with probability proportional to

$$(1-\beta) \, / \, density \, (n) + \beta * goal\text{-}distance\text{-}estimate \, (n) \qquad \text{with } 0 \leq \beta \leq 1.$$

This equation implements a balance between fast-solution search and best-solution search by choosing different values for β. With β near to 0, the choice of a node to be expanded from *OPEN* depends only on the density around it. That is, nodes with lower density will be chosen first, which is the heuristic used in traditional PRM approaches to guaranty the diffusion of nodes and to accelerate the search for a path

[10]. As β approaches 1, the choice of a node to be expanded from *OPEN* will rather depend on its estimated distance to the goal. In this case we are seeking optimality rather than speed.

- To increase the resolution of the roadmap, a new predecessor is randomly generated within a small neighborhood radius (that is, the radius is fixed empirically based on the density of obstacles in the workspace) and added to the list of successors in the roadmap generated so far. The entire list of predecessors is returned.

- Collision is delayed: detection of collisions on the edges between the current node and its predecessors is delayed until a candidate solution is found; if there is a collision, we backtrack. Collisions that have already been detected are stored in the roadmap to avoid redoing them.

- The robot may start executing the first path found. Concurrently, the path continues being improved by re-planning with an increased value of β.

- Changes in the environment (moving obstacles, moving arm, or changes in *dd* for zones) cause updates of the roadmap and re-planning.

We implemented FADPRM as an extension to the Motion Planning Kit (MPK)[10] by changing the definition of PRM to include zones with degrees of desirability and changing the algorithm for searching the PRM with FADPRM. The calculation of a configuration *dd* and a path *dd* is a straightforward extension of collision checking for configurations and path segments. For this, we customized the Proximity Query Package (PQP)[12].

3 Roman Tutor

3.1 Roman Tutor Architecture

Roman Tutor's architecture contains seven main components: the simulator, the FADPRM path planner, the movie generator, the task editor, the student model and the tutoring sub-system.

As most knowledge related to the simulation-based robotic manipulation in *Roman Tutor* is mainly consistent with spatial reasoning, an appropriate structure is needed for the simulator. We equipped our system with the FADPRM path planner, which as we said before will provide a framework to support the reasoning process within the simulator. However, this reasoning base won't be sufficient to bring useful tutoring explanations to guide and orient the astronaut during his manipulations. The level of explanation that could be given here remains very limited because the planner is connected at the basic level of the simulator which is made up essentially of physical components in the environment such as the robot, obstacles, cameras, zones, and some related low-level parameters and variables such as the robot's configuration, its degree of desirability and whether it is colliding or not. This level is equivalent to the structure proposed by Forbus [13]. However a proper use of FADPRM could exploits information in that level to generate very important tutoring feedbacks without any hard-coded structure.

3.2   Roman Tutor User Interface

The *Roman Tutor* interface (Fig. 3) resembles that of the robotic workstation on which the astronaut operates to manipulate the SSRMS. We have three monitors each of them connected to one of the fourteen cameras present on the station. On each monitor, we have buttons and functionalities to move the corresponding camera: Tilt, Pan and Zoom.

SSRMS can be manipulated in two modes: the For mode or the Joint-by-Joint mode. In the For mode, the learner moves the robot starting from his end-effector's position and by commanding him to go forward or backward, left or right and up or down. In the Joint-by-Joint mode, the learner selects a joint in the robot and moves it according to the corresponding link. In the two modes, the manipulation is done incrementally. While manipulating the robot, the astronaut can choose and change the camera in each monitor to have a better sight of the zone he is working in.

Windows at the bottom of the *Roman tutor* interface contain the trace done so far by the learner. Every operation done by the learner is posted on this window: the selection of a new camera in a monitor, the displacement of a camera and the manipulation of the robot in the For/Joint-by-Joint mode. This trace contains also all information relevant to the current state: if there is a collision or not, the coordinates of the End-Effector, the position and the orientation of the cameras (Fig. 3).

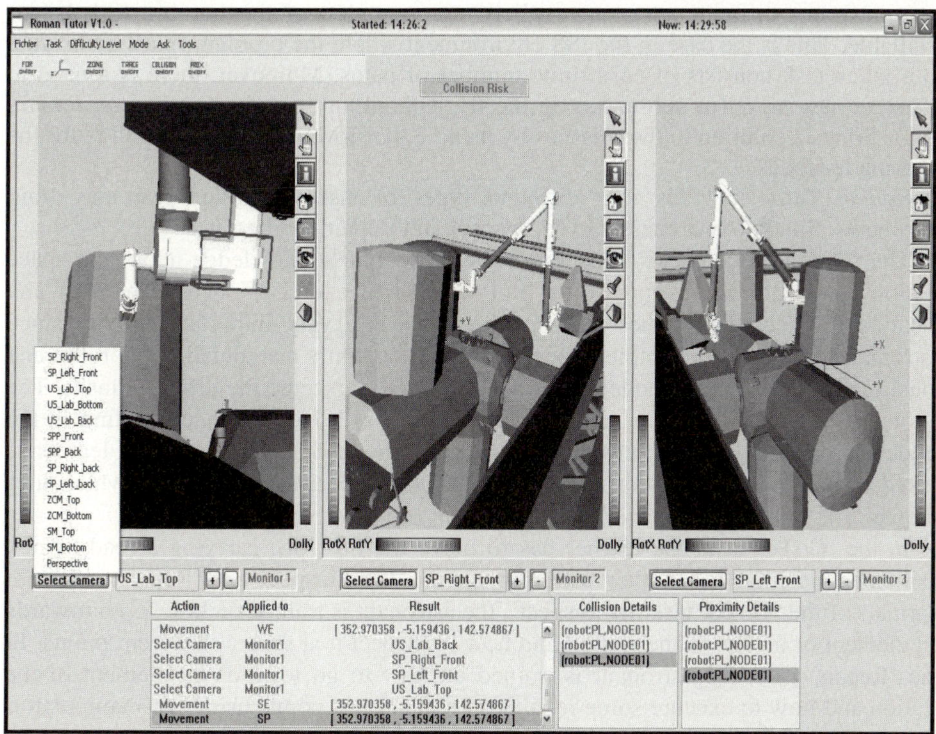

Fig. 3. Roman Tutor User Interface

The Trace window keeps then a continuous track of all operations done so far by the learner. So if he had done a mistake (a collision for example), by examining the Trace window, he will find out to what this was due and he will see what to do to get out of it.

Roman Tutor's interface contains four main menus: Task, Mode, Ask and Tools. From the menu 'Task', the learner chooses one of the several tasks he wants to work on. From the second menu 'Mode', the learner chooses between two different modes: Free and Assisted. In the 'Assisted' mode, the non-cognitive tutor intervenes when needed to support the learning of the student by guiding him or by giving him an illustrated video of the task he has to do. Whereas in the 'Free' mode, the learner relies only on the Trace window to carry on his task. In the two modes, the 'Ask' menu allows the learner to ask different types of questions while executing a task. In the last menu 'Tools', the expert is provided with three different tools that will help him design and validate new tasks to add into the system. These different tools are: the FADPRM Path-Planner, the Movie Generator and the Task Generator.

4   Using FADPRM Path-Planner for the Tutoring Assistance

One of the main goals of an intelligent tutoring system is to actively provide relevant feedback to the student in problem solving situations [3]. This kind of support becomes very difficult when an explicit representation of the training task is not available. This is the case in the ISS environment where the problem space associated to a given task consists of an infinite number of paths. Moreover, there is a need to generate new tasks (or sub-tasks) on the fly without any cognitive structure. *Roman Tutor* brings a solution to these issues by using FADPRM as principal resource for the tutoring feedback.

Roman Tutor includes four different types of tasks on which we may train astronauts: Spatial Awareness, GoTo, Inspect and Repair.

The 'Spatial Awareness' task improves the learner's knowledge about the space station's environment by providing him with some exercises such as naming and locating ISS elements, zones and cameras. This is a very important activity since astronauts don't have a complete view of the station while manipulating the robot and must memorize a spatial model of the ISS in order to execute the different tasks. The tutor can invoke this type of activity when it notices a lack of understanding in the student profile about some environment-related knowledge. In Fig. 4, the learner is asked to name an element of the station and to select the camera from which it is shown.

In the 'GoTo' task, the learner has to move the SSRMS, carrying a load or not, from one position to another different on the ISS. Inspect and Repair tasks are variants of the 'GoTo' task. In 'Inspect', the astronaut is trained on how to go towards an element or a zone in the station and how to inspect it at several different points. In the 'Repair' task, the astronaut is trained on how to go towards an element of the station and how to execute some repairs on it at several points using the manipulator. These "GoTo"-like tasks are well described in the next paragraph.

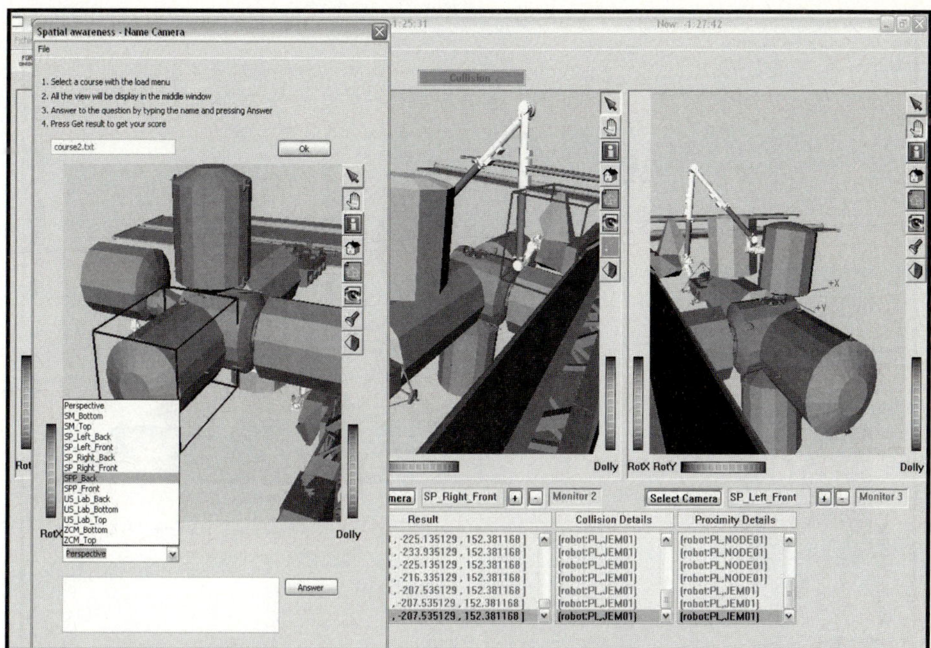

Fig. 4. 'Spatial Awareness' Task in Roman Tutor

During a 'GoTo' task, the non-cognitive *Tutor* uses the anytime capability of the FADPRM path planner to validate incrementally student's action or sequence of actions, give information about the next relevant action or sequence of actions, and generate relevant task demonstration resources using the movie generator. In Fig. 5, the learner is shown an illustration (demonstration) of the task he's working on. The movie is created so that the end-effector will follow the generated path (in red).

RomanTutor gives access to a menu that allows the learner to ask some relevant questions during manipulations. These questions may be of three different forms: How To, What if and Why Not. Several extensions are associated to these different questions. For example, with 'How to', one could have: How to Go To, How to avoid obstacle, How to go through zone. *Roman Tutor* answers How-To questions by generating a path consistent with the best cameras views using FADPRM and by calling the movie generator to build an interactive animation that follows that path. The incremental planning capability of FADPRM is used by *Roman Tutor* to bring answers to the What-If and Why-Not questions. In both cases, *Roman Tutor* provides the learner with relevant illustrations explaining whether his action or sequence of actions is appropriate or out of scope (thus may bring him to a dead end) given the generated plan that corresponds to the correct path.

We see here the importance of having FADPRM as a planner in our system to guide the evolution of the astronaut. By taking into account the disposition of the cameras on the station, we are assured that the proposed plan the learner is following passes through zones that are visible from at least one of the cameras placed on the environment.

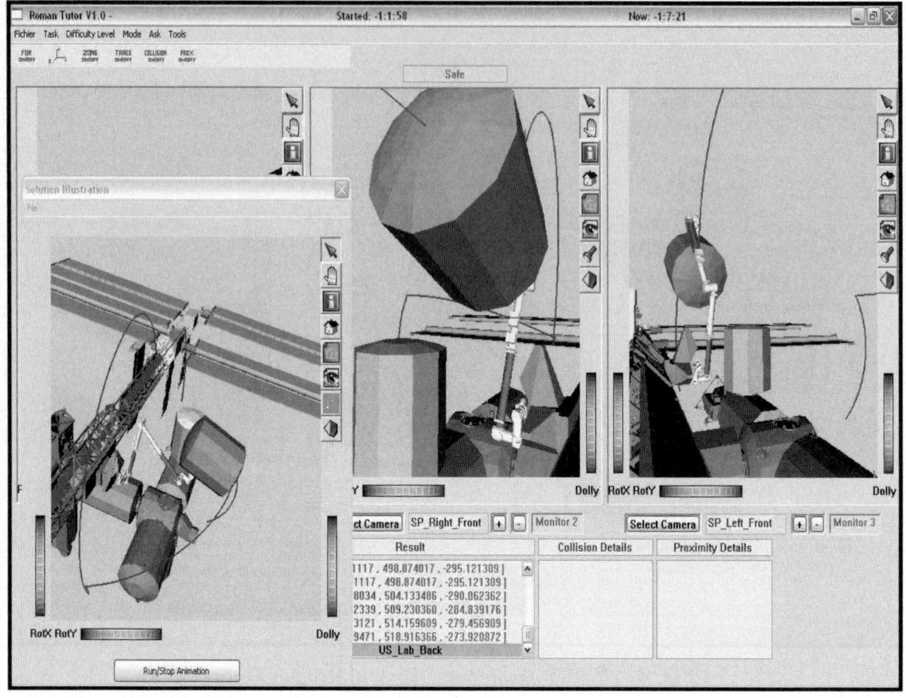

Fig. 5. 'GoTo' Task in Roman Tutor

5   Conclusion

In this paper, we described how a new approach for robot path planning called FADPRM could play an important role in providing tutoring feedback for training on a robot simulator. The capability of our path-planner, built within the simulator's architecture to provide predictions and to determine what manipulations might achieve a desired effect, makes it a useful component in simulation-based training systems. We also, detailed the architecture of the intelligent tutoring system *Roman Tutor* in which FADPRM is integrated. All the components of *Roman Tutor* but the cognitive tutor, are working properly.

This constitutes a very important contribution especially in the field of intelligent tutoring systems: we showed that it is not necessary to plan in advance what feedback to give to the learner or to explicitly create a complex task graph to support the tutoring process.

The next step is to improve the expressiveness of domain knowledge structures under SSRMS to lead to a better diagnosis process of problems experienced by the learner during manipulations. Also, an evaluation of the system will be done in collaboration with the Canadian Spatial Agency.

Acknowledgment. We would like to thank the Canadian Space Agency, The Infotel Group and the Natural Sciences and Engineering Research Council of Canada

(NSERC) for their logistic and financial support. Special thanks to Mahie Khan, Daniel Dubois, Patrick Hohmeyer and Kaufmann Meudja, who contributed in the design of this system. Special thanks also to all members of J.C. Latombe's Laboratory at the University of Stanford for providing as with MPK.

References

1. Forbus, K.: Articulate software for science and engineering education. In Forbus, K., Feltovich, P., and Canas, A. (Eds.) Smart machines in education: The coming revolution in educational technology. AAAI Press (2001)
2. Richard Angros, W. Lewis Johnson, Jeff Rickel, Andrew Scholer: Learning domain knowledge for teaching procedural skills. AAMAS, 1372-1378 (2002)
3. VanLehn, K.: The advantages of Explicity Representing Problem Spaces. User Modeling, Springer Verlag LNAI 2702:3. (2003)
4. Crowley R.S., Medvedeva, O., Jukic, D.: SlideTutor - A model-tracing Intelligent Tutoring System for teaching microscopic diagnosis. Proceedings of the 11th International Conference on Artificial Intelligence in Education (2003)
5. Latombe, J.C.: Robot motion planning. Kluwer Academic Publishers, Boston, MA, (1991)
6. Overmars, M.H.: Recent developments in motion planning. P. Sloot, C. Kenneth Tan, J. Dongarra, A. Hoekstra (Eds.): Computational Science - ICCS 2002, Part III, Springer-Verlag, LNCS 2331, (2002) 3-13
7. LaValle, S. M., Branicky, M. S., Lindemann, S.R.: On the relationship between classical grid search and probabilistic roadmaps. International Journal of Robotics Research 23: 673–692, (2004)
8. Roy, J., Nkambou, R., Kabanza, F.: Supporting spatial awareness in training on a telemanipulator in space. Intelligent Tutoring Systems, LNCS 3220, 860-863, Springer-Verlag Berlin Heidelberg (2004)
9. Belghith, K., Kabanza, F., Hartman, L., Nkambou, R.: Anytime Dynamic Path-Planning with Flexible Probabilistic Roadmaps. In Proc. of IEEE International Conference on Robotics and Automation, ICRA (2006)
10. Sanchez, G., Latombe, J.C.: A single-query bi-directional probabilistic roadmap planner with lazy collision checking. Int. Symposium on Robotics Research (ISRR'01), Lorne, Victoria, Australia, November 2001. Published in Robotics Research: The Tenth Int. Symp. R.A. Jarvis and A. Zelinsky (eds.), Springer Tracts in Advanced Robotics, Springer, 403-417 (2003)
11. Likhachev, M., Ferguson, D., Stentz, A., Thrun, S.:. Anytime Dynamic A*: An Anytime Replanning Algorithme. In Proc. of International Conference on Automated Planning and Scheduling, June (2005)
12. Larsen, E., Gottschalk, S., Lin, M., Manocha, D.: Fast Distance Queries using Rectangular Swept Sphere Volumes. In Proc. of IEEE International Conference on Robotics and Automation, 4:24-28 (2000)
13. Forbus, K.: Using qualitative physics to create articulate educational software. *IEEE Expert*, May/June, 32-41 (1997)

Elaborating the Context of Interactions
in a Tutorial Dialog

Josephine Pelle and Roger Nkambou

Université du Québec à Montréal
Montréal, Québec H3C 3P8, Canada
tchetagni@ciurrier.uqam.ca, nkambou.roger@uqam.ca

Abstract. In Socratic tutorial dialogues the tutor selects the most appropriate question to be asked, based on assumptions about what the learner knows. However, there is no guarantee that the learner will understand the question. Indeed, the assumptions of the tutor are sometimes likely to be inaccurate. In this case, an appropriate action for the tutor is to revise its current GOAL as well as its current dialogue plan. In this paper, we present an instance of this issue in PROLOG-TUTOR, a tutoring system for Logic Programming. Our contribution is an explicit address of the dialog management mechanism which supports the revision of the tutor's intention in a Socratic dialogue. This is done using a combination of the theory of accommodation of communicative acts with the notion of revising intentions.

1   Introduction

In Socratic dialogues, the main goal is to guide the learner toward an understanding of the concepts and the principles which underlie the domain learned. Several types of interactions support tutorial dialogues: explanations ([1, 3]), decompositions ([12]), hinting ([7, 20]), questions ([9]). When questions are asked in a tutorial dialogue, there are two different schemes of intervention: the dialogue is directed by the tutor; the tutor and the learner have equal participation in the dialogue. In the former case, only the tutor is allowed to take the initiative in the dialogue. In this scheme of interaction, the tutor selects the most appropriate question to be asked based on assumptions about what the learner knows ([4, 5]). However, the information contained in the learner model is sometimes unlikely to be accurate. Therefore, there is no guarantee that the learner will understand the question that is asked to him. For that reason, the management of tutoring dialogues should anticipate this kind of situation in order to trigger an appropriate action. In this case one example of appropriate action for the tutor is to revise its current GOAL as well as its current dialogue plan. For the tutor, the intended goal of this revision is to make the learner understand what it meant with the last question asked. In this paper, we present an instance of this issue in PROLOG-TUTOR, a tutoring system for Logic Programming (section 1). We describe a model of dialogue management in order to support the revision of a predefined dialogue plan (section 2). This model uses a combination of the theory of accommodation of communicative acts in information states ([14]) with

M. Ali and R. Dapoigny (Eds.): IEA/AIE 2006, LNAI 4031, pp. 848–858, 2006.

the notion of revising intentions ([2]). We analyze research work related to the revision of dialogue plan in tutorial interactions (section 3). We outline the more general context of research from which this model is taken and we discuss some issues of evaluation with this respect (section 4).

2   Elaborating the Context of a Question in a Tutorial Dialogue

One learning activity in PROLOG-TUTOR is the RESOLUTION of a GOAL given a PROLOG KNOWLEDGE-BASE. In that activity, the learner has to give the solution of such a resolution. If he fails, the goal of PROLOG-TUTOR is to guide him toward the solution. The resolution is a procedural task which consists in the application of a set of principles in order to perform a sequence of appropriate computations. When the learner fails to solve correctly an exercise on Resolution, the tutor engages an articulation process ([19]). The articulation is a tutorial strategy where the tutor takes the learner step-by-step through some reasoning toward the solution or toward the realisation of his own errors. The execution of each step necessitates the elicitation of a skill: applying a principle, recalling a domain statement, etc. The articulation is a generic process. When applied to a procedure, it consists in asking questions to the learner for each step of the procedure. In this way the learner is expected to reflect on the principles that govern the execution of each step, as well as the principles which govern the execution of the overall procedure. There is an implicit way and an explicit way to elicit the learner's reflection through articulation. The implicit way consists in asking him to give the result of the execution of a step. In that case, the tutor assumes that a good execution implies that the learner masters the concepts and the principles that underlie the achievement of this step. The explicit way consists in making the learner explicitly apply the principle of the domain which is most appropriate at the current stage of the procedure (Table 1).

Table 1. Types of questions of Prolog-tutor in articulating a skill

Question that promotes implicit reflection at the first step of a RESOLUTION	Question that promotes explicit reflection at the first step of a RESOLUTION
[T1]: What is the first element in the knowledge base which corresponds to the GOAL grand_father(X,john)	[T1']: Can you unify your GOAL grand_father(john,X) with the Head of the Horn Clause: Grand_father(X,Y):- father(X,Z), father(Z,Y)
[S2]: Grand_father(X,Y):- father(X,Z), father(Z,Y)	[S2']: Yes [T2']: So what will you do next?

In any case, when the learner is unable to answer the question of the tutor, the reaction of the tutor will depend on its pedagogical strategy. We have implemented several scenarios in PROLOG-TUTOR which aim at promoting learner's reflection [19]. In the most basic scenario, the tutor provides an explanation to the learner when he his unable to answer a question.

2.1 Using a Simulated Learner Model to Adapt a Predefined Dialogue Plan

So far, PROLOG-TUTOR uses a simulated learner model in order to choose the next question to ask to the learner. The learner model is drawn upon a Bayesian Network which expresses conditional relationships between the knowledge elements considered in the domain of Logic Programming ([18]). The content of the learner model is a list of knowledge elements, each element being associated with a probability of mastery. In order to choose the next question to ask to the learner, the tutor uses a rule $\mathcal{R}1$ (Table 2).

Table 2. A Rule to choose if a step should be articulated

> **R1:** If $[\min_{i\ \{i\ in\ SkillOfCurrentStep\}}(\text{Probability\_of\_mastery}[i]) > \delta$
> $\Rightarrow$ remove_next_question_from(Private.DialoguePlan)

Table 3. Example of elaboration of the context of a question

Predetermined Dialogue Plan	Adapted Dialogue plan with temporary accommodations	
[T1] What is the first element of your knowledge base which corresponds to the GOAL to prove [S2] grand_father(X,Y):- father(X,Z), father(Z,Y)	T1] What is the first element of your knowledge base which corresponds to the GOAL to prove [S2] grand_father(X,Y):- father(X,Z), father(Z,Y)	

[T3] Right. If you use this prolog-rule, what would you do next?
[S4] Solve the new goals father(X,Z) and father(Z,john)
[T5] Ok. Give me the first solution that you obtain
[S6] X= valery, Z=john.
[T7] Right. And what about father(Z,john)
[S8] Z= stephen
[T8] Not really. The variable Z used in father(X,Z) is the same as the one used in father (Z,john)
....
	[T3 [AdaptPredeterminedDialoguePlan]] Right. What solution do you obtain with your first sub-goal?
	[S4] Don't understand
	
	[T3 [AccomodateCurrentQuestion]] Ok. Your new sub-goals are father(X,Z), father(Z,john)
	[S6] Don't understand
	[T3 [AccomodateCurrentQuestion] When you associate father(X,john) with the prolog-rule:
	  1. unify the GOAL with the head of the rule
	  2. apply the substitutions of the unification to the Tail of the rule
	  3. The facts of the tail of the prolog-rule become your new goals
	  4. In this case, your new goals are father(X,Z) and father(Z,john)
	[S8] .....
		Adaptation of the predetermined plan
		
		Incremental Elaboration of the context of a question

This rule tells that a given step should not be articulated if among the skills associated to that step, the one which has the minimum probability of mastery is *above* a threshold δ. In a real context, this rule takes a certain importance since it allows the tutor to be responsive to the learner's needs: the tutor focuses the articulation of a procedure on the steps which corresponding skills are lacking to the learner. Table 3 illustrates 2 instances of tutorial interactions where one can see the difference between: 1) the sequential articulation of the steps of a procedure based on a predetermined plan and 2) the adaptive articulation of the steps of a procedure, based on the learner model.

2.2   Possible Reasons for the Inaccuracy of the Learner's Model

In PROLOG-TUTOR, the Bayesian network which supports the updating of the learner model is not a temporal Bayesian network. We use a heuristic approach which calculates the mean of all the probabilities obtained for each knowledge element, at each update of the network. More over, the elements of the network as well as their relationships have been defined on the basis of the personal point of view of the author. For that reason, the probabilities that are reported in the student model are likely to be inaccurate. When choosing the next question to ask on the basis of such a model, the learner may not understand the context of this question. This is explained as follows. Let's suppose that the last step that has been articulated with the learner in a procedural task was step I.

Let's also consider that the next step that will be articulated (chosen on the basis of $\mathcal{R}1$) is J, $J \neq I+1$. Thus, when asking the learner to execute step J, he may find himself confused because he is not able to link that step with the last articulated step I. This may happen because the learner does not understand what has happened in the steps that are between I and J. Moreover, even if the learner knows what has happened, he may lack the knowledge which explains the passage through the steps that are between I and J.

2.3   Revision of the Tutor's Intentions and Accommodation of Its Utterance

From the above remarks, we have conceived the tutoring interactions as follows:

If the learner is unable to answer the question of step J while the preceding step is the step I, I≠J-1 then (Fig. 1):

o   The tutor reconsiders its current intention to evolve with the predetermined dialogue plan
o   The tutor revises its current intention and accommodates its utterance:
   ▪ Its new intention is to propose a first elaboration of the context of the current question, expecting that the learner will get a better understanding of the question. The elaboration is minimal first in order to make the student find out by himself the elements of the gap between I and J.
   ▪ After the first Elaboration, the tutor prompts the learner to try again to answer the question that has been asked in the current step (step J). If he fails, the tutor

gives a more detailed elaboration. This process continues until the tutor has given a maximal elaboration.

- When a maximal elaboration has been stated, the tutor gives an explanation of the answer to the question of the current step (step J). Then, it revises again its intention: its purpose is to go back to continue with the higher level dialogue plan, from step J.

3   A Model to Elaborate the Context of a Question in a Tutorial Dialogue

In order to elaborate the context of a question, the tutor uses 3 models. The first model allows the tutor to produce the basic utterances of the dialogue. The second model allows the management of information during the dialogue. The third model defines the rules which govern how the dialogue will evolve.

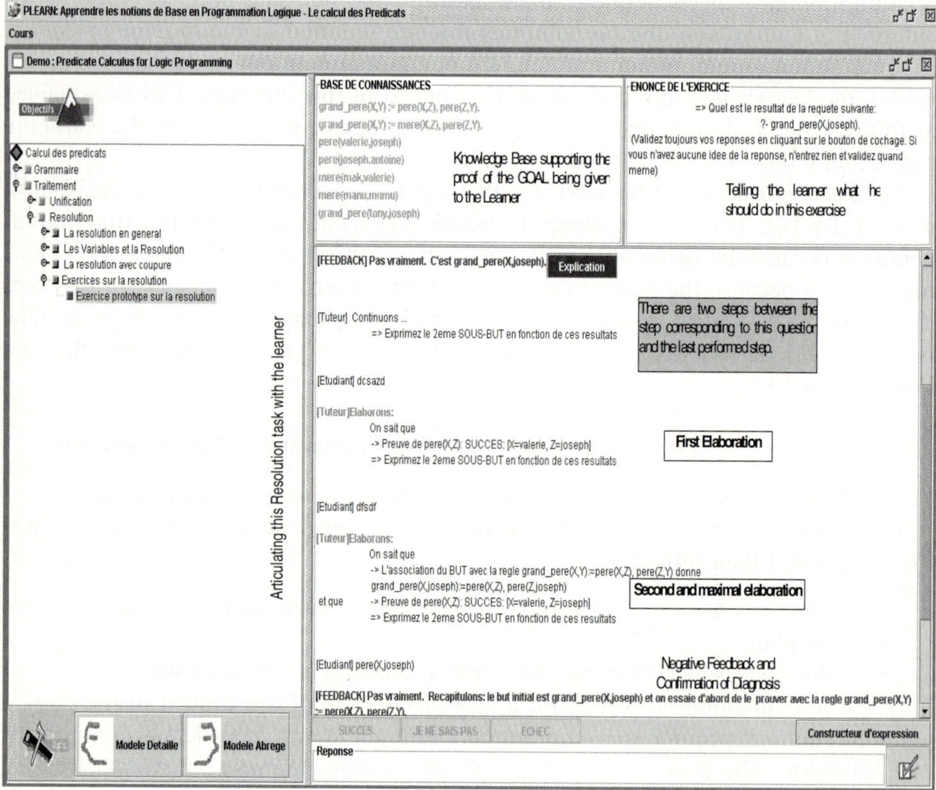

Fig. 1. Example of diagnosis revision trough the elaboration of dialog question in guiding the learner in a "Resolution" task in Logic Programming

3.1 Modeling the Content of the Utterances of the Tutor

This model relates each step I of a procedural task to: 1) the questions that may be asked to the learner and the goal of each of these questions (explicit reflection or implicit reflection); 2) the feedback (positive/negative) that is given to the learner for each type of question; 3) the explanation of the answer to that question in case the learner fails to answer correctly; 4) for each step K<I, an incremental set of contexts, each context elaborating on his predecessor on the actions that have lead from K to I; 5) the set of skills that are elicited in the execution of that step.

To conduct the articulation, a structural model and a contextual model have been defined. The structural model allows the tutor to go trough each step of the task. This model is defined with two data structures: S, the set of steps from which the procedural task is drawn; Ω, a control structure which defines the order of execution of these steps. Thus a procedural task (PT) is defined by the combination $< PT, S, \Omega >$.

The contextual model provides the tutor with the resources necessary to produce the appropriate utterances for each step examined in a tutorial dialogue. For each step S of the procedure, this model comprises three sets: $\{[Q,G]\}$, the set of the questions that are associated with S, with their respective goals; α, a set comprising the expected answer for each question that could be asked in S; $\{\Sigma_{IS}\}$ a set that comprises several sets, each set Σ_{IS} contains some utterances, these utterances correspond to the elaboration of the computations that have happened from step I to S; **Sk,** the set of skills that are associated to S. Then S is defined by the combination $<S, \{[Q,G]\}, \alpha, \Sigma_{IS}, Sk>$.

The utterance in $\Sigma_{(S-1)S}$ is a *default context* and the corresponding utterance recalls the link between the current step (step S) and its predecessor (step $S-1$). For each of the other steps $I < (S-1)$, Σ_{IS} comprises a set of utterances. Each utterance gives more details about what has been computed between I and S. These utterances may be characterized as follows:

- Σ_{IS} (0) is a general summary of the rationale of S. This utterance is used as an introduction by the tutor when passing from step I to step S in the articulation process. Before asking the question in step S, Σ_{IS} (0) is produced in order to maintain a certain coherence in the flow of the dialogue.
- For $[K>I \wedge K<S]$, Σ_{IS} (K) is an explanation of how the output of step K was drown and how it may be used to perform step S.

3.2 Modeling the State of the Tutorial Dialogue

In order to interact with the learner in a tutorial dialogue, the tutor manages a memory that defines the current information state in the system. The notion of information states that we use is an adaptation of the dialogue game board ([10, 11]). The content of an information state is divided between the information that is shared between the dialogue participants and the information that is private to each dialogue participant. The private part is only accessible by the tutor. It contains a representation of the dialogue plan, an agenda and a learner model. The representation of the dialogue plan is a stack which contains a predetermined sequence of steps. These are the steps that will be addressed by the tutor in the articulation process. The top of the stack is the first step of the procedure and the bottom is the last step of the procedure. This sequence is drawn from the structural model of the procedural task that is being articulated. In this case, it is the `resolution of a GOAL` in PROLOG. The `CurrentAgenda` contains the short term goals of the tutor. In order to model explicitly the fact that a predetermined plan of dialogue may change, we have attributed a set of *intentions* to the tutor. These intentions are modeled through the use of `TutorGOALs`.

The learner model is a set of propositions which state the probability of mastery of the learner with respect to a knowledge element in the domain. Each time that the learner answers to a question, his model is updated accordingly: evidences are sent to the Bayesian network. These evidences activate the knowledge elements that are associated with the skills elicited through the currently articulated step.

The shared part of the information state (Table 4) contains the information that both the learner and the tutor can access: the last utterance that the tutor has stated (CTU), the currently articulated step (CS), the learner's answer to the CTU if it is a question (LA) and the last step articulated before the current step (LS).

Table 4. Information state for a tutorial dialogue

```
  Private        DialoguePLAN :   StackSet(Step)
Information       CurrentAgenda:   StackSet(TutorGOALs)
                 LearnerModel :   SET(Prop(KnowledgeElements[Probs]))

  Shared         CTU : Current Tutor Utterance
Information       CS  : Currently Articulated step
                 LA  : Learner answer to QUA
                 LS  : Last step Articulated Before
```

3.3 Modeling the Management of the Tutorial Dialogue: Rules for Dialogue Adaptation and Rules for Dialogue Accommodation

Two types of goals have been defined: EVOLVE and ELABORATE. The goal EVOLVE allows the *dialogue plan to be adaptive* to the learner model (Table 5). Using **R1** (Table 2), the tutor modifies this dialogue plan in order to select the next step that will be articulated. This goal is set when the conditions of the current information state are normal. We consider that these conditions are normal in two cases: 1) the learner's answer to the currently articulated step is correct; 2) the currently articulated step naturally follows (as defined in the structural model of the procedure) the last articulated step. Thus by default, the goal EVOLVE is at the top of the stack which represents the `CurrentAgenda`.

If none of the normal conditions are fulfilled in the current information state of the dialogue, the goal ELABORATE is pushed at the top of the `currentAgenda` (revision of the intention of the tutor, Table 6). The tutor will accommodates CTU in order to elaborate the context of the last question that it has asked, before providing an explanation of the good answer.

Table 5. Rules to adapt the predetermined dialogue plan

Rule	Adapt the predetermined Dialogue Plan
Conditions	`associate(Step,Private.pop(DialoguePLAN));` `maximumProbMastery(Sk(Step)) < `δ
Effect	`push(Private.currentAgenda,  EVOLVE(Step))`

Table 6. Rules to accommodate the utterance of the tutor to the learner needs

Rule	Accommodate the next utterance by setting the tutor goal to ELABORATE

Conditions	`¬ normal(`
	`    evaluateCurrentConditions(Shared.QA,`
	`Shared.CS,  Shared.LS))`

Effect	`Push(Private.currentAgenda,` `ELABORATE(Shared.LS,Shared.CS))`

Table 7. Rules to update the dialogue information state

Rule	Update information state
Conditions	`get(Private.CurrentAgenda)  ==  EVOLVE`

Effect	`updateLS(Shared.CS)`
	`updateCS(pop(Private.DialoguePlan))`
	`getQuestion(Shared.CS,  Shared.CTU)`

Conditions.	`get(Private.CurrentAgenda)  ==  ELABORATE`
Effect	`getContexts(Shared.CS,  Shared.CTU)`

The difference between adaptation and accommodation lies in their respective consequence on the dialogue plan. Adaptation will definitely change the evolvement of the predetermined dialogue plan. Adaptation depends on the model of the learner, rather than on his answer. The notion of accommodation consists in changing temporarily the course of the dialogue. The goal of this change is to take into account the needs of the interlocutor, perceived through one of his utterances ([14]). In accommodation, the global goal does not change, while the focus of the current state of the dialogue may change temporarily. In our particular case, the global goal is to entertain an adaptive dialogue with a learner in order to help him reflect about the solution to a problem. However, if the adaptation is based on assumptions that are not accurate, the goal (focus) becomes – temporarily – the elaboration of the context of an utterance.

There are also update rules which support the updating of the information state after a dialogue move (Table 7).

3.4 Implementation

PROLOG-TUTOR is implemented in Java and includes:

- One class which encodes the structural model of a procedure
- One class which encodes the contextual model for each step of the procedure. This class also encodes all the functions related to the management of this information.
- One class which encodes the information state of the dialogue
- One class which encodes the management of the dialogue
- One library of classes which encode the structure of the Bayesian Network and its updating. This library has been obtained from the work of Cozman[8]
- One class which encodes the management of the updating of the Bayesian network

4 Related Work

Dialogue based tutoring has been investigated from several perspectives. Some systems such as Auto-tutor ([16]) focus on natural language processing issues while modeling several types of hints. Other systems address the formalisation of the hinting process ([20, 21]). The hinting process has also been addressed in an implicit manner in ITS, in the course of student diagnosis([6, 7, 13]). Tutoring dialogues based on the specific articulation of the problem in hand has also been studied ([12, 17]). Moore[15] has showed how an intelligent tutor can refer to past explanations in a tutoring dialogue. Our approach is more inspired from these two frames of research. Our approach differs however in that we have incorporated the notion of context and the notion of intention of the tutor. The hints are associated to the specific state of the dialogue (not that of the resolution of the problem at hand). Therefore, the tutor is aware of what has happened in the past and it can use that information to make hypothesis about the explanation of the learner's difficulties. Moreover, the tutor is explicitly attributed some specific goals. This approach allows an organization of the tutoring dialogue plan in small units of focus that are nested. This also allows the explicit modelling of several kinds of tutoring strategies in the dialogue.

5 Future Work: Using Tutorial Dialogue for the Explicit Promotion of Reflection

In PROLOG-TUTOR, our goal is to propose some models of tutorial dialogues which explicitly promote learner reflection. This paper describes a very specific case of the consequence of such tutorial dialogues. While the ideas in the current paper will not be the direct objects of an evaluation, PROLOG-TUTOR is now in evaluation with respect to the more general goal of promoting explicit reflection. 10 undergraduate students in computer sciences are participating to this evaluation. The goal of this experience is to assess: 1) if the way that questions are asked to the learner promote reflection; 2) if there is reflection, what type of reflexive processes are triggered by these questions (recall, inference, analysis, etc.).

6 Conclusion

This paper has presented how a tutoring dialogue can be adapted and accommodated to fit the learner needs in PROLOG-TUTOR, an ITS for Logic Programming. We have described a set of models inspired from: the dialogue game board model, the theory of the accommodation of dialogue utterances, the notion of intention. These models support a framework which allows a tutor to: 1) adapt a predefined dialogue plan by removing some dialogue steps; 2) accommodate the current dialogue focus in order to elaborate the context of a question that has been asked to the learner. The adaptation is based on the learner model and its goal is to skip the dialogue steps that may be irrelevant for the learner, according to his model. The goal of the elaboration is to revisit the steps that have been skipped, to insure that the learner understands well the context of the current step of the dialogue. This position contributes to similar research that focused on the formalisation of hinting in tutorial dialogue, revisiting past explanation, etc. Our future work concerns the evaluation of the more general framework on which PROLOG-TUTOR is built. This framework comprises a set of model to explicitly promote student's reflection in tutorial dialogues.

References

1. Cawsey, A., *Planning Interactive Explanations.* International Journal of Man-machine Studies, 1993. **38**(2): p. 169-200.
2. Cawsey, A., J. Galliers, G. Logan, S. Reese, and K. Sparck-Jones. *Revising Beliefs and Intentions: A Unified Framework for Agent Interaction.* in *Prospects in artificial intelligence: AISB.* 1993: Amsterdam, IOS Press.
3. Chi, M.T., N. De Leeuv, M. Chiu, H., and C. Lavancher, *Eliciting Self explanations improves understanding.* Cognitive Sciences, 1994. **18**(3): p. 439-477.
4. Clancey, W., J., *Knowledge-Based Tutoring: The Guidon Program.* 1987, Cambridge, Massachusset: MIT Press.
5. Collins, A. and A.L. Stevens, *Goals and strategies of inquiry teachers*, in *Advances in instructional psychology*, R. Glaser, Editor. 1982, Lawrence Erlbaum Assoc.: Hillsdale, NJ. p. 65-119.
6. Conati, C., A. Gertner, and K. VanLehn, *Using Bayesian Networks to Manage Uncertainty in Student Modeling.* Journal of User Modeling and User-Adapted Interaction, 2002. **12**(4): p. 371-417.
7. Corbett, A.T. and J.R. Anderson, *Knowledge Tracing: Modeling the Acquisition of Procedural Knowledge.* User Modeling and User Adapted Interaction, 1995. **4**: p. 253-278.
8. Cozman, F., G., *The JavaBayes system.* The ISBA Bulletin, 2001. **7**(4): p. 16-21.

9. Dimitrova, V., J. Self, and P. Brna. *Involving the Learner in Diagnosis - Potentials and Problems.* in *Tutorial at Web Information Technologies: Research, Education and Commerce,.* 2000. MontPellier, France.

10. Ginzburg, J., *Interrogatives: Questions, facts and dialogue,* in *Handbook of Contemporary Semantic Theory.* 1996, Blackwell: Oxford.

11. Ginzburg, J. *Clarifying utterances.* in *Proceedings of the Twente Workshop on the Formal Semantics and Pragmatics on Dialogues.* 1998.

12. Heffernan, N. and K. Koedinger. *An Intelligent Tutoring System Incorporating a Model of an Experienced Human Tutor International Conference on Intelligent Tutoring System* 2002. Biarritz, France. : Springer Verlag.

13. Koedinger, K., J. Anderson, W. Hadley, and M. Mark, *Intelligent Tutoring Goes To School in the Big City.* Int. Journal of Artificial Intelligence in Education, 1997. **8**: p. 30-43.

14. Larsson, S., R. Cooper, and E. Engdahl. *Question accommodation and information states ind Dialogue.* in *Third Wokshop in Human-Computer Coversation.* 2000. Bellagio.

15. Moore, J. and C. Paris, *Planning Text for Advisory Dialogues.* Computational Linguistics, 1993. **19**(4): p. 651-694.

16. Pearson, N., A. Graesser, R. Kreuz, V. Pomeroy, and T.R. Group, *Simulating human tutor dialog moves in AutoTutor.* International Journal of Artificial Intelligence in Education, 2001. **12**: p. 23-39.

17. Razzaq, L. and H. Heffernan. *Tutorial dialog in an equation solving intelligent tutoring system.* in *Proceedings of 7th Annual Intelligent Tutoring Systems Conference.* 2004. Maceio, Brazil.

18. Tchetagni, J. and R. Nkambou. *A framework for the hierarchical representation of the learner model using Bayesian Networks.* 2002. Biarritz, France: Springer-Verlag.

19. Tchetagni, J., R. Nkambou, and F. Kabanza. *Epistemological Remediation in Intelligent Tutoring Systems.* in *Industrial and Engineering Applications of Artificial Intelligence and Expert Systems.* 2004. Ottawa, Canada.

20. Tsovaltzi, D. and C. Matheson. *Formalising hinting in tutorial dialogues.* in *EDILOG: 6th workshop on the semantics and pragmatics of dialogue.* 2002. Edinburgh.

21. Woolf, B. and T. Murray. *A Framework for Representing Tutorial Discourse.* in *10th joint conference on artificial intelligence.* 1987.

Static Clonal Selection Algorithm Based on Match Range Model

Jungan Chen[1], Dongyong Yang[2], and Feng Liang[1]

[1] Zhejiang Wanli University
Ningbo, Zhejiang, 315100, China
friendcen21@hotmail.com, liangf_hz@hotmail.com
[2] Zhejiang University of Technology, No.6 District, Zhaohui Xincun
Hangzhou, Zhejiang, 310032, China
yangdy@ieee.org

Abstract. Static Clonal Selection Algorithm (SCSA) is proposed to generate detectors to intrusion detection. A gene expression is used to express detector which exists as a form of classification rules. But full match rule is used and the gene expression can not express classification rules with OR operator freely. In this work, by combined the gene expression with partial match rule which is an important component in negative selection algorithm, a new expression which can express classification rules with OR operator is proposed. But the match threshold in match rule is difficult to set. Inspired from the T-cell maturation, a match range model is proposed. Base on this model and new expression proposed, a Static Clonal Selection Algorithm based on Match Range Model is proposed. The proposed algorithm is tested by simulation experiment for self/nonself discrimination. The results show that the proposed algorithm is more effective to generate detector with partial classification rules than SCSA which generates detector with full conjunctive rules with 'and'; match range is self-adapted.

1 Introduction

In human immune system (HIS), the genes of gene library are inherited from the ancestor. Through Baldwin Effect, HIS generates new antibodies used to detect antigens that had attempted to attack ancestor's body. Similarly, the genes of gene library in the artificial immune system (AIS) can be the genes of nonselves and used to generate detector to detect the nonselves which are attempted to attack before. So Static Clonal Selection Algorithm (SCSA) is proposed to generate detectors. When nonself data are gathered, SCSA is used to extract nonself pattern from nonself data and generate detectors which contain nonself pattern without overlapping self patterns [1].

SCSA evolves detectors existing as a form of classification rules which classify nonself from self. Negative Selection Algorithm (NSA) is used to delete detectors which detect any selves. Simple binary expression proposed by De Jong is used in order to encode the conjunctive rule detectors [2]. Each gene which represents an

M. Ali and R. Dapoigny (Eds.): IEA/AIE 2006, LNAI 4031, pp. 859–868, 2006.

attribute of detector phenotype is combined by an "AND" operator. So it is impossible to express classification rules composed of "OR" in SCSA. Also, it is always difficult that full classification rules are extracted from nonselves and survive after NSA processes because full match rule is used in SCSA [1].

In this work, one new detector expression, r-classification which is combined binary expression proposed by De Jong with partial match rule, is proposed. Classification rules composed of "OR" can be expressed by the r-classification. So the algorithm with the r-classification will be more effective to generate detector because the r-classification can express rules with 'or' and do not require to extract full classification rules but extract (r+1) partial rules with 'and' from nonselves. But in r-classification, r is difficult to set.

In this work, inspired from T-cells maturation, a match range model with selfmax and selfmin is proposed. In the match range model, selfmax, selfmin is self-organized because they are evaluated by selves. So a novel idea is inspired, the match range model can be combined with the r-classification, r in the r-classification is replaced by selfmax, selfmin. Based on this idea, a Static Clonal Selection Algorithm based on Match Range Model (SCSA-MRM) is proposed in this work. SCSA-MRM uses genetic algorithm to evolve the detectors with self-adapted match range and extract partial rules from nonselves.

2   Static Clonal Selection Algorithm

2.1   R-Classification and Match Range Model

Match rule is an important component in negative selection algorithm (NSA) [3]. For binary representation, there exist several partial match rules with match threshold r (termed as r-match rule) like hamming, r-contiguous and r-chunks [3][4][5]. Match threshold r makes it possible that a single detector detects more similar nonselves. For example, there is a detector '100110' with r=2. If the match rule is r-contiguous, then '100***' or '*001***' will be detected.

In this work, one new detector expression, r-classification which is combined binary expression proposed by De Jong with r-match rule, is proposed. Classification rules composed of "OR" can be expressed by the r-classification. Detector match nonself when there are (r+1) genes match between them. For example, there is one classification rule such as:

If (Gene 1=TCP or UDP) and (Gene 2=[20,30]) and (Gene 3=0) Then detect nonself. When match threshold r is set to 1 in the r-classification, the rule can be expressed as following three rules with OR:

If (Gene 1=TCP or UDP) and (Gene 2=[20,30]) or (…others…) Then detect nonself;
If (Gene 2=[20,30]) and (Gene 3=0) or (…others…) Then detect nonself;
If (Gene 1=TCP or UDP) and (Gene 3=0) or (…others…) Then detect nonself.

So the algorithm with the r-classification will be more effective to generate detector because the r-classification can express rules with 'or' and do not require to

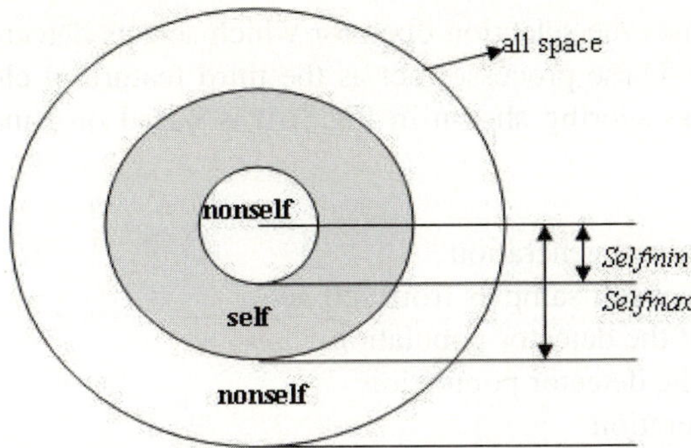

Fig. 1. Match range model

extract full classification rules with 'and' but extract (r+1) partial rules from nonselves. But in the r-classification, r is difficult to set.

In human immune system, T-cells maturation goes through two processes, positive and negative selection [5]. Positive selection requires T-cells to recognize self cells with lower affinity, while T- cells must not recognize self cells with higher affinity in negative selection. So there is a range between lower and higher affinity.

In this work, inspired from T-cells maturation, a match range model shown in Fig.1 is proposed. *Selfmax* is the maximal distance between detector and selves. *Selfmin* is the minimal distance and must be bigger than 0. The range between *selfmin* and *selfmax* belongs to the self space. A nonself is detected when the distance is bigger than *selfmax* or smaller than *selfmin*, which is termed as range match rule. One detector with range match rule will not detect any selves when selfmax,selfmin is set, because every selves is belonged to the range between selfmin and selfmax. So NSA operator can be replaced by setting selfmax,selfmin.

The match range model can be combined with the r-classification, r in the r-classification is replaced by selfmax, selfmin. Based on this idea, a Static Clonal Selection Algorithm based on Match Range Model (SCSA-MRM) is proposed in this work.

2.2 The Model of Algorithm

In human immune system, the main features of the clonal selection theory are [6, 7,8]:

(1) The new cells are copies of their parents (clone) subjected to a mutation mechanism with high rates (somatic hypermutation);
(2) Elimination of newly differentiated lymphocytes carrying self-reactive receptors;
(3) Elimination of newly differentiated lymphocytes carrying low affinity antigenic receptors.

Based on clonal selection theory, the model of SCSA-MRM is shown in Fig.2. In Step.3, the reproduction applies only mutation operator and there are five mutation operators [1], which are coincide to somatic hypermutation in the first feature of clonal selection theory. One parent only product one child.

Step 5~7 simulates the selection operator which selects detectors with high fitness to next generation. These processes act as the third feature of clonal selction theory. Step 5 is the fitness scoring shown in Fig.3; it is based on Binary Immune System Model [9].

maxgen: the maximal generation
S: the rate to select self samples from self set
PSize: the size of the detector population
DETECTORS: the detector population
gen: current generation
1: initialize the detector population
2: For gen=0 to maxgen
3:      children =**reproduction** (only mutation)
4:      DETECTORS = { children $\cup$ DETECTORS }
5:      **Fitness scoring**(DETECTORS)
6:          Rank DETECTORS with fitness from big to small
7:      DETECTORS = Select PSize detectors with higher
fitness from DETECTORS
8: End

Fig. 2. Algorithm of SCSA-MRM

When a subset of antibodies meets many antigens, there is a competition to detect antigens between antibodies. The antibody which detects more antigens will multiply and grow the fastest.

In Fig.3, Step 6~7 means that some detectors randomly meet the nonselves. It is just like antibodies randomly meet antigens. Step 8~19 is the competition to detect the nonself samples. The more nonself samples one detector detect, the higher fitness it has, which means the detector has more chance to multiply. Step 9 is processed in Fig.5 which is to calculate the number of nonselves detected by detector with match range; the distance is based on the gene expression proposed by De Jong [1,2]. Step 17~19 is according to "The antibody in the sample with the highest match score has its match score added to its fitness. The fitness of all other antibodies remains unchanged [9]". The value of C in Step 20 is usually 3[1,9].

Step.2 in Fig.3 is shown in Fig.4 which is used to evaluate the value of tow major parameters of the match model, *selfmax* and *selfmin*, and create the match range. One detector with range match rule will not detect any selves when selfmax,selfmin is set. This process is according to the second feature of clonal selction theory and used to delete detectors which detect any selves, so False Positive (FP) is always equal to 0. In Fig.4, the distance is based on the gene expression proposed by De Jong in Step 5 [1,2]. Step.9 is the process of positive selection. *selfmin* must be bigger than 0, or detector will be deleted, which means that $selfmax$ is equal to the gene length (l) and its fitness is the lowest.

C: the number of times to repeat
DctSample: a sample of DETECTORS
D: the size of DctSample
NonSample: a sample of nonself set
A:the size of NonSample
MaxDetectedNum: the maximal number of nonselves in NonSample detected by detector in DctSample.
MaxSet: the detectors which detect MaxDetectedNum nonselves in NonSample
Hdn[ij]:distance between DctSample[i]and NonSample[j]
DctCount[i]: the number of NonSample detected by DctSample[i]
Fitness[i]: the fitness of DETECTORS[i]
r: the match threshold

Fitness Scoring (DETECTORS)
1: For each detector DETECTORS[i]
2:      **SetSelfminSelfmax**(DETECTORS)
3:      Fitness[i]=0
4: End
5: For Lc=1 to C* the Size of DETECTORS
6:      DctSample is randomly selected from DETECTORS without replacement
7:      NonSample is randomly selected from the nonself set without replacement
8:      For each detector DctSample[i]
9:              DctCount[i] = the number of nonself
                        in NonSample detected by DctSample [i]
10:             If DctCount[i]>MaxDetectedNum then
11:                     MaxDetectedNum= DctCount[i],MaxSet= DctSample[i]
12:             End
13:             If DctCount[i]=MaxDetectedNum then
14:                     MaxSet={MaxSet $\cup$ DctSample[i]}
15:             End
16:     End
17:     For each detector Maxset [k] in Maxset
18:             The fitness of Maxset [k]+= MaxDetectedNum/ Size of MaxSet
19:     End
20: End
21: the processes repeated for (population size×C) times.

Fig. 3. Fitness Scoring of SCSA-MRM

l: the number of bits in detector
SELF: self smaples
Hds[ij]:the distance between DETECTORS[i] and SELF[j]
selfmax[i]:maximal distance between DETECTOR[i] and SELF
selfmin[i]:minimal distance between DETECTOR[i] and SELF
Fitness[i]: the fitness of DETECTORS [i]
SetSelfminSelfmax(DETECTORS)

```
1: Select S*(size of self set) number of SELF  from self set
2: For each detector DETECTORS[i]
3:    selfmax[i]=0, selfmin[i]=1
4:    For each self sample SELF[j]
5:       Compute Hds [ij]
6:       If  Hds [ij]>selfmax[i] then selfmax[i]= Hds [ij]
7:       If  Hds [ij]<selfmin[i] then selfmin[i]= Hds [ij]
8:    End
9:    If selfmin[i]=0 then selfmax[i]=1,Fitness[i]=0
10:End
```

Fig. 4. Setting the *selfmax* and *selfmin*

```
1: DctCount[i]=0
2: For each nonself NonSample[j]
3:      compute Hdn[ij]
4:      if Hdn[ij]>Selfmax or Hdn[ij]<Selfmin then DctCount[i] += 1
5: End
```

Fig. 5. Computation of the number of nonselves detected by detector

2.3 Experiment for Self/Nonself Discrimination

The objective is to understand following:

(1) The comparison between SCSA and SCSA-MRM;
(2) Match range searched by genetic algorithm;
(3) Whether the algorithm is self-adapted.

In this experiment, data set from UCI Repository of machine learning databases is used because two data sets from the UCI are used in JKim's paper [1]. Minimal entropy discretization algorithm is used to discretize these data sets [10].

The first data set is Wisconsin Diagnostic Breast Cancer (WDBC) data which has 30 attributes. The WDBC data is different from the data in JKim's paper which is Wisconsin Breast Cancer Database [1]. It consists of 569 examples with two classes: 'benign', 'malignant'. 357 examples belong to 'benign' and 212 belong to 'malignant'.

The second data set is iris data with 4 attributes which is the same as the data in JKim's paper [1]. It has total 150 examples with three classes: 'Setosa', ' Versicolour', ' Virginica'. Each class has 50 examples.

For the comparison between SCSA and SCSA-MRM, both WDBC data and Iris data are used. In WDBC data, 'malignant' is defined as self set and 'benign' as nonself set. In iris data, 'Virginica' is defined as self set and others as nonself set. Both SCSA and SCSA-MRM runs for ten times with D=5, A=5, S=1, maxgen=500, PSize=10, C=3. The mutate rate of WDBC data is equal to 0.1 and the mutate rate of iris data is equal to 0.2. Resutls are shown in Fig 6, 7.

To illustrate the self-adapted character of SCSA-MRM, Iris data set is used. The algorithm runs for ten times with D=5, A=5, S=1, maxgen=1000, PSize=10, C=3, the mutate rate is equal to 0.2. Before the 500th generation, 'Virginica' is defined as self set and ' Versicolour' is defined as nonself set. After the 500th generation, the data set is changed. 'Virginica' and 'Setosa' are defined as self set. ' Versicolour' is still defined as nonself set. Results are shown in Fig.8.

2.4 Analyze

1. the comparison between SCSA and SCSA-MRM
Fig.6 shows the comparison between SCSA and SCSA-MRM. In (b) TP of two algorithms is almost the same. But in (a), TP of SCSA is equal to 0 which indicate that binary expression proposed by De Jong is not flexible enough to express classification rules with OR and SCSA can not extract full match rules from nonselves within the maximal generation. So SCSA-MRM is better than SCSA and r-classfication rule proposed in this work is effective.

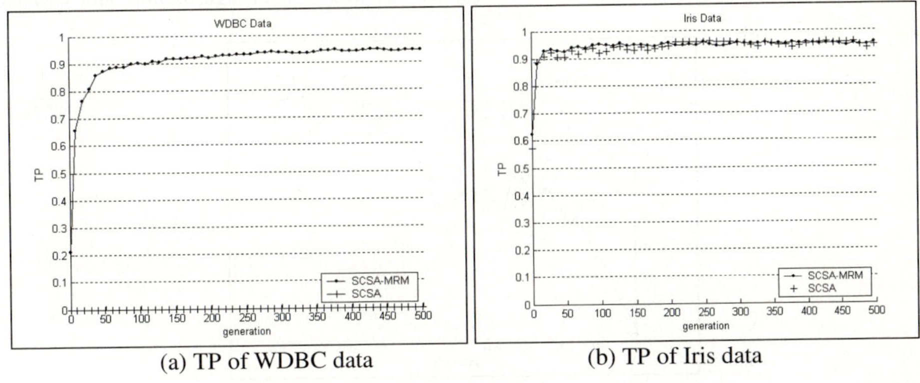

(a) TP of WDBC data   (b) TP of Iris data

Fig. 6. The True Positive of different algorithm

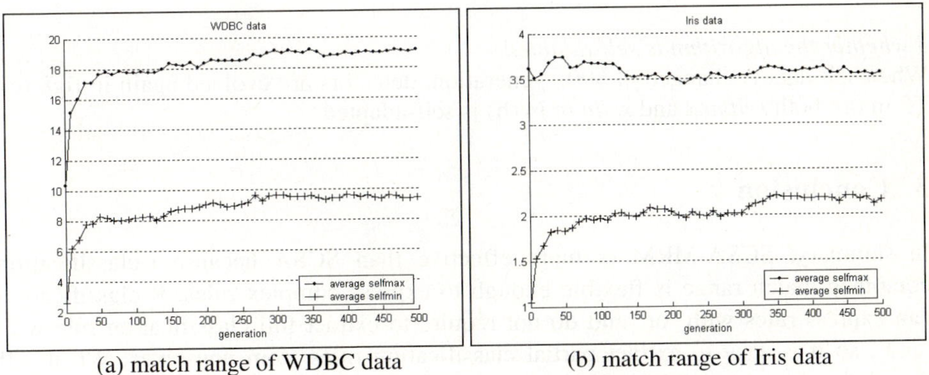

(a) match range of WDBC data   (b) match range of Iris data

Fig. 7. Match Range of SCSA-TM

2 match range searched by genetic algorithm
Fig.7 shows that match range evolve to the optimized range because of clonal selection which is drived by the genetic algorithm. The space which is out of the range between selfmax and selfmin is the nonself space.

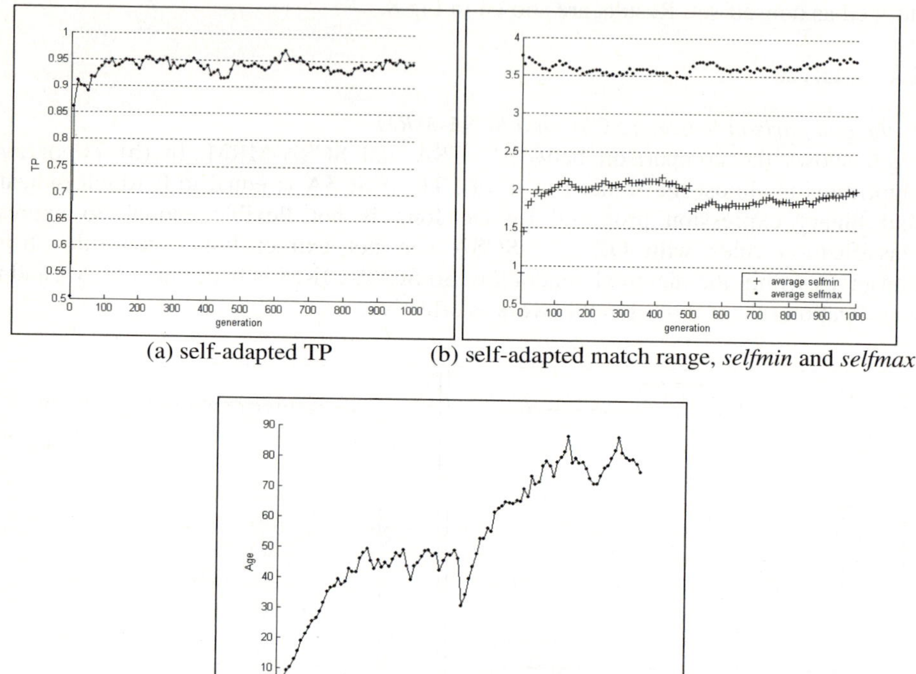

(a) self-adapted TP   (b) self-adapted match range, *selfmin* and *selfmax*

(c) Average Age

Fig. 8. SCSA-MRM

3 whether the algorithm is self-adapted.
When self data is changed at 500th generation, detectors are evolved again in fig8 (c). TP in (a), both *selfmax* and *selfmin* in (b) is self-adapted.

3 Conclusion

In summary, SCSA-MRM is more effective than SCSA because r-classification combined match range is flexible enough to express complex rules. R-classification can express rules with 'or' and do not require to extract full classification rule with 'and', so it is easy to extract partial classification rules from nonselves. When self data is not constant, SCSA-MRM is self-adapted because selfmax and selfmin is evaluated by self data. According to "the different value of r for each detector can fill the potential holes [11]", it is possible to solve the holes problem [11] because there is no match threshold r but the match range in this algorithm. Of course, it is required to research further because experiments are not based on network data and the size of detectors population is not self-adapted when both self and nonself are changed.

Acknowledgements

Thanks for the assistance received by using the UCI Repository of machine learning databases [http://www.ics.uci.edu/~mlearn/MLRepository.html].

References

1. Kim J. W.: Integrating Artificial Immune Algorithms for Intrusion Detection, PhD Thesis,Department of Computer Science, University College London (2002).
2. De Jong, Kenneth A.. William M. Spears, and Diana F. Gordon.: Using Genetic Algorithms for Concept Learning. In Machine Learning (1993) 161-188.
3. Forrest S., Perelson A. S., Allen, L. and Cherukuri, R.: Self-nonself Discrimination in a Computer, Proceedings of the 1994 IEEE Symposium on Research in Security and Privacy, Los Alamos, CA: IEEE Computer Society Press (1994)
4. Hofmeyr S.A.: An Immunological Model of Distributed Detection and its Application to Computer Security, PhD Dissertation, University of New Mexico (1999).
5. Gonzalez F.: A Study of Artificial Immune Systems applied to Anomaly Detection, A Dissertation presented for the Doctor of Philosophy Degree, The University of Memphis (2003).
6. de Castro L. N. and Von Zuben F. J.: Artificial Immune Systems: Part I – Basic Theory and Applications, Technical Report – RT DCA 01/99 (1999)
7. de Castro L. N., Von Zuben F. J.: Learning and Optimization Using the Clonal Selection Principle, IEEE Transactions on Evolutionary Computation, Special Issue on Artificial Immune Systems (2002) 239-251
8. Wenjian L.: Research on Artificial Immune Model and Algorithms Applied to Intrusion Detection, PhD Dissertation, University of Science and Technology of China (2003)
9. Forrest S.,Javornik B., Smith R.E.and Perelson A.S.: Using genetic algorithms to explore pattern recognition in the immune system,Evolutionary Computation (1993) 191-211,
10. Dougherty J., Kohavi R. and Sahami M.: Supervised and unsupervised discretization of continuous features. Available http://robotics.stanford.edu/~ronnyk/disc.ps
11. D'haeseleer P., Forrest S. and Helman P.: A Distributed Approach to Anomaly Detection,,1997, Available http://www.cs.unm.edu/~forrest/isa_papers.htm

Appendix

Parameter (D, A, Mutate Rate) sensitivity of SCSA-MRM is investigated. WDBC data set is used. SCSA-MRM runs for ten times with S=1, maxgen=500, Psize=10, C=3. The results are shown in Fig.9~11.

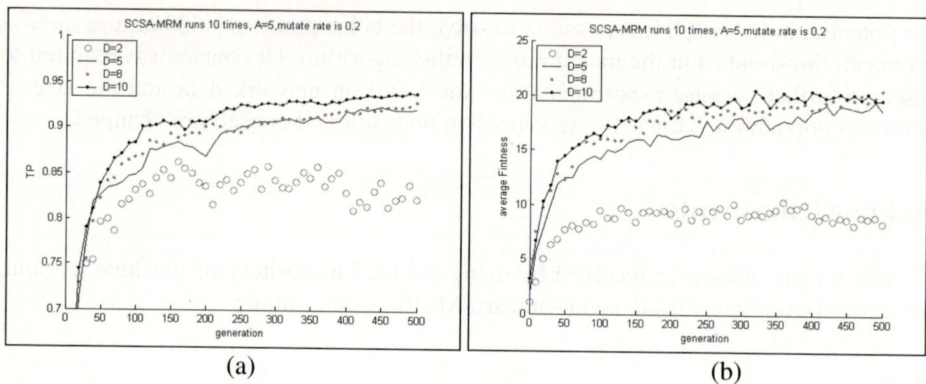

Fig. 9. SCSA-MRM with different D

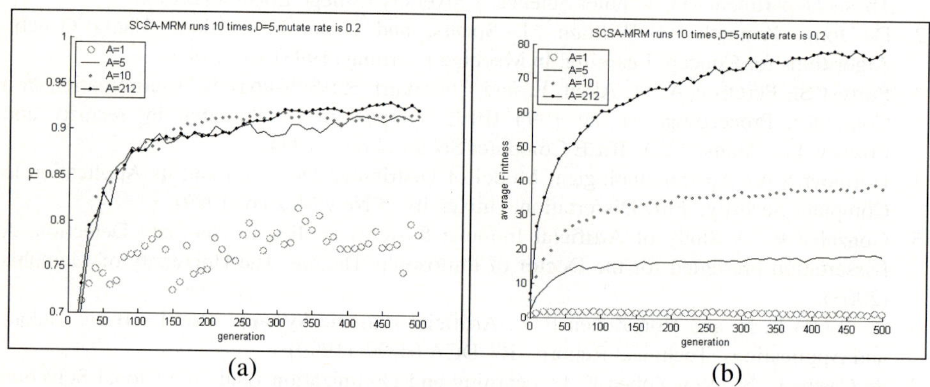

Fig. 10. SCSA-MRM with different A

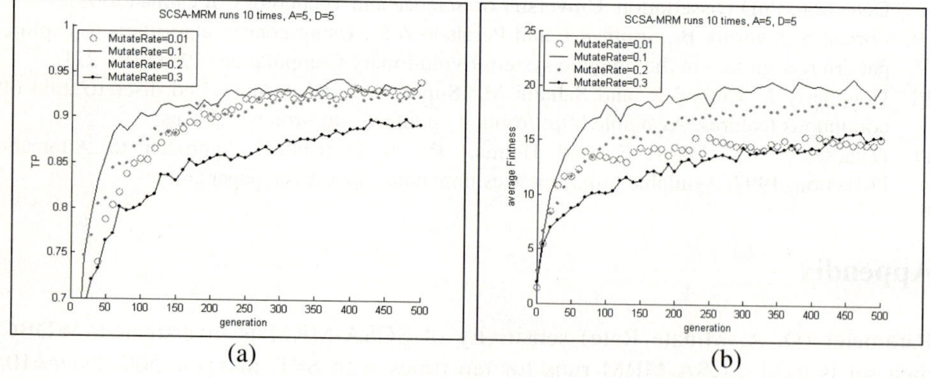

Fig. 11. SCSA-MRM with different Mutate Rate

Diagnosing Faulty Transitions in Recommender User Interface Descriptions

Alexander Felfernig

Computer Science and Manufacturing, University Klagenfurt
A-9020 Klagenfurt, Austria
`alexander.felfernig@uni-klu.ac.at`

Abstract. Complex assortments of products and services offered by online selling platforms require the provision of sales support systems assisting customers in the product selection process. Knowledge-based recommenders are intelligent sales assistance systems which guide online customers through personalized sales dialogs and automatically determine products which conform to their needs and wishes. Such systems have been successfully applied in a number of application domains such as financial services or digital cameras. In this context, the construction of recommender user interfaces is still a challenging task. In many cases faulty models of recommender user interfaces are defined by knowledge engineers and no automated support for debugging such models is available. In this paper we discuss a formal model for defining the intended behaviour of recommender user interfaces and show the application of model-based diagnosis concepts which allow the automated debugging of those definitions. Experiences show that this approach significantly increases the productivity of recommender user interface development and maintenance.

Keywords: knowledge-based recommenders, diagnosis, user interface design.

1 Introduction

Simulating the behaviour of human sales experts, recommender systems [1,4,6,9,12] support customers in the product or service selection process. These technologies are of great importance for making product assortments accessible to online customers without technical product domain knowledge. In this paper we concentrate our discussions on knowledge-based recommenders [1,4] which exploit deep knowledge about the product domain in order to determine products or services fitting to the wishes and needs of the customer. Such representations allow the inclusion of automated debugging mechanisms which support the effective development and maintenance of a recommender application. Two basic aspects have to be considered when implementing a knowledge-based recommender application. Firstly, the relevant set of products has to be identified and transformed into a formal representation, i.e. a recommender knowledge base has to be defined. Such a knowledge base consists of a structural description of the provided set of products, a description of the possible set of customer requirements and a set of constraints restricting the possible combinations of customer requirements and product properties. Secondly, a model of a recommender

M. Ali and R. Dapoigny (Eds.): IEA/AIE 2006, LNAI 4031, pp. 869–878, 2006.

process [4] has to be defined which serves as the basis for personalized dialogs. Knowledge bases and process definitions can be automatically (no programming is needed) translated into an executable advisor, where each state of the process definition corresponds to a Web-page in the generated application [4]. In each state a user can articulate his requirements and depending on the given answers the process control determines the following state. In a final state, product recommendations are displayed, e.g. concrete digital cameras or financial services (savings, bonds, etc.). In this paper we focus on a situation where knowledge engineers develop a model of the user interface of a knowledge-based recommender application. The interfaces of such applications are described by a finite number of states, where state transitions are triggered by user requirements represented by a set of variable settings (see Figure 1).

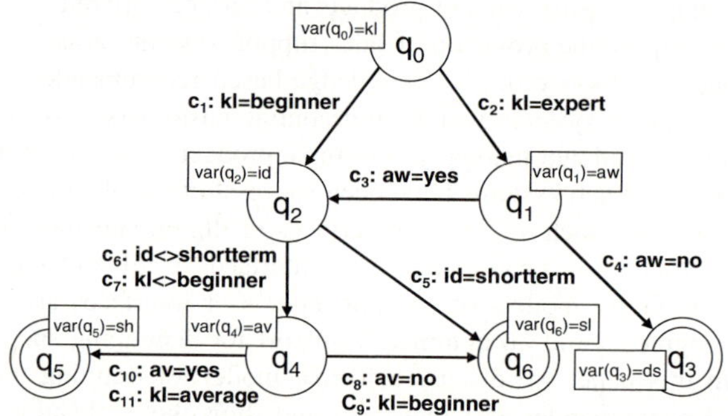

Fig. 1. Example (faulty) process definition. $\{c_1, c_2, ..., c_{11}\}$ are transition conditions between states q_i, var(q_i) represents variables instantiated by the user in state q_i.

Finite state automata [7] can be used for expressing the expected behaviour of a recommender user interface [4]. Typically, customers make decisions by specifying values (requirements) for a subset of a given set of variables. Depending on the answers the automaton changes its state, e.g. an expert (kl = expert) who isn't interested in financial services advisory (aw = no), is forwarded to the state q_3, where a direct product search can be performed, i.e. different subsets of variables are defined by different paths in the automaton. Note that the design in Figure 1 is faulty, since an expert (kl = expert) who wants to be guided by a financial advisory process (aw = yes) and is interested in long-term investments (id = longterm) and doesn't have any available funds (av = no) comes to a standstill at the input of availability (the conditions $\{c_2, c_9\}$ and $\{c_2, c_{11}\}$ are contradictory). In such a situation, mechanisms are needed allowing an effective identification of the sources of inconsistencies. In the following we show how concepts from model-based diagnosis (MBD) [10] are applied for identifying a minimal set of changes allowing consistency recovery in finite state representations of recommender user interfaces. The presented concepts have been implemented within the scope of the Koba4MS[1] [4] project, where finite state models are used to specify the intended behaviour of a recommender user interface.

---

[1] Koba4MS is an acronym for Knowledge-based Advisors for Marketing & Sales (Austrian Research Fund Project 808479).

The remainder of this paper is organized as follows. In Section 2 we introduce the concept of Predicate-Based Finite State Automata (PFSA), a representation formalism for the design of recommender user interfaces. In Section 3 we discuss our approach to the automated debugging of PFSA-based representations using Model-Based Diagnosis (MBD). In Section 4 we present results from evaluating the presented concepts.

2 Finite State Models of Recommender User Interfaces

For the following discussions on the application of model-based diagnosis concepts to the automated debugging of recommender user interface descriptions we introduce a variant of Predicate-Based Finite State Automata (PFSA) [15] (see e.g. Figure 1) which is a natural and compact approach to define state transitions (transitions are defined in terms of domain restrictions of finite domain variables). Note that we restrict our discussions to the case of *acyclic* automata.

Definition 1 (PFSA): we define a Predicate-based Finite State Automaton (PFSA) to be a 6-tuple $(Q, \Sigma, \Pi, E, S, F)$, where

- $Q = \{q_1, q_2, ..., q_j\}$ is a finite set of states, where $var(q_i) = x_i$ is a finite domain variable assigned to q_i, $prec(q_i) = \{\phi_1, \phi_2,..., \phi_m\}$ is the set of preconditions of q_i ($\phi_k = \{c_r, c_s, ..., c_t\} \subseteq \Pi$), $postc(q_i) = \{\psi_1, \psi_2, ..., \psi_n\}$ is the set of postconditions of q_i ($\psi_l = \{c_u, c_v, ..., c_w\} \subseteq \Pi$), and $dom(x_i) = \{x_i=d_{i1}, x_i=d_{i2}, ..., x_i=d_{ip}\}$ denotes the set of possible assignments of x_i, i.e. the domain of x_i.
- $\Sigma = \{x_i = d_{ij} \mid x_i = var(q_i), x_i = d_{ij} \in dom(x_i)\}$ is a finite set of variable assignments (input symbols), the input alphabet.
- $\Pi = \{c_1, c_2, ..., c_q\}$ is a set of constraints (transition conditions) restricting the set of words accepted by the PFSA.
- E is a finite set of transitions $\subseteq Q \times \Pi \times Q$.
- $S \subseteq Q$ is a set of start states.
- $F \subseteq Q$ is a set of final states.   □

Preconditions of a state q_i ($prec(q_i) = \{\phi_1, \phi_2, ..., \phi_m\}$) can be automatically derived from the reachability tree of a Predicate-based Finite State Automaton. Figure 2 depicts the reachability tree for the PFSA of Figure 1. The state q_2 is accessed twice in the reachability tree. The corresponding preconditions ($prec(q_2)$) are derived from the transition conditions of the paths leading to q_2, i.e. $\{\{c_1\}, \{c_2, c_3\}\}$. Similarly, $postc(q_i)$ is the set of postconditions of the state q_i which are as well derived from the reachability tree, e.g. the state q_4 has two postconditions, namely $\{\{c_8, c_9\}, \{c_{10}, c_{11}\}\}$. Example 1 includes a PFSA describing the behaviour of a financial services advisory dialog (the graphical representation is contained in Figure 1). States in the PFSA represent questions which can be posed to customers during an advisory session. Subsequent states in the PFSA are determined depending on the answers given by a customer. We denote the set of input sequences leading to a final state of a PFSA as the accepted language.

In the context of user interface development for recommender applications, supporting concepts are needed which allow the effective identification of faulty transition conditions, e.g. if a sequence of user inputs reaches state q_i, there must exist an extension of this input sequence to a final state of the PFSA. Path expressions are the basis for expressing well-formedness properties on process definitions (see Definition 2).

<table>
<tr><td valign="top">

$Q = \{q_0, q_1, q_2, q_3, q_4, q_5, q_6\}$.
   /* knowledge level of the customer */
$var(q_0) = kl$.
   /* advisory wanted */
$var(q_1) = aw$.
   /* duration of investment */
$var(q_2) = id$.
   /* direct specification of services */

$var(q_3) = ds$.
   /* availability of financial resources*/

$var(q_4) = av$.
   /* high risk products */
$var(q_5) = sh$.
   /* low risk products */
$var(q_6) = sl$.

$dom(kl)=\{kl=beginner, kl=average,$
$kl=expert\}$. $dom(aw)=\{aw=yes, aw=no\}$.
$dom(id)=\{id=shortterm, id=mediumterm,$
      $id=longterm\}$.
$dom(ds)=\{ds=savings,$
$ds=bonds, ds=stockfunds,$
    $ds=singleshares\}$
$dom(av)=\{av=yes, av=no\}$.
$dom(sh)=\{sh=stockfunds, sh=singleshares\}$
.
$dom(sl)=\{sl=savings, sl=bonds\}$.

</td><td valign="top">

$prec(q_0) = \{\{true\}\}$. $prec(q_1) = \{\{c_2\}\}$.
$prec(q_2) = \{\{c_1\}, \{c_2, c_3\}\}$.
$prec(q_3) = \{\{c_2, c_4\}\}$. ...
$postc(q_0) = \{\{c_2, c_4\}, \{c_2, c_3, c_5\},$
       $\{c_2, c_3, c_6, c_7, c_8, c_9\},$
       $\{c_2, c_3, c_6, c_7, c_{10}, c_{11}\},$
       $\{c_1, c_5\}, \{c_1, c_6, c_7, c_8, c_9\},$
       $\{c_1, c_6, c_7, c_{10}, c_{11}\}\}$.
$postc(q_1) = \{\{c_4\}, \{c_3, c_5\},$
       $\{c_3, c_6, c_7, c_8, c_9 \},$
       $\{c_3, c_6, c_7, c_{10}, c_{11}\}\}$.
   ...
$postc(q_4) = \{\{c_8, c_9\}, \{c_{10}, c_{11}\}\}$.
$postc(q_3)=\{\{true\}\}$. $postc(q_5)=\{\{true\}\}$.
$postc(q_6)=\{\{true\}\}$.
$\Sigma = \{kl=beginner, kl=average,$
$kl=expert,$
    $aw=yes, aw=no, ..., sl=savings,$
    $sl=bonds\}$.
$\Pi = \{c_1, c_2, ..., c_{11}\}$.
$E= \{(q_0, \{c_2\}, q_1), (q_0, \{c_1\}, q_2),$
    $(q_1, \{c_4\}, q_3), (q_1, \{c_3\}, q_2),$
    $(q_2, \{c_6, c_7\}, q_4), (q_2, \{c_5\}, q_6),$
    $(q_4, \{c_8, c_9\}, q_6), (q_4, \{c_{10}, c_{11}\},$
$q_5)\}$.
$S= \{q_0\}$.
$F= \{q_3, q_5, q_6\}.\}$

</td></tr>
</table>

Example 1. Predicate-based Finite State Automaton (PFSA)

Definition 2 (consistent path): Let p = $[(q_1, C_1, q_2), (q_2, C_2, q_3), ..., (q_{i-1}, C_{i-1}, q_i)]$ $((q_\alpha, C_\alpha, q_\beta) \in E)$ be a path from a state $q_1 \in S$ to a state $q_i \in Q$. p is consistent (consistent(p)) *iff* $\cup C_j$ is satisfiable.   □

Using the notion of a consistent path we can now introduce the following set of *well-formedness rules* specifying structural properties of a PFSA. These rules are relevant for building knowledge-based recommender applications. Due to the generality of the presented diagnosis approach, we can introduce further well-formedness properties for domain-specific purposes.

A consistent path in a PFSA leading to a state q_i must have a *direct* postcondition, i.e., (q_i, C_i, q_j) propagating the path (i.e. each consistent path must be *extensible*).

Definition 3 (extensible path): Let $p = [(q_1,C_1,q_2), (q_2,C_2,q_3), ..., (q_{i-1},C_{i-1},q_i)]$ be a path from a state $q_1 \in S$ to a state $q_i \in Q - F$. p is extensible (extensible(p)) *iff* $\exists$ (q_i,C_i,q_{i+1}): $C_1 \cup C_2 \cup ... \cup C_{i-1} \cup C_i$ is satisfiable. □

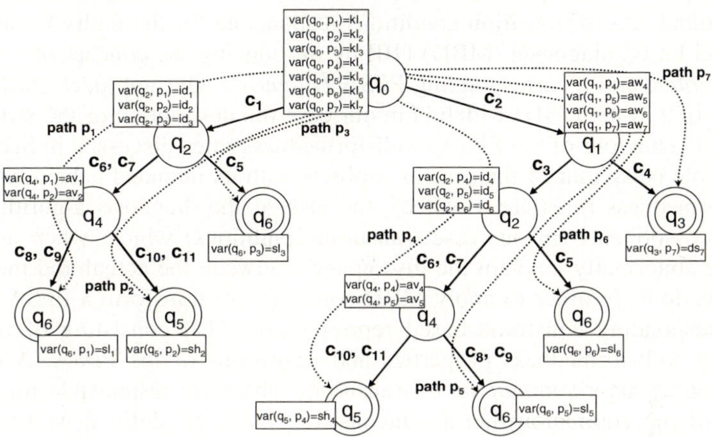

Fig. 2. Reachability tree of a PFSA. The tree represents the expansion of the PFSA shown in Figure 1. {p1, p2, ..., p7} are the possible paths of the PFSA. For each path p_i the corresponding path variables are shown.

A state q_i is a decision point for determining the subsequent state. The selection of subsequent states depends on the definition of the *direct* postconditions for q_i, where each postcondition has to be unique for determining the subsequent state. A state q_i is *deterministic* if each of its postconditions is unique for determining subsequent states.

Definition 4 (deterministic state): Let $p = [(q_1,C_1,q_2), (q_2,C_2,q_3), ..., (q_{i-1},C_{i-1},q_i)]$ be a path from a state $q_1 \in S$ to a state $q_i \in Q - F$. A state (q_i) is deterministic(q_i) *iff* $\forall(q_i,C_{i1},q_j), (q_i,C_{i2},q_k) \in E : C_1 \cup C_2 \cup ... \cup C_{i-1} \cup C_i \cup C_{i2}$ is contradictory $(C_{i1} \neq C_{i2})$. □

All transitions of a PFSA should be *accessible*, i.e. for each transition there exists at least one corresponding path including this transition.

Definition 5 (accessible transition): A transition $t = (q_i,C_i,q_{i+1})$ (postcondition of state q_i) is accessible (accessible(t)) *iff* there exists a path $p = [(q_1,C_1,q_2), (q_2,C_2,q_3), ..., (q_{i-1},C_{i-1},q_i)]$ $(q_1 \in S)$: $C_1 \cup C_2 \cup ... \cup C_{i-1} \cup C_i$ is satisfiable. □

A PFSA is *well-formed*, if the set of defined well-formedness rules is fulfilled.

Definition 6 (well-formed PFSA): A PFSA is well-formed *iff*

- each consistent path $p = [(q_1,C_1,q_2), (q_2,C_2,q_3), ..., (q_{i-1},C_{i-1},q_i)]$ $(q_1 \in S, q_i \in Q - F)$ is extensible to a consistent path $p' = [(q_1,C_1,q_2), (q_2,C_2,q_3), ..., (q_{i-1},C_{i-1},q_i), (q_i,C_i,q_j)]$.
- $\forall q_k \in Q$: deterministic(q_k).
- $\forall t = (q_k,C_k,q_l) \in E$: accessible(t). □

3 Diagnosing Faulty Transitions in User Interface Descriptions

Faulty transition conditions should be identified as soon as possible. Consequently, we need support in the repair of not well-formed PFSAs by an automated identification of minimal sets of transition conditions responsible for the faulty behaviour. We apply model-based diagnosis (MBD) [10] by introducing the concept of a PFSA *Diagnosis Problem* and a corresponding PFSA *Diagnosis*. Our approach starts with the description of a system (SD) which is in our case the description of the structure and the intended behaviour of the PFSA (well-formedness rules discussed in Section 2). If the observable behaviour of the system conflicts with its intended behaviour (some of the well-formedness rules are violated), the task of the diagnosis algorithm is it to determine components (in our case transition conditions) which, when assumed to functioning abnormally, explain the discrepancy between the actual and the intended system behaviour. In order to apply MBD concepts, we transform a PFSA definition into a corresponding constraint-based representation [14] consisting of restrictions representing well-formedness properties and transitions of the PFSA. A calculated diagnosis represents a *minimal* set of transitions which are responsible for the faulty behaviour of the automaton, i.e. are inconsistent with the defined well-formedness properties (see Section 2). Note that there can be different diagnoses providing an explanation for the faulty behaviour of a PFSA. We define a Predicate-based Finite State Automaton Diagnosis Problem (PFSA Diagnosis Problem) as follows.

Definition 7 (PFSA Diagnosis Problem): A PFSA Diagnosis Problem is represented by a tuple (SD, TRANS), where SD = STAT $\cup$ WF. STAT is the structural description of a PFSA represented by a set of finite domain variables. WF is the intended behaviour of a PFSA which is represented by a set of constraints on STAT. Finally, TRANS represents a set of transition conditions. $\quad\square$

The basic elements of a PFSA Diagnosis Problem, i.e., STAT, WF, TRANS, define a corresponding Constraint Satisfaction Problem (CSP) [14]. Solutions for this CSP cover all interaction paths, i.e., accepted runs of the PFSA. In this context, STAT represents a set of finite domain variables related to paths of the reachability tree (the variables of our example PFSA are depicted in Figure 2 and Example 2), e.g. $\{kl_1, id_1, av_1, sl_1\}$ are variables corresponding to the path p_1. Note that the projection of all solutions for the CSP (STAT, WF, TRANS) to e.g. the variables $\{kl_1, id_1, av_1, sl_1\}$ represents input sequences accepted by path p_1.

Example 2 (STAT): STAT = $\{kl_1, id_1, av_1, sl_1, kl_2, id_2, av_2, sh_2, kl_3, id_3, sl_3, kl_4, aw_4, id_4, av_4, sh_4, kl_5, aw_5, id_5, av_5, sl_5, kl_6, aw_6, id_6, sl_6, kl_7, aw_7, ds_7\}$ $\quad\square$

The construction of well-formedness rules (Definitions 3-5) WF = $WF_{extensibility} \cup WF_{accessibility} \cup WF_{determinism}$ is now exemplified by the accessibility rule related to the transition $(q_2, \{c_6, c_7\}, q_4)$ of our example PFSA (see Figure 1).

Example 3 (well-formedness rules for accessibility): $WF_{accessibility} (q_2, \{c_6, c_7\}, q_4) = \{id_1 \neq noval \lor id_2 \neq noval \lor id_4 \neq noval \lor id_5 \neq noval.\}$. $\quad\square$

The transition $(q_2, \{c_6, c_7\}, q_4)$ must be accessible for at least one of the paths p_1, p_2, p_4, p_5, i.e. at least one of the variables id_1, id_2, id_4, id_5 must have a value $\neq$ noval in each solution for the CSP defined by (STAT, WF, TRANS). Since in our case a reachability tree (see e.g. Figure 2) represents the complete expansion of a corresponding PFSA, not all the paths are necessarily consistent. If a path of the reachability tree represents such an illegal trajectory, i.e. no consistent value assignment exists for the corresponding variables, all variables of this path have the assignment noval. This is assured by meta-constraints defined for each path in the reachability tree, e.g. for path p_1: $kl_1 \neq noval \wedge id_1 \neq noval \wedge av_1 \neq noval \wedge sl_1 \neq noval \vee kl_1 = noval \wedge id_1 = noval \wedge av_1 = noval \wedge sl_1 = noval$. An example for the definition of a transition condition (TRANS) is the following (see Example 4). We represent the transition condition c_1 of our example PFSA.

Example 4 (TRANS **for** PFSA): TRANS=$\{c_1$: $(kl_1 = beginner \vee kl_1 = noval) \wedge (kl_2 = beginner \vee kl_2 = noval) \wedge (kl_3 = beginner \vee kl_3 = noval)$. ...$\}$.   □

The condition generated in Example 4 contains those variables belonging to paths including $(q_0, \{c_1\}, q_2)$, i.e. $\{kl_1, kl_2, kl_3\}$ which belong to the paths $\{p_1, p_2, p_3\}$. For the CSP (STAT, WF, TRANS) the possible values of $\{kl_1, kl_2, kl_3\}$ are defined by c_1, i.e. the value can be either *beginner* or *noval* (in the case that the corresponding path is an illegal trajectory). Given a specification of (SD, TRANS), a PFSA Diagnosis is defined as follows.

Definition 8 (PFSA **Diagnosis**): A PFSA Diagnosis for a PFSA Diagnosis Problem (SD, TRANS) is a set S $\subseteq$ TRANS s.t. SD $\cup$ TRANS $-$ S consistent.   □

A diagnosis exists under the assumption that STATS $\cup$ WF is consistent [2]. The calculation of diagnoses is based on the concept of *minimal conflict sets*.

Definition 9 (Conflict Set): a Conflict Set (CS) for (SD, TRANS) is a set $\{c_1, c_2, ..., c_n\} \subseteq$ TRANS, s.t. $\{c_1, c_2, ..., c_n\} \cup$ SD is inconsistent. CS is minimal *iff* $\neg \exists$ CS' $\subset$ CS: conflict set (CS').   □

Algorithm 1 sketches the calculation of diagnoses for a given PFSA.

Algorithm 1: PFSA-Diagnosis (SD, TRANS):
(a) Generate a pruned HSDAG T for the collection of conflict sets induced by transitions of TRANS in breadth-first manner (we generate diagnoses in order of their cardinality). With every theorem prover (TP) call at a node n of T the consistency of (TRANS - H(n) $\cup$ SD) is checked. If there exists an inconsistency, a conflict set CS is returned, otherwise ok is returned. If (TRANS - H(n) $\cup$ SD) is consistent, a corresponding diagnosis H(n) is found.

(b) Return $\{H(n) \mid n$ is a node of T labeled with ok$\}$.

The labelling of the search tree (Hitting Set Directed Acyclic Graph - HSDAG) is based on the labelling of the HSDAG presented in [10]. A node *n* is labelled by a corresponding conflict set CS(n). The set of edge labels from the root to node *n* is denoted to as H(*n*) which represents a corresponding diagnosis (in the case that *n* is a leaf node). Following our example, the conflict sets which are determined by subsequent TP calls are $\{c_2, c_{11}\}$, $\{c_7, c_9\}$, $\{c_2, c_9\}$, and $\{c_1, c_9\}$. One diagnosis for our PFSA is $\{c_2, c_9\}$, i.e., at least $\{c_2, c_9\}$ have to be changed in order to restore consistency of a given PFSA definition.

4 Evaluation

The presented approach to introduce Model-Based Diagnosis (MBD) [10] into the development of knowledge-based recommenders does not change the structure of the user interface supporting the design of recommender processes, but rather complements the existing knowledge acquisition component [4] with concepts supporting the detection of faulty areas in a given PFSA definition. This approach is not restricted to knowledge-based recommendation, but is generally applicable to domains, where a user interface is explicitly defined in terms of a finite state model (in the form of a PFSA). A performance evaluation [2] shows the applicability of the presented algorithm in (interactive) real-world settings. Typically, recommender process definitions consist of about 15-40 states – a size which makes the application of the presented debugging concepts meaningful. In many cases there exist a number of alternative diagnoses explaining the sources of inconsistencies in a given process definition. In this context we will include additional ranking mechanisms for diagnoses which take into account the probability of a transition condition to be faulty (e.g. the probability of a transition condition to be faulty is higher if there exists a large number of incoming paths to the related state). We have compared development efforts related to projects without debugging support for process definitions and with a corresponding debugging support. Our development environment has a logging functionality which stores each activity in the recommender design environment (e.g. change/edit a transition condition, etc.). The projects investigated have a similar structure w.r.t. number of product properties, customer properties, constraints, number of states in the PFSA etc. The observation of time efforts shows that the usage of the debugging concepts can significantly reduce efforts related to the development and maintenance of recommender user interfaces. In order to empirically show the direct positive influence of debugging techniques we have conducted an experiment with ninety-seven participating students all having experiences in developing knowledge-based recommender applications. In this experiment participants were interacting with a web-based application providing the basic functionality of our debugging environment. The participants had to solve the task of identifying a *minimal* set of constraints in given recommender process definitions which should be changed in order to make the process definition consistent with the well-formedness properties presented in this paper. The participants had to propose a set of repair actions which make the process definition consistent with the well-formedness rules. The hypothesis of the experiment was that automated debugging support leads to effort reductions in the detection and repair of faulty transition conditions. The result of the experiment was a significant decrease of time efforts due to the application of the presented debugging concepts (on an average of 36% - time reductions depend on the number of faulty transitions conditions in the process definition). A detailed analysis of the consequences of applying automated debugging concepts in recommender application development is currently ongoing and is in the line of our research focus to improve the effectiveness of recommender application development processes.

5   Related Work

The increasing size and complexity of configuration knowledge bases motivated the application of model-based diagnosis (MBD) [10] in knowledge-based systems development [3]. Similar motivations led to the application of MBD in technical domains such as the development of hardware designs [5], onboard diagnosis for automotive systems [11] and in software development [8]. A value-based model of program execution is introduced in a.o. [8], which is an extension of the approach of debugging imperative languages [5]. Using MBD, the identification of errors is based on source code analysis. Additionally, a set of test cases specifying the expected behaviour of the program is required - this set encompasses concrete values for variables, assertions, reachability constraints for paths, etc. An overview on different applications of model-based diagnosis techniques in software debugging is given in [13]. The representation of the intended behaviour of recommender user interfaces in the form of finite state representations is discussed in [2,4]. This approach is novel in the context of developing knowledge-based applications and, due to its formal foundation, allows an automated translation of the graphical representation into a recommender application. Basically there are three approaches to the implementation of recommender applications. Collaborative Filtering [6,9,12] and Content-based Filtering [9] do not exploit deep knowledge about the product domain. Collaborative Filtering is based on the assumption that customer preferences are correlated, i.e. similar products are recommended to customers with similar interest profiles. Content-based filtering focuses on the analysis of a given set of products already ordered by a customer. Based on this information, products are recommended which resemble products already ordered (products related to similar categories). Additionally, there are a number of approaches combining these basic approaches in order to gain an improved quality of the resulting solutions. Using knowledge-based approaches, the relationship between customer goals and preferences and offered products can be modelled explicitly. An overview on the Koba4MS development environment can be found in [4]. Such model-based knowledge representations are the major precondition for the application of model-based diagnosis [10] discussed in this paper.

6   Conclusions

In this paper we have presented an approach to the automated debugging of recommender process definitions representing the intended behaviour of user interfaces of knowledge-based recommenders. Predicate-based finite state representations are applied in order to model interaction paths of recommender applications. For debugging purposes those finite state automata are translated into a corresponding representation of a constraint satisfaction problem. Results of an experiment show that our approach can significantly increase the productivity of recommender development.

References

[1] Burke, R. Knowledge-based Recommender Systems. *Encyclopedia of Library & Information Systems*, 69, 32, 2000.

[2] Felfernig, A., and Shchekotykhin, K. Debugging User Interface Descriptions of Knowledge-based Recommenders. *Workshop Notes of the IJCAI'05 Workshop on Configuration*, 13–18, 2005.

[3] Felfernig, A., Friedrich, G., Jannach, D., and Stumptner, M. Consistency-based Diagnosis of Configuration Knowledge Bases. *AI Journal* 2, 152, 213–234, 2004.

[4] Felfernig, A. Koba4MS: Selling Complex Products and Services Using Knowledge-Based Recommender Technologies. *7th IEEE International Conference on E-Commerce Technology*, 92–100, 2005.

[5] Friedrich, G., Stumptner, M., and Wotawa, F. Model-based diagnosis of hardware designs. *AI Journal* 111, 2, 3–39, 1999.

[6] Herlocker, J. L., Konstan, J. A., Terveen, L. G., and Riedl, J. T. Evaluating Collaborative Filtering Recommender Systems. *ACM Transactions on Information Systems* 22, 1, 5–53, 2004.

[7] Hopcroft, J., and Ullman, J. Introduction to Automata Theory, Languages, and Computation. Addison-Wesley Publishing Company, Massachusetts, USA, 1979.

[8] Mateis C., Stumptner, M., and Wotawa, F. Modeling Java programs for diagnosis. *14th European Conference on Artificial Intelligence*, 171–175, 2000.

[9] Pazzani, M. A Framework for Collaborative, Content- Based and Demographic Filtering. *Artificial Intelligence Review* 13, 5-6, 393–408, 1999.

[10] Reiter, R. 1987. A theory of diagnosis from first principles. *AI Journal* 23, 1, 57–95, 1987.

[11] Sachenbacher, M., Struss, P., and Carlen, C. A Prototype for Model-Based On-Board Diagnosis of Automotive Systems. *AICOM* 13, 2, 83–97, 2000.

[12] Sarwar, B., Karypis, G., Konstan, J. A., and Riedl, J. T. Item-based collaborative filtering recommendation algorithms. *10th Int. WWW Conference*, 285–295, 2001.

[13] Stumptner, M., and Wotawa, F. A Survey of Intelligent Debugging. *AI Communications* 11, 1, 35–51, 1998.

[14] Tsang, E. Foundations of Constraint Satisfaction. Academic Press, London, 1993.

[15] V.Noord, G., and Gerdemann, D. Finite State Transducers with Predicates and Identities. *Grammars* 4, 3, 263–286, 2001.

An Unsupervised Method for Ranking Translation Words Using a Bilingual Dictionary and WordNet

Kweon Yang Kim[1], Se Young Park[2], and Dong Kwon Hong[3]

[1] School of Computer Engineering, Kyungil University,
33 Buho-ri, Hayang-up Kyungsan-si, Kyungsangpook-do, Korea
kykim@kiu.ac.kr
82-53-850-7287
[2] Dept. of Computer Engineering, Kyungpook National University, Korea
seyoung@mail.knu.ac.kr
82-53-950-5550
[3] Dept. of Computer Engineering, Keimyung University, Korea
dkhong@kmu.ac.kr
82-53-580-5281

Abstract. In the context of machine translation, picking the correct translation for a target word among multiple candidates is an important process. In this paper, we propose an unsupervised method for ranking translation word selection for Korean verbs relying on only a bilingual Korean-English dictionary and WordNet. We focus on deciding which translation of the verb target word is the most appropriate by using a measure of inter-word semantic relatedness through the five extended relations between possible translations pair of target verb and some indicative noun clues. In order to reduce the weight of application of possibly unwanted senses for the noun translation, we rank the weight of possible senses for each noun translation word in advance. The evaluation shows that our method outperforms the default baseline performance and previous works. Moreover, this approach provides an alternative to the supervised corpus based approaches that rely on a large corpus of senses annotated data.

1 Introduction

The task of translation word selection in machine translation is a process to select the correct translation word for a given target word among multiple candidates. The resolution of sense ambiguity and selection of correct translation in non-restricted text are perhaps the great central problem in the context of machine translation. In recent, corpus based solutions for translation word selection have become quite popular. However, theses supervised approaches for selecting translation word heavily rely on the availability of manually created sense tagged or bilingual parallel corpora that they need much of human effort. An alternative approach is to take advantage of the knowledge available in machine readable dictionary[3, 8].

In this paper, we propose an unsupervised method of ranking translation word selection that attempts to select the correct translation word for Korean verbs using

M. Ali and R. Dapoigny (Eds.): IEA/AIE 2006, LNAI 4031, pp. 879 – 888, 2006.

the measure of semantic relatedness that the WordNet similarity package[12] provides. Knowledge sources are extracted from a bilingual Korean-English dictionary and WordNet[5]. From Korean-English dictionary, we first extract the possible English translation words that are corresponding to each sense of given Korean words.

We focus on the semantic relatedness between possible translation words in the view of target language context. Therefore, when investigating senses of possible translation words for a given source language word, we do not know which sense is more appropriate for each translation word. Considering all possible senses for each translation word introduces the application of unwanted senses in the view of source language word that may bring about an incorrect translation word selection. In order to avoid the application of unwanted senses for the noun translation, we rank the weight of possible word senses for each translation word by measuring semantic similarity in WordNet between the translation word and near translation synonyms that are described in a bilingual dictionary. From WordNet, we exploit the knowledge for which the semantic relatedness between the senses of translation words pair for source language words pair is measured.

2 Previous Work

Approaches based on statistical machine translation exploit bilingual parallel corpora or hand-crafted knowledge for selecting translation word[2]. However, as Koehn and Knight[9] pointed out, those knowledge sources are not easily available.

To ease knowledge acquisition, Dagan and Itai[4] have proposed an approach for resolving word sense ambiguity and selecting a translation word using statistical data from a monolingual corpus of target language. They use the statistics on lexical co-occurrence within syntactic relations in a monolingual corpus of target language. Their method can relieve the knowledge acquisition problem by relying on only a monolingual corpus of target language that is sense untagged. However, their method is apt to select an inappropriate translation word because it is based on the simple mapping information between a source word and its possible translation words by using only a bilingual dictionary and a sense untagged target language corpus. When seeing an occurrence of target language word, their method counts word occurrence as a translation word of all the source language words. This can mislead the selection of correct translation word because the translation word also may have several senses from the view of target language.

The source of problem is that this method considers the unnecessary senses of translation words that do not have anything to do with the senses of the original source language word. A possible solution is to use the sense tagged monolingual corpora or bilingual parallel corpora[9, 11]. However, knowledge sources like sense tagged or parallel corpora are generally hard to come by because they need a manual creation. Consider the translation of a Korean phrase "nonmun-ul ssu-da"(that means *write a paper*). In the phrase, noun 'nonmun' has only one sense and has its corresponding translation word *paper* in Korean-English dictionary. However, the translation word *paper* has multiple senses in WordNet. For simplicity's sake, we took into consideration only the first three senses of the translation word *paper* that are explained in the following WordNet entries:

- paper#n#1, {**paper**}
    - a material made of cellulose pulp derived mainly from wood or rags or certain grasses
- paper#n#2, {composition, **paper**, report, theme}
    - an essay. (especially one written as an assignment); "he got an A on his composition"
- paper#n#3, {newspaper, **paper**}
    - a daily or weekly publication on folded sheets; contains news and articles and advertisements; "he read his newspaper at breakfast"

In addition, the Korean verb 'ssu-da' has several translation words such as *write, put on, use, employ, speak*, and etc that are corresponding equivalent to each respective sense in Korean-English dictionary. Table 1 shows the list of combination pairs for possible translation words between 'nonmun' and 'ssu-da'. For this example, the method of Dagan and Itai finds the pairs of possible translation words for source language words using a bilingual dictionary and estimates probabilities of how likely each combination pair of translation words occurs in a target language corpus. We find that an incorrect translation word *use* for a given target word 'ssu-da' is selected because the co-occurrence frequency of pair *use-paper* is dominant in a target language corpus over the pairs of all other translations.

Table 1. Combination pair of translation words with its co-occurrence frequency in the target language corpus

| pair of source words | | pair of translation words | | freq. |
Noun	Verb	Verb	Noun	
'nonmun'	'ssu-da'	*write*	*paper*	22
		put on	*paper*	0
		use	**paper**	**47**
		employ	*paper*	0
		speak	*paper*	0
		…		

Their method fails to select correct translation word for the target word 'ssu-da' as shown in the example of "nonmun-ul ssu-da" because of sense ambiguity of a translation word. The sense of translation word *paper* in almost all of occurrences of *use* and *paper* in target language corpus is used as a first sense of *paper* in WordNet which is not the correct corresponding sense for the source language word 'nonmun'. In consequence, this method selects incorrect translation words pair *use-paper* instead of correct translation words pair *write-paper*.

3 Dictionary Based Approaches

In recent, corpus based solutions for word sense disambiguation have become popular. In general, such approaches rely on the availability of sense tagged corpus that needs a manual creation. An alternative is dictionary-based approaches that take advantage of the information available in machine readable dictionaries or lexical database.

The Lesk algorithm[10] may be identified as a starting point for dictionary based approaches. His algorithm does not require any sense tagged training instances. This approach disambiguates word senses for a particular target word by comparing the dictionary glosses of its possible senses with those of its surrounding words in the context. The target word is assigned the sense whose gloss has the maximum overlap of words with the glosses of its surrounding words. The intuition of this approach is based on two facts that the sense of target word is semantically related to the surrounding words in context and the overlaps of sense glosses reflect the degree of semantic relatedness between senses of a target word and senses of surrounding words in context. Such connections are indicative of the senses in which these words are used rather than not by chance.

The main problem of Lesk algorithm is that dictionary glosses tend to be quite short and may not provide sufficient information to measure of relatedness between a given target word and surrounding words in context. To overcome the limitation of Lesk algorithm based on short definitions, recently Banerjee and Pedersen[1] presented a measure of extended gloss overlaps through the rich network of word sense relations in WordNet rather than simply considering the glosses.

They suggest an extended approach that exploits not only explicit relations through direct links but also implicit relations through indirect links that WordNet provides. In their experiments, they used the seven possible relations such as synset, hypernym, hyponym, holonym, meronym, troponym, and attribute of each word sense in WordNet. In effect, the glosses of surrounding words in the context are expanded to include glosses of theses related words to which they are semantically related through the extended relations in WordNet. This measurement is not restricted by any specific part of speech and can be applied for measurement of relatedness between senses from any part of speech. All of relations that WordNet provides are not equally helpful and the optimal selection of the best relations depends on the application of overlap measurement.

4 Ranking Translation Word Selection

Our algorithm for ranking translation word selection is based on the hypothesis that the correct translation of a target word is highly related to senses of translation words for surrounding clue words. The Korean-English dictionary and WordNet provide good information for mapping from the source language word to possible translation words and mapping from the translation word to word senses. The algorithm first identifies a set of possible translation words for the target word and surrounding clue words using a Korean-English bilingual dictionary.

Figure 1 shows part of the Korean-English bilingual dictionary. Such a bilingual dictionary generally classifies the meaning of an entry word into several senses and groups its translation words and near synonyms by each sense class.

/gisa¹/ 技師
an engineer; a technician
/gisa²/ 記事
an article; an account; news; a statement; a story; a report
/gisa³/ 騎士
a rider; a horseman; an equestrian
/nonmun¹/ 論文
a paper; a treatise; a dissertation; a thesis; "write a paper."

Fig. 1. A part of the Korean-English dictionary

In Korean-English dictionary, each Korean lexical entry word may have multiple senses and there are some corresponding translation words for each sense. In Figure 1, a Korean noun 'gisa' has three senses and has three representative translation words *engineer*, *article*, and *rider* with near synonyms *technician, account, news, statement, story, report, horseman* and *equestrian* according to each sense. In the case of Korean noun 'nonmun' entry, there is only one sense and has one representative translation word *paper* with near synonyms such as *treatise, dissertation,* and *thesis*.

Near synonyms[6] are words that have close senses with the representative translation word for each sense. In addition to sense ambiguity of source language word, the translation word may have multiple senses in WordNet. For example, the translation word *paper* that is corresponding equivalent for source word 'nonmun' has three different noun senses such as paper#n#1, paper#n#2, and paper#n#3 as described in section 2.

In order to reduce the weight of application of possibly unwanted senses for the noun translation word that may bring about incorrect translation word selection, our algorithm needs to decide which sense of the representative translation word is more appropriate for the source language word before we start to compute the score of semantic relatedness between combination pairs of possible senses. Let us suppose that the k-th clue word in a given source language sentence is t_k and the l-th translation of t_k is t_k^l. The weight of m-th sense t_k^{lm} for translation word t_k^l is computed as follows:

$$w(t_k^{lm}) = \frac{\sum_i \max_j sim(t_k^{lm}, NS_i^j(t_k^l))}{\sum_m \sum_i \max_j sim(t_k^{lm}, NS_i^j(t_k^l))}$$

The weight of sense t_k^{lm} is obtained by computing the semantic similarity between the possible senses of the representative translation word and near synonyms(NS) of t_k^l. To get the semantic similarity between two senses, we use the measure proposed by Jiang and Conrath which combines the information contents of each sense and their most specific subsumer that returns the largest set of commonalities between each sense[7]. For the word *paper* that is the translation of a source word 'nonmun', the sense paper#n#2 has higher weight than the sense paper#n#1, because the sense paper#n#2 is more semantically similar to near synonyms of translation word *paper* such as *treatise, dissertation,* and *thesis.*

After the weight of each sense is determined, our algorithm computes the score of semantic relatedness between combination pairs of possible senses. This algorithm selects the translation word of target word that has maximum relatedness using the following equation.

$$\arg \max_i \sum_k \max_{j,l,m} \; related \; (t_0^{ij}, t_k^{lm}) \bullet w(t_k^{lm})$$

This equation computes a relatedness score of each translation word t_0^i for a target word t_0. t_k^{lm} means m-th sense of translation word t_k^l of t_k that is a surrounding clue word.

Two senses are considered to be related semantically when they share a set of words that occur in their respective glosses. The counting of number of overlaps between just gloss words is not likely to find relatedness because they are too short to result in a reliable measure. However, if we consider the glosses and usage examples of all the senses that are connected directly and indirectly to a sense by extended relations, this becomes a larger set of words that can measure relatedness. Rather than simply considering the glosses of the surrounding words in the context, the concept hierarchy of WordNet is exploited to allow for glosses of word senses related to the context words to be compared.

WordNet is a broad coverage, machine readable lexical database widely used in natural language processing. The wide availability of WordNet has led to the development of a number of approaches to word sense disambiguation problem. Each sense of a word is mapped to a synset in WordNet and all synsets in WordNet are linked by a variety of semantic relations. In addition to glosses associated with each sense, WordNet provides many example usages associated with them that play a role of sense tagged training instances. These usage examples and glosses are not likely to be much help because they are short. However, the number of example usages and glosses grow larger by extending through the set of relations that WordNet provides.

In our experiments, we adopt the following extended relations that WordNet provides. Figure 2 shows the five extended relations between noun and verb we employ.

/* noun–verb relation */
syns-syns; syns-glos; syns-exam
glos-syns ; glos-glos; glos-exam
exam-syns; exam-glos; exam-exam

/* coordinate(noun)–verb relation */
syns(coor)-syns; syns(coor)-glos; syns(coor)-exam
glos(coor)-syns; glos(coor)-glos; glos(coor)-exam
exam(coor)-syns; exam(coor)-glos; exam(coor)-exam

/* noun-coordinate(verb) relation */
syns-syns(coor); glos-syns(coor); exam-syns(coor)
syns-glos(coor); glos-glos(coor); exam-glos(coor)
syns-exam(coor); glos-exam(coor); exam-exam(coor)

/* hyponyms(noun)–verb relation */
syns(hypo)-syns; syns(hypo)-glos; syns(hypo)-exam
glos(hypo)-syns; glos(hypo)-glos; glos(hypo)-exam
exam(hypo)-syns; exam(hypo)-glos; exam(hypo)-exam

/* noun–troponyms(verb) relation */
syns-syns(trop); glos-syns(trop); exam-syns(trop)
syns-glos(trop); glos-glos(trop); exam-glos(trop)
syns-exam(trop); glos-exam(trop); exam-exam(trop)

Fig. 2. Extended relations (syns : synsets, glos : definitions, exam : examples, coor : coordinate, hypo : hyponyms, trop : troponyms)

While Pedersen and Banerjee used the immediately surrounding context words, we choose the most relevant words that provide much more indicative clues for selecting correct translation word. The focus in much recent work is on local collocation knowledge including a variety of distance and syntactic relations. For the English tasks, that local collocation knowledge such as n-grams is expected to provide important evidences to resolve sense ambiguity because English is a fixed order language. However, Korean is a partially free order language and therefore the ordering information on surrounding words of the ambiguous word does not provide significantly meaning information for resolving sense ambiguity in Korean.

Korean has some particularities: plenty of inflectional verb endings, postpositions instead of preposition, and so on. The postpositions and verb endings represent syntactic relations such as predicate-arguments, modifier-modified relations. We deal three major predicate-arguments relations: verb-object, verb-locative and verb-instrument relation that construct complement-head structure. The postpositions attached to the noun are either 'ul'/'rul', 'ae', or 'ro'/'uro' that usually represent syntactic relations between the noun and the verb: object, location, and instrument respectively.

We focus the selection of translation word for Korean transitive verbs. Therefore we decided to adopt the three major predicate-argument relations such as noun-'ul'/'rul' (object) + verb, noun-'ae' (locative) + verb, and noun-'ro'/'uro' (instrument) + verb rather than immediate surrounding words to improve the performance of translation word selection.

In order to extract syntactic features, we need a robust syntactic parser. However, the accuracy performance of current parser is not high. Therefore we have taken a simple partial parser by using an only part of speech tagger without robust parsing to identify syntactic relations such as "the first noun with postposition 'ul'/'rul', 'ae', or 'ro'/'uro' to the left or right of target word in context". This provides a better approximation for syntactic relations than just requiring a limited distance between surrounding words in the context, while relying on the availability of part of speech tagger that is simpler and more available than robust syntactic parser. Sometimes it is hard to identify such syntactic relation in the case of embedded sentence. For example, a sentence "gang-i bumram-ha-nun gut-ul mak-da/*keep the river from overflowing*" has the first noun 'gut-ul'(ING) for a verb 'mak-da'. In this case, the algorithm extracts the nominal form 'bumram'/overflow of preceding verb 'bumram-ha'/overflow as a verb-object relation.

5   Experiments and Results

In order to evaluate our algorithm for ranking translation word selection, 1.4 million words Gemong Korean encyclopedia is used as a test data set. Our experiments are performed on ten Korean transitive verbs, 'mak-da', 'ssu-da', 'seu-da', 'jap-da', 'mandul-da', 'nanu-da', 'mut-da', 'bat-da', 'ut-da', and 'jit-da' that appear with high frequency and ambiguity in our experiment corpus.

This data set consists of 12,513 instances each of which contains a sentence with a target verb to be translated. In order to compare our result with the human created answer, human experts have annotated these instances manually with correct translation words in advance.

Table 2. Accuracy of translation word selection

Target Verbs	Instances	Senses	Accuracy(%)			
			Baseline	Lesk	P&B	RTW
'mak-da'	515	7	27	18	38	52
'ssu-da'	2084	9	21	15	41	64
'seu-da'	933	10	40	22	40	47
'jap-da'	560	8	32	20	37	46
'mandul-da'	3573	10	29	18	42	49
'nanu-da'	734	6	45	17	48	63
'mut-da'	585	7	35	18	25	47
'bat-da'	1722	19	38	21	35	49
'ut-da'	881	11	30	17	40	57
'jit-da'	926	13	28	15	36	46
Average	1251	10	33	18	38	52

We define accuracy performance for our evaluation task as the number of correct translations over the number of answers. The results of experiment are summarized in Table 2. The performance of our algorithm was compared with the baseline performance(Baseline) that is achieved by assigning all occurrences to the most frequent translation word. The experimental results show that the accuracy performance of our algorithm(RTW: Ranking Translation Word) performs better than the default baseline(Baseline), original Lesk algorithm(Lesk) and Pedersen and Banerjee's(P&B).

6 Conclusions

In this paper we presented an unsupervised method for ranking translation words based on a bilingual dictionary and WordNet that are easily obtainable knowledge sources. The translation words are selected by measuring semantic relatedness through the five extended relations between possible translations of target word and surrounding clue words in source language text. Considering all possible senses for each translation word introduces the application of unwanted senses in the view of source language word that may bring about an incorrect translation word selection. In order to avoid the application of unwanted senses, we first rank weight of possible word senses for each translation word by measuring semantic similarity in WordNet between the translation word and near synonyms that are described in a bilingual dictionary.

The evaluation suggests that our approach performs better than other approaches including the baseline performance. We report an average accuracy of 52% with ten Korean ambiguous verbs. While the results are generally lower than the supervised approaches that need much of human effort, these results are significant because our approach relies on only a bilingual dictionary and a target language dictionary, therefore it provides an alternative to the supervised approaches that rely on a large corpus of senses annotated data.

Acknowledgements

This work has been supported by grant number(R01-2003-000-10001-0) from the Basic Research Program of Korea Science and Engineering Foundations.

References

1. Banerjee, S. and Pedersen, T.: Extended Gloss Overlaps as a Measure of Semantic Relatedness, Proceedings of the Eighteenth International Joint Conference on Artificial Intelligence (2003) 805-810.
2. Brown, P., Cocke, J., Pietra, V., Peitra, S., Jelinek, F., Lafferty, J., Mercer, R. and Roosin, P.: A Statistical Approach to Machine Translation, Computational Linguistics, Vol. 16, No. 2 (1990) 79-85.
3. Copestake, A., Briscoe, T., Vossen, P., Ageno, A., Casteloon, I., Ribas, G., Rigau, G., Rodriguez, H., and Samiotou, A.: Acquisition of Lexical Translation Relations from MRDs, Machine Translation, Vol. 9, No. 3 (1995) 183-219.
4. Dagan, I. And Itai, A.: Word Sense Disambiguation Using a Second Language Monolingual Corpus, Computational Linguistics, Vol. 20, No. 4 (1994) 563-596.
5. Fellbaum, C. WordNet: An Electronic Lexical Database, MIT Press (1998).

6. Inkpen, D. and Hirst, G.: Automatic Sense Disambiguation of the Near-Synonyms in a Dictionary Entry, Proceedings, Fourth Conference on Intelligent Text Processing and Computational Linguistics (2003) 258-267.
7. Jiang, J. and Conrath, D.: Semantic Similarity based on Corpus Statistics and Lexicon Taxonomy, Proceedings on International Conference on Research in Computational Linguistics (1997) 19-33.
8. Klavans, J. and Tzoukermann, E.: Combining Corpus and Machine Readable Dictionary Data for Building Bilingual Lexicons, Machine Translation, Vol. 10, No. 3 (1996) 1-34.
9. Koehn, P. and Knight K.: Knowledge Sources for Word-Level Translation Models, Empirical Methods in Natural Language Processing Conference (2001) 27-35.
10. Lesk, M.: Automatic Sense Disambiguation Using Machine Readable Dictionaries: how to tell a pine code from an ice cream cone, Proceedings of the Fifth Annual International Conference on Systems Documentations (1986) 24-26.
11. Li, H. and Li, C.: Word Translation Disambiguation Using Bilingual Boostrapping, Computational Linguistics, Vol. 30, No. 1 (2004) 1-22.
12. Patwardhan, S. and Perdersen, T.: The cpan wordnet::similarity package, http://search.cpan.org/~sid/WordNet-Similarity-0.06/ (2005).

Neuro-fuzzy Learning for Automated Incident Detection

M. Viswanathan, S.H. Lee, and Y.K. Yang

College of Software, Kyungwon University,
Bokjeong-Dong, Sujung-Gu, Seongnam-Si,
Kyunggi-Do, South Korea 461-701
{murli, ykyang}@kyungwon.ac.kr

Abstract. Traffic incidents such as vehicle accidents, weather and construction works are a major cause of congestion. Incident detection is thus an important function in freeway and arterial traffic management systems. Most of the large scale and operational incident detection systems make use of data collected from inductive loop detectors. Several new approaches, such as probe vehicles and video image processing tools, have recently been proposed and demonstrated. This research aims at model development for automatic incident detection and travel time estimation employing neuro-fuzzy techniques. As a first step, in this paper we develop an initial model for incident detection using a standard neuro-fuzzy algorithm. In subsequent development we propose a model where the fuzzy rules are themselves extracted from the data using an associative data mining algorithm. The results of the initial experiments suggest that the proposed model has plausible incident detection rates and low false alarm rates. The test results also suggest that the proposed model enhances accuracy of incident detection in an arterial road and can be expected to contribute to formal traffic policy.

Keywords: Neuro-Fuzzy Learning; Automated Incident Detection; Intelligent Traveler Systems; Association Rule Mining.

1 Introduction

Incidents are non-recurring events such as accidents, disabled vehicles, spilled loads, temporary maintenance and construction activities, signal and detector malfunctions, and other special and unusual events that disrupt the normal flow of traffic and cause motorist delay. Incident detection is an important function in freeway and arterial traffic management systems. Issues of traffic policy have also recently changed from traffic management to offer advanced information services to users. Users want to receive correct information about status of road traffic until their destinations. For the reasons mentioned above, numerous investigations are going into research on travel time estimation, incident detection and data fusion. Among these methods, we study models about incident detection.

In the cases where the measured data from traffic observations is applied directly for incident detection, the incident detection contains many false alarms. This is because there are possibilities that the data has noise in itself, due sometimes to traffic detector breakdowns. Furthermore another issue is that the detector itself is measuring different types of data and there can be data from many sources. Therefore, measured

M. Ali and R. Dapoigny (Eds.): IEA/AIE 2006, LNAI 4031, pp. 889 – 897, 2006.

data must go through a data fusion process which aims to merge information from different sources and reduces false alarms. This research uses data of spot speed where outliers of measurement are removed by data fusion [1].

This research is develops an initial model for incident detection using the using the ANFIS (adaptive-network-based fuzzy inference system) neuro-fuzzy algorithm. Fuzzy rules incorporated into the ANFIS algorithm are extracted by a careful analysis of the traffic data which consist of vehicle speed measurements. A futuristic model for the automatic extraction of fuzzy rules is proposed. From experimental analysis we can observe high incident detection rates and low false alarm rates for the current system.

2 Background

The plethora of incident algorithms can be grouped as algorithms based on pattern recognition and statistical methods, algorithms using traffic models and theory, and other hybrid state of the art incident detection methods based on neural networks and fuzzy methods. Among the well-known pattern recognition algorithms are the California algorithm [11, 14, 15] that detected incidents using occupancy rate at specified times, APID algorithm [12, 13, 14, 15] that compares occupancy between two detector areas, and wave analysis, PATREG, and the Monica algorithm. Statistical algorithms include SND and Bayesian algorithms [13, 14] that use probability of incident occurrence through blocked crossroads of downstream traffic. Algorithms using traffic model and theory are Dynamic Algorithms that assumed sudden change in the freeway system to follow predictable patterns due to the integrated relation between speed-density and traffic-density in detection analysis. Additionally based on Catastrophe Theory, the (modified) McMaster Algorithm uses traffic theory as explanation of "Jump" of speed in the operation of freeway that has little change of occupancy. The final group of hybrid algorithms includes Fuzzy Set algorithms, Neural Network Algorithms, Probabilistic Neural Network and Automatic Vehicle Identification Systems [11, 14].

Fuzzy algorithms use reliability and unreliability of deduction as a guiding principle. When the data has unreliability and noise as in the case of the choice of incident decision, fuzzy algorithms would find the most possible decision within boundaries as defined by the fuzzy membership function. Fuzzy membership, differing from 'crisp' 0 and 1 decisions, represents a range of occurrence or likelihood in respect of incidents [2]. Fuzzy rules and fuzzy sets regarding output value of the fuzzy controller are dependent and complement. Fuzzy if-then rules or fuzzy conditional statements are expressions of the form IF A THEN B, where A and B are labels of fuzzy sets characterized by appropriate membership functions [6].

3 Adaptive-Network-Based Fuzzy Inference System

ANFIS (Adaptive-Network-Based Fuzzy Inference System) selects membership function parameters automatically and is thus an adapted fuzzy inference method to data modeling. Given an input/output data set, it constructs a fuzzy inference system that

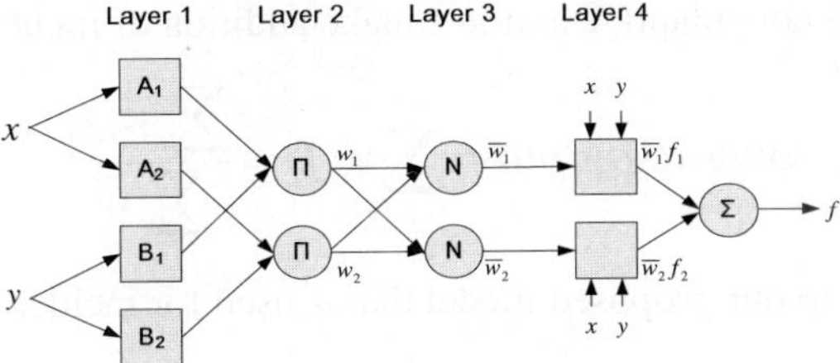

Fig. 1. Structure of Basic ANFIS

controls membership function parameters using back-propagation or combination of least square estimation and the back-propagation algorithm.

In the architectural framework, we assume that there are the two inputs x and y and one output z. We use occupancy and spot speed as input data in this proposed model. ANFIS is an adaptive network which works like the adaptive network simulator of Takagi-Sugeno's fuzzy if-then rules. This adaptive network has a predefined adaptive network topology. The basic topology description is as follows:

layer 1: each node of this layer is adaptive and it's function is:

$$O_i^1 = \mu A_i(x) \tag{1}$$

Where x is input and O is output which represents membership function of input to level linguistic variable. Usually bell membership function is used:

$$\mu A_i(x) = \cfrac{1}{1 + \left[\left(\dfrac{x - c_i}{a_i} \right)^2 \right]^{b_i}} \tag{2}$$

Where ai, bi and ci are parameters set and these are premise parameters.

layer 2: nodes in this layer are not adaptive. They realize only simple multiplication signal of inputs. These outputs represent the firing strength of a rule.

$$w_i = \mu A_i(x) \times \mu B_i(y), \ i = 1, 2 \tag{3}$$

layer 3: nodes in this layer are not adaptive and they calculate a ratio of rule strengths as follows:

$$\overline{w}_i = \frac{w_i}{w_1 + w_2}, \ i = 1, 2 \tag{4}$$

layer 4: nodes in this layer are adaptive and so the transfer function will be as follows:

$$O_i^4 = w_i f_i = wi(p_i x + q_i y + r_i) \tag{5}$$

where pi, qi and ri are consequent parameters.

layer 5: nodes are non-adaptive and just make addition of inputs as follows:

$$O_1^5 = overall\ output = \sum_i w_i f_i = \frac{\sum_i w_i f_i}{\sum_i w_i} \tag{6}$$

We apply ANFIS to our proposed model that is used for incident detection.

4 Generating Fuzzy Classification Rules

As described in the above section the ANFIS system is based on neuro-fuzzy principles. The application of fuzzy if-then rules also improves the interpretability of the results and provides more insight into the classifier structure and decision making process. Therefore we focus on the extraction of fuzzy rule-based classifiers from labeled data describing traffic volumes and other information.

In figure 2 can observe an example of fuzzy membership functions automatically generated by the ANFIS system. However the accuracy of the fuzzy rules produced by this method is low. Therefore, we suggest using an iterative approach for developing fuzzy classifiers as described in [18]. The initial model is derived from the data and subsequently, feature selection and rule-base simplification are applied to reduce the model, while a genetic algorithm is used for parameter optimization.

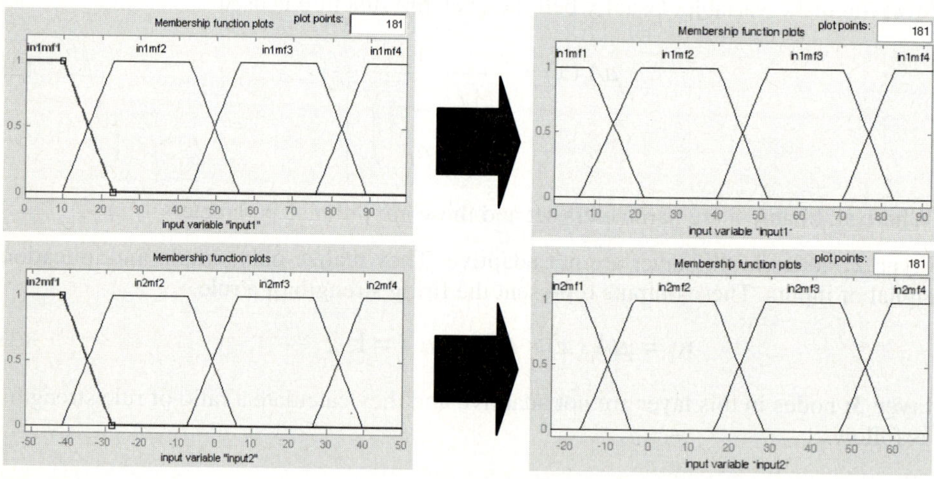

Fig. 2. Fuzzy Rules Generated by ANFIS

It is shown in [18] that compact, accurate and interpretable fuzzy rule-based classifiers can be obtained from labeled observation data in an iterative approach. First, an initial model is derived from the observation data. Secondly, feature selection and rule-base simplification methods are applied to reduce the initial model. Finally, a real-coded genetic algorithm (GA) is applied to optimize the models parameters in order to improve the classification accuracy. The GA can also be applied in a loop together with rule-base simplification. In this case, the GA uses a multi-criterion objective to search not only for model accuracy but also for model redundancy. This redundancy is then exploited to reduce and simplify the rule base. Finally, the GA is applied with a multi-criterion function where the redundancy is suppressed in order to make the rules more distinguishable while preserving the accuracy. The result is a compact fuzzy rule base of low complexity with high classification accuracy.

5   Neuro-fuzzy Algorithm for Incident Detection

The aim of this paper is to adapt the ANFIS algorithm to detect incidents in a scenario where the available input data consists of speed measurements based on moving probe vehicles. Therefore in our case we use ANFIS as the neuro-fuzzy algorithm and input data based on vehicle speed. The speed data is pre-processed to obtain the original speed data and the increase and decrease in acceleration that is calculated through comparison of current speed and past speed.

After calculating the speed rate (increase or decrease in speed) and spot speed, we used this data as inputs and detect incidents through ANFIS using filtered data. Figure 3 demonstrates this process from data collection to incident detection. Fuzzy rules are constructed as follow:

IF AVGSPD is Small and PDSPD is Very SMALL then ouput is Normal

IF AVGSPD is Small and PDSPD is SMALL then ouput is Normal

......

IF AVGSPD is Very Large and PDSPD is Large then ouput is Normal

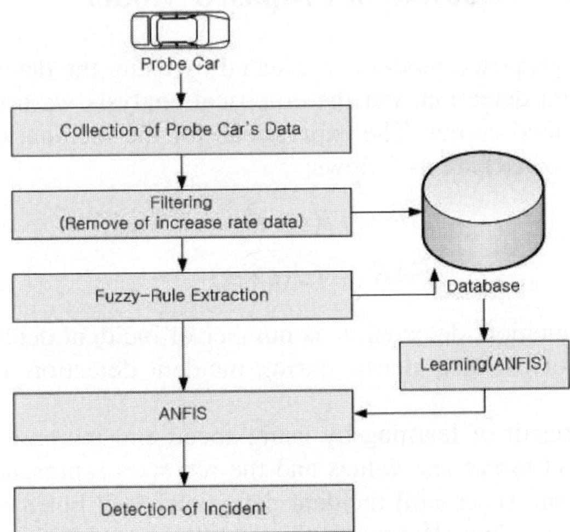

Fig. 3. Architecture of Incident Detection System

First, the two input values which include the rate of change of current speed and average speed in each observation are given to the system. For each value the membership degree is calculated by the fuzzy membership function and these values are passed into the neural network according to the fuzzy rules. The neural network multiply weights to value of all rules and then the resulting values after addition are sent to the output layer. These values undergo de-fuzzification by the fuzzy membership function and the final output value is acquired. The structure of the adapted ANFIS algorithm is shown in figure 4.

Once the error rate of the model reaches 0.01 or the learning has gone through 1350 epochs, the process is terminated.

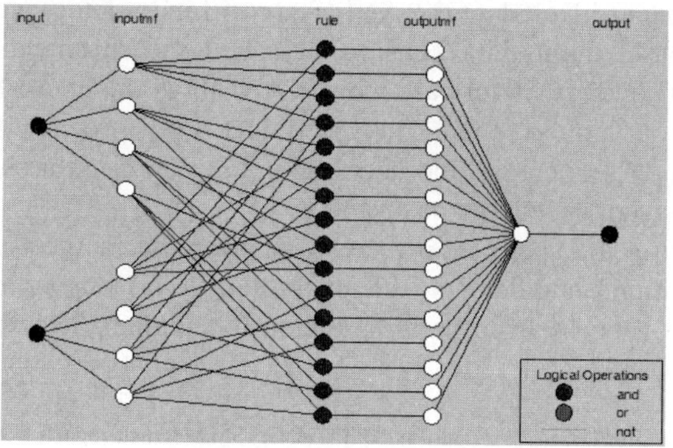

Fig. 4. Structure of ANFIS

6   Performance Evaluation of Proposed Model

Performance of the proposed model is evaluated by using the detection rate and false alarm rate of incident detection. For the empirical analysis we use the spot speed as input data as mentioned earlier. The expressions for the incident detection rate (DR) and false alarm rate (FAR) are as follows:

$$DR = t/(t+t')$$
$$FAR = f/(t \times s)$$

$$(7)$$

t is number of real incident detected, t' is number of incident detection that were undetected, f is number of false alarms during incident detection and s is number of spots.

Figure 5 shows result of learning by using speed and increase and decrease rate. Blue circles represent target test values and the red stars represent the original input data. Figure 5 presents successful incident detection in all but 8 cases when using a data set of 1096 input values. We repeat this experiment with similarly-sized datasets containing traffic speed information for 30 days. Based on the empirical analysis the overall average detection rate is found to be 92.72% and the false alarm rate is approximately 11.54%.

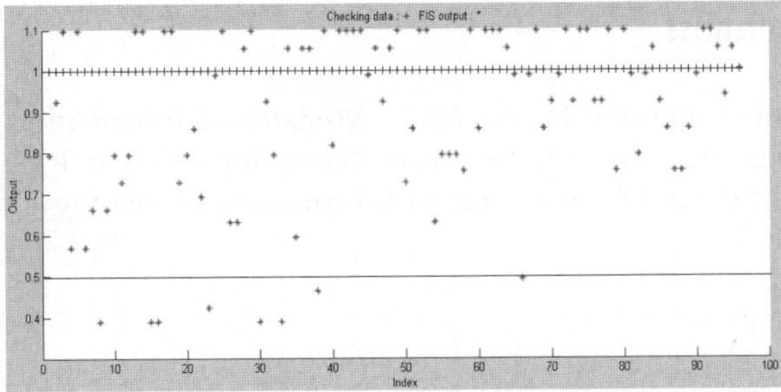

Fig. 5. Result of Learning

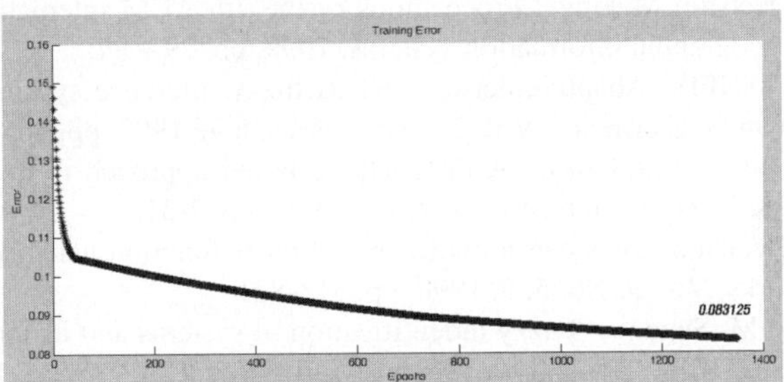

Fig. 6. Error rate in ANFIS

The error is high initially and decreases according to learning volume and as seen from figure 6 is reduced gradually after many learning epochs. It is important to remember that the test data is based on a single information source from GPS-based probe vehicles and therefore it would be optimal to fuse this data with incident information from other sources like fixed detectors. This will be one of our future enhancements to this research work.

7 Summary

This research aims to developed and evaluate a model for incident detection by adapting a neuro-fuzzy algorithm. The available inputs to this system was speed data obtained from a probe car having GPS devices and the change in speed that was calculated through a comparison of current and old data and spot speed. These inputs were given to the ANFIS algorithm which detected the occurrence of an incident. We also propose a method of automatic extraction of fuzzy rules.

As result of performance testing, the detection rate DR of this model was over 92.72% and false alarm rate FAR was around 11.54%. These results suggest that the model is robust and performs well. This model showed high error rate in the case of irregular patterns of input data but low error rate in the case of regular patterns of input data. In the future, we would like enhance the inner structure of the ANFIS algorithm using fuzzy membership functions extracted automatically from the data and include other input measurements in the analysis of traffic flow patterns.

Acknowledgement

This research was supported by the MIC (Ministry of Information and Communication), Korea, under the ITRC (Information Technology Research Center) support program supervised by the IITA (Institute of Information Technology Assessment).

References

1. Keechoo Choi, YounShik Chung, "A Data Fusion Algorithm For Estimating Link Travel Time", Intelligent Transportation Systems Journal, Vol. 7, No. 3-4, 2002, pp. 235 - 260.
2. Ding Zheng, Wolfgang Kainz, "Fuzzy Rule Extraction from GIS Data with a Neural Fuzzy System for Decision Making", Proceedings of the 7th ACM international symposium on Advances in geographic information systems, 1999, pp. 79 – 84.
3. Roger Jang, "ANFIS: Adaptive-network-based fuzzy inference systems", IEEE Trans. on System, Man and Cybernetics, Vol. 23, No. 3, May/June 1993, pp. 665-685.
4. M. Sugeno and T. Yasukawa, "A Fuzzy logic based approach to qualitative modeling," IEEE Trans. on Fuzzy System, Vol. 1, No. 1, 1993, pp. 7-31.
5. M. Kubat, "Decision trees can initialize radial basis function networks," IEEE Trans. on Neural Networks, Vol. 9, No. 5, 5, 1998, pp. 813-821.
6. T. Takagi and M. Sugeno, "Fuzzy indentification of systems and its applications to modeling and control," IEEE Trans. Syst., Man, Cybern., Vol. 15, 1985, pp. 116-132.
7. H. Takagi and I. Hayashi, "NN-driven Fuzzy Reasoning," Int. J. of Approximate Reasoning, Vol. 5, No. 3, 1991, pp. 191-212.
8. Takeshi Yamakawa, " A Neo Fuzzy Neuron and Its Applications to System Identification and Prediction of the System Behavior," Proceeding of the 2nd International Conference on Fuzzy logic & Neural Networks, 1992, pp.477-483.
9. L. A. Zadeh, "Fuzzy Logic", IEEE Computer Society, Vol. 21, 1988, pp. 83-93.
10. Forbes, G. J., "Identifying Incident Congestion", ITE Journal, Vol. 62, No. 6, 1992, pp. 17-22.
11. Dipti Srinivasan, Ruey Long Cheu, Young Peng Poh and Albert Kim Chwee Ng, "Development of an intelligent technique for traffic network incident detection", Engineering Applications of Artificial Intelligence, Vol. 13, Issue 3, 1 June 2000, pp. 311-322.
12. Dipti Srinivasan, Xin Jin and Ruey Long Cheu, "Adaptive neural network models for automatic incident detection on freeways", Neurocomputing, Vol. 64, March 2005, pp. 473-496.
13. N. E. Thomas, "Multi-state and multi-sensor incident detection systems for arterial streets", Transportation Research Part C: Emerging Technologies, Vol. 6, Issues 5-6, 10 December 1998, pp. 337-357.
14. Jiuh-Biing Sheu, "A fuzzy clustering-based approach to automatic freeway incident detection and characterization", Fuzzy Sets and Systems, Vol. 128, Issue 3, 16 June 2002, pp. 377-388.
15. Jiuh-Biing Sheu, "A sequential detection approach to real-time freeway incident detection and characterization", European Journal of Operational Research, Vol. 157, Issue 2, 1 September 2004, pp. 471-485.Kwon, S.W., Lee, K.J. and Vizzini, A.J., "Modeling of Fire-Exposed Composite Structures", *Proceedings of 18th Annual Technical Conference of the American Society for Composites*, Gainesville, Florida, October 2003.

16. Lee, K. and Cho, C., "A Geometrically Nonlinear Nine-Node Solid Shell Element Formulation with Reduced Sensitivity to Mesh Distortion", *Computer Modeling in Engineering and Sciences*, Vol.3, no.3, pp.339-350, 2002.
17. Sun, C.T., *Mechanics of Aircraft Structures,* John Wiley & Sons, Inc, 1988.
18. Johannes A. Roubos, Magne Setnes and Janos Abonyi, Learning fuzzy classification rules from labeled data, Information Sciences, Volume 150, Issues 1-2, March 2003, Pages 77-93.

Intelligent GIS: Automatic Generation of Qualitative Spatial Information

Jimmy A. Lee and Jane Brennan

University of Technology, Sydney, FIT, P.O. Box 123, Broadway NSW 2007, Australia
`janeb@it.uts.edu.au`

Abstract. This paper reports on an extension to Geographic Information Systems (GIS) that can intelligently analyse and record qualitative information of the surrounding area when adding a feature to a map. This recorded qualitative spatial information can be utilised to perform queries such as path generation using landmarks. Although, there is a lot of research on qualitative spatial reasoning, none of the currently available GIS do actually incorporate this kind of functionality. There have been systems developed that do have functions for adding new features, or generating paths; however they do not generally analyse and record, or use, qualitative information. We have implemented a prototype illustrating our approach.

Keywords: Intelligent Systems, Spatial Reasoning, Knowledge Representation, GIS.

1 Introduction

Most Geographic Information System (GIS) computations are quantitative, relying on visualisation tools and user interaction to provide the qualitative insights that users need. Although quantitative representations do allow powerful and efficient calculations, they fall short when users lack information about for example the exact positioning or the geometry of the features involved. It has been recognised that a quantitative approach is an inappropriate representation of human cognition and spatial reasoning (e.g. [7]). Most human reasoning about physical space appears to use a qualitative interpretation of that space. Therefore, purely quantitative methods are inadequate and qualitative methods are essential to effectively represent spatial information.

In recent years, there have been various proposals for spatial descriptions, which are qualitative rather than quantitative to overcome the problem of imprecise spatial information (see [3] for an overview). However, practical applications applying the results of these research efforts are rare. This paper reports on the development of an extension to a GIS. We examined several aspects of GIS functionality in terms of adding qualitative reasoning capabilities to these systems, and included qualitative feature adding and path generation to our GIS extension. When a new feature is added to the map, the system will automatically analyse and record the qualitative information of its surrounding area. This recorded qualitative spatial information will be utilised to perform intelligent queries such as path generation using landmarks. Although, there is a lot of research on qualitative spatial reasoning (QSR), none of the currently

M. Ali and R. Dapoigny (Eds.): IEA/AIE 2006, LNAI 4031, pp. 898–907, 2006.

available GIS do actually incorporate this. There have been systems developed that do have functions for adding new features, or generating paths; however they do not generally analyse and record, or use, qualitative data/information.

A system that did generate qualitative path descriptions is the GRAAD system by Moulin and Kettani [9]. It provides an integrated logical and analogical framework for reasoning about time and space, while generating and describing the paths of a virtual pedestrian in a virtual environment. The analogical framework based on the notion of spatial conceptual map (SCM) specifies a spatial environment; and the logical framework based on a possible worlds approach carries out temporal reasoning and generates plans that are used to compute the virtual pedestrian's displacements in the SCM. It also generates natural language descriptions of the paths. In contrast, our system uses "real world" GIS data and also allows for adding features with qualitative spatial information inferred by the system.

2   Knowledge Representation in GIS

Data in GIS is generally represented in raster or vector format. These files are usually stored in a database together with associated information in the database table. Data in the table can be categorised into two types: quantitative information such as "20" or "40.5" and qualitative information such as "front" or "back". Users can query this information to retrieve particular details such as "which school is on the left of this traffic light". Our extension to GIS allows for qualitative inferences for added features and a qualitative path generation.

Many of the existing GIS do have functions to add features and some also allow for path generation. We reviewed several GIS and found that while all of them had functions to add features, none of them incorporate an intelligent agent to automatically record qualitative information of the surrounding area into the database table. Users would therefore have to enter this information manually. Some systems such as OpenMap® and GRASS® do not even have database tables as they use the Java method to store data. The MapObject® extension of the ArcGIS® package does have a path finding function using shortest path methods. None of the other systems have path generation available. In TakukGIS® and AccuGlobe®, data can also be stored in its GIS database and represented in a database table. There are create/edit feature functions.

2.1 Qualitative Spatial Reasoning in GIS

Research in QSR is motivated by a wide variety of possible application areas such as GIS [5], robotic navigation [8], spatial propositional semantics of natural languages [1, 10], engineering design such as qualitative kinematics [6] and many others. As Cohn [2] points out: *"The principal goal of qualitative reasoning is to represent not only our everyday commonsense knowledge about the physical world, but also the underlying abstractions used by engineers and scientists when they create quantitative models."(p 323)* However, these findings are rarely used in practical applications. The extension we are bringing forward in this paper is, to our knowledge, the first one to actually add a functionality to a GIS that enables the addition of new features coupled with the inference of qualitative spatial information about the surrounding area.

2.2 AccuGlobe®

AccuGlobe® [4] is an ideal GIS software package for prototype implementation, as it is the only user-friendly free GIS software that has create/edit feature functions. The software includes functionality such as zooming, panning, measuring, selecting feature, drawing objects, etc. Information, either quantitative or qualitative, will be stored in a database table. However, when new features are added to the map, the system will not automatically analyse and generate the feature's relation to other objects in the map. Instead, the user has to manually enter the information into the database table.

3 Integrating Qualitative Aspects into GIS

We developed a prototype that integrates qualitative aspects into an existing GIS by allowing features to be added qualitatively. In addition, the prototype automatically analyses, and records qualitative information of the surrounding area. We also developed a road map representation that supports qualitative spatial reasoning based on landmarks, thereby providing an effective tool for path generation.

We used PERL to implement our prototype. AccuGlobe® provides a functionality to export the feature attributes recorded in the shape file to a working directory, and even convert it to an easily readable and editable text file format. The prototype can perform any necessary action to the exported text files, instead of working directly on the shape files. AccuGlobe® will automatically convert the text file to a shape file during the import process. Figure 1 on the previous page shows the framework we used for the prototype.

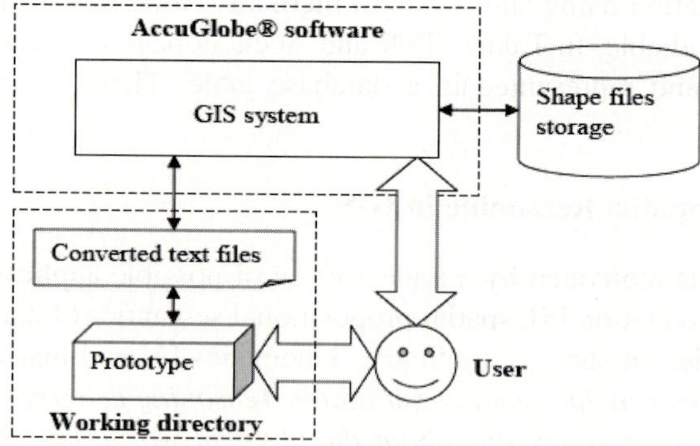

Fig. 1. Integrative framework

3.1 Qualitative Database Table Design

Figure 2 shows a simple example of a database table as used in the shape files, illustrating feature entities and attributes.

The words "Feature", "Type", and "Streetname" in the top row in bold are the feature entities. The words at the bottom row "A", "House", and "Market St" are the feature attributes.

Feature	Type	Streetname
A	House	Market St

Fig. 2. Database table example

3.2 Road Segment Layout

An appropriate road segment layout is very important as the path-finding algorithm generates its way through these road segments. After some trials and testing, we have come up with an easy and effective way to organise these segments. This layout also allows the inference of relative direction relations both when adding features to the map and when generating a path. Roads are generally already divided into segments in GIS data. However, we found it effective to use road intersections as segment dividers. In Figure 3a, there is only one road with no intersection, so there will be only one road segment, which will receive the unique segment id "0". In Figure 3b, there is an intersection between the vertical road and the horizontal road. Therefore the horizontal road will be divided into two different road segments with the ids "0" and "0.1". The vertical road also needs a separate id since it is also a road segment; its id is "1". The layout displayed in Figure 3c follows the same logic.

There is a sequence and meaning for each segment id in order for the path-finding algorithm to work, and to support the inference of qualitative spatial direction relations. Each road segment is either vertical or horizontal. Moreover, all vertical road segments will have segment ids in odd numbers (*before the decimal point*) and all horizontal road segments will have segment ids in even numbers (*before the decimal point*). The numbering always starts at the left or the top for horizontal or vertical road segments respectively. The value before the decimal point is like the Y-axis in a graph having the smallest value at the top and the largest value at the bottom. The value after the decimal point is like the X-axis, with the smallest value on the left and the largest value on the right. Figure 4 shows this pattern clearly by grouping the segments accordingly. This pattern will allow the path-finding algorithm, which will be discussed in sub-section 3.4, to determine which direction to take in order to reach the destination. Any road network can be transformed into this layout because the layout does not consider distances. In practical terms, the road segment layout could be another map layer.

The sample data used for the prototype implementation includes mainly buildings, referred to as address features. In order to fully utilise the road segment layout, address features are issued with "house ids" that start with the value of the segment id on which they are located. Figure 5 illustrates the procedure of assigning house ids.

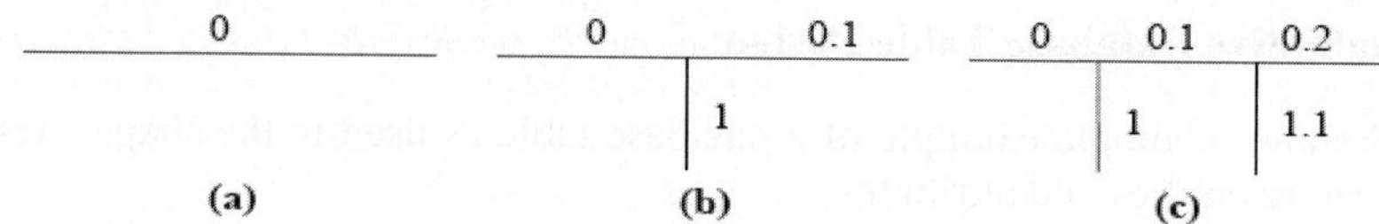

Fig. 3. Division of road segments

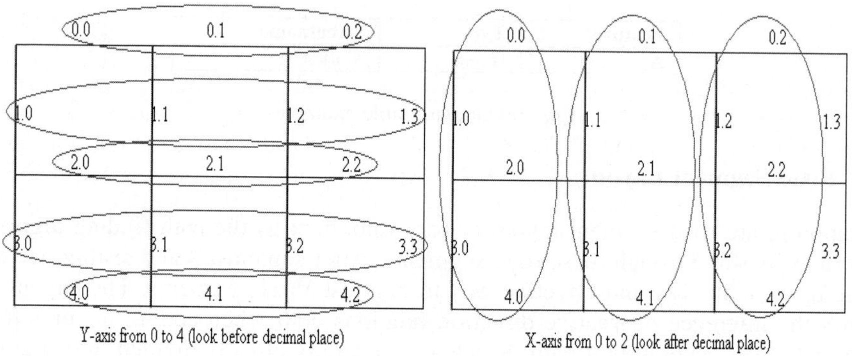

Fig. 4. X and Y-axis pattern in the proposed road segment layout

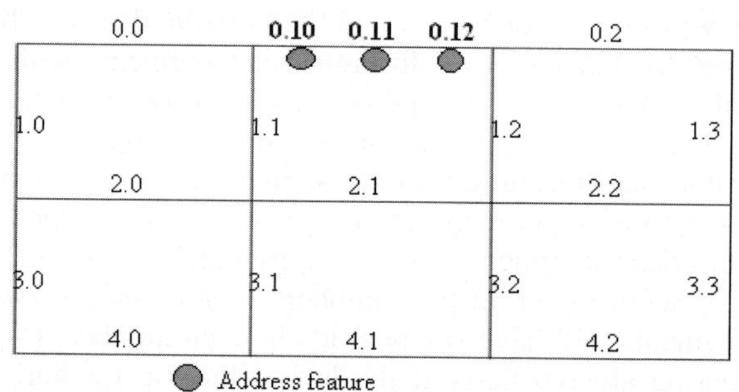

Fig. 5. Address features added to road segment

Suppose that we want to add three address features on a horizontal road segment with segment id "0.1". The left most address feature that is located on this particular road segment will have the house id "0.10". The second left most address feature on the same road segment will have the house id "0.11", and the third left most address feature will have the house id "0.12". They are all preceded by "0.1" to indicate their road segment location. Figure 5 illustrates this clearly, the three address features are added onto the road segment with segment id "0.1". If a new address feature was added between two existing address features such as "0.10" and "0.11", the new house id would be chosen between "0.10" and "0.11", e.g. "0.101".

3.3   Adding Features by Storing and Inferring Qualitative Spatial Relations

We modified the attribute tables of an existing data set in order to accommodate the storage of qualitative relations that can either be entered or inferred. In addition to relative direction relations such as left and right, we also included a small subset of topological relations. In order to resolve any reference frame issues, we presume a bird's eye view. For an address feature on a horizontal path, we will go from left to right, which means the right is always the front and the left is the back. For an address feature on a vertical path, we will go from top to bottom, which means the bottom is always the front and the top is the back.

Figure 6 shows an example of a modified attribute table. If we need to record the qualitative relations of "Feature A" (house id "2.11") with the features of its surrounding area; we have to create new entities for these qualitative relations in the attribute table. With this recorded, qualitative information of the feature's location in relation to other objects can easily be accessed by looking up the attribute table.

The entities "Front", "Back", "Left", "Right", "LeftFrBack", and "RightFrBack" are added to the attribute table, as displayed in Figure 6. We can see that the entity "Right" has a nil attribute value. This is because by turning right at Feature A, there is no feature that can be reached; this is represented by a "nil" in the attribute table.

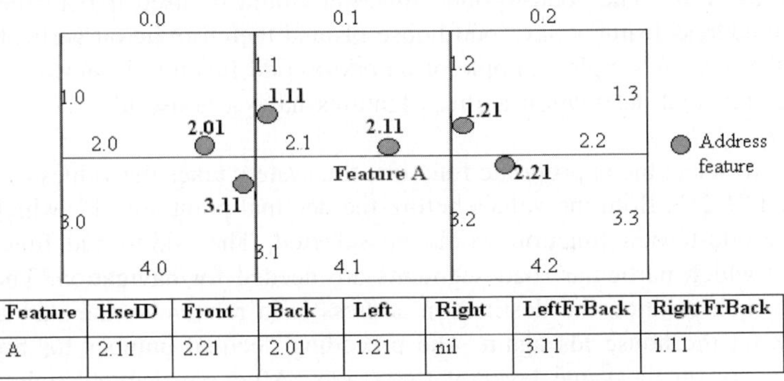

Feature	HseID	Front	Back	Left	Right	LeftFrBack	RightFrBack
A	2.11	2.21	2.01	1.21	nil	3.11	1.11

Fig. 6. Attribute table with added qualitative relations' entities

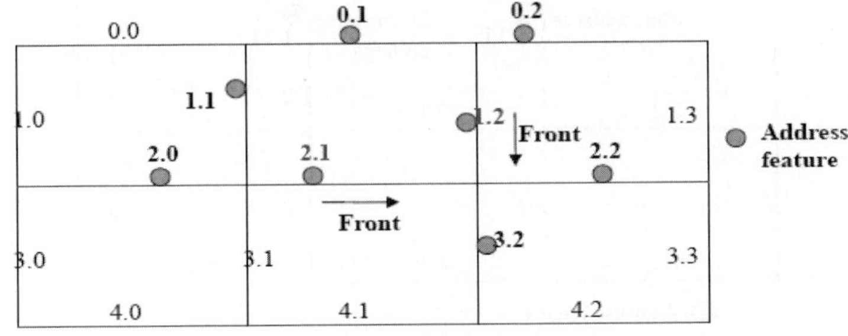

Fig. 7. Qualitative relations of features

Figure 7 illustrates some address features laying on both the vertical path and horizontal path. House id "2.1" is located on a horizontal path and house id "1.2" on a vertical path. The attributes of their qualitative relations with the surrounding features, which can be extracted from the database table, are summarised below Figure 7. If the user goes the other way around, from bottom to top, or right to left, the relations will automatically be transformed (*e.g., the front becomes the back, etc.*) .

Horizontal path (house id "2.1")		**Vertical path (house id "1.2")**	
Front	house id "2.2"	**Front**	house id "3.2"
Back	house id "2.0"	**Back**	Nil
Left	house id "1.2"	**Left**	house id "2.2"
Right	house id "3.2"	**Right**	house id "2.1"
Left from back	Nil	**Left from back**	house id "0.1"
Right from back	house id "1.1"	**Right from back**	house id "0.2"

3.4 Path Finding Algorithm

This section explores the simple path-finding algorithm we developed. Due to our road segmentation into vertical or horizontal segments, we can subset our path-finding algorithm into four functions: "odd-to-odd", "odd-to-even", "even-to-odd" and "even-to-even". The "odd-to-odd" function would be used if both the start and destination address features have odd house ids and therefore lie on vertical road segments in the map. A simple example of an odd-to-odd function is shown in Figure 8, where the start and destination address features have a house id "1.11" and "1.21" respectively.

In order to select the appropriate function, the system takes the values of house ids, "1.11", and "1.21". Both the values before the decimal point are "1", which are odd. Hence, the odd-to-odd function would be selected. The odd-to-odd function itself determines which particular road segments are needed for navigation. The function specifies which position the destination address is in relative to the start address. It will check on the house ids again. The preceding decimal number for both is "1"; hence they lay on the same level of the y-axis. After the decimal point, the start

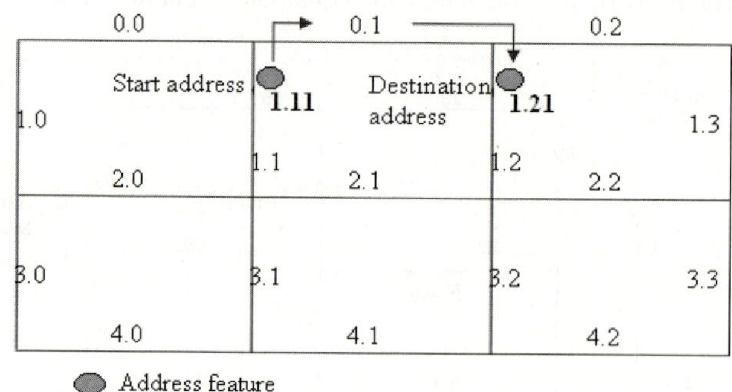

Fig. 8. Odd-to-odd function example

address has a value of "11" and the destination address has a value of "21". The destination address's value is larger than the start address's value on the x-axis; the destination address is therefore on the right of the start address. The results in a path that goes straight to the top, turns right at the next available turn off, then continues to go straight until it finds the right turn with segment id "1.2", along which it can locate the feature address with house id "1.21".

The other functions (e.g. *odd-to-even algorithm*) have the same underlying logic. Mainly they check on the values before and after the decimal points to determine into which direction the path should be generated.

4 Prototype Evaluations

For the software evaluation, we used a photographic image [4] that consists of several layers for different feature types each such as traffic lights, stop signs etc. We have successfully added features to the map qualitatively using topological relations descriptions. The prototype automatically generates and records the feature id, street id, street name, and the qualitative relations with the surrounding area.

4.1 Experimental Details

We tested our GIS extension against several data entries. Once the data was added, we verified information in the database tables for inferred qualitative information. We did this for three different data entry types, namely for the quantitative, simple qualitative and qualitative on different streets addition of features to the map; and subsequently uploaded the newly inferred information into the image map.

The following is an example of a simple qualitative addition of a new feature. When we add an address feature between No.3 and No.4 of Water Street; any further information required by the attribute table is automatically inferred by the system. Figure 9 shows the newly added feature with the reference addresses entered by the user and all the other attributes inferred by the system. The figure also shows the new feature being uploaded into the map.

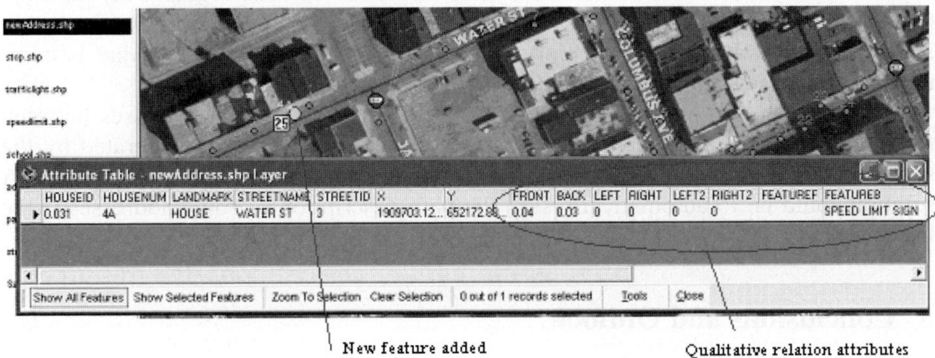

Fig. 9. Added feature to map and feature attributes to database table

We further evaluated the usefulness of our data representation by utilising this qualitative information for path description generation using direction relations and landmarks, as shown in Figure 10. This gave us an additional level of evaluation when doing this with newly added features. Without this qualitative information being recorded, it is not possible to effectively generate a path description as there is no sufficient information about the surrounding area of each feature.

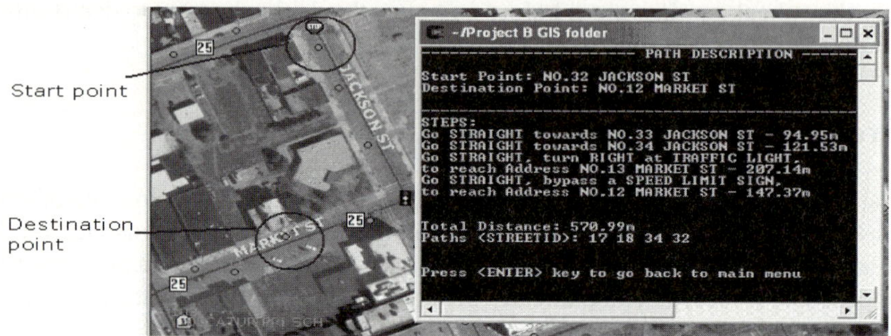

Fig. 10. Path description

4.2   Limitations of the System

Despite its usefulness, our system does also have limitations that need to be discussed. As explained in Section 3.3, for an address feature on a horizontal path, we will go from left to right, which means the right is always the front and the left is the back. For an address feature on a vertical path, we will go from top to bottom, which means the bottom is always the front and the top is the back. There may be a problem if there are two address features lying side by side, one across the street of the other. There is no front, back, left or right relation in this case. Another limitation is the quantitative distance which is currently only used as part of the path generation output, but not during the reasoning process. If we were to use quantitative distance for the path generation, we were again to face problems when data is imprecise.

While every road network can be transformed into our road segment layout theoretically, our system does not yet provide the functionality for such a transformation and relies on manual transformation from existing road network into what is commonly known as "Manhattan Structure".

For the generation of path descriptions, if there is a cluster of addresses between two locations (start and destination locations); the path description generated by the system could be too long to be useful, as every single address would be considered. A solution could be to automatically skip the path description of some addresses if the list is too long.

5   Conclusions and Outlook

In this paper we discussed the possibility of an extension to Geographic Information Systems (GIS) that can intelligently analyse and record qualitative information of the surrounding area when adding a feature to a map. We then presented a prototype implementation of such a system based on a road segment layout and path finding algorithm that not only support spatial reasoning but also allow the automatic inference and storage of qualitative spatial relations when new features are added to a map. This recorded qualitative spatial information can be utilised to perform queries such as path generation using landmarks, this particular function was also implemented in our prototype. An evaluation of the system confirmed the well known assumption that purely quantitative methods are inadequate and qualitative methods are essential to effectively represent spatial information.

Our current prototype is text based, but we are planning a graphical interface to allow user input for feature addition. The path generation still needs to be optimised as it is not necessarily the shortest path. This is a general problem that has received a lot of attention in GIS research.

References

1. Aurnague, M., Vieu, L.: A three-level approach to the semantics of space. C.Zelinsky-Wibbelt (ed.) The semantics of prepositions – from mental processing to natural language processing. Mouton de Gruyter. Berlin (1993)
2. Cohn, A.: The Challenge of Qualitative Spatial Reasoning. ACM Computing Surveys. Vol 27. No.3. (1995) 323-324, UK
3. Cohn A.G., Hazarika S.M.: Qualitative Spatial Representation and Reasoning: An Overview. Fundamenta Informaticae, volume 46, No.1-2, (2001), 2-32
4. DDTI (Digital Data Technologies, Inc.) (2005) http://www.ddti.net
5. Egenhofer, M., Mark, D.: Naïve Geography. Frank and W. Kuhn (eds.) Spatial Information Theory: A theoretical basis for GIS. Proc. COSIT'95. LNCS No. 988. Springer-Verlag (1995) 1-16
6. Faltings, B.: A symbolic approach to qualitative kinematics. Artificial Intelligence. 56(2) (1992)
7. Kuipers, B.: Modeling Spatial Knowledge. Cognitive Science 2 (1978) 129-153
8. Kuipers, B., Byun, Y.: A robot exploration and mapping strategy based on a semantic hierarchy of spatial representations. Journal of Robotics and Autonomous Systems (1991) 47-63
9. Moulin, B., Kettani, D.: Route generation and description using a logical and an analogical framework. Annals of Mathematics and Artificial Intelligence 24. (1998) 155-179
10. Sablayrolles, P.: Spatio-temporal semantics in natural language: the case of motion. M. Aurnague et al. (eds.) Semantics of Time, Space, Movement and Spatio-Temporal Reasoning, Working Papers of the 4th Intl. Workshop (1992) 69-88.

On-Line Learning of a Time Variant System

Fernando Morgado Dias[1], Ana Antunes[1], José Vieira[2], and Alexandre Manuel Mota[3]

[1] Escola Superior de Tecnologia de Setúbal do Instituto Politécnico de Setúbal
Departamento de Engenharia Electrotécnica, Campus do IPS, Estefanilha, 2914-508 Setúbal,
Portugal, Tel.: +351 265 790000
{aantunes, fmdias}@est.ips.pt
[2] Escola Superior de Tecnologia de Castelo Branco,
Departamento de Engenharia Electrotécnica, Av. Empresário, 6000 Castelo Branco,
Portugal, Tel.: +351 272 330300
zevieira@est.ipcb.pt
[3] Departamento de Electrónica e Telecomunicações, Universidade de Aveiro, 3810 - 193 Aveiro
Portugal, Tel.: +351 234 370383
alex@det.ua.pt

Abstract. In the present work a sliding window approach for the Levenberg-Marquardt algorithm is used for on-line modelling a time variant system. The system used is a first order cruise control in which a modification is introduced to change the system gain at some point of operation. The initial control of the cruise control is performed by a PI not particularly optimised but enough to keep the system working within the intended range, which is then replaced by an Artificial Neural Network as soon as it is trained, using an Internal Model Controller loop.

1 Introduction

Among the many algorithms used for training in the field of Artificial Neural Networks (ANNs) the Levenberg-Marquardt has been considered as the most effective one, but its use has been mostly restricted to the off-line training because of the difficulties to implement a true iterative version.

These difficulties come from computing the derivatives for the Hessian matrix, inverting this matrix and computing the region for which the approximation contained in the calculation of the Hessian matrix is valid (the trust region).

In the present work a different approach is suggested: the use of the Levenberg-Marquardt algorithm on-line in a batch version with sliding window and Early Stopping, allowing the use of the Levenberg-Marquardt algorithm in the same way it is used in the off-line approaches. The implementation also uses a hybrid Direct/Specialized evaluation procedure and the final solution is tested with a cruise control system with a time variant gain. The gain is changed in the middle of the experiment to test the capabilities of adaptation of the solution proposed.

Although in most real systems such a time variance does not exist and rather a slow change would be found, this is an extreme situation and if the solution proposed works here it will also be valid for slow variant systems like the ones due to degradation of the systems.

M. Ali and R. Dapoigny (Eds.): IEA/AIE 2006, LNAI 4031, pp. 908–916, 2006.

2   The Newton, Gauss-Newton and Levenberg-Marquardt Algorithms

Starting from the Taylor series approach of second order, for a generic function $F(x)$, the following can be written:

$$F(x_{k+1}) = F(x_k + \triangle x_k) \simeq F(x_k) + G(x, k).\triangle x_k + \frac{1}{2}.\triangle x_k.H(x, k).\triangle x_k \quad (1)$$

where $G(x, k)$ is the gradient of $F(x)$, $\triangle x_k$ is $x_{k+1} - x_k$ and $H(x, k)$ is the Hessian matrix of $F(x)$.

If the derivative of equation 1 in respect to $\triangle x_k$ is taken, equation 1 will be obtained:

$$G(x, k) + H(x, k).\triangle x_k = 0 \quad (2)$$

This equation can be re-written in the following form:

$$\triangle x_k = -H(x, k)^{-1}.G(x, k) \quad (3)$$

The updating rule for the Newton algorithm is then obtained:

$$x_{k+1} = x_k - H(x, k)^{-1}.G(x, k) \quad (4)$$

Considering a generic quadratic function as the objective function to be minimized, as represented in equation 5 for a Multi Input Single Output system (here the iteration index is omitted and i is the index of the outputs):

$$F(x) = \sum_{i=1}^{N} v_i^2(x) \quad (5)$$

The gradient can be expressed in the following form:

$$G(x) = 2.J^T(x).v(x) \quad (6)$$

and the Hessian matrix can be expressed in the following form:

$$H(x) = 2.J^T(x).J(x) + 2.S(x) \quad (7)$$

where $J(x)$ is the Jacobian and $S(x)$ is:

$$S(x) = \sum_{i=1}^{N} v_i(x).\frac{\partial^2 v_i(x)}{\partial x_k.\partial x_j} \quad (8)$$

if it can be assumed that $S(x)$ is small when compared to the product of the Jacobian, then the Hessian matrix can be approximated by the following:

$$H(x) \simeq 2.J^T(x).J(x) \quad (9)$$

This approach gives the Gauss-Newton algorithm:

$$\triangle x_k = - \left[2.J^T(x_k).J(x_k) \right]^{-1} .2.J^T(x_k).v(x_k) \tag{10}$$

One limitation that can happen with this algorithm is that the simplified Hessian matrix might not be invertible. To overcome this problem a modified Hessian matrix can be used:

$$Hm(x) = H(x) + \mu.I \tag{11}$$

where I is the identity matrix and μ is a value such that makes $Hm(x)$ positive definite and therefore can be invertible.

This last change in the Hessian matrix corresponds to the Levenberg-Marquardt algorithm:

$$\triangle x_k = - \left[2.J^T(x_k).J(x_k) + \mu_k I \right]^{-1} .2.J^T(x_k).v(x_k) \tag{12}$$

where μ is now written as μk to show that this value can change during the execution of the algorithm.

The Levenberg-Marquardt algorithm is due to the independent work of both authors in [1] and [2].

The parameter μ_k is the key of the algorithm since it is responsible for stability (when assuring that the Hessian can be inverted) and speed of convergence. It is therefore worth to take a closer look on how to calculate this value.

The modification of the Hessian matrix will only be valid in a neighbourhood of the current iteration. This corresponds to search for the correct update for the next iteration x_{k+1} but restricting this search to $|x - x_k| \leqslant \delta_k$.

There is a relationship between δ_k and μ_k since raising μ_k makes the neighbourhood δ_k diminish [3]. As an exact expression to relate these two parameters is not available, many solutions have been developed.

The one used in the present work was proposed by Fletcher [3] and uses the following expression:

$$r_k = \frac{V_N(x_k) - V_N(x_k + p_k)}{V_N(x_k) - L_k(x_k + p_k)} \tag{13}$$

to obtain a measure of the quality of the approximation. Here V_N is the function to be minimized, L_k is the estimate of that value calculated from the Taylor series of second order and p_k is the search direction, in the present situation, the search direction given by the Levenberg-Marquardt algorithm.

The value of r_k is used in the determination of μ_k according to the following algorithm:

1-Choose the initial values of x_0 e μ_0.
2-Calculate the search direction p_k.
3-If $r_k > 0.75$ then set $\mu_k = \mu_k/2$.
4-If $r_k < 0.25$ then set $\mu_k = 2.\mu_k$.
5-If $V_N(x_k + p_k) < V_N(x_k)$ then the new iteration is accepted.
6-If the stopping condition for the training is not met, return to step 2.

3 On-Line Version

As pointed out before, the difficulties come from computing the derivatives for the Hessian matrix, inverting this matrix and computing the trust region, the region for which the approximation contained in the calculation of the Hessian matrix is valid.

In the literature, some attempts to build on-line versions can be found, namely the work done by Ngia [4] developing a modified iterative Levenberg-Marquardt algorithm which includes the calculation of the trust region and the work in [5] which implements a Levenberg-Marquardt algorithm in sliding window mode for Radial Basis Functions.

3.1 A Double Sliding Window Approach with Early Stopping

The current work is an evolution of the one presented in [6] where an on-line version of the Levenberg-Marquardt algorithm was implemented using a sliding window with Early Stopping and static test set. In the present work two sliding windows are used, one for the training set and another for the evaluation set with all the data being collected on-line. As in the previous work, the Early Stopping technique [7], [8] is used for avoiding the overfitting problem because it is almost mandatory to employ a technique to avoid overtraining when dealing with systems that are subject to noise. The Early Stopping technique was chosen over other techniques that could have been used (like Regularization and Prunning techniques) because it has less computational burden.

The use of two sliding windows will introduce some difficulties since both data sets will be changing during training and evaluation phases. For these two windows it is necessary to decide their relative position. In order to be able to perform Early Stopping in a valid way, it was decided to place the windows in a way that the new samples will go into the test window and the samples that are removed from the test set will go in to the training set according to figure 1.

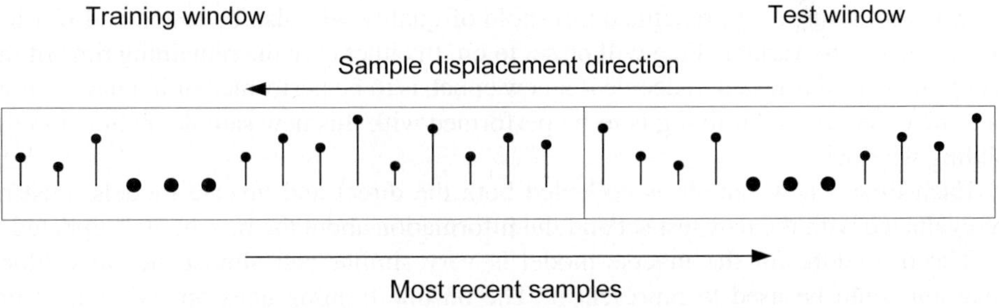

Fig. 1. Relative position of the training and test sets

If the inverse relative position of the two windows was used the samples would be part of the test set after they have been part of the training set and so the objective of evaluating the generalization ability would be somehow faked.

In order to save some of the time necessary to collect all the samples needed to fill both the test and training window, the training is started after some data has been collected but before the windows are both filled. The test window always keeps the same number of samples, while the training window is growing in the initial stage. The choice of maintaining the test window always with the same number of points was taken with the objectives of maintaining this window as stable as possible (since it is responsible for producing the numerical evaluation of the models) and assuming the use of a minimal test window that should not be shortened.

The windows may not change in each training iteration since all the time between sampling is used for training which may permit several training epochs before a new sample is collected. But each time the composition of the windows is changed the test and training errors will probably be subjected to an immediate change that might be interpreted as an overtraining situation. The Early Stopping technique is here used in conjunction with a measure of the best model that is retained for control. Each time there is a change in the windows the values of the best models (direct and inverse) must be re-evaluated because the previous ones, obtained over a different test set, are no longer valid for a direct comparison.

The procedure used for the identification of the direct model on-line is represented in figure 2.

As was already explained, training starts when a predefined amount of points have been collected. After each epoch the ANN is evaluated with a test set. The value of the Mean Square Error (MSE) obtained is used to perform Early Stopping and to retain the best models.

The conditions for overtraining and the maximum number of epochs are then verified. If they are true, the Flag, which indicates that the threshold of quality has been reached, will also be verified and if it is on, the training of the inverse model starts, otherwise the models will be reset since new models need to be prepared. Resetting here means that the model's weights are replaced by random values between -1 and 1 as in used in the initial models.

After testing the conditions for overtraining and the maximum number of epochs, if they are both false, the predefined threshold of quality will also be tested and if it has been reached the variable Flag will be set to on. In either case the remaining time of the sampling period is tested to decide if a new epoch is to be performed or if a new sample is to be collected and training is to be performed with this new sample included in the sliding window.

Each time a new sample is collected both the direct and inverse models must be re-evaluated with the new test set and the information about the best models updated.

The procedure for the inverse model is very similar and almost the same block diagram could be used to represent it. The on-line training goes on switching from direct to inverse model each time a new model is produced. The main difference between the procedure for direct and inverse model lies in the evaluation step. While the direct model is evaluated with a simple test set, the inverse model is evaluated with a control simulation corresponding to the hybrid Direct/Specialized approach for generating inverse models [9].

During the on-line training the NNSYSID [10] and NNCTRL [11] toolboxes for MATLAB were used.

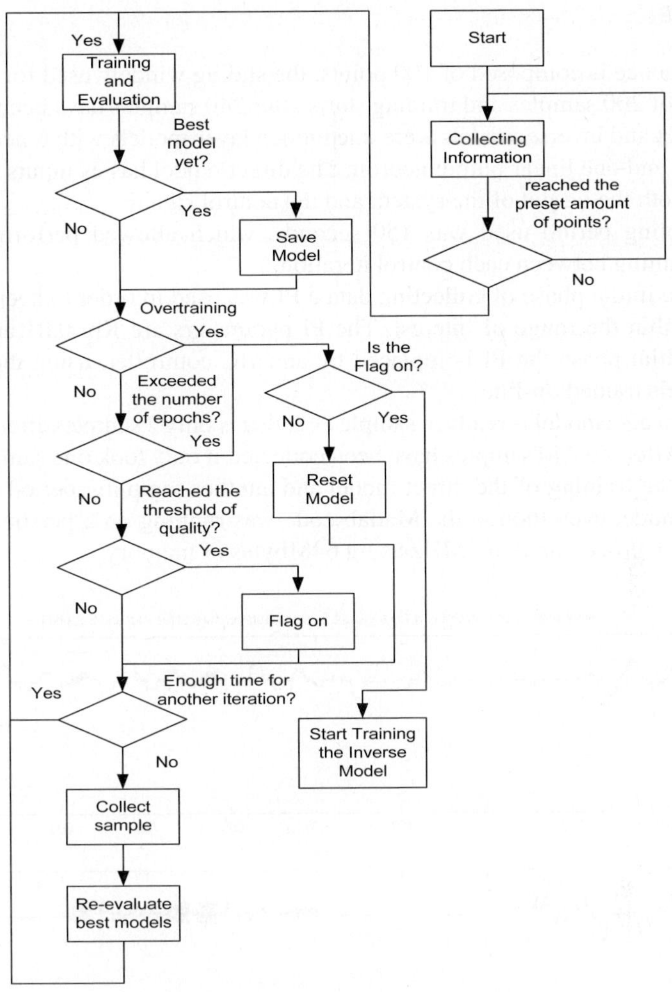

Fig. 2. Block diagram for the identification of a direct model on-line

4   Time Variant System

The time variant system used for this test is a cruise control with a variable gain according to equation 1:

$$\begin{cases} \frac{0.05}{s+0.05} \; if \; sample \leqslant 500 \\ \frac{0.075}{s+0.05} \; if \; sample > 500 \end{cases} \tag{14}$$

that is, the gain is increased 50% after sample 500 is collected. The system used is rather simple but the time variance introduced allows testing the functionality of the algorithm proposed.

5   Results

The test sequence is composed of 100 points, the sliding window used for training has a maximum of 200 samples and training starts after 240 samples have been collected.

Both direct and inverse models were one hidden layer models with 6 neurons on the hidden layer and one linear output neuron. The direct model has as inputs the past two samples of both the output of the system and the control signal.

The sampling period used was 150 seconds, which allowed performing several epochs of training between each control iteration.

During the initial phase of collecting data a PI was used in order to keep the system operating within the range of interest. The PI parameters are Kp=0.01 and Ki=0.01. After this initial phase the PI is replaced by an IMC controller, using the direct and inverse models trained on-line.

The first inverse model is ready at sample 243, that is only 2 samples after the training has started. After the 240 samples have been collected it only took one sampling period to complete the training of the direct model and another sampling period to complete the inverse model even though the Matlab code was running on a personal computer with a Celeron processor at 466MHz using 64Mbytes of memory.

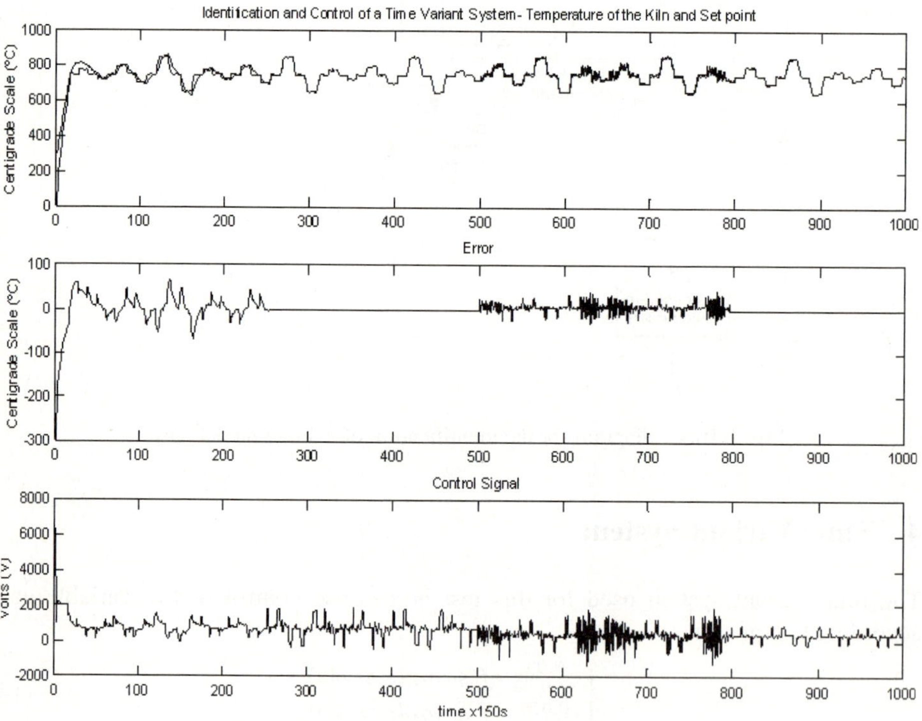

Fig. 3. Result obtained using the IMC control strategy and the proposed on-line learning strategy with a time variant system

As can be seen from figure 3 after the gain is changed the quality of control decreases and a oscilation appears that can reach 20 to 30 degrees.

For a new model to be prepared a test window and a training window with data that belong to the new system need to completed. The necessary points are collected in the next 300 samples. Since the system was changed at sample 500 the renewing of the data in the sliding windows is only complete at sample 800.

During this stage training and evaluation are quite difficult since there is a mixture of data from the two systems, but once the two sliding windows are filled with data from the new system the solution proposed is able to create accurate models: the quality of control is re-established at sample 795.

6   Conclusion

This paper presents on-line identification and control of a time varying system using the Levenberg-Marquardt algorithm in a batch version with two sliding windows and Early Stopping.

The problems pointed out in section 3 to perform Early Stopping under a changing sliding window for the training set were not critical and a good choice of the parameters for identification of the overtraining situation and for the maximum number of iterations for each attempt to create a model were sufficient to obtain reasonable models to perform IMC control.

The PID is here just used to maintain the system in the operating range while data is being collected and is disconnected as soon as the ANN models are ready.

As shown here, even for a noisy system, for which overtraining is a real problem it is possible to create models on-line of acceptable quality as can be concluded from the values presented in table 1.

The artificial time variant system used in this experiment is an extreme situation compared with most real time variant systems, which vary slowly. Nevertheless the successful application of the Levenberg-Marquardt sliding window solution to this situation shows that it will also work for slowly variant systems.

With this artificial time variant system it can be seen that learning is very difficult when the sliding windows contains data from the system previously and after the change. This corresponds to training an ANN with mixed data from two different systems. Once this situation is overcome the models of the new system are rapidly obtained. This problem would not happen for a slow changing system.

The sliding window solution with Early Stopping for the Levenberg-Marquardt algorithm is very interesting since it does not limit the capabilities of the algorithm and overcomes the limitations of application of the traditional solution.

References

1. K. Levenberg, "A method for the solution of certain problems in least squares," *Quart. Appl. Math.*, vol. 2, pp. 164–168, 1944.
2. D. Marquardt, "An algorithm for least -squares estimation of nonlinear parameters," *SIAM J. Appl. Math.*, vol. 11, pp. 431–441, 1963.

3. M. Nørgaard, O. Ravn, N. K. Poulsen, and L. K. Hansen, *Neural Networks for Modelling and Control of Dynamic Systems*, Springer, 2000.
4. Lester S. H. Ngia, *System Modeling Using Basis Functions and Application to Echo Cancelation*, Ph.D. thesis, Department of Signals and Systems School of Electrical and Computer Engineering, Chalmers University of Technology, 2000.
5. P. Ferreira, E. Faria, and A. Ruano, "Neural network models in greenhouse air temperature prediction," *Neurocomputing*, vol. 43, no. 1-4, pp. 51–75, 2002.
6. Fernando Morgado Dias, Ana Antunes, José Vieira, and Alexandre Manuel Mota, "Implementing the levenberg-marquardt algorithm on-line: A sliding window approach with early stopping," *2nd IFAC Workshop on Advanced Fuzzy/Neural Control*, 2004.
7. N. Morgan and H. Bourlard, "Generalization and parameter estimation in feedforward nets: Some experiments.," *Advances in Neural Information Processing Systems, Ed. D.Touretzsky, Morgan Kaufmann*, pp. 630–637, 1990.
8. Jonas Sjöberg, *Non-Linear System Identification with Neural Networks*, Ph.D. thesis, Dept. of Electrical Engineering, Linköping University, Suécia, 1995.
9. Fernando Morgado Dias, Ana Antunes, and Alexandre Mota, "A new hybrid direct/specialized approach for generating inverse neural models," *WSEAS Transactions on Systems*, vol. 3, Issue 4, pp. 1521–1529, 2004.
10. M. Nørgaard, "Neural network based system identification toolbox for use with matlab, version 1.1, technical report," Tech. Rep., Technical University of Denmark, 1996.
11. M. Nørgaard, "Neural network based control system design toolkit for use with matlab, version 1.1, technical report," Tech. Rep., Technical University of Denmark, 1996.

Bioinformatics Integration Framework
for Metabolic Pathway Data-Mining

Tomás Arredondo V.[1], Michael Seeger P.[2], Lioubov Dombrovskaia[3],
Jorge Avarias A.[3], Felipe Calderón B.[3], Diego Candel C.[3], Freddy Muñoz R.[3],
Valeria Latorre R.[2], Loreine Agulló[2], Macarena Cordova H.[2], and Luis Gómez[2]

[1] Departamento de Electrónica
`tarredondo@elo.utfsm.cl`
[2] Millennium Nucleus EMBA, Departamento de Química
[3] Departamento de Informática,
Universidad Técnica Federico Santa María
Av. España 1680, Valparaíso, Chile

Abstract. A vast amount of bioinformatics information is continuously
being introduced to different databases around the world. Handling the
various applications used to study this information present a major data
management and analysis challenge to researchers. The present work
investigates the problem of integrating heterogeneous applications and
databases towards providing a more efficient data-mining environment
for bioinformatics research. A framework is proposed and GeXpert, an
application using the framework towards metabolic pathway determination is introduced. Some sample implementation results are also presented.

1 Introduction

Modern biotechnology aims to provide powerful and beneficial solutions in
diverse areas. Some of the applications of biotechnology include biomedicine,
bioremediation, pollution detection, marker assisted selection of crops, pest management, biochemical engineering and many others [3, 14, 22, 21, 29].

Because of the great interest in biotechnology there has been a proliferation of
separate and disjoint databases, data formats, algorithms and applications. Some
of the many types of databases currently in use include: nucleotide sequences
(e.g. Ensemble, Genbank, DDBJ, EMBL), protein sequences (e.g. SWISS-PROT,
InterPro, PIR, PRF), enzyme databases (e.g. Enzymes), metabolic pathways
(e.g. ERGO, KEGG: Kyoto Encyclopedia of Genes and Genomes database) and
literature references (e.g. PubMed) [1, 4, 11, 6, 23]. The growth in the amount of
information stored has been exponential: since the 1970s, as of April 2004 there
were over 39 billion bases in Entrez NCBI (National Center of Bioinformatics
databases), while the number of abstracts in PubMed has been growing by 10,000
abstracts per week since 2002 [3, 13].

The availability of this data has undoubtedly accelerated biotechnological research. However, because these databases were developed independently and are

M. Ali and R. Dapoigny (Eds.): IEA/AIE 2006, LNAI 4031, pp. 917–926, 2006.
© Springer-Verlag Berlin Heidelberg 2006

managed autonomously, they are highly heterogeneous, hard to cross-reference, and ill-suited to process mixed queries. Also depending on the database being accessed the data in them is stored in a variety of formats including: a host of graphic formats, RAW sequence data, FASTA, PIR, MSF, CLUSTALW, and other text based formats including XML/HTML. Once the desired data is retrieved from the one of the database(s) it typically has to be manually manipulated and addressed to another database or application to perform a required action such as: database and homology search (e.g. BLAST, Entrez), sequence alignment and gene analysis (e.g. ClustalW, T-Coffee, Jalview, GenomeScan, Dialign, Vector NTI, Artemis) [8].

Beneficial application developments would occur more efficiently if the large amounts of biological feature data could be seamlessly integrated with data from literature, databases and applications for data-mining, visualization and analysis. In this paper we present a framework for bioinformatic literature, database, and application integration. An application based of this framework is shown that supports metabolic pathway research within a single easy to use graphical interface with assisting fuzzy logic decision support. To our knowledge, an integration framework encompassing all these areas has not been attempted before. Early results have shown that the integration framework and application could be useful to bioinformatics researchers.

In Section 2, we describe current metabolic pathway research methodology. In Section 3 we describe existing integrating architectures and applications. Section 4 describes the architecture and GeXpert, an application using this framework is introduced. Finally, some conclusions are drawn and directions of future work are presented.

2   Metabolic Pathway Research

For metabolic pathway reconstruction experts have been traditionally used a time intensive iterative process [30]. As part of this process genes first have to be selected as candidates for encoding an enzyme within a potential metabolic pathway within an organism. Their selection then has to be validated with literature references (e.g. non-hypothetical genes in Genbank) and using bioinformatics tools (e.g. BLAST: Basic Local Alignment Search Tool) for finding orthologous genes in various other organisms. Once a candidate gene has been determined, sequence alignment of the candidate gene with the sequence of the organism under study has to be performed in a different application for gene locations (e.g. Vector NTI, ARTEMIS). Once the genes required have been found in the organism then the metabolic pathway has to be confirmed experimentally in the laboratory. For example, using the genome sequence of *Acidithiobacillus ferrooxidans* diverse metabolic pathways have been determined.

One major group of organisms that is currently undergoing metabolic pathways research is bacteria. Bacteria possess the highest metabolic versatility of the three domains of living organisms. This versatility stems from their expansion into different natural niches, a remarkable degree of physiological and genetic adaptability and their evolutionary diversity. Microorganisms play a main role in the carbon cycle and in the removal of natural and man-made waste chemical compounds from the environment [17]. For example, *Burkholderia xenovorans* LB400 is a bacterium capable of degrading a wide range of PCBs [7, 29].

Because of the complex and noisy nature of the data, any selection of candidate genes as part of metabolic pathways is currently only done by human experts prior to biochemical verification. The lack of integration and standards in database, application and file formats is time consuming and forces researchers to develop *ad hoc* data management processes that could be prone to error. In addition, the possibility of using Softcomputing based pattern detection and analysis techniques (e.g. fuzzy logic) have not been fully explored as an aid to the researcher within such environments [1, 23].

3   Integration Architectures

The trend in the field is towards data integration. Research projects continue to generate large amounts of raw data, and this is annotated and correlated with the data in the public databases. The ability to generate new data continues to outpace the ability to verify them in the laboratory and therefore to exploit them. Validation experiments and the ultimate conversion of data to validated knowledge need expert human involvement with the data and in the laboratory, consuming time and resources. Any effort of data and system integration is an attempt towards reducing the time spent by experts unnecessarily which could be better spent in the lab [5, 9, 20].

The biologist or biochemist not only needs to be an expert in his field as well stay up to date with the latest software tools or even develop his own tools to be able to perform his research [16, 28]. One example of these types of tools is BioJava, which is an open source set of Java components such as parsers, file manipulation tools, sequence translation and proteomic components that allow extensive customization but still require the development of source code [25]. The goal should be integrated user-friendly systems that would greatly facilitate the constructive cycle of computational model building and experimental verification for the systematic analysis of an organism [5, 8, 16, 20, 28, 30]. Sun *et al.* [30] have developed a system, IdentiCS, which combines the identification of coding sequences (CDS) with the reconstruction, comparison and visualization of metabolic networks. IdentiCS uses sequences from public databases to perform a BLAST query to a local database with the genome in question. Functional information from the CDSs is used for metabolic reconstruction. One shortcoming is that the system does not incorporate visualization or ORF (Open Reading Frames) selection and it includes only one application for metabolic sequence reconstruction (BLAST).

Information systems for querying, visualization and analysis must be able to integrate data on a large scale. Visualization is one of the key ways of making the researcher work easier. For example, the spatial representation of the genes within the genome shows location of the gene, reading direction and metabolic function. This information is made available by applications such as Vector NTI and Artemis. The function of the gene is interpreted through its product, normally the protein in a metabolic pathway, which description is available from several databases such as KEGG or ERGO [24]. Usually, the metabolic pathways are represented as a flowchart of several levels of abstraction, which are constructed manually. Recent advances on metabolic network visualization include virtual reality use [26], mathematical model development [27], and a modeling language [19]. These techniques synthesize the discovery of genes and are available in databases such as Expasy, but they should be transparent to the researcher by their seamless integration into the research application environment.

The software engineering challenges and opportunities in integrating and visualizing the data are well documented [16, 28]. There are some applications servers that use a SOAP interface to answer queries. Linking such tools into unified working environment is non-trivial and has not been done to date [2]. One recent approach towards human centered integration is BioUse, a web portal developed by the Human Centered Software Engineering Group at Concordia University. BioUse provided an adaptable interface to NCBI, BLAST and ClustalW, which attempted to shield the novice user from unnecessary complexity. As users became increasingly familiar with the application the portal added shortcuts and personalization features for different users (e.g. pharmacologists, microbiologists) [16]. BioUse was limited in scope as a prototype and its website is no longer available. Current research is continued in the CO-DRIVE project but it is not completed yet [10].

4   Integration Framework and Implementation

This project has focused on the development of a framework using open standards towards integrating heterogeneous databases, web services and applications/tools. This framework has been applied in GeXpert, an application for bioinformatics metabolic pathway reconstruction research in bacteria. In addition this application includes the utilization of fuzzy logic for helping in the selection of the best candidate genes or sequences for specified metabolic pathways. Previously, this categorization was typically done in an *ad hoc* manner by manually combining various criteria such as e-value, identities, gaps, positives and score. Fuzzy logic enables an efficiency enhancement by providing an automated sifting mechanism for a very manually intensive bioinformatics procedure currently being performed by researchers.

GeXpert is used to find, build and edit metabolic pathways (central or peripheral), perform protein searches in NCBI, perform nucleotide comparisons of organisms versus the sequenced one (using tblastn). The application can also perform a search of 3D models associated with a protein or enzyme (using the Cn3D viewer), generation of ORF diagrams for the sequenced genome, generation of reports relating to the advance of the project and aid in the selection of BLAST results using T-S-K (Takagi Sugeno Kang) fuzzy logic.

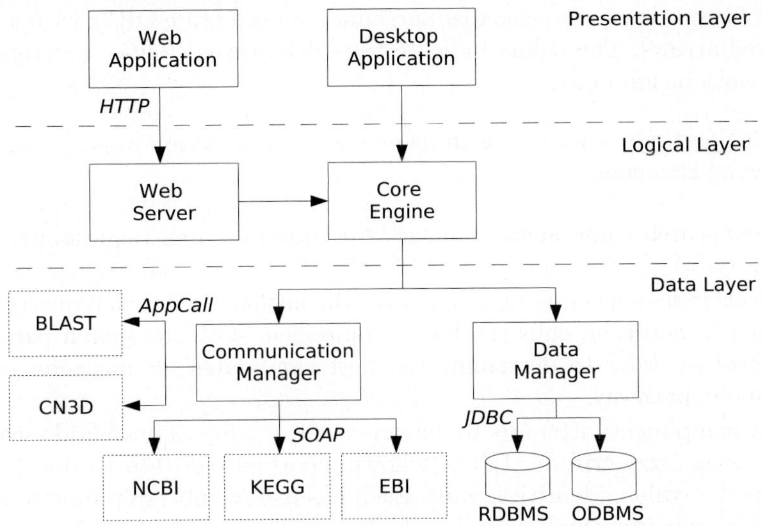

Fig. 1. High level framework architecture

The architecture is implemented in three layers: presentation, logic and data
[18]. As shown in Figure 1, the presentation layer provides for a web based as
well as a desktop based interface to perform the tasks previously mentioned.0

The logical layer consists of a core engine and a web server. The core engine
performs bioinformatic processing functions and uses different tools as required:
BLAST for protein and sequence alignment, ARTEMIS for analysis of nucleotide
sequences, Cn3D for 3D visualization, and a T-S-K fuzzy logic library for candidate sequence selection. The Web Server component provides an HTTP interface
into the GeXpert core engine.

As seen in Figure 1, the data layer includes a communications manager and
a data manager. The communication manager is charged with obtaining data
(protein and nucleotide sequences, metabolic pathways and 3D models) from
various databases and application sources using various protocols (application
calls, TCP/IP, SOAP). The data manager implements data persistence as well
as temporary cache management for all research process related objects.

4.1   Application Implementation: GeXpert

GeXpert [15] is an open source implementation of the framework previously
described. It relies on Eclipse [12] builder for multiplatform support.

The GeXpert desktop application as implemented consists of the following:

- Metabolic pathway editor: tasked with editing or creating metabolic pathways, shows them as directed graphs of enzymes and compounds.
- Protein search viewer: is charged with showing the results of protein searches
  with user specified parameters.
- Nucleotide search viewer: shows nucleotide search results given user specified
  protein/parameters.

– ORF viewer: is used to visualize surrounding nucleotide ORFs with a map of colored arrows. The colors indicate the ORF status (found, indeterminate, erroneous or ignored).

The GeXpert core component implements the application logic. It consists of the following elements:

– Protein search component: manages the protein search requests and its results.
– Nucleotide search component: manages the nucleotide search requests and its results. In addition, calls the Fuzzy component with the search parameters specified in order to determine the best candidates for inclusion into the metabolic pathway.
– Fuzzy component: attempts to determine the quality of nucleotide search results using fuzzy criteria [1].The following normalized (0 to 1 values) criteria are used: e-value, identities, gaps. Each has five membership functions (very low, low, medium, high, very high), the number of rules used is 243 (3^5).
– ORF component: identifies the ORFs present in requested genome region.
– Genome component: manages the requests for genome regions and its results.

GeXpert communications manager receives requests from the GeXpert core module to obtain and translates data from external sources. This module consists of the following subcomponents:

– BLAST component: calls the BLAST application indicating the protein to be analyzed and the organism data base to be used.
– BLAST parser component: translates BLAST results from XML formats into objects.
– Cn3D component: sends three-dimensional (3D) protein models to the Cn3D application for display.
– KEGG component: obtains and translates metabolic pathways received from KEGG.
– NCBI component: performs 3D protein model and document searches from NCBI.
– EBI component: performs searches on proteins and documentation from the EBI (European Bioinformatic Institute) databases.

GeXpert data manager is tasked with load administrating and storage of application data:

– Cache component: in charge of keeping temporary search results to improve throughput. Also implements aging of cache data.
– Application data component: performs data persistence of metabolic paths, 3D protein models, protein searches, nucleotide searches, user configuration data, project configuration for future usage.

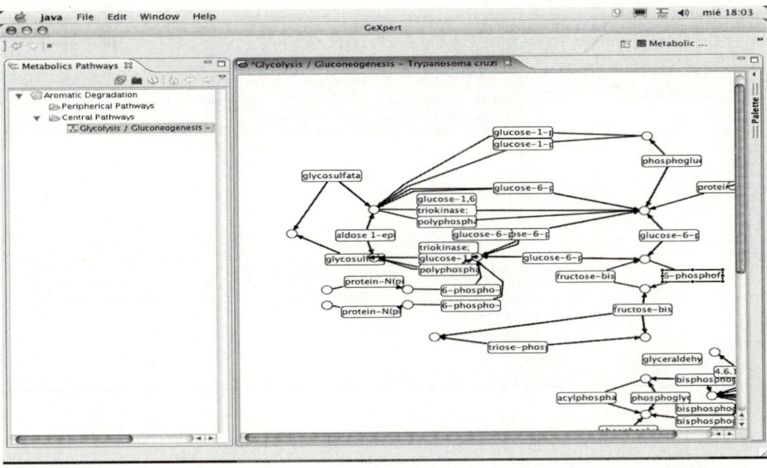

Fig. 2. Metabolic pathway viewer

4.2   Application Implementation: GeXpert User Interface and Workflow

GeXpert is to be used in metabolic pathway research work using a research workflow similar to identiCS [30]. The workflow and some sample screenshots are given:

1. User must provide the sequenced genome of the organism to be studied.
2. The metabolic pathway of interest must be created (can be based on the pathway of a similar organism). In the example in Figure 2, the glycolisis/gluconeogenesis metabolic pathway was imported from KEGG.
3. For each metabolic pathway a key enzyme must be chosen in order to start a detailed search. Each enzyme could be composed of one or more proteins

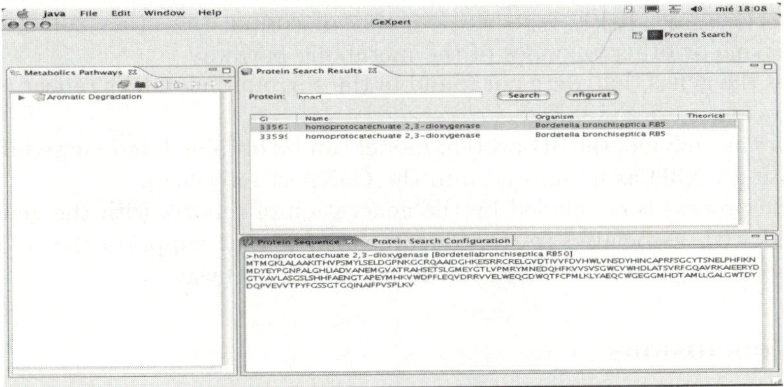

Fig. 3. Protein search viewer

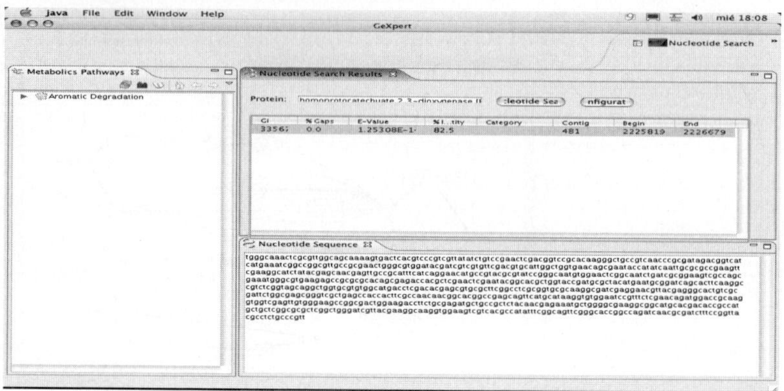

Fig. 4. Nucleotide search viewer

(subunits). Figure 3 shows the result of the search for the protein homoprotocatechuate 2,3-dioxygenase.

4. Perform a search for amino acid sequences (proteins) in other organisms. Translate these sequences into nucleotides (using tblastn) and perform an alignment in the genome of the organism under study. If this search does not give positives results it return to the previous step and search another protein sequence. In Figure 4, we show that the protein homoprotocatechuate 2,3-dioxygenase has been found in the organism under study (*Burkholderia xenovorans* LB400) in the chromosome 2 (contig 481) starting in position 2225819 and ending in region 2226679. Also the system shows the nucleotide sequence for this protein.

5. For a DNA sequence found, visualize the ORF map (using the ORF Viewer) and identify if there is an ORF that contains a large part of said sequence. If this is not the case go back to the previous step and chose another sequence.

6. Verify if the DNA sequence for the ORF found corresponds to the chosen sequence or a similar one (using blastx). If not choose another sequence.

7. Establish as found the ORF of the enzyme subunit and start finding in the surrounding ORFs sequences capable of coding the other subunits of the enzyme or other enzymes of the metabolic pathway.

8. For the genes that were not found in the surrounding ORFs repeat the entire process.

9. For the enzyme, the 3D protein model can be obtained and viewed if it exists (using CN3D as integrated into the GeXpert interface).

10. The process is concluded by the generation of reports with the genes found and with associated related documentation that supports the information about the proteins utilized in the metabolic pathway.

5   Conclusions

The integrated framework approach presented in this paper is an attempt to enhance the efficiency and capability of bioinformatics researchers. GeXpert is a demonstration that the integration framework can be used to implement useful bioinformatics applications. GeXpert has so far shown to be a useful tool for our researchers; it is currently being enhanced for functionality and usability improvements. The current objective of the research group is to use GeXpert in order to discover new metabolic pathways for bacteria [29].

In addition to our short term goals, the following development items are planned for the future: using fuzzy logic in batch mode, web services and a web client, blastx for improved verification of the ORFs determined, multi-user mode to enable multiple users and groups with potentially different roles to share in a common research effort, peer to peer communication to enable the interchange of documents (archives, search results, research items) thus enabling a network of collaboration in different or shared projects, and the use of intelligent/evolutionary algorithms to enable learning based on researcher feedback into GeXpert.

Acknowledgements

This research was partially funded by Fundación Andes.

References

1. Arredondo, T., Neelakanta, P.S., DeGroff, D.: Fuzzy Attributes of a DNA Complex: Development of a Fuzzy Inference Engine for Codon-'Junk' Codon Delineation. Artif. Intell. Med. **35** 1-2 (2005) 87-105
2. Barker, J., Thornton, J.: Software Engineering Challenges in bioinformatics. Proceedings of the 26th International Conference on Software Engineering, IEEE (2004)
3. Bernardi, M., Lapi, M., Leo, P., Loglisci, C.: Mining Generalized Association Rules on Biomedical Literature. In: Moonis, A. Esposito, F. (eds): Innovations in Applied Artificial Intelligence. Lect. Notes Artif. Int. **3353** (2005) 500-509
4. Brown, T.A.: Genomes. John Wiley and Sons, NY (1999)
5. Cary M.P., Bader G.D., Sander C.: Pathway information for systems biology (Review Article). FEBS Lett. **579** (2005) 1815-1820,
6. Claverlie, J.M.: Bioinformatics for Dummies. Wiley Publishing (2003)
7. Cámara, B., Herrera, C., González, M., Couve, E., Hofer, B., Seeger, M.: From PCBs to highly toxic metabolites by the biphenyl pathway. Environ. Microbiol. (6) (2004) 842-850
8. Cohen, J.: Computer Science and Bioinformatics. Commun. ACM **48** (3) (2005) 72-79
9. Costa, M., Collins, R., Anterola, A., Cochrane, F., Davin, L., Lewis, N.: An in silico assessment of gene function and organization of the phenylpropanoid pathway metabolic networks in *Arabidopsis thaliana* and limitations thereof. Phytochem. **64** (2003) 1097-1112
10. CO-Drive project: http://hci.cs.concordia.ca/www/hcse/projects/CO-DRIVE/
11. Durbin, R.: Biological Sequence Analysis, Cambridge, UK (2001)
12. Eclipse project: http://www.eclipse.org
13. Entrez NCBI Database: www.ncbi.nlm.nih.gov/entrez/query.fcgi?db=Nucleotide

14. Gardner, D.,: Using genomics to help predict drug interactions. J Biomed. Inform. **37** (2004) 139-146
15. GeXpert sourceforge page: http://sourceforge.net/projects/gexpert
16. Javahery, H., Seffah, A., Radhakrishnan, T.: Beyond Power: Making Bioinformatics Tools User-Centered. Commun. ACM **47** 11 (2004)
17. Jimenez, J. I., Miambres, B., Garca, J., Daz, E.: Genomic insights in the metabolism of aromatics compounds in Pseudomonas. In: Ramos, J. L. (ed): Pseudomonas, vol. 3. NY: Kluwer Academic Publishers, (2004) 425-462
18. Larman, C.: Applying UML and Patterns: An Introduction to Object-Oriented Analysis and Design and Iterative Development. Prentice Hall PTR (2004)
19. Loew, L. W., Schaff, J. C.: The Virtual Cell: a software environment for computational cell biology. Trends Biotechnol. **19** 10 (2001)
20. Ma H., Zeng A., Reconstruction of metabolic networks from genome data and analysis of their global structure for various organisms. Bioinformatics **19** (2003) 270-277
21. Magalhaes, J., Toussaint, O.: How bioinformatics can help reverse engineer human aging. Aging Res. Rev. **3** (2004) 125-141
22. Molidor, R., Sturn, A., Maurer, M., Trajanosk, Z.: New trends in bioinformatics: from genome sequence to personalized medicine. Exp. Gerontol. **38** (2003) 1031-1036
23. Neelakanta, P.S., Arredondo, T., Pandya, S., DeGroff, D.: Heuristics of AI-Based Search Engines for Massive Bioinformatic Data-Mining: An Example of Codon/Noncodon Delineation Search in a Binary DNA Sequence, Proceeding of IICAI (2003)
24. Papin, J.A., Price, N.D., Wiback, S.J., Fell, D.A., Palsson, B.O.: Metabolic Pathways in the Post-genome Era. Trends Biochem. Sci. **18** 5 (2003)
25. Pocock, M., Down, T., Hubbard, T.: BioJava: Open Source Components for Bioinformatics. ACM SIGBIO Newsletter **20** 2 (2000) 10-12
26. Rojdestvenski, I.: VRML metabolic network visualizer. Comp. Bio. Med. **33** (2003)
27. SBML: Systems Biology Markup Language. http://sbml.org/index.psp
28. Segal, T., Barnard, R.: Let the shoemaker make the shoes - An abstraction layer is needed between bioinformatics analysis, tools, data, and equipment: An agenda for the next 5 years. First Asia-Pacific Bioinformatics Conference, Australia (2003)
29. Seeger, M., Timmis, K. N., Hofer, B.: Bacterial pathways for degradation of polychlorinated biphenyls. Mar. Chem. **58** (1997) 327-333
30. Sun, J., Zeng, A.: IdentiCS - Identification of coding sequence and in silico reconstruction of the metabolic network directly from unannotated low-coverage bacterial genome sequence. BMC Bioinformatics **5:112** (2004)

The Probability Distribution of Distance TSS-TLS Is Organism Characteristic and Can Be Used for Promoter Prediction

Yun Dai[1], Ren Zhang[2], and Yan-Xia Lin[3]

[1] School of Mathematics and Applied Statistics, University of Wollongong, Australia
[2] School of Biological Sciences, University of Wollongong, Australia
[3] School of Mathematics and Applied Statistics, University of Wollongong, Australia

Abstract. Transcription is a complicated process which involves the interactions of promoter *cis*-elements with multiple *trans*-protein factors. The specific interactions rely not only on the specific sequence recognition between the *cis*- and *trans*-factors but also on certain spatial arrangement of the factors in a complex. The relative positioning of involved *cis*-elements provides the framework for such a spatial arrangement. The distance distribution between gene transcription and translation start sites (TSS-TLS) is the subject of the present study to test an assumption that over evolution, the TSS-TLS distance becomes a distinct character for a given organism. Four representative organisms (*Escherichia cloi*, *Saccharomyces cerevisiae*, *Arabidopsis thaliana* and *Homo sapiens*) were chosen to study the probability distribution of the distance TSS-TLS. The statistical results show that the distances distributions vary significantly and are not independent of species. There seems a trend of increased length of the distances from simple prokaryotic to more complicated eukaryotic organisms. With the specific distance distribution data, computational promoter prediction tools can be improved for higher accuracy.

1   Introduction

Transcription initiation is the first and one of the most important control points in regulating gene expression and promoters play a pivotal role in this process of all living organisms. A promoter is the nucleotide acid sequence region upstream of the transcription start site. It includes a core promoter part that governs the basic transcription process and regulatory sequences that control more complicated temporal and spatial expression patterns. It is generally believed that the regulation of transcription relies not only on the specific sequence pattern recognition and interaction between the DNA sequences (*cis*-elements) and other factors (*trans*) but also on their spatial organization during the process. This implies that the *cis*-elements need generally to be located in a defined distance one to the other.

With the vast amount of genomic data available and rapid development of computational tools, there is an increasing advancement in the computational

M. Ali and R. Dapoigny (Eds.): IEA/AIE 2006, LNAI 4031, pp. 927–934, 2006.

techniques to predict promoters, including recognition of promoter region, identification of functional TSS, or both of them [1, 3, 6, 7]. Many algorithms have been developed for the prediction of promoters which vary in performance. In general, the algorithms for promoter recognition can be classified into two groups: the signal-based approach and the content-based approach. There are also methods that combine the both - looking for signals and for regions of specific compositions [6]. Although a great deal of research has been undertaken in the area of promoter recognition, the prediction techniques are still far from satisfactory. Most programs inevitably produce a considerable level of false positives (FPs) at any significant level of true positive (TP) recognition. The promoter recognition systems for large-scale screening require acceptable ratios of TP and FP predictions (i.e. those that maximize the TP recognition while minimize the FP recognition.).

The probability distribution of the distance between transcription start site and translation start site (TSS-TLS) has been studied and utilized in promoter prediction of *E. coli* bacterium, a model prokaryotic organism. It has been demonstrated that, combining with the information of the *E. coli* empirical probability distribution of the distance TSS-TLS, promoter prediction of *E. coli* can be improved significantly [2], using a common neural network promoter prediction tool NNPP2.2 [8, 10]. This has triggered our further interest in examining the TSS-TLS distance distribution in different living organisms with an assumption that over evolution, the TSS-TLS distance will become a distinct character for a given organism. Here, we report our investigation results on four living organisms and discuss the significance and potential application.

2   The Distribution of Distance TSS-TLS

The distance TSS-TLS is defined as the number of base pairs between the TSS and the first nucleotide (A in the case of ATG) of the TLS. For convenience, the following notation will be used in this paper. Given a genome sequence, let s denote the position of TSS of a gene and let $D(s)$ denote the distance (base) between s and its TLS.

D is considered as a random variable and we hypothesize that, for different organisms, the probability distribution of D would be significantly different. For each organism, the distribution of D should have its own special characteristics.

To test our hypothesis, we considered the available data of four different representative organisms in this study: a model bacterium *Escherichia coli* [4], a model monocellular eukaryote yeast *Saccharomyces cerevisiae* [12], a model higher plant *Arabidopsis thaliana* [5] and human *Homo sapiens* [11]. All of them have record on the positions of TSS and TLS identified through laboratory testing.

In genome sequence, sometimes one TLS might correspond to multiple TSS's. Considering the probability distribution of the distance TSS-TLS, all such valid pairs will be counted. Thus, the sample size of genome sequence for each species, *E. coli*, *S. cerevisiae*, *A. thaliana* and *H.sapiens*, are 820, 202, 18958 and 12763 respectively.

Table 1. Summary statistics for distance TSS-TLS of different organisms

	Mean	SD	Median	Kurtosis	Skewness	Min	Max	Sample Size
E. coli	98.37	117.90	56	11.73	2.92	0	920	820
S. cerevisiac	110.78	102.90	68	2.77	1.79	9	481	202
A. thaliana	137.20	134.27	98	32.09	3.58	1	3214	18958
H. sapiens	10904.95	44422.41	353	227.42	12.69	1	1313939	12727

We produce the histogram and smoothed probability density function of the distance TSS-TLS for the four organisms and present them in Figures 1 and 2. Summary statistics for four organisms are given in Table 1.

In Figures 1 and 2, all four organisms have positively-skewed distributions. From Table 1, we note that both of mean and median of the samples increases from *E. Coli* to *S. cerevisiae*, then to *A. thaliana* and finally to *H.sapiens*. Since distributions are positively skewed, the values of median are more meaningful. Additionally, the smoothed density functions for *E. coli* and *S. cerevosiae* have higher and narrower peak than that for *A.thaliana* and *H. sapiens*. This fact can also be seen from the values of sample standard deviation given in Table 1.

Figures 1 and 2 clearly show that the smoothed density functions for the four organisms are significantly different. Since the sample size from each individual organism is reasonably large and the difference between the smoothed density functions are significant, we are confident that the probability distributions of distance TSS-TLS are different from organism to organism. (This can be tested by nonparametric method. Since the case is so clear, such a test is omitted.)

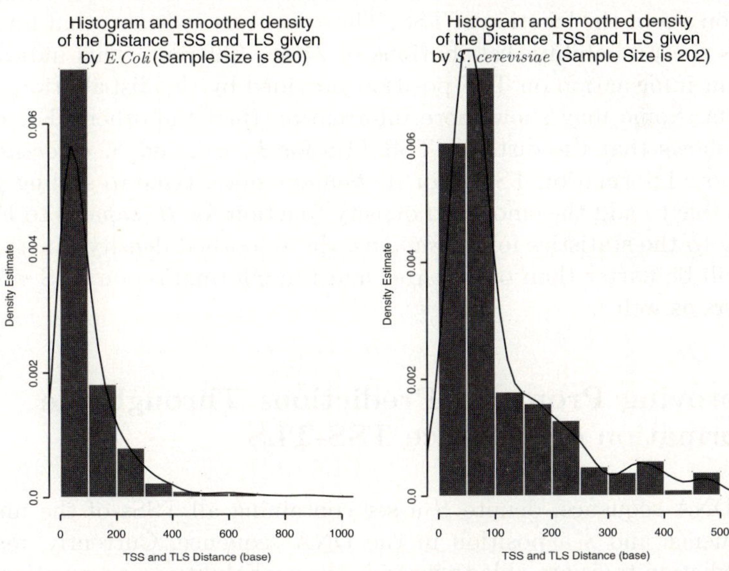

Fig. 1. The histogram and smoothed density of distance TSS-TLS for *E. coli* and *S. cerevisiae*

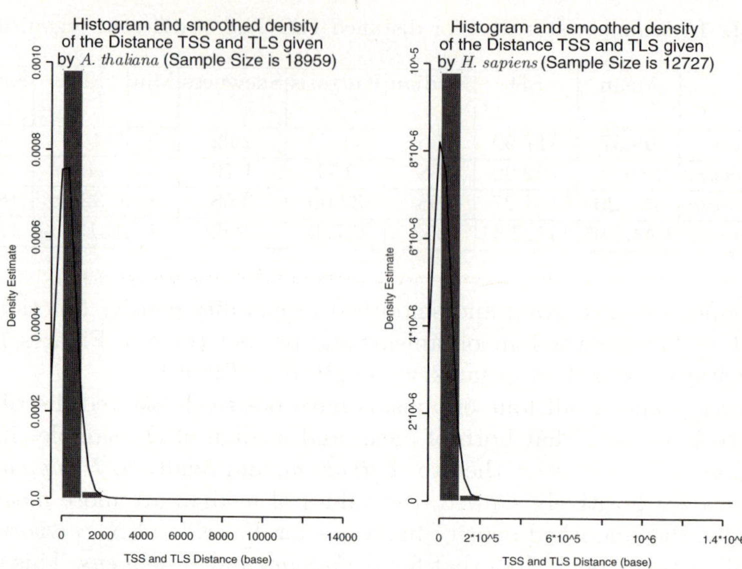

Fig. 2. The histogram and smoothed density of distance TSS-TLS for *A. thaliana* and *H. sapiens*

In summary, the distance TSS-TLS of simple prokaryotes tends to be shorter than that of complicated eukaryotes and the value of the distance TSS-TLS of simple prokaryotes is clustered closely than that of complicated eukaryotes.

Random variable D is related to the TSS position. Therefore, it must contain information about the location of TSS. The above fact indicates that for different organisms the probability distributions of D are different. This indicates that the amount information on TSS position provided by the distribution of D will be different. Some may show more information than the others. For example, Figure 3 shows that the distance TSS-TLS for *E. coli* and *S. cerevisiae* might contain more information TSS than *A. thaliana* does. (Due to scaling problem, we are unable to add the smoothed density function for *H. sapiens* to Figure 3. According to the statistics for *H. sapiens*, the smoothed density function for *H. sapiens* will be flatter than other three and the information on TSS will be less than others as well.).

3   Improving Promoter Predictions Through the Information of Distance TSS-TLS

Given a DNA sequence, denote S a set containing all TSSs of the underlying DNA sequence and s a position in the DNA sequence. Currently, many promoter prediction tools are able to provide the probability s as a position of TSS, i.e. $P(s \in S)$ ($s \in S$ means s is a position for TSS). However, the prediction false positives rate is very high because they are unable to take into account any

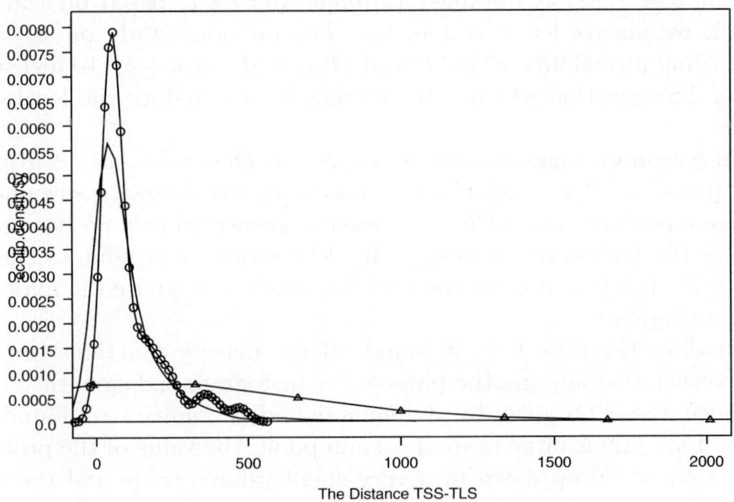

Fig. 3. Comparison of the Smoothed Density of the Distance TSS-TLS for *E. coli*, *S. cerevisiae* and *A. thaliana*

other particular information from the underlying DNA sequence when the tools were developed, for example NNPP2.2 [9, 8, 10].

In previous section, we have demonstrated that different species have different probability distributions for the distance TSS-TLS. Therefore, the information of the distance TSS-TLS should benefit promoter prediction.

In the following we give a formula to show how we combine the probability $P(s \in S)$ with the information of the distance TSS-TLS given by an individual organism to improve TSS prediction for the organism.

Consider the probability that position s is a TSS position and the distance between s and relevant TLS is between in $d - a$ and $d + a$ can be expressed as

$$P(s \in S \text{ and } D(s) \in [d - a, d + a]) \tag{1}$$

where a and d are positive integer and $D(s)$ denotes the distance between s and the TLS associated with s. We suggest to use this joint probability to replace $P(s \in S)$ as a score for the purpose of predicting TSS position.

Probability (1) can be evaluated by using the following formula

$$P(s \in S \text{ and } D(s) \in [d - a, d + a]) = P(s \in S)P(D(s) \in [d - a, d + a]|s \in S). \tag{2}$$

By using the above formula, the estimation of $P(s \in S \text{ and } D(s) \in [d - a, d + a])$ can be obtained subject to the estimation of $P(s \in S)$ and $P(D(s) \in [d - a, d + a]|s \in S)$ being available. The estimation of $P(s \in S)$ can be obtained from other promoter prediction techniques, for example NNPP2.2. The estimation of $P(D(s) \in [d - a, d + a]|s \in S)$, as what have done in [2], can be provided by empirical sample distribution related to the under considered species. If the estimation of $P(s \in S)$ is obtained through NNPP2.2, based on the design of NNPP2.2, we always let $a = 3$ in (1). The previous study on *E. coli* has shown that using probability $P(s \in S$ and $D(s) \in [d - a, d + a])$ to measure the likelihood of TSS position will be able to significantly reduce the level of false positives [2].

The main reason we suggest to use $P(s \in S$ and $D(s) \in [d - a, d + a])$ to predict TSS instead of $P(s \in S)$ alone is based on the following argument. In practice once a position s in a DNA sequence is suspected as a position of TSS, we will study the position s as well as the gene sequence around s. Therefore, while testing if s is a true position of TSS, we should not ignore the information showed in its neighbor.

From our data (Figures 1-2), it found all the density functions are strong positively-skewed. Considering the plots of the histogram and smoothed density of the distance TSS-TLS given by *A. thaliana* and *H. sapiens*, we found, when the distance TSS-TLS is large beyond certain point, the value of the probability density function will drop down to a very small value quickly and the density function provides very limited information for the distribution of the position TSS beyond that point. However, before the point the probability density function of the distance TSS-TLS has a bell shape within a certain range of the distance close to zero. Obviously, this range is varied from species to species, and the centre, the peak and the fitness of the bell shape are different from species to species as well. All of these indicate that the information of the distance TLS-TSS within that range might help the prediction of TSS.

In practice, if we are only interested in predicting TSS within a particular range, formula (2) can be modified as follows

$$P(s \in S,\ D(s) \in [d - a, d + a] \text{ and } D(s) < K)$$
$$= P(s \in S)P(D(s) < K | s \in S)P(D(s) \in [d - a, d + a] | s \in S \text{ and } D(s) < K)$$

$$(3)$$

where the estimation of $P(s \in S)$ can be obtained from other promoter prediction tool, say NNPP2.2; for different spices $P(D(s) < K | s \in S)$ and $P(D(s) \in (d - a, d + a) | s \in S$ and $D(s) < K)$ can be estimated through the sample drawn from the population of the underlying species.

For example, for *A. thaliana* data, K can be chosen as 706. Among *A. thaliana* sample (size 18958), 94.77% TSS have distance TSS-TLS less 706. Since the samples size is very large, we expect that 94.77% is a reasonable estimation of the probability $P(D(s) < 706 | s \in S)$. Considering *A. thaliana* genes with distance TSS-TLS less than 706, Figure 4 (a) gives the histogram diagram which provides the information on conditional probability $P(D(s) \in [d - a, d + a] | s \in S$ and $D(s) < 706)$, where $a = 3$.

Another example is for *H. sapiens*. If K is chosen as 42517, by the same reason above, $P(D(s) < 42517 | s \in S)$ can be estimated through sample, which is about 94%, i.e. approximately 94% *H. sapiens* genes have distance TSS-TLS less than 42517. The histogram diagram for *H. sapiens* sample with distance TSS-TLS < 42517 is given by Figure 4 (b).

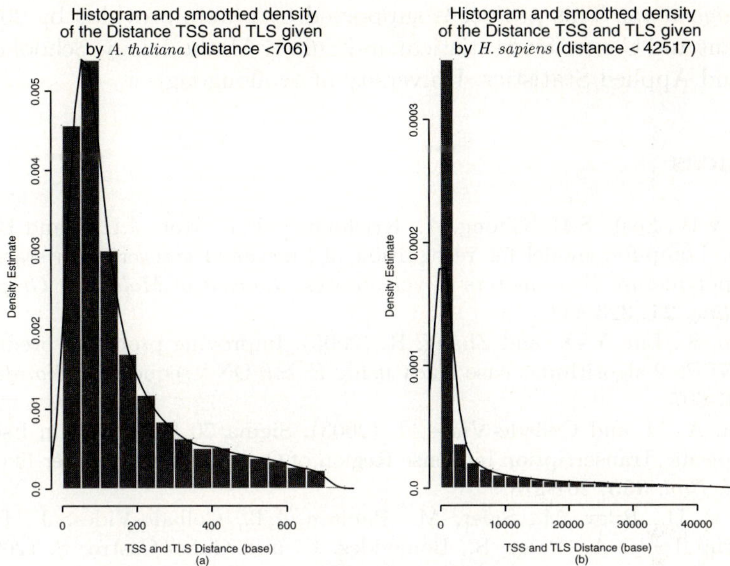

Fig. 4. The histogram and smoothed density of distance TSS-TLS for truncated situations

Figure 4 indicates that the TSS position has strong relationship with the position of its associated TLS when their distance is less than 706 and 42517 for *A. thaliana* and *H. sapiens* respectively. Since, more than 94% the distance TSS-TLS is less than 706 for *A. thaliana* and less than 42517 for *H. sapiens*, it is sufficient to use (3) to predict TSS for *A. thaliana* and *H. sapiens* instead of (2).

4   Conclusion

Statistical analysis shows that the position of the TSS of a gene is not independent of that of the TLS in the gene sequence. Our study also revealed the significant variations among the different organisms tested in the distance distribution of TSS-TLS. The distance is shortest in *E. coli* bacterium and increased to budding yeast, then *Arabidopsis* plant and finally human. Whether these difference reflet certain trend during evolution is worth further investigation. Based on the specific distance distribution data, our previously demonstrated TLS-NNPP method [2] can now be used for predicting promoters in other species including those complicated eukaryotic ones with increased accuracy. The idea developed in this paper can also be used to improve other computational promoter prediction approaches as long as the technique is developed for general situations.

PS. All the data and empirical distributions for the four species studied in this paper are available by contacting any one of the authors.

Acknowledgements. This project is supported by grants provided by 2006 URC Small Grant and Center for Statistical and Survey Methodology, School of Mathematics and Applied Statistics, University of Wollongong.

References

1. Bajic, V.B., Seah, S.H., Chong, A., Krishnan, S.P.T., Koh, J.L.Y. and Brusic, V. (2004). Computer model for recognition of functional transcription start sites in RNA polymerase II promoters of vertebrates. *Journal of Molecular Graphics and Modelling*, **21**, 323-332.
2. Burden, S., Lin, Y.-X. and Zhang, R. (2005). Improving promoter prediction for the NNPP2.2 algorithm: a case study using *E. coli* DNA sequences. *Bioinformatics*, **21**, 601-607.
3. Huerta, A. M. and Collado-Vides, J. (2003). Sigma 70 Promoters in Escherichia coli: Specific Transcrription in Dense Region of Overlapping Promoter-like Singals. *J. Mol. Biol*, **333**, 261-278.
4. Karp, P. D., Riley, M., Saier, M., Paulsen, I.T., Collado-Vides, J., Paley, S., Pellegrini-Toole, A., Paley, S., Bonavides, C. and Gama-Castro, S. (2002). The EcoCyc database. *Nucl. Acids Res.*, **30**, 56-58.
5. Molina, C. and Grotewold, E. (2005). Genome wide analysis of *Arabidopsis* core Promoters. *BMC Genomics*, **6**, 1-12.
6. Ohler, U. and Niemann, H. (2001). Identification and analysis of eukaryotic promoters: recent computational approaches. *Trends in Genetics*, **17**, 56-60.
7. Qiu, P. (2003). Computational approaches for deciphering the transcriptional regulatroy network by promoter analysis. *Biosilico*, **1**, 235-133.
8. Reese, M. (2003). http://www.fruitly.org/seq_tools/promoter.html.
9. Reese, M. and Eeckman, F. (1995). Novel neurla network prediction systems for human promoters and splice sites. *Proceedings of the Workshop on Gene-Finding and Gene Structure PredictionPennsylvania*, Philadelphia, edited by D. Searls, J. Fickett, G. Stormo and M. Noordewier.
10. Reese, M. G. (2001). Application of a time-delay neural network to promoter annotation in the Drosophila melanogaster genome. *Computers and Chemistry*, **26**, 51-56.
11. Suzuki, Y., Yamashita, R., Sugano, S. and Nakai, K. (2004). DBTSS, DataBase of Transcriptional Start Sites: progress report 2004. *Nucleic Acids Research*, **32**, 78-81.
12. Zhu, J. and Zhang, M. Q. (1998). SCPD: a promoter database of the yeast *Saccharomyces cerevisiae. Bioinformatics*, **15**, 607-611.

Protein Stability Engineering in Staphylococcal Nuclease Using an AI-Neural Network Hybrid System and a Genetic Algorithm

Christopher M. Frenz

Department of Biochemistry, New York Medical College, Valhalla, NY 10595
Phone: (914) 714-5635
christopher_frenz@nymc.edu

Abstract. With the recent increases in the use of protein-based therapeutics for the treatment of disease, protein stability engineering is an area of growing importance. Feed forward neural networks are trained to predict mutation induced protein stability changes in Staphylococcal nuclease to an accuracy of 93%. These neural networks are then implemented as part of a larger AI framework that is capable of engineering mutations within a protein sequence to yield the target stability or as the basis for a fitness function of a genetic algorithm capable of producing a population of mutation containing sequences of the desired stability. The AI neural network hybrid and genetic algorithm based approaches are significantly faster than other computational methods of protein engineering and can be utilized for proteins in which structural information is lacking.

1 Introduction

Protein-based therapeutics, like insulin, human growth hormones, and antibodies are being increasingly used as the basis for pharmaceutical treatments. One of the key factors to the success of any protein therapeutic is the stability of the protein, since this has a direct effect on both the active shelf life of the treatment as well as the active life of the treatment within the human body. Thus, in order to maximize the lifespan and effectiveness of a treatment, engineering for increased protein stability is often essential [1]. The stability of a protein is contributed to by a diversity of factors, such as electrostatics, hydrophobicity, and residue packing, and these complex intermolecular interactions often make stability prediction and hence stability engineering a challenge. This is especially true for situations in which multiple mutations are required, since studies have demonstrated that the stability of proteins containing multiple mutations is not always equal to the sum of the stability changes induced by each individual stability change [2]. Furthermore, the challenge of stability engineering is enhanced by the need to maintain the activity of the protein when introducing stabilizing mutations. Current methods rely on structural models to address this by determining which stabilizing mutations produce minimal shifts in the backbone of a given protein fold, in order to ensure that the active site geometry and/or flexibility remains relatively unchanged [3].

M. Ali and R. Dapoigny (Eds.): IEA/AIE 2006, LNAI 4031, pp. 935–942, 2006.
© Springer-Verlag Berlin Heidelberg 2006

Current methods of examining mutation induced protein stability changes include molecular dynamics simulations, which are computationally intensive and the duration of the calculations often make them impractical. Other less computationally intensive methods have involved the statistical analysis of tolerable amino acid substitutions within known elements of tertiary structure or have involved calculations of the electrostatic interactions within the tertiary structure, thereby limiting the applicability of these techniques to computationally known structures [4,5]. Recently a neural network based approached to protein stability prediction was utilized for Staphylococcal nuclease. The input to this network was based on evolutionary-based similarities between residues in the wild type protein sequence and the mutation bearing sequences, rather than tertiary structure, and the technique allowed for the rapid prediction of a protein stability score relative to that of wild-type [6]. Recent studies conducted by Capriotti et al. and Cheng et al. have also demonstrated that machine learning approaches could be utilized to predict mutational effects on protein stabilities from sequence information [7,8]. Each of these approaches utilized support vector machines and was able to predict the effects of single site mutations across a range of proteins. Machine learning based methodologies offer the additional potential advantage of reducing mutation induced effects of activity, if activity screening is utilized during the process of training set creation, since positions, where mutations are shown to have a detrimental effect on activity, could be eliminated at this stage.

This study seeks to apply neural networks trained to predict protein stability to protein stability engineering tasks, by demonstrating an artificial intelligence (AI)-neural network hybrid system that can pinpoint mutations and/or combinations of mutations that will yield a protein of the target stability as well by demonstrating genetic algorithms that can evolve a population of sequences that will yield the desired stability.

2 Methods

2.1 Preparation of Input Patterns

Mutation effects on stability correspond to both the position of the mutation within the protein structure as well as the severity of the mutation at that position. Input pattern were prepared using amino acid similarity tables based on the evolutionary frequency of amino acid substitutions in homologous proteins and derived by Jones et al [9]. The more frequently an amino acid replaces another over evolutionary time, the more similar those amino acids are, and accordingly the greater the similarity between two residues the greater the likelihood that tertiary structure and stability are maintained [7]. Thus, the wild type amino acid sequence was then set as the reference sequence. Each mutation containing sequence was then parsed into its individual residue constituents and its similarity to the wild type residue at the corresponding position calculated as described by Frenz [6]. In this way, an array of similarity values was generated for each sequence. All array/residue positions that were never mutated were then removed, since the stability values of these positions never change and hence would provide no information to the network. The finalized array for any given mutant sequence consisted of the similarity scores obtained for each of the 20 possible mutation sites utilized in the study [6]. The 20 mutation sites were based on staphylococcal nuclease stability data collected by Green & Shortle [10] and are represented by the single residue mutation data shown in Table 1. Green & Shortle utilized guanine hydrochloride denaturation to determine the stability changes induced by amino acid mutations, relative to the wild type. Each of the 20 similarity scores in these reduced arrays was then subsequently input into one of the input neurons of the neural network.

2.2 Neural Network Construction and Training

The type of network that is employed in this study is a feed-forward neural network that learns with adaptive learning rate back-propagation. It consists of three different layers: an input layer, a hidden layer, and an output layer laid out in a 20-6-1 architecture, with each layer fully interconnected to the preceding layer by a weight matrix. The input layer is used to transfer the array of similarity measures into the neural network. A bias is also added to each neuron in the hidden and output layers, which, scales the neurons input values before they pass through the neurons, bipolar sigmoid transfer function. The transfer function for the output unit was a bipolar sigmoid scaled from 0.55 and 1.3, yields a relative stability value that the network

Table 1. Mutation and relative stability data use to train and validate the neural network

Mutation	Relative Stability	Mutation	Relative Stability
WT	1.00	A69T	1.13
I15V	1.05	A90S	1.10
I72V	1.02	I15V+Y85A[1]	1.09
Y85A	1.01	I72V+Y113A[1]	1.10
I92V	1.01	I18M+T33S[1]	1.09
Y113A	0.99	A69T+A90S[1]	1.3
A130G	0.96	L7A+G79S[2]	0.8
L7A	0.89	V23F+L37A[2]	0.73
V23F	0.84	L37A+E75V[2]	0.79
L37A	0.89	T62A+V66L[2]	0.68
T62A	0.88	T62A+G88V[3]	0.69
V66L	0.82	E75V+P117L[3]	0.78
E75V	0.79	P117L+N118D[3]	0.86
G79D	0.87	V23F+A69T[3]	1.17
G79S	0.82	V23F+A90S[4]	1.06
G88V	0.78	L7A+I92V[4]	0.96
P117L	0.92	V23F+A130G[4]	0.76
N118D	0.86	T33S+L37A[4]	1.01
I18M	1.07	V23F+G79S[5]	0.59
T33S	1.09	I15V+L37A[5]	1.01
T62G	1.08	I72V+Y85A[5]	1.07

Superscript Number Indicates Cross-Validation Subset

was trained to associate with the input pattern [6]. The network used in this study was programmed in MATLAB Release 12, utilizing the Neural Network Toolbox.

A training set for the aforementioned neural network was constructed from the mutant sequence and relative stability pairs of Staphylococcal nuclease described by Green & Shortle [10]. Over-training was avoided by using five subsets of the 42 mutant sequences in the training set as cross-validation sequences (Table 1). These subset sequences were removed from the training set and used to determine if over-training had occurred. Training was conducted until the prediction set error dropped below 10^{-2} or stopped improving with continued training epochs. Once this occurred, training was stopped and the validation sequences were input into the neural network. If the network was able to predict the relative stabilities of the mutant validation sequences to within 10% of the target values, the neural network architecture was saved. If the prediction error was off by more than 10% then the network was discarded and a new neural network was trained [6]. Five networks were trained in this manner (one for each subset) and the finalized results were the averages obtained from these 5 networks.

2.3 Artificial Intelligence Construction

The major components of an artificial intelligent system are a knowledge base and a control mechanism that influences how the knowledge in the knowledge base is used to reach a given goal. In the case of AI-neural network hybrid systems trained neural networks are able to serve as a knowledge base component [11]. In this particular case, the five trained neural networks make up the entire knowledge base, since the average of these networks provide an accurate representation of the effects mutational severity and position have upon the stability of staphylococcal nuclease and thus can be considered as encompassing a reasonable body of knowledge upon which further decisions can be made.

The control mechanism of this AI hybrid system utilizes depth first search. The system is initially presented with a target stability range, and begins to engineer a suitable mutant by taking the wild-type sequence and making a mutation within that sequence. This mutated sequence is then input into the neural network and a stability prediction is made. If the prediction is in the target range the sequence is outputted and the calculation completed. If the prediction is outside of the target range, the control mechanism considers whether or not the mutation has brought the stability closer to the target stability. If yes, the mutation is kept and an additional mutation is made in order to attempt to reach the target. If no, the mutation is discarded and another mutation made. This process is repeated until a sequence of the desired stability is reached. The AI logic also allows the maximum number of allowable mutations to be set by the user, and hence the depth first search algorithm will backtrack and consider a path invalid if it cannot reach a solution with a number of mutations that are less than or equal to this cutoff value. This is a desirable feature, since reaching a solution that utilizes only a small number of mutations is less likely to adversely affect the function of the protein. It is also advisable that the protein only be allowed to make mutations in residues that are not highly conserved or crucial for protein function, in order to preserve function.

2.4   Genetic Algorithm Construction

Genetic algorithms allow for the simulation of evolutionary processes *in silico* [11]. For purposes of this simulation each of the twenty residue positions utilized in the neural network was considered a gene and each of the twenty possible amino acids that could occupy that position were considered an allele. The trained neural networks formed the basis of a fitness function in which fitness was defined as an acceptable range of target stabilities. An initial population of 5000 sequences, each containing a single random mutation, was initialized and the fitness function applied to this population. All sequences deemed unfit were removed from the population, and up to 100 randomly chosen sequences that met the fitness criteria were allowed to breed with another a second random member of the population. Breeding generates offspring with a genetic makeup that is comprised of alleles from each parent sequence. For each residue position (gene) there a 50% chance of an allele coming from any one parent. During breeding there is also a 15% chance that a random mutation is introduced in any given gene, which works to simulate genetic drift and helps to ensure that the simulation results in a heterogeneous population at the end. At the end of the breeding step, the fitness function is applied again, and the unfit members removed from the population. Simulations are run for a total of 50 successive generations. At the end of the simulation it is possible to screen the resultant population based on other desired criteria, such as eliminating members of the population that contain more than a maximum allowable number of mutations.

3   Results and Discussion

3.1   Neural Network Results

The neural network is fed both mutant residue similarity information (similarity score) as well as mutant residue position information (location in array). Through training the network is able to learn which positions are most crucial to stability along with the effects of mutation severity at each position. The network learns how multiple inputs work together to produce an output, and in this way learns to associate the multiple mutation patterns with a given stability. Currently an overall accuracy of 92.8% was obtained for 55 Staphylococcal nuclease unknowns and some representative predictions are displayed in Figure 1. Furthermore, the neural networks were able to accurately predict the effects of non-additive mutation combinations, such as L37A/G79S/P117L, which based on the summation of the stability effects of the constituent mutations, should be significantly more destabilizing than observed [6].

In addition to the accuracy of the technique, the other major advantage is that the neural network based predictions are not computationally intensive. Neural network training only takes 3 minutes on a 600 MHz Pentium III processor and unknown predictions are instantaneous. This makes protein engineering in finite time tractable even on a desktop computer, since it enables the artificial intelligence component and genetic algorithms to evaluate hundreds of mutation combinations in a period of several seconds, rather than weeks to months as could be expected from structural based techniques. The other advantage to this neural network based methodology is

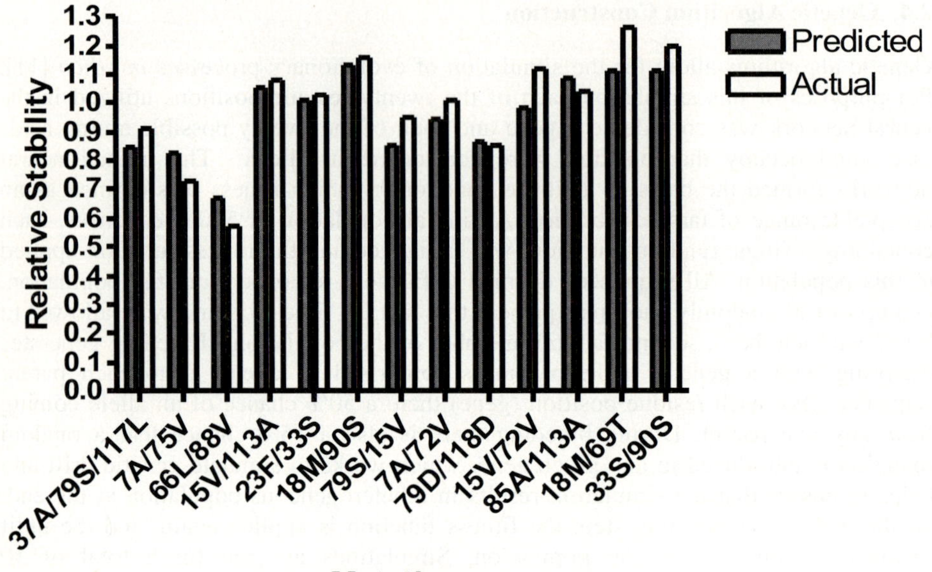

Fig. 1. Representative neural network predictions compared to the values experimentally determined by Green & Shortle [10]

that no explicit structural information is required, which means that this technique is especially viable for situations in which the structure of the target protein remains unknown. The one disadvantage to this technique is that the neural network can only make accurate predictions for residue positions that it was trained to work with. However, with the advent of site directed mutagenesis, a significant number of mutations have already been characterized.

3.2 AI-Neural Network Hybrid Results

The AI neural network hybrid system can be an effective means of engineering protein sequences that correspond to a target stability. When asked to engineer a mutant that has 1.07 times the stability of wild-type with a three mutation maximum the AI-neural network hybrid suggests the mutations T33G/Y113C (Figure 2). This is a probable mutation combination, since T33S mutants are shown to be 1.08 times as stable as wild type and mutation of Y113 to a non-aromatic uncharged residue had no significant effect of stability [10]. Both serine (S) and glycine (G) are aliphatic amino acids with side chains that are shorter in length than threonine (T). When asked to engineer a mutant that has a stability of 0.83 that of wild-type, the hybrid system suggested a G88A mutation, which is also probable, since mutation of G88 to the longer aliphatic amino acid valine destabilizes the protein to 0.79 that of wild-type [10]. Alanine is an aliphatic amino acid that is intermediate in length between glycine and valine and hence it is likely that it is destabilizing but not to the same extent as that of valine.

```
Position:   7 15 18 23 33 37 62 66 69 72 75 79 85 88 90 92 113 117 118 130
Start:      LIIVTLTTAIEGYGAIYPNA
Mutant:     LIIVGLTTAIEGYGAICPNA
Target:     1.07 +/- 0.02
Stability:  1.06111100626469

Start:      LIIVTLTTAIEGYGAIYPNA
Mutant:     LIIVTLTTAIEGYAAIYPNA
Target:     0.83 +/- 0.02
Stability:  0.847678026564103
```

Fig. 2. AI-neural network hybrid output for the engineering of a stabilizing and destabilizing mutant protein sequence

3.3 Genetic Algorithms Results

The genetic algorithm is a more computationally intensive approach than the AI neural network hybrid system, yet it offers the advantage of evolving multiple solutions within the targeted stability range. A representative simulation which requested that the population members have a relative stability have 1.07 ± 2, yielded 72 distinct solutions. In the initial generation, the sequence containing a T33D mutant was determined to be fit, since it yielded a predicted stability of 1.09 times that of wild type, which is probable, since Hydrogen bonding calculations in the Swiss PDB viewer indicate that the aspartate (D) mutant allows for improved H-bonding over threonine. By the end of the simulation, 69% of these sequences contained this single mutation. Additional generations built upon this initial point mutation by incorporating additional mutations into the sequence, which further modified the resultant stability scores to yield sequences whose stabilities encompassed the full range of fit stabilities.

4 Conclusions

Both the AI neural network hybrid and the genetic algorithms are effective methods of protein stability engineering, yet each provides distinct advantages. The depth first search based AI algorithm is less computationally intensive and provides a means of arriving at a single solution to the stability-engineering problem. The genetic algorithm approach is the more computationally intensive approach, yet the populations of sequences generated offers researchers a variety of mutation combinations to choose from, which has the benefit of allowing them to choose the mutation combinations that are best suited for their stability engineering needs. These methodologies illustrate that neural network based methods of protein stability engineering are viable alternatives in cases where structural based methods are not feasible, either due to limitations of processing time or a lack of structural information. The utility of machine learning based approaches for purposes of enzyme engineering is also further supported by recent work in which machine learning based methodologies were used to engineer proteinase K variants with activities up to 45 times that of the wild type enzyme [12]. These findings suggest that machine learning based approaches may be applicable to a diversity of protein engineering tasks and further suggest the potential for machine learning based systems that could be used to simultaneously engineer enhancements in stability and activity.

References

[1] Cleland, J.L., Jones, A.J.S., Craik, C.S.: Introduction to protein engineering. In: Cleland, J.L. & Craik, C.S. (Eds) Protein Engineering: Principles and Practice, Wiley-Liss, NY, (1996) 1-32.

[2] Braxton, S.: Protein engineering for stability. In: Cleland, J.L., Craik, C.S. (Eds.), Protein Engineering: Principles and Practice, Wiley-Liss, NY, (1996) 299-316.

[3] Korkegian, A, Black, M.E., Baker, D., Stoddard, B.L. Computational thermostabilization of an enzyme. Science **308** (2005) 857-860.

[4] Borjesson, U., Hunenberger, P.H.: Effect of mutations involving charged residues on the stability of staphylococcal nuclease: a continuum electrostatics study. Protein Engineering **16** (2003) 831-40.

[5] Topham, C.M., Srinivasan, N., Blundell, T.L.: Prediction of the stability of protein mutants based on structural environment-dependent amino acid substitution and propensity tables. Protein Engineering **10** (1997) 7-21.

[6] Frenz, C.M.: Neural network-based prediction of mutation induced protein stability changes in *Staphylococcal nuclease* at 20 residue positions. Proteins: Structure, Function, Bioinformatics, **59** (2005) 147-151.

[7] Capriotti, E., Fariselli, P., Calabrese, R., Casidio, R.: Predicting protein stability changes from sequences using support vector machines, Bioinformatics **21 Suppl 2** (2005) ii54-ii58.

[8] Cheng, J., Randall, A., Baldi, P.: Prediction of protein stability changes for single-site mutations using support vector machines, Proteins: Structure, Function, Bioinformatics, **62** (2006) 1125-32.

[9] Jones, D.T., Taylor, W.R., Thornton, J.M.: The rapid generation of mutation data matrices from protein sequences. CABIOS **8** (1992) 275-82.

[10] Green, S.M., Shortle, D. Patterns of nonadditivity between pairs of stability mutations in staphylococcal nuclease. Biochemistry **32** (1993) 10131-9.

[11] Tsoukalas, L.H., Zadeh, L.A., Uhrig, R.E., Hines, J.W.: Fuzzy and Neural Approaches in Engineering, Wiley, NY. (1996).

[12] Gustafsson, C., Liao, J., Warmuth, S., Ness, J., Wang, R., Minshull, J.: Engineering proteinase K using machine learning and synthetic genes. PepTalk (2006) Abstract Book.

Identification of Over and Under Expressed Genes Mediating Allergic Asthma

Rajat K. De[1] and Anindya Bhattacharya[2]

[1] Machine Intelligence Unit, Indian Statistical Institute, 203 B. T. Road,
Kolkata 700108, India
`rajat@isical.ac.in`
[2] Department of Computer Science & Engineering, Netaji Subhash Engineering
College, Techno City, Garia, Kolkata 700152, India

Abstract. The present article focuses on identifying some of the genes mediating the development of asthma. Here we apply a pattern recognition based approach to identify the genes those are severely over or under expressed in the allergen samples. The methodology involves clustering on gene expression and fold values followed by determining similarity/dissimilarity among various clusters, and measuring the extent of over/under expression of genes. From this analysis we have identified several genes those have significantly changed their expression values for asthmatic condition, and have reported in the present article. Some of these observations are supported by some earlier investigations. Others have been stayed unnoticed so far, but may play crucial role in mediating the development of asthma.

Keywords: mouse, clustering, fold value, Jaccard score, DB-index.

1   Introduction

Modern genome research, being aided by high-throughput technologies, is producing enormous amount of data that has to be organized, classified and interpreted. In functional genomics, it is increasingly appreciated that various cellular processes are rooted from the dynamic interaction among its many constituents, such as, DNA, RNA, proteins and small molecules. This leads to the emerging of some challenging problems including determination of functions of genes/proteins, interaction among genes/proteins and proteins/proteins, and pathway analysis. Identification of genes whose expression patterns mediate a particular disease is also of great interest.

Asthma is an inflammatory disease that remains poorly understood and hard to control. This disease is characterized by airway hyper reactivity (AHR, defined by exaggerated airflow obstruction in response to bronchoconstrictors), mucus overproduction and chronic eosinophilic inflammation. AHR and mucus overproduction are consistently linked to asthma symptoms and morbidity. Asthma is thought to be mediated by Th2 lymphocytes, which produce a limited repertoire of cytokines, including interleukin-13 (IL-13) [1, 2, 3, 4].

M. Ali and R. Dapoigny (Eds.): IEA/AIE 2006, LNAI 4031, pp. 943–952, 2006.
© Springer-Verlag Berlin Heidelberg 2006

In this article, we report a new methodology based on clustering for identifying a set of genes mediating the development of asthma. These genes are either over expressed or under expressed in the allergen samples as compared to those in normal ones, and are selected from a large set of genes using the methodology involving Partitioning Around Mediod (PAM) [5] and Fuzzy c-means (FCM) [6] clustering algorithms. The methodology of this selection considers oligonucleotide microarray gene expression data GDS958 [7] dealing with expression patterns of as many as 22690 genes of both normal and allergen samples. Clustering algorithms have been applied on gene expression as well as fold values (ratio of expression values of genes in allergen and normal samples). This is followed by determining similarity/dissimilarity among various clusters and also measuring the extent of over/under expression of genes. A set of genes mediating the development of asthma has been newly identified along with those already reported by some earlier investigations [1, 3, 8].

2   Data Description

The oligonucleotide microarray gene expression data (GDS958) that were used here were obtained from lung tissue of mouse [7]. The data set contains samples which had undergone either of the two types of strain, and are termed as Wild Type mouse and IL-13 Knocked Out mouse samples. Each of these Wild Type and IL-13 Knocked Out mouse samples can be either an Allergen sample or a Control sample. Two different types of treatments were used for both Wild Type strain and IL-13 Knocked Out strain: (i) House Dust Mite (HDM) and (ii) Phosphate Buffered Saline (PBS). Allergen samples were obtained from HDM treated Wild Type strain and IL-13 Knocked Out strain, whereas control samples from PBS treated Wild Type strain and IL-13 Knocked Out strain.

Thus we have four different types of sample: (1) HDM treated Wild Type allergen samples, (2) HDM treated IL 13 Knocked Out allergen samples, (3) PBS treated Wild Type control samples and (4) PBS treated IL 13 Knocked Out control samples. In the present investigation, we considered samples undergone only Wild Type strain, *i.e*, (1) HDM treated Wild Type allergen samples and (2) PBS treated Wild Type control samples.

The data set GDS958 contains expression pattern for 22690 genes obtained from six Wild Type samples. Three samples GSM21415, GSM21418 and GSM 21420 are HDM treated Wild Type allergen samples, whereas GSM21422, GSM 21424 and GSM21426 are PBS treated Wild Type control samples. Further information on this data is available at [7]. It is to be mentioned here that the data set contains expression profiles of cytokines including IL-13, IL-4, IL-5 and their receptors known as key mediators for allergen induced immediate development of asthma. This is due to hyperreactivity of the airway and mucus overproduction in the lung as immediate response for house dust mite allergen. The data set is last updated on December 12, 2004, so it is expected to contain recent information.

3   Methodology

The methodology we have used here are based on well known partitioning around medoid (PAM) and fuzzy c-means (FCM) clustering algorithms. Both these algorithms require an expected number k of clusters as input for their execution. For example, if we give $k = 3$ as input, the algorithms partition the entire data set into 3 clusters. Thus selecting a suitable value of k is crucial for these algorithms. In order to find the best k for a set of data points we are going to cluster, we have used a cluster validity index, namely, Davies-Bouldin index (DB-index) [9] which varies with the number of clusters k. Lower the value of DB-index, better is the clustering and vice versa. For details of the clustering algorithms and expression for DB-index, one may refer to [5, 9]. These clustering algorithms have been executed on the (i) expression values of genes given in the data set and (ii) fold values of genes define in Section 3.2.

3.1   Clustering on Expression Values

Clustering on expression value considers gene expression values in both normal (control) and allergen samples. Let there be n number of normal samples and m number of allergen samples. Each of the genes present in the data set is considered as a data point or a pattern. That is, each data point (*i.e.*, each gene) has dimension n for wildtype-normal and m for wildtype-allergen sets. Each of these sets of genes were grouped into k number of clusters using these clustering algorithms. It is to be noted that we select k for which DB-index value attains a minimum. Thus for wildtype-normal samples, we have (say) k_{normal} control clusters $S_1, S_2, \ldots, S_{k_{normal}}$ containing genes with different domains of expression values. Similar is the case for wildtype-allergen samples, where $k_{allergen}$ number of clusters $T_1, T_2, \ldots, T_{k_{allergen}}$ consist of genes with different domains of expression values. The genes in any of these clusters are expected to be co-expressed. On the other hand, genes in different clusters should have different domains of expression values.

Now we find the relationship (*i.e.*, similarity or dissimilarity) between the control and allergen clusters. For this purpose, we use Jaccard score which is widely used in literature [10]. Let us assume that ith control cluster S_i has the highest degree of similarity with jth allergen cluster T_j. Thus it is expected that the domains of expression values of genes in S_i and T_j are similar. If S_i and T_i contain genes in control and allergen samples, respectively, with high expression values, then it is expected that most of the genes (with high expression values) in cluster S_i are present in the cluster T_i. If a gene, say g, is present in T_i but not in S_i then we may infer that the gene g is over expressed in the allergen samples. Thus the genes in the set $(T_i - (S_i \cap T_i))$ are over expressed in the allergen samples. On the other hand, if both T_j and S_j contain genes with low expression values, the presence of gene g in T_j but not in S_j would lead to the inference of the gene g being under expressed in the allergen samples. Thus the set $(T_j - (S_j \cap T_j))$ contains only the genes that are under expressed in the allergen samples.

3.2 Clustering on Fold Values

Apart from the clustering on expression values, genes were grouped by these clustering algorithms on their fold values which are defined below. Let there be n number of control samples and m number of allergen samples, and the expression values of a gene g in ith control sample be c_g^i and that in jth allergen sample be a_g^j. Then the fold value f_g^{ij} of gene g is defined as

$$f_g^{ij} = a_g^j / c_g^i \tag{1}$$

Thus we have mn number of fold values of a gene g. We form an mn-dimensional fold vector $\mathbf{v}_g$ corresponding to gene g as

$$\mathbf{v}_g = [f_g^{11}, f_g^{12}, \ldots, f_g^{ij}, \ldots, f_g^{mn}]^T$$

If fold value f_g^{ij} of a gene g is nearly equal to one, expression values of the gene g in both ith control and jth allergen samples are almost equal. Therefore, we may say that the gene g has no role in mediating the development of asthma. Fold value f_g^{ij} of gene g grater than one (or less than one) indicates that gene g gets over expressed (or under expressed) in jth allergen sample compared to ith control sample. It is to be mentioned here that in an ideal situation if gene g has no role in mediating asthma, the corresponding fold vector would be closed to the vector $\mathbf{v}_0 = [1, 1, \ldots, 1]^T$, where all the components of $\mathbf{v}_0$ are 1.

In order to compute an average extent of over or under expression of genes in an allergen cluster, we have measured Euclidean distance D_{avg} between the corresponding cluster center and $\mathbf{v}_0$, which is given by

$$D_{avg} = \sqrt{||\mathbf{v}_A - \mathbf{v}_0||}$$

Here $\mathbf{v}_A = [v_A^{11}, v_A^{12}, \ldots, v_A^{ij}, \ldots, v_A^{mn}]^T$, $i = 1, 2, \ldots, n$; $j = 1, 2, \ldots, m$ is the center of an allergen cluster. The higher the value of D_{avg}, the higher will be the extent of over or under expression of genes contained in the allergen cluster. Moreover, in order to determine whether D_{avg} indicates an average over or under expression, we use a term $SIGN$ defined as

$$SIGN = \sum_{i=1}^{n} \sum_{j=1}^{m} (v_A^{ij} - 1)$$

If $SIGN > 0$ then D_{avg} indicates an average over expression. On the other hand, if $SIGN < 0$ then D_{avg} indicates an average under expression. For $SIGN > 0$, the highest D_{avg} value indicates that the genes in the allergen cluster get the highest extent of over expression (on an average). Similarly, for $SIGN < 0$, the highest D_{avg} value indicates the highest extent of under expression (on an average).

4 Results and Analysis

Here we identify some genes mediating the development of asthma, by applying the aforesaid methodology based on the clustering algorithms (PAM and FCM) on the gene expression data set GDS958 containing 22690 genes. Some of these genes those are over or under expressed in the allergen samples were not known earlier. The clustering algorithms were applied both on expression values and fold values of genes.

4.1   On Expression Values

In the case of clustering based on expression values of the data set GDS958, the dimension of a data corresponding to a gene in both normal (GSM21422, GSM21424 and GSM21426) and allergen (GSM21415, GSM21418 and GSM 21420) samples is three, as $n = m = 3$. Here we have provided $k = 2$ as input to both these algorithm as DB-index attains its minimum at $k = 2$ for both PAM and FCM (Figure 1). Thus we have obtained two control clusters (S_1 and S_2) and two allergen clusters (T_1 and T_2). We have computed Jaccard score to determine the similarity between control and allergen clusters. We have found, from Jaccard score, that the cluster S_1 is the most similar to T_1 and S_2 to T_2. In fact, the clusters S_1 and T_1 contain genes with low expression values, and S_2 and T_2 contain those with high expression values. Thus we infer that the genes being present in S_1 but not in T_1 are over expressed in the allergen samples. Similarly, the genes in S_2 but not in T_2 are under expressed in the allergen samples.

By applying both PAM and FCM, we have found a few genes, out of the entire set of 22690 genes, which are over expressed in the allergen samples. Some of these observations were already found in [11, 12, 13, 14]. In the present investigation, we have found some new genes including Gpnmb (glycoprotein (transmembrane) nmb), Fxyd4 (FXYD domain-containing ion transport regulator 4), Serpina3n (serine (or cysteine) proteinase inhibitor, clade A, member 3N), Slc26a4 (solute carrier family 26, member 4), Igl-V1 (immunoglobulin lambda chain, variable 1), A430103C15Rik (RIKEN cDNA A430103C15 gene), Igh-4 (immunoglobulin heavy chain 4 (serum IgG1)), AI324046 (expressed sequence AI324046), IgK-V1 (immunoglobulin kappa chain variable 1 (V1)),

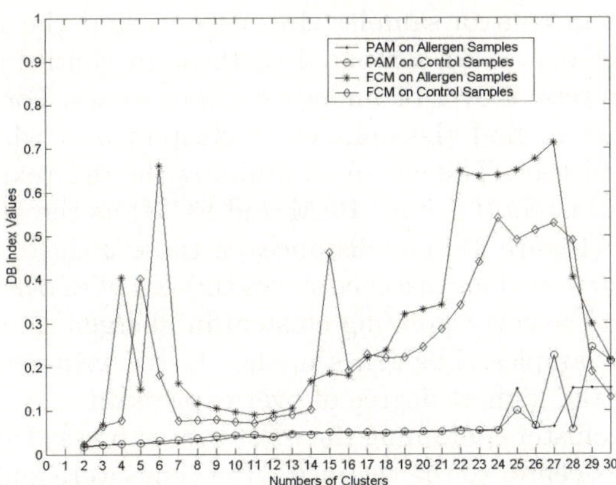

Fig. 1. Variation of DB-index computed on expression values with respect to k

IgK-V5 (immunoglobulin kappa chain variable 5 (V5 family)), Muc5ac (mucin 5, subtypes A and C, tracheobronchial/gastric), which are over expressed in the allergen samples. None of them were previously found responsible for asthma, but in our experiment, very large changes in expression values for all of these genes in the allergen samples suggest that they may have very important role in mediating the development asthma.

Likewise the set of genes that are under expressed includes Ppp1r2 (protein phosphatase 1, regulatory (inhibitor) subunit 2), Cyp2a4 (cytochrome P450, family 2, subfamily a, polypeptide 4), Tncc (troponin C, cardiac/slow skeletal), Dusp16 (dual specificity phosphatase 16), Scnn1b (sodium channel, nonvoltage-gated 1 beta) and Slc7a10 (solute carrier family 7 (cationic amino acid trans-porter, y+ system), member 10) are some of the significantly under expressed genes found in the allergen samples. These genes have newly been found un-der expressed in the allergen samples. Some of the observations that are in accordance with earlier investigations include over expression of Clca3 (chloride channel calcium activated 3) [12], Ear11 (eosinophil-associated, ribonuclease A family, member 11) [8], Sprr2a (small proline-rich protein 2A) [15] in allergen samples.

4.2   On Fold Values

Clustering algorithms were executed on the fold values. Here we are looking for three clusters corresponding to (i) the genes not (over/under) expressed in the allergen samples, (ii) those over expressed in the allergen samples and (iii) those under expressed in the allergen samples. Thus we have considered $k = 3$ as input to these algorithms. It is to be mentioned here that we have three control samples (GSM21422, GSM21424 and GSM 21426), $i.e.$, $n = 3$, and three allergen samples (GSM21415, GSM21418 and GSM21420), $i.e.$, $m = 3$. So the fold vector $\mathbf{v}_g$ of a gene g has the dimension of 9.

It is to be mentioned here that the clusters containing over or under expressed genes may also include those which were not (over or under) expressed much compared to those in control samples. In order to find the genes which were much over or under expressed compared to those in control samples, we have further divided the sets of over or under expressed genes. For this purpose, we have used DB-index to find the number of clusters into which each of these sets to be divided further. The cluster containing the over expressed genes was divided into 2 sub clusters (for both PAM and FCM) as the DB-index attains a minimum at $k = 2$ (Figure 2). The distances of these 2 cluster centers from the vector $\mathbf{v}_0$ were computed. This distance shows the extent of over expression of the genes (contained in the corresponding cluster) in allergen samples as compared to those in control samples. The genes in the cluster with center farthest from the vector $\mathbf{v}_0$ have the highest degree of over expression.

Considering the cluster containing the most over expressed genes, as shown by the distance from its center to the vector $\mathbf{v}_0$, 158 genes were found to be the most over expressed in the allergen samples obtained by both PAM and FCM. Out of these 158 genes, Gpnmb, Fxyd4, Serpina3n, Slc26a4, Igl-V1, A430103C15Rik,

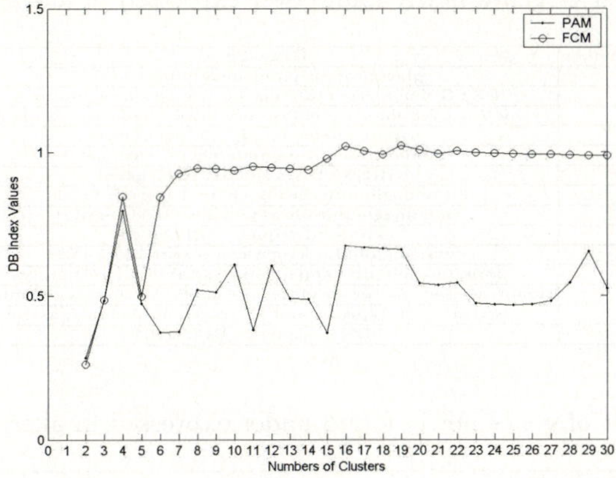

Fig. 2. Variation of DB-index computed on fold values of over expressed genes with respect to k

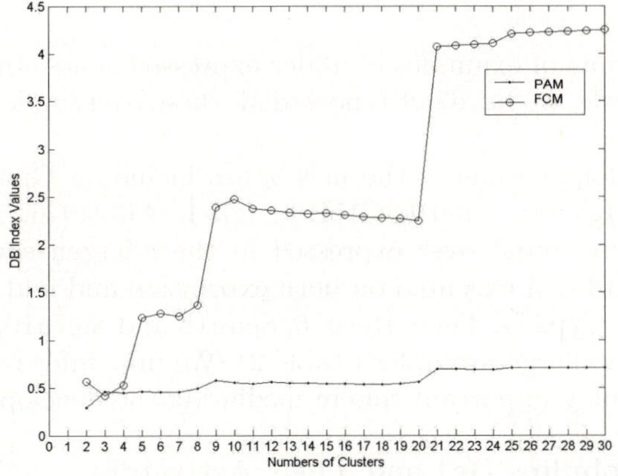

Fig. 3. Variation of DB-index computed on fold values of under expressed genes with respect to k

Igh-4, AI324046, IgK-V1, IgK-V5, Muc5ac are some examples which were also found to be over expressed based on the expression values of the genes.

Similarly, the cluster containing under expressed genes was divided into 2 sub clusters for PAM and 3 sub clusters for FCM, as DB-index attains its minimum at $k = 2$ for PAM and at $k = 3$ for FCM (Figure 3). As in the case of over expressed genes, distances of all the cluster centers from the vector $\mathbf{v}_0$ is computed to check the extent of under expression. The cluster containing the genes having the highest extent of under expression in allergen samples compared to that in control sample is selected based on these distance values. Using the above process based on the distance measure, the farthest cluster is identified. As in the case of clustering based on expression values, Ppp1r2, Cyp2a4, Tncc, Dusp16, Scnn1b

Table 1. List of genes newly found over expressed in allergen samples

GenBank Accession Number	Gene Title	Gene Symbol
NM_053110	glycoprotein (transmembrane) nmb	Gpnmb
NM_033648	FXYD domain-containing ion transport regulator 4	Fxyd4
NM_009252	serine (or cysteine) proteinase inhibitor, clade A, member 3N	Serpina3n
NM_011867	solute carrier family 26, member 4	Slc26a4
AK008145	immunoglobulin lambda chain, variable 1	Igl-V1
BC024402	RIKEN cDNA A430103C15 gene	A430103C15Rik
BC008237	immunoglobulin heavy chain 4 (serum IgG1)	Igh-4
AK007826	immunoglobulin heavy chain (J558 family)	Igh-VJ558
BE687919	expressed sequence AI324046	AI324046
Z95478	immunoglobulin kappa chain variable 1 (V1)	Igk-V1
U29768	immunoglobulin kappa chain variable 5 (V5 family)	Igk-V5
BM250782	tumor necrosis factor receptor sPAM, FCMerfamily, member 9	Tnfrsf9
AK008656	mucin 5, subtypes A and C, tracheobronchial/gastric	Muc5ac
BB113173	cDNA sequence BC032204	BC032204

Table 2. List of genes newly found under expressed in allergen samples

GenBank Accession Number	Gene Title	Gene Symbol
NM_025800	protein phosphatase 1, regulatory (inhibitor) subunit 2	Ppp1r2
NM_007812	cytochrome P450, family 2, subfamily a, polypeptide 4	Cyp2a4
NM_009393	troponin C, cardiac/slow skeletal	Tncc
NM_130447	dual specificity phosphatase 16	Dusp16
NM_011325	sodium channel, nonvoltage-gated 1 beta	Scnn1b
NM_017394	solute carrier family 7 (cationic amino acid transporter, y+ system), member 10	Slc7a10

and Slc7a10 are some of examples of under expressed genes. In order to restrict the size of the article, we have not reported all these over/under expressed genes here.

Thus we have found some of the new genes including Gpnmb, Fxyd4, Serpina3n, Slc26a4, Igl-V1, A430103C15Rik, Igh-4, AI324046, IgK-V1, IgK-V5, Muc5ac which were found over expressed in the allergen samples, by applying both PAM and FCM executed on both expression and fold values (Table 1). Similarly, Ppp1r2, Cyp2a4, Tncc, Dusp16, Scnn1b and Slc7a10 were found to be under expressed in allergen samples (Table 2). We may infer from this fact that these genes must play important role in mediating the development of asthma.

4.3 Immunoglobulins (Ig) and Their Activators

In order to describe how these newly found over expressed genes mediate the development of asthma, we consider immunoglobulins which are well known as mediators of asthma. First of all, let us review various classes and basic structure of immunoglobulins.

Immunoglobulins are glycoprotein molecules that are produced by plasma cells in response to an immunogen and which function as antibodies. An immunoglobulin (Ig) consists of 2 identical light chains (L) and 2 identical heavy chains (H)); at the three-dimensional level. An immunoglobulin (Ig) chain consists of one N-terminal variable domain, V, and one (for an L chain) or several (for an H chain) C-terminal constant domain(s), C. Immunoglobulins can be divided into five different classes, based on differences in the amino acid sequences in the constant region of the heavy chains. They are (1) IgG - Gamma heavy chains, (2) IgM - Mu heavy chains, (3) IgA - Alpha heavy chains, (4) IgD - Delta heavy chains and (5) IgE - Epsilon heavy chains.

(1) *IgK (kappa) genes with light chains*: Here in our analysis we have found IgKV1 and IgKV5 significantly over expressed in asthma samples. These genes are IgK genes and their product constructs N-terminal variable domain of immunoglobulins. (2) *IgL (lambda) genes with light chains*: Similarly, IgLV1 has been found to be significantly over expressed in asthma samples. These genes are IgL genes and their product constructs N-terminal variable domain of immunoglobulins. (3) *IgH ('heavy') genes with heavy chains*: Heavy chains IgH4, IgHVJ558 and AI324046 have also been found to be significantly over expressed in asthma samples. These genes are IgH genes.

Thus these 6 genes take part in construction of immunoglobulin. Immunoglobulin E (IgE), a class of immunoglobulins, was identified as the key molecule in mediating allergic asthma. Production of IgE is significantly increased in allergic asthma condition. Hence increase in expression levels of these 6 genes cause increase in production of immunoglobulins, thereby playing a significant role in mediating allergic asthma.

5   Conclusions

The present investigation demonstrates a pattern recognition based approach for identification of genes mediating the development of asthma. The methodology involves the application of clustering algorithms on expression and fold values of genes, followed by determining similarity/dissimilarity among various clusters and measuring the extent of over and under expression of genes contained in different clusters.

On applying the said methodology, we have identified IL-13, Spp1, Clca3, Ctsk, Ear11, Sprr2a, Chi3l3, Arg1 and Itln genes heavily over expressed in asthma samples. Previous work and biological evidences suggest that these genes are responsible for asthma.

We have identified several new genes, by the methodology applied on both expression and fold values, including Gpnmb, Fxyd4, Serpina3n, Slc26a4, Igl-V1, A430103C15Rik, Igh-4, AI324046, IgK-V1, IgK-V5, Muc5ac that are severely over expressed in allergic asthma condition. Similarly, we have found several genes including Ppp1r2, Cyp2a4, Tncc, Dusp16, Scnn1b, Slc7a10 that are heavily under expressed in asthmatic condition. Therefore, these genes may be considered as mediators for asthma.

References

1. Grunig, G., Warnock, M., Wakil, A.E., Venkayya, R., Brombacher, F., Rennick, D.M., Sheppard, D., Mohrs, M., Donaldson, D.D., Locksley, R.M., Corry, D.B.: Requirement for il-13 independently of il-4 in experimental asthma. Science **282** (1998) 2261–2263
2. Wills-Karp, M., Luyimbazi, J., Xu, X., Schofield, B., Neben, T.Y., Karp, C.L., Donaldson, D.D.: Interleukin-13: Central mediator of allergic asthma. Science **282** (1998) 2258–2261

3. Wills-Karp, M.: Interleukin-13 in asthma pathogenesis. Current Allergy and Asthma Reports **4** (2004) 123–131
4. Welch, J.S., Escoubet-Lozach, L., Sykes, D.B., Liddiard, K., Greaves, D.R., Glass, C.K.: Th2 cytokines and allergic challenge induce ym1 expression in macrophages by a stat6-dependent mechanism. The Journal of Biological Chemistry **277** (2002) 42821–42829
5. Han, J., M.Kamber: Data Mining: Concepts and Techniques. Morgan Kaufmann, CA, USA (2001)
6. Bezdek, J.C.: Pattern Recognition with Fuzzy Objective Function Algorithms. Plenum Press, New York (1981)
7. http://www.ncbi.nlm.nih.gov/projects/geo/gds/gds_browse.cgi?gds=958.
8. Cormier, S.A., Yuan, S., Crosby, J.R., C.A.Protheroe, D.M.Dimina, E.M.Hines, N.A.Lee, J.J.Lee: Th2-mediated pulmonary inflammation leads to the differential expression of ribonuclease genes by alveolar macrophages. American Journal of Respiratory Cell and Molecular Biology **27** (2002) 679–687
9. Davies, D.L., Bouldin, D.W.: A cluster separation measure. IEEE Transactions on Pattern Analysis and Machine Intelligence **1** (1979) 224–227
10. Jain, A.K., Murty, M.N., Flyn, P.J.: Data clustering: A review. ACM Computing Surveys **31** (1999) 264–323
11. Godat, E., Lecaille, F., Desmazes, C., Duchene, S., Weidauer, E., Saftig, P., Bromme, D., Vandier, C., Lalmanach, G.: Cathepsin k: a cysteine protease with unique kinin-degrading properties. Biochemical Journal **383 (Pt 3)** (2004) 501–506
12. Nakanishi, A., Morita, S.: Role of gob-5 in mucus overproduction and airway hyperresponsiveness in asthma. In: Proceedings of the National Academy of Sciences of the United States of America, USA (2001) 5175–5180
13. Vercelli, D.: Arginase: marker, effector, or candidate gene for asthma? The Journal of Clinical Investigation **3** (2003) 1815–1817
14. Zimmermann, N., King, N.E., Laporte, J., Yang, M., Mishra, A., Pope, S.M., Muntel, E.E., Witte, D.P., Pegg, A.A., Foster, P.S., Hamid, Q., Rothenberg, M.E.: Dissection of experimental asthma with dna microarray analysis identifies arginase in asthma pathogenesis. The Journal of Clinical Investigation **3** (2003) 1863–1874
15. Zimmermann, N., Doepker, M., Witte, D., Stringer, K., Fulkerson, P., Pope, S., Brandt, E., Mishra, A., King, N., Nikolaidis, N., Wills-Karp, M., Finkelman, F., Rothenberg, M.: Expression and regulation of small proline-rich protein 2 in allergic inflammation. American Journal of Respiratory Cell and Molecular Biology **32** (2005) 428–435

Correlogram-Based Method for Comparing Biological Sequences

Debasis Mitra[1], Gandhali Samant[1], and Kuntal Sengupta[2]

[1] Department of Computer Sciences
Florida Institute of Technology
Melbourne, Florida, USA
{dmitra, gsamant}@fit.edu
[2] Authentec Corporation
Melbourne, Florida, USA

Abstract. In this article we have proposed an abstract representation for a sequence using a constant sized 3D matrix. Subsequently the representation may be utilized for many analytical purposes. We have attempted to use it for comparing sequences, and analyzed the method's asymptotic complexity. Providing a metric for sequence comparison is an underlying operation to many bioinformatics applications. In order to show the effectiveness of the proposed sequence comparison technique we have generated some phylogeny over two sets of bio-sequences and compared them with the ones available in literature. The results prove that our technique is comparable to the standard ones. The technique, called the correlogram-based method, is borrowed from the image analysis area. We have also done some experiments with synthetically generated sequences in order to compare correlogram-based method with the well-known dynamic programming method. Finally, we have discussed some other possibilities on how our method can be used or extended.

1 Introduction

Sequence comparison constitutes one of the most fundamental operations in many problems in bio-informatics. For this reason many sequence comparison techniques have been developed in the literature sometimes targeting specific problems. In this article we have proposed a novel comparison method and have shown a few of its usages.

Possibly the most accurate sequence comparison technique is the dynamic programming algorithm of Smith and Waterman [1981]. The primary objective of this algorithm is to align two sequences optimally. When the objective is to come up with a distance or a similarity value between two sequences the global alignment provides a mechanism to achieve that. The value of the optimizing function in that case is typically utilized as a similarity parameter. Another popular and efficient sequence comparison method is the BLAST [Altschul, 1990] algorithm. However, its primary purpose is to find homologous longest common sub-sequence between two bio-sequences. BLAST is a problem specific algorithm and is not a competitor to our method.

M. Ali and R. Dapoigny (Eds.): IEA/AIE 2006, LNAI 4031, pp. 953 – 961, 2006.

Our proposed technique is based on a similar method introduced for comparing two images [Huang et al, 1999]. While an image is a two-dimensional organization of the pixels a bio-sequence is a one dimensional organization of characters from a finite set of alphabets (typically nucleic acids or amino acids). We create a mathematical representation of a sequence and subsequently use that representation for the comparison purpose. In the following sections we describe the method (section 2) and some experiments toward using it for sequence comparison (section 3). We conclude with a discussion on a few other possibilities with using the correlogram representations of sequences (section 4).

The concept of correlogram has been used in the field of bioinformatics before. Macchiato et al. [1995] used correlograms to analyze autocorrelation characteristics of active polypeptides. Further, correlograms have been used for analyzing spatial patterns in various experiments, e.g., Bertorelle et al [1995] used correlograms to study DNA diversity. Rosenberg et al [1995] used correlograms in their studies regarding patterns of transitional mutation biases within and among mammalian genomes. However, the representation has not been used for the sequence comparison purposes before.

2   Correlogram and Its Usage in Sequence Comparison

2.1   Correlogram of a Sequence

Let a sequence be indicated by,

$s = a_1 a_2 \ldots a_n$, where $|s|=n$, and for all i, $a_i \in \Sigma$,

Σ is the finite set of alphabets over nucleic acids ({A, T, G, C} for a DNA or {A, U, G, C} for a RNA) or over twenty amino acids for a protein. Let, $|\Sigma| = m$ (m is 4 or 20).

Definition 1. A correlogram for s is a 3-dimensional matrix of size (m x m x d), where $0<d<n$ is a predefined integer (typically between 4 to 7). Both the first two dimensions of the matrix represents the alphabets in Σ, and the third dimension is over the integer index i, $0 \leq i \leq d$. For $x, y \in \Sigma$, and $0 \leq i \leq d$, let $Freq_s (x, y, i)$ be the frequency of occurrence of pairs (x, y) at a distance i, on the sequence s. Each entry of the *Correlogram* matrix for the sequence s, $Corr_s (x, y, i)$ is the normalized frequency, $Freq_s (x, y, i)/ N$, where $N = (n - i)$ is the total number of pairs in the sequence at a distance i.

The normalization is needed to compensate for the sequence length, so that the sequences of different lengths can be subsequently compared. The sequences with greater lengths will have tendency to have higher frequencies of pairs of (x, y)'s.

Example 1. With $\Sigma = \{A, C, G, T\}$, a string $S = AGCTTAGTCT$. The $Freq_s (x, y, 1)$ for the plane with $i =1$ is the following matrix in Figure 2. $Corr_s (x, y, 1)$ plane will have each of these elements divided by 9.

Note that the list of the distances corresponding to the planes of correlograms need not be all the integers between 0 and d ($0 \leq i \leq d$). Rather they could be a predetermined finite set of integers each less than n, the length of the sequence. For example, i could be $\{0, 3, 5, 7, 11\}$. The particular application determines this list.

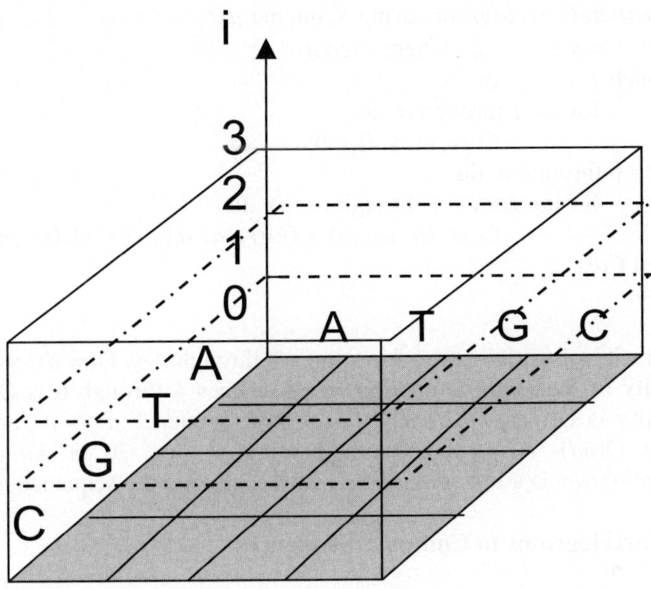

Fig. 1. A shell of a Correlogram over {A,T,G,C} and d=3

	A	T	G	C
A			2/9	
T	1/9	1/9		1/9
G		1/9		1/9
C		2/9		

Fig. 2. A layer for a sample correlogram for S

The correlogram-plane for the distance i=0 is nothing but a normalized histogram representing the normalized frequencies of the occurrences of the characters in the sequence. The corresponding plane (for i=0) is a 2D diagonal matrix.

2.2 Computing Correlogram

The following algorithm computes a correlogram given an input sequence s and a d value.

Algorithm ComputeCorrelogram (string S, integer d)
        // Let, $S = a_1a_2 \ldots a_n$, where each $a_j \in \Sigma$
(1)   for each $x, y \in \Sigma$ do
(2)   for $i = 1$ through d do
(3) $Corr_s (x, y, i) = 0;$
(4)   for $i = 0$ through d do
(5)   for integer $j = 1$ through $(n - i)$ do
(6) $Corr_s (a_j, a_{j+i}, i) = Corr_s (a_j, a_{j+i}, i) + (1/(n-i));$
(7)   return $Corr_s;$
End Algorithm.

The complexity of initialization from lines 1 through 3 is $O(m^2d)$, where $|\Sigma| = m$. The complexity of the main computing loops in lines 4 through 6 is $O(nd)$. So, the total complexity is $O(\max\{m^2d, nd\})$. For a large sequence $n \gg m$, and hence, the complexity is $O(nd)$. Also, since m is a constant ($m= 20$ or 4), and so is d, *ComputeCorrelogram* is a linear algorithm with respect to the sequence length n.

2.3 Using Correlograms to Compare Sequences

Once a sequence is transformed into a correlogram it is possible to measure a distance between two correlograms corresponding to two sequences.

Definition 2: The *distance* between two sequences S and T is $l_{st} = L(Corr_S, Corr_T)$, where the function L is one of the standard *L-norms* of distance metrics.

For L_0-*norm*: $l_{st} = \sum_{x,y\in\Sigma, , 0 \leq i \leq d} |Corr_S (x, y, i) - Corr_T (x, y, i)| / (|S| + |T| +1)$

For L_1-*norm*: $l_{st} = \sqrt{(\sum_{x,y\in\Sigma, , 0 \leq i \leq d} [Corr_S (x, y, i) - Corr_T (x, y, i)]^2)/ (|S| + |T| +1)}$

Higher order *L-norm* distance metrics may be defined accordingly.

Since both the correlogram-matrices are of the same dimension the computation of any of these *L-norm* distances is of the order of $O(m^2d)$. We used L_1-*norm* for our experiments. The distance measure is apparently a metric as evidenced in some of our preliminary experiments (not presented here).

3 Experiments

We have done three sets of experiments in order to study the effectiveness of the correlogram method in the sequence comparison. They are described below.

3.1 Experiments with Synthetic Data

In this set of experiments we compared our proposed technique with Smith-Waterman's [1981] *Dynamic Programming* (DP) method over some synthetically generated sequences. For some experiments, we start with a target sequence S and deform it systematically to S' and measure the distance (or similarity with DP) between the two sequences ($l_{SS'}$) using the two methods (correlogram and DP). In other experiments, we start with two arbitrary sequences $S1$ and $S2$ and deform one of them ($S2$) systematically to $S2'$ and measure how the distance between them ($l_{S1S2'}$) changes with the deformation. Such experiments with synthetic sequences have never been done before, to the best of our knowledge. For the lack of space we will provide some sample results of our experiments from this set [for detail see the Tech Report, Samant et al, 2005]. The same conclusion holds over all such experiments that the Correlogram method is more sensitive to the deformation of a sequence than the DP method.

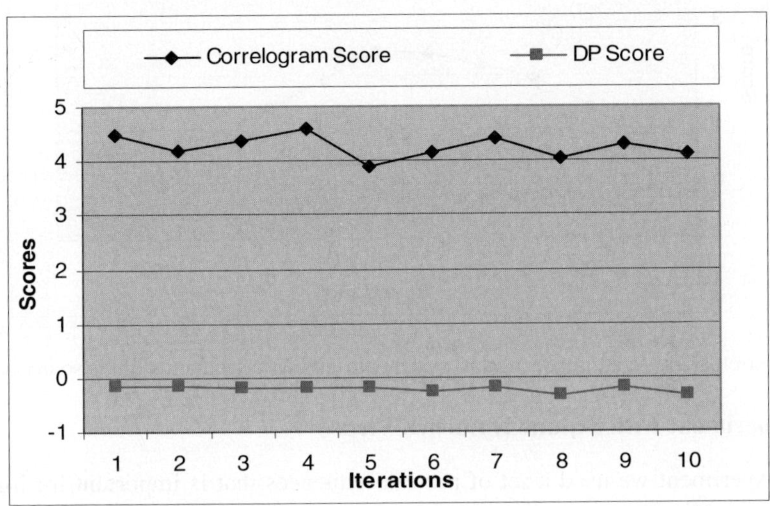

Fig. 3. Correlogram vs. DP scores against character deletion positions (iterations)

Figure 3 shows the result $(l_{S1S2'})$ obtained by deleting a character from the second sequence $S2$. The position j of the deleted character is systematically varied between $1 \leq j \leq n$, for $|S2|=n$. As expected, DP is not very sensitive to the position of the character being deleted, whereas the correlogram method shows some fluctuation as the position progresses over the string $S2$. A cautionary note here is that the absolute values of the two methods should not be compared as the two methods measure different aspects – distances and similarities. Rather their relative change with respect to the control parameter (position of deletion in this experiment) should be compared. Our conclusion is that the correlogram method, overall, is more suitable for comparing sequences when character deletion takes place. This is expected, as we create a richer abstract representation (correlograms) for each of the sequences before we compare the two sequences, *vis a vis* the DP method.

Figure 4 shows the results from a similar experiment where a sequence is wrapped around systematically (first with one character, then with 2 characters, and so on – "iterations" on X-axis in the figure indicates this number), and the distance is measured between the original and the deformed sequence. For example, a wrapping around of string *AGCTTAGTCT* for $i=2$ is, *CTAGCTTAGT*. The higher sensitivity of the correlogram-based method is evidenced in Fig 4 as well. Other experiments, done with systematic character addition, and by reversal of a sequence, also provided the same conclusion as drawn from the character deletion-experiment.

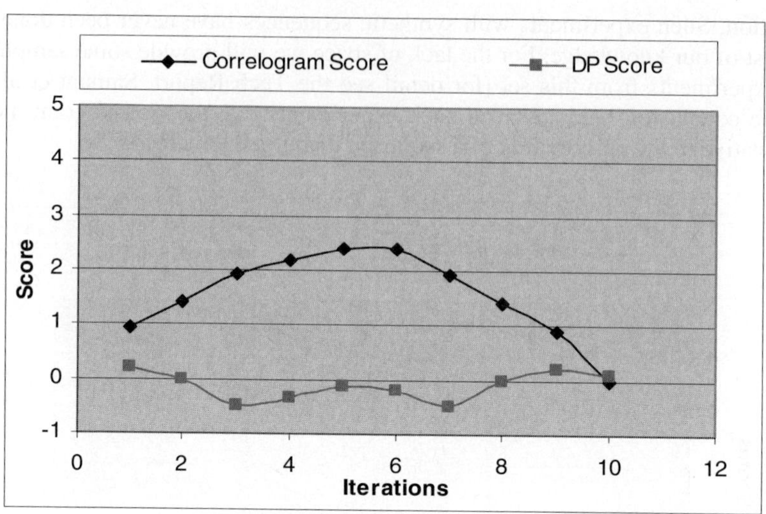

Fig. 4. Correlogram vs. DP scores against systematic circular permutation of the source sequence

3.2 Experiment with Equine Influenza Virus

In this experiment we used a set of protein sequences that is important for immunity of the horse influenza virus. The protein sequences are products of the *hemagglutinin* (HA) gene that has gone through multiple mutations over ten years (1990 through 2000) as the infected horse moved through different parts of the USA. We constructed the phylogeny tree from the distance values generated by the correlogram method and compared the tree with a standard work on the same data available in the literature [Lai et al, 2004].

The Figure 5a and 5b shows the two trees over the set of viruses (SA90/AF197243, SU90/X68437, LM92/X85087, HK92/L27597, KY91/L39918, KY92/L39917, KY94/ L39914, KY95/AF197247, KY96/AF197248, KY97/AF197249, KY98/AF197241, FL93/L39916, FL94/AF197242, AR93/L39913, AR94/AF197245, AR95/AF197244, AR96/AF197246, NY99/AY273167, OK00/AY273168). The first part of each of the elements in this set is the common identifier of the corresponding influenza-A virus, whereas the second part is the respective accession number to the database (EMBL-EBI, European Bioinformatics Institute, *http://www.ebi.ac.uk/cgi-bin/expasyfetch*). The strings are a few hundred characters long. Lai et al [2004] used *GeneTool* version 1.1 (http:// www.biotools.com/products/genetool.html) to generate the distance matrix and then ran the Phylip software (*Neigbor-join* method) from the University of Washington to draw the tree (Fig 4a). We used correlogram method to generate the distance matrix and used the same program from Phylip package (http:// evolution.genetics.washington. edu/phylip.html) for the phylogeny construction. The two trees are small enough to be compared manually. The similarity between the two trees justifies the usability of correlogram method in drawing phylogeny. The minor differences between the two trees necessitate further investigation for their biological significances.

3.3   Experiment with Parvo-Virus

Parvo-virus family resides in the intestines of higher organisms. They are known to cause illness/death of children and are a focus of medical research. The RNA sequences of the viruses of this family from different organisms have been used and we have measured the distances between the sequences using our proposed method. The sequences are from the set: (B19 virus, Bovine parvovirus, Canine parvovirus strain B, Feline panleukopenia virus (strain 193), Murine minute virus (strain MVMI), Porcine parvovirus (strain NADL-2), Raccoon parvovirus, Adeno-associated virus 2, and Galleria mellonella densovirus) studied in the literature [Chapman et al, 1993]. The strings are around 5000 characters long. We have drawn phylogeny tree from the generated distance matrix over the family. Again the striking similarity (Figures 6a and 6b) with Chapman et al's tree proves the strength of the correlogram-based method.

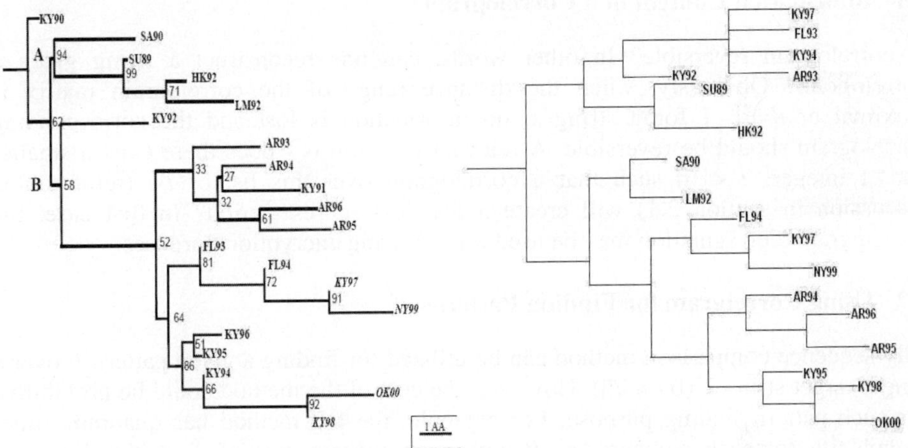

Fig. 5. Phylogeny trees of the Horse Influenza HA1, a. Lai et al (2004), b. Correlogram-based

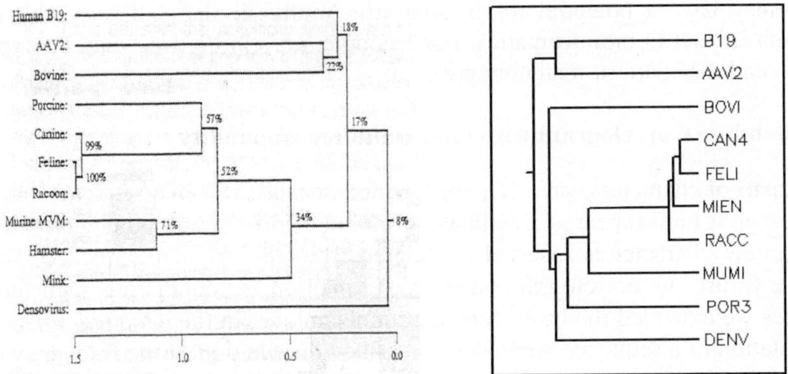

Fig. 6. Phylogeny trees of the Parvovirus RNA sequences, a. Chapman et al (1993), b. Correlogram-based

The two viruses AAV2 and B19 have low sequence similarity and high structural similarity compared to other viruses. Their coming closer to each other in the phylogeny in correlogram-based tree suggests that our proposed method has a stronger capability to classify structures. However, this needs further experimentation to verify.

4 Conclusion and Pointers

In this research we have proposed a new approach toward sequence representation and investigated a few of its capabilities. In order to fully understand the significance of the representation many new questions and challenges need to be addressed. Some of them are posed below.

4.1 Information Content of a Correlogram

Is correlogram reversible? In other words, can one reconstruct a string given a correlogram? Obviously, when the distance range of the correlogram matrix is maximal or $d=|s|$ -1 for a string s, no information is lost and the corresponding correlogram should be reversible. A relevant question is - does there exist a smaller list of integers $i < |s|$ such that a correlogram over this list of i's (refer to the discussion in section 2.1) will create a loss-less representation? In that case, the correlogram representation may be used for the string encryption purposes.

4.2 Using Correlgram for Finding Patterns

Any sequence comparison method can be utilized for finding a given pattern P over a longer target string T ($|T| > |P|$). However, the cost of the method could be prohibitive for such pattern finding purpose. For example, the DP method has quadratic time-complexity for each comparison (P with each subsequence of T of size $|P|$) over scanning the target sequence. We have implemented a modified version of the correlogram method that scans and searches for a pattern over a target sequence in linear time [Samant et al, 2005]. As our experiments indicate that the correlogram method may have a potential for finding structurally similar patterns, it may have significant impact in bioinformatics. For example, *protein docking* may be expedited by such candidate pattern-matching pre-scan.

4.3 Extending Correlogram with Gap Handling Capability

When a pair of characters, say, AG, appears at a distance $i=7$ on a sequence (as A - - - - - - G), then it may appear at a distance 8 or 6 on a corresponding mutated sequence, where a new character is inserted or deleted from the original sequence. With an objective to use the correlogram-based representation for comparing such modified sequences we extended the basic correlogram technique. In this *Gapped-correlogram* representation of a sequence we make a weighted distribution of the frequency counts over the respective adjacent cells of the basic correlogram (over the distance i). Thus, $e1*Freq(x, y, i)$ is added to $Freq(x, y, i+1)$ and to $Freq(x, y, i-1)$, and , $e2*Freq(x, y, i)$

is added to *Freq(x, y, i+2)* and to *Freq(x, y, i-2)*, where $0 < e1, e2 < 1$, are the weight factors. Example *e1* and *e2* may be 0.5 and 0.25 respectively. This type of weighing can be extended to arbitrary number of adjacent cells, not just to two cell-distances. The weight vector itself may be normalized as a probability density distribution that adds up to 1, e.g., *e0+2*(e1+e2)=1* above, where *e0* is the weight factor for *Freq(x, y, i)* itself that was *e0=1* before.

Gapped-correlogram has obvious biological appeal in sequence comparison. However, our preliminary experiments with gapped-correlograms over the problems addressed here did not show any significant difference with the results obtained using the basic correlograms [Samant et al, 2005]. We suspect broader experiments may show some impact.

Acknowledgement. Mavis McKenna provided some data and insight for this work.

References

Altschul, S.F., Gish, W., Miller, W., Myers, E.W. and Lipman, D.J. (1990) "Basic local alignment search tool," *Journal of Molecular. Biology*, 215:403–410.

Bertorelle, G., and Barbujanit, G. (1995) "Analysis of DNA diversity by spatial auto correlation," *Genetics*, Volume 140(2):811-819.

Chapman, M. S., and Rossmann, M. G. (1993) "Structure, Sequence and Function Correlations among Parvoviruses," *Virology*, 194(2):491-508.

Huang, J., Mitra, M., Zhu, W.J. and Zabih, R. (1999), "Image Indexing using color correlograms," *International Journal of Computer Vision*, 35(3), pp 245-268

Lai, A. C.K., Rogers, K. M., Glaser, A., Tudor, L., and Chambers, T. "Alternate circulation of recent equine-2 influenza viruses (H3N8) from two distinct lineages in the United States," Virus Res. (2004) Mar, 15;100(2):159-64.

Macchiato, M. F., Cuomo, V., and Tramontano, A. (1995) "Determination of the autocorrelation orders of proteins," *Genetics*, 140:811-819.

Rosenberg, M. S., Subramanian, S., and Kumar S. (2003) "Patterns of Transitional Mutation Biases Within and Among Mammalian Genomes (2003) Jun;20(6):988-93.

Samant, G., and Mitra, D. (2005) "Correlogram method for ," *Mol Biol Evol.*Comparing Bio-Sequences," *Florida Institute of Technology Technical Report No. CS-2006-01*, http://www.cs.fit.edu/~tr/cs-2006-01.pdf

Smith, T.F., and Waterman, M.S. (1981) "Identification of common molecular sequences," *Journal of Molecular Biology*, 147:195-197.

Learning Genetic Regulatory Network Connectivity from Time Series Data*

Nathan Barker, Chris Myers, and Hiroyuki Kuwahara

University of Utah,
50 S. Central Campus Dr.
Salt Lake City UT, 84112
{barkern, myers, kuwahara}@vlsigroup.ece.utah.edu

Abstract. Recent experimental advances facilitate the collection of time series data that indicate which genes in a cell are expressed. This paper proposes an efficient method to generate the genetic regulatory network inferred from time series data. Our method first encodes the data into levels. Next, it determines the set of potential parents for each gene based upon the probability of the gene's expression increasing. After a subset of potential parents are selected, it determines if any genes in this set may have a combined effect. Finally, the potential sets of parents are competed against each other to determine the final set of parents. The result is a directed graph representation of the genetic network's repression and activation connections. Our results on synthetic data generated from models for several genetic networks with tight feedback are promising.

1 Introduction

High throughput technologies such as cDNA microarrays and oligonucleotide chips can collect *gene expression data* on a large number of genes in parallel which can potentially be used to determine the connectivity of genetic regulatory networks [1]. These techniques measure gene activity and by inference the amount of the protein in the cell produced by each gene. They can be used to gather *time series data* in which a series of measurements of gene activity is taken over a period of time.

Many techniques exist to analyze gene expression data. One approach is *clustering* which groups genes with similar expression patterns [2]. Other approaches modify machine learning algorithms to create Boolean functions that would describe when a gene should be active [3, 4, 5, 6]. Many other methods such as the work by Friedman *et al.* use *Bayesian* analysis to learn genetic networks [7]. These methods consider each gene as a variable in a *joint probability distribution*. If knowledge of gene A's expression level yields information about gene B, the genes are said to be *correlated*. In this case, one gene may be a (potential) *parent* of the other. Recently, Sachs *et al.* applied a Bayesian analysis to find causal connectivities in the human T-cell signaling network [8].

---

* This material is based upon work supported by the National Science Foundation under Grant No. 0331270.

M. Ali and R. Dapoigny (Eds.): IEA/AIE 2006, LNAI 4031, pp. 962–971, 2006.

Unfortunately, Bayesian approaches have several limitations. First, Bayesian approaches often have difficulty determining which gene is the parent and which is the *child*. Second, these approaches rely primarily on correlational data and only use time to separate the data points. Third, these approaches can only be applied to networks that are acyclic. This last one we consider a major limitation since feedback control is a crucial component of genetic regulatory networks.

To address some of these limitations, *Dynamic Bayesian Networks* (DBN) have been introduced which incorporate an aspect of time to allow networks with cycles to be found. One example is the work by Yu *et al.* that uses two different scoring functions to find the best matching network to their data [9]. They first generate a DBN to limit the number of parents considered for a gene since the second step is exponential in the number of parents. Next, the algorithm assigns an *influence score* to each potential connection. To find this score, they build a *cumulative distribution function* (CDF) for the child's potential parents. A CDF is basically a set of bins that indicate the number of times the genes are seen in a given configuration or an earlier one. For example, a configuration may be that proteins produced by all genes are at their highest state. If as the parent's value increases the resulting CDF is more positive than the previous one the parent is considered an activator. If the resulting CDF is more negative, then the parent is considered a repressor. As there can be many different parents and the data can be noisy, each case contributes a vote on the likelihood of activation or repression. To evaluate their method, they generate synthetic data for 10 genetic networks that include 20 genes in which 8 to 12 are connected to at least one other gene. Using this synthetic data, their method is shown to be fairly successful at recovering the initial networks given sufficient data. They still do, however, occasionally have problems determining the direction of influence. Time is also still only used to separate data points. Finally, only two of their networks have any feedback (i.e., cycles), and these cycles are several genes long.

This paper, therefore, presents a new method that targets learning genetic networks with feedback and in particular tight feedback. While this method is similar to the work by Yu *et al.* it differs in several key ways. First, while Yu's method begins with an expensive search for a best fit network, our method begins with a local analysis to determine the best potential parents for each gene. Second, our method utilizes the child's own level in the calculations to further help in determining a child's parent genes. Third, Yu's method neglects the time series nature of the data and simply computes a CDF that represents correlation within each individual experimental data point. Our method considers two sequential time series data points to find the percentage of time a child gene rises in a given configuration. We believe that by utilizing the time series nature of the data, our method can potentially better determine activation and repression behavior especially in the case where there is tight feedback in the network. In other words, we feel that not only the context of when a gene is high or low gives information, but more importantly the context in which it rises. Our method is evaluated using synthetic data generated from models of several genetic networks that include tight feedback. Our results indicate that our method is more successful than Yu's in learning these types of networks.

2 Formalisms

Our method produces a directed graph model of the genetic regulatory network that indicates which gene products activate and repress other genes. A directed graph model is the tuple $\langle S, C \rangle$ where S is the set of species in the network and also the vertices of the graph. Connections between species, or edges in the graph, are represented by $C \subseteq 2^{(S \times I)} \times S$. Each connection, $(P, s) \in C$, is composed of a set of *parents*, P, for a child, s. Each parent in P is paired with its type of influence (i.e., $I = \{a, r\}$ where 'a' represents activation and 'r' represents repression). A directed graph representation of the genes in the phage λ decision network is shown in Figure 1(a) [10]. The 'a' edges are represented by $\rightarrow$ and 'r' edges are represented by $\dashv$. For example, N $\rightarrow$ CII implies that the proteins produced from gene N activate the gene CII. If there are n species, there are an astronomical $2^{4^n n}$ possible network topologies.

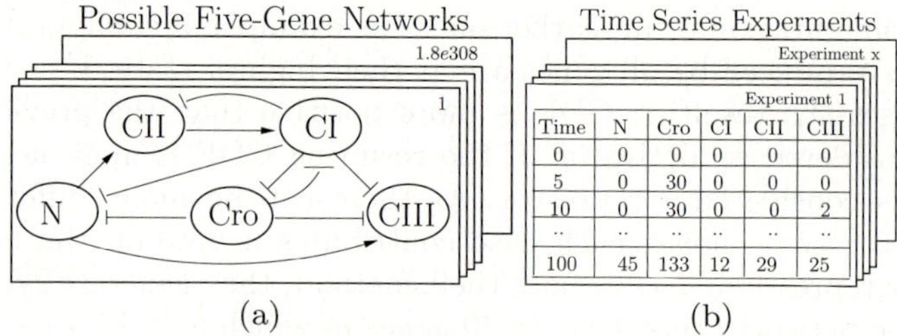

Time	N	Cro	CI	CII	CIII
0	0	0	0	0	0
5	0	30	0	0	0
10	0	30	0	0	2
..	..	..	..	..	..
100	45	133	12	29	25

(a)   (b)

Fig. 1. (a) High level network representation for phage λ. (b) Time series data.

Time series data is assumed to be of the form $D = \langle S, E \rangle$ where S is the set of species (typically proteins or mRNA) that is being monitored, and E is the set of time series data experiments. Each element of E is of the form $\Delta = \langle M, \delta \rangle$, where M is the set of species mutated in the experiment, and δ is the set of data points. A major goal of this work is to integrate results from many different experiments to improve the quality of our predictions. For the best results, time series data should include both wild-type and mutational experiments. A data point $\alpha \in \delta$ is of the form $\alpha = \{\tau, \nu\}$ where $\tau \in \mathbb{R}$ is a time point and $\nu \in \mathbb{R}^{|S|}$ is a vector over S, which includes a value for each species. Time series data collected from microarray data, for example, would provide an expression level for each gene monitored by the microarray. Figure 1(b) shows example time series data.

Our method requires time series data as it is difficult to determine the direction of causality from purely correlational data. Consider for example the 5 gene network shown in Figure 1(a) in which the proteins from gene CII activate CI. With only correlational data it would appear that both CII and CI's proteins are either high or low together. It is, however, difficult to determine which gene activates the other. By adding the element of time, the gene that rose first can be detected, and thus an activation pattern can be determined more easily.

3   Discovering Genetic Networks

The GeneNet algorithm shown in Figure 2 generates a directed graph representation of the connectivity between genes in a genetic network. The main inputs to the GeneNet algorithm are the species, S, and the time series experiments, E. It also takes three optional inputs. The first is the set of initial network connections, C, representing background knowledge about known connections between species used to reduce computational time. The next inputs are the probability thresholds, T, for activation and repression. The final inputs are the encodings, or ranges of time series data values, specified in L for each molecular species. These encodings can be automatically calculated by taking the highest and lowest level of each species and dividing up the state space evenly. They can also be calculated by partitioning the level of each species into equal size bins, which is the default since it appears to be the most effective. The GeneNet algorithm first determines the level encodings if they are not provided and encodes the experimental data into discrete levels for each of the species. Next, each species is considered separately to determine the species (parents) that activate or repress the gene that produces this species (child). If parents are already provided in C for a species, it is skipped. The experiments where the child species is mutated are discarded as these provide no information for this species.

After initial parent genes are selected, the next step is to determine if parent genes act together to influence the child. The last step of the GeneNet algorithm is to determine the most likely parents using the CompetePossibleParents function which considers sets of potential parents together. The result of our method is a new network which includes only those activation or repression edges supported by the experimental data. Currently, our method does not look for self activation or self repression though it does allow for cycles resulting from any other type of feedback. The rest of this section uses the 5 gene network shown in Figure 1 as an example. This network is comprised of the 5 genes involved in the Lysis-Lysogeny decision in the phage λ [10]. The running example focuses on gene $CIII$ as the child gene.

```
GeneNet(Species S, Expts E, NetCon C, Thresholds T, Encodings L)
    (E, L) := EncodeExpts(S, E, L)
    foreach s ∈ S
        if (∗, s) ∉ C
            E' := E − { experiments in which s is mutated }
            C := SelectInitialParents(s, S, E', C, T, L)
            C := CreateMultipleParents(s, S, E', C, T, L)
            C := CompetePossibleParents(s, S, E', C, T, L)
    return ⟨S, C⟩
```

Fig. 2. The GeneNet algorithms

3.1 Scoring Parents

Crucial to each step of the `GeneNet` algorithm is a method to evaluate different potential sets of parents for each child gene. This is accomplished with the `ScoreParents` function, shown in Figure 3, which returns a score representing the likelihood of a parent set of genes activating or repressing a child gene. This score is computed by tallying votes for activation ($votes_a$), repression ($votes_r$), and unrelated ($votes_u$) for each potential level assignment. These votes are initially set to 0. Next, all possible level assignments for the other genes of interest, G, are calculated, and a level assignment, l', is selected. The level assignments for the set of potential parents, P, are also calculated, and a level assignment, l, not equal to l_0 (the lowest level assignment for the parents) is selected. Next, a probability ratio is calculated. The numerator is the probability of the child rising between two consecutive time points given that the parents are at the levels specified by l and the other genes of interest are at the level specified by l'. The denominator is the probability of the child rising when the parents are at their lowest level, l_0, while the other genes are at the levels specified by l'. If this probability ratio, $probRatio$, is larger than the activation threshold, T_a, then there is a vote for this parent set activating the child. If the ratio is smaller than a repression threshold, T_r, then there is a vote for repression. Otherwise, there is a vote for unrelated. The process continues checking each combination of level assignments. When all level assignments have been considered, the score is determined by taking the votes for activation and subtracting the votes for repression and dividing by the total amount of votes obtained. If activation votes outweigh repression votes the score is positive. If repression votes outweigh activation votes the score is negative.

$$
\begin{aligned}
&\textsf{ScoreParents}(s, P, G, E, T, L) \\
&\quad votes_a, votes_r, votes_u := 0 \\
&\quad \textbf{foreach } l' \in levelAssignments(G, L) \\
&\quad\quad \textbf{foreach } l \in (levelAssignments(P, L) - \{l_0\}) \\
&\quad\quad\quad probRatio = \mathcal{P}(s \uparrow \,|\, \nu_P = l, \nu_G = l') / \mathcal{P}(s \uparrow \,|\, \nu_P = l_0, \nu_G = l') \\
&\quad\quad\quad \textbf{if } probRatio > T_a \textbf{ then } votes_a + + \\
&\quad\quad\quad \textbf{else if } probRatio < T_r \textbf{ then } votes_r + + \\
&\quad\quad\quad \textbf{else } votes_u + + \\
&\quad \textbf{return } (votes_a - votes_r)/(votes_a + votes_r + votes_u)
\end{aligned}
$$

Fig. 3. The `ScoreParents` function

Intuitively, if a parent set truly activates a child, then whenever the parents are low, the child should have a lower rising rate between time points than when the parents are high. This should be true regardless of the level of other species in the system. However, if the selected gene is not a parent and the true parents are in the G set, then by fixing the true parents to a low state, the probability of the child rising should not change as the false parent's level is increased.

3.2   Selecting Initial Parent Sets

The `SelectInitialParents` algorithm, shown in Figure 4, is used to select species from the set S as potential parents for the child species s. Every species except the child is considered as a potential parent. The `ScoreParents` function is used to determine if this parent is a potential activator or repressor of the child gene. If the score is higher than the vote threshold, T_v, (default value is 0.5) the parent gene is included in the set of network connections, C, as an activator. If the score is lower than the negative of the vote threshold, T_v, the parent gene is included as a repressor.

```
SelectInitialParents(s, S, E, C, T, L)
    foreach p ∈ S − {s}
        score = ScoreParents(s, {p}, {{s}}, E, T, L)
        if score ≥ T_v  then  C := C ∪ {(({(p, a)}, s)}
        else if score ≤ −T_v  then  C := C ∪ {(({(p, r)}, s)}
    return C
```

Fig. 4. The `SelectInitialParents` algorithm

Considering the gene $CIII$ as the child, the scores obtained for the 4 other genes as parents are shown in Table 1. The result is that N, Cro, and CI are found to potentially repress $CIII$ while CII potentially activates $CIII$. CII, however, is discarded since it does not have a high enough score.

Table 1. Rates and values for potential parents of CIII

N	$Level_0$	$Level_1$	$Level_2$	L_1 / L_0	L_2 / L_0	Votes	Score
CIII $Level_0$	5.4%	2.9%	3.7%	0.53	0.68	$votes_a$ 0	
CIII $Level_1$	9.3%	7.2%	6.7%	0.78	0.72	$votes_r$ 5	
CIII $Level_2$	8.6%	6.4%	6.1%	0.75	0.71	$votes_u$ 1	-0.83
Cro	$Level_0$	$Level_1$	$Level_2$	L_1 / L_0	L_2 / L_0	Votes	Score
CIII $Level_0$	11.5%	1.8%	1.5%	0.16	0.13	$votes_a$ 0	
CIII $Level_1$	14.2%	4.7%	3.1%	0.33	0.23	$votes_r$ 6	
CIII $Level_2$	9.7%	5.0%	4.2%	0.52	0.43	$votes_u$ 0	-1.0
CI	$Level_0$	$Level_1$	$Level_2$	L_1 / L_0	L_2 / L_0	Votes	Score
CIII $Level_0$	19.0%	1.7%	1.0%	0.09	0.05	$votes_a$ 0	
CIII $Level_1$	17.1%	2.6%	1.2%	0.15	0.07	$votes_r$ 6	
CIII $Level_2$	11.6%	2.7%	1.1%	0.23	0.09	$votes_u$ 0	-1.0
CII	$Level_0$	$Level_1$	$Level_2$	L_1 / L_0	L_2 / L_0	Votes	Score
CIII $Level_0$	3.1%	13.7%	-	4.32	-	$votes_a$ 3	
CIII $Level_1$	4.4%	7.4%	12.6%	1.65	2.83	$votes_r$ 2	
CIII $Level_2$	19.4%	5.5%	6.8%	0.28	0.35	$votes_u$ 0	0.2

3.3   Creating Multiple Parent Sets

The `CreateMultipleParents` algorithm, shown in Figure 5, is used to test if two or more parents exert a combined effect on the child gene. The current implementation though is limited to parent sets of size two. The algorithm considers two parent sets, p_1 and p_2, at a time. It first computes the scores for these parent sets (note that this can actually be retrieved from a cache rather than being recomputed and that R() removes a or r from each pair in p_1 and p_2 leaving only the parents). Next, it computes the score for the combination of these two parent sets (i.e., $p_1 \cup p_2$). If the score for the combination is better than both of the simpler parent sets, then this combination is inserted into C and potentially combined again. Finally subsets are removed from the set of parents.

```
CreateMultipleParents(s, S, E, C, T, L)
    foreach (p₁, s) ∈ C
        score₁ := ScoreParents(s, R(p₁), {{s}}, E, T, L)
        foreach (p₂, s) ∈ C − {(p₁, s)}
            score₂ := ScoreParents(s, R(p₂), {{s}}, E, T, L)
            score_b := ScoreParents(s, R(p₁) ∪ R(p₂), {{s}}, E, T, L)
            if abs(score_b) ≥ abs(score₁) and abs(score_b) ≥ abs(score₂) then
                C := C ∪ {(({p₁} ∪ {p₂}), s)}
    C := removeSubsets(C)
    return C
```

Fig. 5. The `CreateMultipleParents` algorithm

Table 2(a) shows the votes and scores for the three different potential parents of $CIII$ as well as the different combinations of parents. For this example, the combination of N and Cro does not have a better score than Cro alone, so it is not retained. The repressor combination of Cro and CI, however, has a score better or equal to each individually, so this combination is retained.

Table 2. Information computed for child CIII

CreateMultipleParents Algorithm

Parents	$votes_a$	$votes_r$	$votes_n$	Score	Retained
N	0	5	1	-0.833	
Cro	0	6	0	-1.0	
CI	0	6	0	-1.0	
N, Cro	0	23	1	-0.958	no
N, CI	0	21	3	-0.875	no
Cro, CI	0	24	0	-1.0	yes

(a)

CompetePossibleParents Algorithm

Parents	$votes_a$	$votes_r$	$votes_n$	score
N	27	12	15	0.27
Cro, CI	0	71	1	-0.98

(b)

3.4   Competing Possible Parent Sets

The `CompetePossibleParents` algorithm in Figure 6 competes parent sets until only one parent set remains. The `getContenders` function returns sets of parents to be competed (for example, the sets with the highest and lowest scores in C). Next, a score is calculated for each contender, q, controlling for the levels of the other contenders (i.e., $Q - \{q\}$). Finally, the scores are compared and the losers, parent sets with scores closest to 0, are removed from C. Also if a parent set's score represents a change in influence (for example, an activator with a negative score), this parent set is removed. This algorithm is run in a tournament fashion to limit the number of configurations which prevents the data from becoming too sparse. The contenders for $CIII$ are $\{N\}$ and $\{Cro, CI\}$. Table 2(b) shows the scores for each set of genes. The winner is the set $\{Cro, CI\}$ so the `GeneNet` algorithm correctly identifies that $CIII$ is repressed by Cro and CI.

```
CompetePossibleParents(s, S, E, C, T, L)
    while |{c ∈ C|c = (∗, s)}| > 1
      Q = getContenders(s, S, E, C, T, L)
      foreach  q ∈ Q
         Scores_q = ScoreParents(s, {q}, (Q − {q}) ∪ {{s}}, E, T, L)
      C := removeLosers(C, Q, Scores)
    return  C
```

Fig. 6. The `CompetePossibleParents` algorithm

4   Results

To evaluate our method, it must be tested on known networks. As there are currently very few known genetic networks, and even fewer with available time series data, we generated synthetic data for the phage λ network and several randomly generated networks. This procedure is shown in Figure 7. The high level description of the gene interactions are translated into a very detailed reaction-based model expressed in the *Systems Biology Markup Language* (SBML). This purely reaction-based model can be simulated stochastically with the U. of Tennessee's *Exact Stochastic Simulator* (ESS). ESS implements an optimized version of Gillespie's *stochastic simulation algorithm* [11] which produces the time evolutions of species in a well-stirred biochemical system. A limited number of time points from this simulation are selected to produce a synthetic time series data run for the original SBML model, which is then used by the `GeneNet` algorithm to construct a network. The original network is compared to the results of our method. As shown in Figure 7, 7 of the 10 arcs in the phage λ network are obtained and no spurious arcs generated. The tool described in [9] recovers 3 of the 10 arcs and reports 3 spurious arcs.

In addition to the phage λ network, our method is examined on 18 synthetic networks inspired by the 4 gene plasmids created by Guet *et al.* [12]. Given 20

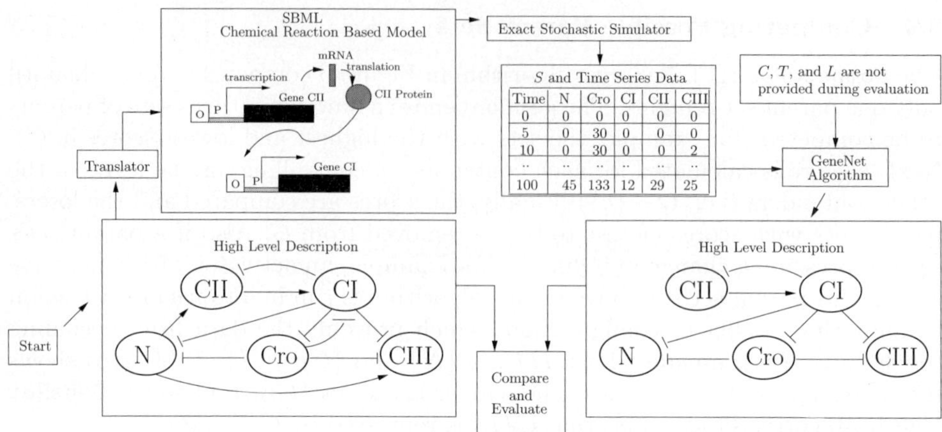

Fig. 7. Data flow for the `GeneNet` algorithm evaluation

Table 3. Results for 10 gene networks

| Number of | GeneNet | | DBN [9] | |
Experiments	Recall	Precision	Recall	Precision
1	26% (26/100)	19% (26/135)	4% (4/100)	15% (4/26)
5	58% (58/100)	46% (58/126)	11% (11/100)	48% (11/23)
10	75% (75/100)	57% (75/132)	14% (14/100)	42% (14/33)
25	82% (82/100)	65% (82/127)	37% (37/100)	47% (37/79)
50	94% (94/100)	70% (94/135)	47% (47/100)	49% (47/96)

experiments with 100 data points generated by ESS for each of these networks, the `GeneNet` algorithm finds all 72 arcs but reports a total of 74. The DBN tool from [9], only finds 33 of the 72 arcs but reports 43 total arcs.

We also created 10 high level 10 gene randomized networks that followed the Guet *et al.* framework. For this example, we also varied the number of experiments where each experiment includes 200 data points. The results are shown in Table 3 using both our `GeneNet` algorithm and Yu's DBN algorithm. The runtimes of the two tools are very similar. Precision difference between algorithms are minimal for the first two cases, but increase as more experiments are added. There are larger differences in recall. For example, the `GeneNet` algorithm finds 26 percent of the arcs using only 1 experiment and nearly 60 percent using only 5 experiments. On the other hand, the DBN algorithm is only able to find 11 percent of the arcs with 5 experiments. With 50 experiments, `GeneNet` finds 94 percent while the DBN method still only finds 47 percent.

5   Discussion

This paper describes a new method for learning connectivities in genetic networks from time-series data using a Bayesian type of analysis. Although the results are promising, there are way to improve them. To reduce noise from the stochasticity of the data a low pass filter can be used. Interpolation can also be used to create intermediate data points to help smooth the data. *Transitive edges*, a special case of extra edges formed from 'shortcuts' when multiple genes are connected by a path, may potentially be removed or marked for later review by graph traversal algorithms. The use of data with interventions (i.e., mutational data) may also significantly improve the results. While our method does allow for cycles as opposed to traditional Bayesian approaches, it does not yet detect self-activation or repression. Finally we plan to apply our method to real experimental data.

Acknowledgments

The authors thank Jing Yu of Duke for providing his software and Michael Samoilov and Adam Arkin of UCBerkeley for their comments on this work.

References

1. Brown, P.A., Botstein, D.: Exploring the new world of the genome with DNA microarrays. Nature Genet. **21** (1999) 33–37
2. Eisen, M.B., Spellman, P.T., Browndagger, P.O., Botstein, D.: Cluster analysis and display of genome-wide expression patterns. Proc. Natl. Acad, Sci, USA **95** (1998) 14863–14868
3. Liang, S., Fuhrman, S., Somogyi, R.: REVEAL, a general reverse engineering algorithm for inference of genetic network architectures. In: Pacific Symposium on Biocomputing. Volume 3. (1998) 18–29
4. Akutsu, T., Miyano, S., Kuhara, S.: Identification of genetic networks from a small number of gene expression patterns under the boolean network model (1999)
5. Ideker, T.E., Thorsson, V., Karp, R.M.: Discovery of regulatory interactions through perturbation: Inference and experimental design (2000)
6. Lähdesmäki, H., Shmulevich, I., Yli-Harja, O.: On learning gene regulatory networks under the boolean network model. Machine Learning **52** (2003) 147–167
7. Friedman, N., Linial, M., Nachman, I., Pe'er, D.: Using bayesian networks to analyze expression data. Journal of Computational Biology **7** (2000) 601–620
8. Sachs, K., Perez, O., Pe'er, D., Lauffenburger, D.A., Nolan, G.P.: Causal protein-signaling networks derived from multiparameter single-cell data. Science **22** (2005) 523–9
9. Yu, J., Smith, V.A., Wang, P.P., Hartemink, A.J., Jarvis, E.D.: Advances to bayesian network inference for generating causal networks from observational biological data. Bioinformatics **20** (2004) 3594–3603
10. Ptashne, M.: A Genetic Switch. Cell Press & Blackwell Scientific Publishing (1992)
11. Gillespie, D.T.: Exact stochastic simulation of coupled chemical reactions. J. Phys. Chem. **81** (1977) 2340–2361
12. Guet, C.C., Elowitz, M.B., Hsing, W., Leibler, S.: Combinatorial synthesis of genetic networks. Science **296** (2002) 1466–1470

On Clustering of Genes

Raja Loganantharaj[1], Satish Cheepala[2], and John Clifford[2]

[1] Bioinformatics Research Lab,University of Louisiana at Lafayette
PO Box 44330, Lafayette, LA 70504
`logan@cacs.louisiana.edu`
[2] Department of Biochemistry and Molecular Biology, LSU Health Sciences Center and
Feist-Weiller Cancer Center, Shreveport, LA 71130

Abstract. The availability of microarray technology at an affordable price makes it possible to determine expression of several thousand genes simultaneously. Gene expression can be clustered so as to infer the regulatory modules and functionality of a gene relative to one or more of the annotated genes of the same cluster. The outcome of clustering depends on the clustering method and the metric being used to measure the distance. In this paper we study the popular hierarchal clustering algorithm and verify how many of the genes in the same cluster share functionality. Further, we will also look into the supervised clustering method for satisfying hypotheses and view how many of these genes are functionally related.

1   Introduction

A gene is the biologic unit of heredity. It is a segment of DNA that contains all the information necessary for the production of a biologically active product (protein or RNA). It is important to study and to understand the regulation and function of genes so as to control or to explain cellular behaviors at the molecular level. A primary regulatory event in the expression of a gene is DNA transcription, the process by which one strand of DNA is copied into an RNA sequence by the basal transcriptional machinery of the cell. Transcription is controlled by a host of DNA-binding transcription factors which, along with associated coactivators or corepressors, bind to specific sequences in the promoter and enhancer regions of the gene [1]. If a pair of genes is up- or down-regulated by the same set of binding factors under the same conditions, they are said to be co-regulated. Such co-regulated genes are expected to contribute to similar cell functions and behaviors [2]. Some of the objectives of microarray analysis include the identification of co-expressed genes, thereby inferring functional relationships. This process is similar to inferring a cause from the effects and therefore the conclusions will only be plausible, but not necessarily be correct.

Clustering is a technique of grouping objects of similar features. Gene expression clustering involves grouping genes of similar or close expression profiles over several different conditions [3]. The expression of a gene under N different conditions may be viewed as a point in an N dimensional space at a location defined by expression values in each dimension (condition). The expression similarity of a pair of genes becomes the spatial proximity of a pair of points corresponding to these genes. The

M. Ali and R. Dapoigny (Eds.): IEA/AIE 2006, LNAI 4031, pp. 972 – 981, 2006.

outcome of gene expression clustering is dependent on the clustering method and on the metric of measuring the distance. The popular metric of measurements being used in microarray analysis include Euclidean distance and Pearson correlation distance. The hierarchal clustering is a popular and a useful unsupervised method to cluster gene expressions [3].

Different clustering methods or different distance measuring metric may result in different outcomes. Several approaches have been used to compare different clustering methods including the following validity indexes: Dunn's, Davies-Bouldin, Silhouette, C, Goodman-Kruskal, Isolation, Jaccard and Rand. All these validation indices are based directly or indirectly on the information used for clustering; hence a method that uses any of these indices does not relate or provide any indication of the effectiveness of meeting the expected outcome of clustering when the expected outcome is in a different parameter space. We are proposing a technique based on the intended purpose of gene clustering, which is to group functionally related genes together. The proposed method is illustrated using the data set that we have created as part of a larger study to determine the cancer suppressive mechanism of a class of chemicals called retinoids.

This paper is organized as follows. We briefly describe the data being used in this study and its preprocessing in section 2. It is followed by gene ontology in section 3. In section 4 we describe supervised and unsupervised clustering. This is followed by results in section 5. In section 6, we summarize and provide concluding remarks.

2   Data and Preprocessing

We have conducted a DNA microarray experiment using the AFFYMETRIX 430 2.0 array, which contains oligonucleotide probe sets representing approximately 39,000 genes. This experiment is part of a larger study to determine the cancer suppressive mechanism of a class of chemicals called retinoids [4]. The major biologically active retinoid is all-trans retinoic acid (ATRA). We have studied the effects of ATRA on skin cancer prevention using the mouse skin 2-stage chemical carcinogenesis protocol. The mouse skin 2-stage chemical carcinogenesis protocol is one of the best-studied models and most informative with regard to understanding molecular mechanisms of carcinogenesis and identifying chemopreventive agents [5]. Skin tumors can be readily induced in this model by the sequential application of a carcinogen, referred to as the initiation stage, followed by repetitive treatment with a noncarcinogenic tumor promoter, referred to as the promotion stage. The initiation stage, accomplished by a single application of the carcinogen dimethylbenzanthracene (DMBA) to the skin, results in a small subset of keratinocytes (skin cells) carrying a mutation in a critical gene(s). The promotion stage requires repeated (twice weekly) application of tumor promoting agents such as 12-O-tetradecanoylphorbol-13-acetate (TPA) that causes the initiated cells to proliferate, eventually producing tumors. ATRA has been shown to be a highly efficient suppressor of tumor initiation and promotion in this model [6].

Here we describe analysis of the gene expression profiles obtained from microarrays for the following mouse skin samples subjected to the 2-stage protocol for 3 weeks; (1) controls treated with acetone solvent alone, (2) TPA (1 µg/application dissolved in 200 μl acetone), (3) ATRA alone (5 μg/application), and (4) TPA plus ATRA. We chose the 3 week time point in the 2-stage protocol, which is 5-7 weeks prior to the appearance of tumors, in order to identify gene expression changes early in the carcinogenic process that may be influenced by ATRA.

Out of the 39,000 genes, 159 were expressed over a factor of 2 after the treatment of TPA compared to normal conditions. This set is called *filtered-genes* and we will use this set for further clustering and processing. Expression values of each gene are normalized in order to compensate for the variations of each gene's absolute expression value. Suppose the expression value of a gene, say g, under a condition, i, is e_{gi}. Then the normalized expression value of e_{gi} becomes $(e_{gi} - \mu)/\sigma$ where μ and σ are respectively the mean and the standard deviation of the expression of the gene g over all the conditions.

3 Gene Ontology

The gene ontology (GO) project [7] provides structured controlled vocabularies to address gene products consistently over several databases including FlyBase (*Drosophila*),the *Saccharomyces* Genome Database (SGD) and the Mouse Genome Database (MGD). The ontology describes gene products in terms of their associated biological processes, cellular components and molecular functions for each annotated gene. Each description of a gene product is arranged in a hierarchy from more general to very specific.

In this work we identify the molecular function of each gene and use the functionality as a measure of success of a cluster. For each gene in the filtered set, we have obtained the GO id and then we have obtained the specific molecular function id. Out of the 159 selected genes, 99 have known functional annotations. These are distributed among several functional groups created by Onto-expression, as shown in Figure 1 [8].

4 Gene Clustering

There are two types of clustering, namely supervised and unsupervised. Supervised clustering is often used to group genes with specific expression patterns. In this experiment, we are interested in sets of genes in two categories: 1.) Those that are upregulated by TPA ($\geq$2-fold) and are oppositely regulated (counter-regulated) when ATRA is coadministered with TPA and 2.) Those genes whose upregulation by TPA remains unaffected by coadministration with ATRA (expression changed $\leq$1.2-fold comparing condition 2 to condition 4). The expression profile of the cluster for the first category is shown in Figure 2. Twenty three genes fit to this category. From the clustering, it is clear that the expression level of genes for skin receiving ATRA treatment alone (condition 3) is scattered, since this condition was not taken into consideration for the supervised learning.

The second category of genes, are upregulated by TPA, but either do not change or are further upregulated upon coadministration of TPA and ATRA, relative to TPA treatment alone. The normalized expression levels for this set of genes are shown in Figure 3.

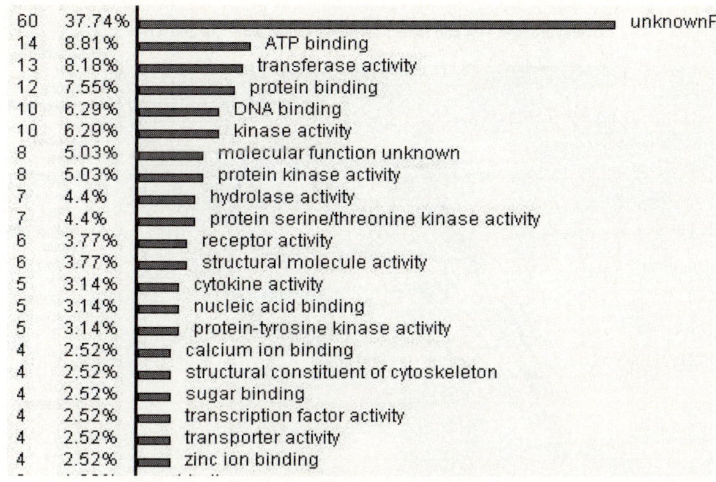

Fig. 1. Functional Distributions of Genes using GO ontology

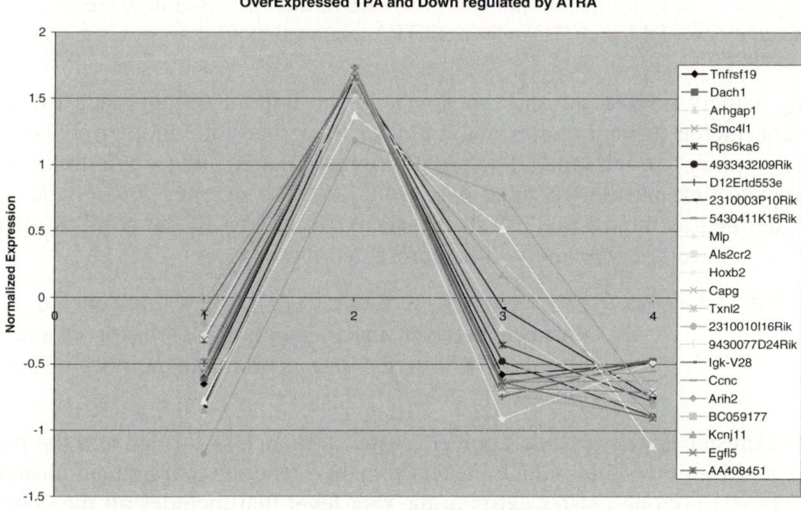

Fig. 2. Supervised clustering of genes that are over expressed by TPA and counter regulated by ATRA

4.1 Unsupervised Clustering

Hierarchical clustering has been successfully used to cluster microarray gene expression data. The data points are represented as hierarchical series of nested clusters and this representation has a single cluster at the root level and each branch leads to a cluster from top to leaf node [9]. There are two ways of building hierarchical

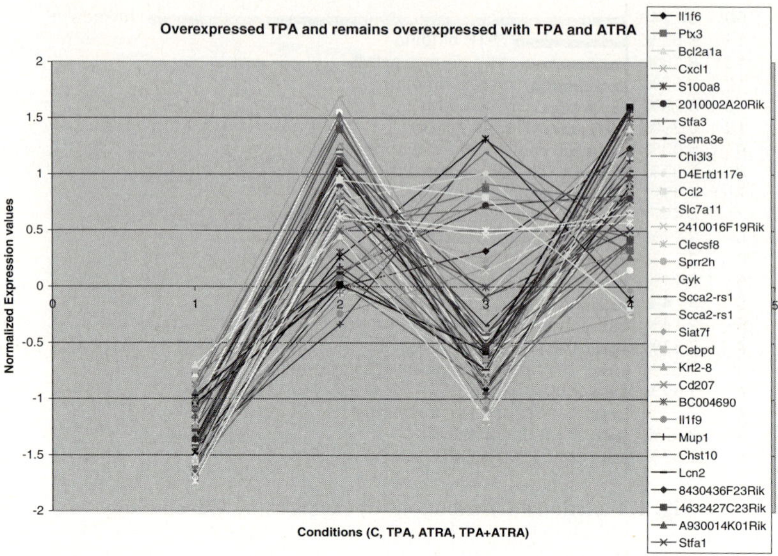

Fig. 3. Expression of genes that do not change, or are further increased in expression with the coadministration of ATRA and TPA relative to TPA treatment alone

clustering namely bottom up and top down. In the bottom up approach every data point is considered to be a cluster and a cluster is merged into another cluster based on their proximity to each other. The proximity measures include single link, average link, complete link and un-weighted pair group. We use *average linkage clustering,* which is defined as the average of all the distances among all the pairs of elements between two clusters, say m and n. It is represented formally as

Average link distance = $\Sigma(d_{ik}|\ e_i \in Cl_m \wedge e_k \in Cl_n)/(|Cl_m| * |Cl_n|)$ where d_{ik} is the distance between the elements e_i of cluster m and e_k of cluster n. $|Cl_r|$ is the size or the total number of genes in cluster Cl_r.

When a cluster is merged into another cluster, a branch is formed and the process continues until no more individual clusters remain. Once the hierarchical cluster tree is constructed, only one cluster exists at the root level that includes all the genes. As we go down the tree each branch indicates divisions of a cluster into more clusters and the measure of closeness among the clusters are also increasing.

The Euclidian distance $d_{i,k}$ between a pair of genes, say g_i and g_k with expression values under n conditions is given by $d_{i,k} = \sqrt{(\Sigma_{m=1,n} (e_{i,m} - e_{k,m})^2)}$ where $e_{i,m}$ is the expression value of gene g_i under the condition m.

We have normalized the expression values of the 159 filtered genes and have created clusters using Hierarchal Clustering Explorer Version 3.5 [10] with the parameters: average linkage clustering with Euclidian distance. As we increase the similarity among the clusters, the number of clusters is also increasing. With the similarity of 0.75 the 159 genes are clustered into 4 groups as shown in Figure 4. As

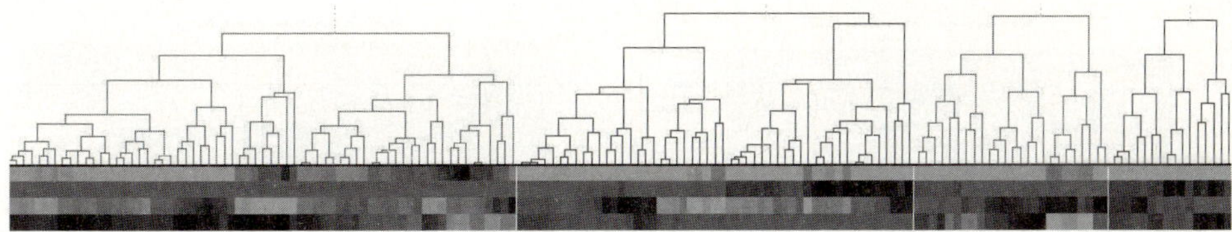

Fig. 4. 4 clusters with similarity of 0.75 (Euclidian distance)

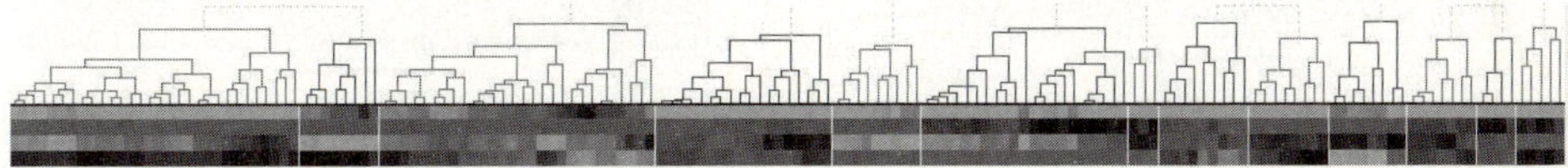

Fig. 5. 13 clusters with similarity of 0.85 (Euclidian distance)

we increase the similarity to 0.85 the genes are further broken down into 13 clusters as shown in Figure 5.

Alternatively, the distance can be based on correlation coefficient. The distance $d_{i,k}$ based on Pearson correlation coefficient between a pair of gene expressions, say g_i and g_k, is given by $d_{i,k} = 1 - \sigma_{i,k}/(\sqrt{(\sigma_i * \sigma_k)})$ where $\sigma_{i,k}$ is the covariance of the gene expression of i and k, and σ_i is the standard deviation of the expression of gene i. With the Pearson distance, the hierarchical clustering resulted in 4 clusters, as shown in Figure 6 when the minimum similarity is set to 0.85.

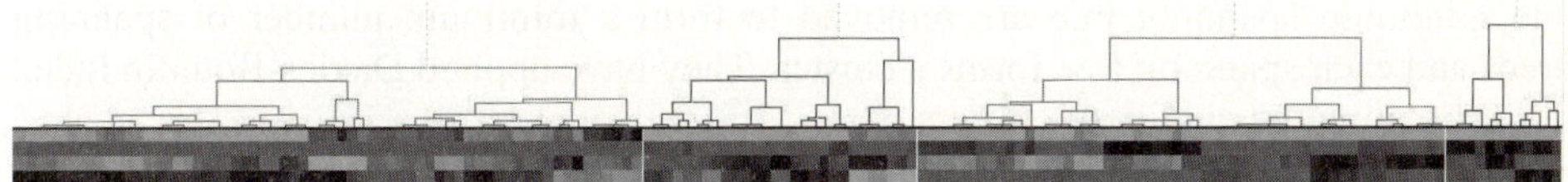

Fig. 6. 4 clusters with similarity of 0.85 (Pearson distance)

The expression profiles of these clusters are shown in Figures from 7 through 10.

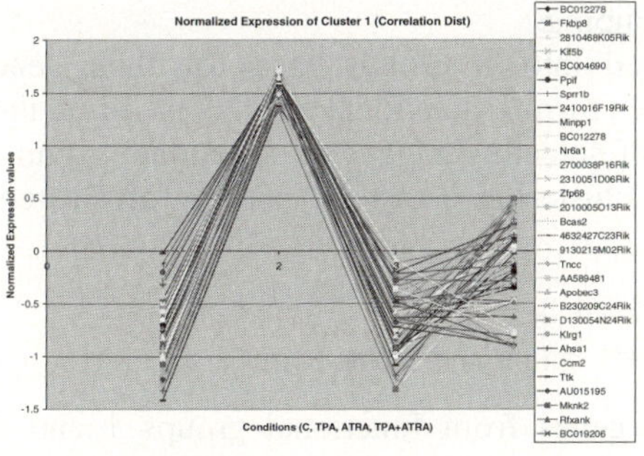
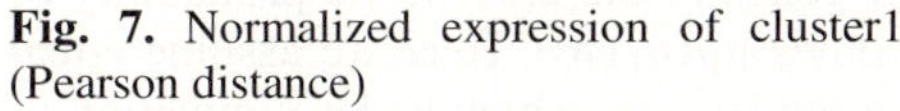

Fig. 7. Normalized expression of cluster1 (Pearson distance)

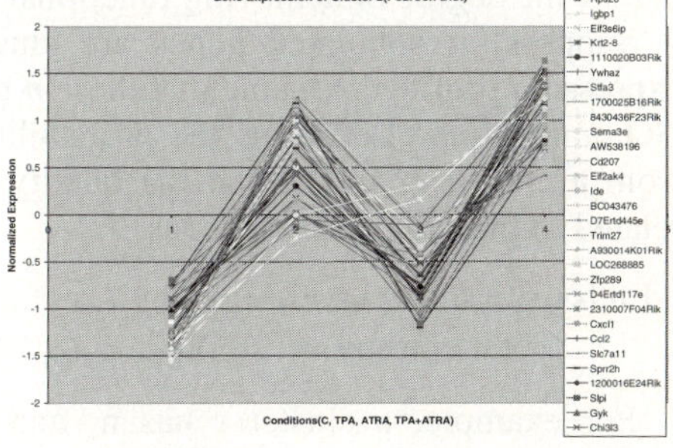

Fig. 8. Normalized expression of cluster2 (Pearson distance)

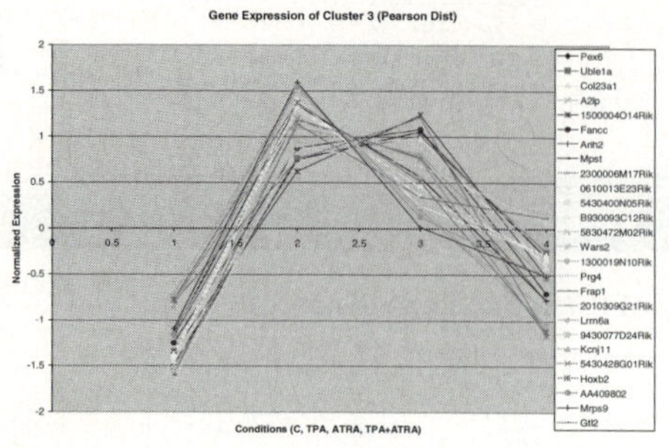

Fig. 9. Normalized expression of cluster 3 (Pearson distance)

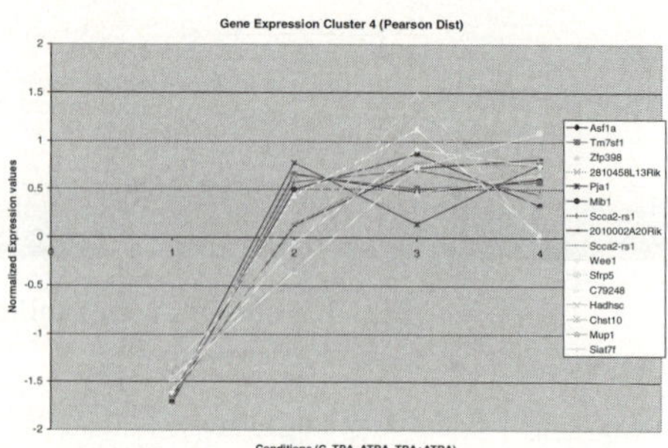

Fig. 10. Normalized expression of cluster 4 (Pearson distance)

4.2 Quality of Clustering

The number of clusters and the content in each cluster are dependent upon the clustering method and the metric being used to measure the distance. Several approaches have been used to compare different clustering methods including the following validity indexes: Dunn's, Davies-Bouldin, Silhouette, C, Goodman-Kruskal, Isolation, Jaccard and Rand. Bolshakova et al. [11] have used some of these indices to compare different proximity measures of hierarchal clustering. Recently, Speer et al. [12] have used GO functional annotations to cluster genes using minimum spanning tree with single link proximity measures. Incompatible links in the minimum spanning tree are removed to form a minimum number of spanning trees and each spanning tree forms a cluster. They have applied Davies-Bouldin index for estimating the quality of clusters.

All the approaches are based directly or indirectly on the information used for clustering and these methods ignore the intended purpose of clustering. DNA microarray expressions are clustered based on their expression profiles, often with the expectation that genes with similar molecular functions group together. In an ideal situation, one to one mapping from a gene expression cluster to a molecular function group is expected. We propose a method based on an expected outcome of clustering, that is, the degree of achieving functional grouping.

Suppose, n annotated genes are clustered into m groups based on their gene expression profiles. Assume that these n genes form k functional clusters based on the GO annotation. Let p_{ir} be the probability of selecting a gene of functional group i from a cluster r. We define the quality of clustering using the entropy of clusters related to functional associations.

$$\text{Entropy of cluster r} = -\Sigma p_{ir}\log_2(p_{ir}) \text{ for } \forall\, i \in 1..k$$
$$\text{Total entropy} = -\Sigma\Sigma p_{ir}\log_2(p_{ir}) \text{ for } \forall\, i \in 1..k \text{ and } \forall\, r \in 1..m$$

For example, a cluster r has n_1 and n_2 genes from functional groups 1 and 2 respectively. Assuming that there are no other genes in the cluster, the probability of selecting a gene from functional group 1 becomes $n_1/(n_1+n_2)$. Here we assume equal probability of distribution. The total entropy of the system, which is the summation of the entropy of all the clusters, provides a measure of the quality of clustering. The lower value of entropy indicates the better quality of clusters. In an ideal situation, if the functional group has a one to one mapping with a cluster, then the total entropy of the system is 0. When we are comparing different clustering methods with different numbers of genes, then we must take the entropy per gene as a measure for comparing the quality of clustering.

5 Results

Out of the filtered 159 genes, 99 have GO functional annotation and we have selected eleven functional groups each containing a minimum of 4 genes. The total functional IDs is 131, indicating that a gene may belong to more than one functional group. The distribution of genes among the functional groups for each cluster, under Pearson correlation distance of hierarchical clustering with similarity 0.85, is shown in Table 1, where fg_r represents the functional group r.

Table 1. Functional distribution of genes (Pearson correlation distance measurement)

Clusters	fg_1	fg_2	fg_3	fg_4	fg_5	fg_6	fg_7	fg_8	fg_9	fg_{10}	fg_{11}
1	9	9	6	6	5	5	2	4	3	2	5
2	3	3	5	2	0	2	2	2	1	4	0
3	4	4	4	5	4	4	5	2	4	3	1
4	1	0	0	1	4	0	1	1	1	0	2

Table 2. Entropy for each clustering method

Clustering Methods	Total Entropy	Number of genes	Entropy per gene
Pearson correlation (4 clusters)	11.48	131	0.088
Euclidian distance (4 clusters)	12.43	131	0.095
Euclidian distance (13 clusters)	27.13	131	0.207
Supervised Learning (2 clusters)	6.645	64	0.104

6 Summary and Discussion

DNA microarray technology allows the study of gene expression patterns of thousands of genes simultaneously under different conditions, so as to understand and to infer which genes are co-regulated, what the potential regulatory mechanisms are, and what functions of co-regulated genes may be. If a pair of genes has a similar expression profile, they are said to be co-expressed, which suggests that these genes can be co-regulated or can have similar molecular functions.

In this work, we have studied the popular hierarchical clustering algorithm for its effectiveness in clustering gene expression. We have investigated supervised and hierarchal clustering with Euclidian distance and Pearson correlation distance. The hierarchal clustering algorithm, with the minimum similarity cut-off point of 0.85 resulted in 4 clusters with Pearson correlation distance. With Euclidian distance, the same similarity cut-off point resulted in 13 clusters, as we have shown in Section 4.1. For comparison, we have also created 4 clusters with Euclidian distance with a similarity cut off point of 0.75.

For measuring or comparing the quality of clusters, several approaches including the following validity indexes have been used: Dunn's, Davies-Bouldin, Silhouette, C, Goodman-Kruskal, Isolation, Jaccard and Rand. Recently, Speer et al. [12] have proposed a clustering method for functional partition based on gene ontology and have used Davis-Bouldin index for validating the clusters. All these validation indices ignore the expected outcome of clustering. We have proposed a technique for measuring the quality of gene clusters that relates to or provides some indication of the intended functional grouping. Our method is based on the concept of entropy of functional groups in each cluster. The total entropy provides a measure of comparing the effectiveness of clustering genes so as to infer functionally related groups. When we are comparing clustering methods with different numbers of genes, the entropy per gene must be used. A small value of entropy per gene indicates better cohesiveness of functional grouping in clusters. In an ideal situation, if the expression cluster yields functional grouping, then the entropy becomes the lowest value 0.

The supervised learning method clustered 64 genes into two groups, where the total entropy is 6.645 and the entropy per gene is 0.104, as shown in Table 2. The hierarchal clustering of genes with Pearson correlation offers the lowest entropy per gene and hence it provides the best clustering metric. Note however that the entropy value is quite high, indicating that co-expressed genes are not always co-functional. This observation is validated by the occurrence of many false positives when inferring co-functionality from co-expression. The method we have proposed is general enough to be used for other purposes, such as measuring co-regulation from co-expression etc. Our investigation is underway for measuring the effectives of gene expression clusters for co-regulation. Further, we are conducting studies to compare our method with other proposed validation methods.

Acknowledgements. The first author thanks the partial support from the Louisiana Governor's Information Technology Initiatives (GITI) for this work.

References

1. Mount, D.W., *Bioinformatics: sequence and genome analysis.* 2nd ed. 2004, Cold Spring Harbor, N.Y.: Cold Spring Harbor Laboratory Press. xii, 692.
2. Jensen, L.J. and S. Knudsen, *Automatic discovery of regulatory patterns in promoter regions based on whole cell expression data and functional annotation.* Bioinformatics, 2000. **16**(4): p. 326-33.
3. Draghici, S., *Data Analysis Tools for DNA Microarrays.* Mathematical Biology and Medcine Series. 2003: Chapman & Hall/CRC.
4. H. Xu, C.S., McCauley E, Coombes K, Xiao L, Fischer SM and Clifford JL, *Chemoprevention of skin carcinogenesis by phenylretinamides: retinoid receptor independent tumor suppression.* Clinical Cancer Research, 2006. **12**(3).
5. DiGiovanni, J., *Multistage carcinogenesis in mouse skin.* Pharmacol Ther, 1992. **54**(1): p. 63-128.

6. Verma, A.K., *Inhibition of both stage I and stage II mouse skin tumour promotion by retinoic acid and the dependence of inhibition of tumor promotion on the duration of retinoic acid treatment.* Cancer Research, 1987. **47**: p. 5097-101.

7. go-ontology, *the gene ontology http://www.geneontology.org/.*

8. Draghici, S., et al., *Global functional profiling of gene expression.* Genomics, 2003: p. 98-104.

9. Eisen, M.B., *Gene Cluster.* p. Hierarchical clustering, self-organizing maps (SOMs), k-means clustering, principal component analysis http://rana.lbl.gov/EisenSoftware.htm.

10. Seo, J., H. Gordish-Dressman, and E.P. Hoffman, *An interactive power analysis tool for microarray hypothesis testing and generation.* Bioinformatics, 2006(in press).

11. Bolshakova, N., F. Azuaje, and P. Cunningham. *An integrated tool for microarray data clustering and cluster validity assessment.* in *Proceedings of the 2004 ACM Symposium on Applied Computing (SAC).* 2004: ACM.

12. Speer, N., C. Spieth, and A. Zell. *A Memetic Clustering Algorithm for the Functional Partition of Genes Based on the Gene Ontology.* in *Proceedings of the 2004 IEEE Symposium on Computational Intelligence in Bioinformatics and Computational Biology (CIBCB 2004).* 2004: IEEE Press.

13. Christian Spieth, F.S., Nora Speer, and Andreas Zell. *Clustering-based Approach to Identify Solutions for the Inference of Regulatory Networks.* 2005.

Towards Automatic Concept Hierarchy Generation
for Specific Knowledge Network

Jian-hua Yeh[1] and Shun-hong Sie[2]

[1] Department of Computer and Information Science, Aletheia University,
Taipei, Taiwan, R.O.C.
`au4290@email.au.edu.tw`
[2] Department of Library and Information Science, Fu Jen Catholic University,
Taipei, Taiwan, R.O.C.
`modify@ms37.hinet.net`

Abstract. This paper discusses the automatic concept hierarchy generation process for specific knowledge network. Traditional concept hierarchy generation uses hierarchical clustering to group similar terms, and the result hierarchy is usually not satisfactory for human being recognition. Human-provided knowledge network presents strong semantic features, but this generation process is both labor-intensive and inconsistent under large scale hierarchy. The method proposed in this paper combines the results of specific knowledge network and automatic concept hierarchy generation, which produces a human-readable, semantic-oriented hierarchy. This generation process can efficiently reduce manual classification efforts, which is an exhausting task for human beings. An evaluation method is also proposed in this paper to verify the quality of the result hierarchy.

Keywords: concept hierarchy, hierarchical clustering, cluster partitioning, tree similarity.

1 Introduction

Manual knowledge network generation has been a labor-intensive work for human beings, since humans are capable of creating semantic hierarchy efficiently. But with growing size of real world concepts and their relationships, it is more difficult for humans to generate and maintain large knowledge networks. Meanwhile, the quality of the knowledge structure is hard to keep because human is not able to keep criteria of creation consistently. Therefore, human-generated knowledge networks are usually difficult to maintain or span, such as web directories, large organization category hierarchies, and so forth. Our experience on constructing government ontology[1] also shows that it is difficult to generate fully semantic-aware concept hierarchy purely replying on traditional data clustering algorithms. So this paper will focus on automatic concept hierarchy generation process with a guided clustering method, called GCC, to reduce human efforts in maintaining large knowledge networks, while keeps a reasonable, consistent semantic quality.

M. Ali and R. Dapoigny (Eds.): IEA/AIE 2006, LNAI 4031, pp. 982 – 989, 2006.

2   Issues of Concept Hierarchy Construction Process

It has been a complex process for human to generate knowledge network (or concept hierarchy) manually. Each concept should be extracted by human first, the dependencies among concepts (including inclusion and subordination) should also be identified, then the hierarchy is able to be created. The whole process can be very complicated, time-consuming and inconsistent since not everyone keeps the same knowledge recognition. Also, even the same person is hard to keep consistent criteria during the hierarchy construction process. After the invention of world-wide web, this problem had gone far more difficult to handle. Portal sites maintaining web directories are suffered from keeping large structure size since it is not practical for human to process huge amount of concepts. The advantage of human-generated knowledge networks is strongly-semantic, but it is only applicable in small-scale domain, such as corporate or personal use. The scalability and consistency problems form a barrier for manual construction of knowledge networks.

While manual construction of knowledge networks has limitations, the automatic hierarchy production researches have gained much attention in recent years [2,3]. Several classification and clustering methods have been proposed to solve the hierarchy generation problem [9-12]. Among these methods, the hierarchical agglomerative clustering (HAC) algorithms [3,4] attracts a lot of attentions since the clustering result is presented in the form of a tree structure, that is, a hierarchy is created. This kind of algorithms has great potential in automatic hierarchy generation since it keeps both scalability and consistency. While this is a promising technology, it still has certain shortage in the current development: the cluster generated by automatic process seldom keeps semantics, since the automatic process based on information retrieval (IR) techniques is usually term-based, but not concept-based. This characteristic causes the clustering result seldom semantic-aware, thus often not acceptable by human being recognition. The automatic generation process can be improved when information retrieval and computational linguistics techniques advance, but for now, it is not applicable to generate high-quality knowledge networks through traditional clustering methods only.

From the discussion above, both of the manual and automatic generation processes are not practical. Therefore, a new hierarchy construction technology should be developed to solve this problem. In this paper, we proposed a hybrid method to help knowledge network (or concept hierarchy) construction. A guided clustering algorithm, called Guided Concept Clustering (GCC), is designed for automatic concept hierarchy generation, while this generation process is supervised and directed to existing semantic hierarchy. The focus of GCC is on generation of scalable and semantic-aware hierarchy.

3   Design Concept of Guided Concept Clustering (GCC)

The design of the proposed method is based on a voting procedure contained in the clustering process. Suppose we are going to generate a concept hierarchy for some concept C with an initial document set $\mathcal{D}$, and the concept hierarchy of concept C which is contained in other existing web directories are fetched in advance. If there

984   J.-h. Yeh and S.-h. Sie

are k networks $\{\mathcal{N}_1, \mathcal{N}_2, ..., \mathcal{N}_k\}$ are fetched, and the underlying document sets $\{\mathcal{DS}_1, \mathcal{DS}_2, ...,\mathcal{DS}_k\}$ corresponding to $\{\mathcal{N}_1, \mathcal{N}_2, ..., \mathcal{N}_k\}$ are identified, each document in set $\mathcal{DS}_i$ (where $i=1, 2, ...,k$) is labeled by its hierarchy path, as shown in Fig. 1. After finishing the labeling process, each document in its document set is carried with hierarchy path information. Next, if the document in initial document set $\mathcal{D}$ also exists in $\mathcal{DS}_i$, the path information is copied as reference. This "attaching" process gives the documents, which appears in other existing hierarchies, votes for latter processing stages. These votes are called document foreign votes (DFVs).

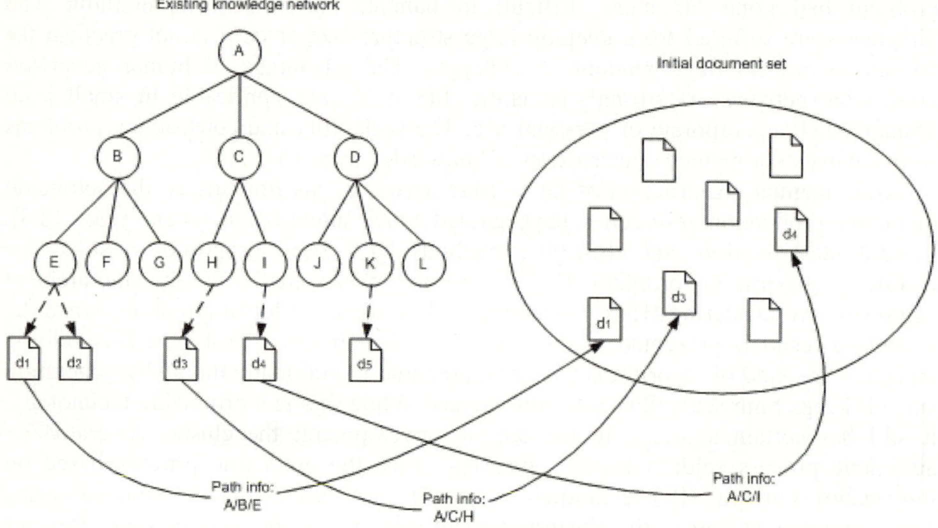

Fig. 1. Labeling process for initial document set

The next step is to apply hierarchical clustering algorithm on the document set $\mathcal{D}$. The clustering algorithm applied here is modified from hierarchical agglomerative clustering (HAC) to incorporate DFV information. The clustering decision function (inter-object distance function) is shown in the following equations:

$$\text{Let } d_u = \{w_{u,1},\cdots, w_{u,n}\} \text{ and } d_v = \{w_{v,1},\cdots, w_{v,n}\}$$

EQ1: be two vectors of correlation values for the document d_u and d_v,

$$w_{u,i} = tf_{u,i} \times idf_i = \frac{freq_{u,i}}{\max freq_{u,i}} \times \log\frac{N}{n_i}$$

the document similarity estimation function is

$$sim_1 = sim(u,v) = \frac{\vec{d}_u \cdot \vec{d}_v}{|\vec{d}_u| \times |\vec{d}_v|} = \frac{\sum_{i=1}^{n} w_{u,i} \times w_{v,i}}{\sqrt{\sum_{i=1}^{n} w_{u,i}^2} \times \sqrt{\sum_{i=1}^{n} w_{v,i}^2}}$$

Let $p_u = \{l_{u,1}, \cdots, l_{u,n}\}$ and $p_v = \{l_{v,1}, \cdots, l_{v,n}\}$

be two path information for the document d_u and d_v,

from root node to leaf node

EQ2: the path similarity estimation function is

$$sim_2 = DFV_{u,i} = \sum_{i=1}^{n} h(l_{u,i}, l_{u,i})$$

where $h(l_{u,i}, l_{u,i}) = \dfrac{1}{n-i}$ if $l_{u,i} = l_{u,i}$, 0 otherwise.

EQ3: The grand similarity estimation function is shown below :

$$sim(u,v) = w_1 sim_1 + w_2 sim_2, 0 \leq w_1 < 1, 0 \leq w_2 < 1, w_1 + w_2 = 1$$

We use **EQ3** as the main decision function for hierarchical agglomerative clustering. In equation 3, the weight parameter can be set individually.

The terminating condition arrives when there is only one cluster exists. Since the root of the existing hierarchy should be the same with target concept C, the root concept of clustering result is certainly converged to C.

The whole concept clustering process is shown in Fig. 2, and the algorithm for the proposed guided clustering method is shown in Fig. 3.

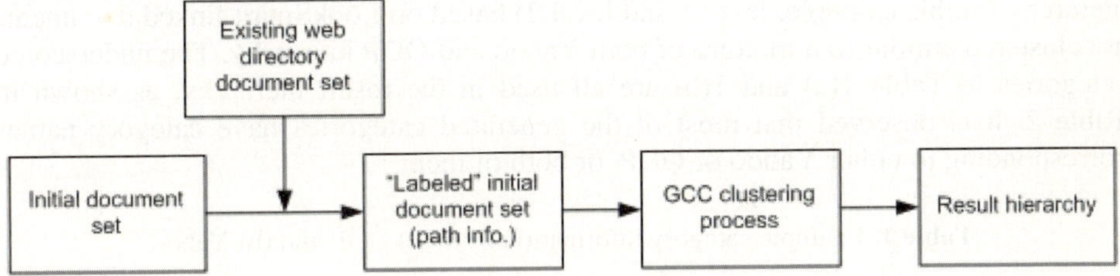

Fig. 2. Cluster construction process

```
procedure GCC
    C_1 = {d_i}, ∀i
    M_1 = sim(C_1, φ)
    k = 1
    while |C_k| > 1 do
        C_{k+1} = cluster(C_k, M_k);
        M_{k+1} = sim(C_{k+1}, M_k);
        k = k + 1;
    end;
    answer = C_k;
end procedure;
```

Fig. 3. Pseudo code for guided concept clustering process

Since the hierarchical clustering algorithm produces a binary tree hierarchy, we apply a cluster partitioning algorithm [7, 15] to produce our final result hierarchy. Besides, we also develop a partition naming strategy to produce proper hierarchy labels with highest frequency terms observed during our clustering process.

In the next section, a real-world experiment is presented to verify our GCC algorithm.

4 Experiment

As a real-world example, a category under LookSmart Web Directory is chosen for our demonstration. Suppose we want to generate a concept hierarchy for organization "Astronomy", which also appears in web directories of Yahoo (yahoo.com) and Open Directory Project (ODP, dmoz.org), both of the partial hierarchies are shown in Table 1. We use documents categorized by the LookSmart Web Directory (looksmart.com) as initial experimental document set (with no hierarchical information included), which contains hierarchies of "Astronomy" for our experiment result evaluation. The hierarchy construction process is shown in the following steps. First, each document in the initial document set is labeled with hierarchy path information in Yahoo or ODP, if possible. Second, the clustering process starts with equal weights for Yahoo and ODP. After clustering process finished, the result hierarchy is shown in Table 2, and the related information is shown in Table 3. In Table 2, it is shown that the result hierarchy (in this example, level 1 and level 2) based on LookSmart linked documents are clustered similar to a mixture of both Yahoo and ODP hierarchy. The underscored categories in Table 1(a) and 1(b) are all used in the result hierarchy, as shown in Table 2. It is observed that most of the generated categories have category names corresponding to either Yahoo or ODP, or both of them.

Table 1. Example category information from (a) ODP and (b) Yahoo

Level1 (Astronomy)	Level2 (Astronomy>Astrophysics, for example)
... Archaeoastronomy@ (95) **Astrophysics**@ (63) Calendars and Timekeeping (47) **Cosmology** (42) **Dark Sky**@ (144) Eclipses, Occultations and Transits (84) Extrasolar Planets (43) Extraterrestrial Life (147) **Galaxies** (54) Interstellar Medium (16) **Personal Pages** (145) Solar System (716) **Star Clusters** (17) Stars (127) ...	Computational Software@ (7) History@ (184) Institutions **Black Holes**@ (63) **Cosmology**@ (42) Neutron Stars@ (24) Stellar Evolution@ (12) ...

(a)   Partial ODP Astronomy category (underscore terms appear in the experiment result)

Table 1. (*continued*)

Level1 (Astronomy)	Level2 (Astronomy>Astrophysics, for example)
... Astronomers (102) Astronomical Calendars (20) **Astrophysics** (127) Auroras@ Comets, Meteors, and Asteroids@ Companies@ Conferences and Events@ Cosmology (113) **Deep Sky** (13) Eclipses@ **Education** (174) Extrasolar Planets (31) FITS (Flexible Image Transport System) (1) **Galaxies** (49) History (16) Humor@ Infrared (11) Interstellar Medium (72) Light Pollution@ News and Media (29) Organizations (23) Pictures (43) Planetaria (62) **Radio Astronomy** (78) Research (248) Scientific Notation@ **SETI (Search for Extraterrestrial Intelligence)**@ Software (14) **Solar System** (987) **Space**@ Stars (222) Telescopes (26) Web Directories (12) **X-Ray** (20) ...	Ask an Expert (3) Conferences (1) **Cosmology**@ **Galaxies** (7) Gamma-Ray Observation (4) Institutes (48) Neutrino Detection@ Observatories@ Relativity@ **Research** (22) **Space Physics**@ Stellar Phenomena@ Surveys (6) Universal Origins@ ...

(b)   Partial Yahoo Astronomy category (underscore terms appear in the experiment result)

To verify the quality of the result concept hierarchy generated by GCC, we refer to several tree similarity measures [13,14]. The similarity measure is shown in Table 4. This result shows the experiment result is over 60% similar to a mixture hierarchy of Yahoo and ODP. In Table 4, the term "structural similarity" shows the portion of result hierarchy concepts shown in the union of ODP and Yahoo hierarchies, and the term "structural difference" shows the portion of result hierarchy concepts missed from the union of ODP and Yahoo hierarchies.

Table 2. Cluster construction result (most categories are classified and have a corresponding category name)

Level1 (Astronomy)	Level2 (Astronomy>Astrophysics)
Astrophysics (ODP/Yahoo) **Cosmology** (ODP) **Dark Sky** (ODP) **Deep Sky** (Yahoo) **Education** (Yahoo) **Galaxies** (ODP/Yahoo) **Personal Pages** (ODP) Reference **Solar System** (Yahoo) **Space** (Yahoo) **Star Clusters** (ODP) **X-Ray** (Yahoo)	**Black Holes** (ODP) **Cosmology** (ODP/Yahoo) **Galaxies** (Yahoo) **Research** (Yahoo) Reference **Space physics** (Yahoo) …

Table 3. Related information for cluster construction result

Hierarchy processed	ODP: Astronomy	Yahoo: Astronomy	Our result: Astronomy
Total node count	3,901	3,016	1,347

Table 4. Structural similarity measure for concept hierarchy construction result

Experiment: w_1=0.6, w_2=0.4 Average-link HAC	Structural similarity with union of ODP & Yahoo	Structural difference from union of ODP & Yahoo
Level1	77.27%	22.73%
Level1&Level2	61.66%	38.34%

5 Conclusion

Though this is the very first step for our guided concept clustering experiment, it is identified that there are still several research issues for us to study to improve our clustering strategy. First of all, the result concept hierarchy is partially learned from the features of existing hierarchies, and the weight distribution for existing hierarchies contribute certain effects to our clustering result, so it is important to study how to decide the weight distribution objectively. Secondly, the comparison with LookSmart hierarchy and our experimental result may show interesting phenomena to indicate the difference viewpoints of ODP/Yahoo and LookSmart directory editors. This issue can be further extended to provide a visualized, comparison tool for user to adjust their manually-generated, shallow concept hierarchy for our GCC algorithm. Thirdly, the labeling process introduced in this paper can be generalized to not only use identical document comparison (including path) but also a more fuzzy strategy to combine both category path information and document similarity, even hyperlinks, anchor texts, and other useful information.

The GCC method presented in this paper adopts the experiences of existing web directories, extracting path information contained and applied to generate new concept hierarchy. This method uses these information as references to guide the formation of target hierarchy, which is both automatic and semantic-aware. This process is able to reduce human efforts efficiently, while keeps semantic quality of generated knowledge network. The GCC algorithm can be used not only in web directories but also other specific domains, such as biology, energy, and other expert domains.

References

1. Chao-chen Chen, Jian-hua Yeh, Shun-hong Sie, "Government Ontology and Thesaurus Construction: A Taiwan Experience", in Proceedings of the 8th International Conference of Asian Digital Libraries (ICADL2005), Bankok, Tailand, December 2005.
2. Jain, A.K. and Dubes, R.C. (1988) Algorithms for clustering data, Prentice Hall.
3. Jain, A.K., Murty, M.N., Flynn, P.J. (1999) Data Clustering: A Review, ACM Computing Surveys, 31, 264-323.
4. Widyantoro, D., Ioerger, T. R., and Yen, J. (2002) An Incremental Approach to Building a Cluster Hierarchy, in Proceedings of the 2002 IEEE International Conference on Data Mining (ICDM-02).
5. San Antonio, Organizing topic-specific web information, Conference on Hypertext and Hypermedia, Texas, United States Pages: 133 – 141, Year of Publication: 2000
6. S. Chakrabarti, B. Dom and P. Indyk "Enhanced hypertext categorization using hyperlinks." Proceedings ACM SIGMOD International Conference on Management of Data (pp.307-318), Seattle, Washington: ACM Press, 1998.
7. S.-L. Chuang and L.-F. Chien, "Automatic query taxonomy generation for information retrieval applications" Online Information Review (OIR), 27(4):243-255, 2003
8. V. Kashyap, C. Ramakrishnan and T. C. Rindflesch, "Towards (Semi-)automatic Generation of Bio-medical Ontologies" Poster Proceedings of the AMIA 2003 Annual Symposium, November, 2003, Washington, DC.
9. Daphne Koller, Mehran Sahami "Hierarchically classifying documents using very few words." Proceedings of ICML-97, 14th International Conference on Machine Learning, 1997.
10. F. Li and Y. Yang. "A loss function analysis for classification methods in text categorization" The Twentith International Conference on Machine Learning (ICML'03), pp472-479, 2003.
11. R.E. Valdes-Perez and etc, "Demonstration of Hierarchical Document Clustering of Digital Library Retrieval Results". Joint Conference on Digital Libraries (JDCL '01), Roanoke, VA (presented as a demonstration), June 24-28, 2001.
12. Y. Yang, J. Zhang and B. Kisiel. "A scalability analysis of classifiers in text categorization" ACM SIGIR'03, pp 96-103, 2003.
13. Bhavsar, V., Boley, H., Yang, L., "A Weighted-Tree Similarity Algorithm for Multi-Agent Systems in E-Business Environments", Computational Intelligence Journal, 20(4), 2004.
14. Tom Morrison, "Similarity Measure Building for Website Recommendation within an Artificial Immune System", Ph.D. Thesis, University of Nottingham, 2003.
15. B. Mirkin., "Mathematical Classification and Clustering", Kluwer, 1996.

An Open and Scalable Framework for Enriching Ontologies with Natural Language Content

Maria Teresa Pazienza and Armando Stellato

AI Research Group, Dept. of Computer Science, Systems and Production
University of Rome, Tor Vergata
Via del Politecnico 1, 00133 Rome, Italy
{pazienza, stellato}@info.uniroma2.it

Abstract. Knowledge Sharing is a crucial issue in the Semantic Web: SW services expose and share knowledge content which arise from distinct languages, locales, and personal perspectives; a great effort has been spent in these years, in the form of Knowledge Representation standards and communication protocols, with the objective of acquiring semantic consensus across distributed applications. However, neither ontology mapping algorithm nor knowledge mediator agent can easily find a way through ontologies as they are organized nowadays: concepts expressed by hardly recognizable labels, lexical ambiguity represented by phenomena like synonymy and polysemy and use of different natural languages which derive from different cultures, all together push for expressing ontological content in a linguistically motivated fashion. This paper presents our approach in establishing a framework for semi-automatic linguistic enrichment of ontologies, which led to the development of Ontoling, a plug-in for the popular ontology development tool Protégé. We describe here its features and design aspects which characterize its current release.

1   Introduction

The scenario offered by the SW (and by the Web in general) is characterized by huge quantities of documents and by users willing to access them. Though machine readability is a primary aim for allowing automatic exchange of data, several SW services like Intelligent Q&A, Semantic Search Engines etc.. still need to recognize and expose knowledge expressed in the sole way humans can easily understand it: natural language. Moreover, the role of different cultures and languages is fundamental in a real World *aWare* Web and, though English is recognized de facto as a "lingua franca" all over the world, much effort must be spent to preserve other idioms expressing different cultures. As a consequence, multilinguality has been cited as one of the six challenges for the Semantic Web [1]. These premises suggest that ontologies as we know them now, should be enriched to cover formally expressed conceptual knowledge as well as to expose its content in a linguistically motivated fashion.

In this paper we introduce our work in establishing a framework for semi-automatic linguistic enrichment of ontologies, which has run through the identification of different categories of linguistic resources and planning their exploitation to augment the linguistic expressivity of ontologies. This effort has lead to the development of

M. Ali and R. Dapoigny (Eds.): IEA/AIE 2006, LNAI 4031, pp. 990–999, 2006.
© Springer-Verlag Berlin Heidelberg 2006

Ontoling[1], a plugin for the popular ontology editing tool Protégé [6]. We describe here the features characterizing its current release and discuss some of the innovations we are planning for the near future.

2 Linguistic Enrichment of Ontologies: Motivation and Desiderata

Whether considering the billions of documents which are currently available on the web, or the millions of users which access to their content, enriching conceptual knowledge with natural language expressivity seems to us a necessary step for realizing true knowledge integration and shareability.

To achieve such an objective, we should reconsider the process of Ontology Development to include the enrichment of semantic content with proper lexical expressions in natural language. Ontology Development tools should reflect this need, supporting users with dedicated interfaces for browsing linguistic resources: these are to be integrated with classic views over knowledge data such as class trees, slot and instance lists, offering a set of functionalities for linguistically enriching concepts and, possibly, for building new ontological knowledge starting from linguistic one.

By considering some of our past experiences [8,9] with knowledge based applications dealing with concepts and their lexicalizations, a few basic functionalities for browsing linguistic resources (from now on, LRs) emerged to be mandatory:

— *Search term definitions (glosses)*
— *Ask for synonyms*
— *Separate different sense of the same term*
— *Explore genus and differentia*
— *Explore resource-specific semantic relations*
  as well as some others for ontology editing:
— *Add synonyms (or translations, for bilingual resources) as additional labels for identifying concepts*
— *Add glosses to concepts description (documentation)*
— *Use notions from linguistic resources to create new concepts*

While ontologies have undergone a process of standardization which culminated, in 2004, with the promotion of OWL [4] as the official ontology language for the semantic web, linguistic resources still maintain heterogeneous formats and follow different models, which make tricky the development of such an interface. In the next two sections we address this problem and propose our solution for integrating available LRs.

3 Lexical Resources, an Overview

"The term linguistic resources refers to (usually large) sets of language data and descriptions in machine readable form, to be used in building, improving, or evaluating natural language (NL) and speech algorithms or systems" [3]. In particular, this definition

---

[1] OntoLing is freely available for download at:http://ai-nlp.info.uniroma2.it/software/OntoLing

includes lexical databases, bilingual dictionaries and terminologies, all resources which may reveal to be necessary in the context of a more linguistic-aware approach to KR. In past years several linguistic resources were developed and made accessible (a few for free), then a wide range of resources is now available, ranging from simple word lists to complex MRDs and thesauruses. These resources largely differentiate upon the explicit linguistic information they expose, which may vary in format, content granularity and motivation (linguistic theories, task or system-oriented scope etc...). Multiple efforts have been spent in the past towards the achievement of a consensus among different theoretical perspectives and systems design approaches.

The Text Encoding Initiative [14] and the LRE-EAGLES (Expert Advisory Group on Linguistic Engineering Standards) project [2] are just a few, bearing the objective of making possible the reuse of existing linguistic resources, promoting the development of new linguistic resources for those languages and domains where they are still not available, and creating cooperative infrastructure to collect, maintain, and disseminate linguistic resources on behalf of the research and development community.

However, at present time, with lack of a standard on existing LRs, it appears evident that desiderata for functionalities which we described in section 2, would depend upon the way these resources had been organized. Often, even a local agreement on the model adopted to describe a given (a series of) resource does not prevent from an incorrect formulation of its content. This is due to the fact that many resources have been initially conceived for humans and not for machines. In some cases [12] synonyms are clustered upon the senses which are related to the particular term being examined, in others [13] they are simply reported as flat lists of terms. In several dictionaries, synonyms are mixed with extended definitions (glosses) in a unpredictable way and it is not possible to automatically distinguish them. Terms reported as synonyms may sometimes not be truly synonyms of the selected term, but may represent more specific or general concepts (this is the case of Microsoft Word synonymy prompter). Of course, the ones mentioned above represent mere dictionaries not adhering to any particular linguistic model, though they may represent valuable resources on their own. A much stronger model is offered by Wordnet [5], which, being a structured lexical database, presents a neat distinction between words, senses and glosses, and is characterized by diverse semantic relations like hypernymy/hyponymy, antonymy etc... Though not being originally realized for computational uses, Word-Net has become a valuable resource in the human language technology and artificial intelligence. Furthermore, the development of WordNets in several other languages [11] has definitively contributed to the diffusion of WordNet schema as a wide accepted model for LRs.

4   Accessing Linguistic Resources: The Linguistic Watermark

To cope with all of these heterogeneous LRs, we introduced the notion of Linguistic Watermark, as the series of characteristics and functionalities which distinguish a particular resource inside our framework. As we can observe from the Class Diagram in Fig. 1, we sketched a sort of classification of *linguistic resources*, with the addition of operational aspects. LRs are in fact structured and described in terms of their features

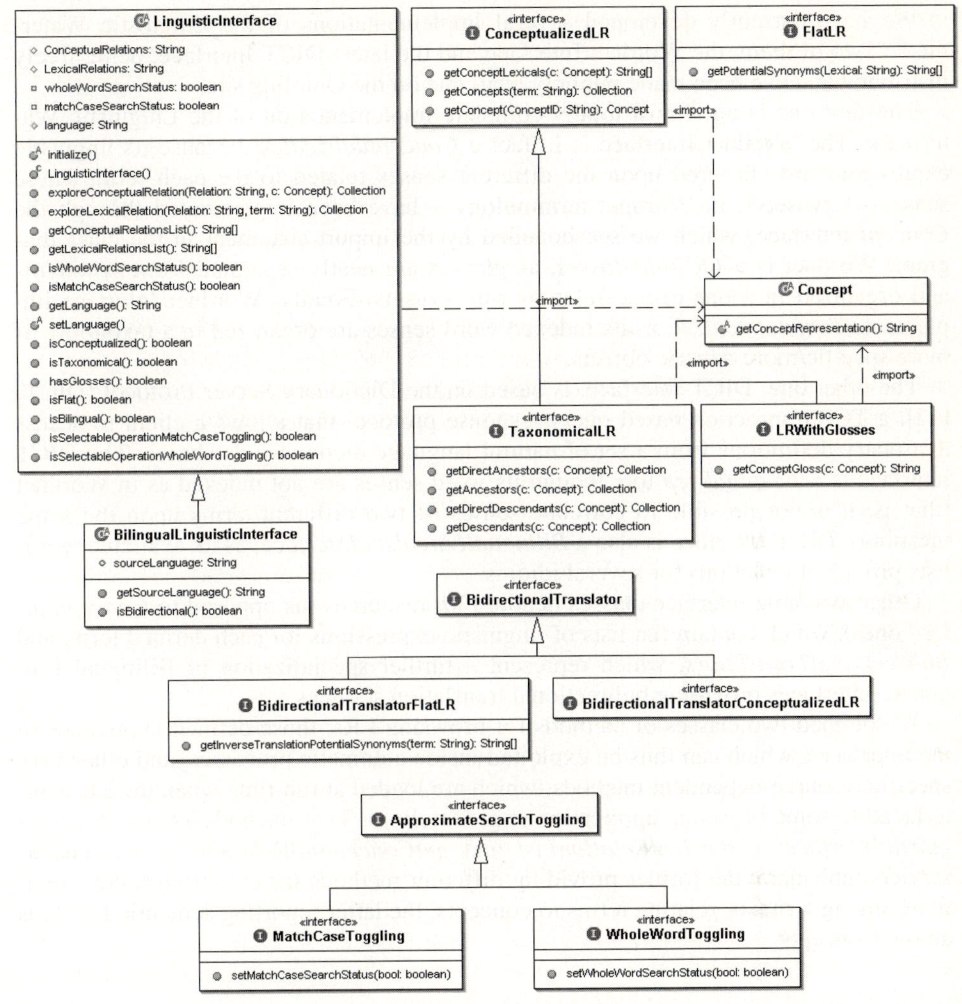

Fig. 1. The Linguistic Watermark

and how their lexical information is organized; the diagram has then been completed with query methods for accessing resource's content.

We thus implemented this schema as a java package on its own, which can externally be imported by any application willing to exploit natural language resources like lexicons and terminologies. The core of the package is composed of an Abstract Class, named *LinguisticInterface*, which is both the locus for a formal description of a given linguistic resource and a service-provider for exposing the resource specific methods. The other abstract classes and interfaces in the package, which can be implemented or not, depending on the profile of the resource being wrapped, provide instead the signatures for known interface methods.

We have currently developed several implementations of the Linguistic Watermark. Two of them, the Wordnet Interface and the latest DICT Interface, being freely distributable, have been made publicly available on the Ontoling site.

The first one is an almost totally complete implementation of the Linguistic Watermark. The Wordnet Interface is in fact a *ConceptualizedLR*, because its linguistic expressions are clustered upon the different senses related to the each term. These senses – "synsets", in Wordnet terminology – have been implemented through the *Concept* interface, which we see bounded by the import statement in the class diagram. Wordnet is a *LRWithGlosses*, as glosses are neatly separated from synonyms and organized in a one-to-one relation with synsets. Finally, Wordnet Interface implements *TaxonomicalLR*, as its indexed word senses are organized in a taxonomy of more specific/more generic objects.

The other one, DICT Interface, is based on the Dictionary Server Protocol (DICT) [12], a TCP transaction based query/response protocol that allows a client to access dictionary definitions from a set of natural language dictionary databases. The DICT interface is *conceptualized* too, though its word senses are not indexed as in Wordnet (that is, it is not possible to correlate senses of two different terms upon the same meaning). DICT Interface is also a *BilingualLinguisticInterface*, as its available word-lists provide translations for several idioms.

Other available interface classes denote *Flat* resources (as opposed to *Conceptualized* ones), which contain flat lists of linguistic expressions for each defined term, and *BidirectionalTranslators*, which represent a further specialization of Bilingual Linguistic Interfaces providing bidirectional translation services.

We defined two classes of methods for browsing LRs: those defined in advance in the interfaces, which can thus be exploited inside automatic processes, and other very specific resource-dependent methods, which are loaded at run-time when the LR is interfaced to some browsing application (e.g. Ontoling). Two methods available in *LinguisticInterface*: *getLexicalRelationList* and *getConceptualRelationList* act thus as service publishers, the former providing different methods for exploring lexical relations among terms or relating terms to concepts, the latter reporting semantic relations among concepts.

5 Ontoling Architecture

The architecture of the Ontoling plugin (see Fig. 2) is based on three main components:

1. the GUI, characterized by the Linguistic Resource browser and the Ontology Enrichment panel
2. the external library *Linguistic Watermark*, which has been presented in the previous section, providing a model for describing linguistic resources
3. the core system

and an additional external component for accessing a given linguistic resource.

This component, which can be loaded at runtime, must implement the classes and interfaces contained in the Linguistic Watermark library, according to the characteristics of the resource which is to be plugged. In the following sections we provide details on the above components.

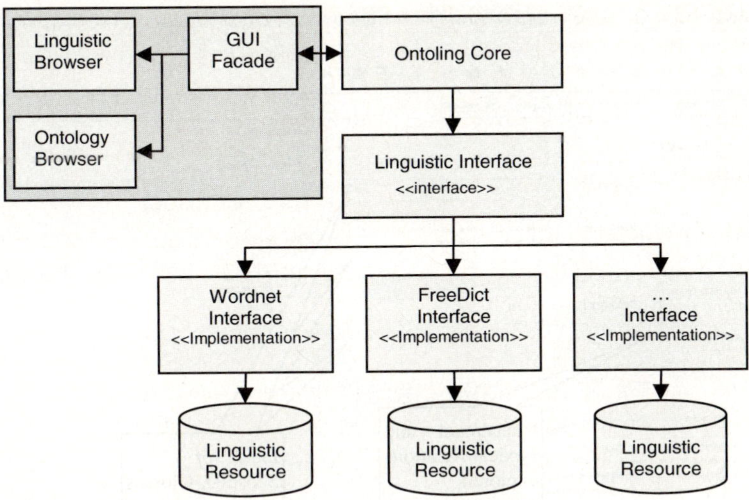

Fig. 2. Ontoling Architecture

5.1 Ontoling Core Application

The core component of the architecture is responsible for interpreting the Watermark of linguistic resources and for exposing those functionalities which suit to their profile. Moreover, the behavior of the whole application is dependant on the nature of the loaded resource and is thus defined at run-time. Several methods for querying LRs and for exposing results have been encapsulated into objects inside a dedicated library of behaviors: when a given LR is loaded, the core module parses its Linguistic Watermark and assigns specific method-objects to each GUI event.

With such an approach, the user is provided with a uniform view over diverse and heterogeneous linguistic resources, as they are described in the Linguistic Watermark ontology, and easily learns how to interact with them (thus familiarizing with their peculiarities) by following a policy which is managed by the system.

For example, with a *flat* resource, a search on a given term will immediately result in a list of (potential) synonyms inside a dedicated box in the GUI; instead, with a *conceptualized* resource, a list of word senses will appear in a results table at first, then it will be browsed to access synonymical expressions related to the selected sense. Analogous adaptive approaches have been followed for many other aspects of the Linguistic Watermark (mono or bidirectional Bilingual Translators, presence of glosses, Taxonomical structures and so on...) sometimes exploding with combinatorial growth.

5.2 Ontoling User Interface

Once activated, the plugin displays two main panels, the Linguistic Browser on the left side, and the Ontology Panel on the right side (see Fig. 3).

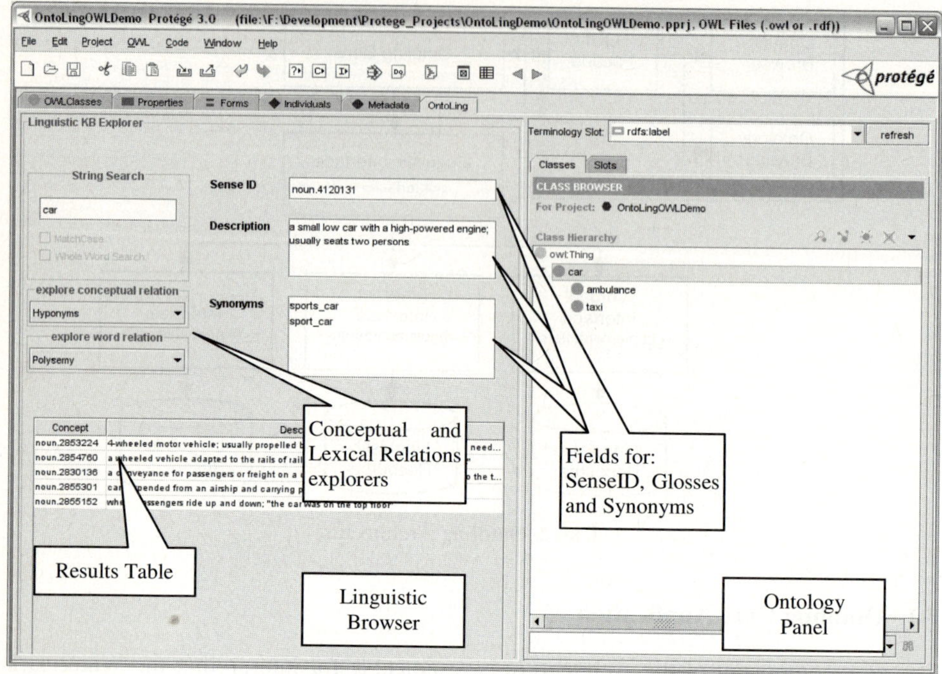

Fig. 3. A screenshot of the Ontoling Plugin

The Linguistic Browser is responsible for letting the user explore the loaded linguistic resource. Fields and tables for searching the LR and for viewing the results, according to the modalities decided by the core component, are made available. The menu boxes on the left of the Linguistic Browser are filled at run time with the methods for exploring LR specific Lexical and Conceptual relations.

The Ontology Panel, on the right, offers a perspective over ontological data in the classic Protégé style. By right-clicking on a frame (class, slot or instance), the typical editing menu appears, with some further options provided by Ontoling to:

1. search the LR by using the frame name as a key
2. change then name of the selected frame to a term selected from the Linguistic Browser
3. add terms selected from the Linguistic Browser as additional labels for the selected frame
4. add glosses as a description for the selected frame
5. add IDs of senses selected from the linguistic browser as additional labels for the frames
6. create a new frame with a term selected from the Linguistic Browser as frame name (identifier)
7. only in class and slot browser: if the LR is a *TaxonomicalLR*, explore hyponyms (up to a chosen level) of the concept selected on the Linguistic Browser and reproduce the tree on the frame browser, starting from the selected frame, if available

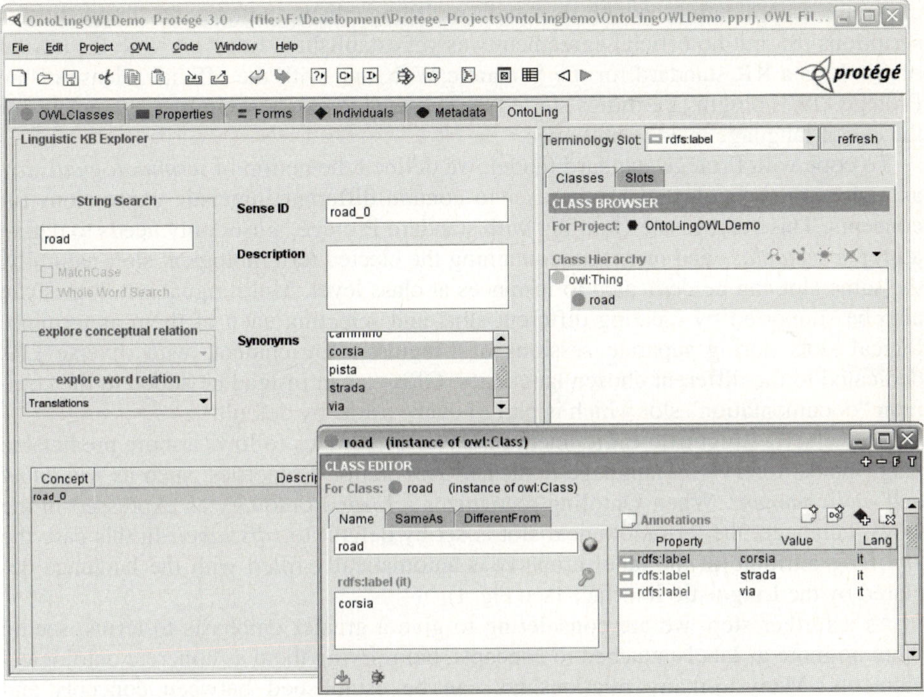

Fig. 4. Enriching an English OWL concept with selected Italian terms

These functionalities allow not only for linguistic enrichment of ontologies, but can be helpful for Ontologists and Knowledge Engineers in creating new ontologies or in improving/modifying existing ones.

Note how functionality 5 has not a rigid linguistic motivation, but is indeed dedicated to those willing to build an artificial controlled vocabulary which contains direct references to the senses of a particular resource.

How terms and glosses are added to the description of ontologies concepts, depends on the ontology model which is being adopted and is explained in detail in the following section.

6 Using Ontoling with Protégé and Protégé OWL

When a frame-based approach was first adopted in Protégé as a knowledge model for representing ontologies and knowledge bases, no explicit effort was dedicated to the representation of possible alternate labels (synonyms) for concepts neither to support the idea of multilingualism in Ontologies. Frame names were almost as equivalent as IDs, and people were only encouraged, as it is common practice in computer programming when addressing variable names, to adopt "meaningful and expressive names" to denote these IDs. The Protégé model was indeed quite strong and expressive, so that every ontology developer could deal with his linguistic needs at a meta-ontological level and find the right place for them. Rare examples exist of Protégé customized applications which deal with multilingualism and/or wider linguistic descriptions [8], but no official agreement was yet established. Later on, with the advent of OWL as a KR standard for the Semantic Web, and with the official release of the Protégé OWL plugin [7], things started to converge towards a minimal agreement for the use of language inside ontologies.

To cope with Protégé standard model, we defined the notion of *terminological slot*, as a slot which is elected by the user to contain different linguistic expressions for concepts. This way, to use Ontoling with standard Protégé, a user only needs to define a proper *metaclass* and *metaslot*, containing the elected terminological slot; naturally, the same slot can be dedicated to instances at class level. Multilingual ontologies can also be supported by creating different slots and selecting each of them as terminological slots during separate sessions of Linguistic Enrichment, with diverse LRs dedicated to the different chosen languages. Glosses can instead be added to the common "documentation" slot which is part of every frame by default.

Conversely, Linguistic Enrichment of OWL Ontologies follows a more predictable path, thanks to OWL's language dedicated Annotation Properties, such as *rdfs:label* and *owl:comment*. When Ontoling recognizes a loaded ontology as expressed in the OWL language, the terminological slot is set by default to *rdfs:label*. In this case the *xml:lang* attribute of the label property is automatically filled with the language declared by the Linguistic Interface (see Fig. 4).

As a further step, we are considering to give a greater emphasis to terms, seeing them no more as labels attached to concepts, but reifying them as concrete ontological elements. Many-to-many relationships can be established between concepts and terms, which can thus be accessed both ways. This approach guarantees greater linguistic awareness over ontological data, and is particularly useful when the conceptual content of Ontologies must be retrieved from documents, user questions and other cases where interaction with natural language content is required. This process is however again far from standardization and thus requires an agreement over the way terms, concepts and their relations are modeled.

7 Conclusions and Future Work

It appears evident that, in a process which has already been widely described and discussed in literature such as Ontology Development, the role of language must not be underestimated. If we believe that knowledge resources will really help in making the Semantic Web dream become true, we have to face the real aspects which characterize the Web as we know it, now.

Thousands of millions of documents which are available on the web are mostly written in natural language; at the same time, people like to interact with computers using even more friendly interfaces, and we do not know better solution than commonly spoken language. A more linguistic awareness could also help semantic search engines in augmenting the retrieval of proper results, or, at least, in excluding information which is not pertinent to the intention behind the submitted query.

In this work we stressed the need of providing a general framework for dealing with heterogeneous linguistic resources and for exploiting their content in the process of ontology development. Different functionalities for augmenting the linguistic expressivity of existing ontologies or for helping users in developing new knowledge resources from scratch have been identified and implemented in the presented Ontoling plugin for Protégé.

Ontoling, with the Wordnet Interface as its first available plugin, has been adopted by a community of users coming from diverse research areas, from pure linguists approaching ontologies, to ontology developers exploiting specific parts of Wordnet's taxonomical structure as a basis for creating their own domain ontology, up to users needing its main functionalities for adding synonyms to concepts of existing ontologies. With the recent release of the DICT Interface we added a little step in assisting multilingual ontology development and we now look forward other available resources (such as [10,11]) to be added to Ontoling plugin library.

References

1. V. R. Benjamins, J. Contreras, O. Corcho and A. Gómez-Pérez. Six Challenges for the Semantic Web. *SIGSEMIS Bulletin*, April 2004
2. N. Calzolari, J. McNaught, and A. Zampolli EAGLES Final Report: EAGLES Editors Introduction. EAG-EB-EI, Pisa, Italy 1996.
3. R. A. Cole, J. Mariani, H. Uszkoreit, A. Zaenen, and V. Zue, Eds. *Survey of the State of the Art in Human Language Technology*, Cambridge University Press, Cambridge, UK, 1997.
4. M. Dean, D. Connolly, F. van Harmelen, J. Hendler, I. Horrocks, D. L. McGuinness, P. F. Patel-Schneider, and L. A. Stein. OWL Web Ontology Language 1.0 Reference, W3C Working Draft 29 July 2002, http://www.w3.org/TR/owl-ref/.
5. Fellbaum, C.: WordNet - An electronic lexical database. MIT Press, (1998).
6. J. Gennari, M. Musen, R. Fergerson, W. Grosso, M. Crubézy, H. Eriksson, N. Noy, and S. Tu. The evolution of Protégé-2000: An environment for knowledge-based systems development. *International Journal of Human-Computer Studies*, 58(1):89–123, 2003.
7. H. Knublauch, R. W. Fergerson, N. F. Noy, M. A. Musen. The Protégé OWL Plugin: An Open Development Environment for Semantic Web Applications *Third International Semantic Web Conference - ISWC 2004*, Hiroshima, Japan. 2004
8. M.T. Pazienza, A. Stellato, M. Vindigni, A. Valarakos, V. Karkaletsis. Ontology integration in a multilingual e-retail system. *HCI International 2003*, Crete, Greece, 2003
9. M. T. Pazienza, A. Stellato, L. Henriksen, P. Paggio, F. M. Zanzotto. Ontology Mapping to support ontology-based question answering. *Proceedings of the second MEANING workshop*. Trento, Italy, February 2005
10. Emanuele Pianta, Luisa Bentivogli, Christian Girardi. MultiWordNet: developing an aligned multilingual database". In Proceedings of the First International Conference on Global WordNet, Mysore, India, January 21-25, 2002
11. P. Vossen. *EuroWordNet: A Multilingual Database with Lexical Semantic Networks*, Kluwer Academic Publishers, Dordrecht, 1998
12. www.dict.org/bin/Dict
13. www.freelang.com
14. www.tei-c.org/

Acquiring an Ontology from the Text
A Legal Case Study

Núria Casellas[1], Aleks Jakulin[2], Joan-Josep Vallbé[1], and Pompeu Casanovas[1]

[1] Institute of Law and Technology, Universitat Autònoma de Barcelona
(Catalonia, Spain)
{nuria.casellas, pep.vallbe, pompeu.casanovas}@uab.es
[2] Jozef Stefan Institute, Ljubljana, Slovenja
aleks.jakulin@ijs.si

Abstract. A topic ontology applies the usual ontological constructs to
the task of annotating the topic of a document. The topic is the highly
summarized essence of the document. The topics are usually chosen intuitively and rarely questioned. However, we have studied several ways
of allocating frequently asked questions from a legal domain into a set
of topical sub-domains. Our criteria were: 1) The sub-domains should
not overlap. 2) The sub-domain should be objectively identifiable from
the words of the text. 3) Which words and grammatical categories can
serve as keywords? 4) Can the structure of sub-domains be induced semi-
automatically from the text itself?

Keywords: ontology acquisition, topic ontology, textual statistics,
legal ontology.

1 Introduction

The work we present in this paper is part of the development within the European SEKT[1] project of the prototype Iuriservice,[2] a web-based application that
retrieves answers to questions raised by newly recruited judges in the Spanish Judiciary. This system offers access to a frequently asked questions (FAQ) database
through a natural language interface, where the judge describes the problem at
hand and the application responds with a list of relevant question-answer pairs
that offer solutions to that particular problem. Within this system, ontologies
are being used to provide a more accurate search than the basic keyword search
[1, 2].

From data gathered through an ethnographic survey [3], a corpus of 756
questions was extracted. Then, with the participation and collaboration of the
General Council of the Judiciary (GCPJ), the questions containing dilemmas
(mostly regarding best-practices during on-duty hours or staff management),

---

[1] http://www.sekt-project.com

[2] Developed by Intelligent Software Components, S.A. (iSOCO, http://www.isoco.-
com) and the Institute of Law and Technology (UAB).

M. Ali and R. Dapoigny (Eds.): IEA/AIE 2006, LNAI 4031, pp. 1000–1013, 2006.

were answered by professionals (the tutors of the Spanish School of the Judiciary). Both, the questions and the answers contained professional knowledge (or lack of professional knowledge) and the purpose of the tool is, thus, the gathering, the maintenance and the distribution of this professional judicial knowledge among the judiciary.

In order to conceptualise that professional and domain dependent knowledge, an ontology was extracted manually from the selection of terms (nouns) and relations (adjectives, verbs) of each of the questions gathered. This ontology is called Ontology of Professional Judicial Knowledge (OPJK) [5, 6].

The classes and instances were extracted manually as the 756 questions' corpus was sufficiently compact to allow manual extraction and, at the time, there was no semi-automatic extraction tool available for Spanish. This ontology is used as the underlying semantic model (OPJK) to compute the input question with natural language processing software (tokenizer, morphological analyser, basic shallow parser and semantic analysis) for retrieving the question-answer pair of FAQ stored within the system [4]. The process of extraction of concepts from the text in order to both model OPJK and show the importance of the source of the data (text) when constructing ontologies of legal professional knowledge has been largely explained in other papers [5].

This paper focuses on the use of this same corpus of questions to model a second ontology, this time a topic ontology, to allow legal sub-domain detection. The sub-domain detection helps with search: if we can detect the topic of a query (such as gender violence), we can offer answers that cover that particular topic. Topic detection does not require the user to be familiar with a specific nomenclature of topics.

First, we will introduce topic ontologies and the manually developed classification into topics (or legal sub-domains) by the legal expert's team. Then, we will describe the analysis of the results provided by a classifier, which results in recommendations on how to prepare the corpus prior to the statistical analysis of the text.

2   A Topic Ontology for the Corpus of Questions

A topic is a semantic annotation of a document that people instinctively use to search and organize information. While we can semantically annotate many facets of a document, the notion of topic covers the document as a whole: it is the conceptualization of the document with the greatest breadth. When we seek information, our primary intention is usually to discover information on the same topic as is the topic of our problem. Topic can be distinguished from other descriptors of a document, such as language, style, punctuation, grammar, reputation, graphical design, author, date, and so on.

The conceptual structure of documents and topics can be mapped to the RDF structure. We will treat both topics and documents to be objects. To associate them, we will use the transitive `hasSubject` predicate to associate a document with its topics. Such a restricted family of ontologies with a somewhat

```
<ptop:Topic rdf:about="#TOP_5">
 <psys:description>Civil: sucesiones</psys:description>
 <ptop:subTopicOf rdf:resource="#TOP_0" />
 <jsikm:hasOntoGenClassProperties rdf:resource="#CLS_PROP_5" />
</ptop:Topic> <jsikm:OntoGenClassProperties rdf:about="#CLS_PROP_5">
 <jsikm:hasCentroidKeywords>herencia, finca, testamento
 </jsikm:hasCentroidKeywords>
 <jsikm:hasSVMKeywords></jsikm:hasSVMKeywords>
</jsikm:OntoGenClassProperties>

<ptop:Document rdf:about="#DOC_8">
 <ptop:hasSubject rdf:resource="#TOP_0" />
 <ptop:hasSubject rdf:resource="#TOP_3" />
 <jsikm:hasOntoGenInstanceProperties rdf:resource="#INST_PROP_8" />
</ptop:Document> <jsikm:OntoGenInstanceProperties
rdf:about="#INST_PROP_8">
 </jsikm:OntoGenInstanceProperties>
```

Fig. 1. An example of the RDF description of topics and documents

different semantics are referred to as topic ontologies to distinguish them from
more general schema ontologies [10]. Fig. 1 shows a description of a topic and
document in the RDF format.

Initially, the team of domain experts identified several sub-domains (topics)
intuitively gathered from the questions. The detection of sub-domains drove, at
the beginning, to a classification of questions into these different sub-domains to
ease the construction of the ontology, which focused, at first, on two specific sub-
domains: on-duty and family issues (containing gender violence and protection
or restraining orders). The manual classification of questions into sub-domains
resulted in the list shown below (see also Fig. 2):

```
1. On-duty                          7. Court office
2. Family issues                    7.1. Organization
2.1. Gender violence                7.2. Civil servants
2.2. Minors                         7.3. Prosecution
2.3. Divorce/separation/custody     7.4. Infrastructure
2.4. Other                          7.5. Security
3. Immigration                      7.6. Informatics
4. Property                         7.7. Experts
5. Sentencing                       7.8. Police and security
5.1. Execution                      7.9. Incompatibilities
5.2. Breach of order/judgment       7.10. Relations with the GCJP
5.3. Form                           7.11. Other
5.4. Notification                   7.12. Lawyers
6. Proceedings                      8. Business Law
6.1. Evidences                      9. Traffic accidents
6.2. Competence                     10. Criminal Law
6.3. Criteria                       10.1. Drugs
                                    10.2. Organized crime
                                    10.3. Theft/Robbery/Burglary
```

Later on, during the manual conceptualization of OPJK, the domain experts
and ontology engineers in the team realised that most of the questions regarding *on-duty* and *family issues* were necessarily related to procedural moments
(phases or acts, *proceedings*). Moreover, *decision-making and judgements* were
also necessarily related to *proceedings* and *gender violence* (included within *family issues*) was necessarily related to *Criminal Law*, thus related to the other sub-
domains being modelled. This fact showed, again intuitively, that the questions

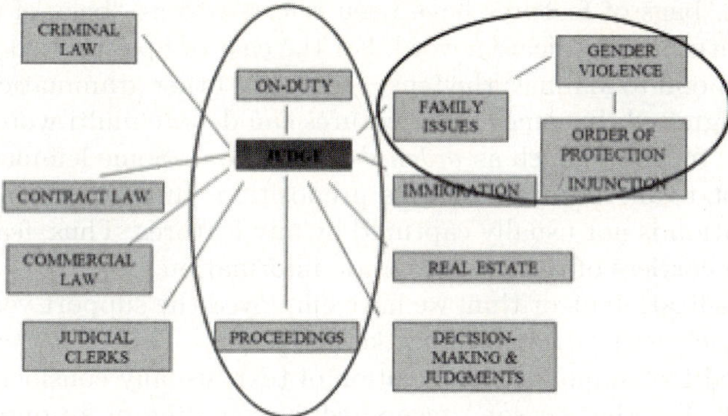

Fig. 2. Screenshot of the intuitively detected sub-domains, where the domains are directly related to the activity of the judge

could have been misclassified and also that the questions could refer to more than just one intuitive sub-domain at the same time.

This intuitive conclusion was confirmed by the results provided by a support vector machine classifier. In simple terms, the classifier attempted to learn by which keywords to distinguish the topics or sub-domains of questions. Ideally, the classifier would automatically, correctly and unambiguously decide what sub-domain a particular question belongs to. In practice, however, the classifier will make mistakes. Some of the mistakes might indicate that the categories are not specified with a sufficient amount of detail. Other mistakes may indicate incorrectly labelled questions, but there might also be questions that can be correctly classified in several ways.

The classifier first analysed the intuitive classification in sub-domains and provided us with two different statistical reports. The first report was a list of keywords for each sub-domain. The list of keywords showed which terms the classifier thought to be in favour or against of that sub-domain. The second report was a diagnosis for each of the intuitively and manually classified questions, listing arguments for or against that classification.

2.1   Operation of the Classifier

The technology needed for topic detection is classification, a ubiquitous technique in machine learning. A classifier (or a classification model) is an automatic detector of topics from documents. Since the classifier cannot work with text directly, the documents are represented with features. Features are concepts that can be easily detected from the text. Normally, the ordering of features is ignored, and we refer to such assumption as "bags of features". Still, we do count the number of appearances of each feature, so each feature is represented as a number proportional to the number of appearances. If the feature was not detected in a document, the number will be zero.

In the past, bags of features have been referred to as "bags of words". It is true that a feature can indicate a word. For the case of Spanish text, the features instead correspond to lemmas: the tense, gender or other grammatical properties of a word are ignored. In some cases, features can denote multi-word expressions with a specific meaning (such as *orden de protección*). Some lemmas are usually considered not to be features, such as prepositions and other function words. Also, punctuation is not usually captured by any features. Thus, features should correspond to carriers of relevant semantic information.

As the classification algorithm, we have employed the support vector machine (SVM) approach with a dot product kernel [12, 8]. This is perhaps the most frequently used technique for classification of text, usually considered to be one of the best [9]. For that reason, unsuccessful grounding of an ontology cannot be blamed on the choice of the classification algorithm, but on the preparation of the data or on the topic ontology.

It is usually insufficient to merely analyze the classification performance of a model. To diagnose the reasons and courses of remedy, we need to examine the problems in more detail. Specifically, we should understand the causes of the errors. Such causes will provide insight about the missing background knowledge which can be introduced manually. To facilitate the analysis, we employ two techniques:

- Identifying the decisive features for each concept.
- Identifying the instances where the concept is not identified correctly.

The SVM classifier encodes each feature with a real-valued variable. All the features are encoded in a feature vector $\boldsymbol{x}$. The sub-domain is encoded with the variable y that takes the value of +1 when the sub-domain is present and -1 when it is absent. The classifier then acts as a function $y = f(\boldsymbol{x})$. SVM with the dot product kernel is associated with a function that takes the following form:

$$f(\boldsymbol{x}) = \begin{cases} -1; & \sum_i \alpha_i y_i (\boldsymbol{x}_i \cdot \boldsymbol{x}) < 0 \\ +1 & \text{otherwise.} \end{cases}$$

Here, $y_i \boldsymbol{x}_i$ are the labelled training instances, and α_i are the parameters of the model. While this sum is over the training instances with nonzero α_i, an alternative is to convert it into a sum over the features [7]. In that case, f takes such a form:

$$f(\boldsymbol{x}) = \begin{cases} -1; & d + \sum_j w_j [\boldsymbol{x}]_j < 0 \\ +1 & \text{otherwise.} \end{cases}$$

Here, $[\boldsymbol{x}]_j$ denotes the j-th dimension of vector $\boldsymbol{x}$. We can interpret the weights w as a degree of importance of each individual feature. However, rare words would appear to have a very high importance, while in fact they only apply to rare cases. Instead, our measure of feature importance for feature j is going to be the net leverage q across all the training instances:

$$q(j) = \sum_i w_j [\boldsymbol{x}_i]_j$$

Positive sign of net leverage will indicate that the particular feature votes in favor of a sub-domain across the whole corpus, and a negative sign will indicate votes against the sub-domain.

While the net leverage allows the overall diagnosis of the corpus, leverage can also be computed only for a particular question. The question may sometimes be misclassified: a question being in the sub-domain but classified as not belonging to the sub-domain is a false negative, while a question not belonging to a sub-domain but classified as being in the sub-domain is a false positive. By examining misclassifications we can see what went wrong, and seek courses of remedy.

Analysis of Keywords. To display the "keywords" of a particular sub-domain, we simply build the classifier to detect the sub-domain. Then, we seek out those features that have the highest net leverage: these features are the 'arguments in favor". The "arguments against" are the features with the lowest negative net leverage.

Analysing the lists of keywords for each sub-domain, the domain experts detected that most terms stated to be in favour had no relevant meaning for that particular sub-domain, some terms stated to be against a sub-domain could actually be relevant for the sub-domain and some terms neither in favour nor against had no more special relation to that particular sub-domain than to another.

```
GUARDIA

Model for  guardia [on-duty] (#q:79)
* Keywords in favor of                       * Keywords against
291.91 ( 170) guardia [on-duty]              139.79 ( 738) .
124.85 ( 119) cadaver [corpse]                73.89 ( 337) caso [case]
108.18 ( 973) ,                               57.73 ( 143) abogado [lawyer]
 80.68 ( 131) asunto [suit]                   48.19 ( 130) menor [minor]
 65.29 ( 146) medico [doctor]                 46.26 ( 318) juicio [trial]
 65.09 ( 250) pedir [to request]              45.28 ( 215) pero [but]
 60.64 ( 117) llamar [to call]                44.59 ( 144) mandar [to order]
 59.66 (  64) traslado [transfer]             43.23 ( 110) seguir [to follow]
 57.74 (  86) levantamiento [corpse removing] 39.64 ( 117) malo [bad/ill]
 52.16 (  51) entrada [entry]                 38.69 ( 110) trato [treatment]
 45.37 (  62) urgente [urgent]                38.34 ( 137) funcionario [civil servant]
 44.65 (  82) en_caso_de [in the case of]     36.97 ( 986) ?
 41.39 ( 207) persona [person]                35.75 ( 149) rapido [fast/quick]
 39.81 ( 186) policia [police]                31.30 ( 105) poner [to put]
 38.77 (  55) registro [search]               31.15 ( 129) ese [that]
 37.50 ( 113) auto [court order]              30.18 (  53) autopsia [autopsy]
 36.77 (  63) social [social]                 28.66 (  80) trabajo [work]
 36.42 (  58) remitir [to refer]              27.76 ( 210) judicial [judicial]
 34.18 ( 156) ante [before]                   27.28 ( 141) delito [offence]
 33.31 ( 325) estar [to be]                   26.08 (  55) telefono [telephone]
```

For example, if we take the example of the on-duty sub-domain (shown above), legal domain experts can identify that on-duty [*guardia*], corpse [*cadaver*], doctor [*medico*], corpse removing [*levantamiento*], entry [*entrada*], urgent [*urgente*], police [*policia*] and search [*registro*] are relevant terms for the on-duty period. However, suit [*asunto*], transfer [*traslado*], person [*persona*], court order [*auto*], social [*social*] and to refer[*remitir*] had no relevant meaning for that particular sub-domain.

Moreover, the list of keywords **against** a particular question being classified into the on-duty sub-domain contains some terms which can be identified by domain experts as being **in favour** of a question belonging to the on-duty sub-domain. The terms *autopsy* [autopsia] and *telephone* [telefono] are especially relevant to on-duty questions as most autopsies and line tappings are requested during on-duty hours. We also have to bear in mind that most on-duty requests are made through a phone call to the judge (who might be home).

Also, some other terms of the list **against** questions being classified into the on-duty sub-domain could be identified as relevant to the on-duty questions but could be relevant to other sub-domains as well. Suit [*caso*], lawyer [*abogado*], minor [*menor*], trial [*juicio*], civil servant [*funcionario*] and offence [*delito*] are relevant keywords to the on-duty sub-domain but also to the family issues sub-domain (minor), to the criminal law sub-domain (offence), to the court office sub-domain (civil servant and lawyer), to the proceedings sub-domain (trial) or to any sub-domain (suit).

A particular feature may be an argument against a sub-domain even if it does appear in the corresponding questions. This can be explained by the fact that the particular feature appears even more frequently in other sub-domains. But as some sub-domains only have a small number of examples (questions), the classifier can make mistakes.

Analysis of Misclassifications. Because all the questions have been manually classified by the experts, we know what is the true classification of a question. If the question is then shown to the classifier, we can check if the automatic classification is consistent with the manual one. If there has been a mistake, we can examine what features were decisive in the classification. We show five features with the highest and five features with the lowest leverage for the wrong classification. Furthermore, we do the same for the correct classification.

The errors may arise for four reasons: overvaluing of arguments in favor of wrong decision and against the correct decision, and undervaluing of arguments in favor of the right decision and arguments against the wrong decision. In practice, the classifier might not detect an important feature, or might detect an irrelevant feature.

When this analysis was related to the analysis made by the same domain experts of the results of the diagnosis for each of the questions originally classified in the on-duty sub-domain, they could detect that:

1. Some on-duty questions had been misclassified in that sub-domain and they clearly belonged to another (see list below).

```
Qué hago con el procedimiento cuando mando análisis de ADN y
tardan casi un año en llegar los resultados?

True=guardia Predicted=proceso/pruebas

* Keywords in favor of guardia        * Keywords against guardia
    0.00 (    0) estar                     1.35 (    4) mandar
    0.00 (    0) juzgar                    0.36 (    6) llegar
    0.00 (    0) unico                     0.06 (    6) ano
    0.00 (    0) guardia                   0.04 (    1) ?
    0.00 (    0) permanente                0.00 (    4) procedimiento
```

```
* Keywords in favor of proceso/pruebas  * Keywords against proceso/pruebas
   2.99 (     6) analisis                   0.32 (     4) procedimiento
   1.85 (     7) casi                       0.04 (     1) ?
   1.85 (     7) adn                        0.00 (     0) estar
   1.29 (     6) ano                        0.00 (     0) juzgar
   1.11 (     6) resultado                  0.00 (     0) unico
```

2. Some on-duty questions were correctly classified into the on-duty period but were also relevant to other sub-domains (see list below).

```
Cómo proceder en aquellos casos en que una mujer
interpone denuncia por malos tratos, pero pide expresamente
que no se acorde ninguna medida de alejamiento?

True=guardia Predicted=familia/violencia_domestica

* Keywords in favor of guardia       * Keywords against guardia
   1.63 (     6) ninguno                 1.55 (     4) trato
   0.88 (     3) pedir                   1.47 (     4) malo
   0.47 (     4) proceder                0.75 (     4) pero
   0.23 (     2) ,                       0.65 (     3) caso
   0.11 (     4) mujer                   0.65 (     5) alejamiento

* Keywords in favor of familia       * Keywords against familia
   5.24 (     4) medida                  1.18 (     4) proceder
   2.85 (     4) malo                    1.06 (     6) ninguno
   2.71 (     4) trato                   1.00 (     3) pedir
   2.66 (     5) alejamiento             0.63 (     5) aquel
   1.79 (     4) denunciar               0.40 (     3) caso
```

3. Some true on-duty questions were shown wrongly to belong to another sub-domain (see list below).

```
Me llaman desde el depósito municipal de cadáveres diciendo
que ha venido la funeraria pidiendo la licencia para llevarse un cadáver.
¿Qué tengo que comprobar antes de darles la licencia? ¿Qué hay que hacer?

True=guardia Predicted=proceso/pruebas

* Keywords in favor of guardia       * Keywords against guardia
   9.60 (     9) cadaver                 5.10 (    13) licencia
   2.25 (     4) llamar                  2.89 (     6) municipal
   0.88 (     3) pedir                   1.99 (     5) deposito
   0.00 (     0) estar                   1.27 (     7) funeraria
   0.00 (     0) juzgar                  1.16 (     5) antes_de

* Keywords in favor of proceso       * Keywords against proceso
   2.87 (    13) licencia                1.63 (     9) cadaver
   0.79 (     5) antes_de                0.78 (     4) dar
   0.60 (     3) pedir                   0.58 (     2) .
   0.59 (     6) municipal               0.33 (     4) venir
   0.35 (     5) deposito                0.28 (     4) llamar
```

In conclusion, the data showed that the classifier encountered several problems in classifying the questions, mostly due to the inefficient original classification. One of the reasons was automatic misclassification, as shown above. However, there was another reason: there was the need to consider the on-duty sub-domain differently. The on-duty sub-domain does not represent a conceptual domain of specific knowledge, it represents a time domain. The on-duty period involves all those questions that happen on a certain time. Therefore, the questions belonging to the on-duty period could and should belong also to the other sub-domains that represent conceptual domains and contain the questions in a certain knowledge area.

Secondly, the classifier misunderstood the relevance of some of the keywords used for argumentation. As stated above, some terms were not relevant for a particular sub-domain. However, the main difficulties were:

1. The usage of complete irrelevant terms for the legal domain (at least on their own) like but [*pero*], to order [*mandar*], to follow [*seguir*], to put [*poner*], that [*ese*], work [*trabajo*]);
2. The inability to capture relevant compound forms. For example: bad/ill [*malo*] and treatment [*trato*] are regarded separately, while they are actually a compound form: bad/ill treatment [*malos tratos*] is a relevant key-phrase, used to identify the questions related to gender violence.

Therefore, a conceptual change was adopted and on-duty was regarded, from that point, as a time domain, rather than a sub-domain in itself. Also the data had to be prepared as to reduce the number of errors.

3   Text Preparation for Ontology Modeling

One of the main principles in Corpus Linguistics is that the analyst has to do his best to avoid as "noise" in the corpus as he can. There are two important operations: to unify all the words with a very similar meaning, and to remove the words that do not carry relevant meaning. The first operation is achieved using stemming, lemmatisation and with thesauri (including WordNet). In stemming, we remove the final few letters of the word that carry grammatical nuances but do not distinguish the meaning. For example, we represent words *dog, dogs, doggy* with *dog+*.

A verb such as *be* may take several forms: *is, are, were, being, be*. During lemmatisation, we replace all these forms that may reflect tense, gender, inflection, irregularity, etc., with the simple canonical one: *be*. While this particular example may seem contrived, other languages, such as Spanish, have many more such examples. Such languages benefit much more from lemmatisation, while English does well already just with stemming [11].

The second important practice is removing the words that are deemed not to carry any relevant meaning for the task of determining sub-domains and topics. Such words (or lemmas) are referred to as *stop words*. There may be two reasons why they are to be ignored. Some words may carry no conceptual meaning on their own (e.g. prepositions, conjunctions, etc). Although a more sophisticated method would be able to gain information from such words, the "bag of words" approach cannot, so such words are mere noise. The second type of words may have meaning on their own, but they do not add any (semantic) value for the purpose of our analysis (e.g. auxiliary verbs). A list of such words is then used to prepare the data before classification.

3.1   Irrelevant Grammatical Categories

In any linguistic corpus we may find many "grammatical" or *function* words that are unlikely to be useful for search. For example, common function words in a text sample in Spanish are *de, la, que, el, en, y, a, los, del,* etc. These words do have important functions in Spanish, but they hardly contribute any useful information for search or topic classification.

The stop words mentioned above (within others) correspond to different grammatical categories and thereby they are to be tagged in diverse ways by the morphological analyser we are using.[3] For instance, *de* [of], *en* [in] and *a* [to] are prepositions [SPS00]; *la* [the, fem.], *el* [the, masc.] are a defined, feminine/masculine, singular articles [TDFS0, TDMS0], *que* [that, which] and *y* [and] are a subordinate [CS00] and a coordinate [CC00] conjunction, and so forth.

The words in our corpora tagged with the following standard codes (corresponding to function words) will be considered stop words. The first two letters of the code are sufficient for their identification, according to EAGLES tags (e.g. TD—, CC–, etc.):

- **Articles, Determiners:** Demonstrative (DD—), Possessive (DP—), Interrogative (DT—), Exclamatory (DE—), Indefinite (DI—)
- **Pronouns:** Personal (PP—), Demonstrative (PD—), Possessive (PX—), Indefinite (PI—), Interrogative (PT—), Relative (PR—)
- **Conjunctions:** Coordinated (CC00), Subordinated (CS00)
- **Interjections:** (I)
- **Prepositions:** Adpositions (SPC-), Prepositions (SPS00)
- **Numerals:** Cardinal (MC–), Ordinal (MO–)
- **Punctuation signs:** (F)

The main category of meaningful words that should be included into the stop word list in order to ease the linguistic treatment are the auxiliary verbs. Some of its forms are in fact removed during the lemmatization process, since all the forms of a verb (including compound ones as *ha hecho* [has done]) are reduced to its infinitive form, so that the auxiliary form *ha* [from *haber* "to have"] is deleted as it functions as an auxiliary verb. Since some errors can be made in this process and some auxiliary verbs can be interpreted by the morphological analyser as full verbs, we propose the elimination *a priori* of all auxiliary verbs. The first two letters of its EAGLES code are VA—.

Another question regarding the classifier is that some verbs like *ser* and *estar* [to be], *tener* [to have something], *haber* [to have, to exist], are used too frequently to have an important value in classification. In other words, neither of these verbs can be seen as defining any special kind of domain, since they may be found in any kind of standard sentence. Our proposal would be to eliminate them also, as we do with the auxiliary verbs. This should be done after the lemmatization [11] —i.e. once the program has reduced all the verbal forms to infinitive— in order to make it easier for the program to identify just the verbal forms *ser, estar, tener* and *haber.*

---

[3] http://garraf.epsevg.upc.es/freeling/

3.2   Words to Be Preserved in the Corpus

In general terms, the words that contribute most to the meaning of a text are nouns and verbs. With the exceptions mentioned above, these kind of words have to be preserved in the corpora in order to perform a good search. The codes are:

1. For verbs (main verbs): VM—
2. For nouns:
   (a) Common nouns: NC—
   (b) Proper nouns: NP—

In reference to the other categories not mentioned so far (adjectives, adverbs and abreviations), we think they should be preserved for some reasons. First, adjectives (AQ—) and substantives (NC— and NP—) —in a broad semantic sense— are considered to form a joint category that some authors call 'noun', which means that the adjective has not always been treated as a completely independent category, for it works as a complement for the sense of the substantive. To delete it would imply a great loss of information.

A typical example of this would be *malos tratos* [ill-treatment], which is formed by an adjective [*malos*] plus a substantive [*tratos*]. Secondly, however its strenght and importance in sense-adding value is not the adjective's (at least in terms of occurrence), adverbs (RG—) are still important for our purposes, because they may add important information about the use (thus the sense) of a verb in many cases. An example of this may be *tramitar urgentemente* [to proceed urgently]. Thirdly, abbreviations (Y) (like *etc.*, but also like *LeCrim* [abbreviated form for referring to the Criminal Code]) are very important for our purposes, since the legal discourse makes a great use of them and can be of great value for classification.

3.3   Domain Dependent Words

The Ontology of Professional Judicial Knowledge (OPJK), introduced above, currently covers the sub-domains of *guardia* [on-duty period], gender violence and procedural law. Currently, it has to be completed with issues from criminal and commercial law. Obviously the words —whether they are concepts or instances— which appear in this ontology ought to be especially taken into account in the classification process. In other words, OPJK ought to be seen (for this purpose) as a statement of relevant linguistic terms that are important for capturing the semantics we care about. This ontology is being built from textual protocols extracted from an extended field work, which *per force* implies a strong relation between words and real data. Moreover, the extraction of the words (concepts and instances) has been made manually, mostly extracted by hand by the legal expert team. Thus the words which appear in OPJK ought to be given some special consideration.

Moreover, as a good number of the terms in OPJK do not correspond to a single word but to a componund form, these compound forms ought to be taken into account as single occurrences and not as two. Typical forms extracted from OPJK are:

- Noun + Preposition + Noun (*juzgado de guardia, diligencia de embargo*, etc.)
- Adjective + Noun (*malos tratos, lesa humanidad,* etc.)
- Noun + Adjective (*documento procesal, enjuiciamiento civil,* etc.)

3.4   Experiments

We have examined the above heuristics in an experiment. We have performed two replications of 10-fold cross validation. The experiments were based on different ways of preparing the text before attempting to ground the ontology. This is expected to reveal where the semantics is hidden. As to summarize the precision (prec) and recall (recall) in a single number, we have used the F-score:

$$\text{F-score} = \frac{2 \times \text{prec} \times \text{recall}}{\text{prec} + \text{recall}}$$

Table 1. A comparison of different processing techniques for text. Best results were obtained by eliminating irrelevant POS categories (P+stop). All the techniques combined (All) was not far behind, and identifying synonyms was found helpful. Prioritizing 'important' words (l+lexicon) and or important POS categories (P+imp) proved less successful - perhaps this was due to our approach of increasing the scale of the important words. But no processing (none) was almost always the worst.

sub-domain	#	None	lemm.	l+lexicon	l+syn	l+stop	P+stop	P+imp	All
1. On-duty	79	0.33	0.23	**0.38**	0.23	0.36	0.37	0.23	0.37
2. Family issues	103	0.31	**0.49**	0.45	0.27	0.45	0.24	0.49	0.24
2.1. Gender violence	62	0.34	0.30	0.43	0.18	**0.47**	0.23	0.29	0.24
2.2. Minors	19	0.00	0.74	0.64	0.38	0.51	0.00	**0.82**	0.00
2.3. Divorce	18	0.00	0.10	0.00	0.20	0.11	0.15	**0.23**	0.15
3. Immigration	26	0.15	0.21	0.06	0.07	**0.24**	0.23	0.20	0.21
4. Property	10	0.14	0.00	**0.18**	0.00	0.00	0.16	0.00	0.00
5. Sentencing	48	0.22	0.32	0.24	0.47	**0.48**	0.43	0.33	0.42
5.1. Execution	40	0.25	0.34	0.29	**0.52**	0.48	0.44	0.35	0.44
6. Proceedings	307	0.49	0.53	0.51	0.54	0.55	**0.59**	0.54	0.59
6.1. Evidence	61	0.13	0.24	0.18	0.28	0.17	**0.32**	0.30	0.29
6.2. Competence	45	0.18	0.12	0.13	0.13	0.18	0.22	0.12	**0.24**
7. Court office	151	0.25	0.24	0.23	0.27	0.25	0.29	0.26	**0.29**
7.1. Organization	40	0.05	0.02	0.00	0.00	0.05	**0.15**	0.02	0.09
7.2. Civil servants	17	0.21	0.10	**0.41**	0.19	0.36	0.21	0.15	0.19
7.3. Experts	20	0.12	0.25	0.48	**0.53**	0.25	0.37	0.36	0.36
7.4. Infrastructure	19	0.00	0.00	0.00	0.00	0.00	**0.10**	0.00	**0.10**
7.6. Informatics	13	0.00	0.07	0.00	**0.19**	0.14	0.07	0.07	0.07
7.12. Lawyers	9	0.00	**0.46**	0.00	0.00	0.00	0.00	**0.46**	0.00
7.10. GCJP	11	0.00	**0.17**	0.00	0.00	**0.17**	**0.17**	**0.17**	**0.17**
7.9. Incompatibilities	14	**0.19**	0.00	**0.19**	0.00	0.00	0.00	0.00	0.00
8. Business law	28	0.38	0.26	0.27	0.30	**0.46**	0.24	0.32	0.24
9. Traffic accidents	11	0.09	**0.31**	0.00	**0.31**	0.00	**0.31**	0.29	**0.31**
10. Criminal law	10	0.00	0.00	0.16	**0.18**	0.00	0.00	0.00	0.00
RANKS		2.89	3.59	3.35	4.26	5.41	**6.07**	4.80	5.62

The higher the F-score, the better the grounding performance. To summarize the F-scores across a number of experiments, we have used the average rank of a particular data-preparation technique across the sub-domains. Each sub-domain had a weight proportional to the number of its instances, as to prevent small sub-domains from exerting too much influence. The higher the rank, the better the method.

Our implementation used the following techniques:

- Lexicon: the words or sequences of words that are deemed to be important have a higher weight in the SVM model. This weighting is done by increasing the scale of the corresponding dimension.
- Synonyms: we replace alternate expressions with a single canonical one.
- Stop words: we remove the terms that correspond to a list of irrelevant words or phrases.
- POS stop: we remove the lemmas that correspond to irrelevant POS categories.
- POS important: we increase the weight of those terms that appear under an important POS category.

The results of the analysis are shown in Table 1. Some infrequent sub-domains were eliminated. We can conclude that POS-based filtering is very successful, and that it helps to establish a list of synonyms. We can also observe that the important word list was especially helpful for the 'On-duty' sub-domain, but not as much for other sub-domains. Also, the lack of success with important words is perhaps due to our way of implementing it with increasing the scale of the variable.

4   Conclusions

In this paper we have explained the construction of a topic ontology from the corpus of questions (obtained by ethnographic field work and related to the Iuriservice prototype developed within the SEKT project). The development started with a manually modelled topic ontology, that was soon disregarded by the evidence given by the classifier. The automatic classification of a set of questions taking into account the previous manual classification resulted in misclassification of questions, and low relevancy of sub-domain keywords. That analysis not only provided some recommendations regarding the sub-domains themselves (on-duty) but also regarding the representation of the text. Thus, the analysis has demonstrated the need to treat the corpus before the automated (or semi-automated) extraction of ontologies to assure better results. In the future we will work on the evaluation of those recommendations and will use a tool (OntoGen) to semi-automatically organize the previously treated corpus of questions into a topic ontology.

Acknowledgements

SEC2001-2581-C02-01 and EU-IST (IP) IST-2003-506826 SEKT.

References

[1] Benjamins, V,R.; Contreras, J.; Blázquez, M.; Rodrigo, L.; Casanovas, P.; Poblet, M. (2004). "The SEKT use legal case components: ontology and architecture", in T.B. Gordon (Ed.), *Legal Knowledge and Information Systems*. Jurix 2004. IOS Press, Amsterdam, 2004, pp. 69-77.

[2] Benjamins V.R.; Casanovas, P. Contreras, J., López-Cobo, J.M.; Lemus, L. (2005). "Iuriservice: An Intelligent Frequently Asked Questions System to Assist Newly Appointed Judges", in V.R. Benjamins et al. *Law and the Semantic Web*, Springer-Verlag, London, Berlin, pp. 205-22.

[3] Casanovas, Pompeu; Poblet, Marta; Casellas, Núria; Vallbé, Joan Josep; Ramos, Francisco; Benjamins, Richard; Blázquez, Mercedes; Rodrigo, Luis; Contreras, Jesús; Gorroñogoitia, Jesús (2005): *D 10.2.1Legal Scenario*. Deliverable WP10 Case Study: Intelligent integrated decision support for legal professionals. SEKT Project (www.sekt-project.com).

[4] Casanovas, P.; Poblet, M.; Casellas, N.; Contreras, J.; Benjamins, V.R.; Blázquez, M. (2005): "Supporting newly-appointed judges: a legal knowledge management case study". *Journal of Knowledge Management*, Vol. 9 No. 5, pp. 7-27.

[5] Casanovas, P.; Casellas, N.; Tempich, C.; Vrandečić, D.; Benjamins, V.R. (2005): "OPJK modeling methodology". Lehman, J.; Biasiotti, M.A.; Francesconi, E.; Sagri, M.T. (eds.): *IAAIL Proceedings*. LOAIT - Legal Ontologies and Artificial Intelligence Techniques. Bologna, June 2005, pp. 121-133.

[6] Casellas, N.; Blázquez, M.; Kiryakov, A.; Casanovas, P.; Benjamins, V.R. (2005). "OPJK into PROTON: legal domain ontology integration into an upper-level ontology". R. Meersman et al. (Eds.): *OTM Workshops 2005*, LNCS 3762. Springer-Verlag Berlin Heidelberg, pp. 846-855.

[7] Jakulin, A., M. Možina, J. Demšar, I. Bratko, B. Zupan. (2005). "Nomograms for visualizing support vector machines". *Proceeding of the eleventh ACM SIGKDD international conference on Knowledge discovery in data mining*. KDD '05.

[8] Joachims T. (1999): "Making large-scale SVM learning practical". In B. Scholkopf, C. Burges, and A. Smola (eds.). *Advances in Kernel Methods - Support Vector Learning*. Cambridge (MA): MIT Press.

[9] Lewis, D. D.; Yang, Y.; Rose, T.; and Li, F. (2004). "RCV1: A New Benchmark Collection for Text Categorization Research". *Journal of Machine Learning Research* 5: 361-397.

[10] Terziev, I., Kiryakov, A., Manov, D. (2004). *D 1.8.1. Base upper-level ontology (BULO) Guidance*, report EU-IST Integrated Project (IP) IST-2003- 506826 SEKT).

[11] Vallbé, J.J.; Martí, M.A.; Fortuna, B.; Jakulin, A.; Mladenić, D.; Casanovas, P. (2005) "Stemming and lemmatisation: improving knowledge management through language processing techniques". Casanovas, P., Bourcier, D., Noriega, P., Cáceres, E., Galindo, F., *The regulation of electronic social systems. Law and the Semantic Web*. Proceedings of the B4-Workshop on Artificial Intelligence and Law. IVR' 05-Granada , May 25th-27th. http://www.lefis.org. XXII World Conference of Philosophy of Law and Social Philosophy. Instituto de Investigaciones Jurídicas, UNAM (México) [In press].

[12] Vapnik, V.N. (1999): *The Nature of Statistical Learning Theory*. Springer- Verlag New York, 2nd edition.

TERMINAE Method and Integration Process for Legal Ontology Building

Sylvie Despres[1] and Sylvie Szulman[2]

[1] CRIP5, Equipe IAD, Université Paris 5
sd@math-info.univ-paris5.fr
[2] LIPN, UMR7030 Université Paris 13
ss@lipn.univ-paris13.fr

Abstract. This paper describes the contruction method of a legal application ontology. This method is based on the merging of micro-ontologies built from European community directives. The TERMINAE construction method from texts enhanced by an alignment process with a core legal ontology is used for building micro-ontologies. A merging process allows constructing the legal ontology.

1 Introduction

This paper presents the contruction method of a legal application ontology. The aim of this ontology is to support the development of formal models of legislation to be used in legal knowledge-based systems. This construction method is based on micro-ontology building and their merging. A micro-ontology refers to a set of concepts and properties describing a domain's restricted context. Each micro-ontology from a European directive is achieved both by using the semi automatic TERMINAE method [3] and by aligning it with a legal core ontology CLO [11]. A core ontology covers a field such as law which may consist of many subdomains like criminal law, private law, European Union law, etc. TERMINAE is based on knowledge elicitation from texts and allows creating a domain model by analyzing a corpus with Natural Language Processing (NLP) tools as for the SEKT project [18]. The method combines knowledge acquisition tools based on linguistics with modeling techniques so as to keep links between models and texts. During the building process [1], it is assumed that: (1) the ontology builder should have a comprehensive knowledge of the domain, so that she/he will be able to decide which terms (nouns, phrases, verbs or adjectives) are domain terms and which concepts and relations are labeled with these domain terms; (2) the ontology builder knows well how the ontology will be used. The alignment process takes place during the micro-ontology construction. [16], [14] and [10] defined ontology alignment as follows: ontology alignment consists in bringing two or more ontologies into mutual agreement, making them consistent and coherent and allowing the aligned ontologies to reuse information one from the other. In alignment, the original ontologies persist, with links established between them. Alignment is usually performed when the ontologies cover complementary domains. The alignment process was performed mostly

M. Ali and R. Dapoigny (Eds.): IEA/AIE 2006, LNAI 4031, pp. 1014–1023, 2006.

by hand, with the TERMINAE tool. Therefore our ontology is structured around CLO. TERMINAE provides easy import of concepts among CLO but doesn't check whether consistency is maintained once the operations are performed. The merging process [8] is achieved on the micro-ontologies. It consists in creating a single coherent ontology from two or more existing ontologies with overlapping parts.

The article is structured as follows: Section 2 describes our ontology construction method; Section 3 implements the method on two European directives around the concepts TRAVAILLEUR (EMPLOYEE), CITOYEN (CITIZEN); Section 4 presents a comparaison with related works. The article ends with a discussion between ontology and text.

2   Construction Method

Our construction method for building the application ontology includes two steps: - building micro-ontologies from texts using TERMINAE and alignment with a core ontology; - merging micro-ontologies obtained at the first step.

2.1   Building Micro-ontologies

Our micro-ontology construction is based on the semi-automatic TERMINAE method enhanced by an alignment process with a core ontology. The interest of the alignment with a top-ontology as DOLCE and a core legal ontology as LRI-Core [5] has been shown in [9]. The legal core ontology concepts constitutes the common conceptual denominators of the field, therefore, normally, their reuse is facilitated. In this work, CLO has been chosen to achieve an alignment from the natural language definition of the concepts. CLO was chosen because it is built from DOLCE and is available in OWL language whereas LRI-Core is still under development.

The TERMINAE method works with the terms that occur in the analyzed texts so as to describe the thus constructed concepts in a formal ontology. This ontology involves two kinds of concepts: terminological and non terminological. The terminological concepts are created through the ontology elaboration process. They are linked to their term occurrences in the corpus through their terminological forms. These forms contain a definition of the concepts in natural language and a list of synonyms. The non terminological concepts are created to structure the ontology. The TERMINAE tool provides material support to the method. Moreover, TERMINAE allows importing and exporting ontologies in OWL language, which aids the alignment and merging processes. SYNTEX [4] is used in the linguistic study activity to obtain the domain terms. The LINGUAE concordancer included in TERMINAE allows pattern recognition. MFD [7] uses association rules to find lexical relations.

2.2   Merging Micro-ontologies

Ontology merging aims to create a unique ontology from the orginal ontologies. The original ontologies will be unified and replaced by the new ontology. Before merging micro-ontologies there has to be a correspondance between the concepts of the ontologies to merge.

[15] define the ontology integration as the iteration of the following steps: (1) find the places in the ontology where they overlap; (2) relate concepts that are semantically close via equivalence and subsumption relations; (3) check the consistency, coherence and non-redundancy of the results.

[16] defined the set of basic operations for ontology merging as: removing a class from the ontology; removing a concept from the list of parent concepts because a more appropriate parent exists in another ontology; adding a concept to the list of parents of the considered class because an appropriate parent concept has been found in another ontology; renaming a concept to conform to naming conventions in another ontology; moving a concept from one ontology to another; removing a slot from the list of slots of a concept because a similar slot was inherited from a new parent concept; moving a slot because it is more appropriately defined in a parent concept; renaming a slot. The problems that arise when merging are the mismatches that may occur between separate ontologies. Ontologies may differ at two levels: language or meta-level (level of the primitives that are used to specify ontologies). In our context, mismatches at the language level do not occur because the micro-ontologies are written in the same language (OWL). The mismatches occur at the ontological and terminological levels.

3   Results

In his section, our first results about the legal application ontology are described. The contruction of this ontology was initiated by using two directives (hereafter refered to as "D-travailleur" and "D-citoyen").

First, the application of the linguistic method (cf 2.1) to the micro-ontology construction from "D-travailleur" is detailed. Then, the micro-ontology established from "D-citoyen" is presented. Finally the merging of these two micro-ontologies is studied.

3.1   Micro-ontology Building

The studied directives were written by the European Union Council which is the first decision organ of the Union. The French version is the support of the linguistic study but we used the English version to translate our examples. The first one is "Council directive 2001/23/EC of 12 March 2001 on the approximation of the laws of the Member States relating to the safeguarding of employees' rights in the event of transfers of undertakings, businesses or parts of undertakings or businesses". The second one is "Council Directive 2004/58/EC on the right of citizens of the Union and their family members to move and reside freely within the territory of the Member States". Henceforth, the "D-travailleur" is used to present our construction method of micro-ontologies.

The Corpus Constitution. The corpus consists of a single text ("D-travailleur") of seven pages (3133 words) selected by jurists. This corpus is imposed, closed and small sized. This small size is not an obstacle to the model elaboration because a directive is self-contained and cohesive.

Linguistic Study. This step consists in selecting the terms and lexical relations that will be modeled. The results of this stage are quite raw and will be further refined. SYNTEX, LINGUAE and MFD are the used tools. SYNTEX yielded 900 candidate-terms. The most used terms were: *travailleur* (*employee*) (56 occurrences), *transfert* (*transfer*) (41 occurrences), *cédant* (*transferor*) (15 occurrences), *cessionnaire* (*transferee*) (14 occurrences). Because we work on a small corpus, there are many hapax (a term which appears only once in the corpus) which are significant and have to be kept such as the syntagm "community charter" of the Fundamental Social Rights or the verb "to abrogate". LINGUAE and MFD tools have been used to explore the relations between central concepts. For example, MFD detects two patterns (notify to transferee, transfer to transferee). Then the relation between transferor and transferee is given by a pattern of LINGUAE (see Figure 1).

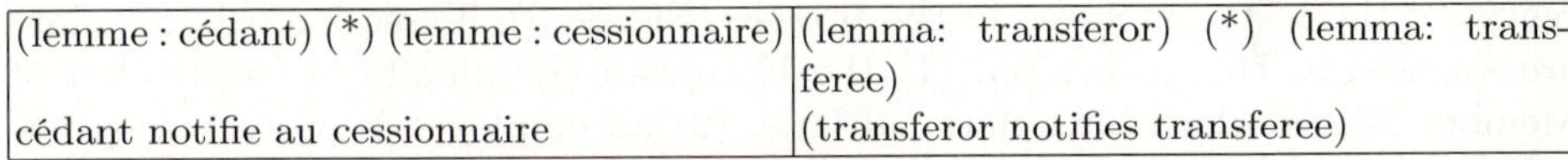

(lemme : cédant) (*) (lemme : cessionnaire)	(lemma: transferor) (*) (lemma: transferee)
cédant notifie au cessionnaire	(transferor notifies transferee)

Fig. 1. Relation study with LINGUAE

Normalization. The normalization step is a semantic study and constitutes a bridge between the lexical and syntactical study toward modeling. It consists in a particular conceptualization process based on corpus analysis. The concept description is based on the semantic analysis of the term occurrences. The semantic interpretation of the terms is driven by expert knowledge and application requirements. The method starts with the study of the central concepts of the model. These central concepts are commanded by the aim of the ontology building namely the description of the TRAVAILLEUR (EMPLOYEE) concept in the context of the outsourcing of his/her enterprise in the European Community. We start with three central concepts (TRAVAILLEUR (EMPLOYEE); TRANSFERT (TRANSFER), LICENCIEMENT(REDUNDANCY)).

a. Modeling bootstrap
From the terminological form of the term bound to a central concept, we find terms and relations describing the concept. Terms are translated into concepts and relations into roles. A natural language definition is either found in the directive or established from term occurrences in the directive. The concept definition is given, in comprehensive form, from the term occurrences found in the text with structural andor functional properties. A structural property references a link toward an ancestor concept (for instance, subsumption link). A functional property describes a domain property between concepts. The following figures

present concept definitions obtained by using the text. Only some definitions are found in the directive. The used syntax simplifies the linguistic expression to remain closer to the ontology language.

* Study of TRAVAILLEUR (EMPLOYEE)
The terminological form involves the following definition found in the directive "D-travailleur"(see Figure 2).

toute personne qui, dans l'état membre concerné est protégé en tant que travailleur dans le cadre de la législation nationale sur l'emploi.	employee shall mean any person who, in the Member State concerned, is protected as an employee under national employment law.

Fig. 2. Definition of the *travailleur* (*employee*) term

The definition of the concept EMPLOYEE has been established from the occurrences of the term *employee* in the text(see Figure 3). Three important points are stressed in this definition: (1) the European community is constituted of Member States which have national laws; (2) an employee is protected by national employment laws; (3) there is no explicit link between national laws and European laws. All these elements have to be represented in the ontology.

TRAVAILLEUR	EMPLOYEE
PROPRIÉTÉS STRUCTURELLES	**STRUCTURAL PROPERTIES**
est une personne	is a person
appartient à une entreprise	belongs to an enterprise
appartient à un Etat membre	belongs to a member state
PROPRIÉTÉS FONCTIONNELLES	**FUNCTIONAL PROPERTIES**
possédant des droits et des intérêts	having rights
ayant des représentants	having representatives
ayant des conditions de travail	having working conditions
est l'objet du transfert de son entreprise	is the object of the transfer of his/her enterprise
est protégée par une législation nationale	is protected by national employment law

Fig. 3. Concept TRAVAILLEUR(EMPLOYEE) definition

b. Modeling consolidation
During the modeling consolidation process, four kinds of activities occur:

- generalization, that is to say, the search of the ancestor concepts. It consists in studying and inserting new concepts along the bottom up axis.
- specialization, that is to say, the search of the child concepts. It consists in studying and inserting new concepts along the top-down axis in respect of differentiation principles [2].

- clustering consists in creating new concepts and regrouping identical properties.
- alignment may occur during these previous activities and requires concept and role meanings. The used ontology is CLO. The domain modeling requires the introduction of non terminological concepts for structuring the ontology. The work according to the top-down axis is dedicated to specialization and differentiation of the concepts already defined. The roles describe the functional properties and some of them restrict the inherited roles.

* Generalization of the EMPLOYEE concept

The EMPLOYEE ancestor concepts are found by working on the ascending axis. The structural properties are the linguistic expressions from which the research of the father concepts is achieved.

The structural property *is a person* leads to the study of the term *person* in the legal domain. In the directive, the term *natural or legal person* exists and is used in the *transferor* definition. Recourse to the expert helped us to create three meanings for this term. Each meaning is represented by a concept. The concepts of NATURALPERSON, LEGALPERSON and NATURALLEGALPERSON are integrated in the micro-ontology.

The linguistic syntagm *employee is a person* is translated into a subsomption link between the EMPLOYEE and NATURALPERSON.

The structural property *belong to* of the EMPLOYEE concept leads to the study of the terms *enterprise* and *member states*. This property is described by the role BELONG TO.

* The study of the functional properties

The functional properties are used for defining the roles. The terms *rights, representatives, working conditions, national employment law* are modeled as concepts in the micro-ontology. These concepts are bound to the EMPLOYEE concept by a role which expresses their linguistic property.

* The role definition

The created bottom-up structuring concept JURIDICALOBJECT gathers all of the juridical concepts described in a directive. It is defined by the role GOVERNED BY which takes its values in the range defined by the SOCIAL-OBJECT concept from CLO. The opposite role TO BE GOVERNED BY has been created.

Lexical properties as *covered by* or *is protected by* that constitute specializations of the property *governed by* (see figure 4) were also used in the text.

Name	Domain concept	Value concept
isGoverned	redundancy	nationalEmploymentLaw
isGoverned	socialObject	juridicalObject
governs	juridicalObject	socialObject
isProtected	employee	nationalEmploymentLaw
belongs to	employee	memberStates

Fig. 4. An excerpt of the defined generic roles

1020   S. Despres and S. Szulman

Therefore a role hierarchy was created between the rolesTO BE GOVERNED BY and TO BE PROTECTED BY.

* The alignment with CLO

An alignment with CLO is achieved for each buttom-up structuration concepts as JURIDICALOBJECT and NATURALPERSON . The NATURALPERSON concept represented in CLO defined by *Cognitive objects have a specific dependence on agentive physical objects (e.g. a natural person)* is identified to the PHYSICALPERSON concept. The DOCUMENT concept represented in CLO defined by *An information realization that realizes (at least) a text* . A subsumption link is defined between the DOCUMENT concept and the JURIDICALOBJECT concept.The figure 5 presents an excerpt of the micro-ontology "D-travailleur".

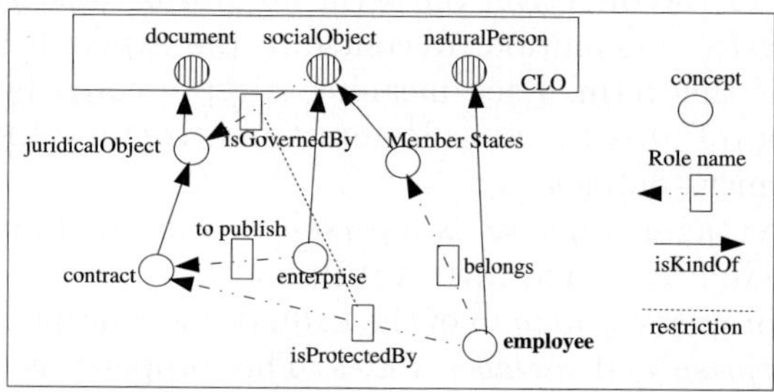

Fig. 5. An excerpt of the worker micro-ontology

"D-citoyen" Micro-ontology Building. The same method has been used to build the "D-citoyen" micro-ontology around the central concepts CITOYEN (citizen), LIBRE CIRCULATION (freely moving), ETATS MEMBRES (Member States). Figure 6 shows an excerpt of this micro-ontology.

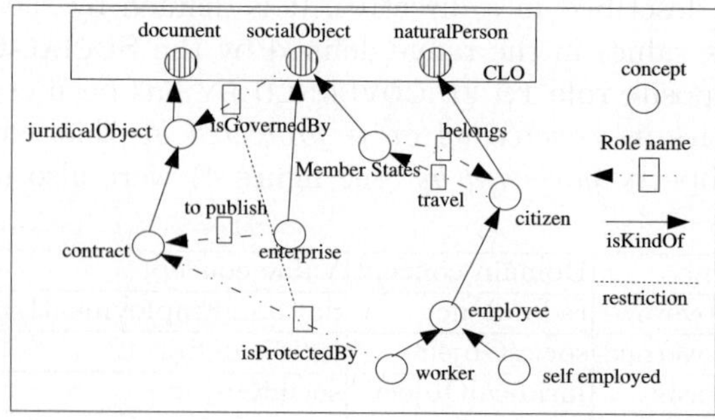

Fig. 6. An excerpt of the citizen micro-ontology

3.2   Merging Micro-ontologies: First Results

For merging union and intersection are the most prominent approaches. In the union approach, the merged ontology is the union of all entities in both source ontologies where differences in the representation of similar concepts have been resolved. In the intersection approach, the merged ontology consists only of the parts of the source ontology which overlap [8].

The aim of this work is to obtain an ontology of the European Union law around the TRAVAILLEUR(WORKER)concept. The jurists' requirements led to the building of a minimal ontology from the merging of micro-ontologies. The merging process is an interesting means both to reveal the inconsistencies between the models used to describe the concepts in the different directives and, if possible, to build a shared model of the studied concepts throughout the directives. Therefore, the intersection approach was chosen to build this ontology.

The merging process for our micro-ontologies is only beginning but some issues already emerge. Our micro-ontologies represent a model of one legal issue of the European law domain. Therefore in order to obtain a unique ontology of the TRAVAILLEUR(WORKER) concept, merging is necessary. The process was achieved with the two above mentionned micro-ontologies as shown in figures 5 and 6. The "D-citoyen" micro-ontology constitutes the reference for the merging process. The two micro-ontologies are written in the same language. Therefore, there are no mismatches at this level. The mismatches occur at the ontological and terminological levels. The merging is around the terms *travailleur (employee)* and *travailleur salarié (worker)*. These two terms refer to the same concept denoted by *travailleur salarié (worker)*. The resort to the terminological form allows the detection of the differences between the definitions associated to these concepts. The results of this study consists in moving the TRAVAILLEUR SALARIÉ (EMPLOYEE) concept from the "D-travailleur" micro-ontology to the "D-citoyen" micro-ontology under the TRAVAILLEUR (WORKER) concept. The generic role *appartient à (belongs to)* attached to the TRAVAILLEUR(EMPLOYEE) concept is removed because it exists at the citizen concept level and it is inherited. The terminological form associated to the WORKER concept contains all linked terms.

4   Comparison with Related Works

Our work is based on texts enhanced by an alignment process and a merging of the resulting micro-ontologies. This approach is clearly different from the legal ontology building presented in [5], [12]. Our approach is the only one in juridical domain that permits the traceability from texts to concepts and relations of ontology building. Thus it presents a great advantage for the management of ontology evolution and normally, it should aid to the enrichment of the constructed ontologies.

Our approach can be compared to the Ontology of Professional Legal Knowledge (OPLK) project [6]. A middle out approach is adopted and NLP tools for the linguistic study are used. By focusing on relations between concepts our method differs from the OPLK project centered on adjectives to construct relations between concepts. The constructed ontologies differ because of the nature of the corpus. If we consider as [17] that juridical language includes several levels: the law-maker's language, the judge's language that interprets the law-maker's language and the language of the jurisprudence, our work is situated at the first level whereas the OPLK project is at the second level since the ontology is built from pragmatic knowledge. In fact, directives constitute normative texts that define objects and doers of the selected reality, and control the EU law.

5   Conclusion

The TERMINAE method gives a central role to the text and permits to establish relations between text and ontology. It differentiates the linguistical and conceptual levels. Therefore terms and concepts are distinct. A terminological network is built from these terms and their linguistical relations. The ontology concepts are built from the terms relevant for the application. The sructural and functional properties are used for elaborating a local concept description. This local concept is linked to a core ontology concepts with an alignment process. During this step, a correspondance is established between a signified of a term and a formal concept. A formalization process such as OntoSpec [13] should permit the alignment between formal concepts.

Acknowledgments

This research was carried out in the context of the specific Action "Ontologie du droit et langages juridiques" (G.Lame) funded by the RTP "Droit et systémes d'information" (Danièle Bourcier). We thank our jurist colleague Nicolas Moisard (IDEA, Centre Juridique de Poitiers) for his collaboration during the project and the validation steps.

References

1. N. Aussenac-Gilles, B. Biébow, and S. Szulman. Revisiting ontology design: a methodology based on corpus analysis. In R. Dieng and O. Corby, editors, *Knowledge Engineering and Knowledge Management : Methods, Models, and Tools. Proc. of the 12th International Conference, (EKAW'2000)*, LNAI 1937, pages 172–188. Springer-Verlag, 2000.

2. B. Bachimont. Engagement sémantique et engagement ontologique : conception et réalisation d'ontologies en ingénierie des connaissances. In J. Charlet, M. Zacklad, G. Kassel, and D. Bourigault, editors, *Ingénierie des Connaissances, évolutions récentes et nouveaux défis*, pages 305–323, Paris, 2000. Eyrolles.

3. B. Biébow and S. Szulman. TERMINAE: A linguistics-based tool for building of a domain ontology. In D. Fensel and R. Studer, editors, *Proc. of the 11th European Workshop (EKAW'99)*, LNAI 1621, pages 49–66. Springer-Verlag, 1999.

4. D. Bourigault and C. Fabre. *Approche linguistique pour l'analyse de corpus*, volume 25, pages 131–151. Université Toulouse Le Mirail, 2000.

5. J. Breuker. Constructing a legal core ontology: LRI-core. In *WONTO'2004*, 2004.

6. P. Casanovas, N. Casellas, C. Tempich, D. Varandecic, and R. Benjamins. OPKJ modeling methodology. In *LOAIT- Legal Ontologies and Artificial Intelligence Techniques*, IAAIL Workshop series, pages 121–133, 2005.

7. V. Ceausu and S. Després. Une approche mixte pour la construction d'une ressource terminologique. In *IC 2004*, pages 211–223, 2004.

8. J. de Bruijn, F. Martin-Recuerda, D. Manov, and M. Ehrig. Technical report.

9. S. Després and S. Szulman. Construction of a legal ontology from a europen community legislative text. In Thomas F. Gordon, editor, *Jurix 2004*, pages 79–88. IOS press, 2004.

10. J. Euzenat, T. Le Bach, J. Barrasa, P. Bouquet, J. De Bo, R. Dieng, M. Ehrig, M. Hauswirth, M. Jarrar, R. Lara, D. Maynard, A. Napoli, G. Stamou, H. Stuckenschmidt, P. Shvaisko, S. Tessaris, S. Van Acker, and I. Zaihrayeu. Technical report.

11. A. Gangemi, A. Prisco, M.T. Sagri, G. Steve, and D. Tiscornia. Some ontological tools to support legal regulatory compliance, with a case study. In *Workshop WORM Core*. LNCS, Springer Verlag, 2003.

12. A. Gangemi, M.-T. Sagri, and D. Tiscornia. *A Constructive Framework for Legal Ontologies*, pages 97–124. LNAI 3369. Springer, 2005.

13. G. Kassel. Une méthode de spécification semi-informelle d'ontologies. In *Actes des 13 èmes journées francophones d'Ingénierie des Connaissances (IC 2002)*, pages 75–87, 2002.

14. M. Klein. Combining and relating ontologies: an analysis of problems solutions. In A. Gomez-Perez, M. Gruninger, H. Stuckenschmidt, and M. Uschold, editors, *Workshop on Ontologies and Information Sharing, IJCAI'01*, pages 309–327, Seattle, USA, 2001.

15. D.L. McGuinness, R. Fikes, J. Rice, and S. Wilder. An environment for merging and testing large ontologies. In *Seventeenth International Conference on Principles of Knowledge Representation And Reasoning KR-2000)*, pages 483–493, 2000.

16. N. Fridman Noy and M.A. Musen. An algorithm for merging and aligning ontologies: Automation and tool support. In *Proc.of the Workshop on Ontology Management at the Sixteenth National Conference on Artificial Intelligence (AAAI-99)*, Orlando, 1999. FL: AAI Press.

17. W. Peters, D. Tiscornia, and M.T. Sagri. The structuring of legal knowledge in lois. In *LOAIT - Legal Ontology and Artificial Intelligence Techniques*.

18. URL: http://www.gate.ac.uk/projects/sekt.

An Approach to Automatic Ontology-Based Annotation of Biomedical Texts

Gayo Diallo, Michel Simonet, and Ana Simonet

Laboratoire TIMC, Université Grenoble 1, Faculté de Médecine,
38700 La Tronche, France
`{gayo.diallo, michel.simonet, ana.simonet}@imag.fr`

Abstract. Sharing and enriching of documents is expected and is made possible nowadays with tools enabling users to perform different kinds of annotations. We propose an Ontology-based approach to automate the semantic annotation of texts; Ontologies are represented in OWL (Web Ontology Language). OWL is supported by Semantic Web tools such as Racer for reasoning purpose and Jena. The tool for automatic semantic annotation supporting word-based and stem-based pre-indexing techniques is presented and its evaluation is made on three medical corpora both in English and French (brain disease area, cardiology and OHSUMED collection). The evaluation shows difference in the results obtained according to the pre-indixng mode used.

1   Introduction

The amount of electronic resources available nowadays is permanently growing, making difficult their organisation and their efficient access. The Semantic web initiative [1] is about adding formal structures and semantics (metadata and knowledge) to web content for easy management and access. To make the resources machine-understandable, it proposes in particular to enrich them with descriptions called annotations.

Annotation tools can be viewed according to the functionalities they implement, which can be classified into three main categories: cataloguing using Dublin Core (DC)[2], textual and conceptual [3]. Annotea [4] and SemTag [5] illustrate those various aspects. Annotea is an outcome of the World Wide Web Consortium (W3C) efforts and mainly deals with textual annotation, i.e., the process of adding pieces of text (comments, examples, questions) to a given document in a collaborative manner. SemTag is a project of the IBM Almaden Research Center and deals with ontology-based automatic semantic annotation, which can be considered as a way to perform concept-based indexing.

Some authors have studied the annotation process following their computational or cognitive aspects. [6]. Up to now, many annotation tools have been conceived for the purpose of indexing. They usually provide semi-automatic procedures (learning algorithm in Melita [7], S-Cream [8]) in addition to manual support (Melita) to hand out semantic annotations. Sometimes, these annotations are only provided manually (Shoe [9], Comma [10]) or together with some cataloguing procedure. In the medical

M. Ali and R. Dapoigny (Eds.): IEA/AIE 2006, LNAI 4031, pp. 1024 – 1033, 2006.

field Health Professionals naturally use textual annotations to link documents and to guide the reading from a document to another (or to a part of document).

In this paper we focus on semantic annotation (also called conceptual annotation) which consists in attaching "semantic labels" to a document or parts of a document, using semantic features provided by a formal knowledge organization called ontology. Using ontologies in the annotation process has a particular benefit: the queries for information retrieval and document annotated share the same vocabulary. We present an approach of automatic conceptual annotation using Natural Language Processing (NLP) technology. This approach extends a tool developed in a previous work, the Noesis Annotation Tool (NAT) [3], which helps manually annotating documents. Regarding conceptual annotation, many tools use NLP in order to automatically extract information from documents (Melita, S-Cream).

The remainder of this paper is organized as follows. In Section 2 we give some preliminaries presenting the manual annotation tool and the domain ontologies used to evaluate our approach. In Section 3 we explain the process of automatic semantic features extraction and present some technical aspects. An evaluation of our approach is presented in Section 4, and Section 5 concludes by discussing future extensions and improvements.

2 Preliminaries

2.1 Noesis Annotation Tool

The NAT (see Fig. 1) has been developed in the context of the NOESIS Project which is an Integrated Project of the European 6th Framework Program (2004 – 2006). Its objective is to build a platform for wide scale integration and visual integration of medical intelligence, with particular emphasis on Knowledge Management and Decision aid.

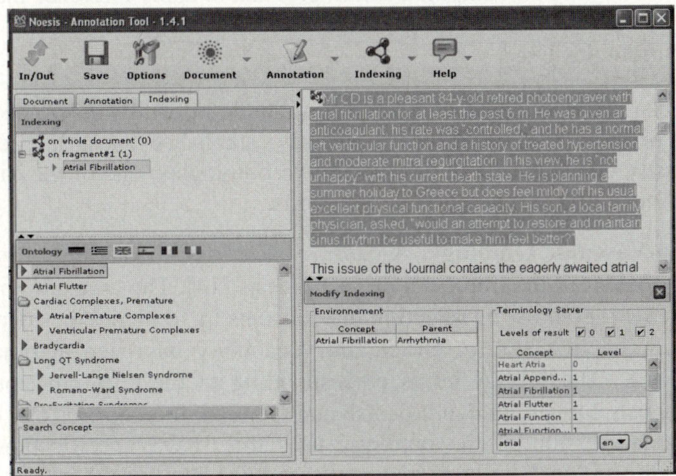

Fig. 1. Noesis Annotation Tool (manual indexing)

The three kinds of annotation considered (cataloging, conceptual and textual) have been implemented in a single tool. One novelty of the Noesis Annotation Tool is the use of a terminology server which, in combination with the ontology, brings a real support for the users' indexing task. This terminology server aims at bridging the gap between the ontology formal language and user's natural language terms. It generally provides candidate concepts for a user's term.

With the current version of the tool, the annotation process (cataloguing, textual, and conceptual) is performed manually. We propose to automate the conceptual annotation through an automatic features extraction process using an ontology.

2.2 Ontology for Automatic Conceptual Annotation

An ontology, as *specification of a conceptualization* [11] may serve to represent and organize the knowledge in specific domain. In this paper ontologies are used for the purpose of conceptual document representation.

The ontology model used here is inspired by the Semantic Document Representation (SDR) module of the UMSIIS approach for unifying the management of structured and informal information sources [12]. UMSIIS distinguishes the domain ontology and the ontologies for defining the terminology used in a specific domain. The model we use relies on three basic elements: concepts, relationships between concepts, and finally terms in two languages (French and English) to manage the multilingual aspects. Each concept is represented by one or several terms (see Fig. 2 and 3). This consideration is important since the algorithm we use is syntax mapping based. We choose the DL-based ontology language, Ontology Web Language (OWL)[1] to represent the model. It provides the necessary elements and is compatible with Semantic Web tools such as Jena API for ontology management and Racer, a DL-based reasoner. Jena [13] is a set of tools developed within the framework of the HP Labs Semantic Web Program project, allowing to manipulate ontologies and to apply inference mechanisms.

2.3 The Ontologies Used

Before we can annotate a text corpus with semantic information, we need to first establish one or more ontologies, or use already-established ones, that define the way we can classify documents. We have used two ontologies: one of the cardio-vascular domain and one of the brain cognitive functions.

The Cardio-Vascular Ontology. A cardio-vascular (CV) ontology has been elaborated in the context of the European project Noesis [14]. The core ontology was taken from the MeSH thesaurus, by selecting the concepts in 10 hierarchies dealing with the CV domain. The first step to enrich the vocabulary has been automatically done through UMLS. The UMLS terms corresponding to the core concepts have been added in English, French, Italian, Spanish and German. It comprises 690 concepts.

The original version of the ontology uses the SKOS specification [15] which provides both *prefLabel* for preferred terms and *altLabel* for other terms. In order to

---

[1] http://www.w3.org/TR/owl-features/

```
<owl:Class rdf:ID='M0001551'>
  <prefLabelEn xml:lang='en'>Aortic Rupture</rdfs:Label >
  <rdfs:label xml:lang='en'>Aortic Ruptures</rdfs:Label >
  <rdfs:label xml:lang='en'>Rupture Aortic</rdfs:Label>
  <rdfs:label xml:lang='en'>Ruptures Aortic</rdfs:Label>
  ...
  <prefLabelFr xml:lang='fr'>Rupture de l'aorte</rdfs:label >
  < rdfs:label xml:lang='fr'>Rupture aortique</rdfs:label >
  < rdfs:label xml:lang='fr'>Rupture aorte</rdfs:label >
  <rdfs:comment>do not coord with rupture spontaneous unless
particularly discussed and then only nim </rdfs:comment>
  <rdfs:isDefinedBy>Tearing of aortic tissue. It may be rupture of
an aneurysm or it may be due to trauma. </rdfs:isDefinedBy>
  <rdfs:subClassOf rdf:resource='#M0026605'/>
  <rdfs:subClassOf rdf:resource='#M0001545'/>
</owl:Class>
```

Fig. 2. Example of a Concept of the Cardio-Vascular Ontology

```
<owl:Class rdf:ID="EfficienceCognitiveGlobale">
    <rdfs:subClassOf>
    <owl:Class rdf:ID="FonctionCognitive"/>
    </rdfs:subClassOf>
    <rdfs:label xml:lang="fr">Efficience Cognitive Globale</rdfs:label>
    <rdfs:subClassOf>
    <owl:Restriction>
    <owl:someValuesFrom> <owl:Class rdfID="TestMemoire"/> </owl:someValuesFrom>
    <owl:onProperty><owl:ObjectProperty rdf:about="#EstTesteePar"/> </owl:onProperty>
    </owl:Restriction>
    ...
    <rdfs:label xml:lang="fr">éfficience cognitive globale</rdfs:label>
</owl:Class>
```

Fig. 3. A Concept of the Brain Cognitive Functions Ontology

provide the same feature (i.e., a preferred term for each language) without using the SKOS specification for simplicity, we have introduced two relations of type « owl:DatatypeProperty » called *« PrefLabelFR »* and *« PrefLabelEn »* for the French and English preferred terms. The other terms of a concept are designated by RDF elements « **rdfs:label** » [16].

The Ontology of Brain Cognitive Functions. In a former project called BC3 (Brain & Heart Knowledge Base) we have designed a functional and an anatomical ontology of the brain. The functional ontology consists of the CAC2 classification of cognitive function of the brain [19] through the subsumption relation. We have migrated to OWL-DL this work and extended it formally in order to take into account the cognitive tests. The anatomical ontology is not used in the present project.

In practice, to determine if a given cognitive function is affected the doctor carries out a set of tests. For example the verbal modality of the cognitive function *"memory"* can be tested by the *"Palm Tree Test"*, *"The verbal fluency test"*, etc. We decided to create two general disjoint concepts: *"CognitiveFunction"* and *"CognitiveTest"* to reflect those two aspects and we have introduced two inverse relations *"IsTestedBy"* and *"Tested"* through the "owl:ObjectProperty", which illustrate the link between a

---

[2] Centre d'Anatomie Cognitive, Hospital of Pitié Salpêtrière, Paris.

cognitive function and a cognitive test and conversely. Both *"IstestedBy"* and *"Tested"* relations are specialised to take into account the different modalities of a cognitive function. Each concept is designed by one or several French or English terms.

We have used the Protégé Editor tool[3] to edit the Ontology and the Racer [18] reasoner to test the consistency of the Ontology (525 concepts).

3 Semantic Annotation Process

The automatic acquisition of semantic features of a domain is an important issue, since it reduces human intervention. The identification of ontology concepts is performed through two distinct phases: a pre-processing phase and a semantic features extraction step.

3.1 Preprocessing Step with Apache Lucene

In order to pre-index corpora, we use Apache Lucene[4], a performance full-featured search engine API implemented in Java which supports both indexing and search of large document collections. The customizability and modular approach of Lucene was essential in the choice of this Information Retrieval tool.

Lucene does not index files but Document objects. To index and then search files, all files must be first converted to Document objects, which we call *Lucene documents* (the basic indexing unit). All the information associated with Lucene documents is stored in units called fields, where each field has its name and textual value (e.g., content, author, etc.). A Lucene module called Index Writer builds a *Token Stream* (a sequence of words*)*, which describes information about the token text. *Token* contains linguistic properties and other information such as the start and end offsets and the type of the string (i.e., the lexical or syntactic class that the token belongs to). Every Lucene token has its own position in the token stream. The task of the Analyzer (which use the Porter Algorithm) is to take a text and provide a stream of tokens. Each analyzer includes one or more tokenizers and may include filters. Lucene provides a French Analyzer that produces stemmed text in French. We have customized this in order to provide root-based and word-based tokens.

Table 1. Token generated following the stem-based and word-based modes

Text	Stem	Word
[...*Mais il existe des difficultés d'attention et un ralentissement qui affectent l'ensemble des activités cognitives...*]	[exist][difficulté][attent][ralent] [affectent] [ensembl] [activité] [cognit]	[existe] [difficultés] [attention] [ralentissement] [affectent] [ensemble] [activités] [cognitives]
[...*It was shown that the percentage stenosis in the coronary arteries measured by coronary angiography was negatively correlated ...*]	[shown][percentag] [stenosi][coronari] [arteri][measur] [coronari][angiographi] [neg] [correl]	[shown][percentage] [stenosis] [coronary] [arteries] [measured] [coronary] [angiography] [negatively] [correlated]

---

[3] http://protege.stanford.edu/index.html.
[4] http://lucene.apache.org.

This step provides a word-based or a stem-based index of the text corpora which we store in a MySQL database.

3.2   The Semantic Features Extraction Step

The semantic features extraction strategy is based on simple phrase identification. Those phrases identified represent the different terms used to design the concepts of the ontology. The entry of this step has four components: the text corpora, the ontology, the stemming mode and finally the target language. Text corpora are treated using the algorithm described in Fig. 4. Each term of a concept is treated according to the analyzer used to build the index in the first step.

The concept weighting is developed using the CF*IDF measure (*concept frequency * inverse document frequency*) which adapts at the concept level the classical TF/IDF method which operates at the term level [19].

We have implemented the semantic features extraction in Java and the semantic index exploration in Python. The Python script uses the HyperGraph[5] source code to

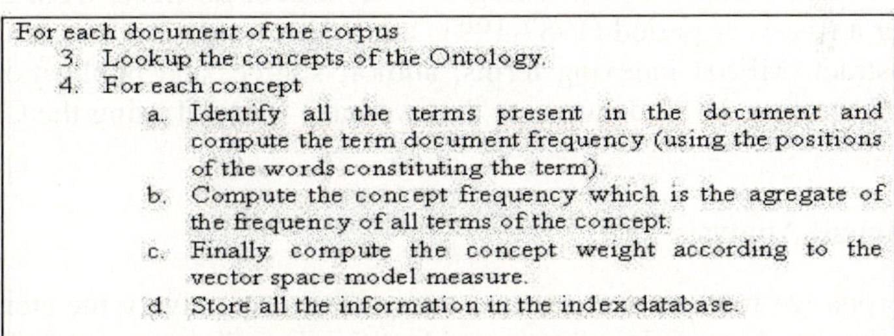

Fig. 4. Algorithm for features extraction

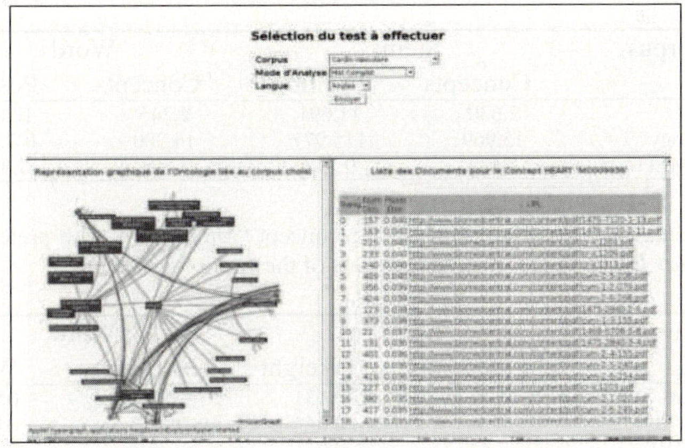

Fig. 5. Semantic Index Visualization

---

[5] http://hypergraph.sourceforge.net

visualize the ontology as a hyperbolic tree to explore the semantic index. The advantage of the hyperbolic view is that users can understand the ontology structure by seeing the relational cross-links between the vertices. Fig. 5 shows a screenshot of the semantic index.

4   Evaluation

4.1   The Corpora

Three corpora have been used to evaluate our approach. The first one, called brain corpus, is composed of 45 medical reports [20] and 285 web pages related to brain obtained through Yahoo! API[6]. The second one is constituted of 430 scientific publications chosen from three journals on cardiology avalaible from BiomedCentral ("*BMC Cardiovascular Disorders*", "*Cardiovascular Diabetology*", "*Cardiovascular Ultrasound*").[7] The last one is a subset of OHSUMED test collection. The OHSUMED test collection is a set of 348,566 references from MEDLINE, the on-line medical information database, consisting of titles and/or abstracts from 270 medical journals over a five-year period (1987-1991) and 101 test queries. The available fields are title, abstract, MESH indexing terms, author, source, and publication type. We have selected the first 2.182 documents that we have indexed using the Cardiovascular Ontology.

4.2   Experiment Analysis

For each corpus we have performed two tests using respectively the stem and word based pre-indexing. The results of concept identification are presented in Table 2.

Table 2. Number of concepts and number of positions by concepts identified according to the two pre-indexing modes

Corpus	Stem		Word	
	Concepts	Positions	Concepts	Positions
Brain	2.630	11.691	2.346	10.606
Cardiology	15.969	115.977	14.380	107.199
OHSUMED	4.492	9.748	3.591	7.372

Table 3. Frequency and Weight (cf.idf) of the concept "*M0025176*" with preferred term "*Peripheral Vascular Diseases*" for three documents of the cardiology corpus

Document	Stem		Word	
	Frequency	Weight	Frequency	Weight
0	4	0.131	2	0.067
141	3	0.044	2	0.030
210	6	0.071	5	0.061

---

[6] http://developer.yahoo.net/.

[7] http://www.biomedcentral.com/.

By examining Table 2 we note that when the stem pre-indexing mode is used, more concepts are identified than with the simple word-based pre-indexing mode. This is due to the fact that each word of ontology term is reduced to its root (stem). For example a concept represented both by singular and a plural form of a term is counted twice when using the stem mode. Taking the cardiology corpus we note that (Table 3) the concept *"M0025176"* with the preferred term *"Peripheral Vascular Diseases"* and as other term *"Peripheral Vascular Disease"* has different frequencies according to the two modes. Taking the brain corpus indexed with the ontology of brain cognitive functions, when the stem mode is used the algorithm associates all the occurrences of the word *"raisonner"* in the corpus with the concept *"Raisonnement"*, as the word *"raisonner"* and *"Raisonnement"* have the same stem. This is a well-known ambiguity due to the use of stemming for text indexing [21].

Contrary to SemTag which implements a disambiguation algorithm called TBD for Taxonomy Based Disambiguation, indexing errors made during the automatic annotation process are to be corrected manually by the NAT. In addition to the situation described above it also may occur that a same term is present in different concepts (typically for the cardiovascular ontology which is enriched by term from UMLS). An example of that is the term "Angiography" which is the preferred term of the concept *"M0001187"* and is an alternative term of "M0001731" (Arteries) and "M0002726" (Blood Vessels).

5   Conclusion and Future Work

In this paper we have presented an approach to automatic features extraction for semantic text annotation using Semantic web technologies and ontologies. This approach may be applied for several biomedical domains as showed by the evaluation. Semantic markup, if present, might serve as indexing terms for a hybrid information retrieval engine (keyword and concept based search). That is, in addition to indexing documents according to the text of their words or stems, we might also index them according to their semantic markup.

The semantic feature extraction time is proportional to the size of ontology; and the process becomes slow for large size ontologies (several hundreds of concepts represented for each by several terms). We hope to improve the processing time by segmenting the ontology into disjoints sub-branches in order to carry out a parallel features extraction.

Only the concepts of the domain ontology are extracted at the present time; the recognition of the named entities will allow a richer description of the documents (e.g., recognition of a cognitive test value). Building an ontology for named entities recognition in medical reports is an ongoing work.

Acknowledgments

This work is partly supported by European Commission (NOESIS project, IST-2002-507960).

References

1. Berners-Lee, T., Hendler, J., Lassila O.: Semantic web. *Scientific American*, 1(1):68-88, (2000)
2. Hillmann D. : Guide d'utilisation du Dublin Core, consulted on 11/29/2005 (http://www.bibl.ulaval.ca/DublinCore/usageguide-20000716fr.htm)
3. Patriarche, R., Gedzelman, S., Diallo, G., Bernhard, D., Bassolet, C.G., Ferriol, S., Girard, A., Mouries, M., Palmer, P., Simonet, A., Simonet, M.: A Tool for Conceptual and Textual Annotation of Documents. e-challenges conference, Ljubljana, 19-21 Oct. (2005)
4. Kahan, J., Koivunen, M.R., Prud'Hommeaux, E., Swick, R.: Annotea : an open RDF Infrastructure for Shared Web Annotations, Proceedings of WWW10, May 1-5 (2001), Hong-Kong, pp. 623-632
5. Dill, S., Eiron, N., Gibson, D., Gruhl, D., Guha, R., Jhingran, A., Kanungo, T., Rajagopalan, S., Tomkins, A., Tomlin, J.A., Zien, J.Y.: SemTag and Seeker: Bootstrapping the Semantic Web via Automated Semantic Annotation. In Proceedings International WWW Conference, Budapest, Hungary (2003)
6. Caussanel J.P., Cahier J.P., Zacklad M., Charlet J. : Les Topic Maps sont-ils un bon candidat pour l'ingénierie du Web Sémantique ?, in Proceedings of IC'2002, Rouen, June (2002)
7. Ciravegna, F., Dingli, A., Petrelli, D., Wilks, Y.: User-system cooperation in document annotation based on information extraction. In Proceedings of the 13th International Conference on Knowledge Engineering and Knowledge Management EKAW02. Sringer Verlag (2002)
8. Handschuh, S., Staab, S., Ciravegna, F.: S-Cream, Semi-Automatic Creation of Metadata. Proc. of the European Conference on Knowledge Acquisition and Management. EKAW*02*. (2002)
9. Heflin, J., Hendler, J. : Searching the web with shoe. In Artifial Intelligence for Web Search. Pages 35-40. AAAI Press, (2000)
10. Gandon, F.: Agents handling annotation distribution in a corporate semantic Web. In Web Intelligence and Agent Systems, IOS Press International Journal (Eds) Jiming Liu, Ning Zhong, Vol.1, Number 1, (2003) pp 23-45, ISSN : 1570-1263 WI Consortium
11. Gruber, T. R. A translation approach to portable ontologies. *Knowledge Acquisition*, 5(2):199-220, (1993)
12. Diallo, G., Simonet, M., Simonet, A., Bringing Together Structured and Unstructured Sources, DEXA'06 Krakow, Poland. Paper submitted.
13. Carroll, J. J., Dickinson, I., Dollin, C., Reynolds, D., Seaborne, A., Wilkinson, K.: "Jena: implementing the semantic web recommendations", in Proceedings of the 13th International World Wide Web Conference, pp. 74 - 83, New York (2004)
14. Gedzelman, S., Simonet, M., Bernhard, D., Diallo, G., Palmer, P.: Building an Ontology of Cardio-Vascular Diseases for Concept-Based Information Retrieval. Computer in Cardiology, Lyon -France (2005)
15. SKOS : Schema for Knowledge Organisation Systems. http://www.w3.org/TR/2005/WD-swbp-skos-core-guide-20050510/
16. Lassila, O., Swick, R.: Ressource Description Framework (RDF) model and syntax specification. W3C Working Draft (1998) http://www.w3.org/TR/WD-rdf-syntax
17. Diallo, G., Bernhard, D., Batrancourt, B., Simonet, M. : Vers une Ontologie anatomo-fonctionnelle du cerveau, Journée Web Sémantique Médicale, Rennes (2003)

18. Haarslev, V., Möller, R.: Racer: A Core Inference Engine for the Semantic Web. In Proceedings of the 2nd International Workshop on Evaluation of Ontology-based Tools (EON2003), located at the 2nd International Semantic Web Conference ISWC 2003, Sanibel Island, Florida, USA, October 20, pages 27–36, (2003)
19. Salton, G., Buckley, C.: Term-weighting approaches in automatic text retrieval. Information Processing and Management, Vol. 24, Issue 5, (1998); 513-523
20. Batrancourt, B.: Modélisation et outils logiciels pour une connaissance anatomo-fonctionnelle du cerveau humain. Thèse de Doctorat, Université Lyon 1 Décembre (2003)
21. Kraaij, W., Pohlmann, R.: Viewing stemming as recall enhancement. In Proc. of SIGIR'96, pp 40-48, Zurich , Switzerland (1996)

Lexical and Conceptual Structures in Ontology

Christophe Roche

Condillac Research Group, LISTIC Lab., University of Savoie, Campus Scientifique,
73376 Le Bourget du Lac cedex, France
`christophe.roche@univ-savoie.fr`
`http://ontology.univ-savoie.fr`

Abstract. From *a stricto sensu* point of view, there is no direct relationship between ontology and text. The former is interesting in conceptualization – as an extra linguistic representation of conceptual knowledge –, when the latter is a matter for linguistics. Nevertheless, ontology and text are more and more connected in particular for ontology acquisition from texts. The main goal of this article, viewed as an introduction for the special session on "Ontology and Text" of the IEA/AIE 06 Conference, is to claim that: "the lexical structure and the conceptual structure in general do not fit". As a matter of fact, writing technical documents remains a linguistic activity which belongs to rhetoric and one of the linguistics' principles is the incompleteness of texts. Even if we can learn a lot of useful information from texts for building conceptual systems, we can not directly consider a word as a lexicalized concept nor the hyponymy relationship as a linguistic translation of the subclass relationship.

1   Introduction

Ontology is a very popular research topic [1], [2], [3] mainly due to what they promise: a way of capturing a shared and common understanding of a domain that can be understood and used as well by humans as programs. Even if there is no really agreement on the meaning of what ontology is, we can resume the most definitions used today by saying that an ontology is a shared description of concepts and relationships of a domain expressed in a computer readable language. At last, everybody agrees on the fact that an ontology can be also considered as a vocabulary of terms with their definition: "*An [explicit] ontology may take a variety of forms, but necessarily it will include a vocabulary of terms and some specification of their meaning (i.e. definitions).*" [4]. Then ontology building raises two main problems: on the first hand a linguistic one with the building of the vocabulary of terms and on the second hand a conceptual one with the definition of concepts. And since we use words for speaking about knowledge, ontology building from texts seems to be a good idea.

2   The Lexical Structure

Domain knowledge is mainly conveyed through scientific and technical texts: we use names for denoting concepts, properties, relationships; and definition of concepts

M. Ali and R. Dapoigny (Eds.): IEA/AIE 2006, LNAI 4031, pp. 1034 – 1041, 2006.

relies on using words: "a voltage relay is a kind of relay", "a Kaplan turbine is a type of propeller turbine in which the pitch of the blades can be changed to improve performance". The words of usage (i.e. the technical words which are used in specialized texts) as their linguistic relationships – lexical or syntactic – more or less translate the knowledge structure.

Let us begin by finding the terms which can denote concepts. Insofar as texts contain linguistic expressions denoting concepts, extracting candidate terms from corpus by automatic text analysis is today an active research domain [5], [6]. Texts are first analyzed from a lexical and syntactic point of view in order to associate to each word its grammatical class and its canonical form. Then linguistic expressions can be automatically extracted using, for example, lexical and syntactic patterns (regular expressions). The "adjective substantive" and "substantive substantive" patterns allow to extract expressions like "electromagnetic relay", "threshold relay", "voltage relay" from a technical corpus about relays. The result, which must be validated by experts, is a lexicon of words considered as concept's names.

This lexicon is structured according to linguistic relationships like hypernymy, hyponymy, synonymy, meronymy and so on. Here too, these linguistic relationships can be "automatically" extracted from the corpus using a syntactic analysis based on verbal patterns, and in particular on the verb "to be": "a voltage relay is a kind of relay", "the three main types of water turbines are Pelton wheels, Francis turbines, and Kaplan or propeller type turbines". We can also use the previously extracted expressions. For example, linguistic expressions made up of several words with the same "queue" (i.e. ending with the same words, e.g. with the same noun) give interesting information about the structure of the lexicon. The following linguistic expressions "voltage relay", "threshold relay', "electromagnetic relay" can be considered as hyponyms of "relay" (in this article, the linguistic expressions will be written between quotation marks) as well as "propeller turbine" and "Kaplan turbine" are hyponyms of "turbine".

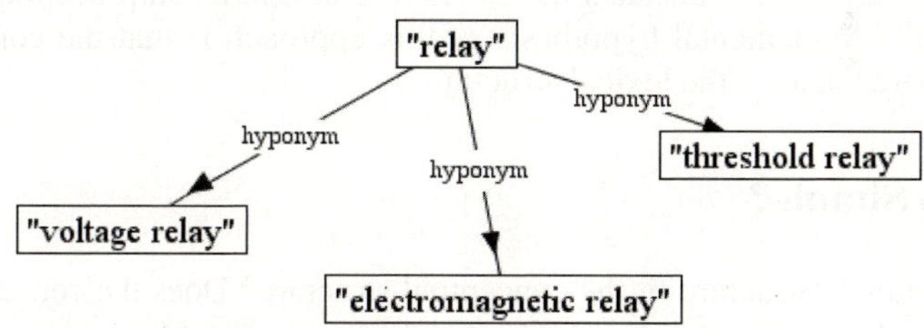

Fig. 1. An example of lexical structure

3   The Conceptual Structure

We have to notice that putting linguistic relationships between linguistic expressions, such hyponymy or synonymy, does not define them. Even if we consider a word, or a set of synonymous words, as a "lexicalised concept" like in Wordnet (a concept is a *synset,* i.e. a set of synonymous words) [7], the words are not defined: a concept is more than a word and an ontology is not a structured lexicon.

If a structured lexicon does not define a conceptual model, its study can bring a lot of useful information for building it. As a matter of fact, the domain conceptualization appears through the words of usage considered as terms denoting concepts and through their lexical structure translating a conceptual structure.

Let us go back to the linguistic expressions made up of several words with the same "queue" (i.e. ending with the same words). From theses data we can extract useful information for building the conceptual structure. The following linguistic expressions "voltage relay", "threshold relay", "on-off relay", if they are considered as lexicalized concepts, denote different kinds of <relay> (let us put linguistic expressions in quotation marks and concept between the lower and upper symbols) linked by a *generalisation – specialisation* (subsumption) relationship. Then, we can represent the denoted concepts and their organisation in a semi-formal formalism as a network of concepts linked by "is a" relationships

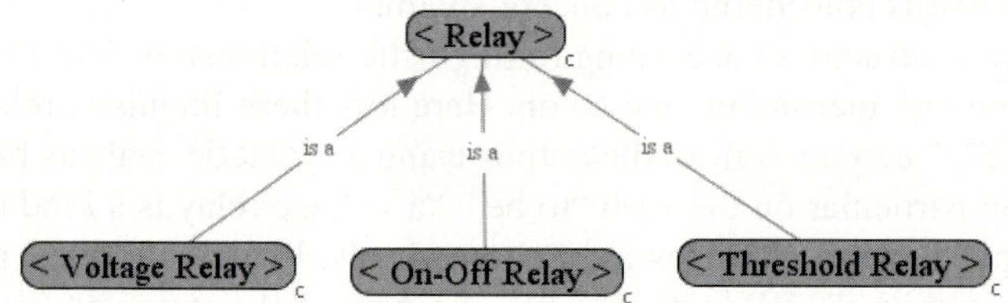

Fig. 2. The conceptual structure corresponding to the lexical structure of figure 1

or in a more formal language:
$$\forall x\ \text{VoltageRelay}\,(x) \rightarrow \text{Relay}\,(x)$$
$$\forall x\ \text{On-OffRelay}\,(x) \rightarrow \text{Relay}\,(x)$$
$$\forall x\ \text{ThresholdRelay}\,(x) \rightarrow \text{Relay}\,(x)$$

Such an approach assumes that a noun denotes a concept when the hyponymy relationship between nouns translates the subsumption relationship between concepts. In few words, the fundamental hypothesis of this approach is that the conceptual structure fits – or translates – the lexical structure.

4   Is It so Simple?

Does the linguistic structure fit the conceptual structure? Does the conceptual structure translate the linguistic structure? Or on the contrary does – or should? – the linguistic structure translate the conceptual structure? These questions are not equivalent. The first one implies that the linguistic and conceptual analyses can be viewed as independent processes and we have a new problem to solve, the one of alignment of the two structures. The second question corresponds to a semasiologic approach where first we find the vocabulary of terms and then define them. When the last question corresponds to an onomasilogic approach, like in terminology [8] [9], whose the main goal is first to define a conceptualization of the world and then to name the concepts.

Ontology building from texts corresponds to a semasiologic approach: we first find terms (mainly nouns) and then define them as concepts. Most of the present works follow the approach we have described, even if the methods and techniques can be more sophisticated (for example in relying on both linguistic and mathematical techniques for extracting candidate terms). But is such a built conceptual structure really sound? and can it be really shared and reused?

Let us go back to the simple example of relays and let us use this conceptualization for a CMS (content management system) application. Documents can be semantically annotated based on this conceptualization [10], it means a document is classified, or indexed, on every concept the content of the document refers to. Then, looking for information about a concept, for example "threshold relay", must return all information about this kind of relay, using if necessary the "is a" inheritance relationship for inferences. But in this case searching information on "threshold relay" does not return any information about "voltage relay". This is not correct. As a matter of fact, for experts, all information about "voltage relay" concerns "threshold relay": if the conceptualization is not wrong, it is not completely correct. Where is the problem?

Working with the experts on their domain conceptualization, independently of the words of usage, it appeared that in fact a <voltage relay> is not a kind of relay in the *same level* than the <on-off relay> or <threshold relay>, but is a kind of <threshold relay> whose the threshold value is voltage. In fact, "voltage relay" is a shortcut for the more complete expression "voltage threshold relay", such a use of linguistic expressions corresponds to a rhetorical figure called a metonymy.

A formal definition of concepts helps us to find the "correct" conceptual structure. As a matter of fact, natural language, even constrained in its syntax and semantics, can not be used for concept definitions. We need a formal language for the definition of a conceptualization – such a "specification of a conceptualisation" is called an ontology [11] –. This is a useful means to escape from the problems raised by the natural language and to reach agreement (indeed, if we accept the hypothetical and deductive approach of the formal system, we are obliged to accept its constructions; it means the domain conceptualization).

The choice of the formal language for the definition of concepts is important. The way we build ontology and define a concept directly depends on the formal language which will be used. Indeed, Knowledge engineer needs an "artificial" but epistemologically founded language which can help him to capture the nature of knowledge[1] independently the way he/she can express it in natural language. In this article we have used a formal language based on the specific-difference theory [12] for which a conceptualization is a system of concepts organized according to their differences (a concept is defined from a previously existing one by adding a specific difference). The difference is then the central notion and the agreement problem is reduced to the agreement on

---

[1] Formal languages are mainly logic-oriented. The concepts are represented as unary predicates when their attributes, or slots, are represented as binary predicates also called roles. Description logic [13] is a good example of logic dedicated to knowledge representation as OWL, the web ontology language [14], is a good example of languages for building ontology based on the W3C philosophy. But logic is a neutral (or flat) language which is not able to represent the different kinds of knowledge: a unary predicate can represent either a concept or a property when binary predicates can represent either attributes (internal relationships) or relationships between concepts (external relationships). The frame representation languages [15], in spite of the criticism of [16], are different in the sense that they allow to directly express the structure of concepts in terms of slots and relationships.

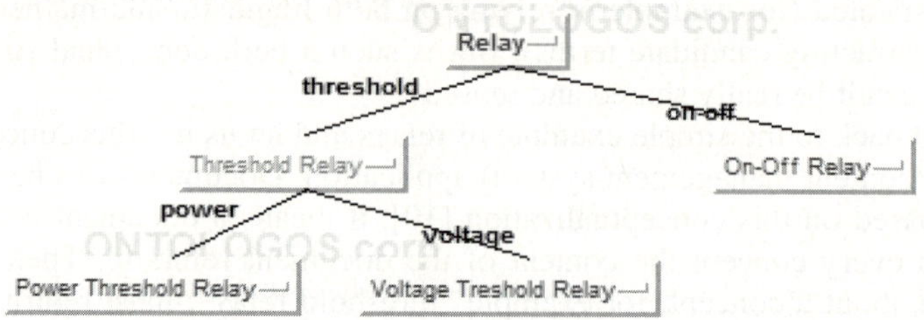

Fig. 3. The "correct" conceptual structure corresponding to the lexical structure of figure 1

differences. Furthermore, everybody can agree with the classical (Aristotelian) definition of a concept: a <voltage threshold relay> is a <threshold relay> whose threshold value is *voltage*, and then on the resulting conceptual structure.

We can notice that the complete and correct linguistic expression for denoting the concept <voltage relay> should be "voltage threshold relay", even if "voltage relay" is an expression of usage which must be take into account in the lexicon[2].

Let us take another example which well illustrates that corpus contains different kinds of knowledge and that a same knowledge – the extra-linguistic conceptualization of the domain – can be expressed in different ways with different linguistic forms.

In a corpus about turbines, we find expressions like:

- "The three main types of water turbines are Pelton wheels, Francis turbines, and Kaplan or propeller type turbines.";
- "A Kaplan turbine is a type of propeller turbine in which the pitch of the blades can be changed to improve performance.";
- "A propeller turbine is a Kaplan turbine with fixed blades…";
- "A Kaplan turbine looks like a propeller turbine…".

So, what kind of ontology can we build from such texts. Is a <Kaplan Turbine> a kind of <Propeller Turbine>? Or on the contrary is a < Propeller Turbine> a kind of <Kaplan Turbine>? Or, as "Kaplan turbine looks like a propeller turbine", is there any subsumption relationship between these two kinds of turbine?

If the previous sentences, taken in their context, are correct since they mainly express a kind of explanation knowledge: "from this point of view, this object is like this one with this difference"; the conceptualization represents a "universal", an invariant knowledge which remains the same whatever the context in which it appears. If the concept's names "Kaplan turbine", "Propeller turbine" can be automatically extracted from corpus, the conceptual structure directly depends on their formal definition and on the way experts conceptualize their domain.

---

[2] The lexicon of a LSP (Language for Special Purpose or Specialized Language) and the vocabulary of concept's names are in fact two different things which should be study independently, and then connected if necessary. Indeed, let us remark that the lexicon of a LSP is made of words of usage which can be polysemic when the concept's names are, by definition, monosemic; as well as hyponymy relationship can be a multiple relation (a same word can have several hypernyms) when the subsumption relationship based on the specific difference theory can not be multiple.

Using the same approach based on the "specific difference" theory, the experts defined the ontology of turbines as described in the following figure, putting in evidence that Kaplan and propeller turbines are similar since they are both kinds of reaction hydraulic turbine with blades, but differ according to the movable of the pitch of the blades.

Note: the "specific difference" ontologies of this article were realized with the OCW (Ontology Craft Workbench) environment of Ontologos corp. (http://www.ontologoscorp.com).

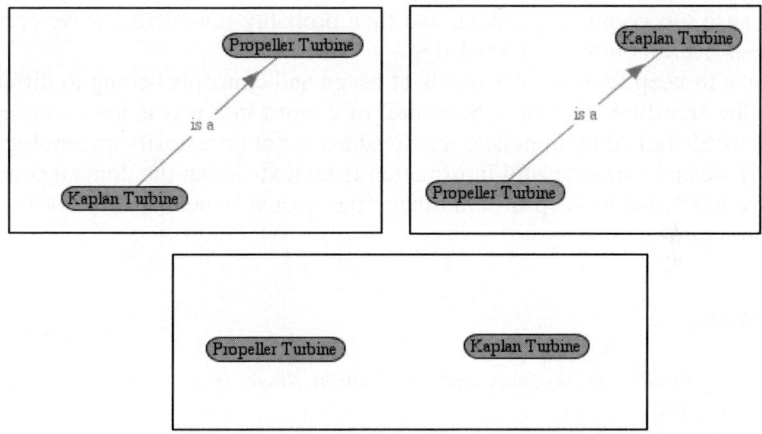

Fig. 4. The possible relationships between Kaplan and Propeller turbines

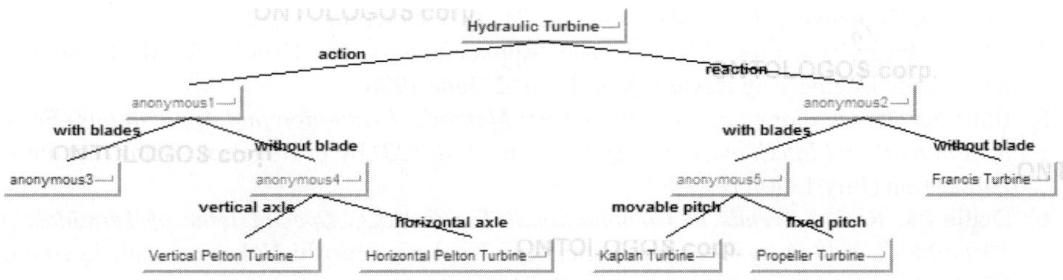

Fig. 5. The "specific difference" ontology of turbines

5   Conclusion

As domain knowledge is mainly conveyed by technical and scientific texts, and since linguistic expressions are used to express this knowledge and to denote concepts and relationships between them, it seems interesting to build ontology – understood as a conceptualization of a domain – from texts.

The knowledge extracted from texts is a linguistic knowledge. The lexical structure is a network of words – can we really consider them as lexicalized concepts? – linked by linguistic relationships like hyponymy, synonymy, etc. This lexical structure is a linguistic "picture" of the conceptual structure of the domain; a picture built in a given and particular context of corpus, which can differ from one context to another.

The lexical structure is not an "isomorphic" translation of the conceptual model. As a matter of fact, texts fall within the language in action. Using rhetorical figures, such as metonymy and ellipse, is a very ordinary practice even for writing technical document. Let us recall the example of "voltage relay" where we use a specific difference for denoting a concept (metonymy principle). Furthermore, one of the principles in textual linguistics, even in technical documents, is the incompleteness of texts. A conceptual model "directly" built from a lexical structure will probably not be reusable, because too corpus-dependent, and then probably not correct if we consider an ontology as a non-contingent knowledge.

We have to keep in mind that words of usage and concepts belong to different disciplines: the signified (signifié – Saussure) of a word in a text is not a concept and a lattice of words linked by linguistic relationships is not necessarily an ontology.

Even if we can extract useful information from texts about the domain conceptualization, we have also to keep in mind that: "the lexical structure does not fit the conceptual structure".

References

1. Staab S.. *Handbook on Ontologies* by Steffen Staab (Editor), Rudi Studer (Editor), Springer, 2004
2. Gomez 04. *Ontological Engineering : with examples from the areas of Knowledge Management, e-Commerce and the Semantic Web* by Asuncion Gomez-Perez, Oscar Corcho, Mariano Fernandez-Lopez Springer, 2004
3. Roche 03. *Ontology: a Survey.* 8th Symposium on Automated Systems Based on Human Skill and Knowledge IFAC, September 22-24 2003, Göteborg, Sweden
4. « Ontologies : Principles, Methods and Applications » M. Ushold & M. Gruninger. Knowledge Engineering Review, Vol. 11, n° 2, June 1996
5. Buitelaar 05. *Ontology Learning from Text: Methods, Evaluation and Applications (Frontiers in Artificial Intelligence and Applications, Vol. 123)* by P. Buitelaar (Editor) Ios Press Publication (July 1, 2005)
6. Daille 04. *Recent Trends in Computational Terminology. Special issue of Terminology 10:1 (2004).* Edited by Béatrice Daille, Kyo Kageura, Hiroshi Nakagawa and Lee-Feng Chien, Benjamins publishing company, 2004 Wordnet.
7. http://wordnet.princeton.edu/
8. *ISO 704: Terminology work - Principles and methods.* International Organization for Standardization. 2000
9. Cabré 99. *Terminology: Theory, methods and applications.* M. Teresa Cabré Castellví, Benjamins publishing company,1999
10. Kiryakov, Popov, Terziev, Manov, and Ognyanoff 05. *Semantic Annotation, Indexing, and Retrieval.*Elsevier's Journal of Web Sematics, Vol. 2, Issue (1), 2005.
11. Gruber 03. *A Translation Approach to Portable Ontology Specifications.* Knowledge Systems Laboratory September 1992 - Technical Report KSL 92-71 Revised April 1993. Appeared in *Knowledge Acquisition*, 5(2):199-220, 199

12. Roche 01. *The 'Specific-Difference' Principle: a Methodology for Building Consensual and Coherent Ontologies*. IC-AI'2001: Las Vegas, USA, June 25-28 2001
13. Baader 03. *The Description Logic Handbook*. Franz Baader, Diego Calvanese, Deborah McGuinness, Daniele Nardi, Peter Patel-Schneider, editors. Cambridge University Press, 2003
14. OWL *Web Ontology Language*: http://www.w3.org/TR/owl-features/
15. Wright, J. M., M. S. Fox, and D. Adam. 84 "SRL/1.5 Users Manual." Technical report;Robotics Institute, Carnegie-Mellon University 1984.
16. Woods 75. *What's in a Link: Foundations for Semantic Networks*. Representation and Understanding: Studies in Cognitive Science, 35-82, edited by D.G. Bobrow and A.M. Collins, New York: Academic Press, 1975.

Discovering Verb Relations in Corpora: Distributional Versus Non-distributional Approaches

Maria Teresa Pazienza[1], Marco Pennacchiotti[1], and Fabio Massimo Zanzotto[2]

[1] University of Roma Tor Vergata, Via del Politecnico 1, Roma, Italy
{pazienza, pennacchiotti}@info.uniroma2.it
[2] DISCo, University of Milano Bicocca, Via B. Arcimboldi 8, Milano, Italy
zanzotto@disco.unimib.it

Abstract. Verbs represent a way in which ontological relationships between concepts and instances are expressed in natural language utterances. Moreover, an organized network of semantically related verbs can play a crucial role in applications. For example, if a Question-Answering system could exploit the direction of the entailment relation win $\rightarrow$ play, it may expand the question "Who played against Liverpool?" with "X won against Liverpool" and it may avoid the expansion of "Who won against Liverpool?" in "X played against Liverpool" that would be wrong. In this paper, we present a survey of the methods proposed to extract verb relations in corpora. These methods can be divided in two classes: those using the Harris distributional hypothesis and those based on point-wise assertions. These methods are analysed and compared.

1 Introduction

Learning domain ontologies (or semantic models) from texts is a largely debated problem that undergoes to different names according to the research area: terminology extraction [1], named entity recognition [2], lexical acquisition, and information extraction [3].

Models for terminology extraction and structuring [1] have always had the aim to extract terms from domain corpora and structuring them in *is-a* hierarchies [4] or different conceptual networks. Terms are strictly related to ontologies as they are the linguistic counterpart of domain concepts.

Named entity extraction as well as information extraction give the possibility of populating ontologies with concept and relationship instances. Traditionally, these techniques are based on a pre-existing semantic model (or ontology) of the domain defining relevant concepts called named entity categories (e.g., `location`, `team`, `person`) and relevant relations between concepts called templates (e.g., `Match(Home,Visitors,Result,Score,Date)`). Given a text, the resulting systems aim to extract named entities, that are instances of the categories, and fillers for the template slots. For example, given the sentence *"Marcus Camby won for NY at the Yankees Stadium"*, these systems have to extract:

M. Ali and R. Dapoigny (Eds.): IEA/AIE 2006, LNAI 4031, pp. 1042–1052, 2006.
© Springer-Verlag Berlin Heidelberg 2006

– 3 named entities: *"Marcus Camby"* as instance of `person`, *"NY"* as instance
  of `team`, and *"Yankees Stadium"* as instance of `location`;
– a partial instance of the `Match` template:

```
Match(New_York_Yankees,-,HomeWinner,-,-)
```

These activities are clearly very difficult. What is written in the sample sentence
is distant with respect to its interpretation according to the template. However,
some systems really achieve good performances in some Information Extraction
tasks [2].

Ontology learning from texts is not then proposing a new challenge to natural
language processing (NLP). It is pushing the scalability of these methods. These
latter give the basis over which more scalable models can be produced.

In particular, verb and verb phrases, one of the linguistic counterpart of ontological relationships between concepts and instances, have been fairly studied.
A clear model of verb semantics could be helpful in determining a clear model
of the relationships between concepts. Relations between verbs play then a very
important role. This will be clarified with an example. Consider the question
"What college did Marcus Camby play for?". A system could find the answer in
the snippet *"Marcus Camby won for Massachusetts"* only if the question verb
play is related to the verb *win* according to some ontological resource even if
play and *win* have a different meaning.

Understanding verb relations and discovering such a relations between verbs in
corpora is a very interesting research field. This can give some insights to model
better ontological resources. Moreover, some results and methods to induce such
relations between verbs from corpora are already available. These are mainly
based on two hypotheses:

– the Harris' Distributional Hypothesis [5]
– the pointwise assertion hypothesis [6]

These two hypotheses originated very different methods for discovering relations
between words in general and between verbs in particular.

The rest of the paper is organised as follows. Sec. 2 shortly revises the possible
verb relations. This give an important view on how relationships between concepts
should be modelled. Sec. 3 and Sec. 4 describe the automatic models to extract these
verb relations from corpora. Sec. 3 and Sec. 4 respectively describes the methods
based on the distributional hypothesis and the pointwise assertion methods.

2   Verb Relations: A Classification

WordNet [7] is a very large lexcial knowledge base. Its organization can give hints
to better understand which relations hold between verbs. Verbs are basically
organized in synonymy sets (*synsets*) and different kinds of semantic relations
can hold between two verbs (i.e., two synsets): *troponymy, causation, backward-
presupposition,* and *temporal inclusion.* All these relations are intended as specific
types of *lexical entailment.* According to the definition in [7] lexical entailment

holds between two verbs v_t and v_h when the sentence *Someone v_t* entails the sentence *Someone v_h* (e.g. *"Someone wins"* entails *"Someone plays"*). Lexical entailment is then an asymmetric relation.

The four types of WordNet lexical entailment can be classified looking at the temporal relation between the entailing verb v_t and the entailed verb v_h.

Troponymy represents the hyponymy relation between verbs. It stands when v_t and v_h are temporally co-extensive, that is, when the actions described by v_t and v_h begin and end at the same times (e.g. *limp→walk*). The relation of *temporal inclusion* captures those entailment pairs in which the action of one verb is temporally included in the action of the other (e.g. *snore→sleep*). *Backward-presupposition* stands when the entailed verb v_h happens before the entailing verb v_t and is necessary for v_t. For example, *win* entails *play* via backward-presupposition as it temporally follows and presupposes *play*. Finally, in *causation* the entailing verb v_t necessarily causes v_h. In this case, the temporal relation is thus inverted with respect to backward-presupposition, since v_t precedes v_h. In causation, v_t is always a causative verb of change, while v_h is a resultative stative verb (e.g. *buy→own*, and *give→have*).

As a final note, it is interesting to notice that the Subject-Verb structure of v_t is preserved in v_h for all forms of lexical entailment. The two verbs have the same subject. The only exception is *causation*: in this case the subject of the entailed verb v_h is usually the object of v_t (e.g., *X give Y → Y have*), as in most cases the subject of v_t carries out an action that changes the state of the object of v_t, that is then described by v_h.

3   Distributional Semantics

3.1   The Harris' Distributional Hypothesis

The Distributional Hypothesis [5] has been fairly explored and exploited in learning similarity between words and between more structured expressions. The hypothesis is the following:

> *Words that tend to occur in the same contexts tend to have similar meanings.*

This seems to be a simple statement but it has given very interesting results. It is a very strong assertion as word semantics is modelled using only contextual information. Target words themselves are only used to select contexts from a corpus.

Trying to formalize, given a set of words W and a set of contexts Ctx drawn from a corpus C, we can define a function that associate the contexts to each subset of words:

$$\mathcal{C} : 2^W \rightarrow 2^{Ctx} \tag{1}$$

The Distributional Hypothesis suggests that the similarity sim_w between two sets of words, W_1 and W_2, is computable as the simililarity sim_{ctx} between the related sets of contexts:

$$sim_w(W_1, W_2) \approx sim_{ctx}(\mathcal{C}(W_1), \mathcal{C}(W_2)) \tag{2}$$

The problem is then how to compute the similarity between contexts. Contexts are generally represented on a feature space $F = F_1 \times ... \times F_n$. As any vector space model, this space hosts also the intensional representation of sets of contexts $\mathcal{I}(Ctx')$ (e.g., their centroids). The function that computes the intesional representations is:

$$\mathcal{I} : 2^{Ctx} \to F \tag{3}$$

The similarity between two sets of contexts (or between their intensional repre-setations) is then computed over the space F. In the following we will use $w \in W$ and $c \in Ctx$ in the similarities to indicate, respectively, the singletons $\{w\}$ and $\{c\}$.

As any other Machine Learning problem, the methods applying this principle differ according to:

- how contexts are represented in features of the space $\mathcal{F}$ (using bag-of-word models, syntactic representations, or semantic models);
- how, evetually, intensional representations of sets of contexts are computed;
- how the similarity measure over contexts is defined.

Before starting the analysis of the method we need to give another classification. This latter depends on how the similarity is used in an algorithm that generates a lexicon of similar words starting from a corpus C. We can distinguish to two ways: a **direct** approach exploit directly the similarity and an **indirect** approach that, working in the context space, select words sharing similar contexts. In the following, we rewiew some of these learning algorithm with respect to this classification.

3.2   Discovering Similarity Using the *Direct* Approach

The **direct** approach is fairly studied and it is applicable when the corpus C is a-priori known. Given a set W of relevant words or linguistic structures, the corpus C is scanned for each element $w \in W$. Contexts for each w are gathered and represented in the feature space $\mathcal{F}$. Pairs (w', w'') in $W \times W$ are ranked according to $sim(w', w'')$ and these are retained as good pairs if their similarity is greater than a threshold α, i.e. $sim(w', w'') > \alpha$. Sometimes, to improve selectiveness this threshold depends on one of the two elements, i.e. $\alpha_{w'}$. The applicability to known corpora depends on two factors. The first is that the set W has to be defined a-priori. This is generally done analysing the frequency, or similar indicators, of the words w in the corpus. The second applicability limitation depends on the fact that the contexts of each w have to be represented in the $\mathcal{F}$ space. This means that the corpus has to be completely scanned. Only after the computation of the similarity between different words can be done.

The general algorithm DH_direct(C), that directly applies the Distributional Hypothesis, is described in the followings. It takes in input a corpus C and return a set of equivalence classes W_i containing words or linguistic sturctures:

DH_direct(C) returns $(W_1,...,W_N)$

Given a corpus C and the releted function C:

1. Let W be the most important elements in C
2. For each $w \in W$:
   (a) retreive all the contexts $C(w)$ and map them in the feature space F
   (b) eventually compute $\mathcal{I}(C(w))$
3. For each $(w_i, w_j) \in W \times W$:
   (a) comupute $sim_{ctx}(C(w_i), C(w_j))$
   (b) if $sim_{ctx}(C(w_i), C(w_j)) > \alpha_{w_i}$ then put w_j in W_i

---

The above algorithm has been largely employed. As we already discussed in the previous sections, the methods differ for the target of the analysis and the feature space in which the similarity is computed.

In [8], the DH_direct has been used to extract similarity between verbs from a single corpus. The elements represented in the feature space F were then intensional representations of verb contexts. The actual features were the determined by the pair $(VerbArg, ArgFiller)$ where $VerbArg$ is one of the possible verb arguments (e.g., the $subject, object, modifier - from, modifier - in, ...$) and $ArgFiller$ is a word sequence. The value of this feature was related to the frequency and the inverse document frequency.

In [9], the algoritm has been used to discover equivalence relations between verbal linguistic expressions connecting two arguments X and Y, e.g. *X solved* $Y \approx X$ *found a solution to* Y. Each one of these verbal linguistic expressions is called pattern p. The idea there was to represent in a feature space the possible filler of the slots X and Y. The feature space represents intensionally a set of contexts of each pattern. The features were (s, w) where s is the slot X or Y and w is a possible word filling the slot. Given a set on contexts where the pattern pat has been found (the set will be called pat as the pattern), the feature values of the $\mathcal{I}(pat)$ are computed as follows:

$$\mathcal{I}_{(s,w)}(pat) = mi(pat, s, w) \tag{4}$$

where $mi(pat, s, w)$ is the point-wise mutual information [10]:

$$mi(pat, s, w) = log \frac{p(pat, s, w)}{p(pat, s)p(s, w)} \tag{5}$$

Probabilities are estimated with the maximun likelihood principle over the corpus. We define the vectors I_s (where s is the slot X or Y) as the vectors having 1 in the feature (s, w) and 0 otherwise. The similarity $sim(p_1, p_2, s)$ between p_1 and p_2 according to the slot s is defined as follows :

$$sim(p_1, p_2, s) = \frac{(\mathcal{I}(p_1) + \mathcal{I}(p_2))I(p_1, p_2)I_s^T}{\mathcal{I}(p_1)I_s^T + \mathcal{I}(p_2)I_s^T} \tag{6}$$

where $I(p_1, p_2)$ is a matrix whose elements on the diagonal are:

$$I_{(s,w),(s,w)}(p_1,p_2) = \begin{cases} 1 \text{ if } \mathcal{I}_{(s,w)}(p_1) > 0 \text{ and } \mathcal{I}_{(s,w)}(p_2) > 0 \\ 0 \text{ otherwise} \end{cases}$$

and elements out of the diagonal are 0. The similarity $sim_p(p_1,p_2)$ between two patterns is then computed as follows:

$$sim_p(p_1,p_2) = \sqrt{sim(p_1,p_2,X) \times sim(p_1,p_2,Y)}. \tag{7}$$

3.3 Anchor-Based Algorithms: *indirect* Approaches

The **indirect** approaches (e.g. [11, 12, 13]) have been proposed to apply the Distributional Hypothesis also when the corpus C is a-priori not known (e.g. the Web that is potentially infinite). The problem there is that the set W can not be computed in advance. If W were somehow given, the more similar words to a word w can be found only when $sim_w(w,w')$ has been computed for each $w' \in W$. This is generally unfeasible due to the large size of the corpus. The pursued idea is the following. Given a seeding set of words or linguistic structures W_S considered similar or realising a unique semantic relation (e.g., the *is-a* relation such as in [11]), a set C_S of prototypical contexts are extracted. Each element c in the set C_S that has some important property is called *anchor* [?]. An anchor highly characterises the contexts where the set of words W_S appears. For each of the element c, it is then possible to derive the set of words:

$$W_c = C^{-1}(\{c' \in CTX | sim_{ctx}(c,c') > \alpha\}) \tag{8}$$

These sets can be used to enrich the original set of word W with similar words. The similarity is always estimated using the similarity between contexts.

DH_indirect$(C,(W_1',...,W_N'))$ returns $(W_1,...,W_N)$

Given a corpus C and the releted function C:

1. For each W_i':
   (a) $W_i = W_i'$:
   (b) For each relevant set $W' \subseteq W_i'$:
      i. compute $I_{W'} = \mathcal{I}(C(W'))$
      ii. extract $W'' =$
          $C^{-1}(\{c' \in CTX | sim_{ctx}(c, I_{W'}) > \alpha\})$
      iii. select the most relevant $W''' \subseteq W''$
      iv. $W_i = W_i \cup W'''$

Hearst [11] by first mined a wide collection of texts to identify, in a set of frequently occurring lexico-syntactic patterns, lexical relations of interest. Main focus was in discovering patterns highlighting hyponymyc lexical relationship between two or more noun phrase in naturally-occurring text. Basic assumption was that the structure of a language can indicate the meanings of lexical items. The problem lies in finding surface linguistic expressions that, frequently and reliably, indicate relations of interest. Limited to hyponymy relation, Hearst identified a set of lexico-syntactic patterns:

- occurring frequently and in several text genres
- recognizable with little or no pre-encoded knowledge

By first these patterns were discovered by observation, then, to find new patterns automatically, a list of terms for which the specified relation hold was gathered. The corpus was mined to find expressions in which these terms occurred near one another. Then commonalities among these environments were extracted and assumed to indicate the relation of interest. Each time the specific list of terms is used as an anchor. Hearst declares the method has been successfull for hyponimy relation, while not for meronymy. Such a different result has been ascribed to the "naming" nature of hyponymy relation.

Ravichandran and Hovy [12] explored the power of surface text patterns for open-domain Question Answering systems. They recognized that in several Q/A systems specific types of answer are expressed by using characteristic phrases (that could be described in regular expressions). They described a pattern-learning algorithm and focused on scaling relation extraction to the Web. In fact with their algorithm it is possible to infer surface patterns from a small set of instance seeds (the anchor in this approach) by extracting substrings relating seeds in corpus sentences. The presence of any variant of the answer term causes the same treatement as for the original answer term. Nevertheless the patterns cannot handle long-distance dependencies. The approach has been tested on several relations providing good results for specific relations (such as birthdate) while lower precision revealed for generic and frequent ones (as is-a and part-of). Also this algorithm is in the line of learning then extracting approach.

Szpektor et al. [13] defined a fully unsupervised learning algorithm for web-based extraction of entailment relations. By assuming that the same meaning can be expressed in a text in a huge variety of surface forms, they focused on acquiring paraphrase patterns that represent different forms in which a certain meaning can be expressed. This approach has been applied to acquire entailment relations from the Web. Paraphrase acquisition results in finding linguistic structures (called templates) sharing the same lexical elements describing the context of a sentence. These lexical elements are used as anchors. Templates extracted from different sentences, while connecting the same anchors, are assumed to paraphrase each other. We recognize a structuring model for which we distinguish between syntactic anchors (such as subject, object, verb) and a context anchor (such as prepositional phrase). Main problems relate to both finding matching anchors and identifying template structure. Specific algorithms have been developed for both problems. A broad range of semantic relations varying from synonymy to more complex entailment have been extracted.

4   Non-distributional Approaches

Since the Distributional Hypothesis [5] suggests equivalence between words, the related methods can discover only symmetric relations. However, consider again the question *"What college did Marcus Camby play for?"*. A system could find the answer in the snippet *"Marcus Camby won for Massachusetts"* as the question verb *play* is related to the verb *win*. The vice-versa is not true. If the question were *"What college did Marcus Camby won for?"*, the snippet *"Marcus Camby played for Massachusetts"* cannot be used. This is why *winnig* entails *playing* but not vice-versa. The relation between *win* and *play* is asymmetric. These kinds of relation cannot be easily discovered using the distributional hypothesis.

The idea that some *point-wise assertions* carry relevant semantic information (as in [6]). This point-wise assertions can be detected at three levels: at the *sentence* level as done in [14], at the level of relations between sentences [15], and, finally, at the level of document as in [16]. In the following sections we will review these methods.

4.1   Single Sentence Patterns

In [14] it has been observed that class-level and word-level selectional preferences [17] offer a very interesting place where to search for these asymmetric entailment relations between verbs. Indeed, selectional preferences indicate an entailment relations between verbs and its arguments. For example, the selectional preference $\{human\}$ *win* may be read as a *smooth* constraint: **if** x is the subject of *win* **then** it is likely that x is a *human*, i.e. $win(x) \rightarrow human(x)$. It follows that selectional preferences like $\{player\}$ *win* may be read as suggesting the entailment relation $win(x) \rightarrow play(x)$.

To exploit the previous principle for entailment detection, we need to find the specific verb selectional preferences. Our method consists of two steps. Firstly, it is necessary to translate the verb selectional expectation in specific Subject-Verb lexico-syntactic patterns ($\mathcal{P}(v_t, v_h)$). Secondly, we need to define a statistical measure ($\mathcal{S}(v_t, v_h)$) that captures the verb preference. This measure will describe how much relations between target verbs (v_t, v_h) are *stable* and commonly agreed.

The above idea requires a Subject-Verb textual entailment lexico-syntactic patterns. It often happens that verbs can undergo an *agentive nominalization,* e.g., *play* vs. *player*. The overall procedure to verify if an entailment between two verbs (v_t, v_h) holds in a point-wise assertion is: *whenever it is possible to apply the agentive nominalization to the hypothesis v_h, scan the corpus to detect those expressions in which the personified hypothesis verb is the subject of a clause governed by the text verb v_t.* Given the two investigated verbs (v_t, v_h) the assertion is formalized in a set of textual entailment lexico-syntactic patterns, that we call *nominalized patterns* $\mathcal{P}_{nom}(v_t, v_h)$. This set will contain the following textual patterns:

$$\mathcal{P}_{agent}(v_t, v_h) =$$
$$\{ \text{``agent}(v_h)|_{number:sing} \quad v_t|_{person:third,tense:present}\text{''},$$

$$\text{``agent}(v_h)|_{number:plur} \quad v_t|_{person:nothird,tense:present}\text{''},$$
$$\text{``agent}(v_h)|_{number:sing} \quad v_t|_{tense:past}\text{''},$$
$$\text{``agent}(v_h)|_{number:plur} \quad v_t|_{tense:past}\text{''}\}$$

where $agent(v)$ is the noun deriving from the personification of the verb v and elements such as $l|_{f_1,...,f_N}$ are the tokens generated from lemmas l by applying constraints expressed via the feature-value pairs $f_1, ..., f_N$. For example, in the case of the verbs *play* and *win*, the related set of textual entailment expressions derived from the patterns are $\mathcal{P}_{nom}(win, play) = \{$ "player wins", "players win", "player won", "players won"$\}$.

Given a pair v_t and v_h we may thus define the following *entailment strength indicator* $\mathcal{S}(v_t, v_h)$. Specifically, the measure $\mathcal{S}_{nom}(v_t, v_h)$ we use is derived from point-wise mutual information [10]:

$$\mathcal{S}_{nom}(v_t, v_h) = log \frac{p(v_t, v_h|nom)}{p(v_t)p(v_h|pers)} \tag{9}$$

where *nom* is the event of having a nominalized textual entailment pattern and *pers* is the event of having an agentive nominalization of verbs.

4.2   Multiple Sentence Patterns

The lexico-syntactic patterns introduced in [15] have been developed to detect six kinds of verb relations: *similarity, strength, antonymy, enablement,* and *happens-before*. Even if, as discussed in [15], these patterns are not specifically defined as entailment detectors, they can be fairly useful for this purpose. In particular, some of these patterns can be use to investigate the *backward-presupposition* entailment. Verb pairs related by backward-presupposition are not completely temporally included one in the other (cf. Sec. 2): the entailed verb v_h precedes the entailing verb v_t. One set of lexical patterns in [15] seem to capture the same idea: the *happens-before* (*hb*) patterns. Indeed, it is used to detect not temporally overlapping verbs, whose relation is semantically very similar to entailment. These patterns in fact show a positive relation with the entailment relation under investigation. The following table reports the *happens-before* lexico-syntactic patterns ($\mathcal{P}_{hb}$) described in [15]:

$$
\begin{aligned}
&\mathcal{P}_{hb}(v_t, v_h) = \\
&\{ \text{``}v_h|_{t:inf} \quad \texttt{and then} \quad v_t|_{t:pres}\text{''}, \\
&\phantom{\{} \text{``}v_h|_{t:inf} \quad \texttt{* and then} \quad v_t|_{t:pres}\text{''}, \\
&\phantom{\{} \text{``}v_h|_{t:past} \quad \texttt{and then} \quad v_t|_{t:pres}\text{''}, \\
&\phantom{\{} \text{``}v_h|_{t:past} \quad \texttt{* and then} \quad v_t|_{t:pres}\text{''}, \\
&\phantom{\{} \text{``}v_h|_{t:inf} \quad \texttt{and later} \quad v_t|_{t:pres}\text{''}, \\
&\phantom{\{} \text{``}v_h|_{t:past} \quad \texttt{and later} \quad v_t|_{t:pres}\text{''}, \\
&\phantom{\{} \text{``}v_h|_{t:inf} \quad \texttt{and subsequently} \quad v_t|_{t:pres}\text{''}, \\
&\phantom{\{} \text{``}v_h|_{t:past} \quad \texttt{and subsequently} \quad v_t|_{t:pres}\text{''}, \\
&\phantom{\{} \text{``}v_h|_{t:inf} \quad \texttt{and eventually} \quad v_t|_{t:pres}\text{''}, \\
&\phantom{\{} \text{``}v_h|_{t:past} \quad \texttt{and eventually} \quad v_t|_{t:pres}\text{''}\}
\end{aligned}
$$

where * is mached with any word. For example, for the classical pair $(v_t, v_h) = (win, play)$, the *happen-before* patterns are realised in $\mathcal{P}_{hb}(win, play) = \{$ "play * and then win", "played and then win", ..., "play and eventually win"$\}$. Also in [15], a mutual-information-related measure is used as statistical indicator. The two methods thus seem to be fairly in line.

4.3 Document Patterns

The other approach we analyse is the "quasi-pattern" used in [16] to capture lexical entailment between two sentences. The pattern has to be discussed in the more general setting of the probabilistic entailment between texts: the *text T* and the *hypothesis H*. The idea is that the implication $T \to H$ holds (with a degree of truth) if the probability that H holds knowing that T holds is higher that the probability that H holds alone, i.e.:

$$p(H|T) > p(H) \tag{10}$$

In [16], words in the two sentences H and T are supposed to be mutually independent: consequently, the previous relation between H and T probabilities holds also for word pairs. Then, a special case can be applied to verb pairs:

$$p(v_h|v_t) > p(v_h) \tag{11}$$

Equation (11) can be interpreted as the result of the following "quasi-pattern": the verbs v_h and v_t should co-occur in the same document. It is thus possible to formalize the idea in *probabilistic entailment "quasi-patterns"* $\mathcal{P}_{pe}$ reported in the following:

$$\mathcal{P}_{pe}(v_t, v_h) =$$
$$\{ \text{``}v_h|_{person:third,t:pres}\text{''} \wedge \text{``}v_t|_{person:third,t:pres}\text{''},$$
$$\text{``}v_h|_{t:past}\text{''} \wedge \text{``}v_t|_{t:past}\text{''},$$
$$\text{``}v_h|_{t:pres\_cont}\text{''} \wedge \text{``}v_t|_{t:pres\_cont}\text{''},$$
$$\text{``}v_h|_{person:nothird,t:pres}\text{''} \wedge \text{``}v_t|_{person:nothird,t:pres}\text{''} \}$$

Also according to [16] point-wise mutual information is a relevant statistical indicator for entailment, as it is strictly related to eq. (11).

5 Conclusions

In this paper, we presented a survey of the methods proposed to extract verb relations in corpora. We tried to demonstate that these standard methods can be divided in two classes: methods using the Harris distributional hypothesis an methods based on point-wise assertions. As ontology learning from texts is not then proposing a new challenge to natural language processing (NLP) but is pushing the scalability of these methods, we believe that reviewing these traditional method can help in building better models for this task.

References

1. Jacquemin, C.: Spotting and Discovering Terms through Natural Language Processing. Massachusetts Institue of Technology, Cambrige, Massachussetts, USA (2001)
2. MUC-7: Proceedings of the seventh message understanding conference (MUC-7). In: Columbia, MD, Morgan Kaufmann (1997)

3. Pazienza, M.T., ed.: Information Extraction. A Multidisciplinary Approach to an Emerging Information Technology. Number 1299 in LNAI. Springer-Verlag, Heidelberg, Germany (1997)
4. Morin, E.: Extraction de liens sémantiques entre termes à partir de corpus de textes techniques. PhD thesis, Univesité de Nantes, Faculté des Sciences et de Techniques (1999)
5. Harris, Z.: Distributional structure. In Katz, J.J., Fodor, J.A., eds.: The Philosophy of Linguistics, New York, Oxford University Press (1964)
6. Robison, H.R.: Computer-detectable semantic structures. Information Storage and Retrieval **6** (1970) 273–288
7. Miller, G.A.: WordNet: A lexical database for English. Communications of the ACM **38** (1995) 39–41
8. Glickman, O., Dagan, I.: Identifying lexical paraphrases from a single corpus: A case study for verbs. In: Proceedings of the International Conference Recent Advances of Natural Language Processing (RANLP-2003), Borovets, Bulgaria (2003)
9. Lin, D., Pantel, P.: DIRT-discovery of inference rules from text. In: Proc. of the ACM Conference on Knowledge Discovery and Data Mining (KDD-01), San Francisco, CA (2001)
10. Church, K.W., Hanks, P.: Word association norms, mutual information and lexicography. In: Proceedings of the 27th Annual Meeting of the Association for Computational Linguistics (ACL), Vancouver, Canada (1989)
11. Hearst, M.A.: Automatic acquisition of hyponyms from large text corpora. In: Proceedings of the 15th International Conference on Computational Linguistics (CoLing-92), Nantes, France (1992)
12. Ravichandran, D., Hovy, E.: Learning surface text patterns for a question answering system. In: Proceedings of the 40th ACL Meeting, Philadelphia, Pennsilvania (2002)
13. Szpektor, I., Tanev, H., Dagan, I., Coppola, B.: Scaling web-based acquisition of entailment relations. In: Proceedings of the 2004 Conference on Empirical Methods in Natural Language Processing, Barcellona, Spain (2004)
14. Zanzotto, F.M., Pazienza, M.T., Pennacchiotti, M.: Discovering entailment relations using textual entailment patterns. In: Proc. of the ACL Workshop on Empirical Modeling of Semantic Equivalence and Entailment, Ann Arbor, Michigan, Association for Computational Linguistics (2005) 13–18
15. Chklovski, T., Pantel, P.: VerbOCEAN: Mining the web for fine-grained semantic verb relations. In: Proceedings of the 2004 Conference on Empirical Methods in Natural Language Processing, Barcellona, Spain (2004)
16. Glickman, O., Dagan, I., Koppel, M.: Web based probabilistic textual entailment. In: Proceedings of the 1st Pascal Challenge Workshop, Southampton, UK (2005)
17. Resnik, P.: Selection and Information: A Class-Based Approach to Lexical Relationships. PhD thesis, Department of Computer and Information Science, University of Pennsylvania (1993)

Modelling Knowledge with ZDoc for the Purposes of Information Retrieval

H. Zinglé

Université de Nice (F)
98, boulevard Edouard Herriot – BP 3209
06204 Nice Cedex 3, France
zingle@unice.fr

Abstract. The paper presents a tool designed for the purpose of information retrieval. It is based on a syntactic-semantic approach of natural language and it exploits the formalism of conceptual graphs for representing the elements of information related to a domain. ZDoc was developed in order to build lexical, semantic and pragmatic resources used to match graphs on documents. It is thus possible either to locate a given information or to list the elements of information contained in a document or in a document flow.

ZDoc is a NLP tool developed in the area of information retrieval on the basis of the syntactic-semantic approach underlying the linguistic workbench ZStation [7][10] from which it is derived. In short, the ZStation is an attempt to facilitate large-scale development of linguistic resources (dictionaries, ontologies, morphologic and syntagmatic grammars) with a special interest in the interpretation of the meaning of utterances, rather than in the calculation of their formal linguistic structure. In the ZStation were also explored different application topics such as word sense disambiguisation, interlingual transfer and document retrieval using linguistic and ontologic knowledge. Despite its interest in the field of research in linguistics and linguistic engineering - in particular with regard to the modelling and the testing of linguistic knowledge - the ZStation reveals to be too complex for operational information retrieval. Like the former experiment with ZTermino [8] - also derived from the ZStation with the intention to help terminology specialists - ZDoc was designed for people working in the field of document retrieval on technical and scientific texts with advanced technology but sparing them an investment in complicated questions in relation with linguistics and knowledge representation.

The underlying principle of ZDoc is that knowledge related to a specific domain (business for example) can be encoded schematically thanks to information schemes. An information scheme is a set of concepts and relations between concepts which are relevant for this domain. In comparison to document retrieval based on keywords (with or without thesaurus) the information retrieval using information schemes reveals to be far more precise. If a document contains the sequence *the new company buys computers* it may be accessed through the non ordered combinations *new ~ company, new ~ buy, new ~ computer, company ~ buy, company ~ computer* and *computer ~ buy*, although only three combinations are meaningful. It seems also obvious that queries using the couples *company ~ buy* and *computer ~ buy* would

M. Ali and R. Dapoigny (Eds.): IEA/AIE 2006, LNAI 4031, pp. 1053 – 1058, 2006.

theoretically select information about companies selling computers as well as about companies buying computers, and why not about computers buying or selling companies. One may consider that linguistic analysis could be of great help in such cases. Nevertheless, the examples like *to buy a company* and *to buy a computer* point out that these sequences have different informative values for an economist, even if both may be reduced to *X buys Y* on a linguistic level. In a similar way *costs grow* and *sales grow* differ in meaning as the information is considered as negative in the first case and as positive in the second one. In addition to these remarks, we have also to take into account that a given information may be expressed in different ways : *to raise rating* is equivalent to *to lift rating* and *to keep rating* has the same meaning as *to maintain rating*.

Conceptual graphs [5][6] appear to be a well suited formalism for representing information schemes. ZDoc uses the technology developed in the ZStation [10] in a more simple way. In short : a conceptual graph is a combination of conceptual nodes (noted in square brackets) connected together by relations (noted in round brackets). A conceptual node is either a concept or a typed concept (or eventually a graph). The symbol ':' is used to associate a concept to the class it belongs to or to quantify a concept. The information that the dollar rises by 2 percent may be represented by following graph :

```
CG-1 [variation : rise]
         ├─(expr)─► [currency : dollar]
         └─(val)─► [percent : @2]
```

The codification [variation : rise] and [currency : dollar] express respectively that [rise] is a kind of [variation] and that [dollar] is a kind of [currency]. The codification [percent : @2] indicates that 2 is the estimated value of the concept of [percent] and represents an extension of the codification of quantification[1].

To raise rating vs. *to lift rating* will be represented by the same graph CG-2

```
CG-2 [process : make]
          └─(obj)─► [variation : positive]
                        └─(expr)─► [rating]
```

as well *as to keep rating* vs. *to maintain rating* by CG-3 below

```
CG-3 [process : make]
          └─(obj)─► [variation : null]
                        └─(expr)─► [rating]
```

---

[1] In the standard theory of conceptual graphs, [company] or [company :*] indicate a generic concept (i.e. any company), [company : #1234] or [company : XLtd] an instance or a named instance of the class company (i.e. a given company), [company : XLtd,YLtd,ZLtd}] an extensive set of companies, [company : {*}] a generic set of companies, [company : {*}@3] a generic subset of 3 companies, [company : {XLtd,Yltd,*} a generic subset of companies including XLtd and Yltd (XLtd, Yltd an other companies), [company : {XLtd,Yltd,*}@5] a generic subset of 5 companies including (XLtd and Yltd).

It is clear that the representation of information based on conceptual graphs is not language dependent. For example, CG-2 applies equally to the French combination *le gouvernement a relevé les taux* as to the English *the government raised rating*. Therefore we consider that the linguistic dependent knowledge (LDK) has to be clearly distinguished from the interlinguisic knowledge (ILK) and that the knowledge modelling must be achieved on the basis of domain expertise. Paraphrase is usually a good way to put conceptual nodes and relations into evidence and to avoid confusions between words and underlying concepts.

ZDoc is programmed in PDC-Visual Prolog as a graphic interface with two fundamental actions : 1) the creation of resources used by the software and 2) the extraction of information which may apply either to a given document or to a set of documents (document flow).

A unique interface is provided for the creation and updating of resources needed for information retrieval, i.e. lexical, semantic and pragmatic resources. Users may browse through the items belonging to each resource and switch from one resource field to another. Experience shows that linguists using this kind of tools need to have an overall approach, as the formalization is splitted over three areas which have to be kept separately.

Lexical resources are built up as a set of lexical units belonging to a specific knowledge domain. For each lexical unit it is necessary – in the current version - to indicate its lemma, the associated concept as well as the associated morphosyntactic variables. If one form is associated to different lemmas or concepts, all configurations have to be defined separately. Experience shows, that this approach is more simple for users than the use of a morphologic grammar based on specifications like in the ZStation[2], as the number of forms are generally reduced. In the new version, which is currently under construction, the users must only input the lemma and its morphosyntactic category and select the morphologic properties from different paradigms generated by the system.

A crucial point here is the selection of the lexical units, as we have to take into account polysemy for the calculation of conceptual graphs. Contrary to what is widely believed, polysemy is not an exception in scientific and technical information. For example, H. Ledouble [4:214] noted that in economic documents from the press agency Reuters the concept of variation of an <economic object> may be expressed in various ways whether the variation concerns an upward or downward movement :

> **<UP>**
> <u>English</u> : *to balloon up, to be up, to boom, to bounce, to climb, to close higher, to close up, to come up, to double, to edge up, to end up, to exceed, to expand, to extend, to fade, to fly high, to fly up, to gain, to grow, to hike, to increase, to jump, to leap, to make progress, to mount, to move up, to open higher, to quadruple, to rally, to rebound, to rise, to soar, to spike higher, to spiral, to surge, to thrive, to trade higher, to triple, to wind up*
> <u>French</u> : *doubler, quadrupler, tripler, décoller, bondir, s'envoler, flamber, rebondir, redécoller, reprendre, gagner, se redresser, accroître, améliorer, augmenter, avancer, croître, gagner, grimper, monter, progresser, remonter*

---

[2] The ZStation uses morphologic prototypes which allow to generate all correct inflected forms for a lexical unit with regard to the associated prototype.

<DOWN>
<u>English</u> : *to be down, to close down, to close lower, to come down, to collapse, to crash, to dip, to dive, to droop, to decrease, to drift lower, to drop, to ease lower, to edge down, to end down, to fall, to lose, to open lower, to pare, to move down, to plummet, to plunge, to shrink, to slide, to slip, to slump, to stall, to trade lower, to underperform, to wane, to weaken, to tumble, to wind down*
<u>French</u> : *chuter, dégonfler, plonger, se tasser, abandonner, céder, perdre, se ralentir, reculer, tomber, céder, chuter*

In addition, the expression of a concept is not limited to a morphosyntactic category. An <UP> variation may be expressed for example by a nominal phrase (English : *recovery*; French : *raffermissement, renforcement, remontée*) as well as by a verbal phrase (English : *to recover;* French : *se raffermir, se renforcer, remonter*).

Lexical formalization within ZDoc is based on corpus analysis using tools like ZText [9] which compile texts into frequency word lists and concordances. The lexical analysis is not limited to single lexical units, but allows also to extract compounds by means of n-gram analysis in association with a linguistic model of compounds.

The semantic resources are built up as a set of concepts belonging to the knowledge domain. Each concept has to be associated to a hyperonym. For example, the concept [dollar] has to be associated to the hyperonym [currency] and the concept [rise] to the hyperonym [variation]. This kind of modelling ontologic knowledge is closer to the lattice of concepts proposed by Sowa [5] than to the ontologies used in the ZStation, where relations between concepts are typed and where multi-inheritance is implemented. We assume that a too fine knowledge representation is generally an obstacle to large-scale formalization achieved by linguists; on the other hand it must be pointed out that knowledge representation is not here a purpose in itself and that the information from lexical and pragmatic resources contribute also to the calculation of information schemes. The analysis of the domain must be done carefully in association with experts. Cadel [1] and Ledouble [4] have demonstrated the benefits of modelling concepts in the field of economy/business in the areas of information retrieval and translation respectively in French and English. For example Cadel [1:150] distinguishes :

- operations (exchange, movements, actions, communication, influence ...)
- modality (approximation, negation ...)
- economic agents (companies, banks, political actors ...)
- products (dividends, benefits, industrial and agronomic products)
- localisation (space, time)
- relations (causality, consequence, implication).

A description of a common ontology obtained by the analysis of comparable corpora in French and English may be found in Cadel & Ledouble [2]. It is clear that the extraction of economic information in a third language will spare this fundamental step, so the major part of the work will essentially consist in the lexical and pragmatic formalization.

Pragmatic resources deal essentially with the definition of information schemes and with the linguistic structures which express them. In other words, it is the area where lexical and semantic knowledge are put in relation so that information takes shape. A dialog box allows users to enter a conceptual graph (with an eventual paraphrase in natural language) and its related linguistic representation in natural language. If a conceptual graph may be expressed in different ways, the related linguistic formulas have to be created. Linguistic structures are matched on graphs through unification over constraints on concepts, lemmas, morphosyntactic variables and values. An important aspect of the calculation of graphs is that we apply here the notion of syntactic-semantic analysis developed in the ZStation [10]. This process does not consist of the derivation of a semantic structure on the basis of the syntactic one, but of the direct calculation of the relations between concepts within the graph by verifying all the specified formal constraints.

The corpus analysis is here very helpful to determine the different linguistic structures expressing a given information scheme. Ledouble [4] has used for this purpose ZText, which allows to list all associations for a word (for example all verbs in relation with a word expressing an economic object). An alternative solution is to use the indexing functions of the ZStation [10:101], specifically the conceptual indexation of corpora using predefined concepts. It is thus possible to obtain directly an index and concordances, for example, for the concept [currency].

The created resources may be exploited either to search for a given information or to extract information from utterances or from documents. In the second case the analysis process produces a list of information elements represented either by conceptual graphs or by paraphrases in natural language. Interesting applications of ZDoc were proposed in the analysis on French [1] and English [4] economic documents furnished by the press agency Reuters. In particular, Cadel and Ledouble [1][2][3] proposed a common ontology on conceptual classes (economic agent, products, operations, movements ...) and information schemes (expressing variations in turnover, expressing trading, expressing influence ...). This double experiment illustrates, in particular, how far intralinguistic knowledge (lexical resources) may be used in combination with interlinguistic knowledge (domain related ontology) by the means of pragmatic interface matching conceptual graphs onto linguistic structures.

References

1. Cadel P. : Utilisation de connaissances linguistiques dans le cadre du traitement documentaire , analyse syntactico-sémantique de documents économiques. Thèse. Université de Nice (2000)
2. Cadel P., Ledouble H. : Extraction of concepts and multilingual information schemes from french and english economic documents. In Proceedings LREC 2000, 1-3 june Athen (2000) 983-986
3. Ledouble H., Cadel P., Kraif O. : Analysis of combinations between economic objects and types of variation in French and English documents. In Proceedings of COMLEX 2000, 22-23 sept. Kato Aicha (2000) 51-54
4. Ledouble H. : Contribution à la traduction de documents économiques anglais, importance de l'extraction et de la représentation du sens. Thèse. Université de Nice (2002)

5. Sowa J. : Conceptual structures : information processing in man and machine. Addison-Wesley (1984)
6. Sowa J. : Knowledge representation, Logical, Philosophical, and Computational Foundations. Brooks/Cole Publishing Co., Pacific Grove, CA. (2000)
7. Zinglé H. : The ZStation workbench and the modelling of linguistic knowledge. In Current Issues in Mathematical Linguistics, Elsevier-NHLS (1994) 423-432
8. Zinglé H. : Acquisition et traitement de données terminologiques avec ZTermino. In Travaux du LILLA, n°2, Nice (1997) 7-22
9. Zinglé H. : ZTEXT, un outil pour l'analyse de corpus. In Travaux du LILLA, n°3, Nice (1998) 69-78
10. Zinglé H. : La modélisation des langues naturelles, aspects théoriques et pratiques. Travaux du LILLA (numéro spécial), université de Nice (1999).

Partially Ordered Template-Based Matching Algorithm for Financial Time Series

Yin Tang

Lab of E-Commerce, Management College, Jinan Univ., GZ 510632, P.R. China
tangyin@tom.com

Abstract. Based on definitions of 1st and 2nd order atomic pattern of time series, this paper deduces n-th order atomic pattern, where partially-ordered relationship within these patterns is discussed. The framework enables more refined comparison between sequences, based on which we propose Template-Based Matching Algorithm. The experimental result has verified its distinct advantages over some similar and classical approaches both in accuracy and performance.

Index Terms: time series, pattern recognition, case-based reasoning, partially order, lattice.

1 Introduction

The futures market is a market of volatility and opportunism, affected by a great many factors like climate, national policy, supply-demand, economical cycle and currency policy, which place enormous difficulties on extrapolation. The work in this paper tries to address the problem in a pattern recognition way under a general assumption that once the same situation happens, the pattern in financial time series will re-occur.

Many approaches for financial time series extrapolation, most of which are based on mathematical models or modern transforming techniques, have been proposed. Classical approaches of time series include Moving Average[1][2], Exponential Smoothing[3], and Box-Jenkins's ARMA and ARIMA[4], Ge and Smith's Deformable Markov Template[5], Bayesian Model[6][7]and some Fuzzy Set Methods[8][9][10], etc.. With the rapid development of computing technology, time series modeling has been away from mathematical way, and turns to dimensional reduction and shape modeling. For instance, Discrete Fourier Transformation [11][12][13][14][15]; Dynamic Time Warping[16] [17] enables the comparison between series of different lengths, dynamically computing the minimum cost of path; Landmark Similarity[18] proposes a new data representation, which maintains a set of minimum features of the sequence, and highly reduces the storage and the computation. Branko Pecar's APRE [19] is a similar attempt to extrapolate the time series in a pattern-recognition way. As for distance measurement, Euclidean Distance treats the sequences as the points in n-th dimensional space, then compute their Euclidean distance, with a complexity of $O(n)$; Goldin and Kanellakis proposed Normalization method[20] which normalizes the mean and the variation, in order to facilitate the comparison.

M. Ali and R. Dapoigny (Eds.): IEA/AIE 2006, LNAI 4031, pp. 1059 – 1070, 2006.

However, these methods have several disadvantages. Some are time-consuming. Some models are either rough or rigid, and unable to fully reflect the market activities. Some of their explanations on similarity measurement are unreasonable and implicit.

Time series consists of a series of variables, each of which has the relationship of Positive, Negative and Zero, with the former one. Branko Pecar's APRE [19] uses "P", "N", "Z" to represent the numerical relationship between current variable and the former one, based on which the APRE performs sequence searching and matching, the criteria of matching includes aggregated computation like mean and standard variation [2]. The approach is relatively rigorous, where two sequences are very much alike but a tiny difference on a single variable will result in a totally different computation, further, a totally different conclusion.

Apart from classical modeling approaches which depend on the assumption of following a certain distribution or a certain kind of mathematical model, the idea we propose in this paper, named Template-Based Matching (TBM), utilizes a set of atomic patterns to match the sequence, based on the fact that similarity is partially ordered. We offer a measuring specification for partially-ordered similarity of the series, and provide an algorithm for time series mining and extrapolating. The algorithm works as reasoning machine, and allows predicting time series based on the case that has occurred.

The rest of the paper is organized as follows: Section 2 discusses how to define 2nd order atomic patterns based on 1st order ones. Section 3 provides an algebraic proof, followed by a distance computing algorithm of the sequences, together with a simple example. Section 4 discusses a whole solution in time series searching and extrapolating, based on the TBM algorithm. The experimental result is presented in section 5. We conclude in section 6.

2 Definition of Atomic Pattern

2.1 1st-Order Atomic Pattern

Definition 1. 1st-order atomic pattern. Let $X'\{x'_i\}$ be the difference series of time series $X\{x_i\}$, define sequence $M\{m_i\}$ as:

$$\text{if } x'_i = \begin{cases} >0 \\ <0 \\ =0 \end{cases}, \text{ then } m_i = \begin{cases} "P" \\ "N" \\ "Z" \end{cases}, \text{ respectively} \tag{1}$$

Here, "P", "N" and "Z" are named as 1st-order time series, $M\{m_i\}$ is called 1st-order basic patterns. As we have seen, 1st-order atomic patterns are simple and rudimentary. However, 1st-order atomic patterns roughly represent the raw one, with loss of inherent information, which is important in similarity measuring. Not only the figure of a time series should be considered, but some other features like maximum point, peak and repeated pattern should be included, where a lot of information is implicated. In our work, we describe not only the relatively increasing relationship between two variables, but also the acceleration, namely, the angle formed by former, current, and latter observation. So, the design should follow the following principles: (1) able to distinguish increase and decrease; (2) able to distinguish positive and negative acceleration in increasing and decreasing; (3) able to distinguish the angle.

2.2 2nd-Order Atomic Pattern

Let $X''\{x''_i\}$ be the difference sequence of $X'\{x'_i\}$, namely the 2nd order difference of $X\{x_i\}$. Sequence $M'\{m'_i\}$ is defined as follows(table 1):

Table 1. Definition of 2nd –Order Atomic patterns

m''_i		Condition	Explanation
PP+	E	$x'_i>0, x'_{i+1}>0, x''_i>0$	accelerated increasing
PP-	C	$x'_i>0, x'_{i+1}>0, x''_i<0$	decelerated increasing
PN	A	$x'_i>0, x'_{i+1}<0$	increasing + decreasing
NN-	K	$x'_i<0, x'_{i+1}<0, x''_i>0$	decelerated decreasing
NN+	I	$x'_i<0, x'_{i+1}<0, x''_i<0$	accelerated decreasing
NP	V	$x'_i<0, x'_{i+1}>0$	decreasing +increasing
PP0	D	$x'_i>0, x'_{i+1}>0, x''_i=0$	increasing
NN0	J	$x'_i<0, x'_{i+1}<0, x''_i=0$	decreasing
ZZ	O	$x'_i=0, x'_{i+1}=0$	zero+zero
ZP	F	$x'_i=0, x'_{i+1}>0$	zero + increasing
ZN	H	$x'_i=0, x'_{i+1}<0$	zero +decreasing
PZ	B	$x'_i>0, x'_{i+1}=0$	increasing +zero
NZ	L	$x'_i<0, x'_{i+1}=0$	decreasing + zero

Here, m'_i is named 2nd-order atomic pattern, $M'\{m'_i\}$ is the series of 2nd order atomic pattern.

Please note that m'_i(PP+, PP-, NN+, NN-) is for convenient presentation in paper work, which enables explicit association to a specific figure. In programming code, it should be a single symbol, as shown in the second column of the table. In addition, "Z" and "ZZ" are practically rare, they are filled when $x_i -x_{i-1}$ is less than a specified small value.

These patterns can bring in good enough result in simple pattern recognition. However, sometime they can not satisfy the requirement of specified applications. As Figure 1 shows, "PZ" and "PN", "PN" and "ZN" seem to have little discrepancy. When it comes to "PZ" and "NN-", we have more and more difference. It will cause problem if we neglect these kinds of situation, that is, among these 13 2nd-order pattern, partial order similarity relationship, rather than linear, ordinal one like "1<2 and 2<3, then 1<3", is mattering.

3 Constructing Higher Order Pattern

3.1 Algebraic Proof

To provide a solid infrastructure for combination of 3rd and higher order patterns, we start from the definition of 1st order patterns.

Let H be the set of 2nd-order atomic patterns, $\prec$ is a relation on the set. For $\forall x, y \in H$, $x \prec y$ is defined as that the included angle of pattern x is less than or equal to the included angle of pattern y. The goal is, hopefully, to prove $\prec$ is a partially ordered relation on set H, then to further define the operators on set H. the H has its upper bound $x \vee y$, the largest included angle of x, y, and its lower bound $x \wedge y$, the smallest included angle of x, y. Where any subset has a least upper bound and a greatest lower bound, there is a complete lattice, whose product generates complete lattice too. Thus, combining the patterns to generate higher order patterns order by order, more and more refined result will be achieved.

For the sake of convenience, we replace these patterns with numerical value, $\{1,-1, 0,.9,-.9\}$ as shown in Fig. 1. The proof is completely equivalent:

(1) DEFINING TWO COMPLETE LATTICES

Suppose a set $S=\{-1,-.9,0,.9,1\}$:

Complete lattice $L_1(S, \prec_2, \cap_2, \cup_2)$, where $\prec_2$ means "greater than or equal to"($\geq$); For any $x,y \in S$, $x \cup_2 y = min(x, y)$, $x \cap_2 y = max(x, y)$;

Complete lattice $L_2(S, \prec_1, \cup_1, \cap_1)$, where $\prec_1$ means "less than or equal to" ($\leq$); For any $x,y \in S$, $x \cup_1 y = max(x, y)$, $x \cap_1 y = min(x, y)$;

(2) DEFINING PRODUCT $L_1 \times L_2$

$L_1 \times L_2 = (S \times S, \prec_\times, \cap_\times, \cup_\times)$, where $(x_1, x_2) \prec_\times (y_1,y_2) <=> x_1 \prec_1 y_1$ and $x_2 \prec_2 y_2 <=> x_1 \geq y_1$ and $x_2 \leq y_2$.

Definition $\cup_\times$ 和 $\cap_\times$: For any (x_1, x_2), $(y_1, y_2) \in S \times S$, $(x_1, x_2) \cup_\times (y_1, y_2) = (min(x_1, y_1), max(x_2, y_2))$, $(x_1, x_2) \cap_\times (y_1, y_2) = (max(x_1, y_1), min(x_2, y_2))$.

The product of the complete lattices generates complete lattice, therefore $L_1 \times L_2$ is complete lattice.

(3) PROOF: $<T, \prec_T>$ IS PARTIALLY ORDERED SET

Let T be a subset of $S \times S$, $\{(-1,1), (0,1), (0.9,1), (1,1), (1,0.9), (1,0), (1,-1), (0,0), (-1,0), (-1,-0.9), (-1,-1), (-0.9,-1), (0,1)\}$. The operator $\prec_\times$ in $L_1 \times L_2$ will be replaced in T with $\prec_T$, T is still a complete lattice $(T, \prec_T, \cap_T, \cup_T)$.

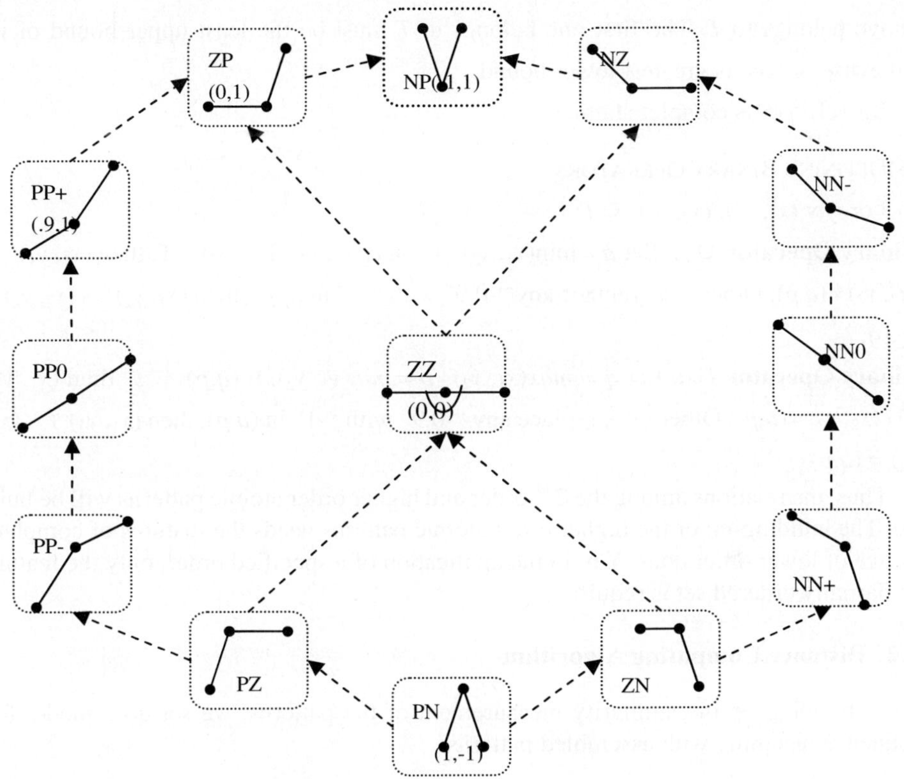

Fig. 1. Partially Ordered Relation among 2nd-order Atomic patterns

Proof: Obviously $\prec_T$ is a relation on set T.

Reflexivity: for any $x \in T$, obviously $x \prec_T x$;

Anti-symmetry: if $x \prec_T y$, namely $x \prec_x y$, and $x \neq y$, then it is impossible for $y \prec_T x$.

Transitivity: if $x \prec_T y$, $y \prec_T z$, then $x \prec_T z$. because $x \prec_T y$, $y \prec_T z$, therefore $x \prec_x y$, $y \prec_x z$, => $x \prec_x z$, => $x \prec_T z$.

So, $<T, \prec_T>$ is partially ordered set.

(4)PROOF, $<T, \leq_T>$ IS COMPLETE LATTICE. Suppose w is a non-empty subset of T, $w=\{(x_1,y_1), (x_2,y_2), \ldots, (x_n,y_n)\}$, obviously $(-1,1)$ is a upper bound of w, let:

$$p= max(y_1, ,y_2, \ldots, y_n) \in \{-1,-0.9,0,0.9,1\}$$

$$q = min(x_1, ,x_2, \ldots, x_n) \in \{-1,-0.9,0,0.9,1\}$$

If $(q,p) \in T$, then (p,q) is the least upper bound of w; If not, suppose $q = .9$, $p = -0.9$, iteratively observe $(.9,0)$, $(.9,.9)$, $(.9,1)$; $(-1,.9)$, $(-1,0)$, $(-1,.9)$, $(-1,1)$, see if any of the above belongs to T. The first one belongs to T must be the least upper bound of w; Likewise, w has its greatest lower bound.

So, $<T, \leq_T>$ is complete lattice.

(5)DEFINING BINARY OPERATORS

For any $(x_1, y_1), (x_2, y_2) \in T$:

Binary Operator $\cup_T$: Let $q = \min(x_1, x_2)$, $p = max(y_1, y_2)$. If $(q,p) \square T$, then $(x_1, y_1) \square T$ $(x_2, y_2) = (q,p)$; Otherwise, replace any "-0.9" with "-1" in (q,p), then $(x_1, y_1) \cup_T (x_2, y_2) = (q,p)$;

Binary Operator $\cap_T$: Let $q = max(x_1, x_2)$, $p = min(y_1, y_2)$. If $(q,p) \in T$, then (x_1, y_1) $\cap_T (x_2, y_2) = (q,p)$; Otherwise, replace any "-0.9" with "-1" in (q,p), then $(x_1, y_1) \cap_T (x_2, y_2) = (q,p)$

Thus, the relations among the 2nd-order and higher order atomic patterns will be built up. The building-up of the higher order atomic patterns needs the features of complete lattice of lower order ones. Yet, in the application of a specified order, only the feature of partially ordered set is required.

3.2 Distance Computing Algorithm

After building up the similarity measurement of the patterns, we set up a model for sequence matching with assembled patterns.

Table 2. Time Series X, Y and their 2nd-order Patterns

x_i	x'_i	x''_i	m'_i	y_i	y'_i	y''_i	n'_i	σ_i
1130				1137.5				
1112	-18	5	NN-	1114.5	-23	11	NN-	0
1099	-13	29	NP	1102.5	-12	14	NP	0
1115	16	-16	PZ	1104.5	2	8.5	PP+	3
1115	0	-20	ZN	1115	10.5	-13	PN	1
1095	-20	7	NN-	1112.5	-2.5	-17.5	NN+	2
1082	-13	26.5	NN-	1092.5	-20	41.5	NP	2
1095.5	13.5	-26	PN	1114	21.5	-58	PN	0
1083	-12.5	10.5	NN-	1077.5	-36.5	38	NP	0
1081	-2	2.5	NP	1079	1.5	21.5	PP+	1
1081.5	0.5	-25.5	PN	1102	23	-56	PN	0
1056.5	-25	13	NN-	1069	-33	18	NN-	0
1044.5	-12	11.5	NN-	1054	-15	3.5	NN-	0
1044	-0.5			1042.5	-11.5			

We define the distance of two atomic patterns as total cost of the path from one to the other in the Haas Map, e.g. the distance from "PN" to "PP+" is 4, the distance from "NN+" and "PP-" is unmeasurable, designated to 6(the maximum distance in the Haas Map). Based on the distances, the similarity of two sequences is calculated according to the formula given below:

$$\sigma = \frac{\sum_{i=2}^{n-1} \sigma_i}{(n-2)*6} \tag{2}$$

Here, σ_i is the distance of each corresponding pattern pair of two sequences ($0 \le \sigma_i \le 6$), n is the length of the sequence. Apparently, $0 \le \sigma \le 1$, when $\sigma = 0$, two sequences have the same shape; when $\sigma = 1$, they are totally different.

Practically, since there are just 13 2nd-order patterns, it is not necessary to dynamically calculate their partially ordered distance. Nevertheless, we can fill the path costs of these patterns into an array or a list (similarity table).

The algorithm is shown below:

```
Input:       sequence   X,   sequence   Y,
similarity table S
Output: σ - the distance of sequence
(1) m = Differnce(X) , m´ = Differnce(m)
(2) n = Differnce(Y) , n´ = Differnce(n)
(3) q = 0
(4) for i =2 to length-1
(5)   p = Lookup(S, m´i ,n´i)
(6)   q = q + p
(7) next i
(8) return σ = q/((1-2)*6)
```

3.3   A Simple Case

Sequence X,Y and their 2nd-order pattern are shown in Table 2, where σ_i at the last column is the distance from x_i, y_i. $\sigma = 0.125$, a conclusion can be made that from the undulating figure, sequence X, Y are fairly similar(Figure 2). To make further conclusion, *Euclidean Distance* can be employed as another criteria.

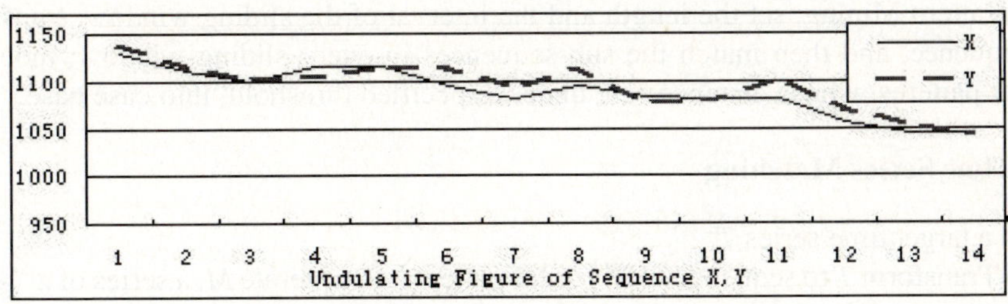

Fig. 2. Undulating Figure of Sequence X , Y

3.4 3rd-Order Patterns

To step further, we can compound the 2nd-order patterns to higher order, and generate 169 3rd-order patterns, which can further refine the similarity assessment and achieve higher accuracy.

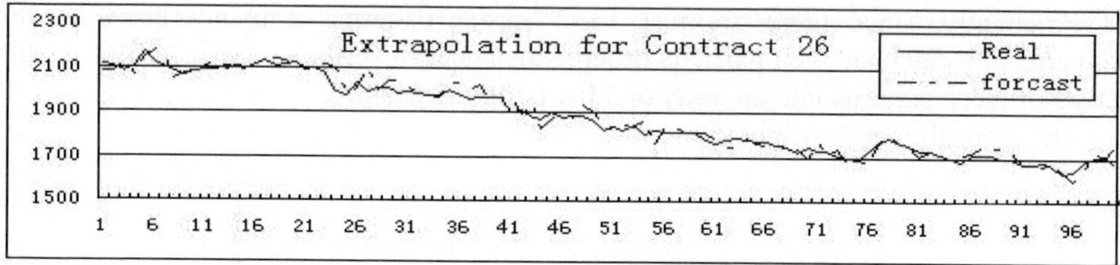

Fig. 3. Extrapolation for Contract 26

In section 2.2, with the complete lattice L_1(T, $\prec_T$, $\cup_T$, $\cap_T$) and L_2(T, $\prec_T$, $\cap_T$, $\cup_T$), we define L(T×T, $\prec$, $\cup$, $\cap$), for any $(x_1, y_1),(x_2,y_2) \in$ T×T, there is $(x_1, x_2) \prec (y_1, y_2)$ <=>$x_1 \prec_T y_1$ and $x_2 \prec_T y_2$. L, named 3rd-order atomic pattern, is also a complete lattice, whose similarity can still be measured by their partial order relations.

Due to the strict time schedule, we just introduced 2nd-order patterns into the extrapolation experiment so far, which brought rather fine result. Promisingly, more accurate result will be carried out if 3rd-order patterns are employed.

4   Template-Based Matching Algorithm

4.1 Time Series Mining

Given time series case base,

(1)Pre-processing: decompose the time series with the techniques like differencing, moving average, etc., into long term trend, periodical fluctuation, seasonal fluctuation, random item, and finally have stationary time series;

(2)Pattern Transforming: transform the time sequence into sequence of 2nd-order patterns;

(3)Pattern Mining: set the length and the interval of the sliding window; transverse the sequence, and then match the sub-sequences in every sliding window; index the similar patterns, whose distances are under a specified threshold, into case base.

4.2 Time Series Matching

Given a target time series T,

(1) Transform T to sequence of 2nd-order patterns, to generate M, a series of 2nd-order patterns;

(2) Set the maximum length l_{max} and the interval of the sliding window; transverse the sequence;

(3) The loop starts from 2 to l_{max}, match each sub-sequence in the sliding window with the source case in time series case base, find out the most familiar one.

4.3 Time Series Extrapolating

After retrieving the time series target cases T', extrapolate the target sequence to a specified length, we will have the result S.

(1) start from the end date of the T', to retrieve the latter part of the sequence, named S', the length required is specified by user;

(2) Calculate the mean and standard deviation of sequence T' and T, the ratio of means and standard deviations will be rendered as the adaptors that transforms S' to S.

(3)Apply the adaptors on S', to have the result S.

5 Experimental Results and Discussion

The experimental dataset is from Chinese futures market from Aug 1996 to Aug 1998. The series consists of 400 observation points, and the first 300 points were used as basis for the initial case. Although most of the comparison methods used does not require a training period, to maintain consistency, the forecasts were produced for all the methods staring with the period 301, ending at the period 400. Error of Relative Mean Average Deviation is measured, shown as follows:

$$RMAD \quad = \frac{\left(\sum_{i=1}^{n} |d_i - d_i'| \right)^2}{n(\overline{X} \cdot \overline{Y})} \tag{3}$$

where n is the length of forecasts(100 points), $\overline{X}$ and $\overline{Y}$ are the average of real values(100 points) respectively, and d_i, d_i' stand for the extrapolated value and real value of these 100 points. The results rendered are given in Table 3.

5.1 Comparative Evaluation

We choose ARMA, DES and APRE as comparative experiment. The value of the smoothing constant was set to 0.5 for alpha in DES. The autocorrelation and partial autocorrelation analysis showed that the time series follows ARIMA (2,1,2).

We show about 100 days extrapolation result of LME COPPER 03 after the *Reference Date*, based on daily data of about 300 out of 400 days before the *Reference Date* (Figure 3).

From the comparative experiment, TBM has twice accuracy as APRE, and outperforms ARMA as well. The error's stable standard deviation also testifies its stability. Due to paper limitation, a part of result for one of the time series (Contract 26) is displayed below:

From the residual ACF and PACF of Contract 26, the residual is random series, which testifies the validity of TBM. The algorithm outperforms classical approaches with relatively high accuracy and stability. In addition, the experimental result also shows that, with the increase of sequence length, the accuracy stably increases.

Table 3. Extrapolation Accuracy with DES, ARIMA, APRE

RMAD	DES	ARIMA	APRE	TBM
TS1	0.0182350	0.0123326	0.013768	0.007688
TS2	0.0120593	0.0092322	0.009229	0.006079
TS3	0.0125862	0.0094235	0.013449	0.007895
TS4	0.0094224	0.0075823	0.008181	0.004972
TS5	0.0157452	0.0125874	0.015637	0.009672
TS6	0.0200363	0.0178742	0.017143	0.009575
TS7	0.0100252	0.0073871	0.008984	0.005034
TS8	0.0014047	0.0102546	0.013196	0.008491
TS9	0.0151426	0.0125871	0.015170	0.00873
TS10	0.0142575	0.0098547	0.012412	0.007974
Aver.	0.0128914	0.010912	0.012717	0.007611
Std. Dev.	2.4766E-05	8.62E-06	8.27706E-06	2.63E-06

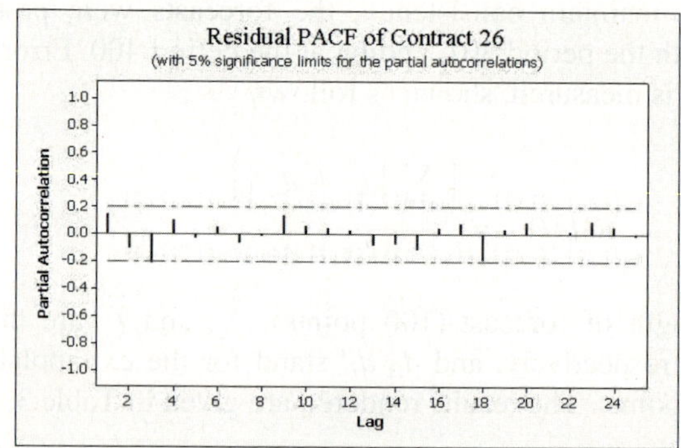

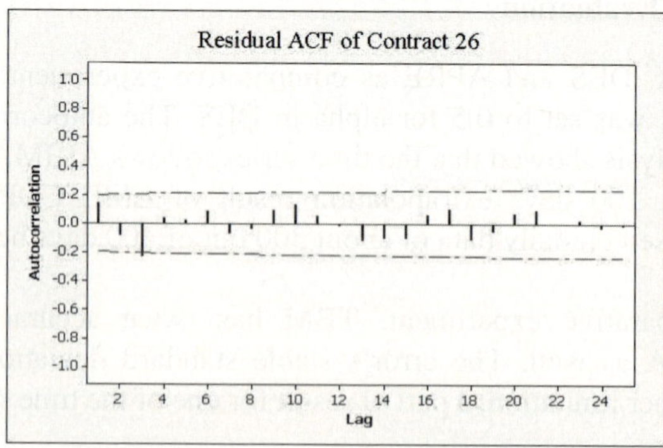

Fig. 4. Residual ACF and PACF for Contract 26 TBM Extrapolating

5.2 Limitations

The study has several limitations. (1) Our research is based on the assumption that, in financial time series the same shape will reoccur when the same condition happens. There is no solid theoretical basis that makes sure the trend of the target time series case can be the basis of forecasting the source time series. the assumption of reoccurence is best applicable in complete market enviornment, and may be not appropriate for non-complete ones. (2) the work is under an assumption that financial time sereis in a same futures market are totally independent, and have no interrelationship. We haven't take into account the inter-actional effect among the time series in the financial market. It is well-known that the assumption is not sufficient in real market. (3)The experimental results support our solution of financial time series well, however, the algorithm has not yet applied on other kinds of time series, which needs further observation.

6 Conclusion

In this paper, based on atomic patterns like "P","N","Z" (which are defined as 1st order atomic patterns), the idea defines binary operation among these 1st order atomic patterns, to further generate 13 2nd-order patterns, and then 169 3rd-order patterns. We examine the partial relationship among these patterns. They are assembled to be a template, with which we match the sequence during similarity mining. According to the partial relationship, matching will probably be more discrepancy-tolerance, but still reasonable. This idea can take into account some segments that are not neglectable. The higher the order is, the more accurate, without any loss of matchable sequences.

This paper offers the definition of 1st-order, 2nd-order and higher order atomic pattern within an integrated theoretical framework, based on which we propose an n-th order atomic pattern template-based matching algorithm (TBM). A solution for time series extrapolation is discussed. The experimental result has verified its distinct advantages over some similar and classical approaches both in accuracy and performance.

This research makes several contributions: (1) the theoretical model enables combination of atomic patterns of specified order. This model can be used as a general framework in similarity assessment in many areas; (2) a fast, simple algorithm is proposed, which facilitates time series extrapolating, with high accuracy and stability.

In sum, our algorithm improves the accuracy of time series extrapolating, especially in futures market, with a reasonable speed. The partially ordered similarity framework can be widely used in many similarity measurement occasions.

References

[1] N. Crato and B.K. Ray (1996) Model selection and forecasting for long-range dependent processes. Journal of Forecasting, 15,p107-125.

[2] Christos Faloutsos, M Ranganathan, Yannis Manolopoulos. Fast Subsequence Matching in Time-Series Database. In Proceedings 1994 ACM SIGMOD Conference, Minneapolis, 1994.

[3] C.C. Holt. Forecasting Seasonal and Trends by Exponentially Weighted Moving Averages, Carnegie Institute of Technology, Pittsburgh, Pennsylvania, 1957.

[4] Box E.P. George & Gwilym M. Jenkins: Time Series Analysis: Forecasting and Control, Holden Day, San Francisco,1970.

[5] Ge and Smyth. Deformable Markov model templates for time-series pattern matching [J]. KDD 2000: 81-90.

[6] M. West and J. Harrison (1997) Basyesian Forecasting and Dynamic Models, 2nd edn. NewYork: Springer.

[7] Jensen V. Finn: An Introduction to Bayesian Networks[M], UCL Press, London, 1996.

[8] Altrock von Constantin: Fuzzy Logic and Neuro Fuzzy Applications Explained, Prentice Hall, Englewood Cliffs, 1995.

[9] Tsoukalas H. Lefteri & Uhrig E. Robert: Fuzzy and Neural Approaches in Engineering, John Wiley, New York, 1997.

[10] Zadeh A. Lotfi, Fu King-Sun, Tanaka Kokichi & Shimura Masamichi (eds): Fuzzy Sets and their Applications to Cognitive and Decision Processes, Academic Press, New York, 1975.

[11] Eamonn J. Keogh, Michael J. Pazzani. "A simple dimensionality reduction technique for fast similarity search in large time series databases." In the Fourth Pacific- Asia Conference on Knowledge Discovery and Data Mining. Kyoto, Japan, 2000.

[12] Eamonn J. Keogh, Michael J. Pazzani: An Indexing Scheme for Fast Similarity Search in Large Time Series Databases. SSDBM 1999: 56-67. 1998.

[13] Eamonn J. Keogh, Kaushik Chakrabarti, Michael J. Pazzani, Sharad Mehrotra: Dimensionality Reduction for Fast Similarity Search in Large Time Series Databases. Knowl. Inf. Syst. 3(3): 263-286 (2001). 2000.

[14] R. Agrawal, K I Lin, IIS Sawhney. Shim K. Fast Similarity Search in the Presence of Noise, Scaling, and translation in Time Series Database. Proc 21st Int'l Conf. VLDB, Sept, 1995, 490-500.

[15] R. Agrawal, C. Faloutsos, A.Swami: Efficient Similarity Search in Sequence Database. Proc 4th Int'l Conf. Foundations of Data Organization and Algorithms, Oct, 1993, 69-84

[16] Eamonn J. Keogh, Michael J. Pazzani. Scaling up Dynamic Time Warping for Datamining Applications, Knowledge Discovery and Data Mining, in ACM 2000 1-58

[17] Berndt and Clifford. Using Dynamic Time Warping to Find Patterns in Time Series. KDD Workshop 1994: 359-370.

[18] Chang-Shing Perng, Haixun Wang, Sylvia R. Zhang, D. Stott Parker. Landmarks- A New Model for Similarity-Based Pattern Querying in Time Series Databases. 16th International Conference on Data Engineering ICDE'2000: 33-42, 2000

[19] Branko Pecar. Case-based Algorithm for Pattern Recognition and Extrapolation [C]. The 7th UK Case-Based Reasoning Workshop, In 22nd SGAI Int'l Conf. on Knowledge Based Systems and Applied Artificial Intelligence, Cambridge, 10-12 December 2002

[20] Goldin, Kanellakis. On Similarity Queries for Time Series Data: Constraint Specification and Implementation. CP 1995, pp137-153.

[21] Davood Rafiei,Alberto O. Mendelson. Querying Time Series Data Based on Similarity. In IEEE TRANS. ON KNOWLEDGE AND DATA ENG., VOL. 12, NO.5, SEP/OCT 2000.

[22] Betty B. Xia. Similarity Search in Time Series Data Sets, M.Sc. thesis, Computing Science, Simon Fraser University, December 1997.

Model and Algebra for Genetic Information of Data*

Deyou Tang[1,2], Jianqing Xi[1,**], and Yubin Guo[1]

[1] School of Computer Science and Engineering, South China University of Technology,
Guangzhou, 510641, China
[2] Department of Computer Science & Technology, Hunan Polytechnic University,
Zhuzhou, 412008, China
deyou_tang@126.com, jianqingxi@163.com, guoyubin@people.com.cn

Abstract. The genetic information of data is the evolution information about data in its lifecycle, and it performs heredity and mutation with the diffusion of data. Managing the genetic information of data has significance to the information discrimination, auditing, tracing and lookup. This paper presents Data Genome Model (DGM) and its algebra to manage the genetic information of data in its lifecycle according to the gene of life. A structure named data genome is used to carry the genetic information of data and querying algebras are defined to manipulate the genetic information.

1 Introduction

Under the environment of complex networks, data is exchanged frequently. In this process, huge amounts of information about the evolution are created. E.g. when data is published, information hiding behind this operation includes the publisher, publishing time, etc. This information has great significance to the incremental utilization of data. Suppose some unhealthy pictures are disseminated in a pure p2p network such as Gnutella[1]. To punish the badman who issues the resource initially, related department has to take long time and much human resource to identify the source step by step. The problem is that no evolution information can be retrieved from the data itself. However, if each item shared in Gnutella has some adjunctive information about the evolution of data such as publisher, propagation path, etc, intelligence agent can do their job through analyzing this information, thus saves much expense. Unfortunately, current data models usually focus on the content or the external characteristic of data, and little attention has been paid to the evolution of data.

Metadata are the data about data in applications. But metadata only expresses the static properties of data, and it doesn't describe the evolution of data.

The concept of "temporal" is used in temporal database to describe history information about data [2]. TXPath model [3] extended the XPath data model to model the history of semi-structured data. The GEM model [4] is a graphical semi-structured

---

* This work is supported by the China Ministry of Education (Grant NoD4109029), Guangdong High-Tech Program (G03B2040770), and Guangdong Natural Science Foundation (B6480598).
** Correspondence author.

M. Ali and R. Dapoigny (Eds.): IEA/AIE 2006, LNAI 4031, pp. 1071–1079, 2006.

temporal data model. These temporal data models use the history information of data effectively, but they don't express the relevancy of different data.

Adoc[5] is a new programming model targeted to collaborative business process integration applications. The concept of "smart distance" was proposed to interweave various dynamic and heterogeneous elements of information system on the base of Adoc[6]. ABO was presented to model the lifecycle of the business entity [7]. However, those methods don't model the evolution of data.

Information Lifecycle Management (ILM) aims at improving system resource utilization and maximizing information value automatically for fixed-content reference data [8][9]. Unfortunately, ILM doesn't take into account the value of evolution information created in data lifecycle.

In this paper, we present Data Genome Model (DGM) to manage the information created in the evolution of data, which is called genetic information. A series of concepts like *data gene, data gene sequence* and *data genome* are introduced to carry the genetic information hierarchically. Data genome algebras are presented to query the genetic information stored in data genomes.

2 Data Genome Model

In biology, the genetic information of life determines the variety and lineage of species, and a genome is the complete set of genetic information that an organism possesses. The genetic information of parents transmits to offspring along with the evolution of life, and different species have different genetic information.

In the evolution of data, information about the evolutionary process are created, including the creator, creation time and descriptive keywords when data is created, the publisher, publishing time and receivers when data is published, the correlation with other data. This kind of information closely correlates with data, and it is created when data is created and deleted when data is deleted. At the same time, it changes with the evolution of data and is different for different phase in the lifecycle of data. Furthermore, it will be transmitted to other data partially or fully in the evolutionary process. As information created in the evolution of data has the above features, we think data has the genetic information too [10]. In this paper, we call this information the genetic information of data and put forward a concept called *data genome* to carry the genetic information of data with genome in biology as reference.

Suppose A is an attribute name of data or operation, and V is its value. We use the concept of data gene, data gene sequence and data genome to carry genetic information for data hierachically. Data gene carries a piece of genetic information for data and describes some characteristics of data at the given condition. Data gene sequence carries the genetic information of a "segment" in the evolution of data. Data genome is "all-sided" to represent the evolution of data and carries genetic information for the whole data.

Definition 1 (Data gene). *A data gene fragment F is a 2-tuple*: $F = (A,V)$, *data gene is the positive closure of F*: $D = F^+ = (A,V)^+$.

Data gene fragment is the minimal unit of genetic information, and the selection of attributes and their domain depends on the situation of applications. Data gene can describe any characteristics of data, for example, it may be a description of *browse* operation or the metadata at the given time. For any data, a whole impression about data at any moment is encoded in the leading data gene.

Definition 2 (Leading data gene). *A leading data gene carries the instant information about data as a whole, denoted as* D_a.

D_a is created when data is created, it holds the global information about data like identifier, title, creator, and so on.

Definition 3 (Data gene sequence). *Data gene sequence is a 2-tuple,* $S=<\$sid, D^+>$, *where* $\$sid$ *is the identifier of the sequence,* D^+ *is the positive closure of data genes that describes the same characteristics of data.*

Usually, we need many data gene sequences to describe the genetic information of data perfectly, and each data gene sequence encodes part of genetic information. The most important data gene sequence is the main data gene sequence.

Definition 4 (Main data gene sequence). *A main data gene sequence* S_m *is a data gene sequence, which describes the global characteristics of data and its evolution.*

S_m includes the leading data gene and data genes carrying the history of those data gene fragments in the leading data gene.

Definition 5 (Data genome). *Data genome DG is a 3-tuple:* $<\$gid, S^+, DG'^* >$, *where* $\$gid$ *is the identifier of data genome,* S^+ *is a positive closure of data gene sequence,* DG' *is a component data genome of DG and* DG'^* *is a Klein closure of* DG'.

In definition 5, $\$gid$ must be unique globally. S^+ has at least one data gene sequence, S_m, and each sequence in it must have different identifer. The component data genome set DG'^* carries genetic information for partial data retrieved from other data sources. Component data genome DG' is a data genome mutated from the data genome of correlated data. In addition, data gene sequences in DG' have main data gene sequence only and the main data gene sequence has a leading data gene only, so do the component data genomes in DG'. Furthermore, for each data genome in DG'^*, there is a sequence in S^+ to record the correlation, whose identifier is equal to the identifier of the component data genome.

Figure 1 is a referenced implementation of data genome for the text file. It is composed of six data gene sequences and two component data genomes. Sequence $\$gid_1$ (Herein, each sequence mentioned belongs to data genome dg) is composed of a leading data gene and two ordinary data genes. From the leading data gene in sequence $\$gid_1$, we can get a whole impression of *Test*. The other two data genes in sequence $\$gid_1$ denote the history of the corresponding data gene fragments in the leading data gene. Sequence $\$sid_3$ carries the genetic information about the history of being edited for data. Data genes in sequence $\$sid_6$ indicate that Tom forwarded this data to Mike and Jane on 06/18/2005 and Mike forwarded this data to Jim on 06/19/2005. Data gene in sequence $\$sid_7$ indicates that Jim browsed this data on 06/20/2005. Sequence $\$gid_2$ is in accordance with component data genome dg_2. The only data gene in sequence $\$gid_2$ denotes that Tom correlated the component data genome to data genome $\$gid_{01}$ on 06/15/2005. Data gene sequence $\$sid_5$ carries the information of operating on the

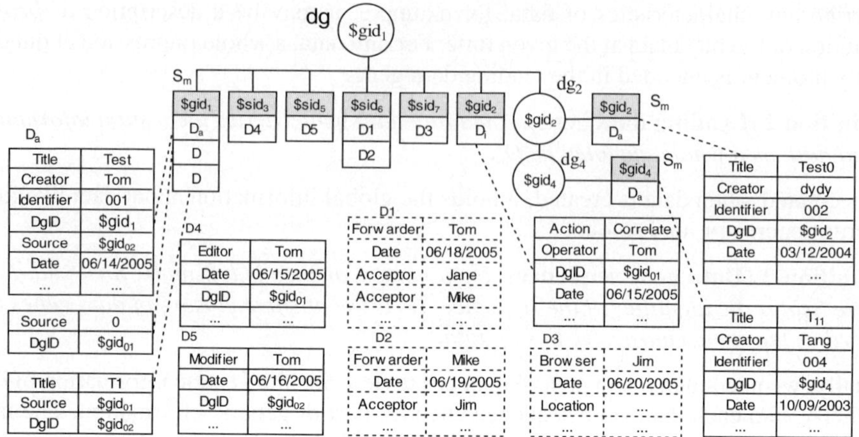

Fig. 1. The structure of data gene, data gene sequence and data genome [1]

leading data gene.Component data genome dg_2 is a sub data genome of data genome of data *Test0*, which means part of genetic information of *Test0* are transmited to *Test*.

Proposition 1. *Each main data gene sequence has a unique leading data gene.*

The leading data gene carries the genetic information of data resembled to metadata. Though all component genomes have their own leading data gene, they are local, and there is only one leading data gene belonging to the whole data. Usually, the structure of this gene is the most complex data gene in a data genome.

Proposition 2. *Each data genome has a unique main data gene sequence.*

The main data gene sequence records the global information of data and its evolution. Comparatively speaking, the main data gene sequence of each component data genome carries the genetic information for part of the data.

Proposition 3. *Each data has a unique data genome to carry its genetic information, and the data genome can be represented as a tree with the data genome as the root, data gene sequences as the leaf nodes and component data genomes as branch nodes.*

The simplest data genome has only two nodes, the root and a leaf, when represented as a tree. Once data correlates to other data, a data genome will be inserted into the component data genome set. Since each data genome has a unique main data gene sequence, we also use the identifier of the data genome to identify the main data gene sequence.

The definitions and propositions presented above give a framework for managing the adjunctive information of data created in its evolution. Since the type of data may vary

---

[1] Dashed lines are used to explain the structure of each data gene. 2). For simplicity, data genes and the *$sid* of each sequence in each data genome are displayed in a table, and different background colors are used to differ them.

from structured (e.g. relational data) to semi-structured (e.g. XML, code collections) to unstructured (word document), we give the privilege of modeling the behaviours of such types of data to users and we give the framwork only.

3 Data Genome Algebra Operations

The data genome algebra includes eight operators, they are *union, intersection, difference, select, project, iterate, filter* and *join*, which in turn are the basis of designing the genetic information querying language. As data gene is the basic operation unit in DGM, the data genome algebra operations are implemented on the base of algebra operations for data genes, which include *union, intersection, difference* and *project*. We introduce some symbols that are used in the remainder of this paper first.

Let G be the set of data genes, $g, g_i, g_j \in G$. Let DG be the set of data genomes, $dg, dg_i, dg_j, dg' \in DG$. $ID(s)$ denotes the identifier of data gene sequence s, $T(s)$ denotes the data genes set of s. $S(dg)$ denotes the set of data gene sequence in dg, $S_m(dg)$ denotes the main data gene sequence of dg, $\psi(dg)$ denotes the component data genome set of dg. $A(g)$ denotes attribute set of data gene g. $\mu_a(f)$ denotes the attribute of data gene fragment f.

Definition 6 (Algebra operations for data gene)
Union, $\cup$

$$g_i \cup g_j = \left\{ f \mid f \in g_i \vee f \in g_j \right\}$$

Intersection, $\cap$

$$g_i \cap g_j = \left\{ f \mid f \in g_i \wedge f \in g_j \right\}$$

Difference, $-$

$$g_i - g_j = \left\{ f \mid f \in g_i \wedge f \notin g_j \right\}$$

Project, π

$$\pi_{A'}(g) = \{ f \mid f \in g \wedge \mu_a(f) \in A' \}$$

Obviously, the result of *union, intersection* and *difference* is a data gene fragment set. Except for the algebra operations for data genes, the other two operations are also the basis of algebra operations for data genome.

Definition7 (Set operations of the main data gene sequence). *Suppose s_i and s_j are different main data gene sequences, and $I(s)$ denotes the leading data gene in the main data gene sequence.*

$$s' = s_i * s_j = \langle \$sid, T(s') \rangle \ where \quad * \in \{\cup, \cap, - \} \ and$$

$$\begin{cases} I(s') = I(s_i) * I(s_j) \\ T(s') = (T(s_i) - \{I(s_i)\}) * (T(s_j) - \{I(s_j)\}) \cup \{I(s')\} \end{cases}$$

Defintion 8 (Concatenation of data gene sequences). *Suppose s_i and s_j are data gene sequences, given the concatenating condition f, then*

$$s' = s_i \underset{f}{\infty} s_j = \langle \$sid, T(s') \rangle \text{ where}$$

$$T(s') = \bigcup (g_i \cup g_j) \quad g_i \in T(s_i) \wedge g_j \in T(s_j) \wedge f(g_i, g_j) = 1$$

The set operation for the main data gene sequence is defined for the set operations of data genomes, while the concatenation operation is defined for the *join* operation of data genomes.

Definition 9 (Algebra operations for data genome). *Let* $s' = S_m(dg')$, $s_i = S_m(dg_i)$, $s_j = S_m(dg_j)$.

Union, $\cup$

$$dg' = dg_i \cup dg_j = \langle \$gid', S(dg'), \psi(dg') \rangle$$

$$where \begin{cases} s' = s_i \cup s_j \\ S(dg') = (S(dg_i) - \{s_i\}) \cup (S(dg_j) - \{s_j\}) \cup \{s'\} \\ \psi(dg') = \psi(dg_i) \cup \psi(dg_j) \end{cases}$$

Intersection, $\cap$

$$dg' = dg_i \cap dg_j = \langle \$gid', S(dg'), \psi(dg') \rangle$$

$$where \begin{cases} s' = s_i \cap s_j \\ S(dg') = (S(dg_i) - \{s_i\}) \cap (S(dg_j) - \{s_j\}) \cup \{s'\} \\ \psi(dg') = \psi(dg_i) \cap \psi(dg_j) \end{cases}$$

Difference, $-$

$$dg' = dg_i - dg_j = \langle \$gid', S(dg'), \psi(dg') \rangle$$

$$where \begin{cases} s' = s_i - s_j \\ S(dg') = (S(dg_i) - \{s_i\}) - (S(dg_j) - \{s_j\}) \cup \{s'\} \\ \psi(dg') = \psi(dg_i) - \psi(dg_j) \end{cases}$$

Select, δ

$$\delta_{sc}(dg) = dg' = \langle \$gid', S(dg'), \phi \rangle$$

$$where\ S(dg') = \{s | s \in S(dg) \wedge sc(s) = true\}$$

Project, π

$$\pi_{A'}(dg) = dg' = \langle \$gid', S(dg'), \phi \rangle$$

$$where\ S(dg') = \left\{ s' | s' = \{\pi_{A'}(g) | g \in s \wedge A' \subseteq A(g)\} \wedge s \in S(dg) \right\}$$

Iterate, λ

$$\lambda_{a[max-iteration]}(dg) = dg' = \langle \$gid', \{s'\}, \phi \rangle$$

$$where\ T(s') = \{g | g \in \bigcup s \wedge s \in S(dg) \wedge a \in A(g)\}$$

$$\cup (\bigcup S(\lambda_{a[max-iteration-1]}(dg'))\quad dg' \notin \psi(dg))$$

Filter, $\mathcal{E}$

$$\mathcal{E}_f(dg) = \bigcup dg' \quad dg' \in \psi(dg) \wedge f(dg') = 1$$

Join, $\bowtie$

$$dg' = dg_i \underset{f}{\bowtie} dg_j = \langle \$gid', S(dg'), \psi(dg') \rangle$$

$$where \begin{cases} S(dg') = \bigcup(s_1 \underset{f}{\infty} s_2) \quad s_1 \in S(dg_i) \wedge s_2 \in S(dg_j) \\ \psi(dg') = \psi(dg_i) \cup \psi(dg_j) \end{cases}$$

Here in above, the result of each operator is a temporary data genome. The operator δ selects data gene sequences from the data gene sequence set of *dg* that satisfies the condition *sc*. Generally, we use this operator to select one data gene sequence from the data genome by refining a right condition. If no condition is specified, this operation will return a data genome without any component data genome.

The operator π filters out data genes whose attribute set is the superset of the given attribute set, gets rid of the redundant attributes and eliminates the repeated data gene for each data gene sequence in *S(dg)*. If no attribute set is specified, this operator will return a null data genome. The operator λ recursively traverses the specified attributes set *a* in the data genome. If no iteration limit is specified, this operation will traverse the whole data genome. If the iteration limit is zero, the temporary data genome will have one data gene sequence consisted of data genes with the given attributes in *S(dg)*. The operator $\mathcal{E}$ selects component data genomes from the data genome with the given filter condition *f*. If no condition is specified, this operator will return the union of all component data genomes in $\psi(dg)$.

In the *join* operation, *f* is a formula specifying the *join predicate*, which is a conjunctive form. Usually, it has the form of $c_1 \wedge c_2 ... \wedge c_n$, where $c_i (i = 1..n)$ has the generic form of $A_1 \otimes A_2$, A_1 and A_2 are attributes belonging to dg_i and dg_j separately, $\otimes$ is a comparison operator. If the operator $\otimes$ is "=", then this operation is an equi-join.

Suppose the structure of data genome for document is defined as the data genome in figure 1. Herein, we give some examples of queries.

Example 1. To query the history of being edited in 2005, including the operator and operation time.

$$\pi_{Editor,Action,Date}(\delta_{Date>12/31/2004 \wedge Date<01/01/2006}(dg))$$

Example 2. To list all data source related to *Test*:

$$\pi_{Title}(\lambda_{Identifier,Title}(dg))$$

Example 3. To list out the creator and creation time of the first correlated data of *Test*:

$$\pi_{Creator,Time}(\mathcal{E}_{\$gid=\$gid2}(dg))$$

Example 4. To list out the common correlated data:

$$\pi_{Title}(\lambda_{Identifier,Title}(dg_1)) \cap \pi_{Title}(\lambda_{Identifier,Title}(dg_2))$$

Example 5. To list out the edit history of T1(suppose the data genome is dg_1), which the operator is the creator of T2(Suppose its data genome is dg_2):

$$\pi_{Editor,Action,Date}dg_1 \underset{dg_1.Editor=dg_2.Creator}{\bowtie} dg_2$$

Definition 9 presents data genome algebras to support the query of genetic information. In fact, we can organize data genomes into a data genome base and perform data mining on it. For example, if we organize data genomes with the same data identifier retrieved from the P2P network into a data genome base, we can mine out the number of contributors, track the distribution, trace the propagation path of each copy, etc.

4   Usages and Applications of DGM

The motivation of DGM is to manage information created in the evolution of data. Due to the limit of space, this paper can't elaborate on the manipulation of data genome and the simulation of its evolution with the evolution of data. The details will be reported in other papers, and we here only give a brief introduction of its usages and list some applications.

Data genome can attach to any types of data and be applied in any information systems if the corresponding information systems have the ability of supporting DGM. For example, when we create a text file in an editor, the editor should create a data genome for the file accordingly. Once the editor saves data, a data gene carrying the operation information is inserted into the corresponding data genome (such as D_4 in figure 1). Moreover, if the file (suppose its data genome is dg) correlates to other file (suppose its data genome is dg'), the editor should mutate dg' as a component data genome of dg, and insert a new data gene sequence that identifier equals to the identifier of the main data sequence of dg' into the data gene sequence set of dg to express the correlation (such as dg_2 and $\$gid_2$ in figure 1).

DGM can be used in information tracking, data mining, information integration, semantic web, and so on. Take information tracking for example, we can find out the source and the propagation path of data instantly using the algebras defined in the previous section or special tools based on data genome. E.g., we can use $\Pi_{Forwarder, Acceptor}(dg)$ to filter out the forwarders and their acceptors in figure 1 and construct a propagation graph based on the result, as shown in figure 2. From figure 2, we know that Tom is the creator of file *Test* and he transmits the file to Mike, and Mike transmits the file to Jim subsequently.

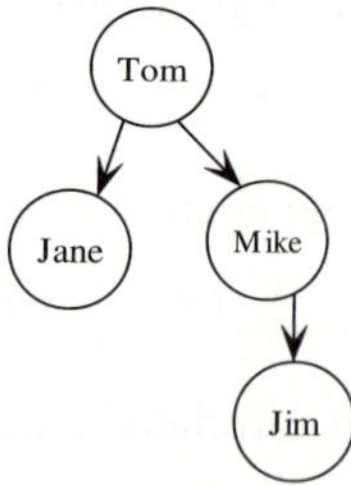

Fig. 2. A propagation graph constructed by Jim

5   Conclusions and Future Works

This paper presents DGM and its algebras to model and manipulate the evolution of data. However, the research of DGM is just underway, and no parallel work has been found yet. This model may be not perfect yet, and much work has to be done to improve this model.

Currently, we are working for the user interfaces of data genome and implementing a file exchange system using the DGM as the base of tracking the lineage of different file appeared in the system. The programming interfaces of data genome include the manipulation interfaces and query interfaces. The data genome manipulation interfaces include creating data genome for any type of data, evolving data genome to synchronize the evolution data, etc. Though we present the algebras of data genome in this paper, we are sure a friendly user programming interfaces is necessary.

In addition, our work can be extended in several ways. First, as we only give a conceptual model for the genetic information of data to date, we plan to design a storage model for DGM recently. Second, we think the number of data gene sequences in a data genome is different for different type of data such as text files, applications, databases etc, so we need to study the metadata of data genome for different type of data. Third, we need to give some tools to mine the value of genetic information more than query language, such as information track system based on DGM, information retrival system with data genome, etc. Moreover, extending DGM to support service is also a prospective direction.

References

1. Gnutella. http://gnutella.wego.com.
2. A. Tansel, J. Clifford, S. Gadia, S. Jajodia, A. Segev, and R.T. Snodgrass, Temporal Databases: Theory, Design, and Implementation, eds.,Benjamin/Cummings, 1994
3. http://www.w3.org/TR/xpath20/
4. C. Combi, B. Oliboni, and E. Quintarelli. A Graph-Based Data Model to Represent Transaction Time in Semistructured Data. DEXA 2004: 559-568
5. S. Kumaran, P. Nandi, T. Heath, K. Bhaskaran, and R. Das. ADoc-Oriented Programming. SAINT 2003: 334-343
6. Y.M. Ye, P. Nandi, and S. Kumaran, Smart Distance for Information Systems: The Concept. IEEE Computational Intelligence Bulletin 2(1), 2003: 25-30
7. P. Nandi, and S. Kumaran. Adaptive Business Objects - A new Component Model for Business Integration. ICEIS (3), 2005: 179-188
8. D. Reiner, G. Press, M. Lenaghan, D. Barta and R. Urmston, Information lifecycle management: the EMC perspective. Proceedings of the 20th International Conference on Data Engineering, 2004:804 - 807
9. Y. Chen. Information Valuation for Information Lifecycle Management, Proceedings of the Second International Conference on Autonomic Computing (ICAC'05), 2005:135 – 146
10. J.Q. Xi, D.Y. Tang, and Y.B. Guo, Data Gene: the Genetic Information Carrier of Data. Computer Engineering (In Chinese, in press).

Forecasting Intermittent Demand by Fuzzy Support Vector Machines

Yukun Bao, Hua Zou, and Zhitao Liu

Department of Management Science and Information System, School of Management,
Huazhong University of Science and Technology, Wuhan 430074, China
yukunbao@mail.hust.edu.cn

Abstract. Intermittent demand appears at random, with many time periods having no demand,which is probably the biggest challenge in the repair and overhaul industry. Exponential smoothing is used when dealing with such kind of demand. Based on it, more improved methods have been studied such as Croston method. This paper proposes a novel method to forecast the intermittent parts demand based on fuzzy support vector machines (FSVM) in regression. Details on data clustering, performance criteria design, kernel function selection are presented and an experimental result is given to show the method's validity.

1 Introduction

A fundamental aspect of supply chain management is accurate demand forecasting. We address the problem of forecasting intermittent (or irregular) demand. Intermittent demand appears at random, with many time periods having no demand [1]. Moreover, when a demand occurs, the request is sometimes for more than a single unit. Items with intermittent demand include service (spare) parts and high-priced capital goods, such as heavy machinery. Such items are often described as "slow moving". Demand that it intermittent is often also "lumpy", meaning that there is great variability among the nonzero value. An example of the difference between intermittent demand data and product demand data that is normal, or "smooth", is illustrated in the tables below:

Table 1. Intermittent Demand Data

Month	1	2	3	4	5	6	7	8	9	10	11	12	13	14	15	16	17
Demand	0	0	**19**	0	0	0	**4**	**18**	**17**	0	0	0	0	0	**3**	0	0

Table 2. Normal, Smooth Demand Data

Month	1	2	3	4	5	6	7	8	9	10	11	12	13	14	15	16	17
Demand	17	20	18	25	30	68	70	41	32	35	66	26	23	25	25	28	36

M. Ali and R. Dapoigny (Eds.): IEA/AIE 2006, LNAI 4031, pp. 1080–1089, 2006.
© Springer-Verlag Berlin Heidelberg 2006

Intermittent demand creates significant problems in the manufacturing and supply environment as far as forecasting and inventory control are concerned. It is not only the variability of the demand size, but also the variability of the demand pattern that make intermittent demand so difficult to forecast [2]. The literature, that includes a relatively small number of proposed forecasting solutions to this demand uncertainty problem, can be found in [3-6]. The single exponential smoothing and the Croston methods are the most frequently used methods for forecasting low and intermittent demands [4,6]. Croston [4] proposed a method that builds demand estimates taking into account both demand size and the interval between demand incidences. Despite the theoretical superiority of such an estimation procedure, empirical evidence suggests modest gains in performance when compared with simpler forecasting techniques; some evidence even suggests losses in performance. On the other hand, Bartezzaghi et al. [3] in their experimental simulation found that EWMA appears applicable only with low levels of lumpiness. Willemain et al. [6] concluded that the Croston method is significantly superior to exponential smoothing under intermittent demand conditions.

Recently, support vector machines (SVMs) was developed by Vapnik and his co-workers [7,8]. With the introduction of Vapnik's -insensitive loss function, SVMs have been extended to solve non-linear regression estimation problems and they have been shown to exhibit excellent performance [7,8].

Since SVMs are formulated for two-class problems, some input points may not be exactly assigned to one of these two classes. Some are more important to be fully assigned to one class so that SVM can separate these points more correctly. Some data points corrupted by noises are less meaningful and the machine should better to discard them. SVM lacks this kind of ability. To solve this problem, Fuzzy support vector machines (FSVM) apply a fuzzy membership to each input point of SVM such that different input points can make different contributions to the learning of decision surface and can enhances the SVM in reducing the effect of outliers and noises in data points [9-11].

Our research focuses on the application of FSVM in regression to make a new attempt to novel forecasting method toward the intermittent demand. The results of experiment indicate that FSVM is effective in improving the accuracy of intermittent demand forecasting compared with the Croston method which has been a widely used method in intermittent demand forecasting.

This paper consists of five sections. Section 2 reviews the most widely used approach for forecasting intermittent demand and indicates its limitation and the direction of further improvement. General principles of FSVM and its application in regression are presented in Section 3, together with the general procedures of applying it. Section 4 presents an experiment concerned with the detailed procedures of how to employing FSVM in regression, involving data set selection, data preprocessing and clustering, kernel function selection and so on. Conclusions and discussion for further research hints are included in the last section.

2   Reviews on Forecasting Intermittent Demand Methods

Generally efforts on forecasting the intermittent demand could fall into two categories. One is to find the distribution function and the other is time series forecasting.

2.1   Demand Distribution Estimation

The inventory control method proposed here relies on the estimation of the distribution of demand for low demand parts. It is necessary to use demand distributions rather than expected values of demand because the intermittent patterns characteristic of low demand parts require a probabilistic approach to forecasting that can be incorporated into an inventory management program. Using the demand distributions, it is possible to manage the inventory to maximize readiness given a fixed inventory budget. Other optimization goals are possible as well.

The chief obstacle to reliable demand distribution estimation is the paucity of historical data available for any typical set of low demand parts. Demand typically occurs in small integer numbers of parts. Some parts may have only 3 or 4 non-zero demands among a large number of zero demand periods. This amount of data is not sufficient to construct a robust probability demand distribution. If a probabilistic model of the demand is available, such as a Weibull model or Poisson model, then it is possible to estimate the demand distribution directly from the model. If an empirical estimate of the demand distribution must derived, through bootstrapping or other means, it is necessary to group the data in a way that generates enough non-zero data points to produce robust demand distribution estimates.

2.2   Croston Method

Croston method falls into the time series forecasting category and is the most widely used method, which could be illustrated as follows.

Let Y_t be the demand occurring during the time period t and X_t be the indicator variable for non-zero demand periods; i.e., $X_t = 1$ when demand occurs at time period t and $X_t = 0$ when no demand occurs. Furthermore, let j_t be number of periods with nonzero demand during interval $[0, t]$ such that $j_t = \sum_{i=1}^{t} X_i$, i.e., j_t is the index of the the non-zero demand. For ease of notation, we will usually drop the subscript t on j . Then we let Y_j^* represent the size of the j th non-zero demand and Q_j the inter-arrival time between Y_{j-1}^* and Y_j^*. Using this notation, we can write $Y_j = X_t Y_j^*$.

Croston method separately forecasts the non-zero demand size and the inter-arrival time between successive demands using simple exponential smoothing (SES), with forecasts being updated only after demand occurrences. Let Z_j and P_j be the forecasts of the $(j+1)_{th}$ demand size and inter-arrival time respectively, based on data up to demand j. Then Croston method gives

$$Z_j = (1 - \alpha) Z_{j-1} + \alpha Y_j^* \tag{1}$$

$$P_j = (1 - \alpha) P_{j-1} + \alpha P_j \tag{2}$$

The smoothing parameter α takes values between 0 and 1 and is assumed to be the same for both Y_j^* and Q_j . Let $l = j_n$ denote the last period of demand. Then the mean demand rate, which used as the h-step ahead forecast for the demand at time $n + h$ is estimated by the ratio

$$\hat{Y}_{n+h} = Z_l \,/\, P_l \tag{3}$$

The assumptions of Croston method could be derived that (1) the distribution of non-zero demand sizes Y_j^* is iid normal;(2) the distribution of inter-arrival times Q_j is iid Geometric; and (3)demand sizes Y_j^* and inter-arrival times Q_j are mutually independent. These assumptions are clearly incorrect, as the assumption of iid data would result in using the simple mean as the forecast, rather than simple exponential smoothing, for both processes. This is the basic reason for more correction and modification toward Croston method.

3   FSVM for Forecasting

In this section we briefly review the description about the idea and formulations of FSVM in regression problem. In regression problem, the effects of the training points are different. It is often that some training points are more important than others, so we apply a fuzzy membership $0 \leq s_i \leq 1$ associated with each training point x_i. This fuzzy membership s_i can be regarded as the attitude of the corresponding training point toward the mapping function and the value $(1 - s_i)$ can be regarded as the attitude of meaningless. In a result, the traditional SVM was extended as FSVM.

Given a set S of data points with associated fuzzy membership

$$(x_1, y_1, s_1) \quad (x_i, y_i, s_i) \tag{4}$$

where $x_i \in R^n$ is the input vector,$y_i \in R$ is the desired value, and a fuzzy membership $\sigma \leq s_i \leq 1$ with $i = 1, ..., n$ and sufficient small $\sigma > 0$. The FSVM regression solves and optimization problem:

$$\min_{\omega, p, \xi, \xi^*} \quad C \sum_{i=1}^{n} s_i(\xi_i + \xi_i^*) + \frac{1}{2}\omega^T \omega$$

$$Subject\ to \begin{cases} y_i - \omega^T \phi(x_i) - b_i \leq \varepsilon + \xi_i, \xi_i \geq 0 \\ \omega^T \phi(x_i) + b_i - y_i \leq \varepsilon + \xi_i^*, \xi_i^* \geq 0 \\ i = 1, ..., n \end{cases} \tag{5}$$

where ϕ is the high dimensional feature space which is non-linearly mapped from the input space x , ξ_i is the upper training error (ξ_i^* is lower), subject to the *varepsilon* -insensitive tube:

$$|y - (\omega^T \phi(x) + b)| \leq \varepsilon \tag{6}$$

The parameters that control the regression performance are the cost of error C, the width of the tube ε, the mapping function $\phi(x)$ and the fuzzy membership s_i. Usually, it is more convenient to solve the dual of Eq.(5) by introducing Lagrange multipliers α_i^*, α_i, and leads to a solution of the form

$$f(x, \alpha_i, \alpha_i^*) = \sum_{i=1}^{n} (\alpha_i - \alpha_i^*) K(x, x_i) + b,$$
$$0 \le \alpha_i^*, \alpha_i \le s_i C \tag{7}$$

In Eq. (7), α_i and α_i^* satisfy the equalities $\alpha_i * \alpha_i^* = 0$, $\alpha_i \ge 0$ and $\alpha_i^* \ge 0$ where i = 1,2,,n and are obtained by maximizing the dual function of Eq. (7) which has the following form:

$$R(a_i, a_i^*) = \sum_{i=1}^{n} y_i (a_i - a_i^*) - \varepsilon \sum_{i=1}^{n} (a_i + a_i^*)$$
$$- \frac{1}{2} \sum_{i=1}^{n} \sum_{j=1}^{n} (a_i - a_i^*) (a_j - a_j^*) K(x_i, x_j) \tag{8}$$

with the constraints

$$\sum_{i=1}^{n} (a_i - a_i^*),$$
$$0 \le a_i \le C, \quad i = 1, 2, \cdots, n$$
$$0 \le a_i^* \le C, \quad i = 1, 2, \cdots, n \tag{9}$$

Based on the Karush-Kuhn-Tucker (KKT) conditions of quadratic programming, only a certain number of coefficients $(a_i - a_i^*)$ in Eq.(5) will assume non-zero values. The data points associated with them have approximation errors equal to or larger than ε and are referred to as support vectors. Generally, the larger the ε, the fewer the number of support vectors and thus the sparser the representation of the solution.

$K(x_i, x_j)$ is defined as the kernel function. The value of the kernel is equal to the inner product of two vectors X_i and X_j in the feature space $\phi(x_i)$ and $\phi(x_j)$, that is, $K(x_i, x_j) = \phi(x_i) * \phi(x_j)$. Any function satisfying Mercer's condition can be used as the kernel function.

From the implementation point of view, training SVMs is equivalent to solving a linearly constrained quadratic programming (QP) with the number of variables twice as that of the training data points. Generally speaking, application of FSVM for forecasting follows the procedures: (1) Transform data to the format of an FSVM and conduct simple scaling on the data; (2) Generate the fuzzy membership; (3) Choose the kernel functions; (4) Use cross-validation to find the best parameter and ; (5) Use the best parameter and to train the whole training set; (6) Test.

4   Experimental Setting

4.1   Data Sets

Forecasting and inventory management for intermittent demand parts is particularly problematic because of the large number of low demand parts that must be considered. As an experiment setting, of 5,000 unique non-repairable spare parts for the Daya Bay Nuclear station in China, over half of those parts have been ordered 10 time or less in the last ten years. While many of these low demand parts are important for the safe operation of the nuclear reactor, it is simply uneconomical to stock enough spares to guarantee that every low demand part will be available when needed.

4.2   Clustering for Data Preprocessing

Clustering is the process of grouping parts with similar demand patterns. There are several methods to cluster data, among which, agglomerative hierarchical clustering and c-means clustering are two typical methods. We have found that demand patterns can be robustly clustered by using cumulative demand patterns. As the cumulative demand patterns avoids problems invoked by the intermittent pattern of incremental demand. Figure 1 shows one of prototype cumulative demand patterns after clustering 4063 low demand spare parts into 10 clusters. Prototype patterns represent the typical demand pattern for each cluster. The cluster size ranges from 34 parts to 241 parts plotted are the $25th$ and $75th$ percentiles of demand gathered from the cumulative demand of the individual parts in each cluster. Clustering was accomplished using a fuzzy c-means (FCM) clustering routine [12]. The generalized objective function subject to the same fuzzy c-partition constraints[13] is:

$$\text{Min } J_m\left(U, V\right) = \sum_{i=1}^{c}\sum_{k=1}^{n}\left(\mu_{ik}\right)^{m}\left\|x_k - v_i\right\|^2 \tag{10}$$

During our experiment, one of the problems associated with clustering is the difficulty in determining the number of clusters, c. Various validity measures have been proposed to determine the optimal number of clusters in order to address this inherent drawback of FCM [13]. In our experiment, the optimal number of terms is defined as the one that has the lowest mean squared error (MSE). The least MSE measure is also used to identify the most appropriate form of membership functions. In summary, the application procedure of the FCM has the following steps:(1) choose $c\left(2 \leq c \leq n\right), m\left(1 < m <\infty\right)$ and initialize the membership matrix. (2) Read in the data set and find the maximum and minimum values. (3) Calculate cluster centers but force the two clusters with the largest and smallest values to take the maximum and minimum domain values. (4) Update the membership matrix (5) Compute the change of each value in the membership matrix and determine whether the maximum change is smaller than the threshold value chosen to stop the iterative process (set at 0.02 throughout this study). If not, return to Step 3. (6) Redistribute erroneous membership

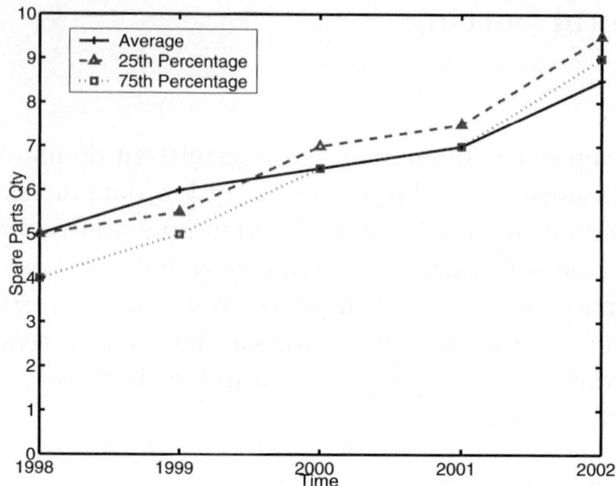

Fig. 1. Cumulative demand pattern of Cluster 1

values to the other two more appropriate terms proportional to their current membership values.

4.3   Defining Fuzzy Membership

It is easy to choose the appropriate fuzzy membership. First, we choose $\sigma > 0$ as the lower bound of fuzzy membership. Second, we make fuzzy membership s_i be a function of time t_i

$$s_i = f(t_i) \tag{11}$$

We suppose the last point x_n be the most important and choose $x_n = f(t_n) = 1$, and the first point x_1 be the most least important and choose $s_1 = f(t_1) = \sigma$. If we want to let fuzzy membership be a linear function of the time, we can select

$$s_i = f(t_i) = \alpha t_i + b = \frac{1 - \sigma}{t_n - t_1} t_i + \frac{t_n \sigma - t_1}{t_n - t_1} \tag{12}$$

If we want to make fuzzy membership be a quadric function of the time, we can select

$$s_i = f(t_i) = \alpha(t_i - b)^2 + c = (1 - \sigma)\left(\frac{t_i - t_1}{t_n - t_1}\right)^2 + \sigma \tag{13}$$

4.4   Kernel Function Parameters Selection

We use general RBF as the kernel function. The RBF kernel nonlinearly maps samples into a higher dimensional space, so it, unlike the linear kernel, can handle the case when the relation between class labels and attributes is nonlinear. Furthermore, the linear kernel is a special case of RBF as (Ref.[14]) shows that the linear kernel with a penalty parameter $\tilde{C}$ has the same performance as the RBF kernel with some parameters (C, γ). In addition, the sigmoid kernel behaves like RBF for certain parameters[15].The second reason is the number of hyper-parameters which influences the complexity of model selection. The polynomial kernel has more hyper-parameters than the RBF kernel. Finally, the RBF kernel has less numerical difficulties. One key point is $0 < K_{ij} \leq 1$ in contrast to polynomial kernels of which kernel values may go to infinity $\left(\gamma x_i^T x_j + r > 1\right)$ or zero $\left(\gamma x_i^T x_j + r < 1\right)$ while the degree is large.

There are two parameters while using RBF kernels: C and γ. It is not known beforehand which C and γ are the best for one problem; consequently some kind of model selection (parameter search) must be done. The goal is to identify good (C, γ) so that the classifier can accurately predict unknown data (i.e., testing data). Note that it may not be useful to achieve high training accuracy (i.e., classifiers accurately predict training data whose class labels are indeed known). Therefore, a common way is to separate training data to two parts of which one is considered unknown in training the classifier. Then the prediction accuracy on this set can more precisely reflect the performance on classifying unknown data. An improved version of this procedure is cross-validation.

We use a grid-search on C and γ using cross-validation. Basically pairs of (C, γ) are tried and the one with the best cross-validation accuracy is picked. We found that trying exponentially growing sequences of C and γ is a practical method to identify good parameters (for example, $C = 2^{-5}, 2^{-3}, \cdots, 2^{15}; \gamma = 2^{-15}, 2^{-13}, \cdots, 2^3$).

4.5   Performance Criteria

The prediction performance is evaluated using the normalized mean squared error (NMSE). NMSE is the measures of the deviation between the actual and predicted values. The smaller the values of NMSE, the closer are the predicted time series values to the actual values. The NMSE of the test set is calculated as follows:

$$\text{NMSE} = \frac{1}{\delta^2 n} \sum_{i=1}^{n} \left(y_i - \hat{y}_i\right)^2, \tag{14}$$

$$\delta^2 = \frac{1}{n-1} \sum_{i=1}^{n} \left(y_i - \overline{y}\right)^2, \tag{15}$$

where n represents the total number of data points in the test set. $\hat{y}_i$ represents the predicted value. $\overline{y}$ denotes the mean of the actual output values. Table 3 shows the NMSE values of different kernel functions compared with Croston method and tells out the best prediction method under our numerical case.

4.6   Experimental Results

Still raise the example of Cluster 1, Figure 2 shows the experimental esults by comparing the forecasting results of actual data, Croston method and FSVM regression. By summing all the clusters' result, SVMs regression method's accuracy is 11.6% higher than Croston method by the computation of standard deviation.

Table 3. NMSE Values of comparative methods

Methods	NMSE
FSVMs_RBF	0.3720
FSVMs_Linear	0.5945
FSVMs_Polynomial	0.6054
Croston	0.5730

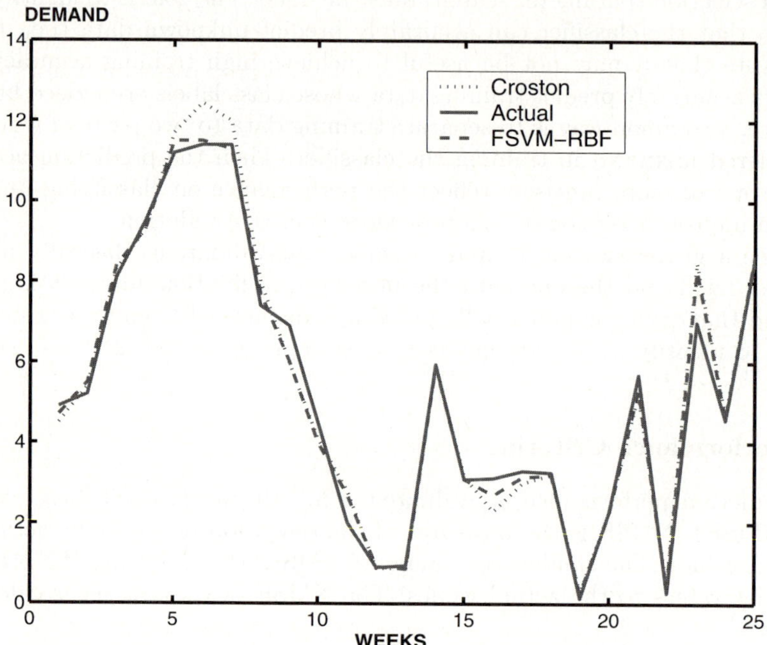

Fig. 2. Forecasting results comparison of Cluster 1

5 Conclusions

The use of FSVM in forecasting intermittent demand is studied in this paper. The study concluded that FSVM provide a promising alternative to forecast the intermittent demand. But further research toward an extremely changing data situation should be done, which means the data fluctuation may affect the performance of this method. In fact, we got confused with the experimental result at the every beginning without the data clustering. Another further research hint is the knowledge priority used in training the sample and determining the function parameters. This is to say, parameters selection is free but affect the performance a lot. A good parameter selection method should be worthy of further research.

Acknowledgements

This research is granted by National Science Foundation of China, No.70401015 and Hubei Provincial Key Social Science Research Center of Information Management.

References

1. Silver, E.A. Operations research in inventory management: A review and critique. Operations Research. **29** (1981) 628-645.
2. Syntetos A.A.,Boylan J.E. On the bias of intermittent demand estimates. International Journal of Production Economics.**71**(2001)457-466.
3. Bartezzaghi E, Verganti R and Zotteri G. A. Simulation framework for forecasting uncertain lumpy demand. International Journal of Production Economics. **59** (1999) 499-510.
4. Croston JD. Forecasting and stock control for intermittent demands. Operational Research Quarterly. **23(3)**(1972)289-303.
5. Rao AV. A comment on: forecasting and stock control for intermittent demands. Operational Research Quarterly. **24(4)**(1973)639-640.
6. Willemain TR, Smart CN, Shockor JH, DeSautels PA. Forecasting intermittent demand in manufacturing: a comparative evaluation of Croston's method. International Journal of Forecasting.**10(4)**(1994)529-538.
7. Vapnik VN, GolowichSE, Smola AJ. Support vector method for function approximation, regression estimation, and signal processing. Advances in Neural Information Processing Systems.**9** (1996)281-7.
8. Vapnik VN. The nature of statistical learning theory. New York: Springer.(1995).
9. Abe, S., & Inoue, T. Fuzzy support vector machines for multi-class problems. Proceedings of the Tenth European symposium on Artificial Neural Networks (ESANN 2002), 113-118.
10. Chun-Fu Lin, Sheng-De Wang, Fuzzy Support Vector Machines, IEEE Trans on Neural Networks.**13(2)**(2002)464-471.
11. Dug H. H, Changha H.. Support vector fuzzy regression machines.Fuzzy Sets and Systems, 138 (2003) 271-281.
12. Medasani S, Kim J, Krishnapuram R. An overview of membership function generation techniques for pattern recognition. International Journal of Approximation Research. **19(2)**, (1998) 391-417.
13. N.R. Pal, J.C. Bezdek. On cluster validity for the fuzzy c-means model. IEEE Trans. Fuzzy Systems. **3(3)** (1995)370-379.
14. Haykin S. Neural networks: a comprehensive foundation. Englewood CliKs, NJ: Prentice Hall. (1999).
15. Zhang GQ, Michael YH. Neural network forecasting of the British Pound US Dollar exchange rate. Omega.**26(4)** (1998)495-506.

Nonlinear Discrete System Stabilisation
by an Evolutionary Neural Network

Wasan Srikasam, Nachol Chaiyaratana, and Suwat Kuntanapreeda

Research and Development Center for Intelligent Systems,
King Mongkut's Institute of Technology North Bangkok,
1518 Piboolsongkram Road, Bangsue, Bangkok 10800, Thailand
sir_tum@yahoo.com, nchl@kmitnb.ac.th, suwat@kmitnb.ac.th

Abstract. This paper presents the application of an evolutionary neural network controller in a stabilisation problem involving an inverted pendulum. It is guaranteed that the resulting closed-loop discrete system is asymptotically stable. The process of training the neural network controller can be treated as a constrained optimisation problem where the equality constraint is derived from the Lyapunov stability criteria. The decision variables in this investigation are made up from the connection weights in the neural network, a positive definite matrix required for the Lyapunov function and matrices for the stability constraint while the objective value is calculated from the closed-loop system performance. The optimisation technique chosen for the task is a variant of genetic algorithms called a cooperative coevolutionary genetic algorithm (CCGA). Two control strategies are explored: model-reference control and optimal control. In the model-reference control, the simulation results indicate that the tracking performance of the system stabilised by the evolutionary neural network is superior to that controlled by a neural network, which is trained via a neural network emulator. In addition, the system stabilised by the evolutionary neural network requires the energy in the level which is comparable to that found in the system that uses a linear quadratic regulator in optimal control. This confirms the usefulness of the CCGA in nonlinear discrete system stabilisation applications.

1   Introduction

Neural network controllers have been successfully applied to various nonlinear systems in the past decades. Since the goals of designing a closed-loop system must always include stability assurance, the need to guarantee the stability of neural network control systems is inevitable. The study into the stabilisation capability of neural network controllers can be divided into three main categories. In the first category, a modification of learning algorithms is made where the search for appropriate connection weights is limited to the space at which the stability can be guaranteed. In the second category, a neural network is used to approximate the behaviour of the nonlinear plant where the network is subsequently used to generate control effort according to a predefined control law or

M. Ali and R. Dapoigny (Eds.): IEA/AIE 2006, LNAI 4031, pp. 1090–1099, 2006.

a stability condition. Finally, in the third category an additional stability condition is introduced where the learning process can be treated as constrained optimisation.

The modification of learning algorithms, which leads to the solution search in the feasible connection weight space only, was first introduced by Sadegh [1] where the stability condition is integrated directly into the weight adaptation algorithm. The concept proposed by Sadegh [1] is subsequently adapted for robotic system control [2]. In addition to the controller role, neural networks have also been used as both observer and controller in a robotic system [3] where a Lyapunov stability condition is utilised during the weight space restriction. Furthermore, the work in this category has also been extended to include the control of discrete systems [4, 5].

In the case where it is desirable to utilise an explicit control law or a stability condition, the training of a neural network to mimic the behaviour of the nonlinear plant is usually carried out. Since the neural network would certainly have a well-defined mathematical structure, the trained neural network can be regulated in a way that a specific control effort can be produced as the network output. The control effort can be generated according to a linear control law that leads to feedback linearisation [6, 7], a control Lyapunov function [8], or an input-to-state stability condition [9].

Another technique, which has also received much attention, is to introduce stability conditions as optimisation constraints during the search for appropriate connection weights. Tanaka [10] has shown that such a technique can be successfully applied in the case that the system can be explained in terms of linear differential inclusions. In later works, Suykens et al. [11] have proposed a stability constraint, which can be applied to any nonlinear systems, for use with recurrent network controllers. In contrast, Kuntanapreeda and Fullmer [12] have proposed a stability constraint for hermitian systems that are controlled by feedforward networks while Ekachaiworasin and Kuntanapreeda [13, 14] have extended the work to cover nonhermitian systems.

From an optimisation viewpoint, the training of a neural network controller usually involves a search in connection weight space where the search objective is defined according to a specific system performance. Although the use of iterative learning algorithms has been successfully applied to the early works mentioned above, it has also been proven that evolutionary computation algorithms are stronger candidates for optimising neural networks [15]. Nonetheless, the application of evolutionary computation for optimising a neural network controller, while also satisfying stability constraints, has rarely been studied. In this paper, a cooperative coevolutionary genetic algorithm or CCGA [16] will be considered for the optimisation of the connection weights in a neural network controller. Specifically, the stability constraint for nonlinear discrete systems developed by Ekachaiworasin and Kuntanapreeda [14] will act as the optimisation constraint. This condition is chosen for this paper since it can be easily integrated into any optimisation techniques.

The organisation of this paper is as follows. In section 2, the architecture of the neural network and the associated stability condition will be explained. In section 3, the description of the CCGA will be given. The application of the CCGA to the task of connection weight optimisation and the performance of neural network controller will be discussed in section 4. Finally, the conclusions will be drawn in section 5.

2   Neural Network and Stability Condition

The architecture of neural network controller, which is chosen for this investigation, is a multilayer perceptron. The network has one hidden layer where the activation function in the hidden node is a hyperbolic tangent function while that in the output node is a linear function. The schematic diagram of the neural network controller is given in Fig. 1. From Fig. 1, it can be seen that each neuron does not have a connection weight that represents a threshold. This means that the input to the activation function is simply a weighted-sum of neuron inputs. In Fig. 1, w_{1ij} represents an element in the connection weight matrix $\mathbf{W}_1$ and reflects the connection weight between the ith neuron in the hidden layer and the jth network input. Similarly, w_{2ij} denotes the connection weight in $\mathbf{W}_2$ and links between the ith output neuron and the jth hidden neuron. Ekachaiworasin and Kuntanapreeda [14] have proven that the network in Fig. 1 can be used as a full-state feedback controller where the associated stability condition, derived from the Lyapunov stability criteria, for the closed-loop discrete system can be described by

$$\mathbf{C}_1 = (\mathbf{A} + a\mathbf{B}\mathbf{W}_2\mathbf{W}_1)^T\mathbf{P}(\mathbf{A} + a\mathbf{B}\mathbf{W}_2\mathbf{W}_1) - \mathbf{P} + \mathbf{q}\mathbf{q}^T + \mathbf{I} = \mathbf{0} \qquad (1)$$

$$\mathbf{C}_2 = (\mathbf{A} + a\mathbf{B}\mathbf{W}_2\mathbf{W}_1)^T\mathbf{P}\mathbf{B}\mathbf{W}_2 + \mathbf{W}_1^T + \mathbf{q}\boldsymbol{\Gamma}^T = \mathbf{0} \qquad (2)$$

$$\mathbf{C}_3 = \mathbf{W}_2^T\mathbf{B}^T\mathbf{P}\mathbf{B}\mathbf{W}_2 + \boldsymbol{\Gamma}\boldsymbol{\Gamma}^T - 2\mathbf{I} = \mathbf{0} \qquad (3)$$

where $\mathbf{A}$ and $\mathbf{B}$ respectively denote system and input matrices of the plant model, which has been linearised around the equilibrium state. In the stability condition, $\mathbf{P}$ is a positive definite symmetric matrix for the Lyapunov function $V = \mathbf{x}^T\mathbf{P}\mathbf{x}$ where $\mathbf{x}$ represents the state vector while $\mathbf{I}$, a, $\mathbf{q}$ and $\boldsymbol{\Gamma}$ are an identity matrix, a constant, a constant matrix and a constant square matrix, respectively. In this paper, a is preset to 0.5. With this condition, the system is guaranteed to be asymptotically stable.

Two types of control strategies are explored in this paper: model-reference control and optimal control. In the model-reference control, the closed-loop behaviour of the system is shaped such that the performances of the system and the reference model are similar. Generally, an error cost function, which is derived from the difference between the performance of the system and that of the reference model, can provide an indication on how the feedback controller should be adjusted. In this investigation, the squared tracking error between the system output and a linear reference model output will be the indicator. In contrast, the cost function for the optimal control is calculated from the energy utilised by the

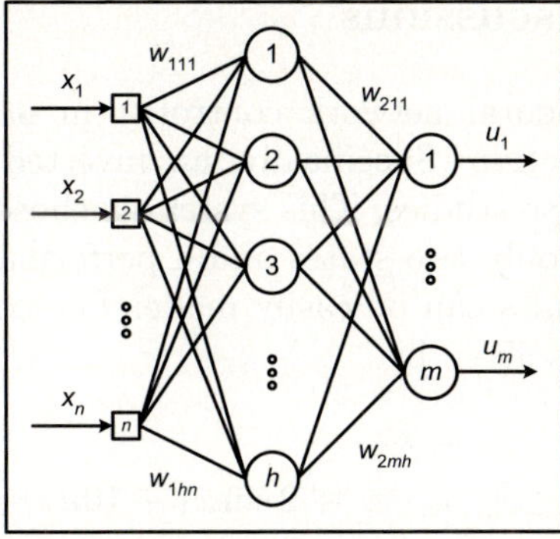

Fig. 1. Architecture of the neural network controller

system during the execution of the control task. Here, the energy is calculated from a quadratic function, which can be described by

$$J_e = \sum_{k=0}^{\infty} (\mathbf{x}^T(k)\mathbf{Q}\mathbf{x}(k) + ru^2(k)) \tag{4}$$

where J_e is the energy cost, $\mathbf{Q}$ is the weighting matrix for the state $\mathbf{x}$ and r is the weighting factor for the control effort u. Both cost functions explained will be parts of fitness functions during the evolution of the neural network controller using a cooperative coevolutionary genetic algorithm.

3   Cooperative Coevolutionary Genetic Algorithm

The cooperative coevolutionary genetic algorithm (CCGA) was first introduced by Potter and De Jong [16]. The CCGA functions by introducing an explicit notion of modularity to the optimisation process. This is done in order to provide reasonable opportunity for complex solutions to evolve in the form of interacting coadapted subcomponents. In brief, the CCGA explores the search space by utilising a population, which contains a number of species or subpopulations. In contrast to other types of genetic algorithm, each species in the CCGA represents a variable or a part of the problem, which requires to be optimised. A combination of an individual from each species will lead to a complete solution to the problem where the fitness value of the complete solution can then be identified. This value of fitness will be assigned to the individual of interest that participates in the formation of the solution. After the fitness values have been assigned to all individuals, the evolution of each species is then commenced using a standard genetic algorithm. The CCGA has been successfully used in a number of problem domains including multivariable function optimisation [16], sequential rule evolution [17], design of a cascade neural network [18] and container loading optimisation [19]. A comprehensive description of the CCGA and the summary of its applications can be found in Potter and De Jong [20].

4   Results and Discussions

The capability of the neural network controller in nonlinear control will be demonstrated in this section. Specifically, an inverted pendulum system will be investigated in the case studies. This system is chosen since it is a regulator control system that has only two states and a performance comparison against previously published results can be easily made. The continuous-time model of the inverted pendulum is given by

$$\dot{x}_1 = x_2$$
$$\dot{x}_2 = -x_2 + 2\sin x_1 + 10u \tag{5}$$

where x_1 is the angular position, x_2 is the angular velocity and u is the control effort. The model is discretised with the sampling interval of 0.05 second. The initial condition of the plant is $\left[\, x_1(0)\ x_2(0) \,\right]^T = \left[\, 1\ 0 \,\right]^T$ while the desired final condition is $\left[\, x_1(k_f)\ x_2(k_f) \,\right]^T = \left[\, 0\ 0 \,\right]^T$ where k_f denotes the final time index. As mentioned earlier in section 2, two control strategies will be explored: model-reference control and optimal control. Since the performance indices for both strategies are described in terms of cost functions, the search objective of the CCGA can be defined as

$$f = \alpha_1 J_c + \alpha_2 \left(\sum_i \sum_j c_{1ij}^2 \right)^{1/2} + \alpha_3 \left(\sum_i \sum_j c_{2ij}^2 \right)^{1/2}$$

$$+\alpha_4 \left(\sum_i \sum_j c_{3ij}^2 \right)^{1/2} + \alpha_5 \left| \left(\sum_i \sum_j c_{1ij}^2 \right)^{1/2} - \left(\sum_i \sum_j c_{2ij}^2 \right)^{1/2} \right|$$

$$+\alpha_6 \left| \left(\sum_i \sum_j c_{2ij}^2 \right)^{1/2} - \left(\sum_i \sum_j c_{3ij}^2 \right)^{1/2} \right|$$

$$+\alpha_7 \left| \left(\sum_i \sum_j c_{1ij}^2 \right)^{1/2} - \left(\sum_i \sum_j c_{3ij}^2 \right)^{1/2} \right| \tag{6}$$

where f is the minimisation objective, J_c is the control cost which can be either the squared tracking error or the energy usage, c_{1ij}, c_{2ij} and c_{3ij} are elements from the stability constraint matrices $\mathbf{C}_1$, $\mathbf{C}_2$ and $\mathbf{C}_3$ as given in equations (1), (2) and (3), respectively and α_i is a weighting factor. It can be clearly seen that the search objective is a weighted-sum between the control cost and the constraint. A desired neural network controller would force the plant to perform according to the strategy employed while the stability condition is also satisfied.

The parameter settings for the multilayer perceptron and the CCGA are given in Table 1. From Table 1, it can be seen that the decision variables for the evolution of the neural network cover both connection weights and variables

Table 1. Parameter settings for the multilayer perceptron and the CCGA

Parameter	Setting and Value
Multilayer Perceptron	
Number of input nodes	2 (Number of feedback states)
Number of hidden nodes	4
Number of output nodes	1
CCGA	
Decision variables	$\mathbf{W}_1$ $(w_{1ij} \in [-2, 2])$, $\mathbf{W}_2$ $(w_{2ij} \in [-2, 2])$, $\mathbf{q}$ $(q_{ij} \in [-2, 2])$, $\mathbf{\Gamma}$ $(\gamma_{ij} \in [-2, 2])$ and $\mathbf{P}$ $(p_{ij} \in [0, 50])$
Number of variables (Number of species)	39
Chromosome representation	Binary chromosome
Chromosome length of a species member	20
Fitness scaling method	Linear scaling
Selection method	Stochastic universal sampling
Crossover method	Uniform crossover with probability $= 0.8$
Mutation method	Bit-flip mutation with probability $= 0.3$
Subpopulation size	100
Number of elitist individuals	1
Number of generations	300
Number of repeated runs	10

from the stability condition. In this work, each decision variable is treated as a species in the CCGA search. In addition, the evolution of the neural network is repeated ten times for each case study where the best result is selected for detailed analysis.

For the purpose of comparison, the performance of the evolutionary neural network for model-reference control will be compared with that of the neural network controller reported in Ekachaiworasin and Kuntanapreeda [14]. In the work by Ekachaiworasin and Kuntanapreeda [14], the model-reference control strategy is also explored. However, an additional neural network emulator is required for the controller training. In brief, a neural network is first trained to emulate the behaviour of the plant. During the training of another neural network for use as the controller, the tracking error between the closed-loop system output and the reference model output is then propagated backward through the neural network emulator where the resulting propagated signal provides an adjustment to the connection weights in the controller. Both evolutionary neural network and neural network controller reported in Ekachaiworasin and Kuntanapreeda [14] are designed such that the resulting closed-loop system behaviour is similar to that of the reference model, which in this study is a linear second order system with the damping ratio $= 0.8$ and the natural frequency $= 3$ rad/s. In contrast to the case study involving model-reference control, the performance of the evolutionary neural network for optimal control will be compared with that of a linear quadratic regulator (LQR). The regulator is designed according to the linearised discrete model of the plant. The comparison will be carried out

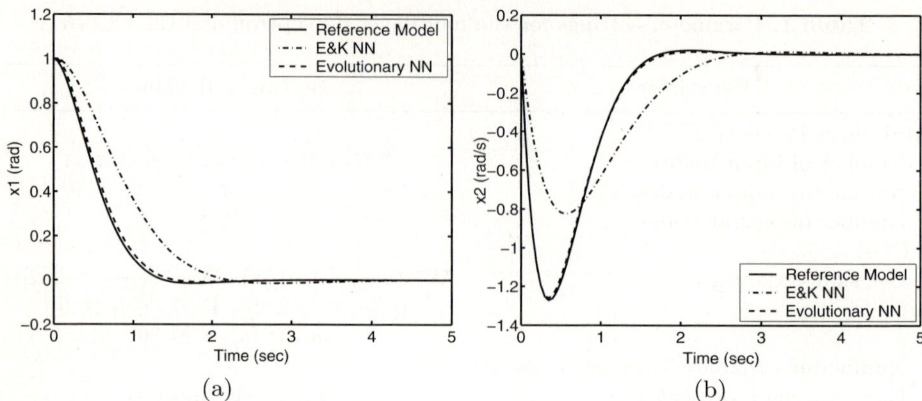

Fig. 2. State trajectory from model-reference control (a) angular position (b) angular velocity

via the monitoring of the energy during the control task execution. The energy cost function is formulated such that the matrix $\mathbf{Q}$ is set to an identity matrix while the parameter r is set to 0.3 for both neural network evolution and linear regulator design.

The performances of the evolutionary neural networks and the techniques selected for comparison for the model-reference control and optimal control are displayed in Figs. 2 and 3, respectively. In addition, the corresponding control cost and constraint are also displayed in Table 2. Firstly, consider the results from the first case study where the strategy employed is model-reference control. It can be clearly seen that the evolutionary neural network is superior to the neural network controller reported in Ekachaiworasin and Kuntanapreeda [14]. The tracking performance of the closed-loop system with the evolutionary neural network is very close to that of the reference model. On the other hand, a significant deviation from the desired response can be observed in the system using the previously reported neural network controller. The numerical results in Table 2 also support this observation where improvements in both squared tracking error and constraint objective are noticeable. These improvements stem from the fact that the use of a neural network emulator, which is previously required during the training of the neural network controller, is no longer necessary in the current implementation. In the early work by Ekachaiworasin and Kuntanapreeda [14], the controller training capability is limited by the ability of the emulator at mimicking the behaviour of the plant. If the emulator cannot truly represent the plant, it would be impossible for the subsequent closed-loop system to behave like the reference model. Since the application of the CCGA as the training algorithm leads to a direct usage of the difference between the closed-loop system and the reference model as the training guidance, the improvements reported are hence not surprising.

The results from the optimal control are now considered. Figure 3 indicates that the state trajectory from the system with the evolutionary neural network

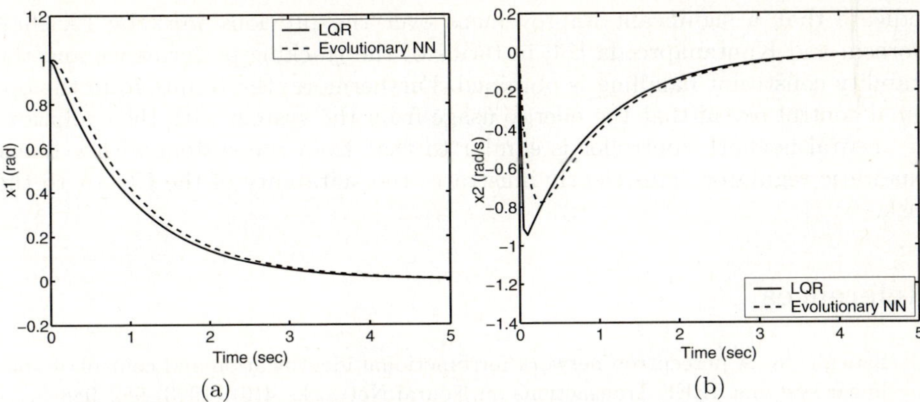

Fig. 3. State trajectory from optimal control (a) angular position (b) angular velocity

Table 2. Control cost and constraint

Strategy	Cost (J_c)	Constraint		
		$\left(\sum_i \sum_j c_{1ij}^2\right)^{1/2}$	$\left(\sum_i \sum_j c_{2ij}^2\right)^{1/2}$	$\left(\sum_i \sum_j c_{3ij}^2\right)^{1/2}$
Model-Reference				
E&K NN	5.136447	0.735667	0.704628	0.265072
Evolutionary NN	0.026669	0.000005	0.000003	0.000006
Optimal Control				
LQR	20.329002	–	–	–
Evolutionary NN	21.704000	0.000029	0.000029	0.000033

controller and that from the system with the LQR are very similar. The energy
usage reported in Table 2 also confirms this similarity where the energy required
by the system with the linear controller is slightly lower. This implies that the
evolved connection weights in the neural network must be close to the true optimal values since the state trajectory obtained approaches the ideally attainable
one.

5   Conclusions

In this paper, the application of neural network controllers in the stabilisation of
a nonlinear discrete system is introduced. The Lyapunov-based stability condition imposed leads to the identification of the feasible connection weight space.
As a result, the training of neural networks can be treated as constrained optimisation where the proposed technique for the task is a cooperative coevolutionary
genetic algorithm (CCGA). Two control strategies, namely model-reference control and optimal control, are investigated where an inverted pendulum system
is utilised in both case studies. The results from the model-reference control

indicate that a significant improvement over the previous work by Ekachai-worasin and Kuntanapreeda [14] in terms of the tracking performance and the stability constraint handling is obtained. Furthermore, the results from the optimal control reveal that the energy usage from the system with the evolutionary neural network controller is similar to that from the system with a linear quadratic regulator. This clearly illustrates the suitability of the CCGA to the task.

References

1. Sadegh, N.: A perceptron network for functional identification and control of nonlinear systems. IEEE Transactions on Neural Networks 4(6) (1993) 982–988
2. Fierro, R., Lewis, F.L.: Control of a nonholonomic mobile robot using neural networks. IEEE Transactions on Neural Networks 9(4) (1998) 589–600
3. Kim, Y.H., Lewis, F.L.: Neural network output feedback control of robot manipulators. IEEE Transactions on Robotics and Automation 15(2) (1999) 301–309
4. Jagannathan, S.: Control of a class of nonlinear discrete-time systems using multilayer neural networks. IEEE Transactions on Neural Networks 12(5) (2001) 1113–1120
5. Zhu, Q., Guo, L.: Stable adaptive neurocontrol for nonlinear discrete-time systems. IEEE Transactions on Neural Networks 15(3) (2004) 653–662
6. He, S., Reif, K., Unbehauen, R.: A neural approach for control of nonlinear systems with feedback linearization. IEEE Transactions on Neural Networks 9(6) (1998) 1409–1421
7. Nam, K.: Stabilization of feedback linearizable systems using a radial basis function network. IEEE Transactions on Automatic Control 44(5) (1999) 1026–1031
8. Kosmatopoulos, E.B.: Universal stabilization using control Lyapunov functions, adaptive derivative feedback, and neural network approximators. IEEE Transactions on Systems, Man, and Cybernetics–Part B: Cybernetics 28(3) (1998) 472–477
9. Sanchez, E.N., Perez, J.P.: Input-to-state stabilization of dynamic neural networks. IEEE Transactions on Systems, Man, and Cybernetics–Part A: Systems and Humans 33(4) (2003) 532–536
10. Tanaka, K.: An approach to stability criteria of neural-network control systems. IEEE Transactions on Neural Networks 7(3) (1996) 629–642
11. Suykens, J.A.K., Vandewalle, J., De Moor, B.: Lur'e systems with multilayer perceptron and recurrent neural networks: Absolute stability and dissipativity. IEEE Transactions on Automatic Control 44(4) (1999) 770–774
12. Kuntanapreeda, S., Fullmer, R.R.: A training rule which guarantees finite-region stability for a class of closed-loop neural-network control systems. IEEE Transactions on Neural Networks 7(3) (1996) 745–751
13. Ekachaiworasin, R., Kuntanapreeda, S.: A training rule which guarantees finite-region stability of neural network closed-loop control: An extension to nonhermitian systems. In: Proceedings of the 2000 IEEE-INNS-ENNS International Joint Conference on Neural Networks, Como, Italy (2000) 325–330
14. Ekachaiworasin, R., Kuntanapreeda, S.: Stabilizing neural network controllers for sampled-data nonlinear systems. In: Mastorakis, N.E. (ed.): Problems in Modern Applied Mathematics. World Scientific and Engineering Society Press, Vouliagmeni, Greece (2000) 282–286

15. Yao, X.: Evolving artificial neural networks. Proceedings of the IEEE **87**(9) (1999) 1423–1447
16. Potter, M.A., De Jong, K.A.: A cooperative coevolutionary approach to function optimization. In: Davidor, Y., Schwefel, H.-P., Männer, R. (eds.): Parallel Problem Solving from Nature–PPSN III. Lecture Notes in Computer Science, Vol. 866. Springer-Verlag, Berlin, Germany (1994) 249–257
17. De Jong, K.A., Potter, M.A.: Evolving complex structures via cooperative coevolution. In: Proceedings of the Fourth Annual Conference on Evolutionary Programming, San Diego, CA (1995) 307–318
18. Potter, M.A., De Jong, K.A.: Evolving neural networks with collaborative species. In: Proceedings of the 1995 Summer Computer Simulation Conference, Ottawa, Canada (1995) 340–345
19. Pimpawat, C., Chaiyaratana, N.: Three-dimensional container loading using a co-operative co-evolutionary genetic algorithm. Applied Artificial Intelligence **18**(7) (2004) 581–601
20. Potter, M.A., De Jong, K.A.: Cooperative coevolution: An architecture for evolving coadapted subcomponents. Evolutionary Computation **8**(1) (2000) 1–29

Genetic Algorithm for Inventory Lot-Sizing with Supplier Selection Under Fuzzy Demand and Costs

Jafar Rezaei[1] and Mansoor Davoodi[2]

[1] Vali-e-Asr University of Rafsanjan, Department of Industrial Management,
Rafsanjan, Kerman, Iran
`Rezaei@vru.ac.ir`
[2] Vali-e-Asr University of Rafsanjan, Department of Computer Sciences,
Rafsanjan, Kerman, Iran

Abstract. In this paper a multi-period inventory lot sizing scenario, where there are multiple products and multiple suppliers, is solved with a Real Parameter Genetic Algorithm. We assume that demand of multiple discrete products is known, not exactly, over a planning horizon and transaction cost is supplier dependent, but does not depend on the variety nor quantity of products involved and holding cost is product-dependent and there are no capacity restrictions and no backlogging is allowed. Because of uncertainties in demand and inventory costs, we consider demand and all costs as fuzzy numbers. The problem is formulated as a fuzzy mixed integer programming and then converted to equivalent crisp decision making problems and is solved with a Real Parameter Genetic Algorithm. Finally, numerical example is provided to illustrate the solution procedure. The results determine what products to order in what quantities with which suppliers in which periods.

1   Introduction

Traditional optimization methods can be classified into two distinct groups: direct and gradient-based methods. In direct search methods, only objective function ($f(x)$) and constraint values ($g_j(x)$) are used to guide the search strategy, whereas gradient-based methods use the first and/or second-order derivatives of the objective function and/or constraints to guide the search process. Since derivative information is not used, the direct search methods are usually slow, requiring many function evaluations for convergence. For the same reason, they can also be applied to many problems without a major change of the algorithm. On the other hand, gradient-based methods quickly converge to an optimal solution, but are not efficient in non-differentiable or discontinuous problems. In addition, there are some common difficulties with most of the traditional direct and gradient-based techniques:

- The convergence to an optimal solution depends on the chosen initial solution.
- Most algorithms tend to get stuck to a suboptimal solution.
- An algorithm efficient in solving one optimization problem may not be efficient in solving a different optimization problem.

M. Ali and R. Dapoigny (Eds.): IEA/AIE 2006, LNAI 4031, pp. 1100–1110, 2006.

– Algorithms are not efficient in handling problems having discrete variables.
– Algorithms cannot be efficiently used on a parallel machine.

Because of the nonlinearities and complex interactions among problem variables often exist in real world optimization problems, the search space may have more than one optimal solutions, of which most are undesired locally optimal solutions having inferior objective function values. When solving these problems, if traditional methods get attracted to any of these locally optimal solutions, there is no escape [1]. To overcome these difficulties, recently Genetic Algorithms (GAs) are used as optimization techniques for decision-making problems. These (c.f. Davis [2], Goldberg [3] and Michalewicz [4]) are adaptive computational procedures modeled on the mechanics of natural genetic systems. They exploit the historical information to speculate on new offspring with expected improved performance (c.f. Goldberg [3] and Pal et al. [5]). These are executed iteratively on a set of coded solutions (called population) with three operators, selection, crossover and mutation. One iteration of these three operators is known as a generation in the parlance of GAs. Since a GA works simultaneously on a set of coded solutions, it has very little chance to get struck at local optima. Here, the resolution of the possible search space is increased by operating on possible solutions and not on the solutions themselves. Further, this search space need not be continuous. Recently, GAs have been applied in different areas like neural network (c.f. Pal et al. [5]), scheduling (c.f. Davis [6]), numerical optimization (c.f.Michalewicz and Janikow [7]), pattern recognition (c.f.Gelsema [8]), inventory classification (Guvenier [9]), fishery modeling (Mardel et. al. [10]), multi criteria flow shop scheduling (Bagchi [11]), inventory control (Mondal and Maiti [12]) etc. Tang and Wang [13], [14] developed an interactive approach for the production problems with quadratic form of fuzzy objective and fuzzy resource constraints and found a family of solutions with acceptable membership degree for the said problem via a GA with mutation along the weighted gradient direction. They also solved a manufacturing problem formulated as a fuzzy non-linear programming problem with penalty coefficients via GA. But, till now, just a few works (c.f. Mondal and Maiti [12], Rezaei and Davoodi [15]) have applied it in the field of inventory control and supply chain management.

With the advent of supply chain management, much attention is now devoted to supplier selection. Rosenthal et al. [16] study a purchasing problem where suppliers offer discounts when a "bundle" of products is bought from them, and one needs to select suppliers for multiple products. A mixed integer programming formulation is presented. Chaudhry et al. [17] consider vendor selection under quality, delivery and capacity constraints and price-break regimes. Ganeshan [18] has presented a model for determining lot sizes that involves multiple suppliers while considering multiple retailers, and consequent demand on a warehouse. Kasilingam and Lee [19] have incorporated the fixed cost of establishing a vendor in a single-period model that includes demand uncertainties and quality considerations in the selection of vendors. In a similar vein, Jayaraman et al. [20] have proposed a supplier selection model that considers quality (in terms of proportion defectives supplied by a supplier), production capacity (this limits the order placed on a supplier), lead-time, and storage capacity limits. This is also a single period model that attaches a 6xedcost to dealing with a supplier. Jayaraman et al. [20] formulate a mixed integer linear programming model to solve the problem.

Basnet and Leung [21] have presented a multi-period supplier selection model that considers demand of multiple products in multiple periods: one or more supplier could be selected in each of these periods for the purchase of products. Alternatively, products could be carried forward to a future period, incurring holding costs. Every time an order is placed on a supplier, a transaction cost is also incurred.

In an inventory system, we consider inventory costs which may be imprecise. On the other hand, the demand may be vaguely defined in a different way. Hence, there is a scope of formulating the inventory control problems with imprecise parameters, resources and objective. Till now, only a few fuzzy inventory models (c.f. Kacprzyk and Staniewski [22], Park [22], Petrovic [24]), Vujosevic et. al [25], Chang et. al [26], Lee et. al [27], Yao et. al [28], Yao et. al [29], Yao et. al [30], Gen et. al [31], Fatemi Ghomi and Rezaei [32] are available in the literature.

In this paper based on Basnet and Leung [21] work a multi-period inventory lot sizing scenario, where there are multiple products and multiple suppliers, is solved with a Real Parameter Genetic Algorithm while demand and all costs are considered as fuzzy numbers.

2 Genetic Algorithm Approach

2.1 Chromosome Syntax Representation

In the multi-product multi-supplier problem, the number of the involved parameters for optimization is large. Traditional binary vectors used to represent the chromosome are not effective in such a large-scale dimension. To overcome this difficulty, a real-number representation is therefore used.

2.2 Initial Population Production

The population initialization technique used in the GA approach is a random real-number initialization that creates a starting GA population filled with randomly generated real-number strings. The population size is set not less than twice the length of the vector of the chromosomes.

2.3 Evaluation and Fitness

Evaluation function plays the same role in GA as that which the environment plays in natural evolution. The objective function value is considered as the evaluation rule of every individual. Sometimes the best and the worst chromosomes will produce almost the same numbers of offspring in the next Population, which cause premature convergence. In this case, the effect of natural section is therefore not obvious. A linear normalization, which converts the evaluations of chromosomes into fitness values, is used here to overcome this problem.

2.4 Parent Selection and Genetic Operators

The purpose of parent selection in GA is to offer additional reproductive chances to those population members that are the fittest. One commonly used technique, the roulette-wheel-selection, is used for this proposed GA. The genetic operators used to perform evaluation are Crossover operator and Mutation operator. Crossover is an extremely important component of GA, which makes it different from all other conventional optimization algorithms. It can recombine the parents and produce offspring as the new individuals. In the proposed GA, Linear crossover is used. Mutation reintroduces diversity into the population when a bit has accidentally taken on a single value everywhere. This prevents the solution from converging to some local optimal solutions; thereby the global optimal solution can be reached. The Random mutation method is used here.

2.5 Termination Criteria and Genetic Parameters Selection

Once the same solution has been continuously obtained by the GA approach for 10 reproduction trials, or the maximum generation is larger than the preset trial times stated in advance, the termination criteria have been reached. The population size is set at 100. The crossover operator is applied with a crossover rate of 90%. This rate of mutation operator is inverse to the standard difference of a generation and is not more than 10% of all the evolution.

3 Formulation and Notation

This paper is built upon Basnet and Leung's [21] work. To avoid any possible confusion, the notations and assumptions utilized in Basnet and Leung are employed in this paper:

D_{it}	demand of product i in period t
P_{ij}	purchase price of product i from supplier j
H_i	holding cost of product i per period
O_j	transaction cost for supplier j
X_{ijt}	number of product i ordered from supplier j in period t
Y_{jt}	1 if an order is placed on supplier j in time period t, 0 otherwise
R_{it}	Inventory of product i, carried over from period t to period t + 1

1. Transaction cost is supplier dependent, but does not depend on the variety and quantity of products involved.
2. There are no capacity restrictions and no backlogging is allowed.
3. Demand of multiple discrete products is known over a planning horizon
4. Holding cost is product-dependent

3.3 Formulation

The total cost (TC) = purchase cost of the products + transaction cost for the suppliers + holding cost for remaining inventory in each period.

$$TC = \sum_i \sum_j \sum_t P_{ij} X_{ijt} + \sum_j \sum_t O_j Y_{jt} + \sum_i \sum_t H_i \left(\sum_{k=1}^{t} \sum_j X_{ijk} - \sum_{k=1}^{t} D_{ik} \right) \tag{1}$$

There are two restrictions for this objective function:

1) All requirements must be filled in the period in which they occur: shortage or backordering is not allowed:

$$R_{it} = \sum_{k=1}^{t} \sum_j X_{ijk} - \sum_{k=1}^{t} D_{ik} \geq 0 \qquad \text{for all } i \text{ and } t \tag{2}$$

2) There is not an order without charging an appropriate transaction cost.

$$\left(\sum_{k=t}^{T} D_{ik} \right) Y_{jt} - X_{ijt} \geq 0 \qquad \text{for all } i, j \text{ and } t \tag{3}$$

The problem is to find number of product i ordered from supplier j in period t so as to minimize the total cost function subject to restrictions and boundary conditions:

$$Min(TC) = \sum_i \sum_j \sum_t P_{ij} X_{ijt} + \sum_j \sum_t O_j Y_{jt} + \sum_i \sum_t H_i \left(\sum_{k=1}^{t} \sum_j X_{ijk} - \sum_{k=1}^{t} D_{ik} \right) \tag{4}$$

$$s.t. \qquad R_{it} \equiv \sum_{k=1}^{t} \sum_j X_{ijk} - \sum_{k=1}^{t} D_{ik} \geq 0 \qquad \text{for all } i \text{ and } t, \tag{5}$$

$$\left(\sum_{k=t}^{T} D_{ik} \right) Y_{jt} - X_{ijt} \geq 0 \qquad \text{for all } i, j \text{ and } t, \tag{6}$$

$$Y_{jt} = 0 \text{ or } 1 \quad \text{for all } j \text{ and } t, \tag{7}$$

$$X_{ijt} \geq 0 \text{ for all } i, j \text{ and } t. \tag{8}$$

When the above objective goal, demand of product i in period t, purchase price of product i from supplier j, holding cost of product i per period and transaction cost for supplier j become fuzzy, the said problem (4-8) is transformed to:

$$Min(\tilde{TC}) = \sum_t \sum_j \sum_t \tilde{P}_{ij} X_{ijt} + \sum_j \sum_t \tilde{O}_j Y_{jt} + \sum_i \sum_t \tilde{H}_i \left(\sum_{k=1}^{t} \sum_j X_{ijk} - \sum_{k=1}^{t} \tilde{D}_{ik} \right) \tag{9}$$

$$s.t. \qquad \tilde{R}_{it} \equiv \sum_{k=1}^{t} \sum_j X_{ijk} - \sum_{k=1}^{t} \tilde{D}_{ik} \geq 0 \qquad \text{for all } i \text{ and } t, \tag{10}$$

$$\left(\sum_{k=t}^{T} \tilde{D}_{ik} \right) Y_{jt} - X_{ijt} \geq 0 \qquad \text{for all } i, j \text{ and } t, \tag{11}$$

$$Y_{jt} = 0 \ or \ 1 \quad \text{for all } j \text{ and } t, \tag{12}$$

$$X_{ijt} \geq 0 \quad \text{for all } i, j \text{ and } t. \tag{13}$$

Following Zimmerman [33], the above fuzzy model reduces to:

$$Max \quad \alpha \tag{14}$$

s.t.

$$\sum_i \sum_j \sum_t (P_{ij} - (1-\alpha)Pp_{ij})X_{ijt} + \sum_j \sum_t (O_j - (1-\alpha)Po_j)Y_{jt}$$
$$+ \sum_i \sum_t (H_i - (1-\alpha)Ph_i)\left(\sum_{k=1}^{t}\sum_j X_{ijk} - \sum_{k=1}^{t}(D_{ik} - (1-\alpha)Pd_{ik})\right) \leq TC_0 + (1-\alpha)Ptc_0, \tag{15}$$

$$\sum_{k=1}^{t}\sum_j X_{ijk} - \sum_{k=1}^{t}(D_{ik} - (1-\alpha)Pd_{ik}) \geq 0 \quad \text{for all } i \text{ and } t, \tag{16}$$

$$\left(\sum_{k=t}^{T}(D_{ik} - (1-\alpha)Pd_{ik})\right)Y_{jt} - X_{ijt} \geq 0 \quad \text{for all } i, j \text{ and } t, \tag{17}$$

$$Y_{jt} = 0 \ or \ 1 \quad \text{for all } j \text{ and } t, \tag{18}$$

$$X_{ijt} \geq 0 \quad \text{for all } i, j \text{ and } t. \tag{19}$$

where Pp_{ij}, Po_j, Ph_i, Pd_{ik} and Ptc_0 are tolerances of P_{ij}, O_j, H_i, D_{ik} and TC_0 respectively and TC_0 is the aspiration level of total cost.

4   Numerical Example

In this section we solved a numerical example of the above fuzzy model using a Real Parameter Genetic Algorithm. We consider a scenario with four products over a planning horizon of five periods whose requirements are as follows: Demands of four products over a planning horizon of five periods are:

Table 1. Demands of four products over a planning horizon of five periods. In each cell, the left number indicates D_{ik} and the right number indicates Pd_{ik}.

Products	Planning Horizon (five periods)				
	1	2	3	4	5
A	(50,10)	(45,8)	(52,7)	(43,8)	(47,8)
B	(35,5)	(40,5)	(38,6)	(35,5)	(42,8)
C	(55,6)	(50,8)	(44,10)	(50,8)	(60,10)
D	(42,7)	(44,5)	(40,6)	(43,8)	(40,5)

There are three suppliers X, Y, Z and their prices are shown in table 2.

Table 2. Price of four products by each of three suppliers X, Y, Z. In each cell, the left number indicates P_{ij} and the right number indicates Pp_{ij} .

Products	Price		
	X	Y	Z
A	(100,8)	(105,10)	(95,6)
B	(80,5)	(80,8)	(78,5)
C	(95,6)	(100,8)	(94,10)
D	(75,5)	(74,5)	(70,6)

Table 3. Transaction cost of three suppliers X, Y, Z. In each cell, the left number indicates O_j and the right number indicates Po_j .

Transaction cost		
X	Y	Z
(500,35)	(550,20)	(480,30)

Table 4. Holding cost of four products A,B,C and D. In each cell, the left number indicates H_i and the right number indicates Ph_i .

Holding Cost			
A	B	C	D
(5,1)	(4,0.5)	(5,0.8)	(3.8,0.4)

Also we considered TC_0 and Ptc_0 as 80000 and 8000 respectively.

4.1 Upper Limits for Decision Variables in GAs

The upper limits for the decision variables X_{ijt} are obtained from the equation (17) as:

$$X_{ijt} \le \sum_{k=t}^{T} (D_{ik} - (1-\alpha)Pd_{ik})Y_{jt} \tag{20}$$

For upper limits, we have considered $Y_{jt} = 1$ and $\alpha = 1$, therefore we have:

$$X_{ijt} \le \sum_{k=t}^{T} (D_{ik} + Pd_{ik}) \tag{21}$$

The results of applying the proposed method are shown as follow:

Table 5. Results for model by GA

	Iteration 90	Iteration 110	Iteration 150	Iteration 180	Iteration 190	Iteration 200
α	0.716	0.7585	0.772	0.802	0.8035	0.82
TC	82266.57	81542.63	81823.62	81547.44	81469.64	81326.81
X_{111}	40	40	40	40	40	40
X_{112}	0	0	0	0	0	0

Table 5. (*Continued*)

X_{113}	53	53	53	53	53	53
X_{114}	0	0	0	0	0	0
X_{115}	0	0	0	0	0	0
X_{121}	0	0	0	0	0	0
X_{122}	23	23	23	23	23	23
X_{123}	0	0	0	0	0	0
X_{124}	0	0	0	0	0	0
X_{125}	3	3	1.5	3	3	3
X_{131}	51	51	51	51	51	51
X_{132}	42	42	42	42	42	42
X_{133}	0	0	0	0	0	0
X_{134}	18	18	18	18	18	18
X_{135}	0	0	0	0	0	0
X_{211}	14	14	14	2.8	3.36	3.36
X_{212}	0	0	0	0	0	0
X_{213}	32	32	44.8	44.8	44.8	44.8
X_{214}	0	0	0	0	0	0
X_{215}	0	0	0	0	0	0
X_{221}	0	0	0	0	0	0
X_{222}	26	26	26	26	26	26
X_{223}	0	0	0	0	0	0
X_{224}	0	0	0	0	0	0
X_{225}	9	9	9	8.1	8.1	4.86
X_{231}	50	50	50	50	50	50
X_{232}	21	21	21	21	25.2	25.2
X_{233}	0	0	0	0	0	0
X_{234}	31	31	31	31	31	31
X_{235}	0	0	0	0	0	0
X_{311}	15	15	15	15	15	15
X_{312}	0	0	0	0	0	0
X_{313}	22	22	22	22	22	22
X_{314}	0	0	0	0	0	0
X_{315}	0	0	0	0	0	0
X_{321}	0	0	0	0	0	0
X_{322}	53	53	53	53	53	53
X_{323}	0	0	0	0	0	0
X_{324}	0	0	0	0	0	0
X_{325}	38	38	30.4	30.4	30.4	30.4
X_{331}	53	53	53	53	53	53
X_{332}	39	39	39	39	39	39
X_{333}	0	0	0	0	0	0
X_{334}	40	40	40	40	40	40
X_{335}	0	0	0	0	0	0

Table 5. (*Continued*)

X_{411}	52	52	52	52	52	52
X_{412}	0	0	0	0	0	0
X_{413}	36	32.4	32.4	32.4	32.4	32.4
X_{414}	0	0	0	0	0	0
X_{415}	0	0	0	0	0	0
X_{421}	0	0	0	0	0	0
X_{422}	9	1.8	1.8	2.5	2.5	3.02
X_{423}	0	0	0	0	0	0
X_{424}	0	0	0	0	0	0
X_{425}	8	8	8	8	8	8
X_{431}	18	18	18	18	18	18
X_{432}	57	57	57	57	57	57
X_{433}	0	0	0	0	0	0
X_{434}	33	33	33	33	31	33
X_{435}	0	0	0	0	0	0

In fuzzy method, only one optimum solution is obtained, whereas, GA gives a series of alternatives along with the optimum one to the decision maker. In all cases, exact optimum solution is not always wanted. As the model has been formulated with vague parameters, the decision maker may choose that solution which suits him best with respect to resources, which will have to be augmented with difficulty.

5 Conclusions

In this paper a multi-period inventory lot sizing scenario, where there are multiple products and multiple suppliers, is solved with a Real Parameter Genetic Algorithm. The proposed method does not require unrealistic assumption about the exact parameter for demand and costs. Therefore, in this paper the cost components and demand are considered as triangular fuzzy numbers. The model has been formulated as Fuzzy Mixed Integer Programming problem and then converted to equivalent crisp decision making problem and solved by a Real Parameter Genetic Algorithm. This methodology can be extended without or with some modifications to the complicated inventory and supply chain models, i.e. models with deterioration, discount, variable replenishment, etc. formulated in crisp, fuzzy or fuzzy-stochastic environments.

References

1. Deb, K.: Multi Objective Optimization Using Evolutionary Algorithms, first edn. John Wiley & Sons, LTD England (2001)
2. Davis, L. (Ed.): Genetic Algorithms and Simulated Annealing. Pitman Publishing, London (1987)
3. Goldberg, D. E.: Genetic Algorithms: Search, Optimization and Machine Learning. Addison Wesley, Massachusetts (1989)

4. Michalewicz, Z.: Genetic Algorithms + Data Structures = Evolution Programs. 3rd edn. Springer-Verlag, Berlin Heidelberg New York (1996)
5. Pal, S. K., De, S., Ghosh, A.: Designing Hopfield Type Networks Using Genetic Algorithms and Its Comparison with Simulated Annealing. Int. J. Patterns Recognition and Artificial Intelligence 11(1997) 447–461
6. Davis, L. (Ed.).: Handbook of Genetic Algorithms. Van Nostrand Reinhold New York (1991)
7. Michalewicz, Z., Janikow, C. Z.: Genetic Algorithms for Numerical Optimization. Statistics and Computing 1 (1991) 75–91
8. Gelsema, E. (Ed.).: Special Issue on Genetic Algorithms, Pattern Recognition Letters, 16 (8) (1995)
9. Guvenir, H. A.: A Genetic Algorithm for Multicriteria Inventory Classification. In Pearson, D. W., Steele, N. C. and Albrecht, R. F (Eds): Artificial Neural Nets and Genetic Algorithms, Proceedings of the Int. Conference, France, Springer-Verlag, Wien, (1995) 6-9
10. Mardle, S., Pasco, S., Tamiz, M.: An Investigation of Genetic Algorithm for the Optimization of Multi Objective Fisheries Bioeconomic Models. Technical report 136, Portsmouth, UK: Center for the Economics and Management of Aquatic Resources, University of Portsmouth (1998)
11. Bagchi, T.: Multi Objective Scheduling by Genetic Algorithm. Kluwer Academic Publishers Boston (1999)
12. Mondal, S., Maiti, M.: Multi-item Fuzzy EOQ Models Using Genetic Algorithm. Computers & Industrial Engineering 44 (2002) 105–117
13. Tang, J., Wang, D.: An Interactive Approach Based on a Genetic Algorithm for a Type of Quadratic Programming Problems with Fuzzy Objective and Resources. Computers and Operations Research, 24(5) (1997) 413–422
14. Tang, J., Wang, D.: A Non-Symmetric Model for Fuzzy non Linear Programming Problems with Penalty Coefficients. Computers and Operations Research, 24(8) (1997) 717–725
15. Rezaei, J., Davoodi, M.: Multi-item Fuzzy Inventory Model with Three Constraints: Genetic Algorithm Approach. In: Zhang, S., Jarvis, R. (eds.): The 18th Australian Joint Conference on Artificial Intelligence. Lecture Notes in Artificial Intelligence, Vol. 3809. Springer-Verlag, Berlin Heidelberg (2005) 1120–1125
16. Rosenthal, EC., Zydiak, JL., Chaudhry SS.: Vendor selection with bundling. Decision Sciences, 26 (1995) 35– 48
17. Chaudhry, SS., Frost, FG., Zydiak, JL.: Vendor selection with price breaks. European J. Operational Research, 70 (1993) 52– 66
18. Ganeshan, R.: Managing supply chain inventories: a multiple retailer, one warehouse, multiple supplier model. Int. J. Production Economics, 59 (1999)341–54
19. Kasilingam, RG., Lee, CP.: Selection of vendors—a mixed integer programming approach. Computers and Industrial Engineering, 31 (1996) 347–50
20. Jayaraman, V., Srivastava, R., Benton, WC.: Supplier selection and order quantity allocation: a comprehensive model. The J. Supply Chain Management, 35 (1999) 50–58
21. Basnet, Ch., Leung, J.M.Y.: Inventory lot-sizing with supplier selection. Computers & Operations Research, 32 (2005) 1–14
22. Kacprzyk, J., Staniewski, P.: Long Term Inventory Policy-Making through Fuzzy Decision Making Models. Fuzzy Sets and Systems 8 (1982) 117–132
23. Park, K. S.: Fuzzy Set theoretic Interpretation of Economic Order Quantity. IEEE Transactions on Systems, Man and Cybernetics 17 (1987) 1082–1087

24. Petrovic, D., Petrovic, R., Vujosevic, M.: Fuzzy Models for the Newsboy Problem. Int. J. Production Economics 45(1996) 435–441
25. Vujosevic, M., Petrovic, D., Petrovic, R.: EOQ Formula when Inventory Cost is Fuzzy. Production Economics 45 (1996)499–504
26. Chang, SC., Yao, J.S., Lee, H.M.: Economic Reorder Point for Fuzzy Backorder Quantity. European J. Operational Research 109 (1998)183–202
27. Lee, H.M., and Yao, J.Sh.: Economic Order Quantity in Fuzzy Sense for Inventory without Backorder Model. Fuzzy Sets and Systems 105(1999)13-31
28. Yao, J.Sh. Change, S.C.h., Su, J.Sh.: Fuzzy Inventory without Backorder for Fuzzy Order Quantity and Fuzzy Total Demand Quantity. Computers & Operations Research 27(2000)935-962
29. Yao, J.S.h., Lee, HM.: Fuzzy Inventory with Backorder for Fuzzy Order Quantity. Information Sciences 93(1996)283-319
30. Yao, J.Sh., Lee, HM.: Fuzzy Inventory with or without Backorder for Order Quantity with Trapezoid Fuzzy Number. Fuzzy Sets and Systems 105(1999)311-337
31. Gen, M., Tsujimura. Y., Zheng, D.: An Application of Fuzzy Set Theory to Inventory Control Models. Computers and industrial Engineering 33(1997)553-556
32. Fatemi Ghomi, S.M.T., Rezaei, J.: Development of a Fuzzy Inventory Control Model with a Real Application. Amirkabir 14(55-D)(2003)924-936
33. Zimmermann, H.J.: Description and Optimization of Fuzzy Systems, Int. J General Systems 2 (4) (1976) 209–215

A Self-tuning Emergency Model of Home Network Environment

Huey-Ming Lee, Shih-Feng Liao, Tsang-Yean Lee, Mu-Hsiu Hsu, and Jin-Shieh Su

Department of Information Management, Chinese Culture University
55, Hwa-Kung Road, Yang-Ming-San, Taipei (11114), Taiwan
hmlee@faculty.pccu.edu.tw,
hf_liao@mail2000.com.tw

Abstract. In this paper, we proposed a self-tuning emergency model of home network environment (SEMHNE). This model can not only tune the scaling factors and membership functions to fit the home network environment but also detect the emergency events automatically. There are three modules in this model, namely, emergency report module (ERM), renewable emergency rule base (RERB), and evolutionary database (EDB). ERM determines the emergency situations by fuzzy inferences and sends the warning message to the users. RERB can provide rules to ERM for inference. EDB can do self-tuning by using genetic algorithm and provide information to ERM for inference. Via this model, our home network environment will become more reliable and safety.

1 Introduction

Since information appliances (IAs) have become available to all in recent years, there are more and more varied IA products appeared. IA plays an important role in home environment. In home network environment, an IA control mechanism can provide the fine control capability of IA devices.

Lee and Huang [8] proposed an IA controlling model (IACM), which can control IA devices through home management broker. Lee et al. [7] came up with the idea of IAs intelligent agent model (IAIA), making home environments more comfortable and convenient. Lee et al. [11] proposed a fuzzy neural network model of information appliances with the functions of self-learning and fuzzy inference, it enables IAIA to maximize efficiency of IAs in a more humane way. Lee et al. [12] proposed an intelligent control model of information appliances (ICMAI) which can not only collect the related users' information appliances preference messages automatically, but also generate the IA control rules by the fuzzy neural network learning. Lee et al. [9] proposed an adaptive exception process model of information appliances (AEPMIA) which can adjust the membership functions to make the reasoning more approximately. Lee et al. [10] proposed an emergency model of home network environment based on genetic algorithm. This model can not only adapt the home network environment by using genetic algorithm but also detect the emergency events automatically. If there is a mechanism which can do the active response of emergency, then we can prevent the serious accident in home network environment.

M. Ali and R. Dapoigny (Eds.): IEA/AIE 2006, LNAI 4031, pp. 1111 – 1118, 2006.
© Springer-Verlag Berlin Heidelberg 2006

In this study, we proposed a self-tuning emergency model of home network environment (SEMHNE). There are three modules in this model, saying emergency report module (ERM), renewable emergency rule base (RERB), and evolutionary database (EDB). RERB provides rules to ERM for inference. ERM determines the emergency situations by fuzzy inferences. EDB can adjust the database by using genetic algorithm and provide information to ERM for inference. Via this model, our home network environment will become more reliable and safety.

2 SEMHNE

In this section, we presented a self-tuning emergency model of information appliances (SEMHNE) under the supervision of IAIA [7], as shown in Fig. 1. There are three modules in SEMHNE, saying emergency report module (ERM), renewable emergency rule base (RERB), and evolutionary database tuner (EDB), as shown in Fig. 2.

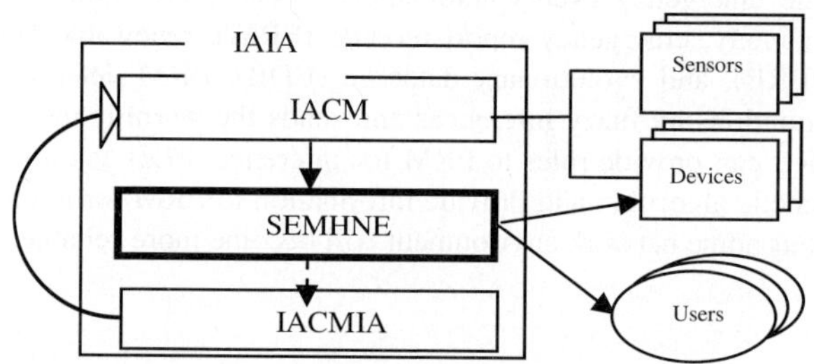

Fig. 1. SEMHNE (Dotted line is normal event)

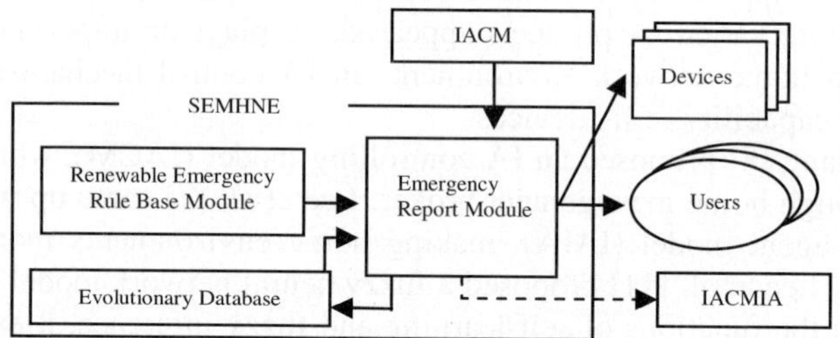

Fig. 2. Architecture of SEMHNE (Dotted line is normal event)

The functions of these modules are as the following:

- RERB: It includes the renewable rule base which is provided by experts and can provide ERM to inference.
- ERM: After receiving the messages from RERB and EDB, ERM can determine the emergency events by using fuzzy inferences. Depending on the inference results, it will send the warning message to users or let it pass by.

♦ EDB: It can tune the scaling factors and membership functions in the database by using genetic algorithm and provide the related messages to ERM for inference.

2.1   ERM

After receiving the messages from IACM, ERM can determine the emergency events by fuzzy inferences and send the warning message to users. There are two components in this module, saying, fuzzy inference component (FIC) and message report component (MRC). FIC can reason the emergency events by fuzzy inference. If the emergency event occurred, MRC would start the devices up and send the warning messages to remote users. If the events are not emergent, FIC will let the messages pass by, as shown in Fig.3.

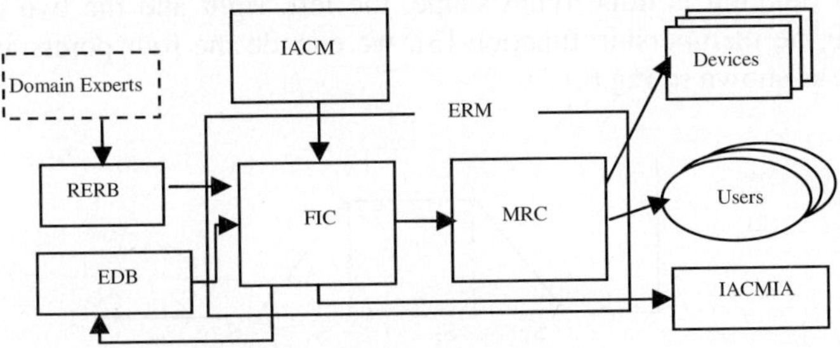

Fig. 3. Architecture of EPM (Dotted line is normal event)

2.2   RERB

There are two components in RERB, saying, update rules component (URC) and emergency rule base (ERB). URC can update ERB by domain experts. ERB can provide ERM to reason the emergency events, as shown in Fig.4.

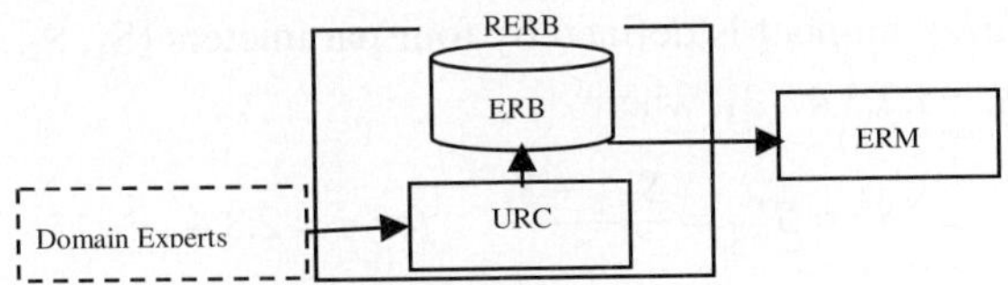

Fig. 4. Architecture of RERB

2.3   EDB

EDB comprises of three components, saying, genetic tuning processor (GTP), reasoning database (RDB) and training data base (TDB). While TDB receives the environment information from ERM, GTP can tune the scaling factors and membership functions in the RDB by using genetic algorithm, as shown in Fig.5.

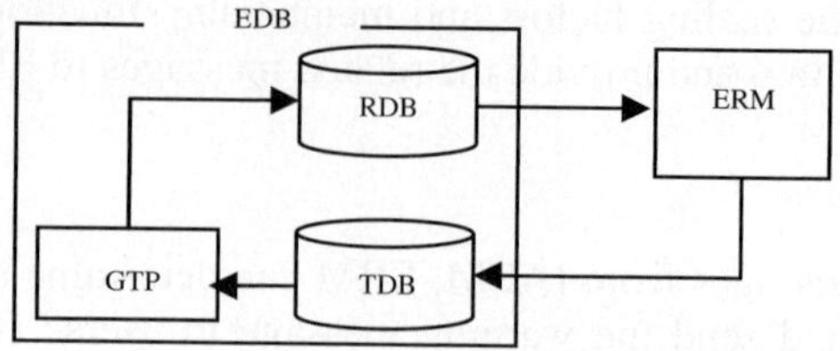

Fig. 5. Architecture of EDB

2.3.1 Tuning Membership Function Process

In order to fit the real situation in home network environment, the proposed model will tune the scaling factors by using genetic algorithm [1, 3]. Since the shape of membership function is trapezoidal shape, the left, right and the two central points parameterize the membership function [3], we encode the four points as genotype in binary code, as shown in Fig.6.

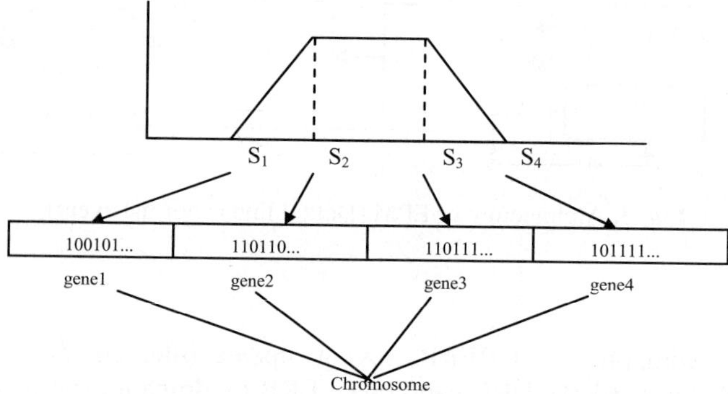

Fig. 6. Initial population encode approach

The trapezoid fuzzy number is defined by four parameters (S_1, S_2, S_3, S_4), $S_k \in [S_k^l, S_k^r], for\ k = 1,2,3,4$ [3], where

$$S_i^l = S_{i-1}^r = \frac{S_{i-1} + S_i}{2} \quad for\ i = 2,3,4$$

$$S_1^l = S_1 - \frac{S_2 - S_1}{2}, S_4^r = S_4 + \frac{S_4 - S_3}{2}$$

Every gene will be produced randomly from the respective interval of its parameter. Then, we can start genetic operator to optimize the membership functions.

2.3.2 Adjusting Scaling Factors Process

In order to get suitable database, we can adjust the scaling factors by using genetic algorithm [1-3]. The adjusting of scaling factors can be regarded as global tuning procedures. The reasoning steps are as shown in Fig.7.

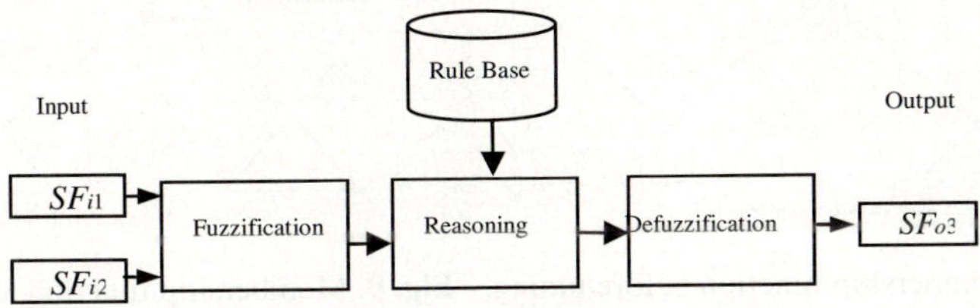

Fig. 7. Fuzzy Inference with scaling factors [6]

Nomenclature:

SF_{i1} : Input scaling factor of parameter 1.

SF_{i2} : Input scaling factor of parameter 2.

SF_{o3} : Input scaling factor of parameter 3.

We set the initial scaling function as Eq. (1)

$$f(x) = \alpha x + \beta \tag{1}$$

Let $\alpha = 1$ and $\beta = 0$, then the tuning fits the real situation.

3   Model Implementation

In order to present the efficacy of this model, we implement this model in this section.

3.1   Practical Environment

For the purpose of ease manipulation, cross-platform, and remote-control capability, we have adopted Java Server Page (JSP) and Java Servlet written Web Server structure, Java 2 Platform, Standard Edition, v1.4.2 API Specification and MATLAB 7.0 are utilized for constructing EEMHNE prototype. Above-mentioned are done with Pentium 4 1.6G desktop that is powered by O/S Windows Professional and Microsoft Access 2002.

3.2   Implementation

We take the membership function of temperature as an example. Also, we set the parameters as followings:

- Population size: 30
- Probability of crossover: $P_c = 0.6$
- Probability of mutation: $P_m = 0.3$
- Selection: roulette wheel
- Elite: enable

The membership function before tuning is shown in Fig.8 and the tuning one is shown in Fig.9.

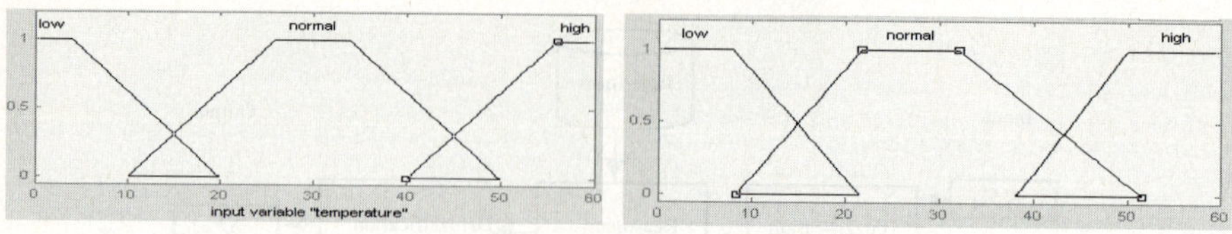

Fig. 8. Membership function before tuning   **Fig. 9.** Membership function after tuning

Next stage, we tune the scaling factors with multiple inputs single output (MISO) system. We set the scaling factors tuning as shown in Table 1:

Table 1. MISO system

Parameter	Labels	Type
Parameter 1	3	input
Parameter 2	5	input
Parameter 3	5	output

- Population size: 200
- Probability of crossover: $P_c = 0.8$
- Probability of mutation: $P_m = 0.1$
- Selection: roulette wheel
- Elite: enable

The tuning results are shown in Table 2:

Table 2. Parameter 1 scaling factors tuning Result

Parameter 1	α	β
Scaling factor	α	β
Before Training	1	0
After Training	1.21	0.25
Parameter 2		
Scaling factor	α	β
Before Training	1	0
After Training	1.12	0.66
Parameter 3		
Scaling factor	α	β
Before Training	1	0
After Training	1.15	0.03

After tuning, our input and output scaling factors will be more suitable for real situation, and the reasoning will be more approximate.

4 Conclusion

At present, there are more and more varied IA products appeared in home network environment. Therefore, emergency process mechanism is the most significant in home network environment. In this study we proposed a self-tuning emergency model of home network environment (SEMHNE). This model can not only do self-tuning to fit the home network environment but also detect the emergency event automatically. Via this model, our home network environment will become more reliable and safety.

Acknowledgement

This work was supported in part by the National Science Council, Republic of China, under grant NSC94-2745-M-034-008-URD.

References

1. Arslan, A., Kaya, M: Determination of fuzzy logic membership functions using genetic algorithm. Fuzzy sets and systems Vol. 118, (2001) 297-306
2. Cordón, O., Herrera, F.: A Three –Stage Evolutionary Process for Learning Descriptive and Approximate Fuzzy-Logic-Controller Knowledge Bases From Examples. International Journal of Approximate Reasoning, Vol.17 (1997) 369-407
3. Cordón, O., Herrera, F., Hoffmann, F., Magdalena, L.: Genetic Fuzzy Systems. World Scientific Publishing Co. (2001)
4. Herrera, F., Lozano, M., and Verdegay, J.L.: Tuning Fuzzy Logic Controller by Genetic Algorithm. International Journal of Approximate Reasoning, Vol.12 (1995) 299-315
5. Jung, C.-H., Ham, C.-S., Lee, K.-I.: A real-time self-tuning fuzzy controller through scaling factor adjustment for the steam generator of NPP. Fuzzy sets and systems Vol. 74 (1995) 53-60
6. Ju, M.-S., Yang, D.-L.: Design of adaptive fuzzy controls based on natural control laws. Fuzzy sets and systems Vol. 81 (1996) 191-204
7. Lee, H.-M., Chen, Y.-C., Chen, J.-J.: The Intelligent Agent Design of Information Appliance. JCIS, 2003, Proceeding of the 7th Join Conference on Information Sciences, Cary. NC. USA, (2003) 1681-1684
8. Lee, H.-M., Huang, J.-H.: The study of IA devices monitoring model, The sixth seminar of the research and practices of information management, (2002) 430-437
9. Lee, H.-M., Liao, S.-F., and Lee, S.-Y.: An Adaptive Exception Process Model of Information Appliances. WSEAS TRANSACTIONS on INFORMATION SCIENCE & APPLICATIONS, Issue 2, Vol. 1 (2004) 778-783
10. Lee, H.-M., Liao, S.-F., and Lee, S.-Y.: An Emergency Model of Home Network Environment Based on Genetic Algorithm. Knowledge-Based Intelligent Information & Engineering Systems, Lecture Note in Artificial Intelligent, Part II, Springer-Verlag, Berlin Heidelberg, LNAI 3682 (2005) 1245-1251
11. Lee, H.-M., Mao, C.-H., and Lee, S.-Y.: A Fuzzy Neural Network of Information Appliance. International Workshop on Fuzzy System & Innovation Computing 2004 (FIC2004), Kitakyushu, Japan, (2004)

12. Lee, H.-M., Mao, C.,-H., Lee, S.-Y.:Intelligent Control Model of Information Appliances. Negoita, M.-G, Howlett, R.-J., Jain, L.-C. (Eds.) Knowledge-Based Intelligent Information and Engineering Systems, Part III, Springer-Verlag, Berlin Heidelberg, LNAI 3215 (2004) 123-128
13. Michalewicz, Z.: Genetic Algorithms + Data Structures = Evolution Programs. 3rd edn. Springer-Verlag, Berlin Heidelberg New York (1996)
14. Randy, L.H., Sue, E.H.: Practical Genetic Algorithm. A Wiley-Interscience Publication (1998)

Simulation Studies of Two-Layer Hopfield Neural Networks for Automatic Wafer Defect Inspection

Chuan-Yu Chang, Hung-Jen Wang, and Si-Yan Lin

Department of Electronic Engineering,
National Yunlin University of Science and Technology, Taiwan
chuanyu@yuntech.edu.tw

Abstract. The occurrence of defect on a wafer may result in losing the yield ratio. The defective regions were usually identified through visual judgment with the aid of a scanning electron microscope. Dozens of people visually check wafers and hand-mark their defective regions leading to a significant amount of personnel cost. In addition, potential misjudgment may introduce due to human fatigue. In this paper, a two-layer Hopfield neural network called the competitive Hopfield wafer-defect detection neural network (CHWDNN) is proposed to detect the defective regions of wafer image. The CHWDNN extends the one-layer 2D Hopfield neural network at the original image plane to a two-layer 3D Hopfield neural network with defect detection to be implemented on its third dimension. With the extended 3D architecture, the network is capable of incorporating a pixel's spatial information into a pixel-classifying procedure. The experimental results show the CHWDNN successfully identifies the defective regions on wafers images with good performances.

1   Introduction

Wafer defect inspection is an essential process before die packaging. The aim of the wafer defect inspection is to detect defective dies and discard them. In general, the inspection methods can be categorized into two types: post-sawing inspection and electric inspection. Electric inspection requires additional space for testing circuits and that way causes the increase of unit cost. With the help of a scanning electron microscope, the defective regions are identified through visual judgment and this is the post-sawing inspection method. Wafers are checked and the defective regions are hand-marked by engineers [1]. However, not only this process can result in considerable personnel costs, but also human fatigue may lead to potential misjudgment.

A number of methods were developed for wafer defect inspection [1-4]. Tobin *et al.* [2] proposed applying image process techniques in co-ordination with database systems for the inspection of wafer defect. It compares the images of the tested dies with those of good ones to find out the defective dies. By this means, however, a variety of templates for different circuits and die images for further processing must be created and therefore loses the flexibility. In addition, incorrect templates may result in mistaken inspection results. Mital *et al.* [3] suggested an automatic wafer pattern inspection system. The inspection system was based on a knowledge database. The knowledge database regulates the geometry and aspects of the assorted regions of

M. Ali and R. Dapoigny (Eds.): IEA/AIE 2006, LNAI 4031, pp. 1119–1126, 2006.

the wafer images. This implies that various patterns need to be collected. Zang *et al.* [4] develop an automatic post-sawing inspection making use of computer vision techniques. This method is limited to boundary defect problems such as die cracks. Besides, this approach would spend thirty minutes per wafer on inspection time. Su *et al.* [1] suggested a neural network approach for semiconductor wafer defect inspection. Three neural learning methods including back propagation (BP), radial basis function (RBF), and learning vector quantization (LVQ) networks, were proposed as well as tested. Nevertheless, all these three neural networks are based on supervised-learning. To be precise, in order to use these neural networks, patterns such as specific defect patterns, predetermined regions, and die boundaries should have be learned. Accordingly, the product flexibility is low. To achieve an efficient inspection, a minor border cut and complex orientation adjusting processes were utilized. These are rather complex and time-consuming processes.

Recently, Chang *et al.* [5] proposed a two-layer Hopfield based neural network (CHEFNN) by including pixel's surrounding spatial information into image edge detection. Therefore, inspired by the concept of CHEFNN, a specific two-layer competitive Hopfield neural network called the competitive Hopfield wafer-defect detection neural network (CHWDNN) is presented for detecting the defective regions of wafer image. With the extended 3-D architecture, the network is capable of incorporating a pixel's spatial information into a pixel-classifying procedure. According to the variance of gray level and sharp irregularity, the CHWDNN classifies the pixel of wafer images into two classes (defect or not). The CHWDNN is zoomed-independent, orientation- independent, i.e. the proposed CHWDNN does not require the zoom parameters and patterns of good dies. In addition, during the inspection process, the proposed CHWDNN does not to adjust image positions and correct circuit templates. Experimental results show the effectiveness and efficiency of the proposed CHWDNN.

2 Two-Layer Competitive Hopfield Neural Network

Wafer defect detection can be considered as a pixel classifying process that assigns pixels to defect points in accordance with their gray-level and spatial information. In this paper, we applied the two-layer Hopfield neural network architecture, proposed a Competitive Hopfield Wafer-defect Detection Neural Network (CHWDNN) for automatic wafer defect inspection, which considers both the local gray level variance and the neighbor-spatial information. The architecture of the CHWDNN is shown in Fig. 1.

The network achieves a stable state when the energy of the Lyapunov function is minimized. The layers of the CHWDNN represent the state of each pixel that indicates if the pixel is a defect point. A neural $V_{x,i,1}$ in layer 1 in a firing state indicates that the pixel locate at (x,i) in the image is defined as a defect point, and a neural $V_{y,j,2}$ in layer 2 in a firing state indicates that the pixel located at (y,j) in the image is identified as a nondefect point.

In order to ensure that the CHWDNN has capability of dealing with spatial information in wafer defect detection, the energy function of CHWDNN must satisfy the following conditions:

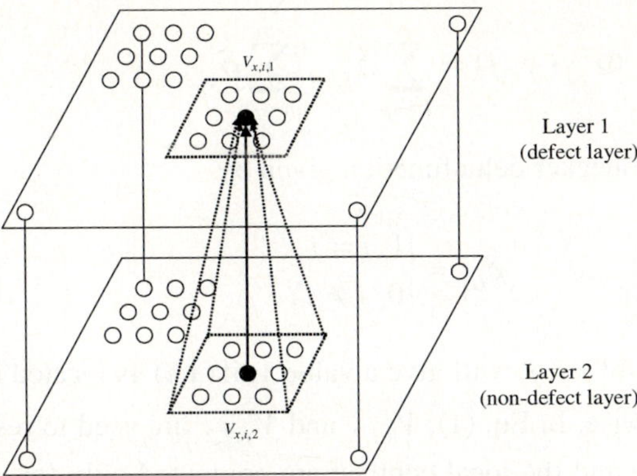

Fig. 1. The architecture of the CHWDNN

First, in the nondefect layer, the normal regions are smoother than the boundary of defective region, and the contrast of normal regions are lower than defect regions. Let $g_{x,i}$ and $g_{y,j}$ denote the gray level of pixels (x,i) and (y,j), respectively. Therefore, assume that a nondefect pixel (x,i) with $V_{x,i,2}=1$ and its surrounding nondefect pixels (y,j) within the neighborhood of (x,i) with $V_{y,j,2}=1$ have the minimum Euclidean distance measure. Then this condition can be characterized as follows:

$$\sum_{x=1}^{N} \sum_{\substack{y=1 \\ (y,j)\neq(x,i)}}^{N} \sum_{i=1}^{N} \sum_{j=1}^{N} \Phi_{x,i}^{p}(y,j)\left(d_{x,i;y,j}+C_{n}^{y,j}\right)V_{x,i,2}V_{y,j,2} \tag{1}$$

where $d_{x,i;y,j}$ is the normalized difference between $g_{x,i}$ and $g_{y,j}$, defined by

$$d_{x,i;y,j} = \left[\frac{g_{x,i}-g_{y,j}}{MAX(G)}\right]^{2}, \tag{2}$$

where $MAX(G)$ denotes the largest gray level of the wafer image. The function $C_{n}^{y,j}$ denotes the contrast value that is located within $n\times n$ area centered at pixel (y,j), defined by

$$C_{n}^{y,j} = \sum_{s=0}^{MAX(G)} \sum_{t=0}^{MAX(G)} |s-t| M_{n}^{y,j}(s,t), \tag{3}$$

where $M_{n}^{y,j}$ denotes the normalized gray-level co-occurrence matrix which is located within a $n\times n$ area centered at pixel (y,j). The function $\Phi_{x,i}^{p}(y,j)$ is a neighborhood function used to specify whether pixel (y,j) is located within a $p\times p$ window area centered at pixel (x,i). The function is defined as

$$\Phi^{p}_{x,i}(y, j) = \sum_{l=-p}^{p} \delta_{j,i+l} \sum_{m=-p}^{p} \delta_{y,x+m} \,, \tag{4}$$

where $\delta_{i,j}$ is the Kronecker delta function given by

$$\delta_{i,j} = \begin{cases} 1 & i = j \\ 0 & i \neq j \,, \end{cases} \tag{5}$$

With this definition $\Phi^{p}_{x,i}(y, j)$ will give a value 1, if (x,i) is located inside the window area, and zero otherwise. In Eq. (1), $V_{x,i,2}$ and $V_{y,j,2}$ are used to restrict that the local gray-level difference and the local contrast are computed only for pixels label by the nondefect layer.

Second, in the non-defect layer, the normal regions trend to regular pattern and have relative bright pattern compared with defective regions. To obtain a more uniform and smooth non-detective regions, this can be represented as:

$$\sum_{x=1}^{N} \sum_{\substack{y=1 \\ (y,j)\neq(x,i)}}^{N} \sum_{i=1}^{N} \sum_{j=1}^{N} \Phi^{q}_{x,i}(y, j)(1 - \overline{g}_{x,i})V_{x,i,2}V_{y,j,2}, \tag{6}$$

where $\overline{g}_{x,i}$ is the normalized $g_{x,i}$, defined by

$$\overline{g}_{x,i} = \left[\frac{g_{x,i}}{MAX(G)} \right], \tag{7}$$

Third, in defect layer, it is easy to perceive that the defective regions trend to darken and concentrated. Therefore, to obtain a more complete and strong detective regions, the criteria is defined by

$$\sum_{x=1}^{N} \sum_{y=1}^{N} \sum_{i=1}^{N} \sum_{j=1}^{N} \Phi^{r}_{x,i}(y, j)\left[\overline{g}_{y,j} + \left(1 - C^{y,j}_{n}\right)\right]V_{x,i,1}V_{y,j,2}, \tag{8}$$

In addition to the constraints mentioned above, the CHWDNN need to satisfy the following two hard conditions to obtain a correct defect detection results:

1. Each pixel can be assigned by one and only one label(defect or not)

$$\sum_{z=1}^{2} V_{x,i,z} = 1. \tag{9}$$

2. All the pixels need to classify. Therefore, the sum of all classified pixel must be

$$\sum_{z=1}^{2} \sum_{x=1}^{N} \sum_{i=1}^{N} V_{x,i,z} = N^{2}. \tag{10}$$

The hard constraints can be completely removed by winner-take-all rule as

$$V = \begin{cases} 1 & \text{if} \quad V = \max\{V_{x,i,1}, V_{x,i,2}\} \\ 0 & \text{otherwise} \end{cases}. \tag{11}$$

Therefore, the objective function of the network for defect detection is obtained as

$$\begin{aligned}
E = \frac{A}{2} \sum_{k=1}^{2} \sum_{z=1}^{2} \sum_{x=1}^{N} \sum_{\substack{y=1 \\ (y,j)\neq(x,i)}}^{N} \sum_{i=1}^{N} \sum_{j=1}^{N} & \left[\left(\frac{A}{2} \Phi_{x,i}^{p}(y,j)\left(d_{x,i;y,j} + C_{n}^{y,j}\right) \right. \right. \\
& \left. + \frac{B}{2} \Phi_{x,i}^{q}(y,j)(1-\overline{g}_{x,i}) \right) \delta_{z,2}\delta_{k,2} \\
& \left. + \frac{C}{2}\left(\overline{g}_{y,j} + (1-C_{n}^{y,j})\right)\delta_{z,2}\delta_{k,1}\Phi_{x,i}^{r}(y,j) \right] V_{x,i,k}V_{y,j,z}.
\end{aligned} \tag{12}$$

Comparing the objection function of the CHWDNN in Eq. (12) and the Lyapunov function of the two-layers Hopfield network, the total input to neuron (x,i,k) is

$$\begin{aligned}
Net_{x,i,k} = -\frac{1}{2} \sum_{z=1}^{2} \sum_{y=1}^{N} \sum_{j=1}^{N} & \left[\left(\frac{A}{2} \Phi_{x,i}^{p}(y,j)\left(d_{x,i;y,j} + C_{n}^{y,j}\right) \right. \right. \\
& \left. + \frac{B}{2} \Phi_{x,i}^{q}(y,j)(1-\overline{g}_{x,i}) \right) \delta_{z,2}\delta_{k,2} \\
& \left. + \frac{C}{2}\left(\overline{g}_{y,j} + (1-C_{n}^{y,j})\right)\delta_{z,2}\delta_{k,1}\Phi_{x,i}^{r}(y,j) \right] V_{y,j,z}.
\end{aligned} \tag{13}$$

3   Experimental Result

In order to verify the proposed CHWDNN could precisely detect defective regions in wafer image, four types of zoomed wafer images (50x and 100x) were used for test. The image size is 640×480 pixels, with each pixel consists of 256 gray levels. The experiments were implemented by C++ Builder on an Intel Pentium IV 2.8GHz processor with 256MB system memory.

Because of space limitation, only two cases of different wafer pattern are demonstrated in Figs. 2 (a-b). To demonstrate that the proposed CHWDNN has good capability of detecting defective regions, the proposed CHWDNN is compare with dynamic thresholding method [6], k-Means clustering, and CHNN method [7]. In the evaluations, the number of clusters is set to 4 for each clustering method to gain the most appreciate detection results. The number of clusters is determined by trial and error.

Figures 3-4 show the detection results of Figs. 2 by various methods. Obviously, the contamination was detection correctly by CHWDNN. Since the color of the bounding pad areas is similar to the contaminations, the other methods could not

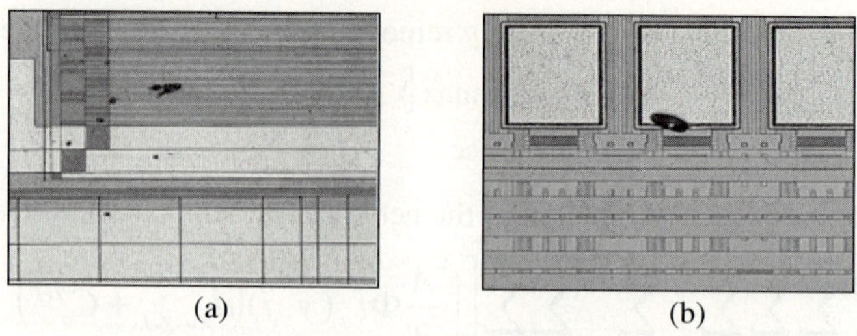

(a)   (b)

Fig. 2. Two wafer images with defective regions

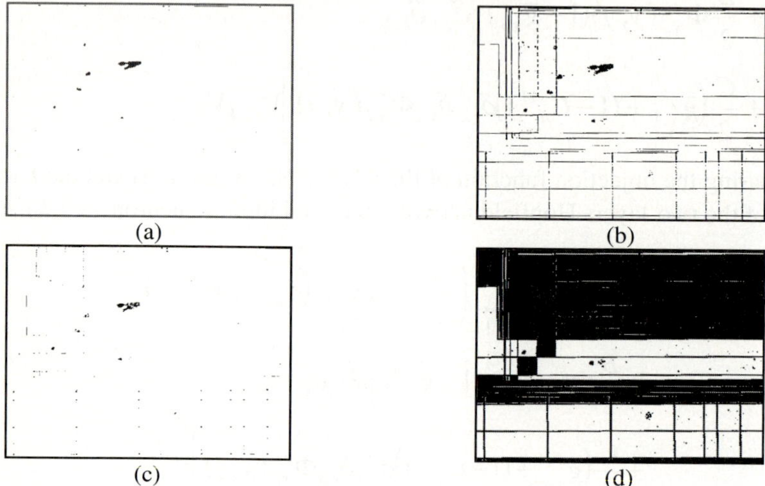

(a)   (b)
(c)   (d)

Fig. 3. Defect inspection results of Fig. 2(a) by (a) proposed CHWDNN, (b) CHNN, (c) k-means, and (d) dynamic thresholding

detect the defective regions correctly, and there were perceived that there existed many over-detection regions.

In order to evaluate the performance of the proposed CHWDNN, we use two measurement equations defined as Eq. (14) [8].

$$Sensitivity = \frac{N_{tp}}{N_p} \text{ and } Specificity = \frac{N_{tn}}{N_n} \tag{14}$$

Let N_p be the total block number of positive ROIs (region of interested) and N_n denote the total block number of negative ROIs. Let N_{tp} be the block number of detection ROIs that contains defective regions and are actually detection. In addition, the N_{fp} is the block number of ROIs which contains no defective regions but are falsely detected. Similarity, the true negative number (N_{tn}) and false negative number (N_{fn}) can be defined by $N_{tn} = N_n - N_{fp}$ and $N_{fn} = N_p - N_{tp}$, respectively.

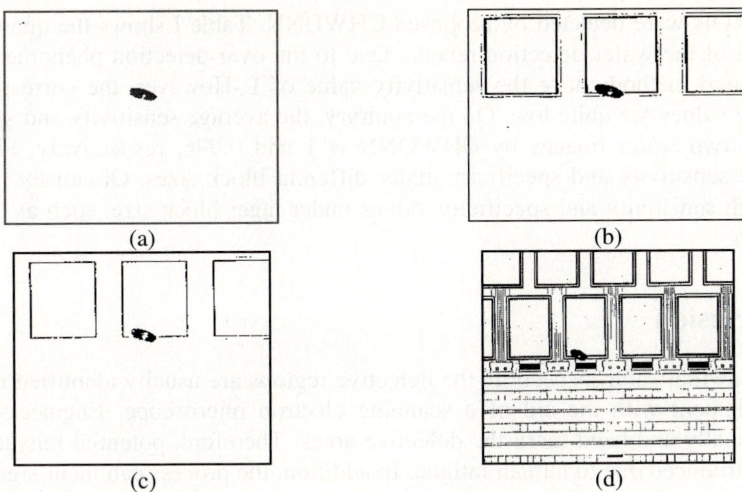

(a)   (b)

(c)   (d)

Fig. 4. Defect inspection results of Fig. 2(b) by (a) proposed CHWDNN, (b) CHNN, (c) k-means, and (d) dynamic thresholding

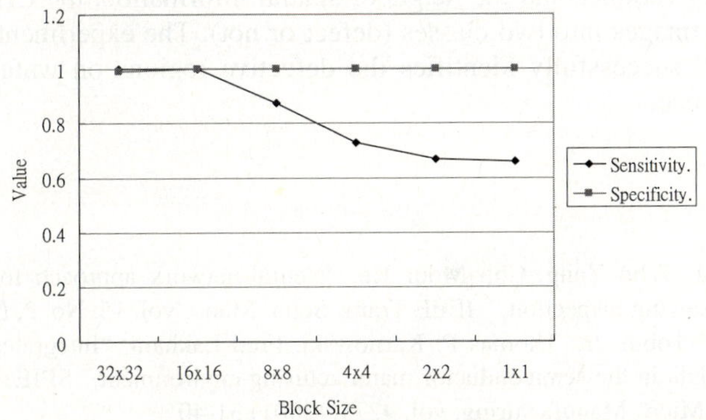

Fig. 5. The sensitivity and specificity values obtained from different block sizes

Table 1. Quantitative comparison results (block size is 32×32)

	CHWDNN		CHNN		k-means		Dynamic thresholding	
	sensitivity	specificity	sensitivity	specificity	sensitivity	specificity	sensitivity	specificity
Fig.2(a)	1	0.997	1	0.0356	1	0.551	1	0.00315
Fig.2(b)	1	0.994	1	0.57	1	0.592	1	0.11824

To quantitative evaluation, both the positive ROI and the detection result are divided into $M \times M$ blocks. One block represents one ROI. If the dimension of wafer image is $N \times N$, then the image can be divided into $(N/M)^2$ ROIs. During the measuring procedure, positive ROIs are hand-marked by experienced testing engineer, and detected ROIs were detected by proposed CHWDNN. Table I shows the quantitative evaluation of the wafer detection results. Due to the over-detection phenomenon, all the compared methods have the sensitivity value of 1. However, the corresponding specificity values are quite low. On the contrary, the average sensitivity and specificity of the two wafer images by CHWDNN is 1 and 0.996, respectively. Figure 5 shows the sensitivity and specificity under different block sizes. Obviously, we can obtain high sensitivity and specificity values under lager block size, such as 32×32 and 16×16.

4 Conclusion

For post-sawing wafer inspection, the defective regions are usually identified through visual judgment with the aid of a scanning electron microscope. Engineers check wafers visually and hand-mark the defective areas. Therefore, potential misjudgment may be introduced due to human fatigue. In addition, the process can incur significant personnel costs. In this paper, a two-layer Hopfield neural network called the competitive Hopfield wafer-defect detection neural network (CHWDNN) is presented for detecting the defective regions automatically. The CHWDNN is capable of incorporating pixel's spatial information into a pixel-classifying procedure. According to the local gray level variance and the neighbor-spatial information, the CHWDNN classified the wafer images into two classes (defect or not). The experimental results show the CHWDNN successfully identifies the defective regions on wafers images with good performance.

References

1. Chao-To Su, Taho Yang, Chir-Mour Ke, "Neural-network approach for Semiconductor wafer post-sawing inspection," IEEE Trans. Semi. Man. , vol. 15, No. 2, (2002) 260-266
2. Kenneth W. Tobin, Jr., Thomas P. Karnowski, Fred Lakhani, "Integrated applications of inspection data in the semiconductor manufacturing environment," SPIE, Metrology-based Control for Micro-Manufacturing, vol. 4275, (2001) 31-40
3. Mital, D.P. Teoh, E.K. "Computer based wafer inspection system," Proceeding of International Conference on Industrial Electronics, Control and Instrumentation, vol. 3, (1991) 2497-2503
4. J.M. Zang, R.M. Lin, and M.J. Wang, "The development of an automatic post-sawing inspection system using computer vision techniques," Computers in Industry, vol. 30, (1999) 51-60
5. Chuan-Yu Chang and Pau-Choo Chung, "Two layer competitive based Hopfield neural network for medical image edge detection," Optical Engineering , vol. 39, no. 3, (2000) 695-703
6. M. Cheriet, J. N. Said, and C. Y. Suen, "A recursive thresholding technique for image segmentation," IEEE Trans. Image Processing, Vol. 7,(1998) 918-921
7. J. S. Lin, K. S. Cheng and C. W. Mao, "The application of competitive Hopfield neural network to medical image segmentation," IEEE Trans. Med. Imag., vol. 15, (1996) 560-567
8. M. G. Penedo, M. J. Carreria, Antonio Mosquera, and D. Cabello, "Computer-Aided Diagnosis: A Neural-Network-Based Approach to Lung Nodule Detection", IEEE Trans. Med. Imag., vol. 17, (1998) 872-880

Supporting Dynamic Supply Networks with Agent-Based Coalitions

Chattrakul Sombattheera and Aditya Ghose

Decision Systems Lab
School of IT and Computer Science, Faculty of Informatics
University of Wollongong, NSW 2500, Australia
{cs50, aditya}@uow.edu.au

Abstract. This work extends our previous work to offer richer support for collaboration across supply networks. The role of agents are divided into three sectors at any point in time: buyers, sellers and LPs. Agents take two steps to form coalitions: *i*) agents in each sector sequencially form primary coalitions in order to increase bargaining power, selling capacity or service efficiency, and *ii*) agents form secondary coalitions across sectors in order to finalize the deal and deliver goods to buyers. We propose a negotiation protocol and deliberation mechanism. The negotiation protocol allows thorough communication among agents within and across sectors. The deliberation mechanism allows agents to consider potential coalition members and attractive payoffs for them. We provide examples of how they can help agents form coalitions successfully.

1 Introduction

The current business environment is characterized by large complex supply networks that are often global in reach and that are highly adaptive, being frequently re-configured to respond to dynamic business contexts. Collaboration across the supply networks is widely recognized as a key prerequisite for supply networks efficiency. Collaboration can be any form of cooperation/coordination among firms (and will be used interchangeably hereafter). The effective deployment of information technology and systems, specially the internet and the web, has made new modes of complex, dynamic yet effective collaboration possible across supply networks. Collaboration in supply networks can take various forms. Suppliers might collaborate to increase selling power or to aggregate capacity. Buyers might collaborate to increase buying power or to reduce logistics costs. LPs might collaborate to increase efficiency in services.

Coalition formation studies the process that rational agents might cooperate to improve individual or social utility. The process involves *i*) deliberation in order to decide with which agents should they cooperate, and *ii*) negotiation in order to exchange information among agents such that they can make decision on cooperation. Once a group of agents unanimously agree to cooperate, they have formed a coalition. Coalition formation research has it's roots in cooperative game theory [1, 2], where the focus of research is how the *coalition value*, which

M. Ali and R. Dapoigny (Eds.): IEA/AIE 2006, LNAI 4031, pp. 1127–1137, 2006.

is the value agents in a coalition jointly created, can be distributed as *payoffs* among the coalition members. In this kind of settings, agents are self-interested, i.e., they seek individually maximal payoffs. They form coalitions when they see opportunity to increase individual payoffs. Coalition formation is ubiquitous in real world settings and can take various forms. We discuss in greater details in section 2.

Coalition formation has been widely studied in supply networks research [3, 4, 5, 6, 7, 8, 9]. A common scenario is coalition formation among buyers, who form coalitions in order to increase their bargaining power and gain some discounts. Such coalitions can be as simple as buying a single good or can be as complex as combinatorial goods [7]. Each agent attempts to seek the most likely formable coalitions and the most attractive payoffs for coalition members in order to reduce the complication in negotiation [10]. These studies solely address the problem of how the discounts achieved from sellers can be distributed among buyers without addressing the delivery cost of the goods. Another common scenario is in logistic domains, where agents are fully cooperative and commonly seek the maximal utility for the system [11, 8]. In this setting, agents cooperatively decide for the optimal solution for the system. The computation for the optimal solution can also computed in centralized fashion when each coalition value is known a priori [8].

We argue that there are missing links in recent coalition formation research in supply networks. Firstly, delivery cost is a serious issue for forming coalitions. Although it is quite common in practice that sellers can provide free delivery for buyers that are located at neighboring locations, disperse geographic proximity of buyers in a coalition can incur an additional delivery cost to those members who are not in such condition. Furthermore, the goods may be sold by themselves without free delivery service being offered at all. Buyers seriously need to take into account such a cost while negotiating with others or they suffer a total high cost. Secondly, the problem of forming coalitions among sellers in response to a large order is an important issue but has been minimally studied [12]. A seller may not be able to cope with the requirement on its own. Thus it is in need of forming a coalition to increase it's selling power. This creates a new model of coalition formation between buyers and sellers that brings various issues into perspective. Lastly, the new model has brought a more complex and challenging problem to which LPs need to react in order to increase their service efficiency. They can seek collaboration with others when they want to increase service or economical efficiency. Hence, collaboration across supply networks can be characterized as highly complex coalitions of buyer(s), seller(s) and LP(s).

This research extends our previous work [13] to offer richer support for dealing with this complexity. In the previous work, buyers, sellers and LPs form primary coalitions simultaneously then try to form secondary coalition across sectors later. This makes the model static and tends to yield low performance. Sellers and logistics providers may not be able to respond to the need of buyers appropriately. This work, buyers form primary coalitions and send their requests to sellers and LPs. Up on receiving the requests, sellers and LPs try to form primary coalitions. Once formed, they can respond to buyers to form secondary coalitions. This makes the model more dynamic and reflects the reality more correctly. In the followings, we describe coalitions in dynamic supply networks. We explain coalition settings in our work and how agents form primary coalitions, which include negotiation among agent of the same sectors and the deliberation mechanism. After that is the explanation of how agents form secondary coalitions across sectors. Lastly, we discuss about related work and conclusion and future work.

2   Coalitions in Dynamic Supply Networks

A *coalition* is a group of agents who unanimously agree to cooperate, e.g., to buy, sell or deliver. Agents are divided according to their roles into buyers, sellers and LPs. The roles of buyer and seller are interchangeable depending on their present activity. An agent can act a seller in a transaction while becomes a buyer in another transaction. Although it is easy to view LPs as sellers, the role of LPs are quite distinct from other sellers that they sell delivery services. Furthermore, the effect of LPs' role can be captured more easily.

A simple example of coalition formation is a small market game [2], where a seller has a good on sale and two buyers are bidding for it. The seller has a value for the good in mind and is unwilling to accept offers below this price, referred to as the seller's *reserve price*. Each buyer also has a private evaluation of the worth of the good and will not pay higher than this worth, called the buyer's *reserve price*. Buyers compete with each other by offering a price for the good to the seller. When a buyer offer a price that the other cannot compete with, that buyer then can buy the good off the seller at that price. This can be viewed as they have reached an agreement to cooperate, i.e., they have formed a coalition to trade the good. The value of a coalition is the difference between the buyers and the sellers reserve prices. The payoffs for both agents are the differences between their reserve prices and the sell price. A simple coalition in supply networks is one where a buyer forms a coalition with a seller and an LP. A more complex of such a coalition involves multiple agents in each sector.

There are multiple distinct drivers for coalition formation. Several small buyers with similar needs coming together to obtain greater bargaining power. Sellers form coalitions with other sellers to aggregate selling power. In some settings, there are legal impediments to certain forms of such coalitions (specifically cartels) in the form of anti-trust laws. However, such coalitions are common for small sellers, such as in agricultural cooperatives (e.g. for micro-producers of dairy products). Sellers sometimes form coalitions to aggregate/augment capabilities. LPs may want to form coalitions to aggregate their service capacities or efficiency. We note that we have only listed the basic drivers. Most real-life supply network coalitions tend to have more than one motivating factor driving their formation. Multiple factors play a role in coalition formation decisions. In the current work, we focus on quantitative factors, e.g., price, delivery cost and lead time. Most decisions typically involve trade-offs among several attributes. One may be willing to pay more for a shorter lead time and vice versa. One may, in some settings, be willing to accept longer lead times for the purpose of getting higher quality. Several other instances of such trade-off are common, but we do not list them all here.

Although negotiation can be either bilateral or multilateral, we can in most instances reduce negotiation to the bilateral case without loss of generality. An agent that stands to benefit the most from forming a coalition usually acts as the coalition *leader*. Firstly, a coalition leader negotiates bilaterally with multiple agents of its own sector to establish a sectoral coalition. An agent might find itself forming a singleton primary coalition because it cannot find suitable coalition members nor there is need to do so. We call this type of coalitions *primary coalition*. Firstly, buyers form primary coalitions and the coalition leaders send request to sellers and LP(s). Interested sellers and LP(s) then form primay coalitions among themselves. The coalition leaders then negotiate across sectors to establish a cross-sectoral coalition involving a coalition of buyer(s), seller(s) and LP(s). We call the type of coalitions *secondary coalition*. This secondary coalition is where the real trade is finalized. The buying leader collects money from its members and pays to the selling leader and LP leader, who in turn distribute among their members. Then the coalitions will break. Members can form coalitions later on should they need to do so. We note that these negotiations must occur within stringent time constraints.

3   Coalition Formation

3.1   Setting

At a point in time, let $B = \{b_1, b_2, \ldots, b_m\}$, $S = \{s_1, s_2, \ldots, s_n\}$ and $L = \{l_1, l_2, \ldots, l_o\}$ are set of agents who act buyers, sellers and LPs respectively. Buyers order goods, $F = \{f_1, f_2, \ldots, f_p\}$, from sellers. LPs distribute the goods over a transportation network, $G = \{V, E\}$, where V is a set of vertices and E is a set of edges, each of which connects a pair of vertices, for them. The location of each buyer b, seller s, and LP l are specified by function $\mathcal{L}_b : B \to V, \mathcal{L}_s : S \to V$, and $\mathcal{L}_l : L \to V$ respectively. These three functions are accessible to all agents. Agents have individual goals and constraints. A goal is represented by the good that an agent may seek to buy or sell. Constraints are the time/deadline and the price at which they wish to conclude the transaction. The amount of a specific good required by a specific buyer is given by $\mathcal{D} : B \times F \to \mathbb{N}^+$, under a budget determined by the function $\mathcal{B} : B \to \mathbb{R}^+$ and a due time, $\mathcal{T} : B \times F \to \mathbb{N}^+$ (here the output of the function denotes the number of time units from some commonly agreed upon origin at which the good is required). The amount of a certain good that a seller can produce is given by $\mathcal{P} : F \times S \to \mathbb{N}^+$. The time it takes to produce a good is determined by $\mathcal{R} : F \times S \to \mathbb{N}^+$. The cost of producing a single unit of good is $\mathcal{C}_P : F \times S \to \mathbb{R}^+$. An LP is initialized with a load capacity, $\mathcal{L} : L \times F \to \mathbb{N}^+$ (thus $\mathcal{L}(l, g)$ denotes the quantity of good g that LP l can ship, if good g was the only l was shipping). The cost of delivery is $\mathcal{C}_D : V \times V \to \mathbb{R}^+$. The time of traveling is $\mathcal{C}_T : V \times V \to \mathbb{N}^+$.

3.2   Forming Primary Coalitions

In the followings, we shall use the notation $\langle x, y, z \rangle$ to designate a collection of a certain kind of vectors. The notation $\langle f, q, t \rangle$, for example, denotes a collection of k requirement vectors $\langle f_i, q_i, t \rangle$, where f_i is a good an agent want to buy, q_i is a quantity that the good is needed for, and t_i is the time by which the good is needed, for all $1 \leq i \leq k$. Similar interpretation applies for the rest of the paper.

Buyer to Buyer Negotiation. A buyer, who wants to buy goods and foresees an opportunity to gain some discounts from buying a large quantity, acts as a coalition leader by negotiating with other buyers. We shall call it the leading buyer. The following is the protocol for forming a coalition of buyers.

1. Every buyer b sends a message $(b, \langle f, q, t \rangle, v, p)$, where b is the identifier of the agent, $\langle f, q, t \rangle$ is a collection of requirements vector, $v \in V$ is the location where the good will be delivered, p is the price, and t is the due time it wants the good to be delivered.
2. Based on it's deliberation, any buyer can act leading buyer, b_0, and initiate the process of forming a primary coalition of buyers. (See section Deliberation for Joining Primary Coalition for more details).
3. Leading buyer b_0 sends a message $(msg, b_0, \langle f, q, t \rangle, v, p, x)$, where msg is the message id, p is the price, and x is the expiry time to potential buyers in it's current best potential coalition.
4. Any buyer, who is satisfied with the offer, sends a message (msg, b, ACK, x) back to b_0 stating that it will wait for a confirmation until time x.
5. Leading buyer b_0 sends message (msg, b_0, ACK) to inform all interested buyers that now the new primary coalition has been formed.
6. Leading buyer b_0 sends message $B2S(msg, b_0, \langle f, q, t \rangle, p)$ to sellers, where $\langle f, q, t \rangle$ is the order details compiled from its members, and t is the available time.
7. At the same time, the leading buyer sends message $B2L(id, b_0, \langle f, q, v, t \rangle, \langle f', q', v', t' \rangle, p)$, where $\langle f, q, v, t \rangle$ and $\langle f', q', v', t' \rangle$ specifies job description for picking up from sellers and delivering the goods to buyers, to LPs.

The leading buyer may find itself being a singleton coalition, i.e., it can not agree with other buyers nor there is need to do so at all. Once the coalition is formed, it can negotiate with sellers and LPs to form secondary coalition by sending messages to them.

Seller to Seller Negotiation. Up on receiving the message from a leading buyer, interested sellers react. If the order is within it's capability, it may form a singleton coalition on its own. If the order is beyond it's capability, it can act as a coalition leader and try to form a coalition of seller in order to increase it's selling power. We shall call it leading seller.

1. Interested sellers send a message $(msg, s, \langle f, q, \mathfrak{p}, \mathfrak{r}, v \rangle)$, where msg is the message id sent by b_0, $\mathfrak{p}$ is specified by function $\mathcal{P}$, $\mathfrak{r}$ is specified by function $\mathcal{R}$, and $\langle f, q, \mathfrak{p}, \mathfrak{r}, v \rangle$ is the list of capability vectors, to all other sellers.

2. Any seller can act leading seller, s_0, and try to form a primary coalition with other sellers. It selects a number of sellers, who might help increasing its selling power (See section Deliberation for Joining Primary Coalition for more details).

3. Leading seller s_0 sends a message $(msg, s_0, \langle s, f, v \rangle, x)$, where $\langle s, f, v \rangle$ is a collection of preferred capability vectors, to selected seller.

4. Any seller, who is satisfied with the offer, replies with the message (msg, s, ACK, x) and waits for the confirmation by time x.

5. Agent s_0 confirms that a primary coalition is formed with the message (msg, s_0, ACK).

The leading seller may find itself being a singleton coalition because it cannot agree with other sellers. It can begin negotiation with the leading buyer to form secondary coalition.

LP to LP Negotiation. Up on receiving the message from leading buyer b_0, interested LPs react. Any interested LP may try to form a primary coalition with other LPs. We shall call such LP leading LP.

1. Every interested LP sends a message $(msg, l, \mathfrak{l}, v)$, where msg is the message id sent by b_0, $\mathfrak{l}$ is the load capacity specified by function $\mathcal{L}$, to all other LPs.

2. Any interested LP can act leading LP, l_0, and try to form a primary coalition with other LPs. It selects a number of LPs, who might help increase its capacity and service efficiency. (See section Deliberation for Joining Primary Coalition for more details).

3. Leading LP l_0 sends a message (msg, l_0, v, x), to agents selected if they would like to form a primary coalition.

4. Any LP, who is satisfied with the offer, replies with the message (msg, l, ACK, x) and waits for the confirmation by time x.

5. Agent l_0 confirms to its primary coalition members with the message (msg, l_0, ACK).

The leading LP may find itself being a singleton coalition. It then can negotiate with the leading buyer b_0 on behalf of it's members to form a secondary coalition.

Deliberation for Joining Primary Coaltion. Agents have a common view when forming primary coalitions: Quality of Coalition (QoC). QoC indicates the likelyhood to achieve the goal of the coalition. The common goal of every agent is to maximize it's payoff. Buyers need members who can help increase bargaining power. Sellers need member who can help increase selling power, which in turn helps maximize their payoffs. LPs needs member who can help increase service efficiency, which in turn helps maximize their payoffs. Based on it status, an agent can create an ideal coalition, the one with the highest QoC. The agent create a template, which is an ideal coalition member of the ideal coalition. Each agent measures the suitability of another agent to the the ideal coalition in terms of the distance between that agent and this template. It uses the distance to rank other agents in a table, which will be used to help select appropriate agents for forming high QoC coalitions. Let $A = \{a_1, a_2, \ldots, a_m\}$ be a set of attributes. Let $B = \{L_1, U_1, L_2, U_2, \ldots, L_m, U_m\}$ be a set of lower bounds and upper bounds of quantitative attributes $a_1, a_2, \ldots, a_m$. A template is a vector $t = \langle q_1, q_2, \ldots, q_m, w_1, w_2 \ldots, w_m \rangle$, where q_i is a quantitative attribute q_j, and w_k is the weight for each a_k of m attributes. The agent a_0, who wants to form a primary coalition, uses the attributes passed over in the first step of the negotiation to measure the distance between other agents and its templates. The closer distance signifies the more suitability for the coalition of the agents. The distance can be considered as the sum of the difference of each pair of corresponding attributes in the template and the agents' attributes. For each attribute, the distance should be 0 if the attribute's value are equal. Otherwise the distance is the multiplication of the difference between the values of corresponding attributes, and the weight for that attribute. Let y_j be the value of attribute j of the template, the distance between an agent and a template can be derived as following:

$$d = \sum_{j=1}^{m} \mathit{Diff}(q_j, y_j) w_m$$

where

$$\mathit{Diff}(q_j, y_j) = \begin{cases} \infty & \text{if } y_j \rangle U_j \text{ or } y_j \langle U_j \\ \frac{q_j - y_j}{q_j - L_j} & \text{if } q_j \rangle y_j \text{ and } y_j \text{ is } \geq L_j \\ \frac{y_j - q_j}{U_j - qj} & \text{if } q_j \langle y_j \text{ and } y_j \text{ is } \leq U_j \\ 0 & \text{if } q_j = y_j \end{cases}$$

Let us consider an example of how this mechanism works. Suppose there are four attributes, $A = \{f, q, p, t\}$, to describe a quality of primary coalition of buyers. Let $B = \{1, 10, 10, 20, 10, 30, 0, 100\}$ be the set of upper and lower bounds for f, q, p and t, respectively. Let $T = \langle 1, 15, 20, 30, \infty, 10, 1, 5 \rangle$ be a template of buyer b_0, who is considering forming a primary coalition. There are two buyers, b_1 and b_2 being considered whether they should be invited to join the coalition. Their attributes, achieved from the messages, are $\{1, 13, 18, 28\}$ and $\{1, 17, 23, 34\}$, respectively. The distance between agent b_1 and template T is

$$\begin{aligned} d_1 &= (0 * \infty) + (2/5) * 10 + (2/10) * 1 + (2/300) * 5 \\ &= 0 + 4 + 0.2 + 0.33 \\ &= 4.53 \end{aligned}$$

The distance between agent b_2 and template T is

$$\begin{aligned} d2 &= (0 * \infty) + (2/5) * 10 + (3/10) * 1 + (4/70) * 5 \\ &= 0 + 4 + 0.3 + 0.57 \\ &= 4.87 \end{aligned}$$

Since 4.53 is less than 4.87, agent b_1 is obviously closer to the template than b_2. Hence, agent b_1 sits higher in the ranking table.

Each agent uses its own ranking table to compute potential primary coalitions, those it might try to form, and keep them in a list. The agent sets up a period of time for deliberation, i.e., generating coalitions and adding them into the list. It computes, for each potential coalition, the aggregrated distance, which is the sum of all members' distance to the template. It then ranks those coalitions by the coalitions' aggregated distance in ascending order. In each potential coalition, the agent computes potential payoffs for the members. The agent considers each potential coalition one by one from the top of the list. For best potential coalition being considered, the agent decides to be a leading agent if it's potential payoff is the greatest. It then follows the primary protocol to negotiate with others. If the agent's potential payoff is not the greatest, it will wait for some time. Up on receiving an invitation message, it computes it's potential payoff and compares it to the potential payoff in the second best potential coalition of it's own list. If the the inviting potential payoff is not lower, the agent accepts the offer, or rejects it otherwise. In case the coalition cannot be formed. The next potential will be considered. More potential coalitions will be computed when needed.

3.3   Secondary Coalitions

A secondary coalition is composed of three primary coalitions: a buyer, a seller and an LP primary coalitions. The negotiation occurs among coalition leaders and within primary coalition members as an ongoing process. They try to agree on their payoffs and tasks (to supply good for sellers and to deliver goods for LPs). Agents who are not satisfied with payoffs being offered may decide to deviate from thier present primary coalitions and try to form new ones.

Buyers to Sellers and LPs. Firstly, leading sellers and leading LPs try to agree on an offer for the corresponding buyer. The negotiation involves their payoffs and tasks.

1. Each member seller evaluates it present capability and sends it's s_0 a message $S2S(msg, b, \langle f, q, t \rangle, p)$ bidding for the supply task.
2. Leading seller s_0 may have to negotiate on good, quantity, time and price with member sellers with message $S2S(id, b, \langle f, q, t \rangle, p)$ until every member seller is satisfied and the total quantity, available time and price is satisfied with the request.
3. Leading seller s_0 accumulates the bids from its member sellers and creates an offer. It then sends message $S2B(msg, s_0, \langle f, q, v, t \rangle, p)$ back to b_0.
4. Similarly, member LP l bids for the task by sending message $L2L(id, \langle f, q, v, t \rangle, \langle f', q', v', t' \rangle, p)$ to its leading LP l_0.
5. Leading LP l_0 may have to negotiate over quantity, pickup location, delivery location, pickup time, delivery time, and price with its member.
6. The leading LP l_0 accumulate all the bid from its members in order to create an offer for the delivery job.
7. It sends a message, i.e., proposal, $(id, s_0, \langle f, q, v, t \rangle, p)$ back to b_0.
8. The leading buyer b_0 accumulate the proposals from the leading sellers and leading LPs and find the best combination of a selling and a LP proposals. It then creates a proposal to its members and sends message $(id, s_0, \langle f, q, v, t \rangle, p)$ to the members.
9. Members who are satisfied with the proposal sends a message (id, s, ACK) to l_0.

10. Members who are not satisfied can negotiate over quantity, time and price by sending message $(id, s, \langle f, q, v, t \rangle, p)$ back to the leading agent.
11. Once all member buyers are satisfied, leading buyer then sends message (id, b_0, ACK) to the selected leading seller and leading LP.
12. The leading buyer, seller, and LP send message $(id, a_0, CONFIRM)$ to their coalition members confirming that the secondary has been formed.

LPs are to pickup the good from sellers and deliver to buyers. Sellers and LPs get paid when the good is delivered. The negotiation within and among primary coalitions can keep going until agents are satisfied or the time is over.

3.4   Decision Mechanism

In our setting, each agent has their individual reserve price. For a buyer, the reserve price r_b is the maximum price he is willing to pay for acquiring a bunch of goods, i.e., including prices of goods and costs of delivery. For a seller, the reserve price r_s is the cost c_p of producing goods and the minimum profit it expects. For an LP, the reserve price r_l would be the estimated cost of operation and the minimum profit it expects. Let $\mathsf{B} \subseteq B, \mathsf{S} \subseteq S,$ and$\mathsf{L} \subseteq L$ be a set of buyers in a primary coalition, a set of sellers in a primary coalition, and a set of LPs in a primary coalition, respectively. For a secondary coalition $\mathsf{C} = \{\mathsf{B}, \mathsf{S}, \mathsf{L}\}$, the reserve price of B is $r_\mathsf{B} = \sum_{b \in B} r_b$, the reserve price of S is $r_\mathsf{S} = \sum_{s \in S} r_s$, and the reserve price of L is $r_\mathsf{L} = \sum_{l \in L} r_l$.

The coalition value of a secondary coalition C is $V_\mathsf{C} = r_\mathsf{B} + r_\mathsf{S} + r_\mathsf{L}$, which is to be distributed among agents. Let $\mathsf{P_S}$ be the price sellers charge buyers. Let $\mathsf{P_L}$ be the price LPs charge buyers. The payoff for buyers in B is $U_\mathsf{B} = r_\mathsf{B} - \mathsf{P_S} - \mathsf{P_L}$. The payoff for sellers in S is $U_\mathsf{S} = \mathsf{P_S} - r_\mathsf{S}$. The payoff for LPs in L is $U_\mathsf{L} = \mathsf{P_L} - r_\mathsf{L}$.

The price each agent use to negotiate may be higher than their reserve prices. There are several solution concepts in coalition formation theory [1], e.g., core, kernel, etc. Knowing biding price of every agent in its primary coalitions, the leading agent can use a fair division of their coalition payoff by using the Shapley value [1] concept. Agents in the primary coalition may find that the shares offered by the leading agent are below than their own reserve price. Hence they may have to deviate from their present primary coalitions.

4   Related Work

Coalition formation is an active research area in multi-agent systems. In addition to analyzing stability and payoff distribution, researchers pay more attention to the formation mechanism, i.e., negotiation protocols among agents and the decision making, or reasoning, of individual agents. Previous work has done some part of our proposing framework as the followings. Tsvetovat et al. [9] studied the formation of buyers in university environment where students buy their text books in group. Li et al. [7] addressed the combinatorial auction in coalition formation. Buyers submit their requests to the mediator who will allocate the good from sellers to them. Goldman et al. [5] searched for a strategy where sellers selected the most profitable deal while buyers looked for the most satisfiable sellers. Kraus et al. [4] proposed a compromise strategy for distributing profits among sellers in order to form coalition quickly. They found that agents who are willing to give away their profits actually earn more. Breban et al. [3] addressed the coalition formation based on trust among agents. Trust is used as a mechanism to enforce agents to commit themselves to the jobs as parts of the coalition. Hyodo et al. [14] addressed the optimal coalitions of buyers and sellers who are located in distributed sites. They deploy genetic algorithm to search for the optimal share over the discount. Klusch et al. [6] addressed problems in static coalition formation and proposed an algorithm for mobile agents to form coalition under dynamic environment. Agents can form overlapping coalitions. The stability is low since agents are allowed to leave their coalitions at any time. Sandholm et al. [8] studied coalition formation of trucks in dispatch centers. There is no work in coalition formation, as we are aware of, that combines buying and delivery.

5   Conclusion and Future Work

This paper proposes a model of agents-based coalitions in dynamic supply networks. In our setting, agents take two steps: i) agents in each sector form loosely-coupled coalitions in order to decrease the complexity of the negotiation, and, ii) agents form coalitions across sectors in order to deliver goods to end customers. We propose a framework, which involves negotiation protocol and decision mechanism. The negotiation protocol allows thorough communication, i.e., buyers to buyers, buyers to sellers, sellers to sellers, buyer to LPs, and LPs to LPs. Since one of the important issues in supply chains is to minimize logistics costs, the aim of our future work is to find a mechanism that helps buyers to manage controlling logistics process rather than leaving it to sellers. We believe that with efficient negotiation protocol and decision making mechanism, the logistics costs can be reduced.

References

1. Kahan, J.P., Rapoport, A.: Theories of Coalition Formation. Lawrence Erlbaum Associates, Hillsdale, New Jersey (1984)
2. Neumann, J.V., Morgenstern, O.: Theory of Games and Economic Behaviour. Princeton University Press, Princeton, New Jersey (1953 (1963 printing))
3. Breban, S., Vassileva, J.: A coalition formation mechanism based on inter-agent trust relationships. In: Proceedings of the first international joint conference on Autonomous agents and multiagent systems, ACM Press (2002) 306–307
4. Kraus, S., Shehory, O., Taase, G.: The advantages of compromising in coalition formation with incomplete information. In: Proc. of AAMAS-2004. (2004)
5. Goldman, C.V., Kraus, S., Shehory, O.: Agent strategies: for sellers to satisfy purchase-orders, for buyers to select sellers. In: . Proceedings of the 10th European Workshop on Modeling Autonomous Agents in a Multiagent World (Maamaw '01), Annecy, France. (2001)

6. Klusch, M., Gerber, A.: Dynamic coalition formation among rational agents. Intelligent Systems, IEEE **17** (2002) 42–47
7. Li, C., Sycara, K.: Algorithms for combinatorial coalition formation and payoff division in an electronic marketplace. Technical Report CMU-RI-TR-01-33, Robotics Institute, Carnegie Mellon University, Pittsburgh, PA (2001)
8. Sandholm, T., Lesser, V.: Coalition Formation among Bounded Rational Agents. 14th International Joint Conference on Artificial Intelligence (1995) 662–669
9. Tsvetovat, M., Sycara, K.: Customer coalitions in the electronic marketplace. In: ACM 2000. (2000)
10. Shehory, O., Kraus, S.: Methods for task allocation via agent coalition formation. Artif. Intell. **101** (1998) 165–200
11. Sandholm, T., Larson, K., Andersson, M., Shehory, O., Tohm, F.: Coalition structure generation with worst case guarantees. Artif. Intell. **111** (1999) 209–238
12. Klusch, M., Contreras, J., Wu, F., Shehory, O.: Coalition formation in a power transmission planning environment. In: Proc. 2. International Conference on Practical Applications of Multi-Agent Systems. (1997)
13. Sombattheera, C., Ghose, A.: Agent-based coalitions in dynamic supply chains. In: Proceedings of The Ninth Pacific Asia Conference on Information Systems. (2005)
14. HYODO, M., MATSUO, T., ITO, T.: An optimal coalition formation algorithm for electronic group buying. In: Proc. of 2003 SICE Annual Conference (SICE2003). (2003)

Reducing Transportation Costs in Distribution Networks

Xi Li[1], Andrew Lim[1], Zhaowei Miao[2], and Brian Rodrigues[3]

[1] Department of IELM, Hong Kong University of Science and Technology,
Clear Water Bay, Hong Kong
[2] School of Computer Science & Engineering, South China University of Technology,
Guang Dong, P.R. China
[3] Lee Kong Chian School of Business, Singapore Management University,
Singapore 178899

Abstract. In this work, we model the conflicting objectives in a distribution network, i.e. trade-offs between transportation costs, inventory and time scheduling requirements. Transportation costs include time costs, truck setup costs, and the number of trucks used. The model is formulated as an integer program and a solution of two-stage metaheuristic is provided. Computational experiments are conducted to test the algorithms.

Keywords: genetic algorithm, heuristic search, inventory, transportation scheduling.

1 Introduction

As companies seek more profitable supply chain management, there has been a desire to optimize distribution networks to reduce logistics costs. This includes finding the best locations for facilities, minimizing inventory, and minimizing transportation costs.

In this work, we focus on reducing transportation costs in distribution networks with the added objective that transshipment centers achieve the quick reshipment goal of crossdocks. In particular, we study trucking consolidation since trucking accounts for 83 percent of freight transportation in the US alone (Wilson 2002). Among companies that have benefited from trucking consolidation, Nabisco Inc., for example, has used consolidation to reduce transportation costs by half, and to bring down inventory levels and improve on delivery (Quinn 1997, Gümüs and Bookbinder 2004).

The model we study has its roots in the classical transshipment problem which is concerned with shipping quantities and routes to be taken through transshipment centers. The problem has been studied in the context of network flow (Hoppe and Tardos 1995) to find the shortest transshipment time. For the general n location transshipment model, Robinson (1990), who developed a large LP by discretizing demand, provided heuristic solutions, while Tayur (1995) used a gradient based approach for the problem, also after discretizing demand.

M. Ali and R. Dapoigny (Eds.): IEA/AIE 2006, LNAI 4031, pp. 1138–1148, 2006.

Although these studies considered inventory and transshipment costs, they did not address time constraints which are present during the transshipment process, for example, constraints imposed by transportation schedules or time window constraints at supply and demand nodes. When time is a critical factor, distribution through crossdocks, which have become synonymous with rapid consolidation and processing, have been studied. Napolitano (2000) has described manufacturing, transportation, distribution, retail and opportunistic crossdocking, all of which have the common feature of consolidation and short cycle times made possible by known pick-up and delivery times. Physical operations which reduce labor costs in LTL crossdocking has been studied by Bartholdi et al. (2000). Some similar work has also been studied by Lim et al. (2005).

The model we study is a global optimization problem which identifies the best choices between the conflicting objectives in distribution network logistics, i.e. trade-offs between transportation costs, inventory and time scheduling requirements at all stages of the supply chain. Transportation costs include time costs, truck setup costs, and the number of trucks used. The model is formulated as an integer program, for which we provide a solution approach which is called two-stage metaheuristic algorithm. Computational experiments are conducted to test the algorithms and comparisons made with exact solutions where these are available.

2   The Model

In this article, any retailer or cluster of retailers at a location supplied directly from the manufacturers or through transshipment centers is referred to as a "customer" (cf. Gümüs and Bookbinder 2004). We refer to transshipment centers and crossdocks by the collective term "crossdock". We assume that each customer is at a predetermined location $k \in \Delta \equiv \{1, ..., m\}$, and demands d_k units of a single product which can be shipped from any manufacturer situated at $i \in \Sigma \equiv \{1, ..., n\}$, either directly or through a crossdock $j \in \mathbf{X} \equiv \{1, ..., l\}$. The value d_k represents the total demand of the retailer or cluster of retailers which are represented by k. Each $i \in \Sigma$, has a supply capacity of s_i units of the product, which can only be shipped (released) in the time window $[b_i^r, e_i^r](i \in \Sigma)$ and must be delivered (accepted) within the time window $[b_k^a, e_k^a](k \in \Delta)$. Also, total supply can meet demand, i.e., $\sum_{i \in \Sigma} s_i \geq \sum_{k \in \Delta} d_k$, and, at each crossdock, a holding cost, given by $h_j(j \in \mathbf{X})$ per unit per time, takes effect. This implicitly allows for shipments to be delayed at crossdocks. Figure 1 illustrates the problem for the multiple -manufacturer, -crossdock and -customer case.

A truck delivering to customers arrives at location following which it can be routed to other locations in the cluster, if required. The delivery routing plan to each retailer in the cluster can be solved separately from the model. This may be preferable since, for example, local trucking vendors provide smaller truck load capacity for short haul delivery and there is no warehousing required. Alternatively, the set of customers can be expanded to include part of or all cluster points. For each truck, we assume variable setup costs which are determined by, for example, location, vendors, and type of freight carried.

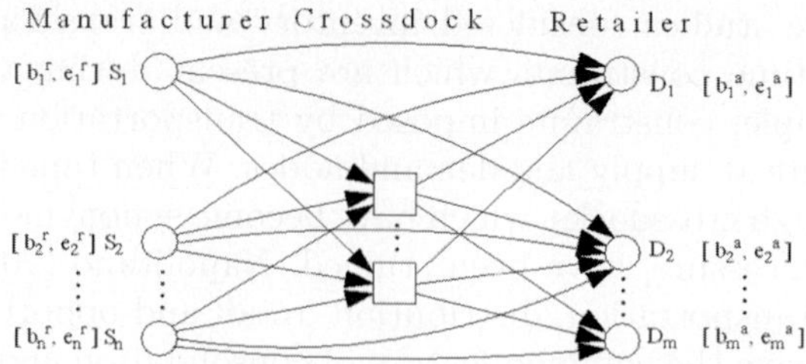

Fig. 1. Distribution network with crossdocks and time windows

In the model, we take the time horizon to be discrete (see Hoppe and Tardos 1995) and given by the non-negative integers, and shipment times can be represented as integers. The following parameters are used:

d_k: the demand quantity of customer $k(k \in \Delta)$
s_i: the available quantity of supplier $i(i \in \Sigma)$
p : setup cost for each truck on arc $(i, k)(i \in \Sigma, k \in \Delta)$
$p^{'}$: setup cost for each truck on arc $(i, j)(i \in \Sigma, j \in \mathbf{X})$
$p^{''}$: setup cost for each truck on arc $(j, k)(j \in \mathbf{X}, k \in \Delta)$
h_j: inventory holding cost per unit product per unit time in crossdock j $(j \in \mathbf{X})$
d_{ik}: total shipping time on arc $(i, k)(i \in \Sigma, k \in \Delta)$
$d^{'}_{ij}$: total shipping time on arc $(i, j)(i \in \Sigma, j \in \mathbf{X})$
$d^{''}_{jk}$: total shipping time on arc $(j, k)(j \in \mathbf{X}, k \in \Delta)$
c_{ik}: shipping cost per unit product per unit time on segment $(i, k)(i \in \Sigma, k \in \Delta)$
$c^{'}_{ij}$: shipping cost per unit product per unit time on segment $(i, j)(i \in \Sigma, j \in \mathbf{X})$
$c^{''}_{jk}$: shipping cost per unit product per unit time on segment $(j, k)(j \in \mathbf{X}, k \in \Delta)$
T_i: set of feasible shipping time points from supplier i, i.e., $T_i = \{b^r_i, b^r_i + 1, ..., e^r_i\}(i \in \Sigma)$
T_{jk}: set of feasible shipping time points from crossdock j to demand point k,
   i.e., $T_{jk} = \{b^a_k - d_{jk}, b^a_k - d_{jk} + 1, ..., e^a_k - d_{jk}\}(j \in \mathbf{X}, k \in \Delta)$
$T^{'}_j$: set of feasible time points at which shipments can arrive at or depart from crossdock j, i.e.
   $T^{'}_j = \{\min_{i \in \Sigma}\{e^r_i + d^{'}_{ij}\}, \min_{i \in \Sigma}\{e^r_i + d^{'}_{ij}\} + 1, ..., \max_{i \in \Sigma}\{b^r_i + d^{'}_{ij}\}\}(j \in \mathbf{X})$
Q: capacity of each truck.

The decision variables required for the model are:

x_{ikt}: quantity of product shipped on arc (i, k) at time $t(i \in \Sigma, k \in \Delta, t \in T_i)$
$x^{'}_{ijt}$: quantity of product shipped on arc (i, j) at time $t(i \in \Sigma, j \in \mathbf{X}, t \in T_i)$
$x^{''}_{jkt}$: quantity of product shipped on arc (j, k) at time $t(j \in \mathbf{X}, k \in \Delta, t \in T_{jk})$
v_{ikt}: number of trucks used on arc (i, k) at time $t(i \in \Sigma, k \in \Delta, t \in T_i)$
$v^{'}_{ijt}$: number of trucks used on arc (i, j) at time $t(i \in \Sigma, j \in \mathbf{X}, t \in T_i)$
$v^{''}_{jkt}$: number of trucks used on arc (j, k) at time $t(j \in \mathbf{X}, k \in \Delta, t \in T_{jk})$
I_{jt}: quantity of inventory in crossdock j at time $t(j \in \mathbf{X}, t \in T^{'}_j)$

The objective in the shipping consolidation problem (SCP) is to minimize the total cost including transportation and inventory costs while satisfying time window constraints. Transportation costs include time costs, truck setup costs and the number of trucks deployed. With the above notation, the SCP can be given by the following integer program:

$$\min \sum_{i \in \Sigma} \sum_{k \in \Delta} \sum_{t \in T_i} (p v_{ikt} + c_{ik} d_{ik} x_{ikt}) + \sum_{i \in \Sigma} \sum_{j \in X} \sum_{t \in T_i} (p' v'_{ijt} + c'_{ij} d'_{ij} x'_{ijt})$$

$$+ \sum_{j \in X} \sum_{k \in \Delta} \sum_{t \in T_{jk}} (p'' v''_{jkt} + c''_{jk} d''_{jk} x''_{jkt}) + \sum_{j \in X} \sum_{t \in T'_j} h_j I_{jt} \tag{1}$$

s.t.

$$\sum_{j \in X} \sum_{t \in T_i} x'_{ijt} + \sum_{k \in \Delta} \sum_{t \in T_i} x_{ikt} \le s_i \quad (i \in \Sigma) \tag{2}$$

$$\sum_{j \in X} \sum_{t \in T_{jk}} x''_{jkt} + \sum_{i \in \Sigma} \sum_{t \in T_i} x_{ikt} = d_k \quad (k \in \Delta) \tag{3}$$

$$I_{j,t-1} + \sum_{i \in \Sigma} x'_{ij,t-d'_{ij}} - \sum_{k \in \Delta} x''_{jkt} = I_{jt} \quad (j \in X, \, t \in T'_j) \tag{4}$$

$$I_{j,t} = 0 \quad (j \in X, \, t = \min_t\{t \in T'_j\} - 1) \tag{5}$$

$$I_{j,t} = 0 \quad (j \in X, \, t = \max_t\{t \in T'_j\}) \tag{6}$$

$$Q(v_{ikt} - 1) < x_{ikt} \le Q v_{ikt} \quad (i \in \Sigma, \, k \in \Delta, \, t \in T_i) \tag{7}$$

$$Q(v'_{ijt} - 1) < x'_{ikt} \le Q v'_{ijt} \quad (i \in \Sigma, \, j \in X, \, t \in T_i) \tag{8}$$

$$Q(v''_{jkt} - 1) < x''_{ikt} \le Q v''_{jkt} \quad (j \in X, \, k \in \Delta, t \in T_{jk}) \tag{9}$$

$$\textit{All decision variables are nonnegative integers} \tag{10}$$

In the objective function, the first term gives direct transportation costs from manufacturers to customers, including all truck setup costs and time costs; the second and third terms are similar to the first, and represent costs between manufacturers and crossdocks and crossdocks and customers, respectively. The last term represents total holding cost. Constraints (2) ensure the total quantity of the product shipped from manufacturers is no greater than the available supply. Similarly, constraints (3) ensure that total quantity of product received meets demand. Constraints (4) require that, for each crossdock, the inventory at time t is equal to the inventory heldover at time $t - 1$ plus the total quantity received at time t minus the quantity shipped out at time t. Constraints (5) and (6) are initial and terminal conditions, respectively, of the inventory level at each cross-dock. Constraints (7), (8) and (9) ensure that the number of trucks used on any route is a minimum.

This problem is $\mathcal{NP}hard$ in strong sense(Miao 2005). In view of the computational complexity of the problem, we provide in the next section, a heuristic approach to its solution.

3   A Two-Stage Heuristic

In attempting to find solutions for the SCP, we need to decide the quantity to be shipped, shipment times and routes to be taken. Once TL quantities are decided, LTL shipments at crossdocks need to consolidated at the manufacturer and crossdock to reduce truck setup costs. The solution approach we take has two components: (1) a full truck load (TL) plan, and (2) a less than truck load (LTL) Plan. This is used in a two-stage heuristic algorithm. In the first, initialization, stage, a solution is found which consists of a TL Plan and a LTL Plan. The TL Plan is found using a network flow algorithm. In a second, iteration, stage, a metaheuristics is used to improve the LTL Plan.

Stage 1: Initialization
A TL Plan is developed, which is used to obtain an initial LTL Plan.

(1)TL Plan
A transportation plan is found by solving a network flow problem determined as follows. Split the demand at each customer into a TL part and a LTL part, and remove the LTL part (remainders) from the demand. Next, form the network G with $|\Sigma|$ supply nodes and $|\Delta|$ customer nodes, without time windows or crossdocks, where the demand is the TL demand obtained in the preceding step and where the supply is unchanged. Each arc in G is taken to be the least cost route available for a TL shipment from a supply node to a demand node, which does not violate time window constraints. Each arc represents a direct route from a manufacturer to a customer, or a route through a crossdock.

A greedy method is utilized to allocate full truck load flow in G to generate the TL Plan. The TL Plan cannot guarantee all demand is satisfied; we leave unsatisfied demand to be satisfied by the LTL Plan.

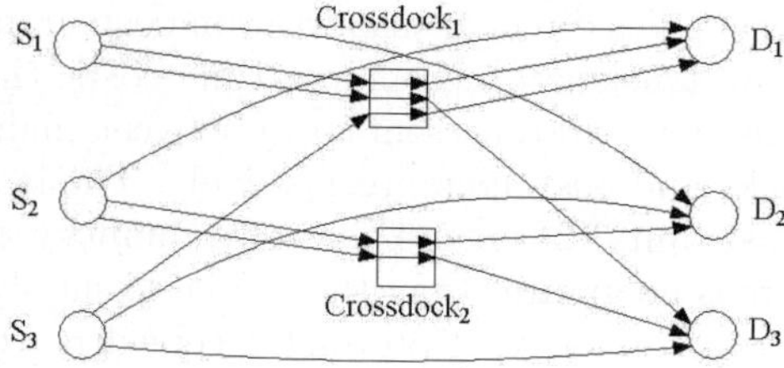

Fig. 2. Example - least cost routes

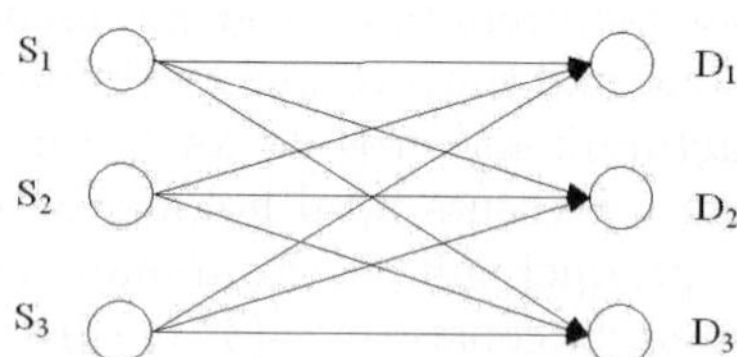

Fig. 3. Network G constructed from Example

To illustrate this, Figure 2 shows a simple example of least cost routes from manufacturers to customers, and Figure 3 shows G constructed from this example. Assume manufacturer nodes, S_1, S_2, S_3, have $s_1 = 103$, $s_2 = 10$, $s_3 = 28$, and customer nodes, D_1, D_2, D_3, have $d_1 = 25$, $d_2 = 27$, $d_3 = 82$, and that the truck capacity $Q = 20$. In G, the demand becomes $d_1' = 20$, $d_2' = 20$, $d_3' = 80$. Assume that transportation costs are such that $C_{11} < C_{12} < C_{13} < C_{33} < \cdots (C_{ik} = $ cost from S_i to D_k on least cost route in Figure 2). Using a greedy method, the resulting transportation plan will be to use one truck from S_1 to D_1 and S_1 to D_2, three trucks from S_1 to D_3, and one truck from S_3 to D_3. Hence, the TL Plan for this example can be represented by: $\{(S_1, Crossdock_1, D_1, 20), (S_1, Directly, D_2, 20), (S_1, Crossdock_1, D_3, 60), (S_3, Directly, D_3, 20)\}$.

Once the TL Plan is decided, it is not altered. Next, we construct an initial LTL Plan.

(2) **LTL Plan**

With a TL Plan in hand, the quantities remaining at supply and demand nodes can be determined. Using the example above, remaining supply and demand is $s_1' = 3$, $s_2' = 10$, $s_3' = 8$, and $d_1'' = 5$, $d_2'' = 7$, $d_3'' = 2$.

Take a *lane* to be an ordered pair of supply and demand nodes and a *route* on a lane to be a crossdock through which shipments pass (possibly empty). Each lane can have multiple routes, i.e., crossdocks through which the product can transit. Take *quantity* to be the number of units of the product shipped on a lane, and let $t1$ be the time the product leaves a supply node, and $t2$ the time the product leaves the crossdock, if it passes through the crossdock. To overcome the difficulty of time window constraints, the LTL Plan is generated lane by lane, i.e., the LTL Plan is represented by $\{(lane_{ik}, route_{ik}, quantity_{ik}, t1_{ik}, t2_{ik}) : i \in \Sigma, k \in \Delta\}$. For example, the element $((1, 2), 1, 13, 7, 12)$ obtained in an LTL Plan indicates that we should ship 13 units of the product from supply node 1 to demand node 2 through crossdock 1, where the time the product leaves the supply node 1 is 7 and the time it leaves crossdock 1 is 12.

Since the TL Plan is fixed, the initial solution depends only on the LTL Plan. This is generated through the following three steps:

Step 1. Preallocate: A plan is found greedily as follows. Sort supply and demand in decreasing order of the remaining quantities and then allocate quantities to be shipped from largest demand to the smallest demand. In the example, $s_1' = 3$, $s_2' = 10$, $s_3' = 8$ and $d_1'' = 5$, $d_2'' = 7$, $d_3'' = 2$; hence $s_2' > s_3' > s_1'$ and $d_2'' > d_1'' > d_3''$. Selecting the largest supply and demand, i.e., $s_2' = 10$ and $d_2'' = 7$, we first satisfy D_2 with S_2, and then satisfy the second largest demand $d_1'' = 5$, so that D_1 is satisfied with the remaining amount 3 at S_2 and the second largest supply at S_3. Continue in this way until all the demand is satisfied. With the assumption that supply is not less than demand, this can always be done and all lanes allocated with flow.

Step 2. Generate a Timetable: With preallocation, once routes are found for each lane, a timetable is constructed taking into account the time window constraints. To avoid holding cost, feasible time intervals at each crossdock for each route of each lane are maintained, i.e., for a route of lane (S_i, D_k), the time the product can remain at crossdock j is calculated according to the time windows at S_i and D_k, the shipping time from S_i to j and from j to D_k.

Step 3. Consolidate: Once a timetable has been constructed, consolidation is made at each supply point and crossdock according to the route and timetable available, and the times $t1$ and $t2$ are determined to complete the plan to obtain a feasible initial solution.

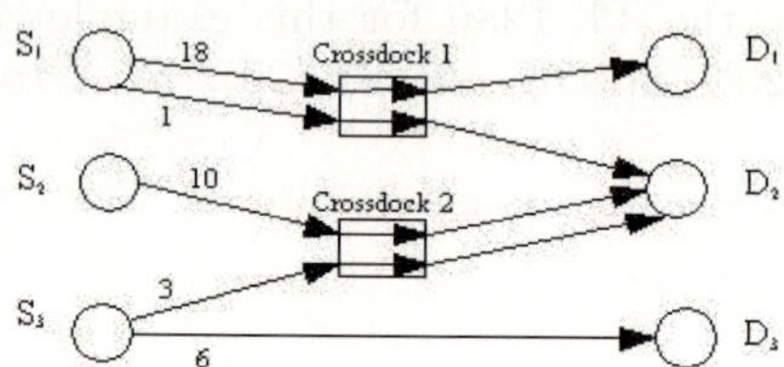

Fig. 4. Consolidation

Figure 4 shows routes and quantities to be shipped in a plan. In this case, flow from S_1 to D_1 and from S_1 to D_2 can be consolidated at S_1, if the time window constraint is not violated, so that there need only be one truck to transport the product from S_1 to Crossdock 1. Similarly, flow from S_2 to D_2 and flow from S_3 to D_2 can be consolidated at Crossdock 2, and there need only be one truck to transport the product from Crossdock 2 to D_2. There may be a holding cost if the product does not arrive crossdock 2 simultaneously, so that the shipment arriving earlier will have to hold for the later shipment. The flow from S_3 to D_3 does not transit any crossdock.

Stage 2: Iteration

Once an initial LTL Plan is found, it can be improved iteratively using a metaheuristic. We chose a genetic algorithm (GA) (Glover and Kochenberger 2003) metaheuristic since it is representative of techniques available. It is used to refine the LTL Plan.

Using GA

Once a TL Plan is generated, a GA can be used to improve the LTL Plan:

Step 1. Each solution is mapped into a sequence $S = (a_1, a_2, \ldots, a_n)$, where n is the number of customers, and S is a permutation of $1, 2, \ldots, n$. The sequence is a customer priority for choosing suppliers. To begin, sequences are generated randomly.

Step 2. Selection: the population is randomly divided into $\frac{M}{2}$ disjoint pairs, where M is the size of the population. Each pair of individuals are used in the crossover step.

Step 3. Crossover: each offspring is generated from its parents with equal probability. Let the parents be $P_1 = (a_1, a_2, \ldots, a_n)$ and $P_2 = (b_1, b_2, \ldots, b_n)$, then, a temporary offspring of P_1 and P_2 is given by $C_{temp} = (rand\,(a_1, b_1),$

$rand\ (a_2, b_2), \ldots, rand\ (a_n, b_n))$ with Prob $(rand\ (a_1, b_1) = a_1) =$ Prob $(rand\ (a_1, b_1) = b_1) = 0.5$.

After crossover, normalize C_{temp} into a permutation of $1, 2, \ldots, n$, by sorting priorities and re-assigning a value from 1 to n to get an offspring C. For example, $C_{temp} = (3, 1, 2, 1)$ becomes $C = (4, 2, 3, 1)$ or $C = (4, 1, 3, 2)$ after normalization.

Step 4. Mutation: a new individual is produced from the offspring by the 2-swap neighborhood with a given probability. For example, $C = (4, 1, 3, 2)$ mutates to $C = (2, 1, 3, 4)$, where the priority of customer 1 and customer 4 is interchanged.

Step 5. Population update: the new individual is inserted into the population replacing one with the highest cost.

4   Computational Experiments

All the algorithms were coded in Java and executed on Intel Pentium(R) 2.8GHz machine with 1024Mb memory. For comparisons, we used CPLEX 8.0 to solve the integer program for the SCP given in Section 3. The test generation process, parameter settings of various methods, and detailed computational results are described in the following sections.

4.1   Test Data Generation

The test cases were generated with three sets of parameters, which were randomly generated using the parameter *param* in a uniform distribution Unif $[\frac{4}{5}param, \frac{6}{5}param]$.

(1) (p, c, h) - (setup cost, transportation cost, inventory holding cost). By setting the ratio of $\frac{p}{c}$, normal setup cost $(\frac{1000}{5})$, high setup cost $(\frac{2000}{5})$, and very high setup cost $(\frac{3000}{5})$ test cases were generated; by setting the ratio for $\frac{p}{h}$, low holding cost $(\frac{1000}{50})$ and high holding cost $(\frac{1000}{300})$ cases were generated.

(2) (q, cap) - (quantity of demand, truck capacity). By setting the ratio of $\frac{q}{cap}$, we generated normal demand quantity $(\frac{30}{20})$, high demand quantity $(\frac{50}{20})$, and very high demand quantity $(\frac{70}{20})$ cases.

Since, in the heuristics, a TL Plan is generated by a network flow algorithm, the performance of the heuristics was tested by setting TL parts to be as small as possible (less than two truck loads) so that the LTL costs contribute more to total cost.

(3) (t, d) - time window and the distances between manufacturers, crossdocks and customers. By setting the ratio of $\frac{t}{d}$, we generated normal time window $(\frac{40}{30})$ and narrow time window $(\frac{20}{30})$ cases. If the time interval used is too wide, time window constraints become unnecessary.

4.2   Results from the Experiments

A test set s-d-cd-attr indicates the number of manufacturers (s), the number of customers (d), the number of crossdocks (cd), and the attributes of the parameters (attr). The basic attribute is normal (n), which means that all three sets

Table 1. Result of general cases

Test set	NF+GA	T_{NF+GA}	CPLEX	T_{CPLEX}
10-20-3-n	227002	4	226127	600
10-40-3-n	456922	8	471217	600
10-50-3-n	571103	10	592163	600
10-60-4-n	691034	16	722602	600
10-80-4-n	919470	22	957030	1200
20-20-4-n	241805	10	233264	600
20-40-4-n	450842	20	468353	600
20-50-4-n	578840	29	598409	600
20-60-4-n	694650	33	721179	1200

have parameters set to normal level as described above. The two-stage heuristic is denoted NF+GA (network flow with GA).

Each test set contains 10 test cases, and the value in the tables are the average cost of all the 10 test cases for each package. T_{NF+GA} and T_{CPLEX} denote running times in seconds.

From table 1, we see that as the number of customers increases, the performance of NF+GA becomes better than CPLEX. And NF+GA require much less time than consumed of the CPLEX.

Using Different Parameters

Setup cost and holding cost. Table 2 gives results for the effect of high (hs) and very high (es) setup costs.

From the table we can see heuristic performs better than CPLEX with high setup cost and extremely high setup cost sets.

The following table 3 shows the heuristic provides superior solutions when compared with CPLEX in almost all packages with high holding cost (h).

Narrow time windows. Table 3 also shows the heuristic outperforms CPLEX in all test packages with narrow time windows (ntw).

Table 2. Result of high setup cost cases

Test set	NF+GA	CPLEX	Test set	NF+GA	CPLEX
10-40-3-hs	559446	569273	10-40-3-es	773072	805238
10-50-3-hs	754346	765658	10-50-3-es	955919	988054
10-60-4-hs	859917	900284	10-60-4-es	1176252	1214280
10-80-4-hs	1247090	1294442	10-80-4-es	1551440	1625256

Table 3. Result of high holding cost and narrow time window cases

Test set	NF+GA	CPLEX	Test set	NF+GA	CPLEX
10-20-3-h	224270	222071	10-20-3-ntw	218593	221497
10-40-3-h	462588	477714	10-40-3-ntw	446453	454824
10-50-3-h	569797	596800	10-50-3-ntw	562514	584205
10-60-4-h	690903	721774	10-60-4-ntw	674903	696020

Table 4. Result of large demand cases

Test set	NF+GA	CPLEX	Test set	NF+GA	CPLEX
10-20-3-lq	<u>527552</u>	545709	10-20-3-eq	<u>774117</u>	788267
10-40-3-lq	<u>986667</u>	1020072	10-40-3-eq	<u>1542854</u>	1604314
10-50-3-lq	<u>1277606</u>	1329626	10-50-3-eq	<u>1929691</u>	2024923
10-60-4-lq	<u>1558303</u>	1642329	10-60-4-eq	<u>2323319</u>	2500889

Large and very large demand. The following table 4 shows the results for large demand (lq) and very large demand (eq) results.

From the table we can see that CPLEX performs unstably, as demand quantity increases. The cost calculated by CPLEX is significantly larger than found by the heuristics. As with the other test packages, the two-stage heuristics performed better than CPLEX for almost all the test sets.

5 Conclusion and Future Work

In this work, we studied a new shipment consolidation problem in distribution networks which include crossdocks with manufacturer and customer time windows. A single product can be shipped directly or through crossdocks, and shipments planned to reduce LTL shipments by consolidation at manufacturers and crossdocks. The problem is formulated as an integer program problem which was shown to be **NP**-hard in strong sense. A two-stage heuristic algorithm, which combines a network flow algorithm and a metaheuristic, was developed to solve the problem. We used a squeaky wheel optimization heuristic and a genetic algorithm to consolidate LTL shipments. The idea behind the heuristics is to split the demand into TL and LTL components. The TL component was solved as network flow problem. In solving the LTL problem, the key point was to represent lanes from manufacturers to customers which are feasible with respect to time windows constraints. This allowed time constraints to be omitted, and the problem reduced, in the next step of the solution procedure. Computational experiments were carried out to compare solutions obtained by CPLEX and the two-stage heuristic. These showed that the heuristic was able to provide better results and required significantly less computing time, while they was more stable than CPLEX.

In future research, it is possible that the multi-commodity consolidation problem, which is more difficult, can be solved.

References

[1] Bartholdi, John J. III and Gue, K. R. (2000)Reducing labor costs in an LTL crossdocking terminal, Operations Research, 48(6) 823-832.

[2] Gümüs, M., Bookbinder, J. H. (2004), Cross-docking and its implication in location-distribution systems, Journal of Business Logistics, 25(2) 199 - 228.

[3] Hoppe, B. and Tardos, E. (1995) The quickest transshipment problem, *In Proceedings of the Sixth Annual ACM-SIAM Symposium on Discrete Algorithms*, San Francisco, California, United States.

[4] Lim, A., Miao, Z., Rodrigues, B. and Xu, Z. (2005) Transshipment through cross-docks with inventory and time windows, *Naval Research Logistics Quarterly*, to appear.

[5] Miao, Z. (2005) Optimization problems in a crossdocking distribution system, Ph.D. thesis, Hong Kong University of Science and Technology.

[6] Napolitano, M. (2000) Making the move to crossdocking, The WERC-sheet, Warehousing Education and Research Council.

[7] Quinn, F. J. (1997) The payoff! *Logistics Management* 36 (12) 37 - 41.

[8] Robinson, L.W. (1990) Optimal and approximate policies in multiperiod, multilocation inventory models with transshipments, *Operations Research* 38 278-295.

[9] Tayur, S. (1995) Computing optimal stock levels for common components in an assembly system, Working paper, Carnegie-Mellon University, USA.

[10] Wilson, R.A. (2002) Transportation in America, 19th edition, Eno Transportation Foundation, Washington, USA.

Application of an Intuitive Novelty Metric for Jet Engine Condition Monitoring

David A. Clifton[1,2], Peter R. Bannister[1], and Lionel Tarassenko[1]

[1] Department of Engineering Science, Oxford University, UK
{davidc, prb, lionel}@robots.ox.ac.uk
[2] Oxford BioSignals Ltd., Magdalen Centre, Oxford Science Park,
Oxford, OX4 4GA, UK

Abstract. Application of novelty detection to a new class of jet engine is considered within this paper, providing a worked example of the steps necessary for constructing a model of normality. Abnormal jet engine vibration signatures are automatically identified with respect to a training set of normal examples. Pre-processing steps suitable for this area of application are investigated. An intuitive metric for assigning novelty scores to patterns is introduced, with benefits for reducing model sensitivity to noise, and in pruning patterns from the model training set.

Keywords: Novelty Detection, Jet Engine Application, Machine Learning.

1   Introduction

Novelty detection, defined to be the identification of departures from normal system behaviour, is appropriate for areas of application in which examples of normal behaviour greatly outnumber examples of abnormal behaviour. The identification of abnormal jet engine vibration data is one such example, in which the majority of available examples are "normal" [12, 3]. This paper describes the application of the *shape analysis* method of novelty detection [9, 5] to a new engine example, investigating the necessary pre-processing steps required to provide accurate classification of abnormal examples from a new class of modern jet engine.

An intuitive novelty metric is introduced for assigning novelty scores to engine examples such that sensitivity of the model of normality to noise in example patterns may be reduced. The novelty metric is used as a basis for meaningful pruning of data from the training set such that a robust model of normality is constructed.

Results from the application of this novelty detection process to the new class of jet engine considered within this investigation are presented, providing evidence of the suitability of the approach in the identification of abnormal engine vibration signatures.

M. Ali and R. Dapoigny (Eds.): IEA/AIE 2006, LNAI 4031, pp. 1149–1158, 2006.
© Springer-Verlag Berlin Heidelberg 2006

2   Data Description

This investigation considers a modern civil jet engine, consisting of several rotating engine *shafts*, mounted concentrically. In normal operation, air enters the *low pressure* ("LP") shaft for compression, passed to the *intermediate pressure* ("IP") and *high pressure* ("HP") shafts for further compression, before ultimately being mixed with aviation fuel for use within the combustion chamber [10]. Vibration energy at the frequency of the fundamental harmonic of vibration associated with each shaft is referred to as the *tracked order* of each shaft [4].

During product testing, engines of the class considered within this investigation perform a controlled two-minute acceleration from idle to maximum speed, followed by a two-minute deceleration back to idle. Vibration amplitude levels of the fundamental tracked orders corresponding to each shaft are recorded during these tests, from which the speed-based vibration signature $a(s)$ is constructed for rotational speeds s of each engine shaft. If $a(s) \leq H$ for all speeds s, where H is a contractual vibration limit, then the engine may be released into service.

The data set used in the investigation described in this article consists of 71 engine examples, initially divided into four sub-sets $D_1 \ldots D_4$, according to their maximum vibration amplitude $\max\{a(s)\}$ compared with the contractual vibration limit H, as shown in Table 1. Note that sub-set D_4 is formed from recordings of engines with seeded fault conditions, in which small masses are deliberately applied to the engine fan blades. These weights are deliberately applied to fan (and sometimes turbine) blades in order to correct any unbalances during rotation of those blades about the shaft to which they are connected. This unbalance is noted by engine manufacturers to result in very large vibration amplitude levels of the LP shaft, with approximately normal behaviour in other shafts. Novelty detection *applied to the IP and HP shafts* should therefore not identify examples from sub-set D_4 as being novel.

Table 1. Data classified according to maximum vibration amplitude

Sub-set	$|D_n|$	Class membership criteria
D_1	29	Examples for which $\max\{a(s)\} < 0.9H$
D_2	15	Examples for which $0.9H \leq \max\{a(s)\} \leq H$
D_3	17	Examples for which $H < \max\{a(s)\}$
D_4	10	Examples in which weights are deliberately applied to the engine fan

3   Quantisation of Vibration Signatures

Increasing dimensionality of data requires exponentially increasing numbers of patterns within the data set used to construct a general model; this is termed the *curse of dimensionality* [1]. In order to avoid this problem, each signature is summarised by a *shape vector* **x**. This is performed by computing a weighted average of the vibration amplitude values $a(s)$ over $D = 10$ speed sub-ranges [9]. The dth dimension of shape vector $\mathbf{x}^d$, for $d = 1 \ldots D$, is defined to be:

$$\mathbf{x}^d = \int_{s_{\min}}^{s_{\max}} a(s)\omega_d(s)ds \qquad (1)$$

in which the vibration amplitude $a(s)$ is integrated over the speed range s : $[s_{\min}\ s_{\max}]$, using weighting functions $\omega_d(s)$, for $d : 1 \ldots D$. The weighting functions used are overlapping trapezoids, as shown in Figure 1.

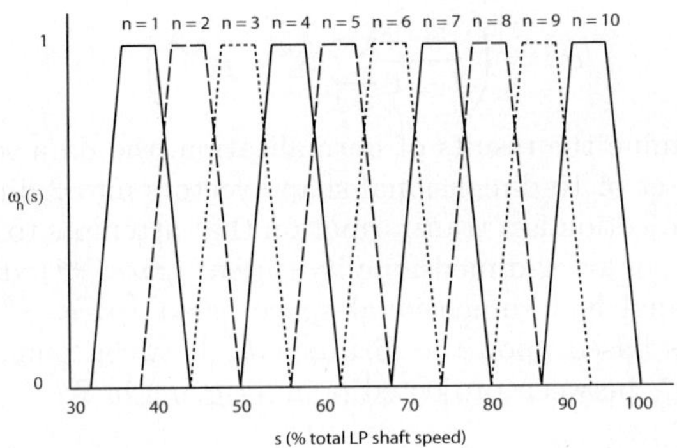

Fig. 1. Example of weighting functions $\omega_d, d : 1 \ldots 10$, used to create shape vectors

4   Normalisation

In order to identify changes in the *shape* of 10-dimensional vectors derived from vibration signatures with respect to a population of normal patterns, regardless of absolute values of vibration amplitude, normalisation is applied. This pre-processing step removes dependence upon absolute amplitudes, whilst preserving information about the general shape of signatures.

Five normalisation methods were investigated [2] for scaling the $d : 1 \ldots 10$ dimensional shape vectors $\{\mathbf{x}_1^d, \mathbf{x}_2^d, \ldots, \mathbf{x}_I^d\}$ constructed from vibration signatures. These normalisation methods are defined in Table 2.

We define the component-wise normalisation function $N(\mathbf{x}_i)$ to be a transformation of the d elements within pattern $\mathbf{x}_i$:

$$N(\mathbf{x}_i) = \frac{\mathbf{x}_i^d - \boldsymbol{\mu}^d}{\boldsymbol{\sigma}^d}, \qquad d = 1 \ldots D \qquad (2)$$

where $(\boldsymbol{\mu}, \boldsymbol{\sigma})$ are vectors of D elements, computed component-wise across all $i = 1 \ldots I$ patterns:

$$\boldsymbol{\mu}^d = \frac{1}{I} \sum_{i=1}^{I} \mathbf{x}_i^d \qquad (3)$$

Table 2. Normalisation methods applied to engine shape vectors

Method	Definition
Energy-based normalisation	$\sum (\mathbf{x}^d)^2 = 1$
Amplitude normalisation	$\sum \mathbf{x}^d = 1$
Unit normalisation	$\max\{\mathbf{x}^d\} = 1$
Zero-mean, unit-variance normalisation	$\mu(\mathbf{x^d}) = 0, \sigma(\mathbf{x^d}) = 1$
Component-wise normalisation	See Eq.(2)

$$\boldsymbol{\sigma}^d = \left(\frac{1}{I-1} \sum_{i=1}^{I} (\mathbf{x}_i^d - \boldsymbol{\mu}^d)^2 \right)^{\frac{1}{2}} \tag{4}$$

In order to examine the results of normalisation, the data set was visualised by projecting the set of 10-dimensional shape vectors into 2 dimensions.

Topographic projection is a transformation that attempts to best preserve, in the projected space of lower-dimensionality (*latent space*, $\mathbb{R}^q$), distances between data in their original high-dimensional space (*data space*, $\mathbb{R}^d$). The *Sammon stress metric*[11] is based upon the distance d_{ij} between points (x_i, x_j) in $\mathbb{R}^d$, and the distance d_{ij}^* between projected points (y_i, y_j) in $\mathbb{R}^q$:

$$E_{\text{sam}} = \sum_{i=1}^{N} \sum_{j>i}^{N} (d_{ij} - d_{ij}^*)^2 \tag{5}$$

in which the distance measure is typically Euclidean. The NeuroScale model [6, 7] trains a radial basis function (*RBF*) neural network to perform the mapping from $\mathbb{R}^d$ to $\mathbb{R}^q$, in which E_{sam} is minimised; i.e. distances between points are best preserved after projection.

A NeuroScale network was used for projecting shape vectors derived from the example data set described previously, with $d = 10$ inputs (corresponding to the number of elements in each shape vector) and $q = 2$ outputs (for 2-dimensional projection).

The projection of the un-normalised vibration signatures from the HP shaft during acceleration manoeuvres, as generated by the NeuroScale network, is shown in Figure 2(a). A new NeuroScale mapping is generated for use with each normalisation scheme, by training a RBF network using data normalised by each method previously considered. The resulting projections from each NeuroScale network are shown in Figure 2(b)-(f). Note that the axes of NeuroScale projections have no units of measurement: they are arbitrary orthogonal axes that allow minimisation of E_{sam}.

The figures show that component-based normalisation provides increase in separation of "abnormal" patterns (sub-set D_3), while the other four normalisation methods result in significant overlap between "normal" and "abnormal" patterns. Thus, component-wise normalisation is used in pre-processing the 10-dimensional shape vectors for this engine data-set.

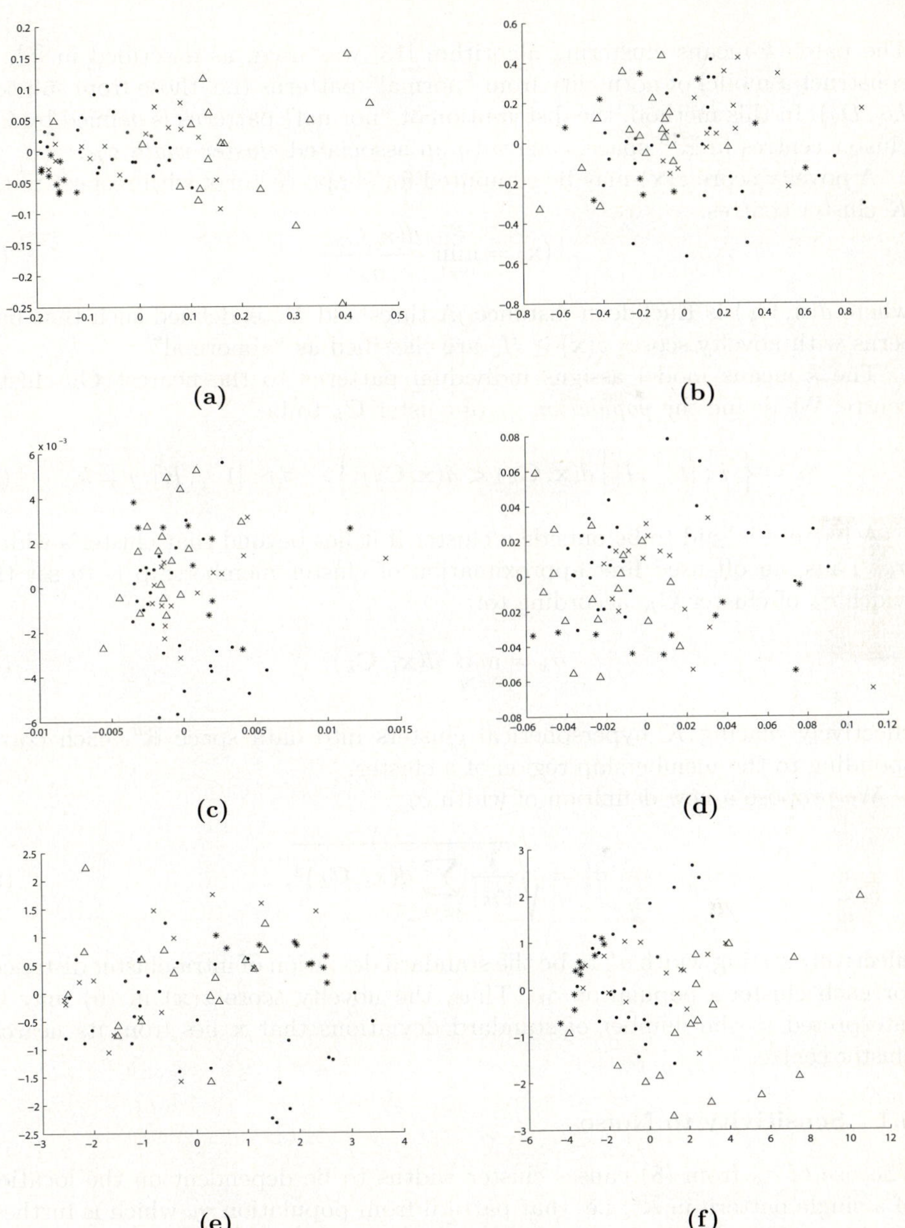

Fig. 2. Projections of HP Shaft Accelerations: (a) un-normalised; (b) unit normalisation; (c) amplitude normalisation; (d) energy-based normalisation; (e) zero-mean, unit-variance normalisation; (f) component-wise normalisation. Data sub-sets $\{D_1 \ldots D_4\}$ are shown by $\{\bullet \ \times \ \triangle \ +\}$, respectively.

5   Modelling Normality

The batch k-means clustering algorithm [13] was used, as described in [8], to construct a model of normality from "normal" patterns (i.e. those from sub-sets D_1, D_2). In this method, the distribution of "normal" patterns is defined by $\mathbf{C}_K$ cluster centres in $\mathbb{R}^{10}$ space, each with an associated *cluster width* σ_K.

A novelty score $z(\mathbf{x})$ may be computed for shape vector $\mathbf{x}$ with respect to the K cluster centres:

$$z(\mathbf{x}) = \min_{k=1}^{K} \frac{d(\mathbf{x}, \mathbf{C}_k)}{\sigma_k} \tag{6}$$

where $d(\mathbf{x}, \mathbf{C}_k)$ is Euclidean distance. A threshold H_z is defined such that patterns with novelty scores $z(\mathbf{x}) \geq H_z$ are classified as "abnormal".

The k-means model assigns individual patterns to the nearest $\mathbf{C}_k$ cluster centre. We define the *population* γ_k of cluster $\mathbf{C}_k$ to be:

$$\gamma_k = \left\{ \, i : [1 \ldots I] \, \middle| \, d(\mathbf{x}, \mathbf{C}_k) < d(\mathbf{x}, \mathbf{C}_j) \, \right\}, \quad \forall j : [1 \ldots K], j \neq k. \tag{7}$$

A pattern is said to be outside a cluster if it lies beyond that cluster's width, σ_k. Thus, an oft-used first approximation of cluster membership is to set the width σ_k of cluster $\mathbf{C}_K$ according to:

$$\sigma_k = \max_{i \in \gamma_k} d(\mathbf{x}_i, \mathbf{C}_k), \tag{8}$$

effectively placing K hyperspherical clusters into data space $\mathbb{R}^d$, each corresponding to the membership region of a cluster.

We propose a new definition of width σ_k:

$$\sigma'_k = \sqrt{\frac{1}{|\gamma_k|} \sum_{i \in \gamma_k} d(\mathbf{x}_i, \mathbf{C}_k)^2}, \tag{9}$$

effectively setting width σ'_k to be the standard deviation of intra-cluster distances for each cluster's population γ_k. Thus, the novelty score $z(\mathbf{x})$ in (6) may be interpreted as the number of standard deviations that $\mathbf{x}$ lies from its nearest cluster centre.

5.1   Sensitivity to Noise

The use of σ_k from (8) causes cluster widths to be dependent on the location of a single pattern in $\mathbb{R}^d$; i.e. that pattern from population γ_k which is furthest from centre $\mathbf{C}_k$. Small variations in the placement of that pattern relative to $\mathbf{C}_k$ can results in considerable variations in σ_k, resulting in poor robustness to noisy data. Furthermore, the cluster width σ_k does not represent the *distribution* of its population of patterns γ_k.

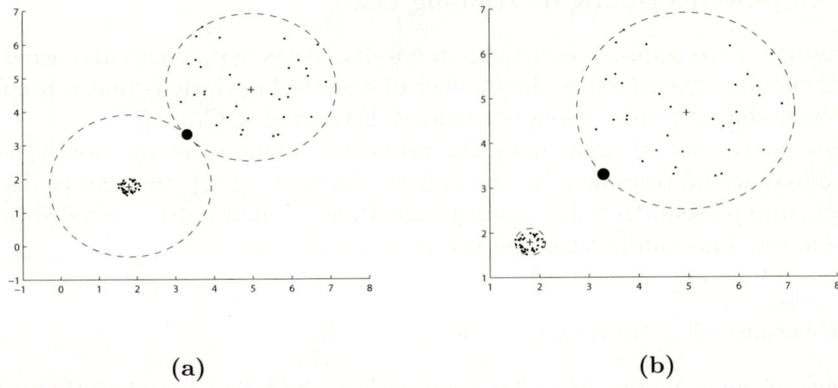

(a)   (b)

Fig. 3. Cluster centre widths calculating using: (a) σ_k; (b) σ'_k. Training patterns and cluster centres are shown by {• +}, respectively. Cluster boundaries are shown by dashed lines. Outlying pattern shown by a large •.

This sensitivity to single patterns can be avoided by:

i. placing cluser centres $\mathbf{C}_k$ using the k-means algorithm, as before;
ii. computing σ'_k using (9);
iii. computing $z(\mathbf{x})$ for all patterns using (6);
iv. re-allocating patterns to cluster populations γ_k according to minimum novelty score using:

$$\gamma_k = \left\{\ i : [1 \ldots I] \ \middle|\ \frac{d(\mathbf{x}), \mathbf{C}_k)}{\sigma'_k} < \frac{d(\mathbf{x}, \mathbf{C}_j)}{\sigma'_k}\ \right\}, \quad \forall j : [1 \ldots K], j \neq k; \quad (10)$$

v. re-computing the final σ'_k using γ_k from the previous step.

This is illustrated in Figure 3, using example data drawn from two circular distributions in $\mathbb{R}^2$, and a single outlying pattern. We refer to these two distributions as p_1 and p_2, appearing in the lower-left and upper-right of Figure 3, respectively. The single outlying pattern, indicated by a large •, lies between p_1 and p_2, and is slightly closer to the centre of the former.

Figure 3(a) shows widths σ_k computed using (8). The outlying pattern has been assigned to $\mathbf{C}_1$, i.e. the cluster centre placed by the k-means algorithms to represent data drawn from p_1. Thus, σ_1 is placed to include all of its population γ_1, and does not closely represent the distribution of the data in γ_1.

Figure 3(b) shows widths σ'_k after the single outlying pattern has been allocated to γ_2, using (10). Thus, $(\mathbf{C}_1, \sigma'_1)$ closely represents distribution p_1, and $(\mathbf{C}_2, \sigma'_2)$ has extended slightly to cover the single outlying pattern.

This illustrates the improvement in model-fit achieved with (9), in which the resulting two cluster centres closely model the underlying distribution from which the example data were drawn. This is beneficial in application to engine vibration data, in which patterns (derived from engine vibration signatures) are subject to noise.

5.2   Improved Pruning of Training Data

The use of (9) to compute σ'_k results in novelty scores $z(\mathbf{x})$, computed using (6), which may be interpreted as the number of standard deviations that $\mathbf{x}$ lies from its closest cluster centre, using normalised distance $d(\mathbf{x}, \mathbf{C}_k)/\sigma'_k$.

This interpretation allowed by the proposed definition of the novelty score $z(\mathbf{x})$ allows initial pruning of patterns from the training set, in order to discard outliers unrepresentative of normality, and which should not be included in the training set. This can be achieved using:

i-v. as before, in 5.1;
vi. discarding all patterns $\mathbf{x}$ for which $z(\mathbf{x}) > H'_z$.

Thus, if, for example $H'_z = 3.0$, all patterns which lie more than three standard deviations from their nearest cluster centre (using normalised distance) are discarded. This corresponds to the intuitive notion of discarding outliers based on their novelty relative to the distribution of the remainder of the data.

6   Results of Application to Example Engine Data

The results of novelty detection using models trained on patterns from each engine shaft may be visualised using NeuroScale projection from $\mathbb{R}^{10}$ onto $\mathbb{R}^2$. Results for the LP and IP shafts are presented.

6.1   LP Shaft Results

Engines that were deliberately unbalanced by attachment of weights to the fan exhibit extremely high vibration amplitude within the LP shaft, as discussed in Section 2. Figure 4 shows a NeuroScale projection of all patterns generated from LP shaft vibration signatures.

6 patterns derived from unbalanced engines (i.e. drawn from sub-set D_4) are contained within the LP shaft data set, all of which are correctly classified "abnormal" by the novelty detection process. The figure shows that they are clearly

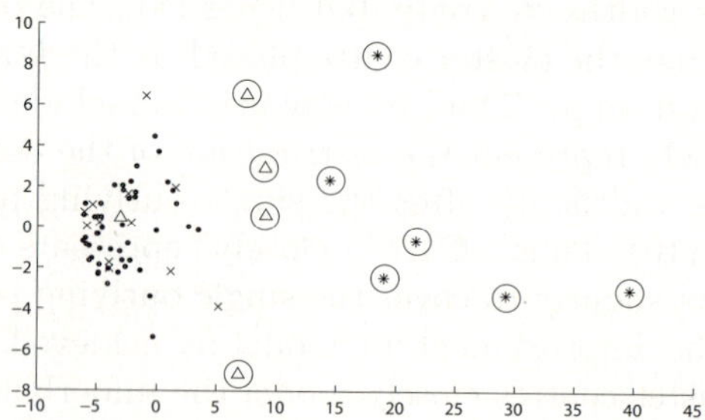

Fig. 4. Projection of all LP shaft patterns. Patterns classified as "abnormal" are circled. Data sub-sets $\{D_1 \ldots D_4\}$ are shown by $\{\bullet \ \times \ \triangle \ *\}$, respectively.

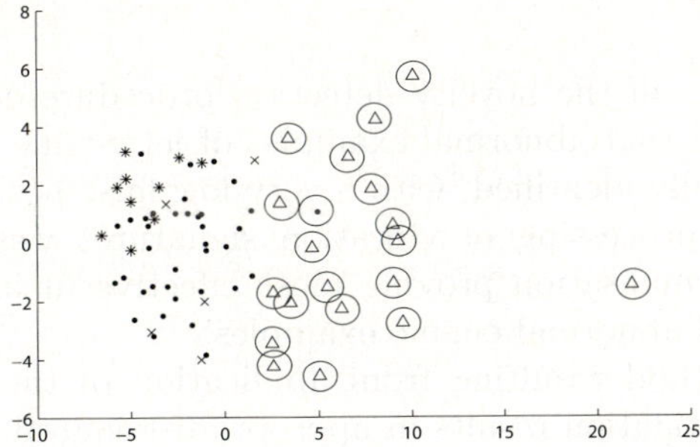

Fig. 5. Projection of all IP shaft patterns. Patterns classified as "abnormal" are circled. Data sub-sets $\{D_1 \ldots D_4\}$ are shown by $\{\bullet \ \times \ \triangle \ *\}$, respectively.

separated from the cluster formed by normal training patterns, supporting the assumption that unbalanced patterns should appear highly abnormal in the LP shaft.

4 of the 5 patterns that form the set of abnormal example patterns for the LP shaft (i.e. drawn from sub-set D_3) are classified "abnormal" with respect to the model. As can be seen from the figure, these 4 patterns classified "abnormal" are clearly separated from the normal patterns.

The remaining pattern of this abnormal class lies in the centre of the normal cluster of patterns. This engine was released into service following pass-off testing (source A), but exceeded the contractual vibration limit for that shaft, placing it within sub-set D_3 (as defined in Section 2). This provides support for the claim that comparison of maximum vibration amplitude to a fixed contractual limit H_a does not provide a reliable indication of abnormality, and that this shape analysis technique can provide better discrimintation between "normal" and "abnormal" engines.

6.2   IP Shaft Results

All abnormal patterns (from sub-set D_3) derived from IP shaft vibration signatures are correctly classified by the novelty detection process, as shown in Figure 5. Obvious separation between "abnormal" and "normal" classes can be seen in the figure.

A single pattern from the "normal" class is classified as "abnormal". This pattern was pruned from the training set prior to training, due to its outlying position relative to the rest of the "normal" patterns.

The figure shows that patterns from sub-set D_4 are not classified as "abnormal" within the IP shaft, following the observation that changes in vibration levels caused by unbalance conditions are localised within LP shaft vibration signatures.

7 Conclusions

Results from the use of the novelty detection procedure described within this investigation showed that abnormal examples of jet engine vibration signatures could be automatically identified, with a very low false-positive rate.

Appropriate pre-processing of vibration signatures was investigated, with component-wise normalisation proving most effective in increasing separation between normal and abnormal engine examples.

The pruning method resulting from application of the novelty metric described in this investigation results in appropriate removal of patterns that are significantly novel with respect to the majority of training patterns. This allows a model of normality to be constructed that closely models vibration signatures taken from normal engines, such that abnormal engine examples are identified.

Acknowledgements. The authors gratefully acknowledge the support of the EPSRC; Dennis King and Mark Walters of Rolls-Royce Plc.; and Nicholas McGrogan of Oxford BioSignals Ltd.

References

1. Bishop, C.: Neural networks for pattern recognition. Oxford University Press (1995)
2. Clifton, D.A.: Condition Monitoring of Gas-Turbine Engines. Department of Engineering Science, University of Oxford, Transfer Report (2005)
3. Hayton, P., Scholkopf, B., Tarassenko, L., Anuzis, P.: Support vector novelty detection applied to jet engine vibration spectra. NIPS Proceedings (2000)
4. Hayton, P., Utete, S., Tarassenko, L.: QUOTE Project Final Report. University of Oxford (2003)
5. Hayton, P., Utete, S., King, D., King, S., Anuzis, P., Tarassenko, L.: Static and dynamic novelty detection methods for jet engine health monitoring. Proc. of the Royal Society (2006)
6. Lowe, D., Tipping, M.E.: Feed-forward neural networks and topographic mappings for exploratory data analysis. Neural Computing and Applications (1996)
7. Nabney, I.T.: NETLAB, algorithms for pattern recognition. Springer (2002)
8. Nairac, A., Corbett-Clark, T.A., Ripley, R.M., Townsend, N.W., Tarassenko, L.: Choosing an appropriate model for novelty detection. IEE 5th International Conference on Artificial Neural Networks (1997)
9. Nairac, A., Townsend N., Carr, R., King, S., Cowley, P., Tarassenko, L.: A system for the analysis of jet engine vibration data. Integrated Computer-Aided Engineering (1999)
10. Rolls-Royce PLC: The jet engine. Renault Publishing (2005)
11. Sammon, JW.: A non-linear mapping for data structure analysis. IEEE Transactions on Computers (1969)
12. Tarassenko, L., Nairac, A., Townsend, N.: Novelty detection. Proc. of NCAF/NSYN (1996)
13. Tarassenko, L.: A guide to neural computing applications. Arnold (1998)

Determination of Storage Locations for Incoming Containers of Uncertain Weight*

Jaeho Kang[1], Kwang Ryel Ryu[1], and Kap Hwan Kim[2]

[1] Department of Computer Engineering, Pusan National University
San 30, Jangjeon-dong, Kumjeong-gu, Busan, 609-735, Korea
{jhkang, krryu}@pusan.ac.kr
[2] Department of Industrial Engineering, Pusan National University
San 30, Jangjeon-dong, Kumjeong-gu, Busan, 609-735, Korea
kapkim@pusan.ac.kr

Abstract. In container terminals, heavier containers are loaded onto a ship before lighter ones to keep the ship balanced. To achieve efficient loading, terminal operators usually classify incoming export containers into a few weight groups and group containers belonging to the same weight group in the same stack. However, since the weight information available at the time of the container's arrival is only an estimate, a stack often includes containers belonging to different weight groups. This mix of weight groups necessitates extra crane works or container re-handlings during the loading process. This paper employs a simulated annealing algorithm to derive a more effective stacking strategy to determine the storage locations of incoming containers of uncertain weight. It also presents a method of using machine learning to reduce occurrences of re-handling by increasing classification accuracy. Experimental results have shown that the proposed methods effectively reduce the number of re-handlings than the traditional same-weight-group-stacking (SWGS) strategy.

1 Introduction

In container terminals, average ship turn-around time is the most important productivity criterion. Container loading and unloading are the two major services provided by terminals, and these services take the majority of available turn-around time. When loading containers, heavier containers must be brought from the yard and loaded onto a ship before the lighter containers are loaded to keep the ship balanced. This weight constraint makes the planning of container loading very difficult. Therefore, terminal operators usually use a more relaxed constraint by grouping containers into a limited number of weight groups and loading them onto the ship in decreasing order (from heaviest to lightest).

However, a container is often misclassified because the weight information provided by the trucking company is not accurate. The true weights of containers

---

* This work was supported by the Regional Research Centers Program (Research Center for Logistics Information Technology), granted by the Korean Ministry of Education Human Resources Development.

are obtained one or two days before the arrival of the ship; by this time, most of the containers destined for the ship have already been stacked. As a result, containers belonging to different weight groups may be piled together, causing extra work in loading. In this situation, a yard crane needs to move a lighter container that has been stacked on top of a heavier container to a temporary location. This temporary container move is a re-handling, and is the major cause of delay in loading. Therefore, the number of re-handlings should be minimized to improve terminal productivity.

Although the traditional stacking strategy (SWGS) is known for causing a large number of re-handlings, terminals have regarded it as the best possible stacking strategy – whether the weight information is accurate or not. There has been little research concerning the re-handlings caused by the inaccuracy of weight information. In this paper, we propose a method of deriving a more effective stacking strategy through the application of a simulated annealing algorithm. Experimental results have shown that stacking strategies derived through our method could more effectively reduce the number of re-handlings than SWGS could. In addition, machine learning is proven to reduce the additional number of re-handlings by increasing classification accuracy.

Section 2 of the paper describes the re-handling problem in a terminal and reviews some related research. Section 3 demonstrates the method of estimating the number of re-handlings caused by inaccurate weight information. The implementation details of determining a more effective stacking strategy are presented in Section 4. In Section 5, the proposed method is tested and the results are summarized. Finally, Section 6 contains our conclusions and outlines topics for future research.

2   Container Re-handing Problem

The storage yard of a container terminal consists of multiple blocks, each having several bays. A bay is made up of several rows of container stacks of a certain maximum height, called tiers. Figure 1(a) presents a top view of a block, about half of which is occupied by the containers to be loaded onto ship 'A.' The containers of the same ports of destination – indicated by 'Hong Kong,' 'Singapore,' and 'Kobe' – are stored at adjacent locations. Since a bay can accommodate only one 20-foot container, the 40-foot containers occupy two consecutive bays. In the figure, the containers belonging to the same weight group are stored in the same bays; this practice does not always occur in reality, but they must at least be stored in the same stack. In most container terminals, the containers are classified in three weight groups: light (L), medium (M), and heavy (H), as indicated in the figure. Figure 1(b) is a cross-sectional view of a block that corresponds to a 4-tier 6-row bay.

Figure 2(a) depicts a bay accommodating only the containers classified to weight group M at the time of their arrival. Figure 2(b) shows the same bay with the containers re-classified based on the correct weight information obtained just before loading time. It turns out that the eight containers indicated by

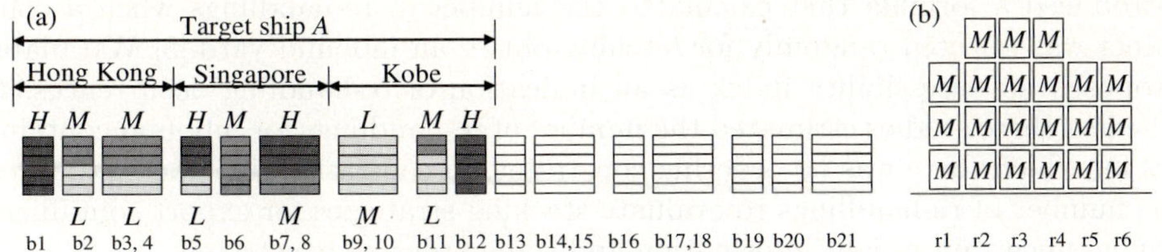

Fig. 1. (a) Top view and (b) cross-sectional view of a block

thick boxes in the figure actually belong to weight groups other than M. The eight shaded containers are those that must be re-handled (i.e., they have to be moved to other locations at the time of loading to fetch out the heavier containers under them). Eight (the number of shaded containers) is the lower bound on the number of required re-handlings. In most cases, we can easily derive a container-loading plan with the required number of re-handlings equal to the lower bound: as more containers are fetched out, more spaces become available for the re-handled containers to be placed without causing any further re-handling. Figure 2(c) reveals the transition of bay status as the containers are fetched out, starting from the initial configuration of Fig. 2(b). In each configuration, the containers to be fetched out are indicated by thick boxes, and those that should be re-handled are shaded. In the sections that follow, we simplify our analysis by assuming that the estimated number of re-handlings for a given bay configuration is always equal to its lower bound.

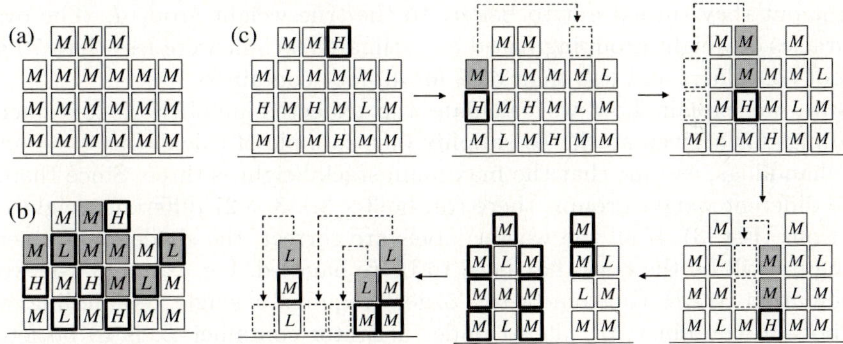

Fig. 2. Status of a bay (a) before and (b) after obtaining the correct weight information, and (c) change of bay status as containers are fetched out for loading

Few studies have focused on reducing the number of re-handlings of export containers with inaccurate weight information. Kim *et al.* derived an optimal stacking strategy for export containers when the weight group classification was always correct.[1] Kim studied the re-handling of inbound containers and derived a formula for estimating the number of required re-handlings.[2] Castilho *et al.*

introduced a formula that calculated the number of re-handlings when a container was selected randomly for fetching out in an inbound yard.[3] Watanabe proposed an accessibility index as an indication of re-handling occurrences.[4] The last three studies estimated the number of re-handlings for inbound containers for which there was no ordering constraint. In contrast, this paper estimates the number of re-handlings to evaluate stacking strategies for export containers having uncertain weight information and some ordering constraints.

3   The Expected Number of Container Re-handlings

Given a stack of containers with the estimated weight groups assigned, we want to calculate the expected number of re-handlings needed to fetch out all the containers from that stack. This expected number later becomes the basis on which we evaluate the stacking results produced by the stacking strategies under investigation. One of the things we need to know to calculate the expected number of re-handlings is the probability distribution of the true weight groups, given an estimated weight group. To obtain this distribution, the record of containers exported for a certain five month period at a real terminal has been analyzed. Table 1 is the confusion matrix of weight grouping of all the 20-foot containers in our record. The numbers in the parentheses next to the group labels L, M, and H in the column and row headings are the proportions of the containers belonging to the respective group. The number in each cell is the proportion of the containers that belonged to a particular estimated weight group and a true weight group. For example, the bold item indicates that 7.1% of all the 20-foot containers had been classified to the weight group M based on the estimated weight but they turned out to belong to the true weight group L. The overall accuracies of weight grouping based on estimated weight were less than 70% for 20-foot containers and less than 65% for 40-foot containers.

Now, we explain how we calculate the expected number of container re-handlings for a given stack. To simplify our example of calculating the number of re-handlings, assume that the maximum stack height is three. Since there are three different weight groups, there can be $3 \times 3 \times 3 = 27$ different weight combinations (Fig. 3). If all the weight labels are correct, the shaded containers in the figure will be the ones that need to be re-handled. For example, the weight combination MLH (bottom-to-top order) requires a single re-handling when the bottom container M, placed under a lighter container L, is to be fetched out.

Suppose we want to calculate the expected number of re-handlings for a stack of three containers with the estimated weight labels LLM. Then the conditional

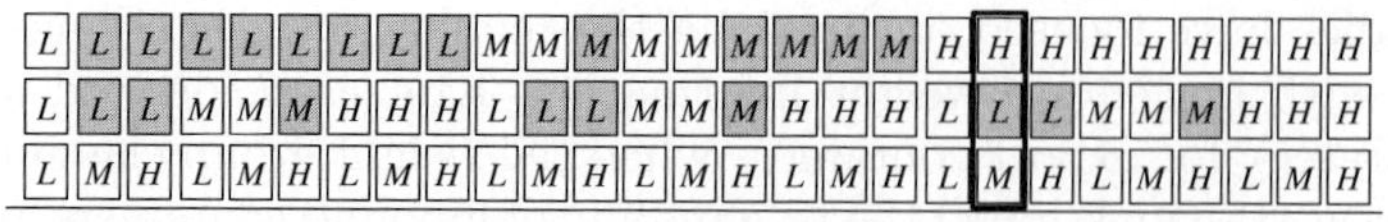

Fig. 3. Twenty-seven possible weight combinations for a stack of height three

Table 1. The confusion matrix for 20-foot containers

Estimated weight group	True weight group		
	$L\,(20.0\%)$	$M\,(23.1\%)$	$H\,(56.9\%)$
$L\,(13.9\%)$	11.1%	2.0%	0.9%
$M\,(39.7\%)$	**7.1%**	17.4%	15.3%
$H\,(46.4\%)$	1.8%	3.8%	40.8%

probability of the true weight combination of this stack to be MLH, given the estimated weight LLM, is

$$p(MLH|LLM) = p(M|L) \cdot p(L|L) \cdot p(H|M). \tag{1}$$

Since the weights of the containers are independent of one another, the conditional probability for a stack can be obtained by multiplying the conditional probabilities for the respective individual containers. From the confusion matrix of Table 1, we see that $p(M|L) = 0.134$, $p(L|L) = 0.8$, and $p(H|M) = 0.383$; thus, $p(MLH|LLM) = 0.041$. If $n(xyz)$ denotes the number of required re-handlings for a stack with true weight labels x, y, and z, the expected number of re-handlings $E[qrs]$ for a stack with estimated weight labels q, r, and s can be calculated by

$$\begin{aligned}
E[qrs] &= \sum_{x,y,z \in \{L,M,H\}} n(xyz) \cdot p(xyz|qrs) \\
&= \sum_{x,y,z \in \{L,M,H\}} n(xyz) \cdot p(x|q) \cdot p(y|r) \cdot p(z|s).
\end{aligned} \tag{2}$$

The above equation can be easily extended to the general case of a stack with an arbitrary height. The lower bound on the expected number of re-handlings for loading all the containers in a bay can be obtained by summing up the expected number of re-handlings of each stack of the bay. This lower bound is used to evaluate the stacking results produced by the stacking strategies under investigation.

4   Deriving Good Stacking Strategies

In this section, we describe the representation of a stacking strategy and explain how we applied a simulated annealing algorithm[5] to the problem of finding a good stacking strategy. We also point out that we can further reduce the number of re-handlings if we increase the accuracy of the weight classification by applying machine learning.

4.1   Representation of a Stacking Strategy

Assuming the maximum stack height of three, there are thirteen possible stack types of different weight combinations (including an empty stack) on which a new container can be placed. Figure 4(a) shows all these stack types, each tagged with a unique index number referring to the particular type. We represent a stacking rule by a permutation of these stack type indexes to indicate the precedence for placing a newly arriving container.

Figure 4(b) depicts an example situation of a bay in which we want to select a stack on top of which we may place a new container. The current state of the bay is represented by a vector $B = (2, 7, X, 10, 6, 4)$, where the numbers are the type indexes of the corresponding stacks and X is an indication that the corresponding stack is full. The figure also shows two different stacking rules s_1 and s_2. According to rule s_1, the best place for a new container is p_1, which is on top of type 2 stack because type 1 stack (which is of higher precedence) cannot be found in the current state of the bay. Similarly, rule s_2 selects p_2 as the best place because it is on top of type 6 stack, which is currently the best type of stack available.

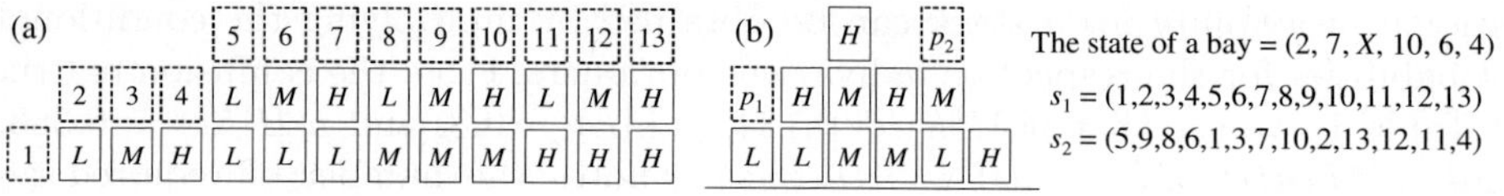

Fig. 4. (a) Thirteen possible 3-tier stack types on which there are empty slots for a newly arriving container to be placed and (b) example of a bay and two stacking strategies

Since the preferred position for an incoming container can be different depending on its estimated weight group, a complete stacking strategy is a triple (s_L, s_M, s_H), where s_e is the stacking rule applicable when the estimated weight group of an incoming container is e. There are more than six billion possible permutations of thirteen stack types; thus, there are more than 10^{29} possible stacking strategies. This number grows exponentially with stack height. Therefore, the problem of finding an optimal stacking strategy is intractable, so a heuristic search might be the only viable solution.

4.2   Searching for a Good Stacking Strategy

Our simulated annealing search starts from a strategy consisting of three randomly generated precedence rules, each for a weight group. Neighbors of a current strategy are generated by randomly picking a precedence rule and then swapping two randomly chosen types of index.

A strategy can be evaluated by calculating the lower bound on the expected number of re-handlings for all possible bay configurations generated by that strategy. However, a strategy can be evaluated only by a simulation because it is infeasible to enumerate all possible bay configurations. Our simulation procedure is as follows. First, a random sequence of containers incoming to a bay is generated according to the probability distribution of the estimated weight groups. The sequence should be long enough to fill up a whole bay. Then the stacking strategy under investigation is applied to place each container in sequence, starting from an empty bay.[1] Finally, once all the containers in the sequence are stacked, we calculate the lower bound on the expected number of re-handlings for that particular bay by applying the method described in the previous section. By repeating this simulation process with randomly generated new sequences for a sufficient number of times, we can get a good estimate of the quality of the stacking strategy. In our experiment, we repeated these simulations ten thousand times per strategy.

4.3 Improving the Accuracy of Weight Grouping Through Learning

Many re-handling situations could be avoided if the weight information given by the trucking companies at the time of container arrival were more accurate. Based on the conjecture that the types of weight errors made are dependent on the trucking companies, we tried to capture the pattern by applying machine learning algorithms. For example, some trucking companies tend to overestimate, while others tend to underestimate the weight of containers. The record obtained from a real container terminal is our data for learning. The containers of the first four months in that record are used for training, and the rest for testing. The attributes for describing each container include the name of the trucking company, the estimated weight in tons (EWT), and a flag indicating whether it is a trans-shipment container. The class value of each container is its true weight group. We tried several machine learning algorithms, including the decision tree[6], naive Bayes, 1R, and PART. By using the estimated weight group given by the learned classifier, we were able to observe some reduction on the number of re-handlings. Detailed results of experiments are given in the next section.

5 Experimental Results

Of the collected record of containers exported for five months in a real container terminal, those for the first four months were used to learn classifiers for weight grouping and to derive stacking strategies. The rest were used to evaluate the derived strategies. Separate experiments were conducted for 20-foot and 40-foot size containers, because they had different confusion matrices. For the learning of weight classification, the data mining tool Weka[7] was used.

In an effort to improve the accuracy of weight grouping, we tried several machine learning algorithms to find a good classifier. Among the algorithms tried, decision tree learning showed the best performance. The accuracies of weight grouping by the decision tree classifier were determined to be 5% higher than that of weight grouping by 'without learning.'

Figure 5 illustrates part of a decision tree generated for 40-foot containers. The attribute CNAME is the name of a trucking company. The decision tree reveals

---

[1] Note, in reality, that the sequence of incoming containers is not known ahead of time although we generate the whole sequence for the simulation purpose. When we are stacking a container, we do not know the type of the container to come in next.

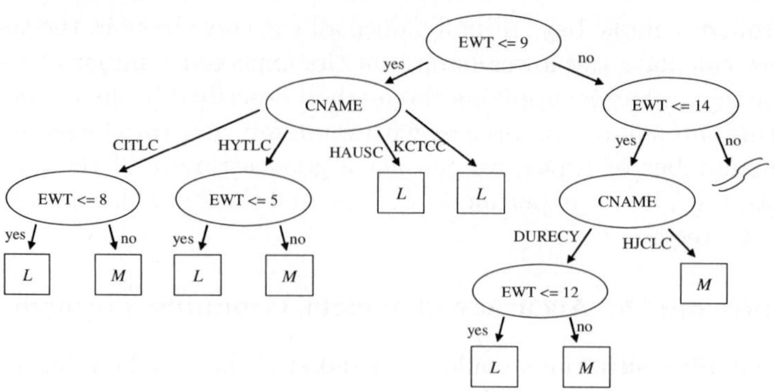

Fig. 5. Part of a decision tree generated for 40-foot containers

tendencies of either overestimating or underestimating the weights, depending on the company. For example, the left part of the tree indicates the containers that actually belong to weight group M, although company CITLC estimated their weights to be between 8 and 9. Note that a 40-foot container of weight less than 10 is regularly classified to weight group L. By using this decision tree, we can compensate for the errors in estimating weight group.

Tables 2 presents the results of experiments performed for a 6-tier 9-row bay, which is used in automated container terminals. We implemented and compared four different stacking strategies, including the one that we propose. SWGS refers to the traditional strategy of stacking the containers of the same weight group on the same stack. DP refers to the stacking strategy derived by dynamic programming, as described in [1]. Note that DP can derive an optimal strategy under the condition that the weight grouping is perfectly correct. Simple-rule positions a newly arriving container using a simple heuristic.[8] The heuristic selects a stack by considering only what the heaviest estimated weight group of the stack is. There are about 90,000 possible such heuristics. All these heuristics are generated and evaluated by simulation and the best one is selected. Since our method uses a simulated annealing algorithm to search for a good strategy, the results differed from experiment to experiment. The numbers in the tables are the averages of the results of five experiments. Our simulated annealing search was terminated if twenty thousand strategies were evaluated or no improvement was observed for one thousand successive moves. The temperature T was initially set to 100.0. After each evaluation, the current temperature T was lowered by subtracting a small fraction of it (i.e., $T \leftarrow T - 0.001 \times T$). The search usually took less than two hours on a Pentium PC with a 1.7GHz Xeon CPU.

The table presents the relative frequencies of re-handlings incurred by different strategies compared to the frequency by SWGS without learning. In all cases, our proposed method showed the best performance. We often observed further reductions of re-handling frequencies when we used a decision tree learned to make a better estimate of the weight group. For the 20-foot containers, however, the performances of SWGS and DP became slightly poorer when a decision tree was used for weight classification. Although the overall accuracy of weight

Table 2. Relative frequencies of re-handlings of different strategies in reference to the frequency by SWGS (without learning) for a 6-tier 9-row bay

Stacking Strategy	20-foot		40-foot	
	Weight Grouping		Weight Grouping	
	Without learning	Decision Tree	Without learning	Decision Tree
SWGS	100.0%	100.5%	100.0%	91.4%
DP	88.5%	89.6%	88.6%	80.2%
Simple rule	73.7%	68.8%	81.6%	75.8%
Proposed method	**70.6%**	**68.9%**	**78.3%**	**72.1%**

classification was improved by the decision tree, the decision tree learned tended to misclassify the real weight group M and H to weight group L more often than the regular weight grouping rule 'without learning'. Since it was likely that the expected number of re-handlings of a stack full of group L containers was higher than that of the stack full of group M or H, the use of such a decision tree might have some negative effects. If we assume that only one container is misclassified and misclassifications to other weight groups are equally likely, the expected number of re-handlings is 1 for stack LLL, 5/6 for MMM, and 2/3 for HHH. The strategies derived by our method somewhat overcame the weakness of the decision tree because the derivation of the strategies was based on the confusion matrix of the decision tree.

Figure 6 reveals a strategy derived by our method without using the learned classifier for weight group estimation. The strategy was for stacking 20-foot containers in a 4-tier 6-row bay. The strategy consisted of three precedence rules, one for each of the three weight groups L, M, and H. Each precedence rule was represented by a sequence of stack types in the order of preference. We were interested in knowing what types of stacks had actually been frequently selected to place the incoming containers of each weight group. Therefore, the figure shows only those stack types that had been selected to place at least 3% of all the containers coming in during the simulation. For example, "8.0%" in the left part of the figure indicates that the number of containers of weight group L that were placed on the ground (i.e., empty stack) was equal to 8.0% of all the containers that came in during the simulation. Overall, we observe that the containers of weight group L were preferred to be placed on empty stacks or on stacks having just one container of weight group L. In contrast, the containers

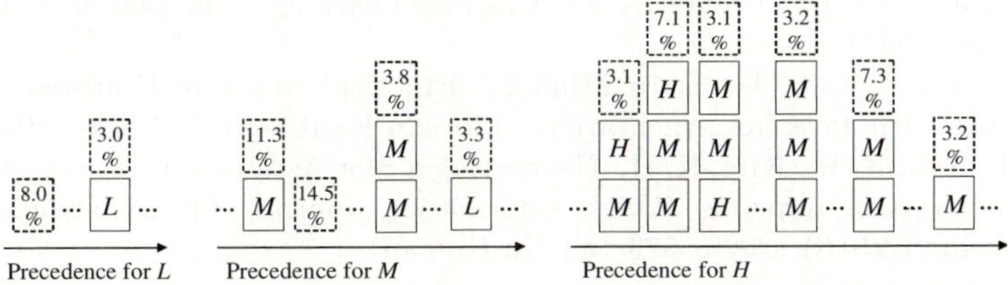

Fig. 6. Strategy derived for stacking 20-foot container in a 4-tier 6-row bay

of weight group H were preferred to be placed on top of stacks of many heavy containers. A somewhat different strategy was derived for the 40-foot containers because the confusion matrix of 40-foot containers was different from that of 20-foot containers. It is noteworthy that yet different strategies were derived if we used the learned classifier for weight group estimation again due to the different confusion matrices.

6   Conclusions

We have presented a method for deriving a strategy for stacking containers with uncertain weight information. Stacking incoming containers according to our strategy can significantly reduce the number of container re-handlings at the time of loading. Since re-handlings occur due to errors in estimated weight groups of containers, we have devised a method that is sensitive to the probability distribution of true weight group, given an estimated weight group. We have implemented a simulated annealing algorithm to find a good stacking strategy within a reasonable time. It was confirmed that the number of re-handlings could be further reduced by improving the accuracy of weight grouping through the use of a learned classifier. The next step of our work will be to apply a cost-sensitive learning for weight classification, since experimental results have shown that improvement of classification accuracy alone does not always lead to reduction of re-handling counts for some stacking strategies.

References

1. Kim, K. H., Park, Y. M., Ryu, K. R.: Deriving Decision Rules to Locate Export Containers in Container Yard. European Journal of Operational Research **124** (2000) 89–101
2. Kim, K. H.: Evaluation of the Number of Rehandles in Container Yards. Computers and Industrial Engineering **32(4)** (1997) 701–711
3. Castilho, B., Daganzo, C. F.: Handling Strategies for Import Containers at Marine Terminals. Transportation Research **27B(2)** (1993) 151–166
4. Watanabe, I.: Characteristics and Analysis Method of Efficiencies of Container Terminal - An Approach to the Optimal Loading/Unloading Method. Container Age (1991) 36–47
5. Aarts, E., Korst, J.: Simulated Annealing, Local Search in Combinatorial Optimization. John Wiley & Sons (1997) 91-120
6. Quinlan, J. R.: C4.5: Programs for Machine Learning. San Mateo, CA, Morgan Kaufmann (1993)
7. Witten, I. H., Frank, E.: Data Mining - Practical Machine Learning Tools and Techniques with Java Implementations. Morgan Kaufmann Publisher (2000)
8. Kang, J., Ryu, K. R., Kim, K. H.: Generating a Slot Assignment Rule for Outbound Containers Having Imprecise Weight Information. Journal of Korean Navigation and Port Research **29(6)** (2005) 573–581 (in Korean)

Fault Diagnostics in Electric Drives Using Machine Learning

Yi L. Murphey[*], M. Abul Masrur[*], and ZhiHang Chen

Abstract. Electric motor and power electronics based inverter are the major components in industrial and automotive electric drives. In this paper we present a fault diagnostics system developed using machine learning technology for detecting and locating multiple classes of faults in an electric drive. A machine learning algorithm has been developed to automatically select a set of representative operating points in the (torque, speed) domain, which in turn is sent to the simulated electric drive model to generate signals for the training of a diagnostic neural network, "Fault Diagnostic Neural Network" (FDNN). We presented our study on two different neural network systems and show that a well-designed hierarchical neural network system is robust in detecting and locating faults in electric drives.

Keywords: intelligent systems, neural networks, machine learning.

1 Introduction

Fault diagnostics for internal combustion (IC) engine vehicles has been well investigated [1,4,10], but not to the same extent for electric or hybrid vehicles. However, there are active researches in electrical system diagnostics [2, 5, 6, 8, 9]. Rule-based expert systems and decision trees are the two traditional diagnostic techniques, but they have serious limitations. A rule-based system often has difficulties in dealing with novel faults and acquiring complete knowledge to build a reliable rule-base, and is system dependent. A decision tree can be very large for a complex system, and it is also system dependent such that even small engineering changes can mean significant updates [2]. More recently model based approaches, fuzzy logic, artificial neural networks (ANN), case based reasoning (CBR) are popular techniques used in various fault diagnostics problems in electrical systems.

Our research is one step more advanced from those published works. Most of the existing diagnostic systems are built to detect a faulty condition against the normal condition. We present an advanced machine learning technology for the development of a robust diagnostic system that has the capability of detecting and locating multiple classes of faults in an electric drive operating at any valid (torque, speed) conditions. The diagnostic system FDNN(Fault Diagnostic Neural Network) is trained with simulation data generated by a robust machine learning algorithm. The diagnostic results provided by FDNN can be used to make a gracefully degradable [6, 8] operation of a faulty drive possible. Experiments were conducted both on the

---

[*] Senior Member, IEEE.

M. Ali and R. Dapoigny (Eds.): IEA/AIE 2006, LNAI 4031, pp. 1169–1178, 2006.

simulated data and the results show that the proposed diagnostic system is very effective in detecting multiple classes of faulty conditions of an inverter in an electric drive operating at any valid (torque, speed) point.

2 Electric Drive Fault Detection Using Signal Analysis and Machine Learning

Figure 1 illustrates our approach to fault diagnostics of an electric drive. "SIM_drive", a simulation model of a field oriented control electric drive with a power electronics based inverter and a 3-phase induction motor(see Figure 2), is developed and implemented using the Matlab-Simulink software. SIM_drive has the capability of simulating normal operation condition of an electric drive as well as the faulty conditions of the open and post-short-circuit faults in an inverter switch. The SIM_drive model operates at any selected (torque, speed) operating point under normal and various faulty conditions. Since in real world an electric drive can operate at different (torque, speed) points, a diagnostic system should be trained to be robust throughout the (torque, speed) domain.

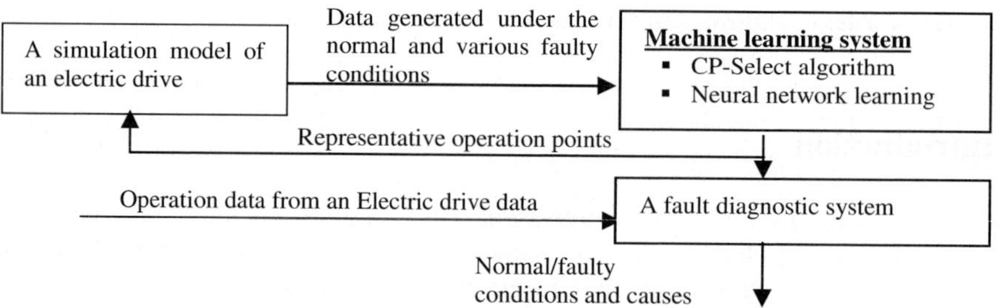

Fig. 1. Illustration of a model based fault diagnostic system driven by machine learning

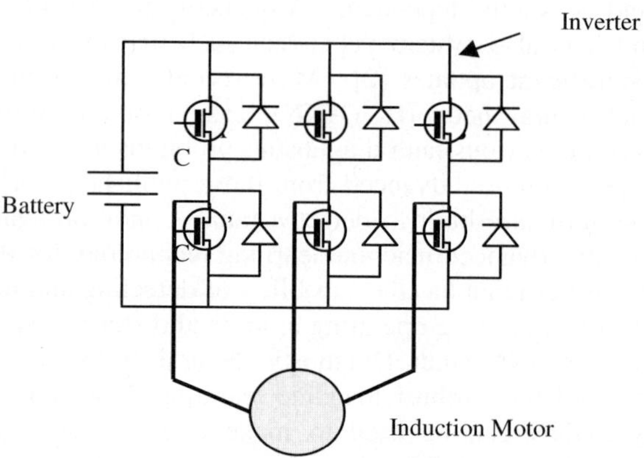

Fig. 2. A a six-switch inverter in a 3-phase electric drive

A machine learning algorithm is developed to select representative operating points from the (torque, speed) domain for use by the SIM_drive model to generate training data. The detail of the SIM_drive can be found in [7]. In this paper we focus on the machine learning system and the fault diagnostic system.

The objective of the machine learning approach is to train a diagnostic system on the representative data so it has the capability of performing accurate fault diagnostics in an electric drive that operates at any valid operating point. The intelligent system used in this research is a multi-class neural network system.

2.1 Multiple Class Fault Detection

We are attempting to develop a robust diagnostic system to detect the faulty cases in the electric drive system shown in Figure 2. The challenges in developing such robust diagnostic systems lie in the fact that it is easier to identify signatures of a faulty condition against the normal condition, whereas signal signatures of one fault against another one are often quite subtle. We model the fault diagnostics in electric drive as a multi-class classification problem.

Figure 3 illustrates the computational steps involved in the signal fault detection system, where the input consists of the input voltages V_{an}, V_{bn}, V_{cn} to the motor, the currents I_a, I_b, I_c, and the motor electro-magnetic torque T_e. The first computational step is to segment the signals and extract the signal features from each segment. The signal segments are then analyzed by an artificial neural network, which is trained on the signals generated by SIM_drive at the parameter points selected by the CP-Select algorithm, a machine learning algorithm. The major research contribution in this paper is the machine learning technology used to train a neural network that can robustly detect and locate faults inside an electric drive operated under any given valid condition.

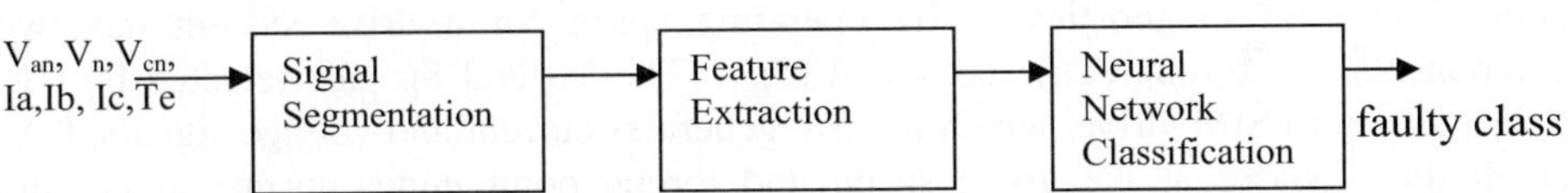

Fig. 3. Major computational steps in a signal fault detection system

2.2 Signal Segmentation and Feature Extraction

Signal fault detection is performed on a segment-by-segment basis. All input signals are segmented using the same fixed sized segments and the two adjacent segments are overlapped in 1/3 of the segment width in order to maintain continuity of information flowing between segments. The basic frequency of the signals is over 80 Hz, and sampling frequency is chosen to be 1000, which is sufficient for this purpose. We chose to use 16 samples in each segment with an overlap of 5 samples between two adjacent segments. A signal of 3000 data samples is segmented into 272 segments. Each signal segment is represented by the following features:

- Max: maximum magnitude of the signal within the segment
- Min: minimum magnitude of the signal within the segment
- Median: median of the signal within the segment
- Mean: mean of the signal within the segment
- Standard deviation: standard deviation of the signal segment
- Zero-frequency component of the power spectrum

The detection of signal faults within a time period requires one segment from each input signal and each segment is represented by the 6 features listed above. Since we have 7 input signals (3 voltage signals, 3 current signals, and 1 torque signal), the combined feature vector to represent a particular state in the electric drive at a particular time is a vector of 42 dimensions. The feature vector is the input to a neural network classifier that determines whether the 7 signals within this time period manifest any fault.

2.3 Smart Selections of Operation Parameters

In an electric drive system, the current and voltage signals behave differently under different operation conditions specified by torque and speed. The issue of smart selection of "control parameters" (also referred to as operating point) in the (torque, speed) domain is important for all electric drive diagnostic systems that are trained on simulated data.

A diagnostic system trained on more representative data is more likely to perform better diagnostics in real world system under any operation condition. We developed a machine learning algorithm, CP-Select (**C**ontrol **P**oint-Select), for the generation of training data for a robust electric drive diagnostic system. The CP-Select algorithm automatically selects representative operating points in a given domain of control parameter (CP) space to generate representative training data for a neural network system for fault diagnostics. The operating space for a drive system has two components, i.e. torque (Tq) and speed (Sp). The Tq and Sp pair selected by CP-Select is sent to SIM_drive, which in turn, generates current and voltage signals, I, V, at all three phases at the given speed and torque point under normal and faulty conditions. Diagnostic features are extracted from these signals and feature vectors are used to train an ANN called FDNN, and the performance of the FDNN is evaluated on a validation data set Tv. If the performance is satisfactory, the algorithm stops, otherwise, more operating points are selected.

The most complicated component in the CP-Select algorithm is ASCP (Automatic Selection of Control parameters). Initially Φ contains the rectangular space that includes all valid torque and speed points used by a real world electric drive. As the process goes on, Φ contains all subspaces from which potential parameters can be selected. The ASCP algorithm repeatedly removes one parameter space from Φ at a time and performs an iterative process until Φ is empty or the performance of the trained FDNN is satisfactory. At each iteration ASCP selects three sets of points, and each set goes through a simulation, training and evaluation process.

The first set of points contains the four corner points and the center point of the current parameter space C_CP and are stored in P_0. The points in P_0 that have not been selected before are sent to SIM_drive to generate new training data. The newly generated training data are combined with the existing ones to form the current training data set, Tr. FDNN is trained on Tr and evaluated on validation data set Tv. If the performance of FDNN on Tv is satisfactory, the process stops. Otherwise it goes on to select the second set of points, which are the interior points of the current parameter space C_CP. The same simulation, training, and evaluation steps are repeated on this set of points. If the performance of FDNN is satisfactory, the process stops. Otherwise the third set of parameters are selected, which contains the four center points on the four sides of C_CP. Again, the same simulation, training and evaluation process is applied to this set of parameters. If the performance of FDNN is satisfactory, the ASCP algorithm stops, otherwise, the current parameter space C_CP is evenly divided into four subspaces CP_1, CP_2, CP_3 and CP_4, which are appended to the parameter space set Φ. All the parameter spaces in Φ are sorted based on the performances of FDNN on the validation points in the space, and the entire process repeats.

2.4 Multi-class Fault Classification Using Artificial Neural Networks (ANN)

Neural networks have been successfully applied to a broad range of problems including engineering diagnosis, pattern classification, intelligent manufacturing, control problems and computer vision. Most of the research in neural networks has been in the development of learning and training algorithms for 2-class classifiers, i.e. classifiers with one output node that represent classes 0 and 1. However, fault diagnostics in electric drive has six classes of single switch faults and three classes of post-short-circuit classes. The most common architectures which have been proposed for multi-class neural networks [11], involve a single neural network with K output nodes, where K is the number of faulty classes, and a system of binary neural networks combined with a posterior decision rule to integrate the results of neural networks. A system of binary neural networks requires separate training of each neural network and each trained neural network generates a decision boundary between one class and all others. The most noticeable limitation in this approach is that the decision boundaries generated by the different 2-class neural network classifiers can have overlapped or uncovered regions in the feature space [11]. For the feature vectors that fall on an overlapped region in the feature space, more than one 2-class classifiers can claim the input as their classes, resulting in ambiguity. The feature vectors falling on the regions that are not claimed by any neural networks will be rejected by all neural networks. As a result the resulting system may not generalize well. Another type of multi-class neural network system is to use a single neural network with k output, where k > 1. This type of the neural network architecture has the advantage of simple training procedure, and only one neural network is trained for all m classes, where m > 2, and, if trained properly a neural network system implemented in this architecture should reduce the ambiguity problem [11].

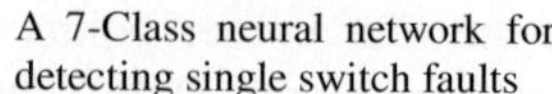

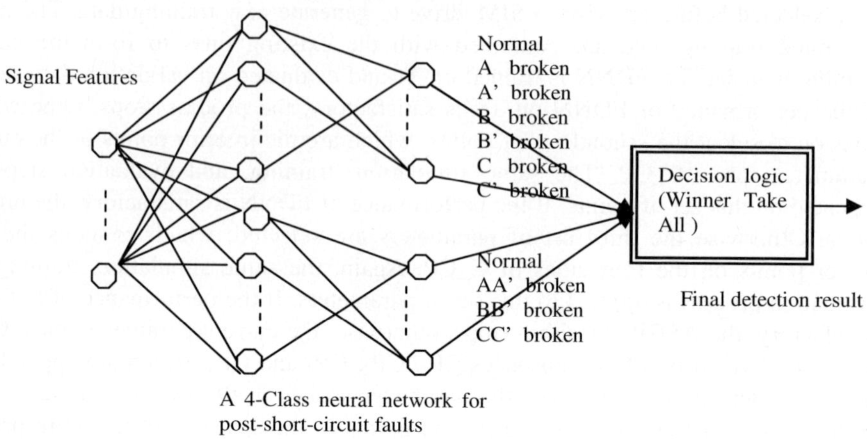

(a) A system of two neural networks for classifying the single switch and short circuit faults in a 3-phase electric drive

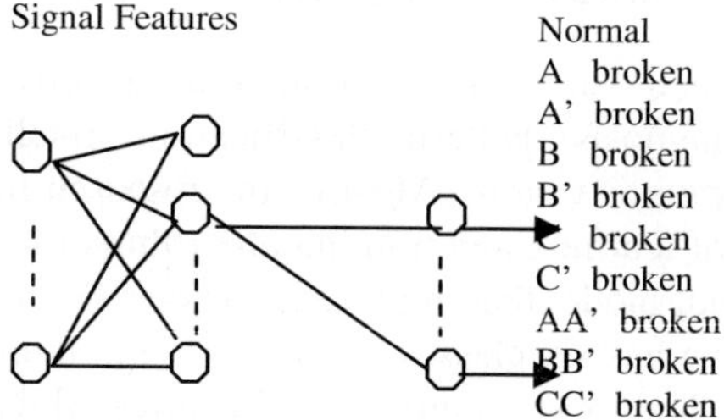

(b) A 10-class single neural network for classifying all 10 classes of faults in a 3-phase electric drive

Fig. 4. Two neural network architectures developed for the fault classification in a in an electric drive

Based on the single neural network architecture, we implemented two different systems of neural networks as illustrated in Figure 4 for the diagnosis of 10 classes of faults in an electric drive: one class represents the normal condition, six classes represent six single switch faults, and the last three classes represent the three post-short-circuit faults. Figure 4 (a) shows a structured diagnostic system consisting of two neural networks, one is trained to classify single switch faults, and the other classifies the post-short-circuit faults, and WTA [11] approach is used to integrate the results from the two neural networks. Figure 4 (b) shows a single neural network trained to classify all 10 classes: normal, six single switch faults, and 3 post-short-circuit faults. One important issue in a multi-class neural network is how to encode the classes in the output nodes of the neural network. In both neural network architectures, we chose to use a "one-hot spot" method described as follows. For a k-class classification problem, we need an output layer of k bits, each class is assigned a unique binary string (codeword) of length k with only 1 bit set to "1" and all other bits are "0." For example if it is a six-class classification problem, class 0 is assigned a codeword of 000001, class 1 is assigned a codeword of 000010, class 2 is assigned of a codeword 000100, etc. The advantage of this encoding is that it gives enough tolerance among different classes. We use the back propagation learning algorithm to train all the neural networks.

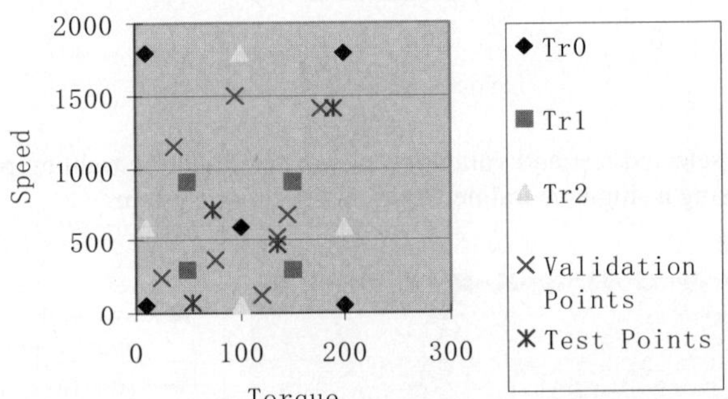

(a) Randomly selected test and validation set, and the train data selected by CP-Select algorithm for classifying single switch faults

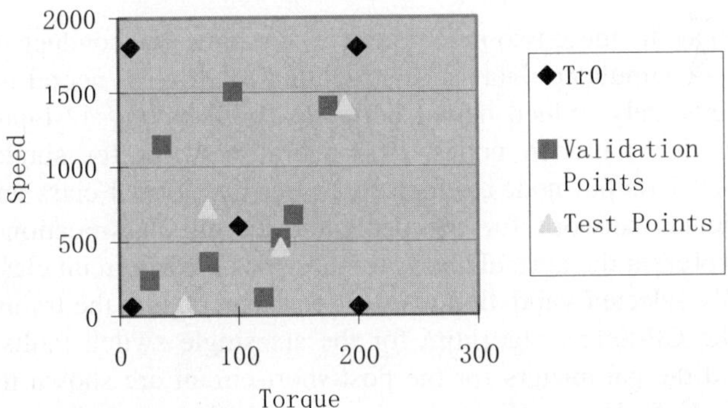

(b) Randomly selected test and validation parameters, and the training parameters selected by the CP-Select for classifying post-short-circuit faults.

Fig. 5. Randomly selected test and validation parameters, and the training parameters selected by the CP-Select for classifying single switch faults and post-short-circuit faults

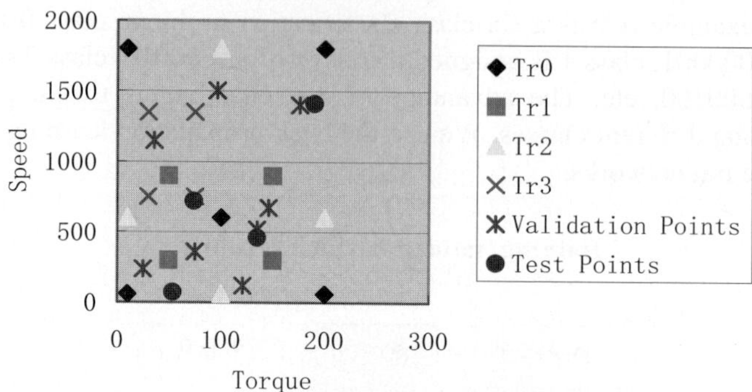

Fig. 6. Randomly selected test and validation parameters, and the training parameters selected by the CP-Select using a single neural network classification system

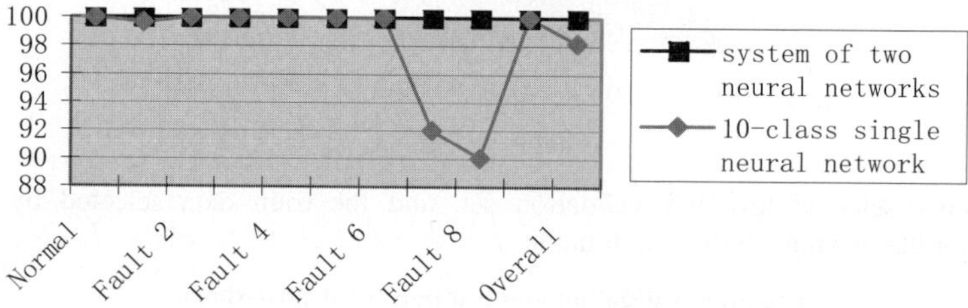

Fig. 7. Performances of two different neural network systems

In order to evaluate these two neural network systems, we conducted the following experiments using simulated data. The structured multi-class neural network system contains two separately trained neural networks, both having 42 input nodes and 1 hidden layer with 20 hidden nodes. The neural network for single switch fault classification has 7 output nodes, which represent the normal class and the 6 faulty classes. The neural network for the post-short-circuit classification has 4 output nodes, which represent the normal class and the 3 post-short-circuit classes.

The randomly selected validation and test parameters, and the training parameters generated by the CP-Select algorithm for the six single switch faults are shown in Figure 5 (a) and the parameters for the post-short-circuit are shown in Figure 5 (b). The single-switch fault classification neural network was trained on the control parameters in Tr_0, Tr_1 and Tr_2 generated by the CP-Select algorithm using 3 iterations as described in section 3.2. The post-short-circuit fault classification neural network was trained on the control parameters in Tr_0 shown in Figure 5 (a), which gave 100% correct performance on the validation data shown in the squared points. Therefore the CP-Select algorithm stopped at the end of the first iteration. The four randomly selected test points are shown in triangular in Figure 5(a).

For the 10-class single neural network system, the CP-Select algorithm generated the training points in four iterations resulting in Tr_0, Tr_1, Tr_2 and Tr_3, which are shown in Figure 6 along with the validation points and test points. The 10-class neural network has 42 input nodes and 1 hidden layer with 20 hidden nodes, and 10 output nodes, where one node represents the normal class, and 6 represent the single switch fault classes, and 3 represent the three post-short-circuit faulty classes. It is trained on the data generated by the SIM_drive using the operating points in $Tr_0 \cup Tr_1 \cup Tr_2 \cup Tr_3$.

The test data for both diagnostic systems were the signals generated by SIM_drive from the same four randomly selected (torque, speed) points. 11320 feature vectors were extracted from these signals among which 6792 data samples contain the six single switch faults, and 3396 contain the three post-short-circuit faults, and 1132 are normal. The performances of these two diagnostic systems on the test data set are shown in Figure 6. The structured diagnostic system correctly detected and located all 9 faulty classes and the normal class with 100% correct detection. The single neural network system correctly detected with 100% all the 6 single switch faults, but detected correctly with only 90% and 92% on test data from the post-short-circuit faulty class 1 and class 2.

3   Summary and Conclusions

We have presented a diagnostic system driven by a machine learning algorithm for multi-class fault detection in an electric drive system with a three phase induction motor. We presented the machine learning algorithm for the smart selection of vehicle operating points from the (torque, speed) space for the use by the simulated model, SIM_drive, to generate representative training data, and a neural network classification system developed and trained on the signals generated at the representative operation conditions for the fault diagnostics of electric drive inverters.

The intelligent diagnostic system trained with machine learning technology has been evaluated by experimental data. We used the test signals generated by the SIM_drive that contain normal and 9 faulty classes. The results show that the proposed intelligent diagnostics approach is very effective in detecting multiple classes of faults in an electric drive inverter. The authors also investigated two different neural network architectures, a structured neural network system and a single neural network. Our finding is that the structured neural network system gives more accurate diagnostics on all 10 classes than the single neural network system.

Acknowledgment

This work is supported in part by a research contract with the U. S. Army TACOM.

References

1. Crossman, J., Guo, H., Murphey, Y., and Cardillo, J., "Automotive Signal Fault Diagnostics: Part I: signal fault analysis, feature extraction, and quasi optimal signal selection," IEEE Transaction on Vehicular, July 2003, Volume 52, Issue 4, July 2003 Page(s):1076 – 1098.
2. Fenton, W., McGinnity, T., and Maguire, L., "Fault diagnosis of electronic systems using intelligent techniques: a review", IEEE Trans. on Systems, Man, and Cybernetics – Pt. C, Vol. 31, No. 3, Aug 2000, pp. 269-281.
3. Huang, W. Y., and Lippmann, R.P., Neural net and traditional classifiers. In D. Z. Anderson (Ed.), Neural Information Processing Systems, pp. 387-396. New York: American Institute of Physics.
4. Gertler, J., Costin, M., Fang, X., Kowalczuk, Z., Kunwer, M., Monajemy, R., "Model Based Diagnosis for Automotive Engines-Algorithm Development and Testing on a production Vehicle", IEEE Trans on Control Systems Technology, Vol. 3, No. 1, pp 61 – 69, 1995,
5. Kim K., and Parlos, A. G., "Induction motor fault diagnosis Based on neuropredictors and wavelet signal processing," IEEE/ASME Transactions on Mechatronics, Vol. 7, No. 2, pp 201 – 219, June 2002.
6. Klima, J., "Analytical investigation of an induction motor drive under inverter fault mode operations", IEE Proc.- Electr. Power Appl., Vol 150, No. 3, May 2003, pp. 255-262.
7. Masrur, M. A., Chen, Z., Zhang, B., Jia, H., and Murphey, Y., "Model-Based Fault Diagnosis in Electric Drives Using Artificial Neural Networks", to appear in the IEEE Trans. On Mechatronics, September, 2005
8. Masrur, M.A.., Xu, X., and Liang, F., "Fault Isolation in an Induction Motor Control System", U.S. Patent 5469351, Nov 1995.
9. Moseler, O., Isermann, R., "Application of Model-Based Fault Detection to a Brushless DC Motor ", IEEE Trans on Industrial Electronics, Vol. 47, No. 5, pp 1015-1020, 2000.
10. Murphey, Y., Guo, H., Crossman, J.., and Coleman, M., "Automotive Signal Diagnostics Using Wavelets and Machine Learning," IEEE Transaction on Vehicular, November, 2000.
11. Ou, G., Murphey, Y., Feldkamp, L., "Multiclass Pattern Classification Using Neural Networks," International Conference on Pattern Recognition, Cambridge, UK, 2004

An Integrated and Flexible Architecture for Planning and Scheduling

Antonio Garrido, Eva Onaindía, and Ma. de Guadalupe García-Hernández

Universidad Politécnica de Valencia
Camino de Vera, s/n, 46071 - Valencia (Spain)
{agarridot, onaindia, magarcia}@dsic.upv.es

Abstract. In this paper we propose an integrated architecture to cope with real-world problems of planning and scheduling. Our approach consists of two specialised processes, one for planning and one for scheduling, which work together in a strong-coupled manner to deal with complex problems that involve time and resource constraints. Besides describing the elements of this approach, we also present its functional behaviour together with an example to show its applicability to real problems.

1 Introduction

The application of AI techniques to automated planning and scheduling is acquiring more and more relevance. The reason behind this is that AI techniques not only help automatise and simplify many tedious tasks but they also provide very adequate mechanisms to improve the quality of plans. Nowadays, AI planning and scheduling techniques are able to deal with real-world problems that require handling duration of tasks, execution costs, resource usage, optimisation criteria, etc. All these ingredients make necessary the use of algorithms to provide action selection together with feasible resource assignments in a countless variety of problems, such as logistics management and distribution, space applications, autonomous vehicle navigation (planetary rovers and observation satellites), manufacturing systems, crisis management, etc. [1].

AI planning aims at determining **which** actions (plan) need to be executed to successfully achieve some goals, which usually entails a complex search process [1]. On the other hand, scheduling aims at determining **when** these actions must be executed and with **which** resources, which usually entails a constraint satisfaction process to validate all the problem constraints. Although many real-world problems include features of both planning and scheduling, these processes have been traditionally hardly related to each other [2]. However, dealing with planning and scheduling in a disunited way does not seem sensible: selecting an action in a plan is usually conditioned to time constraints, resource availability and multiple criteria to be optimised. Consequently, planning and scheduling complement each other perfectly, which clearly motivates the challenge in designing flexible models to integrate planning and scheduling capabilities, particularly considering that they use similar techniques (search in graphs, use of heuristics, management and reasoning of constraints, etc.) [2, 3, 4].

M. Ali and R. Dapoigny (Eds.): IEA/AIE 2006, LNAI 4031, pp. 1179–1188, 2006.
© Springer-Verlag Berlin Heidelberg 2006

This paper presents (what we understand as) a flexible architecture to integrate planning and scheduling, as a model that dynamically interleaves a planner and a scheduler. Hence, our main contributions are: i) the proposal of a general integrated architecture that combines two specialised processes for planning and scheduling; ii) the use of an action network that represents planning causal links and time+resource constraints; iii) the description (and a general algorithm) of the functional behaviour of this integrated architecture; and iv) an example that shows the applicability of this architecture to real-world problems.

2   Modelling Planning and Scheduling Problems: A Brief Review

Solving a planning and scheduling real-world problem in an automated way requires modelling some basic elements, such as:

1. Initial state, with all the information that is true at the beginning of the problem.
2. Goals, with all the facts that must be achieved at the end of the problem.
3. Actions, defined on the problem domain that allow to achieve the goals from the initial state.
4. Available resources, to execute the actions in the plan.
5. Temporal constraints, with additional constraints the plan must satisfy.
6. Metric function, as a multi-criteria function that needs to be optimised.

Although there is not a widely used approach for modelling problems with all these elements, from the planning point of view there exist some proposals to extend planning domain definition languages to deal with scheduling features, such as recent versions of PDDL [5]. For instance, in a planetary rovers problem[1] where rovers navigate a planet surface, finding samples (rocks, soil and images) and communicating them back to a lander, PDDL3 [5] allows us to model: i) actions with duration ((`calibrate ?camera`) takes 5'); ii) actions with local conditions and effects (`calibrate` requires the `?camera` to be `on_board ?rover` just at the *start* of the action); iii) actions with numeric conditions ((`energy ?rover`) needs to be ≥ 10) and effects ((`increase (energy ?rover) 18`)); iv) multi-criteria problem metrics to optimise (minimise the plan makespan and the energy used by `rover0`); and v) other constraints such as deadlines in (sub)goals (`communicate` needs to be performed before 30'), temporal constraints in the form of time windows (`sun` is available in `waypoint1` from 7' to 27'), etc.

However, there still exist some limitations to model hard constraints among actions (`calibrate camera0` must be executed exactly 5' before `calibrate camera1`), finite persistence of action effects (the effect of having a `camera` calibrated only lasts for 10.5'), etc. Despite this, most features of real-world planning/scheduling problems can be currently modelled, at least from an enriched planning point of view [5].

---

[1] More information about this kind of problem can be found in the International Planning Competition at: `http://ipc.icaps-conference.org/`

3   Integrating Planning and Scheduling

When dealing with planning and scheduling problems, different approaches have been traditionally followed [1, 2, 4]; some of them extend planning to cope with scheduling capabilities, whereas others include the planning component into scheduling, by manually providing the set of activities and, usually, the order in which theses activities must be applied. However, the solution does not necessarily imply an embedded planning process into a scheduling one, or vice versa. Our architecture provides a general and flexible model, where both planning and scheduling processes have an important role in the problem solving per se. It is important to note that while designing the architecture, our aim was to come up with a general model where each process is solved by using already existing techniques. There exist many planning and scheduling techniques that, properly combined, can be used for our purpose of creating a cooperative and highly-coupled integrated model of planning and scheduling.

3.1   Description of the Integrated Architecture

Fig. 1 depicts the structure of the integrated architecture for planning and scheduling. The integrated module requires as an input the model of the problem (domain+problem definition). Moreover, a plan (either provided by the user as a set of activities or by a planner), is used as an additional input, which is later

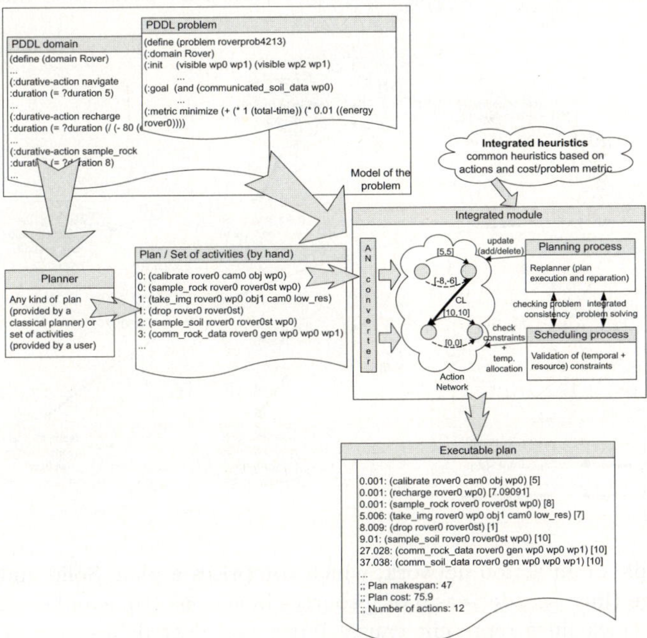

Fig. 1. Structure of the integrated architecture for planning and scheduling

motivated. The integrated module contains an action network (AN) converter that transforms the input plan into a network that represents the plan with its actions, causal links and (temporal+resource) constraints. The planning process updates the action network to make it free of planning conflicts; i.e. it mainly works as a replanner, repairing (adding or deleting) actions in the network when they cannot be executed. The scheduling process mainly works as a validator of constraints and checks the feasibility of the action network and its constraints. However, the scheduler's task is not only to validate the action network, but also to provide the planning process with advice about the conflicting actions and the resources involved in such conflicts. This way, the scheduler helps the planner repair the plan by means of integrated heuristics that allow both processes to take common agreement decisions.

There exist two elements that are essential to establish the foundations of the integrated module: the former concerns the **input** of the module, whereas the latter concerns how the **action network** represents the plan, actions and their constraints. Given the domain and problem definition as the input, the integrated module could start from an empty plan, i.e. generating a plan from scratch. However, it does not seem sensible to tackle such a complex task from scratch when there are many state-of-the-art planners that generate plans very efficiently [6]; so it seems more reasonable to use a given initial plan as a basis. The underlying idea is to use a classical planner, as simple (in terms of expressivity and calculus) and efficient as possible. Note that this does not imply a loss of generality: a plan provided by any planner can be used as an input, and even a plan generated by hand. Also note that this plan does not need to be

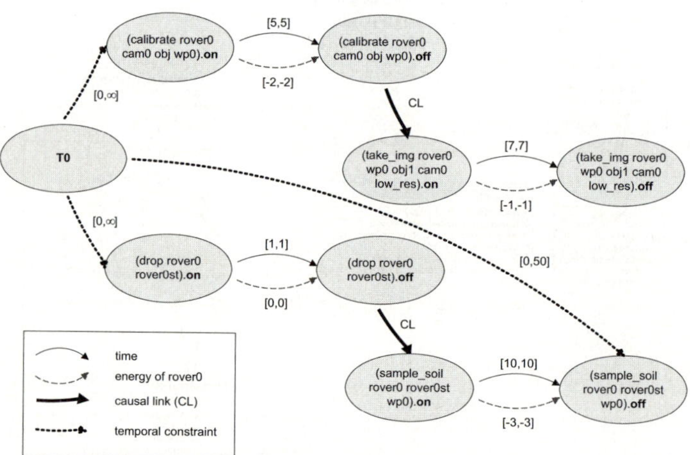

Fig. 2. Example of an action network, which comprises a plan. Solid and dashed lines represent usage (increase/decrease) of resources in actions (time and energy of `rover0`, respectively); thick lines represent causal links; and dotted lines represent temporal constraints. T0 identifies the beginning of time.

executable since the replanner can repair it. This increases the opportunities to use efficient planners as a previous step to the integrated module.

The action network (see Fig. 2) follows the philosophy of temporal constraint networks and (consumable) resource networks (TCN and rCN [7, 8], respectively) to represent actions and constraints on time and resources. Nodes represent timepoints where actions start/end (.on/.off, respectively). There are three types of edges, all of them labelled with an interval, that represent: i) usage of a resource (time is considered as a resource as well) between the .on/.off timepoints of the same action; ii) causal links between timepoints of actions; and iii) temporal constraints between timepoints. For instance, using the planetary rovers problem again, action (`calibrate rover0 cam0 obj wp0`) increases time in 5 units (action duration) and decreases energy of `rover0` in 2 units (note that these values can be also defined by a min-max interval). Action (`calibrate rover0 cam0 obj wp0`)`.off` has a causal link with (`take_img rover0 wp0 obj1 cam0 low_res`)`.on` because the first action generates a proposition *at end* that the second action needs *over all* its execution. Finally, temporal constraints allow to define additional constraints and deadlines between the execution of actions and the beginning of time: (`sample_soil rover0 rover0st wp0`) must finish before time 50.

3.2   Functional Behaviour of the Integrated Architecture

The general scheme with the functional behaviour of the integrated architecture is presented in Algorithm 1. The goal is to revise, both from the planning and scheduling points of view (`rev_PLN` and `rev_SCH`), all actions in the AN to find a conflict-free plan. Selecting one action at a time (step 5), two are the main (planning+scheduling) tasks to perform. One is solve_PLN_conflicts (step 8), i.e. when the plan is not executable due to planning conflicts. This type of conflict is basically caused by unsupported action preconditions or by mutex relations between the actions in the plan. Once the planning conflicts have been solved, the other   task   is   solve_SCH_conflicts   (step   14),   i.e.   when   the   plan   is   not

1: **rev_PLN** ← IS {IS *is a fictitious action that represents the initial state*}
2: **rev_SCH** ← ∅
3: **while** ∃a ∈ AN | a ∉ **rev_SCH do**
4:     {*Planning part; reasoning on causal links*}
5:     a ← earliest action that can be planned (executed) in **AN**
6:     **rev_PLN** ← **rev_PLN** ∪ {a}
7:     **if** number_of_conflicts(**rev_PLN**) > 0 **then**
8:         solve_PLN_conflicts(**rev_PLN**)
9:     {*Scheduling part; reasoning on time and resources*}
10:    **for all** a_i ∈ **rev_PLN** | a_i ∉ **rev_SCH do**
11:        **if** ∃ a consistent allocation of a_i in **rev_SCH then**
12:            **rev_SCH** ← **rev_SCH** ∪ {a_i}
13:        **else**
14:            solve_SCH_conflicts($a_i, \mathcal{R}, quantity, time\_point, Cannot\_acts, Should\_not\_acts, C$)

Algorithm 1. General scheme for integrating planning and scheduling

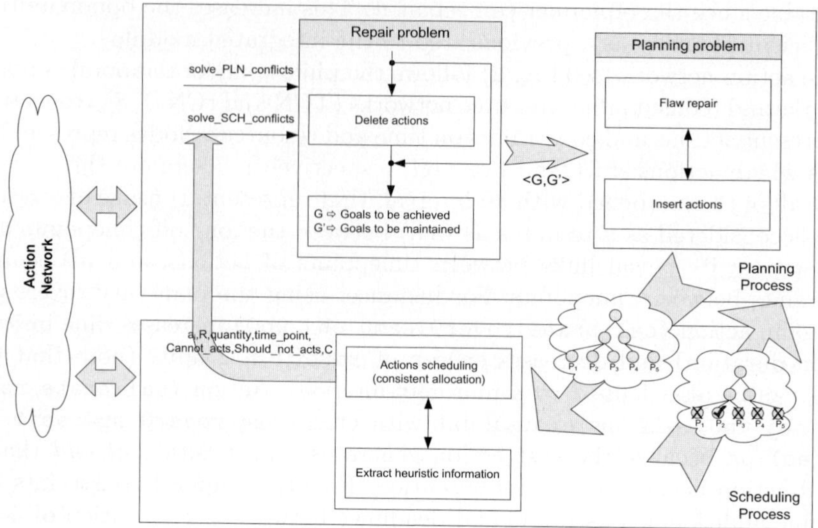

Fig. 3. Subtasks that are *derived* from steps 8 and 14 of Algorithm 1

executable due to time/resources conflicts. In both cases, the planner performs the **same** tasks (see Fig. 3): it converts the original problem into a planning repair problem which is later solved by applying classical planning techniques (flaw repair mechanisms, such as inserting actions to support unsatisfied preconditions). During the process of solving the planning problem, the planner eventually invokes the scheduler to obtain advice and make a better decision about the most convenient planning decision. That is, the scheduler helps the planner focus its search upon those planning alternatives that better accomplish the time/resource objectives/constraints. The key points in this functional behaviour are the two calls (steps 8 and 14 of Algorithm 1) to the planning process and the subtasks derived from them (see Fig. 3):

1. solve_PLN_conflicts. In this case, the planner invokes itself in order to fix the planning conflict in **rev_PLN**. This is the task that requires less heuristic information, entailing fewer decision points, because it means to transforming a planning conflict into a planning repair problem. Hence, the overall idea is how to solve a planning conflict from a planning perspective.
2. solve_SCH_conflicts. Unlike solve_PLN_conflicts, this is a harder task as it implies solving a scheduling conflict through planning. When the scheduler detects a constraint violation due to an oversubscribed resource $\mathcal{R}$, it attempts to find a consistent allocation for actions in **rev_SCH**. The ultimate goal is to find out **when** that resource is needed (at which *time_point*), **how much** is required (*quantity*) and **who** requires it (action a_i). Additionally, the scheduler provides the planner some helpful information on which actions cannot and should not be removed from the AN (*Cannot_acts* and *Should_not_acts*); for instance, a set of actions that must compulsorily be in

the plan, or that support the fulfillment of some time/resource constraints, or that correspond to a sequence of actions already scheduled, etc. Moreover, in order to guide the planning search as much as possible, the scheduler supplies an extra set of constraints ($\mathcal{C}$) that the planner must hold when solving the problem; for instance, do not use more than n units of resource R_j when solving this conflict.

3. The decision criteria to come up with a planning repair problem. After receiving any of the two mentioned calls, the planner analyses the information provided and transforms it into its own terms, i.e. into a planning repair problem (see Fig. 3). The idea is to formulate a repair problem in terms of which subgoals are to be achieved and which ones are to be maintained in the AN. In order to deduce this information, the planner makes use of the information provided by the scheduler and/or its own planning tactics to decide whether it is convenient to delete some actions prior to call the planning solver.

4. The advice provided by the scheduler to focus the planning search process. This stage corresponds to a classical planning solving task. The interesting point here is that the planner will count on the scheduler in order to decide which planning alternative to take on. This way, the planner shows the scheduler the planning decision points (plans $P_1, P_2, \ldots P_5$) and the scheduler determines the best alternative (P_2) from the time/resource perspective.

As a conclusion, this model represents an open collaborative approach where planner and scheduler work together to repair any conflict that arises during the process of building up the plan, no matter the origin of the conflict. Both components work in a strongly-coupled manner taking into account the information/advice provided by the other module (bidirectional communication). Obviously, the planner plays the central role in this collaborative work, though it is intelligently guided by the heuristic information provided by the scheduler.

3.3   Application Example

In this section we will use the rovers problem as an application example to show how our integrated model works. The goal is to have soil, rock and image data communicated. The initial plan, generated by any automated planner is shown in Fig. 4-a, which is subsequently converted into the AN of Fig. 4-b. However, the problem imposes these additional complex constraints: i) actions have different durations and consume energy of `rover0`; ii) the initial energy level of `rover0` is 10; iii) `sun` is available to recharge only in `waypoint1` and `waypoint3`; iv) the subgoal (`have_image objective1`) cannnot be achieved before time 20; v) the effect (`calibrated camera0`) only persists during 30 units; and vi) the goal (`communicated_image`) has a deadline, so it must be achieved before time 40.

Following Algorithm 1, actions are selected from the AN and revised by the planning and scheduling parts. While no planning nor scheduling conflicts arise, the sets `rev_PLN` and `rev_SCH` are updated. This process continues until revising (`comm_image wp0 wp1`) that introduces a scheduling conflict in `rev_SCH` because resource energy becomes oversubscripted: (`comm_image wp0 wp1`) requires

6 units of energy, but only 4 (10-3-2-1) are available. Then, the scheduler executes solve_SCH_conflicts(((comm_image wp0 wp1), (energy rover0), 2 (6-4), (comm_image wp0 wp1).on, {(sample_soil wp0), (take_image cam0 wp0)},∅, {∑(energy rover0) ≤ 10}). Note that *Cannot_acts* contains the actions that need to appear in the plan (they are the only way to achieve certain subgoals), whereas *Should_not_acts* is empty in this case. On the other hand, $\mathcal{C}$ indicates that now energy of rover0 cannot exceed 10 (since this is the initial value). The repair problem solver decides to maintain the same subgoals. Then, the planning solver tries to repair this conflict by inserting actions (recharge wp1) and (recharge wp3), thus creating several alternative plans that may be inserted at different timepoints $(P_1, P_1', \ldots P_3')$, as seen in Fig. 4-b. Since there are several different alternatives, the planner communicates the scheduler these choices and the scheduler verifies their consistency, informing the planner about the best choice to follow. After solving this conflict, the algorithm resumes by studying the next actions in the AN until no more actions need to be revised.

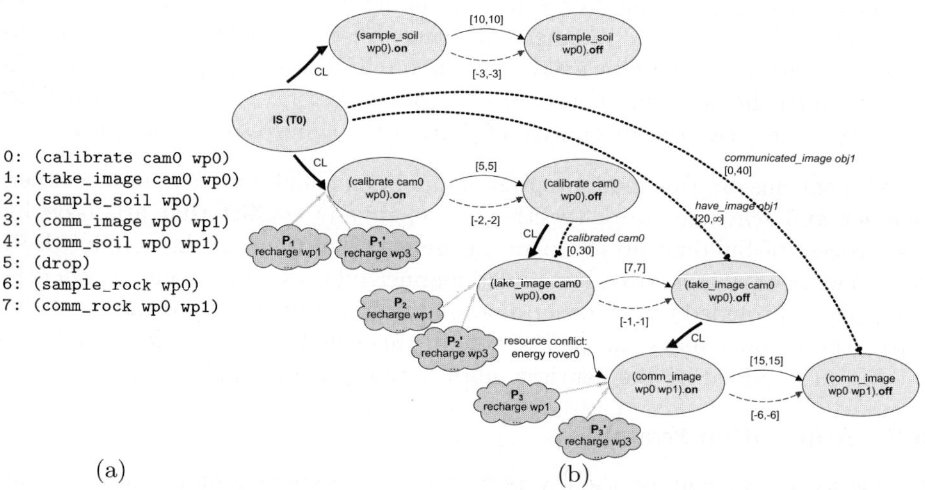

Fig. 4. (a) Initial plan given by an automated planner for the rovers application example; (b) Action network that includes the additional complex problem constraints

4   Discussion Through Related Work

From the AI point of view, there exist two immediate perspectives for solving planning and scheduling problems: a planner can be extended to handle time and resources (temporal planning approach) [1, 9]; or a scheduler can be extended to course some dynamic action selection (planning capabilities embedded within scheduling) [4]. In both cases, the *indistinguishable* mixture of capabilities may increase the complexity of the overall approach, making big problems practically intractable. From the OR point of view, there exist very efficient algorithms to perform the task allocation [10], but modelling the problem and, particularly, finding an initial plan as as set of actions becomes much more difficult. Consequently, the way in which planning and scheduling must be combined has been addressed as an interesting hot topic of research [2].

Although there have been some successful attempts of integrating planning and scheduling, such as HSTS [11] or Aspen [12], they are ad-hoc models designed for solving problems in a particular domain. This loss of generality makes them fail at the time of demonstrating success in other domains. On the contrary, our integrated approach tries to be a general, flexible model that dynamically interleaves planning and scheduling processes (both playing a similar role) to tackle planning problems with a strong and weak component of resource/time management. We combine both processes, separating implementations of planning and scheduling to achieve a bi-modular solver, in which each component deals with the respective sub-problem as presented in [13]: the planner produces a plan while the scheduler enforces the time and resource constraints on this plan, but both work on the basis of the information/advice provided by the other component. This allows us to benefit from their knowledge by separate, such as plan execution and reparation, definition of timepoints, resource allocation, temporal constraint management, etc. Further, it also incorporates the use of common integrated heuristics, reasoning on an action network that combines a TCN with a rCN [7, 8], and an intelligent interaction between both processes.

5   Conclusions

Separating the planning component from the scheduling component when solving real-world problems has shown important drawbacks that are difficult to overcome unless an integrated architecture is used. The key issue about integration is how to level out the roles of both processes. In this paper we have proposed a flexible architecture that makes use of two specialised processes for planning and scheduling under a semi-distributed approach, in opposition to other completely isolated approaches. This way, our approach provides a high flexibility to deal with more complex problems in a more efficient way, since planning features of the problem are managed by a planner, while scheduling features are managed by a scheduler. Further, both processes take advantage of common heuristics and of the advice provided by the other module. For instance, in situations where there exist different planning alternatives, the scheduler can help the planner select the best decision according to scheduling features, such as use of resources, fulfillment of temporal constraints, etc., which are per se difficult to be managed by a planner.

We certainly know there is still some work to be done before achieving a fully automated tool able to solve real-life problems (some decision points and improvements in the planning/scheduling interaction require further investigation). However, the open design of our architecture allows to incorporate new modules to provide extended reasoning on additional aspects of the problem, such as dealing with soft constraints and preferences and including OR algorithms for scheduling, which is part of our current work.

Acknowledgments

This work has been partially supported by the Spanish government project MCyT TIN2005-08945-C06-06 (FEDER).

References

1. Ghallab, M., Nau, D., Traverso, P.: Automated Planning. Theory and Practice. Morgan Kaufmann (2004)
2. Smith, D., Frank, J., Jónsson, A.: Bridging the gap between planning and scheduling. Knowledge Engineering Review **15(1)** (2000) 47–83
3. Bartak, R.: Integrating planning into production scheduling: a formal view. In: Proc. of ICAPS-2004 Workshop on Integrating Planning Into Scheduling. (2004)
4. Smith, S., Zimmerman, T.: Planning tactics within scheduling problems. In: Proc. ICAPS-2004 Workshop on Integrating Planning Into Scheduling. (2004) 83–90
5. Gerevini, A., Long, D.: Plan constraints and preferences in PDDL3. Technical report, University of Brescia, Italy (2005)
6. Edelkamp, S., Hoffmann, J., Littman, M., Younes, H., eds.: Proc. of the International Planning Competition IPC–2004. (2004)
7. Dechter, R., Meiri, I., Pearl, J.: Temporal constraint networks. Artificial Intelligence **49** (1991) 61–95
8. Wallace, R., Freuder, E.: Supporting dispatchability in schedules with consumable resources. Journal of Scheduling **8(1)** (2005) 7–23
9. Gerevini, A., Saetti, A., Serina, I., Toninelli, P.: Planning in PDDL2.2 domains with LPG-TD. In: Proc. ICAPS-2004. (2004) 33–34
10. Winston, W.: Operations Research: Applications and Algorithms. (1994)
11. Muscettola, N.: HSTS: Integrating planning and scheduling. In Zweben, M., Fox, M., eds.: Intelligent Scheduling. Morgan Kaufmann, CA (1994) 169–212
12. Chien, S., *et al.*: ASPEN - automating space mission operations using automated planning and scheduling. In: Proc. SpaceOps 2000. (2000)
13. Pecora, F., Cesta, A.: Evaluating plans through restrictiveness and resource strength. In: Proc. WIPIS of AAAI-2005. (2005)

A Robust RFID-Based Method for Precise Indoor Positioning

Andrew Lim[1,2] and Kaicheng Zhang[1]

[1] Department of Industrial Engineering and Logistics Management
Hong Kong University of Science and Technology
Clear Water Bay, Kowloon, Hong Kong
`{iealim, kczhang}@ust.hk`
[2] School of Computer Science & Engineering
South China University of Technology, Guangdong, PR China

Abstract. A robust method for precise indoor positioning utilizing Radio Frequency Identification (RFID) technology is described. The indoor environment is partitioned into discrete locations, and a set of RFID tags are scattered in the environment. Sample reading patterns of RFID tags are collected at each location by an RFID reader. A pattern recognition and classification method is used, when human, vehicle, or other carrier moves around the environment with an RFID reader, to estimate its physical location based on the reading pattern. The resulting estimation error is within one meter. The method is adaptive to different tag distributions, reader ranges, tag reading defects, and other alterable physical constraints. Results from extensive experiments show that the described method is a robust and cost-saving solution to indoor positioning problems in logistics industry. A provisional US patent is granted on the described method.

Keywords: Intelligent Systems, Systems for Real Life Applications, Indoor Positioning.

1 Introduction

Positioning and location identification are useful in a number of industrial fields. In logistics and transportation domain, the real-time position of each cargo, vehicle carrier, and even human worker can be valuable information. There are growing needs for acquiring high-precision indoor location information at a low cost.

1.1 Background and Related Work

Global Positioning Systems (GPS) has great value in determining the position of a user around the globe. However, for indoor applications, GPS has some problems. First, when it comes to indoor or urban outdoor areas, GPS is not reliable solution due to the poor reception of satellite signals. In addition, indoor applications usually require a much higher precision than that GPS could achieve, sometimes as high as within one meter.

M. Ali and R. Dapoigny (Eds.): IEA/AIE 2006, LNAI 4031, pp. 1189–1199, 2006.
© Springer-Verlag Berlin Heidelberg 2006

Many of the existing Indoor Positioning Systems (IPS) [1] are based on Wireless Local Area Network. Wireless access points are installed in each room and portable receiving device can determine which room it is in when it receives signal from access points. This approach would be useful to determine which room inside a building the tracked subject is in. However the precision is not high enough for logistics applications. Also there will be problem if any of the access points fails to work.

There are other technologies that provide more precise positioning. Wi-Fi, infrared, ultrasonic, or magnetic technologies has been employed in positioning applications such as [2], [3] and [4]. The use of these technologies comes with high-cost. And when comes into industrial environment, the performance may not be good.

Radio Frequency Identification (RFID), a technology invented more than half a century ago, has recently receive overwhelming attention, especially in its use in the logistic applications for cargo tracking and identification. For a comprehensive understanding of RFID, refer to [5]. There has been notably efforts in employing RFID in positioning, both in outdoor applications [3] and indoor applications [6, 7].

1.2   Indoor Positioning – An Industrial Example

Located at the International Container Terminal, SunHing godown, owned by SunHing Group, is one of the largest distribution centers in Hong Kong. Its main operations include receiving goods from various manufacture plants in South China, storing them inside its 11,000 sq ft warehouse, and picking the cargos and loading them into containers, which are then transshipped to various locations in Japan, Europe and the U.S.

The receiving, picking and transferring of cargos within SunHing warehouse are done by more than 20 forklifts. In peak seasons, the operations are quite busy and error in placement or picking could be costly. SunHing believes that an indoor positioning system could be used on its forklifts to enhance its operation accuracy and efficiency.

Usually within a warehouse, a cargo terminal, or a truck depot, we want to know the position of each vehicle. This position information enables the warehouse to have better performance measurement, dynamic job scheduling, and automatic information acquisition. Furthermore, the use of high precision indoor positioning system is not restricted to such logistics application. It could also be used in high precision local navigation system or intelligent system where location-awareness of the mobile agents is required.

2   Our Proposed System

2.1   "Mobile Reader Dispersed Tag" Approach

There exist RFID positioning systems that put tags on mobile agent and place RFID readers at fixed locations [8, 9]. In this approach, when one tag is being read by a reader, the system verdicts that the mobile agent carrying the tag is inside the read range of the particular reader. This approach will be practical for applications in which, mobile agents move around well-partitioned and separated areas through some checkpoints. Readers are normally placed at such checkpoints to detect the movement of the agents. However, when the precision requirement is higher, or the number of checkpoint increases, this "mobile tag fixed reader" approach becomes impractical. Also, the unstable nature of wireless communication, especially of the UHF radio wave communication in industrial environment [10], introduces high error rate when position information of the mobile agent is only based on the reading of one single tag.

Thus, in contrast to "mobile tag fixed reader" method, a "super-distributed tag infrastructure" [11] approach is proposed. In this approach, a large number of passive tags are distributed in the environment, and an RFID reader is carried by each mobile agent. When an agent moves inside the environment, at each location one tag is read and its location determined. Successful applications of such method include [6] and [7]. However, the restriction that only one single tag could be read at any time is too harsh. To place tags on the floor [6, 7] is also inconvenient or infeasible in some industrial applications.

Therefore we propose a new "mobile reader dispersed tag" approach: a large number of tags are dispersed in the environment, allowing more than one tag being read by a reader in the environment. A mobile agent is first placed at designated grid points, or "sample points". "Sample readings" of what tags are read by reader at each point are collected and stored. After that when the agent is moving about in the environment, the real-time reading results are collected and compared against the sample readings; and the location of the agent is classified into one of the sample points with pattern recognition and classification techniques.

2.2   System Overview

Figure 1 illustrates the architecture of our proposed RFID-based indoor positioning system. The system basically contains Dispersed Tags, Mobile Reading and Processing Module, and Backend Server. Dispersed tags are a set of fixed tags distributed in the environment, in this case on the ceiling of the indoor environment. The Mobile Reading and Processing Module is carried by the mobile agent, for instance, a forklift. The module consists of RFID antenna, RFID reader, PDA, and wireless adapter. RFID reader controls antenna, which emits and receives UHF radio waves, and identify the RFID tags inside its reading range. A PDA or a PC is connected to RFID reader, to control the reader and collect the tag reading results. The results are merely on what tags are read in the most recent reading cycle. No additional information, such as signal strength, or direction of tag is required. The processed reading results are then sent through wireless network to the backend server, where classification algorithms convert the reading results to an estimate of the mobile agent's location. The backend information and control server could provide positioning service and control for more than one mobile agent, and can be further integrated into the warehouse management system.

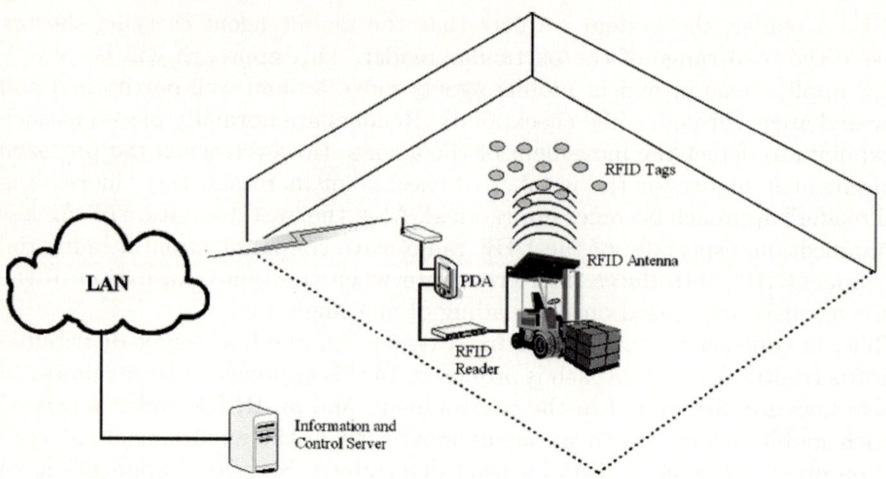

Fig. 1. Architecture of proposed RFID-based indoor positioning system

2.3   Pattern Matching Formulation

We now formulate the positioning problem in the proposed system as a pattern matching process:

First, a set R of m RFID tags, each identified by a 96-, 128-, or 256-bit string, is dispersed in the environment.

Next, we partition the environment into n discrete grid points. The sample data we collect at the ith $(0 \leq i \leq n)$ point is a ternary tuple $S_i = (x_i, y_i, o_i)$, where

x_i is the x-coordinate of ith sample point,

y_i is the y-coordinate of ith sample point, and

o_i a subset of R, is the set of observed RFID tag identification strings at the ith sample point.

Finally we define the input and output of the problem.

Input: A sample data set U collected at n points $\{S_1, S_2, \ldots, S_n\}$, and
A set T of tags observed by a mobile agent at an unknown position, $T \subseteq R$.

Output: An integer j $(1 \leq j \leq n)$, where (x_i, y_i) is the estimated location for T.

3   System Setup and Experiment Design

3.1   System Setup

We set up out proposed system in a quasi-industrial indoor environment in our re-search center. The effective area is a rectangle of size 4.2 m by 8.4 m. This area

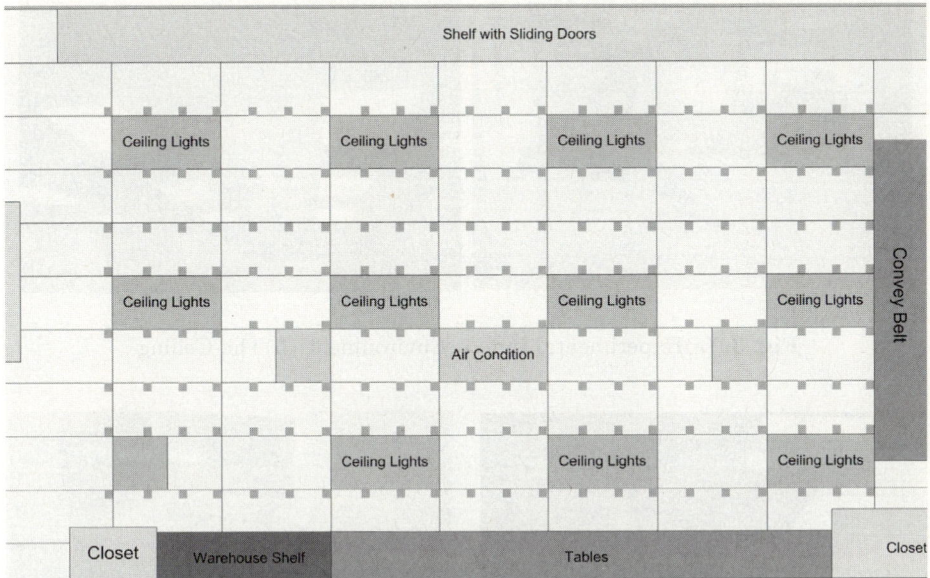

Fig. 2. Floor Plan of Experiment Environment

is partitioned into 7 rows and 7 columns, thus creating 49 grids. The width and length of a grid are not equal. It is made this way so that one grid can perfectly match with one piece of tile on the ceiling. Fig. 2 shows the floor plan of the test environment and the partition. Fig. 3(a) and (b) are photos of the floor and ceiling of the experiment area.

A total number of 176 RFID tags, arranged in 22 columns by 8 rows, are placed onto the ceiling. In Fig. 2, each tag is illustrated by a small square. Each rectangular tile on the ceiling has 4 tags at its vertices and another 4 on its two long sides. The tags used are 4" by 4" Symbol UHF Carton Tag, as shown in Fig. 4.

A simple carrier is built for the experiment as a mobile agent, as shown in Fig. 5. One Symbol AR400 RFID Reader with power supply and two Symbol High Performance Antenna are installed on the carrier. Metal bars are attached to both long and short sides of the carrier to assist in placing the carrier at precise locations. The height and angel of the antenna are adjustable. The reader is connected to a computer that collects the reading results at each location.

3.2   Experiment Design

The main purpose of the experiments is to examine the feasibility of the proposed method as an effective and practical approach for indoor positioning in logistics applications. Also, good algorithms for solving the formulated pattern matching problem are to be discovered. A number of factors related to the performance

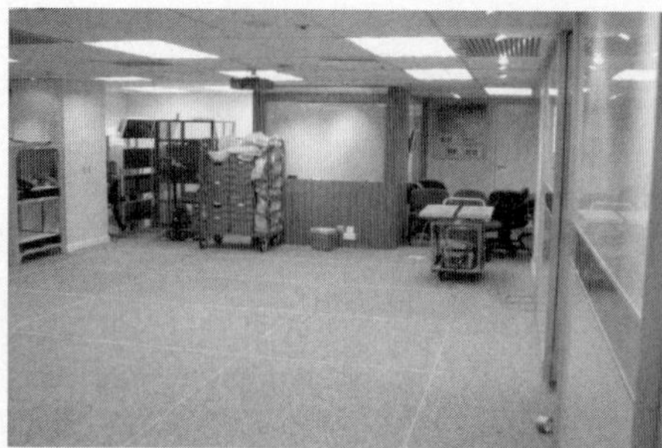 

Fig. 3. (a)Experimental Indoor Environment (b)The Ceiling

Fig. 4. A Tag Placed on the Ceiling

Fig. 5. Mobile Agent with Reader and Antenna

of the system are considered: height, angle, orientation and power level of the antenna, and the density of sample data collection (sampling rate). In total, 7 sets of sample data are collected, as summarized in Table 1.

The standard sample data set U_1 is collected at the center of each partitioned grid, thus having 49 sample points. The standard power level is 255, which is full power. The standard antenna angel is $0°$ with respect to the horizontal plane. The standard antenna height is 77 cm (antenna to ceiling 144.5 cm). The standard orientation of the carrier is facing east (long side of antenna parallel to long side of the rectangular area). U_2 is collected with standard configuration at both center and boundary of each grid, thus having 15×14 points. U_3 through U_6 are sample sets with variations on the power, angel, orientation, and height of the antenna, as described in Table 1. U_7 is the union of U_1 and U_5, introducing another element r_i, the orientation, into the tuple (x_i, y_i, o_i).

Note that, when collecting the readings at every point for each sample set, an additional 9 readings are collected. Together the 10 readings at each point are used as testing set of observations at that point with respect to its sample set. And this testing set is classified against a sample data (normally itself, or a standard sample set) with a pattern matching algorithm to examine the accuracy of the classification or the effect of various alteration on the configuration.

Table 1. Sample Data Sets

Sample Data Sets	Descriptions	Sample Points
U_1–7×7_std	Standard	7×7
U_2–15×14_std	Standard	15×14
U_3–7×7_power192	Power level = 192 (half) 11°	7×7
U_4–7×7_slope11	Slope of antenna 11°	7×7
U_5–7×7_side	Carrier rotated 90° (facing north)	7×7
U_6–7×7_height115	Raised antenna	7×7
U_7–7×7_std_side_mix $U_1 \cup U_5$		7×7×2

4   Pattern Matching Algorithms

We have tested several different algorithms to solve the pattern matching problem formulated in 2.3. Each algorithm runs over all 6 sample data and the results are compared. We find that two algorithms – "Intersection over Union" and "Tag-to-Location Mapping Count' – are able to provide sufficiently good results, as compared to the rest. They are describes in this chapter and the experiment results presented in Chapter 5.

4.1   "Intersection over Union" Algorithm

As in the formulation of the problem in 2.3, the algorithm takes in a sample data set U and an Observation T, and outputs an integer j – the index of the matched pattern. Following are the steps to find such j:

1. For each $S_i \in U$, compute the "similarity" between S_i and T as follows

$$Sim(S_i, T) = \frac{|S_i \cap T|}{|S_i \cup T|} \tag{1}$$

2. Choose j such that $Sim(S_j, T) \geq Sim(S_i, T)$ for all $1 \leq i \leq n$.

Equation (1) merely suggests that the "similarity" between the observation set and a sample set is the quotient of the number of their common elements over the number of their unified elements.

4.2   "Tag-to-Location Mapping Count" Algorithm

The "Tag-to-Location Mapping Count" algorithm matches observation set T to a sample set $S_j \in U$ in the following way:

1. Define tag-to-location mapping, a mapping from a tag id string to a set of integers, which are the indices of the tag's associated sample points.

$$TTL(s) = \{\ p \mid s \in o_p, 1 \leq i \leq n\} \tag{2}$$

2. Given T, for each sample point at (x_i, y_i), compute the mapping count score

$$score(i, T) = \sum_{s \in T} \begin{cases} 0, & \text{if } i \notin TTL(s) \\ 1, & \text{if } i \in TTL(s) \end{cases} \tag{3}$$

3. Choose j such that $score(j, T) \geq score(i, T)$ for all $1 \leq i \leq n$.

Intuitively, (3) suggests that for each tag in an observation, we add one count to every sample point where its corresponding sample set contains the tag. The sample point that receives most count will be considered as solution. Note that, however, this would be faulty when dealing with observations at boundary areas, as Fig. 6 explains. Thus we exclude the boundary points when evaluating the performance of "Tag-to-Location Mapping Count" algorithm.

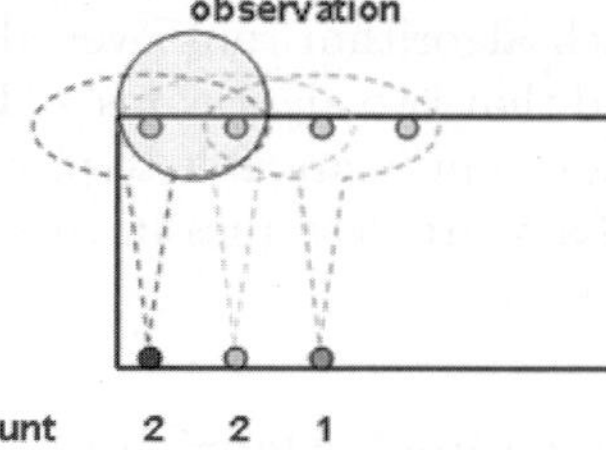

Fig. 6. "Tag-to-Location Mapping Count" Algorithms Runs into Problem with Boundary Cases

5   Experimental Results

5.1   Comparison on Algorithms

To compare the effectiveness of the classification algorithms, 10 readings collected at each point in 7×7 sample data are used as observations and U_1 is used

Table 2. Comparison on Two Algorithms

Sample Data	Test Data	Test Points	"Intersection over Union"		"Tag-to-Location Mapping Count"	
			Errors	Error Rate	Errors	Error Rate
U_1	U_1	250	3	1.2%	1	**0.4%**
U_1	U_3	250	113	45.2%	72	**28.8%**
U_1	U_4	250	5	**2.0%**	36	14.4%
U_1	U_5	250	81	**32.4%**	111	44.4%
U_1	U_6	250	143	57.2%	116	**46.4%**
U_2	U_2	1210	43	**3.55%**	72	5.95%

as sample data set. The reading accuracy are presented in Table 2. Boundary points are excluded for the comparison. Thus for row 1–5, there are $5\times5\times10=250$ test cases. And for row 6, there are $11\times11\times10=1210$ test cases.

We can see that, both algorithms perform well on U_1–7×7_std self-validation test case. Each algorithm outperforms the other in some of the rest test cases. We also observe that change of power, orientation and height of the antenna while using the standard sample data significantly reduces the positioning accuracy.

5.2 Positioning Accuracy of the Proposed Method

Table 3 presents the results of the "Intersection over Union" algorithm running over each same sample data and test data. For all the test cases, our proposed method could provide >97% accuracy in determining the correct position. Furthermore, for the <3% error cases, the average error on x and y is within 0.50 unit with respect to the width and length of one tile, which are within 1 meter.

Table 3. Positioning Accuracy

Sample Data	Test Data	Errors	Test Points	Error Rate
U_1–7×7_std	U_1	11	490	2.24%
U_3–7×7_power192	U_3	2	490	0.41%
U_4–7×7_slope11	U_4	0	490	0.00%
U_5–7×7_side	U_5	5	490	1.02%
U_6–7×7_height115	U_6	2	490	0.41%
U_2–15×14_std	U_2	43	2100	2.05%

5.3 Discussion on Other Factors Related to Accuracy

Through experiment, we also verified that our proposed solution is able to determine the orientation of the carrier by adding an orientation attribute in the sample data tuple, generating sample data U_7. Using it as a sample data, we achieved 2.45% error rate in 7×7_std case and 1.43% 7×7_side case.

From the experiment results, the following recommendations could be made to ensure a high accuracy of the positioning system. First, height and power level of the antenna should be consistent in the whole system. A small change in height or power may lead to big variation on the observation and damage the performance, as one could compare the error rates in Table 2. Second, a slight variation of antenna angle with respect to horizontal plane would not affect the accuracy too much, as shown in Table 2 row 3. This suggests that the method is practical for industrial application where carrier moves on uneven floor in high speed with vibration. Finally, increase on the sampling rate, as we expected, would generally produce higher accuracy (error rate reduced from 2.24% to 1.02% on 7×7_std when sample data changed from 7×7_std to 15×14_std).

6   Conclusions and Future Work

In this paper, we identify the importance of precise indoor positioning problem in industry applications. We propose a new approach – "mobile reader dispersed tag", allowing multiple tags be read each time, to combat the RF-unfriendly environment in real industry workplace. We formulate the positioning problem as pattern matching problem and propose two algorithms that are particular effective. Extensive experiments are carried out and several factors in the system are examined. We conclude that our method achieved >97% positioning accuracy with <1 m error. We also propose a simple approach for identifying the orientation of the carrier in addition to location, which adds on the practicality of the proposed system.

The presented method has several improvements and advantages: It is more precise than existing WLAN-based indoor positioning system. It is low cost solution, since no battery-support is needed for the passive RFID tags, and no information on RF signal strength is required. It is robust to environment noise and tag failure. Finally it provides a way to determine the orientation of the carrier. Future work includes improving of current pattern matching algorithms, possibly with online-learning and reasoning, solving more general 360° orientation problem, and improving the experiment design to estimate the precision of the system on continuous points in the environment.

References

1. Pahlavan, K., Li, X., Makela, J.: Indoor Geolocation Science and Technology. IEEE Com-munications Magazine, Feb. 2002.
2. Hiyama, A., Yamashita, J., Kuzuoka, H., Hirota, K., Hirose, M.: Position Tracking Using Infra-Red Signals for Museum Guiding System. Ubiquitous Computing Systems, Second International Symposium. (UCS 2004).
3. Minami, M., Fukuju, Y., Hirasawa, K., Yokoyama, S., Mizumachi M., Morikawa, H., Ao-yama, T.: DOLPHIN: A Practical Approach for Implementing a Fully Distributed Indoor Ultrasonic Positioning System. Ubiquitous Computing: 6th International Conference (Ubi-Comp 2004).
4. Prigge, E.A., How, J.P.: Signal Architecture for a Distributed Magnetic Local Positioning System. IEEE Sensors Journal, Vol.4, No.6, Dec. 2004.
5. Finkenzeller, K.: RFID Handbook: Fundamentals and Applications in Contactless Smart Cards and Identification, 2nd edition. John Wiley & Sons (2003)
6. Chon, H.D., Jun, S., Jung, H., An, S.W.: Using RFID for Accurate Positioning. Journal of Global Positioning Systems (2004), Vol 3, No.1-2, 32-39
7. Seo, D.S., Won, D., Yang, G.W, Choi, M.S., Kwon, S.J., Park J.W.: A Probabilistic Ap-proach for Mobile Robot Localization under RFID Tag Infrastructures. (Submission) Inter-national Conference on Control, Automation and Systems (ICCAS 2005).
8. Gharpure., C.P.: Orientation Free Radio Frequency Identification Based Navigation in a Robotic Guide for the Visually Impaired. Master Thesis. Utah State University (2004).

9. Borriello, G., Brunette. W., Hall, M., Hartung, C., Tangney, C.: Reminding About Tagged Objects Using Passive RFIDs. Ubiquitous Computing: 6th International Conference (Ubi-Comp 2004).
10. Rappaport, T.S.: Characterization of UHF Multipath Radio Channels in Factory Buildings. IEEE Transactions on Antennas and Propergation, Vol. 37 (1989), No. 8, 1058-1069
11. Bohn, J., Mattern, F.: Super-Distributed RFID Tag Infrastructures. Proc. 2nd European Symposium on Ambient Intelligence (EUSAI 2004)

A Study of Optimal System for Multiple-Constraint Multiple-Container Packing Problems

Jin-Ling Lin[1], Chir-Ho Chang[2], and Jia-Yan Yang[3]

[1] Department of Information Management, Shih-Hsin University
jllin@cc.shu.edu.tw
[2] Dept. of Industrial Management, LungHwa University of Science and Technology
chchang@mail.lhu.edu.tw
[3] Department of Industrial Engineering & Management Information,
Huafan University, 1
M9101005@cat.hfu.edu.tw

Abstract. The proposed research focuses on multiple-container packing problems with considerations of multiple constraints. The space utilization, stability, load bearing, and loading sequence of objects are also considered in order to make results more practicable. Clustering technology and genetic algorithm are combined to solve the proposed problems. At the beginning, clustering algorithm is applied to classify data objects into different groups with varied characteristics, such as dimension of objects, unloading sequence of objects, and capacity of containers. Then, genetic algorithm combines with heuristic rules is used to pack data objects into containers respectively. The stable packing, space utilization, unhindered unloading, and load bear limitation are the major considerations in this stage. A computer system based on the proposed algorithm was developed. Thousands of cases were simulated and analyzed to evaluate the performance of the proposed research and prove the applicability in real world.

1 Introduction

The proposed research stems from the fact that the single container is unable to pack all data objects, therefore lose its practicability in the real world. Besides the space utilization, it is really important to consider constraints such as stability, load bearing, and loading sequence of objects for real world applications. But it is hard to find a literature which discussed these factors together [1], [2], [3].

The K-means clustering algorithm is easy to implement and has a lot of successful applications in the grouping data [4], [5], [6], [7], [8]. Therefore, this proposed paper first applied the K-means clustering algorithm to group data objects with similar dimensions and unloading sequences of objects to be packed [9]. Then genetic algorithm, combined with heuristic rules, is used to pack these objects in the same cluster one by one, respectively [2].

M. Ali and R. Dapoigny (Eds.): IEA/AIE 2006, LNAI 4031, pp. 1200–1210, 2006.

2 Problem Definition

The proposed paper focuses on how to pack n unequal-sized cuboid-shaped data objects into m containers, which can have different dimensions. The container packing problem that we deal with is multiple objectives combined with multiple constraints. Besides the container cost and space utilization, we also take the efficiency of unloading, stability of packing, and load bearing into considers. The details of inputs, limitation, and problem model are described as follows.

2.1 Inputs and Assumptions

The followings information is necessary before using the proposed method to solve multiple-constraint multiple-container packing problems.

a) Objects
Dimensions, weight, load bearing limitation, and unloading sequence of each object to be packed are the inputs information for the proposed system.
b) Containers
Interior size/dimensions and cost of containers to be used for packing are inputs for the proposed system.

In order to work with the proposed method, we put some assumptions on these related objects and containers.

a) Objects
- o Objects to be packed are three-dimension cuboid, whose dimension can be different.
- o The object must keep the top upwards while packing. In other words, objects to be packed can only rotate from side to side.
- o When the center of gravity of an object located on the plane formed by these bearing objects, it satisfies the condition of stability.
b) Containers
- o Containers to be used are three dimension cuboid, whose dimension can be different.
- o The containers can be used in the proposed method are dry containers. It means except exits all of the wall of containers are solid, no way to enlarge or shrink.
- o There is only on exit for a container and it is on the full plane of height by width, which is no longer than length of container.

2.2 Problem Model

The objectives of multiple-container packing problem in the proposed paper are to minimize container cost, maximize space utilization (it is the same as minimize the free space), and minimize unloading overhead, under the constraints of stable packing and load bearing limitation. The corresponding mathematical model for proposed method is shown in Table 1 and these corresponding notations used in the mathematic model are listed as following:

C_i: capacity of container i

$C_{i,l}$, $C_{i,w}$, $C_{i,h}$: length, width, and height of container i

F: objective function value

M: the number of containers needed in order to pack these pre-specified objects

m: the number of different type of containers can be used to pack objects

N: the number of data objects to be packed

N_i: the number of type i container needed in order to pack these pre-specified objects

ni: the number of data objects which are packed into container i

OC_i: the volume of data object i

$OC_{i,j}$:   the volume of data object j which are packed into container i

$OC_{i,l}$, $OC_{i,w}$, $OC_{i,h}$: length, width, and height of data object i

P_i: cost of type i container

$US(O_{i,j})$: loading sequence of data object j in container i

W_c: weight of container cost

W_{su}:   weight of space utilization

W_u: weight of unloading overhead

Table 1. Mathematic model of the proposed problem

$$Minimize$$

$$F = \left(W_c \frac{\sum_{i=1}^{m} N_i P_i - optimal\ (C)}{optimal\ (C)} * 100 \right) + \left(W_{su} \frac{\sum_{i=1}^{M} \left(C_i - \sum_{j=1}^{n_i} OC_{i,j} \right)}{\sum_{i=1}^{M} C_i} * 100 \right) +$$

$$\left(W_u \frac{\sum_{i=1}^{M} \frac{\max_{j=1,...,n_i} (US(O_{i,j})) - \min_{j=1,...,n_i} (US(O_{i,j})) + 1 - n_i}{n_i}}{M} * 100 \right)$$

$$Subject\ to$$

1   $M = \sum_{i=1}^{m} N_i$

2   $N = \sum_{i=1}^{M} n_i$

3   $\max(C_{j,l}, C_{j,w}) \geq \max(OC_{i,l}, OC_{i,w})$ $for\ j = 1,..., M\ \&\ each\ j, i = 1,..., n_i$

4   $\min(C_{j,l}, C_{j,w}) \geq \min(OC_{i,l}, OC_{i,w})$ $for\ j = 1,..., M\ \&\ each\ j, i = 1,..., n_i$

5   $\max_{j=1,...,m}(C_{j,h}) \geq \max_{i=1,...,n_i}(OC_{i,h})$ $for\ j = 1,..., M\ \&\ each\ j, i = 1,..., n_i$

6   $C_{i,h} \geq \sum_{i=1}^{n_i} OC_{i,h}$ $for\ i = 1,..., M\ \&\ each\ j, i = 1,..., n_i$

7   $\forall variables\ are\ interger\ \&\ \geq 1$

8   $W_c + W_{su} + W_u = 1$

The measure of container cost, space utilization, and loading overhead are different, so normalization were done on them. First item denotes the ratio of container cost and optimal container cost, which is the solution of

$$minimize \quad \sum_{i=1}^{m} P_i N_i$$

$$subject\,to \quad \sum_{i=1}^{m} C_i N_i \geq \sum_{i=1}^{N} OC_i \qquad (1)$$

Second term is the percentage of free space. The last term denotes dispersing degree of unloading sequence of objects which will be packed in the same container. Finally, the weight factors, W_c, W_{su}, and W_u, are decided by users according to their needs in the real case.

3 Algorithm Analysis

The packing problem, discussed in this paper, is solved by two stages: a grouping procedure and a packing procedure. In the grouping procedure, K-means method is applied to group objects into different clusters according to the capacity of container, the dimensions of objects, and the unloading sequence of objects. These objects in the same group means they will be packed in the same container. Then, genetic

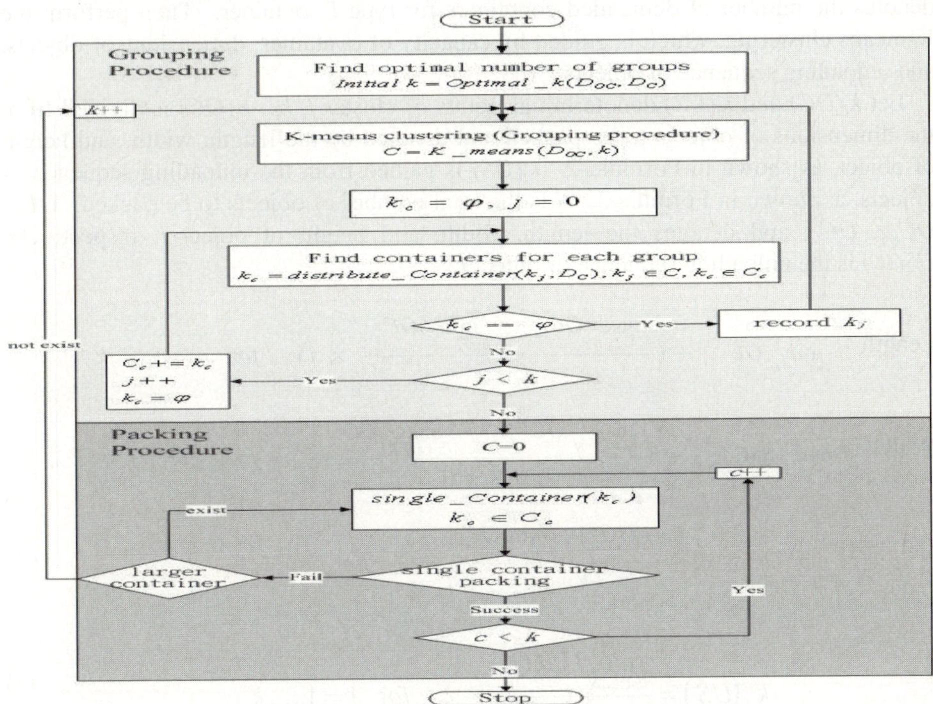

Fig. 1. The procedure of multiple-container packing

algorithm combined with heuristic rules is applied for a single container packing. The details of grouping and packing algorithm are described in Section 3.1 and Section 3.2 respectively. The procedure of the proposed multiple containers packing is shown in Figure 1.

Where

D_{oc}: a list of related information of objects to be packed, information for each object contains dimensions, load bearing limitation, unloading sequence

D_c: a list of related information of different container types, information for each container is cost and capacity

C: a list of grouping information after performing the K-means clustering

C_c: a list of container information for each group

k_j: cluster j, which is a member of C

k_c: containers for current working cluster

3.1 Grouping Algorithm

First, find the demanded number of each kind of container by using the Formula 1. Set k for K-means clustering to the number of demanded containers,

$$Initial \quad k = \sum_{i=1}^{m} N_i$$

where m is the number of different types of containers, N_i denotes the number of demanded containers for type I container. Then perform the K-means clustering, which is guided by capacity of container, dimensions of objects, and unloading sequence of objects.

Let $k_j(OC)$ and $k_j(US)$ denote initial points of cluster j, k_j. $k_j(OC)$ is derived from the dimensions of objects to be packed and denoted by the length, width, and height of object, as shown in Formula 2. $k_j(US)$ is gained from the unloading sequence of objects, as shown in Formula 3. N is the total number of objects to be packed. $OC_{i,l}$, $OC_{i,w}$, $OC_{i,h}$ and denotes the length, width, and height of object i, respectively. $US(O_i)$ is the unloading sequence of object i.

$$Length: \quad \min_{i=1,\ldots,N} OC_{i,l} + \left(\frac{\max\limits_{i=1,\ldots,N} OC_{i,l} - \min\limits_{i=1,\ldots,N} OC_{i,l}}{k+1} \times j\right) \quad for \quad j = 1,\ldots, k$$

$$Width: \quad \min_{i=1,\ldots,N} OC_{i,w} + \left(\frac{\max\limits_{i=1,\ldots,N} OC_{i,w} - \min\limits_{i=1,\ldots,N} OC_{i,w}}{k+1} \times j\right) \quad for \quad j = 1,\ldots, k$$

$$Height: \quad \min_{i=1,\ldots,N} OC_{i,h} + \left(\frac{\max\limits_{i=1,\ldots,N} OC_{i,h} - \min\limits_{i=1,\ldots,N} OC_{i,h}}{k+1} \times j\right) \quad for \quad j = 1,\ldots,k \tag{2}$$

$$k_j(US) = \frac{\max\limits_{i=1,\ldots,N} US(O_i)}{k+1} \times j \quad for \quad j = 1,\ldots,k \tag{3}$$

The degree of approximation between objects and the pivots is measured by two factors: dimension and unloading sequence of objects to be packed. The first one is done by the Euclidean Distance of dimensions of objects. Let i and j denote different points for clustering. The $x_{i,l}$, $x_{i,w}$, and $x_{i,h}$ denote the length, width , and height of point i. The formula to measure degree of approximation of dimensions is shown in Formula 4. The degree of approximation of unloading sequence is measured by difference of unloading sequence.

$$d(i, j) = \sqrt{(x_{i,l} - x_{j,l})^2 + (x_{i,w} - x_{j,w})^2 + (x_{i,h} - x_{j,h})^2} \tag{4}$$

Since the measures of dimensions and unloading sequence are different, we normalize them and use percentage to represent them. Formula 5 shows the normalization, where $OCSimilar\_O_{ij}$ denotes the degree of approximation of dimensions between object i and pivot j. $USSimilar\_O_{ij}$ represents the degree of approximation of unloading sequence between object i and pivot j. W_{su} and W_u, are weight of each term and can be decided by users according to their needs.

$$Similar\_O_{ij} = \left(W_{su} \frac{OCSimilar\_O_{ij}}{\sum_{i=1}^{N} OCSimilar\_O_{ij}} * 100 \right) + \left(W_u \frac{USSimilar\_O_{ij}}{\sum_{i=1}^{N} USSimilar\_O_{ij}} * 100 \right) \tag{5}$$

Objects are classified into clusters depends on the degree of approximation to pivots of clusters. Then the average of degree of approximation of the objects in the same cluster will be used as the new pivot for next generation, as shown in Formula 6. The clustering procedure will be repeated until the stopping criterion, which is set to a predefined number, has been reached.

$$k_j = \left(\frac{\sum_{i=1}^{n_j} (OC_{i,j})}{n_j}, \frac{\sum_{i=1}^{n_j} (US(O_{i,j}))}{n_j} \right), \quad for \ \ j = 1,...,k \tag{6}$$

The procedure following the grouping is to assign containers for each cluster. In this procedure, we choose containers which have not only enough capacity but also minimizing container cost to pack these objects. First, these containers, which have enough capacity to pack objects in the particular cluster, are selected as the candidates. Then pick up one of these candidate containers with the minimal cost. If there is a feasible container to pack objects in the specified cluster, then a signal of success will be returned; otherwise it returns a signal of fail. The procedure of choose appropriate container for a cluster is shown in Figure 2.

3.2 Packing Algorithm

The packing algorithm performs single container packing for each cluster independently right after the grouping procedure. The major algorithm refers previous

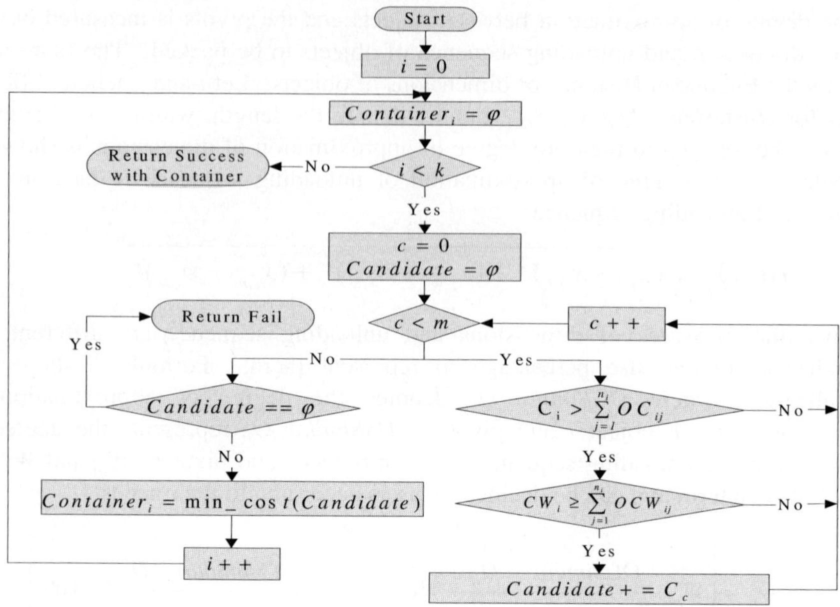

Fig. 2. The procedure of choosing appropriate container for a cluster

works [2]. It uses genetic algorithm combined with heuristic rules to do the single container packing with constraints of load bearing limitation and stable packing.

Each object is assigned a unique number from 1 to n, which is the number of objects to be packed. Genetic algorithm uses these object numbers as genes of individuals. Then, objects are assigned to different layers by heuristic rules based on unloading sequence of objects. In the meantime, multiple-chromosome individual is introduced into genetic operations in order to do crossover and mutation independently for different layers. Finally, heuristic rules, based on constraints of stability and load bearing, are applied to transfer one dimension string into three-dimension packing layout [2].

If it exists that all the objects in a cluster is unable to pack into specified container, the proposed method will redistribute container for the particular cluster. First the algorithm looks for larger capacity, which can pack all objects in the cluster. If the larger capacity container can be found, we choose the container with minimum cost and do the single container packing again. If it is unable to find appropriate container to pack all the objects in the particular container, the initial k value of K-means will increase by 1, then start over again grouping and packing procedure for the new clusters.

4   Simulation and Discussion

In order to evaluate the performance of the proposed method, a computer program was developed based on the proposed algorithm and hundreds of testing cases, which were generated randomly, were simulated. The number of objects for these testing cases is around 100 and types of container are 4~12. From the simulation results, we found the efficiency, which is calculated based on the Formula 1 and the proposed mathematic model in section 2.2, of most of these testing cases is around 80%. The number of generation does not have much effect on the performance when it is over 5, as shown in Figure 3. Because the degree of approximate of objects will be strong after some generations of K-means algorithm and the number of objects in these testing cases is not too many, it is quite reasonable that it doesn't needs too much generation to reach the steady results of clustering. We use three related factors of objective function, such as capacity of container, unloading sequence of objects, and dimensions of objects, as the measure of degree of approximate during the procedure of clustering, so the performance of packing is very high efficiency.

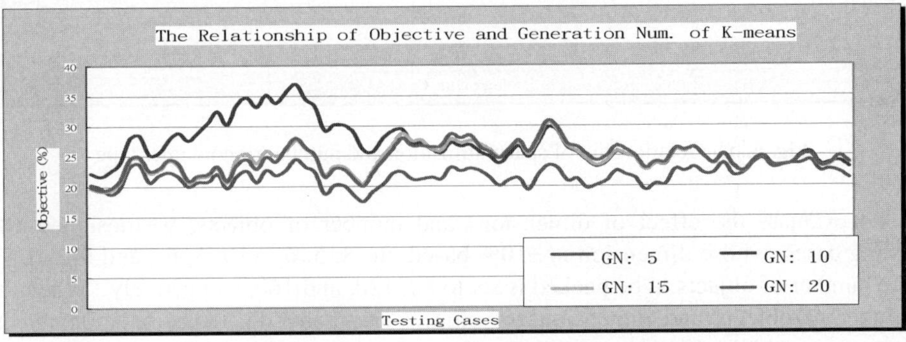

Fig. 3. The relationship of objective and generation number of K-means clustering

From Figure 4, we obviously observed that it has better objective when the weight of container coast is set to 0.25, the weight of free space is set to 0.25, and the weight of loading overhead is set to 0.5. This results show that loading overhead can be satisfied than the other two factors in the objective.

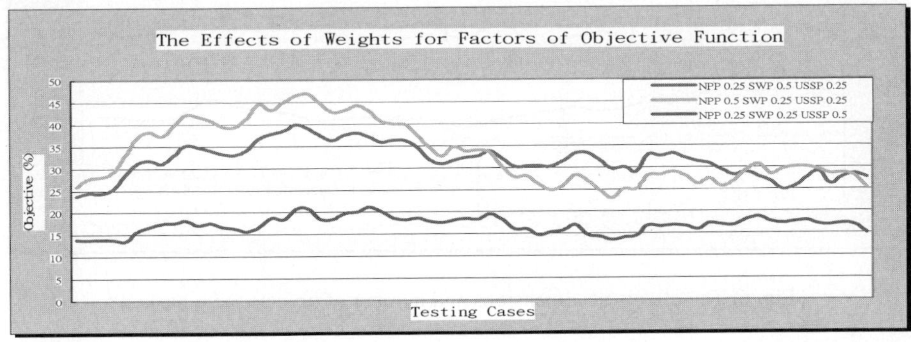

Fig. 4. The effects of weights for factors of objective function

Theoretically, the more types of container it has, the higher efficiency of space utilization has. Since the more type of container, it can choose, the more compact container can be found. From Figure 5, the packing algorithm shows higher efficiency of space utilization when the type of container is more for most of testing cases, but these results is not quite obvious.

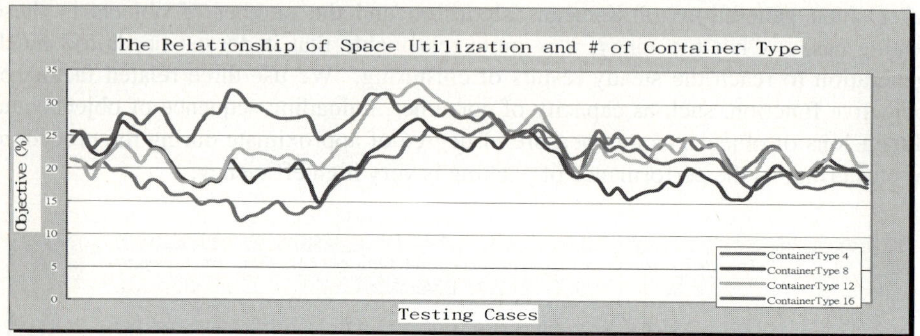

Fig. 5. The relationship of space utilization and number of container type

To evaluate the effect of dimensions and number of objects, we designed 100 testing cases, whose dimension is ±10% based on (8, 5, 6), (10, 5, 6), and (12, 6, 7). The number of objects to be packed is set to 80, 120, and 160, respectively. When the number of objects and dimensions of objects are moderate, the simulation results showed very high efficiency and better than others, as shown in Figure 6. It is also reasonable, because the smaller dimensions of objects are, the more compact packing is. Besides, the more objects to be packed, the more dispersing of unloading sequence of objects is. So when the number of objects and dimensions of objects are moderate, packing will have higher efficiency.

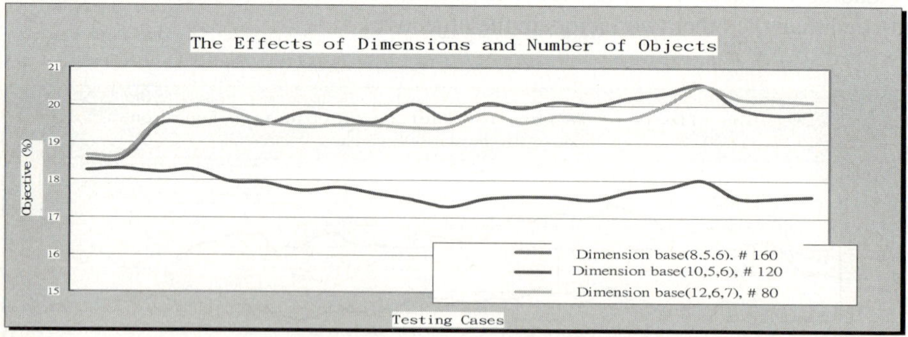

Fig. 6. The effects of dimensions and number of objects to be packed

The last observation is the variation of dimensions among objects. First, use (9, 7, 8) as the dimension base of testing cases. Then generate objects based on the dimension base with 10%, 20%, and 30% adjustment. The number of generation is set to 5 and the number of objects is set to 90. Figure 7 showed the simulation results of these testing cases. It is obvious that the smaller variation percentage of dimensions among objects, the better performance the results have, since the compact packing is more difficult when the dimensions among objects have larger variation.

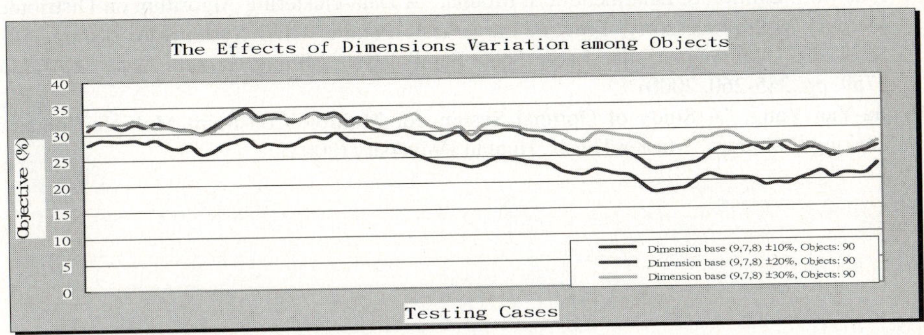

Fig. 7. The effects of dimension variation among objects

5   Conclusion

This research proposed an efficient algorithm to solve multiple-container packing problems with multiple constraints. We are not only consider the space utilization, but also take the load bearing limitation, unloading overhead, and stable packing into considerations.

Besides the algorithm, a computer program based on the proposed algorithm was developed. The computer system is not only a simulation tool for performance analysis, but also a system to provide practical solutions for customer designated multiple-container packing problems. Thousands of cases were simulated and analyzed to evaluate the performance of the proposed research and prove the applicability in real world. The adjustable weight of factors of objective function makes the proposed method more practicable and useful for real world applications.

References

[1] Lin, J. L. & Chang, C. H, "Stability 3D container packing problems," The 5th Automation '98 and International Conference on Production Research, (1998)

[2] Lin, J.L. & Chung, Cheng-Hao, "Solving Multiple-Constraint Container Packing by Heuristically Genetic Algorithm," The 8th Annual International Conference on Industrial Engineering – Theory, Applications and Practice, Nov. 10-12, 2003, Las Vegas, U.S.A., (2003)

[3] Verweij, B., Multiple destination bin packing. *ALCOM-IT Technical Report* (1996)

[4] Bellot, P. and El-Beze, M., A clustering method for information retrieval, Technical Report IR-0199. *Laboratoire d'Informatique d'Avignon* (1999)

[5] Boley, D. Gini, M. Gross, R. Han, E.H. Hastings, K. Karypis, G. Kumar, V. Mobasher B. and Moore J., Partitioning-Based Clustering for Web Document Categorization. *DSSs Journal,* (1999)

[6] Dunham, M., Data Mining: Introductory and Advanced Topics, *Prentice Hall* (2003)

[7] Han, J. and Kamber M., Data Mining: Concepts and Techniques, *Morgan Kafmann Publishers* (2001)

[8] Inderjit S. Dhillon & Dharmendra S. Modha, "A Data-clustering Algorithm on Distributed Memory Multiprocessors," Proc. of Large-scale Parallel KDD Systems Workshop, *ACM SIGKDD*, 1999 August (also Large-Scale Parallel Data Mining, *Lecture Notes in AI*, Vol. 1759, pp. 245-260, 2000)

[9] Jia-Yan Yang, "A Study of Optimal System for Multiple-Constraint Multiple-Container Packing Problems," Master Thesis, Huafan University (2005)

Planning for Intra-block Remarshalling
in a Container Terminal*

Jaeho Kang[1], Myung-Seob Oh[1], Eun Yeong Ahn[1],
Kwang Ryel Ryu[1], and Kap Hwan Kim[2]

[1] Department of Computer Engineering, Pusan National University
San 30, Jangjeon-dong, Kumjeong-gu, Busan, 609-735, Korea
{jhkang, oms1226, tinyahn, krryu}@pusan.ac.kr
[2] Department of Industrial Engineering, Pusan National University
San 30, Jangjeon-dong, Kumjeong-gu, Busan, 609-735, Korea
kapkim@pusan.ac.kr

Abstract. Intra-block remarshalling in a container terminal refers to
the task of rearranging export containers scattered around within a block
into designated target bays of the same block. Since the containers must
be loaded onto a ship following a predetermined order, the rearrangement
should be done in a way that containers to be loaded earlier are placed
on top of those to be loaded later to avoid re-handlings. To minimize
time to complete a remarshalling task, re-handlings should be avoided
during remarshalling. Moreover, when multiple yard cranes are used for
remarshalling, interference between the cranes should be minimized. In
this paper, we present a simulated annealing approach to the efficient
finding of a good intra-block remarshalling plan, which is free from
re-handlings at the time of loading as well as during remarshalling.

1   Introduction

In a container terminal, the efficiency of container loading onto a ship is highly
dependent on the storage location of the containers in the yard. The containers
must be loaded onto the ship in a predetermined loading sequence. Therefore, if
the containers are located adjacently in the yard for successive loading, the travel
distance of yard cranes and service time for container loading can be greatly
reduced. However, gathering containers close to one another is not sufficient
for efficient loading because the loading sequence must be followed. Gathering
containers without considering the sequence may cause a considerable number
of re-handlings at the time of loading because the container to be fetched out at
each time is often found under others. In addition, time required for intra-block
remarshalling must be minimized for efficient use of valuable resources such as
yard cranes. In particular, when multiple yard cranes are used collaboratively
for remarshalling, care must be taken to minimize crane interference.

---

* This work was supported by the Regional Research Centers Program (Research
Center for Logistics Information Technology), granted by the Korean Ministry of
Education Human Resources Development.

M. Ali and R. Dapoigny (Eds.): IEA/AIE 2006, LNAI 4031, pp. 1211–1220, 2006.

For a remarshalling task, cranes have to move tens of containers considering the sequence of container loading and interference between cranes. Therefore, the number of possible crane schedules is very large and finding the optimal one is intractable. Moreover, a crane schedule for remarshalling should be constructed in a reasonable time. In order to solve the scheduling problem efficiently, we applied simulated annealing[1]. Simulated annealing searches for a good partial order among containers to be rearranged that requires less time for remarshalling and does not make any re-handling during remarshalling and loading. A candidate solution expressed in the form of partial order graph does not regard the number of cranes to be used and their detailed movements but it can express a collection of possible re-handling-free total orders of container moves. Each candidate solution is used to construct a full crane schedule by a greedy evaluation heuristic with detailed crane simulation. By the heuristic, container moves are assigned to each crane and an appropriate order of these moves is determined under the constraint of the given partial order graph in a way of minimizing time for remarshalling, taking crane interference into account. The estimated time of the constructed full schedule is used as the quality of the partial order graph. Simulated annealing navigates the search space of partial order graphs using their evaluation results as a compass.

The performance of the evaluation heuristic is adjustable by changing the number of container assignments looked forward in selecting a container for the next assignment. Therefore, under the limited time of scheduling, there are two possible directions of improving the quality of schedule: trying more candidates or constructing a crane schedule with more container assignments looked forward. Experimental results show that a better remarshalling schedule can be obtained by carefully balancing between the two.

The next section explains the remarshalling problem in detail and reviews some related researches. The simulated annealing approach and the evaluation heuristic are presented in Section 3 and 4, respectively. In Section 5, the proposed method is tested and the results are summarized. Finally in Section 6, we give our conclusions and some topics for further research.

2 Intra-block Remarshalling

Intra-block remarshalling is a task of moving a set of target containers to designated bays within a block. We call the bays in which the target containers are located before remarshalling 'source bays' and the empty bays into which the target containers are moved 'target bays.' In Fig. 1, there are two source bays S_1 and S_2 and two target bays T_W and T_G. In this figure, each bay in the block is three rows wide and three tiers high. A bay can contain up to nine containers. Figure 1 also shows cross-sectional views of the source and target bays. A rectangle drawn with a solid line in the source bays is a container. In this example, fourteen target containers need to be moved during remarshalling. The number in each container refers to its order of loading at its target bay and an alphabetic character denotes the target bay for the container.

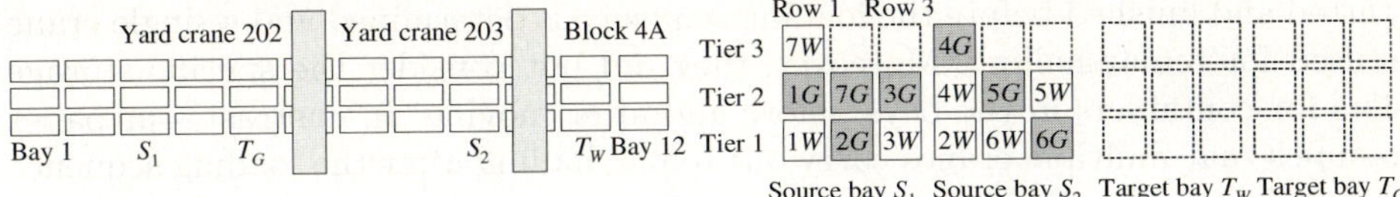

Fig. 1. An example of remarshalling problem

Because a predetermined sequence of container loading in each target bay must be followed, if a container for later loading is moved and stacked on top of an earlier one, the upper container should be moved to a temporary location during container loading. For example, in Fig. 1, if container $4G$ is moved and stacked on top of container $3G$ in one of stacks in T_G, then container $4G$ should be moved to somewhere before container $3G$ is being fetched out for loading. This temporary movement of container is called 're-handling.' Re-handlings incur extra works of yard cranes and delay the work of container loading that is one of the most expensive and time-critical services of container terminals. Therefore, target containers should be moved into their target bays in a manner of avoiding such re-handlings.

For a very simple solution of scheduling cranes for remarshalling, the moves of target containers can be sequenced in the reverse order of container loading. For example, in Fig. 1, a yard crane can move container $7W$ first into its target bay T_W, container $6W$ the next, and so on. However, this approach may cause additional work of yard cranes during remarshalling. For example, in Fig. 1, after moving container $7W$, a yard crane has to move container $5G$ temporarily to some other location before moving container $6W$. Later in the remarshalling, container $5G$ will be moved again to be stacked into its proper target bay. These temporary movements of containers during remarshalling are also called re-handlings and they delay the work of remarshalling that seizes valuable resources such as yard cranes. Therefore, this type of re-handlings should also be avoided to finish remarshalling as early as possible.

A re-handling-free schedule does not incur any re-handling situation during remarshalling as well as during loading. For a schedule to be free of re-handlings, the following two main constraints must be satisfied.

Constraint-Re-handling-Free-In-Loading: After remarshalling, each container should be loaded onto the ship without re-handling.

Constraint-Re-handling-Free-In-Remarshalling: Each container must be moved from its source bay to its target bay without re-handling.

There has been a little research on the issue of remarshalling. Kim and Bae presented a two-stage approach to planning remarshalling.[2] In the first stage, containers to be moved and the target bays of selected containers are determined in a manner of minimizing the number of containers to be moved by considering the given ship profile. In the second stage, the sequence of container moves is determined to minimize crane movements. They assumed that remarshalling is started and finished before the loading sequence is determined and a single crane is used for remarshalling. Moreover, they did not consider the specific storage slots for containers in the bays before and after moving. In contrast, our paper assumes that multiple cranes carry out remarshalling after the loading sequence is determined. Furthermore, we consider the specific storage slots of containers in the bays and interference between cranes.

Some studies have developed strategies that determine a desirable stacking location for each container that comes into the yard. Dekker and Voogd described and compared various stacking strategies.[3] Each stacking strategy is evaluated by a few measures such as the number of re-handling occasions and workload distribution of yard cranes. Kim *et al.* derived a decision rule to locate export containers from an optimal stacking strategy to minimize the number of re-handlings in loading.[4] They assumed that containers are loaded onto a ship in the decreasing order of container weight group. These two studies tried to reduce the number of re-handlings by assigning the location of each container that comes into the yard more carefully. However, re-handlings in loading cannot be avoided completely for various reasons such as imprecise container weight information[5] and insufficient yard storage. Therefore, remarshalling may not be completely removed in most of the practical situations.

Finally, there are studies on crane scheduling particularly when multiple cranes are used in a block. Ng presented a dynamic programming-based heuristic approach to crane scheduling to minimize the waiting time of trucks.[6] Dynamic programming is used to partition the block into ranges in which each crane can move; these ranges help crane interference to be resolved. However, these studies cannot be used to schedule cranes for remarshalling directly because a primitive task of remarshalling is moving a container from one place to another in the same block rather than giving a container to or taking a container from a truck. In addition, there are some order constraints among container moves imposed by the sequence of container loading. Therefore, a crane scheduling method that can efficiently consider the characteristics of remarshalling is required.

3   Using Simulated Annealing for Remarshalling

This section describes a method of deriving a partial order graph from the locations of containers before and after moving. The derived partial order graph is used as an initial solution of simulated annealing. An efficient method of generating valid neighbors from the current partial order graph is also presented in this section.

3.1   Determining Target Locations for Containers

In this sub-section, we present a heuristic method of determining target locations of containers under the two main constraints introduced in the previous section. Figure 2 shows a step-by-step example of the heuristic. In the initial state Fig. 2(a), containers $7W$, $7G$, $3G$, $4G$, $5G$, and $5W$ are located on top of stacks

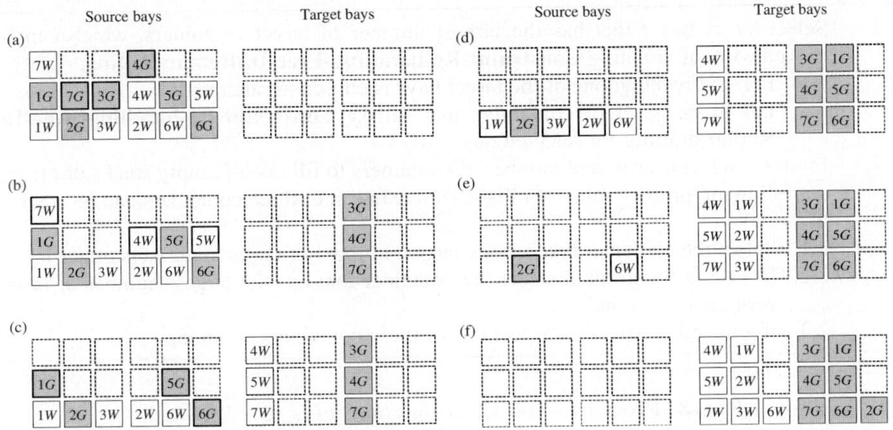

Fig. 2. Example of determining of the target locations of containers

in their source bays. These six containers can be moved to their target bays without violating **Constraint-Re-handling-Free-In-Remarshalling**. From these containers, some to the same target bay can be selected to be moved and stacked without breaking **Constraint-Re-handling-Free-In-Loading**. For example, if $7G$, $4G$, and $5G$ are selected, the order of moves for these selected containers should be $7G \rightarrow 5G \rightarrow 3G$ to satisfy **Constraint-Re-handling-Free-In-Loading**. Although there can be other container selections for a stack, each selection can have only one order of moving if the selected containers belong to the same target bay. Figure 3 shows the detailed procedure of container selection for filling a stack. By the procedure, $4G$, $7G$, and $3G$ are selected, and the order of moves is $7G \rightarrow 4G \rightarrow 3G$. The target locations of the three containers are now fixed. After removing these three containers from the source bays and placing them on a stack in their target bay, the state of bays will be shown as Fig. 2(b). The container selection and placing process is repeated until the target locations of all containers are determined. In this example, the set of containers $\{7W, 5W, 4W\}$ is the next selection, and their order is $7W \rightarrow 5W \rightarrow 4W$. When the target locations of all containers are determined, we can obtain a target configuration defined by the locations of the containers at target bays.

3.2   Deriving Partial Order Graph from the Locations of Containers

Figure 4(a) shows the source configuration defined by the initial positions of containers at the source bays for the remarshalling problem of Fig. 1. The source configuration constrains the order of container moves satisfying **Constraint-Re-handling-Free-In-Remarshalling**. If container c_1 is placed on top of another container c_2 on the same stack in a source configuration, c_1 should be moved to its target bay before c_2 to satisfy **Constraint-Re-handling-Free-In-Remarshalling**. Similarly, a target configuration, which is defined by the

1. Select target bay t that has the largest number of target containers, which can be moved without violating **Constraint-Re-handling-Free-In-Remarshalling**.
    1.1. For tie breaking, one of the target bays is chosen at random
    1.2. Let C_t be a set of containers that satisfy **Constraint-Re-handling-Free-In-Remarshalling** for selected target bay t.
2. From C_t, select a sufficient number of containers to fill one of empty stacks of t using the following priority rules. (In Fig. 2, a maximum of three containers can be stacked in a row)
    2.1. Select the container that has the largest number of target containers under it.
    2.2. If a tie is found, then select the container that has the largest number of target containers for t under it.
    2.3. If a tie still exists, then select one of these containers at random.

Fig. 3. Procedure for selecting containers to fill a stack

positions of containers at the target bays, also restricts the order of moves to fulfill the two main constraints. In a stack of a target configuration, if container c_1 is prior to container c_2 in loading, c_2 must be moved before c_1 so that c_1 should be placed on top of c_2. By combining these two types of ordering constraints imposed by the source and target configurations, a partial order graph can be derived to express all the possible re-handling-free sequences of moves under the two configurations. The derived partial order graph is shown in Fig. 4(c). A solid arrow in the figure represents an order constraint issued by the source configuration, and a dotted arrow is a constraint derived from the target configuration. In our experiment, a derived partial order graph is used for the initial solution of simulated annealing.

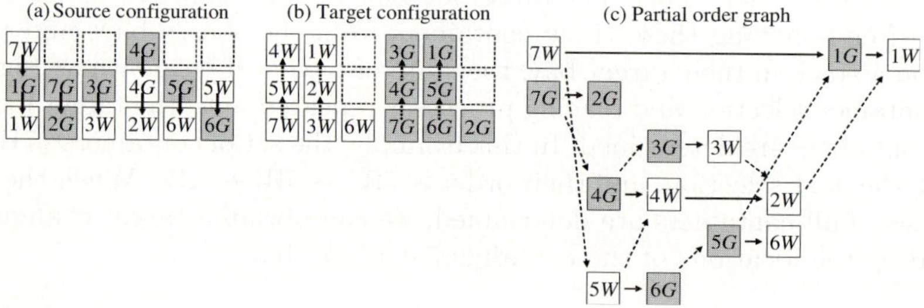

Fig. 4. Partial ordering of container moves

3.3   Generating Neighborhood Solutions

A different partial order graph can be obtained by slightly modifying the current one. Figure 5 shows an example of generating neighbors from the partial order graph in Fig. 4(c). In the graph, two containers on different stacks of the same target bay are selected at random for swapping. After swapping the

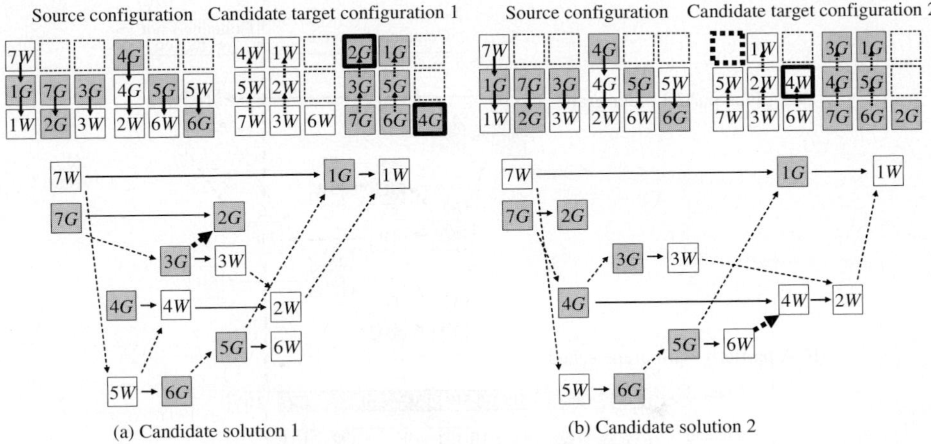

Fig. 5. An example of generating neighbors from the partial order graph in Fig. 4(c)

selected containers, a new partial order graph can be generated. For example, in Fig. 5(a), container $2G$ and $4G$ are selected and a neighbor, which is slightly different with the partial order graph of Fig. 4(c), is obtained. Note that some containers should be reordered in their stacks according to their turns of loading to satisfy **Constraint-Re-handling-Free-In-Loading**. A single container can be transferred to another non-full stack of the same target bay by swapping it with a virtual container as shown in Fig. 5(b).

A container swapping does not always lead to a valid partial order graph. When a cycle exists in a modified graph, no re-handling-free total order can be derived from it. Another swapping is tried to the original graph if the previous swapping introduces a cycle. Cycle detection can be performed in a linear time proportional to the number of containers.[7]

4   Constructing a Schedule from Partial Order Graph

This section presents a detailed description of the evaluation heuristic. The evaluation heuristic constructs an executable crane schedule by assigning each move of container to one of cranes and by determining the order of moves archived by each crane. It also detects crane interference by simulation based on the state-transition-graph model. Figure 6 shows a snapshot of constructing a crane schedule using the heuristic. In this figure, some container moves have been already assigned and currently crane A is moving container $2W$. A new container assignment is required to the idle crane B that just finished the work of moving container $3W$. Under the constraints of the given partial order graph, container $1G$ and $6W$ are two possible containers for the assignment to crane B. The heuristic simulates all the possible container assignments and selects the best-looking one to construct the partially built crane schedule incrementally.

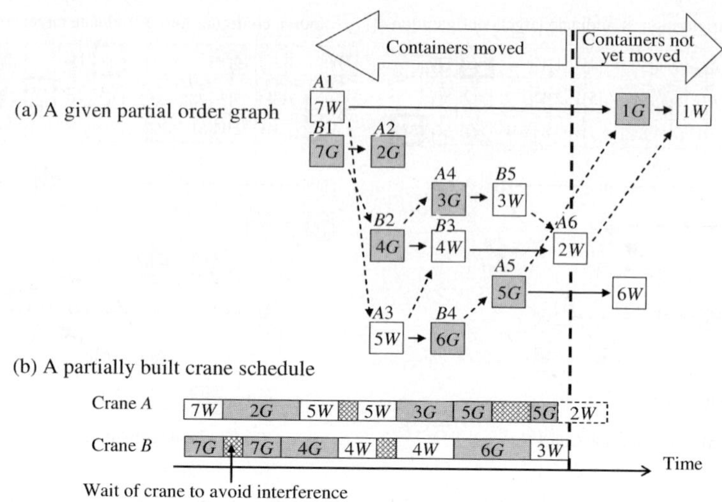

Fig. 6. An example of partially built crane schedule by the evaluation heuristic

The heuristic uses a depth-limited branch-and-bound search[8] to find the best-looking container. Figure 7 shows a tree that was constructed by the heuristic with the maximum depth of four. For each of the containers, there are two possible scenarios of avoiding crane interference when two cranes are used for remarshalling and interference is detected by simulation. Interference between the cranes can be resolved by giving the priority of working to one of the two cranes. The crane that is given the priority works without waiting. In contrast, the other should wait at the location nearest to the crane with priority to avoid interference. Therefore, a node in the tree represents both of crane priority and container assignment. The crane that has priority in each node is expressed in underline face. A node is evaluated by delay time, which is denoted on the right of the node, during the work of moving the assigned container. In Fig. 7, container $1G$ is selected for the assignment of a new container to crane B, and crane A will take the priority in moving container $2W$. The partially built crane schedule of Fig. 6 is expanded by adding the selected container $1G$ to crane B. Another tree search will be performed for the next new container assignment for crane A because crane A will finish its work of moving container $2W$ earlier than crane B. This process is repeated until all the containers are assigned to one of the cranes.

The maximum depth L of the depth-limited search is adjustable. Usually a better crane schedule can be obtained with higher L. However, higher L requires longer time in evaluation and results less trials in the level of simulated annealing if the time for crane scheduling is limited. The results of the experiment show that a better remarshalling schedule can be obtained by adjusting the balance between trying more partial order graphs and evaluating each graph with more forward looking.

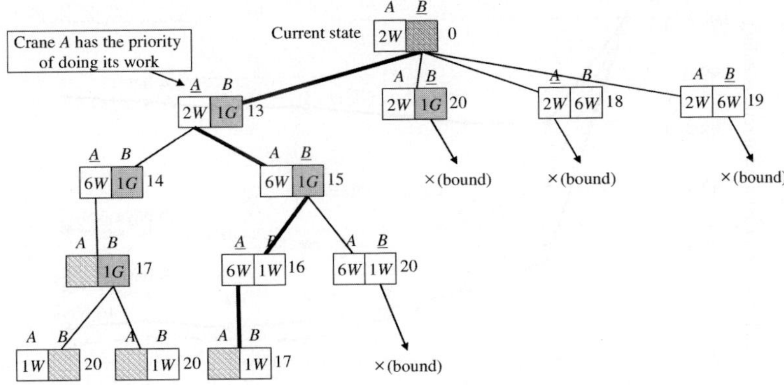

Fig. 7. Depth-limited branch-and-bound for assigning a container to idle crane B

5   Results of Experiment

For the experiment, we chose an environment with 33 bays in a block, each bay consisting of nine rows by six tiers. Two non-crossing cranes were used for remarshalling and the cranes required at least a five-bay gap for suitable working clearance. Four empty target bays are used to stack 196 target containers. Initially, target containers were randomly scattered within the block. Five different scenarios were used to test our approach to problems of various difficulties by changing the crowdness of target containers in the source bays. The time of searching for the remarshalling schedule was limited to 10 minutes. About 15,800 candidate solutions were evaluated in this time limit by depth-limited branch-and-bound with $L = 1$. About 14 candidates were evaluated with $L = 8$ in the same time limit. We also had tried another local-search algorithm, hill-climbing search, which did not show a better performance than simulated annealing. A Pentium PC with 3.2GHz was used for the experiments and each experiment was repeated ten times.

Figure 8 shows the performance of search with different L for each scenario. The graph depicts the relative estimated time of generated remarshalling schedules compared to those generated by search with $L = 1$. It is easily noticeable that higher L does not always give a better remarshalling schedule when the running time is limited. There is a point of balance between the maximum depth in evaluation and the number of evaluations for each scenario.

6   Conclusions

This paper presented a method of generating a remarshalling schedule for multiple cranes. Partial order graph is used to make a schedule to be free of rehandlings, and simulated annealing is applied to minimize time required for remarshalling at the level of partial order graphs. We also presented an evaluation heuristic for constructing a full crane schedule from a partial order graph.

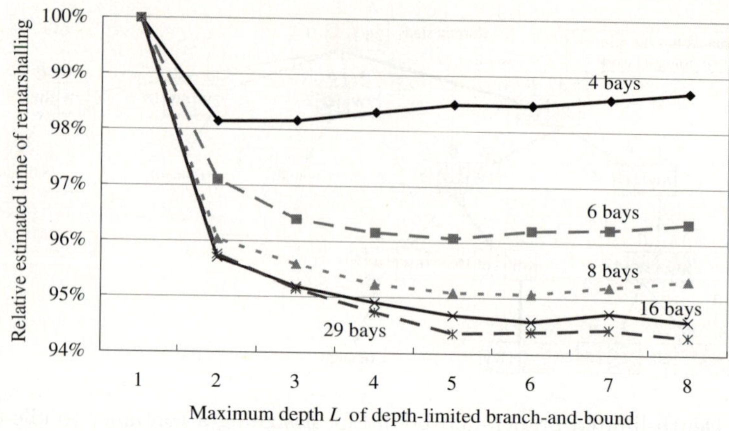

Fig. 8. The relative estimated time of remarshalling with schedules generated by simulated annealing with various maximum depths of evaluation heuristics

Our proposed method can generate an efficient crane schedule in a reasonable time. The results of the experiment show that a better remarshalling schedule can be obtained by carefully adjusting the running time of the evaluation heuristic under a limited time of computation. For further research, we are interested in finding a smart way of generating neighbors by selecting containers to be swapped considering feedback information that can be obtained in the process of applying the evaluation heuristic.

References

1. Aarts, E., Korst, J.: Simulated Annealing. Local Search in Combinatorial Optimization. John Wiley & Sons (1997) 91-120
2. Kim, K. H., Bae, J.-W.: Re-Marshaling Export Containers. Computer and Industrial Engineering **35(3-4)** (1998) 655–658
3. Dekker, R. and Voogd, P.: Advanced methods for container stacking. The Proceeding of International Workshop on Intelligent Logistics Systems (2005) 3–29
4. Kim, K. H., Park, Y. M., Ryu, K. R.: Deriving decision rules to locate export containers in container yards. European Journal of Operational Research, **124** (2000) 89–10
5. Kang, J., Ryu, K. R., Kim, K. H.: Determination of Storage Locations for Incoming Containers of Uncertain Weight. Proceedings of the 19th International Conference on Industrial, Engineering & Other Applications of Applied Intelligent System (2006) 1159–1168
6. Ng, W. C.: Crane scheduling in container yards with inter-crane interference. European Journal of Operational Research **164** (2005) 64–78
7. Nivasch, G.: Cycle Detection Using a Stack. Information Processing Letters **90(3)** (2004) 135–140
8. Russell, S. J., Novrig, P.: Artificial Intelligence: A Modern Approach (second edition) Prentice Hall (2002)

Develop Acceleration Strategy and Estimation Mechanism for Multi-issue Negotiation

Hsin Rau and Chao-Wen Chen

Department of Industrial Engineering, Chung Yuan Christian University
Chungli, Taiwan 320, Republic of China
hsinrau@cycu.edu.tw

Abstract. In recent years, negotiation has become a powerful tool in electronic commerce. When two negotiation parties still have a lot of space to negotiate, little-by-little concession has no benefit to the negotiation process. In order to improve negotiation efficiency, this study proposes a negotiation acceleration strategy to facilitate negotiation. In addition, this paper develops an estimation mechanism with regression technique to estimate the preference of opponent, with which results the joint utility of negotiation can be maximized. Finally, an example is given to illustrate the proposed estimation mechanism.

1 Introduction

Negotiation is a process by means of which agents communicate and compromise to reach mutually beneficial agreements [8]. Recently, negotiation becomes a powerful tool to aid electronic commerce trade. In negotiation strategy, Jennings and Wooldridge [3] considered the negotiation agent should increase the capability of intelligence and learning in order to know the opponent's negotiation attitude. Based on this idea, researchers considered that agents should be able to respond to opponent's actions intelligently and proposed some algorithms or rules to develop new negotiation strategies or tactics [4-10].

Factors in negotiation strategy influencing the negotiation mostly are time, opponent's concession attitude and offer range, etc. However, little-by-little concession has no benefit when two negotiation parties still have a lot of space to negotiate. In order to improve negotiation efficiency, this study extends the negotiation decision functions (NDFs) proposed by Faratin et al. [2] to promote an acceleration strategy to speed up negotiation. In addition, a regression technique is used to estimate the opponent's preference. Moreover, this study uses linear programming to find the maximal joint utility in order to maximize satisfaction. Finally, an example is given to illustrate the proposed methodology.

The rest of this paper is organized as follows. Section 2 briefly introduces negotiation decision functions. Section 3 develops the negotiation acceleration strategy. Section 4 discusses how to estimate opponent's favorite. Section 5 describes the methodology for maximizing utility. Section 6 gives an example for illustration. In the final section, a conclusion is provided.

M. Ali and R. Dapoigny (Eds.): IEA/AIE 2006, LNAI 4031, pp. 1221–1230, 2006.

2 Negotiation Decision Functions

This study extends the negotiation model proposed by Faratin et al. [2]. In their negotiation model, two parties negotiate on one issue or multi-issues, such as price, delivery time, quality, etc. Let $x_j^{a \to b}(t_n)$ be an offer proposed by agent a to agent b for negotiation issue j at time t_n. t_{max}^a is agent a's negotiation deadline. A negotiation thread is denoted as $X_j^{a \to b}(t_n)$, which is a sequence of alternating offers of the form $(x_j^{a \to b}(t_0), x_j^{b \to a}(t_1), x_j^{a \to b}(t_2), \cdots)$. The negotiation is terminated by an acceptance or a withdrawal from either side. Agent a's response at t_n to agent b's offer sent at time t_{n-1} is defined as:

$$I^a(t_n, x_j^{b \to a}(t_{n-1})) = \begin{cases} reject & if\ t_n > t_{max}^a \\ accept & if\ V^a(x_j^{b \to a}(t_{n-1})) \geq V^a(x_j^{a \to b}(t_n)) \\ x_j^{a \to b}(t_n) & otherwise \end{cases} \tag{1}$$

where $x_j^{a \to b}(t_n)$ is the counter offer from agent a to agent b when an offer $x_j^{b \to a}(t_{n-1})$ is not accepted by a.

Agent i (a or b) has a scoring function, $V_j^i : [min_j^i, max_j^i] \to [0,\ 1]$, that gives the score (or utility) agent i assigns a value of issue j in the range of its acceptable values. V_j^i is defined in Eqs.(2) and (3). w_j^a is agent a's weight for issue j, which indicates the importance of issue j for agent a. J is the number of issues.

$$V_j^i(x_j^i) = \begin{cases} (x_j^i - min_j^i)/(max_j^i - min_j^i) & as\ x_j^i\ is\ an\ increasing\ function \\ (max_j^i - x_j^i)/(max_j^i - min_j^i) & as\ x_j^i\ is\ a\ decreasing\ function \end{cases} \tag{2}$$

$$V^a(x) = \sum_{j=1}^{J} w_j^a v_j^a(x_j) \tag{3}$$

The NDFs proposed by Faratin et al. [2] include three tactics: time-dependent, resource-dependent, and behavior-dependent. Moreover, we find that negotiation strategies used mostly relate to time, so we use the time-dependent tactic in this study. The characteristic of time-dependent tactic is that agent gives an offer according to time with concession parameter β, which is described by the concession function $\alpha_j^a(t)$ and offers, as shown in Eqs. (4) and (5).

$$x_j^{a \to b}(t_n) = \begin{cases} x_j^{a \to b}(t_0) + \alpha_j^a(t_n) \times (x_j^{a \to b}(t_{max}^a) - x_j^{a \to b}(t_0)) & if\ x_j^{a \to b}(t_n)\ decreasing \\ x_j^{a \to b}(t_0) + \alpha_j^a(t_n) \times (x_j^{a \to b}(t_{max}^a) - x_j^{a \to b}(t_0)) & if\ x_j^{a \to b}(t_n)\ increasing \end{cases} \tag{4}$$

$$\alpha_j^a(t) = k_j^a + (1 - k_j^a)(\min(t_n, t_{max}^a)/t_{max}^a)^{1/\beta} \tag{5}$$

Time-dependent tactic is divided into three ranges according to the value of β :

(1) $\beta < 1$, it is called as the Boulware tactic, which insists on the offered value until the time is almost exhausted, whereupon it concedes up to the reservation value.
(2) $\beta > 1$, it is called as the Conceder tactic. In this tactic, the agent is willing to concede to its reservation value as quickly as possible.
(3) $\beta = 1$, it is called as the linear tactic. Its behavior is between the above two tactics.

The details can be found in Faratin et al. (1998).

3 Develop a Negotiation Acceleration Strategy

In NDFs, two negotiation agents might spend a lot of time to advance little toward their negotiation settlement. In order to improve this situation, this study proposes a negotiation acceleration strategy for single issue, as expressed in Eq. (6).

$$\alpha_j^a(t_n) = [(\alpha_j^a(t_{n-1})+CTF(t_n))+(1-(\alpha_j^a(t_{n-1})+CTF(t_n)))\times\gamma\times CAF(t_n))]^{\frac{1}{\beta}} \tag{6}$$

where $\gamma \in [0,1]$. CTF is a concession time function and can be defined as the ratio of remaining concession to remaining time, as shown in Eq. (7).

$$CTF(t_n) = \frac{1-\alpha_j^a(t_{n-1})}{t_{max}^a - t_{n-1}} \tag{7}$$

CAF evaluates the distance of current offer between both agents (see Fig. 1) as compared with the distance of initial offer between both agents, as shown in Eq. (8).

$$CAF(t_n) = \begin{cases} \dfrac{x_j^{a\to b}(t_{n-1})-x_j^{b\to a}(t_{n-1})}{x_j^{a\to b}(t_0)-x_j^{b\to a}(t_0)} & if\ x_j^{a\to b}(t_n)\ decreasing \\[4mm] \dfrac{x_j^{b\to a}(t_{n-1})-x_j^{a\to b}(t_{n-1})}{x_j^{a\to b}(t_0)-x_j^{b\to a}(t_0)} & if\ x_j^{a\to b}(t_n)\ increasing \end{cases} \tag{8}$$

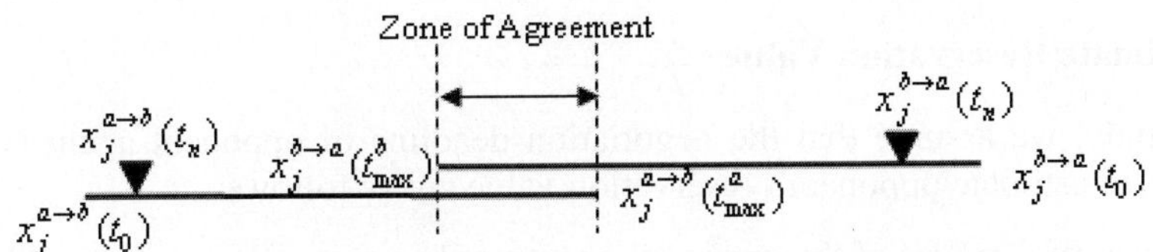

Fig. 1. Illustration of concession acceleration function (CAF)

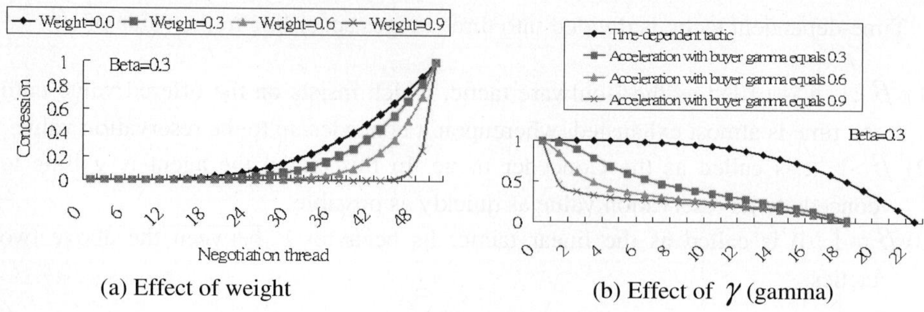

(a) Effect of weight   (b) Effect of γ (gamma)

Fig. 2. Effects of weight and gamma

$CAF \in [-1,1]$. When $x_j^{b \to a}(t_{n-1}) > x_j^{a \to b}(t_{n-1})$, CAF>0 indicates normal concession, whereas CAF<0 presents over-concession. Sometimes an issue with CAF<0 has reached its own settlement; but, it has to wait for other issues to reach the overall settlement together. Parameter γ in Eq.(6) indicates agent's willingness to quickly reach an agreement. When γ =0, $\alpha_j^a(t_n)$ becomes the time-dependent tactic (polynomial function) in the NDFs. As γ increases, the agent enters the zone of agreement quicker. When γ =1, the agent hopes to make a settlement immediately and the offer is the reservation value ($x_j^{a \to b}(t_{max}^a)$ or $x_j^{b \to a}(t_{max}^b)$). For a multi-issue negotiation, we need to take weight into consideration in the negotiation strategy. As shown in Eq. (9), we use an exponential form to express the effect of weight. Using β =0.3 as an example, Fig. 2(a) illustrates the effect of weight on concession. As the weight increases, the agent concedes less. Fig. 2(b) illustrates the effect γ on CAF. CAF decreases quicker as γ increases.

$$\alpha_j^a(t_n)^{\frac{1}{1-w_j^a}} = [(\alpha_j^a(t_{n-1})+CTF(t_n))+(1-(\alpha_j^a(t_{n-1})+CTF(t_n)))\times \gamma$$

$$\times CAF(t_n))]^{\frac{1}{\beta}(\frac{1}{1-w_j^a})}, \ 0 \le w_j^a < 1, \ \gamma \in [0,1]$$

(9)

4   Estimate Opponent's Preference

4.1   Estimate Reservation Value

In this study, we assume that the negotiation deadline of opponent agent is known. The steps to estimate opponent's reservation value are as follows:

(1) Collect offer values of the opponent agent until an arranged negotiation thread.
(2) Normalize the values in (1) with respect to the difference between initial offers.
(3) Collect a number of recent values in (2).

(4) Use an equation with an appropriate order polynomial to fit the scatter diagram with minimal error consideration.
(5) From (4), calculate opponent's reservation value

Based on our experiment, we found a third order polynomial is suitable for tasks done in step (4), in which it needs at least six values to be collected in (3).

4.2 Stop Conditions

During the process of reservation value estimation, we need to set conditions to stop estimation. In this study, we set two stop conditions:

(1) After a number of continuous estimation values is within the predefined range.
(2) An opposite direction for the trend of the decreasing or increasing of the estimation values occurs after an initial period of negotiation.

According to our experiment, if 4 continuous estimation values are in a defined range, we may stop. In the initial period of negotiation, the estimation diverges very much; however, after a period of negotiation, the estimation converges. In our study, condition 2 can be found usually after one fifth of the negotiation deadline.

4.3 Estimate Weights

Once the opponent's reservation value is known, we can estimate the weight of each issue after a sequence of opponent's offers. The procedure is as follows:

(1) Collect offer values of each issue of the opponent until an arranged negotiation thread
(2) Normalize the values in (1) with respect to the difference between opponent's initial offer and reservation value.
(3) Plot scatter diagrams for every two issues.
(4) Use an exponential equation to fit the scatter diagram with minimal error consideration.
(5) From (4), the ratio of two weights for every two issues can be found.
(6) From $\sum_j w_j = 1$, the weight of each issue can be obtained.

In step (5), for any two issues, we can derive simultaneous equations as shown in Eq. (10):

$$\frac{1 - w_X^a}{1 - w_Y^a} = C_{X,Y}, \; X = 1,..,J, \; Y = 1,...,J, \; X \neq Y \tag{10}$$

Considering an example, a buyer estimates a seller's weights. Suppose that there are three issues, and the seller's weights are 0.2, 0.5, and 0.3. According to Eq. (10), we have three sets of equations: issue one and issue two, issue one and issue three, and issue two and issue three. Take set one as an example, we have $C_{1,2} = \dfrac{1 - w_1^a}{1 - w_2^a} = 1.6 \cdot$

The curve is fitted from the scatter diagram that is shown Fig. 3. Then from $C_{1,2}$, $C_{1,3}$, and $C_{2,3}$, we can found the weights w_1, w_2, and w_3.

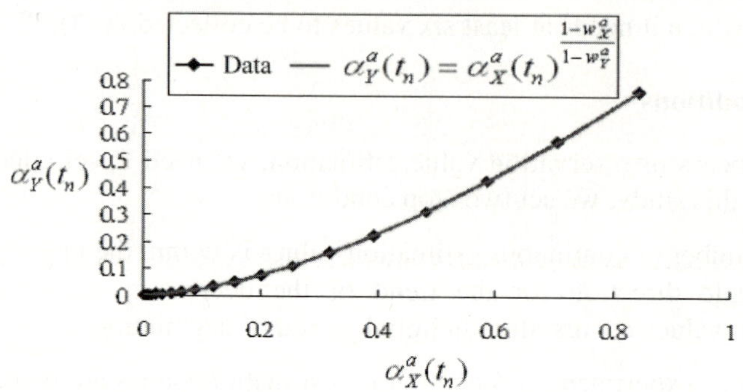

Fig. 3. Concept of estimate weight

5   Utility Maximization

In order to increase the joint utility of negotiation, this study uses the linear programming technique to maximize the opponent's utility (Z) when the utility of the self side is fixed, as shown in Eq. (11). Before doing this, the opponent's weight of each issue must be known beforehand. This explains why the effort is done in the previous section. The objective function in Eq. (11) is agent b's linear combination of weight and scoring function estimated from agent a. Constraints include agent a's linear combination of weight and scoring function and offer range. V is agent a's score.

$$Max\ Z = \begin{cases} \sum_j w_j^b \times \dfrac{x_j^{a \to b}(t_0) - x_j^{b \to a}(t_n)}{x_j^{b \to a}(t_0) - x_j^{b \to a}(t_{max})} & if\ x_j^{b \to a}(t_n)\ decreasing \\[2em] \sum_j w_j^b \times \dfrac{x_j^{a \to b}(t_n) - x_j^{b \to a}(t_0)}{x_j^{b \to a}(t_{max}) - x_j^{b \to a}(t_0)} & if\ x_j^{b \to a}(t_n)\ increasing \end{cases}$$

$$s.t. \begin{cases} \sum_j w_j^a \times \dfrac{x_j^{a \to b}(t_0) - x_j^{a \to b}(t_n)}{x_j^{a \to b}(t_0) - x_j^{a \to b}(t_{max})} = V & if\ x_j^{a \to b}(t_n)\ decreasing \\[2em] \sum_j w_j^a \times \dfrac{x_j^{a \to b}(t_n) - x_j^{a \to b}(t_0)}{x_j^{a \to b}(t_{max}) - x_j^{a \to b}(t_0)} = V & if\ x_j^{a \to b}(t_n)\ increasing \end{cases} \tag{11}$$

$$\begin{cases} x_j^{b \to a}(t_0) \le x_j^{a \to b}(t_n) \le x_j^{a \to b}(t_0) & j = 1,...,J & if\ x_j^{a \to b}(t_n)\ decreasing \\[1em] x_j^{a \to b}(t_0) \le x_j^{a \to b}(t_n) \le x_j^{b \to a}(t_0) & j = 1,...,J & if\ x_j^{a \to b}(t_n)\ increasing \end{cases}$$

Table 1. Parameters used in the example

	Issue	Buyer	Seller
Price	Offer range	[40,100]	[60,120]
	Utility function	Increasing	Decreasing
Due date	Offer range	[2,7]	[5,10]
	Utility function	Increasing	Decreasing
Quantity	Offer range	[100,200]	[150,250]
	Utility function	Increasing	Decreasing

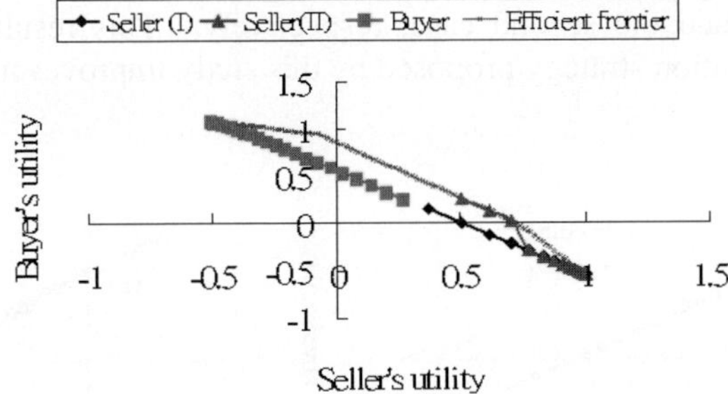

Fig. 4. The effect of utility maximization

Table 2. Compare negotiation process whether the utility maximization is used

Thread	Utility		Utility	
	Buyer	Seller (I)	Buyer	Seller (II)
1	-0.54333	1	-0.54333	1
3	-0.54332	0.99999	-0.54332	0.99999
…	…	…	…	…
37	-0.29249	0.77481	-0.29249	0.77481
39	-0.21537	0.70444	**0.02466**	**0.70444**
41	-0.11865	0.61612	**0.13065**	**0.61612**
43	0.00177	0.50614	**0.26262**	**0.50614**
45	0.15064	0.37022		

Let us use an experiment to discuss the benefit of using the utility maximization. The experiment parameters are shown in Table 1 with $\beta = 0.3$ and weight = [0.2, 0.5, 0.3] for the Seller and $\beta = 1.0$ and weight = [0.4, 0.5, 0.1] for the Buyer. Suppose that the Seller has estimated the Buyer's preference and only the Seller uses the utility maximization. Two cases are that Seller (I) (case I) dose not use utility maximization; but, Seller (II) (case II) starts to use utility maximization when negotiation thread equals 39. The negotiation result is shown in Fig. 4 and Table 2. Bold numbers shown in Table 2 are the offers calculated from utility maximization. We can find that the Buyer's utility becomes higher when the thread reaches 39 if the Seller uses the utility maximization (case II). Moreover, the utility maximization can also make an offer close to the efficient frontier (Pareto), as shown in Fig. 4.

6 Example Illustrations

An example is used here for discussed with parameters shown in Table 1 with $\beta = 0.5$ and $\gamma = 0.5$ for Buyer, and $\beta = 1.0$ and $\gamma = 0.6$ for Seller. Negotiation deadline sets 25 for both agents (thread=50). Under the environment without estimating the opponent's preference, Fig.5 shows the difference between without and with acceleration in a negotiation process, and the negotiation settles at threads 44 and 36 for the first case and the second case, respectively. This result explains that the negotiation acceleration strategy proposed by this study improves negotiation.

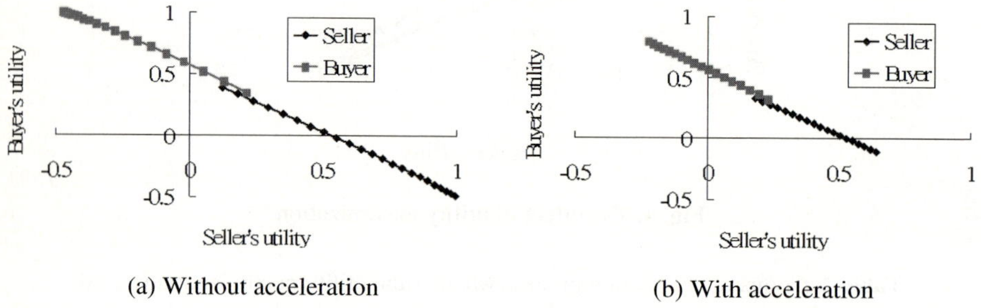

(a) Without acceleration   (b) With acceleration

Fig. 5. Negotiation process without and with acceleration

Table 3. Estimation process of reservation value for each issue

Thread	Price	Due date	Quantity
14	100.0425	7.0021	198.8612
16	100.0338	7.0017	199.0692
18	100.0266	7.0013	199.2475
20			199.3989
22			199.5263

Continuing the previous example but with estimating opponent's preference, Table 3 shows the estimation process, which starts from thread 14. The Buyer's reservation values of price and due date are found to be 100.0266 and 7.0013 at thread 18, and the reservation value of quantity is found to be 199.5263 at thread 22. Comparing with the actual values for three reservation values, (100, 7, 199), it is very close. After all the Buyer's reservation values have been estimated, their weights can be estimated as (0.2, 0.3, 0.5), which are exactly the same as actual values. Once the Buyer's preference is known, we can start the process of utility maximization until the negotiation settles at thread 25. At this moment, the joint utility equals 0.866, which is much better than 0.561 for the case without utility maximization and is close to the best joint utility, 0.953. In Fig.6, we can see Buyer's utility jump from 0.124 to 0.494 at the Seller's side, where the thread is from 21 to 23, as also shown in Table 4.

Table 4. Negotiation process with estimation and utility maximization

	Seller			Buyer	
Thread	Seller's utility	Buyer's utility	Thread	Seller's utility	Buyer's utility
1	0.642	-0.107	2	-0.225	0.793
3	0.620	-0.086	4	-0.206	0.775
13	0.505	0.027	14	-0.099	0.672
15	0.480	0.050	16	-0.074	0.648
17	0.455	0.074	18	-0.049	0.622
19	0.430	0.099	20	-0.022	0.595
21	0.404	0.124	22	0.005	0.567
23	0.378	0.494	24	0.034	0.537
25	0.351	0.514		0.064	0.506

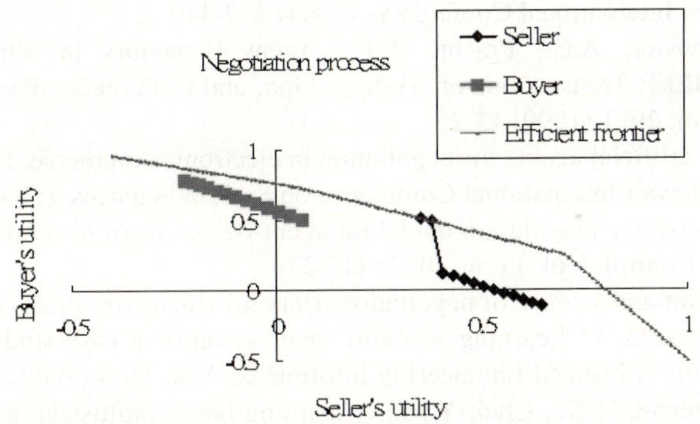

Fig. 6. Negotiation process with estimation and utility maximization

7 Conclusions

Negotiation has been applied to a wide range of industrial and business domains and its electronic format is even essential for electronic commerce. When two negotiation parties are still far away from their settlement, slow concession has no benefit to the negotiation process. In order to speed up the negotiation, this study proposed a negotiation acceleration strategy to facilitate negotiation. In addition, to maximize joint utility, we applied the linear programming technique to maximize the opponent's utility when the self-side's utility is fixed. With this way, we can also attract the opponent to accept the offer early. However, before the utility maximization can be applied, we have to know the opponent's preference. This is why we have to propose the estimation mechanism to estimate the reservation value and the weight for each issue of the opponent. We believe that this study provides several technologies or directions to improve the electronic negotiation process. This study only focuses on the negotiation between two parties; indeed, an extension to multiple parties can be done for the future work.

Acknowledgements

This work is supported in part by the National Science Council of Republic of China under the grant NSC 94-2213-E-033-006.

References

1. Choi, S.P.M., Liu, J., Chan, S.P.: A genetic agent-based negotiation system. Computer Networks. Vol. 37. 2 (2001) 195-204
2. Faratin, P., Sierra, C., Jennings, N.R.: Negotiation decision functions for autonomous agents. Robotics and Autonomous Systems. Vol. 24. 3 (1998) 159-182
3. Jennings, N.R., Wooldridge, M.: Software agents, IEE Review. Vol. 42. 1 (1996) 17-20
4. Li, J., Cao, Y.D.: Bayesian learning in bilateral multi-issue negotiation and its application in MAS-based electronic commerce. Proceedings of Intelligent Agent Technology. IEEE/WIC/ACM International Conference. (2004) 437-440.
5. Krovi, R., Graesser, A.C., Pracht, W.E.: Agent Behaviors in Virtual Negotiation Environments. IEEE Transactions on System, Man, and Cybernetics-Part C: Applications and Reviews. Vol. 29. 1 (1999) 15-25
6. Oliver, J.R.: On artificial agents for negotiation in electronic commerce. Proceedings of the Twenty-Ninth Hawaii International Conference on System Sciences. (1996) 337-346
7. Oprea, M.: An adaptive negotiation model for agent-based electronic commerce. Studies in informatics and Control. Vol. 11. 3 (2002) 217-279
8. Raiffa, H..: The art and science of negotiation. Harvard University Press. (1982)
9. Ren, Z.., Anumba, C. J.: Learning in multi-agent systems: a case study of construction claims negotiation. Advanced Engineering Informatics. Vol. 16. 4 (2002) 265-275.
10. Wang, L.M.., Huang, H.K.., Chai, Y.M.: A learning-based multistage negotiation model. Proceedings of International Conference on Machine Learning and Cybernetics. (2004) 140-145.

Least Squares Support Vector Machines for Bandwidth Reservation in Wireless IP Networks

Jerzy Martyna

Institute of Computer Science, Jagiellonian University, ul. Nawojki 11,
30-072 Cracow, Poland
martyna@softlab.ii.uj.edu.pl

Abstract. Future mobile wireless Internet network will be based on Internet Protocol (IP) version 6. In this paper we describe an approach for obtaining a bandwidth reservation mechanism in the process of handoff in the wireless IP network. In our approach, we adopt the least squares support vector machines (LS-SVM) method to minimize the probability of a new call blocking and the probability of dropping a call during the connection transfer between the cells. Simulation experiments show that in the environments with some types of traffic, a mechanism based on LS-SVM achieves good performance measures in bandwidth reservation.

Keywords: wireless networks, bandwidth reservation, least squares support vector machines.

1   Introduction

As the Internet has grown in size and diversity of applications a two trends have emerged to provide a new perspective. Firstly, to attain mobility, Internet services are achievable by radio access networks. Secondly, to achieve the quality of service (QoS) parameters for different traffic types, such as voice, audio, video, multimedia, are under development. Several traffic types have different characteristics and different QoS demands.

For CAC in wireless cellular networks were proposed some mechanisms. To one of the first solution belongs the fractional *guard channel policy* [16] which determines the number of guard channels for handoffs by considering just the status of the local cell. In the paper by Naghshineh et al. [15], the total bandwidth required for handoff and the existing connections is calculated under the assumptions of the channel holding time and perfect knowledge of the rate of handoff. In the approach presented in the paper by Levine [12], the shadow cluster scheme makes it possible to estimate future resource requirements. However, this method cannot determine the shadow cluster in real networks.

In another scheme given by Lu [14], an algorithm for an indoor management was given. Nevertheless, this scheme does not estimate the channel holding time and therefore cannot be used for bandwidth reservation. In the paper by [3], the user mobility is estimated on the basis of the history of the handoff observed in each cell. The scheme assumes that each mobile user will do handoff to neighboring cells with equal probability in the *mobility-estimate-time-window*. This

M. Ali and R. Dapoigny (Eds.): IEA/AIE 2006, LNAI 4031, pp. 1231–1239, 2006.

assumption may not be accurate in general. In the paper by Liu [13], a hierarchical location-prediction algorithm was introduced. This algorithm was composed of an approximate pattern-matching mechanism that extracts any regular movement pattern to estimate the global intercell direction and of the extended self-learning Kalman filter that deals with random movements by tracking intracell trajectory (local prediction). Nevertheless, the model postulated by Liu is associated with the large number of stored patterns of movements of mobile users.

Recently, the authors of the paper [11] formulated a handoff management scheme using simultanecus multiple bindings that reduces packet loss and generates negligible delays due to the handoff in IP-based third generation cellular systems. In the paper by Kuo [10], the class of staying time, available time, and the class of the mobile host to bandwidth reservation was postulated. However, the presented solution was idealistic since the speed of the mobile host is difficult to detect accurately. On the other hand, Ei-Kadi [6] proposed a scheme in which some bandwidth from multimedia connections for supporting the new calls or handoff connections was borrowed. The borrowed bandwidth is later returned to the original connections as soon as possible to satisfy the QoS requirements.

Motivated by the above discussion, we propose a new bandwidth management scheme in this paper. It consists of a bandwidth reservation scheme in the cellular systems and support vector machines technique to reduce the call-blocking probability of real-time traffic. Our model of cellular system is described by the cellular coverage area in which the location can be easily determined using trigonometric relationships. By means of the use of the fuzzy logic controller for bandwidth estimation we obtained some dependencies which allow us to predict the demand for the bandwidth in all neighbouring cells. We propose the LS-SVM method for the bandwidth prediction in all the cells of the cellular IP network. We also study the accuracy of our LS-SVM method by comparing it with the fuzzy logic controller for bandwidth reservation in wireless IP network.

We recall that the support vector machines (SVM), based on the statistical learning theory, as a powerful new tool for data classification and function estimation, have been introduced by Vapnik [20, 21] and Cortes and Vapnik [4]. SVM map input data into a high dimensional feature space where it may become linearly separable. SVM method was used, among others, by Gong [7] for a multiuser detection in CDMA communications, by Hasegawa [8] for prediction of the Internet traffic. In the paper by Chen [2], the call classification system for AT&T natural dialog system was based on SVMs. Recently, many solutions with SVM methods are implemented in low-cost VLSI chips.

The rest of the paper is organized as follows. In section 2, we describe the proposed fuzzy logic model for bandwidth reservation. Section 3 introduces a support vector machine reservation scheme for problem solving. In section 4, we give some simulation results, which compare the proposed method with the fixed reservation scheme.

2   Fuzzy Logic Controller for Bandwidth Reservation in Wireless IP Networks

This section describes the fuzzy logic model that will be used for bandwidth reservation in cellular wireless IP networks.

Our cellular network model is described by the cellular coverage area in which the cell frontier is defined as the maximum outreach of its base station (BS) transmission (see Fig. 1). Any traffic outside the frontier is of no direct interest to the base station, as it cannot service any of it. The hexagonal regions of each cell represent the region that can be covered by their baseline patterns of coverage. The small rings represent the regions which can only be covered by their own base stations. The shadowed part in the middle represents the forbidden zone (no mobiles in it). For the location of mobile terminal (MT) and movement prediction the standard methods described among others in [1] can be used. In the case when the MT moves from cell 2 to cell 1 and crosses to the shadowed part, the BS_1 will reserve the bandwidth and the BS_2 will release the used bandwidth (see Fig. 2). When the MT goes beyond the darkness area, the base station BS_1 will not reserve the bandwidth and the base station B_2 will release the used bandwidth (see Fig. 2). In the case when the MT goes to the very shadowed area, the three base stations will reserve the bandwidth.

The reservation of bandwidth depends on three factors, namely:

- the probability that the MT will entered the shadowed area,
- the probability that the MT will leave the current cell,
- the speed of movement of the MT.

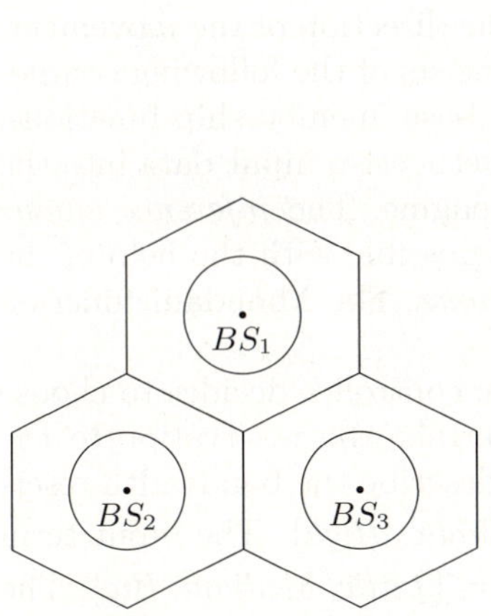

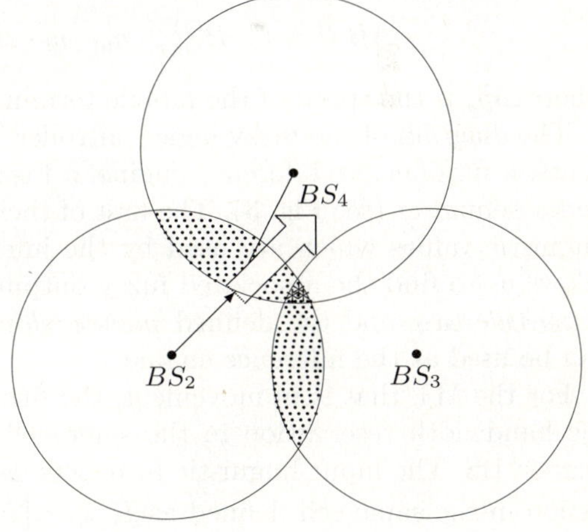

Fig. 1. Cell models used for bandwidth reservation

Fig. 2. Bandwidth reservation after location discovery of mobile terminal and its movement prediction

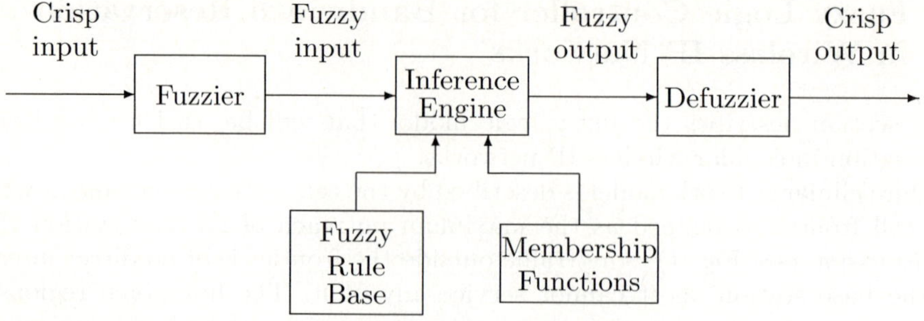

Fig. 3. Schematic diagram of fuzzy logic controller

We present the calculation of the reserved bandwidth that takes all three factors into consideration. Let the MT be in shadowed area and move to cell 1. The amount of the reserved bandwidth for the j-th connection of the MT can be expressed as

$$B^{(j)} = \mathcal{C} \cdot B^{(j)}_{max} \cdot p_m \cdot p_l, \quad j = 1, 2, \ldots, J \tag{1}$$

where $\mathcal{C}$ is the scaling factor, $B^{(j)}_{max}$ is the maximum bandwidth required for the j-th connection of MT, p_m is the probability that the MT will move into the shadowed area, p_l is the probability that the MT will leave the current cell, J the total number of the current connections for the MT. We can give the change of the bandwidth for j-th connection in the current point of the MT in the shadowed area, namely

$$\Delta B^{(j)} = \mathcal{C} \cdot B^{(j)}_{max} \cdot p_m \cdot p_l \cdot \Delta p_s, \quad j = 1, 2, \ldots, J \tag{2}$$

where Δp_s is the speed of the mobile terminal in the direction of the movement.

The diagram of the fuzzy logic controller [17] consists of the following components: a fuzzifier, an inference engine, a fuzzy rule base, membership functions, and a defuzzifer (see Fig. 3). The first of them converts crisp input data into the linguistic values which are used by the inference engine. The *inference engine* allows us to find the associated fuzzy output. It is possible with the help of the *fuzzy rule base* and the defined *membership functions*. The Mamdani function can be used as the inference engine.

For the MT that is in movement, the fuzzy logic controller decides to choose the bandwidth reservation in the same cell or overtake the reservation to the nearest BS. The input linguistic term sets used to describe the bandwidth reservation in the same cell defined as $T^{(c)}_{res} = \{Low,\ Middle,\ High\}$. The input term sets for release the bandwidth in the same cell $T^{(c)}_{rel} = \{Little,\ Medium,\ Big\}$. The term set of the output linguistic variable S (the same cell) is defined $V(S) = \{Reject,\ Weakly\ Accept,\ Accept\}$. Similarly, the term set of the output linguistic variable N (nearest BS) is defined as $V(N) = \{BS,\ Nearest\ BS\}$. The *Nearest BS* variable indicates the switching between the BS stations.

For the estimation of the output data we used the defuzzier which can be given by the ratio:

$$B^{(j)} = \frac{\int (\mu(B_{out}^{(j)}) B_{out}^{(j)}) dB_{out}^{(j)}}{\int \mu(B_{out}) dB_{out}^{(j)}}, \quad j = 1, 2, \ldots, J \tag{3}$$

where $\mu(B_{out}^{(j)})$ is the membership function of the aggregated output.

The reserved bandwidth for the j-th connection in the target cell can be expressed as the product of

$$B_{res}^{(j)} = C_1 \cdot B_1^{(j)}, \quad j = 1, 2, \ldots, J \tag{4}$$

The total bandwidth reserved for the MT in the target cell is given by

$$B_{res} = \sum_{j=1}^{J} B_{res}^{(j)} \tag{5}$$

3   Least Squares Support Vector Machines Method for Bandwidth Reservation in Wireless IP Networks

In this section, we give the overview of the Least Squares SVM method for bandwidth reservation in wireless IP networks.

Let the set $\{(x_i, y_i)\}_{i=1}^{N}$, $x_i \in R^n$, $y_i \in \{-1, +1\}$ be a training data, where x_i is the ith input vector with the known binary target y_i. The original SVM classifier [20] satisfies the following conditions:

$$\begin{cases} w^T \phi(x_i) + b \geq +1 & \text{if } y_i = 1 \\ w^T \phi(x_i) + b \leq -1 & \text{if } y_i = -1 \end{cases} \tag{6}$$

or equivalently

$$y_i[w^T \phi(x_i) + b] - 1 \geq 0, \quad i = 1, 2. \ldots, N \tag{7}$$

where $\phi \colon R^n \to R^m$ is the feature map mapping the input space to a usually high dimensional feature space. The data points are linearly separable by a hyperplane defined by the pair $(w \in R^m, b \in R)$. Thus, the classification function is given by

$$f(x) = sign\{w^T \phi(x) + b\} \tag{8}$$

It is usually not needed to make the assessment with the help of the feature map and it is enough instead to use the kernel function in the original space given by

$$K(x_i, x_j) = \phi(x_i)^T \cdot \phi(x_j) \tag{9}$$

For the violation of Eq. (7) slack variables ξ_i are introduced such that

$$y_i[w^T \phi(x_i) + b] \geq 1 - \xi_i, \quad \xi > 0, \quad i = 1, 2, \ldots, N \tag{10}$$

Thus is considered the following minimization problem:

$$\min_{w,b,\xi} J(w,b,\xi) = \frac{1}{2} \| w \|^2 + C \sum_{i=1}^{N} \xi_i$$

$$\text{subject to} \quad y_i[w^T \phi(x_i) + b] \geq 1 - \xi_i, \quad \xi_i > 0,$$

$$i = 1, 2, \ldots, N, \quad C > 0 \tag{11}$$

where C is a positive constant parameter used to control the tradeoff between the training error and the margin.

The dual of the system (11) as the result of Karush-Kuhn-Tucker (KKT) condition [9] leads to a well-known convex quadratic programming (QP). The solution of the QP problem is slow for large vectors and it is difficult to implement in the on-line adaptive form. Therefore, a modified version of the SVM called the Least Squares SVM (LS-SVM) was proposed by Suykens et al [18].

In the LS-SVM method, the following minimization problem is formulated

$$\min_{w,b,e} J(w,b,e) = \frac{1}{2} w^T w + \gamma \frac{1}{2} \sum_{k=1}^{W} e_k^2$$

$$\text{subject to} \quad y_k[w^T \phi(x_k) + b] = 1 - e_k, \quad k = 1, 2, \ldots, N \tag{12}$$

The corresponding Lagrangian for Eq. (12) is given by

$$L(w,b,e;\alpha) = J(w,b,e) - \sum_{k=1}^{N} \alpha_k \{ y_k[w^T \phi(x_k) + b] - 1 + e_k \} \tag{13}$$

where the α_k are the Langrange multipliers. The optimality condition leads to the following $(N+1) \times (N+1)$ linear system

$$\begin{bmatrix} 0 & Y^T \\ Y & \Omega^* + \gamma^{-1}I \end{bmatrix} \begin{bmatrix} b \\ \alpha \end{bmatrix} = \begin{bmatrix} 0 \\ 1 \end{bmatrix} \tag{14}$$

where
$Z = [\phi(x_1)^T y_1, \ldots, \phi(x_N)^T y_N]$
$Y = [y_1, \ldots, y_N]$
$1 = [1, \ldots, 1]$
$\alpha = [\alpha_1, \ldots, \alpha_N]$
and $\Omega^* = ZZ^T$. Due to the application of Mercer's condition [18] there exists a mapping and an expansion

$$\Omega^*_{kl} = y_k y_l \phi(x_k)^T \phi(x_l) = y_k y_l K(x_k, x_l) \tag{15}$$

Thus, the LS-SVM model for function estimation is given

$$y(x) = \sum_{k=1}^{N} \alpha_k y_k \cdot K(x, x_k) + b \tag{16}$$

where parameters α_k and b are based on the solution to Eqs. (14) and (15). The parameters α_k , b denote the optimal desired weights vector for the bandwidth reservation when the MT crossed the shadowed areas. The parameter y_k contains the information.

In comparison with the standard SVM method, the LS-SVM has a lower computational complexity and memory requirements.

4   Simulation Results

In this section, we give some simulation results presenting the effectiveness of our approach. We compared the proposed LS-SVM bandwidth reservation method with the fuzzy logic controller (FLC) for bandwidth reservation.

Our simulation was restricted to 36 cells in the cellular IP network. In each cell one of the BS station is allocated. Additionally, we assumed that in each cell 100 Mbps were accessible. Each new call is a MT and it will move to one of the six neighbouring cells with equal probability. We assumed that there were two classes of traffic flow, <640 bits, 32 000 bps, 50 ms>, <1280 bits, 64 000 bps, 100 ms>, where each triple defines the burst size of the flow, an average rate of flow, and the end-to-end delay requirement for each class [5]. Each base station can service a traffic flow in any class.

Figures 4 and 5 show the call-blocking probability and the call-dropping probability for two schemes: with the LS-SVM bandwidth reservation method and with the fuzzy logic reservation controller. The depicted graphs illustrate that the proposed LS-SVM method can improve the call-blocking probability ca. by 30% for the low value of call arrival rate and ca. by 100%. for the the high value of call arrival rate, respectively. Analogously, the call-dropping probability is also improved. For the low value of a call arrival rate it is ca. 10% and for the low value of call arrival rate and for the high value of a call arrival it is ca. 30%.

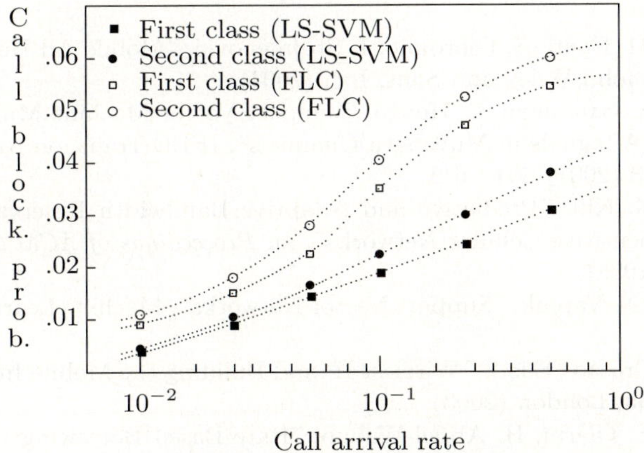

Fig. 4. Call-blocking probability versus call arrival rate

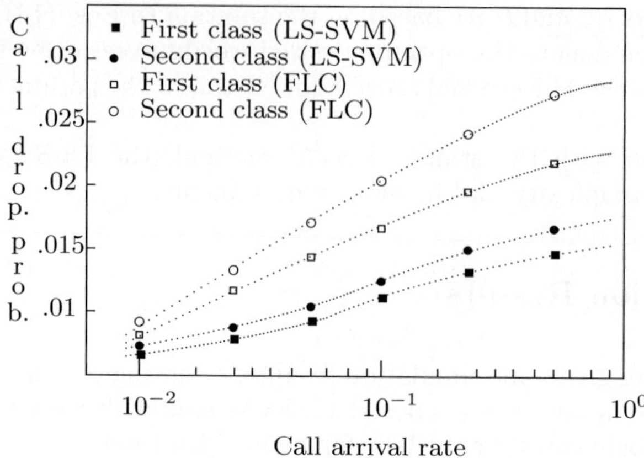

Fig. 5. Call-dropping probability versus call arrival rate

It can also be seen that the bandwidth reservation method is somewhat better for the little traffic flow stream than for the heavily traffic flow stream.

5   Conclusion

In this paper we have established a new scheme for bandwidth reservation in wireless IP networks. We have used the LS-SVM method to determinate the required bandwidth in neighbouring cells. The gained bandwidth reservation show that the LS-SVM method can be a good candidate to effectively improve handoff call-blocking probability and call-dropping probability. However, the investigated method will be compared with other methods of bandwidth reservation.

References

1. S. Basagni, M. Conti, S. Giordano, I. Stojmenović, "Mobile Ad Hoc Networking", IEEE Press, John Wiley and Sons, Inc. (2004).
2. S. Chen, A.K. Samingan, L. Hanzo, "Support Vector Machine Multiuser Receiver for DS-CDMA Signals in Multipath Channels", IEEE Trans. on Neural Networks, Vol. 12, No. 3 (2001) 604 - 611.
3. S. Choi, K.G. Kin, "Predictive and Adaptive Bandwidth Reservation for Handoffs in QoS-Sensitive Cellular Networks", in: *Proceedings of ACM SIGCOMM '98*, Vancouver (1998).
4. C. Cortes, V.N. Vapnik, "Support Vector Networks", Machine Learning, 20, (1995) 273 - 297.
5. S. Dixit, R. Prasad (Eds.), "Wireless IP and Building the Mobile Internet", Artech House, Boston, London (2003).
6. M. Ei-kadi, S. Olariu, H. Abdel-Wahab, "Rate-Based Borrowing Scheme for QoS Provisioning in Multimedia Wireless Networks", IEEE Trans. on Parallel and Distributed Systems, Vol. 13, No. 2 (2002) 156 - 166.

7. X. Gong, A. Kuh, "Support Vector Machine for Multiuser Detection in CDMA Communications", in: *The 33rd Asilomar Conference on Signals, Systems, and Computers*, Vol. 1 (1999) 680 - 684.

8. M. Hasegawa, G. Wu, M. Mizuno, "Applications of Nonlinear Prediction Methods to the Internet Traffic", in: *The 2001 IEEE International Symposium on Circuits and Systems*, Vol. 2 (2001) III-169 - III-172.

9. H. Kuhn, A. Tucker, "Nonlinear Programming", in: *Proceedings of the 2nd Berkeley Symposium on Mathematical Statistics and Probabilistics*, University of California Press (1951) 481 - 492.

10. G.-S. Kuo, P.-C. Ko, M.-L. Kuo, "A Probabilistic Resource Estimation and Semi-Reservation Scheme for Flow-Oriented Multimedia Wireless Networks", IEEE Communications Magazine (2001) 135 - 141.

11. J.-H. Lee, S.-U. Yoon, S.-K. Youm, C.-H. Kang, "An Adaptive Resource Allocation Mechanism Including Fast and Reliable Handoff in IP-Based 3G Wireless Networks", IEEE Personal Communications (2000) 42 - 47.

12. D.A. Levine, I.F. Akyildiz, M. Naghshineh, "A Resource Estimation and Call Admission Algorithm for Wireless Multimedia Networks Using the Shadow Cluster Concept", IEEE/ACM Trans. on Networking, Vol. 5, No. 1 (1997) 1 - 12.

13. T. Liu, P. Bahl, I. Chlamtac, "Mobility Modeling, Location Tracking, and Trajectory Prediction in Wireless ATM Networks", IEEE Journal on Selected Areas in Communications, Vol. 16, No. 6 (1998) 922 - 936.

14. S. Lu, V. Bharghavan, "Adaptive Resource Management Algorithm for Indoor Mobile Computing Environment", in: *Proceedings of ACM SIGCOMM '96*, Stanford, CA, Sept. (1996).

15. M. Naghshineh, M. Schwartz, "Distributed Call Admission Control in Mobile/Wireless Networks", IEEE Journal on Selected Areas in Communications, Vol. 14, No. 4 (1996) 711 - 717.

16. R. Ramjee, R. Nagarajan, D. Towsley, "On Optimal Call Admission Control in Cellular Networks", Wireless Networks Journal, Vol. 3, No. 1 (1997) 29 - 41.

17. Q. Ren, G. Ramamurthy, "A Real-Time Dynamic Connection Admission Controller Based on Traffic Modeling, Measurement and Fuzzy Logic Control", IEEE Journal on Selected Areas in Communications, Vol. 18, No. 2 (2000) 184 - 196.

18. J.A.K. Suykens, T. van Gestel, J. de Brabanter, B. de Moor, J. Vandewalle, "Least Squares Support Vector Machines", World Scientific, New Jersey, London, Singapore, Hong Kong (2002).

19. V.N. Vapnik, "The Nature of Statistical Learning Theory", Springer-Verlag, Berlin, Heidelberg, New York (1995).

20. V.N. Vapnik, "Statistical Learning Theory", John Wiley and Sons, (1998).

21. V.N. Vapnik, "The Support Vector Method of Function Estimation", in: J.A.K. Suykens, J. Vandewolle (Eds.), "Nonlinear Modeling: Advanced Black-box Techniques", Kluwer Academic Publishers, Boston (1998) pp. 55 - 85.

An Ontology-Based Intelligent Agent for Respiratory Waveform Classification

Chang-Shing Lee and Mei-Hui Wang

Department of Computer Science and Information Engineering
National University of Tainan, Tainan, Taiwan
leecs@mail.nutn.edu.tw

Abstract. This paper presents an ontology-based intelligent agent for respiretory waveform classification to help the medical staff with the judging the respiratory waveform from the ventilator. We present the *manual construction tool (MCT)*, the *respiratory waveform ontology (RWO)*, and the *intelligent classification agent (ICA)* to implement the classification of the respiratory waveform. The *MCT* allows the medical experts to construct and store the *fuzzy numbers* of respiratory waveforms to the *RWO*. When the *ICA* receives an input respiratory waveform (*IRW*), it will retrieve the *fuzzy numbers* from the *RWO* to carry out the classification task. Next, the *ICA* will send the classified results to the medical experts to make a confirmation and store the classified results to the *classified waveform repository (CWR)*. The experimental results show that our approach can classify the respiratory waveform effectively and efficiently.

1 Introduction

The research on the ontology has been spread widely to be critical components in the knowledge management, Semantic Web, business-to-business applications, and several other application areas [2]. For example, C. S. Lee *et al.* [8] proposed a fuzzy ontology application to news summarization, M. H. Burstein [4] presented a dynamic invocation of semantic web services using unfamiliar ontologies, A. Hameed *et al.* [6] presented an approach to acquire knowledge and construct multiple experts' ontologies in a uniform way, and R. Navigli *et al.* [9] presented an OntoLearn system for automated ontology learning to extract relevant domain terms from a corpus of text, relate them to appropriate concepts in a general-purpose ontology, and detect taxonomic and other semantic relations among the concepts. C. S. Lee *et al.* [7] proposed an intelligent fuzzy agent for meeting scheduling decision support system.

Currently, for long-term mechanical ventilators (LMVs) patients, the ventilator provides the physician with some vital information such as pressure-time waveform to assist in diagnosis. Besides, the medical staff often needs to spend much of the monitoring and making out a large number of information about patients such as medical history, medicine administered, and the physiological variables. But, for physiological variables, they are continuously generated over time, and generally correspond to physio-pathological processes that require rapid responses. So, P. F'elix *et al.* [5] proposed the FTP (Fuzzy Temporal Profile) model to represent and reason

M. Ali and R. Dapoigny (Eds.): IEA/AIE 2006, LNAI 4031, pp. 1240 – 1248, 2006.

on information concerning the evolution of a physical parameter, and then also study the applicability of this model in the recognition of signal patterns. In addition, because of the development of both the healthcare sciences as well as information technologies, the ICU units handle an ever-increasing amount of signals and parameters, so S. Barror *et al.* [1] proposed a patient supervision system that the fuzzy logic is playing in its designs.

In this paper, we present an ontology-based intelligent agent for respiratory waveform classification. The experimental results show that our approach can work efficiently and effectively for classifying the respiratory waveform. The remainder of this paper is organized as follows. In Section 2, we briefly present the structure of the respiratory waveform ontology. Section 3 introduces the structure of ontology-based intelligent agent for respiratory waveform classification. The experimental results are presented in Section 4. Finally, the conclusions are drawn in Section 5.

2   The Structure of Respiratory Waveform Ontology

In this section, first we briefly introduce the basic fuzzy notions for the *fuzzy number*. If one fuzzy set satisfies the normality and convexity, then this fuzzy set is called the *fuzzy number* [5]. For example, a *fuzzy number* π_C can be denoted by $C = (a,b,c,d), a \leq b \leq c \leq d$, where $[b,c]$ is *core*, $core(C) = \{v \in R \mid \pi_C(v) = 1\}$, and $]a,d[$ is *support*, $supp(C) = \{v \in R \mid \pi_C(v) > 0\}$ [10]. Then, we call a, b, c, and d are the *begin support, begin core, end core,* and *end support,* respectively [10]. Now we give the definition of the *fuzzy number* to generate the possibility distribution of the respiratory waveform slope. A *fuzzy number* $\tilde{M}$ is of *LR-type* if there exist reference functions L, R, and scalars $\alpha > 0$, $\beta > 0$ with

$$\mu_{\tilde{M}}(x) = \begin{cases} L\left(\dfrac{m-x}{\alpha}\right) & x \leq m \\ \\ R\left(\dfrac{x-m}{\beta}\right) & x \geq m \end{cases} \tag{1}$$

where m, called the means value of $\tilde{M}$, is a real number and α and β are called the left and right spreads, respectively. Symbolically $\tilde{M}$ is denoted by $(m, \alpha, \beta)_{LR}$ [11].

Second, we introduce the concepts of the ventilator waveform. Fig. 1 shows the typical *pressure-time* diagram under the volume-controlled and constant flow. From the Fig. 1, the airway *pressure* depends on the alveolar pressure and the total of all airway resistances, and it can be affected by the resistance and compliance values specific to the ventilator and the lung. On inspiration, intra-thoracic volume is increased; this lowers intra-pleural *pressure*, making it more negative and causing the lungs to expand and the air to enter [3]. Consequently, at the beginning of the inspiration, the *pressure* between the point A and B increases dramatically on account of the resistances in the system. Then, after the point B, the *pressure* increases in a

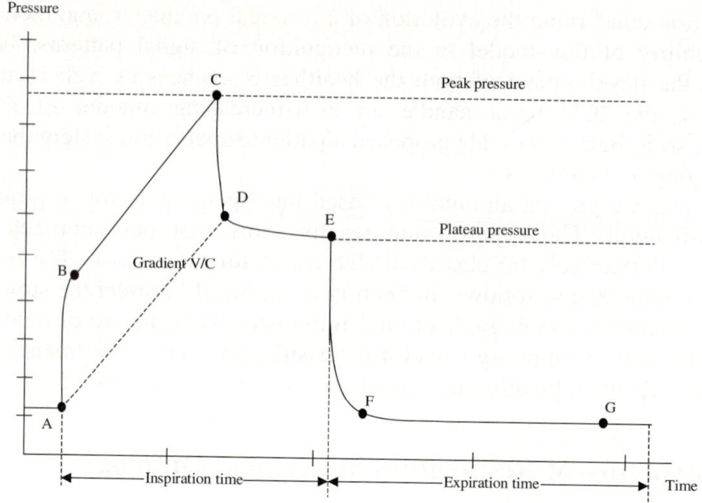

Fig. 1. Pressure-time diagram under the volume-controlled and constant flow

straight line until the peak *pressure* at the point C is reached. At the point C, the ventilator applies the set tidal volume and no further flow is delivered; therefore, the *pressure* quickly falls to the point D, the plateau *pressure*. Then, because of lung recruitment, the *pressure* lightly drops to the point E. In addition, the slope of line A-D will affect the static compliance and it is a key feature when examining the

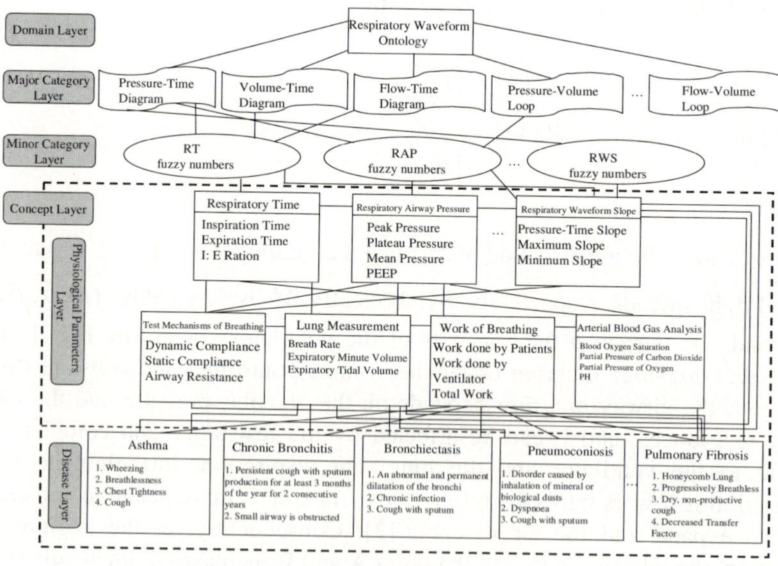

Fig. 2. The structure of the respiratory waveform ontology

patients. On expiration, the muscles of the chest wall relax and the lungs return to their original size by elastic recoil, with the expulsion of air. As a result, the *pressure* exponentially falls to point F, the expiratory-end pressure (EEP) or baseline pressure.

Finally, we introduce the structure of the respiratory waveform ontology, shown as Fig. 2. Included the *domain layer*, *major category layer*, *minor category layer* and *concept layer*, the respiratory waveform ontology is an extended domain ontology of the [8]. The domain name is respiratory waveform ontology, and it consists of several *major categories* such as the pressure-time diagram, volume-time diagram, pressure-time loop, flow-volume loop, and so on. In the *minor category layer*, there are a couple of categories such as the *respiratory time (RT) fuzzy numbers*, *respiratory airway pressure (RAP) fuzzy numbers*, and *respiratory waveform slope (RWS) fuzzy numbers*, and so on. The *concepts layer* is divided into two sub-layers, the *physiological parameters layer* and *disease layer*. The *physiological parameters layer* contains the parameters of the *fuzzy numbers*, such as the *respiratory time, respiratory airway pressure, respiratory waveform slope*, and so on. And, the *disease layer* is with these *fuzzy numbers* like asthma, chronic bronchitis, pulmonary fibrosis, and so on.

3   The Structure of Ontology-Based Intelligent Agent for Respiratory Waveform Classification

In this section, we briefly describe the functionality of the ontology-based intelligent agent for respiratory waveform classification, shown in Fig. 3. There are the *manual construction tool (MCT)*, the *respiratory waveform ontology (RWO)*, and the *intelligent agent (ICA)* proposed to implement the classification of the respiratory waveform. The *MCT* allows the medical experts to construct the parameters of the *standard respiratory waveform (SRW)* such as *RT fuzzy numbers*, and *RAP fuzzy*

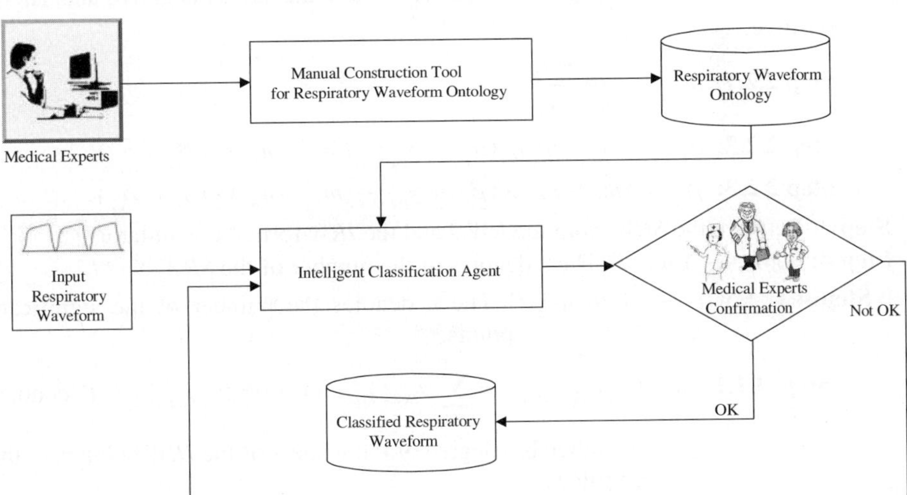

Fig. 3. The structure of the ontology-based intelligent agent for respiratory waveform classification

numbers and then the *respiratory waveform slope* (RWS) *fuzzy numbers* is also automatically constructed. After completing the construction, all of these parameters of the *SRW* are restored to the *RWO*. If the *ICA* receives an *IRW*, based on the information restored in the *RWO*, the *ICA* starts carrying out the classification of the respiratory waveform. Next, the *ICA* sends the classified results to the medical experts to make a confirmation. If the classified results are passed the verification of the medical experts, then they are stored to the *classified waveform repository* (CWR). Otherwise, the *IRW* is sent back to the *ICA* to work again. Below is the algorithm for the *ICA*.

Algorithm for the Intelligent Classification Agent

Step 1: Retrieve the *fuzzy numbers* $\tilde{p}_A$, $\tilde{t}_A$, $\tilde{p}_B$, and $\tilde{t}_B$ from *RWO*

Step 1.1: $\tilde{p}_A = (n_{p_A}, r_{p_A}, \delta_{p_A})_{LR}$

Step 1.2: $\tilde{t}_A = (n_{t_A}, r_{t_A}, \delta_{t_A})_{LR}$

Step 1.3: $\tilde{p}_B = (m_{p_B}, \alpha_{p_B}, \beta_{p_B})_{LR}$

Step 1.4: $\tilde{t}_B = (n_{t_B}, r_{t_B}, \delta_{t_B})_{LR}$

Step 2: Generate $\tilde{s}_{AB} = (m_{s_{AB}}, \alpha_{s_{AB}}, \beta_{s_{AB}})_{LR}$

Step 2.1: Generate the positive slope $\tilde{s}_{AB}$ where the $\Delta\tilde{p}$ is positive and $\Delta\tilde{t}$ is positive.

Step 2.1.1: $m_{s_{AB}} = \dfrac{m_{p_B} - n_{p_A}}{m_{t_B} - n_{t_A}}$

Step 2.1.2: $\alpha_{s_{AB}} = (m_{p_B} - n_{p_A}) \times (\alpha_{t_B} + \delta_{t_A}) + (m_{t_B} - n_{t_A}) \times (\alpha_{p_B} + \delta_{p_A})$

Step 2.1.3: $\beta_{s_{AB}} = (m_{p_B} - n_{p_A}) \times (\beta_{t_B} + \gamma_{t_A}) + (m_{t_B} - n_{t_A}) \times (\beta_{p_B} + \gamma_{p_A})$

Step 2.2: Generate the negative slope $\tilde{s}_{AB}$ where the $\Delta\tilde{p}$ is negative and $\Delta\tilde{t}$ is positive.

Step 2.2.1: $m_{s_{AB}} = \dfrac{m_{p_B} - n_{p_A}}{m_{t_B} - n_{t_A}}$

Step 2.2.2: $\alpha_{s_{AB}} = (m_{t_B} - n_{t_A}) \times (\alpha_{p_B} + \delta_{p_A}) - (m_{p_B} - n_{p_A}) \times (\beta_{t_B} + \gamma_{t_A})$

Step 2.2.3: $\beta_{s_{AB}} = (m_{t_B} - n_{t_A}) \times (\beta_{p_B} + \gamma_{p_A}) - (m_{p_B} - n_{p_A}) \times (\alpha_{t_B} + \delta_{t_A})$

Step 3: Retrieve the *SRW* from the *RWO* and the *IRW* form the ventilator

Step 4: For $k \leftarrow 1$ to c /* The c denotes of the number of the *SRW* S_k.*/

Step 4.1: For $j \leftarrow 1$ to $n\text{-}1$ /* The n denotes the number of the significant points.*/

Step 4.1.1: $total\_\mu_{IRW \in Type\, S_k} = \sum_{j=1}^{n-1} \mu_{IRW \in Type\, S_k}(x_j)$ /* $\mu_{IRW \in Type\, S_k}(x)$ denotes the membership degree of the value x of the *IRW* belongs to the k-th *SRW Type* S_k.

Step 4.2: Normalize the $total\_\mu_{IRW \in Type\, S_k}$ and save it to $\overline{\mu}_{IRW \in Type\, S_k}(x)$.

$$\overline{\mu}_{IRW \in Type\, S_k}(x) = \frac{total\_\mu_{IRW \in Type\, S_k}}{\sum_{j=1}^{n} MAX\{\mu_{IRW \in Type\, S_k}(x_j)\}}$$

Step 5: Run the matching task for *IRW* and *SRW Type1*

If
$$\{(\overline{\mu}_{IRW \in Type\, S_1}(x_{slope}) > \sigma_{S_{AB}}) \wedge (\bigcap_{j=1}^{n}[\mu_{\tilde{p}_j}(x_{p_j})] > \sigma_{p_1}) \wedge$$

$$(\bigcap_{j=1}^{n}[\mu_{\tilde{t}_j}(x_{t_j})] > \sigma_{t_1})\}$$

Then $\mu_{f_1(A)}(y_1) = \bigcap[\overline{\mu}_{IRW \in Type\, S_1}(x_{slope}), \bigcap_{j=1}^{n}[\mu_{\tilde{p}_j}(x_{p_j})], \bigcap_{j=1}^{n}[\mu_{\tilde{t}_j}(x_{t_j})]]$

Step 6: Run the matching task for *IRW* and *SRW Type2*

If
$$\{(\overline{\mu}_{IRW \in Type\, S_2}(x_{slope}) > \sigma_{S_{AB}}) \wedge \qquad (\bigcap_{j=1}^{n}[\mu_{\tilde{p}_j}(x_{p_j})] > \sigma_{p_2}) \wedge$$

$$(\bigcap_{j=1}^{n}[\mu_{\tilde{t}_j}(x_{t_j})] > \sigma_{t_2})\}$$

Then $\mu_{f_2(A)}(y_2) = \bigcap[\overline{\mu}_{IRW \in Type\, S_2}(x_{slope}), \bigcap_{j=1}^{n}[\mu_{\tilde{p}_j}(x_{p_j})], \bigcap_{j=1}^{n}[\mu_{\tilde{t}_j}(x_{t_j})]]$

Step 7: End.

4 Experimental Results

To test the performance of the ontology-based intelligent agent for respiratory wave-form classification, we set up a test experimental environment at National University of Tainan. First, we select two types of respiratory waveforms as the *SRW Type1* and *SRW Type2* denoting the characteristic of the typical *normal waveform* and *highpressure waveform,* respectively. Table1 shows the parameters of *SRW Type1* and *SRW Type2* defined by the medical staff. And, all of the parameters of signification points will be stored to the *RWO.* Second, we design an interface to allow the medical experts to define or tune the *RT fuzzy numbers* and *RAP fuzzy numbers* for the respiratory waveform. Then, the *RWS fuzzy numbers* will be constructed auto-matically. Fig. 4 shows the *MCT* for the *SRW Type1.* Finally, in order to evaluate the accuracy of the *ICA,* we choose the *precision* and *recall* as our criteria. Fig. 5 (a) and Fig. 5 (b) show the *precision* and *recall* versus the number of

Table 1. The parameters of significant points for four types of the *SRW*

SRW	Significant Point (Time: sec, Pressure: cmH2O)						
	A	B	C	D	E	F	G
Type1	(0.2, 6)	(0.3, 22)	(1.1, 44)	(1.2, 31)	(1.9, 29)	(2.2, 6)	(4.4, 6)
Type2	(0.2, 6)	(0.3, 22)	(1.1, 60)	(1.2, 31)	(1.9, 29)	(2.2, 6)	(4.4, 6)

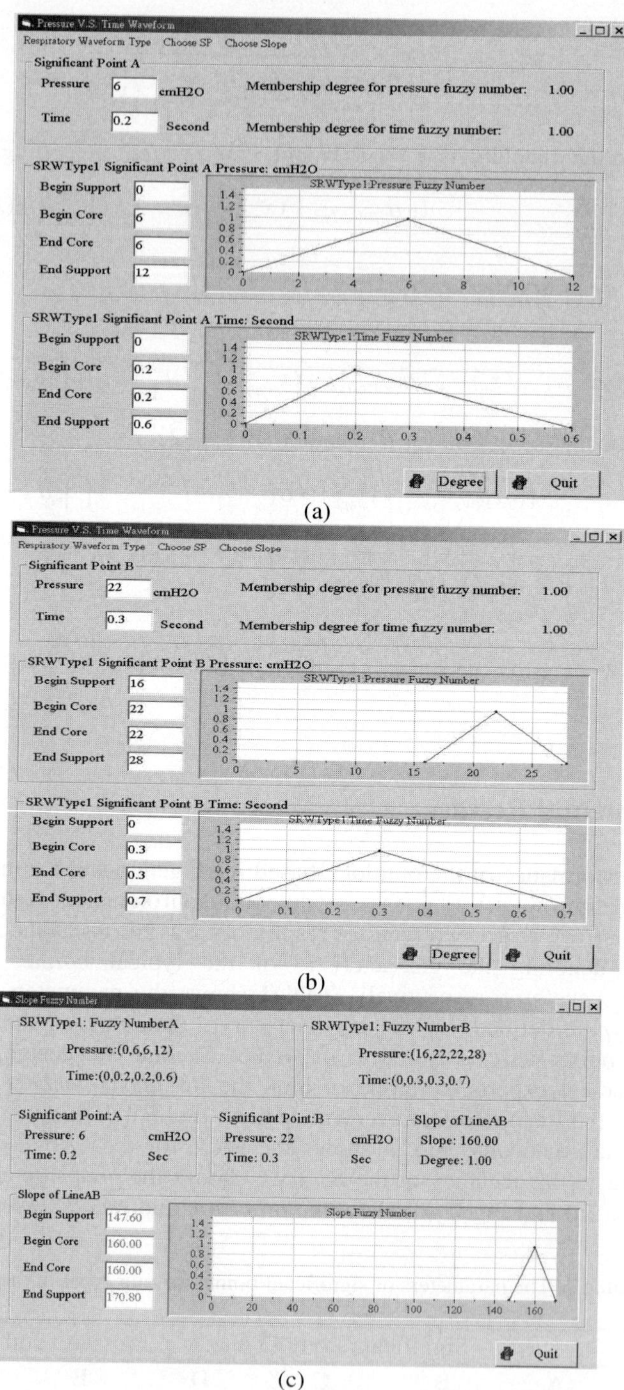

(a)

(b)

(c)

Fig. 4. The manual construction tool of the *RT*, *RAP*, and *RWS fuzzy numbers* for the *SRW Type1*

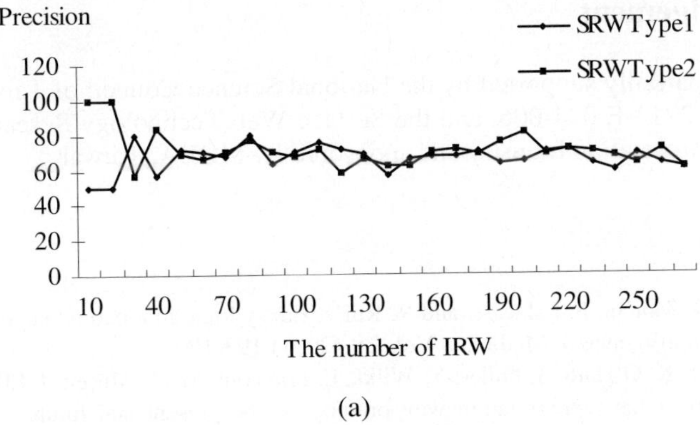

(a)

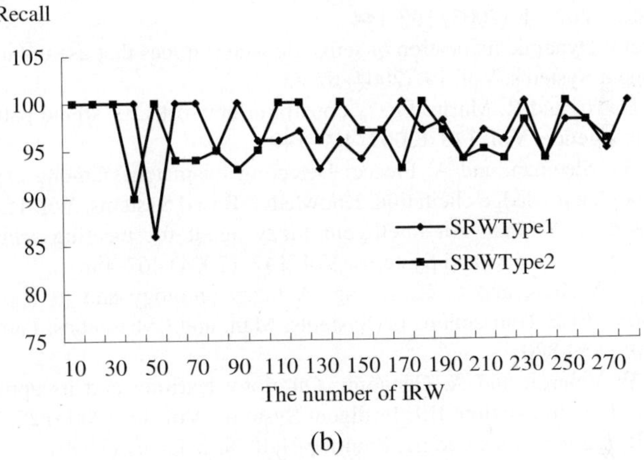

(b)

Fig. 5. The *precision* and *recall* of the *IRW* for the *SRW Type 1* and *SRW Type 2*

IRW curve, respectively, when the threshold $\sigma_{s_{AB}}$ is 0.75. We observe that the average *precision* and *recall* for *SRW Type1* is about 64% and 96%, respectively. And the average *precision* and *recall* for *SRW Type2* is about 68% and 96%, respectively. The experimental results show that our approach can work effectively.

5 Conclusions

In this paper, we present an ontology-based intelligent agent, including *MCT*, *RWO*, and *ICA*, for respiratory waveform classification to help the medical staff with the judging the respiratory waveform from the ventilator. From the experimental results, we observe that the proposed ontology-based intelligent agent applied to classify the respiratory waveform is effectively and efficiently. In the future, we will extend our method to process more different types of *IRW* and semi-automatically construct the *RWO*.

Acknowledgement

This work is partially supported by the National Science Council of Taiwan under the grant NSC94-2213-E-024-006, and the Service Web Technology Research Project of Institute for Information Industry and sponsored by MOEA, Taiwan.

References

1. S. Barro, R. Mar'in, F. Palacios, and R. Rui'z: Fuzzy logic in a patient supervision system, Artificial Intelligence in Medicine. Vol. 21. (2001) 193-199
2. C. Brewster, K. O'Hara, S. Fuller, Y. Wilks, E. Franconi, M. A. Musen. J. Ellman, and S. B. Shum: Knowledge representation with ontologies: the present and future. Vol. 19. (2004) 72-81
3. S. M. Burns: Working with respiratory waveforms: How to Use Bedside Graphics. AACN Clinical Issues. Vol. 14. (2003) 133-144
4. M. H, Burstein: Dynamic invocation of semantic web services that use unfamiliar ontologies. IEEE Intelligent Systems. Vol. 19. (2004) 67-73
5. P. Félix, S. Barro, and R. Marín: Fuzzy constraint networks for signal pattern recognition. Artificial Intelligence. Vol. 148. (2003) 103-140
6. A. Hameed, D. Sleeman, and A. Preece: Detecting mismatches among experts' ontologies acquired through knowledge elicitation. Knowledge-Based Systems. Vol. 15. (2002) 265-273
7. C. S. Lee and C. Y. Pan: An intelligent fuzzy agent for meeting scheduling decision support system. Fuzzy Sets and Systems. Vol. 142. (2004) 467-488
8. C. S. Lee, Z. W. Jian, and L. K. Huang: A fuzzy ontology and its application to news summarization. IEEE Transactions on Systems, Man, and Cybernetics, Part B: Cybernetics. Vol. 35. (2005) 859-880
9. R. Navigli, P. Velardi, and A. Gangemi: Ontology learning and its application to auto-mated terminology translation. IEE Intlligent Systems. Vol. 18. (2003) 22-31
10. J. Yen, and R. Langari: Fuzzy logic. Prentice-Hall, New Jersey (1999)
11. H. -J. Zimmermann: Fuzzy set theory and its applications. Kluwer, Boston (1991)

A New Inductive Learning Method for Multilabel Text Categorization

Yu-Chuan Chang[1], Shyi-Ming Chen[2], and Churn-Jung Liau[3]

[1] Department of Computer Science and Information Engineering
National Taiwan University of Science and Technology
Taipei, Taiwan, R.O.C.
D9315003@mail.ntust.edu.tw
[2] Department of Computer Science and Information Engineering
National Taiwan University of Science and Technology
Taipei, Taiwan, R.O.C.
smchen@et.ntust.edu.tw
[3] Institute of Information Science, Academia Sinica
Taipei, Taiwan, R.O.C.
liaucj@iis.sinica.edu.tw

Abstract. In this paper, we present a new inductive learning method for multi-label text categorization. The proposed method uses a mutual information measure to select terms and constructs document descriptor vectors for each category based on these terms. These document descriptor vectors form a document descriptor matrix. It also uses the document descriptor vectors to construct a document-similarity matrix based on the "cosine similarity measure". It then constructs a term-document relevance matrix by applying the inner product of the document descriptor matrix to the document similarity matrix. The proposed method infers the degree of relevance of the selected terms to construct the category descriptor vector of each category. Then, the relevance score between each category and a testing document is calculated by applying the inner product of its category descriptor vector to the document descriptor vector of the testing document. The maximum relevance score L is then chosen. If the relevance score between a category and the testing document divided by L is not less than a predefined threshold value λ between zero and one, then the document is classified into that category. We also compare the classification accuracy of the proposed method with that of the existing learning methods (i.e., Find Similar, Naïve Bayes, Bayes Nets and Decision Trees) in terms of the break-even point of micro-averaging for categorizing the "Reuters-21578 Aptè split" data set. The proposed method gets a higher average accuracy than the existing methods.

1 Introduction

As the amount of information in the Internet is growing so rapidly, it is difficult for users to find desired information unless it is organized and managed well. Text categorization (TC) is a major research topic in machine learning (ML) and information retrieval (IR) to help users obtain desired information. A document can belong to a

M. Ali and R. Dapoigny (Eds.): IEA/AIE 2006, LNAI 4031, pp. 1249–1258, 2006.

single category, multiple categories, or not belong to any category. The goal of automatic text categorization is to utilize categorized training documents to construct text classifiers, which are then used to classify new documents into appropriate categories automatically. Several machine learning methods have been developed to deal with the text categorization problem, e.g., regression models [10], [17], nearest neighbor classification [16], [18], Bayesian probabilistic approaches [1], [12], [14], decision trees [1], [8], [12], inductive rule learning [1], [6], neural networks [18] and on-line learning [6].

In this paper, we present a new inductive learning method for multilabel text categorization. It uses the mutual information measure [11] for term selection and constructs document descriptor vectors for each category based on the selected terms. These document descriptor vectors form a document descriptor matrix and they are also used to construct a document-similarity matrix based on the cosine similarity measure [2]. It then constructs a term-document relevance matrix by applying the inner product of the document descriptor matrix to the document-similarity matrix. It infers the degree of relevance of the selected terms to construct the category descriptor vector of each category. The relevance score between each category and a testing document is calculated by applying the inner product of its category descriptor vector to the document descriptor vector of the testing document. The maximum relevance score L is then chosen. If the relevance score between a category and the testing document divided by L is not less than a predefined threshold value λ, where $\lambda \in [0, 1]$, then the document is classified into that category. We also compare the classification accuracy of the proposed method with that of the existing learning methods (i.e., Find Similar [13], Decision Trees [5], Naïve Bayes and Bayes Nets [14]) in terms of the break-even point of micro-averaging for categorizing the "Reuters-21578 Aptè split 10 categories" data set [21]. The experimental results show that the proposed method outperforms the existing methods.

2 Preliminaries

Machine learning systems deal with categorization problems by representing samples in terms of features in order to apply machine learning methods to text categorization, documents must be transformed into feature representations. The vector space model [13] is widely used in information retrieval for the representation of documents. In the vector space model, a document is represented as a document descriptor vector of terms and every element in the vector denotes the weight of a term with respect to the document. The learning methods presented in [10] and [17] calculate the tf $\times$ idf term weight for each term. The learning methods presented in [1], [8] and [12] use a binary weight 1 or 0 to represent each index term.

The dimension of a term's space is an important research topic in text categorization. With a high dimension, a classifier over fits training samples, which may be good for classification purposes, but it is not feasible for classifying previously unseen testing samples. The purpose of term selection is to choose relevant terms for document indexing that yield the highest accuracy rates. The simplest term selection method [19] is based on the frequency of a term's occurrence in documents, where only terms that occur in the highest number of documents are retained. Other term selection methods are based on information-theoretic functions, such as the DIA association factor [9], information gain measure [6], [12], chi-square measure [4], and mutual information measure [8], [19]. In recent years, an increasing number of categorization methods have applied the mutual information (MI) measure in term selection [3], [7]. The mutual information score between term t_i and category c is defined by

$$MI(t_i, c) = p(t_i, c) \log_2 \frac{p(t_i, c)}{p(t_i)p(c)}, \tag{1}$$

where $p(t_i, c) = N_C(t_i)/N_C$, $p(t_i) = N(t_i)/N$, $p(c) = N_C/N$, $N_C(t_i)$ denotes the number of occurrences of term t_i in category c, N_C denotes the number of occurrences of all terms in category c, $N(t_i)$ denotes the number of occurrences of term t_i in the collection, and N denotes the number of occurrences of all terms in the collection.

There are some rules for determining the threshold value in multilabel text categorization [15], [16]. The threshold value is used when a document may belong to multiple categories. In this paper, we use a variant of the rank-based thresholding (R-cut) measure [16] to assign text documents into categories. We use the following criterion for multilabel text categorization:

$$\frac{Score(c_i, d)}{L} \geq \lambda, \tag{2}$$

where $Score(c_i, d)$ denotes the relevance score between category c_i and document d, $L = \max_j Score(c_j, d)$ denotes the maximum relevance score, λ is a threshold value that controls the degree of multilabel categorization, and $\lambda \in [0, 1]$. If the relevance score between category c_j and document d divided by L is not less than the threshold value λ, where $\lambda \in [0, 1]$, then the document d is classified into category c_i. The lower the threshold value λ, the more categories a document may belong to. If $\lambda = 0$, then the document belongs to all categories. Thus, the threshold value λ provides us some flexibility to deal with multilabel text categorization problem.

In the following, we briefly review some classifiers [8], namely, Find Similar [13], Decision Trees [5], Naïve Bayes and Bayes Nets [14].

(1) **Find Similar Classifier** [13]: The Find Similar method is a variant of Rocchio's method for relevance feedback, which is often used to expand queries based on the user's relevance feedback. In text classification, Rocchio's method calculates the weight w_t of a term t as follows:

$$w_t = \alpha \cdot w_t + \beta \cdot \frac{\sum_{i \in pos} w_{t,i}}{N_{pos}} + \gamma \cdot \frac{\sum_{i \in neg} w_{t,i}}{N_{neg}}, \tag{3}$$

where w_t denotes the weight of term t, N_{pos} denotes the number of positive documents in the category, N_{neg} denotes the number of negative documents in the category, and α, β and γ are the adjusting parameters. The method finds the representative centroid of the positive documents of each category and classifies a new document by comparing it with the centroid of each category by using a specific similarity measure. In [8],

Dumais *et al.* let $\alpha = 0$, $\beta = 1$ and $\gamma = 0$ and use the Jaccard similarity measure to calculate the degree of similarity between the centroid of each category and a testing document.

(2) **Decision Trees Classifier** [5]: A decision tree (DT) text classifier is a tree in which the internal nodes are labeled by terms, the branches are labeled by weights, and the leaves are labeled by categories. The classifier categorizes a testing document d_j by recursively test the weights of its terms (i.e., the internal nodes) until a leaf node is reached. The label of the leaf node is then assigned to d_j. The main advantage of the decision tree method is that it is easily interpretable by humans.

(3) **Naïve Bayes Classifier** [12]: The Naïve Bayes (NB) classifier (also called the Probabilistic Classifier) is a popular approach for handling classification problems. It uses the joint probability of terms and categories to calculate the probability that the terms of a document belong to certain categories, and then applies the Bayesian Theory to calculate the probability of the document d_j belonging to category c_i:

$$P(d_j \mid c_i) = \prod_{k=1}^{n} P(w_{kj} \mid c_i), \tag{4}$$

$$P(w_{kj} \mid c_i) = \frac{P(w_{kj}, c_i)}{P(c_i)}, \tag{5}$$

where $P(d_j \mid c_i)$ denotes the probability of document d_j belonging to category c_i; $P(w_{kj} \mid c_i)$ denotes the probability of term t_k of document d_j belonging to category c_i, and n denotes the number of terms belonging to document d_j and category c_i. The naïve part of the NB method is the assumption of term independence. This makes NB classifiers far more efficient than non-naïve Bayes methods due to the fact that there is no need to consider the conditional probabilities of terms.

(4) **Bayes Nets Classifier** [14]: In [14], Sahami utilizes the Bayesian network for classification, which relaxes the restrictive assumptions of the Naïve Bayes classifier. A 2-dependence Bayesian classifier allows for the probability that each feature is directly influenced by the appearance/non-appearance of at most two other features.

3   A New Inductive Learning Method for Multilabel Text Categorization

In this section, we present a new inductive learning method for mulitlabel text categorization. The mutual information measure shown in Eq. (1) is used to select the top K terms that have the highest MI scores for a category. Assume there are N documents and K selected terms in category c. We use a K $\times$ N document descriptor matrix to represent the binary weights of the K selected terms in each document. A column in the document descriptor matrix is a document descriptor vector based on the K selected terms. For example, assume that there are 5 documents d_1, d_2, d_3, d_4, d_5 and 4 selected terms t_1, t_2, t_3, t_4 in category c. Fig. 1 shows an example of a 4 $\times$ 5 document descriptor matrix A. Each column of the document descriptor matrix A represents the document descriptor vector of a document. For example, from the second column of the document descriptor matrix A, we can see the document descriptor vector $\overline{d_2}$ of the document d_2, where $\overline{d_2} = \begin{bmatrix} 1 & 0 & 1 & 0 \end{bmatrix}$. It indicates that the terms t_1 and t_3 are appearing in the document d_2 and the terms t_2 and t_4 are not appearing in the document d_2.

$$A = \begin{array}{c} \\ t_1 \\ t_2 \\ t_3 \\ t_4 \end{array} \begin{array}{ccccc} d_1 & d_2 & d_3 & d_4 & d_5 \\ \begin{bmatrix} 1 & 1 & 0 & 1 & 0 \\ 1 & 0 & 1 & 0 & 0 \\ 1 & 1 & 1 & 0 & 1 \\ 1 & 0 & 1 & 0 & 1 \end{bmatrix} \end{array}.$$

Fig. 1. Document descriptor matrix A

We use the "cosine similarity measure" [2] to construct a document-similarity matrix S, shown as follows:

$$S(i, j) = \frac{A(i) \cdot A(j)}{\|A(i)\| \times \|A(j)\|}, \tag{6}$$

where the value of $S(i, j)$ indicates the degree of similarity between document d_i and document d_j, $S(i, j) \in [0, 1]$, and $A(i)$ and $A(j)$ denote the ith and the jth column vectors of the document descriptor matrix A, respectively. For the document descriptor matrix A shown in Fig. 1, we can get its document-similarity matrix S, as shown in Fig. 2.

$$S = \begin{array}{c} \\ d_1 \\ d_2 \\ d_3 \\ d_4 \\ d_5 \end{array} \begin{array}{ccccc} d_1 & d_2 & d_3 & d_4 & d_5 \\ \begin{bmatrix} 1 & 1/\sqrt{2} & \sqrt{3}/2 & 1/2 & 1/\sqrt{2} \\ 1/\sqrt{2} & 1 & 1/\sqrt{6} & 1/\sqrt{2} & 1/2 \\ \sqrt{3}/2 & 1/\sqrt{6} & 1 & 0 & 2/\sqrt{6} \\ 1/2 & 1/\sqrt{2} & 0 & 1 & 0 \\ 1/\sqrt{2} & 1/2 & 2/\sqrt{6} & 0 & 1 \end{bmatrix} \end{array}.$$

Fig. 2. Document-similarity matrix S

We can obtain the term-document relevance matrix R by applying the inner product of the document descriptor matrix A to the document-similarity matrix S, shown as follows:

$$R = A \cdot S, \tag{7}$$

where the value of $R(i, j)$ denotes the relevance degree of term t_i with respect to document d_j. Therefore, for the above example, we can get the term-document relevance matrix R, as shown in Fig. 3.

$$R = \begin{array}{c} \\ t_1 \\ t_2 \\ t_3 \\ t_4 \end{array} \begin{array}{ccccc} d_1 & d_2 & d_3 & d_4 & d_5 \\ \begin{bmatrix} 2.2 & 2.4 & 1.3 & 2.2 & 1.2 \\ 1.9 & 1.1 & 1.9 & 0.5 & 1.5 \\ 3.3 & 2.6 & 3.1 & 1.2 & 3 \\ 2.6 & 1.6 & 2.7 & 0.5 & 2.5 \end{bmatrix} \end{array}.$$

Fig. 3. Term-document relevance matrix R

We use Eq. (8) to get the category descriptor vector $\overline{v}_c$ for category c,

$$\overline{v}_c = R \cdot \overline{1}, \tag{8}$$

where $\overline{1} = [1, 1, ..., 1]^{\mathrm{T}}$. Thus, for the above example, we can get

$$\overline{v}_c = R \cdot \overline{1} = R \cdot \begin{bmatrix} 1 & 1 & 1 & 1 \end{bmatrix}^{\mathrm{T}} = \begin{bmatrix} 9.3 & 6.9 & 13.2 & 9.9 \end{bmatrix}^{\mathrm{T}}.$$

Then, we use the weight-averaged method to normalize $\overline{v}_c$. Thus, for the above example, $\overline{v}_c$ is normalized into $\begin{bmatrix} 0.24 & 0.17 & 0.34 & 0.25 \end{bmatrix}$. Finally, we refine the weight v_{c_i} of the ith term in the category descriptor vector $\overline{v}_c$ into w_{c_i} to obtain the refined category descriptor vector $\overline{w}_c$, where

$$w_{c_i} = v_{c_i} \times \log_2 \frac{|C|}{cf_i}, \tag{9}$$

w_{c_i} denotes the refined weight of the ith term in the refined category descriptor vector $\overline{w}_c$, $|C|$ denotes the number of categories, and cf_i denotes the number of category descriptor vectors containing term t_i. This refinement reduces the weights of the terms that appear in most of the categories and increases the weights of the terms that only appear in a few categories.

Assume that the document descriptor vector of a testing document d_{new} is $\overline{d}_{new}$. We can then apply the inner product to calculate the relevance score $Score(c, d_{new})$ of category c with respect to the testing document d_{new} as follows:

$$Score(c, d_{new}) = \overline{d}_{new} \cdot \overline{w}_c. \tag{10}$$

We calculate the relevance score of each category with respect to d_{new}, rank these relevance scores, and then assign d_{new} to multiple categories according to Eq. (2). In other words, we choose the maximum relevance score L among them. If the relevance score between a category and the testing document divided by L is not less than a predefined threshold value λ, where $\lambda \in [0, 1]$, then the document is classified into that category.

4   Experimental Results

We have implemented the proposed multilabel text categorization method to classify the "Reuters-21578 Aptè split 10 categories" data set [21] using Delphi Version 5.0 on a Pentium 4 PC. The "Aptè split 10 categories" data set contains the 10 top-sized categories obtained from the "Reuters-21578 Aptè split" data set [20], where each category has at least 100 training documents for training a classifier. We chose the "Aptè split 10 categories" data set as our experimental data set, because it accounts 75% of the "Reuters-21578 Aptè split" data set. Table 1 shows the category names of "Aptè split 10 categories", the number of training samples for each category, and the number of testing samples for each category. There are totally 6490 training documents and 2547 testing documents in the "Aptè split 10 categories" data set.

Table 1. The number of training and testinging samples for each category of the "Aptè split 10 categories" data set

Category Names	Number of Training samples	Number of Testing samples
Earn	2877	1087
Acq	1650	719
Money-fx	538	179
Grain	433	149
Crude	389	189
Trade	369	118
Interest	347	131
Wheat	212	71
Ship	197	89
Corn	182	56

Several evaluation criteria for dealing with classification problems have been used in text categorization [15], [16]. The most widely used measures are based on the definitions of precision and recall. If a sample is classified into a category, we call it "positive" with respect to that category. Otherwise, we call it "negative". In this paper, we use the following micro-averaging method [15] to evaluate the recall and the precision of the proposed method, where

$$\text{Recall} = \frac{\sum_{i=1}^{|C|} TP_i}{\sum_{i=1}^{|C|} TP_i + \sum_{i=1}^{|C|} FN_i}, \tag{11}$$

$$\text{Precision} = \frac{\sum_{i=1}^{|C|} TP_i}{\sum_{i=1}^{|C|} TP_i + \sum_{i=1}^{|C|} FP_i}, \tag{12}$$

TP_i denotes the number of correctly classified positive samples for category c_i, FN_i denotes the number of incorrectly classified negative samples for category c_i, FP_i denotes the number of incorrectly classified negative samples for category c_i, and $|C|$ denotes the number of categories.

If the values of the precision and the recall of a classifier can be tuned to the same value, then the value is called the break-even point (BEP) of the system [12]. BEP has been widely used in text categorization evaluations. If the values of the precision and the recall are not exactly equal, we use the average of the nearest precision and recall values as the BEP.

Based on the mutual information measure [11] for term selection, we select the top 300 terms for training classifiers. Table 2 compares the break-even point of the proposed method with those of four existing learning methods [8], namely, Find Similar, Decision Trees, Naïve Bayes and Bayes Nets. From Table 2, we can see that the proposed method gets a higher average accuracy than the existing methods.

Table 2. Breakeven performance for Reuters-21578 Aptè split 10 categories

Methods / Category	Find Similar	Naïve Bayes	Bayes Nets	Decision Trees	The Proposed Method ($\lambda = 0.87$)
Earn	92.9 %	95.9 %	95.8 %	97.8 %	97.5 %
Acq	64.7 %	87.8 %	88.3 %	89.7 %	95.1 %
Money-fx	46.7 %	56.6 %	58.8 %	66.2 %	79.2 %
Grain	67.5 %	78.8 %	81.4 %	85.0 %	84.7 %
Crude	70.1 %	79.5 %	79.6 %	85.0 %	84.4 %
Trade	65.1 %	63.9 %	69.0 %	72.5 %	85 %
Interest	63.4 %	64.9 %	71.3 %	67.1 %	81 %
Ship	49.2 %	85.4 %	84.4 %	74.2 %	85.4 %
Wheat	68.9 %	69.7 %	82.7 %	92.5 %	79.8 %
Corn	48.2 %	65.3 %	76.4 %	91.8 %	78.2 %
Average	64.6 %	81.5 %	85 %	88.4 %	91.3 %

5   Conclusions

In this paper, we have presented a new inductive learning method for multilabel text categorization. The proposed method uses a mutual information measure for term selection and constructs document descriptor vectors for each category based on the selected terms. These document descriptor vectors form a document descriptor matrix and they are also used to construct a document-similarity matrix based on the cosine similarity measure. It then constructs a term-document relevance matrix by applying the inner product of the document descriptor matrix to the document-similarity matrix. The proposed method infers the degree of relevance of the selected terms to construct the category descriptor vector of each category. The relevance score between each category and a testing document is calculated by applying the inner product of its category descriptor vector to the document descriptor vector of the testing document. The maximum relevance score L is then chosen. If the relevance score between a category and the testing document divided by L is not less than a predefined threshold value λ, where $\lambda \in [0, 1]$, then the document is classified into that category. From the experimental results shown in Table 2, we can see that the proposed method gets a higher average accuracy than the existing methods.

Acknowledgements

This work was supported in part by the National Science Council, Republic of China, under Grant NSC 94-2213-E-011-003.

References

[1] Aptè, C., Damerau, F.J., Weiss, S.M.: Automatic Learning of Decision Rules for Text Categorization. ACM Transactions on Information Systems 1 (1997) 233–251

[2] Baeza-Yates, R., Ribeiro-Neto, B.: Modern Information Retrieval. ACM Press, New York (1999)

[3] Bekkerman, R., Ran, E.Y., Tishby, N., Winter, Y.: Distributional Word Clusters vs. Words for Text Categorization. Journal of Machine Learning Research (2003) 1183–1208

[4] Caropreso, M.F., Matwin, S., Sebastiani, F.: A Learner-Independent Evaluation of the Usefulness of Statistical Phrases for Automated Text Categorization. In: Chin, A.G. (eds.): Text Databases and Document Management: Theory and Practice. Idea Group Publishing, Hershey PA (2001) 78–102

[5] Chinkering, D., Heckerman, D., Meek, C.: A Bayesian Approach for Learning Bayesian Networks with Local Structure. Proceedings of Thirteen Conference on Uncertainty in Artificial Intelligence. Morgan Kaufman, San Franscisco California (1997) 80–89

[6] Cohen, W.W., Singer, Y.: Context-Sensitive Learning Methods for Text Categorization. ACM Transactions on Information Systems. 17 (1999) 141–173

[7] Dhillon, I.S., Mallela, S., Kumar, R.: A Divisive Information-Theoretic Feature Clustering Algorithm for Text Classification. Journal of Machine Learning Research 3 (2003) 1265–1287

[8] Dumais, S.T., Platt, J., Heckerman, D., Sahami, M.: Inductive Learning Algorithms and Representation for Text Categorization. Proceedings of CIKM-98, 7th ACM International Conference on Information and Knowledge Management. Bethesda MD (1998) 148–155

[9] Fuhr, N., Buckley, C.: A Probabilistic Learning Approach for Document Indexing. ACM Transactions on Information Systems 9 (1991) 323–248

[10] Fuhr, N., Pfeifer, U.: Probabilistic Information Retrieval as Combination of Abstraction Inductive Learning and Probabilistic Assumptions. ACM Transactions on Information Systems 12 (1994) 92–115

[11] Hankerson. D., Harris, G.A., Johnson, P.D., Jr.: Introduction to Information Theory and Data Compression. CRC Press, Boca Raton Florida. (1998)

[12] Lewis, D.D., Ringuetee, M.: Comparison of Two Learning Algorithms for Text Categorization. Proceedings of the Third Annual Symposium on Document Analysis and Information Retrieval (1994) 81–93

[13] Rocchio, J.J.: Relevance Feedback in Information Retrieval. In Salton G. (eds.): The SMART Retrieval System: Experiments in Automatic Document Processing. Prentice Hall New Jersey (1971) 313–323

[14] Sahami, M.: Learning Limited Dependence Bayesian Classifiers. Proceedings of the Second International Conference on Knowledge Discovery and Data Mining. AAAI Press, (1996) 335–338

[15] Sebastiani, F.: Machine Learning in Automated Text Categorization. ACM Computing Surveys 34 (2002) 1–47

[16] Yang, Y.: An Evaluation of Statistical Approaches to Text Categorization. Information Retrieval 1 (1999) 69–90

[17] Yang, Y., Chute, C.G.: An Example-based Mapping Method for Text Categorization and Retrieval. ACM Transactions on Information Systems 12 (1994) 252–277

[18] Yang, Y., Liu, X.: A Re-examination of Text Categorization Methods. Proceedings of SIGIR-99 22th ACM International Conference on Research and Development in Information Retrieval. Berkeley, California (1999) 42–49

[19] Yang, Y., Pedersen, J.O.: A Comparative Study on Feature Selection in Text Categorization. Proceedings of ICML-97 14th International Conference on Machine Learning. Nashville, TN (1997) 412–420

[20] Reuters-21578 Aptè split data set, http://kdd.ics.uci.edu/data-bases/reuters21578/reuters21578.html

[21] Reuters-21578 Aptè split 10 categories data set, http://ai-nlp.info.uniroma2.it/moschitti/corpora.htm

An Intelligent Customer Retention System

Bong-Horng Chu[1,3], Kai-Chung Hsiao[2], and Cheng-Seen Ho[2,4]

[1] Department of Electronic Engineering, National Taiwan University of Science and Technology, 43 Keelung Road Sec. 4, Taipei 106, Taiwan
ben@ailab2.et.ntust.edu.tw
[2] Department of Computer Science and Information Engineering, National Taiwan University of Science and Technology, 43 Keelung Road Sec. 4, Taipei 106, Taiwan
cheng-seen.ho@ieee.org
[3] Telecommunication Laboratories, Chunghwa Telecom Co., Ltd. 11 Lane 74 Hsin-Yi Road Sec. 4, Taipei, 106, Taiwan
benjamin@cht.com.tw
[4] Department of Electronic Engineering, Hwa Hsia Institute of Technology, 111 Gong Jhuan Road, Chung Ho, Taipei, 235, Taiwan
csho@cc.hwh.edu.tw

Abstract. This paper proposes an intelligent system for handling the customer retention task, which is getting important due to keen competition among companies in many modern industries. Taking wireless telecommunication industry as a target of research, our system first learns an optimized churn predictive model from a historical services database by the decision tree-based technique to support the prediction of defection probability of customers. We then construct a retention policy model which maps clusters of churn attributes to retention policies structured in a retention ontology. The retention policy model supports automatic proposing of suitable retention policies to retain a possible churner provided that he or she is a valuable subscriber. Our experiment shows the learned churn predictive model has around 85% of correctness in tenfold cross-validation. And a preliminary test on proposing suitable package plans shows the retention policy model works equally well as a commercial website. The fact that our system can automatically propose proper retention policies for possible churners according to their specific characteristics is new and important in customer retention study.

1 Introduction

To build customer loyalty and maximize profitability, intelligent techniques for predicting customer churning behaviors are becoming more than necessary in customer relationship management (CRM), especially in the highly competitive wireless telecommunications industry. A study by KPMG about customer defection in the UK reported that 44 percent of UK consumers changed at least one of their key product or service suppliers in 2004 [1]. Analysts have estimated that churning cost wireless service providers in North America and Europe more than four billion US dollars a year [2]. In addition, analysts agreed that acquiring a new customer was many times more expensive than retaining an existing one.

M. Ali and R. Dapoigny (Eds.): IEA/AIE 2006, LNAI 4031, pp. 1259–1269, 2006.

Besides predicting customer defection, proposing appropriate retention policies to retain profitable churners is another significant issue. So far, most of the researchers focus on analyzing customers' behavior and predicting who are likely to churn [3], [4], [5]. There have been, however, no specific researches working on how policies can be made in accord with the churners. Knowing that the reasons of churn are distinct for different people, so are retention policies, by analyzing the specific characteristics of each churner we should be able to provide suitable policy to retain him.

In this paper, we describe an intelligent system for customer retention by suggesting appropriate retention policies for possible churners according to their specific characteristics. In addition to predicting churners, our system deals with customer retention by first constructing an ontology, which contains comprehensive retention policies of various incentives and recommendations to deal with most possible causes of customer defection. It then digs out hidden correlations among the attribute values of the churners, trying to find out the knowledge of how retention policies are related to churn attribute clusters built upon the hidden correlations, which often reveal why a customer defects. The knowledge is then used to automatically propose retention policies for valuable churners. Note that the retention policy ontology we constructed not only can support the construction of specific retention policies but also can help general retention policy design and analysis.

2   Retention Policy Ontology and Historical Services Database

Our system runs in two modes: the learning mode and the application mode. In the learning mode, it learns a churn predictive model and constructs a retention policy model; while in the application mode, it uses the above models to predict whether a customer defects and to propose proper retention policies to retain a potential, valuable churner. Before we further describe how each mode works, we first introduce the construction of our retention policy ontology and the structure of the exemplified historical customer services database.

2.1   Retention Policy Ontology

The retention policy ontology is the key component in our system [6], [7]. To develop the domain ontology, we have done a survey on a variety of policies about CRM in lots of industries and academic papers, from which we analyzed the reasons for subscriber defection, the categories of retention policies, and the potential meaning of each policy [2], [8], [9], [10]. Based on these professional suggestions, we have collected comprehensive retention policies for most types of possible churners.

There are, however, two issues we have to cope with about these collected retention policies. First, they may conflict with one another: each policy has its own specific function but the combination might not always do good things to a churner because of, e.g., mutual exclusion. The second issue is the genera of policies: policies with similar properties should be grouped into the same class to facilitate their usage. We can solve these two issues by constructing a retention policy ontology that can completely categorize all the retention policies into classes and clearly specify the conflicts between them. The ontology is designed to contain five main categories. The *Money* category defines the policies with respect to various fees, the *Service* category specifies the policies associated with value-added services the companies provide, the *Goods* category relates promotion plans that are associated with limited-edition souvenirs or discounted handsets, the *Contact* category lists promising channels in sustaining better communication with subscribers, and the *Quality* category contains the policies of improving quality-of-service, which involves the attitudes of customer service representatives, efficiency of engineering problem-solving, and so forth.

Fig. 1 illustrates the detailed subcategories and the corresponding retention policies of the *Money* category as an example. Note that we further partition the *Money* category into eight different policy clusters, each containing a number of retention policies. A "conflict" relationship is associated with the cluster of *Monthly rental policies* in the figure, which means no two policies of the cluster can be recommended to a possible churner at the same time. Also an "alternative" relationship links the cluster of *Message fees policies* to that of *Monthly rental policies*. It means the policies in either cluster can be proposed for a possible churner, but not both can be chosen at a time. We used Protégé 3.0, which was developed by University of Stanford [11], to build this ontology.

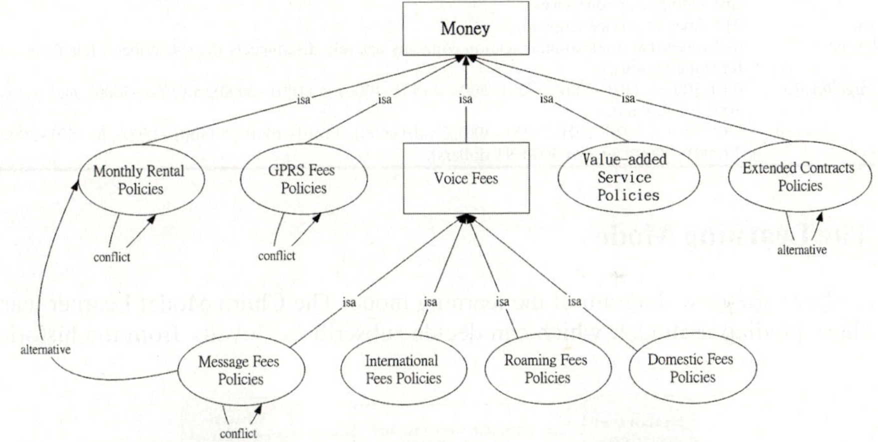

Fig. 1. Part of retention policy ontology about Money category

2.2 Historical Services Database

The historical customer services database of a major telecommunication company in Taiwan is used as our example database. It span for six months and contained information about 63,367 subscribers, each described by hundreds of attributes. Among the attributes, we identify 13 attributes, which we think are most significant in our work. We enumerate the value range of each attribute as shown in Table 1. The following represents an example subscriber data:

   Subscriber A: '15', '8', '3', '2', '4', '7', '1', '3', '0', '0', '1', '2', '2'.

Note that some attributes in our database are numerical, including *Tenure, Average invoice*, and *Average domestic invoice*. They can not be directly used by the decision tree algorithm. We need to divide the range of each such numerical attribute into several intervals whose boundaries are determined according to the subscriber distribution: a cut point is chosen and a boundary is created when the slope of the subscriber distribution curve makes an apparent change.

Table 1. Attributes and their enumerated values in the historical services database

Attribute name	Value enumeration
Zip code	0 (Taipei city), 1 (Keelung), 2 (Taipei county), 3 (Ilan), 4 (Hsinchu city and country), 5 (Taoyuan), 6 (Miaoli), 7 (Taichung city), 8 (Taichung country), 9 (Changhua), 10 (Nantou), 11 (Chiai city and country), 12 (Yunlin), 13 (Tainan city), 14 (Tainan country), 15 (Kaohsiung city), 16 (Kaohsiung country), 17 (Penghu), 18 (Kinmen), 19 (Pingtung), 20 (Taitung), and 21 (Hualien).
Industry code	0 (Public), 1 (Business), 2 (Manufacture), 3 (Finance), 4 (Communication), 5 (Department Store), 6 (Social Service), 7 (Farming and Fishing), 8 (individual), and 9 (Other).
Service center	0 (Site1), 1 (Site2), 2 (Site3), 3 (Site4), 4 (Site5), 5 (Site6), and 6 (Site7).
Tenure	0 (0~4), 1 (5~13), 2 (14~25), 3 26~37), 4 (38~61), and 5 (over 62 months).
Discount type	0 (Government), 1 (Guaranty Free), 2 (Prepaid Card), 3 (Normal), 4 (Enterprise), 5 (Employee), 6 (Military), 7 (Official), 8 (Public Servant), 9 (Alliance), and 10 (Subordinate).
Dealer ID	The ID number (11 Dealers.
Gender	0 (Company), 1 (Male), and 2 (Female).
Package code	0 (Standard), 1 (Economy), 2 (Prepay), 3 (Ultra Low Rate), 4 (Base Rate), 5 (Base Rate plus 100NT), 6 (Base Rate plus 400NT), 7 (Base Rate plus 800NT), 8 (Base Rate plus 1500NT), and 9 (Special Low Rate).
Stop-use	0~9 times that customers actively lay claim to the telecommunication company for temporarily suspending telephone service.
Re-use	0~7 times of service reopening.
Disconnect	0~2 times that a telecommunication company actively disconnects the subscriber's telephone call for some reasons.
Average invoice	0 (0~100), 1 (101~200), 2 (201~500), 3 (501~1000), 4 (1001~2000), 5 (2001~3000), and 6 (over 3001 NT dollars).
Average domestic invoice	0 (0~100), 1 (101~250), 2 (251~400), 3 (401~600), 4 (601~1000), 5 (1001~1500), 6 (1501~2000), 7 (2001~3000), 8 (over 3000 NT dollars).

3   The Learning Mode

Fig. 2 shows the flow diagram of the learning mode. The Churn Model Learner learns the churn predictive model, which can decide subscribers' loyalty from the historical

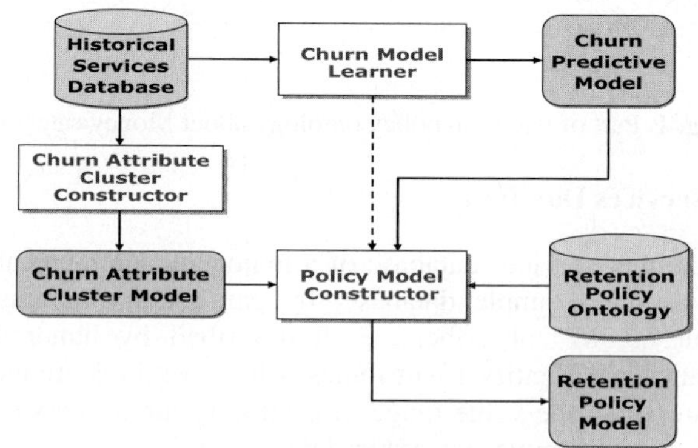

Legend: Dashed line denotes process flow; solid lines denote data flows

Fig. 2. Flow diagram of the learning mode

services database. The Churn Attribute Cluster Constructor discovers hidden correlations among the attribute values of the same database to form the churn attribute cluster model, based upon which and the retention policy ontology, the Policy Model Constructor is able to construct the retention policy model so as to recommend appropriate retention policies for possible churners.

3.1 Churn Model Learner

The Churn Model Learner runs C4.5 algorithm [12], [13] on the historical services database to build a decision tree-represented churn predictive model. As we all know C4.5 doesn't guarantee the created decision tree to be optimal, we thus use the greedy method [14] to optimize the churn predictive model by deleting each attribute one at a time to find out a better accuracy. This process then repeats until no more improvement can be obtained. The remaining attributes are used as the features for churn prediction. Our experiment showed that C4.5 originally produced a decision tree that contained all 13 attributes as listed in Table 1. The follow-up optimization process stopped until the fourth repetition, which produced no further improvement and thus we removed nothing. The previous three repetitions removed *Zip code*, *Industry code*, and *Gender,* respectively. The final churn predictive model thus contained only ten attributes. To our surprise, all the removed attributes belong to the demographic attributes. We therefore conjecture that the demographic-related attributes may not be crucial in deciding subscriber defection in our exemplified database. Fig. 3 shows part of the constructed churn predictive model.

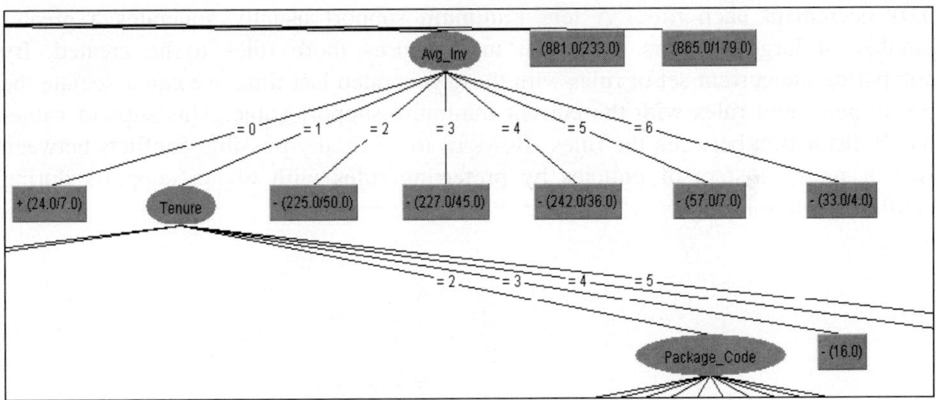

Fig. 3. Churn predictive model (partial)

3.2 Churn Attribute Cluster Constructor

Designing suitable retention policies for possible churners is not an easy task for humans. To do it automatically is even harder. One naïve idea is to provide possible churners with policies according to each single attribute value. It, however, may miss hidden, but significant interactions among attribute values, which can play a key role in explaining why subscribers defect. Our first task is thus to discover how attributes are associated with one another by the association rule mining technique. From the historical services database of all churners, we use Apriori algorithm [15] to mine the association rules, which are in the form of:

Tenure=0 *Average invoice*=2 2480 ==> *Package code*=4 2363 conf: (0.95).

This sample rule means that there are 2,480 churners whose *Tenure* is 0~4 months (code 0) and *Average invoice* is 201~500 NT dollars (code 2), and among whom 2,363 churn because the *Package code* is 4. The confidence of this rule is 0.95. In our experiment, we discovered 12 association rules with the minimum support set to 0.1 and confidence to 0.8. All of the attributes involved in a single rule have to be considered at the same time during the decision of suitable retention policies. In other words, we need to group the antecedents and consequents of a rule into a cluster, and define for it one or several retention policies accordingly. Fig. 4 shows the constructed churn attribute clusters corresponding to these rules. Note that some rules, like Rules 7 and 11, fall into the same group because they contain the same attributes after combination. In the figure some clusters are isolated while others are related by the "*isa*" relationship and form a class hierarchy.

The complete churn attribute cluster model was similarly constructed from 300 association rules, with support from 0.1 down to 0.01 and fixed confidence = 0.8, as partially shown in Fig. 5. This hierarchical model allows us to easily set corresponding policies for two groups that are related by "*isa*". Note that each cluster in the figure is marked with a support value, which is used for conflict resolution. The support values are created by the association rule mining. Specifically, we executed Apriori algorithm ten times starting from support = 0.1 down to support = 0.01 with 0.01 decrement each time. A less minimum support usually generates a greater number of large itemsets, which in turns causes more rules to be created. By comparing the current set of rules with those generated last time, we can associate the newly generated rules with the current minimum support value. This support-value-based distinction between the rules allows us to solve any possible conflicts between two or more clusters of policies by preferring rules with higher supports during conflict resolution.

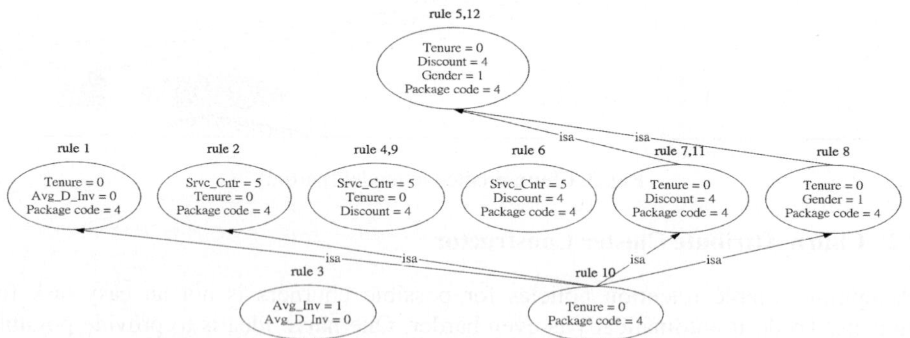

Fig. 4. Churn attribute clusters corresponding to 12 association rules

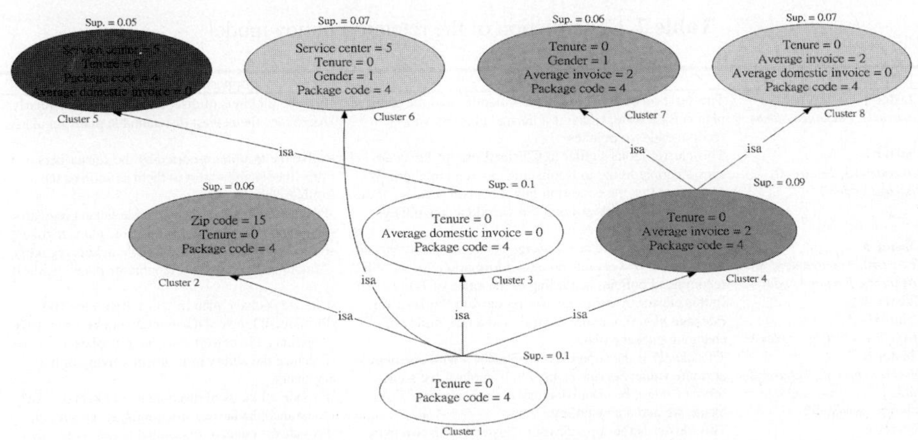

Fig. 5. Part of churn attribute cluster model

There is one issue left: there are some attribute values that could not be properly clustered with other attribute values. It brings in a closely related issue: none of the attribute values of a possible churner can match any pre-clustered group of the churn attribute cluster model. Our solution to the issues is to define proper *nominal policies* for each attribute value that cannot be properly pre-clustered so that we can provide a nominal retention policy for a churner whose major cause of defection is difficult to find, even by an expert.

3.3 Policy Model Constructor

Fig. 6 shows how we construct the retention policy model. First, the attribute values analysis module analyzes the churn attribute cluster model and the attributes that do not appear in the churn attribute cluster model in order to derive any possible explanations. The mapping knowledge construction module then follows the explanations to construct the mappings between the retention policies to each churn attribute cluster or singleton attributes. The policy conflict eliminator finally removes all conflicts from the mappings according to the support values. We take Fig. 5 as an example to demonstrate how we construct the retention policy model, as shown in Table 2 for its churn attribute clusters.

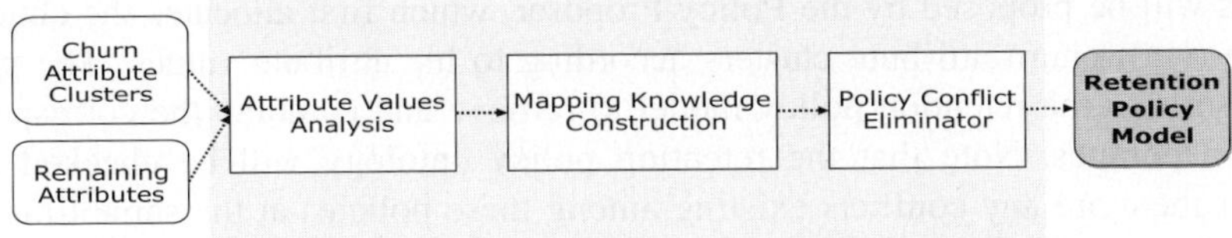

Fig. 6. Retention policy model construction

Table 2. Construction of the retention policy model

Cluster	Explanation	Proposed retention policies
Cluster 1 *Tenure=0, Package code=4*	The duration of use is less than 4 months, and the package plan is Base Rate, which is a normal plan. So we recommend two policies.	-Provide all kinds of discountable tickets regularly. -Announce the newest discountable plans regularly.
Cluster 2 *Zip code=15, Tenure=0, Package code=4*	This cluster looks similar to Cluster 1 except *Zip code* shows people living in Kaohsiung city tend to churn. We conjecture that the condition might happen because of the efficiency of trouble solving. So we add a new policy.	-Solve the troubles reported by the subscribers immediately and report to them as soon as the troubles are cleared. -Provide all kinds of discountable tickets regularly. -Announce the newest discountable plans regularly.
Cluster 3 *Tenure=0, Average domestic invoice=0, Package code=4*	The association between *Average domestic invoice*=0 and *Package code*=4 reveals no new information. So we still recommend policies according to the value of *Tenure*.	-Provide all kinds of discountable tickets regularly. -Announce the newest discountable plans regularly.
Cluster 4 *Tenure=0, Average invoice=2, Package code=4*	In this cluster, *Average invoice* (code=2) is higher than *Package plan* (code=4). We thus add a new policy of changing package plans.	-Change package plan to "Base Rate Plus 100". -Provide all kinds of discountable tickets regularly. -Announce the newest discountable plans regularly.
Cluster 5 *Service center=5, Tenure=0, Package code=4, Average domestic invoice=0*	This cluster is the superclass of Cluster 3 with one more attribute value: *Service center*=5. It implies that some services might be unsatisfactory in service center 5. As a result, we add a new policy.	-Enhance the ability of problem-solving of the engineers. -Provide all kinds of discountable tickets regularly. -Announce the newest discountable plans regularly.
Cluster 6 *Service center=5, Tenure=0, Gender=1, Package code=4*	This cluster is the superclass of Cluster 1 with two more attribute values: *Service center*=5 and *Gender*=1. Unfortunately, it seems that no new information can be discovered from these two attribute values. So we recommend the same policies as for Cluster 1.	-Provide all kinds of discountable tickets regularly. -Announce the newest discountable plans regularly.
Cluster 7 *Tenure=0, Gender=1, Average invoice=2, Package code=4*	This cluster is the superclass of Cluster 4 along with one more attribute value: *Gender*=1, which provides no specific information for policy making. We thus recommend the same policies as for Cluster 4.	-Change package plan to "Base Rate Plus 100". -Provide all kinds of discountable tickets regularly. -Announce the newest discountable plans regularly.
Cluster 8 *Tenure=0, Average invoice=2, Average domestic invoice=0, Package code=4*	This cluster is the superclass of Cluster 4 with one more attribute: *Average domestic invoice*=0. Taking the values of *Average invoice* and *Average domestic invoice* into account, the ratio of the average monthly domestic fees to the average monthly fees is lower than 50 percent. We thus add a new policy.	-Select an appropriate message package plan to suit personal usage. -Provide all kinds of discountable tickets regularly. -Announce the newest discountable plans regularly.

4   The Application Mode

Fig. 7 shows how the application mode works. The Churner Predictor uses the trained churn predictive model to decide the churn possibility of a given subscriber. If the subscriber tends to churner, his/her data will be sent to the Lifetime Customer Value discriminator, which decides whether he/she is a valuable one to retain.

The lifetime value of a possible churner is calculated by Eq. (1).

$$Lifetime\_Customer\_Value = \frac{1}{Churn\_Score} \times Average\_Invoice \tag{1}$$

where *Churn_Score* is the predicted churn rate by the churn predictive model and *Average_Invoice* is the average monthly invoice of a subscriber. If the calculated value is higher than a default lifetime customer value, a suitable set of retention policies will be proposed by the Policy Proposer, which first allocates the churner to some n (n≥0) churn attribute clusters according to his attribute values. The module then resorts to the retention policy model to retrieve and combine the corresponding retention policies. Note that the retention policy ontology will be checked to see whether there are any conflicts existing among these policies at the same time. Only when this check is OK, will the combined retention policies be proposed for the possible churner.

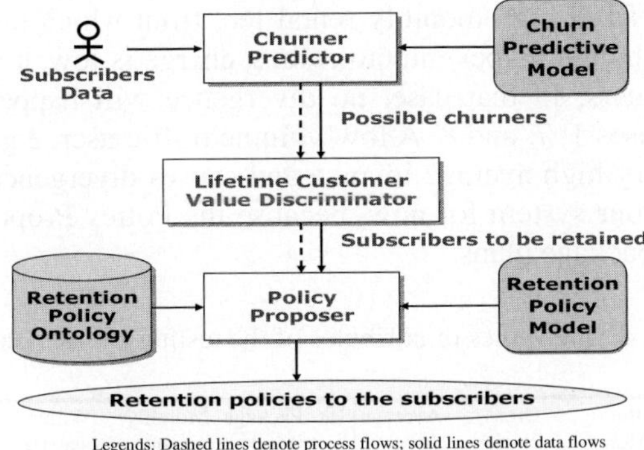

Fig. 7. Flow diagram of the application mode

5   Evaluation

In Table 3 we show the results of tenfold cross-validation on the optimized churn predictive model (Fig. 3). Out of 63,367 subscribers, which contain 24,774 churn instances and 38,593 non-churn instances, 17,668 instances were correctly classified as positive (true positive), and 35,592 instances were correctly classified as negative (true negative). There were 7,106 instances incorrectly classified as negative (false negative) and 2,901 instances incorrectly classified as positive (false positive). On average, the accuracy degree of prediction is 84.21% $\left(\dfrac{17668}{63367} + \dfrac{35692}{63367} = 84.21\% \right)$.

Table 3. Accuracy of the optimized churn predictive model

Churn Prediction		Predicted Class		Total
		+	-	
Actual	+	17,668(27.88%)	7,106(11.21%)	24,774
Class	-	2,901(4.57%)	35,592(56.34%)	38,593
				63,367

As for the evaluation of policy proposing, we found some telecommunication company provides a website to help the subscribers calculate which package plans fit them best [10] and it can be used to partially evaluate how well the automatic policy proposing mechanism in our system does. The input data of the website include: the total call minutes per month, the intra-carrier-call minutes per month, the cross-carrier-call minutes per month.

After normalizing the definition of each package plan of the website to make it the same as ours, we randomly selected 10 churner instances from the historical services database for evaluation. The attribute values of the 10 instances are shown in Table 4. The results of the package plans proposed by the website and our system are shown in Table 5. It shows only case 9 results in different package plans. This divergence is because of the bad correspondence between the package plan selected by customer 9 and his calling minutes. Note that package code 0 stands for the "standard" payment package which has a fixed high monthly rental fee, from which the calling charge is not deductible, even though its per-minute calling charge is low. It is suitable to high-volume traffic customers. In that case, no divergence will happen and our system works as well, e.g., cases 1, 7, and 8. A low-volume traffic user, e.g., case 9, however, will end up with a very high average invoice and causes divergence. This divergence cannot be tackled by our system for now, because the Policy Proposer currently only considers deductible package plans.

Table 4. The values of attributes of the testing churner data

ID	Package code	Monthly usage minutes	Within-carrier counts	Cross-carrier counts	Average invoice	ID	Package code	Monthly usage minutes	Within-carrier counts	Cross-carrier counts	Average invoice
1	0	198	147 (65%)	80 (35%)	4	6	5	90	278 (90%)	31 (10%)	2
2	6	169	84 (30%)	199 (70%)	4	7	0	373	188 (39%)	298 (61%)	5
3	8	545	1164 (77%)	352 (23%)	6	8	0	220	58 (20%)	238 (80%)	4
4	1	639	106 (30%)	253 (70%)	5	9	0	55	164 (100%)	0 (0%)	3
5	4	150	76 (19%)	327 (81%)	4	10	1	42	14 (26%)	40 (74%)	2

Table 5. Comparison of package plans proposed by our system and the website

Customer ID	1	2	3	4	5	6	7	8	9	10
Package plan recommended by our system	7	7	8	8	7	5	8	7	6	4
Package plan recommended by the website	7	7	8	8	7	5	8	7	4	5

6 Conclusions

In this paper we described an intelligent customer retention system which works in two modes. In the learning mode, it learns about potential associations inside the historical services database to construct a churn predictive model. It also creates a churn attribute cluster model by exploiting the correlationships among the attribute values of all churners in the historical services database. The churn attribute cluster model, with the support of the retention policy ontology, allows us to create a retention policy model that maps appropriate retention policies to the clusters. In the application mode, it uses the churn predictive model to calculate the churn probability of a given subscriber. If the subscriber is decided to be a potential churner, it goes one further step to evaluate whether he is valuable to retain. A valuable churner will invoke the system to propose proper retention policies according to the retention policy model. Our experimental results show that the churn predictive model, containing only ten attributes, can reach a high degree of prediction accuracy. A preliminary test on proposing package plans also shows the system works equally well as a commercial website.

The attributes we used to construct the churn predictive model in our system contain much information about the subscribers' background and usage behavior, which explains why we can decide customer defection more objectively and correctly. More factors may also strongly affect the propensities of subscribers. For example, subscriber satisfaction can explain why poor services or inefficient problem solving makes subscribers lose their confidence in the carriers. Frequently checking the complaints of subscribers and figuring out what subscribers really want are indispensable to promote the brand image. Subscriber alliance is another example that the defection of a subscriber to anther carrier is likely to cause a "snow-ball effect", which means that he/she may influence his/her business alliances to follow up. A more intricate investigation of complicated relationships between subscribers is necessary to prevent it from happening.

Acknowledgement

This paper was partly supported by the National Science Council, Taiwan, R.O.C, under grant NSC 94-2213-E-228-006.

References

1. Oceansblue: Accurate Customer Churn Prediction with Information Inventor. Available at: http://www.oceansblue.co.uk/resources/iichurn1.pdf
2. Mozer, M.C., Wolniewicz, R., Grimes, D.B.: Predicting Subscriber's Dissatisfaction and Improving Retention in the Wireless Telecommunications Industry. IEEE Transactions on Neural Networks, Vol. 11, 3 (2000) 690-696
3. Wei, C., Chiu, I.: Turning Telecommunications Call Details to Churn Prediction: A Data Mining Approach. Expert Systems with Applications, Vol. 23, 2 (2002) 103-112
4. Au, W.H., Chan, K.C.C., Yao, X.: A Novel Evolutionary Data Mining Algorithm With Applications to Churn Prediction. IEEE Transactions on Evolutionary Computation, Vol. 7, 6 (2003) 532-545
5. Yan, L., Wolniewicz, R.H., Dodier, R.: Predicting Customer Behavior in Telecommunications. IEEE Intelligent Systems, Vol. 19, 2 (2004) 50-58
6. Uschold, M., Gruninger, M.: ONTOLOGIES: Principles, Methods and Applications. The Knowledge Engineering Review, Vol. 11, 2 (1996) 93-136
7. Fensel, D.: Ontologies: A Silver Bullet for Knowledge Management and Electronic Commerce, Springer (2001)
8. Gerpott, T.J., Rambs, W., Schindler, A.: Customer Retention, Loyalty, and Satisfaction in the German Mobile Cellular Telecommunications Market. Telecommunications Policy, Vol. 25 (2001) 249-269
9. Kin, H.S., Yoon, C.H.: Determinants of Subscriber Churn and Customer Loyalty in the Korean Mobile Telephony Market. Telecommunications Policy, Vol. 28, Issue 9-10 (2004) 751-765
10. Chunghwa Telecom: Best Package Plan Calculation. Available at: http://www.cht.com.tw
11. Stanford Medical Informatics: The Protégé Ontology Editor and Knowledge Acquisition System. Available at: http://protege.stanford.edu
12. Quinlan, J.R.: Induction of Decision Tree. Machine Learning, Vol. 1 (1983) 81-106
13. Quinlan, J.R.: C4.5: Programs for Machine Learning. Morgan Kaufmann, San Mateo CA (1993)
14. Dehne, F., Eavis, T., Rau-Chaplin, A.: Computing Partial Data Cubes for Parallel Data Warehousing Applications. In: Proc. of Euro PVM/MPI 01, Santorini Greece (2001)
15. Agrawal, R., Srikant, R.: Fast Algorithms for Mining Association Rules. In: Proc. of the 20th International Conference on Very Large Databases (1994) 487-499

Software Diagnosis Using Fuzzified Attribute Base on Modified MEPA

Jr-Shian Chen[1,2] and Ching-Hsue Cheng[1]

[1] Department of Information Management, National Yunlin University of Science and Technology, 123, Section 3, University Road, Touliu, Yunlin 640, Taiwan
chcheng@ms.mis.yuntech.edu.tw
[2] Department of Computer Science and Information Management, HUNGKUANG University, No.34, Chung-Chie Road, Shalu, Taichung 433, Taiwan
g9320818@yuntech.edu.tw

Abstract. Currently, there are many data preprocess methods, such as data discretization, data cleaning, data integration and transformation, data reduction ... etc. Concept hierarchies are a form of data discretization that can use for data preprocessing. Using discrete data are usually more compact, shorter and more quickly than using continuous ones. So that we proposed a data discretization method, which is the modified minimize entropy principle approach to fuzzify attribute and then build the classification tree. For verification, two NASA software projects KC2 and JM1 are applied to illustrate our proposed method. We establish a prototype system to discrete data from these projects. The error rate and number of rules show that the proposed approaches are both better than other methods.

1 Introduction

Defective software modules cause software failures, increase development and maintenance costs, and decrease customer satisfaction. Effective defect prediction models can help developers focus quality assurance activities on defect-prone modules and thus improve software quality by using resources more efficiently.

In real-world databases are highly susceptible to noisy, missing, and inconsistent data. Noise is a random error or variance in a measured variable [1]. When decision trees are built, many of the branches may reflect noisy or outlier data. Therefore, data preprocessing steps are very important. There are many methods for data preprocessing. Concept hierarchies are a form of data discretization that can use for data preprocessing. Data discretization has many advantages. Data can be reduced and simplified. Using discrete features are usually more compact, shorter and more accurate than using continuous ones [2]. So that we proposed a modified minimize entropy principle approach on fuzzified attribute and then build the classification tree.

This paper is organized as: The related work is described in section 2. Section 3 will be devoted to study the modified minimize entropy principle approach, and presents our proposed classifier method. Experiment results are shown in Section 4. The final is conclusions.

M. Ali and R. Dapoigny (Eds.): IEA/AIE 2006, LNAI 4031, pp. 1270–1279, 2006.

2 Related Work

In this section, related work include data preprocess, classification decision tree and minimize entropy principle approach.

2.1 Software Diagnosis

Software diagnosis is becoming an important field in software engineering and applications. Defective software modules cause software failures, increase development and maintenance costs, and decrease customer satisfaction. Hence, effective defect diagnosis models can help developers focus quality assurance activities on defect-prone modules and thus improve software quality by using resources more efficiently [3].

2.2 Data Preprocess

In data mining algorithms, the data preprocessing steps are very important. Preprocessing data affects the quality and the efficiency of the data mining algorithms. There are number of data reprocessing techniques. For example: data cleaning [4], data integration and transformation, data reduction [5][6].

Concept hierarchies [7] for numeric attributes can be constructed automatically based on data distribution analysis. Discretization maps similar values into one discrete bin, which can improve predictions by reducing the search space, reducing noise, and by pointing to important data characteristics. Discretization includes the unsupervised and supervised approaches. Unsupervised approaches divided the original feature value range into few equal-length or equal-data-frequency intervals. Supervised method used the maximizing measure involving the predicted variable, e.g. entropy or the chi-square statistics [2]. The entropy–based discretization can reduce the data size. Unlike the other methods, entropy–based discretization uses class information that makes it more likely. The interval boundaries are defined to occur in places that may help classification accuracy.

2.3 Classification Decision Tree ID3 and C4.5

Classification is an important data mining technique. Several classification models have been proposed, e.g. statistical based, distance based, neural network base and decision tree based [8]. A decision tree is a flow-chart-like tree structure, where each internal node denotes a test on an attribute, each branch represents an outcome of the test, and leaf nodes represent class or class distributions [1]. The ID3 [9] is a decision tree algorithm that based on information theory. The basic strategy used by ID3 is to choose splitting attributes with the highest information gain. The concept used to quantify information is called entropy. Entropy is used to measure of information in an attribute.

Assume that have a collection set S of c outcomes then the entropy is defined as

$$H(S) = \sum (-p_i \log_2 p_i) \tag{1}$$

Where p_i the proportion of S belonging to class i.

$Gain(S, A)$ is information gain of example set S on attribute A is defined as

$$Gain(S, A) = H(S) - \sum \frac{|S_v|}{|S|} H(S_v) \qquad (2)$$

and where v is a value of A, $S_v = $ subset of S, $|S_v| = $ number of elements in S_v, $|S| = $ number of elements in S.

   C4.5 is a software extension of the basic ID3 algorithm designed by Quinlan [10] to address the following issues not dealt with by ID3: avoiding overfitting the data, determining how deeply to grow a decision tree, reduced error pruning, rule post-pruning, handling continuous attributes, choosing an appropriate attribute selection measure, handling training data with missing attribute values, handling attributes with differing costs, improving computational efficiency.

2.4 Minimize Entropy Principle Approach(MEPA)

A key goal of entropy minimization analysis is to determine the quantity of information in a given data set. The entropy of a probability distribution is a measure of the uncertainty of the distribution [11]. To subdivide the data into membership functions, establishing the threshold between classes of data is needed. A threshold line can be determined with an entropy minimization screening method, and then start the segmentation process, first into two classes. Therefore, a repeated partitioning with threshold value calculations will allow us to partition the data set into a number of fuzzy sets [12].

   Assume that a threshold value is being seeking for a sample in the range between x1 and x2. An entropy equation is written for the regions [x1, x] and [x, x2], and denote the first region p and the second region q. Entropy with each value of x are expressed as: [13]

$$S(x) = p(x)S_p(x) + q(x)S_q(x) \qquad (3)$$

Where

$$S_p(x) = -[p_1(x)\ln p_1(x) + p_2(x)\ln p_2(x)]$$
$$S_q(x) = -[q_1(x)\ln q_1(x) + q_2(x)\ln q_2(x)] \qquad (4)$$

And

   pk(x) and qk(x) = conditional probabilities that the class k sample is in the region [x1, x1+x] and [x1+x, x2], respectively.

   p(x) and q(x) = probabilities that all samples are in the region [x1, x1+x] and [x1+x, x2], respectively.

$$p(x) + q(x) = 1 \qquad (5)$$

A value of x that gives the minimum entropy is the optimum threshold value. The entropy estimates of pk(x) and qk(x), p(x) and q(x), are calculated as follows: [12]

$$pk(x) = \frac{n_k(x)+1}{n(x)+1} \tag{6}$$

$$qk(x) = \frac{N_k(x)+1}{N(x)+1} \tag{7}$$

$$p(x) = \frac{n(x)}{n} \tag{8}$$

$$q(x) = 1 - p(x) \tag{9}$$

where
nk(x) = number of class k samples located in [x1, x1+x]
n(x) = the total number of samples located in [x1, x1+x]
Nk(x) = number of class k samples located in [x1+x, x2]
N(x) = the total number of samples located in [x1+x, x2]
n = total number of samples in [x1, x2].

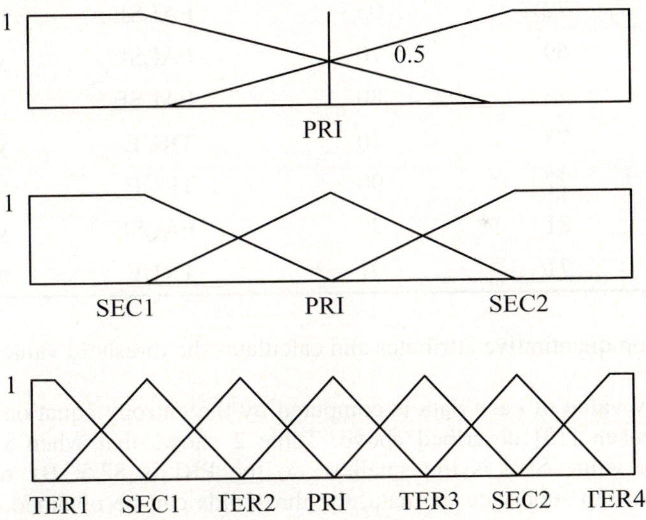

Fig. 1. Partitioning process of Minimize entropy principle approach

Figure 1 shows the partitioning process. While moving x in the region [x1, x2], we calculate the values of entropy for each position of x. The value of x in the region that holds the minimum entropy is called the primary threshold (PRI) value. With repeating this process, secondary threshold values can be determined which denote as SEC1 and SEC2. To develop seven partitions we need tertiary threshold values which denote as TER1, TER2, TER3 and TER4. [8]

3 Proposed Modified MEPA Approach to Fuzzify Attribute

In this section, an approach is described. New approaches are proposed to improve the accuracy rate and reduce number of rules in C4.5 decision tree. The well-known dataset is giving in table 1, that is used to explain these approaches and our proposed method is described as follows:

Table 1. A dataset for play game [8] page 18

outlook	temperature	humidity	Windy	play
sunny	85	85	FALSE	no
sunny	80	90	TRUE	no
overcast	83	86	FALSE	yes
rainy	70	96	FALSE	yes
rainy	68	80	FALSE	yes
rainy	65	70	TRUE	no
overcast	64	65	TRUE	yes
sunny	72	95	FALSE	no
sunny	69	70	FALSE	yes
rainy	75	80	FALSE	yes
sunny	75	70	TRUE	yes
overcast	72	90	TRUE	yes
overcast	81	75	FALSE	yes
rainy	71	91	TRUE	no

Step 1: Partition quantitative attributes and calculates the threshold value (PRI, SEC1, and SEC2).

Entropy value of each data is computed by the entropy equation proposed by Christensen [13] described above. Table 2 shows that when x = 82.5, the entropy value S(x) is the smallest, so the PRI is 82.5. By repeating this procedure to subdivide the data, the thresholds can be obtained, as shown in Table 3.

Step 2: Build membership function.

Using the thresholds from step 1 as the midpoint of triangular fuzzy number, but we modify the first and last membership functions to be trapezoid. When the attribute value is below to SEC1 then the membership degree is equal to 1. That is the same to when attribute value is greater then SEC2. The membership function of minimize entropy principle approach can be established which is shown in Table 3 and Figure 2.

Step 3: Defuzzify the quantity data to determine its linguistic value.

    According to the membership function in step 2, the membership degree of each data is calculated to determine its linguistic value. (see Table 4).

Step 4: Use the C4.5 decision tree classifier to build the model on the dataset.

    Use the linguistic values build the classification decision tree.

Table 2. Example of entropy value calculation for attribute "humidity"

x	$\dfrac{75+80}{2}=77.5$	$\dfrac{80+85}{2}=82.5$	$\dfrac{85+86}{2}=85.5$
$P_1(x)$	$\dfrac{1+1}{5+1}=0.333$	$\dfrac{1+1}{7+1}=0.250$	$\dfrac{2+1}{8+1}=0.333$
$P_2(x)$	$\dfrac{4+1}{5+1}=0.833$	$\dfrac{6+1}{7+1}=0.875$	$\dfrac{6+1}{8+1}=0.778$
$Q_1(x)$	$\dfrac{4+1}{9+1}=0.500$	$\dfrac{4+1}{7+1}=0.625$	$\dfrac{3+1}{6+1}=0.571$
$Q_2(x)$	$\dfrac{5+1}{9+1}=0.600$	$\dfrac{3+1}{7+1}=0.500$	$\dfrac{3+1}{6+1}=0.571$
$P(x)$	$\dfrac{5}{14}=0.357$	$\dfrac{7}{14}=0.500$	$\dfrac{8}{14}=0.571$
$Q(x)$	$\dfrac{9}{14}=0.643$	$\dfrac{7}{14}=0.500$	$\dfrac{6}{14}=0.429$
$S_p(x)$	0.518	0.463	0.562
$S_q(x)$	0.653	0.640	0.640
$S(x)$	0.605	0.552	0.595

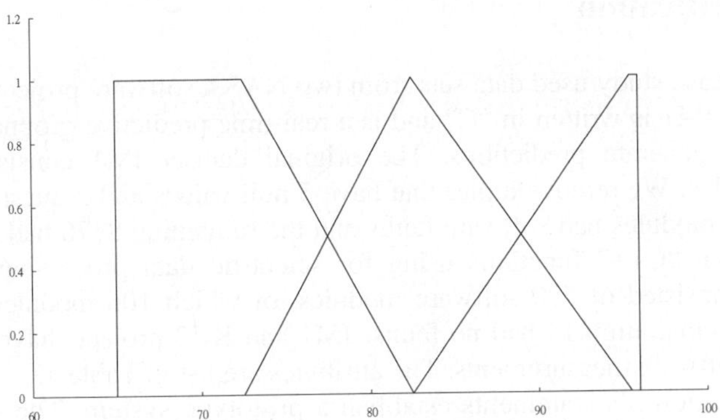

Fig. 2. Membership function of humidity

Table 3. Thresholds of attributes

	min	sec1	pri	Sec2	max
temperature	64	66.5	84	85	85
humidity	65	72.5	82.5	95.5	96

Table 4. Fuzzified attribute base on modified MEPA

temperature	Linguistic value	humidity	Linguistic value
85	high	85	med
80	med	90	high
83	med	86	med
70	low	96	high
68	low	80	med
65	low	70	low
64	low	65	low
72	low	95	high
69	low	70	low
75	low	80	med
75	low	70	low
72	low	90	high
81	med	75	low
71	low	91	high

4 Case Verification

Our empirical case study used data sets from two NASA software projects, labeled JM1 and KC2 [14]. JM1 is written in "C" and is a real-time predictive ground system: Uses simulations to generate predictions. The original dataset JM1 consisted of 10,885 software modules. We remove tuples that have 5 null values and 2 questionable values. The JM1 2102 modules had software faults and the remaining 8776 had no faults. KC2 is the data from "C++" functions using for scientific data processing. The original dataset KC2 consisted of 520 software modules, of which 106 modules had software faults and the remaining 414 had no faults. JM1 and KC2 projects have same with 21 attributes for software measurements. The attributes are list in Table 5.

From the section 3's statements establish a prototype system. The system exploit by the program language Delphi7.0. And then use the system to discrete data and use the linguistic values build the classification decision. The C4.5 classifier used in our studies is Weka open software [15].

The entropy value of each data is computed by equation (3)-(9). By repeating this procedure to partition the data, the thresholds can be obtained, as shown in Table 6.

The proposed approaches are applied to build the classified decision tree on the dataset KC2 and JM1. The C4.5 method is also applied to compare with the proposed approaches. From Table 7, The Error rate and number of rules show that the proposed approaches are better than other methods.

Table 5. Attribute information

no.	Attribute	Attribute information
1	loc	numeric % McCabe's line count of code
2	v(g)	numeric % McCabe "cyclomatic complexity"
3	ev(g)	numeric % McCabe "essential complexity"
4	iv(g)	numeric % McCabe "design complexity"
5	n	numeric % Halstead total operators + operands
6	v	numeric % Halstead "volume"
7	l	numeric % Halstead "program length"
8	d	numeric % Halstead "difficulty"
9	i	numeric % Halstead "intelligence"
10	e	numeric % Halstead "effort"
11	b	numeric % Halstead
12	t	numeric % Halstead's time estimator
13	lOCode	numeric % Halstead's line count
14	lOComment	numeric % Halstead's count of lines of comments
15	lOBlank	numeric % Halstead's count of blank lines
16	lOCodeAndComment	numeric
17	uniq_Op	numeric % unique operators
18	uniq_Opnd	numeric % unique operands
19	total_Op	numeric % total operators
20	total_Opnd	numeric % total operands
21	branchCount	numeric % of the flow graph

Table 6. Thresholds of attributes in KC2 & JM1

	KC2					JM1				
no.	min	sec1	pri	sec2	max	min	sec1	pri	sec2	max
1	1	7.50	31.50	100.50	1275	1	11.50	38.50	93.50	3442
2	1	1.50	6.50	15.50	180	1	1.50	8.50	15.50	470
3	1	3.50	4.50	7.50	125	1	3.50	6.50	12.50	165
4	1	2.50	3.50	8.50	143	1	1.50	4.50	9.50	402
5	1	26.50	72.50	305.50	3982	0	0.50	102.50	295.50	8441
6	0	109.21	354.28	1733.15	33814.56	0	1.00	699.33	2001.57	80843.08
7	0	0.01	0.12	0.34	2	0	0.01	0.06	0.16	1

Table 6. (continued)

8	0	2.93	9.09	24.73	103.53	0	0.50	19.52	26.83	418.2
9	0	24.55	24.73	47.14	415.06	0	1.55	37.29	103.82	569.78
10	0	435.20	3600.08	35401.11	2147483.64	0	4.00	14248.47	41260.17	31079782
11	0	0.04	0.13	0.58	11.27	0	0.16	0.24	0.67	26.95
12	0	24.18	200.01	1966.73	153047.01	0	0.22	791.59	2292.24	1726655
13	0	7.50	23.50	83.00	1107	0	0.50	26.50	67.50	2824
14	0	0.50	1.50	11.00	44	0	0.50	4.50	20.50	344
15	0	1.50	6.50	7.50	121	0	1.50	5.50	11.50	447
16	0	0.50	1.50	3.00	11	0	0.50	1.50	6.50	108
17	1	6.50	11.50	16.50	47	0	0.50	17.50	21.50	411
18	0	9.50	16.50	34.50	325	0	0.50	23.50	55.50	1026
19	1	14.50	80.50	148.00	2469	0	0.50	83.50	198.50	5420
20	0	11.50	49.50	118.50	1513	0	0.50	63.50	326.50	3021
21	1	2.00	12.00	26.00	361	1	2.00	11.50	29.50	826

Table 7. Comparison with the proposed approaches and other model

Approaches	Rforest[16]		C4.5		Proposed Approach	
Dataset	KC2	JM1	KC2	JM1	KC2	JM1
Error rate	23.08%	NA[2]	18.08%	20.45%	17.69%	18.87%
Number of Rules	NA[1]	NA[2]	26	284	17	169
Size of tree	NA[1]	NA[2]	51	567	25	253

Note: The NA[1] denotes no given the answer in this method.
The NA[2] denotes that the method has not use this dataset to experiment.

5 Conclusions

In this paper, we have proposed a new method to classify tree base on fuzzified attribute of modified MEPA. From Table 7, The Error rate and number of rules show that the proposed approaches are better than other methods. We can find that the proposed method has 2 main advantages as follows.

1. Reduce the size of tree and number of rules.
2. Improve the classification accuracy without removing the noise instance.

Future work could focus on the number of membership function used MEPA method, which could be fixed at two, three, and seven …etc. We can consider another flexibility method to build the membership function. That will leave as an area for future research.

Reference

1. J. Han, M. Kamber, Data Mining: Concepts and Techniques, Morgan Kaufmann Publishers, San Francisco(2001)
2. H. Liu, F. Hussain, C. Tan, and M. Dash. Discretization: An enabling technique. Data Mining and Knowledge Discovery, Vol. 6, 4(2002),
3. Norman Fenton and Shari Pfleeger. Software Metrics - A Rigorous and Practical Approach. Chapmann & Hall, London, (1997)
4. Vijayshankar Raman, Joe Hellerstein, Potter's wheel: An interactive data cleaning system. VLDB(2001) ,381-390, Roma, Italy.
5. U. Fayyad, G. P. Shapiro, and P. Smyth, The KDD process for extracting useful knowledge from volumes of data, Communications of the ACM, vol. 39(1996), 27-34
6. S. Mitra, S.K. Pal, p. Mitra, Data mining in soft computing framework: A survey, IEEE Trans. Neural Networks Vol. 13, 1 (2002) 3-14
7. Cai, Y., Cercone, N., and Han, J., Knowledge discovery in databases: an attribute-oriented approach, VLDB (1992) 547-559.
8. MH Dunham, Data Mining: Introductory and Advanced Topics, Prentice Hall, Upper Saddle River, NJ (2003)
9. J. Ross Quinlan, Induction of decision trees. Machine Learning, 1 (1986) 81-106
10. J. Ross Quinlan, C4.5: Programs for Machine Learning, Morgan Kaufmann Publishers, San Mateo, CA (1993)
11. Yager, R. and Filev, D., Template-based fuzzy system modeling, Intelligent and Fuzzy Sys., Vol. 2 (1994) 39-54.
12. Ross, T.J., Fuzzy logic with engineering applications, International edition, McGraw-Hill, USA. (2000)
13. Christensen, R., Entropy minimax sourcebook, Entropy Ltd., Lincoln, MA. (1980)
14. Sayyad Shirabad, J., Menzies, T.J. The PROMISE Repository of Software Engineering Databases. School of Information Technology and Engineering, University of Ottawa, Canada. Available: http://promise.site.uottawa.ca/SERepository(2005)
15. Ian H. Witten, Eibe Frank, Data Mining: Practical machine learning tools and techniques, 2nd Edition, Morgan Kaufmann, San Francisco (2005)
16. Taghi M. Khoshgoftaar, Naeem Seliya, Kehan Gao, Detecting noisy instances with the rule-based classification model, Intelligent Data Analysis, Vol.9, 4 (2005), 347-364

New Methods for Text Categorization Based on a New Feature Selection Method and a New Similarity Measure Between Documents

Li-Wei Lee and Shyi-Ming Chen

Department of Computer Science and Information Engineering
National Taiwan University of Science and Technology
Taipei, Taiwan, R.O.C.
smchen@et.ntust.edu.tw

Abstract. In this paper, we present a new feature selection method based on document frequencies and statistical values. We also present a new similarity measure to calculate the degree of similarity between documents. Based on the proposed feature selection method and the proposed similarity measure between documents, we present three methods for dealing with the Reuters-21578 top 10 categories text categorization. The proposed methods get higher performance for dealing with the Reuters-21578 top 10 categories text categorization than that of the method presented in [4].

1 Introduction

Text categorization is a task of classifying text documents into a predefined number of categories based on classification patterns [3], [22]. The terms appearing in documents are treated as features. One major difficulty in text categorization is the large dimension of the feature space. Therefore, we hope to reduce the dimension of the feature space to get a higher performance for dealing with the text categorization problem. One method for text categorization is based on the feature selection method [3], [4], [21]. Some results from the previous researches show that the semantic feature selection approach affects the performance of text categorization [3], [21]. Some feature selection methods have been presented to deal with a wide range of text categorization tasks, such as Chi-Square test [1], [2], [6], [20], Information Gain (IG) [1], [9], [10], [12], [15], and Mutual Information (MI) [2], [5], [8], [12], [13].

In this paper, we present a new feature selection method based on document frequencies and statistical values to select useful features. We also present a new similarity measure between documents. Based on the proposed feature selection method and the proposed similarity measure between documents, we present three methods for dealing with the Reuters-26578 top 10 categories text categorization. The proposed methods can get higher performance for dealing with the Reuters-26578 top 10 categories text categorization than that of the method presented in [4].

The rest of this paper is organized as follows. In Section 2, we briefly review the previous research for text categorization. In Section 3, we present a new feature selection

M. Ali and R. Dapoigny (Eds.): IEA/AIE 2006, LNAI 4031, pp. 1280–1289, 2006.

method based on document frequencies and statistical values for text categorization. In Section 4, we present a new similarity measure between documents. Based on the proposed feature selection method and the proposed similarity measure between documents, we present three methods to deal with the Reuters-26578 top 10 categories text categorization. In Section 5, we show the experimental results. The conclusions are discussed in Section 6.

2 Preliminaries

In the vector space model [18], documents are usually represented by feature vectors of terms. The task of preprocessing consists of transforming capital letters into lower-cased letters and removing stop words (such as "a", "an", "the", etc.), where words are stemmed by applying the Porter algorithm [17]. The acquired document-term matrix is then transformed into TF-IDF (Term Frequency-Inverse Document Frequency) weights which are normalized by document lengths [19]. After the feature selection process, the dimension of the feature space is reduced and useful features are obtained. Therefore, the feature selection process is a very important task, and it can affect the performance of text categorization.

Assume that F consists of n features f_1, f_2, ..., f_n and assume that S consists of m features s_1, s_2, ..., s_m, where S is a subset of F. The goal of the feature selection process is to choose an optimal subset S of F for text categorization. There are many statistic measures for dealing with the task of feature selection, e.g., Chi-Square [1], [2], [6], [20], Information Gain [1], [9], [10], [12], [15], and Mutual Information [2], [5], [8], [12], [13]. Among these measures, the mutual information measure is the most commonly used measure. It also has a better performance for dealing with the task of feature selection. In the following, we briefly review some feature selection measures, shown as follows:

(1) Chi-Square test [2]: Fix a term t, let the class labels be 0 and 1. Let $k_{i,0}$ denote the number of documents in class i not containing term t and let $k_{i,1}$ denote the number of documents in class i containing term t. This gives us a 2×2 contingency matrix:

$$
\begin{array}{cc|cc}
 & & \multicolumn{2}{c}{I_t} \\
 & & 0 & 1 \\
\hline
 & 0 & k_{00} & k_{01} \\
C & & & \\
 & 1 & k_{10} & k_{11} \\
\end{array}
$$

where C and I_t denote Boolean random variables and $k_{\ell m}$ denotes the number of observations, where $C \in \{0,1\}$ and $I_t \in \{0,1\}$. Let $n = k_{00} + k_{01} + k_{10} + k_{11}$. We can estimate the marginal distribution as follows:

$$\Pr(C = 0) = (k_{00} + k_{01})/n,$$
$$\Pr(C = 1) = (k_{10} + k_{11})/n,$$
$$\Pr(I_t = 0) = (k_{00} + k_{10})/n,$$
$$\Pr(I_t = 1) = (k_{01} + k_{11})/n.$$

The χ^2 test is shown as follows:

$$\chi^2 = \sum_{\ell,m} \frac{(k_{\ell m} - n\,\mathrm{Pr}(C = \ell)\,\mathrm{Pr}(I_t = m))^2}{n\,\mathrm{Pr}(c = \ell)\,\mathrm{Pr}(I_t = m)} = \frac{n(k_{11}k_{00} - k_{10}k_{01})^2}{(k_{11} + k_{10})(k_{01} + k_{00})(k_{11} + k_{01})(k_{10} + k_{00})}. \tag{1}$$

The larger the value of χ^2, the lower is our belief that the independence assumption is upheld by the observed data. In [2], Chakrabarti pointed out that for feature selection, it is adequate to sort terms in decreasing order of their χ^2 values, train several classifiers with a varying number of features, and stopping at the point of maximum accuracy (see [2], pp. 139). The larger the value of χ^2, the higher the priority to choose term t. For more details, please refer to [2].

(2) Information Gain Measure [23], [24]: For the binary document model and two classes (the same as the case of the χ^2 test), the Information Gain (IG) of term t with respect to the two classes can be written as follows:

$$IG(t) = -\sum_{i=0}^{1} P(c_i) \log P(c_i) - \left(-P(t) \sum_{i=0}^{1} P(c_i \mid t) \log P(c_i \mid t) - P(\bar{t}) \sum_{i=0}^{1} P(c_i \mid \bar{t}) \log P(c_i \mid \bar{t}) \right), \tag{2}$$

where
$$P(c_0) = \frac{k_{00} + k_{01}}{k_{00} + k_{01} + k_{10} + k_{11}}, \qquad P(c_1) = \frac{k_{10} + k_{11}}{k_{00} + k_{01} + k_{10} + k_{11}},$$

$$P(t) = \frac{k_{00} + k_{10}}{k_{00} + k_{01} + k_{10} + k_{11}}, \qquad P(\bar{t}) = \frac{k_{01} + k_{11}}{k_{00} + k_{01} + k_{10} + k_{11}}, \qquad P(c_0 \mid t) = \frac{k_{00}}{k_{00} + k_{10}},$$

$$P(c_1 \mid t) = \frac{k_{10}}{k_{00} + k_{10}}, \quad P(c_0 \mid \bar{t}) = \frac{k_{01}}{k_{01} + k_{11}}, \quad \text{and } P(c_1 \mid \bar{t}) = \frac{k_{11}}{k_{01} + k_{11}}.$$

The larger the value of $IG(t)$, the higher the priority to choose term t. For more details, please refer to [23] and [24].

(3) Mutual Information Measure [2]: For the binary document model and two classes (the same as the case of the χ^2 test), the Mutual Information (MI) of term t with respect to the two classes can be written as follows:

$$MI(I_t, C) = \sum_{\ell,m \in \{0,1\}} \frac{k_{\ell,m}}{n} \log \frac{k_{\ell,m}/n}{(k_{\ell,0} + k_{\ell,1})(k_{0,m} + k_{1,m})/n^2}, \tag{3}$$

where $n = k_{00} + k_{01} + k_{10} + k_{11}$. The larger the value of $MI(I_t, C)$, the higher the priority to choose term t. For more details, please refer to [2].

3 A New Feature Selection Method Based on Statistical Values and Document Frequencies

In this section, we present a new feature selection method based on statistical values and document frequencies. Let X and Y be two different classes of documents. The mean values $\mu_{X,t}$ and $\mu_{Y,t}$ of X and Y are $1/|X|(\Sigma_X x_t)$ and $1/|Y|(\Sigma_Y y_t)$, respectively, where x_t denotes the TFIDF of term t in class X and y_t denotes the TFIDF of term t in class Y. Furthermore, the variances σ_X and σ_Y of X and Y are $1/|X|\Sigma_X(x_t - \mu_{X,t})^2$ and $1/|Y|\Sigma_Y(y_t - \mu_{Y,t})^2$, respectively. Let |X| denote the number of documents in the class X and let |Y| denote the number of documents in the class Y. Here, we consider the effect of document frequencies and variances for feature selection. Let $DF(x_t)$ denote the document frequencies of term x_t in the X class and let $DF(y_t)$ denote the document frequency of term y_t in the Y class. The proposed feature selection method is as follows:

$$S(t) = \frac{(DF(x_t)/|X| - DF(y_t)/|Y|)^2}{(1/|X|)\Sigma_X(x_t - \mu_{X,t})^2 + (1/|Y|)\Sigma_Y(y_t - \mu_{Y,t})^2}. \tag{4}$$

The larger the value of S(t), the higher the priority to choose term t.

4 New Methods for Text Classification Based on the Proposed Similarity Measure and the k-NN Approach

Many learning-based approaches have been presented to deal with the task of text categorization, e.g., the k-NN approach [7], [22], [24], support vector machines [5], [14], [24], Naïve Bayes approaches [5], [10], [24], and neural networks [16], [24]. In this paper, we present three classification methods based on the k-NN approach [7], [22], [24] to classify the Reuters-21578 top 10 categories data set.

The k-NN classifier uses the k-nearest training documents with respect to a testing document to calculate the likelihood of categories. The document-document similarity measure used in the k-NN classifier is the most important part for text categorization. Most previous k-NN classifiers use the cosine similarity measure in the vector space model. The cosine similarity measure $\cos(\vec{a}, \vec{b})$, for measuring the degree of similarity between documents a and b is as follows:

$$\cos(\vec{a}, \vec{b}) = \frac{\vec{a} \cdot \vec{b}}{\|\vec{a}\| \cdot \|\vec{b}\|}, \tag{5}$$

where $\cos(\vec{a}, \vec{b}) \in [0,1]$, $\vec{a}$ and $\vec{b}$ denote the vector representation of the documents a and b, respectively. The larger the value of $\cos(\vec{a}, \vec{b})$, the higher the similarity between the documents a and b.

The term weight w_{ij} calculated by TFIDF normalized by document lengths is the most commonly-used method [19] for the cosine similarity measure in the vector space model, where

$$w_{ij} = \frac{TFIDF(t_i, d_j)}{\sqrt{\sum_{k=1}^{|T|} (TFIDF(t_k, d_j))^2}}, \qquad (6)$$

w_{ij} denotes the weight of term i in document j, $|T|$ the total number of terms, and

$$TFIDF(t_i, d_j) = (\text{Term Frequency of Term} \, t_i \, \text{in} \, d_j) \times \log\left(\frac{\text{Number of Documents}}{\text{Document Frequency of Term} \, t_i}\right).$$

A comparison of the three proposed methods with Dona's method [4] is shown in Table 1.

Table 1. A comparison of the three proposed methods with Dona's method

Methods	Dona's method [4]	The first proposed method	The second proposed method	The third proposed method
Feature selection	Mutual Information Measure [2, pp. 139-141]	Mutual Information Measure [2, pp. 139-141]	Mutual Information Measure [2, pp. 139-141]	Formula (4)
Term weight	N/A	Formula (6)	Boolean	Boolean
Similarity measure	N/A	Formula (5)	Formula (7)	Formula (7)
Classifier	Naïve Bayes [24]	k-NN [24]	k-NN [24]	k-NN [24]

In the following, we summarize the three proposed methods as follows:

(A) The First Proposed Method for Text Categorization:

Step 1: Select a predefined number of features based on the Mutual Information (MI) Measure [2] shown in formula (3) to reduce the number of features of each document.
Step 2: Given a testing document, calculate the term weight of the testing document by using formula (6). Find its k-nearest documents among the training documents by using formula (5).
Step 3: The testing document belonging to the category has the largest summing weight.

(B) The Second Proposed Method for Text Categorization:

Step 1: Select a predefined number of features based on the Mutual Information (MI) Measure [2] shown in formula (3) to reduce the number of features of each document.
Step 2: Given a testing document, find its k-nearest documents among the training documents by using the proposed document-document similarity measure described as follows. We use the Boolean method for document representation. Each term weight is either 0 or 1, where 0 means that the term is not appearing and 1 means that it is appearing in the document. Let $M(d_1, d_2)$ denote the number of terms appearing in documents D_1 and D_2, simultaneously. The proposed similarity measure to calculate the degree of similarity $Similarity(d_1, d_2)$ between documents is shown as follows:

$$Similarity(d_1, d_2) = \frac{M(d_1, d_2)}{\sqrt{|d_1| \times |d_2|}}, \tag{7}$$

where $|d_1|$ denotes the number of terms in document d_1 and $|d_2|$ denotes the number of terms in document d_2. Calculate the likelihood of the testing document belonging to each category by summing the weights of its k-nearest documents belonging to the category. For example, assume that there are 3-nearest training documents d_1, d_2, and d_3 of testing document d_4 as shown in Fig. 1. Assume that the degree of similarity between document d_1 and the testing documents d_4 is w_1, the degree of the similarity between document d_2 and the testing document d_4 is w_2, and the degree of similarity between document d_3 and the testing document d_4 is w_3. Then, the summing weights of the documents d_1 and d_2 belonging to Category 1 are equal to $w_1 + w_2$, the weight of d_3 belonging to Category 2 is w_3, if $(w_1 + w_2) < w_3$, then we let the testing document d_4 belong to Category 2.

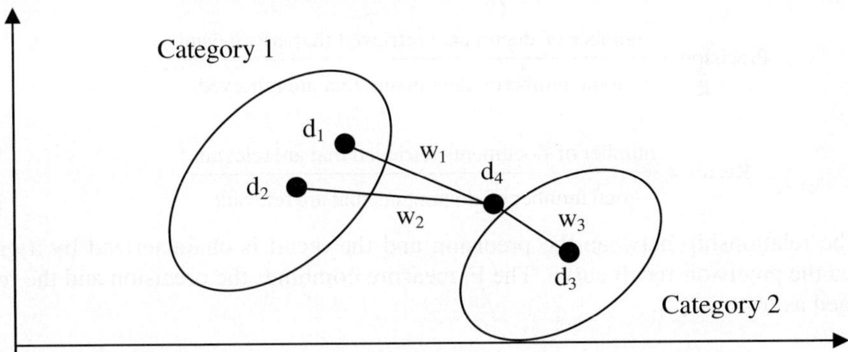

Fig. 1. The 3-nearest training documents of testing document d_4

Step 3: The testing document belonging to the category has the largest summing weight.

(C) The Third Proposed Method for Text Categorization:

Step 1: Select a predefined number of features based on the proposed feature selection method shown in formula (4) to reduce the number of features of each document.
Step 2: The same as **Step 2** of the second proposed method.
Step 3: The testing document belonging to the category has the largest summing weight.

5   Experimental Results

In our experiment, we use the Reuters-21578 "top 10 categories" data set [4], [25] shown in Table 2 for dealing with the text categorization.

Table 2. Top 10 categories of the Reuters-21578 data set [4], [25]

Category	Number of Training Documents	Number of Testing Documents
Earn	2877	1083
Acq	1650	719
Money-fx	538	179
Grain	433	149
Crude	389	189
Trade	368	117
Interest	347	131
Ship	197	89
Wheat	212	71
Corn	181	56
Total	7769	3019

We have implemented the proposed method by using MATLAB version 6.5 on a Pentium 4 PC. We use the Microaveraged F_1 [2] for evaluating the performance of the proposed methods. Precision and Recall are defined as follows [2]:

$$\text{Precision} = \frac{\text{number of documents retrieved that are relevant}}{\text{total numberof documents that are retrieved}}, \tag{8}$$

$$\text{Recall} = \frac{\text{number of documents retrieved that are relevant}}{\text{total number of documents that are relevant}}. \tag{9}$$

The relationship between the precision and the recall is characterized by a graph called the precision-recall curve. The F_1 measure combines the precision and the recall defined as follows [2]:

$$F_1 = \frac{2 \times \text{Precision} \times \text{Recall}}{\text{Precision} + \text{Recall}}. \tag{10}$$

For multiple categories, the precision, the recall, the microaveraged precision, the microaveraged recall, and the microaveraged F_1 are calculated based on the global contingency matrix shown in Table 3, where

$$p_i = \frac{a_i}{a_i + c_i}, \tag{11}$$

$$r_i = \frac{a_i}{a_i + b_i}, \tag{12}$$

$$\text{microaveraged precision} = \frac{A}{A + C} = \frac{\sum_{i=1}^{k} a_i}{\sum_{i=1}^{k} (a_i + c_i)}, \tag{13}$$

$$\text{microaveraged recall} = \frac{A}{A + B} = \frac{\sum_{i=1}^{k} a_i}{\sum_{i=1}^{k} (a_i + b_i)}, \tag{14}$$

$$\text{microaveraged } F_1 = \frac{2 \times \text{microaverage\_precision} \times \text{microaverage\_recall}}{\text{micoraverage\_precision} + \text{microaverage\_recall}}. \tag{15}$$

Table 3. The Contingency Matrix for a Set of Categories [2]

Category $C = \{c_1, c_2, \dots c_{|c|}\}$	Predicted "YES"	Predicted "NO"
Actual class "YES"	$A = \sum_{i}^{|c|} a_i$	$B = \sum_{i}^{|c|} b_i$
Actual class "NO"	$C = \sum_{i}^{|c|} c_i$	$D = \sum_{i}^{|c|} d_i$

In our experiment, we use the proposed three methods (i.e. the first proposed method, the second proposed method and the third proposed method) shown in Table 1 to compare their performance for text categorization with the performance of the method presented in [4]. To compare the proposed three methods with the Dona's Method [4], the microaveraged F_1 is considered for comparing the system performances of different methods for text categorization. Table 4 shows the results of the Retuers-21578 top 10 categories text categorization of the methods. The experimental results show that the proposed three methods (i.e. the first proposed method, the second proposed method and the third proposed method) get higher performances than that of Dona's method [4].

Table 4. A comparison of the performance of categorizing Reuters-21578 top 10 categories data set for different methods

Methods / Categories (F_1 measure)	Dona's method [4]	The first proposed method	The second proposed method	The third proposed method
Earn	98.04	96.82	97.76	97.54
Acq	96.67	89.2	95.43	95.56
Money-fx	76.54	73.13	73.5	73.12
Grain	57.47	57.41	60	59.67
Crude	79.43	70.7	73.68	74.42
Trade	85.60	65.63	70.72	72.44
Interest	73.38	60.97	60.76	65.25
Ship	68.75	84.85	85.71	86.75
Wheat	48.39	39.27	44.25	47.01
Corn	44.02	42.95	38.71	37.57
Microaveraged F_1	74.06	81.99	84.6	84.73

6 Conclusions

In this paper, we have presented a new feature selection method based on document frequencies and statistical values. We also have presented a new similarity measure to calculate the degree of similarity between documents. Based on the proposed feature selection method and the proposed similarity measures between documents, we also have presented three methods to deal with the categorization of the Reuters-21578 top 10 categories data set. The experimental results show that the proposed three methods get higher performance for text categorization than the method presented in [4].

Acknowledgements

The authors would like to thank Professor Yuh-Jye Lee for his help during this research. This work was supported in part by the National Science Council, Republic of China, under grant NSC 94-2213-E-011-003.

References

1. Caropreso, M. F., Matwin, S., Sebastiani, F.: A Learner-Independent Evaluation of the Usefulness of Statistical Phrases for Automated Text Categorization. In: A. G. Chin, eds. Text Databases and Document Management: Theory and Practice, Idea Group Publishing, Hershey, PA (2001) 78–102
2. Chakrabarti, S.: Mining the Web. New York: Morgan Kaufmann (2003) 137–144
3. Chua, S., K, N.: Semantic Feature Selection Using WordNet. Proceedings of the IEEE/WIC/ACM International Conference on Web Intelligence (2004)
4. Doan, S.: An Efficient Feature Selection Using Multi-Criteria in Text Categorization. Proceedings of the IEEE Fourth International Conference on Hybrid Intelligent Systems (2004)
5. Dumais, S. T., Plant, J., Heckerman, D., Sahami, M.: Inductive Learning Algorithms and Representations for Text Categorization. Proceedings of the 7th ACM International Conference on Information and Knowledge Management (1998) 148–155
6. Galavotti, L., Sebastiani, F., Simi, M.: Experiments on the Use of Feature Selection and Negative Evidence in Automated Text Categorization. Proceedings of the 4th European Conference on Research and Advanced Technology for Digital Libraries (2000) 59–68
7. Lam, W., Ho, C. Y.: Using a Generalized Instance Set for Automatic Text Categorization. Proceedings of SIGIR-98 the 21st ACM International Conference on Research and Development in Information Retrieval (1998) 195–202
8. Larkey, L. S., Croft, W. B.: Combining Classifiers in Text Categorization. Proceedings of the 19th ACM International Conference on Research and Development in Information Retrieval (1996) 289–297
9. Larkey, L. S.: Automatic Essay Grading Using Text Categorization Techniques. Proceedings of the 21st ACM International Conference on Research and Development in Information Retrieval (1998) 90–95
10. Lewis, D. D.: An evaluation of phrasal and clustered representations on a text categorization task. Proceedings of the 15th ACM International Conference on Research and Development in Information Retrieval (1992) 37–50
11. Lewis, D. D.: Representation and Learning in Information Retrieval. Ph.D. Dissertation, Department of Computer Science, University of Massachusetts, Amherst, MA (1992)
12. Lewis, D. D.: and Ringuette, M., A Comparison of Two Learning Algorithms for Text Categorization. Proceedings of the 3rd Annual Symposium on Document Analysis and Information Retrieval (1994) 81–93

13. Li, Y. H., Jain, A. K.: Classification of Text Documents, Computer Journal Vol. 41, No. 8 (1998) 537–546
14. Li, H., Yamanishi, K.: Text Classification Using ESC-Based Stochastic Decision Lists. Proceedings of the 8th ACM International Conference on Information and Knowledge Management (1999) 122–130
15. Mladenic, D.: Feature Subset Selection in Text Learning. Proceedings of the 10th European Conference on Machine Learning (1998) 95–100
16. Ng, H. T., Goh, W. B., Low, K. L.: Feature Selection, Perceptron Learning, and a Usability Case Study for Text Categorization. Proceedings of the 20th ACM International Conference on Research and Development in Information Retrieval (1997) 67–73
17. Porter, M. F.: An Algorithm for Suffic Stripping Program. Vol. 14, No. 3 (1980) 130–137
18. Salton, G., Wong, A., Yang, C.: A Vector Space Model for Automatic Indexing. Communications of the ACM, Vol. 18, No. 11 (1975) 613–620
19. Sebastiani, F.: Machine Learning in Automated Text Categorization. ACM Computing Survey, Vol. 34, No. 1 (2002) 1–47
20. Sebastiani, F., Sperduti, A., Valdambrini, N.: An Improved Boosting Algorithm and its Application to Automated Text Categorization. Proceedings of the 9th ACM International Conference on Information and Knowledge Management (2000) 78–85
21. Shima, K., Todoriki, M., Suzuki, A.: SVM-Based Feature Selection of Latent Semantic Features. Pattern Recognition Letters 25 (2004) 1051–1057
22. Yang, Y.: An Evaluation of Statistical Approaches to Text Categorization. Information Retrieval Journal, Vol. 1, No. 1–2, (1999) 69–90
23. Yang, Y. Pedersen, J.: A Comparative Study on Feature Selection in Text Categorization. Proceedings of the 14th International Conference on Machine Learning (1997) 412–420
24. Yang, Y., Liu, X.: A Re-examination of Text Categorization Methods. Proceedings of the SIGIR-99 22nd ACM International Conference on Research and Development in Information Retrieval, Berkeley, CA (1999) 42–49
25. Reuter-21578 Apte Split Data Set, http://kdd.ics.uci.edu/data-bases/reuter21578/reuter221578.html

Using Positive Region to Reduce the Computational Complexity of Discernibility Matrix Method

Feng Honghai[1,2], Zhao Shuo[1], Liu Baoyan[3], He LiYun[3], Yang Bingru[2], and Li Yueli[1]

[1] Hebei Agricultural University, 071001 Baoding, China
honghf@mail.hebau.edu.cn
[2] University of Science and Technology Beijing, 100083 Beijing, China
[3] China Academy of Traditional Chinese Medicine, 100700 Beijing, China

Abstract. Rough set discernibility matrix method is a valid method to attribute reduction. However, it is a NP-hard problem. Up until now, though some methods have been proposed to improve this problem, the case is not improved well. We find that the idea of discernibility matrix can be used to not only the whole data but also partial data. So we present a new algorithm to reduce the computational complexity. Firstly, select a condition attribute C that holds the largest measure of $\gamma(C, D)$ in which the decision attribute D depends on C. Secondly, with the examples in the non-positive region, build a discernibility matrix to create attribute reduction. Thirdly, combine the attributes generated in the above two steps into the attribute reduction set. Additionally, we give a proof of the rationality of our method. The larger the positive region is; the more the complexity is reduced. Four Experimental results indicate that the computational complexity is reduced by 67%, 83%, 41%, and 30% respectively and the reduced attribute sets are the same as the standard discernibility matrix method.

1 Introduction

The rough set theory introduced by Pawlak [1] provides a systematic framework to study the problems arising from imprecise and insufficient knowledge. In a real world information system there may be hundreds of attributes, many of which may be irrelevant to the decision-making. So, knowledge reduction is one of the most important problems in rough set theory. Because an information system may usually have more than one reduction, we always hope to obtain the set of the most concise rules. Unfortunately, it has been shown that finding the minimal reduct of an information system is a NP-hard problem [2]. Therefore, heuristic methods that explore a reduced search space are commonly used for attribute reduction. In these kinds of methods, the measure of significance of every attribute is analyzed, and regard it as a heuristic information in order to decrease search space. WEI has given uncertainty measures in probabilistic rough set using fuzzy entropy of the fuzzy set [3]. Some authors have introduced information-theoretic measures of uncertainty for rough sets [4]. In addition, some authors apply genetic algorithm to find the suboptimal set [5] and use approximation techniques [6] to obtain relative reduct [7], finding relative core and relative knowledge reduction.

M. Ali and R. Dapoigny (Eds.): IEA/AIE 2006, LNAI 4031, pp. 1290–1298, 2006.

2 Concepts of Rough Set

Suppose given two finite, non-empty sets U and A, where U is the universe, and A – a set of attributes. With every attribute $a \in A$ we associate a set V_a, of its values, called the domain of a. Any subset B of A determines a binary relation $I(B)$ on U, which will be called an indiscernibility relation, and is defined as follows:

$xI(B)y$ if and only if $a(x) = a(y)$ for every $a \in A$, where $a(x)$ denotes the value of attribute a for element x.

Obviously $I(B)$ is an equivalence relation. The family of all equivalence classes of $I(B)$, i.e., partition determined by B, will be denoted by $U/IND(B)$; an equivalence class of $IND(B)$, i.e., block of the partition $U/IND(B)$, containing x will be denoted by $B(x)$.

If (x, y) belongs to $IND(B)$ we will say that x and y are *B-indiscernible*. Equivalence classes of the relation $IND(B)$ (or blocks of the partition $U/IND(B)$) are referred to as *B-elementary sets*. In the rough set approach the elementary sets are the basic building blocks (concepts) of our knowledge about reality.

The indiscernibility relation will be used next to define approximations, basic concepts of rough set theory. Approximations can be defined as follows:

$$B_*(X) = \{x \in U : B(x) \subseteq X\}, B^*(X) = \{x \in U : B(x) \cap X \neq \varnothing\},$$

assigning to every subset X of the universe U two sets $B_*(X)$ and $B^*(X)$ called the *B-lower* and the *B-upper approximation* of X, respectively. The set

$$BN_B(X) = B^*(X) - B_*(X)$$

will be referred to as the *B-boundary region* of X.

Sometimes we distinguish in an information table two classes of attributes, called condition denoted by C and decision attributes denoted by D. The coefficient $\gamma(C, D)$ expresses the ratio of all elements of the universe, which can be properly classified to blocks of the partition U/D, employing attributes C.

$$\gamma(C,D) = \frac{|POS_C(D)|}{|U|}, \text{ where } POS_C(D) = \bigcup_{X \in U/I(D)} C_*(X)$$

The expression $POS_C(D)$, called a positive region of the partition $U/IND(D)$ with respect to C, is the set of all elements of U that can be uniquely classified to blocks of the partition $U/IND(D)$, by means of C.

By a discernibility matrix of $B \subseteq A$ denoted $M(B)$ a $n \times n$ matrix is defined as

$$(c_{ij}) = \{a \in B : (x_i) \neq a(x_j)\} \text{ for } i, j = 1,2,\ldots,n .$$

Let us assign to each attribute $a \in B$ a binary Boolean variable $\bar{a}$, and let $\Sigma\delta(x, y)$ denote Boolean sum of all Boolean variables assigned to the set of attributes $\delta(x, y)$. Then the discernibility function can be defined by the formula

$$f(B) = \prod_{(x,y) \in U^2} \{\Sigma\delta(x, y) : (x, y) \in U^2 \text{ and } \delta(x, y) \neq \varnothing\}.$$

The following property establishes the relationship between disjunctive normal form of the function $f(B)$ and the set of all reducts of B.

All constituents in the minimal disjunctive normal form of the function $f(B)$ are all reducts of B.

In order to compute the value core and value reducts for x we can also use the discernibility matrix as defined before and the discernibility function, which must be slightly modified:

$$f^x(B) = \prod_{y \in U} \{ \Sigma \delta(x, y) : y \in U \text{ and } \delta(x, y) \neq \varnothing \}.$$

The D-core is the set of all single element entries of the discernibility matrix $M_D(C)$, i.e.

$$CORE_D(C) = \{ a \in C : c_{ij} = (a), \text{ for some } i, j \}.$$

3 Algorithm

(1) For $(C = 0; C < n; C++)$ // C denotes the condition attributes

   {Using $\gamma(C, D) = \dfrac{|POS_C(D)|}{|U|}$ to calculate $\gamma(C, D)$} // D is the decision attribute.

(2) Sort $\gamma(C, D)$ by size.

(3) Select a condition attribute C that holds the largest measure of $\gamma(C, D)$

(4) With examples in the non-positive region, build another discernibility matrix to induce the other attributes in the attribute reduction set.

(5) Combine the attributes generated in the above two steps into the attribute reduction set.

Below we give a proof of the rationality of the algorithm.

Suppose that condition attribute C holds the largest measure of $\gamma(C, D)$ with which the decision attribute D depends on C, and there are n examples in the positive region of partition of the decision attribute D with respect to the condition attribute C.

Suppose that $U/IND\,(C) = \{A_1, A_2, \cdots A_m\}$, $A_1 = \{a_1, a_2, \cdots a_n\}$, $U/IND\,(D) = \{D_1, D_2, \cdots D_L\}$, for $A_1, A_2, \cdots, A_m$, only $A_1 \subseteq D_1$

Then we can hold

$$POS_C(D) = A_1.$$

The components of the discernibility matrix are denoted by DM.

Every component of the discernibility matrix that discerns the examples in A_1 is denoted by $DM\,(A_1)_i$ which is the combination of condition attributes that discern a_1, $a_2, \cdots, a_n$ from the other examples.

We can affirm that $DM\,(A_1)_i$ must contain the attribute C, that is, $C \in DM\,(A_1)_I$
So

$$\prod DM\,(A_1)_i = C$$

Namely, the result of the Boolean multiplication of the $DM\,(A_1)_i$ is C.

Then with the condition attribute C, a_1, a_2, $\cdots$ a_n can be discerned from the other examples, and with the other condition attributes the other examples can be discerned from each other. Hence for the examples a_1, a_2, $\cdots$ a_n, we can use only the attribute C and the positive knowledge to induce the classification rule, and for the other examples we can build a discernibility matrix to induce the classification rules. So the size of the discernibility matrix is reduced.

For example, Table 1 is the information system of 4 hand-written Chinese characters [8], and Table 2 is the discernibility matrix of the system.

Obviously, $POS_A(Y) = \{7, 8\}$, $POS_B(Y) = \{3, 4, 5\}$, $POS_C(Y) = \{5, 6\}$, so the largest positive region of the partition $U/IND(Y)$ is with respect to B, that is, $\{3, 4, 5\}$ is the largest positive region of the partition $U/IND(Y)$. In the discernibility matrix, the constituents with * are the ones that differentiate examples 3, 4, and 5 from the other examples.

Table 1. The information table of 4 hand-written Chinese characters after discretization

U	A	B	C	D	E	F	Y
1	17	8	5	4	2	1	1
2	18	8	5	3	2	1	1
3	17	9	5	5	2	2	2
4	17	9	5	3	2	1	2
5	18	7	6	4	2	1	3
6	18	8	6	4	3	2	3
7	15	8	5	4	3	2	4
8	16	8	5	5	3	2	4

Table 2. Discernibility matrix of the Table 1

	1	2	3	4	5	6
1						
2						
3	$BDF*$	$ABDF*$				
4	$BD*$	$AB*$				
5	$ABC*$	$BCD*$	$ABCDF*$	$ABCDEF*$		
6	$ACEF$	$CDEF$	$ABCDE*$	$ABCDEF*$		
7	AEF	$ADEF$	$ABDE*$	$ABDEF*$	$ABCEF*$	AC
8	$ADEF$	$ADEF$	$ABE*$	$ABDEF*$	$ABCDEF*$	ACD

We can find that B is the only element in all the constituents with * generated by comparing the examples 3, 4, and 5 with the others, that is, after using Boolean sum and Boolean multiplication to these constituents with * the result is attribute B. In other words, we can use the other examples 1, 2, 6, 7, and 8 to build another discernibility matrix to generate the other constituents with no * to induce the other attributes that will be in the attribute reduction set.

Table 3. The results of the Table 2 after removing the components that contain attribute B

	1	2	3	4	5	6
1						
2						
3	*	*				
4	*	*				
5	*	*	*	*		
6	ACEF	CDEF	*	*		
7	AEF	ADEF	*	*	*	AC
8	ADEF	ADEF	*	*	*	ACD

From Table 3, we can see that all the components with * relate to examples 3, 4, and 5, that is, with the condition attribute B, we can discern the examples 3, 4, and 5 from the other examples and for the other examples we can build a discernibility matrix to get the corresponding attribute reduction.

We can also conclude that the condition attribute B is included in the attribute reduction set determinately.

The reduced condition attribute set contains the least amount of the condition attributes among the all reduced attribute sets generated with standard discernibility matrix method, since the attribute B holds the largest positive region of partition of the decision attribute.

Because attribute B holds the largest positive region of decision attribute, the classification accuracy should be the highest among the all the attribute reduction set generated with standard discernibility matrix attribute reduction method.

4   Hand Written Chinese Character Recognition Experiments

In Table 1, the values of 1, 2, 3, and 4 of attribute Y denote the above 4 hand-written Chinese characters respectively. The features of the Chinese characters are generated with SVD and among all the features, A, B, C, D, E, and F are the ones whose values are not the same after equal-width based discretization.

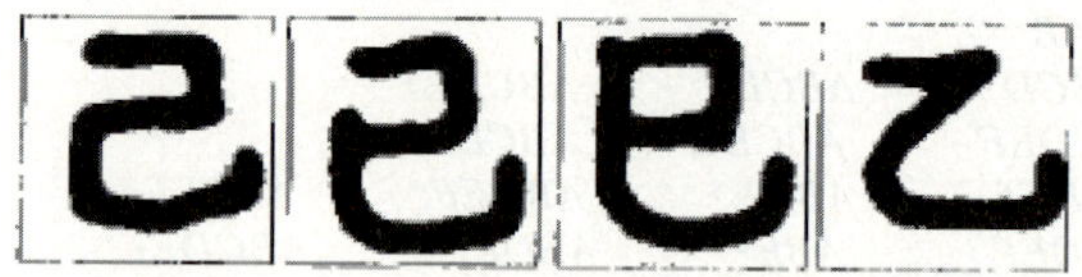

Fig. 1. 4 hand-written Chinese characters

With standard discernibility matrix method, the comparison times between different examples with different decision attribute values are (2*6+ 2*4+2*2)*6=144, namely, examples 1, and 2 should be compared with examples 3, 4, 5, 6, 7, and 8 respectively, following this comparison step, examples 3, and 4 should be compared with 5, 6, 7, and 8 respectively, and examples 5, and 6 should be compared with 7, and 8 respectively.

Table 4. Comparison results of computational complexity of Table 1

	Standard discernibility matrix method	Improved discernibility matrix method
Amount of the examples with Y=1	2	2
amount of the examples with Y=2	2	0
amount of the examples with Y=3	2	1
amount of the examples with Y=4	2	2
amount of the attributes	6	6
times for comparing examples	(2*6+ 2*4+2*2)*6	(2*3+1*2)*6
Ratio	(2*3+1*2) / (2*6+ 2*4+2*2)=8/24=0.33/1	

5 Micronutrients Experiments

The SARS data are the experimental results of micronutrients that are essential in minute amounts for the proper growth and metabolism of human beings. Among them, examples 31~60 are the results of SARS patients and 61~90 are the results of healthy human beings.

Table 5. Left examples after discretization

U	1	2	3	4	5	6	7	C	U	1	2	3	4	5	6	7	C	U	1	2	3	4	5	6	7	C
31	1	1	1	0	1	1	1	0	54	0	0	1	0	0	1	1	0	69	1	1	1	2	2	1	2	1
32	2	1	1	0	1	1	1	0	55	1	0	1	0	1	1	1	0	70	1	2	2	2	2	2	1	1
34	1	1	1	0	1	2	1	0	56	0	1	1	0	0	1	1	0	71	1	1	2	1	1	1	1	1
39	1	1	0	0	0	1	1	0	59	0	0	0	0	0	2	1	0	72	2	1	1	2	2	1	1	1
41	0	1	1	0	0	2	2	0	60	1	2	1	0	1	1	1	0	73	1	1	2	1	2	1	1	1
42	2	1	1	0	1	2	1	0	61	2	1	1	2	2	0	1	1	74	2	1	2	2	2	1	1	1
43	2	1	1	0	2	1	1	0	62	1	1	1	1	1	1	1	1	76	2	1	1	2	1	1	1	1
47	0	1	0	0	0	1	1	0	63	1	1	1	2	1	0	1	1	78	1	1	2	2	2	1	1	1
48	2	1	0	2	1	1	1	0	64	2	1	2	2	1	1	1	1	79	2	2	1	2	2	1	1	1
49	1	1	1	1	1	1	2	0	65	1	1	1	2	1	1	1	1	85	2	1	1	2	1	0	0	1
50	0	1	1	0	0	2	1	0	66	1	1	1	2	1	0	0	1	86	2	1	1	2	2	1	0	1
52	1	1	2	0	1	1	1	0	67	1	1	1	2	2	1	1	1	87	2	1	1	2	2	1	1	1
53	1	1	1	1	1	0	1	0	68	1	1	1	1	1	1	0	1	88	2	1	2	2	2	1	1	1

Attributes "1", "2", "3", "4", "5", "6", "7" denote micronutrient Zn, Cu, Fe, Ca, Mg, K and Na respectively, and decision attribute "C" denotes the class "SARS" and "healthy". $V_C = \{0,1\}$, where "0" denotes "SARS", "1" denotes "healthy". After discretization, some examples become a repeat. The amount of the total examples is reduced from 60 to 39.

$$POS_{Ca}(C) = \{31,32,34,39,41,42,43,47,50,52,54,55,56,59,60\},$$

$$POS_{Fe}(C) = \{39,47,48,59\},\ POS_{Na}(C) = \{66,68,85,86\}$$

Obviously, the largest positive region of the partition U/C is with respect to Ca. With the improved discernibility matrix method, because the examples 31, 32, 34, 39, 41, 42, 43, 47, 50, 52, 54, 55, 56, 59, and 60 are not involved in the comparing step, only three examples 48, 49, and 53 are involved in the comparing step.

Table 6. Comparing results of computational complexity of micronutrients experiments

	Standard discernibility matrix method	Improved discernibility matrix method
amount of the examples with C=0	18	3
amount of the examples with C=1	21	21
amount of the attributes	7	7
times for comparing examples	18*21*7	3*21*7
Ratio	3*21*7/18*21*7=1/6=0.17/1	

With the standard discernibility matrix method, attribute 4 (Ca) is involved in the attribute reduction set, and "Ca=0 → C=0" is involved in the rule set.   So are involved in the improved algorithm. Namely, the rule set is the same.

6   Clinical SARS Data Experiments

From the clinical SARS data set of 501 patients obtained from Beijing in 2003, we find the following rules: (1) T<=37.6°C →1. (2) 37.7°C <=T<=38.6°C →1 or 2. (3)

Table 7. Comparing results of computational complexity of clinical SARS data experiments

Training set	Original training set and standard method	Improved method		
		T<= 37.6°C	37.7<=T<=38.6°C	T>=38.7°C
Total amount of examples	501	26	122	353
Class 1	355	26	92	237
Class 2	135		30	105
Class 3	11			11
Comparing Times	(355*135+355*11+135*11)*47	0	92*30 *47	(237*105+237*11+105*11)*47
	= 53315*47		=2760*47	=28647*47
Total times	53315 *47		31407*47	
Ratio	31407/53315=0.59/1			

T>=38.7°C →1, 2 or 3 (1, 2, and 3 means that the state of illness is slight, serious, and critical respectively). Where T denotes the highest body temperature.

7   Forest Cover Type (UCI) Data Set Experiments

The forest cover type for 30 x 30 meter cells obtained from US Forest Service (USFS) Region 2 Resource Information System (RIS) data. The number of instances (observations) is 581012, the number of attributes is 54, the forest cover type (Cover_Type) designate 7 types (1 to 7). We only take the 44 binary variables into account. From the data set we find that:

"Soil Type 29" =0 → "Cover_Type" = 1, 2, 3, 4, 5, 6, or 7.

"Soil Type 29" =1 → "Cover_Type" = 1, 2, 5, or 7.

So we can divide the whole data set into two parts: "Soil Type 29" =0 and "Soil Type 29" =1.

Table 8. Comparing results of computational complexity of Forest Cover Type (UCI) Data Set

Training set	Original training set and standard method	Improved method	
		"Soil Type 29" =0	"Soil Type 29" =1
Total amount of examples	581012	465766	115246
Class 1	211840	169928	41912
Class 2	283301	211903	71398
Class 3	35754	35754	
Class 4	2747	2747	
Class 5	9493	8362	1131
Class 6	17367	17367	
Class 7	20510	19705	805
Comparing Times	A	B	C
Total times Ratio		(B+C)/A=0.704/1	

Where A=211840*(283301+35754+ 2747+9493+17367+20510)+288301*(35754+ 2747+9493+17367+20510)+35754*(2747+9493+17367+20510)+ 2747*(9493+17367 + 20510) + 9493*(17367+20510)+ 17367*20510=105170508790.

B= 169928*(211903+35754+2747+8362+17367+19705)+ 211903*(35754+2747+ 8362+17367+19705)+35754*(2747+8362+17367+19705)+2747*(8362+17367+19705) + 8362*(17367+19705)+ 17367*19705=70812033350.

C= 41912*(71398+1131+805)+ 71398*(1131+805)+ 1131*805=3212711591.

So the total comparing times ratio is (B+C)/A=0.704/1, namely, the computational complexity is reduced by 30%. And the attribute reduction results are the same as the standard discernibility matrix method theoretically.

8   Conclusions and Discussions

(1) From the four experimental results, with the new algorithm the computational complexities are reduced by 41%, 83%, 67%, and 30% respectively, which shows that the new algorithm is general in reducing the standard discernibility matrix method.

(2) The new algorithm suits the case that the partition of the decision attribute has a larger positive region to a condition attribute. The larger the positive region of the partition of the decision attribute to a condition attribute is, the more the complexity is reduced. That is the reason why the above reduction rates have such a large variance of more than 50%. Of course, the method is not suited to the case where there is not any attribute that holds a positive region of partition of the decision attribute.

(3) The idea of discernibility matrix can be used to not only the whole data but also partial data.

(4) The selected attribute to which the partition $U/IND(D)$ has the largest positive region must be in one of the attribute reduction set generated by the standard discernibility matrix based.

(5) Because the selected attribute holds the largest positive region of decision attribute:

    (a)   The reduced condition attribute set contains the least amount of the condition attributes among all the reduced attribute sets generated with standard discernibility matrix method.

    (b)   The amount of the classification rules is the least.

    (c)   The classification accuracy should be the highest among the all the attribute reduction set generated with standard discernibility matrix attribute reduction method.

References

1.   Pawlak Z.: Rough sets. Int. J. of Computer and Information Science. 11 (1982): 341-356
2.   Wong S K, Ziarko W.:On optimal decision rules in decision tables. Bulletin of Polish Academy of Sciences. 33(1985) 357-362
3.   Duntscb D, Gediga G.: Uncertainly measures of rough set prediction. Artificial Intelligence. 106(1998) 109-137
4.   Beaubouef T, Petry F E and &ora G.: Information-theoretic measures of uncertainty for rough sets and rough relational databases. Information Science. 109(1998) 185-195
5.   Wroblewski, J.: Ensembles of classifiers based on approximate reducts. Fundamenta Informaticae, IOS Press, Netherlands. 47(2001) 351-60
6.   Wroblewski, J. Covering with reducts-a fast algorithm for rule generaten. Rough Sets and Current Trends in Computing. First International Conference, RSCTC'98. Proceedings, (1998) 402-7
7.   Xiao, Jian-Mei. New rough set approach to knowledge reduction in decision table. Proceedings of 2004 International Conference on Machine Learning and Cybernetics, 4 (2004) 2208-2211
8.   Fan Jin-song, Fang Ting-jian. Rough set and SVM based pattern classification method. Pattern Recognition and Artificial Intelligence. 13(2000) 419-423.

A Novel Mining Algorithm for Periodic Clustering Sequential Patterns

Che-Lun Hung[1], Don-Lin Yang[2], Yeh-Ching Chung[1], and Ming-Chuan Hung[2]

[1] Department of Computer Science, Tsing Hua University, 101, Section 2 Kuang Fu Road,
Hsinchu, Taiwan 30013
allen@sslab.cs.nthu.edu.tw, ychung@cs.nthu.edu.tw
[2] Department of Information Engineering and Computer Science, Feng Chia University,
100, Wenhwa Rd., Seatwen, Taichung, Taiwan 40724
{dlyang, mchong}@fcu.edu.tw

Abstract. In knowledge discovery, data mining of time series data has many important applications. Especially, sequential patterns and periodic patterns, which evolved from the association rule, have been applied in many useful practices. This paper presents another useful concept, the periodic clustering sequential (PCS) pattern, which uses clustering to mine valuable information from temporal or serially ordered data in a period of time. For example, one can cluster patients according to symptoms of the illness under study, but this may just result in several clusters with specific symptoms for analyzing the distribution of patients. Adding time series analysis to the above investigation, we can examine the distribution of patients over the same or different seasons. For policymakers, the PCS pattern is more useful than traditional clustering result and provides a more effective support of decision-making.

1 Introduction

With the tremendous growth of data volume and demanding need of knowledge management, data mining has recently become an important research topic and is receiving substantial interest from the areas of both academia and industry. Many data mining technologies have been developed in these past few years, such as the association rule, clustering, and classification, etc. The method of clustering is unsupervised and is based on the similarity of attributes to determine if they are elements of the same cluster [1,2,3,4]. Although clustering is used in many application domains, its time attribute has not been well-researched [5,6,7]. In fact, data attributes are less discussed in data mining, but the consideration of time and time-ordered correlation are becoming more and more popular, especially in the association rule [8,9,10]. There are two popular patterns of time series in data mining, the sequential pattern and periodic pattern [11,12,13,14].

Sequential patterning is a very important technology in temporal databases and is applied in science and finance applications [15,16]. Periodic patterning is equally important and more accurate in analyzing time variations than traditional sequential patterning. Periodic patterns have time slices, but sequential patterns do not. In this

M. Ali and R. Dapoigny (Eds.): IEA/AIE 2006, LNAI 4031, pp. 1299 – 1308, 2006.

paper, we present the mining of periodic clustering sequential (PCS) patterns. It is different from the aforementioned patterns because the PCS pattern is obtained by clustering, whereas the two traditional patterns are from the association rule. The PCS pattern takes advantage of both the sequential and periodic patterns.

We focus on the clustering of varying times, rather than the technology of clustering. The goal is to provide more efficient applications of clustering in time series. The challenge is how to use this new concept, which combines the sequential pattern and the periodic pattern using clustering, in a fast and effective manner. The PCS pattern has two properties, sequential and periodic attributes. In general, the element of time is not considered in clustering because defining the time factor is very difficult. Another reason to disregard time is because it is hard to mine efficiently when many attributes of data and time dimension are considered together. However for the PCS pattern, clusters are made according to the sequence of periods. For example, the attribute values of a cluster that has the highest survival rate may change with season. This will provide better diagnosis support for doctors and help control the symptoms of patients during each season to increase the survival rate.

2   Periodic Clustering Sequential Pattern

Given a time unit $t_i \in T$, $i = 0, \dots, n$, and a time series T, we denote the size of T as L, i.e., $L = Size(T) = |T| = n+1$, and time segment $T_{seg} = [t_i, t_{i+1}]$. A cycle is formed throughout the whole time series being measured, and there exists identical clusters with the same period length in the different time segments. The period length is the size of the time segment when the cycle is being formed. A PCS pattern is based on the cycle with the same period length.

Definition 1 (a cycle)

Given a time series T whose size is L, if period length ι is a positive integer (Z^+), $0 \leq \iota < L$, then $\exists \tau$ and $0 \leq \tau \leq L/\iota$. If $\exists s \in Z^+$ such that $0 \leq s < \iota$, there are identical clusters at the $((\iota . \tau) + s)th$ time unit in the time series T. This is called a cycle, denoted by $\acute{C} = (\iota, s, c)$, where ι is the period length, s is the cyclic position of the period length, and c is the cluster in the cycle. When the period length is known, the cycle can be denoted by $\acute{C} = (s, c)$.

Example 1

After clustering a dataset, we have a time series whose sequence is *abdabcabfabc*. Each letter of the alphabet is the index of a cluster after clustering and is mapped into the position of a Time Cube (see Section 3.1). Note that every first position of the sequence repeats the letter "*a*" starting at offset 0. There is a cycle that can be denoted as $\acute{C}_1 = (3,0,a)$. At the mean time, there are two other cycles $\acute{C}_2 = (3,1,b)$ and $\acute{C}_3 = (6,5,c)$.

Definition 2 (a PCS pattern)

Given a time series T with size L and the period length ι, $0 \leq \iota < L$. If there are v (v > 0) cycles, a PCS pattern P is denoted by $(\iota, v, \hat{C})$, where $\hat{C} = \{(s, c) | \acute{C} = (\iota, s, c)$ for $\forall$ $0 \leq s < v\}$. That is, the combination of all single cycles forms a PCS pattern.

Example 2

Following the time sequence in Example 1, there are two cycles $(3,0,a)$ and $(3,1,b)$, denoted by a^{**} and b^{**} respectively. According to Definition 2, the patterns a^{**} and b^{**} can be denoted as $\hat{C} = \{(0,a),(1,b)\}$, and the combination of $(3,0,a)$ and $(3,1,b)$ forms a PCS pattern, denoted by $(3,2,\{(0,a),(1,b)\})$, or ab^*.

In a time series pattern, every period length has the same cycle. If a cycle $\acute{C} = (\iota, s, c)$ appears in the time series T whose size is L, then the number of occurrences for the cycle $\acute{C}$ is (L/ι). Notice that the PCS pattern defined above refers to the perfect PCS pattern in a time series in the sense that all of the corresponding time units in the series are similar. This is the ideal case. In practice, most applications have noises. Therefore, we need a parameter to indicate the degree of confidence for the PCS pattern.

Definition 3

Suppose there is a cycle $\acute{C} = (\iota, s, c)$ in a time series T of size L. The confidence F of the cycle is the number of times the cycle has appeared. The ideal confidence F is (L/ι).

Notice that a perfect cycle in a time series given in Definition 1 implies $F = 1$. However, a perfect PCS pattern is less common, so we need to define the confidence for full and partial periodic patterns. Usually, a user may provide a minimum confidence threshold, *min_conf*, to indicate the minimum strength of the PCS pattern to be mined. If a PCS pattern is formed, it will satisfy *min_conf* $\times (L/\iota)$, where L is the size of the time series and ι is the period length.

3   An Efficient Mining Algorithm of the PCS Pattern

The main step of the PCS algorithm is to do clustering with time. In order to mine PCS patterns, we construct a Time Cube first. Then, in accordance with the time attribute, which is mapped to a Time-index, we put the clusters into the Time Cube. In this section, we discuss how to construct a Time Cube in our algorithm and how to mine the PCS pattern. The Time Cube is used to create the Periodic Table for discovering candidate PCS patterns.

3.1   Construction of a Time Cube

Time Cubes are used to store clusters after clustering with respect to time. A Time Cube has three dimensions: Cluster-index, Time-index, and Time-period. The goal of using a Time Cube is to produce a Periodic Table, and then verify that if the candidate patterns derived from the Periodic Table are PCS patterns. The Time-period dimension is used to present data in different time periods (e.g., summer quarter, or year 2001); a Time-index is used to indicate the data in each time unit of a period (e.g., the first quarter of year 2001); the Cluster-index discriminates all clusters in every Time-index. Using this structure can save time in verifying the discovered PCS patterns.

1302   C.-L. Hung et al.

Figure 1 shows a Time Cube. It depicts the relationship between time-indices and time-periods. In the next section, we will show how cluster-indices are used to find PCS patterns. Here we use an example to explain how to construct the Time Cube of Figure 1.

Example 3

Assume a stock database contains business information for some companies from 1970-1998, and there are five attributes: stock type, time, the highest stock value of the season, the lowest stock value of the season, and the quantity of trade during the season. Suppose the *min_conf* is 0.75. The Time Cube shown in Figure 1 is a cluster with respect to the time attribute. We use the Time-index to cluster data in separate datasets. The first one is the first season of the first year, and then we do the same step for the second season of the first year, and so on. This process aims at clustering data in different time segments that are independent of each other. When the periodic index becomes the second year, it starts an additional process that compares the cluster of the first season for the first year with that of the first season of the second year. If these two seasons have similar results, it will store the first season of the second year in the same Cluster-index with the first season of the first year. If they are not, then it will be kept in a different Cluster-index.

Assume there exists three clusters in the first season of the first year, and the cluster-indices are a, b, and c, respectively. We compare the three clusters of the first season of the second year with the clusters of the first season of the first year. If all the clusters are different, the clusters of the first season of the second year will be saved with new cluster indices d, e, and f. If two second year clusters are the same as a and b, the cluster indices used in the second year would be a, b, and d. Each dice represents the result of a season in each year after clustering. If it has no cluster in the Cluster-index, it is denoted by 0 in the Time Cube. Otherwise, it is denoted as * in the Time Cube and has at least a cluster with a Cluster-index.

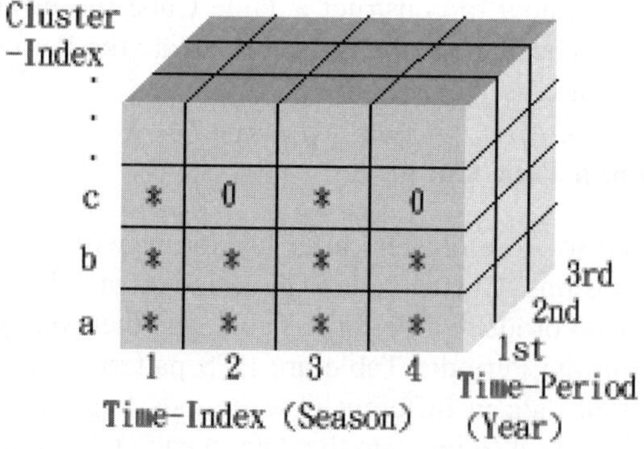

Fig. 1. A time cube

3.2 Construction of a Periodic Table

A Periodic Table is derived from a Time Cube. The table records the number of clusters in the corresponding Cluster-index, indicating that the clusters in each Cluster-index have the same characteristics. The construction of a Periodic Table is shown in Figure 2.

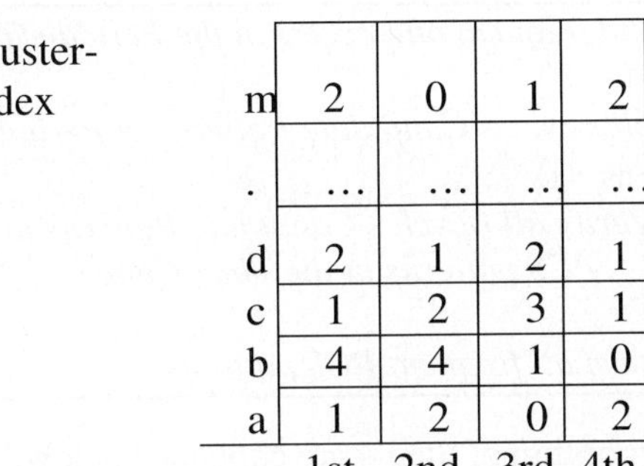

Fig. 2. A Periodic Table

3.3 Mining PCS Patterns

Adopting from the principle of Apriori algorithm [17], we develop the process of finding PCS patterns. First, one-cycle PCS patterns are mined based on the occurrence of patterns in the Periodic Table. A one-cycle PCS pattern comes from Definition 2, $P = (\imath, v, \hat{C})$, where $v = 1$ and period lengthuis the size of the Time-index, such that a one-cycle PCS pattern is formed if the number of occurrences of a pattern P greater than *min_conf*. According to Apriori, for $k \geq 1$, the (k+1)-cycle PCS pattern is derived from the k-cycle PCS pattern, i.e., a (k+1)-cycle is a candidate pattern if all of its k-cycle subsets are k-cycle patterns. All the (k+1)-cycle candidates can be verified by scanning the Time Cube once. Mining the relationship of cluster sequences is the target of the PCS algorithm. The mining process is as follows:

Step 1: Clustering with temporal attribute
The first step is to cluster all valid datasets. One can use the K-mode algorithm or any other appropriate algorithm to cluster a dataset based on the time segment. In this paper, we will not illustrate the process of clustering. The algorithm selection is based on the attributes of datasets.

Step 2: Building a Time Cube
This step puts all clusters from Step 1 into a Time Cube with corresponding Time-indices and Time-periods. After the first round, the clusters of the *nth* time-period will be compared with the clusters of the (n-1)*th* time-period. If there are discrepancies, different cluster-indices will be used for the unmatched clusters of the *nth* time-period.

Step 3: Construction of a Periodic Table
The Time Cube is compressed into a Periodic Table according to the Time-period and the number of clusters that have the same Cluster-indices on the corresponding Time-indices.

Step 4: Mining the PCS pattern

P^1=One-cyclePCSpattern(); /* *Find frequent one-cycles in the Periodic Table* */
  for (i=2 ; i < ι & P^{i-1}≠{ } ; i++)
  {   /* *Create all i-cycles Candidate Patterns in Periodic Table* */
  $PCSC^i$=CreateCandidatePatterns (i)   ;
  P^i=VerifyPattern($PCSC^i$); /* *Verify all i-cycles Candidate Patterns to find frequent*
                             PCS patterns in the Time-Cube   */
  }
  Return all P ;   /* *Return all frequent PCS patterns*   */

The three functions used in the algorithm of Step 4 are explained below.
(1)   One-cyclePCSpattern :

  For i = 0 to Time-Period length - 1
  {
   For j = 0 to Time-Index – 1
    {
     For k = 'a' to Cluster-Index
      $\acute{C}$ (Time-Index, j, k)++;
    }
   if Count of $\acute{C}$ (Time-Index, j, k) >= *min_conf*
     $\acute{C}$ (Time-Index, j, k) is saved in temp;
  } Return temp;

This function finds frequent 1-cycles in the Periodic Table. A 1-cycle can be denoted as   =(ι , s, c) with a confidence no less than *min_conf*, where ι is the period length (the size of the Time-index), s is the cyclic position of the period length, and c is the cluster in the cycle. The confidence is based on the number of clusters in the Periodic Table with a Cluster-index.

Example 4
According to Figure 1 and Figure 2, suppose *min_conf* = 0.75 and the size of the time-period = 4 (there are four months). Any cell with a count no less than 4×0.75 = 3 will pass the test in the Periodic Table. In Figure 2, three 1-cycles of (Time-index = 1, Cluster-index = b), (Time-index = 2, Cluster-index = b), and (Time-index = 3, Cluster-index = c) pass the cycle test. That is, $\acute{C}_0$ = (4, 1, b), $\acute{C}_1$ = (4, 2, b), and $\acute{C}_2$ = (4, 3, c), where $\acute{C}_i$ is denoted as i*th* $\acute{C}$. The output from the algorithm is P^1 = {$PCSC_0^1$ = (4, 1, {(1,b)}), $PCSC_1^1$ = (4, 1,{(2,b)}), $PCSC_2^1$ = (4, 1, {(3,c)}), where PCSC is the candidate PCS pattern and $PCSC_j^i$ is to denote the j*th* candidate pattern in the i*th*-cycle.

(2)   CreateCandidatePatterns :

```
    For j = 0 to P^i-Count − 1
    {
        For l = 1 to P^i-Count
        PCSC_k^i = P_j^i join P_l^i;
        if every element of PCSC_k^i exists in P^i
          k++;
        else
          delete PCSC_k^i;
    }
        return all PCSC_k^i;
```

As in the Apriori algorithm, if a k-cycle is frequent (i.e., passing the *min_conf*), all of its m-cycles for m < k must be frequent as well. Using this property to create a candidate PCS pattern, denoted by $PCSC^i$ where $i \geq 1$, we can form a set of (i-1)-cycle PCS patterns P^{i-1}. This procedure includes two phases: a join phase and a prune phase. The join phase is completed for the (i-1)-cycle PCS pattern set P^{i-1} to form an i-cycle PCSC pattern set $PCSC^i$. The prune phase discards the PCSC patterns in $PCSC^i$ containing some (i-1)-cycle sub-PCS-patterns that are not in P^{i-1}. See Example 5.

Example 5

We continue using the 1-cycle PCS pattern, P^1, obtained in Example 4. The join phase of P^1 and P^1 yields 2-cycle PCSC patterns $PCSC_0^2 = (4, 2, \{(1,b), (2,b)\})$, $PCSC_1^2 = (4, 2, \{(2,b), (3,c)\})$, and $PCSC_2^2 = (4, 2, \{(1,b), (3,c)\})$. Suppose the 2-cycle PCS patterns found after verification are $P_0^2 = PCSC_1^2$ and $P_1^2 = PCSC_2^2$. The only candidate for the 3-cycle PCS pattern formed from P_0^2 and P_1^2 is $PCSC_0^3 = (4, 3, \{(1,b), (2,b), (3,c)\})$. This PCSC pattern is pruned because a sub-pattern of $PCSC_0^3$, $(4, 2, \{(1,b), (2,b)\})$, does not belong to the set of 2-cycle PCS patterns.

(3)   VerifyPattern :

```
    for j = 0 to PCSC_j^i − Count − 1
    {
        for i = 0 to Time-Period length - 1
        {
            if PCSC_j^i appears in each time-slice of the Time Cube
              Count++;
        }
        if Count >= min_conf
          PCSC_j^i is saved in temp;
    }
        return temp;
```

VerifyPattern checks the Time Cube to verify whether or not the pattern posted in the i-cycle PCSC pattern set is frequent. After deriving the i-cycle PCSC patterns, we verify whether such candidates form real i-cycle patterns in the Time Cube. This is done by checking if the number of simultaneous occurrences of the i-cycles in a

PCSC pattern in the time-period is not less than the *min_conf*. When a pattern is confirmed, all of its sub-patterns are eliminated from the pattern lists of fewer cycles.

4   Experimental Results

Since stock research is a good target for time series mining [18], a stock database is used for our experiment. The stock database contains stock exchange information of many companies from 1970-1998, containing approximately 120,000 transactions. After pre-processing the source data, we apply our algorithm to mine PCS patterns for providing decision-making support.

We use the K-mode algorithm in the experiment. First, we transform numeric data to categorical data as shown in Figure 4 by using the transform rules in Figure 5. The fields of the transformed data in Figure 4 (from left to right) are stock id, change rate, open price, highest price, lowest price, trade volume, year, month and week. The date is transformed by using the first week of 1996 as the base. Hence the first week in the first month of 1996 is denoted as "1, 1, 1". The second week is "1, 1, 2".

```
"2016,2,2,2,2,1,1,1,1"
"2207,7,6,6,6,1,1,1,1"
"2014,8,2,2,2,4,1,1,1"
"2006,2,3,3,3,3,1,1,1"
"2012,1,2,2,2,2,1,1,1"
```

Fig. 4. Transformed data

	Change rate (Average)	Open price (Average)	Highest price in a month	Lowest price in a month	Trade volume
1	0%~ -1%	0~10	0~10	0~10	0~500
2	-1%~ -2%	10~20	10~20	10~20	500~1000
3	-2%~ -3%	20~30	20~30	20~30	1000~1500
4	-3%~ -4%	30~40	30~40	30~40	1500~2000
5	-4%~ -5%	40~50	40~50	40~50	2000~2500
6	-5%~ -7%	50~60	50~60	50~60	2500-3000
:	:	:	:	:	:
12	5%~ 7%	110~	110~	110~	5500~

Fig. 5. The transformation rules (Price unit is NT$, Volume unit is 1,000)

Here, the *min_conf* is set to 0.75. So any pattern with a count number not less than 28 × 0.75 = 21 (the database contains twenty-eight years of data, i.e., 112 seasons, and the period length is four because one year has four seasons) will pass the test. In the PCS discovery process, clusters satisfying the *min_conf* are in two segments, the first season and the second season. The number of clusters in the first season is twelve and the number is ten in the second season. The final result is shown in Figure 6.

Time / Item	First season	Second season	Third season	Fourth season
1	7,5,5,5,1	8,2,2,2,2	X	X
2	7,6,6,6,2	3,4,4,4,1	X	X
3	3,4,4,4,1	2,8,2,2,2	X	X
4	4,5,5,5,6	2,2,2,2,8	X	X
5	8,5,5,5,1	7,6,6,6,2	X	X

Fig. 6. The result of 1-cycle PCS patterns

Time / Item	First season	Second season
1	7,5,5,5,1	8,2,2,2,2
2	8,5,5,5,1	3,4,4,4,1
3	3,4,4,4,1	3,4,4,4,1
4	1,5,5,5,1	7,6,6,6,2

Fig. 7. The result of 2-cycle PCS patterns

For the 2-cycle PCS patterns, it can be seen from the Item 1: when cluster {7,5,5,5,1} occurs in the first season, cluster {8,2,2,2,2} is in the second season. Using the transformation rule of Figure 5, categorical data can be converted back to numeric data for the resultant rule. Using the PSC pattern can really provide better decision support for investors and related decision makers.

5 Conclusion and Future Work

In this paper, we present a new concept of time series, the Periodic Clustering Sequential pattern, to illustrate time-related clustering. We develop two mechanisms to use the Time Cube and the Periodic Table, and use the principle of Apriori to make the candidate pattern generation process more efficiently. Although temporal data mining has been applied in many applications, such as the periodic and sequential patterns, the PCS pattern can provide further analysis about time-related clusters.

Presently, we apply the PCS pattern as well as the simplified CS pattern to mine medical information. The attributes come from patient's profiles and examination records. We hope that it can help doctors diagnose patients more effectively. However, more patient data are needed from long-term observations to cluster according to various time periods (such as seasons). In addition, being able to select relevant attributes to illustrate relationship of seasonal illnesses can benefit even more people.

Acknowledgements. This research was partially supported by the National Science Council, Taiwan, under grant number NSC94-2218-E-007-057.

References

1. K. Alsabti, S. Ranka, V. Singh, An Efficient K-Means Clustering Algorithm, PPS/SPDP Workshop on High performance Data Mining, 1997.
2. K. Alsabti, S. Ranka, V. Singh, An Efficient Space-Partitioning Based Algorithm for the K-Means Clustering, 1997.
3. Zhexue Huang, Clustering Large Data Sets With Mixed Numeric and Categorical Values, In Proceedings of The First Pacific-Asia Conference on Knowledge Discovery and Data Mining, Singapore, World Scientific, 1997.
4. Zhexue Huang, A Fast Clustering Algorithm to Cluster Very Large Categorical Data Sets in Data Mining, SIGMOD'97 Data Mining Workshop.
5. Keogh, E., Lin, J., Truppel, W, Clustering of time series subsequences is meaningless: implications for previous and future research. In Data Mining, 2003. ICDM 2003. Third IEEE International Conference, pp. 115-122.
6. Wencai Liu, Yu Luo, Applications of clustering data mining in customer analysis in department store, in Services Systems and Services Management, 2005. Proceedings of ICSSSM '05. 2005 International Conference, pp. 1042-1046.
7. Chun-Hao Chen, Tzung-Pei Hong, Tseng, V.S., Analyzing time-series data by fuzzy data-mining technique. In Granular Computing, 2005 IEEE International Conference, pp. 112-117.
8. Ozden, B.; Ramaswamy, S.; and Silberschatz, A., Cyclic Association Rules. In Proc. Of 1998 Int. Conf. Data Engineering (ICDE'98), pp.412-421, 1998.
9. Chen, X., Petrounias, I. and Heathfield, H., Discovering Temporal Association Rules in Temporal Databases, In Proc. International Workshop on Issues and Applications of Database Technology (IADT'98), pp. 312-319, 1998.
10. Ye, S. and Keane, J.A., Mining Association Rules in Temporal Databases, In Proc. International Conference on Systems, Man and Cybernetics, IEEE, New York. pp.2803-8, 1998.
11. H. Mannila, H. Toivonen, and I. Verkamo, Discovery of Frequent Episodes in Event Sequences, DMKD Journal, 1(3): pp.259-289, 1997.
12. T. Oastes, A family of Algorithms for Finding Temporal Structure in Data, In 6th Workshop on AI and Statistics, 1997.
13. Han, J., Dong, G. and Yin, Y., Efficient Mining of Partial Periodic Patterns in Time Series Database. In Proc. Fifteenth International Conference on Data Engineering, Sydney, Australia. IEEE Computer Society, pp.106-115, 1999.
14. S. Parthasarathy, M. J. Zaki, M. Ogihara, S. Dwarkadas, Incremental and Interactive Sequence Mining, ACM, CIKM'99, 1999.
15. Patel, P., Keogh, E., Lin, J., Lonardi, S., Mining motifs in massive time series databases, In Data Mining, 2002. ICDM 2002. Proceedings. 2002 IEEE International Conference, pp. 370-377.
16. Povinelli, R.J., Xin Feng, A new temporal pattern identification method for characterization and prediction of complex time series events, In 2003 Knowledge and Data Engineering, IEEE Transactions, Vol. 15, No. 2, pp. 339-352.
17. R. Srikant and R. Agrawal, Mining Sequential Patterns: Generalizations and Performance Improvements, In 5th EDBT, 1996.
18. Xiao-Ye Wang, Zheng-Ou Wang, Stock market time series data mining based on regularized neural network and rough set, In Machine Learning and Cybernetics, 2002. Proceedings. 2002 International Conference, pp. 315-318.

Text Mining with Application to Engineering Diagnostics

Liping Huang and Yi Lu Murphey

Department of ECE, 4901 Evergreen Road
Dearborn, Michigan, USA
{yilu, lilyping}@umich.edu

Abstract. Our research focuses on text document mining with an application to engineering diagnostics. In automotive industry, the auto problem descriptions are often used as the first step of a diagnostic process that map the problem descriptions to diagnostic categories such as engine, transmission, electrical, brake, etc. This mapping of problem description to diagnostic categories is currently being done manually by mechanics that perform this task largely based on their memory and experience, which usually lead to lengthy repair processes, less accurate diagnostics and unnecessary part replacement. This paper presents our research in applying text mining technology to the automatic mapping of problem descriptions to the correct diagnostic categories. We present our results through the study on a number of important issues relating to text document classification including term weighting schemes, LSA and similarity functions. A text document categorization system is presented and it has been tested on a large test data collected from auto dealers. Its system performance is very satisfactory.

Keywords: data mining and knowledge, intelligent systems.

1   Introduction

As computers become more powerful, data storage devices become more plentiful, the amount of information in digital form has dramatically increased. Many organizations have been collecting large amounts of information during daily operations, but most of them are unable to extract useful information from the data to improve their operations due to the lack of automatic tools in data mining. In automotive industry there is abundant information available in human language description form that contains valuable vehicle diagnostic knowledge, marketing information, consumer evaluation or satisfaction of certain vehicle models, styles, accessories, etc. We are particularly interested in applying text mining to engineering diagnostics. In automotive industry, several thousand auto problems per week are reported to various dealership shops. In a typical diagnostic process, problems are first described, in casual natural language, by either customers or maintenance technicians. Based on the description, the vehicle problem is assigned with a specific diagnostic code. Each diagnostic code represents a problem category of vehicles, which are used to guide the diagnostic process in search for the true causes of the problems, and help solving automotive problems as well. Problem descriptions are then mapped to diagnostic

M. Ali and R. Dapoigny (Eds.): IEA/AIE 2006, LNAI 4031, pp. 1309–1317, 2006.

categories such as engine, transmission, electrical, etc. The diagnostic code is then used to guide the further diagnosis for the true causes of the vehicle problem within the category. This mapping of problem description to diagnostic categories is currently being done manually by mechanics who perform this task largely based their memory and experience, which usually lead to lengthy repair processes, less accurate diagnostics and unnecessary part replacement. Hence, new techniques are in high demand to correctly and automatically map problem descriptions to problem categories.

Our research is focused on applying text mining technology to automatically categorizing text documents with applications to engineering fault diagnostics. When a customer states his automotive problems, the description, such as there is a noise heard in the engine and the engine runs rough, is probably mapped to different diagnostic codes according to mechanics' experience, which usually point in various directions for the repairing procedure. The text descriptions of vehicles problems pose another challenge: data are often ill-structured and text descriptions often do not follow the English grammar, and often contain many self-invented acronyms and shorthand descriptions. One example is given below.

Customer 1: "WENT ON A SALES ROAD TEST WITH CUST, VEHICLE WOULDNOT START,"
Customer 2: "CHECK CAR WONT START,"
Customer 3: "CK BATTERY HARD TO START."

These three descriptions are expected to be mapped to the same diagnostic category, whose definition typically is: ENGINE WOULD NOT START. From this example we can see a number of problems including synonymy, there are many different ways to describe the same vehicle problem. It is another important task for us to look for the most appropriate code based on multiple symptoms. In addition, we are dealing with other problems such as poor wording and self invented acronyms. Polysemy is also a problem, for example, the word "light" could mean a number of things in vehicle problem descriptions. Finally, there are thousands or more automotive problems reported to the mechanical department every week, manually mapping work by mechanics is time-consuming and error prone. When new codes are generated and added in the diagnostic system with the vehicle development, it requires a longer time for the mechanics to accommodate the system update.

In this paper, we present an automatic text categorization system, DKE&TC (Diagnostic Knowledge Extraction and Text Classification), developed based on vector space model. DKE&TC has two components, DKE is a component that has functions for learning diagnostic categorization knowledge from a corpus of diagnostic text documents. The TC component then applies the learnt knowledge to categorizing a customer's description of vehicle problems to diagnostic codes. We also present our study on a number of important issues relating to text document classification including term weighting schemes, LSA and similarity functions. The proposed system has been trained on more than 200000 documents over mover than 50 diagnostic categories and tested over 6000 documents.

2 DKE&TC: A System for Automatic Learning of Diagnostic Knowledge from Text Documents

In automotive diagnostics, much like other engineering diagnostics, problems of vehicles are organized into different categories. We are trying to develop a system, DKE&TC, that automatically maps a problem description, q, to the correct diagnostic categories. The DKE&TC consists of two stages (see Figure 1), LFT(Learning From Text), and DTC(Diagnostic Text Classification). The LFT system is the machine learning stage that attempts to extract diagnostic knowledge from text documents. The LFT system consists of two major components within our research interest, a Term Category Weight (TCW) matrix and the matrix obtained through the well-known Latent Semantic Analysis (LSA) that uses SVD to obtain a weighted matrix. The output from the LFT system is a matrix representing document categories. The second stage is to transform the input problem description q to document vector and find the best matched diagnostic categories using the matrices generated by the LFT system.

2.1 Learning from Text(LFT)

Learning from Text (LFT) component is developed based on the vector space model(VSM) [1,10,11,12]. It is one of the classic models in the area of information retrieval and text mining. In the vector space model text objects are modeled as elements of a vector space. That is, documents, user query in the model are described as a set of representative keywords called index terms. An index term is simply a word or a token which can help understanding the main theme of the document. After index

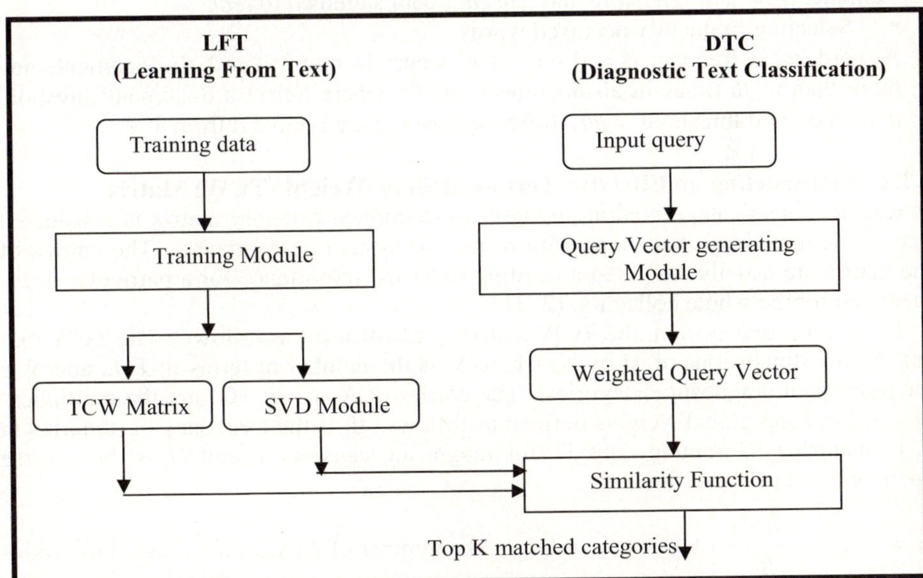

Fig. 1. System architecture of Diagnostic Knowledge Extraction and Text Classification (DKE&TC)

terms are identified and extracted from the document set, they need to be weighted according to their importance for summarizing the contents of a document. There are different ways to compute the index term weight[3]. The most commonly used weight scheme is tf-idf (term frequenc-inverse document frequency). However, depending on document collection, the results of different weight schemes are not quite consistent. After document and query are represented as vectors in the vector space, the document is ranked with respect to the query according to a similarity measure.

LFT consists of two major computational steps, the document indexing, and constructing an effective term by diagnostic category matrix. Let us assume a collection of diagnostic text documents are to be classified into N categories, $(C_1, C_2, \ldots C_N)$, and we have training documents $Tr_1, Tr_2, \ldots, Tr_N$, where Tr_i, contains the training documents belonging to category i, i = 1, ..., N. The following subsections describe the two computational steps.

2.1.1 Document Indexing Process

First we generate an index term list T_L, where each term $t_i \in T\_L$ is extracted from all documents in Tr, where $Tr = Tr_1 \cup \ldots \cup Tr_N$. The T_L is then processed by the following steps:

- Stopping Word (Function Words) Removal:

Since stopping words are unlikely to be useful for document matching, they are removed from T_L. Examples of stopping words: *the, from, to, ...*

- Stemming Words

Morphological variants of the same lexical items are merged into a single root. For example: *leak, leaks, leaking* and *leaked* are all stemmed to *leak*

- Selecting frequently occurred words

A word, *w*, is frequent if and only if it occurs in more than d_th documents and more than *w_th* times in all documents in Tr, where Select a document threshold *d_th* and word threshold *w_th*. Infrequent words are removed from T_L.

2.1.2 Constructing an Effective Term-Category-Weight (TCW) Matrix

In text document categorization, the term by document category matrix is considered one of the most important steps with respect to system performance. The entries of the matrix are usually weighted according to terms' importance for a particular document and for the whole collection [2, 3].

In the proposed system, the TCW matrix is constructed as follows. The TCW matrix A with dimensions of M by N, where M is the number of terms in T_L, and N is the number of diagnostic categories. The entries of A, $a_{i,j} = tf_{ij} * G_i$, are the multiplication of local and global weights defined as follows. tf_{ij} is the frequency of *i*th terms in T_L occurring in training data Tr_j for diagnostic category j, and G_i is the inverse document frequency defined as

$$G_i = \log_2 \left[\frac{ndocs}{df_i} \right] + 1$$

where *ndocs* is the number of documents in the entire train-

ing data Tr, df_i, stands for document frequency of term i, is defined as the total number of documents in Tr that contain term i.

The local weight is used to evaluate the importance of each term in the each category. However sometimes less frequently used terms can be more critical in distinguish one category from another. For example, in a document "check fuel leak, check and advise", term "leak" is probably more meaningful than "check" although "check" occurs more often than "leak". Global weight is therefore introduced to reflect the overall importance of the index term in the whole document collection. The idea is that a term that occurs rarely should have a high weight and frequently occurring terms should be weighted low. Taken to the extreme, stop words such as "the", "an","a", that appear in almost all documents should ideally receive a global weight of 0. The column vectors in TCW matrix A can be interpreted as a representative vector for a diagnostic category.

Another important type of term by diagnostic category matrix is constructed using the latent semantic indexing (LSI) method [4, 5, 6], which is a variant of vector space model. LSI is a statistical model of word usage that permits comparisons of the semantic similarity between pieces of textual information. While assuming the existence of some underlying or "latent" semantic structure according to the overall term usage pattern that is partially obscured by variability in term choice [5], LSA was originally designed to improve the effectiveness of information retrieval methods by performing text retrieval based on the derived "semantic" content of words in a query as opposed to performing direct word matching. This approach avoids some of the problems of synonymy and polysemy. A truncated singular value decomposition (SVD) is used to build a lower dimensional space which is associated with this "latent" semantic structure. Each document and query is mapped into this space. Relevance judgments for the user's query are also performed in this space.

In our model, we decomposed a weighted term frequency matrix A into the product of three matrices [3, 4] , $A = U\Sigma V^{T}$, where $U^{T}U = V^{T}V = I_{n}$ and $\Sigma = diag(\sigma_{1},\cdots,\sigma_{n})$, $\sigma_{i} > 0$ for $1 \le i \le r$, $\sigma_{j} = 0$ for $j \ge r+1$. Matrices U and V contain left and right singular vectors of A, respectively, and diagonal matrix, Σ, contains singular values of A. If only the k largest singular values of Σ are kept along with their corresponding columns in the matrices U and V, we obtain new matrices U_{k},V_{k} with reduced dimension. A rank-k approximation to A is constructed with the following formula: $A \approx A_{k} = U_{k}\Sigma_{k}V_{k}^{T}$. A_{k} is the unique matrix of rank k that is closest in the least squares sense to A.

2.2 Diagnostic Text Classification (DTC)

The DTC component has the following two major computational steps, formulating a query document vector based input problem description, and determining the similarity between the query document and the diagnostic categories. An input problem description, d, is first transformed into a pseudo-document within the reduced term-category space. Namely d is transformed to $\overline{q}$, which is a term vector with the same length M as T_L, and $\overline{q} = (q_{1},...,q_{M})^{T}$, where q_{i} is the frequency of the ith term on T_L occurred in the query document d, i = 1, …, M. The decision on the diagnostic category of $\overline{q}$ is made based on the similarity measure $\overline{q}$ and each column vector of A. Let the column vectors of A be $\overline{a}_j = (a_{1j},...,a_{Mj})^T$, j=1, ..., N, We have investigated three different similarity measures between the query vector $\overline{q}$ and the TCF matrix A. The first similarity function of the query vector and a diagnostic category is measured by the cosine measure [7] denoted as follows:

$$r_j^c(\overline{q},\overline{a}_j) = \frac{\overline{q} \bullet \overline{a}_j}{\|\overline{q}\| \bullet \|\overline{a}_j\|} = \frac{\sum_{i-1}^M q_i a_{ij}}{\sqrt{\sum_{i=1}^M q_i^2 \sum_{i=1}^M a_{ij}^2}}$$

Pearson's correlation coefficient is another measure of extent to which two vectors are related[8]. The formula for Pearson's correlation coefficient takes on many forms. A commonly used formula is shown below:

$$r_j^p(\overline{q},\overline{a}_j) = \frac{M\sum_{i=1}^M q_i a_{ij} - \sum_{i=1}^M q_i \sum_{i=1}^M a_{ij}}{\sqrt{\left[M\sum_{i=1}^M q_i^2 - \left(\sum_{i=1}^M q_i\right)^2\right]\left[M\sum_{i=1}^M a_{ij}^2 - \left(\sum_{i=1}^M a_{ij}\right)^2\right]}}$$

The third measure we investigated in our system is Spearman rank correlation coefficient. It provides a measure of how closely two sets of rankings agree with each other. Spearman rank correlation coefficient is a special case of the Pearson correlation coefficient in which the data are converted to ranks before calculating the coefficient. It can be used when the distribution of the data makes the latter undesirable or misleading [9]. The formula for Spearman's rank correlation coefficient is:

$$r_j^s = 1 - \frac{6\sum_{i=1}^M d_i^2}{M(M^2-1)}$$

where: $\overline{d} = (d_1,...,d_M)^T$ is the difference vector between ranks of corresponding values of $\overline{q}$ and $\overline{a}_j$.

3 Experiment Results

The proposed DKE&TC system has been fully implemented. The LFT program used a training data set of 200,000 documents that describe 54 different categories of auto problems to construct a TCW matrix A with dimensions of 3972x54. Based on the practical consideration, for each input query document d, the DKE&TC finds the three diagnostic categories that best match d. The performance measure is the percentage of the queries in the test set whose true categories are contained in the matched categories returned by DKE&TC.

The performances of DKE&TC system and the SVD system on the test set of 6000 queries are shown in Figure 2 (a). The retrieval performance of SVD is heavily affected by its value of rank K. We explored the effects of varied K values used in SVD and compared it with the DKE&TC's performance. It appears that the best performance was achieved with K equal to 14. However the DKE&TE system outperformed the best SVD system by more than 11%.

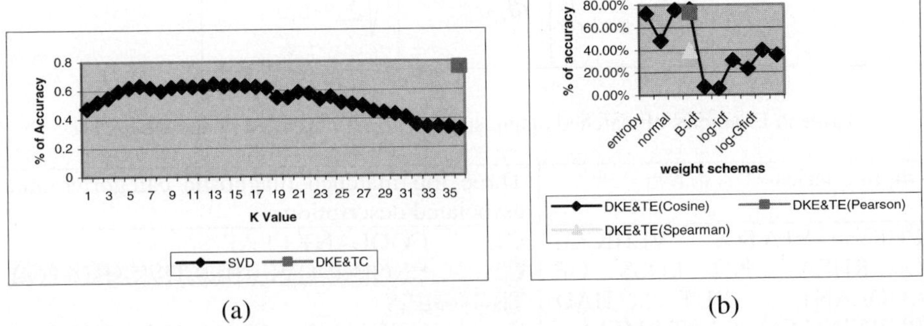

(a)   (b)

Fig. 2. Performance evaluation. (a) Performances of the proposed DKE&TC system vs SVD with various K values. (b) Comparing DKE&TE with various weight schemes and similarity functions.

We also compared the performance of the DKE&TE system with other weighting schemes commonly used in text document categorization and the results are shown in Figure 2(b) along with the performances of the DKE&TC systems that used three different similarity functions, cosine, Pearson, and Spearman. The definition of these weight schemes are defined in Table 1 in which, tf_{ij} is the frequency of term i occurred in document category j, df_i is the total number of document categories in the training data that contain term i, gf_i is global frequency at which term i occurs in the entire training data, ndocs is the total number of document categories in the entire collection. In addition, we define:

$$p_{ij} = \frac{tf_{ij}}{gf_i} \text{, and } \quad B_{ij} = \begin{cases} 0 & \text{if } \text{tf}_{ij} = 0 \\ 1 & \text{if } \text{tf}_{ij} > 0 \end{cases}.$$

Figure 3 shows that the DKE&TC systems used similarity functions of Pearson and cosine gave the best performances.

Table 2 shows three examples of document queries and the diagnostic categories classified by the DKE&TC system. The first column lists the three examples of input queries and the right column lists three top matched diagnostic categories to each input query. The correct categories are highlighted.

Table 1. Definitions of various weight schemes

entropy	Gfidf	Normal	B-idf	B-normal
$\mathrm{tf}_{ij} * \left(1 - \sum_j \dfrac{p_{ij}\log(p_{ij})}{\log(ndocs)}\right)$	$\mathrm{tf}_{ij} * \dfrac{gf_i}{df_i}$	$\mathrm{tf}_{ij} * \sqrt{\dfrac{1}{\sum_j tf_{ij}^2}}$	$B_{ij} * \left(\log\left[\dfrac{ndocs}{df_i}\right]+1\right)$	$B_{ij} * \sqrt{\dfrac{1}{\sum_j tf_{ij}^2}}$
Bg-idf	**Log-entropy**	**log-Gfidf**	**log-norm**	
$\log(\mathrm{tf}_{ij}+1) * \left(\log\left[\dfrac{ndocs}{df_i}\right]+1\right)$	$\log(\mathrm{tf}_{ij}+1) * \left(1 - \sum_j \dfrac{p_{ij}\log(p_{ij})}{\log(ndocs)}\right)$	$\log(\mathrm{tf}_{ij}+1) * \dfrac{gf_i}{df_i}$	$\log(\mathrm{tf}_{ij}+1) * \sqrt{\dfrac{1}{\sum_j tf_{ij}^2}}$	

Table 2. Examples of matched diagnostic categories classified by the DKE&TC

Input queries	Three top matched diagnostic categories and associated description
CUST STATES VEHICLE OVERHEAT NO LOSS OF COOLANT BUT HAD BURNING COOLANT SMELL.	C1: COOLANT LEAK C2: ENGINE OVERHEATS/RADIATOR TROUBLES C3: UNUSUAL EXHAUST SYSTEM ODOR
CUSTOMER STATES CHECK FOR OIL LEAK BETWEEN TRANS. AND ENGINE	C1: ENGINE LEAKS OIL C2: UNDETERMINED ENGINE LEAK C3: TRANSMISSION/CLUTCH FLUID LEAKS
SAYS GETTING SQUEAK NOISE FROM BELT OR BEARING TYPE	C1: ENGINE BELT BREAKING/SLIPPING/SQUEALING C2: ENGINE BELT SLIPPING/SQUEALING C3: ENGINE BELT OFF/FRAYED/COMING APART/BROKEN

4 Conclusion

In this paper, we presented a text document mining system, DKE&TC, developed for the automotive engineering diagnostic application. We presented our research results in a number of important areas including various weighting schemes and similarity functions. Our experiment results show that the proposed system, DKE&TC, outperformed the well-known LSA model and many other weight schemes. We also compared the performance of DKE&TC system with diagnostic engineers on a small data set of 100 queries. The results showed that the DKE&TC system outperformed its human counter part.

Acknowledgment

This work is support in part by a CEEP grant from the College of Engineering and Computer Science at the University of Michigan-Dearborn.

References

1. S.K.M.Wong., V.V.R.a.: A Critical Analysis of Vector Space Model for Information Retrieval. Journal of the Americal Society for Information Science, 1986. **37**(2): p. 279-287.
2. Salton, G.a.B., C.: Term weighting approaches in automatic text retrieval. Information Processing and Management, 1988. **24**(5): p. 513--523.
3. Dumais, S.T.: Enhancing performance in latent semantic indexing (LSI) retrieval, in Technical Report Technical Memorandum. 1990, Bellcore.
4. Berry, M.W., Dumais, S. T., and O'Brien, G. W.: Using linear algebra for intelligent information retrieval. SIAM Review, 1995. **37**(4): p. 573-595.
5. S. Deerwester, S.D., G. Furnas, T. Landauer, and R. Harshman.: Indexing by Latent Semantic Analysis. Journal of the American Society for Information Science, 1990. **41**: p. 391-407.
6. T. K. Landauer, P.W.F., and D. Laham.: Introduction to latent semantic analysis. Discourse Processes, 1998(25): p. 259-284.
7. Michael W. Berry, Z.D., Elizabeth R. Jessup.: Matrices, Vector Spaces, and Information Retrieval. SIAM Review, 1999. **41**(2): p. 335-362.
8. Edwards, A.L.: The Correlation Coefficient. San Francisco, CA: W. H. Freeman, 1976
9. Lehmann, E.L., D'Abrera, H. J. M., Nonparametrics: Statistical Methods Based on Ranks, rev., ed. E. Cliffs. NJ: Prentice-Hall, 1998
10. Baeza-Yates, R., Ribeiro-Neto, B.: Modern Information Retrieval, Addison-Wesley, 1999
11. Gerard Salton and Michael McGill.: Introduction to Modern Information Retrieval. McGraw-Hill, 1983
12. Ana Cardoso-Cachopo, A.L.O.: An Empirical Comparison of Text Categorization Methods. in SPIRE 2003,LNCS, 2003

Handling Incomplete Categorical Data
for Supervised Learning*

Been-Chian Chien[1], Cheng-Feng Lu[2], and Steen J. Hsu[3]

[1] Department of Computer Science and Information Engineering,
National University of Tainan,
33, Sec. 2, Su-Lin St., Tainan 70005, Taiwan, R.O.C.
bcchien@mail.nutn.edu.tw
[2] Department of Information Engineering, I-Shou University,
Kaohsiung 840, Taiwan, R.O.C.
phon@seed.net.tw
[3] Department of Information Management, Ming Hsin University of Science and Technology,
1 Hsin-Hsing Road, Hsin-Fong, Hsin-Chu, Taiwan 304, R.O.C.
steenhsu@mis.must.edu.tw

Abstract. Classification is an important research topic in knowledge discovery. Most of the researches on classification concern that a complete dataset is given as a training dataset and the test data contain all values of attributes without missing. Unfortunately, incomplete data usually exist in real-world applications. In this paper, we propose new handling schemes of learning classification models from incomplete categorical data. Three methods based on rough set theory are developed and discussed for handling incomplete training data. The experiments were made and the results were compared with previous methods making use of a few famous classification models to evaluate the performance of the proposed handling schemes.

1 Introduction

The classification problem is a task of supervised learning that consists of two phases. The learning phase is to learn a classification model from a set of training data with a predefined class for each datum. The classification phase is to classify unknown cases to one of the predefined classes using the learned classification model. Typically, the training data are assumed to be collected completely without loss or error inside. Reliable classification models thus can be learned from the training data and represented in the form of classification rules, decision trees, or mathematical functions. However, incomplete data happen usually in real world applications. An incomplete dataset is that a dataset contains at least one missing value as in Table 1. The symbols '?' in the cases x_5, x_6, x_9 denote missing values. The reasons of producing incomplete data may be caused by a broken machine or mistakenly erased by a person. Generally, the incomplete training data will degrade the learning quality of classification models.

---

* This work was supported in part by the National Science Council of Taiwan, R. O. C., under contract NSC94-2213-E-024-004.

M. Ali and R. Dapoigny (Eds.): IEA/AIE 2006, LNAI 4031, pp. 1318–1328, 2006.

Table 1. A simple incomplete dataset

No.	outlook	temperature	humidity	play
x_1	sunny	L	H	no
x_2	?	H	H	no
x_3	overcast	M	?	yes
x_4	rainy	M	H	yes

In this paper, we investigate the problem of handling incomplete categorical data contained in training datasets for supervised learning. Since the incomplete samples do not provide perfect information for training process, most of traditional supervised learning methods can not deal with incomplete data directly but generate inaccurate classifiers from an incomplete dataset. If the incomplete training data can be tackled well, an effective classification model can be learned. Many methods on dealing with missing values for classification had been proposed in the past decades. The previous researches on handling incomplete data can be generally divided into two strategies:

(1) Ignore the data with missing values inside the dataset. [7][10][13][18][21].
(2) Fill the missing value by an appropriate alternative. [5][8][12][14][17][23].

To learn an effective classification model from incomplete categorical data, we try to overcome the problem of missing values in attributes based on rough set theory. During the learning phase of classification, three methods are proposed to handle the problem of incomplete categorical data based on rough membership functions. The proposed methods transform categorical data into numerical form and replace the missing values with different granular processes based on rough membership.

To evaluate the performance of the proposed handling methods, a few famous classification models, such as GPIZ, SVM, NB and NBTree, were selected to test and compare with C4.5 which handles missing values using information gain. The tested datasets include real and artificial incomplete datasets generated from UCI Machine Learning repository [1]. The experimental results demonstrate that the proposed methods based on rough membership can perform various effects on different classification models.

The remainder of this paper is organized as follows: Section 2 reviews the rough set theory and the related researches of incomplete data. In Section 3, we present the proposed scheme for handling incomplete data. Section 4 describes the experiments and demonstrates the performance of proposed methods combining different classification models. Finally, conclusions and future work are presented.

2   Related Work

2.1   Rough Sets Theory

The rough set theory was proposed by Pawlak in 1982 [19][20] that is an extension of set theory and is well suited to deal with incompleteness and uncertainty. The main advantages of rough set theory are that it does not need any additional information about data and provides a powerful foundation to reveal important structures in data.

Many researches had broadly and successfully applied rough set theory to discover knowledge from incomplete databases [8][10][18][23].

The idea of rough sets is based on the establishment of equivalence classes on a given dataset U, called a universe, and supports two approximations called lower approximation and upper approximation. We give the definitions of the rough set theory as follows:

Let $S = (U, T)$ denote an information table, where U means a non-empty finite set of objects and $T = A \cup C$, A is the set of condition attributes and C is the decision attribute. We then define a *equivalence relation* $R_A(B)$ on S as $R_A(B) = \{(x, y) \mid x, y \in U, \forall A_j \in B, A_j(x) = A_j(y)\}$. We say that objects x and y are indiscernible if the equivalence relation $R_A(B)$ is satisfied on the set U, for all $A_j \in A$ and each $B \subseteq A$. Let $[x]_B$ denote an *equivalence class* of S on $R_A(B)$ and $[U]_B$ denote the set of all equivalence classes $[x]_B$ for $x \in U$. That is, $[x]_B = \{y \mid x\,R_A(B)\,y, \forall x, y \in U\}$ and $[U]_B = \{[x]_B \mid x \in U\}$. Then, the *lower approximation* and *upper approximation* for B on concept X, denoted $B_*(X)$ and $B^*(X)$ are defined as $B_*(X) = \{x \mid x \in U, [x]_B \subseteq X\}$ and $B^*(X) = \{x \mid x \in U$ and $[x]_B \cap X \neq \varnothing\}$, respectively.

For a given concept $X \subseteq U$, a *rough membership function* of X on the set of attributes B is defined as

$$\mu_B^X(x) = \frac{\mid [x]_B \cap X \mid}{\mid [x]_B \mid}, \tag{1}$$

where $\mid [x]_B \cap X \mid$ denotes the cardinality of the set $[x]_B \cap X$. The rough membership value $\mu_B^X(x)$ can be interpreted as the conditional probability that an object x belongs to X, given that the object belongs to $[x]_B$, where $\mu_B^X(x) \in [0, 1]$.

2.2 Review of Incomplete Data Handling

The techniques of supervised learning on incomplete datasets are more difficult than on complete datasets. Designing an effective learning algorithm being able to deal with incomplete datasets is a challenge to researchers. Many previous researches generally were motivated from two strategies: ignoring and repairing.

The first strategy is to ignore the whole record with unknown values or just ignore the missing attribute values. The related researches are enumerated as follows:

(1) *Ignore samples or attributes* [7].
(2) *Ignore the missing attribute values* [10][13][18][21][24].

The second strategy is to use the mechanism of reparation to transforms an incomplete dataset into a complete dataset. The related techniques on handling incomplete categorical data are presented as follows:

(1) *Fill in the missing value manual.*
(2) *Concept most common attribute value* [17].
(3) *Assign all possible values of the attribute* [8][9].
(4) *Use rough set approach to repair missing values* [14][15][23].

The preprocess of handling incomplete data is important and necessary for learning a high-accuracy classification model.

3 Handling Incomplete Data Based on Rough Membership

In this section, we introduce three handling methods for incomplete data based on rough membership. The first method is called *fill in another value* (FIAV). The second and third methods are *fill in all possible value with class* (FIAP-class) and *fill in all possible value with minimum* (FIAP-min), respectively. All the three methods first employ the transformation function based on rough membership of equation (1) for transform categorical data into numerical data. The purpose of the transformation is to transform the categorical attributes into a set of numerical attributes. The transformation function is described as follows:

Given a dataset U having n conditional attributes $A_1, A_2, \dots , A_n$ and a decision attribute C. Let D_i be the domain of A_i, for $1 \leq i \leq n$, and $C = \{C_1, C_2, \dots , C_K\}$, where K is the number of predefined classes. For each object $x_j \in U$, $x_j = (v_{j1}, v_{j2}, \dots , v_{jn})$, where $v_{ji} \in D_i$ stands for the value on attribute A_i of the object x_j.

The idea of transformation is to transform the original categorical attribute A_i into K numerical attributes $\tilde{A}_i$. Let $\tilde{A}_i = (A_{i1}, A_{i2}, \dots , A_{iK})$, where K is the number of predefined classes C and the domains of $A_{i1}, A_{i2}, \dots , A_{iK}$ are in $[0, 1]$. The method of transformation is based on the rough membership function of equation (1).

For an object $x_j \in U$, $x_j = (v_{j1}, v_{j2}, \dots , v_{jn})$, $v_{ji} \in D_i$, the v_{ji} will be transformed into $(w_{jk}, w_{j(k+1)}, \dots , w_{j(k+K-1)})$, $w_{ik} \in [0, 1]$ and $w_{jk} = \mu_{A_i}^{C_1}(x_j)$, $w_{j(k+1)} = \mu_{A_i}^{C_2}(x_j)$, $\dots , w_{j(k+K-1)} = \mu_{A_i}^{C_K}(x_j)$, where

$$\mu_{A_i}^{C_k}(x_j) = \frac{\mid [x_j]_{A_i} \cap [x_j]_{C_k} \mid}{\mid [x_j]_{A_i} \mid}, \text{ if } v_{ji} \in [x_j]_{Ai} \text{ and } x_j \in U. \tag{2}$$

After the transformation, the new dataset U' with attributes $\tilde{A} = \{\tilde{A}_1, \tilde{A}_2, \dots , \tilde{A}_n\}$ is obtained and an object $x_j \in U$, $x_j = (v_{j1}, v_{j2}, \dots , v_{jn})$ will be transformed into y_j, $y_j = (w_{j1}, w_{j2}, \dots , w_{jn'})$, where $n' = q \times K$, q is the number of categorical attributes.

The proposed handling methods are presented in detailed as follows.

FIAV

This method is described as its name; the missing values are filled by an alternate value. For example, we can use 'unknown' value to replace the missing values. Then, the values in categorical attributes are transformed into numerical values. We thus ignore what real values should be in the missing fields and shift to concern about the distribution of 'unknown' value on the decision attribute. We give an example to illustrate this method using the incomplete dataset as shown in Table 1.

Example 1: In Table 1, there are of three categorical attributes: *outlook, temperature* and *humidity* and the decision attribute is *play*. The FIAV method uses the value 'unknown' to replace the symbol '?' as a new attribute value. The symbolic categories in the three attributes become: *outlook*: {sunny, overcast, rainy, unknown}, *temperature*: {L, M, H} and *humidity*: {L, H, unknown}. The number of numerical attributes $n' = 3 \times 2 = 6$. Based on the above equivalence classes, the values in case x_1 after transformation are as follows:

$$w_{11} = \mu_{A_1}^{C_1}(x_1) = 0, \quad w_{12} = \mu_{A_1}^{C_2}(x_1) = 1, \quad w_{13} = \mu_{A_2}^{C_1}(x_1) = 0,$$

$$w_{14} = \mu_{A_2}^{C_2}(x_1) = 1, \quad w_{15} = \mu_{A_3}^{C_1}(x_1) = 0.33, \quad w_{16} = \mu_{A_3}^{C_2}(x_1) = 0.67.$$

So, $y_1 = (w_{11}, w_{12}, w_{13}, w_{14}, w_{15}, w_{16}) = (0, 1, 0, 1, 0.33, 0.67)$. The new dataset U' is generated and shown as Table 2.

Table 2. The results of the transformation of Table 1 using FIAV

No.	outlook		temperature		humidity		play
	w_{j1}	w_{j2}	w_{j3}	w_{j4}	w_{j5}	w_{j6}	C_i
y_1	0	1	0	1	0.33	0.67	no
y_2	0	1	0	1	0.33	0.67	no
y_3	1	0	1	0	1	0	yes
y_4	1	0	1	0	0.33	0.67	yes

FIAP-class

This method assumes that missing values can be any possible values in the attribute. Hence, all possible rough membership values have to be calculated by replacing the missing values with all possible values in that attribute. After all possible rough membership values are derived, the value with the maximum of $\mu_{A_i}^{C_k}(x_j)$ is picked to be the alternate of the missing value for object x_j on attribute A_i, where C_k is the class of object x_j. We give Example 2 to illustrate this method more detailed.

Example 2: In Table 1, the missing values are first replaced by all possible values according to their attributes, e.g. the symbolic categories in the three attributes are: *outlook*: {sunny, overcast, rainy}, *temperature*: {L, M, H} and *humidity*: {L, H}. The object x_2 in attribute *outlook* is replaced by sunny, overcast and rainy. The missing value in the object x_2 will have three sets of possible transformation values corresponding to sunny, overcast and rainy in attribute *outlook*, as follows:

If *outlook* = sunny in case x_2, the values after transformation are
$$w_{21} = \mu_{A_1}^{C_1}(x_2) = 0, \quad w_{22} = \mu_{A_1}^{C_2}(x_2) = 1.$$
If *outlook* = overcast in case x_2, the values after transformation are
$$w_{21} = \mu_{A_1}^{C_1}(x_2) = 0.5, \quad w_{22} = \mu_{A_1}^{C_2}(x_2) = 0.5.$$
If *outlook* = rainy in case x_2, the values after transformation are
$$w_{21} = \mu_{A_1}^{C_1}(x_2) = 0.5, \quad w_{22} = \mu_{A_1}^{C_2}(x_2) = 0.5.$$

Since the class label of the object x_2 is C_2, i.e. *play* = no, we select the set of rough membership values with maximum $\mu_{A_1}^{C_2}(x_2)$ among the three sets (i.e. $w_{21} = 0$ and $w_{22} = 1$) to be the alternate of the missing value on the attribute *outlook*. The other missing values can be also produced by the same procedure and are shown as Table 3.

Table 3. The results of the transformation of Table 1 using FIAP-class

No.	outlook		temperature		humidity		play
	w_{j1}	w_{j2}	w_{j3}	w_{j4}	w_{j5}	w_{j6}	C_i
y_1	0	1	0	1	0.33	0.67	no
y_2	0	1	0	1	0.33	0.67	no
y_3	1	0	1	0	0.50	0.50	yes
y_4	1	0	1	0	0.33	0.67	yes

FIAP-min

This method is similar to the FIAP-class method except the selected rough membership values. FIAP-min selects the minimum of $\mu_{A_i}^{C_k}(x_j)$ as the alternate from the same class instead of the maximum in FIAP-class method. We define the minimum value λ_{jk} as follows

$$\lambda_{jk} = \arg\min_{v_{ji} \in D_i} \left\{ \mu_{A_i = v_{ji}}^{C_k}(x_j) \right\}. \tag{3}$$

Then we use λ_{jk} to replace the missing value w_{jk}. We give Example 3 to show the transformation of FIAP-min on Table 1.

Example 3: As the example of the missing value of object x_2 in Table 1, we first obtain the three sets of transformation values corresponding to sunny, overcast and rainy in the attribute *outlook* as Example 2. Then, we have $\lambda_{21} = \min\{0, 0.5, 0.5\} = 0$ and $\lambda_{22} = \min\{1, 0.5, 0.5\} = 0.5$. Therefore, we replace w_{21} with 0 and w_{22} with 0.5. The same procedure is applied to the other missing values in Table 1 and the result is shown in Table 4.

Table 4. The results of the transformation of Table 1 using FIAP-min

No.	outlook		temperature		humidity		play
	w_{j1}	w_{j2}	w_{j3}	w_{j4}	w_{j5}	w_{j6}	C_i
y_1	0	1	0	1	0.33	0.67	no
y_2	0	0.5	0	1	0.33	0.67	no
y_3	1	0	1	0	0.50	0	yes
y_4	1	0	1	0	0.33	0.67	yes

4 Experiments and Comparison

The experiments was conducted by a PC with 3.4 GHz CPU with 256 MB RAM. For understanding the effect of the proposed methods for supervised learning on incomplete data, we generated incomplete datasets artificially selected from UCI Machine Learning repository [1]. The related information of the selected datasets is summarized in Table 5. The selected datasets were modified to generate the incomplete datasets by randomly selecting a specified percentage of cases to set to be null. However, the generation of missing values still must follow the following constraints:

C1: Each original case retains at least one attribute value.
C2: Each attribute has at least one value left.

Table 5. The selected complete datasets

Datasets	Attributes		Number of Objects	Number of classes
	categorical	numerical		
led7	7	0	3200	10
Lymph	18	0	148	4
tic-tac-toe	9	0	958	2

The performance of the classification scheme is evaluated by the average classification error rate of 10-fold cross validation for 10 runs. Each run works using a new generated incomplete dataset.

In addition to the three proposed methods, we also compare the methods of handling incomplete categorical data with the method of *concept most common attribute value* (CMCAV) in [17]. The selected classification models include a GP-based classifier GPIZ[3], statistical based classifiers Naïve Bayes [6] and NBTree [16]; support vector machines (SVM) [11], and decision tree based classifiers C4.5 [21]. Note that C4.5 was tested on incomplete data directly in the experiment of FIAV because C4.5 has its own mechanism in handling missing values.

The experimental results of classification error rates are listed from Table 6 to Table 8. Table 6 is the classification results of the five classifiers and four incomplete data handling methods on the *led7* dataset. Since the number of data in *led7* is large, we can test higher missing rate up to 30% missing. The NB-based classifiers in this dataset have better classification rate than other classifiers in FIAV and CMCAV methods and the SVM classifier has the best performance in average no matter what handling methods is. Generally, missing data do not influence the classification rate so much in this dataset. Table 7 is the classification results of the five classifiers and four incomplete data handling methods on the *lymph* dataset. This dataset has only 148 objects belonging to four classes. Therefore, only 10 % maximum missing rate can be considered. In this dataset, we found that the FIAP-class method is suitable for non-NB-based classifiers, GPIZ, C4.5 and SVM. The CMCAV method especially provides good classification rates for NB-based classifiers. The error rates on the dataset with missing data are even less than those without missing for NB and NBTree. Table 8 is the classification results of the five classifiers and four incomplete data handling methods on the *tic-tac-toe* dataset. This dataset contains 958 objects and only two classes. The maximum missing rate can be tuned to 30%. The more missing rate increases, the more classification error rate results. We found that NB-based classifiers are terrible bad in this dataset no matter what handling method used. The classifier SVM is fair in this case and the classifier GPIZ is as good as C4.5.

From the experimental results, we obviously knew that no single classifier and handling method can do all data well. Generally, the FIAV method is not an ideal handling method for most of the tested classifiers. The FIAP-class and FIAP-min methods have better classification accuracy than other methods in the GPIZ, C4.5 and

Table 6. The results of classification using incomplete *led7* dataset

Missing rate	FIAV									
	GPIZ		C4.5		SVM		NB		NBTree	
led7	Ave.	S.D.	Ave.	S.D.	Ave.	S.D.	Ave.	S.D.	Ave.	S.D.
0%	27.8	0.9	27.1	0.0	26.6	0.0	26.8	0.0	26.8	0.0
5%	27.6	1.3	27.0	0.3	26.4	0.5	27.0	0.4	26.9	0.5
10%	27.3	1.5	27.3	0.9	26.4	0.7	26.5	0.7	26.9	0.8
20%	27.9	1.9	28.0	1.2	26.4	0.9	26.7	1.0	26.5	0.9
30%	28.5	2.1	29.2	1.4	27.2	1.7	26.9	1.5	26.9	1.7
FIAP-class										
5%	27.5	0.9	26.8	0.2	26.5	0.4	27.3	0.5	27.2	0.5
10%	27.6	1.6	26.9	0.7	26.6	0.9	27.3	0.6	27.2	0.6
20%	27.3	2.2	27.1	1.3	26.5	1.2	27.1	1.3	26.6	1.1
30%	28.0	2.1	27.5	1.4	26.9	2.3	27.5	1.7	27.5	2.1
FIAP-min										
5%	27.9	1.1	27.1	0.4	26.6	0.5	27.2	0.3	26.9	0.4
10%	28.2	1.7	27.3	0.7	26.9	1.1	27.2	0.6	27.0	0.8
20%	28.5	2.1	28.0	1.4	26.8	1.5	26.7	1.0	26.5	0.9
30%	29.3	2.4	29.6	1.6	27.2	1.9	27.1	2.0	26.9	1.7
Concept most common attribute value(CMCAV)										
5%	27.9	0.6	26.7	0.5	26.6	0.5	27.0	0.4	26.9	0.4
10%	28.0	1.4	26.9	0.7	26.6	0.9	27.0	0.6	26.8	0.7
20%	28.6	1.6	27.0	1.4	26.8	1.2	26.8	1.0	26.7	1.1
30%	29.9	2.6	27.6	1.1	27.4	1.6	27.2	1.4	26.8	1.4

Table 7. The results of classification using incomplete *lymph* dataset

Missing rate	FIAV									
	GPIZ		C4.5		SVM		NB		NBTree	
lymph	Ave.	S.D.	Ave.	S.D.	Ave.	S.D.	Ave.	S.D.	Ave.	S.D.
0%	17.9	1.3	22.9	0.0	17.5	0.0	16.9	0.0	14.8	0.0
5%	19.6	2.8	22.5	5.2	17.9	3.4	16.2	1.0	25.4	3.2
10%	20.3	4.4	27.3	6.4	15.3	3.6	13.8	6.0	17.2	7.7
FIAP-class										
5%	16.9	2.1	19.5	4.8	13.6	1.2	18.8	0.8	25.1	1.6
10%	17.6	3.9	14.5	5.9	14.7	2.1	15.9	5.3	26.6	8.1
FIAP-min										
5%	17.3	3.6	23.3	6.2	13.7	2.4	16.3	1.5	24.3	5.4
10%	18.5	6.2	23.2	7.2	14.7	2.1	14.2	7.1	18.5	9.3
Concept most common attribute value(CMCAV)										
5%	20.3	2.5	19.6	2.3	17.3	2.4	12.8	2.7	13.4	2.8
10%	21.2	4.0	24.3	4.6	18.6	3.8	16.9	8.2	19.8	8.1

SVM classification models, and FIAP-class defeats FIAP-min. However, these two methods are not suitable for NB-based classifiers. The CMCAV method obviously is not a good handling method for the GPIZ and the SVM classification models; nevertheless, it provides a good repair for NB-based classifiers.

For the four handling methods, the GPIZ, C4.5 and SVM classifiers combining with the FIAP-class will yield good models for supervised learning. The previous CMCAV method performs fair classification accuracy while combining with NB and

NBTree classification models. Generally, the former models (FIAP-class + GPIZ, C4.5 or SVM) perform better performance than the latter (CMCAV + NB or NBTree). Further, the GPIZ method presents a stable classification rate in average while using the FIAP-class to be the handling method of incomplete data.

5 Conclusion

Supervised learning from incomplete data to learn an effective classification model is more difficult than learning one from complete data. In this paper, we propose three new methods, FIAV, FIAP-class, FIAP-min, based on rough membership to handle the problem of incomplete categorical data. The approach we used is different from previous methods that filled appropriate categorical values for missing data. The novelty of the proposed methods is to transform the categorical data into numerical data and estimate the membership of missing values belonging to each class. Then, the membership values are used to replace the missing values.

The experimental results demonstrate that the proposed method FIAP-class has good performance on GPIZ, SVM and C4.5, but is poor on the NB-based classifiers like NB and NBtree. On the other hand, we found that NB and NBtree have good performance on the CMCAV method. We are also interested in the experimental results that the error rates may decrease when missing rates are larger than 10% or 20% in some datasets. We still analyze and try to explain such a situation using more test data in the future.

Table 8. The results of classification using incomplete *tic-tac-toe* dataset

Missing rate	FIAV									
	GPIZ		C4.5		SVM		NB		NBTree	
tic-tac-toe	Ave.	S.D.	Ave.	S.D.	Ave.	S.D.	Ave.	S.D.	Ave.	S.D.
0%	5.9	0.7	2.60	0.0	19.6	0.0	30.4	0.0	16.0	0.0
5%	7.5	2.1	7.69	1.7	19.9	1.4	36.4	1.4	27.7	2.9
10%	7.4	2.7	8.08	1.3	16.7	2.3	35.1	1.7	26.6	4.0
20%	10.7	4.4	10.6	4.1	18.9	4.4	33.9	4.1	26.9	4.3
30%	13.6	6.3	13.7	5.9	21.4	6.3	33.2	7.4	31.0	6.1
FIAP-class										
5%	6.9	2.3	6.69	1.1	17.0	1.7	36.4	1.3	28.2	1.9
10%	7.3	2.8	6.92	1.4	16.2	2.6	35.0	1.8	28.3	2.1
20%	9.4	4.6	10.2	3.5	16.2	3.1	34.6	3.5	27.0	5.0
30%	15.2	5.5	16.2	6.0	23.2	7.8	34.9	7.9	31.3	5.3
FIAP-min										
5%	7.0	1.2	8.41	1.5	17.2	1.7	36.0	1.2	24.0	3.9
10%	8.2	3.0	8.06	1.7	15.2	2.5	34.8	1.9	24.8	2.8
20%	13.7	3.5	10.9	2.7	18.1	3.6	33.6	3.8	25.7	5.8
30%	17.1	6.7	15.1	6.3	21.8	7.9	32.5	7.6	31.8	3.8
Concept most common attribute value										
5%	7.0	1.9	6.89	1.6	16.3	1.2	34.1	1.1	23.3	1.4
10%	7.4	3.2	8.42	1.3	15.8	2.6	32.7	2.3	19.7	2.8
20%	16.5	4.5	14.5	4.1	22.2	2.6	31.7	4.9	24.1	3.8
30%	18.7	9.0	18.9	8.0	27.1	8.9	31.2	8.7	25.0	8.7

References

1. Blake, C., Keogh E., Merz, C. J.: UCI repository of machine learning database. http://www.ics.uci.edu/~mlearn/MLRepository.html, Irvine, University of California, Department of Information and Computer Science (1998)
2. Chang, C. C., Lin, C. J.: LIBSVM: a library for support vector machines, 2001. Software available at http://www.csie.ntu.edu.tw/~cjlin/libsvm
3. Chien, B. C., Lin, J. Y., Yang, W. P.: Learning effective classifiers with z-value measure based on genetic programming. Pattern Recognition, 37 (2004) 1957-1972
4. Chien, B. C., Yang, J. H., Lin, W. Y.: Generating effective classifiers with supervised learning of genetic programming. Proceedings of the 5th International Conference on Data Warehousing and Knowledge Discovery (2003) 192-201
5. Dempster, P., Laird, N. M., Rubin, D. B.: Maximum-likelihood from incomplete data via the EM algorithm. Journal of the Royal Statistical Society, B39 (1977) 1-38
6. Duda, R. O., Hart, P. E.: Pattern Classification and Scene Analysis. New York: Wiley, John and Sons Incorporated Publishers (1973)
7. Friedman, J. H.: A recursive partitioning decision rule for non-parametric classification. IEEE Transactions on Computer Science (1977) 404-408
8. Grzymala-Busse, J. W.: On the unknown attribute values in learning from examples. Proceedings of the ISMIS-91, 6th International Symposium on Methodologies for Intelligent Systems, Lecture Notes in Artificial Intelligence, Vol. 542, Springer-Verlag, Berlin Heidelberg New York (1991) 368-377
9. Grzymala-Busse, J. W., Hu, M.: A comparison of several approaches to missing attribute values in data mining. Proceedings of the Second International Conference on Rough Sets and Current Trends in Computing (2000) 378-385
10. Grzymala-Busse, J. W.: Rough set strategies to data with missing attribute values. Proceedings of the Workshop on Foundations and New Directions in Data Mining, associated with the third IEEE International Conference on Data Mining (2003) 56-63
11. Gunn, S. R.: Support vector machines for classification and regression. Technical Report, School of Electronics and Computer Science University of Southampton (1998)
12. Han, J., Kamber, M.: Data Mining: Concept and Techniques. Morgan Kaufmann publishers, (2001)
13. Hathaway, R. J., Bezdek, J. C.: Fuzzy c-means clustering of incomplete data, IEEE Transactions on Systems, Man, and Cybernetics-part B: Cybernetics 31(5) (2001)
14. Hong, T. P., Tseng, L. H., Chien, B. C.: Learning fuzzy rules from incomplete numerical data by rough sets. Proceedings of the 2002 IEEE International Conference on Fuzzy Systems (2002) 1438-1443
15. Hong, T. P., Tseng, L. H., Wang, S.-L.: Learning rules from incomplete training examples by rough sets. Expert Systems with Applications 22 (2002) 285-293
16. Kohavi, R.: Scaling up the accuracy of naïve-bayes classifiers: a decision-tree hybrid. Knowledge Discovery & Data Mining, Cambridge/Menlo Park: AAAI Press/MIT Press Publishers (1996) 202-207
17. Koninenko, I., Bratko, K., Roskar,E.: Experiments in automatic learning of medical diagnostic rules. Technical Report, Jozef Stenfan Institute, Ljubljana (1984)
18. Kryszkiewicz, M.: Rough set approach to incomplete information systems. Information Science 112 (1998) 39-49
19. Pawlak, Z.,: Rough sets. International Journal of Computer and Information Sciences 11 (1982) 341-356

20. Pawlak Z., A. Skowron: Rough membership functions, in: R.R. Yager and M. Fedrizzi and J. Kacprzyk (Eds.), Advances in the Dempster-Shafer Theory of Evidence (1994) 251-271
21. Quinlan, J. R.: C4.5: Programs for Machine Learning. San Mateo, California, Morgan Kaufmann Publishers (1993)
22. Singleton, A.: Genetic Programming with C++. http://www.byte.com/art/9402/sec10/art1.htm, Byte (1994) 171-176
23. Slowinski, R., Stefanowski, J.: Handling various types of uncertainty in the rough set approach. Proceedings of the International Workshop on Rough Sets and Knowledge Discovery (1993) 366-376
24. Stefanowski, J., Tsoukias, A.: On the extension of rough sets under incomplete information. Proceeding of the 7th International Workshop on New Directions in Rough Sets, Data Mining, and Granular-Soft Computing (1999) 73-81
25. Witten, H., Frank, E.: Data Mining: Practical machine learning tools with Java implementations. Morgan Kaufmann, San Francisco (2000)

Mining Multiple-Level Association Rules Under the Maximum Constraint of Multiple Minimum Supports

Yeong-Chyi Lee[1], Tzung-Pei Hong[2,*], and Tien-Chin Wang[3]

[1] Department of Information Engineering, I-Shou University, Kaohsiung, 84008, Taiwan
d9003007@stmail.isu.edu.tw
[2] Department of Electrical Engineering, National University of Kaohsiung,
Kaohsiung, 811, Taiwan
tphong@nuk.edu.tw
[3] Department of Information Management, I-Shou University, Kaohsiung, 84008, Taiwan
tcwang@isu.edu.tw

Abstract. In this paper, we propose a multiple-level mining algorithm for discovering association rules from a transaction database with multiple supports of items. Items may have different minimum supports and taxonomic relationships, and the maximum-itemset minimum-taxonomy support constraint is adopted in finding large itemsets. That is, the minimum support for an itemset is set as the maximum of the minimum supports of the items contained in the itemset, while the minimum support of the item at a higher taxonomic concept is set as the minimum of the minimum supports of the items belonging to it. Under the constraint, the characteristic of downward-closure is kept, such that the original Apriori algorithm can easily be extended to find large itemsets. The proposed algorithm adopts a top-down progressively deepening approach to derive large itemsets. An example is also given to demonstrate that the proposed mining algorithm can proceed in a simple and effective way.

1 Introduction

Finding association rules in transaction databases is most commonly seen in data mining. The mined knowledge about the items tending to be purchased together can be passed to managers as a good reference in planning store layout and market policy. Agrawal and his co-workers proposed several mining algorithms based on the concept of large itemsets to find association rules from transaction data [1-4]. Most of the previous approaches set a single minimum support threshold for all the items [3][5][6][7]. In real applications, different items may have different criteria to judge their importance. The support requirements should thus vary with different items. Moreover, setting the minimum support for mining association rules is a dilemma. If it is set too high, many possible rules may be pruned away; on the other hand, if it is set too low, many uninteresting rules may be generated. Liu *et al.* thus proposed an approach for mining association rules with non-uniform minimum support values [10]. Their approach allowed users to specify different minimum supports to different

---

* Corresponding author.

M. Ali and R. Dapoigny (Eds.): IEA/AIE 2006, LNAI 4031, pp. 1329–1338, 2006.

items. Wang *et al.* proposed a mining approach, which allowed the minimum support value of an itemset to be any function of the minimum support values of items contained in the itemset [11]. In the past, we proposed a simple and efficient algorithm based on the Apriori approach to generate large itemsets under the maximum constraints of multiple minimum supports [12][13].

Furthermore, taxonomic relationships among items often appear in real applications. For example, wheat bread and white bread are two kinds of bread. Bread is thus a higher level of concept than wheat bread or white bread. Meanwhile, the association rule "bread → milk" may be more general to decision makers than the rule "wheat bread → juice milk". Discovering association rules at different levels may thus provide more information than that only at a single level [8][9].

In this paper, we thus propose a multiple-level mining algorithm for discovering association rules from a transaction database with multiple minimum-supports of items. It is an extension of our previous approach with taxonomy being considered. Each item is first given a predefined support threshold. The maximum-itemset minimum-taxonomy support constraint is then adopted in finding large itemsets. That is, the minimum support for an itemset is set as the maximum of the minimum supports of the items contained in the itemset, while the minimum support of the item at a higher taxonomic concept is set as the minimum of the minimum supports of the items belonging to it. This is quite consistent with the mathematical concepts of union and intersection. Itemsets can be thought of as item intersection in transactions, and higher-level items as item union. The algorithm then adopts a top-down progressively deepening approach to derive large itemsets.

The remaining parts of this paper are organized as follows. Some related mining algorithms are reviewed in Section 2. The proposed algorithm for mining multiple-level association rules under the maximum-itemset minimum-taxonomy support constraint of multiple minimum supports is described in Section 3. An example to illustrate the proposed algorithm is given in Section 4. Conclusion and discussion are given in Section 5.

2   Review of Related Mining Algorithms

Some related researches about mining multiple-level association rules and mining association rules with multiple minimum supports are reviewed in this section.

2.1   Mining Multiple-Level Association Rules

Previous studies on data mining focused on finding association rules on the single-concept level. However, mining multiple-concept-level rules may lead to discovery of more general and important knowledge from data. Relevant data item taxonomies are usually predefined in real-world applications and can be represented using hierarchy trees. Terminal nodes on the trees represent actual items appearing in transactions; internal nodes represent classes or concepts formed by lower-level nodes. A simple example is given in Figure 1.

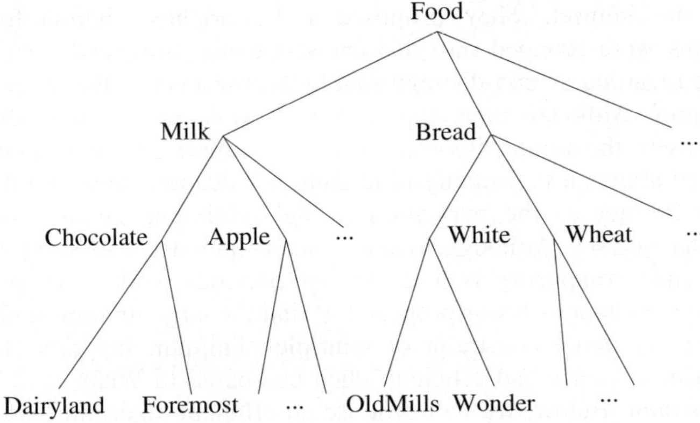

Fig. 1. Taxonomy for the example

In Figure 1, the root node is at level 0, the internal nodes representing categories (such as "Milk") are at level 1, the internal nodes representing flavors (such as "Chocolate") are at level 2, and the terminal nodes representing brands (such as "Foremost") are at level 3. Only terminal nodes appear in transactions.

Han and Fu proposed a method for finding association rules at multiple levels [8]. Nodes in predefined taxonomies are first encoded by sequences of numbers and the symbol "*" according to their positions in the hierarchy tree. For example, the internal node "Milk" in Figure 2 will be represented as 1**, the internal node "Chocolate" as 11*, and the terminal node "Dairyland" as 111. A top-down progressively deepening search approach is then used to mine the rules out.

2.2 Mining Association Rules with Multiple Minimum Supports

In the conventional approaches of mining association rules, minimum supports for all the items or itemsets to be large are set at a single value. However, in real applications, different items may have different criteria to judge its importance. Liu et al. [10] thus proposed an approach for mining association rules with non-uniform minimum support values. Their approach allowed users to specify different minimum supports to different items. The minimum support value of an itemset is defined as the lowest minimum supports among the items in the itemset. This assignment is, however, not always suitable for application requirements. As mentioned above, the minimum support of an item means that the occurrence frequency of the item must be larger than or equal to it for being considered in the next mining steps. If the support of an item is smaller than the support threshold, this item is not worth considering. When the minimum support value of an itemset is defined as the lowest minimum supports of the items in it, the itemset may be large, but items included in it may be small. In this case, it is doubtable whether this itemset is worth considering. It is thus reasonable in some sense that the occurrence frequency of an interesting itemset must be larger than the maximum of the minimum supports of the items contained in it.

Wang et al. [11] then generalized the above idea and allowed the minimum support value of an itemset to be any function of the minimum support values of items contained in the itemset. They proposed a bin-oriented, non-uniform support constraint. Items were grouped into disjoint sets called bins, and items within the same bin were regarded as non-distinguishable with respect to the specification of a minimum support. Although their approach is flexible in assigning the minimum supports to itemsets, the mining algorithm is a little complex due to its generality.

As mentioned above, it is meaningful in some applications to assign the minimum support of an itemset as the maximum of the minimum supports of the items contained in the itemset. Although Wang et al.'s approach can solve this kind of problems, the time complexity is high. In our previous work, a simple algorithm based on the Apriori approach was proposed to find the large-itemsets and association rules under the maximum constraint of multiple minimum supports [12][13]. The proposed algorithm is easy and efficient when compared to Wang et al.'s under the maximum constraint. Below, we will propose an efficient algorithm based on Han's mining approach and our previous approach for multiple-level items under the maximum-itemset minimum-taxonomy support constraint to generate the large itemsets level by level. Some pruning can also be easily done to save the computation time.

3   The Proposed Algorithm

In the proposed algorithm, items may have different minimum supports and taxonomic relationships, and the maximum-itemset minimum-taxonomy support constraint is adopted in finding large itemsets. That is, the minimum support for an itemset is set as the maximum of the minimum supports of the items contained in the itemset, and the minimum support for an item at a higher taxonomic concept is set as the minimum of the minimum supports of the items belonging to it. Under the constraint, the characteristic of downward-closure is kept, such that the original Apriori algorithm can be easily extended to find large itemsets.

The proposed mining algorithm first encodes items (nodes) in a given taxonomy as Han and Fu's approach did [8]. It first handles the items at level 1. The minimum supports of the items at level 1 are set as the minimum of the minimum supports of the items belonging to it. It then finds all large 1-itemsets L_1 from the given transactions by comparing the support of each item with its minimum support. After that, candidate 2-itemsets C_2 can be formed from L_1. Note that the supports of all the large 1-itemsets comprising each candidate 2-itemset must be larger than or equal to the maximum of the minimum supports of them. This feature provides a good pruning effect before the database is scanned for finding large 2-itemsets.

The proposed algorithm then finds all large 2-itemsets L_2 for the given transactions by comparing the support of each candidate 2-itemset with the maximum of the minimum supports of the items contained in it. The same procedure is repeated until all large itemsets have been found. The algorithm then find large itemsets at the next level until all levels have been processed. The details of the proposed mining algorithm under the maximum-itemset minimum-taxonomy support constraint are described below.

The mining algorithm for multiple-level association rules under the maximum-itemset minimum-taxonomy support constraint of multiple minimum supports:

INPUT: A body of n transaction data D, a set of m items, each with a predefined minimum support value, a predefined taxonomy of items in D, a set of membership functions, and a minimum confidence value λ.

OUTPUT: A set of multiple-level association rules under maximum constraint of multiple minimum supports.

STEP 1: Encode the predefined taxonomy using a sequence of numbers and the symbol "*", with the l-th number representing the branch number of a certain item at level l.

STEP 2: Translate the item names in the transaction data according to the encoding scheme.

STEP 3: Set $k = 1$, where k is used to store the level number currently being processed.

STEP 4: Group the items with the same first k digits in each transaction. Use the encoded name to represent the group, and retain only one item when there are more than two items in the same group in a transaction. Denote the j-th group at level k as g_j^k, where $j = 1$ to m^k and m^k is the number of groups at level k.

STEP 5: Calculate the count c_j^k of each group g_j^k at level k as its occurring number in the transaction data set D. The support s_j^k of g_j^k can then be derived as:

$$s_j^k = \frac{c_j^k}{n}.$$

STEP 6: Check whether the support s_j^k of g_j^k is larger than or equal to the threshold τ_j^k that is the minimum of minimum supports of items contained in it. If the support of a group g_j^k satisfies the above condition, put g_j^k in the set of large 1-itemsets (L_1^k) at level k. That is,

$$L_1^k = \{ g_j^k \big| s_j^k \geq \tau_j^k, 1 \leq j \leq m^k \};$$

otherwise, remove all the items in the group from the transactions D.

STEP 7: If L_1^k is null, then set $k = k + 1$ and go to STEP 4; otherwise, do the next step.

STEP 8: Set $r = 2$, where r is used to represent the number of items stored in the current large itemsets.

STEP 9: Generate the candidate set C_r^k from L_{r-1}^k in a way similar to that in the Apriori algorithm [3]. That is, the algorithm first joins L_{r-1}^k and L_{r-1}^k, assuming that r-1 items in the two itemsets are the same and the other one is different. In addition, it is different from the Apriori algorithm in that the supports of all the large (r-1)-itemsets comprising a candidate r-itemset I must be larger than or equal to the maximum (denoted as m_I) of the minimum supports of these large (r-1)-itemsets. Store in C_r^k all the itemsets satisfying the above conditions and with all their sub-r-itemsets in L_{r-1}^k.

STEP 10: If the candidate r-itemsets C_r^k is null, set $k = k + 1$ and go to STEP 4; otherwise, do the next step.

STEP 11: For each newly formed candidate r-itemset I with items $(I_1, I_2, ..., I_r)$ in C_r^k, do the following substeps:

(a) Calculate the count c_I^k of each candidate r-itemset I at level k as its occurring number in the transaction data set. The support of I can then be derived as:

$$s_I = \frac{c_I^k}{n}.$$

(b) Check whether the support s_I of each candidate r-itemset is larger than or equal to τ_I, which is the minimum of minimum supports of items contained in it. If I satisfies the above condition, put it in the set of large r-itemsets (L_r^k) at level k. That is,

$$L_{r+1}^k = \{I | s_I \geq \tau_I\}.$$

STEP 12: If L_r^k is null and k reaches to the level number of the taxonomy, then do the next step; otherwise, if L_r^k is null, then set $k = k + 1$ and go to STEP 4; otherwise, set $r = r + 1$ and go to STEP 9.

STEP 13: Construct the association rules for each large q-itemset I with items $(I_1, I_2, ..., I_q)$, $q \geq 2$, by the following substeps:

(a) Form all possible association rules as follows:

$$I_1 \wedge ... \wedge I_{r-1} \wedge I_{r+1} \wedge ... \wedge I_q \rightarrow I_r, \; r = 1 \text{ to } q.$$

(b) Calculate the confidence values of all association rules by:

$$\frac{s_{I_j}}{s_{I_1 \wedge ... \wedge I_{r-1} \wedge I_{r+1} \wedge ... \wedge I_q}}.$$

STEP 14: Output the rules with confidence values larger than or equal to the predefined confidence value λ.

4 An Example

In this section, a simple example is given to demonstrate the proposed mining algorithm, which generates a set of taxonomic association rules from a given transaction dataset with multiple minimum supports. Assume the transaction dataset includes the ten transactions shown in Table 1. Each transaction consists of two parts, *TID* and *Items*. The field *TID* is used for identifying transactions and the field *Items* lists the items purchased at a transaction. For example, there are three items, plain milk, tea and coke, purchased at transaction *T1*. Assume the predefined taxonomy among the items is shown in Figure 2. All the items fall into three main classes: foods, drinks and alcohol. Foods can be further classified into bread and cookies. There are two kinds of bread, white bread and wheat bread. The other nodes can be explained in the same manner.

Table 1. The ten transactions in this example

TID	Items
T1	plain milk, tea, coke
T2	chocolate biscuits, plain milk, tea
T3	whit bread, chocolate biscuits, red wine, blended whiskey
T4	wheat bread, chocolate biscuits, plain milk, tea
T5	chocolate biscuits, pure malt whiskey, white wine
T6	whit bread, juice milk, tea, coke
T7	chocolate biscuits, plain milk, juice milk, tea
T8	soda cookies, juice milk, coke
T9	soda cookies, coke, blended whiskey
T10	soda cookies, plain milk, tea

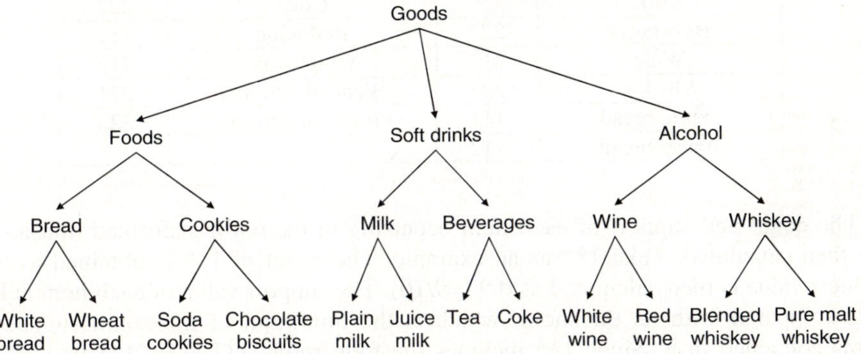

Fig. 2. The predefined taxonomy in this example

Also assume that the predefined minimum support values of items are given in Table 2 and the minimum confidence value is set at 0.85. The proposed mining algorithm for finding association rules with the predefined multiple minimum supports and multiple-level item taxonomy under the maximum-itemset minimum-taxonomy support constraint proceeds as follows.

Table 2. The predefined minimum support values for items

Item	White bread	Wheat bread	Soda cookies	Chocolate biscuits	Plain milk	Juice milk
Min-support	0.4	0.4	0.4	0.7	0.6	0.4
Item	Tea	Coke	Red wine	White wine	Blended whiskey	Pure malt whiskey
Min-support	0.5	0.7	0.4	0.5	0.6	0.4

First of all, each item name is encoded using the predefined taxonomy. The results are shown in Table 3. All transactions shown in Table 1 are encoded using the above encoding scheme. Since $k = 1$, where k is used to store the level number currently being processed, all the items in the transactions are first grouped at level one. For example, the items 112 and 122 are grouped into 1** since their first digits are both 1.

Table 3. Codes of the item names

Item name	Code	Item name	Code
Foods	1**	Soda cookies	121
Drinks	2**	Chocolate biscuits	122
Alcohol	3**	Plain milk	211
Bread	11*	Juice milk	212
Cookies	12*	Tea	221
Milk	21*	Coke	222
Beverages	22*	Red wine	311
Wine	31*	White wine	312
Whiskey	32*	Blended whiskey	321
White bread	111	Pure malt whiskey	322
Wheat bread	112		

The count and support of each item occurring in the ten transformed transactions are then calculated. Take 1** as an example. The count of 1** is obtained as 9. Its support value is then calculated as 0.9 (=9/10). The support value of each item at level 1 is compared with its threshold, which is the minimum of minimum supports of items contained in it. Since 1** includes the four items, 111, 112, 121 and 122, its minimum support is then calculated as min(0.4, 0.4, 0.4, 0.5) according to the minimum supports given in Table 2. The minimum support of 1** is thus 0.4. Since the support value of 1** (=0.9) is larger than its minimum support, 1** is put into the large 1-itemset L_1^1 at level 1. In this example, the set of large 1-itemsets at level 1 is: $L_1^1 = \{\{1**\}, \{2**\}\}$. All the items belonging to 3** (311, 312, 321 and 322) are then removed from the original transaction data set. The candidate set C_2^1 is generated from L_1^1 as $\{1**, 2**\}$. The support of $\{1**, 2**\}$ can then be derived as 0.7. Since the support value of $\{1**, 2**\}$ is larger than the maximum (0.4) of the minimum supports of 1** (0.3) and 2** (0.4), it is thus large at level 1 and is put into the set of large 2-itemsets L_2^1. In this example, $L_2^1 = \{1**, 2**\}$.

The mining processes are then executed for level 2 and level 3. When large itemsets are generated through the process, candidate itemsets may be pruned in the following three cases:

Case 1: The item which belongs to a higher-level small item does not satisfy its own minimum support and can be removed from the original transactions due to the minimum-taxonomy constraint. For example, the items, 111 and 112, belonging to 11*, are pruned since the support of 11* is smaller than its threshold. The original transaction data set is then reformed as a new one without 111 and 112.

Case 2: An itemset is pruned if any of its subset is not in the set of large itemsets. For example, the 2-itemset {11*, 12*} is pruned since 11* is not a large item.

Case 3: An itemset is pruned if any of support values of the items in the itemset is smaller than the maximum of minimum supports of the items contained in it. For example, the two items 122 and 221 at level 3 have support values 0.8 and 0.6, which are respectively larger than their own minimum supports. 122 and 221 are thus large 1-itemsets for level 3. The 2-itemset {122, 221}, formed from them, however, is not likely to be a large itemset, since the support value (0.6) of item 221 is smaller than the maximum (0.7) of minimum supports of these two items. The 2-itemset {122, 221} is thus pruned.

Since the level of the given taxonomy is 3, the association-rule deriving process is then executed. The association rules for each large q-itemsets, $q \geq 2$, are constructed by the following substeps. (a) All possible association rules are formed. (b) The confidence factors of the above association rules are calculated. Take the possible association rule "If 12*, then 21*" as an example. The confidence value for this rule is calculated as:

$$\frac{s_{12* \cup 21*}}{s_{12*}} = \frac{0.5}{0.8} = 0.625 \cdot$$

The confidence values of the above association rules are compared with the predefined confidence threshold λ. Assume the confidence λ is set at 0.85 in this example. The following five association rules are thus output:

1. If 1**, then 2**, with confidence 1.0;
2. If 2**, then 1**, with confidence 0.875;
3. If 21*, then 22*, with confidence 1.0;
4. If 22*, then 21*, with confidence 0.875;
5. If 21* and 12*, then 22*, with confidence 1.0.

The proposed algorithm can thus find the large itemsets level by level without backtracking.

5 Conclusion

Using different criteria to judge the importance of different items and managing taxonomic relationships among items are two issues that usually occur in real mining applications. In this paper, we have proposed a simple and efficient mining algorithm to solve these two issues. In the proposed algorithm, items may have different minimum supports and taxonomic relationships, and the maximum-itemset minimum-taxonomy support constraint which is set as the minimum support for an itemset is set as the maximum of the minimum supports of the items contained in the itemset, while the minimum support of the item at a higher taxonomic concept is set as the minimum of the minimum supports of the items belonging to it. The rational for using the maximum constraint has been well explained and this constraint may be suitable to some mining domains. Under the constraint, the characteristic of downward-closure can be easily kept, such that the original Apriori algorithm can be easily extended to finding large itemsets. The proposed algorithm can thus generate large itemsets from multiple-level items level by level and then derive association rules. Some pruning heuristics have also been adopted in this paper. Due to the minimum-taxonomy constraint, the item with its higher-level item not satisfying the minimum support is removed from the original transactions. The itemset with any of support values of the items contained in it smaller than the maximum of minimum supports of the items is also pruned. These make the proposed algorithm work in a better way.

Acknowledgement

This research was supported by the National Science Council of the Republic of China under contract NSC 94-2213-E-390-005.

References

1. R. Agrawal, T. Imielinksi and A. Swami, "Mining association rules between sets of items in large database," *The ACM SIGMOD Conference,* pp. 207-216, Washington DC, USA, 1993.
2. R. Agrawal, T. Imielinksi and A. Swami, "Database mining: a performance perspective," *IEEE Transactions on Knowledge and Data Engineering,* Vol. 5, No. 6, pp. 914-925, 1993.
3. R. Agrawal and R. Srikant, "Fast algorithm for mining association rules," *The International Conference on Very Large Data Bases*, pp. 487-499, 1994.
4. R. Agrawal and R. Srikant, "Mining sequential patterns," *The Eleventh IEEE International Conference on Data Engineering,* pp. 3-14, 1995.
5. S. Brin, R. Motwani, J. D. Ullman, and S. Tsur, "Dynamic itemset counting and implication rules for market-basket data," *in Proceedings of the 1997 ACM-SIGMOD International Conference in Management of Data*, pp. 207-216, 1997.
6. J. S. Park, M. S. Chen, and P. S. Yu, "An Effective hash-based algorithm for mining association rules," *in Proceedings of the 1995 ACM-SIGMOD International Conference in Management of Data*, pp. 175-186, 1995.
7. A. Savasere, E. Omiecinski, and S. Navathe, "An efficient algorithm for mining association rules in large databases," *in Proceedings of the 21st International Conference in Very Large Data Bases (VLDB'95)*, pp. 432-443, 1995.
8. J. Han and Y. Fu, "Discovery of multiple-level association rules from large databases," *in Proceeding of the 21st International Conference on Very Large Data Bases*, pp. 420-431, 1995.
9. R. Srikant and R. Agrawal, "Mining generalized association rules," *in Proceeding of the 21st International Conference on Very Large Data Bases*, pp. 407-419, 1995.
10. B. Liu, W. Hsu, and Y. Ma, "Mining association rules with multiple minimum supports," *in Proceedings of the 1999 International Conference on Knowledge Discovery and Data Mining*, pp. 337-341, 1999.
11. K. Wang, Y. H and J. Han, "Mining frequent itemsets using support constraints," *in Proceedings of the 26th International Conference on Very Large Data Bases*, pp. 43-52, 2000.
12. Y. C. Lee, T. P. Hong and W. Y. Lin, "Mining fuzzy association rules with multiple minimum supports using maximum constraints", *The Eighth International Conference on Knowledge-Based Intelligent Information and Engineering Systems*, 2004, *Lecture Notes in Computer Science*, Vol. 3214, pp. 1283-1290, 2004.
13. Y. C. Lee, T. P. Hong and W. Y. Lin, "Mining association rules with multiple minimum supports using maximum constraints," *International Journal of Approximate Reasoning*, Vol. 40, No. 1, pp. 44-54, 2005.

A Measure for Data Set Editing by Ordered Projections

Jesús S. Aguilar-Ruiz, Juan A. Nepomuceno,
Norberto Díaz-Díaz, and Isabel Nepomuceno

Bioinformatics Group of Seville,
Pablo de Olavide University and University of Seville, Spain
`direscinf@upo.es, {janepo, ndiaz, isabel}@lsi.us.es`

Abstract. In this paper we study a measure, named *weakness of an example*, which allows us to establish the importance of an example to find representative patterns for the data set editing problem. Our approach consists in reducing the database size without losing information, using algorithm patterns by ordered projections. The idea is to relax the reduction factor with a new parameter, λ, removing all examples of the database whose weakness verify a condition over this λ. We study how to establish this new parameter. Our experiments have been carried out using all databases from UCI-Repository and they show that is possible a size reduction in complex databases without notoriously increase of the error rate.

1 Introduction

Data mining algorithms must work with databases with tends of attributes and thousands of examples when they are used to solve real and specific problems. This kind of databases contain much more information than standard databases, most of them of small size, which are usually used to testing data mining techniques. A lot of time and memory size are necessary to accomplish the final tests on these real databases.

Methodologies based on axis-parallel classifiers are classifiers that provide easy-to-understand decision rules by humans and they are very useful for the expert interest in getting knowledge from databases. These methodologies are the most common among all methodologies used by data mining researchers. If we want to apply one of this type of tools, as C4.5 or k-NN [9], to solve a real problem with a huge amount of data, we should use some method in order to decrease the computational cost of applying these algorithms.

Databases preprocessing techniques are used to reduce the number of examples or attributes as a way of decreasing the size of the database with which we are working. There are two different types of preprocessing techniques: **editing** (reduction of the number of examples by eliminating some of them or finding representatives patterns or calculating prototypes) and **feature selection** (eliminating non-relevant attributes).

M. Ali and R. Dapoigny (Eds.): IEA/AIE 2006, LNAI 4031, pp. 1339–1348, 2006.

Editing methods are related to the nearest neighbours (NN) techniques [4]. For example, in [5], Hart proposed to include in the set of prototypes those examples whose classification is wrong using the nearest neighbour technique; in this way, every member of the main set is closer to a member of the subset of prototypes of the same class than a member of a different class of this subset. In [2] a variant of the previous method is proposed. In [15], Wilson suggests to eliminate the examples which are incorrectly classified with the k-NN algorithm, the works of [13] and [11] follows the same idea. Other variants are based on Voronoi diagrams [7], for example: *Gabriel neighbours* (two examples are Gabriel neighbours if their diametrical sphere does not contain any other examples) or *relative neighbours* [14] (two examples p and q are relative neighbours if for all example x in the set, the following expression is true: $d(p,q) < max\{d(p,x), d(x,q)\}$).

In all previous methods the distances between examples must be calculated, so that, if we are working with n examples with m attributes, the first methods takes a time of $\Theta(mn^2)$, the method proposed in [11] takes $\Theta(mn^2 + n^3)$ and $\Theta(mn^3)$ the methods based on Voronoi diagrams.

We work in this paper in the line proposed by Aguilar-Riquelme-Toro [1], where a first version of editing method by ordered projection technique was introduced. This algorithm works well with continuous attributes. In [10], a second and more elaborated version of this algorithm is proposed and it works simultaneously with continuous and discrete attributes (i.e., nominal attributes) and it conserves the properties of the initial approach. Working with NN-based techniques implies to introduce some initial parameters and defining a distance to calculate the proximity between the different examples of the database. This new method based on ordered projection technique does not need to define any distance and it works with each attribute independently as we will see in the next section. The most important characteristic of this approach to the editing techniques, in addition to the absence of distance calculations, are: the considerable reduction of the number of examples, the lower computational cost $\Theta(mn \log n)$ and the conservation of the decision boundaries (especially interesting for applying classifiers based on axis-parallel decision rules). We are interesting in a measure, the **weakness** of an example, which help us to determine the importance of an example as decision boundary: more weakness implies less relevance. We propose a relaxation to the projection approach eliminating those examples whose weakness is larger than a threshold using a new parameter, λ, in the algorithm.

At the present time some authors think that editing methods are rather old-fashioned because by today's standard technology (even thought today´s data sets are larger) it is not clear whether it is worthwhile to spend the pre-processing time to perform editing. That is why some methods which embedded approaches for (simultaneous) feature selection (or editing) and classification, as SVMs [8], are being used. We are interesting in the study how to relax the projection approach to the editing problem in order to combine this new measure with the parameter of a similar approach to feature selection (eliminating non-relevant attributes), see [12]. A good method (as a new *theory of measure* to preprocessing techniques) to find out the threshold which reduce the number of examples and the number of attributes without losing information in huge databases, would be a great achievement.

In this paper, we show that in more complicated databases we can relax the reduction factor eliminating those examples whose weakness verify a condition over λ. We have dealt with two different databases of the UCI repository [3] (University of California at Irvine), *heart-statlog* database and *ionosphere* database. k-NN (for $k = 1$) and C4.5 classifiers have been used to classify our database before and after applying our editing method POP_λ (patterns by ordered projections). The condition over the weakness of each example has been relaxed gradually in order to study the importance of this measure and the goodness of our method being applied to algorithms based on axis-parallel classifiers. After having determined the threshold using the λ parameter, we carry out the study of it over the different databases of the UCI repository with continuos attributes [3]. A ten-fold cross-validation has been used for each database.

2   Description of the Algorithm

A database with m attributes and n examples can be seen as a space with m dimensions, where each example takes a value in the rank of each attribute and it has a determined class associated. Each attribute represents an axis of this space, with n points or objects inside and each example has a particular label associated with its corresponding class. For example, if our database has two attributes, we will be in a two-dimensional space (attributes are represented by x and y axis respectively) see Figure 1.

As we said in the previous section, our method does not need to define any distance to compare the different examples, we will work with the projection of each example over each axis of the space.

The main idea of the algorithm is the following: if the dimension of the space is d, in order to locate a region (in the context of the example region means hyper-rectangle although our algorithm will work with any hyperplane) of this space with examples with the same class, we will need only $2d$ examples which will define the borders of this region; for example, in order to define a squared in $\mathbb{R}^2$ we only need four points. So that, if we have more than $2d$ examples in the region with the same class, we can eliminate the rest which are inside. Our objective will be to eliminate examples which are not in the boundaries of the region. The way of finding if an example is inner to a region will be studding if it is inner in each corresponding interval in the projection of the region over the different axis of the space.

An *ordered projected sequence* is the sequence formed by the projection of the space onto one particular axis, i.e., a particular attribute. A *partition* is a subsequence formed from one ordered projection sequence which maintains the projection ordered.

We define the **weakness** of an example as the number of times that an example is not a border in a partition (i.e., it is inner to a partition) for every

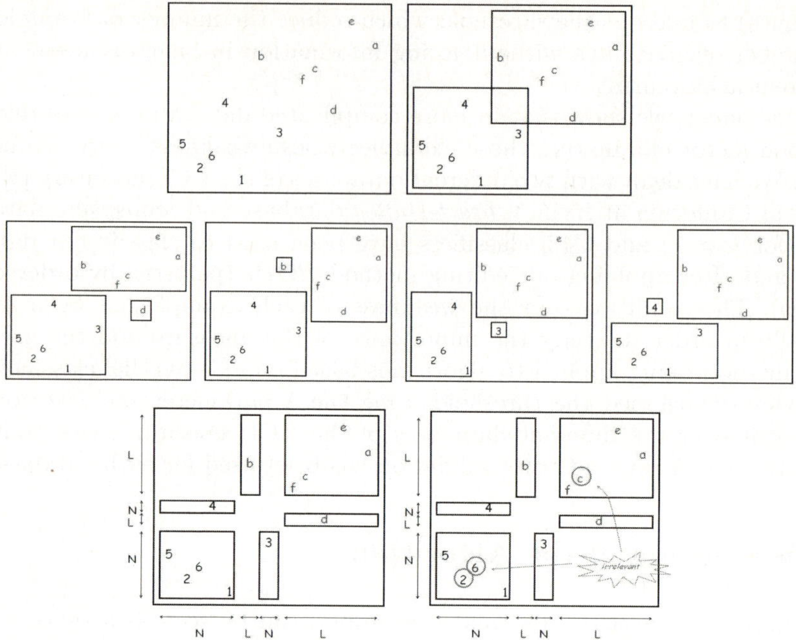

Fig. 1. A two-dimensional database with twelve examples

partition obtained from ordered projected sequences of each attribute. We call
irrelevant examples those examples whose weakness is equal to the number
of attributes.

In order to illustrate the method, we have designed a simple two–dimensional
labelled database. This database is depicted in Figure 1, picture 1, and it contains twelve examples from two different class: N (numbers) and L (letters).
An optimal classifier would obtain two rules, examples with *numbers* label and
letters label, see picture 2 in the Figure 1, with overlapped rules. The classifier
must be hierarchical because it produces overlapped rules. This is no the case of
an axis parallel classifier which does not produce overlapped rules. For example,
C4.5 and many others similar classifiers would produce situations like we can
see in picture 2, 3, 4 and 5 in Figure 1.

The aim of our algorithm is to built regions containing all the examples of the
same class and to eliminate those examples which are not necessaries to define
the regions, that is, those examples which are not in the borders of the regions. If
we consider the situation depicted in picture number 7 in Figure 1, each region
only contains examples of the same class in a maximal way. The projection
of the examples on the abscissa axis, for the first attribute, it will produce four
ordered sequences $\{N, L, N, L\}$ corresponding to $\{[5, 2, 6, 4, 1], [b], [3], [f, c, d, e,
a]\}$. Respectively on the ordinates axis, will produce the sequences $\{N, L, N, L\}$
formed by the examples $\{[1, 2, 6, 5, 3], [d], [4], [f, c, b, a, e]\}$. Each sequence
represents a rectangular region as possible solution of a classifier and initial and

final examples of the sequence (if it has only one, it is simultaneously the initial and the final one) represent the lower and upper values for each coordinate of this rectangle. In this situation, 5 and 1 are border for the first attribute.

According to this figure, the weakness of each examples would be 0 to examples '1', '3' and 'f'; 1 to '4', 'd', 'e', '5', 'b' and 'a'; and 2 to example '2', '6' and 'c'. Last examples have weakness equal to the dimension, therefore they are not necessaries to define the subregions, they are irrelevant examples. So, they are removed from the database, see picture 8 in the Figure 1.

2.1   Algorithm

Given the database E, let be n and n' the initial and the final number of examples $(n \geq n')$, let be m the number of attributes and let be $\lambda \in \mathbb{R}$ the initial parameter to relax the measure of the weakness. The POP_λ-algorithm (algorithm for patterns by projections ordered) is the following:

```
Procedure POP_λ (in: (E_{n×m}, λ), out: E_{n'×m})
for each example e_i ∈ E,i ∈ {1,...,n}
    weakness(e_i) := 0
end for
for each attribute a_j, j ∈ {1,...,m}
    E_j := QuickSort(E_j, a_j) in increasing order
    E_j := ReSort(E_j)
    for each example e_i ∈ E_j, i ∈ {1,...,n}
        if e_i is nor border
            weakness(e_i) := weakness(e_i) + 1
        end if
    end for
end for
for each example e_i ∈ E, i ∈ {1,...,n}
    if weakness(e_i) ≥ m · λ
        remove e_i from E
    end if
end for
end POP_λ
```

The computational cost of POP is $\Theta(mn \log n)$. This cost is much lower than other algorithms proposed in the bibliography, normally $\Theta(mn^2)$.

The algorithm constructs the ordered projected sequence over each axis of the space (attribute) and it calculates the weakness for each example. The value of the projections need to be sorted when we are working with each attribute. We use QuickSort algorithm, [6], and a second sorting, we call it Resort, is made in order to create regions containing examples of the same class in a maximal way. The examples sharing the same value for an attribute are not necessary

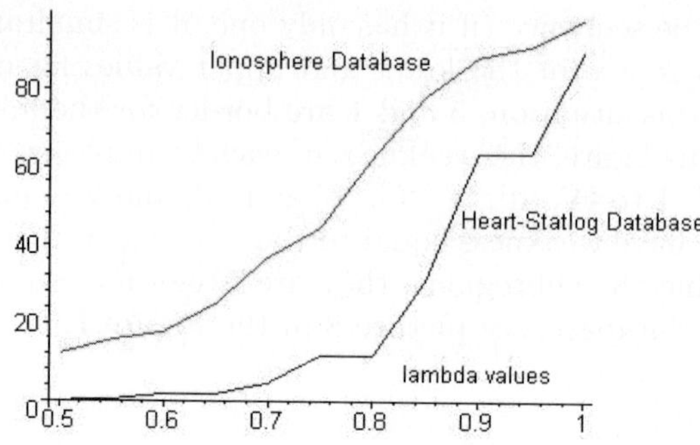

Fig. 2. Applying POP_λ over two different databases. Ordinate axis shows the *percentage of retention*. In abscissa axis different values of the λ parameter.

nearer to those examples that have the same class and have another value. The solution to that problem consists of resorting the interval containing repeated values. The heuristic is applied to obtain the least number of changes of class. Therefore, the algorithm sort by value and, in case of equality, by class (*Resort* sorting). In the case of working with a database with nominal attributes, another more elaborated version of this kind of algorithm could be considered: discrete attributes does not need to be sorted and the weakness of all the examples except one which has the least weakness obtained for the continuous attributes is increased. We are not interesting in this first approach in database with nominal attributes. Finally, examples verifying the condition over λ parameter are eliminated of the database. This parameter permit us to control the level of reduction of our editing method.

3   Experiments

Our tests have been achieved over two different databases: *heart-statlog* database and *ionosphere* database, both obtained from the UCI repository [3]. The main objective is to compare the performance of our editing method when the λ parameter is modified. We have a measure for each example, the weakness of the example, which determines its importance as a decision boundary, we relate this measure with the parameter of our editing algorithm. Our objective is to study how to establish a threshold to eliminate examples of the database, we want to determinate a parameter.

A ten-fold cross-validation is made dividing the database in ten parts and taking blocks of nine parts which are our training set and the other one is the test set. We apply our reducing method to the training set and then, after having applied the corresponding classifier algorithm, we use the test set to validate the process. This operation is realized ten times each one with the different ten subset we have built.

Table 1. Computational Cost in Seconds and Error Rate (*average - standard deviation*) for C4.5 and k-NN (with $k = 1$) algorithms over the different databases obtained with POP_λ

	C4.5				k-NN			
	Heart-Statlog		Ionosphere		Heart-Statlog		Ionosphere	
	CCS	ER $\pm\sigma$	CCS	ER $\pm\sigma$	CCS	ER $\pm\sigma$	CCS	ER $\pm\sigma$
Original	0.08	21.7 ±6.6	0.16	14.3 ±7.9	0.09	24.6 ±8.1	0.06	15.4 ±8.2
POP$_{\lambda=1}$	0.08	24.0 ±6.0	0.18	14.3 ±7.9	0.05	24.8 ±8.6	0.05	16.3 ±8.8
POP$_{\lambda=0.95}$	0.13	20.8±10.8	0.15	15.4 ±8.7	0.05	28.4 ±5.9	0.05	16.8 ±9.3
POP$_{\lambda=0.90}$	0.08	20.8±10.8	0.14	14.8 ±7.7	0.05	28.4 ±5.9	0.05	17.1 ±9.4
POP$_{\lambda=0.85}$	0.05	22.1 ±6.7	0.14	12.0 ±7.2	0.03	24.9±11.4	0.06	17.1 ±9.4
POP$_{\lambda=0.80}$	0.03	27.4±11.4	0.12	14.3 ±6.8	0.02	39.4 ±8.8	0.05	16.3 ±8.9
POP$_{\lambda=0.75}$	0.04	37.4±11.4	0.09	17.7 ±8.1	0.01	39.4 ±8.8	0.05	15.4 ±8.2
POP$_{\lambda=0.70}$	0.03	40.3±14.8	0.08	25.1±14.5	0.01	45.4 ±9.5	0.04	15.7 ±8.5
POP$_{\lambda=0.65}$	0.02	42.0±14.2	0.06	30.2±11.7	0.00	41.3 ±9.5	0.04	19.7±11.5
POP$_{\lambda=0.60}$	0.02	42.0±14.2	0.04	47.2±13.7	0.00	41.3 ±9.5	0.04	24.8±11.2
POP$_{\lambda=0.55}$	0.01	43.0±15.8	0.04	58.3±16.6	0.00	46.6 ±6.5	0.03	44.1 ±9.5
POP$_{\lambda=0.50}$	0.01	9.3$^*\pm18.5$	0.04	53.4±17.0	0.00	42.9 ±7.1	0.03	51.2 ±7.9

We apply POP_λ algorithm with $\lambda \in \{1, 0.95, 0.9, 0.85, 0.8, 0.75, 0.7, 0.65, 0.6, 0.55, 0.5\}$. Figure 2 shows the percentage of retention of our method varying with the different values of λ (100% means that the database has not any reduction)[1]. We notice that both functions are increasing, that is because we have imposed the condition " $weakness(e_i) \geq m \cdot \lambda$" in the algorithm and for each new valor of the parameter, we remove the new examples that verifies the condition and the old ones. If we have put $=$ instead $\geq$, the graphic would not be increasing and the process would not be cumulative. If a group of examples with the same weakness is removed for a value of λ, they will be removed when the parameter decreases. We are interested in relaxing the condition over λ in order to remove examples from the database gradually. A possible threshold could be establish seeing the graphics but we must verify that we do not lose any knowledge in order to make the classification phase.

The results of the classifications using C4.5 and k-NN techniques are shown in Table 1. We presents the CCS, computational cost in seconds, and the ER, error rate, for the original database and the different reduced databases. ER is the classification error produced when the test set validates the model that we have constructed applying the different techniques to the different databases. Values are the average and the standard deviation of complete 10-fold cross-validation (the sum of the 10 experiments for each value obtained). We can observe that the computational cost is decreasing while the lambda value is decreasing too. So, if we found a lambda value less than 1 without losing information, we would manage reduce the database size and the computational cost would decreased too.

---

[1] Percentages of retention for each value of λ are the average of the ten different experiments realized in the 10-fold CV.

The purpose is to study the relevance of POP_λ as a reduction method for the different values of λ. The best situation could be getting the λ which produces the greatest reduction in our database and the least error rate when the classification methods is applied. We observe between $\lambda = 0.85$ and $\lambda = 0.80$ a possible threshold: for $\lambda = 0.80$ the number of examples are removed dramatically from the database and the error rate seems to increase. We have a good candidate to be our threshold. We must verify it and we must study how to establish the valour of the parameter.

In order to proof the goodness of our parameter, in Table 2, we carry out the study of the situation for this two values over all the databases from UCI repository with continuous attributes [3]. We show the percentage of reduction, PR, in order to indicate the number of examples which are removed from the database, values are the average of complete 10-fold cross-validation process. We must consider how the error changes when the database is reduced considerably. Our aim is to ascertain the value of λ which reduce more the database without losing information. For example, for Heart–Statlong, the Error Rate from the original database using C4.5 is 21.7 ± 6.6, but if we apply $POP_{\lambda=0.85}$ (Table 2) the error would be only 22.1 ± 6.7. That is, we have managed to reduce the database in a 68.8% (100-PR) without losing knowledge. If we take the same database and configuration but using k-NN, similar behavior is observed. In general, for $\lambda = 0.85$, databases would be reduced to 61.8% of the original size and error rate would be incremented from 18.6 ± 4.8 to 24.8 ± 5.8 using C4.5, and from 15.4 ± 4.6 to 23.1 ± 5.0 using 1-NN. We have drawn in bold in both tables the data which are relevant according to t-Student statistical distribution.

Paying attention to results obtained with $\lambda = 0.8$ we have to say that although databases was reduced dramatically, the error rate is incremented notably. These Experiments show us how to establish an appropriate value of λ parameter in order to apply the POP_λ algorithm reducing the database up to the limit and conserving the knowledge of the original database.

In summary, we can state that with lambda values minor than 1 it is possible a higher database size reduction without losing information. But this reduction is limited to a 0.85 lambda value. We have established a method to find out a threshold to relax the reduction factor over the algorithm for finding representative patterns for dat aset editing. We have proven the goodness of our level with all the databases of the UCI repository with only continuous attributes.

4   Conclusions

We have defined a new parameter, λ, which helps us to remove all examples in a database which verify a condition over it, its *"weakness* $\geq$(number attributes)$\cdot\lambda$". Therefore we have established a threshold via a measure over each example in order to reduce the number of examples of a database.

After analyzing our approach using some databases from the UCI–Repository, we conclude that it is possible to reduce the database size up to a 40% without losing any knowledge. Furthermore, the computational cost is decreased by allowing to remove examples with weakness less than the number of attributes.

Table 2. Error Rate for C4.5 and k-NN (with $k = 1$) algorithms over databases from UCI repository with continuous attributes. Every database is considered before and after applying POP_λ for $\lambda = 0.85$, for the first table, $\lambda = 0.80$ for the second one. PR is the percentage of reduction of the reduction algorithm.

	C4.5			k-NN		
	Original	$POP_{\lambda=0.85}$		Original	$POP_{\lambda=0.85}$	
Data Base	ER $\pm\sigma$	ER $\pm\sigma$	PR	ER $\pm\sigma$	ER $\pm\sigma$	PR
Heart-Statlog	21.7 ±6.6	22.1 ±6.7	31.2	24.6 ±8.1	**24.9 ± 11.4**	31.2
Ionosphere	14.3 ±7.9	12.0 ±7.2	78.2	15.4 ±8.2	17.1 ±9.4	78.2
Balance-Scale	25.4 ±7.2	**66.0 ± 17.7**	10.8	20.2 ±5.6	**54.0 ± 13.1**	10.8
Breast-W	5.2 ±2.7	**17.0 ± 9.9**	5.2	5.2 ±4.7	**23.2 ± 7.8**	5.2
Bupa	15.4 ±0.0	**42.0 ± 0.0**	42.0	0.0 ±0.0	**22.6 ± 0.0**	42.0
Diabetes	26.4 ±7.3	28.1 ±7.7	55.3	29.6 ±4.0	**35.0 ± 5.8**	55.3
Glass	51.3 ±19	51.4 ±19	97.6	39.8 ±12	39.8 ±12	97.6
Iris	2.0 ±0.0	**12.7 ± 0.0**	26.0	0.0 ±0.0	**3.3 ± 0.0**	26.0
Lung-Cancer	15.6 ±0.0	**9.4 ± 0.0**	96.0	0.0 ±0.0	**3.1 ± 0.0**	96.0
Page-Blocks	1.5 ±0.0	**9.3 ± 0.0**	13.0	0.3 ±5.6	**23.5 ± 3.6**	13.0
Pima-Indians-Diabetes	15.9 ±0.0	**23.6 ± 0.0**	58.0	0.0 ±0.0	**11.9 ± 1.8**	58.0
Segment	3.3 ±1.3	3.8 ±1.5	92.0	3.2 ±1.6	3.2 ±1.6	92.0
Sonar	45.5±19.3	45.5±19.3	100.0	49.4±16.1	49.4±16.1	100.0
Vehicle	27.8 ±3.4	28.2±4.6	88.1	31.9 ±4.6	31.8 ±4.4	88.1
Waveform-5000	25.1 ±1.5	25 ±1.8	97.1	26.8 ±1.5	26.8 ±1.6	97.1
Wine-5000	1.1 ±0.0	1.1 ±0.0	98.0	0.0 ±0.0	0.0 ±0.0	98.0
Average	18.6 ±4.8	24.8 ±5.8	61.8	15.4 ±4.6	23.1 ±5.0	61.8

	C4.5			k-NN		
	Original	$POP_{\lambda=0.80}$		Original	$POP_{\lambda=0.80}$	
Data Base	ER $\pm\sigma$	ER $\pm\sigma$	PR	ER $\pm\sigma$	ER $\pm\sigma$	PR
Heart-Statlog	21.7 ±6.6	**27.4 ± 11.4**	11.7	24.6 ±8.1	**39.4 ± 8.8**	11.7
Ionosphere	14.3 ±7.9	14.3 ±6.8	62.5	15.4 ±8.2	16.3 ±8.9	62.5
Balance-Scale	25.4 ±7.2	**6.0 ± 17.8**	10.8	20.2 ±5.6	**54.0 ± 13.2**	10.8
Breast-W	5.2 ±2.7	**50.4 ± 29**	1.3	5.2 ±4.7	**34.9 ± 9.0**	5.2
Bupa	15.4 ±0.0	**42.0 ± 0.0**	42.0	0.0 ±0.0	**22.6 ± 0.0**	42.0
Diabetes	26.4 ±7.3	**49.5 ± 8.2**	26.4	29.6±4.0	**47.0 ± 4.1**	26.4
Glass	51.3 ±19	52.6±17.5	94.2	39.8±12.0	39.8 ±12	94.2
Iris	2.0 ±0.0	**12.7 ± 0.0**	26.0	0.0 ±0.0	**3.3 ± 0.0**	26.0
Lung-Cancer	15.6 ±0.0	**12.5 ± 0.0**	90.0	0.0 ±0.0	**9.4 ± 0.0**	90.0
Page-Blocks	1.5 ±0.0	**9.3 ± 0.0**	13.0	0.3 ±5.6	**23.6 ± 0.0**	13.0
Pima-Indians-Diabetes	15.9 ±0.0	**48.8 ± 0.0**	28.0	0.0 ±0.0	**32.2 ± 0.0**	13.0
Segment	3.3±1.4	4.1 ±1.5	87.0	3.2 ±1.6	3.7 ±1.5	87.0
Sonar	45.5±19.3	45.5±19.3	100.0	49.4±16.1	49.4±16.1	100.0
Vehicle	27.8 ±3.4	29.0 ±6.4	79.6	31.9 ±4.6	32.8 ±5.3	79.6
Waveform-5000	25.1 ±1.5	25.1 ±1.6	92.6	26.8 ±1.5	26.9 ±1.6	92.6
Wine-5000	1.1 ±0.0	1.1 ±0.0	96.6	0.0 ±0.0	0.0 ±0.0	96.6
Average	18.6 ±4.8	30.6 ±7.5	53.9	15.4 ±4.6	27.2 ±5.0	53.9

In spite of having introduced a new parameter and treating a problem of editing (some authors consider editing is also rather old-fashioned because it is worthwhile to spend the pre-processing time with today´s standard technologies), this paper begins a way to consider the preprocessing problem, such editing as features selection, as a problem of election of two parameters. As a future work, the combination of POP_λ-algorithm with SOAP-algorithm [12] is proposed. Thus we will obtain an algorithm to preprocess a database working with two parameters in order to remove such examples as attributes.

References

1. Aguilar, J.S.; Riquelme, J.C.; Toro, M.: Data set editing by ordered projection, in: Proceedings of the 14th European Conference on Arti2cial Intelligence (ECAI'00), Berlin, Germany, (2000), pp. 251-255.
2. Aha, D.W.; Kibler, D.; Albert, M.K.: Instance-based learning algorithms, Mach. Learning 6 (1991), pp. 37-66.
3. Blake, C.; Merz, E.K.: UCI repository of machine learning databases, (1998).
4. Cover, T. and Hart, P.: Nearest Neighbor Pattern Classification. IEEE Transactions on Information Theory, IT-13 (1) (1967), pp. 21-27.
5. Hart, P.: The condensed nearest neighbor rule, IEEE Trans. Inf. Theory 14 (3) (1968), pp. 515-516.
6. Hoare, C.A.R.: Quicksort, Comput.J. 5 (1) (1962), pp. 10-15.
7. Klee, V.: On the complexity of d-dimensional voronoi diagrams, Arch. Math. 34 (1980), pp. 75-80.
8. Neumann, Julia; Schnörr, Christoph; Steidl, Gabriele: SVM-based Feature Selection by Direct Objective Minimisation Pattern Recognition, Proc. of 26th DAGM Symposium, LNCS, Springer, August (2004).
9. Quinlan, J.R.: C4.5: Programs for Machine Learning, Morgan Kauffmann, San Mateo, CA, (1993).
10. Riquelme, José C.; Aguilar-Ruiz, Jesús S.; Toro, Miguel: Finding representative patterns with ordered projections Pattern Recognition 36 (2003), pp. 1009-1018.
11. Ritter, G.; WoodruI, H.; Lowry, S.; Isenhour, T.: An algorithm for a selective nearest neighbor decision rule, IEEE Trans. Inf. Theory 21 (6) (1975), pp. 665-669.
12. Ruiz, R.; Riquelme, Jose C.; Aguilar-Ruiz, Jesus S.: NLC: A Measure Based on Projections 14th International Conference on Database and Expert Systems Applications, DEXA 2003Lecture Notes in Computer Science, Springer-VerlagPrague, Czech Republic, 1-5 September, (2003).
13. Tomek, I.: An experiment with the edited nearest-neighbor rule, IEEE Trans. Syst. Man Cybern. 6 (6) (1976), pp. 448-452.
14. Toussaint, G.T.: The relative neighborhood graph of a finite planar set, Pattern Recognition 12 (4) (1980), pp. 261-268.
15. Wilson, D.R.; Martinez, T.R.: Improved heterogeneous distance functions, J. Artif. Intell. Res. 6 (1) (1997), pp. 1-34.

Author Index

Lecture Notes in Artificial Intelligence (LNAI)

Vol. 4031: M. Ali, R. Dapoigny (Eds.), Advances in Applied Artificial Intelligence. XXIII, 1353 pages. 2006.

Vol. 4027: H.L. Larsen, G. Pasi, D. Ortiz-Arroyo, T. Andreasen, H. Christiansen (Eds.), Flexible Query Answering Systems. XVIII, 714 pages. 2006.

Vol. 4021: E. André, L. Dybkjær, W. Minker, H. Neumann, M. Weber (Eds.), Perception and Interactive Technologies. XI, 217 pages. 2006.

Vol. 4020: A. Bredenfeld, A. Jacoff, I. Noda, Y. Takahashi, RoboCup 2005: Robot Soccer World Cup IX. XVII, 727 pages. 2006.

Vol. 4013: L. Lamontagne, M. Marchand (Eds.), Advances in Artificial Intelligence. XIII, 564 pages. 2006.

Vol. 4012: T. Washio, A. Sakurai, K. Nakashima, H. Takeda, S. Tojo, M. Yokoo (Eds.), New Frontiers in Artificial Intelligence. XIII, 484 pages. 2006.

Vol. 4005: G. Lugosi, H.U. Simon (Eds.), Learning Theory. XI, 656 pages. 2006.

Vol. 3978: B. Hnich, M. Carlsson, F. Fages, F. Rossi (Eds.), Recent Advances in Constraints. VIII, 179 pages. 2006.

Vol. 3963: O. Dikenelli, M.-P. Gleizes, A. Ricci (Eds.), Engineering Societies in the Agents World VI. XII, 303 pages. 2006.

Vol. 3960: R. Vieira, P. Quaresma, M.d.G.V. Nunes, N.J. Mamede, C. Oliveira, M.C. Dias (Eds.), Computational Processing of the Portuguese Language. XII, 274 pages. 2006.

Vol. 3955: G. Antoniou, G. Potamias, C. Spyropoulos, D. Plexousakis (Eds.), Advances in Artificial Intelligence. XVII, 611 pages. 2006.

Vol. 3946: T.R. Roth-Berghofer, S. Schulz, D.B. Leake (Eds.), Modeling and Retrieval of Context. XI, 149 pages. 2006.

Vol. 3944: J. Quiñonero-Candela, I. Dagan, B. Magnini, F. d'Alché-Buc (Eds.), Machine Learning Challenges. XIII, 462 pages. 2006.

Vol. 3930: D.S. Yeung, Z.-Q. Liu, X.-Z. Wang, H. Yan (Eds.), Advances in Machine Learning and Cybernetics. XXI, 1110 pages. 2006.

Vol. 3918: W.K. Ng, M. Kitsuregawa, J. Li, K. Chang (Eds.), Advances in Knowledge Discovery and Data Mining. XXIV, 879 pages. 2006.

Vol. 3913: O. Boissier, J. Padget, V. Dignum, G. Lindemann, E. Matson, S. Ossowski, J.S. Sichman, J. Vázquez-Salceda (Eds.), Coordination, Organizations, Institutions, and Norms in Multi-Agent Systems. XII, 259 pages. 2006.

Vol. 3910: S.A. Brueckner, G.D.M. Serugendo, D. Hales, F. Zambonelli (Eds.), Engineering Self-Organising Systems. XII, 245 pages. 2006.

Vol. 3904: M. Baldoni, U. Endriss, A. Omicini, P. Torroni (Eds.), Declarative Agent Languages and Technologies III. XII, 245 pages. 2006.

Vol. 3900: F. Toni, P. Torroni (Eds.), Computational Logic in Multi-Agent Systems. XVII, 427 pages. 2006.

Vol. 3899: S. Frintrop, VOCUS: A Visual Attention System for Object Detection and Goal-Directed Search. XIV, 216 pages. 2006.

Vol. 3898: K. Tuyls, P.J. 't Hoen, K. Verbeeck, S. Sen (Eds.), Learning and Adaption in Multi-Agent Systems. X, 217 pages. 2006.

Vol. 3891: J.S. Sichman, L. Antunes (Eds.), Multi-Agent-Based Simulation VI. X, 191 pages. 2006.

Vol. 3890: S.G. Thompson, R. Ghanea-Hercock (Eds.), Defence Applications of Multi-Agent Systems. XII, 141 pages. 2006.

Vol. 3885: V. Torra, Y. Narukawa, A. Valls, J. Domingo-Ferrer (Eds.), Modeling Decisions for Artificial Intelligence. XII, 374 pages. 2006.

Vol. 3881: S. Gibet, N. Courty, J.-F. Kamp (Eds.), Gesture in Human-Computer Interaction and Simulation. XIII, 344 pages. 2006.

Vol. 3874: R. Missaoui, J. Schmidt (Eds.), Formal Concept Analysis. X, 309 pages. 2006.

Vol. 3873: L. Maicher, J. Park (Eds.), Charting the Topic Maps Research and Applications Landscape. VIII, 281 pages. 2006.

Vol. 3863: M. Kohlhase (Ed.), Mathematical Knowledge Management. XI, 405 pages. 2006.

Vol. 3862: R.H. Bordini, M. Dastani, J. Dix, A.E.F. Seghrouchni (Eds.), Programming Multi-Agent Systems. XIV, 267 pages. 2006.

Vol. 3849: I. Bloch, A. Petrosino, A.G.B. Tettamanzi (Eds.), Fuzzy Logic and Applications. XIV, 438 pages. 2006.

Vol. 3848: J.-F. Boulicaut, L. De Raedt, H. Mannila (Eds.), Constraint-Based Mining and Inductive Databases. X, 401 pages. 2006.

Vol. 3847: K.P. Jantke, A. Lunzer, N. Spyratos, Y. Tanaka (Eds.), Federation over the Web. X, 215 pages. 2006.

Vol. 3835: G. Sutcliffe, A. Voronkov (Eds.), Logic for Programming, Artificial Intelligence, and Reasoning. XIV, 744 pages. 2005.

Vol. 3830: D. Weyns, H. V.D. Parunak, F. Michel (Eds.), Environments for Multi-Agent Systems II. VIII, 291 pages. 2006.

Vol. 3817: M. Faundez-Zanuy, L. Janer, A. Esposito, A. Satue-Villar, J. Roure, V. Espinosa-Duro (Eds.), Nonlinear Analyses and Algorithms for Speech Processing. XII, 380 pages. 2006.

Vol. 3814: M. Maybury, O. Stock, W. Wahlster (Eds.), Intelligent Technologies for Interactive Entertainment. XV, 342 pages. 2005.

Vol. 3809: S. Zhang, R. Jarvis (Eds.), AI 2005: Advances in Artificial Intelligence. XXVII, 1344 pages. 2005.

Vol. 3808: C. Bento, A. Cardoso, G. Dias (Eds.), Progress in Artificial Intelligence. XVIII, 704 pages. 2005.

Vol. 3802: Y. Hao, J. Liu, Y.-P. Wang, Y.-m. Cheung, H. Yin, L. Jiao, J. Ma, Y.-C. Jiao (Eds.), Computational Intelligence and Security, Part II. XLII, 1166 pages. 2005.

Vol. 3801: Y. Hao, J. Liu, Y.-P. Wang, Y.-m. Cheung, H. Yin, L. Jiao, J. Ma, Y.-C. Jiao (Eds.), Computational Intelligence and Security, Part I. XLI, 1122 pages. 2005.

Vol. 3789: A. Gelbukh, Á. de Albornoz, H. Terashima-Marín (Eds.), MICAI 2005: Advances in Artificial Intelligence. XXVI, 1198 pages. 2005.

Vol. 3782: K.-D. Althoff, A. Dengel, R. Bergmann, M. Nick, T.R. Roth-Berghofer (Eds.), Professional Knowledge Management. XXIII, 739 pages. 2005.

Vol. 3763: H. Hong, D. Wang (Eds.), Automated Deduction in Geometry. X, 213 pages. 2006.

Vol. 3755: G.J. Williams, S.J. Simoff (Eds.), Data Mining. XI, 331 pages. 2006.

Vol. 3735: A. Hoffmann, H. Motoda, T. Scheffer (Eds.), Discovery Science. XVI, 400 pages. 2005.

Vol. 3734: S. Jain, H.U. Simon, E. Tomita (Eds.), Algorithmic Learning Theory. XII, 490 pages. 2005.

Vol. 3721: A.M. Jorge, L. Torgo, P.B. Brazdil, R. Camacho, J. Gama (Eds.), Knowledge Discovery in Databases: PKDD 2005. XXIII, 719 pages. 2005.

Vol. 3720: J. Gama, R. Camacho, P.B. Brazdil, A.M. Jorge, L. Torgo (Eds.), Machine Learning: ECML 2005. XXIII, 769 pages. 2005.

Vol. 3717: B. Gramlich (Ed.), Frontiers of Combining Systems. X, 321 pages. 2005.

Vol. 3702: B. Beckert (Ed.), Automated Reasoning with Analytic Tableaux and Related Methods. XIII, 343 pages. 2005.

Vol. 3698: U. Furbach (Ed.), KI 2005: Advances in Artificial Intelligence. XIII, 409 pages. 2005.

Vol. 3690: M. Pěchouček, P. Petta, L.Z. Varga (Eds.), Multi-Agent Systems and Applications IV. XVII, 667 pages. 2005.

Vol. 3684: R. Khosla, R.J. Howlett, L.C. Jain (Eds.), Knowledge-Based Intelligent Information and Engineering Systems, Part IV. LXXIX, 933 pages. 2005.

Vol. 3683: R. Khosla, R.J. Howlett, L.C. Jain (Eds.), Knowledge-Based Intelligent Information and Engineering Systems, Part III. LXXX, 1397 pages. 2005.

Vol. 3682: R. Khosla, R.J. Howlett, L.C. Jain (Eds.), Knowledge-Based Intelligent Information and Engineering Systems, Part II. LXXIX, 1371 pages. 2005.

Vol. 3681: R. Khosla, R.J. Howlett, L.C. Jain (Eds.), Knowledge-Based Intelligent Information and Engineering Systems, Part I. LXXX, 1319 pages. 2005.

Vol. 3673: S. Bandini, S. Manzoni (Eds.), AI*IA 2005: Advances in Artificial Intelligence. XIV, 614 pages. 2005.

Vol. 3662: C. Baral, G. Greco, N. Leone, G. Terracina (Eds.), Logic Programming and Nonmonotonic Reasoning. XIII, 454 pages. 2005.

Vol. 3661: T. Panayiotopoulos, J. Gratch, R. Aylett, D. Ballin, P. Olivier, T. Rist (Eds.), Intelligent Virtual Agents. XIII, 506 pages. 2005.

Vol. 3658: V. Matoušek, P. Mautner, T. Pavelka (Eds.), Text, Speech and Dialogue. XV, 460 pages. 2005.

Vol. 3651: R. Dale, K.-F. Wong, J. Su, O.Y. Kwong (Eds.), Natural Language Processing – IJCNLP 2005. XXI, 1031 pages. 2005.

Vol. 3642: D. Ślęzak, J. Yao, J.F. Peters, W. Ziarko, X. Hu (Eds.), Rough Sets, Fuzzy Sets, Data Mining, and Granular Computing, Part II. XXIII, 738 pages. 2005.

Vol. 3641: D. Ślęzak, G. Wang, M. Szczuka, I. Düntsch, Y. Yao (Eds.), Rough Sets, Fuzzy Sets, Data Mining, and Granular Computing, Part I. XXIV, 742 pages. 2005.

Vol. 3635: J.R. Winkler, M. Niranjan, N.D. Lawrence (Eds.), Deterministic and Statistical Methods in Machine Learning. VIII, 341 pages. 2005.

Vol. 3632: R. Nieuwenhuis (Ed.), Automated Deduction – CADE-20. XIII, 459 pages. 2005.

Vol. 3630: M.S. Capcarrère, A.A. Freitas, P.J. Bentley, C.G. Johnson, J. Timmis (Eds.), Advances in Artificial Life. XIX, 949 pages. 2005.

Vol. 3626: B. Ganter, G. Stumme, R. Wille (Eds.), Formal Concept Analysis. X, 349 pages. 2005.

Vol. 3625: S. Kramer, B. Pfahringer (Eds.), Inductive Logic Programming. XIII, 427 pages. 2005.

Vol. 3620: H. Muñoz-Ávila, F. Ricci (Eds.), Case-Based Reasoning Research and Development. XV, 654 pages. 2005.

Vol. 3614: L. Wang, Y. Jin (Eds.), Fuzzy Systems and Knowledge Discovery, Part II. XLI, 1314 pages. 2005.

Vol. 3613: L. Wang, Y. Jin (Eds.), Fuzzy Systems and Knowledge Discovery, Part I. XLI, 1334 pages. 2005.

Vol. 3607: J.-D. Zucker, L. Saitta (Eds.), Abstraction, Reformulation and Approximation. XII, 376 pages. 2005.

Vol. 3601: G. Moro, S. Bergamaschi, K. Aberer (Eds.), Agents and Peer-to-Peer Computing. XII, 245 pages. 2005.

Vol. 3600: F. Wiedijk (Ed.), The Seventeen Provers of the World. XVI, 159 pages. 2006.

Vol. 3596: F. Dau, M.-L. Mugnier, G. Stumme (Eds.), Conceptual Structures: Common Semantics for Sharing Knowledge. XI, 467 pages. 2005.

Vol. 3593: V. Mařík, R. W. Brennan, M. Pěchouček (Eds.), Holonic and Multi-Agent Systems for Manufacturing. XI, 269 pages. 2005.

Vol. 3587: P. Perner, A. Imiya (Eds.), Machine Learning and Data Mining in Pattern Recognition. XVII, 695 pages. 2005.